The Oxford Handbook of Counseling Psychology

OXFORD LIBRARY OF PSYCHOLOGY

Editor-in-Chief PETER E. NATHAN

The Oxford Handbook of Counseling Psychology

Edited by

Elizabeth M. Altmaier

Jo-Ida C. Hansen

OXFORD
UNIVERSITY PRESS

OXFORD
UNIVERSITY PRESS

Oxford University Press, Inc., publishes works that further Oxford University's
objective of excellence in research, scholarship, and education.

Oxford   New York
Auckland   Cape Town   Dar es Salaam   Hong Kong   Karachi
Kuala Lumpur   Madrid   Melbourne   Mexico City   Nairobi
New Delhi   Shanghai   Taipei   Toronto

With offices in
Argentina   Austria   Brazil   Chile   Czech Republic   France   Greece
Guatemala   Hungary   Italy   Japan   Poland   Portugal   Singapore
South Korea   Switzerland   Thailand   Turkey   Ukraine   Vietnam

Published by Oxford University Press, Inc.
198 Madison Avenue, New York, New York 10016
www.oup.com

Library of Congress Cataloging-in-Publication Data

The Oxford handbook of counseling psychology / edited by Elizabeth M. Altmaier, Jo-Ida
C. Hansen.
    p. cm. — (Oxford library of psychology)
  Includes index.
  ISBN-13: 978-0-19-534231-4

1. Counseling psychology—Handbooks, manuals, etc. I. Altmaier, Elizabeth M.
II. Hansen, Jo-Ida C.
  BF636.6.O94 2012
  158.3—dc23   2011027854

SHORT CONTENTS

OXFORD LIBRARY OF PSYCHOLOGY

The *Oxford Library of Psychology*, a landmark series of handbooks, is published by Oxford University Press, one of the world's oldest and most highly respected publishers, with a tradition of publishing significant books in psychology. The ambitious goal of the *Oxford Library of Psychology* is nothing less than to span a vibrant, wide-ranging field and, in so doing, to fill a clear market need.

Encompassing a comprehensive set of handbooks, organized hierarchically, the *Library* incorporates volumes at different levels, each designed to meet a distinct need. At one level are a set of handbooks designed broadly to survey the major subfields of psychology; at another are numerous handbooks that cover important current focal research and scholarly areas of psychology in depth and detail. Planned as a reflection of the dynamism of psychology, the *Library* will grow and expand as psychology itself develops, thereby highlighting significant new research that will impact on the field. Adding to its accessibility and ease of use, the *Library* will be published in print and, later on, electronically.

The *Library* surveys psychology's principal subfields with a set of handbooks that capture the current status and future prospects of those major subdisciplines. This initial set includes handbooks of social and personality psychology, clinical psychology, counseling psychology, school psychology, educational psychology, industrial and organizational psychology, cognitive psychology, cognitive neuroscience, methods and measurements, history, neuropsychology, personality assessment, developmental psychology, and more. Each handbook undertakes to review one of psychology's major subdisciplines with breadth, comprehensiveness, and exemplary scholarship. In addition to these broadly conceived volumes, the *Library* also includes a large number of handbooks designed to explore in depth more specialized areas of scholarship and research, such as stress, health and coping, anxiety and related disorders, cognitive development, or child and adolescent assessment. In contrast to the broad coverage of the subfield handbooks, each of these latter volumes focuses on an especially productive, more highly focused line of scholarship and research. Whether at the broadest or most specific level, however, all of the *Library* handbooks offer synthetic coverage that reviews and evaluates the relevant past and present research and anticipates research in the future. Each handbook in the *Library* includes introductory and concluding chapters written by its editor to provide a roadmap to the handbook's table of contents and to offer informed anticipations of significant future developments in that field.

An undertaking of this scope calls for handbook editors and chapter authors who are established scholars in the areas about which they write. Many of the nation's and world's most productive and best-respected psychologists have agreed to edit *Library* handbooks or write authoritative chapters in their areas of expertise.

For whom has the *Oxford Library of Psychology* been written? Because of its breadth, depth, and accessibility, the *Library* serves a diverse audience, including graduate students in psychology and their faculty mentors, scholars, researchers, and practitioners in psychology and related fields. Each will find in the *Library* the information they seek on the subfield or focal area of psychology in which they work or are interested.

Befitting its commitment to accessibility, each handbook includes a comprehensive index, as well as extensive references to help guide research. And because the *Library* was designed from its inception as an online as well as a print resource, its structure and contents will be readily and rationally searchable online. Further, once the *Library* is released online, the handbooks will be regularly and thoroughly updated.

In summary, the *Oxford Library of Psychology* will grow organically to provide a thoroughly informed perspective on the field of psychology, one that reflects both psychology's dynamism and its increasing interdisciplinarity. Once published electronically, the *Library* is also destined to become a uniquely valuable interactive tool, with extended search and browsing capabilities. As you begin to consult this handbook, we sincerely hope you will share our enthusiasm for the more than 500-year tradition of Oxford University Press for excellence, innovation, and quality, as exemplified by the *Oxford Library of Psychology.*

Peter E. Nathan
Editor-in-Chief
Oxford Library of Psychology

ABOUT THE EDITORS

Elizabeth M. Altmaier

Elizabeth Altmaier is Professor in the Counseling Psychology program in the Department of Psychological and Quantitative Foundations, College of Education, at the University of Iowa, with a joint appointment in the Department of Community and Behavioral Health in the College of Public Health. Dr. Altmaier received her M.A. and Ph.D. in Psychology from The Ohio State University and her B.A. in Psychology from Wheaton College (Ill.). Her research interests are in health psychology, particularly the psychosocial sequelae of treatments for cancer, and in the roles of spirituality and religiosity in recovery from trauma

Jo-Ida C. Hansen

Jo-Ida C. Hansen is Professor in the Department of Psychology and Director of the American Psychological Association–accredited Counseling Psychology Program at the University of Minnesota. She holds an adjunct appointment with the Department of Human Resources and Industrial Relations in the Carlson School of Business, University of Minnesota. She directs the Center for Interest Measurement Research and the Vocational Assessment Clinic, an advanced practicum training site and research laboratory for testing the hypotheses of the Theory of Work Adjustment (TWA). Her awards include the E. K. Strong, Jr. Gold Medal, ACA Extended Research Award, Leona Tyler Award, and Society of Vocational Psychology Lifetime Achievement Award.

CONTRIBUTORS

Saba Rasheed Ali
Department of Psychological and
Quantitative Foundations
University of Iowa
Iowa City, Iowa

Elizabeth M. Altmaier
Department of Psychological and
Quantitative Foundations
University of Iowa
Iowa City, Iowa

Margit I. Berman
Department of Psychiatry
Dartmouth Medical School
Hanover, New Hampshire

Nancy E. Betz
Department of Psychology
The Ohio State University
Columbus, Ohio

Rosie Phillips Bingham
Student Affairs
University of Memphis
Memphis, Tennessee

Robert C. Chope
Department of Counseling
San Francisco State University
San Francisco, California

Kevin O. Cokley
Department of Educational Psychology
University of Texas at Austin
Austin, Texas

Robert K. Conyne
College of Education, Criminal Justice,
and Human Services
University of Cincinnati
Cincinnati, Ohio

Stewart E. Cooper
Department of Psychology
Valparaiso University
Valparaiso, Indiana

Thomas R. Cunningham
Education and Information Division
National Institute for
Occupational Safety and Health
Centers for Disease Control and
Prevention
Cincinnati, Ohio

Gary M. Diamond
Department of Behavioral Sciences
Ben-Gurion University of the Negev
Beer-Sheva, Israel

Michael Duffy
Department of Educational Psychology
Texas A&M University
College Station, Texas

Timothy R. Elliott
Department of Educational Psychology
Texas A&M University
College Station, Texas

Donald E. Eggerth
Education and Information Division
National Institute for
Occupational Safety and Health
Centers for Disease Control and
Prevention
Cincinnati, Ohio

Carolyn Zerbe Enns
Department of Psychology
Cornell College
Mount Vernon, Iowa

Dorothy L. Espelage
Department of Educational Psychology
University of Illinois, Urbana-Champaign
Champaign, Illinois

Ruth E. Fassinger
College of Graduate and
Professional Studies
John F. Kennedy University
Pleasant Hill, California

Nadya A. Fouad
Department of Educational Psychology
University of Wisconsin-Milwaukee
Milwaukee, Wisconsin

Patricia A. Frazier
Department of Psychology
University of Minnesota
Minneapolis, Minnesota

Myrna L. Friedlander
Department of Counseling Psychology
University at Albany, SUNY
Albany, New York

Jairo N. Fuertes
The Derner Institute of Advanced
Psychological Studies
Adelphi University
Garden City, New York

Lawrence H. Gerstein
Department of Counseling Psychology &
Guidance Services, and
Center for Peace and Conflict Studies
Ball State University
Muncie, Indiana

Judy E. Hall
National Register of Health Service
Providers in Psychology
Washington, D.C.

Jo-Ida C. Hansen
Department of Psychology
University of Minnesota
Minneapolis, Minnesota

Robert J. Harmison
Department of Graduate Psychology
James Madison University
Harrisonburg, Virginia

Beth E. Haverkamp
Department of Educational and
Counselling Psychology
University of British Columbia
Vancouver, British Columbia, Canada

Martin Heesacker
Department of Psychology
University of Florida
Gainesville, Florida

Mary Ann Hoffman
Department of Counseling and
Personnel Services
University of Maryland
College Park, Maryland

Arpana G. Inman
Department of Counseling Psychology
Lehigh University
Bethlehem, Pennsylvania

Larry C. James
School of Professional Psychology
Wright State University
Dayton, Ohio

Nicholas Ladany
Department of Educational
Support Services
Loyola Marymount University
Los Angeles, California

Lisa M. Larson
Department of Psychology
Iowa State University
Ames, Iowa

James W. Lichtenberg
Department of Psychology and Research
in Education
University of Kansas
Lawrence, Kansas

William Ming Liu
Department of Psychological and
Quantitative Foundations
University of Iowa
Iowa City, Iowa

Sara Maltzman
County of San Diego Child Welfare
Services
San Diego, California

Melissa L. Morgan
Department of Counseling,
Clinical, & School Psychology
University of California, Santa Barbara
Santa Barbara, California

Bonnie Moradi
Department of Psychology
University of Florida
Gainesville, Florida

Susan L. Morrow
Department of Educational Psychology
University of Utah
Salt Lake City, Utah

Rhoda Olkin
California School of Professional
Psychology
Alliant International University
San Francisco, California

James N. O'Neil
Department of Educational Psychology
University of Connecticut
Storrs, Connecticut

Trent A. Petrie
Department of Psychology
University of North Texas
Denton, Texas

Thomas G. Plante
Department of Psychology
Santa Clara University
Santa Clara, California

Paul V. Poteat
Department of Counseling,
Developmental, and Educational
Psychology
Boston College
Boston, Massachusetts

Jeffrey P. Prince
Department of Counseling &
Psychological Services
University of California, Berkeley
Berkeley, California

Joseph F. Rath
Department of Rehabilitation Medicine
New York University School of Medicine
New York, New York

Sandra L. Shullman
Executive Development Group, LLC
Columbus, Ohio

Jane Swanson
Department of Psychology
Southern Illinois University Carbondale
Carbondale, Illinois

Carl E. Thoresen
School of Education
Stanford University
Stanford, California

Tammi Vacha-Haase
Department of Psychology
Colorado State University
Fort Collins, Colorado

Beverly J. Vandiver
Department of Educational
Psychology, School Psychology,
and Special Education
Pennsylvania State University
University Park, Pennsylvania

Melba J. T. Vasquez
Independent Practice
Austin, Texas

Elizabeth M. Vera
School of Education
Loyola University Chicago
Chicago, Illinois

Janice D. Yoder
Department of Psychology
University of Akron
Akron, Ohio

Stefania Ægisdóttir
Department of Counseling Psychology
and Guidance Services
Ball State University
Muncie, Indiana

CONTENTS

PART 1

Introduction and Overview

A View Across the Life Span of Counseling Psychology

Elizabeth M. Altmaier *and* Saba Rasheed Ali

Abstract

It has been said of psychology, as a discipline, that it has a long past and a short history. This contrast refers to the roots of psychology in philosophy, medicine, and education that date back over several hundred years—and in the case of philosophy and medicine, several thousand. Counseling psychology has deep roots, as well, although its technical birth was in 1952. At that time, the Division of Personnel and Guidance of the American Psychological Association renamed itself the Division of Counseling Psychology. In this chapter, we consider three domains in which our specialty has begun with deep "roots" and has "leafed" out into new ways of thinking about our work with clients and our broader roles in the communities in which we live. These three domains are a focus on building strengths; a holistic, or systems, perspective; and a collaborative, patient-centered model. We trace the development of these domains, noting where, in other parts of this volume, more complete discussion can be found, and we highlight their current explications.

Keywords: values, history, development

Counseling psychology, as a specialty, officially dates to 1952, when the Division of Counseling and Guidance of the American Psychological Association changed its name to the Division of Counseling Psychology, thus formalizing a specialty in psychology that had increasingly differentiated itself from related psychological specialties to form a unique identity. As discussed in many chapters that follow, counseling psychology is one of three original specialties in psychology (the others being clinical psychology and school psychology). Although these specialties differed in their target client population and the activities engaged in by practitioners identified with the specialty, they shared a commitment to client welfare, to the application of scientific knowledge to assessment and intervention, and to training and education. Their differences, however, are significant and continue to this day.

Readers will find this *Handbook* divided into four parts. The first part pertains to foundational knowledge and methods. These chapters concern themselves with the basic interactions of counseling—the counseling relationship, a counselor's assessment of a client, the counselor's choice of interventions—and how theory, research, and professional context influence these interactions over time. Thus, this part covers those critical issues of methodology, ethics and professional issues, and training and supervision that are foundational to all chapters that follow.

From its inception, counseling psychology has emphasized three themes. The first theme is that psychologists work toward a goal larger than that of removing pathology. Rather, counseling psychologists promote positive health through the identification and enhancement of constructive aspects of human functioning, both personal strengths and available resources. The second theme is that clients are best understood in a systems perspective: When conceptualizing persons, counseling psychologists focus on interacting variables, including developmental stage, the person–environment fit, and external systems acting on the person, including family and community. The third theme is that counseling psychologists are collaborative: They are client-centered, using shared relationships, sensitive to the multicultural components of the interaction, to enhance client welfare and outcomes.

In this chapter, each of these themes will be considered in more detail. The purpose is to define a context for the chapters that follow. By considering both the earliest and the most recent iterations of these themes, we hope that the reader will gain a wider view in which to locate the general and specific information contained in the *Handbook* chapters.

Promotion of Health

As a discipline, psychologists respond to clients—whether individuals, couples, groups, or organizations—who face difficulties with their emotional and physical well-being. Are clients best assisted when the difficulty is accurately diagnosed and an intervention is made to reduce or remove the difficulty? Or, are they best served when the assessment and intervention process assists clients in identifying their own personal strengths and resources, then reinforces these strengths and resources within the intervention, so that they can serve to prevent future distress? The response to this question is part of the historical differentiation between clinical and counseling psychology, in which clinical psychology has emphasized diagnosis and treatment of disorders, and counseling psychology has emphasized normal development. Louttit (1939) defined clinical psychology as concerned with diagnosing the nature and extent of psychopathology, with abnormalities present even in "normal" persons. In contrast, Gustad (1953) noted counseling psychology's concern with *hygiology*, with normalities and strengths present even in "abnormal" persons, and with the identification and promotion of adaptive personal tendencies.

However, the specialties are more recently in convergence on the notion of health promotion as well as remediation. Taken from the websites of clinical and counseling psychology are the following definitions (Division of Clinical Psychology, 2010; Division of Counseling Psychology, 2010):

The field of clinical psychology integrates science, theory, and practice to understand, predict, and alleviate maladjustment, disability, and discomfort as well as to promote human adaptation, adjustment, and personal development. Clinical psychology focuses on the intellectual, emotional, biological, psychological, social, and behavioral aspects of human functioning across the lifespan, in varying cultures, and at all socioeconomic levels.

Counseling psychology as a psychological specialty facilitates personal and interpersonal functioning across the lifespan with a focus on emotional, social, vocational, educational, health-related, developmental, and organizational concerns. Through the integration of theory, research, and practice, and with a sensitivity to multicultural issues, this specialty encompasses a broad range of practices that help people improve their well-being, alleviate distress and maladjustment, resolve crises, and increase their ability to live more highly functioning lives. Counseling psychology is unique in its attention both to normal developmental issues and to problems associated with physical, emotional, and mental disorders.

A focus on the promotion of mental health was a vital characteristic of early counseling psychologists, most of whom were operating as guidance specialists during the time between World War I and World War II. These early guidance professionals were concerned with the problems of children and adolescents, particularly those from poor urban environments, who left school early and needed to work to support families but were unable to navigate the work world. Frank Parsons, in particular, focused his efforts on the Civic Service House of Boston, where he assisted students in planning their work future. This foundation for guidance was well received, and national interest in "vocational guidance" increased dramatically. Counseling psychologists of that time were also busy developing curriculum to educate and train the persons who would be guidance specialists in the future.

A second vital focus on health was present in the work of Carl Rogers. Rogers (1940), in contrast to the prevailing therapeutic model of his time, proposed that clients were capable of their own emotional growth and adjustment in the presence of the deeply supportive relationship environment provided by a counselor who was warm, genuine, and fully present to the client. This view contrasted with the notion of the counselor as a removed "expert," whose knowledge would result in a diagnosis of the client and/or the provision of the necessary information to the client for his or her adjustment. Rogers' work was seconded by an early pioneer of counseling psychology, Leona Tyler, who wrote a seminal text in 1953 entitled *The Work of the Counselor*, in which she set forth the proposition that the person and presence of the counselor was more important than counseling content or techniques.

As is clearly detailed in many chapters that follow, counseling psychology has maintained this emphasis on health promotion and has transformed it into a promotion of positive psychology. Notably, this promotion of health by identifying and fostering strengths has expanded beyond the individual to the point at which counseling psychologists maintain an advocacy role for clients and a commitment to fostering social justice in systems, organizations, and communities. Within this contemporary commitment, counseling psychologists use research and theory to identify persons at risk of difficulties and to intervene before serious adversity is present. They also promote client welfare beyond the individuals whom they serve, acting as an advocate for community betterment. And, finally, they are focused on social justice as a necessary and appropriate goal for all clients.

Systems Perspective

As stated previously, counseling psychology emerged as a specialty from the vocational guidance movement. Yet, counseling psychology would eventually branch into many different areas, one of which was the area of career development/vocational psychology. This area of counseling psychology is mostly concerned with helping individuals plan for a career. More recently, vocational psychologists have been more concerned with how to help individuals find and maintain gainful employment in the midst of economic crises and downsizing.

Some of the earliest theories in career development were driven by historical and contextual influences. During the Industrial Revolution, there was a need to assist individuals to find the correct "match" in terms of their skills and a specific job. This could be seen most prominently in factory work, where efficiency was considered paramount. As mentioned previously, Frank Parsons, considered to be the founder of modern vocational psychology, was particularly interested in immigrant youth. Parsons believed that the best way to help immigrant youth find work was to help them find a job that was "a function of the fit between a person's capacities and characteristics on one hand and the requirements of routines of the occupation on the other" (Parsons, 1909). Parsons was a frequent lecturer at a Boston settlement home established to assist neighborhood immigrant residents to develop English fluency and complete high school. His favorite topic was the importance of matching one's abilities to a vocation. Largely, Parson's work was built upon the premise of creating a more efficient society by assisting youth in becoming and *staying* employed in occupations that would provide them with life's necessities and ultimately assist them in transcending poverty.

From Parson's work emerged the trait factor approaches to career planning and development. For example, Holland's (1959) *theory of vocational choice* is centered on the premise that an individual's personality and occupational environments can be matched, and the greater the match, the more successful the person will be in his or her chosen career. Holland developed a series of personality instruments and theoretical positions that outline this model in great detail. Another theory that was developed around the same time was the *theory of work adjustment* (TWA; Dawis, Lofquist, & Weiss, 1968), which is the only major theory that took into account both the needs and interests of the worker, as well as the needs and interests of the work environment. Very briefly, TWA outlines important relationships between the needs of the individuals and the requirements of the particular workplace and the constant adjustment between the two.

More recently, vocational psychologists have been interested in the application of developmental psychology perspectives to career development and to vocational psychology to explain the career development process for disenfranchised groups. For example, Bronfenbrenner's *ecological systems theory* (Bronfenbrenner, 1977) has been used to explain the career development of women in poverty and women of color. Ecological systems theory is a developmental theory that takes into account the multiple systemic influences and interactions that occur for a given individual. Bronfenbrenner asserts that each individual operates within a series of nested systems in which development occurs (e.g., family, culture, government), and that the individual is an active participant in many of these systems and therefore, is not simply acted upon by the system but also influences and changes the environment. This perspective has been used within vocational psychology/counseling psychology to understand the complexity of career development from a multicultural standpoint, and it takes into account that human behavior and development varies depending on the context in which it is occurring. Although Bronfenbrenner's theory has been developed for over 40 years, the application of the model to vocational psychology, career development, and counseling psychology is relatively new.

Collaborative, Client-centered Model

Perhaps the strongest characteristic of counseling psychology, particularly in comparison to the two closely related specialties of clinical and school psychology, is its emphasis on the collaborative nature of the relationship between counselors and clients. A view of the client as working in a collaborative relationship with the counselor carries with it several important components. First, since the client and counselor are working together, the client's view of the nature of his or her distress and its origins carries as much weight as the counselor's view. Thus, the counselor is not the source of information as the expert on the client's condition so much as the counselor facilitates the client's self-exploration, whereby both client and counselor gain valuable insights into the client. Second, the counselor respects the client in the counseling relationship as a partner in both assessment and intervention processes. Clients are not "cured" by counselors; rather, clients work in relationships with counselors to achieve important outcomes, including, as noted above, the identification and promotion of personal and contextual strengths.

Perhaps the earliest explication of these views was in Tyler's 1953 book, referred to earlier. In her writing, she emphasized the individuality of each client and each counselor, and the unique nature of their interaction. Therefore, although technique and knowledge are critical, they are not enough. As Tyler noted in a later edition of her book (1969), "at the heart of the counseling process is a meeting of counselor and client. Whether they meet for 15 or 50 minutes, whether they talk about symptoms, explore feelings, or discuss facts and schedules . . . whatever influence counseling has is related most closely to the nature of the relationship that grows out of this encounter" (p. 33).

A related view of the importance of a collaborative model of counselor and client is the collaborative model of training and education adopted in counseling psychology programs, namely the scientist–practitioner model. This model, established originally at the Boulder Conference, articulated the essential importance of the relationship of science and practice. During graduate education and after, a dual emphasis on the scientist–practitioner model (Altmaier & Claiborn, 1987) allows the integration of both scientific activities and modes of thinking with the art of therapy. Thus, scholarship and practice share reciprocal and essential functions in the advancement of science and clinical work.

This emphasis on collaboration between counselor and client resulted in significant thinking about essential tasks of the counselor, who must be "present" for clients. In particular, how cultural differences between counselor and client influence successful or unsuccessful outcomes were considered. Recently, counseling psychology has been characterized by and differentiated from clinical and school psychology in its emphasis on critical aspects of the multicultural interaction between counselor and client. The second part of this *Handbook* identifies essential elements of multicultural knowledge, attitudes, and skills. As noted in the definition of counseling psychology presented earlier, counseling psychologists carry a sensitivity to multiculturalism into all their activities, ranging from counseling and therapy to testing to research to supervision and training. Much of the current work in the field of psychology in these areas has been accomplished by counseling psychologists. Although *multiculturalism* in its earliest meaning was defined primarily as racial differences between counselor and client, counseling psychology now promotes the view of each encounter between two people as a multicultural encounter. As chapters in this part consider, gender, social class, and sexual minority concerns are examples of cultural encounters in which counseling psychologists have contributed to current knowledge.

Conclusion

Counseling psychology is engaged in exhilarating new directions, as well as continuing time-honored domains of contributions. The fourth and fifth parts of the *Handbook* cover both of these applications. The fourth part considers how counseling psychologists have traditionally assisted clients who are individuals, groups, couples, or families, and who have a variety of identified difficulties. The fifth part identifies "intersections," new areas of practice that have recently developed as counseling psychologists have embraced previously underserved client populations—clients with medical concerns, school-aged children, persons who have experienced trauma—and used both the specialty's roots and its leaves to explicate theories and applications that build on the traditional strengths of counseling psychology in new ways. Increasingly, counseling psychologists operate outside of the borders of the United States, and our last chapter opens the boundaries of our specialty even wider, by identifying the increasing internationalism of counseling psychology.

All of the chapter authors share a deep commitment to our specialty, as well as recognized expertise in the areas they encompass in their chapters. We acknowledge with gratitude their work in bringing historical strengths, current directions, and the exciting future agenda of our specialty.

References

Altmaier, E. M., & Claiborn, C. D. (1987). Some observations on research and science. *Journal of Counseling and Development, 66,* 51.

Bronfenbrenner, U. (1977). Toward an experimental ecology of human development. *American Psychologist, 32,* 513–531.

Dawis, R.V., Lofquist. L. H., & Weiss, D. L. (1968). A theory of work adjustment: A revision. *Minnesota Studies in Vocational Rehabilitation, Vol. 23.*

Division of Clinical Psychology, American Psychological Association. (2010). About clinical psychology. Retrieved from http://www.div12.org/about-clinical-psychology.

Division of Counseling Psychology, American Psychological Association. (2010). About counseling psychologists. Retrieved from http://www.div17.org/students_defining.html.

Gustad, J. W. (1953). The definition of counseling. In R. F. Berdie (Ed.), Roles and relationships in counseling. *Minnesota Studies in Student Personnel Work, No. 3.*

Holland, J. L. (1959). A theory of vocational choice. *Journal of Counseling Psychology, 6,* 35–45.

Louttit, C. M. (1939). The nature of clinical psychology. *Psychological Bulletin, 36,* 361–389.

Parsons, F. (1909). *Choosing a vocation.* Boston: Houghton Mifflin.

Rogers, C. R. (1940). The processes of therapy. *Journal of Consulting Psychology, 4,* 161–164.

Tyler, L. E. (1953). *The work of the counselor.* New York: Appleton-Century-Crofts.

Tyler, L. E. (1969). *The work of the counselor* (3rd ed) Englewood Cliffs, NJ: Prentice-Hall.

Foundations

PART 2

Foundations

Professional Issues

Judy E. Hall

Abstract

After addressing the attributes of a profession, this chapter discusses the requirements for accountability due to the profession's contract with society. The mechanisms of accountability for the profession of psychology—education, training, licensure, and credentialing—are reviewed in the context of counseling psychology. Information on the transition from an input model of education and training to an outcome-driven model is presented. Current challenges in quality assurance are outlined, including distance education, the movement toward competency assessment, and international mobility.

Keywords: accreditation, designation, licensure, credentialing, competency, mobility, distance education, internship, practicum, postdoctoral

In this chapter, the attributes of a profession, its requirements for accountability, and its contract with society are addressed. We focus on the accountability mechanisms and their relationship to professional practice, and as applicable, to counseling psychology. Of great consequence to prospective psychologists are the decisions they make with regard to education, training, licensing, and credentialing; and those are described. Organizations' roles in the development of the profession and today's pressing issues related to distance education, competence, and international mobility are also reviewed.

Professional attributes involve complex activities supported by the efforts of individuals, organizations, and legislative bodies, all of which are committed to ensuring quality assurance for the public. Space does not allow a comprehensive treatment of all the forces, and the reader is encouraged to examine these developments separately.

Definition of a Profession

Psychology is a *profession*. There are many definitions of a profession, but most share four components (Pellegrino, 1991).

First, a profession is based on a systematic body of knowledge, mastered through a broadly defined educational and training process. Second, a profession regulates its own practitioners through a code of ethics and a means of enforcing that code. Third, a profession is characterized by an expectation of all of its members to serve the profession itself, through teaching and mentoring junior members and through other activities that have as their goal the advancement of the profession and the improvement of its contributions to human welfare. Fourth, a profession is held accountable by its implicit contract with the public. The profession agrees to use its special skills and knowledge to promote human and societal welfare. In return for

this promise, the public gives the profession some degree of control over the education and certification of its members.
(Altmaier & Hall, 2008, p. 3)

Thus, as a profession, psychology has certain obligations predicated on its implicit social contract with the public. These obligations often lead to professional issues, and thus are described in the following section.

Professions have what has been called a "special relationship" with society, the essence of which is that professions are given greater autonomy than other social groups. [They] set their own standards, regulate entry into their own ranks, discipline their members, and operate with fewer restraints than the arts, trades, or business. In return, the professions are expected to serve the public good and enforce high standards of conduct and discipline.
(Skrtic, 1991, p. 87)

Thus, a profession is accountable to society in maintaining its status. By carrying out the responsibilities noted, psychology provides assurance to the public that it has purposely considered, developed, and disseminated the methods by which the quality of services is assured. Note that the words *society*, *public*, and *consumer* are used almost interchangeably, so as to be as inclusive as possible. In this chapter, the word *consumer* includes the direct recipient of services by psychologists as well as the prospective student who is a consumer of the education, training, and credentialing processes.

Another example of the importance of terminology is addressed by Ritchie (2008), when he considers the evolution of the *patient* to *client* to *consumer* and the implications of these title changes. He reminds us that the consumer of services has his or her own responsibility to pursue quality by demanding that standards be met through the provision of feedback.

Specialization

Psychology as a profession was initiated with licensure laws, program accreditation, and training conferences. The Boulder Model, named for the location of the conference (Boulder, Colorado, 1949), shaped professional training by establishing the doctorate as the minimum educational requirement for entry into professional practice and the scientist–practitioner model as the desired training model (Raimy, 1950). With the knowledge that was being generated, specialization (focusing on a smaller subset than that encompassed by all of psychology)

was inevitable. At this time, a large number of practitioners were needed to serve the mental health needs of returning World War II veterans. With expansion of psychology's scientific foundation, practitioners began to specialize and to define their areas of specialization (e.g., vocational guidance) and their specialty (typically based on the title of their doctoral program or training site, such as counseling). Even today, after being prepared with broad and general knowledge, skills, and abilities, students often begin to specialize while in their education and training sequence by focusing on populations, theoretical techniques, interventions or locations of practice (e.g., clinics, counseling centers, schools). After licensure, professionals specialize further in the services they provide in order to compete in the marketplace.

Given the historical confusion and lack of agreement on what constitutes specialization, organized psychology asked itself the question, "What is a specialty?" Even though earlier attempts had been made to wrestle with this problem, none was successful. Thus, the American Psychological Association (APA) decided, in 1979, that a consistent set of policies and procedures needed to be developed to identify specialties. This was initiated by the Task Force on Specialty Criteria (TFSC; APA, 1979), with the Subcommittee on Specialization (SOS; Sales, Bricklin, & Hall, 1983, 1984a, b) completing the extensive development of criteria and sample procedures. This effort involved articulating what psychology needed to do that was also developmentally consistent with the history of specialty recognition in medicine, dentistry, and nursing. The basic similarity of psychology and the other three professions is the assumption of a common core of generalist skills and knowledge. Building upon this perspective, the SOS principles and procedures directly impacted on organized psychology's subsequent efforts to define a specialty; this included identifying the parameters of practice, delineating the criteria for recognition/continuation of a specialty and proficiency, and separating the initial recognition principles from the continued recognition principles.

The APA committees/task forces (APA Task Force on Scope and Criteria for Accreditation, Joint Council on Professional Education in Psychology) incorporated these criteria and concepts into their policy documents. Outside of APA, the American Board of Professional Psychology (ABPP) developed its own recognition procedures for new specialties using the SOS principles and procedures

(Bent, Packard, & Goldberg, 1999). In Canada, a task force appointed by the Canadian Psychological Association (CPA) and the Council of Provincial Associations of Psychology (CPAP) built on the work of SOS in its specialty deliberations (Service et al., 1989). In 1993, the APA established the Joint Interim Committee on Recognition of Specialties and Proficiencies in Psychology, which drew representation from outside APA. Its successor, the Commission on Recognition of Specialties and Proficiencies in Professional Psychology (CRSPPP), proposed a set of specialty principles and procedures that were approved by APA as policy (American Psychological Association [APA], 1995). That body continues to review and recommend for approval specialty and proficiency areas in professional psychology. (For current information, see http://www.apa.org/crsppp/rsp.html.)

The APA established the first accreditation process for clinical psychology programs in 1948 (Goodstein & Ross, 1966). To justify its position as a specialty, clinical psychology had both program accreditation standards and the recognition of clinical psychology practitioners by the American Board of Examiners in Professional Psychology (ABEPP). Counseling psychology was only shortly behind in its development as a specialty. The ABEPP awarded its first diploma in Counseling and Guidance in 1947. The first training conference, held at Northwestern University, produced counselor education and training standards (APA Committee on Counselor Training, 1952). The APA accredited its first counseling program in 1950 (Goodstein & Ross, 1966). Much of this programmatic development was stimulated by veterans returning from World War II who needed vocational guidance. Since the numbers returning would strain the usual resources of college counseling centers, federal subsidies for training were made available to these counseling centers, thus providing impetus for the development of counselor training programs. (The distinction between the labels *counseling* and *counseling psychology* was not an issue at that time.) The Department of Medicine and Surgery of the Veterans Administration (VA) instituted a vocational counseling program in its hospitals, so that, by 1958, the VA employed 130 doctoral-level counseling psychologists (Hall & Sales, 2002).

During this period of growth and definition, a committee report from APA Division 17 encouraged members to think of counseling psychology, although still evolving, as a specialty within applied psychology that could be differentiated from clinical psychology (APA Committee on Definition, 1956). In 1961, the Greystone Conference, the second training conference on the preparation of counseling psychologists, was held (Thompson & Super, 1964). Two possible directions for counseling psychology were proposed: one as a sub-specialty of the clinical area, and the other as distinct from clinical and other areas of psychology. The two recommendations were prescient in that counseling psychology, more so than any other area of psychology, is still consummately introspective, comparing itself to its origins in counselor education and vocational guidance (Thompson & Super, 1964) and its practice to clinical psychology (Watkins, 1984).

Indeed, the debate about counseling psychology differing from clinical psychology remains an issue today for some individuals, especially as crossover in practice occurs after graduation and distinction across programs is eroded. But, despite this continued dialogue about counseling psychology's definition within professional psychology, APA's accreditation of counseling programs and board certification by American Board of Professional Psychology (ABPP, formerly ABEPP) justifies its position as a recognized specialty. Counseling psychology, because of its having met many of the characteristics of a recognized specialty, was initially recognized by the APA as a doctoral-level specialty, first through a de facto process and later through a formal de jure process. (See http://www.apa.org/crsppp/counseling.html for its current definition.) For more detail on the history of counseling psychology, see Gelso and Fretz (2001).

Quality Assurance and Accountability of Programs and Individuals

Belonging to a profession includes assuming the responsibility to regulate that profession, both individually and as a group. The various groups in self-regulation of education, training, and credentialing include professional associations that accredit programs (APA/CPA); licensing and credentialing bodies that designate doctoral programs (Association of State and Provincial Psychology Boards [ASPPB] and the National Register of Health Service Providers in Psychology [National Register]); and organizations that designate or approve for listing/membership internship and postdoctoral training programs, such as the Association of Psychology Postdoctoral and Internship Centers (APPIC), Canadian Council of Professional Psychology

Table 2.1. Credentialing Organizations and Their Roles

Competence Level & Scope	Program Evaluation (Designation/Accreditation)	Individual Evaluation (Credentialing)
Basic & Minimal	Criteria-based designation of doctoral programs that produce professional psychologists: *ASPPB/National Register*	Certification of individual's degree/ training in professional psychology: *Universities/Professional Schools*
Basic & Extensive	Criteria-based accreditation of doctoral programs and internships that produce professional psychologists: *Commission on Accreditation (CoA); Canadian Psychological Association Committee on Accreditation* Criteria-based review of internships: *Association of Psychology Post-Doctoral & Internship Centers (APPIC); Canadian Council of Professional Psychology Programs; School Psychology APA Div 16, Council of Directors of Programs in School Psychology and National Association of School Psychologists; National Register of Health Service Providers in Psychology*	License to practice as a professional psychologist: *Regulatory bodies in States, Provinces & Territories in United States & Canada* Credentialing as a health service provider in psychology: *National and Canadian Register of Health Service Providers in Psychology; State Recognition of Health Service Provider*
Traditional Substantive & Specialized	Criteria-based accreditation of postdoctoral programs in professional psychology in traditional substantive & specialized areas: *CoA; Criteria-based Membership of Post Doctoral Training Programs: APPIC*	Board certification through examination of advanced skill in specialty areas: *American Board of Professional Psychology, American Board of Professional Neuropsychology, etc.* Certification bodies for proficiencies: *APA Practice Organization, College of Professional Psychology*

Training Programs (CCPPP), and a joint working group of organizations that review school psychology internships (APA Division 16, National Association of School Psychologists and Council of Directors of School Psychology Programs [CDSPP]) (Go to http://www.ed.psu.edu/educ/espse/school-psychology/internship-directory for a current list.) These organizations and their roles are included in Table 2.1, which is updated from Drum and Hall (1993). Not mentioned are the state or provincial mechanisms that approve doctoral programs for their own jurisdictional purposes, such as in New York State (New York State Doctoral Evaluation Project, 1990).

The accreditation/designation of educational programs, accreditation or approval of internships and postdoctoral residencies, and review of individual psychologists for licensing and credentialing involve multiple national bodies. The first element of regulation relates to the establishment of education and training standards for programs that voluntarily apply for professional recognition. Sometimes, there is a choice for the student. For instance, the developing professional psychologist chooses whether to apply for admission to an accredited or a designated program and to an accredited or designated internship (and if so, approved by whom). At present, 900 doctoral programs, internships, and postdoctoral programs are accredited by the APA Committee on Accreditation (CoA, now Commission on Accreditation) and 36 programs are designated by the ASPPB/National Register as doctoral programs in psychology, but are not APA accredited. The APPIC's membership includes 700 internship program and 126 postdoctoral training programs, including those that are accredited by CoA. The CCPPP has 38 Canadian internship programs as members. These decision points are illustrated in Figure 2.1 and discussed in greater detail in the following sections.

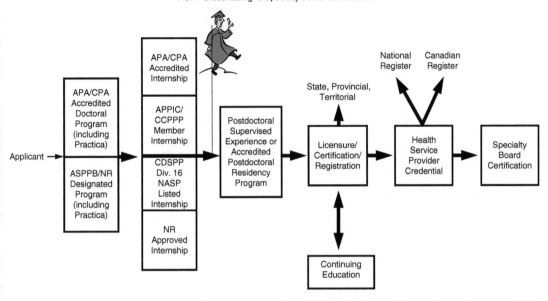

Typical Doctoral Sequence in US & Canada
From Entry into Graduate School to Graduation, Licensure,
HSPP Credentialing & Specialty Board Certification

Fig. 2.1 Typical doctoral sequence in the United States and Canada from entry into graduate school to graduation, licensure, Health Service Provider in Psychology (HSPP) credentialing, and specialty board certification.

Education, Training, Licensure, and Credentialing

The first step in the education and training sequence involves choosing a doctoral program. The potential student asks several questions: What are the approved programs? How can I tell that the program is approved? Will completing that program ensure that I meet the educational requirements for licensure as a psychologist? To answer these questions, the concepts of accreditation (institution and program) and designation (program) are presented.

Accreditation in the United States can be characterized as nongovernmental, voluntary, and self-regulatory. Doctoral education programs in psychology are housed in academic institutions and professional schools. Accreditation assesses these institutions and programs to determine their quality and to provide for continuous improvement. Typically, the term applied to this process is *accreditation*. We also use the term *designation* to apply to the approval of programs. Thus, in the United States, there are accredited institutions, accredited programs, and designated programs. Similarly, there are institutions and programs that are not approved.

Resources for identifying accredited institutions and programs are provided online by the United States Department of Education (USDOE).

Even though the USDOE does not accredit educational institutions and/or programs, it does publish a list of nationally recognized accrediting agencies that are considered reliable authorities as to the quality of education or training provided by the institutions of higher education and the higher education programs they accredit. (The list can be found online at http://www.ed.gov/admins/finaid/accred/accreditation.html#Overview.)

APPROVAL OF INSTITUTIONS AND PROGRAMS

There are two types of accrediting agencies: specialized and institutional. *Institutional accreditation* refers to accreditation of the entire academic institution by one of the regional accrediting authorities recognized by USDOE. These regional accrediting bodies are identified by licensing boards and credentialing organizations as necessary but not sufficient assurers of quality. Laws and regulations for licensing typically refer to the program having to be housed in an institution that is approved by one of the regional accrediting bodies.

Thus, in choosing a program, the student should first verify that the institution is regionally accredited by one of the following bodies. Such institutions are listed online under the regional association that is responsible for that geographic region of the United States.

- Middle States Association of Colleges and Schools, http://www.msache.org
- New England Association of Schools and Colleges, http://www.neasc.org
- North Central Association of Colleges and Schools, http://www.ncahigherlearningcommission.org
- Northwest Commission on Colleges and Universities, http://www.nwccu.org
- Western Association of Schools and Colleges, http://www.wascweb.org
- Southern Association of Colleges and Schools, http://www.sacscoc.org.

After verifying that the institution is regionally accredited, the potential applicant should then determine if the desired program (e.g., clinical, counseling) is approved. Four categories describe doctoral programs in psychology.

Accredited Programs

The first category includes regionally accredited institutions with programs that are *accredited* by the CoA. The CoA accredits doctoral training programs in the specialty areas of clinical, counseling, and school psychology; in other developed practice areas; and a combination of two or three of those specialty areas. (A program may not apply for accreditation in a developed practice area until that area has been added to the scope of accreditation. For more information about CoA accreditation and its purpose and process, see http://www.apa.org/ed/accreditation/accrfaq.html.)

Although regional accreditation is not the term used in Canada, all universities offering doctoral training must be similarly reviewed and approved. The CPA accredits doctoral training programs in the specialty areas of clinical, clinical neuropsychology, school, and counseling psychology. For more information about CPA accreditation and its purposes and process, see http://www.cpa.ca/education/accreditation. Graduates from APA and CPA accredited programs typically meet the educational requirements for licensure and for credentialing in psychology in the United States and Canada.

Designated Programs

The second category includes regionally accredited institutions with programs that are *designated* as psychology programs by the ASPPB/National Register. The ASPPB/National Register Designation Committee reviews doctoral programs in psychology from any specialty area to determine if they meet the "Guidelines for Defining a Doctoral Program in Psychology," typically known as the *designation criteria* (http://www.nationalregister.org/designate.htm). Note that Criterion 1 specifies that programs that are APA/CPA accredited by definition automatically meet the designation criteria. Programs that are not accredited must meet the remaining nine criteria. Graduates from ASPPB/National Register designated programs typically meet the educational requirements for licensing and credentialing in psychology.

Unapproved Programs

The third category addresses regionally accredited institutions with programs that are neither accredited nor designated. Graduates of these programs may not qualify for licensure. In a few states, the applicants may be admitted to the licensing examination on the basis of the institution's regional accreditation. However, these graduates will not qualify for credentialing by the National Register or ABPP. This category may include programs that are so new that they have yet to apply for recognition or ones that have applied and not met the criteria.

Unaccredited Schools

The fourth category is institutions that are not regionally accredited, with a program that is neither APA/CPA accredited nor ASPPB/National Register designated. Graduates from these programs will not qualify for licensure or credentialing (except that graduates of California programs established prior to a change in California statute may be eligible for admission to the California licensure examination, http://www.psychboard.ca.gov/exams/unaccredited.shtml).

The desired outcome for graduates of doctoral education and training programs is preparation for and admission to professional practice. The current APA *Guidelines and Principles for Accreditation of Programs in Professional Psychology* (G&PAPA, 2009) emphasize quality by measuring program goals and outcomes, focusing on competencies rather than curriculum, and stressing self-study rather than external reviews. This shift in emphasis to outcomes was reflected first in the 1996 G&P (APA, 1996).

> That is, while it continued to be appropriate to assess the quality of an institution or program in terms of the appropriateness of its education resources (e.g., faculty, students, facilities, financial support) and processes (e.g., curriculum, methods

of pedagogy, faculty–student relationships) in the context of its mission or goals, it is the final outcomes of an institution or program (e.g., attrition or graduation, demonstrated student learning, faculty productivity) that many argue are ultimately the most accurate measures in assessing quality.

(Nelson, Belar, Grus, & Zlotlow, 2008, p. 19)

However, lack of consistency among the many programs' outcomes and the methods by which they are assessed raises concern for licensing and credentialing bodies and others within the profession of psychology. To counter this concern, advocates of the revised standards point out that—in keeping with the principle that such programs be broad and general—there should be professional competence domains in which all students are prepared. These domains represent the knowledge, skill, and professional function bases of professional practice (e.g., scientific foundations, ethics, and assessment, intervention, and consultation).

A requirement to report student achievement in terms of time to completion, tuition and fees, internship acceptance, attrition, licensure outcomes, and job placement rates became effective January 1, 2007. (See Implementing Regulation C-20 at http://www.apa.org/ed/accreditation/implementregs200524.pdf.) Programs post outcomes on their websites and include this information in other material made available to prospective students. For instance, of great interest is the performance by graduates of doctoral programs on the Examination for Professional Practice in Psychology (known as the EPPP) which is required for licensure in the US and Canada. That information is now posted on the ASPPB web site (go to http://www.ASPPB.org). Mayne, Norcross, and Sayette (2006) also provide program-reported measures to help prospective students evaluate programs in advance of application.

DESIGNATION PROJECT

Licensure laws typically incorporate two paths to meeting educational requirements: accreditation or designation of programs. Designation was created in the late 1970s because of a concern about consistency in the educational curricula in accredited programs and the fact that not all students applying for licensure came from accredited programs. Recognizing that psychology was behind other professions in defining the core curriculum needed to meet the educational requirements for licensure, two national conferences on education and training in psychology convened by the APA and the National Register brought together representatives of organized psychology to establish guidelines for the identification of doctoral programs in psychology for credentialing purposes (Wellner, 1978). This effort intended to present a unified front to state legislatures and to courts as to the educational requirements of a psychologist.

The Guidelines for Defining a Doctoral Program in Psychology were adopted as the educational standard for the National Register and the ASPPB in 1978, were used by the National Register in its development of the Designation Project in 1980 (ASPPB became a partner in that project in 1986), and as a result, had a major impact on licensing and credentialing standards for doctoral programs. They were eventually included in the APA's 1979 accreditation standards (Nelson & Messenger, 2003). For instance, one criterion relates directly to counseling psychology programs: "The program, wherever it may be administratively housed, must be clearly identified as a psychology program. Such a program must specify in pertinent institutional catalogs and brochures its intent to educate and train professional psychologists" (Wellner, 1978). Gelso and Fretz (2001) note that, "the more than 100% increase in the number of APA-accredited programs in counseling psychology from the early 1970s to the late 1980s was directly related to this change. The majority of the newly approved programs were formerly counselor education or counseling and guidance programs in colleges of education" (p. 119).

Although program designation is different from accreditation, both refer to a certification process for programs and training facilities. Designation is the process of reviewing programs, using publically available documentation, to determine if they meet established and public criteria. There is no site visit by peers, such as employed by the CoA. Another distinction is that doctoral programs in any area of psychology may apply for designation (e.g., industrial-organizational psychology), as the focus is on whether the degree program meets the general criteria. Once approved, the program is added to the online list of designated programs and re-reviewed by the ASPPB/National Register Designation Committee at least every 3 years. Although this imprimatur provides assurance to the program applicant, students who are considering enrollment in a doctoral program and intending to practice psychology should still contact the licensing board in the jurisdiction in which they intend to seek licensure to determine any unique education and training requirements. However, typically, the licensing board rules require that the doctoral program be APA/CPA accredited or ASPPB/National Register designated. (All these programs are listed at http://www.nationalregister.org/designate_stsearch.html.)

Practicum

The Association of Psychology Training Clinics (APTC) is the APA-affiliated organization of directors of psychology training clinics. These 115 training clinics offer pre-internship training to clinical, counseling, and school psychology doctoral students. Typically, these clinics are department- or university-based facilities that provide behavioral/mental health services to the community. Other types of training provided in doctoral programs are the practicum that accompany specific courses (e.g., assessment, intervention) Usually, 2 or 3 years of practicum experiences are made available to students by the program. Coming early in graduate school, these are essential training experiences that provide a foundation for professional practice.

The doctoral student needs to have sufficient experiential training to be competitive when applying for internship; this need has led to an increase in the number of practicum hours over the years, with current applicants for internship documenting 1,800–2,000 hours (Association of Psychology Postdoctoral and Internship Centers [APPIC], 2008). The current APA G&P state the following: the applicant must "have completed adequate and appropriate supervised practicum training, which must include face-to-face delivery of professional psychological services." As this criterion no longer specifies a minimum number of hours needed for admission to the internship, students often ask how much is enough. The numbers vary, depending upon the source: academic director versus training director. The percent of time spent in direct service adds another variable when interpreting practicum hours and may place students in a quandary as to what makes them more competitive for internship placement. However, adding on hours is not the solution. In fact, experience is only one of the three factors that help a student secure an acceptable internship (letters of recommendation and the internship application are the other two). Nonetheless, practicum remains a basic requirement that can be fulfilled in a number of ways. With the potential changes at the state level in education and training requirements leading to licensure, it is hoped

that the practicum can be "defined, delineated, and formalized" (Rodolfa, Owen, & Clark, 2007).

Internship

The first internship program in professional psychology was accredited in 1956. Even then, the number of students seeking formal internships was higher than the number of positions available. As a result, students often developed their own training experience "on the job," leading to considerable variability in training. To address this lack of standardization, in 1980, the National Register Appeal Board developed specific internship criteria, which were adapted by the APPIC, APA, and the Council of Doctoral School Psychology Programs (CDSPP) to meet their own needs. (See www.nationalregister.org_internship.pdf for the current National Register criteria.) The major difference between the criterion sets relates to the placement of the internship in the education and training sequence.

Today's internships are intended to provide broad and general education and training and are not classified with a specialty title, such as clinical or counseling psychology. The APPIC, an organization composed of internship and postdoctoral training sites that apply for membership, offers a searchable database containing internships in the United States and Canada. The database indicates if the internship is accredited by APA or CPA, and offers other information, such as the specialization training areas offered (populations, treatment modalities, and specialty areas, such as neuropsychological assessment and intervention, primary care, substance abuse, and geropsychology). APPIC members can indicate the preference given applicants by specialty area of degree. For instance, of the 700 internships listed online as of April 14, 2011, 634 would consider counseling psychologists for internship placement. The current standard for the length of training (e.g., APA, APPIC, National Register) is that the internship must consist of 1 year of full-time training completed in no less than 12 months (for school psychology internships, 10 months) and in no more than 24 months.

The APPIC developed the uniform application for internships (this application went online in 2009) and then, in 1999, initiated the matching process for internship placement, followed in 2011 by a second match for those positions not filled in the initial match. Yearly match statistics are provided to the relevant constituencies, with the most recent results showing 79% of students matched in 2011 (without reference to degree, specialty area of degree, or location of doctoral program) out of a total of 3,899 students. There were 3166 available positions in 2011. Even though new internship positions are created each year, insufficient internship training positions are available to meet the need. Thus, students are experiencing difficulty in obtaining an internship. For several years now, a portion of students have not matched to an internship on the first attempt, now they either move to the second APPIC match or to the Association of Counseling Center Training Agencies (ACCTA) clearinghouse for placement (internship sites that have available positions after the match date). The ACCTA is an organization composed of 150 internships located in college and university counseling centers, the largest single category for internships. (See https://www.accta.net/default.asp for more information.)

For counseling psychology students, a comparable decline in matching rates from 90% (1995–2005) to 78% (2007) was reported on a survey of the members of the Council of Counseling Psychology Programs (CCPTP). Using predictions from training directors on which students would not have matched, Miville, Adams, and Juntunen (2007) believe that a 90% placement rate is achievable for APA-accredited counseling psychology programs. Counseling psychology programs typically admit seven or eight students a year and account for only 10% of the internship applications submitted yearly.

Although many argue that the best resolution to the supply-and-demand problem is admitting fewer students, a program failing to place a reasonable number of students in internships on a consistent basis might constitute "an operational definition of taking too many students" (Stricker, 2008, p. 207). With increasing attention paid to outcomes, doctoral programs are taking more responsibility in helping students locate an internship or are creating captive internships designed for their students. Nonetheless, students must be careful about developing their own experiences, as internships developed outside the scrutiny of an objective, criterion-based organization may not be acceptable for licensing or credentialing. (For a more detailed consideration of the many questions in applying for the internship, interested readers should consult the handbook developed by Williams-Nickelson, Prinstein, and Keilin, 2008).

Postdoctoral Year

The second year of supervised experience typically required for licensure and credentialing is a year of postdoctoral experience. Licensing boards and credentialing organizations have developed their own approval criteria with little commonality other than length. Of concern is whether the experience is supervised by qualified licensed psychologists (for instance, those not qualified would be psychologists in a dual relationship, master's degree psychologists, and psychologists with degrees from unaccredited/unapproved program). With increasing difficulty in achieving an experience that is acceptable from one jurisdiction to another, standardization of the postdoctoral experience requirement was needed.

Concern about postdoctoral experience led to the second conference on postdoctoral training, in 1992, the National Conference on Postdoctoral Fellowship Training in Applied Psychology. This APPIC-sponsored conference, supported by multiple organizations, resulted in draft standards that became the instigating force for organized psychology to work together in solving the quality assurance aspects of the postdoctoral year (Belar, Bieliauskas, Klepac, Stigall, & Zimet, 1993). The first step was the formation of the Inter-Organizational Council for Accreditation of Postdoctoral Programs in Psychology (IOC), consisting of representatives from United States and Canadian organizations concerned with accreditation, credentialing, and licensing, along with the training council representative from each specialty. The purpose was to develop consensual standards and procedures for a postdoctoral accreditation process. Five years later, the APA adopted as policy the postdoctoral accreditation standards (APA, 1996), and it accredited the first two postdoctoral residency training programs in 1997.

Today, postdoctoral residencies may be accredited as programs preparing individuals for practice at an advanced level in the *traditional* practice areas of clinical, counseling, or school psychology (there are currently 30). Other types of postdoctoral residencies may be accredited in *specialty* practice areas (currently 30). Specialty areas that have met the guidelines to be included within the scope of accreditation are clinical child psychology, clinical health psychology, clinical neuropsychology, family psychology, forensic psychology, and rehabilitation psychology.

Finding postdoctoral sites for employment or residency training is also a challenge for graduates. Although electronic mailing lists disseminate information on available positions, there is no matching service such as is provided for internships (APPIC, 2008). The APPIC lists in their online directory 126 postdoctoral programs, 60 of those are APA-accredited residency programs. However, the number of psychologists potentially trained in a year is even smaller than that in internship training, as the number of training positions at each site is usually two. A year (or more) of postdoctoral experience is required by the majority of state licensing bodies, so graduates face a difficult time locating an acceptable, adequately funded postdoctoral experience.

Licensure requirements for the postdoctoral year of experience also vary, so the graduate is advised to determine the specific geographic regulations in advance of signing an employment contract. Then, the specific responsibilities of the site can be included in the negotiations so as to qualify the experience for licensure purposes. Many settings will accommodate a professional's need to acquire experience for licensure purposes, in the hopes of retaining the psychologist after licensure, as this more likely will ensure continuity in service provision to the client population. This is especially true of geographic, demographic, or institutional locations that are classified as underserved (health professional shortage area [HPSA]; see http://hpsafind.hrsa.gov). In general, however, both formal postdoctoral residency training programs and less organized experience, such as supervised employment, meet licensure standards and credentialing requirements for a health service provider in psychology.

Building upon the IOC's success in bringing together a postdoctoral accreditation system for professional psychology, the training councils in professional psychology adopted a similar model when they formed the Council of Chairs of Training Councils (CCTC), consisting of training councils as members and liaisons from licensing and credentialing bodies. The credentialing organizations in professional psychology did the same when they created the Council of Credentialing Organizations in Professional Psychology (CCOPP). The CCOPP's membership consists of the credentialing organizations (including licensure) in the United States, Canada, and now Mexico, with liaisons from the education and training community and graduate students. These organizations were initiated in the 1990s. Like the CoA, which is also interorganizational, the member organizations select the representatives for these important and sometimes policy-recommending bodies. With the many organizations in professional psychology concerned with quality assurance and accountability, and in an era of diminishing resources, interorganizational working groups make the most sense in terms of ensuring essential and relevant representation.

Global universities represent a growth industry, so major universities based in the United States are quickly establishing undergraduate and graduate programs abroad. As a matter of policy, neither the APA nor the CPA accredits programs located outside their own country. However, the ASPPB/National Register Designation Project modified the designation criteria several years ago to permit foreign program review. These programs will be held to the same criteria as programs in the United States and Canada; however, the institution where the program is located must be "accredited by a body that is deemed by ASPPB/National Register Designation Committee to be performing a function equivalent to U.S. regional accrediting bodies." It is likely that approved psychology programs in the United States may decide to offer doctoral education in psychology in foreign countries and will want those programs approved in the United States. If those programs apply for and meet the designation criteria, the key issue will be whether the state and provincial regulatory bodies will find the graduates acceptable on educational grounds.

Licensing and Credentialing

Licensing authorities determine that a psychologist meets state, provincial, or territorial requirements for entry-level, generic practice. Professional licensing has very little to do with the assurance of quality. Although most people assume it does, or wish it did, knowing that a provider is licensed assures one only that the state, province, or territory has determined him or her to possess a *minimum* level of competence. This level of competence is defined as having completed a sequence of education, training, and experience, followed by successful performance on an independent examination of knowledge and skills.

Credentialing and *certification* are terms that are often used interchangeably and usually refer to individual achievement. For instance, the university or professional school certifies to the public that the graduate has met the requirements for the degree by awarding the diploma. Certification typically indicates quality, "especially in the absence of knowledge to the contrary" (Drum & Hall, 1993, p. 151). Credentials for health care professionals are important because "in no other field does a consumer care so much about the quality of services and yet have so little ability to judge quality themselves. . . . Credentials serve as necessary proxies for direct measurement of quality" (Stromberg, 1991, p. 1). Even though credentials signal distinction for a professional, both in terms of services offered as well as in education, training, licensure, and advanced competency, compared to physicians, only a small percentage of psychologists pursue credentials beyond licensure. Credentialing organizations then assess varying levels of specialized education and training, as well as specific competencies or areas of expertise, to determine if the licensee has met national standards, which are often more stringent than licensure requirements.

Credentialing organizations have no requirement to protect the public, yet they play a significant role in this special relationship with consumers. Typically, credentialing organizations conduct primary source verification of credentials (education, training, and licensure). Thus, they provide an independent check on the accuracy and currency of these qualifications. Licensing authorities investigate and adjudicate professional misconduct complaints, and then report the information to professional organizations and credentialing bodies and the federal disciplinary health care databanks. Credentialing bodies may review and take action on disciplinary information and disseminate their actions to the public. Credentialing organizations require psychologists to report disciplinary actions as part of an annual attestation. This process holds the psychologists accountable for professional misconduct. Noting this symbiotic relationship between licensure and credentialing in terms of protecting consumers, Hall (2000) stated that "neither licensing nor certification alone is sufficient . . . [Rather,] both are needed" (pp. 317–318).

Licensure Laws

Licensing laws, established to define the practice of the profession, set educational, training, and examination standards for the profession and assist the consumer in identifying who is qualified to practice the profession. Although this is different from saying that the license assesses quality, the jurisdiction does offer a recourse for complaints against practitioners regarding professional conduct. Presently, 64 jurisdictions in the United States and Canada regulate the practice of psychology or the title of psychologist. Both types of laws attempt to protect the public by clearly identifying who is qualified to practice as a psychologist (practice including title act) or identify him- or herself as a psychologist (title only act).

Stromberg et al. (1988) explained the difference:

Licensure is a process by which individuals are granted permission to perform a defined set of functions. If a professional performs those functions (such as diagnosing or treating behavioral, emotional, or mental disorders) regardless under what name (such as therapist, psychologist, or counselor), he is required to be licensed. In contrast, certification focuses not on the function performed but on the use of a particular professional title (such as psychologist), and it limits its use to individuals who have met specified standards for education, experience and examination performance. (pp. 1–2)

Not all jurisdictions have licensure laws. Many have certification laws, including those labeled as *permissive acts*, requiring the person to be licensed if he or she practices psychology and uses the title. In this volume, the term *license* refers to either type of regulation.

General Licensing Criteria

At present, the various admission requirements for licensure as a psychologist in the United States are similar: a doctoral degree in psychology from an approved program housed in a regionally accreditation institution of higher learning, and 2 years of properly supervised experience, 1 of which may be an internship and the other a year of postdoctoral experience. These requirements are evaluated by each jurisdiction somewhat differently in terms of implementing criteria (e.g., supervisor's qualifications, number of hours on internship), so it is advisable to complete an APA/CPA-accredited or ASPPB/National Register-designated doctoral program; to complete an APA/CPA-accredited internship, if possible; and if not, to seek an internship with an organization that is a member of the APPIC or is developed so that it meets the APPIC, CDSPP, or National Register criteria for internship. In general, it is advisable for any student to acquire the maximum number of hours on internship and in the postdoctoral year (2,000 hours) and to ascertain in advance what is required by the state of intended residency (Hall, Wexelbaum, & Boucher, 2007).

Generic Licensing

Following the tradition of other health care professions, such as medicine, generic licensing has been the model adopted by legislative bodies in seeking to regulate the practice of psychology (Stigall, 1983). This approach assumes that a common body of knowledge, skills, and ability should be mastered prior to entry into the profession, regardless of any specialty area. Using the word *generic* in reference to the license to practice also stems from the fact that any psychologist is eligible to apply for licensure. It does not mean that a licensed psychologist is qualified to practice in any area, as ethics and professional conduct rules restrict practice to within specific areas of expertise. Continuing professional education (CPE) is required by most jurisdictions as a way of ensuring that psychologists remain current with scientific knowledge and applied skills. Criticized by many professionals as unrelated to continuing competence, CPE has face validity from the public perspective and can be a valuable tool for the expansion of practice areas after graduation.

Most graduates of professional psychology programs become licensed as psychologists. The current number of licensed psychologists at the doctoral level is approximately 92,000 (Andrew Boucher, personal communication, July 11, 2008); the exact number is unknown because some psychologists hold more than one license, and some states do not list a degree or differentiate between a master's-level and a doctoral-level psychologist. Licensing criteria are set by each jurisdiction, but have been influenced over time by a series of APA guidelines for state legislation (1955, 1967, 1987 and 2010) and by the ASPPB model for state legislation (1992, 2001 and 2010).

Health Service Provider in Psychology

The National Register was established in 1974 to meet the need for a system by which various insurers, governmental agencies, health services, and other organizations, as well as individual consumers, could identify licensed psychologists who have specific education, training, and supervised experience in health services. Given that licensure was generic, a mechanism was needed that went beyond licensure to identify qualified providers of psychological services, especially given the wide variation in states' requirements. Although licensing was *necessary*, it alone was not sufficient to identify a qualified health care provider.

Both the ABPP and the APA played a role in the establishment of a credential that did provide the *sufficient* information. The APA Board of Professional Affairs formally voted on October 1, 1973, to recommend that the APA request the ABPP to establish a National Register of Health Service Providers in Psychology; on March 1, 1974, the ABPP Board of Trustees voted to implement the project. On June 1, 1974, the initial meeting of the 12-member Council for the National Register of Health Service Providers in Psychology was held, the *Health Service Provider in Psychology* was defined, and the criteria for credentialing were established.

A *Health Service Provider in Psychology* is defined as:

[A] psychologist currently and actively licensed/certified/registered at the independent level in a jurisdiction, who is trained and experienced in the delivery of direct, preventive, assessment and therapeutic intervention services to individuals whose growth, adjustment, or functioning is impaired or to individuals who otherwise seek services.
(National Register of Health Service Providers in Psychology, 2011)

On September 1, 1974, a joint letter from APA President Bandura and National Register Chairman Zimet was sent to 40,000 psychologists soliciting applications for credentialing by the National Register. More than 11,000 licensed psychologists applied and met the criteria during the grandparent period, which ended January 1, 1978.

Note that this more inclusive definition of psychological practice did not refer to a specialty title. However, credentialing by the National Register provided more protection to the consumer seeking psychological services than did a generic license. After the National Register's success, several state licensure boards decided to adopt the criteria for their own provider certification, first in 1978 in Texas, and soon after in eight more states (Indiana, Iowa, Kentucky, Oklahoma, Missouri, Massachusetts, North Carolina, and Tennessee). The National Register also formed the basis for the later development of the Canadian Register in 1985. Today, approximately 11,000 psychologists are credentialed by the National Register as health service providers in psychology, with 1800 credentialed by the Canadian Register (see Wise, Hall, Ritchie & Turner, 2006, for a discussion of both registers).

Clinical Versus Professional Psychologist

The necessity to be inclusive within the area of health care is highlighted by the original federal legislation for Medicare reimbursement. Rather than choosing the term *professional psychologist*, which would have avoided many of the definitional problems that ensued, *clinical psychologist* was selected and predictably defined as someone who graduated from a clinical psychology program. (The intended reference was to psychologists providing health care.) Although this narrower legal definition would have applied to the majority of graduates of professional psychology programs, it would have eliminated many qualified health service psychologists from providing needed services to Medicare patients, such as counseling psychologists. The word *clinical* in other fields is an adjective that distinguishes provision of services from other roles in education and research, such as clinical medicine and clinical social work. This "small c clinical" problem became a major problem in terms of reimbursement for those other qualified psychologists. Many years later, and in response to public comments, the Center for Medicare and Medicaid Services defined clinical psychologists as persons who hold doctoral degrees in psychology and are state licensed at the independent practice level of psychology to furnish diagnostic, assessment, preventive, and therapeutic services (Health Care Financing Administration, 2000).

From the perspective of serving the public's health care needs, psychologists are essential team members in integrated health care. Psychologists serve as behavioral experts, reducing overall medical costs, enabling consumers to adhere to medical regimens, helping physicians make medical decisions on the appropriate medication, and choosing the best behavioral practices for treatment of mental health and addictions. Excellent tools are available to guide the psychologist's choice of the best evidence-based practices (Norcross, Hogan, & Koocher, 2008). In addition, psychologists are essential to the education, training, and practice of physicians and other health care professionals. Although many organized practice settings, such as the United States Department of Veterans Affairs, incorporate an integrated health care model, it is not restricted to institutional practice; it is however, central to the practice of primary care physicians and other group practices seeking to serve patients with a comprehensive approach to health care.

The concept of a health care/health service provider exists throughout health care and is not specific to psychology. However, when the National Register was initiated in 1974, it was a new concept for psychology, partly because of its prior focus on serving the mental health needs of the public. Since then, this definition has been adopted by other professional organizations and state licensing boards. The APA has included health in its mission statement. The broad definition of a health service provider in psychology was developed especially to address psychology's uniqueness as both a profession and a science; this definition does not describe a specialty area, but offers a definition of desired services tied to a doctoral degree in psychology and training (internship and postdoctoral year) in health service. It helped define psychology as essential to the health care system, and in understanding and evaluating the body–mind interrelationship as crucial to

improvement in functioning. Psychologists who complete approved counseling psychology doctoral programs, as well as an internships and postdoctoral experience in health service, are eligible for credentialing as health service providers immediately upon licensure.

Credentialing

In deciding whether to pursue credentialing, it is important to separate credible credentials from those that are not, determine eligibility for credentialing, and evaluate the benefits offered by the credentialing organization. For a full discussion of these issues, see Hall and Boucher (2008). The large number of credentials available to professional psychologists necessitates careful evaluation by the consumer. For example, this author includes a list of 52 different acronyms for specialty and proficiency credentialing organizations in her presentations to doctoral psychology students.

From the public perspective, as Stromberg (1991) noted, "credentialing performs a valuable role by reducing *search costs* for consumers or payers who seek information about the qualifications of a large universe of providers." Credentialing organizations provide a public service by "efficiently disseminating information to the marketplace with respect to the training and expertise of health care providers" (*MacHovec v. Council*, 1985). According to Stromberg (1990), "certification is a process by which government or a private association assesses a person, facility, or program and states publicly that it meets specific standards" (p. 1). These standards are considered to be significant measures. Accreditation and designation are approval mechanisms that refer to the certification of programs, whereas credentialing applies to certification of individuals.

The CCOPP, the organization for credentialing organizations, recently completed a comprehensive sequential analysis of the roles played by the various credentialing organizations in specialization. The conceptual document provides another frame of reference for understanding specialization. (See http://www.nationalregister.org/CCOPP.pdf for more information.)

Once licensed, a psychologist is typically eligible for credentialing as a health service provider in psychology in the United States and Canada, followed by specialty board certification in the United States (few Canadian psychologists seek specialty board certification). Although there are many such certification bodies, only one specifically for counseling psychologists is offered by the ABPP. As of February 17, 2011, there were 166 psychologists with ABPP specialty certification in counseling psychology. Also, of the existent board certification bodies in psychology, only the ABPP is included in a number of state regulations to offer some degree of mobility to its 2948 psychologists (Nancy McDonald, personal communication, February 17, 2011).

The ASPPB offers the certificate of professional qualification (CPQ) to psychologists with five years of licensure experience. As of 3/11/11 the CPQ is held by 2608 licensed psychologists. It was created in 1998 to enhance mobility for licensed psychologists. During its grandparenting period (until 2001), licensed psychologists credentialed by the National Register or ABPP qualified for an expedited review.

Ethical and Professional Conduct
As a doctoral student moves through the sequence, there are repeated opportunities in which issues of being responsible for adhering to scientific and professional ethics arise (e.g., research, practica, internship). Then, as that individual becomes licensed and subsequently credentialed, additional ethical guidelines and professional conduct codes pertain (for instance, annual attestation of any ethical complaints/adjudications). At the time of licensure, the applicant is typically required to be examined about the laws and regulations that apply to practice in that jurisdiction. Licensed professionals are expected to adhere to these ethical and professional conduct codes by virtue of membership in those associations and for renewal of state and national credentials.

The APA (2002) and the CPA (2000) each has its own code of ethics and an ethics committee that educates members and adjudicates complaints. If a professional is licensed in two professions (psychology and counseling), the provisions of both ethics code apply (and may conflict). Ethics and professional conduct is a cornerstone in accountability, and the active monitoring of these responsibilities is itself a responsibility of the profession. Ritchie (2008) addresses this accountability in an excellent chapter while referencing international developments in ethics codes. A comprehensive discussion on this topic is also available in this volume (Vasquez & Bingham, 2011, Chapter 10, this volume).

Challenges to Accountability
Professional educators and practitioners frequently debate the merits of programs housed in distance education or online universities, the current status of the definition and assessment of competencies, and barriers to international mobility. These issues are central to issues of accountability and quality assurance today.

Distance Learning and Online Education
Distance education is a thriving industry, with many companies publicly traded. Investors have seen their stocks increase in value and pay dividends. Historically, higher education was not for profit. That has changed. Other changes relate to the significant and pervasive use of technology in education. According to a survey conducted in 2000–2001, college-level, credit-granting distance education courses are offered at the graduate level by 22% of all institutions. Furthermore, college-level, credit-granting distance education courses are offered at the graduate/first-professional level by 52% of institutions that have graduate/first-professional programs (USDOE National Center for Education Statistics, 2003).

The defining characteristic of distance programs is that students and faculty are geographically dispersed. Because online courses are the most common form of distance education, there is a tendency to assume that distance programs are exclusively provided over the Internet. However, the modalities inherent in distance education are many, including methods involved in campus-based education. Distance learning appeals to those with undergraduate or master's degrees without easy access to traditional residency-based professional schools or university programs and who are unable to move or wish to remain in their geographic location. The typical consumer is the adult learner. However, this group may include students who are either not admitted to or cannot afford tuition in doctoral residency-based programs. Murphy, Levant, Hall, and Glueckauf (2007) report the results of an APA Task Force that examined these issues in 2001, described educators' opinions on best practices, and reviewed the implications of the 1996 CoA accreditation standards for distance education programs.

For those seeking to become professional psychologists, these programs carry considerable risk, as few are approved by licensing bodies for admission to the profession. Such a program faces challenges in ensuring that the scientific foundation in psychology is acquired in an organized sequence that is developmentally complex, that the faculty and students interact effectively with each other, and that outcomes are measured adequately—all at a doctoral level. Integration of the training aspects of education, such as practicum or the laboratory, presents an even greater task within this type of model.

These programs attempt to match (or some would argue exceed) the quality assurance and accountability dimensions inherent in more traditional doctoral programs. A cornerstone of campus-based programs is a mandated residency period. Historically, residency was the mechanism that provided for immersion in the discipline, socialization into the profession, and oversight by a faculty of the developing competencies essential for entry to independent practice (Nelson et al., 2008). Implementing residency in a professional program that is totally online constitutes an even greater challenge. (Jones International University, a totally online university, is now regionally accredited by the North Central Association.)

In 2011, two CoA-accredited programs employ distance education techniques as a major facet of doctoral education. The Philadelphia College of Osteopathic Medicine uses both traditional methods of education and training at a central site and at an extension campus where students meet in traditional classroom formats and interact through teleconferencing. The Fielding Graduate University exemplifies a distributed educational model organized into clusters of students at various sites that also uses electronically mediated instruction. No primarily distance education programs have met the requirements for the ASPPB/National Register designation, although several programs have been evaluated.

The role of distance education programs for psychology is unique among health care professions in which the doctorate is the entry level for professional practice. Medicine and dentistry use distance education programs primarily for upgrading degrees and certifications beyond the entry level. This separates out the important issue of qualification for independent practice from continuing professional education.

Competency Assessment

At the same time that the USDOE underscored a need to improve the quality assurance process involved in higher education, the CoA began to require programs to specify expected, essential competencies and to report information on student learning outcomes. As outcomes vary as a function of the model adopted by the program, what was needed was agreement on the core competencies for psychologists entering independent practice.

Previously, the psychologist was considered ready for independent practice upon completion of a sequence of education and training that included doctoral program, practicum, internship, and post-doctoral year of experience. That sequence was articulated through various model acts from the APA and ASPPB but questioned by various training conferences and in other organized meetings. For instance, could the internship take place after the doctoral degree? Or, was the psychologist ready for independent practice once the doctoral degree was granted?

With the movement toward competency assessment and foundations on which competencies were essential, it was decided to examine carefully the steps in the sequence to determine if one did lead to the other in terms of the acquisition of essential competencies. Multiple factors impacted on these various developments.

Since the original model licensure act (APA, 1955), many changes in doctoral education and training occurred, related to the location of doctoral education, the number of students admitted per year, the extent of the practicum, the diversity of internship experiences, and the increasing adoption of the postdoctoral year as a standard for licensing laws and the variability in licensure rules. The latter led to difficulty in mobility.

Following the creation of the American Psychological Association Graduate Students (APAGS) in 1988, students actively represented their perspective throughout organized psychology. Psychology's status in the health care marketplace, length of training in comparison to other health care professions, problems finding effective and supported internship and postdoctoral training, and the tremendous debt load assumed by some students were identified as critical issues for the profession and a burden for those entering the profession. Thus, in 2000, the APA invited 30 commissioners selected from a wide range of constituencies to a meeting which recommended changes to the sequence of education and training leading to licensure (APA, 2001).

This potential policy change meant that it was very important to define the competencies of licensed psychologists and to determine when in the sequence those were attained. It also shifted the proof of competence from the postdoctoral year to internship completion. Several organizations urged caution in implementing this recommendation without collecting more information. Thus, an agreement was reached to obtain the needed information and to consider the policy change for official approval 5 years later.

Multiple efforts followed. The APPIC sponsored the Competencies Conference in 2002 (Kaslow, 2004; Kaslow et al., 2004). At about the same time, Hatcher and Lassiter's practicum competencies document was drafted as a follow-up to the 2001 APA Education Leadership Conference and approved in 2005 by the relevant constituencies (go to http://www.APTC.org). The APPIC urged the APA to carefully examine the impact of not requiring a year of postdoctoral experience for licensure by convening another conference to develop the benchmarks for competencies at all levels of education and training. If the levels could be integrated and coordinated, and changes to the practicum and the internship made, it was more likely that the proposed change of not requiring the postdoctoral year for a license would succeed.

Thus, in 2006, the APA Council of Representatives approved a change in APA policy, namely that licensure applicants be allowed to complete a sequential, organized, supervised professional experience equivalent to 2 years of full-time training *prior or subsequent* to the granting of the doctoral degree. The policy clarified that, for applicants intending to practice in the health services domain of psychology, one of those 2 years of supervised professional experience was the doctoral internship (APA, 2006). This decision implied that state regulatory bodies should be encouraged to offer applicants a choice of completing required supervised hours either before or after the internship, or some combination of both. This policy did not dismiss the year of postdoctoral experience and reminded us that "postdoctoral education and training remains an important part of the continuing professional development and credentialing process for professional psychologists. Postdoctoral education and training is a foundation for practice improvement, advanced competence, and inter-jurisdictional mobility" (APA, 2006).

Instead of holding a conference, as the APPIC recommended in 2007, the APA Board of Educational Affairs decided to fund a benchmarks workgroup to build upon what had already been completed by the APTC for practicum. A group of 32 psychologists participated in the Assessment of Competencies Benchmarks Work Group and developed a model for defining and measuring competence in professional psychology (APA, 2007).

Because the group was so inclusive, because the rough draft was of high quality, and because the process for further revisions was so open, APPIC did not see a need to establish a separate process devoted exclusively to internship or postdoctoral benchmarks.

(Stephen R. McCutcheon, personal communication, June 30, 2008)

The document is still evolving based upon public comment and continued refinement by various task forces. Interested parties can follow further developments by visiting the CCTC website periodically to look for updates (http://www.psychtrainingcouncils.org/documents.html).

Thus, psychology appears to be in transition, from an input to an output model of quality assurance. Although unlikely to ever relinquish the former completely (degrees remain necessary), considerable time and expertise have been applied toward the latter, with more to come.

PRACTICUM COMPETENCE

The Practicum Competency Outline approved in 2005 describes the baseline competencies needed to enter practicum training and the 11 competency domains that are the focus of that training. Using that outline, psychology training clinics can develop their own competency-based student evaluations (rated as novice, intermediate, or advanced) of the essential practicum competencies. In addition, this methodology can be used to collect objective data about specific training sites, thereby providing a frame of reference for prospective students, and a method for relating the practicum and doctoral program's goals. Updates to the outline will be posted online (http://www.aptc.org).

INTERNSHIP COMPETENCE

Currently, licensing bodies and credentialing organizations view the internship, and in most states, the postdoctoral year of supervised experience, as necessary supplements to the doctoral education in determining readiness for practice. The internship's purpose is to provide developing psychologists with the opportunity to master more skills. Some skills are introduced in practicum; others may be reserved for the internship. The identification and assessment of specific competencies is handled by each internship site, using multiple methods, such as observation of clinical work, apprenticeship to individual mentors, presentations to clinical seminars, and various evaluation tools including self assessment. The internship provides a much more extensive period (1 year full-time or 2 years half-time) for the refinement of competencies than does practicum. At the conclusion of the internship, the director certifies to the licensing/credentialing body the completion of a satisfactory internship experience.

Although programs (doctoral degree and internship) engage in formative evaluations (process) and summative evaluations (outcomes) throughout the education and training sequence, there is no independent performance examination as part of the psychologist licensing process that directly assesses competence in practice. Also, if no postdoctoral year is required for a license, the graduate is deemed qualified for licensure at the successful completion of the internship. The policy change regarding the sequence of education and training leading to licensure has heightened the awareness of internship directors that they are more directly responsible for ascertaining readiness for independent practice. It remains unclear whether this realization means that the training directors will become more vigilant about signing off on the internship as satisfactory only when they have determined that the person is indeed competent.

POSTDOCTORAL COMPETENCE

The third component in the sequence is the year of postdoctoral supervised experience or postdoctoral residency training. The CoA guidelines for accreditation of postdoctoral education and training programs are parallel to those adopted for programs and internships. A judgment is made on the degree to which the program achieves the goals and objectives specified in its training model. It should be "of sufficient breadth to ensure advanced competence as a professional psychologist and of sufficient depth and focus to ensure technical expertise and proficiency in the substantive traditional or specialty practice areas" (APA, 2009, p. 22). The length of the program may vary from 1 year up to 3 for some specialty areas.

The traditional substantive areas include counseling psychology. The specialty practice areas include clinical neuropsychology, clinical child, and rehabilitation psychology. To accomplish the accreditation of specialty postdoctoral residencies, the organizations that represent the specialty each developed their specialty-specific education and training guidelines. These organizations serve on the Council on Specialties (CoS). The CoS was formed upon the recommendation of the IOC, when it ceased operation, as essential to ensuring quality and self-governance in postdoctoral training. (See http://www.cospp.org for more information.) Thus, although

no document parallel to the practicum competencies outline exists for internships or for traditional substantive postdoctoral training, given the continuing dialogue by organized psychology in determining how to assess competencies across the development of the professional, it should emerge.

Prior to this change in policy, Alabama was the only state that allowed independent practice at the doctoral level without requiring a year of postdoctoral experience. Today 11 states offer licensure at the culmination of the doctoral degree, based upon documentation of sufficient supervised experience, including an internship, while in doctoral training. These include Alabama, Arizona, Connecticut, Indiana, Maryland, Ohio, Kentucky, North Dakota, Utah, Washington and Wyoming. For instance, Washington was the first to implement regulations allowing the 2 years to be completed before graduation, with 1 of the years being practicum (or postdoctoral year) and the other an internship. The supervision topics required for the practicum are extensive and may be more complex and difficult to implement than typical for practicum. A careful reading of those criteria is essential if planning to use those practicum hours toward licensure. It is entirely possible that the applicant will find the postdoctoral year of supervised experience more easily satisfied. Completing the postdoctoral year has the added benefit of meeting the requirements for mobility. Regardless of whether it remains linked to the licensure requirements, the postdoctoral experience (before or after licensure) is important for advanced specialization/competency, licensure mobility, and continuing professional development. For instance, credentialing mechanisms such as the CPQ and the National Register require a year of postdoctoral experience (Hall & Boucher, 2003).

International Mobility

We have focused on the United States, and to some degree, Canada, in discussing the professional issues involved in education, training, licensing, and credentialing. However, psychologists increasingly seek employment or training opportunities abroad. For that to happen, at least for licensed psychologists, it is important to understand other countries' perspectives on the preparation of psychologists. There are positive signs that indicate that psychology may be ready to meet the needs of a global population. First, the numbers of psychologists and psychology students are increasing worldwide, and the definition of a psychologist is becoming articulated internationally. At the same time, psychologists are forming organizations within and across borders to promote globalization of practice. Advances in technology make it more likely that expertise can be widely disseminated and services provided across borders.

Countries and geographical regions have developed their own systems of accountability. As psychology operates within a societal context, its manifestation varies considerably from country to country. Some examples of different systems of accountability noted by Altmaier and Hall (2008) follow.

Regulatory

In the United States and Canada, systems of credentialing are regulated by 64 licensing bodies. Mobility mechanisms developed by credentialing organizations (ABPP, ASPPB, Canadian Register and the National Register) assist mobility within and between these two countries, and the Mutual Recognition Agreement promotes mobility for psychologists within Canada. (See http://www.cpa.ca/psychologyincanada/psychologyintheprovincesandterritories for more information.)

Independent

European countries do not adhere to a specific template for regulation of the practice of psychology. Governmental licensing does not exist in all 43 countries. However, compliance with the Bologna Declaration may raise the standard of education offered in universities, which, in turn, may lead to a more universal criterion for the education required for a license (Lunt, 2008).

Collaborative

Australia's system is managed by cooperation between the professional association and the regulatory boards and has a mutual recognition agreement with New Zealand. More importantly, the five states and two territories now implement national licensure (Waring, 2008).

Evolving

Mexico ties federal licensing to a specific degree and a social service requirement. Now under way is a newly established accreditation system and a post-licensure examination with opportunities for specialized certification. Its national licensing is similar to other countries in Central and South America and Spain (Hernández Guzmán & Sanchez-Sosa, 2008).

Psychologists in training today in the United States increasingly seek the opportunity to obtain part of their education and training outside the United States and Canada. These individuals want to be able to qualify for licensure in the United States when they return. Because of the variability in models of education, training, and recognition/licensure outside the United States and Canada, this can be risky to achieve. Currently, there is no guarantee that state licensure boards will accept supervision by an individual who meets the recognition requirements or licensure in another country if not also licensed in the United States. For a thorough review of some of the mechanisms and the challenges to international mobility, see Bullock and Hall (2008).

North American Mobility

Anticipating more global activity due to the North American Free Trade Agreement (NAFTA) signed in 1993, psychologists from the three signatory countries participated for 11 years in the Trilateral Forum on Professional Psychology, primarily to compare structure and process for education and training in the U.S., Canada, and Mexico. Whether or not directly related to those efforts, substantial changes did occur over that time period in Mexico's accreditation and certification process. At the same time, mobility was facilitated for psychologists at the doctoral level between the United States and Canada and within Canada. Mobility has not been achieved between Mexico and the United States and Canada primarily due to an inability to compare outcomes from education and training. Thus, determining comparability of education and training could be solved with competency-based assessments (outcomes).

Beginning in the late 1990s, emphasis was placed on enhancing the mobility of psychologists within the United States. Multiple mechanisms now exist, each with different criteria and purposes, with the foundation being a license to practice psychology in at least one jurisdiction, and the goal to facilitate virtual or geographic mobility (Hall & Boucher, 2003). Such mobility serves a public purpose as well, in that delays in obtaining a license are decreased and faster access to services is provided the public. Often, newly licensed psychologists are most interested in and seeking mobility. (See http://www.nationalregister.org/mobility.htm for up-to-date information.)

A majority of the jurisdictions in the United States and Canada have incorporated one or more mechanisms in laws or regulations permitting psychologists with specialty board certification (ABPP), mobility certificate (CPQ), or health service provider certification (National Register) to expedite their license acquisition in the United States and Canada without waiting or without being examined again, except for a jurisprudence examination. Thus, having mobility or expedited licensure is a major benefit of credentialing, and is reported by early career psychologists as the major reason for applying for credentialing (Hall & Boucher, 2008).

Conclusion

Psychology meets its accountability requirement as a profession in many ways. It reviews and approves education and training programs based upon national criteria using both formative and summative evaluations. It requires professional psychologists to be individually evaluated for licensure and credentialing. These evaluations take place at the state and national level. The move to assess competencies in practicum and internship will assist students in directing their focus on which experiences will make them a more effective psychologist, qualified for independent practice and competitive in the health care marketplace. A similar evolution will eventually occur for postdoctoral training, as it is necessary for advanced competence, mobility, and specialization. Accountability also includes monitoring psychologists' practice to protect the public. Monitoring ethical conduct is supported by the efforts of licensing boards and national credentialing bodies. Ultimately, the profession is accountable to the consumer; self-regulation is the key to meeting this responsibility.

Consumers have opinions about who is best suited to address their issues. Their participation is fostered by the direct representation on policy-establishing and implementing organizations and by direct feedback on the quality of services provided. As pointed out by Stricker, "the rise in consumer voice increases the pressure on psychological groups to self-regulate" (p. 212).

References

Altmaier, E. M., & Hall, J. E. (2008). Introduction to international quality assurance for psychology. In J. E. Hall, & E. M. Altmaier (Eds.), *Global promise: Quality assurance and accountability in professional psychology* (pp. 3–15). New York: Oxford University Press.

American Psychological Association. (1987). Model act for state licensure of psychologists. *American Psychologist, 42,* 696–703.

American Psychological Association. (2002). Ethical principles of psychologists and code of conduct. *American Psychologist, 57,* 1060–1073.

American Psychological Association. (2007). *Competency Benchmarks Work Group.* Retrieved June 28, 2008, from http://www.apa.org/ed/graduate/competency.html.

American Psychological Association. (2010). *Model Act for State Licensure of Psychologists.* http://www.apa.org/about/governance/council/policy/model-act-2010.pdf Accessed March 12, 2011.

American Psychological Association, Committee on Accreditation. (1996). *Guidelines and principles for accreditation of programs in professional psychology.* Washington, DC: Author.

American Psychological Association, Committee on Accreditation. (2009). *Guidelines and principles for accreditation of programs in professional psychology.* Washington, DC: Author.

American Psychological Association, Committee on Counselor Training, Division of Counseling and Guidance. (1952). Recommended standards for training counseling psychologists at the doctoral level. *American Psychologist, 7,* 175–181.

American Psychological Association, Committee on Definition, Division of Counseling Psychology. (1956). Counseling psychology as a specialty. *American Psychologist, 11,* 282–285.

American Psychological Association, Committee on Legislation. (1955). Joint report of the APA and CSPA (Conference of State Psychological Associations). *American Psychologist, 10,* 727–756.

American Psychological Association, Committee on Legislation. (1967). A model for state legislation affecting the practice of psychology 1967: Report of the APA Committee on Legislation. *American Psychologist, 22,* 1095–1103.

American Psychological Association, Council of Representatives. (2006, February). *Minutes.* Washington, DC: Author.

American Psychological Association, Council of Representatives. (1995, February). *Minutes.* Washington, DC: Author.

Association of Psychology Postdoctoral and Internship Centers. (2011). *Match statistics.* Retrieved April 13, 2011, from http://www.appic.org/match/5_2_2_1_10_match_about_statistics_general_2011Comb.html.

Association of Psychology Postdoctoral and Internship Centers. (2008, May). *APPIC e-newsletter.* Retrieved June 24, 2008, from http://appic.org/news/Newsletter/May2008.pdf.

Association of State and Provincial Psychology Boards. (1992). *Model act for licensure of psychologists.* Montgomery, AL: Author.

Association of State and Provincial Psychology Boards. (2001). *Model act of licensure for psychologists.* Montgomery, AL: Author.

Association of State and Provincial Psychology Boards. (2010). *Model act of licensure for psychologists.* Montgomery, AL: Author.

Belar, C. D., Bieliauskas, L. A., Klepac, R. K., Larsen, K. G., Stigall, T. T., & Zimet, C. N. (1993). National Conference on Postdoctoral Training in Professional Psychology. *American Psychologist, 48,* 1284–1289.

Bent, R. J., Packard, R. E., & Goldberg, R. W. (1999). The American Board of Professional Psychology, 1947 to 1997: A historical perspective. *Professional Psychology: Research and Practice, 29,* 65–73.

Bullock, M., & Hall, J. E. (2008). The promotion of international mobility. In J. E. Hall, & E. M. Altmaier (Eds.), *Global* promise: Quality assurance and accountability in professional psychology (pp. 216–231). New York: Oxford University Press.

Canadian Psychological Association. (2002). Accreditation standards and procedures for doctoral programmes and internships in professional psychology. Ottawa, CA: Author. Retrieved June 24, 2008, from http://www.cpa.ca/accreditation.

Canadian Psychological Association. (2000). Canadian code of ethics for psychologists (3rd ed.). Ottawa, CA: Author. Retrieved July 10, 2008, from http://www.cpa.ca/publications.

Drum, D. J., & Hall, J. E. (1993). Psychology's self-regulation and the setting of professional standards. Applied and Preventive Psychology, 2, 151–161.

Gelso, C., & Fretz, B. (2001). Counseling psychology. Orlando, FL: Harcourt Brace.

Goodstein, L. D., & Ross, S. (1966). Accreditation of graduate programs in psychology. American Psychologist, 21, 218–223.

Hall, J. E. (2000). Licensing and credentialing as quality management tools in behavioral health care. In G. Stricker, W. G. Troy, & S. A. Shueman (Eds.), Handbook of quality management in behavioral health (pp. 317–332). New York: Kluwer Academic/Plenum.

Hall, J. E., & Boucher, A. P. (2003). Professional mobility for psychologists: Multiple choices, multiple opportunities. Professional Psychologist: Research and Practice, 34, 463–467.

Hall, J. E., & Boucher, A. P. (2008). Early career psychologists' knowledge of credentialing in professional psychology. Professional Psychology: Research and Practice, 39, 480–487.

Hall, J. E., & Sales, B. D. (2002). Evolution of specialty credentialing in professional psychology. Unpublished manuscript.

Hall, J. E., Wexelbaum, S., & Boucher, A. P. (2007). Doctoral student awareness of licensure, credentialing, and professional organizations in psychology: The 2005 National Register international survey. Training and Education in Professional Psychology, 1, 38–48.

Health Care Financing Administration. (2000). Medicare claims manual, Part 3: Claims processes. Section 2150 clinical psychologists services. Retrieved July 2, 2008, from www.cms.hhs.gov/transmittals/downloads/R1660B3.pdf.

Hernández Guzmán, L., & Sanchez-Sosa, J. J. (2008). Practice and professional regulation of professional psychology in Latin-America. In J. E. Hall, & E. M. Altmaier (Eds.), Global promise: Quality assurance and accountability in professional psychology (pp. 109–127). New York: Oxford University Press.

Kaslow, N. J. (2004). Competencies in professional psychology. American Psychologist, 59, 774–781.

Kaslow, N. J., Borden, K. A., Collins, F. L., Forrest, L., Illfelder-Kaye, J., Nelson, P. D., et al. (2004). Competencies conference: Future directions in education and credentialing in professional psychology. Journal of Clinical Psychology, 80, 699–712.

Lunt, I. (2008). Professional mobility and quality assurance within the European Union. In J. E. Hall, & E. M. Altmaier (Eds.), Global promise: Quality assurance and accountability in professional psychology (pp. 128–139). New York: Oxford University Press.

MacHovec v. Council for the National Register of Health Service Providers in Psychology, 616 F. Supp. 258, 271 (E.D. Va. 1985).

Mayne, T. J., Norcross, J. C., & Sayette, M. A. (2006). Insider's guide to graduate programs in clinical and counseling psychology. New York: Guilford Press.

Miville, M. L., Adams, E. M., & Juntunen, C. L. (2007). Counseling psychology perspectives on the predoctoral internship supply-demand imbalance: Strategies for problem definition and resolution. Training and Education in Professional Psychology, 1, 258–266.

Murphy, M. J., Levant, R. F., Hall, J. E., & Glueckauf, R. L. (2007). Distance education in professional training in psychology. Professional Psychology: Research and Practice, 38, 97–103.

National Register of Health Service Providers in Psychology. (2011). Health service provider in psychology. Retrieved April 14, 2011from http://www.nationalregister.org/about_NR.html.

Nelson, P. D., Belar, C. D., Grus, C. L., & Zlotlow, S. (2008). Quality assessment in higher education through accreditation. In J. E. Hall, & E. M. Altmaier (Eds.), Global promise: Quality assurance and accountability in professional psychology (pp. 16–37). New York: Oxford University Press.

Nelson, P. D., & Messenger, L. C. (2003). Accreditation in psychology and public accountability. In E. M. Altmaier (Ed.), Setting standards in graduate education: Psychology's commitment to excellence in accreditation (pp. 7–38). Washington, DC: American Psychological Association.

New York State Doctoral Evaluation Project. (1990). Doctoral education in psychology. Doctoral Evaluation Project, New York State Education Department, Albany NY 12230.

Norcross, J. C., Hogan, T. P., & Koocher, G. P. (2008). Clinician's guide to evidence-based practices: Mental health and the addictions. New York: Oxford University Press.

Pellegrino, E. D. (1991). Trust and distrust in professional ethics. In E. D. Pellegrino, R. Veatch, & J. Langan (Eds.), Ethics, trust and the professions (pp. 69–89). Washington, DC: Georgetown University Press.

Raimy, V. C. (Ed.). (1950). Training in clinical psychology. New York: Prentice Hall.

Ritchie, P. L.-J. (2008). Codes of ethics, conduct, and standards as vehicles of accountability. In J. E. Hall, & E. M. Altmaier (Eds.), Global promise: Quality assurance and accountability in professional psychology (pp. 73–97). New York: Oxford University Press.

Rodolfo, E. R., Owen, J. J., & Clark, S. (2007). Practicum training hours: Fact and fantasy. Training and Education in Professional Psychology, 1, 64–73.

Sales, B. D., Bricklin, P., & Hall, J. E. (1983). Manual for the identification and continued recognition of proficiencies and new specialties in psychology [Draft report of the subcommittee on specialization]. Washington, DC: American Psychological Association.

Sales, B. D., Bricklin, P., & Hall, J. (1984a). Specialization in psychology: Principles [Draft report of the subcommittee on specialization]. Washington, DC: American Psychological Association.

Sales, B. D., Bricklin, P., & Hall, J. E. (1984b). Specialization in psychology: Procedures [Draft report of the subcommittee on specialization]. Washington, DC: American Psychological Association.

Service, J., Sabourin, M., Catano, V. M., Day, V., Hayes, C., & MacDonald, G. W. (1989). Report of the CPA/CPAP Specialty Designation Task Force. Ottawa, CA: Canadian Psychological Association.

Skrtic, T. M. (1991). *Behind special education: A critical analysis of professional culture and school organization*. Denver: Love.

Stigall, T. T. (1983). Licensing and certification. In B. D. Sales (Ed.), *The professional psychologist's handbook* (pp. 285–337). New York: Plenum.

Stricker, G. (2008). Quality assurance in professional psychology education. In J. E. Hall, & E. M. Altmaier (Eds.), *Global promise: Quality assurance and accountability in professional psychology* (pp. 199–215). New York: Oxford University Press.

Stromberg, C. D. (1990, May). *Associations' certification programs: Legal and operational issues*. Paper presented at the meeting of the American Speech and Hearing Association, Rockville, MD. Unpublished manuscript.

Stromberg, C. D. (1991, April). *Healthcare credentialing: Implications for academic health centers*. Paper presented at the meeting of the Academic Health Centers, Washington, DC. Unpublished manuscript.

Stromberg, C. D., Haggarty, D. J., Liebenluft, R. F., McMillian, M. H., Mishkin, B., Rubin, B. L., et al. (1988). *The psychologist's legal handbook*. Washington, DC: National Register of Health Service Providers in Psychology.

Thompson, A. S., & Super, D. E. (Eds.). (1964). *The professional preparation of counseling psychologists: Report of the 1964 Greystone Conference*. New York: Teachers College.

U.S. Department of Education, National Center for Education Statistics. (2003). *Distance education at degree-granting postsecondary institutions: 2000-2001* (NCES 2003-017). Washington, DC: Author.

Vasquez, M. J. T., & Phillips Bingham, R. (2011). Ethics in counseling psychology. In E. M. Altmaier, & J. C. Hansen (Eds.), *The Oxford handbook of counseling psychology*. New York: Oxford University Press.

Waring, T. (2008). The regulation of psychology in Australia. In J. E. Hall, & E. M. Altmaier (Eds.), *Global promise: Quality assurance and accountability in professional psychology* (pp. 164–185). New York: Oxford University Press.

Watkins, C. E. (1984). Counseling psychology versus clinical psychology: Further explorations on a theme or once more around the "identity" maypole with gusto. *The Counseling Psychologist, 11*, 76–92.

Wellner, A. M. (Ed.). (1978). *Education and credentialing in psychology: Proposal for a national commission in education and credentialing in psychology*. Washington, DC: National Register of Health Service Providers in Psychology.

Williams-Nickelson, C., Prinstein, M. J., & Keilin, W. G. (2008). *Internships in psychology: The APAGS workbook for writing successful applications and finding the right fit*. Washington, DC: American Psychological Association.

Wise, E. H., Hall, J. E., Ritchie, P. L.-J., & Turner, L. C. (2006). The National Register of Health Service Providers in Psychology and the Canadian Register of Health Service Providers in Psychology. In T. J. Vaughn (Ed.), *Psychology licensure and certification: What students need to know*. Washington, DC: American Psychological Association.

The Counseling Relationship

Beth E. Haverkamp

Abstract

Counseling psychology offers a distinctive perspective on the therapeutic relationship, one that is grounded in the discipline's history, values, and professional identity. In the current work, selections from one of the field's pioneers, Leona Tyler, introduce key areas of contemporary research and theory on the counseling relationship. The chapter begins with an examination of early formulations of the therapeutic relationship, the historical context in which they emerged, and early efforts to investigate its role in psychotherapy. Next, enduring themes within relationship research, as well as key contemporary concerns, are surveyed, with an emphasis on the distinctive contributions of counseling psychologists. Closing sections of the chapter identify emerging areas of research, particularly as they relate to traditional counseling psychology concerns, and propose potentially useful avenues for further investigation of the dynamic and interdependent character of counseling relationships.

Keywords: counseling psychology, counseling relationship, therapeutic relationship, therapeutic alliance, history of psychology

[I]t is the relationship with the counselor that makes the difference. . . . It is because of this principle that recent writers on the counseling process are stressing relationships rather than techniques, the general structure of the situation rather than specific rules about what to do and say.

—Leona Tyler, *The Work of the Counselor*
(1953, p. 17)

The field of counseling psychology encompasses extraordinary diversity in research and practice, yet the phenomenon known as "the counseling relationship" has been a source of perennial interest and investigation. Repeated references to the counseling relationship in counseling psychology's self-descriptions (Howard, 1992; Packard, 2009) suggest that the relationship lies at the heart of our field's identity as a specialization within applied psychology and that counseling psychology's perspective

on the relationship is a core element differentiating the field from other areas of applied psychology. Notably, concern with the relationship was visible at the outset of the field's emergence. Leona Tyler, one of the field's pioneers, assigned a central role to the counseling relationship in the three editions of her influential text, *The Work of the Counselor* (1953, 1961, 1969), and her assertion that "it is the relationship with the counselor that makes the difference. . . ." (1953, p. 17), was echoed in Packard's 2008 Leona Tyler Award Address, in which he identified nine core values for counseling psychology; the second of which is, "Positive relationships are a necessary condition for stimulating change in those we seek to help" (2009, p. 622).

Research on the counseling relationship has begun to accelerate and assume new prominence within applied psychology, along with convincing documentation of its role in therapeutic outcomes (see Norcross, 2002a). But, before examining contemporary research on the counseling relationship, it is informative to consider the historical context of counseling psychology's contribution. In this chapter, rather than attempt to address the full spectrum of relationships research (see Norcross, 2002a, for a synthesis), my goal is to present an explicit counseling psychology perspective on the counseling or therapeutic relationship. I propose to do so in three areas: First, for those new to this literature (or for those who may have forgotten), I will examine early formulations of the therapeutic relationship, the historical context in which they emerged, and early efforts to investigate its role in psychotherapy. Second, in discussing key contemporary areas of research on the counseling relationship, there will be an emphasis on the distinctive contributions of counseling psychologists, as well as attention to enduring themes within relationship research. Closing sections of the chapter will identify emerging areas of research on the counseling relationship, particularly as they relate to traditional counseling psychology concerns, and will propose potentially useful avenues for further investigation.

The selections of research and commentary presented in the following sections reflect my view that a unique counseling psychology perspective on the relationship is discernible and that this perspective has influenced the development of counseling psychology as a specialization and continues to be reflected in relationship research being conducted by counseling psychologists. Early writing that emphasized respect for client autonomy, agency, and a focus on client strengths is still visible in newer areas of research, such as social justice (Vera & Speight, 2003) and positive psychology (Lopez et al., 2006; Smith, 2006).

Readers of the current chapter will have an opportunity to consider, for themselves, the roots of counseling psychology's unique perspective on the relationship: Selected quotations from the first edition of Tyler's (1953) *The Work of the Counselor*, are used to introduce key sections. Although the idea of selecting a few key Tyler quotations was appealing from the start, I think readers will share my surprise at the extent to which Leona Tyler's 1953 work remains relevant to contemporary concerns. This chapter summarizes what we have learned, over the past 50 years, about the importance of the counseling relationship in many domains; Tyler's comments remind us that many contemporary conclusions echo assertions advanced at the time when counseling psychology first emerged as a specialization within psychology.

Historical Emergence of a Counseling Psychology Perspective on the Relationship

> Down through the years men have always found that when they have difficult and important decisions to make they can clarify their thinking by talking the problems over with friends whom they trust and respect. . . . that sympathy and understanding make it easier to face these troubles courageously.
> (Tyler, 1953, p.1)

Counseling psychology's formulation of the relationship is often traced to the 1940s and 1950s, coinciding with Carl Rogers' introduction of the influential idea that an accepting relationship with a counselor, characterized by empathy, warmth, and genuineness, is necessary and sufficient for change. Few would disagree that Rogers' (1942, 1957, 1963) contributions constitute the single most important influence on contemporary understandings of the counseling relationship, but it is important to note two earlier influences, both of which emerged in the early years of the 20th century and which continue to be reflected in contemporary perspectives and research on the counseling relationship.

Freudian psychoanalysis contributed the view that change occurs in the context of interaction between analyst and analysand, as well as the observation that, in transference and countertransference, the process is influenced by forces and feelings outside the awareness of client and therapist. Both the processes of therapeutic interaction and the phenomemon of transference/countertransference continue to be a focus of counseling psychology research (e.g., Gelso & Carter, 1994; Gelso & Samstag, 2008).

The vocational guidance movement of the early 1900s, a core forerunner of contemporary counseling psychology, was a second key influence through its focus on the identification of client skills and strengths, not pathology. Parson's early attention to identifying client strengths and capacities as a basis for selecting occupations (Parsons, 1908, cited in Gelso & Fretz, 2001; Lopez et al., 2006) was later reflected in Super's characterization of counseling psychology as emphasizing "a value system aiming at optimum functioning of the individual" (Super, 1955, cited in Samler, 1980, p. 155). Super used the term *hygiology* in arguing that counselors were concerned with client strengths and health, rather than pathology.

With this base—Rogers' attention to an empathic relationship, the Freudian insight that relationship is a dynamic process, and the vocational guidance focus on skills and strengths—counseling psychology formally defined itself as a field (see Whitely, 1980), differentiating itself from clinical psychology, industrial organizational psychology, and school guidance. These distinctions were drawn initially on the basis of work setting and client populations but, before long, could also be characterized by different values and distinctive views of the counselor–client relationship. Super (1955) credited Rogers with making people aware that "one counsels *people* rather than *problems*" (Whitely, 1980, p. 18, italics in original) and went on to note that, "Some clinical psychologists are beginning to say, now that counseling psychology has made clear this surprisingly novel philosophy [attention to strengths/hygiology] and these nonetheless time-honored methods, that clinical psychology made a serious error in defining itself as it did, that it should have been more independent of psychiatric traditions and interests and concerned itself with hygiology as well as pathology" (Whitely, 1980, p. 19).

At this nascent moment in the field's development, Leona Tyler's (1953) *The Work of the Counselor* offered a comprehensive portrait of the new discipline and, by extension, its characterization of the counseling relationship. As noted by Zilber and Osipow (1990), "Tyler integrated many theories in developing her own view . . . her work reflects her own unique blending of the concepts of Carl Rogers, individual differences and psychometrics, psychoanalytic theory, behaviorism, developmental stage theory and existentialism. . . ." (p. 337). Tyler's defining contribution was to effect this integration through the lens of the emerging values and concerns of the new discipline of counseling psychology.

Tyler's core themes can be summarized briefly and, upon first reading, are likely to strike readers as self-evident or not remarkable to any practicing therapist, but they provided one of the first systematic sets of instruction for how a counseling relationship should be conducted. Tyler regarded the relationship itself as central to the whole therapeutic endeavor and was specific about its essential characteristics: The counselor and client must establish a relationship of *safety and trust*; the relational focus includes the *whole person* of the client; the counselor adopts a core focus on *client strengths*, rather than pathology; and counseling activities such as psychological testing or occupational information are employed *within* the counseling relationship and

pursued in ways that do not diminish rapport. Tyler also calls attention to additional aspects of the relationship that continue to be influential in contemporary counseling psychology: Each counseling relationship must focus on the *individual's uniqueness*, a mandate now reflected in the field's emphasis on issues of diversity. In describing how counselors establish relationships, she often reminded readers that "counseling is basically a perceptual skill . . . learning to listen and watch and understand" (p. 35), which foreshadows the cognitive aspects of relationship formation and the subsequent influence of social psychology (e.g., Heppner & Frazier, 1992, Strong, 1978).

Tyler's core themes continue to be visible in comprehensive reviews of relationship research, particularly those contributed by counseling psychologists, and they helped create a template for a counseling psychology perspective on the therapeutic relationship. Those readers who may question the uniqueness of Tyler's counseling psychology perspective—that a warm, safe, respectful counseling relationship is essential to the therapeutic endeavor—are invited to consider an alternate view, also published in 1953. John Dollard who, with Neil Miller, advanced a highly influential synthesis of psychodynamic and behavioral approaches to therapy, produced a text comparable to Tyler's, titled *Steps in Psychotherapy* (Dollard, Auld, & White, 1953). The section, "The role of the therapist," opens as follows:

> We were tempted to refer to the therapist as circling around the embattled patient as an army might circle a citadel awaiting the moment of attack. . . . It is true that there are resistant forces operating within the patient which make it difficult for him to cooperate as he would like to do; but it is equally true that there are strong cooperative forces within the patient which keep him trying and proceeding with therapy. (p. 16)

Although this language will sound harsh to contemporary practitioners, I believe it is important for counseling psychologists to know that our field has been focused on "cooperative forces" all along.

Empiricism: Early Counseling Psychology Research on the Relationship

> It seems to me very important that we do shift over as rapidly as we can to the use of dependable evidence rather than custom and intuition as a basis for judgments as to how counseling should be done. (Tyler, 1953, p. ix)

From the outset of counseling psychology's emergence as a discipline, there was widespread interest in conducting research on the process of counseling and the client–counselor relationship. This stance reflects counseling psychology's enduring tradition of empiricism and, to complete our understanding of counseling psychology's historical perspective on the relationship, this tradition of and some of its early contributions are considered.

Tyler's work reflects a consistent commitment to what we now call *evidence-based practice*. The recommendations offered in her 1953 text were based on the earliest available relationship research; each chapter of *The Work of the Counselor* was followed by a research summary containing examples of early research on the counseling relationship. For example, Seeman (1949, cited in Tyler, 1953), in investigating client response to different counselors, found that, "There were significant differences in the favorableness of the response to different counselors, but they were not related to techniques used. Counselor *responsiveness* seemed to be the quality that produced the favorable reactions" (p. 55). His research illustrates a perennial question, one that previews a contemporary conclusion regarding the distinctive contributions of the counselor (Kim, Wampold, & Bolt, 2006; Wampold, 2007).

Evidence-based practice tends to be associated with outcome research, pursuing questions of "Is the treatment effective?" But a good deal of relationship research is concerned with the counseling process, and counseling psychologists took an early interest in this type of inquiry. A group of eminent counseling psychology researchers (Gelso, Betz, Friedlander, Helms, Hill, Patton, Super, & Wampold, 1988), while noting that process research was not unique to counseling psychology, described process research as "particularly notable" in counseling psychology and as having a "deep and substantial history in our specialty" (p. 388). This group's work alerted me to the pioneering contributions of Francis P. Robinson, of the Ohio State University, and a former president of the American Psychology Association (APA) Division 17, who inaugurated a program of process research in the 1940s. Asserting that "a counselee's willingness to talk is usually symptomatic of a good working relationship between client and counselor" (Carnes & Robinson, 1948, p. 635), Robinson's lab used "typescripts" of counseling sessions to investigate the relationship between the proportion of client talk time and counseling effectiveness.

Evidence of early research interest in the counseling relationship is also found in the inaugural issue of the *Journal of Counseling Psychology* (*JCP*) in 1954. As reported by Wrenn (1966), the first issue of *JCP* included ten research articles, three of which reflect the field's interest in therapist contributions to the counseling relationship: Dipboye's "Analysis of Counselor Style by Discussion Units," Cottle and Lewis' "Personality Characteristics of Counselors: II. Male Counselor Responses to the MMPI and GZTS," and Shaw's "Counseling from the Standpoint of an 'Interactive Conceptualist.'"

Rogers' (1957) description of the "necessary and sufficient" conditions for change had a significant impact on psychology's views of the therapeutic relationship and generated substantive early research on the core conditions of empathy, unconditional positive regard, and genuineness, as well as development of new research tools. Counseling psychologists made noteworthy contributions to investigations of Rogers' hypotheses: A counseling psychologist's dissertation research operationalized the core conditions (Barrett-Leonard, 1959), resulting in the Relationship Inventory, a measure still used in counseling process research (e.g., Heppner, Rosenberg, & Hedgespeth, 1992; Watson & Geller, 2005). Truax and Carhkuff's (1967) five-level observational rating system, the Accurate Empathy Scale, is still used to measure empathic understanding in client–counselor interactions (e.g., Barone et al., 2005).

Research on the counseling process and the role of the counseling relationship also reflects the specialization's openness to theory and research from other areas of psychology, being one of the first areas of counseling psychology research to incorporate ideas drawn from social psychology research. Stanley Strong (1968) drew on Jerome Frank's (1961) characterization of counseling as a social influence process and reformulated Frank's ideas as explicit counselor factors within the counseling relationship. Strong's model identified counselor expertness, perceived attractiveness, and trustworthiness as sources of persuasion. Once a counseling relationship was established in which the client viewed the counselor as influential, the counselor selected an "influence base" which, in his or her judgment, best suited the client's needs (Dixon & Claiborn, 1987). Strong's characterization of the counseling relationship as a social influence process led to a flood of analogue investigations in which variables such as "trustworthiness" and "credibility" were investigated for their relationship to both outcome (e.g., client attitude change; Bergin, 1962) and process factors (e.g., openness to influence; Dell & Schmidt, 1976; Strong & Schmidt, 1970).

Specific counselor factors that are influential in creating effective therapy relationships are surveyed in subsequent sections; this brief historical sketch illustrates the roots of an empirical tradition that continues to infuse counseling psychology's relationship research. Contemporary manifestations of this orientation are reflected in contributions from counseling psychologists to current definitions of "empirically supported relationships," a research-based complement to research on "empirically supported treatments" (see Norcross, 2002b).

Key Formulations of the Counseling Relationship

> The three aspects, understanding, acceptance, and communication, are so inextricably bound up together in the counseling process that it is only for purposes of talking about them that we can single out one at a time. They cannot be separately practiced or learned, and it is inconceivable that a competent counselor could ever be rated high on one and low on the others.
> (Tyler, 1953, p. 23)

A consensus has emerged that the quality of the counseling relationship, across a range of therapeutic approaches and client populations, is a consistent predictor of positive client outcomes (Beutler et al., 2004; Gelso et al., 2005; Horvath, 2001; Lambert & Barley, 2001). In the current edition of the classic resource, *Handbook of Psychotherapy and Behavior Change* (Lambert, 2004), Beutler et al. (2004) note that the 1994 edition had already identified the therapeutic relationship as "among the stronger predictors of treatment outcome" (p. 282). Lambert and Barley (2001) have gone so far as to argue that we now have decades of research demonstrating that the therapeutic relationship is a foundational "curative" component.

These conclusions are supported by a series of meta-analyses (Horvath & Symonds, 1991; Stevens, Hynan, & Allen, 2000) that have produced moderate effect sizes for the association between the therapeutic relationship and outcome. One relatively new conclusion, however, is that the magnitude of the relationship between the quality of the counseling relationship and outcome is less substantial than had been identified previously. Where prior estimates had suggested that 30% of the variance in outcome was attributable to the relationship (Lambert, 1992), more recent reviews (Beutler et al., 2004) have produced mean effect sizes ranging from $r = .22$ ($p < .05$) for a general outcome in

symptom improvement and $r = .17$ ($p < .05$) for targeted symptoms. Reviewers have pointed out that the larger effect sizes were obtained with clients who sought help for more subjective distress (e.g., depression, self-esteem, generalized anxiety), as opposed to diagnosable illness. The implication of this finding for counseling psychologists, whose training tends to be more focused on adjustment concerns, may be that the relationship plays an even greater role in their work than would be true in more clinical or psychiatric settings.

Given the well-established consensus on the importance of the counseling relationship in facilitating client change, the next questions concern the unexplained variance in outcome and can be framed as, "what type of relationship?" and, as "what elements of the relationship?" The first question can be explored by reviewing the findings associated with varying definitions or components of the counseling relationship. The second question, concerning factors that influence relationship development, is addressed in a subsequent section. However, before we can examine the evidence associated with various models of the counseling relationship, it is important to examine some of the definitional challenges associated with this area of research.

Definitional and Conceptual Challenges

> [T]he relationship between two people is something different than the sum of the contributions they make to it.
> (Tyler, 1953, p. 17)

Many researchers would argue that meaningful description rests on precise definition; if we hold to that truism with regard to the counseling relationship, we are in trouble. Gelso and Hayes (1998) have pointed out that, despite agreement on the centrality of the relationship in psychotherapy, there has been a lack of definitional work and few explicit definitions offered. This is not to suggest that there have not been efforts to define the phenomenon but, in each case, the definitions offered have been criticized for either being incomplete, or not being "it." In the 1960s, Carl Rogers expressed his frustration that, "we were all talking about the same experiences, but attaching different words, labels, and descriptions to these experiences. . . . the field of psychotherapy is in a mess" (1963; cited in Patterson, 1966, p. 506). In this section, several influential conceptualizations of the relationship are described briefly to illustrate some of the key definitional issues in this area of theory and research. In a subsequent section, several key formulations, as well as associated research, are considered in greater detail.

One of the most widely cited contemporary definitions of the relationship was developed by Gelso and Carter (1985, 1994), and asserts that "The relationship is the feelings and attitudes that therapist and client have toward one another, and the manner in which these are expressed" (1985, p. 159). This definition was adopted by the APA Division of Psychotherapy Task Force on Empirically Supported Therapy Relationships (see Norcross, 2002) for its comprehensive empirical review of relationship research; as such, it is assuming an influential place in psychology's understanding of the counseling relationship.

The Gelso and Carter definition (1985, 1994) is only one of several formulations that have been influential at some point in the history of relationship research and, in each case, the definitions offered have been criticized. As an initial example, we can consider the model most familiar to counselors, that of Carl Rogers' *person-centered therapy*. Rogers' approach is defined by his view of the relationship, which is considered to be the central mechanism of change and as healing in itself (Gelso & Hayes, 1998). However, Gelso and Hayes (1998) have argued that Rogers equated the relationship with the core conditions of empathy, unconditional regard, and congruence. In their view, the facilitative conditions are more appropriately viewed as factors that help create a relationship, rather than constituting the relationship itself. They also offered the critique that the therapist-offered conditions fail to acknowledge the client's role or contribution to the relationship.

A similar argument could be made regarding Stanley Strong's (1968) social influence model, which presented a view of the counseling relationship derived from social psychological theory. Strong characterized the counseling relationship as a venue for persuasion on the part of the counselor; counselor expertness, attractiveness, and trustworthiness were bases for influence, and the counselor's role was to select the stance best suited to the client's receptivity to influence and, by extension, to adaptive change. Strong's ideas generated extensive research in the 1970s and his contributions expanded the field's understanding of how different therapist characteristics (e.g., trustworthiness) are related to client response. As a model of the relationship, however, his work illustrates the difficulty in separating therapist characteristics and actions from what we would label as the relationship. Similar to Gelso and Hayes' (1998) critique of Rogers, Strong's conditions for influence cannot be equated with the relationship itself.

An influential cluster of definitions for the relationship is associated with the general term *therapeutic alliance*. In contrast to models of the relationship that emphasized therapist contributions, the alliance construct captures an interactive process and recognizes both therapist and client roles. At the same time, it presents some distinctive definitional challenges, particularly with regard to the theoretical roots of the varying formulations. As Horvath and Bedi (2002) point out, variations on the term (e.g., working alliance, helping alliance) represent related but distinct constructs with varying historical antecedents, some with clear roots in psychodynamic thought (e.g., Greenson, 1965, 1967) and others that have become more pantheoretical (e.g., Bordin, 1976). Two influential formulations are those developed by Luborsky and Bordin. Luborsky's (1976) formulation of a type I and type II alliance makes distinctions based on the stage of engagement, with type I referring to initial establishment of the relationship and type II emerging as the work of therapy begins. Bordin, who is most closely associated with the term "working alliance," defined the alliance as a collaboration consisting of three components: a bond between therapist and client, and an agreement on both the goals of therapy and on the tasks pursued. Horvath and Bedi (2002) argue that the common elements in alliance definitions of the relationship have been collaboration and agreement between client and counselor, in contrast to earlier work that was focused on either therapist contributions (e.g., Rogers) or on unconscious distortion (Gelso & Carter, 1985, 1994).

Although definitions based on the therapeutic alliance have shifted attention from therapist factors to an interactive characterization of the relationship, most writers consider the alliance as only one component of the relationship, rather than constituting the whole (Horvath & Bedi, 2002). For Gelso and Carter (1985, 1994), the working alliance is one of three components of the therapeutic relationship, the other two being a transferential component (including therapist countertransference) and a real relationship (Greenson, 1967), with features of genuineness and realistic perception. This tripartite model (see Gelso & Hayes, 1998, Gelso & Samstag, 2008, for extended discussion) offers a more comprehensive characterization of the relationship than the scope of either Rogers' proposal or the alliance literature and has been employed in several influential surveys of relationship research (e.g., Norcross, 2002; Sexton & Whiston, 1994). However, Gelso and Carter's extension in scope has also become the focus of criticism. Hill (1994) has charged that, by going beyond feelings and attitudes to inclusion of their manner of expression, the model becomes overinclusive and could be applied to almost everything that happens in psychotherapy. A related challenge to the model concerns the difficulty in differentiating between the three components, particularly in defining and differentiating the real relationship (Greenberg, 1994; Patton, 1994).

What each of these definitions—and attendant criticisms—reflects is the extreme difficulty of differentiating the counseling relationship from relationship-relevant techniques that a therapist employs (e.g., unconditional regard) and in making clear distinctions between therapist factors, client factors, and the relationship itself. The APA Division of Psychotherapy Task Force on Empirically Supported Therapy Relationships (see Norcross, 2002), in its investigation of relationship factors related to therapy outcome, wrestled with these dilemmas and made a choice to include therapist contributions as distinguishable from the relationship itself. But, with regard to the issue of what a therapist may *do*, they acknowledged the impossibility of fully separating these, noting, "The relationship does not exist apart from what the therapist does in terms of technique, and we cannot imagine any techniques that would not have some relational impact" (Norcross, 2002b, p. 8). And, of course, others would argue that therapist contributions go well beyond "technique" (e.g., Gelso, 2004).

For relationship research to advance, investigators will need to grapple with the fact that, not only are these factors intertwined and reciprocal, they are teleological in character. In other words, they exist within the dimension of *time* and are enacted with *purpose*. Several authors have offered suggestions for a renewed examination of relationship variables; for example, Carter (1994) draws a useful distinction between form and process elements of the relationship. She describes form as those components that exist at a point in time or across people, typically assessed with quantitative methods, and process as "more individualized experiences of

interaction and changes in and through the interaction across time" (p. 79).

My own view is that Carter has captured a critical limitation in our definitions of the relationship, and likely one that has been shaped by the quantitative methods that are familiar to us. Counseling psychology researchers, who have demonstrated openness to qualitative methods and a social constructionist paradigm (see Haverkamp, Morrow, & Ponterotto, 2005), may be uniquely prepared to explore how the dimensions of time and purpose can inform our definitions of the therapeutic relationship.

In the sections that follow, three influential formulations of the relationship are considered, along with illustrative research that has explored their association with client outcomes: Rogers' core conditions of empathy, unconditional positive regard, and congruence; investigations of the relationship as a common factor; and research on the working alliance. Two more recent formulations, those of the real relationship and consideration of the "empirically supported relationship," are also considered. The following discussion cannot offer an exhaustive review but reports current consensual conclusions and draws attention to counseling psychology contributions.

Carl Rogers' Core Therapeutic Conditions

> The value of the basic nondirective technique, reflection of feeling, in stimulating self-exploration has been demonstrated.
> (Tyler, 1953, p. 227)

Graduate students tend to forget that, when Carl Rogers' (1957) proposed that empathy, unconditional positive regard, and congruence were "necessary and sufficient" conditions for therapeutic change, he wanted to advance a testable *hypothesis*, not a "truth claim" or description of fact. Gelso and Hayes (1998) observed that our familiarity with this triad puts us at risk for assuming that there is little more to learn or to say—and, given that Tyler was drawing a similar conclusion in 1953, it is not surprising that many would consider this to be an area where the answers are established. However, although several decades of research have produced a strong consensus as to the positive contribution made by the core conditions, debate and uncertainty continue regarding their relative importance and the mechanisms through which they support change. For example, in 1985, Gelso and Carter evaluated the empirical evidence and concluded that the core conditions cannot be considered either necessary or sufficient, yet a recent review (Bohart, Elliott, Greenberg, & Watson, 2002) advances the idea, with empirical support, that empathy may play a causal role in positive client outcomes, particularly when viewed from the client's perspective. Contemporary researchers continue to explore the role of the facilitative conditions within different therapeutic models (e.g., Watson & Geller, 2005) and client populations (e.g., Chang & Berk, 2009). What cannot be disputed, however, is that Rogers was a remarkably keen observer, as his core therapeutic conditions have continued to be identified as central to an effective counseling relationship (Norcross, 2002a).

Some of the earliest investigations of Rogers' core conditions were conducted by Truax and Carkhuff (1967), who provided some of the first summary evidence for Rogers' formulation of the relationship. These early investigations indicated that, although the association between the individual facilitative conditions and outcome were mixed, more positive results were obtained when the three conditions were treated as an aggregate (Farber & Lane, 2002). This finding, that an aggregate of the core conditions has the greatest predictive power, has continued to gain support. Contemporary investigations have reaffirmed that the association with outcome for the individual core conditions is more variable than for the relationship as a single entity (Farber & Lane, 2002).

Client perception appears to play an important role in the operation of Rogers' core relationship conditions. Work by Batchelor (1988) revealed that clients differ in what they perceive as an empathic response, a point that highlights the necessity of attending to individual differences in clients' experience of the relationship. Lambert and Barley (2002), in a discussion of the facilitative conditions, point to consistent evidence that the more positive associations with outcome are obtained for client-perceived relationship factors, rather than those reported by therapists or observers.

The most compelling contemporary support for the association between Rogers' core conditions and client outcome is presented in the work of the Division 29 Task Force on Empirically Supported Therapy Relationships (Norcross, 2002a). Following their comprehensive review of extant research, the Task Force concluded that the factor of empathy was "demonstrably effective" in promoting positive outcomes and that the factors of congruence/genuineness and positive regard were "promising and probably effective" in facilitating positive change.

The Counseling Relationship as a Common Factor

> There is some evidence that Rogerian, Freudian, and Adlerian therapy situations are more similar, at least in the important matter of the counseling relationship established with the client, than they had been assumed to be.
> (Tyler, 1953, p. 227)

Dare we ask whether psychotherapy researchers are "slow learners?" Tyler's observations in 1953 were empirically based, and Truax and Carkhuff's (1967) review indicated that aggregate measures of the relationship were a stronger predictor than theoretically derived components. Smith and Glass' (1977) classic meta-analysis, which demonstrated both the effectiveness of psychotherapy and the lack of significant differences among treatments, was published over 40 years ago. But, as a field, we have been slow to abandon our faith in the uniqueness of theoretically driven interventions. As Lambert, Garfield, and Bergin (2004) note, "Yet, there is tremendous resistance to accepting this finding as a legitimate one. Numerous interpretations of the data have been given in order to preserve the idea that technical factors have substantial, unique and specific effects" (p. 809). Perhaps in this new century, given the consistent evidence that specific approaches and treatments do not differ in effecting positive client outcomes for most presenting concerns (Lambert, Garfield, & Bergin, 2004), we are ready to "give it up" and learn more about what makes the counseling relationship a critical element of therapeutic success.

The common factors approach can be described as the search for those "active ingredients" that cut across psychotherapeutic approaches, are important in all forms of psychotherapy, and are not linked to the change mechanisms specified by specific theoretical orientations. First advanced by Rosenzweig (1936), the idea of common factors has attracted increased attention as contemporary research continues to document the lack of specificity attached to particular theoretical approaches (Ahn & Wampold, 2001). Various authors have advanced lists of potential common factors (e.g., Greencavage & Norcross, 1990; Stiles, Shapiro, & Elliott, 1986;

Weinberger, 1995). Lambert and Ogles (2004), for example, categorize common factors as support, learning, and action factors. Regardless of the form of categorization for common active ingredients, the counseling relationship is named consistently as an influential factor that crosses theoretical boundaries; Lambert and Ogles (2004) assert that, based on a series of extensive empirical reviews, "Reviewers are virtually unanimous in their opinion that the therapist–patient relationship is critical to positive outcome" (p. 174).

As a common factor, the counseling relationship is frequently operationalized as a constellation of Rogers' core conditions, in contrast to assessing the individual contributions of empathy, unconditional regard, and genuineness. As noted above, there is empirical support for treating them as an aggregate, and Lambert and Ogles (2004) assert that, "Virtually all schools of therapy accept the notion that these [client-centered necessary and sufficient conditions] or related therapist relationship variables are important for significant progress in psychotherapy and, in fact, fundamental in the formation of a working cooperative effort between patient and therapist" (p. 173).

A number of counseling psychology researchers have made important contributions to our understanding of the therapeutic relationship as a common factor. Louis Castonguay, who has emerged as an influential psychotherapy process researcher, conducted comparative research showing that the relationship is associated with outcome more strongly than are specific treatments (e.g., Castonguay, Goldfried, Wiser, & Raue, 1996). Bruce Wampold (2007; Ahn & Wampold, 2001) has been at the forefront of the argument that common factors account for more variance in outcome than do specific techniques. Wampold's work on common factors and the counseling relationship represents several of the themes that have long been central to a counseling psychology perspective; in his program of research, he has used the tools of empiricism to explore the "particularity" of individual counseling relationships, concluding that factors unique to a given relationship are central to the change process. Wampold is not concerned with the relationship as a curative factor in its own right; instead, he has advanced the argument that the relationship with the therapist is critical to the client's engagement in other aspects of the change process, with a particular emphasis on client perceptions of the therapist as a trustworthy guide in exploration of his or her concerns

(Baldwin, Wampold, & Imel, 2007, Wampold, 2007). Readers interested in learning more about this counseling psychologist's perspective are invited to review Wampold (2007).

The broad consensus on the importance of the therapeutic relationship as a common factor has prompted further investigation of the mechanisms through which it may influence positive change. Some of the factors that have been identified as moderators and mediators are discussed in subsequent sections of this chapter.

The Working Alliance

> In this first hour, some kind of relationship must be established. Out of this meeting the client must get something that will make him willing to come back and to put forth the further effort that is required. When this first hour begins, counselor and counselee are strangers; when it ends they must have formed some sort of partnership.
> (Tyler, 1953, p. 24)

Tyler may have underestimated the length of time required to establish a working alliance, as current research indicates that the alliance established by the third session can predict outcome (e.g., Horvath & Symonds, 1991), but it is clear that she appreciated the essential focus on collaboration and partnership that defines the therapeutic alliance.

Horvath and Bedi's (2002) definition of the alliance "refers to the equality and strength of the collaborative relationship between client and therapist in therapy" (p. 41) and includes positive affective and cognitive elements, and an active, conscious, purposeful engagement. They also note that some writers use the terms "alliance" and "counseling/ therapeutic relationship" interchangeably, but point out that there are subtle, yet important differences between these terms. Although the contemporary understanding of the alliance is more pantheoretical, the construct has roots in psychodynamic theory and has produced a range of definitions, with varying emphasis on individual components.

Given the diverse perspectives on this construct, any discussion of findings needs to reference the measures developed to operationalize the alliance. The three measures used most widely are the Penn Helping Alliance (HA) scales (Luborsky, Crits-Cristoph, Alexander, Margolis, & Cohen, 1983), the Vanderbilt Therapeutic Alliance Scale (VTAS; Hartley & Strupp, 1983), and the Working Alliance Inventory (WAI, Horvath, 1981, Horvath & Greenberg, 1986). Horvath and Bedi (2002) report high correlations among the scales cited but emphasize that differences do exist in both the inclusion and weighting of different alliance dimensions. This discussion considers research using the WAI, given its associations with counseling psychology in both its development and ongoing research (Horvath, 1981; Mallinckrodt, 1993, 1996).

The relationship between strength of the working alliance and therapy outcome is now firmly established, across both assessment perspectives (client, therapist, or observer) and across various forms of therapy (Horvath, 2001). Horvath (2005) provides a succinct summary of research to date, noting that, "At the risk of ignoring complexity, a reasonable summary is that the relationships reported across reviews have been quite consistent: the alliance–outcome correlation is moderate but significant (ranges from .22 to .29), clients' assessments tend to be more predictive of outcome than are other sources, early alliance is as good or better predictor of outcome than assessments taken later, and the alliance as measured appears to be related to but not identical to parallel therapeutic gains" (p. 4). Lambert and Barley (2002), following their review of empirical research on the alliance–outcome relationship, noted that therapist contributions to the alliance go beyond provision of the facilitative conditions to include reaching agreement with clients on goals and tasks and to the ability to manage ruptures in the alliance (Hatcher & Barends, 1996; Safran, Muran, & Samstag, 1994).

Contemporary research continues to extend the application of the alliance formulation of the therapeutic relationship to new areas of counseling practice and research, and counseling psychologists are key contributors. As examples, Patton and Kivlighan (1997) used hierarchical linear modeling to explore the relationship between a supervisory working alliance and the working alliance experienced by a trainee's clients and found parallels between a trainee's perceptions of the supervisory alliance and his or her client's perceptions of the working alliance. Bedi (2006) used multivariate concept mapping to understand what factors clients experienced as contributing to the development of the alliance and learned that clients attached importance to both the counselor's personal characteristics and to the physical setting. Friedlander and colleagues (2006, 2008) have investigated alliance formation and its relationship to outcome in family therapy, in which the client perspective on the alliance is represented by multiple family members.

To pursue this work, Friedlander et al. (2006) developed an observational rating tool, the System for Observing Family Therapy Alliances. In recent work (2008), they learned that, in contrast to individual counseling, a strong alliance within the family is more important to treatment success than is an alliance with the counselor.

Another research focus pursued by counseling psychologists has considered whether counselors working in online modalities can establish effective therapeutic alliances. A review published in *The Counseling Psychologist* by Mallen et al. (2005) reported that, at that time, only three studies had investigated this question and had produced mixed results. The authors note that variables related to age and familiarity with online technologies have not been isolated in previous research, making any conclusions highly tentative, and that the absence of nonverbal cues in online environments can increase counselor susceptibility to common stereotypes. In contrast, other research indicates that clients can establish an effective alliance in online counseling (e.g., Cook & Doyle, 2002). Knaevelsrud and Maercker (2006) found that clients seeking online assistance for post-traumatic stress reactions reported positive alliance scores, although there was a variable association between the therapeutic relationship and treatment outcome ($r = .13 – .33$). What may be most noteworthy is the finding that, in a population at risk for premature termination, the alliance was associated with retention in online therapy. The 48 participants in their study had a drop-out rate of 17%, which the authors note contrasts with reported rates of up to 28%.

Although much of the extant research has examined the therapeutic alliance as a predictor of therapy outcome, there has been an increased call to move beyond a direct association. More recently, alliance research has examined the alliance as a mediating variable between provision of Rogers' core conditions and client outcome. As one example, Watson and Geller (2005) used the Relationship Inventory (Barrett-Lennard, 1962), one of the field's earliest measures of Rogers' conditions, and the WAI (Horvath & Greenberg, 1986) to explore mediation in both cognitive-behavioral and process-experiential therapy. Although the two forms of therapy did not differ on measured therapist empathy, acceptance and congruence, the core conditions were related to outcome measures of depression, interpersonal distress, self-esteem and negative attitudes. Importantly, the alliance mediated the relationship between the core conditions and three of the four outcome measures. The authors argued that Rogers' core conditions make their contribution to outcome by fostering a strong working alliance. This point echoes arguments made by other counseling psychology researchers, as noted in a subsequent section on therapist factors in the relationship.

The Real Relationship

> To put on a mask of friendliness to cover hostility, contempt, or plain lack of interest, is to confuse the client, not to help him. Signs of the real feelings will inevitably appear during the interview. . . .
> (Tyler, 1953, p. 27)

A more recent arrival on the theoretical landscape has been Gelso and colleagues' elaboration of the real relationship component of his tripartite model (see Gelso & Samstag, 2008), in which the other components consist of the working alliance and the transferential dimensions of relationship. Gelso (2004) has defined the real relationship as, "the personal relationship existing between two or more people as reflected in the degree to which each is genuine with the other and perceives the other in ways that befit the other" (p. 6), and argues that it both emerges in the first moments of client–counselor interaction and is the base from which a working alliance develops (Gelso et al., 2005).

The importance of the real relationship construct to research on the counseling relationship resides in Gelso et al's. (2005) claim that it plays a unique and significant role in both the counseling process and outcome, across types of therapy, beyond that contributed by variables previously under investigation. Research on the real relationship has been catalyzed by the development of measures to operationalize therapist and client perspectives on the construct (Fuertes et al., 2007; Gelso et al., 2005). To date, the authors report that the real relationship is empirically distinct from the working alliance ($r = .47$, $p < .01$) and demonstrates an independent relationship with session outcome, measured as depth and smoothness of sessions (Gelso et al., 2005).

New ideas often generate controversy, and the claims advanced for the real relationship by Gelso and colleagues are no exception (e.g., Greenberg, 1994; Horvath, 2009). It appears that the primary criticisms are definitional and concerned with the most informative and defensible means of partitioning elements of the relationship, as well as whether conceptual clarity can be achieved in describing the separate components. Greenberg (1994), for example, questioned whether the real relationship, consisting of genuineness and realistic perception, can be differentiated from Rogers' core condition of genuineness. It remains to be seen whether the recent development of measures for the real relationship will generate research that answers the critics.

The Empirically Supported Relationship: Report of the APA Division 29 (Psychotherapy) Task Force

> I still hope that the research summaries . . . will be a help to practicing counselors trying to distinguish between things we do simply because they seem to work well and things we do because of some definite research evidence.
> (Tyler, 1953, p. x)

One of the most significant advances in our understanding of the therapeutic relationship has emerged from the work of a task force established by Division 29 Psychotherapy of the APA (see Norcross, 2002). The task force was commissioned in response to widespread concerns over the emphasis on empirically validated treatments (EVTs, Norcross, 2002b), as advanced by APA Division 12 (clinical psychology; e.g., Chambless & Hollon, 1998) and counseling psychology (Wampold, Lichtenberg, & Waehler, 2002). Now termed *empirically supported treatments*, these lists of therapeutic approaches, with effectiveness demonstrated through randomized clinical trials and manualized treatment, were viewed as emphasizing technique over process factors that have demonstrable impact (Norcross, 2002b). Specifically, the Division 29 Task Force identified three areas that had not received attention: the therapy relationship, the person of the therapist, and the client's characteristics.

The Task Force's goal was to identify therapeutic relationship elements that had sufficient empirical support to qualify as components of an "empirically supported relationship," comparable to the claims of empirically supported treatments (Norcross, 2002a). After 3 years of careful analysis, using clear operational definitions and rigorous selection criteria, the group advanced conclusions and recommendations regarding the empirical evidence for the contribution of various components of therapeutic relationships to positive client outcome. Relationship elements and therapist factors that had accumulated broad and consistent research support were categorized as either "demonstrably effective" or, in cases in which the substantive evidence was positive but still mixed, elements were described as "promising and probably effective."

The conclusions of the Task Force, with regard to "general elements of the therapeutic relationship" (Norcross, 2002a, p. 441), were as follows: Factors with sufficient empirical evidence to be regarded as demonstrably effective included the therapeutic alliance, cohesion in group therapy, empathy, and goal consensus and collaboration. Evidence to support a conclusion of promising and probably effective was found for the factors of positive regard, congruence/genuineness, feedback, repair of alliance ruptures, self-disclosure, management of countertransference, and quality of interpersonal interpretations.

The alert reader will note that many of the factors identified by the Task Force have been cited in the current work as influential components of the various models of the therapeutic relationship. Much of the work reviewed here was considered by the Task Force, and the relevance of its conclusions to counseling psychology is supported by the fact that approximately one-third of the Task Force members are counseling psychologists. The therapeutic relationship, congruent with its now established status as a common factor in change, is an arena in which applied psychologists from diverse specializations are collaborating to understand this most basic element of the psychotherapy process. A summary list cannot begin to capture the depth of investigation that underlies the Task Force conclusions, or to convey the subtle variations or individuating factors that would inform application of these findings. Interested readers are strongly encouraged to consult the full report of the Task Force, which appears in book form (Norcross, 2002a).

Variables That Influence the Counseling Relationship

> Counselors have much to say about "the counseling relationship" and psychoanalysts have had still more to say about "the transference." What has not been stressed enough in all these discussions of "the counseling relationship" or "the transference" is the fact that each relationship has its own individual characteristics; each is unique. It is on these unique characteristics of this particular relationship that the counselor should focus his attention at the beginning.
> (Tyler, 1953, p. 35)

To this point, much of our discussion has treated the counseling relationship as an entity, itself, with little attention to the factors that make each relationship unique, as Tyler so pointedly reminds us.

The following section surveys some of the individuating characteristics that have been investigated as influential in the formation or operation of the counseling relationship. Although researchers have considered factors associated with the therapist, the client, and their reciprocal interaction, the current discussion (for purposes of managing the scope) emphasizes therapist factors. Once again, Leona Tyler's words provide evidence that counseling psychologists have been aware of these factors for a long time, and that contemporary efforts to understand their influence rest on a substantial base of scholarship.

Attachment Style

> It is almost inevitable that attitudes carried over from parent–child relationships should weave themselves into the complex fabric of the counseling relationship.
> (Tyler, p. 41)

A number of psychotherapy researchers have explored the relevance of Bowlby's (1969) and Ainsworth's (1964) work on the attachment of infants to their caregivers, and extensions of this work to adult relationships (Bartholomew, 1994; Bartholomew & Thompson,1995) to characteristics of the counseling relationship (e.g., Mallinckrodt, Gantt, & Coble, 1995). A steady stream of investigation has explored whether client and therapist attachment styles (characterized as anxious, avoidant, or secure) influence either the type or the strength of the counseling relationship, which can also present conditions of emotional vulnerability and stress. In general, investigators have demonstrated that both client and therapist attachment style are important factors in the development and maintenance of the counseling relationship. At the same time, the modest correlations between the range of methods used to operationalize attachment style (e.g., narrative, interview, self-report) mandates caution in assuming that one study's definition of "secure" attachment is comparable to another's (Meyer & Pilkonis, 2002).

There appears to be a consensus that client attachment style plays an important role in the therapeutic relationship, both in ability to form an alliance (Eames & Roth, 2000) and in eliciting different response styles from a therapist (Hardy et al., 1999). Clarkin and Levy (2004), in their summary of the research, suggest a paradox that, although attachment anxiety or avoidance could interfere with establishing a counseling relationship, a preoccupation with intimacy could lead to successful engagement over time, and that the interaction between therapist and client attachment style is important.

Mallinckrodt, a counseling psychologist whose work has been influential in examining the association between attachment style and the alliance, worked with colleagues to develop the Client Attachment to Therapist Scale (CATS; Mallinckrodt et al., 1995). The CATS assesses client attachment to therapists as secure, avoidant, or preoccupied by assessing client perceptions of their therapist as emotionally responsive, disapproving, or rejecting, and the client's wish to feel closer to the therapist. Support for the construct validity of the CATS comes from evidence that clients with difficult family histories experience avoidant-fearful attachment to their therapists (Mallinckrodt, King, & Coble, 1998), whereas those with secure therapeutic attachments experience a stronger working alliance (Mallinckrodt et al., 1995).

In considering the impact of a therapist's attachment style, evidence is emerging that attachment plays an independent role in the form the alliance takes. Some intriguing research indicates that having an attachment style that differs from that of the client is beneficial, in that clients have an opportunity to disconfirm their expectations of relationships with others (e.g., Tyrrell, Dozier, Teague, & Fallot, 1999). Other research indicates that therapists with less secure attachment styles may be prone to respond less empathically (Rubino, Barker, Roth, & Fearson, 2000).

Meyer and Pilkonis (2002) have recommended that researchers investigate attachment as a mediator in the counseling relationship. They offer a compelling rationale, based on Mischel and Shoda's (1995) social cognitive work, that attachment styles be viewed as stable individual factors that are expressed in a context-dependent manner. In other words, a client or therapist with less secure attachment may not act in an "insecure" manner until they perceive a sense of threat or insecurity in the environment. This formulation supports an interactional view of the role of attachment in the therapeutic relationship, one that adds a situational dimension to the current exploration of therapist and client factors.

Countertransference

The counselor's own feelings are bound up in [the relationship]. . . . Inevitably, since he is a sensitive human being, he will react on an immediate unconscious level to subtle indications of hostility in a person he is interviewing. These things will be true no matter how well-integrated a person he is and even if he has set his own personality in order through some thorough-going psychotherapy before beginning his work.
(Tyler, p. 42)

Countertransference occurs when a therapist's reactions to a client are based in the therapist's earlier conflicts or relationships, rather than in the present interaction, and are assumed to be a distortion (Gelso & Carter, 1994). Although the construct of countertransference has roots in psychodynamic thought, other definitions have included all therapist reactions or highlighted its interactive dimension (Gelso & Samstag, 2008). One contemporary, integrative formulation describes it as a component of all therapy relationships (Gelso & Hayes, 1998). Given that countertransference emerges in the context of therapist–client interaction, it needs to be considered as another potentially influential factor in the formation and maintenance of the therapeutic relationship.

There is a longstanding consensus that unrecognized countertransference has negative effects on psychotherapy outcome (Gelso & Hayes, 1998), in part by limiting the therapist's accurate understanding of the client (Lambert & Ogles, 2004; Singer & Luborsky, 1977). As Hayes et al. (1997) noted, "relationships predicated and sustained on illusory perceptions are not likely to succeed in helping clients attain their goals" (p. 151).

Much of the early research on countertransference attempted to identify factors or client types that evoked negative therapist reactions (see Gelso & Hayes, 1998), rather than investigate its role in the therapeutic relationship, and the first links between countertransference and the therapeutic relationship were indirect. In a qualitative investigation, Hill et al. (1996) reported an association between countertransference and client–counselor disagreement and premature termination. Counselors in the study identified their own difficult family histories as contributing to their impasses with clients. As a second example, Hayes and Gelso (1993) and Gelso et al. (1995) found that therapists assessed as high in homophobia exhibited avoidance of important client material presented by analogue gay and lesbian clients. Given that many definitions of the relationship cite therapist–client engagement as a central component, it seems probable that therapist avoidance would have a negative effect on the relationship.

Counseling psychologist Charles Gelso, and a research team with links to the University of Maryland, have been vigorous contributors to research on countertransference, both in explicating definitional issues and in exploring its role in the counseling relationship (see Gelso & Hayes, 2002, for a review). This group has contributed to growing evidence that countertransference influences psychotherapy outcome through its influence on the therapy relationship. In a large-scale field study of therapist trainees (Ligiero & Gelso, 2002), both therapist and supervisor ratings documented a relationship between therapists' negative countertransference behaviors and a less effective working alliance with clients. Interestingly, ratings of therapists' positive countertransference (e.g., being overly friendly or supportive) were associated with lower ratings of the bond component of the alliance.

Another aspect of countertransference research related to the counseling relationship suggests that the therapist's ability to manage countertransference reactions may mediate the countertransference–alliance link. For example, there are demonstrations of a relationship between countertransference and empathic ability (Hayes, Riker, & Ingram, 1997; Peabody & Gelso, 1982), in which greater empathic ability has been associated with both the therapist's recognition and management of countertransference reactions. In a case study of a 13 sessions of psychotherapy, Rosenberger and Hayes (2002) found that the therapist's effectiveness in managing countertransference had positive associations with the client's assessment of their working alliance.

One of the most explicit discussions of the role of countertransference in the relationship comes from Gelso and Hayes' (1998) reflections on their survey of countertransference research. They argued that the negative impact of countertransference may result from its effect in dividing the therapist's attention between his or her internal concerns and the client's concerns. Furthermore, they asserted that countertransference may have an impact on psychotherapy by first influencing the therapist and then, by extension, the relationship. Gelso and Hayes refer to this as "limiting the therapist's instrumentality of self" (p. 100) and argued that its effects will be most noticeable in therapeutic approaches that employ the relationship as a key mechanism of change.

Although the conceptual link between countertransference and the strength of the relationship strikes many as intuitively obvious, there is still scant research to support this claim. Further complicating the picture, several authors have argued that, under certain circumstances, countertransference can be employed to facilitate a counselor's understanding of a client. Finally, it is important to note that countertransference does not operate in isolation; Mohr, Gelso, and Hill (2005) found that, for counselor trainees, countertransference behavior reflected an interaction of both client and counselor attachment style. These initial findings strongly suggest that countertransference, by producing therapist behaviors that interfere with effective engagement, plays a role in the formation and maintenance of therapeutic relationships. However, given the paucity of research, conclusions must remain tentative.

Expectancies and Preferences

[T]he first question he asks himself is, "What are this person's expectations from counseling? What does he think is going to happen? What does he hope to get out of it?"
(Tyler, 1953, p. 36)

Both client and therapist bring their individual expectations to the therapeutic encounter. But, it is within the relationship that expectations have their effect on process and outcome, as that is the arena in which they are either met or not met. Each of us can recall the impact of unmet expectations. For example, the experience of receiving critical supervisory feedback on a counseling session that one considered a success can leave the recipient feeling vulnerable and exposed, perhaps angry, and can raise questions about either oneself or the relationship. Psychologists were quick to note the relevance of expectations to the counseling process and relationship—one of Carl Rogers' students investigated the association between client outcome expectations and observed change (Lipkin, 1954; cited by Arnkoff, Glass, & Shapiro, 2002)—and there has been a lengthy history of research on the role of client expectancies in psychotherapy process and outcome (Clarkin & Levy, 2004).

Early research appeared to support the relevance of client expectations to the development of a strong therapeutic relationship. Clarkin and Levy (2004) report that, in the 1960s, a series of investigations characterized client role expectations as having features such as reciprocity and interdependence, nurturance, and collaboration, as well as characteristics associated with authority and guidance. In 1980, counseling psychologist E. A. Tinsley and colleagues (1980) developed the Expectations About Counseling measure (EAC), based on four empirically derived factors that assessed client anticipation of client personal commitment, counselor provision of Rogers' facilitative conditions, counselor expertise, and counselor nurturance.

Many researchers have pointed out that the congruence, or match, between client and counselor expectations is likely to be most influential. In an early study that surveyed both clients and counselors, Netzky et al. (1982) found that, although both clients and counselors viewed a strong relationship as a central expectation, clients differed from counselors in raising questions that centered on whether the counselor would be trustworthy and respectful. Specifically, clients expected to evaluate counseling based on whether counselors treated them as equals, confronted them when appropriate, and would end counseling if the client was not benefiting.

Several decades of research support a conclusion that client expectancies do have a relationship to therapeutic outcome, although the association appears to be modest and is most likely to be indirect or mediated by third variables (Clarkin & Levy, 2004). Although the therapeutic relationship has been identified as a potential mediator of the correlation between expectations and outcome, very little research has explored the role of client expectations as a direct predictor of the strength of the therapeutic relationship. Several initial studies of actual psychotherapy suggest that expectations may play a significant role. Joyce and Piper (1998) reported a strong association between client expectations and the alliance, whereas two investigations by counseling psychologists Al-Darmaki and Kivlighan (1993) and Tokar et al. (1996) produced mixed findings. More recently, Rizvi et al. (2000, cited in Clarkin & Levy, 2004) found that client expectations, in comparison to therapist variables and problem severity, were the strongest predictor of the therapeutic alliance for clients diagnosed with borderline personality disorder.

Before further discussion, it is useful to consider important distinctions between the various types of expectancies that may operate in a counseling relationship. Garfield (1978) differentiated between the expectations that clients bring into counseling and those that develop out of experience with a specific counselor; both can be influential. A client's initial, positive expectancies for change can be considered a common factor in treatment, and Lambert and Barley (2002) include such expectancies in their category of "placebo effects," assigning as much as 15% of outcome variance to these factors. Alternately, derived expectations, those that emerge in a specific counseling experience, were illustrated in the earlier discussion of how attachment influences relationship formation, in which clients benefited from having a counselor disconfirm their expectations for relational patterns (e.g., Tyrrell et al., 1999).

The area of expectations that has generated the most research is associated with expectations that clients bring to the therapeutic encounter. Highlen and Hill (1984) have pointed out that these initial expectations are probably most influential in the early stages of counseling, before client and therapist have an opportunity to correct or disconfirm erroneous assumptions about what the process may involve. Consistent with this point, client expectations have been consistent predictors for the complementary variables of premature termination and continuation in therapy (Clarkin & Levy, 2004). Specifically, when client expectations for what will happen in psychotherapy are not met, there is a significant increase in premature termination (Hardin, Subich, & Holvey. 1988; Reis & Brown, 1999). Swift and Callahan (2008) note that a large body of literature supports these conclusions; they also describe the magnitude of this issue. According to their review, between 40% and 60% of clients drop out of therapy before any beneficial change is achieved. Furthermore, several authors have pointed directly to unmet client expectations as a key factor in premature termination (e.g., see Wierzbicki & Pekarik, 1993, for a meta-analysis).

One area within the body of research on client expectations that has been catalyzed by work on premature termination is that of expectations held by clients outside the dominant culture. Comas-Diaz (2006) reports earlier research, conducted with colleagues, in which she studied both pretherapy expectations and expectations for therapists that were held by clients of color. Although she found that "people of color have a complex set of expectations related to the cultural variation in the clinician's role" (p. 93), she links this finding to recommendations for managing a multicultural relationship from a position of cultural empathy. In my view, one of the major contributions of Comas-Diaz's work, as well as that of the larger body of work on unmet expectations and premature termination, is that it invites us to reconsider what we are measuring when we investigate client expectations. A brief discussion follows.

As noted above, little research explores a direct link between unmet client expectations and the therapeutic relationship. However, it appears likely that these effects may be partially mediated by relationship factors. Two areas of expectancy research that are directly relevant to the counseling relationship are those focused on role expectations (in contrast to client expectations for therapy effectiveness or outcome) and those focused on client preferences, which refer to therapist characteristics one would choose if given the option. Role expectations refer to the behaviors one expects or considers appropriate in a given encounter and, for clients, can apply to their own behavior or that of the therapist. Therapists undoubtedly hold role expectations, as well; however, the overwhelming emphasis in expectancy research has been on client expectations.

An issue that has not been addressed in the relationship literature, but which may be critical to our understanding, is an examination of the cognitive structure and dynamic influence of expectations. Expectations consist of what we think will, or should, happen and, as an independent construct, appear to have limited predictive power. However, they may represent the tip of a cognitive iceberg, particularly as highly cultural "signs" of the belief structures that give rise to expectations. Similar to other cognitive frames that we use to interpret the world, expectations can arise from preexisting beliefs or prior experience. This formulation has received recent attention from cognitive-behavioral therapists; Leahy (2008), for example, describes the therapeutic relationship as reflecting therapist and client interpersonal schemas. When we measure expectations, we are probably obtaining a window on existing cognitive schemas for how the world "should" work, according to either therapist or client. A similar argument may apply to another construct employed in relationship research, that of "matching" client and therapist on various demographic characteristics; those issues are addressed in a subsequent section that explores research on diversity and the relationship.

For individual clients, an expectation may reflect a belief about themselves ("I don't believe anyone would care about me") or a group to which they belong ("In my experience, people of my sexual orientation may not be accepted"). The real relevance of expectancies to the strength of the counseling relationship may consist in what they tell us about underlying beliefs and attitudes—not only on the part of clients, but also on the part of counselors.

To illustrate this point, it is informative to consider research on client and counselor expectations associated with class and socioeconomic status (SES), as the association between client expectations and premature termination is particularly descriptive of clients in disadvantaged economic circumstances. A body of research on expectations emerged in the 1960s and, although cited sporadically, is largely ignored. Smith (2005), responding to a 2000 APA Resolution on Poverty and Socioeconomic Status, notes that, "Researchers of the 1960s had already established that poor clients terminate treatment prematurely—why, four decades later, does that still constitute the sum of psychology's knowledge about them?" (p. 690). Research conducted in the 1960s and the 1970s is relevant to a discussion of expectations but, to the surprise of some, challenges our assumptions about *therapist* expectations, an area that may be amenable to therapist modification and one likely to have indirect influences on the therapeutic relationship.

In 1971, Graff, Kenig, and Radoff reported that therapists believed that poor people were unlikely to benefit from therapy (expectation) and, in any event, would drop out prematurely (expectation). Lorion's (1973, 1974) significant work on psychotherapy with the poor refuted the notion that the lack of psychotherapeutic effectiveness was attributable to clients' unrealistic expectations about psychotherapy; instead, he made a convincing argument that therapist attitudes and biases (a source of expectations) contributed to treatment failures. In support of this argument, consider research conducted by Jacobs et al. (1972), in which a brief, pre-therapy orientation was provided for poor clients and, for their therapists, a session to enhance awareness of class and cultural factors. Findings indicated that the orientation was associated with significant increases in client continuation in therapy, when both clients and therapists received the orientation, and *if only the therapist received the orientation*. This research did not assess the status of the therapeutic relationship directly, so any connection must be speculative; on the other hand, the fact that a brief intervention for therapists produced positive effects suggests that it had an impact on the connection that therapists established with clients.

Our dominant models of the therapy relationship—the empathy, positive regard, and congruence of Rogers' facilitative conditions and the task, bond, and goal components of the working alliance

(Horvath, 1981)—will surely be undermined if therapist attitudes and biases produce expectations that clients are not engaging in the way they "should" or are expected to. Future research on the role of attitudes and stereotypes, and more research on therapist expectations, may offer promise in advancing this dimension of relationship research. As further context for that effort, we can consider what has been learned about other therapist factors in the formation and maintenance of the therapeutic relationship.

Therapist Factors

> Different personalities inevitably produce differences in the way in which any specified counseling procedure will be used. Two counselors who are attempting to use the same technique may not be producing at all the same psychological effect.
> (Tyler, 1953, p. 291)

An interesting paradox exists in the history of psychotherapy research: From some of the earliest research on counseling outcomes, investigators have hypothesized that outcome would be related to differences in the strength of the counseling relationship and to differences in various therapist characteristics (e.g., level of experience, training, ethnicity), but the two domains were not considered together. Until very recently, little research has examined therapist differences in forming or maintaining the counseling relationship (Baldwin et al., 2007).

The majority of research on therapist characteristics has treated these factors either as independent predictors or as "matching" variables, paired with client demographic characteristics. The most noteworthy conclusion that can be drawn from many decades of research is that therapist characteristics such as age, sex, race/ethnicity, training, skill, experience, and style are poor predictors of outcome (Beutler et al., 2004). When similar variables have been examined as predictors of relationship quality, they have also produced equivocal results but also demonstrate the limitations of treating therapist characteristics as isolated variables. For example, whereas Dunkle and Friedlander (1996) found that therapist experience did not predict strength of the working alliance, Kivlighan et al. (1998) uncovered a more complex association: Overall, therapist experience had no association with relationship strength but, for difficult clients, experienced therapists achieved stronger relationships than did less

experienced therapists. Mallinckrodt and Nelson (1991) identified a series of complex interrelationships between training level and working alliance, and no differences on the bond component of the alliance.

Recognition of the complexity of therapist effects may contribute to what Beutler et al. (2004) have described as a "precipitous decline" (p. 289) in research on therapist variables. Although they express dismay over this shift, the authors also point out that researchers have reconceptualized many of the variables previously employed in investigating therapist characteristics, going beyond observable characteristics such as gender or age to an investigation of associated attitudes or values. For example, contemporary research is investigating "ageism" rather than age, or sex role attitudes rather than biological sex. Similarly, researchers are giving more attention to therapist factors or skill that emerge situationally, rather than generally, such as the earlier point that client attachment style may elicit differential responses from therapists (Hardy et al., 1999). The field does appear to be shifting to greater recognition of interactive and internal therapist factors; some of these domains of research are described below.

THERAPIST INTERPERSONAL STYLE: RECIPROCITY/COMPLEMENTARITY AND CIRCUMPLEX RESEARCH

> Counseling succeeds best when it steers clear of the autocratic attitude on the one hand and the laissez-faire on the other. . . .[and] views it always as a cooperative venture in which the two participants are making contributions of different sorts.
> (Tyler, 1953, p. 102)

One aspect of therapist behavior that has been a focus of relationship research in the past 30 years concerns whether the therapist's interpersonal style provides an effective complement to the client's style; in this domain, complementarity is defined as supporting or confirming a client's preferred style (Sexton & Whiston, 1994). Although there is not a great deal of research in this area, results have generally supported the contention that complementary interpersonal styles between therapist and client are associated with positive relationship development, particularly in the early stages of counseling (Beutler et al., 2004; Caspar, Grossman, Unmussig, & Schramm, 2005; Sexton & Whiston, 1994, Tracey, 1986).

Beutler et al. (2004) reviewed recent research and identified three subcategories of research in this area: investigations of complementarity in interpersonal style; assessments of reciprocal verbal patterns of interaction, focused on how a topic of conversation is negotiated through speaking turns; and investigations of nonverbal or multichannel communication, with an emphasis on the level of correspondence between verbal and nonverbal expression.

The first domain, that of complementarity in interpersonal style, emerged from Leary's (1957) interpersonal circle, which posits that persons on different points of the circle are continually negotiating the two relationship dimensions of control (to assert or submit) and affiliation (to be friendly or hostile). Benjamin (1982), Kiesler (1982), and Wiggins (1982) extended the circumplex model to client–therapist interactions in psychotherapy. Research in this area, including contributions by counseling psychologists (Kivlighan, McGovern, & Corazzini, 1984; Reandeau & Wampold, 1991), generally suggests that complementary styles (e.g., similarity on the friendly–unfriendly dimension and dissimilarity on the dominant–submissive dimensions) are associated with positive relationship development (Tracey, 1986).

In a 1994 review of research, Sexton and Whiston (1994) identified 14 counseling psychology investigations of complementarity, indicating that this has been an area of interest for the field. An illustrative example can be found in research conducted by Terence Tracey, who explored client–counselor reciprocity in negotiating the topic focus of counseling sessions. In a series of investigations between 1985 and 1989, Tracey and colleagues identified several associations between complementarity and the counseling relationship. To cite two examples, they found that high levels of client–counselor agreement on topic determination were associated with continuation in counseling, a finding that was subsequently cross-validated in a new sample (Tracey, 1986), and that more experienced counselors (in comparison to trainees) were more likely to use noncomplementary responses to challenge client's problematic interaction patterns (Tracey & Hayes, 1989). Beutler et al. (2004), summarizing research in this area, noted that, "such findings suggest that a subtle pattern of collaboration and tacit agreement exists between patient and therapist in successful treatment, which may be particularly important in the development of the therapeutic relationship" (p. 244).

Beutler et al. (2004) ended their discussion of complementarity with an expression of concern that this area of research is disappearing; however, their conclusion may have been premature. Recent frustration with static models of the counseling relationship (Angus, March 25, 2009, personal communication) has reactivated interest in more interactive models. A special issue of the journal *Psychotherapy Research* (2005; Vol. 15, 1–2) explored a range of topics identified as germane to complementarity and interaction within the relationship. Among others, these include perspective divergence in the working alliance (Fitzpatrick, Iwakabe, & Stalikas, 2005), nonverbal relationship regulation (Benecke, Peham, & Banniger-Huber, 2005), therapist–client connection in building the alliance (Sexton, Littauer, Sexton, & Tommeras, 2005), and a new model of complementarity in the therapeutic relationship (Caspar et al., 2005). This renewed interest is also reflected in the use of methods not often employed in relationship research; for example, Lepper and Mergenthaler (2007) employed conversation analysis, a qualitative method that applies a contextualized turn-by-turn analysis of talk, to examine the emergence of the therapeutic bond in a single dyad case study.

In anticipating the next 40 years of psychotherapy research, process researcher Lynne Angus predicts that influential therapist effects will reflect the qualities of "responsiveness" and "attunement" (Angus, 2009). Indirect—and somewhat amusing—support for Angus' prediction comes from research that has examined the use of manualized treatment protocols in controlled studies. In these research trials, it appears that the most effective therapists did not conform to the manualized instructions (Strupp & Anderson, 1997) and further, there was a negative correlation between measures of therapist interpersonal skill and ability to learn the manualized approach (Henry, Schacht, Strupp, Butler, & Binder, 1993a; Henry, Strupp, Butler, Schacht, & Binder, 1993b).

The first years of the 21st century produced a rapid escalation of interest in therapist effects, and a growing number of researchers contend that therapist contributions have their effect via their role in forming strong, effective therapeutic relationships (Wampold, 2007). As an example, Lutz and colleagues (2007) studied a naturalistic dataset of 1, 198 clients and 60 therapists and found that, whereas 8% of total outcome variance was attributable to therapist effects, 17% of the variance in clients' rate of improvement was attributable to therapist factors. Although not discussed by the authors, one can speculate that the more we attend to moment-by-moment interaction between client and therapist, the larger the proportion of variance may be. Lutz et al.'s results produced proportions that are very similar to results obtained by other investigators who have begun dismantling therapist contributions to the alliance and to outcome.

Bruce Wampold is a counseling psychologist whose research has brought greater attention to therapist effects. In an APA award address in 2007, he argued that "there is increasing evidence that it is the therapist and not the treatment per se that is responsible for therapeutic change . . . and, it appears that much of the variability among therapists is due to therapists' ability to form a working alliance with a variety of patients" (p. 868). As we move ahead with our efforts to understand the counseling relationship, it is becoming increasingly clear that we must also increase our efforts to understand what is contributed by the individual therapist. As we do so, there is a perennial area of research that receives little attention and is cited rarely in surveys of the therapeutic relationship: that of the therapist's personal adjustment and well-being.

Therapist Well-being, Mental Health, Adjustment

> One can say, for instance, that a counselor should be a very stable, well-adjusted individual himself so that the help he attempts to give others with their problems will not constitute a case of the blind leading the blind. It can just as well be said, however, that a counselor should have experienced anxiety, conflict, and indecision in his own life so that he can understand it in others.
>
> (Tyler, 1953, p. 267)

Although many practitioners would accept the idea that a therapist's level of adjustment or distress could have an impact on the therapeutic encounter, there has been surprisingly little research on this topic, and even less on the relationship between therapist adjustment and the counseling relationship. Beutler et al. (2004) report a very modest positive relationship between therapist well-being and therapeutic outcome, with an average effect size across nine studies of $r = .12$ ($p < .05$). Horvath and Bedi (2002), in their review of research on the working alliance, cite several negative therapist characteristics that have been associated with poor alliance formation: a "take charge" approach

(Lichtenberg et al., 1988), and being perceived as "cold" (Hersoug, Monsen, Havik & Hoglend, 2002) and as irritable (Sexton, 1996).

Although there is little empirical evidence in this area, it is fair to say that our profession holds an assumption that therapist distress or maladjustment can have a negative impact on the counseling relationship. Implicit evidence for this claim comes from our professional ethics codes, which require psychologists to "refrain from initiating an activity when they know or should know that there is a substantial likelihood that their personal problems will prevent them from performing their work-related activities in a competent manner" (American Psychological Association [APA], 2002, Standard 2.06a) and, "When psychologists become aware of personal problems that may interfere with their performing work-related duties adequately, they take appropriate measures, such as obtaining professional consultation or assistance, and determine whether they should limit, suspend, or terminate their work-related duties" (APA, 2002, Standard 2.06b).

A substantial and possibly overlooked body of research may be relevant to the question of how therapist well-being effects the counseling relationship. Given the ubiquity of computerized literature searches driven by author-selected key words, it appears likely that relevant research on this topic has been categorized in other domains and not integrated with relationship research. For example, Nutt-Williams, Hayes, and Fauth (2008) report that, for therapists, there is a consistent positive association between anxiety, negative self-talk, and lower self-assessments of effectiveness. Nutt-Williams and Hill (1996) found that, as trainees increased their level of negative self-talk, clients rated them as less helpful. In a review of counselor supervision literature, Ladany et al. (1999) found that a weaker supervisory working alliance was related to supervisors' lack of adherence to ethical guidelines. Ethical violations can reflect interpersonal difficulties, a hypothesis that gains some support from Nigro's (2004) work: Her qualitative survey of problematic dual relationships ($N = 206$) documented negative consequences in therapists' relationships with clients.

Another area that suggests a connection between therapist factors and relationship quality is the limited research on trainee impairment. In their major contribution and review, Forrest et al. (1999) noted that much of the research has focused on trainees whose impairment is in the area of clinical and interpersonal skills. They further report that "we can assume that most training programs in any 3-year period are probably dealing with four to five impaired or possibly impaired trainees (and) will dismiss one of those trainees" (p. 652).

A student or researcher conducting a search on the key words "therapeutic relationship" would be unlikely to uncover any of the research cited above. This may reflect a tendency to define relationship-relevant research too narrowly. As we learn more about the specificity of therapist contributions to relationship formation and maintenance, factors such as interpersonal skill and ethical adherence are likely to assume a greater role, and merit future research.

Capacity for Relationship: Training and Selection of Counselors and Psychotherapists

> The difficulty is that people with the necessary mental ability and a strong desire to do counseling do not all show the personal characteristics that make for success and satisfaction. It is just these personal characteristics which at present we are not able to analyze or predict.
> (L. Tyler, 1953, p. 267)

The field of relationship research is entering a new era: Psychotherapy researchers have identified the therapeutic relationship as our most consistent predictor of outcome (Horvath & Bedi, 2002; Imel & Wampold, 2008), and further evidence is accumulating that it is the therapist who carries the greatest weight in determining whether an effective relationship will be established. This presents the whole edifice of psychotherapy training with a profound challenge: If the most influential factor *is* the therapist, what is it about the therapist that matters? And, once those characteristics or skills are identified, are they something that can be taught? These may be uncomfortable questions for counseling psychologists. Although Tyler's comments indicate that such questions are not new, we have just begun to address them in a systematic fashion. Our historical values have emphasized the potential for growth in each individual—each trainee—and we may resist the idea that there are trait-like qualities that determine who will, or will not, be effective in developing therapeutic relationships.

At the same time, our legacy of empiricism propels us into an examination of these questions. What little research has been conducted to date presents findings that are challenging, although admittedly tentative and preliminary. Lambert and Ogles (2004), in their review of research investigating the role of training, reported that therapist training had no relationship to outcome or to strength of the therapeutic alliance. However, a therapist or trainee's level of interpersonal skill had a significant and positive relationship with both outcome and the alliance. Despite consistency in results, there are too few studies to draw firm conclusions; one has to wonder why this area has received so little attention.

Several investigators have evaluated the effects of specific training programs, and the results have not been encouraging. Henry et al. (1993a) provided systematic training on development of the alliance but failed to produce gains in therapists' ability to create stronger alliances. Horvath (2005) reported on his own survey of projects designed to train therapists in alliance skills, in which he found that the majority of such efforts failed to demonstrate an association between training and a resulting positive alliance, whether assessed by clients or independent raters. Intriguingly, he also noted that, although few identifiable skills were associated with alliance strength, researchers were successful in identifying personal attributes associated with alliance strength (e.g., flexibility and warmth).

Crits-Cristoph and colleagues (2006) investigated whether training in "alliance-fostering psychotherapy" (p. 268) would enable practicing therapists to enhance their alliance with clients diagnosed with major depressive disorder. Noteworthy as a field study with actual therapists and clients, the increases in alliance ratings for therapists failed to reach significance; further, decreases in alliance scores were observed for two of the five therapists . The authors also noted that therapists varied in their general tendency to form positive alliances and that differences were unrelated to training.

On a more positive note, a series of qualitative investigations conducted with therapist trainees in Norway (e.g., Nerdrum & Ronnestad, 2002, 2004) documented positive outcomes in empathic understanding following an empathy training program. At the same time, qualitative results exploring the trainees' perceptions indicated that many found it stressful and difficult to change their preferred style.

One significant project that has the potential to inform future research on the potential for training in therapist relationship skills is the Collaborative Research Network established by the Society for Psychotherapy Research. A summary report for this large-scale, international project (Orlinsky & Ronnestad; 2005) notes that, among the more than

5,000 therapists who participated, there were four identifiable patterns of engagement with clients: effective, challenging, disengaged, and distressing. Of concern, 17% of respondents reported disengaged relationships and 10% reported distressing engagement. The evidence that 27% of this sample described a stance toward therapeutic engagement that runs counter to descriptions of effective counseling relationships calls to mind some of the research cited earlier: Wampold's findings on the variability in therapist effectiveness and Forrest et al.'s report of the percentage of trainees identified as impaired while still pursuing their education. As Beutler et al. (2004) note, "high levels of therapist well-being cannot be assumed to be present among therapists in research studies. It may be a hidden moderator of many contradictory or inconsistent therapy findings" (p. 276–277). The Orlinsky and Ronnestad (2005) report concludes with some pointed recommendations. In particular, they argue that the available evidence points to the importance of relational skills that students bring to their training experience, as opposed to those that may be developed through supervision, and they recommend that possession of good interpersonal skills become a criterion in selection for psychotherapy training.

Career Psychology and the Counseling Relationship

How would such a job suit Barney?. . . . It is to be noted that [the counselor] has not picked out a job for the client and is not preparing to sell him a new idea. That would be out of keeping with the counseling relationship he has worked hard to create. He is simply insuring that the task the two of them are working on together, the consideration of occupational alternatives and the choice of one, will be carried out as thoroughly and efficiently as possible.
(Tyler, 1953, p. 175)

A longstanding debate has existed within counseling psychology as to whether career and personal counseling constitute independent domains of practice or share much in common. The question is relevant to any discussion of the role of the counseling relationship in career counseling, as one needs to consider whether the compelling findings obtained for its role in psychotherapy and personal counseling can be extended to the career arena. In general, those who have addressed the issue have pointed to commonalities: Crites (1981) described career counseling as an interpersonal process, and

Corbishley and Yost (1989) noted that several aspects of career counseling (e.g., the relationship and client resistance) require a psychological approach. Swanson (1995) argued that the process of career and personal counseling should be regarded as similar, in that both require many of the same skills, including a negotiation of client and counselor roles and a relationship that supports the client's sharing of personal information. A useful resolution to the debate was offered by C. H. Patterson who, in a postretirement interview, remarked that, "Basically, the counselor as an understanding person is the commonality between therapy and career counseling" (Freeman, 1990, p. 297) and, "You still need to think in terms of the core conditions of counseling, whether it is career counseling or not. The core conditions are the principles of any good relationship" (p. 292).

Patterson's reference to the familiar core conditions suggests that the counseling relationship should be considered as central to client change in career counseling. However, few empirical conclusions can be drawn, given that there continues to be a paucity of research in this area. This is a curious state of affairs—not only is career counseling one of the defining domains of counseling psychology, it also reflects some of the strongest applications of our empiricist tradition, in which theory, assessment, and intervention have been subjected to rigorous scrutiny (Fouad, 2007).

The absence of research cannot be attributed to the discipline's failure to call attention to this gap. Swanson, in 1995, issued an urgent call for research on process aspects of career counseling, including the role of the counseling relationship. Her encouragement for additional research continues to be cited (e.g., Whiston & Rahardja, 2008), typically in either the introductory or summary paragraph of an article on career counseling research, by authors who lament the fact that there continues to be little new to report in the process arena. This may be overstating the case to some degree; it is clear that Swanson's call did catalyze new research on the role of the counseling relationship in career counseling, which is reviewed below. However, there continues to be much more to learn.

Overall, the conclusions that can be drawn from the limited research available are that effective career counseling includes operation of a strong counseling relationship or working alliance, and that clients, counselors, and independent observers comment on its importance. However, the association between the relationship and client outcomes is less understood or investigated than is the case in psychotherapy and personal counseling.

Several early investigations used a case study method to investigate relational issues. Kirschner, Hoffman, and Hill (1994) examined seven sessions of successful career counseling with a midlife woman; their critical incident analysis identified an important role for the counseling relationship. Specifically, client and counselor discussions of the counseling relationship were rated as positive critical incidents, whereas avoidance of discussion of the relationship was rated as a negative critical incident. Heppner and Hendricks (1995) conducted a case study of two career clients, one classified as undecided and a second as indecisive and, in the context of assessing the utility of career interventions, determined that the counselor–client relationship was important for both clients. This finding echoes the results of an investigation of career clients who were either moderate or high in distress (Rochlen, Milburn, & Hill, 2004); although the more distressed client desired more active skill training, the two types did not differ in their perceptions of the therapeutic relationship.

In a large-scale, longitudinal field study in Britain, Bimrose et al. (2004, 2005) conducted in-depth case studies of 50 career clients to identify effective career practice and its impact on clients' lives. In the analysis of counselor interventions, both clients and independent raters identified the development of a working alliance as one of four core categories that characterized the career sessions. The project's detailed analysis offers one of the most comprehensive descriptions of career practice available, and its attention to the importance of the counseling relationship in career guidance is noteworthy.

The most direct investigations of the role of the counseling relationship in career counseling have been conducted by Multon and colleagues (Heppner, Multon, Gysbers, Ellis, & Zook, 1998; Multon, Heppner, Gysbers, Zook, & Ellis-Kalton, 2001; Multon, Ellis-Kalton, Heppner, & Gysbers, 2003). In each investigation, the researchers documented the operation of a strong working alliance between career clients and their counselors and found that the strength of the alliance increased across sessions (Heppner et al., 1998; Multon et al., 2001). The strength of the measured alliance is noteworthy; for example, Multon et al. (2003) obtained a mean alliance rating of 71.54, out of a maximum score of 84, with a mean item response of 5.96 on a seven-point Likert scale. Multon and colleagues' findings regarding the relationship between the alliance and

career client outcome have been mixed; the 1998 study failed to find an association, but the 2001 study found that the alliance accounted for 17% of the variance in outcome. Some reviewers (e.g., Whiston & Raharja, 2008) have characterized this as a weak association. However, recent summative reviews of psychotherapy alliance research report an average association between alliance and outcome of .21, with a median effect size of .25 (Horvath & Bedi, 2002), suggesting that the results obtained by Multon et al. are not widely discrepant.

An important program of research conducted by Kim and colleagues has included the counseling relationship among the variables explored in career counseling with Asian American clients. Kim and Atkinson (2002) identified an unexpected association, in that clients who endorsed high levels of Asian values rated an Asian American counselor as more empathic, but rated a European American counselor as more effective. In a further investigation (Li & Kim, 2004), in which a Euro-American counselor offered either directive or nondirective career assistance, the Asian American clients, regardless of their endorsement of Asian values, associated the directive counselor's approach with greater empathy, a stronger alliance, and cultural competence.

In a qualitative study designed to identify influential aspects of the counseling process, Whiston and colleagues (2005) interviewed 12 vocational counseling experts and learned that each considered the counseling relationship to be central to his or her work. Specifically, these counseling experts viewed the relationship as essential for supporting clients in the exploration stage, as well as in forming a trusting base from which they could implement more challenging interventions (e.g., challenging beliefs that interfered with exploration or decision).

As noted previously, there is a very limited body of research that has explored the counseling relationship as a specific factor in career counseling. However, there have been a series of investigations that provide indirect evidence for its role in the career counseling process. Perhaps the most important of these is the global conclusion that emerged from a meta-analysis conducted by Whiston et al. (2003). Based on a comprehensive review, they concluded that counselor-*free* career interventions are significantly less effective that those that include active engagement by a counseling professional. To further elaborate on the indirect evidence that has emerged, several investigations are noted briefly.

Gold et al. (1993) determined that affective components of the career counseling process (e.g., the experience of counselor support and encouragement) were associated with the greatest change in clients' vocational identity. Anderson and Niles (2000), in a study that identified helpful events in career counseling, reported that both counselors and clients cited provision of emotional support as important to client gains. McIlveen (2007) conducted phenomenological research on implementation of a constructivist career assessment and guidance intervention and found that counselors emphasized the importance of embedding the intervention within an established counseling relationship.

Healy (2001) investigated factors that hindered counselor effectiveness in career counseling; the findings indicated that clients reacted negatively to counselors who were perceived as inadequate, as inattentive, and as delivering the results of standardized testing in a mechanistic fashion. Although the counseling relationship was not assessed directly in this study, few would argue that these identified characteristics are compatible with Rogers' core conditions; and, Healy's attention to the importance of attending to relational factors when using standardized assessment provides an introduction to the next topic of interest.

In a final example, Dorn (1988) employed Strong's social influence model in exploring the role of the relationship in career counseling and used the Counselor Rating Form (Barak & LaCrosse, 1975) in process research with a single career client. He found that client ratings of the counselor's Expertness and Trustworthiness were uniformly high across sessions, whereas ratings of the counselor's Attractiveness were high in session 1, dropped in session 3, then increased for session 5. This provides another speculative glimpse of relationship development as a dynamic process, in career as well as personal counseling.

The Counseling Relationship in Standardized Assessment

It is not so many years ago that Bordin and Bixler, thoroughly imbued with the nondirective attitude, first proposed that tests should be chosen by the client rather than by the counselor. At first it seemed to many workers to be a fantastic idea, but as it was tried out it began to seem quite a natural sort of procedure. Its great advantage is that it keeps an essential feature of the situation clear for the counselee—namely, that he is to make the decisions by which the course of his life is to be governed. (Tyler, 1953, p. 143)

A domain of counseling practice that has relevance for our discussion of the counseling relationship, despite a marked absence of research investigation, is the use of standardized testing. The current discussion attempts to catalogue what little research has emerged in this area because, in contrast to many areas of psychotherapy, the counseling psychology approach to the use of standardized assessment represents a clear, historically embedded example of a distinctive counseling psychology approach to practice, one that is wholly grounded in the field's conceptualization of the core relationship between counselor and client. And yet, this is an area virtually ignored by researchers.

Students of the history of applied psychology may recall that expertise in standardized assessment was one of the first and most significant areas of practice that differentiated psychology from the medical domain of psychiatry. Furthermore, counseling psychology was rapidly differentiated from clinical psychology in its endorsement of testing practice that was focused on the needs of the client, and in advocating selection of tests that met client goals, rather than those of persons interested in categorization or diagnosis. As early as 1959, Barbara Kirk and one of her students (Rudikoff & Kirk, 1959) provided guidance to counselors for communicating test information in a manner that clients could comprehend and accept, anticipating a unique counseling psychology perspective on the use of standardized test information.

In 1986, Tinsely and Bradley asserted that the use of testing, and its interpretation, is best viewed as an integral component of the counseling process, rather than as something separate and distinct from other aspects of the work that counselors and clients do together. In 1990, Jane Duckworth advanced a classic formulation of a counseling psychology approach to testing, one that placed the client's concerns in a central role and described how the process of test use was integral to an overarching counseling relationship. If some readers are unfamiliar with this classic reference, I encourage each of you to read Duckworth in its entirety; your practice will be enhanced. As one example, consider Duckworth's advice to counselors on what elements of a test interpretation to address:

Focusing on personal strengths as well as weaknesses leads to a more balanced picture of the individual who is coming in for testing. It also lets clients know that they can assist in their own treatment because they do have strengths . . . [this] approach to testing enlists the power of the client as well as the expertise of the therapist to effect the therapeutic change. The assumption is made that clients can be powerful and solve problems when they have accurate information about themselves. (p. 201)

Other authors have addressed this issue; Prediger and Garfield (1988), in offering a checklist of testing competencies and responsibilities, included the item, "Apply good counseling to test interpretation by attending to the counselee first and the test results second" (p. 53). Although indirect, these established and noteworthy counseling psychology authors and researchers have pointed to the importance of the counseling relationship in effective use of standardized testing.

The activity of communicating test results can be conceptualized as a form of client feedback and Claiborn et al. (2002), in a review of this aspect of the counseling relationship, report that feedback is most likely to be considered within a collaborative therapeutic relationship, and that positive feedback appears to be associated with establishment of strong therapeutic relationships. Furthermore, they note that the therapist's position, conceptualized according to Stan Strong's social influence model of expertness and attractiveness/similarity, plays an important role in client acceptance of test feedback.

In 1997, Finn and Tonsager published a report that described the positive impact of Minnesota Multiphasic Personality Inventory (MMPI) interpretations on clients' sense of self and encouraged the use of tests as an active means of engaging clients in both the therapeutic relationship and the work of psychotherapy. Their work on the potential benefits of test data as an intervention—akin to feedback—continues to be widely cited but, to date, does not appear to have had a significant impact on practice. Curry and Hanson (2010) conducted a national survey of counseling, clinical and school psychology practitioners with respect to both their graduate training and current practice in providing test feedback; one third indicated that their training experience had not prepared them to deliver feedback. Of equal concern from an ethical perspective, only one third reported providing verbal feedback each time tests were administered to clients.

A meta-analysis (Poston and Hanson, 2010) of the impact of psychological assessment as a therapeutic intervention provided robust evidence (Cohen's $d = 0.423$) that standardized testing can have a significant positive impact on the therapeutic process and outcome, "when combined with personalized, collaborative, and highly involving test feedback"

(p. 203). Although readers familiar with the client-centered perspective advocated by Tyler (1959), Kirk (Rudikoff & Kirk, 1959), Tinsley and Bradley (1986) and Duckworth (1990) will not be surprised by the meta-analytic findings, these pioneering authors are virtually invisible in contemporary discussions of how to conduct a collaborative test interpretation to achieve measurable impact on therapy process and outcome. Further, a review conducted for the current discussion identified no research with an explicit focus on the role of the counseling relationship in clients' ability to make constructive use of test data.

One could argue that this is a missed opportunity to elucidate a distinctly counseling psychology perspective on a core therapeutic activity. The use of standardized measures continues to be an important aspect of applied psychology practice and I believe that counseling psychologists, with their distinctive perspective on both the counseling relationship and the use of assessment, could make a significant contribution in elucidating how relationship factors and assessment interact. Whiston et al. (2005) noted that a strong counseling relationship can provide a secure base for client exploration of potentially challenging material and, when used in the service of client goals, tests often provide this sort of information. I encourage researchers to explore the role of the counseling relationship in the domain of standardized assessment and, in particular, as a facilitating factor in counselee acceptance and use of data derived from standardized assessment.

Diversity and the Counseling Relationship

The accepting attitude is the opposite of contempt . . . and, it is a feeling about an *individual*, not about mankind in the abstract. Lofty generalizations about the dignity of personality are irrelevant to it. . . . It is because acceptance is so closely tied to understanding the person as an individual that the two qualities we have stressed cannot be separated, in counseling or anywhere else. (Tyler, 1953, p. 26)

Counseling psychology's distinctive perspective on the therapeutic relationship, as argued previously, is an enactment of values that have long been central to the field's identity. One area where this is particularly germane is the formation of effective therapeutic relationships with clients from diverse backgrounds. This is particularly salient with clients from marginalized or disadvantaged backgrounds, whose cultural or ethnic heritage differs from that of their counselor, or whose religion, sexual orientation, or gender differs from their counselor's life experience. Given that a significant majority of North American psychologists continue to be persons of European, Caucasian heritage, we are basically concerned with the question of whether majority culture practitioners succeed in forming strong relationships with people different from themselves, and whether those relationships promote positive outcomes for clients.

Many have argued that the task of forming strong alliances with clients unlike oneself is an area in which our practice has fallen short of our ideals (e.g., Comas-Dias, 2006; Smith, 2005) but, before examining some of the research conducted in this area, it is worthwhile to note some of the early expressions of our field's commitment to issues of diversity and social justice. Counseling psychology's values and commitment to diversity, if genuine, will be reflected in the types of relationships we construct with clients from diverse backgrounds. The stance that our profession has taken on these issues can provide some insight on the values we aspire to enact.

Despite the moments when we fall far short of our ideals, counseling psychology has played a leadership role in bringing these issues to the attention of the field at large. Roger Myers (2004) traces the field's concern with social justice back to Frank Parsons in the early 1900s, as well as to E.G. Williamson's effort to call attention to "the restrictions on freedom imposed by traditions and custom on racial, religious, or ethnic minority groups" (1965; cited by Myers, 2004, p. 129). In the second half of the 20th century, counseling psychologists understood that acceptance and understanding were not well served by what Tyler called "lofty generalizations" (based largely on the dominant male culture) and began to elucidate principles for practice that addressed the distinctive needs of specific groups. In 1978, the American Psychological Association's Division 17 (Counseling Psychology) approved the *Principles Concerning the Counseling and Psychotherapy of Women* as official policy (Fitzgerald & Nutt, 1986). This contribution was widely influential within the APA and was endorsed by several other divisions. In the 1980s, counseling psychologists began to call attention to cultural diversity and to advocate for guidelines on culturally competent practice (e.g., Sue et al., 1982). These efforts led to APA's *Guidelines on Multicultural Education, Training, Research, Practice, and Organizational Change for Psychologists* (APA, 2003), originating with the work of a joint task force of APA Division 17 (Counseling Psychology) and Division 45 (The Society for the Study of Ethnic Minority Issues). Vasquez (2007), among others, has called attention to the relevance of the *Guidelines* for development of therapeutic relationships with culturally different clients, particularly in calling for therapists to increase their awareness of unconscious beliefs and stereotypic attitudes.

A literature search on "therapeutic relationship" will not produce citations for these important guidelines; at the same time, they are essential for understanding how counseling psychologists regard establishment of an effective relationship with clients whose life history and experience differ from that of the dominant culture. The research review that follows illustrates some of the ways in which these questions have been explored.

Client–Counselor Matching on Demographic Variables

> Most high schools and many colleges arrange for men to take care of the boys and women the girls. There is no evidence, however, that this is the best practice or the one making for best rapport in all cases. . . . Furthermore, these questions are too complex to be thought through on the basis of rapport alone . . . we simply do not know enough about these things to decide wisely. Probably the best procedure . . . is to let the client decide, if counselors of both sexes are available.
> (Tyler, 1953, p. 39)

Some of the earliest investigations of counseling with clients whose ethnicity or culture differed from that of the counselor (who was typically a member of the majority culture) explored the hypothesis that matched dyads—on variables such as gender, race or culture—would produce better outcomes. Several decades of research have not supported this position and, at best, the results for some groups are described as "mixed" (e.g., Comas-Diaz, 2006; Norcross, 2002). In hindsight, the prediction that a match on group membership would be predictive is simplistic. There has been a longstanding awareness (although not always applied) that groups who share the same societal label also have significant within-group differences. More recently, several authors have drawn attention to the necessity of recognizing "multiple identities" and the intersectionality of varied group identifications within a single client (e.g., Cole, 2009; Vasquez et al., 2006).

The issue of multiple identities is particularly important to the question of whether "matching research" can be a productive area for investigating the counseling relationship in diverse populations, as it is difficult to imagine how one could "match" a client on all dimensions that might be relevant to forming a strong counseling relationship. Some cases of multiple identity can present a mix of marginalization and privilege, as in the case of an architect whose progressive disability requires use of a wheelchair and help from a health attendant; this client might "match" a counselor on SES or disability status, but rarely both. Other clients may present multiple forms of marginalization, as in the case of a white lesbian refugee from Eastern Europe. Even beyond the simplistic question of whether a "white" counselor would be the best "match," we cannot assume that a lesbian counselor would be the best person to understand this client's refugee experience. And, neither of these pairings may match the aspect of identity most salient to the client or to the issues she brings to counseling. One of the potential contributions of the multiple identities literature is its capacity to remind us, not only of the more visible forms of diversity that clients may embody, but of the hidden diversities that may play an important role in the formation of the counseling relationship. The literature review conducted for this chapter did not identify any diversity research on the counseling relationship that has incorporated a multiple identities perspective; until we accept this challenge, it is likely that our understanding of the factors influencing relationship development with diverse clients will remain inconclusive. Nevertheless, every summative review on the counseling relationship appears to consider it necessary to discuss the literature on racial/ethnic/gender matching. Typically, this subject becomes the focus of a section or heading, and the reports of mixed and inconclusive results are highly consistent. One can choose to be either intrigued or discouraged by our continued absorption with the topic.

Beutler et al. (2004) note that, although the concept of matching is widely accepted and advocated, there is little empirical evidence to support the recommendation to match clients and counselors on demographic characteristics, particularly with regard to outcome, where results are either equivocal or weakly supportive. Simply stated, client–counselor match does not automatically produce a working alliance that predicts client outcome; Karlsson (2005) attributes the failure to identify consistent associations to both conceptual and methodological problems with matching research. Beutler et al.'s 2004 meta-analysis of 11 studies,

published between 1990 and 2000, found a modest positive effect (mean weighted effect size of $r = .02$), particularly for Asian Americans and Mexican Americans, a finding that is consistent with conclusions reported by Sue and Lam (2002). For our present discussion, it is important to note that the authors found a great deal of heterogeneity in the data which, as they note, suggests that outcomes may be moderated by unidentified third variables. This idea is considered in more detail below.

There is a growing consensus that, although matching does not automatically produce a working alliance that predicts client outcome, it is likely to produce an indirect effect on outcome, particularly for less acculturated clients (e.g., Buetler et al., 2004; Karlsson, 2005; Sue & Lam, 2002). One salient example is the research on matching and therapy drop-out, or the number of sessions completed. A limited number of studies have found that, for African American, Asian American, American Indian, and Latino/Latina and Mexican American clients, matching on racial/ethnic similarity is associated with less likelihood of therapy drop-out. Comas-Diaz (2006) cites research indicating that, in racially similar physician–patient relationships, people of color participate more in their treatment than in racially dissimilar pairings.

As discussed in our examination of the role of expectations in therapy drop-out for low SES clients, the research on racial/ethnic matching and drop-out highlights the need to identify variables that may moderate or mediate these relationships. The following section presents examples of research on therapist, client, or relational characteristics that have been investigated for their role in matching. The studies cited also provide an illustration of Hill's (2005) point that client, therapist, and relationship variables are "inextricably intertwined" (p. 431) and that we lose meaning if we consider them in isolation. Several points are worth noting by way of introduction. First, many of the variables to be considered fall within the first stage of therapy, which Hill labels as one of initial impression formation, the stage at which critical elements of relationship development occur. As noted by Horvath and Bedi (2002), measurement of the therapist alliance is predictive at three sessions.

Second, the following discussion is organized around variables, rather than summarizing findings for groups or populations. This is deliberate; the paucity of research in this area precludes reliable group generalizations or distinctions, and the value of this overview is to suggest variables that are potentially valuable targets for further investigation in many groups.

Third, the categorization of variables as client and therapist factors is necessarily somewhat arbitrary; it is much more likely that these variables exert their effects through an interaction between client and counselor perspectives on each factor described. Those listed as client factors are variables that counselors should take as "given" in a particular counseling relationship. Just as a client's attachment history may challenge or facilitate the counselor's efforts to form a relationship, various diversity factors are inextricable parts of the person with whom a counselor works to form a relationship. Those variables listed as therapist factors represent variables that are most likely to be amenable to some level of therapist control.

Matching Research: Client Factors

[T]here is another whole set of factors affective the structure of the initial relationship—the client's general attitudes toward broad categories of people. These are extremely varied, as human beings classify their fellow-men in all sorts of ways.
(Tyler, 1953, p. 38)

PREFERENCE AND SATISFACTION

The strongest evidence for the value of client–counselor match is found in measures of client satisfaction, as well as the previously noted indirect outcomes, such as continuation in treatment (Sue & Lam, 2002). This is not insignificant, as satisfaction may reflect a client's sense that she has been understood, or that her needs or goals have been met. Regrettably, there is little research to help us understand what constitutes client satisfaction, although a client's preference for the type of counselor she will see appears to be an important factor. For example, research has been consistent in documenting that black clients prefer to work with black therapists (Thompson, Bazile, & Akbar, 2004; Townes, Chavez-Korell, & Cunningham, 2009). However, even this finding is not without complexity; a client's degree of group identification, or racial identity, predicts black American client preferences for a black counselor (Ferguson, Leach, Levy, Nicholson, & Johnson, 2008) and earlier research (Parham & Helms, 1981) found that black clients with pre-encounter racial identity attitudes expressed preferences for white counselors.

In the area of career research. Kim and Atkinson (2002) found that Asian American vocational counseling clients rated their European American counselors more positively than they rated Asian American counselors. The authors found that client ratings of empathy and counselor credibility were associated with the counselors' attention to Asian values; in this sample, the attitudinal variable was more important than a demographic match on race or ethnicity. It appears likely that within-group differences on variables such as racial identity, attitudes and values–for both clients and counselors–are an influential component of client preference and likely moderate the link between group membership, strength of the alliance and outcome.

Research on gender matching has been inconclusive (Sue & Lam, 2002) and the findings of a small but significant outcome effect for female therapists applies to both male and female clients (Bowman, Scogin, Floyd, & McKendree-Smith, 2001). This result calls into question the conclusion that, for female clients, it is the gender match that is associated with greater satisfaction. Zlotnick and colleagues (1998), using National Institute of Mental Health (NIMH) data from the Depression Collaborative Research Program, found that gender match was not related to outcome, or to client perception of therapist empathy. Furthermore, when they examined clients' expectations about whether a male or female therapist would be more helpful, outcomes did not differ based on whether clients were matched or mismatched with the gender they expected to be most helpful.

It should be noted that this area of research has not fully explored whether client satisfaction is mediated by the presenting problem that the client brings to counseling (see the discussion of counselor credibility, below). In matching, the notion of client preference may tap some of the same characteristics that, in Strong's social influence model were classified as "attractiveness," or the sense that a counselor was sufficiently similar to serve as a base of influence or help. Again, the challenge to researchers is to identify what variables, beyond broad demographic categories, may produce this effect.

CULTURE AND LANGUAGE

As noted previously, recent research has documented some modest benefits for matching with Asian American and Mexican American clients (e.g., Beutler et al., 2004; Kim & Atkinson, 2002; Sue & Lam, 2002), and this research has also called attention to the potential roles of language and cultural assumptions and beliefs. Concerning language, Stanley Sue and colleagues (1991) divided

Latino clients based on primary language and found that, for those whose primary language was Spanish, ethnic match was related to drop-out and treatment outcome. Given the wealth of information that must be communicated verbally in "talk therapy," one can easily understand how an ability to differentiate between affect-laden words such as ashamed versus humiliated or disappointed versus devastated might have importance in a client's feeling understood. Sue et al.'s results are salient to the question of developing therapeutic relationships with recent immigrant and refugee clients; these groups are likely to have higher proportions of clients who speak English as a second language. Refugees and immigrants are also populations who are extraordinarily under-represented in psychotherapy research on how ethnicity and culture may influence development of counseling relationships.

In exploring other cultural factors, Nolan Zane, Stanley Sue, and colleagues (2005) have gone beyond purely demographic matching and have explored the "cognitive match" between Asian clients and their therapists. Their work measures counselor and client expectations and perceptions of psychotherapy (e.g., presenting problem, treatment goals) and appears to provide a cultural formulation of the task and goal components of the working alliance. The authors found that cognitive matches between clients and therapists were predictive of outcome and suggest that the cognitive match may account for the finding that ethnically matched therapy dyads complete more sessions. One of their key contributions has been to expand our conceptualization of what may be operating in a purely demographic match to include consideration of other cultural, cognitive, or attitudinal factors that are important in determining the strength of a therapeutic relationship.

In considering this area of research, it is important to note that most counseling psychology research relevant to "diversity" has been concerned with groups that are well established in the United States. In addition to domestic racial-ethnic groups, diversity research has focused on gender, gay/lesbian, and religious groups, but has given little attention to immigrants, refugees, or to clients whose disability status or age may present distinct "cultures" relevant to developing therapeutic relationships. There has also been little attention to an international understanding of diversity, or consideration of how North American conceptualizations of cultural factors may translate to psychotherapy relationships in cultures outside the United States. These groups, or questions about the diversity they represent, are under-represented or wholly absent in psychotherapy research on how ethnicity and culture may influence development of counseling relationships.

One exception to this charge can be found in a study that investigated the working alliance and counselor problem solving style in Taiwanese client–counselor dyads (Wei & Heppner, 2005). In addition to documenting similarities in alliance formation, this work provides a useful example of how culture-specific factors are important in developing a strong counselor–client relationship. For example, both the quantitative and qualitative component of this mixed-method study revealed that counselors' active problem-solving behaviors contributed to client perceptions of counselor helpfulness.

The Wei and Heppner (2005) investigation also provides a conceptual link to earlier counseling psychology research on the therapeutic relationship. As they note, the construct of counselor "credibility" can be conceptualized as client perceptions of counselor expertness, attractiveness, and trustworthiness, variables central to Strong's social influence model (see Hoyt, 1996, for a review). The social influence model has not been used widely to investigate factors that may account for the role of matching in reducing therapy drop-out or increasing client satisfaction; however, it offers a convenient and well-established umbrella for some of the variables associated with therapist factors, as discussed below.

Beyond Matching: Therapist Attitudes and Values

> The capacity for accepting others is a trait far broader than specific training in counseling skills. The counselor's basic attitudes toward human beings are involved, and such basic attitudes are not the product of a year's cultivation or of specific educational experiences. They grow from the responses a person makes to all the experiences of his life. . . .
> (Tyler, 1953, p. 25)

Historically, researchers have given little attention to therapist factors that may influence the process or outcome of psychotherapy with diverse clients (Karlsson, 2005; Leong & Gupta, 2008). This is particularly true for research on therapeutic relationships with cultural or ethnic minority clients. In contrast, literature on therapist attitudes, bias, and stereotypes has demonstrated that therapists hold negative and stereotypic views of clients based on gender, sexual orientation, age, culture, or ethnicity (Beutler et al., 2004). These biases are presumed to have an impact on the process of therapy but little empirical research has investigated their influence on outcome or on the therapeutic relationship. This is another area where evidence related to the counseling relationship appears to be indirect, although two broad areas of therapist attributes that have received attention are therapist beliefs, attitudes, and values, and multicultural knowledge and skills.

Therapist attitudes and values related to a range of diverse populations, reflecting many of the "isms" that embody negative stereotypes of particular groups, have been cited as potential barriers to effective counseling. Similar to Smith's (2005) documentation of negative therapist attitudes toward the poor and low-SES clients, Danziger and Welfel (2000) found that therapists exhibited ageism in holding negative, stereotypic views of older clients. Barrett and McWhirter's (2002) analogue investigation of homophobia in counseling trainees found that those holding more homophobic attitudes viewed gay and lesbian clients more negatively than they did heterosexual clients; male trainees, in particular, were more likely to assign negative adjectives to gay and lesbian clients.

There is evidence that negative attitudes toward client group membership are associated with less empathic responding, a core component of effective relationships. Nelson and Baumgarte (2004) propose that this may be associated with difficulties in perspective taking on the part of the therapist, and report that individuals show less empathy when responding to another's distress when the distress arises from unfamiliar cultural contexts. Given the evidence that therapists are not immune to the negative attitudes that exist in the general population, therapists may experience less empathy for clients whose difficulties arise from unfamiliar life experiences.

The argument that a lack of cultural knowledge may be associated with negative therapist responses receives some support from research conducted by Hayes and Erkis (2000), who found that homophobic attitudes were associated with less empathy and reluctance to work with a gay client, as well as with a tendency to attribute blame and responsibility to HIV-positive clients. For support from the converse position, Constantine, Miville, and Kindaichi (2008), report a series of studies with ethnic minority clients in which therapist empathy was positively associated with client satisfaction with counseling and perceptions of therapist multicultural competence. One potential interpretation would be that, as therapists increased their multicultural knowledge and skill, their perspective taking and empathic abilities also increased. This could address what Comas-Diaz (2006) refers to as "missed empathic opportunities" (p. 84), or instances when a therapist with limited knowledge of the client's culture fails to recognize or address a client's indirect but culturally appropriate introduction of important issues.

A social psychological perspective on the relationship between negative attitudes and the counseling relationship is found in Vasquez' (2007) discussion of how negative behaviors can emerge outside the therapist's awareness. She cites a series of studies by Dovidio et al. (2002), which demonstrated that, when whites interact with persons of different racial background, they exhibit negative nonverbal behaviors. Although the whites report no awareness of their behavior, the ethnic minority participants experienced the interaction as reflecting a negative attitude toward them.

This research is relevant to what have been termed racial "microaggressions," subtle actions that signal power differences in ways that are demeaning and domineering (Fouad & Arrendondo, 2007). This area has begun to receive research attention and appears to offer promise for understanding the process of relationship formation and maintenance. For example, Constantine's (2007) research with black American clients found their perceptions of in-session microaggressions were associated with lower ratings of the working alliance, less satisfaction with counseling, and lower therapist competence.

Therapist attitudes appear to be important contributors to the strength of therapeutic relationships, and the field has begun to explore their operation through the construct of multicultural competence, which includes an awareness of both one's own attitudes and beliefs as well as those of diverse clients (Sue et al., 1982). The area of multicultural competence has generated a significant amount of research but has been criticized for a reliance on survey and analogue research (e.g., Leong & Gupta, 2008). However, in a wide-ranging review, Beutler et al. (2004) concluded that the few studies that use actual clients for investigating culturally sensitive therapist attitudes show promising results, with positive effect sizes (ES) ranging from ES = .12 to .71.

One aspect of multicultural knowledge and skill is the ability to perceive and respond to client expectations for the counseling relationship. As noted previously, there is consistent evidence that clients from many cultural and ethnic groups complete fewer sessions than do majority culture clients, providing indirect evidence that strong relationships had not been established. Many authors have noted that different groups can hold differing expectations and needs for what constitutes a preferred counseling relationship. Although client preferences were discussed in an earlier section, several types of expectations that therapists could act to address are worth noting. Comas-Diaz (2006) asserts that many Latino clients look to their therapists for *familismo*, a sense of being part of a close family or social network, and *platica*, taking time to open a session with small talk in order to establish trust.

Future Directions: New Paradigms, New Methods

> Perhaps we will be closer to the truth if we assume that any personality pattern that permits rich and deep relationships with other human beings to develop is satisfactory. Just as there is no one kind of personality essential to one's functioning as husband or wife, mother or father, lover, neighbor, or friend, so there is no one kind essential to the counselor.
> (Tyler, 1953, pp. 267–268)

In considering the body of relationship research, it is difficult to avoid the impression that our science has focused on a search for "the effective counseling relationship" and has often conceptualized the alliance between client and counselor in rather static terms. However, a good deal of current research has begun to conceptualize the relationship in a more complex form. In the previous discussion, this new attention to complexity was evident in recent work examining the alliance in multicultural counseling through the lens of intersectionality rather than matching on demographic factors (e.g., Vasquez, 2007), in explorations of how a particular attachment style may only be activated under conditions of vulnerability (Meyer & Pilkonis, 2002), or in the discussion of how therapist factors not often examined in alliance research, such as impairment or ethical behavior (e.g., Nigro 2004), may offer useful information.

Two trends have begun to influence relationship research, which I believe offer the potential to expand both our conceptualization and knowledge of this key area of the psychotherapeutic process: qualitative contributions from a social-constructionism paradigm and emerging methods

that permit modeling of complex interactions over time. Building on those ideas, I want to issue an invitation to researchers to explore interdisciplinary research tapping the long tradition of social psychological research on close relationships.

One of the first calls for reconceptualizing the counseling relationship from a social-constructionist perspective was advanced by Sexton and Whiston in 1994. To implement this perspective, they note that, "the primary focus of attention shifts from the identification of components of the counseling relationship to the jointly determined meaning systems developed by the relationship participants" (p. 62). The authors cite a range of studies, available at that time, that were consistent with an interactional perspective. However, in the intervening decades, few researchers have pursued explorations of the more qualitative notions of "meaning" or "purpose." Exceptions can be found in process research conducted from a narrative paradigm and method (e.g., Angus & McLeod, 2004) and in explorations of career counseling as goal-directed action, investigated from an action theory perspective (e.g., Young & Valach, 2009; Young, Valach, & Domene, 2005).

A focus on purpose invites us to consider the function of various elements of the counseling relationship, beyond their identification or level of strength. In describing the operation of common factors in psychotherapy, Lambert and Ogles (2004) note that, "they provide for a cooperative working endeavor in which the patient's increased sense of trust, security, and safety, along with decreases in tension, threat, and anxiety, lead to changes in conceptualizing his or her problems and ultimately in acting differently by reframing fears, taking risks, and working through problems in interpersonal relationships" (p. 173). Or, as Young and Valach (2009) argue in their description of the career counseling process, we must consider the intent of actions that client and counselor undertake, noting that, "this intent is not realized solely by the counselor or the client, but jointly and reflects the goal-directed processes in which they are engaged" (p. 300).

Some methodological advances, pursued from within a post-positivist quantitative framework, reflect an appreciation of the joint, relational character of the counseling relationship. Two examples are offered as illustration. First, the title of a 2007 investigation by counseling psychologist Dennis Kivlighan asks, "Where is the relationship in research on the alliance?" In response, the author presents two statistical approaches for analyzing interdependence in therapeutic dyads. The models are illustrated with alliance and session impact data from 53 client–counselor pairs, and the results identified a shared dyad-level component in the alliance, characterized by mutual influence. The findings, although quantitative, are consistent with the social-constructionist view that the counseling relationship emerges through client–counselor interaction.

A second example of an innovative and relational approach appears in work conducted by Lakey, Cohen, and Neely (2008), who drew upon recent social support research in exploring the unique relational characteristics that emerge in specific therapy dyads. Their analysis was based on prior research indicating that constructs like supportiveness are highly relational; in other words, they are not characteristics of an individual, but of a specific relationship between a provider and recipient. Lakey, Cohen, and Neely's work found strong, statistically significant relational effects for both the working alliance and appraisals of therapist competence, indicating that the most influential factor was the specific relationship, not a uniquely effective therapist or receptive client.

Both Kivlighan (2007) and Lakey, Cohen, and Neely (2008) were investigating relationship concepts that have long been of interest to social psychologists. And, to advance our understanding of counseling relationships further, I believe that our field would benefit from greater familiarity with that body of research. In doing so, we would be repeating a pattern that has characterized past advances in therapy process research, dating back to Strong's (1968) use of social psychological theory in conceptualizing the relationship as an interpersonal influence process. There are several current models that I believe warrant particular attention; although space does not permit detailed description, I encourage interested readers to investigate the work of these authors.

One of the dominant models in current social psychological research is *interdependence theory*, associated with the work of Caryl Rusbult and colleagues (see Rusbult & Van Lange, 2003). This comprehensive model of relationship interaction accords an explicit role for long-term goals and concern for a partner's welfare, as well for social cognitive processes such as attribution, affect, and disposition. Issues such as mutuality and perceived progress toward relationship goals have been examined as predictors of relationship quality (Avivi, Laurenceau, & Carver, 2009) and would appear to have relevance for understanding relationship

dynamics in psychotherapy. Furthermore, interdependence models differentiate between relationship formation and relationship maintenance; research on the latter (e.g., Reis, 2007) has identified a key role for perceived security of the relationship, perhaps comparable to establishment of trust in the counseling dyad.

A second area of investigation with potential application to the dyadic nature of the counseling relationship is that of *relational-independent self construal* (Cross, Bacon, & Morris, 2000), which builds on attention to cultural differences between an interdependent self-in-relationship construal and the group-oriented interdependence more common in collectivist cultures. The authors explored the role of self-construal in relationship development and, specifically, investigated whether a participant's evaluation of a dyadic partner's openness and responsiveness were related to that person's self-construal. Results were positive and confirmed predictions for the role of self-construal in self-disclosure and responsiveness, both qualities that characterize effective counseling relationships.

Finally, social psychologists have been investigating issues of "risk regulation" and emotional self-protection in relationships (e.g., Murray, Holmes, & Collins, 2006). This approach draws on elements of both attachment theory and interdependence theory in exploring the importance of the expectations people hold about a partner's relationship goals. The relevance of this work for psychotherapy relationships is perhaps best illustrated by Baumeister et al.'s (1993) observation (offered with regard to intimate relationships) that the relationships with the greatest potential to satisfy adult needs for connection are precisely those that will evoke the greatest sense of vulnerability and anxiety about rejection. For many clients, progress toward their counseling goals requires a choice to become highly vulnerable, expose troublesome parts of the self, and risk rejection by a therapist.

One can predict that the next advances in relationship research will reflect an increased appreciation for both the complexity and the uniqueness of each dyadic encounter, a stance highly congruent with the earliest expressions of counseling psychology's values as a discipline. Attention to social psychological research on interdependence, methodological advances that help us untangle both shared and independent influences, and a social-constructionist perspective on the meaning clients attach to therapeutic relationships, all hold potential for illuminating what contributes to an effective counseling relationship.

We know that strong relationships are important in counseling; it is time to shift our focus from describing "the relationship" to understanding what facilitates or impedes the therapeutic connection between counselor and client. In doing so, we can be guided by Leona Tyler's observation that effective relationships, like counselor personalities, can take many forms.

Note

1. Leona E. Tyler (1906–1993), the 81st president of the American Psychological Association and long-time faculty member at the University of Oregon, is widely acknowledged as one of counseling psychology's most influential pioneers. The three editions of *The Work of the Counselor* have been described as a leading influence on the development of the counseling profession (Sundberg & Littman, 1994), and the APA Society of Counseling Psychology's most prestigious award is named in her honor. Interested readers are encouraged to consult Zilber and Osipow (1990) or Fassinger (2003) for a biography.

References

Ahn, H., & Wampold, B. E. (2001). Where oh where are the specific ingredients? A meta-analysis of component studies in counseling and psychotherapy. *Journal of Counseling Psychology, 48,* 251–257.

Ainsworth, M. (1964). Patterns of attachment behavior shown by the infant in interaction with his mother. *Merrill-Palmer Quarterly, 10,* 51–58.

Al-Darmaki, F., & Kivlighan, D. M., Jr. (1993). Congruence in client-counselor expectations for relationship and working alliance. *Journal of Counseling Psychology, 40,* 379–384.

American Psychological Association (APA). (2002). Ethical principles of psychologists and code of conduct. *American Psychologist, 57,* 1060–1073.

American Psychological Association (APA). (2003). Guidelines on multicultural education, training, research, practice and organizational change for psychologists. *American Psychologist, 58,* 377–402.

Anderson, W. P., Jr., & Niles, S. G. (2000). Important events in career counseling: Client and counselor perceptions. *Career Development Quarterly, 48,* 251–264.

Angus, L. (2009, March). *Psychotherapy research.* Colloquia presented to the Faculty of Education, University of British Columbia, Vancouver, BC, Canada.

Angus, L., & McLeod, J. (2004). *Handbook of narrative and psychotherapy: Practice, theory and research.* Thousand Oaks, CA: Sage.

Arnkoff, D. B., Glass, C. R., & Shapiro, S. J. (2002). Expectations and preferences. In J. C. Norcross (Ed.), *Psychotherapy relationships that work: Therapist contributions and responsiveness to patients* (pp. 335–356). New York: Oxford University Press.

Avivi, Y. E., Laurenceau, J.-P., & Carver, C. S. (2009). Linking relationship quality to perceived mutuality of relationship goals and perceived goal progress. *Journal of Social and Clinical Psychology, 28,* 137–164.

Baldwin, S. A., Wampold, B. E., & Imel, Z. E. (2007). Untangling the alliance-outcome correlation: Exploring the relative importance of therapist and patient variability in the alliance. *Journal of Consulting and Clinical Psychology, 75,* 842–852.

Barak, A., & LaCrosse, M. B. (1975). Multidimensional perception of counselor behavior. *Journal of Counseling Psychology, 22,* 471–476.

Barone, D. F., Hutchings, P. S., Kimmel, H. J., Traub, H. L., Cooper, J. T., & Marshall, C. M. (2005). Increasing empathic accuracy through practice and feedback in a clinical interviewing course. *Journal of Social and Clinical Psychology, 24,* 156–171.

Barrett, K. A., & McWhirter, B. T. (2002). Counselor trainees' perceptions of clients based on client sexual orientation. *Counselor Education and Supervision, 41,* 219–232.

Barrett-Lennard, G. T. (1962). Dimensions of therapeutic response as causal factors in therapeutic change. *Psychological Monographs: General and Applied, 76*(43, Whole No. 562).

Bartholomew, K. (1994). The assessment of individual differences in adult attachment. *Psychological Inquiry, 5,* 23–27.

Bartholomew, K., & Thompson, J. (1995). The application of attachment theory to counseling psychology. *The Counseling Psychologist, 23,* 484–490.

Batchelor, A. (1988). How clients perceive therapist empathy: A content analysis of "received" empathy. *Psychotherapy, 25,* 227–240.

Baumeister, R. F., Wotman, S. R., & Stilwell, A. M. (1993). Unrequited love: On heartbreak, anger, guilt, scriptlessness and humiliation. *Journal of Personality and Social Psychology, 64,* 377–394.

Bedi, R. P. (2006). Concept mapping the client's perspective on counseling alliance formation. *Journal of Counseling Psychology, 53,* 26–35.

Benecke, C., Peham, D., & Banninger-Huber, E. (2005). Nonverbal relationship regulation in psychotherapy. *Psychotherapy Research, 15,* 81–90.

Benjamin, L. S. (1982). Use of Structural Analysis of Social Behavior (SASB) to guide intervention in psychotherapy. In J. C. Anchin, & D. J. Kiesler (Eds.), *Handbook of interpersonal psychotherapy* (pp. 190–212). New York: Pergamon.

Bergin, A. E. (1962). The effect of dissonant persuasive communications upon changes in a self-referring attitude. *Journal of Personality, 30,* 423–438.

Bergin, A. E., & Garfield, S. L. (1978). *Handbook of psychotherapy and behavior change: An empirical analysis* (2nd ed.). New York: Wiley.

Beutler, L. E., Malik, M., Alimohamed, S., Talebi, H., Noble, S., & Wong, E. (2004). Therapist variables. In M. J. Lambert (Ed.), *Bergin and Garfield's handbook of psychotherapy and behavior change* (5th ed., pp. 227–306). New York: Wiley.

Bimrose, J., Barnes, S.-A., & Hughes, D. (2005). *Effective guidance one year on: Evidence from longitudinal case studies in England.* Coventry: Warwick Institute for Employment Research. Retrieved June 29, 2009, from http://ww2.warwick.ac.uk/fac/soc/ier/publications/bydate/2005/egreportoct05.pdf

Bimrose, J., Barnes, S.-A., Hughes, D., & Orton, M. (2004). *What is effective guidance? Evidence from longitudinal case studies in England.* Coventry: Warwick Institute for Employment Research. Retrieved June 29, 2009, from http://ww2.warwick.ac.uk/fac/soc/ier/publications/bydate/2005/egr2004.pdf

Bohart, A. C., Elliott, R., Greenberg, L. S., & Watson, J. C. (2002). Empathy. In J. C. Norcross (Ed.), *Psychotherapy relationships that work: Therapist contributions and responsiveness to patients* (pp. 89–108). New York: Oxford University Press.

Bordin, E. S. (1976). The generalizability of the psychoanalytic concept of the working alliance. *Psychotherapy: Theory, Research and Practice, 16,* 252–260.

Bowlby, J. (1969). *Attachment and loss*. New York: Basic.

Bowman, D. G., Scogin, F., Floyd, M., & McKendree-Smith, N. (2001). Effect of therapist sex on outcome of psychotherapy: A meta-analysis. *Psychotherapy, 38,* 142–148.

Carnes, E. F., & Robinson, F. P. (1948). The role of client talk in the counseling interview. *Educational and Psychological Measurement, 8,* 635–644.

Carter, J. A. (1994). Refining notions through converging paradigms. *The Counseling Psychologist, 22,* 79–81.

Caspar, F., Grossmann, C., Unmussig, C., & Schramm, E. (2005). Complementary therapeutic relationship: Therapist behavior, interpersonal patterns, and therapeutic effects. *Psychotherapy Research, 15,* 91–102.

Castonguay, L. G., Goldfried, M. R., Wiser, S., & Raue, P. J. (1996). Predicting the effect of cognitive therapy for depression: A study of unique and common factors. *Journal of Consulting and Clinical Psychology, 64,* 497–504.

Chambless, D. L., & Hollon, S. D. (1998). Defining empirically supported therapies. *Journal of Consulting and Clinical Psychology, 64,* 497–504.

Chang, D. F., & Berk, A. (2009). Making cross-racial therapy work: A phenomenological study of clients' experiences of cross-racial therapy. *Journal of Counseling Psychology, 56,* 521–536.

Claiborn, C. D., Goodyear, R. K., & Horner, P. A. (2002). Feedback. In J. C. Norcross (Ed.), *Psychotherapy relationships that work: Therapist contributions and responsiveness to patients* (pp. 217–233). New York: Oxford University Press.

Clarkin, J. F., & Levy, K. N. (2004). The influence of client variables on psychotherapy. In M. J. Lambert (Ed.), *Bergin and Garfield's handbook of psychotherapy and behavior change* (5th ed., pp. 194–226). New York: Wiley.

Cole, E. R. (2009). Intersectionality and research in psychology. *American Psychologist, 64,* 170–180.

Comas-Diaz, L. (2006). Cultural variation in the therapeutic relationship. In C. D. Goodheart, A. E. Kazdin, & R. J. Sternberg (Eds.), *Evidence-based psychotherapy: Where practice and research meet* (pp. 81–105). Washington, DC: American Psychological Association.

Constantine, M. G. (2007). Racial microaggressions against African American clients in cross-racial counseling relationships. *Journal of Counseling Psychology, 54,* 1–16.

Constantine, M. G., Miville, M. L., & Kindaichi, M. M. (2008). Multicultural competence in counseling psychology practice and training. In S. D. Brown, & R. W. Lent (Eds.), *Handbook of counseling psychology* (4th ed., pp. 141–158). Hoboken, NJ: Wiley.

Cook, J. E., & Doyle, C. (2002). Working alliance in online therapy as compared to face-to-face: Preliminary results. *CyberPsychology & Behavior, 5*(2), 95–105. doi:10.1089/109493102753770480.

Corbishley, M. A., & Yost, E. B. (1989). Psychological aspects of career counseling. *Journal of Career Development, 16,* 43–51.

Crites, J. O. (1981). *Career counseling: Models, methods and materials*. New York: McGraw-Hill.

Crits-Christoph, P., Gibbons, M. B. C., Crits-Cristoph, K., Narducci, J., Schamberger, M., & Gallop, R. (2006). Can therapists be trained to improve their alliances? A preliminary study of alliance-forming psychotherapy. *Psychotherapy Research, 16,* 268–281.

Cross, S. E., Bacon, P. L., & Morris, M. L. (2000). The relational-interdependent self-construal and relationships. *Journal of Personality and Social Psychology, 78,* 791–808.

Curry, K. T., & Hanson, W. E. (2010). National survey of psychologists' test feedback training, supervision and practice: A mixed methods study. *Journal of Personality Assessment, 92,* 327–336.

Danzinger, P. R., & Welfel, E. R. (2000). Age, gender and health bias in counselors: An empirical analysis. *Journal of Mental Health Counseling, 22,* 135–149.

Dell, D. M., & Schmidt, L. D. (1976). Behavioral cues to counselor expertness. *Journal of Counseling Psychology, 23,* 197–201.

Dixon, D. N., & Claiborn, C. D. (1987). A social influence approach to counselor supervision. In J. E. Maddux, C. D. Stoltenberg, & R. Rosenwein (Eds.), *Social processes in clinical and counseling psychology* (pp. 83–93). New York: Springer.

Dollard, J., Auld, F., & White, A. M. (1953). *Steps in psychotherapy*. New York: Macmillan.

Dorn, F. J. (1988). Utilizing social influence in career counseling: A case study. *Career Development Quarterly, 36,* 269–280.

Dovidio, J. F., Gaertner, S. L., Kawakami, K., & Hoson, G. (2002). Why can't we just get along? Interpersonal biases and interracial distrust. *Cultural Diversity & Ethnic Minority Psychology, 8,* 88–102.

Duckworth, J. (1990). The counseling approach to the use of testing. *The Counseling Psychologist, 18,* 198–204.

Dunkle, J. H., & Friedlander, M. L. (1996). Contribution of therapist experience and personal characteristics to the working alliance. *Journal of Counseling Psychology, 43,* 456–460.

Eames, V., & Roth, A. (2000). Patient attachment orientation and early working alliance—A study of patient and therapist reports of alliance quality and ruptures. *Psychotherapy Research, 10,* 421–434.

Farber, B. A., & Lane, J. S. (2002). Positive regard. In J. C. Norcross (Ed.), *Psychotherapy relationships that work: Therapist contributions and responsiveness to patients* (pp. 175–194). New York: Oxford University Press.

Fassinger, R. E. (2003). Leona Tyler: Pioneer of possibilities. In G. A. Kimble, & M. Wertheimer (Eds.), *Portraits of pioneers in psychology, vol. 5* (pp. 231–247). Washington, DC: American Psychological Association.

Ferguson, T. M., Leach, M. M., Levy, J. J., Nicholson, B. C., & Johnson, J. D. (2008). Influences on counselor race preferences: Distinguishing Black racial attitudes from Black racial identity. *Journal of Multicultural Counseling and Development, 36,* 66–76.

Finn, S. E., & Tonsager, M. E. (1997). Information-gathering and therapeutic models of assessment: Complementary paradigms. *Psychological Assessment, 9,* 374–375.

Fitzgerald, L. F., & Nutt, R. (1986). The Division 17 principles concerning the counseling/psychotherapy of women: Rationale and implementation. *The Counseling Psychologist, 14,* 180–216.

Fitzpatrick, M. R., Iwakabe, S., & Stalikas, A. (2005). Perspective divergence in the working alliance. *Psychotherapy Research, 15*, 69–80.

Forrest, L., Elman, N., Gizara, S., & Vacha-Haase, T. (1999). Trainee impairment: A review of identification, remediation, dismissal, and legal issues. *The Counseling Psychologist, 27*, 627–686.

Fouad, N. A. (2007). Work and vocational psychology: Theory, research and applications. *Annual Review of Psychology, 58*, 543–564.

Fouad, N. A., & Arrendondo, P. (2007). *Becoming culturally oriented: Practical advice of psychologists and educators.* Washington, DC: American Psychological Association.

Frank, J. D. (1961). *Persuasion and healing.* Baltimore: Johns Hopkins University Press.

Freeman, S. C. (1990). C. H. Patterson on client-centered career counseling: An interview. *The Career Development Quarterly, 38*, 291–301.

Friedlander, M. L., Escudero, V., Horvath, S., Heatherington, L., Cabero, A., & Martens, M. P. (2006). System for observing family therapy alliances: A tool for research and practice. *Journal of Counseling Psychology, 53*, 214–225.

Friedlander, M. L., Lambert, J. E., & de la Pena, C. M. (2008). A step toward disentangling the alliance/improvement cycle in family therapy. *Journal of Counseling Psychology, 55*, 118–124.

Fuertes, J., Mislowack, C., Brown, S., Shovel, G.-A., Wilkinson, S., & Gelso, C. (2007). Correlates of the real relationship in psychotherapy: A study of dyads. *Psychotherapy Research, 17*, 423–430.

Garfield, S. L. (1978). Research on client variables in psychotherapy. In S. L. Garfield, & A. E. Bergin (Eds.), *Handbook of psychotherapy and behavior change* (2nd ed., pp. 191–232). New York: Wiley.

Gelso, C. J. (2004, June). *A theory of the real relationship in psychotherapy.* Paper presented at the International Conference of the Society for Psychotherapy Research, Rome.

Gelso, C. J., Betz, N. E., Friedlander, M. L., Helms, J. E., Hill, C. E., Patton, M. J., Super, D. E., & Wampold, B. E. (1988). Research in counseling psychology: Prospects and recommendations. *The Counseling Psychologist, 16*, 385–406.

Gelso, C. J., & Carter, J. A. (1985). The relationship in counseling and psychotherapy: Components, consequences, and theoretical antecedents. *The Counseling Psychologist, 13*, 155–243.

Gelso, C. J., & Carter, J. A. (1994). Components of the psychotherapy relationship: Their interaction and unfolding during treatment. *Journal of Counseling Psychology, 41*, 296–306.

Gelso, C. J., Fassinger, R. E., Gomez, M. J., & Latts, M. C. (1995). Countertransference reactions to lesbian clients: The role of homophobia, counselor gender, and countertransference management. *Journal of Counseling Psychology, 42*, 356–364.

Gelso, C. J., & Fretz, B. (2001). *Counseling psychology* (2nd ed.). Fort Worth, TX: Harcourt.

Gelso, C. J., & Hayes, J. A. (1998). *The psychotherapy relationship: Theory, research and practice.* New York: Wiley.

Gelso, C. J., & Hayes, J. A. (2002). The management of countertransference. In J. C. Norcross (Ed.), *Psychotherapy relationships that work: Therapist contributions and responsiveness to patients* (pp. 267–283). New York: Oxford University Press.

Gelso, C. J., Kelly, F. A., Fuertes, J. N., Marmarosh, C., Holmes, S. E., Costa, C., & Hancock, G. R. (2005). Measuring the real relationship in psychotherapy: Initial validation of the therapist form. *Journal of Counseling Psychology, 52*, 640–649.

Gelso, C. J., & Samstag, L. W. (2008). A tripartite model of the therapeutic relationship. In S. D. Brown, & R. W. Lent (Eds.), *Handbook of counseling psychology* (4th ed., pp. 267–283). New York: Wiley.

Gold, P. B., Kivlighan, D. M., Jr., Kerr, A. E., & Kramer, L. A. (1993). The structure of students' perceptions of impactful, helpful events in career exploration classes. *Journal of Career Assessment, 1*, 145–161.

Graff, H., Kenig, L., & Radoff, G. (1971). Prejudice of upper class therapists against lower class patients. *Psychiatric Quarterly, 45*, 475–489.

Greenberg, L. S. (1994). What is "real" in the relationship? A comment on Gelso and Carter (1994). *Journal of Counseling Psychology, 41*, 307–309.

Greencavage, L. M., & Norcross, J. C. (1990). Where are the commonalities among the therapeutic common factors? *Professional Psychology: Research and Practice, 21*, 372–378.

Greenson, R. R. (1965). The working alliance and the transference neuroses. *Psychoanalysis Quarterly, 34*, 155–181.

Greenson, R. R. (1967). *Technique and practice of psychoanalysis.* New York: International University Press.

Hardin, S. I., Subich, L. M., & Holvey, J. M. (1988). Expectancies for counseling in relation to premature termination. *Journal of Counseling Psychology, 35*, 37–40.

Hardy, G. E., Aldridge, J., Davidson, C., Rowe, C., Reilly, S., & Shapiro, D. A. (1999). Therapist responsiveness to patient attachment styles and issues observed in patient-identified significant events in psychodynamic-interpersonal psychotherapy. *Psychotherapy Research, 9*, 36–53.

Hartley, D. E., & Strupp, H. H. (1983). The therapeutic alliance: Its relationship to outcome in brief psychotherapy. In J. Masling (Ed.), *Empirical studies in analytic theories* (Vol. 1, pp. 1–37). Hillsdale, NJ: Erlbaum.

Hatcher, R. L., & Barends, A. W. (1996). Patients' view of the alliance in psychotherapy: Exploratory factor analysis of three alliance measures. *Journal of Consulting and Clinical Psychology, 64*, 1326–1336.

Haverkamp, B. E., Morrow, S. L., & Ponterotto, J. G. (Guest Eds.). (2005). Special Issue: Knowledge in context: Qualitative methods in counseling psychology research. *Journal of Counseling Psychology, 52*, 121–260.

Hayes, J. A., & Erkis, A. J. (2000). Therapist homophobia, client sexual orientation, and source of client HIV infection as predictors of therapist reactions to clients with HIV. *Journal of Counseling Psychology, 47*, 71–78.

Hayes, J. A., & Gelso, C. J. (1993). Counselors' discomfort with gay and HIV-infected clients. *Journal of Counseling Psychology, 40*, 86–93.

Hayes, J. A., Riker, J. R., & Ingram, K. M. (1997). Countertransference behavior and management in brief counseling: A field study. *Psychotherapy Research, 7*, 145–153.

Healy, C. C. (2001). A follow-up of adult career counseling clients of a university extension center. *Career Development Quarterly, 49*, 363–373.

Henry, W. P., Schacht, T. E., Strupp, H. H., Butler, S. F., & Binder, J. L. (1993a). Effects of training in time-limited dynamic psychotherapy: Mediators of therapists' responses to training. *Journal of Consulting and Clinical Psychology, 61,* 441–447.

Henry, W. P., Strupp, H. H., Butler, S. F., Schacht, T. E., & Binder, J. L. (1993b). Effects of training in time-limited dynamic psychotherapy: Changes in therapist behavior. *Journal of Consulting and Clinical Psychology, 61,* 434–430.

Heppner, M. J., & Hendricks, F. (1995). A process and outcome study examining career indecision and indecisiveness. *Journal of Counseling and Development, 73,* 426–437.

Heppner, M. J., Multon, K. D., Gysbers, N. C., Ellis, C. A., & Zook, C. E. (1998). The relationship of trainee self-efficacy to the process and outcome of career counseling. *Journal of Counseling Psychology, 45,* 393–402.

Heppner, P. P., & Frazier, P. A. (1992). Social psychological processes in psychotherapy: Extrapolating basic research to counseling psychology. In S. D. Brown, & R. W. Lent (Eds.), *Handbook of counseling psychology* (2nd ed., pp. 141–176). New York: Wiley.

Heppner, P. P., Rosenberg, J. I., & Hedgespeth, J. (1992). Three methods in measuring the therapeutic process: Clients' and counselors' constructions of the therapeutic process versus actual therapeutic events. *Journal of Counseling Psychology, 39,* 20–31.

Hersoug, A. G., Monsen, J. T., Havik, O. E., & Hoglend, P. (2002). Quality of early working alliance in psychotherapy: Diagnoses, relationship, and intrapsychic variables as predictors. *Psychotherapy and Psychosomatics, 71,* 18–27.

Highlen, P. S., & Hill, C. E. (1984). Factors affecting client change in individual counseling: Current status and theoretical speculations. In S. D. Brown, & R. W. Lent (Eds.), *Handbook of counseling psychology* (pp. 334–396). New York: Wiley.

Hill, C. E. (1994). What is the therapeutic relationship? A reaction to Sexton and Whiston. *The Counseling Psychologist, 22,* 90–97.

Hill, C. E. (2005). Therapist techniques, client involvement, and the therapeutic relationship: Inextricably intertwined in the therapy process. *Psychotherapy: Theory, Research, Practice, Training, 42,* 431–442.

Hill, C. E., Nutt-Williams, E., Heaton, K. J., Thompson, B. J., & Rhodes, R. H. (1996). Therapist recall of impasses in long-term psychotherapy: A qualitative analysis. *Journal of Counseling Psychology, 43,* 207–217.

Horvath, A. O. (1981). *An exploratory study of the working alliance: Its measurement and relationship to outcome.* Unpublished doctoral dissertation, University of British Columbia, Vancouver, Canada.

Horvath, A. O. (2001). The alliance. *Psychotherapy: Theory, Research, Practice, Training, 38,* 365–372.

Horvath, A. O. (2005). The therapeutic relationship: Research and theory. *Psychotherapy Research, 15,* 3–7.

Horvath, A. O. (2009). How *real* is the "real relationship?" *Psychotherapy Research, 19,* 273–277.

Horvath, A. O., & Bedi, R. P. (2002). The alliance. In J. C. Norcross (Ed.), *Psychotherapy relationships that work: Therapist contributions and responsiveness to patients* (pp. 37–69). New York: Oxford University Press.

Horvath, A. O., & Greenberg, L. S. (1986). Development of the working alliance inventory. In L. S. Greenberg, & W. M. Pinsof (Eds.), *The psychotherapeutic process: A research handbook* (pp. 529–556). New York: Guilford.

Horvath, A. O., & Symonds, B. D. (1991). Relation between working alliance and outcome in psychotherapy: A meta-analysis. *Journal of Counseling Psychology, 38,* 139–149.

Howard, G. S. (1992). Behold our creation! What counseling psychology has become and might yet become. *Journal of Counseling Psychology, 39,* 419–442.

Hoyt, W. T. (1996). Antecedents and effects of perceived therapist credibility: A meta-analysis. *Journal of Counseling Psychology, 43,* 430–447.

Imel, Z. E., & Wampold, B. E. (2008). The importance of treatment and the science of common factors in psychotherapy. In S. D. Brown, & R. W. Lent (Eds.), *Handbook of counseling psychology* (4th ed., pp. 249–266). New York: Wiley.

Jacobs, D., Charles, E., Jacobs, T., Weinstein, H., & Mann, D. (1972). Preparation for treatment of the disadvantaged patient: Effects on disposition and outcome. *American Journal of Orthopsychiatry, 42,* 666–674.

Joyce, A. S., & Piper, W. E. (1998). Expectancy, the therapeutic alliance, and treatment outcome in short-term individual psychotherapy. *Journal of Psychotherapy Practice and Research, 7,* 236–248.

Karlsson, R. (2005). Ethnic matching between therapist and patient in psychotherapy: An overview of findings, together with methodological and conceptual issues. *Cultural Diversity and Ethnic Minority Psychology, 11,* 113–129.

Kiesler, D. J. (1982). Interpersonal theory for personality and psychotherapy. In J. C. Anchin, & D. J. Kiesler (Eds.), *Handbook of interpersonal psychotherapy* (pp. 3–24). New York: Pergamon.

Kim, B. S. K., & Atkinson, D. R. (2002). Asian American client adherence to Asian cultural values, counselor expression of cultural values, counselor ethnicity and career counseling process. *Journal of Counseling Psychology, 49,* 3–13.

Kim, D. M., Wampold, B. E., & Bolt, D. M. (2006). Therapist effects in psychotherapy: A random effects modeling of the NIMH TDCRP data. *Psychotherapy Research, 16,* 161–172.

Kirschner, T., Hoffman, M. A., & Hill, C. E. (1994). Case study of the process and outcome of career counseling. *Journal of Counseling Psychology, 41,* 216–226.

Kivlighan, D. M., Jr. (2007). Where is the relationship in research on the alliance? Two methods for analyzing dyadic data. *Journal of Counseling Psychology, 54,* 423–433.

Kivlighan, D. M., Jr., McGovern, T. V., & Corazzini, J. G. (1984). Effects of content and timing of structuring interventions on group therapy process and outcome. *Journal of Counseling Psychology, 31,* 363–370.

Kivlighan, D. M., Jr., Patton, M. J., & Foote, D. (1998). Moderating effects of client attachment on the counselor experience-working alliance relationship. *Journal of Counseling Psychology, 45,* 274–278.

Knaevelsrud, C., & Maercker, A. (2006). Does the quality of the working alliance predict treatment outcome in online psychotherapy for traumatized patients? *Journal of Medical Internet Research, 8*(4), e31. Published online December 19, 2006. doi: 10.2196/jmir.8.4.e31.

Ladany, N., Lehrman-Waterman, D., Molinaro, M., & Wolgast, B. (1999). Psychotherapy supervisor ethical practices: Adherence to guidelines, the supervisory working alliance, and supervisee satisfaction. *The Counseling Psychologist, 27,* 443–475.

Lakey, B., Cohen, J. L., & Neely, L. C. (2008). Perceived support and relational effects in psychotherapy process constructs. *Journal of Counseling Psychology, 55,* 209–220.

Lambert, M. J. (1992). Psychotherapy outcome research: Implications for integrative and eclectic therapists. In J. C. Norcross, & M. R. Goldfried (Eds.), *Handbook of psychotherapy integration* (pp. 94–129). New York: Basic Books.

Lambert, M. J. (Ed.). (2004). *Bergin and Garfield's handbook of psychotherapy and behavior change* (5th ed.). New York: Wiley.

Lambert, M. J., & Barley, D. E. (2001). Research summary on the therapeutic relationship and psychotherapy outcome. *Psychotherapy: Theory, Research, Practice, Training, 38,* 357–361.

Lambert, M. J., & Barley, D. E. (2002). Research summary. In J. C. Norcross (Ed.), *Psychotherapy relationships that work: Therapist contributions and responsiveness to patients* (pp. 17–32). New York: Oxford University Press.

Lambert, M. J., Garfield, S. L., & Bergin, A. E. (2004). Overview, trends and future issues. In M. J. Lambert (Ed.), *Bergin and Garfield's handbook of psychotherapy and behavior change* (5th ed., pp. 805–821). New York: Wiley.

Lambert, M. J., & Ogles, B. M. (2004). The efficacy and effectiveness of psychotherapy. In M. J. Lambert (Ed.), *Bergin and Garfield's handbook of psychotherapy and behavior change* (5th ed., pp. 139–193). New York: Wiley.

Leahy, R. L. (2008). The therapeutic relationship in cognitive-behavioral therapy. *Behavioral and cognitive psychotherapy, 36,* 769–777.

Leary, T. (1957). *Interpersonal diagnosis of personality.* New York: Roland.

Leong, F. T. L., & Gupta, A. (2008). Culture and race in counseling and psychotherapy: A critical review of the literature. In S. D. Brown, & R. W. Lent (Eds.), *Handbook of counseling psychology* (4th ed., pp. 320–337). Hoboken, NJ: Wiley.

Lepper, G., & Mergenthaler, E. (2007). Therapeutic collaboration: How does it work? *Psychotherapy Research, 17,* 576–587.

Li, L. C., & Kim B. S. K. (2004). Effects of counseling style and client adherence to Asian cultural values on counseling process with Asian American college students. *Journal of Counseling Psychology, 51,* 158–167.

Lichtenberg, J. W., Wettersten, K. B., Mull, H., Moberly, R. L., Merkey, K. B., & Corey, A. T. (1988). Relationship and control as correlates of psychotherapy quality and outcome. *Journal of Consulting and Clinical Psychology, 45,* 322–337.

Ligiero, D. P., & Gelso, C. J. (2002). Countertransference, attachment, and the working alliance: The therapist's contribution. *Psychotherapy: Theory, Research, Practice, Training, 39,* 3–11.

Lopez, S. J., Magyar-Moe, J. L., Petersen, S. E., Ryder, J. A., Krieshok, T. S., O'Byrne, K. K., et al. (2006). Counseling psychology's focus on positive aspects of human functioning. *The Counseling Psychologist, 34,* 205–227.

Lorion, R. P. (1973). Socioeconomic status and traditional treatment approaches reconsidered. *Psychological Bulletin, 79,* 263–270.

Lorion, R. P. (1974). Patient and therapist variables in the treatment of low-income patients. *Psychological Bulletin, 81,* 344–354.

Luborsky, L. (1976). Helping alliances in psychotherapy. In J. L. Cleghorn (Ed.), *Successful psychotherapy* (pp. 92–116). New York: Bruner/Mazel.

Luborsky, L., Crits-Cristoph, P., Alexander, L., Margolis, M., & Cohen, M. (1983). Two helping alliance methods for predicting outcomes of psychotherapy: A counting signs vs. a global rating method. *Journal of Nervous and Mental Disease, 171,* 480–491.

Lutz, W., Leon, S. C., Martinovich, Z., Lyons, J. S., & Stiles, W. B. (2007). Therapist effects in outpatient psychotherapy: A three-level growth curve approach. *Journal of Counseling Psychology, 54,* 32–39.

Mallen, M. J., Vogel, D. L., Rochlen, A. B., & Day, S. X. (2005). On-line counseling: Reviewing the literature from a counseling psychology framework. *The Counseling Psychologist, 33,* 819–871.

Mallinckrodt, B. (1993). Session impact, working alliance, and treatment outcome in brief counseling. *Journal of Counseling Psychology, 40,* 25–32.

Mallinckrodt, B. (1996). Change in working alliance, social support, and psychological symptoms in brief therapy. *Journal of Counseling Psychology, 43,* 448–455.

Mallinckrodt, B., Gantt, D. L., & Coble, H. M. (1995). Attachment patterns in the psychotherapy relationship: Development of the Patient Attachment to Therapist Scale. *Journal of Counseling Psychology, 42,* 307–317.

Mallinckrodt, B., King, J. L., & Coble, H. M. (1998). Family dysfunction, alexithymia, and client attachment to therapist. *Journal of Counseling Psychology, 45,* 497–504.

Malllinckrodt, B., & Nelson, M. L. (1991). Counselor training level and the formation of the psychotherapeutic working alliance. *Journal of Counseling Psychology, 38,* 133–138.

McIlveen, P. (2007). Counsellors' personal experience and appraisal of My Career Chapter. In 16th National Conference of the Australian Association of Career Counsellors. April, 2007, Perth, Australia. Retrieved June 21, 2009, from http://eprints.usq.edu.au/2549.

Meyer, B., & Pilkonis, P. A. (2002). Attachment style. In J. C. Norcross (Ed.), *Psychotherapy relationships that work: Therapist contributions and responsiveness to patients* (pp. 367–382). New York: Oxford University Press.

Mischel, W., & Shoda, Y. (1995). A cognitive-affective system theory of personality: Reconceptualizing situations, dispositions, dynamics, and invariance in personality structure. *Psychological Review, 102,* 248–268.

Mohr, J. J., Gelso, C. J., & Hill, C. E. (2005). Client and counselor-trainee attachment as predictors of session evaluation and countertransference behavior in first counseling sessions. *Journal of Counseling Psychology, 52,* 298–309.

Multon, K. D., Ellis-Kalton, C. A., Heppner, M. J., & Gysbers, N. C. (2003). The relationship between counselor verbal response modes and the working alliance in career counseling. *Career Development Quarterly, 51,* 259–273.

Multon, K. D., Heppner, M. J., Gysbers, N. C., Zook, C., & Ellis-Kalton, C. A. (2001). Client psychological distress: An important factor in career counseling. *Career Development Quarterly, 49,* 324–335.

Murray, S. L., Holmes, J. G., & Collins, N. L. (2006). Optimizing assurance: The risk-regulation system in relationships. *Psychological Bulletin, 132,* 641–666.

Myers, R. A. (2004). Conferring as a way of knowing. *The Counseling Psychologist, 32,* 128–133.

Nelson, D. W., & Baumgarte, R. (2004). Cross cultural misunderstandings reduce empathic responding. *Journal of Applied Social Psychology, 34*, 391–401.

Nerdrum, P., & Ronnestad, M. H. (2002). The trainees' perspective: A qualitative study of learning empathic communication in Norway. *The Counseling Psychologist, 30*, 609–629.

Nerdrum, P., & Ronnestad, M. H. (2004). Changes in therapists' conceptualization and practice of therapy following empathy training. *The Clinical Supervisor, 22*, 37–61.

Netzky, W., Davidson, J., & Crunkleton, A. (1982). Pertinent consumer issues in choosing a counseling professional. *Journal of Counseling Psychology, 29*, 406–413.

Nigro, T. (2004). Counselors' experiences with problematic dual relationships. *Ethics and Behavior, 14*, 51–64.

Norcross, J. C. (Ed.). (2002). *Psychotherapy relationships that work: Therapist contributions and responsiveness to patients.* New York: Oxford University Press.

Norcross, J. C. (2002b). Empirically supported therapy relationships. In J. C. Norcross (Ed.), *Psychotherapy relationships that work: Therapist contributions and responsiveness to patients* (pp. 3–16). New York: Oxford University Press.

Nutt-Willliams, E., Hayes, J. A., & Fauth, J. (2008). Therapist self-awareness: Interdisciplinary connections and future directions. In S. D. Brown, & R. W. Lent (Eds.), *Handbook of counseling psychology* (4th ed., pp. 303–319). Hoboken, NJ: Wiley.

Nutt-Willliams, E., & Hill, C. E. (1996). The relationship between self-talk and therapy process variables for novice therapists. *Journal of Counseling Psychology, 43*, 170–177.

Orlinsky, D. E., & Ronnestad, M. H. (2005). *How psychotherapists develop: A study of therapeutic work and professional growth.* Washington, DC: American Psychological Association.

Packard, T. (2009). The 2008 Leona Tyler Award address: Core values that distinguish counseling psychology: Personal and professional perspectives. *The Counseling Psychologist, 37*, 610–624.

Parham, T. A., & Helms, J. E. (1981). The influence of Black students' racial identity attitudes on preferences for counselor's race. *Journal of Counseling Psychology, 28*, 250–257.

Patterson, C. H. (1966). *Theories of counseling and psychotherapy.* New York: Harper & Row.

Patton, M. J. (1994). Components of the counseling relationship–An evolving model: Comment on Gelso and Carter (1994). *Journal of Counseling Psychology, 41*, 313–314.

Patton, M. J., & Kivlighan, D. M., Jr. (1997). Relevance of the supervisory alliance to the counseling alliance and to treatment adherence in counselor training. *Journal of Counseling Psychology, 44*, 108–115.

Peabody, S. A., & Gelso, C. J. (1982). Countertransference and empathy: The complex relationship between two divergent concepts in counseling. *Journal of Counseling Psychology, 29*, 240–245.

Poston, J. M., & Hanson, W. E. (2010). Meta-analysis of psychological assessment as a therapeutic intervention. *Psychological Assessment, 22*, 203–212.

Prediger, D. J., & Garfield, N. (1988). Testing competencies and responsibilities: A checklist for counselors. In J. T. Kapes, & M. M. Mastie (Eds.), *A counselors' guide to career assessment instruments* (2nd ed.). Alexandria, VA: National Career Development Association.

Reandeau, S. G., & Wampold, B. E. (1991). Relationship of power and involvement of working alliance: A multiple-case sequential analysis of brief therapy. *Journal of Counseling Psychology, 38*, 107–114.

Reis, H. T. (2007, August). What social psychologists would like to tell clinicians about close relationships. Division 8 Presidential Address, presented at the annual meetings of the American Psychological Association, San Francisco.

Reis, B. F., & Brown, L. G. (1999). Reducing psychotherapy dropouts: Maximizing perspective convergence in the therapeutic dyad. *Psychotherapy: Theory, Research, Practice, Training, 36*, 123–136.

Rochlen, A. B., Milburn, L., & Hill, C. E. (2004). Examining the process and outcome of career counseling for different types of career counseling clients. *Journal of Career Development, 30*, 263–275.

Rogers, C. R. (1942). *Counseling and psychotherapy.* Boston: Houghton-Mifflin.

Rogers, C. R. (1957). The necessary and sufficient conditions of therapeutic personality change. *Journal of Consulting Psychology, 21*, 95–103.

Rogers, C. R. (1963). Psychotherapy today or where do we go from here? *American Psychologist, 17*, 5–16.

Rosenberger, E. W., & Hayes, J. A. (2002). Origins, consequences, and management of countertransference: A case study. *Journal of Counseling Psychology, 49*, 221–232.

Rosenzweig, S. (1936). Some implicit common factors in diverse methods of psychotherapy. *American Journal of Orthopsychiatry, 6*, 412–415.

Rubino, G., Barker, C., Roth, T., & Fearon, P. (2000). Therapist empathy and depth of interpretation in response to potential alliance ruptures: The role of therapist and patient attachment styles. *Psychotherapy Research, 10*, 408–420.

Rudikoff, L. C., & Kirk, B. A. (1959). Test interpretation in counseling. *Journal of Counseling Psychology, 6*, 224–229.

Rusbult, C. E., & VanLange, P. A. M. (2003). Interdependence and relationships. *Annual Review of Psychology, 54*, 351–375.

Safran, J. D., Muran, J. C., & Samstag, L. W. (1994). Resolving therapeutic alliance ruptures: A task analytic investigation. In A. O. Horvath, & L. S. Greenberg (Eds.), *The working alliance: Theory, research and practice* (pp. 225–255). New York: Wiley.

Samler, J. (1980). Where do counseling psychologists work? What do they do? What should they do? In J. M. Whitely (Ed.), *The history of counseling psychology.* Monterey, CA: Brooks-Cole. (Original work published 1964).

Sexton, H. (1996). Process, life events, and symptomatic change in brief eclectic psychotherapy. *Journal of Consulting and Clinical Psychology, 64*, 1358–1365.

Sexton, H., Littauer, H., Sexton, A., & Tommeras, E. (2005). Building an alliance: Early therapy process and the client-therapist connection. *Psychotherapy Process, 15*, 103–116.

Sexton, T. L., & Whiston, S. C. (1994). The status of the counseling relationship: An empirical review, theoretical implications, and research directions. *The Counseling Psychologist, 22*, 6–78.

Singer, B. A., & Luborsky, L. (1977). Countertransference: The status of clinical versus quantitative research. In A. S. Gurman, & A. M. Razdin (Eds.), *Effective psychotherapy: Handbook of research* (pp. 433–451). New York: Pergamon Press.

Smith, E. J. (2006). The strength-based counseling model. *The Counseling Psychologist, 34*, 13–79.

Smith, L. (2005). Psychotherapy, classism, and the poor: Conspicuous by their absence. *American Psychologist, 60*, 687–696.

Smith, M. L., & Glass, G. V. (1977). Meta-analysis of psychotherapy outcome studies. *American Psychologist, 39*, 752–760.

Stevens, S. E., Hynan, M. T., & Allen, M. (2000). A meta-analysis of common factors and specific treatment effects across the outcome domains of the phase model of psychotherapy. *Clinical Psychology: Science and Practice, 7*, 273–290.

Stiles, W. B., Shapiro, D. A., & Elliott, R. (1986). Are all psychotherapies equivalent? *American Psychologist, 41*, 165–180.

Strong, S. R. (1968). Counseling: An interpersonal influence process. *Journal of Counseling Psychology, 15*, 215–224.

Strong, S. R. (1978). Social psychological approach to psychotherapy research. In S. Garfield, & A. E. Bergin (Eds.), *Handbook of psychotherapy and behavior change* (2nd ed., pp. 101–136). New York: Wiley.

Strong, S. R., & Schmidt, L. D. (1970). Trustworthiness and influence in counseling. *Journal of Counseling Psychology, 17*, 197–204.

Strupp, H. H., & Anderson, T. (1997). On the limitations of therapy manuals. *Clinical Psychology: Science and Practice, 4*, 76–82.

Sue, D. W., Bernier, J. B., Duran, M., Feinberg, L., Pederson, P., Smith, E., et al. (1982). Position paper: Cross-cultural counseling competencies. *The Counseling Psychologist, 10*, 45–52.

Sue, D. W., & Lam, A. G. (2002). Cultural and demographic diversity. In J. C. Norcross (Ed.), *Psychotherapy relationships that work: Therapist contributions and responsiveness to patients* (pp. 401–421). New York: Oxford University Press.

Sue, S., Fujino, D. C., Hu, L. T., Takeuchi, D. T., & Zane, N. W. S. (1991). Community mental health services for ethnic minority groups: A test of the cultural responsiveness hypothesis. *Journal of Consulting and Clinical Psychology, 59*, 533–540.

Sundberg, N. D., & Littman, R. A. (1994). Leona Elizabeth Tyler (1906-1993). *American Psychologist, 49*, 211–212.

Super, D. E. (1955). Transition: From vocational guidance to counseling psychology. *Journal of Counseling Psychology, 2*, 3–9.

Swanson, J. L. (1995). The process and outcome of career counseling. In W. B. Walsh, & S. H. Osipow (Eds.), *The handbook of vocational psychology* (pp. 217–259). Mahwah, NJ: Erlbaum.

Swift, J. K., & Callahan, J. L. (2008). A delay discounting measure of great expectations and the effectiveness of psychotherapy. *Professional Psychology: Research and Practice, 39*, 581–588.

Thompson, V. L. S., Bazile, A., & Akbar, M. (2004). African Americans' perceptions of psychotherapy and psychotherapists. *Professional Psychology: Research and Practice, 35*, 19–26.

Tinsley, H. E. A., & Bradley, R. W. (1986). Test interpretation. *Journal of Counseling Psychology, 64*, 462–466.

Tinsley, H. E. A., Workman, K. R., & Kass, R. A. (1980). Factor analysis of the domain of client expectations about counseling. *Journal of Counseling Psychology, 27*, 561–570.

Tokar, D. M., Hardin, S. I., Adams, E. M., & Brandel, I. W. (1996). Clients' expectations about counseling and perceptions of the working alliance. *Journal of College Student Psychotherapy, 11*, 9–26.

Townes, D. L., Chavez-Korell, S., & Cunningham, N. J. (2009). Re-examining the relationships between racial identity, cultural mistrust, help-seeking attitudes, and preference for a Black counselor. *Journal of Counseling Psychology, 56*, 330–336.

Tracey, T. J. (1986). Interactional correlates of premature termination. *Journal of Consulting and Clinical Psychology, 54*, 784–788.

Tracey, T. J., & Hays, K. (1989). Therapist complementarity as a function of experience and client stimuli. *Psychotherapy, 26*, 462–468.

Truax, C. B., & Carkhuff, R. R. (1967). *Toward effective counseling and psychotherapy.* Chicago: Aldine.

Tyler, L. E. (1953). *The work of the counselor.* New York: Appleton-Century-Crofts.

Tyrrell, C. L., Dozier, M., Teague, G. B., & Fallot, R. D. (1999). Effective treatment relationships for persons with serious psychiatric disorders: The importance of attachment states of mind. *Journal of Consulting and Clinical Psychology, 67*, 723–733.

Vasquez, M. J. T. (2007). Cultural difference and the therapeutic alliance: An evidence-based analysis. *American Psychologist, 62*, 878–885.

Vasquez, M. J. T., Lott, B., Garcia-Vasquez, E., Grant, S. K., Iwamasa, G. Y., Molina, L. E., et al. (2006). Personal reflections: Barriers and strategies in increasing diversity in psychology. *American Psychologist, 61*, 157–172.

Vera, E. M., & Speight, S. L. (2003). Multicultural competence, social justice, and counseling psychology: Expanding our roles. *The Counseling Psychologist, 31*, 253–272.

Wampold, B. E. (2007). Psychotherapy: "The" humanistic (and effective) treatment. *American Psychologist, 62*, 857–874.

Wampold, B. E., Lichtenberg, J. W., & Waehler, C. A. (2002). Principles of empirically supported interventions in counseling psychology. *The Counseling Psychologist, 30*, 197–217.

Watson, J. C., & Geller, S. (2005). An examination of the relations among empathy, unconditional positive regard and congruence in cognitive-behavioral and process-experiential psychotherapy. *Psychotherapy Research, 15*, 25–33.

Wei, M., & Heppner, P. P. (2005). Counselor and client predictors of the initial working alliance: A replication and extension to Taiwanese client-counselor dyads. *The Counseling Psychologist, 33*, 51–71.

Weinberger, J. (1995). Common factors aren't so common: The common factors dilemma. *Clinical Psychology: Science and Practice, 2*, 45–69.

Whiston, S. C., Brecheisen, B. K., & Stephens, J. (2003). Does treatment modality affect career counseling effectiveness? *Journal of Vocational Behavior, 62*, 390–410.

Whiston, S. C., Lindeman, D. L., Rahardja, D., & Reed, J. H. (2005). Career counseling process: A qualitative analysis of experts' cases. *Journal of Career Assessment, 13*, 169–187.

Whiston, S. C., & Rahardja, D. (2008). Vocational counseling process and outcome. In S. D. Brown, & R. W. Lent (Eds.), *Handbook of counseling psychology* (4th ed., pp. 444–461). Hoboken, NJ: Wiley.

Whitely, J. M. (Ed.). (1980). *The history of counseling psychology.* Monterey, CA: Brooks-Cole.

Wierzbicki, M., & Pekarik, G. (1993). A meta-analysis of psychotherapy dropout. *Professional Psychology: Research and Practice, 24,* 190–195.

Wiggins, J. S. (1982). Circumplex models of interpersonal behavior in clinical psychology. In P. C. Kendall, & J. N. Butcher (Eds.), *Handbook of research methods in clinical psychology* (pp. 183–221). New York: Wiley.

Wrenn, C. J. (1966). Birth and early childhood of a journal. *Journal of Counseling Psychology, 13,* 485–488.

Young, R. A., & Valach, L. (2009). Evaluating the process and outcomes of vocational counseling: An action theory perspective. *L'Orientation Scolaire et Professionnelle, 38,* 281–306.

Young, R. A., Valach, L., & Domene, J. F. (2005). The action-project method in counseling psychology. *Journal of Counseling Psychology, 52,* 215–223.

Zane, N., Sue, S., Chang, J., Huang, L., Huang, J., Lowe, S., et al. (2005). Beyond ethnic match: Effects of client-therapist cognitive match in problem perception, coping orientation, and therapy goals on treatment outcomes. *Journal of Community Psychology, 33,* 569–585.

Zilber, S. M., & Osipow, S. H. (1990). Leona E. Tyler. In A. N. O'Connell, & N. F. Russo (Eds.), *Women in psychology: A bio-bibliographic sourcebook* (pp. 335–341). Washington, DC: American Psychological Association.

Zlotnick, C., Elkin, I., & Shea, M. T. (1998). Does the gender of a patient or the gender of a therapist affect the treatment of patients with major depression? *Journal of Consulting and Clinical Psychology, 66,* 655–659.

Theory and Research for Counseling Interventions

Martin Heesacker *and* James W. Lichtenberg

Abstract

This chapter describes the role of psychological theory and its relation to counseling practice, with a special emphasis on counseling psychology's unique opportunity to enhance the integration of science and practice in psychology. Improving science–practice integration is presented as critical to fulfilling counseling psychology's claim that its interventions are science-based. The chapter discusses psychological theory generally, and the pathways (both scientific and clinical) through which theory influences counseling interventions. It reviews both the theoretical and research bases of treatment, with a particular focus on how treatments are evaluated. This includes a focus on efficacy, effectiveness, and meta-analytic studies, and how new treatments develop and are accepted by the field; and a focus on differences between practitioners and researchers in their acceptance of treatments as established practice. Matching specific, theoretically distinct, evidence-based treatments to specific client problems is contrasted with the theory-integrating, common factors approach. The chapter closes with a series of future directions for reducing the science–practice gap in counseling psychology.

Keywords: science–practice integration, theory and meta-theory, treatment efficacy and effectiveness, empirically supported interventions, common factors

The disconnect between much of clinical practice and the advances in psychological science is an unconscionable embarrassment for many reasons, and a case of professional cognitive dissonance with heavy costs.

—Mischel, 2009, p. i

The author of the chapter's opening quote, Walter Mischel, is one of psychology's most respected theorists and researchers, and so it should come as no surprise that his influence extends beyond psychology. His 2009 editorial in a major psychological journal triggered an editorial in *Nature* entitled "Psychology: A Reality Check," which sent a similar message throughout the scientific community: "There is a moral imperative to turn the craft of psychology—in danger of falling, Freud-like, out of fashion—into a robust and valued science informed by the best available research and economic evidence" (Abbot, 2009, p. 847). Echoing the alarms sounded by Mischel and Abbot, a recent science column by Sharon Begley in *Newsweek* magazine entitled "Ignoring the Evidence: Why Do Psychologists Reject Science?" (http://www.newsweek.com/id/216506) sent the message to the American public that psychological psychotherapy is not science-based. This message, distributed to ever-widening groups of psychology's stakeholders, challenges a fundamental tenet of the discipline: Namely, that psychological interventions are applications of psychological science.

Notwithstanding the above criticisms of psychological psychotherapy, counseling psychology has a unique and important opportunity to move forward as an applied specialty by fostering the integration of the science and practice that may be less available to other applied specialties in psychology.

It is the purpose of this chapter to review current issues in counseling theory and intervention practices to facilitate a positive, creative, comprehensive, and productive dialog that will result in a more complete integration of science and practice in counseling psychology. This, in turn, will serve as a model for other specialties, highlighting effective ways to address the important disciplinary challenge of the integration of the science and practice of psychology and the furthering of a science-based profession.

Theory As the Key to Science–Practice Integration

> There is nothing more practical than a good theory. (Kurt Lewin, 1952, p. 169).

The key premise of this chapter is that psychological *theory* holds perhaps the greatest promise for the successful integration of counseling psychology science and practice. Theory is what researchers and practitioners have in common: Researchers often are drawn to theory development and validation, whereas practitioners often are drawn to the application of theory. Ideally, researchers and practitioners work in tandem to produce knowledge that helps the common good (see Cialdini's [1980] full cycle social psychology for a description of the reciprocal relationship between researchers and practitioners in theory development, refinement, validation, and application). Because a valuing of theory is what counseling psychology's researchers and practitioners share, allocating effort toward understanding the state of the theoretical art and addressing the challenges researchers and practitioners face with regard to theory is likely to pay the richest dividends by maximizing the link between counseling psychology's science and its practice.

In this chapter, we discuss the nature and development of theories within psychology generally and the translation of theories into counseling interventions. In the process, we will be addressing both the theoretical and scientific bases of treatment, how new treatments develop, and how they come to be accepted by the specialty. We will also address documented differences between practitioners and researchers with regard to acceptance of treatments as established practice. All of this will be done with respect for differing perspectives and contexts, and in the service of facilitating the complete integration of counseling psychology science and practice, knowing that the process will be imperfect and ongoing.

What we will *not* do is ascribe antiscience motives to practitioners of counseling psychology or antipractice motives to researchers in counseling psychology. Unfortunately, for practical reasons, we will not have the space to review specific theories *per se*. That is done in other chapters in this volume and in other publications. Instead, our focus will remain on the broader landscape of science–practice integration.

What Is a Theory?

Counseling interventions are mostly based on scholarly theories (Brooks-Harris, 2008, p. 4), but what *is* a theory? A theory (also known as a *symbolic model*, according to Ford and Urban, 1998, p. 6) is a description of some aspect of the natural world. This description can be verbal, mathematical, or both. A scientific theory is presented in a manner that allows its utility to be assessed by comparing the description to empirical observation. The assessment of theory by comparing its description to empirical observation is called the *scientific method*, and it is through this method that theory is validated. Theory and method often operate recursively in science.

Scientific theories can be basic or applied. *Basic theories* describe elements of the natural world that may or may not have any direct application to the betterment of the natural world, but instead have as their primary objective a better understanding of nature—whether practically useful or not. Basic theories have often been developed and tested without regard to application, and yet basic theories often later trigger important applications. In contrast to basic theory, *applied theory* seeks to describe aspects of the natural world that can be applied to create a benefit or reduce a cost. For example, Schachter and Singer's (1962) two-factor theory of emotion is a basic theory that posits that emotion results from one's cognitive processing and assessing of one's physiological responses. On the other hand, Albert Ellis' rational emotive behavior therapy theory (Ellis & Dryden, 2007) is an applied theory that describes how unwanted emotion may be reduced or eliminated by disciplining oneself to cognitively process experience rationally.

Why Does Theory Matter?

Other than the fact that most counseling interventions are theory-based, why do counseling psychologists care about theory? As mentioned earlier, theory provides an excellent pathway through which the work of scientists and practitioners can be complementary. This is true for four reasons. First, personality theories and other behavior-relevant basic science theories often tie very closely to theories of psychotherapy. For example, Carl Rogers' (1957) self theory, a basic science theory, ties closely to his theory of psychotherapy, which endeavors to provide the conditions under which a client's ideal self may be realized fully. Another example is John Holland's theory of vocational behavior (Holland, 1997). Holland's work emphasizes person-by-environment fit, that in turn ties closely with his theory of career counseling, which endeavors to provide clients with insights regarding their work and career interests and aspirations, and to match those with jobs and careers.

A second reason that theory can reduce the scientist–practitioner divide is that a theory is, in essence, a story. Likewise, clients very frequently tell stories as part of therapy, and psychotherapists frequently work with, challenge, and help alter the narratives or stories that may contribute to or sustain client dysfunction.

There is a third reason theory may reduce this divide between researchers and practitioners of counseling psychology. Theory represents a common factor among scholars of psychology. Likewise, theory represents a coherent narrative about the nature of change and the nature of problems and problem resolution, and thus constitutes a common factor across nearly all recognized psychotherapeutic approaches.

A final reason why a focus on theory may reduce the science–practice divide is that theory, as discussed earlier, appeals to both scientists and practitioners. The process of direct service delivery (e.g., intense, personal interactions; ambiguity of outcome) is generally less appealing to researchers than to practitioners. Likewise, the process of psychological research (e.g., research design, advances in statistical analyses) often is less interesting to practitioners than to researchers. In contrast, a focus on theory, especially on narrative theory, holds interest and appeal for both groups.

Appealing to both scientists and practitioners are a host of important *intellectual* reasons for a theory focus. Perhaps the most important of these is that theory provides causal explanations that are critical for effective counseling and psychotherapy. These causal explanations include explanations for how clients developed into the people they are, and how they developed the functions and dysfunctions they present in counseling. They also include explanations of how and under what conditions clients change from dysfunctional behavior and to more functional behavior. Virtually every major theory of psychotherapy describes client development and the processes and conditions for change.

How Theory Influences Practice

According to Ford and Urban (1998, p. 6), "A set of transformation rules is required to map the meaning of the symbol onto the phenomenon represented [in a theory] because their relationship is completely arbitrary." In practice, this means that theories must be transformed into specific interventions. *Constructs* that are part of a theory have to be transformed into action. Descriptions of *processes* posited by a theory likewise must be transformed into specific actions or measures. These operationalizations of theory are required for theory to translate into practice. Likewise, operationalization is required for scientific assessment of the utility and validity of a theory.

So, psychotherapy practice can be understood as the advancement of theory by transforming theory into practice. In turn, observations resulting from the transformation of theory into practice inform theory and often provide necessary correction to theory (see Cialdini, 1980).

The importance of this process of theory to operation (or intervention) and back to theory cannot be overstated. A theory is no better than the quality of the operations used to implement and evaluate it. A psychotherapeutic approach that is judged to be ineffective may be judged that way for three distinguishable reasons: the theory is wrong, the operationalization of the theory is wrong, and/or the measures of the theory's effectiveness are invalid. Likewise, theories of psychotherapy can wrongly be judged to be valid if the operationalization was unfaithful to the theory and yet the operation produced a beneficial outcome, or if the measures of the theory's effectiveness are invalid and yet inaccurately yielded results that indicate client improvement. Again, collaboration between scientists and practitioners, this time on how to operationalize theory so that it improves practice, is essential in reducing the science–practice divide.

Addressing Theory-related Challenges

Having opined that focusing on theory is arguably the best approach to maximizing the link between counseling psychology's science and its practice, we must also readily admit that counseling psychology has to address and overcome two theory-related challenges to achieve that goal: the proliferation of theories, which is a challenge because it creates a psychotherapeutic Tower of Babble, in which counseling psychologists do not enjoy a common conceptual language; and what has come to be known as the *common factors perspective*, which is a challenge to the notion that specific theories and their posited change mechanisms even matter in psychotherapeutic intervention and change.

OVERCOMING CHALLENGES ASSOCIATED WITH THEORY PROLIFERATION

An interesting and perplexing theory-related challenge involves the proliferation of theories that exist in the field, with their concomitant interventions and techniques. In the mid-1960s, Garfield (writing in 1989) collected a list of over 60 different approaches to therapy—each grounded in some more or less explicitly stated theory explaining the nature and bases for clients' psychological problems and the mechanisms by which change in those problems could be effected. A few years later, a report of the Research Task Force of the National Institute of Mental Health (NIMH, 1975) noted over 130 different types of psychotherapy. Five years after that, Herink (1980) published an account of over 200 different forms of therapy, and within 6 years of Herink's publication, Kazdin (1986) referred to over 400 different therapeutic techniques! Although it is not clear whether the list of theories in counseling and psychotherapy has gotten bigger or smaller, it *is* clear that counseling theories exist in a welter of forms and with a variety of different conceptual and empirical justifications. The diversity-valuing ethic at the heart of counseling psychology allows the counseling psychologist to embrace this nearly incomprehensible diversity, even while recognizing that some theories are better scientifically supported than others and that some are more readily useful in application than others.

Diversity celebration notwithstanding, the proliferation of theories constitutes a real challenge to science–practice integration and must be addressed. One approach to proliferation begins by asking which core assumptions and intellectual roots may unite subgroups of theories of counseling and psychotherapy. It is our perspective that theories of counseling and psychotherapy, like other scientific theories, emerge from and are embedded in broader meta-theories, which often reflect the zeitgeist prevalent in the era of their development. By *meta-theory*, we are referring to certain structural properties of the theories they subsume—properties including the basic assumptions and types of laws proposed, the determinants of behavior, units of analysis, issues concerning the consistency/specificity of behavior, developmental/contemporaneous parameters of the theory, and strategies of research. In the history of science, meta-theories have been referred to as *paradigms* (Kuhn, 1970).

These structural properties, viewed in combination, form the bases of a variety of different theories of and approaches to counseling and psychotherapy that populate the field—theories and approaches that are often discontinuous and incompatible with one another in significant ways. When considering the diversity of theories, it is not possible to know which one best represents a true picture of human functioning, but what *is* possible to acknowledge is that different groups of theories reflect often radically different ways of construing human events. In short, these construal differences determine what can be observed and what practicing counseling psychologists decide to do about those observations.

Three meta-theoretical positions provide architecture for understanding more simply the welter of theories within counseling and psychotherapy. These three meta-theoretical positions are typically labeled *personologism, situationism*, and *interactionism* (Endler & Magnusson, 1976). Bowers (1973) has noted that there is a chronological order to their appearance, with each representing the zeitgeist of its historical period, and with each intended to serve a corrective function with regard to challenges unmet by the previously held view. As mechanisms of change, theories of counseling and psychotherapy derive from, or at least are reflective of, these three meta-theoretical positions. Although it is tempting to view each of these positions as representing a discrete and homogeneous cluster, there are notable differences among the theories and models subsumed within each perspective, despite certain fundamental paradigmatic structural similarities among them.

Personologism or the *personological paradigm* (B = f P) represents the earliest meta-theoretical position. Characteristic of this paradigm is the assumption that behavior (B) is a function (f) of the person (P). This is the position that Cronbach (1957) identified as *correlational psychology*, but which could be construed in other terms, such as differential psychology, trait psychology, and psychodynamic theory. The common element in this paradigm is the attribution of internal, dispositional, "psychodynamic" factors as the primary causal determinants of behavior.

Although there are a variety of different dispositional domains (e.g., aptitudes and traits) and constructs (e.g., psychoanalytic constructs), as well as methodological differences within each of the theories subsumed under this meta-theory, certain consistent consequences have followed from this particular paradigm: First, the concept of causality is essentially a linear, unidirectional one emanating from some internal source. Behavior is primarily "pushed" from within. Second, the types of laws derived are of a response–response (R–R) variety, with the intent being to discover consistent individual response patterns across different situations—with inconsistent response patterns usually attributed to the presence of a higher-order or more genotypic trait (Allport, 1966). And third, although the units of analysis may vary in conceptual size and clarity across theories within this paradigm, they invariably involve some internal, dispositional system of intervening or mediating constructs such as traits, needs, cognitive abilities, dynamic constructs (instincts).

As Endler and Magnusson (1976) suggest, the B = fP paradigm has had a tremendous impact in personality research, particularly in the myriad of person measurement strategies. Consequently, the measurement of alleged R–R consistencies has had enormous effects in the applied areas of counseling, selection, classification, and psychodiagnosis (e.g., the assessment of vocational interests, personality traits and dispositions, needs, aptitudes, and abilities).

Situationism or the *situational paradigm* (B = fE) is the second meta-theoretical paradigm, appearing partly in reaction to the inadequacies of the personological paradigm. Situationism stipulates that behavior (B) is a function (f) of factors in the environment (E) or situations in which people find themselves. This is the position that Cronbach (1957) identified as *experimental psychology*, with its primary intent being to explain behavioral variability as a function of differences in environmental conditions. In contrast to the B = fP paradigm, which searches for consistency in response patterns across situations, the situational paradigm assumes that human behavior is considerably malleable, with the behaviors or forms of behavior that people take being primarily a function of external stimulus factors. It is a structure that has been somewhat slower in developing, but as Moos (1973, 1974) described, a number of different systems utilize quite different units of analysis developed to describe environmental factors (e.g., contingencies of reinforcement, environmental "presses," and organizational patterns).

As a general research approach, situationism concerns itself with treatment differences, rather than individual differences. In effect, Cronbach (1957) has noted that both personologism and situationism have an affinity for the variables that the other view ignores. However, they are similar in the sense of being linear, unidirectional models of attributing causality, the only difference being the *source* of cause. In the situational view, the source is external and behavior is "pulled" from the organism; hence laws of the S–R type result.

In a more applied and strategic sense, this view typically frames questions that address "what treatment conditions are more effective in producing X?" Treatments, of course, can be construed in a variety of ways, ranging from complex educational/therapeutic conditions and manipulations of single independent variables in highly controlled experimental designs, to traits of others as external sources of influence.

Perhaps the most specific applications of this paradigm to the domain of counseling have been the behavior therapies—the application of general learning theory principles (operant, respondent, and social modeling) to the amelioration of behavioral problems and disorders. In each case—be it the application of respondent conditioning principles to the extinction of a school phobia, operant conditioning principles to the shaping of career exploration behaviors, or modeling for increasing social skill behaviors—counseling constitutes the "experiment," and the counselor's intervention constitutes the "experimental treatment." The counselor in essence controls, manipulates, determines, and causes (in accord with the professed learning principles invoked) the change in the client's behavior. It is the counselor, serving as a benevolent and therapeutic (albeit deterministic) environment, who *causes* the client to change.

A situationist has a perspective on events that is radically different from that of the personologist. The view of the personologist is that the counselor, although providing certain "core" therapeutic conditions, is *not* the cause of client change per se; rather that change is generated by (or pushed from) the client as a consequence of the client's own intrapersonal dynamics, traits, dispositions, and self-actualizing tendencies. Viewing the same change phenomena, the situationist holds that the core conditions, as well as other counselor behaviors, elicit, modify, determine, and cause the behavior change of the client. That is, to a situationist, the situation, not the client, determines client change (Truax, 1966).

Although many counseling psychologists reject the mechanistic formalisms of situationism as expressed in the behavior therapies, the B = fE paradigm may find its way into their reasoning in more subtle ways. As Powers (1973a) notes; "A humanistic (counselor) . . . may reject the idea that painful stimuli act on a passive nervous system to cause an organ to secrete adrenalin, but he may be perfectly willing to say that stress acts on a person to make him anxious" (p. 1).

Running throughout this particular psychological paradigm (frequently referred to as *scientific psychology*) is a particular concept of cause and effect. The cause, the immediate physical cause of what a person does, lies outside the person. Whether what is outside the client is the family, school, or some other environment to which the cause and maintenance of a client's disturbance or dysfunction is attributed, or whether what is outside the client is a benevolent other attempting to change the client in some "therapeutic" direction, the assumption is that the best the client can do is to modulate the connections from the stimulus (environment/situation) that is the cause, to the behavior or behavior change that is the effect. In the best tradition of experimental psychology, the strategy for research and practice in counseling with this paradigm is to determine the "main effects" of treatments—with little or no regard to individual differences among clients.

The *interactional paradigm* (B = f Person × Situation) can, in certain respects, be regarded as a synthesis of the personological and situational paradigms (i.e., it considers the interaction of person and situational factors as the main source of behavioral variation). Although the most recent of the three meta-theoretical paradigms, the interactional paradigm is not a new general meta-theory, as Ekehammar's (1974) historical review points out. Its application to and integration into counseling psychology has come about through the work of personality psychologists (Bowers, 1973; Endler & Magnusson, 1976; Harvey, Hunt, & Schroder, 1961; Mischel, 1976), counseling process researchers (Hertel, 1972; Lichtenberg & Hummel, 1976; Raush, 1965; Tracey, 1993), therapy practitioners (Cashdan, 1973; Claiborn & Lichtenberg, 1989; Haley, 1963; Strong & Claiborn, 1982; Watzlawick, Weakland, & Fisch, 1974), and family and marital researchers and practitioners (Madanes, 1981; Raush, Barry, Hertel, & Swain, 1974; Watzlawick & Weakland, 1977).

Although variations on the interactional paradigm may employ different units of analysis and do so in differing theoretical domains, they nonetheless have a core commonality in their concept of causality. These views all posit a mutual and reciprocal (interactive) system of causality or influence between the person and environment, such that causality is not a function of one or the other but a process of mutual constraint or influence. A logical consequence of this view is that the behavior of any individual may vary in its consistency, depending upon the nature of the individual and the situation in which the individual is performing. Thus, the focus is not on simple R–R or S–R consistencies, but on patterns or systems of behavioral chains that may be relatively stable within any given person–environment combination but which also may show different patterns between other person–environment combinations (i.e., there may be instability across combinations) (see Claiborn & Lichtenberg, 1989). The paradigm of interactionism reflects a cybernetic, closed-loop feedback model in as much as "responses are dependent on present and past stimuli in a way determined by the current organization of the nervous system . . . But it is equally true that stimuli depend on responses according to the current organization of the environment and the body in which the nervous system resides" (Powers, 1973b, p. 351).

In short, behavioral variation represents an adaptive process that is governed by feedback emanating from the interaction of both internal and external sources. Consequently, the model of the person is not one of being strictly internally driven or externally controlled but one of simultaneously being influenced as well as being influential. From this view, the usual dichotomies of internal–external, proactive–reactive, and the like are rendered nonsensical.

OVERCOMING CHALLENGES ASSOCIATED WITH A COMMON FACTORS PERSPECTIVE

The previous section of the chapter described, compared, and contrasted three meta-theoretical paradigms. The goal of the section was to show how these meta-theoretical paradigms can be used to categorize the welter of existing theories into a much smaller number of more manageable groups, thus facilitating the link between science and practice. In this section we discuss what is arguably the most important theoretical challenge facing counseling psychologists in recent times—the call to turn away from concentrating on specific psychotherapy theories, and focus instead on an integrating and superordinate meta-theoretical perspective known as the *common factors perspective*. This challenge comes from several sources. Meta-analyses of psychotherapy outcome studies (e.g., Smith & Glass, 1977), common factors approaches (e.g., Frank & Frank, 1991), and critiques of the randomized clinical trials approach to empirically supported treatments (ESTs; e.g., Wampold, 2001) raise important questions regarding the validity of theoretical claims concerning how client psychotherapeutic change occurs in therapy and the sources of that therapeutic change.

Meta-analyses have revealed that, generally speaking, psychotherapies based on very different and often incompatible claims regarding client development and the nature of client change nonetheless perform similarly to one another on key client outcome variables. Moreover, meta-analytic evidence fails to support the notion that tailoring the theory to the specific type of client and type of presenting problem improves psychotherapy outcomes. The common factors perspective emphasizes that non-specific and contextual factors, rather than factors unique to a particular theory, are largely responsible for client change. The common factors perspective raises the possibility that the specifics that distinguish one theory (or meta-theory) from another are largely irrelevant to whether theory-based psychotherapy is effective (see Baker, McFall, & Shoham, 2009 for an alternate perspective on common factors). Wampold's (2001) critique of randomized clinical trials of theory-based psychotherapies is based on the finding that the favorability of psychotherapy outcomes was *uncorrelated* with the level of the ostensible "active ingredient" of change posited by the theory. In other words, whether clients got better or worse was unaffected by whether the therapy had been successful in engaging the client in those processes that the theory holds to be required for change. These findings present important issues on which counseling psychology scientists *and* practitioners must collaborate as they grapple with the role and nature of theory in psychotherapy. Furthermore, these findings suggest that research efforts should switch from trying to determine which therapeutic approach is "the best approach" to trying to understand why the current wide array of theory-based therapies fail to produce differential outcomes, why matching treatments to client concerns has failed to enhance outcomes, and why putative mechanisms of client change have not been reliably associated with differential psychotherapeutic outcomes. These questions are of critical importance in the science and practice of counseling psychology. Cooperation among, not Balkanization of, scientists and practitioners of counseling psychology is required to understand and respond effectively to these provocative and challenging findings.

Science–Practice Integration Challenges Associated with Therapeutic Outcomes

EYSENCK'S INITIAL OUTCOME STUDY

A notable first attempt to examine the evidence on the effects of therapy was conducted in 1952, by Hans J. Eysenck. The evaluation of the efficacy of therapy requires that the effects of treatment be compared with a no-treatment control group. To conduct his evaluation, Eysenck compared the outcomes found in 24 studies of psychodynamic and eclectic psychotherapy with spontaneous remission rates (i.e., rate of improvement in client functioning—the remission of symptoms—without benefit of therapeutic intervention) using two control groups. The control or comparison groups used consisted of severely neurotic clients receiving mainly custodial care in a state mental hospital and disability claimants who had been treated by general practitioners. The results of Eysenck's study were disconcerting, finding that clients who received psychodynamic or eclectic therapy improved less than did those in his control/comparison no-treatment condition. Not only did it appear that therapy was ineffective—it might actually be harmful. The alarm one might experience in response to today's widely publicized concern about the scientific basis of psychotherapy is but an echo of the alarm psychologists undoubtedly experienced with the publication of Eysenck's findings.

EFFICACY VERSUS EFFECTIVENESS

The determination of therapy outcomes involves a variety of issues and considerations. Efficacy and effectiveness are two ways in which the outcome of counseling and psychotherapy are discussed. *Efficacy* refers to the therapeutic benefits found in comparing the treatment and a no-treatment control group within the context of a controlled clinical study. In contrast, *effectiveness* refers to the benefits of therapy that occur in the context of actual counseling practice. In the former instance, the question is whether a treatment or intervention is found to achieve a greater benefit for clients than no treatment. If so, the treatment is said to be "efficacious." In the latter instance, the question is how effective is counseling for those clients who seek and receive treatment within the community.

It has been argued that clinical studies create an artificial context in which the therapy that takes place is not characteristic of how treatments are provided in actual practice with actual clients. Consequently, finding that a treatment is efficacious cannot be assumed to mean that it is effective (i.e., will be beneficial to clients in practice settings). Although there is merit in this criticism, effectiveness findings are generally compromised by the absence of a control group within a practice setting against which to compare client therapeutic gains. As a result, it may not be possible to determine whether the benefits derived by clients receiving counseling in community settings are the result of the treatment or of some extraneous factors.

In the consideration of counseling and psychotherapy outcomes, it is important to ask, "When is an outcome significant?" The significance of therapy outcomes can be evaluated in several ways. Outcomes can be evaluated for their statistical significance, and they can be evaluated for their clinical significance or clinical relevance.

STATISTICAL SIGNIFICANCE

Two types of statistical significance may be considered when evaluating therapy outcomes. The first has to do with differences between or among treatment groups. The second has to do with the changes experienced by individuals within those groups.

Between-group differences are examined by comparing the outcomes of two different approaches to therapy (e.g., a new approach to therapy vs. an established approach), or by comparing the outcome of a specific therapeutic approach with a placebo treatment or a nontreatment (wait-list) group (i.e., a control group). Whatever the comparison, if the research is designed to rule out extraneous factors as competing explanations for the change, statistical procedures may be used to determine whether the observed differences that appear between groups (i.e., their respective outcomes) can reasonably be attributed to differences in the administered treatments, or whether it is more reasonable to conclude that the differences are due to chance (e.g., sampling differences). If the difference between the outcomes of the treatment group and the comparison group is in the expected direction and unlikely to be due to chance sampling differences, then we may conclude that the difference is statistically significant. In other words, the treatment group was more efficacious and yielded a statistically better outcome than did the comparison group.

Although the treatment outcome of one group may differ significantly from that of another group, this does not necessarily mean that the change that occurred was itself significant. Indeed, it is conceivable that the treatment group did not change at all, but rather that the comparison group became significantly worse, relative to the treatment group. To evaluate the statistical significance of change within the treatment group (i.e., the statistical significance of its outcome), a different approach is needed. In this approach, a group's pretreatment performance on some relevant outcome variable is evaluated against its post-treatment performance on the same variable. If the difference between the pre- and post-treatment assessments is in the expected direction and not attributable to chance differences in the measurement of the outcome variable (measurement error), then the change (or outcome) is said to be statistically significant.

CLINICAL SIGNIFICANCE

The statistical significance of outcome research findings can provide empirical support for different treatment approaches, but Ogles, Lambert, and Masters (1996) noted that "statistically significant differences between groups do not necessarily indicate meaningful or clinically significant differences between groups or for individuals within the groups" (p. 77). That is to say, although the treatment outcome for one group may differ from that of another and be in the desired direction, such a finding may not be *clinically* meaningful. For example, although a treatment for depression might produce in a group of clients therapeutic change that is significantly different statistically from that of a placebo treatment, this does not necessarily mean that those who received the treatment are no longer depressed or are experiencing a better quality of life. Furthermore, a statistically significant within-group pre–post difference does not necessarily mean that the individuals who received the treatment are meaningfully improved. It simply means that their post-treatment scores are reliably different from their pretreatment scores.

Several approaches to the evaluation of clinically relevant change have been proposed. Researchers have suggested that evidence that treated clients are indistinguishable from a nondisturbed reference group is probably the most convincing evidence of clinically meaningful change. This notion has been extended to a proposed standardized statistical method involving two criteria for assessing clinical significance (Jacobson & Truax, 1991). First, the treated client should be more likely identifiable as a member within a distribution of healthy persons than of a distribution of disturbed or troubled individuals. Second, the client change must be reliable; that is, it must be large enough that the pre-to post-treatment change cannot be attributable to measurement error—a criterion for which they have developed a *reliable change index* that can be statistically computed. Notwithstanding the above discussion, statistical significance, rather than clinical significance, is the manner in which outcome efficacy is generally reported.

META-ANALYSIS

Eysenck's (1952) study was not without critiques, as the study suffered from serious design problems. Responding to the challenge to therapy implied by Eysenck's study, numerous reviews of aggregated efficacy studies of counseling and psychotherapy were conducted during the 1960s and 1970s. Although having their own methodological problems, these subsequent studies generally contradicted those of Eysenck and instead yielded findings supportive of therapy's efficacy.

Over the years, examinations of the efficacy of counseling and psychotherapy have reached different and even contradictory conclusions. It is noteworthy that these earlier reviews of the outcome literature often lacked objectivity and replicability. They generally involved narrative descriptions of each study included in the review, an evaluation of the results in terms of the type of evidence offered with respect to therapy outcome, and then an implicit summing up of the findings to render an overall conclusion about therapy's effectiveness. However, with the hundreds of outcome studies now available for consideration in concluding therapy's effectiveness (outcome), how to turn the thousands of pieces of evidence that derive from all of these studies into an integrated summary of the benefits of counseling and psychotherapy is problematic.

Although a single outcome study will reveal information about the benefits received by the participants of that study, the answer to the broad question, such as "Is counseling/psychotherapy effective?" requires the examination of the body of research that has addressed this question. More recent inquiries into therapy efficacy have used the statistical method of meta-analysis to examine the aggregated results of hundreds of different studies that have compared counseling/psychotherapy with a control group. Briefly, meta-analysis consists of a set of statistical procedures that allow researchers to gain a comprehensive picture of the research on a research question and an unbiased answer to the research question. Through meta-analysis, outcome data from many individual counseling and psychotherapy outcome studies are systematically aggregated, allowing the findings to be analyzed to achieve an answer to the larger question of whether therapy is effective. Unlike the research methods used in individual studies, for which the client/participants serve as data points for analysis, meta-analysis uses the summary statistics from individual studies as the data points for analysis. Although not without detractors, meta-analytic procedures provide a methodology to assemble an overall picture of therapy's effectiveness (relative to no therapy or a placebo treatment) and allow investigators to compare studies using different approaches to therapy to investigate the relative efficacy of different treatments.

The first meta-analysis of the outcome of psychotherapy was conducted by Smith and Glass (1977). They analyzed the results of 375 published and unpublished therapy outcome studies. The results of their study produced an effect size of .68, which suggests that an average client receiving therapy would be better off (i.e., improved) than 75% of untreated (control group) clients. Although their results suggest that a proportion (34%) of untreated clients also improved (i.e., spontaneous remission), the success rate for those receiving treatment was 66%, leading them to conclude that the research showed the beneficial effects of counseling.

As with the challenges to Eysenck's methodology and findings, there have been critics of and challenges to Smith and Glass' meta-analytic findings. Subsequent meta-analyses of the therapy outcome literature have challenged the validity of those criticisms, while at the same time providing rather convincing support for the absolute efficacy of counseling and psychotherapy. Therapy is not effective for every one who seeks it, but the likelihood of someone benefitting from therapy is high, and outcomes are generally much better than for those left untreated.

The finding that a particular treatment is effective or efficacious is *not* compelling evidence that the theory is correct; rather, it is only evidence that the treatment worked. Why the treatment works—its mechanism of change—and whether that comports with the theory presumed as the basis for the treatment is an entirely different matter (Horan, 1980; Kiesler, 1966).

An unfortunate tendency of intervention developers is to cite literature that supports the *efficacy* of their interventions as also supporting the role of the theorized causal *mechanisms* of their interventions. Findings that support an intervention's efficacy may simply reflect the influence of common or nonspecific factors in producing the change. As Wampold, Lichtenberg, and Waehler (2005) noted, "Attributions of causality to specific ingredients of an intervention should be made only if the evidence supports such attributions. Relative efficacy does not necessarily imply that the superiority of an intervention was due to the specific ingredients; similarly, superiority to a placebo control does not imply effectiveness of specific ingredients. The efficacy of unique ingredients must be demonstrated by positing and verifying a psychological process. Verification can be made by examining mediating variables, establishing parametric relationships (e.g., increased ingredients or better implemented ingredients relate to better outcomes), or using other appropriate methods" (p. 34). Identifying those particular aspects of an intervention that are responsible for outcomes is particularly difficult because interventions are complex amalgams of ingredients delivered in an interpersonal context that varies from client to client and from instance to instance (Wampold, 1997, 2001).

ABSOLUTE VERSUS RELATIVE
TREATMENT EFFICACY

Whether considering efficacy or effectiveness, or statistical or clinical significance, there are two primary approaches to examining the question of whether an intervention "works." The first of these is to examine the *absolute* efficacy or effectiveness of the treatment. The question is this: Is this treatment better than no treatment or a placebo? If clients do not reliably improve as a result of the intervention, then the treatment should be abandoned; it is either worthless or harmful.

In light of the proliferation of approaches to therapy, it is also reasonable to ask whether some approaches are *better* than others. Such a question addresses the *relative* efficacy of different treatments. Specifically: "Does Treatment X produce a better outcome than Treatment Y?" In contrast to the evaluation of the absolute efficacy of a treatment ("Is Treatment X better than no treatment?"), one evaluates the relative efficacy of different approaches to counseling and psychology by contrasting one treatment with another. An examination of the relative efficacy of a treatment presumes that the absolute efficacy of the treatment has been established (because it makes no sense to contrast a worthless treatment against an established, efficacious treatment to see which is better). The results of such a study can be that the treatment is found to be better than, equivalent to, or worse than the established treatment.

Although a history of comparative outcome reviews reveals mixed results regarding the outcome superiority of various counseling and psychotherapy approaches, contemporary meta-analytic reviews of the comparative outcome research reach a conclusion remarkably similar to that reached by Rosenzweig (1936)—quoting the Dodo in *Alice in Wonderland*, who proclaimed, after much thought, following the Caucus race "*Everybody* has won, and *all* must have prizes" (italics in the text, Carroll, 1865/2001, p. 18). In their proportions of clients who improve by the end of therapy, differences between various forms of therapy are generally insignificant, but consistent with the absolute efficacy outcome finding already noted—that is, across different established approaches to counseling and psychotherapy, efficacy appears to be uniform.

MATCHING CLIENTS WITH TREATMENTS:
THE EMPIRICALLY SUPPORTED
TREATMENT APPROACH

Because the results of treatment comparison studies suggest little in the way of outcome differences between different approaches to counseling and psychotherapy, it is reasonable to speculate that outcome differences might exist for different therapies, depending on the problems/disorders toward which they were applied. Such a supposition is reflected in the question of what treatment works best for what specific problem. The implication in this question is that the comparison of various treatment outcomes is too gross a comparison to capture meaningful differences among therapy approaches for specific types of presenting concerns. Instead, it may be that one approach is best for treating depression, while another is best for treating anxiety, while yet another is best for treating eating disorders, and so on. In this regard, detractors of the finding of uniform treatment efficacy contend that the lack of findings of superiority for certain various treatments is the result of researchers failing to take into consideration the effect of different treatments on different client problems or concerns.

The vast array of approaches to therapy has already been noted. Similarly, there are many different sorts of concerns, problems, and disorders that clients present to counselors and therapists. A cross-tabulation of treatments by disorders would be enormous. Adding therapist, client, and circumstantial variables to this mix would result in an impossibly large number of combinations for researchers to test and compare, and for counselors and therapists to master.

Notwithstanding the enormity of the challenge posed by considering disorder-specific therapy, an increasingly large body of research supports the efficacy of particular treatments for particular problems. These studies provided the evidentiary basis for what are referred to as *empirically supported treatments*. The results of meta-analyses comparing different treatment approaches for different problems, however, generally do not support an interpretation that certain treatments are more effective than others for specific client problem areas.

In light of the proliferation of counseling approaches, irrespective of the diversity of theoretical notions upon which the variety of counseling interventions purportedly are based, it is reasonable to ask whether some forms of therapy are "better" (i.e., more effective) than others, or at least better (or at least more appropriate) for some problems or clients. The question would seem to argue for a sort of treatment matrix within which treatments would be associated with different client characteristics—e.g., the nature of the client's problem or disorder, the client's age, gender, or cultural background.

The matrix idea is an attractive one—indeed, a responsible one—for practice psychology, resembling the way in which medicine is understood to be practiced; namely, by matching the medical treatment to the patient's medical condition. Although Paul (1967) is generally credited with first posing the matrix, in reality it may have been articulated first by a counseling psychologist in the *Journal of Counseling Psychology*.

> The agenda for counseling then must be to provide answers to this question:
>> For clients desiring help on each type of problem of concern to the counselor
>>> What techniques and procedures,
>>> When used by what kind of counselors,
>>> With which type of clients,
>>> For how long,
>>> And in what sequence,
>>> Will produce which types of behavior change?
>
> The overriding task of our profession must be to use our highly developed understanding of client problems and concerns to generate new and more effective ways of being of service. (Krumboltz, 1965, p. 226).

Such a question suggests a treatment selection paradigm according to which an intervention would be selected for a particular client from a cell or set of cells within a multidimensional matrix (e.g., treatment by therapist by client by problems by setting; Stiles, Shapiro, & Elliott, 1986).

Such a paradigm has for decades driven clinical research in psychology, and now drives an important (albeit contentious) movement toward the identification and promulgation of empirically supported inventions (American Psychological Association, 2005; Task Force on Promotion and Dissemination of Psychological Procedures, 1995). The thrust of the movement is to identify those interventions whose efficacy for particular diagnostic groups is supported by empirical research. The proliferation of interventions seems to match and therefore be justified by the proliferation of *Diagnostic and Statistical Manual* (DSM) disorders.

COMMON FACTORS

As discussed already, therapy (generically) is robust in its efficacy, but different types of therapy do not appear to produce different types or degrees of benefit for clients. This is not to say that certain therapies applied to certain problems or disorders do not work; rather, the result of multiple meta-analyses (beginning with Smith, Glass, & Miller [1980] through Wampold [2001]) demonstrate that different approaches to therapy seems to produce comparable outcomes. From this finding has emerged the perspective that factors common across therapies and nonspecific to any particular approach hold the key to treatment efficacy.

This thesis, initially based upon an arm-chair analysis of the irreducible minimum variables in any counseling or psychotherapy interaction between two persons, was first proposed by Rosenzweig in 1936, as we wrote earlier. Understandably, the notion that there were common therapeutic features across different approaches to therapy could not have been proffered much earlier than this. But, as noted by Wampold (2001), by the 1930s, the variety of psychoanalytic therapies—each claiming therapeutic success and interpreting this success as evidence supporting its respective theory and interventions—had proliferated to the point that process and outcome comparisons across therapies were not only possible but inevitable.

Rosenzweig went on to suggest that, although factors specific to particular therapeutic approaches may contribute to their efficacy, a reasonable explanation for the apparent equivalence of the sometimes vastly different orientations and interventions was the presence of "certain unrecognized factors . . . that may be even more important than those being purposely employed" (p. 412). His position, one that has been reflected by others over the past nearly 75 years, was that these basic factors, common to every form of therapy, play essentially the same role in every therapy model and account for whatever positive results are obtained by any of them.

To be sure, the proponents of each of the various individual theories and approaches to counseling and psychotherapy believed that their theories and interventions captured the essence (and commonalities) of therapeutic change. Indeed, it was not uncommon for the proponents of particular theories and approaches to situate other theories and approaches within their own framework and to claim (implicitly) that the specific therapeutic factors of other therapeutic approaches were not only common to, but also explained by, their own framework. Shoben (1949), for example, argued that psychotherapy was fundamentally a problem in learning theory, and he proposed a conceptualization of therapy in terms of then-current behavior theory. Dollard and Miller (1950) and Alexander (1963) did essentially the same, recasting psychoanalytic psychotherapy in terms of a common set of learning theory principles. And Krasner (1962) offered the notion that, across diverse approaches to therapy, the therapist functioned as a "social reinforcement machine" (p. 61).

But these theory-specific common factors were not exclusively learning or behavioral factors. Fromm-Reichmann (1950) proposed a set of general psychoanalytic principles of intensive psychotherapy that were presumed to apply across successful approaches to therapy. Rogers (1957) proposed a general set of relationship principles that he believed to be common across effective counseling and psychotherapy (also see Truax & Carkhuff, 1967). Others (e.g., Cashdan, 1973; Haley, 1963; Strong & Claiborn, 1982) have proposed that it is through the resolution of interpersonal control conflicts that therapeutic change takes place.

Defining commonalities among diverse approaches to therapy by reframing them into the language of a specific therapy is one way to explain the finding of different approaches yielding similar (positive) outcomes. But recasting the specific ingredients of one approach into the language of another is not what Rosenzweig (1936) was proposing and it is not what is generally meant when discussing "common factors." Common factors are not theory- or approach-specific, and to suggest that psychoanalysis is really nothing but behavior therapy misses the point. The various approaches to counseling and psychotherapy *are* different—in theory and in their implementation. So, how is it that they seem

to yield similar outcomes? What do they have in common?

Schofield (1964) has suggested that, to identify common factors across various forms of therapy, it may be most reasonable to start with a clear idea of their explicit differences. To the extent that individual systems of therapy have an articulated theory, it is easy to point out differences among them at the level of theory. But, as Schofield has noted, psychotherapy theories only have an indirect impact on clients. What clients experience are the theories filtered through and by therapists who differ in how faithfully and effectively they understand and translate any particular theory into practice. Not surprisingly, evidence suggests that the *therapist* may be at least as important in psychotherapeutic outcomes as his or her theoretical approach (e.g., Crits-Christoph & Mintz, 1991; Whitehorn & Betz, 1960).

Although differences between theories need not be paralleled by notable differences in therapeutic techniques, there is evidence to suggest that theory-based treatments can be distinguished by the processes used and that these differences are quite consistent with the various theories underlying these approaches (e.g., DeRubeis, Hollon, Evans, & Bermis, 1982; Luborsky, Woody, McLellan, O'Brien, & Rosenzweig, 1982; also see Wampold, 2001). Various theories of counseling and psychotherapy can be distinguished by what must be present or occur and by what must not be present or may not occur (e.g., reinforcement must occur in behavior modification but cannot in client-centered therapy; dream interpretation must occur psychoanalysis but cannot occur in cognitive-behavior therapy). There is also evidence, however, of considerable variability in the implementation of specific types of therapy, even when that therapy has been manualized (Malik, Beutler, Alimohamed, Gallagher-Thompson, & Thompson, 2001).

Granting the theoretical and procedural distinctiveness of different approaches to counseling, one factor common to all formal systems of therapy is that there is some theory—some more or less highly explicated theoretical formulation of client troubles (psychopathology) and the therapeutic process—and it has been suggested by Frank (1961), Hobbs (1962), Rosenzweig (1936), and Schofield (1964), among others, that some sort of *systematic ideology* may be an essential *contextual element* in successful therapy (see Wampold, 2001). "Whether the therapist talks in terms of psychoanalysis or Christian Science is from this point of view relatively unimportant as compared with the formal consistency with which the doctrine employed is adhered to, for by virtue of this consistency the patient receives a schema for achieving some sort and degree of personality organization" (Rosenzweig, 1936, p. 415, cited in Wampold, 2001, p. 26).

Examining the broad outlines of therapy, other structural properties emerge that are unavoidably common to all form of counseling. These common factors do not contribute to differences in the conduct of the therapy, and they cannot explain any difference in results that might be demonstrated by different approaches. But it is the contention of the proponents of a common factors perspective that these common factors may well account for most of the positive results that each of the various schools of therapy claim.

The specific common factors proffered as accounting for therapeutic results have been "numerous and varied" (Patterson, 1989). And, as a result of different authors focusing on different levels and aspects of the counseling enterprise, diverse conceptualizations of the commonalities across different therapies have emerged. Historically, these conceptualizations are of several types: therapist factors, client factors, relationship factors, and contextual factors—this latter conceptualization being a sort of meta-conceptualization subsuming and integrating the other three.

Therapist Factors

Therapist factors—broadly defined as attitudes, qualities, and conditions provided by therapists in their relationships with clients—are qualities embodied by therapists that cut across different schools despite their differences in response modes, techniques, and verbal content. Stiles et al. (1986) proposed two broad categories of these factors: warm involvement with the client, and the communication of a new perspective on the client's person and situation (p. 172). Perhaps the best known example of the warm involvement factor is the triad of necessary and sufficient conditions proposed by Rogers (1957). The new perspective factor was described by Frank (1973) as the process by which the therapist provides the client with a new *assumptive word*.

Client Factors

Within this group of common factors are the notions that (a) clients enter therapy sharing a common "ailment" and motivation (Frank [1973] describes this as a sense of demoralization), and (b) the client involvement (focusing and experiencing

[Gendlin, 1970, 1978]), self-disclosure (Jourard, 1971), and expectancies (e.g., Frank, 1982; Goldstein, 1962; Schofield, 1964) are critical to successful therapy.

Relationship Factors

This group of common factors includes the elements defining the therapeutic alliance (also called *the working* or *helping alliance*). In general, such an alliance is distinguished by three aspects: an emotional bond between the client and therapist, the quality of the client and counselor involvement in the tasks of therapy, and the concordance between the client and the therapist on the goals of counseling (Bordin, 1979). Also included in this group of factors would be the status differential of the counselor and client (Frank, 1973; Haley, 1963; Schofield, 1964).

Contextual Factors

Historically, Rosenzweig's contextual perspective on counseling and psychotherapy was the first common factors model proposed. Others articulating this perspective have been Frank (1961, 1973, 1982; Frank & Frank, 1991), Hobbs (1962), and Schofield (1964)—and more recently and empirically, Wampold (2001). A contextual model of therapy (Wampold, 2001) subsumes and integrates many of the features or components presented as therapist, client, and relationship common factors. Although presented somewhat uniquely by each of its various proponents, four features have been proposed as common to or shared by all forms of counseling and psychotherapy and that create the context for therapeutic change. These include the following:

1. *A special relationship between the client and the therapist.* This has been described as "an emotionally charged, confiding relationship with a helping person" (Frank, 1982), but has been considered also to include features such as a status differential between the therapist and client, in which the therapist is in an ascendant (and socially sanctioned) helping position relative to the client; the client's confidence in the therapist's competence and desire to be of help; the client's expectation of help; and the controlled, circumscribed, and limited nature of the relationship (see Hobbs, 1962; Schofield, 1964).

2. *A healing setting.* Such a setting sets counseling and therapy apart from the client's other environments, sanctioning the locale as "place of healing" (Frank, 1973, p. 326), heightening the therapist's prestige and status

differential, and providing a safe and protected place for self-examination, emotional expression, and other tasks of therapy.

3. *A rationale or "myth" that provides a plausible explanation for the client's symptoms and distress.* This rationale (also described as a *systematic ideology* [Schofield, 1964] or more routinely as a *theory of psychotherapy*) additionally prescribes a therapeutic "ritual" or the series of tasks and procedures to be implemented by the client and therapist.

4. *A therapeutic ritual or set of procedures or tasks prescribed (or informed) by the theory.* This ritual and these procedures characterize the therapy process. They may include such diverse activities as gradual exposure/extinction procedures, catharsis, disputing irrational beliefs, primal screaming, dream interpretation, free association, selective reinforcement, and role playing.

It is with particular regard to Features 3 and 4 that the various approaches to therapy are distinguished, and it is at this level of analysis that each of the several hundred approaches to therapy are most clearly differentiated. Nevertheless, it is the contention of subscribers to a common factors perspective that it is not the specific theory, rationale, or myth, or the specific therapeutic procedures or ritual that are important. Rather, it is held that a client's symptomatic and emotional relief derives from the fact that an explanation for the client's symptoms and distress is provided to the client by a caring, trustworthy, experienced *socially sanctioned healer* within a *designated healing setting* and followed by the implementation of a conceptually consistent set of procedures applied *as therapy* to the client's problems.

Together, these factors—common across the various approaches to counseling and psychotherapy—are presumed to influence client attitudes and behavior in certain common and consistent ways, including providing new opportunities for cognitive and behavioral learning; enhancing the client's hope/expectancy of relief; providing success experiences that enhance the client's sense of efficacy, mastery, and competence; combating and helping overcome the client's sense of demoralization and alienation; and arousing the client emotionally.

The common factors perspective is now considered one of three central thrusts of the *psychotherapy integration movement* (Grencavage & Norcross, 1990), a direction within therapy that is considered by some to be one of most significant and potentially important trends in psychotherapy research,

and one addressed routinely in contemporary reviews of psychotherapy (e.g., Lambert & Bergin, 1994). Most recently, the common factors perspective (reflected as a contextual model of therapy) has achieved considerable empirical prominence as a result of Wampold's carefully documented deconstruction of the specific factors view of therapy, the view that is driving the current EST movement.

Notwithstanding the evidence for common factors, the fact remains that a proliferation of approaches to therapy all claim distinctive differences. How are those differences to be characterized? Acknowledging a commonality among theories/approaches, Wampold has proposed that a given approach to therapy is distinctive to the extent that there are actions carried out in the therapy that are *unique* and *essential* to the approach. These he refers to these as the "specific ingredients" of the approach—those aspects of the therapy that differentiate it from other approaches and represent the *sine qua non* of that approach. These specific ingredients stand in contrast to factors common across different approaches to therapy. Within that approach may also be found actions that are *essential* but *not* unique to the approach, actions that are *acceptable* but *not necessary* to the approach, as well as actions that are *proscribed* by the approach. These elements—unique/essential, shared/essential, acceptable but not necessary, and proscribed occur at different levels of abstraction in theory and practice.

HOW NEW TREATMENTS DEVELOP AND ARE ACCEPTED BY THE FIELD

As we noted at the outset of this chapter, perhaps the most important issue in applied psychology is the very deep schism between psychologists who believe strongly that science must always and absolutely buttress everything done clinically (e.g., Cummings & Donohue, 2009, pp. 128–129; McFall, 1991; Yalom, 1985, p. 537) and those scholars and practitioners who believe that reality dictates a reliance on *other* sources of information, such as clinical experience, context, and intuition, in addition to—and sometimes instead of—science (e.g., Davison & Lazarus, 1995; Levant, 2004). People often view the science-central position as espoused *only* by scientists, which is not true. Likewise, people view the pluralist position as espoused *only* by practitioners, which, likewise, is not true. Still, it only makes sense that scientists would mostly espouse the science-central position and that practitioners would advocate reliance on their experience.

As Levant (2004) has insightfully noted, "Since this [one's position on the centrality of science] is a matter of faith rather than reason, arguments would seem to be pointless" (p. 219). So, the matter will not be resolved in this or probably in any other treatise. Nonetheless, the science-centrality issue largely defines or at least powerfully frames nearly every major issue related to counseling theories. Readers will have seen specific examples of this issue in play throughout the chapter, as well as in the sections that follow.

THE SCIENTIFIC PATHWAY

There appear to be, in essence, two stories of how new treatments develop: one scientific, one clinical. The scientific story is reflected in a spate of articles about how to develop manualized treatments (e.g., Carroll, & Neuro, 2002; Rounsaville, Carroll, & Onken, 2001) and in this description by Alan Kazdin: "Systematic desensitization for the treatment of anxiety and cognitive therapy for the treatment of depression began with conceptual models that explained how the therapies worked, generated hypotheses that could be tested, and fostered scores of studies on the models" (Kazdin, 2009, p. 276). One interesting omission in these scientific accounts is the description of how these systematic developments come to be embraced and implemented by practitioners. Some evidence that we discuss suggests that often they are not. On the other hand, psychotherapy researchers have synthesized three preexisting models into a set of best practices for dissemination of treatments (Stirman, Crits-Christoph, & DeRubeis, 2004). How effective these best practices prove to be remains to be seen.

THE CLINICAL PATHWAY

The second story of how new treatments develop, the clinical one, is reflected in the stories of theorists like Francine Shapiro, who developed eye movement desensitization and reprocessing (EMDR) by accident (Maiberger, 2009, p. 33) and Bill Miller, whose motivational interviewing resulted from him slowly noticing something that he later came to learn was clinically significant (Treasure, 2004): "Motivational interviewing was conceived when Miller, a psychologist from the USA, sat with colleagues from Norway and described what sort of therapeutic approach worked for people with alcohol problems. The process of discovery may have been like the technique itself: a gradual process of listening, reflecting to check understanding, and clarification" (p. 331). In contrast to the scientific story, these clinical stories are more human and messy. The truth about treatment development and acceptance is multifaceted, ranging from the intentional to the fortuitous. Despite, or perhaps because of, that messiness, Davison and Lazarus (1995) observed "that most new methods have come from the work of creative practitioners [not from scientists]" (p. 96).

We found no research addressing Yalom's observation that "Unfortunately, the adaption [adoption] of a new method is generally a function of the vigor, the persuasiveness, or the charisma of its proponent. . . ." (Yalom, 1985, p. 537). That is not to say Yalom was wrong, but only to say it remains a hypothesis untested, yet worth testing. The one consistent principle that seems to influence whether treatments are accepted and implemented is easy accessibility, with "easy" defined in multiple ways. It could be defined as *intellectually* easy. So, treatments based on the epistemology a therapist already relies on appear to be more readily accepted (e.g., Neimeyer & Morton, 1997). A survey of 2,607 practitioners suggested that the biggest factor reported in adopting a new treatment was its similarity to currently used treatments (Cook, Schnurr, Biyanova, & Coyne, 2009). Similarity makes a new treatment easier to understand and use. Treatments that do not require practitioners to extrapolate from scientific studies appear to be more readily accepted (e.g., Stewart & Chambless, 2007). Reading a case study that uses the treatment is easier than extrapolating from scientific studies testing the treatment. Treatments presented in case studies have been reported to be accepted more readily (Cook et al., 2009). Nearly *all* therapists who underwent organization-wide, mandated training in new treatments reported adopting the new treatments (Squires, Gumbley, & Storti, 2008). It is easy to use something you have just been required to learn.

This ease-of-use factor has been identified as an important one in the adoption of technological advances, generally. Christiansen (1997) demonstrated that a very important factor in the adoption of new technologies is how much easier they make peoples' lives. Technologies that are easier to use, cheaper, and simpler get selected over those currently in use. This holds true even if the new technology fails to produce better results than the established technology.

Results of a practitioner survey conducted by Cook et al. (2009) suggest that the psychotherapies taught in graduate school strongly influence the approaches therapists adopt subsequently, a finding similar to the mandated-training effect reported by Squires et al. (2008). The Commission on Accreditation of the American Psychological Association now requires students from accredited doctoral programs and predoctoral internships to demonstrate knowledge of and competence in ESTs. When coupled with Cook et al.'s (2009) finding on the influence of graduate school training and another finding of theirs that many practitioners do not engage in evidence-based practice, this Commission requirement suggests that practice will become more evidence based as today's students become tomorrow's practitioners. Psychiatry has gone a step further, requiring that psychiatry residents be competent in five specified, evidence-based psychotherapies (Mellman & Beresin, 2003). An informal survey of Canadian psychiatry residency programs suggests that important advances in training have resulted from psychiatry's emphasis on demonstrating competency in evidence-based practice (Ravitz & Silver, 2004).

Less is known regarding those factors associated with the *sustained* use of a newly adopted therapy. In a recent survey of practitioners described earlier, practitioners reported that they were more likely to continue using new approaches when they felt effective using them, enjoyed conducting therapy using them, when their clients appeared to like the new approaches, and when clients reported improvement as a result of the new approach (Cook et al., 2009).

Challenges Related to Accepting Treatments As Established Practice

EPISTEMIC STYLE DIFFERENCES

There is little empirical research regarding how researchers and practitioners view each other's work (Weisz & Addis, 2006); however, evidence *does* exist regarding factors that influence practitioners' selections of treatments. Several studies suggest that client and therapist epistemic style guides the selection of and responsiveness to psychotherapeutic approaches. One example of this work is by Neimeyer and Morton (1997), whose data suggest that cross-cutting the issue of empirical support may be the therapist's *epistemic* style. With no information provided regarding a treatment's level of empirical support, therapists with a rationalist epistemology reported a preference for behavior treatments over others, whereas therapists with a constructivist epistemology reported a preference for constructivist approaches over others. These studies raise the possibility that therapists select

approaches and interventions based on their beliefs about the nature of knowledge, rather than based on empirical support for any given treatment. Going further, these findings might help to explain the scientist–practitioner divide. Perhaps researchers tend to be rationalists, whereas practitioners may tend more toward constructivist and other nonrationalist epistemologies, so they tend not to adopt the rationalist approaches championed by researchers. This epistemic divide may be one way to understand the common complaint of practitioners that psychotherapy research lacks relevance to practice. In 1995, Persons suggested six potential reasons that practitioners do not adopt validated treatments: psychologists receive little training in ESTs; psychologists receive extensive training in nonempirically supported treatments; some practitioners are not invested in reading the outcome literature; research findings are difficult for practitioners to use, perhaps because the writing is inaccessible; many practitioners believe that all psychotherapies are equally effective; and consumers are not informed. Practitioners' difficulties in applying research findings to their clients may be the greatest difficulty in traversing the hypothesized epistemic divide.

WEAKNESSES IN SCIENCE

Scholars, beginning with Lakatos (1968) and Meehl (1978, 1990), have suggested that theorists and theoretical researchers are unwilling to discard unsupported theories. Lakatos, for example, decried the lack of falsifiability in Freudian theory as reflecting "intellectual dishonesty" (p. 150). Meehl's primary concerns included that psychotherapeutic and other "soft" psychological theories are not abandoned by scientists when they have been disproved, but only when they become boring (Meehl, 1978, p. 807). In a 1990 paper, Meehl decried the misguided use of null hypothesis statistical testing to demonstrate the validity of a psychological theory when, he argued, given that "everything correlates with everything," significant findings often simply reflect sufficient statistical power to detect the ubiquitous correlational clutter that Meehl argued is characteristic of psychological research. In short, to Meehl, these significance tests are sham demonstrations of validity. So, in addition to the issue of practical relevance raised by practitioners, Meehl has questioned the scientific validity of much psychological—and, by extension—psychotherapeutic research. More recently, evaluations of published randomized clinical trials of psychotherapy techniques (which are viewed by many as the evidentiary gold standard) suggest that nearly *all* have fallen short of the criteria described in widely accepted guidelines regarding the proper execution of such trials (Cook, Hoffmann, Coyne, & Palmer, 2007; Spring, Pagoto, Knatterud, Kozak, & Hedeker, 2007). Finally, the vast majority of research on psychotherapy tests linear effects, whereas practitioners may often observe curvilinear and even recursive behavioral processes at work (see Collins, 2006; Hayes, Laurenceau, Feldman, Strauss, & Cardaciotto, 2007; Laurenceau, Hayes, & Feldman, 2007).

DIFFICULTY IN UNDERSTANDING

A far more prosaic but probably more influential factor than epistemology or quality of the science is the degree of clarity with which ESTs are presented. Mirroring results regarding adoption of treatment approaches more generally, results from several studies converge in supporting the notion that the clearer the presentation of the treatment and its implementation, the more readily ESTs are adopted by practitioners. The highest reported level of adoption of ESTs came from a study in which entire agencies signed on for direct training in ESTs for all of their staff members, in which case 96% of practitioners were reported to have adopted ESTs in their practices (Squires et al., 2008). Interestingly, this 96% reported compliance rate may have come at a cost. Research by Henry, Strupp, Butler, Schacht, and Binder (1993) found that therapists who complied most fully with manualized treatment training also showed the greatest reduction in empathic sensitivity.

Raine, Sanderson, Hutchings, Carter, Larkin, and Black (2004) found that when practitioners were randomly assigned to receive a summary of the research evidence, they recommended evidence-based treatments 60% of the time, and when they received no summary, they only recommended evidence-based treatments 42% of the time. Correlational evidence is consistent with evidence from intervention studies. Morrow-Bradley and Elliott (1986) surveyed APA Psychotherapy Division members and, with a 72.7% rate of return, found that 48% reported that their direct experience with clients was the most important source of information, whereas only 10% reported that information from research was most useful. Less than a fourth of those sampled reported relying on research, even for difficult cases (similar findings were reported by Stewart and Chambless [2007] for independent practitioners). So, when difficulty in understanding ESTs was removed or reduced, practitioners used them. When given a choice, practitioners reported most frequently relying on what is most familiar— namely, one's direct experience. Cook, Biyanova, and Coyne (2009) made a related point that variability in the extent of scientific training across mental health professions represents a barrier to some practitioners in understanding and using empirical research reports. This point is mirrored in research by Mullen and Bacon (2003), who reported that social workers lack the scientific background of psychologists and therefore relied on professional consensus rather than empirical support in selecting treatments. These findings suggest that reducing the science–practice gap may require the transformation of clinical science into readily teachable formats.

LACK OF A COMMON CONCEPTUAL FOCUS

Another challenge in accepting treatments as established practice involves the notion that scientists may have a problem and problem-resolution focus whereas practitioners may have a person focus, focusing more heavily on the particular client receiving treatment than on the nature of the problem and the nature of change. A potential pathway for reducing the gap between scientists and practitioners therefore is through personality psychology. In their article articulating five fundamental principles for an integrative science of personality, McAdams and Pals (2006) suggested that "psychopathology and problems in living can be conceived as operating with respect to different levels of personality" and "clinical and counseling psychologists may find in ... [personality psychology] an organizational scheme for sorting through what aspects of personality should be targeted for change in psychotherapy" (p. 214). The notion is that personality scientists and psychotherapists may be able to work together through a shared focus on personality, and may do so more effectively than in the past. Adopting this approach mirrors a suggestion made by Trierweiler (2006), namely, that the scientist–practitioner divide should be traversed by an adoption of a set of common methods. Trierweiler has argued that currently, practice methodologies focus on the individual whereas research methodologies focus on the group. Davison and Lazarus (1995) made a related point as they championed the use of case studies in clinical science.

Another potential pathway for creating a common conceptual focus and thereby reducing the scientist–practitioner divide comes from Jeff Brooks-Harris' book, *Integrative Multitheoretical Psychotherapy* (2008). Brooks-Harris clearly articulated specific skills and strategies associated with seven major psychotherapy theories, dividing them both by theory and by whether they address thoughts, feelings, actions, or cultural context. Brooks-Harris' scheme constitutes a potential psychotherapy Rosetta Stone, allowing and even inviting dialogue between and among scientists and practitioners, united in a common language that links theories with specific skills and strategies, with systems (the thought system, the feeling system, and so on; see also Beutler & Harwood, 2000, for a forerunner approach). Each of the three meta-theories we described earlier is represented in at least one of Brooks-Harris' seven major psychotherapy theories. So, linking Brooks-Harris' work with that of Endler and Magnusson (1976) provides the opportunity to link meta-theories to theories and theories to specific skills. Brooks-Harris (2008) provided between 12 and 15 specific strategies for each of the seven theories, with descriptions of each strategy. Table 4.1 provides three example skills for each theory, to give readers some sense of how Brooks-Harris translated theories into specific skills and links each theory to its meta-theory. Readers are encouraged to consult Brooks-Harris (2008, Appendix B) for a comprehensive and detailed list of specific skills. Some of Brooks-Harris' specific skills appear to reflect a different meta-theory from the one generally reflected by a specific theory. For example, behavioral psychotherapy reflects situationism, yet one of the specific behavioral skills noted by Brooks-Harris (2009, p. 487) is "Fostering Acceptance," which appears to reflect personologism. Nonetheless, connecting meta-theories with theories, and connecting theories with specific skills, is useful in spite of, and perhaps because of, the epistemic complexity these connections reveal.

Future Directions

This chapter has presented material on the theory and research that underlay counseling interventions, with a special emphasis on reducing the gap between science and practice. What follows are 13 specific future directions for reducing the science–practice gap in counseling psychology, based on material covered in this chapter.

1. Most importantly, in the future do not delay in allocating significant professional resources in addressing the science–practice gap in counseling psychology. Both the public (http://www.newsweek.com/id/216506, retrieved October 23, 2009) and the community of scientists (Abbot, 2009) have been told recently that psychological practice lacks a scientific basis, thus seriously undermining the specialty's credibility with critically important stakeholders and raising troubling concerns about the discipline. Practitioners in private practice are strongly

Table 4.1.   Meta-theories, Theories, and Example Skills

Meta-theory	Theory	Example Skills
Personologism	Cognitive	Identifying thoughts, Clarifying the impact of thoughts, challenging irrational beliefs
Personologism	Experiential-Humanistic	Identifying feelings, clarifying the impact of feelings, encouraging expression of feelings
Personologism/ Interactionism	Psychodynamic-Interpersonal	Listening to narratives, identifying relationship themes, observing the therapeutic relationship
Situationism	Behavioral	Illuminating reinforcement and conditioning, determining baselines, establishing schedules of reinforcement
Situationism	Multicultural-Feminist	Viewing clients culturally, highlighting oppression and privilege, supporting social action
Interactionism	Biopsychosocial	Exploring the effect of biology on psychological functioning, recognizing the influence of psychological functioning on health, considering the interaction between health and relationships
Interactionism	Systemic-Constructivist	Understanding problems within their social context, viewing families as systems, searching for multigenerational patterns

encouraged to emphasize science-focused training in their continuing education, and those in clinics are encouraged to make use of relevant scientific articles with regard to challenging clinical cases at case conferences. Practitioners in various settings are encourage to provide feedback to authors and journal editors regarding scientific articles they find particularly helpful and, in contrast, those they find particularly frustrating to apply. In turn, researchers are encouraged to refocus at least a part of their research programs to ensure that they are addressing practice-relevant research questions. They may also wish to have practitioner colleagues review research plans and manuscripts for their relevance and utility to practice. Internships and doctoral training programs may want to focus a portion of their research–practice integration on identifying and reducing gaps between research and practice in their training.

2. Avoid future Balkanization of science and practice positions, favoring instead approaches that appreciate and utilize the differing gifts of scientists and practitioners, as well as the differing and valuable perspectives afforded by scientific and practice contexts. Doctoral training programs, in particular, should actively foster dialogue among faculty members and practicum supervisors, and include participation from program students whenever possible. Counseling psychology conferences should feature programming that highlights the complementarity of scientific and practice knowledge, skills, and abilities. Researchers should partner with practitioners in the conduct of research, and practitioners should partner with researchers in analyzing cases and developing treatment plans.

3. Remain realistically optimistic about the chances for success of substantially reducing counseling psychology's science–practice gap, recognizing that future science–practice integration will necessarily remain an incomplete and ongoing process. In the same way that attaining multicultural competence, softening rigid gender role prescriptions, and recognizing the injustices triggered by marginalization remain "works in progress," counseling psychologists (both practitioners and researchers) need to adopt a similar perspective regarding the science–practice gap. Graduate training, continuing education, and convention programming can all be directed to helping people stay aware of the unresolved issue, while remaining optimistic about the future.

4. Focus future science–practice integration efforts on theory and meta-theory. Theoretical perspectives arguably hold the greatest promise for uniting researchers and practitioners in a common interest and in complementary professional activities. Graduate programs in counseling psychology should emphasize and highlight learning and applying theory and meta-theory as a part of both the academic training and the practice training of students. They should develop theory- and meta-theory–based proximal outcomes for assessing graduate training. Furthermore, counseling psychology's leadership is encouraged to assure that continuing education offerings and convention programming emphasize *theoretical* integration of research and practice and to consider asking the American Board of Professional Psychology (ABPP) to emphasize a demonstration of science–practice integration at the theoretical level for all board certification in counseling psychology.

5. Broaden one's perspectives beyond a specific theory and instead operate within a meta-theoretical/paradigmatic model, such as personologism, situationism, or interactionism, in order to overcome the challenges posed to reducing the science–practice divide by the welter of differing theories. This broadening will allow more meaningful future interactions between and among a wider array of scientists and practitioners. For example, graduate training programs could require demonstration of competence in understanding theories from at least two of the three meta-theoretical approaches, as could state licensing boards. Special issues of primary counseling psychology journals could be devoted to helping readers transition from theory-orientation to a meta-theoretical orientation.

6. As an alternative to an undisciplined eclecticism in either science or practice, and as a way to reduce the science–practice gap, adopt one or more specific theories—or, preferably, adopt a meta-theory or a common factors approach to guide one's counseling psychology science, practice, and professional interactions. Undisciplined eclecticism could be identified in training program documents, in specialty accreditation guidelines, in counseling psychology best practices documents, and in accreditation guidelines as something to be avoided in practice, in research, in training graduate students, and in postdoctoral continuing education.

Accreditation of doctoral training programs and internships could require demonstration of competence in understanding and applying specific theories, meta-theories, and/or common factors approaches in practice and research.

7. Accept and appreciate the differing information produced by controlled studies of psychotherapy (which assess *efficacy* and provide insight regarding cause and effect) and studies of the benefits resulting from psychological interventions in naturalistic settings (which assess *effectiveness* and provide insight regarding external generalizability of approaches). Counseling psychology training program documents should reflect the importance of doctoral training regarding both efficacy and effectiveness.

8. In addition to statistical significance, appreciate the importance of clinical significance, to reduce counseling psychology's science–practice gap. For example, in the reviews and critiques of each other's work, researchers must respect practitioners' concerns that a statistically reliable change in a client's functioning may translate to remarkably little in terms of clinically meaningful change in a client's level functioning. At the same time, practitioners need to understand that empirically demonstrated, statistically significant change is reliable, meaningful, and not trivial.

9. Understand meta-analysis as a psychotherapy outcome assessment method, along with the major findings produced by this technique and the limitations of this approach and of the findings it produces. In this regard, graduate programs should attend to recent developments in expectations for graduate training in evidence-based practice that require students to be conversant with the most common methods used to examine the outcomes of therapeutic factors and interventions (e.g., efficacy studies, effectiveness studies, meta-analytic studies) and the conclusions drawn from this research. Practitioners, as the consumers and users of psychotherapy research, are urged to understand and appreciate that appropriately aggregated research findings provide a stronger and more reliable picture of the state of the research support underlying their practices and provide the best basis for evidence-based practice.

10. Appreciate the differing outcome information produced by assessment of the absolute versus relative efficacy of an intervention and where each type of information is most useful. Notwithstanding evidence for the notion that therapy provides greater benefits for clients than no therapy and that different approaches to therapy are surprisingly similar in their outcomes, we recommend that, in the training of practitioners, graduate programs assure that students understand that the information deriving from outcome research does not support the notion that anything they do will necessarily be beneficial to clients nor that their clinical practices are necessarily as good as those of anyone else.

11. Understand treatment-matching approaches and the EST outcome methods, along with the major findings produced using these approaches, as well as the limitations of these approaches. In particular, graduate programs in counseling psychology, regardless of bias toward a common/contextual factors orientation to practice, need to assure that students understand and appreciate that clients may be differentially responsive to different types of empirically supported interventions and therapy styles, and that the most effective approach to therapy may require therapists to match their approaches to their clients.

12. Understand and appreciate the strengths and limitations of both the scientific and the clinical pathways through which new treatments are developed and accepted. Both researchers and practitioners have a role in the development of new treatments. New treatments emerge from thoughtfully building on and extrapolating from theory, and researchers contribute to the development and acceptance of new treatments through such scientific pathways. But new treatments also emerge as a result of the thoughtful reflective practice of clinicians. Treatments emerging via scientific pathways require clinical validation and effectiveness studies. Treatments emerging from clinical experience require scientific validation and efficacy studies. In this regard, graduate training programs need to orient their students, both as practitioners and as researchers, to understand and embrace the reciprocal and complementary nature of science and practice in the development, refinement, and adoption of new therapeutic interventions.

13. Accept, understand, and in the future work to resolve the epistemic style differences, science weaknesses, challenges in understanding science, and the lack of shared conceptual foci that constitute continuing barriers to accepting science-based treatments as established practice. Therapy researchers and practitioners may differ

in the manner in which they view evidence for the effectiveness of interventions, but neither has "immaculate perception." Each perspective has its limits and is prone to bias, but they share a common concern for the improvement of the human condition. And, whether it comes about through their graduate education or as a function of an open-minded approach to the profession, practitioners and researchers, rather than focusing on the liabilities of their different perspectives, both are urged to look for the synergy and complementarity of their views and how their different perspectives collectively may enhance their respective efforts.

Acknowledgments

The authors wish to acknowledge with gratitude the insights of Jeff E. Brooks-Harris regarding ways that psychotherapy treatments develop and gain acceptance, the insights of Timothy R. Elliot regarding nonlinearity in psychotherapeutic change, the library research conducted by Sean Loughridge, and especially the library research and analysis conducted by Zaday Sanchez, which were most helpful in completing this chapter. The contributions of the two authors were approximately equal.

References

Abbott, A. (2009). Psychology: A reality check. *Nature, 461*(7266), 847.

Alexander, F. (1963). The dynamics of psychotherapy in the light of learning theory. *American Journal of Psychiatry, 201*, 440–448.

Allport, G. (1966). Traits revisited. *American Psychologist, 21*, 1810.

American Psychological Association. (2005). Policy statement on evidence-based practice in psychology. Retrieved October 26th, 2009, from http://www2.apa.org/practice/ebpstatement.pdf.

Baker, T. B., McFall, R. M., & Shoham, V. (2009). Current status and future prospects of clinical psychology: Toward a scientifically principled approach to mental and behavioral health care. *Psychological Science in the Public Interest, 9*(2), 67–103.

Beutler, L., & Harwood, T. M. (2000). *Prescriptive psychotherapy: A practical guide to treatment selection.* New York: Oxford.

Bordin, E. (1979). The generalizability of the psychoanalytic concept of working alliance. *Psychotherapy: Theory, Research and Practice, 16*, 252–260.

Bowers, K. (1973). Situationism in psychology: An analysis and critique. *Psychological Review, 80*, 307–336.

Brooks-Harris, J. E. (2008). *Integrative multitheoretical psychotherapy.* Boston: Houghton Mifflin.

Carroll, L. (2001). *Alice's adventures in wonderland.* London: Macmillan. Mineola, NY: Dover. (Original work published 1865).

Carroll, K. M., & Nuro, K. F. (2002). One size cannot fit all: A stage model for psychotherapy manual development. *Clinical Psychology: Science and Practice, 9*(4), 396–406.

Cashdan, S. (1973). *Interactional psychotherapy.* New York: Grune & Stratton.

Christensen, C. M. (1997). *The innovator's dilemma: When new technologies cause great firms to fall.* Boston: Harvard Business School Press.

Cialdini, R. B. (1980). Full-cycle social psychology. In L. Bickman (Ed.), *Applied social psychology annual* Vol. 1 (pp. 21–47). Beverly Hills, CA: Sage Publications.

Claiborn, C. D., & Lichtenberg, J. W. (1989). Interactional counseling. *The Counseling Psychologist, 17*, 355–453.

Collins, L. M. (2006). Analysis of longitudinal data: The integration of theoretical model, temporal design, and statistical model. *Annual Review of Psychology, 57*, 505–528.

Cook, J. M., Biyanova, T., & Coyne, J. C. (2009). Influential psychotherapy figures, authors, and books: An internet survey. *Psychotherapy Theory, Research, Practice, Training, 46*, 42–51.

Cook, J. M., Hoffmann, K., Coyne, J. C., & Palmer, S. C. (2007). Reporting of randomized clinical trials in the Journal of Consulting and Clinical Psychology 1992 and 2002: Before CONSORT and beyond. *Scientific Review of Mental Health Practice, 5*(1), 69–80.

Cook, J. M., Schnurr, P. P., Biyanova, T., & Coyne, J. C. (2009). Apples don't fall far from the tree: Influences on psychotherapists' adoption and sustained use of new therapies. *American Psychiatric Services, 60*(5), 671–676.

Crits-Christoph, P., & Mintz, J. (1991). Implications of therapist effects for the design and analysis of comparative studies of psychotherapies. *Journal of Consulting and Clinical Psychology, 59*, 20–26.

Cronbach, L. J. (1957). The two disciplines of scientific psychology. *American Psychologist, 12*, 671–683.

Cummings, N. A., & O'Donohue, W. T. (2009). *Eleven blunders that cripple psychotherapy in America: A remedial unblundering.* New York: Routledge.

Davison, G. C., & Lazarus, A. A. (1995). The dialectics of science and practice. In S. C. Hayes, V. M. Follette, R. M. Dawes, & K. E. Grady (Eds.), *Scientific standards of psychological practice: Issues and recommendations* (pp. 95–120). Reno, NV: Context Press.

DeRubeis, R., Hollon, S., Evans, M., & Bermis, K. (1982). Can psychotherapies for depression be discriminated? A systematic investigation of cognitive therapy and interpersonal therapy. *Journal of Consulting and Clinical Psychology, 50*, 744–756.

Dollard, J., & Miller, N. (1950). *Personality and psychotherapy.* New York: McGraw-Hill.

Ekehammar, B. (1974). Interactionism in personality from a historical perspective. *Psychological Review, 81*, 1026–1048.

Ellis, A., & Dryden, W. (2007). *The practice of rational emotive behavior therapy.* New York: Springer.

Endler, N., & Magnusson, D. (1976). Toward an interactional psychology of personality. *Psychological Bulletin, 83*, 956–974.

Eysenck, H. J. (1952). The effects of psychotherapy. *Quarterly Bulletin of the British Psychological Society, 3*, 41.

Ford, D. H., Urban, H. B., & Ford, D. H. (1998). *Contemporary models of psychotherapy: A comparative analysis* (2nd ed.). Hoboken, NJ: John Wiley & Sons.

Frank, J. (1961). *Persuasion and healing.* Baltimore: Johns-Hopkins.

Frank, J. (1973). *Persuasion and healing* (2nd ed.). Baltimore: Johns-Hopkins.

Frank, J. (1982). Therapeutic components shared by all psychotherapies. In J. Harvey, & M. Parks (Eds.), *Psychotherapy research and behavior change* Vol. 1 (pp. 9–37). Washington, DC: American Psychological Association.

Frank, J., & Frank, J. (1991). *Persuasion and healing* (3rd ed.). Baltimore: Johns-Hopkins.

Fromm-Reichman, F. (1950). *The principles of intensive psychotherapy*. Chicago: University of Chicago Press.

Garfield, S. (1989). *The practice of brief psychotherapy*. Elmsford, NY: Pergamon.

Gendlin, E. T. (1970). A theory of personality change. In J. Hart, & T. Tomlinson (Eds.), *New directions in client-centered therapy* (pp. 129–173). Boston: Houghton-Mifflin.

Gendlin, E. T. (1978). *Focusing*. New York: Bantam.

Goldstein, A. (1962). *Therapist-patient expectancies in psychology*. New York: Pergamon.

Grencavage, L., & Norcross, J. (1990). Where are the commonalities among the therapeutic common factors? *Professional Psychology: Research and Practice, 21*, 372–378.

Haley, J. (1963). *Strategies of psychotherapy*. New York: Grune & Stratton.

Harvey, O., Hunt, D., & Schroder, H. (1961). *Conceptual systems and personality organization*. New York: Wiley.

Hayes, A. M., Laurenceau, J., Feldman, G., Strauss, J. L., & Cardaciotto, L. A. (2007). Change is not always linear: The study of nonlinear and discontinuous patterns of change in psychotherapy. *Clinical Psychology Review, 27*, 715–723.

Henry, W. P., Strupp, H. H., Butler, S. F., Schacht, T. E., & Binder, J. L. (1993). Effects of training in time-limited dynamic psychotherapy: Changes in therapists' behavior. *Journal of Consulting and Clinical Psychology, 61*, 434–440.

Herink, R. (Ed.). (1980). *The psychotherapy handbook: The A to Z guide to more than 250 different therapies in use today*. New York: New American Library.

Hertel, R. (1972). Application of stochastic process analysis to the study of psychotherapeutic process. *Psychological Bulletin, 77*, 421–430.

Hobbs, N. (1962). Sources of gain in psychotherapy. *American Psychologist, 17*, 18–34.

Holland, J. L. (1997). *Making vocational choices: A theory of vocational personalities and work environments* (3rd ed.). Odessa, FL: Psychological Assessment Resources.

Horan, J. J. (1980). Experimentation in counseling and psychotherapy. Part I: New myths about old realities. *Educational Researcher, 9*, 5–10.

Jacobson, N. S., & Truax, P. (1991). Clinical significance: A statistical approach to defining meaningful change in psychotherapy research. *Journal of Consulting and Clinical Psychology, 59*, 12–19.

Jourard, J. (1971). *Self-disclosure*. New York: Wiley.

Kazdin, A. E. (1986). Comparative outcome studies in psychotherapy: Methodological issues and strategies. *Journal of Consulting and Clinical Psychology, 54*, 95–105.

Kazdin, A. E. (2009). Bridging science and practice to improve patient care. *American Psychologist, 64*, 276–278.

Kiesler, R. (1966). Some myths of psychotherapy research and the search for a paradigm. *Psychological Bulletin, 65*, 110–136.

Krasner, L. (1962). The therapist as a social reinforcement machine. In H. Strupp, & L. Luborsky (Eds.), *Research in psychotherapy* Vol. II (pp. 61–94). Washington, DC: American Psychological Association.

Krumboltz, J. D. (1965). The agenda for counseling. *Journal of Counseling Psychology, 12*(3), 226.

Kuhn, T. (1970). *The structure of scientific revolutions*. Chicago: University of Chicago Press.

Lakatos, I. (1968). Criticism and the methodology of scientific research programmes, *Proceedings of the Aristotelian Society, New Series* (69), 149–186. New York: Blackwell Publishing on behalf of The Aristotelian Society.

Lambert, M., & Bergin, A. (1994). The effectiveness of psychotherapy. In A. Bergin, & S. Garfield (Eds.), *Handbook of psychotherapy and behavior change* (4th ed.). New York: Wiley.

Laurenceau, J., Hayes, A. M., & Feldman, G. C. (2007). Some methodological and statistical issues in the study of change processes in psychotherapy. *Clinical Psychology Review, 27*, 682–695.

Levant, R. F. (2004). The empirically validated treatments movement: A practitioner/educator perspective. *Clinical Psychology: Science and Practice, 11*(2), 219–224.

Lewin, K. (1952). *Field theory in social science: Selected theoretical papers by Kurt Lewin*. London: Tavistock.

Lichtenberg, J. W., & Hummel, T. (1976). Counseling as stochastic process: Fitting a Markov chain model to initial counseling interviews. *Journal of Counseling Psychology, 23*, 310–315.

Luborsky, L., Woody, G. E., McLellan, A. T., O'Brien, C. P., & Rosenzweig, J. (1982). Can independent judges recognize different psychotherapies? An experience with manual-guided therapies. *Journal of Consulting and Clinical Psychology, 30*, 49–62.

Madanes, C. (1981). *Strategic family therapy*. San Francisco: Jossey-Bass.

Maiberger, B. (2009). *EMDR essentials: A guide for clients and therapists*. New York: W. W. Norton.

Malik, M., Beutler, L., Alimohamed, S., Gallagher-Thompson, D., & Thompson, L. (2001). *Are all cognitive therapies alike? A comparison of cognitive and non-cognitive therapy process and implications for the application of empirically supported treatments*. Unpublished manuscript. University of California-Santa Barbara.

McAdams, D. P., & Pals, J. L. (2006). A new Big Five: Fundamental principles for an integrative science of personality. *American Psychologist, 61*(3), 204–217.

McFall, R. M. (1991). Manifesto for a science of clinical psychology. *Clinical Psychologist, 44*(6), 75–88.

Meehl, P. E. (1978). Theoretical risks and tabular asterisks: Sir Karl, Sir Ronald, and the slow progress of soft psychology. *Journal of Consulting & Clinical Psychology, 46*, 806–834.

Meehl, P. E. (1990). Appraising and amending theories: The strategy of Lakatosian defense and two principles that warrant it, *Psychological Inquiry, 1*(2), 108–141.

Mellman, L. A., & Beresin, E. (2003). Psychotherapy competencies: Development and implementation. *Academic Psychiatry, 27*, 149–153.

Mischel, W. (1976). *Introduction to personality*. New York: Holt, Rinehart & Winston.

Mischel, W. (2009). Editorial: Connecting clinical practice to scientific progress. *Psychological Science in the Public Interest, 9*(2), i–ii.

Moos, R. (1973). Conceptualizations of human environments. *American Psychologist, 28*, 652–665.

Moos, R. (1974). Psychological environments. *American Psychologist, 29*, 179–188.

Morrow-Bradley, C., & Elliott, R. (1986). Utilization of psychotherapy research by practicing psychotherapists. *American Psychologist, 41*(2), 188–197.

Mullen, E. J., & Bacon, W. F. (2003). Practitioner adoption and implementation of evidence-based effective treatments and issues of quality control. In A. Rosen, & E. K. Proctor (Eds.), *Developing practice guidelines for social work interventions: Issues, methods, and a research agenda* (pp. 223–235). New York: Columbia University Press.

National Institute of Mental Health (NIMH). (1975). *Report of the Research Task Force of the National Institute of Mental Health: Research in the service of mental health* (No. ADM 75–236). Rockville, MD: DHEW Publications.

Neimeyer, G. J., & Morton, R. J. (1997). Personal epistemologies and preferences for rationalist versus constructivist psychotherapies. *Journal of Constructivist Psychology, 10*(2), 109–123.

Ogles, B. M., Lambert, M. J., & Masters, K. S. (1996). *Assessing outcome in clinical practice.* Needham Heights, MA: Allyn & Bacon.

Patterson, C. (1989). Foundations for a systematic eclecticism in psychotherapy. *Psychotherapy, 25*, 171–181.

Paul, G. (1967). Strategy of outcome research in psychotherapy. *Journal of Consulting and Clinical Psychology, 64*, 973–982.

Persons, J. B. (1995). Why practicing psychologists are slow to adopt empirically-validated treatments. In S. C. Hayes, V. M. Follette, R. M. Dawes, & K. E. Grady (Eds.), *Scientific standards of psychological practice: Issues and recommendations* (pp. 141–161). Reno, NV: Context Press.

Powers, W. (1973a). *Behavior: The control of perception.* Chicago: Aldine.

Powers, W. (1973b). Feedback: Beyond behaviorism. *Science, 179*, 351–356.

Raine, R., Sanderson, C., Hutchings, A., Carter, S., Larkin, K., & Black, N. (2004). An experimental study of determinants of group judgments in clinical guideline development. *Lancet, 354*, 429–437.

Raush, H. (1965). Interaction sequences. *Journal of Personality and Social Psychology, 2*, 487–499.

Raush, H., Barry, W., Hertel, R., & Swain, M. (1974). *Communication, conflict, and marriage.* San Francisco: Jossey-Bass.

Ravitz, P., & Silver, I. (2004). Advances in psychotherapy education. *Canadian Journal of Psychiatry, 49*, 230–237.

Rogers, C. (1957). The necessary and sufficient conditions of therapeutic personality change. *Journal of Consulting Psychology, 21*, 95–103.

Rosenzweig, S. (1936). Some implicit common factors in diverse methods of psychotherapy. *American Journal of Orthopsychiatry, 6*, 412–415.

Rounsaville, B. J., Carroll, K. M., & Onken, L. S. (2001). A stage model of behavioral therapies research: Getting started and moving on from stage I. *Clinical Psychology: Science and Practice, 8*(2), 133–142.

Schachter, S., & Singer, J. E. (1962). Cognitive, social and physiological determinants of emotional state. *Psychological Review, 69*, 379–399.

Schofield, W. (1964). *Psychotherapy: The purchase of friendship.* Englewood Cliffs, NJ: Prentice-Hall.

Shoben, E. J. (1949). Psychotherapy as a problem in learning theory. *Psychological Bulletin, 46*, 366–392.

Smith, M. L., & Glass, G. V. (1977). Meta-analysis of psychotherapy outcome studies. *American Psychologist, 32*, 752–760.

Smith, M. L., Glass, G. V., & Miller, T. L. (1980). *Benefits of psychotherapy.* Baltimore: Johns Hopkins University Press.

Spring, B., Pagoto, S., Knatterud, G., Kozak, A., & Hedeker, D. (2007). Examination of the analytic quality of behavioral health randomized clinical trials. *Journal of Clinical Psychology, 63*(1), 53–71.

Squires, D. D., Gumbley, S. J., & Storti, S. A. (2008). Training substance abuse treatment organizations to adopt evidence-based practices: The Addiction Technology Transfer Center of New England Science to Service Laboratory. *Journal of Substance Abuse Treatment, 34*, 293–301.

Stewart, R. E., & Chambless, D. L. (2007). Does psychotherapy research inform treatment decisions in private practice? *Journal of Clinical Psychology, 63*(3), 267–281.

Stiles, W., Shapiro, D., & Elliott, R. (1986). "Are all psychotherapies equivalent?" *American Psychologist, 41*, 165–180.

Stirman, S. W., Crits-Christoph, P., & DeRubeis, R. J. (2004). Achieving successful dissemination of empirically supported psychotherapies: A synthesis of dissemination theory. *Clinical Psychology: Science and Practice, 11*(4), 343–351.

Strong, S., & Claiborn, C. (1982). *Change through interaction: Social psychological processes of counseling and psychotherapy.* New York: Wiley.

Task Force on Promotion and Dissemination of Psychological Procedures. (1995). Training in and dissemination of empirically validated treatments: Report and recommendations. *The Clinical Psychologist, 48*(1), 3–23.

Tracey, T. J. (1993). An interpersonal stage model of the therapeutic process. *Journal of Counseling Psychology, 40*, 1–14.

Treasure, J. (2004). Motivational interviewing. *Advances in Psychiatric Treatment, 10*, 331–337.

Trierweiler, S. J. (2006). Training the next generation of psychologist clinicians: Good judgment and methodological realism at the interface between science and practice. In C. D. Goodheart, A. E. Kazdin, & R. J. Sternberg (Eds.), *Evidence-based psychotherapy: Where practice and research meet* (pp. 211–238). Washington, DC: American Psychological Association.

Truax, C. B. (1966). Reinforcement and nonreinforcement in Rogerian psychotherapy. *Journal of Abnormal Psychology, 71*, 1–9.

Truax, C. B., & Carkhuff, R. (1967). *Toward effective counseling and psychotherapy.* Chicago: Aldine.

Wampold, B. E. (1997). Methodological problems in identifying efficacious psychotherapies. *Psychotherapy Research, 7*, 21–43.

Wampold, B. E. (2001). *The great psychotherapy debate: Models, methods and findings.* Mahwah, NJ: Erlbaum.

Wampold, B. E., Lichtenberg, J. W., & Waehler, C. A. (2005). A broader perspective: Counseling psychology's emphasis on evidence. *Journal of Contemporary Psychotherapy, 35*(1), 27–38.

Watzlawick, P., & Weakland, J. (1977). *The interactional view.* New York: Norton.

Watzlawick, P., Weakland, J., & Fisch, R. (1974). *Change.* New York: Norton.

Weisz, J. R., & Addis, M. E. (2006). The research-practice tango and other choreographic challenges: Using and testing evidence-based psychotherapies in clinical care settings. In C. D. Goodheart, A. E. Kazdin, & R. J. Sternberg (Eds.), *Evidence-based psychotherapy: Where practice and research meet* (pp. 179–206). Washington, DC: American Psychological Association.

Whitehorn, J., & Betz, B. (1960). Further studies of the doctor as a crucial variable in the outcome of treatment with schizophrenic patients. *American Journal of Psychiatry, 117*, 215–223.

Yalom, I. D. (1985). *The theory and practice of group psychotherapy* (3rd ed.). New York: Basic Books.

Process and Outcomes in Counseling and Psychotherapy

Sara Maltzman

Abstract

This chapter reviews process and outcome research in counseling and psychotherapy. An overview of the research is described in its historical context. The imperative for evaluating mediator and moderator variables is described. The interactional influence between methodology and outcome research is discussed in the context of conclusions and causal inferences drawn from various methodologies and analyses. In particular, the contribution of meta-analytic techniques is discussed. Last, the medical and common factors contextual models are discussed. The biopsychosocial model is suggested as an alternative model. Specific applications of the biospsychosocial model to process and outcome research are described. A biopsychosocial understanding of attachment and resilience is offered as a framework for facilitating process and outcome research and an understanding of psychosocial flourishing.

Keywords: process, outcome, common factors, contextual model, biopsychosocial, attachment, resilience, flourishing

This chapter reviews issues in process and outcome research in counseling and psychotherapy. The extant literature in these areas is enormous, and specific areas related to process and outcome (e.g., the counseling relationship, theories and interventions, and methodologies) are covered in detail in other chapters of this *Handbook*. For these reasons, this chapter takes a broader perspective. It provides an overview of the research in its historical context by describing sociopolitical influences that have shaped research in counseling and psychotherapy process and outcome over the past 30 years. It then traces the evolution of the research from treatment efficacy studies to effectiveness studies and the imperative for evaluating mediator (process) and moderator (input) variables. The interactional influence between methodology and outcome research is discussed in the context of what conclusions and causal inferences can be drawn from various methodologies and analyses. In particular,

the contribution of meta-analytic techniques is discussed.

Last, this chapter reviews and discusses the medical and common factors contextual models that have been described in the literature. The biopsychosocial model is suggested as an alternative model that offers a superior conceptual framework for explicating treatment effectiveness and the contributions of process and input variables. Specific examples are provided regarding possible applications of the biopsychosocial model. A biopsychosocial conceptualization of attachment and resilience is offered as a framework for future directions in process and outcome research.

Definitions of Terms
Therapist, Client, and Treatment

To simplify nomenclature and for consistency, this chapter will use *therapist* to designate psychologists and other licensed mental health professionals engaged in the provision of counseling and psychotherapy. *Client* will be used rather than "patient," consistent with the principles of client empowerment and a collaborative approach that minimizes the inherent power differential. *Treatment* refers to counseling and psychotherapy interventions that meet Kendal and Beidas' (2007) criteria for *empirically based* or *empirically supported* interventions designed to target specified aspects of the presenting concern or disorder. *Intervention* is a broader term that includes other professional activities, such as assessment and case conceptualization, which are used within counseling and psychotherapy paradigms.

Moderator (Input) and Mediator (Process) Variables

Laurenceau, Hayes, and Feldman (2007) describe input (moderator) and process (mediator) variables as follows: *moderators* of change are variables that define and predict who will benefit from treatment and under what conditions. *Mediator (process)* variables explain the *why* and *how* change occurs (Laurenceau, Hayes, & Feldman, 2007). Variables originating outside of the therapeutic setting can be external events (extra-therapy variables) or intraindividual characteristics (input variables). These external (extra-therapy) variables may directly or indirectly impact the client and the client's presentation in therapy (e.g., natural disasters or personal life events). *Moderator* variables are input variables such as client expectancies, personality, and severity of illness (Hill & Corbett, 1993; Hill & Williams, 2000). However, intraindividual characteristics may or may not be relatively stable over time. Gender, age, socioeconomic status, ethnic, cultural, and religious identity tend to be conceptualized as stable characteristics, although that can change based on the particular research question. Age, for example, has its own associated developmental limitations, tasks, and opportunities. Gender is not immutable, and gender-related issues may become a focus in therapy. Socioeconomic status may contribute to both the therapist and client's worldview and can change dramatically as a consequence of mental illness or external economic forces. Additionally, client and therapist expectations, attitudes, and subjective levels of distress are additional input variables that originate outside of the therapeutic dyad. However, these particular variables often are the subject of research, either as process or outcome variables,

depending upon the particular hypothesis and topic of study (Hill & Corbett, 1993).

Process variables include client and therapist behaviors within the therapeutic setting, and the therapist–client interaction (Hill & Corbett, 1993; Hill & Williams, 2000). These behaviors include overt and covert thoughts and feelings (i.e., they may or may not be directly observable). Examples include therapist attitudes and expertise, the "dose" of treatment, and the interaction among these variables (Hill & Corbett, 1993; Hill & Williams, 2000). There is consensus that evaluation of moderator and mediator variables within the counseling and psychotherapeutic process is critical to understanding mechanisms of change (Westen, Novotny, & Thompson-Brenner, 2004). Such studies also are necessary for developing appropriate paradigms for flexibly implementing empirically supported treatments (ESTs) in naturalistic settings (Kazdin, 2008). Kazdin (2007, 2008) and others have called for the increased use of qualitative methods to explicate these relationships.

Outcome Variables

Outcomes are defined as changes that may be directly, or indirectly, the result of the treatment (Hill & Corbett, 1993). What constitutes "change" has been defined in a variety of ways: client satisfaction with treatment, mutual termination (presumably after treatment goals have been achieved) versus premature termination (unilateral termination by the client), reduction in symptomatology as assessed by client and/or therapist report, and/or improvement in psychosocial functioning as determined by client, therapist, or collateral report. These outcomes can be evaluated at varying points in time relative to treatment termination. *Initial response* refers to outcome at termination; *sustained response* refers to assessment of positive treatment effects at follow-up intervals (Westen & Morrison, 2001). Outcome also can be measured session-by-session to assess for dose–response effects and associated client input variables that may be influencing treatment process (Stulz, Lutz, Leach, Lucock, & Barkham, 2007).

The potential blurring of process and outcome variables is evident by these descriptions. The same variable can be considered a process or outcome variable depending on the research question and methodology.

Efficacy and Effectiveness

Efficacy has been used to describe treatment outcomes determined in controlled trials, ideally randomized controlled trials (RCTs). Treatments are compared to no-treatment controls (e.g., wait-list conditions) or other treatments. The goal is to control, to the greatest degree possible, for variability in settings, treatment delivery, therapist variables, and client input variables. The ideal RCT for determining efficacy includes standardized (e.g., manualized) treatments to control for intragroup variability in delivery. The purpose of efficacy studies is to identify treatments that causally contribute to positive outcomes (Seligman, 1995; Westen & Morrison, 2001). Wampold (2000) further distinguished *absolute efficacy* studies, in which treatments are compared with a control group, from *relative efficacy* studies, in which two or more treatments are directly compared; these studies typically include a control group, as well. The most common criticism of efficacy studies is that the "real world" is not so neat. Clients tend to present with multiple psychological and/or physical complaints that impact treatment delivery or outcome; private practice and mental health clinics are not run with the same degree of structure and control as is the clinical laboratory in terms of exposure to other clients and extra-therapy events.

Effectiveness studies evaluate treatments in the "real world": the generalizability of efficacy to naturalistic settings that include heterogeneous client populations with comorbid presentations (Seligman, 1995; Westen & Morrison, 2001). Thus, effectiveness studies increase the external validity of results because they reflect "real-world" conditions. For example, treatment delivery in naturalistic settings may vary in length, whereas treatment delivery within an RTC tends to be of predetermined length. Because conditions are not well controlled, it is more difficult to infer causal mechanisms in naturalistic settings. On the other hand, the artificial constraints of RTCs can attenuate treatment effectiveness. For example, Westen and Morrison (2001) noted that duration of treatment for depression in naturalistic settings is approximately 6 months when cognitive-behavioral therapy (CBT) is utilized, and longer for other modalities, assuming there are no imposed external limitations (e.g., managed care constraints). Treatment duration approximately doubles when there is co-morbidity (Westen & Morrison, 2001).

Thus, artificially constraining treatment to a specified duration in efficacy studies can potentially attenuate treatment effectiveness and result in a type II error due to an inadequate trial of treatment.

History and Sociopolitical Context of Process and Outcome Research

The need to demonstrate psychological treatment efficacy and effectiveness took on a greater sense of urgency in the 1970s in the context of the debate regarding the economic feasibility of national health insurance. There was no consensus among psychologists that reimbursement for psychological treatments under such insurance was fiscally feasible or even appropriate.

Arguments by psychologists against reimbursement centered on three issues: treatment could not be cost-effectively financed, treatment could not be adequately monitored to prevent fiduciary abuse, and treatment in outpatient private practice was dominated by psychiatrists serving primarily the middle and upper socioeconomic (SES) classes who were seeking self-fulfillment (McSweeny, 1977; Strupp & Hadley, 1977). This last issue was central to the expressed concerns because the Community Mental Health Centers Act of 1963, which mandated the development of public mental health services to meet the needs of the poor, had not successfully bridged the quality gap between services accessible by upper and lower SES clients. One reason was that public mental health centers tended to be staffed by less educated and trained therapists. Not only was there a quality gap in service delivery, but the values promoted by private therapists tended to reflect those of the middle-class, focusing on the exploration of feelings, thoughts, intentions, and motivation of clients who did not experience the severity of symptoms and distress exhibited by lower SES clients. Thus, carte blanche reimbursement for psychological treatments would not benefit the general American public nor their overall health; rather, it would amount to the subsidy of treatment for the rich by the poor (Cummings, 1977).

Arguments supporting reimbursement cited the overutilization of medical services by clients suffering psychological and emotional distress. Cummings (1977) reported that "60% of physician visits . . . are from sufferers of emotional distress rather than organic illness" (p. 711). Therefore, the cost of covering psychological treatment should be offset by greater savings through decreased medical utilization.

This tied psychological treatment for mental health concerns to the amelioration of medical health concerns and reductions in medical care costs (Olbrisch, 1977; Strupp & Hadley, 1977).

Rapprochement between these divergent perspectives was achieved through agreement and recognition that clear standards were needed against which treatments could be evaluated.

Within this context, the American Psychological Association (APA) Task Force on Standards for Service Facilities published the first revision of the 1974 *Standards for Providers of Psychological Services* (1977). The goal of this revision was to develop uniform standards for practicing psychologists regardless of specialty, setting, or reimbursement. These standards specifically noted the goal of ensuring uniform quality across both the public and private sectors. Although the standards were developed in the context of justifying reimbursement, there was a clear message that the ultimate goal was to ensure that the public's best interests were met.

The 1977 standards specified that citizens accessing private and public mental health services should be afforded the same quality of care under similar regulatory safeguards in both domains, and that these services should address clients' needs without undue financial hardship (i.e., treatment must be cost-effective). These standards (1977) reflected the consensus that reimbursement guidelines should disallow payment for treatments that were not clearly specified, supported by evidence, or that were focused on "obvious class biases, such as existential crises and ennui. . . ." rather than on "real" (quotes in original) psychological problems that disrupt basic psychosocial functioning (McSweeny, 1977, p. 725). They also acknowledged the many stakeholders in this debate–psychologists, client, society, government–all of whom would have a unique perspective on what "effectiveness" meant.

In summary, the 1977 standards and consensus in the professional community supported the following requirements:

• Treatment should focus on rehabilitative, ameliorative strategies rather than self-fulfillment and self-actualization.
• Treatment should have demonstrated effectiveness as a prerequisite for reimbursement.
• Therapists should be held accountable for the effectiveness of their services.
• Treatment should be equally available to clients across the socioeconomic spectrum and should be of equal quality and effectiveness for all clients served.
• Effective treatment should mitigate the misutilization or overutilization of medical care.
• Psychological treatments should be integrated with physical health, both in its approach toward improving physical health and in preventing disease.

Meta-Analysis and Treatment Efficacy

Within the above historical context, the Smith and Glass meta-analysis (1977) reflected the contemporaneous sociopolitical zeitgeist. It provided the first evidence of treatment efficacy that addressed some of the core themes outlined above in the debate regarding inclusion of psychological treatments in a national insurance plan. The interventions included in the study addressed psychosocial functioning and core issues relevant to the broader population. Treatment goals targeted maladaptive behaviors, feelings, values, and attitudes (Smith & Glass, 1977). What Smith and Glass did not include was as important as what they did include. They eschewed interventions associated with higher-SES clients by excluding interventions that tended to last longer and thus were associated with financial drain, and excluded outcomes that pertained to self-fulfillment and self-actualization. They also excluded interventions that were not grounded in psychological principles (e.g., drug therapies, occupational therapy), as well as interventions provided by individuals who were unqualified to understand and apply these psychological principles in practice (e.g., peer counselors). Thus, the data met fundamental criteria around which professional consensus had been built. The study justified reimbursement. It not only represented a methodological first, it was a sociopolitical boost for establishing psychological interventions as legitimate treatment for improving psychosocial functioning.

The Smith and Glass study (1977) may be one of the most widely cited works in psychology (668 citations as of May 1, 2011, as noted in APA PsychNET), underscoring its significance in the field. Methodologically, it was the first published meta-analysis of individual outcome studies, and it is cited for this significance. It included all studies that evaluated treatment outcomes, published and unpublished, that had utilized at least one treatment condition compared with a no-treatment control group or second treatment condition. It also was the first study to determine effect sizes for treatment outcome in each study, which leveled the playing field across varying types of treatments and thus allowed for direct comparisons; and it attempted to draw causal inferences among study characteristics (such as therapist training) and treatment outcome. Thus, it attempted to determine treatment efficacy as well as assess the contributions of process and input variables on outcome. For these reasons, the Smith and Glass (1977) meta-analysis represented a promising methodology of choice for many investigators. Its legacy continues to influence process and outcome research today.

The results of the Smith and Glass (1977) meta-analysis were not universally applauded. Issues were raised by several investigators. Wilson and Rachman (1983) pointed out two primary shortcomings: Smith and Glass (1977) omitted many "well-controlled" studies, particularly in the area of behavior therapy, without apparent reason or documented rationale; and methodological rigor was not a criterion for inclusion in the meta-analysis. For example, Smith and Glass (1977) included theses and unpublished documents. Their meta-analysis also categorized study variables in arbitrary ways: internal validity was categorized as high, medium, or low depending on whether the study included "randomization, low mortality [*high*]; more than one [unspecified] threat to internal validity [*medium*]; no matching of pretest information to equate groups [*low*]" (p. 755). Client diagnosis was categorized for the sake of analysis as either "neurotic" or "psychotic." Smith and Glass created four categories for assigning levels of client–therapist similarity: College students: *very similar*; Neurotic adults: *moderately similar*; Juveniles, minorities: *moderately dissimilar*; Hospitalized, chronic adults, disturbed children, prisoners: *very dissimilar*.

For the above reasons, the Smith and Glass (1977) meta-analysis evaluated outcomes on only the broadest level, using a study sample that disregarded methodological rigor and which did not, claims to the contrary, have the ability to compare the relative efficacy of specific interventions for specific presenting concerns. It also serves as an illustration for the potential for bias in meta-analyses vis à vis decision making regarding study inclusion and exclusion criteria and coding schemes.

At the time of the Smith and Glass (1977) study, the establishment of a national health insurance plan appeared to be imminent. For example, Olbrisch (1977) noted that such a plan "will come into being, a nearly certain result of growing recognition that access to adequate health care is an essential human right" (p. 761). However, to date, the United States still does not have universal health coverage, and parity for mental health coverage did not occur until 2008, with the passing of the Paul Wellstone and Pete Domenici Mental Health Parity and Addiction Equity Act. The Act requires health insurance plans that offer mental health coverage to provide that coverage on par with financial and treatment coverage offered for other physical illnesses. This underscores the continuing sociopolitical imperative to demonstrate psychological treatment effectiveness.

The Development of Treatment Standards

The debate regarding national health insurance, and whether mental health interventions should be included, continued into the 1990's and provided the context for the development of the APA Division 12 Task Force on the Promotion and Dissemination of Psychological Procedures. The goal of the Task Force was to develop empirical standards for the evaluation of intervention effectiveness, specifically treatment efficacy (Beutler, 1998). Psychologists agreed that if we offer treatments that ameliorate, improve, or enhance psychosocial functioning, it is logical that this effectiveness should be demonstrable and reportable. A shift toward managed health care during the previous 20 years appeared to include a shift toward cost containment as the primary criterion of effectiveness, to the neglect of demonstrated efficacy. This increased the incentive for psychology to establish empirically derived criteria for defining treatment efficacy as the critical component of effectiveness. If psychology failed to develop these criteria, there was concern that the promotion of short-sighted and short-term cost-savings (i.e., medication only) over more effective treatments (e.g., behavioral treatments, medication plus psychotherapy) might prevail.

The Division 12 Task Force (DIV12TF) published efficacy criteria and a list of treatments–"finite and incomplete"–that met these criteria (Beutler, 1998). Prior to these efforts, it was generally accepted that therapists were held to the principle of the *community standard* and/or the principle of the *respectable minority*. Both reflected subjectivity that allowed for the practice of treatments that could be ineffective or even harmful, as long as the treatment was practiced with frequency within a given community (*principle of the community standard*) or was consistent with the theoretical orientation or model that met the criteria of having "definite principles" and at least six followers (*principle of the respectable minority*). Both principles were established by case law pertaining to malpractice allegations or contested managed care policies, rather than by the evaluation of empirical data (Beutler, 1998). Beutler noted that the criteria published in 1995 by the Task Force were adapted from the criteria used by the Federal Drug Administration (FDA), again paralleling the increased pressure on both medicine and psychology to demonstrate effectiveness.

In addition to the sociopolitical pressures regarding reimbursement, there was a clear call to ensure that psychological treatments served the public welfare and represented the best of psychology as a science, rather than therapist bias or comfort level (Kendall, 1998). Therefore, treatments promoted as effective had to be gauged against standardized criteria to minimize the potential for investigator bias, allegiance, or (financial) interest to influence research results (Kendall, 1998). At the same time, there was recognition that one size does not fit all, and that various treatment evaluation methodologies would be required to address the effects and interactions known to influence outcome, such as therapist and client characteristics.

Chambless and Hollon (1998) clarified and more clearly operationalized the criteria published in the DIV12TF report. They defined three levels of efficacy: *possibly efficacious* treatments have demonstrated superiority in one study (for single-case experiments the sample size must be three or greater); *efficacious* treatments have demonstrated superiority in at least two independent research settings (for single-case experiments, the sample size must be three or greater at each site); and *efficacious and specific* treatments have demonstrated superiority beyond comparison with a no-treatment control group in at least two independent settings; its superiority must be demonstrated in comparison with an alternative treatment or a placebo treatment (either medication or psychological).

In response to the publication of the DIV12TF Report (1995; as cited in Beutler, 1998), the Society for Counseling Psychology (Division 17 of the APA) convened a Special Task Group (STG) to develop criteria and standards regarding evidence-based practice that reflected the historical perspective and values of counseling psychology (Wampold, Lichtenberg, & Waehler, 2002). The DIV17STG report (2002) described seven principles regarding "empirically supported interventions," rather than

following the lead of Division 12 and listing treatments that met a set of well-defined criteria. This decision was based on the reluctance to unintentionally promote the misuse of the list by managed care systems for reimbursement decision making, and to implicitly ascribe to a deficit-based model, such as reflected by the DIV12TF report, which focused on *Diagnostic and Statistical Manual* (DSM) diagnoses and the amelioration of psychopathology. In contrast, the DIV17STG report noted counseling psychology's strengths-based philosophy focusing on personal growth and enhancement across the continuum of "normal" psychosocial functioning. Another contribution of the DIV17STG report was the inclusion of Principle 2, which recognized the importance of client input variables: cultural/ethnic diversity, attitudes, values, and other characteristics representing individual differences that have an impact on the choice of treatment.

The DIV17STG report diverged from the DIV12TF report (1995) in a few other significant ways. The former required that causal attribution for specific treatment ingredients could only be made if the evidence was "persuasive," a criterion described as more "stringent" than the criteria set by DIV12TF without an apparent trade-off in increased clinical significance (Chambless, 2002). Additionally, the DIV17STG Principle 7 allowed therapists greater latitude in treatment utilization. Principle 7: Outcomes Should Be Assessed Locally and Freedom of Choice Should Be Recognized states: "Although local decisions should be guided by the critical application of empirical results, as discussed above, outcomes should be monitored at the local level" (p. 210). When considering Principles 2 and 7 together, the DIV17STG report suggested an increased latitude and therapist discretion in treatment application unless this higher standard of efficacy could be met. Thus, both divisional reports made substantial contributions to defining the criteria for ESTs. However, there also were significant differences in the concerns described as the foci of treatment, standards for evaluating treatments, and the allowable discretion at the therapist level.

Subsequent to the publication of these divisional standards, the APA 2005 Presidential Task Force on Evidence-Based Practice was convened and developed a consensus paper (2006) that clearly articulated the parallel development of evidence-based practice in psychology and medicine. Evidence-based practice in psychology was defined by the 2005 Presidential Task Force as "the integration of the best available research with clinical expertise in the context of patient characteristics, culture, and preferences" (p. 273), adapting the definition of evidence-based practice published by the Institute of Medicine in 2001 (Task Force, 2006). Both definitions allow flexibility in treatment application, specifically noting the need to consider client context and input variables. The Task Force also noted the varying levels of established treatment efficacy or effectiveness across specific concerns and disorders.

Effectiveness does not only mean that a causal relationship between treatment and outcome has been empirically demonstrated. It also requires demonstration of cost effectiveness and accountability on the part of the therapist. These forces have served as incentives for the development of several lines of process and outcome research, as will be discussed below. These forces are not purely negative when seen from the perspective of the client as consumer. For example, the advent of hospital and medical group "report cards" has been lauded by consumer groups as a positive step in monitoring health care providers and identifying those services and facilities that rank high on quality standards, effectiveness, and service. Reporting morbidity and mortality rates, medication errors, and iatrogenic illnesses allows for objective evaluation of health services and empowers the public to make informed choices. The same issues regarding the need to assess effectiveness across diverse populations, with which psychology has struggled for over 30 years, have already been raised in this context.

For these reasons, the APA Task Force report (2006) recommendations included the call for various types of research designs to balance the issues of external and internal validity. It also repeated the need to evaluate evidence that is not restricted to efficacy, but rather contributes to overall assessment of effectiveness, namely cost effectiveness, treatment utilization, cost–benefit, and epidemiological data. They noted that different types of studies are required for the evaluation of these different types of evidence. Randomized controlled trials (and their logical equivalents) were cited as the standard for drawing causal inference regarding intervention effects, and meta-analyses are cited as a means for synthesizing results across studies. The list of acceptable designs reflected differences in methodology as well as differences in research goals. It included qualitative research designs, such as single-case and systematic case studies, experimental single-case designs, effectiveness studies in naturalistic settings, and studies evaluating the relationship between process and treatment outcome.

The APA Task Force report (2006) specifically noted two types of studies for evaluating specific interventions: efficacy and clinical utility. Efficacy has been discussed above. *Clinical utility* refers to the generalization (external validation) of an efficacious intervention, in which its applicability and feasibility for use in that particular setting is evaluated. Its applicability and feasibility include the assessment of the treatment's cost effectiveness and the cost–benefits associated with implementation across diverse therapists, clients, and settings and the interactions among these variables (moderating effects). Feedback loops for clients and therapists across the course of treatment, development of practice research networks, the need for developing professional consensus regarding the research evidence necessary to discredit treatments, and research on the prevention of risk behaviors and psychological disorders also were listed by the Task Force as priorities for future research.

The APA Presidential Task Force (2006) distinguished ESTs from the more general concept of evidence-based practice in psychology (EBPP). *Empirically supported treatments* have demonstrated efficacy with a particular client population experiencing a particular presenting concern. *Evidence-based practice in psychology* (EBPP) refers to a broader range of psychological services and interventions (e.g., assessment, case conceptualization) that include, but are not limited to, specific treatments. These interventions are derived through the integration of converging and varying types of evidence with the therapist's expertise, resulting in the formulation that is acceptable to, and consistent with, the client's values and psychosocial context. The APA Task Force noted that efficacy data are sparse or nonexistent for many psychological disorders and concerns. Under these conditions, the therapist would integrate psychological principles, the best known research data, and best clinical judgment to develop an appropriate treatment.

Evidence-based Practice, Empirically Based Treatments, and Empirically Supported Treatments

The above discussion exemplifies how different terms have been used to describe different levels of research support for treatments and interventions: evidence-based practice in psychology, empirically supported interventions (EVIs), evidence-based treatments (EBTs), etc. Because of this confusing variability in nomenclature and what each term signifies regarding relative research strength, Kendall and Beidas (2007) provided definitions of terms used to denote varying levels of empirical support. Specifically, *evidence-based practice* (EBP), *empirically based treatments* (EBTs), and *ESTs* are used to describe treatments that have received research support, but the distinctions among these terms have been blurred at times. These authors defined them as reflecting increasing levels of scientific control.

Evidence-based practice refers to the integration of scientific principles (e.g., principles of operant conditioning) with clinical judgment. As such, it reflects the interaction of the application of these principles with the specific characteristics of the client. This represents the most flexibility in research design and applied practice. *Empirically based treatments* (EBTs) include specific components that are based in, and derived from, empirical data about the presenting concern or disorder. As such, the treatment is based in scientific principles and is designed to target aspects or symptoms of the presenting concern that have been identified through experimental research to be an inherent aspect of the presentation. The specifics of this intervention are devised by the therapist and may be *idiographic*–determined on a case by case basis. An EST consists of clearly specified components. Through RCT, controlled single-case experiment, or equivalent time-series design, it has been found to be superior to alternative treatment, placebo control, or a no-treatment control group. The treatment must be manualized (or its equivalent vis à vis the logical sequencing of components and application), the client sample must be homogeneous regarding the presenting concern that is the target of treatment, and valid and reliable measures must be used for the assessment of the presenting concern for inclusion in the study, as well as for the assessment of treatment outcome (Kendall & Beidas, 2007).

Treatment fidelity refers to the implementation and application of a treatment with a client as it was designed and described in the treatment manual (or equivalent). Fidelity checks guard against the potential for selective implementation of some components but not others. Additionally, they assist in preventing or minimizing the natural but unintentional "drift" in the treatment application over time if adherence to the manual guidelines is not routinely checked. However, it is a misrepresentation to infer that manuals are rigid and prescriptive in intrasession requirements and client–therapist interactions. The best manualized treatments acknowledge and accommodate the necessary therapist skills required to ensure appropriate matching with the client's presentation and characteristics. Thus, there is room for flexibility within fidelity (Kendall & Beidas, 2007).

Efficacy Versus Effectiveness

A consensus has been reached that a variety of research designs are required to evaluate treatment ingredients, process–outcome relationships for identifying mechanisms of change, and therapist or client variables and the interactions among these factors. Process variables, input variables, and the interactions among them contribute to treatment outcomes. In fact, these factors are significant and necessitate continued research to explicate these relationships. It is in the evaluation of clinical utility for treatments of established efficacy that process and input variables become critical.

Qualitative research, single-case experimental designs, effectiveness research in naturalistic settings, and meta-analysis for synthesizing results, testing hypotheses, and estimating effect sizes were endorsed by the APA Task Force (2006). The design depends on the research question and the relative degree of internal or external validity required (APA Task Force, 2006; Westen & Morrison, 2001). The Task Force identified directions for future research, emphasizing studies evaluating the generalizability of efficacious treatments, client × treatment interactions, and both efficacy and effectiveness studies with diverse populations (age, gender, culture, ethnicity, disability status, sexual orientation, children and youths at different developmental stages, and older adults). Thus, the report recognized the importance of evaluating both therapist and client process and input variables.

The APA Task Force (2006) did not state that meta-analysis was appropriate for identifying whether specific ingredients across treatments were causally related to outcomes. What the APA Task Force did state was that APA policy recognized two accepted methods for evaluating the research on specific treatments. These methods were efficacy studies utilizing RCTs, and clinical utility studies evaluating the generalizability of an efficacious treatment to the setting in which it will be used, including its applicability, feasibility, and usefulness in that particular setting.

When the issue is demonstrating relative efficacy among treatments for a specific concern in a well-defined population, RCTs are the standard for scientific rigor. Under these conditions, RCTs have identified treatments with superior efficacy. For example, Chambless & Ollendick (2001) noted that two independent RCTs reported that exposure plus response prevention was statistically superior to progressive muscle relaxation for the treatment of adult anxiety disorder. In another RCT conducted by Borkovec and Costello (1993), both CBT and applied relaxation were statistically and clinically superior to nondirective therapy post-treatment in a sample of adults treated for generalized anxiety disorder. At 1-year follow-up, only CBT demonstrated maintenance of statistically and clinically significant change. Randomized controlled trials also have identified the superiority of CBT in comparison with nondirective, supportive therapy for the treatment of depression among children and adolescents (Chambless & Ollendick, 2001). Exposure-based therapy also has been identified as a superior treatment for phobias and posttraumatic stress disorder (PTSD), even in very complicated cases with severe PTSD and comorbidity, in comparison with relaxation training and eye movement desensitization and reprocessing (EMDR; Taylor et al., 2003).

However, Lam and Sue (2001) and Bernal and Scharron-Del-Rió (2001) noted the dearth of research evaluating treatment outcomes for diverse populations. Bernal and Scharron-Del-Rió suggested a combination of qualitative and quantitative research designs that address discovery and hypothesis testing, in an iterative process that emphasizes external and internal validity, in turn. One example of a cultural adaptation of an EST was an evaluation of narrative exposure therapy (NET) for refugees exposed to war-related trauma who still lived in unsafe environments (i.e., refugee camps; Neuner, Schauer, Klaschik, Karunakara, & Elbert, 2004). This study evaluated NET as a brief, culturally acceptable intervention that could be delivered by local staff who typically would not have backgrounds in therapy or research. Although the treatments were administered by Caucasian psychologists or graduate students from Konstanz University in Germany, rather than by therapists from the community, there were many methodological strengths: Only one prospective client declined to participate (indicating acceptability of intervention description and rationale), utilization of local community members as research assistants or translators was successful (i.e., the study was embedded within the community to the extent feasible), therapists were trained in three interventions with equally plausible rationales, and there

was continuing supervision of therapists to ensure treatment fidelity.

This study by Neuner, Schauer, Klaschik, Karunakara, and Elbert (2004) compared a culturally adapted effective treatment for decreasing PTSD-related symptomatology with supportive counseling (to control for nonspecific treatment effects) and a one-session psychoeducational intervention (control group). It is particularly significant that an RCT was successfully implemented in a war-torn, traumatized Sudanese refugee community, the people of whom were uprooted from their homes and living in Imvepi, a Northern Ugandan refugee settlement. Symptoms and health status were assessed at pretreatment, post-treatment, and at 4-month and 1-year follow-up. Treatment duration with NET or supportive counseling was four sessions. Results were mixed. Clients in all groups improved somewhat during the 1-year post-treatment. The NET group showed more improvement in comparison with the supportive counseling and control conditions, but 50% of these individuals still evidenced severe psychological disturbance, and effect sizes did not indicate superior effectiveness of NET. This is not surprising because the study participants were still living in the same desperate circumstances.

However, one notable difference among study groups was that the majority of the NET participants managed to leave the refugee camp within 1 year of treatment, whereas participants in the other conditions did not. Data collected at 1-year follow-up indicated that 93% of study participants reported experiencing or witnessing one or more additional traumatic events during that year. However, the participants who left the camp reported a significantly lower mean number of traumatic events in comparison with refugees who did not leave (Neuner et al., 2004). This appeared to be due to the fact that the NET participants moved to places that were safer and/or more amenable to finding work or sustenance. In the context of the biopsychosocial model described below, one might hypothesize that NET sufficiently increased emotion regulation through the reduction of chronic hyperarousal. This reduction facilitated increased executive functioning that mediated the planning required to successfully leave the refugee camp.

Evaluating Treatment Effectiveness
Evaluating ESTs under naturalistic conditions to ascertain effectiveness and clinical utility has proven to be more challenging than evaluating efficacy

under controlled conditions. This is particularly true with clients who present with multiple concerns and complicated presentations (see Ruscio & Holohan, 2006, for an excellent discussion of these issues). Efficacy studies, by definition, control extraneous variables (setting, process, and input variables) to the greatest extent feasible. Inclusion and exclusion criteria are strict, typically eliminating clients with comorbid psychological concerns, although comorbidity is the rule, not the exception, in the community (Westen, Novotny, & Thompson-Brenner, 2004). Benchmarking is one analytical strategy developed for bridging this gap.

The goal of *benchmarking* is to utilize treatment outcome data from RCT efficacy studies as a standard of reference for evaluating the effectiveness of these treatments when administered in naturalistic (clinic) settings. Benchmarking is the direct comparison of pre- and post-treatment data of treatments with established efficacy with the pre- and post-treatment data of the same treatment administered in a naturalistic (clinic) setting. Benchmarking studies have identified equivalency between a treatment's efficacy and its effectiveness, thus indicating generalizability (e.g., Hunsley & Lee, 2007; Minami, Wampold, Serlin, Hamilton, & Kircher, 2008). However, issues concerning this strategy include inherent potential for bias regarding which studies to include in calculating benchmarks and heterogeneity across diagnoses, client input characteristics, and outcome measures, and the inability to identify specific components causally related to outcomes.

Treatment Implementation at the Case Level

A significant issue in the literature is the dissemination of an efficacious treatment at the "real-world" level. In the clinic and private practice, therapists are faced with decisions regarding whether and how to implement and administer treatments of known efficacy with a particular client. The waters are particularly muddy when the treatment has not been evaluated with the client's population in terms of age, culture, ethnicity, or other characteristics as described by the APA Presidential Task Force report (2006). Client expectations and personality are additional input variables that might not be readily apparent to the therapist, but which could influence treatment outcome.

To what extent a therapist should adhere to a treatment of known efficacy when these client characteristics are diverse, complex, or unknown, has been an issue of debate (Goldfried & Eubanks-Carter, 2004; Ruscio & Holohan, 2006). Issues include how and to what extent a therapist should administer manualized treatments. Running throughout this discussion regarding generalizability and clinical utility is a philosophical question regarding models. Some investigators question the utility of RCTs for defining efficacy. The primary concern is that RCTs reflect rigidity in the extent to which conditions (and client presentations) are controlled and that therefore they do not and cannot develop treatments applicable to real-world practice; in other words, the paradigm is too artificial and restrictive, as evidenced in part by limiting inclusion to clients who meet DSM criteria. This was a primary objection and concern noted in the DIV17STG report (2002). The RCT paradigm is seen as being consistent with a medical model that reflects a categorical, reductionistic taxonomy rather than a paradigm that acknowledges dimensional continua of functioning (Goldfried & Eubanks-Carter, 2004). Therefore, adherence to manualized treatment is viewed as adherence to this medical model.

These differences in perspective are highlighted when considering theoretical models for organizing the data and directing future research, as discussed below in this chapter. From a balanced perspective, the issue is how to extract what is learned through RCTs regarding efficacy and apply that adaptively to meet the client's needs (Kazdin, 2008; Kendall & Beidas, 2007; cf. Westen, Novotny, & Thompson-Brenner, 2004). More generally, how will therapists reconcile the best research evidence (nomothetic data) with their particular client at that particular point in time? This represents, at a basic level, the conflict between clinical and actuarial (statistical) prediction (Lutz et al., 2006; Meehl, 1954). A treatment of known efficacy, flexibly applied (and the operable word is "flexibly") should have a higher probability of positive treatment outcome in comparison with clinical "expertise" integrated to an unknown extent with knowledge of psychological principles. However, as Kazdin noted, there are no models or algorithms for determining how to adapt an efficacious treatment flexibly but with fidelity (Kazdin, 2008). Without paradigms or decision rules, there remains the potential for reverting to the principle of community standard or the principle of the respectable minority on one hand and, on the other hand, there is the potential for rigid adherence to a treatment that disregards individual differences and threatens the therapeutic process and alliance. Closer collaboration between researchers and therapists is required to address these issues. In particular, practice must inform research, as suggested by the community therapist networks described and advocated by the APA Presidential Task Force report (2006).

Process–Outcome Research: The Shape of Change and Dose–Response

Pre- and post-test assessments of symptom reduction and functionality are inadequate for assessing change because they do not explicate the contributions of moderator and mediator variables. Yet, understanding these effects is critical for establishing effectiveness across diverse groups and, for the therapist, within the single case over time. A comprehensive review of advances in quantitative and qualitative methods for assessing change associated with moderator and mediator variables is beyond the scope of this chapter. However, a few promising trends are noted below.

Several analytic approaches assess change longitudinally over the course of treatment. This is accomplished by sampling client status frequently and then plotting progress over time. These analytic techniques include individual growth curve modeling, growth mixture modeling, dynamical systems modeling (Laurenceau, Hayes, & Feldman, 2007; Stulz, Lutz, Leach, Lucock, & Barkham, 2007), survival analysis (Anderson & Lambert, 2001; Corning & Malofeeva, 2004), and case-based time-series analysis (Borckardt et al., 2008). These techniques identify changes in rate of progress in treatment over time, thus facilitating the ability to identify which process and input variables contribute causally to change during treatment. These *client-focused* approaches utilize either a rationally derived model to detect clinically significant change or an empirically driven decision model (e.g., nearest-neighbors method; Lutz et al., 2006) to statistically estimate growth curves across treatment phases to predict client outcome. At the single-case level, therapists can assess change over time as treatment progresses. This assists the therapist in objectively evaluating the dose (intensity) of treatment, and in detecting problems related to moderator or mediator variables that must be addressed in treatment.

The use of case-based time-series analysis was described by Borckardt et al. (2008), who noted an advantage of this design is the ease of implementation in clinic or private practice settings. Case-based time-series analysis allows the assessment of change by treatment phase. Client status on multiple measures of symptomatology and functioning are sampled frequently during baseline, treatment, discharge, and follow-up. These measures can include client, therapist, and/or collateral report.

One way of utilizing survival analysis is to determine how many sessions (i.e., dose) are required to achieve clinically significant change (response). Survival analysis can detect moderator variables (e.g., severity of illness) that contribute to outcome and what "dose" of treatment is required for positive outcome for each group (Anderson & Lambert, 2001). Survival analysis also has been used to identify factors contributing to poor outcome, defined as premature termination (Corning & Malofeeva, 2004).

Corning and Malofeeva (2004) noted that attempts to predict poor outcome, defined as premature termination, have been particularly problematic. Psychotherapy is a longitudinal process; therefore, termination after one session should not be treated statistically the same as termination after ten sessions because the causal factors are not likely to be the same. For example, symptom severity and the quality of the therapeutic relationship can change over time, and not necessarily in a linear fashion. Additionally, some cases may terminate for external reasons (college graduation) that are irrelevant to progress in counseling and achievement of mutually agreed upon goals. The advantages of survival analysis is that it can include static moderator variables that vary across clients but not over time, moderator variables that vary over time but not across clients, and predictor variables that vary across time and across clients (e.g., number of sessions completed at any point in time). Survival analysis also can statistically address *censored* cases that have unknown termination points; that is, those that continue beyond the conclusion of data collection or, conversely, those that terminate for arbitrarily imposed reasons unrelated to the therapeutic process. Multiple types of termination also can be evaluated simultaneously using survival analysis via a competing risks analysis. *Competing risks* assesses the relationship of the predictor variables to different types of events simultaneously, such as different types of termination: premature, mutual, and arbitrary.

Assessing change and dose–response during counseling and psychotherapy requires a case-level approach with immediate feedback. Such an approach can be utilized at the case level and then aggregated across clients to assess for treatment effectiveness. It also can be used by therapists facing the dilemma of incorporating treatments whose efficacy has been evaluated via group differences to case-specific treatment with a particular client (i.e., implementing treatment with flexibility within fidelity; Kendall & Beidas, 2007). Client-focused systems for monitoring progress can facilitate the therapist's awareness of a negative response to treatment in an objective manner, so that modifications in treatment or process can be made (Whipple et al., 2003).

Whipple et al. (2003) reported that, in previous studies, feedback about client nonresponders facilitated the therapist's ability to keep the client in therapy and prevent premature termination. For these nonresponders, staying in therapy longer was associated with a better outcome in comparison with nonresponders whose therapists did not receive feedback. However, this improvement was not clinically significant. Feedback regarding clients who were responding to treatment allowed the therapist to decrease the number of sessions without negatively impacting outcome. These results suggested that additional feedback information was necessary to prevent premature termination and promote positive outcome in nonresponders and poor responders.

In a subsequent study at a university counseling center (Whipple et al., 2003), a sample of 981 clients (mean age = 23 years; 66% female, 86% Caucasian) participated in a study evaluating the effectiveness of clinical support tools (CSTs) in improving clinical outcome in treatment nonresponders. The CSTs were organized in a decision tree format. They were hypothesized to assist the therapist in identifying specific moderator variables (readiness to change, level of social support), mediator variables (quality of the therapeutic alliance), and the evaluation of alternative, appropriate psychological and/or psychotropic treatment options for clients who were not progressing as expected in therapy (Whipple et al., 2003). Essentially, the CSTs formalized therapist decision-making as part of the therapeutic process. One component of the CSTs assessed psychological concerns (Subjective Discomfort, Interpersonal Relationships, and Social Role Performance) as measured by the Outcome Questionnaire-45 (OQ-45; Lambert et al., 1996, as cited in Anderson & Lambert, 2001). This study indicated that more nonresponders and poor responders whose therapists received feedback on client progress and utilized the CSTs achieved "reliable" or clinically significant improvement and were less likely to be rated as deteriorated at therapy termination.

The specific value of the OQ-45 is that it can be used in effectiveness studies of various designs (survival analysis, case-based time-series). It provides immediate feedback to the therapist, who can then identify "signal" cases (clients failing to respond) for further attention to process variables and "dosing" (Lambert, Hansen, & Finch, 2001). For this reason, it is an example of an objective method for assessing response to treatment for the purpose of facilitating positive outcome that is amenable for use by the private practice therapist. It also serves as an option for assessing clinical utility and accountability at the therapist level. Such instruments could potentially facilitate science–practice dialogue and enrichment of the knowledge base through the objective collection of data by therapists (APA Presidential Task Force, 2006; Persons, 2007).

Length of Treatment

The length of treatment required to reach mutually agreed upon goals has been an issue of continuing debate. Particularly in the age of managed care and imposed time limits, there are ethical as well as clinical reasons for carefully evaluating how much treatment is necessary and sufficient to attain initial positive outcome and to maintain gains. This question is directly tied to dose–response evaluation. Unfortunately, no clear guidelines have emerged to date. Baldwin, Berkeljon, Atkins, Olsen, and Nielsen (2009) attempted to identify the length of necessary and sufficient treatment by evaluating two competing hypotheses: the *dose–effect* model, in which the client's improvement is causally and positively related to the number of treatment sessions but the rate of change slows across time (i.e., negatively accelerates) versus the *good-enough level* (GEL) model, which predicts that clients stay in therapy until they have reached a "good enough" level of improvement, as determined in collaboration with their therapist. Therefore, the number of sessions (dose) will vary as a function of the amenability ("malleability") of the presenting concern to treatment.

The GEL model predicts that sufficient change has occurred for each client at time of mutual termination, although the number of sessions will vary across clients. Furthermore, change is independent of the number of sessions attended, and rate of change is faster for clients who terminate after fewer sessions in comparison with clients who remain in psychotherapy longer before achieving good enough improvement. Participants in the

Baldwin, Berkeljon, Atkins, Olsen, and Nielsen (2009) study were 4,676 clients seen at a university counseling center. Demographics were as follows: client mean age: 22.3; gender: 62% female, marital status: 65% single; ethnicity: Caucasian 88%, Hispanic 5%, Asian 2%, Pacific Islander 1%. The proportion of clients with a particular initial diagnosis varied: adjustment disorder 38%, mood disorders 25%; anxiety disorders 12%, eating disorders 5%. Twenty percent received other diagnoses. Archival OQ-45s completed at the initial session were reviewed to determine baseline level of distress. Data were included for analyses if the baseline total OQ-45 score was over 63 and the client improved by 14 or more points by termination, representing a reliable and clinically significant improvement (RCSI).

Data for 2,985 clients met the OQ-45 baseline criterion for inclusion in the analyses. Of these, 1,242 (41.6%) met the outcome criterion for RCSI. Results indicated that change over time was accelerated for clients who participated in fewer sessions, compared with clients who stayed longer in psychotherapy (Baldwin et al., 2009). In other words, the results appeared to support the GEL model: Under naturalistic conditions in which there was no apparent imposition of termination that created artificial, censored cases, clients stayed in treatment until they achieve therapeutic gain. Those who improve more rapidly will participate in counseling or psychotherapy for a shorter length of time. However, it is important to note that less than 50% of the clinically distressed clients had met the RCSI criterion by therapy termination. The identification of moderator and mediator variables that impacted the counseling and psychotherapy process could not be addressed in this study. Clearly, elucidation of these variables would be critical for understanding the suboptimal therapeutic outcome for the majority of these clients.

Return to Meta-Analysis: What It Is and What It Isn't

The use of meta-analytic techniques will be discussed in more detail because they are at the core of the discussion regarding relative treatment efficacy. The promotion of meta-analysis as an objective technique and methodology has hinged on its putative ability to statistically control for moderator and mediator variables that contribute to inconsistent findings across individual studies. These include differences in outcome measures, control conditions, treatment plausibility, and researcher allegiance. However, as described above, meta-analytic techniques are not immune to bias because of the inherent subjectivity involved in deriving the decision rules for study inclusion/exclusion, nor are they immune to allegiance issues (Westen & Morrison, 2001).

Several investigators (e.g., Ahn & Wampold, 2001; Lambert, 2005; Wampold, 2001) cite meta-analytic results as demonstrating equivalent efficacy for treatments utilized for a variety of client populations and presenting concerns, thus providing support for a common factors model of treatment outcome. This equivalence has been labeled the *Dodo bird effect* (Rosenzweig, 1936, as cited in Wampold et al., 1997). The Dodo bird effect references the dodo bird in Alice in Wonderland who declared that everyone had won and therefore "all must have prizes" (as cited in Wampold et al., 1997, p. 203), and reflects their conclusion that all psychological treatments are essentially equivalent in efficacy. Wampold and colleagues (Ahn & Wampold, 2001; Wampold, 2000) have described this reported equivalence as a failing so significant that it "weakens support for psychotherapy as a mental health treatment rather than strengthens it" (Wampold et al., 1997, p. 211). They further state that psychologists should accept that treatments are not analogous to medications: There is no one-to-one relationship between psychological concern/distress and intervention in the same way that there is a one-to-one relationship between disease and medication. They further posit that investigators who report differential efficacy across treatments (i.e., "specific ingredients" proponents) adhere to a medical model (described below).

It is clear that meta-analytic techniques have improved over the past 30 years and that researchers utilizing meta-analysis have attempted to respond to the concerns expressed by critiques of these techniques, as described above in this chapter (e.g., Wilson & Rachman, 1983). Meta-analyses have clearly established the absolute efficacy of counseling and psychotherapy treatments (Wampold, 2000).

On the other hand, meta-analysis, by virtue of its logic and methodology, requires the collapsing of client, treatment, and therapist variables, thus preventing the ability to identify relative efficacy among treatments; that is, specific differences and interactions among them (Beutler, 2002; Craighead, Sheets, & Bjornsson, 2005). Wampold (2000) stated:

> Because the evidence is presented at the meta-analytic level, evidence for a particular ingredient is precluded. The purpose of this

review [Wampold, 2000] is to establish whether the outcome data generally support common factors or specific ingredients (or both) as determinants of the well-documented general efficacy of counseling and psychotherapy. (p. 719)

The methodology of meta-analysis, which has advantages for synthesizing data, also is its limitation: the inability to assess for differential effectiveness across treatments. This inability is not the same as equivalence, and it is faulty logic to thus assume that the results must be attributable to "common factors" (e.g., Kazdin, 2005). As Wampold et al. (1997) noted regarding the results of that meta-analysis:

> As is the case with the primary studies, the results reference average effects; but it is not appropriate to conclude that every treatment is equally effective with every patient. The results of this meta-analysis suggest that the efficacy of the treatments is comparable, not that the treatments are interchangeable. (p. 211)

These comments underscore the point that when meta-analyses collapse data across various client populations and treatments, they are unable to assess for potential differential efficacy. In contrast with the tendency to collapse across populations and treatments, Siev and Chambless (2007) directly compared the efficacy of cognitive therapy and relaxation training for panic disorder (PD) and generalized anxiety disorder (GAD) in two meta-analyses of five studies each. Each meta-analysis directly evaluated specific components for a clearly defined disorder. These authors found no difference in efficacy in treating GAD, but did find cognitive therapy superior to relaxation training in the treatment of PD. The included studies had crossed therapists with treatments, controlling therapist effects (allegiance, bias, experience) that have been hypothesized to represent common factors responsible for treatment efficacy (rather than specific treatment components; e.g., Wampold, 2001). The authors also noted, consistent with comments above, that their meta-analysis could not address causal mechanisms (Siev & Chambless, 2007). The utility was in demonstrating superior efficacy in a "head-to-head" comparison. This meta-analysis demonstrated that, if only studies with fairly homogeneous and equivalent client samples and interventions are included, meta-analysis appears able to determine differential efficacy. However, even under these conditions, it cannot identify causal mechanisms. Therefore, the

fundamental clinical question: "What treatment, by whom, is most effective with this individual with that specific problem under which set of circumstances" (Paul, 1967, p. 111, as cited by Wilson & Rachman, 1983) cannot be answered through meta-analytic inquiry.

As can be seen from this discussion, the debate regarding the appropriate use of meta-analytic techniques and the interpretation of meta-analytic results has been the running undercurrent of the argument regarding treatment efficacy, comparative superiority and, ultimately, differential effectiveness (e.g., Crits-Christoph, 1997; Howard, Krause, Saunders, & Kopta, 1997; Maltzman, S., 2001).

Meta-analysis and the Common Factors Model

The common factors model was derived from meta-analytic results that were interpreted as indicating treatment equivalence. The model is predicated on the assumption that insignificant (statistical and clinical) variance in outcome is attributable to specific treatment components per se. It proposes that most variance in treatment outcome is accounted for by common (mediator and/or moderator) variables, rather than components specific to a particular treatment (e.g., Lambert, 2005; Wampold, 2001). Wampold (2001) described a common factors model as inconsistent with a medical model, in which specific treatment components causally contribute to outcome. Several investigators agree that nonspecific factors, in addition to specific treatment components, are causally related to outcome.

However, there is debate regarding whether specific treatment components contribute at all to outcome and how nonspecific common factors are conceptualized. For example, Craighead, Sheets, and Bjornsson (2005) reviewed the superiority of specific treatment components for specific presenting problems, such as PD. They acknowledged the contribution of nonspecific effects but pointed out that these effects are "nonspecific" only because they have not yet been elucidated. They identify the therapeutic alliance and therapist variables as clear contributors to outcome that require further investigation.

The Medical Model

As noted above, some investigators who support a common factors model have described psychologists who reject the notion of equivalence across treatments as adherents of the *medical model*. Wampold and colleagues (Wampold, Ahn, &

Coleman, 2001; Imel & Wampold, 2008) have described the model as including five components:

> (a) The client presents with a disorder, problem, or complaint; (b) there exists a psychological explanation for the disorder, problem, or complaint; (c) the theoretical conceptualization and knowledge are sufficient to posit a psychological mechanism of change; (d) the therapist administers a set of therapeutic ingredients that are logically derived from the psychological explanation and the mechanism of change; and (e) the benefits of psychotherapy are due, for the most part, to the specific ingredients. The last component, which is often referred to as specificity, is critical to the medical model of psychotherapy and gives primacy to the specific ingredients rather than common or contextual factors.
> (Wampold, Ahn, & Coleman, 2001, p. 268)

This model reflects traditional medical practice, which historically has ignored psychosocial influences in health presentation. Traditional medical practice also has been noted for deficiencies in interpersonal communication skills and subjective biases that have created barriers to treatment. The issue is whether this medical model can be extrapolated directly to psychology: Does it reflect current research and practice? The first component of the medical model as described above implies agreement with the notion of single-problem presentation—a lack of comorbidity, such as dual diagnosis (e.g., mental illness and substance abuse), or multiple problems (e.g., chronic health concerns and marital issues). However, that runs counter to much of the literature in psychology as documented above in this chapter. Single-problem presentations are not reflective of typical real-world client populations (e.g., Westen & Morrison, 2001). It is generally recognized that most clients present with more than one problem or diagnosable mental health concern, and that certain problems also tend to co-occur in certain populations (e.g., Cutuli, Chaplin, Gillham, Reivich, & Seligman, 2006). Second, the description of this medical model appears to ignore the roles of moderator (input) and mediator (process) variables as contributors to treatment process and outcome. Historically, psychology also has described and acknowledged the interactions and influences among physiological, social, environmental, and psychological influences across subdisciplines (e.g., Alcorn, 1991; Altmaier, 1991; APA Presidential Task Force, 2006; Bronfenbrenner,1977; Nomura, Chemtob, Fifer, Newcorn, & Brooks-Gunn, 2006;

Peterson & Elliott, 2008; Ruphuy, 1977; Sameroff & Rosenblum, 2006; Thoresen & Eagleston, 1985).

Other aspects of the medical model, not included in the five components described above, also have been criticized by psychologists. The traditional patient–physician relationship inherent to this model reflects an unequal power hierarchy and promotes the role of patient as the passive, unquestioning recipient of treatment: "The good patient is passive, cooperative, dependent, uncomplaining, and willing to suffer in silence" (Chrisler & O'Hea, 2000, p. 325). Physician racism, sexism, and homophobia have historically impeded clients' access to prompt and/or optimal physical health care (Chrisler & O'Hea, 2000; Meyerowitz, Bull, & Perez, 2000; O'Hanlan, 2000). These characteristics of the medical model have been rejected in psychology, and by counseling psychology in particular.

For these reasons, the medical model still may have relevance in describing pertinent issues within medicine, but it would be difficult to find current adherents within psychology. In spite of this, there appears to be a tendency to describe investigators who acknowledge biological components in mental illness or substance abuse, or who question a common factors model, as adherents to this medical model. For example, Imel and Wampold (2008) cited a few specific, older studies of treatment for alcohol dependence to make this point (Project Match Research Group, 1997; Sobell & Sobell, 1973). Imel and Wampold (2008) wrote:

> More than 20 years ago, Mark and Linda Sobell (Sobell & Sobell, 1973) demonstrated that a regimen of controlled drinking was at least as effective as an abstinence based program, which was counter to the dominant abstinence-based models of treatment. . . . The Sobells' conclusion that training in moderation was as effective as abstinence was subjected to an unprecedented level of criticism (e.g., congressional hearings) by advocates of the disease model of alcoholism (see Pendery, Maltzman, & West, 1982). Although the Sobells were eventually vindicated from [sic] any wrong-doing, controlled drinking has never gained wide acceptance in the United States. (p. 251)

Imel and Wampold used the above example to argue that adherence to a "disease" model of alcoholism (requiring abstinence) was the same as adherence to their definition of the medical model. They suggested that psychologists ignored and rejected the Sobell and Sobell (1973a) data because the results of their study were not consistent with the disease model of alcoholism. This is a confusing argument because alcohol dependence is a disorder with known biological and genetic components (e.g., Cloninger, 1987; Enoch, 2006; Nie et al., 2004).

The Sobell and Sobell (1973a) study generated significant controversy. Because Imel and Wampold (2008) raised the issues again, it warrants discussion. This study was conducted at Patton State Hospital. Participants were 40 clients characterized as "gamma" (physically dependent) alcoholics, all of whom were judged to be appropriate for learning controlled drinking strategies via an experimental operant conditioning paradigm. The Sobells reported that they had conducted a RCT in which 20 of these clients were assigned to the abstinence arm and 20 were assigned to the experimental (controlled drinking) condition. In the experimental condition, clients were taught controlled drinking strategies via 17 individualized behavior therapy sessions at a simulated bar in the hospital. Over the course of treatment, clients had access to alcoholic drinks of variable alcohol content (3%–43%) of varying amounts and strength ("straight" vs. "mixed" drinks). Clients received aversion conditioning via electric shock during some sessions for "inappropriate drinking behaviors" (1973a, p. 56). After completion of treatment and discharge from hospital, clients and collaterals were contacted every 3–4 weeks for a 2-year follow-up period. The primary outcome measure was "days functioning well": the sum of abstinent + controlled drinking days vs. days not functioning well: sum of drunken days + days incarcerated in prison or hospital secondary to drinking.

Sobell and Sobell (1973b) reported that, at the end of the Year 1 follow-up period, clients assigned to the controlled drinking arm experienced significantly more "functioning well" days in comparison with the clients assigned to the abstinence arm. Similar results were reported at the end of the Year 2 follow-up period (Pendery, Maltzman, & West, 1982). Pendery, Maltzman, and West (1982) conducted an independent follow-up study with the cooperation of Patton State Hospital. These investigators located and interviewed all clients assigned to the controlled drinking condition and their collaterals during the period 1976–1979, with intermittent contact continuing until 1981. They also located collateral, objective documentation (e.g., hospital records, drunk driving arrests, jail records) to verify client status. What these authors reported was that Patton State Hospital records documented rehospitalization of 13 of the 20 controlled drinking clients within 1 year of discharge from the study. Ten were readmitted to Patton; three were admitted to other hospitals.

The follow-up data reported by Pendery, Maltzman, and West (1982) differed substantially from the results reported by the Sobells (e.g., 1973b). Clients assigned to controlled drinking fared very poorly. By the 1981 conclusion of this follow-up study, six controlled drinking clients were abstaining completely from alcohol; four of these stopped drinking after multiple rehospitalizations related to alcohol abuse. Four clients in the controlled drinking condition died alcohol-related deaths. The interested reader is referred to this 1982 report for a detailed description of each client's trajectory post-discharge from the controlled drinking study. Pendery, Maltzman, and West (1982) refrained from discussing methodological discrepancies between their and the Sobells' reports, stating their preference to address treatment outcome issues instead. However, it is these methodological questions that resulted in consequent hearings. Therefore, it is inaccurate to attribute the contradictions in these studies' conclusions to theoretical bias.

Imel and Wampold (2008) described results reported by the Project Match Research Group (1997) as indicating "no evidence of differences among treatments" (p. 251) for alcohol abuse and dependence. What is notable is that abstinence during a 1-year post-treatment follow-up period was one of two dependent variables in this study. The second dependent variable, drinks per drinking day, was used as a measure of drinking severity. However, abstinence appeared to be the desired outcome of treatment. Imel and Wampold did not criticize the use of abstinence as an outcome measure as adherence to a medical model. Rather, they cited the Project Match Research Group data as indicating equivalence among alcohol treatments (i.e., as support for a common factors model), without noting that abstinence was an outcome measure. Thus, Imel and Wampold criticized proponents of abstinence and a "disease" model of alcoholism as reflecting theoretical bias and a medical model in their first example, yet refrained from criticizing abstinence as a goal in their second example.

The suggestion that the Project Match Research Group study (1997) provided support for a common factors model is questionable. The Project Match study evaluated the *matching hypothesis*: It matched clients to treatment based on specified a priori client attributes (moderator variables). The study consisted of two parallel arms: One arm consisted of clients who entered aftercare post-discharge from hospital or day treatment for alcohol abuse or dependence. The second arm consisted of outpatient clients who had not been hospitalized or treated in intensive day rehabilitation. Although these clients also met DSM-III-R criteria for alcohol abuse or dependence, the fact that they did not require hospitalization or intensive day treatment suggests that these clients evidenced less disease severity. Both parallel studies included three conditions consisting of individual therapy provided over a 12-week period. These conditions were cognitive-behavioral coping skills training (CBT), motivational enhancement therapy (MET), or a 12-step facilitation (TSF) therapy that encouraged participation in a 12-step program.

The CBT and TSF treatments were delivered weekly; the MET was delivered in four sessions at the first, second, sixth, and twelfth week. The study described all three conditions as "treatments." However, the MET and TSF conditions were not treatments, per se, as noted by the Project Match Research Group authors (1997). Both conditions were designed to promote the client's participation in alcohol treatment. Effectiveness of a 12-step intervention, such as Alcoholics Anonymous (AA), was not assessed. Client engagement in activities intrinsic to 12-step programs, such as AA meeting attendance and obtaining a sponsor, also was not assessed. The authors noted that clients in all three conditions in both study arms were exposed to AA "and a 12-step approach" (p. 24). They also commented that: "Direct comparisons between treatments are difficult because the MET intervention consisted of fewer sessions over the 12-week period and TSF clients were encouraged to attend AA meetings in addition to the 12 individual treatment sessions" (p. 13).

The primary focus of the Project Match Research Group 1997 study was the evaluation of client matching as a moderator of treatment effectiveness. The authors reported that there was no clear advantage to matching clients to treatment. In general, client matching did not appear to improve number of abstinent days across conditions. However, they reported that clients low in psychiatric severity in the outpatient study had more abstinent days after TSF than did clients assigned to CBT at 1 year post-treatment. There was no advantage for TSF in clients exhibiting moderate to high

psychopathology (Project Match Research Group, 1997).

The above review of the Sobell and Sobell (1973) and Project Match Research Group (1997) studies helps clarify why they were not viewed as providing definitive data for rejecting abstinence as the treatment goal nor for accepting treatment equivalence in the substance abuse field.

The Biopsychosocial Model

Although psychology was debating whether psychological treatments should be covered by national health insurance, Engel (1977) published perhaps the earliest call for an integrated biopsychosocial model to address "medicine's crisis [due to] adherence to a model of disease no longer adequate for the scientific tasks and social responsibilities of either medicine or psychiatry" (p. 129) and which Engel described as reductionistic. He described the need for a biopsychosocial model "that would account for the reality of diabetes and schizophrenia as human experiences as well as disease abstractions" (p. 131). Although Engel used schizophrenia and diabetes as exemplars for application of a biopsychosocial perspective, there were clear implications for research and practice across the continuum of psychological functioning. In fact, Engel's position was not inconsistent with the 1977 revision of the 1974 American Psychological Association *Standards for Providers of Psychological Services*, which acknowledged an interaction between psychology and medicine.

Although Engel's challenge has been hailed as a "landmark" publication (Biderman, Yeheskel, & Herman, 2005), the transition within medicine to a biopsychosocial perspective has been slow and inconsistent. Progress has been made in teaching medical students communication skills and psychosocial history taking. However, the concept of relationship (alliance) building with patients as a core component of treatment has not been as accepted (Suchman, 2005). There are some examples of a biopsychosocial approach. These include an increased acknowledgment of individual differences within medicine, particularly in response to medications. There have been attempts to incorporate a biopsychosocial model in treating major mental illness, such as schizophrenia and chronic, debilitating major depression (e.g., the Texas Medication Algorithm Project; Rush et al., 1999, 2003). A comprehensive, biopsychosocial approach has been incorporated in the research and treatment of persistent pain (e.g., Axford, Heron, Ross, &

Victor, 2008; Daniel et al., 2008). Some health maintenance organizations advertise a commitment to facilitating and promoting psychosocial interventions (e.g., lifestyle changes) to facilitate achievement or maintenance of medical treatment goals. However, these initiatives do not appear to reflect medicine as generally practiced in the United States.

Various reasons have been offered for the limited incorporation of a biopsychosocial approach in medicine. These include a lack of medical student training, financial imperatives on new physicians to limit time with patients to maximize billings, and difficulties with implementation due to an inadequate clinical model for assessing psychosocial factors (Weston, 2005). A more disturbing and sobering perspective was offered by Stein (2005), who placed Engel's paper in a historical context of particular interest to psychology:

> Historically, it is essential (and ironic) to remember that by 1977, when George Engel published his celebrated paper in *Science* advancing the BPS [biospsychosocial] model, mainstream American psychiatry was already retreating from, if not repudiating, its brief liaison with behavioral science and becoming increasingly biomedical (largely pharmacological). This cultural lure of what many in American biomedicine call "real science" or "hard science" promised higher status than anything associated with the "softer" behavioral and social sciences. Even practitioners of family medicine– many of whose early leaders embraced an integrative model that encompassed the patient's personality, family, culture, community, and relationship with the physician–have not escaped this intense gravitational pull. (pp. 440–441)

Stein's description of psychiatry's "retreat" into the "hard science" of biomedicine, particularly psychopharmacology, in the 1970s underscores the concerns expressed by psychologists at that time, in particular the imperative to empirically evaluate and validate the efficacy of psychological treatments. Since then, psychopharmacology has become increasingly utilized and popularized as a "quick fix," with the goal of symptom amelioration, often to the exclusion of addressing the root causes of many psychological concerns.

In contrast to medicine, over the past 30–40 years, psychology has increasingly utilized a biopsychosocial perspective in many subdisciplines of research and practice. This has advantageously positioned psychologists to develop treatments that

can be linked to "hard" science by developing theories and constructs based on neurophysiological data and validated with physiological measures, as described below. Additionally, psychology has a long history of developing treatments for promoting health and wellness, in addition to ameliorating or eliminating psychological distress and mental illness. In particular, counseling psychology has developed strong research interests in positive psychology, resilience, and mental health promotion (Lopez & Edwards, 2008; Robbins & Kliewer, 2000). These have been described as primary requirements for a comprehensive approach to mental health and mental health services (Keyes, 2007). Because these foci are preventive and proactive, they have a clear advantage over a deficit-based, narrowly focused medical model. These interests and foci are promoted and furthered by a biopsychosocial approach, examples of which are offered below.

One obstacle to incorporating a biopsychosocial perspective more broadly within psychology and across the sciences may be the explosion of research and data facilitated by technological advances over the last 30 years. This subsequently resulted in the need for increased specialization within fields. A consequence of this is an observed intellectual "silo effect," with suboptimal cross-threading of research and multidisciplinary collaboration. In spite of this, there are particular areas within psychology in which the biopsychosocial model has been evident, such as psychoneuroimmunology, and developmental, rehabilitation, and health psychology (including counseling health psychology; e.g., Chwalisz & Obasi, 2008; Hoffman & Driscoll, 2000; Maltzman, S., 2005).

A Biopsychosocial Approach to Process and Outcome Research

A biopsychosocial model is promising for process and outcome research because it promotes the incorporation of research across disciplines such as epidemiology, neurophysiology, and genetics to generate integrated models of mental and physical health. This integration provides a more detailed and comprehensive explication of causal mechanisms as well as the opportunity to evaluate the effects of moderator and mediator variables. This approach also increases scientific rigor through the integration of biological correlates of observed behavior (Melchert, 2007). This moves psychology from its position as an inherently "soft" science that historically has relied on the imprecise measurement of latent constructs. Such an approach required controlling the effects of moderator and mediator variables that could have explanatory power (Meehl, 1978). This arguably has impaired psychology's ability to adequately evaluate treatment efficacy and effectiveness. Thus, working from a biopsychosocial paradigm has the potential for facilitating the adaptation of efficacious treatments to the needs of diverse clients seen in diverse practice settings.

The biopsychosocial model is consistent with the goals of counseling psychology because it facilitates research and practice in life enhancement strategies, resilience, and flourishing rather than focusing only on ameliorating mental illness. It also is consistent with the historical foundations and values of counseling psychology because it recognizes client values, worldviews, and individual differences as necessary components in conceptualizing research hypotheses and in treatment administration. Thus, a biopsychosocial approach is congruent with counseling psychology in acknowledging the interactive influences among biological, psychological, and social influences on psychosocial functioning and well-being.

BIOLOGICAL INDICATORS OF TREATMENT EFFECTIVENESS

Neuroimaging studies provide one potential, albeit expensive, method for assessing treatment efficacy; some examples of neuroimaging studies are described below. Another promising method for obtaining convergent biological data is the assessment of immune system functioning, which is an indicator of emotional well-being as well as physical health. For example, assessment of proinflammatory cytokines could be one methodological strategy for assessing treatment outcome (Kiecolt-Glaser, Page, Marucha, MacCallum, & Glaser, 1998). The release of stress hormones in response to acute or chronic stressors is associated with anxiety and depression. Therefore, endocrinological measures (e.g., epinephrine levels and cortisol diurnal patterns and levels), described elsewhere in this chapter, are additional examples of biological indicators that could be used to assess treatment outcome (e.g., Kiecolt-Glaser, Bane, Glaser, & Malarkey, 2003; Fisher, Gunnar, Dozier, Bruce, & Pears, 2006). Biological measures offer an opportunity to explicate treatment outcome by serving as direct, objective measures of response to treatment over time; measures for validating less intrusive or less expensive indicators for assessing outcome, such as self-report instruments; and components of a multitrait–multimethod matrix for the validation of latent constructs.

The Contextual Model from a Biopsychosocial Perspective

Wampold and colleagues (e.g., Imel & Wampold, 2008; Wampold, 2001) have proposed a common factors model called the *contextual model*. The Cartesian conceptualization of mind–body dualism is utilized to explain the distinctions between the specific effects of medical treatments on the body (soma) versus the nonspecific, common effects of psychotherapy in general on the mind (psyche). The contextual model describes treatment outcome in counseling and psychotherapy as consistent with a placebo effect. This means that the psychotherapeutic intervention causally contributes to outcome because the client is provided with a culturally and contextually acceptable explanation for the distress and an acceptable rationale and intervention for treatment. The contextual model acknowledges the therapeutic alliance as the means by which psychological interventions exert their effects as placebos. The model hypothesizes that the effectiveness of the alliance is due to the following components: (a) a "healing," therapeutic relationship that (b) is "emotionally charged" and which the client expects will continue to develop over time through the disclosure of personal and sensitive material; (c) the client believes that the therapist is working in the client's best interests and will help the client, at least partly because (d) the therapist offers an explanation for the intervention that is plausible and consistent with the client's worldview and because the intervention (e) includes a "ritual" or procedure that has face validity for the client because it is consistent with the plausible explanation and rationale offered for the intervention and because it requires the active participation of both the client and therapist. Wampold (2001) minimizes the contribution of "neurobiological" processes, describing them as relevant only to understanding the etiology of major mental illness (e.g., schizophrenia); a "neurobiological model" of psychotherapy is described as "reductionistic."

However, the contextual model is limited in its heuristic value for hypothesis testing and ability to suggest methodological strategies. It assumes independent relationships between physical–medical and emotional–psychological functioning (i.e., mind–body dualism). An integration of research from other disciplines, such as neuroscience, provides a more complete understanding of the phenomena of interest and suggests methodologies for testing the contextual model itself.

An example of this is a review of the meta-analysis by Wampold, Minami, Tierney, Baskin, and Bhati (2005) from a cross-disciplinary perspective. This meta-analysis reanalyzed data from an earlier meta-analysis by Hróbjartsson and Gøtzschse (2001). Hróbjartsson and Gøtzschse evaluated the size of the placebo effect comparing active treatment versus placebo treatment versus no-treatment conditions; both psychological and physical disorders were included in their analysis. The goal was to evaluate the clinical utility of the placebo response rather than evaluating its use as a control condition in randomized clinical trials per se. Studies utilizing dichotomous or continuous outcome variables for either subjective and/or objective measures of improvement were included in the analysis. Forty conditions were represented in the studies, including hypertension, asthma, smoking, alcohol abuse, herpes simplex infection, depression, schizophrenia, anxiety, phobia, "fecal soiling," enuresis, epilepsy, carpal tunnel syndrome, Parkinson's disease, Alzheimer's disease, "marital discord," bacterial infection, pain, nausea, and "undiagnosed ailments" (Hróbjartsson & Gøtzschse, 2001). Acute (venipuncture), subacute (postoperative) and chronic (rheumatoid arthritis, fibromyalgia) pain conditions of both nociceptive and neuropathic origin were included.

Hróbjartsson and Gøtzschse (2001) reported no significant effect for placebo in comparison with no treatment, although there was significant heterogeneity across trials. They noted that these results were found for three presenting concerns evaluated in at least three independent studies with dichotomous outcomes (depression, relapse after smoking cessation, and nausea), as well as in studies of five presenting concerns (anxiety, insomnia, asthma, hypertension, and pain) evaluated in at least three independent studies with continuous outcome variables (Hróbjartsson & Gøtzschse, 2001). A statistically significant effect for placebo (vs. no treatment) was found only for pain intensity as measured by visual analogue scale, although the authors did not indicate whether there were differential effects based on pain type (nociceptive or neuropathic; acute vs. persistent/chronic).

Papakostas and Daras (2001), commenting on the Hróbjartsson and Gøtzschse meta-analysis, noted the beliefs held in the medical community regarding which types of concerns are most amenable to a placebo response: "Generally, the presence of anxiety and pain, the involvement of the autonomic nervous system, and the immunobiochemical processes are believed to respond favorably to placebo, whereas hyperacute illnesses (i.e., heart attack), chronic degenerative diseases, or hereditary diseases are expected to resist" (Papakostas & Daras, 2001, pp. 1620–1621). They also noted that "the establishment of predictable placebo response patterns to particular disorders has been proven difficult. . . ." (p. 1620).

Consistent with Wampold et al.'s (2005) position, Papakostas and Daras (2001) described the placebo (nonspecific) response as the patient's response to a healing environment. Where Papkostas and Daras differed from the conclusions later drawn by Wampold et al. is that the former authors stated that a multidisciplinary research approach for elucidating this nonspecific response is "mandatory." They called for the evaluation of moderator and mediator variables in medical practice, similar to the evaluation by psychologists of moderator and mediator variables in process and outcome research. In contrast, Wampold et al. attributed a nonspecific (placebo) response to context and culture and described these effects as the only causal factor contributing to outcome.

Wampold et al. (2005) noted that the implication of Hróbjartsson and Gøtzschse's (2001) meta-analysis was that the placebo effect was expected to have the same potential impact on the outcome measures of interest across trials, irrespective of the presenting concern. They reanalyzed the Hróbjartsson and Gøtzschse data, hypothesizing that the presenting conditions were not equally amenable to a placebo response (i.e., "psychological factors"). As defined by the contextual model, the potential for identifying a "true" placebo response was attenuated in the Hróbjartsson and Gøtzschse meta-analysis because the studies were not differentially weighted based on the relative potential for influence by placebo. For this reason, Wampold et al. classified the studies as "definitely amenable," "possibly amenable," or "not amenable" to psychological factors based on the disorder being treated. The raters were five doctoral students in counseling psychology. The categorization of all the conditions included in the meta-analysis were not included in the paper but the authors listed examples of each category as follows: "definitely amenable": insomnia, depression, and chronic pain; "possibly amenable": acute pain, chemotherapy-induced nausea, and asthma; and "not amenable": bacterial infection and anemia. The authors did not describe the criteria used to determine why, for example, acute pain was "less amenable" to "psychological factors" than was chronic pain or why bacterial infection was deemed "not amenable."

The results of their reanalysis indicated a large placebo effect (Wampold et al., 2005). However, if research from neuroscience and psychoneuroimmunology is considered, the conceptualization of these presenting concerns and their "amenability" to psychological factors likely would be very different, as would the generation of the decision rules for the meta-analysis. For example, both psychological and physiological processes influence the perception of both acute and chronic pain (Basbaum & Jessell, 2000; Finniss, Kaptchuk, Miller, & Benedetti, 2010), and emotional distress influences susceptibility to infection and wound healing time (Kiecolt-Glaser & Glaser, 2002). Therefore, differential amenability to psychological factors becomes a less tenable assumption and rationale for differentially weighting studies. Thus, the original meta-analysis and subsequent reanalysis together serve as an example of the extent to which methodology and results can be influenced by the knowledge base used for theory building and hypothesis testing.

THE CONTEXTUAL MODEL AND THE PLACEBO EFFECT

As noted above, the *placebo effect* is a primary tenet of the contextual model of psychotherapy. It was described by Wampold et al. (2005) as the incidental aspects of the psychological treatment that are common to most, if not all, of these treatments. These incidental components are what contribute causally to a positive outcome, whereas the predefined, specific components of treatment are more or less irrelevant to treatment outcome. However, a cross-disciplinary approach integrating research from neuroscience questions this assumption. There are data from studies utilizing magnetic resonance imaging (MRI), positron emission tomography (PET), and functional MRI (fMRI) that suggest that the placebo effect is similar to the neurophysiological effects of psychotropic medications, and that these effects are distinguishable from the neurophysiological effects of psychotherapy. Some research in this area is described and summarized below.

Goldapple et al. (2004) evaluated glucose metabolism, as assessed by PET at baseline and at the end of 15–20 individualized sessions of CBT. Participants included 11 women and six men with mean scores of 20 (standard deviation = 3) on the 17-item Hamilton Depression Rating Scale (HAM-D). Participants met DSM-III or DSM-IV criteria for

major depressive episode, as assessed by the Structured Clinical Interview. Treatment was conducted by therapists expert in manual-based CBT. Fourteen of the 17 participants completed treatment. Of these, nine participants evidenced a decrease of 50% or more on the HAM-D; the remaining five evidenced a decrease of at least 35% on the HAM-D. The PETs at treatment completion indicated, among other changes, decreases in dorsolateral prefrontal cortex metabolism; the authors did not indicate whether this change was bilateral.

Goldapple et al. (2004) also compared these baseline and endpoint PETs with scans completed in a prior study evaluating the effects of paroxetine (a serotonin-specific reuptake inhibitor; SSRI) in depression, as assessed by the HAM-D. They noted no differences in glucose metabolism between the CBT and paroxetine conditions at baseline. They also noted some similarities in the neuroanatomical sites impacted by CBT and paroxetine, as evidenced by PET at endpoint, although these effects were in opposite directions. Goldapple et al. also reported changes specific to CBT. These included decreased metabolism in the medial frontal, orbital frontal, anterior and dorsal midcingulate areas of the frontal lobe in comparison with medication. They also noted that past evaluations of medication placebo and fluoxetine (another SSRI) suggested that placebo most closely mimicked the response to active medication, in contrast to the effects of CBT reported in their current study (2004).

Benedetti, Mayberg, Wager, Stohler, and Zubieta (2005) summarized research evaluating the effects of fluoxetine in a placebo-controlled study across drug responders/nonresponders and placebo responders/nonresponders over a 6-week period as assessed by PET. The PET scans were acquired at baseline (before treatment) and after 1 and 6 weeks of treatment. Increased glucose metabolism was noted in prefrontal cortex and posterior cingulate gyrus in both the fluoxetine and placebo groups, indicating a similar clinical response in both groups after 6 weeks of treatment. However, the magnitude of change for the fluoxetine-treated group was generally larger in comparison with the placebo group. There also were additional, unique areas impacted by fluoxetine in comparison with placebo. There were no regional changes in activation unique to placebo.

Benedetti et al. (2005) further hypothesized that if the activation of brain areas common to both fluoxetine and placebo were due to a placebo effect, described as "nonspecific psychological effects" rather than a specific active ingredient in fluoxetine, similar but hypothetically more robust changes in the same brain areas would be expected secondary to completion of formal psychological treatment. To test this hypothesis, they compared the PET results from the fluoxetine–placebo study with PET scans from the Goldapple et al. (2004) study evaluating CBT and two studies evaluating interpersonal therapy (IPT; Brody et al., 2001; Martin et al., 2001). Benedetti et al. noted distinct differences in the activation patterns between the medication and placebo PET scans in comparison with the scans from the psychotherapy studies. Cognitive behavioral therapy and IPT were associated with decreases in prefrontal cortical activation, whereas there were additional regional effects specific to each intervention. They also noted that response to CBT was observed in brain regions not affected by medication, including the dorsal anterior cingulate gyrus, and the orbital frontal and medial frontal cortex. These authors concluded: "These findings suggest that the placebo changes are unlikely attributable to passive psychotherapy effects but rather specific effects attributable to the effects of expectation and conditioning facilitated by the psychosocial context of the trial" (p. 10397). They further noted:

> The change patterns seen with these specific psychotherapies provide preliminary evidence refuting the hypothesis that placebo response is mediated by changes in a common antidepressant response pathway. These findings additionally suggest that placebo response is also not the result of uncontrolled, nonspecific psychological treatment effects.
> (Benedetti, Mayberg, Wager, Stohler, & Zubieta, 2005, p. 10398)

The studies by Martin et al. (2001) and Brody et al. (2001) were cited as key data by Benedetti, Mayberg, Wager, Stohler, and Zubieta (2005). However, when they were published, an accompanying commentary by Thase (2001) noted potential confounds and methodological issues. These included nonrandomized group assignment–Brody et al. assigned participants based on their preference and Martin et al. randomized 23 of 28 participants (82%)–and nonequivalence between groups at baseline. The ITP-assigned participants in Brody et al. appeared to have a longer history of depression (onset at an earlier age), more prior treatment, higher baseline symptom severity scores, and a

higher proportion of participants with positive family histories. Thus, group assignment was skewed in favor of medication treatment. Thase also commented that differential efficacy may exist between medication and psychotherapy depending on the nature of the specific symptomatology and the presumed neurophysiology mediating the symptoms.

Kennedy et al. (2007) evaluated glucose metabolism via PET in a randomized trial comparing 16 weeks of venlafaxine, a serotonin-noradrenergic reuptake inhibitor (SNRI) with 16 weeks of CBT. There were 12 participants in each condition. These investigators reported similar response rates in each group: 9/12 in the venlafaxine condition; 7/12 in the CBT condition. Thirteen men and 18 women who met DSM-IV-TR criteria for a major depressive disorder and who were experiencing a current major depressive episode, as assessed by the Structured Clinical Interview and a minimum score of 20 on the 17-item HAM-D, were included. The CBT-assigned participants received weekly individualized outpatient treatment from therapists with extensive experience providing manual-based CBT. Participants in the venlafaxine condition received 75 mg of medication daily for the first 2 weeks; this was titrated up to a target dose of 150–225 mg. Data from five participants in the CBT condition and two participants from the venlafaxine condition were excluded because they failed to complete a second PET scan and at least 8 weeks of treatment. This resulted in a final $N = 12$ in each condition. There were no statistically significant differences on the HAM-D between groups at baseline or endpoint. Responders in both groups exhibited similar decreases in symptomatology, as assessed by HAM-D scores. There also were no statistically significant differences in glucose metabolism between groups at baseline. However, the second PETs in treatment responders evidenced similar changes in glucose metabolism across both groups in comparison with baseline. These included decreased metabolic activity in the orbitofrontal cortex bilaterally, the right dorsomedial prefrontal cortex, and left dorsomedial prefrontal cortex. An increase in glucose metabolism in the right lateral inferior occipital cortex also was observed in responders in both conditions. There also were changes in glucose metabolism that were unique to each condition. Similarly, nonresponders in both conditions evidenced some similar patterns in glucose metabolism at endpoint, yet there also were unique changes specific to each condition. Some overlap also occurred between metabolic changes seen in nonresponders in both groups and the responders in both groups; specifically, decreased glucose metabolism was seen in the left lateral orbital prefrontal cortex (Kennedy et al., 2007).

Synthesizing and interpreting the above data is both complicated and confusing. As noted above, neuroimaging studies are subject to the same methodological concerns that arise in psychological research. These include random assignment and equivalence in baseline measures across conditions. There also is the potential for interpreting averaged results across clients as clinically significant findings when, in fact, they may represent "noise" attributable to measurement error. Additionally, differences in the neurophysiological effects of various psychotropic medications may be attributable to the differences in the neurotransmitters and systems they were designed to target. Similarly, some of the differences observed between CBT and IPT may reflect differential effectiveness mediated by differences in treatment specificity. Alternatively, the very specific, often unilateral neurophysiological effects observed across psychotherapies and medications may be due to methodological differences and may ultimately be minimized with increasing methodological rigor.

Although acknowledging these concerns, there appear to be four emerging trends when summarizing the accumulating data: medication and psychotherapy appear to share some neurophysiological effects associated with effectiveness in treating depression; medication and psychotherapy appear to each have some unique neurophysiological effects associated with treating depression; the neurophysiological effects of placebo appear to be measurable and to mimic, to a lesser degree, the effects of active ingredients in an SSRI; and the neurophysiological effects of placebo appear to be distinct from the neurophysiological effects of psychotherapy.

Consistent with the position of Wampold et al. (2005), Papakostas and Daras (2001), and Craighead, Sheets, and Bjornsson (2005), the neuroimaging studies just described suggest that nonspecific effects are associated with treatment effectiveness for depression. They also support Wampold et al.'s (2005) hypothesis that these nonspecific effects are consistent with a placebo effect. This placebo effect is the client's response to a healing environment and reflects, at least in part, the expectation that treatment will be effective. However, in contrast to the conclusions of Wampold et al. (2005), the neuroimaging data suggest that these nonspecific placebo effects are distinct from the effects of psychotherapy. The neuroimaging data also suggest that the effects of psychotherapy may be specific and distinguishable in comparison with pharmacotherapy. Thus, the data support the goals of process and outcome research in elucidating the contributions of moderator variables and variables associated with the therapeutic process and alliance (e.g., Craighead, Sheets, & Bjornsson, 2005). Additionally, these data question the validity of the major tenet of the contextual model (and of a common factors interpretation in general), which is that treatment efficacy is mediated only by a placebo effect.

PLACEBO AND PROCESS RESEARCH

In the context of process research, the neuroimaging data described by Benedetti, Mayberg, Wager, Stohler, and Zubieta (2005) above suggest that individual differences exist in susceptibility to the influences of the treatment context. These influences appeared to be independent of the specific, active ingredients, suggesting a moderator influence. The data also have implications for evaluating the therapeutic relationship and psychotherapy process in promoting client engagement and preventing premature termination. Historically, the placebo has been conceptualized in negative terms. For example, Papakostas and Daras (2001) noted that placebo has been described as a "deceptive" therapy (p. 1614). However, reconceptualizing placebo as representing the treatment impact of moderator and mediator variables reframes the construct more positively. Placebo may represent the neurophysiological mechanisms by which moderator and mediator variables contribute adjunctively to psychotherapy treatment effectiveness. One goal of process and outcome research might be to delineate how this effect can be maximized.

Assessment of Moderator Variables
Client and Therapist Temperament and Personality

Temperament and personality are two moderator variables that may impact treatment process and outcome. *Temperament* is defined for this discussion as stable, physiologically based individual differences in emotion, attention, and arousal that essentially are present from birth (Strelau, 1994). Some researchers include individual differences in motivation as another aspect of temperament (e.g., Bates, 1989, as cited in Rothbart, Derryberry, & Posner, 1994), whereas others (e.g., Strelau, 1994) include motivation among the broader range of differences associated with personality. Both temperament and personality are viewed as enduring characteristics across the lifespan. Eastern European and Russian investigators have historically focused on theories of temperament. This research can be traced back to Pavlov's proposed typology based on his observations of stable, enduring individual differences in conditional learning and response inhibition among dogs in his laboratory (Teplov, 1964). However, some researchers appear to have used the terms "temperament" and "personality" interchangeably (e.g., Gray, 1964). Western psychologists have focused primarily on the construct of personality, typically when studying individual differences in adult humans. "Temperament" is referenced when studying biologically based differences in infants and young children, particularly individual differences in reactivity to social stimuli and levels of arousal (e.g., Gunnar, 1994).

There exists fairly substantive and robust research support for the construction of *personality* as consisting of five factors: neuroticism, extraversion, openness to experience, agreeableness, and conscientiousness (e.g., McCrae & Costa, 1997). These five factors have been confirmed cross-culturally. Consistent gender differences also have been identified cross-culturally, with the magnitude of the difference increasing with increases in measured gender equality and national health and wealth (Costa, Terracciano, & McCrae, 2001; McCrae et al., 2004; Schmitt, Realo, Vocacek, & Allik, 2008).

Individual differences in temperament and personality can moderate the therapeutic process. For example, Beutler, Rocco, Moleiro, and Talebi (2001) reviewed the literature on the moderating and mediating effects of trait-like resistance on treatment. From a biopsychosocial perspective of emotion regulation (described below), one hypothesis is that observed resistance is a reflection of increased emotional reactivity mediated by chronic hypervigilance and hyperarousal to current or past stressors. This interpretation is supported by data indicating that levels of stress hormones have been associated with a decreased threshold for aggressive behavior, as well as a decreased ability to attend, concentrate, learn, self-monitor, and self-reflect (Dishion & Connell, 2006; Lewis, Granic, & Lamm, 2006). This impairs the client's ability to address treatment goals due to a compromised ability to attend, concentrate, and engage in functions mediated by the prefrontal cortex. Thus, the client is less able to process the material or develop insight.

Capacity for insight is a potential moderator variable, but also potentially a mediator variable in psychotherapy. The capacity for insight and self-understanding has been associated with positive treatment outcome (Hill & Knox, 2008). If this capacity moderates the ability to benefit from treatment, psychotherapeutic interventions targeted to increase these abilities could potentiate positive treatment outcome. Because the ability to utilize insight and self-reflection is inversely related to emotional reactivity, as described above, treatments or process strategies that target emotional reactivity as the initial treatment goal would be an important initial step toward addressing and achieving longer-term, designated treatment goals.

Identifying clients with impaired capacity for insight secondary to increased emotional reactivity could theoretically be an important part of the assessment process. This hypothesis is consistent with the conclusions of Beutler, Rocco, Moleiro, and Talebi (2001), which suggested nondirective treatment is more effective with resistant, reactive clients in comparison with directive treatments. Addressing the client's needs in such a hierarchical manner would hypothetically require longer-term psychotherapy. Thus, increased emotional reactivity and a requisite hierarchical therapy model might be two predictors of psychotherapy length.

Attachment and Self-regulation: Implications for Process and Outcome Research

A recent and significant trend in counseling psychology is the interest in attachment constructs, their implications regarding the client's and/or therapist's attachment style, and these effects on the therapeutic alliance.

Childhood Attachment Styles

The quality of the primary attachment relationship developed in childhood has been associated with the quality of later interpersonal peer relationships. Bernier and Dozier (2002) cited research indicating that preschoolers with secure attachment histories are more empathic, more effective at conflict resolution, better at accurately interpreting social cues, and initiate more play than do peers with other types of attachment histories. Additionally, children with avoidant attachment histories exhibited more hostility, bullying, and scapegoating behaviors in comparison with other children, children with resistant attachment histories were more likely to be victimized by peers, and children with disorganized attachment as assessed in infancy were more likely to aggress against peers in preschool and into later childhood (Bernier & Dozier, 2002). Therefore, the data suggest that the attachment developed in infancy and early childhood may be reflective of enduring relationship patterns across childhood and potentially into adult peer relationships.

Childhood Development of Self-regulatory Systems

Development of the primary attachment relationship appears to be causally related to the development of self-regulatory systems and resilience. Regulation of emotional reactivity and impulsivity is gradual and is not fully developed until late adolescence or young adulthood. Development of self-regulation is moderated, in part, by the child's resilience. *Resilience* refers to protective factors that reduce poor outcomes under conditions of adversity and risk (Greenberg, 2006) and has been described as positive adaptation in the face of severe adversity (Sameroff & Rosenblum, 2006). An individual's resilience reflects three interactive influences: intraindividual (temperament, cognitive abilities), quality of social relationships (e.g., the relationship with the primary caregiver, and the quality of the broader environment, such as school and neighborhood (Greenberg, 2006). Intraindividual resilience refers to the ability to self-regulate in two broad areas. *Emotion self-regulation* is the ability to cope adaptively and inhibit inappropriate emotional/behavioral responses to stressors. *Cognitive self-regulation* is the ability to focus attention and concentration to facilitate learning (Dishion & Connell, 2006).

Children exposed to proximal adversity, such as physical abuse, sexual abuse, emotional abuse, and/or neglect are at higher risk for neurodevelopmental delays in emotion regulation and associated cognitive regulation. The experience of such severe adversities by young children has been reliably related to disrupted and atypical diurnal cortisol levels. These atypical cortisol patterns reflect dysregulation of the hypothalamic-pituitary-adrenal cortex (HPA) axis that mediates the response to stressors and the release of stress-related hormones (Fisher, Gunnar, Dozier, Bruce, & Pears, 2006). Dysregulation of the HPA axis impacts the neurophysiological functioning of areas with bidirectional communication with the HPA axis including the amygdala, orbitofrontal cortex, and medial prefrontal cortex.

Functions mediated by these structures and affected by chronic stressors include: the degree to which emotional significance is attached to stimuli, particularly social stimuli; the ability to avoid or inhibit responses in anticipation of negative consequences; the ability to select appropriately among competing choices; the ability to self-monitor performance; and the ability to learn new material (Lewis, Granic, & Lamm, 2006). Emotion and cognitive regulation are inextricably intertwined. When a child with emotion dysregulation perceives a threat, executive functions mediated by the prefrontal cortex are decreased. Arousal and vigilance, mediated by the limbic and autonomic nervous systems, predominate. Individuals who have experienced chronic stressors and adversity develop a lower threshold for this chronic hyperarousal. They are more likely to misperceive social stimuli and react in maladaptive ways. Thus, a lowered threshold for arousal and the experience of chronic hyperarousal are associated with difficulties in attention, memory, and learning (Mayes, 2006).

What is significant from an attachment perspective is that abuse and neglect, as well as removal from the home if that is necessary to protect the child, represent disruptions in relationships with a primary caregiver (Fisher et al., 2006).

Childhood Interventions for Promoting Self-regulation and Coping

Coping has been defined as the conscious, mindful effort to regulate the emotional, cognitive, behavioral, physiological, and environmental impact of stressors or adversity (Compas, 2006). Coping is an executive function mediated by the prefrontal cortex. Factors that promote emotion regulation also promote coping. Two interventions evaluated for infants, toddlers, and preschoolers in foster care were designed to target the neurodevelopment of emotion regulation and promote coping. These interventions focused on caregiver interactive style with infants and toddlers in one study, and preschoolers in another. These interventions emphasized the role of the foster caregiver as a buffer for the child's experience of adversity. The primary hypotheses were that positive interactive experiences can impact and modify the neural bases of self-regulation, and that these modifications can reverse negative effects of adversity (Fisher, Gunnar, Dozier, Bruce, & Pears, 2006). In other words, the caregiver provided the treatment through the primary social relationship with the child. The interactive style was designed to facilitate the child's ability to attach adaptively. The goal was to promote the caregiver's ability to respond to the distress signals of infants and toddlers, even when the signals were unclear or ambiguous; respond in a sensitive and respectful style; and follow the child's lead. Caregivers of preschoolers were supported to respond in a consistent manner and to respond contingently to the child's behavior by positively reinforcing positive behavior and setting limits for negative behavior (Fisher et al., 2006). Evaluation of these interventions indicated normalized HPA function, as assessed by salivary cortisol levels (Fisher et al., 2006).

Implications of Self-regulation Research for Adult Counseling and Psychotherapy

The ability to self-regulate has been researched primarily in infants, toddlers, and preschoolers who have experienced abuse and neglect and are therefore at higher risk for life-long mental health concerns. However, there are data suggesting that even experimentally induced stressors can have profound effects in adults. These effects are similar to the cognitive dysregulation and difficulties with executive functioning described in dysregulated children. Whitson and Galinsky (2008) summarized six studies, each of which evaluated the effects of perceived lack of control on illusory pattern perception. In each study, adult participants who were in the lack-of-control condition were statistically more likely to perceive patterns in stimuli or behavior when, in fact, none existed. An opportunity to participate in a standardized self-affirmation procedure after the lack-of-control manipulation but prior to stimulus exposure negated the effects of the lack-of-control manipulation. Whitson and Galinsky interpreted these data as indicating a strong, innate motivation in humans to make sense of their perceptual world, and that the need to create organization increases when individuals perceive a loss of control. Thus, perceived lack of control can result in an increased probability to misperceive sensory and social stimuli. The authors noted that these results have implications for psychotherapeutic processes and treatments.

The simple addition of a self-affirmation procedure could be viewed as consistent with the caregiver interventions reported by Fisher, Gunnar, Dozier, Bruce, and Pears (2006). Taken together, these data have implications for process and outcome research, particularly regarding the role of the therapeutic relationship.

EMOTION REGULATION AS A TREATMENT GOAL

As discussed above, decreasing emotional reactivity to social stimuli and increasing emotion regulation hypothetically may be an appropriate treatment goal for some clients. For example, endocrinological data (stress hormone levels) predicted marital satisfaction and marriage dissolution 10 years later in a sample of newlyweds married 1 year or less at the time of baseline assessment (Kiecolt-Glaser, Bane, Glaser, & Malarkey, 2003). Marital interactive style, personality, and marital satisfaction at baseline were not related to marital status 10 years later. Exaggerated daytime and nighttime fluctuations in epinephrine levels at baseline predicted marital status; individuals with statistically significant higher daytime levels and lower nighttime levels were more likely to be divorced 10 years later in comparison with individuals whose levels did not vary as widely. These data suggest that emotional reactivity may be an important moderator variable. When considered with the data reported by Dishion and Connell (2006) and Lewis, Granic, and Lamm (2006) regarding the relationship between stress hormones and a decreased threshold for aggressive behavior, these data suggest that modification of emotion regulation may be an appropriate treatment goal in and of itself.

The Therapeutic Alliance from an Attachment Perspective

Henry, Schacht, and Strupp (1990) conceptualized the therapeutic alliance from the theoretical perspective of interpersonal introjection. The *introject* is the internalization of the manner in which one was treated by others in early interpersonal relationships. Although stable, the introject is modifiable over the life span. The therapeutic alliance, as an interpersonal process between client and therapist, is hypothesized by these investigators as reflecting the therapist's past treatment by important others. Expanding on this conceptualization, Hilliard, Henry, and Strupp (2000) attempted to evaluate a model in which the therapist's and client's early parental relationships were hypothesized to impact treatment outcome, directly and/or indirectly, through the therapeutic process. These authors reported that data provided tentative support for these hypotheses. Based on self-report, clients' early parental relations appeared to directly and indirectly influence outcome, whereas the therapists' self-reported early parental relationships appeared to directly influence the therapy process. Meyer and Pilkonis (2001) reviewed research assessing the relationships among attachment styles of adult clients and therapists and their moderating effects on the therapeutic process. Attachment styles were assessed with either semistructured interviews, such as the Adult Attachment Interview (AAI), or self-report instruments. The AAI is based on Bowlby's research on infant attachment and Ainsworth's research on adult attachment style as assessed via direct observation of infant–parent interaction (Main, Hesse, & Goldwyn, 2008). It is a qualitative measure consisting of 20 questions that include, but are not limited to, the assessment of the respondent's perceptions (thoughts and feelings) of their own experience with primary caregivers, how these experiences affected adult personality, and the experience of major losses (Main, Hesse, & Goldwyn, 2008; Steele & Steele, 2008). Meyer and Pilkonis (2001) concluded that both client and therapist attachment styles, based on childhood attachment relationships, likely are important moderators of the therapeutic process. This conclusion was echoed by Eagle (2006), who also reviewed attachment research and noted that client and therapist attachment styles may moderate both the therapeutic process and outcome.

THE THERAPEUTIC ALLIANCE AND THE REAL RELATIONSHIP

Theoretically, increasing emotion and cognitive regulation could be achieved by addressing the client's preestablished attachment style. Attaining this goal could be a prerequisite for addressing other presenting concerns that create emotional distress or psychosocial dissatisfaction for the client. This implies that the therapeutic relationship becomes a corrective experience, similarly to the caregiver interventions described by the Fisher, Gunnar, Dozier, Bruce, and Pears (2006) study.

Gelso and colleagues have described the concept of the *real relationship* as the underlying connection between therapist and client. It consists of two basic elements, genuineness and realism, each of which can vary along the dimensions of magnitude and valance (Gelso & Samstag, 2008). *Genuineness* is defined as the ability to be present and authentic with others, whereas *realism* pertains to "the experiencing or perceiving the other in ways that befit him or her, rather than as projections of wished for or feared others (i.e., transference)" (Gelso & Samstag, 2008, p. 276). These investigators hypothesized that it is the real relationship, rather than the therapeutic alliance, that mediates treatment outcome. This perspective may be viewed from an attachment perspective as the therapist's ability to respond to the client's attachment needs (Eagle, 2006). This ability could hypothetically be a core requirement of the therapeutic process. Failure to

achieve this relationship could be predictive of premature termination, alliance rupture, and/or resistance to the therapeutic process. The AAI, or a self-report instrument validated against the AAI and/or biological indicators of stress reactivity, might be a useful approach for assessing a client's attachment style and, potentially, ability to emotionally regulate. This information could inform the therapeutic relationship as well as identify whether short-term goals should include decreasing emotional reactivity and the promotion of emotion regulation.

Resilience, Positive Psychology, and Psychosocial Flourishing

Counseling psychologists have been interested in the constructs of attachment and resilience to further an understanding of the emotionally healthy, self-actualized adult (Lopez, F. & Brennan, 2000). Understanding the client's presentation from an emotion and cognitive regulation perspective supports a strengths-based approach, consistent with the tenets of positive psychology (Lopez, S. & Kerr, 2006) and the values of counseling psychology. Secure attachment promotes resilience within the context of significant adversity and the ability to mindfully cope with acute and chronic stressors. Yet, attachment style alone is insufficient to explain why some individuals flourish in spite of significant adversity, why some individuals appear to succumb to the effects of adversity, or why some later overcome these effects and function well.

Assessment of moderator variables such as temperament, personality, and emotion and cognitive regulation, in addition to attachment style, could elucidate what core variables contribute to psychological resilience and psychosocial flourishing. Complex interaction effects appear to exist among these variables and the social and environmental factors impacting a particular individual (Greenberg, 2006; Werner, 2005). The emerging field of behavioral epigenetics, which explores the effects of social experience on neurobiological processes across the lifespan, may elucidate these interactions (e.g., Bagot & Meaney, 2010; Champagne & Curley, 2009; Curley, Jensen, Mashoodh, & Champagne, 2011). Whether, and to what extent, emotion regulation can be moderated via the therapeutic relationship remains an empirical question. The degree to which emotion regulation reflects a stable congenital individual difference in temperament may be the extent to which self-regulation is modifiable via the therapeutic relationship or specific treatment components.

Data discussed in this chapter suggest that the ability to utilize executive functions, such as the capacity for insight, empathy, the conscious allocation of attentional resources for planning, and the ability to self-evaluate performance, are potential core components necessary for utilizing adaptive coping strategies. Additionally, the data suggest that strategies for maximizing self-regulation, resilience, perceived control, and mindful coping may promote self-actualization and flourishing. These hypotheses are supported by data from longitudinal studies described by Werner and colleagues (as summarized in Werner, 2005).

Conclusion

This chapter traced the development of process and outcome research over the past 30 years. This research is grounded in the premise that all clients are entitled to the highest quality of psychological treatment available for addressing their particular concerns. Counseling psychology historically has been in the forefront of process and outcome research. A cross-disciplinary, biospsychosocial perspective has significant heuristic value for explicating treatment effectiveness, as well as moderator and mediator variables of the counseling and psychotherapy process. The potential applications of the biopsychosocial perspective described in this chapter suggest a more positive prognosis for facilitating positive change and personal growth in individuals who have experienced severe adversity than that voiced by Arbona and Coleman (2008). In their review of the literature on risk and resilience, Arbona and Coleman commented that perhaps only policy and community-level changes that reduce or eliminate the root causes of social adversity would be sufficient to facilitate resilience and adaptive coping in severely impacted individuals.

As a qualitative extension and complement to the amelioration of emotional distress and dysregulation, counseling psychology promotes mental health flourishing from a strengths-based perspective. A strengths-based perspective is supported by a cross-disciplinary biopsychosocial model that emphasizes human potential. The constructs of resilience and attachment offer a paradigm for integrating cross-disciplinary research to explicate psychological flourishing from a resilience perspective.

Future Directions

The biopsychosocial model emphasizes a cross-disciplinary approach to research. Ideally, a multi-disciplinary team of researchers would collaborate on design and methodology, applying the expertise of each member. That is not often feasible in many environments, particularly those not associated with a university. However, what is feasible is the integration of cross-disciplinary research when conceptualizing and developing research hypotheses, thus informing the counseling psychologist's decision making regarding design and methodology. Future directions in research suggested in this chapter include:

• Evaluating temperament and personality as moderator variables in outcome research
• Evaluating client resistance in psychotherapy as a manifestation of emotional reactivity mediated by chronic hypervigilance and hyperarousal
• Exploring the relationship between capacity for insight and emotional reactivity
• Testing a hierarchical therapy model based on the client's pretreatment level of emotional reactivity
• Validating self-report instruments for the assessment of treatment outcome against biological markers
• Exploring components of executive functioning as moderators of psychosocial flourishing.

References

Ahn, H., & Wampold, B. E. (2001). Where oh where are the specific ingredients? A meta-analysis of component studies in counseling and psychotherapy. *Journal of Counseling Psychology, 48*, 251–257.

Alcorn, J. D. (1991). Counseling psychology and health applications. *The Counseling Psychologist, 19*, 325–341.

Altmaier, E. M. (1991). Research and practice roles for counseling psychologists in health care settings. *The Counseling Psychologist, 19*, 342–364.

Anderson, E. M., & Lambert, M. J. (2001). A survival analysis of clinically significant change in outpatient psychotherapy. *Journal of Clinical Psychology, 57*, 875–888.

APA Presidential Task Force on Evidence-Based Practice. (2006). Evidence-based practice in psychology. *American Psychologist, 61*, 271–285.

Arbona, C., & Coleman, N. (2008). Risk and resilience. In S. D. Brown, & R. W. Lent (Eds.), *Handbook of counseling psychology* (4th ed., pp. 483–499). New York: John Wiley & Sons.

Axford, J., Heron, C., Ross, F., & Victor, C. R. (2008). Management of knee osteoarthritis in primary care: Pain and depression are the major obstacles. *Journal of Psychosomatic Research, 64*, 461–467.

Bagot, R. C., & Meaney, M. J. (2010). Epigenetics and the biological basis of gene × environment interactions. *Journal of the American Academy of Child & Adolescent Psychiatry, 49*, 752–771. doi:10.1016/j.jaac.2010.06.001.

Baldwin, S. A., Berkeljon, A., Atkins, D. C., Olsen, J. A., & Nielsen, S. L. (2009). Rates of change in naturalistic psychotherapy: Contrasting Dose-Effect and Good-Enough level models of change. *Journal of Consulting and Clinical Psychology, 77*, 203–211.

Basbaum, A. I., & Jessell, T. M. (2000). The perception of pain. In E. R. Kandel, J. H. Schwartz, & T. M. Jessell (Eds.), *Principles of neural science* (pp. 472–491). New York: McGraw-Hill.

Benedetti, F., Mayberg, H. S., Wager, T. D., Stohler, C. S., Zubieta, J.-K. (2005). Neurobiological mechanisms of the placebo effect. *The Journal of Neuroscience, 25*, 10390–10402. doi:10.1523/JNEUROSCI.3458-05.2005.

Bernal, G., & Scharron-Del-Rió, M. R. (2001). Are empirically supported treatments valid for ethnic minorities? Toward an alternative approach for treatment research. *Cultural Diversity and Ethnic Minority Psychology, 7*, 328–342.

Bernier, A., & Dozier, M. (2002). The client-counselor match and the corrective emotional experience: Evidence from interpersonal and attachment research. *Psychotherapy: Theory/Research/Practice/Training, 39*, 32–43.

Beutler, L. E. (1998). Identifying empirically supported treatments: What if we didn't? *Journal of Consulting and Clinical Psychology, 66*, 113–120.

Beutler, L. E. (2002). The dodo bird is extinct. *Clinical Psychology: Science and Practice, 9*, 30–34.

Beutler, L. E., Rocco, F., Moleiro, C. M., & Talebi, H. (2001). Resistance. *Psychotherapy, 38*, 431–436.

Biderman, A., Yeheskel, A., & Herman, J. (2005). The biopsychosocial model–have we made any progress since 1977?. *Families, Systems, & Health, 23*, 379–386.

Borckardt, J. J., Nash, M. R., Murphy, M. D., Moore, M., Shaw, D., & O'Neil, P. (2008). Clinical practice as natural laboratory for psychotherapy research: A guide to case-based time-series analysis. *American Psychologist, 63*, 77–95.

Borkovec, T. D., & Costello, E. (1993). Efficacy of applied relaxation and cognitive-behavioral therapy in the treatment of generalized anxiety disorder. *Journal of Consulting and Clinical Psychology, 61*, 611–619. doi:10.1037/0022-006X.61.4.611.

Brody, A. L., Saxena, S., Stoessel, P., Gillies, L. A., Fairbanks, L. A., Alborzian, S., et al. (2001). Regional brain metabolic changes in patients with major depression treated with either paroxetine or interpersonal therapy. *Archives of General Psychiatry, 58*, 631–640.

Bronfenbrenner, U. (1977). Toward an experimental ecology of human development. *American Psychologist, 32*, 513–531.

Chambless, D. L. (2002). Identification of empirically supported counseling psychology interventions: Commentary. *The Counseling Psychologist, 30*, 302–308.

Chambless, D. L., & Hollon, S. D. (1998). Defining empirically supported therapies. *Journal of Consulting and Clinical Psychology, 66*, 7–18.

Chambless, D. L., & Ollendick, T. H. (2001). Empirically supported psychological interventions: Controversies and evidence. *Annual Review of Psychology, 52*, 685–716.

Champagne, F. A., & Curley, J. P. (2009). Epigenetic mechanisms mediating the long-term effects of maternal care on development. *Neuroscience and Biobehavioral Reviews, 33*, 593–600. doi:10.1016/j.neubiorev.2007.10.009.

Chrisler, J. C., & O'Hea, E. L. (2000). Gender, culture, and autoimmune disorders. In R. M. Eisler, & M. Hersen (Eds.), *Handbook of gender, culture, and health* (pp. 321–342). New York: Lawrence Erlbaum.

Chwalisz, K., & Obasi, E. (2008). Promoting health and preventing and reducing disease. In S. D. Brown, & R. W. Lent (Eds.), *Handbook of counseling psychology* (4th ed., pp. 517–534). New York: John Wiley & Sons.

Cloninger, C. R. (1987). Neurogenetic adaptive mechanisms in alcoholism. *Science, 236*, 410–416.

Committee on Standards for Providers of Psychological Services (1977). Standards for providers of psychological services. *American Psychologist, 32*, 495–505. doi:10.1037/0003-066X.32.6.495.

Compas, B. E. (2006). Psychobiological processes of stress and coping: Implications for resilience in children and adolescents–Comments on the papers of Romeo & McEwen and Fisher et al. In B. M. Lester, A. Masten, & B. McEwen (Eds.), *Annals of the New York Academy of Sciences: Vol. 1094. Resilience in Children* (pp. 226–234). New York: New York Academy of Sciences.

Corning, A. F., & Malofeeva, E. V. (2004). The application of survival analysis to the study of psychotherapy termination. *Journal of Counseling Psychology, 51*, 354–367.

Costa, P. T., Jr., Terracciano, A., & McCrae, R. R. (2001). Gender differences in personality traits across cultures: Robust and surprising findings. *Journal of Personality and Social Psychology, 81*, 322–331.

Craighead, W. E., Sheets, E. S., & Bjornsson, A. S. (2005). Specificity and nonspecificity in psychotherapy. *Clinical Psychology: Science and Practice, 12*, 189–193.

Crits-Christoph, P. (1997). Limitations of the Dodo bird verdict and the role of clinical trials in psychotherapy research: Comment on Wampold et al. (1997). *Psychological Bulletin, 122*, 216–220.

Cummings, N. A. (1977). The anatomy of psychotherapy under national health insurance. *American Psychologist, 32*, 711–718.

Curley, J. P., Jensen, C. L., Mashoodh, R., & Champagne, F. A. (2011). Social influences on neurobiology and behavior: Epigenetic effects during development. *Psychoneuroendocrinology, 36*, 352–371. doi: 10.1016/j.psyneuen.2010.06.005

Cutuli, J. J., Chaplin, T. M., Gillham, J. E., Reivich, K. J., & Seligman, M. E. P. (2006). Preventing co-occurring depression symptoms in adolescents with conduct problems: The Penn resiliency program. In B. M. Lester, A. Masten, & B. McEwen (Eds.), *Annals of the New York Academy of Sciences: Vol. 1094. Resilience in children* (pp. 282–286). New York: New York Academy of Sciences.

Daniel, H. C., Narewska, J., Serpell, M., Hoggart, B., Johnson, R., & Rice, A. S C. (2008). Comparison of psychological and physical function in neuropathic pain and nociceptive pain: Implications for cognitive behavioral pain management programs. *European Journal of Pain, 12*, 731–741.

Dishion, T. J., & Connell, A. (2006). Adolescents' resilience as a self-regulatory process: Promising themes for linking intervention with developmental science. In B. M. Lester, A. Masten, & B. McEwen (Eds.), *Annals of the New York Academy of Sciences: Vol. 1094. Resilience in children* (pp. 125–138). New York: New York Academy of Sciences.

Eagle, M. N. (2006). Attachment, psychotherapy, and assessment: A commentary. *Journal of Consulting and Clinical Psychology, 74*, 1086–1097.

Engel, G. L. (1977). The need for a new medical model: A challenge for biomedicine. *Science, 196*, 129–136.

Enoch, M.-A. (2006). Genetic and environmental influences on the development of alcoholism: Resilience vs. risk.

In B. M. Lester, A. Masten, & B. McEwen (Eds.), *Annals of the New York Academy of Sciences: Vol. 1094. Resilience in children* (pp. 193–201). New York: New York Academy of Sciences.

Finniss, D. G., Kaptchuk, T. J., Miller, F., & Benedetti, F. (2010). Biological, clinical, and ethical advances of placebo effects. *The Lancet, 375,* 686–695. doi:10.1016/S0140-6736(09)61706-2.

Fisher, P. A., Gunnar, M. R., Dozier, M., Bruce, J., & Pears, K. C. (2006). Effects of therapeutic interventions for foster children on behavioral problems, caregiver attachment, and stress regulatory neural systems. In B. M. Lester, A. Masten, & B. McEwen (Eds.), *Annals of the New York Academy of Sciences: Vol. 1094. Resilience in children* (pp. 215–225). New York: New York Academy of Sciences.

Gelso, C. J., & Samstag, L. W. (2008). A tripartite model of the therapeutic relationship. In S. D. Brown, & R. W. Lent (Eds.), *Handbook of counseling psychology* (4th ed., pp. 267–283). New York: Wiley and Sons.

Goldapple, K., Segal, Z., Garson, C., Lau, M., Bieling, P., Kennedy, S., & Mayberg, H. (2004). Modulation of cortical-limbic pathways in major depression. *Archives of General Psychiatry, 61,* 34–41.

Goldfried, M. R., & Eubanks-Carter, C. (2004). On the need for a new psychotherapy research paradigm: Comment on Westen, Novotny, and Thompson-Brenner (2004). *Psychological Bulletin, 130,* 669–673.

Gray, J. A. (1964). Strength of the nervous system as a dimension of personality in man. In J. A. Gray (Ed.), *Pavlov's Typology* (pp. 157–287). Oxford, England: Pergamon Press Ltd.

Greenberg, M. T. (2006). Promoting resilience in children and youth: Preventive interventions and their interface with neuroscience. In B. M. Lester, A. Masten, & B. McEwen (Eds.), *Annals of the New York Academy of Sciences: Vol. 1094. Resilience in children* (pp. 139–150). New York: New York Academy of Sciences.

Gunnar, M. R. (1994). Psychoendocrine studies of temperament and stress in early childhood: Expanding current models. In J. E. Bates, & T. D. Wachs (Eds.), *Temperament: Individual differences at the interface of biology and behavior* (pp. 175–198). Washington, DC: American Psychological Association.

Henry, W. P., Schacht, T. E., & Strupp, H. H. (1990). Patient and therapist introject, interpersonal process, and differential treatment outcome. *Journal of Consulting and Clinical Psychology, 58,* 768–774. doi: 10.1037/0022-006X.58.6.768.

Hill, C. E., & Corbett, M. M. (1993). A perspective on the history of process and outcome research in counseling psychology. *Journal of Counseling Psychology, 40,* 3–24.

Hill, C. E., & Knox, S. (2008). Facilitating insight in counseling and psychotherapy. In S. D. Brown, & R. W. Lent (Eds.), *Handbook of counseling psychology* (4th ed., pp. 284–302). New York: Wiley and Sons.

Hill, C. E., & Williams, E. N. (2000). The process of individual therapy. In S. D. Brown, & R. W. Lent (Eds.), *Handbook of counseling psychology* (3rd ed., pp. 670–710). New York: Wiley and Sons.

Hilliard, R. B., Henry, W. P., & Strupp, H. H. (2000). An interpersonal model of psychotherapy: Linking patient and therapist developmental history, therapeutic process, and types of outcome. *Journal of Consulting and Clinical Psychology, 68,* 125–133.

Hoffman, M. A., & Driscoll, J. M. (2000). Health promotion and disease prevention: A concentric biopsychosocial model of health status. In S. D. Brown, & R. W. Lent (Eds.), *Handbook of counseling psychology* (3rd ed., 532–567). New York: Wiley.

Howard, K. I., Krause, M. S., Saunders, S. M., & Kopta, S.M. (1997). Trials and tribulations in the meta-analysis of treatment differences: Comment on Wampold et al. (1997). *Psychological Bulletin, 122,* 221–225.

Hróbjartsson, A., & Gøtzsche, P. (2001). Is the placebo powerless? An analysis of clinical trials comparing placebo with no treatment. *New England Journal of Medicine, 344,* 1594–1602.

Hunsley, J., & Lee, C. M. (2007). Research-informed benchmarks for psychological treatments: Efficacy studies, effectiveness studies, and beyond. *Professional Psychology: Research and Practice, 38,* 21–33.

Imel, Z. E., & Wampold, B. E. (2008). The importance of treatment and the science of common factors in psychotherapy. In S. D. Brown, & R. W. Lent (Eds.), *Handbook of Counseling Psychology* (4th ed., pp. 249–266). New York: John Wiley & Sons.

Kazdin, A. E. (2005). Treatment outcomes, common factors, and continued neglect of mechanisms of change. *Clinical Psychology: Science and Practice, 12,* 184–188.

Kazdin, A. E. (2007). Mediators and mechanisms of change in psychotherapy research. *Annual Review of Clinical Psychology, 3,* 1–27.

Kazdin, A. E. (2008). Evidence-based treatment and practice: New opportunities to bridge clinical research and practice, enhance the knowledge base, and improve patient care. *American Psychologist, 63,* 146–159.

Kendall, P. C. (1998). Empirically supported psychological therapies. *Journal of Consulting and Clinical Psychology, 66,* 3–6.

Kendall, P. C., & Beidas, R. S. (2007). Smoothing the trail for dissemination of evidence-based practices for youth: Flexibility within fidelity. *Professional Psychology: Research and Practice, 38,* 13–20.

Kennedy, S. H., Konarski, J. Z., Segal, A. V., Lau, M. A., Bieling, P. J., McIntyre, R. S., & Mayberg, H. S. (2007). Differences in brain glucose metabolism between responders to CBT and venlafaxine in a 16-week randomized controlled trial. *American Journal of Psychiatry, 164,* 778–788.

Keyes, C. L. M. (2007). Promoting and protecting mental health as flourishing: A complementary strategy for improving national mental health. *American Psychologist, 62,* 95–108.

Kiecolt-Glaser, J. K., & Glaser, R. (2002). Depression and immune function: Central pathways to morbidity and mortality. *Journal of Psychosomatic Research, 53,* 873–876.

Kiecolt-Glaser, J. K., Bane, C., Glaser, R., & Malarkey, W. B. (2003). Love, marriage, and divorce: Newlyweds' stress hormones foreshadow relationship changes. *Journal of Consulting and Clinical Psychology, 71,* 176–188.

Kiecolt-Glaser, J. K., Page, G. G., Marucha, P. T., MacCallum, R. C., & Glaser, R. (1998). Psychological influences on surgical recovery: Perspectives from psychoneuroimmunology. *American Psychologist, 53,* 1209–1218.

Lam, A. G., & Sue, S. (2001). Client diversity. *Psychotherapy, 38,* 479–486.

Lambert, M. J. (2005). Early response in psychotherapy: Further evidence for the importance of common factors rather than "placebo effects." *Journal of Clinical Psychology, 61,* 855–869.

Lambert, M. J., Hansen, N. B., & Finch, A. E. (2001). Patient-focused research: Using patient outcome data to enhance treatment effects. *Journal of Consulting and Clinical Psychology*, *69*, 159–172.

Laurenceau, J.-P., Hayes, A. M., & Feldman, G. C. (2007). Some methodological and statistical issues in the study of change processes in psychotherapy. *Clinical Psychology Review*, *27*, 682–695.

Lewis, M. D., Granic, I., & Lamm, C. (2006). Behavioral differences in aggressive children linked with neural mechanisms of emotion regulation. In B. M. Lester, A. Masten, & B. McEwen (Eds.), *Annals of the New York Academy of Sciences: Vol. 1094. Resilience in children* (pp. 164–177). New York: New York Academy of Sciences.

Lopez, F. G., & Brennan, K. A. (2000). Dynamic processes underlying adult attachment organization: Toward an attachment theoretical perspective on the healthy and effective self. *Journal of Counseling Psychology*, *47*, 283–300.

Lopez, S. J., & Edwards, L. M. (2008). The interface of counseling psychology and positive psychology: Assessing and promoting strengths. In S. D. Brown, & R. W. Lent (Eds.), *Handbook of counseling psychology* (4th ed., pp. 86–99). New York: John Wiley & Sons.

Lopez, S. J., & Kerr, B. A. (2006). An open source approach to creating positive psychological practice: A comment on Wong's strengths-centered therapy. *Psychotherapy: Theory, Research, Practice, Training*, *43*, 147–150.

Lutz, W., Lambert, M. J., Harmon, S. C., Tschitsaz, A., Schürch, E., & Stulz, N. (2006). The probability of treatment success, failure and duration–What can be learned from empirical data to support decision making in clinical practice? *Clinical Psychology and Psychotherapy*, *13*, 223–232.

Main, M., Hesse, E., & Goldwin, R. (2008). Studying differences in language usage in recounting attachment history: An introduction to the AAI. In H. Steele, & M. Steele (Eds.), *Clinical applications of the Adult Attachment Interview* (pp. 31–68). New York: Guilford Press.

Maltzman, S. (2001). The specific ingredients are in the match: Comments on Ahn and Wampold (2001). *Journal of Counseling Psychology*, *48*, 258–261.

Maltzman, S. (Spring 2005). Addressing the impact of environmental toxins. *Counseling For Health*. Retrieved from http://www.apa.org/divisions/div17/sections/health/News.html.

Martin, S. D., Martin, E., Rai, S. S., Richardson, M. A., & Royall, R. (2001). Brain blood flow changes in depressed patients treated with interpersonal psychotherapy or venlafaxine hydrochloride. *Archives of General Psychiatry*, *58*, 641–648.

Mayes, L. C. (2006). Arousal regulation, emotional flexibility, medial amygdale function, and the impact of early experience: Comments on the paper of Lewis et al. In B. M. Lester, A. Masten, & B. McEwen (Eds.), *Annals of the New York Academy of Sciences: Vol. 1094. Resilience in children* (pp. 178–192). New York: New York Academy of Sciences.

McCrae, R. R., & Costa, P. T., Jr. (1997). Personality trait structure as a human universal. *American Psychologist*, *52*, 509–516.

McCrae, R. R., Costa, P. T., Jr., Martin, T. A., Oryol, V. E., Rukavishnikov, A. A., Senin, I. G., et al. (2004). Consensual validation of personality traits across cultures. *Journal of Research in Personality*, *38*, 179–201.

McSweeny, A. J. (1977). Including psychotherapy in national health insurance. *American Psychologist*, *32*(9), 722–730.

Meehl, P. E. (1954). *Clinical vs. statistical prediction: A theoretical analysis and a review of the evidence.* Minneapolis: University of Minnesota Press.

Meehl, P. E. (1978). Theoretical risks and tabular asterisks: Sir Karl, Sir Ronald, and the slow progress of soft psychology. *Journal of Consulting and Clinical Psychology*, *46*, 806–834.

Melchert, T. P. (2007). Strengthening the scientific foundations of professional psychology: Time for the next steps. *Professional Psychology: Research and Practice*, *38*, 34–43.

Meyer, B., & Pilkonis, P. A. (2001). Attachment style. *Psychotherapy*, *38*, 466–472.

Meyerwitz, B. E., Bull, A. A., & Perez, M. A. (2000). Cancers common in women. In R. M. Eisler, & M. Hersen (Eds.), *Handbook of gender, culture, and health* (pp. 197–225). New York: Lawrence Erlbaum.

Minami, T., Wampold, B. E., Serlin, R. C., Hamilton, E. G., & Kircher, J. C. (2008). Benchmarking the effectiveness of psychotherapy treatment for adult depression in a managed care environment: A preliminary study. *Journal of Consulting and Clinical Psychology*, *76*, 116–124.

Neuner, F., Schauer, M., Klaschik, C., Karunakara, U., & Elbert, T. (2004). A comparison of narrative exposure therapy, supportive counseling, and psychoeducation for treating posttraumatic stress disorder in an African refugee settlement. *Journal of Consulting and Clinical Psychology*, *72*(4), 579–587.

Nie, Z., Schweitzer, P., Roberts, A. J., Madamba, S. G., Moore, S. D., Siggins, G. R. (2004). Ethanol augments GABAergic transmission in the central amygdala via CRF1 receptors. *Science*, *303*, 1512–1514.

Nomura, Y., Chemtob, C. M., Fifer, W. P., Newcorn, J. H., & Brooks-Gunn, J. (2006). Additive interaction of child abuse and perinatal risk as signs of resiliency in adulthood. In B. M. Lester, A. Masten, & B. McEwen (Eds.), *Annals of the New York Academy of Sciences: Vol. 1094. Resilience in children* (pp. 330–334). New York: New York Academy of Sciences.

O'Hanlan, K. (2000). Health concerns of lesbians. In R. M. Eisler, & M. Hersen (Eds.), *Handbook of gender, culture, and health* (pp. 377–404). New York: Lawrence Erlbaum.

Olbrisch, M. E. (1977). Psychotherapeutic interventions in physical health: Effectiveness and economic efficiency. *American Psychologist*, *32*, 761–777.

Papakostas, Y. G., & Daras, M. D. (2001). Placebos, placebo effect, and the response to the healing situation: The evolution of a concept. *Epilepsia*, *42*, 1614–1625.

Pendery, M. L., Maltzman, I. M., & West, L. J. (1982). Controlled drinking by alcoholics? New findings and a reevaluation of a major affirmative study. *Science*, *217*, 169–175.

Persons, J. B. (2007). Psychotherapists collect data during routine clinical work that can contribute to knowledge about mechanisms of change in psychotherapy. *Clinical Psychology: Science and Practice*, *14*, 244–246.

Peterson, D. B., & Elliott, T. R. (2008). Advances in conceptualizing and studying disability. In S. D. Brown, & R. W. Lent (Eds.), *Handbook of counseling psychology* (4th ed., pp. 212–230). New York: John Wiley & Sons.

Project Match Research Group. (1997). Matching alcoholism treatments to client heterogeneity: Project MATCH postreatment drinking outcomes. *Journal of Studies on Alcohol*, *58*, 7–29.

Robbins, S. B., & Kliewer, W. L. (2000). Advances in theory and research on subjective well- being. In S. D. Brown, & R. W. Lent (Eds.), *Handbook of counseling psychology* (3rd ed., pp. 310–345). New York: Wiley and Sons.

Rothbart, M. K., Derryberry, D., & Posner, M. I. (1994). A psychobiological approach to the development of temperament. In J. E. Bates, & T. D. Wachs (Eds.), *Temperament: Individual differences at the interface of biology and behavior* (pp. 83–116). Washington, DC: American Psychological Association.

Ruphuy, R. S. (1977). Psychology and medicine. A new approach for community health development. *American Psychologist, 32*, 910–913.

Ruscio, A. M., & Holohan, D. R. (2006). Applying empirically supported treatments to complex cases: Ethical, empirical, and practical considerations. *Clinical Psychology: Science and Practice, 13*, 146–162.

Rush, A. J., Rago, W. V., Crismon, M. L., Toprac, M. G., Shon, S. P., Suppes, T., et al. (1999). Medication treatment of the severely and persistently mentally ill: The Texas Medication Algorithm Project. *Journal of Clinical Psychiatry, 60*, 284–291.

Rush, A. J., Crismon, M. L., Kashner, T. M., Toprac, M. G., Carmody, T. J., Trivedi, M. H., et al. (2003). Texas Medication Algorithm Project, Phase 3 (TMAP-3): Rationale and study design. *Journal of Clinical Psychiatry, 64*, 357–369.

Sameroff, A. J., & Rosenblum, K. L. (2006). Psychosocial constraints on the development of resilience. In B. M. Lester, A. Masten, & B. McEwen (Eds.), *Annals of the New York Academy of Sciences: Vol. 1094. Resilience in children* (pp. 116–124). New York: New York Academy of Sciences.

Schmitt, D. P., Realo, A., Voracek, M., & Allik, J. (2008). Why can't a man be more like a woman? Sex differences in Big 5 personality traits across 55 cultures. *Journal of Personality and Social Psychology, 94*, 168–182.

Seligman, M. E. P. (1995). The effectiveness of psychotherapy: The Consumer Reports study. *American Psychologist, 50*, 965–974.

Siev, J., & Chambless, D. L. (2007). Specificity of treatment effects: Cognitive therapy and relaxation for generalized anxiety and panic disorders. *Journal of Consulting and Clinical Psychology, 75*, 513–522.

Smith, M. L., & Glass, G. V. (1977). Meta-analysis of psychotherapy outcome studies. *American Psychologist, 32*, 752–760.

Sobell, M. B., & Sobell, L. C. (1973a). Individualized behavior therapy for alcoholics. *Behavior Therapy, 4*, 49–72.

Sobell, M. B., & Sobell, L. C. (1973b). Alcoholics treated by individualized behavior therapy: One year treatment outcome. *Behaviour Research and Therapy, 11*, 599–618.

Steele, H., & Steele, M. (2008). Ten clinical uses of the Adult Attachment Interview. In H. Steele, & M. Steele (Eds.), *Clinical applications of the Adult Attachment Interview* (pp. 3–30). New York: Guilford Press.

Stein, H. F. (2005). It ain't necessarily so: The many faces of the biopsychosocial model. *Families, Systems, & Health, 23*, 440–443.

Strelau, J. (1994). The concepts of arousal and arousability as used in temperament studies. In J. E. Bates, & T. D. Wachs (Eds.), *Temperament: Individual differences at the interface of biology and behavior* (pp. 117–141). Washington, DC: American Psychological Association.

Strupp, H. H., & Hadley, S. W. (1977). A tripartite model of mental health and therapeutic outcomes: With special reference to negative effects in psychotherapy. *American Psychologist, 32*, 187–196.

Stulz, N., Lutz, W., Leach, C., Lucock, M., & Barkham, M. (2007). Shapes of early change in psychotherapy under routine outpatient conditions. *Journal of Consulting and Clinical Psychology, 75*, 864–874.

Suchman, A. L. (2005). The current state of the biopsychosocial approach. *Families, Systems, & Health, 23*, 450–452.

Task Force on Standards for Service Facilities, American Psychological Association Council of Representatives. (1977). Standards for providers of psychological services. *American Psychologist, 32*, 495–505.

Taylor, S., Thordarson, D. S., Maxfield, L., Fedoroff, I. C., Lovell, K., & Ogrodniczuk, J. (2003). Comparative efficacy, speed, and adverse effects of three PTSD treatments: Exposure therapy, EMDR, and relaxation training. *Journal of Consulting and Clinical Psychology, 71*(2), 330–338.

Teplov, B. M. (1964). Problems in the study of general types of higher nervous activity in man and animals. In J. A. Gray (Ed.), *Pavlov's Typology* (pp. 3–153). Oxford, England: Pergamon Press Ltd.

Thase, M. E. (2001). Commentary: Neuroimaging profiles and the differential therapies of depression. *Archives of General Psychiatry, 58*, 651–653.

Thoresen, C. E., & Eagleston, J. R. (1985). Counseling for health. *The Counseling Psychologist, 13*, 15–87.

Wampold, B. E. (2000). Outcomes of individual counseling and psychotherapy: Empirical evidence addressing two fundamental questions. In S. D. Brown, & R. W. Lent (Eds.), *Handbook of counseling psychology* (3rd ed., pp. 711–739). New York: Wiley and Sons.

Wampold, B. E. (2001). Contextualizing psychotherapy as a healing practice: Culture, history, and methods. *Applied & Preventive Psychology, 10*, 69–86.

Wampold, B. E., Ahn, H., & Coleman, H. L. K. (2001). Medical model as metaphor: Old habits die hard. *Journal of Counseling Psychology, 48*, 268–273.

Wampold, B. E., Lichtenberg, J. W., & Waehler, C. A. (2002). Principles of empirically supported interventions in counseling psychology. *The Counseling Psychologist, 30*, 197–217.

Wampold, B. E., Minami, T., Tierney, S. C., Baskin, T. W., & Bhati, K. S. (2005). The placebo is powerful: Estimating placebo effects in medicine and psychotherapy from randomized clinical trials. *Journal of Clinical Psychology, 61*, 835–854.

Wampold, B. E., Mondin, G. W., Moody, M., & Ahn, H. (1997). The flat earth as a metaphor for the evidence for uniform efficacy of bona fide psychotherapies: Reply to Crits-Christoph (1997) and Howard et al. (1997). *Psychological Bulletin, 122*, 226–230.

Wampold, B. E., Mondin, G. W., Moody, M., Stich, F., Benson, K., Ahn, H. (1997). A meta- analysis of outcome studies comparing bona fide psychotherapies: Empirically, "all must have prizes." *Psychological Bulletin, 122*, 203–215.

Werner, E. E. (2005). Resilience research: Past, present, and future. In R. DeV. Peters, B. Leadbeater, & R. J. McMahon (Eds.), *Resilience in children, families, and communities: Linking context to practice and policy* (pp. 3–11). New York: Kluwer Academic/Plenum Publishers.

Westen, D., & Morrison, K. (2001). A multidimensional meta-analysis of treatments for depression, panic, and generalized anxiety disorder: An empirical examination of the status of empirically supported therapies. *Journal of Consulting and Clinical Psychology, 69*, 875–899.

Westen, D., Novotny, C. M., & Thompson-Brenner, H. (2004). The empirical status of empirically supported psychotherapies: Assumptions, findings, and reporting in controlled clinical trials. *Psychological Bulletin, 130*, 631–663.

Weston, W. W. (2005). Patient-centered medicine: A guide to the biopsychosocial model. *Families, Systems, & Health, 23*, 387–405.

Whipple, J. L., Lambert, M. J., Vermeersch, D. A., Smart, D. W., Nielsen, S. L., & Hawkins, E. J. (2003). Improving the effects of psychotherapy: The use of early identification of treatment failure and problem-solving strategies in routine practice. *Journal of Counseling Psychology, 50*, 59–68.

Whitson, J. A., & Galinsky, A. D. (2008). Lacking control increases illusory pattern perception. *Science, 322*, 115–117.

Wilson, G. T., & Rachman, S. J. (1983). Meta-analysis and the evaluation of psychotherapy outcome: Limitations and liabilities. *Journal of Consulting and Clinical Psychology, 51*, 54–64.

Further Reading

Bates, J. E., & Wachs, T. D. (Eds.). (1994). *Temperament: Individual differences at the interface of biology and behavior.* Washington, DC: American Psychological Association.

Lester, B. M., Masten, A., & McEwen, B. (Eds.). (2006). *Annals of the New York Academy of Sciences: Vol. 1094. Resilience in children.* New York: New York Academy of Sciences.

Peters, R. DeV., Leadbeater, B., & McMahon, R. J. (Eds.). (2005). *Resilience in children, families, and communities: Linking context to practice and policy.* New York: Kluwer Academic/Plenum Publishers.

Steele, H., & Steele, M. (Eds.). (2008). *Clinical applications of the Adult Attachment Interview.* New York: Guilford Press.

Worklife Across the Lifespan

Lisa M. Larson

Abstract

An extensive literature search across the spectrum of vocational psychology was conducted using the time frame of 1991–2008 and resulted in 47 quantitative reviews (i.e., meta-analyses). First, theories of vocational psychology are presented including John Holland's (1997) and René Dawis and Loyd Lofquist's (1984; Dawis, 2005) theory of work adjustment person–environment fit (P–E fit) models; Lent, Brown, and Hackett (1994) social cognitive career theory; the social learning theory of John Krumboltz (1990); Donald Super's career construction theory (Super, 1992); and L. S. Gottfredson's (1999) circumscription theory. Next, vocational outcomes of young people (the development of interests, educational and occupational aspirations, educational achievement, and career choice) and wage-earning adults (job search, job entry, job performance, job satisfaction, career success, and mental health outcomes) are reviewed. The last two major sections concern diverse groups (women and racially and ethnically diverse groups) and individual differences (cognitive ability, personality, and interests) as predictors of vocational outcomes.

Keywords: educational and occupational aspirations, career choice, job search, job satisfaction, job performance, cognitive ability, personality, interests, women, diverse groups

Vocational psychology. . . . is the behavioral study of the worklife, the study of people's behavior in choosing, preparing for, entering, progressing in, and finally retiring from one's life work. Each of these verbs represents a variable that ranges from negative to positive; for example "choosing" can extend from a default or accidental to a well informed, fully rational choice, and "progressing" includes regressing. And "life work" can be more than one kind of activity.

—Dawis, 1996, p. 229

Dawis' definition of vocational psychology addresses the broad outcomes across the lifespan that includes both positive and negative outcomes, and paid and unpaid work, although paid work is emphasized. This definition emphasizes vocational psychology's concern with processes as well as with outcomes. As the title of the chapter implies, these outcomes

encompass both educational and work environments. The person predictors of vocational outcomes range from status variables, such as sex and ethnicity, to individual differences, such as interests, to more domain-specific person variables such as self-efficacy (SE). The environmental predictors range from distal variables, such as socioeconomic status (SES) or tracking in school, to proximal variables. Within industrial/organizational (I/O) psychology, proximal variables include taxonomies of the work environment (i.e., work design characteristics [e.g., job complexity], social characteristics [e.g., supervisor support], and work context characteristics [e.g., work conditions]). Within counseling psychology, the proximal variables are support (e.g., social support or parent support) or barriers (e.g., discrimination or harassment). Mediators that explain part or all of the relation between the predictor and the vocational outcome (e.g., SE, job stress) have been examined. Moderators that alter the relation of the predictor and the vocational outcomes were also examined (e.g., job complexity moderated the influence of SE on performance type of study [Judge, Jackson, Shaw, Scott, & Rich, 2007]).

Vocational psychology theories attempt to explain a wide range of vocational outcomes across children, adolescents, and adults. Donald Super's career construction theory (Super, 1992) concerns career development across the lifespan, whereas L. S. Gottfredson's (1999) circumscription theory emphasizes the impact of sex roles and occupational prestige on the ways in which children and adolescents ultimately narrow their career choices. Lent, Brown, and Hackett (1994) adapted Bandura's (1986) social cognitive theory to explain academic performance, development of interests, and career choice. The social learning theory of John Krumboltz (1990) focuses on how the person's learning experiences, shaped by the environment, impact her or his career choices and guide future career counseling. John Holland's (1997) person–environment fit (P–E fit) model presents a hexagonal structure of interests and a corresponding hexagonal structure of work environments that predict choice, satisfaction, and tenure. René Dawis and Loyd Lofquist's (1984; Dawis, 2005) theory of work adjustment (TWA) is the predominant P–E fit theory that examines the satisfaction of the employee and the satisfaction of the employer (i.e., *satisfactoriness*), as well as work outcomes like tenure and adjustment.

History

Vocational psychology has deep and enduring roots. One root is the individual difference tradition (Thorndike, 1911), in which people vary systematically on a range of traits; by knowing that information, educators could help teach each individual (Walsh & Savickas, 2005). The individual difference tradition also spawned the measurement of intelligence, followed by the measurement of interests and aptitudes at premier academic institutions like Teachers College, Columbia University. Here, James Mckeen Cattell, E. L. Thorndike, and Robert S. Woodsworth mentored Harry Hollingsworth, who published the first vocational psychology textbook in 1916. Hollingsworth was also important as a mentor as well, having mentored E. K. Strong. Another critical academic institution in our history was the Carnegie Institute of Technology; it became the first institution to offer an applied psychology department and to hire a well-known applied psychologist, Walter Dill Scott, who developed the first occupational aptitude test.

A second root, the vocational guidance movement, was fueled by the transformation of an agricultural society into a manufacturing society. As people moved to the cities, there was a societal need to help educate and train young men and place them into employment (e.g., Young Men's Christian Association employment bureaus and classes). Frank Parsons (1909) emerged from the vocational guidance movement and was the first to articulate the P–E fit model that continues to dominate the field (Walsh & Savickas, 2005).

A third root in vocational psychology concerns the engagement of the pioneers of vocational psychology in both world war efforts. During World War I, offshoots of the field flourished, namely aptitude testing (Army Alpha and Army Beta group intelligence tests), the development of performance ratings of officers, and the development of qualification criteria for hundreds of military jobs (Savickas & Baker, 2005). After World War I, vocational testing exploded, leading to the development of the Strong's Vocational Interest Blank (Strong, 1927) and the predominance of the P–E fit orientation in the field. During World War II, vocational psychologists helped classify 9 million men through the Army General Classification Test (Savickas & Baker, 2005). Moreover, vocational psychologists across 30 universities generated research to study military problems. Air force psychologists were involved in selecting, classifying, and training Air Force personnel. (Donald Super was one of those psychologists.)

A fourth root in vocational psychology concerned the schism in the 1930s between applied psychologists focused on selection and adjustment, and the applied psychologists focused on vocational guidance. The former group persuaded employers that well-adjusted workers were more productive, thus shifting the lens to industry rather than to the individual (Savickas & Baker, 2005). Vocational guidance psychologists continued to focus on the individual. Besides a schism as to who the client was (industry vs. the individual), there was also a schism between applied psychologists who remained in academia and researched vocational choices of high school students and college students versus applied psychologists who worked in industry and clinics and concerned themselves with the application of psychology to business and industry. The selection and adjustment psychologists, as a group, were ultimately excluded from joining the American Psychological Association (APA) due to being viewed as unscientific; this led them to form their own professional organization (the American Association of Applied Psychology) (Savickas & Baker, 2005). The vocational guidance psychologists, as part of the APA, remained at universities. This schism persists, with work adjustment and job selection literature quite distinct from the vocational choice literature. The final root for vocational psychology concerns the explosion of career theory in the 1950s, during which most of the predominant theories were developed and first presented.

Organization of the Chapter

The first section of the chapter is organized by the major theories in the field. Those that have received attention in the form of reviews or meta-analyses will receive the most attention. The next section is devoted to vocational outcomes (e.g., vocational choice) and vocational processes (vocational exploration, career decision making) that precede entry into the workforce and involve young people in educational settings (i.e., children, adolescents, and college students). The third section concerns employed adults and is organized by vocational outcomes (e.g., job satisfaction). The fourth section of the chapter will identify integrative vocational psychology reviews focused exclusively on the multicultural variables of sex, race and ethnicity, and culture. The fifth section of the chapter will be directed toward individual differences, since this area has been one of the most prolific arenas of investigation. In the final section, I will identify fruitful research directions for the next generation of vocational psychologists.

Search Criteria

An extensive literature search was conducted using the time frame of 1991 to 2008. Three approaches were used. First, all relevant handbooks were located. Second, the search involved pairings of vocational terms with one of two terms "meta-analysis" or "review." Third, relevant journals were searched to identify any vocational reviews or meta-analyses that might have been missed in the literature search. The literature search yielded more meta-analyses than conceptual reviews. Meta-analysis is a statistical technique that empirically condenses the effect sizes of the relation of two variables into a correlation ranging from 0 to 1. The meta-analyses that were reviewed were across multiple disciplines (e.g., counseling psychology,

I/O psychology). Only correlations equal to or larger than .20 will be reported.

Theories
Overview

Theories continue to be prominent in vocational psychology and to evolve. The P–E fit theories those in which attributes of the person and attributes of the environment are complementary. The key characteristics of the person and the environment vary across these theories, and the definition of the environment varies. In these theories, the influence of the person is bidirectional. These theories assume that positive vocational outcomes occur as a result of the match between the person and the environment. René Dawis and Lloyd Lofquist's (1984) theory and John Holland's (1997) theory are the dominant P–E fit theories. The other dominant theory is Lent, Brown, and Hackett's social cognitive career theory (SCCT; Lent et al., 1994). This theory is rooted in social learning theory (Bandura, 1977) and social cognitive theory (Bandura, 1982, 1986). The SCCT also involves interaction between the person and environment; in addition, the person's actions are viewed as more than the outcome of the P–E interaction. Thus, Bandura's social cognitive theory is embedded in triadic causality (person, environment, and actions) rather than bidirectional causality in which one's actions are viewed as a function of P–E fit. Self-efficacy is the determining mechanism in career-related activities. John Krumboltz's theory, reflecting more emphasis on social learning theory will also be discussed. Two developmental theories, Super's career construction theory and L. S. Gottfredson's circumscription and compromise theory, will also be described, with major terms identified. Finally, sociological theories will be briefly reviewed.

The largest number of reviews was located for social cognitive career theory and reviews of SE in particular. Holland's hexagonal structure and the congruence construct also yielded large-scale studies. Dawis' and Lofquist's TWA was indirectly related to much of the research that will be presented later in the chapter concerning adult outcomes, including job satisfaction, job performance, and career success. Some of Gottfredson's constructs, particularly occupational prestige and sex-role socialization, will be discussed under the section pertaining to children. Career construction theory does not lend itself as well to empirical reviews and, not surprisingly, none was found. However, several chapters were located elucidating Super's theory.

Theory of Work Adjustment

The TWA (Dawis & Lofquist, 1984), which originated in the 1950s, is a P–E fit theory that focuses on adults in the work environment. The theory explains job satisfaction, job performance, and job tenure. The theory is derived so that the employee is at the center of the theory, with the focus placed on her or his satisfaction and adjustment on the job. The employer is also at the center of the theory, with the employer's satisfaction with the employee's performance labeled as satisfactoriness. The theory is anchored in the assumption that the employee's satisfaction and satisfactoriness intertwine to produce beneficial work outcomes for both (Dawis, 2005). The broader theory derived from TWA extends beyond work to encompass other environments and is labeled the *person–environment–correspondence theory* (PEC; Dawis, 2005). The PEC theory is based on a harmonious relationship (correspondence) between the person and the environment, and has been used as a unifying theory in the field (Savickas & Lent, 1994). The focus of this chapter will be on TWA, although the overlap with PEC is extensive.

The important attributes of the person are his or her needs and abilities. Needs are defined as work values and include achievement, comfort, status, altruism, safety, and autonomy (Dawis, 2002, 2005). The person's abilities are general dimensions that underlie groups of acquired skills (i.e., behavior sequences emitted in response to a task) (Dawis, 2005). The TWA theorist measures skills as to the repeatability of the behavior sequence, energy expenditure, speed of performance, and difficulty of the task. The attributes of the environment correspond with the person's needs and skills. The environment's capacity to meet a person's needs is called a *reinforcer* (Dawis, 2002). Reinforcers are the aspects of the task that fulfill the person's needs or meets her or his important work values (e.g., a person values achievement, and the task offers achievement). The environment's skill requirements are those skills necessary for the satisfactory execution of the job duties.

The correspondence between the person and environment predicts job satisfaction and job tenure. The theory can be used to predict the person's satisfaction with the job (satisfaction) or can be used to predict the employer's satisfaction with the employee (satisfactoriness). A person is satisfied to the extent that her or his needs and work values are met on the job. For example, if the employee values autonomy, and the job can provide sufficient autonomy, then the employee will be satisfied. Likewise, the employer is satisfied with the worker (satisfactoriness) to the extent that the employee performs the necessary job requirements. The TWA predicts outcomes derived from both satisfaction and satisfactoriness. The degree to which an employee is satisfied will determine whether the employee stays (job tenure) or quits the job. The degree to which an employer is satisfied with the employee (satisfactoriness) will determine whether the employee is promoted, transferred, retained, or fired. Other outcomes that may concern TWA scholars include productivity, profit, morale, mental health, turnover or retention rates, and accident or safety records (Dawis, 2002, 2005). Occupational choice is also an outcome, although rarely discussed (Dawis, 2002, 2005). The person examines the costs and benefits for a range of occupations by examining his or her values attached to certain occupations and the skills required for those occupations; the person chooses the best fit among multiple options.

The TWA identifies temporal process dimensions (personality style and adjustment style) that are distinct from the more structural person and environment attributes. The first four personality style dimensions describe how people interact with the work environment over time. These personality styles are celerity or speed with which an individual initiates interaction with the environment (quickness), pace or activity level of one's interaction with the environment (intensity), the pace of interaction with the environment (e.g., steady, cyclical, or erratic; pattern), and the sustainability of the interaction with the environment (endurance).

The remaining temporal process dimensions concern four adjustment styles that describe different ways people adjust to various degrees of dissatisfaction in a job (discorrespondence). Initially, people vary as to their flexibility, defined as the ability to tolerate a mismatch between needs and rewards. After time, the person becomes dissatisfied and tries to change either self (reactive adjustment) or job (active adjustment). Finally, perseverance is used to describe the duration of the adjustment behavior; that is, how long the person is in a state of discorrespondence.

In general, support is strong for TWA's first three propositions concerning the role of satisfaction and satisfactoriness (i.e., subjective job performance), in work adjustment (e.g., intentions to quit [negative]), and the prediction of satisfaction and satisfactoriness (Dawis, 2002). First, work adjustment at any time is indicated by concurrent levels of the person's satisfaction and the person's satisfactoriness. Second, the person's satisfaction is predicted from how well reinforcers in the work environment meet the person's needs (provided that person's abilities match the job's requirements). Third, satisfactoriness is predicted from how well the person's abilities match what the job requires (provided that the reinforcers in the job match the person's needs).

There is also support for the tenure propositions, particularly the relation of satisfaction to tenure (Dawis, 2005). These concern propositions six through eight. One proposition states that the probability that the person will quit is inversely related to the person's satisfaction. Second, the probability that the employer will fire the person is inversely related to the person's satisfactoriness. Third, tenure is predicted from both the person's satisfaction and satisfactoriness.

The rest of the theory's propositions have either received mixed reviews or have been minimally examined. For example, the little-known personality style and adjustment style variables have been under-researched (Dawis, 2005; Hesketh, 2001; Hesketh & Griffin, 2005).

Person–Environment Fit

John Holland's (1997) theory continues to dominate the landscape of vocational psychology. This P–E fit theory originated by Holland in the 1950s (Holland, 1959) has shaped how many psychologists think about vocational psychology. The theory elaborates on Frank Parsons' original idea of matching people's skills to the job. Holland's (1997) theory states that people search for environments that let them exercise their skills and abilities, express their attitudes and values, and take on agreeable problems and roles. Finally, behavior is determined by an interaction between the person and the environment (Holland, 1997). The assumption is that, when there is a good match between the person and the environment, people are more likely to make better vocational choices and be better adjusted.

Holland integrated theory and practice and identified six vocational personality/interests types that can adequately capture most people. Arranged around a hexagon, these six types capture each type's characteristics, self-descriptions, and occupations, and are labeled, in order, realistic (mechanical, practical, working with ones hands, being outdoors), investigative (scientific, analytic, problem-solving), artistic (creative, musical, originator), social (serving/helping others), enterprising (persuading/managing others), and conventional (organizing/working with

data/numbers) forming a well-known acronym, RIASEC (Holland, 1997). The types are measured with a myriad of well-known assessment tools, such as the 2005 Strong Interest Inventory (SII; Donnay, Morris, Schaubhut, & Thompson, 2005) (see Swanson, 2011, Chapter 8, this volume). The theory asserts that people can be described according to the extent to which they identify with each of those six types. This results in a Holland three-letter code, in which the first letter of each type is used (e.g., RIC would represent a person whose highest score was the Realistic type followed by the next highest score, the Investigative type, followed by the third highest score, the Conventional type).

The environment can also be described by these same six types, arranged in the same hexagonal configuration. The environment's six types are derived in two ways, based either on the preponderance of people in that work setting from a particular type (e.g., most accountants' first letter in their Holland code is Conventional) or based on the most common activities performed in that work environment (e.g., predominant activities in an accounting firm are data management and processing). The environment is usually considered the work environment but could be the intended environment or the academic environment (e.g., academic department). Holland code types for the environment have been linked to the Occupational Information Network (O*NET). The O*NET system serves as the nation's primary source of occupational information, providing comprehensive information on key attributes and characteristics of workers and occupations; this database can be easily accessed online.

Four theoretical assumptions in Holland's theory are based on four diagnostic indicators: congruence, consistency, differentiation, and vocational identity. The first fundamental indicator in Holland's (1997) theory, labeled congruence, describes the degree to which the person's Holland code and environment's code are similar. A highly congruent person would be someone whose three-letter Holland code matches the Holland code for the environment. The congruence index is used to determine the degree of P–E fit (see Swanson, 2011, Chapter 8, this volume).

The second fundamental indicator in Holland's (1997) theory, labeled consistency, describes the relation of the six personality/interest types to each other. The arrangement of the six types around a hexagon, the RIASEC, is important to the theory in terms of determining consistency. A highly consistent three-letter Holland code would be one in which three types are close to one another on the hexagon. The first letters of each of the six types are described as the RIASEC; thus, a person whose code type is ASE would be a very consistent code type because the top three scores are representing three types that are right next to each other on the hexagon.

The third fundamental indicator in Holland's (1997) theory, labeled differentiation, describes the distinctness of the personality/interest type (Spokane & Cruza-Guet, 2005). Differentiation is operationalized as the person's highest minus the lowest score among the six types, or among the three scores comprising the three-letter code (Spokane & Cruza-Guet, 2005). The most differentiated profile would be one in which the person could be described predominantly as one type on the hexagon and the least differentiated profile would be a flat profile (i.e., the person's scores across the RIASEC would be within a range of one or two points).

The final fundamental indicator, labeled vocational identity, refers to the degree to which a person has a clear "picture of one's goals, interests, and talents" (Holland, 1997, p. 5). A person with a high degree of identity would have a profile that is consistent, differentiated, and congruent. This person will likely do competent work, be satisfied and personally effective, and engage in appropriate social and educational behavior (Holland, 1997, p. 40). The theory (Holland, 1997) also allows for the work environment to be described in terms of the same parallel constructs (work environment consistency, differentiation, and identity) (Spokane & Cruza-Guet, 2005).

Many of Holland's (1997) propositions have been supported. First, six types can describe a person's work personalities or interests. Second, they are arranged in a circumplex (Day & Rounds, 1998), and this circumplex structure holds for U.S. racial and ethnic minorities (Day & Rounds, 1998). Day and Rounds (1998) found structural equivalence across samples of African American, Mexican American, Asian American, Native American, and Caucasian American groups (N = 49,450) students using the UNIACT. An analysis by Darcy and Tracey (2007) from the American College Testing database across time (grades 8, 10, and 12, N = 69,987) shows that the RIASEC order is consistent with the data, and that it is consistent for both boys and girls and across the three age periods. However, they did not find equal spacing across the RIASEC types; there was more space between realistic and conventional types and between artistic and social types, and less space between social and enterprising types. Cross-culturally, support for the circumplex model is mixed. According to Long and Tracey's (2006) analysis on 29 independent RIASEC correlation matrices across Chinese participants, Holland's circumplex model did not fit the data well, although the RIASEC ordering was present. The ordering was consistent across instrument, age (middle school, college, adult), sex, and region (mainland China, Taiwan, Hong Kong). More space than anticipated by the theory existed between realistic and conventional and between artistic and investigative. Gati's (1991) model, Rounds and Tracey's (1996), and Liu and Rounds' (2003) modified octant rating (circumplex with eight points with an unidentified type between realistic and conventional and between investigative and artistic) fit the Chinese data better than did the six evenly spaced points on the hexagon. Rounds and Tracey (1996) examined 96 RIASEC samples from U.S. racial and ethnic minorities (n = 16), U.S. white European samples (n = 4), and samples from 19 countries including Australia, Brazil, Canada, Columbia, France, Guyana, Iceland, Indonesia, Israel, Japan, Malaysia, Mexico, New Zealand, Pakistan, Papua New Guinea, Paraguay, Portugal, and Taiwan. They compared the structural equivalence of RIASEC models to U.S. matrices generated from 77 RIASEC matrices reported by Tracey and Rounds (1993). Rounds and Tracey (1996) found that Holland's circular order model was not supported, but Gati's three-group partition (realistic/investigative, artistic/social, and enterprising/conventional) and the authors' alternative three-class partition (realistic/investigative, artistic, and social/enterprising/conventional) were supported. The U.S. racial and ethnic minority samples did not yield a good fit across all three models.

Support for Holland's assumption that congruence leads to better adjustment, satisfaction, and performance seems mixed. Congruence, when assessed using an index, did not significantly relate to job satisfaction in the most recent meta-analysis on the topic (Tsabari, Tziner, & Meier, 2005; N = 6557, k = 53, ρ = .17, which includes 0 in the 95% confidence interval [CI]). There does seem to be evidence that people who change jobs move in a congruent direction (Spokane & Cruza-Guet, 2005). The ability to make congruent choices may be mediated by adjustment variables like anxiety or depression, or by the importance a person places on identification with a group (Spokane & Cruza-Guet,

2005). Finally, people seem to have difficulty identifying congruent occupational options, seeking congruent accurate information, evaluating options that are congruent, and engaging in effective entry behaviors (Spokane & Cruza-Guet, 2005).

Some researchers use a different way to measure congruence through continuous scores on the SII across Holland's hexagon for the P measure and educational major or occupation as the E measure. Researchers have shown interests across the RIASEC to be predictive of choice of major that is parallel or consistent with the interest profile (Gasser, Larson, & Borgen, 2007; Harmon, Hansen, Borgen, & Hammer, 1994) and choice of occupation (e.g., Ackerman & Beier, 2003; Donnay & Borgen, 1996; Donnay et al., 2005; Harmon et al., 1994).

Holland's assumption concerning consistency (having a Holland three-letter code with the strongest types being closer to each other on Holland's hexagon) and differentiation (spikes on Holland profile rather than a flat profile across all six types) leading to positive vocational outcomes has not been clearly demonstrated. However, one intriguing study showed in a hierarchical regression analyses, separated by sex, that the interaction of differentiation with agreeableness and conscientiousness explained statistically significant variance in work performance for men, and that the interaction of congruence with agreeableness, artistic, and social subscales was significantly related to work performance in women (Kieffer, Schinka, & Curtiss, 2004).

Social Cognitive Career Theory

Built upon Betz and Hackett's earlier work on career SE of women in nontraditional domains, Lent, Brown, and Hackett (1994) adapted Bandura's (1977, 1986) social cognitive theory to the vocational psychology domain. Their theory sees SE as the driving force to explain the development of interests, academic and career choice, and performance and persistence in educational and occupational pursuits (Lent et al., 1994).

The theory is anchored in the construct, SE. Self-efficacy is defined as "people's judgments of their capabilities to organize and execute courses of action required to attain designated types of performances" (Bandura, 1986, p. 391). Lent and colleagues incorporated Bandura's four sources of SE into SCCT. They were mastery, modeling, social persuasion, and physiological arousal (anxiety). They identified two other key sociocognitive mechanisms in their model, namely outcome expectations and goals. Outcome expectations (OE) were defined as people's personal

beliefs about probable response outcomes (Lent et al., 1994) and were classified by Bandura as physical (e.g., monetary), social (e.g., approval), and self-evaluative (e.g., self-satisfaction). Goals were defined as the determination to engage in a particular activity or to affect a particular future outcome (Bandura, 1986). For SCCT, expressed choices, career plans, decisions, occupational aspirations are all forms of goals. In SCCT, distinction is made between a choice goal (an intention to act) and a choice action (having made a selection or choice). In this model, SE is the mediator between thought and action, between knowing what to do and executing the action or choice (Bandura, 1986).

The social cognitive model in general and SCCT in particular has three key actors; namely, the person, the proximal environment, and the person's actions. The person variables, referred to as *human agency*, are his or her motivational, emotional, and cognitive processes. The person's actions include not only his academic and vocational performance but also his choices (e.g., choice of occupation) (Bandura, 1986; Lent et al., 1994). The interplay among the person's agency, his or her actions, and the environment are dynamic and reciprocal. In this context, three vocational outcomes are prescribed, all of which are intricately linked with the other.

The first set of outcomes predicted in SCCT is the development of vocational interests. As exogenous variables, the four sources of SE are postulated to directly impact SE and outcome expectations, which in turn directly affect vocational interests. Self-efficacy and outcome expectancies are postulated to directly and indirectly affect intentions/ goals, activity selection and practice, and performance attainments. Interests are posited to directly influence intentions/goals and indirectly influence activity selection and practice, and performance attainments. Intentions/goals are thought to directly influence activity selection and practice and indirectly influence performance attainments. Activity selection and practice is thought to directly influence performance attainments. Performance attainments cycle back to influence the sources of SE (Lent et al., 1994).

The second set of outcomes predicted is career-related choice behaviors. In this model, person inputs (e.g., gender, ethnicity) and background are exogenous variables that predict learning experiences and contextual influences proximal to the choice behavior. Learning experiences are posited to impact SE and outcome expectations, which in turn directly influence interests, choice goals, and choice actions and indirectly influence performance domains and attainments. Interests directly affect choice goals and indirectly affect choice actions and performance domains and attainments. Contextual influences that are proximal to choice behaviors are thought to moderate the relation of interests and choice goals and moderate the relation of choice goals and choice actions (Lent, 2005). Choice goals directly affect choice actions and indirectly affect performance domains and attainments. Choice actions directly affect performance domains and attainments. Performance domains and attainments cycle back to directly influence learning experiences.

The third set of outcomes predicted is performance and persistence in educational and occupational pursuits (Lent et al., 1994). In this model, the exogenous variable is ability/past performance, which directly affects SE and outcome expectations and performance attainment level. Self-efficacy and outcome expectations directly affect performance goals/subgoals and indirectly affect performance attainment level. Performance goals/subgoals are thought to directly affect performance attainment level. Performance attainment level then cycles back to directly influence future performance (Lent et al., 1994).

Four meta-analyses were located that specifically examined SCCT. The findings will be presented in order of the presentation of the three models; namely, the development of interests, then career-related choice, and then academic achievement. In all the studies, SE was domain-specific not generalized SE.

DEVELOPMENT OF INTERESTS

Regarding interest development, SE seems to strongly relate to interests when parallel content domains exist (Rottinghaus, Larson, & Borgen, 2003). In their meta-analyses ($k = 60$, $N = 39,154$), academic SE (e.g., math, art) correlated strongly with academic interests; vocational SE across the RIASEC correlated strongly with interests across the RIASEC (rs ranged from .51 to .69). Age, sex, and measure moderated the effect somewhat. Men yielded slightly higher SE–interests (SE–I) relations than did females; older versus younger samples yielded slightly higher SE–I relations, and the Campbell Interest and Skill Survey (Campbell, Hyne, & Nilsen, 1992) versus the SII yielded higher SE–I relations especially for the social, enterprising, and conventional domains. These studies were not experimental, so cause cannot be established.

Self-efficacy also appears to contribute to mathematics and/or science course interests after outcome expectancies have been partialed out (Young et al., 2004). Their meta-analyses concerned the relations of mathematics and science outcome expectancies with other sociocognitive constructs, including SE ($k = 10$; $N = 3331$). Young and colleagues reported in their review that studies using structural equation modeling consistently showed both direct and indirect effects of SE on mathematics course interests. Finally, SE has also been shown to moderately relate to course intentions, with Lent and colleagues (1994) reporting an effect size of $r = .40$.

Finally, there is some evidence that SE relates to the four sources of SE. Lent and colleagues (1994) in their meta-analysis of three studies presented the following effect sizes: $r = .51$ for mastery, $r = .20$ for modeling, $r = .28$ for social persuasion, and $r = -.40$ for emotional arousal.

In the model of the development of interests, outcome expectancies are also an important construct. Consistent with the model, outcome expectations have also been shown to relate strongly to SE (Lent et al., 1994; Young, et al., 2004 Lent and colleagues (1994) reported an effect size of $r = .49$, whereas Young and colleagues (2004) reported a very similar effect size for the mathematics domain of $r = .45$ ($k = 7$, $N = 1208$) and $r = .41$ ($k = 4$; $N = 2456$) for the mathematics/science domains combined. Also supporting the SCCT model, outcome expectancies have also been shown to be strongly related to interests based on these same two meta-analyses (Lent et al., 1994; Young et al., 2004). The relation of outcome expectancy and interests was reported by Lent and colleagues to be a moderate effect size ($r = .52$); Young and colleagues reported a similar effect size of .54 for the mathematics/science domain across ten samples with an N of 3,331 (Note: Lent et al. did not report number of samples or sample size.) Finally, both meta-analyses reported a linkage of outcome expectancies with intentions. Lent and colleagues referred to them as *choice goals* (i.e., expressed choice, intentions, and range of occupational considerations) related to outcome expectancies $r = .42$. Young and colleagues reported a correlation of $r = .50$ for mathematics outcome expectancies and course intentions ($k = 4$, $N = 774$). Young and colleagues reported in their review that studies using structural equation modeling consistently showed both direct and indirect effects of outcome expectations on mathematics course interests. Moreover, Young and colleagues also reported across eight studies that mathematics/science outcome expectancies and interests uniquely predicted mathematics course intentions.

Although sources of SE (i.e., mastery, modeling, social persuasion, and lowering anxiety) are postulated to increase SE (Bandura, 1986), Lent et al. (1994) identified the first three of these sources (mastery, modeling, and social persuasion) as impacting outcome expectancies, in that they provide the reinforcing consequences that lead a person to expect more positive outcomes in the future. Young and colleagues reported evidence ($k = 3$, $N = 391$) that mathematics outcome expectancies did relate moderately to perceived mastery in mathematics ($r = .48$), modeling ($r = .41$), social persuasion ($r = .50$), and anxiety ($r = -.47$). Although the model presumes that mastery would be the strongest source among the four sources, Young and colleagues did not find differential effect sizes across the four sources in relating to mathematics outcome expectancies.

Although the theory presents SE as partly determining the development of interests, some empirical evidence has emerged that suggests the pathway is bidirectional. That is, SE may be partly determined by interests. First, the reciprocal relation of SE and interests has been demonstrated (Nauta, Kahn, Angell, & Cantarelli, 2002; Tracey, 2002). Second, interests are in part inherited traits, with at least 40%–50% of the variance being genetic (e.g., Betsworth et al., 1994; Gottfredson, 1999; Moloney, Bouchard, & Segal, 1991; Waller, Lykken, & Tellegen, 1995). Third, interests appear stable over many years (Hansen & Swanson, 1983; Low & Rounds, 2007; Rottinghaus, Coon, Gaffey, & Zytowski, 2007; Strong, 1955; Swanson & Hansen, 1988). Furthermore, in a meta-analysis ($k = 66$, $N = 23,665$), Low, Yoon, Roberts, and Rounds (2005) provided convincing evidence that interests remain relatively unchanged in adolescence and increased dramatically during the college years, and then remained stable for the next two decades. Stability was measured using both rank order and profile correlations. Interests, in part, motivate people to seek out activities in their environment and avoid other activities in their environment and determine if, whether, and to what extent efficacy in some domains develop. Silvia (2006) sees initial interest (distinct from interests) as an emotion that, through attributional processes and key variables of task difficulty, interacts over time to create enduring interests. He argues for more experimental research (e.g., Silvia, 2003) testing under what conditions confidence

may elicit interests and what psychological processes (e.g., attributional processes) may be involved.

CAREER-RELATED CHOICE

The second model concerns the prediction of career-related choices. Lent and colleagues (1994) in their meta-analyses reported that choice goals were moderately related to SE ($r = .40$), outcome expectations ($r = .42$), and interests ($r = .60$). Young, and colleagues (2004) showed mathematics/science outcome expectations to be moderately related to intentions ($r = .50$). Across several studies, Young and colleagues (2004) also reported that outcome expectancies are unique predictors of course intentions above and beyond SE, and that outcome expectancies may mediate the relation of SE and course intentions. Young and colleagues also showed evidence that course interests directly affected course intentions after other sociocognitive variables were controlled.

Besides the meta-analyses, multiple studies have shown SE to be predictive of choice of major (e.g., Larson, Wei, Wu, Borgen, & Bailey, 2007), occupation (e.g., Betz et al., 2003; Rottinghaus, Betz, & Borgen, 2003), and educational aspirations (e.g., Rottinghaus, Betz, et al., 2003; Rottinghaus, Lindley, Green, & Borgen, 2002). Likewise, researchers have shown interests to be predictive of choice of major (Gasser et al., 2007; Harmon et al., 1994) and choice of occupation (e.g., Ackerman & Beier, 2003; Donnay & Borgen, 1996; Donnay et al., 2005; Harmon et al., 1994). Self-efficacy combined with interests has also been shown to be predictive of choice of major (e.g., Betz, Harmon, & Borgen, 1996; Larson, Wu, Bailey, Borgen, & Gasser, 2010) and occupation (e.g., Betz, et al., 1996, 2003; Donnay & Borgen, 1999). The SCCT theory postulates that SE is domain specific. Consistent with the theory, a number of studies have consistently shown evidence that specific versus general RIASEC domains of SE and interest domains of SE and confidence are significantly more predictive of career-related goals and choice actions such as educational major, choice of occupation, and educational aspiration (e.g., Betz et al., 2003; Donnay & Borgen, 1996, 1999; Gasser et al., 2007; Larson, Wu, et al., 2010; Rottinghaus et al., 2002; Rottinghaus, Betz et al., 2003).

ACADEMIC PERFORMANCE ATTAINMENT

The third model concerns academic performance. Self-efficacy appears to significantly predict academic performance ($r = .34$) based on Multon,

Brown, and Lent's (1991; $k = 18$, $N = 1,194$) findings. Moderators revealed that the relation was stronger for younger versus older students, for low- versus high-complexity tasks, and for subject versus standardized tests. Finally, the relation was strong for post-test rather than pretest measurement of SE. Young and colleagues' meta-analytic findings concerning subsequent mathematics grades are consistent with Multon and colleagues findings. Young and colleagues reported an effect size of .24 for outcome expectancies and subsequent mathematics grades. Studies examining the unique contribution of outcome expectancies after SE has been controlled for have found that only SE uniquely contributes to subsequent academic achievement (Lent, Lopez, & Bieschke, 1993; Tilley, 2002).

Other Theories

SOCIAL LEARNING THEORY OF CAREER CHOICE AND COUNSELING

John Krumboltz's social learning theory of career decision making and counseling (Krumboltz, Mitchell, & Jones, 1976; Mitchell & Krumboltz, 1990, 1996) focuses on how individuals learn from interactions with the environment in making career choices. It also tries to address the origin of career choice. The emphasis is on instrumental learning (reinforcement and punishment) and associative learning (a neutral stimulus is paired with an emotionally laden one). Mitchell and Krumboltz (1996) outline four factors that influence a person's career path. The first factor that influences career decision making by interacting with the environment is the person's innate genetic endowment and any special abilities the person may possess. The second factor that influences career decision making is environmental conditions and events, broken up into 12 categories: job opportunities, social policies, rewards for some occupations, labor laws, physical events, natural resources, technological developments, changes in social organization, family training and resources, educational system, neighborhood influences, and community influences. The third and most important factor influencing career decision making has to do with learning experiences (i.e., instrumental and associative learning). Instrumental learning includes antecedents (e.g., innate ability and environmental conditions), covert and overt behaviors, and immediate or delayed consequences. Associative learning occurs when two stimuli are paired (e.g., smiles become associated with approval). The fourth factor in career decision making is called *task approach skills* (i.e., skills one brings to a task, such as

expectations about performance, work habits, emotional responses).

These four factors (innate abilities, environmental conditions, learning experiences, and task approach skills) interact over time to result in generalizations about self (self-observation generalizations) and the world (worldview generalizations). Six hypotheses predict a person's preference for (or avoidance of) an occupation to the extent that she or he has: succeeded (or failed) at tasks typical of the occupation; role models have been reinforced (or not reinforced) for those activities; and someone has spoken positively (or negatively) to him or her about that career (Mitchell & Krumboltz, 1996).

CAREER CONSTRUCTION THEORY

The career construction theory (Super, 1992; Super, Savickas, & Super, 1996) covers career development across the lifespan. In this theory, the people's own subjective meaning of their experiences moves to the forefront in the form of the narrative. People are believed to construct their careers by imposing meaning on their vocational behaviors and occupational experiences. These constructions are elicited from the career counselor in the form of stories or narratives (Savickas, 2005).

Three key constructs to be gleaned from the person's narrative are his or her vocational personality, life themes, and career adaptability. One's vocational personality is the objective and subjective P–E fit. The objective P–E fit concerns the information gleaned from the range of career assessments regarding the person and the environment (e.g., Holland code, classification of occupation according to Holland's RIASEC). The objective P–E fit includes the individual's career-related needs, abilities, values, and interests (Savickas, 2005). The subjective P–E fit encompasses the ideographic personal ideas about the self, work, and life. One's vocational personality concerns the "what" regarding vocational development.

People's life themes, referred to as the "why," are their ideas of the kind of people they are, the way in which their preferred or current occupations reflects their self-concepts, and the way in which work is reflective of the self. Vocational development is the process of trying to improve the P–E fit, express the self, and give back to the community (Savickas, 2005).

Career adaptability is defined as how people construct their careers. It consists of the attitudes, behaviors, and competencies a person uses in fitting the self to work that suits the person. In this theory, the interaction of P–E fit is emphasized; that is, the coping process. Savickas sees career adaptability as a "psychosocial construct that denotes an individual's readiness and resources for coping with current and imminent vocational development tasks, occupational transitions, and personal traumas" (Savickas, 2005, p. 51).

To be career adaptive, Savickas (2002, 2005) identifies four dimensions that must be addressed: becoming concerned about one's future as a worker, increasing personal control over one's vocational future, displaying curiosity by exploring possible selves and future scenarios, and strengthening confidence to pursue his or her aspirations. Career concern, the first dimension, incorporates planfulness and foresight into career planning by having the individual connect the past to the future, by being optimistic and future oriented. Career control, the second dimension, means the person and others believe he or she is responsible for constructing his or her career. Career curiosity, the third dimension, means the person is inquisitive about options and explores the fit between self and the world of work. Career confidence, the final dimension, reflects anticipation of success in encountering challenges and overcoming obstacles. Savickas (2005) provides an excellent case study example in which the reader can see an illustration of how a career counselor examines one's vocational personality, life themes, and career adaptability by engaging in a person's narrative. The counselor becomes an active player in helping to shape the narrative.

Savickas (2002) elucidates propositions of Super's theory, which emphasizes individual development rather than an individual difference view. The first three propositions anchor the theory in developmental contextualism; that is, that people construct their careers within a particular context. Life space is defined as a set of social roles. One's occupation is seen as a core role for most people. Career pattern is defined as a sequence and duration of work positions determined by parents, person's education, abilities, traits, self-concepts, and adaptability in transaction with opportunities presented by society (Savickas, 2002).

The next propositions integrate the individual difference tradition into the model. The theory states that the variation across people's attributes, such as ability, interests, and values, and the diversity across occupations and occupational requirements ensure considerable variation as to which occupations people seek out. Occupational success depends on the extent to which the person finds the work role an adequate outlet for his or her predominant vocational characteristics.

The next propositions concern the development of vocational self-concepts defined as "symbolic representations that are personally constructed, interpersonally conditioned, and linguistically communicated" (Savickas, 2002, p. 161). The propositions concerning vocational self-concepts are as follows. Job satisfaction depends on the degree the person has implemented his or her vocational self-concepts. The process of career construction is developing and implementing vocational self-concepts in work roles. Self-concepts develop through interaction. These vocational self-concepts become increasingly stable, although they can change with time and experience.

The last set of propositions concerns the progression of developmental tasks across time. People experience a maxicycle of career stages across time, labeled as periods of growth, exploration, establishment, management, and disengagement. Each stage is subdivided into periods marked by vocational development tasks that are social expectations. Minicyles of the stages occur when moving from one stage to the next. Vocational maturity is a psychosocial construct that denotes the degree of development along the stages. Crites (1978) defined vocational maturity as five attitudes about career decision making; namely, decisiveness, involvement, independence, orientation, and compromise. One proposition defines career adaptability (i.e., how one constructs a career). Career construction is prompted by vocational development tasks and produced by responses to these tasks (Savickas, 2002).

The theory's scholars have generated some research and attracted a number of practitioners. No meta-analyses or recent conceptual reviews of the theory were located. The propositions of the theory have received some support using data post hoc. Scholars agree that the theory does a good job of describing vocational development and does capture, after the fact, the integration of empirical data (Savickas, 2002).

OCCUPATIONAL CIRCUMSCRIPTION AND COMPROMISE THEORY

Occupational circumscription and compromise theory (L. S. Gottfredson, 1996, 1999) "focuses on how young people gradually come to recognize and deal with or fail to deal with the array of vocational choices their society provides" (L. S. Gottfredson, 2005, p. 71). Key concepts in the theory include self-concept (i.e., one's public and private view of self [L. S. Gottfredson, 2002]), images of occupations (i.e., occupational stereotypes), cognitive maps of occupations (sex type by prestige level, organization of occupations [L. S. Gottfredson, 2002]), compatibility (P–E fit), accessibility of occupations (realistic and available occupations), occupational aspirations (joint product of compatibility and accessibility), and social space (range of alternative within the cognitive map that person considers acceptable [L. S. Gottfredson, 2002]). Circumscription is the process by which youth narrow their range or zone of acceptable alternatives (L. S. Gottfredson, 2002). Compromise is the process by which youth give up their most preferred choices for less compatible choices that they perceive as more accessible (L. S. Gottfredson, 2002). Gottfredson also identified four stages corresponding to preschool (orientation to size and power), elementary school (orientation to sex roles), middle school (orientation to social valuation), and high school and beyond (orientation to internal, unique self).

Gottfredson's model has generated research particularly concerning occupational prestige and sex role socialization in children and adolescents (L. S. Gottfredson, 1999, 2002, 2005). Some researchers have found evidence supporting circumscription, while other researchers have found evidence that does not support compromise (L. S. Gottfredson, 2005). More research is needed that yields contrasting hypotheses for this theory in contrast with other theories such as social cognitive theory (L. S. Gottfredson, 2005). The literature search did not yield reviews or meta-analyses.

SOCIOLOGICAL THEORIES
Sociological theories of vocational choice development emphasize societal factors that directly and indirectly impact socioeconomic inequality and mobility. Examples include occupational prestige, parents' SES, parents' education, and structural features of secondary course preparation, like college tracks versus vocational tracks. These societal factors are moved to the foreground while person variables are in the background (Johnson & Mortimer, 2002). Occupational choice became of interest to sociologists as a context for studying intergenerational mobility. Over time, sociological theories that tried to explain how the prestige level of different occupations differs across people have incorporated sex, ethnicity, community size, number of siblings, and family of origin features.

Discrimination of women and racial and ethnic minorities has been incorporated into understanding the attainment process.

The strength of sociological approaches to career choice and development has been the central role of the social context outside the person as impacting the process. Some of the most important social contexts include cross-national differences in the structure of education and work (e.g., U.S. youth receive general high school diplomas vs. German youth, who are tracked to either the university or apprenticeships), structural features of schools (e.g., inequities in access to college preparation courses, differential learning due to tracking, quality differences in schools), and structural features of organizations (e.g., formal hiring procedures vs. informal procedures result in more or less hiring of racial and ethnic minority workers). Sociological factors thought to influence occupational attainment include the family (SES, occupation, work values, conditions of employment, and access to opportunities), adolescent employment, and community labor market conditions.

In the next section, the literature has been organized by vocational outcomes (e.g., vocational choice) and vocational processes (e.g., career decision making) that precede entry into the workforce. The population of interest includes children, adolescents, and college students.

Vocational Outcomes and Processes of Young People

The description of the history of vocational psychology already mentioned the split between vocational guidance of adolescents and college students and the work adjustment of employed adults. The literature concerning adolescents and college students focused on the processes and outcomes preceding entry into the workforce. The setting is the educational environment, with the majority of the samples being high school students and college students. The outcomes evolve as the child matures. The development of vocational interests, educational aspirations, and occupational aspirations are salient beginning in childhood. Educational attainment for all levels of schooling sets the stage for subsequent education and career advancement and hence is a salient vocational outcome. In college, choice of educational major and tentative career choice are important outcomes. The processes include the precursors to those aspirations, achievement, and choices, including exploration and the decision-making process. In the past 10 years, enough studies have been directed toward children so that several conceptual reviews have organized this literature (Hartung, Porfeli, & Vondracek, 2005; Watson & McMahan, 2005). Vocational outcomes will be presented first, including the development of interests, educational aspirations, occupational aspirations, educational achievement, and vocational choice. Vocational processes will be presented last, including career exploration and awareness, career decision making/career maturity, and decision making styles.

Vocational Outcomes

DEVELOPMENT OF INTERESTS

Given the enormous attention interests have received in vocational psychology, little work has focused on the interests of children, with notable exceptions (e.g., Tracey, 2002). Some evidence shows that there are few differences across U.S. racial and ethnic groups in terms of structure, stability, and content of interests for middle school students (Davison-Avilés & Spokane, 1999) and high school students (Day & Rounds, 1998; Day, Rounds, & Swaney, 1998). The hexagonal structure of interests posited by Holland's (1997) theory emerges more clearly for college students than for elementary and middle school students (Tracey & Ward, 1998). Socialization and occupational gender stereotyping appear to influence the occupations children prefer (e.g., Oppenheimer, 1991) and the extent to which those interests are traditionally feminine or masculine (e.g., Barak, Feldman, & Noy, 1991). Tracey (2002) showed that self-perceived competence in an activity predicted level of interests in that activity. The reverse was also true; level of interests predicted perceived competence in the activity. Denissen, Zarrett, and Eceles (2007), in a longitudinal study of 1,000 children between grades 1 and 12, showed a similar linkage between interests in English, math, science, sports, and instrumental music and self-perceived competence in those subjects. They provided evidence that the correlation increased over time, which they referred to as *longitudinal coupling*.

EDUCATIONAL ASPIRATIONS

Educational aspirations are defined as the impressions formed about academic abilities and the highest level of education an individual would like to attain (Rojewski, 2005). They are strongly related to occupational aspirations, seem stable from eighth grade on (Rojewski & Kim, 2003), and are thought to be the bedrock of occupational choice (Rojewski, 2005).

Educational aspirations appear to influence career choice because the higher the educational aspiration, the more opportunities are available to obtain a higher educational degree, which in turn increases occupational opportunities. These educational aspirations do not simply concern postsecondary aspirations but concern aspirations in middle school and high school to pursue college-bound math and science courses. Educational achievement likewise opens (or closes) doors of opportunity, which, in turn, leads to higher (or lower) educational and occupational aspirations. Rojewski and Yang (1997), for example, showed that achievement in grade 8 had a modest positive influence on occupational aspirations. In a sample of adolescents sampled first in eighth grade and then 2 years after high school graduation, two results were clear from their structural equation modeling. The students' occupational aspirations 2 years after high school were influenced more by academic achievement and educational aspirations in grade 8 than by anticipated occupational attainment in grade 8 (Rojewski & Kim, 2003).

OCCUPATIONAL ASPIRATIONS

Occupational aspirations can be defined as an individual's expressed career-related goals or choices (Johnson, 1995). Current aspirations predict future occupational aspirations and occupational choices. E. K. Strong, Jr., as early as 1955 showed that occupational aspirations of first-year college students predicted occupational attainment 19 years later ($r = .69$). Aspirations have been differentiated from occupational expectations, which reflect what occupations people realistically expect to enter. Gottfredson's theory (L. S. Gottfredson, 1999, 2002, 2005) identifies two processes, circumscription and compromise, which account for the discrepancy between aspirations and expectations. Aspirations may be compromised when people do not feel they have the ability to be successful, think the educational requirements are out of reach, believe their aspirations are not supported by family or friends, or perceive barriers regarding entry into or success in their occupational aspirations (Rojewski, 2005).

Several theories account for the development of occupational aspirations. Super's stage of career exploration is characterized by a gradual narrowing of career options from fantasizing to identifying tentative options (Super, 1992). Social cognitive career theory does not explicitly address occupational aspirations; rather, it identifies career goals and educational goals, which are dynamically impacted by SE, outcome expectancies, and interests as well as past performance attainments. Circumscription and compromise theory (L. S. Gottfredson, 2002) purports that children compromise their "ideal" aspirations by incorporating the salient barriers and reality of their situations to achieve an accessible realistic expectation. The circumscription process occurs when expectations are narrowed by eliminating options that do not fit with people's occupational self-concepts. These processes begin in the early stages, incorporating prestige and sex role stereotyping. Sociological theories posit that the link between occupational aspirations and occupational attainment are determined more by social forces (e.g., SES) than by personal forces (e.g., ambition) (Rojewski, 2005).

Occupational aspirations appear to develop in early childhood and become more realistic and stable over time (Rojewski & Kim, 2003; Rojewski & Yang, 1997). Studies have shown that half of children aged 8 and 11 years old reported stable aspirations 8 months later (Trice, 1991; Rojewski, 1997). Change is also common, and most often occurs within the same prestige level (e.g., doctor to lawyer or plumber to electrician) rather than higher or lower prestige (e.g., McNulty & Borgen, 1988). If aspirations across prestige levels occur, the change seems more likely to be from lower to higher prestige (Rojewski, 2005).

Sex, race and ethnicity, SES, and miscellaneous variables have been investigated as influencing occupational aspirations. Across multiple studies, sex continues to emerge as impacting occupational aspirations (Rojowski, 2005). It seems that children as young as age 4 report sex-based occupational preferences (Trice & Rush, 1995). Fantasy aspirations for girls compared to boys increased more proportionally from second grade (10% more) to 12th grade (20% more) (Helwig, 1998a,b, 2001, 2004). Females were more likely to have high- and low-prestige aspirations, whereas males were more likely to aspire to moderate-prestige jobs (see Rojewski, 2005). Despite higher aspirations, females' actual career expectations may not be consistent with those high aspirations. For example, females may restrict their range of potential occupations at an early age and may narrow their expectations downward over time (e.g., Hansen, 1994; Wahl & Blackhurst, 2000). Likewise, it appears that girls' aspirations and expectations may diverge, such that their aspirations are high while their actual expectations are

more traditional across both Hispanic (Arbona & Novy, 1991) and Caucasian girls (Arbona & Novy, 1991; Davey & Stoppard, 1993).

The literature regarding ethnicity has shown mixed results when other variables are not controlled (see Rojewski, 2005). It may be that SES or sex is a more powerful predictor than ethnicity regarding occupational aspirations (Arbona & Novy, 1991; Rojewski, 2005). For example, Arbona and Novy (1991) showed no differences across Hispanics and Caucasians, but did find sex differences, with girls having more social and conventional occupational aspirations whereas boys had more realistic and investigative occupational aspirations. Socioeconomic status was reported to moderate the effects of race/ethnicity on occupational aspirations (Rojewski & Yang, 1997).

A longitudinal study by Cook, Church, Ajanaku, and Shadish (1996) looked at career expectations and career aspirations over time of African American inner-city boys and Caucasian boys, sampling the children at second, fourth, sixth, and eighth grades. As the inner-city African American boys group ($n = 110$) aged, the gap widened between their own expectations and aspirations. Cook and colleagues (1996) reported that the relation between SES and age with occupational expectations was mediated by residing with both parents, having role models, and anticipating obstacles.

Across multiple studies, higher SES is directly or indirectly related to higher educational and occupational aspirations (e.g., Rojewski & Yang, 1997; Wahl & Blackhurst, 2000). A host of other variables have also been examined as to their influence on occupational aspirations. One variable that has consistently emerged is the role of the parents and families. Barber and Ecles (1992) showed that maternal employment, family processes, and parental expectations directly affected adolescents' values, self-concept, and achievement, which in turn, influenced educational and occupational aspirations.

EDUCATIONAL ACHIEVEMENT

The successful progression of children, adolescents, and college students through school and college is an important vocational outcome. Several clear predictors within the child (i.e., person predictors) have emerged in this literature. Cognitive ability appears to be a potent predictor of educational achievement (Benbow & Stanley, 1996; Snow, 1996). A recent meta-analysis examined graduate business students' academic success. The predictors were undergraduate grade point average (GPA) and the aptitude test required for graduate degrees in business schools, the Graduate Management Admission Test (GMAT) (Kuncel, Credé, & Thomas, 2007). They showed that both predictors combined contribute unique and substantial variance in predicting first-year graduate GPA and overall GPA of graduate students. In a meta-analysis of 58 studies with German-speaking samples, the Big Five personality factor conscientiousness was positively related to academic grades (Trapmann, Hell, Hirn, & Schuler, 2007). This finding is similar to the meta-analysis conducted by Barrick and Mount (1991) that showed conscientiousness to be the only Big Five factor related to job performance. None of the other Big Five factors related to educational achievement. The meta-analyses concerning the social cognitive career theory by Lent and colleagues (1994) presented earlier in the chapter showed that SE (Multon et al., 1991) and outcome expectancies (Young et al., 2004) were predictors of educational achievement. However, it appears that outcome expectancies do not predict academic grades in analyses in which SE is entered first in the regression equation (Lent et al., 1993; Tilley, 2002). In sum, cognitive ability, prior educational success (i.e., GPA), conscientiousness, and SE seem substantive contributors of educational attainment.

Besides person predictors, the role of parental involvement in educational achievement has been sufficiently researched to warrant several meta-analyses. Fan and Chen (2001), across 25 studies, found parental involvement overall (i.e., collapsing aspiration for child's education, communication, supervision, participation, and other) related (ρ = .25) to academic achievement (i.e., collapsing specific subject grades, GPA, combined grades). The specific parental involvement dimension of parental aspirations/expectations for child's education, in particular related to academic achievement (ρ = .40), whereas parental home supervision (e.g., rules concerning television watching and homework) did not relate (ρ = .09). Also, parental involvement overall was moderately related to general achievement like GPA (ρ = .33) and only somewhat related to achievement in specific domains (ρ ranges from .15 to .18) (Fan & Chen, 2001).

Rosenzweig (2001), examining 34 studies and 438 independent findings, found that seven positive parenting practices, when combined, accounted for 16.3% of the variance in educational attainment defined as standardized achievement tests, grades, GPAs, teacher tests and ratings, and orientation toward school. These seven practices were each significantly related to educational attainment: aspirations

and grade expectations (r = .29, 50 findings); parent engagement (i.e., interested and knowledgeable about child's life, spending time with child, active involvement, monitoring progress, positive attention to child-rearing) (r = .19, 25 findings); authoritative parenting (i.e., being demanding and yet responsive to children's needs and requests, showing warmth, clear standards, encouraging verbal exchanges, social responsibility, psychological autonomy) (r = .20, 22 findings), autonomy support (i.e., degree to which parents value and use techniques that encourage independent problem solving, choice, and participation in decisions) (r = .23, 12 findings), emotional support (i.e., showing personal love and compassion, initiating and receiving positive physical contact with child, accepting child for who she or he is) (r = .28, 6 findings), providing resources and learning experiences (i.e., establishing and supporting a positive learning environment at home, cultural enrichment) (r = .25, 10 findings), and specific parent participation activities in school (i.e., participating in decision making councils or frequency of participation in volunteer activities at the school) (r = .32, 6 findings).

Significant moderators included SES, grade level, and ethnicity. Socioeconomic status (low, middle, high, mixed) was influential for high and low levels but less so for the middle level (Rosenzweig, 2001). The relations of school success with the following parent involvement variables were significantly stronger for the low-SES children compared to other levels: parent participation in school, emotional support, aspirations for educational attainment, engagement, and providing resources and learning experiences. The relation of educational attainment and authoritative parenting was significantly stronger for high-SES children. The relation of educational attainment and parental engagement was significantly higher for middle-class children. Grade level (elementary, middle, and high school) was also a significant moderator. The relation of educational attainment and the seven positive parenting practices was strongest for the elementary level, weaker for the middle school level, and lowest for the high school level. Finally, ethnicity (white, African American, Asian American, Latino American, and other) emerged as a significant moderator. Only five of the seven positive parenting practices emerged as significant in a regression equation for Asian American and Latino American students: parental engagement, authoritative parenting, parent participation in school, aspirations for educational attainment and grade expectations, and providing resources and learning experiences. Autonomy support and emotional support were not as supportive for these two groups compared to whites and the "other" category. For African American children, autonomy support was not related to educational attainment; the other six positive parenting practices were significantly related to educational attainment (Rosenzweig, 2001).

Finally, Jeynes (2007) conducted a meta-analysis locating 52 studies that examined Hedges' g as the effect size unit of educational achievement in comparing samples of urban secondary school students who had parental involvement (i.e., expectations, parental style [extent to which parent demonstrated a supportive and helpful parenting approach], parent–child communication, monitoring homework) versus those who did not have parental involvement. Educational achievement was defined as grades, standardized tests, and other measures like teacher rating scales and indices of academic attitudes and behaviors. The effect size overall was $g = .53$; those parents who were more involved as opposed to less involved had children who were more academically successful by one-half of a standard deviation unit. Race did not moderate the effect size.

VOCATIONAL CHOICE

Vocational choice can be defined as a decision to choose a particular educational major, a particular job, or a particular career or occupation. In the literature, occupational and career choice are used synonymously, although the former term has been seen as more inclusive of a broader array of occupations across prestige level. Moreover, occupational choice is more anchored to a particular point in time, whereas career choice could be interpreted as a process that occurs across time. Choice of job is quite specific to one point in time and may or may not imply stability over time. Young adults' early entry into the workforce or entry into lower-prestige jobs may be best seen as actions of necessity rather than as something they aspire to or freely choose. In this section, the term *occupational choice* refers to occupations unless otherwise noted. Factors contributing to occupational choice have been extensively studied in vocational psychology for many years. Different theories emphasize different determinants of choice and have received variable amounts of support.

Holland's theory explains occupational choice as congruence between the person's primary interests and the occupational environment. A clear picture emerges regarding congruence from over 40 years of evidence: "what we know is that people choose, achieve, remain in, and are satisfied with their occupations for reasons other than congruence" (Phillips & Jome, 2005, p. 131). The point is that congruence accounts for very little explanatory power in why people choose and remain in their jobs.

Gottfredson's theory (L. S. Gottfredson, 1999, 2002, 2005) assumes that occupational choice comes about through a process, whereby occupational prestige and sex role stereotyping over time result in a narrowing of occupations under consideration. This theory has received mixed support (Phillips & Jome, 2005). People do share similar cognitive structures of the occupational world. Constructs of sex-role stereotyping, occupational prestige, and interests have been shown to be important in career choice (e.g., Leung & Plake, 1990). However, sex-based stereotypes appear to be learned earlier than posited in the theory (e.g., Henderson, Hesketh, & Tuffin, 1988). Also inconsistent with the theory is that girls perceive more flexibility than boys in the gender tradition of occupations they consider (e.g., Henderson et al., 1988). Moreover, occupational alternatives seem to expand rather than narrow over time, which is also inconsistent with the theory. One difficulty that may account for some of the mixed findings concerns the inability to untangle some levels of prestige, sex roles, and interests (Phillips & Jome, 2005). For example, it is hard to identify high-prestige, traditionally feminine occupations across the six Holland types.

Social cognitive career theory has received considerable support in the prediction of vocational choice. High scores on SE measures for the six Holland types have been shown to discriminate among educational major choices (Betz, et al., 1996; Larson et al., 2007; Lent, 2005) and among occupational choices (e.g., Donnay & Borgen, 1999; Lent, 2005). Basic dimensions of confidence have also been shown to differentiate educational major choice (Rottinghaus, Betz, et al., 2003) and occupational choice (Betz et al., 2003). Interests have long been shown to discriminate among educational major choices (e.g., Rottinghaus et al., 2002) and occupational choice (e.g., Donnay & Borgen, 1996; Harmon et al., 1994). Self-efficacy and outcome expectancies have also been shown to relate to career choice partly through interests (Lent, 2005).

SUMMARY

It is clear that social cognitive constructs, predominantly SE, are being widely researched as outcomes and as predictors. Self-efficacy is predicted by the four sources of SE. Self-efficacy across the six Holland types seem to predict and be predictive of vocational interests. Self-efficacy and outcome expectancies across academic domains are seem to be Choice goals seem to be predicted by SE, outcome expectancies, and interests within the respective domain. The prediction of choice goals across academic domains has received some attention. Interests continue to receive enormous amounts of attention as outcomes of SE, as predictors of career choice, and as an individual difference variable. The literature concerning the structure of interests cross-culturally is impressive. Educational aspirations have received some attention as an outcome with sociocognitive variables like SE and interests as predictors. Occupational aspirations are influenced by past achievement and past educational aspirations, as well as by parents' influences, gender, and SES. Finally, academic performance is clearly predicted by cognitive ability, SE, and parental involvement. It also seems that SES, grade level, and ethnicity alter the relation of parental involvement and academic success.

Vocational Processes

CAREER EXPLORATION AND AWARENESS

Few recent studies have sampled children and focused on career exploration and awareness. The findings are tentative and come from individual studies (Hartung et al., 2005). It seems children aged 10–12 engage in dynamic career exploration and increasingly work for pay outside the home as they enter middle school (e.g., Entwisle, Alexander, Olson, & Ross, 1999). Parents may be more important than peers by age 12 in the career exploration process (Hartung et al., 2005). Career awareness has been examined by determining what children know about various occupations. It seems clear that children by the age of 10 know about occupations. Moreover and not surprisingly, brighter children may know more about occupations than those peers who are less bright. It also seems that how much career information children and adolescents learn is impacted by SES. For example, poverty reduces the amount of career knowledge children have acquired (Weinger, 1998). Two studies conducted 25 years apart found that few job options, lower SES, and ethnicity accounted for the most variance in predicting less occupational knowledge in 180 children (Jordan, 1976; Jordan & Pope, 2001). Researchers have noted that children's knowledge does increase with age, but also have noted that children's occupational stereotypes may not

evaporate with more accurate knowledge over time (Watson & McMahon, 2005). In one study, Hispanic ninth graders did reduced stereotyped attitudes toward careers after career interventions. However, children with stereotyped attitudes distorted counter-stereotyped information (Haas & Sullivan, 1991).

In terms of gender, it seems girls are aware of work–family balance at a younger age than are boys, yet this may also impact girls' choices about careers. For example, girls as young as the sixth grade compared to boys incorporated more diverse life roles in terms of how they viewed work and family, as well as other life roles (Curry, Trew, Turner, & Hunter, 1994). At the same time, girls may consider fewer career options than boys and also are more decided about their careers than are boys; it may be that the girls' decisions are premature and lacking in specificity and careful planning (McMahon & Patton, 1997).

CAREER DECISION MAKING
AND CAREER MATURITY

Several theories identify decision making stages as well as related factors thought to be involved in the decision making process. Tiedeman's model (Super, Tiedeman, & Borow, 1961; Tiedeman, 1979; Tiedeman & O'Hara, 1963) identifies the stages of exploring, crystallizing choice, and clarifying choice by putting it into action. Harren (1979) extended Tiedeman's model to include person and contextual factors. These stages were labeled awareness, planning, commitment, and implementation. Krumboltz and Hamel (1977) created the DECIDES model standing for define, establish plan, clarify values, identify alternatives, eliminate alternatives, and starting action. Katz (1966) and Pitz and Harren (1980) proposed expected utility models that posit that the best decisions are those that include comprehensive information gathering and the weighing of probable outcomes and desired utilities of options. Gati (1986) created the sequential elimination model as an adaptation to the expected utility models. Gati's model has individuals eliminate alternatives in arriving at an optimal choice. There is weak support for these models in the literature, primarily because it appears that people do not follow a systematic logical progression in their career decision making, as the theories propose (Phillips, 1997; Phillips & Jome, 2005).

Difficulties in making vocational decisions have been investigated by categorizing subtypes of undecided students. Researchers have identified subtypes of career indecision ranging from needing more information to chronically indecisive regardless of information received (e.g., Chartrand, Martin, Robbins, & McAuliffe, 1994). Measures have been developed to assess indecision, such as the Careers Factors Inventory (Chartrand et al., 1994); these measures have been used to assist career counselors in working with undecided students and used to assist researchers in identifying correlates of career indecision, such as neuroticism and lack of confidence (Phillips & Jome, 2005).

Career maturity or vocational maturity, most commonly identified with Super's (1992) model, was defined by Super and Jordaan (1973) as "readiness to cope with developmental tasks of one's life stage, to make socially required career decisions, and to cope appropriately with the tasks which society confronts the developing youth and adult" (p. 4). Vocational maturity is often linked to career decision making and assumes children will make more mature decisions as they age (e.g., more decisive, involved, independent, oriented, and able to compromise). Walls (2000) did find that children's accuracy of occupational knowledge increased as they got older. It may be that children who have made a choice have a stronger vocational identity. Vondracek, Silbereisen, Reitzle, and Wiesner (1999) showed, in a sample of German children aged 10–13, that career maturity was higher in children who had made a vocational choice than for those who had not made a choice. It also seems that parents play a role in the timing of making a vocational choice. Evidence of occupational stereotyping that biases occupational preference was noted (Hartung et al., 2005). The good news is that gender stereotyping of occupations may have declined with successive generations of children, especially for girls (Watson & McMahon, 2005). Other societal influences that appear to have some influence on vocational preferences were parents, the school, media, and the home environment (Hartung et al., 2005). For example, parental support had an impact on the timing of vocational preferences (Walls, 2000).

DECISION MAKING STYLES

Most research in this area concerns Harren's three decision-making styles; namely, rational, intuitive, and dependent styles. The rational style is posited to be the most efficient for making deliberative choices, although the research is mixed. Results concerning career maturity were inconclusive. Phillips, Christopher-Sisk, and Gravino (2001) have used a relational continuum to describe decision making

styles; that is, a taxonomy of how young people make decisions in a relational context. Scholars are now speculating that the "best" decision making style may depend on the context.

Vocational Outcomes of Wage Earning Adults
Overview

Many theories have been used to explain the range of vocational outcomes concerning adults in the world of work. The theories have bridged counseling psychology, industrial/organizational psychology, and social/personality psychology. Holland's (1997) P–E fit theory and Dawis and Lofquist's TWA (Dawis, 2002, 2005; Dawis & Lofquist, 1984) have been the predominant theories from counseling psychology. Work motivation theories have been dominant in I/O psychology. Work motivation is viewed as a "set of energetic forces that originate both within as well as beyond an individual's being to initiate work-related behavior and to determine its form, direction, intensity, and duration" (Pinder, 1998, p. 11). Social psychology's contribution has come in the adaptation of mini-theories that explain why certain antecedents or mediator/moderators may have an impact on a particular vocational outcome. Two examples include attribution theory (i.e., job satisfaction or performance is based, in part, on how the person attributes his or her situation [My job satisfaction is based on my hard work versus the whims of the organization]) and expectancy theory (i.e., satisfaction is produced by the reinforcers that follow performance).

The theories highlight different processes and outcomes. Holland's theory is most commonly seen as identifying congruence as an antecedent of job satisfaction and subsequent work adjustment. Dawis' TWA focuses on the complementary outcomes of job satisfaction and satisfactoriness (job satisfaction from employer's perspective). Dawis identifies processes that the person uses to stay within an organization when the P–E fit is in a state of discorrespondence (Dawis, 2005). These include flexibility (tolerating mismatch), reactive adjustment (change self), active adjustment (change the job), and perseverance (duration of discorrespondence). His theory can be used to examine tenure and negative indicators like intentions to quit and quitting. Work motivation theory identifies person characteristics that motivate the person to choose, persist, and be successful in the job (Latham & Pinder, 2005). Social psychology theories focus on the explanation for a particular relation. For example, expectancy theories would explain how job performance leads to job satisfaction because satisfaction follows from the rewards produced by performance.

Outcomes

Since 1990, researchers have extensively examined the contribution of antecedents or predictors on a wide range of vocational outcomes. The vocational outcomes in this section are frequently multifaceted and often measured by more than one method. The organization of this section will be by outcomes organized logically by how they occur sequentially in people's lives. The outcomes are job search behaviors and job search outcomes, job satisfaction, job attitudes, organizational citizenship behavior (defined as behaviors that facilitate the core aspects of the job), job performance, counterproductive work behaviors, turnover intentions/intentions to quit, quitting/turnover, absenteeism, withdrawal, career success, negative mental health outcomes, and life satisfaction and well-being. When a construct is both a predictor and an outcome (e.g., job satisfaction is an outcome and a predictor of job performance), the construct will be discussed separately as an outcome and also as an antecedent of another outcome.

JOB SEARCH BEHAVIORS AND
JOB SEARCH OUTCOMES

Job search behaviors can be defined as a purposive, volitional pattern of action that begins with the identification and commitment to pursuing an employment goal (Kanfer, Wanberg, & Kantrowitz, 2001). Most authors had measured only frequency (how many times the person engaged in job search behaviors) or effort (how many hours the person engaged in job search activities over a specific time period). In the meta-analyses, Kanfer and colleagues (2001) defined job search behaviors as both frequency and effort. Kanfer and colleagues defined job search outcome in three ways: job status (I have/do not have a job), job search duration, and number of job offers. In their meta-analyses ($k = 82$, $N = 21,898$), Kanfer and colleagues investigated the contribution of sets of antecedents that influence both job search behaviors and the job search outcome. The antecedents were personality traits, generalized expectancies, self-evaluations, situational antecedents (motives [financial need and employment commitment] and social support), and demographic variables. They will be reviewed in that order, starting with the prediction of job search behaviors followed by job search outcomes.

Personality is thought to have an impact on the job search through the engagement of different search strategies and the extent to which people use proactive job search behaviors (Kanfer et al., 2001). Job search behaviors (measures of frequency of job search activities or time spent searching were used) were related to extraversion ($\rho = .46$), openness ($\rho = .27$), and conscientiousness ($\rho = .38$) (Kanfer et al., 2001).

Generalized expectancies are thought to have an impact on job search behaviors through their influence on both problem-and emotion-focused coping. The two antecedents in this category—locus of control and optimism—were not predictive of job search behaviors. However, self-evaluations were predictive of job search behaviors, namely SE ($\rho = .27$) and self-esteem ($\rho = .27$). Self-evaluations were thought to have an impact on job search behaviors through their influence on persistence when difficulty increases (Kanfer et al., 2001).

Situational antecedents were also modestly related to job search behaviors, including motives of financial need ($\rho = .21$) and employment commitment, defined as the belief that having a job is very important ($\rho = .29$) and social support ($\rho = .24$). Motives are thought to influence job search behaviors by influencing job search effort and intensity, and social support is thought to influence job search behaviors as a way of coping with negative aspects of the job search by receiving advice in the short term and encouragement in the long run (Kanfer et al., 2001). None of the demographic variables influenced job search behaviors, including age, gender, education, race, and job tenure.

The antecedents, in general were less predictive of job search outcomes (i.e., job status, number of offers, and duration of search) than of job search behaviors (i.e., three dimensions labeled intensity of effort, content duration, and temporal-persistence). There were also less data on job search outcomes than on job search behaviors as criterion variables. Job search behaviors modestly related to job status (i.e., having a job) ($\rho = .21$) and number of offers ($\rho = .28$). Neuroticism was modestly related to number of offers ($\rho = -.22$). Extraversion, openness, and agreeableness modestly related to number of job offers in the only study that measured both job offers and those traits ($rs = .41, .28, .29$) (Kanfer et al., 2001). Interestingly, conscientiousness, which was measured more frequently, showed no relation with job search outcomes. Generalized expectancies were not predictive of job search outcomes. Self-evaluation was related; self-esteem was modestly related to the duration of the search ($\rho = -.24$), and SE was modestly related to the number of offers ($\rho = .28$). The situational antecedent of motive was not related to job search outcomes, whereas the social antecedent of social support was moderately related to job status ($\rho = .30$). Demographic variables were not related to the job search outcomes.

JOB SATISFACTION

Job satisfaction is defined as a "pleasurable or positive emotional state resulting from the appraisal of one's job or job experiences" (Locke, 1978, p. 1300). Job satisfaction has been most frequently measured by the Job Descriptive Index (Smith, Kendall, & Hulin, 1969) and the Minnesota Job Questionnaire (Weiss, Dawis, & England, 1967).

Surprisingly, one salient predictor of job satisfaction may be a genetic influence. Arvey, Bouchard, Segal, and Abraham (1989) presented evidence with monozygotic twins reared together versus apart that job satisfaction was dispositional, and as much as 30% of the variance was inherited. This may partially explain the strong relationship of job satisfaction with life satisfaction (Fritzsche & Parrish, 2005).

One class of job satisfaction predictors has been dispositional traits ranging from broad traits to a specific trait, locus of control. Connolly and Viswesvaran (2000), in their meta-analyses, were interested in the interaction of negative and positive affectivity with job satisfaction. They also examined a third trait labeled *affective disposition*, defined as the "tendency to respond to classes of environmental stimuli in a predetermined affect-based manner" (Judge & Hulin, 1993). Their meta-analyses ($N = 6233$, $k = .27$) did find moderate relations of job satisfaction with positive affectivity ($\rho = .49$), negative affectivity ($\rho = -.33$), and affective disposition ($\rho = .36$). The next study was the examination of the Big Five personality factors as antecedents of job satisfaction. Judge, Heller, and Mount (2002), in their meta-analyses ($N = 24527$, $k = 163$), reported small effect sizes concerning the relation of job satisfaction with neuroticism ($\rho = -.29$), extraversion ($\rho = .25$), and conscientiousness ($\rho = .26$). Finally, locus of control has also been examined as a specific dispositional attribute; it was shown to correlate with job satisfaction at about .20 (Fritzsche & Parrish, 2005).

Holland's supposition concerning congruence as predictive of job satisfaction has received considerable attention. The most recent meta-analyses was conducted Tsabari and colleagues (2005;

$N = 6557$, $k = 53$). The congruence–job satisfaction relation was .17, which included 0 in the 95% CI. In other words, there was no relation. Owings and Fritzsche (2000) suspect that one reason for the weak relation of congruence and job satisfaction may be that job satisfaction often includes domains that are not directly related to environmental congruence, such as pay or coworkers. Another reason may be that job satisfaction measures aspects of satisfaction other than the tasks associated with one of the six domains of Holland's RIASEC (Spokane & Cruza-Guet, 2005). Tsabari and colleagues (2005) did find that the correlation was influenced by several moderators. First, the correlation varied by vocational type. Only social types on Holland's RIASEC hexagon did not include 0 in the 95% CI, although the effect was small ($\rho = .11$). The correlation also varied by the congruence index used. The strongest congruence index was the Lachan index, with $\rho = .22$ with a 95% CI ranging from .18 to .25. Finally, the correlation varied by interest questionnaire; the relation was .09 when the General Occupational Themes from the SII were used, compared to the relation being .20 when the Self-Directed Search was used.

Dik (2006) also found moderators of the congruence–job satisfaction relation in a sample of employed young adults. Congruence was associated more with job satisfaction for participants who placed less importance on their jobs and who perceived less opportunity for active involvement in their work. Congruence was associated more with intrinsic job satisfaction than with overall job satisfaction. The modified C index (Eggerth & Andrew, 2006) resulted in a higher mean congruence score and had larger congruence–satisfaction correlations compared to other congruence indices' correlations with satisfaction (Dik, 2006).

Within the I/O literature, the environment has been defined as the organization, rather than by Holland's six types. Person–organization fit has also been shown to be an antecedent of job satisfaction. Verquer, Beehr, and Wagner (2003), in their meta-analysis ($k = 21$), reported an effect size of $\rho = .28$. Type of fit, method of calculating fit, dimension of fit, and use of established measure moderated the relation. Saks and Ashforth (1997) also reported a significant relation between person–organization fit and job satisfaction.

Other antecedents of job satisfaction have been examined. Perceived organizational support positively relates to job satisfaction with a strong effect size ($\rho = .62$) (Rhoades & Eisenberger, 2002; $k = 73$,

N = 13,719). A second meta-analyses (Podsakoff, LePine, & LePine, 2007; k = 183; N = 20, 943) differentiated stressors into hindrance stressors, which consist of role ambiguity, organization politics, and job security concerns, from challenge stressors, which consist of levels of workload, time pressure, job scope, and responsibilities. In Podsakoff and colleagues' model, hindrance and challenge stressors were thought to have an impact on job satisfaction directly and indirectly through strain. Hindrance stressors (i.e., role ambiguity, organization politics, and job security concerns) were significantly related to job satisfaction (ρ = −.57); challenge stressors were not related to job satisfaction.

Meta-analyses have been conducted on specific populations, namely, nurses and people employed part-time versus full-time. Zangaro and Soeken (2007; k = 31, N = 14,567) examined nurses' job satisfaction and only reported uncorrected correlations. They identified three antecedents of job satisfaction yielding medium effects. They were the relation of job satisfaction with autonomy (r = .30), job stress (r = −.43), and nurse-physician collaboration (r = .37). Thorsteinson (2003), in his meta-analysis (k = 38, N = 51, 231), examined whether part-time workers versus full-time workers would differ in job satisfaction. Thorsteinson reported no significant differences between part-time versus full-time workers on either global job satisfaction or any of the facets of job satisfaction.

JOB ATTITUDES

Although job satisfaction was examined individually, job satisfaction has also been considered as part of a larger constellation of job attitudes. From this perspective, job attitudes include positive attitudes toward the job (job satisfaction and affective commitment [employee's emotional attachment to, identification with, and involvement in the organization]) and negative attitudes toward the job (burnout and turnover intentions). Thoresen, Kaplan, Barsky, Warren, and Chermont (2003), in their meta-analyses (k = 205, N = 62,527), hoped to elucidate the role of emotions in predicting job attitudes. First, they differentiated affect into two dimensions: namely, positive and negative affect. They expected that job attitudes and performances that are positive and negative should differentially relate accordingly to indices of positive and negative affect. However, their meta-analyses did not support this. Positive affectivity and negative affectivity related moderately with job satisfaction (ρs = .34, −.34), affective commitment (ρs = .35, −.27), depersonalization

(ρs = −.27, .47), and personal accomplishment (ρs = .49, −.34), and somewhat with turnover intentions (ρs = −.17, .28). Positive and negative affectivity did seem to differentially relate to emotional exhaustion (ρs = −.32, .62).

Second, Thoresen and colleagues (2003) were interested in differentiating the role of dispositional traits of affectivity from more state-like affect. They speculated that an argument could be made that trait affectivity should be more influential than state affect because work attitudes have accumulated over time; thus, trait affectivity that is consistent across many situations would have had a cumulative effect on job attitudes. On the other hand, state affect could be argued to be more influential because it is more proximal to job attitudes. Their findings showed little difference between the relation of job attitudes with trait measures versus state affect measures. Another meta-analysis by Rhoades and Eisenberger (2002) examined perceived organizational support as contributing to job attitudes. Perceived organizational support was defined as employees' belief that the organization values their contribution and cares about their well-being (Rhoades & Eisenberger, 2002; k = 73, N = 13,719). Job attitudes included organizational commitment (affective commitment and continuance commitment [resulting from accumulated personal interests binding one to the organization; Meyer & Allen, 1997]), job-related affect (job satisfaction and positive mood at work [general emotional state without a specific object; George, 1989]) job involvement (identification with and interest in the specific work one performs; O'Driscoll & Randall, 1999), strains (aversive psychological and psychosomatic reactions), desire to remain on the job, and intentions to quit. Rhoades and Eisenberger (2002), in their meta-analysis, showed that perceived organizational support was moderately related to all of the job attitudes including job satisfaction (ρ = .62), positive mood at work (ρ = .49), job involvement (ρ = .39), strain (ρ = −.32), desire to remain with organization (ρ = .66), and turnover intentions (ρ = −.51).

The final meta-analysis that examined job attitudes as outcomes was that by Humphrey, Nahrgang, and Morgeson (2007). They were interested in how much job characteristics, social characteristics, and work context characteristics influenced job attitudes. The job attitudes included satisfaction with the job, growth, supervisor, coworkers, compensation, and promotion. Job attitudes also included organizational commitment, job involvement, and internal work motivation.

The job characteristics included autonomy (freedom an individual has in carrying out work), skill variety (the extent to which an individual must use different skills to execute his or her job), task variety (extent to which an individual performs different tasks), task significance (extent to which a job impacts others' lives), task identity (extent to which an individual can complete a whole piece of work), feedback from the job (extent to which a job imparts information about an individual's performance), information processing (extent to which a job necessitates an incumbent to focus on and manage information), job complexity (extent to which a job is multifaceted and difficult to perform), specialization (extent to which a job involves the performance of tasks requiring specific knowledge and skill), and problem solving (extent to which a job requires the production of unique solutions or ideas). Social characteristics included interdependence (extent to which a job is contingent on others' work and other jobs are dependent on the work of the focal job), feedback from others (extent to which other organizational members provide performance information), social support (extent to which a job provides opportunities for getting assistance and advice from either supervisors or coworkers), and interaction outside the organization (extent to which a job requires person to communicate with people outside the organization). Work context characteristics include physical demands (amount of physical activity or effort necessary for a job) and work conditions (aspects of the work environment such as health hazards, temperature, and noise). The studies that measured work demands included only job satisfaction.

Satisfaction with the job and satisfaction with growth opportunities were moderately correlated above |.20| with all the work characteristics and social characteristics except satisfaction with growth was not related to feedback from others. Job satisfaction was also modestly correlated above |.20| with work demands. Satisfaction with the supervisor and coworkers was correlated above |.20| with work characteristics except task identity and with social characteristics. Satisfaction with compensation was only correlated above |.20| with the work characteristics of autonomy and feedback from the job and the social characteristics of feedback from others. Satisfaction with promotion was correlated above |.20| only with the work characteristics of task variety and feedback from the job and the social characteristic of feedback from others. Organizational commitment was moderately correlated with all work characteristics and all social characteristics.

Job involvement correlated with all work characteristics except task identity and none of the social characteristics. Internal work motivation correlated with all work characteristics except task identity and all social characteristics except social support (Humphrey et al., 2007).

ORGANIZATIONAL COMMITMENT

Organizational commitment has been defined as consisting of three components; namely, affective commitment (identification with and attachment to the organization), continuance commitment (resulting from accumulated personal interests binding one to the organization), and normative commitment (sense of obligation to remain with the organization; Meyer & Allen, 1997). Several meta-analyses identify some antecedents of organizational commitment. The first antecedent identified was job satisfaction. One meta-analyses ($N = 39,187$ $k = 112$) by Harrison, Newman, and Roth (2006) showed organizational commitment to be strongly related to job satisfaction ($\rho = .60$). A second antecedent, perceived organizational support (support in the organizational environment), also was strongly related to organizational commitment ($\rho = .67$), as shown by Rhoades and Eisenberger (2002) in their meta-analysis ($k = 73$, $N = 13,719$). Person–organization fit has also been shown in a meta-analysis to be an antecedent of organizational commitment (Verquer et al., 2003; $\rho = .31$). An additional antecedent, hindrance stressors (i.e., role ambiguity, organization politics, and job security concerns), was identified in Podsakoff, LePine, and LePine's (2007) meta-analyses. They showed hindrance stressors (and not challenge stressors) significantly related to organizational commitment ($\rho = -.52$). Finally, part-time versus full-time job status did not differ by organizational commitment (Thorsteinson, 2003).

GLOBAL JOB PERFORMANCE

Job performance has been defined in either a broad, global way or based on separating job performance into two facets. The global job performance assessment has dominated and has often been measured as a subjective global rating (e.g., supervisor ratings) and an objective global rating (e.g., salary or productivity). Job performance will be specified as either a global rating (subjective and/or objective) or instrumental performance. The predictors or antecedents thought to influence global job performance will be presented in the following order: cognitive abilities and job knowledge, personality, SE, job satisfaction, and additional antecedents.

Cognitive abilities and job knowledge, although seldom researched in counseling psychology, have long been examined as an antecedent of work performance in I/O psychology (Borman et al., 2003; Hough & Oswald, 2000). The general factor in intelligence, referred to as the *g* factor, is predictive of job knowledge, job performance, and training performance (e.g., Hunter & Hunter, 1984; Judge et al., 2007; Levine, Spector, Menon, Narayanan, & Cannon-Bowers, 1996; Schmidt & Hunter, 1998) with the influence strongest for high-complexity roles (see Bormon et al., 2003). Research findings accumulated over 85 years, primarily in the United States, suggest that a general cognitive ability test plus a structured interview is highly predictive of future job performance (Schmidt & Hunter, 1998). The potency of cognitive ability as a predictor of job performance is cross-culturally robust. This relation of cognitive ability to job performance and job training was supported in a meta-analysis using only German samples (ks = 9, 90, Ns = 7,46,11,969) with ρ values of .534 and .467 (Hülsheger, Maier, & Stumpp, 2007). A meta-analysis using only British samples (Bertua, Anderson, & Salgado, 2005; k = 283, 223, Ns = 1,32,62,75,311) found similar strong relations of cognitive abilities and specific abilities relating to job performance and training success (ρs = .50, .48). Salgado and colleagues (2003) widened the cross-cultural meta-analytic examination to 11 European countries (ks = 19, 15, Ns = 1,93,62,897) to examine the relation of cognitive ability with job performance and job training across occupational groups. They also found similar moderate to large relations between cognitive ability and job performance (ρs range from .24 [police] to .67 [manager]; and training success (ρs range from .25 [police] to .74 [engineer]). As with American studies, job complexity moderated the relation to both outcomes, in that more cognitively complex positions yielded a stronger relation (Salgado et al., 2003). Job knowledge is also predictive of job performance and training performance, especially in conditions of high job-test similarity (ρs = .62, .76) (Borman et al., 2003).

Personality traits have gained prominence as antecedents of job performance. One well-known meta-analysis is Barrick and Mount's (1991) meta-analysis (k= 162, N = 23,994) of the Big Five and objective and subjective indices of job performance. Objective indices were productivity, salary, turnover, tenure, and status change. Subjective ratings were supervisor ratings. Five occupational groups were examined; namely, professionals, police, managers, sales people,

skilled workers, and semiskilled workers. Conscientiousness was related to job performance across three criteria (job proficiency, training proficiency, personnel data) with ρs ranging from .20 to .23. When the subjective supervisory data was separated from the objective data (i.e., turnover/tenure, productivity data, status change, and salary), the supervisor ratings yielded a higher relation (ρ = .26) than the mean of the objective ratings (ρ = .10). Extraversion and openness to experience yielded relations with training proficiency of ρs =.26 and .25, respectively.

Researchers continue to examine the role of conscientiousness in job performance. Dudley, Orvis, Lebiecki, and Cortina's (2006) meta-analysis (k = 42, N = 7,342) examined if facets of conscientiousness (achievement, dependability, order, and cautiousness) related to indices of job performance beyond the general trait of conscientiousness. In this study, prior meta-analytic estimates were included. Given the lower internal consistency estimates in subscales, the uncorrected rs rather than the population estimates are reported. None of the facets was related to overall job performance (rs ranged from-01 to .13). Likewise, the facets did not relate to task performance (rs ranged from .06 to .13).

Three meta-analyses have examined the relation of SE (not generalized SE) to predict job performance (Judge et al., 2007; Sadri & Robertson, 1993; Stajkovic & Luthans, 1998). Sadri and Robertson (k = 16, N = 1,658) showed that SE was related to performance overall (ρ = .40) and behavioral intentions (ρ = .34). Stajkovic and Luthans (1998) added more studies to those located in 1993 by Sadri and Robertson (k = 157, N = 21,616) and found a relation of SE and performance overall of ρ = .36. They identified several moderators of that relation. The magnitude of the relation was strongest for simple tasks, decreasing for moderate and high task complexity. The relation of SE and performance was also lower in magnitude for field settings (r = .37) compared to lab settings (r = .60). Judge and colleagues (2007), in the final meta-analysis, used prior meta-analytic estimates and computed some that were not reported in the literature. They examined whether the relation of SE and performance would be attenuated after the relation of performance and distal influences—namely, the Big Five, ability, and experience—had been taken into account. These authors showed that the contribution of SE to work-related performance is much smaller once the distal variables were controlled. Self-efficacy's standardized regression coefficient was .13 in the prediction of work performance and nonsignificant. Significant unique predictors of work performance were cognitive ability (β = .52), conscientiousness (β = .26), and experience (β = .26). Collectively, the Big Five, experience, and cognitive ability and SE accounted for 46% of the variance in work performance. Significant predictors of SE were cognitive ability, conscientiousness, extraversion, emotional stability, and experience.

One of the most discussed predictors of global job performance is job satisfaction. Harrison and colleagues (2006) found a robust relation between job satisfaction and job performance (ρ = .30). Judge, Thoresen, Bono, and Patton (2001), in their meta-analysis (k =312, N = 54,417), showed job satisfaction and global job performance to be related ρ = .30. (The uncorrected relation was .18.) Judge and colleagues (2001) presented seven alternative models of the possible explanatory relation of job satisfaction and job performance with each predicting the other, no relation, no relation due to a third variable, and a model showing reciprocal influence.

Situational antecedents of job performance were looked at extensively by Humphrey and colleagues (2007). In their meta-analysis (k = 259, N = 2,19,625), they divided situational antecedents into motivational work characteristics (e.g., task variety), social characteristics (e.g., social support), and work context characteristics (working conditions). Job performance was defined subjectively (e.g., supervisor ratings) and objectively (e.g., salary). No motivational, social, or work context characteristics in the work environment predicted objective performance. Motivational (autonomy, task variety, task significance, feedback from the job, and job complexity) and social (feedback from other) characteristics in the work environment related to subjective performance (ρs range from .20 to .37).

Person–organizational fit models have been shown to be predictive of job performance. Hoffman and Woehr (2006), in their meta-analyses (k = 24), reported significant effect sizes of person–organization fit indices that related positively to both objective measures of job performance (ρ = .25) and subjective measures of job performance (ρ = .26).

INSTRUMENTAL JOB PERFORMANCE
The two facets of job performance (instrumental performance and contextual performance) have received increasing attention. Instrumental performance, also called *focal performance*, in role behaviors or task performance has been defined as behavior forming the core of the job. An example of instrumental performance would be productivity (number of articles published). Contextual performance, most commonly called *organizational citizenship behavior* (OCB), has been defined as supporting the core of the job. An example of OCB would be the willingness to serve on committees or assist other workers. The examination of OCB will be reviewed immediately after instrumental job performance. Several meta-analyses have examined instrumental job performance or task performance as distinct from global job performance. Task performance was positively related to perceived organizational support (ρ = .18) (Rhoades & Eisenberger, 2002; k = 73, N = 13,719). Trust was also related to task performance (ρ = .33) (Colquitt, Scott, & LePine, 2007; k = 132, N = 7,284).

ORGANIZATIONAL CITIZENSHIP BEHAVIOR
Organizational citizenship behavior has also been called *contextual performance* or *interpersonal facilitation*. Some studies have reported the antecedents of OCBs as distinct from task performance.

Regarding personality traits, Dudley and colleagues (2006) in their meta-analysis examined if the facets of conscientiousness (i.e., achievement, dependability, order, and cautiousness) related to interpersonal facilitation. The relation of the facet scores with interpersonal facilitation yielded nominal uncorrected correlations.

Harrison and colleagues (2006) showed OCB to be related to job satisfaction (ρ = .28), organizational commitment (ρ = .25), and focal performance or task performance (ρ = .23). The relation of OCB with job satisfaction is very similar to the findings reported by Organ and Ryan (1995) in their earlier meta-analysis.

Several other predictors have been examined. Person–organizational fit models have been shown to be predictive of OCB (ρ = .21) (Hoffman & Woehr, 2006). Perceived organizational support was positively related to extra role job performance (i.e., OCB) (ρ =.22) in Rhoades and Eisenberger's (2002) meta-analyses. Trust was related to OCB (ρ = .27) in Colquitt and colleagues' meta-analysis.

Some authors have conceptualized OCB as multifaceted, and have identified five facets; namely, altruism toward individuals, compliance (labeled conscientiousness), sportsmanship (not complaining), courtesy (consulting with others before acting), and civic virtue (keeping up with matters that affect the organization). LePine, Erez, and Johnson (2002), in their meta-analyses, showed that OCB facets did not differentially relate to predictors. Moreover, the OCB facets correlated highly with each other. All five facets related to predictors around .20 (job satisfaction, organizational commitment, fairness, leader support, and the Big Five conscientiousness). LePine and colleagues then tried dividing the five facets into two facets, namely OCB-Interpersonal (courtesy and altruism) and OCB-Organizational (sportsmanship, civic virtue, and compliance), and still the results yielded no differentiation. The global measure of OCB correlated highest with outcomes: job satisfaction (ρ = .31), organizational commitment (ρ = .32), fairness (ρ = .31), leader support (ρ = .41), and conscientiousness (ρ = .13) (LePine et al., 2002).

Dalal (2005) examined the relation of OCB and counterproductive work behaviors in his meta-analysis (k = 49; N = 16,721). He theorized the explanatory mechanism of the relation between OCB and counterproductive work behaviors (CWB) on the one hand and organizational justice, job satisfaction, and organizational commitment on the other. Employees respond to working conditions that are satisfying and workplace processes that are fair by behaving in ways that benefit the organization and/or others (OCB). However, if employees are dissatisfied and feel workplace processes are not fair, then they behave in ways that are not helpful (CWB). The relation of OCB and CWB was ρ = –.32 (Dalal, 2005). The two constructs were split into two separate constructs, an interpersonal OCB and an organizational OCB, and an interpersonal CWB and an organizational CWB. Only the OCB-O and the CWB-O were related (ρ = –.33) (Dalal, 2005).

Dalal (2005) also examined antecedents of OCB and CWB. Significant OCB antecedents were organizational commitment (ρ = .28), organizational justice (ρ = .20), conscientiousness (ρ = .23), and positive affect (ρ = .34). Job satisfaction and negative affect were not significant antecedents. He theorized that positive affect and negative affect should have an impact on OCB and CWB because affect is arousal that entices action, with positive affect leading to constructive action and negative affect leading to destructive action. The results suggest that positive and negative affect may operate differently on the two constructs.

COUNTERPRODUCTIVE WORK BEHAVIORS

These negative work outcomes have received some attention. In the meta-analysis reported earlier, Dalal (2005) reported several antecedents that related

above .20 to CWBs. These included job satisfaction (ρ = –.37), organizational commitment (ρ = –.36), organizational justice (ρ = –.25), conscientiousness (ρ = –.38) (the uncorrected correlation was much smaller, r = .2), positive affect (ρ = –.34), and negative affect (ρ = .41). Dudley and colleagues (2006) reported a similar correlation for CWBs and conscientiousness with an uncorrected correlation of –.16 and a ρ = –.26. The facet scale, dependability, was also modestly related to CWBs (r = –.21; ρ = –.34). Colquitt and colleagues (2007) recently showed trust to negatively relate to CWBs (ρ = –. 33).

TURNOVER INTENTIONS/INTENTION TO QUIT

Intentions to quit are defined as one's desire or willingness to leave an organization. The theory of reasoned action (Ajzen, 2002) explains intentions as the mechanism that leads to the action of quitting. This vocational outcome has received considerable attention in meta-analyses. In terms of affective antecedents, Thoreson and colleagues (2003) in their meta-analysis showed intentions to quit to be related to negative affectivity (ρ = .28) but not to positive affectivity. One situational antecedent among many examined was shown to relate to turnover intentions, namely a social antecedent (feedback from others) (ρ = .34). Person–organization fit has also been shown to be an antecedent of intentions to quit (Verquer et al., 2003) (ρ = –.21). Perceived organizational support relates strongly to turnover intentions, with a ρ = –.51 (Rhoades & Eisenberger, 2002). Hindrance stressors also strongly related to turnover intentions (ρ = .49), as reported by Podsakoff and colleagues (2007) in their meta-analysis. It appears that part-time versus full-time workers are no more or less likely to have intentions of leaving their job (Thorsteinson, 2003).

WITHDRAWAL BEHAVIORS

Withdrawal behaviors are identified as those that pull employees away from the organization and are often seen as precursors to quitting. Two meta-analyses were located concerning withdrawal behaviors. Perceived organizational support did relate to withdrawal behavior (ρ = –.26) (Rhoades & Eisenberger, 2002). Hindrance stressors were also related to withdrawal behaviors (ρ = .22) in Podsakoff and colleagues' meta-analysis (2007).

QUITTING/TURNOVER

This outcome has been used as one behavioral negative job outcome. Several meta-analyses examined turnover or quitting. It seems turnover is negatively related to job satisfaction (ρ = −19), organizational commitment (ρ = −.22), contextual performance (ρ = −.22) and absenteeism (ρ = −.26). Person–organizational fit models have been shown to be predictive of turnover (ρ = .26) (Hoffman & Woehr, 2006). Perceived organizational support did not relate to turnover (Rhoades & Eisenberger, 2002), but hindrance stressors did relate to turnover (ρ = .23), as shown by Podsakoff and colleagues' (2007) meta-analysis. One creative suggestion in the literature concerning the examination of turnover as a construct was made by Griffeth, Steel, Allen, and Bryan (2005). They suggested that scholars needed to measure perceived job alternatives if a person quits the job. Their intent was to capture positive reasons for leaving a job rather than only negative reasons (e.g., lack of organizational support). They proceeded to develop such a measure, titled the Employment Opportunity Index (Griffeth et al., 2005).

LATENESS

Lateness has rarely been investigated in meta-analyses. Harrison and colleagues (2006) found no relation with job satisfaction, organizational commitment, or contextual performance. Lateness was negatively related to focal performance (i.e., task performance) (ρ = −.26) and absenteeism (ρ = −.29).

ABSENTEEISM

Absenteeism appears to be unrelated to many vocational antecedents. No relation was identified between absenteeism and job satisfaction (Harrison et al., 2006), organizational commitment (Harrison et al., 2006), motivational work characteristics, social characteristics (social support), or work context characteristics in the work environment (Humphrey et al., 2007). These results suggest that absenteeism perhaps should be viewed not as absence per se, but rather as a process in which workers are drawn away from the workplace by valued features of their nonwork environment (Fritzsche & Parrish, 2005).

CAREER SUCCESS

One outcome that cuts across any given job is career success. Career success can be defined as the accumulated positive work outcomes and psychological outcomes resulting from one's work experiences (Seibert & Kraimer, 2001). In their meta-analysis (k = 52, N = 45,293), Ng, Eby, Sorensen, and Feldman (2005) operationalized career success as

objective (i.e., salary attainment, number of promotions) and subjective (job satisfaction, career satisfaction). They examined four sets of predictors: human capital (e.g., amount of work experience or knowledge); organizational sponsorship, defined as the extent to which the organization provides special assistance to employees to facilitate their career success (Dreher & Ash, 1990); sociodemographic variables; and stable individual differences. Each of these predictors will be discussed in order by examining the outcomes of objective career success first, followed by subjective career success.

Objective career success was measured in the meta-analyses by Ng and colleagues (2005) as salary attainment and number of promotions. The number of promotions was predicted by one organizational sponsorship variable—namely, training and skill development opportunities (ρ = .23) (Ng et al., 2005). Salary attainment had several significant predictors across all four sets of predictors. Salary attainment was modestly related to human capital, including hours worked (ρ = .24), organizational tenure (ρ = .20), work experience (ρ = .27), and educational level (ρ = .29). Salary attainment was also modestly related to organizational sponsorship, including career sponsorship (ρ = .22) and training and skill development opportunities (ρ = .24). Salary attainment was related to one sociodemographic variable, age (ρ = .26), and one individual difference variable, cognitive ability (ρ = .27). Salary attainment was below the cutoff of |.20| but in women modestly had lower salaries than men (ρ = .18).

Subjective career success in the Ng and colleagues (2005) study was predicted by some human capital variables, almost all the organizational sponsorship variables, and several individual difference variables. Career satisfaction was predicted by two human capital variables, hours worked (ρ = .22) and political knowledge and skills (ρ = .28). Satisfaction was predicted by three organizational sponsorship variables; namely, career sponsorship (ρ = .44), supervisor support (ρ = .46), and training and skill development opportunities (ρ = .38). Career satisfaction was negatively related to neuroticism (ρ = −.36), and was positively related to extraversion (ρ = .27), proactivity (ρ = .38), and locus of control (ρ = .47).

NEGATIVE MENTAL HEALTH OUTCOMES

Negative mental health outcomes identified from this literature search included anxiety, stress, overload, burnout, and strain. Humphrey and colleagues' (2007) meta-analysis identified specific work characteristics categorized as motivational, social, or work context features of the job environment as being potential antecedents of anxiety, stress, overload, and emotional exhaustion. Anxiety was related to motivational antecedents (i.e., feedback from the job) and social antecedents (i.e., feedback from others) in the work environment (ρs = −.32, −.23). Stress was related to motivational antecedents (autonomy), social antecedents (social support, feedback from other), and work context antecedents (work conditions) in the work environment (ρs range from −.26 to −.42). Overload was related to motivational antecedents (task variety, and job complexity) in the work environment (ρs =.38, .59). Emotional exhaustion from burnout was related to motivational antecedents (autonomy, task significance, task identify) and social antecedents (social support) in the work environment (ρ = −.28 to −.34).

Burnout's three facets, emotional exhaustion, depersonalization, and personal accomplishment were examined in two meta-analyses. Thoreson and colleagues (2003) related positive affect and negative affect to emotional exhaustion (ρs = −.32, .54), depersonalization (ρs = −.27, .39), and personal accomplishment (ρs = .49, −.27). Halbesleben (2006) found that social support did not yield different relations across the three burnout dimensions.

Finally, strain was examined as an outcome of hindrance stressors and challenge stressors in Podsakoff and colleagues' (2007) meta-analysis. Hindrance stressors predicted strain (ρ = .56), as did challenge stressors (ρ = .40) (Podsakoff et al., 2007).

LIFE SATISFACTION AND WELL-BEING

Life satisfaction positively relates to job satisfaction. This positive relation provides support for the spillover model, which says that happiness in one area of life spills over into other areas of life (Fritzsche & Parrish, 2005). Likewise, life satisfaction relates to the Big Five factors in a similar way that job satisfaction relates to the Big Five, with the exception of openness (DeNeve & Cooper, 1998; Judge et al., 2002). In Judge and colleagues' (2002) meta-analysis, life satisfaction and job satisfaction correlated negatively with neuroticism (ρs = −.30, −.29), and positively correlated with extraversion (ρs = .22, .25), openness (ρs = .18, 02), agreeableness ρs = .17, 21), and conscientiousness (ρs = .26, .28).

Wellbeing, also known as subjective well-being, is defined by Diener (2000) as the way in which

people assess their lives both at the moment and over longer periods. Life satisfaction is included as one indicator of well-being, as is work satisfaction and family satisfaction (Walsh & Eggerth, 2005). Research studies have accumulated showing that two of the Big Five are clear predictors of well-being; namely, emotional stability (negative loading on neuroticism) and extraversion. DeNeve and Cooper (1998), in their meta-analysis, showed, in fact, that all of the Big Five factors (emotional stability for neuroticism) were positively related to subjective well-being (k = 197; N = 42,171) . Walsh and Eggerth (2005) presented evidence showing that adults who are in more congruent careers experience more subjective well-being. Lent (2004) reviewed well-being as a construct and differentiated well-being into subjective well-being as defined by Diener (2000) and psychological well-being defined as "the striving for perfection that represents the realization of one's true potential" (Ryff, 1995, p. 100).

Vocational Psychology and Diverse Groups
Overview

Vocational psychology has a rich tradition of examining the vocational issues affecting women (e.g., see reviews by Borgen, 1991; Buboltz, Ebberwein, Watkins, & Savickas, 1995; London & Greller, 1991; Loscocco & Roschelle, 1991). Race and ethnicity have been salient in vocational psychology for many years, with the emphasis on multicultural training and attention to local norms for career assessment. However, issues related to race and ethnicity have become more prominent in the field. The positive development in the field is that researchers are collecting data specific to different racial and ethnic groups, and career counselors are generating tailored interventions specific to different groups, rather than collapsing across racial and ethnic groups. In the literature search, some reviews and meta-analyses were identified concerning gender and race and ethnicity.

Gender

Changing demographics of women will be discussed first, followed by barriers and supports for women. Issues pertaining to sex and schooling, work–family conflict, and sexual harassment will also be examined.

DEMOGRAPHICS

Some statistics paint a picture of women in the United States that words cannot. First, 75% of women aged 25 to 44 work outside the home, and 71% of mothers of children under 18 work outside the home (2006 Current Population Survey Annual Social and Economic Supplement). Second, the probability is 90% that a woman will work outside the home during her lifetime (Betz, 2006). Women work because they have to; in fact, they earn a third of their family's total income (Bureau of Labor Statistics, 2007). Third, the average marriage lasts 7 years (Betz, 2006). Moreover, there are 12 million single parents in the United States, and most of them are women. One in four children live in a single-parent household (2007 Current Population Survey). Three out of four of the elderly poor are women (Betz, 2006). In short, even if a woman does spend some of her adult years out of the workforce, it is probable that most of her time will be in the workforce. The reality is, women, like men, need to work (Betz, 2006).

Although American society often gives women the message that work will be a stressor for them in their multiple roles (e.g., mothers, workers), research has shown that paid work outside the home is a protective factor against women's depression (Betz, 2006). The most satisfied women were employed, and the least satisfied women were homemakers. In fact, women who were married and not working were the most distressed among married women (Betz, 2006).

BARRIERS

Girls and women face barriers in the workforce. Employed women are paid 80% of what employed men are paid (Bureau of Labor Statistics, 2007). The pay gap is greatest for older versus younger women, and greater for white women compared to white men. Women continue to dominate lower-paying jobs. The inadequacy of the parental leave policy is one workforce barrier that may contribute to women's dominance in lower-paying jobs. The Center for Economic and Policy Research issued a report in September 2008 that provided evidence that the United States had the least generous family leave policies of the 21 countries examined (Ray, Gornick, & Schmitt, 2008). These structural practices regarding childrearing contribute to mothers' (and fathers') experience of role overload.

Educational barriers are also present. Girls may experience the "null environment" in educational classrooms, meaning that teachers may not encourage and support them (Betz, 2006). Sexual harassment continues to be a barrier for girls and women (Betz, 2006). Occupational and gender stereotypes may lead girls to be less interested in the physical sciences, engineering, and technology. Girls take fewer technology/engineering courses in high school (Science and Engineering Indicators, 2008), and then proceed to college where they earned only 22% of computer science bachelor's degrees, 20% of engineering bachelor's degrees, and 21% of physics bachelor's degrees in 2005 (Science and Engineering Indicators, 2008). Not surprisingly, given those statistics, college women compared to college men report lower SE in computer science, using technology, mechanical, and science SE compared to men (Betz, 2006; Fassinger, 2005). Moreover, college women compared to college men report less vocational interests in the mechanical domain and computer hardware and software domains (Donnay et al., 2005).

Girls and women are reaching parity in some traditionally male domains within the high school classroom, and this carries on into higher education. High school girls, compared to boys, have completed more advanced biology courses and more chemistry courses, and have completed equal amounts of coursework in advanced math courses included trigonometry, pre-calculus, statistics, calculus, and advanced placement calculus (Science and Engineering Indicators, 2008). Moreover, in college, women earned 51% of the bachelor's degrees in agricultural sciences, 62% of the degrees in biological sciences, and 52% of the degrees in chemistry (Science and Engineering Indicators, 2008). However, these gains are not reflected in the percentage of women faculty in those disciplines.

Russell (2006) suggested that the field needed career development theories in business settings that addressed the career preparation, career entry, and career progression of women, while also taking into consideration the reality of marriage or committed relationships, pregnancy, and childrearing. She identified a number of barriers, including insufficient mentoring, being frequently not placed in positions sequenced for advancement, inadequate attention to long-range goals, lack of a supportive spouse, and the glass ceiling preventing most women from achieving top positions.

Women of color experience the barriers listed above, but they also suffer the double jeopardy of discrimination and racism (Worthington, Flores, & Navarro, 2005). Oppression in the workplace and in society at large contributes to their stress levels (Fassinger, 2005). There are some notable differences in the barriers across different ethnic groups. For example, African American women have long been in the workforce, but find themselves shut out of higher-paying or more prestigious jobs due to the glass ceiling and due to discrimination and lack of societal supports, such as day care and affordable health care. Mexican American women may be more likely than women from other ethnic groups to be dealing with sex role stereotypes and the extended family's expectations, and perhaps their own expectations, of needing to be exclusively focused on the family (Betz, 2006).

SUPPORTS

Girls and women's career development and work adjustment can be facilitated by a variety of support structures within the educational system, family, and job. Parental support and parent availability are crucial to girls' educational success. Support for career adjustment includes having a supportive spouse, supportive coworkers, and employers. Organizational and structural changes to allow women to meet the demands of work and family are essential. These changes could include job flexibility, job sharing, parental leave with pay, affordable day care, time off for family responsibilities, and telecommuting. Some of these structural changes are being implemented systematically at institutions of higher learning across the country. For example, the National Science Foundation has awarded over 40 institutions institutional 5-year grants geared toward transforming the culture of those institutions to make them more conducive to the hiring and retention of women faculty in the sciences, technologies, engineering, and mathematics departments. Internal supports, such as a sense of agency combined with communion or expressiveness, are also crucial. Other internal supports include persistence, passion for one's work, coping efficacy, and a sense of connection with others (Betz, 2006).

SCHOOLING

Education is the foundation upon which career success is built. Women earn more college degrees than do men, and a record number of women are earning law, medical, and business degrees (Meece & Scantelbury, 2006). Girls also outperform boys in almost all school subjects, with the exception of high school physics. Yet, in spite of these achievements, disparities continue to exist for girls in primary and secondary schools due to some schools supporting climates conducive for verbal abuse of girls, sexual harassment, and discrimination against girls who are lesbian, bisexual, or transsexual (Kahle, Meece, & Scantelbury, 2000).

Meece and Scantelbury (2006) identify multiple issues salient for girls' success in education and subsequently, in their careers. Within the school setting, most girls attending school observe that the majority of women are teachers, secretaries, or nurses, whereas the majority of men are administrators, coaches, or custodians. The proportion of male characters continues to outnumber female characters in basal readers (Fleming, 2000). Boys seem to continue to initiate more interaction with teachers, and teachers call on boys more frequently (e.g., Altermatt, Jovanovic, & Perry, 1998). Girls drop out of high school at a lower percentage than do boys (28% vs. 36%) but are less likely to return if they do drop out. In spite of girls' and boys' academic achievement being identical, by elementary school, girls rate themselves higher in verbal, social, and reading abilities and lower in math, physical science, and sports abilities; boys rate themselves in the opposite direction. Some girls' self-esteem may drop from elementary to middle school. Girls from different racial and ethnic groups receive different messages from mothers as they mature. For example, African American mothers expect daughters to be self-reliant, resourceful, and attain autonomy (Collins, 1998). These girls are more likely than their male peers to earn a higher GPA, finish high school, attend college, and enter white-collar careers (Weiler, 2000). In contrast, Latina girls, especially those who are economically disadvantaged, are less likely to extend education past high school and are more likely to move into low-paying positions (Kahle et al., 2000).

WORK–FAMILY CONFLICT

Work–family conflict research cannot be adequately reviewed here. Readers are directed to Chapter 29 of this volume (Eggerth & Cunningham, 2011) for more detailed information, as well as for meta-analyses of the topic (e.g., Allen, Herst, Bruck, & Sutton, 2000; Kossek & Ozeki, 1998; Mesmer-Magnus & Viswesvaran, 2005). Two of the most recent reviews on the topic are discussed here. Work–family conflict has been examined as two constructs referred to as *work interference with the family* (WIF) and *family interference with work* (FIW). The antecedents for these two consequences have been separated into work variables (job involvement, hours spent at work, work support, schedule flexibility, and job stress) and nonwork variables (family/nonwork involvement, hours of nonwork, family support, family stress, family conflict, number of children, age of youngest child, marital status, spousal employment), and demographic variables (sex, income, and coping style). The meta-analysis (k = 61, N = 7,034) by Byron (2005) showed that WIF was related above |.20| to all the work variables except job involvement (ρs range from +/– .26 to .48) and family stress and family conflict (ρs = .30, .35). The FIW construct was related above |.20| with the work variables schedule flexibility and job stress (ρs = .29, .29), and nonwork variables (family/nonwork involvement, hours of nonwork, family stress, family conflict, and age of youngest child) with ρs ranging from +/– .21 to .32. Gender yielded a non-zero relation with both WIF and FIW, but its effect was marginal (ρs = –.03, .12). However, gender and being a parent did moderate the relation between job stress and WIF and FIW. Specifically, when there were more parents in the sample, women experienced more WIF and FIW than did men; when there were fewer parents in the sample, men experienced more WIF and FIW than did women. Also single parents had more WIF and FIW than did parents who were married; married and single employees without children had similar levels of WIF and FIW.

Ford, Heinen, and Langkamer (2007) examined many of the same variables in their meta-analysis (k = 120, N = 42,804). Like Byron (2005), they found job stress, work support, and work hours to be related above |.20| to WIF (ρs range from +/– .25 to .56.) They also did not find job involvement to be related above |.20| to WIF. The prediction of FIW with family variables was similar to Byron regarding the predictors family stress and family conflict (ρs = .27, .26), but not family hours and family support. They also showed that WIF contributed additional variance (2%) to family dissatisfaction after family variables were controlled for; FIW did not contribute additional variance to job dissatisfaction after work variables were controlled for. Like the Byron meta-analysis, gender exerted few direct effects on WIF or FIW; however, sex had an impact on the job stress–family satisfaction relation such that, for women, job stress had a smaller negative correlation with family satisfaction than for men. Also, the percentage of the sample that had children was a moderator between work hours and family satisfaction, such that work stressors had a strong negative effect on family satisfaction for individuals with children. Both studies imply that parenthood, marital status, and gender need to be considered as moderators in the relation of work and family antecedents on WIF and satisfaction.

WORKPLACE HARASSMENT

Workplace harassment is a major concern for men and especially women with regard to their quality of life at work. Bowling and Beehr (2006), in their meta-analysis (k = 90, N = 17,663), present an attributional model identifying the antecedents and consequences of workplace harassment. The model explains why negative consequences occur both to the self (blaming self leading to negative mental health outcomes), the perpetrator (blaming perpetrator impacting organizational justice), and the organization (blaming organization impacting individual performance outcomes). The model presents the norm of reciprocity and attributional processes of either blaming the organization and/or blaming the self as a means of explaining the processes involved in the consequences of workplace harassment. In their meta-analysis, Bowling and Beehr reported workplace harassment related to some antecedents of harassment (i.e., role conflict, role ambiguity, role overload, work constraints, and victim negative affectivity) with ρs ranging from |.25 to .53|. (Sex was not related to workplace harassment.)

The consequences of workplace harassment included negative impact on the victim's well-being and on his or her job performance. Specifically, workplace harassment was negatively correlated with the victim's well-being (i.e., positive emotions at work, self-esteem, life satisfaction, job satisfaction, organizational commitment), with ρs ranging from –.21 to .–39. Workplace harassment was positively related to negative indices of well-being (i.e., generic strain, anxiety, depression, burnout, frustration, negative emotions at work, and physical symptoms), with ρs ranging from .31 to .46. Workplace harassment was positively related to the victim's negative performance outcomes (CWBs, turnover intentions) (ρs = .29, .30), and negatively related to organizational justice (ρ = –.35). Finally, Bowling and Beehr showed that workplace harassment added incremental validity to the prediction of the consequences of harassment after other stressors had been controlled.

Race and Ethnicity

Two reviews and four meta-analyses, all of which were published in the past 5 years, suggest vitality and integrative efforts occurring in the field exclusively focused on racial and ethnic groups and vocational psychology. In addition, one large-scale study is included that has examined the structure of interests across racial and ethnic groups in the United

States (Day & Rounds, 1998). Career choice will be discussed first, followed by the structure of interests, then job satisfaction and job performance. Finally, workplace learning and development will be briefly discussed.

CAREER CHOICE VARIABLES

Culture and choice variables were examined by Fouad and Byars-Winston (2005). In their meta-analysis, they located 16 studies that examined either career aspirations, perceptions of opportunities and barriers, and tasks related to decision making and exploration with a sample size of 19,611 high school or college students. Career aspirations/career choice did not differ between racial and ethnic groups ($g = .01$). (Hedge's g is very similar to Cohen's d). Career exploration/career decision making also did not differ between groups ($g = .23$, $\rho > .05$). Career expectations and perceptions of opportunities and barriers did differ across racial and ethnic groups ($g = .38$, $\rho < .02$). The CI was large, ranging from .06 to .69. Racial/ethnic minorities perceived fewer career opportunities and more career barriers than did white individuals.

STRUCTURE OF INTERESTS

The structure of interests does not appear to differ across African Americans, Mexican Americans, Asian Americans, Native Americans, and Caucasians; ($N = 49,450$). This finding comes from a definitive article by Day and Rounds (1998), who examined the circular structure of Holland's six vocational types using the Revised Unisex Edition of the ACT Interest Inventory (UNIACT; Swaney, 1995). These findings concerned students going to college, although similar results were found for tenth-grade students regardless of whether they were going to college (Day et al., 1998).

JOB PERFORMANCE

McKay and McDaniel (2006) is the most recent meta-analysis ($k = 97$, N = 1,09,974) comparing African Americans and Caucasians in terms of job performance. Their dataset includes many of the same studies that Roth, Huffcutt, and Bobko (2003) reviewed, so the focus will be on McKay and McDaniel's review. The effect size used in this study was Cohen's d. Medium effects or larger ($d \geq .5$) will be discussed to allow the reader to focus on salient effects. McKay and McDaniel examined the following outcomes: task performance, contextual performance, personality-applied social skills, on the job training, overall job performance, work samples, job knowledge tests, absenteeism, salary, promotion, accidents, and commendations–reprimands. Of those 12 criteria, only one outcome—namely, job knowledge tests—was notably different for African Americans and Caucasians ($d = .53$, with a 90% CI of .33 to .74). Caucasians scored higher on job knowledge tests than did African Americans. Caucasians and African Americans' means did not differ more than $d = .5$ on the dimensions of task performance, contextual performance, personality-applied social skills, on the job training, overall job performance, work samples, absenteeism, salary, promotion, accidents, and commendations–reprimands. Turnover was also not significantly different.

WORKPLACE CAREER DEVELOPMENT, PROMOTION, AND PERFORMANCE APPRAISALS

Brooks and Clunis (2007) reviewed research over the past 25 years in the U.S. workforce. Career development, promotion, and performance appraisals were three of the seven topics. Research concerning Asian Americans and Latinos was much more limited than African American studies.

Career development articles mostly focused on supports, barriers, and strategies. Supports identified included opportunity for feedback, access to information, interactive learning processes, and conducive environments. Barriers for African Americans included structural factors in the workplace (e.g., lack of diversity), existence of a "good old boy" network, lack of mentoring, and lack of adequate succession planning, prejudice, stereotypes, and discrimination (Palmer & Johnson-Bailey, 2005). Also, African Americans were more likely to be denied training requests, be steered away from management track titles, be discouraged from seeking professional promotion opportunities, and have the requirements increased regarding promotion (Brooks & Clunis, 2007). Models focused on women are insufficient for African American women. Coping strategies that have been used successfully by women include networking, education and training, career self-management, mentoring, and supervisor support. Hispanic men and women's chance of promotion centered on English fluency, whereas the non-Hispanic whites' chance of promotion centered on years of education (Mundra, Moellmer, & Lopez-Aqueres, 2003).

Performance attainments have been examined in terms of bias in the ratings of employees based on rater race. Most of the studies were atheoretical. Most studies show African Americans to be at a disadvantage regarding promotion, regardless of rank, and theories suggest that some workplaces may have embedded practices and policies that may inadvertently be discriminatory (e.g., extraversion of worker positively influencing ratings having nothing to do with extraversion).

ASIAN AMERICAN CAREER DEVELOPMENT

Asian Americans, compared to other ethnic groups, may be more encouraged by family members to pursue occupations in the sciences and to pursue advanced degrees (Leong & Gupta, 2007). It seems that Asian Americans may express more investigative interests than creative or enterprising interests (Leung, Ivey, & Suzuki, 1994). A report from the Division of Science Resources Statistics within the National Science Foundation in 2008 showed that Asian Americans, compared to other racial and ethnic groups (i.e., white, non-Hispanic and black, non-Hispanic) were enrolled in more pre-calculus, calculus, advanced placement calculus, chemistry, and physics courses during high school. Compared to other groups, they were twice as likely to choose an engineering discipline. Within the sciences, Asian Americans chose biology and computer science more than did their white counterparts. For those Asian Americans who earn a college degree, 50% of them earn science and engineering degrees. For non-Asian Americans earning a college degree, about 33% of them earn science and engineering degrees (Science and Engineering Indicators, 2008). A higher proportion of them compared to white counterparts aspire to either a doctorate or medical degree. Interestingly, Asian Americans, especially women, aspire to more male-dominated occupations than do their European American counterparts (Leong & Gupta, 2007). The imbalance of college degrees across Holland's typology shows up in studies concerning the career choices of Asian Americans and the occupations they select. Asian Americans were over-represented in career choices that were in the realistic and investigative domains according to Holland's typology (Tang, Fouad, & Smith, 1999). This is consistent with the findings that Asian Americans in the workforce seem to be over-represented in medicine and under-represented as managers (Leong & Gupta, 2007).

Asian American's values have been examined across individual studies with no consensus. Chinese American children's most important values in one study were money and task satisfaction (Leong & Tata, 1990). Occupational prestige was important in a second study (Leung et al., 1994). A third study found Asian American college students valued more extrinsic rewards and security compared to their white counterparts (Leong, 1991). One study found Asian Americans lower in career maturity compared to white counterparts (Hardin, Leong, & Osipow, 2001). The authors noted that career maturity implies independent decision making (Crites, 1978); the interdependent decision making valued in an Asian context implies more career immaturity (Hardin et al., 2001).

Work adjustment and vocational problems have been noted both for Asian immigrants and Asian Americans in general. Immigration may result in lower occupational prestige (Cheng, 1996). Language issues and acculturative stress are common for first-generation Asian Americans (Matsuoka & Ryujin, 1989). As employed Asian Americans become acculturated, their job satisfaction seems to increase (Leong, 2001). However, even with Asian Americans who are not immigrants or first-generation Americans, it appears that Asian Americans as a group, compared to a group of European Americans, were less satisfied with their jobs (Weaver, 2000). One reason for lower job satisfaction may be that Asian Americans in the workforce may report being more underemployed than white counterparts (Madamba & De Jong, 1997). They also may be experiencing more social anxiety than white counterparts (e.g., Hardin & Leong, 2005), which may also contribute to job dissatisfaction. Finally, Asian Americans may be experiencing additional financial strain if caring for an extended family (Leong & Gupta, 2007).

Within the work setting, Asian Americans have been shown to suffer discrimination. For example, Asian Americans, compared to Caucasians, were not selected by classmates to be team managers in mini-assessment centers set up in organizational behavior classes (Cheng, 1996). Occupational stereotyping was demonstrated by Leong and Hayes (1990), who showed respondents thought Asian Americans were more likely to be successful as computer scientists, engineers, and mathematicians and less likely to be successful as insurance sales people. Occupational discrimination has also been documented against Asian American scientists and engineers within U.S. universities (National Science Foundation, 2004) and against women physicians (Corbie-Smith, Frank, Nickens, & Elon, 1999).

More research is needed in all these areas, and the research needs to move beyond descriptive research to identify underlying processes that may explain racism and discrimination. The focus on cultural moderators such as cultural identity, acculturation, and SES will be much more illuminating than simply describing differences between various groups (Leong & Gupta, 2007).

ASIAN AMERICAN EDUCATIONAL EXPERIENCE. Asian Americans' educational experience can be split into positive and negative outcomes. Often viewed as the model minority, evidence has accumulated to verify that their academic successes are mostly comparable to European Americans and greater than other American racial and ethnic minority groups like Native Americans, Hispanics, and African Americans (Tseng, Chao, & Padmawjaja, 2007). Based on large, nationally represented samples collected over years (Tseung et al., 2007), academic achievement in third grade (Rathbun, West, & Germino-Hausken, 2004), middle school (Kao, 1995; Kao, Tienda, & Schneider, 1996), and high school (National Center for Educational Statistics, 2001, 2002, 2003a,b) was demonstrated to be comparable to European Americans and superior to other racial and ethnic minority groups after controlling for contextual variables (e.g., SES, sex). Asian Americans and European Americans, in comparison to other ethnic groups, reported lower percentages of high school dropout rates, higher undergraduate graduation rates, and higher standardized test scores in mathematics (Tseng et al., 2007).

The negative outcomes that Asian Americans experience occur outside the classroom and often are due to racism that results in peers resorting to verbal abuse, physical harassment, and intimidation (e.g., Juvonen, Nishina, & Graham, 2000; Kao, 1995). This behavior is interwoven with SES, immigration status, language elitism ("In America, everyone should speak English"), and peers resenting positive teacher reactions toward Asian Americans (Gibson, 1988; Tseng et al., 2007).

Vocational Psychology and Individual Differences

> We inherit dispositions, not destinies. Life 'vocational' outcomes are consequences of lifetimes of behavior choices. The choices are guided by our dispositional tendencies and the tendencies find expression within environmental opportunities that we actively create.
> (Rose, 1995, p. 648)

This quote clearly explains how dispositional tendencies—namely, individual differences—are interwoven into the vocational outcomes that have

been discussed in this chapter. The quote also amplifies how the educational and vocational choices people make beginning in childhood and continuing throughout adulthood are impacted by individual differences. That is perhaps why vocational psychology is rooted in the individual difference tradition in psychology. Moreover, the quote reflects counseling psychology's emphasis on the individuality of each student and client. The foundation of individual difference research lies in the understanding that people differ in magnitude of any characteristic they possess (Dawis, 2005) and that the range is five to six standard deviations or more (Dawis, 2005; Lubinski, 2000) compared to the much smaller (most often less than Cohen's d of .5) effect size of group differences (e.g., sex differences and racial and ethnic differences).

Not surprisingly, individual differences, especially interests and personality traits, repeatedly emerged as salient predictors of vocational outcomes like educational aspirations, career choice, affective commitment in the job, job satisfaction, job performance, intentions to quit, CWBs, career success, career satisfaction, and mental health outcomes (e.g., Lubinski, 2000). A discussion of individual differences needs to start with a foundation in heritability. Following heritability, cognitive ability, personality traits, interests, and values will be reviewed as they pertain to vocational outcomes. Finally, integrative work in which more than one individual difference variable is examined will be presented.

Heritability

Heritability can be defined as the proportion of variance in an observed trait that can be traced to genetic variation in the population (L. S. Gottfredson, 2002). It can range from 0% of the variance in a trait due to genetics—meaning the variation is all due to nurture or the environment—to 100% of the variance in a trait due to genetics—meaning that the variation is all due to nature. Scholars in vocational psychology have begun to acknowledge the accumulated evidence across multiple studies that children are born predisposed toward certain traits, attitudes, and behaviors (Gottfredson, 2002).

For the domain of vocational psychology, the facts accumulating about heritability are startling. The variation in interests due to nature appears to be about 40% (Betsworth et al., 1994; Lykken, Bouchard, McGue, & Tellegen, 1993). The heritability of personality traits appears to be around 50% (Tellegen et al., 1988), whereas the heritability of cognitive abilities appear to be around 70%

(Bouchard, 1998). Work values appear to be also partly due to nature, although the variance due to genetic variation is lower than interests, personality, and cognitive abilities, around 35% (Arvey, McCall, Bouchard, Taubman, & Cavanaugh (1994). Self-rated competence across academic and social domains appears to be influenced by nature as well, with a 50%–60% heritability estimate reported (McGuire, Neiderhiser, Reiss, Hetherington, & Plomin, 1994). Interestingly, some vocational outcomes appear to also be substantially influenced by nature, including level of education (60%–70%), occupation (50%), and income (40%–50%) (L. S. Gottfredson, 2002). Finally, overall job satisfaction appears to be partially attributed to nature, with a heritability estimate of 30% (Arvey et al., 1994).

The influence of nature extends beyond the person to interaction with the environment. Behavioral geneticists have come to understand that the environmental social context of the person is also in part due to nature, based on the people in the environment. "Behavioral genetic research consistently shows that family environment, peer groups, social support, and life events often show as much genetic influence as do measures of personality" (Plomin, DeFries, McClearn, & Rutter, 1997, pp. 203–204). People have differential susceptibility to the same environment based on their internal predispositions. Nonshared (environmental influences not shared by siblings such as peer groups), rather than shared, environmental influences have an impact on the development of general traits. In sum, vocational psychologists need to better understand the processes involved in how and why and in what contexts individual difference variables have the most impact on vocational psychology (L. S. Gottfredson, 2002).

Ability

Cognitive ability has been identified in many of the theories of vocational psychology. Dawis postulates in his TWA that cognitive ability is the general dimension that underlies groups of acquired skills. The work environment requires particular skills of the individual for the job to be satisfied with the person, or for the person to achieve satisfactoriness (Dawis, 2005). Holland's theory (1997) includes ability as part of the broad definition of the person including their interests, skills, abilities, and values. Likewise, Super, in the career construction theory, hypothesizes that one's vocational personality includes abilities. In SCCT, Lent and colleagues

(1994) predict performance and persistence in educational and occupational pursuits (Lent et al., 1994). One of the exogenous variables is ability, which directly affects SE and outcome expectations and performance attainment level. Krumboltz' social learning theory (e.g., Mitchell & Krumboltz, 1996) also sees cognitive ability as an antecedent to instrumental learning.

Cognitive ability, measured most commonly by the g factor, is a major attribute in educational achievement (Benbow & Stanley, 1996; Snow, 1996). Cognitive ability is also a potent attribute in job performance and job training (e.g., Hunter & Hunter, 1984; Judge et al., 2007; Levine et al., 1996; Schmidt & Hunter, 1998). Moreover, the more complex the job or training demands, the more important cognitive ability becomes. These results have also been supported cross-culturally with German samples (Hülsheger et al., 2007), British samples (Bertua et al., 2005), and samples from 11 European countries (Salgado et al., 2003).

Cognitive ability has also been shown to overshadow the contribution of SE in the prediction of work performance. Judge and colleagues (2007), in their meta-analysis, examined whether the relation of SE and performance would be attenuated after the relation of performance and distal influences, namely the Big Five, ability, and experience, were taken into account. Self-efficacy's standardized regression coefficient was nonsignificant ($\beta = 13$) in the prediction of work performance, whereas cognitive ability ($\beta = .52$), conscientiousness ($\beta = .26$), and experience ($\beta = .26$) were significant. In that same meta-analyses, Judge and colleagues also showed cognitive ability ($r = .20$) to be predictive of SE itself.

Finally, cognitive ability was shown to be an antecedent in objective career success (i.e., salary) in a meta-analysis (Ng et al., 2005). In fact, salary was related above .20 to only one individual difference variable; namely, cognitive ability ($\rho = .27$; Ng et al., 2005). Ng and colleagues (2005) did not find cognitive ability related to the other objective indicator of career success; namely, number of promotions.

The general g factor appears quite salient in important vocational outcomes. As Lubinski (2000) clarifies, the measures of cognitive ability seem to capture one's ability to learn as long as cognitive ability refers to ability to learn complex processes and skills and that a different mix of those constituents may be required in different learning tasks and settings.

Interests

Interests seem to be stable dispositional tendencies that guide, direct, and maintain one's actions toward certain activities and away from other activities (Low & Rounds, 2006). In many vocational psychology theories, interests have played a central role. The most obvious example is Holland's P–E fit theory, in which interests form the core of the person side of the equation, and the match occurs when a person seeks out an environment that allows her or him to express interests in a compatible educational or work environment. In SCCT, interests become the criterion variable, with SE and outcome expectations hypothesized as the primary determinants of the development of interests over time (Lent et al., 1994). In Super's career construction model, interests are part of the objective P–E fit aspect of the vocational personality (Savickas, 2005).

Interests have been one of the most researched constructs in vocational psychology. This may be due to the early construction of E. K. Strong's Vocational Interest Blank (1927) and the popularity of Holland's hexagonal structure of interests. It seems clear that interests are, in large part, due to nature (e.g., Betsworth et al., 1994) and that they are relatively stable across time (e.g., Hansen & Swanson, 1983; Low & Rounds, 2007; Low et al., 2005; Rottinghaus et al., 2007; Strong, 1955). Interests also appear to be robust for single individuals over time (Low & Rounds, 2006) and stable in the relative placement of individuals within a group (Low & Rounds, 2006). In fact, there is some evidence that interests may be more stable than personality, despite the assumption of many scholars that personality traits are the developmental antecedents of interests. Low and Rounds (2006) reported stability coefficients for interests that were consistently more stable than the personality traits' stability coefficients reported in Roberts and DelVecchio (2000) across ages 12 to 40. Moreover, the structure of interests seems to be circular (the six dimensions are not equidistant and may not be all inclusive), with the six dimensions of Holland representing an excellent typology across multiple racial and ethnic groups in the United States (Armstrong, Hubert, & Rounds, 2003; Day & Rounds, 1998), across men and women in the United States (e.g., G. D. Gottfredson, 1999; Low & Rounds, 2006), and cross-culturally (Low & Rounds, 2006; Rounds & Tracey, 1996).

Interests, despite their stability, do interact with the near environment to yield changes in interest patterns (G. D. Gottfredson, 1999). Environmental influences include parents' actions in what activities they offer and reinforce to children (manual labor not reinforced as career choice in homes with professional parents). Other influences include teachers who encourage learning or engage the student (Meece & Scantlebury, 2006). Mastery, modeling, feedback, and responsiveness to the context (women being encouraged to be primary caretaker for small children) may encourage or discourage certain interests (Betz, 2006). Social and cultural influences are potent, as illustrated by the scarcity of women in the U.S. Senate and House of Representatives.

Interests have been studied as outcomes of personality traits, SE, and outcome expectancies. Scholars have ascertained that some personality traits overlap with some of Holland's six interests (Barrick, Mount, & Gupta, 2003; Larson, Rottinghaus, & Borgen, 2002) and that specific facets of personality predict specific interests (Staggs, Larson, & Borgen, 2003; Sullivan & Hansen, 2004). Self-efficacy across Holland's hexagon and across specific academic domains has been moderately predictive of parallel interests (Rottinghaus, Larson, et al., 2003). Interests have also been shown to influence SE bidirectionally (Nauta et al., 2002; Tracey, 2002). Domain-specific outcome expectations, particularly in math/science domains, have been predictive of parallel domains of interests (Lent et al., 1994: Young et al., 2004).

Interests have been shown to be potent predictors of other vocational outcomes. The most well-known outcome is educational major and career choice. Vocational interests across Holland's hexagon have shown to be robust in discriminating among diverse educational majors (Gasser et al., 2007; Harmon et al., 1994) and among diverse occupational choices (e.g., Ackerman & Beier, 2003; Donnay & Borgen, 1996; Donnay et al., 2005; Harmon et al., 1994). Basic domains of interests (e.g., Basic Interest Scales of the Strong) compared to the six Holland domains have been shown to be superior predictors of both educational major and occupational choice (e.g., Betz et al., 2003; Donnay & Borgen, 1996, 1999; Gasser et al., 2007; Larson, Wu, et al., 2010; Rottinghaus, Betz et al., 2003). Interests across Holland's dimensions have also been shown to be predictive of educational aspirations (Rottinghaus et al., 2002).

Finally, a specific type of vocational interest—namely, interest in math/science content—has been shown to predict course intentions (Young et al., 2004). Course interests remained significant predictors of intentions even after parallel outcome expectations were controlled (Young et al., 2004). Researchers have paid less attention to the role of interests as antecedents to job outcomes. One meta-analysis (Hunter & Hunter, 1984) did report a nominal mean correlation of interests with job performance ($r = .10$).

Personality Traits

As opposed to interests that move people toward or away from activities, personality traits appear to affect how a person copes with or adapts to an environment (Low & Rounds, 2006). Interestingly, personality traits are not central in any of the well-known vocational psychology theories and are, at best, distal exogenous predictors in some models, like SCCT (Lent et al., 1994).

Personality traits have received enormous attention in their motivational role as antecedents of a host of vocational outcomes. This is surely due to the popularity of research involving the Big Five and negative and positive affectivity. Positive and negative affectivity (labeled most recently by Tellegen [2000] as positive emotional temperament and negative emotional temperament) are viewed as alternative higher-order affective dimensions to the Big Five. These two superordinate factors, along with a third factor, constraint, were conceptualized by Auke Tellegen (1982, 2000) and measured by the Multidimensional Personality Questionnaire (MPQ; Tellegen, 1982, 2000; Tellegen & Waller, 2008). The constraint factor captures behavioral regulation. Under these three factors are 11 primary traits (Tellegen, 2000) labeled well-being (happiness), achievement (works hard), social potency (forceful and decisive), social closeness (sociability), absorption (entranced by evocative sights and sounds), stress reaction (worry, vulnerable), aggression (victimizer), alienation (victim), control (cautious, careful), traditionalism (social conservative), and harm-avoidance (chooses safe and boring over danger). There is very little overlap among these traits, and strong psychometric properties exist behind each one.

There has been a resurgence of scholars examining personality traits in interest development and career choice of college students (e.g., Ackerman & Beier, 2003; Larson & Borgen, 2006; Larson et al., 2007; Staggs et al., 2003; Sullivan & Hansen, 2004). Several studies examined choice of major, contribution of personality traits in specific interests, and relation of personality traits and SE.

Regarding choice of major, Larson and colleagues (2007) showed that the Big Five contributed somewhat to differentiating among Taiwanese college students who had chosen one of four majors, namely, accounting, engineering, counseling, or finance. For example, female counseling majors were more agreeable and less conventional than were female finance majors. Male counseling majors were more agreeable and less neurotic than were the male finance majors. Ackerman and Beier (2003) also found that personality traits were part of a set of trait complexes (composite traits of ability, interests, and personality traits) that differentiated among adults' retrospective undergraduate college majors.

Regarding the influence of personality traits on specific interests, Staggs and colleagues (2003), showed in a hierarchical multiple regression that primary personality traits more specific than the Big Five or the Big Three (Tellegen, 2000) were significantly predictive of some basic interests even after the variance due to the salient general trait had been removed. For example, after removing variation due to constraint, harm-avoidance scores (person who scores low tends to prefer excitement and danger; avoids safe activities because they are tedious [Tellegen, 2000]) contributed an additional 17% of the variance in the prediction of scores on the Strong Basic Interest Scale, mechanical activities. Sullivan and Hansen (2004) showed that facet scales of the Big Five captured most of the variance in some Basic Interest Scales, leaving no significant variation due to the Big Five traits. For example, they showed that the openness scores did not add unique variance to the prediction of the five artistic Basic Interest scales (music/performing arts, art/design, writing, international activities, fashion, and culinary arts) after the variation due to one of openness' facet scales, the aesthetics facet scale, had been removed.

Finally, Larson and Borgen (2006) wanted to ascertain the relation of dimensions of vocational SE (or confidence) across Holland's hexagon and Tellegen's Big Three and his 11 primary traits (Tellegen, 2000). Across four samples of college students, they found positive emotional temperament related substantially to all of Holland's SE dimensions except conventional confidence (*r*s range from .19 to .66). Moreover, social potency was associated with artistic, social, and enterprising confidence (*r*s range from .24 to .66). Achievement correlated with investigative and enterprising confidence (*r*s range from .19 to .34); well-being correlated with social and enterprising confidence (*r*s range from .20 to .33); and social closeness correlated with social confidence (*rs* range from .19 to .28) (Larson & Borgen, 2006). Larson and Borgen's results suggest clearly that vocational confidence across Holland's interest types is related to broad and specific personality traits. A study by Judge and colleagues (2007) found similar results that suggest that SE needs to be untangled from personality traits. Judge and colleagues examined work outcomes and showed that the specific contribution of task-specific SE to work-related performance was much smaller once the distal variables, including the Big Five, were controlled. Conscientiousness, extraversion, and emotional stability were significant unique predictors of SE.

In the adult literature, personality traits were significant predictors of job search behaviors, job satisfaction, global job performance, and training proficiency. The personality traits include positive and negative affectivity, neuroticism, extraversion, openness to new experiences, agreeableness, and conscientiousness.

Positive affectivity was shown to be a positive antecedent, whereas negative affectivity was shown to be a negative antecedent to job satisfaction (ρs = .49, −.33, Connolly & Viswesvaran, 2000; ρs = .34, −34, Thoresen et al., 2003); affective commitment (ρ = .36; Connolly & Viswesvaran, 2000; ρs = .35, −.27, Thoresen et al., 2003); and personal accomplishment (ρs = .49, −.34; Thoresen et al., 2003). Conversely, positive affectivity was shown to be negatively related, whereas negative affectivity was shown to be positively related to turnover intentions (ρs = −.17, 28, Thoresen et al., 2003); emotional exhaustion (ρs = −.32, .62, Thoresen et al., 2003); and depersonalization (ρs = −.27, .47, Thoresen et al., 2003). Future scholars need to examine the relation of more specific traits beyond the overarching dimensions of positive and negative affectivity. Tellegen's 11 primary traits would be excellent specific traits to examine in the future work adjustment literature.

The Big Five personality traits have been examined extensively in the adult literature. One or more of the Big Five have been significant predictors of job search behaviors, number of job offers, job satisfaction, global subjective ratings of job performance, training proficiency, CWBs, career satisfaction, and life satisfaction. Neuroticism, for example, was shown to be a negative antecedent to job satisfaction (ρ = −.29, Judge et al., 2002), life satisfaction (ρ = −.30; Judge et al., 2002), and career satisfaction (ρ = −.36; Ng et al., 2005). Extraversion was shown to be an antecedent to job search

behaviors (frequency of activities or time spent searching) (ρ = .46, Kanfer et al., 2001); number of job offers (ρ = .41, Kanfer et al., 2001); job satisfaction (ρ = .25; Judge et al., 2002); training proficiency (ρ = .26; Judge et al., 2002); career satisfaction (ρ = .27; Ng et al., 2005); and life satisfaction (ρ = .22; Judge et al., 2002).

Openness was shown to be an antecedent to job search behaviors (ρ = .27, Kanfer et al., 2001); number of job offers (ρ = .28, Kanfer et al., 2001); job satisfaction (ρ = .29; Judge et al., 2002); and training proficiency (ρ = .25; Judge et al., 2002). Agreeableness was predictive of number of job offers (ρ = .29, Kanfer et al., 2001). Conscientiousness was shown to be predictive of job search behaviors (ρ = .38; Kanfer et al., 2001); job satisfaction (ρ = .26, Judge et al., 2002); subjective job performance (supervisor ratings) (ρ = .26; Judge et al., 2002); CWBs (ρs = −.39, −.26, Dalal, 2005; Dudley et al., 2006; and life satisfaction (ρ = .26; Judge et al., 2002). Conscientiousness remained a significant predictor of job performance even after accounting for experience, cognitive ability, and SE (conscientiousness, β = .26; Judge et al., 2007).

Needs, Work Values, and Goals

Needs and values have not received the attention in counseling psychology that they deserve. However, Rounds and Armstrong (2005) provided an excellent overview of this area. They identify work values as shared interpretations of what people want and expect from work. Needs, compared to values, are defined as more biological, and Rounds and Armstrong use Murray's concept of needs as being how individuals feel, behave, or react. In contrast, values are conceptualized as more cognitive in comparison to needs. In TWA, work values are categorized in the domains of achievement, comfort, status, altruism, safety, and autonomy (Dawis, 2002, 2005). Work motivation theories (Latham & Pinder, 2005) attempt to explain the context and processes that account for an individual's energy, direction of effort, and maintenance of that effort in a work setting. Latham and Pinder (2005) list several individual studies that have shown that work values relate to job satisfaction, job choice, tenure, commitment and cohesion, intention to quit, turnover, and self-report ratings of teamwork (e.g., Dawis, 1991; Kristof, 1996; Ronen, 1994).

Other constructs mentioned in work motivation research that affect job performance include self-monitoring strategies, self-regulating strategies (goal setting), core self-evaluations, and goal orientation.

I found one meta-analysis by Judge and Ilies (2002) that examined three indicators of performance evaluation (goal-setting, expectancy, and SE motivation) and their relation to the Big Five. They showed goal setting motivation to be related to neuroticism ($\rho = -.29$), agreeableness ($\rho = -.29$), and conscientiousness ($\rho = .28$). Expectancy motivation was related to neuroticism ($\rho = -.29$) and conscientiousness ($\rho = .23$). Self-efficacy motivation was related to neuroticism ($\rho = -.35$), extraversion ($\rho = .33$), openness ($\rho = -.20$), and conscientiousness ($\rho = .22$).

Integration Across Ability, Personality, and Interests: Cross-fertilization

The scholarship concerning the overlap among attributes has been burgeoning in the past 10 years. On the counseling psychology side, the role of personality traits has led to ongoing dialogue about the role of personality in training students (Walsh, 2001; Walsh & Eggerth, 2005) and the role of personality and interests in optimal human functioning (e.g., Borgen & Harmon, 1996; Borgen & Lindley, 2003). Empirical studies have emerged investigating personality and interests (e.g., Ackerman & Beier, 2003; Lindley & Borgen, 2000; Staggs et al., 2003; Sullivan & Hansen, 2004) and personality and confidence (e.g., Betz, Borgen, & Harmon, 2006; Larson & Borgen, 2006). Mount, Barrick, Scullen, and Rounds (2005) identified underlying higher-order dimensions that captured the overlap of interests and personality. Ackerman (1996) articulated a theory of adult intellectual development that explains how people accumulate knowledge over time based on personality, interest, and cognitive abilities interrelations. He anchored the theory in a seminal work produced in partnership with Heggestad (Ackerman & Heggestad, 1997), in which they articulated an integrated framework that reconsiders the uniqueness of abilities, interests, and personality. Finally, several quantitative reviews have moved the field ahead (Barrick, Mount & Gupta, 2003; Larson, Rottinghaus, & Borgen, 2002; Staggs, Larson, & Borgen, 2007).

Interests and Personality Overlap

Three meta-analyses have converged to provide an excellent grasp of the extent of overlap between the Big Six (interests) and the Big Five. Larson and colleagues (2002) conducted a meta-analysis ($k = 12$, $N = 2,571$). Of the 30 interests–personality (I–P) relations, five appeared to be substantial for both men and women across the six Holland types. They were artistic interests–openness ($r = .48$),

enterprising interests–extraversion ($r = .41$), social interests–extraversion ($r = .31$), investigative interests–openness ($r = .28$), and social interests–agreeableness ($r = .19$). Type of measure and sex interaction moderated one additional relation. Conventional interests–conscientiousness was related .25 to .33 for men and for women who took the Self-Directed Search. For women who took the SII, the relation was not present ($r = .07$).

Barrick and colleagues (2003), using a broader, more diverse sample, reached essentially the same conclusions regarding the relation of the Big Six and the Big Five. Their significant I–P relations were artistic interests–openness ($\rho = .39$), enterprising interests–extraversion ($\rho = .41$), social interests–extraversion ($\rho = .29$), investigative interests–openness ($\rho = .25$), social interests–agreeableness ($\rho = .15$), and conventional interests–conscientiousness ($\rho = .19$).

Finally, Staggs and colleagues (2007) corroborated the Big Six–Big Five relations using meta-analyses ($k = 5$, $N = 2,023$). Instead of the Big Five model, they used Tellegen's Big Three and his 11 primary traits. Five of those primary traits had previously been identified as marker scales for the Big Five: stress reaction for neuroticism, social potency or social closeness for extraversion, absorption for openness, aggression (inversely) for agreeableness, and control for conscientiousness (Blake & Sackett, 1999; Church, 1994; Tellegen & Waller, 2008). The substantive I–P relations were artistic interests–absorption (openness) ($r = .44$), enterprising interests–social potency (extraversion) ($r = .36$), social interests–social closeness (extraversion) ($r = .29$), and social interests–aggression (inverse of agreeableness) ($r = -.22$). The investigative interests–absorption (openness) relation was null ($r = .15$). Tellegen's measures differentiated extraversion into social potency (power), social closeness (love/affiliation), and control (vs. impulsivity) (Tellegen & Waller, 2008). Staggs and colleagues' (2003) meta-analysis illustrated clearly how separating the love/affiliation/warmth from social influence/power was useful in clarifying the overlap of extraversion and vocational interests. Social closeness relates to social interests but not enterprising interests, whereas social potency relates to enterprising interests but not social interests.

Mount and colleagues (2005) used meta-analyses to identify a higher-order structure of the interests–personality overlap. Cluster analysis and nonmetric multidimensional scaling were used to identify three dimensions that explained relations among the 11 attributes: interests versus personality traits, striving for accomplishment versus striving for personal growth, and interacting with people versus interacting with things.

Trait Complexes

Ackerman and Heggestad (1997) reconceptualized how many scholars now think of cognitive ability, interests, and personality. That is, they encouraged scholars to think of them in a rearranged way, according to four trait complexes rather than general and specific abilities, six domains of interests, and five domains of personality (Big Five) or the 11 traits identified by Tellegen (1982, 2000). In their seminal work, they presented meta-analytic evidence showing that cognitive abilities and personality traits (the Big Five and the 11 primary traits identified by Tellegen [1982, 2000]) could be integrated across these four trait complexes. In addition, they speculated without data as to where Holland's Big Six interests would be located. The four trait complexes are labeled science/math, intellectual/cultural, social, and clerical/conventional. They provided evidence that the cognitive ability of fluid intelligence, visual perception, and math reasoning would be located within the science/math complex; no personality traits were identified as being in this complex. They speculated that realistic and investigative interests would be located here. Next, the intellectual/cultural complex included the cognitive abilities of ideational fluency, crystallized intelligence, and knowledge and achievement and the personality traits of openness (Big Five) and absorption (11 primary traits). They speculated that artistic and some investigative interests would be located in this complex. Next, the social complex was shown to include no cognitive abilities and was anchored by the personality traits of extraversion (Big Five) and social potency and well-being (primary traits). They speculated that social and enterprising interests would fall within the social complex. Finally, within the clerical/conventional complex, the cognitive ability, perceptual speed, was located along with the personality traits of conscientiousness (Big Five), and control and traditionalism (11 primary traits) were located. They placed Holland's conventional interests in this complex.

The meta-analyses that came after Ackerman and Heggestad's seminal (1997) article supported many of their hypothesized interests–personality linkages using Holland's Big Six and the Big Five personality traits. These I–P linkages from the meta-analyses included artistic interests and openness,

investigative interests and openness, social interests and extraversion, enterprising interests and extraversion, and conventional interests with conscientiousness (excluding women who completed the SII) (Barrick et al., 2003; Larson et al., 2002). Like Ackerman and Heggestad, these two groups of scholars also did not find realistic interests to be linked to the Big Five. Finally, Staggs and colleagues (2007) provided meta-analytic interests–personality linkages using Tellegen's 11 primary traits. They were the first to show in a meta-analysis that the science/math trait complex may include personality traits not included in the Big Five; namely, harm-avoidance and achievement. Both of these traits related to realistic interests. Moreover, they provided support for the proposed I–P linkages made by Ackerman and Heggestad using the 11 primary traits including artistic interests and absorption, social potency and enterprising interests (not social interests), social interests (not enterprising interests) and well-being. They did not find I–P linkages in the clerical/conventional trait complex; that is, conventional interests were not related to control and traditionalism as Ackerman and Heggestad had proposed.

Staggs and colleagues (2007) went one step beyond the prior meta-analyses and provided, for the first time, meta-analytic I–P linkages that were quite specific. They examined the linkages between the Big Six and the 25 basic dimensions of interests from the Basic Interest Scales of the SII (Harmon et al., 1994) with Tellegen's 11 primary traits. For example, artistic interests are separated into writing, art, music/drama, applied arts, and culinary arts, and realistic interests are separated into mechanical, agricultural, military, and athletic interests. Using these meta-analytic estimates, they revised Ackerman and Heggestad's (1997) tentative I–P linkages located in each of their four trait complexes. Figure 6.1 shows the hypothesized meta-analytic I–P relations made by Staggs and colleagues (2007). The personality traits are in capital letters, and Holland's typology is abbreviated to form the RIASEC. Conventional [C] is left off since there were no conventional I–P relations above |.20|. Their r values are shown on Figure 6.1. The dotted lines represent those I–P linkages that were negative. Within the science/math complex, they found realistic interests and mechanical and agricultural interests, in particular, to be negatively linked with harm-avoidance (choosing boredom over danger) (rs range from −.21 to −.31) and investigative interests and science interests, in particular, to be positively linked to achievement (rs = .27, .21). Within the intellectual/cultural

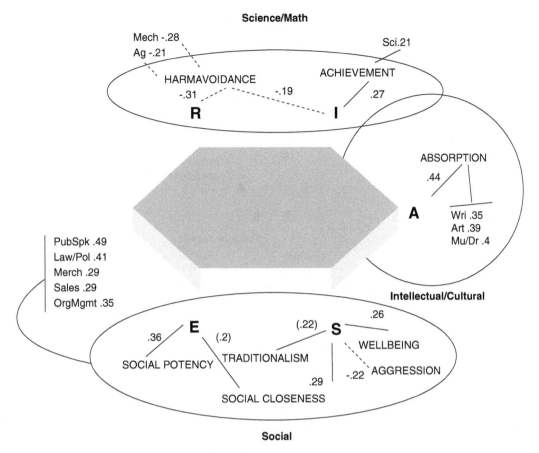

Fig. 6.1 Hypothesized MPQ and Strong Meta-analytic Findings.
Reprinted with permission from Journal of Career Assessment.

complex, absorption was positively related to general and specific artistic interests (*rs* range from .35 to .44). Within the social complex, social and enterprising interests were differentiated based on the former being related positively to well-being (dispositional happiness) and negatively related to aggression, and the latter being related to social potency (forceful, dominant, charming). Social potency was also positively related to specific enterprising interests (public speaking, law/politics, merchandising, sales, and organizational management) with *rs* ranging from .29 to .49.

Figure 6.2 shows additional specific I–P linkages that were not hypothesized in which the I–P correlations were .2 or greater. Similar to Figure 6.1, dotted lines represent negative relations. In the science/math complex, additional I–P linkages not posited by Ackerman and Heggestad (1997) emerged; interests in military activities were negatively related to harm-avoidance and positively related to aggression. Math interests were positively

related to achievement. In the intellectual/cultural complex, interests in applied arts, nature, and social service were positively related to absorption. Within the social complex, a large number of specific I–P linkages of |.2| or greater were reported. The particular linkages provide more evidence that enterprising interests and social interests are uniquely linked with different constellations of personality traits. For example, the Basic Interest Scales that are listed as social interests related negatively to aggression; none of the Basic Interest Scales that were listed as enterprising interests related negatively to aggression. It also appears that the personality trait of well-being is related to primarily specific social interests but also was linked to athletics, a realistic interest, and culinary arts, an artistic interest. Finally, Staggs and colleagues also provide evidence in both figures that traditionalism may need to be moved from the clerical/conventional complex to the social complex. Sex was not found to be a substantial moderator of I–P correlations.

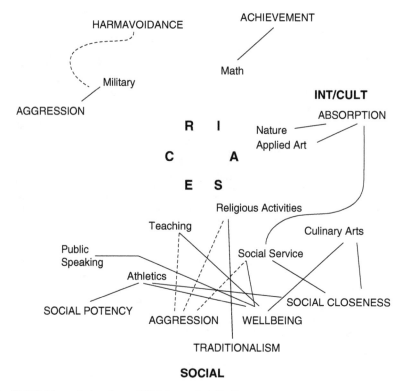

Fig. 6.2 Additional MPQ Primary Scales - Strong BISs Meta-analytic Findings.
Reprinted with permission from Journal of Career Assessment.

Looking Back and Looking Ahead

Since Frank Parsons' (1909) publication, *Choosing a Vocation*, which many consider to be the birth of vocational psychology, the field has evolved and been transformed by the societal forces that shaped psychology in general and vocational psychology in particular. Scholars have summarized the most recent past by celebrating the contributions of the grand masters of vocational psychology, like Donald Super, John Holland, and René Dawis, and more recently Sam Osipow (Borgen, 1991; Barak & Leong, 2001), and by reviewing trends in the journals (e.g., Borgen, 1991; London & Greller, 1991; Watkins & Savickas, 1990), and trends in the field (Dawis, 1996; Lee, Mitchell, & Sablynski, 1999; Loscocco & Roschelle, 1991).

Vocational psychology's vision is a mosaic with diverse viewpoints. Scholars do not speak with one voice. Some argue that vocational psychology needs to break away from counseling psychology and form its own specialty (e.g., Tinsley, 2001), or that vocational psychology needs to be more scientific and grounded in measurement and basic psychology

(e.g., G. D. Gottfredson, 2001; Hesketh, 2001; Vondracek, 2001). Some argue that vocational psychology needs to be more grounded in the multicultural zeitgeist of the day and focus more on those who have not had a voice in the literature (e.g., Blustein, 2001; Fouad, 2001; Subich, 2001).

The separation of the literature dealing with youth and college students versus wage-earning adults has been clearly established, based partly on tradition and partly on different outcomes and processes. Cross-fertilization is occurring, however, with the school-to-work efforts in counseling psychology and the work of scholars in integrating personality, interests, values, and abilities. Multicultural scholars and feminist scholars writing about vocational issues dealing with discrimination, sexual harassment, worklife–family balance are also crossing the divide.

The field is vibrant and thriving. Multiple scholars in counseling psychology, I/O psychology, organizational psychology, and applied and individual differences psychology are generating research, educating the next generation, and disseminating findings.

Also, more longitudinal studies are being conducted. Books and book chapters proliferate that serve to inform and energize new and old scholars alike. A number of scholarly journals are devoted exclusively to vocational psychology. Vocational counselors continue to provide assistance to university clients, high school clients, and elementary students as they explore the world of work, learn about themselves, and develop aspirations, goals, and initial choices about what to study and what activities to pursue. Psychologists in work settings provide assistance to employees, employers, and the public at large regarding how wage earners can be both productive and well adjusted.

As scholars, our first task is to generate new knowledge concerning vocational psychology. That new knowledge needs to build on prior findings and also provide new lines of inquiry. Ideally, vocational theories should fall out of favor due to lack of support for the propositions rather than simply neglect. Likewise, vocational theories that are widely used and accepted should continue to be rigorously examined and anchored in science. For example, scholars need to examine the proposition that congruence defined by a congruence index leads to job satisfaction and tenure; the empirical support is absent. It may be that unexamined moderators are present or that measures of job satisfaction are theoretically inappropriate. Nonetheless, scholars need to either give up on the proposition that congruence as defined by a congruence index leads to job satisfaction or discover under what conditions that proposition holds true. To generate new knowledge, all research methods need to be utilized. The literature search yielded insufficient findings anchored in experimental or quasi-experimental design. Experimental design has many strengths, particularly in maintaining strong internal validity. It is hard to eliminate alternative hypotheses without a proportion of findings being anchored in experimental or quasi-experimental design. Experimental studies may be particularly well-suited to examine potential mechanisms that may explain well-established linkages. For example, if SE and interests are moderately to strongly related, and interests are 40% genetic, then what mechanisms initially lead children to pursue certain activities that they lack confidence in because they have never attempted the activity? Is it curiosity? More research is needed that examines how general variables (e.g., personality traits) are applied to and mediated by task- and situation-specific variables in affecting performance, and how these variables are moderated and affect situational

structuring and choice (Locke & Latham, 2004). Also, some traits have a direct impact on performance (like ability), and vocational psychologists need to understand when and why this occurs (Latham & Pinder, 2005).

Our second task, as vocational scholars, is to integrate existing knowledge. Scholars need to continue to generate more quantitative reviews in the form of meta-analyses. In searching the literature base, it became apparent that the number of meta-analyses concerning children's and adolescents' vocational development was sparse in comparison to meta-analyses concerning adults in the workforce and/or individual differences, especially personality. The 47 meta-analyses that were located in researching this chapter could be organized according to the sections: wage-earning adults (17), individual differences (16), diverse groups (6), achievement (5), children/adolescents/college students other than achievement (3). The scarcity of quantitative reviews may be one reason the vocational psychology of career choice and vocational development is not more integrated into the larger psychological domain.

Vocational scholars need to generate more conceptual reviews as well. The positive news is that many conceptual reviews are being published in various handbooks and texts. Integrating knowledge within particular domains of the field allows scholars to coalesce what is known and what new directions of inquiry to pursue. It also gives scholars opportunities to discard aspects of theories that are not supported by evidence. For example, congruence and job satisfaction's relation is either insignificant or too small to be practical. Scholars need to consider moderators or be more precise about what might be going on through the use of moderators (Dik, 2006).

The third task is to disseminate information learned in vocational psychology to a range of audiences. Career counselors need research findings to continue to update and upgrade their knowledge base and skills. Vocational clients need the most parsimonious and empirically grounded theories, measures, and tools to assist them in their learning, choosing, and working. Psychology undergraduates need to be informed of vocational psychology in introductory psychology courses, as well as in other advanced-level courses, such as individual difference courses, personality courses, and specialized courses in vocational psychology or counseling psychology.

The fourth task is to inform other areas and be informed by those areas. Because the field is vast and scholars can only be well-informed in their particular niches, it is crucial that we inform other scholars within and outside vocational psychology. Vocational psychology will benefit from increasing its visible contribution to psychology, so that the body of work cross-pollinates with related fields like industrial/organizational, clinical psychology, social psychology, and developmental psychology (Vondracek, 2001). Vocational researchers need to continue to learn broadly from areas within and outside our own niches, so that we can continue to see with fresh eyes and new perspectives. The strongest benefit of counseling psychology's commitment to multiculturalism is the understanding that seeing research from many dimensions adds breadth and depth and allows us to be more helpful to clients.

Acknowledgments

I would like to thank the following undergraduate research assistants who have assisted in literature searches, organization, and building references: Sara Tiedman, Lisa Bildeaux, Steven Mahan, Arnold Kong, Katrina Field, and Chris Demaria. A special thanks goes to my graduate advisee, Tsui-Feng Wu, who serves as my lab director. Appreciation goes to her for her supervision of the undergraduate research assistants, and her coordination and assistance with multiple tasks involved in bringing this chapter to fruition. A final thanks goes to my husband, Art Konar, who lovingly supported me throughout this endeavor.

References

Ackerman, P. L. (1996). Intelligence as process and knowledge: An integration for adult development and application. In W. A. Rogers, A. D. Fisk, & N. Walker (Eds.), *Aging and skilled performance: Advances in theory and applications* (pp. 139–156). Hillsdale, NJ: Lawrence Erlbaum Associates.

Ackerman, P. L., & Beier, M. E. (2003). Intelligence, personality, and interests in the career choice process. *Journal of Career Assessment, 11,* 205–218.

Ackerman, P. L., & Heggestad, E. D. (1997). Intelligence, personality, and interests: Evidence for overlapping traits. *Psychological Bulletin, 121,* 219–245.

Ajzen, I. (2002). Perceived behavioral control, self-efficacy, locus of control, and the theory of planned behavior. *Journal of Applied Social Psychology, 32,* 665–683.

Allen, T. D., Herst, D. E. L., Bruck, C. S., & Sutton, M. (2000). Consequences associated with work-to-family conflict: A review and agenda for future research. *Journal of Occupational Health Psychology, 5,* 278–308.

Altermatt, E. R., Jovanovic, J., & Perry, M. (1998). Bias or responsivity? Sex and achievement-level effects on teachers' classroom questioning practices. *Journal of Educational Psychology, 90,* 516–527.

Arbona, C., & Novy, D. M. (1991). Career aspirations and the expectations of Black, Mexican American, and White students. *Career Development Quarterly, 39,* 231–239.

Armstrong, P. I., Hubert, L., & Rounds, J. (2003). Circular unidimensional scaling: A new look at group differences in interest structure. *Journal of Counseling Psychology, 50,* 297–308.

Arvey, R. D., Bouchard, T. J., Jr., Segal, N. L., & Abraham, L. M. (1989). Job satisfaction: Environmental and genetic components. *Journal of Applied Psychology, 74,* 187–192.

Arvey, R. D., McCall, B. P., Bouchard, T. J., Jr., Taubman, P., & Cavanaugh, M. A. (1994). Genetic influences on job satisfaction and work values. *Personality and Individual Differences, 17,* 21–33.

Bandura, A. (1977). Self-efficacy: Toward a unifying theory of behavioral change. *Psychological Review, 84,* 191–215.

Bandura, A. (1982). Self-efficacy mechanism in human agency. *American Psychologist, 37,* 122–147.

Bandura, A. (1986). *Social foundations of thought and action: A social cognitive theory.* Englewood Cliffs, NJ: Prentice-Hall.

Barak, A., Feldman, S., & Noy, A. (1991). Traditionality of children's interests as related to their parents' gender stereotypes and traditionality of occupations. *Sex Roles, 24,* 511–524.

Barak, A., & Leong, F. (2001). *Contemporary models in vocational psychology: A volume in honor of Samuel H. Osipow.* New York: Routledge.

Barber, B. L., & Eccles, J. S. (1992). Long-term influence of divorce and single parenting on adolescent family-related and work-related values, behaviors, and aspirations. *Psychological Bulletin, 111,* 108–126.

Barrick, M. R., & Mount, M. K. (1991). The Big Five personality dimensions and job performance: A meta-analysis. *Personnel Psychology, 44,* 1–26.

Barrick, M. R., Mount, M. K., & Gupta, R. (2003). Meta-analysis of the relationship between the Five-Factor Model of personality and Holland's occupational types. *Personnel Psychology, 56,* 45–74.

Benbow, C. P., & Stanley, J. C. (1996). Inequity in equity: How "equity" can lead to inequity for high-potential students. *Psychological Public Policy and Law, 2,* 249–292.

Bertua, C., Anderson, N., & Salgado, J. F. (2005). The predictive validity of cognitive ability tests: A UK meta-analysis. *Journal of Occupational and Organizational Psychology, 78,* 387–409.

Betsworth, D. G., Bouchard, T. J., Cooper, C. R., Grotevant, H. D., Hansen, J. C., Scarr, S., & Weinberg, R. A. (1994). Genetic and environmental influences on vocational interests assessed using adoptive and biological families and twins reared apart and together. *Journal of Vocational Behavior, 44,* 263–278.

Betz, N. (2006). Basic issues and concepts in the career development and counseling of women. In W. B. Walsh, & M. J. Heppner (Eds.), *Handbook of career counseling for women* (2nd ed., pp. 45–74). Mahwah, NJ: Lawrence Erlbaum Associates.

Betz, N. E., Borgen, F. H., & Harmon, L. W. (2006). Vocational confidence and personality in the prediction of occupational group membership. *Journal of Career Assessment, 14,* 36–55.

Betz, N. E., Borgen, F. H., Rottinghaus, P., Paulsen, A., Halper, C. R., & Harmon, L. W. (2003). The Expanded Skills Confidence Inventory: Measuring basic dimensions of vocational activity. *Journal of Vocational Behavior, 62,* 76–100.

Betz, N. E., Harmon, L. W., & Borgen, F. H. (1996). The relationships of self-efficacy for the Holland themes to gender, occupational group membership, and vocational interests. *Journal of Counseling Psychology, 43,* 90–98.

Blake, R. J., & Sackett, S. A. (1999). Holland's typology and the Five-Factor Model: A rational-empirical analysis. *Journal of Career Assessment, 7*, 249–279.

Blustein, D. L. (2001). Extending the reach of vocational psychology: Toward an inclusive and integrated psychology of working. *Journal of Vocational Behavior, 59*, 171–182.

Borgen, F. H. (1991). Megatrends and milestones in vocational behavior: A 20-year counseling psychology retrospective. *Journal of Vocational Behavior, 39*, 263–290.

Borgen, F. H., & Harmon, L. W. (1996). Linking interest assessment and personality theory: An example of convergence between practice and theory. In M. L. Savickas, & W. B. Walsh (Eds.), *Handbook of career counseling theory and practice* (pp. 251–266). Palo Alto, CA: Davies-Black.

Borgen, F. H., & Lindley, L. D. (2003). Individuality and optimal health functioning: Interests, self-efficacy, and personality. In W. B. Walsh (Ed.), *Counseling psychology and optimal human functioning* (pp. 55–91). Mahwah, NJ: Lawrence Erlbaum Associates.

Borman, W. C., Hedge, J. W., Ferstl, K. L., Kaufman, J. D., Farmer, W. L., & Bearden, R. M. (2003). Current directions and issues in personnel selection and classification. In J. J. Martocchio, & G. R. Ferris (Eds.), *Research in personnel and human resources management* (pp. 287–355). Oxford, UK: Elsevier Science Ltd.

Bouchard, T. J., Jr. (1998). Genetic and environmental influences on adult intelligence and special mental abilities. *Human biology, 70*, 257–279.

Bowling, N. A., & Beehr, T. A. (2006). Workplace harassment from the victim's perspective: A theoretical model and meta-analysis. *Journal of Applied Psychology, 91*, 998–1012.

Brooks, A. K., & Clunis, T. (2007). Where to now? Race and ethnicity in workplace learning and development research: 1980–2005. *Human Resource Development Quarterly, 18*, 229–252.

Buboltz, W. C., Ebberwein, C., Watkins, C. E., & Savickas, M. L. (1995). A comparison of the content, authors, and institutions represented in the Career Development Quarterly and the Journal of Vocational Behavior. *Journal of Vocational Behavior, 46*, 216–226.

Bureau of Labor Statistics (BLS). (2007). *Women in the labor force: A datebook.* Retrieved from http://www.bls.gov/cps/wlf-datebook2007.htm.

Bureau of Labor Statistics (BLS). (2006). *Current population survey annual social and economic supplement.* Retrieved from http://www.bls.gov/cps/.

Bureau of Labor Statistics (BLS). (2007). *Current population survey.* Retrieved from http://www.bls.gov/cps/.

Byron, K. (2005). A meta-analytic review of work-family conflict and its antecedents. *Journal of Social Psychology, 135*, 483–497.

Campbell, D. P., Hyne, S. A., & Nilsen, D. L. (1992). *Manual for the Campbell Interest and Skills Survey: CISS.* Minneapolis: National Computer Systems.

Chartrand, J. M., Martin, W. F., Robbins, S. B., & McAuliffe, G. J. (1994). Testing a level versus an interactional view of career indecision. *Journal of Career Assessment, 2*, 55–69.

Cheng, C. (1996). We choose not to compete: The "merit" discourse in the selection process, and Asian and Asian American men and their masculinity. In C. Cheng (Ed.), *Masculinities in organizations* (pp. 177–200). Thousand Oaks, CA: Sage.

Church, A. T. (1994). Relating the Tellegen and Five-Factor models of personality structure. *Journal of Personality and Social Psychology, 67*(5), 898–909.

Collins, P. H. (1998). The social construction of Black feminist thought. In K. A. Myers, C. D. Anderson, & B. J. Risman (Eds.), *Feminist foundations: Toward transforming sociology.* (pp. 371–396). Thousand Oaks, CA: Sage Publications.

Colquitt, J. A., Scott, B. A., & LePine, J. A. (2007). Trust, trustworthiness, and trust propensity: A meta-analytic test of their unique relationships with risk taking and job performance. *Journal of Applied Psychology, 92*, 909–927.

Connolly, J. J., & Viswesvaran, C. (2000). The role of affectivity in job satisfaction: A meta-analysis. *Personality and Individual Differences, 29*, 265–281.

Cook, T. D., Church, M. B., Ajanaku, S., & Shadish, W. R., Jr. (1996). The development of occupational aspirations and expectations among inner-city boys. *Child Development, 67*, 3368–3385.

Corbie-Smith, G., Frank, E., Nickens, H. W., & Elon, L. (1999). Prevalences and correlates of ethnic harassment in the U. S. Women Physicians' Health Study. *Academic Medicine, 74*, 695–701.

Crites, J. O. (1978). *Career maturity inventory: Administration and use manual.* Monterey, CA: McGraw-Hill.

Curry, C., Trew, K., Turner, I., & Hunter, J. (1994). The effect of life domains on girls' possible selves. *Adolescence, 29*, 133–150.

Dalal, R. S. (2005). A meta-analysis of the relationship between organizational citizenship behavior and counterproductive work behavior. *Journal of Applied Psychology, 90*, 1241–1255.

Darcy, M. U. A., & Tracey, T. J. G. (2007). Circumplex structure of Holland's RIASEC interests across gender and time. *Journal of Counseling Psychology, 54*, 17–31.

Davey, F. H., & Stoppard, J. M. (1993). Some factors affecting the occupational expectations of female adolescents. *Journal of Vocational Behavior, 43*, 235–250.

Davison Avilés, R., & Spokane, A. R. (1999). The vocational interests of Hispanic, African American, and White middle school students. *Measurement and Evaluation in Counseling and Development, 32*, 138–148.

Dawis, R. V. (1991). Vocational interests, values, and preferences. In M. D. Dunnette, & L. M. Hough (Eds.), *Handbook of industrial and organizational psychology* (2nd ed., pp. 833–871). Palo Alto, CA: Consulting Psychologists Press.

Dawis, R. V. (1996). Vocational psychology, vocational adjustment, and the workforce: Some familiar and unanticipated consequences. *Psychology, Public Policy, and Law, 2*, 229–248.

Dawis, R. V. (2002). Person-environment-correspondence theory. In D. Brown (Ed.), *Career choice and development* (4th ed., pp. 427–464). San Francisco: Jossey-Bass.

Dawis, R. V. (2005). The Minnesota theory of work adjustment. In S. D. Brown, & R. W. Lent (Eds.), *Career development and counseling: Putting theory and research to work* (pp. 3–23). Hoboken, NJ: John Wiley & Sons.

Dawis, R. V., & Lofquist, L. (1984). *A psychological theory of work adjustment.* Minneapolis: University of Minnesota Press.

Day, S. X., & Rounds, J. (1998). Universality of vocational interest structure among racial and ethnic minorities. *American Psychologist, 53*, 728–736.

Day, S. X., Rounds, J., & Swaney, K. (1998). The structure of vocational interests for diverse racial-ethnic groups. *Psychological Science, 9*, 40–44.

DeNeve, K. M., & Cooper, H. (1998). The happy personality: A meta-analysis of 137 personality traits and subjective well-being. *Psychological Bulletin, 124,* 197–229.

Denissen, J. J. A., Zarrett, N. R., & Eccles, J. S. (2007). I like to do it, I'm able, and I know I am: Longitudinal couplings between domain-specific achievement, self-concept, and interest. *Child Development, 78,* 430–437.

Diener, E. (2000). The science of happiness and a proposal for a national index. *American Psychologist, 55,* 34–43.

Dik, B. J. (2006). *Moderators of the Holland-type congruence-satisfaction and congruence- performance relations.* Doctoral dissertation, University of Minnesota-Minneapolis.

Donnay, D. A. C., & Borgen, F. H. (1996). Validity, structure, and content of the 1994 Strong Interest Inventory. *Journal of Counseling Psychology, 43,* 275–291.

Donnay, D. A., & Borgen, F. H. (1999). The incremental validity of vocational self-efficacy: An examination of interest, self-efficacy, and occupation. *Journal of Counseling Psychology, 46,* 432–447.

Donnay, D. A., Morris, M. L., Schaubhut, N. A., & Thompson, R. C. (2005). *Strong Interest Inventory manual: Research, development and strategies for interpretation.* Palo Alto, CA: Counseling Psychology Press.

Dreher, G. F., & Ash, R. A. (1990). A comparative study of mentoring among men and women in managerial, professional, and technical positions. *Journal of Applied Psychology, 75,* 539–546.

Dudley, N. M., Orvis, K. A., Lebiecki, J. E., & Cortina, J. M. (2006). A meta-analytic investigation of conscientiousness in the prediction of job performance: Examining the intercorrelations and the incremental validity of narrow traits. *Journal of Applied Psychology, 91,* 40–57.

Eggerth, D. E., & Andrew, M. E. (2006). Modifying the C index for use with Holland codes of unequal length. *Journal of Career Assessment, 14,* 267–275.

Eggerth, D. E., & Cunningham, T. R. (2011). Counseling psychology and occupational health psychology. In E. M. Altmaier, & J. C. Hansen (Eds.), *The Oxford handbook of counseling psychology.* New York: Oxford University Press.

Entwisle, D. R., Alexander, K. L., Olson, L. S., & Ross, K. (1999). Paid work in early adolescence: Developmental and ethnic patterns. *Journal of Early Adolescence, 19,* 363–388.

Fan, X., & Chen, M. (2001). Parental involvement and students' academic achievement: A meta-analysis. *Educational Psychology Review, 13,* 1–22.

Fassinger, R. E. (2005). Theoretical issues in the study of women's career development: Building bridges in a brave new world. In W. B. Walsh, & M. L. Savickas (Eds.), *Handbook of vocational psychology* (3rd ed., pp. 85–124). Mahwah, NJ: Lawrence Erlbaum Associates.

Fleming, P. (2000). Three decades of educational progress and continuing barriers for women and girls. *Equity and excellence in education, 33,* 74–79.

Ford, M. T., Heinen, B. A., & Langkamer, K. L. (2007). Work and family satisfaction and conflict: A meta-analysis of cross-domain relations. *Journal of Applied Psychology, 92,* 57–80.

Fouad, N. A. (2001). The future of vocational psychology: Aiming high. *Journal of Vocational Behavior, 59,* 183–191.

Fouad, N. A., & Byars-Winston, A. M. (2005). Cultural context of career choice: Meta-analysis of race/ethnicity differences. *The Career Development Quarterly, 53,* 223–233.

Fritzsche, B. A., & Parrish, T. J. (2005). Theories and Research on Job Satisfaction. In S. D. Brown, & R. W. Lent (Eds.), *Career Development and Counseling: Putting Theory and Research to Work* (pp. 180–202). Hoboken, NJ: John Wiley & Sons.

Gasser, C. E., Larson, L. M., & Borgen, F. H. (2007). Concurrent validity of the 2005 strong interest inventory: An examination of gender and major field of study. *Journal of Career Assessment, 15,* 23–43.

Gati, I. (1986). Making career decisions: A sequential elimination approach. *Journal of Counseling Psychology, 33,* 408–417.

Gati, I. (1991). Career counselors' perception of the structure of vocational interests. *Journal of Counseling Psychology, 38,* 175–181.

George, J. M. (1989). Mood and absence. *Journal of Applied Psychology, 74,* 317–324.

Gibson, M. A. (1988). *Accommodation without assimilation.* Ithaca, NY: Cornell University Press.

Gottfredson, G. D. (1999). John L. Holland's contributions to vocational psychology: A review and evaluation. *Journal of Vocational Behavior, 55,* 15–40.

Gottfredson, G. D. (2001). Fostering the scientific practice of vocational psychology. *Journal of Vocational Behavior, 59,* 192–202.

Gottfredson, L. S. (1996). Gottfredson's theory of circumscription and compromise. In D. Brown, & L. Brooks (Eds.), *Career choice and development* (3rd ed., pp. 179–232). San Francisco: Jossey-Bass.

Gottfredson, L. S. (1999). The nature and nurture of vocational interests. In M. L. Savickas, & A. R. Spokane (Eds.), *Vocational interests: Meaning, measurement, and counseling use* (pp. 57–85). Palo Alto, CA: Davies-Black.

Gottfredson, L. S. (2002). Gottfredson's theory of circumscription, compromise and self-creation. In D. Brown (Ed.), *Career choice and development* (4th ed., pp. 85–148). San Francisco: Jossey-Bass.

Gottfredson, L. S. (2005). Applying Gottfredson's theory of circumscription and compromise in career guidance and counseling. In S. D. Brown, & R. W. Lent (Eds.), *Career development and counseling: Putting theory and research to work* (pp. 71–100). Hoboken, NJ: John Wiley & Sons.

Griffeth, R. W., Steel, R. P., Allen, D. G., & Bryan, N. (2005). The development of a multidimensional measure of job market cognitions: The employment opportunity index (EOI). *Journal of Applied Psychology, 90,* 335–349.

Haas, N. S., & Sullivan, H. (1991). Use of ethnically matched role models in career materials for Hispanic students. *Contemporary Educational Psychology, 16,* 272–278.

Halbesleben, J. R. B. (2006). Sources of social support and burnout: A meta-analytic test of the conservation of resources model. *Journal of Applied Psychology, 91,* 1134–1145.

Hansen, J. C., & Swanson, J. L. (1983). Stability of interests and the predictive and concurrent validity of the 1981 Strong-Campbell Interest Inventory for college majors. *Journal of Counseling Psychology, 30,* 194–201.

Hanson, S. L. (1994). Lost talent: Unrealized educational aspirations and expectations among U.S. youth. *Sociology of Education, 67,* 159–183.

Hardin, E. E., & Leong, F. T. L. (2005). Optimism and pessimism as mediators of the relations between self-discrepancies and distress among Asian and European Americans. *Journal of Counseling Psychology, 52,* 25–35.

Hardin, E. E., Leong, F. T. L., & Osipow, S. H. (2001). Cultural relativity in the conceptualization of career maturity. *Journal of Vocational Behavior, 58*, 36–52.

Harmon, L. W., Hansen, J. C., Borgen, F. H., & Hammer, A. L. (1994). *Applications and technical guide for the Strong Interest Inventory*. Palo Alto, CA: Consulting Psychologists Press.

Harren, V. A. (1979). Research with the assessment of career decision making. *Character Potential: A Record of Research, 9*, 63–69.

Harrison, D. A., Newman, D. A., & Roth, P. L. (2006). How important are job attitudes? Meta-analytic comparisons of integrative behavioral outcomes and time sequences. *Academy of Management Journal, 49*, 305–325.

Hartung, P. J., Porfeli, E. J., & Vondracek, F. W. (2005). Child vocational development: A review and reconsideration. *Journal of Vocational Behavior, 66*, 385–419.

Helwig, A. A. (1998a). Developmental and sex differences in workers' functions of occupational aspirations of a longitudinal sample of elementary school children. *Psychological Reports, 82*, 915–921.

Helwig, A. A. (1998b). Occupational aspirations of a longitudinal sample from second to sixth grade. *Journal of Career Development, 24*, 247–265.

Helwig, A. A. (2001). A test of Gottfredson's theory using a ten-year longitudinal study. *Journal of Career Development, 28*, 77–95.

Helwig, A. A. (2004). A ten-year longitudinal study of the career development of students: Summary findings. *Journal of Counseling and Development, 82*, 1–4.

Henderson, S., Hesketh, B., & Tuffin, K. (1988). A test of Gottfredson's theory of circumscription. *Journal of Vocational Behavior, 32*, 37–48.

Hesketh, B. (2001). Adapting vocational psychology to cope with change. *Journal of Vocational Behavior, 59*, 203–212.

Hesketh, B., & Griffin, B. (2005). Work adjustment. In W. B. Walsh, & M. L. Savickas (Eds.), *Handbook of vocational psychology* (pp. 245–266). Mahwah, NJ: Lawrence Erlbaum Associates.

Hoffman, B. J., & Woehr, D. J. (2006). A quantitative review of the relationship between person-organization fit and behavioral outcomes. *Journal of Vocational Behavior, 68*, 389–399.

Holland, J. L. (1959). A theory of vocational choice. *Journal of Counseling Psychology, 6*, 35–44.

Holland, J. L. (1997). *Making vocational choices: A theory of vocational personalities and work environments* (3rd ed.). Odessa, FL: Psychological Assessment Resources.

Hough, L. M., & Oswald, F. L. (2000). Personnel selection: Looking toward the future—Remembering the past. *Annual Review of Psychology, 51*, 631–664.

Hülsheger, U. R., Maier, G. W., & Stumpp, T. (2007). Validity of general mental ability for the prediction of job performance and training success in Germany: A meta-analysis. *International Journal of Selection and Assessment, 15*, 3–18.

Humphrey, S. E., Nahrgang, J. D., & Morgeson, F. P. (2007). Integrating motivational, social, and contextual work design features: A meta-analytic summary and theoretical extension of the work design literature. *Journal of Applied Psychology, 92*, 1332–1356.

Hunter, J. E., & Hunter, R. F. (1984). Validity and utility of alternate predictors of performance. *Psychological Bulletin, 96*, 72–98.

Jeynes, W. H. (2007). The relationship between parental involvement and urban secondary school student academic achievement: A meta-analysis. *Urban Education, 42*, 82–110.

Johnson, L. (1995). A multidimensional analysis of the vocational aspirations of college students. *Measurement and Evaluation in Counseling and Development, 28*, 25–44.

Johnson, M. K., & Mortimer, J. T. (2002). Career choice and development from a sociological perspective. In D. Brown (Ed.), *Career choice and development* (4th ed., pp. 37–84). San Francisco: Jossey-Bass.

Jordan, T. E. (1976). Preschool influences on occupational knowledge of seven-year-olds: A prospective study. *Journal of Experimental Education, 44*, 27–37.

Jordan, T. E., & Pope, M. L. (2001). Developmental antecedents to adolescents' occupational knowledge: A 17-year prospective study. *Journal of Vocational Behavior, 58*, 279–292.

Judge, T. A., Heller, D., & Mount, M. K. (2002). Five-Factor Model of personality and job satisfaction: A meta-analysis. *Journal of Applied Psychology, 87*, 530–541.

Judge, T. A., & Hulin, C. L. (1993). Job satisfaction as a reflection of disposition: A multiple source causal analysis. *Organizational Behavior and Human Decision Processes, 56*, 388–421.

Judge, T. A., & Ilies, R. (2002). Relationship of personality to performance motivation: A meta-analytic review. *Journal of Applied Psychology, 87*, 797–807.

Judge, T. A., Jackson, C. L., Shaw, J. C., Scott, B. A., & Rich, B. L. (2007). Self-efficacy and work-related performance: The integral role of individual differences. *Journal of Applied Psychology, 92*, 107–127.

Judge, T. A., Thoresen, C. J., Bono, J. E., & Patton, G. K. (2001). The job satisfaction-job performance relationship: A qualitative and quantitative review. *Psychological Bulletin, 127*, 376–407.

Juvonen, J., Nishina, A., & Graham, S. (2000). Peer harassment, psychological adjustment, and school functioning in early adolescence. *Journal of Educational Psychology, 92*, 349–359.

Kahle, J., Meece, J., & Scantlebury, K. (2000). Urban African-American middle school science students: Does standards-based teaching make a difference? *Journal of Research in Science Teaching, 37*, 1019–1041.

Kanfer, R., Wanberg, C. R., & Kantrowitz, T. M. (2001). Job search and employment: A personality-motivational analysis and meta-analytic review. *Journal of Applied Psychology, 86*, 837–855.

Kao, G. (1995). Asian Americans as model minorities? A look at their academic performance. *American Journal of Education, 103*, 121–159.

Kao, G., Tienda, M., & Schneider, B. (1996). Racial and ethnic variation in academic performance. In A. M. Pallas (Ed.), *Research in sociology of education and socialization, 11*, 263–297.

Katz, M. R. (1966). A model of guidance for career decision-making. *Vocational Guidance Quarterly, 15*, 2–10.

Kieffer, K. M., Schinka, J. A., & Curtiss, G. (2004). Person-environment congruence and personality domains in the prediction of job performance and work quality. *Journal of Counseling Psychology, 51*, 168–177.

Kossek, E. E., & Ozeki, C. (1998). Work-family conflict, policies, and the job-life satisfaction relationship: A review and directions for future organizational behavior-human resources research. *Journal of Applied Psychology, 83*, 139–149.

Kristof, A. L. (1996). Person-organization fit: An integrative review of its conceptualizations, measurement, and implications. *Personnel Psychology, 49*, 1–49.

Krumboltz, J. D., & Hamel, D. A. (1977). *Guide to career decision making skills*. New York: College Entrance Examination Board.

Krumboltz, J. D., Mitchell, A. M., & Jones, G. B. (1976). A social learning theory of career selection. *The Counseling Psychologist, 6*, 71–81.

Krumboltz, J. D., & Nichols, C. W. (1990). Integrating the social learning theory of career decision making. In W. B. Walsh, & S. H. Osipow (Eds.), *Career counseling: Contemporary topics in vocational psychology* (pp. 159–192). Hillsdale, NJ: Erlbaum.

Kuncel, N. R., Credé, M., & Thomas, L. L. (2007). A meta-analysis of the predictive validity of the graduate management admission test (GMT) and undergraduate grade point average (UGPA) for graduate student academic performance. *Academy of Management, Learning, and Education, 6*, 51–68.

Larson, L. M., & Borgen, F. H. (2006). Do personality traits contribute to vocational self-efficacy. *Journal of Career Assessment, 14*, 295–311.

Larson, L. M., Rottinghaus, P. J., & Borgen, F. H. (2002). Meta-analyses of Big Six interests and Big Five personality variables. *Journal of Vocational Behavior, 61*, 217–239.

Larson, L. M., Wei, M., Wu, T.-F., Borgen, F. H., & Bailey, D. C. (2007). Discriminating among educational majors and career aspirations in Taiwanese undergraduates: The contribution of personality and self-efficacy. *Journal of Counseling Psychology, 54*, 395–408.

Larson, L. M., Wu, T. F., Bailey, D. C., Borgen, F. H., & Gasser, C. E. (2010). Male and female college students' educational majors: The contribution of basic vocational cofidence and interests. *Journal of Career Assessment, 18*, 16–33.

Latham, G. P., & Pinder, C. C. (2005). Work motivation theory and research at the dawn of the twenty-first century. *Annual Review of Psychology, 56*, 485–516.

Lee, T. W., Mitchell, T. R., & Sablynski, C. J. (1999). Qualitative research in organizational and vocational psychology, 1979–1999. *Journal of Vocational Behavior, 55*, 161–187.

Lent, R. W. (2004). Toward a unifying theoretical and practical perspective on well-being and psychosocial adjustment. *Journal of Counseling Psychology, 51*, 482–509.

Lent, R. W. (2005). A social cognitive view of career development and counseling. In S. D. Brown, & R.W. Lent (Eds.), *Career development and counseling: Putting theory and research to work* (pp. 101–127). Hoboken, NJ: John Wiley & Sons.

Lent, R. W., Brown, S. D., & Hackett, G. (1994). Toward a unifying social cognitive theory of career and academic interest, choice, and performance. *Journal of Vocational Behavior, 45*, 79–122.

Lent, R. W., Lopez, F. G., & Bieschke, K. J. (1993). Predicting mathematics-related choice and success behaviors: Test of an expanded social cognitive model. *Journal of Vocational Behavior, 42*, 223–236.

Leong, F. T. L. (1991). Career development attributes and occupational values of Asian American and White American college students. *Career Development Quarterly, 39*, 221–230.

Leong, F. T. L. (2001). The role of acculturation in the career adjustment of Asian American workers: A test of Leong and Chou's (1994) formulations. *Cultural Diversity & Ethnic Minority Psychology, 7*, 262–273.

Leong, F. T. L., & Gupta, A. (2007). Career development and vocational behaviors of Asian Americans. In F. T. L. Leong, A. G. Inman, A. Ebreo, L. H. Yang, L. Kinoshita, & M. Fu (Eds.), *Handbook of Asian American psychology* (2nd ed., pp. 159–178). Thousand Oaks, CA: Sage.

Leong, F. T. L., & Hayes, T. J. (1990). Occupational stereotyping of Asian Americans. *Career Development Quarterly, 39*, 143–154.

Leong, F. T. L., & Tata, S. P. (1990). Sex and acculturation differences in occupational values among Chinese-American children. *Journal of Counseling Psychology, 37*, 208–212.

LePine, J. A., Erez, A., & Johnson, D. E. (2002). The nature and dimensionality of organizational citizenship behavior: A critical review and meta-analysis. *Journal of Applied Psychology, 87*, 52–65.

Leung, S. A., Ivy, D., & Suzuki, L. (1994). Factors affecting the career aspirations of Asian Americans. *Journal of Counseling and Development, 72*, 404–410.

Leung, S. A., & Plake, B. S. (1990). A choice dilemma approach for examining the relative importance of sex type and prestige preferences in the process of career choice compromise. *Journal of Counseling Psychology, 37*, 399–406.

Levine, E. L., Spector, P. E., Menon, S., Narayanan, L., & Cannon-Bowers, J. (1996). Validity generalization for cognitive, psychomotor, and perceptual tests for craft jobs in the utility industry. *Human Performance, 9*, 1–22.

Lindley, L., & Borgen, F. H. (2000). Personal style scales of the Strong Interest Inventory: Linking personality and interests. *Journal of Vocational Behavior, 57*, 22–41.

Liu, C., & Rounds, J. (2003). Evaluating the structure of vocational interests in China, *Acta Psychologica Sinica, 35*, 411–418.

Locke, E. A. (1978). Job satisfaction reconsidered: Reconsidered. *American Psychologist, 33*, 854–855.

Locke, E. A., & Latham, G. P. (2004). What should we do about motivation theory? Six recommendations for the twenty-first century. *Academy of Management Review, 29*, 388–403.

London, M., & Greller, M. M. (1991). Demographic trends and vocational behavior: A twenty year retrospective and agenda for the 1990s. *Journal of Vocational Behavior, 38*, 125–164.

Long, L., & Tracey, T. J. G. (2006). Structure of RIASEC scores in China: A structural meta-analysis. *Journal of Vocational Behavior, 68*, 39–51.

Loscocco, K. A., & Roschelle, A. R. (1991). Influences on the quality of work and nonwork life: Two decades in review. *Journal of Vocational Behavior, 39*, 182–225.

Low, K. S. D., & Rounds, J. (2006). Vocational interests: Bridging person and environment. In D. Segal, & J. Thomas (Eds.), *Comprehensive handbook of personality and psychopathology, Volume I: Personality and every day functioning* (pp. 251–267). New York: Wiley.

Low, K. S. D., & Rounds, J. (2007). Interest change and continuity from early adolescence to middle adulthood. *International Journal for Educational and Vocational Guidance, 7*, 23–36.

Low, K. S. D., Yoon, M., Roberts, B. W., & Rounds, J. (2005). The stability of vocational interests from early adolescence to middle adulthood: A quantitative review of longitudinal studies. *Psychological Bulletin, 131*, 713–737.

Lubinski, D. (2000). Scientific and social significance of assessing individual differences: Sinking shafts at a few critical points. *Annual Review of Psychology, 51*, 405–444.

Lykken, D. T., Bouchard, T. J., McGue, M., & Tellegen, A. (1993). Heritability of interests: A twin study. *Journal of Applied Psychology, 78*, 649–661.

Madamba, A. B., & De Jong, G. F. (1997). Job mismatch among Asians in the United States: Ethnic group comparisons. *Social Science Quarterly, 78*, 524–542.

Matsuoka, J. K., & Ryujin, D. H. (1989). Vietnamese refugees: An analysis of contemporary adjustment issues. *Journal of Applied Social Sciences, 14,* 23–45.

McGuire, S., Neiderhiser, J. M., Reeiss, D., Hetherington, E. M., & Plomin, R. (1994). Genetic and environmental influences on perceptions of self-worth and competence in adolescence: A study of twins, full siblings, and step-siblings. *Child Development, 65,* 785–799.

McKay, P. F., & McDaniel, M. A. (2006). A reexamination of Black-White mean differences in work performance: More data, more moderators. *Journal of Applied Psychology, 91,* 538–554.

McMahon, M., & Patton, W. (1997). Gender differences in children and adolescents' perceptions of influences on their career development. *School Counselor, 44,* 368–376.

McNulty, W. B., & Borgen, W. A. (1988). Career expectations and aspirations of adolescents. *Journal of Vocational Behavior, 33,* 217–224.

Meece, J. L., & Scantlebury, K. (2006). Gender and schooling: Progress and persistent barriers. In J. Worell, & C. D. Goodheart (Eds.), *Handbook of girls' and women's psychological health: Gender and well-being across the lifespan* (pp. 283–291). New York: Oxford University Press.

Mesmer-Magnus, J. R., & Viswesvaran, C. (2005). Convergence between measures of work-to-family and family-to-work conflict: A meta-analytic examination. *Journal of Vocational Behavior, 67,* 215–232.

Meyer, J. P., & Allen, N. J. (1997). *Commitment in the workplace: Theory, research, and application.* Thousand Oaks, CA: Sage.

Mitchell, L. K., & Krumboltz, J. D. (1990). Social learning approach to career decision making: Krumboltz's theory. In D. Brown, & L. Brooks (Eds.), *Career choice and development* (2nd ed., pp. 145–196). San Francisco: Jossey-Bass.

Mitchell, L. K., & Krumboltz, J. D. (1996). Krumboltz's learning theory of career choice and counseling. In D. Brown, & L. Brooks (Eds.), *Career choice and development* (3rd ed., pp. 233–280). San Francisco: Jossey-Bass.

Moloney, D. P., Bouchard, T. J., & Segal, N. L. (1991). A genetic and environmental analysis of the vocational interests of monozygotic and dizygotic twins reared apart. *Journal of Vocational Behavior, 39,* 76–109.

Mount, M. K., Barrick, M. R., Scullen, S. M., & Rounds, J. (2005). Higher-order dimensions of the Big Five personality traits and the big six vocational interest types. *Personnel Psychology, 58,* 447–478.

Multon, K. D., Brown, S. D., & Lent, R. W. (1991). Relation of self-efficacy beliefs to academic outcomes: A meta-analytic investigation. *Journal of Counseling Psychology, 38,* 30–38.

Mundra, K., Moellmer, A., & Lopez-Aqueres, W. (2003). Investigating Hispanic underrepresentation in managerial and professional occupations. *Hispanic Journal of Behavioral Sciences, 25,* 513–529.

National Center for Education Statistics. (2001). *The National Assessment of Educational Progress (NAEP). The nation's report card: Mathematics 2000.* U.S. Department of Education, Office of Educational Research and Improvement. Washington, DC. Author.

National Center for Education Statistics. (2002). *The National Assessment of Educational Progress (NAEP). The nation's report card: Science highlights 2000.* U.S. Department of Education, Institute of Educational Sciences. Washington, DC: Author.

National Center for Education Statistics. (2003a). *The National Assessment of Educational Progress (NAEP). The nation's report card: Reading highlights 2002. 2002 reading trends differ by grade.* U.S. Department of Education, Institute of Education Sciences. Washington, DC: Author.

National Center for Education Statistics. (2003b). *The National Assessment of Educational Progress (NAEP). The nation's report card: Writing highlights 2002. Fourth and eight grade students make gains in writing since 1998.* U.S. Department of Education, Institute of Education Sciences. Washington, DC: Author.

National Science Foundation (NSF). (2004). *Women, minorities, and persons with disabilities in science and engineering* (Report No. NSF04–317). Washington, DC: Author.

National Science Foundation (NSF). (2008). *Science and engineering indicators* (Report No. NSB 06–01). Washington, DC: Author.

Nauta, M. M., Kahn, J. H., Angell, J. W., & Cantarelli, E. A. (2002). Identifying the antecedent in the relation between career interests and self-efficacy: Is it one, the other, or both? *Journal of Counseling Psychology, 49,* 290–301.

Ng, T. W. H., Eby, L. T., Sorensen, K. L., & Feldman, D. C. (2005). Predictors of objective and subjective career success. A meta-analysis. *Personnel Psychology, 58,* 367–408.

O'Driscoll, M. P., & Randall, D. M. (1999). Perceived organizational support, satisfaction with rewards, and employee job involvement and organizational commitment. *Applied Psychology: An International Review, 48,* 197–209.

Oppenheimer, L. (1991). Determinants of action: An organismic and holistic approach. In L. Oppenheimer, & J. Valsiner (Eds.), *The origins of action: Interdisciplinary and international perspectives* (pp. 37–63). New York: Springer–Verlag.

Organ, D. W., & Ryan, K. (1995). A meta-analytic review of attitudinal and dispositional predictors of organizational citizenship behavior. *Personnel Psychology, 48,* 775–802.

Owings, S. R., & Fritzsche, B. A. (2000). *The relationship between person-environment congruence and job satisfaction.* Poster session presented at the annual meeting of the Society for Industrial and Organizational Psychology, New Orleans, LA.

Palmer, G., & Johnson-Bailey, J. (2005). The career development of African Americans in the areas of training and organizational development. *Human Resource Planning, 28,* 1–12.

Park, S. E., & Harrison, A. A. (1995). Career-related interests and values, perceived control, and acculturation of Asian American and Caucasian-American college students. *Journal of Applied Social Psychology, 25,* 1184–1203.

Parsons, F. (1909). *Choosing a vocation.* Boston: Houghton Mifflin.

Phillips, S. D. (1997). Toward an expanded definition of adaptive decision making. *The Career Development Quarterly, 45,* 275–287.

Phillips, S. D., Christopher-Sisk, E. K., & Gravino, K. L. (2001). Making career decisions in a relational context. *The Counseling Psychologist, 29,* 193–213.

Phillips, S. D., & Jome, L. M. (2005). Vocational choices: What do we know? What do we need to know? In W. B. Walsh, & M. L. Savickas (Eds.), *Handbook of vocational psychology* (3rd ed., pp. 127–154). Mahwah, NJ: Lawrence Erlbaum Associates.

Phillips, S. D., Savickas, M. L., & Lent, R. W. (1994). Choice and change: Convergence from the decision-making perspective. In S. D. Phillips (Ed.), *Convergence in career development theories: Implications for science and practice* (pp. 155–163). Palo Alto, CA: CPP.

Pinder, C. C. (1998). *Work motivation in organizational behavior.* Upper Saddle River, NJ: Prentice Hall.

Pitz, G. F., & Harren, V. A. (1980). An analysis of career decision making from the point of view of information processing and decision theory. *Journal of Vocational Behavior, 16*, 320–346.

Plomin, R., DeFries, J. C., McClearn, G. E., & Rutter, M. (1997). *Behavior genetics* (3rd ed., pp. 203–204). New York: Freeman.

Podsakoff, N. P., LePine, J. A., & LePine, M. A. (2007). Differential challenge stressor-hindrance stressor relationships with job attitudes, turnover intentions, turnover, and withdrawal behavior: A meta-analysis. *Journal of Applied Psychology, 92*, 438–454.

Rathbun, A., West, J., & Germino-Hausken, E. (2004). *From kindergarten through third grade* (NCES Report No. 2004–2007). Washington, DC: National Center for Education Statistics.

Ray, R., Gornick, J. C., & Schmitt, J. (2008, September). *Parental leave policies in 21 countries: Assessing generosity and gender equality. Center for Economic and Policy Research Report*. Retrieved from www.cepr.net/documents/publicatons/parental_2008_09.pdf.

Rhoades, L., & Eisenberger, R. (2002). Perceived organizational support: A review of the literature. *Journal of Applied Psychology, 87*, 698–714.

Roberts, B. W., & DelVecchio, W. F. (2000). The rank-order consistency of personality from childhood to old age: A quantitative review of longitudinal studies. *Psychological Bulletin, 126*, 3–25.

Rojewski, J. W. (1997). Characteristics of students who express stable or undecided occupational expectations during early adolescents. *Journal of Career Assessment, 5*, 1–20.

Rojewski, J. W. (2005). Occupational aspirations: Constructs, meanings, and application. In S. D. Brown, & R. W. Lent (Eds.), *Career development and counseling: Putting theory and research to work* (pp. 131–154). Hoboken, NJ: John Wiley & Sons.

Rojewski, J. W., & Kim, H. (2003). Career choice patterns and behavior of work-bound youth during early adolescence. *Journal of Career Development, 30*, 89–108.

Rojewski, J. W., & Yang, B. (1997). Longitudinal analysis of select influences on adolescents' occupational aspirations. *Journal of Vocational Behavior, 51*, 375–410.

Ronen, S. T. (1994). An underlying structure of motivational need taxonomies: A cross-cultural confirmation. In H. C. Triandis, M. D. Dunnette, & L. M. Hough (Eds.), *Handbook of industrial and organizational psychology* (2nd ed., pp. 241–269). Palo Alto, CA: Consulting Psychologists Press.

Rose, R. J. (1995). Genes and human behavior. *Annual Review of Psychology, 46*, 625–654.

Rosenzweig, C. (2001). *A meta-analysis of parenting and school success: The role of parents in promoting students' academic performance*. Paper presented at the American Educational Research Association National Convention, Seattle, Washington.

Roth, P. L., Huffcutt, A. I., & Bobko, P. (2003). Ethnic group differences in measures of job performance: A new meta-analysis. *Journal of Applied Psychology, 88*, 694–706.

Rottinghaus, P. J., Betz, N. E., & Borgen, F. H. (2003). Validity of parallel measures of vocational interests and confidence. *Journal of Career Assessment, 11*, 355–378.

Rottinghaus, P. J., Coon, K. L., Gaffey, A. R., & Zytowski, D. G. (2007). Thirty-year stability and predictive validity of vocational interests. *Journal of Career Assessment, 15*, 5–22.

Rottinghaus, P. J., Larson, L. M., & Borgen, F. H. (2003). Theoretical and empirical linkages of self-efficacy and interests. *Journal of Vocational Behavior, 62*, 221–236.

Rottinghaus, P. J., Lindley, L. D., Green, M. A., & Borgen, F. H. (2002). Educational aspirations: The contribution of personality, self-efficacy, and interests. *Journal of Vocational Behavior, 61*, 1–19.

Rounds, J., & Armstrong, P. I. (2005). Assessment of needs and values. In S. D. Brown, & R. W. Lent (Eds.), *Career development and counseling: Putting theory and research to work* (pp. 305–329). Hoboken, NJ: Wiley.

Rounds, J., & Tracey, T. J. (1996). Cross-cultural structural equivalence of RIASEC models and measures. *Journal of Counseling Psychology, 43*, 310–329.

Russell, J. E. A. (2006). Career counseling for women in management. In W. B. Walsh, & M. J. Heppner (Eds.), *Handbook of career counseling for women* (2nd ed., pp. 453–512). Mahwah, NJ: Lawrence Erlbaum Associates.

Ryff, C. D. (1995). Psychological well-being in adult life. *Current Directions in Psychological Science, 4*, 99–104.

Sadri, G., & Robertson, I. T. (1993). Self-efficacy and work-related behaviour: A review and meta-analysis. *Applied Psychology: An International Review, 42*, 139–152.

Saks, A. M., & Ashforth, B. E. (1997). A longitudinal investigation of the relationships between job information sources, applicant perceptions of fit, and work outcomes. *Personnel Psychology, 50*, 395–426.

Salgado, J. F., Anderson, N., Moscoso, S., Bertua, C., de Fruyt, F., & Rolland, J. P. (2003). A meta-analytic study of general mental ability validity for different occupations in the European community. *Journal of Applied Psychology, 88*, 1068–1081.

Savickas, M. L. (2002). Career construction: A developmental theory of vocational behavior. In D. Brown (Ed.), *Career choice and development* (4th ed., pp. 149–205). San Francisco: Jossey-Bass.

Savickas, M. L. (2005). The theory and practice of career construction. In S. D. Brown, & R. W. Lent (Eds.), *Career development and counseling: Putting theory and research to work* (pp. 42–70). Hoboken, NJ: John Wiley & Sons.

Savickas, M. L., & Baker, D. B. (2005). The history of vocational psychology: Antecedents, origin and early development. In B. Walsh, & M. Savickas (Eds.), *Handbook of vocational psychology* (3rd ed.). Mahwah, NJ.: Lawrence Erlbaum Associates.

Savickas, M. L., & Lent, R. W. (1994). *Convergence in career development theories: Implications for science and practice*. Palo Alto, CA: CPP.

Schmidt, F. L., & Hunter, J. E. (1998). The validity and utility of selection methods in personnel psychology: Practice and theoretical implications of 85 years of research findings. *Psychological Bulletin, 124*, 262–274.

Seibert, S. E., & Kraimer, M. L. (2001). The Five-Factor Model of personality and career success. *Journal of Vocational Behavior, 58*, 1–21.

Silvia, P. J. (2003). Self-efficacy and interest: Experimental studies of optimal incompetence. *Journal of Vocational Behavior, 62*, 237–249.

Silvia, P. J. (2006). Exploring the psychology of interest. New York: Oxford University Press.

Smith, P. C., Kendall, L. M., & Hulin, C. L. (1969). *The measurement of satisfaction in work and retirement: A strategy for the study of attitudes*. Oxford, England: Rand McNally.

Snow, R. E. (1996). Aptitude development and education. *Psychological Public Policy and Law, 3*, 536–560.

Spokane, A. R., & Cruza-Guet, M. C. (2005). Holland's theory of vocational personalities in work environments. In D. Brown, & R. W. Lent (Eds.), *Career development and counseling: Putting theory and research to work* (pp. 24–41). Hoboken, NJ: John Wiley & Sons.

Staggs, G. D., Larson, L. M., & Borgen, F. H. (2003). Convergence of specific factors in vocational interests and personality. *Journal of Career Assessment, 11*, 243–261.

Staggs, G. D., Larson, L. M., & Borgen, F. H. (2007). Convergence of personality and interests: Meta-analysis of the multidimensional personality questionnaire and the strong interest inventory. *Journal of Career Assessment, 15*, 423–445.

Stajkovic, A. D., & Luthans, F. (1998). Self-efficacy and work-related performance: A meta-analysis. *Psychological Bulletin, 124*, 240–261.

Strong, E. K., Jr. (1927). *Vocational interest blank*. Palo Alto, CA: Stanford University Press.

Strong, E. K., Jr. (1955). *Vocational interests 18 years after college*. Minneapolis, MN: University of Minnesota Press.

Subich, L. M. (2001). Dynamic forces in the growth and change of vocational psychology. *Journal of Vocational Behavior, 59*, 235–242.

Sullivan, B. A., & Hansen, J. C. (2004). Mapping associations between interests and personality: Toward a conceptual understanding of individual differences in vocational behavior. *Journal Counseling Psychology, 51*, 287–298.

Super, D. E. (1992). Toward a comprehensive theory of career development. In D. H. Montross, & C. J. Shinkman (Eds.), *Career development: Theory and practice* (pp. 35–64). Springfield, IL: Charles C Thomas.

Super, D. E., & Jordaan, J. P. (1973). Career development theory. *British Journal of Guidance and Counselling, 1*, 3–16.

Super, D. E., Savickas, M. L., & Super, C. M. (1996). The life-span, life-space approach to careers. In D. Brown, & L. Brooks (Eds.), *Career choice and development* (pp. 121–178). San Francisco: Jossey-Bass.

Super, D. E., Tiedeman, D. V., & Borow, H. (1961). Vocational development: A symposium. *Personnel & Guidance Journal, 40*, 11–25.

Swaney, K. B. (1995). *Technical manual: Revised Unisex Edition of the ACT Interest Inventory (UNIACT)*. Iowa City, IA: ACT.

Swanson, J. L. (2011). Measurement and assessment in counseling psychology. In E. M. Altmaier, & J. C. Hansen (Eds.), *The Oxford handbook of counseling psychology*. New York: Oxford University Press.

Swanson, J. L., & Hansen, J. C. (1988). Stability of vocational interests over 4-year, 8-year, and 12-year intervals. *Journal of Vocational Behavior, 33*, 185–202.

Tang, M., Fouad, N. A., & Smith, P. L. (1999). Asian Americans' career choices: A path model to examine factors influencing their career choices. *Journal of Vocational Behavior, 54*, 142–157.

Tellegen, A. (1982). *Brief manual for the multidimensional personality questionnaire*. Unpublished manuscript, University of Minnesota, Minneapolis, Minnesota.

Tellegen, A. (2000). *Manual for the Multidimensional Personality Questionnaire*. Minneapolis: University of Minnesota Press.

Tellegen, A., Lykken, D. T., Bouchard, T. J., Wilcox, K. J., Segal, N. L., & Rich, S. (1988). Personality similarity in twins reared apart and together. *Journal of Personality and Social Psychology, 54*, 1031–1039.

Tellegen, A., & Waller, N. G. (2008). Exploring personality through test construction: Development of the multidimensional personality questionnaire. In G. J. Boyle, G. Mathews, & D. H. Saklofske (Eds.), *The SAGE handbook of personality theory and assessment. Personality measurement and testing* Vol. 2 (pp. 261–292). Thousand Oaks, CA: Safe.

Thoresen, C. J., Kaplan, S. A., Barsky, A. P., Warren, C. R., & Chermont, K. (2003). The affective underpinnings of job perceptions and attitudes: A meta-analytic review and integration. *Psychological Bulletin, 129*, 914–945.

Thorndike, E. L. (1911). *Individuality*. Boston: Houghton-Mifflin.

Thorsteinson, T. J. (2003). Job attitudes of part-time vs. full-time workers: A meta-analytic review. *Journal of Occupational and Organizational Psychology, 76*, 151–177.

Tiedeman, D. V. (1979). *Career development: Designing our career machines*. New York: Character Research Press.

Tiedeman, D. V., & O'Hara, R. P. (1963). *Career development: Choice and adjustment*. New York: College Entrance Examination Board.

Tilley, B. (June, 2002). *The validation of the educational outcome expectancy scale*. Unpublished master's thesis, Iowa State University, Ames, Iowa.

Tinsley, H. E. A. (2001). Marginalization of vocational psychology. *Journal of Vocational Behavior, 59*, 243–251.

Tracey, T. J. G. (2002). Development of interests and competency beliefs: A 1-year longitudinal study of fifth- to eighth-grade students using the ICA-R and structural equation modeling. *Journal of Counseling Psychology, 49*, 148–163.

Tracey, T. J. G., & Rounds, J. (1993). Evaluating Holland's and Gati's vocational-interest models: A structural meta-analysis. *Psychological Bulletin, 113*, 229–246.

Tracey, T. J. G., & Ward, C. C. (1998). The structure of children's interests and competence perceptions. *Journal of Counseling Psychology, 45*, 290–303.

Trapmann, S., Hell, B., Hirn, J. O. W., & Schuler, H. (2007). Meta-analysis of the relationship between the Big Five and academic success at university. *Zeitschrift für Psychologie/ Journal of Psychology, 215*, 132–151.

Trice, A. D. (1991). Stability of children's career aspirations. *Journal of Genetic Psychology, 152*, 137–139.

Trice, A. D., & Rush, K. (1995). Sex-stereotyping in four-year-olds' occupational aspirations. *Perceptual and Motor Skills, 81*, 701–702.

Tsabari, O., Tziner, A., & Meir, E. I. (2005). Updated meta-analysis on the relationship between congruence and satisfaction. *Journal of Career Assessment, 13*, 216–232.

Tseng, V., Chao, R. K., Padmawidijaja, I. A. (2007). Asian Americans' educational experiences. In F. T. L. Leong, A. G. Inman, A. Ebreo, L. H. Yang, L. Kinoshita, & M. Fu (Eds.), *Handbook of Asian American psychology* (2nd ed., pp. 105–123). Thousand Oaks, CA: Sage.

Verquer, M. L., Beehr, T. A., & Wagner, S. H. (2003). A meta-analysis of relations between person-organization fit and work attitudes. *Journal of Vocational Behavior, 63*, 473–489.

Vondracek, F. W. (2001). The developmental perspective in vocational psychology. *Journal of Vocational Behavior, 59*, 252–261.

Vondracek, F. W., Silbereisen, R. K., Reitzle, M., & Wiesner, M. (1999). Vocational preferences of early adolescents: Their development in social context. *Journal of Adolescent Research, 14*, 267–288.

Wahl, R. T., & Blackhurst, A. (2000). Factors affecting the occupational and educational aspirations of children and adolescents. *Professional Counseling, 3*, 367–374.

Waller, N. G., Lykken, D. T., & Tellegen, A. (1995). Occupational interests, leisure time interests, and personality: Three domains or one? Findings from the Minnesota twin registry. In D. Lubinski, & R. V. Dawis (Eds.), *Assessing individual differences in human behavior: New concepts, methods, and findings* (pp. 233–259). Palo Alto, CA: Davies Black.

Walls, R. T. (2000). Vocational cognition: Accuracy of 3rd-, 6th-, 9th-, and 12th-grade students. *Journal of Vocational Behavior, 56*, 137–144.

Walsh, W. B. (2001). The changing nature of the science of vocational psychology. *Journal of Vocational Behavior, 59*, 262–274.

Walsh, W. B., & Eggerth, D. E. (2005). Vocational psychology and personality: The relationship of the Five-Factor Model to job performance and job satisfaction. In W. B. Walsh, & M. L. Savickas (Eds.), *Handbook of vocational psychology: Theory, research, and practice* (3rd ed., pp. 267–295). Mahwah, NJ: Lawrence Erlbaum Associates.

Walsh, W. B., & Savickas, M. L. (Eds.). (2005). *Handbook of vocational psychology: Theory, research, and practice* (3rd ed.). Mahwah, NJ: Lawrence Erlbaum Associates.

Watkins, C. E., Jr., & Savickas, M. L. (1990). Psychodynamic career counseling. In W. B. Walsh, & S. H. Osipow (Eds.), *Career counseling: Contemporary topics in vocational psychology* (pp. 79–116). Hillsdale, NJ: Lawrence Erlbaum Associates.

Watson, M., & McMahon, M. (2005). Children's career development: A research review from a learning perspective. *Journal of Vocational Behavior, 67*, 119–132.

Weaver, C. N. (2000). Work attitudes of Asian Americans. *North American Journal of Psychology, 2*, 209–218.

Weiler, J. D. (2000). *Codes and contradictions: Race, gender identity and schooling* (pp. 46). Albany, NY: State University of New York Press.

Weinger, S. (1998). Children living in poverty: Their perception of career opportunities. *Families in Society: The Journal of Contemporary Human Services, 79*, 320–330.

Weiss, D. J., Dawis, R. V., & England, G. W. (1967). Manual for the Minnesota Satisfaction Questionnaire. *Minnesota Studies in Vocational Rehabilitation, 22*, 120.

Worthington, R. L., Flores, L. Y., & Navarro, R. L. (2005). Career development in context: Research with people of color. In S. D. Brown, & R. W. Lent (Eds.), *Career development and counseling: Putting theory and research to work* (pp. 225–252). Hoboken, NJ: John Wiley & Sons.

Young, K., Bailey, D., Boysen, G., Quinn, A., Robinson, R. Ruxton, B., Seeman, J., Spencer, K., & Larson, L. M. (2004, August). *Outcome Expectancy in the Career and Academic Domain: A Review.* Poster presented at the American Psychological Association National Convention, Honolulu, Hawaii.

Zangaro, G. A., & Soeken, K. L. (2007). A meta-analysis of studies of nurses' job satisfaction. *Research in Nursing & Health, 30*, 445–458.

Training and Supervision

Nicholas Ladany *and* Arpana G. Inman

Abstract

Training and supervision theory and research is reviewed, specifically in relation to counselor education and training linked to the development of therapist competence, and supervision. Counselor competence is defined and reviewed along three areas: knowledge, self-awareness, and skills. Multiple areas of supervision are examined: history of supervision; predominant, theoretical models of supervision; supervisor techniques; the supervisory relationship; multicultural diversity; supervisor self-disclosure; supervisor countertransference; supervisee development; supervisee and supervisor nondisclosures; sexual attraction; supervision ethics; parallel process; client outcome; evaluation; supervisee competence; supervisee and supervisor professional competence problems; harmful supervision; supervisor training and competence; and specialized methods and topic areas of supervision. Throughout the chapter, we provide future research directions and practice implications for each training and supervision area reviewed. We conclude with some ideas about why training and supervision fails, fails to succeed, succeeds to fail, and succeeds.

Keywords: supervision, training, education

The single most important function of graduate education in counseling psychology is training students in the art and science of counseling/psychotherapy. It is the reason why graduate programs exist. Even so, the empirical and theoretical literature on training has lagged far behind counseling process and outcome variables, as well as other areas of counseling and psychotherapy traditionally linked with counseling psychology (e.g., career, multiculturalism, etc.). But, like these traditional areas, counseling psychologists have been the prime movers and shakers when it comes to training and supervision theory and research. As such, training and supervision is arguably a core foundational subfield of counseling psychology and is the focus of this chapter.

The purpose of this chapter is to synthesize our theoretical and empirical knowledge of training and supervision, and reciprocally offer research and practice implications based on this review. We divide the chapter into two broad sections: counselor education and training linked to the development of therapist competence; and supervision, the primary endeavor used in graduate education to impart therapeutic competence.

Counselor Education and Training

Keeping with its scientist–practitioner roots (Wampold, Lichtenberg, & Waehler, 2002), a major focus in the training of counseling psychology students has been on didactic-experiential education, in which students receive coursework and experiential training to facilitate the development of counseling competence. Counseling competence, broadly speaking, has been "understood to mean that a professional is qualified, capable, and able to understand and do certain things in an appropriate and effective manner" (Rodolfa et al., 2005; p. 348).

The ability to engage in several professional activities or domains (e.g., diagnosis and assessment, application of ethical standards, translating research to practice, and practicing cultural diversity) has been noted to encompass this general sense of competence.

Some of the earliest work related to highlighting domains of competence has been attributed to the National Council for Schools and Programs of Professional Psychology (NCSPP), Joint Council on Professional Education in Psychology (Stigall et al., 1990), and the Committee on Accreditation (Commission on Accreditation, 2007). In recent years, the emphasis on counselor competence has received greater attention due to the increasing emphasis on service accountability (Rodolfa et al., 2005); this is reflected in the American Psychological Association (APA) Ethical Principles and Code of Conduct (APA, 2002) and the Guidelines and Principles for the Accreditation of Programs in Professional Psychology initiated in 1996 with targeted changes made in 2002 (Committee on Accreditation, 2007). Within this context, many have highlighted foundational competency domains (e.g., knowledge in areas of research methodologies, cultural diversity) needed to acquire functional competences (e.g., knowledge, values, and skills needed to perform the tasks) (Rodolfa et al., 2005). Although counselors have to develop several functional domains of competence (e.g., diagnosis and assessment, intervention, research), there is a general agreement that counselor competence is defined as a counselor's ability to effectively integrate a knowledge base, one's personal and professional beliefs and attitudes, and appropriate skills that influence the effective practice of various domains (Epstein & Hundert, 2002; Meier, 1993; McIlvried & Bent, 2003, Rodolfa et al., 2005). In sum, we define counseling competence to include three subconstructs—knowledge, self-awareness, and skills—and use this definition to frame our discussion of counselor education and training.

Knowledge

According to the Guidelines and Principles for the Accreditation of Programs in Professional Psychology (Committee on Accreditation, 1996, 2002), doctoral graduate training programs are required to provide didactic training to afford students the opportunity to gain knowledge about the basic competencies necessary to provide psychological services. Based in part on Rodolfa et al.'s (2005) cube model for competency development, we believe that the knowledge dimension of competence can

be categorized as consisting of six scientifically based knowledge domains: foundations of psychology, research methods, counseling approaches, supervision and consultation, cultural diversity, and ethics. Courses specific to these domains have typically been offered to meet the knowledge requirements.

Gaining knowledge in foundations of psychology involves an understanding of how cognitive, biological, and affective bases of behaviors influence an individual's functioning. Research methods and evaluation have been addressed through a diversity of courses (e.g., statistics, research methods, univariate and multivariate statistics, and qualitative analyses) that tap into different methodologies and approaches. Counseling approaches have encompassed aspects related to assessment and interventions with coursework related to psychological, vocational, personality, and intellectual assessment. In addition, counseling interventions, geared toward helping to alleviate suffering and to promote well-being of individuals, have utilized courses that emphasize traditional counseling theories, psychopathology, lifespan development, group and family counseling approaches and modalities, and empirically supported therapies. Empirically validated therapies are specialized interventions that have been deemed as efficacious for treating specific psychological disorders (Waehler, Kalodner, Wampold, & Lichtenberg, 2000). In a related fashion, the APA (2000) has developed specific guidelines for incorporating these treatments into the training of graduate students. However, the lack of attention to diversity issues (i.e., the idea that one size does not fit all) has raised some concerns over such treatment approaches (Waehler et al., 2000).

Supervision and consultation is a fourth knowledge domain that has been deemed important. Specifically, supervision has been identified as one of the top five crucial areas of training and professional activities for psychologists (Robiner & Schofield, 1990) and is discussed further later in the chapter. In a related fashion, consultation, which is the ability to provide expert guidance in the service of client needs, as well as relate effectively within different systems, has been identified as a related competency area. Specific courses on supervision and professional development have been used to impart knowledge particular to each of these areas. In recent years, greater attention has been paid to the knowledge domain of cultural diversity, whereby counselors in training are expected to gain knowledge of different cultural communities, appreciate the uniqueness of clients and their cultures, understand the intersection of power and privilege inherent in multiple identities (Anderson & Collins, 2007; Carter & Qureshi, 1995; Pederson 1991), and understand culture-specific forms of healing (Ancis & Rasheed Ali, 2005; Pederson, 1991, 1999). A recent focus in the field has been on developing a social justice agenda that broadens the multicultural emphasis. Finally, the knowledge domain of ethics pertains to professionalism and is rooted in ethics courses and professional development courses. The basic assumption is that students who have achieved proficiency in these knowledge domains will, in part, have the foundation upon which to learn counseling skills.

- *Research to practice*: Educators have a tradition of keeping with tradition, which is the reason why these domains have changed little over time. They are encouraged to consider the means by which they test student knowledge (e.g., comprehensive exams, portfolios, etc.) and empirically determine the efficacy of these assessment methods.
- *Future research*: Multiple courses have been identified that tap into foundational competencies. It is important to examine the extent to which this knowledge indeed serves as a foundation to therapist skill acquisition.

Self-awareness

Engaging in self-assessment or self-reflective practice has been identified as a core foundational component of competent practice (Committee on Accreditation, 1996, 2002). Researchers (Bennet-Levy, 2001; Boswell & Castonguay, 2007) strongly recommend that trainees engage in systematic self-reflections as a way to gain a deeper understanding of the therapeutic role, the change process, and the specific theoretical models being used. Although self-reflection has been identified as an important factor (Eells, 1997) and is consistent with certain theoretical approaches (e.g., psychodynamic), a major emphasis on self-awareness has been limited in training programs. The one caveat is the knowledge domain of multiculturalism (Richardson & Molinaro, 1996), in which specific attention to how one's identities (e.g., race, gender) may influence one's worldview is attended to. Instructional techniques used to develop these competencies have included personal genograms (Ivey, Ivey, & Simek-Morgan, 1993), autobiographical essays (Arredondo & Arciniega, 2001), self-reflective journals (Burnett, & Meacham, 2002), cultural immersion exercises

(Arredondo et al., 1996), triad training model (Pedersen, 1994), and racial-cultural labs (Carter, 2003). Other approaches have included reading about identity development (Arredondo et al., 1996) and culture- and class-bound values of traditional psychotherapies (Ancis & Rasheed Ali, 2005), reacting to critical incidents in cross-cultural interactions (i.e., Intercultural Sensitizer; Leong & Kim, 1991), and teaching students to perceive situations from the perspectives of the "other community members" (intercultural assimilator model; Fiedler, Mitchell, & Triandis, 1971). However, the extent to which these approaches have been generalized and integrated with other knowledge areas seems marginal at best. Given the importance of self-awareness to a counselor's professional development, it would seem prudent to begin importing more of these approaches to other knowledge domains. For example, in a counseling theories course, having students apply a particular construct to their personal lives (e.g., journaling on an issue that is an unfinished business) can not only help create greater personal awareness, but also help the student translate theory to practice. Similarly, in a career assessment course, having trainees develop a career genogram in which they can symbolically represent career decisions and choices made in their own families can help generate multiple perspectives on their own career development.

- *Research to practice*: Developing self-awareness involves a critical self-assessment of one's beliefs, values, and behaviors that may influence one's work. Developing such self-criticality can help trainees integrate multiple perspectives, maintain flexibility in their thinking, tolerate ambiguity, and suspend judgment (Elder & Paul, 1994; Granello et al., 2008, Watkins, 1995).
- *Future research*: Although the role of self-awareness within the context of multicultural issues has been explored, additional work is needed to examine the impact and outcomes of developing self-awareness through other knowledge domains.

Counseling and Psychotherapy Skills

Skills cover a broad array of day-to-day activities (e.g., assessment, diagnosis, conceptualization and intervention, consultation, evaluation, advocacy) provided by counselors to their clients. These have been identified as functional competencies needed to perform the role of a psychologist (Rodolfo et al., 2005). In the past, functional competencies or skills were typically based in conceptualizations that evolved from theoretical frameworks (e.g., psychodynamic theory), suggesting that what happens in the therapy session is directly related to the therapist's theoretical orientation. However, the uniform efficacy of all psychotherapies noted originally by Rosenzweig (1936) and the endorsement of common factors across therapeutic approaches (Wampold, Mondin, Moody, Stich, Benson, & Ahn, 1997) has resulted in focusing on the pattern of contextualized variables or factors that influence therapeutic process. As such, in recent years, greater emphasis has been placed on examining the overt and covert client–therapist behaviors and, in particular, facilitating students' development of these overt–covert helping skills (e.g., reflection, open-ended questions, etc.) (Hill, 2004). In fact, the late 1960s and early 1970s saw the initial development of systematic and structured training models that focused on teaching counseling trainees these helping skills. Varying in learning philosophies (Nerdrum & Ronnestad, 2002), methods for training (e.g., rating scales, video and audio taped feedback), and empirical support, four approaches received the greatest attention: human resource training (HTR; Carkhuff, 1971), microcounseling (MC; Ivey, 1971), interpersonal process recall (IPR; Kagan, 1984), and Hill's helping skills model (Hill, 2004; see Ladany & Inman, 2008, for a review of these models). What these four models share in common is a focus on the moment-to-moment interactions that highlight the discrete helping skills needed to engage in the therapeutic process.

Based on Hill's (1982, 1986) and Stiles (1979, 1986) frameworks, Ladany, Walker, Pate-Carolan, and Gray Evans (2008) offered a framework that conceptualizes therapy skills along four levels: (1) nonverbal behaviors (e.g., eye contact, arms crossed), (2) response modes (i.e., how something is said and what is said), (3) covert processes (internal thought and feelings experienced by the dyad), and (4) therapeutic strategies and techniques (i.e., theoretically driven techniques, such as dream interpretation, empty chair technique). These four levels not only highlight aspects relevant to the four training models (e.g., Hill's helping skills model) but go beyond the models to provide a clinically driven, conceptual framework.

LEVEL 1: NONVERBAL BEHAVIORS
It has been suggested that at least 60% of what we communicate when talking directly with others is through paralanguage or nonverbals (Sue & Sue, 2003).

Nonverbal behaviors such as gestures, facial expressions, head nods, glances, changes in tone of voice, keeping an open body posture are critical ways that alter or emphasize what we say and do. These nonverbal forms of communication provide a depth to the emotions underlying one's experience and are often more important than what is being said orally. These nonverbals become all the more important in cultural contexts, when communication patterns may vary across communities. The nonverbal behaviors highlighted as an important skill in several of the training models (e.g., HTR, MC, Hill's helping skills model) and developed to teach trainees helping skills (e.g., nonverbal attending used by Carkhuff, 1971, and based on Rogers,' 1957 work) emphasize the importance of nonverbal behaviors. For example, *microcounseling skills training* (Ivey, 1971) proposes a meta-theory of counseling and uses four training components (instruction, modeling, practice, and feedback) to teach a hierarchy of interviewing skills that include nonverbal attending behaviors. The emphasis on nonverbal behaviors also comes through in Hill's three-stage (e.g., exploration, insight, and action) theoretically integrated approach. Specifically, the exploration stage, informed by client-centered therapeutic tenets, focuses on empathy, warmth, and positive regard, aspects often projected thorough nonverbal behaviors.

LEVEL 2: RESPONSE MODES
According to Ladany et al., (2008), there are two types of response modes. The first relates to the type of verbal exchange or how one communicates. For example, a therapist may use an open-ended question with a client: "What brings you here today?" The second type of response mode refers to the content of the verbal exchange or what one communicates. Thus, the open-ended question ("What brings you here today?") may be labeled as the therapist's attempts at exploring the client's reasons for treatment. Whereas therapist verbal response modes (e.g., open or closed questions, direct guidance, confrontation, pointing out incongruence, approval, paraphrase, interpretation, and therapist self-disclosure) are pantheoretical, theoretical orientation has been noted to influence therapists' choice of response mode (e.g., psychodynamic therapists use interpretation more often than do behavioral therapists). Like therapists, clients also engage in a parallel system of response modes (e.g., resistance, agreement, affective exploration, cognitive-behavioral exploration, insight, and therapeutic changes). Continuing with

the example, the client uses the invitation of the open question to open up and share her or his reasons for coming to treatment. Both forms of verbal exchanges are important in highlighting different perspectives on the same issue. These response modes not only highlight the interpersonal and dialectic nature of counseling but also help us understand the relationship between the process (what is being said) and outcome (why something happened) of a session. The focus on response modes is not only particular to Hill's helping skills model but is highlighted in the HTR model's focus on advanced empathy (e.g., interpretation, self-disclosure, immediacy) and direct guidance skills (e.g., problem solving, decision making), the use of a hierarchy of skills (reflection of feelings) in MC, and reflecting on the different processes that hamper or facilitate the therapeutic process in the IPR model.

LEVEL 3: COVERT PROCESSES

A lot that goes on in the therapeutic process often is not readily observable but significantly affects the therapeutic work. These covert processes can operate for both the therapist and the client. For instance, Hill (2001) identified helper intentions (e.g., limit setting, support, focus, instilling hope, educating, intensifying feelings) that may underlie a particular response mode (e.g., challenge, information gathering) and that are clinically meaningful and engaged in by the therapist. Similarly, client covert processes may include feeling understood, supported, unstuck, or being scared and confused, to name a few. In addition, another form of covert process that both therapists and clients engage in relates to nondisclosures or secrets that can dramatically influence the therapeutic process (Hill, 2001). These issues have also been highlighted in the various models that have been developed for counselor development. For instance, focusing on interpersonal dynamics in the counseling process, IPR uses a unique recall process whereby an "inquirer" has trainees review and reflect on those in-session thoughts, feelings, and bodily sensations that may have interfered with the therapeutic process (Kagan, 1984). Similarly in Hill's three-stage model, the insight stage, founded in psychodynamic-interpersonal theories, focuses on the covert processes that are salient to the therapeutic process.

LEVEL 4: THERAPEUTIC STRATEGIES AND TECHNIQUES

Often based in theoretical frameworks, therapeutic strategies and techniques have evolved out of a translation of theory to practice. A major assumption underlying this premise has been that therapeutic process is theory driven (e.g., psychodynamic theory emphasizes insight and catharsis). Due to this premise, therapeutic strategies and techniques tended to be largely examined within the context of theoretical integration and technical eclecticism. However, with researchers endorsing some common factors across therapeutic approaches as central to the therapy process (Luborsky, Singer & Luborsky, 1975; Smith, Glass, & Miller, 1980; Wampold et al., 1997), therapeutic strategies and techniques are also currently seen to be embedded in common therapist–client factors. For instance, Hill's three-stage model of helping skills integrated three of the most common theoretical orientations (humanistic, psychodynamic, and cognitive-behavioral) each of which not only draws on typical therapist–client covert and overt response modes but also conceptually contextualizes the counseling process. Specifically, based on client-centered theory, exploration involves counselors exploring client's thoughts and feelings about a particular problem. In the psychodynamic and interpersonally based insight stage, counselors help clients construct new and deeper meanings for their problems. Finally, in the action stage, based in cognitive and behavioral theories, counselors work with clients to change their feelings, thoughts, and behaviors related to the problem. Throughout this process, the focus is on therapists building and maintaining a good working relationship/alliance with their clients.

Learning helping skills has been considered important and necessary in most training programs. Yet, it is interesting to note that much of this training tends to occur in one or at the most two classes that emphasize helping skills, the adequacy of which may leave many students short of proficient levels of skill acquisition. Moreover, these skills are not generally integrated throughout the different knowledge domains. For instance, a course on counseling theories or family counseling may include a lab component. A course in group counseling may include a simulated group or observation of group processes using an existing group, or a program may have a specific course on helping skills that focuses on discrete skills. Frequently, by engaging in role plays with other peer counselors, the simulated experiences are the precursor to student practica and internships, but these fall short of providing a realistic experience for these trainees. Furthermore, these courses and training may be too close to the practicum experience to allow for a thorough evaluation of the student's readiness for a practicum.

- *Research to practice*: Educators may want to begin with helping skills and determine whether students are proficient enough to move to a beginning practicum. As it stands, the vast majority of students make it past pre-practicum courses, which points to problems with evaluation criteria, rather than the field uniquely attracting a disproportionate number of proficient students. In addition, counselor educators may want to reconsider the disproportionate balance of knowledge, self-awareness, and skills, specifically increasing the attention to self-awareness and skills.

- *Future research*: What is enough in terms of helping skills acquisition? Researchers would do well to develop serious and rigorous methods for assessing skill acquisition at an early stage of professional development, prior to working with actual clients.

Supervision

Supervision is arguably the most important activity related to the development of therapeutic competence, particularly if importance is determined based on the amount of energy and resources devoted to an aspect of learning. After all, most content area courses in a doctoral counseling psychology curriculum consist of one or two semesters of coursework, whereas supervised experiences typically last 2–3 years, followed by a year-long internship. Yet, compared to these other areas, which we spend considerably less attention to in graduate school, supervision theory and research is limited. The reasons for this are unclear, although they include, in part, the difficulty of conducting quality and rigorous research (Ellis & Ladany, 1997), limited theoretical formulations, the tradition of non-inclusion in curricula, and limited accreditation attention and requirements (e.g., the APA does not require didactic-practica in supervision).

Historically, the earliest roots of supervision can be traced to the field of social work in the late 1800s as part of the Charity Organization Societies (Kadushin & Harkness, 2002; Munson, 2002). In these societies, agents/social workers were trained in the context of apprenticeships, in which supervisors provided periodic individual meetings to multiple supervisees. In 1902, Freud provided an initial context for the provision of analyzing the analyst (Goodyear & Guzzardo, 2000), and by 1925, supervision was required for the first time as a training requirement (Kugler, 1995). Initial attempts at developing supervision theory were largely based on models of psychotherapy (Ekstein & Wallerstein, 1958). In the 1980s, supervision shifted from psychotherapy-based models of supervision to models created for supervision proper (Bernard, 2005). During this same period, empirical work in supervision began to flourish, or at least began to be seen in the literature, typically with less than a dozen empirical studies published per year. The three fields most connected with supervision research were, and continue to be, counseling psychology, counselor education, and social work (Ellis, Ladany, Krengel, & Schult, 1996).

Over the past three decades, the result of supervision theory and research can perhaps best be described as what happens when a bag of flour is thrown into a swimming pool from a high diving board. There are some areas of concentration, but there are also many areas of single drops, and large swaths where no flour has landed. To be sure, a few attempts have been made to address supervision in a comprehensive fashion via theoretical formulations and programmatic research, but it is clear that there is much work to be done.

The rest of this section is devoted to two primary areas: theoretical formulations of supervision and supervisor techniques, and variables in supervision that are believed to be most salient to supervision process and to outcome based on the attention they have received in the empirical, theoretical, and practice literature. Following these reviews, we offer theory and/or research to practice recommendations and suggestions for future research. The bulk of the review is based on individual supervision of individual therapy. This focused review is not to imply that other forms of supervision are less important or relevant to counseling psychologists. The reality is that this additional literature base is at its earliest stages (i.e., some practice writings and very few, if any, empirical studies) and has a great deal of catching up to do before it can be reviewed in a substantive manner. For this review, we broadly define individual supervision as a dyadic activity whereby the supervisor facilitates the provision of feedback to the supervisee, which is based on the interpersonal communication between both members of the dyad and can pertain to the work in supervision, the supervisee, the supervisee's clients, or the supervisor.

Theoretical Models of Supervision

There are arguably three leading models of supervision (Westefeld, 2009), all of which were developed by counseling psychologists: the *integrated developmental model* (IDM; Stoltenberg, McNeill, & Delworth, 1998), the *systems approach to supervision* (SAS; Holloway, 1995), and the *critical events model of supervision* (CES; Ladany, Friedlander, & Nelson, 2005). Expanding upon Westefeld's (2009) and Ladany and Inman's (2008) rationale for identifying these supervision models, they share common features that make them stand out among other models: they are comprehensive, are empirically based, are derived and developed for supervision, can be used pantheoretically with diverse theoretical approaches to counseling and psychotherapy, offer testable hypotheses, are descriptive and prescriptive, and are practitioner-friendly and applicable.

Before attending further to these three aforementioned models, it is important to further consider what makes these models unique and important for discussion. As indicated previously, up until the 1980s, most models of supervision were geared toward and linked to specific theoretical approaches to counseling and psychotherapy. This habit continues to the present (e.g., Hyman, 2008), however, we believe there are four fundamental problems with psychotherapy-based and theoretically linked models of supervision. First, the models often do not fully recognize aspects of supervision that are uniquely different from that of psychotherapy (e.g., supervision, unlike psychotherapy is generally involuntary, evaluative, and didactic). Second, psychotherapy-based models of supervision vary widely in their adherence or link to constructs associated with the psychotherapy model to which they are tied (e.g., how does one "teach" psychoanalysis via psychoanalysis?). Third, these psychotherapy-based models often ignore or lose sight of the integrative nature of the counseling and supervision enterprise (Wampold, 2001). In the worst cases. it is like fitting a square peg into a round hole, and everything gets jammed into a triangle (aka, The Client). Fourth, psychotherapy-based models have little empirical foundation and have rarely been studied. In all, although we agree that psychotherapy models offer constructs that can be useful in supervision (as do pedagogies of teaching), basing a model of supervision on a particular psychotherapy offers too many shortcomings to warrant a high quality rating and endorsement.

We should also recognize that a number of models developed for supervision—perhaps best described as "mini-models"—attend to supervisory phenomena in a much more circumscribed manner than the aforementioned comprehensive models. These mini-models have attended to supervision variables,

techniques, or processes such as interpersonal process recall (Kagan, 1984), supervisor competencies (Falender & Shafranske, 2004; Ancis & Ladany, 2010 in press), reflective learning (Ward & House, 1998), Socratic supervision (Overholser, 2004), supervisor self-disclosure (Ladany & Walker, 2003), and cognitive development (Blocher, 1983).

Many of these circumscribed models have influenced and were integrated within the comprehensive models. For example, Hogan's (1964), as well as Littrel, Lee-Bordin, and Lorenz's (1979) developmental models were precursors of Stoltenberg et al.'s (1998) IDM, Bernard's (1979) discrimination model is linked to Holloway's (1995) SAS, and Bordin's (1983) model of the supervisory working alliance served as the foundation for Ladany et al.'s (2005) CES. In subsequent sections, we provide for each model an overview of the theoretical propositions, identify and define the primary constructs, review strengths and weaknesses, summarize past research and offer future research suggestions, and provide practice recommendations.

INTEGRATED DEVELOPMENTAL MODEL

The foundational assumption of the IDM (Stoltenberg, McNeill, & Delworth, 1998) is that supervisees typically grow in a developmental fashion that can be tracked and observed by supervisors. The model offers a complex interplay between supervisee structures of professional growth and domains of clinical practice, from which supervisee developmental level is assessed and determined. The overriding structures that change developmentally include: self and other awareness (e.g., high anxiety to low anxiety), motivation (e.g., high, fluctuating, and then stable), and autonomy (e.g., dependence to independence). The primary domains of clinical activity include intervention skills competence (e.g., confidence in modality of therapy), assessment techniques (e.g., using vocational or personality instruments), interpersonal assessment (e.g., assessing the client's interpersonal dynamics), client conceptualization (e.g., diagnosis), individual differences (e.g., cultural differences), theoretical orientation (e.g., psychotherapy approach), treatment plans and goals (e.g., organization of treatment), and professional ethics (e.g., integration of personal and professional ethics). Depending on the assessed supervisee developmental level and the training environment, educators or supervisors choose to provide a variety of interventions and mechanisms. Interventions can be facilitative, prescriptive, conceptual, or catalytic. Mechanisms include supervisory processes such as observations, skills training, role-playing, and group supervision.

A primary task for the supervisor is to assess supervisees on their structures within particular domains. Supervisees can function at high or low levels, depending on the domain of clinical activity. Supervisees can then be classified as Level 1, Level 2, Level 3, or Level 3i. For example, Level 1 supervisees tend to be highly motivated, highly anxious, require a focus on skill acquisition, are dependent on the supervisor, need structure, should be minimally confronted, have limited self-awareness, and have difficulty seeing strengths and weaknesses. As supervisees progress through the levels, and as they develop skills across multiple domains, they eventually reach Level 3i, where integration occurs. At this point, they are considered master therapists, something the authors do not believe occurs often. In the IDM model, the supervisory relationship is seen as an important component. For example, IDM postulates how the supervisor should approach the relationship with the supervisee (e.g., supervisors need to be prepared with supervisee's in Level 2, who will likely create more conflictual relationships than those in other levels). Although identified as important by the IDM model, how the relationship is defined is unclear.

A clear strength of the IDM is that it added much complexity and detail to earlier developmental models, which were short of content. In addition, the IDM has evolved over time, and its assumptions have been modified. Moreover, the developmental framework seems to appeal to supervisor practitioners. Nonetheless, the IDM has been critiqued on a couple of grounds (Chang & O'Hara, 2010 in press). First, empirical support for specific aspects of the model are limited (e.g., Ramos-Sanchez et al., 2002). Second, the integration of multicultural issues is limited, specifically, the manner in which multicultural issues influence the interaction between the supervisor and supervisee. Finally, it is unclear if supervisors are able to use the IDM as more than a general heuristic devise (e.g., supervisees change over time), rather than as a prescriptive or theoretical template for working with supervisees (e.g., change their approach based on a moment-to-moment, multilayer assessment of the supervisee). Moreover, within the model, supervisors are assumed to be generally competent and equipped to supervise, an assertion that may be suspect (Ladany, 2002).

• *Theory to practice*: The IDM offers practitioners a theoretical lens through which to assess supervisees developmental needs and match these needs with techniques to help supervisees develop into more competent clinicians.

• *Future research*: The development of reliable and valid instrumentation will be necessary to test many of the model's assumptions. Specifically, instruments need to be developed that attend to the multilevel nature of supervisees, which accounts for supervisee structures and domains of clinical activity.

SYSTEMS APPROACH TO SUPERVISION

The SAS (Holloway, 1995) has been categorized as a type of "social role model" of supervision (Bernard & Goodyear, 2009). Social role models generally highlight the roles that supervisors play in the context of supervision. Bernard's (1979, 1997) discrimination model is one of the earliest developed social role models, and it can be credited with highlighting and popularizing the commonly referred to supervisor roles of teacher, counselor, and consultant. Holloway's SAS expanded upon Bernard's model and conceptualized supervision as a seven-factor enterprise. The supervisory relationship is considered the core factor; it consists of supervisory power, as well as interpersonal intimacy and attachment between the supervisor and supervisee. Moreover, the supervisory relationship is seen as passing through phases (e.g., beginning, mature) and involves a negotiated goals contract between the supervisor and supervisee.

Two factors are used to determine supervision process: supervisor functions (i.e., monitoring/evaluating, advising/instructing, modeling, consulting, and supporting/sharing), and supervision tasks (i.e., counseling skill, case conceptualization, professional role, emotional awareness, and self-evaluation). Together, these functions and tasks offer the supervisor a way to identify what is happening in supervision at any point in time. Specifically, the supervisor should be able to assess her or his function in relation to the task at hand, thereby identifying the type of supervisory process that is occurring.

Additional factors, all of which are contextual in nature, include the client (i.e., client characteristics, identified problems and diagnosis, counseling relationship), the trainee (i.e., experience in counseling, theoretical orientation to counseling, learning needs and style, cultural characteristics, and self-presentation), the supervisor (professional experience, role in supervision, theoretical orientation to counseling, cultural characteristics, and self-presentation), and the institution (agency clientele, organizational structure and climate, professional ethics and standards).

The SAS is a very far-reaching model that relies on a comprehensive understanding of multiple factors and the interplay among factors. Unique to the model is its recognition of institutional factors that influence the supervisory work and could, at times, trump all other factors in relation to the training a supervisee receives. The SAS does well to include the relationship as a core factor; however, how it is created and maintained is not clearly discussed. An important critique of the model's adequacy is that it has spawned virtually no empirical work since inception. Like any strong theory, its utility and credibility will be based on the extent to which it can be empirically tested, verified, and modified.

• *Theory to practice*: The SAS provides supervisor practitioners with the additional lens of institutional factors to take into consideration when understanding supervisory work.

• *Future research*: An important contribution of the SAS is its predictions about functions and tasks in supervision. Similar to other interpersonal coding schemes (e.g., structural analysis of social behavior, Benjamin, 1996), researchers could develop a coding system for functions and tasks in supervision, then test the extent to which these functions and tasks adequately describe supervisory process and indeed predict supervision outcomes.

CRITICAL EVENTS IN SUPERVISION

The fundamental assumption of the CES (Ladany et al., 2005) is that supervision can be broken down into meaningful critical events of learning that can take place within a session or across multiple sessions. Over time, authors of the CES approach have identified what are believed to be the most common critical events in supervision. These include remediating skill difficulties and deficits, heightening multicultural awareness, negotiating role conflicts, working through countertransference, managing sexual attraction, repairing gender-related misunderstandings, addressing problematic supervisee emotions and behaviors, facilitating supervisee insight, and facilitating a supervisee correction relational experience.

The CES is intended to be pantheoretical in nature and proposes that all critical events have in common four components: the supervisory working alliance, a marker, the task environment, and a resolution. The *supervisory working alliance* is deemed the foundation of the model and is based on Bordin's (1983) model of the supervisory working alliance. The supervisory working alliance consists of three components: mutual agreement between the supervisee and supervisor about the goals of supervision (e.g., increase skill set), mutual agreement between the supervisee and supervisor about the tasks of supervision (e.g., review audio recordings), and an emotional bond between the supervisee and supervisor consisting of mutual trust, respect, liking, and caring. The supervisory working alliance is developed via listening, reflections, and empathy, as well as through negotiations between the supervisee and supervisor about the tasks and goals of supervision that best meet the supervisee's needs.

The second component of the CES, the *marker*, consists of a supervisee statement or behavior (e.g., supervisee asks for guidance on a technique, supervisee chronically arrives late for supervision, supervisee expresses frustration at supervisor or client) that signals to the supervisor that a critical event may be initiating. Once the marker is identified, the supervisory dyad enter what is called the *task environment*, whereby the supervisor can engage in a selection of interaction sequences, which in essence are techniques intended to assist the supervisee. Interaction sequences include focus on the supervisory alliance, focus on the therapeutic process, exploration of feelings, focus on countertransference, attention to parallel processes, focus on self-efficacy, normalization of experience, focus on skill, assessment of knowledge, focus on multicultural awareness, and focus on evaluation. The selection of the number and frequency of interaction sequences depends on the critical event.

At the conclusion of the task environment (i.e., the series of interaction sequences), the critical event (e.g., managing sexual attraction) ends with a resolution or mini-outcome (e.g., increased awareness of sexual attraction). These outcomes consist of a change (from enhancing to declining) in self-awareness, knowledge, skills, or the supervisory working alliance.

A strength of the CES is that the theory offers practitioners a meaningful set of supervision-based outcomes that can be empirically tested in a relatively straightforward manner. In addition, it attends to managing and working with specific multicultural issues, such as gender, race, and sexual orientation. Of all the aspects of the model, the supervisory working alliance has been investigated the most extensively (over a dozen empirical articles), and its utility and importance in supervision seems quite evident. That said, the model's newness means that the empirical work that has tested its efficacy is limited, particularly the interaction sequences hypothesized for particular events. Furthermore, the model does not address events deemed "noncritical," such as when the supervisor asks the supervisee to spend extensive time on case overview. In addition, critical events currently absent from the model may need to be considered in future work.

- *Theory to practice*: The CES model offers a prescriptive approach to handling a variety of issues in supervision, such as how to handle supervisees with professional competence problems. In addition, it offers supervisors an enhanced awareness of the types and range of supervisor techniques available in the supervision context.

- *Future research*: The CES approach was designed intentionally to allow and promote empirical testing. The basic empirical approach would be to identify a critical event (e.g., upon supervisee or supervisor reflection, via video recording) and assess the supervisory alliance, the marker, interaction sequences, and resolution (e.g., from perspectives of the supervisor, supervisor, and/or observer rating) to determine the extent to which the components hypothesized occur as predicted.

Supervisor Techniques

Similar to therapist skills, supervisor skills can be viewed as falling along four levels: nonverbal behaviors (e.g., head nods, nonverbal tracking, etc.), response modes (e.g., reflection of feelings, demonstrate understanding, etc.), covert processes (e.g., intentions and reactions), and theoretical strategies and techniques (e.g., IDM, SAS, CES) (Ladany et al., 2008). We have already discussed three theoretical models that offer broad and overarching strategies, as well as specific theoretically consistent techniques associated with each of the models. In addition, other stand-alone techniques have been developed specifically for supervision that are either couched in a mini-model or could be deemed pantheoretical in nature. Bernard and Goodyear (2009) and Walker (2010) present a series of supervision techniques that expand upon the aforementioned theoretically based techniques; these include interpersonal process recall (Kagan & Kagan, 1997),

the supervision genogram (Aten, Madson, & Kruse, 2008), processing multicultural issues (e.g., Gatmon et al., 2001), managing countertransference (Ladany et al., 2008), supervisor self-disclosure (Ladany & Walker, 2003), structured peer group supervision (Borders, 1991), contracting (Munson, 2002), reading assignments (Munson, 2002), journaling (Griffith & Frieden, 2000; Guiffrida, 2005; Knowles et al., 2007), self-reflection (Neufeldt, 1999), and live observation (Bernard & Goodyear, 2009).

Among the supervision techniques developed, *interpersonal process recall* (IPR; Kagan & Kagan, 1997) is arguably the only technique that clearly provided an educational method and that was empirically tested in a programmatic manner (e.g., Kagan, 1980; Kagan & Krathwohl, 1967; Kingdon, 1975). The basic elements of IPR include: the supervisee and supervisor review audio recording of counseling sessions, impromptu stopping of the recording can be made by either member of the dyad, and the supervisor facilitates supervisee self-reflection and analysis of the counseling work. Once the reflection phase is complete, the recording is listened to again, and the process repeats itself. Although IPR has been well-defined and used in many counseling training programs, current research on its efficacy has been minimal.

- *Research to practice*: A number of techniques have been published for supervisor use. Supervisor practitioners are encouraged to become aware of these techniques to broaden their repertoire of skills.

- *Future research*: Supervisor techniques have been prescribed, but there is limited research testing their efficacy. To that end, it will be important to determine the efficacy of supervisor techniques and specifically address the proximal and distal supervision outcomes that are anticipated.

Supervision Variables

As supervision theory began to develop in the early 1980s, so did empirical work. Since that time, the publication output of supervision research typically consists of less than a dozen articles published per year. This relatively low publication rate (as compared to counseling and psychotherapy research) has been attributed to limited samples available, the difficulty in obtaining perspectives from a multiperson unit (i.e., supervisee, supervisor, clients), and the limited number of supervision researchers interested in programmatic work (Ladany & Inman, 2008).

That said, we identified clusters of literature on particular variables, on which at least a modicum of loosely tied-together programmatic work has been conducted. Our review expanded recent reviews (Inman & Ladany, 2008; Ladany & Inman, 2008) and consists of studies from multiple psychotherapy disciplines, including counseling psychology and counselor education (the two disciplines with the largest concentration of research literature in supervision), as well as social work and clinical psychology. Although our review extends back to the 1970s, our focus tends to be on research publications over the past two decades, as that seems to be when the most rigorous research was conducted.

The Supervisory Relationship

According to the literature, the term "relationship" in the supervisory context can mean many things (Chen & Bernstein, 2000; Efstation, Patton, & Kardash, 1990; Ellis & Ladany, 1997; Heppner & Handley, 1981; Holloway & Wampold, 1983; Schact, Howe, & Berman, 1989). Often it is left to the reader's conception and is largely undefined. At other times, it has been defined in an all-inclusive fashion, essentially referring to all that occurs in supervision. Given the relationship's central role in supervision, it is surprising how little attention has been given to actually defining it, and how it has been studied in such a haphazard and obfuscatory fashion. Presumably, a good definition of the supervisory relationship would define what it is, indicate how it is strengthened and weakened, and provide a link between the relationship and outcomes in a relatively orthogonal fashion. Arguably, the definition that does this best is Bordin's (1983) model of the supervisory working alliance. In addition, his model has been the definition most extensively tested in the literature (in over a dozen studies), and his model is well-suited for clinical applicability (Wood, 2005).

As noted previously, Bordin (1983) conceptualized the supervisory working alliance as consisting of three components: agreement on the goals of supervision (e.g., mastery of skills, increasing conceptualization ability, increasing awareness of one's self in the counseling process, maintaining ethics, etc.), agreement on the tasks of supervision (e.g., feedback on reports, provide alternative conceptualizations, have supervisee select the topics of discussion for supervision, etc.), and an emotional bond (e.g., mutual caring, respecting, trusting). Bordin's model was a reconceptualized and extended version of his model of the therapeutic working

alliance (Bordin, 1979). Similar to his therapeutic alliance, Bordin (1983) believed that it was not the specific goals or tasks that were agreed upon that were important; rather, it was the agreement itself that was most critical. Hence, the scale developed to measure the supervisory working alliance (Bahrick, 1989), which was based on the scale for the therapeutic working alliance (Horvath & Greenberg, 1986), assessed the extent to which goals and tasks were agreed upon (e.g., "My supervisor and I agree upon the goals of supervision"), rather than examining specific goals and tasks.

Bordin regarded the "mutual" nature of the components to be most critical. He thought the goals of the supervisee and supervisor needed to be congruent; otherwise, the work in supervision could not be done. Bordin also indicated some additional processes that were important to establish a strong alliance, which included empathizing with the supervisee, diffusing the hierarchical status between the supervisee and supervisor, and balancing critical feedback with recognizing supervisee strengths.

The supervisory working alliance has been empirically examined across a variety of studies. Results from these investigations have found that a stronger supervisory working alliance was related to more advanced racial identity interactions (Ladany, Brittan-Powell, & Pannu, 1997), increased supervisor self-disclosure (Ladany & Lehrman-Waterman, 1999), supervisee satisfaction (Inman, 2006; Ladany, Ellis, Friedlander, & Stern, 1999), clearer goal-setting and feedback (Lehrman-Waterman & Ladany, 2001), greater supervisor attractiveness and interpersonal sensitivity (Ladany, Walker, & Melincoff, 2001), and supportive gender-related events (Walker, Ladany, & Pate-Carolan, 2007). Moreover, a weaker supervisory working alliance has been found to predict greater supervisee role conflict and ambiguity (Ladany & Friedlander, 1995); less supervisor multicultural competence (Inman, 2006); insecure supervisor attachment styles (Riggs & Bretz, 2006); negative supervisory experiences (Ramso-Sanchez et al., 2002); greater anxiety, nondisclosure, and less willingness to disclose (Mehr, Ladany, & Caskie, in preparation); and less supervisor adherence to ethical behaviors (Ladany, Lehrman-Waterman, Molinaro, & Wolgast, 1999). Furthermore, the supervisory working alliance can change over time, for better and for worse (Ladany et al., 2008). Recently, there has been a debate about the psychometric strengths of the Supervisory Work Alliance (SWAI) scale, such as whether the scale should be used as a single-score measure, a three-subscale measure, or a shortened measure (Ellis, Russin, & Deihl, 2003; Inman, 2006).

• *Research to practice*: The supervisory alliance has been considered the foundation upon which effective supervision is based (Ladany, 2005). To that end, supervisors are encouraged to consider the alliance as a figure–ground-type construct, such that it is highlighted early in the relationship, and when conflicts arise in the relationship, and/or when it is strong enough to engage in other supervisory work, it recedes into the background.

• *Future research*: Although Bordin's (1983) model seems to be a solid construct to define the supervisory relationship, reformulation and modification of the model based on theoretical and empirical grounds should occur (Ladany & Inman, 2008). Moreover, additional models of the supervisory relationship may shed light on aspects not attended to by Bordin, and in fact, may offer a stronger construct for future study (Ellis, Russin, & Deihl, 2003).

Multicultural Diversity

The literature related to multicultural supervision has given us an understanding of two overarching areas of multicultural work: handling general multicultural issues and handling specific multicultural issues. In relation to managing general multicultural issues, a number of researchers have found that supervisees learn from and appreciate the discussion of diversity in supervision (Dressel, Consoli, Kim, & Atkinson, 2007; Duan, & Roehlke, 2001 Fukuyama, 1994; Hird, Cavaleri, Dulko, Felice, & Ho, 2001; Killian, 2001 Kleintjes and Swartz, 1996; Lawless, Gale, & Bacigalupe, 2001).

Authors have also identified and studied specific multicultural issues in supervision, most of which has dealt with gender, race, sexual orientation, and nationality. In the realm of race, the results of racial matching in relation to supervision process and outcome have been equivocal (Cook & Helms, 1988; Hilton, Russell, & Salmi 1995; McRoy, Freeman, Logan, & Blackman, 1986; Vander Kolk, 1974), however, racial identity seems to be a more promising variable in predicting process and outcome (Ladany, Brittan-Powell, & Pannu, 1997). In addition, evidence suggests that supervisees value the discussion of racial issues in supervision (Kleintjes & Swartz, 1996) and focusing supervisees on race in a case conceptualization leads them to include racial

issues in the conceptualization (Ladany et al., 1997).

Burkard et al. (2006), via a qualitative design, cleverly teased out the differences between culturally responsive supervision and culturally unresponsive supervision. Supervisors who were culturally responsive tended to create a safe space for discussing cultural issues and to share their own professional struggles with supervisees. Alternatively, supervisors who were culturally unresponsive tended to demonstrate a lack of cultural self-awareness, use stereotypical explanations, minimize cultural issues, and engage in gender, racial, and sexual orientation bias. In addition, supervisees of color experienced culturally unresponsive supervision more frequently than did white supervisees. In an interesting blend of qualitative and analog methodology, Utsey, Gernat, and Hammar (2005) sampled white supervisees and found they were uncomfortable discussing racial issues. In addition, Constantine and Sue (2007) in their qualitative study, found that black supervisees experienced multiple types of microaggressions (e.g., invalidating racial concerns) from their white supervisors.

In terms of gender and supervision, early studies of gender matching in relation to supervision process and outcome demonstrated equivocal results (Behling, Curtis, & Foster, 1988; Gloria, Hird, & Tao, 2008; Goodyear, 1990; Jordan, 2007; Sells, Goodyear, Lichtenberg, & Polkinghorne, 1997; Petty & Odewahn, 1983; Putney, Worthington, & McCullough, 1992; Schiavone & Jessell, 1988; Stenack & Dye, 1983; Worthington & Stern, 1985). However, more refined investigations found the extent to which a supervisor was task-or relationship-oriented, as well as displayed power messages, varied depending on the gender of the supervisor and supervisee (Nelson & Holloway, 1990; Robyak, Goodyear, & Prange, 1987; Sells, Goodyear, Lichtenberg, & Polkinghorne, 1997). In addition, Szymanski (2005) found that feminist identity was related to feminist supervision practices, and Fong and Borders (1985) offered evidence that sex role orientation was a better predictor of counseling skills than was gender in counseling skills training. Finally, Walker, Ladany, and Pate-Carolan (2007) found that supervisors facilitated roughly equal numbers of supportive and unsupportive gender-related events. In all, these studies point to the fact that gender issues continue to be relevant in supervision.

There continues to be a notable gap in the empirical literature addressing sexual orientation and supervision. Only two studies have been conducted that consider sexual orientation in supervision. Newman, Bogo, and Daly (2008) found that supervisees who are lesbian, gay, bisexual, or transgender (LGBT) found self-disclosing their sexual orientation to their supervisors a useful enterprise when they felt safe enough to do so. Sherry, Whilde, and Patton (2005) surveyed directors of training and found most thought that sexual orientation issues were discussed at some point during practicum and supervision experiences. However, it was unclear what the extent and quality of these discussions were. Without a doubt, further scholarship is warranted in this understudied area of knowledge.

One emerging feature of the multicultural work has been the recognition that psychological variables, such as racial identity or gender identity, are more predictive of cultural competence than are simple nominal variables such as race or sex. In addition, identity has been associated with the self-awareness component of competence for both supervisees and supervisors. Ladany and Ancis (2010, in press) offered a revised theoretical model (the *heuristic model of nonoppressive interpersonal development*; HMNID) for conceptualizing multicultural identities in both counseling and supervision. Based on a variety of identity models (e.g., Cass, 1979; Helms, 1990; Sodowsky, Kwan, & Pannu, 1995), the HMNID sets out to give supervisees and supervisors a way of conceptualizing multiple identities (i.e., gender, race, sexual orientation, ethnicity, disability, and socioeconomic status) in the client–counselor–supervisor triad. For each demographic variable, people pass through phases of identity development (i.e., adaptation, incongruence, exploration, and integration) that vary depending on whether the identity in question is related to a socially oppressed group (e.g., Asian American) or a socially privileged group (e.g., white). Each supervisee–supervisor or client–counselor dyad can be defined based on the interpersonal relationship type that is present: progressive, in which the supervisor is at a more advanced identity phase than the supervisee; parallel-advanced, in which the supervisor and supervisee are at comparable and advanced identity phases; parallel-delayed, in which the supervisor and supervisee are at comparable and delayed identity phases; and regressive, in which the supervisee is at a more advanced identity phase than the supervisor. Preliminary research (e.g., Constantine, Warren, & Miville, 2005; Ladany, Brittan-Powell, & Pannu, 1997) has shown that identity interactions can predict perceived

multicultural competence development, but additional work is needed.

Most recently, the area of nationality and international issues has been brought to the fore in relation to diversity and supervision (Nilsson & Anderson, 2004). There are two ways to consider international issues: (1) non-U.S. nationality of at least one of the members of the client–counselor–supervisor triad (Mori, Inman, & Caskie, 2009; Nilsson & Anderson, 2004; Nilsson & Wang, 2009) and (2) supervision in international contexts (e.g., Orlinsky & Ronnestad, 2005). In terms of nationality issues, supervisors are encouraged to consider the effects of language, acculturation, and role ambiguity on counseling self-efficacy (Mori et al., 2009; Nilsson & Anderson, 2004; Nilsson & Wang, 2009). In relation to supervision in international contexts, an examination of practices can be quite enlightening and sometimes shed light on issues in which U.S.-based training is lacking. For example, supervision in Great Britain is considered a lifelong professional development activity, whereas in the United States, supervision is primary advocated for in the context of graduate training and, at most, a couple of years beyond. Broadening the U.S.-based view of supervision is strongly suggested.

- *Research to practice*: Supervisors are encouraged to look beyond simple nominal variables such as gender and race, and consider the role of identity in their supervisees and in themselves.
- *Future research*: The research has indicated that supervisors are too often providing biased and multiculturally incompetent supervision (e.g., sexism, racism, etc.). Additional work is sorely needed to examine the impact that these biased supervisory approaches have on the development of supervisees.

Supervisor Self-disclosure

Supervisor self-disclosure has received attention in recent years because of its purported influence on the supervisory relationship, evaluation on the supervisee, and supervision outcome (Farber, 2006; Yourman, 2003). The literature has supported these contentions and shown that supervisors self-disclose more when they perceived the need to normalize the supervisee's experience or when they witness the supervisee struggling. Furthermore, supervisor self-disclosure also tends to occur within a positive supervisory relationship and leads to positive effects on supervisees (Knox, Burkard, Edwards,

Smith, & Schlosser, 2008). Moreover, the types of supervisor self-disclosures have ranged from helpful to unhelpful and included personal issues, struggles, successes, and reactions to the supervisee's clients (Ladany & Lehrman-Waterman, 1999). Based on the empirical work, Ladany and Walker (2003) hypothesized the conditions under which supervisor self-disclosure would be most to least powerful. Specifically, they posited that the content of supervisor self-disclosures could be considered along three personalization dimensions: (1) discordant to congruent, (2) nonintimate to intimate, and (3) in the service of the supervisor or in the service of the supervisee, the latter of each dimension representing more powerful self-disclosures that would lead to strengthening the supervisory alliance, increased supervisee self-disclosure, and greater supervisee edification.

• *Research to practice*: More does not always indicate better when it comes to supervisor self-disclosure. We suggest that supervisors examine the intentionality of their self-disclosures and assess the kinds of impacts these self-disclosures have on their supervisees.

• *Future research*: Researchers are encouraged to identify and assess the proximal outcomes of supervisor self-disclosures.

Supervisor Countertransference

Supervisor countertransference, also dubbed "supertransference" (Teitelbaum, 1990), has been recognized in the theoretical literature for some time (Ackerman, 1953; Altschuler & Katz, 2002; Anastasopoulous & Tsiantis, 1999; Issacharoff, 1984; Lower, 1972; Strean, 2000). However, it has been studied only in a limited fashion. Via a qualitative investigation, Ladany, Constantine, Miller, Erickson, and Muse-Burke (2000) defined supervisor countertransference as "an exaggerated, unrealistic, irrational, or distorted reaction related to a supervisor's work with a trainee. This reaction may include feelings, thoughts, and behaviors that are likely to be in response to both the trainee's interpersonal style and the supervisor's unresolved personal issues and may also be in response to trainee–supervision environmental interactions, problematic client–trainee interactions, trainee–supervisor interactions, or supervisor–supervision environment interactions" (p. 111; Ladany et al., 2000). In a separate investigation, Ladany et al. (2008) identified negative supervisor countertransference thoughts, feelings, and behaviors (e.g., distraction

by external events, less engagement, more or less authoritativeness) and positive supervisor countertransference thoughts, feelings, and behaviors (e.g., identification with the supervisee, engaged in rapport building, provided support). These limited investigations offer a pantheoretical look at the ways in which supervisor countertransference may be operating and influencing supervision process and outcome.

• *Research to practice*: Supervisors would do well to consider the role that their personal biases may influence the supervision and counseling work.

• *Future research*: Given the limited study that supervisor countertransference has received, replication and extension along the qualitative and quantitative lines is in order. Furthermore, the development of measures of the construct would benefit future investigations.

Supervisee Development

The research on supervisee development was primarily conducted in the 1980s and early 1990s (e.g., Borders, 1990; Ellis, 1991; Friedlander & Snyder, 1983; McNeill, Stoltenberg, & Pierce, 1985; Wiley & Ray, 1986; Winter & Holloway, 1991), and over the last decade has been largely left unattended (Ladany & Inman, 2008). Supervisee development has been predominately defined based on some type of supervisee experience variable (e.g., type of practicum setting, years of experience). These investigations have been critiqued on a variety of grounds (e.g., relied on self-report and cross-sectional data) and have offered equivocal results (Ellis & Ladany, 1997). The results have varied; perhaps the two conclusions that can be drawn is that sometimes supervisees see themselves change with experience and sometimes supervisors have different perceptions when they supervise supervisees with different amounts of experience (e.g., the beginning practicum supervisee needs lots of guidance). That said, these general conclusions should be considered in light of reviews that have demonstrated that experience is a better predictor of *confidence* than *competence* (Garb, 1989).

• *Research to practice*: Although it may be heuristically appealing for supervisors to view supervisees through a developmental lens, they are encouraged not to engage in simplistic developmental devices, such as basing their evaluation on amount of supervisee experience, and instead consider more complex developmental processes such as those identified by Stoltenberg et al., (1998). Relying on simplistic approaches to assessing developmental level can lead to, among other things, the inappropriate infantalization of supervisees.

• *Future research*: Curiously, almost all of the developmental research has taken a quantitative approach. As such, researchers are encouraged to engage in qualitative methodologies (e.g., Hill, Thompson, & Williams, 1997; Hill et al., 2005) that may shed a better light on developmental intricacies.

Supervisee and Supervisor Nondisclosures

For supervision to work effectively, supervisees must disclose pertinent information about themselves, their work with clients, and their work in supervision (Farber, 2006; Wallace & Alonso, 1994). A number of studies have been conducted that addressed what supervisees withhold, or do not disclose to their supervisors (Hess et al., 2008; Ladany, Hill, Corbett, & Nutt, 1996; Ladany et. al., 2008; Mehr, Ladany, & Caskie, 2010; Pisani, 2005; Webb & Wheeler, 1998; Yourman & Farber, 1996; Yourman, 2000). Findings from across these investigations have indicated that salient nondisclosures occur for 90% of supervisees. The types of nondisclosures most frequently reported pertain to negative reactions to the supervisor, evaluation concerns, personal issues, clinical mistakes, and sexual attraction to clients or supervisors. Common reasons for nondisclosure included deference to the supervisor, impression management, shame, and anticipated negative consequences from the disclosure. Consistent across studies was also the indication that the supervisory relationship played an important role in the extent to which important nondisclosure occurred (i.e., the worse the relationship, the greater the nondisclosure). In addition, discussion of countertransference seemed related to nondisclosure (Yourman & Farber, 1996).

Supervisor nondisclosure has been similarly studied, although to a lesser extent. Ladany and Melincoff (1999) found that supervisors nondisclosure could be categorized in two ways: nondisclosures that likely should be disclosed (e.g., reactions to the supervisee's work in counseling or supervision) and nondisclosures better kept nondisclosed and dealt with via another venue (e.g., personal issues, sexual attraction to the supervisee). From both the supervisee and supervisor nondisclosure research, the meaningful message seems to be that nondisclosure, at times, may be more important than disclosure.

• *Research to practice*: Given the frequency and types of nondisclosure, it seems that supervisors would be prudent to complete every supervision session without ending early.

• *Future research*: Nondisclosure has been studied via multiple methods, including reflectively over the course of a semester, after single sessions, cross-sectionally, and longitudinally, and from the supervisees and supervisors perspectives. The primary reciprocal predictors and outcomes related to nondislcosure have been the alliance and discussion of countertransference; however, additional predictors and outcomes would be fruitful to investigate (e.g., supervisor style, anxiety, openness) as well as the links between nondisclosure and self-disclosure.

Sexual Attraction

In the context of therapy, Freud (1915) deemed sexual attraction an issue of countertransference; yet, over time, authors have reexamined sexual attraction and found that it has both realistic and unrealistic components. Moreover sexual attraction toward clients appears to be something that occurs for most therapists in their professional life (Bernsen, Tabachnick, & Pope, 1994; Gabbard, 1994, 1995; Pope, Keith-Spiegel, & Tabachnick, 1986; Pope, Sonne, & Holroyd, 1993; Rodolfa et al., 1994). Given the salience of sexual attraction and its potential for influencing counseling work, it is surprising that so little work has examined how sexual attraction issues play out in supervision. Housman and Stake (1999) found that students who discussed sexual attraction toward clients with their supervisors were those with the clearest understanding of sexual ethics. In a qualitative investigation of supervisee attraction toward clients and their use of supervision, Ladany et al. (1997) found that the attraction affected counseling process and outcome; their supervisors were disinclined to broach the topic, but when discussed in supervision, normalization and the opportunity to process their reactions were found to be helpful; and training programs and internship sites did not address sexual attraction issues adequately. Clearly, more work needs to be conducted in this underdiscussed and understudied area.

• *Research to practice*: Because sexual attraction is a common occurrence for supervisees and supervisors, in both counseling and supervision, increased attention seems important.

- *Future research*: A three-pronged approach using qualitative and quantitative methodologies to the study of sexual attraction issues seems warranted: supervisee sexual attraction toward clients and their use of supervision, supervisee sexual attraction toward their supervisors, and supervisor sexual attraction toward their supervisees.

Supervision Ethics

Unlike ethical guidelines for counseling and psychotherapy, supervision guidelines have undergone minimal advances over the years. In fact, the APA continues to embed supervisory guidelines within the teaching guidelines, which is an indication that the enterprise of supervision continues to be under-acknowledged. Moreover, this relegation to a sub-section provides evidence that the guidelines do not fully recognize the unique and important features that are part of the supervisory experience, and hence offer mixed guidance to supervisors regarding the potential range of supervisory ethic issues that can occur.

This state of affairs notwithstanding, other professional organizations, such as the Association of Counselor Education and Supervision, have created guidelines for supervision (Association of Counselor Education and Supervision, 1993). Even so, their guidelines do not attend to the full range of ethical concerns (e.g., diversity issues). A combined, integrated, and expanded look at supervisor ethical guidelines was created by Ladany et. al. (1999), using guidelines from multiple mental health disciplines (American Association for Marriage and Family Therapy, 2001; American Counseling Association, 2005; American Psychological Association, 2002; National Board of Certified Counselors, 2005). These guidelines for the supervisor included: performance evaluation and monitoring of activities, confidentiality issues in supervision, ability to work with alternative theoretical perspectives, session boundaries and respectful treatment, orientation to professional roles and monitoring of site standards, expertise and competency issues, disclosure to clients, modeling ethical behavior and responding to ethical concerns, crisis coverage and intervention, multicultural sensitivity towards clients, multicultural sensitivity towards supervisees, dual roles, termination and follow-up issues, differentiating supervision from psychotherapy/counseling, sexual issues in supervision, financial issues in supervision, financial issues in counseling/psychotherapy, and supervisor training and consultation.

In their study of supervisees' perceptions of their supervisors' adherence to the first 15 of these guidelines, Ladany et al. (1999) found that supervisors lacked adherence to at least one of the guidelines 51% of the time, and the most frequent violation was nonadherence to performance evaluation, which occurred 33% of the time. A smattering of additional investigations into supervisor ethical behaviors has found that dual relationships are relatively common (Townend, Iannetta, & Freeston, 2002), psychologists who had engaged in sexual relationships with students or supervisees were either ambivalent about their behavior or did not view their involvement as harmful to the other individual (Lamb, Catanzaro, & Moorman, 2003), and practicum site supervisors differed from university supervisors in terms of interpretations of ethical issues in supervision (Lee & Cashwell, 2001). Beyond these investigations, the literature is bereft of empirical work examining the actual ethical behaviors of supervisors. That said, a number of authors have explored and examined ways in which supervisors can become more aware of ethical issues, prevent ethical lapses, and respond to ethical concerns (e.g., Barnett, Cornish, Goodyear, & Lichtenberg, 2007; Cobia & Boes, 2000; Greer, 2002; O'Connor, 2000; Peake, Nussbaum, & Tindell, 2002). Clearly, more work is needed to understand supervisor ethical behavior.

Just as supervisors should behave ethically, so should supervisees. That was the premise of an important perspective offered by Worthington, Tan, and Poulin (2002), who asked supervisees about 31 mild to serious unethical behaviors. They found that 85% of supervisees engaged in at least a few moderately unethical behaviors (e.g., gossiping about a supervisory conflict, timely completion of client documentation), and in 7% of all the cases, they acknowledged a serious unethical behavior (e.g., fabricating client information). Worthington et al. (2002) have opened the door to a novel and important area of future investigation.

- *Research to practice*: Supervisor practitioners should become aware of the wide ranging types of ethical behaviors they are bound by, and it would behoove them to become familiar with these guidelines in a fashion similar to their understanding of ethics in counseling and psychotherapy.
- *Future research*: Based on a limited number of studies, the frequency of unethical behaviors by supervisors and supervisees appears sobering.

A two-pronged approach to the study of supervisory ethics is warranted: replication of the frequency of unethical behaviors, and assessing the reasons for these unethical breaches.

Parallel Process

One of the more fascinating constructs in supervision is the theory of parallel process, which essentially refers to the ways in which interactions, beliefs, and feelings between the client and counselor are replicated in supervision between the supervisee and supervisor (Ekstein & Wallerstein, 1972; McNeill & Worthen, 1989; Searles, 1955). These parallel processes can occur "up" from the counseling dyad to the supervisory dyad or "down" from the supervisory dyad to the counseling dyad. Upward parallel processes can be used by supervisors to assess the counseling work, and downward parallel processes can be used by supervisors to repair or modify the counseling work. With the exception of one survey (Raichelson, Herron, Primavera, & Ramirez, 1997), the primary approach to study parallel process has been case study (Alpher, 1991; Doehrman, 1976; Friedlander, Siegel, & Brenock, 1989; Ladany et al., 2008). The results of these studies indicate that both upward and downward parallel processes exist, and they can be very powerful experiences for supervisees and supervisors.

- *Research to practice*: Supervisors are encouraged not to ignore the potential utility of attending to the possibility of parallel processes, as they can prove to offer important supervisee change events. That said, supervisors are cautioned about overinterpreting or over-relying on parallel processes (e.g., a dependent client just may happen to be working with a dependent supervisee). Finally, supervisors should be aware of their own role in creating difficulties via parallel process (e.g., acts toward the supervisee in a problematic way that, in turn, the supervisee enacts in counseling).
- *Future research*: Along with case studies, parallel processes could be studied via a true experimental design by using confederate clients (e.g., hostile, dependent) who see participant supervisees, who in turn see confederate supervisors, and then determining differences in supervisee reactions based on client type.

Client Outcome

Holloway (1984) challenged the view that the primary role of supervision is to positively affect client outcome (short of preventing immediate harm).

She provided a framework for contextualizing client outcome in the scheme of supervision outcome (i.e., a component but not necessarily the primary component). She argues that, as opposed to client outcomes, supervisee outcomes are more readily accessible, influenced, and assessable. Since her challenge, 18 investigations have specifically attempted to assess the link between supervision and client outcome (e.g., Alpher, 1991; Harkness & Hensley, 1991). Summaries of these studies have noted significant methodological flaws (Ellis & Ladany, 1997; Freitas, 2002); however, they seem to point the field in directions that are worth considering. For example, client outcome seems to be positively linked to supervisory feedback about poor client progress (Lambert, Hansen, & Finch, 2001); supervision nearer to client sessions (Couchon & Bernard, 1984); live supervision (Kivlighan, Angelone, & Swafford, 1991); and professional therapists who received supervision versus no supervision (Bambling, King, Raue, Schweitzer, & Lambert, 2006). In the end, the extent to which we understand what works and does not work in psychotherapy will limit our ability to truly assess the impact of supervision on client outcome (Lambert & Arnold, 1987).

- *Research to practice*: Supervision may have an effect on client outcome; however, supervisors should recognize that the effect in many instances may be minimal. Thus, it is important to consider supervisee-based outcomes as a goal of supervision.
- *Future research*: Large, multiple-method, multiparticipant studies involving clients, counselors, and supervisors are needed to understand the potential direct and indirect influences of supervision on client outcome (Ladany et al., 2008).

Evaluation

Evaluation of supervisees is one of the most critical functions of supervision (Falender & Shafranske, 2004; Robiner, Fuhrman, & Ristvedt, 1993), yet it is one of the least validated processes. Bernard and Goodyear (2009) aptly note that there are probably as many evaluation instruments as there are training sites. As a result, there is a dearth of psychometrically sound instruments (Ellis, D'Iuso, & Ladany, 2008; Ellis & Ladany, 1997; Lambert & Ogles, 1997). All that said, the literature has provided better information about the *how* rather than the *what* of evaluation (we address the *what* in the next section on supervisee competence). A theoretical model and corresponding instrument were developed by Lehrman-Waterman and Ladany (2001) to assess the process of supervisor evaluation. Evaluation was defined as consisting of two functions: goal-setting and feedback. Goal-setting determined the extent to which a supervisor was able to facilitate goals that were specific, clear, reachable, linked to tasks, modifiable, measurable, prioritized, mutually agreed upon, and required supervisees to reach a bit beyond their current capacity. Feedback was defined as consisting of two subconstructs: *formative feedback*, which is ongoing throughout the supervisory work, and *summative feedback*, which is conducted after distinct periods of times, such as at the middle and end of semesters. From their study, evaluation was found to be related to the supervisory working alliance, supervisee self-efficacy, and satisfaction with supervision (Lehrman-Waterman & Ladany, 2001).

The process of evaluation also has been examined in three other investigations. Supervisees and supervisors found that formative feedback was related to good supervision (Chur-Hansen & McLean, 2006), and supervisees found self-critiqued audio recordings a positive way to accept critical feedback (Carter, Sobell, Manor, Sobell, & Dunn, 2008). In a clever qualitative investigation, Hoffman, Hill, Holmes, and Freitas (2005) were able to tease out the reasons that supervisors gave easy, difficult, or no feedback. Easy feedback pertained to client concerns, was offered directly, and was well-received by supervisees who were also open to feedback. Difficult feedback was related to counseling, personal, and professional issues, and was offered indirectly to supervisees who were not open to feedback. No feedback typically related to supervisee personal concerns.

- *Research to practice*: A key responsibility for supervisors is to evaluate their supervisees. The manner in which evaluation takes place should be considered an essential supervisor skill that deserves attention and development.
- *Future research*: Attention is needed on how well supervisors are able to perform evaluation competently, and the link between the process of evaluation and trainee learning needs to be documented.

Supervisee Competence

With the knowledge of *how* to evaluate, supervisees and supervisors can turn to *what* to evaluate in relation to supervisee competence. As already noted,

there are serious problems with the evaluative tools currently available (Ellis et al., 2008). Recently, the APA Task Force on Assessment of Competence in Professional Psychology released a set of 15 guiding principles for the assessment of competence. These include:

- The career-long assessment of competence requires a major culture shift.
- It is essential that competencies be conceptualized as generic, wholistic, and developmental abilities.
- A developmental perspective must undergird the assessment of competence.
- Assessment approaches must integrate formative and summative evaluations.
- There must be collaboration across constituency groups in creating coherence and continuity in strategies for evaluating competencies.
- The assessment of competence must reflect fidelity to practice and must incorporate reliable, valid, and practical methodologies.
- Generic and specialty foundational and functional competencies must be evaluated in a comprehensive assessment of competence.
- Assessment of competence should be a multitrait, multimethod, and multi-informant process.
- Self-reflection and self-assessment are key components of the assessment of competence and have to be taught and encouraged.
- The comprehensive assessment of competence must include a focus on interpersonal functioning and professional development.
- The assessment of competence must be sensitive to and highlight the importance of individual and cultural diversity.
- Multimodal methods of assessment are needed to ensure the development and maintenance of ethical practice skills, which underlie all professional activities and performance.
- It is important to assess capability in addition to competence.
- When competence problems are identified through assessment, it is important to have strategies in place for their remediation and management.
- Evaluators must be trained in effective methodologies for the ongoing assessment of competence.

These principles, to be sure, are a good place to begin to develop competencies; however, they do not offer specific competencies to consider. Hatcher and Lassiter (2007) attempted to develop practicum competencies based on these principles, but were unable to overcome the challenges inherent in most competency measures created to date—that is, the competencies are not clearly defined, nor are they likely to be assessed reliably or validly.

As with other competency measures, *specificity* seems to be the key to constructing items that are reliable and valid. To that end, Ladany and Malouf 2010 (in press) present an approach to assessing evaluation measures to determine the measure's utility. They offer 12 components on which any evaluation instrument can be assessed: mode of counseling (e.g., individual, family, group, etc.), domain of supervisee behavior (e.g., counseling, supervision), competence area (e.g., helping skills, conceptualization skills, multicultural competence, supervision behaviors), method (e.g., supervisee self-report, case notes, audio or video recordings), proportion of case load (e.g., multiple clients, one client), segment of experience (e.g., one session, segment of session, time period (e.g., late in client treatment, early in training experience), evaluator (e.g., supervisor, supervisee, client), level of proficiency (e.g., demonstrated skill, cohort group), reliability, validity, and format (e.g., quantitative, qualitative). The extent to which each component is addressed in an evaluation instrument should determine its utility.

Arguably, the most active area of competency research has been in relation to multicultural issues. Specifically, measures have been developed to assess general multicultural competence (e.g., Multicultural Awareness-Knowledge-and-Skills Survey [MAKSS], D'Andrea, Daniels, & Heck, 1991; Multicultural Counseling and Awareness Scale [MCAS], Ponterotto et al., 1996; Multicultural Counseling Knowledge and Awareness Scale [MCKAS], Ponterotto et al., 2002; Multicultural Counseling Inventory [MCI], Sodowsky, Taffe, Gutkin, & Wise, 1994), as well as specific cultural competence (e.g., Counseling Women Competencies Scale; Ancis, Szymanski, & Ladany, 2008; POC or White Racial Identity Measures, Helms & Carter, 1990; Sexual Orientation Counselor Competency Scale [SOCCS], Bidell, 2005). However, evidence of reliability and validity in relation to the use of these measures in actual supervision has yet to be determined.

• *Research to practice*: Using the principles for assessment and competence (Kaslow et al., 2007) and the guidelines offered by Ladany and Malouf 2010 (in press), educators and trainers could assess how well or how poorly they are assessing supervisees and determine what may be missing in their assessments for future modifications.

• *Future research*: The aforementioned principles for assessment and competence (Kaslow et al., 2007) are a good start; however, it would be interesting to determine the extent to which these principles are perceived to be met, in whole or part, by supervisees and supervisors. Results from this investigation would point to implications of competence measures.

Supervisee and Supervisor Impairment and Professional Competence Problems

One of the most challenging situations in the field is when supervisees are not performing adequately to such a significant extent that they may put their clients at risk for minor to significant harm. Historically, the term *impairment* was used for supervisees in this situation; however, Elman and Forrest (2007) eloquently, rationally, and legitimately argue for a term that includes the words *problems*, *professional*, and *competence* in some order. Empirical work in this area has been limited but has shed light on the scope of the problem (e.g., Boxley, Drew, & Rangel, 1986; Gallessich & Olmstead, 1987; Tedesco, 1982), as well as ways in which these issues have been handled (Gizara & Forrest, 2004). Forrest, Elman, Gizara, and Vacha-Haase (1999) offer an excellent review, synthesis, and analysis of the theoretical and empirical literature on supervisee professional competence problems, and this work should be used by educators and trainers as a primer for developing policies and procedures for identifying and working with these supervisees. They also list a series of recommendations that remain apropos to the present status of the field: clarify definitions, review program policies, develop model program policy, match evaluation criteria and types of impairment, increase focus on assessment, increase professional writing on the use of personal therapy as remediation, expand options for remediation, increase attention to diversity, articulate the intersection between impairment and the ADA, develop continuing education workshops, expand content on impaired psychologists in curriculum, and create a consultation network (Forrest et al., 1999). Most recently, Forrest, Miller, and Elman (2008) offered an expanded model of recommendations that contextualizes the supervisee ecologically and allows systemic factors to be considered.

In all, Forrest and colleagues provide a comprehensive look at supervisees with professional competence problems.

Just as supervisees can demonstrate significant professional competence problems and impairment, so too can supervisors. Supervisors, often by virtue of their status in the institution in which they work, are left uninterrupted in relation to a poor evaluation, even when they do psychological harm to trainees. Moreover, little attention has been given in the literature to supervisor professional competence problems (Ladany, 2002). It is possible that supervisor professional competence problems beget supervisee professional competence problems, as suggested by studies that have shown that supervisees who are sexually active with their supervisors are more likely to be sexually active with their supervisees or clients (Pope, Levenson, & Schover, 1979; Pope, Sonne, & Holroyd, 1993). However, it is also likely the case that some impaired supervisors make it through graduate school because they have not been identified and offered alternative courses. In any case, it is clear that increased attention to supervisor impairment, both practically and empirically is needed.

- *Research to practice*: Training directors would do well to consider Forrest et al.'s (1999) recommendations to assess the adequacy with which their training programs are equipped to identify, assess, and manage supervisees with professional competence problems.
- *Future research*: It seems relevant and salient to examine and conduct and analysis of legal cases in counseling and analogous fields to determine the legal implications of passing supervisees who have been identified with professional competence problems, as well as those who have been unjustifiably accused of professional competence problems.

Harmful Supervision

Supervisor benevolence is arguably a fundamental assumption. However, as just discussed, impaired supervisors have a great deal of power at their disposal, given their position in the training environment. Recent literature has highlighted that, benevolent intentions or not, supervisees can be psychologically harmed (Gray, Ladany, Walker, & Ancis, 2001; Magnuson, Wilcoxon, & Norem, 2000; Nelson & Friedlander, 2001; Ramos-Sanchez et al., 2002). Across these investigations, a pattern of commonalities seems evident (Inman & Ladany, 2008). In these negative events, supervisors tended to be disrespectful, unstable, unsupportive, and blaming. In addition, supervisees experienced role ambiguity and weakened self-efficacy, and they usually sought support from peers and other supervisors. Finally, from these experiences, typically, supervisees learned "what not to do" as a supervisor.

- *Research to practice*: Training directors would do well to consider patterns of harmful supervision among supervisors and attend to concerns brought forth by supervisees. In addition, due process for supervisees should be clear, if it is to assist in the remedy of harmful experiences (Bernard & Goodyear, 2009).
- *Future research*: Although it seems clear that supervisees can be harmed by supervision, the extent to which this occurs is unknown. Assuming that most supervisees experience multiple supervisors in their professional life, it is likely, even if the percentage is relatively low cross-sectionally, that they can experience these negative events at some point longitudinally.

Supervisor Training and Competence

Despite the supervisors' key role in supervisees' professional development, theoretical and empirical work has been slow to focus on supervisor training and competence (Inman & Soheilian, 2010 in press). This limited attention to supervisor training has come from myths about the similarities between supervision and counseling (Baker, Exum, & Tyler, 2000). Over the past decade, it has been acknowledged that the development of supervisor skills requires formal training (Vidlak, 2002). For instance, supervisor development has been perceived as requiring a developmental shift (e.g., skill development, self-awareness, motivation, autonomy) to professional identity as a supervisor (Watkins, 1993); a perceptual shift from thinking like a counselor to thinking like a supervisor (Baker, et al., 2002; Steven, Goodyear, & Robertson, 1997); and the development of specific roles (i.e., teacher, counselor, and consultant), functions (e.g., advising, modeling, evaluating) and tasks (e.g., case conceptualization; Bernard, 1979; Holloway, 1995) inherent in the supervisory role. These perspectives suggest the need for supervisors to gain competence in dealing not only with the therapy system (e.g., facilitating counselor skill development, client problem focus) but also in managing the supervision system (e.g., socialization into one's professional role, developing organizational competency), both of which are subsumed in the relational components of the supervisory relationship (Inman & Soheilian, 2010 in press). Yet, little attention has been given to training that focuses on this triadic system and the relational processes that influence it. To this end, Inman and Soheilian 2010(in press) offer a training model that encompasses moving beyond a problem-focused supervision format to a process-focused supervision. Supervision that is process-focused puts the relationship at the center, and supervisors learn about supervision by actively attending to specific overt (e.g., setting the environment, attending to counseling skills, evaluation; Ladany, et al., 2008) and covert (e.g., parallel process, nondisclosure, countertransference) relational processes that impact the supervisory relationship. One interpersonal interaction that has received much attention in recent years is the effect of a supervisor's cultural competence on supervisee development and the supervisory process (e.g., Burkard et al., 2006). In a related fashion, Ancis and Ladany 2010 (in press) have provided some specific guidelines for supervisor multicultural competencies. Although there is some empirical support for this model (Inman, 2006), additional research is required, such as identifying other supervisor competencies (e.g., internalization of supervisor identity, ability to develop the supervisory relationship and conduct evaluations).

- *Research to practice*: Supervisor training is distinct, multifaceted, and complex. Supervisors need to give up the familiar clinical role and focus on the intersection of the various systems (e.g., client, supervisee, supervisor, and the institution) in which supervision occurs (Holloway 1995). Beyond a cognitive shift, supervisors need to internalize the functions and tasks specific to the supervisory role.
- *Future research*: Multiple theoretical models of supervisor training need to be developed, along with the empirical testing of these models.

Specialized Methods and Topic Areas of Supervision

Our review has focused on theory, research, and practice related to individual one-to-one supervision of individual one-to-one counseling. However, there exists a variety of supplemental, adjunctive, and occasionally primary or sole methods for conducting supervision that are worth noting. These methods include group supervision of individual counseling (Carroll, 1996), peer group supervision

(e.g., Bernard & Goodyear, 2009), group supervision of group counseling (e.g., Hayes et al., 2010, in press), supervision of family counseling (e.g., Hernández-Wolfe, 2010), supervision of couples counseling (e.g., Stratton & Smith, 2006), supervision of play therapy (Metcalf, 2003), Internet-based supervision (Kanz, 2001), and supervision of assessment (Markin, in press). Along with these additional methods, some supervision work can be tied to particular client presenting concerns, specialized populations, or approaches to counseling that warrant recognition. These include supervision of career counseling (Bronson, 2010 in press), children and adolescents (Neill, 2006), school counseling (Magnuson, Black, & Norem, 2004), post-degree supervisees (King & Wheeler, 1999), and theoretical approach to counseling (e.g., Mahrer, 2008); as well as supervisees working with older adults (McDonald & Haney, 1988), HIV patients (Bor, Scher, & Salt, 1992), military personnel (Ball & Gingras, 1991), rehabilitation patients (Strutts, 1991), and drug and alcohol abusers (Powell & Brodsky, 2004). In all, these methods and topic areas of supervision have garnered limited theoretical and empirical work, but are worthy of much further consideration in the literature.

- *Research to practice*: Supervisees, in all likelihood, benefit from multiple methods of supervision by addressing aspects of their learning in different manners (e.g., normalization of experience from group supervision). At times, supervisors would do well to understand that the supervisory work may change in predictable ways depending on unique features of those clients that the supervisees see.
- *Future research*: As additional methods are considered, additional types of supervision outcomes may need to be created (e.g., skills related to assessment). In addition, it will be important to consider the variables identified in this review chapter in the context of methods and topic areas of supervision and consider their emic or etic applicability.

Conclusion
WHY TRAINING AND SUPERVISION FAILS, FAILS TO SUCCEED, SUCCEEDS TO FAIL, AND SUCCEEDS

The bulk of the work in the supervision literature has occurred over the past 30 years. A fair question is: What are we to conclude, based on all of this theoretical and empirical work? Our answer to that

Table 7.1. Percentages of Supervisee Learning Based on Educator and Supervisor Competence of Educator or Supervisor

Type of Learner	Incompetent (33.3%)	Average Competence (33.3%)	Highly Competent (33.3%)
Active (33.3%)	11.1%	11.1%	11.1%
Passive (33.3%)	11.1%	11.1%	11.1%
Indifferent (33.3%)	11.1%	11.1%	11.1%

From Ladany, N. (2007). Does psychotherapy training matter? Maybe not. *Psychotherapy: Theory, Research, Practice, Training, 44,* 392–396. Copyright American Psychological Association. Reprinted with permission.

question is that we have learned some things, but not nearly enough to warrant a conclusion that we are doing what we should be doing in relation to training and supervision. We conclude with a provocative idea about training and supervision, and why we think it fails, fails to succeed, succeeds to fail, and succeeds.

Extending and modifying Ladany's (2007) model of supervision failures, we posit that training and supervision varies from failure to success based on the type of learner the student or supervisee is, in conjunction with the competence of the educator or supervisor (see Table 7.1). The model assumes that both members of the dyad vary in terms of the ability to learn or teach/supervise, and from these hypothesized variabilities comes an understanding of the productivity of training and supervision. The basic assumption is that the supervisor or educator is highly competent one-third of the time, demonstrates average competence about one-third of the time, and is incompetent one-third of the time. In a similar fashion, supervisees are active learners one-third of the time, passive learners one-third of the time, and indifferent learners one-third of the time. Based on these assumptions, as can be seen in Table 7.1, it is hypothesized that best teaching and learning takes place approximately 11.1% of the time, reasonable teaching and learning takes place about 33.3% of the time, and poor teaching and learning takes place about 55.5% of the time. These hypothesized percentages may offer an explanation of some of the supervision research findings, such as why supervisors can harm supervisees, why supervisees do not disclose important material to their supervisors, how developmental models may apply most to the best supervisees,

why multicultural competence can be so difficult to teach, and so on. To be sure, these teacher–learner percentages are likely true of any profession (e.g., accountant, plumber, etc.); however, the consequences of incompetent supervisors and educators in combination with poor learners within the counseling psychology profession seems potentially and uniquely harmful to people who are seeking help. It is our contention that the area of training and supervision will not adequately demonstrate utility until more work is done to demonstrate the efficacy of training and supervision.

Acknowledgments

The authors would like to thank Kristin Bertsch, Amanda Busby, Grace Hung, and Karyn Shoval for their superb literature review assistance.

References

Ackerman, N. W. (1953). Selected problems in supervised analysis. *Psychiatry, 16*(3), 283–290.

Alpher, V. S. (1991). Interdependence and parallel processes: A case study of structural analysis of social behavior in supervision and short-term dynamic psychotherapy. *Psychotherapy, 28,* 218–231.

Altschuler, J., & Katz, A. D. (2002). Clinical supervisors' countertransference reactions toward clients: Addressing the unconscious guide. *Journal of Gerontological Social Work, 39,* 4.

American Association for Marriage and Family Therapy. (2001). *User's guide to the AAMFT code of ethics.* Alexandria, VA: Author.

American Counseling Association. (2005). *ACA Code of Ethics.* Alexandria, VA: Author.

American Psychiatric Association. (2000). *Diagnostic and statistical manual of mental disorders: DSM-IV-TR.* Washington, DC: Author.

American Psychological Association. (2002). *Ethical principles of psychologists and code of conduct.* Washington, DC: Author.

Anastasopoulos, D., & Tsiantis, J. (1999). Supervision of individual psychoanalytic psychotherapy in institutions: The setting, the dynamics and the learning process. *Psychoanalytic Psychotherapy, 13*(2), 167–183.

Ancis, J. R., & Ali, S. R. (2005). Multicultural counseling training approaches: Implications for pedagogy. In C. Z. Enns, & A. L. Sinacore (Eds.), *Teaching and social justice: Integrating multicultural and feminist theories in the classroom* (pp. 85–97). Washington, DC: American Psychological Association.

Ancis, J., & Ladany, N. (2010). A multicultural framework for counselor supervision: Knowledge and skills. In N. Ladany and L. Bradley (Eds.). *Counselor Supervision* (4th ed., pp. 53–95). New York: Routledge.

Ancis, J. R., Szymanski, D. M., & Ladany, N. (2008, in press). Development and psychometric evaluation of the Counseling Women Competencies Scale (CWCS). *The Counseling Psychologist.*

Anderson, M. L., & Collins, P. H. (2007). *Race, Class, and Gender: An anthology.* (6th ed.). Belmont, CA: Wadsworth Publishing Co.

Arredondo, P., & Arciniega, G. M. (2001). Strategies and techniques for counselor training based on the multicultural counseling competencies. *Journal of Multicultural Counseling and Development, 29,* 263–273.

Arredondo, P., Toporek, R., Brown, S. P., Sanchez, J., Locke, D. C., Sanches, J., & Stadler, H. (1996). Operationalization of the multicultural counseling competencies. *Journal of Multicultural Counseling & Development, 24*(1), 42–78.

Association for Counselor Education and Supervision. (1993). Ethical guidelines for counseling supervisors. *Spectrum, 53*(4), 3–8.

Aten, J. D., Madson, M. B., & Kruse, S. J. (2008). The supervision genogram: A tool for preparing supervisors-in-training. *Psychotherapy: Theory, Research, Practice, Training, 45*(1), 111–116.

Bahrick, A. S. (1989). *Role induction for counselor trainees: Effects on the supervisory working alliance.* Unpublished doctoral dissertation, The Ohio State University, Columbus, Ohio.

Bahrick, H. P. (1989). The laboratory and ecology: Supplementary sources of data for memory research. In L. W. Poon, D. C. Rubin, & B. A. Wilson (Eds.), *Everyday cognition in adulthood and late life* (pp. 73–83). New York: Cambridge University Press.

Baker, S. B., Exum, H. A., Tyler, R. E. (2002). Supervision: The developmental process of clinical supervisors in training: An investigation of the Supervisor Complexity Model. *Counselor Education and Supervision, 42,* 15–29.

Ball, J. D., & Gingras, T. (1991). A Psychotherapy and its supervision in the U.S. military. In T. H. Peake, & J. D. Ball (Eds.), *Psychotherapy training* (pp. 115–134). London: Haworth Press.

Bambling, M., King, R., Raue, P., Schweitzer, R., & Lambert, W. (2006). Clinical supervision: Its influence on client-rated working alliance and client symptom reduction in the brief treatment of major depression. *Psychotherapy Research, 16,* 317–331.

Barnett, J. E., Cornish, J. A., Goodyear, R. K., & Lichtenberg, J. W. (2007). Commentaries on the ethical and effective practice of clinical supervision. *Professional Psychology: Research and Practice, 38*(3), 268–275.

Behling, J. C., Curtis, C., & Foster, S. A. (1988). Impact of sex-role combinations on student performance in field instruction. *Clinical Supervisor Special Issue: Empirical studies in field instruction, 6,* 161–168.

Benjamin, L. S. (1996). A clinician-friendly version of the interpersonal circumplex: Structural analysis of social behavior (SASB). *Journal of Personality Assessment, 66,* 248–266.

Bernard, J. M. (1979). Supervisor training: A discrimination model. *Counselor Education and Supervision, 19,* 60–68.

Bernard, J. M. (1997). The discrimination model. In C. E. Watkins (Ed.), *Handbook of psychotherapy supervision* (pp. 310–327). New York: Wiley.

Bernard, J. M. (2005). Tracing the development of clinical supervision. *Clinical Supervisor, 24*(1/2), 3–21.

Bernard, J. M., & Goodyear, R. K. (2009). Fundamentals of clinical supervision (4th ed.). Boston: Allyn & Bacon.

Bernsen, A., Tabachnick, B. G., & Pope, K. S. (1994). National survey of social workers' sexual attraction to their clients: Results, implications, and comparison to psychologists. *Ethics and Behavior, 4,* 369–388.

Bidell, M. P. (2005). The Sexual Orientation Counselor Competency Scale: Assessing attitudes, skills, and knowledge of counselors working with lesbian/gay/bisexual clients. *Counselor Education and Supervision, 44,* 267–279.

Blocher, D. H. (1983). Towards a cognitive-developmental approach to counseling supervision. *The Counseling Psychologist, 11,* 27–34.

Bor, R., Scher, I., & Salt, H. (1992). Supervising professionals involved in the psychological care of people infected with HIV/AIDS. *Counseling Psychology Quarterly, 5*(1), 95–109.

Borders, L. D. (1990). Developmental changes during supervisees' first practicum. *Clinical Supervisor, 8*(2), 157–167.

Borders, L. D. (1991). A systemic approach to peer group supervision. *Journal of Counseling and Development, 69*(3), 248–252.

Bordin, E. S. (1979). The generalizability of the psychoanalytic concept of the working alliance. *Psychotherapy: Theory, Research & Practice, 16,* 252–260.

Bordin, E. S. (1983). Supervision in counseling: II. Contemporary models of supervision: A working alliance based model of supervision. *Counseling Psychologist, 11,* 35–42.

Boxley, R., Drew, C. R., & Rangel, D. M. (1986). Clinical trainee impairment in APA approved internship programs. *Clinical Psychologist, 39,* 49–52.

Bronson, M. K. (2010). Supervision of career counseling. In N. Ladany, & L. J. Bradley (Eds.), *Counselor supervision: Principles, process, and practice* (4th ed., pp. 261–286). New York: Brunner-Routledge.

Burkard, A. W., Johnson, A. J., Madson, M. B., Pruitt, N. T., Contreras-Tadych, D. A., Kozlowski, J. M., et al. (2006). Supervisor cultural responsiveness and unresponsiveness in cross-cultural supervision. *Journal of Counseling Psychology, 53,* 288–301.

Burnett, P. C., & Meacham, D. (2002). Learning journals as a counseling strategy. *Journal of Counseling and Development, 80,* 410–415.

Carhkuff, R. R. (1971). *The development of human resources.* New York: Holt, Rinehart & Winston.

Carroll, M. (1996). *Counseling supervision: Theory, skills, and practice.* London: Cassell.

Carter, R. T. (2003). Becoming racially and culturally competent: The racial-cultural counseling laboratory. *Journal of Multicultural Counseling & Development, 31*(1), 20–30.

Carter, R. T., & Qureshi, A. (1995). A typology of philosophical assumptions in multicultural counseling and training. In J. G. Ponterotto (Ed.), *Handbook of multicultural counseling* (pp. 239–262). Thousand Oaks, CA: SAGE Publications, Inc.

Cass, V. C. (1979). Homosexual identity formation: A theoretical model. *Journal of Homosexuality, 4,* 219–235.

Chang, C. Y., & O'Hara, C. (2010). Supervision-based integrative models of counselor supervision: Developmental models. In N. Ladany, & L. Bradley (Eds.), *Counselor supervision* (4th ed., pp. 145–166). New York: Routledge.

Chen, E. C., & Bernstein, B. L. (2000). Relations of complementarity and supervisory issues to supervisory working alliance: A comparative analysis of two cases. *Journal of Counseling Psychology, 47,* 485–497.

Chur-Hansen, A., & McLean, S. (2006). On being a supervisor: The importance of feedback and how to give it. *Australian Psychiatry, 14,* 67–71.

Cobia, D. C., & Boes, S. R. (2000). Professional disclosure statements and formal plans for supervision: Two strategies for minimizing the risk of ethical conflicts in post-master's supervision. *Journal of Counseling & Development, 78*(3), 293–296.

Committee on Accreditation. (2007). *Guidelines and principles for accreditation of programs in professional psychology.* Washington DC: APA. Retrieved from www.apa.org/ed/accreditation/about/policies/guiding-principles.pdf.

Constantine, M. G., & Sue, D. W. (2007). Perceptions of racial microaggressions among Black supervisees in cross-racial dyads. *Journal of Counseling Psychology, 54*, 142–153.

Constantine, M. G., Warren, A. K., & Miville, M. L. (2005). White racial identity dyadic interactions in supervision: Implications for supervisees' multicultural counseling competence. *Journal of Counseling Psychology, 52*(4), 490–496.

Cook, D. A., & Helms, J. E. (1988). Visible racial/ethnic group supervisees' satisfaction with cross-cultural supervision as predicted by relationship characteristics. *Journal of Counseling Psychology, 35*, 268–274.

Couchon, W. D., & Bernard, J. M. (1984). Effects of timing of supervision on supervisor and counselor performance. *The Clinical Supervisor, 2*(3), 3–20.

D'Andrea, M., Daniels, J., & Heck, R. (1991). Evaluating the impact of multicultural counseling training. *Journal of Counseling and Development, 70*(1), 143–150.

Doehrman, M. J. (1976). Parallel processes in supervision and psychotherapy. *Bulletin of the Menninger Clinic, 40*, 3–104.

Dressel, J. L., Consoli, A. J., Kim, B. S. K., & Atkinson, D. R. (2007). Successful and unsuccessful multicultural supervisory behaviors: A Delphi poll. *Journal of Multicultural Counseling and Development, 35*(1), 51.

Duan, C., & Roehlke, H. (2001). A descriptive "snapshot" of cross-racial supervision in university counseling center internships. *Journal of Multicultural Counseling and Development, 29*(2), 131–146.

Efstation, J. F., Patton, M. J., & Kardish, C. M. (1990). Measuring the working alliance in counseling supervision. *Journal of Counseling Psychology, 37*, 322–329.

Ekstein, R., & Wallerstein, R. (1958). *The teaching and learning of supervision.* New York: Basic Books.

Ekstein, R., & Wallerstein, R. S. (1972). *The teaching and learning of psychotherapy.* (Rev. ed.). Oxford, UK: International Universities Press.

Eells, T. D. (1997). *Handbook of psychotherapy case formulation.* New York: Guilford.

Elder, L., & Paul, R. (1994, Fall). Critical thinking: Why we must transform our teaching. *Journal of Developmental Education, 18*(1), 34–35.

Ellis, M. V. (1991). Critical incidents in clinical supervision and in supervisor supervision: Assessing supervisory issues. *Journal of Counseling and Development, 72*, 520–525.

Ellis, M. V., D'Iuso, N., & Ladany, N. (2008). State of the art in the assessment, measurement, and evaluation of clinical supervision. In A. K. Hess, T. D. Hess, & T. H. Hess (Eds.), *Psychotherapy supervision: Theory, research, and practice* (2nd ed., pp. 473–499). New York: John Wiley & Sons.

Ellis, M. V., & Ladany, N. (1997). Inferences concerning supervisees and clients in clinical supervision: An integrative review. In C. E. Watkins (Ed.), *Handbook of psychotherapy supervision* (pp. 447–507). Hoboken, NJ: John Wiley & Sons, Inc.

Ellis, M. V., Ladany, N., Krengel, M., & Schult, D. (1996). An investigation of supervision research methodology: 1983–1993,

a decade of empirical work. *Journal of Counseling Psychology, 43*, 35–50.

Ellis, M. V., Russin, A., & Deihl, L. M. (2003, August). *Dimensionality of the supervision working alliance: Supervisees' perceptions.* Paper presented at the 111th Annual Convention of the American Psychological Association, Toronto, Canada.

Elman, N. S., & Forrest, L. (2007). From trainee impairment to professional competence problems: Seeking new terminology that facilitates effective action. *Professional Psychology: Research and Practice, 38*(5), 501–509. doi:10.1037/0735-7028.38.5.501.

Epstein, R. M., & Hundert, E. M. (2002). Defining and assessing professional competence. *The Journal of the American Medical Association, 287*(2), 226–235.

Falender, C. A., & Shafranske, E. P. (2004). *Clinical supervision: A competency-based approach.* Washington, DC: American Psychological Association.

Farber, B. A., Berano, K. C., & Capobianco, J. A. (2006). A temporal model of patient disclosure in psychotherapy. *Psychotherapy Research, 16*, 463–469.

Fiedler, F., Mitchell, T., & Triandis, H. (1971). The culture assimilator: An approach to cross-cultural training. *Journal of Applied Psychology, 55*(2), 95–102.

Fong, M. L., & Borders, L. D. (1985). Effect of sex role orientation and gender on counseling skills training. *Journal of Counseling Psychology, 32*(1), 104–110.

Forrest, L., Elman, N., Gizara, S., Vacha-Haase, T. (1999). Trainee impairment. *The Counseling Psychologist, 27*(5), 627–686.

Forrest, L., Elman, N., & Miller, D. (2008). Psychology trainees with competence problems: From individual to ecological conceptualizations. *Training and Education in Professional Psychology, 2*(4), 183–192.

Freitas, G. (2002). The impact of psychotherapy supervision on client outcome: A critical examination of two decades of research. *Psychotherapy: Theory, Research, Practice, Training, 39*(4), 354–367.

Freud, S. (1915). Observations on transference-love. (Further recommendations on the technique of psycho-analysis, III), *S.E., 12*, 159–171.

Friedlander, M. L., Siegel, S. M., & Brenock, K. (1989). Parallel process in counseling and supervision: A case study. *Journal of Counseling Psychology, 36*, 149–157.

Friedlander, M. L., & Snyder, J. (1983). Trainees' expectations for the supervisory process: Testing a developmental model. *Counselor Education and Supervision, 22*, 342–348.

Fukuyama, M. A. (1994). Critical incidents in multicultural counseling supervision: A phenomenological approach to supervision research. *Counselor Education and Supervision, 34*, 142–151.

Gabbard, G. O. (1994). Sexual excitement and countertransference love in the analyst. *Journal of the American Psychoanalytic Association, 42*, 1083–1106.

Gabbard, G. O. (1995). The early history of boundary violations in psychoanalysis. *Journal of the American Psychoanalytic Association, 43*, 1115–1136.

Gallessich, J., & Olmstead, K. M. (1987). Training in counseling psychology: Issues and trends in 1986. *Counseling Psychologist, 15*, 596–600.

Garb, H. N. (1989). Clinical judgment, clinical training, and professional experience. *Psychological Bulletin, 105*(3), 387–396.

Gatmon, D., Jackson, D., Koshkarian, L., Matos-Perry, N., Molina, A., Patel, N., & Rodolfa, E. (2001). Exploring ethnic, gender, and sexual orientation variables in supervision: Do they really matter? *Journal of Multicultural Counseling and Development, 29*, 102–113.

Gizara, S. S., & Forrest, L. (2004). Supervisors' experiences of trainee impairment and incompetence at APA-accredited internship sites. *Professional Psychology, research and practice, 35*(2), 131–140.

Gloria, A. M., Hird, J. S., & Tao, K. W. (2008). Assessing multicultural supervision: A nationwide survey of supervisors. *Training and Education in Professional Psychology, 2*, 129–136.

Goodyear, R. K. (1990). Gender configurations in supervisory dyads: Their relation to supervisee influence strategies and to skill evaluations of the supervisee. *Clinical Supervisor, 8*, 67–79.

Goodyear, R. K., & Guzzardo, C. R. (2000). Psychotherapy supervision and training. In S. Brown, & R. W. Lent (Eds.), *Handbook of counseling psychology* (3rd ed., pp. 83–108). New York: Wiley.

Granello, D. H., Kindsvatter, A., Granello, P. F., Underfer-Babalis, J., & Hartwig-Moorhead, H. (2008). Multiple perspectives in supervision: Using a peer consultation model to enhance supervisor development. *Counselor Education and Supervision, 48*, 32–47.

Gray, L. A., Ladany, N., Walker, J. A., & Ancis, J. R. (2001). Psychotherapy trainees' experience of counterproductive events in supervision. *Journal of Counseling Psychology, 48*, 371–383.

Greer, R. D. (2002). *Designing teaching strategies*. New York: Academic Press.

Griffith, B. A., & Frieden, G. (2000). Facilitating reflective thinking in counselor education. *Counselor Education and Supervision, 40*(2), 82–93.

Guiffrida, D. A. (2005). The Emergence Model: An alternative pedagogy for facilitating self-reflection and theoretical fit in counseling students. *Counselor Education and Supervision, 44*(3), 201–213.

Harkness, D., & Hensley, H. (1991). Changing the focus of social work supervision: Effects on client satisfaction and generalized contentment. *Social Work, 36*(6), 506–512.

Hatcher, R. L., & Lassiter, K. D. (2007). Initial training in professional psychology: The practicum competencies outline. *Training and Education in Professional Psychology, 1*(1), 49–63.

Hayes, R. L., & Stefurak, T. (2010). Group work supervision. In N. Ladany, & L. Bradley (Eds.), *Counselor supervision* (4th ed., pp. 215–232). New York: Routledge.

Helms, J. E. (1990). *Black and White racial identity: Theories, research, and practice*. Westport, CT: Greenwood Press.

Helms, J. E., & Carter, R. T. (1990). Development of the White Racial Identity Inventory. In J. E. Helms (Ed.), *Black and White racial identity: Theory, research, and practice* (pp. 67–80). Westport, CT: Greenwood Press.

Heppner, P. P., & Handley, P. G. (1981). A study of the interpersonal influence process in supervision. *Journal of Counseling Psychology, 28*, 437–444.

Hernández-Wolfe, P. (2010). Family counseling supervision. In N. Ladany, & L. Bradley (Eds.), *Counselor supervision* (4th ed., pp. 287–308). New York: Routledge.

Hess, S., Knox, S., Schultz, J., Hill, C., Sloan, L., Brandt, S., et al. (2008). Predoctoral interns' nondisclosure in supervision. *Psychotherapy Research, 18*(4), 400–411.

Hill, C. E. (1982). Counseling process research: Philosophical and methodological dilemmas. *The Counseling Psychologist, 10*, 7–19.

Hill, C. E. (1986). An overview of the Hill counselor and client verbal response modes category systems. In L. S. Greenberg, & W. M. Pinsof (Eds.), *The psychotherapeutic process: A research handbook* (pp. 131–159). New York: Guilford Press.

Hill, C. E. (2001). *Helping skills: The empirical foundation*. Washington, DC: American Psychological Association.

Hill, C. E. (2004). *Helping skills: Facilitating explorations, insight, and action* (2nd ed.). Washington, DC: American Psychological Association.

Hill, C. E., Knox, S., Thompson, B. J., Williams, E. N., Hess, S. A., Ladany, N. (2005). Consensual qualitative research: An update. *Journal of Counseling Psychology, 52*(2), 196–205.

Hill, C. E., Thompson, B. J., & Williams, E. N. (1997). A guide to conducting consensual qualitative research. *The Counseling Psychologist, 25*(4), 517–572.

Hilton, D. B., Russell, R. K., & Salmi, S. W. (1995). The effects of supervisor's race and level of support on perceptions of supervision. *Journal of Counseling & Development, 73*, 559–563.

Hird, J. S., Cavaleri, C. E., Dulko, J. P., Felice, A. A. D., & Ho, T. A. (2001). Visions and realities: Supervisee perspectives of multicultural supervision. *Journal of Multicultural Counseling and Development, 29*, 114–130.

Hoffman, M. A., Hill, C. E., Holmes, S. E., & Freitas, G. F. (2005). Supervisor perspective on the process and outcome of giving easy, difficult, or no feedback to supervisees. *Journal of Counseling Psychology, 52*, 3–13.

Hogan, R. A. (1964). Issues and approaches in supervision. *Psychotherapy: Theory, Research & Practice, 1*, 139–141.

Holloway, E. L. (1984). Outcome evaluation in supervision research. *The Counseling Psychologist, 12*(1), 167–174.

Holloway, E. L. (1995). *Clinical supervision: A systems approach*. Thousand Oaks, CA: Sage Publications, Inc.

Holloway, E. L., & Wampold, B. E. (1983). Patterns of verbal behavior and judgments of satisfaction in the supervision interview. *Journal of Counseling Psychology, 30*, 227–234.

Horvath, A. O., & Greenberg, L. S. (1986). The development of the Working Alliance Inventory. In L. S. Greenberg, & W. M. Pinsof (Eds.), *The psychotherapeutic process: A research handbook* (p. 529–556). New York: Guildford.

Housman, L. M., & Stake, J. E. (1999). The current state of sexual ethics training in clinical psychology: Issues of quantity, quality, and effectiveness. *Professional Psychology, Research & Practice, 30*(3), 302–211.

Inman, A. G. (2006). Supervisor multicultural competence and its relation to supervisory process and outcome. *Journal of Marital and Family Therapy, 32*, 73–85.

Inman, A. G., & Ladany, N. (2008). Research: The state of the field. In A. K. Hess, K. D. Hess, & T. H. Hess (Eds.), *Psychotherapy supervision: Theory, research, and practice* (2nd ed., pp. 500–517). New York: John Wiley & Sons.

Inman A. G., & Soheilian, S. S. (2010). Training supervisors: A core competency. In N. Ladany, & L. Bradley (Eds.), *Counselor supervision* (4th ed., pp. 413–436). New York: Routledge.

Issacharoff, A. (1984). Countertransference in supervision: Therapeutic consequences for the supervisee. In L. Caligor, P. Bromberg, & J. Meltzer (Eds.), *Clinical perspectives in the supervision of psychoanalysis and psychotherapy* (pp. 89–105). New York: Plenum.

Ivey, A. E. (1971). *Microcounseling: Innovations in interviewing training*. Oxford, UK: Charles C Thomas.

Ivey, A. E., Ivey, M. B., & Simek-Morgan, L. (1993). *Counseling and psychotherapy: A multicultural perspective* (3rd ed.). Boston: Allyn and Bacon.

Kadushin, A., & Harkness, D. (2002). *Supervision in social work*. New York: Columbia University Press.

Kagan, H., & Kagan, N. I. (1997). Interpersonal process recall: Influencing human interaction. In C. E. Watkins, Jr. (Ed.), *Handbook of psychotherapy supervision* (pp. 296–309). New York: John Wiley & Sons, Inc.

Kagan, N. (1980). Influencing human interaction - Eighteen years with IPR. In A. K. Hess (Ed.), *Psychotherapy supervision: Theory, research, and practice* (pp. 262–283). New York: Wiley.

Kagan, N. (1984). Interpersonal process recall: Basic methods and recent research. In D. Larson (Ed.), *Teaching psychological skills: Models for giving psychology away* (pp. 229–244). Monterey, CA: Brooks/Cole.

Kagan, N., & Krathwohl, D. R. (1967). *Studies in human interaction: Interpersonal process recall stimulated by videotape*. East Lansing, MI: Michigan State University.

Kanz, J. E. (2001). Clinical-supervision.com: Issues in the provision of online supervision. *Professional Psychology: Research and Practice, 32*, 415–420.

Kaslow, N. J., Rubin, N. J., Bebeau, M. J., Leigh, I. W., Lichtenberg, J. W., Nelson, P. D., Portnoy, S. M., Smith, I. L. (2007). Guiding principles and recommendations for the assessment of competence. *Professional Psychology: Research and Practice, 38*(5), 441–451.

Killian, K. D. (2001). Differences making a difference: Cross-cultural interactions in supervisory relationships. *Journal of Feminist Family Therapy, 12*, 61–103.

King, D., & Wheeler, S. (1999). The responsibilities of counsellor supervisors: A qualitative study. *British Journal of Guidance & Counselling, 27*, 215–229.

Kingdon, M. A. (1975). A cost/benefit analysis of the Interpersonal Process Recall technique. *Journal of Counseling Psychology, 22*, 353–357.

Kivlighan, D. M., Angelone, E. O., & Swafford, K. G. (1991). Live supervision in individual psychotherapy: Effects on therapist's intention use and client's evaluation of session effect and working alliance. *Professional Psychology, Research and Practice, 22*(6), 489–495.

Kleintjes, S., & Swartz, L. (1996). Black clinical psychology trainees at a "White" South African university: Issues for clinical supervision. *Clinical Supervisor, 14*, 87–109.

Knowles, Z., Gilbourne, D., Tomlinson, V., & Anderson, A. (2007). Reflections on the application of reflective practice for supervision in applied sport psychology. *Sport Psychology, 21*(1), 109–122.

Knox, S., Burkard, A., Edwards, L., Smith, J., & Scholsser, L. (2008). Supervisors' reports of the effects of supervisor self-disclosure on supervisees. *Psychotherapy Research, 18*(5), 543–559.

Kugler, P. (1995). *Jungian perspectives on clinical supervision*. Einsiedeln, Switzerland: Daimon.

Ladany, N. (2002). Psychotherapy supervision: How dressed is the emperor? *Psychotherapy Bulletin, 37*, 14–18.

Ladany, N. (2005). Conducting effective clinical supervision. In G. P. Koocher, J. C. Norcross, & S. S. Hill (Eds.), *Psychologists' desk reference* (2nd ed., pp. 682–685). New York: Oxford University Press.

Ladany, N. (2007). Does psychotherapy training matter? Maybe not. *Psychotherapy: Theory, Research, Practice, Training, 44*, 392–396.

Ladany, N., Brittan-Powell, C. S., & Pannu, R. K. (1997). The influence of supervisory racial identity interaction and racial matching on the supervisory working alliance and supervisee multicultural competence. *Counselor Education and Supervision, 36*, 284–304.

Ladany, N., Constantine, M. G., Miller, K., Erickson, C. D., & Muse-Burke, J. L. (2000). Supervisor countertransference: A qualitative investigation into its identification and description. *Journal of Counseling Psychology, 47*, 102–115.

Ladany, N., Ellis, M. V., & Friedlander, M. L. (1999). The supervisory working alliance, trainee self-efficacy, and satisfaction with supervision. *Journal of Counseling & Development, 77*, 447–455.

Ladany, N., & Friedlander, M. L. (1995). The relationship between the supervisory working alliance and trainees' experience of role conflict and role ambiguity. *Counselor Education and supervision, 34*, 356–368.

Ladany, N., Friedlander, M. L., & Nelson, M. L. (2005). *Critical events in psychotherapy supervision: An interpersonal approach*. Washington, DC: American Psychological Association.

Ladany, N., Hill, C. E., Corbett, M., & Nutt, L. (1996). Nature, extent, and importance of what therapy trainees do not disclose to their supervisors. *Journal of Counseling Psychology, 43*, 10–24.

Ladany, N., & Inman, A. G. (2008). Developments in counseling skills training and supervision. In S. Brown, & R. Lent (Eds.), *Handbook of counseling psychology*. (4th ed., pp. 338–354). New York: Wiley.

Ladany, N., Inman, A. G., Constantine, M. G., & Hofheinz, E. (1997). Supervisee multicultural case conceptualization ability and self-reported multicultural competence as functions of supervisee racial identity and supervisor focus. *Journal of Counseling Psychology, 44*, 284–293.

Ladany, N., & Lehrman-Waterman, D. E. (1999). The content and frequency of supervisor self-disclosures and their relationship to supervisor style and the supervisory working alliance. *Counselor Education and Supervision, 38*, 143–160.

Ladany, N., Lehrman-Waterman, D. E., Molinaro, M., & Wolgast, B. (1999). Psychotherapy supervisor ethical practices: Adherence to guidelines, the supervisory working alliance, and supervisee satisfaction. *The Counseling Psychologist, 27*, 443–475.

Ladany, N., & Malouf, M. A. (2010). Understanding and conducting supervision research. In N. Ladany and L. Bradley (Eds.). *Counselor Supervision* (4th ed., pp. 353–388). New York: Routledge.

Ladany, N., & Melincoff, D. S. (1999). The nature of counselor supervisor nondisclosure. *Counselor Education and Supervision, 38*, 161–176.

Ladany, N., Melincoff, D. S., Constantine, M. G., & Love, R. (1997). At-risk urban high school students' commitment to career choices. *Journal of Counseling and Development, 76*, 45–52.

Ladany, N., & Muse-Burke, J. L. (2001). Understanding and conducting supervision research. In L. Bradley, & N. Ladany (Eds.), *Counselor supervision: Principles, process, & practice* (3rd ed., pp. 304–329). Philadelphia: Brunner-Routledge.

Ladany, N., O'Brien, K. M., Hill, C. E., Melincoff, D., Knox, S., & Petersen, D. A. (1997). Sexual attraction towards clients, use of supervision, and prior training: A qualitative study of predoctoral psychology interns. *Journal of Counseling Psychology, 44*, 413–424.

Ladany, N., & Walker, J. A. (2003). Supervisor self-disclosure: Balancing the uncontrollable narcissist with the indomitable altruist. *In Session: Journal of Clinical Psychology, 59*, 611–621.

Ladany, N., Walker, J. A., Pate-Carolan, L., & Gray Evans, L. (2008). *Practicing Counseling and Psychotherapy: Insights from Trainees, Clients, and Supervisors.* New York: Routledge.

Lamb, D. H., Catanzaro, S. J., & Moorman, A. S. (2003). Psychologists reflect on their sexual relationships with clients, supervisees and students: Occurrence, impact, rationales, and collegial intervention. *Professional Psychology: Research and Practice, 34*(1), 102–107.

Lambert, M. J., & Arnold, R. C. (1987). Research and the supervisory process. *Professional Psychology, Research and Practice, 18*(3), 217–224.

Lambert, M. J., Hansen, N. B., & Finch, A. E. (2001). Patient-focused research: Using patient outcome data to enhance treatment effects. *Journal of Consulting and Clinical Psychology, 69*, 159–172.

Lambert, M. J., & Ogles, B. M. (1997). The effectiveness of psychotherapy supervision. In C. E. Watkins (Ed.), *Handbook of psychotherapy supervision.* (pp. 421–446). Hoboken, NJ: John Wiley & Sons, Inc.

Lawless, J. J., Gale, J. E., & Bacigalupe, G. (2001). The discourse of race and culture in family therapy supervision: A conversation analysis. *Contemporary Family Therapy, 23*, 181–197.

Lee, R. W., & Cashwell, C. S. (2001). Ethical issues in counseling supervision: A comparison of university and site supervisors. *Clinical Supervisor, 20*(2), 91–100.

Lehrman-Waterman, D., & Ladany, N. (2001). Development and validation of the evaluation process within supervision inventory. *Journal of Counseling Psychology, 48*, 168–177.

Leong, F. T. L., & Kim, H. H. W. (1991). Going beyond cultural sensitivity on the road to multiculturalism: Using the intercultural sensitizer as a counselor training tool. *Journal of Counseling & Development, 70*(1), 112–118.

Littrell, J. M., Lee-Borden, N., & Lorenz, J. A. (1979). A developmental framework for counseling supervision. *Counselor Education and Supervision, 19*, 119–136.

Lower, R. B. (1972). Countertransference resistances in the supervisory situation. *American Journal of Psychiatry, 129*, 156–160.

Luborsky, L., Singer, B., & Luborsky, L. (1975). Comparative studies of psychotherapies: Is it true that "Everyone has won and all must have prizes"? *Archives of General Psychiatry, 32*, 995–1008.

Magnuson, S., Black, L. L., Norem, K. (2004). Supervising school counselors and interns: Resources for site supervisors. *Journal of Professional Counseling, Practice, Theory, & Research, 32*(2), 4–15.

Magnuson, S., Wilcoxon, S. A., & Norem, K. (2000). A profile of lousy supervision: Experienced counselors' perspectives. *Counselor Education and Supervision, 39*(3), 189–202.

Mahrer, A. R. (2008). Supervision and training of experiential psychotherapists. In A. K. Hess, K. D. Hess, T. H. Hess, A. K. Hess, K. D. Hess, T. H. Hess (Eds.), *Psychotherapy supervision: Theory, research, and practice* (2nd ed., 137–156). Hoboken, NJ: John Wiley & Sons Inc. Retrieved from EBSCOhost.

McDonald, P. A., & Haney, H. (1988). *Counseling the older adult: A training manual in clinical gerontology* (2nd ed.). Lexington, MA: Lexington Books.

McIlvried, J., & Bent, R. (2003). *Core competencies: Current and future perspectives.* Paper presented at the annual midwinter conference of the National Council of Schools and Programs of Professional Psychology, Scottsdale, AZ.

McNeill, B. W., Stoltenberg, C. D., & Pierce, R. A. (1985). Supervisees' perceptions of their development: A test of the counselor complexity model. *Journal of counseling psychology, 32*(4), 630–633.

McNeill, B. W., & Worthen, V. (1989). The parallel process in psychotherapy supervision. *Professional Psychology: Research and Practice, 20*, 329–333.

McRoy, R. G., Freeman, E. M., & Logan, S. (1986). Strategies for teaching students about termination. *Clinical Supervisor, 4*, 45–56.

Mehr, K. E., Ladany, N., & Caskie, G. I. L. (2010). Trainee nondisclosure in supervision. *Counselling and Psychotherapy Research, 10*, 103–113.

Meier, S. T. (1993). Revitalizing the measurement curriculum: Four approaches for emphasis in graduate education. *American Psychologist, 48*, 886–891.

Metcalf, L. M. (2003). Countertransference among play therapists: Implications for the therapist development and supervision. *The Association for Play Therapy, 12*(2), 31–48.

Mori, Y., Inman, A. G., & Caskie, G. (2009). Supervising international students: Relationship between acculturation, supervisor multicultural competence, cultural discussions, and supervision satisfaction. *Training and Education in Professional Psychology, 3*, 10–18.

Munson, C. E. (2002). *Handbook of clinical social work supervision.* New York: Haworth Press.

National Board For Certified Counselors. (2005). *Code of ethics.* Greensboro, NC: Author.

Neill, T. K. (2006). *Helping others help children: Clinical supervision of child psychotherapy.* Washington, DC: American Psychological Association.

Nelson, M. L., & Friedlander, M. L. (2001). A close look at conflictual supervisory relationships: The trainee's perspective. *Journal of Counseling Psychology, 48*, 384–395.

Nelson, M. L., & Holloway, E. L. (1990). Relation of gender to power and involvement in supervision. *Journal of Counseling Psychology, 37*, 473–481.

Nerdrum, P., & Rønnestad, M. H. (2002). The trainees' perspective: A qualitative study of learning empathic communication in Norway. *The Counseling Psychologist, 30*, 609–629.

Neufeldt, S. A. (1999). *Supervision strategies for the first practicum* (2nd ed.). Alexandria, VA: American Counseling Association.

Newman, P. A., Bogo, M., & Daley, A. (2008). Self-disclosure of sexual orientation in social work field education: Field instructor and lesbian and gay student perspectives. *The Clinical Supervisor, 27*(2), 215–237. doi:10.1080/07325220802487881.

Nilsson, J. E., & Anderson, M. Z. (2004). Supervising international students: The role of acculturation, role ambiguity, and multicultural discussions. *Professional Psychology: Research and Practice, 35*, 306–312.

O'Connor, B. P. (2000). Reasons for less than ideal psychotherapy supervision. *The Clinical Supervisor, 19*(2), 173–183. doi:10.1300/J001v19n02_10.

Orlinsky, D. E., & Ronnestad, M. H. (2005). *How psychotherapists develop: A study of therapeutic work and professional growth.* Washington, DC: American Psychological Association.

Overholser, J. C. (2004). The four pillars of psychotherapy supervision. *Clinical Supervisor, 23,* 1–13.

Peake, T. H., Nussbaum, B. D., & Tindell, S. D. (2002). Clinical and counseling supervision references: Trends and needs. *Psychotherapy: Theory, Research, Practice, Training, 39,* 114–125.

Pedersen, P. (1994). Simulating the client's internal dialogue as a counselor training technique. *Simulation & Gaming, 25*(1), 40–50.

Pederson, P. B. (1991). Multiculturalism as a fourth force in counseling. *Journal of Counseling & Development, Special Issue.*

Pederson, P. B. (1999). *Multiculturalism as a fourth force in counseling.* Philadelphia: Brunner/Mazel.

Petty, M. M., & Odewahn, C. A. (1983). Supervisory behavior and sex role stereotypes in human service organizations. *The Clinical Supervisor, 1,* 13–20.

Pisani, A. (2005). Talk to Me: Supervisee disclosure in supervision. *Smith College Studies in Social Work, 75*(1), 29–47.

Ponterotto, J. G., Gretchen, D., Utsey, S. O., Rieger, B. P., & Austin, R. (2002). A revision of the Multicultural Counseling Awareness Scale. *Journal of Multicultural Counseling & Development, 30*(3), 153–181.

Ponterotto, J. G., Rieger, B. P., Barrett, A., Harris, G., Sparks, R., Sanchez, C. M., & Magids, D. (1996). Development and initial validation of the Multicultural Counseling Awareness Scale. In G. R. Sodowsky, & J. C. Impara (Eds.), *Multicultural assessment in counseling and clinical psychology* (pp. 247–282). Lincoln, NE: Buros Institute of Mental Measurements.

Pope, K. S., Levenson, H., Schover, L. R. (1979). Sexual intimacy in psychology training: Results and implications of a national survey. *The American Psychologist, 34*(8), 682–289.

Pope, K. S., Sonne, J. L., & Holroyd, J. (1993). *Sexual feelings in psychotherapy: Explorations for therapists and therapists-in-training.* Washington, DC: American Psychological Association.

Pope, S., Keith-Spiegel, P., & Tabachnick, B. (1986). Sexual attraction to clients: The human therapist and the (sometimes) inhuman training system. *American Psychologist, 41,* 147–158.

Powell, D. J., & Brodsky, A. (2004). *Clinical supervision in alcohol and drug abuse counseling: Principles, models, methods* (Rev. ed.). San Francisco: Jossey-Bass.

Putne, M. W., Worthington, E. L., & McCullough, M. E. (1992). Effects of supervisor and supervisee theoretical orientation and supervisor-supervisee matching on interns' perceptions supervision. *Journal of Counseling Psychology, 39,* 258–265.

Raichelson, S. H., Herron, W. G., Primavera, L. H., & Ramirez, S. M. (1997). Incidence and effects of parallel process in psychotherapy supervision. *Clinical Supervisor, 15,* 37–48.

Ramos-Sanchez, L., Esnil, E., Goodwin, A., Riggs, S., Touster, L. O., Wright, L. K., et al. (2002). Negative supervisory events: Effects on supervision satisfaction and supervisory alliance. *Professional Psychology: Research and Practice, 33*(2), 197–202.

Richardson, T. Q., & Molinaro, K. L. (1996). White counselor self-awareness: A prerequisite for multicultural competence. *Journal of Counseling & Development, 74,* 238–242.

Riggs, S., & Bretz, K. (2006). Attachment processes in the supervisory relationship: An exploratory investigation. *Professional Psychology: Research and Practice, 37,* 558–566.

Robiner, W., Fuhrman, M., & Ristvedt, S. (1993). Evaluation difficulties in supervising psychology interns. *The Clinical Psychologist, 46,* 3–13.

Robiner, W. N., & Schofield, W. (1990). References on supervision in clinical and counseling psychology. *Professional Psychology: Research and Practice, 21*(4), 297–312.

Robyak, J. E., Goodyear, R. K., & Prange, M. (1987). Effects of supervisors' sex, focus, and experience on preferences for interpersonal power bases. *Counselor Education and Supervision, 26,* 299–309.

Rodolfa, E., Bent, R., Eisman, E., Nelson, P., Rehm, L., & Ritchi, P. (2005). A cube model for competency development: Implications for psychology educators and regulators. *Professional Psychology: Research and Practice, 36,* 347–354.

Rodolfa, E., Hall, T., Holms, V., Davena, A., Komatz, D., Antunez, M., & Hall, A. (1994). The management of sexual feelings in therapy. *Professional Psychology: Research and Practice, 25,* 168–172.

Rogers, C. R. (1957). The necessary and sufficient conditions of therapeutic personality change. *Journal of Consulting Psychology, 21,* 95–103.

Rosenzweig, S. (1936). Some implicit common factors in diverse methods of psychotherapy. *American Journal of Orthopsychiatry, 6,* 412–415.

Schacht, A. J., Howe, H. E., & Berman, J. J. (1989). Supervisor facilitative conditions and effectiveness as perceived by thinking- and feeling-type supervisees. *Psychotherapy: Theory, Research, Practice, Trainin, 26,* 475–483.

Schiavone, C. D., & Jessell, J. C. (1988). Influence of attributed expertness and gender in counselor supervision. *Counselor Education and Supervision, 28,* 29–42.

Searles, H. F. (1955). The informational value of the supervisor's emotional experiences. *Psychiatry, 18*(2), 135–146.

Sells, J. N., Goodyear, R. K., Lichtenberg, J. W., & Polkinghorne, D. E. (1997). Relationship of supervisor and trainee gender to in-session verbal behavior and ratings of trainee skills. *Journal of Counseling Psychology, 44,* 406–412.

Sherry, A., Whilde, M. R., & Patton, J. (2005). Gay, lesbian, and bisexual training competencies in American Psychological Association accredited graduate programs. *Psychotherapy: Theory, Research, Practice, Training, 42,* 116–120.

Smith, M., Glass, G., & Miller, T. (1980). *The benefits of psychotherapy.* Baltimore: Johns Hopkins.

Sobell, L., Manor, H. L., Sobell, M. B., & Dum, M. (2008). Self-critiques of audiotaped therapy sessions: A motivational procedure for facilitating feedback during supervision. *Training and Education in Professional Psychology, 2*(3), 151–155. doi:10.1037/1931-3918.2.3.151.

Sodowsky, G. R., Kwan, K. L. K., & Pannu, R. (1995). Ethnic identity of Asians in the United States. In J. G. Ponterotto, J. M. Casas, L. A. Suzuki, & C. M. Alexander (Eds.), *Handbook of multicultural counseling* (pp. 123 154). Thousand Oaks, CA: Sage.

Sodowsky, G. R., Taffe, R. C., Gutkin, T., & Wise, S. L. (1994). Development of the Multicultural Counseling Inventory: A self-report measure of multicultural competencies. *Journal of Counseling Psychology, 41,* 137–148.

Stenack, R. J., & Dye, H. A. (1983). Practicum supervision roles: Effects on supervisee statements. *Counselor Education and Supervision, 23*, 157–168.

Stevens, D. T., Goodyear, R. K., & Robertson, P. (1997). Supervisor development: An exploratory study in changes in stance and emphasis. *Clinical Supervisor, 16*, 73–88.

Stigall, T., Bourg, E., Bricklin, P., Kovacs, A., Larsen, K., Lorion, R., et al. (1990). *Report of the Joint Council on Professional Education in Psychology*. Baton Rouge, LA: Land and Land Printers.

Stiles, W. B. (1979). Verbal response modes and psychotherapeutic technique. *Psychiatry, 42*, 49–62.

Stiles, W. B. (1986). Development of a taxonomy of verbal response modes. In W. M. Pinsof (Ed.), *The psychotherapeutic process: A research handbook* (pp. 161–199). New York: The Guilford Press.

Stoltenberg, C. D., McNeill, B., & Delworth, U. (1998). *IDM supervision: An integrated developmental model for supervising counselors and therapists*. San Francisco: Jossey-Bass.

Stratton, J. S., & Smith, R. D. (2006). Supervision of couples cases. *Psychotherapy: Theory, Research, Practice, Training, 43*, 337–348.

Strean, H. S. (2000). Resolving therapeutic impasses by using the supervisor's countertransference. *Clinical Social Work Journal, 28*(3), 263–279.

Stutts, M. L. (1991). Supervision in comprehensive rehabilitation settings: The terrain and the traveler. In T. H. Peake, & J. D. Ball (Eds.), *Psychotherapy training* (pp. 115–134). London: Haworth Press.

Sue, D. W., & Sue, D. (2003). *Counseling the culturally diverse: Theory and practice* (4th ed.). New York: Wiley.

Szymanski, D. M. (2005). Feminist identity and theories as correlates of feminist supervision practices. *The Counseling Psychologist, 33*, 739–747.

Tedesco, J. F. (1982). Premature termination of psychology interns. *Professional Psychology: Research and Practice, 13*, 695–698.

Teitelbaum, S. H. (1990). The impact of psychoanalytic supervision on the development of professional identity: Introduction. *Psychoanalysis & Psychotherapy Special Issue: The supervision of the psychoanalytic process, 8*, 3–4.

Townend, M., Iannetta, L., & Freeston, M. H. (2002). Clinical supervision in practice: A survey of UK cognitive behavioural psychotherapists accredited by the BABCP. *Behavioural and Cognitive Psychotherapy, 30*(4), 485–500.

Utsey, S. O., Hammar, L., & Gernat, C. A. (2005). Examining the reactions of White, Black, and Latino/a counseling psychologists to a study of racial issues in counseling and supervision dyads. *The Counseling Psychologist, 33*, 565–573.

Vander Kolk, C. J. (1974). The relationship of personality, values, and race to anticipation of the supervisory relationship. *Rehabilitation, 18*, 41–46.

Vidlak, N. W. (January 1, 2002). *Identifying important factors in supervisor development: An examination of supervisor experience, training, and attributes*. ETD collection for University of Nebraska - Lincoln. Paper AAI3055295. Retrieved from http://digitalcommons.unl.edu/dissertations/AAI3055295.

Waehler, C. A., Kalodner, C. R., Wampold, B. E., & Lichtenberg, J. W. (2000). Empirically supported treatments (ESTs) in perspective. *The Counseling Psychologist, 28*(5), 657–671.

Walker, J., Ladany, N., & Pate-Carolan, L. (2007). Gender-related events in psychotherapy supervision: Female trainee perspectives. *Counselling and Psychotherapy Research, 7*, 12–18.

Wallace, E., & Alonso, A. (1994). *Clinical Perspectives on psychotherapy supervision*. Arlington, VA: American Psychiatric Publishing.

Wampold, B. E. (2001). *The great psychotherapy debate: Models, methods, and findings*. Mahwah, NJ: Lawrence Erlbaum Associates.

Wampold, B. E., Lichtenberg, J. W., & Waehler, C. A. (2002). Principles of empirically supported interventions in counseling psychology. *Counseling Psychologist, 30*(2), 197–217.

Wampold, B. E., Mondin, G. W., Moody, M., Stich, F., Benson, K., & Ahn, H. (1997). A meta-analysis of outcome studies comparing bona fide psychotherapies: Empirically, "all must have prizes." *Psychological Bulletin, 122*, 203–225.

Ward, C. C., & House, R. M. (1998). Counseling supervision: A reflective model. *Counselor Education and Supervision, 38*, 23–33.

Watkins, C. E., Jr. (1993). Development of the psychotherapy supervisor: Concepts, assumptions, and hypotheses of the supervisor complexity model. *American Journal of Psychotherapy, 47*(1), 58–74.

Watkins, C. E., Jr. (1995). Researching psychotherapy supervisor development: Four key considerations. *The Clinical Supervisor, 13*(2), 111–118.

Westefeld, J. S. (2009). Supervision of psychotherapy: Models, issues, and recommendations. *The Counseling Psychologist, 37*(2), 296–316. doi:10.1177/0011000008316657

Measurement and Assessment
in Counseling Psychology

Jane L. Swanson

Abstract

In this chapter, I present two broad topics: psychological measurement, or the process of assigning numbers to observations to quantify important characteristics of individuals, and the use of testing and assessment within counseling psychology. The first half of the chapter describes principles of measurement, including methods of scale and test development and evaluating the psychometric characteristics of tests (reliability and validity). The second half focuses on the use of testing and assessment, including models of assessment within counseling psychology, various types of commonly used assessment tools, computer-assisted and Internet-based assessment, gender and diversity issues, considerations in the selection and use of assessment in counseling, and professional and ethical issues.

Keywords: assessment, testing, validity, reliability, individual differences

The psychological test was the invention that revolutionized psychological science, comparable in its impact to the telescope in physics and the microscope in biology. It opened up a new world for psychology to explore. . . . [It] is the technological innovation from psychology that has had the greatest effect on society.

—Dawis, 1992, p. 10

The principles of measurement and assessment provide the bedrock on which scientific and applied psychology has been built. From the standpoint of theory and research, measuring constructs is fundamental to understanding the laws governing human behavior, whether one is interested in social relationships, career development, or cognitive growth and decline. From the standpoint of applied psychology, measuring the important characteristics of an individual aids in diagnosis and treatment. Measurement and assessment allow us to compare individuals to one another, to communicate important information to and about others, and to make decisions about individuals on the basis of objective rather than subjective information.

The purpose of this chapter is to present a broad overview of the interconnected topics of *measurement, testing* and *assessment,* beginning with the philosophical foundation of the study of *individual differences.* The subsequent section of the chapter consists of a discussion of key principles of psychological measurement, followed by a consideration of the practice of testing and assessment in counseling psychology.

The Individual Differences Tradition in Psychology

The study of individual differences emerged in psychology at the end of the 19th century through the influences of Charles Darwin, who focused on differences among individuals within a species as the basis for natural selection and evolution, and Francis Galton, who developed ways to quantify differences among individuals. In response to a practical problem that needed a solution, Alfred Binet applied the study of individual differences to the development of the first successful psychological test that would become the prototype for all later psychological tests (Dawis, 1992).

The psychology of individual differences continued to develop early in the 20th century, particularly as the field of applied psychology gained ground. The two growing specialties within American applied psychology—educational psychology and industrial psychology—were focused on the study of individual differences at school and at work (Dawis, 1992), and many of the proponents of individual differences methods and analyses were aligned with these fields.

A primary purpose of the study of individual differences is to describe, in quantitative ways, how individuals and groups vary on important psychological attributes. This quantitative description is addressed by the field of *psychometrics* or psychological measurement. A second purpose of the study of individual differences is to examine factors that are related to these differences, their antecedents or causes, and their outcomes or consequences; this purpose is reflected in much of the research conducted within counseling psychology.

The study of individual differences in the 20th century led to focused attention on psychological measurement, or psychometric theory and principles. The concept of *co-relation*, as proposed by Galton and refined by Pearson into the contemporary *correlation coefficient*, provided the method of quantifying the association between two separate variables and thus offered a significant advance in the study of individual differences. The correlation coefficient became central to the development of psychological tests (Dawis, 1992). These methods and their philosophical underpinnings led to what Cronbach (1957) called the "two disciplines" of scientific psychology—the correlational and experimental approaches to the study of human behavior—which treat variation among individuals in fundamentally different ways: Experimental psychology focused on minimizing individual differences, treating them as error in an otherwise carefully controlled experimental treatment, whereas correlational psychology focused on describing and predicting such individual differences. Measurement theory and assessment practice both developed to describe individual differences and to use them to predict other behavior and to make decisions about individuals.

The individual differences tradition has been particularly influential in the history of counseling psychology as a professional specialty. First and foremost is that it offered a "technology for client assessment" (Dawis, 1992, p. 11), which was intertwined with the early development of vocational guidance and counseling through the mechanism of assessing interests, abilities, and personality, as well as the characteristics of occupations (Dawis, 1992; Hansen, 2005; Parsons, 1909). Dawis (1992) described the influence of the "individual differences point of view in assessment," which included an emphasis on quantitative assessment of individuals, along multiple dimensions, stated in relative (vs. absolute) and actuarial (likelihood) terms.

Psychological Measurement, Psychological Testing, and Psychological Assessment

What are the connections between testing, assessment, and measurement? Because these terms are overlapping, and sometimes used interchangeably, it is useful to begin with a definition of each. As just described, all three of these terms and activities are related to the study of individual differences. *Measurement* is at the root of it all, as the field of psychometrics provides the principles that guide the development of specific tests and assessment procedures, as well as provides the framework for evaluating the quality of information obtained about individuals and the purposes to which the information will be put.

Briefly, *assessment* is "a broad array of evaluative procedures that yield information about a person," with testing as a subset or as one component of assessment activities, using a standardized measurement instrument that yields scores based on the structured gathering of data (Neukrug & Fawcett, 2006, p. 3). *Testing*, in and of itself, entails "little or no continuing relationship or legally defined responsibility between examinee and examiner" (Matarazzo, 1990, p. 1000). Assessment, on the other hand, involves a one-to-one clinician–client relationship, "an activity by which the clinician integrates test findings with information from the personal, educational, and occupational histories as well as from the findings of other clinicians" (Matarazzo, 1990, p. 1011).

For the purpose of the present chapter, the term *test* is used when referring to a specific instrument or class of instruments, and *assessment* is used when referring to the broader endeavor. Tests (and, more broadly, assessments) are used in many different settings and for many different purposes. Tests are used in educational settings, to make decisions about instruction and grading, admissions and placement, counseling and guidance, curriculum, and educational policy. They are used in organizational settings, for pre-employment screening, selection and placement decisions, and performance appraisal, and in legal and forensic settings, to provide information for decisions such as mental competency or child custody. Tests also are used in clinical and counseling settings, to gather information related to diagnosis, to plan therapeutic interventions, and to measure therapeutic change. All of these purposes represent the use of testing to solve a wide range of practical problems, a reflection of the history and evolution of testing in general (Anastasi & Urbina, 1997; McIntire & Miller, 2007). To be useful in solving problems, however, any test must meet psychometric standards, and test users must understand the principles of psychological measurement.

Fundamental Principles of Psychological Measurement
Definition and Purpose of Measurement
Measurement is a set of "rules for assigning symbols to objects" (Nunnally & Bernstein, 1994, p. 3), or "the process of assigning numbers according to certain agreed-upon rules" (Walsh & Betz, 2001, p. 15). These "rules" imply that there is an explicit procedure for assigning numbers that can be consistently applied to different individuals, and by different individuals. In some cases, these rules are quite evident, such as the process of using a tape measure to quantify a person's height, whereas in other cases, the rules are not at all obvious, such as how to quantify a person's self-esteem or level of multicultural competence. Most of what is measured in counseling psychology falls into the latter category, and so it is particularly crucial to understand principles of psychological measurement.

Measurement has been called "*the* major problem in psychology" because it is not possible to test a theory unless its components can be adequately measured. Furthermore, psychology as a science "can progress no faster than the measurement of its key variables" (Nunnally & Bernstein, 1994, p. 6).

What are we attempting to measure? In counseling psychology (as in most areas of psychology), we are typically interested in attributes or characteristics of individuals that are not directly observable, such as self-esteem, depression, psychopathology, multicultural competence, or work values. We act as if these are tangible features of an individual, similar to their height, weight, eye color—but these attributes are *hypothetical constructs*, something that we believe to exist but which we cannot directly see. Measurement thus becomes a process of assigning numbers to individuals by devising ways of inferring the unobservable construct through a series of careful and systematic observations of an individual's behavior.

Why is it important to assign numbers to observations about an individual? Measurement procedures are used for many purposes, including the research and theory building activities that lead to scientific advances (Nunnally & Bernstein, 1994). For the purpose of this chapter, though, the focus is on those aspects of measurement that lead to standardized testing and assessment, which in turn lead to therapeutic interventions and client change. In this context, quantifying characteristics of individuals allows a comparison of individuals to one another and to a standard or benchmark, but this serves an intermediate goal. The ultimate goal is typically to choose a treatment, to measure change, to assist clients in some way. But none of these intermediate or ultimate goals is achievable without accurate measurement—without assigning numbers in a way that is precise and standardized.

All efforts to measure something must begin by carefully defining the construct of interest. For example, what, specifically, do we mean by self-esteem? How does this definition overlap with other constructs, such as self-efficacy or self-confidence? In defining a construct, it is important to be precise, narrow, and parsimonious in definition. Note that this definition is at the hypothetical or theoretical (that is, unobservable) level. In a classic paper, Cronbach and Meehl (1955) defined a *construct* as "some postulated attribute of people, assumed to be reflected in test performance" (p. 283). This construct occurs within a *nomological network*, "the interlocking system of laws which constitute a theory" (p. 290). Laws within a nomological network "may relate (a) observable properties or quantities to each other; or (b) theoretical constructs to observables; or (c) different theoretical constructs to one another" (p. 290). For a construct to be "scientifically admissible," it must be located within a nomological network with at least some components that have defined "observables," some evidence of the hypothetical construct.

The next step in measurement is to determine how to *operationalize* the construct—how to translate from the hypothetical to the observable. For example, given a well-articulated definition of self-esteem, how would we infer an individual's level of self-esteem? In psychology, these "observables" are some samples of behavior. Items on a test serve as samples of behavior, and thus are a way to operationalize the construct in question. These observations, an individual's response to items, then need to be converted into numbers and combined into scales.

The purpose of assigning numbers to observations is to infer some *quantity* of an attribute, or to determine whether individuals fall into the same or different *categories* in terms of some attribute (Nunnally & Bernstein, 1994). The characteristics and rules of these numbers (or scales) themselves vary, and are classified as four *levels of measurement* (Stevens, 1951, cited in Nunnally & Bernstein, 1994): nominal, ordinal, interval, or ratio. Each successive type allows greater flexibility in what may be done with the numbers and the conclusions that may be reached.

Nominal scales are the most basic, in which numbers are used to classify, name, or identify individuals by groups to which they belong (Walsh & Betz, 2001); a nominal scale contains rules for deciding whether two individuals are equivalent or not equivalent (Nunnally & Bernstein, 1994) in terms of sharing a critical property, for example, they are both female. The numbers serve as labels, do not have meaning in and of themselves, do not imply an order, and no mathematical operations (that is, addition, subtraction, multiplication, or division) may be applied. Other examples are numbers assigned to runners in a marathon, telephone numbers, or social security numbers: A runner with #23 does not possess less of a characteristic than a runner with #40, and adding phone numbers together would not yield any useful information. Categorizing individuals via nominal scales may lead to useful conclusions, but the numbers used to represent group members are essentially irrelevant to such a conclusion. For example, researchers may assign a numerical value to racial/ethnic group membership during the coding phase of data entry, but those numbers may be used only for description via frequency distributions; using them to compute an average is not meaningful (and could be misleading).

With *ordinal* scales, numbers are assigned to indicate rank or order from highest to lowest; an ordinal scale contains rules for deciding whether one individual is greater than or less than another individual on some characteristic. Ordinal scales thus reflect the property of magnitude or "moreness" (Kaplan & Saccuzzo, 2009), but not how much of that characteristic the individual possesses nor how much the two individuals differ in terms of the characteristic. For example, the first-place medal awarded to the winner of a swim meet does not provide any information about the differences among participants, simply that this particular individual had a faster time than the second-place finisher. Other examples include a student's rank within her graduating class, or a client's three-letter code on the Self-Directed Search. Some statistical tools have been developed to use with rank-order scores, but one cannot perform any other mathematical operation on them, such as adding or subtracting. The numbers in ordinal scales thus represent meaning (as compared to nominal scales); however, the number assigned to an individual may not reflect much about the measured attribute itself, but rather only the relative standing of the individual compared to other individuals—or the relative standing of a specific characteristic of that individual compared to other characteristics of that same individual. As such, the numbers need to be interpreted carefully. For example, knowing that a student is ranked fourth in her class does not say how well she performed in absolute terms, just how well she performed relative to her classmates. Likewise, knowing that a client's score on the work value of "security" is higher than his score on the value of "income" does not reveal information about the absolute value of either of these constructs.

Interval scales define a specific unit of measurement, and presume that the distances between numerical points are equal; for example, the difference between 20° and 30° Fahrenheit is the same as the difference between 50° and 60° Fahrenheit. In addition to knowing the rank order of individuals (evident with ordinal scales), interval scales permit addition and subtraction, and therefore it is possible to perform linear transformations. The mathematical operation of division is not allowed because it requires an exact known zero point, which cannot be assumed about interval-level scales. We cannot say that 60°F is "twice as warm" as 30°F because there is no exact zero point (even though there is an assigned zero point on the Fahrenheit temperature scale). Because it is possible to add or subtract interval scale numbers, it is also permissible to compute means, standard deviations, and correlation coefficients, thus allowing a description of distributions of numbers such as test scores. It is also possible to translate raw scores into different kinds of derived scores through linear transformations. Numbers in interval scales thus allow far greater interpretation than nominal or ordinal scales. For example, interval scale numbers may be transformed into T scores (i.e., scores that have been converted, so that the distribution has a mean of 50 and standard deviation of 10), so that they are more readily interpreted by test users. Likewise, means and standard deviations may be obtained from interval-level data, providing useful summary information about scale or sample distributions. Furthermore, a wide range of statistical analysis techniques may be applied to interval-level scales.

Finally, *ratio* scales also assume equal intervals between numbers, but with the additional property of having an exact zero point, a "rational" or true zero rather than an arbitrary one, which reflects a true absence of the characteristic (Nunnally & Bernstein, 1994). Numbers derived on a ratio scale permit use of all mathematical operations, including multiplication and division, and so it is possible to express relative numbers as ratios. Examples are height, weight, and volume: An individual who weighs 200 pounds is twice as heavy as one who weighs 100 pounds. Few psychological measurements qualify as ratio-level scales; those that do are expressed in physical units, such as galvanic skin response, electroencephalogram tracings, or response time (Walsh & Betz, 2001). However, Nunnally and Bernstein (1994) advised that ratio scales are "rarely needed to address the most common needs of scaling . . . defining an interval is very important, but ordering is the most crucial concept" (Nunnally & Bernstein, 1994, p. 18).

To summarize, consider the way in which numbers are used in a horse race. Multiple numbers might be used with any specific horse: A number is assigned to the horse to distinguish it from other horses (nominal), the horse finishes the race in a specific place relative to other horses (ordinal), and the track posts the elapsed time in the race (ratio): Horse #7 may be in second place with a time of 3 minutes and 25 seconds, representing three different uses of numbers. Level of measurement is crucial to understand because the level determines which mathematical operations are permissible to apply to the resultant numbers, and therefore, ultimately what can be done to the numbers to make them useful to the consumer of assessment results (clients, counselors, researchers).

Test Construction

Development of a psychological test involves applying the principles of measurement to a specific task. Test construction, when done well and thoroughly, is a complex process with a number of iterative steps (Dawis, 1987; Walsh & Betz, 2001). Briefly, the starting point is to define the construct

of interest. Then, a large pool of potential items is developed that encompasses the full range of the defined construct, and this initial pool of items is administered to a large sample, the "development sample." Next, the original item pool is refined through factor analysis, expert judgment, item analysis, and other considerations, and the revised measure is administered to a new sample; this step may be repeated to further refine the focus of the test. The final step is to look for evidence of reliability and validity, and develop norms. These steps, simplified here, can be very time consuming, and frequently measures that are developed for a particular research purpose (vs. as a published test) entail abbreviated development and testing of the initial item pool, and do not carry out the final step related to reliability, validity, and normative information. A commercially available published test, however, will include the information outlined in these steps.

METHODS OF CONSTRUCTING PSYCHOLOGICAL TESTS

There are three primary methods of developing psychological tests: rational/theoretical, empirical, and factor-analytic. The *rational* or *theoretical* approach assumes that item content directly reflects the construct being measured, and so each item shows a logical relationship to the construct. The process of test development thus evolves in a "rational" or logical manner: The construct is clearly and thoroughly defined, the test developer writes items that directly reflect the construct, item analysis is used to hone the measure, and, as a result, the scores are directly interpretable—the name of the scale has led to the content of the items and thus guides interpretation of an individual's score (Walsh & Betz, 2001).

The *empirical* approach to test construction uses a different starting point, a defined criterion group (this approach is also called the *external criterion* method; Dawis, 1987). Items are chosen for a measure based on their ability to differentiate among groups of people that are hypothesized or shown to differ on the characteristic of interest; in other words, the item's ability to predict membership in the criterion group. The actual content of the item plays a lesser (or no) role. Two examples are the Minnesota Multiphasic Personality Inventory (MMPI-2) and the Occupational Scales of the Strong Interest Inventory, both of which rely on contrast groups to select items for scales. For example, the Architect scale on the Strong was developed by identifying a sample of architects, administering a set of items to them, comparing their responses to a general reference group, and then selecting the items that show substantial differences between the architects and the general group. These items are then assembled into a scale. Interpretation of empirically derived scales is not as straightforward as rationally derived scales, since the content of the items may have no obvious or logical connection to the construct and are likely to be more heterogeneous. Interpretation of an individual's score is best conceptualized as degree of similarity to the criterion group's responses, rather than as level or amount of the scale's content. Although more difficult to interpret, empirically derived scales can have great practical utility due to their ability to predict important criteria, which is one goal of psychological assessment (Hansen, 1999; Walsh & Betz, 2001).

Factor-analytic scale construction begins with a large pool of items and uses the statistical technique of factor analysis to determine the "best" items to include in the measure. This method is useful in developing a set of scales, each of which is internally consistent and relatively independent from the other scales. Factor analysis is used to identify dimensions underlying a set of data, in this case, items. Items that show the highest loadings on each factor are chosen for a specific scale.

These three primary methods of test construction are not necessarily mutually exclusive, and a combination of methods may be used in the process of developing a psychological test. For example, Jackson (1977, as cited in Hansen, 1999) described the use of a *sequential* method, beginning with a rational/theoretical approach to develop items for his interest inventory, followed by statistical methods to select items and refine scales.

ITEM FORMATS

Items on psychological tests take several different forms. Tests that measure cognitive ability or achievement are most likely to be multiple-choice or true–false items. Most other psychological tests are designed to measure constructs that are attitudes, such as interests, values, or personality. Items could be formatted so that the test taker indicates his or her level of endorsement on a 5-point scale, or chooses his or her most preferred statement from a pair or trio of options, or rank orders a group of statements or words (Dawis, 1987; Walsh & Betz, 2001).

ITEM ANALYSES

Item analysis is a crucial part of the process of developing a test, and is used to identify and select the best items from the initial pool of items or in subsequent revisions, in term of each item's reliability and validity. Two item-analysis indices were developed in the context of achievement tests or other tests with right–wrong answers: item difficulty and item discrimination. An item's *difficulty* refers to the proportion of people who respond correctly (or in a defined direction) to an item, and thus reflects how easy or difficult an item is relative to other available items. Item difficulty is expressed as a proportion, or p value. An item that is answered correctly by only 20% of people ($p = .20$) is considered much more difficult than an item that is answered correctly by 90% of people ($p = .90$). Once item difficulty values are determined, then the test developer may choose items based on varying difficulty, depending on the purpose of the test. Generally, test items are chosen to represent an appropriate level of difficulty for the group to whom it will be given, and to yield a wide distribution of scores, suggesting that items should be chosen across the range of difficulty levels (Walsh & Betz, 2001). If all of the items chosen have high p levels (the items are too easy), then a "ceiling" effect is likely to occur, in which scores will be clustered at the high end of the distribution. Similarly, if all of the items chosen have low p levels (the items are too hard), then a "floor" effect is likely to occur, in which scores will be clustered at the low end of the distribution. In either case, the test will not distinguish among individuals, thus providing little useful information about individual differences.

An item's "difficulty" is most obvious in classroom or achievement tests; however, the concept is also useful to consider in attitude (or other trait) measures that do not have right–wrong answers. In the case of an item with a 5-point Likert-type scale, ranging from "strongly disagree" to "strongly agree," the item's "difficulty" would be the mean score across the sample (e.g., 3.75 on a 5-point scale). Recall that one of the fundamental purposes of measurement is to quantify individual differences to use in decision making and prediction. So, a measure that produces a restricted distribution of scores is less useful than one that produces a wide distribution of scores. For example, if all of the items in a measure of self-esteem are strongly endorsed in one direction by most people, then the resultant measure will not provide any useful information about individuals, and, thus, will not add any new information to what is already known.

The second index computed during item analysis is an item's *discrimination*, defined as the extent to which responses to any individual item are related to the scores on the measure as a whole. If an item is not related to the total score (or, worse, negatively related), then its relationship to the construct being measured is suspect. Item discrimination is related to a test's internal consistency reliability (to be discussed later). An item's discrimination index is typically calculated as the correlation between the item and the total score (the item–total correlation), and the test developer will want to select those items with the highest levels of discrimination.

Test developers also examine interitem correlations, which are related to a test's internal consistency reliability. Each item should be correlated with every other item that is purported to measure the same construct, and so the test developer is particularly alert to negative correlations or low positive correlations. If a measure contains two or more subscales, measuring different constructs, then each item should be correlated with other items on the same subscale, and not correlated with items on other subscales.

The development of item response theory (IRT) has brought new concepts to item analysis, specifically, the use of *item characteristic curves* (ICC) to evaluate the suitability of different items for a test. An ICC is a graph of the probability of answering an item correctly (or in a defined way) given different levels of the underlying trait, thus providing a picture of the item's difficulty and how well it discriminates among people at different trait levels, independent of the specific sample or test used. ICCs are important in adaptive testing, in which test takers are given different sets of items depending on their trait level, thus providing a more efficient and precise way to measure a particular trait. ICCs also can be used to evaluate item (or test) performance for different groups through *differential item functioning* (DIF), and therefore can identify potential bias in test items (Bolt & Rounds, 2000; McIntire & Miller, 2007).

TEST NORMS

Most psychological tests incorporate some type of *norms*, which provide information on which an individual's performance may be compared, or a way of "making meaning out of raw scores" (Neukrug & Fawcett, 2006, p. 65). *Raw scores* are typically a straightforward summing of an individual's responses, whether correct answers (such as in classroom tests or ability measures), "keyed" responses (such as in interest or personality measures), or level of agreement or endorsement (such as in attitude surveys). Raw scores may be useful in some situations, but typically they are converted to a score that provides more information about an individual's standing. Norms thus provide a frame of reference in which to interpret an individual's score, most frequently by comparing an individual's raw score to a reference group of people (Walsh & Betz, 2001).

Norms may be based on characteristics of individuals that change over time in predictable ways (such as age- or grade-related norms) or characteristics that classify individuals (such as sex or occupation). Several features of norms are crucial for the test user to understand. First and foremost is whether the norms on which scores are based are appropriate for the specific individual taking the test; some assessments cannot be scored without demographic information (such as age and sex) about the test taker, so that the appropriate norm group may be applied. Age- or grade-related norms could provide substantially different results if the incorrect norm group is used.

Norms are developed by identifying an appropriate, representative sample of individuals, the *normative* or *standardization sample*. Test developers should include a thorough description of the normative sample in the manual for a published test. The normative sample must be clearly defined, and determined on the basis of appropriateness for the ultimate use of the test. For example, if a test will be used with college students, then the normative sample must be representative of the population of college students for whom the test will be used, in terms of factors such as age, sex, race/ethnicity, class standing, and the context of assessment. Several different normative samples may be necessary to adequately provide the appropriate frame of reference for test takers.

There are several possible ways to convert raw scores to normed scores. Two of the most typical are percentiles and standard scores, both of which rely on the distributions of scores within the normative sample to provide an interpretive framework for individuals' scores. *Percentile scores* refer to how many people in a distribution fall below a specific score. For example, if 65% of people in the normative sample obtained scores below 40, then a score of 40 is considered to be at the 65th percentile. This example demonstrates the utility of norms— although there is no inherent meaning in a score of 40 (what was the range of scores, and how does this score fall within that range?), a percentile score of 65 provides more meaning (the individual's score is in the top 35% of scores). Raw scores are transformed to percentile scores by constructing a frequency distribution of the raw scores in the original normative sample and determining, for each possible raw score, the percentage of individuals who score at or below that point, or the *percentile equivalent*.

Percentiles are not the same as percentages. A percentage is not a normed score, but rather is another way of communicating a raw score; for example, receiving 25 correct on a 50-item achievement test could be expressed as a 50% score. However, that 50% correct could be equivalent to the 75th percentile (on a very difficult test) or a 25th percentile (on a very easy test), or any other percentile score, depending on how other people scored on the same test.

One disadvantage of percentile scores is that they are not interval-level data; in other words, the difference between the 20th and 30th percentile may not be the same as the difference between the 70th and 80th percentile, in terms of the raw scores underlying the percentile distribution. Percentile score differences in the center of the distribution usually reflect small differences in raw scores, whereas percentile score differences at the extreme ends of the distribution usually reflect large differences in raw scores. Although this is usually not a major factor in using percentile scores, it is important to keep in mind.

A second method of raw-score-to-normed-score conversion is via the use of *standard scores*. Standard scores are the most common way of expressing normed scores, and there are actually a few different variations of standard scores. Like percentiles, standard scores also use the raw score distribution within the normative sample to provide an interpretive frame of reference for an individual's score, in this case by expressing an individual's score in terms of its distance from the mean or average of the distribution, using standard deviation units. Converting raw scores to standard scores uses a linear transformation of the form $Y = AX + B$, where A and B are constants based on the distribution of scores in the normative sample. Standard scores reflect the characteristics of the distribution of the normative sample, allow a variety of transformations to suit the user, and can be directly interpreted as distance from the mean of the normative sample.

Calculating a z score is one form of standard score. A raw score is converted to a z score by subtracting it from the mean of the sample distribution, and then dividing by the standard deviation of the sample. In other words, z scores are calculated so that the mean of the distribution equals 0, and scores range from -3.0 to +3.0. Thus, negative z scores are below the mean, and positive z scores are above the mean of the normative sample; a score of +1.0 is exactly 1 standard deviation above the mean, and so z-scores may be directly interpreted in terms of the distance of a score from the mean in standard deviation units.

A disadvantage of z scores is the use of negative numbers, and of non–whole numbers, and so other forms of standard scores are frequently used. For example, T scores are commonly used in measures such as the Strong Interest Inventory and the MMPI. T scores are an extension of z scores, where the mean has been set to 50 and the standard deviation to 10, by multiplying the z score by 10 and adding 50 ($T = 10z + 50$). The resultant scores are more user-friendly to interpret. A general form of this formula can be used to derive any type of standard score: The desired standard deviation is multiplied by the z score and added to the desired mean. For example, consider SAT scores used in college admissions and GRE scores used in graduate school admissions. Both use the formula $100z + 500$ to derive scores, so that the resultant mean is 500 and the standard deviation is 100.

Considering these ways of calculating normed scores highlights the critical nature of the normative sample itself. Yet, too often, test users neglect to thoroughly consider the normative sample underlying clients' test scores. Consider, for example, the different types of conclusions that might result if a high school freshman's achievement test raw score was compared to ninth-grade norms versus twelfth-grade norms. In the former case, her raw score might convert to a 90th percentile score, whereas in the latter case, the same raw score might convert to a 65th percentile equivalent. Similarly, comparing a client's score on an interest inventory to a same-sex rather than a combined-sex norm group may influence the type of career options suggested. As noted earlier, test developers may present multiple scores based on different normative samples (such as same-sex and combined-sex groups), or national, state, or local norms (such as achievement test results).

The discussion of normed scores thus far has focused on the information they convey about an individual's score relative to other people in the norm group. Another advantage of normed scores is that they allow other types of comparisons, within and across individuals. Results can be compared across test-takers who take the same test but receive scores based on different norm groups; for example, two high school students in different grades could be compared using the percentile scores they received on the basis of the grade-appropriate norms. Similarly, an individual could be compared at two different times on the basis of those grade-appropriate norms, such as a student who receives an 80th percentile score in a fifth-grade reading test (using fifth-grade norms), and a 30th percentile score in sixth grade (using sixth-grade norms). Another useful comparison would be two scores for one person at a single point in time, such as comparing the percentile scores for two subscales of the ACT score to determine relative strengths across content areas.

In addition to norm-referenced test scores, which compare an individual's performance or standing to a defined group of individuals, some tests are considered *criterion-referenced* tests. In contrast to norm-referenced scores, criterion-referenced test scores compare an individual's performance to a predefined level or standard. Examples are the test used for licensure as a psychologist (the Examination for Professional Practice in Psychology, EPPP), and school-based testing under the No Child Left Behind legislation. In each case, an individual receives a score, but the ultimate outcome is that he or she either passes or fails, either meets or does not meet the standard.

Psychometric Characteristics of Psychological Tests

An assessment instrument is only as good as its psychometric characteristics, most notably, its reliability and validity, and development of a test should include plans to provide reliability and validity evidence. *Reliability* refers to the dependability of measurement: Will a test-taker get the same results across different forms and different times? *Validity* refers to the utility of assessment, whether the test is truly measuring what it claims to measure. A bathroom scale is reliable if it yields the same weight when an individual steps on it five times in a row; it is valid if the number displayed corresponds to one's actual weight. The point of using a bathroom scale is to determine one's weight at any given time, to compare weights of two family members, or to monitor changes in one's weight over time. If the number displayed fluctuates (within a short time interval), or if it does not correspond to "true" weight, then the scale loses its utility: It cannot be trusted to produce a meaningful number to use for the defined purpose of the scale. Similarly, if an instrument is designed to produce an assessment of

a psychological characteristic, such as depression, then random fluctuation in the results, or, worse yet, no connection between the results and "true" depression, render the instrument unusable. Unfortunately, however, determining the utility of an assessment instrument is more difficult than determining the utility of a bathroom scale: Psychological constructs, unlike physical ones, are not visible nor tangible. How do we determine the presence of depression?

MEASUREMENT THEORY

Many of the principles of measurement rely on *classical test theory*, but more recent developments in measurement, particularly IRT, have influenced the way that tests are developed and evaluated (Bolt & Rounds, 2000; Embretson, 1996). Two other theories, domain sampling theory and generalizability theory, also contribute to an understanding of a test's reliability and validity.

Classical Test Theory

Estimating reliability relies on *classical test score theory*, which describes what occurs when we attempt to measure something unobservable. Essentially, we assume that each person has a "true score" on the attribute in question, which is inferred from the score obtained on a relevant measure—or an individual's "observed score." Any imperfection in the measuring procedures leads to a discrepancy between a person's observed and true scores, referred to as *measurement error*. Classical test theory denotes this relationship as $X = T + E$, where an individual's observed score (X) is the sum of his or her true score (T) plus measurement error (E). Thus, every observed score consists of two components, true score and error. Error is assumed to be random, an assumption that is important to methods of estimating reliability. If error is indeed random, then the accumulation of repeated measures should converge on the true score. An individual's true score will not change with repeated measurements, whereas the random errors of measurement will vary.

Item Response Theory

In contrast to classical test theory, IRT focuses on the interaction between the individuals and test items, modeling people and items on the same underlying or latent trait. The original applications of IRT were related to the latent trait of ability, but now IRT models have been extended to include personality and attitudes.

A major advantage of IRT models is *computer-adaptive testing*, in which a provisional score can be calculated after each item, and the next item to be administered is chosen from all remaining items so that it provides the most information about the test taker. The degree of precision also can be determined after each item. This method of administering test items is considerably more efficient in most cases, since test takers are not taking items that provide little information (i.e., are too easy or too difficult). Many achievement and aptitude tests are now based on IRT models, including the Graduate Record Exam (GRE), Law School Admissions Test (LSAT), and the SAT (Bolt & Rounds, 2000; Tinsley, 2000).

Domain Sampling Theory
In developing a test of a particular construct, it is useful to think of a hypothetical universe or domain of possible test items for that construct, from which a random sample will be chosen for the test. This is the premise of *domain sampling theory*, and true score is conceptualized as the result if the entire domain of items could be administered (Nunnally & Bernstein, 1994). A contribution of domain sampling theory is the idea that the larger the sample of items selected for the test, the more likely that test will represent the underlying true characteristic, so that reliability increases as length of test increases.

Generalizability Theory
An extension of classical test theory, generalizability theory analyzes multiple sources of error and allows an evaluation of random sampling error and systematic error. Generalizability theory is useful in situations in which multiple judges evaluate a number of individuals on multiple dimensions (Bolt & Rounds, 2000; Hoyt & Melby, 1999; Nunnally & Bernstein, 1994).

TEST RELIABILITY
Reliability is defined as "the degree to which test scores are free from errors of measurement" (American Educational Research Association, American Psychological Association, National Council on Measurement in Education [AERA, APA, NCME], 1999, p. 180), or the "consistency or dependability of the measurement tool" (Bolt & Rounds, 2000, p. 156). Since all psychological measurement includes error—the discrepancy between the measurement and the "true" score—then determining the accuracy of a measure involves estimating how much error exists. Because reliability is such an important attribute of an assessment instrument, test developers should conduct studies related to reliability as they devise new inventories, and test publishers should clearly report reliability for test consumers to evaluate.

Error is inevitable from a number of different sources, and the objective in developing a reliable test is to minimize the impact of error on test scores (Walsh & Betz, 2001). Error includes effects due to (1) *time*, such as fluctuations in test performance over time due to carryover or practice effects (which are separate from change over time due to "real" change in the true score); (2) *test content*, in which items selected do not adequately represent the domain; (3) *examiner or scorer error*, through incorrect administration or scoring of the test, such as giving too much time on the GRE or reading the instructions incorrectly; (4) the *situation* in which the testing occurs, including fluctuation in environmental conditions such as noise, light, or temperature; and (5) *examinee factors*, such as sickness, fatigue, or lack of motivation. Through the test construction process, there are ways to reduce error in testing and therefore make measures more reliable, including writing items clearly, making instructions easy to understand, closely following instructions for administering tests, making rules for subjective scoring as explicit as possible, and training raters (Nunnally & Bernstein, 1994; Walsh & Betz, 2001).

Estimating Reliability
Because there are different sources of error, many factors contribute to an observed score differing from the true score. Consequently, there are several different ways of estimating reliability, which reflect these different sources of variation: test–retest, parallel forms, split-half, and internal consistency. Moreover, any given test could be described by more than one type of reliability coefficient, which may differ from one another and across different samples and conditions (Walsh & Betz, 2001).

Test–retest reliability reflects the consistency of results for the same measure given at two different times, and is most appropriate for characteristics that are not expected to change over time; it is frequently referred to as the "coefficient of stability." To calculate test–retest reliability, the same individuals are administered the same measure at two different times, separated by a time interval of typically not less than 1 week. Scores on the first administration are correlated with scores on the second administration, and the resultant correlation coefficient reflects the degree to which individuals in the group receive similar scores relative to other individuals in the group.

An important consideration in evaluating test–retest reliability is the possibility of practice or carryover effects, which occur when the second administration of a measure is influenced by the first administration. These effects may overestimate the true reliability of a measure, particularly if individuals are differentially affected by the amount of carryover effects. A related consideration is the amount of time that elapses between the first and second administrations of a measure: Too short, and carryover effects will be more likely to occur; too long, and other factors are likely to decrease reliability, such as real change in the characteristic over time.

Another important consideration in evaluating test–retest reliability coefficients is whether they are an appropriate indicator of reliability for the particular construct being measured. If the trait or characteristic itself is not expected to be stable over time—that is, if it is expected to change, whether in a normal development progression or due to some type of intervention—then test–retest reliability may not be appropriate. Test users should pay attention to the time interval associated with a reported test–retest reliability coefficient, and evaluate the coefficient in light of the elapsed time and the nature of the characteristic being measured.

Parallel forms or *alternate forms reliability* uses two different yet equivalent forms of a specific test to estimate reliability, assuming that items comprising the two forms have been carefully drawn from the same larger domain defined by the construct. The two forms may be given at the same time, which eliminates some forms of error and therefore is considered a more rigorous form of reliability estimation (Kaplan & Saccuzzo, 2009). This type of reliability obviously requires development of two different forms of the same measure. The reliability index is the correlation coefficient between the two different forms given to the same group of individuals. The forms must be as equivalent as possible, including the same number and type of items, and the same level of difficulty (in the case of achievement/ability tests). The two forms should be administered in counterbalanced order (i.e., half of the sample receives Form A first, whereas the other half of the sample receives Form B first) to minimize the impact of carryover effects due to fatigue, decreased attention or motivation, or practice.

Split-half reliability is related to the alternate forms version. Instead of developing two separate forms of a measure, split-half reliability is computed by administering a measure in its entirety, then splitting the items into two sets and correlating the two scores that result. Like alternate forms reliability, split-half reliability focuses on the error associated with the content within an instrument, and eliminates the error associated with the time interval in test–retest reliability. A primary consideration with split-half reliability is determining how best to divide the items into two halves: The goal is to end up with two equivalent halves, similar to the process of developing alternate forms of a measure. Several approaches are used to divide items, such as assigning the odd-numbered items to one set and the even-numbered items to another set, or using a random numbers table. Items should not be divided into first and second halves, because this would introduce error due to carryover effects such as practice, fatigue, and motivation. The coefficient that results from correlating two halves of a test, however, is essentially an estimate of the reliability of each half. Generally speaking, longer tests (with more items) are more reliable than shorter tests (with fewer items), and so the initial split-half coefficient is likely to be an underestimate of the reliability of the whole test. To adjust for this underestimate, a calculation known as the *Spearman-Brown formula* is used to estimate the reliability for the entire test.

Internal consistency reliability may be considered a logical extension of alternate forms and split-half reliability in that these two previous estimates of reliability are based on similarity between specifically defined sets of items (Walsh & Betz, 2001). Internal consistency reliability reflects the degree to which each item on a test is measuring the same thing as every other item on the same test, or a test's homogeneity. To determine a test's internal consistency, the test is given once to a group of individuals, and then the interitem consistency is calculated, most commonly via Cronbach's coefficient α, or the Kuder-Richardson-20 (KR-20) for dichotomous items.

Internal consistency reliability is the most frequently cited type of reliability, perhaps due to the relative ease of determining an index such as coefficient α: The test is given once in its entirety to one group of individuals, and the coefficient is easily obtained via computer statistical packages such as IBM's SPSS statistical package. However, coefficient α is not always an appropriate estimate of reliability, particularly for broadly defined constructs, and the coefficient as a reflection of a measure's unidimensionality may be overstated (Cortina, 1993; Schmitt, 1996).

Evaluating Reliability Evidence

Evaluation of reliability evidence for any specific test begins with a review of the purpose of the test and the nature of the construct that the test is designed to measure. Each type of reliability estimate (test–retest, parallel forms, split-half, and internal consistency) rests on different assumptions about which sources of error are most important to control, and so test users need to be aware of the information conveyed by different reliability coefficients.

Reliability coefficients may be interpreted in several different ways (Hansen, 1999; Walsh & Betz, 2001). A coefficient can be interpreted as the proportion of observed score variance that is "true" rather than "error" variance; for example, a reliability coefficient of .85 could be interpreted as 85% of the variance due to true score and 15% due to error. This perspective is used in determining *standard error of measurement* (SEM), an index that reflects the relative size of the error component for an individual taking a given measure. The SEM provides an estimate of how close an individual's observed score is to his or her true score. The formula incorporates a test's reliability coefficient, plus the standard deviation (or spread) of scores on the test, and reliability is inversely related to the standard error of measurement: The higher the reliability coefficient, the smaller the SEM, and thus, the more confidence that can be placed in an individual's observed score as being close to his or her true score. Calculating the SEM also provides a way to construct a *confidence interval* around an individual's test score, thus indicating the probability that the true score is within a certain range around the observed score. The smaller the SEM (and, the higher the reliability), the tighter the confidence interval around the observed score.

How reliable is reliable? It depends on the construct being measured, the characteristics of the test itself, and the planned use of the test. Very high reliability would be expected for a test that is very narrow in focus; measures of complex constructs may not appear as reliable. If a test is being used to make major decisions about people's lives, the test ought to be very reliable. The SEM can be extremely useful when looking at one person's score, particularly in relation to an important decision.

Reliability coefficients provided by test publishers also must be evaluated in the context of the use of the test: If the samples used to estimate reliability do not generalize to the individuals for whom the test will be used, then it is advisable to carry out local reliability calculations (Hansen, 1999; Kaplan & Saccuzzo, 2009).

What should a test developer or test user do if a test evinces low reliability? At the test development stage, reliability can be improved by adding more items and increasing the length of the test, or by examining item analyses and eliminating items that are deflating reliability due to low interitem correlations, or dividing the items into multiple subscales. Test–retest reliability coefficients should be high, particularly over short time intervals; coefficients lower than expected raise questions about the construct, the measure, or both.

TEST VALIDITY

Validity refers to the "scientific utility of a measuring instrument . . . in terms of how well it measures what it purports to measure" (Nunnally & Bernstein, 1994, p. 83). Three broad categories of validity are content validity, criterion-related validity, and construct validity, although some authors have argued that all types of validity really boil down to construct validity (Messick, 1995; Nunnally & Bernstein, 1994).

Establishing validity for a measure is based on empirical evidence, which is accumulated and replicated over a variety of investigations and circumstances. Furthermore, a measure itself is not "validated"; rather, the *use* of a measure is validated. Validity is "not an inherent property of the test itself, but rather with respect to a particular interpretation or use of the test" (Bolt & Rounds, 2000, p. 161).

Content Validity

Content validity refers to how well the specific sample of items represents the entire domain of interest and is often viewed as an essential first step in establishing the validity of a measure (Walsh & Betz, 2001). In developing a test, one can think of a universe of possible items from which to sample to assess a particular attribute. Again, it is crucial to carefully define the construct of interest before the universe of content can be defined. This is most obvious when discussing an achievement test over a particular topic (e.g., calculus), but is important in the construction of any measure. Evidence to support content validity may be achieved directly by including expert judges' ratings of content during test development, as well as indirectly through evidence of internal consistency reliability, which indicates that each item measures the same domain as other items (although it does not directly demonstrate validity).

Criterion-related Validity

Criterion-related validity refers to the extent to which a measure of a specific attribute is associated with some external or independent indicator (the "criterion") of the same attribute; for example, whether a measure of depression correlates with an independent diagnosis of depression. Criterion-related validity takes two forms that vary in terms of the temporal relationship of the measure and the criterion. If the predictive measure and the criterion occur at the same time, then we speak of *concurrent validity*, such as in the example related to depression. If the criterion occurs some time after the predictive measure, then we speak of *predictive validity*, such as if a measure of depression is correlated with a diagnosis obtained 3 months later.

Evidence to support criterion-related validity typically is either correlational evidence between the predictor measure and a criterion variable, or observed differences among criterion groups. In the example of depression, correlational support might come from clients' ratings of their behavior, and group-difference support could come from average test scores obtained from two groups on the basis of their diagnoses.

Construct Validity

Construct validation is the "process of gathering data to support our contention that this test . . . is actually a reflection of the construct or attribute it is designed to reflect" (Walsh & Betz, p. 64). A systematic investigation of the construct validity of a measure must occur within the broader nomological network (Cronbach & Meehl, 1955) and involve a clear specification of the range of expected "observables" related to the construct, how these observables measure the same or different things, and examine how a measure correlates with similar or different measures (Nunnally & Bernstein, 1994).

Evidence in support of construct validity takes many forms and is ideally focused on both *convergent* and *discriminant* evidence, or the relation of a measure to other measures that should, and should not, be related. For example, a new measure of depression would be expected to be strongly correlated with an existing measure of depression (convergent) but weakly correlated with a measure of a construct thought to be unrelated to depression, such as attachment style (discriminant). Convergent and discriminant validity are important to keep in mind because of our tendency to focus on convergent validity in determining content, criterion-related, and construct validity, but it is important to also provide evidence of discriminant validity. If a new measure is too strongly related to something that it should not be, then doubt is cast on the measure.

Campbell and Fiske (1959) developed a method of examining the convergent and discriminant evidence, using a matrix that combines multiple measures of the same construct and of different constructs. They also discussed the concept of *method variance*, a form of error that introduces a spurious relationship between two measures existing solely because of the way in which the information is obtained. Method variance artificially inflates the observed correlation between two measures, thus overestimating convergent validity and underestimating discriminant validity. Two different ways of measuring the same construct should yield higher correlations than the same way of measuring two different constructs. For example, a student's career certainty assessed via a self-report paper-and-pencil measure should be more highly correlated with an advisor's rating of the student's certainty than it is with a self-report measure of anxiety.

To disentangle the effects of method variance, Campbell and Fiske (1959) devised a *multitrait-multimethod matrix*, which compares correlations between measures of at least two different attributes measured in at least two different ways. The matrix is constructed with three different types of coefficients—reliability coefficients (same construct using same type of measurement), convergent validity coefficients (same construct using different types of measurement), and discriminant validity coefficients (different constructs using the same type of measurement, and different constructs using different types of measurement). Test validity is supported when the convergent validity coefficients are higher than discriminant validity coefficients. Although Campbell and Fiske's (1959) method of comparison relied on visual inspection of the coefficients, more recent methods involve the use of confirmatory factor analysis to evaluate the coefficients.

Other Aspects of Validity

Before investing a substantial amount of time and money in developing an assessment instrument, it is important to determine whether the test adds enough information to justify the expense. Sechrest (1963) referred to this as *incremental validity*: Does the test improve the accuracy of a prediction or decision that would be made without the test? Incremental validity does not necessarily correspond to the test's validity per se, but must be considered in the context of other methods of prediction. Incremental validity is related to the *base rate* of an event (Meehl & Rosen, 1955, cited in Walsh & Betz, 2001), which refers to the proportion of people who are expected to be in a certain category. If 80% of any and all students who begin college successfully finish their freshman year, then selection of any specific student to admit to college will be correct 80% of the time (if the defined outcome is measured as completion of freshman year). If the base rate of an event is already high, then adding the use of a test for selection will not improve the accuracy of prediction by very much. If, on the other hand, the base rate of an event is low—say only 20% of the general population would complete freshman year—then a selection tool could substantially improve the accuracy of predicting which students to admit. Thus, incremental validity is the "extent to which a test can improve the accuracy of prediction beyond that possible by simply using base-rate data" (Walsh & Betz, p. 69).

Another term used in the context of validity is "face validity," or whether the test *appears* to measure what it is designed to measure. Face validity is not considered a type of validity, and demonstrating face validity is not a requirement for a test to be judged as valid. However, face validity is useful to consider as it relates to the perceptions of the test taker or to the general public. If a test does not appear to be measuring what the test taker believes it does, then this may become an additional source of error variance in the test-taking process. For example, if a student arrives to take a specialized graduate school admissions test to be admitted to a doctoral program in psychology (such as the GRE) and finds items related to American history, he or she may question the relevance of the test—and may be upset or annoyed enough to not do as well as he or she could otherwise. The test may have a high degree of predictive validity (that is, students with high scores on the American history test do well in psychology doctoral study), but the test itself does not have face validity. Lack of face validity thus affects test takers, but also may influence administrators who decide whether or not to use tests for a specific purpose.

Exploration validity is a recent concept related to test construction and validation, and, like face validity, is not a standard form of validity. Exploration validity has been discussed most extensively within vocational assessment, and refers to the "power" of an inventory to stimulate an individual to pursue additional career exploration activities after receiving test results (Randahl, Hansen, & Haverkamp, 1993). Similarly, Messick (1995) proposed the idea of *consequential validity*, or the intended and unintended consequences of test use. Messick argued that validity is a feature of a test interpretation rather than of the test itself, and so emphasized the importance of examining the actions that are based on test use. Finally, Walsh and Betz (2001) discuss *interpretive validity*, or the premise that the test results and interpretation are presented in a useful and valid manner.

Evaluating Validity Evidence

The process of validating a measure is ongoing; it is not possible to say that a test has a specific amount of validity, or that it has been "validated." As Fouad (1999) noted, "counselors cannot merely look up the validity coefficients of an inventory in a test manual . . . counselors need to know what evidence is available about the validity of an instrument for particular populations, for particular settings, and at a particular time" (p. 193).

Validity evidence may be found in varied places. Unlike reliability, which is typically clearly labeled in journal articles, validity evidence may be less obvious. Because validity evidence is continually accruing, it may be found in any subsequent study that uses a measure. For example, a new measure developed to assess career adaptability may be accompanied by adequate details regarding its development, reliability information, and some initial concurrent or construct validity. However, any subsequent study that uses the scale has potential implications for the validity of the measure, such as results among groups that would be expected given the definition of career adaptability, or correlations with other measures of related and unrelated constructs, or changes in test scores due to relevant interventions. Any of these results may contribute to validity evidence for a measure.

A final comment about the psychometric characteristics of a test pertains to the relationship between reliability and validity. A perfectly reliable test may not be valid; conversely, a test cannot be valid if it is not reliable. If a new test designed to measure extroversion has excellent test–retest reliability over a 2-week period and high internal consistency reliability, it might be judged to be a reliable measure. However, if scores on the test do not relate to other measures of extroversion, or are not useful predictors of relevant behavior, then the measure has little utility: It may be reliable but not valid. On the other hand, if the same test does predict useful behavior, but it does not measure the construct consistently at different times, then it also has little utility: It cannot be valid if it is not reliable. Said another way, reliability sets an upper limit on validity. Thus, test developers and test users need to pay attention to both reliability and validity, and how they relate to one another.

Testing and Assessment in Counseling Psychology

Assessment has long held a central role in professional psychology (Camara, Nathan, & Puente, 2000), although its implementation differs among specialty areas, due in part to the disparate historical roots of the specialties early in the 20th century. Clinical psychology as a discipline emerged from the mental health movement and psychoanalytic psychology, and has placed a continuing emphasis on psychopathology and the assessment of intellectual and personality functioning (Cobb et al., 2004; Morgan & Cohen, 2008). Counseling psychology, on the other hand, emerged from the vocational guidance movement, developed in the environment of educational institutions, and has placed a continuing emphasis on assessment of career and developmental concerns in well-functioning individuals.

These traditional differences between the two specialties remain in terms of training, students' career aspirations, internship placements, and eventual work settings: Counseling psychology trainees and professionals are more likely to be found in university counseling centers, whereas those in clinical psychology are more likely to be found in medical settings (Cassin, Singer, Dobson, & Altmaier, 2007; Morgan & Cohen, 2008; Neimeyer, Bowman, & Stewart, 2001; Neimeyer, Rice, & Keilin, 2009). Furthermore, differences between the two specialties are exhibited in choice of theoretical orientations: Counseling psychology trainees are more likely to indicate interpersonal and humanistic/existential orientations and less likely to indicate cognitive-behavioral, behavioral, and biological orientations, than are clinical psychology trainees (Cassin et al., 2007).

Because of the differing historical roots, the roles and practices of assessment have evolved in different directions within the two specialties. Clinical psychologists are more likely to do formal comprehensive assessment apart from treatment, usually before treatment commences, and assessment may constitute a substantial part of a practitioner's professional activity. Counseling psychologists, on the other hand, are more likely to conduct briefer forms of assessment, integrate assessment into therapy, and approach assessment from a compensatory and strengths-based perspective (Campbell, 2000; Dawis, 1992; Duckworth, 1990). Training in clinical psychology is more likely to include assessment of children and neuropsychological assessment, and training in counseling psychology is more likely to include vocational assessment (Agresti, 1992; Cobb et al., 2004; Larson & Agresti, 1992; May & Scott, 1991; Ryan, Lopez, & Lichtenberg, 1999).

In spite of the aforementioned divergences, the specialties of counseling psychology and clinical psychology actually do share many common features, and their gradual convergence has created new opportunities and practice settings for both counseling and clinical psychologists, and differences in the use of tests and assessment may be lessening. Discussions of merging the training of the two specialties have been ongoing, with recent calls for combined or integrated doctoral training (Cobb et al., 2004).

Models of Assessment in Counseling Psychology

The current practice of assessment in counseling psychology varies widely, from the traditional use of testing as an integrated part of career counseling, in which clients frequently expect to participate in testing, to full-scale evaluation in medical or forensic settings, with specific referral questions that are addressed in written reports to relevant parties.

The unique aspects of counseling psychology's approach to the use of testing were outlined 20 years ago by Duckworth (1990); in contrast to other applied specialties, counseling psychologists tend to use testing to enhance short-term therapy, focus on developmental issues, facilitate problem solving, assist with decision making, and, provide psychoeducational opportunities for clients. She further described the "counseling psychological approach" to testing, in which testing is done for the benefit of the client *and* the therapist, testing is done to generate information for both the client *and* counselor, the client needs to be an active participant, the client is assumed to be able to profit from the testing process, testing should focus on both strengths and weaknesses, the test taker is more likely to be "normal," clients are capable of change, vocational tests are important part of assessment, and the goal of testing is empowerment of the test taker (Duckworth, 1990).

Duckworth's observations still hold today, perhaps most noticeably in testing and assessment conducted as part of career counseling. It could be argued that there are now *two* different models of assessment within the specialty of counseling psychology, one that focuses on the use of tests in counseling with career and/or "normal" developmental adjustment as its primary focus (a "traditional" model), and one that focuses on what might be considered a clinical psychology application of assessment (a "diagnostic" model). In fact, for the purpose of the present chapter, it is useful to consider assessment used within the context of career or developmentally-oriented counseling as fundamentally different from assessment outside of such a context. It seems misleading to classify career assessment together with other types of assessment, because the goals, procedures, and outcomes differ substantially. For example, Duckworth's (1990) depiction of the client as an active part of testing decisions, and the client and counselor as being equal beneficiaries of testing outcomes is very apparent in the use of career assessment, more so than in other areas. If a client comes to therapy to deal with depression, assessment may be used but will not be a primary focus as it is in career counseling.

Dividing the use of assessment in counseling psychology into two models is not intended to further any schism between "career" and "personal" (or noncareer) counseling (Swanson, 2002). Rather, discussion of two models allows a more precise consideration of how assessment is implemented within different professional settings in which counseling psychologists find themselves. The further that counseling psychology has expanded the scope of its professional activities, the more that the model of assessment has diverged into two forms, one of which resembles the way in which clinical psychologists do assessment. Previous writing about assessment within counseling psychology has focused on career assessment, or assessment in general, but rarely both, perhaps because of the differing models that underlie assessment.

THE "TRADITIONAL" CAREER/ DEVELOPMENTAL MODEL

As described at the beginning of this chapter, counseling psychology was heavily influenced by the psychology of individual differences, and a major contribution of this approach was the technology for client assessment and the individual differences point of view in assessment (Dawis, 1992). This is particularly evident in the earliest uses of assessment in counseling psychology, namely, in the vocational/career realm. As counseling psychology expanded its scope, the range of tests and assessment used also expanded.

The traditional model encompasses an image of a psychologist working in a collaborative relationship with an "intact" client who can engage in and benefit from assessment. This model, in its current form, allows more flexibility in the range of acceptable assessment methods. For example, Hartung (2005) discussed a merging of quantitative and qualitative methods of obtaining information, proposing such an approach as an "optimum approach to career assessment and counseling" (p. 378), and Walsh (2001) echoed the need to go beyond traditional assessment to consider "idiographic, qualitative, and other creative approaches to assessing multiple aspects of both people and the contexts" (p. 271).

Moreover, discussion of how to integrate assessment into counseling occurs primarily within the realm of career counseling, because nowhere else is it as central to the role and purpose of counseling. This is not to succumb to the "career-counseling-as-testing" mindset warned by Hartung (2005), in which testing is viewed as *the* equivalent of counseling; rather, it highlights the level of skill necessary to effectively integrate test and nontest sources of information in a way that is maximally effective for clients' goals (Tinsley & Bradley, 1986).

A "CONTEMPORARY" PSYCHODIAGNOSTIC MODEL

As counseling psychologists share professional activities and work environments with clinical psychologists, their methods and uses of assessment will continue to converge, as reflected in this contemporary psychodiagnostic model. In this view, appropriate uses of assessment are to describe current functioning, confirm or disconfirm impressions formed through other sources of information, identify therapeutic goals, highlight issues likely to emerge in treatment, recommend forms of intervention, offer prognoses, assist in differential diagnosis, evaluate success of interventions, identify emerging therapeutic issues, and provide feedback as a therapeutic intervention in itself (Meyer et al., 2001, p. 129).

An advantage of considering this model of assessment is that it clearly acknowledges the degree of overlap in training, professional activities, and work settings for professional psychologists, regardless of the choice of specialty. In other words, the counseling and clinical psychology distinction is less evident in the noncareer side of counseling.

Conceptualizing two models of assessment within counseling psychology may assist with further discussion of the types of assessment and their uses. It should be acknowledged, however, that this obscures a wide segment of assessment that occurs somewhere in between the two models, particularly because of the demonstrated specialty differences in theoretical orientations and work settings noted earlier, which undoubtedly affect assessment practice.

Types of Assessment

It may be helpful to revisit the distinction between testing and assessment. Psychological testing has been defined as a "relatively straightforward process wherein a particular scale is administered to obtain a specific score, [to which] a descriptive meaning can be applied . . . on the basis of normative, nomothetic findings" (Meyer et al., 2001, p. 143). Psychological assessment, in contrast, "is concerned with the clinician who takes a variety of test scores, generally obtained from multiple test methods, and considers the data in the context of history, referral information, and observed behavior to understand the person being evaluated, to answer the referral questions, and then to communicate findings to the patient, his or her significant others, and referral sources" (Meyer et al., 2001, p. 143). To illustrate, Meyer et al. (2001) distinguished between the *nomothetic* meaning in testing and the *idiographic* nature of assessment, in which the same score on an intelligence test subscale may have very different meanings: The nomothetic interpretation is that the client possesses "average" skills, whereas the idiographic interpretation is of change, such as decline after a head injury or improvement during rehabilitation.

A further reminder from the discussion of testing versus assessment is that tests are used in the assessment process, but not all assessment procedures are tests. "Assessment" covers a variety of techniques and procedures; thus far, the focus has been on "tests," but there are other methods of assessment as well.

This section includes an overview of several different categories of assessment, according to the construct that is being assessed. These categories cover a range of assessment formats, including structured or "formal" assessment, qualitative or informal assessment, interviews, and structured interviews, as well as the role of examiner and examinee. Because many tests are available, and because in-depth assessment information and training is beyond the scope of the present chapter, the presentation here will be cursory.

Career/Vocational Testing

Vocational testing has long been the bailiwick of counseling psychologists, although other applied specialties such as industrial/organizational psychologists, school psychologists, and clinical psychologists also may use such testing. The most typical venue for using career assessment is in the context of career counseling, as well as in educational or other group interventions. By far, the most common type of vocational testing is assessment of *interests*, such as with the Strong Interest Inventory, the Self-Directed Search, or the Kuder (Hansen, 2005). The construct of *values* also is frequently assessed with instruments such as the Minnesota Importance Questionnaire (MIQ) or Super's Work Values Inventory (Rounds & Armstrong, 2005). *Ability* assessment may occur via objective measures such as the Armed Services Vocational Aptitude Battery (ASVAB) or the O*NET Ability Profiler (Ryan Krane & Tirre, 2005), although self-estimates of abilities are more commonly used, such as the Kuder Skills Assessment and ACT's Inventory of Work-Relevant Abilities. Other constructs, such as self-efficacy, career adaptability, and career indecision, have gained attention in the past few decades (Swanson & D'Achiardi, 2005). Career assessment is most amenable to the recommendations of Duckworth (1990), regarding the involvement of the client in all aspects of assessment. Moreover, assessment is perhaps best considered as an intervention in and of itself within career counseling, and qualitative methods of assessment have grown in popularity of use. For example, card sorts are frequently used during career counseling sessions as a tool to discuss a client's interests, values, or skills (Swanson & Fouad, 2010).

ASSESSMENT OF COGNITIVE ABILITY: INTELLIGENCE/APTITUDE/ACHIEVEMENT

Aptitude is defined as the capacity to learn, and aptitude measures include a wide range of experiences and content, and typically are developed with criterion-related validity as a key goal

(Kaplan & Saccuzzo, 2009). These tests are used to predict one's ability to profit from or be successful in some future situation. Tests of scholastic aptitude include the ACT, SAT, the general tests of the GRE, and Miller Analogies Test (MAT), as well as test batteries that measure multiple aptitudes, such as the General Aptitude Test Battery (GATB), Differential Aptitude Test (DAT), and the ASVAB.

Achievement refers to what has already been learned, usually in a known or controlled set of experiences, and measures of achievement are developed via strong content validation procedures with clearly defined domains of content (Kaplan & Saccuzzo, 2009). Achievement tests are designed to assess what an individual has mastered (in contrast to intelligence tests, which measure ability or capability). Commonly used tests include the Wide Range Achievement Test (WRAT-4) and the Wechsler Individual Achievement Test (WIAT-II), the advanced subject area tests of the GRE, and the Medical College Admissions Test (MCAT).

Intelligence is typically thought of as general intellectual ability, although different theoretical perspectives have been proposed, and the concept of "intelligence" has been debated since Binet's first test. Intelligence is typically measured via individual tests administered one-on-one by a trained assessor, such as the Wechsler tests: the Wechsler Adult Intelligence Scale (WAIS-III), the Wechsler Intelligence Scale for Children (WISC-IV), and the Wechsler Preschool and Primary Scale of Intelligence (WPPSI-III). Similarly, the Stanford-Binet is individually administered; the test consists of one form that extends over the entire lifespan. Other tests of intelligence include the Kaufman Assessment Battery for Children (KABC-II) and the Kaufman Brief Intelligence Test (KBIT-II), and the Woodcock-Johnson (Anastasi & Urbina, 1997; Goldfinger & Pomerantz, 2010).

NEUROPSYCHOLOGICAL ASSESSMENT

Neuropsychological assessment has historically been performed primarily by clinical psychologists, but counseling psychologists are increasingly involved in this type of assessment (Larson & Agresti, 1992; Ryan, Lopez, & Lichtenberg, 1999). Neuropsychological assessment is used to identify cognitive dysfunction or brain damage, and serves a number of different purposes (Hebben & Milberg, 2002). A primary function is to describe and identify changes in psychological functioning, in terms of cognition, affect, and/or behavior. Relatedly, it is used to determine the extent and location of damage within the brain, to determine the causes or correlates of change, to assess changes over time and develop a prognosis, to determine the cause and progression of a disease, and to determine whether rehabilitation is occurring. Results of neuropsychological assessment can offer guidelines for rehabilitation and education, for medical professionals and family members. Full neuropsychological batteries, such as the Halstead-Reitan Neuropsychological Battery (HRB) and the Luria-Nebraska Neuropsychological Battery, require substantial training to administer and interpret. In many situations, a suitable alternative to a full battery is to use a brief neuropsychological screening, such as the Bender Visual-Motor Gestalt Test.

PERSONALITY ASSESSMENT

Psychologists have been interested in personality assessment since early in the history of psychological assessment. Personality is typically considered as the "relatively stable and distinctive patterns of behavior that characterize an individual and his or her reactions to the environment" (Kaplan & Saccuzzo, 2009, p. 334), although there are many different ways of measuring personality. Personality assessment has developed according to several different paradigms, depending on the theoretical view of the components and structure of personality (Wiggins, 2003), with psychodynamic, interpersonal, multivariate, and empirical paradigms producing the most commonly used measures.

Personality tests are classified as objective or projective. *Objective* tests are similar to other types of psychological tests, with a set of items to which clients respond, from which quantitative, normed scores are derived. The most common objective tests of personality are the MMPI-2, the Personality Assessment Inventory (PAI), the Millon Clinical Multiaxial Inventory (MCMI-III), the California Psychological Inventory (CPI-III), the 16PF, and the NEO Personality Inventory (NEO-PI). These inventories yield scores on a set of scales, the content of which varies across the inventories according to the paradigm underlying the measure.

In *projective* tests, an individual responds to some type of ambiguous or unstructured stimuli, and the responses are assumed to reveal something about his or her personality. Scoring and interpretation of projective personality tests are less standardized than for objective tests, although scoring protocols have been developed to increase the reliability and validity of these measures. The most common projective tests are the Rorschach Inkblot

Method, the Thematic Apperception Test (TAT), the Rotter Incomplete Sentences Blank, and the Kinetic Family Drawing (Goldfinger & Pomerantz, 2010). Despite controversy surrounding the use of projective tests, they are among the most extensively used tests (Camara, Nathan, & Puente, 2000; Groth-Marnat, 1999).

DIAGNOSTIC ASSESSMENT AND INTERVENTION PLANNING

As noted earlier, intervention/treatment planning is one of the primary purposes of assessment (Meyer et al., 2001), particularly in the psychodiagnostic model of assessment. The increasing role of managed care has put pressure on psychologists to provide more efficacious services, and to justify the services that they do provide (Antony & Barlow, 2002). The link between assessment and interventions is particularly evident in empirically supported treatments, in which specific diagnoses lead to specific interventions. Spengler, Strohmer, Dixon, and Shivy (1995), with elaboration by Meier (1999), presented a model linking conceptualization, assessment, intervention, and analysis of intervention effects in a reciprocal feedback loop.

Brief screening assessments are frequently used as part of intake procedures in university counseling center, community mental health agencies, and primary care settings (Bufka, Crawford, & Levitt, 2002) and include measures such as the PAI. In addition to broad screening measures, diagnostic measures are designed to identify problems in specific areas, such as eating disorders, attention deficit disorders, depression, anxiety, or suicidality. Frequently, cutoff scores are used to determine diagnosis, such as on the Beck Depression Inventory (BDI), in which specific score ranges are associated with diagnoses of "minimal," "mild," or "moderate" depression.

SYMPTOM AND BEHAVIOR CHECKLISTS

Checklists differ in format from other types of assessment in that they consist of a list of problems, behaviors, or symptoms, and test-takers indicate those that apply to them. Checklists may be comprehensive or targeted to a few areas of behavior, they may be used as screening devices, and they may be completed by people other than the client, such as by parents or teachers. The Symptom Checklist-90 (SCL-90-R) and the Child Behavior Checklist (CBCL) are two examples of broad-based checklists. The BDI-II, Beck Anxiety Inventory (BAI), and Eating Disorder Inventory

(EDI-3) are self-report measures that target specific symptoms or problems (Goldfinger & Pomerantz, 2010).

BEHAVIORAL ASSESSMENT

Behavioral or cognitive-behavioral assessment is particularly useful in identifying problematic behavior, the context in which it occurs, and a treatment plan for modifying the behavior. The goal of the assessment, then, is not so much to understand causes of the behavior, but to identify specific conditions in which the behavior occurs. According to Kaplan and Saccuzzo (2009), several important differences exist between "traditional" and behavioral assessment: the target and goal of the assessment (underlying cause vs. disordered behavior), the importance of specifying symptoms (superficial vs. focus of treatment), assessment (indirectly vs. directly related to treatment), and theory (medical model vs. behavioral model). An important component of behavioral assessment is to determine whether the problem behavior is an excess or a deficit; in other words, whether the goal is to decrease or increase a specific behavior. Some measures have been developed for specific problem behaviors, including the Fear Survey Schedule, the Irrational Beliefs Test, and the Assertive Behavior Survey Schedule.

ASSESSMENT/DIAGNOSTIC INTERVIEWS

Interviews can serve as valuable assessment tools and are used for the purposes of diagnosis and treatment planning. Interviews take many different forms, such as intake interviews, diagnostic interviews, mental status exams, crisis interviews, and assessment interviews. Interviews also may be conducted not only with the client, but also with parents, guardians, and other collateral informants (Goldfinger & Pomerantz, 2010; Groth-Marnat, 1999). Similar to tests, interviews are a method for gathering data, are used to make predictions, are evaluated in terms of reliability and validity, can be group or individual, can be structured or unstructured, and have a defined purpose (Kaplan & Saccuzzo, 2009).

In some sense, all therapeutic sessions could be considered assessment or diagnostic interviews, in that the therapist is continually gathering information for use in making predictions about in-session or later behavior. The use of standardized or structured clinical interviews as a form of assessment has grown substantially in the past several decades (Kaplan & Saccuzzo, 2009; Summerfeldt

& Antony, 2002). Structured interviews include a specific set of questions presented in a particular order, with administrative procedures to ensure standardization. Many structured interviews also have scoring procedures with norms. One commonly used structured interview protocol is the Structured Clinical Interview (SCID), originally developed for the *Diagnostic and Statistical Manual, Third Edition, Revised* (DSM-III-R) and subsequently revised for the DSM-IV.

Like standardized tests, structured interviews have important psychometric features to be considered. In the case of diagnostic interviews, reliability refers to consistency or replicability of measurement and stability of diagnostic outcomes (Summerfeldt & Antony, 2002): Essentially, do the same diagnoses result from multiple psychologists using the interview protocol? The reliability of a diagnostic interview is most frequently evaluated via *inter-rater reliability*, in which two or more independent evaluators rate identical interview material. A statistic called Cohen's κ is used to quantify the degree of agreement between two raters; κ can range from -1.00 (perfect disagreement) to +1.00 (perfect agreement), with 0 indicating agreement equivalent to chance. The reliability of diagnostic interviews is an excellent reminder that reliability is not a feature of the instrument per se, but rather is dependent on the context in which the assessment occurs.

Structured diagnostic interview protocols have been developed for specific psychological disorders, such as the Anxiety Disorders Interview Schedule (ADIS-IV; Brown, Di Nardo, & Barlow, 1994), or for a broad range of disorders, such as the Structured Clinical Interview (SCID), which has separate forms for Axis I and Axis II disorders, as well as for research purposes.

Computer-assisted and Internet-based Assessment

Computer-assisted assessment has been around for several decades, and many inventories previously administered via paper-and-pencil formats are now available via desktop computer or the Internet. A new set of issues arises with assessment that is made available online. Such assessment is burgeoning, due to the explosive growth of individuals' access to the Internet (nearly 75% of people in the United States had access to the Internet in 2008, up from 44% in 2000, www.internetworldstats.com); and, because of the promise of "better, faster, and cheaper services and products" common to the Internet (Naglieri et al., 2004, p. 151). A whole host of issues arise regarding Internet-based assessment, some of which could not (and cannot) be anticipated, as technology and popular culture change and evolve in unpredictable ways. Assessment on the Internet ranges from traditional tests converted to web-based platforms to the equivalent of a magazine quiz, and vary in terms of their content, quality, and function (Buchanan, 2002).

The APA Task Force on Psychological Testing on the Internet (Naglieri et al., 2004) provided a useful overview of pertinent issues. They noted advantages of Internet testing, such as accessibility for clients in rural settings, those without transportation or with physical limitations; greater accuracy in scoring and suitability for using IRT models; and assessing abilities or skills not easily assessed via paper-and-pencil tests (e.g., musical aptitude). Several key problems include (a) ensuring test–client integrity (is the client the person actually taking the test?), which increases in importance when the goals of test taker differ from the goals of test user, such as with employment testing; (b) test security, in terms of access to client information, test scores, and test materials, such as preventing unauthorized copying of test material that is presented online; (c) issues for special populations, in which lack of equal access to technology may result in poorer test performance for some groups, or contextual factors may interact with Internet test performance; and (d) ethical issues unique to Internet testing (to be discussed in a later section).

Returning once again to the distinction between testing and assessment, Naglieri et al. (2004) concluded that most of what is available on the Internet is testing, not assessment: "*Testing* refers to the administration, scoring, and perhaps the interpretation of individual test scores by applying a descriptive meaning based on normative, nomothetic data . . . with the focus on the test itself"; whereas, "in *psychological assessment*, the emphasis is typically on the person being assessed and the referral questions, rather than on specific test results" (Naglieri, 2004, p. 153). Some of the negative consequences of Internet testing are due to the fact that they do not occur within a broader assessment context, or with the assistance of a psychologist or other trained professional.

GENDER AND DIVERSITY ISSUES IN ASSESSMENT

Discussions of assessment with diverse clientele have changed substantially in the past few decades—these issues have become more mainstream, perhaps due to the pressing nature of psychologists' preparation to work with diverse clients given changes in demographics. On the other hand, the issues themselves have not changed. As Fouad and Chan (1999) noted a decade earlier, psychologists often take tests developed and normed for one group and apply them to another group. And, although test developers are more savvy to the need to include culture, language, and gender in the development and norming of tests, ultimately it is up to the individual psychologist to be aware of the multitude of issues surrounding use of an established assessment instrument with *any* client, but particularly with clients who historically have been outside of the mainstream.

It is useful to consider these issues from the perspective of *multiculturalism* or *cultural pluralism* (Fouad & Chan, 1999; Leong, 2000)—the belief that the dominant or mainstream culture in the United States is but one of many that coexist. This perspective changes the lenses through which we view assessment with diverse clients because the dominant culture no longer serves as the standard of "normal" against which other cultures are judged as deviations from that standard (Fouad & Chan, 1999). Moreover, it is important to consider interactions among cultural dimensions, as individuals have multiple group identities, such as gender and race/ethnicity.

Two factors are of particular importance. The first is test bias—its sources, implications, and recommended solutions—which has been a topic of heated discussion. The *Standards for Educational and Psychological Testing* recommends that item or performance differences among groups be researched as soon as possible, and that test developers design inventories to eliminate or minimize such bias (AERA, 1991). Betz (2000) identified three types of test bias: *content* bias, observable at the item level, in which a difference exists between groups in the probability of individuals with the same level of ability answering an item correctly; *internal structure* or factorial bias, in which the structure of test items or scales differs across groups, raising questions of whether the test can be interpreted as the same for each group; and *predictive* or selection bias, in which a difference in prediction is observed across groups, typically evaluated via regression lines that are used to predict successful performance in a target behavior. Potential test bias has been identified in every form of psychological assessment, and test developers have taken a number of different strategies to address it, including within-group norming, adjusting scores, and separate cutoff scores.

The second factor is the context of assessment—the cultural competence of the counselor, the relationship between counselor and client, and the client's attitudes toward testing (Fouad & Chan, 1999). Recent research regarding the impact of stereotype threat (Steele & Aronson, 1995) suggests that heightened awareness of one's group membership, whether gender, race, or age, can have negative effects on test performance (Hess, Hinson, & Hodges, 2009; Nguyen & Ryan, 2008). Psychologists must be aware of the impact of the context of assessment throughout all aspects, including selection, administration, and interpretation of psychological tests.

Fortunately, many resources are available to guide psychologists in the selection and interpretation of tests and assessments with a diverse range of clients. The American Psychological Association (APA), for example, has created several compendia of references for practitioners, including the use of testing and neuropsychological assessment with racial/ethnic minorities, cross-culturally, linguistic minorities, women, and people with disabilities (Committee on Ethnic Minority Affairs, 2000; Committee on Psychological Tests and Assessment, 2002a, b). Furthermore, authors such as Fernandez, Boccaccini, and Noland (2007) provide guidance to practitioners selecting tests that have been translated into Spanish, which is likely to be useful, given the escalating increase in Spanish-speaking clients.

Psychologists' use of tests/assessment with culturally diverse individuals also is related to ethical standards and practice guidelines. The *APA Ethical Principles of Psychologists* (APA, 2002) cautions psychologists to use assessment instruments with established reliability and validity for the population being tested, and appropriate for a client's language preference. Similarly, the *Standards for Educational and Psychological Testing* (AERA, APA, NCME, 1999) provides guidelines regarding assessment with individuals of diverse linguistic backgrounds. At the very least, test users must be aware of the material provided by test developers regarding the gender, race/ethnicity, and other cultural factors of the clients with whom they work. Psychologists also need to be familiar with the *Guidelines on Multicultural Education, Training, Research, Practice, and Organizational Changes for Psychologists* (APA, 2003). In addition to knowledge about reliability and validity, psychologists need to use assessment instruments with demonstrated measurement equivalence—including not only linguistic equivalence (appropriate translations into target languages), but also conceptual and functional equivalence—whether the assessed constructs have the same meaning and serve the same function across cultures (APA, 2003).

Use of Assessment

Responsible use of assessment includes several types of decisions: deciding whether to use assessment, what specific tests to use, how to use assessment given the specific context, and interpreting and reporting test results.

DECIDING WHETHER TO USE ASSESSMENT

Psychologists should be able to "furnish a sound rationale for their work and explain the expected benefits of an assessment, as well as the anticipated cost" (Meyer et al., 2001, p. 129). Psychologists' own views of assessment vary, from those who eschew testing to those who use it routinely with all clients. Testing may be viewed as an invasion of a client's privacy, not to mention a substantial investment in terms of time and money. Yates and Taub (2003) describe procedures for determining the cost-effectiveness and cost–benefit of assessment; expected cost–benefit ratios may vary from person to person, and so must be evaluated in the context of the individual.

In recent years, the practice of assessment has come under scrutiny from third-party payers, and reimbursement policies have influenced the frequency and type of assessment that psychologists use (Camara, Nathan, & Puente, 2000; Cashel, 2002; Meyer et al., 2001; Turchik, Karpenko, Hammers, & McNamara, 2007). Thus, psychologists will need to give thought to their decisions about whether to use assessment, and be prepared to provide a rationale to clients and other parties.

SELECTION OF ASSESSMENT

The scientist–practitioner approach in counseling psychology is evident in the selection and use of assessment results. Selecting a test for use with a specific client entails determining the client's goals and choosing instruments to reach these goals, on the basis of available research and knowledge about assessment instruments. Allison, Lichtenberg, and Goodyear (1999) offered a brief checklist of important psychometric information that a practitioner should know before selecting an instrument: what information is available in the existing literature about a particular measure, including the primary criticisms; how the test was developed, with implications for interpretation for a particular client; the available reliability and validity data for the test; applicability of the test norms for a given client; and, groups for whom the test might produce biased results, and the nature of these biases. Information about assessment is available from a number of sources, including graduate-level coursework, assessment-focused journals, the *Mental Measurement Yearbook*, information on the APA website, and test manuals.

Psychologists who work in agencies or other organizations may have little input about selection of assessment instruments, at least at the global level. That is, the agency may have purchased certain inventories for practitioners' use, and so the individual practitioner will use what is available. On the other hand, the practitioner may have control over whether the assessment is used, or may have several options from which to choose. For example, a career counselor may have access to both the Strong Interest Inventory and the Self-Directed Search, and may choose to use either or neither.

Another scenario exists in which all clients in an agency are administered a screening inventory as part of intake, such as the PAI. In this case, the individual practitioner does not control the assessment selection process, but still must be well-informed about characteristics of the inventory and its interpretation.

USING ASSESSMENT RESULTS IN COUNSELING

Test interpretation can be viewed as a process that extends throughout the entire interaction between therapist and client, beginning with an informed selection of appropriate assessment instruments and ending with termination of therapy. In other words, "interpretation" is not limited to the specific points in time that a psychologist is explaining test results to a client, but rather, is an integrative process.

Goodyear and Lichtenberg (1999) outlined three overlapping definitions and sequential steps of test interpretation. First, the psychologist makes sense of the test data. This is reminiscent of the distinction between testing and assessment, in which the latter is the synthesizing of the data obtained from multiple tests that may include inconsistencies or contradictions, or may result in the whole picture being more than the sum of its parts. Second, data obtained from the test(s), and implications of these data, are presented to the consumer, most frequently the client him- or herself. This is the most commonly used definition of test interpretation (Goodyear & Lichtenberg, 1999). Finally, the third aspect of test interpretation is the client (or other consumer) making meaning of the test data and deriving implications from the data.

Although the technical aspects of testing may be systematically covered in graduate coursework, how to actually interpret tests with clients may receive less attention. Tinsley and Bradley (1986) offered two guiding principles: first, that test interpretation not be viewed as a discrete activity but conceptualized as part of the ongoing counseling process and integrated into the flow of counseling; and second, that tests are best thought of as structured interviews that provide an efficient source of information about clients. Furthermore, they recommended practical pointers for interpreting tests with clients, including remembering clients' goals, keeping the test precision in mind, minimizing defensive reactions, avoiding jargon, encouraging feedback, and being sensitive to the impact of information contained in test profiles. Other authors have reminded therapists not to lose sight of rapport-building and basic counseling skills while conducting test interpretation (Campbell, 2000).

A useful interpretive strategy is to consider assessment as a rich source of information for generating ideas and hypotheses about clients. As Tyler (1984) noted, "what test scores give us are *clues* to be followed . . . the scores mean something, but in order to know what we must consider each individual case in an empathic way, combining test evidence with everything else we know about the person" (Tyler, 1984, p. 50). This approach builds on the idea that therapists develop hypotheses and "working models" of clients throughout the therapy process (Maloney & Ward, 1976, in Goodyear & Lichtenberg, 1999; Swanson & Fouad, 2010; Walborn, 1996). Psychologists use all available sources of information to generate hypotheses, and may select certain assessment instruments because they provide information relevant to their hypotheses. Consistencies and inconsistencies can be identified across several sources of information (Swanson & Fouad, 2010).

As Goodyear and Lichtenberg (1999) noted, "test interpretation can have real consequences" (p. 2), including decisions about diagnosis, treatment planning, hiring, career choice, occupational classification, custody, and so on. These decisions often have a clinical intent, with the goal of helping the client. However, at times, the decisions have a gatekeeping or administrative intent. In these cases, the assessment and subsequent interpretation is made on behalf of "an entity that wants guidance in making a judgment about a person being evaluated" (Goodyear & Lichtenberg, 1999, p. 2); as a consequence, the results may or may not be helpful to the person who is being evaluated. Moreover, the person requesting the assessment and the person being assessed may have different goals and desired outcomes, highlighting the need to carefully define the audience that will receive the interpretation.

It is important to remember that the consumer most frequently is a client who has taken tests as part of a counseling relationship, and has been involved in the decision making about testing (Duckworth, 1990). A prime example within counseling psychology is a client who is engaged in career counseling, in which formal assessment is a typical intervention. However, as implied earlier, the consumer may be another individual or agency who wants information about a client, such as a judge, attorney, or human resources manager. Regardless of who the consumer is, eventually he or she will attempt to make sense of the test data and decide what the implications are for him- or herself (Goodyear & Lichtenberg, 1999).

With these issues in mind, what is the goal of test interpretation? First, psychologists interpret tests to make diagnoses and plan interventions. The psychologist him- or herself may be considered the primary consumer in this case, particularly if they are providing psychotherapy, because the tests are used to guide their work with the client. All mental health professionals "assess" their clients' level of functioning as they formulate the best course of action; formal testing provides more structured data for doing so. A second purpose of test interpretation is, as noted earlier, for psychologists to interpret the results of tests directly to clients. Goodyear and Lichtenberg (1999) argued that psychologists have an ethical imperative, given that tests are intrusive and have consequences; therefore, clients have the right to know the results of their tests. Tests may be interpreted to clients to help them monitor their progress, such as repeated testing to document change throughout therapy, or to facilitate choice, such as in the practice of career counseling. Assessment plays such a central role in the delivery of career counseling that test interpretation is an intervention.

Despite the importance of interpreting tests directly to clients, there is little evidence regarding the impact or effectiveness of test interpretation itself (Goodyear, 1990; Tinsley & Chu, 1999). In fact, Tinsley and Chu (1999), reviewing literature related to the interpretation of vocational interest inventories, described the empirical foundation for this activity as "shockingly inadequate" (p. 259).

A third purpose of test interpretation is psychologists interpreting test data to a third party, most frequently in the form of a written report. Although traditionally the domain of clinical psychology, the distinctions have eroded, so that counseling psychologists are also engaged in third-party test interpretation. The psychologist's role is as a consultant, typically responding to a specific referral question raised by the third party about the client. This purpose of test interpretation raises ethical issues about who is the client and what the psychologist's responsibilities are toward the person being tested.

The manner in which assessment results are used may relate to the two models discussed earlier, the traditional or contemporary models of assessment within counseling psychology. Relevant to the latter model, Goldfinger and Pomerantz (2010) offer a six-step model for assessment, beginning with the *referral* and an analysis of the *context of the referral*: who requested the assessment, what are the goals, who will receive the information, what are the implicit and explicit questions to be addressed? Next, the psychologist determines the *information* necessary to address the referral question, and then *gathers, scores, and interprets data*. Based on these data, the psychologist *draws conclusions* in relation to the referral question, and *communicates the findings* to the primary (and secondary) audiences.

Training, Professional, and Ethical Issues

The first portion of this chapter focused on psychometric theory and procedures, as a precursor to understanding the selection and use of assessment instruments. Training in psychometric concepts has been identified as crucial for counseling psychologists due to their joint roles as test administrators and test interpreters (Bolt & Rounds, 2000), as well as for general training in research methodology, statistics, and measurement (Aiken, West, Sechrest, & Reno, 1990). In addition, counseling psychology training needs to include attention to the professional standards and guidelines related to the use of assessment.

STANDARDS AND GUIDELINES

It is imperative that psychologists be aware of the range of standards and guidelines related to assessment, including the *Code of Fair Testing Practices in Education* (Joint Committee on Testing Practices, 2004), *Standards for Educational and Psychological Testing* (AERA, APA, NCME, 1999), APA's *Ethical Principles of Psychologists and Code of Conduct* (APA, 2002), and APA's *Guidelines for Test User Qualifications* (Turner, DeMers, Fox, & Reed, 2001).

The APA has focused on the qualifications of those who use psychological tests, in reaction to concerns that doctoral programs were providing insufficient training related to statistics and measurement (Aiken et al., 1990). As defined by the APA, the term *test user qualifications* refers to "the combination of knowledge, skills, abilities, training, experience, and where appropriate, practice credentials" considered desirable for responsible use of psychological tests (Turner et al., 2001, p. 1099). Furthermore, the APA focused on the qualifications of test users because growing concerns about problems associated with test use seemed to be related to the competence of individuals using tests, rather than with the quality of test materials or practices of test developers. In other words, regardless of the quality of the test itself, tests can easily be misused by practitioners, through inappropriate selection, administration, interpretation, and conclusions (Betz, 2000; Turner et al., 2001). Early efforts to monitor the qualifications of test users were developed by the APA in 1954, and classified tests according to their level of complexity: Level A tests (such as achievement tests) could be administered, scored, and interpreted by nonpsychologists; Level B tests (such as the Strong Interest Inventory) require knowledge of technical aspects of test construction and so users needed to have advanced coursework; Level C tests (such as the WAIS and MMPI) require an advanced degree in psychology and/or licensure (Betz, 2000).

Consistent with discussion earlier in this chapter, the APA *Guidelines for Test Users* clearly acknowledged that psychological tests must be viewed within the broader context of assessment, which necessarily entails a "complex activity requiring the interplay of knowledge of psychometric concepts with expertise in an area of professional practice or application" (Turner et al., 2001, p. 1100). The *Guidelines* include two types of qualifications for test users: general psychometric knowledge and skills, and specific qualifications for particular settings or purposes. General knowledge and skills include (a) psychometric and measurement knowledge (descriptive statistics, reliability and measurement error, validity and meaning of test scores, normative interpretation of test scores, selection of appropriate tests, and test administration procedures); (b) ethnic, racial, cultural, gender, age, and linguistic variables; (c) testing individuals with disabilities; and (d) supervised experience. Within each of these categories, the authors provided detailed lists of crucial knowledge and skills. The second type of qualifications pertains to specific contexts, including six different purposes of tests (classification, description, prediction, intervention planning, tracking, and training and supervision) within five diverse contexts (employment, education, career and vocational counseling, health care, and forensic). Clearly, all of these purposes and contexts are relevant to the practice of assessment within counseling psychology.

ETHICAL ISSUES

The APA *Ethical Principles of Psychologists and Code of Conduct* devotes one of its ten ethical standards specifically to matters related to assessment. This standard includes guidelines specifying the following:

(a) *Bases for assessment* (Standard 9.01): Psychologists base their recommendations or diagnoses on sufficient information, and only after conducting an examination of the individual that is adequate to support such recommendations. If recommendations are made based solely on a review of records, then the limits are explained.

(b) *Appropriate use* of assessment (Standard 9.02): Psychologists use assessment tools in a manner that is appropriate given the available research, use instruments with established reliability and validity for the given population (or, in the absence of psychometric evidence, note the limits of the instrument), and use assessment appropriate to an individual's language preference and competence.

(c) *Informed consent* (Standard 9.03): Psychologists obtain clients' informed consent for assessment; informed consent will include the nature of the assessment, fees, the role of third parties, and limits of confidentiality. Several situations may obviate the need for informed consent, such as when testing is mandated by law, is implied because testing is a routine activity (e.g., within an educational or employment context), or if a purpose of the testing is to evaluate decisional capacity. Additional issues regarding informed consent

are addressed by Standard 3.10 of the *Ethical Principles*.

(d) *Release of test data* (Standard 9.04): Psychologists provide test data (defined as item responses, scale scores, and notes/recordings) to clients or others as specified in a client release document. Psychologists may choose not to release test data to protect clients or others from harm or misuse of data. In the absence of a client release, psychologists release test data only as required by law or court order.

(e) *Test construction* (Standard 9.05): Psychologists who develop tests or assessment procedures use appropriate psychometric procedures and knowledge.

(f) *Interpretation of results* (Standard 9.06): When interpreting test results, psychologists take into account the purpose of the assessment, as well as contextual factors related to test-taking and the test-taker, that might influence the accuracy or direction of the interpretation. They also indicate any significant limitations of their interpretations.

(g) *Assessment by unqualified individuals* (Standard 9.07): Psychologists do not promote the use of assessment tools by people who are not qualified, except as used in training with appropriate supervision.

(h) *Obsolete tests and outdated test results* (Standard 9.08): Psychologists do not base recommendations or decisions on data or tests that are outdated for the current purpose.

(i) *Test scoring and interpretation services* (Standard 9.09): Psychologists who offer assessment services to other professionals provide an accurate description of the purpose, psychometric properties, and applications of the assessment; psychologists who select others' services do so on the basis of evidence of validity; and, psychologists retain responsibility for the use of assessment even if they use others' services.

(j) *Explaining assessment results* (Standard 9.10): Psychologists ensure that the results are explained to the test-taker, unless there are specific predetermined reasons not to do so (such as security screenings or forensic evaluations).

(k) *Maintaining test security* (Standard 9.11): Psychologists maintain the integrity and security of test materials (instruments, manuals, and protocols).

In addition to these components of Standard 9, other standards in the *Ethical Principles* are relevant to assessment, such as Standard 2 (Competence) and Standard 4 (Privacy and Confidentiality), as described next.

Competence

Standards 2.01 and 2.03 pertain to boundaries of competence, and maintaining competence. These standards state that psychologists provide services with populations and in areas only within the boundaries of their competence, based on education, training, experience, consultation, or study. Psychologists planning to provide services involving populations or techniques that are new to them pursue relevant education, training, or experience. Furthermore, psychologists continue to develop and maintain competence (APA, 2002). Issues of competence thus are particularly important when psychologists use a test or assessment procedure that is new on the market, recently revised, or new to them.

Confidentiality and Privacy

Generally, *privacy* refers to the individual's right to control access to information about him- or herself. Privacy is the right to be left alone. On the other hand, *confidentiality* refers to how private information provided by an individual will be protected by the recipient of that information, in this case, a psychologist. Confidentiality is also shaped by legal considerations, which may vary by state.

Standard 4 of the *Ethical Principles* addresses confidentiality and privacy. Psychologists have a "primary obligation and take reasonable precautions to protect confidentiality information obtained through or stored in any medium" (Standard 4.01, APA, 2002, p. 1066) and discuss the limits of confidentiality with clients. Psychologists also minimize intrusions on privacy, by including in reports only that information that is directly relevant to the purpose of the report (Standard 4.04).

Ethical Issues Related to Use of the Internet in Assessment

With the increase in Internet-based assessment, issues of privacy and confidentiality become more complicated and more crucial. For example, a client may take an assessment online, upload his or her responses to a scoring service, which then scores and sends the results electronically to the psychologist, who stores or downloads the scores and materials. Each of these transfer or storage points opens the possibility of a breach of confidentiality, and psychologists using these mechanisms should be aware of the security measures in place, as well as the limits to security. For example, an APA Task Force on Psychological Testing on the Internet recommended the use of a three-tier server model, in which the test system has three independent servers, one each for the Internet, the test, and the database, with appropriate firewalls and other security measures (Naglieri et al., 2004).

Internet-based assessment also raises additional concerns related to many aspects of the ethical standard related to assessment. Access to the Internet has led to an explosive proliferation of information and access to materials that were previously unavailable. New concerns are emerging regarding use of Internet tests by unqualified individuals, appropriate release of test data, interpretation of test results, test security, and outdated test materials (Bartram, 2006; Naglieri et al., 2004). A recent example was provided by LoBello and Zachar (2007), who documented sales of current and obsolete test materials (including the WAIS, WISC, MMPI, and Rorschach) on Internet auction sites such as eBay. Although the existing *Ethical Principles* provide guidance, monitoring compliance to the principles is becoming more difficult given the growth of Internet services.

Additional Ethical and Professional Issues

The APA *Ethical Principles* provide broad guidance related to testing and assessment (as well as other professional activities). In addition, there are many unique situations that psychologists encounter regarding ethical dilemmas in testing. For example, Turchik, Karpenko, Hammers, and McNamara (2007) described several examples for practitioners working in rural or economically depressed areas: "What should a practitioner do when a third-party payer denies authorization for a needed neuropsychological assessment? How does a clinic director decide which tests to purchase and still stay within the clinic's limited budget? What does a small rural community do when there are no practitioners trained to provide psychological assessment?" (Turchik et al., 2007, p. 158).

The examples provided by Turchik et al. (2007) are a reminder that ethical dilemmas are just that—dilemmas—and the guidelines are just that— guidelines. Although "ethical principles dictate that psychologists provide services that are in the best interests of their patients" (Meyer et al., 2001, p. 129), frequently competing interests or needs are difficult to resolve.

An additional professional issue regards the importance of ongoing training that occurs after completion of the doctoral degree. Many of the tests and assessments used by counseling psychologists are stalwarts, some used for many decades (such as the MMPI or Strong Interest Inventory). However, test developers frequently update the test materials—test items, scales, norms, interpretive materials—and psychologists must be aware of these changes and update their own training and preparation.

Future Directions in Testing and Assessment

What does the future hold for the development and use of psychological tests and assessment? Several trends are worth noting. The first is the often-cited changing demographic characteristics and continued cultural and linguistic diversification of the U.S. population. In addition, there is increasing diversity on other important individual difference variables that will have implications for testing and assessment, such as age and disability. Considering such diversification from the perspective of multiculturalism and acknowledging multiple group identities presents somewhat of a conundrum: Although it is clearly important to develop and validate the use of tests for diverse individuals, at what point does this become an unrealistic goal, given the wide range of test users?

The second trend is globalization, which has major implications for the use of psychological tests both in the United States and internationally (Bartram, 2006; DeBell, 2006). Globalization presents similar issues to those discussed related to changing demographics, such as linguistic and cultural equivalence of existing and newly developed tests. Furthermore, the "internationalization of testing" (Bartram, 2006) is a direct result of the explosive growth of the Internet, erasing the borders between countries as well as between national rules and regulations regarding the use of testing.

The third trend is increasing technology, particularly Internet assessment and computerized assessment (Bartram, 2006; Naglieri et al., 2004; Tippins et al., 2006). Coupled with the previously discussed trend of globalization, expanded technology raises intriguing questions about the delivery infrastructure of assessment; relationships among test publishers, test users, and test takers; and unproctored testing and assessment (Bartram, 2006; Tippins et al., 2006).

These trends, as well as other issues, such as the evolving impact of managed care, serve to highlight the importance of knowledge regarding testing and assessment. Understanding the key underlying principles of measurement will prepare psychologists for using assessment in their work, today and in the future.

References

Agresti, A. A. (1992). Integrating neuropsychological training into a counseling psychology curriculum. *The Counseling Psychologist, 20*, 605–619.

Aiken, L. S., West, S. G., Sechrest, L., & Reno, R. R. (1990). Graduate training in statistics, methodology, and measurement in psychology: A survey of PhD programs in North America. *American Psychologist, 45*, 721–734.

Allison, R. D., Lichtenberg, J. W., & Goodyear, R. K. (1999). Science and the practice of test interpretation. In J. W. Lichtenberg, & R. K. Goodyear (Eds.), *Scientist-practitioner perspectives on test interpretation* (pp. 167–182). Needham Heights, MA: Allyn and Bacon.

American Educational Research Association, American Psychological Association, National Council on Measurement in Education (AERA, APA, NCME). (1999). *Standards for educational and psychological testing*. Washington, DC: AERA.

American Psychological Association (APA). (2002). Ethical principles of psychologists and code of conduct. *American Psychologist, 47*, 1597–1611. Retrieved from http://www.apa.org/ethics/code2002.html.

American Psychological Association (APA). (2003). Guidelines on multicultural education, training, research, practice, and organizational change for psychologists. *American Psychologist, 58*, 377–402.

Anastasi, A., & Urbina, S. (1997). *Psychological testing* (7th ed.). Upper Saddle River, NJ: Prentice-Hall.

Antony, M. M., & Barlow, D. H. (Eds.). (2002). *Handbook of assessment and treatment planning for psychological disorders*. New York: Guilford.

Bartram, D. (2006). The internationalization of testing and new models of test delivery on the Internet. *International Journal of Testing, 6*, 121–131.

Betz, N. E. (2000). Contemporary issues in testing use. In C. E. Watkins, Jr., & V. L. Campbell (Eds.), *Testing and assessment in counseling practice* (2nd ed., pp. 481–516). Mahwah, NJ: Lawrence Erlbaum.

Bolt, D. M., & Rounds, J. (2000). Advances in psychometric theory and methods. In S. D. Brown, & R. W. Lent (Eds.), *Handbook of counseling psychology* (3rd ed., pp. 140–176). New York: Wiley.

Brown, T. A., Di Nardo, P. A., & Barlow, D. H. (1994). *Anxiety Disorders Interview Schedule for DSM-IV (ADIS-IV)*. San Antonio, TX: Psychological Corporation.

Buchanan, T. (2002). Online assessment: Desirable or dangerous? *Professional Psychology: Research and Practice, 33*, 148–154.

Bufka, L. F., Crawford, J. I., Levitt, J. T. (2002). Brief screening assessments for managed care and primary care. In M. M. Antony, & D. H. Barlow (Eds.), *Handbook of assessment and treatment planning for psychological disorders*. New York: Guilford.

Camara, W., Nathan, J., & Puente, A. (2000). Psychological test usage: Implications in professional psychology. *Professional Psychology: Research and Practice, 31*, 141–154.

Campbell, D. T., & Fiske, D. W. (1959). Convergent and discriminant validation by the multitrait-multimethod matrix. *Psychological Bulletin, 56*, 81–105.

Campbell, V. L. (2000). A framework for using tests in counseling. In C. E. Watkins, Jr., & V. L. Campbell (Eds.), *Testing and assessment in counseling practice* (2nd ed., pp. 3–13). Mahwah, NJ: Lawrence Erlbaum.

Cashel, M. L. (2002). Child and adolescent psychological assessment: Current clinical practices and the impact of managed care. *Professional Psychology: Research and Practice, 33*, 446–453.

Cassin, S. E., Singer, A. R., Dobson, K. S., & Altmaier, E. M. (2007). Professional interests and career aspirations of graduate students in professional psychology: An exploratory survey. *Training and Education in Professional Psychology, 1*, 26–37.

Cobb, H. C., Reeve, R. E., Shealy, C. N., Norcross, J. C., Schare, M. L., Rodolfa, E. R., et al. (2004). Overlap among clinical, counseling, and school psychology: Implications for the profession and combined-integrated training. *Journal of Clinical Psychology, 60*, 939–955.

Committee on Ethnic Minority Affairs, Committee on Psychological Tests and Assessment. (2000). *Relevant literature addressing testing and assessment of cultural, ethnic, and linguistically diverse populations.* Washington, DC: Author. Retrieved May 2, 2009, from http://www.apa.org/science/minority_testing_ref.pdf.

Committee on Psychological Tests and Assessment. (2002a). *Books and chapters pertaining to neuropsychological assessment cross-culturally, with minorities, and with non-English speaking individuals.* Washington, DC: Author. Retrieved May 2, 2009, from http://www.apa.org/science/neuropsych_minority_cit.pdf.

Committee on Psychological Tests and Assessment. (2002b). *References on testing of people of color, women, language minorities, and people with disabilities.* Washington, DC: Author. Retrieved May 2, 2009, from http://www.apa.org/science/women_and_dis_ref.pdf.

Cortina, J. M. (1993). What is coefficient alpha? An examination of theory and applications. *Journal of Applied Psychology, 78*, 98–104.

Cronbach, L. J. (1957). The two disciplines of scientific psychology. *American Psychologist, 12*, 671–684.

Cronbach, L. J., & Meehl, P. E. (1955). Construct validity in psychological tests. *Psychological Bulletin, 52*, 281–302.

Dawis, R. V. (1987). Scale construction. *Journal of Counseling Psychology, 34*, 481–489.

Dawis, R. V. (1992). The individual differences tradition in counseling psychology. *Journal of Counseling Psychology, 39*, 7–19.

DeBell, C. (2006). What all applied psychologists should know about work. *Professional Psychology: Research and Practice, 37*, 325–333.

Duckworth, J. (1990). The counseling approach to the use of testing. *The Counseling Psychologist, 18*, 198–204.

Embretson, S. E. (1996). The new rules of measurement. *Psychological Assessment, 8*, 341–349.

Fernandez, K., Boccaccini, M. T., & Noland, R. M. (2007). Professionally responsible test selection for Spanish-speaking clients: A four-step approach for identifying and selecting translated tests. *Professional Psychology: Research and Practice, 38*, 363–374.

Fouad, N. A. (1999). Validity evidence for interest inventories. In M. L. Savickas, & A. R. Spokane (Eds.), *Vocational interests* (pp. 193–209). Palo Alto, CA: Davies-Black.

Fouad, N. A., & Chan, P. M. (1999). Gender and ethnicity: Influence on test interpretation and reception. In J. W. Lichtenberg, & R. K. Goodyear (Eds.), *Scientist-practitioner perspectives on test interpretation* (pp. 31–58). Needham Heights, MA: Allyn and Bacon.

Goldfinger, K., & Pomerantz, A. M. (2010). *Psychological assessment and report writing.* Thousand Oaks, CA: Sage.

Goodyear, R. K. (1990). Research on the effects of test interpretation: A review. *The Counseling Psychologist, 18*, 240–257.

Goodyear, R. K., & Lichtenberg, J. W. (1999). A scientist-practitioner perspective on test interpretation. In J. W. Lichtenberg, & R. K. Goodyear (Eds.), *Scientist-practitioner perspectives on test interpretation* (pp. 1–14). Needham Heights, MA: Allyn and Bacon.

Groth-Marnat, G. (1999). *Handbook of psychological assessment* (3rd ed.). New York: Wiley.

Hansen, J. C. (1999). Test psychometrics. In J. W. Lichtenberg, & R. K. Goodyear (Eds.), *Scientist-practitioner perspectives on test interpretation* (pp. 15–30). Needham Heights, MA: Allyn and Bacon.

Hansen, J. C. (2005). Assessment of interests. In S. D. Brown, & R. W. Lent (Eds.), *Career development and counseling: Putting theory and research to work* (pp. 281–304). New York: Wiley.

Hartung, P. J. (2005). Integrated career assessment and counseling: Mindsets, models, and methods. In W. B. Walsh, & M. L. Savickas (Eds.), *Handbook of vocational psychology* (3rd ed., pp. 371–395). Mahwah, NJ: Lawrence Erlbaum.

Hebben, N., & Milberg, W. (2002). *Essentials of neuropsychological assessment.* New York: Wiley.

Hess, T. M., Hinson, J. T., & Hodges, E. A. (2009). Moderators of and mechanisms underlying stereotype threat effects on old adults' memory performance. *Experimental Aging Research, 35*, 153–177.

Hoyt, W. T., & Melby J. N. (1999). Dependability of measurement in counseling psychology: An introduction to generalizability theory. *The Counseling Psychologist, 27*, 325–352.

Joint Committee on Testing Practices. (2004). *Code of fair testing practices in education.* Washington, DC: Author.

Kaplan, R. M., & Saccuzzo, D. P. (2009). *Psychological testing: Principles, applications, and issues* (7th ed.). Belmont, CA: Wadsworth/Thomson.

Larson, P. C., & Agresti, A. A. (1992). Counseling psychology and neuropsychology: An overview. *The Counseling Psychologist, 20*, 549–555.

Leong, F. T. L. (2000). Cultural pluralism. In A. E. Kazdin (Ed.), *Encyclopedia of psychology* Vol 2 (pp. 387–389). Washington, DC: American Psychological Association.

LoBello, S. G., & Zachar, P. (2007). Psychological test sales and Internet auctions: Ethical considerations for dealing with obsolete or unwanted test materials. *Professional Psychology: Research and Practice, 38*, 68–70.

Matarazzo, J. D. (1990). Psychological assessment versus psychological testing: Validation from Binet to the school, clinic, and courtroom. *American Psychologist, 45*, 999–1017.

May, T. M., & Scott, K. J. (1991). Assessment in counseling psychology: Do we practice what we teach? *The Counseling Psychologist, 19*, 396–413.

McIntire, S. A., & Miller, L. A. (2007). *Foundations of psychological testing: A practical approach* (2nd ed.). Thousand Oaks, CA: Sage.

Meehl, P. E., & Rosen, A. (1955). Antecedent probability and the efficiency of psychometric signs, patterns, or cutting scores. *Psychological Bulletin, 52*, 194–216.

Meier, S. T. (1999). Training the practitioner-scientist: Bridging case conceptualization, assessment, and intervention. *The Counseling Psychologist, 27*, 846–869.

Messick, S. (1995). Validity of psychological assessment: Validation of inferences from persons' responses and performances on scientific inquiry into score meaning. *American Psychologist, 50*, 741–749.

Meyer, G. J., Finn, S. E., Eyde, L. D., Kay, G. G., Moreland, K. L., Dies, R. R., et al. (2001). Psychological testing and psychological assessment: A review of evidence and issues. *American Psychologist, 56*, 128–165.

Morgan, R. D., & Cohen, L. M. (2008). Clinical and counseling psychology: Can differences be gleaned from printed recruiting materials? *Training and Education in Professional Psychology, 2*, 156–164.

Naglieri, J. A., Drasgow, F., Schmit, M., Handler, L., Prifitera, A., Margolis, A., Veslasquez, R. (2004). Psychological testing on the Internet: New problems, old issues. *American Psychologist, 59*, 150–162.

Neimeyer, G. J., Bowman, J., & Stewart, A. E. (2001). Internship and initial job placements in counseling psychology: A 26-year retrospective. *The Counseling Psychologist, 29*, 763–780.

Neimeyer, G. J., Rice, K. G., & Keilin, W. G. (2009). Internship placements: Similarities and differences between clinical and counseling psychology programs. *Training and Education in Professional Psychology, 3*, 47–52.

Neukrug, E. S., & Fawcett, R. C. (2006). *Essentials of testing and assessment: A practical guide for counselors, social workers, and psychologists.* Belmont, CA: Brooks/Cole.

Nguyen, H.-H. D., & Ryan, A. M. (2008). Does stereotype threat affect test performance of minorities and women? A meta-analysis of experimental evidence. *Journal of Applied Psychology, 93*, 1314–1334.

Nunnally, J. C., & Bernstein, I. H. (1994). *Psychometric theory* (3rd ed.). New York: McGraw-Hill.

Parsons, F. (1989). *Choosing a vocation.* Garrett Park, MD: Garrett Park Press. (Original work published 1909).

Randahl, G. J., Hansen, J. C., & Haverkamp, B. E. (1993). Instrumental behaviors following test administration and interpretation: Exploration validity of the Strong Interest Inventory. *Journal of Counseling & Development, 71*, 435–439.

Rounds, J. B., & Armstrong, P. I. (2005). Assessment of needs and values. In S. D. Brown, & R. W. Lent (Eds.), *Career development and counseling: Putting theory and research to work* (pp. 305–329). New York: Wiley.

Ryan Krane, N. E., & Tirre, W. C. (2005). Ability assessment in career counseling. In S. D. Brown, & R. W. Lent (Eds.), *Career development and counseling: Putting theory and research to work* (pp. 330–352). New York: Wiley.

Ryan, J. J., Lopez, S. J., & Lichtenberg, J. W. (1999). Neuropsychological training in APA-accredited counseling psychology programs. *The Counseling Psychologist, 27*, 435–442.

Schmitt, N. (1996). Uses and abuses of coefficient alpha. *Psychological Assessment, 8*, 350–353.

Sechrest, L. (1963). Incremental validity. *Educational and Psychological Measurement, 23*, 153–158.

Spengler, P. M., Strohmer, D. C., Dixon, D. N., & Shivy, V. A. (1995). A scientist-practitioner model of psychological assessment: Implications for training, practice and research. *The Counseling Psychologist, 23*, 506–534.

Steele, C. M., & Aronson, J. (1995). Stereotype threat and the intellectual test performance of African Americans. *Journal of Personality and Social Psychology, 69*, 797–811.

Summerfeldt, L. J., & Antony, M. M. (2002). Structured and semistructured diagnostic interviews. In M. M. Antony, & D. H. Barlow (Eds.), *Handbook of assessment and treatment planning for psychological disorders* (pp. 3–37). New York: Guilford Press.

Swanson, J. L. (2002). Understanding the complexity of clients' lives: Infusing a truly integrative career-personal perspective into graduate training. *The Counseling Psychologist, 30*, 815–832.

Swanson, J. L., & D'Achiardi, C. (2005). Beyond interests, needs/values, and abilities: Assessing other important career constructs over the life span. In S. D. Brown, & R. W. Lent (Eds.), *Career development and counseling: Putting theory and research to work* (pp. 353–381). New York: Wiley.

Swanson, J. L., & Fouad, N. A. (2010). *Career theory and practice: Learning through case studies* (2nd ed.). Thousand Oaks, CA: Sage.

Tinsley, H. E. A. (2000). Technological magic, social change, and counseling rituals: The future of career assessment. *Journal of Career Assessment, 8*, 339–350.

Tinsley, H. E. A., & Bradley, R. W. (1986). Test interpretation. *Journal of Counseling & Development, 64*, 462–466.

Tinsley, H. E. A., & Chu, S. (1999). Research on test and interest inventory interpretation outcomes. In M. L. Savickas, & A. R. Spokane (Eds.), *Vocational interests* (pp. 257–276). Palo Alto, CA: Davies-Black.

Tippins, N. T., Beaty, J., Drasgow, F., Gibson, W. M., Pearlman, K., Segall, D. O., & Shepherd, W. (2006). Unproctored Internet testing in employment settings. *Personnel Psychology, 59*, 189–225.

Turchik, J. A., Karpenko, V., Hammers, D., & McNamara, J. R. (2007). Practical and ethical assessment issues in rural, impoverished, and managed care settings. *Professional Psychology: Research and Practice, 38*, 158–168.

Turner, S. M., DeMers, S. T., Fox, H. R., & Reed, G. M. (2001). APA's guidelines for test user qualifications. *American Psychologist, 56*, 1099–1113.

Tyler, L. E. (1984). What tests don't measure. *Journal of Counseling & Development, 63*, 48–50.

United States of America Internet usage and broadband usage report. Retrieved May 20, 2009, from http://www.internetworldstats.com/am/us.htm.

Walborn, F. S. (1996). *Process variables: Four common elements of counseling and psychotherapy.* Pacific Grove, CA: Brooks/Cole.

Walsh, W. B. (2001). The changing nature of the science of vocational psychology. *Journal of Vocational Behavior, 59*, 262–274.

Walsh, W. B., & Betz, N. E. (2001). *Tests and assessment* (4th ed.). Upper Saddle River, NJ: Prentice-Hall.

Wiggins, J. S. (2003). *Paradigms of personality assessment.* New York: Guilford.

Yates, B. T., & Taub, J. (2003). Assessing the costs, benefits, cost-effectiveness, and cost-benefit of psychological assessment: We should, we can, and here's how. *Psychological Assessment, 15*, 478–495.

Methodologies in Counseling Psychology

Nancy E. Betz *and* Ruth E. Fassinger

Abstract

This chapter reviews quantitative and qualitative methodologies most frequently used in counseling psychology research. We begin with a review of the paradigmatic bases and epistemological stances of quantitative and qualitative research, followed by overviews of both approaches to empirical research in counseling psychology. In these overviews, our goal is to provide a broad conceptual understanding of the "why" of these methods. Among the quantitative methods receiving attention are analysis of variance (ANOVA) and multivariate analysis of variance (MANOVA), factor analysis, structural equation modeling, and discriminant analysis. We include discussion of such qualitative methods as grounded theory, narratology, phenomenology, ethnography, and participatory action research. Important general issues in designing qualitative studies are also discussed. The chapter concludes with a discussion of mixed methods in research and the importance of knowledge of both major approaches in order to maximally utilize findings from our rich and diverse counseling psychology literature.

Keywords: quantitative research methods, qualitative research methods, methods in counseling psychology research

All research in counseling psychology is based on the fundamental principle that we learn about people—their thoughts, feelings, and behaviors—by "observing" them in some systematic manner. Certainly, we learn much about people from the processes of informal observation, as might be the case when we watch someone interact at a party and make inferences about his or her social skills. But to advance science, our observations must be done under conditions that include some sort of control over the process of gathering those observations. The observations can be gained in a variety of ways: via formalized assessments or measures, from interviews or other kinds of narratives, through structured viewing and tracking of behavior, or even from cultural artifacts that provide information about the phenomenon of interest.

Broadly speaking, observations can be divided into those yielding numeric representations and those yielding linguistic representations, and each offers a unique and heuristically valuable approach to explaining the phenomenon of interest. The manner in which we examine the observations to make sense of them is determined by the nature of those observations, and science provides us with a wide variety of methods from which to choose. These methods are the subject of this chapter.

In this chapter, we begin with a review of the paradigmatic bases and epistemological stances of quantitative and qualitative research, followed by overviews of both approaches to empirical research in counseling psychology. In these reviews, our goal is to provide a broad conceptual understanding of the "why" of these methods rather than a detailed technical "how-to" description of any method. We note that our somewhat differential coverage of quantitative and qualitative approaches in the chapter reflects the disproportionate attention to quantitative methods currently seen in our field, an empirical imbalance that we hope will be rectified over the next decade. We also point out that, although we cover quantitative and qualitative approaches separately in this chapter for ease in presentation, combining these approaches can yield the most informative programs of research over time. Thus, we conclude the chapter with a brief discussion of mixed methods research and of future directions in research methodology.

Paradigmatic Bases and Epistemological Stances of Qualitative Research

Ponterotto (2002, 2005) has written cogently about the paradigmatic bases and epistemological stances underlying quantitative and qualitative research in counseling psychology, using a four-category system that distinguishes among positivist, post-positivist, constructivist-interpretivist, and critical-ideological paradigms. Beginning with several concepts integral to the philosophy of science, Ponterotto (2005) outlines the major premises of the four paradigms based on their assumptions regarding ontology (nature of reality), epistemology (acquisition of knowledge), axiology (role of values), rhetorical structure (language of research), and methodology (research procedures). Generally, it can be said that positivist and post-positivist paradigms most often undergird quantitative research, whereas constructivist-interpretivist and critical-ideological paradigms most often form the foundation for qualitative research. However, these distinctions are not completely orthogonal; the post-positivist position, for example, can typify the work of some qualitative as well as quantitative researchers, and some of the specific "qualitative" approaches (e.g., participatory action research, ethnography) may incorporate different forms of quantitative data if appropriate to the goals of the study.

Positivist and Post-positivist Paradigms

Positivism is often called the "received view" in psychology (Guba & Lincoln, 1994, cited in Ponterotto, 2005). It is based on the theory-driven, hypothesis-testing, deductive methods of the natural sciences, and involves a controlled approach to generating hypotheses about a phenomenon of interest, collecting carefully measured observations, testing hypotheses for verification using descriptive and inferential statistics, and producing general theories and cause-and-effect models that seek to predict and control the phenomenon under investigation. Ontologically, positivism assumes an objective reality that can be apprehended and measured, and epistemologically, it posits separation between the researcher and the participant, so that the researcher can maintain objectivity in knowing. Axiologically, it presumes the absence of values in research, and methodologically, it focuses on discovering reality as accurately and dispassionately as possible (hence the emphasis on experimentation and quasi-experimentation, as well as psychometric rigor). Finally, its rhetorical structure of detachment, neutrality, and third-person voice is aimed at capturing the objectivity that has characterized the entire research endeavor.

Post-positivism shares much in common with positivism, the main distinction being that post-positivism assumes human fallibility and, ontologically, accepts a true reality that can be apprehended and measured only imperfectly. Epistemologically, axiologically, methodologically, and rhetorically, the ideal of objectivity, the assumption of researcher–participant independence, the prevention of values from entering research, the controlled use of the hypothetico-deductive method, and the detached scientific voice, respectively, are acknowledged as goals that may be realized only imperfectly in actual practice. For this reason, the post-positivist paradigm embraces theory falsification rather than verification, while maintaining the remainder of the positivist assumptive structure. Both the positivist and post-positivist paradigms stand in contrast to the two broad classes of qualitative research paradigms described below

Constructivist-Interpretivist Paradigms

In contrast to the ontological assumption of a fixed, external, measurable reality that can be apprehended, the constructivist-interpretivist paradigm assumes a relativist notion of multiple, equally valid realities that are constructed in the minds of actors and observers; that is, there is no objective reality that exists apart from the person who is either experiencing or processing the reality, or both. Thus, any account of a phenomenon is necessarily an experientially driven, co-constructed account influenced by the narrator/actor/participant and the listener/observer/researcher, both of whom bring their unique interpretive lenses (shaped by context, history, individual differences, and other forces) to the co-constructed account, which itself is created within a particular experiential context. Epistemologically speaking, then, there cannot be separation between the participant and the researcher, as the process of coming to know and understand is a transactional process that relies on the relationship between them and their mutual construction and interpretation of a lived experience. Imperative to building the kind of relationship that facilitates a full and detailed sharing of lived experience is connection to and entry into the participant's world on the part of the researcher; thus, methodologically, the research process often involves intense and prolonged contact between researchers and participants, utilizing narrative, observational, contextual, historical, and other kinds of data that reveal deep or hidden aspects of the lived experiences under investigation.

It should be obvious that the role of the researcher differs markedly in this paradigm from the positivist or post-positivist researcher position. Researcher subjectivity in a constructivist-interpretivist paradigm is not only acknowledged but becomes an integral part of the research process. Axiologically, values are acknowledged as important, but "bracketed" so that they do not unduly influence the lived experience or the perception of that experience being shared and documented, and researcher reflexivity (in the form of deep reflection, self-monitoring, and immersion in the participant's world) is vitally important to maintaining the integrity of the researcher–participant relationship. Rhetorically, the intense involvement of both the researcher and the participant in the constructivist-interpretivist research process is captured in first-person language, detailed descriptions of how interpretations were generated, direct quotations from the primary data sources (e.g., narratives), and personal reflections of the researcher, including statements regarding values and expectations that likely influenced the work.

Critical-Ideological Paradigms

The critical-ideological paradigm shares a great deal of its assumptive structure with the constructivist-interpretivist paradigm, upon which it is built. However, it is more radical in its goals, which include disruption of the power inequalities of the societal status quo and the liberation and transformation of individual lives. Ontologically, it assumes relativist, constructed realities, but it focuses on historically and societally situated power relations that permeate those realities, and it seeks to dismantle the power structures that have been socially constructed to oppress particular groups of people (e.g., women, people of color, sexual minorities).

Epistemologically, the mutual, transactional relationship between participant and researcher embedded in the constructivist-interpretivist paradigm is presumed but expanded to a more dialectical aim of "inciting transformation in the participants that leads to group empowerment and emancipation from oppression" (Ponterotto, 2005, p. 131). Thus, axiologically speaking, values on the part of the researcher not only are acknowledged and described, but become the driving force behind the ultimate goal of social change.

As might be expected in an approach in which research constitutes a social intervention, the constructivist-interpretivist methodological practice of deeply connecting to individuals to document their lived experiences becomes liberationist in the critical-ideological paradigm. As such, the researcher joins with participants not only as a reflective, empathic chronicler of their lived experiences, but as a passionate advocate for the social change that would empower and emancipate them. This kind of approach necessitates much more prolonged engagement between researchers and participants than is typical in behavioral research and often results in deeply forged alliances that are maintained long after the formal research project has ended. The advocacy stance on the part of the researcher also is reflected in the rhetorical structures used in critical-ideological research, which include description of the societal (interpersonal and intergroup relationships, institutional, community, and policy) changes that resulted or are expected to result from the research.

The constructivist-interpretivist and critical-ideological paradigms give rise to and subsume most of the specific qualitative approaches being used in psychology currently. Although qualitative approaches share some basic philosophical and epistemological premises, each of the extant approaches has features that distinguish it from other approaches. However, some approaches are more fully developed and articulated than others, leading qualitative researchers to borrow and combine aspects of other approaches (e.g., coding procedures, interviewing techniques) in the implementation of studies that may emanate from very different philosophical and epistemological foundations and goals. In addition, a host of contextual factors shape the practical application of qualitative research aims, such as academic publish-or-perish institutional structures, lack of qualitative expertise and training in most graduate programs, and lack of resources or support for the kind of sustained effort considered ideal in these approaches. Thus, the variability among approaches (as well as the specific philosophical underpinnings of a study) may be masked by compromises in conducting the actual study.

Because qualitative approaches differ substantially based on their particular paradigms and epistemological assumptions throughout all phases of the research (and the closer the adherence to core tenets of the approaches, the greater the differences), every qualitative research project must begin with a thoughtful consideration of these issues (Denzin & Lincoln, 2000; Patton, 2002; Ponterotto, 2002, 2005). Quantitative approaches, on the other hand, because they tend to share in common a positivist or post-positivist paradigm involving hypothetico-deductive theory verification or theory falsification methods, find their variability in approach primarily in the kinds of measurement (e.g., interval or categorical) and statistical analyses (e.g., correlation or analysis of variance) utilized. In the following section, we provide an overview of quantitative methods.

Quantitative Methods

As noted above, quantitative methods are based on positivist or post-positivist epistemologies in which theories are used to guide hypothesis generation and hypothesis testing regarding phenomena of interest. Hypotheses are examined using carefully defined and obtained empirical observations, which are assumed to represent important abstract constructs. These hypotheses are tested using descriptive and inferential statistics. The usefulness of quantitative methods depends on the quality of the observational data, which in this case refers to the quality of measurement. Measurement is the process by which we assign numbers to observations, usually of human characteristics or behaviors. Measures (scores) could be derived from a vocational interest inventory, from a measure of depressive symptoms, from a measure of client's liking for the therapist, or from an index of problematic eating behaviors. What is essential is the quality of measurement, usually grounded in the concepts of reliability and validity. Without reliable and valid measures, further data analysis is futile, a waste of time. Detailed discussion of the quality of measures is outside the scope of this chapter, but see the chapter by Swanson (2011, Chapter 8, this volume).

The next sections will summarize different types of data analysis using quantitative methods. It is important to note that complete coverage of statistical methods would require several textbooks, obviously beyond the scope of this chapter. We cover the most commonly used methods in counseling psychology research and refer readers to well-known introductory statistics books and to advanced volumes such as Tabachnick and Fidell's (2007) excellent text *Using Multivariate Statistics*.

Describing Observations

Two basic areas of introductory statistics are scales of measurement (Stevens, 1951) and descriptive statistics, and they will be mentioned here only briefly. Scales of measurement—nominal, ordinal, interval, and ratio—are important because our use of quantitative methods often depends on the kind of data we have. Nominal, or categorical, scales do not actually represent measurement but rather category membership, for example gender or marital status. Next in level of measurement is the ordinal scale, or rank orders. League standings in baseball and class rank are ordinal scales. These numbers have a "greater than" or "less than" quality, but the intervals between numbers are not necessarily (or even usually) equal. Next in level is the interval scale, in which not only order but interval size are presumed to be meaningful. Most test data are interval scale data. Finally, ratio scales have a true zero point as well as ordinal meaning and the assumption of equal intervals. Ratio scales are often found in the physical or psychophysical sciences.

Basic descriptive statistics are also important—in their eagerness to move to inferential statistics, many researchers underemphasize the basic importance of descriptive statistics, or how the numbers "look." If we recall that numbers reflect the observations of people, basic summary descriptions of those numbers become interesting. Observations can be described using frequency distributions (numbers of observations at each score point or score interval, often called histograms [bar diagrams] or frequency polygons). The most important frequency distribution is the *normal distribution*, or *bell curve*, which has certain very useful properties, most especially predicted percentages of cases that fall above and below each z score point on the normal curve. These points are used in determining such critical statistics as standard error of measurement and standard error of estimate.

The best known descriptive statistics are measures of *central tendency* and *variability*. Measures of central tendency include the arithmetic mean, median, and mode, and indices of variability include the range, the variance, and the standard deviation (the square root of the variance). Descriptive statistics are important in and of themselves. For example, we may want to answer the question, "How depressed are college students at our university?" Not only the mean score on our measure of depression but the range and variance of scores are critical information—for example, how many of our students are at risk of suicidal thoughts or behavior? We usually compare score means across gender or race/ethnicity, for which we need group standard deviations as well as means. We may want to compare the scores of a new sample with the original normative sample. We may want to compare the scores of those receiving an intervention to those in a control group. Thus, the mean, variance, and standard deviation are fundamental to many types of analysis.

Inferential Statistics—Group Differences

When we want to compare means—such as those of women and men, normative versus new samples, or those of treatment versus control groups—we usually begin with the assumption that we are examining a sample or samples from a population/populations. Only in very rare instances would we assume that we have assessed the entire population, and we will not deal with that possibility here. Because we are assessing samples from populations, we are using inferential statistics, making educated guesses about population parameters from sample statistics. In doing this, we assume that a population parameter has a sampling distribution with a mean and standard deviation, and that sample values taken from the population will array themselves around the population mean—this array of values is known as the *sampling distribution*. Generally speaking, the larger the standard deviation of the sampling distribution, the more variation in means we will have when sampling from that distribution. The key question for our statistical methods—*t*-tests, analysis of variance (ANOVA) and multivariate analysis of variance (MANOVA)—is to estimate the probability that the means have come from the same versus different populations (we do not refer to *z* tests here because they assume that we have sampled the entire population).

SUM OF SQUARES

Before proceeding, it may be helpful to review the concept of sum of squares (SS), which is critical to the variance calculations required by all these tests. Recall that a sample has a mean that is an estimate of the population parameter. And it has variability

of individual scores around that mean. The wider the variability, the greater will be the variance, or its positive square root, the standard deviation. The variance and standard deviation are based on the sum of squared deviations of individual values from the sample mean, divided by the degrees of freedom, generally n-1 to reflect that the mean used is the sample rather than the population mean. The concept of SS is very important in ANOVA and regression as well, as it is a basis of the general linear model (GLM) fundamental to many of our statistical methods.

THE *t* TEST

Given the above, we begin with a null hypothesis, which usually is that group means are not different from each other. The test statistic, in this case *t*, is the difference between our two means divided by the standard error of the difference. This latter value is the combined standard deviations divided by the combined degrees of freedom. Most computer programs will give the value of *t* for both pooled and separate variances—pooled variance estimates are appropriate if it can be assumed the two population variances are equal. Normally, the statistical software will provide as an option a test of homogeneity of variance, often Levene's test, Hartley's F max test (Kanji, 1993), or Bartlett's test (see Glass & Hopkins, 1984; Kanji, 1993). If the hypothesis of homogeneity of variance is rejected, then the separate variance estimates must be used.

The obtained value of *t* is taken to the table of percentile points of the *t* distribution, sometimes called the *critical values* of the *t* distribution. Using the degrees of freedom, we determine the critical value for rejection of the null Ho at the prescribed value of α—for example, if our two groups each had an N of 21, then our *df* would be 40 and the critical values of *t* are 2.021 ($p < .05$), 2.704 ($p < .01$), and 3.551 ($p < .001$). As sample sizes increase, *t* approaches the value of *z*. At $df =$ infinity, the critical *t* at .05 is 1.96, which is also the .05 critical value for the *z* statistic.

CONFIDENCE INTERVALS AND EFFECT SIZES

In addition to acceptance or rejection of the null hypothesis, we should compute both confidence intervals and effect sizes. There has been much criticism of null hypothesis significance testing (NHST) based on the fact that it allows us only to reject a null hypothesis (which usually is not what we actually want to know), at an arbitrary and necessarily dichotomous level, instead of giving us a probability that our desired hypothesis is true. Cohen (1994) argues that what we want to know is, "Given these data, what is the probability that Ho is true?" but that what it actually indicates is, "Given that Ho is true that is the probability of these (or more extreme) data?" (p. 997).

Confidence intervals improve hypothesis testing by providing estimates of the range of values that likely includes the true population value. When based on a t test, the confidence interval is the mean difference plus or minus a value computed as the critical value of t, multiplied by the standard error of the difference. Thus, we derive a confidence interval that contains the true (population) difference with a probability of 1- p; if that interval includes zero, then we have not rejected the null hypothesis of no difference between the means.

Also, because the statistical significance of t tests is dependent on sample size, we could find that a trivial difference in means was statistically significant but practically unimportant. Likewise, we might overlook a potentially important difference if small sample sizes prevented it from reaching statistical significance. Because of this, it is always advisable to also calculate effect size, an index of the importance of the difference or, as noted by Kirk (1996) "practical significance." There are several indices of effect size in terms of standardized mean differences, most commonly Cohen's (1969) d and Glass' (1976) δ. Cohen's d is the mean difference divided by the combined (pooled) standard deviation. It essentially can be interpreted as the size of the difference in standard deviation units, and is directly related to the amount of overlap between two score distributions. Greater effect size equals less overlap between the distributions. With caution, in that all interpretations must be based on the context and purposes of the research, Cohen (1988) recommended the following ranges of d: .20 to .50 is a small to medium effect, .50 to .80 is a medium to large effect, and over .80 is a large effect. There is not a one-to-one correspondence between statistical significance and effect size—a difference can be statistically significant but not practically important and vice versa.

Effect size is especially important since a difference of a given magnitude can be more or less important based on the overall spread of the score distributions. Assume we have a mean difference of 5 score points between men and women; if the standard deviation of the combined distributions is 10, we have an effect size (d) of .5, what Cohen would describe as a moderately large effect. But if the

standard deviation were 30, d would be .17, less than what Cohen would require for a small effect. In the first case, the difference is one-half a standard deviation, but in the second case it is only one-sixth a standard deviation.

One major use of effect size data is in the technique of *meta-analysis*, first coined by Glass (1976). Meta-analysis is used to quantitatively summarize the findings of many studies of the same general topic. In the case of mean differences, we often use it to summarize a number of studies of a treatment versus a control group. In the classic study of Smith and Glass (1977), 833 comparisons of psychotherapy treatment versus control groups were done, yielding a definitive conclusion of the effectiveness of psychotherapy. Meta-analysis involves searching the literature for all relevant studies, extracting the statistic of interest (in this case the effect size of a comparison of means) and then averaging the effect sizes across studies, often weighted by sample size or, in some cases, by judgments of the quality of the studies. Meta-analyses can also be done within subgroups, such as gender or race/ethnicity; in the case of Smith and Glass (1977), analyses were done for each theoretical approach to therapy. Readers may consult Glass (2006) for a comprehensive discussion of how to conduct a meta-analysis.

ANOVA is used to simultaneously test the differences between two or more means. When there are only two means, its results are identical to those from a t test, but it is more versatile in that three or more means can be tested for difference simultaneously. The null hypothesis is that the population means (μ) are equal: $\mu1 = \mu2 = \mu3$, etc. This is also called an *omnibus test of the equality of means*.

The method of ANOVA utilizes the decomposition of variance components. In a simple one-way analysis of variance, when there is only one independent variable, the total variance is the sum of the variance between treatment and the variance within treatments. We estimate these using the concept of sums of squares mentioned previously. The total SS is the squared deviation of each score in the entire set from the grand mean of all the scores. The *SS Between* is the SS from the squared deviation of each group mean from the grand mean, and the *SS Within* is the sum of squares of each individual's score from the mean of his or her group.

To convert these into variances we obtain the mean squares (MS) by dividing the SS by the degrees of freedom, usually shown as the Greek letter ν. For the between-group SS, ν is J–1, where J is the number of groups, and for the within-group SS,

v is $n-J-1$, where n is the total sample size and J is again the number of groups. The test statistic F, is MSB/MSW, or the between-group variance divided by the within-group variance. We take this value to the F table using the df of 1 and 17. The closer the value of F is to 1.0, the less likely it is to be statistically significant—if the MSB/MSW is close to 1, then we can assume that they are estimating the same variance, the population variance, and that the groups do not differ from each other. If the value of F is statistically significant, we can reject the null hypothesis of group mean equality. Note that, if there are three or more groups, a significant result does not tell us specifically which groups are different from each other—that is examined using post hoc tests of means, such as the Tukey, Tukey-B, and Scheffe tests.

Next in complexity to one-way ANOVA is two- or more-way ANOVA, used with factorial designs. A factorial design involves two or more independent variables, for example type of treatment and gender. The IVs can be manipulated or formed into "natural groups" (such as gender or ethnicity, groups, which existed a priori and are not manipulated). When each level of one IV is paired with each level of the other, we call it a *completely crossed design*. This is probably the most commonly used factorial design, although there are many others—see research design texts (e.g., Heppner, Wampold, & Kivlighan, 2008) for possibilities. A two-way ANOVA can provide one or more main effects and/or an interaction effect.

In a two-way ANOVA, we calculate the MS for each independent variable and the MS for the interaction between the independent variables. Each MS is divided by MSW(within) to get the F for that effect. These are taken to the appropriate cell in the F table to determine whether we accept or reject the null hypothesis for that effect. Again, with an interaction or any main effect involving more than two levels, we must do post hoc tests.

EFFECT SIZES

In the same way that we use effect sizes to evaluate the practical importance of the differences when we have done t tests, effect sizes also should be provided for ANOVA and MANOVA. The effect sizes we use here are in terms of variance accounted for, which is also known as strength of association. η^2 is the proportion of sample total variance that is attributable to an effect in an ANOVA design. It is the ratio of effect variance to total variance; Cohen (1988) suggests that $\eta^2 = .01, .09$, and $.25$ correspond to small,

medium, and large effect sizes, respectively. ω^2 estimates the effect size in the population (Tabachnick & Fidell, 2007). The intraclass correlation also can be used as an index of effect size in ANOVA models.

Vacha-Haase and Thompson (2004) provide an excellent table summarizing strategies for obtaining effect sizes for different analyses using IBM's SPSS software suite (p. 477).

CONFIDENCE INTERVALS FOR EFFECT SIZES

There are two final important trends to mention in hypothesis testing. First, the American Psychological Association (APA) Task Force on Statistical Inference included as a recommendation that confidence intervals be provided for effect sizes themselves (see Tabachnick & Fidell, 2007, and Vacha-Haase & Thompson, 2004, for further details). Moreover, some journal editors are now recommending that the statistic called $prep$ (probability of replication) should be reported instead of the p itself. The $prep$ is the probability of replicating an effect and is itself a function of the effect size and the sample size (Killeen, 2005). The value of $prep$ is inversely related to p—for example, in a given study, p values of .05, .01, and .001 might correspond respectively to $prep$ values of .88, .95, and .99 (Killeen, 2005). Note that $prep$ is a positive way of attaching a probability to the likelihood that we will find the same effect again, instead of a statistical sign that we should reject a null hypothesis.

MANOVA is appropriate when we have several dependent variables (DVs). Using the logic of type 1 error, rejecting the null hypothesis at $p < .05$ means that there is a .05 chance of error, that is, of falsely rejecting the null hypothesis. When we do several tests at the .05 level, we compound that probability of error—we have what is called "experiment-wise error" or "family-wise error." With two DVs, the error rate is approximately .10, and with five DVs it is .23 (see Haase & Ellis, 1987, for the formula). Clearly, these levels of experiment-wise error will lead to excessive type 1 error.

One method of correction for this error is known as the *Bonferroni correction*, which sets the per comparison level of α at approximately α/p, where p equals the number of dependent variables (Tabachnick & Fidell, 2007). This correction is adequate if the variables are not correlated, or if they are highly correlated, but it is not preferable if the variables are mildly correlated, which will be true in most cases. In these cases, MANOVA can be used. It controls the experiment-wise error at the original α, .05, .01, or .001, whatever probability had been determined as the critical value. Like ANOVA, MANOVA can involve only one factor or it can involve a factorial design with two or more IVs. The analysis yields a multivariate F based on an "omnibus" or simultaneous tests of means, which describes the probability of type 1 error over all the tests made. If the multivariate F is statistically significant, we may proceed to examine the univariate F statistics, the same as those we would receive in a univariate ANOVA, to determine which dependent variables are contributing to the significant overall F. The F statistics in MANOVA are provided by one or more of four statistical tests—Wilkes' λ, Pillai's trace, Hotelling's trace, and Roy's criterion (see Haase & Ellis, 1987).

Describing Relationships

Methods for studying relationships between and among variables have at least two important uses within psychology. The most basic use is to further the understanding of human behavior by helping to elucidate the interrelationships of behavior, personality, and functioning. Another important use is that of prediction; when we understand relationships, we can use them to predict future behavior. The study of relationships, including those used in prediction, begins with the topics of correlation and regression. The ideas of association, or covariation, are fundamental in science, including psychology. Many of our quantitative methods are based on the study of relationships.

The index of correlation we use depends on the nature of our variables, but the best known and most frequently used is the Pearson product moment correlation r. This statistic describes the relationship between two interval scale variables, and its calculation is based on the cross-products of the deviation of each score from its own mean. These values can be positive in value, indicating that, as one variable becomes large, the other one does as well; negative, indicating that larger values of one are associated with smaller values of the other; or zero, meaning that there is no association between the two variables. Pearson correlations range from 1 to −1, and it is the absolute value of the correlation that indicates its strength—a correlation of −.5 is as strong as one of .5.

Correlations can be interpreted in terms of statistical significance, percentage of variance accounted for, and effect size. Statistical significance when applied to a correlation means that the correlation is statistically different from zero. The null hypothesis

for a correlation is that the population parameter ρ is equal to 0. All statistics texts contain a table that presents this as a function of sample size—the larger the sample size, the smaller an r must be to be statistically different from zero. For example with an N of 100, a correlation of .20 is significant at $p < .05$, whereas if the N were 1,000, a correlation of .06 would be significant at that level. As with all hypothesis testing, we specify the level of type 1 error we are willing to tolerate, and test our hypothesis at the .05, .01, or .001 levels. If the N is large enough, very small correlations can be statistically significant. For example, the critical value of r ($p < .01$) in a sample of 10,000 is .02.

The latter is an example of a case in which a statistically significant value may be practically insignificant. The square of the r is the coefficient of determination, which is the percentage of variance shared by the two variables. Thus, a correlation of .10, when squared, is .01, meaning that only 1% of the variance is shared between the two variables, and 99% of their variance is not shared. Under most circumstances, this would be a trivial association. In the example given above, the statically significant correlation of .02 when N = 10,000, we are accounting for only an infinitesimal .0004% (4/10 of 1%) of the shared variance between the two variables.

In addition to the percent of shared variance, practical importance also is reflected by effect size, as it is with the description of mean differences in t tests and ANOVA. The value of r is itself an established index of effect size, and its interpretation is based on its relationship to the most common measures of effect size, such as Cohen's d (1988). Cohen (1992) attaches values of r of .10, .30, and .50 to small, medium, and large effect sizes, respectively, but it should be recalled that these describe, respectively, only 1%, 9%, and 25% of the shared variance.

Table 9.1 contains a matrix of correlations among eight personality variables measured by the Healthy Personality Inventory (Borgen & Betz, 2008), an inventory designed to reflect the emphasis on positive psychology and the healthy personality. The table provides the bivariate correlations among the eight variables. As is standard practice, no values are shown for the diagonal, as they are 1.0 (the correlation of a variable with itself, although in some cases the value of coefficient α is shown instead). The table is bilaterally symmetric, so it is necessary to show only the upper or lower diagonal. In some cases, values for one gender are shown above the diagonal, and those for the other gender are shown

Table 9.1. Intercorrelations among Eight Scales of the Healthy Personality Inventory (Borgen & Betz, 2008)

Variable	1.	2.	3.	4.	5.	6.	7.	8.
1. Confident		.51	.44	.71	.37	.50	.28	.58
2. Organized			.68	.72	.17	.34	.03	.26
3. Detail-oriented				.66	.20	.38	.12	.27
4. Goal-directed					.30	.51	.20	.47
5. Outgoing						.66	.56	.65
6. Energetic							.47	.58
7. Adventurous								.71
8. Assertive								

Values for 206 college students. For an N of 206, values of *r* of .14, 18, and .23 are significant at the .05, .01, and .001 levels, respectively, for a two-tailed test.

below the diagonal. Values of *r* that are statistically significant for an N of 206 are provided in a note below the table.

It is important to note four cautions. The value of *r* reflects only linear relationships. If there is curvilinearity in the relationship, then the relationship is better described by the statistic η. Second, the value of the correlation coefficient will be restricted if there is restriction in range in either or both of the two variables being studied. If there is little variability in the scores, there is less chance for changes on one to be reflected by changes in the other. There are formulas for corrections for restriction in range (see Hogan, 2007, p. 122), and these are often used in predictive validity studies (see Sireci & Talento-Miller, 2006). But unless there is some reasonable expectation that score ranges can be increased, then this correction is unduly optimistic and not reflective of what actual relationships will be found in the data.

A third caution is that we must resist the temptation to conclude that a statistically significant correlation is "significantly larger" than a nonsignificant correlation. For example, if we had an N of 50, a correlation of .28 would be significant (at $p < .05$), whereas one of .25 would not be statistically significant, yet they are *not* statistically different from each other. This must be tested by the *z* test for the significance of the difference between two values of ρ (see Glass & Hopkins, 1996).

Finally, correlation does not imply causation. Correlation reflects the covariation among two variables, but does not allow any assumptions about

whether or not one causes the other or whether both are caused by a third (or more) variable. For example, we might find that depression and loneliness are correlated. We could postulate that depression leads to loneliness, that loneliness makes people depressed, or that some third variable like low self-esteem or perceived social inadequacy causes both depression and loneliness. Other research designs (e.g., experimental examinations of treatments for low self-esteem, depression, or loneliness, or structural equation modeling) are required to address questions of causality.

OTHER CORRELATION COEFFICIENTS

Although *r* is the most commonly used index of correlation, a number of others are suitable when one or both variables are not interval in nature. ϕ is often used with two categorical variables, whereas the contingency coefficient is used with two polychotomous variables (categorical variables with more than two categories, such as marital status or race/ethnicity). The relationship between a dichotomous variable (such as right–wrong or true–false answers) and a continuous variable, such as total test score, is indexed by the point-biserial coefficient if we assume a true dichotomy, or the biserial coefficient, which assumes that the dichotomous answer actually reflects an underlying continuum and is therefore dichotomized. The biserial is not a Pearson product moment *r*, so its absolute value can exceed 1.0. Correlations between data, when both sets of numbers are ordinal, can be computed using the Spearman rank correlation (see Glass & Hopkins, 1996).

Regression

Although the most basic reason for studying covariation is to understand the myriad relationships in human behavior, characteristics, and functioning, in many settings these relationships also are used to predict behavior, and in these cases we use the method of regression. One of the oldest uses of regression is based on the relationship between high school grades and performance in college. Using a scatter plot, we could place the predictor variable, high school grades, on the horizontal axis and the criterion, college grade point average (GPA), on the vertical axis. The relationship between these two sets of scores would be described by Pearson's *r*. A regression equation is an equation for a line $Y' = bX + a$, where X is the value of the predictor variable and Y' is the predicted value of the criterion. In this equation, the *a* is the Y intercept, the value of Y where the regression line crosses the y axis or, in other words, the value of y corresponding to an X of 0. The b is the slope of the line and is a direct function of the correlation r between X and Y. The slope of the line is the rate of change in Y as a function of changes in X. Given the formula $Y' = bX + a$, we can estimate a person's score on the criterion variable, given his or her score on the predictor variable. The regression line is known as the "line of best fit" and is determined mathematically as that equation which minimizes the errors of prediction of the criterion from the predictor. In new samples, we then could use this equation to make predictions of collegiate performance from high school GPA.

Multiple Regression

In many cases, we wish to use multiple predictor variables to predict a criterion—the simplest example of this is the use of both scholastic aptitude test scores and high school GPA to predict college GPA. In this case, the formula for a line is generalized to multiple predictors and takes the form $Y' = b_1X_1 + b_2X_2 + \ldots b_nX_n + a$. The quality of prediction is based on the strength of the multiple correlation coefficient R, describing the relationship between a linear composite or summary of the predictor variables and the criterion variable Y. And R^2, like r^2, is referred to as the *coefficient of determination.*

Variables can be entered into a regression analysis in several different ways. In simultaneous entry, all variables are entered together, and each is evaluated according to what it adds after the other variables have been accounted for. In sequential or hierarchical regression, variables are entered in a specific order as determined by the researcher. In stepwise regression, variables are entered one at a time according to statistical criteria—forward, backward, and stepwise entry can be used (see Tabachnick & Fidell, 2007).

Regardless of the method of variable entry utilized, weights in the equation should be cross-validated. Because multiple regression is a maximization procedure, meaning that it selects the weights that will maximize predictive efficacy in that particular sample, it is subject to shrinkage in subsequent samples. Therefore it is recommended that the equation be cross-validated. This is done by dividing the original sample in two, with the development sample being larger (see Tabachnick & Fidell, 2007). In the cross validation step, the predictive weights derived for the first sample are applied to the second sample, and the resulting R^2 determined. The second R^2 is probably a more realistic estimate of the predictive power of the set of variables. The method of double cross validation involves separately obtaining an original set of weights on each half of the sample, and then applying the within sample weights to the other sample. The average of the two R^2 is probably a good estimate of the predictive efficacy of the variable set.

Meta-analysis

Meta-analysis, described previously in the discussion of group differences, is used frequently in the study of predictive validity. We use meta-analysis in this context to summarize across many predictive validity studies—the summary if we do find evidence for predictive validity across studies is often called "validity generalization." For example, DeNeve and Cooper (1998) published a meta-analysis of 1,538 correlation coefficients from 148 studies of the relationships of 137 personality variables to measures of subjective well being. In brief, they found that Big Five Neuroticism was the strongest (negative) predictor of life satisfaction and happiness and the strongest predictor of negative affect. The strongest predictors of positive affect were Big Five Extraversion and Agreeableness.

Moderators and Mediators

Two other types of variables often are used in predictive and other correlational studies—moderator variables and mediator variables. Perhaps because the two terms are similar and/or perhaps because they both involve a "third variable" that influences the interpretation and meaning of a bivariate correlation, these terms are often confused or are assumed to be equivalent. This is not the case.

As mentioned, both moderators and mediators are third variables that can be involved in examining the relationship between two other variables. A *moderator* (see Frazier, Tix, & Barron, 2004) is a third variable that influences the strength of relationship of two other variables to each other but is not related itself to either one. That third variable can be categorical, such as gender, or interval, such as job satisfaction. For example, two variables may be more strongly related in women than in men or more strongly related in more highly versus less highly satisfied workers. A moderator in ANOVA terms is an interaction in which the effect of one variable depends on the level of the other. It may be suggested that a moderator leads to "differential predictability" of criterion from predictor variables.

The analytic methods used to identify moderators include the z test comparison of two correlations after conversion to Fisher's Z (see Glass & Hopkins, 1996) and moderated multiple regression (see Tabachnick & Fidell, 2007). Shown in Figure 9.1A is a hypothetical example wherein social support moderates the relationship between stress and distress. It is postulated that, for people high in social support, the correlation between stress and distress is lower than for those low in social support. The moderator effect is shown by an arrow leading down to the arrow showing the relationship between stress and distress. Suppose that, for high support individuals, the correlation is only .10, whereas for low support individuals it is higher, .50. If these are shown to differ significantly using the z test following transformation to Fisher's Z, then we can conclude a moderator effect for social support in this study. Moderator effects should always be replicated and the search for them should be based on theoretical considerations rather than "data snooping."

A *mediator* is a variable that represents the generative mechanism by which one variable affects another (Baron & Kenny, 1986). In this case, we have a relationship between two variables, but we postulate that the intervening mechanism is the relationship of each with a third variable, the mediator. Figure 9.1B shows a postulated mediator relationship for the same variables shown in Figure 9.1A. Say, for example, that we postulate that stress causes people to avoid social support, which causes them distress. If the relationship between stress and distress is significantly reduced when the path to social support is considered, we may have a mediator. Baron and Kenny postulate that finding a mediator requires four steps (shown in the figure): (1) that the predictor is related to the criterion (c); (2) that the predictor is related to the mediator (a); (3) that the mediator is related to the criterion

or outcome (b); and (4) that the strength of the relationship between predictor and criterion is significantly reduced (c') after the variance due to the mediator is removed. This can be tested using multiple regression, structural equation modeling, or the Sobel (1982) test, a handy and easy-to-use test available online (e.g., www.quantpsy.org), or as a subroutine of SPSS and other software.

Discriminant Analysis
Discriminant analysis is a topic that could be covered either in the section on MANOVA or in this section on multiple regression in that it has purposes and procedures similar to both (see Sherry, 2006, for an extended description of discriminant analysis). Probably the most common use of discriminant analysis is the use of multiple predictor variables to predict a categorical criterion—thus, it is like multiple regression except that the criterion variable is categorical rather than continuous. It is like MANOVA in that it tells us which of a set of variables differs significantly as a function of group membership. Probably its most frequent use would be to use a set of predictor variables to predict success versus failure, for example, in a job training program or in completion of a college degree. Like regression, it yields a set of weights that are applied to the predictors to yield the maximally predictive composite of scores to predict group membership.

As another possibility, discriminant analysis could be used as a follow-up to a significant MANOVA. MANOVA tells us whether or not a set of variables significantly differentiates two or more groups, controlling for the experiment-wise error by giving us a multivariate F. Post hoc univariate tests tell us for which variables significant group differences exist, but they do not tell us which variables contribute

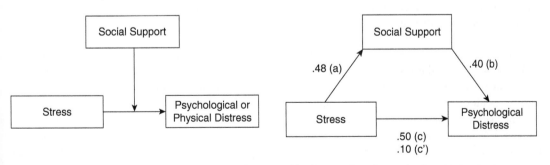

Fig. 9.1 (**A**) Hypothetical example of social support as moderator variable. (**B**) Hypothetical example of social support as mediator variable.

most strongly to the overall group separation. Discriminant analysis will give us discriminant weights, analogous to regression weights, which will tell us the strongest contributors to the group differences. Effect sizes could be used with the MANOVA to determine the variables leading to the largest differences between the groups, but that method would not control for the intercorrelations among the predictors.

Like MANOVA, discriminant analysis requires a set of two or more variables for two or more groups. The method of analysis involves a search for the linear equation that best differentiates the groups, so it is (like multiple regression) a maximization procedure and must be cross-validated. The analysis yields at least one discriminant function, analogous to a regression equation, which contains a set of β weights that are applied to the variables. Like β weights in regression, the weights indicate the importance of the variables in separation, or differentiating, the groups. The maximum number of discriminant functions is the number of groups minus 1 or the number of predictors, whichever is smaller. Of the discriminant functions, none, one, or more can be statistically significant. If not significant, then the function is not making a meaningful contribution to our understanding of group differences.

For predictive purposes, the weights are applied to each individual's scores and compared with what are termed *group centroids* to estimate the probabilities of group membership. If the discriminant weights are applied to the mean scores within each group, the results, two or more centroids, depending on the number of groups differentiated, will be maximally separate from each other. We assign each individual's score composite to the closest centroid. The number of correct versus incorrect assignments is known as the "hit rate" and is compared to the probability of correct assignment by chance. For example if we have three groups of equal size, the probability of making correct assignments by chance is .333. To the extent that the discriminant weights can improve on that, which we examine using the z test for the difference between proportions (Glass & Hopkins, 1996), the discriminant function is enhancing prediction. Cross-validation can be done using a holdout sample, double cross validation, and the "jackknife" method. In the latter method, one case is held out at a time, and the discriminant function is calculated based on the remaining cases. The weights are applied to the case held out to make a group assignment. This is done for each case, and

the probability of correct classification is based on the cumulative number of correct classifications across all cases.

An excellent example of the use of discriminant analysis in counseling psychology research is the study of Larson, Wei, Wu, Borgen, and Bailey (2007) of the degree to which personality and confidence measures differentiated four college major groups in 312 Taiwanese college students. Personality and confidence measures each differentiated the college major groups well, but the combination of both significantly improved prediction beyond either set used alone.

Other Related Analyses

Less often used in counseling psychology research but worth knowing about are logistic regression and multiway frequency analysis (MFA; or its extension, log-linear analysis). Both are used with data in which some or all are categorical. Logistic regression (see Tabachnick & Fidell, 2007, for a full description) is used to predict a categorical dependent variable (criterion) from a set of interval and/or categorical variables. It is used extensively in the medical field. For example, gender and whether or not a smoker (both categorical), and body mass index and amount of exercise per week (both interval scale), could be used to predict whether or not someone has a heart attack before age 50. Logistic regression is similar to discriminant analysis except that the latter uses only continuous predictor variables (unless categorical variables are dummy coded, e.g., assigning 1 to female and 2 to male).

Multiway frequency analysis, or an extension called *log-linear analysis*, is used to examine the relationships among multiple categorical variables. If we have only two categorical variables, we use the χ-square test of independence to investigate the relationship (vs. independence) between the two variables. For example, we could examine the relationship between gender and whether or not a student dropped out of college before finishing. If we have three or more categorical variables (for example, race/ethnicity and whether or not the student is a first-generation college student in addition to gender and completion of college), we would use MFA. For more information on all of these methods see Tabachnick and Fidell (2007).

Finally, one problem which is common to all quantitative data analyses is the problem of missing data. Several recent papers (Schafer & Graham, 2002; Sterner, 2011) have detailed the types of missing data and methods for handling each type.

Usually less problematic are those instances where missing data are assumed to occur at random, while more serious problems may be caused in instances where there is non-randomness, or systematicity, in the missing data – for example if missing data is significantly more likely among one gender or ethnic group than the other gender or another ethnic group. These articles provide excellent suggestions for handling missing data in all of these cases and provide recommendations for statistical software that can be useful in each of these cases.

Examining Structure and Dimensionality

FACTOR ANALYSIS

Factor analysis has been one of the most widely used analytical procedures in psychological research. It began with the work of Charles Spearman (1904) on the structure of mental abilities. He developed a mathematical model specifying that ability tests were composed of two factors—a general ability factor (g) and a specific factor (s). Factor analysis has grown into a family of methods that enable us to study the structure and dimensionality of measures and of sets of variables. For example, we could use factor analysis to determine dimensions underlying several indices of social behavior or to ask how many underlying dimensions of personality there are in a new measure we have constructed. In recent years, factor analytic methods have been differentiated as exploratory factor analyses (EFA) and confirmatory factor analyses (CFA).

Exploratory Factor Analysis

As defined by Fabrigar, Wegener, MacCallum, and Strahan (1999): "The primary purpose of EFA is to arrive at a more parsimonious conceptual understanding of a set of measured variables by determining the number and nature of common factors needed to account for the pattern of correlations among the measured variables" (p. 275). Exploratory factor analysis is used when the researcher has no a priori theories about the structure of the measure or construct, or when a priori theories have not been supported by confirmatory factor analyses. The method utilizes a matrix of either correlations or covariances describing the relationships among the variables to be analyzed. The variables can be measures or items, for each of which there is a matrix of scores for a sample of people. The correlation or covariance matrix is a symmetrical matrix showing the relationships of each variable with every other variable (or item).

Given such a matrix, software from packages such as SPSS, SAS, CEFA, BMDP, Systat, or RAMONA are used to do the analyses. However, any EFA involves a sequential series of considerations that will determine the results of the analysis. These considerations are the nature of the variables and sample, the appropriate method of analysis, method of factor extraction, number of factors to extract, and method of rotation. In addition, the interpretation or naming of the factors and the decision as to whether or not to compute factor scores follow the analyses themselves.

ASSUMPTIONS REGARDING THE DATA

In both EFA and CFA, certain assumptions about the data are necessary. First, quality solutions result only from quality data—measures (or items, if it is to be a factor analysis of an item set) must be carefully selected to represent a defined domain of interest (Fabrigar et al., 1999). Just as in scale construction itself, the quality of the scale depends on the care put into defining the construct or domain of interest. There should be evidence for item or scale reliability. MacCallum, Widman, Zhang, and Hong (1999) suggest that, if one has an idea of the common factors to be represented, three to five measured variables (MVs) per factor will provide stable and interpretable results. If the researcher does not have hypotheses about the number of common factors, then the domain of variables should be delineated carefully and as many of those variables as possible included in the study. The data should be interval or quasi-interval in nature and be normally distributed, although the latter criterion depends on the method of factor extraction used. Some researchers have found that both EFA and CFA are relatively robust in the face of non-normality. However, less biased fit indices and more interpretable and more replicable solutions may follow when data are normally distributed.

SAMPLE SIZE AND VARIABLE INDEPENDENCE

Although there has been much discussion of necessary sample sizes for factor analysis, a generally accepted guideline is five to ten participants per variable or item, if the analysis is at the item level (Joreskog & Sorbom, 2008). If sample sizes are larger than that, they may be divided into subsamples, so that the solution can be replicated. However, other authors have demonstrated that when common factors are overdetermined (three or four variables per factor) and communalities are high (averaging at least .70), smaller sample sizes (e.g., N = 100) are often sufficient (MacCallum et al., 1999). When the reverse is true—that is, factors are less well determined or communalities are lower—even very large sample sizes (up to N = 800) may not be sufficient. It is clear there are no simple answers to the question of sample size.

METHODS OF FACTOR EXTRACTION

It is necessary at the outset to differentiate two different types of analysis: principal components analysis (PCA) and factor analysis (EFA or CFA). The major difference between them is that PCA analyzes all the variance among the variables, both common and unique, where unique variance includes that specific to the variable and also error variance. It is designed to rescale the original variables into a new set of components that can be equal in number to the original set but that are now uncorrelated with each other. It is not designed to elucidate underlying structure or latent variables (LVs) but to rescale or reassign the variables in the analysis. Generally speaking, it is not considered a method of factor analysis (Fabrigar et al., 1999), but if the researcher's goal is to determine the linear composite of variables that retains as much information as possible from the original set of variables, then PCA is appropriate. An example of an appropriate use would be analysis of a large set of vocational interest items, where the purpose was to assign them to interest scales, retaining as much variance as possible from the original set.

If the purpose of the analysis is to more parsimoniously describe the underlying dimensions common to a set of variables, also known as the *underlying LVs*, then common variance analysis is much more appropriate. The common factor model is implemented by model-fitting methods, also known as *factor extraction techniques*. The major ones are maximum likelihood (ML) and principal axis factoring (PAF). All use only common variance in the estimation of communalities. The advantage of ML procedures is that they are accompanied by a large number of fit indices that can be used to evaluate the goodness of fit of the factor model to the data (see Browne, Cudeck, Tateneni, & Mels, 2004). However, they also require the assumption of multivariate normality. Principal axis factoring does not require such distributional assumptions but also provides fewer fit indices.

Although PCA places 1's in the diagonal of the correlation matrix, common FA uses a communality estimate in the diagonal, where commonality refers to the shared *common* variance of that variable with other variables in the set. There are several commonality estimates typically used, including the largest correlation of a variable with any other variable in the set, the squared multiple correlation (SMC) of the variable with the remaining variables, and iterated estimates based on preliminary SMCs.

NUMBER OF FACTORS TO EXTRACT

The decision regarding the number of factors to extract should be based on a balance of parsimony with theoretical meaningfulness. In theory, we want to arrive at a smaller number of fundamental LVs, but we also want those LVs to be important and to accurately define the domain of interest. Especially if our goal is to explore a reduced number of factors that reflect underlying LVs, it is pointless to extract minor or trivial factors. However, researchers generally agree that it is more problematic to underfactor (to select too few factors) than to overfactor—in the former case, we may overlook important aspects of the behavioral domain, whereas in the latter case, we may simply end up focusing on an unimportant or trivial aspect of behavior.

There are several approaches to determining how many factors to extract, all of them in some way attempting to operationalize factor importance, as we only want to extract important factors. One basis for decisions is how much variance a factor accounts for. A variable's contribution to a factor is represented by the square of the factor loading (factor loadings are analogous to correlations, which, when squared, represent the proportion of variance accounted for). In an unrotated solution, the factor contribution is known as the *eigenvalue*. The best known and most commonly used is the Kaiser-Guttman criterion (Gorsuch, 1983), in which factors having eigenvalues greater than 1 are extracted. This method is appropriate only for PCA or for other methods where 1's are in the diagonal (such as α or image FA) and should not be used in common factor analyses where communality estimates are in the diagonal. This is the default in some statistical packages, although it tends to lead to overfactoring (more than an optimal number of components or factors) (Zwick & Velicer, 1986).

A frequently used method is the *scree plot* (Zwick & Velicer, 1986), in which the values of the eigenvalues are plotted, in order of factor extraction, on the vertical axis. The point at which the plot levels out (or the slope of the line approaches zero) is where factoring should stop. Common sense should be used, however, as there may be cases in which the scree plot would lead to the inclusion of factors with eigenvalues below 1.0. In some cases, there is no clear leveling off, or there is more than one leveling off point. A logical criterion for number of factors to extract is to include only factors having at least two or three variables loading highly on them. If only one variable loads on a factor, then it is questionable whether that variable reflects an underlying latent dimension. Other methods include parallel analysis (Hayton, Allen, & Scarpello, 2004) and root mean square error of approximation (RMSEA; Steiger, 1990), in which maximum likelihood estimation is used to extract factors (see also Browne & Cudeck, 1993).

ROTATION

The results of a factor analysis yield solutions based on mathematical maximization procedures, rather than solutions that are psychologically or intuitively satisfying. Factor rotation is designed to lead to a more interpretable set of factors. Methods of rotation are generally classified as orthogonal or oblique. An *orthogonal rotation* yields factors that are uncorrelated, whereas an *oblique rotation* allows factors to be correlated.

To understand rotation methods, it is necessary to understand Thurstone's (1947) concept of *simple structure*. Simple structure defines a maximal interpretability and simplicity of a factor structure, such that each factor is described by less than the total number of variables, and each variable should be described by only one factor. Ideally, each factor should be loaded on by at least two but fewer than a majority of variables.

Orthogonal rotational methods include varimax and quartimax; *varimax* (Kaiser, 1958) is regarded as the best orthogonal rotation (Fabrigar et al., 1999) and is often the default in computer packages. Comparing the two, varimax is more likely to "spread out" the variance across factors, reducing the predominance of the general factor or of specific factors and increasing the number of common factors (factors on which a few variables load strongly). *Quartimax* has the opposite effect—emphasizing general and specific factors and de-emphasizing common factors.

Oblique rotations are generally considered preferable because they allow correlated factors, and the reality is that most psychological variables are at least partially correlated naturally. If the factors are truly uncorrelated, oblique rotations will yield an orthogonal set of factors. Oblique rotations provide the correlations among factors and, therefore, second-order factor analyses, where the factor intercorrelations are themselves factor analyzed to examine high-order structures. Oblique rotations include *direct oblimin* and *promax*. Most quantitative researchers view direct oblimin as preferable because the mathematical functions minimized (and maximized) in factor rotation are made explicit (Browne, 2001).

Regardless of which method of rotation is used, a matrix of factor structure coefficients will result that is different from the coefficients generated before rotation. The structure coefficients represent the correlations between the variables and the factors. For clarity of interpretation, it is best if the coefficients are either large or very small (near zero). The rule of thumb is to retain on a factor any variable with a loading of .40 or greater, although there may be instances where loadings as small as .30 or as large as .50 are determined as the minimum (Floyd & Widaman, 1995). A loading of .40 indicates a reasonably strong contribution of the variable to determining the "nature" of that factor.

Another feature of the results will be the percentage of variance accounted for by each factor and the total percentage of variance accounted for by the solution. A general rule is that, to meaningfully explain the interrelationships in the data, a factor structure should account for from 50% to 80% of the common variance. If factors 1 and 2 account for 40% and 20% of the variance and factor 3 accounts for only 2% of the variance, we may decide that factor 3 is too trivial to divert attention from the two more significant factors.

Table 9.2 shows the factor matrix resulting when principal axis factor analysis is applied to the correlation matrix shown in Table 9.1, the eight variables from the Healthy Personality Inventory. Direct oblimin (an oblique) rotation was used. Using the decision criterion that factors with eigenvalues over 1.0 should be retained led to the retention of two factors with eigenvalues of 4.1 and 1.8, respectively; two factors were also indicated by the scree plot. Table 9.2 shows the resulting factor structure matrix. The most important factor in terms of variance accounted for is shown first—this factor accounts for 47% of the common variance. The second factor accounts for an additional 18% of the common variance. For the factor loadings shown for each variable on the two factors, larger loadings mean that the variable is more important to the definition of the factor. As we used oblique rotation, we allowed the factors to be correlated (they correlate $r = .37$). It is most useful to name the factors based on the variables that load highly on them. Thus, in

Table 9.2. Factor loadings of eight scales of the HPI

HPI Scales	Factors and Factor Loadings	
	Factor 1	Factor 2
Confident	**.68**	.53
Organized	**.84**	.20
Detail-oriented	**.74**	.25
Goal-oriented	**.91**	.43
Outgoing	.29	**.78**
Energetic	.50	**.71**
Adventurous	.14	**.75**
Assertive	.42	**.88**

N = 206; Highest loading of each scale on a factor is shown. Factor 1 accounts for 47% of the common variance, whereas factor 2 accounts for an additional 18% of the common variance. Factor 1 was named Productivity Styles, whereas Factor 2 was named Interpersonal styles. From Borgen, F. H., & Betz, N. E. (2008). Career self-efficacy and personality: Linking career confidence and the healthy personality. *Journal of Career Assessment, 16*, 22–43.

the example shown, Factor 1 was named Productivity Styles, as it had strong loadings from the variables of Confident, Organized, Detail Oriented, and Goal Directed; and Factor 2 was named Interpersonal Styles, as it included Outgoing, Energetic, Adventurous, and Assertive.

Scores on the factors themselves also can be computed. Factor scores are useful if we wish to predict some type of criterion behavior from a concise set of factor scores. For example, assume that we have a battery of 15 ability tests—verbal ability, math ability, and spatial ability—that we wish to use to predict job performance. When calculated in the same sample, the factor score can be computed as the sum of the score on each variable multiplied by its weight on the factor(s) on which it loads significantly. However, since factor analysis is a maximization procedure, if used in subsequent samples, it has been shown that simple unit weighting of all the variables loading on a factor provides more stable results (Gorsuch, 1983).

Confirmatory Factor Analysis

Confirmatory factor analysis is used when we have an a priori hypothesis about the structure or dimensionality of the data or domain of behavior. There are several different types of such uses. One use is to examine the factor structure and/or construct validity of a scale or a set of measures: If a measure is postulated to have three underlying factors, we could use CFA to verify (or not) that structure.

The first step in CFA is to specify the model to be tested; that is, we specify which measures should load on which factor. In many cases, the CFA was preceded by an EFA to get an idea of the factor structure of the domain in question, and this structure is then tested using CFA. Hypotheses about relationships (of items or measures to factors or among factors) are operationalized in the model, usually with Thurstone's simple structure in mind. We typically desire high loadings of items on one and only one factor, and specification of a factor by a few strongly loading items. In some cases, we postulate that one or more factors may be correlated.

Statistical software is used to compare the estimated covariance matrix of the specified model to the actual matrix of covariances found in the data. A number of possible software programs are available; all of these software packages are updated periodically. They include the SPSS subroutine AMOS (which must be purchased separately from the standard package), LISREL (Joreskog & Sorbom, 2008), EQS (Bentler, 1995), and Mplus (Methuen & Methuen, 1998). According to Kahn (2006), the latter three yield comparable results for a CFA, although Mplus may have more user-friendly syntax and also provides other multivariate analyses not available on other packages.

A number of fit indices are available to evaluate the fit of the model to the data. Fit indices indicate how well the actual covariances (relationships) in the data correspond to those in the hypothesized model (see Kahn, 2006, for a full explanation). The traditional χ-square test of goodness of fit is best known and indicates the differences between the model-hypothesized covariances and those found in the data; the larger the value of the χ-square statistic, the greater the discrepancy between the hypothesized and actual models. Thus, a statistically significant χ-square indicates a lack of fit of the hypothesized model to the data. But the χ-square statistic is highly sensitive to large sample sizes and/ or a large number of observed variables and often leads to the rejection of models that are good, if not perfect. One solution to this problem is the χ-square test of close fit (not perfect) developed by Brown and Cudeck (1993). This index seems to perform better across a range of sample sizes and models.

Other fit indices are not adversely affected by sample size. These include the Bentler-Bonnett non-normed fit index (NNFI; also known as the Tucker Lewis index) and the Comparative Fit Index

(CFI). Using criteria suggested by Browne and Cudeck (1993) and Hu and Bentler (1999), models with CFI and NNFI (TLI) of at or above .95 indicate an excellent fit, whereas those between .90 and .94 indicate an adequate fit. The standardized root mean-squared residual (SRMR) and the RMSEA (Bentler, 1995) are other fit indices; for these indices, values at or below .05 indicate an excellent fit while those between .06 and .10 indicate an adequate fit. Confidence intervals also are provided for the RMSEA. Most authors (e.g., McCallum & Austin, 2000) recommend using multiple fit indices, paying particular attention to the RMSEA due to its sensitivity and its provision of a confidence interval.

Although it makes intuitive sense that CFA would be used most often to confirm structures (tentatively) established using EFA, there are instances in which the reverse sequence can be put to good use. One example of the latter can be found in Forester, Kahn, and Hesson-McInnis (2004), who reported the results of confirmatory and exploratory factor analyses of three previously published inventories of research self-efficacy. Using a sample of 1,004 graduate students in applied psychology programs, Forester et al. began with a CFA of each of the inventories separately, finding poor fit of each to its postulated factor structure. They then used EFA to evaluate the structure of the combined total of 107 items from the three inventories, arriving at a four-factor structure in which 58 items loaded at least .50 on one and only one factor. Of course, the next logical step in this research effort would be to return to CFA to examine whether the four-factor structure holds in new samples.

Confirmatory factor analysis also is well-suited to comparing factor structures in new demographic groups or across groups (such as gender or race/ethnicity). Often, EFA will have been used to derive a factor structure in original normative samples dominated by white males (particularly in older instruments), so it is crucial to demonstrations of construct validity that the factor structure be validated, or explored anew, in other groups with which we wish to use the measure(s). Kashubeck-West, Coker, Awad, Stinson, Bledman, and Mintz (2008), for example, found, using CFA, that factor structures in three inventories of body image and eating behavior that had been derived from white samples demonstrated poor fit in samples of African American women. They subsequently used EFA to explore the factor structure in the African American samples.

Multidimensional Scaling

Although used less frequently that factor analysis, the structure of a set of variables or items also can be described by multidimensional scaling (MDS). Multidimensional scaling provides the structure of variables in multidimensional (usually two-dimensional) space. Analysis of proximity or similarity data (which can be represented as correlations between variables) yields a series of points in two dimensional space, where each point represents a variable or item and the closeness of the points represents the variables' similarity to each other. A good example of the use of MDS in counseling psychology research is the work of Hansen, Dik, and Zhou (2008). They analyzed 20 leisure interest scales using both EFA and nonmetric MDS and found two dimensions of leisure interests in college students and retirees—expressive-instrumental (e.g., arts and crafts vs. individual sports) and affiliative–nonaffiliative (e.g., shopping vs. gardening). With MDS, each leisure interest can be described on these two dimensions. For example, shopping would be a more affiliative expressive activity, whereas arts and crafts would be an expressive but less affiliative activity; team sports would be instrumental and affiliative, whereas building and repairing would be instrumental but less affiliative. For more information about MDS, readers may consult Fitzgerald and Hubert (1987).

Examining Causal Models
Structural Equation Models

Structural equation modeling is actually a family of methods that subsumes many of the methods we have discussed so far. In the general case, it is a method of statistically testing a network of interrelationships among variables. It subsumes multiple regression analysis and confirmatory factor analysis but also includes path analysis and testing of full structural equation models. To understand the distinctions among these methods, it is useful to define two possible components of a structural model.

Elements and Path Diagrams

The elements of a structural model are MVs, usually shown as squares or rectangles, and LVs, usually shown as ellipses or circles. Measured variables are (as they sound) those that are measured directly, whereas LVs are unobservable constructs. In addition to measured and latent variables, the model must postulate relationships among variables, including error terms. These relationships are

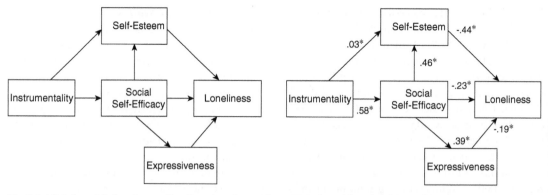

Fig. 9.2 (**A**) Path model of predictors of loneliness in college students. (**B**) Path model predicted 45% of the variance in loneliness. From Hermann, K. (2005). Path models of the relationships of instrumentality and expressiveness, social self-efficacy, and self-esteem to depressive symptoms in college students. Unpublished Ph.D. Dissertation, Department of Psychology, Ohio State University.

represented as unidirectional (one-way) and bidirectional (two-way) arrows. The values assigned to or resulting from directional relationships are regression coefficients, whereas those for nondirectional relationships are covariances (or correlations if variables are standardized). Variables in the model can be endogenous or exogenous. Endogenous (dependent) variables are those in which there is a directional influence to the variable from one or more other variables in the system. Exogenous (independent) variables are those that do not have directional influence from within the system; their influences may be unknown or may not be of interest in the current model.

The simplest model is a path model, for which each LV is directly measured—thus, this actually models relationships among a series of measures (and directional relationships are shown using arrows).

A sample path model is shown in Figure 9.2A, where the researcher (Hermann, 2005) was examining variables related to loneliness in college students. Note that all variables are shown as rectangles, as the model does not incorporate latent variables; that is, each variable is assumed to be measured fully by one scale. Note also that only instrumentality in this model is exogenous—all other variables are endogenous; that is, they are postulated to be predicted by variables earlier in the model.

A full structural model consists of two parts: a measurement model, which represents the relationships of LVs and their indicators; and a structural model, which represents the interrelationships between LVs, both independent and dependent. In a full structural equation model (SEM), the measurement model is tested first to evaluate the fidelity by which the measures are valid indicators of the

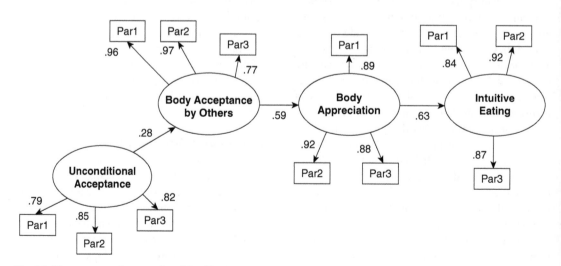

Fig. 9.3 Measurement and structural models of intuitive eating.

construct; following that, the full structural model is tested (see Figure 9.3 for an example of a full structural model).

The steps in SEM are (1) model specification, (2) identification, (3) estimation, and (4) modification (Schumaker & Lomax, 2004). In the first step, the researcher hypothesizes the relationships (including lack of relationship) among all variables. As in CFA, relationships between variables, also known as *parameters* or *paths*, must be either specified in advance or determined from the analysis of the correlation or covariance matrix. A free parameter is one whose value is unknown and must be estimated, whereas a fixed parameter is one we determine in advance; the latter also is known as a *constrained parameter* (Weston & Gore, 2006). Three types of parameters are necessary in a structural model. First, *direct effects parameters* specify relationships between a LV and its postulated MVs (known as *factor loadings*) and between LVs (known as *path coefficients*). To scale the MVs, it is common to set one of the factor loadings for each LV at 1.0, which has the effect of standardizing the set. Parameters other than those set at 1.0 need to be estimated (shown as asterisks). Error terms for dependent measured and latent variables also must be either fixed or estimated, and covariances among exogenous variables are specified as parameters as well.

MODEL IDENTIFICATION

This refers to the relationship between the number of parameters to be estimated and the number of data points in the correlation or covariance matrix. The number of elements in a correlation matrix is equal to the number of variables k by the following formula: $[k(k + 1)]/2$; if there are six variables, there are $[6(7)]/2 = 21$ elements in the matrix. Subtracting the number of parameters to be estimated from the number of elements yields the degrees of freedom for the analysis—if it is positive, the model is said to be overidentified, which is the optimal situation.

ESTIMATION

Structural equation modeling software is needed to estimate the free parameters and provide fit indices for the fit of the postulated model to the data. This software includes the same software programs used with CFA, including LISREL, AMOS (SPSS), Mplus, and EQS. Most programs describe path coefficients as either standardized β weights or unstandardized β weights, including standard errors, analogous to the results of a regression analysis. The statistical significance of weights can be computed

(or may be provided by the software), and the sizes of standardized weights may be compared directly as indicators of relative importance.

The worth of the model tested can be evaluated by the significance and size of the path coefficients (indicating the strength of relationships among the variables), the amount of variance accounted for in endogenous variables, and indices of model fit. Like CFA, fit indices include the χ-square goodness of fit, in which a nonsignificant value is indicative of fit, and the χ-square test of close fit, postulated to be a more realistic examination of fit. Other indices are the NNFI (Tucker-Lewis Index), CFI, RMSEA, and SRMR (see Weston & Gore, 2006, p. 742, for full descriptions). Criteria for good and adequate fit were described previously for CFA, but it is important to recognize that fit indices do not always agree with one another, so the use of multiple indicators of fit is recommended (MacCallum & Austin, 2000).

Figure 9.2B shows the results of simple path analysis of the model presented in Figure 9.2A using a sample of 696 college students (Herman, 2005). The path coefficients are regression coefficients showing relationships ranging from .58 (between instrumentality and social self-efficacy) and –.44 (between self-efficacy and loneliness) to as small as .03 (between instrumentality and self-esteem). All paths except the latter were statistically significant in testing this model. Results concerning the fit of the model were mixed, with acceptable values of RMSEA, NNFI, and CFI, but a statistically significant χ-square (which, it should be recalled, is sensitive to large sample sizes). Further testing indicated that the model demonstrated a good fit in males (N = 346) but an inadequate fit in females (N = 350) (see Hermann & Betz, 2006, for the final published findings).

Figure 9.3 presents an example of a full structural equation model of intuitive eating developed and tested by Avalos (2005). Three indicators (or parcels of items) were constructed from the scales measuring each LV following the recommendations of Russell, Kahn, Spoth, and Altmaier (1998). Parcels were constructed by using EFA to derive the loadings of scale items on a single factor—items were successively assigned to the three parcels from highest to lowest loadings, so that the quality of the parcels as measures of the LVs is roughly comparable.

The measurement and structural components of the model were tested in 461 college women. Testing of the measurement model using CFA indicated fit indices ranging from adequate fit (RMSEA = .060) to excellent fit (CFI = .982, TLI = .975, and SRMR = .041). All indicators/item parcels loaded significantly on their latent factors, suggesting that all latent factors were adequately measured. The paths from the LVs to the parcels indicate the parcel loadings—in essence the factor saturation of each parcel; as can be seen, all parcels loaded highly on their respective LVs. Fit indices for the structural model also were adequate (RMSEA = .058) to excellent (CFI = .982; TLI = .977, SRMR = .046). All paths between LVs were statistically significant and ranged from .28 to .63. Thus, this is a plausible model (although not the only plausible model that could be hypothesized), and it shows a possible causal pathway by which variables related to acceptance can facilitative intuitive eating.

MODIFICATION INDICES

When the model is not fitting optimally (one or more of the fit indices indicates poor or inadequate fit), some researchers use modification indices to attempt to improve it. Done through what is known as a *specification search*, two major modification indices are the Wald test, which uses a χ-square difference test to indicate any (non-zero) paths that might profitably be eliminated, and the Lagrange multiplier (LM) test, which uses a χ-square difference test to indicate any new paths that would significantly improve the model if added (Bentler, 1995).

MacCallum, Roznowski, and Necowitz (1992) suggested that, to avoid a data-driven model that capitalizes too much on sample specificity, only changes that are theoretically meaningful, based on prior evidence, should be made. And because modification of structural equation models based on statistical indices has been challenged as data-driven and often unstable across samples, it is important to cross-validate the modified model (MacCallum & Austin, 2000). This is done using calibration and validation samples, of which the first should be about two-thirds of the entire sample to provide stable initial parameter estimates.

Structural equation modeling can be used to compare models, for example, by testing models across populations (e.g., Fassinger, 1990; Lent et al., 2005). Standard error of the mean also can be used to examine longitudinal designs (e.g., Tracey, 2008) and to explore experimental designs more generally (see Russell, Kahn, Spoth, & Altmaier, 1998).

Summary

It should be clear to readers that many analytic methods are appropriate for use with a variety of kinds of quantitative data. Careful consideration of the purposes of the research and the type of data at hand or accessible will facilitate meaningful and useful analyses. In the following section, we turn to qualitative research methods.

Qualitative Methods

Qualitative approaches to research increasingly are being used in counseling psychology, resulting in what Ponterotto (2005) described as "a gradual paradigm shift from a primary reliance on quantitative methods to a more balanced reliance on quantitative and qualitative methods" (p. 126). In contrast to the nomothetic perspective of quantitative approaches, which seeks to identify large-scale normative patterns and universal laws, qualitative approaches take an idiographic perspective, focusing instead on in-depth understanding of the lived experiences of individuals or small groups. As outlined in the first half of this chapter, quantitative methods rely on quantifying carefully measured observations amassed from large samples (with some measure of control over the variables as the ideal) and statistically analyzing data to produce models of relationship and prediction thought to apply to the general population. Qualitative methods, on the other hand, rely on detailed or "thick" description of context-specific phenomena, most typically as narratives voiced by relatively small numbers of persons, with transparent interpretation by the researcher into descriptions, summaries, stories, or theories thought to capture the complexity of the phenomena under investigation. In quantitative research, the researcher seeks to remain distant and objective to avoid contaminating the data gathering process, such that the data stand as accurately as possible as a representation of an assumed reality apart from the researcher. In qualitative research, however, data collection occurs through the relationship between the researcher and the participant(s) in a co-creative process, and consideration of the subjectivity of the researcher is woven deliberately into every phase of the research process.

Thus, the perspectives, purposes, processes, and products of qualitative research are very different from those of quantitative research, and they require different mind sets and different standards for assessing quality and rigor. Readers should keep these complexities in mind in reviewing the following section, in which we present brief overviews of the most commonly used qualitative approaches within psychology and/or those most likely to enter the repertoire of counseling psychologists. We note that these do not represent the full range of qualitative approaches available; discourse analysis and case study methods, for example, offer considerable possibilities in counseling psychology (the former in studying counseling interactions and the latter in organizational consultation, for example), but they do not appear to have been embraced within our field at this time. We also note that, due to space limitations, we simply present broad descriptions of some of the distinctive features of these approaches, and readers should consult several excellent handbooks and overviews of qualitative methods (e.g., Camic, Rhodes, & Yardley, 2003; Creswell et al., 2007; Denzin & Lincoln, 2000; Patton, 2002; Ponterotto, Haverkamp, & Morrow, 2005) to learn about these and other methods in greater detail.

Common Qualitative Research Methods
GROUNDED THEORY
Rooted in sociology and symbolic interactionism, grounded theory is a highly influential qualitative approach that is widely used throughout the health, social, and behavioral sciences, including counseling psychology (Charmaz, 2000; Fassinger, 2005; Henwood & Pigeon, 2003; Rennie, 2000). Developed by Glaser and Strauss (1967) and further articulated by these researchers and colleagues (e.g., Glaser, 1992, 2000; Strauss, 1987; Strauss & Corbin, 1998), grounded theory is so named because its aim is to produce theories that are "grounded" in participants' lived experiences within a social context. The central question of grounded theory is: "What theory emerges from systematic comparative analysis and is grounded in fieldwork so as to explain what has been and is observed?" (Patton, 2002, p. 133).

Theory-building takes place inductively and iteratively using a method of "constant comparison," in which data collection, coding, conceptualizing, and theorizing occur concurrently in a process of continually comparing new data to emerging concepts until theoretical saturation is reached (no new information is being generated); at this point, data collection/analysis ends and relationships among the emergent constructs are articulated in the form of an innovative theoretical statement about the behavior under investigation. Data usually consist of detailed narratives obtained in extensive interviews with participants, although other forms of data (e.g., observations, archival documents, case notes) can be used as well. The relationship between the researcher and the participant forms the foundation for the participant's deep

sharing of the lived experience, and there is an expectation that participants' perspectives and feedback will be included throughout the process of data analysis and theory articulation, thus ensuring that the theory remains grounded in the participant's lived experiences (Charmaz, 2000; Fassinger, 2005; Henwood & Pigeon, 2003).

Although there is some debate about the appropriate paradigmatic home for grounded theory, it most often is presented as a constructivist-interpretivist approach (Charmaz, 2000; Fassinger, 2005; Henwood & Pigeon, 2003). This makes sense, given its ontological and epistemological assumptions that researchers and participants will, through their relationships, co-construct accounts of the deep meanings of subjectively experienced realities, as well as its axiological and methodological foci on revealing, recording, and monitoring the expectations and interpretive lenses of the researcher. However, Fassinger (2005) has argued that the considerable flexibility of the grounded theory approach allows for its conceptualization and use across a broad paradigmatic range, from, for example, a post-positivist attempt to triangulate quantitative data to the liberationist aims of giving voice to and empowering marginalized populations characterized by the critical-ideological paradigm.

Fassinger (2005) further asserts that grounded theory can serve as a paradigmatic bridge for researchers. It allows those researchers holding fast to positivist and post-positivist empirical values to begin to venture into more naturalistic territory using the highly specified, rigorous analysis procedures of grounded theory. On the other hand, those who are oriented toward radical social reformation can find in this approach a means to tackle some of society's most challenging problems. The adaptability of grounded theory is particularly well-suited to counseling psychology, as exemplified by the wide range of studies in our field that have used this approach successfully. Examples include the work of Fassinger and her colleagues (Gomez et al., 2001; Noonan et al., 2004; Richie et al., 1997), as well as Morrow and Smith (1995), Rennie (1994) and Kinnier, Tribbensee, Rose, and Vaughan (2001).

NARRATOLOGY
Although narratives and narrative analysis techniques are used widely in many different approaches to qualitative research, Hoshmand (2005) uses the term "narratology" to denote a distinct qualitative perspective that is informed by narrative theory. Shaped broadly by the work of narrative theorists

such as Foucault and Ricouer and articulated within psychology by Polkinghorne (1998, 2005) and others, the narratological approach to research is "concerned with the structure, content, and function of the stories that we tell each other and ourselves in social interaction" (Murray, 2003, p. 95). Its central question is: "What does this narrative or story reveal about the person and the world from which it came? How can this narrative be interpreted to understand and illuminate the life and culture that created it?" (Patton, 2002, p. 133).

Narratology relies on a "narrative mode of understanding" human experience (Hoshmand, 2005, p. 180) in which the researcher interrogates narratives of individuals' lived experiences for the story-like elements that underlie those narratives. In this approach, narratives are considered to be storied accounts of experience that have an internal, developmental coherence containing plot-like elements, thematic meanings, self-presentational style aspects, and temporal and causal sequences, and are mediated by culture, historical time, and other contextual elements. Narratological inquiry seeks both to understand narratives as well as to construct storied accounts of particular lived phenomena. Data may consist of documents already rendered in narrative form (e.g., interviews, oral histories, biographies, journals) or may be more loosely organized pieces of information (e.g., chronological events, observations, cultural artifacts) that will be translated into narrative form by the researcher in the data analysis process. Analyzing data may take several forms (e.g., linguistic/literary, grounded, contextual), but each approaches the narrative holistically within its social context, and arranges its elements into a coherently and chronologically sequenced account of experience (Hoshmand, 2005; Murray, 2003).

Hoshmand (2005) asserts that narratological research approaches are still evolving, and that what exist currently to guide researchers are simply concepts and principles rather than a unified method per se. Paradigmatically, narratological approaches appear to be constructivist-interpretivist in their reliance on the co-construction of the storied account and the importance of researcher positionality. However, Hoshmand (2005) distinguishes the narrative mode of understanding, which is focused on "descriptive and discovery-oriented research involving configural patterns of interpretation and a part-to-whole logic of argumentation" (p. 181), from the "paradigmatic mode of interpretation brought to bear on narrative data such as the

theorizing stage of grounded theory" (p. 181), reinforcing the difference between narrative analysis and narratological inquiry. The focus of the narratological approach on the formation and expression of individual and cultural identity through story also renders it particularly useful for multicultural research, an area of interest to many counseling psychologists. Examples include Winter and Daniluk (2004) and Hardy, Barkham, Field, Elliott, and Shapiro (1998).

ETHNOGRAPHY

Spawned from cultural anthropology at the turn of the 20th century, including such giants as Boas and Malinowski, ethnography has found its way slowly into contemporary psychology, highlighted recently for counseling psychologists by Suzuki and her colleagues (Suzuki, Ahluwalia, Mattis, & Quizon, 2005). Focused on groups of people within their cultures and communities, the central question of ethnography is: "What is the culture of this group of people?" (Patton, 2002, p. 132).

The ethnographic approach focuses on studying the cultural and community life (behaviors, language, artifacts) of individuals, and relies on the researcher functioning as a participant-observer in extensive fieldwork under conditions of prolonged engagement with the community (e.g., 6 months to 2 years or more). Interviewing and direct observation are the chief means of data collection, although archival records, surveys, and other documentation may be used as well. The end product of ethnographic research is the creation of narratives that are thought to capture the lived experiences of people in their complex cultural contexts, an aim that is consistent with and amenable to the multicultural emphasis within counseling psychology (Miller, Hengst, & Wang, 2003; Suzuki et al., 2005).

Ethnographic approaches can span the paradigmatic spectrum from post-positivist methods that rely largely on observations and quantitatively organized data (particularly in seeking out negative cases or contradictory information) to critical-ideological aims of giving voice to and thus empowering marginalized populations, especially if used in multicultural research in counseling psychology, as advocated by Suzuki et al. (2005). However, in its ideal form, ethnography probably most closely fits the constructivist-interpretivist paradigm in its epistemological focus on the awareness of the "subjectivities" and "guesthood" of the researcher, a position of genuine connection with participants balanced by enough distance to avoid compromising data collection or interpretation (Miller et al., 2003).

Indeed, one of the most intense debates within the ethnography literature concerns how and to what extent the insider or outsider status of the researcher influences the investigation, a debate that focuses, at its heart, on the relative roles of researchers and participants in co-constructing the final account of the lived experience under investigation (Miller et al., 2003; Suzuki et al., 2005). From a methodological perspective, the expectation that cultural immersion and a reflexive research stance will produce narratives and observational data that constitute an accurate or true reflection of lived cultural experience implicitly recognizes the subjectivity of the researcher in the co-construction of the account (as well as the need to monitor that subjectivity). Moreover, the assumption that ethnographers will decide upon "skill sets, material goods, or resources that they can and will *gift* to the community" (Suzuki et al., 2005, p. 211; italics ours) also acknowledges the distance of the researcher even in the final procedural stages of a study that may have involved months or years of connection with participants.

The many types of ethnographic approaches available to researchers (e.g., memoir, life history, narrative ethnography, auto-ethnography) suggest wide variability in types of data and methods of interpreting those data (Miller et al., 2003; Suzuki et al., 2005). Moreover, aspects of the ethnographic approach can be found in similar research methods that may be more familiar to counseling psychology researchers (e.g., community-based research). These approaches offer considerable heuristic value, particularly in multicultural counseling psychology research. Examples, can be found in Miller, Wang, Sandel, and Cho (2002), Pipher (2002), and Suzuki, Prendes-Lintel, Wertlieb, and Stallings (1999).

PHENOMENOLOGY

Rooted in the work of philosopher Edmund Husserl and the later American phenomenological and existential psychologists, the phenomenological approach has as its central question: "What is the meaning, structure, and essence of the lived experience of this phenomenon for this person or group of people?" (Patton, 2002, p. 132). Phenomenology is a descriptive method of investigating the life-worlds of individuals, wherein the researcher "attempts to grasp the essence of the individual's life experience through imaginative variation" (Wertz, 2005, p. 172).

In this approach, the researcher seeks to enter empathically into the participant's life-world to understand and communicate the subjective meaning of an individual's lived experience. This is accomplished through a reflective process of suspending assumptions and biases and focusing on a phenomenon itself, then imaginatively varying concrete instances of the phenomena to distill their essential features, culminating in a description that is thought to portray the essence of that lived experience (Giorgi & Giorgi, 2003; Wertz, 2005). This kind of "intentional analysis begins with a situation just as it has been experienced—with all its various meanings—and reflectively explicates the experiential processes through which the situation is lived" (Wertz, 2005, p. 169).

Data are collected as descriptions, and although typically they are direct verbal or written accounts from participants and others who interact with and/or know participants or can provide some kind of insight on the phenomenon under investigation, data also may consist of other forms of expression such as drawings, fictional accounts, poetry, and the like. Analysis consists of generating "situated descriptions" of the participant's experience, organized sequentially or thematically, that then are mined for underlying psychological meanings and processes. The descriptions finally are synthesized into a case study representation that can be considered together with other cases to locate general themes and experiences, as well as variations in "knowledge of types" (Wertz, 2005, p. 173). The final product is a context-bound descriptive presentation of the psychological structure of participants' experiences in a specific life domain (Giorgi & Giorgi, 2003; Wertz, 2005).

Wertz (2005) locates phenomenology as the historical birthplace of contemporary qualitative research, and yet he also distinguishes phenomenology from other qualitative approaches in its unwavering commitment to bracketing researcher presuppositions and biases and its singular emphasis on pure description. Giorgi and Giorgi (2003) argue that phenomenology as a method is distinct from phenomenology as a philosophical endeavor, and it generally is acknowledged that phenomenology shares many procedural elements with other qualitative approaches (e.g., Giorgi & Giorgi, 2003; Wertz, 2005). As a very well-established research approach (including an entire curriculum devoted to phenomenology at Duquesne University), and one with high relevance to many areas of psychology, phenomenology has much to offer counseling psychologists. Examples can be found in Arminio (2001), Friedman, Friedlander, and Blustein (2005), and Muller and Thompson (2003).

PARTICIPATORY ACTION RESEARCH

Emanating from the work of Kurt Lewin (Fine et al., 2003) and embodied in the writings of liberationists such as Frantz Fanon and Paulo Friere (Kidd & Kral, 2005), participatory action research is widely used in community psychology, as well as in other social science fields. Participatory action research (PAR; Fine et al., 2003; Kidd & Kral, 2005) has as its goal the creation of knowledge that directly benefits a group or community (typically marginalized, disenfranchised, or disempowered in some way) through political and social empowerment. Its central question is: How are systems of power and privilege manifested in the lived experiences of this person or group of people, and how can knowledge be gained and used to raise consciousness, emancipate, and empower this person and group?

It is an approach in which researchers and participants work collaboratively over an extended period of time to assess a need or problem in a particular social group, gather and analyze data, and implement results aimed at the "conscientization" (raising consciousness) of and giving voice to individual participants, such that their collective empowerment leads directly to social action and change. Participatory action research takes an unabashedly political stance, and, ideally, the values of the researcher and the participants mesh to drive the social change agenda. The involvement of the researcher is prolonged and intensive, and the success of a PAR project is judged by the manner and extent of changes that have occurred in the lives of participants (Fine et al., 2003; Kidd & Kral, 2005).

Although PAR clearly fits within the critical-ideological paradigm, based on its focus on power relations and structural inequality, in its goals of individual and group empowerment and social change, and its positioning of the researcher as a collaborator, it actually is more of a hybrid approach in many of its features. Data in a PAR project can take virtually any form (including quantitative surveys and statistical analyses of archival data), and its final products may include a wide range of artifacts, such as position papers, policy statements, charts and tables, records, and even speaking or lobbying activities. Kidd and Kral (2005) assert that PAR is not actually a method but rather is "the creation of

a context in which knowledge development and change might occur—much like building a factory in which tools may be made rather than necessarily using tools already at hand" (p. 187). In this sense, PAR is much like organizational consultation in its collaborative approach to assessing needs, gathering data about what is happening in the collective, ensuring that all are given voice in articulating problems and determining future directions, and building readiness for implementation of clearly specified changes and goals.

Almost all experts in PAR note its challenges in practical use, including lack of time and resources for the prolonged engagement that PAR requires, resistance within traditional psychology to the overtly radical change agenda PAR espouses, and deeply entrenched societal and professional disrespect and disdain for the stigmatized, disenfranchised groups that PAR usually seeks to empower. Moreover, lack of knowledge and training in the PAR approach, and the emotional and psychological energy PAR requires from researchers (including the need for flexibility, good group management skills, and the ability to share power) make it difficult for some researchers, particularly novices. Finally, the volatile and changing nature of social groups and social problems can render the research-intervention goal of PAR a moving target, and there are often contextual barriers that make community participation and change extraordinarily difficult. Nevertheless, PAR is well-suited to the diversity and social justice focus within counseling psychology, and it provides unprecedented ways to enact the scientist–practitioner–advocate model of professionalism (Fassinger, 2001; Fassinger & O'Brien, 2000) becoming ever more popular in our field. Examples include Leff, Costigan, and Power (2004), O'Neill, Small, and Strachan (2003), and Fine et al. (2003).

OTHER

In this final section on the various qualitative methods, we include two approaches developed by counseling psychologists that are (so far) used by small groups of researchers confined to counseling psychology. These approaches are *consensual qualitative research* developed by Hill and her colleagues (CQR; Hill, Knox, Thompson, Williams, Hess, & Ladany, 2005) and the *action-project method* of Young and his colleagues (Young, Valach, & Domene, 2005).

Consensual qualitative research, the better known of the two approaches, was developed in the mid-1990s in an effort to create an easy-to-use method of summarizing narrative data, and it has been used primarily in counseling-related investigations to date. Most qualitative methods assume, implicitly or explicitly, that more than one researcher will be participating in data gathering and/or data coding, monitoring, and interpretation. Consensual qualitative research, however, clearly delineates a team approach to collecting data through structured interviews (or counseling sessions) that are consistent across participants, with systematic coding and summarizing of data utilizing interjudge ratings, discussion, and consensus.

Hill and colleagues have claimed that CQR fits within a constructivist-interpretivist paradigm (Hill et al., 2005), but there is considerable disagreement on this point. Most experts acknowledge that it is strongly post-positivist in its use of theoretically or empirically generated structures for framing the study and starting the coding process, its reliance on consistency across participants in data gathering (including the search for negative cases or disconfirming evidence), its goal of achieving inter-rater agreement in coding, its quantitatively oriented analytic techniques and rhetorical structures, and its overall attempt to maintain researcher objectivity as much as possible throughout the research process. Indeed, it bears considerable similarity to simple content analysis in its aims and procedures. Nevertheless, it offers clearly specified procedures and a substantial number of model studies (especially related to counseling processes) for those interested in undertaking their own investigations. Moreover, it provides a viable starting point for researchers interested in qualitative techniques but needing more gradual movement in that direction. An example is Juntunen, Barraclough, Broneck, Seibel, Winrow, and Morin (2001).

The action-project method (Young, Valach, & Domene, 2005) is based in action theory and concerns itself with intentional, goal-directed behavior. It utilizes a three-dimensional model of action that incorporates perspectives on action and levels of action organization into four action systems: individual action, joint action, the action project, and the career (Young et al., 2005, p. 217). Individual and joint actions are short-term, everyday occurrences that cumulatively compose the longer-term "project" in their common themes and goals, which, in turn, results in a long-term organization of projects into a "career" of action that has significant importance in one's life.

Young et al. (2005) insist that the action-project method does not fit into any of the existing qualitative paradigms, but rather "represents a unique epistemology and research paradigm" (p. 218). Certainly, the data collection procedures in the action-project method are distinctive and worth noting. They can include several taped dialogues over an extended period of time (e.g., 6 months) in which each subsequently is replayed and commented upon separately by each participant, the data coded and summarized for distribution back to the participants, supplemented by journal entries, phone conversations, and electronic communications. All of these data are captured in an analysis that is fed back to participants in what is essentially a behavioral intervention, a process that may be repeated many times with the same participants in the course of a study. Indeed, the action-project approach resembles a highly specified behavioral counseling process, and it is not surprising that it offers considerable utility in understanding interpersonal interactions and their impact on the goals and behaviors of the individuals involved. Counseling psychologists with strong interests in the integration of science and practice might find the action-project method especially compelling. An example is found in Young et al. (1997).

Basic Issues to Consider in Qualitative Research

Regardless of the specific qualitative approach a researcher decides to adopt, there are a number of basic issues and challenges with which every researcher must grapple. In this section, we review sampling, data collection, researcher role, data analysis and communication, evaluation, and ethical considerations in conducting qualitative inquiry. Although we present these issues separately, it is important to remember that these decisions are inextricably linked paradigmatically, ontologically, epistemologically, axiologically, methodologically, and rhetorically.

SAMPLING

Quantitative sampling strategies, because they are focused on generalizing findings, always are aimed at isolating a clearly bounded group of observations (represented numerically) that is sizable enough to support statistical inferences regarding the overall population of interest. In qualitative research, however, the goal is an in-depth understanding of the meaning of a particular life experience to those who live it, and data most often consist of narratives, observations, field notes, researcher journals, and other kinds of data that are represented (primarily) linguistically. Sample size depends entirely upon saturating the data set—that is, collecting enough data to satisfy the judgment of the researcher that no new information would be gained by additional cases. Thus, sample sizes in terms of actual participants typically are much smaller in qualitative than in quantitative studies, but the data sets themselves are much larger and more complex.

Given the aim of in-depth understanding, sampling in qualitative inquiry is always "purposeful," that is, to select participants who will provide the most "information-rich" accounts of the phenomena of interest (Patton, 2002, p. 239). The purposes in "purposeful" sampling can be quite varied, depending on the focus of the research. Patton (2002), for example, includes 15 different types of sampling strategies that may be of interest to qualitative researchers, including maximum variation, homogeneous, extreme case, snowball, intensity, typical case, critical case, disconfirming case, and other kinds of sampling.

Qualitative sampling also is criterion-based, in that specific criteria used in selecting participants are based on the research questions that guide the inquiry as well as the particular qualitative approach being used (Creswell, Hanson, Clark, & Morales, 2007; Morrow, 2007). In a phenomenological study, for example, the sample may consist of a small group of individuals who share a very specific common experience (e.g., priests accused of sexual abuse), whereas a participatory action research approach may call for a sample that includes an entire community or organization (e.g., a shelter providing services for women victimized by partner violence). In addition, there are decisions to be made about the extent and kind of contact with participants, ranging from one single lengthy interview with follow-up contact to immersion in and observation of a community over several years. These decisions about who will participate in the study and what the length and nature of the contact will be also determine how the process of actually gathering data will occur.

DATA COLLECTION

As the goal of data collection in qualitative inquiry is to ensure that all information relevant to understanding a particular phenomenon is obtained (i.e., the data set is saturated), the process of gathering data often is both prolonged and iterative. Because interviews, observations, extensive field notes, cultural artifacts, and other similar kinds of documentation form the corpus of data, it is not unusual for months and even years to be devoted to data collection. Moreover, most qualitative methods assume some sort of additional contact with participants to verify the researcher's interpretations during the analysis process, creating an iterative cycle of data collection, researcher analysis, participant feedback, additional data collection and/or analysis, and repeated feedback from participants until no new information is emerging from the process.

Much has been written about the primary data tool in qualitative research: the individual interview. Researchers must conceptualize and articulate their interview strategy in terms of length, depth, kinds of open-ended questions, degree of structure, degree and kind of probing for sensitive information, ways of ensuring that participants' words and ideas are being captured, and ways of monitoring their own reactivity. Patton (2002, as but one example) includes detailed discussion of theoretical and practical issues in planning and conducting interviews, including sections on focus groups and cross-cultural interviewing, as well as numerous tables and checklists. It is imperative that counseling psychologists undertaking qualitative research for the first time consult such resources, as there may be a tendency to assume that competent clinical interviewing skills fully prepare one for conducting interviews aimed at gathering data for research purposes. However, the roles of scientist and helper are very different, and, although good clinical skills may facilitate the kind of relationship-building that is critical to the success of any interview, acquiring an in-depth understanding for research purposes requires a different mindset and approach than coming to understand an individual therapeutically (an ethical issue to which we return below).

Because data collection in qualitative research is implemented in a deeply interpersonal manner, the researcher also must consider when and how entry into the research context will occur and how trust and rapport will be established. Again, the form that this process takes is determined largely by the qualitative approach being used. If interviews with participants who have no connection to one another constitute the primary means of data collection, then the task becomes one of establishing credibility and trust with people one individual at a time. But if data collection includes multiple interviews, behavioral observations, and scrutiny of organizational documents within a group of highly interconnected individuals, then the task of entry into the organization, identification of key informants, rapport-building, and role clarification will be considerably more complex. Similarly, exit from the research context also is driven by approach; a study that utilized single isolated interviewees requires a different kind of process of following up and sharing findings than does a study of an entire community in which multiple stakeholders desire a product they can use to initiate political redress of identified problems. Of course, these different approaches to relationship-based data collection also have important implications for the role and stance of the researcher.

RESEARCHER ROLE

Implementing interpersonally based inquiry requires a different researcher stance than that taken in most quantitatively based studies, in which the goals are appropriate distance, control, and avoidance of researcher contamination of data. Because qualitative research relies on co-constructed representations of lived experience, the researcher is rendered both a participant and an observer in the investigative process, with values, assumptions, and world views that must be made conscious and articulated clearly. As both participants and observers, researchers must grapple with the tension inherent in those roles, including the extent to which they want to function emically (as insiders) or etically (as outsiders), the degree to which they want their observations to be overt or more covert and less obvious, the amount of self-disclosure and collaboration they will offer, the expectation of entry into a long-term or more short-term relationship with participants, and the extent to which they will function as catalysts for change (Fine, 1992, 2007; Morrow, 2007; Patton, 2002).

Clearly, a research approach that requires interpersonal connection as its foundation and squarely places the researcher within that connection calls for a researcher stance that differs markedly from the distanced position of quantitative approaches. Researcher "reflexivity" is the term used most often to capture this stance (e.g., Marecek, 2003; Morrow, 2005, 2007), and refers to the capacity to use own one's experiences, thoughts, and feelings, to recognize and understand one's own perspectives and world views, and to actively and constantly reflect upon the ways in which those might influence one's experience of observing, collecting, understanding, interpreting, and communicating data. Rennie (2004, cited in Morrow, 2005) described reflexivity as self-awareness and agency within that self-awareness. Moreover, reflexivity is not just about the self; it also includes deep reflection about those

studied, the intended and unintended audiences for the inquiry, and the cultural and historical context in which the scientific endeavor occurs. Fine (1992) captured the complexity of the reflexive stance in her description of qualitative researchers as "self-conscious, critical, and participatory analysts, engaged with but still distinct from [their] informants" (p. 254).

In actual practice, researcher reflexivity is facilitated through a variety of strategies that are articulated somewhat differently depending on the particular qualitative approach being used. These strategies may include publicly articulating one's biases through researcher-as-instrument statements, bracketing and monitoring one's biases, being rigorously subjective in one's observations and interpretations, keeping and using field notes throughout the research process, continuously separating description from interpretation and judgment, using thick description to ensure remaining close to participants' experiences, maintaining an appropriate balance between participation and observation, returning again and again to the data and/or participants to verify one's interpretations, memoing or keeping a journal throughout the course of the study, and using external auditors or teams of multiple researchers to maintain systems of peer checking and review (Morrow, 2005). Researcher reflexivity is important throughout the entire inquiry, but it is especially critical during the process of analyzing, interpreting, and communicating the data in the study.

ANALYSIS, INTERPRETATION, AND COMMUNICATION OF DATA

As noted earlier, qualitative approaches differ in the extent to which systematic analytic principles have been detailed in specific how-to formats. However, all offer conceptual delineations of data analyses that parallel the core paradigmatic assumptions of the approach. Thus, a grounded theory analysis moves the researcher through a system of coding and constantly comparing data to an end point of generating an emergent theory grounded in the lived experiences of the participants. A narratological researcher, on the other hand, will (re)arrange narratives into a chronologically and psychologically coherent, storied account of lived experience. Participatory action researchers involve the constituent group(s) in making sense of the data and consciously use the data to mobilize individuals and the community into actions aimed at social change.

Regardless of specific approach, all qualitative methods rely heavily on researcher reflexivity in the analysis process. This reflexive stance compels a continual return to and immersion in the data—not only the narratives or other data gathered from participants, but also the memos, journals, field notes, research team notes, and other documentation of the extensive and intensive process of rigorous thinking that has occurred throughout the inquiry. Thus, six or eight interview transcripts alone (totaling, at minimum, about 150 pages of text) will generate hundreds more pages of an analysis record and audit trail. Moreover, it can be assumed that many hundreds of hours will be devoted to reading, coding, (re)arranging, thematizing or propertizing, theorizing, (re)checking, obtaining feedback, and discussing the data. When other kinds of data are added (e.g., behavioral observations, artifacts, historical records), the sheer size and complexity of the data set becomes quite challenging, and it should be clear why continually interrogating the data corpus is an absolute necessity in qualitative research.

Capturing the enormity and complexity of the data analysis process for purposes of communicating findings also is extremely challenging, and not particularly well-suited to the length and format constraints of most scholarly journals (Morrow, 2005). Morrow (2005) has provided a cogent guide to writing publishable versions of qualitative inquiries, and many excellent studies have been published in counseling psychology journals despite the difficulties. Unfortunately, the brevity of most published accounts belies the extensive work that undergirds those studies and provides limited information about why particular conceptual, sampling, data collection, or analytic decisions were made, thus offering little basis for judging the quality of the research.

EVALUATING QUALITATIVE RESEARCH

Because qualitative and quantitative research emanate from different paradigmatic assumptions, the criteria for judging the quality and rigor of quantitative research simply do not apply to qualitative studies. Attempts have been made to describe evaluation criteria for qualitative studies that parallel the quantitative criteria of validity, reliability, generalizability, and objectivity (probably developed, at least in part, to make qualitative work more acceptable to the positivist researchers comprising most editorial and review boards). However, Morrow (2005) argues that such criteria do not mean or

accomplish the same things, and that qualitative studies are more appropriately evaluated using standards that are congruent internally with what qualitative research seeks to do. Morrow advises the development and use of "intrinsic standards of trustworthiness that have emerged more directly from the qualitative endeavor" (2005, p. 252).

Key to discussions of evaluating the rigor of qualitative research is the concept of trustworthiness or credibility (Morrow, 2005). A comprehensive evaluation framework offered by Morrow (2005) outlines four overarching or "transcendent" criteria (p. 250), so termed because they transcend the particular requirements of any specific approach and apply to the evaluation of all qualitative inquiry. The first criterion for judging the trustworthiness of a study is social validity, or the social value of the project. The second criterion addresses the way in which the study handles subjectivity and reflexivity on the part of the researcher, so that the reader can determine whether the participants' accounts are being honored or whether the findings merely or predominantly reflect the opinions of the researcher. Morrow (2005) advises that, regardless of paradigmatic and axiological approach (i.e., whether researcher subjectivity is bracketed and monitored or incorporated as a driving force in the study), researchers must make their implicit assumptions and biases fully and clearly explicit to themselves and to all others.

The third criterion for judging the trustworthiness of a study lies in the adequacy of the data. Because sample size has little to do with the richness, breadth, and depth of qualitative research data, the study must demonstrate other forms of evidence that the data are maximally informative. Such evidence might include information-rich cases, appropriate sampling, saturated data sets, lengthy and open-ended interviews, feedback from participants, multiple data types and sources, field notes indicating rapport with participants, and inclusion of discrepant or disconfirming cases. The fourth criterion for evaluating the trustworthiness of the inquiry is the adequacy of the interpretation. There must be clear evidence of immersion in the data set during analysis, the use of a specified analytic framework and analytic memos, and a balance in the writing between the interpretations of the researcher and the direct words of the participants (Morrow, 2005).

In addition to these four transcendent criteria, Morrow (2005) also includes criteria that are more specific to the paradigm that undergirds a particular study. In a constructivist/interpretivist study, for example, the additional criteria of fairness, authenticity, and meaning would be important, whereas a critical/ideological study would be expected to include those criteria but also demonstrate consequential and transgressive evidence. Finally, regardless of approach, the trustworthiness of a study also must include evidence that the researcher attended to the social and ethical issues inherent in that study.

ETHICS, POLITICS, AND SOCIAL RESPONSIBILITY

Social, political, and ethical considerations are not pertinent uniquely to qualitative inquiry, as all research is embedded in a sociopolitical and scientific context and therefore must attend to issues of social power, researcher responsibility, protection of people from harm, and potential (mis) use of findings. However, "[b]ecause qualitative methods are highly personal and interpersonal, because naturalistic inquiry takes the researcher into the real world where people live and work, and because in-depth interviewing opens up what is inside people—qualitative inquiry may be more intrusive and involve greater reactivity than surveys, tests, and other quantitative approaches" (Patton, 2002, p. 407). That is, relationship-based methods create unique challenges in the implementation of the standard ethical requirements of the scientific enterprise, and they "increase both the likelihood of 'ethically relevant moments' and the ambiguity of how, or whether, specific ethical standards apply to the question at hand" (Haverkamp, 2005, p. 148).

The relational focus of qualitative inquiry also is buttressed by the use of linguistically based data, which offer researchers considerable interpretive latitude. However, those constructions typically are supported by participant verification which, in turn, is obtained through repeated and prolonged contact. In addition, qualitative inquiry transforms the notion of research benefit where, particularly in the critical/ideological approach, outcomes of a study must include direct benefit to participants in the form of knowledge and empowerment. Finally, the very process of qualitative research has ethical implications, as its flexibility, fluidity, and changeability necessitate ethical decision making repeatedly throughout the entire inquiry process.

Many discussions of ethical, political, and social issues in qualitative research may be found in the literature (e.g., Fine, 1999, 2007; Haverkamp, 2005; Marecek, 2003; Morrow, 2007). Haverkamp (2005) offers a particularly useful discussion for counseling psychologists, recommending a synthesis of virtue ethics, principle ethics, and an ethic of care, all of which are central to graduate training in our field and thus known to counseling psychologists. Haverkamp (2005) calls for "professional reflexivity" (p. 152), the ethical counterpart to research reflexivity, which refers to a conscious consideration of the ways in which our social roles, skills, and knowledge base may influence our research practices, including relationships with participants. Professional reflexivity is the cornerstone of competence, and Haverkamp (2005) notes that professionally reflexive competence includes not only expertise in the populations and topics we wish to investigate, but also in the qualitative methods that we will use in the investigation.

Probably the most widely discussed ethical issue in qualitative research involves researcher boundaries and the complexities inherent in multiple relationships with participants. The deep and prolonged engagement between researcher and participants; the centrality of the researcher's positionality and values; the public and individual perceptions and expectations of psychologists as healers; the skills of clinically trained psychologists in eliciting deeply private and even unconscious information; the co-creation of the meaning, interpretation, and form of the research product; and the focus of much qualitative inquiry on marginalized and disempowered social or cultural groups elicit a host of complex ethical issues that have clear social and political ramifications. Such issues include dual relationships, conflicts of roles and interests, confidentiality, informed consent, coercion, fiduciary responsibility, and use of professional and social power.

Although detailed discussion of these issues is well beyond the scope of this chapter, we return to the concept of trustworthiness, noted above as the primary criterion for evaluating the quality of a study. Haverkamp (2005) argues that trustworthiness does not pertain only to the rigor of methods used in a study, but that it "is an inherently relational construct with relevance for multiple dimensions of the research enterprise" (p. 146). Trustworthiness in the realm of ethics recognizes the potential vulnerability of participants involved in qualitative inquiry, and it reminds researchers that they must maintain constant vigilance in their responsibility to protect participants from harm. Fine (2007) extends this notion into the arena of political and social responsibility by urging a deeper kind of responsibility upon counseling psychologists. She asks that we consider the harm implicit in oppressive social structures and protect our participants by refusing to perpetuate their narratives of denial, blame, or victimization. Fine asserts that we "bear responsibility to theorize that which may not be spoken by those most vulnerable, or, for different reasons, by those most privileged" (p. 472), a clarion call for the kind of qualitative inquiry that also becomes individual and social intervention.

Mixed Methods and Future Prospects

It should be clear that both quantitative and qualitative methods have much to offer in understanding the kinds of issues of interest to most counseling psychologists—relationships, work, counseling, culture, health, and the like. It is our position that mixing these methods in creative ways offers much potential in solving some of the thorniest problems in our field today, and we urge researchers to consider mixed method approaches.

That being said, it is also true that quantitative and qualitative methods may not necessarily mesh well or complement one another within one study. Because they utilize different paradigms, different conceptions of researcher role, different approaches to interacting with participants, different ways of unearthing information, and different articulations of the research enterprise, the outcomes of qualitative and qualitative methods may be not only disparate but wholly incompatible. Dealing with this fundamental gap requires great caution and care, and it may be easier to alternate quantitative and qualitative approaches across studies within an ongoing program of research over many years, shifting the approach to illuminate different aspects of the same research problem (Ponterotto & Grieger, 2007).

Several authors have offered perspectives on the challenges and possibilities of mixed-methods approaches. Marecek (2003) offers a less polarized view of quantitative and qualitative methods, suggesting that the tension is not that one approach produces greater truth than the other, but that they offer different kinds of truths, and researchers must determine which truth is of greatest interest to them in understanding a particular phenomenon. In addition, she observes that any research approach, regardless of paradigmatic and methodological underpinnings, can be used oppressively or dismissively by researchers, and that no particular method

guarantees appropriate handling of social justice goals or redress of social ills. Patton (2002) offers an assortment of possibilities that mix research design, measurement, and analysis in creative approaches to specific problems.

Ponterotto and Grieger (1999, 2007) suggest that, just as psychologists can learn to embrace different cultures and languages and become bicultural, researchers can learn to be facile in both quantitative and qualitative inquiry and become bicultural or "merged" in their research identity (1999, p. 59), termed "bimethodological" (2007, p. 408). These authors argue that the flexibility of a merged identity produces scientific richness, but they caution that becoming truly bicultural methodologically requires immersion in the unfamiliar culture—that is, counseling psychologists must actively undertake qualitative research to learn qualitative research. Ponterotto and Grieger (1999) describe in detail two mixed-methods studies that they judge to be of high quality (Jick, 1983, and Blustein et al., 1997), demonstrating how the researchers successfully navigated the complexities of contrasting paradigmatic approaches, and explaining how and why a mixed-methods approach was effective in these particular investigations. The work of Fassinger and her colleagues in women's career development provides an example of the use of both quantitative (e.g., Fassinger, 1990) and qualitative (e.g., Gomez et al., 2001) approaches in different studies over time to explicate a vocational process. These examples may be of help to counseling psychologists wishing to stretch their scientific competence and work toward becoming more bimethodological.

Conclusion

In concluding this chapter, we express hope that more researchers will embrace the notion of using mixed methods in their research programs. In some cases, this "mixing" may be done by one researcher—within one study or over time in a programmatic series of studies designed to enhance understanding of some phenomenon of interest. In other cases, groups of researchers may combine their efforts, some engaged in qualitative and others in quantitative investigations of a particular problem. In all cases, we assert that researchers must become competent in any method they wish to use, and that, at the same time, we all become conversant enough in both quantitative and qualitative research approaches to appreciate their significant and unique contributions to scholarly progress.

References

AMOS. Structural equation modeling software. [Software]. Available from www.spss.com/Amos/.

Arminio, J. (2001). Exploring the nature of race-related guilt. *Journal of Multicultural Counseling and Development, 29*, 239–252.

Avalos, L. (2005). *An initial examination of a model of intuitive eating.* Unpublished honors thesis, Department of Psychology, the Ohio State University.

Baron, R. M., & Kenny, D. A. (1986). The moderator-mediator variable distinction in social psychological research. *Journal of Personality and Social Psychology, 51*, 1173–1182.

Bentler, P. (1995). EQS: Structural equation modeling software. [Software]. Available from Multivariate Software: www.mvsoft.com/.

Blustein, D. L., Phillips, S. D., Jobin-Davis, K., Finkelberg, S. L., & Rourke, A. E. (1997). A theory- building investigation of the school-to-work transition. *The Counseling Psychologist, 25*, 364–402.

Borgen, F. H., & Betz, N. E. (2008). Career self-efficacy and personality: Linking career confidence and the healthy personality. *Journal of Career Assessment, 16*, 22–43.

Browne, M. (2001). An overview of analytic rotation in exploratory factor analysis. *Multivariate Behavioral Research, 36*, 111–150.

Browne, M., & Cudeck, R. (1993). Alternative ways of assessing model fit. In K. A. Bollen, & J. Long (Eds.), *Testing structural equation models* (pp 136–162). Newbury Park, CA: Sage.

Browne, M., Cudeck, R., Tateneni, K., & Mels, G. (2004). *Comprehensive exploratory factor analysis (CEFA). Computer software and manual.* Retrieved from http://faculty.psy.ohio-sttae.edu/browne/software.php.

Charmaz, K. (2000). Grounded theory: Objectivist and constructivist methods. In N. K. Denzin, & Y. S. Lincoln (Eds.), *Handbook of qualitative research* (2nd ed., pp. 509–536). Thousand Oaks, CA: Sage Publications.

Cohen, J. (1969). *Statistical power analyses for the behavioral sciences.* New York: Academic Press.

Cohen, J. (1988). *Statistical power analyses for the behavioral sciences* (2nd ed.). Hillsdale, NJ: Erlbaum.

Cohen, J. (1992). A power primer. *Psychological Bulletin, 112*, 155–159.

Cohen, J. (1994). The earth is round (p < .05). *American Psychologist, 49*, 997–1003.

Creswell, J. W., Hanson, W. E., Plano Clark, V. L., & Morales, A. (2007). Qualitative research designs: Selection and implementation. *The Counseling Psychologist, 35*(2), 236–264.

DeNeve, K. M., & Cooper, H. (1998). The happy personality. *Psychological Bulletin, 124*, 197–229.

Denzin, N. K., & Lincoln, Y. S. (2000). *Handbook of qualitative research* (2nd ed.). Thousand Oaks, CA: Sage Publications.

Fabrigar, L. R., Wegener, D. T., MacCallum, R. C., & Starhan, E. J. (1999). Evaluating the use of exploratory factor analysis in psychological research. *Psychological Methods, 4*, 272–299.

Fassinger, R. E. (1990). Causal models of career choice in two samples of college women. *Journal of Vocational Behavior, 36*, 225–248.

Fassinger, R. E. (2001). *On remodeling the master's house: Tools for dismantling sticky floors and glass ceilings.* Invited keynote address, Fifth Biennial Conference of the Society for Vocational Psychology, Houston, TX.

Fassinger, R. E. (2005). Paradigms, praxis, problems, and promise: Grounded theory in counseling psychology research. *Journal of Counseling Psychology, 52*, 156–166.

Fassinger, R. E., & O'Brien, K. M. (2000). Career counseling with college women: A scientist-practitioner-advocate model of intervention. In D. Luzzo (Ed.), *Career development of college students: Translating theory and research into practice* (pp. 253–265). Washington, DC: American Psychological Association Books.

Fine, M. (2007). Expanding the methodological imagination. *The Counseling Psychologist, 35*, 459–473.

Fine, M., Torre, M. E., Boudin, K., Bowen, I., Clark, J., Hylton, D., et al. (2003). Participatory action research: From within and beyond prison bars. In P. M. Camic, J. E. Rhodes, & L. Yardley (Eds.), *Qualitative research in psychology: Expanding perspectives in methodology and design* (pp. 173–198). Washington, DC: American Psychological Association Books.

Fitzgerald, L. F., & Hubert, L. J. (1987). Multidimensional scaling: Some possibilities for counseling psychology. *Journal of Counseling Psychology, 34*, 469–480.

Forester, M., Kahn, J., & Hesson-McInnis, M. (2004). Factor structure of three measures of research self-efficacy. *Journal of Career Assessment, 12*, 3–16.

Frazier, P. A., Tix, A. P., & Barron, K. E. (2004). Testing moderator and mediator effects in counseling psychology research. *Journal of Counseling Psychology, 51*, 115–134.

Friedman, M. L., Friedlander, M. L., & Blustein, D. L. (2005). Toward an understanding of Jewish identity: A phenomenological study. *Journal of Counseling Psychology, 52*, 77–83.

Giorgi, A. P., & Giorgi, B. M. (2003). The descriptive phenomenological psychological model. In P. M. Camic, J. E. Rhodes, & L. Yardley (Eds.), *Qualitative research in psychology: Expanding perspectives in methodology and design* (pp. 243–274). Washington, DC: American Psychological Association Books.

Glaser, B. G. (1992). *Basics of grounded theory analysis: Emergence vs. forcing.* Mill Valley, CA: Sociology Press.

Glaser, B. G. (2000). The future of grounded theory. *Grounded Theory Review, 1*, 1–8.

Glaser, B. G., & Strauss, A. L. (1967). *The discovery of grounded theory: Strategies for qualitative research.* Chicago: Aldine.

Glass, G. V. (1976). Primary, secondary, and meta-analysis of research. *Educational Researcher, 5*, 3–8.

Glass, G. V. (2006). Meta-analysis: Quantitative synthesis of research findings. In J. Green, G. Camilli, & P. Elmore (Eds.), *Handbook of complementary methods in education research* (pp. 427–438). Mahwah, NJ: Erlbaum.

Glass, G. V., & Hopkins, K. (1996). *Statistical methods in psychology and education* (3rd ed.). Englewood Cliffs, NJ: Prentice Hall.

Gomez, M. J., Fassinger, R. E., Prosser, J., Cooke, K., Mejia, B., & Luna, J. (2001). Voces abriendo caminos (voices forging paths): A qualitative study of the career development of notable Latinas. *Journal of Counseling Psychology, 48*, 286–300.

Gorsuch, R. L. (1983). *Factor analysis* (2nd ed.). Hillsdale, NJ: Erlbaum.

Haase, R. F., & Ellis, M. V. (1987). Multivariate analysis of variance. *Journal of Counseling Psychology, 34*, 404–413.

Hansen, J. C., Dik, B., & Zhou, S. (2008). An examination of the structure of leisure interests in college students, working age adults, and retirees. *Journal of Counseling Psychology, 55*, 133–145.

Hardy, G. E., Barkham, M., Field, S. D., Elliott, R., & Shapiro, D. A. (1998). Whineging versus working: Comprehensive process analysis of a "vague awareness" event in psychodynamic-interpersonal therapy. *Psychotherapy Research, 8*, 334–353.

Haverkamp, B. E. (2005). Ethical perspectives on qualitative research in applied psychology. *Journal of Counseling Psychology, 52*(2), 146–155.

Hayton, J. C., Allen, D. G., Scarpello, V. (2004). Factor retention decisions in exploratory factor analysis: A tutorial on parallel analysis. *Organizational Research Methods, 7*, 191–205.

Henwood, K., & Pidgeon, N. (2003). Grounded theory in psychological research. In P. M. Camic, J. E. Rhodes, & L. Yardley (Eds.), *Qualitative research in psychology: Expanding perspectives in methodology and design* (pp. 131–156). Washington, DC: American Psychological Association Books.

Heppner, P., Wampold, B., & Kivlighan, D. (2008). *Research design in counseling* (4th ed.). Belmont, CA: Brooks-Cole.

Hermann, K. (2005). *Path models of the relationships of instrumentality and expressiveness, social self-efficacy, and self-esteem to depressive symptoms in college students.* Unpublished PhD Dissertation, Department of Psychology, Ohio State University.

Hermann, K., & Betz, N. E. (2006). Path models of the relationships of instrumentality and expressiveness, social self-efficacy, and self-esteem to depressive symptoms in college students. *Journal of Social and Clinical Psychology, 25*, 1086–1106.

Hill, C. E., Knox, S., Thompson, B. J., Williams, E. N., Hess, S. A., Ladany, N. (2005). Consensual qualitative research: An update. *Journal of Counseling Psychology, 52*(2), 196–205.

Hogan, T. P. (2007). *Psychological testing: A practical introduction* (2nd ed.). New York: Wiley.

Hoshmand, L. T. (2005). Narratology, cultural psychology, and counseling research. *Journal of Counseling Psychology, 52*(2), 178–186.

Hu, L., & Bentler, P. (1999). Cutoff criteria for fit indexes in covariance structure analysis: Conventional criteria versus new alternatives. *Structural Equation Modeling, 6*, 1–55.

Jick, T. D. (1983). Mixing qualitative and quantitative methods: Triangulation in action. In J. Van Maanen (Ed.), *Qualitative methodology* (pp. 135–148). Beverly Hills, CA: Sage.

Joreskog, K. G., & Sorbom, D. (2008). *LISREL 8.8.* [Software]. Lincolnwood IL: Scientific Software. Retrieved from www.ssicentral.com/lisrel/new.html.

Juntunen, C. L., Barraclough, D. J., Broneck, C. L., Seibel, G. A., Winrow, S. A., & Morin, P. M. (2001). American Indian perspectives on the career journey. *Journal of Counseling Psychology, 48*, 274–285.

Kahn, J. H. (2006). Factor analysis in counseling psychology research, training, and practice. *The Counseling Psychologist, 34*, 684–718, inside back cover.

Kanji, G. K. (1993). *100 statistical tests.* Newbury Park, CA: Sage.

Kashubeck-West, S., Coker, A. D., Awad, G. H., Hix, R. D., Bledman, R. A., & Mintz, L. (2008, August). *Psychometric evaluation of body image measures in African American women.* Poster presented at the meeting of the American Psychological Association, Boston, MA.

Kidd, S. A., & Kral, M. J. (2005). Practicing participatory action research. *Journal of Counseling Psychology, 52*, 187–195.

Killeen, P. R. (2005). An alternative to null-hypothesis significance tests. *Psychological Science, 16*, 345–353.

Kinnier, R. T., Tribbensee, N. E., Rose, C. A., & Vaughan, S. M. (2001). In the final analysis: More wisdom from people who have faced death. *Journal of Counseling & Development, 79*, 187–195.

Kirk, R. (1996). Practical significance: A concept whose time has come. *Educational and Psychological Measurement, 56*, 746–759.

Larson, L., Wei, M., Wu, T., Borgen, F., & Bailey, D. (2007). Discriminating among educational majors and career aspirations in Taiwanese undergraduates. *Journal of Counseling Psychology, 54*, 395–408.

Leff, S. S., Costigan, T., & Power, T. J. (2004). Using participatory research to develop a playground-based prevention program. *Journal of School Psychology, 42*, 3–21.

Lent, R. W., Brown, S. D., Sheu, H.-B., Schmidt, J., Brenner, B., Gloster, C., et al. (2005). Social cognitive predictors of academic interest and goals in engineering: Utility for women and students at historically Black universities. *Journal of Counseling Psychology, 52*, 84–92.

MacCallum, R. C., & Austin, J. (2000). Applications of structural equation modeling in psychological research. *Annual Review of Psychology, 51*, 201–226.

MacCallum, R., Roznowski, M., & Necowitz, L. (1992). Model modifications in covariance structure analysis: The problem of capitalization on chance. *Psychological Bulletin, 111*, 490–504.

MacCallum, R. C., Widaman, K. F., Zhang, S., & Hong, S. (1999). Sample size in factor analysis. *Psychological Methods, 4*, 84–89.

Marecek, J. (2003). Dancing through minefields: Toward a qualitative stance in psychology. In P. M. Camic, J. E. Rhodes, & L. Yardley (Eds.), *Qualitative research in psychology: Expanding perspectives in methodology and design* (pp. 49–70). Washington, DC: American Psychological Association Books.

Miller, P. J., Hengst, J. A., & Wang, S. (2003). Ethnographic methods: Applications from developmental cultural psychology. In P. M. Camic, J. E. Rhodes, & L. Yardley (Eds.), *Qualitative research in psychology: Expanding perspectives in methodology and design* (pp. 49–70). Washington, DC: American Psychological Association Books.

Morrow, S. L. (2005). Quality and trustworthiness in qualitative research in counseling psychology. *Journal of Counseling Psychology, 52*(2), 250–260.

Morrow, S. L. (2007). Qualitative research in counseling psychology: Conceptual foundations. *The Counseling Psychologist, 35*(2), 209–235.

Morrow, S. L., & Smith, M. L. (1995). Constructions of survival and coping by women who have survived childhood sexual abuse. *Journal of Counseling Psychology, 42*, 24–33.

Murray, M. (2003). Narrative psychology and narrative analysis. In P. M. Camic, J. E. Rhodes, & L. Yardley (Eds.), *Qualitative research in psychology: Expanding perspectives in methodology and design.* Washington, DC: American Psychological Association Books.

Muthen, L. K., & Muthen, B. O. (2006). *Mplus users guide* (4th ed.). Los Angeles: Muthen and Muthen. Retrieved from www.statmodel.com/company.shtml.

Noonan, B. M., Gallor, S., Hensler-McGinnis, N., Fassinger, R. E., Wang, S., & Goodman, J. (2004). Challenge and success: A qualitative study of the career development of highly achieving women with physical and sensory disabilities. *Journal of Counseling Psychology, 51*, 68–80.

Patton, M. Q. (2002). *Qualitative research & evaluation methods* (3rd ed.). Thousand Oaks, CA: Sage Publications.

Polkinghorne, D. (2005). Language and meaning: Data collection in qualitative research. *Journal of Counseling Psychology, 52*, 137–145.

Ponterotto, J. G. (2005). Qualitative research in counseling psychology: A primer on research paradigms and philosophy of science. *Journal of Counseling Psychology, 52*(2), 126–136.

Ponterotto, J. G., & Grieger, I. (1999). Merging qualitative and quantitative perspectives in a research identity. In M. Kopala, & L. A. Suzuki (Eds.), *Using qualitative methods in psychology* (pp. 49–61.). Thousand Oaks, CA: Sage Publications.

Ponterotto, J. G., & Grieger, I. (2007). Effectively communicating qualitative research. *The Counseling Psychologist, 35*(3), 431–458.

Rennie, D. L. (1994). Clients' deference in psychotherapy. *Journal of Counseling Psychology, 41*, 427–437.

Rennie, D. L. (2000). Grounded theory methodology as methodological hermeneutics. *Theory & Psychology, 10*(4), 481–502.

Rennie, D. L. (2004). Anglo-North American qualitative counseling and psychotherapy research. *Psychotherapy Research, 14*, 37–55.

Richie, B. S., Fassinger, R. E., Linns, S., Johnson, J., Prosser, J., & Robinson, S. (1997). Persistence, connection, and passion: A qualitative study of the career development of highly achieving African American/Black and White women. *Journal of Counseling Psychology, 44*, 133–148.

Russell, D., Kahn, J., Spoth, R., & Altmaier, E. (1998). Analyzing data from experimental studies. *Journal of Counseling Psychology, 45*, 18–29.

Schafer, J. L., & Graham, J. W. (2002). Missing data: Our view of the state of the art. *Psychological Methods, 7*, 147–177.

Schumaker, R. E., & Lomax, R. G. (2004). *A beginner's guide to structural equation modeling.* Mahwah, NJ: Lawrence Erlbaum.

Sherry, A. (2006). Discriminant analysis in counseling psychology research. *The Counseling Psychologist, 34*, 661–683.

Sireci, S. G., & Talento-Miller, E. (2006). Evaluating the predictive validity of Graduate Management Admissions Test scores. *Educational and Psychological Measurement, 66*, 305–317.

Smith, M. L., & Glass, G. V. (1977). Meta-analysis of psychotherapy outcome studies. *American Psychologist, 32*, 752–760.

Sobel, M. E. (1982). Asymptotic intervals for indirect effects in structural equation models. In S. Leinhart (Ed.), *Sociological methodology* (pp. 290–312). San Francisco: Jossey-Bass.

Spearman, C. (1904). General intelligence: Objectively defined and measured. *American Journal of Psychology, 15*, 201–293.

Steiger, J. H. (1990). Structural model evaluation and modification: An interval estimation approach. *Multivariate Behavioral Research, 25*, 173–180.

Sterner, W. R. (2011). What is missing in counseling research? Reporting missing data. *Journal of Counseling and Development, 89*, 56–63.

Stevens, S. S. (1951). *Handbook of experimental psychology.* New York: Wiley.

Strauss, A. L. (1987). *Qualitative analysis for social scientists.* New York: Cambridge University Press.

Strauss, A. L., & Corbin, J. (1998). *Basics of qualitative research: Techniques and procedures for developing grounded theory* (2nd ed.). Thousand Oaks, CA: Sage Publications.

Suzuki, L. A., Ahluwalia, M. K., Mattis, J. S., & Quizon, C. A. (2005). Ethnography in counseling psychology research: Possibilities for application. *Journal of Counseling Psychology, 52*, 206–214.

Suzuki, L. A., Prendes-Lintel, M., Wertlieb, L., & Stallings, A. (1999). Exploring multicultural issues using qualitative methods. In M. Kopala, & L. A. Suzuki (Eds.), *Using qualitative methods in psychology* (pp. 123–134). Thousand Oaks, CA: Sage Publications.

Swanson, J. L. (2011). Measurement and assessment in counseling psychology. In E. M. Altmaier, & J. C. Hansen (Eds.), *The Oxford handbook of counseling psychology.* New York: Oxford University Press.

Tabachnick, B. G., & Fidell, L. S. (2007). *Using multivariate statistics* (5th ed.). New York: Harper Collins College Publishers.

Thurstone, L. L. (1947). *Multiple factor analysis.* Chicago: University of Chicago Press.

Tracey, T. J. G. (2008). Adherence to RIASEC structure as a key career decision construct. *Journal of Counseling Psychology, 55*, 146–157.

Vacha-Haase, T., & Thompson, B. (2004). How to estimate and interpret various effect sizes. *Journal of Counseling Psychology, 51*, 473–481.

Wertz, F. J. (2005). Phenomenological research methods for counseling psychology. *Journal of Counseling Psychology, 52*, 167–177.

Weston, R., & Gore, P. (2006). A brief guide to structural equation modeling. *The Counseling Psychologist, 34*, 719–751.

Wilkinson, L., & Task Force on Statistical Inference. (1999). Statistical methods in psychology journals: Guidelines and explanations. *American Psychologist, 54*, 594–604.

Young, R. A., Valach, L., & Domene, J. E. (2005). The action-project method in counseling psychology. *Journal of Counseling Psychology, 52*(2), 215–223.

Young, R. A., Valach, L., Paseluihko, M. A., Dover, C., Matthes, G. E., Paproski, D., et al. (1997). The joint action of parents and adolescents in conversation about career. *Career Development Quarterly, 46*, 72–86.

Zwick, W. R., & Velicer, W. F. (1986). A comparison of five rules for determining the number of components to retain. *Psychological Bulletin, 99*, 432–442.

Ethics in Counseling Psychology

Melba J. T. Vasquez *and* Rosie Phillips Bingham

Abstract

This chapter focuses on the contributions that counseling psychology has made to the evolution of professional ethics. Kitchener's moral principles and Meara, Schmidt, and Day's (1996) virtue ethics are examples of contributors whose work has influenced the ethics discourse. Changes to the 2002 American Psychological Association's Ethical Principles of Psychologists and Code of Conduct are discussed, as are mechanisms for accountability and key areas of concern for psychologists. Counseling psychology's unique contribution to social justice as an ethical imperative is addressed, and an ethical decision-making model is suggested. Finally, future directions in ethics, especially in regard to the social milieu, are described, including the direction of ethics training.

Keywords: ethics, virtue ethics, moral principles, counseling psychology, social justice, practice guidelines, accountability, ethics education, ethical decision making

In this chapter, we discuss the evolution of the American Psychological Association (APA) ethics codes, including an overview of counseling psychologists' contribution to the ethics discourse, such as Kitchener's (1984, 2000) moral principles and Meara, Schmidt, and Day's (1996) virtue ethics. Throughout the chapter, we discuss changes to the APA 2002 Ethical Principles of Psychologists and Code of Conduct. We describe the mechanisms for accountability, and identify key areas of concern based on the areas of most common violation by psychologists. We suggest a decision-making model for use with ethical dilemmas. We also discuss counseling psychology's unique contribution to social justice as an ethical imperative, and describe several of the aspirational guidelines that have been developed in large part through the contributions of various counseling psychologists. The final section identifies our concluding thoughts on key dilemmas yet to be fully addressed in the ethical realm of professional responsibilities and ethics education.

Counseling Psychologists and the Ethics Codes

The influence of counseling psychologists on the development of the last couple of revisions of the APA Ethical Principles of Psychologists and Code of Conduct (1992, 2002) has been significant, although counseling psychologists were not involved in the early development of the ethical discourse for various reasons. The Division of Counseling Psychology was founded in 1943, as Division 17 of the American Psychological Association with the name of Division of Counseling and Guidance. The first tentative draft of an APA ethics code occurred in 1951. The early drafters of the code were operating in a climate that questioned the need for an ethics code (Hall, 1952). The APA Ethics Committee was founded in 1938, 46 years after the APA was founded. Given the increasing ethical questions and dilemmas in the profession, the APA Council of Representatives adopted the first official Ethical Standards for Psychologists in 1953. The current

Ethical Principles of Psychologists and Code of Conduct (APA, 2002) is the tenth revision, and was amended in 2010.

During the development of the first APA Ethics Code, counseling psychology was very inwardly focused on establishing itself as a discipline, to the extent that it even concerned itself with finding an appropriate name. The professionals of the time worked to distinguish counseling psychology from clinical psychology and to establish it as a viable discipline. Several national counseling psychology conferences, including the 1951 Northwestern Conference, the 1964 Greystone Conference, and the 1987 Atlanta Conference, firmly solidified counseling psychology as a legitimate field of study in psychology. During the conferences, there appears to have been minimal attention paid to discussions of ethics.

Although there are no reported major publications on ethics from these early counseling psychology conferences, there were discussions of issues that would have bearing on the content of later ethics codes and guidelines. As early as the Northwestern Conference in 1951, the discourse referred to the need for counseling psychologists to be concerned with culture (APA, 1952). The Greystone Conference was specifically charged to examine emerging diversity in the field (Thompson & Super, 1964). Participants of the 1987 Atlanta Conference identified five major areas of concern, including the call for more multicultural research and the integration of diversity, gender, and multiculturalism throughout the curricula and training. In 2001, the Houston Conference on counseling psychology firmly and definitively staked a claim in the discipline's commitment to social justice and acknowledged the implications of that commitment. In addition to the general focus of helping individuals with emotional and psychological problems, Bingham (2002) surmised that counseling psychology had these four foci: multiculturalism, because culture is important and there is more than one culture; social justice, because of the emphasis on development and growth and environmental/ situation influences; vocational issues, because counseling psychology has long held vocational issues as one of the core components of the field; and fostering human strengths, because counseling psychology unequivocally proclaims a focus on "healthy aspects and strengths of clients." These were some major themes that have been addressed in more recent versions of the ethics code, which includes diversity issues such as sexual harassment and unfair discrimination.

Although the counseling psychology conferences did not address ethics per se, several counseling psychologists have promoted key concepts in the field of ethics. Schmidt and Meara (1984) provided a framework for understanding ethical, legal, and professional issues for counseling psychology. Their framework for discussing these issues through the lens of human services, research, teaching/training, and public policy provided a useful method for effectively writing about and discussing ethics across the rather broad counseling psychology specialty. The Schmidt and Meara (1984) contribution served as an ethics educational tool for counseling psychologists and as a reminder that counseling psychology was a young field, struggling for credibility and legitimacy. The authors clarified certain areas, such as the difference between privileged communication and confidential communication. In their roles as educators for counseling psychologists, they also highlighted portions of the Ethics Code that dealt with matters such as informed consent, confidentiality with clients and research subjects, sexual exploitation and sexual harassment, research subjects and the role of deceit and debriefing, and so on.

It is interesting to note that the Schmidt and Meara (1984) contribution reflects some of counseling psychology's struggle for identity and legitimacy in the early years. In several sections in which the authors highlighted the ethical concerns for clients and students, they also offered cautions that the consequences of certain behaviors could adversely affect counseling psychology as a whole. For example, Schmidt and Meara (1984) cautioned, "If the belief developed that counseling psychologists misled subjects in their research, doubts might also arise over their treatment of clients in counseling relationships. This clearly is to be avoided, both for the sake of the individual and the profession at large" (p. 69). Schmidt and Meara (1984) also talked about the "reputation and credibility of counseling psychologists" when they discussed the role and ethics of placebo treatments in research.

Evidence that counseling psychology was a young field was reflected in the Schmidt and Meara (1984) statements that very few counseling psychologists were called as expert witnesses. Fretz and Mills (1980) indicated that, throughout the 1970s, counseling psychology was fairly closed and insular. These statements may explain why the Schmidt and Meara (1984) contribution was written in such a way that it served almost as a primer on ethics.

During the time that Schmidt and Meara (1984) were concerned with writing about ethics for counseling psychologists, it is important to note that at least two other substantive developments were taking root in the field. One focused on women. The Division 17 Ad Hoc Committee was formed in 1970. The committee developed a set of principles for counseling and therapy with women (Farmer, 2002), Also at the close of the 1970s, the Division adopted a position paper on cross-cultural competencies (Sue et al., 1982). These two documents represented the cementing of part of counseling psychology's identity and its focus on multiculturalism and social justice. These two documents were significant contributions, and serve as forerunners to the APA's development and adoption of guidelines in these two areas: The APA Guidelines on Multicultural Education, Training, Research, Practice, and Organizational Change for Psychologists (APA, 2003), and the APA Guidelines for Psychological Practice with Girls and Women (APA, 2007). Counseling psychologists were key authors in the development of these and other important guidelines, which provide guidance in the provision of the highest quality of care. Such guidelines are important because they have implications for ethical standards to speak to competence and admonitions against discrimination.

In 1992, Fretz and Simon (1992) summarized views that indicated a maturing of counseling psychologists on matters of ethics. The discussion moved toward what it means to be an ethical person, rather than focusing more narrowly on the codes that provided the essential rules about ethical conduct. By 1992, the APA Ethics Code had been through several revisions, including those that ended APA's restrictive practices on advertising. However, other challenges to the 1981 code resulted in the courts' ruling that the code was so ambiguous that it was difficult to apply. So, although the mindset of counseling psychologists had undergone an ethical maturing process, the code was about to experience a major revision.

Perhaps Fretz and Simon (1992) could depart from the more explanatory focus on the content of the Ethics Code because Hall (1987) had reported that 85% of all APA accredited programs had some form of ethics education. Welfel and Lipsitz (1984) maintained that knowledge was not enough to produce an ethical psychologist. Furthermore, Fretz and Simon (1992) reported that there had been significant increases in the number of ethics articles and books being published. More significantly, a number of counseling psychologists had begun to make notable forays into the ethics literature. Kitchener and Anderson (2000) suggested that "The intensified involvement of state legislatures to regulate psychology, the increased number of civil suits filed against psychologists, and the public's increased awareness and expectations that psychologists act ethically calls for the profession to see good counseling, research, and training as impossible without good or virtuous ethical behavior" (Kitchener & Anderson, 2000, p. 75).

Several counseling psychologists have indeed made significant contributions to the literature on psychological ethics. Karen Kitchener (1984, 2000) adapted the Beauchamp and Childress (1979) conceptualization of principle ethics for decision making in medicine to the field of psychology. Beauchamp and Childress conceptualized the principles of autonomy, nonmalefience, beneficence, and justice as well-established standards for bioethical medicine in the United States. Kitchener (1984) added the principle of fidelity and applied those to psychology ethics. Since then, those principles have shaped the general principles of the APA's Ethical Principles of Psychology and Code of Conduct (1992, 2002). These principles are particularly helpful in resolving ethical dilemmas. Ethical dilemmas evolve when ethical principles sometimes compete against each other, or an ethical principle may conflict with law. Kitchener (1984, 2000) suggested that a critical-evaluative level or moral reasoning could be developed by applying the five ethical principles as a foundation for ethical decision making in psychology. These principles are often used in society to establish policy, such as in the court system. The APA 2002 Ethics Code was reorganized so that the introductory General Principles are more consistent with these bioethical principles. Thus, we see that counseling psychology has had an enduring impact on the APA Ethics Code.

Meara, Schmidt, and Day (1996) have also had an impact on the conceptualization of ethics in psychology. They described how virtue ethics focuses on character traits and nonobligatory ideals that facilitate the development of ethical individuals. They suggested that these were complementary ethical perspectives that helped provide a coherent structure for enhancing the ethical competence of psychologists and counselors and the level of public trust in the character and actions of these professions and their members. Virtue ethics, rooted in the narratives, aspirations, and ideals of specific communities, can be particularly helpful to professionals in discerning appropriate ethical conduct in multicultural settings and interactions.

Meara and her colleagues (Meara, Schmidt, & Day, 1996, Jordan & Meara, 1990) moved the ethics discussion beyond codification, rules, and regulations to a focus on the person, rather than on cognitive analyses such as those embodied in the principled ethics described by Kitchener. Jordan and Meara (1990) championed a message about the kind of ethical persons counseling psychologists should be. Such discussions led Fretz and Simon (1992) to assert that training programs would need to move beyond the mere teaching of ethics content to more foundational discussion of ethics philosophy and ethical decision-making models. Another implication has been validation of the attention to the selection of students into the field of counseling psychology. That is, that character is a critical element in ethical behavior and that the selection of future psychologists should assess for those aspects of character that support ethical behavior.

Like Schmidt and Meara (1984), Fretz and Simon (1992) highlighted ethical issues that were receiving considerable attention at the close of 1980s. These issues included informed consent in supervision, research, and professional writing. Furthermore, as the human immunodeficiency virus/acquired immune deficiency syndrome (HIV/AIDS) epidemic burst onto the scene, new problems of confidentiality arose regarding the relationship, obligations, and responsibility of the counseling psychologist to an HIV-infected client who maintained a physical relationship with a person to whom the client had not disclosed his or her HIV status. Fretz and Simon (1992) also raised issues of a client's right to end his or her own life. These authors were making it clear that ethical issues were becoming more nuanced and complex. In addition, the number of cases being referred to the APA Ethics Committee experienced a steep rise. It seemed that counseling psychologists and clients were becoming more ethically sophisticated and more aware of problems in the field. Fretz and Simon (1992) also conveyed their understanding of the increasing importance of cultural diversity and the implication of cultural competence as a key ethical requirement.

In 1992, the Ethics Code underwent a major revision. This revision occurred in part because consumers and psychologists were beginning to understand the complexities of psychological relationships, raising more questions about the impact of psychologists' behaviors and their consequences in psychotherapy, research, educational, and other business settings. There was growing diversity in the U.S. demographics and in the clientele seeking psychological services. These changes occurred at a time when society was becoming more litigious. The number of cases brought before the APA ethics committees and state psychology boards increased, and the number of suits filed against psychologists rose dramatically. Additionally, more psychologists were objecting to sanctions being imposed by ethics bodies. Change was needed. The 1992 revision of the ethics code was designed to be a utilitarian document that would provide simple, straightforward, and direct guidance to psychologists (Canter, Bennett, Jones, & Nagy, 1994). Principled ethics, like those espoused by Kitchener, were deemed ambiguous and therefore were separated out as aspirational and not enforceable. The code then delineated a series of topically divided declarative statements that would act as enforceable standards.

Kitchener and Anderson (2000) raised the question of whether such a collection of standards could help an individual become a truly ethical counseling psychologist. They argued for the inclusion of virtue ethics in the training of counseling psychologists. Virtue ethics had been proposed by Meara (1996) to examine the characteristics, emotions, motivation, prudence, and moral habits of individuals. Kitchener and Anderson maintained that "Moral behavior is complex; these philosophical and psychologically sophisticated models are necessary to understand it" (p. 72.) Of course, such models were considered far too complex to include in an ethics code.

But Kitchener and Anderson (2000) advocated for counseling psychologists to at least include such training in educational programs and then research their effectiveness. The authors seemed to be concerned about the fact that no such research was being conducted in psychology. They did report on Bebeau's (1994) work with dental students, whose data indicated that moral sensitivity and reasoning can be improved with training. Kitchener and Anderson believed that such research is necessary for counseling psychology students because data suggests that, even after an ethics course, students will still make serious errors in deciding on ethical issues (Fly, vanBark, Weinman, Kitchener, & Lang, 1997). Furthermore, they pointed to the increasing complexity of multiple relationships; the complication of competence, bias, and justice at the intersection of race, ethnicity, and gender; and even the problems of confidentiality in various settings as examples of why a simple compendium of utilitarian standards was insufficient in today's psychological environment. Kitchener and Anderson (2000) made such a compelling argument for virtue ethics that it was clear that the ethics code would shortly require another revision.

Werth, Cummings, and Thompson (2008) provided an overview of select ethical and legal issues affecting counseling psychologists, including risk management and competence. They focused on the APA Ethics Code, professional regulations, state statutes, and federal laws. They emphasized the importance of consultation and exposure to the literature in order to monitor competence and biases in every professional situation. Werth et al. and other counseling psychologists cited here challenged the profession to view ethics as more than a codification of rules and regulations. They demonstrated that ethics must be pervasive in all that psychologists do, if they are to be competent and accountable.

Thus, counseling psychologists have contributed to the discourse and direction of professional ethics in psychology. Considerations of key professional obligations are integrated into the fabric of counseling psychology teaching, training and supervision, our publications, and in the research and practice of psychology.

Mechanisms of Accountability

Four major mechanisms hold psychologists and other mental health professionals accountable to an explicit set of professional standards and legal requirements, including professional ethics committees, state licensing boards, civil malpractice courts, and criminal courts. Although considerable overlap exists, each of these mechanisms may use different formulations of standards. Our profession has a social contract with society, based on attitudes of mutual respect and trust, that the discipline will do everything it can to assure that its members will act ethically in conducting the affairs of the profession within society. The "contract" implies a commitment to place the welfare of society and individual members of the society above the welfare of the discipline and its professionals. So, psychologists have a higher duty of care to members of society than the general duty of care that all members of society have to each other, including taking care that psychologists not abuse power, and in fact use it to help others. This is the basis on which mechanisms of accountability are established; that is, to be committed to ensuring that professions meet

minimal standards as their members carry out their work, and that those who are served by professionals are protected from harm in the case of incompetent, negligent, and/or unscrupulous practitioners (Pope & Vasquez, 2007). Counseling psychologists may have an even higher duty of care because of our emphasis on social justice. A commitment to social justice implies that the discipline is intentional and purposeful in its attention to issues of relationships, justice, and fairness for all individuals. So, although the accountability mechanism ensures that the profession meets minimal standards, the social justice emphasis suggests that counseling psychologists must challenge themselves to go beyond these minimum requirements.

The APA Ethics Code and Areas of Concern

Pope and Vasquez (2007) reported a compilation of data from the major areas of most frequently reported disciplinary action as described by the APA Ethics Committee, the Association of State and Provincial Psychology Boards (ASPPB), and the APA Insurance Trust. Based on those data, we will describe issues involved in the following categories: multiple relationships, including sexual intimacy/sexual misconduct and nonsexual boundary violations; confidentiality; insurance and fees; record keeping; child custody; and terminations.

Multiple Relationships: Sexual Misconduct and Nonsexual Boundary Violations

Sexual intimacies with current clients/patients have been explicitly prohibited since the 1977 APA Ethics Code; however, the standard of practice prior to that inclusion precluded a sexual relationship between therapist and client. The prohibition had been indirectly implied by other standards before that time (Pope &Vasquez, 2007). Several of the general principles and standards in the 2002 Ethics Code prohibit sexual relationships and involvements with clients and students.

General Principle A, Beneficence and Nonmaleficence, states that, "psychologists strive to benefit those with whom they work and take care to do no harm" (APA, p. 1062). Psychologists are cautioned to avoid inflicting intentional harm and not to engage in actions that risk harming others. Ethics Code Standard 10.05 most directly addresses sexual intimacies with current therapy clients/patients, and 10.08 prohibits sexual intimacies with former therapy clients and patients for at least 2 years after termination of professional services. Even then, the burden is on the psychologist to demonstrate that no exploitation exists, based on several factors. Standard 10.06, a new standard in the 2002 Ethics Code, prohibits sexual intimacies with relatives or significant others of current therapy clients/patients, and 10.07 prohibits therapy with former sexual partners. Other standards relevant to the prohibition include 3.04, Avoiding Harm, and 3.08 Exploitative Relationships. In addition, Ethics Code Standard 7.07 prohibits sexual relationships with students and supervisees over whom psychologists have or are likely to have evaluative authority.

The evidence is clear that sexual contact with clients/patients and students has a high potential for harm, partly because the power differential and influence that psychologists possess result in exploitation of the vulnerabilities of those with whom they work (Pope & Vasquez, 2007). It also harms the public image of psychologists, and the prevalence of sexual involvement of mental health providers with clients/patients has resulted in an increasing criminalization of this behavior in over half of the states in the United States (Haspel, Jorgenson, Wincze, & Parsons, 1997). Sex with clients is the highest risk behavior in which a psychologist can engage. The behavior is risky in terms of the reported harm to clients/patients, as well as in the risk to the psychologist. At one point, sexual impropriety constituted over half (53.2%) of all costs of violations for professional liability insurance for psychologists, although a recent APA Insurance Trust evaluation reported that the percentage of claims for sexual misconduct had decreased, based on a "snapshot" review of the data (Bruce Bennett, personal correspondence, December 19, 2005). Hopefully, this means that psychologists have taken to heart the risks such relationships pose to clients and to themselves.

Self-awareness is a key to avoidance. We all have to accept the fact that psychologists can become emotionally and sexually attracted to a client. In one survey, 87% of all therapists (95% of men, 75% of women) reported that they have been attracted to their clients, at least on occasion (Bernsen, Tabachnick, & Pope, 1994; Pope, Keith-Spiegel, & Tabachnick, 1986)). Social psychological literature informs us that "proximity" is the most salient variable predicting who gets together with whom. The skill of managing romantic/sexual feelings toward clients throughout the course of therapy can help identify inappropriate feelings of attraction toward clients.

A complicating issue is that, although the Ethics Code does not prohibit nonsexual touching, risk management strategies encourage psychologists to be cautious about how easily touch can be misunderstood as a sexual overture by some clients/patients, perhaps particularly those with a history of incest or other similar violations. Cultural and theoretical orientations also inform this behavior; for example, some clients and therapists have cultural or other orientations that allow for nonsexual hugs, handshakes, or other forms of affectionate communication. Because of cultural variations in behavior around matters such as touching, it is recommended that psychologists must be knowledgeable about relevant guidelines (for example, the Guidelines for Psychological Practice with Girls and Women, APA, 2007, and the Multicultural Guidelines, APA, 2003) that provide further direction on appropriate therapist behavior.

It is important to note that "sex therapy" does not include romantic or erotic interaction between the therapist and client/patient, although it may involve communication about explicitly sexual information, instructions, or readings. Psychologists must still be cautious because clients/patients may perceive comments as erotic, without regard to the psychologist's intent. The use of sexual surrogates is controversial, but if the psychologist endorses the use of surrogates, the surrogate may *never* be the psychologist.

Judgments about nonsexual dual or multiple relationships are more complex for all psychologists. The new Ethics Code acknowledges that not all multiple or dual relationships are problematic, or avoidable. These behaviors are *not* specifically prohibited. Instead, in Standard 3.05, Multiple Relationships, psychologists are warned to avoid relationships that, "could reasonably be expected to impair the psychologist's objectivity, competence, or effectiveness in performing his or her functions as a psychologist, or otherwise risk exploitation or harm to the person with whom the professional relationship exists"(APA, 2002, p. 1065). Authors of the code tried to indicate the risk factors and situations that can lead to risk of harm. However, "Multiple relationships that would not reasonably be expected to cause impairment or risk exploitation or harm are not unethical" (APA, 2002, p. 1065). It is important to note that most risk management guidelines would strongly discourage even the appearance of a conflict.

Kitchener (2000) relied on social role therapy to explain the problems with multiple role relationships. Responsibilities, needs, and expectations are very different with a business partner than with a client, for example. Trying to maintain two different roles with someone, especially a client, increases the potential for misunderstanding and harm because the incompatibility of all these expectations is higher. As the obligations of different roles diverge, the potential for divided loyalties and loss of objectivity increases. As the power and prestige difference increases, so does the potential for exploitation and lowered objectivity and autonomy of the consumer.

Confidentiality

Confidentiality, privacy, and privilege are three overlapping concepts. In almost all states, privilege belongs to the client. Confidentiality, considered a primary ethical obligation, is a commitment to clients, research participants, and others that private information will not be divulged without their consent. This obligation is embedded in the moral principles of autonomy, fidelity, beneficence, and nonmaleficence. Individuals have the right to make decisions about those with whom they wish to share private information and those from whom they wish to withhold it (Kitchener, 2000).

With some exceptions, only the client can permit the therapist to release records to others. Psychologists sometimes have the obligation to ascertain whether the client is clear about the potential consequences of the release of such records, but the client holds the legal privilege. Psychologists have the ethical and legal obligation to maintain the confidentiality of records, including after the death of a client. Privacy speaks to the responsibility to share only that information that is vital to the purpose of the release of the information, such as to managed care utilization reviewers, when one has the client's signed release to do so. Key topics related to confidentiality are the exceptions to confidentiality, coping with subpoenas and compelled testimony, and the obligation of informed consent.

Exceptions to Confidentiality

One of the common conflicts or dilemmas that arises from the two moral principles of nonmaleficence and autonomy occurs in the situation in which the right to privacy and confidentiality conflicts with the restriction that autonomous rights do not extend to infringing on the autonomous rights of others. Several limits to confidentiality exist, and it is the psychologist's responsibility to inform clients of those limits. Exceptions to confidentiality encompass situations in which the client is a danger to self or others (e.g., the Tarasoff

decision, including the duty to warn and/or protect a third party from a threatening client) and the legal responsibility to report child, elderly, or disability abuse. Limits of confidentiality generally exist if the client files suit against the therapist for breach of duty, or if a court order requires disclosure.

Bongar (1992) suggested that suicidal clients are the most stressful of all clinical endeavors. A national survey found that psychologists responded to the loss of a patient to suicide in a manner akin to the death of a family member. Psychologists have a greater than 20% chance of losing a patient to suicide at some time during their professional careers. Psychiatrists have a 50% chance of losing a patient to suicide. Rudd, Joiner, and Rajab (2001) identified a trend of increasing attention to the assessment and treatment of suicidal behavior. This reflects a heightened level of awareness of the complexity of the issues—clinical, ethical, and legal—facing clinicians when working with suicidal patients. Most would argue that the main goal of suicidal therapy (therapy for suicide prevention) is to defuse the potentially lethal situation, and that to hold to the principle of confidentiality is contradictory to a basic tenets of an ethical psychotherapeutic relationship and the principle of helping clients.

Bongar (1992) suggested that therapists have a professional duty to take appropriate affirmative measures to prevent patients from harming themselves, including communicating with families about the specifics of a patient's case, attempting to ameliorate toxic family interactions with the patient, or mobilizing support from the family and significant others. However, the scope of the disclosure should be limited to what is necessary to provide appropriate care; thus, for example, disclosures made in good faith while seeking a civil commitment for the patient would largely be protected.

Psychologists also have ethical and legal obligations to address the situation if a client is a danger to others. The nature of the legal obligations varies from state to state, and it is critical for practitioners to be familiar with the requirements of their state practice laws. In 1974, the California Supreme Court issued an opinion stating that California therapists have a *duty to warn* potential victims of their patients' threats of violence (*Tarasoff* I), rather than simply doing something with the client, such as hospitalization or arrest. Two years later, the Court revised its opinion to state that California therapists have a duty to *protect* potential victims if their clients are dangerous (*Tarasoff* II). This legal responsibility conflicts with the obligation to maintain confidentiality. An additional issue is that the prediction of dangerousness is still a problematic one for most therapists. Various states are increasingly adopting the duty to protect, but with variations in some of the specifics. Some states indicate that mental health providers may warn or protect potential victims, or take other actions such as notifying officials. It is vital that each therapist become familiar with the requirements and obligations of his or her jurisdiction.

Coping with Subpoenas or Compelled Testimony for Client Records or Test Data

The concerns involved with coping with subpoenas or compelled testimony for client records or test data was addressed by APA's Committee on Legal Issues (American Psychological Association Committee on Legal Issues [APA COLI], 1996). Members of COLI prepared an article in response to a large number of inquires. As a general principle of law, all citizens are required to provide information necessary for deciding issues before a court; the trier of fact is a judge or jury. The basic assumption is that the more relevant information available, the fairer the decision. Subpoenas (legal commands to provide testimony) or *subpoenas duces tecum* (legal commands to appear and bring along specific documents) are issued to obtain relevant material. A psychologist must respond to a subpoena in a timely matter, but the request may be modified or made void or invalid if the client chooses not to provide a release. Federal law and most state jurisdictions allow the client to prevent confidential material from being communicated. However, a court order to provide testimony or produce documents must be honored regardless of client's preference, or the psychologist may be held in contempt of court. So, if a client provides a release, or if a court order is issued, psychologists are required to release therapy notes, process notes, client information forms, billing records, and other information, unless the psychologist engages in attempts to quash the order.

Strategies for dealing with subpoenas include verifying whether it is enforceable. A recommendation is to have an attorney review it and to contact the client in question to ensure that he fully understands that he is putting his entire file into the public record. Often, the client wishes the records to be released. In either case, the psychologist must obtain a written consent and make sure that the client understands the purposes and scope of disclosure. A psychologist may wish to negotiate with the requester and/or may also wish to seek a ruling from the court, preferably through the client's attorney, or with the psychologist's attorney.

In addition to requests for compelled testimony and subpoenas for client records, test data may also be requested. The Committee on Psychological Tests and Assessment of the APA published a "Statement on the Disclosure of Test Data" that was then incorporated as an addendum into the same article that addressed strategies for dealing with subpoenas (APA COLI, 1996). The statement was developed as a result of confusion regarding what is ethical and/or legal in the release of test data. A release from a client did not at the time resolve the potential confidentiality claims of third parties, such as test publishers, and psychologists continued to hold obligations to withhold test data or protocols. Such dilemmas have been very controversial in a number of cases, especially when courts want to see items related to IQ testing of particular populations. Attorneys sometimes misuse test data, for example, by selecting specific responses to the Minnesota Multiphasic Personality Index (MMPI) and asking questions about the client's/patients specific responses to specific items (e.g., "I have engaged in strange sexual behaviors," asked of a sexual harassment complainant). The Task Force for revisions of the 2002 Ethics Code struggled with this issue more than any other. Forensic psychologists tended to want protection/support for withholding test data; other practitioners wanted to avoid the expense of hiring attorneys to protect test publishers and the validity of the tests, since the information is readily available through libraries and other sources. The new Standard 9.04, Release of Test Data, defined test data as "raw and scaled scores, client/patient responses to test questions or stimuli, and psychologists' notes and recordings concerning client/patient statements and behavior during an examination. Those portions of test materials that include client/patient responses are included in the definition of *test data.*" The APA Ethics Code (2002) Standard 9.04 Release of Test Data essentially states that psychologists may provide test data upon client/patient release, or may refrain from doing so if they judge that substantial harm, misuse, or misrepresentation of the data may occur.

Informed Consent

Related to the issue of confidentiality is the issue of informed consent. Emerging issues in informed consent include duty to assess and protect against client dangerousness (to self and others), obligations to third parties (third-party payers, managed care, etc.), and issues of deception. The primary moral principle underlying the obligation to obtain informed consent involves the promotion of autonomy. Any procedure performed on or on behalf of a patient without his or her consent diminishes the patient's autonomy or capacity to act in a free and self-determining manner. Therefore, giving the person an opportunity to make a choice emphasizes his or her autonomy.

Pope and Vasquez (2007) suggested that information provided during the consent process will differ according to the professional service, whether it is an assessment, psychotherapy, forensic evaluation, or the like. They suggested the following questions to address in a form, as well as on an ongoing basis (informed consent is an ongoing process):

• Does the client understand who is providing the service, the *clinician's qualifications*, and whether supervision is involved?
• Does the client understand the reason for the initial session (self-initiated, court-or physician-referred)?
• Does the client understand the nature, extent, and possible consequences of the services the clinician is offering?
• Does the client understand the degree to which there may be alternatives to the services provided by the clinician?
• Does the client understand actual or potential limitations to the services (a managed care plan's limitation of four to six sessions unless a major mental illness diagnosis is given); does the client understand how services may be terminated?
• Does the client understand fee policies and procedures, including information about missed or canceled appointments, use of fee collection services, etc.?
• Does the client understand policies and procedures concerning access to the clinician, to those providing coverage for the clinician, and to emergency services? For example, under what conditions, if any, will a therapist be available by phone between sessions?
• Does the client understand limits to confidentiality in situations involving partner, family, or group psychotherapy? Does the client understand the conditions under which the clinician might be required to disclose information to an insurance company, utilization reviewers, the police, child protective services, the courts?

The information should be presented in a language reasonably understandable to the client/patient.

Consent may be written or oral, but in any case, must be documented by the psychologist. Psychologists who are "covered entities" under the Health Insurance Portability and Accountability Act (HIPAA) must also provide clients/patients with written information (Notice of Privacy Practices) about their rights regarding the use and disclosure of their health information, including information about their rights to access to their protected health information (PHI), excluding psychotherapy notes. Other information should include explanations of the uses and disclosures of the PHI, their individual rights, and the psychologist's legal duties in regard to the PHI. The APA Practice Directorate and APA Insurance Trust have developed authorization model Notice of Privacy Practice forms to be compatible with the laws governing practice in each state; these are available at http://apa.org/practice and http://apait.org/hipaa.

Custody Evaluations
Professionals get into trouble with child custody evaluations in a number of ways. The paramount obligation in custody evaluations is to assess and report factors that affect the best psychological interests of the child. Moral principles involved include Principle A, Beneficence and Nonmaleficence, which involves helping others and doing no harm, and Principle B, Fidelity, which involves honest communication and obligation to fulfill certain functions. Principle E, Respect for People's Rights and Dignity is involved because the therapist must respect parental rights to share in the raising of their children. Generally, a forensic child custody expert is employed to evaluate all persons involved. The biggest error psychotherapists make is to testify on behalf of their client, and to make negative comments about the other parent without ever having seen, diagnosed, or assessed that other parent. It is not recommended that psychotherapists (as opposed to objective child custody evaluators) serve as the evaluator, since objectivity will always be a challenge in such cases.

According to Ackerman and Ackerman (1997), 90% of divorce custody situations agree to a restructuring arrangement. However, when a dispute occurs, the court must help to determine the relative allocation of decision-making authority and the physical contact each parent will have with the child. The courts typically apply a "best interest of the child" standard in determining this restructuring of rights and responsibilities. Psychologists are thus called upon to provide a competent, objective, impartial assessment. Often, in these disputes, one of the two parties will be unhappy with the results and blame the psychologist. Therefore, those who are called upon to testify and/or who provide assessment services for child custody evaluations must be clear about duties and responsibilities. Although specific instructions about custody evaluations are not provided in the ethics code, several principles apply. The APA Guidelines for Child Custody Evaluations in Divorce Proceedings (APA, 2004) provide helpful guidance.

Insurance and Fee Problems

Insurance fraud is a major area of violation, including billing insurance for services delivered by others; billing insurance for missed sessions; waiving copayments (this may be an option on an individual basis in most states, but not as a rule, and the option may have a requirement to inform the third party); billing couple, family, or group sessions as individual sessions; falsifying diagnostic categories to fit reimbursement criteria; and changing the date of the onset of the client's episode or the beginning of therapy to fit third-party reimbursement criteria, to try to prevent denial of services based on preexisting condition. Often, well-meaning therapists try to provide financial relief by, in effect, colluding with a client to violate the client's contract with his insurance company. Although continuously frustrated by insurance companies, psychologists must fight those battles in the legislature through organizational advocacy efforts—or potentially end up in trouble with insurance companies and the law. Such dilemmas are also a therapeutic issue in that, if this ethic is violated, psychologists model and communicate lack of respect for the role of honesty and fidelity in relationships.

It is critical to ensure the accuracy of billings and payments. Record keeping and documentation from a billing and payment frame of reference may include the reflection of transactions with private insurance companies, managed care companies, government entities including Medicare and Medicaid, individual client billing, organizational billing, and forms of presenting services rendered, date of service, treatment, diagnosis, and other information requested. Accurate and understandable records that can explain the essential elements of services rendered are an excellent protection against misinterpretations of services and resulting difficulties in billing questions and payment. The amount and type of information included in records for billing and payment can be challenging to determine. Psychologists may be asked for information for billing purposes that would not otherwise be included in the record and which the psychologist may think is detrimental to the welfare of the client. Therefore it becomes necessary for the psychologist to accurately provide details for billing purposes while at the same time not including statements that would potentially harm the client.

Record Keeping

Several obligations are involved in the new clear requirement to maintain records. The APA (2002) Ethics Code Standard 6.01 requires for the first time that records be kept in written form. The Committee on Professional Practice & Standards (COPPS) of the APA published guidelines regarding the maintenance of records in 1993 and updated them in 2007. The Guidelines were revised by the COPPS, partly to incorporate the HIPAA guidelines; these new guidelines were approved by the APA Council of Representatives in 2007.

The content of psychotherapy notes should minimally include identifying data, dates of services, types of services, fees, any assessment, plan for intervention, consultation, summary reports, and/or testing reports, supporting data, and any release of information obtained. It is also recommended that a record be made of any unusual struggles and dilemmas that surface during the therapeutic process as part of an overall risk management strategy. The HIPAA legislation allows for two sets of notes: one with basic information, and another set with the therapist's process notes. Notes for psychotherapy group, family, and relationship therapy should also be kept. Complications regarding confidentiality can surface. Most recommend that group therapy notes be kept per individual, in order to maintain confidentiality of other group members should the records be requested.

The Freedom of Information Act (1966) is a law requiring that U.S. government agencies release their records to the public on request, unless the information sought falls into a category specifically exempted, such as national security, an individual's right to privacy, or internal agency management. This typically means that clients legally have access to their records. Various options are provided by therapists—reviewing notes in a session(s) for therapeutic benefit is one option, as is the provision of a summary. Ultimately, if clients choose to obtain their notes, they can do so. However, most jurisdictional administrative practice laws have a clause that allows psychologists to withhold notes if they may be deemed harmful to the client.

States, provinces, and territories vary in the period of time that psychologists are required to maintain records. The revised APA Record Keeping Guidelines (2007) suggest retaining full records for no less than 7 years after the last date of service delivery for adults or until 3 years after a minor reaches the age of majority, whichever is longest, or the number of years required by one's licensing board, whichever is longest. Jurisdictional licensing boards, other state and federal laws, and institutional requirements may determine the length of time that psychologists must keep records. Psychologists should always retain the complete record to comply with the more stringent of the applicable requirements. Psychologists may legally destroy their records after that time, but psychologists may at times wish to keep some records longer than the length required, for example, in situation in which records may be sought to illuminate some future legal issue, or when a minor may have long-term developmental difficulties.

It is wise to make arrangements for the storage of records when leaving one's practice, and/or in case of disability or death. Arrangements should be made so that, in the case of death, someone, preferably a mental health professional, knows how to access information about current clients and notify them. With clients' permission, some psychologists make reciprocal arrangements with colleagues to exchange lists of patients' names, phone numbers, and information about their treatment. In case of death or incapacitation, the covering therapist would notify patients/clients, and serve as a referral person or "bridge therapist" for continuation of care, and to deal with the death or incapacitation of the therapist. Some therapists arrange for a notice to be placed in the newspaper, informing former clients of the death and letting them know who holds their records.

Terminations

Terminations are an important part of the therapeutic process, and there are ethical responsibilities to termination appropriately. Research indicates that 30% to 57% of all psychotherapy patients drop out prematurely (Garfield, 1994). Premature termination is a vexing problem and a subject of research investigation (Vasquez, Bingham, & Barnett, 2008). Some clients/patients simply stop coming, despite the recommendation of a "pretermination counseling process," and do not get the benefit of that process. Multiple factors influence how long a client/patient remains in psychotherapy. What are those factors, and what can be done to facilitate successful separations and psychotherapeutic terminations?

Vasquez, Bingham, and Barnett (2008) provided practice recommendations for helping to ensure the clinically appropriate and effective termination of each client.

At the beginning of psychotherapy, and throughout the treatment, psychologists have responsibilities to provide informed consent about psychotherapy. That is, clients/patients should be educated about the process of psychotherapy, including the factors involved in deciding when to stop. Ending therapy usually depends on the nature of the case, the condition of the client/patient, the evolution and attainment of goals as set forth by the client/patient and psychotherapist, and the client's/patient's financial situation (either personal or managed care limitations).

Ethical responsibilities include the responsibility to terminate when the client/patient no longer needs the service, isn't benefiting, or is being harmed by the service (APA 2002 Ethical Principles of Psychologists and Code of Conduct Standard 10.10a). Psychologists are also required to make reasonable efforts to provide pretermination counseling and suggest alternative service providers as appropriate (APA Standards 10.10c, 10.09 and 3.12). A new APA Ethics Code standard indicates that therapists have the right to terminate psychotherapy when threatened (10.10b). It is probably not appropriate to terminate when a client is in crisis. Some clients are able to easily announce that they are ready to stop coming, or that their employer has switched insurance providers, and that they'd like the current psychologist's help to choose their next therapist from their new provider list. Others may be panicked at the notion of stopping without appropriate preparation.

The issue becomes complex if the psychotherapist perceives that the treatment is progressing well, and the client/patient either is not clear about how long to continue, or no longer wishes to continue, but has difficulty raising the issue. Often, these clients just stop coming. They either indicate that they will call to schedule the next appointment, or cancel and do not reschedule. In addition, many people currently utilize psychotherapy in short installments, "stop out" for a while, and later return to either the same practitioner, or to another. A key psychotherapeutic strategy is to review the presenting concerns, goals, and progress from time to time. This helps clarify how much has been accomplished, as well as what still needs to be addressed, and whether the client/patient and psychotherapist collaboratively wish to continue or not. When clients who seem successfully engaged in psycho-therapy stop coming, a note or call to provide them with options can yield helpful and interesting information.

Counseling Psychology's Unique Contribution of Social Justice As an Ethical Imperative

Counseling psychology has a long history of interest and commitment to social justice and multicultural issues (Ivey & Collins, 2003), and it has moved to the forefront to join community and liberation psychologists in engaging more systematically in social justice work (Goodman et al., 2004; Vera & Speight, 2003). Goodman et al. (2004) conceptualized the social justice work of counseling psychologists as scholarship and professional action designed to change societal values, structures, policies, and practices, such that disadvantaged or marginalized groups gain increased access to these tools of self-determination. Goodman et al. (2004) drew upon an ecological model of social analysis to propose that social justice work occurs on three different levels, including the micro level (individuals and families); the meso level (including communities and organization); and the macro level (including social structures, ideologies, and policies). The authors also proposed several tenets, derived from feminist and multicultural counseling theories and including ongoing self-examination, sharing power, giving voice, facilitating consciousness raising, building on strengths, and giving clients with the tools to work toward social change. The authors provided an illustration of a thoughtful process for developing, managing, and evaluating a faculty-led collaboration with community-based projects as a training experience in social justice.

An application of the micro level is the emphasis on cultural competence in the psychotherapeutic process. Cultural competence is no longer a marginal topic of interest, and cultural competence in today's mental health care environment requires far more knowledge and sophistication on the part of the professional. It is becoming part of the mainstream fundamental knowledge and skill set required for effective practice. Therefore, multicultural competency is a core social justice value, as well as an ethical responsibility. Diversity training in general should be more incorporated into the fabric of training programs, continuing education, and life-long learning for psychologists (Vasquez, 2009).

Vera and Speight (2003) argued that counseling psychology's operationalization of multicultural competence must be grounded in a commitment to social justice that includes an expansion of professional activities beyond counseling and psychotherapy. Vera and Speight (2003) suggested that engaging in advocacy, prevention, and outreach are activities critical to social justice efforts. They suggested that grounding teaching and research in collaborative and social action processes are ways to expand roles.

Toporek and Williams (2006) believe that even the most recent 2002 APA Ethics Code needs to be revised because it does not provide enough guidance for the social justice philosophy of counseling psychologists. The 2001 National Conference on Counseling Psychology advocated for social justice as a primary foundation of the field. The Social Justice Ethics Work Group from the conference defined social justice as:

> A concept that advocates engaging individuals as co-participants in decisions which directly affect their lives; it involves taking some action, and educating individuals in order to open possibilities, and to act with value and respect for individuals and their group identities, considering power differentials in all areas of counseling practice and research.
> (Blustein, Elman, & Gerstein, 2001, p. 9)

Toporek and Williams (2006) argued that, implied in this definition, are the themes of respect, responsibility, and action. They then looked at the ethical issues of competence, multiple relationships, informed consent, and the do-no-harm tenet through the social justice principles of respect, responsibility and action. The authors concluded that, although attention to these issues was implicit in some of the 2002 APA Ethics Code principles, the language was not explicit enough and therefore did not provide enough guidance to counseling psychologists. For example, because a social justice approach would dictate that a counseling psychologist should intervene on behalf of a client to end discrimination or oppression, the client and therapist could work together outside the counseling office and the traditional counseling hour. The client and counselor could inadvertently end up in a dual relationship, and the client may not be fully informed of the possible consequences of such action or alliance. Toporek and Williams argued that the APA Ethics Code did not provide enough guidance to the therapist about how to make a virtuous social justice–oriented ethical decision.

Toporek and Williams (2006) did advise that more guidance could be found in other codes, such as those of the Association of Black Psychologists and the National Association of Social Workers. These codes go far beyond those of the APA code in directing psychologists about advocacy matters. The NASW Ethics Code 6.04 even states, for example, that "Social workers should engage in social and political action. . . ." (NASW, 1996). At best, the APA code relegates such strong statements to the nonenforceable aspirational principles section of the ethics document. Structural limitations, such as the APA's tax status as a c(3) is limiting in that regard; NASW maintains a c(6) tax status, which allows for more political advocacy.

Counseling psychologists may find more help by reviewing the various practice guidelines that are designed to help practitioners across specializations to provide ethically competent service. The guidelines include the Guidelines for Psychological Practice with Girls and Women (APA, 2007); Guidelines for Psychotherapy with Lesbian, Gay, and Bisexual Clients (APA, 2000); Guidelines on Multicultural Education, Training, Research, Practice and Organizational Change for Psychologists (APA, 2003); and Guidelines for Psychological Practice with Older Adults (APA, 2004). All of these guidelines tend to have social justice themes, and counseling psychologists were intimately involved in drafting most of these documents. The guidelines for practice with girls and women, for example, were spearheaded by a joint group from the Society of Counseling Psychology (Division 17) and the Society for the Psychology of Women (Division 35), and the guidelines for practice with racial/ethnic minorities by a joint task group from Division 17 and the Society for the Psychological Study of Ethnic Minority Issues (Division 45). These guidelines tend to have a social justice emphasis that addresses issues of marginalization, discrimination, and oppression for certain groups, and the responsibilities that psychologists have to monitor those concerns in their work with clients. In the introduction to the guidelines for girls and women, for example, is the statement that "the changing and increasingly complex life experiences of girls and women and the intersection of their gender roles with ethnicity, sexual orientation, ability, SES etc. demonstrate compelling evidence and need for professional guidance for helping psychologists (a) avoid harm in psychological practice with girls and women, (b) improve research, teaching, consultation, and psychotherapeutic and counseling training and practice; and (c) develop and enhance treatment efforts, research, prevention, teaching and other areas of practice that will benefit women and girls" (see http://www.apa.org/about/division/girlsandwomen.pdf). So, while Toporek and Williams maintain that the APA Ethics Code does not provide sufficient guidance for ethical decision making, guidelines such as those listed above can be used to enhance a psychologist's ethical decision-making process and competence in providing the highest standard of care to members of certain groups.

Decision-making Models

Using the APA Ethics Code and all of the guidelines listed above, can one arrive at an ethical decision? Clearly Jordan and Meara (1990) and Kitchener and Anderson (2000) would argue that one must combine knowledge gleaned from all of the standards, principles, and guidelines with one's virtuous character. Kitchener (2000) suggested that information about the situation and one's ordinary moral sense leads to an immediate level of impressions, but that a critical-evaluative level of decision making, including ethical rules (codes, guidelines, laws) combined with foundational ethical principles and ethical theory is important. Kitchener proposed the following five foundational moral principles as essential to making virtuous ethical decisions:

- *Autonomy*: Psychologists must make free decisions, understand the consequences, and treat others in the same way. This means a fundamental respect for the rights of others to make choices, unless those choices infringe on the rights of others.
- *Nonmaleficence*: Above all psychologists must not do harm. This generally means neither inflicting intentional harm nor engaging in actions that risk harming others.
- *Beneficence*: Psychologists must strive to do good or benefit others. At its core, psychology is committed to contributing to the health and welfare of others.
- *Justice*: Psychologists must treat all fairly and equally and be concerned with issues of social justice.
- *Fidelity*: Psychologist must strive for truth, honor, faithfulness, and loyalty. Fidelity is at the core of the fiduciary relationship between psychologists and the people with whom they work.

Models for ethical decision making tend to list steps that an individual might follow when a dilemma arises. The Ethics Resource Center (http://www.ethics.org/decision-making-model.asp) uses a six-step model entitled The PLUS Decision-Making Model. PLUS is a mnemonic for Policies,

Legal, Universal, and Self. PLUS is applied at steps 1, 3, and 6. At step 1, the problem is identified and the therapist asks whether there are policy issues, legal issues, universal principles, and values to consider, especially of his or her professional organization. In addition, the therapist considers self issues of rightness, goodness, or fairness. At step 2, the therapist lists alternative solutions to the dilemma. Step 3 requires that the therapist evaluates the alternatives using PLUS questions. Step 4 asks for a decision. Step 5 is implementation, and step 6 is an evaluation of the decision, again using PLUS questions. This model further advises the use of empathy, patience, integrity, and courage.

Other decision-making models essentially follow the same step-wise pattern (Bersoff, 1995; Canter et al., 1994; Clabon & Morris, 2004; Koocher & Keith-Spiegel, 1998). Psychologists often argue that knowing the Ethics Code, their jurisdictional administrative and practice laws, and guidelines provide a good starting point for making an ethical decisions. They sometimes add a step that suggests consulting with a trusted colleague, ethics expert, or mental health attorney on the matter. These two suggestions would fit in well with any of the decision-making models that were reviewed for this chapter. Welfel (2002) proposed a ten-step model that begins with becoming ethically sensitive as the first step and includes, at step 7, consultation with a supervisor or respected colleague. Houser, Wilczenski, and Ham (2006) declared that few if any of these decision-making models have been empirically investigated or grounded in theory. They argued that one thing missing from the models is context. Houser et al. (2006) asserted that ethic codes and ethical models are generally lists of rules and principles that are stated as if they exist in a cultural vacuum. They believe that, to make ethical decisions, ethical decision-making models must be situated in a cultural context and there must be a general understanding of various worldviews. Also, the ethics must have some theoretical underpinnings.

Basically, it is important for counseling psychologists to develop a plan for ethical decision making before an ethical dilemma occurs. We recommend these steps:

1. Regularly review the APA Ethics Code and be knowledgeable and/or review your jurisdictional rules. It is helpful to refer to relevant guidelines as endorsed by the APA.

2. Define and understand the ethical dilemma. Why is the situation problematic?

What principles, rules, laws, or obligations are at issue? One's theoretical orientation may sometimes enter into the conceptualization of the problem, and sometimes it is important to try to distinguish between a therapeutic issue/dilemma and whether the dilemma potentially reaches the threshold of a potential ethical and/or legal violation.

3. Understand the key moral principles in psychology, as described above, and apply those principles.

4. Determine alternative solutions. If the options increase the potential for harm, the psychologist should increase vigilance and attention. Whose interests are involved in the problem? What would be the positive and negative consequences of each choice?

5. Consult with others to help clarify the issues. Ethics experts and/or ethics bodies can be helpful. Consider whether there is a need for legal advice from lawyers who specialize in mental health law.

6. Decide on a solution based on the code, the culture, your moral principles, and your understanding of probable consequences. Document the process and the results. Keeping track of the process through documentation can help one remain clear about the elements of the problem, the options and potential consequences, the guidance provided by others, and the rationale for the decision.

Clabon and Morris (2004) claim that making good ethical decisions helps to build character. Hopefully good character helps to make virtuous ethical decisions.

Concluding Thoughts on Ethical Dilemmas and Ethics Education

Counseling psychologists have had significant input into the evolution of professional ethics in psychology, and we provided a brief summary of those contributions. In addition, we described the various methods of accountability in our profession, and identified key areas of vulnerability for psychologists in ethical practice, including multiple relationships, confidentiality, custody evaluations, insurance and fee problems, record keeping, and terminations. Finally, we described the role of counseling psychology in promoting social justice as an ethical imperative. The following section identifies our concluding thoughts on key dilemmas yet to be fully addressed in the ethical realm of professional responsibilities and ethics education.

The social milieu affects the ethics code. Over time, society has dealt with cultural and legal issues such as discrimination, sexual harassment, divorce. These topics influence changes in the ethics code, and the code changes as society changes. With the advent of the World Wide Web, the Internet, e-mail, listservs, blogs, and chat rooms, social issues and conditions are communicated far more rapidly and therefore pressure may emerge for the ethics code to change more frequently.

For example, during the United States' war with Iraq, serious questions were raised about the role psychologists should play in the interrogation of detainees from the war, especially if individuals were being held in places considered illegal. The United States entered into war against the Taliban in Afghanistan in 2002, and into war with Iraq in 2003. As a result of these wars, many individuals were imprisoned or "detained" at Guantanamo Bay, Cuba, and in Abu Ghraib, in Iraq. Subsequent to their detainment, numerous allegations were made of detainee abuse and illegal detention. Questions arose regarding the role of psychologists in assisting the government in questioning detainees, providing psychological services to these individuals, and consulting with the government about these matters; it was even questioned if it was legal for psychologists to work in some of these facilities. Psychologists and members of the public turned to the APA Ethics Code and the Ethics Committee for guidance. Some thought they found answers in the code; others thought the code was left wanting. Counseling psychologists were actively involved on the APA governing bodies, the Council of Representatives, and the Board of Directors as the organization grappled with ethical, legal, and professional questions about the detainee issue. Some were involved in the actual intervention to ensure that interrogations were conducted in safe, moral, and effective ways (James, 2008).

The answer to whether or not the code provided sufficient guidance is beyond the scope of this chapter. However, the situation did shine light on the need for guiding ethical principles and standards, and the need for effective ethical decision-making models and processes. Psychologists and members of the public demanded that the ethics code provide much more direction about the role of psychologists. Their demands led to a referendum on the matter. The APA Public Affairs Office released this announcement about the APA members' approval of the petition resolution on detainee settings (September 17, 2008 from http://www.apa.org/releases/petition0908.html):

> The petition resolution stating that psychologists may not work in settings where "persons are held outside of, or in violation of, either International Law (e.g., the UN Convention Against Torture and the Geneva Conventions) or the U.S. Constitution (where appropriate), unless they are working directly for the persons being detained or for an independent third party working to protect human rights" was approved by a vote of the APA membership.
> The final vote tally was 8,792 voting in favor of the resolution; 6,157 voting against the resolution. To become policy, a petition resolution needs to be approved by a majority of those members voting.
> Per the Association's Rules and Bylaws, the resolution became official APA policy as of the Association's August 2009 annual convention.
> The approval of the petition resolution represented a significant change in APA's policy regarding the involvement of psychologists in interrogations. The petition resolution limits the roles of psychologists in certain defined settings where persons are detained to working directly for detainees or for an independent third party to protect human rights, or to providing treatment to other military personnel.
> This resolution expanded on the 2007 APA resolution, which called on the U.S. government to ban at least 19 specific abusive interrogation techniques, including waterboarding, that are regarded as torture by international standards. The 2007 resolution also recognized that "torture and other cruel, inhuman or degrading treatment or punishment can result not only from the behavior of individuals, but also from the conditions of confinement," and expressed "grave concern over settings in which detainees are deprived of adequate protection of their human rights."
> APA will continue to call upon the Department of Defense and Congress to safeguard the welfare and human rights of detainees held outside of the United States and to investigate their treatment to ensure the highest ethical standards are being upheld.

The question remains as to whether and how the ethics code reflects the dictates of the referendum and how quickly the code can change if necessary. These situations are likely to become even more prevalent as members of the profession look to the Ethics Code and relevant policy development for guidance.

Several other key dilemmas and issues are yet to be fully addressed in the profession, and thus comprise "future directions." Those include the use of the Internet or other electronic communication methods, practicing across jurisdictional boundaries, distance learning, testing for continued competencies for initial licensure, and for expansion of practice into emerging areas.

The use of telecommunications and information technology to provide assessment, diagnosis, and intervention (psychotherapy, forensic and consultation services) information has increased in the past few years. Yet, clear guidelines have not been developed. Pope and Vasquez (2005) suggested the importance of confidentiality in considering the location of computers, as well as the use of "strong" passwords, encryption (software that adds an extra layer of protection and safeguards), firewalls (software or hardware to help prevent break-ins), and other technological safeguards. Other challenges include the importance of being aware of standard ethical, regulatory, and legal obligations if work crosses jurisdictional boundaries. Questions asked by DeMers, Van Horne, and Rodolfa (2008) include: How will an emergency be handled? What are the limits of confidentiality? How are the HIPAA regulations (1996) applicable? How are charges and payments handled? Will professional liability insurance cover practice across jurisdictional lines? How will a complaint be handled?

Distance education has rapidly expanded, and this has implications for the definition of quality assurance and regulation of student performance. The APA (2006) Accreditation Guidelines and Principles require that each student serves a minimum of 3 full-time academic years of graduate study, at least 2 of which must be at the institution from which the doctoral degree is granted, and at least 1 year of which must be in "full-time residence or the equivalent thereof" (p. 10). This requirement is assumed to allow for faculty and supervisors to assess student competence. The dilemma of providing greater flexibility in meeting residency requirements versus the obligation to assess student competency is an ethical challenge and responsibility to be faced by psychology education in the future.

Assessment of competency has been an issue and theme in the profession for the past few years. The Association of Psychology Postdoctoral and Internship Centers (APPIC) sponsored a Competencies Conference that focused on the identification of the mutually agreed upon set of competencies underlying professional psychology practice (Kaslow et al., 2004). One of the issues is whether a competency-based approach to the assessment of progress through training and readiness for practice, as well as for expansion of practice into emerging areas, might be applied. Continuing education and life-long learning for the ethical requirement to maintain and develop competence is a goal embraced by professionals. The potential requirement of some kind of demonstration of competence in the knowledge, judgment, and technical and interpersonal skills relevant to a therapist's job throughout his or her career is more controversial (DeMers et al., 2008).

What is the future role of education in ensuring that counseling psychologists receive quality ethical training and that programs produce ethical psychologists? The future of the teaching of psychological ethics will continue to evolve, as psychology evolves as a growing field. Ethics education requires the ability to help learners "think well about doing good" (Kitchener, 2000). For example, vignettes and case presentations help us all think through dilemmas. The reality is that a particular dilemma may have a different outcome depending on various factors (e.g., therapist factors, client factors, theoretical orientation, etc.). Teaching the distinctions and overlaps, for example, between ethics and the law, ethics and values, ethics and professional behavior, ethics and conscience are important to promote critical thinking and understanding (Kitchener, 2000). Promoting knowledge of ethical theory, foundational ethical principles and values, ethical rules, and related laws in order to develop a critical evaluative judgment that involves evaluation, analysis, and reasoned judgment are important tasks of ethics education.

Meara and her colleagues, who emphasize virtue ethics, seem to suggest that educational programs must seek to select ethical students to be a part of each incoming class. The challenge is that there is no evidence that psychologists know how to select ethical individuals. There is some evidence to suggest that one can improve ethical decision making. It could be that programs must be more intentional in training those skills. Forrest, Elman, Gizara, and Vacha-Haase (1999) suggest various issues involved in evaluating and ensuring the competence and professional behavior of trainees in professional psychology training programs and internships. This is a start in the academy's responsibility in ensuring the production of ethical, competent professionals.

Most state licensure laws now require that psychologist obtain some hours of ethics training during each licensure reissue period. Such practice suggests that educational programs might want to consider offering more ethics training. It may be that we should seek to have ethics education integrated into most of the courses that are taught, rather than the addition of one course on legal and ethical issues. Ethics could be included in counseling theories courses, marriage and family courses, multicultural courses, and more. We encourage more intentional training experiences at all levels of training and for life-long learning.

References

Ackerman, M. J., & Ackerman, M. C. (1997). Custody evaluation practices: A survey of experienced professionals (revisited). *Professional Psychology: Research and Practice, 28*, 137–145.

American Psychological Association. (2002). Ethical principles of psychologists and code of conduct. *American Psychologist, 57*, 1060–1073. Retrieved from www.apa.org/ethics.

American Psychological Association. (2010). *Ethical principles of psychologists and code of conduct with the 2010 amendments.* Retrieved from http://www.apa.org/ethics/code/index.aspx.

American Psychological Association. (1994). Guidelines for child custody evaluations in divorce proceedings. *American Psychologist, 49*, 677–680.

American Psychological Association. (2007). *Guidelines for psychological practice with girls and women: A joint task force of APA Divisions 17 and 35.* Retrieved November 2, 2008, from http://www.apa.org/about/division/girlsandwomen.pdf.

American Psychologial Association (2004). Guidelines for psychological practice with older adults. *American Psychologist, 59*(4), 236–260.

American Psychological Association. (2003). Guidelines on multicultural education, training, research, practice, and organizational change for psychologists. *American Psychologist, 58*, 377–402.

American Psychological Association. (2003). *Guidelines for psychological practice with older adults.* Retrieved from http://www.apa.org/practice/Guidelines_for_Psychological_Practice_with_Older_Adults.pdf.

American Psychological Association. (2000). Guidelines for psychotherapy with lesbian, gay and bisexual clients. *American Psychologist, 55*, 1440–1451.

American Psychological Association. (2007). *Record keeping guidelines.* Retrieved November 2, 2008, from http://apapractice.org/apo/insider/professional/apaapproved/revised_apa_record.html.

American Psychological Association. (2006, August 9). *Resolution against torture and other cruel, inhuman, and degrading treatment or punishment.* Retrieved from http://www.apa.org/about/governance/council/policy/chapter-3.aspx.

American Psychological Association Committee on Legal Issues. (1996). Strategies for private practitioners coping with subpoenas or compelled testimony for client records or test data. *Professional Psychology: Research and Practice, 27*, 245–251.

Beauchamp, T. L., & Childress, J. F. (1979). *Principles of biomedical ethics.* Oxford, UK: Oxford University Press.

Bebeau, M. J. (1995). Can ethics be taught? A look aat the evidence: Revisited. *The New York State Dental Journal, 50*, 51–57.

Bernsen, A., Tabachnick, B. G., & Pope, K. S. (1994). National survey of social workers' sexual attraction to their clients: Results, implications, and comparison to psychologists. *Ethics and Behavior, 4*, 369–388.

Bersoff, D. (1995). *Ethical conflicts in psychology.* Washington, DC: American Psychological Association.

Bingham, R. P. (2002). The issue may be the integration of personal and career issues, A reaction to "The reintegrating of vocational psychology and counseling psychology." *The Counseling Psychologist, 30*, 933–936.

Blustein, D., Elman, N., & Gerstein, L. (2001, August). *Executive report: Social action groups National Counseling Psychology Conference.* Houston, TX: Authors.

Bongar, B. (1992). *Suicide: Guidelines for assessment, management, & treatment.* New York: Oxford University Press.

Canter, M. B., Bennett, B. E., Jones, S. E., Nagy, T. F. (1994). Ethics for psychologists: A commentary on the APA ethics code. Washington, DC: American Psychological Association.

Clabon, S., & Morris, J. F. (2004). A consensus model for making ethical decisions in a less-than-ideal world. The ASHA Leader.

DeMers, S. T., Van Horne, B. A., & Rodolfa, E. R. (2008). Changes in training and practice of psychologists: Current challenges for licensing boards. *Professional Psychology: Research and Practice, 29*, 473–479.

Ethics Resource Center. *The PLUS decision making model.* Retrieved October 23, 2008 from http://www.ethics.org/decision-making-model.asp.

Farmer, H. (2002). Focus on division 17's Committee on Women/Section for the Advancement of Women (SAW) 1970–2030: Achievement challenges. *The Counseling Psychologist, 30*, 417–440.

Fly, B. J., van Bark, W. P., Weinman, L., Kitchener, K. S., & Lanf, P. R. (1997). Ethical transgressions of psychology graduate students: Critical incidents with implications for training. *Professional Psychology: Research and Practice, 28*, 492–495.

Forrest, L., Elman, N., Gizara, S., Vacha-Haase, T. (1999). Trainee impairment: A review of identification, dismissal, and legal issues. *The Counseling Psychologist, 27*, 627–686.

Fretz, B. R. & Mills, D. H. (1980). *Licensing and certification of psychologists and counselors: A guide to current policies, procesures and legislation.* San Francisco: Jossey-Bass.

Fretz, B. R., & Simon, N. P. (1992). Professional issues in counseling psychology: Continuity, change, and challenge. In S. D. Brown, & R. W. Lent (Eds.), *Handbook of counseling psychology* (2nd ed., pp. 3–36). New York: Wiley.

Garfield, S. L. (1994). Research on client variables in psychotherapy. In A. E. Bergen, & S. L. Garfield (Eds.), *Handbook of psychotherapy and behavior change* (4th ed., pp. 190–228). New York: Wiley.

Goodman, L. A., Liang, B., Helms, J. E., Latta, R. E., Sparks, E., & Weintraub, S. R. (2004). Training counseling psychologists as social justice agents: Feminist and multicultural principles in action. *The Counseling Psychologist, 32*, 793–837.

Hall, C. S. (1952). Crooks, codes, and cant. *American Psychologist, 7*, 430–431.

Hall, J. E. (1987). Gender-related ethical dilemmas and ethics education. *Professional Psychology: Research and Practice, 18,* 573–579.

Haspel, K. C., Jorgenson, L. M., Wincze, J. P., & Parsons, J. P. (1997). Legislative intervention regarding sexual misconduct: An overview. *Professional Psychology: Research and Practice, 28,* 58–62.

Houser, R., Wilczenski, F. L., & Ham, M. (2006). *Culturally relevant ethical decision-making in counseling.* Thousand Oaks, CA: Sage.

Ivey, A. E., & Collins, N. M. (2003). Social justice: A long-term challenge for counseling psychology. *The Counseling Psychologist, 31,* 290–298.

James, L. C. (2008). *Fixing hell: An army psychologist confronts Abu Ghraib.* New York: Grand Central Publishing.

Jordan, A. E., & Meara, N. M. (1990). Ethics and the professional practice of psychologists. *Professional Psychology: Research and Practice, 21,* 107–114.

Kaslow, N. J., Borden, K. A., Collins, F. L., Forrest, L., Illfelder-Kaye, J., Nelson, P. D., et al. (2004). Competencies conference: Future directions in education and credentialing in professional psychology. *Journal of Clinical Psychology, 60,* 699–712.

Kitchener, K. S. (1984). Intuition, critical evaluation and ethical principles: The foundation for ethical decisions in counseling psychology. *The Counseling Psychologist, 12,* 43–55.

Kitchener, K. S. (2000). *Foundations of ethical practice, research, and teaching in psychology.* Mahwah, NJ: Lawrence Erlbaum Associates.

Kitchener, K. S., & Anderson, S. K. (2000). Ethical issues in counseling psychology: Old themes—New problems. In S. D. Brown, & R. W. Lent (Eds.), *Handbook of counseling psychology* (3rd ed., pp. 50–82). New York: Wiley.

Koocher, G. P., & Keith-Spiegel, P. (1998). *Ethics in psychology: Professionals standards and cases* (2nd ed.). New York: Oxford University Press.

Meara, N., Schmidt, L., & Day, J. (1996). Principles and virtues: A foundation for ethical decisions, policies, and character. *The Counseling Psychologist, 24,* 4–77.

National Association of Social Workers. (1996). *Code of ethics of the National Association of Social Workers.* Retrieved on November 2, 2008, from http://www.socialworkers.org/pubs/code/code.asp.

Pope, K. S., Keith-Spiegel, P., & Tabachnick, B. G. (1986). Sexual attraction to patients: The human therapist and the (sometimes) inhuman training system. *American Psychologist, 41,* 147–158.

Pope, K. S., & Vasquez, M. J. T. (2007). *Ethics in psychotherapy and counseling: A practical guide* (3rd ed.). San Francisco: Jossey-Bass/John Wiley.

Pope, K., & Vasquez, M. J. T. (2005). *How to survive and thrive as a therapist: Information, ideas and resources for psychologists in practice.* Washington, DC: American Psychological Association.

Rudd, M. D., Joiner, T., & Rajab, M. H. (2001). *Treating suicidal behavior: An effective, time-limited approach.* New York: Guilford Press.

Schmidt, L. D., & Meara, N. M. (1984). Ethical, professional and legal issues in counseling psychology. In S. D. Brown, & R. W. Lent (Eds.), *Handbook of counseling psychology.* New York: Wiley.

Sue, D. W., Bernier, J. E., Durran, A., Feinberg, L., Pedersen, P., Smith, E., & Vasquez-Nutall, E. (1982). Position paper: Cross-cultural counseling competencies. *The Counseling Psychologist, 10,* 45–52.

Thompson, A. S., & Super, D. E. (Eds.). (1964). *The professional preparation of counseling psychologists (Greystone Conference).* New York: Columbia University. Teachers College, Bureau of Publications.

Toporek, R. L., & Williams, R. A. (2006). Ethics and professional issues related to the practice of social justice in counseling psychology. In R. L. Toporek, L. H. Gerstein, N. A. Fouad, G. Roysircar, & T. Israel (Eds.), *Handbook for social justice in counseling psychology: Leadership, vision, and action.* Thousand Oaks, CA: Sage.

Vasquez, J. J. T. (2009). Ethics in multicultural counseling practice. In J. G. Ponterotto, J. M. Casas, L. A. Suzuki, & C. M. Alexander (Eds.). Handbook of Multicultural Counseling (3rd ed., pp. 127–136). Thousand Oaks, CA: Sage.

Vasquez, M. J. T., Bingham, R. P., Barnett, J. E. (2008). Psychotherapy termination: Clinical and ethical responsibilities. *Journal of Clinical Psychology: In Session, 64,* 653–665.

Vera, E. M., & Speight, S. L. (2003). Multicultural competence, social justice and counseling psychology: Expanding our roles. *The Counseling Psychologist, 31,* 253–272.

Werth, J. L., Cummings, D. L., & Thompson, M. N. (2008). Legal and ethical issues affecting counseling psychologists. In S. D. Brown, & R. W. Lent (Eds.), *Handbook of counseling psychology* (4th ed., pp. 3–20).

Welfel, E. (2002). *Ethics in counseling and psychotherapy: Standards, research and emerging issues.* Pacific Grove, CA: Brooks/Cole.

Welfel, E. R., & Lipsitz, M. E. (1984). The ethical behavior of professional psychologists: A critical analysis of the research. *The Counseling Psychologist, 12*(3), 31–42.

Further Reading

Campbell, L., Vasquez, M. J. T., Behnke, S., & Kinscherff, R. (in press). *APA ethics code commentary and case illustrations.* Washington, DC: American Psychological Association.

Fisher, C. B. (2003). *Decoding the ethics code: A practical guide for psychologists.* Thousand Oaks, CA: Sage.

Knapp, S., & VandeCreek, L. (2003). *A guide to the 2002 revision of the American Psychological Association's ethics code.* Sarasota, FL: Professional Resource Press.

Nagy, T. F. (2005). *Ethics in plain English: An illustrative casebook for psychologists* (2nd ed.). Washington, DC: American Psychological Association.

PART 3

Contextual Perspectives

Ethnic and Racial Identity

Kevin O. Cokley *and* Beverly J. Vandiver

Abstract

This chapter discusses the significance of racial and ethnic identity to the work of counseling psychologists and surveys historical and contemporary models of ethnic and racial identity. Many racial identity models, including white identity, minority identity, and people of color racial identity, were greatly influenced by the developmental thrust of early black identity models, in particular the Nigrescence model. Ethnic identity models were influenced by social identity theory as well as by developmental theories. The reliable and valid measurement of ethnic and racial identity remains an area of great interest and concern. Ethnic and racial identity are complex, multidimensional constructs whose influences are just starting to be understood. Nevertheless, there remains much to learn about the mechanisms through which ethnic and racial identity influence behavior and well-being.

Keywords: racial identity, ethnic identity, black identity, white identity, minority identity, people of color, nigrescence

More than any other event in our nation's history, the campaign for the 2008 Democratic presidential nomination sparked a national dialogue and debate about ethnic and racial identity. At the center of this debate was the Democratic nominee and now President, Barack Obama, whose ethnic and racial identity was a point of intrigue among Americans across racial, ethnic, and political lines. Questions such as "Is he too black?" or "Is he black enough?" were asked as racial identity litmus tests. Although Obama's biracial heritage challenges conventional notions of racial and ethnic identity, he has consistently self-identified as being African American, because he says that he is viewed and treated as a black man. Obama's self-identification underscores the complexity of ethnic and racial identity, because he can rightfully claim to be as "white" as he can "black"; however, the combination of his phenotype and the lingering influence of the United States' history of the "one-drop rule" make his self-identification as "black" or "African American"

more acceptable. Whatever people think of his identity, the election of the first black president of the United States will likely have a psychological impact on the racial and ethnic identity development of ethnic minorities for years to come.

Over the past 20 years, the discipline of counseling psychology has increasingly become defined by its scholarly focus on multicultural issues in psychology, especially race. It is therefore not surprising that a counseling psychologist, Joseph Ponterotto, published the first content analyses with a multicultural focus (Ponterotto, 1986, 1988; Ponterotto & Sabnani, 1989). The purpose of the 1989 study was to "identify the most influential (i.e., frequently cited) books, book chapters, conceptual/theoretical articles, empirical studies, and scholars in the multicultural counseling field" (Ponterotto & Sabnani, 1989, p. 24). Among the results reported was the finding that the classic article by Thomas Parham and Janet Helms (1981) on the topic of racial identity was the most cited empirical article.

Ponterotto concluded that the conceptual focus on racial identity development, particularly as it pertained to blacks, was among the three most influential themes in multicultural research and practice.

In an invited response to a series of articles on multicultural education and training, Ponterotto (1998) also identified racial identity development as an important area that needs further research. The fact that Ponterotto spent more than double the amount of written space addressing research needs related to racial identity development compared to other areas in multicultural counseling training underscored the importance of counseling psychologists gaining a better understanding of racial identity.

Cokley et al. (1999) conducted a content analysis to provide insight about where racial identity articles were being published most frequently, as well as to identify the individuals who had been the most prolific researchers of this topic over a 20-year period. Results revealed that approximately two out of every three racial identity articles (64%) published over the past 20 years had been published in the three counseling psychology–oriented journals. The greatest number of empirical articles was published in the *Journal of Counseling Psychology* (*JCP*), whereas the greatest number of conceptual or theoretical articles was published in *The Counseling Psychologist* (*TCP*). Ninety percent of the top 16 contributors to the racial identity literature were identified as counseling psychologists.

At this point, it should be apparent that there has been far more discussion of racial identity compared to ethnic identity. An examination of the counseling psychology literature reveals several noteworthy observations on comparisons of ethnic versus racial identity. The first article that included ethnic identity as a variable was published in *JCP* (Chang, Yeh, & Krumboltz, 2001). The first article that focused on ethnic identity was published in *JCP* (Lee, 2003). Excluding a 2007 special issue on ethnic and racial identity measurement, a total of 13 articles that focus on or involve ethnic identity have been published in *JCP* since 2001. Ten of these published articles have involved Asian American participants, two involved African American participants, and one involved Mexican American participants. By comparison, the first article that focused on racial identity was published in *JCP* in 1981 (Parham & Helms, 1981). Excluding the 2007 special issue, since 1981, there have been 29 articles that have focused on or involved racial identity. All but one of the published racial identity articles involved African American or European American participants. The first article that focused on ethnic identity in *TCP* was published in 2001 (Pizarro & Vera, 2001). Since 2001, only two articles have been published in *TCP* that substantively address ethnic identity. By comparison, the first article published in *TCP* that focused on racial identity was published in 1989 (Parham, 1989). Since 1989, 22 articles have been published in *TCP* focusing on some aspect of racial identity. This brief survey of the literature indicates that racial identity has been a much more popular construct for counseling psychologists than has ethnic identity.

The reasons for this predisposition toward racial versus ethnic identity are not altogether clear. Some scholars have made arguments against the construct of ethnicity that include it being ill-defined and simply a euphemism for the more emotionally laden term, *race* (Helms, 1990; Helms & Talleyrand, 1997). This logic would presumably be extended to the correlate of ethnic identity.

The disproportionate focus of racial versus ethnic identity articles has largely not been commented on by scholars in the discipline, perhaps because the constructs are seen to be more similar than different. We draw attention to this phenomenon because reviewing the extant literature reveals two obvious themes that will necessarily shape the approach in this chapter. First, racial identity research is overwhelmingly conducted with African American and European American samples, whereas the majority of ethnic identity studies are conducted with Asian American and Latino samples. Racial identity theories appear to rely on a binary black–white racial relations model as the paradigmatic experience for all ethnic groups. Although the history of slavery, segregation, and the Civil Rights Movement logically inform racial identity models for African Americans and European Americans, it is not clear whether they are adequate for understanding the experiences, cultural psychology, and "racial identity" of ethnic groups who are not "black" or "white." In spite of attempts to apply a racial identity model to all racial and ethnic minority groups (e.g., Atkinson, Morten, & Sue's minority identity development; Helms' people of color (POC) racial identity model; Sue & Sue's racial/cultural identity model), racial identity studies are still overwhelmingly conducted with African Americans, and to a lesser degree European American samples, and to an even lesser degree with Asian American samples. Consistent with this reality, the discussion of racial identity models focuses disproportionately on black and white identity, whereas the discussion of ethnic identity is broader in scope.

Given the centrality of racial identity research among counseling psychologists, it is no surprise that the *Oxford Handbook of Counseling Psychology* would dedicate an entire chapter to this topic. Although previous handbooks of counseling psychology incorporate racial identity in chapters that focus on racial and ethnic variables in counseling (Brown & Lent, 1992), race and social class (Brown & Lent, 2000), and multicultural psychology and research (Brown & Lent, 2008), none dedicates an entire chapter to racial identity. This chapter surveys historical and contemporary models of racial and ethnic identity. The chapter will begin with an overview of theories and models of racial identity, then move on to discuss black racial identity (BRI), minority identity/POC racial identity, white racial identity (WRI), roots of ethnic identity and social identity theory, ethnic identity, implications for counseling, measurement issues for racial identity, and measurement issues for ethnic identity. The chapter concludes with a look at future research directions.

Overview of Theories and Models of Racial Identity

A summary and review are provided of the most influential and prevalent theories and models of racial identity in that they significantly advanced one or more areas of the social sciences: theory, application, measurement, and research. Numerous stage models, such as those by Cross (1971), Thomas (1971), Jackson (1976), and Millones (1980), described the impact of a social movement via the process of transformation from Negro into black (for more historical details, see Cross, 1991; Helms, 1990). To underscore the commonality of these models, Cross (1978) labeled them *Nigrescence* (a term derived from the French) models—the "process of becoming black" (p. 108). Starting with the most influential black identity development models, we summarize and review the Nigrescence models of Thomas (1971) and Cross (1971). The Thomas model provides a historical perspective of racial identity theorizing. Cross' impact has spanned over 30 years. One of the most forward thinkers of racial identity theories, Cross has revised and expanded his Nigrescence model to parallel the evolving cultural climate over time. His thinking anchors the past with the present. The evolution of Cross' model is provided, followed by a review of Atkinson et al.'s (1979) minority identity

development model, which is an extension of Nigrescence to other racial minorities. Then Helms' (1990, 1995) modification and expansion of Cross' 1971 Nigrescence model is summarized, followed by a review of her POC model (Helms, 1995), a synthesis of Cross' (1971) and Atkinson et al.'s (1989) work. Helms' impact on the racial identity work in the social sciences, especially counseling psychology, has been tremendous. Next, Sellers et al.'s (1998) multidimensional model of racial identity is reviewed. Sellers' impact on racial identity is also significant, in large part because of the productivity of his racial identity lab. We conclude this section on racial identity by providing a review of the most influential white identity models, starting with the developmental models first proposed by Hardiman (1979) and Helms (1990), and ending with the attitudinal model of white racial consciousness (LaFleur, Rowe, & Leach, 2002; Rowe, Bennett, & Atkinson, 1994), which emerged as an alternative to Helms' development model and led to several notable debates about conceptualizing and measuring racial identity.

From Negromachy to "Boys No More"

No discussion of historical models of racial identity would be complete without referencing the contributions of Charles Thomas. At the 1968 American Psychological Association's annual convention, Thomas along with several other black psychologists formed the Association of Black Psychologists (ABPsi), and Thomas served as the first co-president. Before the articulation of his Negromachy model (Thomas, 1971) and the now classic Nigresence model (Cross, 1970, 1971; Hall & Cross, 1970), Thomas published a relatively unknown article that laid the groundwork for his and arguably other racial identity models to follow (Thomas, 1969). In that article, which reflected the gendered/sexist language of the times, Thomas discussed how the vestiges of slavery and oppressive social policies contributed to the breakdown and disintegration of black families. Thomas argued that the cultural climate for black people supported the belief that "white is right" (p. 39), and he asked the reader to reflect on the long period of time that black people "accommodated and internalized their astoundingly oppressive society" (p. 39). Without explicitly identifying the causal mechanisms or developmental antecedents, Thomas described a new sense of blackness, which he compared to "one's first physical encounter" or a "deep religious conversion" (p. 40). He indicated that this new sense of blackness could occur when an individual was "able to refer to himself as black in public," or when a lady could wear a natural hair style, or when an individual could comfortably wear "Afro-American clothes." Finally, Thomas characterized black people as "boys no more" (p. 40) because they were discovering a collective group awareness, which could be understood as occurring in a developmental fashion.

Building on this article, Thomas (1971) wrote the more cited and better known book *Boys No More*. In this book, Thomas gave form to his 1969 musings by introducing the term *Negromachy*, which he described as a psychological illness of preconscious blacks characterized by confusion of self-worth and being dependent on white society for self-definition. According to Thomas, the antidote to Negromachy was a succession of five stages, which would lead to a new sense of blackness. The first stage, withdrawal, required blacks to voluntarily withdraw themselves from traditional relationships with whites in order to resolve power imbalances. The second stage, testifying, was characterized by blacks testifying about all the pain they had endured in denying their humanity. In the third stage, information processing, individuals started to process the new information they were receiving about their black cultural heritage. The third stage led to the fourth stage, activity, in which blacks became active in a group or organization as a way to become connected to the larger black experience. Finally, in the transcendental stage, blacks transcend the various social identities that divide people (e.g., race, sex, social class) and see themselves as part of humanity.

Nigrescence Models

As a clinical psychology doctoral student in the 1960s, William Cross was very interested in how the social turbulence of the Civil Rights Movement and the Black Power Movement impacted black people. He noted and later documented what he believed to be a progression or stages of black consciousness, which he labeled *Nigrescence*. There have been three iterations of the Cross Nigrescence models: the 1971 version, now called the original model (NT-O; Cross); the 1991 version, called the revised model (NT-R; Cross); and the current versions, called the expanded model (NT-E; Cross & Vandiver, 2001; Worrell, Cross, & Vandiver, 2001). The original five-stage model is well known, chronicling the movement from an initial adherence to dominant cultural values by blacks (pre-encounter)

to black acceptance and activism (internalization-commitment). Due to limitation in space, the original and revised models are not presented here. Readers are referred to the seminal article "The Negro-to-Black Conversion Experience" (Cross, 1971) and the book *Shades of Black* (Cross, 1991) that delineate clearly both models. For an in-depth understanding of the expanded model, see Cross and Vandiver (2001), and for earlier critiques of Nigrescence models, see the 1989 special issue of TCP on Nigrescence and Reginald Jones' (1998) edited book *African American Identity Development*. The expanded Nigrescence theory contains six elements, which have emerged in Cross' writings in the past decade: (a) the structure of the self-concept; (b) the exemplars of black identities; (c) identity socialization from infancy to early adulthood; (d) adult identity conversion; (e) recycling; and (f) daily strategies to manage racial encounters. A brief review of the expanded Nigrescence model (points a, b, d, and e) and the key assumptions that demarcate it from the original model are presented here.

The revised model was based on five changes made to the original Nigrescence model, which are now fundamental to the expanded Nigrescence model. One, Nigrescence shifted from a stage model (developmental) to an experiential process, although developmental elements were more present in the revised model than in the current model. Two, personality was separated from social identity. Three, a shift was made from the stage process to the specification of exemplars of black racial identities in each stage and the respecification of other exemplars. Four, a linear relationship was no longer made between the stages and psychological functioning. And five, racial identity was not due solely to the oppressive or discriminatory aspects of society (Parham, 1989), but could occur for a variety of reasons.

Cross shifted the focus on racial identity from "becoming black" to "being black" by creating exemplars of black attitudes and incorporating the recycling mechanism, proposed by Parham (1989). The stage model now reflects experiences of blackness, which may or may not be sequential. Individuals may go through a series of experiences in developing a black identity, but not every black person will automatically start with a pre-encounter racial identity. Thus, recycling to encounter can occur at any stage, leading to a deeper processing of an individual's racial identity. Although Cross and colleagues (Cross & Vandiver, 2001; Worrell et al., 2001) continue to use terminology (stage model) that implies a developmental process, it isn't clear whether the terms are used to maintain a continuity across the models or whether both represent experiential and developmental processes.

Cross (1991) contended in the revised model that self-concept is made up of two components: personal identity (PI) and reference group orientation (RGO). Reference group orientation refers to an individual's preference for social affiliation, whereas PI reflects the unique aspects of an individual, including personality traits and psychological functioning such as self-esteem, happiness, depression, and anxiety. The focus of the Nigrescence model is not on PI, but RGO—the social identity of the individual, which includes the importance of race (race salience; Cross, 1991).

Each stage contains multiple racial attitudes, bound together by a core essence but reflecting unique RGO characteristics. No assumptions are made about a specific process from one attitude to another within or across stages. Thus, the focus of the expanded model is on the attitudinal aspects of RGO. The five-stage process remains the same if the focus is on the Nigrescence process that a black adult might undergo in developing a black identity, but a developmental process is not assumed. The original stage names are still used for continuity and underscore a theme that identities share within each stage. When the focus is on the exemplars of attitudes, only the stages/themes of preencounter, immersion-emersion, and internationalization are used. A racial attitude is not associated with encounter, as it is transitory in nature (Cross & Vandiver, 2001). The expanded theory underscores that an indefinite universe of black identities are representative of the themes of each stage/theme (Cross & Vandiver, 2001).

The racial identity exemplars, first noted in the NT-R, have been further fleshed out, resulting in the delineation of nine racial identities, two more than in NT-R (Vandiver, Fhagen-Smith, Cokley, Cross, & Worrell, 2001; Worrell et al., 2001). Three identities, instead of two (assimilation and anti-black) in the revised model, now make up the pre-encounter stage: assimilation, miseducation, and self-hatred. All reflect the endorsement of a mainstream social identity, but for different reasons. Pre-encounter assimilation refers to a pro-American RGO (low race salience, but high salience to other cultural aspects—e.g., social class, religion, etc.). Miseducation (moderate negative race salience) refers to the stereotypical views that individuals

adopt about other blacks. Self-hatred (high negative race salience) characterizes the individual who personally rejects being black.

Immersion-emersion consists of the same two attitudes described in the revised model. Intense black involvement refers to the idealized immersion into black culture, whereas the anti-white attitude reflects an individual's intense dislike of white culture. Four racial attitudes make up internalization: black nationalist, biculturalist, multiculturalist inclusive—all in the revised model—plus the addition of multiculturalist racial. All attitudes have a high positive race salience for being black. The only difference is the number of cultural identities that is salient, which in turn influences the focus of the individuals. Black nationalists focus solely on being black and the empowerment of other blacks. Biculturalists focus on being black, plus have another salient cultural identity (e.g., gender or American). And multiculturalists focus on multiple salient cultural identities (i.e., black, female, lesbian) and on building coalitions with other cultural groups. The difference between the multiculturalists is the extent of cultural inclusion. A multiculturalist racial connotation refers to blacks whose identity revolves around being black in relation to other racial minority groups. Their RGO does not extend to non–racial minority groups such as gays/lesbians or well-informed whites. In contrast, those with a multiculturalist inclusive identity build coalitions with anyone who is interested in working toward social equity.

Blacks with internalization attitudes are not expected to have a higher self-concept or psychological functioning than those with immersion-emersion or pre-encounter assimilation attitudes. Only individuals with a pre-encounter self-hatred attitude (the negative merger of PI and RGO) are expected to suffer from low self-esteem, as they hate themselves for being black. Thus, no difference in psychological functioning is expected between individuals if they express a preference for one reference group over another, except if they have a deep disdain for being black. Someone with a black nationalist identity could be just as depressed as someone with a pre-encounter assimilation identity.

Evaluation

It is to Cross' (1971, 1991; Cross & Vandiver, 2001) credit that he continues to innovate the Nigrescence model, modifying it based on an accumulation of evidence and critique. There is a growing body of research on the NT-E using the Cross Racial Identity Scale (CRIS; Vandiver et al., 2000), with a host of sociocultural (RGO and PI) variables, such as acculturation, psychological health, academic adjustment, and ethnic identity. The accumulated research will in time determine the efficacy of the expanded theory, in whole or in part. Despite the burgeoning research using the CRIS, some of the findings must be viewed with caution, as common flaws have occurred across the research process such as drawing the wrong conclusions due to using the 1971 model (NT-O) and misusing the CRIS (separate subscale use).

Two issues may explain this state in the literature. One, conceptual confusion appears to exist about the expanded model. Although Cross' model is still called Nigrescence and the stages are still included, the model is no longer the original model and is not developmental. Scholars still write as if the original Nigrescence model is in force and invoke developmental terminology (e.g., internalization is a higher level than pre-encounter). Two, the original Nigrescence model has intuitive appeal (R. Bingham, personal communication, February 16, 2008; Stevenson, 1998). The stage process makes intuitive sense to people because psychological health and self-worth should be linearly linked to internalizing a black identity. However, the empirical evidence doesn't support these common-sense premises (Cross, 1991; Cross & Vandiver, 2001). Perhaps it is time for a sea change in the terminology (i.e., cease using *Nigrescence* and *stages*) used to describe the current Cross model. This shift might result in facilitating best practice of the theory/model. Currently, the most noteworthy support for the expanded model has been the identification of four cluster patterns, which parallel the exemplars in the model (Vandiver, Korell, & Miller, 2007; Worrell, Vandiver, Schaefer, Cross, & Fhagen-Smith, 2006): assimilated, immersion, Afrocentric, and multiculturalist. More work is needed in theorizing about BRI, as the cultural world continues to change racially and sociopolitically. Cross' BRI model is only one perspective in addressing the complexity of identity.

Janet Helms' Models: Nigrescence and Beyond

Helms (1995) has developed an overarching theory of racial identity development, with the understanding that the process is applicable to all racial beings. Three separate models were developed to capture the differences in their racial experiences

and history: black, white, and people of color. These three models share several common features. One, the racial identity process is described in terms of *status*, replacing the term *stage*, to reflect the dynamic and complex cognitive, affective, and behavioral processes that guide the person in interpreting racial information. Using stage seemed to imply a static condition that was mutually exclusive of the other stages. Two, individuals still undergo a developmental sequence of ego differentiation and have available within their identity a repertoire of all ego statuses. The most dominant status is the one usually expressed, but other statuses may be strong enough for individuals to access when necessary. Three, content of the statuses will vary based on the sociocultural experiences, including power differences, of one's racial group. Four, ego statuses will vary in maturation, from simplistic unexamined ones to more complex and dynamic ones, and will emerge based on the need to cope and digest meaningful experiences. Reliance on external sources for identity reflects less mature ego statuses, whereas more mature ego statuses represent a personal discovery and integration process of an internalized identity. Five, schemata are the behavioral manifestations of statuses and are what is tapped on paper-and-pencil measures. A reciprocal process is assumed to exist between the relevant schemata and statuses, strengthening or weakening each other depending on use. Finally, each status is defined by an "underlying cognitive-emotional information-processing strategy" (Helms, 1995, p. 187), which is assumed to be the same regardless of the era in which the person was socialized (Helms, 1995). Readers should review Helms (1990, 1995), and Thompson and Carter (1997) for an in-depth understanding of Helms' models.

Black Racial Identity

Helms (1990) modified and extended Cross' original Nigrescence model to create another model of BRI. The number of statuses was reduced from five to four: pre-encounter, encounter, immersion/emersion, and internalizations. Each status represents a separate racial perspective and differs in PI, RGO, and ascribed identity. Within each status, Helms elaborated that two bimodal forms of expression existed. The original pre-encounter status is an active expression of blacks intentionally idealizing whites and denigrating blacks. In the passive mode, considered the healthier of the two, the individual actively assimilates the dominant worldview to earn acceptance and status, while unconsciously accepting the established racial stereotypes. Conscious awareness of the need to discard being pro-white and to find another is the first mode of expression in encounter, whereas the struggle to find a new identity, comprised of a mixture of feelings, reflects the other mode of expression. Helms maintained Cross' depiction of immersion-emersion (the active immersion into black culture vs. the withdrawal into a supportive black environment to resolve identity). The first mode of expression in internalization is the blend of one's PI with a newly found positive black identity. Internalization-commitment is now the second mode of expression in internalization, in which commitment to a black identity is evidenced through social activism. More nuanced details of Helms' black identity model are presented in Helms (1990) and Carter (1995).

EVALUATION
This model is intriguing in that Helms, early on, advanced nuances (modes of expression) at each of the stages that most scholars are unaware of. The specifics of her model are typically overlooked, as most scholars use the Black Racial Identity Attitude Scale (BRIAS; Helms & Parham, 1996), which is based on Cross' (1971) model. No research exists in support of Helms' model, although it is likely that the first modes of expression in pre-encounter and internalization are measured in the BRIAS. It is not clear what modes of expression are tapped in the BRIAS for encounter and immersion-emersion. Like all Nigrescence models, Helms' model has been criticized on specific aspects, which will be summarized once at the end of the section. The issue at this point is whether Helms still views this model as viable, given the lack of measurement of it and the development of the POC model, which includes blacks.

People of Color
The POC model is a synthesis of Cross' original Nigrescence model and Atkinson's et al. (1989) minority identity development. Helms (1995) uses the term *people of color* to refer "to those persons whose ostensible ancestry is at least in part African, Asian, Indigenous, and/or combinations of these groups and/or white or European ancestry" (p. 189). The underlying assumption of the model is that people of color have internalized societal racial stereotypes and that the central goal of racial identity development is to overcome the internalized racism. Five ego statuses describe this maturation

process: conformity (pre-encounter), dissonance (encounter), immersion/emersion, internalization, and integrative awareness. Ego statuses parallel the process of the original Nigrescence model from accepting white standards and devaluating own-group values to accepting own racial identity and willingness to collaborate with others. The difference is that the process is now written in the context for other racial/ethnic minorities.

EVALUATION
Combining the Nigrescence and the minority identity development models reflect the forward thinking that Helms (1994) had about racial identity development. The inclusion of other racial/ethnic minorities recognized that discrimination wasn't reserved just for blacks. Limitations common to all models are discussed below, but a unique concern is whether the same racial identity process is common to all racial/ethnic minorities. Furthermore, whites are the comparison group for internalized racism. What about the racism that occurs between racial/ethnic minorities (e.g., Cubans and blacks; blacks and Koreans)? Does racism between racial/ethnic minorities have an impact on racial identity development, or does only the white hegemony count at this point? Some research has been conducted on the POC model using the People of Color Racial Identity Attitudes Scale (PRIAS; Helms, 1995). Despite the lengthy existence of the model (at least a decade), research is just emerging on it. Its value will depend on the psychometric adequacy of the PRIAS, which is just beginning to be tested.

White Racial Identity
Helms (1990, 1995) contends that whites are consciously or unconsciously socialized to assume that they are racially superior, thus giving whites the privilege to ignore or deny their race. Thus, developing a positive WRI requires overcoming the influence of racism, accepting the sociopolitical nature of whiteness, and personally acknowledging the racial equality of others, as well as identifying as a racial being (Helms, 1990, 1995). Six ego statuses, differing in the degree of acceptance of racism and whiteness, delineate the maturation process of WRI: contact, disintegration, reintegration, pseudo-independence, immersion-emersion, and autonomy. The contact status is characterized by whites' "obliviousness to racism," in which they are satisfied with the status quo. Sustained exposure to racial/ethnic minorities may lead to the development of

the disintegration status, which includes increased awareness of racial differences and concomitant feelings of anxiety in making sense of racial issues. The reintegration status emerges when individuals resolve these racial ambiguities by acknowledging their whiteness and adopting the two-belief system of white superiority-racial/minority inferiority. Unless fixated in this status, poignant events may precipitate whites to requestion their racist beliefs. If successful, whites adopt the pseudo-independence status, an intellectual definition of positive white identity and the acceptance of other racial/ethnic groups. Movement into the immersion-emersion status involves developing a personal definition of whiteness, which includes questioning racist beliefs and racial stereotypes. The final status is autonomy and involves the internalization of a positive WRI in which one actively does not oppress another, but seeks to build cross-racial relationships. These statuses reflect two phases of white identity development: the abandonment of racism, which includes the first three statuses (contact, disintegration, and reintegration), and the acceptance/internalization of a nonracist white identity, which covers the last three statuses (pseudo-independence, immersion-emersion, and autonomy).

EVALUATION

Comments in this section are pertinent to all of the racial identity models, with many of the comments pointed to WRI. Helms' contribution to the field of psychology on racial identity has been enormous. She has stimulated work on racial identity in several ways: the development of her own and other racial identity models (e.g., Rowe et al., 1994; Sabnani, Ponterotto, & Borodovsky, 1991), the development of her own and other racial and ethnic identity scales, and the development of a racial identity interaction model (Helms, 1984, 1990). However, major criticisms have been made about all of the models. One, they don't fit the criteria for a developmental model (Leach, Behrens, & LaFleur, 2002; Rowe et al., 1994; Stokes, Murray, Chavez, & Peacock, 1998). Despite shifting from not using the term *stage* to using *statuses*, the developmental process is still believed to be embedded in the model. Two, the focus is not on white identity, but on how whites view other racial/ethnic minorities (Fischer & Moradi, 2001; Hardiman, 2001; Leach et al., 2002; Rowe et al., 1994). Thus, the theory is considered prescriptive (chronicling what whites need to do to overcome being racist) instead of descriptive—describing the attitudes and process

of being white (Hardiman, 2001). Three, it has been questioned whether the process of white identity development parallels the development of racial/ethnic minorities. Four, as a result, the theory is considered to be a "gross oversimplification" of the process of becoming white. Hardiman (1991, pp. 116–117) contends that, "white identity development might entail different processes for individuals raised in all- or mostly white environments, and whites who were raised in close proximity to people of color." At the same time, white racial consciousness scholars (Leach et al., 2002; Rowe et al., 1994, 1995) have criticized the white racial model for being too complex and exhaustive, containing an answer for any aspect of racial identity development. Thus, none of the models can ever truly be confirmed (fully measured) nor disconfirmed, as there will always be missing elements or conditional premises in explaining mixed empirical findings. Despite these criticisms and issues about the psychometric adequacy of the White Racial Identity Attitudes Scale (Helms & Carter, 1990), empirical findings have provided support for an overarching aspect of white identity (Behrens, 1997; Swanson, Tokar, & Davis, 1994). In conclusion, Helms' models are at a crossroads. Should the models be revised, or should the process of whites accepting other racial/minorities or racial minorities accepting their racial identity remain the same? Does the social era or the racial composition of the United States matter?

Multidimensional Model of Racial Identity

Thus far, the review of the literature has focused primarily on the contributions of counseling psychologists and clinical psychologists (e.g., Charles Thomas, William Cross). Counseling psychologists have especially been instrumental in conducting empirical research to advance our understanding of racial identity. However, interest in the racial identity of African Americans has a much longer history in psychology than the contributions of counseling psychology, dating back to the early "Negro" self-concept and racial identification studies (Clark & Clark, 1939; Horowitz, 1939; Kardiner & Ovesey, 1951). These studies were conducted by social psychologists who were interested in understanding the psychological impact of having a stigmatized racial identity.

As racial identity research increased through the 1990s, concerns were expressed about inconsistencies in the literature. These inconsistencies were attributed to "mainstream" versus "underground" approaches to the study of African American or BRI (Sellers, Smith, Shelton, Rowley, & Chavous, 1998). Mainstream approaches assume that the oppression of white racism has resulted in blacks internalizing a negative black self-concept and having a stigmatized racial identity (Sellers et al, 1998). Underground approaches emphasize the role of history and culture in understanding what it means to be black. According to Sellers et al., mainstream approaches place more emphasis on the stigma of being black than on the experiential aspects associated with history and culture related to what it means to be black. On the other hand, underground approaches offer different perspectives about what it means to be black, but have not generated a lot of empirical support for the internal processes hypothesized to undergird the development of a black identity. Finally, mainstream approaches focus more on the process and structure of racial identity, whereas underground approaches focus more on the qualitative aspects of racial identity.

In an attempt to integrate the best of both approaches, Sellers et al. proposed a new theoretical framework for understanding black identity, the Multidimensional Model of Racial Identity (MMRI). The MMRI is informed by social identity theories that state that social identities are influenced by situations as well as by relatively stable properties of the individual (Stryker & Serpe, 1982, 1994). According to Sellers et al., the theoretical framework of the MMRI allows for the reconciliation of inconsistencies in the literature. The MMRI starts with the supposition that race is one of a number of salient social identities for African Americans, and not necessarily the most important. Instead of assuming that race is an important social identity for African Americans, the MMRI asks two questions: How important is race in the individual's perception of self? What does it mean to be a member of this racial group (Sellers et al., 1998)?

Four empirically testable assumptions form the foundation of the MMRI. The assumptions are that identities are situationally influenced and also stable properties of the individual, individuals have a number of hierarchically ordered identities, peoples' perceptions of their racial identity is the most valid indicator of their identity, and the status of an individual's racial identity is of primary concern, as opposed to the development of the racial identity. A particularly noteworthy difference between the MMRI and underground approaches (such as the various permutations of the Nigrescence model) is that the MMRI does not assume that any racial

identity status is inherently good or bad. Instead, the framework of the MMRI allows for the possibility that certain identities may be more likely to be associated with more positive outcomes. However, even if this is the case, it is still important for empirical research that the identity be kept separate from the outcome.

In addition to these four testable assumptions, the MMRI consists of four dimensions that concentrate on both the qualitative meaning and significance of race in the self-concepts of African Americans (Sellers et al., 1998). The four dimensions consist of racial salience, racial centrality, racial regard, and racial ideology. *Racial salience* "refers to the extent to which one's race is a relevant part of one's self-concept at a particular moment or in a particular situation" (Sellers et al., 1998, p. 24). This dimension assumes that race is more salient for African Americans in certain situations than in others. For example, regardless of how important race is to an individual's self-concept, being the only black person in a meeting where a racist joke is told using a racial epithet would most likely make race a salient part of the individual's self-concept at that moment. *Racial centrality* "refers to the extent to which a person normatively defines himself or herself with regard to race" (Sellers et al., 1998, p. 25). This dimension addresses how central race is to an individual's identity. For example, the individual who sees being black as an important part of her or his self-concept is higher on racial centrality than is the individual who does not. *Racial regard* "refers to a person's affective and evaluative judgment of her or his race in terms of positive–negative valence" (Sellers et al., 1998, p. 26). This dimension examines how positively or negatively an individual feels about being black, and is included because this is a theme of much of the psychological literature on African Americans. The racial regard dimension consists of both private regard and public regard. *Private regard* refers to how individuals feel about being black, as well as how they feel about other blacks. *Public regard* refers to how much individuals feel that others hold positive or negative views toward or about blacks. *Racial ideology* "is composed of the individual's beliefs, opinions, and attitudes with respect to the way she or he feels that the members of the race should act" (Sellers et al., 1998, p. 27).

Historically, at least four dominant racial ideologies have been embraced by African Americans. These four ideologies have been incorporated into the MMRI and include the nationalist philosophy, the oppressed minority philosophy, the assimilation philosophy, and the humanist philosophy. A nationalist ideology is characterized by a strong belief in the uniqueness of the black experience, self-determination with no interference from other racial groups, and an increased likelihood of participating in black organizations. An oppressed minority ideology is characterized by a belief in the similarities between blacks and other marginalized and disenfranchised minorities. An assimilationist ideology is characterized by the belief that African Americans are similar to other groups in American society, and as such should work within the system to effect change. Finally, a humanist ideology is characterized by the belief in the similarities between humans, and that individuals should not be simply reduced to their race, gender, class, or other social identity.

As mentioned previously, the MMRI does not view any dimension of racial identity as being inherently positive or negative. It attempts to remove evaluation or judgment from the beliefs and attitudes individuals have about being black. This is perhaps the most striking difference between the MMRI and both mainstream and underground approaches. Conducting research using the MMRI does not mean that negative outcomes, such as low self-esteem, depression, or poor academic performance, are not legitimate areas of research inquiry. It simply means, as Sellers et al. (1998) state, that the negative outcomes should be not defined as part of the dimensions of racial identity themselves, because this becomes a tautological problem. Although not explicitly mentioned, these concerns seem to be more applicable to Cross's (1971) original Nigrescence model, in which pre-encounter attitudes were initially seen as anti-black and pro-white, with the implication being that blacks who exhibited these attitudes were self-hating and suffering from low self-esteem. However, in a comprehensive review of the literature, Cross (1991) had already concluded that psychological functioning, such as self-esteem, should not be automatically linked to racial identity attitudes, and with the assistance of his colleagues (Vandiver et al., 2001), he sought to empirically support his evolved thinking. Thus, Sellers et al.'s concerns, while well-founded, do not seem to accurately reflect the evolution of Cross's thinking and his revised and expanded Nigrescence models.

One final observation that should be pointed out and that has relevance to this issue concerns disciplinary and historical influences on the development of these models. Namely, at its core, the MMRI is a social psychological theory of identity developed by social psychologists whose orientations are as contemporary social scientists living in a post Civil Rights and Black Power era. They did not live through segregation and the Black Is Beautiful era. By contrast, the Nigrescence model was developed by a clinical psychology doctoral student living and experiencing the turbulence of the 1960s Civil Rights and Black Power era. The concern for many black social scientists during that era was for black liberation, which by definition assumed that black people were oppressed and needed to be liberated. The *zeitgeist* of those times clearly impacted the ideological thrust of the Nigrescence model. This, combined with a clinical psychology student's orientation toward mental health, made it quite natural to link self-esteem to an individual's racial identity attitudes. It might be argued that the MMRI places no explicit value on dimensions of racial identity because its authors were fortunate enough to not live through the racially turbulent times of the 1960s. There is not a sense of urgency in the MMRI or resoluteness of purpose, because the MMRI is essentially descriptive in scope rather than prescriptive. In other words, there is no desired endpoint because the MMRI seeks only to capture and describe the dimensions of black identity. In spite of its theoretical sophistication, it is perhaps because of this orientation that the MMRI has not resonated very strongly with counseling psychologists. A review of the counseling psychology literature reveals that the MMRI has largely not been utilized by counseling psychologists. In fact, outside of one study published by the first author (Cokley, 1999), the authors are not aware of any counseling psychologists who have published studies utilizing the MMRI as their theoretical framework for racial identity.

Minority Identity (Racial/Cultural Identity) Development

In 1979, Atkinson, Morten, and Sue developed the minority identity development model (MID) for the purpose of assisting mental health professionals in working better with racial minorities. Based on the BRI models of Cross (1971) and Jackson (1976), and the authors' clinical experience in working with minority clients, the MID was applied to all racial/ethnic minority groups, such as blacks, Latinos, and Asian Americans, because of their common experience of oppression, even though sociopolitical experiences varied. Several premises undergird the model: it is not a theory of personality development; it is a developmental stage model; the stages are not discrete, but continuous; and everyone may not go through all the stages in a lifetime, possibly remaining in only one stage. There is no prerequisite that individuals must go through the lower stages first, that there is an irreversible sequence to reach the higher stages, and that the higher stages represent more valued attitudes (Atkinson et al., 1979).

The five MID stages are conformity, dissonance, resistance and immersion, introspection, and synergetic articulation and awareness. The essence of each stage is similar to the original Nigrescence model: individuals in conformity start with a preference for dominant culture and denigration of their own culture only to undergo transformation in appreciating their own culture and have a more discerning view about other cultures (synergetic). The stages' content has remained the same for almost 30 years (Atkinson, 2003; Atkinson et al., 1979) with only minor changes. Sue and Sue (1990) renamed the MID the racial/cultural identity development (R/CID) model and changed the name of the fifth stage to *integrative awareness*, which has been extended in subsequent editions of the text (1999, 2003, 2008). Sue and Sue (1990) also applied the model to white identity development, crafting the description to reflect change from a dominant (ethnocentric) identity to developing a nonracist identity. Atkinson et al. (1998) and Atkinson (2003), however, have continued to present the original model, absent the modifications made by Sue and Sue. For a detailed review of the MID or R/CID models, the reader is referred to the citations listed above.

Evaluation

The primary strength of the model is its universality, as it is appropriate to describe the cultural identity development of all individuals, including whites. Also, the model was designed for counselors in understanding the racial/minority identity development of their clients. However, through six editions of the text *Counseling American Minorities: A Cross-Cultural Perspective* from 1979 (Atkinson et al.) to 2003 (Atkinson), the basic tenets of the model have remained the same, except for changes noted above (Sue & Sue, 2008). Substantive changes in U.S. sociocultural landscape have not been taken into account. The model continues to be described as developmental, even though it doesn't meet stage criteria (Stokes et al., 1998).

Finally, continued use of the MID (R/CID) model is primarily based on intuitive appeal and anecdotal clinical data, with little empirical support—a status acknowledged by Atkinson et al. (1993). A perusal of PsychINFO for use of the model in the psychological literature resulted in 14 articles, spanning 1983 to 2005: six dissertations—half quantitative (Fernandez, 1989; Lim, 2002; Lott-Harrison, 1999) and half conceptual or qualitative (DeJesus-Rueff, 1986; Pak, 2005; Ponpipom, 1997). In some articles, the MID was applied to various counseling modalities (Barrett, 1990; D'Andrea & Daniels, 1996; Sue, 1989; Thomas, 1985). Two published quantitative studies reported relationships between MID level and preference for counselors (Morten & Atkinson, 1983), and between MID level and psychological help-seeking in Polish immigrants in the United Kingdom (Bassaly & Macallan, 2006). Both studies created a measure of MID, but no standard measure has been developed that could be used across racial/ethnic groups.

Helms and Carter (1986, 1990) developed the Visible/Racial Identity Attitudes Scale ([VIAS] and noted by other acronyms as well) to measure four to five attitudes on the MID, depending on the version used. Some version of the VIAS has been used up to 2000, and the findings have been in keeping with theory. For example, increased racial awareness (fifth stage) has been linked to increased career maturity in Asian Americans (Carter & Constantine, 2000), and positive racial identity has been associated with achieved ego identity in Hispanic Americans (e.g., Miville & Helms, 1996). However, it is unclear whether this scale is viable, as limited psychometric research has been conducted or reported (Kohatsu & Richardson, 1996), or that it will continue to be used, since another scale has evolved from the VIAS to measure the people of color model (Helms, 1995), which is a fusion of the original Nigrescence and MID models. If not, what is the implication of continuing to use a theory without sustained or clear empirical support?

White Identity Development

Hardiman (1982) developed what is considered the earliest model of white identity development (WID) in order to shift the focus from the victims of racial oppression to the oppressors of racism and to describe the process of whites developing a nonracist identity. An underlying assumption of the model is that no one can "escape the racist socialization," as it is a "by-product of living within . . . institutional and cultural racism"

(Hardiman, 2001, p. 111). Using autobiographical data of white writers and influenced by the early BRI models, Hardiman offered a five-stage model of WRI development, which has been updated (Hardiman, 1994; Hardiman & Jackson, 1992): no social consciousness of race or naivete, acceptance, resistance, redefinition, and internalization. The first stage, no social consciousness of race or naïveté, begins and ends in early childhood and is characterized by a lack of awareness or understanding of the meaning or value of race. In stage 2, acceptance, whites have unconsciously internalized racism and a status of privilege. Movement to stage 3, resistance, is marked by an individual's questioning of mainstream racial views and the onset of rejecting racist ideology and becoming an activist. Feelings of guilt and shame are prevalent. Individuals begin to take responsibility for being white (a new white identity) in stage four, redefinition. And, in the final stage, internalization, this new white identity is integrated into all aspects of an individual's life. Transition from one stage to the next is articulated in the model.

Evaluation

In an analysis of the model, Hardiman (2001, p. 122) contends that the major contribution of the WID model has been "the decentering of whiteness and the marking of whites as a race that should be the subject of study." She also indicates that, in the fields of counseling psychology and education, the model has had a major impact toward reducing racism and bias in practice and in influencing the development of other cultural models. Hardiman (2001) offered several problems with the WID model: white identity is seen through the lens of racial minorities instead of how whites identify with being white, the model represents the racial identity development of those who become antiracist activists, and the model is not based on empirical research. Hardiman (2001, p. 112) stated, "It is a gross oversimplification to say that WID defined the racial identity experience for all whites in the United States." To date, no empirical research has been published or found to support the model. Rather, Hardiman (2001) viewed the model as a "prescription of what whites needed to do" (p. 113) to develop a nonoppressor white identity.

White Racial Consciousness

White racial consciousness (WRC) represents a collection of racial attitudes white Americans have

"toward racial/minority group members . . . identifiable and recognized as non-white" (Rowe, Behrens, & Leach, 1995, p. 225). These attitudes are acquired in the same manner as other attitudes and are not viewed as personality traits, but represent clusters of attitudes held by whites. Each cluster represents a describable set of related attitudes, which are called *types*. Individuals can possibly have attitudes representative of more than one type, but it is assumed that most people can be classified as holding one type of white racial consciousness. White racial consciousness emerged as an alternative model in response to concerns about the conceptual underpinnings of the WRI development (WRID) models, most notably Helms' (1990, 1995) model. Major criticisms cited by the WRC developers (Rowe & Atkinson, 1995; Rowe et al., 1994) about the WRID models include the inappropriate use of developmental concepts to describe the movement between stages/statuses, a minority identity model to create a white identity model, and the label of white identity when focus of the model is not on awareness of a white identity but reflects varying levels of awareness about other racial/minorities (Rowe et al., 1995, p. 224).

Rowe et al. (1994) originally proposed seven types of WRC attitudes. These types were clustered on two dimensions, exploration and commitment, terms adapted from Phinney's (1989) work on ethnic identity and used for ease of delineating the types of attitudes. *Exploration* refers to the extent to which individuals examine racial/ethnic minority issues or not, and *commitment* refers to the extent to which an individual adopts a specific attitude about racial/ethnic minority issues. Three types of attitudes reflect either no exploration or commitment to racial/ethnic minority issues: avoidant, dependent, and dissonant. Individuals with avoidant-type attitudes do not explore or commit to racial/ethnic minority concerns or consider their own race. People with dependent-type attitudes commit to others' (i.e., family or friends) views about racial/ethnic concerns, superficially endorsing one without personally exploring their own attitudes. Dissonant-type attitudes accrue to individuals who have explored various attitudes about these concerns, but who do not commit to a point of view. Individuals may take a dissonant attitude when they are in transition from one racial attitude to another. These three attitude types are labeled as *unachieved white racial consciousness* status "because the attitudes are not securely integrated into the belief structure of the individual" (Rowe et al., 1995, p. 227).

In contrast, *achieved white racial consciousness* status refers to individuals who have explored and committed to a specific attitude about racial/ethnic minority issues and are exemplified in four types: conflictive, dominative, integrative, and reactive. Individuals with a conflictive-type attitude do not support overt discrimination toward racial/ethnic minorities, but also do not think it is fair to have systematic programs (i.e., affirmative action) that would give advantages to minorities. The attitudes of dominative-type individuals are that whites are inherently superior to racial/ethnic minorities and, as a result, are entitled to be in charge and dominate nonmajority people. Integrative-type attitudes describe those whites who are secure in their whiteness, are comfortable interacting with racial/ethnic minorities, and value a fair and culturally diverse society. Reactive types are sensitive to the inequities in society and feel guilty and responsible for discrimination, potentially romanticizing minority plights and operating in a paternalistic manner (Rowe et al., 1994, 1995).

Although the achieved-type attitudes are considered fairly stable, dissonance experiences are considered the likely process that results in an individual's movement from one achieved-status attitude type to another. As tension and conflict are necessary to produce a change, the dissonant-type attitude is considered the likely conduit when individuals with an unachieved-status attitude move to an achieved-status attitude. Dissonance is not necessary between the unachieved-status type attitudes because the views have not been internalized (Rowe et al., 1994, 1995).

A measure was developed to tap the WRC attitude types, the preliminary form of the Oklahoma Racial Attitude Scale (ORAS-P; Choney & Behrens, 1996). Validation work (Behrens, Leach, Franz, & LaFleur, 1999; Pope-Davis, Dings, Stone, & Vandiver, 1995; Pope-Davis, Vandiver, & Stone, 1999; Summerson, 1997 on the ORAS-P to measure the WRC type attitudes resulted in the reconceptualization of the model (LaFleur, Rowe, & Leach, 2002) and the emergence of the standard form of the Oklahoma Racial Attitude Scale (ORAS; LaFleur, Leach, & Rowe, 2003). In the reconceptualized model, three major changes were made. One, dominative, integrative, conflictive, and reactive type attitudes were reoriented based on one of two racial themes that had been identified through factor analysis. Dominative and integrative type attitudes are now viewed as a bipolar dimension best reflecting the theme of racial acceptance. On one end of the dimension, white individuals with a dominative-type attitude have a highly negative view of other racial/ethnic groups and are not accepting of other races/ethnicities. The other end of the dimension best describes whites with a positive/accepting accepting attitude toward racial/ethnic minorities (integrative-type attitude). Also sharing a common theme is the conflictive and reactive type attitudes. Individuals with either type of attitudes do not condone racial discrimination, but their stance for racial justice—the common theme shared between the types—is different. Those with a conflictive-type attitude do not want whites to be at an unfair advantage and therefore do not think it is racially just to support any programs that support racial/ethnic minorities. Whereas individuals with a reactive-type attitude believe that whites have been privileged and believe is it racially just to support programs for racial/ethnic minorities that would realign the status quo. Although these two type attitudes reflect a common theme, unlike dominative and integrative, they are treated as separate constructs psychometrically. Thus, racial acceptance and racial justice provide an orientation to three types of attitudes: dominative/integrative, conflictive, and reactive (LaFleur et al., 2002).

Two, labeling the types of attitudes as achieved and unachieved statuses is no longer necessary. The original purpose for having unachieved types of racial attitudes was to identify those who had not explored and committed to a racial attitude. LaFleur, Rowe, and Leach (2002, p. 151) stated, "In truth, the scores on the unachieved scales do not reflect racial attitude content." Three, the previously labeled unachieved attitudes are now considered attitudes of commitment and are labeled as such. These attitudes reflect the extent of commitment toward a racial attitude by individuals either expressing no concern (avoidant), relying on others (dependent), or being uncertain (dissonant). Thus, scales representative of these attitudes on the ORAS are to be used as "indices of one's expressed commitment to the four types of racial attitudes" (LaFleur et al., p. 151). For an in-depth reading of the WRC model and reconceptualization, see LaFleur et al. (2002), Leach, Behrens, and LaFleur (2002), and Rowe et al. (1994, 1995).

Evaluation

In regards to the WRC model (LaFleur et al., 2002; Rowe et al., 1994, 1995) Ponterotto (2006, p. 101) says it best: "One great strength of the Rowe et al. (1994, 1995) white racial consciousness model is that it has been closely linked to empirical research at the outset." Empirical studies (Pope-Davis et al., 1995, 1999; Summerson, 1997) conducted independently of the WRC researchers were taken seriously, resulting in the stimulation of further empirical studies on the ORAP-P and the reconceptualization of WRC. Another strength of the WRC is the use of a typology model and its general clarity. Although these models can be viewed as stereotypical and simplistic, the WRC extends the early development of type models (e.g., Gaertner, 1976; Kovel, 1970) on white racial attitudes through theory and empirical work. By using the term *attitude type*, the developers have been cautious to avoid stereotyping individuals based on a score on a scale. It is clear that the model reflects a unidimensional view of attitudes and describes types of attitudes that are commonly held by whites, which have as their basis empirical verification (Leach et al., 2002). More clarity, however, is needed in the model about the relationship between the racial orientation attitudes (dominative/integrative, conflictive, and reactive) and the commitment attitudes. Labeling the avoidant, dissonant, and dependent attitudes with the term *commitment* may be misleading as it is unclear in the reconceptualized model how they operate in relation to the racial orientations. Embedded in the model is the notion of attitude change, in which the process may be viewed as similar to what is found in the social psychology literature. This process may need to be made more explicit, so that it isn't viewed as a developmental process (Block & Carter, 1996).

The revised WRC model has received some empirical support. Four dissertations were found that used the ORAS. One study (Schmidt, 2007) found that the reactive attitude type was associated with higher levels of ego development, whereas lower ego development was linked to the avoidant attitude type. The remaining studies focused on white racial attitudes to multicultural education/ training and various professional groups. Loya (2007) reported that approximately a third of professional social workers' responses to the ORAS had categorized them as holding a negative racial attitude type (e.g., dominative). College students taking a multicultural education course had increased reactive attitudes over time than did those students taking a general education course (Weathersby, 2005). Furthermore, women were found to have higher reactive attitudes than were men, and men had higher dominative and conflictive attitudes than did women. Fierstien (2004) also found

that integrative and reactive attitudes were associated with cultural awareness, whereas conflictive attitudes were negatively associated with cultural awareness.

These findings are promising, especially for the potential impact on multicultural education and training, but continued systematic research is needed. For example, is changing attitudes enough? Does attitudinal change actually lead to behavioral changes in the interactions and cultural lifestyle of people? One of the criticisms of WRI models is their use of minority identity development models to create a model about whites' racial attitudes (Rowe et al., 1994, 1995). Is there a relationship between racial attitudes and RGO—social affiliation patterns? No assumptions are made in the WRC model about racial attitudes and psychological adjustment. Rowe and his colleagues (1994, 1995, LaFleur et al., 2002; Leach et al., 2002) have contended that the WRC model is fundamentally different from the WRI models, especially Helms' (1990, 1995). However, Block and Carter (1996) have refuted that contention, deeming the WRC a variant of WRI. Both views have been supported in that Pope-Davis et al. (1999) found that the WRI measure, the WRAIS, and the WRC measure, the ORAS-P, tapped similar and dissimilar constructs. As the current WRC measure, the ORAS, is different from the preliminary form, further research is needed to demonstrate the differences between the WRI and WRC models, not only through scale work but in examining the WRC constructs in relation to various sociocorrelates. It is important to illuminate more clearly how whites view racial/ ethnic minorities, as societal views about race/ ethnicity continue to change. Another significant step in WRC research would be to examine how whites view other whites holding different racial attitudes from their own. Such perspective taking research might have implications in better understanding whites' racial attitudes about themselves and others.

Roots of Ethnic Identity: Social Identity Theory

As previously mentioned, ethnic identity has a much briefer history in counseling psychology compared to racial identity. However, scholarly interest in ethnic identity has a much longer history outside of counseling psychology, with social psychological roots that can be traced back to the social identity theory of Henri Tajfel (1978). Tajfel defines social identity as "that part of the individuals' self-concept which derives from their knowledge of their membership of a social group (or groups) together with the value and emotional significance of that membership (Tajfel, 1981, p. 255). Tajfel along with his student John Turner (Tajfel & Turner, 1979) sought to explain how and why social groups formed, and how social identity contributed to intergroup relations, especially conflicts. Tajfel and Turner proposed that individuals identify with groups for several reasons, and these reasons make up the four elements of social identity theory: categorization, identification, comparison, and psychological distinctiveness. According to social identity theory, individuals have a natural tendency to categorize themselves into in-groups and out-groups, and identifying with in-groups boosts self-esteem. Social identity theory posits that individuals also tend to compare their in-groups with out-groups, with the outcome often being a more positive evaluation or a favorable bias toward their in-groups. Individuals want the groups to which they belong to be distinct from, and positively compared to, groups to which they do not belong. Thus, social identity theory was created to understand the psychology of intergroup discrimination and prejudice.

The social identities of ethnic minorities have been characterized as one of two American prototypes: assimilation and the remnants of legalized discrimination (Sears, Fu, Henry, & Bui, 2003). The assimilation prototype is based largely on European immigrants, and involves a reduction of ethnically or culturally based traits (e.g., fluency in language, intraethnic friendships) while exhibiting an increase in behaviors (e.g., interethnic marriage and interethnic friendships) that fall in line with the American ideology of the melting pot. The remnants of legalized discrimination prototype is based primarily on the African American experience, with people who have a unique American experience that includes slavery and Jim Crow segregation before experiencing equal rights (Sears et al.). The uniqueness of the African American experience is also evidenced by blacks being the targets of the most negative racial attitudes and of having the lowest rates of intermarriage among all ethnic groups (Sears et al., 2000).

Ethnic Identity

Ethnic identity is one of the most researched social identities in the social science literature (Galkina, n.d.). Although ethnic identity is a popular social identity among social scientists, ethnicity remains an elusive and difficult construct to define (Cokley, 2007; Helms & Talleyrand, 1997). The difficulty in defining ethnicity is due in part to its history of instability and malleability. Cokley, citing the Office of Management and Budget (1995), gave Asian Indians as one example of this malleability because they have been classified as Hindus, white, and Asian or Pacific Islander in various census counts during the 20th century. The malleability of ethnicity, and by extension its corollary ethnic identity, have contributed to the lack of a cohesive, general theoretical framework for understanding ethnic identity (Galkina, n.d.). However, an argument can be made that a general theory of ethnic identity may be theoretically and methodologically impractical because the development of ethnic identity across ethnic groups differs with respect to social context, cultural experiences, historical context, and values (Cokley; 2007; Galkina, n.d.). Nevertheless, there is an interest in developing a general theoretical framework for understanding ethnic identity. The most influential work in this area has been the program of research conducted by Jean Phinney.

Ethnicity and Ethnic Identity

One of Phinney's most important conceptual contributions was unpacking the construct of ethnicity (Phinney, 1996). In her seminal article, Phinney acknowledged the growing importance of ethnicity in American life and wanted to more clearly understand what ethnicity meant, so that there could be a clearer understanding of how ethnic group membership impacted psychological outcomes. Phinney believed that ethnicity was psychologically important, and she identified three aspects that contributed to its psychological importance. These three aspects included ethnicity as culture, ethnicity as identity, and ethnicity as minority status. Ethnicity as culture refers to the norms, values, attitudes, and behaviors that characterize and are embraced by an ethnic group. Ethnicity as identity refers to the strength of identification an individual has with her or his ethnic group. Ethnicity as minority status refers to the experiences of ethnic groups of color living in a country in which they have been historically marginalized, under-represented, and discriminated against. She concludes by suggesting that researchers should discontinue the practice of treating ethnicity as a simple categorical variable rather than as a complex, multidimensional construct. Individuals who are truly interested in the psychological implications of ethnicity are best served by examining one of the three dimensions that she identified. In her own line of research, Phinney has chosen to focus on ethnicity as identity, otherwise known as ethnic identity.

The first major review of ethnic identity research was conducted by Phinney (1990). In that review, Phinney characterized the ethnic identity literature as "fragmentary" and "inconclusive," in large part because researchers from different disciplines were largely unaware of each other's work, so there was often duplication of effort; follow-up studies were rarely undertaken to improve instruments or elaborate on concepts; and (3) there was no generally agreed upon definition of ethnic identity. One obvious tendency in the review was the interchangeable usage of the terms ethnic identity and racial identity. Phinney has made the argument that ethnicity and race should be combined into a superordinate construct because ethnicity subsumes race (Phinney, 1990, 1996). Her assumption is that ethnic identity and racial identity are essentially the same construct. This assumption has sparked debate and disagreement in the field by several scholars (Cokley, 2005; Helms & Talleyrand, 1997; Parham, 2002). Although not providing a general definition of ethnic identity, Phinney (1990) identified important aspects of ethnic identity that included self-identification, belonging and commitment, sense of shared attitudes and values, attitudes toward one's group, and cultural aspects such as language, behavior, values, and knowledge of group history.

Phinney next sought to identify the major conceptual frameworks used to study ethnic identity. She identified social identity theory, acculturation and culture conflict, and identity formation as the major conceptual frameworks; however, it should also be noted that she identified approximately 25% of the studies as having no theoretical framework. Social identity theory and identity formation (e.g., Cross's Nigrescence model) have already been briefly reviewed, so we will turn our attention to acculturation. Phinney indicated that ethnic identity is only meaningful "in situations in which two or more ethnic groups are in contact over a period of time" (p. 501). This is noteworthy because in countries that are relatively ethnically homogeneous, such as Greece, South Korea, and Japan, ethnic identity is not a particularly salient concept. Phinney further indicated that very little distinction has been made between ethnic identity and acculturation. For purposes of conceptual clarity, ethnic identity can be thought of as one aspect of acculturation, and is most appropriately

conceptualized at the individual level, whereas acculturation is conceptualized at the group level (Phinney, 1990). Phinney makes the case that acculturation should be used as a framework for understanding and studying ethnic identity. Using Berry et al.'s (1986) acculturation framework, Phinney (1990) stated that an individual could have a strong or weak identification with his or her ethnic group, while also having a strong or weak identification with the majority group. Individuals who strongly identify with both the majority group and their ethnic group are acculturated or bicultural. Individuals who strongly identify with the majority group and weakly identify with their ethnic group are assimilated. Individuals who weakly identify with the majority group but strongly identify with their ethnic group are separated and dissociated. Individuals who weakly identify with both the majority group and their ethnic group are marginalized. Culture conflict becomes an issue as ethnic groups come into contact with each other, and this conflict influences ethnic identity formation (Phinney, 1990).

Ethnic Identity and Developmental Theory

Although Phinney's conceptualization of ethnic identity can be considered a framework and perhaps a model, there remain questions about whether her formulation can truly be considered a theory. Additionally, there remains a question of whether Phinney's conceptualization of ethnic identity remains true to its Eriksonian influences (Umana-Taylor, Yazedijian, & Bamaca-Gomez, 2004). In the first article that includes a thorough critique of Phinney's theoretical work, Umana-Taylor et al. review Phinney's operationalization of ethnic identity to determine to what degree it is consistent with Erikson's theory of identity formation vis à vis Marcia's (1980, 1994) operationalization (i.e., four identity statuses of diffused, foreclosed, moratorium, and achieved). Umana-Taylor points out that Erikson's (1968) theory of identity formation emphasizes exploration and commitment as central elements of identity formation. They further argued that Erikson's theory does not assume that commitment to an identity was always or necessarily positive. Commitment simply means that identity exploration has been resolved. Next, they cited Marcia's four identity statuses, which operationalized the work of Erikson. Characterizing Phinney's work on ethnic identity as a three-stage model, they briefly reviewed Phinney's (1989) article, which used a qualitative methodology to code interviews of adolescents. The results were three identifiable "stages": diffusion/foreclosure, moratorium, and achieved. The first stage, diffusion/foreclosure, characterizes individuals who have not really critically thought about or explored their ethnic identity. Instead, they have simply internalized the dominant society's view of them, or they have never been exposed to other ethnic groups. The second stage, moratorium, characterizes individuals who have begun to explore their ethnic identity. The third stage, achievement, characterizes individuals who have resolved their feelings about their ethnic identity and what it means to them.

The crux of Umana-Taylor's critique of Phinney's work lies in what she sees as a discrepancy between Phinney's theoretical model of ethnic identity and the way she measures ethnic identity. These measurement issues form the basis of Umana-Taylor's conceptualization of ethnic identity and will be addressed later in the chapter.

Implications for Counseling

Ethnic and racial identity research should not simply be conducted for the sake of conducting research. Theoretical debates and disagreements about measurement issues should be waged to ultimately improve counseling outcomes for all ethnic and racial groups. As Cokley (2007) noted, racial and ethnic identity research should be evaluated, in part, on the development of efficacious clinical interventions. A review of the literature regarding racial and ethnic identity and counseling implications reveals three interesting trends. First, a disproportionate amount of this research has focused either on the racial identity attitudes of white counselors in training (e.g., Burkard, Ponterotto, Reynolds, & Alfonso, 1999; Burkard, Juarez-Huffaker, & Ajmere, 2003; Carter & Helms, 1992; Constantine, 2002; Constantine, Warren, & Miville, 2005; Middleton et al., 2005; Ottavi, Pope-Davis, & Dings, 1994; Utsey & Gernat, 2002) or the racial identity attitudes of black students and clients (e.g., Carter & Helms, 1992; Ford, Harris III, & Schuerger, 1993; Franklin, 1999; Hargrow, 2001; Ponterotto, Anderson, & Grieger, 1986; Richardson & Helms, 1994) with very little interest in other groups (e.g., Alvarez & Kimura, 2001). The second trend is that the majority of this research has been published in counselor education journals such as the *Journal of Counseling and Development*, the *Journal of Multicultural Counseling and Development*, *Counselor Education and Supervision*, and the *Journal of Mental Health Counseling*, with

relatively little work being published in the *JCP* or the TCP. The third trend is that relatively little work has been done on ethnic identity and counseling implications (e.g., Bowen, Christensen, Powers, Graves, & Anderson, 1998; McNeill et al., 2001; Yeh & Hwang, 2000).

Regarding the first trend, a logical area of inquiry is how the racial identity attitudes of both the client and the counselor interact to impact therapy. A question that arises is whether clients whose racial identity attitudes reflect a predominant outlook or worldview would be better matches for counselors who share conceptually similar racial identity attitudes. For example, would a black client who holds predominantly pre-encounter attitudes be best matched with a white counselor who holds predominantly contact racial identity attitudes? The question is a difficult one to answer, and does not easily lend itself to empirical investigation. Along these lines, do racial identity attitudes, especially WRI attitudes, impact the therapeutic working alliance, as asserted by prominent multicultural scholars (e.g., Helms, 1984; Sue & Sue, 1990)?

The first (and perhaps only) attempt to incorporate racial identity attitudes into a typology of counseling relationships was offered by Helms' black–white interactional model (1984). In that typology, Helms describes four relationship types involving black and WRI development: parallel, progressive, regressive, and crossed. A *parallel relationship* is characterized by the counselor and client having similar racial identity attitudes. A *progressive relationship* is characterized by the counselor being at least one stage more advanced than the client. A *regressive relationship* is characterized by the client being at least one stage more advanced than the counselor. A *crossed relationship* is characterized by the counselor and client having opposite racial identity attitudes toward blacks and whites (i.e., whites have more positive attitudes toward blacks and blacks have more positive attitudes toward whites). The premise of Helms' interactional model is that the four different relationship types are "associated with different counselor cognitive and behavioral strategies, client reactions, and both participants' experience of the sessions and affective responses" (Carter & Helms, p. 196).

Using participants who were workshop attendees, Carter and Helms (1992) tested Helms' typology using several measures, including the Racial Identity Attitude Scale and the White Racial Identity Attitudes Inventory. Based on the highest percentile scores, counselor–client pair types were assigned to one of the four relationship types, which included various racial combinations (i.e., black therapist and black client; white therapist and white client; white therapist and white client; and black therapist and white client). Carter and Helms (1992) emphasize that racial identity attitudes, rather than race, were used to classify relationship types. The end result was 17 parallel relationships, seven progressive relationships, nine regressive relationships, and no crossed relationships. Conducting multiple correlation analyses between client reactions, therapist intentions, session evaluation, and affective measures, they found evidence for differential significant correlations among the relationship types. In spite of the methodological limitations of conducting multiple, sample-dependent correlation analyses that increase the possibility of type I errors (which they acknowledged), Carter and Helms concluded that the study provided evidence that black and WRI attitudes can be used to understand counseling interactions.

In one of the few empirical tests of Helms' interactional model, Constantine, Warren, and Miville (2005) examined 50 supervisory dyads that consisted of white supervisors and white supervisees. They hypothesized that supervisees in parallel-high and progressive racial supervision dyads would report greater multicultural counseling competency and demonstrate better multicultural case conceptualization than would supervisees in regressive and parallel-low racial supervision dyads. They found support for three of their hypotheses (with the exception being the regressive racial supervision dyad), and concluded that there was support for Helms' interactional model. In their discussion, they point out the negative consequences of white counselors who are low in racial consciousness (i.e., have less sophisticated racial identity attitudes). These negative consequences include dismissing or devaluing racial and cultural issues presented in supervision or counseling relationships, the higher likelihood of clinical misdiagnosis because of lack of awareness and understanding of cultural issues, and developing inadequate treatment plans that do not address important cultural issues (Constantine et al., 2005).

Another popular area of inquiry has been to examine the relationship of WRI with multicultural counseling competencies. Several studies have shown that more "mature" or "sophisticated" WRI attitudes are positively associated with self-reported multicultural counseling competencies

(Constantine, 2002; Ottavi, Pope-Davis, & Dings, 1994; Middleton et al., 2005). Emphasis is placed on self-reported because it is entirely possible, and in fact probable, that individuals overestimated their degree of multicultural counseling competence. Research has shown that four self-reported multicultural competency instruments are significantly correlated with a measure of social desirability, and once social desirability is controlled for none of these measures was significantly related to multicultural counseling case conceptualization (Constantine & Ladany, 2000). Therefore, it is still not clear whether more "sophisticated" WRI attitudes are truly related to higher multicultural counseling competencies.

In perhaps the most detailed discussion of the counseling implications of racial identity to date, Franklin (1999) examined the role of racial identity development using a single case example of an African American man. Avoiding the temptation to simply and formulaically apply Cross's Nigrescence stages to the case example, Franklin writes an intricate narrative about how general race awareness and race consciousness can be viewed as a healthy and adaptive response to racism and racialized environments. Franklin makes the observation that what is missing from racial identity development theory, relevant to clinical work, is understanding about the individual's intrapsychic process when race is made salient. Nevertheless, he argues that racial identity development is a protective factor against racism. Encounters of racism and discrimination, while harmful, often result in African Americans engaging in a "sanity check" (Franklin, 1999, p. 781) that involves discussing racist or racialized experiences with each other to receive support and validation. These sanity checks, followed by validation, foster personal resilience. In the case example, Franklin describes his client as having attitudes that were consistent with the immersion-emersion ego profile (e.g., being reactive and outspoken about racial slights and discrimination). His client was angry because of a racialized incident he experienced with a white woman on an elevator. His anger came from his awareness and knowledge of the history of racial oppression that has impacted African Americans, and knowing that no matter how he presented himself he will always be feared because he is a black man. His sanity check was discussing the incident with another African American man who, because of his difference in temperament and style, offered a more forgiving perspective. Franklin deduces that his client's colleague exhibited a racial identity ego profile consistent with either the latter phase of the immersion-emersion ego profile or the internalization ego profile. This article was a sophisticated application of how racial identity development theory can be used with other culturally relevant themes to enhance the counseling process and clinical interventions with African Americans.

It is clear that much more work needs to be conducted to better understand the clinical implications of racial and ethnic identity. It might be generally stated that clients with strong ethnic and racial identities may feel dissatisfaction and frustration with counselors who either ignore or are not comfortable with addressing racial identity issues. Similarly, counselors who have strong ethnic and racial identities may also feel frustration with clients who are at low levels of racial or ethnic identity, and deny or minimize the impact of racial/ethnic discrimination in their lives. In either case, it is still not well known exactly how the racial and/or ethnic identity of the client and counselor impacts a counseling session.

Measurement Issues for Racial Identity

The popularity of racial identity models has resulted in a proliferation of racial identity measures. Predictably, the increased attention to racial identity models has resulted in closer scrutiny of racial identity instruments, in which psychometric concerns have contributed to some of the most intense scholarly debates in this area of research.

Black Racial Identity Attitudes Scales

THEORETICAL BASE AND SCALE

The BRIAS (formerly RIAS-B; Parham & Helms, 1981; Helms & Parham, 1996) is designed to measure four of the five BRI attitudes as delineated in the original Nigrescence model (Cross, 1971): pre-encounter, encounter, immersion-emersion, and internalization. The first BRIAS, Form A, contains 30 items and is based on the Q-sort items created by Hall, Cross, and Freedle (1972). Two subsequent BRIAS versions were developed, another 30-item one, Form B (factor analytically derived) and a 50-item Long Form to increase the internal consistency estimates of the BRIAS scores (Helms & Parham, 1996).

Instructions for taking the measures as well as the rating range of 5 points (1 = *Strongly Disagree* to 5 = *Strongly Agree*) are the same for all versions. The forms, as also observed by Fischer and Moradi (2001), are not equivalent, and some of the items

belong to multiple subscales or different subscales, depending on the version used. Individual subscale scores are computed, but no total score is given. Higher scores on any of the subscale indicate an endorsement of the specific racial identity attitude.

PSYCHOMETRIC BASE

Limited methodological information is available on the scale development of the BRAIS. Form A was developed with a sample of 58 black college students in the Midwest (Helms, 1990), and across three samples, reliability estimates ranged from .50 (encounter) to .80 (internalization; Helms & Parham, 1996). A four-factor solution of Form A resulted in the creation of Form B (Helms & Parham, 1996), which was based on two samples of black college students (Helms & Parham, 1996). Exploratory factor analyses (EFA) criteria were not reported. Additional construct validity was based on the correlational pattern between parallel scales of the BRIAS and Developmental Inventory of Black Consciousness (DIBC; Milliones, 1980; Grace, 1984). Internal consistency scores of the BRIAS subscales, compiled from previous reviews, reveal the following: .37 to .72 for Form A (Sabnani & Ponterotto, 1992); .41 to .79 for Form B (Fischer & Moradi, 2001; Sabnani & Ponterotto, 1992); and .27 to .86 for the Long Form (Fischer & Moradi, 2001; Sabnani & Ponterotto, 1992). Score reliability of the encounter subscale on any of the forms has been the most variable: .27 to .72. Factor analysis of the BRIAS forms has provided support for three of the four subscales, but not encounter (Form A; Ponterotto & Wise, 1987; Form B; Yanico, Swanson, & Tokar, 1994; Long Form; Stevenson, 1995; Tokar & Fischer, 1998). The amount of total variance accounted for has been small, ranging from 20% (Yanico et al., 1994) to 30.5% (Ponterotto & Wise, 1987). The four-factor structure tested through confirmatory factor analysis has not been supported (e.g., goodness of fit index [GFI] = .65; comparative fit index [CFI] = .48, standardized root mean square residual [SRMR] = .012; Tokar & Fischer, 1998). Two studies (Tokar & Fischer, 1998; Yanico et al., 1994) also reported a restriction in range of scores on pre-encounter and internalization, with more respondents disagreeing with the pre-encounter items and more agreeing with the internalization items. Also, a social desirability methods effect was found to structurally contaminate the pre-encounter construct in the Long form (Fischer, Tokar, & Serna, 1998). Numerous studies have been noted in providing support or mixed support for convergent and discriminant validity of the BRIAS (Fischer & Moradi, 2001; Fischer et al., 1998; Ponterotto, Fuertes, & Chen, 2000; Sabnani & Ponterotto, 1992) to an array of sociocultural variables (i.e., psychological health, racism, self-esteem, counselor preference, and vocational variables). Findings, however, have been met with caution due to the psychometric concerns of the measure.

For the past 20 years, ongoing psychometric evaluations of the BRIAS have raised concerns about its viability as a measure (Cokley, 2007; Fischer & Moradi, 2001; Fischer et al., 1998; Lemon & Waehler, 1996; Ponterotto, Fuertes, & Chen, 2000; Ponterotto & Wise, 1987; Sabnani & Ponterotto, 1992; Stokes et al., 1998; Tokar & Fischer, 1998; Yanico et al., 1994). However, Helms (1996, 1997, 1999, 2005, 2007; Helms, Henze, Sass, & Mifsud, 2006) has questioned the adequacy of classical test theory methods in capturing the validity of complex and dynamic racial identity constructs. Cokley (2007), in response, notes that the primary problems with the measurement of racial identity lie in the rigid allegiance to an established ideology about racial identity and its outcome when it is measured.

EVALUATION

The BRIAS has been the most used racial identity measure over the past 25 years. At the time of its development, the BRIAS offered an avenue for social scientists to test models of racial identity and to move cultural research beyond using racial classification as the primary predictor of cultural and psychological issues. The accumulated evidence indicates that the BRIAS is no longer a viable instrument for two major reasons. One, the scales have not substantially changed since their development, despite the evaluation of their psychometric limitations. Two, the theory to which the scale is grounded is outdated. Is the original Nigrescence model viable 37 years later? In fact, the RIAS scales do not tap the advances that Helms made to the Nigrescence model (see the review on Helms' BRI model). As sociopolitical issues of the world have evolved, blacks in America have changed as well. The viability of any incarnations of the RIAS must be based on new iterations of the theory, as well as the scales. Using the additional statistical methods that Helms (2007) has highlighted, as well as the increased use of sound qualitative research methods as recommended by Ponterotto et al. (2001)—in essence a multimethod approach to racial identity—might

prove fruitful in understanding better the complexity and measurement of BRI in relation to critical counseling psychology issues.

Cross Racial Identity Scale

THEORETICAL BASE

The CRIS (Vandiver et al., 2000) was developed over a 5-year period across six phases of scale work and is designed to measure racial identity attitudes *only* articulated in the expanded Nigrescence model (Cross & Vandiver, 2001). Three attitudes are not included in the scale. Validity work continues on the immersion-emersion intense black involvement and internalization multiculturalist racial measures. The biculturalist attitude is not measured due to its linkage to the multiculturalist inclusive attitude and the limitations in empirically delineating the two constructs well (Cross & Vandiver, 2001; Vandiver et al., 2001, 2002). Finally, a developmental process is not assumed or measured in the CRIS.

SCALE

The 40-item CRIS consists of six subscales, which are composed of five items each (30 scorable items): pre-encounter assimilation, miseducation, and self-hatred; immersion-emersion anti-white; and internationalization Afrocentric and multiculturalist inclusive. Ten filler items, which are not scorable, are dispersed throughout the scale "to minimize response bias and to diminish the obviousness of the CRIS items" (Cross & Vandiver, 2001, p. 387). Respondents are asked to rate each statement on a 7-point Likert scale from 1 (strongly disagree) to 7 (strongly agree). Scoring and interpretations are summarized by Cross and Vandiver (2001) and are delineated in the second edition of the CRIS manual (Worrell, Vandiver, & Cross, 2004). Strict guidelines are provided in using the CRIS. Modifications in wording, which is crucial in the design of the scale, are not permitted as these invalidate scores obtained. Also, no total CRIS score can be created, and the six subscale scores are used together unless construct validity work is being conducted. Thus, multivariate analyses are the expected statistical procedures to use. The CRIS is designed as a multidimensional scale, which is believed to reflect the view that racial identity attitudes are complex and cannot be reflected by one score.

PSYCHOMETRIC BASE

Establishing psychometric support for the CRIS is ongoing, but the initial validity findings provide strong support for its use. For a detailed account of the scale development process, readers are directed to the July 2001 special issue of the *Journal of Multicultural Counseling and Development* (Cross & Vandiver, 2001; Vandiver & Worrell, 2001; Vandiver et al., 2002). Cronbach's α for the final version of the CRIS ranged from .78 (miseducation) to .89 (anti-white), subscale intercorrelations ranged from |.01| to |.55| (anti-white and Afrocentric). Structural validity was established through a series of exploratory factor analyses (EFA) and supported through confirmatory factor analyses (CFA; CFI = .94; root mean square error of approximation [RMSEA] 90% confidence interval [CI] = .043, .055). Initial convergent validity was based on correlations between the CRIS subscales and the subscales of the Multidimensional Inventory of black Identity (MIBI; Sellers et al., 1998), another measure of BRI. Discriminant validity was based on no statistically significant correlation between social desirability, self-esteem, and the Big Five and most of the CRIS subscales. However, the expected pattern between the CRIS subscales and global self-esteem (Rosenberg Self-Esteem; Rosenberg, 1965) was supported: Only a meaningful relationship was found between high self-hatred scores and low global self-esteem scores.

RECENT VALIDITY WORK

Since the initial validity work, 11 other validity studies have been conducted on the CRIS and approximately 25 dissertations, via PsychInfo, were found that have used the CRIS. Adequacy of score reliabilities for the CRIS across nine studies have been supported, with values ranging from .70 (assimilation) to .89 (self-hatred and anti-white; Worrell &Watson; 2008), and test–retest reliabilities over a 6-week period have been found to range from .73 (multiculturalist) to .86 (assimilation; Vandiver, 2007). Four structural validity studies, using EFAs with different populations, have replicated the expected six-factor solution: a middle and high school sample (Gardner-Kit & Worrell, 2007), a sample of college students (Simmons, Worrell, & Berry, in press), a sample of college students and adults (Helm, 2002), and an adult sample (Worrell, Vandiver, Cross, & Fhagen-Smith, 2004). Using CFA, Worrell and Watson (in press) also supported the six-factor structure (CFI = .94; RMSEA = .037).

Several convergent validity studies have provided mixed support for the CRIS and the expanded model. The CRIS and MIBI seem to tap similar

constructs of black attitudes, as well as different constructs (Helm, 2002). Cokley (2002) found that negative and positive black stereotypes were correlated to CRIS attitudes. Simmons et al. (in press) found support for Afrocentric, multiculturalist inclusive and self-hatred based on the correlational pattern between the African Self-Consciousness Scale (Baldwin & Bell, 1982), MIBI (Sellers, Rowley, Chavous, Shelton, & Smith, 1997), and the CRIS. Two studies examined the construct validity between the CRIS and Multigroup Ethnic Identity Measure (MEIM; Phinney, 1992) scores. Worrell and Gardner-Kit (2006) found two patterns between the measures: black/racial ethnic identification and grounded multiculturalism, as did Cokley (2005) between racial identity (CRIS), ethnic identity, Afrocentric values, and stereotyping of blacks: a nonracialized ethnic identity and a racialized ethnic identity. Most recent work on the CRIS focuses on its application. Worrell's (2008) cross-sectional analysis of CRIS scores across three age groups (adolescents, emerging adults, and adults) supported factorial congruence among the six factors and reported similarities and differences in CRIS across age groups. As noted earlier, cluster analyses of the CRIS scores (Vandiver et al., 2007; Worrell et al., 2006) have resulted in finding four clusters replicated across four samples and may have implications in how the CRIS is scored, interpreted, and used.

EVALUATION

Alexander and Suzuki (2001) complimented the CRIS for its orthogonal subscales, and the strong reliability and validity of the subscale scores, but were concerned that the encounter and internalization-commitment stages were not measured, thus limiting the full measurement of NT-E. Recently, several reviews of racial and ethnic identity measurements have evaluated the psychometric strengths of the CRIS (Burkard & Ponterotto, 2008; Cokley, 2007; Ponterotto & Park-Taylor, 2007), highlighting it as an example of best practice in scale development. Despite the kudos, continued work is needed on the CRIS. Several studies have raised questions about the definitional clarity and validity of the Afrocentric (Cokley, 2002, 2005, Helm, 2002) and multiculturalist (Helm, 2002) subscales. Does the Afrocentric subscale actually measure the Afrocentric construct or something else, such as racialized stereotyping? More construct work is needed in understanding the relationship between ethnic and racial identity, given that the CRIS taps a specific racial identity and the MEIM taps a broad perspective of ethnicity. Longitudinal studies are needed to understand the process of racial identity development (Worrell, 2008) and its connection to parent–child racial socialization (Stevenson, 1998; Worrell, 2008). As the makeup of blacks (the influx of people from the Caribbean and Africa and increased numbers of biracial and multiracial children) in America change, examining self-labeling and racial identity is another needed area of study. The racial makeup of blacks, as well as the racial/ethnic makeup of the U.S. population as a whole, may have implications in the wording of items in the CRIS and its subsequent revalidation.

Multidimensional Inventory of Black Identity

THEORETICAL BASE AND SCALE

The MIBI (Sellers et., 1997) is a 56-item instrument designed to measure BRI as articulated in the MMRI (Sellers et al., 1998). The model consists of seven dimensions made up of four ideologies (i.e., nationalist, assimilationist, humanist, and oppressed minority), private regard, public regard, and racial centrality. Although researchers can use all 56 items, much of the research conducted by Sellers and his colleagues has used only specific subscales in accord with the research questions being asked. This usage is consistent with social psychological approaches, but stands in contrast to the use of racial identity instruments in counseling psychology, in which the authors discourage the sole use of any single subscale.

Instructions for completing MIBI include completing a set of items based on a 7-point Likert scale, with response options ranging from 1 (strongly disagree) to 7 (strongly agree). Higher scores on any of the subscales indicate an endorsement of the specific racial identity attitude.

PSYCHOMETRIC BASE

The original psychometric study conducted by Sellers et al. (1997) reported an exploratory factor analysis of a 71-item instrument. Sellers et al. attempted to find a three-factor solution to correspond with the three stable dimensions (i.e., centrality, ideology, and regard) proposed by the MMRI, but the initial exploratory factor analysis resulted in Kaiser-Meyer-Olkin (KMO) values of less than .60. Therefore, the factor analysis reported in the 1997 article was only conducted on the ideology subscales. Based on the results of the factor analysis, the "final" version of the MIBI

included 51 items that made up four ideology subscales, the centrality subscale, and the private regard subscale. The public regard subscale was dropped due to only having two items. Reliability estimates ranged from .60 to .79. Predictive validity was determined by finding that several race-related behaviors (e.g., having an African American best friend, enrolling in Black Studies classes, interracial contact) were related to the MIBI dimensions in theoretically predictable ways. In an attempt to conduct a more rigorous psychometric study, Cokley and Helm (2001) conducted a CFA on a 56-item version of the MIBI. Unlike Sellers et al. (1997), Cokley and Helm conducted the CFA on all of the items, rather than on the three dimensions (i.e., centrality, ideology, and regard) separately. Thus, the data were fit to the seven-dimensional MMRI. The initial fit index values were poor (i.e., normed factor index [NFI] = .53, CFI = .68, SRMR = .097). Modification of the model based on several misfitting parameters only slightly improved the fit index values (i.e., NFI = .56, CFI = .71, SRMR = .09). Concurrent validity was demonstrated through theoretically consistent relationships with the African Self-Consciousness Scale. Reliability estimates ranged from .72 to .83.

EVALUATION

The MIBI represents a viable alternative with which to study racial identity with African Americans. As pointed out by Cokley (2007), it is important to approach the study of racial identity using different models and instruments. The centrality and private regard subscales are particularly useful for researchers interested in a brief assessment of racial identity. However, concerns still remain about the construct validity of the assimilationist and nationalist subscales. As an item analysis by Cokley and Helm (2001) revealed, attempts to place items into specific racial identity dimensions by individuals familiar with the model produced mixed results, which at least partially explained why the CFA results were mediocre. Issues of definitional and theoretical clarity surrounding the four ideologies remain, and a review of the literature reveals that Sellers et al. have yet to respond, either theoretically or empirically, to the concerns raised. As mentioned earlier, counseling psychologists have not often used the MIBI in research (except as support for validity in scale development), most likely because its theoretical foundation does not easily lend itself to mental health applications. Nevertheless, the MIBI could easily be applied to other areas germane to counseling psychology, such as career counseling, vocational psychology, and academic achievement.

People of Color Identity Attitude Scale

THEORETICAL BASE AND SCALE

The PRIAS (Helms, 1995) is a 50-item scale designed to measure the racial identity attitudes of Asian, black, Hispanic, and American Indians, as delineated in the POC racial identity model (Helms, 1995). Four subscales make up the PRIAS: conformity (minimization of race; 11 items); dissonance (confusion and beginning awareness of race; 14 items); immersion-emersion (idealization of one's racial group; 15 items); and internalization (intellectualized view about race; 10 items). The internalization subscale also contains items reflective of the fifth status, integrative awareness in the POC model (Lo, 2005). Items are rated on a 5-point Likert scale (*Strongly Disagree* = 1 to *Strongly Agree* = 5), and four subscale scores are computed instead of a total score. Higher subscale score indicates higher preference for the specific racial attitude.

PSYCHOMETRIC BASE

The PRIAS evolved from an earlier racial identity measure called the Visible Racial/Ethnic Identity Attitude Scale (VIAS; Helms & Carter, 1985), which was formerly called the Cultural Identity Attitudes Scale (CIAS; Helms & Carter, 1990). At this time, no published summary of the scale development of the PRIAS and its psychometric properties exists. Several studies have used the measure and provide some information about its validity (Alvarez, Juang, & Liang, 2006; Bianchi, Zea, Belgrave, & Echeverry, 2002; Bryant & Baker, 2003; Chen, LePhuoc, Guzman, Rude, & Dodd, 2006; Juni, Bresnan, & Vescio, 2006; Liu, 2002; Lo, 2005). Cronbach's α have ranged from .61 (conformity) to .86 (internalization/integrative) and are based on samples of various racial/ethnic groups, such as Asian Americans, black Brazilians, Lumbee Native Americans, and Hispanic Americans. Most subscale intercorrelations have ranged between .20 and .30, with the largest correlations usually between conformity and dissonance (e.g., .49 or .53). Three exploratory factor analyses have been reported on the PRIAS. Two studies (Lumbee Indians; Bryant & Baker, 2003; mixture of racial groups; Lo, 2005) reported a four-factor solution that accounted for 19% and 37% of the total variance, respectively; used an outdated factor selection method (eigenvalue rule of 1); and had numerous items (12–20) with complex loadings. One cluster analysis, using Asian American adults, has been conducted and supports a four-cluster solution, reflective of the named subscales (Chen et al., 2006). Several published studies and over a dozen dissertations have used the PRIAS, providing support or partial support for the PRIAS constructs and expected relationships: self-esteem (Bianchi et al., 2002; Yacoubian, 2004), ethnicity-related stress (Lo, 2005), racism-related stress and color-blind attitudes (Chen et al., 2006), racial socialization and racism (Alvarez et al., 2006), and gender role conflict and male role norms (Liu, 2002). No meaningful correlations were found between the PRIAS and a social desirability measure.

EVALUATION

The strength of the PRIAS is that it is grounded in theory, but one of its limitations is that it is measuring only four of the five statuses delineated in the POC model. Integrative awareness items have been folded into the internalization subscale. More clarity is needed in understanding what the internalization subscale is measuring. Score reliability and validity seem to reflect reasonable estimates, but some concerns exist about the structural validity. One, outdated factor retention criteria were used; two, the factor structures accounted for a small percent of the total variance; and three, approximately 25%–40% of the items had complex loadings on other factors, thus blurring the dimensionality of the constructs. As a result, other factor analytic studies are warranted, using diverse samples as well as same race/ethnic samples. Although this scale has been in existence in some iteration for almost 20 years, more empirical work, and possibly revisions, on the PRIAS is needed to ensure that the findings obtained are reliable and valid.

White Racial Identity Attitudes Scale

THEORETICAL BASE AND SCALE

The White Racial Identity Attitudes Scale (WRIAS; Helms & Carter, 1990) was originally designed to measure the five stages, now statuses, of WRI development proposed by Helms (1984): contact, disintegration, reintegration, pseudo-independence, and autonomy. Another stage (immersion-emersion) was added, resulting in a six-stage model (Helms & Carter, 1990). The WRIAS is composed of 50 items, 10 items per subscale, and all items are rated on a 5-point Likert scale (1 = *Strongly Disagree* to 5 = *Strongly Agree*). Subscale scores are computed, but no total score. Higher scores on any of the subscales indicate an endorsement of the specific racial identity attitude. The content of the items focuses on whites' perceptions of and interactions with blacks.

PSYCHOMETRIC BASE

No information is available on the development and selection of items for the WRIAS, other than that the scale was rationally derived and that items had to have "a minimum item-total subscale correlation with its own scale of .30" (Helms & Carter, 1990, p. 68). The initial psychometric findings were based on a pilot study and two other studies with white college students. In the pilot study, internal consistency reliability estimates for the WRIAS subscale scores were reported to be above .90 (Helms & Carter, 1990). Score reliability estimates, however, in the subsequent studies were all below .90, with the lowest for contact (.55–.67), pseudo-independence (.65–.71), and autonomy (.65–.67). Subscale intercorrelations ranged from |.20| to |.72|, with the highest correlation between the disintegration and reintegration subscales. A principal components analysis conducted on the WRIAS, using a varimax rotation and the eigenvalue rule of one, identified 11 factors. No rationale was provided for interpreting an 11-factor solution and its relationship to the scale's five subscales. Additional evidence for construct validity was based on the WRIAS subscales correlated with other measures of personality constructs (i. e., anxiety, interpersonal behaviors, reaction to counselor interventions), all in the direction expected theoretically.

Several studies (Alexander, 1992; Behrens, 1997; Helms, 1999; Lemon & Waehler, 1996; Mercer & Cunningham, 2003; Pope-Davis et al., 1999; Swanson et al., 1994; Tokar & Swanson, 1991) have reported score reliabilities ranging from .33 to .67 for contact, .75 to .81 for disintegrative, .74 to .88 for reintegrative, .60 to .72 for pseudo-independence, and .53 to .71 for autonomy. In a meta-analysis of 22 studies, Behrens (1997) found that the average score reliabilities for the WRIAS subscales fell within the ranges listed above. High intercorrelations have been found between the disintegrative and reintegrative subscales, and between the pseudo-independence and autonomy subscales (Behrens, 1997, Jome, 2000; Mercer & Cunningham, 2003; Tokar & Swanson, 1991). Exploratory factor analyses have found either a four-factor (Mercer & Cunningham, 2003) or five-factor (Alexander, 1992; Neuger, 2002; Swanson et al., 1994) solution, but none was in keeping with the expected five-factor structure. What has been found is a bipolar factor pattern reflective of the two phases of WRI development: abandoning racism and becoming nonracist (Pope-Davis et al., 1999; Swanson et al.). Confirmatory factor analyses have been problematic to conduct on the WRIAS items, resulting in inadmissible solutions for the five-factor model (Alexander, 1992; Behrens, 1997) or poor fit models (e.g., one-factor model CFI = .67 and .72; root mean square residual [RMSR] = .08 and .07; Behrens, 1997). Expected relationships have been found between the WRIAS and numerous sociocultural variables (e.g., interracial comfort, multicultural competencies skills, and psychological health; Fischer & Moradi, 2001; Ponterotto et al., 2000). No serious confound has been found between social desirability and the WRIAS (Jome, 2000; Kurtzweil, 1996). A viable explanation offered for this paradoxical pattern—poor structural validity, but still evidence for validity—is that the WRIAS does measure an overarching construct of positive and negative racial attitudes (Behrens, 1997; Fischer & Moradi, 2001; Rowe et al., 1995).

EVALUATION

The value of the WRIAS is its theoretical base and the implication of its content, bringing tangible attention to the construct of WRI beyond what any theory could do. The items do not tap white identity, but rather whites' views of being white in relation to blacks (Fischer & Moradi, 2001; Hardiman, 2001). Reviewers have been clear about the inadequacy of the WRIAS and its continued use as-is (Behrens, 1997; Behrens & Rowe, 1997; Fischer & Moradi, 2001). As indicated earlier, Helms (1997, 1999, 2007; Helms et al., 2006) and Carter (1997) contend that the negative evaluations of the scale are due to existing methodological and environmental issues when studying a construct as complex as racial identity. Other scholars (Behrens, 1997; Behrens & Rowe, 1997; Cokley, 2007) have noted that these issues do not explain totally the psychometric problems of the WRIAS. The potential of the theory (Behrens & Rowe, 1997, Ponterotto et al., 2000; Swanson et al., 1994) and its measurement have been noted, resulting in the call for further testing and revisions (Ponterotto et al., 2000; Swanson et al., 1994). The accumulated evidence indicates the potential presence of the superordinate phases (abandonment of racism and acceptance of nonracist attitude; Helms, 1995). The scale with revisions could still tap a multidimensional construct, evidenced in the recent iteration of the

White Racial Consciousness Development Scale-Revised (WRCD-R; Lee et al., 2007), which is designed to measure four white racial attitudes of Helms' (1984) model. Reviews of the psychometric properties of the WRCDS-R are promising (Burkard & Ponterotto, 2008; Ponterotto & Park-Taylor, 2007).

White Racial Consciousness

White racial consciousness represents a collection of racial attitudes that white Americans have "toward racial/minority group members" (Rowe, Behrens, & Leach, 1995, p. 225). These attitudes, acquired in the same manner as other attitudes, are not personality traits, but clusters of attitudes held by whites. Each cluster represents a describable set of related attitudes called types. Individuals can have attitudes representative of more than one type, but most people can be classified as holding one type of white racial consciousness. White racial consciousness emerged as an alternative model in response to concerns about the conceptual underpinnings of the WRID models, most notably Helms' (1990, 1995) model.

A preliminary form of the Oklahoma Racial Attitude Scale (ORAS-P; Choney & Behrens, 1996) was developed to tap the WRC attitude types, but validation work (Behrens et al., 1999; Pope-Davis et al., 1995; Pope-Davis, Vandiver, & Stone, 1999; Summerson, 1997) on the scale resulted in the reconceptualization of the model (LaFleur et al., 2002) and the emergence of the standard form of the Oklahoma Racial Attitude Scale (ORAS; LaFleur et al., 2003). In the reconceptualized model, three major changes were made. First, dominative, integrative, conflictive, and reactive type attitudes were reoriented based on one of two racial themes that had been identified through factor analysis. Dominative (negative view of nonwhites) and integrative (positive view of nonwhites) type attitudes are now viewed as a bipolar dimension best reflecting the theme of racial acceptance. Also sharing a common theme of racial justice are the conflictive- and reactive-type attitudes, with those having a conflictive-type attitude not wanting whites to be at an unfair advantage versus those with a reactive-type attitude taking a pro-racial/ethnic minority stance. Although these two type attitudes reflect a common theme, they are treated as separate constructs psychometrically. Second, labeling the types of attitudes as achieved and unachieved statuses is no longer necessary. Third, the previously labeled unachieved attitudes are now considered attitudes of commitment toward a racial attitude by individuals either expressing no concern (avoidant), relying on others (dependent), or being uncertain (dissonant). Thus, scales representative of these attitudes on the ORAS are to be used as "indices of one's expressed commitment to the four types of racial attitudes" (LaFleur et al, 2002, p. 151). For an in-depth reading of the WRC model and reconceptualization, see LaFleur et al. 2002, Leach, Behrens, and LaFleur (2002), and Rowe et al. (1994, 1995).

EVALUATION

"One great strength of the Rowe et al. (1994, 1995) white racial consciousness model is that it has been closely linked to empirical research at the outset" (Ponterotto, 2006, p. 101). Empirical studies were used to revise the model and the scale. Another strength of the WRC is the use of a typology model and its general clarity, extending the early development of type models (e.g., Gaertner, 1976; Kovel, 1970) on white racial attitudes through theory and empirical work. More clarity, however, is needed in the model about the relationship between the racial orientation attitudes (dominative/integrative, conflictive, and reactive) and the commitment attitudes. Labeling the avoidant, dissonant, and dependent attitudes with the term *commitment* seems misleading, as it is unclear how they operate in relation to the racial orientations. The revised WRC model has received some empirical support in the publication of four dissertations. The reactive attitude type was found associated with higher levels of ego development, and lower ego development was linked to the avoidant attitude type (Schmidt, 2007). College students reported increased reactive attitudes when taking a multicultural education class (Weathersby, 2005). And integrative and reactive attitudes were associated with cultural awareness, whereas conflictive attitudes were negatively associated with cultural awareness (Fierstien, 2004). These findings are promising, especially concerning their potential impact on multicultural education and training, but continued systematic research is needed.

Oklahoma Racial Attitude Scale

THEORETICAL BASE AND SCALE

The ORAS (LaFleur et al., 2003) is a 35-item scale designed to measure the white racial consciousness construct as delineated in the revised conceptualization of WRC (LaFleur et al., 2002). Six subscales make up the ORAS—dominative/integrative (10 items), a bipolar measure of racial acceptance, ranging from negative view of racial minorities to acceptance; conflictive (seven items), preferential treatment for whites; reactive (seven items), preferential treatment for racial minorities—and three commitment indices tap being unconcerned (avoidant [three items]), being uncertain (dissonant [four items]), or relying on the views of others (dependent [three items]).

Items are rated on a 5-point scale (*Strongly Disagree* =1 to *Strongly Agree* = 5), in which the first item is not scored, but the remaining 34 are. LaFleur et al. (2003) specify in the ORAS manual the computation and scoring of the scales. For the bipolar dominative/integrative scale, dominative items are reverse-scored, with lower scores representing the dominative view and the higher scores representing the integrative attitude. For the other five scales, higher scores indicate the higher preference for that specific attitude.

PSYCHOMETRIC BASE

The 50-item ORAS-P (Choney & Behrens, 1996) was originally designed to measure seven types of attitudes, delineated earlier in the WRC model (Rowe et al., 1994, 1995). High correlations existed between the achieved scales (conflictive and reactive, and dominative and integrative), but the CFA findings supported a seven- instead of a five-factor model (Choney & Behrens, 1996). However, a subsequent study (Pope-Davis, Vandiver, & Stone, 1999) examining both the WRIAS (Helms & Carter, 1990) and ORAS-P items in the same EFA and CFA failed to support separate factors for the achieved scales. Further work on the ORAS-P led to the reformulation of the WRC model and the creation of a standard measure called the ORAS (LaFleur et al., 2002).

Psychometric evidence for the ORAS, as delineated in the ORAS manual (LaFleur et al., 2003), is based on the findings of two studies. Cronbach's α for the ORAS scales were all above .70, except for the avoidant scale (.60). Correlations between the ORAS scales ranged from .00 to $-.57$ (dominative/integrative and conflictive). Convergent and discriminant validity of the ORAS was based on correlations among three scales on the Interpersonal Reactivity Index (Davis, 1980). Correlations between the ORAS and a social desirability measure were below .30. Structural validity of the ORAS across both studies indicated that the fit indices for the six-factor model were similar (AGFI = 86 vs. CFI = .86; RMSR = .08 vs. RMSEA = .04, .05) and more viable than a seven-factor model (r = .87

between dominative and integrative). In the six-factor model, the largest correlation was $-.68$ between conflictive and dominative/integrative (LaFleur et al., 2003). Marcell (2005) examined the structural validity of the ORAS and found results similar to those above—the six-factor model was the best fitting model tested, even though the fit did not meet the expected standards (CFI < .90).

EVALUATION

Fischer and Moradi's (2001) evaluation of the ORAS is fitting. The strengths of the ORAS are in its grounding in theory and the reciprocal iteration of theory and scale based on empirical findings. It is still unclear what role the commitment scales play in the interpretation of the racial attitudes. If these scales do not play a major role in understanding or interpreting the racial attitudes, it might be best to drop them. Further psychometric evidence is needed on the ORAS, as the fit indices are below the expected guidelines (CFI > .90). There are no published studies using the ORAS, but several dissertations have used the ORAS in examining racial attitudes in relation to various sociocultural aspects.

Measurement Issues for Ethnic Identity

Unlike racial identity, which has multiple competing models and instruments, ethnic identity research has been dominated by the use of one measure. However, growing theoretical and psychometric concerns over the adequacy of the most used measure of ethnic identity has resulted in the development of another promising measure.

Multigroup Ethnic Identity Measure

The most utilized and researched measure of ethnic identity is Phinney's MEIM (1992). The MEIM was created as a measure of ethnic identity that could be used across ethnic groups because Phinney believed that ethnic identity was relevant to all groups. In reviewing the literature to identify components of ethnic identity, Phinney identified self-identification, ethnic behaviors and practices, affirmation and belonging, and ethnic identity achievement. Regarding ethnic behaviors and practices, she noted that the majority of measures of ethnic identity focused on ethnic behaviors and practices, which was good for studying individual ethnic groups but not ideal for studying different ethnic groups. Phinney also believe that attitudes toward other ethnic groups, although not formally a part of ethnic identity, were important inasmuch as they may interact with ethnic identity and thereby influence it. In constructing the MEIM, Phinney was especially interested in whether the components of ethnic identity were part of a global factor or were instead independent aspects of ethnic identity (Phinney, 1992). Through an iterative process of scale construction, Phinney administered a 14-item version that measured what she believed to be three components of ethnic identity: affirmation and sense of belonging (measured with five items), ethnic identity achievement (measured with seven items), and ethnic behaviors and practices (measured with two items). Phinney also administered a six-item scale to measure attitudes toward other groups. The results of a principal axis factor analysis with a high school sample initially resulted in three factors, but because of interpretability issues, two of the factors were collapsed into one. The result was two factors, with all the items measuring ethnic identity loading on one factor while the remaining six items all loaded on the second factor. This approach is tautological because the factor of ethnic identity is used as a part of the definition of ethnic identity (Cokley, 2007). The principal axis factor analysis with the college sample initially resulted in five factors, but high intercorrelations among the factors resulted in Phinney again identifying two factors that were similar to the high school sample. The results of the factor analyses from both samples led Phinney to conclude that ethnic identity consists of a single factor, whereas other-group orientation constitutes a separate factor. Even though the factor analyses did not provide strong evidence for the three hypothesized components of ethnic identity, Phinney nevertheless calculated correlations among the three components and, unsurprisingly, found high intercorrelations. She concluded that the intercorrelations "provide further support for the results of the factor analysis in suggesting a unified construct of ethnic identity (consisting of three interrelated components) that is distinct from other-group orientation" (Phinney, 1992, p. 167). This statement is methodologically ambiguous because, although it seems to indicate that ethnic identity consists of one factor, it also gives the impression that ethnic identity can be examined using the three hypothesized components. Phinney's conclusions and subsequent use of the scale have influenced the entire field of ethnic identity, with most researchers choosing to compute a single score of ethnic identity. This usage has led to concern among some researchers regarding the importance of examining the specific aspects of

ethnic identity (e.g., Lee & Yoo, 2004; Umana-Taylor et al., 2004).

Earlier, it was stated that Umana-Taylor's critique of Phinney's work lies primarily in what she sees as a discrepancy between Phinney's theoretical model of ethnic identity (informed by Erikson and Marcia) and the way ethnic identity is operationalized by the MEIM. In Erikson's theory of identity development (1968), the eight developmental stages are each characterized by a crisis or conflict. Each crisis or conflict must be successfully resolved before progression to the next stage of identity can take place. Resolution of each stage can either be positive and satisfactory, or negative and unsatisfactory. An unsatisfactory resolution of the stage has negative implications for the development of self-concept. Marcia (1980) built upon Erikson's work by theorizing that identity achievement occurs once an individual has experienced and resolved a crisis by committing to a certain role, value, or perspective. It is important to note that identity achievement from the perspectives of Erikson and Marcia does not necessarily mean affirming that aspect of identity. It simply means that one has thoroughly reflected on what that identity means. The individual may affirm it, or may choose not to affirm it. With this understanding of Erikson and Marcia, Umana-Taylor argues that the scoring and use of Phinney's MEIM are inconsistent with identity achievement as theorized by Erikson and Marcia. Specifically, items from the affirmation component (e.g., "I have a lot of pride in my ethnic group and its accomplishments") are summed with items from the achievement component (e.g., "I have spent time trying to find out about my own ethnic group, such as its history, traditions, and customs") and behaviors component (e.g., "I participate in cultural practices of my own group, such as special food, music, or customs") to create a total score. However, use of a total score obscures the unique contributions of each component and essentially indicates that an individual has an achieved ethnic identity by affirming it. In short, a better and more refined understanding of ethnic identity and its correlates and associated outcomes will occur by examining the distinct components as opposed to combining them into one total score (Umana-Taylor et al., 2004).

Ethnic Identity Scale

In response to these aforementioned concerns about the MEIM, Umana-Taylor et al. created the Ethnic Identity Scale (EIS). Two studies were conducted using samples of college and high school students. The first study submitted the original 46-item measure to an exploratory and confirmatory factor analysis, and the second study examined the psychometric properties of the resultant measure. Results from the first study yielded eight initial factors, of which a three-factor solution was ultimately retained. The result was a 22-item measure consisting of subscales for exploration, affirmation, and resolution. Construct validity of the EIS was established through the differential intercorrelations of the subscales, which was consistent with theoretical expectations. A stronger correlation existed between exploration and resolution than between affirmation and exploration or affirmation and resolution, leading the authors to conclude that it can not be assumed that "individuals will feel positively about their ethnicity just because they have explored their ethnicity and/or feel that they have resolved how they feel about their ethnicity" (Umana-Taylor et al., 2004, p. 23). The follow-up confirmatory factor analysis indicated a poor fit of the model to the data. Five items were removed because of significant residuals, resulting in a 17-item measure. The second study used the 17-item measure of the EIS that consisted of three subscales: exploration (measured with seven items), resolution (measured with four items), and affirmation (measured with six items). All three subscales yielded scores that were adequately reliable and differentially correlated with familial ethnic socialization and self-esteem. These findings lend support to their contention that the dimensions of ethnic identity are differentially associated with various outcomes.

Future Research Directions

Racial identity research, although not the sole province of counseling psychology, has experienced the most heated debates and arguably reached its most sophisticated understanding through the efforts of counseling psychologists. Ethnic identity research has a shorter history in counseling psychology research, but recent trends indicate a rise in interest over the last few years. Counseling psychology, more than any other area of applied psychology, has engaged in intense scholarly studies and debates over racial and ethnic identity. This is evidenced by special issues of TCP (1989, 1994) and the JCP (2007) being devoted to racial and ethnic identity, as well as the numerous articles published in both journals that have focused on various aspects of racial and ethnic identity theory and measurement. It can be confidently stated that an informed understanding of ethnic and racial identity is an integral part of the foundation of knowledge that counseling psychologists are expected to have.

Changes in the U.S. population and lifestyles indicate that racial identity is changing, with counseling psychology being required to follow social trends to accurately understand Americans in the 21st century. Four trends briefly summarized here seem to be influencing the meaning of racial identity in the U.S. and its measurement: U.S. racial classifications, multiracial people, the hip-hop generation, and immigration.

In 2000, U.S. Census allowed respondents to select one or more races to self-identify or to note their belonging to the category of "Some Other Race." Race is not treated as a static category and ethnicity is no longer considered exclusive of race (U.S. Census, 2000). This fluid treatment of racial and ethnic classifications means that those who are from interracial unions no longer have to choose one race, and that race and ethnicity may not be reflective of separate constructs or realities (Cross & Cross, 2008). Roughly 18.5 million people identified, as part of or as their only race response, as "Some Other Race," with the majority writing in a specific Hispanic origin for the 2000 census.

The birth of children from interracial unions has increased and has been made more public. A number of biracial/multiracial identity models were developed in the 1990s to capture the overt acknowledgment of the existence of these individuals (e.g., Kerwin & Ponterotto, 1995; Poston, 1990; Root, 1999). Societal pressure still exists for these children with any minority heritage to identify as being minority (Root, 1999). Waters (2000, p. 1736) reported that "intermarried parents filling out the census form simplify their children's ancestries," where approximately 40% do not report the logical combination of racial backgrounds, but report the race of only one parent. What impact do these variables and related ones have on racial socialization and subsequent racial identity?

Hip-hop culture emerged out of the post-Civil Rights era (mid-1960s and 1970), with racial tensions as the backdrop due to the continued marginalization (e.g., segregation and the right to vote) of blacks despite overt signs of equality. The messages behind the movement were "come as you are" and "we are family" (Herc, 2005, p. xi), indicative of one's individual and collective identities. Each new generation of youth has added to the hip-hop identity. Its positive aspects (e.g., commerce, expression of individuality, and messages about sociopolitical realities) have been overshadowed by its negative impact, with adults of previous generations sharply critical of its music form, content, fashion statement, and general lifestyle (George, 1998). Despite its critics, hip-hop culture has been in existence for at least 30 years, and its influence is pervasive, ever-changing, and expanding. The focus of the early hip-hop generation (born between 1965–1984) is on social responsibility, while younger generations continue to reinvent hip-hop (George, 1998).

So, what do counseling psychologists know of the hip-hop generation? Psychological research on the hip-hop generation and racial identity is needed. A brief search in PsychInfo revealed 112 publications (84 in journals, four books, three conference proceedings, and 17 dissertations) from 1990 to 2008 when the term "hip-hop" was used as the key words. No articles on hip-hop were found in any of the mainstream psychology journals such as the JCP, *Journal of Personality and Social Psychology*, or *Journal of Black Psychology*. Most publications on hip-hop have come from arts and humanities, as the four main aspects (rapping, Djing, graffiti art, and dancing) said to define hip-hop culture reflect both (George, 1998). But hip-hop is more than art; it is a dominant influence on all spheres of life in countries around the world (e.g., England, Japan, Germany, Chile, etc.; George, 1998). Is racial identity, regardless of the era, the same for all, as defined by Cross, Helms, or Sellers? Some aspects of hip-hop seem to reflect black nationalism; other aspects seem to reflect a multicultural one. With its mainstream popularity, what role does it play in white or Asian identity?

More research on the impact of legal and illegal immigration on racial identity is needed. According to Passel (2005) of the Pew Hispanic Center, as of March 2004, approximately 81% of undocumented migrants have come from Latin American countries (57% from Mexico), with the remaining percent of undocumented individuals in the United States coming from the rest of the world (i.e., 9% from Asia, 6% from Europe and Canada, and 4% from other countries). Approximately one in six are estimated to be minors, with most falling between the ages of 18 and 39, and about 60% are men. These statistics are presented to highlight several reasons why research is needed in this area. One, less than 4% of the undocumented migrants are from countries in which the predominant population represents the African diaspora. For centuries, legal immigration of Africans and Caribbeans to the United States has been difficult, even when political strife in their countries (e.g., Darfur and Haiti) was and is clearly evident. In contrast, Cubans have had political refugee status. What implications do immigration policies have on the changing nature of race and racial identity?

As ethnic identity research continues to increase in counseling psychology, researchers must be mindful that ethnic identity is a multidimensional rather than a unidimensional construct. Although both Phinney and Umana-Taylor agree with this in theory, only Umana-Taylor consistently incorporates this perspective in her program of research. This is because Phinney views the multiple dimensions as interrelated, whereas Umana-Taylor views them as independent dimensions. Regardless of the perspective taken, relatively little is still known about how the different dimensions of ethnic identity relate to specific outcomes. Umana-Taylor et al. (2004) point out that previous studies that found modest positive relations between ethnic identity and self-esteem are limited because they used MEIM total scores rather than examine individual MEIM subscales. They argue that this method introduces error, and ultimately may weaken the relationship. It may very well be the case that observed relationships with specific outcomes will depend on which aspect of ethnic identity is assessed. Future ethnic identity research must explore the specific linkages of ethnic identity with various outcomes.

Furthermore, debates around the conceptualization, measurement, and operationalization of ethnic identity will no doubt continue. At least one prominent scholar has controversially asserted that there is no evidence that ethnic identity has actually been measured (Helms, 2007, personal communication). Future research should continue to refine the theoretical underpinnings of ethnic identity, paying particular attention to delineating where it both converges with and diverges from racial identity. Special attention should be paid to a more robust operationalization of the content (e.g., cultural practices and experiences) of ethnic identity. Although both the MEIM and EIS include items that measure cultural experiences, multiple experiences are combined into a single item, which is never ideal by test construction standards (e.g., "I participate in cultural practices of my own group, such as special food, music, or customs" and "I have experienced things that reflect my ethnicity, such as eating food, listening to music, and watching movies"). Current ethnic identity measures should be revised, or new ethnic identity measures should be created, to include more individual items that reflect cultural practices and experiences related to ethnic identity (Alba, 1990). A more robust measurement of ethnic identity will certainly advance our understanding of this construct.

One of the most important areas of future research is to advance a better understanding of how ethnic identity changes over time. Being informed by the developmental models of Erikson and Marcia, more longitudinal research needs to be conducted that charts the fluctuations of ethnic identity. Numerous questions remain about the development of ethnic identity. Are there psychological antecedents to an increase or decrease in ethnic identity? Does a change in the political climate impact ethnic identity, and if so, in what ways? Does an individual's ethnic identity change from childhood to adolescence to adulthood? Do major life events (e.g., birth, weddings, death) impact ethnic identity? Are individuals who have certain experiences (e.g., higher education, international travel) more likely to explore and reflect on their ethnic identity compared to individuals who do not have these experiences? Do certain experiences shorten or lengthen ethnic identity formation? Counseling psychologists know a lot about the correlates of ethnic identity, but virtually nothing about developmental issues of ethnic identity over the course of a lifetime.

Conclusion

As evidenced in the brief reviews about racial classification, multiracial individuals, hip-hop culture, and immigration, race and ethnicity, and by extension racial and ethnic identity, will continue to have an impact on the lives of Americans. With increasing advances in technology, as well as the decreasing proximity between people of diverse backgrounds, the heterogeneity within a racial and ethnic group is becoming more pronounced. Each new generation of Americans is experiencing different aspects of American and global cultures. The generational aspects of social identity may become more demarcated as the ability to "be global" changes what it means to have a local identity.

Ethnic and racial identity are both complex, multidimensional constructs whose influences in various areas (e.g., mental health, career development, academic achievement) are just starting to be understood. Nevertheless, there remains much to learn about the specific mechanisms through which ethnic and racial identity influence behavior and well-being.

References

Alba, R. D. (1990). Ethnic identity: The transformation of White America. New Haven, CT: Yale University Press.

Alvarez, A. N., Juang, L., & Liang, C. T. H. (2006). Asian Americans and racism: When bad things happen to "model minorities." *Cultural Diversity and Ethnic Minority Psychology*, *12*, 477–492.

Alvarez, A. N., & Kimura, E. F. (2001). Asian Americans and racial identity: Dealing with racism and snowballs. *Journal of Mental Health Counseling*, *23*, 192–206.

Alexander, C. M. (1992). Construct validity and reliability of the White Racial Identity Attitude Scale (WRIAS). *Dissertation Abstracts International*, *53*(11A), 3799.

Alexander, C. M., & Suzuki, L. A. (2001). Measurement of multicultural constructs: Integration and research directions. In J. G. Ponterotto, J. M. Casas, L. A. Suzuki, & C. M. Alexander (Eds.), *Handbook of multicultural counseling* (2nd ed., pp. 499–506). Thousand Oaks, CA: Sage.

Atkinson, D. R. (Ed.). (2003). *Counseling American minorities: A cross-cultural perspective* (6th ed.). Dubuque, IA: McGraw Hill.

Atkinson, D. R., Morten, G., & Sue, D. W. (Eds.). (1979). *Counseling American minorities: A cross-cultural perspective*. Dubuque, IA: Wm. C. Brown.

Atkinson, D. R., Morten, G., & Sue, D. W. (Eds.). (1989). *Counseling American minorities: A cross-cultural perspective* (3rd ed.). Dubuque, IA: Wm. C. Brown.

Atkinson, D. R., Morten, G., & Sue, D. W. (Eds.). (1993). *Counseling American minorities: A cross-cultural perspective* (4th ed.). Dubuque, IA: Wm. C. Brown.

Atkinson, D. R., Morten, G., & Sue, D. W. (Eds.). (1998). *Counseling American minorities: A cross-cultural perspective* (5th ed.). Dubuque, IA: McGraw Hill.

Baldwin, J. A., & Bell, Y. R. (1982). *The African Self-Consciousness Scale manual*. Unpublished manuscript, Florida A & AM University, Tallahassee, FL.

Barrett, S. E. (1990). Paths toward diversity: An intrapsychic perspective. *Women & Therapy*, *8*(1–2), 41–52.

Bassaly, A., & Macallan, H. (2006). Willingness to use psychological help among Polish immigrants in the UK. *Counselling Psychology Review*, *21*(4), 19–27.

Behrens, J. (1997). Does the White Racial Identity Attitude Scale measure racial identity? *Journal of Counseling Psychology*, *44*, 3–12.

Behrens, J. T., Leach, M. M., Franz, S., & LaFleur, N. K. (1999, August). *Revising the Oklahoma Racial Attitudes Scale: Work in progress*. Poster session presented at the meeting of the American Psychological Association, Boston, MA.

Behrens, J. T., & Rowe, W. (1997). Measuring White racial identity: A reply to Helms (1997). *Journal of Counseling Psychology*, *44*, 17–19.

Berry, J., Trimble, J., & Olmedo, E. (1986). Assessment of acculturation. In W. Lonner, & J. Berry (Eds.), Field methods in cross-cultural research (pp. 291–324). Newbury Park, CA: Sage.

Bianchi, F. T., Zea, M. C., Belgrave, F. Z., & Echeverry, J. J. (2002). Racial identity and self- esteem among Black Brazilian men: Race matters in Brazil too! *Cultural Diversity and Ethnic Minority Psychology*, *8*, 157–169.

Bowen, D. J., Christensen, C. L., Powers, D., Graves, D. R., & Anderson, C. A. M. (1998). Effects of counseling and ethnic identity on perceived risk and cancer worry in African American women. *Journal of Clinical Psychology in Medical Settings*, *5*, 365–379.

Brown, S. D., & Lent, R. W. (1992). *Handbook of counseling psychology* (2nd ed.). Hoboken, NJ: John Wiley & Sons.

Brown, S. D., & Lent, R. W. (2000). *Handbook of counseling psychology* (3rd ed.). Hoboken, NJ: John Wiley & Sons.

Brown, S. D., & Lent, R. W. (2008). *Handbook of counseling psychology* (4th ed.). Hoboken, NJ: John Wiley & Sons.

Bryant, A., Jr., & Baker, S. B. (2003). The feasibility of constructing profiles of Native Americans from the People of Color Identity Attitude Scale: A brief report. *Measurement and Evaluation in Counseling and Development, 36*, 2–8.

Burkard, A. W., Juarez-Huffaker, M., & Ajmere, K. (2003). White racial identity attitudes as a predictor of client perceptions of cross-cultural working alliances. *Journal of Multicultural Counseling and Development, 31*, 226–244.

Burkard, A. W., & Ponterotto, J. G. (2008). Cultural identity, racial identity, and multicultural personality. In L. Suzuki, & J. G. Ponterotto (Eds.), *Handbook of multicultural assessment: Clinical, psychological, and educational applications* (3rd ed., pp. 52–72). San Francisco: John Wiley & Sons, Inc.

Burkard, A. W., Ponterotto, J. G., Reynolds, A. L., & Alfonso, V. C. (1999). White counselor trainees' racial identity and working alliance perceptions. *Journal of Counseling & Development, 77*, 324–329.

Carter, R. T. (1995). *The influence of race and racial identity in psychotherapy: Toward a racially inclusive model.* New York: John Wiley & Sons.

Carter, R. T., & Constantine, M. G. (2000). Career maturity, life role salience, and racial/ethnic identity in Black and Asian American college students. *Journal of Career Assessment, 8*, 173–187.

Carter, R. T., & Helms, J. E. (1992). The counseling process as defined by relationship types: A test of Helms' interactional model. *Journal of Multicultural Counseling and Development, 20*, 181–201.

Chang, T., Yeh, C. J., Krumboltz, J. D. (2001). Process and outcome evaluation of an on-line support for Asian American male college students. *Journal of Counseling Psychology, 48*, 319–329.

Chen, G. A., Lephuoc, P., Guzman, M. R., Rude, S., & Dodd, B. G. (2006). Exploring Asian American racial identity. *Cultural Diversity and Ethnic Minority Psychology, 12*, 461–476.

Choney, S. K., & Behrens, J. T. (1996). Development of the Oklahoma Racial Attitudes Scale: Preliminary form (ORAS-P). In G. R. Sodowsky, & J. Impara (Eds.), *Multicultural assessment in counseling and clinical psychology* (pp. 225–240). Lincoln, NE: Buros Institute of Mental Measurements.

Clark, K. B., & Clark, M. P. (1939). The development of consciousness of self and the emergence of racial identification in Negro pre-school children. *Journal of Social Psychology, 10*, 591–599.

Cokley, K. (1999). Reconceptualizing the impact of college racial composition on African American students' racial identity. *Journal of College Student Development, 40*, 235–246.

Cokley, K. O. (2002). Testing Cross's revised racial identity model: An examination of the relationship between racial identity and internalized racialism. *Journal of Counseling Psychology, 49*, 476–483.

Cokley, K. O. (2005). Racial(ized) identity, ethnic identity, and Afrocentric values: Conceptual and methodological challenges in understanding African American identity. *Journal of Counseling Psychology, 52*, 517–526.

Cokley, K. O. (2007). Critical issues in the measurement of ethnic and racial identity: A referendum on the state of the field. *Journal of Counseling Psychology, 54*, 224–239.

Cokley, K. O., & Helm, K. (2001). Testing the construct validity of scores on the Multidimensional Inventory of Black Identity. *Measurement and Evaluation in Counseling and Development, 34*, 80–95.

Cokley, K. O., Komarraju, M., Patel, N., Muhammad, G., Daniels, K., & Banet, M. (1999). *Where are racial identity articles most published? A content analysis of journals and authors from 1980–1999.* Unpublished manuscript.

Constantine, M. G. (2002). Racism attitudes, White racial identity attitudes, and multicultural counseling competence in school counselor trainees. *Counselor Education & Supervision, 41*, 162–174.

Constantine, M. G., & Ladany, N. (2000). Self-report multicultural counseling competence scales: Their relation to social desirability attitudes and multicultural case conceptualization ability. *Journal of Counseling Psychology, 47*, 155–164.

Constantine, M. G., Warren, A. K., & Miville, M. (2005). White racial identity dyadic interactions in supervision: Implications for supervisees' multicultural counseling competence. *Journal of Counseling Psychology, 52*, 490–496.

Cross, W. E., Jr. (1970, April). *The Black experience viewed as a process: A crude model for Black self-actualization.* Paper presented at the 34th Annual Meeting of the Association of Social and Behavioral Scientists, Tallahassee, Florida.

Cross, W. E., Jr. (1971). The Negro-to-Black conversion experience: Toward a psychology of Black liberation. *Black World, 20*, 13–27.

Cross, W. E., Jr. (1978). The Cross and Thomas models of psychological nigrescence. *Journal of Black Psychology, 5*, 13–19.

Cross, W. E., Jr. (1991). *Shades of black.* Philadelphia: Temple University Press.

Cross, W. E., Jr., & Cross, T. B. (2008). The big picture: Theorizing self-concept structure and construal. In P. B. Pedersen, J. G. Draguns, W. J. Lonner, & J. E. Trimble (Eds.), *Counseling across cultures* (6th ed., pp. 73–88). Thousand Oaks, CA: Sage.

Cross, W. E., Jr., & Vandiver, B. J. (2001). Nigrescence theory and measurement: Introducing the Cross Racial Identity Scale (CRIS). In J. G. Ponterotto, J. M. Casas, L. A. Suzuki, & C. M. Alexander (Eds.), *Handbook of multicultural counseling* (2nd ed., pp. 371–393). Thousand Oaks, CA: Sage.

D'Andrea, M., & Daniels, J. (1996). Promoting peace in our schools: Developmental, preventive, and multicultural considerations. *School Counselor, 44*(1), 55–64.

Davis, M. H. (1980). A multidimensional approach to individual differences in empathy. *JASA Catalog of Selected Documents in Psychology, 10*, 85.

DeJesus-Rueff, R. (1986). An exploratory study of ego identity status and ethnic identity among mainland Puerto Rican female adolescents. *Dissertation Abstracts International, 47*(1-A), 124–125.

Erikson, E. H. (1968). *Identity: Youth and crisis.* New York: Norton.

Fernandez, R. M. (1989). An empirical test of the minority identity development model with Cuban-Americans. *Dissertation Abstracts International, 49*(9-B), 4035.

Fierstien, J. R. (2004). An exploration of relationships between cultural awareness, White racial consciousness, and referrals to child study teams. *Dissertation Abstracts International: Section B: The Sciences and Engineering, 64*(9-B), 4676.

Fischer, A. R., & Moradi, B. (2001). Racial and ethnic identity: Recent developments and needed directions. In J. G. Ponterotto, J. M. Casas, L. A. Suzuki, & C. M. Alexander (Eds.), *Handbook of multicultural counseling* (2nd ed., pp. 341–370). Thousand Oaks, CA: Sage.

Fischer, A. R., Tokar, D. M., & Serna, G. S. (1998). Validity and construct contamination of the Racial Identity Attitude Scale—Long form. *Journal of Counseling Psychology, 45*, 212–224.

Ford, D. Y., Harris, D., III, & Schuerger, J. M. (1993). Racial identity development among gifted Black students: Counseling issues and concerns. *Journal of Counseling & Development, 71*, 409–417.

Franklin, A. J. (1999). Invisibility syndrome and racial identity development in psychotherapy and counseling African American men. *The Counseling Psychologist, 27*, 761–793.

Gaertner, S. L. (1976). Nonreactive measures in racial attitude research: A focus on liberals. In P. A. Katz (Ed.), *Towards the elimination of racism.* New York: Pergamon.

Galkina, H. (n.d.). *Theoretical approaches to ethnic identity.* Retrieved June 30, 2008, from http://sincronia.cucsh.udg. mx/galkina.html.

Gardner-Kitt, D. L., & Worrell, F. C. (2007). Measuring nigrescence attitudes in school-aged adolescents. *Journal of Adolescence, 30*, 187–202.

George, N. (1998). *Hip hop America.* New York: Viking.

Grace, C. A. (1984). The relationship between racial identity attitudes and choice of typical and atypical occupations among Black college students. *Dissertation Abstracts International, 45*(2-B), 722.

Hall, W. S., & Cross, W. E., Jr. (1970). *The formation of an ego identity in black Americans: Toward a conceptualization of stages in coming to terms with self.* Paper presented at the Annual Meeting of the National Association of Black Psychologists, Miami Beach, Florida.

Hall, W. S., Cross, W. E., & Freedle, R. (1972). Stages in the development of Black awareness: An empirical investigation. In R. L. Jones (Ed.), *Black psychology* (pp. 156–165). New York: Harper & Row.

Hardiman, R. (1982). White identity development: A process oriented model for describing the racial consciousness of White Americans. *Dissertation Abstracts International, 43*(1-A), 104.

Hardiman, R. (1994). White racial identity development in the United States. In E. P. Salett, & D. R. Koslow (Eds.), *Race, ethnicity, and self: Identity in multicultural perspective* (pp. 117–140). Washington, DC: National Multicultural Institute.

Hardiman, R. (2001). Reflections on White identity development theory. In C. L. Wijeyesinghe, & B. W. Jackson (Eds.), *New perspectives on racial identity development: A theoretical and practical anthology* (pp. 108–128). New York: New York University Press.

Hardiman, R., & Jackson, B. W. (1992). Racial identity development: Understanding racial dynamics in college classrooms and on campus. In M. Adams (Ed.), *Promoting diversity in college classrooms: Innovative responses for the curriculum, faculty, and institutions* (pp. 21–37). San Francisco: Jossey-Bass.

Hargrow, A. M. (2001). Racial identity development: The case of Mr. X., an African American. *Journal of Mental Health Counseling, 23*, 222–237.

Helms, J. E. (1984). Toward a theoretical explanation of the effects of race on counseling: A Black and White model. *The Counseling Psychologist, 12*, 153–165.

Helms, J. E. (1990). *Black and White racial identity: Theory, research, and practice.* New York: Greenwood Press.

Helms, J. E. (1990). The measurement of Black racial identity attitudes. In J. E. Helms (Ed.), *Black and White racial identity: Theory, research and practice* (pp. 34–47). New York: Greenwood.

Helms, J. E. (1994). Racial identity and assessment. *Journal of Career Assessment, 2*, 199–209.

Helms, J. E. (1995a). An update of Helms' White and People of Color Racial Identity models. In J. G. Ponterotto, J. M. Casas, L. A. Suzuki, & C. M. Alexander (Eds.), *Handbook of multicultural counseling* (pp. 181–198). Thousand Oaks, CA: Sage.

Helms, J. E. (1995b). *The People of Color (POC) Racial Identity Attitude Scale.* Unpublished manuscript. University of Maryland, College Park, MD.

Helms, J. E. (1996). Toward a methodology for measuring and assessing "racial" as distinguished from "ethnic" identity. In G. R. Sodowsky, & J. Impara (Eds.), *Multicultural assessment in counseling and clinical psychology* (pp. 143–192). Lincoln, NE: Buros Institute of Mental Measurements.

Helms, J. E. (1997). Implications of Behrens (1997) for the validity of the White Racial Identity Attitude Scale. *Journal of Counseling Psychology, 44*, 13–16.

Helms, J. E. (1999). Another meta-analysis of the White Racial Identity Attitude Scale's Cronbach alphas: Implications for validity. *Measurement & Evaluation in Counseling & Development, 32*, 122–137.

Helms, J. E. (2005). Challenging some misuses of reliability as reflected in evaluations of the White Racial Identity Scale (WRIAS). In R. T. Carter (Ed.), *Handbook of racial-cultural psychology and counseling: Theory and research* Vol. 1 (pp. 360–390). New York: John Wiley & Sons.

Helms, J. E. (2007). Some better practices for measuring racial and ethnic identity constructs. *Journal of Counseling Psychology, 54*, 235–246.

Helms, J. E., & Carter, R. T. (1986). *Manual for the Visible Racial/Ethnic Identity Attitude Scale.* University of Maryland, College Park, MD: Authors.

Helms, J. E., & Carter, R. T. (1990). *A preliminary overview of the Cultural Identity Attitude Scale.* Unpublished manuscript.

Helms, J. E., & Carter, R. T. (1990). Development of the White Racial Identity Inventory. In J. E. Helms (Ed.), *Black and White racial identity: Theory, research, and practice* (pp. 67–80). Westport, CT: Greenwood.

Helms, J. E., Henze, K. T., Sass, T. L., & Mifsud, V. A. (2006). Treating Cronbach's alpha reliability coefficients as data in counseling research. *The Counseling Psychologist, 34*, 630–660.

Helms, J. E., & Parham, T. A. (1996). The development of the Racial Identity Attitude Scale. In R. L. Jones (Ed.), *Handbook of tests and measurements for Black populations* Vol. 2 (pp. 167–174). Hampton, VA: Cobb & Henry.

Helms, J. E., & Talleyrand, R. M. (1997). Race is not ethnicity. *American Psychologist, 52*, 1246–1247.

Helm, K. M. (2002). A theoretical and psychometric analysis of the revised Black racial identity development model and the multidimensional model of racial identity: Outcomes on the Revised African American Acculturation Scale-33.

Dissertation Abstracts International: Section B: The Sciences and Engineering, 62(10-B), 4833.

Herc, D. J. K. (2005). Introduction. In J. Chang (Ed.), *Can't stop won't stop: A history of the hip hop generation* (pp. xi–xiii). New York: St. Martin's Press.

Horowitz, R. (1939). Racial aspects of self-identification in nursery school children. *Journal of Psychology, 7*, 91–99.

Jackson, B. W. (1976). Black identity development. In L. H. Golubchick, & B. Persky (Eds.), *Urban, social, and educational issues* (pp. 158–164). Dubuque, IA: Kendall/Hunt.

Jones, R. L. (Ed.). (1998). *African American identity development.* Hampton, VA: Cobb & Henry Publishers.

Jome, L. M. (2000). Construct validity of the White Racial Identity Attitude *Dissertation Abstracts International: Section B: The Sciences and Engineering, 61*(2-B), 1133.

Juni, S., Bresnan, M. W., & Vescio, C. F. (2006). Reliability of a modified People of Color Identity Attitude Scale and a White Racial Identity Attitude Scale for a sample of master's counseling students. *Psychological Reports, 98*, 809–818.

Kardiner, A., & Ovesey, L. (1951). *The mark of oppression.* New York: Norton.

Kerwin, C., & Ponterotto, J. G. (1995). Biracial identity development: Theory and research. In J. G. Ponterotto, J. M. Casas, L. A. Suzuki, & C. M. Alexander (Eds.), *Handbook of multicultural counseling* (pp. 199–217). Thousand Oaks, CA: Sage.

Kohatsu, E. L., & Richardson, T. Q. (1996). Racial and ethnic identity. In L. A. Suzuki, P. J. Meller, & J. G. Ponterotto (Eds.), *Handbook of multicultural assessment: Clinical, psychological, and educational applications* (pp. 611–650). San Francisco: Jossey-Bass.

Kovel, J. (1970). *White racism: A psychohistory.* New York: Pantheon Books.

Kurtzweil, P. L. (1996). The influence of life experience and social desirability on the development and measurement of White racial identity attitudes. *Dissertation Abstracts International: Section B: The Sciences and Engineering, 56*(10-B), 5836.

LaFleur, N. K., Leach, M. M., & Rowe, W. (2003). *Manual: Oklahoma Racial Attitudes Scale.* Unpublished manuscript.

LaFleur, N. K., Rowe, W., & Leach, M. M. (2002). Reconceptualizing White racial consciousness. *Journal of Multicultural Counseling and Development, 30*, 148–152.

Leach, M. M., Behrens, J. T., & LaFleur, N. K. (2002). White racial identity and white racial consciousness: Similarities, differences, and recommendations. *Journal of Multicultural Counseling and Development, 30*, 66–80.

Lee, R. M. (2003). Do ethnic identity and other-group orientation protect against discrimination for Asian Americans? *Journal of Counseling Psychology, 50*, 133–141.

Lee, S. M., Puig, A., Pasquarella-Daley, L., Denny, G., Rai, A. A., Dallape, A., & Parker, W. M. (2007). Revising the White Racial Consciousness Development Scale. *Measurement and Evaluation in Counseling and Development, 39*, 194–208.

Lemon, R. L., & Waehler, C. A. (1996). A test of stability and construct validity of the Black Racial Identity Scale, Form B (RIAS_B) and the White Racial Identity Attitude Scale (WRIAS). *Measurement and Evaluation in Counseling and Development, 29*, 77–85.

Lim, B. A. (2002). The role of experience and integrative complexity in ethnic identity Development. *Dissertation Abstracts International, 62*(11-B), 5430.

Liu, W. M. (2002). Exploring the lives of Asian American men: Racial identity, male role norms, gender conflict, and prejudicial attitudes. *Psychology of Men & Masculinity, 3*, 107–118.

Lo, H. W. (2005). Construct validity of the People of Color Racial Identity Attitude Scale. *Dissertation Abstracts International Section A: Humanities and Social Sciences, 65*(9-A), 3289.

Lott-Harrison, S. L. (1999). Racial and cultural identity development of African-American and Puerto Rican individuals: Same process, different content? *Dissertation Abstracts International, 59*(10-B), 5600.

Loya, M. (2007). Racial attitudes and cultural awareness in white social workers: A cross-sectional, correlational study. *Dissertation Abstracts International Section A, 68*, Retrieved from EBSCO*host*.

Marcia, J. E. (1980). Identity in adolescence. In J. Adelson (Ed.), *Handbook of adolescent psychology* (pp. 159–187). New York: Wiley.

Marcia, J. E. (1994). The empirical study of ego identity. In H. A. Bosma, T. G. Graafsma, H. D. Grotevant, & D. J. de Levita (Eds.), *Identity and development: An interdisciplinary approach* (4th ed., pp. 281–321). Belmont, CA: Wadsworth.

McNeill, B. W., Prieto, L. R., Niemann, Y. F., Pizarro, M., Vera, E. M., & Gomez, S. P. (2001). Current directions in Chicana/o psychology. *The Counseling Psychologist, 29*, 5–17.

Mercer, S. H., & Cunningham, M. (2003). Racial identity in White American college students: Issues of conceptualization and measurement. *Journal of College Student Development, 44*, 217–230.

Middleton, R. A., Stadler, H. A., Simpson, C., Guo, Y., Brown, M. J., Crow, G., et al. (2005). Mental health practitioners: The relationship between White racial identity attitudes and self-reported multicultural counseling competencies. *Journal of Counseling & Development, 83*, 444–456.

Milliones, J. (1980). Construction of a black consciousness measure: Psychotherapeutic implications. *Psychotherapy: Theory, Research, and Practice, 17*, 175–182.

Miville, M. L., & Helms, J. E. (1996). *Exploring relationships of cultural, gender, and ego identity among Latinos/as.* Poster presentation at the annual meeting of the American Psychological Association, Toronto, Canada.

Morten, G., & Atkinson, D. R. (1983). Minority identity development and preference for counselor race. *Journal of Negro Education, 52*(2), 156–161.

Neuger, D. A. (2002). Underlying dimensions of White racial attitudes. *Dissertation Abstracts International: Section B: The Sciences and Engineering, 63*(3-B), 1610.

Office of Management and Budget. (1995). *Standards for the classification of federal data on race and ethnicity.* Retrieved March 29, 2006, from http://www.whitehouse.gov/omb/fedreg/race-ethnicity/html.

Ottavi, T. M., Pope-Davis, D. B., & Dings, J. G. (1994). Relationship between White racial identity attitudes and self-reported multicultural counseling competencies. *Journal of Counseling Psychology, 41*, 149–154.

Pak, J. H. (2005). Narrative analysis of Korean American women's acculturation and changing self. *Dissertation Abstracts International, 66*(6-B), 3421.

Parham, T. A. (1989). Cycles of psychological nigrescence. *The Counseling Psychologist, 17*, 187–226.

Parham, T. A. (Ed.). (2002). *Counseling persons of African descent: Raising the bar of practitioner competence.* Thousand Oaks, CA: Sage.

Parham, T. A., & Helms, J. E. (1981). The influence of Black students' racial identity attitudes on preference for counselor's race. *Journal of Counseling Psychology, 28,* 250–258.

Passel, J. S. (2005). *Estimates of the size and characteristics of the undocumented population.* Washington, DC: Pew Hispanic Center. Retrieved April 20, 2008, from http://pewhispanic.org/reports/archive/Report.

Phinney, J. S. (1989). Stages of ethnic identity development in minority group adolescents. *Journal of Early Adolescence, 9,* 34–49.

Phinney, J. S. (1990). Ethnic identity in adolescents and adults: Review of research. *Psychological Bulletin, 108,* 499–514.

Phinney, J. S. (1992). The Multigroup Ethnic Identity Measure: A new scale for use with diverse groups. *Journal of Adolescent Research, 7,* 156–176.

Pizarro, M., & Vera, E. M. (2001). Chicana/o ethnic identity research: Lessons for researchers and counselors. *Counseling Psychologist, 29,* 91–117.

Ponpipom, A. (1997). Asian-American ethnic identity development: Contributing factors, assessment, and implications for psychotherapy. *Dissertations Abstracts International, 58*(1-B), 0425.

Ponterotto, J. G. (1986). A content analysis of the Journal of Multicultural Counseling and Development. *Journal of Multicultural Counseling and Development, 14,* 98–107.

Ponterotto, J. G. (1988). *Cross-cultural research in the Journal of Counseling Psychology: A content analysis and methodological critique.* Unpublished manuscript.

Ponterotto, J. G. (1989). Expanding directions for racial identity research. *The Counseling Psychologist, 17,* 264–272.

Ponterotto, J. G. (1998). Charting a course for research in multicultural counseling training. *The Counseling Psychologist, 26,* 43–68.

Ponterotto, J. G., Anderson, W. H., & Grieger, I. Z. (1986). Black students' attitudes toward counseling as a function of racial identity. *Journal of Non-White Concerns in Personnel & Guidance, 14,* 50–59.

Ponterotto, J. G., Casas, J. M., Suzuki, L., & Alexander, C. M. (2001). *Handbook of Multicultural Counseling.* Thousand Oaks, CA: Sage.

Ponterotto, J. G., Fuertes, J. N., & Chen, E. C. (2000). Models of multicultural counseling. In S. D. Brown, & R. W. Lent (Eds.), *Handbook of counseling psychology* (3rd ed., pp. 639–669). New York: John Wiley & Sons.

Ponterotto, J. G., & Park-Taylor, J. (2007). Racial and ethnic identity theory, measurement, and research in counseling psychology: Present status and future directions. *Journal of Counseling Psychology, 54,* 282–294.

Ponterotto, J. G., & Sabnani, H. B. (1989). "Classics" in multicultural counseling: A systematic five-year content analysis. *Journal of Multicultural Counseling and Development, 17,* 23–37.

Ponterotto, J. G., Utsey, S. O., & Pedersen, P. B. (2006). *Preventing prejudice: A guide for counselors, educators, and parents* (2nd ed.). Thousand Oaks, CA: Sage.

Ponterotto, J. G., & Wise, S. L. (1987). Construct validity study of the Racial Identity Attitude Scale. *Journal of Counseling Psychology, 34,* 218–223.

Pope-Davis, D. B., Dings, J. G., Stone, G. L., & Vandiver, B. (1995, August). *White racial identity attitude development: A comparison of two instruments.* Poster session presented at the meeting of the American Psychological Association, New York.

Pope-Davis, D. B., Vandiver, B. J., & Stone, G. L. (1999). White racial identity attitude development: A psychometric examination of two instruments. *Journal of Counseling Psychology, 46*(1), 70–79.

Poston, W. S. C. (1990). The biracial identity development model: A needed addition. *Journal of Counseling and Development, 69,* 152–155.

Richardson, T. Q., & Helms, J. E. (1994). The relationship of the racial identity attitudes of Black men to perceptions of "parallel" counseling dyads. *Journal of Counseling & Development, 73,* 172–177.

Root, M. P. P. (1999). The biracial baby boom: Understanding ecological constructions of racial identity in the 21st century. In R. H. Sheets, & E. R. Hollins (Eds.), *Racial and ethnic identity in school practices: Aspects of human development* (pp. 67–89). Mahwah, NJ: Lawrence Erlbaum.

Rosenberg, M. (1965). *Society and the adolescent self-image.* Princeton, NJ: Princeton University Press.

Rowe, W., Behrens, J. T., & Leach, M. M. (1995). Racial/ethnic identity and racial consciousness: Looking back and looking forward. In J. G. Ponterotto, J. M. Casas, L. A. Suzuki, & C. M. Alexander (Eds.), *Handbook of multicultural counseling* (pp. 218–235). Thousand Oaks, CA: Sage.

Rowe, W., Bennett, S. K., & Atkinson, D. R. (1994). White racial identity models: A critique and alternative proposal. *The Counseling Psychologist, 22,* 129–146.

Sabnani, H. B., & Ponterotto, J. G. (1992). Racial/ethnic minority-specific instrumentation in counseling research: A review, critique, and recommendations. *Measurement and Evaluation in Counseling and Development, 24,* 161–187.

Sabnani, H. B., Ponterotto, J. G., & Borodovsky, L. G. (1991). White racial identity development and cross-cultural counselor training: A stage model. *The Counseling Psychologist, 19,* 76–102.

Schmidt, C. (2007). Racial/ethnic identity formation and ego development. *Dissertation Abstracts International Section A: Humanities and Social Sciences, 68*(1-A), 96.

Sears, D. O., Fu, M., Henry, P. J., & Bui, K. (2003). The origins and persistence of ethnic identity among the "New Immigrant" groups. *Social Psychology Quarterly, 66,* 419–437.

Sellers, R. M., Rowley, S. A. J., Chavous, T. M., Shelton, J. N., & Smith, M. A. (1997). Multidimensional Inventory of Black Identity: A preliminary investigation of reliability and construct validity. *Journal of Personality and Social Psychology, 73,* 805–815.

Sellers, R. M., Smith, M. A., Shelton, J. N., Rowley, S. A., & Chavous, T. M. (1998). Multidimensional model of racial identity: A reconceptualization of African-American racial identity. *Personality and Social Psychology Review, 2,* 18–39.

Simmons, C., Worrell, F. C., & Berry, J. M. (in press). Psychometric properties of scores on three Black racial identity scales. *Assessment.*

Stevenson, H. C., Jr. (1995). Relationship of adolescent perceptions of racial socialization to racial identity. *Journal of Black Psychology, 21,* 49–70.

Stevenson, H. C., Jr. (1998). The confluence of "both-and" in Black racial identity theory: Response to Stokes, Murray, Chavez and Peacock. In R. L. Jones (Ed.), *African American identity development* (pp. 151–157). Hampton, VA: Cobb & Henry Publishers.

Stokes, J. E., Murray, C. B., Chavez, D., & Peacock, M. J. (1998). Cross' stage model revisited: An analysis of theoretical formulations and empirical evidence. In R. L. Jones (Ed.), *African American identity development* (pp. 121–140). Hampton, VA: Cobb & Henry Publishers.

Stryker, S., & Serpe, R. T. (1982). Commitment, identity salience and role behavior. In W. Ickes, & E. Knowles (Eds.), *Personality, roles, and social behavior* (pp. 199–218). New York: Springer-Verlag.

Stryker, S., & Serpe, R. T. (1994). Identity salience and psychological centrality: Equivalent, overlapping, or complementary concepts? *Social Psychology Quarterly, 57,* 16–35.

Sue, D. W. (1989). Racial/cultural identity development among Asian-Americans: Counseling/therapy implications. *AAPA Journal, 13*(1), 80–86.

Sue, D. W., & Sue, D. (1990). *Counseling the culturally different: Theory and practice* (2nd ed.). New York: Wiley & Sons.

Sue, D. W., & Sue, D. (2008). *Counseling the culturally diverse: Theory and practice* (5th ed.). New York: Wiley & Sons.

Summerson, M. T. (1997). White racial consciousness and preference for counselor ethnicity in White undergraduate students. *Dissertation Abstracts International: Section B: The Sciences and Engineering, 57*(11-B), 7238.

Swanson, J. L., Tokar, D. M., & Davis, L. E. (1994). Content and construct validity of the White Racial Identity Attitude Scale. *Journal of Vocational Behavior, 44,* 198–217.

Tajfel, H. (Ed.). (1978). *Differentiation between social groups: Studies in the social psychology of intergroup relations.* London: Academic Press.

Tajfel, H., & Turner, J. C. (1979). An integrative theory of intergroup conflict. In W. G. Austin, & S. Worchel (Eds.), *The social psychology of intergroup relations* (pp. 94–109). Monterey, CA: Brooks-Cole.

Thomas, C. W. (1969). Boys no more: Some social psychological aspects of the new Black ethic. *The American Behavioral Scientist, 12,* 38–42.

Thomas, C. W. (1971). *Boys no more.* Beverly Hills, CA: Glencoe Press.

Thomas, R. E. (1985). Counseling diverse adults through transitions. *Journal of Employment Counseling, 22*(3), 124–127.

Thompson, C. E., & Carter, R. T. (1997). An overview and elaboration of Helms' racial identity development theory. In C. E. Thompson, & R. T. Carter (Eds.), *Racial identity theory: Applications to individual, group, and organizational interventions* (pp. 15–32). Mahwah, NJ: Lawrence Erlbaum Associates, Inc.

Tokar, D. M., & Fischer, A. R. (1998). Psychometric analysis of the Racial Identity Attitude Scale—Long form. *Measurement and Evaluation in Counseling and Development, 31,* 138–149.

Tokar, D. M., & Swanson, J. L. (1991). An investigation of the validity of Helms' (1984) model of White racial identity. *Journal of Counseling Psychology, 38,* 296–301.

U. S. Census Bureau. (2001). *The census 2000 brief overview of race and Hispanic origin.* Retrieved June 15, 2008, from http://www.census.gov/prod/2001pubs/c2kbr01–1.pdf.

Umana-Taylor, A. J., Yazedijian, A., & Bamaca-Gomez, M. (2004). Developing the Ethnic Identity Scale using social identity perspectives. *Identity: An International Journal of Theory and Research, 4,* 9–38.

Utsey, S. O., & Gernat, C. A. (2002). White racial identity attitudes and the ego defense mechanisms used by White counselor trainees in racially provocative counseling situations. *Journal of Counseling & Development, 80,* 475–483.

Vandiver, B. J. (2007, August). *Examining the reliability of the CRIS scores.* Poster session presented at the annual conference of the American Psychological Association, San Francisco, CA.

Vandiver, B. J., Cross, W. E., Jr., Fhagen-Smith, P. E., Worrell, F. C., Swim, J. K., &. Caldwell, L. D. (2000). *The Cross Racial Identity Scale.* State College, PA: Author.

Vandiver, B. J., Cross, W. E., Jr., Worrell, F. C., & Fhagen-Smith, P. E. (2002). Validating the Cross Racial Identity Scale (CRIS). *Journal of Counseling Psychology, 49,* 71–85.

Vandiver, B. J., Fhagen-Smith, P. E., Cokley, K. O., Cross, W. E., Jr., & Worrell, F. C. (2001). Cross' nigrescence model: From theory to scale to theory. *Journal of Multicultural Counseling and Development, 29,* 174–200.

Vandiver, B. J., Korell, S. C., & Miller, A. R. (2007). *CRIS cluster project.* State College, PA: Author.

Vandiver, B. J., & Worrell, F. C. (Eds.). (2001). Psychological nigrescence revisited: Theory and research [special issue]. *Journal of Multicultural Counseling and Development, 29,* 165–213.

Waters, M. C. (2000). Immigration, intermarriage, and the challenges of measuring racial/ethnic identities. *American Journal of Public Health, 90,* 1735–1737.

Weathersby, A. (2005). The effects of multicultural education on white racial consciousness. *Dissertation Abstracts International: Section B: The Sciences and Engineering, 65*(9 B), 4901.

Worrell, F. C. (2008). Nigrescence attitudes in adolescence, emerging adulthood, and adulthood. *Journal of Black Psychology, 34,* 156–178.

Worrell, F. C., Cross, W. E., Jr., & Vandiver, B. J. (2001). Nigrescence theory: Current status and challenges for the future. *Journal of Multicultural Counseling and Development, 29,* 201–209.

Worrell, F. C., & Gardner-Kitt, D. L. (2006). The relationship between racial and ethnic identity in Black adolescents: The Cross Racial Identity Scale (CRIS) and the Multigroup Ethnic Identity Measure (MEIM). *Identity: An International Journal of Theory and Research, 6,* 293–315.

Worrell, F. C., Vandiver, B. J., & Cross, W. E. (2004). *The Cross Racial Identity Scale: Technical manual* (2nd. ed.). Berkeley, CA: Author.

Worrell, F. C., Vandiver, B. J., Cross, W. E., Jr., & Fhagen-Smith, P. (2004). Reliability and structural validity of the Cross Racial Identity Scale scores in a sample of African American adults. *Journal of Black Psychology, 30,* 489–505.

Worrell, F. C., Vandiver, B. J., Schaefer, B. A., Cross, W. E., & Fhagen-Smith, P. E. (2006). Generalizing nigrescence profiles: Cluster analyses of Cross Racial Identity Scale (CRIS) scores in three independent samples. *The Counseling Psychologist, 34,* 519–547.

Worrell, F. C., & Watson, S. (2008). A confirmatory factor analysis of Cross Racial Identity Scale (CRIS) scores: Testing the expanded nigrescence model. *Educational and Psychological Measurement, 68,* 1041–1058.

Yacoubian, V. V. (2004). Assessment of racial identity and self-esteem in an Armenian American population. *Dissertation Abstracts International: Section B: The Sciences and Engineering, 64*(12-B), 6382.

Yanico, B. J., Swanson, J. L., & Tokar, D. M. (1994). A psychometric investigation of the Black Racial Identity Attitude Scale—Form B. *Journal of Vocational Behavior, 44,* 218–234.

Yeh, C. J., & Hwang, M. Y. (2000). Interdependence in ethnic identity and self: Implications for theory and practice. *Journal of Counseling & Development, 78,* 420–429.

Developing a Social Class and Classism Consciousness

William Ming Liu

Abstract

Current methods in psychology to study and understand social class are problematic because using objective indicators of income, education, and occupation may not capture the meaningfulness of social class in a person's life. I argue for psychologists to shift to a subjective approach to social class and classism. I revise the social class worldview model-revised (SCWM-R) (Liu, 2001, 2002; Liu & Ali, 2008) and elaborate on a complementary framework embedded within the SCWM-R titled the social class and classism consciousness model (SCCC). The SCCC explores the ways in which individuals come to see themselves as socially classed persons. The SCCC has ten levels of social class consciousness ranging from being unconscious about social class to being self-conscious to being social class conscious. I present clinical and research implications and suggests future directions for research concerning social class and classism in psychology.

Keywords: social class, classism, consciousness, worldview

The social class worldview model (SCWM) (Liu, 2001, 2006; Liu & Ali, 2008; Liu, Ali, et al., 2004; Liu, Soleck, Hopps, Dunston, & Pickett, 2004) was created as a subjective and phenomenological approach to understanding an individual's experiences of and perspectives about social class and classism. Significant research suggested the utility of a subjective understanding of social class and socioeconomic status (SES) (Adler, Boyce, Chesney, Folman, & Syme, 1993; Cohen et al., 2008; Ostrove, Adler, Kuppermann, & Washington, 2000; Sapolsky, 2005) that moved beyond using only sociodemographic indicators of income, education, and occupation as descriptors of social class and SES. It was important for psychologists to move beyond these sociological indices of social class and SES because, although these indicators provided some help in categorizing individuals into discreet groupings (e.g., middle-class), these sociodemographic indices tended to be unhelpful in providing clarity or a deeper understanding of an individual's

experiences with social class and SES (Brown, Fukunaga, Umemoto, & Wicker, 1996; Fouad & Brown, 2001; Frable, 1997). The SCWM was a framework in which psychologists could integrate an individual's contexts, experiences, and worldview, to help psychologists explore and understand social class and classism (American Psychological Association [APA], 2007; Liu, 2001; Liu & Ali, 2008).

The SCWM is a wholly subjectively based approach to understanding and exploring social class and classism, but one implicit assumption of the SCWM is that individuals understood and could discuss social class in their lives. That is, the SCWM assumed that individuals already were conscious and aware of themselves as a socially classed person and were able to discuss the meaning and importance of social class in their lives. Invariably, however, social class awareness varies since exposure to and familiarity with social class issues are not consistent across individuals. Thus, it was necessary to develop a framework to explore the ways in which social class awareness and consciousness develop. The purpose of this chapter is to develop a central construct in the SCWM that focuses on how individuals think of themselves as socially classed persons. That is, I will explore how people develop a social class and classism consciousness. To do so, this chapter will first present problems in our current understanding and use of the terms *social class* and *socioeconomic status*. Second, I operationalize two key constructs: class and status, and differentiates between social class and SES. Third, I present a model for developing a social class and classism consciousness (SCCC). Finally, I discuss clinical and training implications and presents suggestions for future research directions for social class issues and this model.

The Problem with Current Uses of Social Class and Socioeconomic Status

Psychologists' problems with understanding social class, classism, and SES stem from poor operationalization of terms and variables and generally an atheoretical use of social class and SES in research (Brown et al., 1996; Duncan & Magnuson, 2003; Ensminger & Fothergill, 2003; Liberatos, Link, & Kelsey, 1988; Liu & Ali, 2008; Oakes & Rossi, 2003). Liu (2001, 2006; Liu & Ali, 2008; Liu, Ali, et al. 2004) suggests that the importing of sociological devices and frameworks to understand social class and SES at the individual level has been problematic for research and practice. Although income, education, and occupation are frequently used as individual indicators and as a means to aggregate people into social class groups (e.g., lower-class), no evidence suggests that these indicators affect any particular social class group (Brown et al., 1996).

Attempts to make meaning of these different groupings only created greater confusion. One typical strategy was to use income, education, and occupation and create a series of pseudo social class groupings (Liu & Ali, 2008). This approach only produced an unlimited number and type of social class striations (e.g., lower-working class, middle-working class, working-class). But because these groupings were unlinked to any particular theory or rationale, these social class striations were idiosyncratic to each researcher and practically meaningless between researchers.

A similar problem arose when clinicians discussed the social class of individuals. What does it mean for a clinician to describe a client as "middle-class?" What is the clinician drawing upon to make this description, and what is being attributed to the client? How are clinicians to make sense of these sociodemographic descriptions? The likely problem of using social class in clinical practice becomes more difficult as clinicians conceptualize a client's sociodemographic characteristics or attempt to discuss "social class" with the client. This sociodemographic approach would likely limit the discussion to issues of income, education, or occupation, but may not provide clinicians with a "roadmap" to explore other issues such as classism, inequality, affluence, power, or privilege (Liu, Pickett, & Ivey, 2007).

Moreover, by unlinking measurement from theory, categories such as middle- or upper-class lose their qualitative saliency. That is, by making the focus on creating different social class or SES striations within an economic hierarchy, the meaningful concerns of power, privilege, access to resources, and inequality are lost in favor of a focus on accurate in objective indices. Wright (2002) argues that traditional social class critiques from Max Weber and Karl Marx were focused on qualitative groups such as "capitalists and workers, debtors and creditors" (p. 839) rather than on names such as "upper, upper-middle, middle, lower-middle" classes (p. 839). Although somewhat antiquated in terms and constructs, Wright's critique is valid in that, rather than explicating the power and privilege for those in the upper classes, the current discussion in psychology may mostly be nominal and revolve around demographic characteristics, such as income or educational level. Consequently, upper class becomes just another group with inferred privileges versus a group with explicit privileges and experiences. In effect, current uses of social class or SES have been diminished with regard to their political meaning. A corollary would be to study race and discuss racism, but then limiting the discussion to describing racism as events without the emotional valence associated with each event, thereby potentially neutralizing its interpersonal meaning.

Contributing to these problems is terms such as social class and SES can simultaneously be meaningless levels of measurement, and be meaningful levels of measurement for different groups. Moreover, different indices may have different meanings for individuals depending on their context, time of life, and demands and expectations. For instance, a social class and SES economic hierarchy implies a continuum of low (usually the impoverished) and high (usually those possessing the most wealth). The assumption is that an economic hierarchy exists as a ratio level of measurement (with an absolute zero). Many of the current economic hierarchies have some baseline with zero or "poor" at the bottom, usually dictated by the amount of one's income. The belief by some researchers may be that, with appropriate measures and methods, one may be able to perfectly assess objective indices and create a baseline with equal steps throughout the hierarchy (Pollack et al., 2007). But, in a modern economy, there are several problems with these assumptions. First, for some individuals, there certainly is an absolute zero (no income, no equity, no opportunities, or limited access to additional resources). For these individuals, the felt loss of a single dollar is perceived much more severely than for those in a higher social class group (Tyszka & Przybyszewski, 2006). And, there are real and meaningful educational, health, occupational, and life consequences attributed to being poor (Hopps & Liu, 2006). But for others, "zero" is a relative term depending on the indicator or measure. For example, one could have no income but live on an inheritance or on interest from investments; one could have negative equity but still have wealth elsewhere; and opportunities and access to additional resources are likely related to the quality and extensiveness of social networks (Lin, 1999), which may vary by individual. Thus, a single measure with the assumed "zero baseline" may not accurately assess persons across the social class and SES continuum. Additionally, for individuals for whom income is only one factor in their overall self-assessment of wealth, the amount of their actual cash-on-hand is minor compared to other indices and assets that reflect their position and status.

Second, "distance" is relative. Clearly objective indicators may show discrete distances between income level and education, for instance. Increments of $10,000 in a demographic form suggest that income distance is absolute and not relative. But research suggests that these differences vary in meaning (Pingle & Mitchell, 2002; Solnick & Hemenway, 1998). People typically compare themselves on income within their peer group and not necessarily across income groups. Thus, individuals making $45,000–$55,000 may recognize how discrete differences in levels of income translate to minor increases in their monthly paycheck. These individuals may recognize someone making several million dollars, but the perceived "steps" to that level are less likely to be seen in $10,000 increments than as someone making "several million dollars." That is, people may compare themselves with peers around them within a given context, but there may be income "cutoffs" between the individual and the next higher or lower income group. Thus, in measuring a person's income, it may be necessary to have individuals indicate their income, but to also demarcate the boundaries of their income group. This may give researchers a sense of the income level of a particular group of participants, and it may give clinicians an indication of what individuals consider their normative group. But meaningfulness of one's income may also be different. The meaningfulness of increasing income may also represent a type of dose-response curve (in which a dose equals amount of income and the curve is related to specific outcome measures). That is, income may be differentially meaningful depending on the individual and for what the income is used (i.e., leisure, material objects, savings, debt).

Furthermore, because income, education, and occupation are independently meaningful and linked to different social class outcome variables (e.g., health, happiness, satisfaction) (Duncan, 1988), and because of the notorious problem of inaccurate reporting of data such as personal income or the emotional reactivity associated with reporting income (Croizet & Claire, 1998), researchers have generally been more focused on how to accurately measure social class rather than on determining what each variable means to the individual. Attempts have been made to shift from discrete single variables to aggregate constructs, such as wealth or affluence. Yet, even in these larger constructs, aggregating these variables still rests primarily on the accurate reports of income, assets, and other wealth estimates by individuals (Pollack et al., 2007), or the number and type of possessions (e.g., "Does your family own a car, van, or truck?" [Family Affluence Scale]) (Currie, Elton, Todd, & Platt, 1997).

But if individuals were to accurately report all of their demographic data, what would that mean to our understanding of a person's social class or SES (Offer, 2006)? Liu and his colleagues made a necessary critique of existing paradigms around the measurement and use of social class and SES in psychology, but the extent of these critiques was insufficient. Psychologists do have problems in measuring income, educational level, and occupation, but these variables—much like any other demographic variable, such as race or gender—have no inherent value or meaning besides what the individual or researcher ascribes to them. Thus, it is necessary to capture the individual meaning related to each indicator rather than to seek accuracy or verisimilitude. If we examine income for instance, it is most meaningful to the individual as "relative income" in comparison to others in his or her peer group (Pingle & Mitchell, 2002; Solnick & Hemenway, 1998). Therefore, understanding a $100,000 income may depend on the individual's taxes, neighborhood, the material objects his or her peers possess, and the size of the home, for instance (Fletcher, 2001; The Wall Street Journal, 2001). A similar problem may exist for educational level. Although degrees and ranks are stable among institutions, the meaning of degrees and educational level will vary. For example, an individual's doctorate from an accredited online college is likely to be very different from a doctorate from Harvard University. The individuals in these two examples are likely to recognize and imbue their degrees with different levels of prestige and will employ this educational prestige differently depending on the context. For instance, the individual with the online degree may, with people who may not be familiar with doctoral education, promote the degree, but among those with Ivy League educations, the online degree may not be promoted. Further potentially moderating these attributions to academic level may be the age at which the individual receives the degree (i.e., younger age with advanced degrees may indicate higher intelligence), if the individual is a first-generation student, and possibly the person's race and gender—none of which is considered in a question about educational level.

Finally, for occupations, prestige is usually the implied value when categorizing certain jobs as lower-, middle-, or upper-class. A prestige index assumes that every individual possesses the same or similar perspective on all jobs and their relative value. However, occupational prestige may also vary between contexts and geographic region (Ali & McWhirter, 2006; Blustein, 2006) such that, in some situations, a traditional intergenerational occupation (i.e., coal mining) may possibly be just as prestigious as a college professorship. Similarly, to ascribe prestige on a given occupation is to assume that an individual would have full knowledge of any specific occupation along the prestige hierarchy. Yet, it may be fair to speculate that there may be some high-status and high-prestige occupations that are not esteemed by persons unfamiliar with those jobs. This unfamiliarity problem may also become worse as middle- and upper-class occupations proliferate in specizations within disciplines, while lower- and working-class occupations remain relatively stable in titles and job responsibilities.

Since no research has examined how different social class groups value the hierarchy of occupations, it is uncertain why one occupational prestige index would be used in all situations and populations.

SOCIO- OR IDIO-CLASS?

The use of income or educational level has been confounded and has led several researchers to explore the potential for a subjective approach to understanding an individual's perspective on social class and SES. One popular method used in various studies of SES and health revolves around using a "ladder." Research participants are presented with a ten-rung ladder and given instructions to:

> Think of this ladder as presenting where people stand in the United States. At the top of the ladder are the people who are the best off. . . . At the bottom are the people who are the worst off. . . . The higher up you are on the ladder, the closer you are to the people at the very top and the lower you are, the closer you are to the people at the very bottom. . . . (Ostrove et al., 2000, p. 614)

Findings generally show that people, even in dire economic circumstances such as homelessness, are likely to have better self-rated health and potentially more favorable outcomes if they consider themselves higher on the ladder than do those who rate themselves lower on the ladder (Adler, Epel, Castellazzo, & Ickovics, 2000). These findings do not refute the social class and health gradient, wherein better objective health is related to one's higher position (Adler et al., 1993; Singh & Siahpush, 2006) or contradict research findings on the causal relationship between poverty and poorer mental and physical health (Costello, Compton, Keeler, & Angold, 2003; Gallo, Bogart, Vranceanu, & Matthews, 2005; Gallo & Matthews, 1999, 2003; Gallo, Smith, & Cox, 2006; Geronimus, Bound, Waidmann, Hillemeier, & Burns, 1996). Instead, the "ladder" research suggests that individuals will vary in making meaning of objective circumstances, and that within-group variation exists even among those in abject situations.

Since people vary in their interpretation of economic situations and their social class standing, this is not to suggest that "socio" should become *idio-class* or *idioeconomic status*. The study and exploration of social class and classism cannot be divorced from the individual's context and the interrelationships that support and challenge a particular social class worldview. Yet, since the original nominal term *socioeconomic* was used by Lester Ward in 1883 to link the social and economic spheres of people's lives (Jones & McMillan, 2001), psychologists have concocted various synonyms to understand the individual-level social class experience and perspective. In one study, Liu, Ali et al. (2004) reviewed three counseling journals for use of social class in research. Liu, Ali et al. found approximately 448 words linked to the constructs of social class, classism, and SES. These terms varied from single variables, such as educational level, to aggregates, such as "school-lunch" or "welfare" participants. The common theme in most studies was to use these variables as demographic or categorical variables (socio) rather than asking the participants about their perception of being in "school-lunch" or "welfare" programs (idio).

As psychologists, the general focus is on the individual experiences and understanding, rather than on the macro level. With social class or SES, the different levels of society (e.g., mesosystem, macrosystem) (Bronfenbrenner, 1986) may be used to inform the individual's current experiences (Liu & Ali, 2008). Liu and Ali show that understanding how issues such as unemployment, materialism, policies on poverty, and community violence, for instance, are directly related to issues such as the individual's self-esteem, stress level, coping styles, and intimate relationships, to name a few. Moreover, the "socio" issues related to an individual's social class perspectives and experiences implicate the ways in which society constructs meaning, imbues value, and marginalizes people and materials. Thus, it is still meaningful to focus on "social" class and "socio" economic status rather than on an idiographic approach.

A Subjective Approach to Social Class and Classism

A subjective approach to social class and SES represents a shift from current paradigms of understanding these two constructs. Liu and his colleagues (Liu & Ali, 2008; Liu, Ali et al., 2004) felt that psychologists needed to transform social class and SES into meaningful psychological variables, constructs, and theories. For instance, psychologists interested in racial or cultural issues within a specific population focus their research on theory-based constructs, such as racial identity and acculturation. Psychologists do not study specifically race or immigration. Instead, psychologists address racial identity or acculturation, and in effect, the individual's experiences with racism, migration, and cultural adaptation are measured and explored. Similarly with social class and SES, psychologists should operationalize these as psychological constructs, such as identity, acculturation, dissonance, worldview, and roles, to name a few.

Regardless of the theory and psychological dimension, focusing on the individual-level experience does not negate or diminish the larger sociopolitical (e.g., the unequal distribution of power), sociohistorical (e.g., biased and inaccurate histories of peoples), and sociostructural (e.g., legal, education, and economic systems) forces that marginalize and oppress peoples (Liu & Ali, 2005). Liu and Pope-Davis (2003a, 2003b) believe that a subjective approach also allows psychologists to explore the complex networks of power that potentially reinforce and perpetuate economic inequality. Rather than addressing only binary approaches to economic disadvantage (Smith, 2005, 2006; Smith, Foley, & Chaney, 2008), which creates procrustean groups of powerful and powerless, Liu and Pope-Davis (2003a) suggest that it would be advantageous for psychologists to understand the ways in which people negotiate power and privilege, and the ways in which power and inequality are produced and recreated (Liu et al., 2007).

CLASS AND STATUS

Heretofore, I have discussed social class and SES as similar constructs. In part, this reflects the general atheoretical problems related to operationalizing both social class and SES (Liberatos et al., 1988; Oakes & Rossi, 2003). But social class and SES could represent different but related aspects of understanding a person's experiences with his or her economic spheres of life. In a similar way, Weberian and Marxian notions differ, in that Weberian analysis focuses on life chances and Marxian analysis focuses on exploitation (Wright, 2002). Liu, Ali et al. (2004) already provided a nonexhaustive discussion of the potential differences between social class and SES. In their description, individuals discussed within the framework of social class are part of an economic hierarchy with in- and out-groups; with the out-groups (e.g., people in lower social positions) being the targets of derision and marginalization. Liu, Ali et al. suggest that a critical function within the social class framework is "group awareness" (p. 8) and class consciousness. Being aware of one's belonging within a particular social class group (Wright, 2002) and the need to protect and reinforce the group, is the root of classism. Therefore, a "class" is an economic group within which an individual belongs, and the individual perceives material (i.e., types of belongings, neighborhood) and nonmaterial (i.e., educational level) boundaries. The individual may observe other "classes" that are perceived to be, in a subjective hierarchy, higher, lower, and at the same place (i.e., lateral) as the individual's own class. Social class mobility is possible, but only through the comprehension of the other class's norms, values, and culture; that is, each class is perceived to have its own culture, and the further away the social class group is from the current position, the more dissonant or unfamiliar the culture is to the individual. Consequently, classism is an employed behavior and attitude, and an expected consequence as the individual attempts to navigate within and between classes.

With SES, Liu, Ali et al. (2004) suggest that the individual's place within an economic hierarchy is temporary and mobile. The difference between social class and SES may be that individuals in an SES framework are not expected to share any group consciousness. Rather, the individual is an independent actor in a dynamically fluid economic environment. Status, as the name implies, focuses on the current perceived economic place of the individual. Perceived inequality in access to resources, for instance, may be congruent within this approach. Inequality may be a consequence of classism, but one cannot employ "unequalness." In both frameworks, social class and SES, income, educational level, occupational prestige, power, and access to resources may be perceived to have different functions. Within the social class framework, these variables may be aspects that the individual possesses and uses to maintain her social class position and the boundaries of the group. Within a SES framework, these same variables may be perceived as facets for social mobility. But these are not exhaustive categorizations of social class and SES. Instead, this is an attempt to operationalize variables that are often conflated with each other or used synonymously.

I use the term *social class* and *classism* hereafter since the constructs are inherently linked, and the hypothesis that individuals perceive different "classes" is an important assumption for the SCWM. Additionally, the nominal term *classism* is widely accepted to represent marginalizing behaviors and attitudes based on perceived economic variations (Lott, 2002; Smith et al., 2008). Social class and classism are conceptualized as interdependent constructs similar to race and racism. Research on and around issues of classism, economic marginalization, and economically motivated negative interpersonal behavior and attitudes generally suggests negative

effects related to classism (Croizet & Claire, 1998; Croizet, Desert, Dutrevis, & Leyens, 2001; De Vogli, Ferrie, Chandola, Kivimaki, & Marmot, 2007; Miller, 2001; Vohs, Mead, & Goode, 2006). The SCWM is an individual's "worldview" about social class, or the beliefs, attitudes, and values an individual uses to interpret her economic situations and conditions. These beliefs, attitudes, and values stem from the person's socialization experiences with family, friends, and peers, as well as the larger economic culture, and the worldview helps the individual make sense of the expectations and demands of these groups (Liu, Ali et al., 2004). This worldview also interprets experiences of classism and shapes the ways in which individuals use classism to maintain their perceived social class position.

The Social Class Worldview Model – Revised

The original SCWM (Liu, 2001, 2002) was developed as a theoretical framework that shifts the psychological discourse around social class away from the stratification and sociological paradigms that have permeated much of the theoretical and empirical literature. The SCWM provides a theoretical model, a heuristic that integrates both social class and classism and allows psychologists a means by which to explore the subjective social class experiences of individuals. *Worldview* is used as the psychological construct from which social class is understood by the individual. The SCWM is meant as a way to model, frame, and understand social class behaviors, attitudes, and cognitions and is comprised of multiple components; consequently, there is no one measure that adequately assesses the entire model. The SCWM (Liu, 2001, 2002; Liu & Arguello, 2006; Liu & Ali, 2008) is comprised of three components that are theoretically linked in a feedback system to help the individual maintain homeostasis or a positive sense of self within his or her social class. The first assumption of the SCWM is that people are motivated to maintain a sense of normality within their perceived social class group. Individuals' motivations are to perceive and act on the world in ways similar to those of their peers and cohort, and if successful, they achieve a sense of homeostasis. Disequilibrium occurs when new demands and expectations are exacted on the individual, and the person must configure behaviors, resources, and attitudes to reestablish his or her homeostasis. For instance, disequilibrium may occur when new materialistic demands are placed on a person, such as a new car or a larger home. If the individual believes these new materialistic expectations are a part of being normal in his social class group, then he will act in ways to obtain these new objects. A second assumption of the SCWM is that people live within different economic cultures (ECs), neighborhoods, or communities within which the individual seeks social class position and status. For instance, ECs vary, such that no one unitary "middle-class" group exists, but rather many "middle-class" groups or ECs. There are not necessarily any real geographic or material boundaries demarcating these ECs, but certainly for some individuals, an EC may be a certain neighborhood or community with familial roots, economic markers (e.g., gated communities), or particular setting (e.g., school or work).

These different ECs vary with regard to expectations and demands on a person. In one EC, physical attributes may be highly valued, and individuals in that EC may feel pressure to develop and maintain physical attributes and features. Athletes, for instance, may find themselves in ECs in which physicality is valued above other resources, and physical prowess is a type of capital (resource) employed to maintain one's social class position. Another example may be professors, for whom intellectual abilities are favored and social capital (one's social network) is equally important to nurture. Thus, an EC is important because it shapes the expectations and demands an individual experiences with regard to accumulating and using certain kinds of capital or resources. Within the SCWM, there are three types of capital to accumulate: cultural capital (aesthetics important in the EC), social capital (important relationships), and human capital (important physical or intellectual skills).

The second component is the worldview, or the lens through which the individual attempts to understand these different capital demands and how these resources are to be used. The individual's worldview is comprised of socialization messages from parents and peers. Another group that provides socialization messages is the group to which the individual aspires (e.g., upper-class groups). Other components of the worldview are an individual's materialistic attitudes, perceived social class–congruent behaviors (e.g., etiquette, accent), and lifestyle considerations, such as the way a person spends his or her time (e.g., leisure, work, vacations). These aspects of the worldview are not all equally salient but vary depending on the EC. Depending on the individual's EC, one of these dimensions will be prominent and be the likely way through which the world is experienced and perceived. For instance,

an individual may live in an EC in which social network capital is highly valued, and one way that the individual believes (and is reinforced) these interpersonal relationships are developed is through material possessions. Thus, for this person, others are valued for "what they have," the self is valued for what is possessed, and a motivational factor is the accumulation of belongings as a way to maintain one's social class position.

The final component is classism. In the SCWM, classism is both interpreted and used by the individual to maintain one's social class. Classism, therefore, is both employed by the individual to gain resources and is similarly experienced by the individual when interacting with people from perceived different social class groups. For example, if it were important in an EC to maintain social capital and social networks through the exclusion of individuals believed to be from "upper-class" groups, then the labeling of those perceived to be "elitist" would be a form of upward classism. These forms of classism are in some ways independent of the objective social class position of the individual, such that one could be from an upper social class group (defined by extreme wealth, high education, and prestigious occupation), but still characterize someone similarly as "elitist" or a "snob." Upward classism is one of four types of classism in the SCWM. The four types of classism are: downward (against those perceived to be in a lower social class), upward (against those perceived to be in a higher group, such that others in that group are labeled snobs or elitists), lateral (against those perceived to be in a similar group and may be experienced as pressure to keep up with the Joneses because the Joneses keep reminding you), and internalized (against the self for not being able to maintain one's social class position).

Although downward classism has been largely recognized as a dominant form of oppression and a principal factor related to inequality (Smith, 2005, 2006, 2008; Smith et al., 2008), Liu and Ali (2008) and Liu and Pope-Davis (2003a) have argued that classism, much like other forms of oppression and marginalization, has to be conceptualized as a network of power relationships and that this oppressive web is nurtured by any and all forms of classism. And, although the effects of downward classism and inequality are pernicious, upward and lateral classisms help to reinforce and feed the interpersonal prejudices and biases that solidify discrimination against those who are poor.

Internalized classism is but one form of proposed classism. Internalized classism is not just the introjections of negative stereotypes about being poor. Instead, internalized classism, as part of the SCWM, is conceptualized as the feelings of anxiety, depression, or inadequacy resulting from one's inability to maintain one's social status. Internalized classism is not classism to be used against others, as is lateral or downward classism. This redefinition of internalized classism represents a slight revision to the SCWM and posits that internalized classism is always activated as a result of experiences with upward, downward, or lateral classism, and not simply activated when the individual is unable to meet the expectations of his or her EC. More specifically, internalized classism is an intrapsychic classism experience that is triggered when new social class demands and expectations are placed on the individual or when resources are inadequate to meet one's current social class standing (see Figure 12.1). For instance, Liu posits that internalized classism is regularly triggered when new products (e.g., cars, computers) are introduced and meant to appeal to the individual's EC. As people within the EC purchase the product, lateral classism may be exerted and experienced by the individual (i.e., keeping up with others in one's cohort). The effect of lateral classism is to remind individuals what is necessary to maintain one's social class position. Internalized classism is always enacted internally (i.e., feelings of

inadequacy, anxiety) as the individual recognizes that he or she is deficient. At issue, and most importantly, is whether the individual possesses the capacity to meet these new demands. If the opportunity and capacity exists, then the individual may obtain the possession and maintain homeostasis. If the individual is unable, then the person is in a state of disequilibrium and must find some means to reinstate equilibrium (e.g., purchasing the material object on credit) or potentially shift the EC within which these demands originate.

Internalized classism helps psychologists potentially understand the relationships between the individual experiencing internalized classism and his or her relationships and mental health. For instance, as Liu (2002) speculated in his discussion of social class and men, internalized classism may be a factor related to the despair, depression, and anxiety men experience when they lose their job. It is not only the loss of the "breadwinner" status (Kimmel, 1996); the job loss also means the man is unable to maintain his social class position. Liu also speculates that internalized classism is possibly one aspect related to adjustment disorders for first-generation college students. As these men and women enter college and universities and begin interacting with students across the social class spectrum, they may begin to experience internalized classism related to

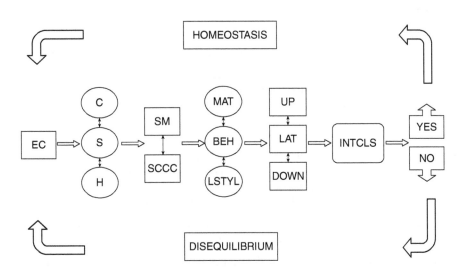

Note. EC = Economic Culture; C = Cultural Capital; S = Social Capital; H = Human Capital; SM = Socialization Messages; SCCC = Social Class and Classism Consciousness; MAT = Material Possessions; BEH = Social Class Behaviors; LSTYL = Social Class Lifestyle; UP = Upward Classism; LAT = Lateral Classism; DOWN = Downward Classism; and INTCLS = Internalized Classism.

Fig. 12.1 The Social Class Worldview Model – Revised EC, economic culture; C, cultural capital; S, social capital; H, human capital; SM, socialization messages; SCCC, social class and classism consciousness; MAT, material possessions; BEH, social class behaviors; LSTYL, social class lifestyle; UP, upward classism; LAT, lateral classism; DOWN, downward classism; and INTCLS, internalized classism.

Table 12.1. Social Class Interventions Using the Social Class Worldview Model

The social class interventions are targeted toward the client's experiences of classism. Upward, downward, lateral, and internalized classisms are the focus of the therapist. Through collaboration, the client is helped to gain

insight about his or her experiences of classism, worldview, and the pressures he or she experience as a part of an economic culture.

The client is helped to identify situations in which certain feelings are tied to classism experiences.

Empathy by the therapist toward the client's classism experiences is important.

The therapist challenges the client's irrational cognitions about his or her social status and what he or she needs to do to maintain or achieve a social status.

The therapist helps the client integrate his or her history with his or her current situation.

The client is encouraged to develop self-efficacy in coping and managing his or her situation.

Step 1—Help the Client identify and Understand his or her Economic Culture

Sample query: Tell me what kind of pressure you feel/experience as you try to keep up with your friends.
Identify answers that touch on cultural, social, and human capital pressures/expectations.

Step 2—Help the client identify the social class messages he or she receive(d)

Sample query: What would your parent(s)/peers say about your current situation?
How would your parent(s)/peers help you resolve your current situation?
List the ways in which you are acting to live out messages given to you by your parent(s)/peers.
Tell me about your peer group. Your support network.
Identify answers that focus on strong/salient cultural socialization messages still running in the client's mind, which drive the client's behavior and attitudes.

Step 2a—Help the client identify social class behaviors, lifestyles, and material possessions that are salient to the client in his or her current situation

Sample query: Tell me how you imagine your life.
How would you ideally be spending your time?
What do others have that you want?
What do you notice about how other people act/behave that you like?
Identify answers that pinpoint the client's materialism values; how he has changed his lifestyle to fit into a new group, and how he has changed his behavior to belong in a new group.

Step 3—Identify the client's experiences with classism and move toward developing an adaptive, realistic, and healthy expectation about him- or herself

Sample query: Do people look down on you?
Do you look down on others who are not like you?
What do your peers expect from you to maintain your status with them?
What does it feel like for you when you can't keep up with your peers? What do you do?
Identify answers that express high social class expectations and the negative consequences related to not meeting specific demands. Additionally, in what ways is the client participating in classism to maintain her social class standing?

Step 4—Help the client integrate his or her experiences of classism

Sample query: Now that we've started talking about all these aspects of your social class experience, tell me what it means to you?
What are you aware of about yourself that you didn't know before we started?
Identify an ability to understand and integrate the social class discussions into other aspects of the client's life.

Step 4a—Help the client take action and make changes in his or her life

Sample query: What is the one thing you could do to change your awareness, situation, or perception?
Identify an ability to make personal changes in the client's life.

new social norms and values. Especially pertinent for first-generation college students from working- or lower-class backgrounds are distinct pressures toward obtaining new material goods and products. Certainly, some material purchases are practical (i.e., computer), but others may be disguises that allow this particular student to "pass" for a social class group (i.e., clothes, iPod). It may be no surprise then that credit card use may often start in college (Roberts & Jone's, 2005). Unfortunately, focusing on material objects to cope with interpersonal issues and conflicts is ineffective and may only further exacerbate the interpersonal problems by adding on financial burdens.

This framework has been used to guide the exploration of an individual's social class experiences and worldview (American Psychological Association [APA], 2007; Liu & Ali, 2008; Liu & Arguello, 2006). Clinicians are encouraged to explore the three interrelated components as a means to help the person develop insight about his or her experiences and to develop healthy coping and skills to navigate his or her economic culture and environment. For example, Table 12.1 outlines the general structure clinical work uses when integrating the framework from the original SCWM.

One aspect identified but not previously explored in the SCWM is the assumption that individuals, upon exploring their social class worldview and experiences, would have little trouble understanding and conceptualizing social class as a system and themselves within that system. In the original version of the SCWM, Liu (2001, 2002) put at the center of the model the notion that individuals vary in their social class consciousness. It is true that, within the SCWM, socialization messages from family and friends are related to one's social class consciousness; however, the SCWM did not specify how social class consciousness was related to the worldview. It became clear that, depending on the depth and interest in social class among friends and family, one might imagine that a person in an environment rich with discussions about merit, social class, inequality, and wealth would be much more aware of being a socially classed person than would an individual living in an environment in which these topics were taboo. Therefore, in the current iteration of the SCWM – R, social class consciousness is considered a variable related to socialization messages.

In considering how social class consciousness develops and evolves for a person, research and theoretical literature from other areas of identity development provides some guidance. The research in other areas of racial identity development, for instance, suggests that people may experience themselves and others differently depending on their levels of cognitive maturity and sophistication about race and racism, how well they integrate and internalize their burgeoning sense of themselves as a racial person, and how well they conceptualize experiences around racism. Therefore, as clinicians explore social class and classism with a client, they should be prepared for the various ways in which an individual may respond to seeing him- or herself as a social class being, new information about social class and classism, and a new perspective on classism experiences. To account for these changes that a person experiences, the social class and classism consciousness model is presented.

Developing Social Class and Classism Consciousness

"I am bourgeois. I am deliberately so" (Marai, 1972/2000, p. 7). The character in *The Right Man* speaks about his willingness to remain faithful to others in his social class; an awareness of himself and others who share a similar socioeconomic place in society. This self-awareness or consciousness of self and others is the central construct of the Social Class and Classism Consciousness (SCCC) framework. The individual develops a sense of him- or herself, an awareness, or consciousness of him- or herself as a socially classed person. Becoming aware of being a socially classed individual is dependent on becoming aware of social class and classism experiences, and allows the individual to be introspective about his or her experiences, to recognize him- or herself in these experiences, and to potentially deliberate about how social class is used in that person's life (Nelson, 1996). One impetus for the SCCC arose from my clinical experiences using the SCWM with clients. When I walked through various questions within each component of the SCWM, it became evident that clients presented with varying levels of understanding related to how they perceived themselves as socially classed individuals and with social class and classism issues. Thus, before exploring the worldview of clients, I found it necessary to understand the individual's level of social class consciousness. Additionally, I used the SCCC framework to conceptualize clients' ever-developing awareness as they constantly came into contact with new information or experiences and made social class self-discoveries. The SCCC model is a descriptive framework outlining the various levels of social class and classism consciousness.

In the SCCC, there are three levels, starting with no social class consciousness to the second level of social class self-consciousness, to the last level of social class consciousness. Among the three levels are ten statuses: unawareness, status position saliency, questioning, exploration and justification, despair, the world is just, intellectualized anger and frustration, reinvestment, engagement, and equilibration (see Table 12.2). These changes also occur regardless of one's objective situation (e.g., income level) since these are intrapsychic and are supposed to be personally meaningful.

At the beginning level of no social class consciousness, the individual who is largely unaware of social class in his or her life is considered to have no social class consciousness. This is not to say that the individual is devoid of all awareness, but rather that the individual does not possess a complex or sophisticated understanding and awareness of how social class operates in his or her life. At this first level, the frameworks typically used are those introjected from one's environment (e.g., media), friends, or family. Parroting these introjects is a characteristic of this first level. For instance, the individual may not question the myth of meritocracy but believe in it wholesale. As the individual gains more experience, he or she may start to recognize economic differences and begin to see him- or herself as a socially

Table 12.2. Social Class and Classism Consciousness Model Levels and Statuses (SCCC)

No social class consciousness
Unawareness
Status position saliency
Questioning
Social class self-consciousness
Exploration and justification
Despair
The world is just
Intellectualized anger and frustration
Social class consciousness
Reinvestment
Engagement
Equilibration

classed person, but the rudimentary social class schema is ineffective in exploring, explaining, or comprehending these new social class experiences. Consequently, the individual may generate questions about these new experiences but not have the capacity to answer these questions.

At the second level of social class self-consciousness, the individual begins to develop a self-consciousness and sensitivity to social class and classism. Self-consciousness is meant here to characterize a person who is acutely sensitive to his or her context and environment and how he or she may be perceived, but does not possess the requisite cognitive complexity to decipher how power, privilege, and inequality operate in one's life. In essence, the individual knows that something is happening but does not know what is happening or how it is happening. This current social class self-consciousness is an inward-focused approach to understanding social class and classism, and he or she is primarily interested in exploring and comprehending what he or she already knows. For instance, if the person was socialized to believe in the notion of meritocracy, then one is likely to start with exploring and justifying this belief system. Certainly, some evidence may be found to support the belief, and disqualifying information is recognized but often minimized. The individual may come to despair that alternative ways of explaining how social class operates in one's life are simply insufficient and conclude that the economic world is largely just. This approach categorizes the world dichotomously as either economically good or bad, and it is just for those who work to achieve. Some individuals may rest at this level of consciousness since it makes relative sense of the world and does not require an individual to change attitudes or behaviors. Others, however, may attempt to understand themselves as socially classed beings by taking an alternative approach. Rather than seeing themselves as beneficiaries of a just economic world, they may focus on the inequalities and disadvantages resulting from the current economic system. This last status of social class self-consciousness may resemble a shift from an inward focus to larger sociostructural and economic injustice or inequality (outward). This last status represents an intellectualized approach to these issues and may marshal feelings of anger and frustration. Intellectualized is purposefully used here to identify a defensive and personally protective approach to social class and classism and not necessarily an intellectual approach to these same issues. At this status, the person still focuses on large (macro) concerns and envisions broad social movements but does not necessarily comprehend the steps toward these larger social actions. Consequently, individuals at this status are easily frustrated and may turn away from further social action because, as they begin to see the enormity of the issues and problems, they become overwhelmed and believe these problems are intractable. At this status, social class and classism is focused on "other" exploration rather than "self" exploration.

At the final level of social class consciousness, social class consciousness is developed and explored, and the individual shifts the focus of social class and classism toward the self. Rather than focusing on answering questions about social class and classism, however, he or she is interested in understanding how he or she impacts others as a socially classed person. This final level represents a focus of the socially classed self in relation to socially classed others and vice versa. As the person understands these interpersonal interactions around social class and classism, he or she may find personally meaningful ways to positively impact the lives of others. The individual may start to engage in individual (micro) activities and explore macro-level involvements that are connected to these activities. For instance, an individual active at the micro level may be concerned with donating food items to a local food bank and may find macro-level involvements that address issues of diet, food access, and nutrition. The assumption here is that there are many ways that economic inequality may be addressed, but people find personally meaningful ways to contribute and engage in these issues. Eventually, the last status assumes that the individual has some sophistication and complexity in understanding him- or herself as a socially classed person and how social class and classism operates. The individual is able to approach issues of inequality, for instance, with some reason and equilibrium and is capable of considering multiple sides to an issue or concern. Because he or she is able to comprehend these issues with more complexity, the individual is also potentially better able to make better decisions with his or her life in relation to shifting EC demands and experiences with classism, especially feelings of internalized classism.

Within each level, there are four relational components of the self, peers, others, and society. These relational components are meant to identify how an individual in these different statuses may perceive and possibly interact with others. Each of the ten levels represents different ways in which

the individual comes to understand social class and classism and him- or herself as a socially classed individual. The four relational components are ways in which the individual sees him- or herself (self), the perception and relationship with peers (peers), the perception of how other people outside the immediate social class group operate within the social class system and how the individual relates to these "others," and how society operates around social class and the individual's connection to them. Table 12.3 describes and outlines each level.

The SCCC resembles a developmental model in that there are less sophisticated or unaware statuses (i.e., unaware) and more complex and aware statuses (i.e., equilibration). I posit that any person would first need to experience or process through all the statuses in some hierarchical order since it would make sense that these social class–based schemas would need to be created before an individual has an ability to use them. Access to these schemas could come from experience or from socialization messages. For instance, someone coming from a family who discusses social class may have some sophistication in understanding the pressures of social class in his or her life. After having access to these statuses, there may be dominant or preferential ways of understanding the social class world, and it is also possible that all these statuses are always active, but in different levels or in auxiliary positions. That is, people possibly may and do shift between the statuses as a consequence of new social class and classism experiences and discourse within significant relationships. For illustration, the first-generation college student experiencing pressures to purchase new material objects to maintain a social class position may start as being unaware of being a socially classed person but, as a result of these new expectations, begin to understand that there are those around him or her with more and less. The student may realize that his or her social class position is important and meaningful, and begin to make changes in his or her life to accommodate these new demands. It is also possible that this same student, at some later point, may be using equilibration as a dominant status and may not succumb to new material demands as quickly or easily. The purpose of the SCCC was to provide the clinician and client with a framework to understand the possible changes in self- and other-awareness stemming from an exploration of social class and classism experiences. The SCCC is presented as a linear model with discrete levels, and it assumes that individuals become increasingly more complex in the

Table 12.3. Social Class and Classism Consciousness Model

Status	Definition	Self-perception	Perception of Peers	Perception of Others	Perception of Society
Unawareness	Social class is not a salient part of one's worldview. There is recognition of inequality, of rich and poor, but no real conceptualization of how social systems may work to create inequality. Overall, there may be a belief in the myth of meritocracy and an acceptance of personal and other peoples' unqualified privileges and entitlements.	The self is an independent actor in the social class system.	Peers are perceived to reflect and endorse the individual's worldview and are believed to share a similar unaware worldview.	Some recognition that there are higher and lower "others" but no acknowledgement that the individual is also part of a larger economic system.	The larger sociostructural system works neutrally. People get what they deserve. The individual believes that there are some unfair advantages but not so much to unbalance the system.
Status Position Saliency	The individual recognizes people in higher and lower groups, and the individual is aware that he or she may belong to a social class group.	The individual generally sees him- or herself as belonging to a social class group and begins to recognize the boundaries of his or her social class group.	Peers are part of the individual's social class group and the individual recognizes peers who may belong to other social class groups.	The individual perceives of multiple social class groups within which others belong and these groups are stratified but the individual is unclear what creates the hierarchy, stratification, or inequality.	The larger society is recognized to be comprised of higher and lower social class groups, some of which deserve esteem and others deserve derision.
Questioning	The individual questions the role of social class in his or her life. The questions may create anxieties and tensions related to how social class operates in the individual's life and the larger society.	Some dissonance about the individual's role in social class and inequality; generally unsure what social class and classism means, but some burgeoning recognition that social class exists and operates. The individual may also question how he or she came to his or her particular social class position.	Beginning sense that the individual and his or her cohort have certain social class boundaries which still seem diffuse and unclear and some recognition that the peer group has boundaries.	Steady recognition that there are social class in-groups and out-groups.	Still greatly unsure how the larger sociostructural system of social class operates but some sense that status considerations are important parts of one's experience.

Exploration and Justification	The individual seeks out knowledge and experiences to answer these questions. The individual is primarily interested in finding support for his or her previously held beliefs about how social class functions and the role it plays in his or her life.	The self is unsure and is vulnerable, but the individual is willing to explore answers that may support his or her already existing, albeit tenuous worldview.	Peers and the cohort group are sought out for answers but a growing recognition that the peer group may be an unreliable source of information.	Other people are unreliable because they do not "understand" the individual's experiences and perspectives and are likely to challenge the individual too much.	A growing sense that society "must" be just and inequality "must" be a "natural" product of people's efforts.
Despair	The individual resigns him- or herself to believing there is no escape from the current circumstances. For instance, an individual in poverty may believe he or she cannot move beyond his or her situation.	The self is perceived as impotent against the current situation; the individual does not believe he or she possesses the skills to overcome his or her situation.	Peers are regarded in a similar situation and peers may be the target of anger if they try to deviate (improve) their current situation.	People are not interested in helping you cope with the situation better.	There are rich and poor and society is made to make the rich richer and the poor poorer.
The World Is Just	The individual is resigned to accepting inequality and the rationalization that people get what they deserve. The individual is interested in his or her own privilege, entitlements, and status attainment.	Because the world is unchangeable, it is important to look out for oneself.	Peers are sought out who reinforce this same worldview. Usually people reinforce the individual's current social class position or who are interested in upward mobility.	Other people have not worked hard enough or made the right "life choices" to succeed.	Society is just and inequality is a natural product and process.

(Continued)

Table 12.3. (Continued)

Status	Definition	Self-perception	Perception of Peers	Perception of Others	Perception of Society
Intellectualized Anger and Frustration	As the individual explores his or her questions around social class, classism, and inequality, the individual becomes angry and frustrated at the state of inequality. The individual becomes increasingly interested in addressing economic inequality. The individual likely attempts to involve him- or herself in broad and far-reaching activities that are outside his or her ability to intervene and understand. There is no introspection and deep consideration about poverty and inequality except reactive anger and frustration.	The self is blameless, and it is others and society who created inequality, and it is the individual who must "correct" the injustices.	Interested in seeking out other groups and expanding their peer group to find additional support for their experiences and growing perspective. Peers are expected to reflect the individual's worldview about inequality.	Others are categorized into oppressed and oppressors—with the oppressed being those in poverty and low income situations. Others are also encouraged to fight against inequality.	Society is unjust and must be corrected—usually through some revolutionary action. Large social action is sought.
Reinvestment	The individual investigates social class, classism, and inequality again in his or her own personal life and explores how his or her actions impact others. The individual is interested in finding ways to understand social class in his or her own world.	The individual recognizes that he or she is engaged in unequal, unjust, and sometimes classicist actions. The individual recognizes these actions having negative impacts on others. He or she begins to connect individual behavior to possibly larger social problems.	The individual observes how peers also enact social class and classism. Peers are being evaluated on their social class consciousness.	Rather than focusing on society at large, the individual focuses on his or her surrounding environment. The individual's interest is the immediate context within which social class and classism are enacted and how their individual behaviors may make an impact.	Society is recognized to be comprised of smaller contexts. These smaller contexts are the ways in which society may be changed to be more equitable.

Engagement	The individual is actively involved in social class, inequality, and poverty issues in his or her world. The individual is testing his or her developing awareness of being a socially classed person.	The individual recognizes the importance of being vigilant against inequality and that social class operates all around. The individual is intentional and deliberate about how he or she acts in certain contexts, and is sensitive to social class differences.	New peer groups may be sought that reinforce this growing new consciousness. Dissonance and conflict may still exist as the individual shifts away from old friends to new networks. Anxiety may increase from these new experiences.	It is important to find way to help people in one's community/neighborhood. It is also important to support other causes against classism.	Society is largely unjust and classici and marginalizing of people from poverty and the poor. The whole of society cannot be changed immediately, but it is important to be a part of or start a process of change.
Equilibration	The individual is able to complexly explore and understand the role of social class in his or her world. The individual struggles for equilibrium when trying to figure out issues of poverty/injustice.	The individual recognizes that he or she is constantly negotiating privilege and power, and there are some times and contexts in which he or she has and uses the privilege, and others in which he or she does not or cannot exercise privilege.	The individual has multiple groups of friends and peers which reflect their complex understanding of social class. The individual has some ability to move between and within each of these groups.	The individual recognizes people in different strata and sees the privileges, power, and limits of each group. He or she recognizes the fluidity of these groups and how context changes the quality of each group.	Society is not an independent entity or organism outside the individual, and the individual can only make changes through constant vigilance in combating classism.

ways in which they process social class information and the ways in which they regard themselves and others. The SCCC is presented as a hierarchy for this presentation, but it is possible that these levels may also be present in every individual but with varying degrees of salience and importance. Additionally, individuals certainly may move between each level in any order. Finally, becoming conscious about social class and being aware of oneself as a socially classed person is not a singular event. Rather, individuals are constantly confronted with and must struggle through always becoming social class conscious. Thus, individuals may constantly cycle through these levels. For psychologists, working with clients on social class issues necessarily means making the client aware of being a socially classed person. To adequately approach and discuss these issues with clients, it is important to be at a similar or higher level of understanding than the client. That is, to help clients develop their own awareness and consciousness, it is important that the clinician be at a higher level of social class consciousness than the client. Being incongruent in levels of social class consciousness could potentially be related to therapeutic problems such as impasses or ruptures in the therapeutic relationship (Liu & Pope-Davis, 2005).

Conclusion

The psychology of social class and classism needs to focus on the personal and lived experiences of individuals and their perspectives on themselves and others. As I have argued, the current use of sociodemographic variables is insufficient in accessing and exploring these socially classed experiences and perspectives. Instead of providing illumination in social class, the use of income, education, and occupation to stratify individuals into social class groups or to place them on an economic hierarchy may only create confusion as researchers and clinicians disentangle methodology from phenomenology. Generally, the research seems to indicate that subjective approaches, even a simple question of placing an "X" on a ten-rung ladder, may be more helpful in explicating a person's social class self-awareness and appraisal than an extensive questionnaire. It seems that, as research by Adler et al. (2000) and Ostrove et al. (2000) suggests, it is how the individual conceptualizes him- or herself as a socially classed individual within an economic system that is important in understanding certain relationships, such as self-rated health. One additional benefit from taking a subjective approach to understanding social class

and classism is the potential incorporation of other aspects of the client's identity. For instance, throughout this chapter, race and gender were not specifically discussed. In part, a review of the social class literature on race and gender is far too extensive for this chapter and has been conducted elsewhere (Liu, 2002; Liu, Hernandez, Mahmood, & Stinson, 2006). But using a subjective approach to social class, clinicians and researchers are likely more able to discuss the interrelationships of social class and race or classism and racism. Although the SCWM (Liu, 2001; Liu & Ali, 2008) provides a heuristic from which to explore the individual's perceptions and experiences about social class and classism, the ways in which individuals come to see themselves as a socially classed persons were unexplored. This chapter presents the SCCC as a complementary framework to the SCWM. The SCCC was developed from my own clinical experiences, and the experiences and perspectives that clients discussed when their worldview was queried. The SCCC is comprised of ten levels of social class consciousness that range from unawareness to a balanced perspective on social class. Within each level are four relational components that are hypothetical ways in which the individual views him- or herself, peers, others, and society with regard to the developing social class awareness. I hope this will be a useful tool in social class–based clinical practice and research, and a helpful alternative to the sociodemographic approach to social class and classism.

Training Implications

The SCWM is laid out as a framework to help clinicians and clinicians in training work with clients to explore, understand, and integrate social class and classism experiences. The sample queries provided in Table 12.1 are meant to be exemplar questions that clinicians may use with clients, and these questions may also help supervisors work more effectively with trainees in developing their competencies around social class and classism (Liu & Pope-Davis, 2005b). But, along with assisting trainees in their work with clients, the SCWM and the SCCC are important ways in which trainees may be guided in understanding their own social class experiences and the ways in which trainees understand themselves as socially classed persons.

I posit that, within the SCWM, classism experiences are critical in shaping one's social class consciousness and how the individual may interact and relate to others. Classism, especially early traumatic experiences of classism, may have enduring affects on the individual and shape self and other perceptions and interactions. For instance, the multicultural competency literature generally encourages trainees to explore and understand how privilege shapes one's worldview. Trainees unaware of the impact of privilege may assume clients to have had experiences, access to resources (i.e., long-term health care), or a similar upward-mobility preference that may minimize or distort a presenting issue. In a similar way, classism has to be explored and understood by the trainee. A trainee with an early or traumatic experience with inequality or classism, such as losing one's home or being teased or bullied for not dressing correctly (i.e., fashionably), for instance, may harbor a prejudice against those perceived to be from higher social class backgrounds (i.e., upward classism), or they may be especially sensitive to lateral classism (i.e., keeping up with the Joneses). These experiences with classism are important since these therapists may work with clients perceived to be from higher social class backgrounds and potentially treat them less well than they do other clients.

In working with trainees to understand their worldview or consciousness around social class and classism, it is important to consider the varying ways in which trainees may understand themselves to be socially classed persons. For instance, the trainee who had an early bullying experience in grade school for wearing hand-me-down clothes may harbor deep feelings of hurt, and may regard these as "just bullying experiences" rather than related to social class. Thus, this trainee may be unaware of social class in his or her life, even though the bullying was a form of classism and in part related to the social class background of the trainee. It may be obvious to the supervisor that these connections exist, but the supervisor should not be surprised that this trainee does not see the apparent links. The trainee may not be fully aware of his poor treatment of clients from perceived higher social class backgrounds.

Working with trainees from a social class and classism informed approach also necessitates that the supervisor receive training and education. There are a number of references, articles, books, and chapters from which to choose, and these resources should provide the supervisor with adequate knowledge about social class and classism. The more important and critical work for the supervisor is to also develop an understanding and awareness to the impact of social class and classism in his or her own life. Similar to the trainee, clinical supervisors could

also have experiences of classism that could distort and color the supervisory relationship with a trainee or affect the ways and type of supervisory direction and instruction. For instance, a supervisor who comes from an upper-class background may have had experiences of upward classism (i.e., being called a snob or elitist) directed at him or her during graduate school. Consequently, the supervisor may develop a sensitivity toward any markers, behaviors, or attitudes that may indicate his or her upper-class upbringing. When the supervisor works with trainees who come from working-class backgrounds and experiences, the supervisor may try to overidentify with the supervisee; rather than challenge and confront the supervisee, the supervisor colludes with or minimizes the trainee's mistakes.

For training, the SCWM and SCCC allow clinicians to first develop self-awareness around social class and classism. Before working with a client, this self-awareness has to focus on not only understanding these concerns but also on developing a capacity and ability to articulate how social class and classism affected the clinician. Similar to becoming multiculturally competent with race or gender, clinicians need to develop a familiarity and comfort with discussing topics that are generally considered taboo for public conversation. Because social class and classism are relatively unfamiliar topics of discussion, it is critical to nurture conversations with clinicians. In these discussions, instructors and supervisors should be mindful of how the SCWM and SCCC statuses are operating for clinicians, and how they are conceptualizing and discussing social class and classism. As clinicians become more comfortable with these topics, it may be inevitable that clinicians will feel comfortable introducing these topics into psychotherapy.

Future Directions
Throughout this chapter, I addressed the importance of exploring the ways in which people conceptualize social class and classism and begin to see themselves as socially classed individuals. These are theoretical notions on how people see their social class world. But important work remains in research and theory development. Future directions for social class and classism work in counseling and psychology may include the following questions:

How does counseling psychology research move beyond objective indices and social class demographic proxy variables?

In what ways may subjective and phenomenological approaches to social class and classism be used to develop, improve, and implement public policy focused on inequality?

How may we shift the discussion about social class and classism to encompass the entire range of economic experiences (e.g., from affluent to poor)?

How might issues around social class, classism, and inequality be better infused in current training?

References

Adler, N. E., Boyce, W. T., Chesney, M., Folkman, S., & Syme, L. (1993). Socioeconomic inequalities in health: No easy solution. *Journal of the American Medical Association, 269,* 3140–3145.

Adler, N. E., Epel, E. S., Castellazzo, G., & Ickovics, J. R. (2000). Relationship of subjective and objective social status with psychological and physiological functioning: Preliminary data in healthy white women. *Health Psychology, 19,* 586–592.

Ali, S. R., & McWhirter, E. H. (2006). Rural Appalachian Youth's Vocational/Educational Post-secondary Aspirations: Applying Social Cognitive Career Theory. *Journal of Career Development, 33,* 87–111.

American Psychological Association. (2007). *Taskforce report on socioeconomic status.* Retrieved January 31, 2007, from www2.apa.org/pi/SES_task_force_report.pdf.

Blustein, D. L. (2006). *The psychology of working: A new perspective for career development, counseling, and public policy.* Mahwah, NJ: Lawrence Erlbaum.

Bronfenbrenner, U. (1986). Ecology of the family as a context for human development: Research perspectives. *Developmental Psychology, 22,* 723–742.

Brown, M. T., Fukunaga, C., Umemoto, D., & Wicker, L. (1996). Annual review, 1990–1996: Social class, work, and retirement behavior. *Journal of Vocational Behavior, 49,* 159–189.

Cohen, S., Alper, C. M., Doyle, W. J., Adler, N., Treanor, J. J., & Turner, R. B. (2008). Objective and subjective socioeconomic status and susceptibility to the common cold. *Health Psychology, 27,* 269–274.

Costello, E. J., Compton, S. N., Keeler, G., & Angold, A. (2003). Relationships between poverty and psychopathology: A natural experiment. *Journal of the American Medical Association, 290,* 2023–2029.

Croizet, J. C., & Claire, T. (1998). Extending the concept of stereotype threat to social class: The intellectual underperformance of students from low socioeconomic backgrounds. *Personality and Social Psychology Bulletin, 24,* 588–594.

Croizet, J. C., Desert, M., Dutrevis, M., & Leyens, J. P. (2001). Stereotype threat, social class, gender, and academic underachievement: When our reputation catches up with us and takes over. *Social Psychology and Education, 4,* 295–310.

Currie, C. E., Elton, R. A., Todd, J., & Platt, S. (1997). Indicators of socioeconomic status for adolescents: The WHO Health Behaviour in School-aged Children Survey. *Health Education Research, 12*(3), 385–397.

De Vogli, R., Ferrie, J. E., Chandola, T., Kivimaki, M., & Marmot, M. G. (2007). Unfairness and health: Evidence from the Whitehall II study. *Journal of Epidemiological Community Health, 61,* 513–518.

Duncan, G. J. (1988). The volatility of family income over the life course. In P. Baltes, & R. M. Lerner (Eds.), *Life span development and behavior* Vol. 9 (pp. 317–358). Hillsdale, NJ: Erlbaum.

Duncan, G. J., & Magnuson, K. A. (2003). Off with Hollingshead: Socioeconomic resources, parenting, and child development. In M. H. Bornstein, & R. H. Bradley (Eds.), *Socioeconomic status, parenting, and child development* (pp. 83–106). Hillsdale, NJ: Erlbaum.

Ensminger, M. E., & Fothergill, K. E. (2003). A decade of measuring SES: What it tells us and where to go from here. In M. H. Bornstein, & R. H. Bradley (Eds.), *Socioeconomic status, parenting, and child development* (pp. 13–27). Hillsdale, NJ: Erlbaum.

Fouad, N. A., & Brown, M. T. (2001). Role of race and social class in development: Implications for counseling psychology. In S. D. Brown, & R. W. Lent (Eds.), *Handbook of counseling psychology* (pp. 379–408). New York: Wiley.

Fletcher, J. (2001, March 16). When a million isn't enough. *The Wall Street Journal,* p. W1, W14.

Frable, D. E. S. (1997). Gender, racial, ethnic, sexual, and class identities. *Annual Review Psychology, 48,* 139–162.

Gallo, L. C., Bogart, L. M., Vranceanu, A. M., & Matthews, K. A. (2005). Socioeconomic status, resources, psychological experiences, and emotional responses: A test of the reserve capacity model. *Journal of Personality and Social Psychology, 88,* 386–399.

Gallo, L. C., & Matthews, K. A. (1999). Do negative emotions mediate the association between socioeconomic status and health? *Annals of the New York Academy of Sciences, 896,* 226–245.

Gallo, L. C., & Matthews, K. A. (2003). Understanding the association between socioeconomic status and physical health: Do negative emotions play a role? *Psychological Bulletin, 129,* 10–51.

Gallo, L. C., Smith, T. W., & Cox, C. M. (2006). Socioeconomic status, psychosocial processes, and perceived health: An interpersonal perspective. *Annals of Behavioral Medicine, 31,* 109–119.

Geronimus, A. T., Bound, J., Waidmann, T. A., Hillemeier, M. M., & Burns, P. B. (1996). Excess mortality among blacks and whites in the United States. *New England Journal of Medicine, 355,* 1552–1558.

Hopps, J., & Liu, W. M. (2006). Working for social justice from within the health care system: The role of social class in psychology. In R. L. Toporek, L. H. Gerstein, N. A. Fouad, G. Roysircar, & T. Israel (Eds.), *Handbook for social justice in counseling psychology: Leadership, vision, and action* (pp. 318–337). Thousand Oaks, CA: Sage.

Jones, F. L., & McMillan, J. (2001). Scoring occupational categories for social research: A review of current practice, with Australian examples. *Work, Employment and Society, 15,* 539–563.

Kimmel, M. (1996). *Manhood in America: A cultural history.* New York: Free Press.

Lachman, M. E., & Weaver, S. L. (1998). The sense of control as a moderator of social class differences in health and well-being. *Journal of Personality and Social Psychology, 74,* 763–773.

Liberatos, P., Link, B. G., & Kelsey, J. L. (1988). The measurement of social class in epidemiology. *Epidemiologic Reviews, 10,* 87–121.

Lin, N. (1999). Social networks and status attainment. *Annual Review of Sociology, 25,* 467–487.

Liu, W. M. (2001). Expanding our understanding of multiculturalism: Developing a social class worldview model. In D. B. Pope-Davis, & H. L. K. Coleman (Eds.), *The intersection of race, class, and gender in counseling psychology* (pp. 127–170). Thousand Oaks, CA: Sage.

Liu, W. M. (2002). The social class-related experiences of men: Integrating theory and practice. *Professional Psychology: Research and Practice, 33,* 355–360.

Liu, W. M. (2006). Classism is much more complex. *American Psychologist, 61,* 337–338.

Liu, W. M., & Ali, S. R. (2005). Addressing social class and classism in vocational theory and practice: Extending the emancipatory communitarian approach. *The Counseling Psychologist, 33,* 189–196.

Liu, W. M., & Ali, S. R. (2008). Social class and classism: Understanding the impact of poverty and inequality. In S. D. Brown, & R. W. Lent (Eds.), Handbook of counseling psychology 4th edition. New York: Wiley.

Liu, W. M., Ali, S. R., Soleck, G., Hopps, J., Dunston, K., & Pickett, T., Jr. (2004). Using social class in counseling psychology research. *Journal of Counseling Psychology, 51,* 3–18.

Liu, W. M., & Arguello, J. (2006). Social class and classism in counseling. *Counseling and Human Development, 39*(3), 1–12.

Liu, W. M., Fridman, A., & Hall, T. (in press). Social class and school counseling. In H. L. K. Coleman, & C. Yeh (Eds.), *Handbook of school counseling.* New York: Erlbaum.

Liu, W. M., Hernandez, J., Mahmood, A., & Stinson, R. (2006). The link between poverty, classism, and racism in mental health. In D. W. Sue, & M. G. Constantine (Eds.), *Racism as a barrier to cultural competence in mental health and educational settings* (pp. 65–86). Hoboken, NJ: Wiley.

Liu, W. M., Pickett, T., Jr., & Ivey, A. E. (2007). White middle-class privilege: Social class bias and implications for training and practice. *Journal of Multicultural Counseling and Development, 35,* 194–207.

Liu, W. M., & Pope-Davis, D. B. (2003a). Moving from diversity to multiculturalism: Exploring power and the implications for psychology. In D. B. Pope-Davis, H. L. K. Coleman, W. M. Liu, & R. L. Toporek (Eds.), *Handbook of multicultural competencies in counseling and psychology* (pp. 90–102). Thousand Oaks, CA: Sage.

Liu, W. M., & Pope-Davis, D. B. (2003b). Understanding classism to effect personal change. In T. B. Smith (Ed.), *Practicing multiculturalism: Internalizing and affirming diversity in counseling and psychology* (pp. 294–310). New York: Allyn & Bacon.

Liu, W. M., & Pope-Davis, D. B. (2005). The Working alliance, therapy ruptures and impasses, and counseling competencies: Implications for counselor training and education. In R. T. Carter (Ed.) *Handbook of racial-cultural psychology and counseling* Vol. 2. (pp. 148–167). New York: John Wiley and Sons.

Liu, W. M., Soleck, G., Hopps, J., Dunston, K., & Pickett, T. (2004). A new framework to understand social class in counseling: The social class worldview and modern classism theory. *Journal of Multicultural Counseling and Development, 32,* 95–122.

Lott, B. (2002). Cognitive and behavioral distancing from the poor. *American Psychologist, 57,* 100–110.

Marai, S. (2000). *Memoir of Hungary, 1944–1948* (A. Tezla, Trans.). Corvina, Budapest: Central European University Press. (Original work published 1972).

Miller, D. T. (2001). Disrespect and the experience of injustice. *Annual Review of Psychology, 52,* 527–553.

Nelson, T. O. (1996). Consciousness and metacognition. *American Psychologist, 51,* 102–116.

Oakes, J. M., & Rossi, P. H. (2003). The measurement of SES in health research: Current practice and steps toward a new approach. *Social Science and Medicine, 56,* 769–784.

Offer, A. (2006). *The challenge of affluence: Self-control and well-being in the United States and Britain since 1950.* New York: Oxford.

Ostrove, J. M., Adler, N. E., Kuppermann, M., & Washington, A. E. (2000). Objective and subjective assessments of socioeconomic status and their relationship to self-rated health in an ethnically diverse sample of pregnant women. *Health Psychology, 19,* 613–618.

Pollack, C. E., Chideya, S., Cubbin, C., Williams, B., Dekker, M., & Braveman, P. (2007). Should health studies measure wealth? A systematic review. *American Journal of Preventive Medicine, 33,* 250–264.

Pingle, M., & Mitchell, M. (2002). What motivates positional concerns for income? *Journal of Economic Psychology, 23,* 127–148.

Roberts, J. A., & Jones, E. (2005). Money attitudes, credit card use, and compulsive buying among American college students. *Journal of Consumer Affairs, 35,* 213–240.

Sapolsky, R. (2005, December). Sick of poverty. *Scientific American, 293*(6), 92–99.

Singh, G. K., & Siahpush, M. (2006). Widening socioeconomic inequalities in US life expectancy, 1980–2000. *International Journal of Epidemiology, 35,* 969–979.

Smith, L. (2005). Psychotherapy, classism, and the poor: Conspicuous by their absence. *American Psychologist, 60,* 687–696.

Smith, L. (2006). Addressing classism, extending multicultural competence, and serving the poor. *American Psychologist, 61,* 338–339.

Smith, L. (2008). Positioning classism with counseling psychology's social justice agenda. *The Counseling Psychologist, 36,* 895–924.

Smith, L., Foley, P. F., & Chaney, M. P. (2008). Addressing classism, ableism, and heterosexism in counselor education. *Journal of Counseling and Development, 86,* 303–309.

Solnick, S. J., & Hemenway, D. (1998). Is more always better?: A survey on positional concerns. *Journal of Economic Behavior & Organization, 37,* 373–383.

The Wall Street Journal. (2001, March 16). *The Dow Jones rich index.* p. W14.

Tyszka, T., & Przybyszewski, K. (2006). Cognitive and affective factors affecting currency perception. *Journal of Economic Psychology, 27,* 518–530.

Vohs, K. D., Mead, N. L., & Goode, M. R. (2006). The psychological consequences of money. *Science, 314,* 1154–1156.

Wright, E.O. (2002). The shadow of exploitation in Weber's class analysis. *American Sociological Review, 67,* 832–853.

The Psychology of Women

Bonnie Moradi *and* Janice D. Yoder

Abstract

In this chapter, we describe theory and research that highlights connections between the social contexts of women's lives and women's intrapersonal and interpersonal functioning. Specifically, in the first section of the chapter, we discuss how women's social contexts are shaped by gender and its intersections with other social categories and by sexism expressed as prejudice, stereotyping, and discrimination. Next, we discuss women's mental health, with attention to the interplay of gender with psychological disorders and the role of sexist discrimination in women's mental health. In the third section, we focus on women's relationships, starting with the socializing relationships of childhood, turning to intimate relationships in adulthood, and then discussing the role of power in women's relationships. Finally, we review research on women's identities, focusing on feminist, lesbian, and womanist identity models. We conclude this chapter with a call to counseling psychologists to adopt the feminist understanding that women's well-being depends on both their personal and their sociopolitical empowerment.

Keywords: women, gender, sexism, feminist psychology, psychology of women, sexist discrimination, women's mental health, women's identity, women's relationships

To better understand women as women, counseling psychologists need to look outside individual women themselves to the gendered social context in which all women live their lives. Certainly, how these contexts affect individuals is highly personalized, but there is common ground that brings all women together, both as a single group and as subgroups designated by other intersecting social markers, such as race/ethnicity, sexual orientation, age, and physical ability. Feminists have captured this understanding in the activist insight that "the personal is political." Guided by this perspective, in this chapter, we aim to highlight connections between the social contexts of women's lives and women's intrapersonal and interpersonal functioning.

Specifically, in the first section of the chapter, we discuss how women's social contexts are shaped

by gender and its intersections with other social categories and by sexism expressed as prejudice, stereotyping, and discrimination. Next, we discuss women's mental health, with attention paid to the interplay of gender with psychological disorders and the role of sexist discrimination in women's mental health. In the third section, we examine women's relationships, starting with the socializing relationships of childhood, turning to intimate relationships in adulthood, and then discussing the role of power in women's relationships. Finally, we review research on women's identities, focusing on feminist, lesbian, and womanist identity models. We conclude this chapter with a call to counseling psychologists to adopt the feminist understanding that women's well-being depends on both their personal and their sociopolitical empowerment.

Women in Social Context

Social psychologists define social context as the social environment in which individual behaviors occur and can work to produce or constrain other behavior (Ross & Nisbett, 1991). In this chapter, we contend that this social context is ubiquitously gendered, although more or less obviously so. This global truism begins with the simple process of social categorization.

Social Categorization

Social categorization refers to the essential human propensity to cognitively sort people into groups based on perceived common properties (Hampson, 1988). Sex, along with age and race/ethnicity, is a primary category (Schneider, 2004) that we use so seamlessly in our everyday lives that we often sort people into groups without awareness or effort (Ito & Urland, 2003). Indeed, sex is so important as a social marker that we find it disconcerting when we cannot readily identify an individual's sex (Butler, 1990). Typically without definitive proof of another's biological sex, we rely on social indicators of femaleness and maleness, that is, gender. Thus, social constructionists like Judith Butler (1990) argue that gender is something we actively *do* in our everyday lives (expressed in our choice of clothes, hair styles, mannerisms, etc.) to ensure that we do not confuse others. One side effect of this constructed exaggeration of femaleness or maleness is heightened gender polarization, that is, perceptions that women and men are "opposites" (Bem, 1993).

In addition to undermining the fundamental shared humanness that connects women with men, using femaleness as a social representation glosses over an individual's unique qualities, such as her hopes, dreams, and feelings, and instead establishes expectations about what is appropriate or good and inappropriate or bad; that is, gendered injunctive norms (Eagly & Karau, 2002). Given that these gender-linked expectations are formed within a generally patriarchal culture, being female comes with less power and privilege than does being male (Johnson, 2006). With men's conferred dominance over women comes greater access to resources and rewards (Ridgeway, 1991), greater power in interpersonal relationships (Felmlee, 1994), and more privileges in the workplace and in politics (Lips, 1991). In sum, being female is commonly regarded as essentially different from being male (subjective essentialism; Prentice & Miller, 2007) and of lower social status, thus immersing women and men in fundamentally different gendered social contexts that necessarily affect their social interactions (Deaux & Major, 1987).

INTERSECTIONALITY

Although humans' propensity to categorize lays the groundwork for us to think (Woll, 2002), the process of grouping people together brings with it the pitfall of ignoring or underestimating within-group diversity—the individual differences that distinguish among individuals within the general category of women. Additionally, although gender is a very potent social representation through which others label each of us, it is not the only social marker others use (Loden & Rosener, 1991). Rather, each of us is shaped by an interlocking set of social representations, including our race/ethnicity, age, sexual orientation, religion, education, income, physical attributes, and so on. Each of these markers brings with it either social privilege or oppression, and each contributes to the complex social contexts through which we pass every day, sometimes benefiting us and at other times disadvantaging us. None of these markers stands alone; they are interlocking or intersecting (West & Fenstermaker, 1995).

SYSTEMS OF INEQUALITY

Social categorization describes the role that individuals play in creating and maintaining the contextual status quo, a status quo that is ubiquitously gendered. A second building block focuses on understanding the systems of inequality that structure our interpersonal, organizational, and societal contexts. The fundamental human propensity to sort people into social hierarchies, in which some groups are privileged at the expense of others, is captured in social dominance theory (Pratto, Sidanius, & Levin, 2006). Within this framework, gender and age are the key markers for two universal hierarchical systems in which women, children, and the elderly are relegated to less powerful statuses. The third category of systems, arbitrary sets, develops social hierarchies based on other socially constructed characteristics such as race, ethnicity, and sexual orientation. Interestingly, these arbitrary sets also may involve a gendered component; for example, these systems are frequently used by men to dominate other men (in addition to women and children). A central point for our discussion that emerges from social dominance theory is that these systems of inequality are produced and maintained by prejudices and discrimination at multiple levels of intergroup analysis, expanding in scope from the individual to the interpersonal, organizational, and societal levels. These interlocking systems are strengthened to the degree that individuals endorse legitimizing myths that appear consensual, serve to justify the existing social structure, and are expressed in values, attitudes, beliefs, stereotyping, and cultural ideologies.

Four basic points about systems of inequality will help inform our discussion (Johnson, 2006). First, one must be a member of an oppressed social category to be affected by that oppression. For example, regarding sexism, although masculinity, especially hypermasculinity, has documented costs for men, such as negative health consequences (Good & Sherrod, 2001), on balance, the costs of being male are far overshadowed by the benefits. Peter Blood and his colleagues (1995, p. 159) captured this point succinctly: "However much men are hurt by sex roles in this country [USA], the fact remains that they are not systematically denied power simply because of being born a certain sex, as women are." Second, few people are universally oppressed. Given the wide diversity of social markers used to categorize people, very few of us escape being unjustly privileged by some marker in some contexts. Third, having privilege is not the equivalent of being oppressive; and fourth, being oppressed does not eliminate the possibility of being oppressive. Although social categories likely affect how people treat each other, what individuals actually do within their social category is their individual responsibility.

Sexism in Social Contexts

This basic understanding of how social categorization, intersectionality, and systems of inequality construct each individual's social context helps us better explore the concept of, and women's experiences with, sexism. Sexism directed at women is the oppression or limiting of women "through a vast network of everyday practices, attitudes, assumptions, behaviors, and institutional rules" (Young, 1992, p. 180). There are three related, but conceptually distinct aspects to sexism: sexist stereotyping, sexist prejudice, and sexist discrimination (Lott, 1995).

SEXIST STEREOTYPING

Although the specific contents of gender stereotypes may change over time (Diekman & Eagly, 2000), Fiske and her colleagues (2002) have identified the underlying mechanisms that drive the process of gender stereotyping. They reason that the contents of gender stereotypes can be filtered down to two underlying dimensions: warmth (which includes the communal expressiveness of feminine traits, the traditional roles of homemaker and sexy woman, and the female-dominated occupations) and competence (which includes the agentic instrumentality of masculine traits, the roles of athlete/lesbian, businesswoman, and feminist, and the male-dominated occupations). Seeing a group as "warm" originates from regarding its members as noncompetitive and nonthreatening. Regarding a group as "competent" reflects perceptions of its members' higher status. The reason these seemingly benign gender stereotypes become sexist is that none of the traits, real roles, and occupations associated with actual women engender perceptions of both warmth and competence. Thus women, unlike men, are left to choose between being liked or respected. That is, women become targets of sexist stereotyping, which by definition, is directed toward women and restricts them to less powerful and/or disliked roles.

A common example of this trade-off for women is the stereotypically incompatible roles of mother (warmth) with employment (competence). In the eyes of college student raters, when professional women took on the role of mother, these women traded perceived competence for perceived warmth (Cuddy, Fiske, & Glick, 2004). In contrast, professional men who became fathers gained in warmth without any reduction in their perceived competence. This difference in perceptions of professional mothers and fathers was not inconsequential for women. Rather, raters predicted less interest in hiring, promoting, and educating professional mothers, establishing a connection between sexist stereotyping and sexist discrimination.

SEXIST PREJUDICE

Sexist stereotyping describes the process of ascribing traits, roles, and occupations to women and often goes hand-in-hand with sexist prejudice; that is, attitudes that serve to oppress women and girls. The attitudes that most typically affect women relate to the stereotypic choice of being either warm or competent. Women who are stereotyped as warm, but not competent (e.g., housewives, the elderly) face paternalistic prejudice, which is characterized by pity and sympathy (Cuddy, Norton, & Fiske, 2005). Alternatively, women who are regarded as competent, but not warm (e.g., feminists, professionals) are challenged by envious prejudice, which blends grudging admiration with envy and jealousy. Each combination is neither completely positive nor completely negative, but rather reflects ambivalence (Glick & Fiske, 1996).

Generally, prejudice reflects antipathy toward its targets, and one component of sexist prejudice (hostile sexism) indeed expresses overtly disparaging attitudes (e.g., "Women seek to gain power by getting control over men"; item from the Ambivalent Sexism Inventory) (Glick & Fiske, 2001). More intuitively challenging to understand is benevolent sexism, which on its face appears positive. Benevolent sexism takes three forms: heterosexual intimacy (e.g., "No matter how accomplished he is, a man is not truly complete as a person unless he has the love of a woman"), gender differentiation (e.g., "Many women have a quality of purity that few men possess"), and protective paternalism (e.g., "A good woman should be set on a pedestal by her man"). The distinguishing marker for benevolent sexism is that it ultimately works to restrict women to limited roles. For example, although a "good" woman deserves adoration, who decides which women are good, and what do women need to do to remain in good standing? Like hostile prejudice, benevolent sexism reflects a view of women as likeable or competent, but not both.

The "carrot" and "stick" implications of benevolent sexism become clear in both group and individual research. At the broadest level, Glick, Fiske, and colleagues' (2000) comparison of 19 countries revealed that as men's hostile sexism increased so did women's endorsement of benevolent sexism. Similarly, individual women who were led to believe that research documented men's negative attitudes toward women expressed stronger benevolently sexist attitudes than did women who were assigned randomly to either positive or no information conditions (Fischer, 2006). Both studies suggest that hostile and benevolent sexism are linked, function differently, and work together to perpetuate a power hierarchy in which men dominate (Goodwin & Fiske, 2001).

SEXIST DISCRIMINATION
Sexist discrimination describes overtly negative acts directed toward women and girls because they are female, as well as patronizing acts that assert male superiority. These acts can include extreme forms of violence against specific women as well as less pronounced, yet insidious everyday forms that are virtually universal. Our focus first is on the latter, and then we will return to the former.

Generally, sexist discrimination encompasses three forms: blatant sexist discrimination that is intentional, visible, and easily documented; covert sexist discrimination that is hidden, purposeful, and often maliciously motivated; and subtle sexist discrimination, the most common type, that may pass unnoticed, may be unintentional, and is always difficult to document and remedy (Benokraitis (1997). Illustrative examples of each are sexist language and jokes (blatant), discrete and intentional sabotage of women's work (covert), and protective paternalism and back-handed compliments (subtle).

At least two measures have been developed to assess women's experiences with sexist discrimination in general: The Schedule of Sexist Events (Klonoff & Landrine, 1995) and a 25-item measure of exposure to daily sexist events (Swim, Cohen, & Hyers, 1998). A general conclusion across studies that use these measures is that women's experiences with sexist discrimination are virtually universal (Moradi & DeBlaere, 2010). Additionally, internal consistency reliabilities tend to be stronger within context-specific clusters of discriminatory experiences, and more specific subordinate constructs have been well defined and researched. These specific contexts include sexist discrimination based on appearance (e.g., body objectification, discussed later), in relationships, in the workplace, and toward women as a group.

Interpersonal Discrimination
In day-to-day relationships, Lott (1995) describes interpersonal sexist discrimination as attempts to separate from women through exclusion, avoidance, and physical distancing. Research on interpersonal sexist discrimination documented that judges paid more attention to arguments made by male, as compared to female, lawyers (MacCorquodale & Jensen, 1993); that participants taking memory tests remembered the names of more famous men than women (Banaji & Greenwald, 1994); and that male students with female instructors signing up for class extra credit disrespectfully procrastinated more than the other student–teacher combinations (Louie & Tom, 2005).

Workplace Discrimination
In the workplace, findings with general measures of sexist discrimination converge with the more fully developed literature on sexual harassment. In the workplace, harassment can involve obvious abuses of power (quid pro quo harassment) or take on more covert and subtle forms to create a chilling educational or work climate (hostile work environment harassment), such that the latter fits with our focus here on everyday discrimination. Similar to other forms of male violence against women, the

prevalence of sexual harassment is high (likely 50%; Fitzgerald, 1993). Importantly, prevalence rates likely reflect underestimates of sexual harassment because targets commonly fail to label behaviors that meet criteria for defining harassment as harassment (Koss, Goodman, Browne, Fitzgerald, Keita, & Russo, 1994), and ambiguities surround what constitutes "unwanted" and "nonconsensual" (key elements in the definition of sexual harassment) behaviors (Muehlenhard, Powch, Phelps, & Giusti, 1992). In terms of responses to harassment, some women blame themselves and minimize the severity of their experiences (Kelly & Radford, 1996), discrepancies exist between how hypothetical targets think they would respond (e.g., confrontation) compared to how most targets actually respond (e.g., endurance, denial, detachment, and illusory control) (Fitzgerald, Swan, & Fischer, 1995), and some women's resilience challenges definitions that demand devastation as necessary for legal restitution.

Discrimination and Violence

There is a subtle stepwise progression from the seemingly minor daily hassles of being female captured in examples of interpersonal sexist discrimination to more obviously troublesome instances of sexual harassment in the workplace to even more destructive forms of male violence against women. Although it certainly would be sensationalistic to propose that people can readily move from daily slights directed toward women to despicable forms of violent misogyny toward women as a group, as well as toward individual women in the forms of battering and rape, the social psychological literature on aggression clearly documents how major atrocities like genocide (Staub, 1989) build on a series of increasingly violent actions. This continuum of increasing acceptance of, and engagement in, aggression serves to gradually disempower its targets and draws on two important processes: polarization (i.e., regarding the target of violence as different from me) and objectification (i.e., regarding the target as not human).

Gender polarization is commonly assumed and reinforced when differences between women and men are regarded as inherent and natural (i.e., subjectively essentialized; Prentice & Miller, 2007), when masculinity and femininity are exaggerated, when we fall back on gender stereotyping to think about and react to individuals, when subtly sexist jokes highlight and perpetuate gender differences, when gender roles become rigid and strictly enforced, and so on (Yoder, 2007, p. 340).

These common beliefs and activities can lay the groundwork to take the next step toward dehumanizing or objectifying women: calling women degrading names, judging and ogling women's bodies, ridiculing and harassing women, trying to control women, and so on. Both steps build to set the context for the possibility of escalated violence.

There is growing piecemeal evidence to support these proposed linkages, although theoretically based, programmatic research is sorely needed. For example, college men who enjoyed sexist humor also were found to harbor destructive rape attitudes as well as report a higher likelihood of using sexual coercion (Ryan & Kanjorski, 1998). This relationship is mutually reinforcing: college men exposed to a confederate who engaged in sexual harassment or who was generally sexist subsequently told more sexist jokes to a female student (Angelone, Hirschman, Suniga, Armey, & Armelie, 2005). Furthermore, male sexual aggressiveness has been connected to exaggerations of the masculine gender role or hypermasculinity (Driscoll, Kelly, & Henderson, 1998; Franchina, Eisler, & Moore, 2001; Murnen, Wright, & Kaluzny, 2002; Weisbuch, Beal, & O'Neal, 1999), reasserting masculinity (Eisler, Franchina, Moore, Honeycutt, & Rhatigan, 2000; Messerschmidt, 2000), and the masculine ideal of control and dominance (Anderson & Umberson, 2001; Reitz, 1999). Similarly, men's openly sexist attitudes have been associated with tolerance of sexual harassment (Russell & Trigg, 2004) as well as with men's rape proclivity and misperceptions that rape victims really "wanted it" (Abrams, Viki, Masser, & Bohner, 2003). In fact, a meta-analysis of 72 studies of beliefs in rape myths found greater rape myth acceptance among people endorsing traditional, polarized gender roles and harboring adversarial sexual beliefs (Anderson, Cooper, & Okamura, 1997). Furthermore, these linkages are not confined to men: some women help perpetuate rape myths through their own distrust of, and hostility toward, women (Cowan, 2000).

All forms of male violence against women (including sexual harassment, sexual abuse, and male partner abuse) share several recurrent themes (Yoder, 2007). First, understanding them is compromised by definitional ambiguities about what constitutes "unwanted" and "nonconsensual" behaviors (Muehlenhard et al., 1992) and language that can mask their severity (McHugh, Frieze, & Browne, 1993). For example, "family violence" implies equal intent to harm, equal perceived vulnerability, and equal harm—equality rarely achieved in male violence against women (Gordon, 2000)—and passive-voice language (e.g., "she was beaten"), which fails to acknowledge the responsibility of the perpetrator (Lamb & Koen, 1995). Second, these ambiguities often serve to invalidate and make invisible women's experiences (Parrot & Bechhofer, 1991), even at times for women themselves (e.g., unacknowledged date rape victims who confine their definition of rape to stranger rape) (Kahn, Mathie, & Torgler, 1994). Still, carefully collected data establish some realistic estimates of abuse prevalence across American women's lifetimes: 15% for rape and sexual assault among adult women (Rozee & Koss, 2001) and 21%–34% for physical assault by an intimate adult partner (Browne, 1993; Randall & Haskell, 1995). Finally, although even women may minimize the violence in their experiences as a way to cope with their trauma (Kelly & Radford, 1996; Koss, Figueredo, Bell, Tharan, & Tromp, 1996), all of these forms of trauma have serious physical and psychological consequences that heighten women's distress and jeopardize their well-being. Common psychological outcomes resulting from male violence against women include reduced self-esteem, heightened feelings of helplessness and entrapment, self-blame, depression, anxiety, psychological numbing, and fear (for example, see Goodman, Koss, & Russo, 1993; Koss, 1990). Indeed, these consequences can spill over onto all women, even those not the immediate targets of violence, because women, not men, live their everyday lives under the constant threat of these forms of psychological, physical, and sexual abuse (Hollander, 2001; Thompson & Norris, 1992).

Women's Mental Health in Context

As the previous section illustrates, examining gender and sexism in social context lays a foundation for understanding women's mental health. Understanding the processes of social categorization and intersectionality and the structure of systems of inequality makes it clear that there is no genderless person (Wise & Rafferty, 1982) and no generic woman (Landrine, 1985). Thus, every client comes to therapy, and every therapeutic interaction takes place, within a gendered context that includes automatically activated expectations (Devine, 1989) that, if left unexamined, can become detrimentally self-fulfilling (Skrypnek & Snyder, 1982). Social categorization reminds counseling psychologists that gender matters; the intersections of social representations make it clear that one's own experiences

cannot explain another's; and systems of inequality highlight how power differentials and status implications attached to gender cannot be ignored. In sum, these understandings provide a cogent rationale for considering women's mental health within the gendered social contexts described thus far, and engaging in feminist psychotherapy (see Enns chapter).

Gender and Psychological Disorders

The lifetime prevalence of having a psychological disorder appears to be similar for women and men (Kessler et al., 2005), but gender differences are found in the rates of some specific psychological disorders. For example, women appear to be at greater risk for anxiety and mood disorders; men, for impulse control and substance use disorders (Kessler et al., 2005). Such gender differences may be shaped by essential gender differences in disorder prevalence, but additional factors may contribute to these observed gender differences as well. For example, an important limitation of available gender ratio data is that they are typically drawn from nonprobability samples and can therefore reflect sampling bias rather than actual gender differences in the population (Hartung & Widiger, 1998).

An additional consideration is that diagnostic criteria for many psychological disorders may be gendered. For instance, the *Diagnostic and Statistical Manual* (DSM) diagnostic criteria for depression and personality disorders have been shown to evoke gender (and other demographic) categorization in undergraduate students (Landrine, 1988, 1989). Such gender stereotyped disorders may contribute to under-reporting symptoms that transgress stereotypic gender roles (e.g., Bekker, 1996; Sigmon et al., 2005). Relatedly, therapists may make gender-stereotypical diagnoses more readily than gender-nonstereotypic diagnoses. For instance, Potts and colleagues (1991) found that medical and mental health practitioners diagnosed depression more frequently among women than among men in patient groups who both did, and did not, meet criteria for depression. Thus, depression was overdiagnosed among women who were not depressed and underdiagnosed among men who were depressed. Similarly, in an analogue study, Robertson and Fitzgerald (1990) found that therapists were more likely to diagnose a videotaped male actor with a severe mood disorder if he described his professed "happy" marriage as nontraditional compared to traditional. Thus, any real gender differences in the prevalence of specific psychological disorders must be interpreted in the context of potential gender stereotyping of the disorders themselves, as well as of resultant biases in reporting symptoms and diagnosing disorders.

An additional consideration is that some disorders may actually reflect extremes of feminine gender role socialization. For instance, Gelfond (1991) conducted an exploratory comparison of independent, average, and agoraphobic women. The independent and average women were categorized as such based on their high or average scores on a measure of independent travel and activity. The agoraphobic group scored low on this measure, self-identified as phobic, and scored as phobic on the Brief Symptom Inventory (BSI). Gelfond noted substantial similarities between the "average" and "agoraphobic" women. Specifically, she found that over half of the women designated as average scored near the clinical range for agoraphobia (on the BSI), and these average women were similar to agoraphobic women in their negative attitudes about traveling alone, limited directional skills, and low use of recreational resources. In contrast, independent women did not share these characteristics. Thus, "average" and "agoraphobic" women were similar in their symptoms as well as in terms of the attitudes, skills, and behaviors assessed by Gelfond. Gelfond suggested that these similarities were rooted in the contexts of women's lives (e.g., learning experiences, fear of crime) rather than in intrapsychic factors, and that agoraphobia might reflect the extremes of women's learning histories.

A related issue is that the DSM may pathologize feminine gender socialization more so than masculine gender socialization. To illustrate this point, Caplan (1995) submitted "Delusional Dominating Personality Disorder" for DSM consideration. Designed to reflect extremes of stereotypic masculinity, this "disorder" included characteristics such as the inability to establish and maintain interpersonal relationships, inability to identify and express feelings, and difficulty expressing empathy. This fictitious disorder was never seriously considered for inclusion in the DSM. By contrast, "Self-defeating Personality Disorder," which placed responsibility for interpersonal mistreatment with the target and included feminine stereotypic criteria such as unsolicited self-sacrifice, was slated for inclusion in the DSM-III. It was withdrawn only after a public outcry charging that it blamed survivors of abuse, mostly women, for being abused (Caplan & Gans, 1991). As this example illustrates, ignoring the contexts of women's lives, including the continuum of sexism from subtle gender role expectations to violence, can lead to pathologizing women for the consequences of those contexts.

Sexist Discrimination and Women's Mental Health

A growing body of research reveals the connection between various manifestations of sexist discrimination and women's mental health. Paralleling our earlier discussion, we discuss potential mental health implications of everyday interpersonal sexism, sexism in the workplace, and discrimination and violence, adding a fourth section to explore sexual objectification.

INTERPERSONAL DISCRIMINATION

Kobrynowicz and Branscombe (1997) found that women's perceptions of sexist discrimination directed toward women in general were associated with depressive symptoms. Numerous studies also have linked women's reports of personal experiences of sexist events, across the past year or over their lifetime, with a range of psychological symptoms and overall psychological distress; this link has been supported with predominantly white and African American samples, college and community samples, predominantly heterosexual and lesbian and bisexual samples, and with women seeking counseling services (e.g., Berg, 2006; Fischer & Holz, 2007; Landrine, Klonoff, Gibbs, Manning, & Lund, 1995; Moradi & Funderburk, 2006; Moradi & Subich, 2002a, 2003; Szymanski, 2005a). Although most studies examined retrospective reports of women's experiences of sexism, Swim and associates' (2001) conducted a 2-week diary study and found that the number of daily sexist hassles reported by college women predicted their end-of-day anger and anxiety. Collectively, these studies suggest that sexist discrimination, from the global to the long-term to the daily, is associated with psychological distress.

WORKPLACE DISCRIMINATION

These patterns of association between discrimination and distress are also documented for workplace harassment. Women's experiences of sexual harassment have been related to anxiety attacks, headaches, sleep disturbances, gastrointestinal disorders, nausea, weight loss or gain, and crying spells (Crull, 1982; Gutek, 1985) and can lead to body dissatisfaction and disordered eating (Harned, 2000). Women targets of sexual harassment described fear, anger, anxiety, depression, self-questioning, and self-blame (Koss, 1990); their confidence can be shaken (Satterfield & Muehlenhard, 1997); their job satisfaction may be undermined (Chan, Tang, & Chan, 1999); and their perceptions of academic climate can deteriorate (Cortina, Swan, Fitzgerald, & Waldo, 1998). Furthermore, the effects of workplace mistreatment, including non–gender-specific derogation, sexist treatment, and sexual harassment, can be additive, leading to more negative work and psychophysical health outcomes when combined (Lim & Cortina, 2005).

DISCRIMINATION AND VIOLENCE

As we saw earlier, workplace sexual harassment falls along a broader continuum of sexist discrimination that ranges from everyday interpersonal hassles and exclusion to severe forms of male violence against women (e.g., sexual assault to femicide). The relationship of various forms of sexism with mental health outcomes can be understood through Root's (1992) dimensions of stressful trauma. Insidious trauma results from being devalued because of an individual characteristic, such as gender, and it has obvious connections with interpersonal sexist discrimination. At the other extreme, direct trauma results from being forced to commit an atrocity or from maliciously perpetrated violence directly targeting an individual, with the latter relating here to victims of sexual harassment, sexual assault, and battering. Although the DSM diagnosis of Post-Traumatic Stress Disorder captures the situational context for trauma, the remaining intrapsychic DSM diagnoses do not, and observed connections between these diagnoses and trauma are growing.

For example, violence and trauma have been linked to women's depression (Cutler & Nolen-Hoeksema, 1991; Hamilton & Jensvold, 1992) as well as to personality disorders (Lerman, 1996). Histories of sexual abuse and other violence were over-represented among women in substance abuse programs (Teets, 1995), and incest rates were found to be higher among alcoholic than nonalcoholic women (Beckman, 1994). In studies of women with eating disorders, sexual abuse or rape was reported in half or more cases, with sexual assault experiences emerging at even higher levels (over 75%) in inpatient samples (Root, 1991; Tripp & Petrie, 2001) and with recovery rates diminished among women with a history of chronic physical and sexual abuse (Hesse-Biber, Marino, & Watts-Roy, 1999). Sexual abuse has been connected with somatization disorders (Morrison, 1989), psychotic

disorders (Darves-Bornoz, Lemperiere, Degiovanni, & Gaillard, 1995), and bodily self-harm (Shaw, 2002). In sum, sexism as a form of trauma has strong implications for women's distress and well-being.

SEXUAL OBJECTIFICATION

Sexual objectification is a specific manifestation of sexism that has received increasing attention in research on women's mental health. Messages that equate girls' and women's value with white heterosexual standards of beauty, thinness, and sexual availability to men are an omnipresent part of girls' and women's socialization in Western cultures (APA Task Force on the Sexualization of Girls, 2007) and with increasing globalization, are being exported to non-Western cultures (Becker, 2004). These messages communicate standards that most girls and women cannot achieve; indeed, the term *normative discontent* has been used to capture women's near ubiquitous dissatisfaction with their bodies (Rodin, Silberstein, & Striegel-Moore; 1984). Fredrickson and Roberts (1997) offered objectification theory as a framework for explaining how women's socialization and body dissatisfaction can contribute to mental health problems that have higher prevalence among women than among men.

Objectification theory posits that women's life experiences and socialization include routine exposure to sexual objectification from external sources (Fredrickson & Roberts, 1997), and diary studies support sexual objectification as a dimension of daily experiences of sexism in women's lives (Swim, Hyers, Cohen, & Ferguson, 2001). Within the objectification theory framework, sexual objectification experiences are thought to socialize girls and women to treat themselves, to varying degrees, as objects to be looked upon and evaluated based upon bodily appearance (Fredrickson & Roberts, 1997). This individualized internalization of an observer's perspective upon one's own body is called *self-objectification*. Self-objectification is manifested at its extreme by persistent body surveillance, or the act of "habitual monitoring of the body's outward appearance" (Fredrickson & Roberts, 1997, p. 180). Appearance-focused self-objectification and manifest body surveillance parallel McKinley and Hyde's (1996) earlier conceptualization of body surveillance as a component of objectified body consciousness.

High levels of self-objectification and manifest body surveillance are posited to promote body shame resultant from perceived failure to meet an internalized or cultural appearance standard; increase anxiety about physical safety and about when and how one's body will be evaluated; reduce awareness of internal bodily states, such as satiety and physiological sexual arousal; and interrupt cognitive processing and flow experiences or what Csikszentmihalyi (1982, 1990) described as "rare moments during which we feel we are truly living, uncontrolled by others, creative and joyful" (Fredrickson & Roberts, 1997, p. 183). Objectification theory proposes that this chain of relations—from external sexual objectification to internalized self-objectification and body surveillance, to increased body shame and anxiety, reduced internal bodily awareness, and disrupted flow—can exacerbate women's risks for depression, sexual dysfunction, and eating disorders (Fredrickson & Roberts, 1997).

Since its publication, research on objectification theory has proliferated and supported the direct and indirect relations of sexual objectification experiences, self-objectification/body surveillance, and body shame with eating disorder and depressive symptomatology (for review, see Moradi & Huang, 2008). Importantly, some of these aspects of the theory also have been tested and supported with women who identified as African American (Buchanan, Fischer, Tokar, & Yoder, 2008), Deaf or hearing impaired (Moradi & Rottenstein, 2007), and lesbian (Kozee, Tylka, Augustus-Horvath, & Denchik, 2007). These latter studies also point to the importance of considering group-specific variables, such as skin tone surveillance (Buchanan et al., 2008), and Deaf cultural identity attitudes (Moradi & Rottenstein, 2007). In addition, contexts-heightening self-objectification (e.g., wearing a swimsuit in front of a full-length mirror, even in private) have been shown to inhibit women's performance in math and other concentration-related tasks (e.g., Fredrickson, Roberts, Noll, Quinn, & Twenge, 1998; Quinn, Kallen, Twenge, & Fredrickson, 2006). By contrast, research is limited on other objectification theory variables (e.g., sexual dysfunction). Still, objectification theory provides an integrative framework for understanding how women's socialization can be translated into psychological risk factors and symptomatology. Consistent with feminist conceptualizations, research on objectification theory points to changes needed at the societal level (e.g., reducing the sexual objectification of women) and also highlights potentially useful strategies at the individual level (e.g., resisting internalized self-objectification) to reduce women's psychological distress.

Girls and Women in Relationships

Our argument that to understand an individual one must take into strong consideration that individual's social context challenges us to closely examine girls' and women's relationships as the most immediate forms of everyday social interaction. Furthermore, given our interest in power, privilege, and oppression as driving forces in a general system of social inequality, it becomes important to examine how girls and boys, women and men operate within a system of differential power and status. Here, we will look at girls and women in the context of their interpersonal relationships, starting with the socializing relationships of childhood, then turning to intimate relationships in adulthood.

Girls and Socialization Practices

A comprehensive model of gender development that explores the differentiation of girls and boys is offered by Bussey and Bandura (1999; 2004). In general, these sociocognitive theorists regard gender socialization as the combination of a child's learning through socializing agents (e.g., parents, schools, media, and peers) with the child's own cognitive processing and within a general cultural context. It is the embeddedness of socialization within a child's culture, in this case a culture that emphasizes gender polarization (Bem, 1993), that shapes each child's ways of thinking (e.g., gender schema), that leads to the self-regulation of behavior (e.g., reproducing what is normative for one's gender), and that influences self-efficacy. Indeed, children's actions are so context-dependent that they have been shown to vary according to the salience of gender in specific contexts (Messner, 2000).

Lips (2002) synthesized the massive body of research on gender differentiated socialization practices and outcomes to identify the pervasive meta-message conveyed by girls' socialization experiences. She argues that girls are raised in a culture that prepares them for powerlessness. Although both girls and boys begin with the potential to develop wings and take flight, typically girls' socialization experiences clip their wings by teaching them habits of silence, self-doubt, and acquiescence. In contrast, boys learn to achieve mastery over tasks and are empowered to influence others. In sum, socialization practices work to maintain the status quo of gendered systems of inequality.

Although the literature exploring specific socialization practices is vast, some recent examples provide background for Lips' conclusion and its continued relevance. For example, parents allowed boys greater risk-taking (Morrongiello & Hogg, 2004); fathers commonly told sons family stories with autonomy themes (Fiese & Skillman, 2000), whereas mothers often included emotional references in their conversations with daughters (Flannagan & Perese, 1998); and computer games that target male audiences emphasized efficacy (Whitley, 1997). In their comprehensive review of the gendered lessons taught in schools, the Sadkers (1994) concluded that girls learned to speak quietly, to defer to boys, to value neatness over innovation, and to stress appearance over intelligence. In the media, "bad" cartoon characters deviated from gender stereotypes (Ogletree, Martinez, Turner, & Mason, 2004), birth announcements heralded happiness for girls and pride for sons (Gonsalez & Koestner, 2005), and even books touted as "nonsexist" described girls' personalities, domestic chores, and leisure activities using feminine stereotyping (Diekman & Murnen, 2004). Among peers, the more girls played only with other girls, the more they engaged in gender-stereotypic behavior (Martin & Fabes, 2001).

Indeed, one of the strongest, overarching patterns researchers have identified in the socialization of girls and boys is the typicality of sex-segregated play and preferences (Ruble & Martin, 1998). Paralleling the sex segregated world of employment (Padavic & Reskin, 2002), girls are drawn to playing with other girls (rather than actively avoiding boys) (Maccoby, 1990). The reasons why girls oftentimes find girls more appealing than boys are intriguing. Girls tend to share the belief that feelings are important (in contrast to boys' valuing of shared activities and interests), and girls' interactional style typically is marked by cooperation, politeness, and interaction with others (as opposed to being focused on dominance and restrictive interaction) (Neppl & Murray, 1997; Voss, 1997). In-group evaluation bias is strong among both sexes, and girls' valuation of gender equality tends to strengthen across elementary through middle school (whereas boys' weakens) (Ruble & Martin, 1998). Finally, children simply like peers better when they play stereotypically with same-sex friends (Colwell & Lindsey, 2005). The results of these peer preferences then is that girls and boys grow up in strikingly different social contexts.

Finally, a major component of sociocognitive theory is self-efficacy, the belief that one has the capabilities to produce positive outcomes for oneself. The generalized, long-term effect of cultural preparedness for powerlessness may be a small to moderate difference in adult women's and men's self-esteem (Kling, Hyde, Showers, & Buswell, 1999). Even more germane to our argument here is the persistent superiority of men's self-reported agency or instrumentality; that is, how much an individual believes she or he can take charge of and accomplish goals independently (Helgeson, 1994).

Women in Intimate Relationships

Worell (1988) describes the defining features of close relationships: They are expected to endure over time and to provide each individual with respect, intimacy, caring, concern, support, and affection. Specific romantic attachments go beyond general close relationships to include sexual passion, exclusiveness, and commitment. The degree to which romantic attachments live up to an individual's expectations, preferences, and conceptualization of what constitutes a good relationship is reflected in relationship satisfaction, which in turn is positively associated with psychological and physical well-being. Supportive relationships enhance an individual's responses to stress, self-esteem, feelings of self-efficacy, reported happiness, and resistance to loneliness, depression, and serious illness (Worell, 1988).

MULTIPLE ROLES

Romantic attachments are one piece of the myriad of interpersonal relationships that compose a healthy individual's life. Two views of women's multiple roles envision them as engendering either scarcity or enhancement (Barnett & Hyde, 2001). The scarcity hypothesis posits that more roles bring conflict based in both competing time demands and spillover from one role to another. In contrast, the enhancement hypothesis contends that multiple roles invigorate individuals and can even serve as buffers against undesirable consequences when troubles emerge in any one role or subset of roles (Crosby, 1991). The common application of these ideas to women's lives concentrates on women's employment, partner, and parental roles.

For most women, role conflict and enhancement coexist. For example, Rankin (1993) studied 118 employed mothers of preschoolers aged 23–43 months. Most described their lives as stressful, citing lack of time, child-related problems, and maternal guilt. Simultaneously, these women reported personal benefits, financial rewards, and improved family lives as the result of their multiple roles. Febbraro (2003) offers an insightful resolution to these trade-offs that acknowledges both conflict and enhancement by calling on structural accommodations in the workplace rather than personal role redefinition or unrealistic reactive role behavior (i.e., being a do-it-all superwoman) (also see Tiedje, 2004). These structural changes can include less stressful flexible work schedules (Matsui, Ohsawa, & Onglatco, 1995), autonomy to be absent from work (Moen & Forest, 1990), supportive supervisors and workplace cultures, opportunities for advancement (Galinsky, Bond, & Friedman, 1996), and maternity leave (Hyde, Klein, Essex, & Clark, 1995). Unfortunately, though, women's real-life choices often force them to make more family-role accommodations than work-role redefinitions (Matsui et al., 1995).

However, even within the often unyielding constraints of workplace demands, the negative consequences of multiple roles can be mitigated by having strong social supports, both instrumental and emotional. For example, Ozer (1995) found that a woman's belief in her ability to enlist the help of her spouse for childcare predicted well-being and reduced distress. Family emotional support reduced women's family-related stress, which in turn lowered family-to-work interference (Bernas & Major, 2000) and contributed to women's sense of mastery, which then enhanced well-being (Martire, Stephens, & Townsend, 1998).

MAKING RELATIONSHIPS WORK FOR WOMEN
The next obvious question then becomes how to make relationships work for women. Popular self-help books focused on women's intimate relationships promulgate three general myths: women do not know what will make them happy in a relationship (ignorance); women lack the skills to initiate and maintain satisfying relationships (incompetence); and the gender polarity between women and men in heterosexual relationships makes them basically incompatible (Worell, 1988). Not surprisingly, the more adults were exposed to these popular myths through the media, the more dysfunctional and unrealistic were their beliefs about romantic attachments (Shapiro & Kroeger, 1991). Despite the popular wisdom that women do not know what they want in relationships, researchers find that they actually do: Quite simply put, women want intimacy and equality.

Intimacy and Sexuality
Popular wisdom often portrays women as seeking genuine intimacy through their sexuality, as opposed to men's simplistic and hedonistic pleasure-seeking.

A large-scale study of 445 women and 457 men lent some credibility to this speculation by finding that, indeed, women attached less importance to pure pleasure, conquest, and relief of tension through sexual activities (Leigh, 1989). However, a closer look at the data revealed that, although women did rank emotional closeness first and men gave pleasure their top priority for engaging in sexual behaviors, regardless of sexual orientation, men ranked attachment as a close second. Furthermore, men rated pleasing their partner as more important than women did. Additional research concluded that how women and men think about their own sexuality (i.e., their sexual schema) (Andersen, Cyranowski, J.M., & Espindle, 1999), as well as about sexually related terms (Noland, Daley, Drolet, Fetro, McCormack Brown, Hassell, & McDermott, 2004), was remarkably similar.

As for sexual attitudes and behaviors, Oliver and Hyde's (1993) meta-analysis found widespread similarities between women and men, with the largest singular differences being men's considerably more permissive attitudes about casual sexual behaviors and higher rates of masturbation. Moreover, looking across the 1960s through the 1980s, gender differences in sexual attitudes and behaviors narrowed considerably.

Gentry (1998) asked undergraduates to evaluate a hypothetical woman or man who was portrayed as either monogamous or engaged in multiple heterosexual relationships, as well as enacted low, moderate, or high levels of sexual activity. On overt measures, women targets were treated similarly to men, such that both female and male promiscuous and highly active targets were disparaged. Women preferred the woman target described as below average in sexual activity in contrast to men's preference for the more active stimulus woman, who was regarded as liberal and assertive. Taken together, these studies describe a newly evolving, complex image of sexuality that combines permissive expressed attitudes and some overt acceptance of sexually assertive women.

Additional studies, however, raise the specter that the traditional double standard of women's and men's sexuality has not fully disappeared. For example, undergraduate students concocted a stronger justification of love for an extramarital partner when the transgression was committed by a woman than by a man (Sprecher, Regan, & McKinney, 1998). Women pornography actors were rated more harshly than were men (Evans-DeCicco & Cowan, 2001), and unobtrusive observations of Wisconsin's procedures for establishing paternity and child support uncovered that women were questioned far more extensively about their sexual practices and partners than were men (Monson, 1997). Paralleling the pattern we have seen overall for sexist discrimination, the double standard for women's and men's sexuality may simply have shifted from more overt to more covert and subtle expressions.

Our discussion thus far has examined sexual attitudes and behaviors of and about women relative to men. But, women's sexuality must also be considered on its own terms, beyond phallocentirc definitions of sex that render women's experiences of sexual behavior, pleasure, and orgasm implicit or even inconsequential in the sexual script (see Fassinger & Arseneau, 2008). To this end, attention to women's same-sex sexuality can inform understanding of women's sexuality in general. For example, available data suggest that the most prevalent dating script among lesbians is a friendship script, in which a friendship grows and is gradually expressed sexually (Rose & Zand, 2000). Also, sexuality between women may not be focused on a single act of "sex" but rather on a sexual episode comprised of a range of behaviors that might or might not result in orgasm(s) (Fassinger & Arseneau, 2008; Rose, 2000). Such conceptualizations challenge us to think about a broad range of sexual behaviors that constitute sexual episodes in a range of relationship contexts for women.

Egalitarian Relationships
Turning to the second quality women seek in their romantic attachments, equality, egalitarianism is now rated as more desirable in marriage than it was 40 years ago, reaching almost universal levels among college students (Gilbert & Rader, 2001). In addition, women who see themselves as an equal partner in their marriage reported higher relationship satisfaction and were less likely to resort to using power strategies to get their way (Donaghue & Fallon, 2003). However, true behavioral equality appears to be achieved in only a minority of marriages (Steil, 1997). Rather, women perform a disproportionate share of household labor (Bond, Thompson, Galinsky, & Prottas, 2003; Thomas, 2002) regardless of socioeconomic class (Wright, 1992) and race/ethnicity (John & Shelton, 1997). Imbalances also appear in women's general caregiving (Gerstel & Gallagher, 2001) and in the caretaking of children. Mothers average over 11 more hours each week of child care than do fathers (Bond et al., 2003), about 5.8 waking hours of every day, a contribution that

has remained stable from 1965 through 1998 (Bianchi, 2000). Becoming a first-time parent commonly reshapes women's home (increases) and employment (reduces) lives, whereas men's lives remain virtually unaltered (Sanchez & Thomas, 1997).

Recurrent themes of intimacy and equality are also central in lesbians' descriptions of their romantic attachments. For example, Eldridge and Gilbert's (1990) extensive nationwide survey of 275 dual-employed couples concluded that, despite folk wisdom to the contrary, lesbian relationships were stable, enduring, and committed, although often largely invisible to outsiders. Relationship satisfaction was related not only to sexual intimacy, but also to recreational (common interests) and to intellectual intimacy, although not with social intimacy (possibly a causality of secrecy). Unlike both gay male and heterosexual partners, lesbian partners tend to perform an equal number of household tasks (Kurdek, 1993). Beyond simple household contributions, lesbian couples mention equality of influence as a core goal (Eldridge & Gilbert, 1990) and actually use bilateral influence strategies (Rosenbluth & Steil, 1995) and psychologically intimate communication (Mackey, Diemer, & O'Brien, 2000) to achieve relationship equality and hence relational satisfaction.

Power in Women's Relationships
As we saw previously in our discussion of social dominance theory and systems of inequality, a core point for understanding women in context concerns their relatively disempowered intergroup status in relation with men. Although generally regarded as influencing broad sociopolitical issues, social dominance theory contextualizes how these macroscopic forces penetrate into the most intimate and proximal of women's relationships.

Starting with women's sexuality, interpersonal power and sexual communication affect the safe sexual practices of African American (Bowleg, Lucas, & Tschann, 2004) and European American heterosexually active adolescents (Gutierrez, Oh, & Gillmore, 2000) and Mexican-born married women (de Snyder, Acevedo, Diaz-Perez, & Saldivar-Guaduno, 2000). In one study of sexual decision making, only 12% of couples in which the man made the decision used condoms more than half the time. This figure jumped to 49% when women made the decision and to 32% when both partners decided (Osmond et al., 1993). Through all these factors runs a strand of power: the more powerful person, both personally and interpersonally, controls how sexuality is practiced (Amaro, Raj, & Reed, 2001; Quina, Harlow, Morokoff, Burkholder, & Deiter, 2000). Thus, violence and risk-taking prevention programs aimed at women must foster women's empowerment in negotiating sexual encounters and in ending those that put them at risk (Croteau, Nero, & Prosser, 1993).

Power in an intimate relationship involves two key dimensions that may be important in communication about safe sexual practices: relationship control and decision-making dominance (Pulerwitz, Gortmaker, & DeJong, 2000). Relationship control is exercised when women project that their male partner's response to them will include violence and/or anger, both within and outside the sexual arena. For example, nonsexual signs of relationship control include doing what one's partner wants to do most of the time and having a partner dictate what one wears. Decision-making dominance includes deciding with whose friends the couple interacts, whether they engage in sexual relations, and what they do together. Further research is needed to directly tie these dimensions to sexual risk-taking, although at this time the empirical and theoretical foundation for expecting such linkages is strong.

Although there is much overlap between lesbians' and heterosexual women's dating scripts and relational desires for intimacy and equality, one of the most glaring differences is in the more commonly achieved egalitarianism among lesbians (Eldridge & Gilbert, 1990; Klinkenberg & Rose, 1994). Certainly there are multiple bases for power differentials in all relationships (e.g., being more emotionally invested); however, compared to heterosexual relationships, the internal workings of lesbians' relationships are freed from the gendered system of inequality. This comparison also highlights the largely subtle and invisible ways in which heterosexual relationships support and reflect the general gender system of social dominance. Thus, to understand heterosexual women in the context of their intimate relationships, it becomes important to understand the balance of power between partners.

Whether or not women's greater earnings can offset men's social power is unclear. For example, Steil and Weltman's (1991) study with women earning at least one-third more than their spouses found that women still performed more than their equal share of domestic labor, but had more influence in decision-making. Other studies, such as Pyke and

Coltrane's (1996), associated enhanced earnings with more household sharing. Not surprisingly, the less emotionally involved partner in a relationship has more power, and that partner is more commonly the man (Sprecher & Felmlee, 1997). Lennon and Rosenfield (1994) found that women who had fewer alternatives to marriage because of limited economic resources, in contrast to more independent women, were more likely to view unequal divisions of labor as fair. Although caregiving certainly enriches people's lives, it rarely benefits the caregiver with anything exchangeable and thus does not confer power to women (Pratto & Walker, 2004).

One of the most puzzling paradoxes of this literature is women's depressed entitlement, the finding that women often perceive objectively imbalanced domestic contributions as fair (Thompson, 1991). Major (1993) concluded that this apparent inconsistency could be explained by considering women's comparison group of other women, not men themselves. In addition, women who compared themselves to normative standards of what women should do felt inadequate despite their disproportionate overcontributions. Alternatively, women who compared their husband's level of participation to their own inputs, rather than to those of other men, had husbands who contributed more (Hawkins, Marshall, & Meiners, 1995).

However, if we consider depressed entitlement within the global context of social dominance theory, then we might expect depressed entitlement to be related to gendered power differentials. Indeed, this linkage was established by Hogue and Yoder (2003) in their experimental examination of women's depressed entitlement in self-pay. The gap between women's underpayment relative to men's allocation in a control condition disappeared when women's status was raised through either gender- or education-related status manipulations. Furthermore, in a vignette study examining domestic contributions, Swearingen-Hilker and Yoder (2002) showed that raters' endorsement of hostile sexism was associated with viewing men's household undercontributions as fair, thus serving as a legitimating attitude supportive of the gendered system of inequality.

Although women generally may feel less unfairly treated than might objectively be predicted, those women who do perceive inequities suffer in terms of heightened distress, marital dissatisfaction (Golding, 1990; Robinson & Spitze, 1992), and depression (Bird, 1999). This may be one reason why women try to deny, rationalize away (Blain, 1994), or work out ways to juggle excessive demands (Hessing, 1994) rather than admit that unfairness threatens their marriage. Shifting to a more positive interpretation, women exhibited a stronger sense of fairness if men participated, if the couple actively decided together how to allocate chores, and if they felt their labor was appreciated (Hawkins et al., 1995). Indeed, women who get what they desire (e.g., interpersonal gratification) were unlikely to sense injustice (Thompson, 1991).

In sum, egalitarian marital relationships are embedded in a more global context of social dominance that works against their realization, despite women's clear valuation of and benefits from them. Weitzman's (1994) review of research on multiple-role realism concluded that although many college women wanted to combine work and family in their own future projections and were aware of the existence of multiple-role conflict, they did not expect it to be problematic in their own lives. Instead, personal, relationship, and even financial satisfaction was enhanced to the extent that women and men directly confronted these issues. Egalitarian sharing does not just happen in relationships; rather, it is actively constructed by committed and vigilant partners (Blaisure & Allen, 1995). Tangri and Jenkins (1997) found that women who expected work–family conflict and prepared accordingly— by asserting their career intentions with their spouse, by postponing child-bearing, and by having fewer children—experienced less marital conflict than did those who failed to acknowledge potential problems.

Women's Identities
Shifting our focus from women in relationships to a focus on women themselves brings us to models of group identity that outline women's sense of self as a member of the group "women." Models of group identity have been proposed for various stigmatized, marginalized, and oppressed populations. Group identity is important to counseling psychologists' research and practice because it is linked with important outcomes including psychological distress and well-being, academic achievement, interpersonal relationships, and civic and social engagement (for review, see Ashmore, Deaux, & McLaughlin-Volpe, 2004). In their review of the literature, Ashmore and coauthors (2004) articulated the various elements of group identity that have been the focus of prior scholarship. These elements are self-categorization as a member of the group; evaluation of the group (one's own and

others'); importance of group membership to self-definition; attachment and connection with the group; embeddedness of the collective identity in one's everyday relationships; behavioral involvements with the collective identity; and view of the characteristics, ideology, and narrative of the group as self-relevant. Several identity models have been proposed to capture these elements of group identity for women. We review three prominent models here, with emphasis on empirical findings that elucidate their relevance for women's experiences and mental health: Downing and Roush's (1985) model of feminist identity development, McCarn and Fassinger's (1996) model of lesbian identity formation, and Helms' (1990, as cited in Carter & Parks, 1996; Ossana, Helms, & Leonard, 1992) model of womanist identity development.

Feminist Identity Development
There are many philosophies of feminism, and feminism itself is an evolving construct (Frieze & McHugh, 1998; Henley, Spalding, & Kosta, 2000). Nevertheless, most feminisms and feminists are "united by a belief that unequal and inferior social status of women is unjust and needs to be changed" (Jaggar, 1983, p. 322). Consistent with this position, Russo (1998) found that about 90% of women who identified as feminists desired equal distribution of power between women and men in government, business, industry, and family. Importantly, many individuals hold feminist values and attitudes without self-identifying as feminist (e.g., Williams & Wittig, 1997; Zucker, 2004). Thus, researchers have investigated the correlates of "feminism" using various operationalizations, including feminist self-identification, but also pro-feminism or feminist attitudes, and egalitarian attitudes about the rights and roles of women relative to men. Downing and Roush's (1985) model of feminist identity development connects feminist attitudes and values (independent of feminist self-identification) with attitudes about oneself as a woman.

Informed by Cross's (1971) model of racial identity development, Downing and Roush (1985) initially proposed a developmental process. But, as with other identity development models, feminist identity development has been operationalized as a set of nonlinear attitudes that reflect profiles, rather than stages of feminist identity (see Moradi & Subich, 2002b; Moradi, Subich, & Phillips, 2002b). The set of five feminist identity attitudes ranges from a denial of cultural discrimination against women to an understanding of such discrimination and commitment to social justice. Specifically, *passive acceptance* is characterized by unexamined acceptance of traditional gender roles and denial of individual, institutional, and cultural discrimination against oneself and women in general. One or more events (e.g., consciousness raising group, a college class, workplace discrimination) can catalyze *revelation* or a realization about sexism, which is usually accompanied by feelings of anger toward a sexist society and feelings of guilt about one's own participation in the systematic oppression of women. *Embeddedness and emanation* encompasses seeking immersion in women's cultures and communities (e.g., taking women's studies courses, becoming involved in women's support groups), often idealizing such cultures and communities, as well as approaching men cautiously. *Synthesis* involves integrating feminist consciousness with other aspects of a positive self-concept and replacing dichotomous thinking about women and men with an individual differences approach. Finally, *active commitment* reflects a commitment to working toward societal change and eliminating oppression.

Downing and Roush's (1985) model was initially operationalized with the Feminist Identity Development Scale (Bargad & Hyde, 1991), which assessed all five feminist identity attitudes, and the Feminist Identity Scale (Rickard, 1989), which measured all but active commitment attitudes. Responding to psychometric concerns about each of these measures, Fischer and colleagues (2000) developed the Feminist Identity Composite (FIC), which integrated the FIDS and the FIS to capitalize on their psychometric strengths. Although some psychometric limitations remain with each of these instruments (see Moradi & Subich, 2002b), they have been used to explore linkages of feminist identity attitudes with a range of variables relevant to counseling psychologists. For example, prior research indicates that passive acceptance scores are related negatively, whereas revelation, embeddedness-emanation, synthesis, and active commitment scores are generally related positively with perceptions of sexism (e.g., Fischer & Good, 1994; Fischer et al., 2000; Moradi & Subich, 2002a, 2002b), activism in women's organizations (e.g., Fischer et al., 2000; White, Strube, & Fisher, 1998), and egalitarian attitudes (Fischer & Good, 1994; Yoder, Perry, & Saal, 2007). Passive acceptance may also underlie the link between egalitarian marital role expectations and assertiveness regarding sexual initiation and safer sex practices (Yoder et al., 2007).

Feminist identity attitudes have been linked with women's mental health as well. For example, synthesis and active commitment scores are associated with higher levels of empowerment and psychological well-being, whereas revelation and passive acceptance scores are related to lower levels of these mental health indicators (Peterson, Grippo, & Tantleff-Dunn, 2008; Saunders & Kashubeck-West, 2006). Furthermore, passive acceptance and revelation scores have been linked with greater psychological distress (Moradi & Subich, 2002a). Importantly, Fischer and Good (2004) found that the relation of revelation with distress was mediated in part by state anger. Thus, consistent with feminist identity development theory, the anger experienced as part of revelation can be associated with distress.

Although findings related to general distress and well-being indicators are consistent with feminist identity development theory, studies that have focused specifically on body image and eating problems have found mixed support for relations between feminist identity attitudes and body image and eating problems (Cash, Ancis, & Strachan, 1997; Snyder & Hasbourck, 1996). However, a recent intervention study found expected connections between body image improvement and feminist identity attitudes. Specifically, for participants exposed to a body image intervention grounded in feminist theory, improvements in body image were associated with increased synthesis and decreased passive acceptance (Peterson, Tantleff-Dunn, & Bedwell, 2006).

In addition to their direct links with mental health indicators, some feminist identity attitudes have been found to moderate links of perceived sexism with psychological symptomatology. For instance, level of passive acceptance moderated the link between perceived experiences of sexism and psychological distress such that the sexism–distress link was stronger for women with high passive acceptance scores than for women with low passive acceptance scores (Moradi & Subich, 2002a). Similarly, levels of synthesis and active commitment moderated the relation between perceived experiences of sexism and disordered eating, such that the sexism-disordered eating relation was positive for women with low levels of synthesis and active commitment, but nonsignificant for women with high levels of these feminist identity attitudes. Thus, low passive acceptance and high synthesis and active commitment attitudes may buffer the link of perceived sexism with some psychological symptoms.

An important caveat to the literature reviewed here is that most research on the feminist identity development model has been conducted with predominantly young white women of unknown sexual orientation. But, a few notable exceptions exist. For instance, with a sample of African American women, White and coauthors (1998) found that feminist identity attitudes were associated in expected directions with parallel racial identity development attitudes. In another study, Flores, Carrubba, and Good (2006) found that levels and factor structure of feminist identity attitudes for Mexican American adolescent girls differed from those found in other studies with primarily white and mostly college student samples, with the pattern of findings suggesting higher revelation and active commitment scores for Mexican American girls. Within the context of this limited sample diversity, scholars have called for greater attention to how feminist identity attitudes may intersect with racial/ethnic, sexual orientation, and other identities (e.g., Moradi, Subich, & Phillips, 2002a, b; Vandiver, 2002).

Also of importance to counseling psychologists are studies of feminist identity attitudes among therapists and clinical supervisors. Among therapists, passive acceptance scores were related negatively, and revelation and synthesis scores were related positively, with reported use of feminist therapy behaviors, and revelation emerged as the best predictor of self-identification as a feminist therapist (Juntunen, Atkinson, Reyes, & Gutierrez, 1994). Similarly, among clinical supervisors, passive acceptance scores were associated negatively, whereas revelation, embeddedness-emanation, and active commitment scores were associated positively, with self-reported feminist supervision practices (Szymanski, 2005b). Thus, practitioners' feminist identity attitudes appear to be related to self-reported counseling and supervision practices.

The demonstrated relations of feminist identity attitudes with women's mental health suggest that reducing passive acceptance, increasing synthesis and active commitment, and helping women work through revelation might realize educational and intervention goals. Similarly, reducing passive acceptance and increasing other feminist identity attitudes might be fruitful in education and training aiming to promote feminist therapy and supervision behaviors. The good news is that change in feminist identity attitudes is possible, as demonstrated by evidence of the effectiveness of various training approaches. For instance, Worell and colleagues (1999) assessed the feminist identity attitudes of graduate students in a large midsouthern university. They found some baseline differences between graduate programs, such that master's and doctoral degree students in what they called a "gender aware" counseling psychology program reported lower passive acceptance and higher embeddedness-emanation and active commitment scores than did similar students in school or educational psychology programs. They also found evidence suggesting that level of training is associated with shifts in feminist identity attitudes. Specifically, revelation scores were higher for doctoral students than for master's students in the counseling psychology program. By contrast, revelation scores were lower for doctoral students than for master's students in the noncounseling psychology programs (Worell, Stilwell, Oakley, & Robinson, 1999). Thus, greater training in a gender-aware program may increase revelation, and interestingly, training in not specifically gender-aware programs may reduce revelation.

This interpretation should be balanced, however, with the possibility that students who are drawn to and remain in a gender-aware program are more inclined to increase revelation attitudes than those who do not choose to train in such programs. The possible selection bias across groups is eliminated by short-term longitudinal studies that observe the same individuals before and after an intervention. For example, Yoder and associates (2007) found that, across five different psychology of women classes, passive acceptance scores decreased and the other four feminist identity attitude scores increased from the beginning to the end of the course. These studies suggest that feminist identity attitudes are responsive to training and education.

Lesbian Identity Formation

McCarn and Fassinger (1996) proposed a model of lesbian identity formation that teases apart individual sexual identity formation processes from group membership and sociopolitical identity formation processes. McCarn and Fassinger (1996) deemed this distinction important for acknowledging that, for lesbian (and gay and bisexual) persons, limited public identification or political activism does not signify "unhealthy" or "low" identity development. Rather, choices regarding sexual minority identity disclosure and political activism are shaped by contextual realities, including prejudice and discrimination in family, workplace, and other contexts. McCarn and Fassinger (1996) proposed four phases of individual and group membership identity formation: *awareness, exploration, deepening/commitment*, and *internalization/synthesis*. They emphasized that these phases may not necessarily occur in a linear or stage-wise progression; instead, they could be continuous and circular. Furthermore, phases of individual and group membership branches of identity formation are not necessarily simultaneous.

Individual sexual identity formation begins with an awareness of feeling different from the heterosexual norm. Exploration consists of active examination of erotic feeling for women (or a particular woman). Deepening/commitment involves clarity about one's sexuality and crystallization of one's sexual identity (e.g., lesbian, bisexual). Finally, internalization/synthesis reflects feeling comfortable and fulfilled with one's sexual identity. For group membership identity, identity formation begins with awareness that different sexual orientations exist and heterosexuality is not universal. Exploration involves examining one's position among sexual minority people and communities by acquiring more knowledge about and exploring one's attitudes toward these groups. Deepening/commitment includes engaging with and valuing sexual minority communities, and recognizing shared experiences of prejudice and stigmatization with those communities. Finally, internalization/synthesis reflects a sense of acceptance and fulfillment with one's group membership identity across contexts. McCarn and Fassinger's (1996) model has been operationalized with the Lesbian Identity Questionnaire (LIQ; see Swann & Spivey, 2004; Tomlinson & Fassinger, 2003), which was developed to assess the aforementioned four phases of individual sexual identity and group membership identity formation. Later efforts to conceptualize and operationalize sexual identity have yielded support for the model as well (e.g., Worthington, Navarro, Savoy, & Hampton, 2008), and the model and instrument have been modified and validated with gay men (Fassinger & Miller 1996).

Using the LIQ, researchers have found support for the distinctive relations of individual sexual identity and group membership identity phases with mental health indicators. For example, with predominantly white lesbian women, self-esteem was correlated negatively with levels of group membership identity formation awareness, exploration, and deepening/commitment, but it was uncorrelated with these phases of individual sexual identity formation (Swann & Spivey, 2004). By contrast,

self-esteem was correlated positively with synthesis/internalization levels for both individual sexual identity and group membership identity formation (Swann & Spivey, 2004). This pattern of findings is consistent with the notion that individual and sociopolitical identity have distinct implications for self-esteem. Specifically, high awareness, exploration, and commitment to a marginalized sociopolitical identity may be associated with self-esteem costs. By contrast, individual and group membership synthesis and internalization, which are markers of self-acceptance and fulfillment, may be associated with self-esteem benefits.

McCarn and Fassinger's (1996) proposed lesbian identity formation phases also have been linked with self-perceptions of positive functioning in terms of vocational development and within the campus climate. Specifically, in a sample of predominantly white, college-age lesbian, bisexual, and questioning women, self-perceptions of more advanced vocational development (i.e., greater sense of vocational clarity, interest, and efficacy) were correlated positively with scores on the internalization/synthesis phase of both individual sexual identity and group membership identity (Tomlinson & Fassinger, 2003). Furthermore, perceptions of a supportive campus climate (i.e., quality of faculty–student relations, feelings of acceptance, fair treatment, safety and security, and academic competence) were correlated positively with scores on the internalization/synthesis phase of individual sexual identity, and correlated negatively with scores on the exploration/commitment phase of both individual sexual identity and group membership identity (Tomlinson & Fassinger, 2003). Thus, greater exploration/commitment in both branches of identity formation was associated with perceptions of a less supportive campus climate, suggesting that perceived contextual challenges may heighten or be heightened by individual and group identity exploration/commitment. By contrast, as with the previously described positive associations with self-esteem, scores on the synthesis/internalization phase of both branches of identity formation were associated with positive perceptions of vocational development and campus climate. As such, greater synthesis/internationalization of individual and group membership identity appears to be associated with positive functioning across various domains. To broaden understanding of the mental health correlates of lesbian identity formation phases, research is needed to build on the findings described here, and investigate the links of McCarn and Fassinger's (1996) proposed identity formation phases with psychological symptomatology and other aspects of functioning.

Womanist Identity Development

Consistent with the distinction that McCarn and Fassinger (1996) made between individual and sociopolitical identity formation, Helms' (1990, as cited in Carter & Parks, 1996; Ossana et al., 1992) proposed the *womanist identity development* model to focus on the process of self-definition as a woman, without entangling it with feminist sociopolitical identification or activism. Specifically, according to Ossana et al. (1992), womanist identity development involves moving from an externally based sociocultural or sociopolitical definition of oneself as a woman to an internally based self-definition; this process is posited to be similar across diverse groups of women (e.g., in terms of race/ethnicity, social class).

Descriptions of Helms' four womanist identity development model stages—*pre-encounter, encounter, immersion-emersion,* and *internalization*—were initially published by Ossana et al. (1992) and Carter and Parks (1996). As with other developmental models, conceptualizations of womanist identity development have shifted from a stage-wise progression to a set of attitudes that can occur simultaneously, cyclically, or in other nonlinear fashions (Moradi, 2005; Moradi, Yoder, & Berendsen, 2004). Pre-encounter involves denial of societal oppression of women and conformity to rigid social norms that privilege men over women. Encounter occurs when new information or experiences challenge a preencounter lens, awareness of sexism and identification with womanhood is heightened, and alternative conceptualizations of the roles of women and men are explored. Immersion-emersion involves an initial phase during which women are idealized and patriarchal definitions of woman's roles are rejected, and a second phase during which there is a search for positive definitions of womanhood and affiliation with other women. Finally, internalization reflects the integration of an internally defined positive view of womanhood into one's identity "without undue dependence on either sexist societal norms or the antithetical positions of the women's movement" (Carter & Parks, 1996, p. 74).

It is important to note that, despite the aim to distinguish womanist identity development from feminist identity development, both models involve a shift in consciousness from denial of women's oppression to an acknowledgment of such oppression and exploration, synthesis, and internalization of alternatives to oppressive roles; and neither model presumes adoption of feminist self-identification. Indeed, in data with African American and white women, moderate to high correlations have emerged between parallel womanist and feminist identity development attitudes (Boisnier, 2003; Hoffman, 2006).

The womanist identity development model has been operationalized with the Womanist Identity Attitudes Scale (WIAS), which has four subscales corresponding to the four womanist identity attitudes (see Moradi et al., 2004; Ossana, 1986). As with measures of feminist identity development and other identity development models, psychometric concerns about the WIAS have been noted (see Moradi et al., 2004). Nevertheless, research with the WIAS has yielded some theoretically consistent findings that are important for counseling psychology research and practice. For example, consistent with the proposition that womanist identity development is similar across diverse groups of women, black and white women did not differ in mean levels or intercorrelations of womanist identity subscales (Moradi et al., 2004). Also, with both black and white women, pre-encounter scores were correlated negatively with egalitarian attitudes toward women and correlated positively with sexist attitudes, and internalization scores were correlated positively with egalitarian attitudes toward women (Moradi et al., 2004). But, contrary to expectation, encounter and immersion-emersion scores were generally uncorrelated with egalitarian and sexist attitudes.

Like feminist identity attitudes and lesbian identity phases, womanist identity attitudes have been associated with mental health indicators (for review, see Moradi, 2005). Specifically, with samples of African American/black women, black South African women, and predominantly white women, indicators of well-being, such as self-esteem and self-efficacy, generally have been linked negatively with pre-encounter, encounter, and immersion-emersion scores and positively with internalization scores (e.g., Boisnier, 2003; Letlaka-Rennert, Luswazi, Helms, & Zea, 1997; Ossana et al., 1992; Poindexter-Cameron & Robinson, 1997). Also, pre-encounter and immersion-emersion scores were related to external locus of control in a sample of black South African women (Letlaka-Rennert et al., 1997), and immersion-emersion scores were correlated negatively, whereas internalization scores were correlated positively, with life satisfaction in a sample of African American/black women (Constantine & Watt, 2002). In terms of psychological distress, Carter and Parks (1996) found that, for white women, pre-encounter, encounter, and immersion-emersion scores were related positively with psychological symptomatology, but relations between womanist identity attitudes and symptomatology did not emerge for black women in their sample. This differential pattern may have been due to the substantially smaller sample size for black women than for white women.

Womanist identity attitudes also have been examined in relation to racial identity attitudes for African American/black and white women. Poindexter-Cameron and Robinson (1997) found that African American women's womanist and racial identity pre-encounter, immersion-emersion, and internalization scores (but not encounter) were correlated positively. Parks et al. (1996) examined covariation between womanist and racial identity attitudes for African American/black and white women using canonical correlation. They found significant covariation for African American/black women but not for white women. Specifically, for African American/black women, womanist and racial identity encounter and internalization scores loaded positively, whereas womanist and racial identity pre-encounter and immersion-emersion scores loaded negatively, on the canonical root. This pattern of findings suggests some parallels in racial and womanist identity attitudes for African American/black women, but not necessarily for white women. Parks et al. (1996) reasoned that such a parallel would be expected for African American/black women because, for them, womanist and racial identity development involve socioculturally marginalized identities, whereas for white women, racial identity development involves a socioculturally privileged identity.

Finally, in a study that examined the relations of both womanist and feminist identity attitudes with ethnic identity in a racially/ethnically diverse sample, Hoffman (2006) found that revelation, embeddedness-emanation, and active commitment feminist identity scores and immersion-emersion womanist identity scores each were correlated positively with an indicator of ethnic identity exploration and commitment (Hoffman, 2006). Thus, in a sample of women of various racial/ethnic backgrounds, feminist and womanist identity attitudes that reflect heightened awareness of gender oppression were associated with greater exploration of and commitment to ethnic identity. This pattern

of findings highlights the importance of attending to intersections of identities when considering women's gender-related identity formation (e.g., Moradi et al., 2002a, b; Vandiver, 2002). Indeed, the concept of *womanist consciousness* was coined (e.g., Brown, 1989; Walker, 1983) to reflects the view that racial, gender, and other oppressions and identities as inextricably linked. Measures have been developed to assess womanist consciousness (e.g., Henley, Meng, O'Brien, McCarthy, & Sockloskie, 1998; King, 2003), but, research on womanist consciousness, including its implications for women's mental health, remains needed.

Distinguishing Group Identity and Group Consciousness

Gurin and Townsend (1986) distinguished women's awareness of and feelings about being a woman (group identity) from ideology about the group's sociopolitical position (group consciousness). Specifically, group identity includes perceived similarity between the self and the group, sense of common fate with the group, and the centrality of group membership to self-concept. For sociopolitically subordinate groups, group consciousness includes sense of collective discontent about the group's position, perceived legitimacy or illegitimacy of that position, and belief about the necessity of collective action to improve the group's condition. Data gathered in the 1970s an 1980s from nationally representative samples of women yielded low to moderate correlations among these group identity and group consciousness dimensions, suggesting that they are related but distinct dimensions (Gurin & Townsend, 1986).

Gurin (1985) found that women's group identity and consciousness levels were generally lower than those of African American, older adult, and blue-collar samples. Gurin (1985) suggested that contextual factors may serve as barriers to women's group identity and consciousness. For example, familial connections and social segregation foster high levels of in-group interaction and intimacy among racial/ethnic, social class, and some other groups. But, as children, siblings, parents, and romantic partners, most women's lives are inextricably linked with men's. These connections foster a sense of shared values, common fate, and intimacy between women and men. In addition, the ubiquity of sexism and the fact that it is often perpetrated by intimate relations (e.g., parents, partners) can make sexism seem normative and forgivable rather than unjust. Thus, the contexts of women's lives may impede group identity and consciousness. This perspective also suggests, however, that women's connections with other women and women's communities might foster group identity and consciousness. Interestingly, the role of women's connections with other women has not received much attention in research on the three identity models reviewed in this section.

Of the identity models reviewed here, McCarn and Fassinger's (1996) model clearly distinguishes group identity from group consciousness, with individual sexual identity reflecting the former and group membership identity reflecting the latter construct. The feminist and womanist identity development models, however, seem to capture mostly group consciousness; although embeddedness-emanation and immersion-emersion include the similarity and centrality aspects of group identity. As such, Gurin and colleagues' framework suggests some interesting questions about feminist and womanist identity models. For example, should these models be refined to more clearly separate group identity and group consciousness? Would group identity and group consciousness aspects of feminist and womanist identity have different implications for women's mental health? How do women's connections with other women relate to feminist, womanist, and lesbian identity? These questions arise from attending to how the context of women's lives may shape and be shaped by their sense of being a woman and its sociopolitical meaning.

A Call for Feminist Thinking

Because the goals of counseling psychology include minimizing psychological distress and maximizing well-being in people's everyday lives, we took care in each section of this chapter to draw linkages to these outcomes for women as often as the existing literature would allow. We made the sweeping case that women and women's experiences take place within a surrounding social context that is not only often different for women and men, but also value-laden, such that gender itself is confounded with power and status. We found evidence of these gendered power differences in sexist treatment directed toward women, in evaluations of women's mental health, in women's relationships, and in women's own attitudes and identities. The recurring theme across all of these areas of research is that women's well-being is continually challenged simply by being women in a patriarchal culture.

This analysis readily leads to an understanding that women's psychological health and well-being depends, at least in part, on personal empowerment (Gibbs & Fuery, 1994; Worell & Remer, 1992). There is an extensive body of research reviewed by Helgeson (1994) clearly linking personal agency or instrumentality with overall well-being, including reduced depression, lower anxiety, elevated self-esteem, fewer health complaints, and mitigated distress. Similar associations between well-being and empowerment are evident in the interpersonal spheres of women's family and work relationships. For example, heterosexual women who expect to have to grapple with work–family conflict in their intimate relationships and prepare for this inevitable conflict by asserting their career intentions with their partner, by postponing childbearing, and by having fewer children tend to experience less marital conflict than do women who fail to acknowledge potential problems (Tangri & Jenkins, 1997). Indeed successful egalitarian couples understand that they need to be vigilant and work hard to realize equality in their relationship (Blaisure & Allen, 1995; Knudson-Martin & Mahoney, 2005). Women are more likely to report achieving sexual satisfaction if they feel empowered by their own personal agency to initiate sexual contact more often, and to express their sexual needs clearly in their primary relationships (Mosher & Danoff-Burg, 2005). In the workplace, women need to first establish their legitimacy in order to effectively influence their coworkers (Ridgeway, 2001; Yoder, Schleicher, & McDonald, 1998). Having the supports provided by a higher-status mentor helps build women's own power and resources (Dreher & Ash, 1990), which in turn promotes their global job satisfaction (Mobley, Jaret, Marsh, & Lim, 1994). Masculinizing information about job candidates for male-type occupations can help level the playing field for women applicants (Glick, Zion, & Nelson, 1988). In general, adopting status-enhancing strategies in masculinized, hierarchal work contexts can enhance women's leadership effectiveness (Yoder, 2001).

A complete understanding of women's empowerment, both personal and relational, must regard empowerment as more of a process than as a static thing to be achieved, then taken for granted (Browne, 1995). The view of empowerment that works for women focuses on power as energy, potential, and competence, not on traditional definitions of power as domination, coercion, and competition. Furthermore, the empowerment of women cannot be confined to these individual and relational arenas alone, but rather must extend to changing broader social and political contexts through collective social activism (Kitzinger, 1991; Riger, 2000). Too often, psychologists have focused on personal and relational empowerment without making this necessary connection to social activism (Kravetz & Marecek, 1996; Marecek & Hare-Mustin, 1991; Parvin & Biaggio, 1991). Nowhere is this point clearer than in definitions and practice of feminist therapy, a topic discussed in Carol Enns' chapter in this volume (Enns, 2011, Chapter 16, this volume). By reviewing the ways in which the contexts of women's lives can shape their functioning and mental health, the present chapter underscores the importance of feminist therapy in meeting the mental health needs of women, along with social justice efforts to transform the damaging aspects of the contexts of women's lives.

Future Directions

Throughout this chapter, we have offered an integrative summary of available research and highlighted specific needs for further research when appropriate. In this final section, we outline broad directions for advancing psychological scholarship with and about women. In each of the following areas, we see a need for articulating theoretical frameworks that integrate available data and outline directions for future investigation.

Central to each of the proceeding directions for scholarship are questions about how multiple social categories (e.g., age, ethnicity, race, sexual orientation, socioeconomic status) intersect with gender. Thus, our first recommendation is that the diversity of women's experiences should be the point of initiating inquiry, rather than a dimension that is considered as an "add on" after white, presumably heterosexual, often young and middle class women are considered. To this end, theory and research with women of diverse backgrounds is integral to advancing a complete psychology of women (Yoder & Kahn, 1993), and such scholarship should always articulate which group(s) of women are the focus of study.

Understanding women's experiences and improving their functioning can be advanced by moving from a focus on internal, enduring characteristics to external, modifiable aspects of social contexts that shape behaviors by and toward women. For example, social psychological literature has established that the power, status, and resources associated with gender, rather than gender itself, shape behaviors (Ridgeway & Smith-Lovin, 1999). Similarly, gender stereotypic expectations are

self-fulfilling in that they elicit stereotype-consistent behaviors (e.g., Skrypnek & Snyder, 1982). These examples highlight the power of social situations and point to the promise of identifying modifiable aspects of social context that can improve women's experiences and functioning.

Longitudinal and experimental research is needed to reveal causal directions in the relations of sexist stereotypes, prejudice, and discrimination with outcome variables. Research is also needed to elucidate how stereotypes, prejudice, and discrimination against women manifest when they intersect with other social category dimensions. For instance, across subgroups of women, what are shared and unique manifestations of sexist discrimination? How does sexist discrimination function with other forms of discrimination in shaping women's experiences across domains (e.g., mental health, physical health, work and career development)?

Theoretically grounded and empirically informed interventions programs aiming to prevent and reduce stereotypes, prejudice, and discrimination against women need to be developed and evaluated. Data on the long-term effectiveness of such interventions is particularly important.

Connections along the continuum of subtle and everyday to violent and acute manifestations of sexism need to be better understood. For instance, what factors prevent or promote expressions of subtle sexism and their translation to more blatant sexism, or even violence? Within this continuum, are there developmental processes that can be interrupted to prevent the escalation of sexism?

What we know about potential biases in DSM diagnostic criteria and their use in clinical practice suggests the need for counseling psychologists (along with other stakeholders) to evaluate if and how DSM criteria should be used to maximize their utility and minimize their harm to women and men. In addition, training approaches that reduce clinician bias need to be developed, evaluated, and disseminated.

Available data on the socialization of girls and boys underscore the omnipresence of disempowering messages to girls. Within this context, research is needed to understand girls' positive functioning despite sexist socialization. For example, what conditions help girls and boys to resist sexist socialization? What factors promote girls' self-efficacy, positive body image, career aspirations, and resilience in other domains?

Available research about women's relationships points to factors that can hinder or promote relationship satisfaction and quality across domains (e.g., romantic, workplace). Many of these factors revolve around managing and sharing power. An important future direction is to explicitly articulate and study the role of power in women's relationships. How do women and their relationship partners view, assert, and manage power in their relationships, and how do these approaches relate to relationship quality and satisfaction?

Efforts are needed to integrate existing group identity development models. What are the areas of overlap and redundancy across models? What are the unique dimensions of various models? And, what elements of group identity and collective consciousness are captured and not captured by available models? Such efforts are important for consolidating available theory and data and also for identifying directions for developing a fuller understanding of women's group identity and collective consciousness.

The recommendations offered thus far focus on advancing scholarship. But, at the heart of a feminist psychology of women is a commitment to reducing and ultimately eliminating sexism and other forms of oppression that hinder women's (and men's) potential. The scholarship reviewed in this chapter illustrates the social justice implications of psychological theory and research. But, psychologists need to move beyond being producers and consumers of research. Thus, our final recommendation is for efforts to translate research findings about women's experiences into individual and group counseling interventions, training for researchers and mental health practitioners, public education programs, and public policy. Articulations of how to engage in such translation can help to move the field toward fulfilling its social justice promise.

References

Abrams, D., Viki, G. T., Masser, B., & Bohner, G. (2003). Perceptions of stranger and acquaintance rape: The role of benevolent and hostile sexism in victim blame and rape proclivity. *Journal of Personality and Social Psychology, 84*, 111–125.

Amaro, H., Raj, A., & Reed, E. (2001). Women's sexual health: The need for feminist analyses in public health in the Decade of Behavior. *Psychology of Women Quarterly, 25*, 324–334.

Andersen, B. L., Cyranowski, J. M., & Espindle, D. (1999). Women's sexual self-schema. *Journal of Personality and Social Psychology, 76*, 645–661.

Anderson, K. B., Cooper, H., & Okamura, L. (1997). Individual differences and attitudes toward rape: A meta-analytic review. *Personality and Social Psychology Bulletin, 23*, 295–315.

Anderson, K. L., & Umberson, D. (2001). Gendering violence: Masculinity and power in men's accounts of domestic violence. *Gender & Society, 15*, 358–380.

Angelone, D. J., Hirschman, R., Suniga, S., Armey, M., & Armelie, A. (2005). The influence of peer interactions on sexually oriented joke telling. *Sex Roles, 52*, 187–199.

Ashmore, R. D., Deaux, K., & McLaughlin-Volpe, T. (2004). An organizing framework for collective identity: Articulation and significance of multidimensionality. *Psychological Bulletin, 130*, 80–114.

Banaji, M. R., & Greenwald, A. G. (1994). Implicit stereotyping and prejudice. In M. P. Zanna, & J. M. Olson (Eds.), *The psychology of prejudice: The Ontario symposium* Vol. 7 (pp. 55–76). Hillsdale, NJ: Erlbaum.

Bargad, A., & Hyde, J. S. (1991). Women's studies: A study of feminist identity development in women. *Psychology of Women Quarterly, 15*, 181–201.

Barnett, R. C., & Hyde, J. S. (2001). Women, men, work, and family: An expansionist theory. *American Psychologist, 56*, 781–796.

Becker, A. E. (2004). Television disordered eating, and young women in Fiji: Negotiating body image and identity during rapid social change. *Culture, Medicine and Psychiatry, 28*, 533–559.

Beckman, L. J. (1994). Treatment needs of women with alcohol problems. *Alcohol Health and Research World, 18*, 206–211.

Bekker, M. H. J. (1996). Agoraphobia and gender: A review. *Clinical Psychology Review, 16*, 129–146.

Bem, S. L. (1993). *The lenses of gender: Transforming the debate on sexual inequality*. New Haven, CT: Yale.

Benokraitis, N. V. (1997). Sex discrimination in the 21st century. In N. V. Benokraitis (Ed.), *Subtle sexism: Current practice and prospects for change* (pp. 5–33). Thousand Oaks, CA: Sage.

Berg, S. H. (2006). Everyday sexism and posttraumatic stress disorder in women: A correlational study. *Violence Against Women, 12*, 970–988.

Bernas, K. H., & Major, D. A. (2000). Contributors to stress resistance: Testing a model of women's work-family conflict. *Psychology of Women Quarterly, 24*, 170–178.

Bianchi, S. (2000). Maternal employment and time with children: Dramatic change and surprising continuity. *Demography, 37*, 401–414.

Bird, C. E. (1999). Gender, household labor, and psychological distress: The impact of the amount and division of housework. *Journal of Health and Social Behavior, 40*, 32–45.

Blain, J. (1994). Discourses of agency and domestic labor: Family discourse and gendered practice in dual-earner families. *Journal of Family Issues, 15*, 515–549.

Blaisure, K. R., & Allen, K. R. (1995). Feminists and the ideology and practice of marital equality. *Journal of Marriage and the Family, 57*, 5–19.

Blood, P., Tuttle, A., & Lakey, G. (1995). Understanding and fighting sexism: A call to men. In M. L. Andersen & P. H. Collins (Eds.), *Race, class, and gender: An anthology* (2nd ed., pp. 154–161). Belmont, CA: Wadsworth.

Boisnier, A. D. (2003). Race and women's identity development: Distinguishing between feminism and womanism among Black and White women. *Sex Roles, 49*, 211–218.

Bond, J. T., Thompson, C., Galinsky, E., & Prottas, D. (2003). *Highlights of the 2002 national study on the changing workforce* (No. 3). New York: Families and Work Institute.

Bowleg, L., Lucas, K. J., & Tschann, J. M. (2004). "The ball was always in his court": An exploratory analysis of relationship scripts, sexual scripts, and condom use among African American women. *Psychology of Women Quarterly, 28,* 70–82.

Brown, E. B. (1989). Womanist consciousness: Maggie Lena Walker and the Independent Order of St. Luke. *Signs, 14,* 610–633.

Browne, A. (1993). Violence against women by male partners: Prevalence, outcomes, and policy implications. *American Psychologist, 48,* 1077–1087.

Browne, C. V. (1995). Empowerment in social work practice with older women. *Social Work, 40,* 358–364.

Buchanan, T. S., Fischer, A. R., Tokar, D. M., & Yoder, J. D. (2008). Testing a culture-specific extension of objectification theory regarding African American women's body image. *The Counseling Psychologist, 36,* 697–718.

Bussey, K., & Bandura, A. (1999). Social cognitive theory of gender development and differentiation. *Psychological Review, 106,* 676–713.

Bussey, K., & Bandura, A. (2004). Social cognitive theory of gender development and functioning. In A. Eagly, et al. (Eds.), *The psychology of gender* (2nd ed., pp. 92–119). New York: Guilford.

Butler, J. (1990). *Gender trouble: Feminism and the subversion of identity.* New York: Routledge.

Caplan, P. J. (1995). *They say you're crazy: How the world's most powerful psychiatrists decide who's normal.* Reading, MA: Addison-Wesley.

Caplan, P. J., & Gans, M. (1991). Is there empirical evidence for the category of "self-defeating personality disorder"? *Feminism & Psychology, 1,* 263–278.

Carter, R. T., & Parks, E. E. (1996). Womanist identity and mental health. *Journal of Counseling and Development, 74,* 484–489.

Cash, T. E., Ancis, J. R., & Strachan, M. D. (1997). Gender attitudes, feminist identity, and body image among college women. *Sex Roles, 36,* 433–447.

Chan, D. K., Tang, C. S., & Chan, W. (1999). Sexual harassment: A preliminary analysis of its effects on Hong Kong Chinese women in the workplace and academia. *Psychology of Women Quarterly, 23,* 661–672.

Colwell, M. J., & Lindsey, E. W. (2005). Preschool children's pretend and physical play and sex of play partner: Connections to peer competence. *Sex Roles, 52,* 497–509.

Constantine, M. G., & Watt, S. K. (2002). Cultural congruity, womanist identity attitudes, and life satisfaction among African American college women attending historically Black and predominantly White institutions. *Journal of College Student Development, 43,* 184–194.

Cortina, L. M., Swan, S., Fitzgerald, L. F., & Waldo, C. (1998). Sexual harassment and assault: Chilling the climate for women in academia. *Psychology of Women Quarterly, 22,* 419–441.

Cowan, G. (2000). Women's hostility toward women and rape and sexual harassment myths. *Violence Against Women, 6,* 238–246.

Crosby, F. J. (1991). *Juggling: The unexpected advantages of balancing career and home for women and their families.* New York: Free Press.

Cross, W. E. (1971). Negro-to-Black conversion experience: Toward a psychology of Black liberation. *Black World, 20*(9), 13–27.

Croteau, J. M., Nero, C. I., & Prosser, D. J. (1993). Social and cultural sensitivity in group-specific HIV and AIDS programming. *Journal of Counseling and Development, 71,* 290–296.

Crull, P. (1982). Stress effects of sexual harassment on the job: Implications for counseling. *American Journal of Orthopsychiatry, 52,* 539–544.

Csikszentmihalyi, M. (1982). Toward a psychology of optimal experience. In L. Wheeler (Ed.), *Review of personality and social psychology.* Beverly Hills, CA: Sage.

Csikszentmihalyi, M. (1990). *Flow: The psychology of optimal experience.* New York: Harper Perennial.

Cuddy, A. J. C., Fiske, S. T., & Glick, P. (2004). When professionals become mothers, warmth doesn't cut the ice. *Journal of Social Issues, 60*(4), 701–718.

Cuddy, A. J. C., Norton, M. I., & Fiske, S. T. (2005). This old stereotype: The pervasiveness and persistence of the elderly stereotype. *Journal of Social Issues, 61*(2), 267–285.

Cutler, S. E., & Nolen-Hoeksema, S. (1991). Accounting for sex differences in depression through female victimization: Childhood sexual abuse. *Sex Roles, 24,* 425–438.

Darves-Bornoz, J. M., Lemperiere, T., Degiovanni, A., & Gaillard, P. (1995). Sexual victimization in women with schizophrenia and bipolar disorder. *Social Psychiatry and Psychiatric Epidemiology, 30,* 78–84.

de Snyder, V. N. S., Acevedo, A., Diaz-Perez, M. J., & Saldivar-Guaduno, A. (2000). Understanding the sexuality of Mexican-born women and their risk for HIV/AIDS. *Psychology of Women Quarterly, 24,* 100–109.

Deaux, K., & Major, B. (1987). Putting gender into context: An interactive model of gender-related behavior. *Psychological Bulletin, 94,* 369–389.

Devine, P. G. (1989). Stereotypes and prejudice: Their automatic and controlled components. *Journal of Personality and Social Psychology, 56,* 5–18.

Diekman, A. B., & Eagly, A. H. (2000). Stereotypes as dynamic constructs: Women and men of the past, present, and future. *Personality and Social Psychology Bulletin, 26,* 1171–1188.

Diekman, A. B., & Murnen, S. K. (2004). Learning to be little women and little men: The inequitable gender equality of nonsexist children's literature. *Sex Roles, 50,* 373–385.

Donaghue, N., & Fallon, B. J. (2003). Gender-role self-stereotyping and the relationship between equity and satisfaction in close relationships. *Sex Roles, 48,* 217–230.

Downing, N. E., & Roush, K. L. (1985). From passive acceptance to active commitment: A model of feminist identity development for women. *The Counseling Psychologist, 13,* 695–709.

Dreher, G. F., & Ash, R. A. (1990). A comparative study of mentoring among men and women in managerial, professional, and technical positions. *Journal of Applied Psychology, 75,* 539–546.

Driscoll, D. M., Kelly, J. R., & Henderson, W. L. (1998). Can perceivers identify likelihood to sexually harass? *Sex Roles, 38,* 557–588.

Eagly, A. H., & Karau, S. J. (2002). Role congruity theory of prejudice toward female leaders. *Psychological Review, 109,* 573–598.

Eisler, R. M., Franchina, J. J., Moore, T. M., Honeycutt, H. G., & Rhatigan, D. L. (2000). Masculine gender role stress and intimate abuse: Effects of gender relevance of conflict situations on men's attributions and affective responses. *Psychology of Men and Masculinity, 1,* 30–36.

Eldridge, N. S., & Gilbert, L. A. (1990). Correlates of relationship satisfaction in lesbian couples. *Psychology of Women Quarterly, 14*, 43–62.

Enns, C. Z. (2011). Feminist approaches to counseling. In E. M. Altmaier, & J. C. Hansen (Eds.), *The Oxford handbook of counseling psychology*. New York: Oxford University Press.

Evans-DeCicco, J. A., & Cowan, G. (2001). Attitudes toward pornography and the characteristics attributed to pornography actors. *Sex Roles, 44*, 351–361.

Fassinger, R. E., & Arseneau, J. R. (2008). Diverse women's sexualities. In F. L. Denmark (Ed.), *Psychology of Women: A handbook of issues and theories* (2nd ed., pp. 484–505). Westport, CT: Praeger Publishers/Greenwood Publishing.

Fassinger, R. E., & Miller, B. A. (1996). Validation of an inclusive model of sexual minority identity formation on a sample of gay men. *Journal of Homosexuality, 32*, 53–78.

Febbraro, A. R. (2003). Alpha and beta bias in research on labour and love: The case of enhancement versus scarcity. *Feminism & Psychology, 13*, 210–223.

Felmlee, D. H. (1994). Who's on top? Power in romantic relationships. *Sex Roles, 31*, 275–295.

Fiese, B. H., & Skillman, G. (2000). Gender differences in family stories: Moderating influence of parent gender role and child gender. *Sex Roles, 43*, 267–283.

Fischer, A. R. (2006). Women's benevolent sexism as reaction to hostility. *Psychology of Women Quarterly, 30*, 410–416.

Fischer, A. R., & Good, G. E. (1994). Gender, self, and others: Perceptions of the campus environment. *Journal of Counseling Psychology, 41*, 343–355.

Fischer, A. R., & Good, G. E. (2004). Women's feminist consciousness, anger, and psychological distress. *Journal of Counseling Psychology, 51*, 437–446.

Fischer, A. R., & Holz, K. B. (2007). Perceived discrimination and women's psychological distress: The roles of collective and personal self-esteem. *Journal of Counseling Psychology, 54*, 154–164.

Fischer, A. R., Tokar, D. M., Mergl, M. M., Good, G. E., Hill, M. S., & Blum, S. A. (2000). Assessing women's feminist identity development: Studies of convergent, discriminant, and structural validity. *Psychology of Women Quarterly, 24*, 15–29.

Fiske, S. T., Cuddy, A. J. C., Glick, P., & Xu, J. (2002). A model of (often mixed) stereotype content: Competence and warmth respectively follow from perceived status and competition. *Journal of Personality and Social Psychology, 82*, 878–902.

Fitzgerald, L. F. (1993). Sex harassment: Violence against women in the workplace. *American Psychologist, 48*, 1070–1076.

Fitzgerald, L. F., Swan, S., & Fischer, K. (1995). Why didn't she just report him? The psychological and legal implications of women's responses to sexual harassment. *Journal of Social Issues, 51*(1), 117–138.

Flannagan, D., & Perese, S. (1998). Emotional references in mother-daughter and mother-son dyads' conversations about school. *Sex Roles, 39*, 353–367.

Flores, L. Y., Carrubba, M. D., & Good, G. E. (2006). Feminism and Mexican American adolescent women: Examining the psychometric properties of two measures. *Hispanic Journal of Behavioral Sciences, 28*, 48–64.

Franchina, J. J., Eisler, R. M., & Moore, T. M. (2001). Masculine gender role stress and intimate abuse: Effects of masculine gender relevance of dating situations and female threat on men's attributions and affective responses. *Psychology of Men and Masculinity, 2*, 34–41.

Fredrickson, B. L., & Roberts, T. (1997). Objectification theory: Toward understanding women's lived experiences and mental health risks. *Psychology of Women Quarterly, 21*, 173–206.

Fredrickson, B. L., Roberts, T., Noll, S. M., Quinn, D. M., & Twenge, J. M. (1998). That swimsuit becomes you: Sex differences in self-objectification, restrained eating, and math performance. *Journal of Personality and Social Psychology, 75*, 269–284.

Frieze, I. H., & McHugh, M. C. (1998). Measuring feminism and gender role attitudes. *Psychology of Women Quarterly, 22*, 349–352.

Galinsky, E., Bond, J. T., & Friedman, D. E. (1996). The role of employers in addressing the needs of employed parents. *Journal of Social Issues, 52*(3), 111–136.

Gelfond, M. (1991). Reconceptualizing agoraphobia: A case study of epistemological bias in clinical research. *Feminism & Psychology, 1*, 247–262.

Gentry, M. (1998). The sexual double standard: The influence of number of relationships and level of sexual activity on judgments of women. *Psychology of Women Quarterly, 22*, 505–511.

Gerstel, N., & Gallagher, S. K. (2001). Men's caregiving: Gender and the contingent character of care. *Gender & Society, 15*, 197–217.

Gibbs, J. T., & Fuery, D. (1994). Mental health and well-being of Black women toward strategies of empowerment. *American Journal of Community Psychology, 22*, 559–582.

Gilbert, L. A., & Rader, J. (2001). Current perspectives on women's adult roles: Work, family, and life. In R. K. Unger (Ed.), *Handbook of the psychology of women and gender* (pp. 156–169). New York: Wiley.

Glick, P., & Fiske, S. T. (1996). The Ambivalent Sexism Inventory: Differentiating hostile and benevolent sexism. *Journal of Personality and Social Psychology, 70*, 491–512.

Glick, P., & Fiske, S. T. (2001). An ambivalent alliance: Hostile and benevolent sexism as complementary justifications for gender inequality. *American Psychologist, 56*, 109–118.

Glick, P., Fiske, S., Mladinic, A., Saiz, J. L., Abrams, D., Masser, B., et al. (2000). Beyond prejudice as simple antipathy: Hostile and benevolent sexism across cultures. *Journal of Personality and Social Psychology, 79*, 763–775.

Glick, P., Zion, C., & Nelson, C. (1988). What mediates sex discrimination in hiring decisions? *Journal of Personality and Social Psychology, 55*, 178–186.

Golding, J. M. (1990). Division of household labor, strain, and depressive symptoms among Mexican Americans and non-Hispanic Whites. *Psychology of Women Quarterly, 14*, 103–117.

Gonzalez, A. Q., & Koestner, R. (2005). Parental preference for sex of newborn as reflected in positive affect in birth announcements. *Sex Roles, 52*, 407–411.

Goodman, L. A., Koss, M. P., & Russo, N. F. (1993). Violence against women: Physical and mental health effects: Part 1. Research findings. *Applied and Preventive Psychology, 2*, 79–89.

Gordon, M. (2000). Definitional issues in violence against women: Surveillance and research from a violence research perspective. *Violence Against Women, 6*, 747–783.

Good, G. E., & Sherrod, N. B. (2001). The psychology of men and masculinity: Research status and future directions.

In R. K. Unger (Ed.), *Handbook of the psychology of women and gender* (pp. 201–214). New York: Wiley.

Goodwin, S. A., & Fiske, S. T. (2001). Power and gender: The double-edged sword of ambivalence. In R. K. Unger (Ed.), *Handbook of the psychology of women and gender* (pp. 358–366). New York: Wiley.

Gurin, P. (1985). Women's gender consciousness. *Public Opinion Quarterly, 49,* 143–163.

Gurin, P., & Townsend, A. (1986). Properties of gender identity and their implications for gender consciousness. *British Journal of Social Psychology, 25,* 139–148.

Gutek, B. A. (1985). *Sex and the workplace.* San Francisco, CA: Jossey-Bass.

Gutierrez, L., Oh, H. J., & Gillmore, M. R. (2000). Toward an understanding of (em)power(ment) for HIV/AIDS prevention with adolescent women. *Sex Roles, 42,* 581–611.

Hamilton, J. A., & Jensvold, M. (1992). Personality, psychopathology, and depression in women. In L. S. Brown, & M. Ballou (Eds.), *Personality and psychopathology: Feminist reappraisals* (pp. 116–143). New York: Guilford.

Hampson, S. E. (1988). The dynamics of categorization and impression formation. In T. K. Srull, & R. S. Wyer, Jr. (Eds.), *Advances in social cognition: Vol 1: A dual process model of impression formation* (pp. 77–82). Hillsdale, NJ: Erlbaum.

Harned, M. S. (2000). Harassed bodies: An examination of the relationships among women's experiences of sexual harassment, body image and eating disturbances. *Psychology of Women Quarterly, 24,* 336–348.

Hartung, C. M., & Widiger, T. A. (1998). Gender differences in the diagnosis of mental disorders: Conclusions and controversies of the DSM-IV. *Psychological Bulletin, 123,* 260–278.

Hawkins, A. J., Marshall, C. M., & Meiners, K. M. (1995). Exploring wives' sense of fairness about family work: An initial test of the distributive justice framework. *Journal of Family Issues, 16,* 693–721.

Helgeson, V. S. (1994). Relation of agency and communion to well-being: Evidence and potential explanations. *Psychological Bulletin, 116,* 412–428.

Henley, N. M., Meng, K., O'Brien, D., McCarthy, W. J., & Sockloskie, R. J. (1998). Developing a scale to measure the diversity of feminist attitudes. *Psychology of Women Quarterly, 22,* 317–348.

Henley, N. M., Spalding, L. R., & Kosta, A. (2000). Development of the short form of the Feminist Perspectives Scale. *Psychology of Women Quarterly, 24,* 254–256.

Hesse-Biber, S., Marino, M., & Watts-Roy, D. (1999). A longitudinal study of eating disorders among college women: Factors that influence recovery. *Gender & Society, 13,* 385–408.

Hessing, M. (1994). More than clockwork: Women's time management in their combined workload. *Sociological Perspectives, 37,* 611–633.

Hoffman, R. M. (2006). Gender self-definition and gender self-acceptance in women: Intersections with feminist, womanist, and ethnic identities. *Journal of Counseling & Development, 84,* 358–372.

Hogue, M., & Yoder, J. D. (2003). The role of status in producing depressed entitlement in women's and men's pay allocations. *Psychology of Women Quarterly, 27*(4), 330–337.

Hollander, J. A. (2001). Vulnerability and dangerousness: The construction of gender through conversation about violence. *Gender & Society, 15,* 83–109.

Hyde, J. S., Klein, M. H., Essex, M. J., & Clark, R. (1995). Maternity leave and women's mental health. *Psychology of Women Quarterly, 19,* 257–285.

Ito, T. A., & Urland, R. (2003). Race and gender on the brain: Electrocortical measures of attention to the race and gender of multiply categorizable individuals. *Journal of Personality and Social Psychology, 85,* 616–626.

Jaggar, A. (1983). Political philosophies of women's liberation. In L. Richardson, & V. Taylor (Eds.), *Feminist frontiers: Rethinking sex, gender, and society* (pp. 322–329). New York: Random House.

John, D., & Shelton, B. A. (1997). The production of gender among Black and White women and men: The case of household labor. *Sex Roles, 36,* 171–193.

Johnson, A. G. (2006). *Privilege, power, and difference* (2nd ed.). New York: McGraw Hill.

Juntunen, C. L., Atkinson, D. R., Reyes, C., & Gutierrez, M. (1994). Feminist identity and feminist therapy behaviors of women psychotherapists. *Psychotherapy, 31,* 327–333.

Kahn, A. S., Mathie, V. A., & Torgler, C. (1994). Rape scripts and rape acknowledgment. *Psychology of Women Quarterly, 18,* 53–66.

Kelly, L., & Radford, J. (1996). "Nothing really happened": The invalidation of women's experiences of sexual violence. In M. Hester, L. Kelly, & J. Radford (Eds.), *Women, violence and male power* (pp. 19–33). Bristol, PA: Open University Press.

Kessler, R. C., Berglund, P., Demler, O., Jin, R., Merikangas, K. R., & Walters, E. E. (2005). Lifetime prevalence and age-of-onset- distributions of DSM-IV disorders in the National Comorbidity Survey Replication. *Archives of General Psychiatry, 62,* 593–602.

King, K. R. (2003). Do you see what I see? Effects of group consciousness on African American women's attributions to prejudice. *Psychology of Women Quarterly, 27,* 17–30.

Kitzinger, C. (1991). Feminism, psychology, and the paradox of power. *Feminism & Psychology, 1,* 111–129.

Kling, K. C., Hyde, J. S., Showers, C. J., & Buswell, B. N. (1999). Gender differences in self-esteem: A meta-analysis. *Psychological Bulletin, 125,* 470–500.

Klinkenberg, D., & Rose, S. (1994). Dating scripts of gay men and lesbians. *Journal of Homosexuality, 26,* 23–35.

Klonoff, E. A., & Landrine, H. (1995). The Schedule of Sexist Events: A measure of lifetime and recent sexist discrimination in women's lives. *Psychology of Women Quarterly, 19,* 439–472.

Knudson-Martin, C., & Mahoney, A. R. (2005). Moving beyond gender: Processes that create relationship equality. *Journal of Marital & Family Therapy, 31,* 235–246.

Kobrynowicz, D., & Branscombe, N. R. (1997). Who considers themselves victims of discrimination? Individual difference predictors of perceived gender discrimination in women and men. *Psychology of Women Quarterly, 21,* 347–363.

Koss, M. P. (1990). The women's mental health research agenda: Violence against women. *American Psychologist, 45,* 374–380.

Koss, M. P., Figueredo, A. J., Bell, I., Tharan, M., & Tromp, M. (1996). Traumatic memory characteristics: A cross-validated mediational model of response to rape among employed women. *Journal of Abnormal Psychology, 105,* 1–12.

Koss, M. P., Goodman, L. A., Browne, A., Fitzgerald, L. F., Keita, G. P., & Russo, N. F. (1994). *No safe haven: Male violence against women at home, at work, and in the community.* Washington, DC: American Psychological Association.

Kozee, H. B., Tylka, T. L., Augustus-Horvath, C. L., & Denchik, A. (2007). Development and psychometric evaluation of the Interpersonal Sexual Objectification Scale. *Psychology of Women Quarterly, 31,* 176–189.

Kravetz, D., & Marecek, J. (1996). The personal is political: A feminist agenda for group psychotherapy research. In B. DeChant (Ed.), *Women and group psychotherapy: Theory and practice* (pp. 351–369). New York: Guilford.

Kurdek, L. A. (1993). The allocation of household labor in gay, lesbian, and heterosexual married couples. *Journal of Social Issues, 49*(3), 127–139.

Lamb, S., & Keon, S. (1995). Blaming the perpetrator: Language that distorts reality in newspaper articles on men battering women. *Psychology of Women Quarterly, 19,* 209–220.

Landrine, H. (1985). Race x class stereotypes of women. *Sex Roles, 13,* 65–75.

Landrine, H. (1988). Depression and stereotypes of women: Preliminary empirical analyses of the gender-role hypothesis. *Sex Roles, 19,* 527–541.

Landrine, H. (1989). The politics of personality disorder. *Psychology of Women Quarterly, 13,* 325–339.

Landrine, H., Klonoff, E. A., Gibbs, J., Manning, V., & Lund, M. (1995). Physical and psychiatric correlates of gender discrimination: An application of the Schedule of Sexist Events. *Psychology of Women Quarterly, 19,* 473–492.

Leigh, B. C. (1989). Reasons for having and avoiding sex: Gender, sexual orientation, and relationship to sexual behavior. *Journal of Sex Research, 26,* 199–209.

Lennon, M. C., & Rosenfield, S. (1994). Relative fairness and the division of housework: The importance of options. *American Journal of Sociology, 100,* 506–531.

Lerman, H. (1996). *Pigeonholing women's misery: A history and critical analysis of the psychodiagnosis of women in the twentieth century.* New York: Basic.

Letlaka-Rennert, K., Luswazi, P., Helms, J. E., & Zea, M. C. (1997). Does the womanist identity model predict aspects of psychological functioning in Black South African women? *South African Journal of Psychology, 27,* 236–243.

Lim, S., & Cortina, L. M. (2005). Interpersonal mistreatment in the workplace: The interface and impact of general incivility and sexual harassment. *Journal of Applied Psychology, 90,* 483–496.

Lips, H. M. (1991). *Women, men, and power.* Mountain View, CA: Mayfield.

Lips, H. M. (2002). Female powerlessness: Still a case of "cultural preparedness"? In A. E. Hunter & C. Forden (Eds.), *Readings in the psychology of gender* (pp. 19–37). Boston, MA: Allyn & Bacon.

Loden, M., & Rosener, J. B. (1991). *Workforce America: Managing employee diversity as a vital resource.* Homewood, IL: Business One Irwin.

Lott, B. (1995). Distancing from women: Interpersonal sexist discrimination. In B. Lott, & D. Maluso (Eds.), *The social psychology of interpersonal discrimination* (pp. 12–49). New York: Guilford.

Louie, T. A., & Tom, G. (2005). Timely completion of class requirements: Effects of student and faculty gender. *Sex Roles, 52,* 245–250.

Maccoby, E. E. (1990). Gender and relationships: A developmental account. *American Psychologist, 45,* 513–520.

MacCorquodale, P., & Jensen, G. (1993). Women in the law: Partners or tokens? *Gender & Society, 7,* 582–593.

Mackey, R. A., Diemer, M. A., & O'Brien, B. A. (2000). Psychological intimacy in the lasting relationships of heterosexual and same-gender couples. *Sex Roles, 43,* 201–227.

Major, B. (1993). Gender, entitlement, and the distribution of family labor. *Journal of Social Issues, 49*(3), 141–159.

Marecek, J., & Hare-Mustin, R. T. (1991). A short history of the future: Feminism and clinical psychology. *Psychology of Women Quarterly, 15,* 521–536.

Martin, C. L., & Fabes, R. A. (2001). The stability and consequences of young children's same-sex peer interactions. *Developmental Psychology, 37,* 431–446.

Martire, L. M., Stephens, M. A., & Townsend, A. L. (1998). Emotional support and well-being of midlife women: Role-specific mastery as a mediational mechanism. *Psychology & Aging, 13,* 396–404.

Matsui, T., Ohsawa, T., & Onglatco, M. (1995). Work-family conflict and the stress-buffering effects of husband support and coping behavior among Japanese married working women. *Journal of Vocational Behavior, 47,* 178–192.

McCarn, S. R., & Fassinger, R. E. (1996). Revisioning sexual minority identity formation: A new model of lesbian identity and its implications for counseling and research. *The Counseling Psychologist, 24,* 508–534.

McHugh, M. C., Frieze, I. H., & Browne, A. (1993). Research on battered women and their assailants. In M. Paludi, & F. Denmark (Eds.), *Handbook on the psychology of women* (pp. 513–552). New York: Greenwood Press.

McKinley, N. M., & Hyde, J. S. (1996). The Objectified Body Consciousness Scale: Development and validation. *Psychology of Women Quarterly, 20,* 181–215.

Messerschmidt, J. W. (2000). Becoming "real men": Adolescent masculinity challenges and sexual violence. *Men and Masculinities, 2,* 286–307.

Messner, M. A. (2000). Barbie girls versus sea monsters: Children constructing gender. *Gender & Society, 14,* 765–784.

Mobley, G. M., Jaret, C., Marsh, K., & Lim, Y. (1994). Mentoring, job satisfaction, gender, and the legal profession. *Sex Roles, 31,* 79–98.

Moen, P., & Forest, K. B. (1990). Working parents, workplace supports, and well-being: The Swedish experience. *Social Psychology Quarterly, 53,* 117–131.

Monson, R. A. (1997). State-ing sex and gender: Collecting information from mothers and fathers in paternity cases. *Gender & Society, 11,* 279–295.

Moradi, B. (2005). Advancing womanist identity development: Where we are and where we need to go. *The Counseling Psychologist, 33,* 225–253.

Moradi, B., & DeBlaere, C. (2010). Women's experiences of sexist discrimination: Review of research and directions for centralizing race, ethnicity, and culture. In H. Landrine & N. F. Russo (Eds.), *Handbook of Diversity in Feminist Psychology* (pp. 173–210). New York: Springer.

Moradi, B., & Funderburk, J. R. (2006). Roles of perceived sexist events and perceived social support in the mental health of women seeking counseling. *Journal of Counseling Psychology, 53,* 464–473.

Moradi, B., & Huang, Y. P. (2008). Objectification theory and psychology of women: A decade of advances and future directions. *Psychology of Women Quarterly, 32,* 377–398.

Moradi, B., & Rottenstein, A. (2007). Objectification theory and deaf cultural identity attitudes: Roles in deaf women's eating disorder symptomatology. *Journal of Counseling Psychology, 54,* 178–188.

Moradi, B., & Subich, L. M. (2002a). Perceived sexist events and feminist identity development attitudes: Links to women's psychological distress. *The Counseling Psychologist, 30,* 44–65.

Moradi, B., & Subich, L. M. (2002b). Feminist identity development measures: Comparing the psychometrics of three instruments. *The Counseling Psychologist, 30,* 66–86.

Moradi, B., & Subich, L. M. (2003). A concomitant examination of the relations of perceived racist and sexist events to psychological distress for African American women. *The Counseling Psychologist, 31,* 451–469.

Moradi, B., & Subich, L. M. (2004). Examining the moderating role of self-esteem in the link between experiences of perceived sexist events in psychological distress. *Journal of Counseling Psychology, 51,* 50–56.

Moradi, B., Subich, L. M., & Phillips, J. (2002a). Beyond revisiting: Moving feminist identity development ahead. *The Counseling Psychologist, 30,* 103–109.

Moradi, B., Subich, L. M., & Phillips, J. (2002b). Revisiting feminist identity development theory, research, and practice. *The Counseling Psychologist, 30,* 6–44.

Moradi, B., Yoder, J. D., & Berendsen, L. L. (2004). An evaluation of the psychometric properties of the Womanist Identity Attitudes scale. *Sex Roles, 50,* 253–266.

Morrison, J. (1989). Childhood sexual histories of women with somatization disorder. *American Journal of Psychiatry, 146,* 239–241.

Morrongiello, B. A., & Hogg, K. (2004). Mothers' reactions to children misbehaving in ways that can lead to injury: Implications for gender differences in children's risk taking and injuries. *Sex Roles, 50,* 103–118.

Mosher, C. E., & Danoff-Burg, S. (2005). Agentic and communal personality traits: Relations to attitudes toward sex and sexual experiences. *Sex Roles, 52,* 121–129.

Muehlenhard, C. L., Powch, I. G., Phelps, J. L., & Giusti, L. M. (1992). Definitions of rape: Scientific and political implications. *Journal of Social Issues, 48*(1), 23–44.

Murnen, S. K., Wright, C., & Kaluzny, G. (2002). If "boys will be boys," then girls will be victims? A meta-analytic review of the research that relates masculine ideology to sexual aggression. *Sex Roles, 46,* 359–375.

Neppl, T. K., & Murray, A. D. (1997). Social dominance and play patterns among preschoolers: Gender comparisons. *Sex Roles, 36,* 381–393.

Noland, V. J., Daley, E. M., Drolet, J. C., Fetro, J. V., McCormack Brown, K. R., Hassell, C. D., & McDermott, R. J. (2004). Connotative interpretations of sexuality-related terms. *Sex Roles, 51,* 523–534.

Ogletree, S. M., Martinez, C. N., Turner, T. R., & Mason, B. (2004). Pokemon: Exploring the role of gender. *Sex Roles, 50,* 851–859.

Oliver, M. B., & Hyde, J. S. (1993). Gender differences in sexuality: A meta-analysis. *Psychological Bulletin, 114,* 29–51.

Osmond, M. W., Wambach, K. G., Harrison, D. F., Byers, J., Levine, P. Imershein, A., & Quadango, D. M. (1993). The multiple jeopardy of race, class, and gender for AIDS risk among women. *Gender & Society, 7,* 99–120.

Ossana, S. M. (1986). *The relationship between women's perceptions of the campus environment and self-esteem as moderated by women's identity attitudes.* Unpublished master's thesis, University of Maryland, College Park.

Ossana, S. M., Helms, J. E., & Leonard, M. M. (1992). Do "womanist" identity attitudes influence college women's self-esteem and perceptions of environmental bias? *Journal of Counseling and Development, 70,* 402–408.

Ozer, E. M. (1995). The impact of childcare responsibility and self-efficacy on the psychological health of professional working mothers. *Psychology of Women Quarterly, 19,* 315–335.

Padavic, I., & Reskin, B. (2002). *Women and men at work* (2nd ed.). Thousand Oaks, CA: Pine Forge.

Parks, E. E., Carter, R. T., & Gushue, G. V. (1996). At the crossroads: Racial and womanist identity development in Black and White women. *Journal of Counseling and Development, 74,* 624–631.

Parrot, A., & Bechhofer, L. (Eds.) (1991). *Acquaintance rape: The hidden crime.* New York: Wiley.

Parvin, R., & Biaggio, M. K. (1991). Paradoxes in the practice of feminist therapy. *Women & Therapy, 11*(2), 3–12.

Peterson, R. D, Grippo, K. P., & Tantleff-Dunn, S. (2008). Empowerment and powerlessness: A closer look at the relationship between feminism, body image and eating disturbance. *Sex Roles, 58,* 639–648.

Peterson, R. D., Tantleff-Dunn, S., & Bedwell, J. S. (2006). The effects of exposure to feminist ideology on women's body image. *Body Image, 3,* 237–246.

Poindexter-Cameron, J. M., & Robinson, T. L. (1997). Relationships among racial identity attitudes, womanist identity attitudes, and self-esteem in African American college women. *Journal of College Student Development, 38,* 288–296.

Potts, M. K., Burnam, M. A., & Wells, K. B. (1991). Gender differences in depression detection: A comparison of clinician diagnosis and standardized assessment. *Psychological Assessment, 3,* 609–615.

Pratto, F., & Walker, A. (2004). The bases of gendered power. In A. H. Eagly, A. E. Beall, & R. J. Sternberg (Eds.), *The psychology of gender* (2nd ed., pp. 242–268). New York: Guilford.

Pratto, F., Sidanius, J., & Levin, S. (2006). Social dominance theory and the dynamics of intergroup relations: Taking stock and looking forward. *European Review of Social Psychology, 17,* 271–320.

Prentice, A. D., & Miller, T. D. (2007). Psychological essentialism of human categories. *Association for Psychological Science, 16,* 202–206.

Pulerwitz, J., Gortmaker, S. L., & DeJong, W. (2000). Measuring sexual relationship power in HIV/STD research. *Sex Roles, 42,* 637–660.

Pyke, K., & Coltrane, S. (1996). Entitlement, obligation, and gratitude in family work. *Journal of Family Issues, 17,* 61–82.

Quina, K., Harlow, L. L., Morokoff, P. J., Burkholder, G., & Deiter, P. J. (2000). Sexual communication in relationships: When words speak louder than actions. *Sex Roles, 42,* 523–549.

Quinn, D. M., Kallen, R. W., Twenge, J. M., & Fredrickson, B. L. (2006). The disruptive effect of self-objectification on performance. *Psychology of Women Quarterly, 30,* 59–64.

Randall, M., & Haskell, L. (1995). Sexual violence in women's lives: Findings from the Women's Safety Project, a community-based survey. *Violence Against Women, 1,* 6–31.

Rankin, E. D. (1993). Stresses and rewards experienced by employed mothers. *Health Care for Women International, 14,* 527–537.

Reitz, R. R. (1999). Batterers' experiences of being violent: A phenomenological study. *Psychology of Women Quarterly, 23,* 143–165.

Rickard, K. M. (1989). The relationship of self-monitored dating behaviors to level of feminist identity on the feminist identity scale. *Sex Roles, 20*, 213–226.

Ridgeway, C. L. (1991). The social construction of status value: Gender and other nominal characteristics. *Social Forces, 70*, 367–386.

Ridgeway, C. L. (2001). Gender, status, and leadership. *Journal of Social Issues, 57*(4), 637–655.

Ridgeway, C. L., & Smith-Lovin, L. (1999). The gender system and interaction. *Annual Review of Sociology, 25*, 191–216.

Riger, S. (2000). From snapshots to videotape: New directions in research on gender differences. In S. Riger (Ed.), *Transforming psychology: Gender in theory and practice* (pp. 39–51). New York: Oxford.

Robertson, J., & Fitzgerald, L. F. (1990). The (mis)treatment of men: Effects of client gender role and life-style on diagnosis and attribution of pathology. *Journal of Counseling Psychology, 37*, 3–9.

Robinson, J., & Spitze, G. (1992). Whistle while you work? The effect of household task performance on women's and men's well-being. *Social Science Quarterly, 73*, 844–861.

Rodin, J., Silberstein, L., & Striegel-Moore, R. (1984). Women and weight: A normative discontent. *Nebraska Symposium on Motivation, 32*, 267–307.

Root, M. P. P. (1991). Persistent, disordered eating as a gender-specific, post-traumatic stress response to sexual assault. *Psychotherapy, 28*, 96–102.

Root, M. P. P. (1992). Reconstructing the impact of trauma on personality. In L. S. Brown, & M. Ballou (Eds.), *Personality and psychopathology: Feminist reappraisals* (pp. 229–265). New York: Guilford.

Rose, S. (2000). Heterosexism and the study of women's romantic and friend relationships. *Journal of Social Issues, 56*, 315–328.

Rose, S., & Zand, D. (2000). Lesbian dating and courtship from young adulthood to midlife. *Journal of Gay & Lesbian Social Services: Issues in Practice, Policy & Research, 11*, 77–104.

Rosenbluth, S. C., & Steil, J. M. (1995). Predictors of intimacy for women in heterosexual and homosexual couples. *Journal of Social and Personal Relationships, 12*, 163–175.

Ross, L., & Nisbett, R. E. (1991). *The person and the situation: Perspectives of social psychology*. New York: McGraw-Hill.

Rozee, P. D., & Koss, M. P. (2001). Rape: A century of resistance. *Psychology of Women Quarterly, 25*, 295–311.

Ruble, D. N., & Martin, C. L. (1998). Gender development. In W. Damon (Series Ed.), & N. Eisenberg (Ed.), *Handbook of child psychology: Vol. 3. Social, emotional, and personality development* (5th ed., pp. 933–1016). New York: Wiley.

Russell, B. L., & Trigg, K. Y. (2004). Tolerance of sexual harassment: An examination of gender differences, ambivalent sexism, social dominance, and gender roles. *Sex Roles, 50*, 565–573.

Russo, N. F. (1998). Measuring feminist attitudes: Just what does it mean to be a feminist? *Psychology of Women Quarterly, 22*, 313–315.

Ryan, K. M., & Kanjorski, J. (1998). The enjoyment of sexist humor, rape attitudes, and relationship aggression in college students. *Sex Roles, 38*, 743–756.

Sadker, M., & Sadker, D. (1994). *Failing at fairness: How America's schools cheat girls*. New York: Macmillan.

Sanchez, L., & Thomson, E. (1997). Becoming mothers and fathers: Parenthood, gender, and the division of labor. *Gender & Society, 11*, 747–772.

Satterfield, A. T., & Muehlenhard, C. L. (1997). Shaken confidence: The effects of an authority figure's flirtatiousness on women's and men's self-rated creativity. *Psychology of Women Quarterly, 21*, 395–416.

Saunders, K. J., & Kashubeck-West, S. (2006). The relations among feminist identity development, gender-role orientation, and psychological well-being in women. *Psychology of Women Quarterly, 30*, 199–211.

Schneider, D. J. (2004). *The psychology of stereotyping*. New York: Guilford.

Shapiro, J., & Kroeger, L. (1991). Is life just a romantic novel? The relationship between attitudes about intimate relationships and the popular media. *American Journal of Family Therapy, 19*, 226–236.

Shaw, S. N. (2002). Shifting conversations on girls' and women's self-injury: An analysis of the clinical literature in historical context. *Feminism & Psychology, 12*, 191–219.

Sigmon, S. T., Pells, J. J., Boulard, N. E., Whitcomb-Smith, S., Edenfield, T. M., Herman, B. A., et al. (2005). Gender differences in self-reports of depression: The response bias hypothesis revisited. *Sex Roles, 53*, 401–411.

Skrypnek, B. J., & Snyder, M. (1982). On the self-perpetuating nature of stereotypes about women and men. *Journal of Experimental Social Psychology, 18*, 277–291.

Snyder, R., & Hasbrouck, L. (1996). Feminist identity, gender traits, and symptoms of disturbed eating among college women. *Psychology of Women Quarterly, 20*, 593–598.

Sprecher, S., & Felmlee, D. (1997). The balance of power in romantic heterosexual couples over time from "his" and "her" perspectives. *Sex Roles, 37*, 361–379.

Sprecher, S., Regan, P. C., & McKinney, K. (1998). Beliefs about the outcomes of extramarital sexual relationships as a function of the gender of the "cheating spouse." *Sex Roles, 38*, 301–311.

Staub, E. (1989). *The roots of evil: The origins of genocide and other group violence*. Cambridge, UK: Cambridge University Press.

Steil, J. M. (1997). *Marital equality: Its relationship to the well-being of husbands and wives*. Thousand Oaks, CA: Sage.

Steil, J. M., & Weltman, K. (1991). Marital inequality: The importance of resources, personal attributes, and social norms on career valuing and the allocation of domestic responsibilities. *Sex Roles, 24*, 161–179.

Swann, S. K., & Spivey, C. A. (2004). The relationship between self-esteem and lesbian identity during adolescence. *Child & Adolescent Social Work Journal, 21*, 629–646.

Swearingen-Hilker, N., & Yoder, J. D. (2002). Understanding the context of unbalanced domestic contributions: The influence of perceiver's attitudes, target's gender, and presentational format. *Sex Roles, 46*, 91–98.

Swim, J. K., Cohen, L. L., & Hyers, L. L. (1998). Experiencing everyday prejudice and discrimination. In J. K. Swim, & C. Stangor (Eds.), *Prejudice: The target's perspective* (pp. 37–60). San Diego: Academic Press.

Swim, J. K., Hyers, L. L., Cohen, L. L., & Ferguson, M. J. (2001). Everyday sexism: Evidence for its incidence, nature, and psychological impact from three daily diary studies. *Journal of Social Issues, 57*, 31–53.

Szymanski, D. M. (2005a). Heterosexism and sexism as correlates of psychological distress in lesbians. *Journal of Counseling and Development, 83*, 355–360.

Szymanski, D. M. (2005b). Feminist identity theories as correlates of feminist supervision practices. *The Counseling Psychologist, 33*, 729–747.

Tangri, S. S., & Jenkins, S. R. (1997). Why expecting conflict is good. *Sex Roles, 36*, 725–746.

Teets, J. M. (1995). Childhood sexual trauma of chemically dependent women. *Journal of Psychoactive Drugs, 27*, 231–238.

Thomas, S. (2002). The personal is the political: Antecedents of gendered choices of elected representatives. *Sex Roles, 47*, 343–353.

Thompson, L. (1991). Family work: Women's sense of fairness. *Journal of Family Issues, 12*, 181–196.

Thompson, M. P., & Norris, F. H. (1992). Crime, social status, and alienation. *American Journal of Community Psychology, 1*, 97–119.

Tiedje, L. B. (2004). Processes of change in work/home incompatibilities: Employed mothers 1986–1999. *Journal of Social Issues, 60*(4), 787–800.

Tomlinson, M. J., & Fassinger, R. E. (2003). Career development, lesbian identity development, and campus climate among lesbian college students. *Journal of College Student Development, 44*, 845–860.

Tripp, M. M., & Petrie, T. A. (2001). Sexual abuse and eating disorders: A test of a conceptual model. *Sex Roles, 44*, 17–32.

Vandiver, B. J. (2002). What do we know and where do we go? *The Counseling Psychologist, 30*, 96–104.

Voss, L. S. (1997). Teasing, disputing, and playing: Cross-gender interactions and space utilization among first and third graders. *Gender & Society, 11*, 238–256.

Walker, A. (1983). *In search of our mother's garden.* New York: Harcourt.

Weisbuch, M., Beal, D., & O'Neal, E. C. (1999). How masculine ought I be? Men's masculinity and aggression. *Sex Roles, 40*, 583–592.

Weitzman, L. M. (1994). Multiple-role realism: A theoretical framework for the process of planning to combine career and family roles. *Applied & Preventive Psychology, 3*, 15–25.

West, C., & Fenstermaker, S. (1995). Doing difference. *Gender & Society, 9*, 8–37.

White, A. M., Strube, M. J., & Fisher, S. (1998). A black feminist model of rape myth acceptance. *Psychology of Women Quarterly, 22*, 157–173.

Whitley, B. E. (1997). Gender differences in computer-related attitudes and behavior: A meta-analysis. *Computers in Human Behavior, 13*, 1–22.

Williams, R., & Wittig, M. A. (1997). "I'm not a feminist, but . . .": Factors contributing to the discrepancy between pro-feminist orientation and feminist social identity. *Sex Roles, 37*, 885–904.

Wise, E., & Rafferty, J. (1982). Sex bias and language. *Sex Roles, 8*, 1189–1196.

Woll, S. (2002). *Everyday thinking: Memory, reasoning, and judgment in the real world.* Mahwah, NJ: Erlbaum.

Worell, J. (1988). Women's satisfaction in close relationships. *Clinical Psychology Review, 8*, 477–498.

Worell, J., & Remer, P. (1992). *Feminist perspectives in therapy: An empowerment model for women.* New York: Wiley.

Worell, J., Stilwell, D., Oakley, D., & Robinson, D. (1999). Educating about women and gender: Cognitive, personal and professional outcomes. *Psychology of Women Quarterly, 23*, 797–811.

Worthington, R. L., Navarro, R. L., Savoy, H. B., & Hampton, D. (2008). Development, reliability and validity of the Measure of Sexual Identity Exploration and Commitment (MoSIEC). *Developmental Psychology, 44*, 22–33.

Wright, D. (1992). Impediments to safer heterosexual sex: A review of research with young people. *AIDS Care, 4*, 11–23.

Yoder, J. D. (2001). Making leadership work more effectively for women. *Journal of Social Issues, 57*(4), 815–828.

Yoder, J. D. (2007). *Women and gender: Making a difference.* Cornwall-on-Hudson, NY: Sloan.

Yoder, J. D., Fischer, A. R., Kahn, A. S., & Groden, J. (2007). Changes in students' explanations for gender differences after taking a Psychology of Women class: More constructionist and less essentialist. *Psychology of Women Quarterly, 31*, 415–425.

Yoder, J. D., & Kahn, A. S. (1993). Working toward an inclusive psychology of women. *American Psychologist, 48*, 846–850.

Yoder, J. D., Perry, R. L., & Saal, E. I. (2007). What good is a feminist identity? Women's feminist identification and role expectations for intimate and sexual relationships. *Sex Roles, 57*, 365–372.

Yoder, J. D., Schleicher, T. L., & McDonald, T. W. (1998). Empowering token women leaders: The importance of organizationally legitimated credibility. *Psychology of Women Quarterly, 22*, 209–222.

Young, I. M. (1992). Five faces of oppression. In T. E. Wartenberg (Ed.), *Rethinking power* (pp. 174–195). Albany, NY: State University of New York Press.

Zucker, A. N. (2004). Disavowing social identities: What it means when women say "I'm not a feminist but . . ." *Psychology of Women Quarterly, 28*, 423–435.

The Psychology of Men

James M. O'Neil

Abstract

The status of the psychology of men in 2010 is assessed in terms of empirical research and knowledge about men in therapy. A brief historical context for the psychology of men over the past decades is presented. Men's problems are reviewed from the survey research and the most frequently referenced paradigms in the psychology of men. Empirical research studies are examined that assess whether masculinity ideology, gender role conflict/stress, and other masculinity constructs are correlated with men's psychological problems. The results strongly suggest that masculinity conflicts are significantly related to men's psychological and interpersonal problems. The clinical knowledge on men as clients is reviewed in the context of published paradigms that treat men in therapy. The chapter concludes with recommendations for more complex research designs, greater emphasis on diversity, more evidence-based interventions with men, and more extensive training and teaching about the psychology of men in counseling psychology. The overall status of the psychology of men is "alive and well" but more elaborate theoretical paradigms and focused empirical research are needed for the psychology of men to significantly affect counseling psychology and mainstream psychology.

Keywords: men, masculinity, counseling psychology, gender

Over the last 30 years, the psychology of men has emerged as a recognized discipline in the social sciences. The feminist's movements of the 1970s were the primary stimuli for activating the psychology of men. As women deconstructed their gender roles, men began to do the same. How sexism negatively affected women raised significant questions about how sexist norms affect men. The Men's Liberation Movement was the precursor to the psychology of men (Pleck & Pleck, 1980), and in the early 1970s social scientists began to discuss men's roles. Six seminal books were published from 1974 to 1977 that gave men's liberation a national prominence (David & Brannon, 1976, Farrell, 1974; Fasteau, 1974; Goldberg, 1977; Nichols, 1975; Pleck & Sawyer, 1974). Additional publications appeared in scholarly journals that established an early rationale for the psychology of men

(Harrison, 1978; Lewis & Pleck, 1979; Levinson, Darrow, Klein, Levinson, & McKee, 1978; Skovholt, Gormally, Schauble, & Davis, 1978).

Counseling psychology was one of the first American Psychological Association (APA) divisions to recognize the importance of the psychology of men. A special issue of *The Counseling Psychologist* (*TCP*), titled "Counseling Men" (Skovholt et al., 1978) introduced men's issues to counseling psychology. The special issue was the field's first statement about men, and established the psychology of men as a legitimate area of scientific and clinical importance. During the 1980s, continued efforts were made to explore the psychology of men. Brooks and Levant (1998) document the activities of psychologists during this formative period in the psychology of men. Most notably was a special issue in the *Personnel and Guidance Journal* on "Counseling

Men" (Scher, 1981) and the *Handbook of Counseling and Psychotherapy with Men* (Scher, Stevens, Good, & Eichenfield, 1987). In 1991, the Special Interest Group (SIG) on Men, Masculinity and Men's Studies was formed in Division 17 to better coordinate activities related to the psychology of men.

During the 1990 APA Boston convention, a group of 50 psychologists met to discuss institutionalizing the psychology of men as an official division of the APA (Brooks & Levant, 1998). There was consensus that the psychology of men deserved official recognition within the APA. In 1995, after 5 years of lobbying, the APA endorsed the Society for the Psychological Study of Men and Masculinity (SPSMM) as an official division in APA. As SPSMM was becoming an APA Division, different factions in the men's movement (Mythopoetic and Men's Right's groups) became active in communicating their positions about men's roles and rights (Kimmel, 1995). The American Men's Studies Association was formed in 1988, and new journals like the *Journal of Men's Studies* and *Men and Masculinities* were created. In 2000, SPSMM published the *Psychology of Men and Masculinity*, the first empirical journal devoted to the psychology of men, and in 2007, *Thymos: Journal of Boyhood Studies* was the first journal devoted to research on boys.

The psychology of men is a new discipline and in its early stages of defining its identity and purpose. Like most new disciplines, the psychology of men is experiencing growing pains as it defines its mission and desired impact. Over the past 10 years, the published literature in the psychology of men has been substantial, but the discipline suffers from few theories and measures to conceptualize the diversity of men's attitudes, problems, and potentialities. Furthermore, much of the empirical research has not been applied to clinical interventions with men. Therefore, knowledge about doing therapy with men is in its early stages of development.

Goals of the Chapter, Limitations, and Literature Search Process

The overall goal of this chapter is to review the status of the psychology of men, with specific attention paid to theory, research, and clinical practice with men. The eight goals of this chapter are to briefly review the historical and contemporary views of men and masculinity, to report men's problems as they are described in the literature, to summarize the main theories and concepts in the psychology of men, to review the empirical research that has correlated masculinity ideology and gender role

conflict/stress with men's psychological and interpersonal problems, to review the research on men as clients, to summarize assessment approaches for therapists who counsel men, to summarize the recommendations on therapeutic processes with men, and to discuss future directions for the study of men and masculinity. The first three sections of the chapter give historical, theoretical, and contextual overviews on the psychology of men. The next two sections review the empirical research that assesses how masculinity conflicts relate to men's psychological problems and what is known about men as clients. The following two sections focus on recommended assessment approaches and therapeutic processes with men. The final section of the chapter enumerates nine critical directions for the future study of men and masculinity.

Over a 2-year period, an exhaustive literature review was conducted to synthesize the psychology of men's theory and research. Defined strategies of review were employed. First, a review of the major journals in men's studies and the psychology of men was conducted. Theory and empirical research studies were read and organized on grid sheets to determine major concepts and empirical areas that currently define the psychology of men. The grid sheets were then sorted into various groupings to facilitate the analysis of the findings. Separate sorts were implemented for the eight goals of the chapter. Additional sorts were made for specific topic areas. Written summaries of each sorting were completed to establish the current knowledge of the psychology of men in theory, research, and clinical practice. All the findings of the review are not summarized here. Priority is given to published manuscripts and thematic topics consistently appearing in the literature. The review is also limited to publications in the psychology of men that have research and clinical relevance to advance service delivery for men.

Historical Background and Contemporary Status of the Psychology of Men

The history of masculinity documents how social, economic, and political factors have shaped men' lives. Historical analyses of masculinity have been made by authors over various time periods (Blazina, 2003; Doyle, 1995; Dubbert, 1979; Kimmel, 2006; Pleck & Pleck, 1980; Rotundo, 1993; Smiler, 2004). Most historical analyses describe how social, political, and economic developments shape the understanding of men's lives. Kimmel's (2006) cultural history of manhood concludes that men's problems and defensiveness today "lie deep in our nation's past" (p. 1). He traces the idea of men testing and proving their masculinity from the early part of the 19th century and concludes that this single premise continues to affect contemporary men's lives. Kimmel argues "that the quest for manhood—the effort to achieve, to demonstrate, to prove our masculinity—has been one of the formative and persistent experiences in men's lives" (p. 3). This historical analysis is important because proving one's masculinity has powerful psychological significance in explaining men's contemporary problems.

Kimmel is correct in stating that American men have not had a history of themselves as men. In almost all of the published historical analyses, men's personal experiences with their gender roles have not been explained. Famous men's lives have been studied, but analyses of the average men's experiences with their gender roles have gone unexplored. Whether men from previous generations felt gender role conflict and strain in their interpersonal and work roles is unclear from the historical analyses. Little historical documentation exists on how men coped with changing gender roles or whether they even consciously thought about them in any significant ways. Most historians do acknowledge that American middle-class men had to "contend with a paradigmatic revolution in self-perception during the nineteenth and twentieth centuries" (Dubbert, 1979, p. 9). These paradigm shifts continue today in men's lives. Scholars are now assessing men's psychological experience of their gender roles with scholarly rigor not witnessed before in human history. Therapists should consider this past history when examining men's contemporary dilemmas in therapy.

Capturing the evolution of the psychology of men over decades is easier than summarizing the current state of men's lives. Contemporary conceptions of masculinity are complex because of differences based on race, class, age, ethnicity, religion, nationality, and sexual orientation. Many contextual and diversity factors influence how men define themselves. The current state of masculinity in the United States is best described as diverse and in constant transition or flux. Furthermore, like the women's movement of the 1970s, men's issues have stimulated cultural and political clashes between feminists and traditionalists, as well as divisions within the men's movements. These ideological conflicts have rarely advanced our knowledge, and have sometimes polarized groups in unproductive ways (Kimmel, 1995).

From my literature review, one issue crystalized. The scholarly study of men's lives has a short history in psychology. Only in the last 15 years has psychology specifically focused on men's psychological processes. The study of ordinary men's lives has been neglected in psychology. One wonders why. What has contributed to the limited study of men's emotional and interpersonal lives? Have patriarchal structures been so strong (or maybe so vulnerable) that the study of men's lives threatens the status quo? The gradual emergence of the psychology of men over the last three decades has brought men's issues into psychological focus. Theoretical and empirical advances have explained how sexism negatively affects male development. How restricted gender roles affect men's lives now has a firm base in psychology. The damaging effects of patriarchal sexism on men and women are now social justice issues for many psychologists doing research or providing clinical services.

Men's Problems: Is There a Crises in America?

Survey data on men's psychological problems are quite limited. Only two large epidemiological studies of men's problems were found (Robin & Reiger, 1991; Kessler & Walters, 2002). Cochran (2005) reviews the base rates of mental disorders of men in these two large-scale surveys. According to Cochran's analysis, men are at the highest risk for alcohol and drug abuse and dependency over the lifespan. Between 31% and 47% of all men will develop a substance abuse problem over the lifetime. Additionally, these surveys indicate that lifetime prevalence rates for men's psychological problems are: depressive disorder (3. 6%–12.7%), antisocial personality disorder (4.5%–5.8%), generalized anxiety disorder (2.4%–3.6%), and bipolar disorder (1.1%–1.6%). Conspicuously absent in the literature are many large-scale studies that evaluate men's problems with their gender roles.

Beyond these epidemiological studies, numerous authors indicate that boys and men have serious physical and emotional problems (Glicken, 2005; Courtenay, 1998; 2000a, b; Robin & Reiger, 1991). Courtenay (1998) reports that men in the United States, on average, die 7 years younger than women and have higher death rates for all leading causes of death (DHHS, 1996a). Men commit suicide 4 to 15 times more often than do women (Cochran & Rabinowitz, 2000; Murphy, 1998). Seven of 10 of the most common infectious diseases in the United States are higher among men compared to women

(CDC, 1997). Seventy-five percent of people under the age of 65 who die from heart attacks are men (American Heart Association [AHA], 1994). Surveys indicate that lifetime prevalence estimates for alcohol and drug dependency is approximately 30% for men (Robins & Reiger, 1991). This means that 1 of 3 men will have a problem with drugs and alcohol during their lives. Courtenay (1998) reports that for males 1-to 24 years old, 75% of the deaths each year are from fatal injuries. This accounts for over 80% of all deaths among this age group. Sixty-seven percent of all men experience some kind of problem with violence during their lives, mostly by other men (U.S. Census Department, 1998; Glicken, 2005). Thirty-five percent of boys who are aged 15–17 years are below grade level in school (United States Census Bureau, 2005), and boys are three times more likely to be enrolled in a special education class compared to girls. Twelve percent of males who are 18 to 24 years old are high school dropouts (United States Census Bureau, 2003), 37% of 12th grade boys score below basic levels on standardized writing tests (Persky, Daane, & Jin, 2003), and 16% of school-aged boys have been diagnosed with attention deficit disorder (Center for Disease Control, 2005). Finally, 80% of boys report being bullied at least once, and 12% of high school boys report being threatened or injured with a weapon on school property (Center for Disease Control, 2007).

The statistics on boy's and men's lives are sobering when taken to heart. The temptation is to deny or explain away these statistics as distorted or exaggerated numbers. The statistics are from reliable sources and capture the truth about boy's and men's lives. Levant (1997) and Brooks (1998) argue that a masculinity crisis exists with men and the reported statistics document it. Based on my review, the statistics also verify a "boy crisis" that is serious and real (Hall, 1999; Hoff Sommer, 2000; O'Neil & Lujan, 2009; Pollack, 1998a; Kindlon & Thompson, 1999; Tyre, 2006; Von Drehle, 2007). Denial exists about boy's and men's problems in our society. Telling the truth about men's gender role issues can threatens the status quo and people who endorse traditional gender role values. Furthermore, if the data were taken seriously, calls to action (O'Neil & Lujan, 2009) would significantly alter educational practices and family socialization processes.

The critical question is whether men and boys have these problems because of socialized gender roles. During the 1970s and 1980s, the men's liberation writers argued that gender roles played a crucial part in the development of men's problems. Arguments were made about the "hazards of being male" (Goldberg, 1977) and that gender roles could be dangerous to men's mental health (Harrison, 1978). In the 1970s and 1980s, very little empirical support existed for these propositions.

One of the critical questions in this chapter is whether gender roles, masculinity ideology, and gender role conflict and stress are empirically related to boy's and men's problems. In the next section, theories and paradigms about men and masculinity are summarized. A review of the current paradigms on men and masculinity is necessary to evaluate the current status of empirical research and the clinical knowledge in the psychology of men.

Paradigms on Men, Masculinity, and Gender Role Conflict

Overall, a lack of unified concepts about men exist in the psychology of men. Currently, no well developed theories address how men's gender role socialization occurs and how it affects men's lives. The psychology of men has been primarily atheoretical and suffers from having only a few paradigms that explain men's problems and potentialities. Theoretical perspectives on men have been published but represent general extrapolations from the psychoanalytic and social psychological theories. For example, Wong (1982) reviewed nine psychoanalytic theorists that describe the developmental dynamics of male gender role identity. More recently, Kilmartin (2007) reviewed how biological, sociobiological, psychoanalytic, and ego psychology theories may contribute to the formation of men's gender roles. Furthermore, he reviewed relevant conceptualization from social learning, humanistic, and existential theories that provide insights into male development. A useful review of theoretical perspectives that explain men's gender roles and masculinity was completed by Addis and Cohane (2005). They reviewed four gender/masculinity paradigms that convey the different ways to understand men's gender roles. The four paradigms included psychodynamic, social learning, social constructionist, and feminist perspectives. This analysis is important because for each paradigm specific directions are given for future research and intervention.

These reviews have advanced the psychology of men by providing insights on how boys and men may develop their gender roles. More critical thought is needed on how the different masculinity paradigms relate to both research and clinical practice. The current paradigms do not provide comprehensive, coherent, or heuristic frameworks to understand male development over the lifespan. Second, they do not adequately explain how men develop problems from restrictive gender roles, nor do they suggest how to help men overcome them.

Another way to evaluate the status of theory in the psychology of men is to focus on the controversial issues discussed and the most widely referenced paradigms used in past empirical research. There have been scholarly critiques of theoretical issues related to essentialism, the gender role identity paradigm, and the social constructivist view of gender roles (Addis & Cohane, 2005; Kilmartin, 2007; Pleck, 1981; 1995). Criticism of previous psychodynamic theorists (Freud, Jung, Alder, and Horney) indicate that they were primarily concerned with the unconscious aspect of masculinity conflicts and viewed male femininity as an intrapsychic problems (O'Neil, 2008). There has been endorsement of the notion of hegemonic masculinity that originated in sociology (Connell, 1995). Masculinity ideology has been the most prominent conceptualization describing the attitudes, values, and norms that boys and men learn (Levant et al., 1992; Mahalik et al., 2003b; Pleck, 1995). Masculinity ideology has been the stimulus for considerable research in the psychology of men. Furthermore, the gender role strain paradigm (Pleck, 1981, 1995), gender role conflict (O'Neil, 2008), and gender role stress (Eisler, 1995) are currently the most widely used theoretical models to explain the negative consequences of men's gender roles.

In all of these paradigms, developmental perspectives that explain both dysfunctional and healthy development in men have been lacking (Smiler, 2004). There has been criticism that men's problems have not been contextualized. This means that studies have not considered the situational, demographic, and diversity contingencies that have negatively affected individual men's lives (O'Neil, 2008a,b; Smiler, 2004). How biological factors may affect male attitudes and behaviors over the lifespan has been given limited attention. Furthermore, there have been very few interdisciplinary dialogues about masculinity between psychologists and other scholars in other disciplines like medicine, sociology, history, and religious studies. Finally, the psychology of men has been preoccupied with describing the male role and identifying men's problems, rather studying men's potentials and the positive aspects of being a man (O'Neil & Lujan, 2008). Unfortunately, the emergence of positive psychology has yet to make any significant difference in the psychology of men.

Current Paradigms and Concepts in the Psychology of Men

For the purpose of this review, the most frequently cited paradigms and concepts in the psychology of men are reviewed. Six theoretical areas have dominated the psychology of men: hegemonic masculinity; masculinity ideology, masculine norms, and masculine conformity; gender role strain paradigm; gender role conflict paradigm; masculine gender role stress paradigm; reference group identity paradigm, and fear of femininity or antifemininity. A brief summary of these concepts is summarized below as a context to understanding the current research and to formulate ways to help boys and men in therapy.

HEGEMONIC MASCULINITY PARADIGM

Hegemonic masculinity is a consistently cited concept to understand men and masculinity (Connell, 1995; Connell & Messerschmidt, 2005). *Hegemony* is a cultural dynamic in which one group claims and sustains a leading position in social life. Hegemonic masculinity is a set of practices that permit men's dominance over women. Hegemonic masculinity includes gender practices that legitimatize patriarchal values and guarantee the dominant position of some men over others and the subordination of women. Hegemonic masculinity is the normative ideal of masculinity to which men are suppose to aspire. Connell indicates that hegemonic masculinity is not the most prevalent masculinity but the most socially endorsed, and it represents the most honored way to be a man. Therefore, many men define themselves in relation to hegemonic masculinity. Men can receive benefits from this kind of masculinity without being dominant and therefore endorse complicit acceptance of hegemonic dominance over women. Qualities that define hegemonic masculinity include aggressiveness, strength, drive, ambition, and self-reliance. There are currently no measures of hegemonic masculinity.

MASCULINITY IDEOLOGY AND CONFORMITY AND HYPERMASCULINITY PARADIGMS

Masculinity ideology describes how men are socialized to masculine stereotypes. Masculinity ideology has been operationalized by the concepts of masculine norms and roles (Levant et al., 1992; Thompson & Pleck 1986), and masculine conformity and nonconformity (Mahalik et al., 2003). Masculinity ideology represents the primary values and standards that define, restrict, and negatively affect boy's and men's lives (Levant et al., 1992; Mahalik et al., 2003b;

Pleck, 1995; Pleck, Sonenstein, & Ku, 1993; Thompson & Pleck, 1995). Masculinity ideology refers "to beliefs about the importance of men adhering to culturally defined standards for male behavior" (Pleck, 1995, p. 19). Masculinity ideology involves "the individual's endorsement and internalization of cultural belief systems about masculinity and male gender, rooted in the structural relationships between the sexes" (Pleck, 1995, p. 19). Masculinity ideologies can be restrictive because gender roles can have negative consequences for men and can be dysfunctional in their interpersonal relationships. The negative outcomes of adhering to or deviating from culturally defined and restrictive masculinity ideologies result in gender role conflict and strain (O'Neil, 2008; Pleck, 1995). Internalizing rigid masculinity ideologies can produce distorted gender role schemas (Mahalik, 1999a, 2001a; O'Neil & Nadeau, 1999) and patterns of gender role conflict that are potentially damaging to men and others.

Gender role norms provide guidance for both sexes on how to act, think, and feel but also can restrict men and women from certain behaviors that are considered inappropriate (Mahalik et al., 2005). One of the most widely cited typologies of masculinity ideology represents traditional masculinity themes including: antifemininity–no sissy stuff, status and achievement–the big wheel, inexpressiveness and independence–the sturdy oak, and adventurousness and aggressiveness–give 'em hell (David & Brannon, 1976). Thompson and Pleck (1986) have operationally defined the masculine norms of status, toughness, and antifemininity, whereas Levant et al. (1992) conceptualize the following aspects of traditional masculinity: avoidance of femininity, fear and hatred of homosexuals, self-reliance, aggression, achievement/status, nonrelational attitudes toward sex, and restrictive emotionality.

Conformity to masculine norms is defined as meeting societal expectations of masculinity in one's public or private life, whereas nonconformity to masculine norms is defined as not meeting these societal expectations (Mahalik et al., 2003b). Mahalik's conformity paradigm is based on both societal and individual men's masculine expectancies that are either accepted (conformity) or rejected (nonconformity). The male norms of conformity include winning, emotional control, risk taking, violence, dominance, playboy, self-reliance, primacy of work, power over women, disdain for homosexuality, and the pursuit of status.

Hypermasculinity has been defined as an exaggeration of traditional male stereotypes that includes callous attitudes toward women and sexual behavior, the perception that violence is manly, and that danger is exciting (Mosher & Sirkin, 1984; Mosher & Tomkins, 1988). Hypermasculinity is like masculinity ideology but takes a more extreme form (Mosher & Tomkins, 1988). Burk, Burkhart, and Sikorski (2004) expand the definition of hypermasculinity by providing more emphasis on men's personal power and how fear and anger are associated with interpersonal violence. They define hypermasculinity as exhibiting exaggerated traditional male gender roles that include super-valuation of competitive and aggressive activities and the devaluation of cooperative, care-taking behaviors. They indicate that status and self-reliance are highly valued, and interpersonal violence, dominance of others, and sensation-seeking behavior are necessary to being considered male. Women are seen as sex objects and are to be pursued as conquests.

Scales that measure masculinity ideologies, norms, and hypermasculinity include Brannon Masculinity Scale (BMS; Brannon & Juni, 1984), Masculine Role Norms Scale (MRNS; Thompson & Pleck, 1986), Male Role Norm Inventory (MRNI; Levant et al., 1992), Conformity to Masculine Norm Inventory (CMNI; Mahalik et al., 2003b), Adolescent Masculinity Ideology in Relationship Scale (AMIRS, Chu, Porche, & Tolman, 2005), Hypermasculine Inventory (HMI, Mosher & Sirkin, 1984), and the Auburn Differential Masculinity Inventory (ADMI, Burk et al., 2004). One of the critical questions of this review is whether empirical research indicates that masculinity ideology, masculine norms, and hypermasculinity relate to negative outcomes for men, women, and children.

PLECK'S GENDER ROLE STRAIN PARADIGM
Joseph Pleck's gender role strain paradigm describes how restrictive gender roles can be detrimental to psychological health (Garnets & Pleck, 1979; Pleck, 1981, 1995). Gender role strain has been a dominant paradigm in the psychology of men and has been explained in two separate statements. First, Pleck specified ten gender role strain propositions (Pleck, 1981). The propositions implied that gender roles are defined by gender role stereotypes, are contradictory and inconsistent, and are violated by many individuals. Pleck also states that violating gender role stereotypes is common and can lead to social condemnation and negative evaluations from others. Furthermore, he hypothesized that

overconformity to the stereotypes has more severe consequences for males than females but that prescribed gender roles are psychologically dysfunctional for both sexes in their works and family roles.

Pleck's second theoretical statement specified three subtypes of male gender role strain: discrepancy strain, trauma strain, and dysfunction strain (Pleck, 1995). *Discrepancy strain* implied that stereotypic gender role standards exist and that individuals attempt to conform to them in varying degrees. Pleck's assumption was that "not conforming to these standards has negative consequences for self-esteem and other outcomes reflecting psychological well-being because of negative social feedback as well as internalized negative self judgments" (Pleck, 1995, p. 13). This assumption suggests that nonconformity to masculinity ideology can produce negative feeling in self (gender role self-devaluations) because of people's negative judgments. Not conforming to these gender role norms can cause devaluation from others, self-devaluations, and attempts to compensate for the discrepancies through exaggerated masculine behaviors, sometimes referred to as *machismo*. Researchers have attempted to empirically assess discrepancy strain (Liu, Rochlen, & Mohr, 2005; Nabavi, 2004), and this form of gender role strain holds promise for future research.

Gender role trauma strain results from traumatic experiences during men's gender role socialization that can have serious negative consequences (Pleck, 1995). Gender role trauma has not been fully conceptualized in the literature, but theorists have discussed boys' separation from mothers and having an absent fathers as traumatizing (Levant, 1995; Pollack, 1992). How gender role trauma strain and men's conflicts interact has not been fully established. There has been discussions about men as victims (Brooks & Good, 2001b, O'Neil, 2008) and how gender role socialization can be traumatizing (Brooks, 1998; Lisak, 2001). Gender role conflict has also been hypothesized to be traumatizing to boys and men during gender role socialization (O'Neil, 1981, 2008). How trauma and masculine socialization interact is now being discussed without some of the political sensitivities of the past. Therefore, Pleck's trauma strain and how it relates to men's problems are likely to be an important topic in future decades.

Dysfunction strain is Pleck's third subtype and implies that the fulfillment of gender roles norms can have negative consequences. Pleck (1995) indicates that the "fulfillment of gender role standards can have negative consequences because the behavior and characteristics these standards prescribe can be inherently dysfunctional in the sense of being associated with negative outcomes either for the male himself or for others" (pp. 16–17). This is what early men's liberation writers meant when they discussed the "hazards of being male" (Goldberg, 1977) or that the "male gender role may be dangerous to your health" (Harrison, 1978). Pleck's dysfunction strain has theoretical relevance to men's gender role conflict and stress because this subtype implies negative outcomes from endorsing restrictive gender role norms.

GENDER ROLE CONFLICT PARADIGM AND RESEARCH

Gender role conflict (GRC) has been defined in a series of theoretical statements and empirical studies (O'Neil, 1981a, b, 1982, 1990, 2006, 2008a, b, c; O'Neil & Egan, 1993; O'Neil & Fishman, 1992; O'Neil, Fishman, Kinsella-Shaw, 1987; O'Neil, Good, & Holmes, 1995; O'Neil, Helm, Gable, David, & Wrightsman, 1986; O'Neil & Nadeau, 1999). Gender role conflict is defined as a psychological state in which socialized gender roles have negative consequences for the person or others. Gender role conflict occurs when rigid, sexist, or restrictive gender roles result in restriction, devaluation, or violation of others or self (O'Neil et al., 1995). The ultimate outcome of GRC is the restriction of a person's human potential or the restriction of another person's potential. Gender role conflict is operationally defined by four psychological domains, numerous situational contexts, and three personal experiences. The domains, contexts, and experience of GRC represent the complexity of GRC in people's lives, and each is defined below.

The psychological domains of GRC imply cognitive, affective, unconscious, or behavioral problems caused by socialized gender roles learned in sexist and patriarchal societies. The four domains of GRC include: *cognitive*, how we think about gender roles; *affective*, how we feel about gender roles; *behavioral*, how we act, respond, and interact with others and ourselves because of gender roles; and *unconscious*, how gender role dynamics beyond our awareness affect our behavior and produce conflicts (O'Neil et al., 1986, 1995). Furthermore, GRC occurs in situational contexts when men experience a gender role transition or face difficult developmental tasks over the lifespan (O'Neil & Egan, 1992a, b; O'Neil & Fishman, 1992; O'Neil, et al., 1987, 1995);

deviate from or violate gender role norms of masculinity ideology (Levant et al., 1992; Mahalik et al., 2003b; Pleck, 1981, 1995); try to meet or fail to meet gender role norms of masculinity ideology; experience discrepancies between their real self-concepts and their ideal self-concepts, based on gender role stereotypes and masculinity ideology (Garnets & Pleck, 1979; Liu et al., 2005); personally devalue, restrict, or violate themselves for failing to meet masculinity ideology norms (O'Neil, 1990; O'Neil et al., 1995); experience personal devaluations, restrictions, and violations from others for conforming to or deviating from masculinity ideology (O'Neil, 1981b, 1990; O'Neil et al., 1995); and personally devalue, restrict, or violate others because of their deviation from or conformity to masculinity ideology norms (O'Neil, 1990; O'Neil & Egan 1993). The complexity of these situational contexts can be reduced to four categories: GRC caused by gender role transitions, GRC experienced intrapersonally (within the man), GRC expressed toward others interpersonally, and GRC experienced from others (O'Neil, 1990).

Understanding gender role transitions is critical to understanding men's gender role conflict. Gender role transitions are events in a man's gender role development that alter or challenge his gender role self-assumptions and consequently produce GRC or positive life changes (O'Neil & Fishman; 1992; O'Neil et al., 1987; O'Neil & Egan, 1992b). Examples of gender role transitions are entering school, puberty, getting married, becoming a father, or losing one's father.

Gender role conflict in an intrapersonal context is the private experience of negative emotions and thoughts when experiencing gender role devaluations, restrictions, and violations. Gender role conflict expressed toward others occurs when men's gender role problems result in devaluing, restricting, or violating someone else. Gender role conflict from others occurs when someone devalues, restricts, or violates another person who deviates from or conforms to masculinity ideology and norms.

The personal experience of GRC constitutes the negative consequences of conforming to, deviating from, or violating the gender role norms of masculinity ideology. Three personal experiences of GRC (devaluations, restrictions, and violations) are operationally defined. Gender role devaluations are negative critiques of self or others when conforming to, deviating from, or violating stereotypic gender role norms of masculinity ideology. Devaluations result in lessening of personal status, stature,

or positive regard. Gender role restrictions occur when confining others or oneself to stereotypic norms of masculinity ideology. Restrictions result in controlling people's behavior, limiting one's personal potential, and decreasing human freedom. Gender role violations result from harming oneself, harming others, or being harmed by others when deviating from or conforming to gender role norms of masculinity ideology. To be violated is to be victimized and abused, causing psychological and physical pain. Gender role violations is a similar concept to Pleck's gender role trauma strain because it implies that experiences with gender roles can have severe, negative outcomes in terms of psychological functioning. According to GRC theory, gender role restrictions, devaluations, and violations have a direct negative impact on men's interpersonal, career, family, and health lives (O'Neil, 1981a, b, 1982, 1990; O'Neil & Egan, 1993; O'Neil et al., 1995; O'Neil & Nadeau, 1999). Furthermore, the cognitive, affective, behavioral, and unconscious domains of GRC relate to men's problems with depression, anxiety, self-esteem, homophobia, restricted emotionality, communication problems, intimacy, marital conflict, violence toward women, health problems, and substance abuse. The empirical question is whether any research shows that GRC relates to these negative consequences for men.

Four patterns of GRC have been measured using the 37-item Gender Role Conflict Scale (GRCS, O'Neil et al., 1986; O'Neil, 2008; O'Neil, et al., 1995). The four patterns are success/power/competition (SPC), restrictive emotionality (RE); restrictive affectionate behavior between men (RABBM), and conflict between work and family relations (CBWFR). RE is defined as having restrictions and fears about expressing one's feelings, as well as restrictions in finding words to express basic emotions. RABBM represents restrictions in expressing one's feelings and thoughts with other men and difficulty touching other men. The third factor, SPC, describes personal attitudes about success pursued through competition and power. CBWFR reflects experiencing restrictions in balancing work, school, and family relations resulting in health problems, overwork, stress, and a lack of leisure and relaxation.

THE FEAR OF FEMININITY AND ANTIFEMININITY (NO SISSY STUFF) PARADIGMS

Fears about femininity have been consistently mentioned as central to understanding men's experience with their gender roles. Men's conscious and unconscious fears of femininity have existed in the theoretical literature for many years (Blazina, 1997, 2003; Boehm, 1930; David & Brannon, 1976; Freud, 1937; Hays, 1964; Horney, 1967; Jung, 1953; Lederer, 1968; Levinson et al., 1978; Menninger, 1970; Norton, 1997). The fear of femininity consists of strong, negative emotions associated with stereotypic feminine values, attitudes, and behaviors. These fears are learned in early childhood when gender role identity is being shaped by parents, peers, and societal values. The dynamics of fearing are not well understood and many times are unconscious to the man (Jung, 1959). When a man fears his feminine side, he really fears that others will see him as stereotypically feminine (e.g. weak, dependent, submissive) rather than positively masculine. This is not an unreasonable fear since certain aspects of femininity are devalued in society. Men are cognizant that women's femininity is sometimes devalued by other men, and they attempt to avoid situations in which they could also be devalued. The cost of showing stereotypic feminine qualities could be disrespect, failure, and emasculation. These are risky costs for the man who wants to actualize masculinity ideologies and prove his masculinity (Kimmel, 2005).

A similar concept to the fear of femininity is the antifemininity ("no sissy stuff") conceptualization (David & Brannon, 1976). Antifemininity suggests a stigma associated with all stereotypical feminine characteristics and qualities. Specifically, this concept suggests that the fear of femininity is learned by early anxiety of being considered a girl, sissy, or feminine; a rule dictating that a "real man" must never resemble a woman or possess feminine characteristics; openness and vulnerability being considered unmasculine; and fear of being seen as a homosexual. Many times, antifemininity is reinforced by parents. Parents are concerned about how well boys conform to masculine norms, and fathers are particularly concerned if their sons manifest feminine qualities. Boys learn to avoid most stereotypic feminine qualities when experiencing parent's displeasure at their deviation from masculine norms. Consequently, the male socialization process can produce a life-long aversion to any quality thought to be feminine, constant striving for the ways to be masculine, an inexpressive male image that prohibits open expression of feelings and feminine characteristics, and an emotional and physical distance between men because of feared homosexuality. Therefore, boys learn to reject and repress the feminine part of their personalities at an early age.

Subscales of the MRNS (Thompson & Pleck, 1986) and the MRNI (Levant et al., 1992) measure aspects of antifemininity. Furthermore, all of O'Neil's patterns of gender role conflict have been theoretically linked to the fear of femininity (O'Neil, 1981a,b, 1982; O'Neil et al., 1986) and operationalized through the GRCS (O'Neil et al., 1986).

EILSER'S MASCULINE GENDER ROLE STRESS PARADIGM

Richard Eisler has developed a theory of masculine gender role stress (Eilser, 1995). Overall, the paradigm suggests that men are required to adhere to culturally approved masculinity ideology that may have dysfunctional health outcomes. He discusses three theoretical perspectives in defining the gender role stress paradigm, including Bem's (1981) gender schema theory, Pleck's (1981) gender role strain paradigm, and Lazarus' theory-based measurement of stress (Lazarus & Folkman, 1984). The paradigm consists of five propositions including that sociocultural contingencies reinforce masculine behavior and punish feminine behavior, resulting in gender role cognitive schemas for boys and men; masculine gender role schema are used by men to assess threats and challenges and to choose ways to cope; men have different commitments to culturally accepted models of masculinity that vary from full endorsement of traditional masculine norms to a complete abandonment of these norms; masculine gender role stress occurs when there is full endorsement of culturally approved masculine schemas that limit ways to cope in particular situations; and masculine gender role stress occurs when a man believes that he is not living up to culturally endorsed masculine gender role behavior. Based on these propositions, the Masculine Gender Role Stress Scale (MGRSS) was developed (Eilser, 1995; Eisler & Skidmore, 1987). The MGRSS measures the following areas of gender role stress: physical inadequacy, emotional inexpressiveness, subordination to women, intellectual inferiority, and performance failure.

MALE REFERENCE GROUP IDENTITY PARADIGM

Jay Wade has developed a paradigm of male reference group identity (Wade, 2008; Wade & Gelso, 1998). This paradigm suggests that differences in men's attitudes and behaviors may be due to male reference group identity dependence. He defines this as ". . . . the "extent to which males are dependent on a reference group for their gender role self-concepts (Wade & Gelso, 1998, p. 384)." The theory suggests that the male reference group is the purveyor of masculine culture and affects differences in men's definitions of masculinity. Three male reference group identity–dependent statuses are defined by a man's feelings of psychological relatedness to other men: no reference group defined as a lack of psychological relatedness to other men; the reference group–dependent status, meaning that there is psychological relatedness to some men and not others; and the reference group–nondependent, in which there is psychological relatedness to all men. The Reference Group Identity Dependence Scale (RGIDS, Wade & Gelso, 1998) measures male reference group identity. Research has shown that the three reference group statuses are related to masculine ideology and GRC (Wade, 2008; Wade & Brittan-Powell, 2001; Wade & Gelso, 1998).

Summary of the Paradigms

How the masculinity paradigms discussed above overlap or deviate from each other has gone unexplained. Analyses of how these theoretical concepts overlap and diverge could bring greater coherence to the psychology of men. One of the future challenges is to create more expansive operational definitions for these concepts. For example, it is important to understand how the macrosocietal concept of hegemonic masculinity relates to the personal aspects of learning masculinity ideology and experiencing GRC and stress. Men's GRCs need to be better conceptualized from a larger social structural and feminist perspective by giving more attention to how power, societal patriarchy, and institutional sexism operate in men's lives (Enns, 2008).

The paradigms are also limited in explaining how diversity variables affect men's lives. A coherent, multicultural approach to men's diversity does not exist in the psychology of men. Very little has been written on how race, class, ethnicity, nationality, age, religion, and sexual orientation affect male socialization. In a previous paper (O'Neil, 2008), I indicated that: "The assumption that a single masculinity exists (i.e., white, middle-class, heterosexual, American) is erroneous, short sighted, and biased. Race, class, age, ethnicity, sexual orientation, religious orientation, nationality, and other variables are assumed to affect men's experience of GRC. Exactly how these diversity variables affects men is one of the most crucial issues to be assessed in the psychology of men and counseling psychology" (pp. 381–382). Thompson, Pleck, and Ferrara (1992) amplified this point by indicating that "we are largely unfamiliar with how age, generation,

sexual orientation, class, race, and ethnicity differentially structure the form and content of men's lives and the standards of masculinity to which they adhere" (p. 602).

Additionally, the role of biology, the politically incorrect factor in gender studies for so long, needs much more attention from theoreticians if we are to discern the complex dynamics of nature and nurture in men's lives. Finally, more theorizing is needed on men's lives contextually. Both developmental and social psychologists indicate that the study of gender roles needs to be contextualized (Eckes & Trautner, 2000; Smiler, 2004; Trautner & Eckes, 2000). Contextualism is defined by how human experience is shaped by many factors operating in concert with each other (Lerner, 1992). A contextual analysis implies studying people in real-life situations and the dynamic interaction between individuals and the multiple contexts in which they live. Knowledge is obtained by assessing the interplay between the person and the environment. Contextualism is concerned with how ecological factors dynamically operate to shape experience, and how biological, cultural, psychological, interpersonal, spiritual, political, and social context affect behavior. Therefore, theorizing about the psychology of men needs to become more contextual because gender roles are activated by many personal, societal, racial, cultural, political, religious, and situational contingencies (Deaux & Majors, 1987). Without contextual knowledge, the psychology of men cannot move past its limited theoretical base.

Research In The Psychology of Men: What do We Know Empirically?

Research programs in the psychology of men parallel the emerging paradigms and psychometric scales that assess masculinity ideologies and conflicts. Research programs are now identified with the following perspectives: masculinity ideology, GRC and stress, hypermasculinity, and reference group dependence identity. Four research questions are discussed in this section of the chapter: Does evidence exist that masculinity ideology relates to men's psychological and interpersonal problems? Does evidence exist that GRC and stress relate to men's psychological and interpersonal problems? Does evidence exist that hypermasculinity and reference group identity dependence relate to masculinity conflicts? Does evidence exist that GRC and masculinity ideology relate to adolescent's boys' problems?

To answer these questions, a literature review was completed of published studies that assessed whether masculinity constructs and GRCs have negative psychological consequences for men and boys. Empirical studies that used the following ten measures were reviewed: the MRNS (Thompson & Pleck, 1986), MRNI (Levant et al., 1992), CMNI (Mahalik et al., 2003b), MGRSS (Eisler & Skidmore, 1987), GRCS (O'Neil, 2008; O'Neil et al., 1986), GRC Scale for Adolescents (GRCS-A; Blazina, Pisecco, & O'Neil, 2005), AMIRS (Chu et al., 2005), HMI (Mosher & Sirkin, 1984), ADMI (Burk et al., 2004), and RGIDS (Wade & Gelso, 1998).

The studies were analyzed to determine whether men's psychological and interpersonal problems have been statistically correlated with each scale. The goal of this literature search was to develop an overall summary of the significant empirical relationships between masculinity scales and men's and boy's problems. Significant statistical relationships were defined as any correlational tests at less than the .05 level between any scale (or any of its subscales) and a psychological and interpersonal variable. Given the complexity of reporting measures' subscales, only overall relationships between each scale and dependent measures are reported.

Table 14.1 summarizes the studies reviewed for ten published masculinity scales. The author and the name of the scale are given first, followed by the names of the subscales and number of studies reviewed. For each scale, the dependent variables that significantly correlate with men's psychological and interpersonal processes are enumerated. Two hundred forty-nine studies were reviewed. References to the individual studies summarized in Table 14.1 are available from the author upon request.

The summary of the masculinity ideology scales (MRNS, CMNI, and MRNI) indicate that attitudes about masculinity have been statistically correlated with a wide variety of psychological and interpersonal problems in 26 studies. Over 58 dependent variables related to men's problems have been significantly correlated with masculinity ideology, norms, and conformity.

A similar pattern is evident with the GRCS and MGRSS studies. The ten MGRSS studies correlated with 19 dependent variables, and the 200 GRCS studies correlated with 87 separate indices of men's personal and interpersonal problems. A more complete summary of the GRCS studies over the last 25 years can be found in O'Neil (2008b).

The four studies using hypermasculinity scales (HMI and ADMI) suggest that extremes in masculinity ideology are significantly correlated with 25 separate variables that represent even more dangerous and hostile interpersonal behaviors of men. Furthermore, three studies using the RGIDS found relationships between reference group status and eight male problems. Finally, for adolescent boys, the three studies using the GRCS-A and AMIRS found indications that masculinity problems and GRC related to 17 negative outcomes.

Summary of Masculinity Ideology, Gender Role Conflict and Stress, and Other Masculinity Constructs

The results in Table 14.1 represent the first summary of empirical research that correlates studies measuring masculinity ideology, masculine gender role stress, and GRC with men's psychological and interpersonal problems. The results of the 249 studies in Table 14.1 provide a rather convincing case that masculinity ideology, GRC and stress, and other masculinity measures have significant relationships to men's and boy's psychological and interpersonal problems. Overall, the results across many studies point to masculinity ideology and GRCs relating to negative psychological attitudes toward women and gays, dangerous risk-taking with sex and health issues, substance use and abuse, psychological stress and strain, negative attitudes toward help-seeking, delinquent behavior, low self-esteem, hostility and aggression, higher blood pressure levels, depression, anxiety, marital and family problems, and violent attitudes toward women. The hazards of being male appear to empirically related to men's attitudes about their masculinity and gender roles.

The results of this analysis shed light on male problem areas documented by the epidemiological surveys discussed earlier in the chapter. The surveys and other statistical data indicated that men's and boy's problems included substance abuse, depression, anxiety, learning problems, threats, bullying, and violence. In answering the earlier question on whether men's problems are related to socialized gender roles, the answer based on the correlational data, is an absolute yes.

There are some limitations to these findings. All of the results reported were statistically significant ($p < .05$), but it is unclear how much of the variance in men's problems relates to masculinity ideology and GRC and stress. Future meta-analyses could assess the exact effect sizes for these studies. Furthermore, these studies are simple correlational studies and do not account for the effects

Table 14.1. Men's Psychological and Interpersonal Problem Areas That Significantly Correlate With Ten Major Masculinity Measures

---

1. Thompson and Pleck's Male Role Norm Scale (MRNS)

Subscales: Status Norm; Toughness Norm; Antifemininity Norm
Number of Studies: 9

Men's Problems Significantly Correlated with the MRNS:

Negative Attitudes Lesbians; Hostile Sexism; Negative Attitude Toward Women; Opposition to the ERA; Preference for Virgin Wife; Ethnic Belonging; Suspension from School; Drinking and Use of Drugs; Being Picked Up by Police; Being Sexually Active; Coercive Sex; Increased Sexual Risk; Loneliness; Separation-Individuation Problems; Restricted Affectionate Behavior Between Men; Fear of Appearing Feminine; Antigay Attitudes; Overt Hostility and Aggression; Adversarial Sexual Beliefs; Rape Myths; Psychological Violence.

---

2. Mahalik's Conformity to Male Role Inventory (CMNI)

Subscales: Winning; Emotional Control; Risk Taking; Violence; Power over Women; Dominance; Playboy; Self-Reliance; Primacy of Work; Disdain for Homosexuals; Pursuit of Status; Total Conformity.
Number of Studies: 13

Men's Problems Significantly Correlated with the CMNI:

Positive Relations with Others; Unhealthy Alcohol Use; Neglecting Preventive Skin Care; Health Screenings; Not Seeking Help with Emotional Difficulties; Not Going to Health Care Appointments; Getting Into Physical Fights; Difficulty Managing Anger; Taking Risks; Risky Behavior with Automobiles and Sexual Practices; Substance Use; Marijuana Use; Binge Drinking; Responses to Depression; Health Risks; Few Health Promotion Behaviors; Sexism; Health-Promotion Behaviors; Internalized Homophobia; Masculine Body Ideal Distress; Poor Sexual Functioning; Racial Identity: Pre-encounter Phase; Lower Self-esteem; Psychological Distress; Attitudes About Help-seeking; Shocks Given During Competition.

---

3. Levant's Male Role Norms Inventory (MRNI)

Subscales: Avoidance of Femininity; Fear and Hatred of Homosexuals; Self-Reliance; Aggression; Achievement/Status; Non Relational Attitudes Toward Sex; Restrictive Emotionality.
Number of Studies: 4

Men's Problems Significantly Correlated with the MRNI:
Alexithymia; Negative Attitudes About Racial Identity and Women's Equality; Attitudes Toward Condoning Sexual Harassment of Women; Racial Group Marginalization; Ethnocentrism; Negative Attitudes Toward Help-seeking.

---

4. Eisler's Masculine Gender Role Stress Scale (MGRSS)

Subscales: Physical Inadequacy; Emotional Inexpressiveness; Subordination to Women; Intellectual Inferiority; Performance Failure.
Number of Studies: 10

Men's Problems Significantly Correlated with the MGRSS:
Increases in Systolic Blood Pressure; Impaired Cognitive Performance; Higher State Anger; Negative Intent Attributions; Verbal Aggression; Greater Negative Intent; Greater Irritation, Anger, Jealousy, and Aggression; Anger; Increases in Anxiety; Poorer Health Habits; Greater Systolic Blood Pressure; Lower Work Satisfaction; Negative Attributions and Negative Affect; Verbal Aggression; Alexithymia; Social Support; Overt Hostility and Aggression; Controlling Behaviors; Fearful Attachment.

---

5. O'Neil's Gender Role Conflict Scale (GRCS)

Subscales: Success, Power and Competition; Restrictive Emotionality; Restrictive Affectionate Behavior Between Men; Conflict Between Work and Family Relations.
Number of Studies: 203

(*Continued*)

Table 14.1. Continued

Men's Problems Significantly Correlated with the GRCS:

Self-esteem; Anxiety; Depression; Stress; Shame; Help Seeking Attitudes; Alexithymia; Alcohol and Substance Use and Abuse; Hopelessness; Coping; Psychological Strain; Traditional Gender Role Attitudes; Machismo; Psychological Well-Being; Homonegativity; Self-Silencing; Body Image; Family Problems; Family Stress; Conduct Problems; Problems with Anger; Physical Strain; Health Risk Taking; Problem Solving Attitudes; Anger; Suicide; Physical Health Problems; Drive for Muscularity; Interpersonal Problems and Competence; Self-Disclosure; Shyness; Attachment; Intimacy; Friendship; Marital Satisfaction; Family Enmeshment/Disengagement; Family Conflict/Avoidance; Family Cohesion; Fathering Self Efficacy; Parenting Satisfaction; Women's Psychological Health; Women's Depression and Anxiety; Women's Marital Happiness and Adjustment; Women's Negative Affect; Couple's Marital Adjustment and Depressive Symptoms; Gender Role Stereotyping; Stereotypic Beliefs About Man's Emotions; Attitudes Toward Women; Sex Role Egalitarianism; Racial Bias; Attitudes Toward African Americans; Anti-Gay Attitudes and Beliefs; Homophobia; Abusive Attitudes and Behaviors; Hostile Sexism; Hostility Toward Women; Attitudes Toward Sexual Harassment; Rape Myth Attitudes; Dating Violence; Sexual Aggression and Coercion; Men's Entitlement; Victim Blaming; Violence Against Women and Other Men.

6. Mosher and Sirkin's Hypermasculinity Inventory (HMI)

Subscales: Violence; Danger; and Calloused Sex
Number of Studies: 1

Men's Problems Significantly Correlated with the HMI:
Self-Reported Drug Use; Aggressive Behavior; Dangerous Driving Following Alcohol Consumptions; Delinquent Behaviors During High School Years.

7. Burk, Burkhart and Sikorksi's Auburn Differential Masculinity Inventory (ADMI)

Subscales: Hypermasculinity; Sexual Identity; Dominance and Aggression; Conservative Masculinity; Devaluation of Emotion.
Number of Studies: 3

Men's Problems Significantly Correlated with the ADMI:
Hostility Toward Women; Antisocial Practices; Negative Self-esteem; Sensation Seeking; Anxiety; Anger; Contempt; Acceptance of Interpersonal Violence; Beliefs that Women are Manipulators; Hedonism; Not Loving; Social Acceptance; Dominance; Sexual Competence; Consensual Sexual Experiences; Ignoring Partner's Protests to Obtain Sex; Use of Low Physical Force to Obtain Sex; Desired Orgasms Per Week; Number of Sexual Partners; Likelihood to Use Force to Obtain Sex; Likelihood to Commit Rape; Negative Sexual Satisfaction.

8. Wade and Gelso's Reference Group Identity Dependence Scale (RGIDS)

Subscales: Reference Group Nondependent; No Reference Group; Reference Group Dependent
Number of Studies: 3

Men's Problems Significantly Correlated with the RGIDS:
Identity Diffusion; Social Anxiety; Low Self-Esteem; Anxiety; Depression; Negative Attitudes About Racial Diversity and Women's Equality; Positive Attitudes Toward Sexual Harassment; Health Related Behaviors; and Personal Wellness.

9. Chu, Porche, and Tolman's Adolescent Masculinity Ideology Relationships Scale (AMIRS)

Single Scale: Adolescent Masculinity Ideology in Relationships
Number of Studies: 1

Boy's Problems Significantly Correlated with the AMIRS:
Restrictive Emotionality; Inhibited Affection; Exaggerated Self-Reliance; Negative Attitudes Toward Women; Low Self-esteem; Acting Out; GRC; Need for Achievement and Success; Restrictive Affectionate Behavior Between Men; Status and Anti-femininity Norms; Engaging in Sexual Relations.

10. Blazina, Pisecco, and O'Neil's GRC Scale for Adolescents (GRCS-A)

Subscales: Restricted Affection Between Men; Restrictive Emotionality; Conflict Between Work, School, and Family; Need for Success and Achievement.
Number of Studies: 2

Boy's Problems Significantly Correlated with the GRCS-A:
Emotional, Family, and Anger Management Problems; Conduct Problems; Family Stress; Emotional and Psychological Stress; Masculinity Ideology; Anti-femininity Norms; Sexual Relations.

of moderator or mediator variables (Heppner, 1995; O'Neil, 2008b). Future studies will need to employ more sophisticated methodologies to assess how third variables increase, decrease, or mediate relationships between gender role issues and men's psychological and interpersonal problems. Finally, the analyses of the studies in Table 14.1 do not address whether there are differences between men of different races, classes, ages, ethnicities, religions, nationalities, or sexual orientations. Future analyses should assess these potential differences related to men's diversity.

Empirical Research on Men As Clients and the Psychotherapeutic Process

Little research has been completed on male clients and the psychotherapeutic process (Good & Sherrod, 2001). Only recently have psychologists begun to explore how to do therapy with men. The lack of clinical research may be related to the discipline's difficulty in formulating significant questions about men's therapy. New therapeutic concepts about men may need to be developed, and traditional therapeutic approaches may need to be examined or reconsidered. Overall, the theoretical concepts discussed earlier (masculinity ideology, gender role stress, GRC, etc.) have not been assessed in a therapeutic context. The clinical research that does exist is primarily on client's GRC (O'Neil, 2008b). Seven studies have assessed whether client's GRC relates to men's psychological problems and processes (Coonerty-Femiano, Katzman, Femiano, Gemar, & Toner, 2001; Cusack, Deane, Wilson, & Ciarrochi, 2006; Good, Robertson, Fitzgerald, Stevens, & Bartels, 1996; Hayes & Mahalik, 2000; Mertens, 2000; Noyes, 2004; Van Delft, 1998). Two studies found that male counseling center clients' GRC significantly relates to psychological distress, hostility, compulsiveness, social discomfort, paranoia, psychoticism, obsessive-compulsivity, and interpersonal sensitivity (Good et al., 1996; Hayes & Mahalik, 2000). Comparisons of clients' and nonclients' GRC has been made. Four studies have found that clients experience more RE and RABBM than do nonclients (Burke, 2000; Coonerty-Femiano et al., 2001; Mertens, 2000; Van Delft, 1998). Furthermore, clients' RE has been found to be inversely related to perception of treatment helpfulness (Cusack et al., 2006), and clients who experienced sexual abuse reported significantly greater RE and CBWFR than did nonabused clients (Thomson, 1995).

Studies on nonclient, male students also have clinical relevance in understanding men in therapy. Students' GRC have been associated with psychological defenses, treatment fearfulness, perceptions of counselors, and expectations about counseling (Englar-Carlson, 2001; Englar-Carlson, & Vandiver, 2001; Schaub & Williams, 2007; Wisch, Mahalik, Hayes, & Nutt, 1995). One study found that men's psychological defenses and GRC were related (Mahalik, Cournoyer, DeFranc, Cherry, & Napolitano, 1998). Additionally, SPC, RE, and RABBM were significantly related to immature and neurotic defenses (projection, denial, and isolation), and SPC and RE predicted defenses that are turned against others. Gender role conflict has also significantly predicted treatment fearfulness (Englar-Carlson & Vandiver, 2001), and men with higher GRC have rated counselors as significantly less expert and trustworthy (Wisch et al., 1995). Furthermore, men who reported RE, RABBM, and SPC had significantly higher expectations of the counselor as an expert and lower self-expectations for taking responsibility in counseling (Schaub & Williams, 2007).

Little research has been completed on how gender roles affect men's career attitudes and behaviors. This is puzzling, given that men's work has been defined as primary to male identity and self-worth. Four studies have assessed how GRC relates to men's career attitudes and needs (Dodson & Borders, 2006; Jome & Tokar, 1997; Rochlen, Blazina, & Rajhunathan, 2002; Rochlen & O'Brien, 2002). In two studies, men with higher GRC reported greater career counseling stigma, decreased willingness to engage in career counseling, and greater needs for self-clarity, career information, and assistance with career indecisiveness (Rochlen & O'Brien, 2002; Rochlen et al., 2002). Additionally, GRC appears to be more evident with career traditional men and also to predict career choice traditionality (Jome & Tokar, 1997; Tokar & Jome, 1998).

Therapists' biases against men have been documented (Robertson & Fitzgerald, 1990) but not widely studied. Therapists' GRC and their negative judgments of male clients have been assessed in two studies (Hayes, 1985; Wisch & Mahalik, 1999). Therapists with high RABBM reported significantly less liking of male clients, less empathy with nontraditional male clients, and more maladjustment for nontraditional male clients (Hayes, 1985). Therapists reporting SPC and RABBM had significantly less liking for, empathy with, and comfort with male clients and were less willing to see clients who were homosexuals, angry, but not sad (Wisch & Mahalik, 1999). Furthermore, therapists with significantly less RABBM were more comfortable seeing a homosexual client and reported better prognosis for him in therapy. In both of these studies, RABBM related to therapists' biases about clients who were nontraditional or homosexual. These studies suggest that counselors may need additional training on men's issues (Wester & Vogel, 2002) to examine their biases about men who deviate from or conform to masculinity ideology.

Psychoeducational interventions have tested whether men's masculine attitudes and conflicts can be changed. Empirically tested programs indicate that men can change their GRC and dysfunctional attitudes about gender roles (Davis & Liddell, 2002; Kearney, King, & Rochlen, 2004; Schwartz & Waldo, 2003; Schwartz, Waldo, & Higgins, 2004). These psychoeducational interventions have changed men's GRC related to dating violence (Schwartz, Magee, Griffin, & Dupius, 2004), partner abuse (Schwartz & Waldo, 2003), rape prevention (Davis & Liddell, 2002), and sexual harassment (Kearney et al., 2004). Most of these programs assessed short-term change and used attitudinal measures. Whether these treatments have long-term impact on men's behaviors is still unclear.

Summary of Empirical Research on Men and Therapy

The review of the clinical literature supports Cochran's (2005) conclusion: "The psychology of men as distinct practice and research area has yet to generate controlled studies demonstrating differential effectiveness of specific treatments with men" (p. 650). Research on men in therapy is in the early stages of development. Few researchers have specified focused clinical questions that could be pursued through research. How masculinity ideology and GRC relate to the therapeutic processes is just now emerging as a critical area of research. Some evidence exists that clients report GRC with greater frequency than nonclients. Only a few studies have assessed whether clients' problems are specifically related to masculinity or GRCs. There are no counseling studies on clients from varied racial, ethnic, cultural backgrounds, or on those who have different sexual orientations. The finding that therapists who have GRC have clinical biases may suggest that counseling psychology may need to expand its training agenda to the psychology of men (O'Neil, 2008b; Wester & Vogel, 2002). Assessment of both clients' and therapists' GRC should be a fertile area for future clinical research. Furthermore, there are very few documented ways to treat men's problems such as depression, restrictive emotionality, and obsession with power and control. Case studies of men in therapy (Blazina, 2004; Englar-Carlson & Stevens, 2006; Mahalik, 1999a; O'Neil, 2006) currently provide the best evidence of effective therapy approaches and processes. Psychoeducational interventions have documented that men's GRC can be altered, but the mechanism that cause the change have not been studied.

Therapeutic Assessment in the Psychology of Men: The Current Status

Over the last decade, more information has been published on assessing men in therapy. In this section, assessment, as it relates to traditional diagnostic categories is discussed and how multiculturalism relates to therapeutic appraisal is reviewed. The published diagnostic schemas, typologies, and problems areas are summarized.

Dilemmas, Bias, and Evidence-based Assessment

For many years, the literature on men's therapy was exclusively focused on describing male problems or what is wrong with men. Recently, how these problems relate to therapeutic assessment has received more attention from various perspectives. Glicken (2005) indicates that "diagnosing male problems seem particularly fraught with ambiguity, worker bias, and politically correct notions of men as dysfunctional without question" (p. 67). A critical question is to determine how accurately men's psychological problems are captured by conventional diagnostic criteria (Rochlen, 2005). For example, questions have been raised whether men's depression can be understood using the *Diagnostic and Statistical Manual* (DSM-IV) criteria (Addis, 2008). Authors have speculated that men may present "masked depression" because of how defenses may operate to keep symptoms covert (Addis, 2008; Cochran & Rabinowitz, 2000; Lynch & Kilmartin, 1999; Magovcevic & Addis, 2008; Pollack, 1998b; Real, 1997). Cochran and Rabinowitz (2003) propose that masked depression be assessed as male anger, alcohol and substance abuse, somatic complaints, interpersonal conflicts, and a host of other problems.

Therapists' bias toward men is another critical assessment area for therapists. Stereotyping and having biases about men are probably as frequent as they were with women in the 1970s (Brodsky & Holroyd, 1975) and therefore need to be monitored by therapists (Gilbert & Scher, 1999; Glicken, 2005). Gilbert and Scher (1999) indicate that therapists' biases against men can occur in the following six ways: encouraging clients' independence and discouraging emotions and feelings in relationships; failing to recognize the costs of equating personal power with sexual power over women; alienating men from their children by associating caring with weakness; encouraging and modeling autonomy, success, and competition; leaving unchallenged the exaggerated importance of male sexual power in terms of personal meaning; and reinforcing homophobia and heterosexism. No effective assessment can exist if therapists hold conscious or unconscious biases about men. More research is needed to document whether and specifically which biases exist against men in order to determine how these may affect the therapeutic process.

Masculine-sensitive, evidence-based assessment has been recommended by Cochran (2005). Using a prevailing practice paradigm (Sackett, Straus, Richardson, Rosenberg, & Hayne, 2000), Cochran enumerates three kinds of information critical to assessing men including: research-based evidence pertaining to diagnosis and treatment, recommendations based on clinical expertise, and patient values or preferences. This approach combines processes of evidence-based practice with gender-sensitive expertise emerging in the psychology of men. Cochran (2005) calls for greater research on evidence-based treatment of men, particularly using masculine GRC and stress constructs.

Assessment and Multiculturalism

No adequate assessment can also be completed without a multicultural framework that assesses diversity variables and the role of oppression in men's lives (O'Neil, 2008b; Wester, 2008a). All men and women are systemically oppressed by patriarchal values that interact with all forms of oppression. Making this oppression visible by explaining how people suffer from discrimination is one of the primary goals of feminists and other activists. As mentioned earlier, masculinity and gender roles are multidimensional constructs affected by many political, racial, ethnic, age, class, religious, and sexual orientation variables. The psychology of men has recognized the importance of honoring the

diversity of men who come to therapy (Liu, 2005; Wester, 2008a,b). Knowledge of how men's gender roles vary by race, ethnicity, nationality, religion, and sexual orientation is evolving slowly in the psychology of men. The assumption that a single masculinity exists is the ultimate stereotypic bias and an illusion of the status quo. Race, class, age, ethnicity, sexual orientation, religious orientation, nationality, and other variables affect every man's personal experience in life and are critically important during the therapy process. Exactly how these diversity variables affect men is one of the most crucial issues in the psychology of men and counseling psychology.

Liu (2005) recommends a multicultural perspective, so that therapists could recognize their biases and negative expectancies of men from diverse backgrounds. The guidelines on multicultural education have been accepted by psychology (APA, 2003) but they have not been integrated with our current knowledge about men. The development of the multicultural competencies with men from diverse backgrounds could become an important diversity agenda for counseling psychology. Contributions to diversity by counseling psychology have significantly expanded American psychology's overall view of multiculturalism. Therefore, counseling psychology could take the next step in integrating diversity and multiculturalism with the psychology of gender roles. This integration would give prominence to the complexity of how male and female gender roles interact with racial, ethnic, class, age, religious, and sexual orientation variables. The psychology of men cannot be a credible force in psychology until there is a greater commitment to understanding diversity, multiculturalism, and oppression in men's lives.

Diagnostic Schemas, Typologies, and Problem Areas

Four diagnostic schemas to assess men have been previously published (O'Neil, 1990, 2006, 2008b; O'Neil & Lujan 2010; Rabinowitz & Cochran, 2002). These diagnostic schemas have been developed to assess men and help therapists better conceptualize clinical interventions. My own diagnostic schema (O'Neil, 2008b) has seven assessment domains including therapist's self-assessment; diversity and oppression; men's defenses; men's emotionality and restrictive emotionality; men's distorted schemas about masculinity ideology; men's patterns of GRC and gender role devaluations, restrictions, and violations; and men's needs for information, psychoeducation, and preventive programs. This diagnostic schema emanates from the GRC research program, but only limited data exist on its validity or utility. In the future, this diagnostic schema needs to be empirically validated using evidence-based research.

The second assessment paradigm focuses on appraising fathers or father–son, father–daughter relationships in the context of GRC (O'Neil & Lujan, 2010. Overt and covert contexts to assess men's fathering problems are discussed in the contexts of masculinity ideology, unfinished business with one's own father, and the *father wound*. The same diagnostic areas found in O'Neil (2008b) are applied to assess men's fathering or past father wounds. This new paradigm suggests that fathering can be a critical assessment area for therapists helping men with their GRC.

Rabinowitz and Cochran (2002) outline a heuristic, theoretically derived model for assessing men's problems that integrates psychodynamic perspectives of men with masculine GRC research. Four intersecting dimensions of male psychological conflict are outlined including: assessing how male clients' relational experiences relate to the managing of their dependency strivings and needs in relationships; assessing ways that clients learn to manage their feelings of sadness, grief, and loss; assessing the extent to which clients develop a healthy set of masculine behavior and values; and assessing the balance between doing and being. The model has four interacting and overlapping dimensions of male psychological experience including the assessment of men's psychological history, formative experiences, cultural upbringing, and current functioning. The dimensions of this assessment model provide a very useful and comprehensive framework to assess men in therapy.

Other typologies for assessing men in therapy are emerging in the psychology of men. Pollack proposes the Major Depressive Disorder-Male Type and Disorder of the Self: Male Type as diagnostic categories (Pollack, 1998b, 2001). Depressive Disorder-Male Type has 12 symptoms that include interpersonal withdrawal, over involvement in work, denial of pain, autonomy, denial of emotions, substance abuse, changes in sexual interests, mood problems, and weight or sleep disorders to just name a few. The Disorder of the Self: Male Type includes the following symptoms: affective–intellectual splits, anger, rage, or repressive personality, loss of vulnerability, sexualized self-object yearnings, shame-sensitive or shame phobic, blunting

of empathic recognition, alexithymia, unconscious self-criticism, perfectionism, workaholism, inability to grieve or mourn, and vulnerability to substance abuse and depression. Full explanations for these diagnostic symptoms are found elsewhere (Pollack, 1995, 1998b) and represent how new diagnostic categories are changing how men's problems are understood.

Other clinical researchers have developed other typologies that relate to assessing men. Seven masculine scripts have been defined and reflect potential assessment areas. These include men as strong and silent, tough guy, give 'em hell, playboy, homophobic, winner, and independent (Mahalik, Good, & Englar Carlson, 2003a). Furthermore, critical male problem areas have been defined that include depression, anxiety, stress, sexual dysfunction, substance abuse, toughness, violence, and rape (Good & Sherrod (2001). In a similar way, Gilbert and Scher (1999) describe critical male problems as discrepancy strain, male emotional restrictiveness, male shame, dysfunction strain, male prerogative, and violence against women. Additionally, recommendations have been made to assess men's distorted cognitive schemas about masculinity (O'Neil & Nadeau, 1999; Mahalik, 1999a, 2001a). Cognitive schemas about masculinity represent how men think about gender roles in the context of masculinity ideology, norms, and conformity (Levant et al., 1992; Mahalik et al., 2003b; Mooney, 1998; Pleck, 1995; Thompson et al., 1992). Distorted cognitive schemas are exaggerated thoughts and feelings about masculinity ideology in a man's life (O'Neil & Nadeau, 1999). Distorted cognitive schemas occur when men experience pressure, fear, or anxiety about meeting (or failing to meet) stereotypic notions of masculinity. Mahalik (1999) recommends that cognitive distortions be assessed in the following areas: success, power, emotional control, fearlessness, self-reliance, primacy of work, playboy, and disdain of homosexuals.

The status of assessing men in therapy appears to be progressing, but much is still unknown. There are the unanswered questions about whether stereotypes and bias against men actually exist in therapy. Also, evidence-based, gender-sensitive assessment is endorsed by the experts, as is incorporating a multicultural framework into any therapy with men. Numerous assessment paradigms exist, but none has been tested for utility and effectiveness. The assessment of men in therapy could be strengthened with further case studies and both qualitative and quantitative research.

Therapy Processes and Therapeutic Interventions for Men
Major Textbooks and Conceptualization of Men's Therapy

Seven publications have contributed significantly to our knowledge about therapy with men and boys (Brooks, 1998; Brooks & Good, 2001a; Englar-Carlson & Stevens, 2006; Horne & Kiselica, 1999; Glicken, 2005; Pollack & Levant, 1998, Rabinowitz & Cochran, 2002). A full review of these publications is not possible, but each provides valuable information on the critical issues with men's therapy. Most notably is *The New Handbook of Psychotherapy and Counseling with Men* (Brooks & Good, 2001a). This two-volume resource includes 39 chapters that represent a comprehensive guide to men's problems and treatment approaches. Furthermore, Pollack and Levant's (1998) edited book *The New Psychotherapy with Men* is also a valuable collection of chapters that distill the dilemmas and new possibilities with men's therapy. Every chapter develops new ideas about men's therapy that have clinical applications. There are chapters on psychoanalytic and cognitive behavior therapy, depression, shame, and approaches to African American, gay, and bisexual men. *A New Psychotherapy for Traditional Men* (Brooks, 1998) provides an excellent orientation to why men need therapy, and how to effectively implement interventions that work. Brooks presents seven basic principles of psychotherapy with traditional men that have therapeutic depth and practical approaches. Englar-Carlson and Stevens (2006) have assembled the first therapy casebook on men. The 14 case studies provide an excellent analyses of how actual therapy has been conducted by experienced therapists. Horne and Kiselica's (1999) text on counseling adolescent boys describes the developmental dilemmas of male youth, and how adaptive and maladaptive male development is shaped by complex interaction of biological, cultural, and economic forces. This book has a wealth of information on counseling boys in a variety of settings. The clinical knowledge in these seven texts has significantly expanded our understanding about doing therapy with men and boys, but more elaboration may be needed for evidence-based treatments to be designed and tested.

Many other authors have published important manuscripts that have focused on specific topics about men's therapy. Therapeutic topics related to men's therapy have focused on the fragile masculine self (Blazina, 2001), men's cognitive distortions (Mahalik, 1999a; 2001a), masculinity scripts (Mahalik, Good, & Englar-Carlson, 2003a), men's depression (Cochran & Rabinowitz, 2003), clinical practice with men (Rochlen, 2005), men's emotional behavior (Wong & Rochlen, 2005), men's interpersonal psychotherapy (Mahalik, 1999b, 2001b), evidence-based assessment of men (Cochran, 2005), and training for counselors of men (Wester & Vogel, 2002). Taken collectively, these publications have made men's therapy credible in psychology, but convincing men to seek help remains a critical challenge.

Why Don't Men Use Therapy Services? Negative Attitudes Toward Help-seeking

One of the most critical mental health problems in the United States is men's underutilization of therapy services. How to convince men to actually show up for therapy may be as difficult as helping them. The research indicates that men have problems but prefer to solve them on their own. Men's underutilization of mental health services is one of the most consistent themes in the help-seeking literature (Addis & Mahalik, 2003; Blazina & Watkins, 1996; Good, Dell, & Mintz, 1989; Mahalik, Good, & Englar-Carlson, 2003). Estimates on who uses therapy vary, but Vessey and Howard (1993) indicate that only about one-third of clients are men. Robertson (2001) indicates that the ratio of male and female clients in North America is "about one to two, with one male visit for every two or more female visits" (pp. 147–148). Clinical researchers indicate that this underutilization is caused by the incongruence of therapy processes with the rigid norms of masculinity (Brooks, 1998; Robertson & Fitzgerald, 1992). Campbell (1996) enumerates the masculinity issues that contribute to underutilization of therapy services, including men's achievement and goal orientation, restricted emotions, independence, self-reliance, instrumentality, and worries about getting close to others, particularly other men. Rochlen (2005) indicates that more information is needed on how clinicians can address the critical problem of incongruence between restrictive norms and the psychotherapeutic process.

Negative attitudes toward help-seeking have been found to be a central reason why men underutilize therapy services (Addis & Mahalik, 2003). Research indicates that men's negative attitudes toward help-seeking relates to GRC. O'Neil (2008) reported 17 studies indicating that men's GRC significantly relates to negative attitudes toward seeking psychological help. Knowledge about the significant relationship between attitudes toward help-seeking and GRC are critical for therapists since negative attitudes have been empirically documented across race, age, sexual orientation, and nationality groups. Gender role conflict's significant relationship with negative help-seeking attitudes makes conceptual sense based on the rigid standards of masculinity ideology that boys and men learn. For many men, expressing feelings and vulnerabilities and giving up some power and control may be violations of their masculinity ideology that threaten their male identity. Therapists can use the help-seeking research to facilitate men's adjustment in therapy and to be more vigilant to premature terminations.

Based on the past help-seeking research, Rochlen and Hoyer (2005) discussed how to effectively publicize services for men using a social marketing perspective. They suggest that descriptions of mental health services for men should use less psychologically loaded words and descriptions. Research does support using promotional information that is less threatening or that sounds less clinical. Three studies have assessed men's GRC and men's preferences for help using varied counseling brochures (Blazina & Marks, 2001; Robertson & Fitzgerald, 1992; Rochlen, McKelley, & Pituch, 2006). The results of these studies indicate that men reporting high GRC were significantly more likely to prefer a non-traditional counseling brochure (i.e., describing workshops or classes) over a direct service counseling brochure, and that power issues are related to seeking help. Future marketing brochures should be tested that define counseling as empowering and a sign of masculine strength and courage.

In summary, there is considerable evidence that GRC significantly relates to men's negative attitudes about seeking help. Whether these results explain the critical reasons why men do not seek help is still unclear. What is also unknown from these studies are the specific fears and reservations men have when talking about their problems. Do men fear loss of control and power by entering therapy? Does the distorted notion that "real men solve problem on their own" keep them away? Does resistance to seeking help relate to homophobia and fears about being "feminized" through therapy? Men's resistance to seeking help is now being researched with the *Barriers to Help-Seeking Measure* (Mansfield, Addis, & Courtenay, 2005). Through this research and more positive marketing of men's services, the stigma that men associate with seeking help can decrease.

Treatment Models in Men's Therapy

As with assessment, the methods and models of therapy with men are few, and the various treatment recommendations lack coherence and clarity. Two comprehensive approaches have been defined that provide concrete direction for men's therapy (Brooks, 1998; Rabinowitz & Cochran, 2002). Rabinowitz and Cochran's (2002) *Deepening Psychotherapy with Men* is the most comprehensive treatment paradigm currently in the psychology of men. This book provides detailed therapeutic methods based on theory and research that can guide effective therapy with men. They integrate psychoanalytic and gender role strain formulations that actually translate to into concrete interventions with men. They recommend "deepening psychotherapy," defined as uncovering and elucidating masculine-specific conflicts experienced on an emotional level. They conceptualize four psychological dynamics that are part of deepening men's psychotherapy, including assessment of men's psychodynamic, developmental, and GRC/stress issues; recognition of male dependence, prohibition related to emotions, grief, sadness, and loss; focus on masculine-specific self-structure and gender role identity; and recognition that men's action orientation (doing) can conflict with discomfort with being. Moreover, they provide 43 different interventions for treating men in therapy that emanate from five different theoretical frameworks. This paradigm is the most developed approach in the literature for doing therapy with men.

Another therapeutic contribution is the *New Psychotherapy with Traditional Men* (Brooks, 1998). This text is practical, coherent, and detailed. The core of Brooks' psychotherapeutic approach comprises seven core elements that guide therapy with men. These core elements include countering resistance, valuing traditional men, assessing men's problems in the context of gender awareness, accommodating the "good ol' boy" style, evoking men's emotional pain, recognizing masculine heritage, and challenging men to change. Within these core areas are nine other critical approaches for doing therapy with men : selling therapy; avoiding pitfalls; envisioning a sequence of change; digging, prodding, and provoking; holding and focusing; showing and modeling; using experiential exercises; inciting and escalating tensions; and using therapeutic silence. Brook's therapeutic concepts provide therapists with a very useful approach when doing therapy with men.

In addition to these two major contributions, 25 other publications provide overall approaches for doing therapy with men. Table 14.2 enumerates over 80 therapeutic approaches and their publication citations. This table allows researchers and practitioners to locate specific therapeutic approaches that interest them. On the left side of Table 14.2 are the specific therapeutic approaches categorized in the following six categories: gender-aware, gender-sensitive approaches; gender-aware, gender-sensitive, contextual problem assessment; multicultural consciousness and assessment; expectancies and assumptions of therapists; therapeutic processes with men; and techniques, skills, and approaches with men. A complete elaboration of the approaches enumerated in Table 14.2 is beyond the scope of the chapter. Some overall analyses of the approaches in Table 14.2 are given below.

Strong consensus exists that gender-aware and -sensitive approaches are critical when doing therapy with men. If men's sexist gender role socialization is harmful and sometimes traumatic (O'Neil, 1981a, b, 2008b; Brooks & Good, 2001b; Lisak, 2001; Pleck, 1995), then focusing on distorted notions of masculinity and femininity and GRC would be critical to therapeutic healing. The many gender-related approaches enumerated in Table 14.2 document that the psychology of men recognizes that boys and men are gendered beings. The call for gender-aware therapy 20 years ago by Good, Gilbert, and Scher (1990) has been heard in the psychology of men. How well gender-aware therapy is understood in other clinical disciplines is unclear. How many therapists utilize gender-aware approaches in their therapy and at what level of effectiveness is a critical empirical question.

Furthermore, over 24 assessment areas have been specified on how to make appraisals of men in therapy (see Table 14.2). Collectively, these assessment areas do represent a new and emerging way to evaluate men that deviates from standard DSM-IV criteria and other traditional paradigms. Furthermore, there is also support for including men or maleness as a multicultural variable in therapy. Interventions with men have been excluded from multicultural competencies (Liu, 2005). Of course, gender has been included in the multicultural competencies but exactly what that means for men has gone unspecified. The recommendations in Table 14.2 support full understanding of masculinity, maleness, and boys' and men's gender role socialization processes as important multicultural competencies. Multicultural assessment of white men should be included in this assessment, but even more important is the multicultural issues for men of color, immigrant men, gay and transgendered people, and men from different classes (both the wealthy and the poor). The training of multiculturally competent therapists of men has emerging support in the literature and therefore should be a vital topic in the decades ahead.

The experts indicate that the assumptions or expectancies that therapists make about male clients are important considerations. What is still lacking is the assessment of clients' expectations of therapy. This is particularly important in regards to men's negative attitudes toward help-seeking and the incongruence between traditional forms of therapy and men's socialization to restrictive gender roles. A careful examination of how clients' masculinity ideology and GRC contribute to negative stigma about therapy is a critical issue for therapists of men.

All the therapeutic approaches in Table 14.2 have been discussed in the context of men's problems with their sexist gender role socialization. Brooks (1998) and Rabinowitz and Cochran 2002) provide the most vital information about doing therapy with men that transcends traditional approaches to therapy. With the exception of these two approaches, many of the processes listed in Table 14.2 do not significantly differ from general recommendations for men or women in therapy. Maybe this reflects the belief that no unique processes are needed for men. It is more likely, however, that we do not have enough knowledge to generate unique therapeutic processes for men. We do not know enough about how masculinity ideology and GRC interact in the psychotherapeutic processes. For example, a strong case can be made that homophobia, power, and control are universal issues with men in therapy and should be addressed directly or indirectly by therapists. To make this assumption is one thing, but to fully understand it in the interactive, psychotherapeutic moment with a client is quite different and much more complex and important.

There are many unanswered questions about men's therapy. Are there therapeutic approaches that are unique to men's therapy? Should there be separate clinical approaches for men compared to women? How does diversity competency (Miville et al., 2009) relate to working with men from different racial, ethnic, religious, age, and sexual orientations categories? Is a new and gender-informed kind of therapy developing in the psychology of men? If so, what are its unique components and processes? What exactly is the current status of doing therapy with men? Understanding men's psychotherapeutic processes should be a growth area in the psychology of men in the coming decades.

Table 14.2. Therapy Approaches for Men Recommended by Published Authors

Therapeutic Approaches	References
Gender-Aware, Gender-Sensitive Approaches	
Regard conceptions of gender as integral to counseling	Good, Gilbert, & Scher, 1990
Consider problems within their societal context	Good, Gilbert, & Scher, 1990
Actively change gender injustices experienced by men and women	Good, Gilbert, & Scher, 1990
Emphasize the development of collaborative therapeutic relationships	Good, Gilbert, & Scher, 1990
Respect clients' freedom to choose	Good, Gilbert, & Scher, 1990
Understand the worldviews of men Recognize how patriarchal structures harm men	Good, Thompson, & Braithwaite, 2005; Liu, 2005
Accommodate and respect men's gender role values and masculine styles	Brooks, 1998
Value traditional men	Brooks, 1998
Help men yield to system pressures	Brooks, 2001
Gender-Aware, Gender-Sensitive Contextual Problem Assessment	
Assess one's own biases, values, about men	Mahalik, Good, Englar- Carlson, 2003a; O'Neil, 2008; Liu, 2005
Assess one's own knowledge about the psychology of men	O'Neil, 2008; O'Neil & Lujan, 2010
Assess men's expectancies of therapeutic process	Mahalik, Good, & Englar-Carlson, 2003a
Assess formative family and cultural heritage in context of gender roles	Rabinowitz & Cochran, 2002; O'Neil, 2008
Assess maladaptive patterns from family of origin and psychological history in context of gender roles	Rabinowitz & Cochran, 2002
Assess family system and interpersonal interactions	Lazur, 1998; Philpot, 2001
Assess using a gender role analysis	Englar-Carlson, 2006
Assess a portal (central focus or focal conflict)	Rabinowitz & Cochran, 2002
Assessing conformity and nonconformity to male norms	Mahalik, Talmadge, Locke, & Scott, 2005
Assessing men's wounds	Rabinowitz & Cochran, 2002;
Assess the father wound	O'Neil & Lujan, 2010
Assess overt and covert fathering contexts	O'Neil & Lujan, 2010
Assess how clients manage dependency needs, sadness, grief, and loss	Rabinowitz & Cochran, 2002
Assess cognitive distortion, explore illogical thoughts, modify biased thought with rationality	Mahalik, 1991, 2001;O'Neil, 2008, 1990, 2006; Mooney, 1998
Assess fathering roles and relationships with father	O'Neil & Lujan, 2010
Assess masculine-specific scripts and self- structures	Rabinowitz & Cochran, 2002; Mahalik, Good, & Englar-Carlson, 2003

(Continued)

Table 14.2. Continued

Therapeutic Approaches	References
Contextual Problem Assessment Continued	
Assessing and working with shame	Krugman, 1998
Assess body language	Rabinowitz & Cochran, 2002
Assessing defenses and resistance	O'Neil, 2008; Mahalik, 2008; Good & Mintz, 2001; Johnson, 2001
Assess emotionality and alexithymia	O'Neil, 2008
Assess need for psychological information	O'Neil, 2008; Levant 1998
Assess men's health needs	Courtenay, 2001
Assess men's patterns of GRC	O'Neil, 1990, 2008
Assess diversity & oppression in men's lives	O'Neil, 2008,; Good, Thompson, Braithwaite, 2005
Multicultural Consciousness and Assessment	
Recognize that therapy is cross-cultural for men	Good, Thompson, & Braitwaite, 2005; Glicken, 2005
Recognize the culture of therapy is in conflict with traditional masculine socialization	Good, Thompson, & Braitwaite, 2005; Glicken, 2005
Consider the culture of traditional masculinity in the context of therapy	Good, Thompson, & Braitwaite, 2005; Glicken, 2005
Recognize that therapy with men is about changing cultural values	Good, Thompson, & Braitwaite, 2005; Glicken, 2005
Develop culturally appropriate intervention strategies and techniques	Good, Thompson, & Braitwaite, 2005; Glicken, 2005
Respect men's gender role values and cultural context	Good, Thompson, & Braitwaite, 2005; Glicken, 2005
Recognize that men are different than women	Good, Thompson, & Braitwaite, 2005; Glicken, 2005
Assess one's own bias and stereotypes about men who are different than you	O'Neil, 2008
Assess men's experience with oppression and discrimination	O'Neil, 2008
Assess the invisibility syndrome for men who are victims of racism or other forms of oppression	Franklin, 1998
Assess men's experience with microaggressions	Franklin, 1998
Therapist self-interrogation and self-confrontation of their racist socialization	Caldwell & White, 2001
Expectancies and Assumptions of Therapists	
Assume men's pain and vulnerability	Brooks, 1998; Brooks, 2001
Define therapy as problem solving with men	Glicken, 2005
Normalize therapy as positive; selling therapy	Brooks, 1998
Respect men's readiness to change	Brooks, 2001
Recognize men's ambivalence about therapy	Good, Thompson, & Braithwaite, 2005

(Continued)

Table 14.2. Continued

Therapeutic Approaches	References
Expectancies and Assumption of Therapists Continued	
Define male socialization in positive ways	Glicken, 2005
Therapeutic Processes with Men	
Work collaboratively	Glicken, 2005
Develop culturally appropriate interventions, strategies, and techniques	Good, Thomson, & Brathwaite, 2005
Balance assessment and connection in early parts of therapy	Cochran & Rabinowitz, 2002
Structure therapy	Glicken, 2005
Focus on men's strengths	Glicken, 2005
Recognize that trust develops slowly with men	Glicken, 2005
Focus on areas of change: emotions, cognitions, behaviors, interpersonal relationships	Good & Mintz, 2001
Counter and work through resistance	Good & Mintz, 2001; Glicken, 2005; Brooks, 1998; Rabinowitz & Cochran (2002)
Avoid power struggles and psychological labeling	Glicken, 2005
Avoid pitfalls Brooks, 1998	Brooks, 1998
Stimulate and evoke men's emotional pain	Brooks, 1998
Inciting and escalating tensions	Brooks, 1998
Envision a sequence of change	Brooks, 1998
Digging, prodding, and provoking	Brooks, 1998
Holding and focusing	Brooks, 1998
Help clients balance "doing with being"	Rabinowitz & Cochran, 2002
Work with transference and countertransference	Good & Mintz, 2001,; Johnson, 2001,; Gilbert & Scher, 2001, Good, Thomson, & Brathwaite, 2005; Rabinowitz & Cochran, 2002
Develop effective terminations	Good & Mintz, 2001; Rabinowitz & Cochran, 2002
Techniques, Skills, and Approaches With Men	
Rabinowitz and Cohran's 43 approaches across psychoanalytic, jungian, existential, self-psychology, person-centered, experiential, transpersonal, and spiritual forms of deepening psychotherapy with men	Rabinowitz & Cochran, 2002
Educate about how cognitive thoughts, feelings, behaviors interrelate	Mahalik, 1999a, 2001
Use language that men will understand	Robertson, 2001
Help clients develop a healthy set of masculine values and behaviors	Rabinowitz & Cochran, 2002; Cochran, 2002
Use humor, humility, metaphors, and self-disclosure	Kiselica, 2001; Glicken, 2005

(Continued)

Table 14.2. Continued

Therapeutic Approaches	References
Techniques, Skills, and Approaches With Men Continued	
Use bibliotherapy and experiential exercise: novels, poetry, films, and music	Glicken, 2005; Rabinowitz & Cochran, 2002; Good & Mintz, 2002; Brooks, 1998
Showing and modeling	Brooks, 1998
Challenging men to change	Brooks, 1998
Therapeutic silence	Brooks, 1998
Enumerate change patterns	Good & Mintz, 2001
Humanize vulnerability and pain	Courtenay, 2001
Use motivational interviewing and enhancement	Isenhart, 2001; Good, Thomson, & Brathwaite, 2008
Use gender inquiry	Philpot, 2001
Defining healthy manhood	Courtenay, 2001

All therapists of men should consider Brook's (1998) guidelines and Rabinowitz and Cochran's (2002) 43 therapeutic skill/techniques across eight theoretical areas. These approaches open up a multitude of ways to help therapists who are struggling with men's resistance, defensiveness, or dilemmas that have been reached in therapy. The rest of the skills in Table 14.2 have a cognitive, behavioral, and humanistic emphasis but very few of them have been tested for effectiveness. Therefore, teams of clinicians and researchers should collaborate in designing research that promotes evidence-based assessment and treatment (Cochran, 2005).

Summary of Therapy Process and Treatment Interventions for Men

Over the last 10 years, knowledge about men's therapy has expanded significantly. Some diagnostic paradigms and guidelines exist, and at least two comprehensive approaches to men's therapy have been discussed in the literature (Brook, 1998; Rabinowitz & Cochran, 2002) What is unclear is whether these guidelines are being used by practitioners. Beyond these approaches, the literature on men's therapy is underdeveloped and scattered across various journal articles, books, and other publications. Very few empirically based or theoretically robust models of men's therapy currently exist (Good & Sherrod, 2001). There has been limited amount of research on clients or how actual therapeutic process work with men.

Experts on men's therapy indicate that challenges exist in assessing men's problems. Numerous authors indicate that men's problems may be "masked" or do not fit traditional diagnostic categories (Magovcevic & Addis, 2008; Pollack, 1998b, 2001; Rabinowitz & Cochran, 2002). Other critical issues include how to get men to use psychological services, and how to effectively market men's services. How to redefine help-seeking and the therapeutic process so that men use mental health services remains a critical challenge in the psychology of men. Furthermore, no therapeutic paradigm currently exists that assesses men across different races, classes, ages, ethnicities, nationalities, and sexual orientations. Biases and discrimination against men during therapy because of their sex, race, religion, sexual orientation, or nationality have not been studied. The initial diagnostic criteria to assess men are in the earlier stages of development and primarily based on clinical experience. Evidence-based assessment has been recommended (Cochran, 2005), but this kind of appraisal requires operational definitions of men's problems and potentials. Therefore, more clearly defined therapeutic concepts need to be developed that can be tested empirically.

Almost all of the theorists define therapy with men using gender-sensitive approaches (Good, Gilbert, & Scher, 1990). It is now recognized that patriarchal sexism can harm men in significant ways. Consequently, men's therapy should include how gender role values contribute to men's problems. Numerous theorists suggest psychodynamic and cognitive behavioral approaches in the context of men's gender role development (Mooney, 1998; Pollack, 1995, 1998b; Rabinowitz &

Cochran, 2002). The misdiagnosis of men and the limitations of previous diagnostic schemas are currently being discussed. The literature also underscores men's resistance, ambivalence, and defensiveness about therapy, and the incongruence between the client's gender role socialization and traditional approaches to therapy. Clinical processes to uncover men's problems are emphasized and, as in all therapies, a trusting relationship is considered critical. Special male symptoms are identified as central to men's problems including dependency, emotional restrictiveness, sadness, grief, loss, power, control, vulnerability, and pain. There are recommendations to focus on men's strengths, and to avoid power conflicts and psychological labels. Empowering men and using experiential exercises to promote men's growth are considered important to therapeutic effectiveness.

Future Directions in the Psychology of Men: Theory, Research, Clinical Practice and Training

The psychology of men has witnessed much scholarly activity since it was officially recognized by American psychology in 1995. For the discipline to mature and impact the rest of psychology, new agendas need to be pursued. Below are eight agendas to advance the research and clinical practice in the psychology of men.

New Research Directions

Empirical evidence now exists documenting that men's and boy's gender roles have negative psychological consequences (Good, Wallace, & Borst, 1994; Levant & Richmond, 2007; O'Neil 2008b). The relationship between masculinity ideology and GRC and stress to men's psychological problems has been documented in hundreds of studies (see Table 14.1). How, why, and when men experience these conflicts with their masculinity is the next critical contextual question. More complex studies that assess contextual variables are needed if the psychology of men is to make a significant contribution to society. This implies moving past simple correlational studies to moderator and mediator analyses that assess how third variables interact with men's experience with their gender roles (Heppner, 1995; O'Neil, 2008b,c). In previous papers, a contextual research agenda for GRC (O'Neil, 2008b,c) was delineated that could easily be adapted to masculinity ideology and any other constructs in the psychology of men.

Furthermore, studies need to use more behavioral measures and be conducted in laboratory and real-life situations. Eisler's (1995) research program and Breiding's research studies (Breiding, 2004; Breiding, Windle, & Smith, 2008) provide excellent examples of real-life, situational research. More behavioral measures and laboratory-based studies are needed when studying masculinity ideology, fears of femininity, and GRC. Studies that assess actual violations of masculine norms (Bosson, Taylor, & Prewitt-Freilino, 2006) are needed to understand how "gender role threats" activate men's psychological problems and hypermasculinity. More qualitative research and case studies that capture the complexity of male behavior are needed. The qualitative research is needed to better conceptualize men's lives and develop more comprehensive concepts than those reviewed in the chapter.

Diversity, Racial and Ethnic Identity, and International Men

Discovering how racial and ethnic identities interact with the internalization of masculinity ideology and gender-related conflict and stress needs to be a high priority in the future. Research and theory on how racial identity, racism, and other forms of discrimination relate to men's problems is essential to understanding how the larger social system is implicated in patriarchal dynamics (Carter, Williams, Juby, & Buckley, 2005; Enns, 2008; Heppner & Heppner, 2008; O'Neil, 2008b). Studies that assess men who have been victimized by societal or personal oppression need to be conducted. Furthermore, men who victimize others need to be vigorously studied if we are to slow and eliminate the senseless amount of victimization that men inflict on human beings in our world. Additionally, how acculturation stress interacts with masculinity conflicts is particularly relevant for the millions of immigrant men and women entering our country. Another important diversity issue is how the psychology of men can engage researchers, therapists, and colleagues around the world in collaborative efforts (Connell, 2003; Blazina & Shen-Miller, 2011; O'Neil, 2011). Counseling psychology has been a leader in international networking, and the psychology of men could be an attractive discipline to many countries that identify with Division 17. My literature review of the GRC research found over 60 empirical studies on men from 24 different countries. Therefore, research networks on men are developing around the world, but no official mechanism exists to promote collaborations of international researchers in the psychology of men.

Future Directions for Understanding Men's Therapy and Psychological Assessment

Recommendations to improve men's therapy and psychological assessment are difficult to specify. The current literature on men's therapy is promising, but overall the paradigms are preliminary and general. Almost all of the paradigms and approaches lack the rigors of empirical tests and evidence-based examination. Furthermore, I found in my review very few recommendations for future research on men's therapy. In many ways, it appears that scholars have not been able to specify the critical research questions needed to study men's therapy. One approach to remedy this situation would be to take the emerging therapeutic models (Brooks, 1998; Brooks, 2001, Glicken, 2005; Good & Mintz, 2001; Good, Thompson, & Braithwaite, 2000; Mahalik, 1999a, 2001a; Rabinowitz & Cochran, 2002) and make them more operational for possible empirical tests. More case studies (Englar-Carlson & Stevens, 2006) and qualitative research may be needed to generate important therapeutic questions. Scientists and practitioners need to work together to generate a comprehensive research program assessing therapeutic interventions that are effective with all men, but particularly with men from diverse backgrounds.

Masculinity and Preventing Men's Violence

One of the most critical issues in the psychology of men is documenting what causes men's violence against women, children, and other men (Harway & O'Neil, 1999; O'Neil & Nadeau, 1999). Physical violence is everyone's fear in our current society, and men are the primary victimizers. Many discussions on men's violence become consumed in legitimate anger, blame, defensiveness, and outright helplessness, given the enormity and heaviness of the problem. Psychologists need to lead the way past these understandable but unfortunate emotions with research and preventive programs. One way to do this is to generate masculinity hypotheses about men's violence (O'Neil & Nadeau, 1999). For example, how, when, and why does masculinity ideology and GRC stimulate threat, intimidation, and violent retaliation by men? The research cited in Table 14.1 indicates that masculinity ideology and GRC and stress are significantly correlated with negative and angry attitudes toward others, coercive

and abusive behavior and violence, and aggression. Furthermore, more study is needed on how men's oppressive and discriminatory experiences stimulate violence toward others. How men's emotional and psychological processes contribute to violence deserves increased research studies and preventive programming.

Marketing Psychological Services for Men and Developing Prevention Programs

This chapter documents that men have serious problems from gender roles but do not use therapeutic services to remediate them. Discovering how to more effectively market services for men and change negative attitudes toward help-seeking needs to be a primary agenda in the psychology of men. Demystifying help-seeking and making therapy services attractive requires creative interventions and "thinking outside the box." Help-seeking by men has been distorted by patriarchal structures that deny men the right to have human vulnerabilities to life's inevitable problems. This is one of the saddest outcomes of modern patriarchy. Men are socialized to have problems because of sexist and patriarchal values, and simultaneously denied help by the very same system that causes the problems. Variables that mediate negative help-seeking attitudes need to be studied by researchers. For example, it has been found that men's GRC and negative attitudes toward help-seeking are mediated by difficulties disclosing distressing information and the self-stigma associated with seeking counseling (Pederson & Vogel, 2007). This research finding supports developing preventive interventions that describe the positive power of self-disclosure and the origins of stigma about men seeking help. For example, it may be that the advantages of therapy and self-disclosure need to be more publicized with men.

Another study found that encouragement to seek help or knowing someone who had sought help were related to more positive expectations about mental health services and help-seeking (Vogel, Wade, Wester, Larson, & Hackler, 2007). These results suggest that social networks that endorse help-seeking or specific individuals who have sought help can be influential in mediating resistance to seeking help. This kind of mediation research holds promise because it assesses the potential factors that can change men's attitudes toward help-seeking. Based on this research, testimonials of therapy by past clients may be very valuable in helping resistant men seek the help that they need. Active experimentation with unique ways to help men break through their fears of being helped are critical to any prevention agenda in the psychology of men.

Promoting the Psychology of Boys

The psychology of boys has been slow to develop as a speciality in the psychology of men. The publication of specific books on boys (Horne & Kiselica, 1999; Pollack, 1998a) and media debates about "boys crises" (Hall, 1999; Hoff Sommer, 2000; Pollack, 1998a; Kindlon & Thompson, 1999; Tyre, 2006; Von Drehle, 2007) have now given the psychology of boys a central place in the psychology of men. There is a great need to accelerate our efforts to create and evaluate prevention programming for boys in public schools and in the community (O'Neil & Lujan, 2009). First, we need to create a curriculum that boys can use to promote their psychological development. Suggestions on how to enter public schools and how to develop user-friendly curriculum that focuses on both life skills and masculinity conflicts have been suggested (O'Neil & Lujan, 2009). An important aspect of the development of boy's psychology is understanding the multiplicity of factors in families, schools, and peer groups that shape male gender role identity.

Many parents and educators are unaware of how sexism and restrictive gender roles negatively affect boy's lives. There is denial about boy's problems that emanate from sexist stereotypes. The axiom "boys will be boys" is frequently used to ignore significant problems of male youth. The assumption that boys will outgrow their problems is seriously flawed because it represents a superficial assessment of boy's lives, and does not capture the deeper and unidentified sources of boys' GRCs. A call to action to prevent boys' problems has been issued (O'Neil & Lujan, 2009) but will require much effort and commitment by progressive educators.

Interventions and Research on Men's Health Issues

Courtenay's (2000a,b) call to action for men's health issues is one of the most important areas for researcher and practitioners to pursue in the future. To pursue men's health issues, the psychology of men must venture into how the biological bases of behavior interact with psychological and gender-related factors for men. How masculinity ideology and GRC moderate and mediate men's physical problems deserves more expansive conceptualization

(O'Neil, 2008b). Courtenay's (2000c) health agenda for men includes over 30 male behaviors that increase men's risk of disease, injury, and death. Teams of psychologists could work with teams of medical experts in developing preventive interventions and research that literally have life-and-death implications for men.

Promoting Positive and Healthy Masculinity

The psychology of men needs to emphasis more healthy criteria for being male. The psychology of men has primarily focused on men's problems, rather than on men potentials and possibilities. Paradigms of positive masculinity are needed to describe men's strengths and how to transcend sexist stereotypes (O'Neil, 2008; O'Neil & Lujan, 2009). Patterns of positive masculinity can help men and boys learn alternatives to sexist attitudes and behaviors that cause GRC. Programming could emphasize what constitutes "healthy masculinity." Men's strengths and potentialities could focus on themes such as responsibility, courage, altruism, resiliency, service, protection of others, social justice, positive fathering, perseverance, generativity, and nonviolent problem solving. Positive masculinity moves away from what is wrong with boys and men by identifying the qualities that empower males to improve themselves and society. Programs and research on healthy masculinity could change the common misperception that the psychology of men is about documenting what is wrong with boys and men. Attention to healthy masculinity could attract more psychologists to the psychology of men as a critical discipline committed to social justice for both men and women.

Training and Teaching the Psychology of Men

The APA training programs in counseling psychology and other mental health specialties can be instrumental in promoting the psychology of men. Recently an entire issue of *The Counseling Psychologist* recommended that race, ethnic, and gender issues be better integrated into our training programs (*TCP*, 2009; Miller, Forrest, Elman, 2009; Miville et al., 2009). Gender and masculinity issues were mentioned as important training areas, but no recommendations were given on how to teach the psychology of men.

In published papers spanning over 25 years, I advocated that the psychology of men become a priority in counseling training programs (O'Neil,

1981a, b, 1982, 1990, 2008b). In the early years, limited empirical research existed for this training. As this review demonstrates, strong empirical evidence now exists indicating that masculinity attitudes and conflicts are related to men's poor mental health and significant interpersonal problems. The research reviewed here supports increased attention on men's problems in our training programs, in the context of masculinity ideology and GRC. Furthermore, sufficient knowledge exists on men's therapy to justify coursework specifically focused on techniques and skills when counseling men.

Teaching the psychology of men can become a priority training issues in counseling psychology. Survey research indicates that the psychology of men has not been included in counseling psychology training, even though there is high interest and positive belief in its value (Mellinger & Liu, 2006). What is unclear is whether counseling psychology will address men's issues with the same vigor that women's issues were addressed over the past three decades. Furthermore, analyses have indicated that gender has been conspicuously lacking in the training literature for both sexes (Silverstein, 2006). What curriculum and skills should be taught therapists and psychoeducators remains unclear, but methods of teaching the psychology of men are being explored (O'Neil, 2004; O'Neil, Addis, Kilmartin, & Mahalik, 2004). Ultimately, training standards for boys and men will need to be integrated with multicultural competencies (Liu, 2005). Teaching the psychology of men and training needs to become part of diversity competence (Alberta & Wood, 2009 ; Miville et al., 2009) for counseling psychology to move beyond the traditional approaches to training clinicians, professors, and researchers. The future of the psychology of men rests with the next generations of researchers and practitioners who teach and train psychologists about men's problems and potentials.

Conclusion
Final Thoughts on the Status of the Psychology of Men in 2010

The overall status of the psychology of men in 2010 is healthy and vibrant. The number of publications cited in this review is evidence that the psychology of men is growing and expanding. Some critical issues need to be addressed if the psychology of men is to fully explain how patriarchal norms negatively affect men, women, and children. For the first time, empirical evidence reviewed in this chapter documents that masculinity ideology and conformity, GRC and stress, and other masculinity constructs significantly contribute to men's and boys' mental health problems. These data deserve more attention in psychology and a call to action is strongly recommended to better serve boys and men.

References

Addis, M. (2008). Gender and depression in men. *Clinical Psychology: Science and Practice, 15,* 153–168.

Addis, M. E., & Cohane, G. H. (2005). Social scientific paradigms of masculinity and their implications for research and practice in men's mental health. *Journal of Clinical Psychology, 61,* 1–15.

Addis, M. E., & Mahalik, J. R. (2003). Men, masculinity, and the context of help seeking. *American Psychologist, 58,* 5–14.

Alberta, A. J., & Wood, A. H. (2009). A practical skills model for effectively engaging clients in multicultural settings. *The Counseling Psychologist, 37,* 564–579.

American Heart Association (1994). Heart and stroke facts: 1995. Statistical Supplement. Dallas: author.

American Psychological Association (2003). Guidelines on multicultural education, training, research, practice, and organizational change for psychologists. *American Psychologist, 58,* 377–402.

Anderson, A. J. (1998). Treating anger in Africn American men. In W. S. Pollack & R. F. Levant (Eds.) New psychotherapy for men (pp. 239–258). New York: John Wiley & Sons Inc.

Bem, S. (1981). Gender schema theory: A cognitive account of sex typing *Psychological Review, 88,* 354–364.

Blazina, C. (1997). The fear of the feminine in the western psyche and the masculine task of disidentification: Their effect on the development of masculine gender role conflict. *Journal of Men's Studies, 6,* 55–68.

Blazina, C. (2001). Analytic psychology and gender role conflict: The development of the fragile masculine self. *Psychotherapy, 38,* 50–59.

Blazina, C. (2003). *The cultural myth of masculinity.* Westport, CT: Praeger.

Blazina, C. (2004). Gender role conflict and disidentification process: Two cases studies on fragile masculine self. *The Journal of Men's Studies, 12,* 151–161.

Blazina, C., & Marks, I. (2001). College men's affective reactions to individual therapy, psychoeducation workshops, and men's support group brochures: The influence of gender role conflict and power dynamics upon help seeking attitudes. *Psychotherapy, 38,* 297–305.

Blazina, C., Pisecco, S., & O'Neil, J. M. (2005). An adaptation of the Gender Role Conflict Scale for adolescents: Psychometric issues and correlates with psychological distress. *Psychology of Men and Masculinity, 6,* 39–45.

Blazina, C., & Shen-Miller, D. S. (Eds.) (2011). An international psychology of men: Theoretical advances, case studies, and clinical innovations. New York: Routledge.

Blazina, C., & Watkins, C. E. (1996). Masculine gender role conflict: Effects on college men's psychological well-being, chemical substance usage, and attitudes toward help-seeking. *Journal of Counseling Psychology, 43,* 461–465.

Boehn, F. (1930). The femininity-complex in men. *International Journal of Psychoanalysis, 11,* 444–469.

Bosson, J. K., Taylor, J. N., & Prewitt-Freilino, J. L. (2006). Gender role violations and identity misclassification: The roles of audience and actor variables. *Sex Roles, 55,* 13–24.

Brannon, R., & Juni, S. (1984). A scale for measuring attitudes toward masculinity. *JSAS*.

Breiding, M. J. (2004). Observed hostility and observed dominance as mediators of the relationship between husbands' gender role conflict and wives' outcomes. *Journal of Counseling Psychology, 51*, 429–436.

Breiding, M. J., Wundle, C. R., & Smith, D. A. (2008). Interspousal criticism: A behavioral mediator between husband's gender role conflict and wife's adjustment. *Sex Roles, 59*, 880–888.

Brodsky, A., & Holroyd, J. (1975). Report of the Task Force on Sex Bias and Sex-role Stereotyping in Psychotherapeutic Practice. *American Psychologist, 30*, 1169–1175.

Brooks, G. R. (1998). *A new psychotherapy for traditional men*. San Francisco: Jossey-Bass.

Brooks, G. R. (2001). Counseling and psychotherapy for male military veterans. In G. Brooks & G. E. Good (Eds.), *The new handbook of psychotherapy and Counseling with men: A comprehensive guide to settings, problems, and treatment approaches* (pp. 206–225). Vol. 1, San Francisco: Jossey-Bass.

Brooks, G. R., & Good, G. E. (Eds.). (2001a). *The new handbook of psychotherapy and counseling with men: A comprehensive guide to settings, problems, and treatment approaches*. San Francisco: Jossey-Bass.

Brooks, G. R., & Good, G. E. (2001b). Introduction. In G. R. Brooks & G. E. Good (Eds.), *The new handbook of psychotherapy and counseling with men: A comprehensive guide to settings, problems, and treatment approaches* (pp. 3–21). San Francisco, CA: Jossey-Bass.

Brooks, G. R., & Levant, R. F. (1998). A history of division 51 (the Society for the Psychological Study of Men and Masculinity). In D. A. Dewsbury (Ed.) *Unification through division: Histories of the Divisions of the American Psychological Association*, volume III (pp. 197–222). Washington, DC: APA Books.

Burke, K. (2000). *Gender role conflict and psychological well being: An exploratrion in men enrolled to attend an initatory weekend*. Unpublished master thesis. University of Maryland, Baltimore County.

Burk, L. R., Burkhart, B. R., & Sikorski, J. F. (2004). Construction and preliminary validation of the Auburn Differential Masculinity Inventory. *Psychology of Men and Masculinity, 5*, 4–17.

Campbell, J. L. (1996). Traditional men in therapy: Obstacles and recommendations. *Journal of Psychological Practice, 2*, 40–45.

Carter, R. T., Williams, B., Juby, H. L., & Buckley, T. R. (2005). Racial identity as mediator of the relationship between gender role conflict and severity of psychological symptoms in Black, Latino, and Asian men. *Sex Roles 53*, 473–486.

Center for Disease Control (CDC). (1997). Demographic differences in notifiable infections disease morbidity–United States, 1992–1994. *Morbidity and Mortality Weekly Report, 46*(28), 637–641.

Center for Disease Control (CDC). (2005). Mental health in the United States: Prevalence of Diagnosis and medication treatment for attention-deficit hyperactivity disorder–United States, 2003. Center for Disease Control and Prevention, Atlanta, GA. 54(34), 842–847.

Center for Disease Control (CDC). (2006). Quick stats–Excessive alcohol use and risks to men's health, Center for Disease Control and Prevention, Atlanta, GA.

Center for Disease Control (CDC). (2007). Facts at a glance: Youth Violence Center for Disease Control Center for Disease Control and Prevention, Atlanta, GA.

Chu, J. Y., Porche, M. V., Tolman, D. L. (2005). The Adolescent Masculinity Ideology in Relationships Scale. *Men and Masculinities, 8*, 93–115.

Cochran, S. V., & Rabinowitz, F. (2000). *Men and depression: Clinical and empirical perspectives*. San Diego, CA: Academic Press.

Cochran, S. V., & Rabinowitz, F. (2003). Gender-sensitive recommendations for assessment and treatment of depression in men. *Professional Psychology: Research and Practice, 34*, 132–140.

Cochran, S.V. (2005). Evidence based assessment with men. *Journal Clinical Psychology. 61*, 649–660. *Professional Psychology: Research, and Practice, 30*, 5–13.

Connell, R. W. (1995). *Masculinities*. Cambridge, U K: Polity Press.

Connell, R. W. (2003). Masculinities, change, and conflict in global society: Thinking about the future of men's studies. *Journal of Men's Studies, 11*, 249–266.

Connell, R. W., & Messerschmidt, J. W. (2005). Hegemonic masculinity: Rethinking the concept. *Gender and Society, 19*, 829–859.

Coonerty-Femiano, A. M., Katzman, M. A., Femiano, S., Gemar, M., & Toner, B. (2001, August). *Gender role conflict in male survivors of childhood abuse*. Paper presented at the American Psychological Association, San Francisco, CA.

Courtenay, W. H. (1998). College men's health: An overview and a call to action. *Journal of American College Health, 46*, 279–290.

Courtenay, W. H. (2000a). Engending health: A social constructionist examination of men's health beliefs and behaviors. *Psychology of Men and Masculinity, 1*, 4–15.

Courtenay, W. H. (2000b). Teaming up for the new men's health movement. *Journal of Men's Studies, 8*, 387–392.

Courtenay, W. H. (2000c). Behavioral factors associated with disease, injury, and death among men: Evidence and implication for prevention. *Journal of Men's Studies, 9*, 81–142.

Courtenay, W. H. (2001). Counseling men in medical settings: The six-point health plan. In G. R. Brooks & G. E. Good (Eds.) *The new handbook of psychotherapy and counseling with men: A comprehensive guide to settings, problems, and treatment approaches.*, Vol 1 (pp. 59–91), San Francisco, CA: Jossey-Bass.

Cusack, J., Deane, F. P., Wilson, C. J., & Ciarrochi, J. (2006). Emotional expression, perception of therapy, and help seeking intentions in men attending therapy services. *Psychology of Men and Masculinity, 7*, 69–82.

David, D., & Brannon, R. (Eds.). (1976). *The forty-nine percent majority*. Reading, MA.: Addison-Wesley.

Davis, T. L., & Liddell, D. L. (2002). Getting inside the house: The effectiveness of a rape prevention program for college fraternity men. *Journal of College Student Development, 43*, 35–50.

Deaux, K., & Majors, B. (1987). Putting gender in context: An integrative model of gender-related behavior. *Psychological Review, 94*, 369–389.

Department of Health and Human Services (1996). Report of final mortality statistics, 1994. Monthly Vital Statistics, Report 45, Suppl. 3., Hyattsville, MD: Published Health Services.

Dodson, T., & Borders, D. (2006). Men in traditional and nontraditional careers: Gender role attitudes, gender role conflict, and job satisfaction. *Career Development Quarterly*, 54, 283–296.

Doyle, J. A. (1995). *The male experience*. Dubuque, IA: Brown & Benchmark.

Dubbert, J. L. (1979). *A man's place: Masculinity in transition*. Englewood Cliffs: N. J.: Prentice-Hall.

Eckes, T., & Trauter, H. M. (2000). *The developmental social psychology of gender*. Mahwah, NJ: Lawrence Erlbaum Associates Publishers.

Eisler, R. M. (1995). The relationship between masculine gender role stress and men's health risk: The validation of a construct. In R. F. Levant & W. S. Pollack (Eds.), *The new psychology of men* (pp. 207–225) New York: Basic Books.

Eisler, R. M. & Skidman, J. R. (1987). Masculine gender role stress: Scale development and component factors in appraisal of stressful situations. *Behavior Modifications*, 1, 123–136.

Englar-Carlson, M., & Stevens, M. A. (Eds.). (2006). *In the room with men: A casebook of therapeutic change*. Washington, DC: APA Books.

Englar-Carlson, M., & Vandiver, B. (2001, August). Gender role conflict, help seeking, and treatment fearfulness. In J. M. O'Neil & G. E. Good (Chairs). *Gender role conflict research: Testing new constructs and dimensions empirically*. Symposium conducted at the annual meeting of the American psychology Association, San Francisco.

Englar-Carlson, M. (2001). Two causal models of white male psychological help-seeking attitudes and preferences for psychotherapy. (Doctoral dissertation, Penn State University, 2001). *Dissertation Abstracts International*, 58, 1599.

Enns, C. Z. (2008). Toward a complexity paradigm for understanding gender role conflict. *The Counseling Psychologist*, 36, 446–454.

Farrell, W. (1974). *The liberated man*. New York: Bantam Books.

Fasteau, M. F. (1974). *The male machine*. New York: McGraw Hill.

Freud, S. (1937). Analysis terminable and interminable. In P. Rieff (Ed.), *Freud: Therapy and techniques*. (pp. 233–271). New York: Macmillan.

Garnets, L., & Pleck, J. (1979). Sex role identity, androgyny, and sex role transcendence: A sex role strain analysis. *Psychology of Women Quarterly*, 3, 270–283.

Gilbert, L. A., & Scher, M. (1999). *Gender and sex in counseling and psychotherapy*. Boston, MA.: Allyn & Bacon.

Glicken, M. D. (2005). *Working with troubled men: A contemporary practitioner's guide*. Mahwah, NJ: Lawrence Erlbaum Associates.

Goldberg, H. (1977). *The hazards of being male*. New York: New American Library.

Good, G. E., Dell, D. M., & Mintz, L. B. (1989). Male role and gender role conflict: Relations to help seeking in men. *Journal of Counseling Psychology*, 36, 295–300.

Good, G. E., Gilbert, L. A., & Scher, M. (1990). Gender aware therapy: A synthesis of feminist therapy and knowledge about gender. *Journal of Counseling and Development*, 68, 376–380.

Good, G. E., & Mintz, L. B. (2001). Integrative therapy for men. In G. R. Brooks & G. E. Good (Eds.), *The new handbook of psychotherapy and counseling with men: A comprehensive guide to settings, problems, and treatment approaches*, Vol.2 (pp. 582–602). San Francisco, CA: Jossey-Bass.

Good, G. E., Robertson, J. M., Fitzgerald, L. F., Stevens, M., & Bartels, K. M. (1996). The relation between masculine role conflict and psychological distress in male university counseling center clients. *Journal of Counseling and Development*, 75, 44–49.

Good, G. E., & Sherrod, N. B. (2001). Men's problems and effective treatments: Theory and empirical support. In G. Brooks & G. E. Good (Eds.), *The new handbook of psychotherapy and counseling with men: A comprehensive guide to settings, problems, and treatment approaches* Vol. 1 (pp. 22–40). San Francisco: Jossey-Bass.

Good, G. E., Thomson, D. A., & Brathwaite, A. D. (2005). *Journal of Clinical Psychology*, 61, 697–708.

Good, G. E., Wallace, D. L., & Borst, T. S. (1994). Masculinity research: A review and critique. *Applied and Preventive Psychology*, 3, 1.

Hall, S. S. (1999). The trouble life of boys. *The New York Times Magazine*, August 22, 1999. pp. 31–65.

Harrison, J. (1978). Warning: The male sex role may be dangerous to your health. *Journal of Social Issues*, 34, 65–86.

Harway, M., & O'Neil J. M. (Eds.). (1999). *What causes men's violence against women?* Thousand Oaks, CA: Sage Publications.

Hayes, J. A., & Mahalik, J. R. (2000). Gender role conflict and psychological distress in male counseling center clients. *Psychology of Men and Masculinity*, 2, 116–125.

Hayes, M. M. (1985). Counselor sex-role values and effects on attitudes toward, and treatment of non-traditional male clients. (Doctoral dissertation, Ohio State University, 1985). *Dissertation Abstracts International*, 45, 3072.

Hays, H. R. (1964). *The dangerous sex: The myth of feminine evil*. New York: Pocket Books.

Heppner, P. P. (1995). On gender role conflict in men: Future directions and implications for counseling. *Journal of Counseling Psychology*, 42, 20–23.

Heppner, P. P., & Heppner, M. J. (2008). The gender role conflict literature: Fruits of sustained commitment. *The Counseling Psychologist*, 36, 455–461.

Hoff Sommer, C. (2000). *The war against boys: How feminism is harming our young men*. New York: Simon & Schuster.

Horne, A. M., & Kiselica, M. S. (1999). *Handbook of counseling boys and adolescent males: A practitioner's guide*. Thousand Oaks, CA: Sage Publications.

Horney, K. (1967). *Feminine psychology*. New York: Norton.

Jome, L. M., & Tokar, D. M. (1997). Dimensions of masculinity and major choice traditionality. *Journal of Vocational Behavior*, 52, 120–134.

Johnson, N. G. (2001). Women helping men: Strengths of and barriers to women therapists working with men clients. In G. R. Brooks & G. E. Good (Eds.) *The new handbook of psychotherapy and counseling with men: A comprehensive guide to settings, problems, and treatment approaches* Vol. 2 (pp. 696–718), San Francisco, CA: Jossey-Bass.

Jung, K. (1953). *Animus and anima*. Collected Works, vol. 7, New York: Pantheon.

Jung, K. (1959). *Concerning archetypes, with special reference to the anima concept (1954)*. Collected Works, Vol. 9, Part I. New York: Pantheon.

Kearney, L., King, E. B., & Rochlen, A. B. (2004). Male gender role conflict, sexual harassment tolerance, and efficacy of a psychoeducative training program. *Psychology of Men and Masculinity*, 5, 72–82.

Kessler. R. C., & Walters, E. (2002). The national comorbidity survey. In M. T. Tsuang & M. Tohen (Eds.) *Psychiatric Epidemiology*, Second edition, (pp. 343–362). New York: Wiley.

Kilmartin, C. T. (2007). *The masculine self*. (Third Edition) Cornwall-on-Hudson, New York: Sloan Publishing.

Kimmel, M. S. (Ed.). (1995). *The politics of manhood: Profeminist men respond to the mythopoetic movement (and the mythopoetic leaders answer*. Philadelphia: Temple University Press.

Kimmel, M. S. (2006). *Manhood in America: A contextual history*. New York: Oxford University Press.

Kindlon, D. F., & Thompson, M. (1999). *Raising Cain: Protecting the emotional life of boys*. New York: Ballantine Books.

Lazar, R. F. (1998). Men in family: A family system's approach to treating men. In W. S. Pollack & R. F. Levant (Eds.) *New psychotherapy for men* (pp. 127–144). New York: John Wiley & Sons Inc.

Lazarus, R. S., & Folkman, S. (1984). Stress, appraisal, and coping. New York: Springer.

Lederer, W. (1968). *The fear of women*. New York: Harcourt, Brace, Jovanovich.

Lerner, R. M. (1992). *Developmental systems theory: An integrative approach*. Newbury Park, CA: Sage.

Levant, R. F. (1995). Toward the reconstruction of masculinity. In R. F., Levant & W. S. Pollack (Eds.), *A new psychology of men*. (229–251). New York: Basic Books.

Levant, R. F. (1997). The masculinity crises. *The Journal of Men's Studies*, 5, 221–231.

Levant, R. F., Hirsch, L., Celentano, E., Cozza, T., Hill, S., MacRachorn, M., et al. (1992). The male role: An investigation of contemporary norms. *Journal of Mental Health Counseling*, 14, 325–337.

Levant, R. F., & Richmond, K. (2007). A review of research on masculinity ideologies using the Male Norm Inventory. *The Journal of Men's Studies*, 15, 130–146.

Levinson, D. J., Darrow, C. N., Klein, E. B., Levinson, M. H., & McKee, B. (1978). *The season's of a man's life*. New York: Ballantine Books.

Lewis, R. A., & Pleck, J. H. (Eds.). (1979). Special issue: Men's roles in the family. *The Family Coordinator*, 28, 429–646.

Lisak, D. (2001). Male survivors of trauma. In G. R. Brooks & G. E. Good (Eds.), The new handbook of psychotherapy and counseling with men: A comprehensive guide to settings, problems, and treatment approaches (pp. 263–277). San Francisco, CA: Josses-Bass.

Liu, W. M. (2005). The study of men and masculinity as an important multicultural competency consideration. *Journal of Clinical Psychology*, 61, (Wiley.Com) DOI: 10 1002/ jclp.20/02.

Liu, W. M., Rochlen, A. B., & Mohr, J. (2005). Real and ideal gender role conflict: Exploring psychological distress among men. *Psychology of Men and Masculinity*, 6, 137–148.

Lynch, J., & Kilmartin, C. T. (1999). *The pain behind the mask: Overcoming masculine depression*. Binghamton, New York: Haworth.

Magovcevic, M., & Addis, M. (2008). The Masculine Depression Scale: Development and psychometric evaluation. *Psychology of Men and Masculinity*, 9, 117–132.

Mahalik, J. R. (1999a). Incorporating a gender role strain perspective in assessing and treating men's cognitive distortions. *Professional Psychology: Research and Practice*, 30, 333–340.

Mahalik, J. R. (1999b). Interpersonal psychotherapy with men who experience gender role conflict. *Professional Psychology: Research, and Practice*, 30, 5–13.

Mahalik, J. R. (2001a). Cognitive therapy for men. In G. R. Brooks & G. E. Good (Eds.), The new handbook of psychotherapy and counseling with men: A comprehensive guide to settings, problems, and treatment approaches, Vol. 2 (pp. 544–564). San Francisco, CA: Jossey-Bass.

Mahalik, J. R. (2001b). Interpersonal therapy for men. In G. R. Brooks & G. E. Good (Eds.), The new handbook of psychotherapy and counseling with men: A comprehensive guide to settings, problems, and treatment approaches, Vol. 2 (pp. 565–581). San Francisco, CA: Jossey-Bass.

Mahalik, J. R., Cournoyer, R., DeFranc, W., Cherry, M., & Napolitano, J. M. (1998). Gender role conflict: Predictors of men's utilization of psychological defenses. *Journal of Counseling Psychology*, 45, 247–255.

Mahalik, J. R., Good, G. E., & Englar-Carlson, M. (2003a). Masculinity scripts, presenting concerns, and help seeking: Implications for practice and training. *Professional Psychology: Research and Practice*, 34, 123–131.

Mahalik, J. R., Locke, B. D., Ludlow, L. H., Diemer, M. A., Scott, R. P., Gottfried, M., et al. (2003b). Development of the Conformity to Masculine Norms Inventory. *Psychology of Men and Masculinity*, 4, 3–25.

Mahalik, J. R., Morray, E. B., Coonerty-Femiano, A., Ludlow, L. H., Slattery, S.M., & Smiler, A. (2005). Development of the Conformity to Feminine Norms Inventory. *Sex Roles*, 52, 417–435.

Mansfield, A. K., Addis, M. E., & Courtenay, W. (2005). Measurement of men's help seeking: Development and evaluation of the Barriers to Help Seeking Scale. *Psychology of Men and Masculinity*, 6, 95–108.

Mellinger, T. N., & Liu, W.M. (2006). Men's issues in doctoral training: A survey of Counseling Psychology Programs. *Professional Psychology, Research, and Practice*, 37, 196–204.

Menninger, K. (1970). *Love against hate*. New York: Harcourt, Brace, Jovanovich.

Mertens, C. E. (2000). Male gender role conflict in depressed versus nondepressed medical populations (Doctoral dissertation, University of Iowa, 2000). *Dissertation Abstract International*, 61, 3068.

Miller, D. D, Forrest, L., & Elman, N. S. (2009). Training directors' conceptualizations of the intersection of diversity and trainee competence problems: A preliminary analysis. *The Counseling Psychologist*, 37, 482–518.

Miville, M. L., Changming, D., Nutt, R. L., Waehler, C. A., Suzuki, L., Pistole, M. C., Arredondo, P., Duffy, M., Mejia, B. X., Corpus, M, (2009). Integrating practice guidelines into professional training: Implications for diversity competence. *The Counseling Psychologist*, 37, 519–563.

Mooney, T. F. (1998). Cognitive behavior therapy for men. In W. S. Pollack & R. F. Levant (Eds.) *New psychotherapy for men* (pp. 57–82). New York: John Wiley & Sons, Inc.

Mosher, D. L., & Sirkin, M. (1984). Measuring a macho personality constellation. *Journal of Research in Personality*, 13, 150–163.

Mosher, D. L., & Tomkins, S. S. (1988). Scripting the macho male: Hypermasculine socialization and enculturation. *The Journal of Sex Research*, 25, 60–84.

Nabavi, R. (2004). The "Masculinity Attitudes, Stress, and Conformity Questionnaire (MASC)": A new measure for studying psychology of men (Doctoral dissertation, Alliant International University, 2004). *Dissertation Abstracts International*, 65, 2641.

Nichols, J. (1975). *Men liberation: A new definition of masculinity*. New York: Penguin.

Norton, J. (1997). Deconstructing the fear of femininity. *Feminism & Psychology*, 7, 441–447.

Noyes, B. B. (2004). Gender role conflict as a predictor of therapy outcome. Unpublished masters thesis, The University of Utah.

O'Neil, J. M. (1981a). Male sex-role conflict, sexism, and masculinity: Implications for men, women, and the counseling psychologist. *The Counseling Psychologist, 9,* 61–80.

O'Neil, J. M. (1981b). Patterns of gender role conflict and strain: Sexism and fear of femininity in men's lives. *Personnel and Guidance Journal, 60,* 203–210.

O'Neil, J. M. (1982). Gender role conflict and strain in men's lives: Implications for psychiatrists, psychologists, and other human service providers. In K. Solomon & N. B. Levy (Eds.), *Men in transition: Changing male roles, theory, and therapy* (pp. 5–44). New York: Plenum Publishing Co.

O'Neil, J. M. (1990). Assessing men's gender role conflict. In D. Moore & F. Leafgren (Eds.), *Men in conflict: Problem solving strategies and interventions* (pp. 23–38). Alexandria, VA: American Association for Counseling and Development.

O'Neil, J. M. (2004b). Special Focus: Teaching the Psychology of Men. *SPSMM Bulletin, 10,* 20–71.

O'Neil, J. M. (2006). Helping Jack heal his emotional wounds: The gender role conflict diagnostic schema. In M. Englar-Carlson & M. Stevens (Eds.), *In the therapy room with men: A casebook about psychotherapeutic process and change with male clients* (pp. 259–284). Washington, DC: American Psychological Association.

O'Neil, J. M. (2008a). Special issue. Men's gender conflict: 25 year research summary. *The Counseling Psychologist, 36,* 358–476.

O'Neil, J. M. (2008b). Special Issue: Summarizing Twenty-five years of research on men's gender role conflict using the Gender Role Conflict Scale: New research paradigms and clinical implications. *The Counseling Psychologist. 36,* 358–445.

O'Neil, J. M. (2008c). Complexity, contextualism, and multiculturalism: Responses to the critiques and future directions for the gender role conflict research program. *The Counseling Psychologist, 36,* 469–476.

O'Neil, J. M. (2011). Exploring the psychology of Russian men with Russian psychologists during my fulbright scholarship in the former soviet union. In C. Blazina, C. & D. S. Shen-Miller, (Eds.). *An international psychology of men: Theoretical advances, case studies, and clinical innovations.* (pp. 361–383). New York: Routledge.

O'Neil, J. M., Addis, M., Kilmartin, C., Mahalik, J. (2004). Teaching the Psychology of Men: A potential growth area for psychology and Division 51: A report from the APA Honolulu convention. *SPSMM Bulletin, 10,* 36–47.

O'Neil, J. M., & Egan, J. (1992a). Men's and women's gender role journeys: Metaphor for healing, transition, and transformation. In B. Wainrib (Ed.), *Gender issues across the life cycle.* (pp. 107–123). New York: Springer Publishing Co.

O'Neil, J. M., & Egan, J. (1992b). Men's gender role transitions over the life span: Transformations and fears of femininity. *Journal of Mental Health Counseling 14,* 305–324.

O'Neil, J. M., & Egan, J. (1993). Abuses of power against women: Sexism, gender role conflict, and psychological violence. In E. Cook (Ed.), *Women, relationships, and power: Implications for counseling* (pp. 49–78). Alexandria, VA: ACA Press.

O'Neil, J. M., & Fishman, D. (1992). Adult men's career transitions and gender role themes. In H. D. Lee & Z. B. Leibowitz (Eds.), *Adult career development: Concepts, issues, and Practices* (2nd ed., pp. 132–162). Alexandria, VA: ACA Press.

O'Neil, J. M., Fishman, D. M., & Kinsella-Shaw, M. (1987). Dual-career couples' career transitions and normative dilemmas: A preliminary assessment model. *The Counseling Psychologist, 15*(1), 50–96.

O'Neil, J. M., Good, G. E., & Holmes, S. (1995). Fifteen years of theory and research on men's gender role conflict: New paradigms for empirical research. In R. Levant & W. Pollack (Eds.), *The new psychology of men* (pp. 164–206). New York: Basic Books.

O'Neil, J. M., Helm, B., Gable, R., David, L., & Wrightsman, L. (1986). Gender role conflict scale (GRCS): College men's fears of femininity. *Sex Roles, 14,* 335–350.

O'Neil, J. M., & Lujan, M. L. (2009). Preventing boy's problems in schools through psychoeducational programming: A call to action. *Psychology in the Schools, 46,* 257–266.

O'Neil, J. M. & Lujan, M. L. (2010). An assessment paradigm for fathers and men in therapy using gender role conflict theory. In C. Z. Oren & D. C. Oren (Eds.) *Counseling fathers* (pp. 49–71). New York: Routledge.

O'Neil, J. M., & Nadeau, R. A. (1999). Men's gender-role conflict, defense mechanism, and self-protective defensive strategies: Explaining men's violence against women from a gender-role socialization perspective. In M. Harway & J. M. O'Neil (Eds.), *What causes men's violence against women?* (pp. 89–116). Thousand Oaks, CA: Sage Publications.

Pederson, E. L., & Vogel, D. L. (2007). Male gender role conflict and willingness to seek counseling: Testing a mediation model on college-aged men. *Journal of Counseling Psychology, 54,* 373–384.

Persky, H. R., Daane, M. C., & Jin, Y. (2003). The nation's report card: Writing 2002. National Center for Educational Statistics, Washington, DC.

Pleck, E. H., & Pleck, J. H. (1980). *The American man.* Englewood Cliffs, NJ: Prentice-Hall Inc.

Pleck, J. (1981). *The myth of masculinity.* Cambridge, MA: MIT Press.

Pleck, J. H. (1995). The gender role strain paradigm: An update. In R. F. Levant & W. S. Pollack (Eds.), *A new psychology of men* (pp. 11–32). New York: Basic Books.

Pleck, J. H., & Sawyer, J. (1974). *Men and masculinity.* Englewood Cliffs, NJ: Prentice Hall.

Pleck, J. H., Sonenstein, F. L., & Ku, L. C. (1993). Masculinity ideology and its correlates. In S. Oskamp & M. Costanzo (Eds.), *Gender issues in social psychology* (pp. 85–110). Newbury Park, CA: Sage Publications.

Pollack, W. (1995). No man is an island: Toward a new psychoanalytic psychology of men. In R. Levant & W. Pollack (Eds.), *A new psychology of men* (pp. 33–67). New York: Basic Books.

Pollack, W. (1998a). *Real boys: Rescuing our sons from the myths of boyhood.* New York: Random House.

Pollack, W. S. (1998b). Mourning, melancholia, and masculinity: Recognizing and treating depression in men. In W. S. Pollack & R. F. Levant (Eds.), *New psychotherapy with men.* (pp. 147–166), New York: Wiley.

Pollack, W. S. (1992). Should men treat women? Dilemmas for the male psychotherapist and psychoanalytic and developmental perspectives. *Ethics and Behavior, 2,* 39–49.

Pollack, W. S. (2000). *Real boys' voices.* New York: Random House.

Pollack, W. S. (2001). "Masked men": New psychoanalytically oriented treatment models for adult and young men. In G. Brooks & G. E. Good (Eds.), *The new handbook of psychotherapy and counseling with men: A comprehensive guide to settings, problems, and treatment approaches* (pp. 525–543). San Francisco: Jossey-Bass.

Pollack, W. S., & Levant, R. F. (1998). *New psychotherapies for men.* New York: Wiley.

Rabinowitz, F. E., & Cochran, S. V. (2002). *Deepening psychotherapy with men*. Washington, DC: American Psychological Association.

Real, T. (1997). *O don't want to talk about it: Overcoming the legacy of male depression*. New York: Fireside.

Robertson, J. M. (2001). Counseling men in college settings. In G. Brooks & G. E. Good (Eds.), *The new handbook of psychotherapy and counseling with men: A comprehensive guide to settings, problems, and treatment approaches* Vol. 1 (pp. 146–169). San Francisco: Jossey-Bass.

Robertson, J. M., & Fitzgerald, L. F. (1990). The (mis) treatment of men: Effects of client gender role and life-style on diagnosis and attribution of pathology. *Journal of Counseling Psychology, 37*, 3–9.

Robertson, J. M., & Fitzgerald, L. F. (1992). Overcoming the masculine mystique: Preferences for alternative forms of assistance among men who avoid counseling. *Journal of Counseling Psychology, 39*, 240–246.

Robin, L., & Reiger, D. (1991). *Psychiatric disorders in America*, New York: Free Press.

Rochlen, A. B. (2005). Men in (and out) of therapy: Central concepts, emerging directions, and remaining challenges. *Journal of Clinical Psychology*, published online. Wiley Interscience, *10*, 1002, 1–5.

Rochlen, A. B., Blazina, C., & Raghunathan, R. (2002). Gender role conflict, attitudes toward career counseling, career decision making, and perceptions of career advertising brochures. *Psychology of Men and Masculinity, 3*, 127–137.

Rochlen, A. B., & Hoyer, W. D. (2005). Marketing mental health to men: Theoretical and practical consideration. *Journal of Clinical Psychology, 61*, 675–684 (Wiley.com) DOI: 10 1002/jclp.20102.

Rochlen, A. B., McKelley, R. A., & Pituch, K. A. (2006). A preliminary examination of the "Real Men. Real Depression" campaign. *Psychology of Men and Masculinity, 7*, 1–13.

Rochlen, A. B., & O'Brien, K. M. (2002). The relation of male gender role conflict and attitudes toward career counseling to interest in and preference for career counseling styles. *Psychology of Men and Masculinity, 3*, 9–21.

Rotundo, E. A. (1993). *American manhood: Transformation in masculinity from the revolution to the modern era*. New York: Basic Books.

Sackett, D. L., Straus, S. E., Richardson, W. S., Rosenberg, W., & Haynes, R. B. (2000). *Evidence based medicine: How to practice and teach* (2nd ed.) London: Churchill, Livingston.

Schaub, M., & Williams, C. (2007). Examining the relations between masculine gender role conflict and men's expectations about counseling. *Psychology of Men and Masculinity, 8*, 40–52.

Scher, M. (Ed.). (1981). Special Issue: Counseling men. *Personnel and Guidance Journal, 60*, 198–264.

Scher, M., Stevens, M., Good, G. E., & Eichenfield, G. (Eds.). (1987). *Handbook of counseling and psychotherapy with men*. Newbury Park, CA: Sage.

Schwartz, J. P., Magee, M. M., Griffin, L. D., Dupius, W. (2004). Effects of a group preventive intervention on risk and protective factors related to dating violence. *Group Dynamics: Theory, Research, and Practice, 8*, 221–231.

Schwartz, J. P., & Waldo, M. (2003). Reducing gender role conflict among men attending partner abuse prevention. *Journal for Specialist in Group Work, 20*, 1–15.

Silverstein, L. B. (2006). Integrating feminism and multiculturalism: Scientific fact or science fiction? *Professional Psychology: Research and Practice, 37*, 21–28.

Skovholt, T., Gormally, J., Schauble, P., & Davis, R. (Eds.). (1978). Counseling men [Special Issue]. *The Counseling Psychologist, 7*.

Smiler, A. P. (2004). Thirty years after the discovery of gender: Psychological concept and measures of masculinity. *Sex Roles, 50*, 15–26.

Thompson, E. H., & Pleck, J. H. (1986). The structure of the male norms. *American Behavioral Scientist, 29*, 531–543.

Thompson, E. H., & Pleck, J. H. (1995). Masculinity ideologies: A review of research instrumentation on men and masculinities. In R. Levant & W. Pollack (Eds.), *A new psychology of men* (pp. 129–163). New York: Basic Books.

Thompson, E. H., Pleck, J. H., & Ferrera, D. L. (1992). Men and masculinity: Scales for masculinity ideology and masculinity-related constructs. *Sex Roles, 27* (11/12), 573–607.

Thomson, P. (1995). Men's sexual abuse: Object relations, gender role conflict, and guilt. (Doctoral dissertation, Adelphi University, 1995). *Dissertation Abstracts International, 56*, 3467.

Tokar, D. M., & Jome, L. M. (1998). Masculinity, vocational interests, and career choice traditionality: Evidence for a fully mediated model. *Journal of Counseling Psychology, 45*, 424–435.

Trautner, H. M., & Eckes, T. (2000). Putting gender development into context: Problems and prospects. In T. Eckes & H. Trautner (Eds.), *The developmental social psychology of gender* (pp. 419–435). Mahwah, NJ: Lawrence Erlbaum.

Tyre, P. (2006). The trouble with boys. TIME Magazine, pp. 44–52.

United States Census Department. (1998). United States Census Department Report. Washington, DC: Author.

United States Census Bureau. (2005). School enrollment–social and economic characteristics of students: October, 2003, May 2005. U.S. Census Bureau, U.S. Department of Commerce, Economic and Statistical Administration, Washington, DC: Author.

Van Delft, C. W. (1998). *Gender role conflict and psychological distress in army men*. Unpublished Master's thesis, University of Maryland.

Vessey, J., & Howard, K. (1993). Who seeks psychotherapy? *Psychotherapy, 30*, 546–553.

Vogel, D. L., Wade, N. G., Wester, S. R., Larson, L., & Hackler, A. H. (2007). Seeking help from a mental health professional: The influence of one's social network. *Journal of Clinical Psychology, 63*, 233–245.

Von Drehle, D. (2007). The Boys are all right. TIME Magazine, pp. 38–47.

Wade, J. C. (2008). Masculinity ideology, male reference group identity dependence, and African American men's health related attitudes and behaviors. *Psychology of Men and Masculinity, 9*, 5–16.

Wade, J. C., & Brittan-Powell, C. (2001). Men's attitude toward race and gender equity: The importance of *masculinity ideology, gender-related traits, and reference group identity dependence. Psychology of Men and Masculinity, 2*, 42–50.

Wade, J. C., & Gelso, C. J. (1998). Reference group identity dependence scale: A measure of male identity. *The Counseling Psychologist, 26*, 384–412.

Wester, S. R. (2008a). Male gender role conflict and multiculturalism: Implications for counseling psychology. *The Counseling Psychologist. 35*, 294–324.

Wester, S. R. (2008b). Thinking complexly about men, gender role conflict, and Counseling Psychology. *The Counseling Psychologist, 36*, 462–468.

Wester, S. R., & Vogel, D. L. (2002). Working with masculine mystique: Male gender role conflict, counseling self-efficacy and the training of male psychologists. *Professional Psychology, Research, and Practice, 33*, 370–376.

Wisch, A., & Mahalik, J. R. (1999). Male therapists' clinical bias: Influence of client gender roles and therapist gender role conflict. *Journal of Counseling Psychology, 46*, 51–60.

Wisch, A. F., Mahalik, J. R., Hayes, J. A., & Nutt, E. A. (1995). The impact of gender role conflict and counseling technique on psychological help seeking men. *Sex Roles, 33*, 77–89.

Wong, M. R. (1982). Psychoanalytic-developmental theory and the development of male gender role identity. In K. Soloman & N. B. Levy (Eds.) *Men in transition: Theory and therapy* (pp. 5–44).

Wong, Y. J., & Rochlen, A. B. (2005). Demystifying men's emotional behavior: New directions and implications for counseling and research. *Psychology of Men and Masculinity, 6*, 62–72.

Further Readings

Blazina, C., & Shen-Miller, D. S. (2011). *An international psychology of men: Theoretical advances, case studies, and clinical innovations*. New York: Routledge.

Brooks, G. R. (2010). *Beyond the crisis of masculinity: A transtheoretical model for male-friendly therapy*. Washington, DC: American Psychological Association. (Not reviewed in this chapter but recommended)

Brooks, G. R., & Good, G. E. (Eds.). (2001a). *The new handbook of psychotherapy and counseling with men: A comprehensive guide to settings, problems, and treatment approaches*. San Francisco: Jossey-Bass.

Englar-Carlson, M., & Stevens, M. A. (Eds.). (2006). *In the room with men: A casebook of therapeutic change*. Washington, DC: APA Books.

Kilmartin, C. T. (2007). *The masculine self*. (Third Edition) Cornwall-on-Hudson, New York: Sloan Publishing.

Levant, R. F., & Pollack, W. S. (1995). *The new psychology of men*. New York: Basic Books.

O'Neil, J. M. (2008). Special Issue: Summarizing Twenty-five years of research on men's gender role conflict using the Gender Role Conflict Scale: New research paradigms and clinical implications. *The Counseling Psychologist. 36*, 358–445.

Rabinowitz, F. E. & Cochran, S. V. (2002). *Deepening psychotherapy with men*. Washington, DC: American Psychological Association.

Sexual Orientations and Identities

Susan L. Morrow

Abstract

This chapter addresses critical issues for counseling psychologists regarding sexual minority people. The first section lays the groundwork for the chapter by defining relevant terms and framing sexual orientations and identities in a social constructionist context. Then, assumptions and values of counseling psychologists that are relevant to lesbian, gay, bisexual, and transgender (LGBT) orientations and identities are clarified. The second section of the chapter focuses on research issues with LGBT people. Next, the chapter explores sexual orientations and identities in the identity development process and in coming out. Finally, it addresses LGBT-affirmative counseling and psychotherapy, including multicultural competence in working with sexual minorities, relationship and family issues, spiritual and religious issues, and multiple identities and intersections. It ends with a call for activism on the part of counseling psychologists and identifies future directions for counseling psychology research and practice.

Keywords: lesbian, gay, bisexual, transgender, LGBT, sexual minority, sexual orientation, sexual identity

Since our entry into the field of lesbian, gay, and bisexual (LGB) psychologies in the early 1990s, counseling psychologists have been major contributors to the evolution of lesbian, gay, bisexual, and transgender (LGBT) research and practice in psychology. Several themes have emerged, including a move from pathology to affirmation, LGBT-affirmative practice, developmental issues, and intersections of identities and contexts (Croteau, Bieschke, Fassinger, & Manning, 2008).

To understand LGBT issues relative to counseling psychology, it is important to examine the context and rationale for addressing sexual orientations and identities in our field. Counseling psychologists actively entered the dialog about sexual orientations and identities with the publication of a landmark special issue of *The Counseling Psychologist* (*TCP*) in 1991, edited by Fassinger (1991a), on lesbian/gay affirmative counseling practice. This came 16 years after the American

Psychological Association (APA) issued a statement deploring discrimination against lesbian women and gay men and urging the repeal of discriminatory legislation against them (Conger, 1975), and 35 years after the first article on LGB issues appeared in the *Journal of Counseling Psychology* (Haselkorn, 1956). The special issue of *TCP* included an overview of the then-current issues related to research and practice with lesbian women and gay men (Fassinger, 1991b); affirmative psychotherapy with lesbian women (Browning, Reynolds, & Dworkin, 1991) and gay men (Shannon & Woods, 1991); training issues for therapists working with lesbian women and gay men (Buhrke & Douce, 1991); and work and career issues of lesbian women (Morgan & Brown, 1991).

Additionally, although gender was addressed as a "special populations" issue in the first and second editions of Brown and Lent's (1984, 1992) *Handbook of Counseling Psychology*, it was not until the third and fourth editions (Brown & Lent, 2000, 2008) that sexual orientations and identities were included. Thus, counseling psychologists were slow on the uptake of addressing LGBT issues in psychology; we have, however, since our serious entry into the dialogue, been major contributors to research and scholarship in this area. In addition to the 1991 special issue of *TCP*, the field has seen three additional major contribution issues of *TCP*, as well as numerous empirical articles and recent special issues of the *Journal of Counseling Psychology (JCP)* on "Advances in Research with Sexual Minority People" (2009) and of *TCP* on "Research with Lesbian, Gay, and Bisexual People of Color" (Moradi, DeBlaere, & Huang, 2010a). In addition, counseling psychologists have been active contributors to LGB scholarship in psychology journals outside counseling psychology.

Nonetheless, Croteau et al. (2008) challenged the role of counseling psychologists in adequately dealing with issues related to sexual minority people, noting that our entry into the study of sexual orientation came late. And, although counseling psychology takes an affirmative and nonpathologizing stance toward LGBT people, this stance tends to be "often shallow, affirming that 'gay is okay' but failing to promote advocacy that would change systemic inequalities and heterosexist norms" (Croteau et al., 2008, p. 196; see also Bieschke, Croteau, Lark, & Vandiver, 2005). Croteau et al. called for a new paradigm to address the complexities of intersecting identities and contextual factors (such as race, class, and gender), to include the experiences of bisexual and transgender people, and to examine multiple pathways toward developing identity.

This chapter will attempt to address those concerns. To begin, in this introductory section, I have included a section on definitions and dilemmas related to the language used to describe sexual orientations and identities that honors the complexity and fluidity of diverse, evolving, and self-defining sexual minority people.

Language: Definitions and Dilemmas

Over time, language and definitions related to sexual orientations and identities have expanded and evolved and continue to do so at a rapid rate. This chapter takes a social constructionist view of gender and sexual orientation (Hare-Mustin & Marecek, 1990), arguing that our working definitions of women and men, lesbian women and gay men, bisexual women and men, transgender individuals, and other gendered and sexual categories are overwhelmingly determined by social as opposed to biological factors. This perspective is in direct contrast with an essentialist perspective, which views gender and sexual orientation as immutable characteristics often attached to biology (Broido, 2000). As I will discuss later, individuals with biological characteristics of female or male sex who deviate from their expected gender roles are often subject to persecution, regardless of their sexual orientation. As Fukuyama and Ferguson (2000) argued, "Homophobia . . . has been used as a means to enforce traditional gender role behavior" (p. 85). Thus, gender and sexuality are magnificently confounded, and contemporary research often magnifies, rather than necessarily clarifying, the confusion over the relationships between the two (Fassinger, 2000).

In her in-depth discussion of the intersections of sex, gender, and sexuality, Fassinger (2000) provided concise definitions and a critical analysis of terminology addressing sex, gender, sexuality, and identity. At biological, psychological, and sociopolitical levels, these intersections and definitions are relevant to understanding the psychology of sexual orientations and identities. Biological sex is often confounded with gender, creating confusion and misunderstanding on the part of medical and psychological professionals, as well as the lay public. When a child is born, numerous factors come into play that determine how that child will be responded to, interpersonally and culturally, as well as how that child will come to a self-identity. Often, the first thing new parents look at when an infant slips from the womb is the genitalia. With unambiguous genitalia, medical professionals and parents make a decision that the child is a boy or a girl based on external appearance, and the socialization process begins from that point (it may have begun even earlier if the parents knew the sex of the child prior to birth). With ambiguous genitalia, chromosomal configuration, gonads, internal reproductive structures, external genitalia, hormonal secretions, sex assigned at birth, and psychological sex or gender identity all come into play to define what is commonly thought of as the child's biological sex (Shively & DeSecco, 1993) and determine how that child is responded to as a gendered being. Thus, the apparent or assigned biological sex of a child at birth determines how future socialization will proceed, regardless of whether the child's biological sex is congruent with that child's emergent gender identity. As Fassinger (2000) argued,

"Societal preoccupation with categorizing people as males or females suggests difficulty in making sense of those who do not fit neatly into these two categories (e.g., intersexed or transgendered individuals), and general resistance to viewing human sexuality on the continuum that is generally thought to characterize this trait (Bohan, 1996; Fausto-Sterling, 1998)" (p. 347).

A number of circumstances have converged to create confusion about terminology used to describe the broad umbrella of human sexuality, particularly related to sexual orientations and identities (Moradi, Mohr, Worthington, & Fassinger, 2009). Imprecise use of language has led to the terms *sex* and *gender* being used interchangeably. Essentialist perspectives on sex would have us believe that there are two biological sexes, male and female. In fact, 1 in 2,000 babies are born intersexed, with both female and male characteristics (Green, 2000). They are part of a larger *transgender* or *gender variant* population comprised of individuals whose biological, behavioral, or psychological make-up runs counter to traditional notions of gender roles (Moradi et al., 2009). These individuals may identify as "transsexual, gender queer, genderblend, drag king, drag queen, and androgyne" (Moradi et al., 2009, p. 7), as well as male-to-female (MTF) transsexuals or transwomen, female-to-male (FTM) transsexuals or transmen; or they may reject labels and not identify at all.

In addition to confusion about sex and gender, a historical confusion regarding gender expression and sexual orientation has led to myths and stereotypes about people who "transgress" traditional gender roles (Fassinger & Arseneau, 2007). Thus, parents worry when their little boys are not masculine enough, or when their little tomboys don't reject their pigtails in favor of dresses at the proper age. The underlying fears expressed over these departures from accepted gender roles center around the belief that the child will grow up to be gay or lesbian. So common is this confusion that gender-nontraditional youth and adults are subject to anti-gay violence, even if they are heterosexual. As Moradi et al. (2009) noted, "Both same-sex-oriented and other-sex-oriented people exhibit both same-sex and other-sex behavior" (p. 7).

A complex set of biological and cultural factors determine a person's gender identity, as well as one's sexual orientation. *Sexual orientation* refers to an individual's sexual attraction to women, men, or both (Bailey, 2003). The term *sexual orientation* may more accurately be viewed as shorthand for sexual and affectional orientation (Shively & De Cecco, 1993). Although traditionally sexual orientation has been seen along a bipolar continuum with heterosexuality at one end and homosexuality at the other, and bisexuality in the middle of the continuum (Kinsey, Pomeroy, & Martin, 1948; Kinsey, Pomeroy, Martin, & Gebhard, 1953), there are multiple dimensions to a person's sexual orientation, including sexual attraction, desire, fantasy, feelings of romantic love, actual sexual behaviors and history, relationship history, community of support, patterns of intimacy, and even political affiliations (Fassinger, 2000). Furthermore, an individual may be only situationally engaged in a sexual or affectional relationship with a person of the same sex (e.g., while in a sex-segregated environment such as prison) or may have a more enduring orientation (Keys, 2002).

Sexual orientation identity relates to the way in which an individual defines her or his sexual orientation. The term *sexual identity* has typically been used to describe sexual orientation identity; however, properly used, *sexual identity* refers to one's identity regarding the full range of the "broadest dimensions of human sexual behavior, such as sexual values and mores, sexual needs and preferences for sexual activities, and preferred modes of sexual expression" (Moradi et al., 2009, p. 6). *Sexual orientation identity* may or may not be congruent with sexual orientation itself (Bailey, 2003). For example, a young woman may have dated men throughout high school, then fallen in love with her college roommate. The two may engage in a romantic and sexual relationship while still identifying themselves as heterosexual, either relating romantically only to each other or continuing to relate to men as well. Cultural variables may also be at play in identity (DeBlaere, Brewster, Sarkees, & Moradi, 2010). For example, Latino and African American men may have sex with both men and women but not identify as gay or bisexual (Wolitski, Jones, Wasserman, & Smith, 2006). In addition, active or receptive (top/bottom) sexual behaviors may be more defining than sex of partner in some Latin American communities (Zea, Reisen, & Díaz, 2003). Among some American Indian communities, individuals who are either gender-nontraditional or who engage in same-gender sexual behavior may be referred to as "two spirit" (Adams & Phillips, 2006). Consistent with numerous cross-cultural examples of the blending of concepts of gender roles and sexual orientation identities, women in Thailand whose sexual orientation is to other women are referred to as *thoms* (similar to the concept of "tomboys") and *dees* ("ladies"). Thoms, although having masculine characteristics, also value feminine, nurturing behaviors, and may see themselves as a third sex (Thaweesit, 2004).

Sexual orientation identities can be very confusing to the uninitiated (and even to those who are members of those communities), and definitions and preferences for labels—or for no labels at all—are constantly in flux. The terms *heterosexual, bisexual*, and *homosexual* have been used consistently over time, but although they may provide a somewhat accurate description of sexual orientations (especially when placed on continua), they often do not adequately express sexual orientation identities. *Heterosexuality* describes the orientation of being sexually or affectionally attracted to a person of the opposite sex, and a heterosexual person may also be described as *straight*. Some heterosexual people prefer not to be called "straight" because of the implications that such an identity is rigid, giving rise to the slogan, "Straight but Not Narrow" espoused by some progressive heterosexual people. *Homosexuality* is the term that has been used over time to describe people whose sexual and affectional orientations are toward individuals of the same sex. The term *homosexual*, although commonly used, has fallen into disfavor among many lesbian, gay, and bisexual activists because of its medical and pejorative history and implications. Terms used to describe people who are attracted to members of their same sex include *gay, gay men, gay women, lesbian, same-sex attracted (SSA), men who have sex with men (MSM)*, and *women who have sex with women (WSW)*, along with numerous "code" labels that enable people in their respective communities to communicate with one another. Just as it is difficult for the culturally sensitive counselor or researcher to know the most accessible and appropriate terms to use to describe various cultural groups, this plethora of terms is fraught with confusion and contradiction. Some individuals who are attracted to members of their same sex do not identify as gay or lesbian, sometimes because of fear and sometimes because they do not identify with what they think of as "the gay (or lesbian) community." This may be particularly the case for individuals who experience religious conflict over their sexual orientation. Conversely, "out and proud" lesbians and gay men may be offended at being called "same-sex attracted" because of its association with religious conservatism. The terms MSM and WSW may be unappealing to many gay men and lesbian women, as historically gay and lesbian people

have been seen as primarily sexual; resistance to these labels comes from their insistence on being viewed as whole people. The term *sexual and affectional orientation* has become a preferred way to describe sexual orientation because it does not imply that same sex-attracted people are only sexual. Despite the inadequacy of selecting terminology to describe people according to their preferences, I will, for the most part, use the terms *lesbian* and *gay* to describe predominantly same-sex attracted women and men in this chapter, except when discussing individuals in religious conflict or others who acknowledge same-sex attractions but actively reject the terms.

Bisexuality has been a much-neglected topic in the counseling psychology literature. Bisexual women and men are individuals whose sexual and affectional orientations are toward both women and men. Their attractions may be equally strong toward both genders, or they may be more strongly attracted to one gender or the other. It may be more accurate to say that bisexual individuals are attracted to people, not genders (Diamond, 2008). Historically, with the emergence of an affirmative approach toward lesbians and gay men, bisexuality was viewed as a "stage" along the path to successfully "coming out" as gay or lesbian; individuals who expressed a bisexual identity were seen as having foreclosed on a healthy resolution of their presumed lesbian or gay identity (Fox, 1996). This view reflected the dichotomous perspective on sexual orientation articulated by Kinsey and his colleagues (1948, 1953), as well as the psychoanalytic view that human beings were predisposed to bisexuality in childhood and evolved into healthy heterosexuality as adults. Bisexuality in adults, then, was seen as an arrested state of development (Fox, 1996). Even after the American Psychiatric Association (followed later by the American Psychological Association) removed homosexuality from its diagnostic list of disorders, pathologizing views of bisexuality persisted. However, just as research on homosexuality has failed to find a link to pathology, research on bisexuality has also failed to find such a link. In fact, bisexuals have been found to have high self-esteem, positive self-concept, assertiveness, and cognitive flexibility (Fox, 1996).

Complicating any discussion of sexual orientations and identities is the debate about so-called *sexual preference*. People have asked for decades whether sexual orientation is innate or acquired, as well as if it can be changed. Unfortunately, political agendas have led this debate, with gay activists arguing that, because sexual orientation is biological and stable, lesbians and gay men cannot be "blamed" for their orientations. Led primarily by the religious right, the view that sexual orientation is chosen, or at least acquired, is used to illustrate that it can also be changed. Each side calls upon the "science" that supports its position. As Bailey (2003) suggested, this argument is largely unproductive, because research into hormonal and neuroendocrine contributors to sexual orientation has not been conclusive. The more important question regards the motives of those who promote the different perspectives and the consequences that these debates have for lesbian, gay, and bisexual people in their family, religious, occupational, and social lives.

Confounding discussions of sexual orientations and identities are recent theory and research regarding the fluidity of sexual orientation (Diamond, 2000). In a study of lesbian, bisexual, and "unlabeled" same-sex-attracted women, Diamond found that half of women changed their sexual orientation identities in a 2-year period, although their attractions changed very little. Based on her longitudinal research, Diamond (2005) identified subtypes of women who experienced attractions to women: Those who had maintained consistent lesbian identifications over an 8-year span, whom she described as *stable lesbians*; those who had alternated between lesbian and nonlesbian labels, described as *fluid lesbians*; and *stable nonlesbians*, who had never adopted the label of lesbian. The notion of fluidity does not necessarily deny a biological component. Diamond (2008) views "sexual feelings and experiences as simultaneously embedded in both physical–biological and sociocultural contexts" (p. 22) and suggests that women's sexual attractions are more influenced by environmental processes than are those of men. It should also be noted that, according to Diamond (2008), many, but not all, women who experience attractions to other women have fluid identities, leaving a significant number who were stable lesbians. The stability or instability of sexual orientation identities is highly political. At a time when the religious right insists that sexual orientation is a choice and therefore subject to change, many sexual minorities are forced to defend the stability of their gay or lesbian orientations. Despite evidence of fluidity in women, many lesbians and the majority of gay men experience their same-sex orientations as immutable. Many who have made attempts to change their orientations through conversion therapies have spoken of the harms they endured both during and long after such therapies (Beckstead & Morrow, 2004; Shidlo & Schroeder, 2002).

Transgender issues add further complexity to the discussion of sexual orientations and identities. The term *transgender* may be seen as an umbrella term that encompasses a broad range of gender-variant experiences, behaviors, and bodies in which individuals' gender expression, behaviors, or bodies differ from traditional notions of masculinity or femininity (Lev, 2007; Sánchez & Vilain, 2009), including "cross-dressers, transsexuals and transgenderists, male-to-female transsexuals (MTFs), female-to-male transsexuals (FTMs), androgynes, feminine gay men, butch lesbians, drag queens [and kings], heterosexual as well as gender-bent queers, . . . two-spirit and intersex people," (Lev, p. 151) and eunuchs (Vale et al., in press; Wassersug & Johnson, 2007). Transsexual individuals are those whose physical bodies do not represent what they experience as their true sex (Lev), and they may or may not seek sexual reassignment. They are properly referred to by the gender designation (man, woman) and pronouns that fit the gender they experience as true for them or toward which they are transitioning. Thus, a FTM transsexual would be referred to as a man (or sometimes transman). So strongly are gender and sexual orientation blurred in our culture that transgender status has historically been conflated with sexual orientation, so that male cross-dressers have been thought of as gay, as have gender-nonconforming heterosexuals been assumed to be gay or lesbian. However, cross-dressers may be heterosexual, and gender expression is not necessarily related to sexual orientation.

Queer, like transgender, is an umbrella term that is sometimes used to cover the universe of LGBTQIA (Lesbian-Gay-Bisexual-Transgender-Queer-Intersex-Ally) or LGBTQQIA (to include "Questioning") individuals and communities. What is common across this universe is gender "transgression" (Fassinger & Arseneau, 2007), even though the specific demonstrations of gender nonconformity are highly variable and subject to different consequences in society at large, as well as in the medical and psychological arenas. The term "queer" was historically used pejoratively to describe LGB people; LGB activists reclaimed the term in order to dismantle its power and use it to express pride. Its current usage, in addition to being the umbrella described above, has emerged within queer theory and describes individuals and a movement that attempt to deconstruct and undermine gendered categories (Carroll & Gilroy, 2001). Thus, an individual identifying as gender-queer may identify as other than a man or a woman, as both male and female, or as neither; or the individual may reject the gender binary altogether.

In some sense, the contradictions and dilemmas identified above reflect the challenges in dealing adequately with constructs of sexual orientations and identities, as we are faced with constantly changing terminology couched in an essentialist context while trying to talk meaningfully about individuals, groups, and communities that are overwhelmingly diverse and constantly changing. Given these dilemmas, it is important to point out that individuals may or may not find the terminology that is used to describe their experience relevant or even acceptable. Thus, counseling psychologists face particular challenges as they attempt to find a common language among themselves and with their research participants and clients. These challenges will be further addressed in subsequent sections of this chapter. Next, in striving for greater clarity, I articulate some underlying values and assumptions in counseling psychology related to sexual orientations and identities and sexual minority people that ground this chapter.

Assumptions and Values Underlying This Chapter

A number of premises underlie the perspectives of counseling psychology regarding sexual orientations and identities and LGBT people. These premises are not without contradictions. In this section, I address the individual in context, violence in the lives of LGBT people, and the mental health treatment of LGBT people.

The Individual in Context

Despite our historical valuing of context, counseling psychologists have a tendency to "psychologize" and decontextualize the behaviors, emotions, and experiences of the human beings we counsel and study. Even LGBT-affirmative therapists adhere to stage models to describe the development of LGB individuals, and therapists who advocate for transsexual clients are forced to use the *Diagnostic and Statistical Manual* (DSM; American Psychiatric Association, 2000b) diagnosis of gender identity disorder to support their clients' process of sexual reassignment. In psychologizing the experiences of LGBT individuals, we run the risk of ignoring the contexts of their lives, as well as of pathologizing them. Two core counseling psychology values thus are violated: viewing human beings from a positive perspective as individuals who are coping with life stressors, and viewing individuals in the context of their lives.

Wrenn's (1962) concern about the culturally encapsulated counselor is still relevant today, despite counseling psychology's commitments to multiculturalism and social justice. Our field's commitment to looking at the individual in her or his cultural context is a core value of counseling psychology, and it is important that we not lose sight of what this means in the lives of LGBT people. Social movements have accomplished great things. But, just as we do not live in a "postracial" society with the election of a black president of the United States, LGBT people—despite significant gains—continue to face barriers to employment and parenthood; rejection by families, churches, and communities; and violence.

The cultural and political contexts of the lives of LGBT people in the United States are filled with contradictions. On the one hand, media increasingly portray sexual minorities in a positive light and as the complex human beings that they are. In urban areas and on the Internet, increasing numbers and diversity of support networks are available for LGBT people from their teens to old age. In a few jurisdictions, same-sex marriages, civil unions, and adoptions have passed into law. At the same time, conservative political backlash has frequently pulled the civil rights rug out from under the feet of LGBT people and families. California's Proposition 8, restricting marriage to opposite-sex couples, was a massive blow to same-sex couples and their families everywhere. According to DOMA Watch (http://www.domawatch.org/index.php, retrieved June 6, 2010), an organization dedicated to keeping the public aware of the legal issues related to the Defense of Marriage Acts (DOMA), 37 states have such acts on their books, whereas 30 have actual constitutional amendments to restrict marriage to one man and one woman. These U.S. trends are interesting in light of increasing acceptance of same-sex marriage in many other countries. Spain, a largely Catholic country, was the third country in the world to legalize same-sex marriage in 2005.

Other contemporary sociopolitico-cultural climate issues include ongoing controversy over the "Don't Ask—Don't Tell" (DADT; "House passes," 2010) military policy in which, since the passage of Department of Defense (DOD) Directive 1304.26 introduced by President Bill Clinton in 1993, military personnel are not to be pursued regarding information about their sexual orientations. Originally seen as a step forward in the rights of LGB women and men in the military, it left in place the longstanding policy that homosexuality is incompatible with military service (DOD Directive 1332.14, 1982). At present, the U.S. House of Representatives and the Senate Armed Forces Committee have both voted in favor of repealing DADT ("House Passes," 2010).

Despite notable progress, the civil liberties of LGBT people continue to be challenged. Conservative backlash is strong, and violence against sexual minorities is a serious problem worldwide.

Violence in the Lives of LGBT People

The history of violence toward individuals whose sexual orientation is toward individuals of their own gender is shocking. Both Europe and the United States have early histories of castrating, mutilating, or putting to death people who engaged in same-sex sexual behaviors. Between 5,000 and 15,000 homosexuals were put to death in Nazi prison camps in World War II (Herek, Berrill, & Berrill, 1992). By the early 1990s, increasing numbers of lesbian women and gay men were out of the closet, accompanied by rapidly increasing anti-gay and lesbian violence (Herek et al., 1992). The National Gay and Lesbian Task Force (http://www.thetaskforce.org/issues/hate_crimes_main_page) reported that, after 27 years of antiviolence work by the NGLTF, President Barack Obama signed into law the Matthew Shepard and James Byrd, Jr. Hate Crimes Prevention Act, which extended hate crimes legislation in the United States to include sexual orientation and gender identity, on October 28, 2009. In November 2009, the National Transgender Discrimination Survey, conducted by the National Center for Transgender Equality and the NGLTF, found that transgender people had double the rate of unemployment, near universal harassment on the job, significant losses of jobs and careers, high rates of poverty, and significant housing insecurity (http://www.thetaskforce.org/downloads/reports/fact_sheets/transsurvey_prelim_findings.pdf). Despite true gains in the quality of life for LGBT people in the United States and many parts of the world, in most areas of the country, sexual minorities can be fired from their jobs without recourse, as well as face discrimination in housing, health care, and family-related processes such as marriage, custody, and adoption. Furthermore, violence or fear of violence continues to be commonplace. These concerns have clear relevance to counseling psychologists.

Mental Health Treatment of LGBT People

A look at the mental health maltreatment of lesbian and gay people is eye-opening. For most of the history of psychiatric and psychological perspectives on same-sex orientations, people who were attracted to or had sex with people of the same sex were viewed as mentally disturbed. Freud held an ambivalent attitude toward homosexuality, insisting that it was not an illness (although seeing it as resulting from arrested sexual development) and, for his time, adopting an affirmative stance toward homosexuals (Rothblum, 2000). On the one hand, he considered humans as psychologically bisexual; on the other, he believed that homosexual feelings should be sublimated and pursued treatments to help his patients do so (Rothblum, 2000). Current-day conversion therapists built upon psychoanalytic theory; however, they do not agree with Freud that people are innately bisexual, instead viewing homosexuality as pathological and a result of faulty parent– (especially mother–) child relationships. Conversion (also known as "reparative" or "reorientation") therapies have been demonstrated to be ineffective and often harmful (Haldeman, 1994; 2004); however, they continue to be used, particularly by conservative, religiously oriented practitioners (Beckstead & Israel, 2007). In addition to psychoanalytically based approaches to same-sex attractions, efforts to "cure" homosexuality have included surgeries, electroconvulsive treatments, hormonal therapies, and behavioral and cognitive behavioral treatments (Morrow & Beckstead, 2004). In 1973 and 1975, respectively, the American Psychiatric Association and the American Psychological Association declassified homosexuality as a mental disorder; and, at present, most mental health professions have issued statements confirming the view that lesbian, gay, and bisexual orientations and identities are no more or less pathological than are heterosexual ones and condemning conversion therapy theory and practice.

Affirmative mental health treatment of transsexual individuals has lagged behind that of LGB people and at present is caught in a dilemma. Most medical and mental health professionals are shamefully un- or undereducated about the needs of transsexuals, leading to maltreatment ranging from microaggressions to overt discrimination (Korrell & Lorah, 2007). Yet, these same mental health professionals may be called upon to assist transsexual clients in meeting psychological criteria for proceeding with medical treatments for sexual reassignment. Counseling psychologists and their transsexual clients seeking medical interventions face a values-based challenge. As multiculturally competent counseling psychologists, we do not view LGBT people through a lens of pathology; however, for those transsexual people who seek sexual reassignment treatment, the psychologist is called upon to diagnose the individual with gender identity disorder. Korrell and Lorah predicted that many therapists will work with at least one transgender client at some point, and that many more will see family members of transgender people. To date, the only mental health organization that has developed guidelines for working with transgender/transsexual people is the Association of Lesbian, Gay, Bisexual, and Transgender Issues in Counseling (ALGBTIC; 2009); these guidelines were approved by the American Counseling Association (ACA) Governing Council in November, 2009.

The context for LGBT people might seem grim, and at times it is. Despite the decline in violent crime in the United States in recent years and growing visibility and acceptance of LGBT people in the culture at large, violence against LGBT people continues to rise. The successful passage of the Matthew Shepard and James Byrd, Jr. Hate Crimes Prevention Act was a milestone in the effort to end this violence. Resistance to equal rights for LGBT people in the United States and elsewhere appears to have increased with the virulence of the religious right (Herek, 2004); yet, LGBT people and their allies are undaunted in their fight for fair treatment for all. For many young people, particularly in larger urban areas, sexual orientation appears to be a "nonissue," as youth of all genders and sexual orientations identify as queer in unity and solidarity (Jacobson & Donatone, 2009).

Understanding the context of the lives of LGBT people is a central part of cultural competence in research, teaching, and practice with these populations. The issues that are relevant to counseling psychologists related to sexual orientations and identities are many, and an exhaustive coverage is not possible. Thus, I have selected what I consider to be critical issues for counseling psychologists, either because they are areas that have been addressed by counseling psychologists or are part of the core foci of our discipline. They include research issues on LGBT people; developmental issues, including identities and coming out; and LGBT-affirmative counseling and psychotherapy, including issues of multiculturalism and intersectionality.

Research Issues on LGBT People

Research on LGBT issues has evolved over time since Evelyn Hooker's (1957) seminal research demonstrating that homosexuality was not correlated with psychopathology. However, attitudes, even in psychology, change slowly; and, in 1977, Morin found that most published research still viewed homosexuality from an illness model. In 1991, the *American Psychologist* published an article by Herek, Kimmel, Amaro, and Melton on heterosexist bias in research. *Heterosexist bias* was defined as "conceptualizing human experience in strictly heterosexual terms and consequently ignoring, invalidating, or derogating homosexual behaviors and sexual orientation, and lesbian, gay, and bisexual relationships and lifestyles" (p. 958). This article—a report from the American Psychological Association Task Force on Nonheterosexist Research convened in 1985 by the Board for Social and Ethical Responsibility in Psychology—addressed the scientific, social, and ethical consequences of heterosexist bias, raised questions for researchers interested in evaluating heterosexist bias in their own research, and made recommendations for reducing heterosexist bias in research, publishing, and academe. The authors addressed issues of sampling bias, research design and procedures, protection of research participants, and interpreting and reporting results. These guidelines have relevance 20 years later and could productively be implemented by counseling psychology researchers and educators today.

More recently, the *JCP* published a special issue on "Advances in Research with Sexual Minority People" (2009). In their lead article, in addition to describing the difficulties with conceptualizing and defining sexual minorities addressed above, Moradi et al. (2009) outlined current challenges in sexual minority research and offered suggestions for consideration in future research. These challenges fall into seven areas: construct-related issues, issues related to population(s) of interest, internal validity, external and ecological validity, measurement, procedural issues, and writing.

Construct-related Issues

Research on sexual minority people is complicated by the many definitional problems described above, as well as because researchers have used a variety of terms (e.g., homophobia, heterosexism, heteronormativity, homonegativity) to capture a particular phenomenon or population group, as well as using the same term (e.g., internalized heterosexism) to mean somewhat different things. This lack of consistency can lead to difficulty in comparing the findings of different studies (Frost & Meyer, 2009). Moradi et al. (2009) also argued that the "conceptual breadth of constructs of interest" (p. 11) needed greater attention in LGBT research. Clarity about whether to investigate variables (e.g., social support) at a broader, more global level or a more specific, LGBT-focused level will contribute to more meaningful outcomes. Citing Reise, Waller, and Comrey (2000), Moradi et al. pointed out that "narrower constructs tend to be more effective in predicting specific outcomes, whereas global constructs tend to be better at predicting complex and multifaceted outcomes" (p. 11). Moradi et al. also recommended that researchers investigating sexual minority issues consider conducting multilevel analyses, including within-person, between-person, and larger social-unit levels. For example, heterosexism may vary within individuals according to the contexts in which they find themselves (Levitt et al., 2009); it may be explored as a between-person variable (Szymanski, 2009), or it may be investigated at a larger, systemic level (Rostosky, Riggle, Horne, & Miller, 2009).

Issues Related to Population(s) of Interest

Given the complexity and ambiguity that surrounds describing sexual minority people, as well as the tremendous variation in their experiences and identities, it is important to clearly identify the population of interest in relation to research question and sampling procedures (Moradi et al., 2009). Many within-group differences (e.g., related to race/ethnicity/culture) may impact the results of a study, even when the population appears to be carefully identified. Moradi et al. recommended careful consideration of what dimensions of sexual minority status are of interest in formulating a research question.

Issues Related to Internal Validity

Moradi et al. (2009) recommended greater diversity in research approaches on sexual minority people, expressing concern about the use of cross-sectional data to test directional hypotheses. They suggested considering experimental and repeated measures designs to test causal hypotheses. Furthermore, they recommended longitudinal research designs to investigate developmental processes, such as identity and vocational development.

External and Ecological Validity

A number of problems regarding external and ecological validity confront investigators conducting research on sexual minorities. Over time, one of the most common critiques of sampling bias in such research has been the difficulty of obtaining a representative sample, as sexual minority status and the accompanying stigma may prevent more closeted

individuals from learning about or being willing to participate in studies geared toward LGBT people (Herek et al., 1991). Furthermore, cultural variables related to sexual orientation identity, such as those described above, may negatively impact participation of sexual minority people of color (Moradi et al., 2009). Meyer and Wilson (2009) identified challenges and recommended principles to guide sampling with LGB populations.

Measurement

A considerable number of measurement challenges confront researchers on LGBT issues (Moradi et al., 2009). These concerns include the applicability of existing measures to sexual minority people on whom psychometric evidence is absent; validity problems with an instrument created for use with one sexual minority population and then applied to another; heterosexist language in measures developed for heterosexual people; problems with attempting to investigate constructs for which measures have yet to be constructed; and challenges with using older instruments to measure constructs that are rapidly changing. Of particular concern is the tendency on the part of some scholars to "add 'B' and stir," assuming that measures that reflect the realities of lesbian women and gay men will be equally applicable to bisexual women and men. The confounding of sexual orientation (LGB) and sexual identity (including transgender issues) addressed earlier has further complicated this problem. Moradi et al. (2009) recommended accurately assessing sexual orientation and gender identities when recruiting and measuring sexual minority constructs, as well as developing "standards regarding core constructs to assess in sexual minority research" and "measures to assess those constructs" (p. 15).

Procedural Issues

The stigmatization and marginalization of sexual minority people is a theme that runs throughout research considerations with LGBT populations. The sociopolitical context of such research complicates the process, from the formulation of the research question to the dissemination of the results. Because of past and sometimes current research abuses of marginalized groups, including sexual minorities, LGBT people may experience what Sue and Sue (1999) termed "cultural paranoia" directed toward traditional researchers, in which past injuries within and outside the research setting may engender wariness on the part of potential research participants. Alternatively, sexual minority people, weary of the silence surrounding their lives, may be eager to contribute to research that will cast them, their lives, and their communities in a positive light. Moradi et al. recommended that researchers carefully consider and minimize the potential risks to participants of participating in research and conduct pilot studies to increase sensitivity to participant needs. In addition, recognizing the unique circumstances that may affect honest responding, researchers can work to build collaborative relationships that will increase trust on the part of participants. Finally, the authors suggested that researchers "give back" to participants and their communities.

Writing

As described above, clear communication in the form of precisely defining terms and constructs; clearly stating research questions; and carefully describing sampling, recruitment, and procedures can provide the basis for the accurate and meaningful reporting of findings (Moradi et al., 2009). Keeping in mind the sociopolitical nature of research with sexual minority people, it is essential to understand the ways in which research findings can be misinterpreted and abused by those with conservative agendas (Gonsiorek, 1991). Moradi et al. recommended that researchers "anticipate and clarify points that could be misunderstood or distorted by readers and/or the media" (p. 17).

As articulated by Worthington and Navarro (2003), Croteau et al. (2008), and Moradi et al. (2009), a major concern at this juncture in counseling psychology is to address the intersectionality of various statuses and identities, in particular LGB people of color, in order to take research on sexual minorities to a more inclusive and complex arena. The authors of a major contribution of *TCP* (Moradi, DeBlaere, & Huang, 2010b) have responded to this call by further addressing the invisibility of LGB people of color and making recommendations for centralizing the experiences of LGB people of color in counseling psychology. Although it is certainly the case that stigma surrounding sexual minorities in communities of color may contribute somewhat to the invisibility of LGB people of color, Moradi et al. (2010b) argued that "LGB people of color have been leaders in LGB organizations" (p. 323) over time and have been visible contributors to LGB communities and to social change efforts. However, their visibility in these arenas has not been reflected in the literature on LGB people of color; overall, race/ethnicity has

been greatly under-reported in the literature on sexual orientation, and sexual orientation has been under-reported in studies of people of color (Moradi et al., 2010b).

Sexual Orientations and Identities: Development and Coming Out

According to Croteau et al. (2008), sexual identity theory is counseling psychology's "most-studied concept" in relation to LGBT people. Sexual identity development is the "process by which individuals develop a psychological sense of themselves that embraces their sexual orientation amidst pervasive societal heterosexism and sexual prejudice" (p. 196). Models have been developed to understand the identity formation process of lesbian women and gay men, bisexual women and men, and transsexual individuals.

Lesbian and Gay Identity Development

Cass (1979) theorized six stages of sexual identity development for lesbian and gay people: *identity confusion*, characterized by growing awareness of one's homosexuality and a sense of incongruence with one's prior identity or sense of morality; *identity comparison*, in which the individual tentatively adopts a homosexual identity and experiences a sense of being different from the heterosexual majority; *identity tolerance*, in which the individual still experiences ambivalence but becomes more committed to a homosexual identity; *identity acceptance*, in which the individual has increasing contact with other lesbian and gay people and experiences feeling "normal"; *identity pride*, in which the individual holds other gay and lesbian people in high regard and devalues heterosexual people and associated values; and, finally, *identity synthesis*, in which the individual continues to feel pride but no longer devalues heterosexuality per se and is able to integrate her or his sexual orientation identity with the rest of life. At any time, the individual may foreclose on her or his identity.

Coleman (1982) also proposed a stage theory model, including *pre-coming out*, when individuals feel "different" but do not understand why; *coming out*, when they acknowledge their homosexual feelings (corresponding to Cass's identity confusion); *exploration*, consisting of experimentation and greater openness (corresponding to Cass's identity tolerance); *first relationships*; and *integration* (corresponding to Cass's identity synthesis). Coleman warned that this linear, progressive model was simplistic and may not accurately capture reality; however, it could be useful for clinicians in understanding underlying dynamics of identity development.

Cass's (1979) and Coleman's (1982) models have been criticized more recently for being overly simplistic and decontextualized (Fassinger & Arseneau, 2007; McCarn & Fassinger, 1996); however, they provided the field with important tools to understand identity development and the process of "coming out of the closet" for lesbian and gay people. Reading the original articles, along with Coleman's (1978) review of the treatment literature and proposal for a nonpathologizing approach to psychotherapy with lesbians and gay men, provides an excellent historical grounding for understanding just how far we have come.

Contemporary theories are more contextual as well as inclusive of women, bisexual women and men, and transgender people (Lev, 2007; Potoczniak, 2007; Sophie, 1986) and of intersections of race, ethnicity, and culture with sexual orientations and identities (Fukuyama & Ferguson, 2000; Greene, 2000). Sophie critiqued stage models of identity development proposed by Cass (1979) and Coleman (1982), as well as others from whose work Sophie synthesized a general stage model consisting of *first awareness, testing and exploration, identity acceptance*, and *identity integration*. She assessed this model in terms of its applicability to lesbians based on her longitudinal interview-based qualitative study with 14 college-aged lesbian women. She found that, although her participants experienced some of the stages proposed by theorists, there were serious limitations to their applicability. In particular, her participants appeared not to follow a linear path through stages, demonstrating more fluidity than accounted for by stage theories. Sophie also emphasized the importance of contextual factors, as her participants had also benefitted from the results of the gay liberation movement, noting that "the development of lesbian identity is extremely sensitive to variations in the prevailing attitudes toward homosexuality and in the availability of others who support a positive view of relations between women" (p. 50).

Striving for greater complexity and contextuality, McCarn and Fassinger (1996) further critiqued existing stage models, particularly for conflating individual and social aspects of identity, and proposed an inclusive model of sexual identity formation in lesbian women, hypothesizing two separate, but reciprocal, developmental processes, *individual sexual identity* and *group membership identity*.

These are referred to as phases to imply "greater flexibility and circularity" (Fassinger & Miller, 1996, p. 56) than rigid stage models. Although similar in some ways to other models, the McCarn and Fassinger model does not view disclosure as evidence of developmental progression because of the profound impact that an oppressive context may have on disclosure. For example, a teacher in a conservative area may feel proud to be lesbian or gay but make a decision not to risk her or his career by being open in the workplace or community. Developmental tasks within each identity process (individual sexual identity, group membership identity) include *awareness* (Individual: feeling "different," experiencing confusion; Group: of the reality of varied sexual orientations); *exploration* (Individual: of erotic feelings toward same-sex individuals; Group: of oneself in relation to lesbian/gay people); *deepening/commitment* (Individual: deepening of self-knowledge, commitment to choices about sexuality; Group: to involvement with lesbian/gay people, understanding the realities of oppression); and *internalization/synthesis* (Individual: of love for same-sex individuals, identity; Group: of one's identity as a member of lesbian/gay community, across contexts). Although the two processes (individual and group-oriented) are related and may enhance one another, individuals may proceed in different ways and at different paces through them. This model has received considerable research support for both lesbian women (McCarn & Fassinger, 1996) and gay men (Fassinger & Miller, 1996), as well as for lesbian women and gay men of color (Risco, 2008; Risco & Fassinger, 2007).

Bisexual Identity Development

The early development of stage theories of lesbian and gay identity development was characterized either by ignoring bisexuality or considering bisexuality a "transitional identity" in the evolution of a mature, stable lesbian or gay identity (Rust, 2007). Finally, in the 1980s, researchers began to view bisexuality as a legitimate identity in and of itself. Despite evidence to the contrary, many theorists continue to view sexual identity as a fixed point toward which sexual minority individuals develop (Rust, 2007). On the contrary, Weinberg, Williams, and Pryor (2001) proposed a developmental model culminating in continued uncertainty following the adoption of a bisexual identity, thereby normalizing a "mature state of identity flux" (Rust, 2007, p. 4). Research by Diamond (1998, 2008) suggests that, for women in particular, sexual orientation is quite fluid, thus reinforcing Rust's concept of identity flux. Furthermore, investigating whether bisexuality was (a) a transitional stage as described above, (b) a "third" sexual orientation (in addition to heterosexual and lesbian/gay, or (c) a clear example of sexual fluidity in human beings, Diamond (2008) found support for (b) and (c), but not (a). In particular, she proposed an integrated model describing bisexual women's identity in which "bisexuality may best be interpreted as a stable pattern of attraction to both sexes in which the *specific* balance of same-sex to other-sex desires necessarily varies according to interpersonal and situational factors" (p. 12). Based on her findings, Diamond argued that, contrary to common wisdom, "identity *change* is more common that identity *stability*" (p. 13). Research by Stokes, McKirnan, and Burzette (1993); Stokes, Damon, and McKirnan (1997); Dickson, Paul, and Herbison (2003); and Weinberg et al. (1994) have also found evidence of fluidity in men; Weinberg et al. noted the impact of both relationships and situational factors in bisexual men's attractions and behaviors.

Rust (2007) found a number of ways in which bisexual women and men experienced changes in their sexual orientation identities. For some, identity change was a personal process in which people became more deeply self-aware and redefined their sexual orientation based on this new awareness. Although this process appears similar to the traditional "coming-out" process experienced by lesbians and gay men, it differs in that bisexuals do not reject their prior attractions to opposite-sex people, and many may experience a second coming-out after having been lesbian- or gay-identified. In addition, for some, taking on the identity of bisexuality provided a more flexible identity in which to experience and express their sexuality without having to continually reconstruct their identities. Rust also found that, for some individuals, a sociopolitical context in which bisexuality became a possibility for them provided the impetus for identifying as bisexual. For some individuals, a bisexual identity can be a political statement. Although a reflection of their honest feelings and attractions, some choose to make a statement of solidarity with other bisexuals by "coming out" as bisexual.

Alternative identities also arise as individuals define and construct themselves (Rust, 2007). One example is reclaiming the term *queer*, formerly a pejorative term. According to Rust:

"[Q]ueer" identity . . . is a well-developed, nuanced identity within the sexual minority community.

It represents a challenge to traditional dichotomous notions of sex (female, male), gender (woman, man), and sexuality (homo-, heterosexual). It reconstructs bisexuality, commonly conceptualized as a hybrid combination of homo- and heterosexuality, by calling into question the distinction between these two forms of gendered sexuality. "Queer" is about crossing, blurring, and erasing boundaries, both conceptual and political. (p. 16)

Thus, bisexual identity tends to challenge traditional developmental stage theories of identity development and, in doing so, provides a paradigm for greater creativity and flexibility in conceptualizing sexual minority identity.

Transgender/Transsexual Identity Development

To understand the identity development of gender variant or transgender people, it is important to place it in a cultural context (Lev, 2007). Today's emphasis on hormonal treatments and surgical interventions places transsexuals squarely in a medical model in many people's minds. However, transgender people have lived their lives throughout history and across cultures, sometimes given legitimate positions in their societies and, at other times, passing for members of the other sex (Lev, 2007). In the current cultural climate, the intersections of medical, psychological, and activist agendas complicate the identity development process of transgender people.

In the process of coming to terms with one's gender identity, a trans person may also be in a position in which a redefinition of sexual orientation is necessary (Gagné, Tewksbury, & McGaughey, 1997). In their research with transgender individuals (MTF transsexuals and male cross-dressers), Gagné et al. identified a number of processes through which their participants transited—which resemble developmental stage theories that have been developed for LGB people—beginning with early experiences of "not fitting" or wanting to be a girl or woman. Some experienced these feelings and desires as children, whereas others became aware of their dissatisfaction with their assigned gender in adolescence or adulthood. Some, rather than wanting to be, felt they actually *were* women or girls in the wrong bodies. These experiences were accompanied by confusion, especially if they were given less-than-supportive messages by others. Many experimented with cross-gender behavior and dress, usually in secret. This period was followed by a process of coming out to self as they found names for their feelings and learned that there were others with the same experiences. At this time, a search for authenticity became important. This was also accompanied for many by a period of questioning their sexual orientations. Because transgender role models are scarce, many sought information and confirmation from media or on the Internet. Finally, these transgender individuals made decisions about coming out to others and developed strategies for managing their identities in the various facets of their lives. This enabled them to try out and legitimize their emerging identities. These activities, along with finding support groups, facilitated identity resolution, including making decisions about whether to "pass" as an individual of the new gender and a desire to contribute to the positive development of other transgender people (Gagné et al., 1997).

Lev (2007) suggested a stage-developmental model for transgender people considering sex reassignment. This model consists of six stages: awareness, seeking information/reaching out, disclosure to significant others, exploration (identity and self-labeling), exploration (transition issues/possible body modification), and integration (acceptance and post-transition issues). Lev's model is illustrative of the move away from a medicalized, pathologizing lens to one that honors sexual diversity.

Intersecting Identities

A caution is in order regarding identity models, as individuals develop with multiple identities, some privileged and some not. Thus, a white lesbian woman will be privileged because of her skin color but will be in a nondominant position as a lesbian and a woman. In the case of changing identities, a woman may conceive of herself as heterosexual and then fall in love with another woman, thus transiting from a majority to minority sexual orientation identity. A female-to-male transsexual may experience greater discrimination because of his transsexual status (especially if it is obvious), but may find himself taken more seriously in the workplace as a man. Multiple oppressed identities can be confusing, as often the individual does not know whether she or he is being oppressed based on race/ethnicity, gender, sexual orientation, or another intersecting status or identity such as socioeconomic class, disability, age, or physical appearance. Thus, many of the foregoing models are highly simplified ways to attempt to understand what sexual minority people experience as they develop positive

and healthy self-concepts. Nonetheless, they set the stage for multiculturally competent practice when working with sexual minority people.

LGBTQ Affirmative Counseling and Psychotherapy

Affirmative counseling and psychotherapy with sexual minority people is based on the premise that healthy human beings hold a wide variety of identities and attractions; relate in many different ways as lovers, spouses, or life partners; and express themselves sexually with an array of possibilities. LGBT-affirmative counselors and therapists challenge the medicalization and pathologizing of sexual orientations and identities and work as allies to LGB people within and without the mental health setting. In addition, these therapists are committed to developing competence in their work with LGB clients.

Multicultural Competence in Counseling Sexual Minorities

At the heart of ethical practice when counseling sexual minorities is the therapist's deep commitment to becoming culturally competent. The counseling psychology literature has applied multicultural counseling competencies to LGBT counseling (Fassinger & Sperber-Richie, 1997) as well as developing knowledge, attitude, and skills-based competencies (Israel, Ketz, Detrie, Burke, & Shulman, 2003). Bidell (2005) developed the Sexual Orientation Counselor Competency Scale (SOCCS), also based on multicultural models. Dillon and Worthington (2003) developed the Lesbian, Gay, and Bisexual Affirmative Counseling Self-Efficacy Inventory (LGB-CSI), which measured application of knowledge, advocacy skills, awareness, relationship, and assessment. Professional organizations have been active in developing competency-based guidelines for working with sexual minority people.

COMPETENCE IN THERAPEUTIC WORK WITH LGB CLIENTS

At the core of competent practice with LGB clients are the guidelines published by the American Psychological Association Division 44/Committee on Lesbian, Gay, and Bisexual Concerns Joint Task Force on Guidelines for Psychotherapy with Lesbian, Gay, and Bisexual Clients (Division 44, 2000). These 16 guidelines are organized into four main categories: attitudes toward homosexuality and bisexuality, relationships and families, issues of diversity, and education. A brief synopsis of these guidelines follows.

Psychologists who are competent to work with LGB individuals first examine their attitudes toward homosexuality and bisexuality (Division 44, 2000). They know from the research literature that neither homosexuality nor bisexuality is suggestive of mental illness. They are also aware of their own homonegative biases and limits of their knowledge, so that they know when to consult or refer. Furthermore, they understand the effects of stigma, prejudice, discrimination, and violence on LGB people, and they work to be aware of how a lack of or inaccurate information and prejudice affect client presentation, their own attitudes and behaviors, and the therapy relationship and process.

LGB people experience unique challenges in the areas of relationships and families, not because of inherent differences between them and heterosexuals, but because of society's treatment of them. Therapists working with LGB people—and even LGB people themselves—may, because of the lack of legitimacy in society, fail to recognize the importance of or fully respect LGB relationships and families. Competent therapists recognize both the similarities and differences between LGB and heterosexual relationships. Unique issues such as coming out to families and friends, gender socialization, reproduction, and child custody make expertise in this area essential when conducting relationship and family counseling. In addition, the stress and distress experienced by LGB individuals and couples and their families that arise from the politics of same-sex marriage require special attention (Arm, Horne, & Levitt, 2009; Levitt et al., 2009; Rostosky et al., 2009). Familiarity with the research on children of LGB parents and LGB parenting is essential to combat prejudices long held by the majority of society (Division 44, 2000). It is also important to understand the varied family structures of LGB people, particularly when many families of origin have rejected their LGB children.

Issues of diversity, or intersections of identities, are essential to understand to provide competent services to LGB clients (Division 44, 2000). In particular, LGB people of color may experience dual isolation from and marginalization by LGB communities and their families and communities of color. In a similar fashion, bisexual people may be unable to fully fit into either heterosexual or lesbian/gay communities, given the lingering stereotypes about bisexuality. Both LGB youth and older adults also experience unique challenges. Adolescents who have been rejected by their families are at greater risk for homelessness, HIV, substance abuse, violence,

and suicide. Older LGB adults may have come out during a time prior to or during the feminist and LGB movements, with varying influences depending on the time frame of coming out and various cohort effects; they also may face stigma and invisibility as they attempt to access services for older adults. LGB people with disabilities comprise another population that is uniquely affected. Many support systems for LGB people may be inaccessible to LGB people with disabilities, and LGB communities may be less than welcoming of people with disabilities.

Ongoing education is essential to address many of the gaps between policy and practice related to LGB people (Division 44, 2000). Training and supervision must incorporate current knowledge about LGB issues, and counseling psychologists need to be committed to their own ongoing training, supervision, consultation, and continuing education in this area. Competent counselors and therapists also make themselves aware of mental health and community resources for their LGB clients.

COMPETENCE IN THERAPEUTIC WORK WITH TRANSGENDER CLIENTS

Although many of the guidelines designed for competent counseling with LGB people are applicable to competence in working with transgender people, they were not developed with transgender clients in mind. Thus, ALGBTIC (2009) of the American Counseling Association developed a document outlining competencies for counseling with transgender clients based on a "wellness, resilience, and strengths-based approach" (p. 2) that is consistent with the values of counseling psychology. The competencies were developed using the multicultural knowledge, skills, and awareness model (KSA) developed by Sue, Arredondo, and McDavis (1992). Key competency areas and illustrative competencies include:

1. *Human growth and development*: "Affirm that all persons have the potential to live full functioning and emotionally healthy lives throughout their lifespan while embracing the full spectrum of gender identity expression, gender presentation, and gender diversity beyond the male-female binary" (ALGBTIC, 2009, p. 6).

2. *Social and cultural foundations*: "Understand the importance of using appropriate language (e.g., correct name and pronouns) with

transgender clients; be aware that language in the transgender community is constantly evolving and varies from person to person; seek to be aware of new terms and definitions within the transgender community; honor clients' definitions of their own gender; seek to use language that is the least restrictive in terms of gender (e.g., using client's name as opposed to assuming what pronouns the clients assert are gender affirming); recognize that language has historically been used to oppress and discriminate against transgender people; understand that the counselor is in a position of power and should model respect for the client's declared vocabulary" (p. 8).

3. *Helping relationships*: "Understand that attempts by the counselor to alter or change gender identities and/or the sexual orientation of transgender clients across the lifespan may be detrimental, life-threatening, and are not empirically supported; whereas counseling approaches that are affirmative of these identities are supported by research, best practices, and professional organizations" (p. 9).

4. *Group work*: "Recognize the impact of power, privilege, and oppression within the group especially among the counselor and members and between members of advantaged and marginalized groups" (p. 11).

5. *Professional orientation*: "Understand and be aware that there has been a history of heterosexism and gender bias in the Diagnostic and Statistical Manual (DSM). For instance, counselors should have knowledge that homosexuality was previously categorized as a mental disorder and that currently 'Gender Identity Disorder' remains in the DSM" (p. 12).

6. *Career and lifestyle development competencies*: "Recognize that existing career development theories, career assessment tools, employment applications, and career counseling interventions contain language, theory, and constructs that may be oppressive to transgender and gender-conforming individuals. . . . Acknowledge the potential problems associated with career assessment instruments that have not been normed for the transgender community" (p. 13).

7. *Appraisal*: "Consider in the differential diagnosis process how the effects of stigma, oppression, and discrimination contribute to psychological symptoms, but do not necessarily indicate pathology for transgender individuals. Consider these effects when collaboratively deciding client's readiness for body modifications" (p. 15).

8. *Research*: "Recognize research is never free of positive or negative bias by identifying the potential influence personal values, gender bias, and heterosexism may have on the research process (e.g., participant selection, data gathering, interpretation of data, reporting of results, DSM diagnosis of Gender Identity Disorder), and seek to address these biases in the best manner possible" (p. 17).

These eight competencies are merely a sample of the 103 competencies contained in the ALGBTIC document; thus, a careful reading of the document as a whole will help a clinician assess her or his own knowledge, awareness, and skills in this area. In addition, therapists should have some basic under-standing of the processes in which transsexual clients who wish to transition to their gender of fit must engage. Not all transgender individuals are interested in gender reassignment; and "transsexual people make a wide range of choices as they attempt to find alignment between sex and gender" (Korell & Lorah, 2007, p. 272), including doing nothing, dressing in the clothing of the preferred gender, and choosing hormonal and/or sex reassignment surgical (SRS) procedures. Those who choose (and are able to afford) SRS follow recommendations of the World Professional Association for Transgender Health (WPATH) Standards of Care, previously known as the Harry Benjamin International Gender Dysphoria (HBIGD) Standards of Care (Meyer et al., 2001). These Standards clarify psychiatric, psychological, medical, and surgical management of gender identity disorders and are essential knowl-edge for mental health professionals working with transgender clients.

Affirmative therapies for sexual minority people are grounded in the competencies described above. In addition, I recommend that counseling psychol-ogy practitioners and educators seek Safe Zone training to provide a basic understanding of some of the history and constructs that affect the lives of LGBT people. Safe Zone training is offered through many university and community LGBT/ Pride centers across the country. Although space does not permit extensive coverage of all that coun-seling psychologists need to know to be effective counselors and therapists for sexual minority people, the following section addresses a few issues that have been addressed by counseling psychologists.

Issues in Counseling LGBT Clients

Lesbian and gay people utilize mental health services at a somewhat higher rate than do heterosexual people (Bieschke, McClanahan, Tozer, Grzegorek, & Park, 2000; Biescke, Paul, & Blasko, 2007). These findings undoubtedly reflect distress on the part of individuals seeking to work out their identities in an oppressive culture (Cochran, Sullivan, & Mays, 2003); however, they likely also indicate that LGB people hold positive perceptions of the helpfulness of therapy, particularly if it is conducted in an affirmative way (Bieschke et al., 2000, 2007).

Relationships and Families

Croteau et al. (2008) urged counseling psychologists to focus greater attention on LGB couples, relationships, marriage, family, and parenting. Although LGB couples and families are challenged by many of the same issues that confront heterosexual people, the legal and social policy contexts in which LGB people find themselves have extraordinary consequences in their everyday lives (Patterson, 2007). Despite greater acceptance of LGB people by mainstream Americans (Herek, 2003) and increasing legal victories for same-sex couples (Patterson), few jurisdictions have passed civil unions or domestic partner protections or benefits for unmarried couples, and the religious right has mounted a largely successful campaign nationally to reverse the very few marriage rights victories that have passed (Patterson, 2007; Rostosky et al., 2009). The success of these campaigns to refuse marriage rights to same-sex partners has resulted in high levels of minority stress and psychological distress, not only for same-sex partners who wish to marry, but for sexual minorities as a whole, due to the acceleration of epithets and judgments directed against them (Rostosky et al.). Thus, counseling psychology practitioners are called on to be aware of the impact of these experiences on the self-esteem of their sexual minority clients. Rostosky et al. emphasized the importance of counselors and therapists being aware of the social context and assisting their clients in managing stigma during these inflammatory political times. In addition, therapists must help their LGB clients balance the "dual dangers of engagement with GLBT advocacy and self-protection through withdrawal" (Levitt et al., 2009, p. 67), encouraging self-acceptance and advocating for clients to find social supports to combat

"isolation, discrimination, and aggression and to fight for social justice" (p. 67). Counselors and therapists should also be aware that, even though same-sex couples experience stress and distress as a result of anti-marriage initiatives, not all desire to marry (Warner, 1999). Thus, counseling psychologists should not make assumptions about a couple's degree of commitment based on the parties' decisions about marriage.

Because of the paucity of legal and social support for same-sex marriage, LGB people are at risk as prospective or current parents (Patterson, 2007). Many LGB parents have children from heterosexual marriages, and it is still not uncommon in divorce situations for the heterosexual parent to use the courts to take custody from the nonheterosexual parent. Although legal guidelines exist to facilitate fairness in these decisions, LGB parents are still at risk of losing their children because of prejudice in the judicial system (Patterson, 2007). These decisions fly in the face of extensive research indicating that children of lesbian women and gay men fare as well as those of heterosexual parents developmentally and in terms of their adjustment (Patterson, 2006).

Same-sex couples who wish to have children are faced with decisions about how to have biological children (through heterosexual intercourse or alternative insemination) or to adopt. These options are fraught with complexity and may not be supported in some jurisdictions. Same-sex adoptions have been pursued legally in many states (Human Rights Campaign, 2010); however, the lack of favorable rulings in a number of states leave many children without legal ties to both of their parents (Patterson, 2007).

Therapists are challenged to keep in mind the social context of the parents and prospective parents with whom they work. Decision-making on the part of same-sex couples may take place in the context of certain legal restrictions, with which the therapist should become familiar. Good parenting becomes complicated as parents make decisions about how to relate to medical and school personnel. Grief over loss of children through custody battles is exacerbated by groundless attacks on the nonheterosexual parent's morality and fitness to parent. Conversely, the creativity that is often required of same-sex parents to manage barriers may lend itself to greater flexibility and creativity in parenting. Thus, a supportive, strengths-based approach to helping LGB parents negotiate the parenting process is essential.

Recent research has also focused on biological and extended families of LGB people. Patterson (2007) acknowledged the complexities involved in LGB people's relationships with their families of origin. If the LGB individual elects not to disclose her or his sexual orientation to the family of origin, or if her or his family refuses to acknowledge or support the LGB child's sexual orientation, partner, or family, the LGB person may distance emotionally from the extended family (Savin-Williams, 2003). Alternatively, LGBT families of origin who were supportive of their LGBT children were negatively impacted by anti-LGBT legislation in terms of their own personal relationships, physical and mental health, feelings about their country, and their hopes for the future (Arm et al., 2009). These experiences continue to reinforce the importance of practice being informed by an awareness of the sociopolitical climate.

Spiritual and Religious Issues

Spiritual and religious concerns have gained increasing attention in multicultural counseling, and LGBT people face challenges in this regard. Heterosexuality and the nuclear family—and consequently adherence to rigid gender roles—form the basis for many conservative and orthodox religious teachings. Thus, sexual minorities may find themselves under attack from religious organizations, and they may have internalized the heteronegative teachings of their families and religious communities. For many people of color, their religious communities may be inseparable from their cultures. Thus, counselors and psychotherapists will encounter same-sex attracted people in religious or spiritual conflict with their religious traditions. For some, their religious/spiritual selves are as much an identity as other cultural identities, and clients are no more able to separate themselves from their religious/spiritual identities than clients of color can from their ethnic identities.

The American Psychological Association (1998) has taken the relatively moderate stance that therapists must advise clients that scientific evidence supporting conversion therapy does not exist. Other professional associations, such as the ACA (Whitman, Glosoff, Kocet, & Tarvydas, 2006), the ALGBIC (2010), and the American Psychiatric Association (2000a), maintain a stronger stance, advising against attempts to change clients' sexual orientations, particularly until more evidence exists to support such treatments, and urging counselors to inform clients wishing to change their sexual

orientations of the lack of evidence for efficacy and the potential harms of these treatments. Based on descriptive data (Beckstead & Morrow, 2004; Shidlo & Schroeder, 2002) and clinical experience and advice (Haldeman, 2001; 2004), Beckstead and Israel (2007) stated, "Given that the positive aspects found in conversion therapy (such as religious validation, reframing, behavioral strategies, and group work) can be found in most effective therapies, and given that the potential exists for significant harms from conversion ideology and interventions, it is unnecessary and unethical to provide such therapy" (p. 229).

Effective therapy with same sex-attracted clients in religious conflict must begin with the therapist, whether religious or an LGB person or ally, holding client autonomy as a central ethical tenet and closely examining her or his biases and assumptions. Such a therapist will be aware both of religious/spiritual resources as well as resources to provide clients with positive perspectives of living openly lesbian, gay, or bisexual lives. Clients need information about the distinction between sexual orientation, identity, and behavior, so that they can form realistic goals for therapy and for their lives. They also need to know that they may make life choices that later need to be revisited. Thus, the therapist must be able to provide a holding space for the ambivalence and ambiguity that surrounds what is often a long and rocky road toward a tenuous peace of mind for the client. Above all, the therapist has a moral and ethical responsibility to value and respect the many selves that the client brings to counseling—the spiritual self, the sexual self, and the other possible selves that intersect the religious/spiritual/sexual self.

Multicultural Issues and Intersections

Although, for purposes of simplicity, I have used fairly restricted terminology (LGBT) to discuss sexual orientation and identity issues, those terms do not necessarily describe the experiences of diverse groups of sexual minority people. Across cultures, same-sex attractions and gender variance are viewed through different lenses. DeBlaere et al. (2010) gave several examples of terms used in various cultures and contexts to describe alternative sexual and gender orientations: *down low* (Latino and African American men who have sex with both women and men and do not identify as gay); *girlfriend* or *sister* (terms used by African American women that describe an important woman-to-woman relationship but that may or may not designate a romantic or sexual relationship); *homo thugs* (tough young men in African American communities who have sex with men); *mati-ism* (African term for women who have sex with women); *same-gender loving* (Latino or African American term to describe same-gender sexual relating without identifying as gay); *top/bottom* (term used by Latino gay and bisexual men that distinguishes between the more insertive, and thus more masculine, and the more receptive, or more "gay," partner); *two spirit* (people in some American Indian cultures who live the gender role of the opposite sex and may engage in same-sex sexual behaviors); and terms such as *Warias* (Indonesian), *Kathoey* (Thai), *Bayot* (Filipino), and *Fa'fafine* (Polynesian) (Asian-Pacific terms for people who "cross traditional gender and sexual lines" p. 334). Therapists working with clients from diverse cultures do well to follow the client's lead and language when exploring the meanings of gendered and sexual orientations and identities.

It should be noted that the whole notion of sexual identity is a culture-bound construct that may have limited or no value when working with clients from cultures in which sexuality is not perceived as a source of identity (Rust, 1996). Depending on the client's culture of origin, along with her or his level of acculturation, achieving an identity based on sexuality may or may not be salient.

This is relevant not only to counseling clients of color or from non-European American cultures, but across age cohorts as well. Older same-sex-attracted clients may identify as *homosexual*; those who came out or became activists via feminism or the LGB movement may be most comfortable with the terms *lesbian, gay*, or *bisexual;* and young people of various sexual orientations—including some heterosexual—may prefer the term *queer.*

The paucity of scholarship on intersections of sexual and gender orientations with other diverse identities—race/ethnicity, age, disability, socioeconomic status, and others—require counseling psychologists to synthesize and integrate multiple literatures to provide competent services to a diverse clientele. Despite calls for greater attention to intersecting identities (Croteau et al., 2008), counseling psychology is still at the brink of grasping the full implications of this challenge. LGB people are disproportionately below the poverty line and/or homeless (Albelda, Lee Badgett, Schneebaum, & Gates, 2009), stemming from a complex interaction of factors, including being rejected by families while young, experiencing discrimination in educational and employment systems, and, for women, the likelihood that—as single women or couples—their income is reflective of women in general and they are likely to be raising children. Transgender individuals are universally concerned about employment issues (Korrell & Lorah, 2007) as well. Thus, the very fact of being LGBT puts an individual at risk for lower socioeconomic status. For people of color, who are often also systemically and systematically economically oppressed, being LGBT may further increase their risk of economic disadvantage. These intersections of sexual/gender orientation, race/ethnicity, socioeconomic class, and sometimes gender illustrate how intersections complicate the lives of LGBT people exponentially, given other oppressed statuses. Youth or older age, also associated with lower income levels, may also come into play to create stress and distress for LGBT clients.

Multiple identities, and thus multiple layers of oppression, require multiple coping strategies on the part of the individuals who hold them (Fukuyama & Ferguson, 2000). They also demand diligence on the part of the counselor or therapist working with LGBT people with multiple identities. As noted above, the meanings of sexual and gender orientations across cultures can differ widely. In addition, an individual's visibility or invisibility as a member of each identity group, as well as the salience of each identity in a particular context, are important variables as the individual negotiates her or his identities in various communities (Fukuyama & Ferguson, 2000). Therapists must assist their clients in examining the multiple layers of oppression that impact them, as well as, when possible, to distinguish the sources (racism, sexism, homonegativity, etc.) of oppression. An LGBT person dealing with a single layer of oppression (e.g., a European American, able-bodied, gay man of means) may need support from a counselor to deal with internalized oppression directed toward him as a gay person; a lesbian woman of color has at least three identity statuses to negotiate, and not being clear why she is being targeted creates additional challenges. The therapist must also be on guard not to assume that a client has only one identity status, as many statuses (sexual or gender orientation, religion, class, and certain disabilities) are invisible until the client shares them. Fukayama and Ferguson recommended qualitative research methods to further elaborate the experiences and understand the needs of individuals with multiple cultural identities.

I have barely scratched the surface of LGBT counseling issues for counseling psychologists. Numerous other topics and issues have, because of space constraints, been omitted in this chapter. They are nonetheless important issues for counseling psychologists and deserve passing attention before concluding.

Vocational issues are a key concern of counseling psychologists. Croteau, Anderson, Distefano, and Kampa-Kokesch (2000) identified five primary areas of study in vocational psychology of LGBT people as LGB identity development; discrimination and workplace climate (e.g., Chung, 2001); managing sexual identity at work; influences of societal messages on occupational interests, choices, and perceptions; and career interventions (Chung, 2003a, 2003b). Croteau et al. (2008) further identified three recent trends in the research literature: nondiscrimination policies; LGBT-affirmative workplace environments; and heterosexism, homophobia/homonegativity, and discrimination in workplace. They warned that vocational psychology of LGBT people has not attended to people of color. This is in keeping with their observations about research overall on LGBT people.

Counseling psychologists have also been leaders in studying supervision and training, including counselor supervision, mentoring, trainee attitudes, counseling skills, and LGBT issues in the training process (Croteau et al., 2008). Croteau et al. noted that efforts are being made to provide LGBT-affirmative training, but these training interventions need to be investigated systematically. Halpert, Reinhardt, and Toohey (2007) proposed a theoretical model of LGB-affirmative supervision; however, there have been no published empirical studies to date. In this area, as in others discussed in this chapter, further research is needed on transgender issues in training as well as training issues that are culturally sensitive.

Conclusion
Future Directions
The overwhelming breadth of critical issues surrounding sexual orientations and identities for counseling psychologists made it necessary to neglect a number of important issues when writing this chapter. Future scholarship should expand on the issues I have identified above; in addition, I join Croteau et al. (2008) in calling for more scholarship in counseling psychology on couples/relationships/families/parenting, adolescents and school safety, and aging and gerontology. In addition, we need greater attention to bisexual and transgender issues and to the intersections of gender, race/ethnicity/culture, class, disability, and other identity statuses.

Future directions for counseling psychology in the arena of sexual orientations and identities encompass research and scholarship, practice, and social advocacy. I conclude by addressing each of these issues below.

Research and Scholarship on Sexual Orientations and Identities
Counseling psychologists have led the field in many areas of research and scholarship concerning LGBT people and have called for more rigorous attention to areas that have been neglected in the past. Future directions for research and scholarship include:

• *Expanded research on LGBT people of multiply marginalized statuses*, including race/class/culture, socioeconomic factors, differing physical and mental abilities, age, and religious and spiritual orientations. It is also important to study LGBTQ issues over time in the context of different geographies and cohorts. Identity development pathways of sexual minorities from different groups need to be identified and understood. In addition, research is needed to better understand the intersections of sexual orientations and identities with other marginalized or oppressed statuses. This includes research on the effects of dual minority stress. Qualitative, multilevel, and contextual analyses are needed to understand the complexity of these intersections. More effective recruitment approaches are needed to access sexual minority people of under-represented cultures. Counseling psychologists conducting LGBT research need to become more committed to giving voice to invisible sexual minorities across doubly and multiply marginalized groups.

• *Spiritual and religious concerns.* Counseling psychologists need to continue to conduct rigorous qualitative and quantitative research to better understand the intersection of spiritual/religious and sexual orientation identities and provide competent services to individuals who are dealing with conflicts in this area. Continued research on the effects of conversion treatments are necessary; in particular, ongoing research is needed to demonstrate the harms of such treatments and lead to more stringent guidelines regarding reorientation approaches.

• *Research on neglected areas* such as couples, relationships, marriage, family, adoption, childbirth, and parenting. Sexual minority people experience unique challenges in all of these areas, and continued research is needed to pave the way to counseling interventions and social advocacy.

• *Vocational research,* particularly related to LGB identity and career development; discrimination and workplace climate; nondiscrimination policies; LGBT-affirmative workplace environments; managing sexual identity at work; influences of societal messages on occupational interests, choices, and perceptions; and career interventions.

Counseling, Supervision, and Training

Future directions for counseling psychologists in counseling, supervision, and training range from general issues of competence to more specific concerns. Counseling psychologists have been effective in moving the field forward in this area; however, more work is needed.

• Efforts are being made to provide LGBT-affirmative training, but these training interventions need to be investigated systematically and applied more broadly. Training programs and continuing education opportunities need to be developed to provide counseling psychologists with the awareness, knowledge, and skills to intervene beyond the individual level to promote social justice for LGBT people. Although progress has been made in this area regarding training in LGB issues, transgender concerns have been sorely neglected. Competencies need to be defined, and procedures for assessing competency developed and implemented.

• The current state of treatment for transsexual people who wish to pursue gender reassignment requires that therapists and clients operate within a medical model that pathologizes the client's desires to change gender. As this model contradicts basic counseling psychology values, new models that support change but do not pathologize the client are needed.

• Effective counseling and psychotherapy approaches are needed to assist clients in religious or spiritual conflict about their sexual orientations. Because many sexual minority people have been rejected by or left their religious homes, competent spiritual counseling is important to help them negotiate this aspect of their lives. In addition, effective training and supervision models are needed to assure competence in students whose religious beliefs may be at odds with LGB-affirmative therapy approaches.

• As this chapter was going to press, the news media reported a number of suicides of gay youth who had been bullied by peers or "outed" over social networks. Intervention programs that address bullying, in particular that targeted at sexual minority and gender nontraditional youth, as well as research and intervention related to the impact of the Internet—positive, neutral, and negative—is necessary to bring a contemporary and relevant perspective to these issues.

Social Advocacy

Social advocacy cannot really be separated from research, scholarship, counseling, supervision, and training. Using a scientist-practitioner-social justice advocate model, our research and training must also serve our social justice agenda.

• Counseling psychologists, in concert with members of other social justice-oriented divisions of the American Psychological Association, have made great strides in creating an environment of fairness and equality for people of traditionally marginalized and oppressed groups, including LGBT people—but our work is not yet complete. Counseling psychologists can assist in developing or implementing guidelines for working with transgender people. We can also continue to address accreditation guidelines to prevent discrimination against sexual minorities and to affect training on LGBT issues. Counseling psychologists have served and continue to serve in positions of leadership not only in the Society of Counseling Psychology, but in other divisions as well as in the highest reaches of American Psychological Association governance. Ongoing mentorship for leadership in American Psychological Association and elsewhere should be a top priority for counseling psychology.

• Counseling psychologists need to be active in social issues that affect sexual minority people. Recently, the news media reported that the Church of Jesus Christ of Latter-day Saints (LDS, or Mormon, church) had removed language from its *Church Handbook of Instructions* for leaders in the church that disparaged same-sex attractions; instead, celibate gay Mormons are to be allowed to be active members and participate fully in the church (Stack, 2010), although the church will still not support monogamous same-sex unions. Because religious groups such as the LDS church hold tremendous political power (e.g., the LDS church gave tremendous sums of money to support

Proposition 8 in California), counseling psychologists must take an active stance against bad science and religious bigotry that negatively affect LGBT people. Pivotal issues at this time include marriage, domestic partner, and parental rights as well as "Don't Ask, Don't Tell" policies in the military.

I echo Rostosky et al. (2009) in identifying engagement in social activism as a healing factor for many clients. I would also add that activism can serve as a healing factor for counseling psychology researchers who study and therapists who work with LGBT people, as we counseling psychologists are subject to vicarious traumatization or secondary traumatic stress (Brown, 2008) as we work with people who are targets of prejudice, oppression, and violence. I concur with Rostosky et al. in that, in addition to providing effective training in LGBT issues, training programs can teach skills for addressing social injustice. As counseling psychologists, we have the opportunity to use our leadership to influence change in our profession, our communities, and the world.

References

Adams, H., & Phillips, L. (2006). Experiences of two-spirit lesbian and gay Native Americans: An argument for standpoint theory in identity research. *Identity, 6*, 273–291.

Albelda, R., Lee Badgett, M. V., Schneebaum, A., & Gates, G. J. (2009). *Poverty in the lesbian, gay, and bisexual community.* Los Angeles: UCLA School of Law, Williams Institute.

American Psychiatric Association (2000a). Commission on Psychotherapy by Psychiatrists (COPP). Position statement on therapies focused on attempts to change sexual orientation (reparative or conversion therapies). *American Journal of Psychiatry, 157*, 1719–1721.

American Psychiatric Association. (2000b). *Diagnostic and statistical manual of mental disorders DSM-IV-TR* (4th ed., Text Revision). Arlington, VA: American Psychiatric Publishing.

American Psychological Association. (1998). Appropriate therapeutic responses to sexual orientation in the proceedings of the American Psychological Association, Incorporated, for the legislative year 1997. *American Psychologist, 53*, 882–939.

Arm, J. R., Horne, S. G., & Levitt, H. M. (2009). Negotiating connection to GLBT experience: Family members' experience of anti-GLBT movements and policies. *Journal of Counseling Psychology, 56*, 82–96.

Association of Lesbian, Gay, Bisexual, and Transgender Issues in Counseling. (2009). *Competencies for counseling with transgender clients.* Alexandria, VA: Author.

Association of Lesbian, Gay, Bisexual, and Transgender Issues in Counseling. (2010). Statement from ALGBTIC Division on Conversion Therapy. Retrieved July 18, 2010, from http://www.algbtic.org/resources/tfct.htm.

Bailey, J. M. (2003). Biological perspectives on sexual orientation. In L. D. Garnets & D. C. Kimmel (Eds.), *Psychological*

perspectives on lesbian, gay, and bisexual experiences (2nd ed., pp. 50–85). New York: Columbia University Press.

Beckstead, A. L., & Israel, T. (2007). Affirmative counseling and psychotherapy focused on issues related to sexual orientation conflicts. In K. J. Bieschke, R. M. Perez, & Kurt A. DeBord (Eds.), *Handbook of counseling and psychotherapy with lesbian, gay, bisexual, and transgender clients* (2nd ed., pp. 221–244). Washington, DC: American Psychological Association.

Beckstead, A. L., & Morrow, S. L. (2004). Mormon clients' experiences of conversion therapy: The need for a new treatment approach. *The Counseling Psychologist, 32*, 651–691.

Bidell, M. P. (2005). The Sexual Orientation Counselor Competency Scale: Assessing attitudes, skills, and knowledge of counselors working with lesbian, gay, and bisexual clients. *Counselor Education and Supervision, 44*, 267–279.

Bieschke, K. J., Croteau, J. M., Lark, J. S., & Vandiver, B. J. (2005). Toward a discourse of sexual orientation equity in the counseling professions. In J. M. Croteau, J. S. Lark, M. A. Lidderdale, & Y. B. Chung (Eds.), *Deconstructing heterosexism in the counseling professions: A narrative approach* (pp. 189–210). Thousand Oaks, CA: Sage.

Bieschke, K. J., McClanahan, M., Tozer, E., Grzegorek, J. L., & Park, J. (2000). Programmatic research on the treatment of lesbian, gay, and bisexual clients: The past, the present, and the course for the future. In R. M. Perez, K. A. DeBord, & K. J. Bieschke (Eds.), *Handbook of counseling and psychotherapy with lesbian, gay, and bisexual clients* (pp. 309–336). Washington, DC: American Psychological Association.

Bieschke, K. J., Paul, P. L., & Blasko, K. A. (2007). Review of empirical research focused on the experience of lesbian, gay, and bisexual clients in counseling and psychotherapy. In K. J. Bieschke, R. M. Perez, & K. A. DeBord (Eds.), *Handbook of counseling and psychotherapy with lesbian, gay, bisexual, and transgender clients* (2nd ed., pp. 293–316). Washington, DC: American Psychological Association.

Bieschke, K. J., Perez, R. M., & DeBord, K. A. (Eds.). (2007). *Handbook of counseling and psychotherapy with lesbian, gay, bisexual, and transgender clients* (2nd ed.). Washington, DC: American Psychological Association.

Bohan, J. S. (1996). *Psychology and sexual orientation: Coming to terms.* New York: Routledge & Kegan Paul.

Broido, E. M. (2000). Constructing identity: The nature and meaning of lesbian, gay, and bisexual identities. In R. M. Perez, K. A. DeBord, & K. J. Bieschke (Eds.), *Handbook of counseling and psychotherapy with lesbian, gay, and bisexual clients* (pp. 13–33). Washington, DC: American Psychological Association.

Brown, L. S. (2008). *Cultural competence in trauma therapy: Beyond the flashback.* Washington, DC: American Psychological Association.

Brown, S. D., & Lent, R. W. (Eds.). (1984). *Handbook of counseling psychology.* New York: Wiley.

Brown, S. D., & Lent, R. W. (Eds.). (1992). *Handbook of counseling psychology* (2nd ed.). New York: Wiley.

Brown, S. D., & Lent, R. W. (Eds.). (2000). *Handbook of counseling psychology* (3rd ed.). New York: Wiley.

Brown, S. D., & Lent, R. W. (Eds.). (2008). *Handbook of counseling psychology* (4th ed.). New York: Wiley.

Browning, C., Reynolds, A. L., & Dworkin, S. H. (1991). Affirmative psychotherapy for lesbian women. *The Counseling Psychologist, 19*, 177–196.

Buhrke, R. A., & Douce, L. A. (1991). Training issues for counseling psychologists in working with lesbian women and gay men. *The Counseling Psychologist, 19*, 216–234.

Carroll, L., & Gilroy, P. J. (2001). Teaching "outside the box": Incorporating queer theory in counselor education. *Journal of Humanistic Counseling, Education & Development, 40*, 49–58.

Cass, V. C. (1979). Homosexual identity formation: A theoretical model. *Journal of Homosexuality, 4*, 219–236.

Chung, Y. B. (2001). Work discrimination and coping strategies: Conceptual frameworks for counseling lesbian, gay, and bisexual clients. *Career Development Quarterly, 50*, 33–44.

Chung, Y. B. (2003a). Career counseling with lesbian, gay, bisexual, and transgendered persons: The next decade. *Career Development Quarterly, 52*, 78–86.

Chung, Y. B. (2003b). Ethical and professional issues in career assessment with lesbian, gay, and bisexual persons. *Journal of Career Assessment, 11*, 96–112.

Cochran, S. D., Sullivan, J. G., & Mays, V. M. (2003). Prevalence of mental disorders, psychological distress, and mental health services use among lesbian, gay, and bisexual adults in the United States. *Journal of Consulting and Clinical Psychology, 71*, 53–61.

Coleman, E. (1978). Toward a new model of homosexuality: A review. *Journal of Homosexuality, 3*, 345–359.

Coleman, E. (1982). Developmental stages of the coming-out process. *Journal of Homosexuality, 7*(2), 31–43. Beverly Hills: Sage.

Conger, J. J. (1975). Proceedings of the American Psychological Association, Incorporated, for the year 1974: Minutes of the Annual meeting of the Council of Representatives. *American Psychologist, 30*, 620–651.

Croteau, J. M, Anderson, M. Z., Distefano, T. M., & Kampa-Kokesch, S. (2000). Lesbian, gay, and bisexual vocational psychology: Reviewing and planning construction. In R. M. Perez, K. A. DeBord, & K. J. Bieschke (Eds.), *Handbook of counseling and psychotherapy with lesbian, gay, and bisexual clients* (pp. 383–408). Washington, DC: American Psychological Association.

Croteau, J. M., Bieschke, K. J., Fassinger, R. E., & Manning, J. L. (2008). Counseling psychology and sexual orientation: History, selective trends, and future directions. In S. D. Brown and R. W. Lent (Eds.), *Handbook of counseling* (4th ed., pp. 194–211). Hoboken, NJ: Wiley.

DeBlaere, C., Brewster, M. E., Sarkees, A., & Moradi, B. (2010). Conducting research with LGB people of color: Methodological challenges and strategies. *The Counseling Psychologist, 38*, 331–362.

Diamond, L. M. (1998). Development of sexual orientation among adolescent and young adult women. *Developmental Psychology, 34*, 1085–1095.

Diamond, L. M. (2000). Sexual identity, attractions, and behavior among young sexual-minority women over a 2-year period. *Developmental Psychology, 36*, 241–250.

Diamond, L. M. (2005). A new view of lesbian subtypes: Stable versus fluid identity trajectories over an 8-year period. *Psychology of Women Quarterly, 29*, 119–128.

Diamond, L. M. (2008). *Sexual fluidity: Understanding women's love and desire.* Cambridge: Harvard University Press.

Dickson, N., Paul, C., & Herbison, P. (2003). Same-sex attraction in a birth cohort: Prevalence and persistence in early adulthood. *Social Science & Medicine, 56*, 1607–1615.

Dillon, F. R., & Worthington, R. L. (2003). The Lesbian, Gay, and Bisexual Affirmative Counseling Self-Efficacy Inventory (LGB-CSI): Development, validation, and training implications. *Journal of Counseling Psychology, 50*, 235–251.

Division 44/Committee on Lesbian, Gay, Bisexual Concerns Joint Task Force on Guidelines for Psychotherapy with Lesbian, Gay, and Bisexual Clients. (2000). Guidelines for psychotherapy with lesbian, gay, and bisexual clients. *American Psychologist, 55*, 1440–1151.

Fassinger, R. E. (Ed.). (1991a). Counseling lesbian women and gay men [Special issue]. *The Counseling Psychologist, 19*(2).

Fassinger, R. E. (1991b). The hidden minority: Issues and challenges in working with lesbian women and gay men. *The Counseling Psychologist, 19*, 157–176.

Fassinger, R. E. (2000). Gender and sexuality in human development: Implications for prevention and advocacy in counseling psychology. In S. D. Brown & R. W. Lent (Eds.), *Handbook of counseling psychology* (3rd ed., pp. 346–378). New York: Wiley.

Fassinger, R. E., & Arseneau, J. R. (2007). "I'd rather get wet than be under that umbrella": Differentiating the experiences and identities of lesbian, gay, bisexual, and transgender people. In K. J. Bieschke, R. M. Perez, & K. A. DeBord (Eds.), *Handbook of counseling and psychotherapy with lesbian, gay, bisexual, and transgender clients* (2nd ed., pp. 19–50). Washington, DC: American Psychological Association.

Fassinger, R. E., & Miller, B. A. (1996). Validation of an inclusive model of sexual minority identity formation on a sample of gay men. *Journal of Homosexuality, 32*, 53–78.

Fassinger, R. E., & Sperber-Richie, B. (1997). Sex matters: Gender and sexual orientation training for multicultural counseling competency. In D. B. Pope-Davis & H. L. K. Coleman (Eds.), *Multicultural counseling competencies: Assessment, education and training, and supervision* (pp. 83–110). Thousand Oaks, CA: Sage.

Fausto-Sterling, A. (1998). The five sexes: Why male and female are not enough. In D. L. Anselmi & A. L. Law (Eds.), *Questions of gender: Perspectives and paradoxes* (pp. 24–28). Boston: McGraw-Hill.

Fox, R. C. (1996). Bisexuality in perspective: A review of theory and research. In Firestein (Ed.), *Bisexuality: The psychology and politics of an invisible minority* (pp. 3–50). Thousand Oaks, CA: Sage.

Frost, D. M., & Meyer, I. H. (2009). Internalized homophobia and relationship quality among lesbians, gay men, and bisexuals. *Journal of Counseling Psychology, 56*, 97–109.

Fukuyama, M. A., & Ferguson, A. D. (2000). Lesbian, gay, and bisexual people of color: Understanding cultural complexity and managing multiple oppressions. In R. M. Perez, K. A. DeBord, & K. J. Bieschke (Eds.), *Handbook of counseling and psychotherapy with lesbian, gay, and bisexual transgender clients* (pp. 81–106). Washington, DC: American Psychological Association.

Gagné, P., Tewksbury, R., & McGaughey, D. (1997). Coming out and crossing over: Identity formation and proclamation in a transgender community. *Gender and Society, 11*, 478–508.

Gonsiorek, J. C. (1991). The empirical basis for the demise of the illness model of homosexuality. In J. Gonsiorek & J. Weinrich (Eds.), *Homosexuality: Research implications for public policy* (pp. 115–136). Thousand Oaks, CA: Sage.

Greene, B. (2000). Beyond heterosexism and across the cultural divide: Developing an inclusive lesbian, gay, and bisexual psychology: A look to the future. In B. Greene (Ed.), *Education, research, and practice in lesbian, gay, bisexual, and transgendered psychology* (pp. 1–45). Thousand Oaks, CA: Sage.

Green, J. (2000). *Introduction to transgender issues.* Washington, DC: National Gay and Lesbian Task Force.

Haldeman, D. C. (1994). The practice and ethics of sexual orientation conversion therapy. *Journal of Consulting and Clinical Psychology, 62,* 221–727.

Haldeman, D. C. (2001). Therapeutic antidotes: Helping gay and bisexual men recover from conversion therapies. *Journal of Gay & Lesbian Psychotherapy, 5*(3–4), 117–130.

Haldeman, D. C. (2004). When sexual and religious orientation collide: Considerations in working with conflicted same-sex attracted male clients. *The Counseling Psychologist, 32,* 691–715.

Halpert, S. C., Reinhardt, B., & Toohey, M. J. (2007). Affirmative clinical supervision. In K. J. Bieschke, R. M. Perez, & K. A. DeBord (Eds.), *Handbook of counseling and psychotherapy with lesbian, gay, bisexual, and transgender clients* (2nd ed., pp. 241–258). Washington, DC: American Psychological Association.

Hare-Mustin, R. T.; Marecek, J. (1990). Gender and the meaning of difference: Postmodernism and psychology. In R. T. Hare-Mustin & J. Marecek (Eds.), *Making a difference: Psychology and the construction of gender* (pp. 22–64). New Haven, CT: Yale University Press.

Haselkorn, H. (1956). The vocational interests of a group of male homosexuals. *Journal of Counseling Psychology, 3,* 8–11.

Herek, G. M. (2003). *Sexual prejudice: Prevalence.* Retrieved July 18, 2010, from http://psychology.ucdavis.edu/rainbow/html/prej_prev.html.

Herek, G. M. (2004). Beyond "homophobia": Thinking about sexual prejudice and stigma in the twenty-first century. *Sexuality Research and Social Policy, 1*(2), 6–24.

Herek, G. M., Berrill, K., & Berrill, K. T. (1992). *Hate crimes: Confronting violence against lesbians and gay men.* Newbury Park, CA: Sage.

Herek, G. M., Kimmel, D. C., Amaro, H., & Melton, G. B. (1991). Avoiding heterosexist bias in psychological research. *American Psychologist, 46,* 957–963.

Hooker, E. (1957). The adjustment of the male overt homosexual. *Journal of Projective Techniques, 21,* 18–31.

House passes "Don't ask, don't tell" repeal amendment, Senate bill advances. (2010, June 23). *The Huffington Post.* Retrieved June 23, 2010, from http://www.huffingtonpost.com/2010/05/27/senate-armed-services-com_n_592782.html.

Human Rights Campaign. (2010). *Documenting discrimination.* Retrieved July 18, 2010, from http://www.hrc.org/issues/parenting.asp.

Israel, T., Ketz, K., Detrie, P. M., Burke, M. C., & Shulman, J. L. (2003). Identifying counselor competencies for working with lesbian, gay, and bisexual clients. *Journal of Gay and Lesbian Psychotherapy, 7,* 3–21.

Jacobson, B., & Donatone, B. (2009). Homoflexibles, omnisexuals, and genderqueers: Group work with queer youth in cyberspace and face-to-face. *Group, 33,* 223–234.

Journal of Counseling Psychology. (2009). Advances in research with sexual minority people. [Special issue]. *Journal of Counseling Psychology, 56*(1).

Keys, D. P. (2002). Instrumental sexual scripting: An examination of gender-role fluidity in the correctional institution. *Journal of Contemporary Criminal Justice, 18,* 258–278.

Kinsey, A. C., Pomeroy, W. B., & Martin, C. E. (1948). *Sexual behavior in the human male.* Philadelphia: W. B. Saunders.

Kinsey, A. C., Pomeroy, W. B., Martin, C. E., & Gebhard, P. H. (1953). *Sexual behavior in the human female.* Philadelphia: W. B. Saunders.

Korrell, S. C., & Lorah, P. (2007). An overview of affirmative psychotherapy and counseling with transgender clients. In K. J. Bieschke, R. M. Perez, & K. A. DeBord (Eds.), *Handbook of counseling and psychotherapy with lesbian, gay, bisexual, and transgender clients* (2nd ed., pp. 271–288). Washington, DC: American Psychological Association.

Lev, A. I. (2007). Transgender communities: Developing identity through connection. In K. J. Bieschke, R. M. Perez, & K. A. DeBord (Eds.), *Handbook of counseling and psychotherapy with lesbian, gay, bisexual, and transgender clients* (2nd ed., pp. 147–176). Washington, DC: American Psychological Association.

Levitt, H. M., Ovrebo, E., Anderson-Cleveland, M. B., Leone, C., Jae, Y. J., & Arm, J. R., et al. (2009). Balancing dangers: GLBT experience in the time of anti-GLBT legislation. *Journal of Counseling Psychology, 56,* 67–81.

McCarn, S. R., Fassinger, R. E. (1996). Revisioning sexual minority identity formation: A new model of lesbian identity and its implications for counseling and research. *The Counseling Psychologist, 24,* 508–534.

Meyer, I. H., & Wilson, P. A. (2009). Sampling lesbian, gay, and bisexual populations. *Journal of Counseling Psychology, 56,* 23–31.

Meyer, W. J. III, Bockting, W. O., Cohen-Kettenis, P. T., Coleman, E., Di Ceglie, D., Devor, H., et al. (2001). *The standards of care for gender identity disorders* (6th ed.). Minneapolis: Harry Benjamin International Gender Dysphoria Association.

Moradi, B., DeBlaere, C., & Huang, Y. (Eds.). (2010a). Research with Lesbian, Gay, and Bisexual people of color [Special issue]. *The Counseling Psychologist, 38.*

Moradi, B., DeBlaere, C., & Huang, Y. (Eds.). (2010b). Centralizing the experiences of LGB people of color in counseling psychology. *The Counseling Psychologist, 38,* 322–330.

Moradi, B., Mohr, J. J., Worthington, R. L., & Fassinger, R. E. (2009). Counseling psychology research on sexual (orientation) minority issues: Conceptual and methodological challenges and opportunities. *Journal of Counseling Psychology, 56,* 5–22.

Morgan, K. S., & Brown, L. S. (1991). Lesbian career development, work behavior, and vocational counseling. *The Counseling Psychologist, 19,* 273–291.

Morin, S. F. (1977). Heterosexual bias in psychological research on lesbianism and male homosexuality. *American Psychologist, 32,* 629–637.

Morrow, S. L., & Beckstead, A. L. (2004). Conversion therapies for same-sex attracted clients in religious conflict: Context, predisposing factors, and implications for therapy. *The Counseling Psychologist, 32,* 641–650.

Patterson, C. J. (2006). Children of lesbian and gay parents. *Current Directions in Psychological Science, 15,* 241–244.

Patterson, C. J. (2007). Lesbian and gay family issues in the context of changing legal and social policy environments. In K. J. Bieschke, R. M. Perez, & K. A. DeBord (Eds.), *Handbook of counseling and psychotherapy with lesbian, gay, bisexual, and transgender clients* (2nd ed., pp. 359–377). Washington, DC: American Psychological Association.

Potoczniak, D. J. (2007). Development of bisexual men's identities and relationships. In K. J. Bieschke, R. M. Perez, & K. A. DeBord (Eds.), *Handbook of counseling and psychotherapy with lesbian, gay, bisexual, and transgender clients* (2nd ed., pp. 119–146). Washington, DC: American Psychological Association.

Reise, S. P., Waller, N. G., & Comrey, A. L. (2000). Factor analysis and scale revision. *Psychological Assessment, 12,* 287–297.

Risco, C. M. (2008). *Evaluation of a culturally inclusive model of sexual minority identity formation* (Unpublished master's thesis). University of Maryland, College Park, MD.

Risco, C., & Fassinger, R. E. (2007). *Exploring identity processes for LGB people of color: Validation of a dual-trajectory model of sexual minority development.* Unpublished manuscript, University of Maryland.

Rostosky, S. S., Riggle, E. D. B., Horne, S. G., & Miller, A. D. (2009). Marriage amendments and psychological distress in lesbian, gay, and bisexual (LGB) adults. *Journal of Counseling Psychology, 56,* 56–66.

Rothblum, E. D. (2000). "Somewhere in Des Moines or San Antonio": Historical perspectives on lesbian, gay, and bisexual mental health. In R. M. Perez, K. A., DeBord, & K. J. Bieschke (Eds.), *Handbook of counseling and psychotherapy with lesbian, gay, and bisexual clients* (pp. 57–79). Washington, DC: American Psychological Association.

Rust, P. C. (1996). Managing multiple identities: Diversity among bisexual women and men. In B. A. Firestein (Ed.), *Bisexuality: The psychology and politics of an invisible minority* (pp. 53–83). Thousand Oaks, CA: Sage.

Rust, P. C. R. (2007). The construction and reconstruction of bisexuality. In B. Firestein (Ed.), *Becoming visible: Counseling bisexuals across the lifespan* (pp. 3–27). New York: Columbia University Press.

Sánchez, F. J., & Vilain, E. (2009). Collective self-esteem as a coping resource for male-to-female transsexuals. *Journal of Counseling Psychology, 56,* 202–209.

Savin-Williams, R. C. (2003). Lesbian, gay and bisexual youths' relationships with their parents. In L. D. Garnets & D. C. Kimmel (Eds.), *Psychological perspectives on lesbian, gay, and bisexual experiences* (2nd ed., pp. 299–326). New York: Columbia University Press.

Shannon, J. W., & Woods, W. J. (1991). Affirmative psychotherapy for gay men. *The Counseling Psychologist, 19,* 197–215.

Shidlo, A., & Schroeder, M. (2002). Changing sexual orientation: A consumers' report. *Professional Psychology: Research and Practice, 33,* 249–259.

Shively, M. G., & De Cecco, J. P. (1993). Components of sexual identity. In L. Garnets & D. C. Kimmel (Eds.), *Psychological perspectives on lesbian and gay male experiences.* New York: Columbia University Press.

Sophie, J. (1986). A critical examination of stage theories of lesbian identity development. *Journal of Homosexuality, 12,* 39–51.

Stack, P. F. (2010, November 11). Updated LDS handbook softens language on gays. *The Salt Lake Tribune.* Retrieved from http://www.sltrib.com/sltrib/home/50658721-76/church-behavior-homosexual-gay.html.csp.

Stokes, J. P., Damon, W., & McKirnan, D. J. (1997). Predictors of movement toward homosexuality: A longitudinal study of bisexual men. *Journal of Sex Research, 34,* 304–312.

Stokes, J. P., McKirnan, D., & Burzette, R. (1993). Sexual behavior, condom use, disclosure of sexuality, and stability of sexual orientation in bisexual men. *Journal of Sex Research, 30,* 203–213.

Sue, D. W., Arredondo, P., & McDavis, R. J. (1992). Multicultural counseling competencies and standards: A call to the profession. *Journal of Counseling & Development, 70,* 477–486.

Sue, D. W., & Sue, D. (1999). *Counseling the culturally different: Theory and practice* (3rd ed.). New York: Wiley.

Szymanski, D. M. (2009). Examining potential moderators of the link between heterosexist events and gay and bisexual men's psychological distress. *Journal of Counseling Psychology, 56,* 142–151.

Thaweesit, S. (2004). The fluidity of Thai women's gendered and sexual subjectivities. *Culture, Health, & Sexuality, 6,* 205–219.

Vale, K., Johnson, T. W., Jansen, M. S., Lawson, B. K., Lieberman, T., Willette, K. H., & Wassersug, R. J. (In press). The development of standards of care for individuals with a male-to-eunuch gender identity disorder. *International Journal of Transgenderism, 12.*

Warner, M. (1999). Beyond gay marriage. In M. Warner, *The trouble with normal: Sex, politics, and the ethics of queer life.* New York: Free Press.

Wassersug, R., & Johnson, T. (2007). Modern-day eunuchs: motivations for and consequences of contemporary castration. *Perspectives in Biology and Medicine, 50,* 544–546.

Weinberg, M. S., Williams, C. J., & Pryor, D. W. (1994). *Dual attraction: Understanding bisexuality.* New York: Oxford University Press.

Weinberg, M. S., Williams, C. J., & Pryor, D. W. (2001). Bisexuals at midlife: Commitment, salience, and identity. *Journal of Contemporary Ethnography 30*(2), 180–208.

Whitman, H. L., Glosoff, M., Kocet, M., & Tarvydas, V. (2006). Ethical issues related to conversion or reparative therapy. Retrieved July 18, 2010 from http://www.counseling.org/PressRoom/NewsReleases.aspx?AGuid=b68aba97-2f08-40-c2-a400-0630765f72f4.

Wolitski, R. J., Jones, K. T., Wassserman, J. L, & Smith, J. C. (2006). Self-identification as "down low" among men who have sex with men (MSM) from 12 US cities. *AIDS and Behavior, 10,* 519–529.

Worthington, R. L., & Navarro, R. L. (2003). Pathways to the future: Analyzing the contents of a content analysis. *The Counseling Psychologist, 31,* 85–92.

Wrenn, C. G. (1962). The culturally encapsulated counselor. *Harvard Educational Review, 32,* 444–449.

Zea, M. C., Reisen, C. A., & Díaz, R. M. (2003). Methodological issues in research on sexual behavior with Latino gay and bisexual men. *American Journal of Community Psychology, 31,* 281–291.

Further Reading

Advances in Research with Sexual Minority People. (2009). [Special issue]. *Journal of Counseling Psychology, 56*(1).

Association of Lesbian, Gay, Bisexual, and Transgender Issues in Counseling. (2009). *Competencies for counseling with transgender clients.* Alexandria, VA: Author.

Bieschke, K. J., Perez, R. M., & DeBord, K. A. (Eds., 2007). *Handbook of counseling and psychotherapy with lesbian, gay, bisexual, and transgender clients* (2nd ed.). Washington, DC: American Psychological Association.

Division 44/Committee on Lesbian, Gay, and Bisexual Concerns Joint Task Force on Guidelines for Psychotherapy with Lesbian, Gay, and Bisexual Clients. (2000). Guidelines for psychotherapy with lesbian, gay, and bisexual clients. *American Psychologist, 55,* 1440–1151.

Meyer, W. J. III, Bockting, W. O., Cohen-Kettenis, P. T., Coleman, E., Di Ceglie, D., Devor, H., et al. (2001). *The standards of care for gender identity disorders* (6th ed.). Minneapolis: Harry Benjamin International Gender Dysphoria Association.

Moradi, B., DeBlaere, C., & Huang, Y. (Eds.). (2010). Research with lesbian, gay, and bisexual people of color. [Special issue]. *The Counseling Psychologist, 38*(3).

Perez, R. M., DeBord, K. A., & Bieschke, K. J. (2000). *Handbook of counseling and psychotherapy with lesbian, gay, and bisexual clients.* Washington, DC: American Psychological Association.

Feminist Approaches to Counseling

Carolyn Zerbe Enns

Abstract

This chapter summarizes central values and features of feminist counseling. It discusses feminist theories that support feminist counseling, characteristics of an egalitarian feminist therapy relationship, and the ways in which feminist counselors enact the maxim "the personal is political." A biopsychosocial, ecological approach to assessment and conceptualization is proposed. The chapter articulates ways in which feminist counseling operates from a social justice perspective informed by locational, intersectional, and multicultural frameworks, as well as approaches that are attentive to the diverse gender and social identities of clients. Examples of feminist counseling as an integrative approach are provided. Future directions include building linkages across social justice approaches and practicing feminist values in a changing society, in counseling men, and in global contexts.

Keywords: the personal is political, social justice, feminist counseling, feminist theory, gender counseling, counseling relationship, egalitarian, multicultural, social identity, biopsychosocial, ecological, social identity

Feminist therapy emerged in the midst of second-wave feminist activism during the 1960s and 1970s (Contratto & Rossier, 2005; Kaschak, 1981). The first forms of feminist counseling and therapy were modeled after consciousness-raising groups, which were created as a vehicle for exploring women's experiences of sexism and discrimination, and building commitment to social and political activism. Participants soon discovered that these ad hoc groups also offered therapeutic and personal growth benefits, assisted women in making connections between the personal and political realities of their lives, and fostered visions of mental health based on egalitarian roles (Brodsky, 1977; Kravetz, 1978).

In parallel developments, feminist psychologists identified biases within personality theories and research (Barrett, Berg, Eaton, & Pomeroy, 1974; Weisstein, 1970), double standards of mental heath that overvalued "masculine" attributes and devalued "feminine" attributes (Broverman, Broverman,

Clarkson, Rosenkrantz, & Vogel, 1970), psychotherapy relationships in which the therapist defined reality for the client (Chesler, 1972), and diagnostic practices that contributed to the labeling of persons without regard to the contexts in which they experienced distress (Kaplan, 1983). Extended definitions and principles of feminist counseling and psychotherapy were constructed during the mid-1970s and 1980s (e.g., Brodsky, 1980; Greenspan, 1983; Rawlings & Carter, 1977; Sturdivant, 1980).

During its 40-year evolution, feminist counseling has grown from a critique of psychotherapy practice to a well-developed approach that is embedded within the rich research and theoretical foundation of the feminist psychology of women and gender (e.g., Crawford, 2006; Matlin, 2008; Yoder, 2007) and featured in a variety of introductory counseling texts (e.g., Corey, 2009; Murdock, 2008; Sharf, 2008). Feminist therapists have also contributed to a wider consensus about values, ethics, and consumer rights in counseling. For example, feminist psychologists were among the first to call for informed consent practices and increased attention to the rights of clients (Hare-Mustin, Marecek, Kaplan, & Liss-Levinson, 1979). Feminist counselors brought attention to the ethical problems of violence and abuse in relationships, boundary violations in psychotherapy, careless and harmful diagnostic practices, gender role strains that limited development, and a monocultural model of mental health. They also proposed aspirational approaches to ethics (Brabeck, 2000; Brown & Brodsky, 1992; Feminist Therapy Institute [FTI] 2000; Vasquez, 2003). Most recently, many of the values and contributions of feminist psychologists have informed the American Psychological Association's (APA) Guidelines for Psychological Practice with Girls and Women (2007).

Since its earliest days, feminist counseling has been described as a large umbrella or awning that supports a flexible scaffold for organizing philosophical assumptions about human experience, personal and social change, and approaches to seeking knowledge (Brown, 2010; Rawlings & Carter, 1977). This overarching structure provides a foundation for social justice–oriented practice; is embedded in interdisciplinary scholarship and activism; and encompasses personal, interpersonal, collective, and sociocultural transformation. It is informed by scholarship about multiculturalism, the study of oppression in its many forms (e.g., racism, sexism, heterosexism, classism, ageism, ableism), and methods for challenging and transcending biases and discrimination. Feminist counseling represents an integrative and technically eclectic approach that can be compatible with many approaches to psychotherapy, prevention, and social activism. Feminist counseling is informed by values that are most consistently reflected in how one thinks about distress and change, rather than in specific counselor behaviors. It is "a sensibility, a political and aesthetic center that informs a work pervasively" (Luepnitz, 1988, p. 231), and "not a prescription or technique" (Brown & Brodsky, 1992, p. 51). As a result, feminist counseling holds affinity with theories that are attentive to the diversity and complexity of women's and men's lives, recognize the intricate connections between the internal and external worlds of all people, and give voice to the worldviews and perspectives of those who experience discrimination and oppression.

This chapter provides a glimpse of central values and features of feminist counseling and includes a historical perspective on feminist theories that inform feminist counseling. Following a discussion of the counseling relationship, it uses "the personal is political" as an organizer for summarizing major characteristics. Later sections of the chapter illustrate several ways in which feminist counseling operates as an integrative approach. It concludes with a brief discussion of new directions and issues in feminist counseling. The themes discussed in this chapter are informed by the APA (2007) Guidelines for Psychological Practice with Girls and Women (referred to hereafter as the 2007 Guidelines); the APA (2003) Guidelines on Multicultural Education and Training, Research, Practice, and Organization Change for Psychologists; and the APA (2000) Guidelines for Psychotherapy with Lesbian, Gay, and Bisexual Clients.

Values and Foundations of Feminist Counseling

In her landmark description, Gilbert (1980) identified two core features of feminist therapy: the personal is political, and the psychotherapy relationship is egalitarian. During the past 30 years, feminist practitioners have elaborated substantially on these tenets, and most of the central values of feminist therapy can still be organized around these two major themes (Ballou, Hill, & West, 2008; Worell & Remer, 2003). The phrases "the personal is political" and the "the political is personal" emphasize the systemic, sociocultural, and ecological perspectives that are central to feminist concepts of distress and change. These phrases also highlight the importance of consciousness-raising and empowerment at individual, interpersonal, and societal levels. The egalitarian relationship represents the context in which feminist values are modeled and enacted, and new forms of behavior are practiced and affirmed. Egalitarian relationships are also valued as goals and outcomes of feminist counseling (Ballou & West, 2000; Brown, 1994, 2010; Enns, 2004; Worell & Remer, 2003; Wyche & Rice, 1997).

As feminist counseling has matured, a third theme of diversity has become central to practice. Feminist counseling is informed by multicultural, intersectional, and locational perspectives that conceptualize identities and experience as complex, changing, and socially constructed (American Psychological Association [APA], 2007; Porter, 2005; Shields, 2008; Stewart & McDermott, 2004; Worell & Remer, 2003). Porter (2005) uses the repetition of one word—"location, location, location" (p. 144)—to highlight three central positionalities or perspectives that are brought to the counseling context by the theorist, the therapist, and the client. Contemporary feminist therapists seek to be attentive to the multiple and diverse realities, roles, and needs of women and men in a 21st-century world.

The premises of multiracial feminism (Zinn & Dill, 1996) and critical race feminism (Wing, 2000) are helpful for framing the wide range of interlocking identities, inequalities, privileges, and realities that contribute to the construction of gender. Gender, class, race, sexuality, ability, and a variety of additional social identities are experienced differently, depending on one's position in a "matrix of domination" (Collins, 2000) and one's access to social privilege and power. These interlocking features are not separable but operate simultaneously and uniquely to shape an individual's experience. Each element of identity, such as religion, sexual orientation, or nationality, shapes how other aspects of self are experienced, and the salience of any one dimension may vary across contexts (Wing, 2000). Furthermore, privilege and oppression are not "always or never" experiences. As the foreground and background of various identities shift across contexts, a person may experience privilege in one situation (e.g., due to light skin color, heterosexual orientation, or middle-class status) and discrimination in another setting (e.g., gender-based bias in a setting in which a person is the only woman). This locational perspective is not only relevant to women, but also to men and boys of all classes, genders, and races. In addition, all groups are characterized by within-group diversity (Shields, 2008; Stewart & McDermott, 2004).

Visual cues, such as skin color or body size, may also modify experiences of gendered privilege and oppression. For example, discrimination on the basis of skin color, including skin tone, often permeates class, gender, and sexual identities and life experiences (Higginbotham, 1992; Root, 1995). Thus, for many women of color, racism is a more everyday and virulent experience than is sexism, and may be magnified by a variety of microaggressions that can have powerful negative effects on well-being, but may be discounted or minimized by perpetrators (Sue et al., 2007). Alternatively, the invisibility associated with statuses, such as a lesbian identity, can also contribute to complex decisions about "coming out," which are likely to affect experiences of oppression and privilege (Stein, 1997). Although gender is a powerful social cue associated with privilege and power, gender cannot be assumed to be the primary, most significant, or unifying form of oppression that links all women and girls (e.g., Espín & Gawelek, 1992; Comas-Díaz & Greene, 1994).

Feminist Theory and Feminist Counseling

Feminist theories have developed along a parallel course that intersects with and complements feminist counseling practice. Although feminist counselors share an endorsement of the three principles identified in the previous section, these commitments are interpreted in multiple ways, depending on the feminist theoretical orientation that a counselor chooses either implicitly or explicitly. Because these theoretical positions mark major areas of "nonconsensus" within feminist counseling (Ballou & Gabalac, 1985), it is important to briefly discuss their development and the ways in which they have informed feminist counseling. More detailed discussions of feminist theory and psychology can be found in Enns (2004) and Enns and Sinacore (2005).

Second-wave Feminisms and Feminist Practice

During the early years of feminist counseling, various civil rights movements, including antipsychiatry and radical psychiatry traditions, challenged the very structure of society and its mental health professions (Ballou et al., 2008). Most feminist theories addressed four themes: the description of gendered oppression, why and how power differences and oppression exist and are perpetuated, the goals of feminism or what "should be," and strategies for eliminating injustice and changing reality (Bunch, 1987). Many second-wave feminist theorists developed comprehensive explanations or "grand theories" (Jaggar, 2008) about why oppression occurs and how inequality can be eliminated. The theories that gained the widest recognition and prominence included liberal feminism, socialist feminism, radical feminism, and cultural feminism.

In general, liberal feminist theorists and activists have worked to reform existing institutions rather than question their underlying foundations. They emphasize equal opportunity, personal initiative, and fair treatment of individuals. The impact of liberal feminist thought can be found in a variety of research and therapeutic approaches that emphasize "nonsexist" therapy and a "questioning" perspective within psychology (Ballou & Gabalac, 1985; Rawlings & Carter, 1977). Consistent with liberal feminism, these approaches focus on efforts to eliminate biases in treatment and research, disentangle myths about individual gender differences, treat clients and research participants equitably, and enhance the objectivity with which researchers and therapists approach their work (McHugh, Koeske, & Frieze, 1986).

Second-wave radical feminist theorists proposed that gender-based oppression is the original and most pervasive form of oppression. According to radical theorists, gender oppression appears in all cultures. It is often manifested through the exploitation of women's sexuality, such as through violence against women, the imposition of heterosexual norms, and the control of women's reproductive physiology (Jaggar & Rothenberg, 1993). Theorists have called for the dismantling of patriarchal power at its roots and a reconstruction of society, to be accomplished by abolishing gender and sex roles and replacing them with new possibilities that are free of gender stereotypes and mandates (Kaschak, 1981; Lorber, 2005; Tong, 2008).

Radical approaches that challenge institutional structures have been closely connected to consciousness-raising activities, but the deep application of radical principles has not been compatible with well-established disciplines, including professional and academic psychology (Ballou & Gabalac, 1985; Crowley-Long, 1998). Many second-wave grassroots antiviolence programs, such as domestic violence shelters and antirape programs, were built on radical feminist principles and offered therapeutic services consistent with a radical egalitarian approach that rejected the use of diagnosis, relied on forms of psychotherapy informed by consciousness-raising practices, incorporated peer support among survivors/victims, and emphasized organizational decision-making based on consensus and social activism as a cornerstone of counseling (Enns, 1992; Kaschak, 1981). Burstow's (1992) enduring radical antipsychiatry approach highlights ways in which *woman* is reduced to a body that is beautified, objectified, sexualized, exploited, and violated. She rejects the use of psychotropic medications, and places priority on practical assistance, advocacy, and social change. Others operating from a radical perspective have argued that all psychotherapy, including feminist counseling, places the burden of change on individuals, and is inconsistent with an emphasis on social change (e.g., Kitzinger & Perkins, 1993).

Socialist feminist theorists have shared radical feminist beliefs that social structures need to be dismantled and transformed. In contrast to those who view gender as a fundamental focus of oppression, socialist feminists generated an integrated analysis of race/ethnicity, class/economics, and gender to explain social problems, and emphasized the importance of understanding intersecting forms of inequality (Tong, 2008). Socialist feminist theories also became a foundation for some second-wave women of color feminisms (e.g., Combahee River Collective, 1982).

Feminist practice rooted in radical and socialist principles has occurred most frequently in grassroots, community-based feminist organizations. Early practices were based on group process, informal connections, advocacy for women as a group, volunteerism, and decision-making by consensus. Over time, these organizations increasingly emphasized meeting the individual needs of clients and implemented more formal, hierarchical organizational and decision-making structures that supported efforts to acquire government funding (Kravetz, 2004; Metzendorf, 2005). With external funding came requirements for grassroots agencies to provide "professional" services and to be accountable to funding agencies. As a result of these changes and the growing power of formal diagnosis to dictate the terms of psychotherapy, organizations that rely on radical and socialist practices have decreased in number and become less visible.

A fourth second-wave feminism, cultural feminism, has focused on transforming individuals and the larger culture by challenging the hegemony or dominance of individualistic "masculine" values such as autonomy, independence, and self-sufficiency. A major goal of cultural feminism is to revalue and infuse "feminine" and relationally oriented values throughout the culture (Donovan, 2000). Women's historic roles as nurturers and mothers are seen as important foundations for new social structures based on nonviolence and cooperation. Some cultural feminists began their feminist journey as radical feminists and adopted a radical-cultural position as they moved toward supporting women's institutions and alternative autonomous communities (e.g., bookstores, music festivals, lesbian communities) that were designed to model options for living based on women's strengths (Rudy, 2001; Taylor, Whittier, & Pelak, 2001). Others gravitated toward a cultural feminist perspective after being exposed to the writings of feminist philosophers, psychologists, and scholars who challenged traditional and patriarchal values embedded in academic disciplines (Robb, 2006).

Psychological approaches with the greatest similarity to cultural feminist values have sought to revalue "women's way's of knowing" (e.g., Belenky,

Clinchy, Goldberger, & Tarule, 1986) or women's relational self (e.g., Gilligan, 1982; Miller, 1976), and have often emphasized a unique mother–daughter bond that fosters connection and growth (e.g., Eichenbaum & Orbach, 1983). Within feminist circles, Gilligan's (1982) book on women's "different voice" received wide acclaim as well as criticism (Becker, 2005). Efforts to increase awareness of options for gaining empowerment through participation in the development of others offered a corrective to psychological theories that emphasized autonomy to the exclusion of relational themes, and became a source of inspiration for many who identified themselves as feminist therapists. Others viewed these relational models as encouraging romantic oversimplification of women's experience (Kerber, 1986) or a reintroduction of the "cult of true womanhood" (Luria, 1986, p. 320).

Some of the most influential theoretical and practice-oriented contributions in feminist therapy are referred to as *relational-cultural theory* (e.g., West, 2005), and were inspired in large part by woman-centered psychological theories that bear resemblance to cultural feminist thought. Over time, these approaches have expanded and increasingly centralized the lives of diverse groups of women (Goldberger, 1996; Jenkins, 2000; Turner, 1997; West, 2005). In general, relational-cultural feminist therapists frame connection and mutual empathy as the source of mental health and identify disconnection as a major cause of problems (Miller & Stiver, 1997).

Jaggar (2008) described second-wave rival theories and their "bold conjectures" as "so ambitious that they were massively underdetermined by the available data" (p. 193). Despite their limitations, these theories spawned concepts and language that raised consciousness about a wide range of gendered social problems, such as date and acquaintance rape, sexual harassment, domestic violence, the second shift, comparable worth, the feminization of poverty, heterosexism, and sexual objectification. Second-wave theories remain influential, but feminist psychologists are less likely to be influenced by a single position. In an effort to address gaps within specific theories, they are more likely to endorse hybrid options that integrate multiple perspectives.

Although some elements of all second-wave feminisms can be seen within feminist psychology, the impact of liberal feminism has been more enduring, perhaps because of its compatibility with institutionalized social science (Crowley-Long, 1998). Various studies also reveal that many women who do not self-identify as feminist often endorse liberal feminist beliefs (e.g., Aronson, 2003; Quinn & Radtke, 2006; Zucker, 2004). These individuals are sometimes referred to as egalitarians, lifestyle feminists, or "I'm not a feminist, but . . ." women, and may be responsive to feminist counseling practices based on liberal feminist thought.

Diversification and Locational Third-wave Feminisms

By the mid 1980s and early 1990s, theories inspired by cultural feminism and other related second-wave approaches were often identified as "essentialist." They were often criticized for drawing generalizations about the "universal woman," and were characterized as being inattentive to the standpoints, life challenges, and survival needs of women of color (Jaggar, 2008; Thompson, 1998). An essentialist position was defined as treating gendered behaviors as "fundamental attributes" (Bohan, 1993, p. 7) that are persistent and "resident within the individual" (p. 6). In contrast, constructionist alternatives were often posited as preferred alternatives, and these conceptualize gender as "doing," as a byproduct of activity and interactions within a social context, and as attentive to differences among people. Antiessentialist critiques examined the ways in which the lives of white, middle-class women had become normative within feminist theory and often led to the erasure of differences among women. Within psychology, theories about women's relational self and "ways of knowing" (e.g., Belenky et al., 1986; Gilligan, 1982) were sometimes seen as oversimplifying gender or even seeking to replace "woman as inferior" models with "woman as superior" options (Tavris, 1992).

Also criticized were empirical methods that tended to reduce the complexity of gender to binary categories, as well as approaches that obscured the complex dynamics of oppression and detracted from strength and coping perspectives by relying on a "woman as victim" discourse (Lamb, 1999). Finally, approaches that drew arbitrary or artificial distinctions between the "personal and the political," or social and individual manifestations of distress, were perceived as ignoring myriad ways in which the political and personal interact in people's lives (Cosgrove, 2002; Hurtado, 1989). Corrective efforts tended to emerge in two forms: postmodern feminist perspectives, and a variety of "diversity" approaches that focused on the standpoints of women of color and lesbian women.

Although theories and activism by and for women of color had been crucial to second-wave feminism (Smith, 1983; Thompson, 2002), the voices of women of color feminists and lesbians were sometimes marginalized or overlooked. Along with growing awareness of the inadequacy of previous theories, the perspectives of women of color and lesbians have been increasingly centralized within feminist psychology. As noted by Butler (2000), when the lives of women with diverse life experiences, sexual orientations, and ethnicities are placed at the center of inquiry, the lives of privileged persons are more likely to be decentered and "we raise our awareness and understand of the experiences of all women either implicitly or directly" (p. 177).

A variety of standpoint feminisms, which were authored by and highlighted the "herstories" and lives of specific groups of women, featured Black feminist thought (e.g., Collins, 2000), Chicana feminism (e.g., Bernal, 1998; Hurtado, 2003), Asian feminisms (e.g., Asian Women United of California, 1997; Nam, 2001), and lesbian feminism (e.g., Garber, 2001; Ross, 1995; Rudy, 2001). Other theorists emphasized the complex interactions of statuses and identities in their discussions of multiracial feminism (Zinn & Dill, 1996), critical race feminism (Wing, 2000), antiracist feminism (Calliste, Dei, & Aguilar, 2000), queer theory (Garber, 2001; Weed & Schor, 1997), Third World feminism (Mohanty, Russo, & Torres, 1991), and global/transnational feminisms (Basu, 1995). Within feminist psychology, the voices of women of color theorists and psychologists such as Jean Chin, Lillian Comas-Díaz, Oliva Espín, Beverly Greene, Maria Root, and Carolyn West have been influential in centralizing perspectives that emphasize the integration of sexuality, race, colonialism, indigenous healing practices, and immigration status (Barrett et al., 2005; Chin, 2000; Comas-Díaz, 2000; Comas-Díaz & Greene, 1994; Espín, 1999; Root, 1992, 1995; Jackson & Greene, 2000; West, 2002). Locational themes, an intersectional perspective, and a multicultural framework have become cornerstones of contemporary feminist counseling practice (Enns, 2010; Enns & Byars-Winston, 2010).

In other developments, many critiques of the 1980s and 1990s relied heavily on "deconstruction," which involves examining the implied meanings of texts and concepts, such as the underlying assumptions about truth, reality, language, and the self, and how these suppositions imbue concepts with power and authority (Flax, 1987). Postmodern feminists argued that it is impossible to create knowledge that is ahistorical, universal, or context free. Postmodern feminisms provided feminist psychologists with tools for asking meta-theoretical questions about the role and function of theory and practice, and became a mechanism for supporting less all-encompassing or "grand" theories and more modest approaches to feminism (Enns, 2004). Postmodern reality (including feminist reality) is viewed as invented and negotiated in social relationships and historical contexts, and reproduced through power relationships.

Of particular interest to postmodern feminists is the manner in which language reveals power relationships, which are often communicated as bipolar and polarized concepts (e.g., strong vs. weak). The deconstruction of language reveals, for example, that when masculine is compared to feminine, or objective is placed beside subjective, the first word in a pair typically assumes primacy or is more highly valued than the second term. Multiple, nonoppositional, or integrative ways of constructing social reality become obscured (Scott, 1988). Deconstruction challenges existing power relationships and reveals that binary constructs such as heterosexual–homosexual, white–black, and masculine–feminine are creations that only have meaning when they are viewed as dichotomous entities.

Some authors have expressed concern that postmodern thought can result in a slide into relativism, in which all realities are placed into question (Alcoff, 1988). Despite concerns about its inability to offer universal, enduring truths and a united rationale for pursuing social change, postmodernism has become increasingly accepted as a reminder of the complexity of gender and related intersecting identities, as well as the ways in which power structures evolve over time. Gergen (2001) proposed that postmodern theory provides us with tools for critiquing narrow ways of conducting science and constructing theory; encouraging psychologists to practice reflexivity, which involves ongoing self-reflection and self-questioning about the limitations of our perspectives; and recognizing the role of values and language in knowledge construction.

Recent locational and postmodern feminisms speak to the importance of relying on flexible feminisms that recognize wide-ranging social identities without exaggerating differences or seeing difference as divisive (Friedman, 1998). These feminisms are also marked by engagement with multiculturalism, cultural studies, postcolonial studies, queer theory, and transnational and poststructual views (Brown, 1994; Enns, 2004). Many contemporary feminist therapists draw on these perspectives to create integrative, flexible frameworks that can be modified.

A postmodern outlook has also been incorporated within third-wave feminism, an approach that is often endorsed by the daughters and sons of second-wave feminists who have benefited from the higher levels of equality earned by previous generations (Peltola, Milkie, & Presser, 2004). Self-identified third-wave feminists tend to resist "politically correct" elements of second-wave feminism. Instead, they tend to adopt strategic, hybrid, and flexible approaches, and seek to apply the most appropriate feminist lens for the specific need or occasion. Their goals include expanding what it means to be feminist, transcending seeming contradictions among feminist theories, and becoming more global in orientation (Heywood & Drake, 1997). Their activist efforts focus on a wide range of causes (e.g., AIDS, racism, poverty, violence against women) and often rely on personal stories, cyberspace, Internet "zines," and unique forms of grassroots projects to communicate about feminist issues (Baumgardner & Richards, 2000, 2005; Dicker & Piepmeier, 2003; Hernández & Rehman, 2002). Body image and body self-acceptance are also identified as revealing political implications of the personal (Rubin & Nemeroff, 2001). Feminist approaches to eating disorders and trauma are especially relevant to third-wave feminist counseling applications.

The Feminist Therapist and the Counseling Relationship

From its earliest days, feminist counselors have emphasized the importance of egalitarian relationships. In her influential critique, Chesler (1972) characterized the traditional therapeutic relationship as that of patriarch and patient and "just one more instance of an unequal relationship, just one more opportunity to be rewarded for expressing distress and to be 'helped' by being (expertly) dominated" (p. 140). To redefine this relationship, the feminist therapist became a "supporter and believer" (Brodsky, 1976, p. 376) of women's competence and worked toward sharing power and responsibility with clients (Marecek & Kravetz, 1977). Rawlings and Carter (1977) also recommended forming counseling contracts that specified goals, supported client autonomy, and limited the likelihood that the therapist could manipulate the client. Feminist therapists' attentiveness to client and therapist responsibilities led to increased awareness throughout psychology of ethical issues regarding informed consent, collaboration, and power dynamics (Ballou & Hill, 2008).

Transparency on the part of the feminist therapist is another foundational concept. Feminist therapists are encouraged to provide appropriate levels of information about their values in order to convey respect for the client's right to full disclosure about the therapist's approach, ensure that therapists do not inadvertently bring limited self-awareness or hidden agendas to the working alliance, and provide a basis for clients to become full partners (Hare-Mustin et al., 1979). Despite these stated values, Marecek and Kravetz's (1998) qualitative study revealed that feminist therapists sometimes reported concealing their feminist values from clients, fearing that disclosure might limit their effectiveness or credibility, or might lead to loss of business. Marecek and Kravetz argued that withholding such information can be a form of dishonesty, may convey a patronizing attitude, or reveal limited respect for clients' abilities to think for themselves.

Although egalitarian values are central to feminist concepts of growth, power differences are inevitable in relationships in which one person has studied psychological and social issues, gained professional credentials, and built knowledge based on substantial experience. The adoption of "undifferentiated egalitarianism," which involves the belief that the erasure of all power differences is possible, can lead to the blurring of boundaries, inappropriate role reversals, and carelessness about the therapist's responsibilities to the client (Brown, 1991; FTI, 2000). The feminist counselor is attentive to the levels and forms of self-disclosure that are in the best interests of the client. For example, she or he may avoid communicating information that may overwhelm the client, or may be of limited use to the client who is in crisis (Wyche & Rice, 1997).

Feminist counselors have also raised consciousness about abuses of power within psychotherapy, such as sexual harassment and sexual victimization (FTI, 2000). Cognizant of the importance of relationship integrity, some feminist therapists have found traditional rule-oriented approaches to multiple relationships to be overly rigid or even inhumane (Marecek & Kravetz, 1998). The FTI (2000) Code of Ethics uses the phrase "overlapping relationships" to convey the reality that multiple relationships are sometimes unavoidable. The feminist counselor takes care to monitor any overlapping relationships, and works to support best interests of the client. The counselor also ensures that therapeutic interactions are not sexualized.

The importance of relational facets of the counseling relationship was documented by Rader and

Gilbert's (2005) study of 42 female therapists and their clients. This study revealed that feminist therapists (19 persons) were more likely than counselors who did not identify themselves as feminists (15 individuals) to report using power-sharing behaviors and to show higher levels of agreement with feminist attitudes. Clients who worked with these feminist therapists described their therapists as using power-sharing behaviors to a greater degree than did clients who were paired with counselors who did not identify themselves as feminist. These two groups of therapists (feminist and those who did not identify themselves as feminist) showed similar levels of endorsement of feminist therapy behaviors and techniques. Furthermore, clients who worked with both groups of therapists did not differ with regard to their perceptions of their therapists' use of collaborative behaviors with clients. The absence of difference in the area of reported collaborative behaviors may reflect the growing value placed on collaboration across contemporary psychotherapy approaches. The lack of difference with regard to reported therapy behaviors is consistent with the definition of feminist therapy as a set of attitudes and beliefs rather than techniques.

A second study examined therapists' endorsement of feminist therapy behaviors associated with three factors: the personal is political, empowerment, and assertiveness/autonomy (Moradi, Fischer, Hill, Jome, & Blum, 2000). Whereas self-identification as a feminist therapist predicted endorsement of the first two groups of behaviors (the personal is political and empowerment), it did not predict a greater emphasis on assertiveness and autonomy. Although assertive behaviors are often identified as a component of feminist empowerment (e.g., Worell, 2001), assertive behaviors are also valued goals of many nonsexist therapies, and thus, may not reflect unique features of the feminist counseling relationship.

More specific findings (Moradi et al., 2000) revealed that, compared to therapists who did not identify themselves as feminist (60 persons), self-identified feminist therapists (15 individuals) were more likely to report paying attention to clients' experiences of oppression and discrimination, assuming a collaborative role with clients, and supporting self-esteem by focusing on positive and unique qualities of clients. When asked about their feminist behaviors with women clients, feminist therapists were more likely to report reframing clients' definitions of problems to include socialization explanations. When asked about their work

with men, feminist therapists were more likely to report supporting men's efforts to expand behaviors beyond traditional gender roles. No differences were found in self-reports about unconditional positive regard or empathy.

Another study, based on a survey of 108 family therapists, revealed that, although general endorsement of feminist therapy behaviors was high, a minority (35%) identified feminist therapy as a guiding orientation (25% of 40 men and 40% of 68 women). In addition, self-identification as a feminist therapist and exposure to gender-sensitive training experiences were associated with higher levels of reported use of feminist therapy behaviors (Dankoski, Penn, Carlson, & Hecker, 1998). Similarly, a survey of male therapists found that 24% of 81 respondents identified themselves as feminist therapists. These therapists scored higher than did nonfeminist male therapists on scales that assessed attitudes toward gender roles and feminism as well as endorsement of feminist therapeutic behaviors (Szymanski, Baird, & Kornman, 2002).

Several studies have used qualitative approaches to explore counselors' perceptions of core feminist relationship behaviors. Hill and Ballou (1998) completed a content analysis of 35 feminist therapists' responses to open-ended questions that asked counselors to describe how they had made the "substance or ongoing dialogue of therapy feminist" (p. 7). A majority of responses focused on how therapists showed sensitivity to issues of power in the counseling relationship. The second most frequent theme emphasized sociocultural and structural causes of distress. Other themes included a valuing of the reality and priorities of clients, providing an integrated analysis of the interlocking matrix of oppression (e.g., sexism, sizism, racism), and valuing both overt and subtle social change goals. Another qualitative study of 13 self-identified feminist family therapists (Whipple, 1996) identified the following priorities of therapists: the formation of collaborative, nonhierarchical relationships; exploration of gender and egalitarianism in relationships; and empowerment and the affirmation of women.

Finally, Chester and Bretherton's (2001) study of 140 feminist counselors made use of a checklist of feminist counseling characteristics. Over 90% of respondents identified the following as essential: knowledge of sex-role stereotyping and lifespan issues of women, belief in the ability of women to reach their potential, acknowledgment of the sociocultural aspects of women's problems, and encouraging women to value themselves on their own terms.

A common finding of these studies is that feminist counselors share perceptions that sociocultural contributors to distress are central to assessment and counseling (the personal is political), and that valuing the personhood, perspectives, strengths, and growth alternatives of clients is crucial (empowerment). All studies reveal that the egalitarian, collaborative counseling relationship and respect for clients are perceived as central to the counseling relationship. The next section turns to a more specific discussion of central features of feminist counseling.

The Personal Is Political

The notion that the personal is political informs the feminist therapist's overall worldview, as well as his or her goals and interventions. Feminist therapy shares the values of critical psychology (Prilleltensky & Nelson, 2002), including an interest in deconstructing and challenging power structures both within and beyond psychology; an analysis of oppression, which can be defined as "a state of symmetric power relations characterized by domination, subordination, and resistance" (p. 13); an emphasis on liberation, which involves resisting oppressive influences; and the goal of well-being that balances personal, relational, and collective needs. Each of these themes is reflected in feminist therapy's conceptualization of "the personal is political" and its corollary, the "political is personal."

External Forces and Psychological Distress

Rawlings and Carter's (1977) classic definition of feminist psychotherapy declared that "the primary source of women's pathology is social, not personal: external, not internal" (p. 55). Since that time, there has been growing awareness that both intrapsychic issues and external forces contribute to distress; however, an emphasis on sociocultural forces remains central to feminist analysis. The following paragraphs illustrate some of the ways in which biases and "isms" may contribute to distress and/or lowered achievement.

Studies have found that psychological distress is related to perceived sexist, racist, and heterosexist experiences and the degree to which personal stress is experienced in response to these events and psychological distress (e.g., Klonoff, Landrine, & Campbell, 2000; Moradi & Subich, 2003; Moradi & Funderburk, 2006; Szymanski, 2005). Self-esteem may play a role in these links. Moradi and Subich (2004) found a significant association between psychological distress and perceived sexist events for women with low self-esteem, but not for

women with high self-esteem. More recently, Fischer and Holz's (2007) study found initial support for a sequence in which public and private collective self-esteem, as well as personal self-esteem mediated relationships between perceived sexist discrimination and both depression and anxiety symptoms.

Although the literature on sexism, racism, and other "isms" reveals that blatant forms of prejudice have decreased during recent decades (Campbell, Schellengerg, & Senn, 1997), contemporary forms of sexism, racism, and related biases have taken on more clandestine forms that are often referred to as *modern racism* and *sexism*, or *unintentional* or *symbolic racism* and *sexism* (Dovidio, Gaertner, Kawakami, & Hodson, 2002; Gaertner & Dovidio, 2005; Swim, Aikin, Hall, & Hunter, 1995). *Stereotype threat*, which involves the internalization of stereotypes about a marginalized social identity (e.g., gender or race), has also been shown to generate anxiety, affect working memory, and result in significant negative decrements on performance (Osborne, 2001; Schmader & Johns, 2003; Spencer, Steele, & Quinn, 1999).

Theory and research on ambivalent sexism (Glick & Fiske, 2001) reveals that sexism consists of two forms: hostile sexism and benevolent sexism. Although hostile sexism is blatant and is recognized easily, benevolent sexism is more subtle, can be associated with warmth and praise for women who fulfill traditional communal roles, and may be linked to patronizing behaviors. This set of attitudes and behaviors is not easily recognized as sexist; and instead, it is frequently unchallenged and may contribute to increased justification of restrictive gender relations (Barreto & Ellemers, 2005; Jost & Kay, 2005). Benevolent sexism, but not hostile sexism, has also been shown to have a negative impact on performance (Dardenne, Dumont, & Bollier, 2007). The person experiencing benevolent sexism typically feels that she is viewed as having limited competence, but the behavioral cues are ambiguous, and it is difficult to conclude whether the behavior in question is sexist or merely polite. Self-doubt, mental intrusions, and preoccupation with one's performance appear to be mechanisms through which benevolent sexism may operate in performance situations. Fischer (2006) also found that benevolent sexism can also become a type of self-protective or defensive strategy that may be used by women who encounter another person's negative attitudes about women. In other words, endorsing benevolent sexist beliefs (e.g., that women should be cherished by men or are morally superior to men) allows women to maintain at least some level of self-esteem in the face of restrictive attitudes.

Taken together, contemporary theory and research indicate that perceived and subtle discrimination are associated with psychological distress, lowered self-esteem, decreased performance or achievement, or the adoption of subtle biases toward other women. The exploration of these issues in the feminist counseling context may help the client reframe her or his experience, identify how her or his internalized problems have wider "political" implications, restore the client's self-esteem, and help the client plan active, self-affirming responses to these challenges. A more extended discussion of these issues can be found in Moradi and Yoder (2011; Chapter 13, this volume).

In addition to the "ordinary" external challenges identified above, a variety of gendered traumatic stressors related to interpersonal traumas, such as rape, battering, and sexual abuse, are summarized in the APA (2007) Guidelines. These traumatic stressors are associated with posttraumatic stress reactions, depression, and anxiety. The Guidelines also document a variety of biases and discrimination related to health systems, education, the workplace, religious institutions, the workplace, legal systems, and the family. Each of these external factors is related to women's and girls' distress.

A Strength and Coping Perspective

Long before positive psychologists Seligman and Csikszentihihalyi (2000) called for an end to the "exclusive focus on pathology" (p. 5) as well as human weakness, suffering, and disorder, feminist psychologists advocated a strength and coping perspective for women as "enactors, not victims" (Reid & Kelly, 1994). Klein (1976) declared: "Not all symptoms are neurotic. Pain in response to a bad situation is adaptive, not pathological" (p. 90). Building on this positive reframing of "pathology," feminist counselors argue that many symptoms have functional, coping, or survival value as individuals negotiate difficult challenges (Greenspan, 1983). A major goal of the feminist therapist is to find the kernel of health embedded in behaviors that may be defined as pathological, and to help clients undo a "patient identity" by redirecting perceived weaknesses into strengths that that can enhance well-being and alter oppressive circumstances. This version of positive psychology emphasizes the development of strength, resilience, and optimism that is also grounded in a realistic assessment of challenges.

As noted by the APA Guidelines (2007), "Being attentive to the strengths and personal resources of girls and women may also help decrease the likelihood of committing inadvertent biases, overemphasizing problematic aspects of behavior, or pathologizing adaptive behaviors" (p. 964). Some of the pathways for developing resources in younger women and girls include education and positive attitudes toward academic activities, positive peer and adult relationships, supportive and flexible family systems, opportunities for problem-solving skill development, supportive and flexible family systems, experiences with growth-promoting community groups, and other satisfying skill-building activities (Worell, 2006).

Effective coping in the midst of obstacles is an important theme in the works of many feminists of color. For example, Anzaldúa (1987) described the ways in which women of color develop *la facultad*, a survival skill that is informed by experiences of marginalization, discrimination, and outsider status. *La facultad* facilitates efficient perception of power dynamics in everyday experiences and allows one to "adjust quickly and gracefully to changing (and often threatening) circumstances" (Moya, 2001, p. 469). Although the creative survival skills of women of color have facilitated their ability to withstand economic, social, and sexual exploitation, these skills can also be associated with substantial emotional costs. West (1995) notes, for example, that the Mammy stereotype reinforces the notion that black women are capable of contributing endlessly to the needs of others without encountering negative outcomes. Feelings of being overburdened experienced by this "strong black woman" may be rendered invisible. As noted by bell hooks (1981), endurance and strength should not be confused with opportunities for growth and transformation. A strengths-based perspective must lead to opportunities for thriving.

The concept of posttraumatic growth, which is defined as "the experience of positive change that occurs as a result of the struggle with highly challenging life crises" (p. 1) is also relevant to feminist counseling. Posttraumatic growth includes a deeper appreciation of life and a redirection of priorities. It may include increased warmth and intimacy in relationships, an expanded view of personal strength, the identification of new directions for the future, and the development of a more spiritual perspective (Tedeschi & Calhoun, 2004). Within feminist psychology, an emphasis on posttraumatic growth can be seen most consistently in discussions of recovery and empowerment following interpersonal violence and trauma. It includes meaning-making following trauma and generating possibilities for participating in social change. A study of female survivors of childhood sexual abuse (Lev-Wiesel, Amir, & Besser, 2005) found that posttraumatic stress disorder and posttraumatic growth coexisted. Studies of battered women (e.g., Humphreys, 2003; Werner-Wilson, Zimmerman, & Whalen, 2000) have also revealed that high levels of physical and psychological distress can be accompanied by resourcefulness and resilience. By emphasizing strengths, feminist counselors help clients expand existing skills, as well as acknowledge the reality and relevance of their pain.

Assessment and Conceptualization in Feminist Counseling

Since its earliest days, feminist therapists have been skeptical about the value of traditional diagnosis, which is exemplified by Rawlings and Carter's (1977) declaration that "the therapist does not use diagnostic labels" (p. 62). Instead, feminist counselors were encouraged to use behavior analysis, sex/gender role analysis, and other context-based assessments, thus ensuring that assessment emphasized client strengths and resources as well as deficit behaviors. At the time when these early statements were made, the *Diagnostic and Statistical Manual of Mental Disorders* was a 134-page document (DSM-II, American Psychiatric Association [APA], 1968) and represented "a mildly annoying formality required for insurance reimbursement" (Wylie, 1995, p. 23). In contrast, the current edition of the DSM (DSM-IV-TR, APA, 2000) is a massive tome that exceeds 900 pages. Avoiding the use of formal diagnosis in the current era of managed care has become extraordinarily difficult (Ballou et al., 2008).

Over time, feminist counselors have criticized DSM-based diagnoses for many reasons, including its overemphasis on intrapsychic symptoms and inattentiveness to contextual factors; tendency to reinforce gender, cultural, and race-based stereotypes (especially the personality disorders); arbitrary criteria for conceptualizing disorders; adjustment versus change focus; scientific inadequacies; tendency to "pigeonhole" misery rather than offering creative ways of addressing pain; and tendency to reinforce or extend the values of powerful psychiatric, medical, and pharmaceutical establishments (e.g., Caplan & Cosgrove, 2004; Eriksen & Kress, 2005; Lerman, 1996). Feminist counselors' distrust of formal diagnosis is also consistent with the views

of counselors who practice narrative, humanistic, and existential psychotherapies. These approaches share the critique that DSM diagnosis can reduce the client to a label, pathologize difference, limit the counselor's or client's vision to the lens provided by DSM criteria, decrease attentiveness to strengths, and even elicit client behaviors consistent with diagnostic checklists (Rigazio-DiGilio, 2000; Winslade, Crockett, & Monk, 1997; Yalom, 2002).

Although diagnosis has been used cautiously by feminist counselors, the 1980 addition of posttraumatic stress disorder (PTSD) to the DSM was welcomed by many feminist counselors as a nonstigmatizing diagnosis consistent with feminist models (e.g., Walker, 1979, battered woman syndrome) that would normalize clients' reactions to interpersonal abuse, violence, and other external causes of distress (Brown, 2004). Compared to diagnoses that lend themselves to victim blaming (e.g., borderline personality disorder), PTSD seemed to offer feminist therapists "a rhetorical resource for voicing their objection, as feminists, to conventional diagnoses and the medical model" (Marecek, 1999, p. 162). When diagnostic criteria for PTSD were broadened (APA, 1994), some feminist therapists found the category even more attractive, assuming that it would reflect more accurately the regularity with which intimate violence occurs, and might allow more individuals to gain access to needed services (Brown, 2004).

Becker (2004) argued, however, that using disease-based labels to normalize reactions to trauma is illogical when greater energy could be directed toward the prevention of circumstances that contribute to trauma. Furthermore, the expanded version of PTSD has the potential to become a "catch all" category that contributes to greater medicalization. For example, biological factors, such as hormonal differences, have been hypothesized as accounting for a portion of the 2:1 ratio of women to men who meet the criteria for this diagnosis (Wolfe & Kimerling, 1997). In addition, the DSM category does not allow for full consideration of the ways in which insidious and prolonged interpersonal trauma may affect the person (Courtois, 2004), nor does it lend adequate insight about how racism, sexism, heterosexism, ageism, classism, and cultural factors may affect posttraumatic reactions (Sanchez-Hucles & Hudgins, 2001). The PTSD example points to the complexity of conceptualizing problems adequately when diagnostic options are embedded within powerful institutional frameworks. Some feminists have proposed alternatives for understanding reactions to trauma and include Brown's (1992) oppression artifact disorder, Root's (1992) insidious trauma model, and Herman's (1992) complex posttraumatic stress syndrome.

Despite concern about the potentially negative impact of many diagnostic categories, contemporary feminist counselors are less likely than early feminist therapists to reject DSM-based diagnosis, but see such diagnosis as only a starting point for conducting assessment. Brown (2006, 2010) recommended "subversion" as a strategy for undermining traditional diagnosis. Although the feminist therapist is likely to provide a diagnosis required by an insurance company, often in consultation with the client, the feminist counselor also highlights multiple layers of experience and meaning that inform distress, such as developmental factors, coping strategies the client uses to deal with power and powerlessness, the competencies and strengths of the client, her or his social identities and locations, and dysfunctional and supportive aspects of the client's context. A holistic biopsychosocial perspective is valued.

Of particular value to biopsychosocial assessment is a feminist ecological perspective, which facilitates the assessment of the complex systems that surround the individual (Ballou, Matsumoto, & Wagner, 2002; Bronfenbrenner & Morris, 2006). These systems encompass the individual's *microsystem*, which includes the various familial, spiritual, educational, and other support systems; *the mesosystem*, or interactions among the structures of the microsystem; the *exosystem*, which consists of social, governmental, legal, and political institutions and policies with which a person may not have direct contact but have an impact on a person's privileges, opportunities, oppression, and general flexibility of movement; and the *macrosystem*, which reflects cultural values, worldviews, ideologies, and global influences. The manner in which the client's social identities (e.g., race, class, gender, disability) intersect with these systems is also relevant to an ecologically valid understanding of a client's problems and strengths.

Feminist assessment is also embedded within a developmental approach (APA, 2007). Research conducted by feminist psychologists and summarized in a variety of psychology of women and gender texts (e.g., Crawford, 2006; Matlin, 2012; Yoder, 2007) has enriched our understanding of diverse gender-related biological, social, and psychological development. A developmental approach helps normalize life transitions and decreases the likelihood of pathologizing adjustments that may seem problematic on the surface, but may represent temporary life course corrections. For example, important biopsychosocial developmental realities relevant to reproduction include menarche, sexual development, sexual health practices, pregnancy, birth control, abortion, fertility/infertility, childbirth, postpartum reactions, and menopause. Each of these experiences mark changes in a woman's or girl's life and may be associated with enhanced possibilities as well as challenge and difficulty (APA, 2007). The negotiation of these reproductive experiences is also related to the timing of developmental changes, individual differences in priorities, and the degree to which these reproductive events are associated with supportive or complicated relationship, environmental, and cultural realities. Using a developmental approach supports and complements the strengths-based perspective discussed earlier.

A hallmark of feminist counseling is social identity analysis, which was originally referred to as *sex role analysis* (Kaschak, 1981; Rawlings & Carter, 1977). This personalized assessment is designed to clarify how a person's socialization, privileges, oppressions, life phase issues, multiple social identities, and current environmental realties may influence the client and his or her interactions within an ecological network. This context includes, but is not limited to, the client's family, educational environment, religious experience, peer relationships and groups, work settings, immigration/acculturation experiences, and cultural contexts (Brown, 1990). Open-ended questions about social identities can be integrated with tools such as power analysis (Worell & Remer, 2003) or a cultural genogram (Vasquez, & Magraw, 2005). Major goals include identifying ways in which external forces are internalized as strengths or limitations, considering how public and private aspects of the self interact, and exploring ways in which the personal is political and the personal is political within a person's larger ecological context. This knowledge contributes to a deeper understanding of the self, decreased self-blame and discouragement, and greater knowledge for becoming an active change agent on one's own behalf.

Assessment of feminist development can be included within social identity analysis. Persons who adopt a feminist identity tend to navigate a series of developmental stages that begin with passive acceptance of dominant cultural values and lack of awareness of gender identity issues. However, a crisis phase of "revelation," can be triggered by direct experiences of bias, developmental transitions, or general awareness of oppression that may be facilitated by educational experience. The recognition of unfair treatment and bias (e.g., sexism and racism) is typically followed by the desire to test and reinforce one's emerging awareness through interactions with like-minded individuals. Feminist identity evolves over time and culminates in a phase of active commitment to a nonsexist world (Downing & Rousch, 1985).

Feminist identification and activism are also predicted by exposure to feminism through life experiences, participating in women's and gender studies courses, and social changes and milieu of childhood and adulthood (e.g., Liss, Crawford, & Popp, 2004; Reid & Purcell, 2004; Stake, 2007; Zucker & Stewart, 2007). Research reveals that early phases of development (e.g., denial of sexism) are associated with higher levels of psychological distress (Moradi & Subich, 2002), and feminist identification is related to psychological well-being (Saunders & Kashubeck-West, 2006; Yakushko, 2007). See Moradi and Yoder (2011; Chapter 13, this volume) for more information.

Feminist identity development often intersects with other social identities, such as lesbian, racial/ethnic, womanist, and white identity (Hoffman, 2006; Jones & McEwen, 2000; Ossana, Helms, & Leonard, 1992; Parks, Carter, & Gushue, 1996; Reynolds & Pope, 1991). A person's ability to work through the implications and challenges associated with multiple identities is likely to be influenced by the degree to which various identities are related or can be integrated, the person's life events and transitions, the salience and visibility of identity domains, the relevance of these identities to current developmental experiences, the extent to which identities are associated with oppression or privilege, and family or cultural background (Stewart & McDermott, 2004; Suyemoto, 2002).

The feminist counselor is prepared to use interventions that address these developmental concerns (McNamara & Rickard, 1989; Rederstorff & Levendosky, 2007). At the earliest phases of feminist identity development, clients may prefer a relatively traditional relationship. Counselors may support development by asking open-ended questions that facilitate clients' awareness of how their multiple social identities are related to presenting concerns. During middle phases of development, more active interventions, such as social and gender identity analysis, anger work, and self-disclosure, may be especially beneficial for addressing issues marked by greater awareness of biases, privileges,

and "isms." As clients gain more complex and meaningful understandings of their feminist and other intersecting social identities, they are likely to benefit from interventions that support concrete decision making and action-oriented responses (McNamara & Rickard, 1989; Rederstorff & Levendosky, 2007). Being mindful of the complexity and multidimensionality of social identity throughout assessment and intervention is crucial. Finally, it is important to note that womanist and/or feminist identity development may be experienced in unique ways that may not conform to this pattern (Park et al., 1996; Zucker & Stewart, 2007).

Empowerment and Social Activism

The concept of "empowerment" defies easy definition, in part because the term has become a "sanitized buzz-word" (Cheater, 1999, p. 1) or an almost mandatory term for the mission statements of many human service organizations (Pease, 2002). The term empowerment is appropriated by persons with dramatically different ideologies to support diverse philosophies about "helping people gain control over their own lives" (Pease, 2002, p. 136). Some suggest that the rhetoric of "empowerment" is in danger of losing its radical potential. Use of the term may project an "illusion of equality" (p. 138) without posing any real challenge to oppressive power structures. Thus, clarification of feminist empowerment practice is important.

Feminist theorists, as well as critical and liberation theorists, speak of the importance of consciousness-raising or *conscientização* as a foundation for personal empowerment and activism. Consciousness-raising involves using knowledge about personal distress, inequality, and stigmatization to inform self-awareness, healing, and activism. Similarly, *conscientização* or conscientization, is defined as "learning to perceive social, political, and economic contradictions, and to take action against the oppressive elements of reality" (Freire, 1970, p. 19). Through involvement in consciousness-raising or conscientization, participants learn to recognize systems of oppression, articulate their roles and positions in these systems, and devise concrete responses (Burbules & Berk, 1999). Feminist empowerment entails helping individuals see themselves as active agents in personal, interpersonal, and sociopolitical contexts and includes analyzing how social power structures contribute to feelings of powerlessness and distorted, negative self-perceptions in an unequal world; exploring how individuals can learn to experience power in personal, interpersonal, and institutional domains; and applying advocacy skills in the service of social justice (Morrow & Hawxhurst, 1998). The new interpretive framework associated with empowerment can be liberating in and of itself, but also becomes the foundation for developing personal and social action plans.

Consciousness raising and conscientization lead to greater understanding about how the "personal is political." In addition, "the public is *personally* political" (Hurtado, 1989, p. 849). Hurtado's reframing of the familiar maxim is consistent with the realities of many people of color and poor people whose personal lives have been so restricted by social policies and institutionalized racism/sexism that it is difficult to create private lives on their own terms. Whereas many middle-class white women experience at least some choice (e.g., choosing whether to work for monetary remuneration), less privileged women may not have such options. These variations in experience need to be understood when considering the personal meaning of consciousness-raising.

A feminist definition of empowerment is typically seen as inconsistent with "power over," which relies on dominance, coercion, and oppression. "Power within" is associated with a sense of inner strength that allows one to make sound decisions, "power to" suggests a capacity to act in a manner that is respectful of oneself and others, and "power with" implies an ability to cooperate and make connections with others in enacting personal and social change (Smith & Douglas, 1990). Miller and Cummins' (1992) study of women's definitions revealed that these participants distinguished between "control over," which included power over people and resources, and "personal authority" (p. 419). Respondents tended to define personal authority as experiencing self-control or engaging in self-enhancing activity, such as gaining knowledge or feeling physically healthy.

Worell (2001) proposed ten goals of empowerment: self-esteem and self-valuing, positive daily functioning, gender and culture awareness, perceived self-efficacy and control, self-nurturing capacities, problems-solving skills, behavioral flexibility, assertiveness, the ability to access and use community resources, and participation in social activism. The Personal Progress Scale (Worell & Remer, 2003) can be used to assess progress toward many of these goals. Another approach, the relational-cultural model, identifies relational connections and mutual empathy as leading to mutual empowerment and resilience (Miller & Stiver, 1997). Mutual empowerment consists of five aspects: zest, or vitality and energy that comes from emotional connection; action and the motivation to use "relational interplay" to behave in new ways, greater knowledge about oneself and others; an increased sense of worth based on relational connection; and a desire for additional growth-facilitating connections with others. Consistent with a postmodern perspective, Becker (2005) cautioned that feminist therapists emphasizing a relational approach can fall prey to dichotomous or binary thinking about complex concepts such as relatedness and autonomy, which should be seen as informing each other rather than standing in opposition to each other.

Although original descriptions identified the goal of feminist therapy as "social and political change" (Rawlings & Carter, 1977, p. 56), there is lack of consensus about the importance of social activism (Ballou & Gabalac, 1985). Marecek and Kravetz's (1998) in-depth interviews with 25 practitioners revealed that these therapists typically emphasized "inner power" (p. 22), "private and static" (p. 22) aspects of empowerment, and "personal fulfillment through a process of private discovery, without regard to social or political change" (p. 21). The empowerment strategies identified by these therapists included: creating a climate of respect and acceptance, encouraging clients to co-direct the psychotherapy process, using self-disclosure to increase awareness and model possibilities, and encouraging clients to participate in assessment by assisting in the selection of a diagnostic label. Although research participants spoke of the political and social changes needed for achieving equality, they "did not overtly challenge systems of power operating in society" (p. 26). Becker (2005) suggested that when empowerment is personalized and not connected to macro-level change, "therapeutic feminism" (p. 139) can contribute to the myth that women's problems are more personal and medical than political.

Recent social justice developments within counseling psychology reinforce social change perspectives in feminist counseling. The APA (2007) Guidelines recommend knowledge and use of community, mental health, and education resources for girls and women (Guideline 10). In addition, psychologists "are encouraged to understand and work to change institutional and systemic bias that may impact girls and women" (Guideline 11, p. 969). An ongoing challenge for the 21st century involves identifying and implementing meaningful social action activities. Activism is an important priority of many third-wave feminists (e.g., Baumgardner & Richards 2000, 2005; Labaton & Martin, 2004), and this commitment may facilitate higher levels of involvement in political action among third-wave feminist therapists. Consistent with third-wave perspectives, new forms of activism are likely to be more diverse and less obvious expressions of activism than those associated with second-wave feminism.

Feminist Counseling As an Integrative Approach

Feminist psychotherapy is a theoretically integrative and technically eclectic approach. Feminist counselors link their foundation in feminist values to various psychotherapy systems. No limits are placed on what frameworks are appropriate, provided these systems do not support biases or limit human potential. Worell and Remer (2003) identified areas feminist counselors should consider when examining the compatibility of theories, including potential sources of bias in historical development, theoretical concepts, assumptions about clients' problems, forms of assessment, psychotherapy techniques, and the respective roles of counselor and client. When potential conflicts are identified, counselors explore how biased aspects of theories can be restructured and transformed within a feminist framework. Considering the fit between psychotherapy approaches and the counselor's specific feminist and multicultural theoretical worldview is also important (Enns, 2004). Although it is not possible to provide extensive illustrations of feminist counseling as an integrative approach, the next section provides several examples: feminist narrative therapy and feminist trauma treatment.

Feminist Narrative Therapy As Theoretical Integration

Narrative therapy is often identified as a postmodern therapy that lends itself to integration with feminist counseling because of their theoretical similarities (e.g., Brown, 2007; Gremillion, 2004; Lee, 1997). Consistent with the priorities of feminist counselors, narrative therapists attempt to understand clients' "insider" positions by paying close attention to the ways in which clients internalize dominant cultural messages that limit their agency and confine them to less than optimal functioning. Therapists do not look for externally validated definitions of problems or for "correct" interpretations or solutions. Instead, they emphasize the capacities of clients to generate their own solutions and to make sense of their challenges

in light of personal realities or "truths." A major goal of narrative therapists is to work collaboratively with clients in a series of co-authoring activities designed to disrupt and defy the power of culture, and to help clients reclaim or reauthor their lives according to empowering metaphors (Maisel, Epston, & Borden, 2004). Clients are viewed as major characters of their lives who actively create meaning by weaving together the past, present, and future in a coherent life story or narrative.

Narrative therapists avoid "totalizing" language, which refers to any effort to assign a single, all-encompassing description to a client's problems or identity. Therapists also reject totalizing terms such as diagnosis, resistance, and denial, "which grant precedence to 'regimes of truth over clients' knowledge of their lives" (Winslade et al., 1997, p. 56), or tend to place blame on individuals and discount their personal expertise about themselves. Clients are encouraged to develop more complex views of themselves and their options. From a narrative therapy perspective, "therapeutic practices are never 'objective,' or culturally neutral, because they help reconfigure persons' lives and relationships in particular social contexts" (Gremillion, 2004, p. 183). This feature is consistent with "the personal is political" and a feminist emphasis on an ecological framework for understanding distress and change.

The narrative therapy technique of externalization involves deconstructing a problem by helping separate the client from "being" the problem. Externalizing a problem includes distancing oneself from a problem-saturated story and self-definition, which may include self-labeling, self-blame, the adoption of a "victim" identity, or internalized oppression. Energy is redirected toward devising a counterplot associated with hope, possibility, and creative alternatives for change (Gremillion, 2004; Miller, Cardona, & Hardin, 2006). Narrative therapy and externalization are closely related to the strength and coping-based focus of feminist counseling, an emphasis on reframing problems, and the concept of empowerment. Similar to feminist practice, the counselor and client conceptualize an issue as a "problem story" that is reinforced by dominant cultural understandings of gender roles, ideal bodies, or a "proper self."

Authors have proposed specific feminist narrative approaches for working with eating disorders (Brown, 2007; Gremillion, 2004; Maisel et al., 2004) and sexual assault (Miller et al., 2006). For example, an eating disorder can be described as a vindictive entity that is supported by cultural myths and attacks unsuspecting individuals. The goal of counseling is to "empower the 'insider' and weaken (and ultimately destroy) the dangerous external foes of anorexia and bulimia" (Strife, 2006, p. 121). However, some feminist theories of eating disorders (see Gilbert & Thompson, 1996) note that eating preoccupations can represent efforts to gain control rather than merely reveal powerlessness in the face of a vindictive opponent. Thus, feminist therapists point out the value of integrating narrative approaches with feminist models that reflect a wider range of meanings associated with women's bodies and eating (Brown, 2007). In the case of sexual assault, a narrative therapy approach begins with the telling of the client's story, which is followed by deconstructing societal messages about victims. Using externalization, clients identify oppressive social messages, which contribute to the silencing of victims and the shame and self-denigration that often accompany assault. This process paves the way for resisting negative messages and creating a new story (Miller et al., 2006).

To summarize, narrative therapies and feminist therapy share an emphasis on collaboration and co-authoring strategies for change. Similar to feminist therapy, narrative therapists avoid formal diagnostic language because it tends to give greater priority to an external, "professional" truth than to the client's reality. Both approaches encourage clients to act as their own best experts and to generate creative solutions. Furthermore, both approaches seek to decrease clients' self-blame by understanding how external factors or definitions influence the person's distress. In contrast to most feminist counseling approaches, narrative approaches place less emphasis on implications for social change and social activism. Thus, social identity analysis, power analysis, and social change perspectives can be used to enhance narrative therapy within a feminist framework.

Feminist Approaches to Trauma

Feminist approaches to trauma include theoretical models, such as those focusing on insidious traumatization (Root, 1992) and betrayal trauma (Freyd, 1996), as well as diagnostic models such as battered women's syndrome (Walker, 1979), complex posttraumatic stress disorder (Herman, 1992), and oppression artifact disorder (Brown, 1992). Feminist therapists have also developed multiple intervention approaches such as Harvey's (1996) ecological model, Walker's (1994) survivor therapy, Courtois' (2000) approach to working with sexual abuse memories,

Herman's (1992) phase-based model of working with long-term prolonged abuse, and Worell and Remer's (2003) empowerment model.

The various feminist trauma approaches share some common themes, including an understanding that trauma must be understood from an individual's subjective frame of reference, which is likely to be shaped by the person's multiple identities and experiences with discrimination (Brown, 2004). In the case of rape trauma, for example, the feminist therapist facilitates a client's examination of the cultural, gender role, and racial myths that contribute to victim blaming, as well as unequal power dynamics and socialization experiences that contribute to self-blame (West, 2002; Worell & Remer, 2003). Feminist therapists give visibility to the ways in which violence is gendered, bring a sociocultural and contextual analysis to trauma, and emphasize the importance of empowerment (Brown, 2004). Empowerment includes recovering a sense of personal power and efficacy as a survivor rather than as a victim, and, when appropriate, engaging in social change on behalf of other victims of violence (Worell & Remer, 2003).

Most feminist models address the challenges of working through traumatic memories and dealing with posttraumatic reactions, and recommend the use of empirically supported interventions for helping clients cope with symptoms of distress related to rape, child sexual abuse, and other traumas. In this way, feminist counselors draw on technically eclectic strategies for linking a feminist perspective with approaches such as cognitive behavioral therapies (CBT; Ford, Courtois, Steele, van der Hart, & Nijenhuis, 2005). For example, cognitive processing therapy (CPT) for sexual assault victims (Resick & Schnicke, 1993) combines successive writing assignments that expose clients to trauma memories. In addition, cognitive restructuring components focus on themes of safety, trust, power, esteem, and intimacy. Foa and Rothbaum's (1998) CBT intervention for rape, interpersonal trauma, and PTSD holds many similarities to CPT and integrates both prolonged exposure (PE) and stress inoculation training within a structured intervention program. This CBT approach is designed to facilitate the emotional processing and reorganization of trauma; challenge unhelpful cognitions; and help clients establish schemas that enhance a sense of personal efficacy and competence, control, and meaning.

The efficacy of both approaches has been well-supported, and researchers exploring both CBT and

CPT approaches have often worked collaboratively (e.g., Resick, Nishith, Weaver, Astin, & Feuer, 2002; Schnurr et al., 2007). Findings related to both CBT and CPT have shown that combined PE and cognitive restructuring treatments do not show superior outcomes over options that rely on PE alone or cognitive restructuring alone (Foa & Rauch, 2004; Foa et al., 2005; Resick et al., 2002; Resick, Galovski, Uhlmansiek, Scher, Clum, & Youn-Xu, 2008). Other CBT options for working with posttraumatic symptoms and interpersonal affect regulation therapy options are reviewed by Ford et al. (2005). Brown (2002) also recommends the integration of eye movement desensitization and reprocessing within a feminist therapy approach.

In addition to using technically integrative options with nonsexist approaches, such as those described above, it is also important for the feminist counselor to explore the theoretical connections between feminist counseling and CBT. During the first decades of feminist therapy, CBT approaches were often integrated with assertiveness and other group skills training programs, and framed as resocialization tools that would allow women to become aware of their interpersonal rights; challenge self-beliefs that limited their options; and adopt direct forms of self-expression to increase self-confidence, empowerment, and influence over their environments (e.g., Fodor, 1988; Jakubowski, 1977). These CBT interventions are based on a gender-neutral perspective. They also acknowledge the role that environments and external factors place on human development, and emphasize the importance of a collaborative client–therapist relationship (Enns, 2003; Worell & Remer, 2003).

After initial enthusiasm, observers noted that CBT approaches needed to be modified to be integrated effectively with feminist values. First, traditional CBT interventions emphasize individual change, and methods for addressing wider ecological issues that limit personal choices (e.g., sexual harassment, patterns of interruption in conversation) may be ignored (Fodor, 1988; Kantrowitz & Ballou, 1992). Second, CBT approaches provide no critical examination of androcentric assumptions that tend to prioritize rationality over emotion. Labeling a client's cognitions as "irrational" or "distorted" may deny the client's reality, which may include traumatic events or more insidious social conditions that may contribute to cognitions that limit one's perspective or wear down one's ability to challenge others directly. Even "feminist" assertiveness programs may fall short of the goals of feminist therapy because of the underlying assumption that the use of assertive skills will naturally lead to successful interpersonal outcomes, and that human rights can be defined independently from the complex gender and cultural injunctions that shape perceptions of rights. With modification, however, CBT tools can be integrated with more contextually valid approaches that consider the interpersonal and social realities of participants and the costs and benefits of any specific course of action (Enns, 2003). It should be noted that CBT interventions have also been effectively integrated with feminist eating disorder interventions, depression, and anxiety.

Because feminist counseling represents a worldview or system for organizing one's thinking about interventions rather than a specific technique-oriented approach, feminist counseling does not lend itself to traditional outcome research. However, feminist therapists seek to employ techniques that have been supported by research, especially outcome research relevant to gender-related concerns. It can be argued, therefore, that feminist therapists are practicing empirically supported or empirically validated counseling when they operate from a well-articulated theoretical and technically integrative approach that is informed by research. The APA Guidelines (2007) also call on psychologists to implement approaches that have been demonstrated to facilitate women's and girls' efforts to negotiate developmental transitions, resolve life challenges, and achieve positive outcomes. The Guidelines identify a wide range of approaches (e.g., family therapies, humanistic therapies) that can be integrated within a feminist framework.

Conclusion
Future Directions
Feminist counseling and psychotherapy approaches emerged approximately 40 years ago to facilitate work with women who had been disenfranchised by traditional psychotherapy. Over time, feminist therapy has become a broadly based social justice approach that combines knowledge from multiple disciplines in an intersectional and locational perspective that is attentive to the multidimensional social identities of clients. Feminist counseling approaches have been enriched by a range of feminist theories (e.g., body objectification, violence) and integrative approaches for working with highly challenging problems and social change issues (Brown, 2010). This chapter concludes with a brief identification of four challenges and recent directions: implementing feminist counseling approaches

within changing (and sometimes conservative) cultural contexts, building solid working alliances that decenter positions of privilege and centralize knowledge based in diversity, applying feminist frameworks to interventions with boys and men, and exploring possibilities for global partnerships.

In general, research reveals that, although feminist values and change efforts are often viewed positively, individuals are often disinclined to identify themselves as feminist (Aronson, 2003; Quinn & Radtke, 2006; Zucker, 2004). Furthermore, some therapists who endorse many feminist counseling behaviors are hesitant to claim the label "feminist" (e.g., Dankoski et al., 1998), and some self-identified feminist therapists avoid using this label with clients because of potential business consequences (Marecek & Kravetz, 1998). Still others appear uncomfortable with a feminist counseling commitment to social activism and prefer the "neutrality" of providing individual counseling services informed by feminism without making a more radical, social change commitment (Morrow et al., 2006). Claims that we have entered a "post-feminist" era further complicate the challenges of working as a feminist counselor in the 21st century.

Despite the concerns identified above and popular media sources that claim the erosion of feminist values, a variety of researchers note that feminism remains a vibrant force, but that each generation may need to define feminism in ways that are most meaningful to contemporary contexts (Hall & Rodriguez, 2003; Peltola et al., 2004). Similarly, feminist therapy needs to be seen as a living, evolving, flexible approach. The theoretical and practice contributions of second-and third-generation feminist therapists will become especially important to this evolution.

A recent working group (Mansour, Gosset, Elder, Averill, & Morrow, 2008) discussed challenges for practicing feminist multicultural therapy in conservative contexts. The group identified a list of strategies, which included seeking mentoring and networking opportunities, resisting discouragement and isolation by seeking out support and consultation groups, being well-grounded in research about the costs of discrimination and oppression, emphasizing patience and persistence, building collaborative alliances with others who share social justice goals, and placing priority on advocacy and social activism and advocacy. These suggestions reaffirm goals that date back to the earliest days of feminist therapy, and also point to the types of environments that are likely to nurture the contributions of future feminist therapy theorists.

Second, it is also important to acknowledge painful conflicts within feminism that have contributed to the disavowal of a feminist label. For example, many women of color prefer to self-identify as "womanist" and remain wary because of white feminists' historical inattentiveness to their own privileged status, tendency to generalize research and theory based on white women's lives to all women, and limited awareness that leads to difficulty in acting on the egalitarian values they claim (Bowman et al., 2001). Important directions for the future include developing truly inclusive forms of feminist practice that centralize diversities among individuals, building alliances that involve implementing stated values, and expanding on feminist multicultural counseling models.

An emphasis on intersectionality and the inseparability of multiple social identities will be especially useful for transcending past limitations of feminist theory and practice. Shields (2008) noted that, although intersectionality has become an accepted concept for approaching the study of gender, methods that are useful for implementing intersectional research and practice have lagged behind. Cole (2008) recommends the use of coalitions that foster connections across differences as a central feature for future work related to intersectionality. The National Multicultural Conference and Summit (NCMS) has become one setting in which "difficult dialogues" about interrelationships across race/ethnicity, gender, sexual orientation gender, and other social identities have been fostered, and is an important base for coalition building (Sue, Bingham, Porché-Burke, & Vasquez, 1999). Building approaches that integrate feminist approaches with other social justice undertakings can be facilitated in other environments that resemble the NCMS and that feature face-to-face dialogue.

A third development is the growth of approaches for working with men and masculinity. The accumulation of 25 years of research and theory on male gender role conflict (GRC) and its implications for counseling has resulted in a robust body of literature (O'Neil, 2008). To date, however, much of the research literature on male GRC has emphasized individual and interpersonal aspects and costs of GRC for men. This literature has only addressed the implications of gender as a system of power relations to a limited degree. Theory and research relevant to male GRC and its consequences can be further enhanced through the use of intersectional, social structural analyses that are becoming increasingly central within feminist psychology (Stewart &

McDermott, 2004). Similarly, depression and other psychological issues of men and women have been linked to gender-related challenges. Integrating research on relationships between depression and conformity to masculinity norms (e.g., Mahalik & Rochlen, 2006) and feminine communal norms (e.g., Mazure, Keita, & Blehar, 2002) will allow for a more complete understanding of how gender-related cultural expectations may affect both men and women. By placing both female and male gender issues within ecological frameworks that address individual, interpersonal, and social structural dimensions, it will become increasingly possible to build useful connections between the rich, parallel literatures supporting the psychologies of men and women (Enns, 2008).

Exploring parallels between feminist or gender-aware therapy by and/or for men and women is likely to be another productive avenue. Previous research about the attitudes and practices of male feminist therapists (Baird, Szymanski, & Ruebelt, 2007; Szymanski, Baird, & Kornman, 2002) suggests that the attitudes and self-reported behaviors of male feminist therapists are similar to those of self-identified female feminist therapists. A recent qualitative study (Baird et al., 2007) identified some of the important formative experiences for these men as including personal experiences with social change movements, personal relationships with women and others who had influenced their individual and professional development, professional training and experiences relevant to feminism and multiculturalism, and awareness of male privilege and political aspects of psychology (e.g., diagnostic practices, feelings of isolation and difference from other men), among others. Brown's (2010) recent book identifies feminist therapy as "not for women only." Building on that theme, further explorations of the intersections between feminist psychotherapies for men and women merit attention (Philpot, Brooks, Lusterman, & Nutt, 1997).

A fourth area for future development is the global practice of feminist counseling. The problems for which individuals seek feminist counseling, such as violence and gendered oppression, are global concerns, and there are growing efforts to link feminist counselors and activists across national boundaries as co-learners, co-mentors, and co-constructors of knowledge (Enns, 2004; Horne & Mathews, 2006; Norsworthy & Khuankaew, 2004, 2006). Western psychologies are often exported to other parts of the globe with minimal consideration of cultural factors (APA, 2004; Norsworthy & Khuankaew, 2006;

Rice & Ballou, 2002), and there will be many challenges ahead as Western feminists work toward implementing mutually enriching partnerships that truly enact the egalitarian values they espouse, and act as learners who are respectful of indigenous forms of expertise.

Western feminists have often been slow to recognize forms of privilege and power that may cloud their thinking, including the power to "orientalize, exoticize, ethnicize, racialize, or sexualize members of other nations or groups" (Mackie, 2001, p. 182). To create an egalitarian transnational psychology of women, it will be necessary to "shift the axis" and emphasize "world traveling" (Lugones, 1987). *World traveling* consists of three interrelated awareness-building activities that focus on seeking insight about cultural practices that have created "us" (e.g., recognizing how systems of oppression have influenced the West, and how these oppressions may parallel or be different from experiences of people around the globe), looking at "what it is to be ourselves in their eyes" (p. 18) (e.g., by understanding our country's role in colonization and how we may inadvertently perpetuate colonizing attitudes in our relationships with others), and working toward seeing people from various parts of the world as they see themselves. World traveling calls for an attitude of humility and a willingness to value the expertise of women as they speak in their own voices. Through egalitarian interaction, North American feminists may gain new lenses for evaluating Western feminist models and therapies and learning from the insights and practices of theorists and practitioners around the globe.

In light of these issues, participants in a recent working group on global aspects of feminist practice (Enns & Machizawa, 2008) noted that feminist therapy concepts such as consciousness-raising, empowerment, identity development, personal goals, personal power, assertiveness, and collaboration, are typically embedded in Western indigenous, individualistic frameworks and need to be deconstructed and transformed to be relevant beyond North American borders. Furthermore, the hegemony of English and expectations that our partners will communicate in English limit opportunities for full power-sharing collaborations. Third, although problems such as violence and gendered oppression are universal, these issues are manifested through specific cultural lenses that are shaped by many factors such as colonial histories, imperialism, religious beliefs, family structures, educational options, ethnicity, economic realities, and legal and governmental systems. The "insider" perspectives and expertise of transnational feminists are essential for understanding the complexity of issues in specific contexts and intervening effectively at both individual and social change levels. The APA Resolution on Gender and Culture Awareness in Psychology (2004) provides initial direction and calls on psychologists to build respect for pluralism and cultural difference (without implicitly condoning gendered oppressions), incorporate an analysis of power and the reduction of power asymmetries in partnerships, implement a critical analysis of Western perspectives, and emphasize the sociocultural realities that influence individual realities (Rice & Ballou, 2002).

The principles of feminist counseling approaches are well-established. As we move further into the 21st century, the applications of feminist counseling will continue to diversify. As the purview of feminist therapy has grown, new directions have emerged, and new possibilities for integrating feminist values with other frameworks in psychology are multiplying. During the past 40 years, great progress toward achieving equality has occurred, and these gains have the potential to benefit the mental health of all. However, the resurgence of old oppressions and the emergence of more subtle forms of discrimination call for even more creative feminist counseling responses and social change efforts. New cultural issues continue to emerge in a world in which oppression also intersects with new technologies, media forces, and global conflict (APA, 2007). A major challenge involves reinforcing core values of feminist thought while recognizing the diversity of human experience that calls for flexibility in the application of these values, and the need to respond to new gender-related opportunities and problems that emerge in this rapidly changing society.

References

Alcoff, L. (1988). Cultural feminism versus post-structuralism: The identity crisis in feminist theory. *Signs: Journal of Women in Culture and Society, 13*, 405–436.

American Psychiatric Association. (1968). *Diagnostic and statistical manual of mental disorders* (2nd ed.). Washington, DC: Author.

American Psychiatric Association. (1994). *Diagnostic and statistical manual of mental disorders* (4th ed.). Washington, DC: Author.

American Psychiatric Association. (2000). *Diagnostic and statistical manual of mental disorders* (DSM-IV-TR, 4th ed., text revision). Washington, DC: Author.

American Psychological Association. (2000). Guidelines for psychotherapy with lesbian, gay, and bisexual clients. *American Psychologist, 55*, 1440–1451.

American Psychological Association. (2003). Guidelines on multicultural education, training, research, practice, and organizational change for psychologists. *American Psychologist, 58*, 377–402.

American Psychological Association. (2004). *Resolution on culture and gender awareness in international psychology.* Washington, DC: Author.

American Psychological Association. (2007). Guidelines for psychological practice with girls and women. *American Psychologist, 62*, 949–979.

Anzaldúa, G. (1987). *Borderlands, la frontera: The new mestiza.* San Francisco: Aunt Lute Books.

Aronson, P. (2003). Feminists or "postfeminists"? Young women's attitudes toward feminism and gender relations. *Gender and Society, 17*, 903–922.

Asian Women United of California (Eds.). (1997). *Making more waves: New writings by Asian American women.* Boston: Beacon.

Baird, M. K., Szymanski, D. M., & Ruebelt, S. G. (2007). Feminist identity development and practice among male therapists. *Psychology of Men and Masculinity, 8*, 67–78.

Ballou, M., & Gabalac, N. W. (1985). *A feminist position on mental health.* Springfield, IL: C. C. Thomas.

Ballou, M., & Hill, M. (2008). The context of therapy: Theory. In M. Ballou, M. Hill, & C. West (Eds.), *Feminist therapy: Theory and practice* (pp. 1–8). New York: Springer.

Ballou, M., Hill, M., & West, C. (Eds.). (2008). *Feminist therapy: Theory and practice.* New York: Springer.

Ballou, M., Matsumoto, A., & Wagner, M. (2002). Toward a feminist ecological theory of human nature: Theory building in response to real-world dynamics. In M. Ballou and L. S. Brown (Eds.), *Rethinking mental health and disorder: Feminist perspectives* (pp. 99–141). New York: Guilford Press.

Ballou, M., & West, C. (2000). Feminist therapy approaches. In M. Biaggio & M. Hersen (Eds.), *Issues in the psychology of women* (pp. 273–297). New York: Kluwer Academic/Plenum.

Barreto, M., & Ellemers, N. (2005). The burden of benevolent sexism: How it contributes to the maintenance of gender inequalities. *European Journal of Social Psychology, 35*, 633–642.

Barrett, C. J., Berg, P. I., Eaton, E. M., & Pomeroy, E. L. (1974). Implications of women's liberation and the future of psychotherapy. *Psychotherapy: Theory, Research and Practice, 11*, 11–15.

Barrett, S. E., Chin, J. L., Comas-Díaz, L., Espín, O, Greene, B., & McGoldrick, M. (2005). Multicultural feminist therapy: Theory in context. *Women and Therapy, 28*, 27–61.

Basu, A. (Ed.). (1995). *The challenge of local feminisms: Women's movements in global perspective.* Boulder: Westview Press.

Baumgardner, J., & Richards, A. (2000). *Manifesta: Young women, feminism, and the future.* New York: Farrar, Straus, & Giroux.

Baumgardner, J., & Richards, A. (2005). *Grassroots: A field guide for feminist activism.* New York: Farrar, Straus and Giroux.

Becker, D. (2004). Post-traumatic stress disorder. In P. M. Caplan & L. Cosgrove (Eds.), *Bias in psychiatric diagnosis* (pp. 207–212). Lanham, MD: Rowman & Littlefield.

Becker, D. (2005). *The myth of empowerment: Women and the therapeutic culture in America.* New York: New York University Press.

Belenky, M. J., Clinchy, B. M., Goldberger, N. R., & Tarule, J. M. (1986). *Women's ways of knowing*. New York: Basic Books.

Bernal, D. D. (1998). Using a Chicana feminist epistemology in educational research. *Harvard Educational Review, 68*, 555–579.

Bohan, J. S. (1993). Regarding gender: Essentialism, constructionism, and feminist psychology. *Psychology of Women Quarterly, 17*, 5–21.

Bowman, S. L., Rasheed, S., Ferris, J., Thompson, D. A., McRae, M., & Weitzman, L. (2001). Interface of feminism and multiculturalism: Where are the women of color? In J. G. Ponterotto, J. M. Casas, L. A. Suzuki, & C. A. Alexander (Eds.), *Handbook of multicultural counseling* (2nd ed., pp. 779–798). Thousand Oaks, CA: Sage.

Brabeck, M. (Ed.). (2000). *Practicing feminist ethics in psychology*. Washington, DC: American Psychological Association.

Brodsky, A. (1976). The consciousness-raising group as a model for therapy with women. In S. Cox (Ed.s), *Female psychology: The emerging self* (pp. 372–377). Chicago: Science Research Associates.

Brodsky, A. (1977). Therapeutic aspects of consciousness-raising groups. In E. I. Rawlings & D. K. Carter (Eds.), *Psychotherapy for women* (pp. 300–309). Springfield, IL: C. C. Thomas.

Brodsky, A. (1980). A decade of feminist influence on psychotherapy. *Psychology of Women Quarterly, 4*, 331–343.

Bronfenbrenner, U., & Morris, P. A. (2006). The bioecological model of human development. In R. M. Lerner (Ed.), *Handbook of child psychology: Vol.1. Theoretical models of human development* (6th ed., pp. 793–828). Hoboken, NJ: Wiley.

Broverman, I. K., Broverman, D. M., Clarkson, F., Rosenkrantz, P., & Vogel, S. (1970). Sex-role stereotyping and clinical judgments of mental health. *Journal of Consulting and Clinical Psychology, 45*, 250–256.

Brown, C. (2007). Talking body talk: Merging feminist and narrative approaches to practice. In C. Brown & T. Augusta-Scott (Eds.), *Narrative therapy: Making meaning, making lives* (pp. 269–302). Thousand Oaks, CA: Sage.

Brown, L. S. (1990). Taking account of gender in the clinical assessment interview. *Professional Psychology: Research and Practice, 21*, 12–17.

Brown, L. S. (1991). Ethical issues in feminist therapy: Selected topics. *Psychology of Women Quarterly, 15*, 323–336.

Brown, L. S. (1992). A feminist critique of the personality disorders. In L. S. Brown & M. Ballou (Eds.), *Personality and psychopathology: Feminist reappraisals* (pp. 206–228). New York: Guilford.

Brown, L. S. (1994). *Subversive dialogues: Theory in feminist therapy*. New York: Basic Books.

Brown, L. S. (2002). Feminist therapy and EMDR: Theory meets practice. In F. Shapiro (Eds.), *EMDT as an integrative psychotherapy approach* (pp. 263–288). Washington, DC: American Psychological Association.

Brown, L. S. (2004). Feminist paradigms of trauma treatment. *Psychotherapy: Theory, Research, Practice, Training, 41*, 464–471.

Brown, L. S. (2006). Still subversive after all these years: The relevance of feminist therapy in the age of evidence-based practice. *Psychology of Women Quarterly, 30*, 15–24.

Brown, L. S. (2010). *Feminist therapy*. Washington, DC: American Psychological Association Press.

Brown, L. S., & Brodsky, A. M. (1992). The future of feminist therapy. *Psychotherapy: Theory, Research, & Practice, 29*, 51–57.

Bunch, C. (1987). *Passionate politics: Feminist theory in action*. New York: St. Martin's Press.

Burbules, N. C., & Berk, R. (1999). Critical thinking and critical pedagogy: Relations, differences, and limits. In R. S. Popkewitz & L. Fendler (Eds.), *Critical theories in education: Changing terrains of knowledge and politics* (pp. 45–65). New York: Routledge.

Burstow, B. (1992). *Radical feminist therapy: Working in the context of violence*. Newbury Park, CA: Sage.

Butler, J. E. (2000). Transforming the curriculum: Teaching about women of color. In J. A. Banks & C. A. M. Banks (Eds.), *Multicultural education: Issues and perspectives* (4th ed., pp. 174–193). New York: Wiley.

Calliste, A. M., Dei, G. J. S., & Agular, M. (Eds.). (2000). *Anti-racism feminism: Critical race and gender studies*. Halifax, Nova Scotia, Canada: Fernwood Publishing.

Campbell, B., Schellenberg, E. G., & Senn, C. Y. (1997). Evaluating measures of contemporary sexism. *Psychology of Women Quarterly, 21*, 89–102.

Caplan, P., & Cosgrove, L. (Eds.). (2004). *Bias in psychiatric diagnosis*. Lanham, MD: Rowman & Littlefield.

Cheater, A. P. (1999). *Anthropology of power: Empowerment and disempowerment in changing structures*. New York: Routledge.

Chesler, P. (1972). *Women and madness*. New York: Doubleday.

Chester, A., & Bretherton, D. (2001). What makes feminist counseling feminist? *Feminism and Psychology, 11*, 527–545.

Chin, J. L. (Ed.). (2000). *Relationships among Asian American women*. Washington, DC: American Psychological Association.

Cole, E. R. (2008). Coalitions as a model for intersectionality: From practice to theory. *Sex Roles, 59*, 443–453.

Collins, P. H. (2000). *Black feminist thought: Knowledge, consciousness, and the politics of empowerment* (2nd ed.). New York: Routledge.

Comas-Díaz, L. (2000). An ethnopolitical approach to working with people of color. *American Psychologist, 55*, 1319–1325.

Comas-Díaz, L., & Greene, B. (1994). *Women of color: Integrating ethnic and gender identities in psychotherapy*. New York: Guilford Press.

Combahee River Collective. (1982). A Black feminist statement. In G. T. Hull, P. B. Scott, & B. Smith (Eds.), *All the women are white, all the Blacks are men, but some of us are brave* (pp. 13–22). Old Westbury, NY: The Feminist Press.

Contratto, S., & Rossier, J. (2005). Early trends in feminist therapy theory and practice. *Women and Therapy, 28*(3/4), 7–26.

Corey, G. (2009). *Theory and practice of counseling and psychotherapy* (8th ed.). Belmont, CA: Wadsworth.

Cosgrove, L. (2002). Resisting essentialism in feminist therapy theory: Some epistemological considerations. *Women and Therapy, 25*(1), 89–112.

Courtois, C. (2000). *Recollections of sexual abuse*. New York: Norton.

Courtois, C. A. (2004). Complex trauma, complex reactions: Assessment and treatment. *Psychotherapy: Theory, Research, Practice, Training, 41*, 412–425.

Crawford, M. (2006). *Transformations: Women, gender, and psychology*. Boston: McGraw-Hill.

Crowley-Long, K. (1998). Making room for many feminisms: The dominance of the liberal political perspective in the psychology of women course. *Psychology of Women Quarterly, 22*, 113–130.

Dankoski, M. E., Penn, C. D., Carlson, T. D., & Hecker, L. L. (1998). What's in a name? A study of family therapists' use and acceptance of the feminist perspective. *American Journal of Family Therapy, 26*, 95–104.

Dardenne, B., Dumont, M., & Bollier, T. (2007). Insidious dangers of benevolent sexism: Consequences for women's performance. *Journal of Personality and Social Psychology, 93*, 764–779.

Dicker, R., & Piepmeier, A. (2003). *Catching a wave: Reclaiming feminism for the 21st century.* Boston: Northeastern University Press.

Donovan, J. (2000). *Feminist theory: The intellectual traditional of American feminism* (3rd ed.). New York: F. Ungar.

Dovidio, J. F., Gaertner, S. L., Kawakami, K., & Hodson, G. (2002). Why can't we just get along? Interpersonal biases and interracial distrust. *Cultural Diversity and Ethnic Minority Psychology, 8*, 88–102.

Downing, N. E., & Roush, K. L. (1985). From passive acceptance to active commitment: A model of feminist identity development for women. *Counseling psychologist, 13*, 695–709.

Eichenbaum, L., & Orbach, S. (1983). *Understanding women: A feminist psychoanalytic approach.* New York: Basic Books.

Enns, C. Z. (1992). Toward integrating feminist psychotherapy and feminist philosophy. *Professional Psychology: Research and Practice, 23*, 453–466.

Enns, C. Z. (2003). Contemporary adaptations of traditional approaches to the counseling of women. In M. Kopala, & M. A. Keitel (Eds.), *Handbook of counseling women* (pp. 3–21). Thousand Oaks, CA: Sage.

Enns, C. Z. (2004). *Feminist theories and feminist psychotherapies: Origins, themes, and diversity* (2nd ed.). New York: Haworth.

Enns, C. Z. (2008). Toward a complexity paradigm for understanding gender role conflict. *The Counseling Psychologist, 36*, 446–454.

Enns, C. Z. (2010). Locational feminisms and feminist social identity analysis. *Professional Psychology: Research and Practice, 41*, 333–339.

Enns, C. Z., & Byars-Winston, A. (2010). Multicultural feminist therapy. In H. Landrine & N. F. Russo (Eds.), *Handbook of diversity in feminist psychology* (pp. 367–388). New York: Springer.

Enns, C. Z., & Machizawa, S. (2008, March). *Psychological practice with women and girls: Global perspectives.* Working group conducted at the 2008 International Counseling Psychology Conference, Chicago, Illinois.

Enns, C. Z., & Sinacore, A. L. (Eds.). (2005). *Teaching and social justice: Integrating multicultural and feminist theories in the classroom.* Washington DC: American Psychological Association.

Eriksen, K., & Kress, V. E. (2005). *Beyond the DSM story: Ethical quandaries, challenges, and best practices.* Thousand Oaks, CA: Sage.

Espín, O. M. (1999). *Women crossing boundaries: A psychology of immigration and transformations of sexuality.* New York: Routledge.

Espín, O. M., & Gawelek, M.A. (1992). Women's diversity: Ethnicity, race, class, and gender in theories of feminist psychology. In L. S. Brown & M. Ballou (Eds.), *Personality and psychopathology: Feminist reappraisals* (pp. 88–107). New York: Norton.

Feminist Therapy Institute. (2000). *Feminist therapy code of ethics* (revised, 1999). San Francisco: Feminist Therapy Institute.

Fischer, A. R. (2006). Women's benevolent sexism as reaction to hostility. *Psychology of Women Quarterly, 30*, 410–416.

Fischer, A. R., & Holz, K. B. (2007). Perceived discrimination and women's psychological distress: The roles of collective and personal self-esteem. *Journal of Counseling Psychology, 54*, 154–164.

Flax, J. (1987). Postmodernism and gender relations in feminist theory. *Signs: Journal of Women in Culture and Society, 12*, 621–643.

Foa, E. B., Hembree, E. A., Cahill, S. P., Rauch, S. A. M., Riggs, D. S., Feeny, N. C., & Yadin, E. (2005). Randomized trial of prolonged exposure for posttraumatic stress disorder with and without cognitive restructuring: Outcome at academic and community clinics. *Journal of Consulting and Clinical Psychology, 73*, 953–964.

Foa, E. B., & Rauch, S. A. M. (2004). Cognitive changes during prolonged exposure versus prolonged exposure plus cognitive restructuring in female assault survivors with posttraumatic stress disorder. *Journal of Consulting and Clinical Psychology, 72*, 879–884.

Foa, E. B., & Rothbaum, B. O. (1998). *Treating the trauma of rape: Cognitive behavioral therapy for PTSD.* New York: Guilford Press.

Fodor, I. G. (1988). Cognitive behavior therapy. Evaluation of theory and practice for addressing women's issues. In M. A. Dutton-Douglas & L. E. Walker (Eds.), *Feminist psychotherapies: Integration of therapeutic and feminist systems* (pp. 91–117). Norwood, NJ: Ablex.

Ford, J. D., Courtois, C. A., Steele, K., van der Hart, O. (2005). Treatment of complex posttraumatic self-dysregulation. *Journal of Traumatic Stress, 18*, 437–447.

Freire, P. (1970). *Pedagogy of the oppressed.* (M. B. Ramos, Trans.). New York: Seabury Press.

Freyd, J. J. (1996). *Betrayal trauma: The logic of forgetting abuse.* Cambridge, MA: Harvard University Press.

Friedman, S. S. (1998). *Mappings: Feminism and the cultural geographies of encounter.* Princeton, NJ: Princeton University Press.

Gaertner, S. L., & Dovidio, J. F. (2005). Understanding and addressing contemporary racism: From aversive racism to the common group identity model. *Journal of Social Issues, 61*, 615–639.

Garber, L. (2001). *Identity poetics: Race, class, and the lesbian-feminist roots of queer theory.* New York: Columbia University Press.

Gergen, M. (2001). *Feminist reconstructions in psychology.* Thousand Oaks, CA: Sage.

Gilbert, L. A. (1980). Feminist therapy. In A. Brodsky & R. T. Hare-Mustin (Eds.), *Women and psychotherapy* (pp. 245–265). New York: Guilford Press.

Gilbert, S., & Thompson, J. K. (1996). Feminist explanations of the development of eating disorders: Common themes, research findings, and methodological issues. *Clinical Psychology: Science and Practice, 3*, 183–202.

Gilligan, C. (1982). *In a different voice.* Cambridge, MA: Harvard University Press.

Glick, P., & Fiske, S. T. (2001). An ambivalent alliance: Hostile and benevolent sexism as complementary justifications for gender inequality. *American Psychologist, 56*, 109–118.

Goldberger, N. R. (1996). Cultural imperatives and diversity in ways of knowing. In N. R. Goldberger & J. M. Tarule (Eds.), *Knowledge, difference, and power: Essays inspired by "Women's Ways of Knowing"* (pp. 335–371). New York: Basic Books.

Greenspan, M. (1983). *A new approach to women and therapy.* New York: McGraw-Hill.

Gremillion, H. (2004). Unpacking essentialisms in therapy: Lessons for feminist approaches from narrative work. *Journal of Constructivist Psychology, 17*, 173–200.

Hall, E. J., & Rodriguez, M. S. (2003). The myth of postfeminism. *Gender and Society, 17*, 878–902.

Hare-Mustin, R. T., Marecek, J., Kaplan, A. G., & Liss-Levinson, N. (1979). Rights of clients, responsibilities of therapists. *American Psychologist, 34*, 3–16.

Harvey, M. R. (1996). An ecological view of psychological trauma and trauma recovery. *Journal of Traumatic Stress, 9*, 3–24.

Herman, J. L. (1992). *Trauma and recovery: The aftermath of violence.* New York: Basic Books.

Hernández, D., & Rehman, B. (2002). *Colonize this! Young women of color on today's feminism.* Emeryville, CA: Seal Press.

Heywood, L., & Drake, J. (Eds.). (1997). *Third wave agenda: Being feminist, doing feminism.* Minneapolis: University of Minnesota Press.

Higgenbotham, E. B. (1992). African American women's history and the metalanguage of race. *Signs: Journal of Women in Culture and Society, 17*, 251–274.

Hill, M., & Ballou, M. (1998). Making therapy feminist: A practice survey. *Women and Therapy, 21*(2), 1–16.

Hoffman, R. M. (2006). Gender self-definition and gender self-acceptance in women: Intersections with feminist, womanist, and ethnic identities. *Journal of Counseling and Development, 84*, 358–372.

hooks, b. (1981). *Ain't I a woman.* Boston: South End Press.

Horne, S. G., & Mathews, S. S. (2006). A social justice approach to international collaborative consultation. In R. L. Toporek, L. H. Gerstein, N. A. Fouad, G. Roysircar, & T. Israel (Eds.), *Handbook for social justice in counseling psychology* (pp. 388–405). Thousand Oaks, CA: Sage.

Humphreys, J. (2003). Resilience in sheltered battered women. *Issues in Mental Health Nursing, 24*, 137–152.

Hurtado, A. (1989). Relating to privilege: Seduction and rejection in the subordination of white women and women of color. *Signs: Journal of Women in Culture an Society, 14*, 833–855.

Hurtado, A. (2003). *Voicing Chicana feminisms: Young women speak out on sexuality and identity.* New York: New York University Press.

Jackson, L. C., & Greene, B. (Eds.). (2000). *Psychotherapy with African American Women: Innovations in psychodynamic perspectives and practice.* New York: Guilford Press.

Jaggar, A. M. (Ed.). (2008). *Just methods: An interdisciplinary feminist reader.* Boulder, CO: Paradigm.

Jaggar, A. M., & Rothenberg, P. S. (1993). *Feminist frameworks: Alternative theoretical accounts of the relations between women and men* (3rd ed.). New York: McGraw-Hill.

Jakubowski, P. A. (1977). Assertion training for women. In E. I. Rawlings & D. K. Carter (Eds.), *Psychotherapy for women* (pp. 147–190). Springfield, IL: Charles C. Thomas.

Jenkins, Y. M. (2000). The Stone Center theoretical approach revisited: Applications for African American women. In L. C. Jackson & B. Greene (Eds.), *Psychotherapy with African American women* (pp. 62–81). New York: Guilford.

Jones, S. R., & McEwen, M. K. (2000). A conceptual model of multiple dimensions of identity. *Journal of College Student Development, 41*, 405–414.

Jost, J. T., & Kay, A. C. (2005). Exposure to benevolent sexism and complementary gender stereotypes: Consequences for specific and diffuse forms of system justification. *Journal of Personality and Social Psychology, 88*, 498–509.

Kantrowitz, R. E., & Ballou, M. (1992). A feminist critique of cognitive-behavioral therapy. In L. S. Brown & M. Ballou (Eds.), *Personality and psychopathology: Feminist reappraisals* (pp. 70–87). New York: Guilford.

Kaplan, M. (1983). A woman's view of DSM-III. *American Psychologist, 38*, 786–792.

Kaschak, E. (1981). Feminist psychotherapy: The first decade. In S. Cox (Ed.), *Female psychology: The emerging self* (pp. 387–400). New York: St. Martin's Press.

Kerber, L. K. (1986). Some cautionary words for historians. *Signs: Journal of Women in Culture and Society, 11*, 304–310.

Kitzinger, C., & Perkins, R. (1993). *Changing our minds: Lesbian feminism and psychology.* New York: New York University Press.

Klein, M. H. (1976). Feminist concepts of therapy outcome. *Psychotherapy: Theory, Research and Practice, 13*, 89–95.

Klonoff, E. A., Landrine, H., & Campbell, R. (2000). Sexist discrimination may account for well-known gender differences in psychiatric symptoms. *Psychology of Women Quarterly, 24*, 93–99.

Kravetz, D. (1978). Consciousness-raising groups in the 1970s. *Psychology of Women Quarterly, 3*, 168–186.

Kravetz, D. (2004). *Tales from the trenches: Politics and practice in feminist service organizations.* Dallas, TX: University Press of America.

Labaton, V., & Martin, D. L. (2004). *The fire this time: Young activists and the new feminism.* New York: Anchor Books.

Lamb, S. (Ed.). (1999). *New versions of victims: Feminists struggle with the concept.* New York: New York University Press.

Lee, J. (1997). Women re-authoring their lives through feminist narrative therapy. *Women and Therapy, 20* (3), 1–22.

Lerman, H. (1996). *Pigeonholing women's misery.* New York: Basic Books.

Lev-Wiesel, R., Amir, M., & Besser, A. (2005). Posttraumatic growth among female survivors of childhood sexual abuse in relation to perpetrator identity. *Journal of Loss and Trauma, 10*, 7–17.

Liss, M., Crawford, M., & Popp, D. (2004). Predictors and correlates of collective action. *Sex Roles, 50*, 771–779.

Lorber, J. (2005). *Gender inequality: Feminist theories and politics* (3rd ed.). Los Angeles: Roxbury.

Luepnitz, D.A. (1988). *The family interpreted.* New York: Basic Books.

Lugones, M. (1987). Playfulness, "world"-travelling and loving perception. *Hypatia, 2*(2), 3–19.

Luria, Z. (1986). A methodological critique. *Signs: Journal of Women in Culture and Society, 11*, 316–321.

Mackie, V. (2001). The language of globalization, transnationality and feminism. *International Feminist Journal of Politics, 3*(2), 180–206.

Mahalik, J. R., & Rochlen, A. B. (2006). Men's likely responses to clinical depression: What are they and do masculinity norms predict them? *Sex Roles, 55*, 659–667.

Maisel, R., Epston, D., & Borden, A. (2004). *Biting the hand that starves you: Inspiring resistance to anorexia/bulimia.* New York: Norton.

Mansour, E., Gosset, E., Elder, W., Averill, L., & Morrow, S. (2008, March). *Practicing feminist multicultural therapy in conservative environments.* Working group conducted at the 2008 International Counseling Psychology Conference, Chicago, Illinois.

Marecek, J. (1999). Trauma talk in feminist clinical practice. In S. Lamb (Ed.), *New versions of victims: Feminist struggle with the concept* (pp. 158–182). New York: New York University Press.

Marecek, J., & Kravetz, D. (1977). Women and mental health: A review of feminist change efforts. *Psychiatry, 40*, 323–329.

Marecek, J., & Kravetz, D. (1998). Power and agency in feminist therapy. In I. B. Seu & C. Heenan (Eds.), *Feminism and Psychotherapy* (pp. 13–29). London: Sage.

Matlin, M. W. (2012). *The psychology of women* (7th ed.). Belmont, CA: Wadsworth.

Mazure, C. M., Keita, G. P., & Glehar, M. C. (2002). *Summit on women and depression: Proceedings and recommendations.* Washington, DC: American Psychological Association.

McHugh, M. C., Koeske, R. D., & Frieze, I. H. (1986). Issues to consider in conducting nonsexist research: A guide for researchers. *American Psychologist, 41,* 879–890.

Moradi, B., & Subich, L. M. (2002). Perceived sexist events and feminist identity development attitudes: Links to women's psychological distress. *The Counseling Psychologist, 30,* 44–65.

McNamara, K., & Rickard, K. M. (1989). Feminist identity development: Implications for feminist therapy with women. *Journal of Counseling and Development, 68,* 184–189.

Metzendorf, D. (2005). *The evolution of feminist organizations: An organizational study.* Lanham, MD: University Press of America.

Miller, C. L., & Cummins, A. G. (1992). An examination of women's perspectives on power. *Psychology of Women Quarterly, 16,* 415–428.

Miller, J. B. (1976). *Toward a new psychology of women.* Boston: Beacon Press.

Miller, B. J., Cardona, J. R. P., & Hardin, M. (2006). The use of narrative therapy and internal family systems with survivors of childhood sexual abuse: Examining issues related to loss and oppression. *Journal of Feminist Family therapy, 18*(4), 1–27.

Miller, J. B., & Stiver, I. P. (1997). *The healing connection: How women form relationship in therapy and in life.* Boston: Beacon Press.

Mohanty, C. T., Russo, A., & Torres, L. (1991). *Third world women and the politics of feminism.* Bloomington, IN: Indiana University Press.

Moradi, B., Fischer, A. R., Hill, M. S., Jome, L. M., & Blum, S. A. (2000). Does "feminist" plus "therapist" equal "feminist therapist"? *Psychology of Women Quarterly, 24,* 285–296.

Moradi, B., & Funderburk, J. R. (2006). Roles of perceived sexist events and perceived social support in the mental health of women seeking counseling. *Journal of Counseling Psychology, 53,* 4634–4473.

Moradi, B., & Subich, L. M. (2003). A concomitant examination of the relations of perceived racist and sexist events to psychological distress for African American women. *The Counseling Psychologist, 31,* 451–469.

Moradi, B., & Subich, L. M. (2004). Examining the moderating role of self-esteem in the link between experiences of perceived sexist events and psychological distress. *Journal of Counseling Psychology, 51,* 50–56.

Moradi, B., & Yoder, J. D. (2011). The psychology of girls and women. In E. M. Altmaier, & J. C. Hansen (Eds.), *The Oxford handbook of counseling psychology.* New York: Oxford University Press.

Morrow, S. L., & Hawxhurst, D. M. (1998). Feminist therapy: Integrating political analysis in counseling and psychotherapy. *Women and Therapy, 21* (2), 37–50.

Morrow, S. L., Hawxhurst, D. M., Montes de Vegas, A. Y., Abousleman, T. M., & Castañeda, C. L. (2006). Toward a radical feminist multicultural therapy: Renewing a commitment to activism. In R. L. Toporek, L. H. Gerstein, N. A. Fouad, G. Roysircar, & T. Israel (Eds.), *Handbook for social justice in counseling psychology* (pp. 231–247). Thousand Oaks, CA: Sage.

Moya, P. M. L. (2001). Chicana feminism and postmodernist theory. *Signs: Journal of Women in Culture and Society, 26,* 441–483.

Murdock, N. (2008). *Theories of counseling and psychotherapy: A case approach* (2nd ed.). Old Tappan, NJ: Prentice-Hall.

Nam, V. (2001). *Yell-oh girls: Emerging voices explore culture, identity, and growing up Asian American.* New York: HarperCollins.

Norsworthy, K. L., & Khuankaew, O. (2004). Women of Burma speak out: Workshops to deconstruct gender-based violence and build systems of peace and justice. *The Journal for Specialists in Group Work, 29,* 259–283.

Norsworthy, K. L., & Khuankaew, O. (2006). Bringing social justice to international practices of counseling psychology. In R. L. Toporek, L. H. Gerstein, N. A. Fouad, G. Roysircar, & T. Israel (Eds.), *Handbook for social justice in counseling psychology* (pp. 421–441). Thousand Oaks, CA: Sage.

O'Neil, J. M. (2008). Summarizing 25 years of research on men's gender role conflict using the gender role conflict scale: New research paradigms and clinical implications. *The Counseling Psychologist, 36,* 358–445.

Osborne, J. W. (2001). Testing stereotype threat: Does anxiety explain race and sex differences in achievement? *Contemporary Educational Psychology, 26,* 291–310.

Ossana, S. M., Helms, J. E., & Leonard, M. M. (1992). Do "womanist" identity attitudes influence college women's self-esteem and perceptions of environmental bias? *Journal of Counseling and Development, 70,* 402–408.

Parks, E. E., Carter, R. T., & Gushue, G. V. (1996). At the crossroads: Racial and womanist identity development in Black and White women. *Journal of Counseling and Development, 74,* 624–631.

Pease, B. (2002). Rethinking empowerment: A postmodern reappraisal for emancipatory practice. *British Journal of Social Work, 32,* 135–147.

Peltola, P., Milkie, M. A., & Presser, S. (2004). The "feminist" mystique: Feminist identity in three generations of women. *Gender and Society, 18,* 122–144.

Philpot, C. L., Brooks, G. R., Lusterman, D. D., & Nutt, R. L. (1997). *Bridging separate gender worlds: Why men and women clash and how therapists can bring them together.* Washington, DC: American Psychological Association.

Porter, N. (2005). Location, location, location: Contributions of contemporary feminist theorists to therapy theory and practice. *Women and Therapy, 28*(3/4), 143–160.

Prilleltensky, I., & Nelson, G. (2002). *Doing psychology critically: Making a difference in diverse settings.* New York: Palgrave Macmillan.

Quinn, J. E. A., & Radtke, H. L. (2006). Dilemmatic negotiations: the (un)tenability of feminist identity. *Psychology of Women Quarterly, 30,* 187–198.

Rader, J., & Gilbert, L. A. (2005). The egalitarian relationship in feminist therapy. *Psychology of Women Quarterly, 29,* 427–435.

Rawlings, E., & Carter, D. (1977). Feminist and nonsexist psychotherapy. In E. I. Rawlings & D. K. Carter (Eds.), *Psychotherapy for women* (pp. 49–76). Springfield, IL: C. C. Thomas.

Rederstorff, J. C., & Levendosky, A. A. (2007). Clinical applications of feminist identity development: An illustrative case study. *Clinical Case Studies, 6*(2), 119–130.

Reid, A., & Purcell, N. (2004). Pathways to feminist identification. *Sex Roles, 50,* 759–769.

Reid, P. T., & Kelly, E. (1994). Research on women of color: From ignorance to awareness. *Psychology of Women Quarterly, 18*, 477–486.

Resick, P. A., & Schnicke, M. (1993). *Cognitive processing therapy for rape victims: A treatment manual.* Thousand Oaks, CA: Sage.

Resick, P. A., Galovski, T. E., Uhlmansiek, M. O., Scher, C. D., Clum, G. A., & Young-Xu, Y. (2008). A randomized clinical trial to dismantle components of cognitive processing therapy for posttraumatic stress disorder in female victims of interpersonal violence. *Journal of Consulting and Clinical Psychology, 76*, 243–258.

Resick, P. A., Nishith, P., Weaver, T. L., Astin, M. C., & Feuer, C. A. (2002). A comparison of cognitive-processing therapy with prolonged exposure and a waiting condition for the treatment of chronic posttraumatic stress disorder in female rape victims. *Journal of Consulting and Clinical Psychology, 70*, 867–879.

Reynolds, A. L., & Pope, R. L. (1991). The complexities of diversity: Exploring multiple oppressions. *Journal of Counseling and Development, 70*, 174–180.

Rice, J., & Ballou, M. (2002). *Cultural and gender awareness in international psychology.* Washington, DC: American Psychological Association, Division 52, International Psychology, International Committee for Women.

Rigazio-DiGilio, S. A. (2000). Relational diagnosis: A coconstructive-developmental perspective on assessment and treatment. *Journal of Clinical Psychology: Psychotherapy in Practice, 56*, 1017–1036.

Robb, C. (2006). *This changes everything: The relational revolution in psychology.* New York: Farrar, Straus & Giroux.

Root, M. P. P. (1992). Reconstructing the impact of trauma on personality. In L. S. Brown & M. Ballou (Eds.), *Personality and psychopathology: Feminist reappraisals* (pp. 229–265). New York: Guilford.

Root, M. P. (Ed.) (1995). *The multiracial experience: Racial borderlands as the new frontier.* Thousand Oaks, CA: Sage.

Ross, B. (1995). *The house that Jill built: A lesbian nation in formation.* Toronto, ON: University of Toronto Press.

Rubin, L., & Nemeroff, C. (2001). Feminism's third wave: Surfing to oblivion? *Women and Therapy, 23* (2), 91–104.

Rudy, K. (2001). Radical feminism, lesbian separatism, and queer theory. *Feminist Studies, 27*, 191–222.

Sanchez-Hucles, J., & Hudgins, P. (2001). Trauma across diverse settings. In J. Worell (Ed.), *Encyclopedia of women and gender* Vol. 2 (pp. 1151–1168). San Diego, CA: Academic Press.

Saunders, K. J., & Kashubeck-West, S. (2006). The relations among feminist identity development, gender-role orientation, and psychological well-being in women. *Psychology of Women Quarterly, 30*, 199–211.

Schmader, T., & Johns, M. (2003). Converging evidence that stereotype threat reduces working memory capacity. *Journal of Personality and Social Psychology, 85*, 3440–3452.

Schnurr, P. P., Friedman, M. J., Engel, C. C., Foa, E. B., Shea, M. T., Chow, B. K., Resick, P. A., Thurston, V., Orsillo, S. M., Haug, R., Turner, C., Turner, C., & Bernardy, N. (2007). Cognitive behavioral therapy for posttraumatic stress disorder in women: A randomized controlled trial. *Journal of the American Medical Association, 297*, 820–830.

Scott, J. W. (1988). Deconstructing equality-versus-difference: Or, the uses of poststructuralist theory for feminism. *Feminist Studies, 14* (1), 35–50.

Seligman, M. E. P., & Csikszentmihalyi, M. (2000). Positive psychology: An introduction. *American Psychologist, 55*, 5–14.

Sharf, R. S. (2008). *Theories of psychotherapy and counseling: Concepts and cases* (4th ed.). Belmont, CA: Wadsworth.

Shields, S. A. (2008). Gender: An intersectionality perspective. *Sex Roles, 59*, 301–311.

Smith, A., & Douglas, M. A. (1990). Empowerment as an ethical imperative. In H. Lerman & N. Porter (Eds.), *Feminist ethics in psychotherapy* (pp. 43–50). New York: Springer.

Smith, B. (Ed.). (1983). *Home girls: A Black feminist anthology.* New York: Kitchen Table, Women of Color Press.

Spencer, S. J., Steele, C. M., & Quinn, D. M. (1999). Stereotype threat and women's math performance. *Journal of Experimental Social Psychology, 35*, 4–28.

Stake, J. E. (2007). Predictors of change in feminist activism through women's and gender studies. *Sex Roles, 57*, 43–54.

Stein, A. (1997). *Sex and sensibility: Stories of a lesbian generation.* Berkeley, CA: University of California Press.

Stewart, A., & McDermott, C. (2004). Gender in psychology. *Annual Review of Psychology, 55*, 519–544.

Strife, S. (2006). Anti-anorexia/bulimia: Finding the voice of resistance. *Psychology of Women Quarterly, 30*, 121–122.

Sturdivant, S. (1980). *Therapy with women.* New York: Springer Publishing Co.

Sue, D. W., Bingham, R., Porché-Burke, L., & Vasquez, M. (1999). The diversification of psychology: A multicultural revolution. *American Psychologist, 54*, 1061–1069.

Sue, D. W., Capodilupo, C. M., Torino, G. C., Bucceri, J. M., Holder, A. M. B., Nadal, K. L., & Esquilin, M. (2007). Racial microaggressions in everyday life: Implications for clinical practice.

Suyemoto, K. L. (2002). Constructing identities: A feminist, culturally contextualized alternative to "personality." In M. Ballou & L. S. Brown (Eds.), *Rethinking mental health and disorder: Feminist perspectives* (pp. 71–98). New York: Guilford.

Swim, J. K., Aikin, K. J., Hall, W. S., & Hunter, B. A. (1995). Sexism and racism: Old fashioned and modern prejudices. *Journal of Personality and Social Psychology, 68*, 199–214.

Szymanski, D. M. (2005). Heterosexism and sexism as correlates of psychological distress in lesbians. *Journal of Counseling and Development, 83*, 355–360.

Szymanski, D. M., Baird, M. K., & Kornman, C. L. (2002). The feminist male therapist: Attitudes and practices for the 21st century. *Psychology of Men and Masculinity, 3*, 22–27.

Tavris, C. (1992). *The mismeasure of woman.* New York: Simon & Schuster.

Taylor, V., Whittier, N., & Pelak, C. F. (2001). The women's movement: Persistence through transformation. In L. Richardson, V. Taylow, & N. Whittier (Eds.), *Feminist frontiers* (5th ed., pp. 559–574). New York: McGraw-Hill.

Tedeschi, R. G., & Calhoun, L. G. (2004). Posttraumatic growth: Conceptual foundations and empirical evidence. *Psychological Inquiry, 15*, 1–18.

Thompson, A. (1998). Not the color purple: Black feminist lessons for educational caring. *Harvard Educational Review, 68*, 522–554.

Thompson, B. (2002). Multiracial feminism: Recasting the chronology of second wave feminism. *Feminist Studies, 28*, 337–355.

Tong, R. (2008). *Feminist thought: A more comprehensive introduction* (3rd ed.). Boulder, CO: Westview Press.

Turner, C. W. (1997). Clinical applications of the Stone Center theoretical approach to minority women. In J. V. Jordan (Ed.), *Women's growth in diversity: More writings from the Stone Center* (pp. 74–90). New York: Guilford.

Vasquez, H., & Magraw, S. (2005). Building relationships across privilege: Becoming an ally in the therapeutic relationship. In M. P. Mirkin, K. L. Suyemoto, & B. F. Okun (Eds.), *Psychotherapy with women: Exploring diverse contexts and identities* (pp. 64–83). New York: Guilford.

Vasquez, M. J. T. (2003). Ethical responsibilities in therapy: A feminist perspective. In M. Kopala & M. A. Keitel, *Handbook of counseling women* (pp. 557–573). Thousand Oaks, CA: Sage.

Walker, L. E.A. (1979). *The battered woman*. New York: Harper & Row.

Walker, L.E. A. (1994). *Abused women and survivor therapy*. Washington, DC: American Psychological Association.

Weed, E., & Schor, N. (Eds.). (1997). *Feminism meets queer theory*. Bloomington, IN: Indiana University Press.

Weisstein, N. (1970). Kinder, kuche, kirche as scientific law: Psychology constructs the female. In R. Morgan (Ed.), *Sisterhood is powerful* (pp. 205–219). New York: Vintage Books.

Werner-Wilson, R. J., Zimmerman, R. S., & Whalen, D. (2000). Resilient response to battering. *Contemporary Family Therapy: An International Journal, 22,* 161–188.

West, C. M. (1995). Mammy, Sapphire, and Jezebel: Historical images of black women and their implications for psychotherapy. *Psychotherapy: Theory, Research, and Practice, 32,* 458–466.

West, C. M. (2002). *Violence in the lives of Black women: Battered, black, and blue*. New York: Haworth Press.

West, C. K. (2005). The map of relational-cultural theory. *Women and Therapy, 28*(3/4), 93–110.

Whipple, V. (1996). Developing an identity as a feminist family therapist: Implications for training. *Journal of Marital and Family Therapy, 22,* 381–396.

Wing, A. K. (Ed.). (2000). *Global critical race feminism: An international reader*. New York: New York University Press.

Winslade, J., Crocket, K., & Monk, G. (1997). The therapeutic relationship. In G. Monk, J. Winslade, K. Crocket, & D. Epston (Eds.), *Narrative therapy in practice: The archaeology of hope* (pp. 53–81). San Francisco: Jossey-Bass.

Wolfe, J., & Kimerling, R. (1997). Gender issues in the assessment of posttraumatic stress disorder. In J. P. Wilson & T. M. Keane (Eds.), *Assessing psychological trauma and PTSD* (pp. 192–237). New York: Guilford.

Worell, J. (2001). Feminist interventions: Accountability beyond symptom reduction. *Psychology of Women Quarterly, 25,* 335–343.

Worell, J. (2006). Pathways to healthy development: Sources of strength and empowerment. In J. Worell & C. D. Goodheart (Eds.), *Handbook of girls' and women's psychological health* (pp. 25–35). New York: Oxford University Press.

Worell, J., & Remer, P. (2003). *Feminist perspectives in therapy: Empowering diverse women* (2nd ed.). New York: Wiley.

Wyche, K. F., & Rice, J. K. Feminist therapy: From dialogue to tenets. In J. Worell & N. G. Johnson (Eds.), *Shaping the future of feminist psychology* (pp. 57–71). Washington, DC: American Psychological Association.

Wylie, M. S. (1995). Diagnosing for dollars? *Psychotherapy Networker, 19*(3), 23–33, 65–66.

Yakushko, O. (2007). Do feminist women feel better about their lives? Examining patterns of feminist identity development and women's subjective well-being. *Sex Roles, 57,* 223–234.

Yalom, I. D. (2002). *The gift of therapy*. New York: HarperCollins.

Yoder, J. D. (2007). *Women and gender: Making a difference* (3rd ed.). Cornwall-on-Hudson, NY: Sloan.

Zinn, M. B., & Dill, B. T. (1996). Theorizing difference from multiracial feminism. *Feminist Studies, 22,* 321–331.

Zucker, A. N. (2004). Disavowing social identities: What it means when women say, "I'm not a feminist, but . . ." *Psychology of Women Quarterly, 28,* 423–435.

Zucker, A. N., & Stewart, A. J. (2007). Growing up and growing older: Feminism as a context for women's lives. *Psychology of Women Quarterly, 31,* 137–145.

Further Reading

American Psychological Association. (2007). Guidelines for psychological practice with girls and women. *American Psychologist, 62,* 949–979.

Ballou, M., Hill, M., & West, C. (Eds.). (2008). *Feminist therapy theory and practice: A contemporary perspective*. New York: Springer.

Brown, L. S. (1994). *Subversive dialogues: Theory in feminist therapy*. New York: Basic Books.

Brown, L. S. (2010). *Feminist therapy*. Washington, DC: American Psychological Association Press.

Enns, C. Z. (2004). Feminist theories and feminist psychotherapies: Origins, themes, and diversity (2nd ed.). New York: Haworth.

Evans, K. M., Kincade, E. A., & Seem, S. R. (2011). *Introduction to feminist therapy: Strategies for social and individual change*. Thousand Oaks, CA: Sage.

Hill, M., & Ballou, M. (2005). *The foundation and future of feminist therapy*. New York: Haworth.

Kopala, M., & Keitel, M. A. (Eds.). (2003). *Handbook of counseling women*. Thousand Oaks, CA: Sage.

Landrine, H., & Russo, N. F. (Eds.). (2010). *Handbook of diversity in feminist psychology*. New York: Springer.

Worell, J., & Goodheart, C. D. (Eds.). (2006). *Handbook of girls' and women's psychological health*. New York: Oxford.

Worell, J., & Remer, P. (2003). *Feminist perspectives in therapy: Empowering diverse women* (2nd ed.). New York: Wiley.

Disability: A Primer for Therapists

Rhoda Olkin

Abstract

This chapter is an overview of the concepts critical to an understanding of disability. A social justice perspective underlies all four topics areas. Topics covered include, first, conceptualizing disability, including models of disability, common disability experiences, legal issues relevant to persons with disabilities, and sociocultural and familial factors for persons with disabilities. Next, issues related to counseling individuals with disabilities are discussed. In particular, *disability-affirmative therapy* is described, along with a template for key questions to explore with clients. Special issues in training and supervision are discussed from two perspectives: when the client or when the therapist is the person with a disability. Future issues to be illuminated and explored include abuse as a cause of disability, bicultural partnerships between a person with and a person without a disability, and outcome studies of therapy with persons with disabilities; finally, a research agenda is proposed.

Keywords: disability, handicap, impairment, disability-affirmative therapy, psychotherapy, counseling, sociocultural experiences, social justice

This chapter is intended to introduce, in a relatively short space, all of the key concepts necessary for a basic understanding of disability. The purpose is to acquaint readers with sufficient conceptual foundations to build competence in counseling individuals and families with disabilities. A skill set, under the umbrella of *disability-affirmative therapy* (D-AT; Olkin, 1999, 2008), is introduced. Although it is not possible to convey the full richness of disability experiences nor the range of knowledge and skills necessary for cultural competence, it is hoped that readers will feel enabled to undertake clinical work with clients with disabilities. Part of this empowerment will come from knowing that you can make mistakes in therapy with your clients with disabilities and yet recover from them. Only when you are free to make mistakes are you free to engage in the work.

In this chapter, I explore how disability affects the counseling relationship, countertransference, and the therapeutic work itself. To do this, I first review basic disability concepts. These concepts include models of disability, common disability experiences, and legal and sociocultural influences on persons with disabilities. Next, I turn to a model for counseling individuals with disabilities called disability-affirmative therapy (Olkin, 1999, 2008). Finally, special issues in training and supervision are presented, followed by future clinical issues needing further research and explication.

Defining Disability

In this section and throughout this chapter, it is important to remember that disabilities are not always visible to others, and persons with hidden disabilities can encounter special types of problems. Additionally, we need to keep in mind that the rate of disability in the United States is rising, due to aging of the population, the dramatic increase in rate of diabetes, and as a result of continuing wars in the Middle East (Smith, Foley, & Chaney, 2008).

Many different words are used to describe disability, often as if these words are interchangeable. The most commonly used terms are *disability, handicap*, and *impairment*. These words have different meanings, and understanding the differences in terminology illuminates how disability is variously conceptualized.

An *impairment* refers to the cause of a functional difference (e.g., arthritis). A *handicap* is the way that the impairment affects functioning (e.g., limited use of one arm and hand and reduced hand strength). The *disability* is found in the mismatch between functioning and the environment (e.g., need to type without access to voice dictation software). The impairment and handicap are about the person, but the disability is about the environment; thus, as environments change, disability can range from pronounced to moot.

Definitions of disability are evolving, and can be found in a variety of sources (Brown, DeLeon, Loftis, & Scherer, 2008). One place to start in defining disability is with the World Health Organization's (WHO) International Classification of Functioning, Disability, and Health (WHO, 2001). First, one can think of the functioning of various body functions. These include mental, sensory, and speech functions. Body systems include cardiovascular, hematological, immunological, respiratory, digestive, metabolic, endocrine, genitourinary, and reproductive systems, as well as neuromusculoskeletal, movement, and skin systems (WHO, 2001). Any of these systems and functions can work differently, be impaired or inhibited, or even work counterproductively. A second way of thinking about what is altered in disability is to consider the types of activities in which humans participate, and how disability affects these activities. These activities include learning, applying knowledge, communication, mobility, self-care, interpersonal relationships, social interactions, domestic life, and community involvement (WHO, 2001). A third way to think about disability is to describe the assistance that enables participation by an individual. These might include use of a product (e.g., speech board) or technology (e.g., electric wheelchair), changes to the environment (e.g., ramps and curb cuts), or support from other persons (e.g., financial management). Each of these methods of defining disability has value in particular contexts. In medical venues, understanding of body systems and functions might be most helpful. In educational settings, the second method of focusing on activities may be most useful. In working toward the goal of community integration, understanding needed levels of assistance with activities of daily living would be most germane.

From this, we see that there is no universal definition of disability. Rather, disability is a fluid concept that can only be defined by the context in which it is occurs. In this way, disability is said to be a social construct. In fact, the WHO states that health and disability are not opposites but equally part of the human experience:

> It acknowledges that every human being can experience a decrement in health and thereby experience some degree of disability. Disability is not something that only happens to a minority of humanity. The ICF thus "mainstreams" the experience of disability and recognises it as a universal human experience. By shifting the focus from cause to impact it places all health conditions on an equal footing, allowing them to be compared using a common metric—the ruler of health and disability. Furthermore ICF takes into account the social aspects of disability and does not see disability only as "medical" or "biological" dysfunction. By including Contextual Factors, in which environmental factors are listed, ICF allows to record the impact of the environment on the person's functioning. (Accessed June 3, 2008 from http://www.who.int/classifications/icf/en/)

A legal definition of disability is different from any of those described above. In the United States, the legal definition that was part of the Rehabilitation Act (1973) has remained the same in subsequent legislation, notably in the Americans with Disabilities Act (1990). In these laws "disability means, with respect to an individual–(a) A physical or mental impairment that substantially limits one or more of the major life activities of such individual; (B) A record of such an impairment, or (C) Being regarded as having such an impairment." Note that the law incorporates the concepts of body systems (*physical or mental impairment*), functioning (*substantially limits*), and perception (*being regarding as having such an impairment*). However, there have been ardent legal discussions over the meanings of key phrases, particularly "substantially limits" and "major life activities." (See section on Laws.)

Models of Disability

Various ways of conceptualizing disability have been hypothesized, but a three-model system seems to capture clinically useful ways of understanding how our clients view their disabilities. These three models are the moral, medical, and social models (Asch & Rousso, 1985; Florian, 1982; Olkin, 1999, 2007;

Rose, 1997). The *moral model* posits that disability is a manifestation of spiritual, moral, religious, or personal weaknesses or strengths, either in this life or past lives. In such a view, a client might say that a baby was born with a deformity because the mother encountered evil during the pregnancy. Alternately, the client might say that this baby was born with a deformity because the mother has a special relationship with the deity who deemed her capable of raising such a child. Thus, the event itself (a baby with a deformity) is not in itself good or bad, but rather is interpreted positively or negatively, but all within the lens of morality. Healing comes from within spiritual, moral, or religious beliefs. In the *medical model*, the disability is viewed as a defect in one or more bodily parts or functions (as in the first method of defining disability proposed by the WHO). Such a defect may stem from behaviors related to health (e.g., poor dental hygiene) or unrelated to health (e.g., a car accident), from heredity (e.g., albinism), injury (e.g., a diving accident), or environment (e.g., exposure to lead), but are considered to be medical problems best attended to within the general medical service delivery system. Some blame may be attached to the disability (not getting vaccinated, taking risks, having a type A personality), but generally the stigma and shame of disability often associated with the moral model is alleviated in the medical model. However, the role of the person with a disability is that of a patient or client who is expected to participate in recovery and rehabilitation.

The *social model* is a paradigm shift from the moral and medical models. In the social model, disability is a social construct, created by the interaction or a mismatch of the person and the environment, rather than being located solely within the person. From this perspective, an impairment has no valence, but rather is evaluated in terms of its interaction with the physical, socioeconomic, and interpersonal environments. For example, using a wheelchair for mobility is not denigrated as inferior to walking, but rather as an alternate method of locomotion. The use of the wheelchair becomes problematic when the environment poses barriers (stairs, absence of curb cuts, narrow passageways), many of which are readily remediable, and when interpersonal interactions convey inferiority (pulling young children out of the way, making disparaging comments, failing to make eye contact).

Table 17.1 shows a comparison of the moral, medical, and social models. Each model is explored in terms of how it makes meaning of disability, the moral implications that stem from the meaning, sample ideas associated with the model, origins of the model, goals and providers of intervention, and both the benefits and deficits of each model. Each model prevails in certain settings. The moral model is most prevalent in Eastern cultures, whereas the medical model prevails in North America and Western Europe, including in their medical service delivery systems and professional literature. The social model is prevalent within disability rights movements, embedded in many civil rights laws in the United States and England, and underlies the WHO and some other global and governmental agencies.

A critical question is whether knowing about these models helps with our understanding of clients and of the counseling process with clients with disabilities. First, we have to consider whether clients have been informed about the models and their differences. Second, we need to know if we should teach clients about these models, and, if so, we need ways of explaining these models to clients. Third, we have to evaluate the client's beliefs related to these models. Fourth, we need to examine in what ways the client receives the benefits and/or the deficits of the model. And fifth, we need to explore whether a shift in models is desirable and, if so, feasible. Let us take these questions one at a time.

Do clients know about these models? Generally speaking, I would say that most people, with or without disabilities, have not been introduced to the idea of different ways of conceptualizing disability. Disability is not a topic in standard curricula or daily discourse. It is safest to assume that some of the ideas promulgated in the models are new to clients.

Unfortunately, they are also new ideas to therapists. Undergraduate students are mostly likely to learn about disability as part of abnormal psychology, if they learn about it at all. A content analysis of undergraduate textbooks regarding content on diversity was unable to include disability because textbook coverage on disability was too sparse for any meaningful analysis (Hogben & Waterman, 1997). The picture is hardly better in graduate psychology training (Kemp & Mallinckrodt, 1996; Olkin & Pledger, 2003). Analysis of one graduate program's training curriculum revealed that physical disability received the lowest amount of coverage of seven areas of diversity (Bluestone, Stokes, & Kuba, 1996). In a study of the required curriculum at all graduate clinical and counseling psychology programs accredited by the American Psychological Association, the modal number of courses on

Table 17.1. Comparison of the Moral, Medical and Social Models of Disability

	Moral Model	Medical Model	Social Model
Meaning of disability	Disability is a manifestation of moral lapse, sins, failure of faith, or evil; alternatively, it is a test of faith or honor.	A defect in or failure of a bodily system that is inherently abnormal and pathological.	Disability is a social construct. Problems reside in the environment that fails to accommodate people with disabilities, and in the mismatch between person and environment.
Moral implications	If viewed as a moral mark, the disability brings shame to the person with the disability and to his or her family. Alternatively, it is a reminder of having been chosen or saved.	A medical abnormality due to genetics, bad health habits, person's behavior.	Society has failed a segment of its citizens, and oppresses them.
Sample ideas	"God gives us only what we can bear" or "There's a reason I was chosen to have this disability."	Clinical descriptions of "patients" in medical terminology; isolation of body parts.	"Nothing about us without us." "Civil rights, not charity."
Origins	Oldest model and still most prevalent worldwide.	Mid-19th century Most common model in U.S. Entrenched in most rehabilitation clinics and journals.	In 1975, with the demonstrations by people with disabilities in support of the yet-unsigned Rehabilitation Act.
Goals of intervention	Spiritual or divine; acceptance.	"Cure" or amelioration of the disability to the greatest extent possible.	Political, economic, social, and policy systems; increased access and inclusion.
Benefits of model	An acceptance of being selected, a special relationship with God, a sense of greater purpose to the disability.	A lessened sense of shame and stigma Faith in medical intervention. Spurs medical and technological advances.	Promotes integration of the disability into the self. A sense of community and pride. Depathologizing of disability.
Negative effects	Shame, ostracism, need to conceal the disability or person with the disability.	Paternalistic; promotes benevolence and charity. Services *for* but not *by* people with disabilities.	Powerlessness in the face of needed broad social and political changes. Challenges to prevailing ideas.

disability was zero (Olkin & Pledger, 2003). Data from 1989, just prior to the passage of the Americans with Disabilities Act (ADA), and 1999, 9 years after passage of the ADA, showed that the situation had gotten slightly worse. In 1999, "only 11% of programs had at least one course on disability (less than in 1989). Furthermore, this disability course was most likely to be on 'exceptional' children, learning disabilities, or mental retardation—courses that generally reflect the medical model of disability. Only 7 out of 210 programs had a course on psychosocial aspects of disability, i.e., courses more likely to reflect

the social model of disability espoused in disability studies" (Olkin & Pledger, 2003, p. 297).

Within psychology, disability is relegated to rehabilitation psychology (Smart & Smart, 2006), which has kept the focus more on acquired and acute conditions (e.g., traumatic brain injury, spinal cord injury) and medical settings. However, most of the over 53 million persons in the United States with a disability are not in such settings, and if they seek psychological treatment, it is most likely to be in an outpatient setting and delivered by a therapist who was not trained in rehabilitation counseling.

Therefore, the lack of graduate training on disability is a serious problem resulting in lack of availability of therapists competent in disability culture and affirming therapy (Smart & Smart, 2006). If therapists are not familiar with the models of disability, they are unable to discuss them with clients. Nor can they assess their clients' views of disability. And, potentially more damagingly, they are not attuned to the necessity of matching their language and treatment approach to the client's model.

Should we teach clients with disabilities about these models? This is an intricate clinical question that cannot receive a blanket answer. So, the answer is: It depends. For some clients, it can be helpful to elucidate the ways in which they are thinking about disability. This can be compared and contrasted with how the educational or medical systems might be responding to disability. Bringing these issues to light can help families find ways to communicate better with professionals, understand how professionals communicate with them, and create understanding of differences in perspectives and opinions. Furthermore, the person with a disability and his or her family may not agree about their models of disability; teaching about models can be a useful way to elicit and elucidate similarities and differences in how each family member views the disability. For other clients, examining models of disability is too abstract an idea that can detract from the symptoms and problems for which they seek treatment. Keep in mind, however, the caveat that most therapists are not trained in models of disability; it is imperative that therapists first become familiar with the three models and have a chance to explore and understand their own responses to disability in light of these models, so that they are better equipped to discuss them with clients.

How do we evaluate clients' beliefs about disability? There is no scale extant to assess a client's model of disability. Such a scale would need to inquire about beliefs related to the nature of the "problem" of disability, where the "problem" is located, and potential remediators of the "problem." Guber (2007) endeavored to create such a scale, taking as his starting point client questions posed by Olkin (1999; see Table 17.2). He was hampered in his efforts by lack of consensus on which models to use, what they mean, and whether they are valid. There are myriad factors affecting one's belief system related to disability, including current age and age of disability onset, socioeconomic status, national origin, religion, family history with disability, level of impairment, placement in special education or use of resource room and/or assistant, use of reasonable accommodations in school or work, and visibility of the disability. Any scale that elicited a client's model of disability could potentially assess these factors, but in and of themselves they would not lead to any scores on the three models.

There is no reason to assume that clients would fit neatly into one and only one model. It is probable that many clients would straddle more than one model, would be en route from one model to another, or hold contradictory ideas (see Table 17.3 for a hypothetical array of models ascribed to by any one client). The combination of the moral and medical, or the medical and social models seems psychologically consistent, whereas the simultaneous holding of the moral and social models seems at odds, and theoretically would cause cognitive dissonance such that one would have to reconcile the opposing beliefs by shedding one set or the other. This turns out not to be the case. In a study using interviews (in Cantonese) with 12 immigrant Chinese families of lower socioeconomic status about their beliefs related to their child with a disability (usually autism), the modal perspective was a hybrid of the moral and social models (Wong, 2008). For example, a father might say that the son's autism was caused by evil spirits, and in the next sentence state his conviction that his son has rights under the law and that the father must assert those rights with the school.

In what ways does the client receive benefits or negative effects of the model(s)? Whichever individual model or hybrid of models the client believes in leads to the potential for beneficial and/or negative consequences. The moral model may bring shame and dishonor, anger at the deity, a sense of purposelessness. Conversely, it may strengthen beliefs, foster awareness of the preciousness of life, or create meaning in an otherwise random event. The medical model may counter shame by medicalizing the disability, foster support among persons with similar impairments, and provide technical and medical advances that improve the daily lives of people with disabilities. Alternatively, the medical model can create passiveness, reinforce the role of receiver rather than active participant or leader, and de-emphasize the socioeconomic and political barriers for persons with disabilities. The social model promotes independence and interdependence, creates a disability community, empowers individuals and groups, and promotes sociopolitical change. However, it can create schisms in beliefs within the family, enable hopelessness in the face of massive

Table 17.2. Assessing the Client's Model of Disability

Model	Questions to Ask Yourself
Moral Model:	* Do you feel shame or embarrassment about your disability? * Do you feel you bring dishonor to the family? * Do you try to hide and minimize the disability as much as possible? * Do you try to make as few demands on others as possible, because it's "your problem" and hence your responsibility? * Do you try to make your disability inconspicuous? * Do you think your disability is a test of your faith, or as a way for you to prove your faith? * Do you think your disability is a punishment for your or your family's failings?
Medical Model:	* Compared to Franklin Delano Roosevelt (FDR)'s time, do you think that life for persons with disabilities has improved considerably? * Do you think FDR wouldn't have to hide his disability today? * Do you try to make as few demands on others as possible because you think you should be able to find a way to do it yourself? * Do you dress in ways that maximize your positive features and minimize the visibility of the disability? * Do you believe that the major goals of research should be to prevent disabilities and find cures for those who already have disabilities? * Do you think that persons with disabilities do best when they are fully integrated into the nondisabled community?
Minority Model:	* Do you identify yourself as part of a minority group of persons with disabilities? * Do you feel kinship and belonging with other persons with disabilities? * Do you think that not enough is being done to assure rights of persons with disabilities? * When policies and legislation are new, do you evaluate them in terms of their effects on persons with disabilities? * Do you think the major goals of research should be to improve the lives of persons with disabilities by changing policies, procedures, funding, and laws? * Do you think that persons with disabilities do best when they are free to associate in both the disabled and nondisabled communities, as bicultural people?

Table reprinted with permission from Halstead, L. (1998).

societal changes that are needed, and detract from self-examination in the fostering of social examination. As we see from these descriptions of potential benefits or drawbacks, models in and of themselves are not positive or negative, but can be either or both for any individual.

Table 17.3. Theoretical Patterns in Ascribing to One or More of the Three Models of Disability

	Moral	Medical	Social
Moral	1	4	6
Medical	4	2	5
Social	6	5	3

1, 2, and 3 are pure models. (moral, medical, or social)
4 is a hybrid of moral and medical models.
5 is a hybrid of medical and social models.
6 is a hybrid of moral and social models.
7 (not shown) is a hybrid of all three models.

Is a shift in models clinically desirable, and if so, is it feasible? As discussed later in this chapter, in D-AT, the therapist should ascribe to the social model. However, we should not insist on any particular model for our clients. Rather, we need to help them realize the benefits and decrease the deficits that come from the model they believe in. However, some clients have been raised to believe in a particular model (most often the moral or medical model) and wish to question those beliefs. Other clients become exposed to ideas through the disability community, which leads to reevaluation of beliefs. Additionally, parents often want assistance in thinking about how to raise their children with disabilities. For these and other reasons, it can be useful to explore models of disability with clients. Making the models explicit can help in elucidating how doctors and other medical professionals, educational systems, national organizations, and support groups think and talk about disability, and how this fits for the family.

How does a therapist help a client who wishes to change models do so? This is an untested empirical question. My own clinical experience suggests that repeated exposure to the ideas and groups that espouse a particular model is the most effective. Changing models is not an intellectual exercise, but one that goes to the heart of self-concept, self-evaluation, and core beliefs, and can be an intensely emotional journey for persons with disabilities.

Common Disability Experiences

This section addresses some of the commonalities in experiences for people with disabilities. Although disabilities vary widely, there still is some universality in experiences of being a person with a disability in most cultures. The key issues addressed here are how disability affects others' perceptions of the person and attitudes toward disability, language used to discuss disability, affective prescriptions and prohibitions, personal boundaries, awareness of vulnerability, and managing stigma.

Perceptions and Attitudes

"If there is a disability community, then its foundation rests on this communal experience, whose essential components are not the disability per se, but the interpersonal and psychosocial experiences that result from being a persons with disabilities" (Olkin, 1999, p. 54). Research on attitudes toward disability and persons with disabilities is important because the attitudes of others are an important influence on the behavior and lives of people with disabilities. Although attitudes toward disability are "complex and multifaceted" (Yuker, 1988, p. xiii), it must be acknowledged that, across many cultures, disability often is associated with negative characteristics (Chan, Lam, Wong, Leung, & Fang, 1988; Florian, 1982; Saetermoe, Scattone, & Kim, 2001; Westbrook, Legg, & Pennay, 1993). In many situations in which a person with a disability is first encountered, the disability is viewed as a *central characteristic* (Asch, 1946), such that the one characteristic of disability comes to unduly influence the impression formation. There is potentially a fundamental negative bias toward disability (Wright, 1988). Wright posits that if three conditions exist (a salient characteristic, a negative valence associated with that salient characteristic, and ambiguity or vagueness of context), then the fundamental negative bias is elicited. Disability is a salient characteristic, and one that is associated with negative characteristics.

Vagueness comes from lack of other information about the person, the context, the nature or the cause of the disability.

A concept closely related to central characteristic is the concept of *spread*, which "refers to the power of single characteristics to evoke inferences about a person" (Wright, 1983, p. 32). When given a limited amount of information about another person, the central characteristic, in this case disability, is allowed to color perceptions of unrelated areas. If the central characteristic is viewed positively (e.g., warmth, masculinity, intelligence), then the spread is likewise positive. But in the case of disability, if the disability is seen as a negative characteristic, the spread is negative. Interestingly, participants in a study on spread were able to give a logical progression of their ideas from the central characteristic to the other characteristics to which it spread (Mussen & Barker, 1944; Ray, 1946).

Just as a disability is used by others to form impressions, known characteristics about a person are said to be explained by a disability. For example, someone who is shy might be said to be so because he has cerebral palsy; someone who excels at work might be thought of as overcompensating for a disability. Both positive and negative traits can be pathologized when ascribed to a disability. One effect of spread is that the disability itself is seen as more pervasive than it often is. Thus, a man who is blind gets talked to loudly by a waitress, as if his hearing also was impaired, or a woman in a wheelchair gets asked if she can sign her name on a credit card receipt, as if the two things are related.

People with disabilities are not immune to the strait-jacket of attractiveness found in many societies. They are judged on attractiveness, as are others, but the disability itself may affect the assessment of attractiveness. Furthermore, the disability may cause body and facial movements that can be misinterpreted by others (e.g., a person with disability-related fatigue may give short answers to questions, a person with muscle spasms may make random movements). One problem is that the body can be seen as a window into the soul. This is a common literary and fictional device, using a physical manifestation to denote a character trait, a way to shorthand the revealing of a person's personality. This works in literature; in life it does not.

Language Used to Discuss and Describe Disability

In an important early study, the terms "blindness" and "physical handicap" elicited more negative responses than the terms "blind people" and "physically handicapped people" (Whiteman & Lukoff, 1965, as cited in Wright, 1988). It seems that inserting the person into the image of the disability is important in changing perceptions. As such, people-first language has become the desired norm in the United States and Canada (it differs in other countries). Such language utilizes phrases such as "person using a wheelchair," "person with schizophrenia," "persons with blindness," as opposed to a "wheelchair-bound person," "a schizophrenic," or "the blind." This may seem like mere semantics, but in fact the use of language not only reflects but also influences our perceptions.

A word commonly associated with disability in the professional literature is *burden*. This is seen in phrases such as caregiver burden, the burden of autism on families, the financial burden of disability, the burden of schizophrenia on the mental health system, etc. The idea is that people with disabilities are costly to society in financial and personal terms. The obvious next question is then: Are people with disabilities too costly? Are the costs worth it? Note that costs associated with preventing disability are viewed differently (e.g., in prevention of birth defects) than are costs associated with assistance for people with disabilities (e.g., personal assistance, physical changes for accessibility, more mental health services). This difference is reflected in one of the slogans of the disability rights movement, which would like to see a higher percentage of funds spent on improving the quality of life of persons with disabilities: Care, not cure.

Affective Prescriptions and Prohibitions

In her seminal books on physical disability, Wright discussed the *requirement of mourning* for people with disabilities (Wright, 1960, 1983). There is myriad literature conceptualizing disability as a loss, and from this stems the notion that the loss must be mourned. Disability is viewed as a tragedy, and persons experiencing tragedies must be in mourning. Two problems stem from this requirement of mourning. One is that depression is viewed as normative, when in fact it is not the modal response to disability (Olkin, 2004). Depression in a person with a disability, whether that disability is new or ongoing, should be treated as aggressively as depression in a person without a disability. Second, when the person with the disability is not depressed, sad, or in mourning, others profess amazement and ascribe superhuman qualities to that person. If one is not sad in situations in which others think one

should be sad, then one clearly is exceptional. This might be called the "requirement of pluckiness." Both of these requirements (mourning and pluckiness) are prescriptions for what people with disabilities should feel, and more importantly are dictates for how they should behave.

Part of the mandate for pluckiness is the requirement of gratitude. Accessibility and accommodations are seen as *special needs*; that is, needs for only a few, not for everyone, not normal. Thus, if changes are made just for people with disabilities, and these changes are necessitated by needs that are special, then people with disabilities should be grateful for the changes. People with disabilities are expected to be grateful—for having survived, for not having worse conditions, for the people who hold open doors for them, for the ramp that goes to an entrance in the back of the building, for the lifts on buses.

Along with these prescriptions of mourning, pluckiness, and gratitude is the prohibition against anger about any issues related to the disability. The goal of rehabilitation, in addition to any physical or cognitive work, is to help the person adjust to being a person with a disability. Anger denotes maladjustment of the person, a failure to reach acceptance of the disability. This prohibition has two problems. One is that acceptance of the disability is an illusory goal. One lives with a disability, and some days are diamonds, some days are stones. Changes in the disability due to time and/or aging or reinjury necessitate readjustment; new insights or experiences lead to reevaluation; new relationships require renegotiations. In other words, adjustment implies that disability is static, when instead it is a lifelong affair that is fluid and mercurial. The second problem with the prohibition against anger is that any manifested anger is decontextualized. Typically, people with disabilities experience multiple events in any given day that a person without a disability might not. These might include pain, fatigue, extra tasks or time necessitated by the disability. Other events relate to interactions with the social and physical environment such as inaccessibility, stigma, discrimination, prejudice. These events can be considered *microaggressions* (Sue, Capodilupo, & Holder, 2008; Sue, Nadal, Capodilupo, Lin, Torino, & Rivera, 2008) in the daily lives of people with disabilities. One of these events may lead the person with a disability to feel angry on one day but sanguine on another day. But the anger, seen from the outside, is perceived only in relation to the one event that led to the anger, not in relation to the myriad events that went by without much notice. This is an issue common to minorities of various types, resulting in an internal experience different from what is seen externally; behaviors are judged by others by the externals only, and usually ascribed to traits of the person (what social psychology calls the *fundamental attribution error*). It is probable that, just as for people of color (Sue, 2010), these daily microaggressions lead to psychological distress for people with disabilities. If a person with a disability tries to conform to nondisabled norms and standards, this too could lead to psychological stress.

Personal Boundaries

The body has its boundaries, and disability seems to distort other people's sense of boundaries in a paradoxical way. On one hand, people with disabilities may be touched less, due to stigma or fear of contagion. People with certain conditions (cancer, AIDS, intellectual disabilities), especially, say that others are loathe to touch them. On the other hand, they may be touched in situations in which a nondisabled person would not be—the elbow of a blind woman grabbed to help her across the street, the cup of coffee taken away for refill without asking from a man sitting in a wheelchair, the pat on the head of a person using a scooter, picking up a little person.

Using assistive devices presents another set of issues about touch. Generally, people don't come up to another person and feel the glasses on his face, or rub her belly, or pat adults on the head. But there is something about assistive devices that seems to erase these body boundaries. Someone might lean on the arm of a wheelchair, or allow her child to climb on the scooter, or grab an interesting device to look at it, or play with a machine. Since these devices are part of the body boundary of the person who uses them, touching the device is akin to touching the person's body. This is all right if that is the nature of the relationship, but otherwise it can feel like an intrusion.

Awareness of Vulnerability

Disability often implies that something went wrong. It might be loss of oxygen during birth, or ear infections in infancy, a car accident, a heart valve problem, an illness with lasting effects, a stroke. Some of these causes are hereditary, some are related to lifestyle, some are contagious, some happen in an instant. What they share is the stamp of a certain randomness to life, a roll of the dice that made one household have two children with polio while the household next door went unscathed, a young woman gets breast cancer while her sisters do not, a drunk driver hits the car to his right and leaves the one to the left untouched. Thus, having a disability can bring an awareness of vulnerability, or what can happen to the body and the mind due to seemingly random events. Some people might easily shrug this knowledge off, but others may find it brings an ever-present awareness that sits just behind them, a bit off to the side. Examples might be the man who is blind in one eye who seems overly protective of his eye with vision, or the woman with a systemic disability who leaves her job in the prison because she is afraid of getting hurt, or the student who wants to rush through all her work for the quarter before she has a flare up of her Crohn's disease, or the mother with multiple sclerosis who is afraid her baby will die of sudden infant death syndrome. What is a rational fear, and how do we decide?

Just as the person with a disability has to come to terms with vulnerability, persons without disabilities want to find reasons for the disability that could not apply to themselves. Furthermore, the more severe the disability, the greater the tendency to find unique causative factors (Walster, 1966). Whether it is that someone failed to get a vaccine, or they weren't careful enough drivers, or they led an unhealthy lifestyle, others would like to attach a cause to the disability. The alternative—namely, that disability is sometimes random (a genetic mutation), or bad luck (struck by a drunk driver), or lies completely outside personal control (living in neighborhoods with higher levels of toxins)—is scary. These alternatives imply that disability can happen in an instant, and to anyone. This is precisely the case, and people with disabilities often have had this knowledge foisted upon them, whereas people without disabilities find cognitive maneuvers to distance themselves from this certainty.

Managing Stigma

Disability is a characteristic that is salient, stigmatized, and which creates a negative spread effect (Dembo, Leviton, & Wright, 1956/1975). As discussed earlier, spread is the tendency to view the disability as more pervasive than it is, as if the disability affected all aspects of the person. Similarly, unrelated characteristics of the person with a disability are ascribed to the disability. Furthermore, stigma can be associated with the ideas others have about causes of the disability. As discussed above, persons find reasons for another's disability that precludes the possibility of that disability occurring to themselves. Some of those reasons may be negative personal traits ascribed to the person with a disability, such as negligence, carelessness, irresponsibility, or deleterious beliefs (e.g., against vaccines). These negative traits then create a further desire for distancing from the person with the disability. All of these issues—stigma, spread effects, assumptions of causality—create the need for the person with the disability to be skilled in managing the interpersonal and social aspects of disability. This is an incredible social burden on people with disabilities.

Legal and Sociocultural Influences on Disability

Legions of laws have been written in the United States related to disability, covering housing, air travel, ground travel, taxes, and more. In this section, I discuss the three most important in terms of their range of applicability and implications, and consider what they do and do not provide. These three laws are the Rehabilitation Act (1973), the Individuals with Disabilities Education Act (1975) and its reauthorizations (currently, Individuals with Disabilities Education Improvement Act of 2004), and the Americans with Disabilities Act (ADA, 1990).

Laws can take the lead in changing attitudes and behaviors. Desegregation is a prime example of how federal legislation (*Brown v. Board of Education of Topeka, KS*, 1954) can lead to far-reaching sociological changes. And, as we see with desegregation, laws can create opportunities, provide equitable resources, and address equal access (i.e., outlaw discrimination), but they cannot eradicate prejudice and stigma, or, in the case of the Brown decision, racism. We need to keep this example in mind as we examine the three disability laws.

The *Rehabilitation Act*, sections 503 (affirmative action) and 504 (accessibility of places and services), passed in 1973 and set the stage for much of the legislation that followed. It included a definition of disability (see previous section on definitions of disability), and this definition was used again for the ADA. The Rehabilitation Act prescribed affirmative action and nondiscrimination in all institutions receiving federal funding. This includes virtually every college, university, and hospital, thus ensuring greater access to many public institutions. But it did not affect private institutions that did not receive federal funding, such as restaurants, theaters, or department stores—the places and things that comprise the daily lives of people. Nonetheless, it set the stage for more encompassing legislation to follow, and delineated an important principle—namely,

that people with disabilities were a class of persons in need of laws regarding nondiscrimination.

Around the same time, the *Education of All Handicapped Children Act* (1975) was passed by congress, and subsequently reauthorized and renamed the *Individuals with Disabilities Education Act* (IDEA, 2004). The IDEA sets forth certain principles that are critical to equity for people with disabilities. One is the principle of *least restrictive environment*. In most cases, the least restrictive environment is considered to be in the classroom with peers without disabilities. So, this principle encompasses the notion of inclusion; that the least restrictive environment is one that is not separate. Another principle is inclusion of persons with disabilities or their representatives (in this case, parents) in decision making about the person with the disability. A third principle is that plans are individualized to the person with a disability. The *Individualized Education Plan* (IEP) is the bedrock of IDEA, and suggests that there is no single modification or accommodation that works for all (or even most). A fourth principle is the interdisciplinary team approach to modifications and accommodations, thereby not locating disability within one field of specialization.

The ADA (1990) was passed after considerable committee review and revisions. One impetus for the ADA was a Harris Poll (1985) that indicated a 66% unemployment rate among people with disabilities, and that 70% of respondents had not gone to a restaurant or movie in the past year because of a disability and problems with accessibility. The Rehabilitation Act (1973) did not address public places, and the variety of places that were potentially inaccessible to some people with disabilities included housing, employment, transportation, communication systems, recreational facilities, voting places, libraries, and public services. Thus, a more far-reaching law was necessary to remove major barriers in the daily lives of people with disabilities. The beginning section of the ADA noted that historically "society has tended to isolate and segregate individuals with disabilities, and . . . such forms of discrimination . . . continue to be a serious and pervasive social problem" (www.apta.org/ada/adalaw.html).

The ADA has five Titles, addressing *Employment* (Title I), *Public Services* (Title II), *Public Accommodations and Services Operated by Private Entities* (Title III), *Telecommunications* (Title IV), and *Miscellaneous* (V). In Title I a "qualified individual with a disability" is defined as "an individual with a disability who, with or without reasonable accommodations, can perform the essential functions of the employment positions . . . consideration shall be given to the employer's judgment as to what functions of a job are essential." There is no requirement to hire a person with a disability who is not qualified for the particular job, or who cannot perform an essential task of the job. The ability to define the essential functions are presumed to rest with the employer. Some examples may be clear-cut. For example, a professor's ability to evaluate students' work is an essential function of being an instructor; writing the evaluation by hand or entering it into a computer could be performed by an assistant without compromising the task. A different example is a graduate student who procures an internship at a Veteran's Administration Medical Center (VAMC). All interns are required to rotate through three settings during the year, one of which must be neuropsychological assessment. A blind student who requests an accommodation to stay longer at the other two settings and bypass the neuropsychological assessment placement may be met with resistance. Several factors are important to consider in this latter case. First, the ADA is not triggered unless the person with the disability does two things: identifies him- or herself as a person with a disability, and requests a reasonable accommodation. This is an important difference from IDEA, which is an entitlement law; the ADA is a civil rights law. Second, the ADA specifically states that the person with the disability must be included in the process of deriving reasonable accommodations. However, the final decision for an accommodation is left to the employer, who is not required to choose the optimal accommodation, but only one that works. So, the VAMC might decide that the student should take a different third placement to substitute for the neuropsychological assessment placement, even though the student feels that, because a visual impairment can slow acclimation to a setting, it would be preferable to stay at one setting longer. Note that the accommodation in this case accrues no costs (and 70% of reasonable accommodations in the workplace cost under $500), but rather a change in procedure. This is an important factor as it involves attitudes, beliefs about the role of interns and psychologists, and determination of the essential functions of an intern, all of which are areas in which reasonable people can disagree.

The list of places to which the ADA applies is long. It includes employment settings, buses, paratransit systems, trains, lodging, museums, libraries, zoos, day care centers, private schools, homeless shelters, half-way houses, banks, recreational areas, voting places, gas stations, department stores, repair shops, bakeries. (Note that religious organizations are exempt from the ADA, except for those religious organizations that accept federal funding, such as church-affiliated colleges, or are open to the public, such as a room that is used by Girl Scouts.) It would seem that the ADA provides a means of legal recourse to redress discrimination. However, as vital and as far-reaching as the ADA is, we need to examine what it is not. Additionally, numerous U.S. Supreme Court decisions have substantively weakened the ADA. The most potentially damaging of these (*Toyota v. Williams*, 2002) sent the decision back to a lower court because it was not clear that the woman involved was a person with a disability—she had only demonstrated limitations at the workplace, and work was not believed by the courts to be a *major life function*!

One major factor in the ADA is the notion of whether separate is equal. Although other civil rights laws clearly embrace the philosophy that forced separation is tantamount to segregation, the ADA (and the IDEA) allows for separate services, access, and systems. For example, a transit service only for people with disabilities (often called paratransit or some such equivalent) is prevalent in the United States. Entrances to a restaurant or other public site may be separate, with a sign near the building noting the entrance that persons with disabilities who require accessibly should use. It is hard, in the 21st century, to imagine a sign that would single out any other groups for a requirement of a separate line, entrance, or system, and be tolerated. But because the access needs of people with disabilities can be different from those of persons without a disability, such separateness is not only tolerated but sanctioned by law. A more equitable solution would be to make accessibility inherent in all design, such that there would be no need for separation of a class of persons.

Each of the laws just discussed views people with disabilities as a class in need of special protection and civil rights laws. This shifts the view of disability from that of disability as defect or abnormality, as it has traditionally been viewed (Olkin & Pledger, 2003; Reid & Knight, 2006), to that of a dimension of difference which is part of the multicultural spectrum (Smith et al., 2008). As I turn to discussing counseling with people with disabilities, this multicultural and social justice perspective dominates, as it does for counseling with other members of diverse but marginalized groups (D'Andrea & Heckman, 2008).

Counseling Individuals with Disabilities

In this section I outline the key aspects of D-AT and briefly present a template for understanding and conceptualizing clients with disabilities (Olkin 2008).

The essential tenets of D-AT are these:

- The therapist should ascribe to the social model of disability; this presumes a social justice orientation to counseling and psychotherapy.
- The client may ascribe to any one model or combination of models.
- Therapy between an able-bodied therapist and a client with a disability is cross-cultural therapy.
- No one therapeutic approach or theory of therapy predominates. D-AT is meant to be incorporated into the therapist's own theory.
- A template for questions to consider about clients can help therapists systematically understand the relevant disability history and issues.
- The case formulation should neither overinflate nor underestimate the role of disability in the client's life and problems.
- There is no such thing as *adjustment* to disability; rather there is *response* to disability, which is fluid, evanescent, and malleable.
- Therapists will need to have skills in working with professionals in other disciplines, such as education, nursing, occupational and physical therapy, and medicine.

The D-AT Template

As in all cross-cultural counseling, necessary aspects for the therapist are awareness of the importance of culture, an appreciation of one's limits of knowledge, receptivity to a culture different from one's own, knowledge about social oppression as it relates to specific groups, and an orientation towards social justice (D'Andrea & Heckman, 2008). Systemic and institutional factors that promote D-AT are organizational support, a mission statement consistent with D-AT, appropriate in-service evaluation and training, and valuing of diversity as exemplified in a diverse staff (Whealin & Ruzek, 2008). Additionally, specific skills are important in D-AT. This section walks the reader through five areas that are embedded in D-AT. These include special knowledge areas (developmental history as affected by a disability, models of disability, disability community and culture, and psychosocial issues); using the models of disability clinically; making treatment accessible; case formulation; and being culturally affirmative. For each of these areas, a list of questions that a clinician might ask or consider is given in Table 17.4.

SPECIAL KNOWLEDGE AREAS

Clinicians virtually always take a history of their clients, and doing so is one part of D-AT. The difference is in examining the developmental and personal/family history in light of the disability. In addition to the usual history-taking questions, one would include a medical history, such as the onset of the disability, any surgeries, hospitalizations or other periods of separation from parents, and changes in the disability or the treatment (e.g., leg braces, casts, new glass eyes, hearing implants). Along with the medical history, the therapist should note the psychosocial concomitants of that history. For example, if a child had surgery in the middle of second grade and was absent from school for 3 months, what were the reactions of peers when the client returned to school, how did siblings respond to the absence and reunification, how did parents and teachers handle it, and what was the take-home message (some might say *schemas*) of the experience for the client? Also embedded in the medical history is how the family conceptualizes disability and pain, the medical delivery service system, and treatment.

In addition to a medical history, the educational history should be assessed. Important factors include whether the child was mainstreamed in a regular classroom, used an aide, went to a resource room, or was bused elsewhere, and how much time was spent with other children with disabilities. Within these details are important clues to the model of disability, but also indications of what the client believes is abnormal, atypical, unusual, or pathological about the self, and about disability per se.

USING THE MODELS OF DISABILITY CLINICALLY

There are no studies on what models clients believe in, how belief in one or more models is related to mental health and functioning, and whether using the models of disability in therapy can help the therapeutic process. In the absence of such data, I can surmise that an appropriate match between the client's beliefs and the therapist's intervention would be a critical factor in the therapeutic alliance and possibly in treatment outcome. Although I have stated categorically that the therapist should hold the social model of disability, this is about the awareness of the therapist of disability as a social

Table 17.4.   Potential Questions for Clinicians and Clients

Topic Area	Questions for Clients	Questions for Clinicians
Special Knowledge Areas: Developmental history Models of disability Disability community/culture Psychosocial issues	What is my personal, family, medical, educational, social, religious/spiritual, and economic history? What is the role of my disability in each of these areas? In my friendships and relationships, what role does my disability play?	Am I asking the client about everything I usually do, or am I omitting some areas I believe are less relevant (e.g., sports, sexuality, occupational history)? Can I bring up disability before the client does? Are there questions I'm afraid to ask? Why?
Using the Models of Disability	See Table 17.2	See Table 17.2. Also: Do I view people with disabilities as constituting a minority group? Is disability an abnormality or part of human difference? Do I espouse social justice as an integral part of therapy?
Making Treatment Accessible	Does this therapist get flustered when she or he learns that I have a disability? Has the therapist thought in advance about what might be the needs of someone with my type of disability? Does the therapist seem free to talk about disability openly? Does she or he take some responsibility for learning about disability on her or his own?	Is there handicapped parking, a ramp or curb cut, a wheel-chair accessible bathroom with grab bars? Do addresses/rooms have Braille signage? Am I near a bus stop? Do I have materials in alternate formats (online, large print)? Can I schedule appointments at times of day to accommodate fatigue?
Case Formulation	How central a role does disability play in my life? Can I list both positive and negative outcomes of having a disability? Am I still striving for some ephemeral level of adjustment to disability?	Can I view disability as fostering resilience? Have I made disability the most important factor in the history? If I write the three to five most important factors in this person's life, where would disability fall? Am I using disability to explain features of the client? Am I downplaying the role of stigma, discrimination, prejudice?
Being Culturally Affirmative	Who are other people *like me*? Do I understand disability pride? Do I shun or embrace other people with disabilities? Do I keep up with major events affecting people with disabilities? Are there disability magazines or websites or listservs I read?	Are there disability magazines, websites or listservs I read or know about and can introduce the client to? Do I believe it is psychologically healthy for the person to know other people with disabilities? Are there positive disability images in the arts (movies, exhibits, dance, theater) I can introduce a client to?

construct; familiarity with disability history, concepts, culture, and community; and an affirming approach to clients. The language the therapist uses to discuss disability and the intervention methods must match the client's belief system. For example, if a mother describes her son as having right hemiplegia and a learning disability, she is describing the son's functional impairments. Think about the effect on the mother that the following questions might have: *Does your son play with other children with disabilities? What is your belief about the cause of your son's disability? Have you consulted anyone (a priest, a doctor, a shaman, a herbalist, a resource teacher) about how to treat your son's disability? What kind of future do you imagine for you son?* These are all good questions, and the answers will teach the therapist much about the mother's belief system and model of disability. But note that the questions are worded such that they do not presume any of the models of disability, but leave answers free to come from any of the models.

MAKING TREATMENT ACCESSIBLE

Imagine a client who uses a wheelchair calling for a first appointment. The client asks if your office is accessible. What is your answer? The most helpful answer might not be a simple yes or no, but rather a description (e.g., there is handicapped parking close by, a bus stops a block away and there are curb cuts, the bathroom has a handicapped stall with grab bars and room for front or side transfer, there are no steps into the building, the office is wheelchair accessible). Go through this same exercise for a client with a visual impairment, or a Deaf client. As you will note, the meaning of *accessible* changes quite a bit for different types of disabilities. So we see that accessible is not a fixed state. Some of the accessibility issues are about the facility. Others are about written materials, and others are about process. For example, some clients may need shorter sessions (e.g., a person with an intellectual disability who fatigues), others may need particular times of day (e.g., later in the day to accommodate a morning routine), or accommodations in sessions (written homework, reminder cards). The types of changes noted above don't alter the fundamental aspects of therapy. Testing, however, can be more profoundly altered in making accommodations. The first question has to be whether the test is appropriate, and second whether it is in an accessible format for the person with a particular disability. The third question is whether there are norms for persons with similar disabilities, and if items on the test can skew scores due to disability (e.g., a question about energy, when the person has multiple sclerosis). And the fourth question is whether the accommodations have changed the fundamental nature of what is being tested. These are not readily answerable questions, but should be considered carefully, and possible consultation should be sought when assessing a person with a disability.

Accessible treatment also can be thought of as integrated treatment. Often, the person with a disability, especially the child with a disability, is treated in multiple settings by professionals from different disciplines. The therapist may need to be the one who collects all relevant data and makes meaning of the whole. Facility in communicating with professionals in a variety of disciplines is a valuable and necessary skill (Lollar, 2008).

CASE FORMULATION

The fundamental skill in being culturally receptive is the facility to incorporate the disability into the case formulation without overinflating or underestimating the role of the disability. It is important to set aside any question of who the person might be without the disability—this is tantamount to asking who the person would be if that person were another person. The disability, even if new, is an integral part of the client. For a new or sudden onset of disability, the impairment may be experienced as alien. Often this is encouraged in the medical delivery service system. (Note Kaiser Permanente's radio ad: *I have cancer, it doesn't have me.* The idea is that the cancer is a separate entity, apart from the person.) This may be a good model for illnesses such as cancer (Rolland, 1994), especially one which could disappear with treatment. The idea is that the impairment is a thing separate from the essence of the person. But this does not work for disability—a permanent condition that will affect the person's functioning, incur stigma, and alter relationships. Such a disability needs to be incorporated into the sense of self, as one facet, but not necessarily the defining one. This idea of incorporating the disability but not making it overly central is, in deriving a case formulation, the very task for the therapist as well. A core question in formulation is: Why does *this* client have *this* problem, and why is he or she seeking treatment *now*? Does the history explain how the current functioning developed? What is maintaining the current functioning? What issues are seen in the relationship with others and with the therapist? Can the case formulation make some predictions about problem areas and future functioning? What are the person's strengths?

If the therapist makes a list of symptoms, behaviors, mood, cognitions, beliefs, functioning, and prognosis, and another list of positive traits and behaviors (initiative, creativity, humor, values, morality, insight, independence, intimacy, and positive relationships), the disability should be examined in relation to each of these areas. In addressing each of these areas, how relevant and salient are disability issues? In the summary of the client, the therapist can state that this is a client who has this set of problems, which were learned by this set of circumstances, and which are maintained by this current set of circumstances. Is disability a factor in the current set of problems? Is it part of the learning history? Is disability an element of maintaining problematic behaviors, thoughts, or mood? All of us are shaped by our heredity, environment, parenting, learning history, personality, traumas and experiences. Disability can be a major or a minor part of each of these, and either a synergistically crucial element or merely part of the background.

The idea of using a template to assess clients from a marginalized group has been suggested by others. For example, the RESPECTFUL[1] model (D'Andrea & Daniels, 2001) and the developmental counseling and therapy model (Ivey & Ivey, 1999) both have counselors use a holistic framework for developing a case formulation of clients. What these models share is an awareness of how marginalized status can impact every aspect of a person's background and current life, and suggestions of a systematic way of organizing the inquiry about a client and the resulting data from the client. These models go beyond diagnosis to case formulation. However, in putting more stock in social justice (and injustice) and the reality factors of marginalization, these models shift from a medical model, in which the locus of the problem resides in the client, to a case formulation model, in which multiple factors are involved in psychosocial distress (Zalaquett, Fuerth, Stein, Ivey, & Ivey, 2008).

BEING CULTURALLY AFFIRMATIVE

Disability community and culture is a relatively new idea (Hahn, 1993, 1999; Olkin, 2005; Peters, 2000). More recently, the ideas of disability pride, affiliation with a disability community, and a culture unique to the disability community have become more accepted. This is not to say that most children or even adults with disabilities are aware of the disability community and culture, nor a part of it. But therapists need this awareness, because without it they are unable to introduce it to the client,

or to even assess where the client stands with regard to it.

Not all clients with disabilities want to or need to be part of the disability culture and community. To force this would be as wrong as to ignore it. But it is important that clients with disabilities be aware of resources, supports, information, and places where responses to the disability will not be negative. It is helpful if therapists can recommend books, magazines, listservs, movies, organizations, and community resources relevant to the type of disability the client has. Families of children with disability and those with newly diagnosed disabilities especially can use assistance in finding resources.

Special Issues in Training and Supervision

Two sets of issues will be examined in this section. One set focuses on how to best train all students in how to work with clients with disabilities, and what issues are likely to emerge in supervision when the student without a disability is working with a client with a disability. The second set of issues is about training and supervising the student with a disability.

STUDENTS WITHOUT DISABILITIES

As discussed above in the section on models of disability, few graduate students in counseling or clinical psychology receive training in disability history or culture, working with clients with disabilities, or disability-affirmative clinical processes. To compound the problem, the student is likely to be supervised by a therapist equally untrained in working with clients with disabilities. Issues that are likely to arise are aversion to disability, self-consciousness about the therapist's own body, and use of language, hesitancy, ignorance, and becoming "deskilled" (i.e., forgetting what skills one possesses in the fluster over the presence of disability; Heller & Harris, 1987, p. 60). These issues cover attitudes, knowledge, and skills; thus, supervision has to address all three of these areas. Although there is a tendency to want to address attitudes first, I believe that arming students with knowledge and equipping them with skills should be the first line of training. When students feel more competent, they can achieve greater self-efficacy and have more psychoemotional freedom to address their own attitudes and prejudices. Additionally, getting to know their client with a disability better, as a fuller person, will help put disability into perspective. And, therapists are more likely to be helpful to their clients with disabilities when they feel knowledgeable, capable, appropriate, and affirming in understanding and working with clients' disability identities (Israel, Gorcheva, Walther, Sulzner, & Cohen, 2008).

Although there is scant literature on positive aspects of disability, borrowing from literature on gay or lesbian persons (Riggle, Whitman, Olson, Rostosky, & Strong, 2008), areas to be explored are belonging to a community (of people with similar or other types of disabilities), creating families of choice (of people who are affirmative about the disability), forging strong connections with others in the disability community, serving as a positive role model to other people with disabilities, developing empathy and compassion for others, greater flexibility in gender roles, and involvement in social justice and disability rights activism. In supervision of students without disabilities, the student should be encouraged to keep these positives in mind and see how they might be assessed, developed, and strengthened in therapy.

If the supervisor feels ill-prepared to teach the trainee about disability, this is an opportunity to model how to address gaps in one's skills. Two books are especially geared to helping therapists both in training and in the field increase their knowledge and skills with regard to clients with disabilities (Mackelprang & Salsgiver, 1999; Olkin, 1999).

STUDENTS WITH DISABILITIES

Trainees with disabilities are more likely than those without disabilities to possess knowledge about disability that will be helpful in their provision of treatment to clients with disabilities. It could be instructive to observe their interactions with clients to cull skills that could be transferable through training to students without disabilities (Dillon, Worthington, Soth-McNett, & Schwartz, 2008). But students with disabilities are not immune to the pervasive negative social messages about disability, and they may feel negatively or conflicted about their own disability. We should not assume disability knowledge or skills just because the trainee has a disability.

Trainees with disabilities being supervised by a professional without a disability may find that the supervisor's attitudes toward and beliefs about disability are manifest in supervision. Supervision, like therapy, has to put disability in perspective without overemphasizing it or ignoring it. One problem that can happen is that the supervisor projects onto clients his or her own difficulties with disability, and insists that clients will be put off by the therapist with a disability, or protective of the therapist, or unable to genuinely discuss the disability.

When the supervisor asks the student about clients' reactions, it may well be that the clients have not expressed any particular reactions. This can lead the unbelieving supervisor to accuse the student of being in denial, or unable to handle open discussion of disability with clients. This is a no-win situation for the student, because any further objections seemingly are proof of denial. In such cases, direct observation of sessions (through one-way mirrors or on video tape) can help supervisor and supervisee look together at a session for signs of unaddressed disability issues. It is important that the supervisor is available and supportive, disability-affirmative with the student, and genuine in mentorship (Israel et al., 2008), so that exploration of the impact of the student's disability on therapy can be openly and nondefensively explored in a cooperative manner.

Future Issues in Disability

In a dissertation on how to evaluate clients' models of disability (Guber, 2007), the following two questions were posed: What are the most salient clinical manifestations of each model of disability? What are the more common clinical manifestations of the three models of disability? Guber (2007) took questions from Olkin (1999) and expanded on them, then got several rounds of feedback from professionals in rehabilitation and other persons with disability expertise as he refined the set of questions. He found that there was no consensus on the validity of the three models of disability as useful constructs, nor on the clinical utility of these, or any other, models of disability. One concern is whether the models of disability overly simplify the general complexity of responses to disability. As Guber (2007) points out, understanding a client's model of disability is not diagnostic, nor does it dictate intervention.

Outside of rehabilitation settings, we know remarkably little about therapy with clients with disabilities. We need basic information on the types of problems for which clients with disabilities seek therapy, and whether they are any more or less likely to seek treatment than are clients without disabilities. Numerous potential presenting problems are more germane to clients with disabilities that could use further exploration. One is the area of pain, which can greatly impact quality of life (Lee, Chronister, & Bishop, 2008). Chronic pain patients for whom there is no known medical cause may differ from persons with disabilities for whom pain is a part of their condition, but the similarities and differences have not been systematically studied.

Fatigue is a major component of many disabilities, and we need data to guide how to help clients manage a lifestyle when fatigue forces a never-ending series of choices about how to best spend one's limited energies. Employment, and the disheartening unemployment rate among persons with disabilities, has not improved since passage of the ADA (Lehmann & Crimando, 2008) and begs guidance on how to ameliorate the situation. Employment tends to lead to positive outcomes such as reduced poverty, more socialization, and the greater probability of partnering, and thus is a critical area of intervention for people with disabilities. How can we help achieve those outcomes in the absence of employment? Adjustment to earlier-than-desired retirement or part-time employment is another area in need of exploration, as is aging with a disability (as opposed to aging and then acquiring a disability). The development of intimate relationships between a person with and a person without a disability has received remarkably little attention.

Elsewhere, Olkin and Pledger (2003) identified eight disability areas in need of further research. A slightly modified list would include care versus cure (universal design, visitability laws, personal assistant services, assistive technology, supported living environments, job access, and economic policy); disability in the context of other demographic variables, especially other marginalized statuses[2]; abuse of people with disabilities and disability as a result of abuse; romance, dating, and mating patterns for persons with disabilities; fertility, pregnancy, and childbirth; parenting with a disability; how to best foster and promote a positive disability identity; appropriate assessment and diagnosis of clients with disabilities; and using the models of disability in clinical practice.

Some of these are topics best suited for research within disability studies and interdisciplinary fields. But disability studies is not the venue for clinical research, which should remain within counseling and psychology. The needs for clinical research on disability are legion, as there are many unaddressed questions. The move toward evidence-based practice, the dictates of insurance reimbursement, and the necessity of training culturally competent therapists all prescribe that more research with direct application to counseling and therapy be undertaken. There needs to be a conference or collaborative effort within psychology to embrace disability studies and, within a social justice framework and including the voices of people with disabilities,

to set the research agenda for the coming decade. This is not the same as a rehabilitation psychology agenda, but rather an agenda for training in all graduate counseling and clinical psychology programs, dissertations related to therapy with people with disabilities, and research to address basic questions regarding such therapy. These basic questions include rates of use of psychotherapy by people with disabilities, with what types of disabilities, and for what types of problems; satisfaction and factors in satisfaction with the therapeutic process; correlations of premature drop-out; and impact of therapy on presenting problems. The criticisms of other outcome studies conducted with diverse populations must be addressed, such as threats to internal validity and problems in sample selection (Sue, 1999).

Studies are needed on D-AT, including how to teach D-AT, how best to incorporate D-AT into different theories of therapy, and D-AT outcome studies. Evidence-based practices need to be verified with this population, which has generally been excluded from outcome studies (Olkin & Taliaferro, 2005). Barriers to treatment need to be explicated and eradicated to the greatest extent possible.

"Quality of life" is one catch phrase of our times. The effects of stigma, prejudice, and discrimination are expected to take their toll on quality of life. What lessons can we learn from people with disabilities about stigma management, coping with prejudice, and survival in the face of daily discrimination? How can we take those lessons and use them with our clients who are less adept at these skills? The fields of counseling and psychology have much to offer in the area of disability, as long as it is seen as a worthy and fruitful area of inquiry. Of course, none of this can happen without a substantial boost in the priority level of disability as an area for psychology to address, and concomitant funding for research in this area.

Conclusion

Disability has been a neglected area within mainstream clinical and counseling psychology. This chapter has addressed conceptualizations of disability; counseling people with disabilities, in particular, using the D-AT model; training and supervision of students with and without disabilities; and research necessary to guide future clinical work with clients with disabilities. A thread that ties all these areas together is a social justice approach to understanding and working with a highly marginalized and disadvantaged group of potential clients.

Notes

1. RESPECTFUL: R = religious/spiritual issues; E = economic class issues; S = sexual identity issues; P = psychological development issues; C = chronological issues, T = trauma and threats to well-being; F = family issues; U = unique physical issues; L = language and location of residence issues.

2. For some relatively recent work on disability and specific ethnicities or sexual orientation, see: Asbury, C., Walker, S., Belgrave, F., Maholmes, V., & Green, L., 1994; Asbury, C. A., Walker, S., Maholmes, V., Rackley, R., & White, S., 1992; Bae & Kung, 2000; Balcazar, Keys, & Suarez-Balcazar, 2001; Becker, Stuifbergen, & Tinkle, 1997; Belgrave, 1998; Choi & Wynne, 2000; Guter & Killacky, 2004; Ino & Glicken, 1999; Hajat, Lucas, & Kington, 2000; Hanna & Rogovsky, 1991; Hwang, 1997; Fine & Asch, 1988; Jarama, Reyst, Rodriguez, Belgrave, & Zea, 1997; Jones, Atkin, & Ahmad, 2001; Krause, Coker, Charlifue, & Whiteneck, 1999; Marshall, 2001; Olkin, 2006; O'Toole & Bregante, 1993; Parkin & Nosek, 2001; Serafica, 1999; Shah, 1997; Smart & Smart, 1992, 1993, 1997; Tews & Merali, 2008; Tezzoni, McCarthy, Davis, Harris-David, O'Day, 2001; Whitfield & Lloyd, 2008.

References

Americans with Disabilities Act. (1990). Public Law 101-336, 42 U.S.C. 1211, 12112.

Asbury, C., Walker, S., Belgrave, F., Maholmes, V., & Green, L. (1994). Psychosocial, cultural, and accessibility factors associated with participation of African-Americans in rehabilitation. *Rehabilitation Psychology, 39*(2), 113–121.

Asbury, C. A., Walker, S., Maholmes, V., Rackley, R., & White, S. (1992). *Disability prevalence & demographic association among race/ethnic minority populations in the United States: Implications for the 21st century.* Washington, DC: Howard Univ. RTC for Access to Rehab. & Economic Opportunity.

Asch, S. E. (1946). Forming impressions of personality. *Journal of Abnormal and Social Psychology, 41*, 258–290.

Asch, A., & Rousso, H. (1985). Clinicians with disabilities: Theoretical and clinical issues. *Psychiatry, 48*, 1–12.

Bae, S., & Kung, W. W. (2000). Family intervention for Asian Americans with a schizophrenic patient in the family. *American Journal of Orthopsychiatry, 70*(4), 532–541.

Balcazar, F. E., Keys, C. B., & Suarez-Balcazar, Y. (2001). Empowering Latinos with disabilities to address issues of independent living and disability rights: A capacity-building approach. *Journal of Prevention and Intervention in the Community, 21*(2), 53–70.

Becker, H., Stuifbergen, A., Tinkle, M. (1997). Reproductive health care experiences of women with physical disabilities: A qualitative study. *Archives of Physical Medicine and Rehabilitation, 78*(12), S26–S33.

Belgrave, F. Z. (1998). *Psychosocial aspects of chronic illness and disability among African Americans.* Westport, CT: Auburn House.

Bluestone, H. H., Stokes, A., & Kuba, S. A. (1996). Toward an integrated program design: Evaluating the status of diversity training in a graduate school curriculum. *Professional Psychology: Research & Practice, 27*, 394–400.

Brown, K. S., DeLeon, P. H., Loftis, C. W., & Scherer, M. J. (2008). Rehabilitation psychology: Realizing the true potential. *Rehabilitation Psychology, 53*, 111–121.

Chan, F., Lam, C. S., Wong, D., Leung, P., & Fang, X. (1988). Counseling Chinese-Americans with disabilities. *Journal of Applied Rehabilitation Counseling, 19*(4), 21–25.

Choi, K., & Wynne, M. E. (2000). Providing services to Asian Americans with developmental disabilities and their families: Mainstream service providers' perspectives. *Community Mental Health Journal, 36*, 589–595.

D'Andrea, M., & Heckman, E. F. (2008). Contributing to the ongoing evolution of the multicultural counseling movement: An introduction to the special issue. *Journal of Counseling and Development, 86*, 259–260.

Dembo, T., Leviton, G. L., & Wright, B. A. (1956/1975). Adjustment to misfortune: A problem of social-psychological rehabilitation. *Artificial Limbs, 3*, 4–62. (Reprinted in Rehabilitation Psychology, 1975, 2, 1–100.)

Dillon, F. R., Worthington, R. L., Soth-McNett, A. M., & Schwartz, S. J. (2008). Gender and sexual identity-based predictors of lesbian, gay, and bisexual affirmative counseling self-efficacy. *Professional Psychology: Research & Practice, 39*, 353–360.

Fine, M., & Asch, A. (Eds.). (1988). *Women with disabilities: Essays in psychology, culture, and politics.* Philadelphia: Temple University Press.

Florian, V. (1982). Cross-cultural differences in attitudes towards disabled persons. *International Journal of Intercultural Relations, 6*, 291–299.

Guter, B., & Killacky, J. R. (Eds.). (2004). *Queer crips: Disabled gay men and their stories.* New York: Harrington Park Press.

Hahn, H. (1993). Can disability be beautiful? In M. Nagler (Ed.), *Perspectives in disability* (pp. 217–226). Palo Alto, CA: Health Markets Research.

Hajat, A., Lucas, J. B., & Kington, R. (2000). Health outcomes among Hispanic subgroups: Data from the NHIS, 1992–95. *Advance Data, 310*, 1–14.

Hanna, W. J., & Rogovsky, B. (1991). Women with disabilities: Two handicaps plus. *Disability, Handicap & Society, 6*(1), 49–63.

Heller, B. W., & Harris, R. I. (1987). Special considerations in the psychological assessment of hearing impaired persons. In B. W. Heller, L. M. Flohr, & L. S. Zegans (Eds.), *Psychosocial interventions with sensorially disabled persons* (pp. 53–77). Orlando, FL: Grune & Stratton.

Hogben, M., & Waterman, C. K. (1997). Are all of your students represented in their textbooks? A content analysis of coverage of diversity issues in introductory psychology textbooks. *Teaching of Psychology, 24*, 95–100.

Hwang, K. (1997). Living with a disability: A woman's perspective. In M. L. Sipski & C. J. Alexander (Eds.), *Sexual function in people with disability and chronic illness: A health practitioner's guide* (pp. 119–130). Gaithersburg, MD: Aspen.

Individuals with Disabilities Education Improvement Act of 2004, 20 U.S.C. § 1400 *et seq.* (2004).

Ino, S. M., & Glicken, M. D. (1999). Treating Asian American clients in crisis: A collectivist approach. *Smith College Studies in Social Work, 69*(3), 525–533.

Israel, T., Gorcheva, R., Walther, W., Sulzner, J. M, & Cohen, J. (2008). Therapists' helpful and unhelpful situations with LGBT clients: An exploratory study. *Professional Psychology: Research & Practice, 39*, 361–368.

Ivey, A. E., & Ivey, M. B. (1999). Toward a developmental diagnostic and statistical manual: The vitality of a contextual framework. *Journal of Counseling & Development, 77*, 484–490.

Jarama, S. L., Reyst, H., Rodriguez, M., Belgrave, F. Z., & Zea, M. C. (1998). Psychosocial adjustment among Central American immigrants with disabilities: An exploratory study. *Cultural Diversity and Mental Health, 4*(2), 115–125.

Jones, L., Atkin, K., & Ahmad, W. I. U. (2001). Supporting Asian deaf young people and their families: The role of professionals and services. *Disability and Society, 16*(1), 51–70.

Kemp, N. T., & Mallinckrodt, B. (1996). Impact of professional training on case conceptualization of clients with a disability. *Professional Psychology: Research and Practice, 27*, 378–385.

Krause, J. S., Coker, J. L., Charlifue, S., & Whiteneck, G. G. (1999). Depression and subjective well-being among 97 American Indians with spinal cord injury: A descriptive study. *Rehabilitation Psychology, 44*(4), 354–372.

Lee, G. K., Chronister, J., & Bishop, M. (2008). The effects of psychosocial factors on quality of life among individuals with chronic pain. *Rehabilitation Counseling, 51*, 177–189.

Lehmann, I., & Crimando, W. (2008). Unintended consequences of state and federal antidiscrimination and Family Medical Leave legislation on the employment rates of persons with disabilities. *Rehabilitation Counseling, 51*, 159–169.

Lollar, D. (2008). Rehabilitation psychology and public health: Commonalities, barriers, and bridges. *Rehabilitation Psychology, 53*, 122–127.

Mackelprang, R. W., & Salsgiver, R. O. (1999). *Disability: A diversity model approach in human service practice*. Belmont, CA: Wadsworth Publishing Company.

Marshall, C. A. (Ed.). (2001). Rehabilitation and American Indians with disabilities: A handbook for administrators, practitioners, and researchers. *Rehabilitation Education, 16*(1), 103–104.

Mussen, P. H., & Barker, R. (1944). Attitudes toward cripples. *Journal of Abnormal and Social Psychology, 39*, 351–355.

Olkin, R. (1999). What psychotherapists should know about disability. New York: Guilford.

Olkin, R. (2004). Disability and depression. In S. L. Welner & F. Haseltine (Eds.), *Welner's guide to the care of women with disabilities* (pp. 279–300). Philadelphia: Lippincott Williams & Wilkins.

Olkin, R. (2005). *Disability culture: A baker's dozen*. Newsletter of the Contra Costa County Psychological Association.

Olkin, R. (2006). Persons of color with disabilities. In M. Constantine (Ed.), *Clinical practice with people of color: A guide to becoming culturally competent*. New York: Teacher's College Press.

Olkin, R. (2008). Disability-Affirmative Therapy and case formulation: A template for understanding disability in a clinical context. *Counseling & Human Development, 39*(8), 1–20.

Olkin, R. (2009). Disability-Affirmative Therapy. In I. Marini & M. Stebnicki (Eds.), *Professional Counselors' Desk Reference* (pp. 355–370). NY: Springer.

Olkin, R., & Pledger, C. (2003). Can disability studies and psychology join hands? *American Psychologist, 58*(4), 296–304.

Olkin, R., & Taliaferro, G. (2005). Evidence-based practices have ignored people with disabilities; Dialogue. In J. Norcross, L. Beutler, & R. Levant (Eds.), *Evidence-based practices in mental health* (pp. 353–359; 365–367). Washington, DC: APA.

O'Toole, C., & Bregante, J. (1993). Disabled lesbians: Multicultural realities. In M. Nagler (Ed.), *Perspectives on disability*. Palo Alto, CA: Health Markets Research.

Parkin, E. K., & Nosek, M. A. (2001). Collectivism versus independence: Perceptions of independent living and independent living services by Hispanic Americans and Asian Americans with disabilities. *Rehabilitation Education, 15*(4), 375–394.

Peters, S. (2000). Is there a disability culture? A syncretisation of three possible world views. *Disability & Society, 15*(4), 583–601.

Ray, M. H. (1946). *The effect of crippled appearance on personality judgment*. Unpublished master's thesis, Stanford University. Rehabilitation Act of 1973, Public law 93-112.

Reid, D. K., & Knight, M. G. (2006). Disability justifies exclusion of minority students: A critical history grounded in disability studies. *Educational Researcher, 35*, 18–23.

Riggle, E. D. B., Whitman, J. S., Olson, A., Rostosky, S. S., & Strong, S. (2008). The positive aspects of being a lesbian or gay man. *Professional Psychology: Research & Practice, 39*, 210–217.

Rolland, J. (1994). *Families, illness and disability*. New York: Basic Books.

Rose, A. (1997). "Who causes the blind to see": disability and quality of religious life. *Disability and Society, 12*(3), 395–405.

Saetermoe, C., Scattone, D., & Kim, K. (2001). Ethnicity and the stigma of disabilities. *Psychology and Health, 16*, 699–713.

Serafica, F. C. (1999). Clinical interventions and prevention for Asian American children and families: Current status and needed research. *Applied and Preventive Psychology, 8*, 143–152.

Smart, J. F., & Smart, D. W. (1992). Cultural issues in the rehabilitation of Hispanics. *Journal of Rehabilitation, 58*(2), 29–37.

Smart, J. F. & Smart, D. W. (1993). The rehabilitation of Hispanics with disabilities: Sociocultural constraints. *Rehabilitation Education, 7*, 167–184.

Smart, J. F., & Smart, D. W. (1997). The racial-ethnic demography of disability. *Journal of Rehabilitation, 63*(4), 9–15.

Smart, J. F., & Smart, D. W. (2006). Models of disability: Implications for the counseling profession. *Journal of Counseling & Development, 84*, 29–40.

Smith, L., Foley, P. F., & Chaney, M. P. (2008). Addressing classism, ableism, and heterosexism in counselor education. *Journal of Counseling and Development, 86*, 303–309.

Sue, D. W. (2010). *Microaggressions in everyday life: Race, gender, and sexual orientation*. Hoboken, NJ: John Wiley and Sons.

Sue, D. W., Capodilupo, C. M., & Holden, A. M. B. (2008). Racial microaggressions in the life experience of black Americans. *Professional Psychology: Research & Practice, 39*, 329–336.

Sue, D. W., Nadal, K. L., Capodilupo, C. M., Lin, A. I., Torino, G. C., & Rivera, D. P. (2008). Racial microaggressions against black Americans: Implications for counseling. *Journal of Counseling and Development, 86*, 330–338.

Sue, S. (1999). Science, ethnicity, and bias: Where have we gone wrong? *American Psychologist, 54*, 1070–1077.

Tews, L., & Merali, N. (2008). Helping Chinese parents understand and support children with learning disabilities. *Professional Psychology: Research & Practice, 39*, 137–144.

Tezzoni, L. I., McCarthy, E. P., Davis, R. B., Harris-David, L., O'Day, B. (2001). Use of screening and preventive services among women with disabilities. *American Journal of Medical Quality, 16*(4), 135–144. *Toyota Motor MFG., KY., Inc. v. Williams*, 534 U.S. 184 (2002).

Walster, E. (1966). Assignment of responsibility for an accident. *Journal of Personality and Social Psychology, 3*, 73–79.

Westbrook, M. T., Legge, V., & Pennay, M. (1993). Attitudes towards disabilities in multi-cultural society. *Social Science and Medicine, 36*, 615–623.

Whealin, J. M., & Ruzek, J. (2008). Program evaluation for organizational cultural competence in mental health practices. *Professional Psychology: Research & Practice, 39*, 320–328.

Whitfield, H. W., & Lloyd, R. (2008). American Indians/Native Alaskans with traumatic brain injury: Examining the impairments of traumatic brain injury, disparities in service provision, and employment outcomes. *Rehabilitation Counseling, 51*, 190–192.

Wong, D. (2008). *Beliefs of immigrant Chinese families with children with disabilities: An investigation of three theoretical models of disability*. Unpublished doctoral dissertation, California School of Professional Psychology at Alliant International University, San Francisco.

World Health Organization (2001). *International classification of functioning, disability, and health*. Geneva, Switzerland: Author.

Wright, B. A. (1960). *Physical disability: A psychological approach*. New York: Harper & Row.

Wright, B. A. (1983). *Physical disability: A psychosocial approach* (2nd ed.). New York: Harper & Row.

Wright, B. A. (1988). *Attitudes and the fundamental negative bias: Conditions and corrections*. (pp. 3–21). In H. E. Yuker (Ed.), Attitudes toward person with disabilities. New York: Springer.

Yuker, H. E. (Ed.) (1988). *Attitudes toward persons with disabilities*. New York: Springer.

Zalaquett, C. P., Fuerth, K. M., Stein, C., Ivey, A. E., & Ivey, M. B. (2008). Reframing the DSM-IV-TR from a multicultural/social justice perspective. *Journal of Counseling and Development, 86*, 364–371.

Counseling Psychologists Working with Older Adults

Tammi Vacha-Haase *and* Michael Duffy

Abstract

This chapter explores the relationship between counseling psychology and working with older adults. A brief overview of the increasing expansion and core areas within the aging population is provided, with focus on aging in society, intergenerational family, and issues of diversity. Clinical work with older adults is addressed, highlighting later-life issues, as well as engaging in psychotherapy and assessment with older adults. In the final section, opportunities for counseling psychologists are outlined, with recommendations for the expansion of traditional areas for counseling psychology, as well as relatively newer areas such as quality of life, pain management, and end-of-life treatment.

Keywords: geropsychology, older adult, counseling psychology, training counseling psychologists, career opportunities

An exciting and increasing area of opportunity for counseling psychology comes with the growing numbers of older adults. Not only is "America graying," but the mental health needs of the older population are expanding and becoming more apparent than ever before in history. The population growth of those over 65 years of age can be attributed to the aging of baby boomer generation, as well as an increase in the average lifespan (Centers for Disease Control and Prevention, 2007). People are living longer, with a current average life expectancy of over 78 years (Kung, Hoyert, Xu, & Murphy, 2008). Although old age has typically been defined as over 65 years, additional terminology has emerged with the increasing lifespan, categorizing adults over 65 but under the age of 75 as the "young-old," those aged 75 to 85 as the "old-old," and those over age 85 as the "oldest old." With advances in medicine and public health, people are not only living longer, but continuing to be in reasonably good health for the majority of their years.

Much has been written about the later years of the lifespan, with attention often given to the physical decline and challenges that come with age.

However, current trends are returning to a more positive outlook of older adulthood, with increased focus on the optimizing of healthy aging. Rowe and Kahn (1998) popularized the term *successful aging*, and Hill (2005) expanded on Seligman and Csikszentmihalyi's (2000) work in positive psychology, bringing to center stage the movement of *positive aging*. Recognizing aging as involving a "state of mind," Hill (2005) identified four characteristics to living a longer and higher-quality life. These included the importance of coping with age-related decline; choosing a lifestyle to preserve well-being; maintaining cognitive, emotional, and behavioral flexibility; and, focusing on the positives, rather than the negatives, of the aging process.

Although not inevitable with aging, there is often a decline of physical health, with an increase of chronic medical problems such as arthritis, high blood pressure, and late-onset diabetes. As a group, older adults tend to visit physicians more frequently than do younger adults, and approximately 87% of older adult patients regularly see a primary care physician (Ross, 2005). Unfortunately, declining health status is magnified for diverse elders, as the health of older adults of racial and ethnic minorities lags far behind that of nonminority populations. Data from the 2004 National Health Interview Survey (NHIS) indicated that 39% of non-Hispanic white adults aged 65 years or older reported very good or excellent health, compared with 24% of non-Hispanic blacks and 29% of Hispanics.

A longstanding debate has focused on the mental health of older adults, with an ongoing assertion that old age, in comparison to youth, brings about higher rates of depression and anxiety. However, it is now generally accepted that older adults actually have a lower incidence of anxiety (Brenes, Knudson, McCall, Williamson, Mille, & Stanley, 2008) and depression (Fiske, Wetherell, & Gatz, 2009) than do younger adult groups, perhaps a testimony to the increasing resilience that comes from a lifetime of coping with and resolving problems.

However, a recent comprehensive study of older adults found that 6% reported 14 or more days each month of poor mental health due to stress, depression, or problems with emotions, with the prevalence of frequent mental distress lower among non-Hispanic whites (5.9%) and Asians and Pacific Islanders (6.1%) compared with Native Americans and Alaska Natives (8.4%), non-Hispanic blacks (9.8%), and Hispanics (11.2%) (CDC, 2007). A review of the literature over the past decade estimates that mental health disorders among the elderly range from 18% to 28%, and if current prevalence rates for mental disorders are applied, more than 7.5 million older Americans are suffering from afflictions that require the professional services of psychologists. If these older individuals are residents of long-term care (LTC) facilities or nursing homes, the estimates are even higher, with the prevalence of psychiatric disorders in nursing homes for older adults ranging from 50% to 90% (Chandler & Chandler, 1988; Rovner et al., 1990; Rovner et al., 1986; Tariot, Podgorski, Blazina, & Leibovici, 1993).

Relatively few options are available for older adults to obtain psychological treatment (Yang & Jackson, 1998), especially for the increasingly large number who have diminishing resources. Mental health utilization studies show a low access of older adults to community mental health centers across the United States, with estimated utilization by older adults comprising only 4% of total outpatient mental health visits (Karlin & Duffy, 2006). With the downsizing and closing of public state psychiatric facilities, nursing homes have increasingly become the new inpatient psychiatric hospitals for older adults

(Schmidt et al., 1977). Unfortunately, LTC facilities have not been traditionally well equipped (Lombardo, 1994) or adequately financed or staffed to provide psychological or psychiatric services to older adults, leaving unmet the mental health needs for the majority of LTC residents (Moak & Borson, 2000).

Perhaps the greatest untold story today is the effect of an aging population on families. It has been well established that caring for a sick relative promotes increased stress and burden for the caregiver (Gatz, Bengtson, & Blum, 1990; Zarit, Johansson, & Jarrott, 1998). When caregivers are elderly and caring for their spouses with dementia, the stress of this undertaking may be compounded, and marital satisfaction lessened as the degree of perceived caregiver burden increases (Fitzpatrick & Vacha-Haase, in press). However, it is often middle-generation adults, particularly middle-generation women, who struggle with caregiving for older parents who have an increasing incidence of chronic medical and mental health concerns.

Who Will Provide Needed Mental Health Services?

There has been little change over the past several decades regarding the number of psychologists interested in working with older adults (Qualls, Segal, Norman, Niederehe, & Gallagher-Thompson, 2002). Research has consistently found that only a few, between 1% and 4% of psychologists surveyed, were either interested in or specializing in working with the elderly (Gatz, Karel, & Wolkenstein, 1991; Koder & Helmes, 2008). Clearly, not all psychologists will specialize in older adults, nor will they all require specific training (Knight, Karel, Hinrichsen, Qualls, & Duffy, 2009). However, given changing demographics, the majority of psychologists will eventually treat an older client. With the increase in the number of grandparents raising grandchildren, even those specializing in children and adolescents will encounter older adults in need of mental health services. Unfortunately, according to a 2002 survey of American Psychological Association (APA) practicing psychologists, less than 30% have been exposed to course work in geropsychology, and less than 20% have completed practicum or supervised clinical experience (Qualls et al., 2002).

Unfortunately, the attention paid to an older population by counseling psychologists is limited if publication within professional journals is representative of the degree that a field includes older adults in its training, research, and clinical interest. Werth and his colleagues (Werth, Kopera-Frye, Blevins,

& Bossick, 2003) reviewed all published articles from 1991 to 2000 in counseling psychology's leading journals, *The Counseling Psychologist* (*TCP*) and *The Journal of Counseling Psychology* (*JCP*), to explore the extent of older adult representation in these professional publications. The final results identified a lack of published material focusing on older adults, an outcome similar to previous reviews of *JCP* (Munley, 1974; Scherman & Doan, 1985). However, the authors added the following caveat: "although *JCP* and *TCP* have not shown significant attention to geropsychological research and practice, this is not to insinuate that such work is not being conducted by counseling psychologists. There are a number of researchers and practitioners who integrate gerontology with counseling psychology in research and practice. The bottom line, however, is that their contributions to the literature are not being published in counseling psychology's premiere journals" (Werth et al., 2003; p. 805).

Counseling psychology provides a "natural" fit for being involved with older adults through research, treatment, training, outreach, and advocacy. The profession's strengths-based approach to human behavior provides a positive psychological emphasis in both gaining knowledge and working with elders. The valuing of diversity and social justice embedded within counseling psychology creates a meaningful and significant framework from which to contribute to the rapidly growing older adult population. And counseling psychology's emphasis on a developmental model for both human behavior and emerging problems appears highly congruent with geropsychology.

Core Areas in Geropsychology

Geropsychology encompasses a multitude of areas, each intersecting with the other. While areas intersect, they are also sufficiently distinct in focus and research contributions that this chapter defines them separately: the life span approach to development, an approach to development that optimizes compensation as a focus, aging viewed as gains or declines, and the challenges posed by physical illnesses and limitations.

Geropsychologists have been very prominent in lifespan development research, extending the range of developmental phases to include later life and contributing to the understanding of the classic nature versus nurture debate. This includes recognition that the biological and organic blueprint plays a central role in development. In the mid-1980s, Raymond Cattell indicated that the variance of

personality characteristics biologically based and inherited in the range of 30%. His notable summary statement was based on his extensive research, as well as that of other personality psychologists (Hettema & Deary, 1993). But this leaves a significant 70% of human behavior that is highly influenced by social, physical, and environmental variables. It might be said that, although one cannot change a kangaroo into an elephant, it is possible to improve the kangaroo! The simple divide of biological and environmental factors in development has moved from a simple dualism to an interactive and process model of the relationship of the organism and environment in human development. Not only do genetics and the environment interact in complex ways, but the individual actively participates in his or her own development. In turn, part of that participation is influenced by the enduring personality make-up of the person, including such features as resilience (Eisold, 2005), which has a distinct influence on the unfolding development of the older person. So, personality characteristics not only influence but are in turn influenced; biology is not static but dynamic and plastic. This plasticity in human capacity is also recognized in the world of neurobiology, in which neuropsychological studies reveal that the brain is not a static instrument but is in dynamic interaction with the total environment including innate characteristics, interpersonal interactions, and the ongoing influences of life (Whitbourne, 2005). Such dynamic and process-oriented views of human development strongly support a role for intervention and counseling in the lives of older adults. It is clear that human persons are not victims of biology but rather are positively shaped by temperamental factors that allow them to adapt, change, and move in positive and health-giving directions (Hill, 2005).

Finally, a major contribution to lifespan developmental understanding is Erik Erickson's (Erikson, 1959, 1963) lifespan psychological theory. He focused on *internal* development, such as trust, intimacy, and identity issues, whereas much previous developmental psychology is probably best described as describing developmental *behavior*. Erickson focused on the development of the person's internal psychological world. His addition of the late life stage of ego integrity versus despair brought his understanding of the lifespan full circle. His recognition that development of ego integrity is threatened by chronic illness and increasing body preoccupation in some persons is critical to understanding late-onset somatic complaints. These various developmental stages or themes are in fact not linear but recursive; older adults continue to revisit issues of intimacy, trust, and identity development throughout the life cycle (Christianson & Palvovitz, 1998). In general there is a strengthening of the sense of self as an individual moves through life. Erickson's work is compatible with the internal development processes enshrined in the tradition of counseling psychology. It provides a model for counseling psychologists to understand and intervene effectively in the developmental processes of older adults.

A major theoretical contribution within the tradition of lifespan development is the *selection optimization compensation* (SOC) developmental model (Baltes & Baltes, 1990), which clearly fits with a dynamic and realistic view of late-life development. In developing the SOC model, the authors suggested that development involves not only acquisition and maturation, but also decomposition and decline of life processes and competencies. Thus, there is a need to proactively offset age-related losses. In this model, S (Selection) involves choosing realistic and attainable goals and skills in later life that are compatible with functional level. O (Optimization) focuses on enhancing competencies that are active and available to the older person, and C (Compensation) develops new skills and strategies to cope with actual or predictable losses.

The compensatory emphasis given in the SOC model and also the actual documented medical conditions that are prevalent in late life emphasize that everyone will age and die, and not before likely experiencing a selection of chronic illnesses. This reality-based view is sometimes at odds with a "Pollyanna" view, in which aging is seen as unequivocally positive. For many years in the early stages of professional gerontology, researchers and policy analysts were rightfully bent on counteracting common negative stereotypic views of aging. These negative stereotypes accepted static inherent physical and psychological limitations and therefore did not invite active intervention.

Although many older adults live full and healthy lives up to the time of their deaths, there are also many who suffer from advancing mental and physical problems with older age. For example, arthritis, a painful, chronic stiffing of joints is common, with over one-half of adults over the age of 65 suffering from this disease. Diabetes, caused by blood levels of glucose being too high, can lead to dangerous health problems in older adults including kidney failure, vision loss, and neuropathy. Although cancer can develop at any age, older adults are also more likely to experience this disease. Osteoporosis, often considered a "silent" disease, as symptoms may not be initially noticed, weakens the bones, increasing risks for a fracture or break. High blood pressure, or hypertension, is often referred to as the "silent killer" of the elderly due to the lack of identifiable symptoms; left unidentified or treated, high blood pressure can lead to stroke, heart disease, and kidney failure.

Another critical dimension of deteriorating health in older adults is through cognitive changes and decline. Understanding the normal and pathological changes in brain function in late life is a vast, complex, and still little understood area. It is certainly true that not all memory problems, for example, are a sign of approaching dementia; by the same token, however, memory loss can be an initial stage of the dementing process. Estimates of the presence of dementia in older adults suggest that approximately 50% of adults over the age of 85 will develop some dementing process, either of the Alzheimer's type, vascular dementia, or subcortical dementias such as Parkinson's or Huntington's dementia (Corrada, Brookmeyer, Berlau, Paganini-Hill, & Kawas, 2008). It is also critical to be aware of reversible dementias, such as those associated with delirium or with medical disorders such as pernicious anemia, thyroid imbalance, or even severe constipation (Clarfield, 2005).

The skills of psychologists are pertinent in both understanding and interacting with older persons with dementing disorders, as well as simply working with the age-related minimal memory dysfunction that normatively accompanies aging. A risk of comorbid anxiety and depression is associated with dementia, often with the unintended "emotional abandonment" by family and even professional staff. There is a critical need for counseling psychologists to understand that the loss of logical language processes in dementing disorder does not mean the loss of emotional life of the older adult. It is unfortunately common that, when younger adults identify cognitive impairment in older adults, they begin to give up trying to communicate and distance themselves emotionally (Duffy, 1999b). A simple example is the frequent short-term loss of speech in a stroke victim; all too often, emotional abandonment occurs when family members, even spouses, who are no longer able to have usual conversation with their older relative begin to ignore and often lessen the frequency of visits. It is as if the stroke victim is encased in a "glass coffin," from which they cannot communicate but can see and appreciate that they are not abandoned by love ones. At a time like this, the most critical intervention is to "keep talking" (Duffy, 1999b) even though the conversation is not appreciated logically by the impaired older adult.

Changes and decline in later life also affect couple relationships. The aging of the body often involves changes in sexuality and sexual responsiveness. Although sexual beings throughout life, there is a gradual decline in sexual performance and sometimes also in sexual interest for both genders. Such changes as decreases in testosterone (men) and estrogen and progesterone (women), increased size of the prostate (men), and decrease in vaginal lubrication (women) frequently result in slowed or weaker response at excitement and orgasmic phases, respectively (Zeiss & Zeiss, 1999). Although these changes are factual and should be realistically appreciated, it is also important to develop strategies that are compatible, for example, with the SOC model, which focuses on optimization and compensation for losses. Couples may benefit from counseling that helps adapt to changing sexual patterns and develop adaptive sexual behaviors in tune with changed physiological conditions. Sexuality needs also be handled sensitively in long-term care settings, with ongoing staff education to promote understanding and acceptance of older adult sexual intimacy (Martin & Vacha-Haase, in press). This is true even in residents with dementia, as advanced cognitive impairment does not preclude emotional and sexual responsiveness (Duffy, 1999b). Disturbed sexual behavior, however, in long-term care settings can become intrusive on other residents as well as professional staff, and sensitive but firm management is required.

The Intergenerational Family

With the aging demographics, especially the increases in the "old-old," family structures are becoming increasing complex. As mentioned earlier, the stress on intergenerational families is perhaps the greatest untold story in contemporary society, especially with stress on family caregivers increasing incrementally. Increasing survival of older adults has meant increases in the frequency of extended multigenerational family systems. Whereas the two- or three-generation family would have been normative in earlier years, it is now common to find four or even five generations coexisting in the multigenerational family (Matthews & Sun, 2006). Add in a 50% divorce and remarriage rate and the complexity escalates, for example, with a child having up to eight (sometimes competing!) grandparents.

The social and psychological implications of this complex structure and attendant social problems are obvious. The focal point of this stress is sometimes referred to as the *sandwich generation*. This refers to middle-generational women who may be responsible for up to two younger generations (e.g., a 25-year-old adult child and a 2-year-old grandchild) and potentially two older generations (e.g., a 70-year-old mother and a 90-year-old grandmother). This middle generation, often a woman, is a heroine in coping with both caregiving situations, but can also be identified as a victim of the economic, domestic, health, and psychological pressures involved in caregiving. Bear in mind also, that an increasing number of these middle-generation women are now working outside the home, so that their lives involve a double role of worker and caregiver.

However, this situation should not be taken to imply a negative view of the extended family. It also does not necessarily imply a lack of connection or decline in the extended family. This popularized view of decline in sociological views during the 1960s suggested that modern, highly mobile culture presaged the decline of the extended family. In contrast, studies by social gerontologists in the last 20 years have clearly indicated a continuing and meaningful contact between members of the extended family, even as it becomes more complex. For example, Shanas (1979) found that about 85% of older adults have weekly contact with an immediate family member, and indeed a full 65% have a daily contact with a family member.

Furthermore, it is important to note that incidence of contact, either physically or electronically, does not fully capture the quality and interior importance of relationships. Even with distant older parents, the importance and quality of the relationship is not simply correlated with the degree of contact. It is now known that the psychological significance of parental relationships continues late into adult life and continues throughout the later phases of the extended family (Pillemer & McCartney, 1991). Psychological connections with parents are simply too strong (even when negative) to be discounted.

In a similar vein, a mythology has developed about families abandoning older adults to LTC facilities or nursing homes. In fact, this behavior is quite rare and is present in perhaps 5%–10% of largely dysfunctional families. Note that this figure is consistent with the presence of family and severe personality pathology that exists in the population as a whole (Kessler et al., 1994). In other words, families largely do not abandon older parents, and indeed, the issue of caring for older parents is typically an issue of great emotional sensitivity, not to mention pain and stress.

Clearly, there is a role for active intervention by counseling psychologists in these extended family systems. Although society is indebted to the family therapy movement of the 1960s and beyond, traditional family therapy was largely concerned with the nuclear family (mom, dad, and kids) and had little awareness of the critical emotional connections that exist with older parents in the extended family. Family therapy methods with multigenerational families need to be flexible and multimodal and deal with the pragmatic constraints of distance. Often, family members might be reached only through telephone and conference-call connections and background information gained from family members at a distance. In a specific example, it is likely that, in some cases, the most effective treatment of depression in an older adult will involve a strategic "therapeutic" phone call to an absent family member with whom the older adult feels emotionally disconnected. Late life is a time for resolution of unfinished family business, and the "ticking clock of death" is often a signal for families to reach out to one another in caring and in forgiveness.

The increasing presence of older adults within contemporary society has a large-scale societal effect, as well as consequences in the more intimate clinical areas discussed above. Not only is the older individual threatened economically in terms of the adequacy of Social Security payments, Medicare, Medicaid, and the depletion of private retirement homes, but there is also a societal impact. With the increasing older adult population, policy makers and social strategists recognize that the extension of the human lifespan has significant social, economic, and political impact. For example, Medicare, the universal healthcare system for older adults, provides as much as 65% of the income of those in average acute and long-term care hospitalizations (MedPac, 2008). It is also noteworthy that, in the current national fiscal woes, Medicare is under fairly routine pressure to reduce reimbursements, with subsequent loss of physician providers for older adults: As of now, only 38% of family physicians remain Medicare providers (Xakellis, 2004).

However, older adults are a considerable force, socially and politically, and in more recent years have become increasingly organized for political action. The American Association of Retired Persons (AARP) is an influential political advocate for the well-being—financially, medically, and socially—of older adults. A very common misconception about late life is that older adults are homogeneous in their political and social views. In fact, there is increasing heterogeneity among persons as they age. Traditionally, politicians understood this and often felt there was no "power block" that must demand their attention. However, with the ascendance of AARP, Gray Panthers (a national group of older adults committed to aging social and advocacy issues), and like organizations, politicians now take serious notice of organized political advocacy in Washington, D.C. on behalf of older adults. In terms of sheer numbers, older adults form a strong lobby when they stand behind any given issue.

Work, retirement, and leisure issues also have a large personal and economic effect on society. Although the age limit requirements of mandatory retirement have frequently been raised, older adults still frequently choose to seek retirement and greater opportunity for family time and leisure. In rural and agrarian societies, it has been noted that there is only a limited concept of retirement for example, as the farmer continues to work until finally physically unable to manage the physical demands of work (Cavanaugh, 1997). In urban societies, however, retirement has become a norm and has been increasingly studied as a topic within social gerontology. Clearly, counseling psychologists place a special emphasis on the psychological importance and patterns of vocational choice and work. The emphasis on workplace psychology and the various patterns of retirement is much needed since older adults are inclined to "escape" the world of work into a retirement in a manner that is often ill-considered economically, socially, and psychologically. Naïve assumptions that happiness will be gained by either staying in the workforce or "sitting on the balcony and looking out to sea" are often the victims of later harsh reality. Not only are individual personality differences relevant, but cultural and ethnic influences also need to be taken into account as a vocational psychology of retirement is developed. In addition, gender differences in retirees are critical. It has been often noted that women tend to do better in retirement (Mandal & Roe, 2008) because they retain connections with friends and family members, and often become the "family kin keeper" who updates the address book and sends the holiday cards. Men, on the other hand, frequently become increasingly isolated and vulnerable to subsequent depression. It is conjectured that this pattern of isolation contributes to older white males having the second highest suicide rate across the lifespan (Conwell & Thompson, 2008). Ethnic and cultural differences may explain the fact that older men in other ethnic groups are less isolated and affected by such processes.

Diversity in Aging

With the baby boom cohort aging, the elderly population will not only increase, but racial and ethnic diversity will continue to enlarge with this population expansion (United States Census, 2003). For example, in 2000, Latinos represented 12.5% of the nation's population, but only 5% of those were over 65. For African Americans, the average growth for those over age 65 is about 31%.

Although fundamental similarities exist in developmental trajectories, individual and group development is significantly influenced by gender, sexual orientation, and cultural and ethnic experiences. There are notable differences between African American, Anglo, and Mexican American aging processes in terms of cultural patterns, family priorities, and caregiving (Morales, 1999). The intersection of age with ethnicity also signals a significant change in socioeconomic status, specifically in access to material resources. Older adult members of most ethnic groups are poorer than Anglo elderly, although decreased resources characterize older adults in general. Older African Americans often experience a significant poverty that is the product of past and present racial discrimination that kept them from well-paying jobs (Atchely, 1994). They tend to have significantly poorer health status than do Anglo elderly, with several chronic conditions, such as heart disease and cancer (Thorson, 1995).

Hispanic Americans represent several different heritage groups, including Mexican, Cuban, and Puerto Rican, as well as several Latin American cultures, all of which have considerable intercultural variations. A key issue with older Hispanic Americans is the length of time living in the United States. Language differences are often the cause of discrimination, and many older Mexican American adults, for example, are monolingual and rely on younger bilingual family members to deal with daily affairs.

There are approximately 5,00,000 older adults of Asian or Pacific Islander descent in the United States, a category composed of widely disparate groups differing in racial, cultural, religious, and language characteristics: Japanese, Indian, Chinese, Korean, Filipino, Hawaiian, and Southeast Asian peoples. The differences are also economic, with Chinese and Japanese older adults having occupational and economic backgrounds similar to European Americans, whereas Filipino older adults have largely worked in poor and unskilled jobs (Cavanaugh, 1997).

The smallest ethnic minority group older adults are the earliest U.S. citizens, Native Americans. Although the tribes have some degree of official independence, living on a reservation involves a paternalistic system that often cuts a person off from the resources available to other older adults. Although Native Americans often escape typical European ailments such as heart disease, they are vulnerable to alcoholism, diabetes, accidents, and poor life expectancy; less than 42% reach age 65 (Thorson, 1995). Not unrelated is the very limited quality of the health and mental health services provided on reservations.

Within these ethnic groups, there are differences between rural and urban settings. Rural families have tended to assume care for older parents, whereas urban families, often involved in a corporate workday, have relied on nursing homes as a part of the caregiving system. There are ethnic and cultural differences in the role and place of the older adult within the extended family and within society. In some cultures, the Anglo culture being the most typical, the significance of the role of older adults, socially and politically, diminishes over time. This is in contrast to other ethnic groups, such as Native Americans, in which age is considered to give a special role in society and the family as advisor, wisdom bearer, and consultant.

In addition to racial or ethnic diversity, older adults must be understood within the context of gender issues (Smith & Baltes, 1998). Older women experience unique social challenges (Crose, 1999; Davenport, 1999), as they are more likely to live below the poverty line, have significantly less income than their male counterparts, live alone, and experience some form of disability while outliving their partners. Older men also face unique challenges (Huyck & Gutmann, 1999; Vacha-Haase, Wester, & Christianson, in press), including loss of independence and power, social isolation, and increased emotional distress with higher likelihood of suicide completion.

An area of diversity that has received little attention within society is the presence of gay and lesbian older adults (OLGBTs). Estimates suggest that there are approximately 3 million gay elders currently living in the Unites States; by 2030, there will be up to 6 million lesbian and gay seniors (National Gay and Lesbian Task Force, 2009). In earlier cohorts of older adults, sexual orientation was largely invisible, although it was likely present in the same degree as in contemporary society. As the years pass, later cohorts will most likely deal with sexual orientation diversity with greater comfort and openness. In fact, a recent study found that the more interaction older adults had with gay men or lesbian women, the higher their comfort level in interacting with gay and lesbian peers. It is highly likely that the transformations in the social meaning of marriage and legal unions happening today will influence the acceptance of sexual orientation diversity among future older adults.

Another related area interfacing with all of these diversities is religious belief and adherence. The importance of spirituality and indeed religious adherence increases with age, probably in relationship to a parallel increase in introspection or interiority that has been identified with later phases of the life cycle. Religious belief is a critical area of differentiation and importance among older adults and is also an embedded factor within ethnic identity and sexual orientation.

Finally, an area of diversity that is critical in the lives of older adults is the presence of disability, which intersects across aging, gender, and minority status. Disability of mobility, sensory processes (vision, hearing), language (post stroke), and cognition (dementia or other mental limitations) are reported by 4.8 million older adults (National Institutes of Health, 2006). This does not take into account the many disabling effects of the chronic health problems endemic in late life. Again, these data are also influenced by the intersection of ethnic minority status, in which African Americans and Hispanics are disproportionately represented among disabled older persons (Song, Chang, Tirodkar, Chang, Manheim, & Dunlop, 2007). Also, it is known that abusive behavior, often by family members, shows an increase toward disabled and therefore more vulnerable disabled older adults (Drayton-Hargrove, 2000).

All of these areas of diversity among older adults require a knowledgeable and calibrated approach in providing counseling and psychological services. This requires a familiarity with the issues discussed above and also the application of sensitive listening and attending skills that can grasp the specific concerns of the individual older person.

Clinical Work with an Older Adult Population

Working with older adults who are experiencing emotional distress starts with an underlying knowledge of normal aging, and differentiation of when symptoms go outside the overall norms. The older adult population, more than any other, has the highest coexistence of physical and emotional ailments. An accurate diagnosis and follow-up treatment calls for an investigative approach, looking at the entire picture in order to answer, "To what extent is this disturbance due to psychological, environmental, or physical factors?" Older adults experience a number of mental disorders, many which are highlighted below. An expanded review of mental health issues affecting older adults is offered through an extensive literature review completed by the Surgeon General (U.S. Department of Health and Human Services, 1999).

All too often older individuals, their family members, and even professionals mistakenly accept depression as a normal part of the aging process. This belief is especially unfortunate for those who first develop depression late in life, when such resignation can prevent the individual from receiving effective care. Research suggests an increasing risk of depression with age, as statistics indicatethe prevalence of depression is 8% to 16% in community-dwelling older persons (Weyerer et al., 2008). However, it is not age, per se, that causes depression, but rather impairment in physical health and the perceptions of health status. It is important to distinguish that increased risk of depression is due to decreased health, and not directly to age; physically healthy, normal functioning older adults are at no greater risk of depression than are younger adults. However, complicating the diagnosis of depression is often the overlap of symptoms of a chronic illness, progressive dementia, or the propensity for somatic symptoms. Older adults experiencing a mental disorder tend to approach their medical providers with persistent physical symptoms including headaches, gastrointestinal problems, and chronic pain, which often leads to depressed states among the elderly being neglected, underdiagnosed, and undertreated (Lebowitz et al., 1997; NIH Consensus Development Panel on Depression in Late Life, 1992).

Older Americans are disproportionately likely to die by suicide: Representing only 12% of the U.S. population, nonetheless individuals aged 65 and older accounted for 16% of all suicide deaths in 2004 (Centers for Disease Control and Prevention, NationalCenter for Injury Prevention and Control, 2005).Recent research has indicated that suicide is most related to physical illness, with older white men over the age of 85 being most at risk for completion (Centers for Disease Control and Prevention,

National Center for Injury Prevention and Control, 2005).

It is critical to distinguish between later-life patients expressing suicidal ideation due to depression and those indicating they are "ready to die." Many older adults who are not suffering from depression will openly state, "I wish it was my time," or more directly indicate that they would like to die. Upon further exploration, the majority of these older adults are identifying that they have enjoyed a full and productive life, and view their death in somewhat objective and realistic terms. As one 83-year-old woman summarized, "I know I have more years behind me than I do ahead of me. I am ready to go when it's my time."

Anxiety disorders, or the "silent geriatric giant," remain one of the most common psychiatric disorders of later life (Cassidy & Rector, 2008). More than 10% of adults aged 55 years and older meet criteria for an anxiety disorder in 1 year (Flint, 1994). However, actual occurrence may be even higher given its coexistence with depression, medical disorders, and dementia, although issues in relation to comorbidity and the nature of anxiety in old age remain unresolved (Bryant, Jackson, & Ames, 2008). In fact, numerous medical conditions such as chronic obstructive pulmonary disease, hypertension, overactive thyroid, and Parkinson's disease can mimic or even cause symptoms of anxiety. The same can be seen as side effects of various medications, both prescription and over-the-counter.

Alcohol use among older adults is thought to be one of the fastest growing health problems in the country, and is the third leading health problem among Americans 55 years of age and older (King, Van Hasselt, & Segal, 1994). Although alcohol abuse among seniors has only recently begun to receive adequate empirical attention (Substance Abuse and Mental Health Services Administration, 2005), it is clear that older adults are at a higher risk for developing alcohol-related problems as age modifies the body's responses to alcohol, including the manner and rate of absorption, distribution, and excretion.

Although prescription medication abuse affects many Americans, a concerning trend can be seen among older adults that suggests that prescription abuse is on the rise. Persons 65 years of age and older account for approximately 33% of all medications prescribed in the United States, and older patients are more likely to be prescribed long-term and multiple prescriptions, which could lead to unintentional misuse (Special Committee on Aging, 1987).

Because of their high rates of comorbid illnesses, changes in drug metabolism with age, and the potential for drug interactions, prescription and over-the-counter drug abuse and misuse can have more adverse health outcomes. In addition, older adults have the poorest rates of compliance with directions for taking medication (Glantz & Leshner, 2000).

The misuse of alcohol or prescription medications by older adults has been viewed as the "invisible epidemic" both in the literature and in practice. Addiction to alcohol or prescription medications can also be missed due to the client's reduced social and occupational functioning. Signs may more often present as poor self-care, unexplained falls, malnutrition, and medical illnesses. Older adults may attempt to cope with challenges by drinking alcohol or misusing prescription medications, rather than seeking psychological treatment; they may routinely use pharmacological interventions to deal with feelings of depression or physical pain, which then leads to an addiction or abuse problem.

Unfortunately, problems resulting from substance abuse may be missed due to the attitudes held by psychologists as well as other health practitioners. Clinicians may be likely to avoid the topic of alcohol or drug use because it can be a difficult topic to discuss with older patients. There may be a misguided belief that it is not necessary to screen for substance-related problems in older adults because these patients cannot be treated "successfully," or that the time and energy required to treat substance abuse is too great for patients who are so close to the end of their lifespans (Sharp & Vacha-Haase, in press).

Given the numerous life changes experienced by older adults, many elderly clients may present with situational difficulties or adjustment issues. These may include loss, death and dying, physical and mental health changes, chronic illness and disability, and debilitating pain. End-of-life issues are often at the forefront of the older client's presenting problems. Although choices for preferences at the end of life have received increasing recognition, they are often neglected and perhaps even ignored by family members. Having these conversations is the best way to protect one's autonomy in many unpredictable situations.

Similar to younger adults, an older adult population also includes those with a personality disorder. Current estimates suggest that approximately 10% of community-dwelling older adults exhibit a personality disorder (Widiger & Seidlitz, 2002). When a personality disorder is suspected, it is important to establish that these characteristics and behaviors were present in earlier adulthood, and cannot be better accounted for at this time by physiological causes such as neurological disease (e.g., multiple sclerosis, Parkinson's disease), a stroke, or dementia. Personality changes often precede or accompany several neurological or medical conditions that have higher prevalence rates in older adulthood (Balsis, Carpenter, & Storandt, 2005). In addition, consistent problematic behavioral symptoms being reported must be verified to ensure that these inflexible behaviors are longstanding, and neither an outcome of the current situation or due to a crisis, nor reactions to severe prolonged stress. Zweig (2008) provided an overview for empirically informed assessment of personality disorder in older adults.

Working with behavioral difficulties in older adults is an emerging area in which psychologists can provide assessment and intervention. These clients are often found living in communities, such as assisted living or LTC facilities (Snyder, Chen, & Vacha-Haase, 2007). Behaviors such as agitation, yelling or shouting, or inappropriate sexual activities are best managed through a behavioral modification or environmental approach. Pharmacological treatments for behaviors are generally ill advised and often not effective. Clinicians are expanding their expertise in working with older adults who are increasingly cognitively impaired (Logsdon, McCurry, & Teri, 2007).

Research consistently supports the decrease of memory and speed of thought processing with age, but with little agreement on the specific domains or timing of cognitive decline (Lindenberger & Ghisletta, 2009). Although few 80-year-olds would deny changes in their cognitive functioning compared to when they were 40, cognitive change is predominated by individual differences. For some people, decline occurs rapidly and appears extreme. For others, decline may be a slow and gradual process, or may not appear to occur at all until late life. It seems that cognitive decline in late life is not as extensive or as devastating as once thought.

The most natural or benign memory loss is referred to as *age-associated memory impairment*, and predominantly occurs in many people over the age of 50, who must work harder to remember things. Mild cognitive impairment (MCI) is an advancing memory deficit, but one that does not meet criteria for diagnosis of dementia (Petersen et al., 2001). It is the transitionary stage between age-related memory changes and more serious problems associated with dementia. Mild cognitive impairment is

characterized by difficulties remembering names, following a conversation, or misplacing things; increased difficulty in complex planning may also occur above and beyond normal changes with age. The person is generally aware of the increasing "senior moments," but is able to successfully compensate for the cognitive decline.

The number of older adults experiencing MCI who go on to be diagnosed with dementia is not well known. However, as noted previously, many older adults will be diagnosed with dementia, a chronic decrease in memory in addition to impairment in at least one other area of thought process, including impaired judgment, problemsolving, emotional regulation, or language ability (American Psychiatric Association, 1994). *Dementia* is an overarching descriptive term, describing a number of symptoms affecting the thought process. A number of disorders cause dementia, with Alzheimer's disease being the most common type for people over the age of 65. *Vascular dementia* is another common type of dementia, caused by cerebrovascular or cardiovascular problems—usually strokes. A third type of dementia frequently seen in the elderly is that of *Lewy body dementia*, often linked with neurological disorders such as Parkinson's disease.

Created by an APA presidential task force, the Guidelines for the Evaluation of Dementia and Age-Related Cognitive Decline (American Psychological Association [APA], 1998) was the first effort to provide an overview of the knowledge, skill, and unique ethical issues related to assessing cognitive changes. More recently, APA partnered with the American Bar Association Commission on Law and Aging to author the *Assessment of Older Adults with Diminished Capacity: A Handbook for Psychologists* (American Bar Association and APA, 2008). Not only does this handbook include helpful legal definitions and practical information regarding assessing varying capacities (e.g., sexual, driving, financial, medical), but it provides a listing and description of cognitive functioning and corresponding neuropsychological assessments to use in evaluations.

Psychological Interventions

The core of effectively working with older adults in both psychotherapy and assessment is a strong foundation of basic clinical skills (Duffy, 1992), with modifications made to meet the unique complexity of needs in the later-life client (Knight et al., 2009). When working with later-life clients, counseling psychologists most likely will interact with professionals from other specialties, including physicians, nurses, social workers, dieticians, and physical and occupational therapists. In addition to a myriad of health care providers, extended family members and other caregivers may also be involved in the client's care.

It is well known that older adults are at risk for physical and mental decline, with potential problems of vision, hearing, mobility, or cognitive slowing. If hearing is a challenge, the therapist may want to speak slightly lower, louder, and slower, remembering that maintaining eye contact is vital. Materials printed in a larger font are often useful, as is paying particular attention to lighting, temperature control, appropriate seating (avoiding chairs that are too low and difficult to get up out of), and ease of accessibility (with a walker, cane, or wheelchair).

The majority of counseling psychologists working with older adults will provide psychological services such as individual talk therapy, group therapy, psychological assessment, neuropsychological evaluation, and staff or family education. Regardless of the method of service delivery, clarifying the presenting problem and differential diagnosis are essential to effective intervention. For example, a psychologist completing an intake with a client presenting with symptoms of anxiety should rule out medical causes, in addition to recent cognitive and personality changes. Appropriate interventions will not only be varied given the clinical problem, but also influenced by the context and characteristics of the person. For example, even if the diagnosis and context are similar, the psychological intervention may be different if the client is a retired African American university professor versus a migrant farm worker. Even if they have both just been diagnosed with terminal cancer, a 95-year-old Hispanic women living independently in the community will require a different approach than will a 77-year-old man who is bedridden in a LTC facility.

At times, interactions with an older adult client may be somewhat informal, taking on a "conversational" quality. In response to clinical questions, some older adults may offer additional information, sometimes with a "story-telling" quality. For example, a specific question about appetite may solicit a response that includes preferences for cooking, increased stomach problems, and associated bowel problems, with a summary, "I just don't have an appetite anymore."

When working with older adults, attention to vocabulary and use of specific words calls for additional consideration. Many current, commonly used words may have little meaning for older adults (e.g., "hooking up," "awesome," or "hanging out"). Use of general psychological terms such as "depression," "anxiety," "cognitive impairment," and "dementia" may cause unnecessary concern to the older adult, and on occasion even initial denial of symptoms. Older clients may tend to say that they are "feeling blue," "not felt like myself lately," or "been down in the dumps." More anxious clients may state they have "felt more on edge lately" or experienced a "hard time relaxing." Client reaction to terminology is determined not only by age, but also by education level, cohort, religious preference, culture, and geographical surroundings.

Critical to working with older adults is avoiding "elder speak." That is, speaking too loud or slow to an older adult who does not having a hearing impairment, treating them like children, or using a term of endearment such as "sweetie," "honey," or "dear." Although perhaps meant in a positive way, recent research indicates that elder speak is more likely to be experienced as an insult, supporting negative views of aging, and possibly even increasing negative health consequences (Collins, 2008; Lelenad, 2008; Ryan, Giles, Bartolucci, & Henwood, 1986; Ryan, Hummert, & Boich, 1995). One resource offering further guidance in communicating with older adults is *Talking with Your Older Patient: A Clinician's Handbook* (National Institute of Aging, 2009).

In addition, a significant part of working with older adults is self-awareness, in particular being conscious of one's own biases. Skilled clinicians are aware of personal preconceptions, while being sensitive to the within-group differences of older adults (Crowther & Zeiss, 2003). Even in today's society, many myths and stigmas are attached to growing older, leading to misinformation and "ageism." Older people are often thought of as being "all alike," and often mistakenly portrayed as being weak, fragile, senile, asexual, and incompetent.

A number of individual psychotherapeutic interventions have been offered in effective treatment with older adults, including interpersonal psychotherapy (Hinrichsen, 2008), cognitive-behavioral treatments (e.g., Knight & Satre, 2006; Stanley, Beck, & Glassco, 1996), and reminiscence therapy (Fielden, 1992). However, in an extensive review, Scogin and McElreath (1994) suggested that no single modality of psychological intervention is most effective for older adults. Although the best intervention for mental disorders faced by older adults is not currently known, it is recognized that older adults do benefit from both individual psychotherapy (Scogin & McElreath, 1994) and group treatment (Payne & Marcus, 2008). Research also suggests that older adults find psychological intervention to be an acceptable treatment (Lebowitz et al., 1997), despite identifiable barriers such as physical access, financial resources, cognitive limitations, and attitudinal issues (Yang & Jackson, 1998).

Although significant progress is being made regarding empirically supported treatments (ESTs) or evidence-based practice (EBPP) for older clients, this research remains in its infancy. Future clinicians will undoubtedly have access to more specific treatments as research continues to expand with older adult populations. A significant contribution was provided recently in a special section on evidence-based psychological treatment for older adults, published in *Psychology and Aging* in 2007. Scogin (2007) and his colleagues provided reviews of psychological treatment for anxiety (Ayers, Sorrell, Thorp, & Wetherell, 2007), insomnia (McCurry, Logsdon, Teri, & Vitiello, 2007), and behavior disturbances among older adults suffering from dementia (Logsdon et al., 2007). An additional article (Gallagher-Thompson & Coon, 2007) reviewed treatment strategies for family caregivers of older adults.

Not only is psychological treatment effective (Scogin & McElreath, 1994), but negative side effects of this type of intervention are limited (Sperry, 1995). Given that, on average, older adults between 60 to 65 fill 13.6 prescriptions per year, and those 80 to 84 years old average 18.2 prescriptions per year (American Society of Consultant Pharmacist, 2003), pharmacological intervention for mental disorders significantly increases the risk for adverse interactions (Arnold, 2008). Research has shown that, with mild clinical depression, psychotherapy is as effective as chemical intervention and has no adverse side effects (Sperry, 1995). For more severe depression, treatment is most successful if psychotherapy is utilized in addition to medication, as this can drastically reduce the noncompliance rate of medication use as well as contribute to longer-lasting change (Little et al., 1998; Reynolds et al., 1999).

Cognitive Assessment and Neuropsychological Evaluation
Although many of the important aspects of clinical assessment would be similar regardless of client age (e.g., psychometric properties of the instrument), a number of areas are also unique to working with older adults. A number of neuropsychological

screening instruments are available, ranging from those that are broad, to those that are more specific or narrow in nature. Regardless of the specific measurement chosen, it is important to be sensitive to normative information based on older samples, keeping in mind the limits of using assessment instruments created for younger persons with older adults, but without adequate standardization.

In addition to cognitive screening, assessment of an older adult's "capacity" or "diminished capacity" for decision making in a specific area may become the focus. In these situations, the aim is to be specific in regards to the situational or contextual capacity, asking, "Does the patient have capacity for _____?" (e.g., making a will, doing own finances, or making medical decision). Unfortunately, there is no "golden standard" or universal criteria for judging capacity, as it is contextual (which does not easily allow for one standard) and can change over time. The focus is on the client's functional ability, rather than the diagnosis, as a diagnosis by itself cannot determine capacity. In general, capacity is assessed in four main areas: medical (is the patient able to understand the medical procedure, by comprehending risk, benefit, and choice?); financial (what is the client's financial performance in handling change, paying bills, etc.? Is he or she able to act in his or her own best interest, with proper judgment about financial matters?); contractual (does the patient have the ability to comprehend the situation?); and, testamentary (is this person able to make a will; does he or she have a basic understanding of what a will is, who the heirs are, what constitutes his or her assets, and a plan for distribution?)

Training Counseling Psychologists to Work with Older Adults
Graduate training in professional psychology continues to be under pressure to respond to the growing number of elderly and their mental health needs (e.g., Fretz, 1993; Hinrichsen, Myers, & Stewart, 2000; Jacobs & Formati, 1998; Qualls, 1998). A previous survey determined that only 16 to 20 clinical and counseling psychology programs offered specialized training in aging (Blieszner, 1994). Hinrichsen, Myers, and Stewart (2000) identified 65 doctoral internship sites training in clinical geropsychology.

In 2004, the geropsychology training offered in APA-accredited counseling psychology programs was explored (Vacha-Haase, 2004). Written material from all accredited doctoral programs in counseling psychology (*n* = 73), as well as program websites for all accredited programs, were used to compile information in the following areas for each program: number of core faculty, number of faculty with "geriatrics" listed as an interest area, the availability of specializing in geropsychology, type of training offered in geropsychology, and whether coursework in geropsychology was offered on the university campus. Results indicated that 12% of the programs offered training in geropsychology through options such as a minor, concentration, track, or adaptation to the student's area of interest. In addition, another 8% of the programs offered coursework, such as a seminar or workshop focusing on geriatrics. According to written materials, counseling programs identified having from no faculty up to three faculty with an interest in geriatrics, either through their research or clinical work. The average number of faculty per program with geriatric interest was less than 1%.

Anecdotally, many have speculated that working with older adults is not viewed as interesting or exciting for faculty and students in counseling psychology programs. Others have focused on what is believed to be a limited amount of available interventions (e.g., only neuropsychological assessment services) or the idea that an older client cannot be "fixed" or "saved" or "really helped," as can a younger client. And, finally, others have focused strictly on economical issues, indicating low reimbursement rates for trained geropsychologists.

Although these misrepresentations are unfortunate, perhaps the last is of greatest concern, given that, over the past few years, Medicare reimbursement has been financially competitive with managed care companies' reimbursement rates. In July 2008, Congress provided for Medicare coinsurance parity for Medicare patients when it enacted the Medicare Improvements for Patients and Providers Act (MIPPA). Under MIPPA, mental health services will enjoy an 80%–20% split in coinsurance by 2014, with the phase-in to coinsurance parity for outpatient mental health services scheduled to begin in January 2010.

Over the past decade, a number of initiatives within the APA have produced guidance for practice and training in geropsychology. As a valuable product of the APA Interdivisional Task Force on Professional Geropsychology, the APA Guidelines for Psychological Practice with Older Adults (APA, 2004) were built on the profession's ethical guidelines, providing a background repertoire of academic and clinical knowledge in the field of aging. Rather than specific methods that must be followed, the document outlined areas of knowledge and clinical skills considered imperative to those working with an older population.

More recently, the Pike's Peak model for training in professional geropsychology (Knight et al., 2009) outlined options at the doctoral, internship, postdoctoral, and postlicensure level of training. Specifically, the Pike's Peak document focused on competencies that relate to attitudes toward older adults (e.g., combating stereotypical, ageist attitudes), knowledge (e.g., biological and psychological dimensions), and skills (e.g., assessment, psychotherapy, and consultation) in working with older adults. Also included in these competencies were age-specific informed consent and confidentiality guidelines, skills in capacity and competence evaluation, end-of-life decision making, and elder abuse and neglect. Complementing the training model, the Pike's Peak Geropsychology Knowledge and Skill Assessment Tool (Council of Professional Geropsychology Training Programs, CoPGTP, 2008) is a competency evaluation measure, providing ratings across levels (e.g., novice, intermediate, advanced, proficient, expert). The assessment scale assumes that the acquisition of competency in geropsychology is developmental in nature, and thus appropriate for both the graduate student in a specialized geropsychology program as well for the seasoned general practitioner attending continuing education workshops. The tool can be accessed at: http://www.uccs.edu/~cpgtp/Pikes%2520Peak%2520Evaluation%2520Tool%25201.1.pdf.

The Council of Professional Geropsychology Training Programs (http://www.usc.edu/programs/cpgtp/) was established in 2006. Now with over 30 members, CoPGTP includes programs and individuals that provide geropsychology training in psychology graduate, internship, and postdoctoral programs as well training to postlicensure psychologists. CoPGTP is committed to the promotion of excellence in and the development of high-quality training programs in professional geropsychology. CoPGTP is especially interested in facilitating access to resources in the acquisition of geropsychology knowledge and skill competencies during formal training at doctoral, internship, and postdoctoral levels, as well as among licensed psychologists who want to acquire this specialty later in their careers.

In response to impediments to increasing the numbers of trained clinicians working with older adults, the importance of clinical "exposure" to older clients and age-related course content within training programs has been noted (Koder & Helmes, 2008), with suggestions such as integration of content focusing on older adults into existing curriculum and offering a specialized geropsychology course (Hinrichsen, 2000). The following section describes a practicum model that is designed to give intensive geropsychology experience to counseling psychology doctoral students (Duffy, 1992; Qualls, Duffy, & Crose, 1995).

Doctoral students are offered the opportunity to take this practicum in geropsychology after the conclusion of their basic counseling practicum training. After initial orientation, class meetings are located in the various LTC facilities, retirement communities, or rehabilitation hospitals in which the practicum students are placed. Each week, the class rotates around these various facilities, utilizing rounds-type supervision, in which the instructor and students visit the practicum students' various older clients in their rooms using a naturalistic "home visit" format. One hour of the 3-hour group class period is devoted to a didactic and experiential presentation of a specific clinical topic as it relates to working with older adults, such as depression and aging, intergenerational family therapy, dementia assessment, and the like. These topics frequently involve a videotape of the instructor demonstrating the topic or relevant skill. Each week, students who do not receive supervision in the live, supervised rounds receive individual supervision focused on audio tape recordings, with special attention paid to dynamic and process aspects of their individual interactions with clients. Supervision, therefore, is experiential and involves two modalities: the first is the live group supervision in the resident's room, where the instructor/supervisor models and stimulates discussion with the resident, with increasing responsibility given to the supervisee. This is a group activity in which other members of the class are present and learn from the events. The second modality is individual, dynamic, process-oriented supervision based on audio tapes as available, and focusing on individual dynamics between the therapist and the client.

This type of intensive practicum training at the predoctoral level is usually quite engaging to students, even those who were hesitant to take part initially. An important gain is losing the inhibition that is understandably present when a 22-year-old student deals with an 85-year-old client. Also, a pragmatic effect of this kind of practicum experience is to give students a decided advantage in applying for internship positions that require either specific training in geropsychology or in general health psychology.

Counseling Psychology and Opportunity Within Geropsychology

Perhaps no other area offers counseling psychologists so many growing opportunities in today's healthcarefield as does the expanding need for those skilled in working with older adults. Many vibrant, well-established areas within counseling psychology have remained virtually untapped in application to an older population, leaving ample opportunity for counseling psychologists to expand their role with older adults.

One of counseling psychology's most senior and principal components, vocational psychology and career development (Brown & Lent, 2000; Gelso & Fretz, 2001), is an optimal example poised for expansion with an older population. As mentioned earlier, "second-time-around" careers are on the increase, and the topic is in much need of theoretical understanding, as well as vigorous research and practical applications. Many current vocational theories could be utilized to shed light on older adults who wish to return to the workforce after retiring from their initial occupation. Retirement is another area ripe for significant contributions from counseling psychology. In the general literature, the majority of the focus in retirement planning has traditionally been placed on financial preparation, with little attention given to other themes, such as identity changes or emotional experience. Counseling psychology's interest and expertise in vocational psychology could easily be extended into a critical understanding of retirement's dynamics and processes.

More specifically, the monumental contributions of Holland (1966, 1973, 1984) and Super (1957, 1963, 1980, 1994) have much to offer when extended into increasing the understanding of retirement satisfaction and possibly other later-life experiences. Holland's theory proposed that individuals tend to thrive in environments consistent with their personality types, and noted that stability and achievement depend on the congruence between one's personality and environment. Although he was referring to vocational satisfaction, these assertions would appear to be relevant to activities involving retirement choices, and even conceivably be extended for use in guidance when choosing living arrangements and making end-of-life decisions. Over a decade ago, Walsh and Chartrand (1994) called for the expansion of the person–environment (PE) interaction paradigm. Counseling psychologists could effectively increase efforts in extending this theory to retirement choices or to the choice of elder living environments, such assisted-living or LTC facilities.

Super's developmental focus on social context (life space) and self-concept also have a natural extension to older adults. In explaining his lifespan approach, while focusing on the differential salience of life roles during the life cycle, Super (1980) included the end of the lifespan, with one of the nine roles being "Pensioner" and a possible theater as "retirement community or home." His belief that "the more a person's abilities and interests find ready and temporally compatible outlets in the full range of the activities engaged in, the more successful and satisfied that person will be" (p. 287) seems to be as relevant to retirement and later years as it does to the vocational choice and career pattern to which he was actually referring.

Counseling psychology's strengths-based approach is a natural fit for the expanding need of a society that is increasingly focused on prevention in healthcare, capitalizing on the three roles identified as central throughout the history of the specialty—remedial (assisting people to remediate problems), prevention, and educative-developmental (Gelso & Fretz, 2001). With factors such as obesity and high-risk behaviors, such as smoking and substance abuse, implicated in health decline, counseling psychologists have much to contribute to the systematic provision of programmatic treatments.

Counseling psychologists can also be influential in increased disease management. In January 2002 (APA, 2002) codes for health and behavior assessment and intervention services (e.g., H & B codes) could be applied to behavioral, social, and psychophysiological procedures for the prevention, treatment, or management of physical health problems. Thus, psychologists are able to bill for services provided to patients who have a physical health diagnosis, rather than a mental health diagnosis, thus allowing a blend of physical and psychological services delivery. Through engaging in a comprehensive approach to patient care, the H & B codes pertain to psychological intervention that allows clients to improve health and functioning in a multitude of ways. For example, psychologists may focus on helping clients to engage in behaviors that help promote their health through supporting compliance to treatment or by providing motivation for various prescribed treatments. Psychologists may facilitate patient adjustment to physical illness, or address behaviors that keeps patients from effectively engaging in treatment. Some of the H & B services involve circumstances and behaviors related to food and eating, in which a psychologist can help to refine the dietary regimen to make it more palatable to the patient. H & B codes are also utilized in some circumstances in which, due to cognitive impairment, verbal psychotherapy is not an option, but in which significant psychological contributions will facilitate recovery or rehabilitation.

Assessment is another area in which counseling psychology can continue to expand upon its strengths. Not only is neuropsychological evaluation of great need, but so too is personality and behavioral assessment, including functional analysis. The individual approach to behavioral assessment allows for the unique causes of an individual's behaviors to be monitored, through a number of multiple methods and sources congruent with the expertise of counseling psychology. Through functional analysis, the attention to explaining the relationship between behavior and its causes facilitates the formulation of unique, context-specific and client-centered treatment plans that will lead to the greatest improvement. Because behavioral assessment is conceptually based and methodologically diverse, it is well suited for a wide range of clinical and research applications for describing and explaining behaviors among the diverse older adult population.

Counseling psychologists will also find much room for their expertise in the area of education and training. For over a decade, there has been a warning regarding the lack of professionals, including psychologists, trained to work with older patients. Thus, those who have a knowledge base for working with older adults will be in great demand as other mental health providers seek relevant education and training experiences. As noted above, working with older adults requires an interdisciplinary approach. This, too, provides challenges, as professionals must to learn how to collaborate effectively with one another. In addition, other healthcare fields will need skill sets for working with older adults, including basic knowledge of normal aging and development, as well as appropriate and sensitive interview techniques and skills in interacting with older adults. For example, those providing direct care, such as nurses and nursing assistants, can benefit from increased education (Brescian & Vacha-Haase, in press). Fields outside of healthcare will undoubtedly interact with a growing older adult population and also require specialized training. These groups include police officers, sales people, and even teachers who are working with grandparents raising grandchildren (Smith, Dannison, & Vacha-Haase, 1998).

Counseling psychology's foothold on inclusiveness and sensitivity to multicultural issues provides another example of areas of opportunity, given the increasing diversity among the older adult population. Whether it is through culturally sensitive training or prevention, treatment programs for the elderly, or advocacy for the needs for an older adult population, counseling psychology has much to offer regarding not only valuing differences, but understanding them and incorporating them into daily life.

At its most basic level, counseling psychology embraces social justice and advocacy by promoting the inclusion of and increased competence in working with older adults in both research and clinical settings. As counseling psychologists continue to enhance their involvement with social justice, social action, and advocacy, older adults can receive support, and ageism can be opposed at all levels. Recognition of social and economical issues, both individually and within society, emphasizes the aim for equity and fair distribution of resources for older adults. Older adults and their families can be empowered to seek the resources and support they require to maintain dignity and basic human rights.

At the organizational level, just as racism is addressed through changing institutional policies to promote advocacy against it (Arredondo et al., 1996), counseling psychologists can help to address institutional ageism. For example, counseling psychologists might call for fair practices for older adults in the workplace; increased accessibility to health care for the poorest of older adults; and support of human rights, such as privacy while in a nursing home, or the right for older LGTB individuals to name life-long partners as executors of their power of attorney or have the same visitation rights as heterosexual couples. They can promote these changes through organizing community agency partnership, influencing the legislative process, and increasing their role in policy setting in regards to the welfare of older adults. Counseling psychologists can call for the profession to be more activist oriented (Toporek, Gerstein, Fouad, Roysircar, & Israel, 2006), questioning a system that disempowers an older adult's choice in areas such as preference for housing, medical treatment, or end-of-life decisions.

Counseling psychologists are well situated to meet the needs of healthy older adults interested in prolonging a high quality of life. This generation is the first of many to be more health minded, and more open to psychological intervention, outreach, and prevention. Neuroscience is uncovering techniques to prevent cognitive decline, and creative services such as memory-enhancing programs, will no doubt be sought after by older generations that focus on brain fitness and increasingly know that "if you don't use it, you lose it." As noted above, prevention programs, including those that promote weight loss or a decrease in high-risk behaviors, will most likely be in high demand. Counseling psychologists can provide a positive impact by encouraging older adults to adopt healthier behaviors and obtain regular health screenings that can reduce the risk for many chronic diseases and help decrease the health disparities that currently exist.

At the other end of the health continuum, there is need for counseling psychologists who are willing to work with the most frail and demented elderly. Psychologists have only begun to scratch the surface of the psychological interventions that can be provided to increase quality of life for those with dementia, as well as to provide support for their caregivers and family (Duffy, 1999a, 2005, 2006), including diverse and culturally sensitive approaches (Borrayo, Goldwaser, Vacha-Haase, & Hepburn, 2007). A critical role for counseling psychologists has emerged in the need to enhance care for institutionalized elders, as LTC settings pose a particular challenge to the maintenance of mental health, given that physical and social conditions have a pervasive and continuing effect on residents.

The future also holds ample opportunity for counseling psychologists to be influential in continuing to provide progressive care through more effective pain management. Whether through behavioral changes in the early stages of an older adult's life, or through pain management techniques to ease severe or chronic pain, psychological intervention has much to offer.

Counseling psychologists can also play a prominent role in providing holistic, culturally sensitive end-of-life care. Utilizing their strengths-based approach and embracing the value of individual differences, counseling psychologists can ultimately help both older adults and their families during the dying process. Given that two states (Oregon and Washington) now have legalized physician-assisted suicide, which allows physicians to prescribe a lethal dose of drugs for mentally competent patients with less than 6 months to live, the focus on choices at the end of life is more prominent than ever.

The employment opportunities for working with older adults are likely to expand. For example, Veteran Administration (VA) hospitals will not only continue to rely on doctoral-level psychologists, but most likely will continue to enlarge its programs for frailer, declining older adults, offering assistance through home and long-term care environments. Additional government opportunities will surface as increased focus is given to women (male patrons have been the main recipients of VA care) and families.

Additional opportunities will continue to emerge from independent practice, both within the community on an outpatient basis, as well as through older adult living communities. Given that those living in independent and assisted-living facilities are often among the least cared for adults, these communities are in need of psychological services, including prevention programs. In addition, the need for psychologists in LTC settings will continue to exist and most likely expand.

The aging of the U.S. population is one of the major societal occurrences in the 21st century. More than ever before, focus is on the process of healthy aging, highlighting the optimal physical, mental, and social well-being and functioning of older adults. Encapsulated within the increasing older population comes both grave challenges and momentous opportunity. There is much that counseling psychologists can do to contribute to the number of older adults who will live longer, high-quality, productive, and independent lives. The profession's strengths-based, developmental approach, steeped within sensitivity to multiculturalism and social advocacy, highlights the important contributions possible to this rapidly aging and diverse population. Counseling psychologists are encouraged to include older adults in their practice, theory development, and research, and strive to combat ageism at all levels, being active in the support of equity and empowerment for all older adults.

References

American Bar Association and the American Psychological Association. (2008). Assessment of older adults with diminished capacity: A handbook for psychologists. Retrieved from http://www.apa.org/pi/aging/capacity_psychologist_handbook.pdf.

American Psychiatric Association. (1994). Diagnostic and statistical manual of mental disorders (4th ed.). Washington, DC: American Psychiatric Association.

American Psychological Association (APA). (2002). APA Practice directorate announces new health and behavior CPT codes. Retrieved from http://www.apa.org/practice/cpt_2002.html.

American Psychological Association (APA). (2004). Guidelines for psychological practice with older adults. American Psychologist, 59, 236–260.

American Psychological Association, Presidential Task Force on the Assessment of Age-Consistent Memory Decline and Dementia. (1998). Guidelines for the evaluation of dementia and age-related cognitive decline. Washington, DC: American Psychological Association.

American Society of Consultant Pharmacist. (2003). Seniors at risk: Medication-related problems among older Americans. Alexandria, VA: American Society of Consultant Pharmacists Research and Education Foundation.

Arnold, M. (2008). Polypharmacy and older adults: A role for psychology and psychologists. Professional Psychology: Research and Practice, 39, 283–289.

Arredondo, P., Toporek, R., Brown, S. P., Jones, J., et al. (1996). Operationalization of the multicultural counseling competencies. Journal of Multicultural Counseling & Development, 24, 42–78.

Atchley, Robert. (1994). Social forces and aging. Belmont, CA: Wadsworth Publishing.

Ayers, C. R., Sorrell, J. T., Thorp, S. R., & Wetherell, J. L. (2007). Evidenced-based psychological treatments for late-life anxiety. Psychology and Aging, 22, 8–17.

Balsis, S., Carpenter, B. D., & Storandt, M. (2005). Personality change precedes clinical diagnosis of dementia of the Alzheimer type. Journal of Gerontology: Psychological Sciences, 60, 98–101.

Baltes, P. B., & Baltes, M. M. (1990). Psychological perspectives on successful aging: A model of selective optimization with compensation. In P. B. Baltes and M. M. Baltes (Eds.), Successful aging: Perspectives from the behavioral sciences. New York: Cambridge University Press.

Blieszner, R. (1994). Doctoral programs in adult development and aging. Washington, DC: American Psychological Association, Division 20.

Borrayo, E. A., Goldwaser, G., Vacha-Haase, T., & Hepburn, K. W. (2007). An inquiry into Latino caregivers' experience caring for older adults with Alzheimer's disease and related dementias. Journal of Applied Gerontology, 26, 486–505.

Brenes, G. A., Knudson, M., McCall, W. V., Williamson, J. D., Mille, M. E., & Stanley, M. A. (2008). Age and racial differences in the presentation and treatment of Generalized Anxiety Disorder in primary care. Journal of Anxiety Disorders, 22, 1128–1136.

Brescian, N. E., & Vacha-Haase, T. (2007, August). Certified nursing assistants in long-term care: Exploring the relationship between locus of control and patient aggression. Poster session presented at the meeting of the American Psychological Association, San Francisco, CA.

Brown, S. D., & Lent, R. W. (2000). Handbook of counseling psychology. New York: John Wiley & Sons.

Bryant, C., Jackson, H., & Ames, D. (2008). The prevalence of anxiety in older adults: Methodological issues and a review of the literature. Journal of Affective Disorders, 109, 233–250.

Cassidy, K., & Rector, N. A. (2008). The silent geriatric giant: Anxiety disorders in late life. Geriatrics Aging, 11, 150–156.

Cavanaugh, J. C. (1997). Adult development and aging (3rd. ed.). New York: Brooks/ColePublishing Company.

Centers for Disease Control and Prevention, National Center for Injury Prevention and Control. Web-based Injury Statistics Query and Reporting System (WISQARS) [online]. (2005). Retrieved January 31, 2007 from www.cdc.gov/ncipc/wisqars.

Center for Disease Control and Prevention. (2007). The state of aging and health in America. Retrieved January 18, 2009 from www.cdc.gov/aging/pdf/saha_2007.pdf.

Chandler, J. D., & Chandler, J. E. (1988). The prevalence of neuropsychiatric disorders in a nursing home population. *Journal of Geriatric Psychiatry Neurology, 1,* 71–76.

Christianson, S. L., & Palvovitz, R. (1998). Exploring Erikson's psychosocial theory of development: Generativity and its relationship to paternal identity, intimacy, and involvement in childcare. *The Journal of Men's Studies, 7*(1), 133–156.

Clarfield, A. M. (2005). Reversible dementia the implications of a fall in prevalence. *Age and Ageing, 34,* 544–545.

Collins, A. T. (2008, July 28). "Baby talk" irritates Alzheimer's patients: Caregivers for the elderly should avoid certain patterns of speech. *ABC Medical Unit.* Retrieved from http://abcnews.go.com/Health/ActiveAging/story?id=5452861&page=1.

Conwell, Y., & Thompson, C. (2008). Suicidal behavior in elders. *Psychiatric Clinics of North America, 3,* 333–356.

Corrada, M. M., Brookmeyer, R., Berlau, D., Paganini-Hill, A., & Kawas, C. H. (2008). Prevalence of dementia after age 90: Results from the 90+ study. *Neurology,* July. Online.

Council of Professional Geropsychology Training Programs. (2008). *Pikes Peaks Geropsychology Knowledge and Skill Assessment Tool.* Retrieved from http://www.uccs.edu/~cpgtp/Pikes%2520Peak%2520Evaluation%2520Tool%25201.1.pd.

Crose, R. (1999). Addressing late life developmental issues for women: Body image, sexuality and intimacy. In M. Duffy (Ed.), *Handbook of counseling and psychotherapy with older adults.* New York: Wiley.

Crowther, M. R., & Zeiss, A. M. (2003). Aging and mental health. In J. S. Mio & G. Y. Iwamasa (Eds.), *Culturally diverse mental health: The challenge of research and resistance* (pp. 309–322). New York: Brunner-Routledge.

Drayton-Hargrove, S. (2000). Assessing abuse of disabled older adults: A family systems approach. *Rehabilitation Nursing, 25,* 136–140.

Davenport, D. (1999). Dynamics and treatment of middle generation women: Heroines and victims of multigenerational families. In M. Duffy (Ed.), *Handbook of counseling and psychotherapy with older adults.* New York: Wiley.

Duffy, M. (1992). A multimethod model for practicum and clinical supervision in nursing homes. *Counselor Education and Supervision, 32,* 61–69.

Duffy, M. (1999a). Using process dimensions in psychotherapy: The case of the older adult. In M. Duffy (Ed.), *Handbook of counseling and psychotherapy with older adults.* New York: Wiley.

Duffy, M. (1999b). Reaching the person behind the dementia: Treating co-morbid affective disorders through subvocal and non-verbal strategies. In M. Duffy (Ed.), *Handbook of counseling and psychotherapy with older adults.* New York: Wiley.

Duffy, M. (2005). Strategies for working with women with dementia. In F. K. Trotman and C. Brody (Eds.), *Women therapists working with older women.* New York: Springer.

Duffy, M. (2006). Psychotherapeutic interventions for older persons with dementing disorders. In C. Brody, *Strategies for therapy with the elderly:Living with hope and meaning* (2nd ed.). New York: Springer.

Eisold, B. K. (2005). Notes on lifelong resilience: Perceptual and personality factors implicit in the creation of a particular adaptive style, *Psychoanalytic Psychology, 22,* 411–425.

Erickson, E. H. (1959). Identity and the life cycle: Selected papers. *Psychological Issues Monographs, 1,* 1–177.

Erikson, E. H. (1963). *Childhood and society.* New York: Norton.

Fielden, M. A. (1992). Depression in older adults: Psychological and psychosocial approaches. *British Journal of Social Work, 22,* 291–307.

Fiske, A., Wetherell, J. L., & Gatz, M. (2009). Depression in older adults. *Annual Review of Clinical Psychology, 5,* 363–389.

Fitzpatrick, K., E., & Vacha-Haase, T. (in press). Marital satisfaction and resilience in caregivers of spouses with dementia. *Clinical Gerontologist, 33,* 165–180

Flint, A. J. (1994). Epidemiology and comorbidity of anxiety disorders in the elderly. *American Journal of Psychiatry, 151,* 640–649.

Fretz, B. R. (1993). Counseling psychology: A transformation for the third age. *The Counseling Psychologist, 21,* 154–170.

Gallagher-Thompson, D., & Coon, D. W. (2007). Evidence-based psychological treatments for distress in family caregivers of older adults. *Psychology and Aging, 22,* 37–51.

Gatz, M., Bengtson, V. L., & Blum, M. J. (1990). Caregiving families. In J. E. Birren & K. W. Schaie (Eds.), *Handbook of the psychology of aging* (3rd ed., pp. 404–426). San Diego, CA: Academic Press.

Gatz, M., Karel, M. J., & Wolkenstein, B. (1991). Survey of providers of psychological services to older adults. *Professional Psychology: Research and Practice, 22,* 413–415.

Gelso, C., & Fretz, B. (2001). *Counseling psychology* (2nd ed.). Orlando, FL: Harcourt College.

Glantz, M. D. & Leshner, A. I. (2000). Drug abuse and developmental psychopathology. *Development and Psychopathology, 12,* 795–814.

Hettema, J., & Deary, I. J. (1993). *Foundations of personality: Proceedings of the NATO Advanced Research Workshop on Basic Issues in Personality.* New York: Springer.

Hill, R. D. (2005). *Positive aging: A guide for mental health professionals and consumers.* New York: W. W. Norton.

Hinrichsen, G. A. (2000). Knowledge of and interest in geropsychology among psychology trainees: *Professional Psychology: Research and Practice, 31,* 442–445.

Hinrichsen, G. A. (2008). Interpersonal psychotherapy for late life depression: Current status and new applications. *Journal of Rational-Emotive & Cognitive-Behavior Therapy, 26,* 263–275.

Hinrichsen, G. A., Myers, D. S., & Stewart, D. (2000). Doctoral internship training opportunities in clinical psychology. *Professional Psychology: Research and Practice, 31,* 88–92.

Holland, J. L. (1966). *The psychology of vocational choice: A theory of personality types and model environments.* Waltham, MA: Blaisdell.

Holland, J. L. (1973). *Making vocational choices: A theory of careers.* Englewood Cliffs, NJ: Prentice-Hall.

Holland, J. L. (1984). *Making vocational choices: A theory of careers* (2nd ed.). Englewood Cliffs, NJ: Prentice-Hall.

Huyck, M. H., & Gutmann, D. L. (1999). Developmental issues in psychotherapy with older men. In M. Duffy (Ed.), *Handbook of counseling and psychotherapy with older adults.* New York: Wiley.

Jacobs, S. C., & Formati, M. J. (1998). Older adults and geriatrics. In S. Roth-Roemer, S. E. R. Kurpius, & C. Carmin (Eds.), *The emerging role of counseling psychology in health care* (pp. 309–329). New York: W.W. Norton.

Karlin, B. E., & Duffy, M. (2006). Geriatric mental health policy: Impact on service delivery and directions for effecting change. *Professional Psychology: Research and Practice.*

Kessler, R. C., McGonagle, K. A., Zhao, S., Nelson, C. B., Hughes, M., Eshleman, S., et al. (1994). Lifetime and

12-month prevalence of DSM-III-R psychiatric disorders in the United States. *Archives of General Psychiatry. 51*, 8–19.

King, C., Van Hasselt, V., & Segal, D. (1994). Diagnosis and assessment of substance abuse in older adults: Current strategies and issues. *Addictive Behaviors, 19*, 41–55.

Knight, B. G., & Satre, D. D. (2006). Cognitive behavioral psychotherapy with older adults. *Clinical Psychology: Science and Practice, 6*, 188–203.

Knight, B. G., Karel, M. J., Hinrichsen, G. A., Qualls, S. H., & Duffy, M. (2009). Pikes Peak model for training in professional psychology. *The American Psychologist, 64*, 205–214.

Koder, D. A., & Helmes, E. (2008). Predictors of working with older adults in an Australian psychologist sample: Revisiting the influence of contact. *Professional Psychology: Research and Practice, 39*, 276–282.

Lebowitz, B. D., Pearson, J. L., Schneider, L. S., Reynolds III, C. F., Alexopoulos, G. S., Bruce, M. L., et al. (1997). Diagnosis and treatment of depression in late life: Consensus statement update. *Journal of the American Medical Association, 278*, 1186–1190.

Leland, J. (2008, October 6). In "sweetie" and "dear," a hurt for the elderly. *The New York Times.* Retrieved from http://www.nytimes.com/2008/10/07/us/07aging.html?_r=3&ref=health&oref=slogin&oref=slogin.

Lindenberger, U., & Ghisletta, P. (2009). Cognitive and sensory declines in old age. *Psychology and Aging, 24*, 1–16.

Little, J. T., Reynolds III, C. F., Dew, M. A., Frank, E., Begley, A. E., Miller, et al. (1998). How common is resistance to treatment in recurrent, nonpsychotic geriatric depression? *American Journal of Psychiatry, 155*, 1035–1038.

Logsdon, R. G., McCurry, S. M., & Teri, L. (2007). Evidenced-based psychological treatments for disruptive behaviors in individuals with dementia. *Psychology and Aging, 22*, 28–36.

Lombardo, N. E. (1994). *Barriers to mental health services for nursing home residents.* Washington, DC: American Association of Retired Persons.

Martin, K. L., & Vacha-Haase, T. (in press). Staff perceptions of resident sexual contact in long-term care facilities.

Matthews, S. H., & Sun, R. (2006). Incidence of four-generation family lineages: Is timing of fertility or mortality a better explanation? *The Journals of Gerontology Series B: Psychological Sciences and Social Sciences, 61*, S99–S106.

McCurry, S. M., Logsdon, R. G., Teri, L., & Vitiello, M. V. (2007). Evidenced-based psychological treatments for insomnia in older adults. *Psychology and Aging, 22*, 18–27.

MedPac. (2008). Long-term care hospitals payment system. Washington, DC: MedPac Retrieved at: www.medpac.gov/documents/MedPAC_Payment_Basics_08_LTCH.pdf.

Moak, G., & Borson, S. (2000). Mental health services in long-term care: Still an unmet need. *American Journal of Geriatric Psychiatry, 8*, 96–100.

Mandal, B., & Roe, B. (2008). Job loss, retirement and the mental health of older Americans. *Journal of Mental Health Policy and Economics, 11*, 167–176.

Morales, P. (1999). The impact of cultural differences in psychotherapy with older clients: Sensitive issues and strategies. In M. Duffy (Ed.), *Handbook of counseling and psychotherapy with older adults.* New York: Wiley.

Munley, P. H. (1974). A content analysis of the *Journal of Counseling Psychology. Journal of Counseling Psychology, 21*, 305–310.

National Gay and Lesbian Task Force. (2009). Aging. Retrieved from http://www.thetaskforce.org/issues/aging.

National Institute of Aging. (2009). Talking with your older patient: A clinician's handbook. Retrieved from http://www.nia.nih.gov/HealthInformation/Publications/ClinicianHB.

National Institutes of Health Consensus Development Panel on Depression in Late Life. (1992). Diagnosis and treatment of depression in late life. *Journal of the American Medical Association, 268*, 1018–1024.

National Institutes of Health. (2006). *Disability in older adults: Fact sheet.* Washington, DC: National Institutes of Health.

Payne, K. T., & Marcus, D. K. (2008). The efficacy of group psychotherapy for older adult clients: A meta-analysis. *Group Dynamics: Theory, Research, and Practice, 12*, 268–278.

Petersen, R. C., Doody, R., Kurz, A., Mohs, R. C., Morris, J. C., Rabins, P. V., et al. (2001). Current concepts in mild cognitive impairment. *Archives of Neurology, 58*, 1985–1992.

Pillemer, K, & McCartney, K. (Eds.). (1991). Parent-Child Relations Throughout Life. Hillsdale, NJ: Lawrence Erlbaum.

Qualls, S. H. (1998). Training in geropsychology: Preparing to meet the demand. *Professional Psychology: Research and Practice, 29*, 23–28.

Qualls, S., Duffy, M., & Crose, R. (1995). Supervision in community practicum settings. In *Handbook of Clinical Geropsychology.* Washington, DC: The American Psychological Association.

Qualls, S. H., Segal, D. L., Norman, S., Niederehe, G., & Gallagher-Thompson, D. (2002). Psychologists in practice with older adults: Current patterns, sources of training, and need for continuing education. *Professional Psychology: Research and Practice, 33*, 435–442.

Reynolds III, C. F., Frank, E., Perel, J. M., Imber, S. D., Cornes, C., Miller Mazumdar, S., et al. (1999). Nortriptyline and interpersonal psychotherapy as maintenance therapies for recurrent major depression: a randomized controlled trial in patients older than 59 years. *Journal of the American Medical Association, 28*, 39–45.

Ross, S. (2005). Alcohol use disorders in the elderly. *Primary Psychiatry, 12*, 32–40.

Rovner, B. W., German, P. S., Broadhead, J., et al. (1990). The prevalence and management of dementia and other psychiatric disorders in nursing homes. *International Psychogeriatrics, 2*, 13–24.

Rovner, B. W., Kafonek, S., Filipp, L., et al. (1986). Prevalence of mental illness in a community nursing home. *American Journal of Psychiatry, 143*, 1446–1449.

Rowe, J. W., & Kahn, R. L. (1998). *Successful Aging.* New York: Pantheon.

Ryan, E. B., Giles, H., Bartolucci, R. Y., & Henwood, K. (1986). Psycholinguistic and social psychological components of communication by and with the elderly. *Language and Communication, 6*, 1–24.

Ryan, E. B., Hummert, M. L., & Boich, L. (1995). Communication predicaments of aging: Patronizing behavior toward older adults. *Journal of Language Social Psychology, 14*, 144–166.

Scherman, A., & Doan, R. E., Jr. (1985). Subjects, designs, and generalizations in Volumes 25–29 of the *Journal of Counseling Psychology. Journal of Counseling Psychology, 32*, 272–276.

Schmidt, L. J., Rheinhardt, A. M., Kane, R. L., et al. (1977). The mentally ill in nursing homes: New backwards in the community. *Archives of General Psychiatry, 34*, 687–691.

Scogin, F. (2007). Introduction to the special section on evidenced-based psychological treatments for older adults. *Psychology and Aging, 22*, 1–3.

Scogin, F., & McElreath, L. (1994). Efficacy of psychosocial treatments for geriatric depression: A quantitative review. *Journal of Consulting and Clinical Psychology, 62*, 1, 69–74.

Seligman, M. E. P., & Csikszentmihalyi, M. (2000). Positive psychology: An introduction. *American Psychologist, 55*, 5–14.

Shanas, E. (1979). The family as a social support system in old age. *The Gerontologist, 19*: 169–174.

Smith, J., & Baltes, M. M. (1998). The role of gender in very old age: Profiles of functioning and everyday life patterns. *Psychology and Aging, 13*, 676–695.

Smith, A. B., Dannison, L., & Vacha-Haase, T. (1998). When "Grandma" is "Mom": What today's teachers need to know. *Childhood Education, 75*, 12–16.

Snyder, L. A., Chen, P. Y., & Vacha-Haase, T. (2007). Underreporting aggressive incidents from geriatric patients by certified nursing assistants. *Violence and Victims, 22*, 367–379.

Song, J., Chang, H. J., Tirodkar, M., Chang, R. W., Manheim, L. M., & Dunlop, D. D. (2007). Racial/ethnic differences in activities of daily living disability in older adults with arthritis. *Arthritis Care and Research* (doi: 10.1002/art.22906).

Special Committee on Aging. (1987). *Medicare prescription drug issues. Report to the Chairman, Special Committee on Aging.* Washington, DC: General Accounting Office.

Sperry, L. (1995). Psychopharmacology and psychotherapy. New York: Psychology Press.

Stanley, M. A., Beck, J. G., & Glassco, J. D. (1996). Treatment of generalized anxiety in older adults: A preliminary comparison of cognitive-behavioral and supportive approaches. *Behavior Therapy, 27*, 565–581.

Substance Abuse and Mental Health Services Administration. (2005). National survey on drug use and health. Rockville, MD: U.S. Department of Health and Human Services.

Super, D. E. (1957). *The psychology of careers.* New York: Harper, New York.

Super, D. E. (1963). Self-concepts in vocational development. In D. E. Super, R. Starishevsky, N. Matlin, & J. P. Jordaan (Eds.), *Career development: Self-concept theory* (pp. 1–16). College Entrance Examination Board. New York.

Super, D. E. (1980). A life-span, life-space approach to career development, *Journal of Vocational Behavior, 16*, 282–298.

Super, D. E. (1994). A life span, life space perspective on convergence. In M. L. Savickas & R. W. Lent (Eds.), *Convergence in career development theories: Implications for science and practice.* (pp. 63–74). Palo Alto: Consulting Psychologists Press.

Tariot, P. N., Podgorski, C. A., Blazina, L., & Leibovici, A. (1993). Mental disorders in the nursing home: Another perspective. *American Journal of Psychiatry, 150*, 1063–1069.

Thorson, J. A. (1995). *Aging in a changing society.* Belmont, CA: Wadsworth.

Toporek, R., Gerstein, L., Fouad, N., Roysircar, G., & Israel, T. (Eds.). (2006). Handbook of social justice in counseling psychology. New York: Sage.

United States Census. (2003). *Statistical abstract of the United States.* Washington, DC: US Bureau of the Census.

United States Census Bureau. (2001). The 65 years and over population: 2000. Retrieved from http://www.census.gov/prod/2001pubs/c2kbr01–10.pdf.

US Department of Health and Human Services. (1999). Mental health: A report of the surgeon general. Retried from http://www.surgeongeneral.gov/library/mentalhealth/home.html.

Vacha-Haase, T. (2004). Counseling psychology and geropsychology training. Unpublished manuscript.

Vacha-Haase, T., Wester, S. R., & Christianson, H. (in press). Psychotherapy with Older Men. New York: Routledge.

Walsh, W. B., & Chartrand, J. M. (1994). Emerging directions of person-environment fit. In M. L. Savickas & R. W. Lent(Eds.), Convergence in career development theories (pp. 187–195). Palo Alto, CA: CPP Books.

Werth, J. L., Kopera-Frye, K., Blevins, D., & Bossick, B. (2003). Older adult representation in the Counseling Psychology literature. *The Counseling* Psychologist, *31*, 789–814.

Weyerer, S., Eifflaender-Gorfer, S., Kšhler, L., Jessen, F., Maier, W., Fuchs, A. (2008). Prevalence and risk factors for depression in non-demented primary care attenders aged 75 years and older. *Journal of Affective Disorders, 111*(2-3), 153–163.

Whitbourne, S. R. (2005). *Adult development and aging.* New York: John Wiley & Sons.

Widiger, T. A., & Seidlitz, L. (2002). Personality, psychopathology, and aging. *Journal of Research in Personality, 36*, 335–362.

Xakellis, G. C. (2004). Who provides care to medicare beneficiaries and what settings do they use? *The Journal of the American Board of Family Practice, 17*, 384–387.

Yang, J. A., & Jackson, C. L. (1998). Overcoming obstacles in providing mental health treatment to older adults. *Psychotherapy, 35*, 498–505.

Zarit, S. H., Johansson, L., & Jarrott, S. E. (1998). Family caregiving: Stresses, social programs, and clinical interventions. In I. H. Nordhus, G. R. VandenBos, S. Berg, & P. Fromholt (Eds.), *Clinical geropsychology* (pp. 345–360). Washington, DC: American Psychological Association.

Zeiss. A. M., & Zeiss, R. A. (1999). Sexual dysfunction: Using an interdisciplinary team to combine cognitive-behavioral and medical approaches. In M. Duffy (Ed.), *Handbook of counseling and psychotherapy with older adults* (pp. 294–313). New York: Wiley.

Zweig, R. A. (2008). Personality disorder in older adults: Assessment challenges and strategies. *Professional Psychology: Research and Practice, 39*, 298–305.

Further Reading

Duffy, M. (Ed.). (1999). *Handbook of counseling and psychotherapy with older adults.* New York: Wiley.

Hill, R. D. (2005). *Positive aging: A guide for mental health professionals and consumers.* New York: W. W. Norton.

Molinari, V. (Ed.). (2000). *Professional psychology in long term care.* New York: Hatherleigh.

Norris, M. P., Molinari, V., & Ogland-Hand (Eds.). (2002). *Emerging trends in psychological practice in long term care.* New York: The Haworth Press, Inc.

Vacha-Haase, T., Wester, S. R., & Christianson, H. (2010). *Psychotherapy with older men.* New York: Routledge.

PART 4

Applications

Individual Counseling As an Intervention

Mary Ann Hoffman

Abstract

Individual counseling is the primary intervention of the practice component of the scientist–practitioner model and a frequent focus of research related to the scientific component. A timeline of historical events shaping individual counseling is presented, followed by an examination of commonalities across schools of therapy that define this intervention. These include why clients seek counseling; the therapeutic relationship; client expectancies; micro-skills; facilitating emotions, insight, and change in counseling; phases of counseling; and extra-therapeutic factors. The role of theory, with its focus on specific or unique effects, is examined and contrasted to the common factors approach. Conclusions and recommendations for future research are presented, including those areas in which there is some degree of consensus (e.g., need for research on the role of the relationship and insight) and areas in which there is divergence (e.g., specific or unique factors vs. common factors; transferability of evidence-based treatments to clinical settings; single theory vs. integrationist approaches).

Keywords: counseling, psychotherapy, therapeutic relationship, client expectancies, micro-skills, emotion-focused therapy, insight, therapeutic efficacy, common factors, specific factors, termination

Individual counseling is arguably the cornerstone of counseling psychology. Not only does it represent the primary intervention of the practitioner component of counseling psychology, but key aspects, such as process and outcome, comprise a large portion of the scholarly work representing the scientific aspect of the scientist–practitioner model. Graduate training devotes considerable time to mastering this intervention, and approximately half of members of the Society of Counseling Psychology report that they work in practice settings in which many likely utilize individual counseling as an intervention (American Psychological Association [APA], 2004). Yet, surprisingly, a review of the literature yields relatively few studies when the terms *individual counseling or psychotherapy* are entered into search engines, in contrast to those that appear for the many *components* of individual counseling, such as process, outcome, and the therapeutic relationship.

More is known about these components of individual counseling than about how they interact to form the sum of this intervention. To wit, the most highly cited literature reviews in the past 20 years have focused on components such as counseling process and outcome (e.g., Hill & Williams, 2008), the relationship or therapeutic alliance (e.g., Gelso & Carter, 1985), the process of therapy (e.g., Hill & Williams, 2000; Orlinsky & Howard, 1986), and treatment effects/outcome (e.g., Grissom, 1996; Wampold et al., 1997).

Paradoxically, at the same time that research has focused on the common *components* of individual counseling that are present across orientations (e.g., the therapeutic relationship), the number of purportedly distinct theories or systems of psychotherapy have proliferated. Beginning with psychoanalytic approaches in the early 1900s, relatively few systems of psychotherapy existed in the first part of the century. But, by the late 1950s, Harper (1959) had identified 36 systems of psychotherapy, most of which were individual approaches. Today, it is estimated that over 400 therapies exist, with all claiming unique characteristics and successful outcomes (Prochaska & Norcross, 2007). The staggering proliferation of systems of therapy might suggest that theoretical constructs and strategies unique to each system play the most important role in potentiating the effectiveness of individual counseling. Yet, research to date has provided more support for common factors in contrast to the specific or unique factors of these various therapies. One of the biggest debates today is not *whether* individual psychotherapy is effective but *why* and *how*.

Historical and Contemporary Factors Influencing Individual Counseling, with an Emphasis on Counseling Psychology

A complete history of individual counseling as an intervention is beyond the scope of this paper. In fact, some years ago, Jerome Frank (1982) noted that it would take over 250 pages to provide a historical *review* of the development of individual counseling, beginning with Freud, moving to the evolution of behavioral and humanistic approaches, and then moving to cognitive and affective approaches. With the more recent advent of feminist and multicultural theories that focus on sociopolitical forces, constructivist theories, and integrationist approaches, a historical review is an even more daunting undertaking. The *zeitgeist* of the time is one thread that has defined this evolution in schools of therapy. The timeline below presents significant events and trends that have shaped individual counseling including events, with special relevance to the development of counseling psychology:

- 1900: Sigmund Freud published *Interpretation of Dreams*, marking the beginning of psychoanalytic thought (Freud, 1953). Individual therapy is focused on the intrapsychic world of client and viewed as a "one-person" approach
- 1910–1930s: Key followers of Freud left his psychoanalytic group to form variations on this school of therapy (neo-Freudians); e.g., Alfred Adler, Carl Jung, Karen Horney.
- 1942: Humanistic focus begins with Carl Rogers' publication of *Counseling and Psychotherapy*. Individual therapy moves toward constructivism and a "two-person" approach.
- 1949: Boulder Conference outlined scientist–practitioner model of psychology

(led by development of clinical psychology and Veterans Administration role in training).
- 1951: Carl Rogers publishes *Client-centered Therapy* (Rogers, 1951), leading to emergence of humanist approaches including those of Abraham Maslow and Fritz Perls. Northwestern Conference on the Training of Counseling Psychologists (Division 17, Counseling and Guidance); terms "'counseling psychology'" and "'counseling psychologist'" introduced; defined focus as on adaptive versus maladaptive behavior across lifespan and on prevention (Super, 1955).
- 1952: Hans Eysenck's review of research concludes that therapy is no more effective than spontaneous remission. Division 17's name is changed to the Division of Counseling Psychology (see Munley, Duncan, McDonnell, & Sauer, 2004).
- 1953: B.F. Skinner outlined his theory of behavioral therapy (although behavioral approaches began in the 1920s).
- 1954: *Journal of Counseling Psychology* (JCP) begun Milton E. Hahn, Harold G. Seashore, Donald E. Super, and C. Gilbert Wrenn (see Wrenn, 1966).
- 1957: Albert Ellis and rational emotive behavior therapy are at forefront of cognitive therapies that emerged through next two decades (e.g., Aaron Beck).
- 1960s–1970s: Beginnings of contemporary psychodynamic approaches based on attachment theory (John Bowlby) and self-psychology theory (Hans Kohut).
- 1964: Greyston Conference (Division of Counseling Psychology) solidified identity and training of counseling psychologists (Thompson & Super, 1964).
- 1969: John Whiteley founded *The Counseling Psychologist* (TCP).
- 1977: Albert Bandura leads emergence of social learning theory, with move away from behaviorist and psychodynamic perspectives. Meta-analysis supports the efficacy of psychotherapy (Smith & Glass, 1977; does therapy work?).
- 1982: Carol Gilligan published *In a Different Voice* (Gilligan, 1982), on feminist psychology, and leads the way for feminist therapies.
- 1986: Albert Bandura continued to expand his work to social cognitive theory.
- 1987: Atlanta Conference (counseling psychology's third national conference) affirms value of the scientist–practitioner/

scientist–professional model; strengths including prevention; lifespan development; importance of culture, ethnicity, gender, and diversity (Kagan et al., 1988, p. 351).

• 1990s:- Narrative and other constructivist approaches develop (e.g., Michael White). Multicultural theories develop (e.g., Stanley Sue and Derald Wing Sue). Integrative and eclectic approaches begin to predominate over single-therapy models (e.g., John Norcross, Paul Wachtel, Arnold Lazarus). Evidence-based practice movement emerges (how and why does therapy work?).

• 2001: Houston's Fourth National Counseling Psychology Conference (emphasis on social justice) is held.

• 2003: Division 17 changes name to The Society of Counseling Psychology.

• 2008: Chicago International Counseling Conference (globalization of training, practice, and research) is held.

What we do know now is that individual counseling is quite effective. Since the publication of Eysenck's (1952) review of 24 studies that concluded that psychotherapy is no more effective than remission following no treatment in samples of neurotic clients, a number of meta-analyses and randomly controlled treatment studies across decades of research have clearly established the efficacy of psychotherapy in the treatment of clients with various diagnoses and presenting concerns (Elkin, Shea, Watkins, Imber, Sotsky, S. M, Collins, J. F., et al., 1989; Lambert & Bergin, 1994; Lipsey & Wilson, 1993; McNeilly & Howard, 1991; Orlinsky, Rønnestad, & Willutzki, 2004; Roth & Fonagy, 2005; Smith & Glass, 1977).

However, successful therapies of various orientations are described similarly by clients, suggesting that some common elements account for positive outcomes across therapeutic schools and systems (Lambert & Ogles, 2004). Jerome Frank was among the first to identify the importance of common processes across therapies based on his decades of research (1982). His classic paper continues to be persuasive in light of more recent research that has consistently found that common factors contribute to positive therapy outcomes. His findings remain timely in light of the current debate between common and specific factors and the efficacy of psychotherapy.

These identified common factors typically include the development of a therapeutic alliance, clients' positive expectancies about therapy, the opportunity for catharsis, self-awareness and insight, and the acquisition and practice of new behaviors. Proponents of the common factors model take the view that active ingredients shared by most systems of psychotherapy account for the majority of the variance in effective outcomes (e.g., Frank & Frank, 1991; Patterson, 1984; Wampold, 2001).

On the other side of the debate are proponents of the view that factors that are unique or specific to various theories or schools of therapy contribute to outcome beyond that accounted for by common factors (e.g., Crits-Christoph, 1997; Garfield, 1991); most of these researchers support the generic model that views outcomes as coming from a complex interaction of common and specific factors (e.g., Beutler & Harwood, 2002).

Currently, we know considerably less about outcome variance attributable to the *specific* ingredients of various treatments and approaches (Wampold, 2001; Wampold & Brown, 2005). For example, the relative contribution of specific methods effects to counseling outcomes is difficult to ascertain, as findings have been inconsistent across studies. Cognitive therapy is one of the best established approaches for successfully treating depression (Hollon & Beck, 2004). Yet, it is unclear whether changes in cognitions *mediate* changes in depression and anxiety or if some other mechanism of change is responsible for outcomes (e.g., Burns & Spangler, 2001). In sum, although we know that certain counseling processes contribute to the efficacy of therapy, the mechanisms that explain the *how* and *why* of positive outcomes are not yet well understood (Kazdin, 2006).

Because of the overwhelming number of theoretical systems of therapy and the current support for common factors across theories, the overarching framework for this chapter will be to examine individual counseling as an intervention drawing from commonalities that have been found in the literature. The chapter will begin by defining relevant terms; then, the reasons why clients seek therapy will be examined. Next, sections on therapeutic commonalities, including the therapeutic relationship, client expectancies, micro-counseling skills, the role of catharsis and emotion, insight and self-awareness, and facilitating action and change, will be examined. This will be followed by an examination of the roles of theory and specific factors, the phases of counseling, and a look at the effect of extra-therapeutic factors. Because many topics in this chapter overlap with other chapters in this *Handbook*, the emphasis will be on individual counseling as an intervention. Finally, conclusions and future directions will be discussed.

Definition of Terms

Client will be used instead of *patient*, consistent with the positive, adaptive approach to psychological issues consistent with counseling psychology. *Counselor* or *therapist* will be used to designate counseling psychologists as the target population of mental health professionals providing services. *Counseling, psychotherapy,* and *therapy* will be used interchangeably to refer to individual counseling as an intervention.

Despite being a widely used type of intervention, a review of the literature provides surprisingly few definitions of individual counseling. The hundreds of theories and systems of psychotherapy that exist today make defining individual therapy challenging. The definition of individual counseling used in this chapter is modified from Norcross (1990, p. 218). Because his definition was not limited to individual psychotherapy, modifications are in parentheses.

Psychotherapy is the informed and intentional application (by a trained counselor or therapist) of clinical methods and interpersonal stances derived from established psychological principles for the purpose of assisting (the client) to modify behaviors, cognitions, emotions, and/or other personal characteristics in directions that (the counselor and client mutually) deem desirable.

This definition is pantheoretical, in that *psychological principles* can refer to specific theoretical strategies and/or to the relationship as the mechanism of change. Unlike informal help from friends and family members, psychotherapy is a planned intervention between a trained counselor using established approaches to assist the client who is seeking help. An important part of this definition is that the counselor and client collaborate and mutually agree on the focus and the goals of the therapy.

Although this is a contemporary definition of counseling and psychotherapy, this definition is in line as well with the original doctoral training report, which identified the roles and functions of counseling psychologists as being to facilitate optimal development of the individual across levels of psychological adjustment but with an emphasis on those individuals in the normal range of adjustment and on the positive and preventative (APA, 1952a; Munley, Duncan, McDonnel, & Sauer, 2004). Although individual counseling need not occur face-to-fact, the focus of this chapter will be on this type of individual psychotherapy.

Why Do Clients Seek Counseling?

Why do people seek counseling? This is an important question but a difficult one to answer. For example, clients might present with multiple concerns, such as anxiety, relationship issues, and social anxiety, making it difficult to capture specific reasons for seeking therapy; much of the research on this topic is based on college student populations that may differ from other populations, and many studies do not examine clinical populations but instead examine the *attitudes* toward help-seeking of respondents who are *not* seeking psychotherapy, to determine their likelihood of seeking counseling.

We do know that interpersonal or relationship issues are the most common reasons for seeking counseling, followed by mood concerns such as depression and anxiety. In addition, several other factors have been found that contribute to seeking counseling in actual clients, including prior success with help-seeking (e.g., Deane & Todd, 1996), level of psychological distress (e.g., Deane & Chamberlain, 1994), and being female (e.g., Cohen, Guttmann, & Lazar, 1998). Yet, such studies typically account for about 25% of the variance associated with help-seeking (Vogel & Wester, 2003).

Attitudes toward help-seeking provide another way to understand why people may or may not be open to seeking counseling. In a series of two studies, predictors of seeking psychological services were examined (Vogel, Wester, Wei, & Boysen, 2005). Study 1 examined the role of attitudes in mediating the relationship between psychological factors previously identified in the literature on help-seeking (e.g., distress, self-concealment, anticipated utility, anticipated risk) and intent to seek help for specific psychological problems (interpersonal, academic, and drugs). Psychological factors and attitudes predicted 62% of the variance in intent to seek help for interpersonal problems but only 18% of the variance for drug problems. Attitudes toward counseling mediated relationships between most of the psychological factors and intentions to seek help. Study 2 extended this research by examining the relationship of having experienced a psychological stressor (e.g., abuse or severe loss) to attitudes toward help-seeking. Results showed that significantly more of those who had experienced a psychological stressor sought counseling during the time period of data collection (about 20%) versus only about 8% who did not report having experienced a significant stressor. This finding lends support to previous findings that psychological distress is a common reason for seeking counseling, although these results and those of other studies have shown that distress does not consistently predict help-seeking. It is interesting that Study 2 also found that those who had experienced psychological distress were more likely to seek psychological services but also were more likely to anticipate the risks of disclosing emotions. This finding is consistent with other studies (e.g., Kushner & Sher, 1989) that have found that psychological distress was positively related to both the likelihood of seeking counseling *and* to greater fears and anxiety about seeking treatment.

Researchers have also studied factors that contribute to the *avoidance* of therapy or that decrease the likelihood that an individual will seek counseling or will lead to premature termination. Identified avoidance factors include a fear of treatment (Deane & Chamberlain, 1994; Deane & Todd, 1996), a wish to conceal distressing or shameful personal information (Cepeda-Benito & Short, 1998; Kelly & Achter, 1995), and a desire to avoid experiencing an increase in painful feelings (Komiya, Good, & Sherrod, 2000).

Using structural equation modeling, Vogel, Wade, and Hackler (2008) found that the anticipated risks and benefits of therapy fully mediated the relationship between feelings about emotional expression and attitudes toward help-seeking *and* willingness to seek help. This study suggests that potential clients may first consider the risks and benefits of seeking therapy, which may in turn affect their feelings about emotional expression (e.g., comfort/discomfort) and willingness to seek help.

Drawing from this literature, clients typically seek counseling because of psychological distress due to the persistence of concerns exacerbated by ineffective or maladaptive emotions, thoughts, or behaviors and the wish to find new, more effective ways to respond to difficult experiences. But important caveats must be added: The client must believe or expect that counseling will be helpful, must believe that the benefits outweigh the risks, must have the skills to manage disclosure, must be able to experience painful emotions (cathart) in reaction to the clinical material; and must be motivated to translate what is learned in therapy into making changes outside of therapy. In other words, clients most often seek therapy when their beliefs in the benefits are sufficient to overcome the barriers (Hill, 2004).

This leads to another important question about what clients *want* to occur as a result of seeking therapy. In a study of clients seeking therapy at a university counseling center, immediately after each intake interview, both clients and therapists were asked to respond to 14 "wants" or things that they hoped would happen as a result of counseling or believed that their client wanted to happen (Sacuzzo, 1975). Three items or wants were endorsed by nearly all of the clients: "Get help in talking about what is really troubling me," "Understand the reasons behind my feelings and behavior," and "Have someone respond to me on a person-to-person basis." Both clients and therapists were in high agreement about the underlying dimensions of client wants, and three major themes emerged for both samples: self-exploration, catharsis, and encouragement. These client wants are similar to commonalities of individual therapy across theoretical orientations and systems identified by meta-analytic studies.

Developing a Facilitative Therapeutic Relationship

One of the primary reasons clients seek therapy is to "have someone respond to me on a person-to-person basis" (Sacuzzo, 1975). Decades of research demonstrate that individual therapy is, at its core, an interpersonal process in which a main curative component or element is the therapeutic relationship created by the counselor and the client. Both the counselor and the client bring important aspects of themselves to the relationship and together co-create the therapeutic alliance. The view of the therapeutic relationship has moved from Freud's and other early psychoanalysts view of it as a "one-person" approach, with the therapist being an observer of what unfolds from deep within the client, to the more contemporary view of the relationship as a "two-person" dyadic, co-constructed alliance (Wachtel, 2008). The two-person view acknowledges that the counselor will have an impact on the client and, in turn, the client will have an impact on the counselor.

Based on a multidisciplinary review of the relationship in therapy initiated by Division 29 of the American Psychological Association, 11 elements and eight processes that occur within the framework of the therapeutic relationship were identified (see Norcross, 2002). These elements included the alliance, empathy, goal consensus and collaboration, cohesion, positive regard, congruence, feedback, repair of alliance ruptures, self-disclosure, management of countertransference, and relational interpretation. Despite overlap on some of these elements, agreement on conceptual aggregation has not occurred, nor has a conceptual model evolved that could unify these elements into an overarching framework.

Several researchers have attempted to create such cohesive models, but consensus on these frameworks has not occurred. For example, Gelso and colleagues describe a tripartite model of the therapeutic relationship that posits that every psychotherapy relationship consists to some degree of a working alliance, a transference–countertransference configuration, and a real relationship (Gelso & Carter, 1985; Gelso & Samstag, 2008). Although the tripartite model has a number of advocates, some believe that transference and countertransference cannot be kept distinct from alliance (e.g., Meissner, 1992); the distinctiveness between the three parts has not been established, and some believe that the transference–countertransference configuration, with its attention to the unconscious, is not necessary to understanding the client–therapist relationship. For these and other reasons, the vast majority of research published on the therapeutic relationship has not yet adopted a consistent overarching model.

Yet, as Gelso and Carter (1985) note in their seminal review of the literature in this area, the therapeutic relationship is widely viewed as playing a key role in nearly all therapies, regardless of theoretical orientation. Some therapies view the relationship as the sine qua non of effective therapy, in that it is the mechanism that contributes most directly to change, whereas others believe it plays a key role in *facilitating* the application of strategies and techniques that lead to change. For example, in studies of the effects of cognitive therapy on depression, although compliance with the requirements of the cognitive elements of the treatment predicted success, so did the quality of the therapeutic relationship (Burns & Nolen-Hoeksema, 1991, 1992). As defined by Gelso and Carter (1985, p. 159), the relationship is "the feelings and attitudes that counseling participants have toward one another, and the manner in which these are expressed."

There is widespread agreement and evidence that the counselor–client relationship is related to positive outcomes in most, if not all, types of therapy. In their review of the literature on psychotherapy process and outcome, Orlinsky, Grawe, and Parks (1994) cite five process variables that have consistently shown robust relationships with outcome. One of these is the overall quality of the therapeutic relationship. Yet, the vast majority of studies have actually examined only one aspect of

the therapeutic relationship—the working alliance. Because another chapter in this *Handbook* is devoted to the therapeutic relationship, this chapter will limit its focus to the therapeutic alliance and its role in individual counseling.

The therapeutic or working alliance is often viewed as being comprised of three components: goals, tasks, and bonds (Bordin, 1979; Horvath & Greenberg, 1986; Horvath & Symonds, 1991). Although there is some question about the distinctiveness of these three components, there is much support for the relationship of the working alliance to positive counseling outcomes. Randomized clinical trials repeatedly find that a positive alliance is one of the best predictors of outcome. For example, Krupnick, Sotsky, Simmons, Moyer, et al. (1996) found that the therapeutic alliance was predictive of treatment success across all treatments for depression, based on data from the large-scale National Institute of Mental Health Treatment of Depression Collaborative Research Program. Nearly 300 empirical process and outcome studies published over a recent 10-year period have demonstrated that the relationship, most commonly conceptualized as the working alliance, has shown the most consistent and robust association between counseling process and outcome (Orlinsky et al., 2004).

A number of meta-analytic studies have demonstrated this relationship as well. A meta-analytic study of 20 datasets examining the relationship between the working alliance and therapeutic outcomes found a moderate relationship between good working alliance (especially from the client's perspective) and positive outcomes (Horvath & Symonds, 1991). More recently, Martin, Garske, and Davis (2000) analyzed data from 79 studies and concluded that the results "indicated that the overall relation of therapeutic alliance with outcome is moderate, but consistent . . . [and that] . . . the relation of alliance and outcome does not appear to be influenced by other moderator variables. . . ." (p. 438). Overall, meta-analyses have found small to medium effect sizes for the effect of the therapeutic alliance on outcome (e.g., Horvath & Symonds, 1991; Norcross & Wampold, 2011).

Another consistent finding in the research in this area is the positive association between scores on measures of early treatment alliance and outcome (Horvath & Symonds, 1991), despite the variety of alliance conceptualizations and instruments used to measure it (Horvath & Greenberg, 1994). For example, Bordin's (1994) pantheoretical view of the therapeutic alliance emphasizes agreement between the client and counselor on tasks and goals, as well as a sense of bonding. In contrast, Luborsky (1994) conceptualized the alliance from a psychodynamic perspective having two parts: the client experiencing the therapist as helpful, and the client sensing that therapy is a collaborative effort. Despite these differences in conceptualization of the alliance, research on both Luborsky's and Bordin's views has consistently found that alliance predicts outcome. What is less clear is the relationship of the therapeutic alliance to outcome in later sessions.

This issue is sometimes framed in the debate about whether alliance is best viewed as the consequence of effects that have already occurred (e.g., Crits-Christoph et al., 2006) or as having a direct effect on outcome. However, research has shown that, when improvement up to the point of alliance measurement is controlled, alliance predicts outcome, thus suggesting that alliance has a direct effect on outcome (Barber, Connolly, Crits-Christoph, Gladis, & Siqueland, 2000). "These findings suggest that alliance might have a direct effect on outcome as opposed to simply being a consequence of improvements that have already occurred because of a positive attitude toward treatment and the therapist" (Crits-Christoph et al., 2006, p. 269).

What is important about this research is that it supports the importance of the therapeutic alliance as a change factor in counseling. It is clear from other studies cited in this chapter that early alliance is predictive of outcome. Less is known about the pattern of the alliance over time in the relationship. Research examining the stability of the alliance across therapy suggests that greater benefit may occur when the alliance is nonstable and nonlinear. For example, Kivlighan and Shaughnessy (2000) found that curvilinear U-shaped alliances were associated with better outcome than were linear. In a replication and extension of this study, Stiles et al. (2004) found support for the U-shaped pattern in a subset of the clients, but found no main effect differences for alliance patterns. Some have speculated that the experience of alliance rupture followed by alliance repair provides opportunities for clients to learn about how to manage painful interpersonal situations in a more productive manner (e.g., Safran & Muran, 1996, 2000). These two studies on the patterning of the alliance suggest that the alliance may not follow a linear pattern of development and may serve as a means for managing therapeutic ruptures and repairs, which are viewed as an important process in helping clients manage relationship ruptures outside of therapy. These two studies also show the complexities inherent in studying the therapeutic alliance, as the manner in which it evolves and develops likely differs among counselor–client dyads, thus making it difficult to capture using typical research methodologies.

Although the importance of the therapeutic alliance to outcome has been well established, many things about this complex process are still unknown.

In a paper examining the therapeutic alliance in a historical context, Horvath (2006) notes several challenges that have persisted over the years and have received limited research in this area: the absence of a clear definition of the alliance, the lack of a broad consensus about the alliance's relation to other aspects of the therapeutic relationship, and the need to more clearly specify the role and function of the alliance throughout the phases of treatment. Regarding the definitional issue, what is the *nature* of the therapeutic alliance? Is it *intrapersonal* (as would be suggested by psychodynamic scholars who posit that transference–countertransference plays an essential role), or is it better described as an *interpersonal* process, with an emphasis on collaboration (in line with more recent views of transference, such as those proposed by self-psychology and interpersonal therapists). Evidence appears to support both these perspectives, which suggests that the therapeutic alliance can be described as both an intrapersonal and an interpersonal process.

Moving to Horvath's second issue, whether the role of the alliance in the therapeutic process is as an active versus facilitative ingredient of change, remains unclear. There is consistent support that the alliance early in therapy predicts therapeutic outcomes, and it appears that the relationship continues to play a role in outcome throughout therapy; however, the manner in which this occurs as therapy progresses is less clear (Horvath, 2006). Disruptions and ruptures invariably occur in therapy, and the manner in which these are addressed likely affects both the relationship and outcome. Finally, some characteristics of the client and the counselor that contribute to the therapeutic relationship have been identified, but research on other factors has been mixed. As important as it seems to identify client and therapist variables that contribute to the therapeutic relationship and to the overall efficacy of counseling across therapies, relatively few have been identified. For example, Grencavage and Norcross' (1990) common factors study found that only 6% of the commonalities identified by researchers were client factors, and 21% were therapist factors.

The most consistent findings for client characteristics that contribute to outcome are motivation for change (client actively seeking help), positive expectancies, and level of distress. Those commonalities identified for therapists that are linked to positive outcomes are ability to enhance hope and increase expectancies, empathy, warmth and positive regard, acceptance, and what was referred to as general positive characteristics (e.g., Frank, 1982; Grencavage & Norcross, 1990).

Facilitating Positive Expectancies

Client expectancies have been positively linked to both seeking *and* persisting in counseling. For example, people are more likely to seek counseling if they are ready to change and believe that the intervention will help them make desired changes. Clients who have had a prior positive counseling experience have more positive expectancies about counseling and are more likely to seek therapy in the future (e.g., Deane & Todd, 1996). Based on an analysis of over 100 studies of psychotherapy occurring over decades of research, Lambert and Barley (2001) estimated that expectancies accounted for about 15% of the variance in counseling outcome. Moreover, client expectancies have been found to predict attrition from counseling. Pretreatment expectancies were examined during intake in a sample of adults seeking counseling at a training clinic utilizing the Psychotherapy Expectancy Inventory–Revised (PEI–R) (Aubuchon-Endsley & Callahan, 2009). Results showed that clients who scored outside the reference range were seven times more likely to subsequently terminate treatment prematurely than were those who scored within the reference range. This finding suggests that client expectancies prior to beginning therapy affect their persistence in counseling.

However, findings from research on the relationship between expectations and process variables, specifically the alliance, have been mixed. In part, this has been attributed to inadequate measurement of expectations (see Arnkoff, Glass, Shapiro, & Norcross, 2002). One consistent finding is that clients' expectations regarding their commitment to therapy contribute to developing an alliance early in treatment. For example, client expectancies that they will play an active, collaborative role in counseling predict the task, bond, and goal dimensions of the working alliance (Patterson, Uhlin, & Anderson, 2008; Tokar, Hardin, Adams, & Brandel, 1996). The vast majority of the research on counseling expectancies focuses on the client and minimizes the role of the therapist or of the therapeutic relationship in shaping expectancies. Yet, counselors play a key role in activating and shaping expectations. Positive expectancies are sometimes described as being similar to a placebo effect (Lambert & Barley, 2001). Yet, the interpersonal nature of counseling goes well beyond administering the classic placebo pill to activate positive expectancies.

From the very first sessions, counselors strengthen client expectations, activate hope, and shape expectations to the treatment in a variety of ways (Frank & Frank, 1991). Presenting one's credentials, describing one's treatment approach, providing a rationale for the approach, and suggesting that one has used it successfully before with clients with similar issues are just a few of the ways that counselors communicate expectancies about the outcome of the therapy. In the National Institute of Mental Health Treatment of Depression Collaborative Research study, expectancies of clients (who completed treatment) and therapists were examined (Meyer et al., 2002). Clients who expected therapy to be effective engaged more constructively during their sessions and had better therapy outcomes. Therapists' positive expectancies for client improvement predicted better outcomes as well.

An intriguing aspect of expectancies that has been documented in the medical field but ignored in the counseling literature is the *nocebo* effect on expectancies of benefit from a treatment. Just as the placebo effect refers to benefits produced by aspects of a treatment that should have no effect (e.g., the classic sugar pill), the nocebo effect refers to the opposite effect, in which clients (or counselors) presume the worst and expect that a counseling intervention will not be effective. This may occur when a client does not believe that a therapeutic approach will be effective, or when a therapist believes that a particular client cannot benefit from an approach. Nocebo effects have been described in the medical field when the patient (or physician) believes that something will go wrong (Barsky, Saintfort, Rogers, & Borus, 2002). For example, patients who believed that they were prone to heart disease were four times more likely to die from a heart attack, and those who expected to die during surgery were more likely to do so. Barksy et al. (2002) concluded that a low expectancy for treatment success is the central characteristic of medical patients who are most likely to experience the nocebo effect. This parallels the findings in the psychotherapy literature that low expectations for counseling success predict premature termination and poorer outcomes.

Micro-skills: Facilitating Process and Outcome

Just as the therapeutic relationship is a component of all therapies, facilitates what happens during counseling sessions, and contributes to outcome as well, so too do micro-skills. Counselors across theoretical orientations use micro-skills to get information, show support and understanding, clarify emotions and thoughts, promote self-awareness and insight, and reinforce change (Hill & O'Grady, 1985). Perhaps the best known and most highly researched model or taxonomy of micro-skills or helping skills in counseling is that of Clara Hill (e.g., Hill, 2001, 2004). In addition to the taxonomy of helping skills, Hill has developed a three-stage model of the helping process that integrates these helping skills into each stage. The taxonomy of helping skills is pantheoretical. Across theories and systems, research has supported the presence of these helping skills, albeit utilized to different extents in various theoretical perspectives, as being among the essential tools that therapists use to facilitate the counseling process and to express their intentions (Hill, 2001). Given the extent of this literature, a brief overview will be presented in this chapter, and the reader is referred to several key writings by Hill and colleagues (Hill, 2001, 2004; Hill & Knox, 2008).

Hill's three-stage model of helping includes exploration (establishing rapport, encouraging clients to tell their story, exploring clients' thoughts and feelings, and facilitating arousal of emotions and affect), insight (constructing new awareness and insight—including the client's role in feelings, thoughts, and behaviors—and addressing issues in the therapeutic relationship), and action (deciding and implementing action based on exploration and insight). The underlying philosophy of this model is that certain helping skills are more likely to be utilized in each stage, and these represent counselor intentions to achieve the goals of that stage. For example, in the exploration stage, common micro-skills are attending, open-ended questions, restatement, reflection, and probes. In a study of these counselor behaviors on discussion of feelings in undergraduate volunteer clients in a single helping session, Hill and Gormally (1977) found that probes resulted in more discussion of feelings than did either reflections or restatements, whereas no effects were found for nonverbal behaviors. Although exploration-stage skills are essential in exploring client issues and establishing rapport, mastery of these basic skills is assumed to be in the repertoire of counselors and rarely explored in the recent literature.

Helping skills that Hill associates with the insight stage of her model include the advanced skills of challenge, interpretation, self-disclosure, and immediacy. Research on these skills has been steady over several decades. Hoffman-Graff (1977) and Hoffman and Spencer (1978) found that clients perceived therapist self-disclosure to be most helpful when it normalized the presenting concern for clients and when it represented nonimmediate (past) information about the therapist. Similar findings were found in a qualitative study of clients currently in long-term therapy (Knox, Hess, Petersen, & Hill, 1997). Clients reported that helpful instances of therapist self-disclosure occurred when they believed that their therapists' intentions were to normalize or reassure them and when the disclosure was based on personal nonimmediate information about the therapists. Positive outcomes reported by these clients included insight or new perspective, normalization, and reassurance.

Interpretation is another helping skill that has been discussed extensively in both the clinical and empirical literature. In examining therapists' interpretations on the outcome of dynamic therapy, Crits-Cristoph, Cooper, and Luborsky (1988) found the accuracy of these interpretations in terms of core conflictual themes was of interest. Results indicated that accuracy regarding core relationship themes was significantly related to outcome, even when controlling for the quality of the therapeutic alliance. Other hypotheses were not supported, which leads to an important caveat about the difficulty of studying helping behaviors. As noted by Hill (2004, p. 59), "research on helping skills is very difficult because the helping process is complex and research methods for studying this process are crude."

Irrespective of theoretical framework, all counselors utilize micro-skills to facilitate the therapeutic alliance, engage the client in the process of change, explore client issues, promote awareness and insight, and facilitate change. A critical aspect of utilizing micro-skills, and one that has been related to both theoretical orientation and outcomes, is the intention of the therapist in utilizing a particular helping skill or response mode (see Hill & Williams, 2000). For example, a psychodynamic therapist might use a probe to encourage client insight, whereas a cognitive therapist might use this same micro-skill to gain more detailed information to use in targeting maladaptive thoughts. Overall, counselors' intentions and response modes fit their theoretical orientation; helping skills have a small, but significant impact on immediate outcome during sessions; and some skills, such as interpretation and self-disclosure, have been found to be generally related to process and outcome but are used infrequently.

Experiencing and Regulating Affect in Individual Therapy

Facilitation of emotional arousal is another commonality of all or most psychotherapeutic approaches, and it appears to be a prerequisite to cognitive and behavioral changes (see Grencavage & Norcross, 1990). Emotional distress is a consequence or cause of the problems that bring clients to therapy, and amelioration or management of this distress is one of the most wished-for outcomes. According to Leslie Greenberg, the preeminent scholar on the role of emotion in psychotherapy, all therapeutic approaches converge on a "shared view of emotion as a rapid-action, adaptive, control system that orients people to the relevance that events in their environment have to their well-being" (Greenberg, 2008, p. 51). His view is that emotions are adaptive resources and that overregulation is often problematic. Emotional reactions create tendencies to act and to process in specific ways in response to events. In other words, emotions are intimately tied to meaning systems. Frequently, emotional reactions to interpersonal and environmental events are ineffective and troubling and an important signal that something needs to be addressed (Foa, Riggs, Massie, & Yarczower, 1995; Greenberg, 2002; Linehan et al., 2002). *Catharsis* or relief from troubling emotions typically begins in the first sessions of therapy, when clients first tell their story and experience positive responses from the therapist, such as empathy and normalization.

The belief that exploring painful emotions in the holding environment of the therapeutic relationship can lead to positive changes is not a new idea (e.g., Kohut, 1977; Rogers, 1951). A good therapeutic relationship has long been viewed as the vehicle for emotional processing, given the widely recognized link between both the alliance and empathy and outcome (Greenberg, Elliott, Watson, & Bohart, 2001). In fact, the working alliance appears to mediate emotional arousal and processing, in that high arousal predicted good session outcome, but only when there was a strong alliance (Beutler, Clarkin, & Bongar, 2000; Iwakabe, Rogan, & Stalikas, 2000). A recent study explored

this issue further by examining the relationship of varying amounts of emotional arousal to therapeutic outcomes (Carryer, J. & Greenberg, L.S., 2011). After controlling for therapeutic alliance, the authors concluded that too much or too little heightened arousal was less effective than moderate levels in predicting therapeutic outcome.

Recent research on the role of emotion in therapy has moved beyond the notion of the therapeutic relationship as a holding environment for processing distressing feelings to other processes of change that can occur when working with emotions. Research suggests that not all emotions serve the same function and that therapists may need to work with different emotional processes in different ways. For example, work with a client who under-regulates emotions would differ from therapy with a client who typically over-regulates emotions. Based on his review of the empirical literature on the role of emotion in therapy, Greenberg and colleagues have identified five principles or processes of change: emotion awareness, expression of emotion, emotional regulation, reflection on emotion, and emotional transformation or changing emotion by using emotion. Each of these processes of change will be briefly reviewed (Greenberg, 2002; Greenberg & Watson, 2005).

The most basic goal of emotional change is helping clients gain *emotional awareness*. One of the basic skills taught to beginning therapists is to help clients identify and label their emotions. Five levels of emotional awareness have been identified by Lane and Schwartz (1992), with the most basic being awareness of physical sensations followed by action tendencies (e.g., responding quickly with anger to a variety of situations), single emotions, recognizing blends of emotion (e.g., loss and anxiety), and the capacity to view the emotional experiences of self and other in a complex manner.

Emotional expression has an effect on affect, cognitions, physical well-being, and interpersonal interactions. Emotional expression in therapy has been shown to predict unique variance in solving interpersonal problems (Greenberg & Malcolm, 2002).

Emotion regulation refers to mechanisms that individuals use to help soothe and regulate distress. A positive therapeutic relationship has been found to provide an empathic, validating, and safe environment for emotional regulation (Bohart & Greenberg, 1997), especially for clients who have difficulty with self-regulation (Linehan et al., 2002). Empathy from a therapist is one of the most basic tools used to help a client learn to self-soothe and gain emotional equilibrium (Greenberg, Auszra, & Herrmann, 2007). Beyond empathy, therapeutic interventions such as meditation and helping clients gain self-compassion are helpful in reducing overwhelming core emotions (Teasdale et al., 2000).

Reflection on emotion in therapy is an important way for clients to gain information, create new meaning, and develop new narratives to explain their experiences and to shape future events (Greenberg & Angus, 2004; Pennebaker, 1995). For example, putting traumatic emotional experiences into words is one way of assimilating these experiences into one's view of oneself and lessening distress (Elliott, Llewelyn, Firth-Cozens, Margison, Shapiro, & Hardy, 1990; Van der Kolk, 1995). According to research by Elliott et al. (1990), this process occurs as new schemata developed by the therapist and client are used to gradually assimilate painful feelings, leading to increased self-awareness and less distress. Utilizing a technique based on clients writing about their emotional experiences, Pennebaker and colleagues have shown that this type of writing can have positive effects on psychological and physical well-being (e.g., Pennebaker, 1995).

A novel and recent view of emotional change is the notion of *emotion transformation*. Greenberg (2002) describes this as the process of changing emotion with emotion. In other words, a maladaptive or negative emotion can be managed by addressing it with a more adaptive emotion. In research based on Frederickson's *broaden-and-build hypothesis*, the incompatibility of positive emotions with negative emotions has been found to undo deleterious effects (Frederickson, 2001). For example, helping clients experience positive emotions from an experience that created negative emotions may promote better outcomes by helping them bounce back. This does not entail simply telling clients to think positive thoughts, but rather helps them to evoke a meaningful alternate experience that counteracts their negative feelings. For example, a counselor might assist a client who is faced with a life-threatening disease and is experiencing fear and anger to explore an alternate view of his situation (e.g., the opportunity to reprioritize what is most important in his life; to reconnect with people who have been sources of social support in the past; to use his experience to assist others facing a similar experience), which leads to positive emotions that help counteract the negative emotions.

Facilitating New Perspectives and Insight

Understanding our feelings, thoughts, and behaviors and the manner in which they connect to experiences in our lives provides a sense of meaning and mastery (Frank & Frank, 1991). From the client's perspective, to "understand the reasons behind my feelings and behavior" was one of the most important expectations hoped for in therapy (Sacuzzo, 1975). This process has been referred to variously as insight (Hill, 2004; Hill, Castonguay, et al., 2007), consciousness raising (Prochaska & Norcross, 2007), and constructing new awareness (Hill, 2002), and is a component of most, if not all, therapies. When asked "What is insight?" a panel of experts (Hill, Castonguay, et al., 2007) defined it as "a conscious meaning shift involving new connections" (p. 441). More explicitly, insight is conscious; involves something new, such as seeing something in a new light; involves making connections between things that had previously seemed to be disparate (e.g., a past reaction to an event is connected to a present reaction); and involves causality (e.g., understanding the reasons for the intensity of a present emotional reaction) (Hill & Knox, 2008).

A number of studies have found that insight occurs in therapy through methods ranging from examining expressions of insight during sessions to post-session reports of helpful events that could be classified as insight. In-session findings on client expressions of judged insight show that it occurs across different types of therapies (but less frequently than other behaviors, such as exploration), that it remains inconclusive as to whether it changes across sessions in a systematic fashion, and that it seems to occur more frequently in insight-oriented therapies such as psychodynamic approaches (Hill & Knox, 2008). One limitation of these studies was that insight attainment was assessed by judges and based on single events that occurred in therapy.

In contrast, more compelling evidence for the importance of insight has been found in studies that have examined this construct as a client-rated helpful event in therapy or as a post-session measure of insight attainment. A number of studies have asked clients to rate the most helpful event in their therapy. For example, Elliott and James (1989) found that self-understanding/insight was rated most often as the most helpful event in a review of 21 studies. In a study assessing results from a set of eight studies of dream interpretation, Hill and Goates (2004) found that the level of client-reported gains in insight was consistently more than a standard deviation higher than insight levels reported by clients in sessions in which they did not work on dreams. The finding that insight seemed to occur at a higher rate in dream interpretation sessions is in line with the research suggesting that clients participating in psychodynamic sessions are rated as higher in insight, in that both of these therapy modalities have a strong focus on gaining insight.

The most compelling evidence for the role of insight in individual therapy comes from studies examining changes in insight as a therapeutic outcome. Hill and Knox (2008) calculated effect sizes for changes in insight that occurred over time in therapy in a series of studies ranging in methodologies and utilizing both client- and judge-rated insight. In two different case studies of therapist immediacy, clients showed medium to large gains in self-understanding (Kasper, Hill, & Kivlighan, 2008; Hill et al., 2006). Judge-rated increases in insight in a series of dream work studies showed medium effects across eight samples of clients in six different studies (Hill & Knox, 2008). Overall, studies examining insight utilizing a range of methodologies have consistently found gains in insight ranging from small to large effects. Several issues remain unclear from current research: the role that client insight plays across theoretical orientations, the best way to measure client insight (e.g., client vs. judge-rated; in-session vs. post-therapy), and the pattern of change for insight across therapy.

What leads to insight in therapy? Several specific therapist interventions have been linked to client attainment of insight. Therapist probes for insight have been found to lead to client insight across multiple studies (e.g., Baumann & Hill, 2008; Hill, Knox, Hess, Crook-Lyon, et al., 2007). Findings for therapist interpretation have been mixed (see Hill & Knox, 2008). Several other counselor interventions have been linked to client insight in multiple studies, including confrontation, paraphrasing, and open questions (Hill & Knox, 2008). Based on their research and clinical experience, a panel of experts were asked to reflect on what leads to insight in therapy (Hill, Castanguay et al., 2007). Panelists agreed that clients are more likely to gain insight if they are psychologically minded, demonstrate a higher level of cognitive ability, lack defensiveness, exhibit low levels of psychopathology, and show a readiness or motivation to achieve insight. Belief in the importance of insight was identified as an important therapist factor that facilitates insight. Environmental factors were noted as well, including social support and having others in one's life to provide reliable feedback about the client's behavior or effect on others.

Finally, how does insight affect therapeutic outcomes? Kivlighan, Multon, and Patton (2000) found a significant negative relationship between target complaints and judge-rated insight. Specifically, increases in client insight preceded symptom reduction (but symptom reduction did not in turn lead to insight). However, findings of other studies have been mixed. In their review of studies examining the relationship between insight and therapy outcome, Hill and Knox (2008) found that six studies found this relationship and four did not. They attributed these inconsistent findings to the great variation in the manner that insight is assessed, different measures of outcome, and the different types of therapy (e.g., dream work, psychodynamic) examined. Despite the mixed findings about the role of awareness and insight in individual counseling, two factors are compelling. First, clients expect that they will learn new perspectives and insight when they seek counseling. And second, although the results of this body of literature are mixed, they are in the direction of positive or nonsignificant effects, rather than deleterious effects. This suggests that problems in measurement are impeding examination of this complex process of change and that the role of insight in therapy is an important change process for further examination.

Facilitating Action and Change

The wish to alleviate psychological distress caused by emotions, thoughts, or behaviors is a common reason for seeking counseling (e.g., Vogel et al., 2005). Although insight alone can result in change, sometimes insight represents simply the first step in the change process. A client may need to take action to achieve goals or to solidify insight or self-awareness (Hill, 2004). According to Hill's (2004) three-stage model of helping, during the action stage of counseling, therapists move to a more collaborative role with clients as they explore options and ways for change to occur. Commonly used counseling skills include giving information, feedback, process advisement, direct guidance, and disclosures about strategies.

Seeking counseling may represent one of the early stages in client change, according to Prochaska and DiClemente's (2005) transtheoretical model of readiness to change. The contemplation of making changes precedes actually making preparations for taking action and then initiating the action. Once clients identify changes they would like to make, they often practice new behaviors, thoughts, and reactions, both during the counseling session and outside the session. Getting feedback and support from the therapist is an important part of enhancing the client's sense of mastery and self-efficacy (Frank, 1982). Moreover, maintaining changes by managing demoralization due to lack of success or preventing and managing relapse is another function that occurs in therapy.

How do people who receive counseling change compared with those who do not receive counseling? What *types* of changes occur as a result of counseling? And, what are the processes or mechanisms of change? The first question will be addressed by a brief overview of literature on the overall efficacy of counseling; in other words, do those who receive counseling do better than those who do not?

Overall Efficacy of Counseling

In 1977, Smith and Glass were the first to use meta-analysis to analyze the results of multiple studies on counseling process and outcome. They found a medium to large effect size, meaning that about 75% of those receiving counseling did better than those who had not received counseling. This result has been supported by numerous meta-analyses since the Smith and Glass study, and results have typically concluded that the effect size for the efficacy of psychotherapy is large and that common factors account for more of the variance in outcomes than do specific techniques or theoretical approaches (e.g., Lambert & Bergin, 1994; Lipsey & Wilson, 1993; Wampold, 2001). Depending on criteria for inclusion, meta-analyses of the effectiveness of therapy may include designs ranging from analogue studies to clients in clinical settings, and may include outcomes including personality traits, interpersonal behaviors, and affective ratings.

A study conducted by *Consumer Reports* magazine (*CR*; 1995; Seligman, 1995) asked readers who had received psychotherapy to answer several questions about their experience. Results found that most (2,900 responded) reported that they received benefits from therapy and were satisfied with their treatment. Differences in effectiveness were not found between type of therapy, more improvement was reported for long- versus short-term therapy, and respondents reported that psychotherapy alone was just as effective as medication plus psychotherapy. Despite limitations in the design of the survey (e.g., no control group, no consideration of spontaneous remission, assessing outcome from only the client's perspective), the findings are important because they reflect the public's view of the benefits and effectiveness of therapy (Seligman, 1995, 1996).

In fact, consumer satisfaction and perceived benefit should be viewed as important indices of counseling efficacy. In summary, in terms of a global view of the efficacy of therapy, numerous studies have found that those who receive therapy do better than those who do not on outcome measures, they perceive that they benefit, and they are satisfied with therapy.

Types of Changes That Occur in Counseling

The second question to be examined is "What *types* of changes occur as a result of counseling?" Clients typically seek counseling because of ongoing psychological distress due to persistent concerns exacerbated by ineffective or maladaptive emotions, thoughts, or behaviors, and because they wish to be happier and to manage their lives more effectively. Therefore, the issue of what types of changes occur is important. This brief overview will discuss some of the more robust findings on types of changes that occur.

CHANGES THAT AMELIORATE DISTRESSING AND PAINFUL EMOTIONS

Depression and anxiety are the most common distressing emotions that clients wish to change in counseling. The identification of efficacious treatments for anxiety disorders has been more successful than for any other major diagnostic class (e.g. Roth & Fonagy, 2005). In their review of psychological treatments for this class of concerns, Barlow and Lehman (1996) stated, "Evidence now exists on the effectiveness (i.e., efficacy) of psychosocial treatment approaches for every anxiety disorder when compared with no treatment or credible psychosocial placebos" (p. 727). Thus, clients seeking counseling for specific anxiety disorders such as social anxiety, generalized anxiety disorder (GAD), and posttraumatic stress disorder (PTSD) can expect some degree of relief from interventions that have been found to be efficacious.

Social anxiety is one of the most prevalent diagnosable disorders and is common in settings in which counseling psychologists work, such as university counseling centers. Although both exposure and cognitive restructuring have both been shown to be efficacious, there is a developing consensus that a combination of the two is most beneficial (see Barlow & Lehman, 1996). Anxiety and GAD are prevalent client concerns as well, and are often difficult to ameliorate. Applied relaxation (Borkovec & Costello, 1993) has been shown to be effective with GAD, and recent research on other applied relaxation techniques, such as meditation and mindfulness, will likely prove efficacious as well. Another approach that shows promise in treating anxiety and other mood disorders is well-being therapy (WBT), which is based on Ryff's (1989) six dimensions of psychological well-being: autonomy, personal growth, environmental mastery, purpose in life, positive relations, and self-acceptance. For clients with anxiety disorders, studies have documented the efficacy of this psychotherapeutic intervention in improving on all six dimensions (see Fava, Rafanelli, Cazzaro, Conti, & Grandi, 1998; Rafanelli et al., 2000).

Depression is another mood disorder that is common in clients seeking counseling. Cognitive therapy, which focuses on altering the maladaptive thoughts, beliefs, attitudes, and behaviors that cause and maintain depression, has been found to be effective in treating depression (e.g., DeRubeis et al., 1990; Whisman, Miller, Norman, & Keitner, 1991). However, the exact mechanisms of change in cognitive therapy are not known, and whether it is more effective than other interventions is unknown. In sharp contrast to viewing maladaptive cognitions as the cause of depressive symptoms, psychodynamic-interpersonal therapy (IPT) has been shown to be as effective as cognitive therapy in treating depression (e.g. Barkham et al., 1996; Elkin et al., 1989). This approach views interpersonal problems as the cause of depression, and counseling focuses on improving interpersonal deficits. A final example of the efficacious treatment of depressive symptoms in therapy is based on a positive psychology intervention that utilizes activities aimed at facilitating positive feelings, behaviors, and cognitions, with the goals of increasing well-being and ameliorating depression. A meta-analysis of 51 studies utilizing this approach with 4,266 individuals (Sin & Lyubomirsky, 2009) found that positive psychology interventions significantly enhance well-being and decrease depressive symptoms.

Changes That Improve Quality of Life

Improved quality of life is an important and meaningful change in counseling. Studies have consistently found that therapy increases scores on quality of life indices, such as subjective well-being and happiness. One of the few studies to examine subjective well-being and to show the *why* of change through identifying mediators was a phase therapy model by Howard, Lueger, Maling, and Martinovich (l993). Three phases of therapy were examined in psychotherapy clients to track improvement in subjective well-being and to see its relationship to symptom improvement. Howard et al. (1993) found that improvement in subjective well-being precedes and is likely a necessary condition for reduction in symptomatic distress. In turn, symptomatic improvement precedes and is likely a necessary condition for improvement in life functioning.

Examining clients' reports of positive changes in quality of life over the course of a variety of types of therapies and client concerns, five studies using a common assessment battery were combined (Crits-Christoph et al., 2008). The purpose of this study was to evaluate change in positive quality of life (assessed at intake, termination, and 6 and 12 months post-treatment), to see if these changes resulted in symptom change. Results showed that positive quality of life improved moderately over the course of psychotherapy and was maintained at follow-up. Changes in quality of life were moderately related to changes in symptoms and interpersonal functioning. However, the amount of change in positive quality of life varied considerably by disorder, in that those with major depressive disorder and generalized panic disorder changed the most and those with panic disorder changed the least.

The types of changes that have been described are simply representative examples and not inclusive of other types of changes that have often been found. Other common changes include improved interpersonal relationships; benefit-finding following traumatic experiences; lifestyle changes, such as changes in self-care; and self-modification of problematic behaviors, such as smoking and not exercising.

Mediators and Mechanisms of Change in Counseling

"What are the mechanisms of change in therapy?" asks the question of *why* change occurs in successful therapies—or what mechanisms result in change. This is important to address, given current economic and political forces that press for evidence that certain therapies are efficacious in addressing specific client concerns (see APA, 1995). Furthermore, from the perspective of advancing the field, Kazdin (2006) states that understanding therapeutic change mechanisms will maximize therapeutic change and enhance generalization of treatment study results to clinical practice.

Kopta, Lueger, Saunders, and Howard (1999) suggest that this area of research will advance only if three critical questions are addressed: Which psychotherapies work as *specified* (e.g., according to theory) under controlled conditions? Which psychotherapies work as *practiced* in actual clinical settings? And, which psychotherapies work most *efficiently*? These questions are essential to address for the future of individual therapy. Kopta et al. (1999) posit that creative, randomly controlled treatment studies that are able to distinguish unique active ingredients can address the first question: Which psychotherapies work as specified (e.g. Jacobson et al., 1996)? To address the second question, they conclude that dose–effect studies can identify the change mechanisms of different types of therapy that affect outcomes for clients in real clinical settings. Efficiency of therapy can also be examined using dose–effect strategies that show rate of improvement using statistical techniques such as growth curves (rather than the change scores typically used). Recent research on the mediators of change and dose–effects of change utilize these design and statistical approaches to identify unique active ingredients (e.g., Baldwin, Berkeljon, Atkins, Olsen, & Nielsen, 2009; Harwood, Beutler, Castillo, & Karno, 2006; Hofmann, 2000).

The most important question emerging from the research on mechanisms of change in therapy is whether results from evidence-based treatment findings translate into clinical practice (sometimes defined as *evidence-based practice*). As noted by the American Psychological Association Presidential Task Force on Evidence-Based Practice (2006), psychotherapeutic treatment effects found in highly controlled contexts like randomly controlled treatment studies may not translate to similar findings in clinical practice settings. Specifically, key conditions and characteristics of treatment studies (e.g., therapist and client characteristics, treatment, and contexts) frequently differ from those in clinical practice (see Hoagwood, Hibbs, Brent, & Jensen, 1995; Kazdin, 2008). Generalizability of findings from evidence-based treatments and other gaps between research and practice must be bridged, so that both research and practice contribute to understanding how and why clients change in therapy (see Kazdin, 2008).

Moving Through the Phases of Individual Counseling

Change is often associated with the end of therapy, but different types of changes occur across all phases of therapy. For example, amelioration of painful feelings and thoughts may occur in the early or middle phases of counseling and may be necessary before the client can move on to more global changes, such as increases in happiness, improved interpersonal skills, and subjective well-being. These types of changes might then generalize outside of therapy in the form of increased social support, better intimate relationships, and greater life satisfaction.

Individual counseling is often conceptualized as encompassing three phases: beginning phase, working phase, and termination phase. During the beginning phase, clients tell their story, the therapeutic alliance is established, expectancies are discussed and facilitated, concerns to explore are identified, and goals are mutually determined. The working or middle phase of counseling includes managing and exploring emotions, gaining new awareness and insight, learning new perspectives and skills, and persisting in the face of painful emotions and slow progress or setbacks. The termination phase includes internalizing and transferring what has been learned to other environments outside of counseling, managing extra-therapeutic factors that might impede change, and managing relapse and setbacks. This section will examine factors that relate to premature termination and to continuance in counseling, indices of improvement that occur as therapy progresses, dose–effects of treatment duration, and the termination process.

Beginning Phase of Counseling

One of the findings across numerous studies is that treatment duration relates positively to outcomes (Orlinksy et al., 1994), and the likelihood of accomplishing therapeutic goals is lessened in premature termination. Planned termination typically occurs following the working phases of counseling. Yet, a meta-analysis of 125 studies found that a mean of 47% of clients drop out of therapy prematurely (Wierzbicki & Pekarik, 1993). A large portion of these clients terminated against their therapists' advice after just one session (Deane, 1991), and most dropped out of counseling prior to completing their therapeutic goals (e.g., Garfield, 1986; Pekarik, 1992).

In their meta-analysis, Wierzbicki and Pekarik (1993) found significant effect sizes for three client demographic variables (low education, low income, and ethnic or racial minority status) in predicting higher dropout rates. Lower dropout rates were found when therapist judgment was used to define dropout rather than number of sessions. Client (nondemographic), therapist, and problem characteristics were not predictive of dropout.

Utilizing Bandura's (1986) social cognitive theory to predict client motivation and attrition in counseling, measures of self-efficacy regarding counseling-related tasks, outcome expectations, motivation, distress level, state anxiety, and self-esteem were completed by university counseling center clients at intake (Longo, Lent, & Brown, 1994). Self-efficacy and outcome expectations each explained unique variation in both motivation and client return status. Client characteristics, such as state anxiety and self-esteem, were not related to the outcome variables.

These findings are important because duration of treatment may be predictive of positive therapy outcomes (Orlinsky et al., 1994) Moreover, unlike client demographics, variables related to premature termination, such as self-efficacy and readiness to change, are often modifiable. In addition, because the type or intensity of symptomatology does not consistently predict continuation or dropout, other factors are important to consider.

Working Phase of Counseling

In a study examining the relationship of readiness to change to predicting termination and continuation status in therapy, nearly 92% of clients were correctly classified as premature terminators, appropriate terminators, or therapy continuers (Brogan, Prochaska, & Prochaska, 1999). Specifically, the best predictors of termination status and continuation status were high endorsement of contemplation and low endorsement of precontemplation in terms of readiness to change, and high expectations of utilitarian gains from therapy.

Dose–effect studies are another way to look at the gains that clients make in counseling during the working phase. Most of these studies have examined grouped client data (rather than individual growth curves of clients with specific concerns) and have found that duration or amount (dose) of therapy leads to better outcomes. For example, an overview of studies shows that, for most clinical issues, 16 sessions of therapy provide at least a 50% chance for recovery to normal functioning (Barkham et al., 1996; Kadera, Lambert, & Andrews, 1996; Kopta, Howard, Lowry, & Beutler, 1994), and 26 to 58 sessions (Kadera et al., 1996; Kopta et al., 1994) improve success to about 75%. It is important to note that *patterns* of improvement across sessions in these studies (e.g., Kadera et al., 1996) vary substantially for specific clients and may not follow a linear trend, which may have implications at the clinical level.

Other studies have looked at both the number of sessions and symptomatology at intake to examine outcome. Examining clients' responses to counseling using both pretreatment and post-treatment measures is another way to examine client characteristics, number of sessions, dropout, and change (Snell, Mallinckrodt, Hill, & Lambert, 2001). A follow-up survey was sent to clients who had received one or more counseling sessions at a university counseling center 10 months after termination. Likelihood of clinically significant change depended on the number of sessions received, but the pattern of change was not linear. For example, some achieved significant change after eight sessions, and 50% did after 16 sessions. However certain client personality characteristics were associated with needing fewer sessions to achieve reliable change.

Symptomatic *recovery* is another way to determine that a client is ready to move from the working phase of counseling to termination. Using a dosage model in which the effect of dose was the probability of recovery, client-reported psychological symptoms were grouped into three categories (Kopta et al., 1994). On average, chronic distress symptoms responded to treatment most quickly, whereas character-based symptoms had the slowest response. Across doses, clients exhibiting acute distress symptoms showed the highest average response. Similar to other studies reported in this section, the typical outpatient needed about a year of psychotherapy (doses) to have a 75% chance of symptomatic recovery.

Termination Stage of Counseling

Studies of termination following the working phase of counseling have examined affective reactions and behaviors associated with this phase of counseling. Private-practice clients' perspectives on reasons for termination and their relationship to demographic and treatment variables and to satisfaction with therapy were examined using quantitative and qualitative analyses (Roe, Dekel, Harel, & Fennig, 2006). Based on quantitative results, the most frequent reasons for termination were accomplishment of goals, circumstantial constraints, and dissatisfaction with therapy. Client satisfaction with therapy was positively related to positive reasons for termination. Qualitative results showed two additional reasons for termination, which were viewed as positive outcomes: the client's involvement in new, meaningful relationships and the client's need for increased independence.

Termination represents an ending to what is often a significant relationship. Using the metaphor of *termination as loss*, Marx and Gelso (1987) examined client-reported affective reactions and behaviors in a sample of former university counseling center clients. Most reported being satisfied with the termination experience, and the set of loss-related variables did not predict satisfaction. However, a smaller cluster of these loss-related variables was predictive of the importance that clients placed on discussing their feelings about ending the therapy with counselors.

Boyer and Hoffman (1993) examined the termination process from the therapist's perspective using the metaphor of *termination as loss*. Affective reactions to termination as a function of counselor loss history and perceived client sensitivity to loss were examined in a sample of licensed psychologists. Counselor loss history (age at time of most significant loss, past grief reactions, and present grief reactions) was a significant predictor of counselor anxiety and depression during termination. Perceived client sensitivity to loss (sensitivity to loss and experiencing of other losses at time of termination) was a significant predictor of counselor anxiety during termination when the effect of counselor loss history was partialed out. Counselor task satisfaction during termination was not predicted by counselor loss history or by perceived client sensitivity to loss. This study is unique in that the results support the view that the termination process is affected by both counselor and client variables related to loss.

Utilizing Theory in Individual Counseling: Specific and Unique Factors

It is difficult to imagine conducting counseling without a theoretical framework to use in conceptualizing expected processes and outcomes. Although great progress has been made in empirically demonstrating the efficacy of individual therapy, less is known about *why* and *how* it works. This is especially the case when considering the specific factors associated with various theories and schools of therapy (see Kazdin, 2006). Because training in counseling and the practice of psychotherapy is based in part on adherence to specific theoretical orientations, debate centers on whether the different theories and systems each contain unique active ingredients that contribute to positive outcomes beyond those that have been attributed to common factors, such as the therapeutic relationship. The unique ingredients theory posits that different schools of psychotherapy produce different specific effects for different types of clients with different

sets of concerns. Because the common ingredients perspective has received support over decades of research (see Ahn & Wampold, 2001; Wampold, 2001), the question becomes: Is it important to demonstrate specific ingredients or effects? Because this issue is discussed extensively in the chapter in this *Handbook* on counseling process and outcome, here, we briefly overview two key issues.

One part of the answer to this question rests on the role that theory plays in the implementation of individual counseling as an intervention. A common reason that clients seek therapy is to gain awareness of and insight into their concerns. It is difficult to think of this occurring absent the therapist using theory as a roadmap to form a conceptual schema for making sense of the causes of a client's distress, to explain or express this rationale to the client, and to provide a method or strategy consistent with the rationale for relieving it (Frank, 1961; Frank & Frank, 1991). Theoretical choice reflects the therapist's beliefs about how and why problems occur and the conditions that allow change to occur, as well as the therapist's worldview and values. Clients often seek therapies that match their beliefs and worldview as well.

Utilizing a theoretical rationale not only helps the therapist structure what occurs in therapy, but supports therapist efficacy and influence and increases client confidence in the therapeutic work. As noted throughout this chapter, learning to identify and name affective, cognitive, and behavioral reactions allows clients to develop a framework of awareness and understanding that helps them transfer what they learn in therapy.

The second issue to address is whether theories or schools of therapy must do more than provide a roadmap for counseling. Proponents of the specific ingredients model posit that it is necessary to demonstrate that those components that are unique to a system or theoretical approach are responsible for meaningful therapeutic gains. Most who support this view acknowledge the important role that common factors (such as the relationship) play in client improvement, but view this as occurring in some combination with the unique ingredients of the therapeutic approach (e.g., Crits-Christoph, 1997).

Accepting the common ingredients theory in its entirety creates several critical dilemmas: It makes it more difficult to distinguish how psychotherapy differs from other helping interventions that include common ingredients such as a helping relationship, it calls into question the value of teaching and implementing systems of therapy that require specific steps and processes if those cannot be supported empirically, and it might discourage the development of new, more effective theoretically based interventions (see Ahn & Wampold, 2001). Most important, there is evidence that specific effects contribute meaningfully to the outcome of therapy, although less is known about the specific manner in which they do so. For example, Lambert and Barley (2001) derived estimates of the contribution of various components of psychotherapy to psychotherapeutic outcomes and estimated that 15% of outcome is due to specific techniques.

Although research suggests that specific effects account for a meaningful amount of variance in outcome, the empirical support for common ingredients continues to surpass the support for effective unique ingredients. Several of the reasons that have been suggested for the difficulties in establishing support for unique ingredients are that clients rarely seek therapy for a single presenting concern (e.g., depression); even clients with the same presenting concern may vary in meaningful ways in terms of how that concern is expressed; the interpersonal nature of therapy leads to constant change, based on the dyadic interchange; therapists may self-correct based on this dyadic interchange; interventions have multiple components, and it may be difficult to identify that component that is necessary for change; and current research methodologies typically used may not be optimal for identifying the effects of unique ingredients.

It is important to note that recent research, especially on cognitive-based therapies and on certain client concerns (such as anxiety and worry), have shown some success in identifying unique ingredients related to outcome (e.g., Borkovec, Newman, Pincus, & Lyttle, 2002; Foa, Rothbuam, & Furr, 2003). Foa et al. (2003) reviewed studies that compared exposure therapy for PTSD to other treatments. Results showed that exposure therapy is highly effective and that attempting to augment it with other treatments appears to diminish its effectiveness through dilution. This suggests that exposure therapy contains sufficient and perhaps necessary ingredients for change.

In a similar study, Borkovec et al. (2002) conducted a component analysis of cognitive-behavioral therapy for GAD by assigning clients to one of three treatments: applied relaxation and self-control desensitization, cognitive therapy, or a combination of these methods. All treatments resulted in significant improvement (e.g., no longer meeting diagnostic criteria for GAD) in anxiety and depression that was maintained at a 2-year follow-up, and no significant differences in outcome were found between treatments. Borkovec et al. (2002) concluded that the absence of significant differences between treatments may have been due to strong effects produced by each component condition. Finally, interpersonal difficulties remaining at post-therapy in a subset of clients were negatively associated with improvement, suggesting the possible utility of adding interpersonal treatment to cognitive-behavioral therapy to increase therapeutic effectiveness.

Another important issue in how therapists view theory in their work is the trend in psychotherapy to move away from a single theoretical orientation perspective and toward integration, in which empirically supported active ingredients from various theories are identified and brought together under a single, more generic overarching theoretical umbrella. A related trend is a move toward *eclecticism*, which can be expressed in several ways, including combining two or more theoretical orientations or conceptualizing client dynamics from one orientation but utilizing interventions from one or more other orientations. Currently, more therapists describe their theoretical orientation as eclectic or integrative, rather than following any single orientation (Norcross, Bike, & Evans, 2009), with 34% of counseling psychologists identifying themselves in this manner.

Early proponents of an integrative approach concluded that behind the specific methods of various theories were commonalities that contributed to outcomes (e.g., Frank, 1982). More recent proponents of this approach have argued that the unique but only partially effective strengths of various schools can be combined into more effective therapies that fit into one of four categories: common factors, technical eclecticism, theoretical integration, or assimilative integration (Stricker, 2008; Wachtel, 2000). The movement toward eclecticism and integrationism represents both a disenchantment with the utility of single-theory approaches and a recognition of the value of the planned integration of two or more approaches. Despite the appeal of eclecticism and integrative approaches for most clinicians, definitional issues remain challenging, and this perspective can run contrary to evidence-based, manualized treatment approaches.

Extra-therapeutic Factors Effects on Individual Counseling

To this point, the focus has been on what occurs within the context of the individual counseling.

An area that has received limited attention is what happens outside of therapy, both in terms of what the client brings to therapy and what happens to the client once he or she leaves the counseling session. Psychotherapy is just one of many influences that affect clients' lives, typically occupying only 1 hour a week for a limited duration. As Jerome Frank so aptly stated, "What goes on between sessions may be more important in determining outcome than what occurs in sessions" (Frank, 1982, p. 13). Environmental factors that may influence ongoing therapy include social support, work, and fortuitous (and not so fortuitous) events. For example, as the client begins to change, so must his or her environment, which changes the status quo. Other environmental characteristics, such as social and political factors, can exert a powerful influence on clients as well. For example, feminist and multicultural theories have long recognized the role of sociopolitical and cultural factors such as oppression, privilege, stigma, and culture in affecting client outcomes (e.g., Brown, Sue, & Sue, 2003). In other words, environmental factors at times support client changes and at other times undermine these changes in ways that facilitate or hinder transferability of therapeutic changes.

In addition, client background variables influence the effectiveness of therapy. These include personality variables, beliefs and values, cultural values, and readiness to change. Based on their review of psychotherapy research, Lambert and Barley (2001) concluded that extra-therapeutic factors account for about 40% of outcome variance. Despite the importance of extra-therapeutic factors to therapy outcomes, the literature in this area is relatively sparse. In part, this may be because an unlimited number of extra-therapeutic factors may affect therapy. It is difficult to identify and separate these factors to study their unique contribution to therapy process and outcome.

Examples of client characteristics and environmental factors will illustrate the importance of extra-therapeutic factors. Reviews of the literature have identified several personality variables that clients bring to therapy and that are related to successful counseling outcomes (e.g. Luborsky, Chandler, Auerbach, Cohen, & Bachrach, 1971). In Luborsky and colleagues classic review of over 100 studies on psychotherapy, personality variables most predictive of positive therapy outcome were level of initial personality functioning, motivation/expectations for therapy, and history of previous psychotherapy. Somatic concerns and defensiveness were predictive of more negative therapy outcomes.

A series of two studies examined five areas of clients' environment (life adjustment, external support, alternative counsel, current stress events, and logistical barriers) that were hypothesized to influence continuation or premature termination from therapy (Cross & Warren, 1984). Participants were continuers and terminators from an outpatient clinic. The only variable that differentiated these two groups of clients was that continuers reported access to more individuals in the community (such as spouses) with whom they received informal support in conjunction with therapy. This study supports the importance of significant others outside of therapy supporting the client while in therapy. Although research has identified the importance of extra-therapeutic factors to therapy continuation and outcome, far less is known about their myriad effects and their relationships to process and outcome than is known about other therapeutic components.

Conclusion
Future Directions
Individual counseling as an intervention has been shown by over 30 years of research to be effective, beneficial, and satisfying. Much has been learned about the efficacy of psychotherapy and the commonalities that contribute to change across therapies, and progress has been made in understanding the how, what, and why of counseling outcomes. Yet, many challenges remain, ranging from a need for a greater understanding of commonalities in counseling (e.g., the therapeutic relationship), to the search for effective, unique ingredients in counseling, to how much therapy is needed to lead to good outcomes. This chapter ends with recommendations for future directions in research that are relevant to the effective practice of individual counseling.

• Although a large body of research has shown that certain common factors or commonalities across therapies are effective, important areas of inquiry on these factors remain. For example, the relationship is widely viewed as a component of counseling that has direct effects on outcomes, or one that can, at other times, facilitate the application of therapeutic specific factors, which in turn have outcome effects. Yet, work remains in defining the therapeutic relationship because most research focuses on one only aspect—the therapeutic alliance. What are the components of the therapeutic relationship? Given the contextual, dyadic, and dynamic nature of the relationship, is it best viewed in its entirety rather than in its component parts? For example, can the transference–countertransference configuration and the real relationship be viewed separately from the therapeutic relationship?

• Client expectancies about psychotherapy prior to seeking counseling or that are facilitated during therapy by the counselor are another commonality factor. Most research focuses on client pretherapy expectancies, with far fewer studies examining *how* counselors facilitate expectancies. Clients typically seek counseling expecting it will be helpful, yet nearly half terminate prematurely (often after just one session), before their goals can be fully met. What role do expectancies play in continuance in counseling? And, how do counselors influence expectancies?

• Experiencing and regulating emotions represents another commonality across therapies that predicts successful outcomes. To date, cognitive therapies have been studied most frequently and have shown the greatest efficacy across the widest range of problem areas related to affect regulation. Recent research on emotion-focused therapy shows promise to move the field forward in a different direction, based on its success with concerns ranging from depression to forgiveness (see Greenberg, 2008; Greenberg, Warwar, & Malcolm, 2008). Moreover, emotion-focused therapy is in line with a growing interest in positive emotions, such as compassion and forgiveness.

• Insight and self-awareness is another common factor of counseling. One of the primary reasons clients give for seeking counseling is to understand the reasons behind their feelings, thoughts, and behaviors. Yet, a panel of experts found it difficult to reach consensus on a definition of insight and to describe how it manifests in therapy and how it relates to outcomes (Hill, Castonguay, et al., 2007). A fruitful area for future research is a greater understanding of *how* clients obtain insight and understanding and how that facilitates the process and outcome of counseling.

• Many believe that research should continue to focus on identifying the mechanisms of change, by determining which specific or unique effects serve as mediators of therapeutic outcome. Yet, this has proved challenging. Cognitive therapies have been studied most often, and although these approaches have been found to be efficacious across

a range of client concerns, research has shown limited success in identifying mediators of change. Some proponents of unique effects posit that this may be resolved through the use of different design and data analytic methodologies (e.g., growth curves) to identify mediators, which seems the most promising direction for future research in this area (e.g., Kazdin, 2007).

• In contrast, integrative researchers advocate moving away from evidence-based treatments based on narrowly defined diagnostic criteria and step-by-step treatment manuals. They recommend alternative treatment paradigms that use integrative approaches, including a focus on the two-person relationship and on contextual factors that more closely approximate clinical practice (Wachtel, 2000, 2008).

• A pressing concern recognized by proponents of both common and specific factors approaches is the importance of finding treatment evidence utilizing actual clinical contexts, or what is referred to as evidence-based practice (Howard et al., 1993; Kazdin, 2009; Seligman, 1996; Wachtel, 2000). Unlike the typical protocol for evidence-based treatment, in the clinical context, decisions are made by individual therapists based on their expertise, their judgment of the evidence they see in their sessions, and their view of their client and their relationship with the client. In contrast, commonly cited limitations of most randomized clinical trials are that they do not study clients in real settings, adherence to manualized treatments may limit responsiveness to contextual concerns, and narrow definitions for client inclusion limit generalizability to clinical samples, where clients typically present with multiple concerns.

• A related issue that warrants more research is therapist use of self-correcting processes to enhance responsiveness to client reactions to therapy and to achieve better outcomes. Lambert and colleagues have conducted a series of studies examining the effects of providing therapists with client feedback during psychotherapy (e.g., Lambert et al., 2001). Results show that feedback reduces premature dropout, improves outcome relative to nonfeedback conditions, and facilitates clinically significant change. In addition, feedback to therapists may reduce the number of therapy sessions without reducing positive client outcomes. This is an interesting direction for future research as it may address two important needs in this area: efficacy and efficiency.

• The efficiency and effectiveness of psychotherapy are important areas for future research due to concerns with cost containment and competition with biological psychiatry, which asserts that medication is less expensive, faster, and more effective. Which psychotherapies are both effective and efficient, and for whom? One of the best but underutilized research designs to examine these questions uses dose–effect strategies that utilize growth curves rather than change scores and that provide an index of the rate of improvement for either groups or subsets of clients.

• Another area of surprisingly little research is that on extra-therapeutic effects that affect who seeks counseling, who remains in counseling, and therapy outcomes. This research has primarily focused on identifying client characteristics that predict better outcomes, such as motivation to change, expectancies, and nondefensiveness. In contrast, less attention has focused on environmental factors that affect therapy outcomes, such as social support, oppression, and logistical barriers.

• Termination continues to be defined as the ending of therapy in the majority of research and scholarly writings. Several researchers have questioned this view of the finality of termination, yet few studies have examined other models (e.g., Cummings, 2001; Wachtel, 2002). For example, counseling could be viewed as an adaptive and preventative intervention that clients pursue intermittently throughout their lifetimes, in contrast to the view that they continue in therapy until they are "cured" or "done."

• A focus on adaptive functioning and prevention across the lifetime is in line with the current interest in positive psychology. Researchers are examining interventions that focus on client strengths rather than deficits. Examples include interventions that facilitate well-being, benefit-finding following traumatic events, and positive emotions such as forgiveness and gratitude (Malcolm, Warwar, & Greenberg, 2005).

• An important change affecting individual counseling is the movement away from single-theory orientations to theoretical integrationism and eclecticism. Although both dissatisfaction with single theories and appreciation for points of convergence between two or more theories drive this change, there is little consensus about what integrationism looks like. Future research needs to examine the manner in which therapists combine theories and intervention strategies, and their effectiveness.

• Face-to-face individual counseling was the focus of this chapter. Yet, the use of online technologies such as the Internet, Skype, and teleconferencing are being utilized with a variety of settings, modalities, and client populations (see Casper & Berger, 2005; Mallen, Vogel, Rochlen, & Day, 2005). Research is at the nascent stage with these technologies, and many issues, such as the client types and problems for which this is effective and the ethical guidelines related to "remote counseling" remain unresolved.

References

Ahn, H., & Wampold, B. E. (2001). Where oh where are the specific ingredients? A meta-analysis of component studies in counseling and psychotherapy. *Journal of Counseling Psychology, 48*(3), 251–257.

American Psychological Association, Division if Counseling, Guidance, & Committee on American Psychological Association. (2004). *2002 APA Directory survey.* (Table 3, Current major field of APA members by membership status, 2002). Compiled by APA Research Office. Washington, DC: American Psychological Association.

American Psychological Association Presidential Task Force on Evidence-Based Practice. (2006). Evidence-based practice in psychology. *American Psychologist, 61*, 271–285.

Arnkoff, D. B., Glass, C. R., Shapiro, S. J., & Norcross, J. C. (2002). Expectations and preferences *Psychotherapy relationships that work: Therapist contributions and responsiveness to patients.* (pp. 335–356). New York: Oxford University Press.

Aubuchon-Endsley, N. L., & Callahan, J. L. (2009). The hour of departure: Predicting attrition in the training clinic from role expectancies. *Training and Education in Professional Psychology, 3*(2), 120–126.

Baldwin, S. A., Berkeljon, A., Atkins, D. C., Olsen, J. A., & Nielsen, S. L. (2009). Rates of change in naturalistic psychotherapy: Contrasting dose-effect and good-enough level models of change. *Journal of Consulting and Clinical Psychology, 77*(2), 203–211.

Bandura, A. (1986). *Social foundations of thought and action: A social cognitive theory.* New York: Prentice-Hall.

Barber, J. P., Connolly, M. B., Crits-Christoph, P., Gladis, L., & Siqueland, L. (2000). Alliance predicts patients' outcome beyond in-treatment change in symptoms. *Journal of Consulting and Clinical Psychology, 68*(6), 1027–1032.

Barkham, M., Rees, A., Shapiro, D. A., Stiles, W. B., Agnew, R. M., Halstead, J., et al. (1996). Outcomes of time-limited psychotherapy in applied settings: Replicating the Second Sheffield Psychotherapy Project. *Journal of Consulting and Clinical Psychology, 64*(5), 1079–1085.

Barlow, D. H., & Lehman, C. L. (1996). Advances in the psychosocial treatment of anxiety disorders: Implications for national health care. *Archives of General Psychiatry, 53*(8), 727–735.

Barsky, A. J., Saintfort, R., Rogers, M. P., & Borus, J. F. (2002). Nonspecific Medication Side Effects and the Nocebo Phenomenon. *JAMA, 287*(5), 622–627.

Baumann, E., & Hill, C. E. (2008). The attainment of insight in the insight stage of the Hill dream model: The influence of client reactance and therapist interventions. *Dreaming*, *18*(2), 127–137.

Beutler, L. E., Clarkin, J. F., & Bongar, B. (2000). *Guidelines for the systematic treatment of the depressed patient*. New York: Oxford University Press.

Beutler, L. E., & Harwood, T. M. (2002). What is and can be attributed to the therapeutic relationship? *Journal of Contemporary Psychotherapy, 32*(1), 25–33.

Bohart, A. C., & Greenberg, L. S. (1997). *Empathy reconsidered: new directions in psychotherapy* (1st ed.). Washington, DC: American Psychological Association.

Bordin, E. S. (1979). The generalizability of the psychoanalytic concept of the working alliance. *Psychotherapy: Theory, Research & Practice, 16*(3), 252–260.

Bordin, E. S. (1994). Theory and research on the therapeutic working alliance: New directions. In A. O. Horvath, & L. S. Greenberg (Eds.), *The working alliance: Theory, research, and practice* (pp. 13–37). New York: Wiley.

Borkovec, T. D., & Costello, E. (1993). Efficacy of applied relaxation and cognitive-behavioral therapy in the treatment of generalized anxiety disorder. *Journal of Consulting and Clinical Psychology, 61*(4), 611–619.

Borkovec, T. D., Newman, M. G., Pincus, A. L., & Lytle, R. (2002). A component analysis of cognitive-behavioral therapy for generalized anxiety disorder and the role of interpersonal problems. *Journal of Consulting and Clinical Psychology, 70*, 288–298.

Boyer, S. P., & Hoffman, M. A. (1993). Counselor affective reactions to termination: Impact of counselor loss history and perceived client sensitivity to loss. *Journal of Counseling Psychology, 40*, 271–277.

Brogan, M. M., Prochaska, J. O., & Prochaska, J. M. (1999). Predicting termination and continuation status in psychotherapy using the transtheoretical model. *Psychotherapy: Theory, Research, Practice, Training, 36*(2), 105–113.

Brown, L. S. (1994). *Subversive dialogues: Theory in feminist therapy*. New York: Basic Books.

Burns, D. D., & Nolen-Hoeksema, S. (1991). Coping styles, homework compliance, and the effectiveness of cognitive-behavioral therapy. *Journal of Consulting and Clinical Psychology, 59*(2), 305–311.

Burns, D. D., & Spangler, D. L. (2001). Do changes in dysfunctional attitudes mediate changes in depression and anxiety in cognitive behavioral therapy. *Behavior Therapy, 32*, 337–369.

Carryer, J. R. & Greenberg, L. S. (2010). Optimal levels of emotional arousal in experiential therapy of depression. *Journal of Consulting and Clinical Psychology, 78*(2), 190–199.

Caspar, F., & Berger, T. (2005). The future is bright: How can we optimize online counseling, and how can we know whether we have done so? *Counseling Psychologist, 33*, 900–909.

Cepeda-Benito, A., & Short, P. (1998). Self-concealment, avoidance of psychological services, and perceived likelihood of seeking professional help. *Journal of Counseling Psychology, 45*(1), 58–64.

Cohen, B.-Z., Guttmann, D., & Lazar, A. (1998). The willingness to seek help: A cross-national comparison. *Cross-Cultural Research: The Journal of Comparative Social Science, 32*(4), 342–357.

Crits-Christoph, P. (1997). Limitations of the dodo bird verdict and the role of clinical trials in psychotherapy research: Comment on Wampold et al. (1997). *Psychological Bulletin, 122*(3), 216–220.

Crits-Christoph, P., Connolly Gibbons, M. B., Crits-Christoph, K., Narducci, J., Schamberger, M., & Gallop, R. (2006). Can therapists be trained to improve their alliances? A preliminary study of alliance-fostering psychotherapy. *Psychotherapy Research, 16*(3), 268–281.

Crits-Christoph, P., Connolly Gibbons, M. B., Ring-Kurtz, S., Gallop, R., Stirman, S., Present, J., et al. (2008). Changes in positive quality of life over the course of psychotherapy. *Psychotherapy: Theory, Research, Practice, Training, 45*, 419–430.

Crits-Christoph, P., Cooper, A., & Luborsky, L. (1988). The accuracy of therapists' interpretations and the outcome of dynamic psychotherapy. *Journal of Consulting and Clinical Psychology, 56*(4), 490–495.

Cross, D. G., & Warren, C. E. (1984). Environmental factors associated with continuers and terminators in adult outpatient psychotherapy. *British Journal of Medical Psychology, 57*(4), 363–369.

Cummings, N. A. (2001). Interruption, not termination: The model from focused, intermittent psychotherapy throughout the life cycle. *Journal of Psychotherapy in Independent Practice, 3*, 3–18.

Deane, F. P. (1991). Attendance and drop-out from outpatient psychotherapy in New Zealand. *Community Mental Health in New Zealand, 6*, 34–51.

Deane, F. P., & Chamberlain, K. (1994). Treatment fearfulness and distress as predictors of professional psychological help-seeking. *British Journal of Guidance & Counselling, 22*(2), 207–217.

Deane, F. P., & Todd, D. M. (1996). Attitudes and intentions to seek professional psychological help for personal problems or suicidal thinking. *Journal of College Student Psychotherapy, 10*(4), 45–59.

DeRubeis, R. J., Evans, M. D., Hollon, S. D., Garvey, M. J., Grove, W. M., & Tuason, V. B. (1990). How does cognitive therapy work? Cognitive change and symptom change in cognitive therapy and pharmacotherapy for depression. *Journal of Consulting and Clinical Psychology, 58*(6), 862–869.

Elkin, I., Shea, M. T., Watkins, J. T., Imber, S. D., Sotsky, S. M, Collins, J. F., et al. (1989). National Institute of Mental Health Treatment of Depression Collaborative Research Program: General effectiveness of treatments. *Archives of General Psychiatry, 46*(11), 971–982.

Elliott, R., & James, E. (1989). Varieties of client experience in psychotherapy: An analysis of the literature. *Clinical Psychology Review, 9*(4), 443–467.

Elliott, R., Llewelyn, S., Firth-Cozens, J., Margison, F., Shapiro, D., & Hardy, G. (1990). Assimilation of problematic experiences by clients in psychotherapy. *Psychotherapy, 27*, 411–420.

Fava, G. A., Rafanelli, C., Cazzaro, M., Conti, S., & Grandi, S. (1998). Well-being therapy: A novel psychotherapeutic approach for residual symptoms of affective disorders. *Psychological Medicine, 28*(2), 475–480.

Foa, E. B., Riggs, D. S., Massie, E. D., & Yarczower, M. (1995). The impact of fear activation and anger on the efficacy of exposure treatment for PTSD. *Behavior Therapy, 26*, 487–499.

Foa, E. B., Rothbaum, B. O., & Furr, J. M. (2003). Augmenting exposure therapy with other CBT procedures. *Psychiatric Annals, 33*, 47–53.

Frank, J. D. (1961). *Persuasion and healing: A comparative study of psychotherapy*. Baltimore: Johns Hopkins University Press.

Frank, J. D. (1982/1989). Therapeutic components shared by all psychotherapies. In J. H. Harvey, & M. M. Parks (Eds.), *Psychotherapy research and behavior change. Master lecture series* Vol. 1 (pp. 9–37). Washington, DC: American Psychological Association.

Frank, J. D., & Frank, J. B. (1991). *Persuasion and healing: A comparative study of psychotherapy* (3rd ed.). Baltimore: Johns Hopkins University Press.

Frederickson, B. (2001). The role of positive emotions in positive psychology: The broaden-and-build theory of positive emotions. *American Psychologist, 56*, 218–226.

Freud, S. (1953). *The interpretation of dreams* Vols. 4–5. London: Hogarth Press. (Original work published 1900).

Garfield, S. L. (1986). Research on client variables in psychotherapy. In S. L. Garfield, & G. Bergin (Eds.), *Handbook of psychotherapy and behavior change* (3rd ed., pp. 213–256). New York: John Wiley.

Garfield, S. L. (1991). Psychotherapy models and outcome research. *Am Psychol, 46*(12), 1350–1351.

Gelso, C. J., & Carter, J. A. (1985). The relationship in counseling and psychotherapy: Components, consequences, and theoretical antecedents. *Counselling Psychologist, 2*, 155–243.

Gelso, C. J., & Samstag, L. W. (2008). A tripartite model of the therapeutic relationship. In S. Brown, & R. Lent (Eds.), *Handbook of counseling psychology* (4th ed., pp. 267–283). New York: Wiley.

Gilligan, C. (1982). *In a different voice: Psychological theory and women's development*. Cambridge, MA: Harvard University Press.

Greenberg, L. J., Warwar, S. H., & Malcolm, W. M. (2008). Differential effects of emotion-focused therapy and psychoeducation in facilitating forgiveness and letting go of emotional injuries. *Journal of Counseling Psychology, 55*, 185–196.

Greenberg, L. S. (2002). *Emotion-focused therapy: Coaching clients to work through their feelings*. Washington, DC: APA Press.

Greenberg, L. S., & Angus, L. (2004). The contributions of emotion process to narrative change in psychotherapy: A dialectical–constructivist perspective. In L. E. Angus, & J. McLeod (Eds.), *Handbook of narrative psychotherapy: Practice, theory, and research* (pp. 331–350). Thousand Oaks, CA: Sage.

Greenberg, L. S., Auszra, L., & Herrmann, I. R. (2007). The relationship among emotional productivity, emotional arousal and outcome in experiential therapy of depression. *Psychotherapy Research, 17*(4), 482–493.

Greenberg, L. S., Elliott, R., Watson, J. C., & Bohart, A. (2001). Empathy. *Psychotherapy: Theory, Research, Practice, Training, 38*, 380–384.

Greenberg, L. S., & Malcolm, W. (2002). Resolving unfinished business: Relating process to outcome. *Journal of Consulting and Clinical Psychology, 70*, 406–416.

Greenberg, L. S., & Watson, J. (2005). *Emotion-focused therapy of depression*. Washington, DC: APA Press.

Grencavage, L. M., & Norcross, J. C. (1990). Where are the commonalities among the therapeutic common factors? *Professional Psychology: Research and Practice, 21*, 372–378.

Grissom, R. J. (1996). The magical number .7 ± .2: Meta-meta-analysis of the probability of superior outcome in comparisons involving therapy, placebo, and control. *Journal of Consulting and Clinical Psychology, 64*(5), 973–982.

Harper, R. A. (1959). *Psychoanalysis and psychotherapy: 36 systems*. Englewood Cliffs, NJ: Prentice Hall.

Harwood, T. M., Beutler, L. E., Castillo, S., & Karno, M. (2006). Common and specific effects of couples treatment for alcoholism: A test of the generic model of psychotherapy. *Psychology and Psychotherapy: Theory, Research and Practice, 79*(3), 365–384.

Hill, C. E. (2001). *Helping skills: The empirical foundation*. Washington, DC: American Psychological Association.

Hill, C. E. (2004). *Helping skills: Facilitating exploration, insight, and action* (2nd ed.). Washington, DC: American Psychological Association.

Hill, C. E., Castonguay, L. G., Angus, L., Arnkoff, D. B., Barber, J. P., Bohart, A. C., et al. (2007). Insight in psychotherapy: Definitions, processes, consequences, and research directions. In L. G. Castonguay, & C. E. Hill (Eds.), *Insight in psychotherapy* (pp. 441–454). Washington, DC: American Psychological Association.

Hill, C. E., Crook-Lyon, R. E., Hess, S. A., Goates-Jones, M., Roffman, M., Stahl, J., et al. (2006). Prediction of session process and outcome in the Hill dream model: Contributions of client characteristics and the process of the three stages. *Dreaming, 16*(3), 159–185.

Hill, C. E., & Goates, M. K. (2004). Research on the Hill Cognitive-Experiential Dream Model. In C. E. Hill (Ed.). *Dream work in therapy: Facilitating exploration, insight, and action* (pp. 245–288). Washington, DC: American Psychological Association.

Hill, C. E., & Gormally, J. (1977). Effects of reflection, restatement, probe, and nonverbal behaviors on client affect. *Journal of Counseling Psychology, 24*, 92–97.

Hill, C. E., & Knox, S. (2008). Facilitating insight in counseling and psychotherapy. In S. Brown, & R. Lent (Eds.), *Handbook of counseling psychology* (4th ed., pp. 284–302). New York: Wiley.

Hill, C. E., Knox, S., Hess, S. A., Crook-Lyon, R. E., Goates-Jones, M. K., Sim, W., et al. (2007). The attainment of insight in the Hill Dream Model: A case study. *Insight in Psychotherapy, 18*, 200–215.

Hill, C. E., & O'Grady, K. E. (1985). List of therapist intentions illustrated in a case study and with therapists of varying theoretical orientations. *Journal of Counseling Psychology, 32*(1), 193–22.

Hill, C. E., Williams, E. N. (2000). The process of individual therapy. In S. Brown, & R. Lent (Eds.), *Handbook of counseling psychology* (3rd ed., pp. 670–710). Hoboken, NJ: John Wiley & Sons, Inc.

Hoffman-Graff, M. A. (1977). Interviewer use of positive and negative self-disclosure and interviewer-subject sex pairing. *Journal of Counseling Psychology, 24*(3), 184–190.

Hofmann, S. G. (2000). Treatment of social phobia: Potential mediators and moderators. *Clinical Psychology: Science and Practice, 7*, 3–16.

Hollon, S. D., & Beck, A. T. (2004). Cognitive and cognitive behavioral therapies. In M. J. Lambert (Ed.), *Bergin and Garfield's handbook of psychotherapy and behavior change* (5th ed., pp. 447–492). New York: Wiley.

Horvath, A. O. (2006). The alliance in context: Accomplishments, challenges, and future directions. *Psychotherapy: Theory, Research, Practice, Training, 43*(3), 258–263.

Horvath, A. O., & Greenberg, L. S. (1986). The development of the Working Alliance Inventory. In L. S. Greenberg, & W. E. Pinsof (Eds.), *The psychotherapeutic process: A research handbook*. New York: The Guilford Press.

Horvath, A. O., & Greenberg, L. S. (1994). *The Working alliance: theory, research, and practice*. New York: Wiley.

Horvath, A. O., & Symonds, B. D. (1991). Relation between working alliance and outcome in psychotherapy: A meta-analysis. *Journal of Counseling Psychology, 38*(2), 139–149.

Howard, K. I., Lueger, R. J., Maling, M. S., & Martinovich, Z. (1993). A phase model of psychotherapy outcome: Causal mediation of change. *Journal of Consulting and Clinical Psychology, 61*(4), 678–685.

Iwakabe, S., Rogan, K., & Stalikas, A. (2000). The relationship between client emotional expressions, therapist interventions, and the working alliance: An exploration of eight emotional expression events. *Journal of Psychotherapy Integration, 10*, 375–402.

Kadera, S. W., Lambert, M. J., & Andrews, A. A. (1996). How much therapy is really enough? A session-by-session analysis of the psychotherapy dose-effect relationship. *Journal of Psychotherapy Practice & Research, 5*(2), 132–151.

Kagan, N., Armsworth, M. W., Altmaier, E. M., Dowd, E. T., et al. (1988). Professional practice of counseling psychology in various settings. *Counseling Psychologist, 16*(3), 347–365.

Kasper, L. B., Hill, C. E., & Kivlighan, D. M., Jr. (2008). Therapist immediacy in brief psychotherapy: Case study I. *Psychotherapy: Theory, Research, Practice, Training, 45*(3), 281–297.

Kazdin, A. E. (2006). Mechanisms of change in psychotherapy: Advances, breakthroughs, and cutting-edge research (do not yet exist). In R. R. Bootzin, & P. E. McKnight (Eds.), *Strengthening research methodology: Psychological measurement and evaluation* (pp. 77–101). Washington, DC: American Psychological Association.

Kazdin, A. E. (2007). Mediators and mechanisms of change in psychotherapy research. *Annual Review of Clinical Psychology, 3*, 1–27.

Kazdin, A. E. (2008). Evidence-based treatment and practice: New opportunities to bridge clinical research and practice, enhance the knowledge base, and improve patient care. *American Psychologist, 63*, 146–159.

Kelly, A. E., & Achter, J. A. (1995). Self-concealment and attitudes toward counseling in university students. *Journal of Counseling Psychology, 42*(1), 40–46.

Kivlighan, D. M., Jr., Multon, K. D., & Patton, M. J. (2000). Insight and symptom reduction in time-limited psychoanalytic counseling. *Journal of Counseling Psychology, 47*(1), 50–58.

Kivlighan, D. M., Jr., & Shaughnessy, P. (2000). Patterns of working alliance development: A typology of client's working alliance ratings. *Journal of Counseling Psychology, 47*, 362–371.

Knox, S., Hess, S. A., Petersen, D. A., Hill, C. E., et al. (1997). A qualitative analysis of client perceptions of the effects of helpful therapist self-disclosure in long-term therapy. *Journal of Counseling Psychology, 44*(3), 274–283.

Kohut, H. (1977). *The restoration of the self*. New York: International Universities Press.

Komiya, N., Good, G. E., & Sherrod, N. B. (2000). Emotional openness as a predictor of college students' attitudes toward seeking psychological help. *Journal of Counseling Psychology, 47*(1), 138–143.

Kopta, S. M., Howard, K. I., Lowry, J. L., & Beutler, L. E. (1994). Patterns of symptomatic recovery in psychotherapy. *Journal of Consulting and Clinical Psychology, 62*(5), 1009–1016.

Kopta, S. M., Lueger, R. J., Saunders, S. M., & Howard, K. I. (1999). Individual psychotherapy outcome and process research: Challenges leading to greater turmoil or a positive transition? *Annual Review of Psychology, 50*, 441–469.

Krupnick, J. L., Sotsky, S. M., Simmens, S., Moyer, J., Elkin, I., Watkins, J., et al. (1996). The role of the therapeutic alliance in psychotherapy and pharmacotherapy outcome: Findings in the National Institute of Mental Health Treatment of Depression Collaborative Research Program. *Journal of Consulting and Clinical Psychology, 64*(3), 532–539.

Kushner, M. G., & Sher, K. J. (1989). Fears of psychological treatment and its relation to mental health service avoidance. *Professional Psychology: Research and Practice, 20*, 251–257.

Lambert, M. J., & Barley, D. E. (2001). Research summary on the therapeutic relationship and psychotherapy outcome. *Psychotherapy: Theory, Research, Practice, Training, 38*(4), 357–361.

Lambert, M. J., Bergin, A. E., & Garfield, S. L. (1994). The effectiveness of psychotherapy. In A. E. Bergin & S. L. Garfield (Eds.), *Handbook of psychotherapy and behavior change* (4th ed., pp. 143–189). New York: Wiley.

Lambert, M. J., & Ogles, B. M. (2004). The efficacy and effectiveness of psychotherapy. In M. Lambert (Ed.), *Bergin and Garfield's handbook of psychotherapy and behavior change* (5th ed., pp. 139–193). New York: Wiley.

Lambert, M. J., Whipple, J. L., Smart, D. W., Vermeersch, D. A., Nielsen, S. L., & Hawkins, E. J. (2001). The effects of providing therapists with feedback on patient progress during psychotherapy: Are outcomes enhanced? *Psychotherapy Research, 11*(1), 49–68.

Lane, R. D., & Schwartz, G. E. (1992). Levels of emotional awareness: Implications for psychotherapeutic integration. *Journal of Psychotherapy Integration, 2*, 1–18.

Linehan, M., Dimeff, L. A., Reynolds, S. K., Comtois, K. A., Welch, S. S., Heagerty, P., et al. (2002). Dialectal behavior therapy versus comprehensive validation therapy plus 12-step for the treatment of opioid dependent women meeting criteria for borderline personality disorder. *Drug and Alcohol Dependence, 67*(1), 13–26.

Lipsey, M. W., & Wilson, D. B. (1993). The efficacy of psychological, educational, and behavioral treatment: Confirmation from meta-analysis. *American Psychologist, 48*, 1181–1209.

Luborsky, L., Chandler, M., Aurbach, A. H., Cohen, J., & Bachrach, H. M. (1971). Factors influencing the outcome of psychotherapy: A review of quantitative research. *Psychological Bulletin, 75*(3), 145–185.

Luborsky, L., Horvath, A. O., & Greenberg, L. S. (1994). Therapeutic alliances as predictors of psychotherapy outcomes: Factors explaining the predictive success. In A. O. Horvath and L.S. Greenberg (Eds.) *The working alliance: Theory, research, and practice* (pp. 38–50). Oxford, England: John Wiley & Sons.

Malcolm, W., Warwar, S., & Greenberg, L. (2005). Facilitating forgiveness in individual therapy as an approach to resolving interpersonal injuries. In E. L. Worthington, Jr. (Ed.),

The handbook of forgiveness (pp. 379–393). New York: Routledge.

Mallen, M. J., Vogel, D. L., Rochlen, A. B., & Day, S. X. (2005). Online counseling: Reviewing the literature from a counseling psychology framework. *Counseling Psychologist, 33*, 819–871.

Martin, D. J., Garske, J. P., & Davis, K. M. (2000). Relation of the therapeutic alliance with outcome and other variables: A meta-analytic review. *Journal of Consulting and Clinical Psychology, 68*, 438–450.

Marx, J. A., & Gelso, C. J. (1987). Termination of individual counseling in a university counseling center. *Journal of Counseling Psychology, 34*(1), 3–9.

McNeilly, C. L., & Howard, K. I. (1991). The effects of psychotherapy: A reevaluation based on dosage. *Psychotherapy Research, 1*(1), 74–78.

Meisnner, W. W. (1992). The concept of the therapeutic alliance. *Journal of the American Psychoanalytic Association, 40*(4), 1059–1087.

Meyer, B., Pilkonis, P. A., Krupnick, J. L., Egan, M. K., Simmens, S. J., & Sotsky, S. M. (2002). Treatment expectancies, patient alliance and outcome: Further analyses from the National Institute of Mental Health Treatment of Depression Collaborative Research Program. *Journal of Consulting and Clinical Psychology, 70*(4), 1051–1055.

Munley, P. H., Duncan, L. E., McDonnell, K. A., & Sauer, E. M. (2004). Counseling psychology in the United States of America. *Counselling Psychology Quarterly, 17*(3), 247–271.

Norcross, J. C. (1990). An eclectic definition of psychotherapy. In J. K. Zeig, & W. M. Munion (Eds.), *What is psychotherapy?* San Francisco: Jossey-Bass.

Norcross, J. C. (2002). Empirically supported therapy relationships. In J. C. Norcross (Ed.), *Psychotherapy relationships that work: Therapist contributions and responsiveness to patients* (pp. 3–16). New York: Oxford University Press.

Norcross, J. C., Bike, D. H., & Evans, K. L. (2009). The therapist's therapist: A replication and extension 20 years later. *Psychotherapy: Theory, Research, Practice, Training, 46*(1), 32–41.

Norcross, J. C. & Wampold, B. E. (2011). Evidence-based therapy relationships: Research conclusions and clinical practices. *Psychotherapy, 48*(1), 98–102.

Orlinsky, D. E., Grawe, K., & Parks, B. K. (1994). Process and outcome in psychotherapy: Noch einmal. In A. E. Bergin, & S. L. Garfield (Eds), *Handbook of psychotherapy and behavior change* (4th ed., pp. 270–376). New York: John Wiley & Sons.

Orlinsky, D. E., & Howard, K. I. (1986). The psychological interior of psychotherapy: Explorations with the therapy session report questionnaires. In L. S. Greenberg, & W. M. Pinsof (Eds.), *The psychotherapeutic process: A research handbook*. New York: Guilford.

Orlinsky, D. E., Rønnestad, M. H., Willutzki, U. (2004). Fifty years of psychotherapy process outcomes and research: Continuity and change. In M. J. Lambert (Ed.), *Bergin and Garfield's handbook of psychotherapy and behavior change*, (5th ed., pp. 307–393). New York: Wiley.

Patterson, C. H. (1984). Empathy, warmth, and genuineness in psychotherapy: A review of reviews. *Psychotherapy: Theory, Research, Practice, Training, 21*(4), 431–438.

Pekarik, G. (1992). Posttreatment adjustment of clients who drop out early vs. late in treatment. *Journal of Clinical Psychology, 48*, 378–387.

Pennebaker, J. W. (1995). Emotion, disclosure, and health: An overview. In J. W. Pennebaker (Ed.) *Emotion, disclosure, & health* (pp. 3–10). Washington, DC: American Psychological Association.

Prochaska, J. O., DiClemente, C. C., Norcross, J. C., & Goldfried, M. R. (2005). The transtheoretical approach. In J. C. Norcross & M. R. Goldfried (Eds.) *Handbook of psychotherapy integration* (2nd ed., pp. 147–171). New York: Oxford University Press.

Prochaska, J. O., & Norcross, J. C. (2007). *Systems of psychotherapy: a transtheoretical analysis* (6th ed.). Belmont, CA: Thomson Brooks/Cole Pub.

Rafanelli, C., Park, S. K., Ruini, C., Ottolini, F., Cazzaro, M., & Fava, G. A. (2000). Rating well-being and distress. *Stress Medicine, 16*(1), 55–61.

Roe, D., Dekel, R., Harel, G., & Fennig, S. (2006). Clients' reasons for terminating psychotherapy: A quantitative and qualitative inquiry. *Psychology and Psychotherapy: Theory, Research and Practice, 79*(4), 529–538.

Rogers, C. R. (1951). *Client-centered therapy*. Boston: Houghton Mifflin.

Roth, A., & Fonagy, P. (2005). *What works for whom: A critical review of psychotherapy research.* (2nd ed.). New York: Guilford Press.

Ryff, C. D. (1989). Happiness is everything, or is it? Explorations on the meaning of psychological well-being. *Journal of Personality and Social Psychology, 57*(6), 1069–1081.

Sacuzzo, D. P. (1975). What patients want from counseling and psychotherapy. *Journal of Clinical Psychology, 31*(3), 471–475.

Safran, J. D., & Muran, J. C. (1996). The resolution of ruptures in the therapeutic alliance. *Journal of Consulting and Clinical Psychology, 64*, 447–458.

Safran, J. D., & Muran, J. C. (2000). *Negotiating the therapeutic alliance: A relational treatment guide*. New York: Guilford Press.

Seligman, M. E. P. (1995). The effectiveness of psychotherapy: The Consumer Reports study. *American Psychologist, 50*(12), 965–974.

Seligman, M. E. P. (1996). Science as an ally of practice. *American Psychologist, 51*(10), 1072–1079.

Smith, M. L., & Glass, G. V. (1977). Meta-analysis of psychotherapy outcome studies. *American Psychologist, 32*(9), 752–760.

Snell, M. N., Mallinckrodt, B., Hill, R. D., & Lambert, M. J. (2001). Predicting counseling center clients' response to counseling: A 1-year follow-up. *Journal of Counseling Psychology, 48*(4), 463–473.

Stiles, W. B., Glick, M. J., Osatuke, K., Hardy, G. E., Shapiro, D. A., Agnew-Davies, R., et al. (2004). Patterns of alliance development and the rupture-repair hypothesis: Are productive relationships U-shaped or V-shaped). *Journal of Counseling Psychology, 51*, 81–92.

Stricker, G. (2008). Milestones in psychotherapy integration. *Psychotherapy Bulletin, 43*, 25–28.

Sue, D. W., & Sue, D. (2003). *Counseling the culturally diverse: Theory and practice* (4th ed.). New York: Houghton Mifflin.

Sin, N., & Lyubomirsky, S. (2009). Enhancing well-being and alleviating depressive symptoms with positive psychology interventions: A practice- friendly meta-analysis. *Journal of clinical psychology: In session, 55*, 467–487.

Super, D. E. (1955). Transition: From vocational guidance to counseling psychology. *Journal of Counseling Psychology, 2*, 3–9.

Teasdale, J. D., Segal, Z. V., Williams, J. M. G., Ridgeway, V. A., Soulsby, J. M., & Lau, M. A. (2000). Prevention of relapse/recurrence in major depression by mindfulness-based cognitive therapy. *Journal of Consulting and Clinical Psychology, 68,* 615–623.

Thompson, S. D., & Super, D. E. (Eds.). (1964). *The professional preparation of counseling psychologists: Report of the 1964 Greyston Conference.* New York: Bureau of Publications, Teachers College, Columbia University.

Tokar, D. M., Hardin, S. I., Adams, E. M., & Brandel, I. W. (1996). Clients' expectations about counseling and perceptions of the working alliance. *Journal of College Student Psychotherapy, 11*(2), 9–26.

Van der Kolk, B. A. (1995). The body keeps the score: Memory and the evolving psychobiology of posttraumatic stress. *Harvard Review of Psychiatry, 1,* 253–265.

Vogel, D. L., Wade, N. G., & Hackler, A. H. (2008). Emotional expression and the decision to seek therapy: The mediating roles of the anticipated benefits and risks. *Journal of Social & Clinical Psychology, 27*(3), 254–278.

Vogel, D. L., & Wester, S. R. (2003). To seek help or not to seek help: The risks of self-disclosure. *Journal of Counseling Psychology, 50*(3), 351–361.

Vogel, D. L., Wester, S. R., Wei, M., & Boysen, G. A. (2005). The Role of Outcome Expectations and Attitudes on Decisions to Seek Professional Help. *Journal of Counseling Psychology, 52*(4), 459–470. doi:10.1037/0022-0167.52.4.459.

Wachtel, P. (2000). Integrative psychotherapy. In A. E. Kazdin (Ed.), *Encyclopedia of psychology* Vol. 4 (pp. 315–318). Washington, DC: American Psychological Association.

Wachtel, P. (2008). *Relational theory and the practice of psychotherapy.* New York: Guilford Press.

Wachtel, P. L. (2002). Termination of therapy: An effort at integration. *Journal of Psychotherapy Integration, 12,* 373–383.

Wampold, B. E. (1997). Methodological problems in identifying efficacious psychotherapies. *Psychotherapy Research, 7*(1), 21–43.

Wampold, B. E. (2001). *The great psychotherapy debate: Models, methods, and findings.* Mahwah, NJ: Lawrence Erlbaum Associates.

Wampold, B. E., & Brown, G. S. J. (2005). Estimating variability in outcomes attributable to therapists: A naturalistic study of outcomes in managed care. *Journal of Consulting and Clinical Psychology, 73*(5), 914–923.

Wampold, B. E., Mondin, G. W., Moody, M., Stich, F., Benson, K., & Ahn, H. -N. (1997). A meta-analysis of outcome studies comparing bona fide psychotherapies: Empirically, "all must have prizes." *Psychological Bulletin, 122*(3), 203–215.

Whisman, M. A., Miller, I. W., Norman, W. H., & Keitner, G. I. (1991). Cognitive therapy with depressed inpatients: Specific effects on dysfunctional cognitions. *Journal of Consulting and Clinical Psychology, 59*(2), 282–288.

Wierzbicki, M., & Pekarik, G. (1993). A meta-analysis of psychotherapy dropout. *Professional Psychology: Research and Practice, 24,* 190–195.

Wrenn, C. G. (1966). Birth and early childhood of a journal. *Journal of Counseling Psychology, 13,* 485–488.

Prevention and Psychoeducation in Counseling Psychology

Melissa L. Morgan *and* Elizabeth M. Vera

Abstract

The history of prevention and its long role in counseling psychology are discussed in this chapter. Traditional definitions of primary, secondary, and tertiary prevention are provided, as well as newer definitions that insist that true prevention must occur before the onset of a diagnosable disorder. We further discuss what constitutes a successful prevention program, prevention's role in training in counseling psychology programs, and selected examples of recent prevention programs. Finally, the closely related construct of psychoeducation is discussed, along with applications of best practice in this area. Application to current societal problems is provided.

Keywords: prevention, psychoeducation, counseling psychology mission, remediation alternative, counselor roles

Prevention is an intuitively appealing approach to the maintenance of well-being for people around the world. Numerous daily activities are intended to prevent a host of health problems. For example, we wear seat belts, take vitamins, exercise regularly, and watch what we eat, all in an effort to maintain our health and well-being (Conyne, 2004). However, activities aimed at the prevention of mental health problems, such as actions taken to reduce substance abuse, depression, and suicide, are less widely accepted and understood in the general population. Even among mental health professionals, prevention activities may be less frequently adopted for use with clients. Counseling psychology, however, is one of the mental health professions that has historically been a proponent of prevention. In this chapter, we examine the role of counseling psychologists in contemporary prevention research, practice, and training; describe qualities of effective prevention programs; and suggest future directions for the field of prevention. We also review the use of psychoeducation in the field of counseling psychology, a topic that is closely related to prevention.

What Is Prevention?

Several definitions for prevention currently exist in the literature, based on multiple conceptualizations of the term. Prevention has historically been subdivided into three categories: primary, secondary, and tertiary. *Primary prevention* has been defined as that which reduces the incidence of new cases of a designated disorder (Albee, 1983). *Secondary prevention* targets populations exhibiting early symptoms, with the purpose of preventing further symptoms (Durlak, 1997), and *tertiary prevention* aims to reduce the effects of existing problems (Caplan, 1964).

The three levels of prevention can be illustrated with a relevant problem, binge drinking on college campuses. An example of primary prevention of binge drinking is teaching students refusal skills that would help them to resist peer pressure to drink. Providing students with such skills would ostensibly prevent them from ever beginning patterns of drinking that would include binge drinking. Thus, any emergence of the problem could be effectively circumvented, and new cases of this problem would be decreased.

Providing education to students who had exhibited early warning signs of binge drinking (possibly through public intoxication arrests or self-report) about the nature of addiction is an example of secondary prevention. These students, who exhibit early symptoms of substance abuse already, or have at least been noted to have an increased propensity for binge drinking, would be targeted for intervention, and the goal would be to prevent further episodes of binge drinking or other serious symptoms of substance abuse from developing.

Finally, using a 12-step program as a form of relapse prevention for binge drinking would be an example of tertiary prevention. In this case, the substance abuse has already become a problem for the individual, and the prevention effort is designed to remediate the effects of the problem on the person and to help him/her avoid any future incidents.

To further exemplify these concepts in the public health realm, the recommendation that we all eat five servings of fruits and vegetables per day to reduce the *occurrence* of poor health and nutrition is a primary prevention initiative. Educating individuals who may have evidenced patterns of unhealthy eating already about nutrition and dietary changes is a secondary prevention initiative, and providing nutritional supplements and a set diet to remediate existing nutrition problems is an example of tertiary prevention. In each of these illustrations, what differentiates the three types of prevention is the extent to which problems have already appeared for the target audience of the intervention.

More recently, theorists within the field of medicine have proposed that true preventive interventions are only those which occur before the onset of a diagnosable disorder. Specifically, they recommend use of the terms *universal preventive interventions* to characterize activities targeting general public or nonindividual audiences, *selective preventive interventions* to describe those activities that focus on specific populations that have been identified as being at risk, and *indicated preventive interventions* to classify those interventions targeting high-risk individuals with current symptoms or biological markers that do not yet meet diagnostic criteria (Munoz, Mrazek, & Haggerty, 1996). To connect these terms to the aforementioned example, the recommendation to all to eat five servings of fruits and vegetables per day could be classified as a universal preventive intervention, providing diet information to those identified as at risk for nutritional disorders is a selective preventive intervention, and providing vitamins and specific diet recommendations to

people who have symptoms of nutrition problems but have not yet been identified as having nutritional disorders is an indicated preventive intervention. Note that in all of the examples for this specific model of conceptualizing prevention, the problem (in this case, diagnosed nutritional disorder) has not yet actually occurred.

Romano and Hage (2000) classify prevention in a way that encompasses several major strands of previous conceptualizations of the construct. They posit prevention as consisting of interventions that have one or more of the following characteristics: stopping a problem from ever occurring; delaying the onset of a problem behavior; reducing the impact of an existing problem behavior; strengthening knowledge, attitudes, and behaviors that promote emotional and physical well-being; and/or supporting institutional, community, and government policies that promote physical and emotional well-being. This definition is a broader, more inclusive way of thinking about prevention activities. To return to the binge drinking example, a prevention program meeting these criteria might either prevent, delay, or reduce the impact of binge drinking, educate on the strengths-based behaviors surrounding non–binge drinking, and/or be in line with school policy promoting student wellness.

Finally, Robert Conyne, a pioneer in the field of prevention, has proposed the following definition:

> Prevention is a goal for both everyday life and
> for service delivery, through which people become
> empowered to interact effectively and appropriately
> within varying levels of systems (micro, meso, exo,
> and macro) and settings (individual, family, school,
> community, work). Preventive application can
> yield a reduction in the occurrence of new
> cases of a problem, in the duration and severity of
> incipient problems, and it can promote strengths
> and optimal human functioning.
> (Conyne, 2004, p. 25)

For the purposes of this chapter, we will primarily discuss primary and secondary prevention programs. These interventions may occur at any of the levels defined by Munoz, Mrazek, and Haggerty (1996).

History of Prevention

The concept of prevention has been traced back to ancient civilizations, drawing from such sources as Greek philosophers and folk wisdom (Spaulding & Balch, 1983). Prevention has been a longstanding topic in the professional literature of many fields in the United States. In the field of public health, for example, attention has often been given to specific, targeted outreach programs related to specific disorders (i.e., obesity, HIV, sexually transmitted diseases). Along with this focus has been an emphasis on addressing inequalities in health care. In 1979, for example, the public health field initiated an ongoing public health agenda, "Healthy People 2010," for increasing quality of life and eliminating health disparities (Romano & Hage, 2000). In a recent Institute of Medicine brief by the Committee on Assuring the Health of the Public in the 21st Century, a new call and new recommendations were made to focus prevention efforts on communities, to take into account socioeconomic inequities, and to create political policies that address issues such as education, adequate housing, a living wage, and clean air (National Academy of Sciences, 2002).

Primary prevention's role within the field of psychology and mental health as a whole has been sporadic, although several significant events have taken place. In 1976, the National Institute of Mental Health declared that primary prevention was an idea whose time had come (Klein & Goldston, 1977), and by the 1980s, many programs had been developed that utilized primary prevention. Because some felt that these programs were not always tied to evidence of their effectiveness, however, a general skepticism arose about primary prevention as practiced by psychologists (Conyne, 1991). The American Psychological Association (APA) responded to this skepticism by creating a task force for Promotion, Prevention, and Intervention Alternatives in Psychology to identify effective prevention programs. Several common characteristics of these programs were delineated (Conyne, 1991), resulting in the manual *14 Ounces of Prevention* (Price, Cowen, Lorion, & Ramos-McKay, 1988). In 2003, APA President Martin Seligman created a second APA task force on prevention, entitled Prevention: Promoting Strength, Resilience, and Health in Young People. This task force synthesized prevention knowledge and offered prevention practice guidelines in a special issue of the *American Psychologist* (2003).

Despite the occurrence of these significant events, one issue that has perhaps slowed the progress of prevention activities from being more incorporated into the field of psychology as a whole is disagreement on the definition of what constitutes a prevention activity. In 1991, at the National Institute of Mental Health (NIMH)-sponsored

National Prevention Conference, the term *prevention science* was coined. This term was put forth as a descriptor of previous prevention studies that exclusively focused on reduction of risk factors for mental disorders. The Institute of Medicine differentiated between "prevention activities" and "promotion activities," stating that promotion activities are not included in the spectrum of prevention activities because they "focus on the enhancement of well-being" rather than intervening "to prevent psychological or social problems or mental disorders" (Mrazek & Haggerty, 1994, p. 27). Many in the field of psychology felt this designation was limiting (Masten & Coatsworth, 1998), including APA President Seligman's task force. In 2003, an issue of the *American Psychologist* was devoted to presenting empirically based prevention studies with children and youths, in which prevention is conceptualized as encompassing activities that focus on enhancement of well-being, as well as prevention of psychological disorders.

Prevention and Counseling Psychology

Prevention has long been a central component in the identity of counseling psychology, and can be traced back to the vocational guidance movement and the mental health and hygiene efforts of the early 1900s in the United States. The vocational guidance movement, spurred by Frank Parsons, looked at the match between worker and societal needs to allow workers to be more productive, satisfied, and able to contribute to societal solutions (Conyne, 1987; Gelso & Fretz, 1992). In the mental health movement, Clifford Beers called for improved treatment and prevention of mental illness (Romano & Hage, 2000). Despite this long-standing historical and philosophical commitment to well-being and prevention in the field as a whole, the actual practice of prevention has ebbed and flowed. Calls have been made through the years to more fully integrate prevention into the identity of counseling psychologists, a proposition that essentially calls counseling psychology back to its roots. Hurdles such as the debate over an evidence-based practice approach within the field of psychology as a whole have caused counseling psychologists to periodically contemplate their unique contribution to the field, and whether such a perspective takes us further from our roots of commitment to prevention, multiculturalism, and social justice (Hage, 2003).

A Special Interest Group for Prevention and Public Interest was formed by Division 17 (Society of Counseling Psychology) of the APA in the early

1990s, and in 2000, Romano and Hage proposed a prevention-based agenda for the field, which outlined the goals of utilizing systemic and integrative models, targeting children and youth for early intervention, emphasizing sensitivity to diversity, and advocating for more thorough training in prevention interventions. In the same issue of *The Counseling Psychologist* (2000), Conyne proposed a resolution to formally incorporate prevention into counseling psychology. Prevention has also been specifically called for in therapy practices, with Lewis and Lewis (1981) outlining skills needed by counselors engaging in primary prevention counseling (Conyne, 1997).

Prevention Training in Counseling Psychology Programs

Although it has been argued by some counseling psychologists that specialized training in prevention is not needed in graduate programs (as students already learn skills such as effective communication and knowledge of theoretical models of change in therapeutic training; Conyne, 2004), some graduate training programs within counseling psychology have begun to emphasize specific training in prevention. This commitment is evidenced by practicum settings related to prevention activities, opportunities for faculty and student prevention practice and research, emphasis on theoretical change models, courses on prevention methodology, and an emphasis on strengths and resilience perspectives in working with clients (Romano & Hage, 2000). Such efforts, however, are not the norm. Most training programs still emphasize individual remediation of psychological disorders, and funding sources still seem to prefer individualized rather than systemically based preventive interventions (Roche & Sadowski, 1996).

There is recent evidence that the commitment to training in prevention may be increasing in the field, however. *The Counseling Psychologist* has published two special issues on prevention. "Best Practice Guidelines on Prevention" (2007) and "Culturally Relevant Prevention" (2007) provide comprehensive summaries of how to design prevention programs and how to integrate cultural relevance into such efforts, respectively. These contributions are significant since the journal had not published an issue focused on prevention since 2000. Notwithstanding the significance of these special issues, no current database demonstrates the level of commitment that training programs have to preparing their students to engage in careers that include prevention. For example, it is unknown what percentage of training programs either require or offer classes on the topic. It is also unknown to what extent practicum or internship programs include prevention activities as required elements. So, at best, these special issues might indicate that a critical mass of scholars is now arguing for the inclusion of prevention training in doctoral curricula.

Successful Prevention Programs

What constitutes a successful prevention program? Cowen (1984) stressed that any good prevention program must include thoughtful planning and be founded on a "generative base," derived from theory and research. Such theoretical bases can come from a variety of sources, including positive psychology, behavioral theories, and ecological frameworks. All of these frameworks should be culturally informed, as a frequently cited downfall of prevention activities is a lack of cultural relevance. One way that cultural relevance can be successfully accomplished is to engage in collaborative, community-based programs in which the participants are stakeholders in the process and help to plan the program components (Vera et al., 2007). Key factors in this process include addressing existing community structures that perpetuate inequality and not focusing exclusively on the individual participants themselves, as this may have the result of placing undeserved blame and responsibility on the individual and not the system or environment (Prilletensky, 1997; Vera & Reese, 2000).

Operating from a theoretically and culturally informed base helps program leaders to choose an appropriate direction for the project. This, in combination with collaborative involvement from community constituents, can be a good starting point for the development of culturally responsive programs, which must include both addressing "surface structure modifications" and "deep structure modifications," according to Resnicow, Solar, Breathwaite, Ahluwalia, and Butler (2000). Examples of surface structure modifications would include the translation of interventions into the primary language of the participants, whereas deep structure modifications would increase perceptions of "face validity" or relevance of a program's goals to the needs of the participants. We return to a discussion of this issue in the section on psychoeducation.

In their work, Hage et al. (2007) outlined several overarching goals that have been found to contribute to effective prevention programming. They point out that such programs must include risk reduction, use methods to increase strengths in community or individuals, and have social justice as a goal. Risk factors to be reduced may include those at the individual or systemic level. These efforts are differentiated from treatment efforts in that treatment addresses symptoms, thereby possibly alleviating some distress, but not reducing risk per se because it does not reduce the occurrence of new cases. When risk is not reduced, prevention programs will fail to address prominent societal health disparities among people of different races, ethnicities, and socioeconomic levels—a philosophical goal of prevention work that is representative of social justice.

Increasing strengths or well-being in communities of individuals consists of promoting awareness of existing assets and providing ways to capitalize on these strengths. Promotion of well-being via a focus on strengths promotion has been found to be both cost effective and psychologically beneficial for individuals and societies (Albee & Ryan-Finn, 1993). Finally, social justice–oriented prevention programs often focus on social policy change (which is a component of social justice). Successful examples of this in the United States include the women's movement, Social Security, and Medicare programs (Hage et al., 2007). Such programs are essentially examples of distributive justice interventions which, by changing opportunities, strive to prevent the development of mental health problems associated with injustice (e.g., sexism, classism). Although there is still undoubtedly much more that needs to be done to combat oppression in this society, such policies often indicate a willingness at the macro level to begin this process.

Recommendations for the more structural aspects of effective prevention programs call for initiatives to be comprehensive, utilize varied teaching methods, have sufficient dosage or program intensity, build positive relationships for participants, give good staff training, and have sufficient program evaluation components (Nation et al., 2003). Comprehensive programs are those that address multiple factors across multiple contexts. In other words, rather than a narrow focus on one prevention strategy and one problem behavior (e.g., teaching conflict resolution to reduce violence), comprehensive prevention programs use several different types of interventions that may take place in a variety of settings and affect a range of problem behaviors. It has been shown that such comprehensive approaches to prevention are the most effective for reducing or preventing problem behaviors (Nation et al., 2003). An example of

a comprehensive prevention program will be presented later in this chapter.

Similarly, varied teaching methods have been found to increase the chances of successfully reaching more participants and increasing positive outcomes of prevention programs. The range of effective teaching methods typically include some type of focused skill set development (e.g., using role plays or modeling), which varies across type of intervention program. Promoting strong relationships, particularly with at least one adult, have been associated with positive outcomes for prevention in children, in contrast with prevention programs that rely solely on peer evaluation and mentorship (Grossman & Tierney, 1998). Well-trained prevention personnel or staff help to ensure a successful and effective prevention program. Finally, issues such as timing, competent and culturally sensitive interventions, and supervision of the program all contribute in crucial ways to the success of a prevention program (Lewis, Battistich, & Schaps, 1990).

The research methodology by which prevention programs are developed and evaluated should be carefully considered, as it has been noted that processes that contribute to social change are not easily measured with only experimental or quasi-experimental designs (Prillentensky & Nelson, 1997). Another concern is that, with the use of randomized, control-group designs, although they are often preferred for federally funded projects (Biglan et al., 2003), it can be difficult to reconcile the design of the evaluation with the needs of the community (Reese & Vera, 2007). Specifically, it can be difficult to convince underserved communities of the value of no-treatment or delayed-treatment control groups, when the goal of community leaders may be to obtain as many services for as many individuals as possible.

Qualitative or mixed methodological studies may therefore be more easily utilized to address community needs. Such types of research have the advantage of being able to more fully address cultural contexts and to more deeply understand the participant's perspective. First of all, qualitative methodology, such as semistructured interviewing, allows the researcher to get the perspective of the participant and therefore gain context for any interventions, thereby helping to increase the chances that any resulting program will be responsive to community, rather than only researcher needs. Second, in qualitative studies, each participant is given a distinctly individual voice, which increases the feeling of involvement of participants and possibly increases participant investment in the project, as well as avoids the above-mentioned problems associated with no-treatment or delayed-treatment quantitative designs. Certain types of qualitative research, such as *participatory action research*, stress both collaboration with participants and a social justice agenda (Creswell, 2007), and are thus particularly well suited to prevention activities.

For example, in utilizing a participatory action research approach for a qualitative study involving recent immigrants to the United States, interview data and observations collected would give information on the process of immigration for the participants at a very detailed level. Such specific information could be invaluable in gaining the "inside perspective" needed to inform effective political and social change in this area. For example, if a participant discussed the specific difficulty of obtaining community connections when he or she first arrived in the United States, then the interviewer might ask what would have been helpful to the immigrant to address this problem of social support. The participant's response could potentially provide valuable information for informing prevention programs for recent immigrants (Morgan, 2006).

Ethics is a final, very important, consideration in the development of an effective prevention program. Because prevention programs often deal with a system, many ethical considerations and possible negative impacts may not be initially obvious. In addition to considering the issues of informed consent and competency, some particular areas of possible negative impact include publicly identifying a stigmatized group (Bloom, 1993), targeting behaviors that serve a protective purpose for the community (Pope, 1990), and long-term negative impact on the community even though short-term impact is positive (Brown & Liao, 1999). For example, if parents in a low-income neighborhood choose to keep their children indoors most of the time because of a lack of neighborhood safety, and a prevention program focuses on building a green space to bring children outside more, there may be short-term gain in the children having a place to play, but long-term harm in that more children fall victim to random gang violence. Again, designing collaborative, community-based programs, in which participants actively engage with researchers in the discussion of such topics, helps to address concerning issues effectively from the beginning of the research process. In this case, neighborhood participants would likely be able to alert researchers to the possible long-term consequences of providing an attractive green space before the program was even implemented, thus saving time and money and making the goals of the program much more relevant to the community.

Recent Prevention Literature/Programs: An Update

In general, increased attention has been paid to prevention in the psychology field in the last 5 to 10 years. In 2003, a special issue of *The American Psychologist* was devoted to "Prevention that Works for Children and Youth." An outgrowth of APA President Martin Seligman's emphasis on positive psychology (i.e., a focus on more strengths-based psychological approaches and research), this journal issue highlighted the state of prevention with children and youths in the past several years. Major themes included advocacy for the integration of science and prevention (Biglan, Mrazek, Carnine, & Flay, 2003), more effective evaluation of prevention programs and the need for more results-based accountability (Wandersman & Florin, 2003), a highlight of prevention work being done in various contexts, such as health care settings, schools, and family environments (Kumpfer & Alvarado, 2003; Greenberg, Weissberg, O'Brien, Zins, Fredericks, Resnik, & Elias, 2003; Johnson & Millstein, 2003), and the state of federal prevention funding for children (Ripple & Zigler, 2003).

The recent literature on prevention in the field of counseling psychology has frequently contained an emphasis on cultural relevance, and, in fact, culturally relevant prevention is where the field of counseling psychology seems to have made the greatest contribution within the prevention arena. In the 2007 issue of *The Counseling Psychologist* that focused on "Culturally Relevant Prevention," a call was made for counseling psychologists to continue to devise and implement prevention programs that are truly multicultural in nature, not in name only. Specifically, both cultural relevance (i.e., the extent to which outcomes are consistent with beliefs, values, and desired outcomes of a particular community; see Kumpfer, Alvarado, Smith, & Bellamy, 2002; Nation et al., 2003) and cultural competence (i.e., a standard that calls for the program administrators to have the required training and experience to work with a specific population; see Lopez, 1997) were discussed as being necessary for a culturally relevant prevention program (Reese & Vera, 2007). Another theme of the issue was the need to bring together social justice, prevention, and multiculturalism, which are each components of the identity of a counseling psychologist. More frequent attempts to merge these efforts in research and literature was suggested as one way to begin to approach this goal of integration (Adams, 2007). Several prevention programs based in the United States were highlighted throughout the issue. Each program focused on health, educational, and/or familial outcomes designed to reduce disparities. Another issue of *The Counseling Psychologist* focused on "Best Practices in Prevention" and was discussed extensively earlier in this chapter.

On the international front and within the broader psychological and academic realms, several recent prevention studies have also highlighted cultural issues and contain examples of many of the elements of successful prevention efforts discussed previously in this chapter. In an international program for preventing human immunodeficiency virus/sexually transmitted disease (HIV/STD) for married men in urban poor communities in India, for example, both a community-based research and programming and a multidisciplinary approach (psychologists, anthropologists, microbiologists, and educators) was utilized. The mixed methodological study was grounded in a philosophy of transdisciplinary research and was funded by a grant from the U.S. National Institute of Mental Health (NIMH) grant, thus providing an example of community-based, collaborative prevention programming that received external funding (Schensul, Nastasi, & Verma, 2006).

In another recent international and cross-culturally collaborative project, Brazilian professionals designed a program to prevent child abuse in Rio de Janeiro. This endeavor included interviewing child protective professionals to explore their beliefs about what would be needed in an effective program for preventing child abuse in Rio de Janeiro, obtaining their input on necessary systemic change (i.e., utilizing qualitative methodology), and providing training that evolved from a larger nine-country initiative sponsored by the International Society for the Prevention of Child Abuse and Neglect (IPSCAN) and that incorporated the views of these Brazilian child protective professionals (Lidchi, 2007).

The final example of recent international prevention efforts is a program developed in the United States that was adapted for use in Russia. The Reconnecting Youth (RY) drug use prevention program developed at the University of Washington was utilized with youth in Moscow through funding by the National Institute on Drug Abuse. In their adaptation, the program administrators used focus groups to better understand the viewpoint of youths in Moscow and to incorporate this understanding into their cross-cultural adaptation. Materials for the program were all translated and back-translated, and an iterative consultation process was utilized in which cultural linguistic advisors and cross-cultural consultants gave input on the cultural appropriateness on the program. The adapted program was used to successfully decrease identified risk factors and increase protective factors in the Russian youths (Tsarouk, Thompson, Herting, Walsh, & Randell, 2006).

These examples demonstrate current and successful prevention projects that encompass many of the traits of effective programs discussed in this chapter. Since counseling psychology is a discipline not specifically represented in all countries (Leong & Leach, 2007), the international programs described here exemplify work being done in other disciplines within the area of prevention in general.

Psychoeducation

Psychoeducation is a topic closely related to prevention in the literature. Within the history of counseling psychology, psychoeducation has always been considered a staple of the field and, in fact, is identified as one of the defining themes of the profession (Gelso & Fretz, 1992). Within the history of the mental health professions, psychoeducation has played an important role in the treatment of many psychological problems. Authier (1977) documents various influences on the field of psychology that have contributed to the emergence of psychoeducational approaches. Among these influences is the community mental health movement of the 1960s, during which time the feasibility of a remedial approach as a hallmark of mental health services was questioned (Hobbs, 1964). It was thought that teaching people the skills they would need to avoid psychological symptoms (e.g., coping techniques, parenting approaches) was a more productive role for mental health professionals. However, some scholars trace the history of psychoeducation as far back as Alfred Adler, who, in the 1920s, gave public demonstrations of counseling with families to educate the community about healthy family functioning (Carlson, 2006).

More recent literature has defined psychoeducation as "among the most effective of evidence-based practices that have emerged in both clinical trials and community settings" (p. 205) (Lukens & McFarlane, 2004). Many working definitions of psychoeducation exist in the literature. For the purposes of this chapter, psychoeducation will be defined as an intervention approach that integrates psychotherapeutic and educational components (Lukens & McFarlane, 2004) and that can be used in both remedial and preventative contexts. Dixon (1999) argued that psychoeducation embodies a paradigm of empowerment and collaboration that stresses competence-building and coping, and builds on the strengths of the client. Rather than solely focusing on the amelioration or prevention of symptoms, psychoeducation focuses on health promotion, viewing clients as learners and therapists as teachers.

Psychoeducation has become a widespread approach to the treatment of a variety of psychological problems. For example, recent reviews of the literature and meta-analyses have been published on the use of psychoeducation in the treatment and/or prevention of eating disorders (Fingeret et al., 2006), bipolar disorders (Rouget & Aubry, 2006), teenage suicide (Portzky & van Heering, 2006), and bullying (Newman-Carlson & Horne, 2004). As a result of accumulating evidence, psychoeducation is now seen as an important component in treating a variety of medical problems, where it is used to enhance treatment compliance and prevent disease progression. Recent mandates at both the federal and international levels have pushed to include psychoeducation as a focal point in treatment for schizophrenia and other mental illnesses, and these efforts are backed by national policy makers (President's New Freedom Commission on Mental Health, 2003) as well as influential family self-help groups such as the National Alliance for the Mentally Ill (NAMI) (Lehman & Steinwachs, 1998; McEvoy, Scheifler, & Frances, 1999).

In the remainder of this section, a sample of psychoeducational best practices in the prevention of three psychological problems will be presented, along with a discussion of several important considerations in the development and evaluation of psychoeducational interventions. Finally, the role and preparation of the counselor as psychoeducator will be presented.

Psychoeducation Best Practices in Adolescent Suicide Prevention, Bullying, and Eating Disorders

ADOLESCENT SUICIDE PREVENTION

Psychoeducation programs have been the most popular forms of adolescent suicide prevention (Portzky & van Heeringen, 2006). Psychoeducation reduces suicidality mainly by increasing adolescents' understanding of symptoms of suicidal ideation/intent and by promoting help-seeking behavior (Aseltine & Martino, 2004). As such, the intended positive outcomes of such programs are an increased ability to detect suicidal symptoms in self and others and an increased willingness to reach out for help for oneself, or for friends and family who may be suicidal. However, few studies have shown a decrease in the incidence of suicide attempts in connection with such programs. Critics of these psychoeducational prevention programs have argued that it is important to design programs that alter knowledge and attitudes that will translate into behavioral changes.

One recent psychoeducational prevention program that was able to demonstrate a reduction in suicidal behavior was Signs of Suicide (SOS) (Aseltine & DeMartino, 2004), the focus of which is on peer education and intervention. Peer intervention as a focus of adolescent suicide prevention programs is rooted in studies that have found that adolescents communicate distress more often and more easily with their friends than with family members or other concerned adults (Kalafat & Elias, 1995). The content of SOS includes providing information about incidence rates of suicide attempts and completions, presenting data on risk and protective factors, and describing what is called the "suicide process." The suicide process involves the progression of suicidality from ideation to attempts to completion (van Heeringen, 2001). The model is used in psychoeducation because it implies the possibility of intervention and help being valuable at multiple points in the process.

The peer intervention component of the program teaches participants to recognize warning signs of suicidal ideation and behavior, and teaches appropriate strategies of intervention (i.e., active listening, encouragement of help-seeking). Finally, such programs also identify school- and community-based resources, such as school counselors. The objective of this program is to help adolescents better monitor their friends and peers for signs of suicidal ideation or intent *and* to increase the likelihood that such signs will be reported to adults capable of providing help. Although psychoeducational suicide prevention programs may not be optimal for use with actively suicidal teens, they appear to be an appropriate intervention to change peers' awareness of and ability to identify those who may be at risk from among their peer groups (Portzky & van Heeringen, 2006).

BULLYING

In the research on bullying, psychoeducational programs that have adopted social learning theoretical underpinnings have been in use for over 30 years (Olweus, 1978). One of the most commonly used psychoeducational prevention programs based on learning theory to date, Bully Busters (Newman, Horne, & Bartolomucci, 2000) was designed to instruct teachers in elementary schools to acquire the skills and knowledge to better confront bullying and victimization in their classrooms. As role models, teachers play a powerful role in what their students learn about norms regarding bullying, as documented by previous research (Wilezenski et al., 1994). If teachers ignore or tolerate bullying as normative behavior, it teaches children to do the same.

The Bully Busters program is taught to teachers in three sessions and has seven content areas including increasing awareness of bullying, recognizing bullies and victims, teaching potential interventions, assisting victims appropriately, preventing bullying behavior, and promoting healthy coping skills. The program was offered to the teachers as part of a school-based in-service session. The results of a controlled experiment found that teachers who participated in the program were more self-efficacious in regard to identifying bullies and victims, and had acquired a greater repertoire of intervention skills than were teachers who did not participate in the program. In terms of long-term change, such programs have been found to reduce incidents of bullying in the school by as much as 50% (Newman et al., 2000).

As is the case with suicide psychoeducation prevention programs, the emphasis in the majority of the bullying psychoeducational prevention programs is on raising awareness and empowering individuals who have special access to the perpetrators and victims. Although some psychoeducational programs target individuals who may be at risk for such problems (e.g., potential victims, suicidal youth), such programs have ignored the role of significant others in the prevention of these problems. By including a wider scope of participants, rather than simply attempting to identify and work with only depressed youth, bullies, or victims, these programs have a systemic philosophical underpinning whereby the power of the environment in shaping individuals' behavior is not only affirmed, but is the target of the intervention. Although it is probably the case that bullying or adolescent suicidal attempts will never be completely eliminated from the experience of children, programs that attempt to change school and peer climates have been shown to be very promising.

EATING DISORDERS

Although the aforementioned programs have aimed to influence important significant others as agents of change, the majority of eating disorders psychoeducational prevention programs have targeted individuals, namely girls, and have focused on changing unhealthy thinking that can lead to eating disorder symptomatology. A large number of programs have been designed with such objectives in mind. However, recently, there has been some controversy over these programs. One area of debate revolves around potential iatrogenic effects of incorporating descriptive information about eating disorders into an intervention. O'Dea and Abraham (2000) argued against the inclusion of such psychoeducational material by warning of the potential for glamorizing and normalizing eating disorders and introducing young people to dangerous methods of weight control. Fortunately, a recent meta-analysis found no evidence of this effect on program participants (Fingeret, Warren, Cepeda-Benito, & Gleaves, 2006).

The content of psychoeducational approaches to eating disorders prevention typically includes information about healthy nutrition and diet; body satisfaction; idealization of thinness; the dangers of overexercising, binging, and purging; and other symptoms of eating disorders. Evaluations of these programs have found that participants generally demonstrate an increase in knowledge from pre- to post-test, changes in levels of body satisfaction are typically minimal, and providing information about symptoms of eating disorders does not result in an increase in unhealthy behaviors, such as excessive exercising or purging.

One of the most interesting recent findings from a meta-analysis conducted by Fingeret et al. (2006) is that specific program content differences are not related to significant effect size differences. Rather, what does account for larger effect sizes in such programs is targeting participants who are at higher-risk for eating disorders, using interactive and multiple-session formats, and working with girls who are over 15 years of age. Additionally, the authors found that purely psychoeducational approaches were equally as effective in influencing knowledge, eating patterns, and body dissatisfaction as were interventions that incorporated a cognitive-behavioral therapy component.

In general, it appears that good evidence supports the use of psychoeducation to prevent eating disorders and related symptoms. The research in this area in particular suggests that targeting specific audiences may be an important element in maximizing the effects of such interventions. The research that identifies moderators of effect sizes—or who responds most dramatically to psychoeducational interventions—is a critical area for future studies in a variety of content areas. This type of information not only will be helpful in terms of maximizing the cost effectiveness of such interventions, but it is also critical to tailoring programs to specific audiences who may be in greatest need.

Developing and Evaluating Psychoeducational Interventions

What makes for a "good" psychoeducation prevention program? The answer to this question in many ways parallels the discussion contained earlier in this chapter on what constitutes effective preventative interventions. For example, good psychoeducation models are based on research and theory; are delivered by trained, competent professionals; are developmentally appropriate; are well-timed; and are culturally relevant to the participants. In many ways, good psychoeducation programs are similar to good psychotherapeutic interventions. The primary differences, however, often lie within the context of delivery and the outcomes measures.

Psychoeducation can and does occur on an individual level. However, to be most cost effective and to capitalize on the benefits of group counseling, most psychoeducation occurs with groups of individuals. For example, parenting groups, stress management workshops, job search clubs, and biofeedback training are typically taught to groups of individuals who share characteristics, have common needs, and can provide important support to one another. The objectives of many psychoeducational programs are often to promote healthy development or adjustment, rather than to solely stave off psychopathology (Carlson, 2006). Although the prevention of pathology may be an added benefit of the interventions, these programs are rarely evaluated based on such criteria.

For example, a good parenting program might be based on learning theory, offered to parents early in the process (i.e., while their children are very young), and have goals to increase parents' knowledge of the developmental needs of their children

and to encourage the use of positive parenting techniques (i.e., positive reinforcement) (Carlson, 2006). A long-term benefit of such a program may be to reduce incidents of child abuse; if the program was offered to parents who might be at risk of such behavior, the program would be an example of secondary prevention. However, a program might also be able to demonstrate its effectiveness by tracking changes in participants' knowledge base and intentions regarding parenting. In the case of psychoeducation that is used to increase compliance to medical treatment, evaluations may also be based on incidence rates of relapse, disease complication, and other measures of compliance.

One of the most critical characteristics of effective psychoeducation, however, is its perceived relevance to the participants. This perception is often a function of the extent to which the program has cultural relevance to the targeted audience. *Cultural relevance* refers to the extent to which interventions are consistent with the values, beliefs, and desired outcomes of a particular community (Kumpfer, Alvarado, Smith, & Bellamy, 2002; Nation et al., 2003). Nation et al. (2003) argued that prevention program relevance, to which psychoeducation program relevance is related, is a function of the extent to which a community's norms, cultural beliefs, and practices have been integrated into program content, its delivery, and evaluation. Kumpfer et al. (2002) argued that including cultural relevance in prevention programs improves recruitment, retention, and outcome effectiveness.

One of the superficial ways that cultural adaptations have been made in many past prevention efforts has been what Resnicow, Solar, Braithwaite, Ahluwalia, and Butler (2000) termed "surface structure modifications." As previously discussed, such efforts could include translating intervention materials into the primary language of the participants or hiring program staff who have ethnic backgrounds similar to those of the participants. Such modifications may be one important aspect of cultural adaptation. It may be highly advantageous to have program participants communicate with program staff in their first languages or to interact with staff of the same ethnicity and/or gender. However, when program content does not reflect the reality of the participants' experience, interventions delivered by racially or linguistically similar staff will not make the program relevant or, more importantly, effective.

Rather than surface modifications, "deep structure modifications" (Resnicow et al., 2003) often determine the cultural relevance of prevention programs. Often, the adaptations required for a prevention program to be culturally relevant result in a program that may be substantively different from its prototype. Dryfoos (1990), Lerner (1995), and Reiss and Price (1996), among others, have suggested that the most effective, culturally relevant prevention and psychoeducation programs include the target program participants in the planning, implementation, and evaluation of the program.

As discussed with prevention programming, if this approach is followed, the content of the psychoeducation program may not only become more relevant, but the very structure of the program may look significantly different from a program designed for a culturally dissimilar population. Although a preponderance of the literature suggests that a relationship with the target community is a key to acquiring cultural knowledge, there is still a need for large-scale epidemiological research that identifies risk factors and how they affect particular communities. Such studies must be designed carefully and their findings examined responsibly, to assist prevention researchers and practitioners in more accurately understanding the communities in which they work.

Psychologists As Psychoeducators

Watkins (1985) argued that psychologists must be given distinct training in psychoeducation and should not assume that their more general training in counseling and psychotherapy has prepared them for this important type of service delivery. More specifically, he argued that at least three types of training are necessary for psychologists who wish to be competent psychoeducators. One, psychologists must be trained with the skills to seek out the psychological knowledge that is relevant to the identified problem. Two, psychologists must be trained in program development and evaluation skills. Three, psychologists must be capable of communicating program content effectively. Watkins argued that, although many psychologists gain training and experience in the first skill—seeking out appropriate psychological knowledge—few are trained sufficiently in the latter two skills. Each of these skill development areas will be discussed in greater detail below.

Obtaining appropriate knowledge on the development of specific psychological problems (e.g., eating disorders) requires that psychologists know where to find literature on the etiology and development of particular problems and that they become familiar with literature on risk and protective factors associated with such disorders. Rutter (1987) defines risk and protective factors as variables that are likely to increase and minimize the emergence of a particular problem, respectively. Many epidemiological studies that identify risk and protective factors are conducted by researchers who are not psychologists. Therefore, it is important that psychologists consult multidisciplinary sources of information in their searches, particularly for topics that may be more frequently researched by public health professionals or psychiatrists.

The second skill set, program development and evaluation, is usually a matter of consulting the literature on existing programs rather than developing programs from scratch. A number of empirically supported psychoeducational approaches to bullying, for example, could be adapted to new community groups. However, the importance of cultural relevance in the development of psychoeducation cannot be overemphasized. Often, psychoeducational programs that were developed on majority populations are not generalizable to minority populations. This has been discussed in detail previously in this chapter.

The third skill set involves the ability to effectively communicate information to the program's participants. This not only involves the ability to be an effective lecturer and group facilitator, but it also involves the ability to use developmentally appropriate language and to find common ways of communicating often complex psychological constructs. For example, discussing self-esteem with first graders is very different from doing so with adults. Since most first graders would not use or be familiar with the term "self-esteem," it would be important for psychoeducators to adjust their language appropriately. Using the phrase "feeling good about who you are" or "loving yourself" might be more appropriate ways to communicate the construct of self-esteem to children. Being able to avoid jargon and consistently defining terms in one's presentation is a key component of effective psychoeducation.

Also, assuming that a great deal of psychoeducation takes place in group, not individual settings, it is important for psychologists to be capable of processing group dynamics and facilitating productive group discussion during psychoeducational programs. Since there is no guarantee of confidentiality during most psychoeducational sessions, it is also critical that psychologists monitor and focus group discussions such that participants do not become too vulnerable, which is a major divergence from the role of counselor or therapist. Often, despite one's efforts, participants in psychoeducational programs can border on disclosing things about themselves that would be more appropriate for therapy sessions.

The issue of how counselors-in-training can acquire such skill sets is the topic of considerable debate in the literature. Most programs in counseling psychology and other related fields find it challenging to add courses or required experiences to their already lengthy curricula. However, it has been argued that creating flexibility in course content and the type of practica experiences we offer our students could be a great first step in broadening graduates' skill sets. Adams (2007), for example, argued that there are many core content areas within most programs where prevention and psychoeducational experiences could be included as course assignments or as service-learning opportunities. As was the case with providing training experiences for prevention (discussed previously in this chapter), many adaptations to current curricula are feasible.

Example of a Comprehensive Psychoeducational Prevention Program

In this final section, we provide an example of a comprehensive psychoeducational prevention program that includes both individual and environmental approaches and incorporates many of the elements of effective psychoeducational prevention discussed in this chapter.

Project Northland addresses the prevention of substance abuse in adolescents; it utilized psychoeducation and operated at both the individual and systemic levels (Perry et al., 2002). This long-term project took place in northeastern Minnesota, an area shown to be particularly at risk for alcohol use. The project was conducted in three phases and utilized a variety of interventions in different contexts. Interventions included the development of social-behavioral classroom curricula (i.e., an example of psychoeducation in prevention), parent involvement programs, peer leadership opportunities, and community task forces. The goal of the program was to empower community residents to sustain their own substance abuse prevention program for adolescents (Perry et al., 2002).

Participants for Project Northland were recruited through school district superintendents beginning in 1991 and resulted in all adolescents in the graduating class of 1998 (sixth graders in 1991) in 24 public school districts in the northeastern Minnesota counties taking part in the study. For Phase 1 of the project, participants were divided randomly into two groups, the Education Program (for whom participant interventions began in 1991) or the Delayed Program (for whom participant interventions began in 1994) condition. Student self-report surveys were given when participants began the study, and after each year of subsequent involvement (i.e., sixth, seventh, and eighth grades). Parent surveys (conducted via telephone), interviews of community leaders, observation of potential underage drinking (using confederates as underage buyers), and a survey of alcohol salespeople were also conducted (Perry et al., 1993).

To address prevention at an individual level, students were given two self-report surveys, one consisting of questions on students' knowledge of alcohol, attitudes and expectations about drinking, family rules about drinking, the presence of alcohol in a students' environment, and problematic alcohol use, and the other consisting of assessment of psychosocial risk factors related to early alcohol use, including some items from the drug problems scale of the Minnesota Multiphasic Personality Inventory for Adolescents (MMPI-A) (Perry et al., 2002).

To address systemic and environmental needs for change, community task forces were organized through identifying community leaders interested in prevention during the community leader interviews. These leaders formed groups that identified major community problems related to teen alcohol abuse, and developed and implemented a community policy action plan. Task forces focused on such topics as educating merchants about legal consequences of underage sales and ways of avoiding them, and the development and enforcement of alcohol-related school policies.

The Interim Phase of the project (1994–1996) consisted of a five-session classroom psychoeducation component called "Shifting Gears." Students began this in the ninth grade and discussed topics such as drinking and driving, tactics of alcohol advertising, and effective coping in the face of these pressures.

Phase 2 (1996–1998), begun when students were in the eleventh grade, entailed implementation of classroom curriculum on social and legal consequences of drinking, parent education programs, a media campaign focused on not providing alcohol to people under age 21, peer action teams that developed campaigns for their classmates not to drink, and community action teams focused on decreasing access to alcohol among high school students (Perry et al., 2002).

Results of the 7-year project included students in the participating schools being significantly less likely to have increased tendency to use alcohol, to be influenced by peers to use alcohol, and to have decreased self-efficacy to use alcohol (i.e., maintain a higher self-efficacy about refusal). Parents in the intervention programs were also less permissive than those not in the programs. Researchers gained valuable information about ideal developmental levels (i.e., earlier is more effective than later) for substance abuse prevention in adolescents and the increased effectiveness of multilevel and context interventions (Perry et al., 2002).

We present the Project Northland prevention project as one example of effective prevention programming, not as the sole way of doing effective prevention work. As discussed previously, effective prevention programs can look quite different from each other, depending on the populations involved and the prevention goals. This project incorporated both individual and community approaches, with attention to policy change. It was quite comprehensive, utilizing multiple contexts for interventions. The program obtained cultural relevance through community collaboration and provided positive relationships for its participants to build upon in the future. Methodologically, the program used both qualitative and quantitative approaches, providing data at varying levels of depth that were beneficial in program planning. Altogether, it met many of the "ideal goals" of a well-executed and informative psychoeducational prevention program.

Future Directions

The areas of prevention and psychoeducation, as well as the counseling psychologists who work within these specialty areas, have made some progress in recent years toward increasing awareness of our need for such activities in our daily work lives. As outlined above, several important counseling psychology venues have begun to publish more literature in this area, and some specialized training in prevention is beginning to take place in our graduate programs. All of these advancements can be seen as evidence of the field's interest in and commitment to effective prevention work. Nevertheless, we still have many important lessons to learn from our sister disciplines, and there is much more to be done if prevention work is to become a consistently sustained part of the overall identity of counseling psychologists. We make the following suggestions toward the accomplishment of this important goal.

- *Training.* Despite the efforts by some training programs mentioned above, the existence of consistent prevention training in graduate programs is probably not widespread. We strongly suggest that, much in the way that sensitivity to multicultural issues has been successfully integrated into aspects of all courses in many programs, the "meta-lens" of prevention be utilized as an element of the framework for thinking about any coursework. This would mean introducing the concepts of prevention to students immediately during their training, exposing them to various concrete models of effective and ethical prevention programs, then following-up with continued reinforcement of this way of thinking about issues (i.e., from a preventive perspective) in every course. Such training would also include incorporating prevention activities into practicum settings and experiences, so that students may apply the ideas they have learned. In this way, prevention could be taught as a central component of our identity, much in the way that issues of social justice have come to be emphasized by many programs (Adams, 2007).

- *Collaboration.* As exemplified in the international prevention studies described above, there can be great benefit in cross-cultural and cross-disciplinary collaboration. Such alliances serve to enhance the ability of practitioners to take different perspectives and to enrich the final product of the program. It therefore seems a worthy goal, as we continue to incorporate prevention more solidly into our identity as counseling psychologists, to increase efforts for such collaborations, whether domestic or international. This process parallels the process of collaborative participant participation, and has many of the same benefits. It is important to think of this process broadly and creatively, as all collaborations may not look the same. This flexibility should affect both logistical and theoretical aspects of the project. For example, an international collaboration may be framed in public health theory (particularly given this field's longstanding contributions to the area).

- *Evaluation.* Counseling psychologists need to continue to work on ways to effectively evaluate prevention and psychoeducation programs. As discussed, this can be quite difficult, as we do not want "empirical outcome evaluation" to take precedence over community needs. In other words, we must continue to think about what constitutes a "successful program," not just in terms of practical steps to take for the programming, but in how we can balance this with social justice and cultural responsiveness. This may mean utilizing more nontraditional forms of program evaluation or incorporating the evaluation component into the program itself, in a way that aids the participants in self-reflection while also being of benefit to the researcher (i.e., is a mutually beneficial component of the program to all involved parties).

Conclusion

We seem to still be at a crossroads for truly incorporating prevention work into our identities as counseling psychologists. With the newly minted guidelines for best practices in prevention, counseling psychologists now have detailed plans for how good prevention can occur. With our values of social justice and multiculturalism, we have lenses through which we can teach and look for implementations of these programs that are consistent with our professional identities. What remains is for more counseling psychologists to awaken to and embrace prevention as part of their identity and to go out and put it into practice, teach future counseling psychologists to do the same, and thereby change the course of problem behavior and mental health issues. We feel that the issues of training, collaboration, and evaluation must be addressed for this to successfully occur.

References

Adams, E. (2007). Moving from contemplation to preparation: Is counseling psychology ready to embrace culturally responsive prevention? *The Counseling Psychologist, 35*(6), 840–849.

Albee, G. (1983). Psychopathology, prevention, and the just society. *Journal of Primary Prevention, 4*, 5–36.

Albee, G. W., & Ryan-Finn, K. D. (1993). An overview of primary prevention. *Journal of Counseling and Development, 72*, 115–123.

Aseltine, R., & DeMartino, R. (2004). An outcome evaluation of the SOS suicide prevention program. *American Journal of Public Health, 94*, 446–451.

Authier, J. (1977). The psychoeducation model: Definition, contemporary roots and content. *Canadian Counsellor, 12*, 15–22.

Biglan, A., Mrazek, P. J., Carnine, D., & Flay, B. R. (2003). The integration of research and practice in prevention of youth problem behaviors. *American Psychologist, 58*, 433–440.

Bloom, M. (1993). Toward a code of ethics from primary prevention. *Journal of Primary Prevention, 13*, 173–182.

Brown, C. H., & Liao, J. (1999). Principles for designing randomized preventive trials in mental health: An emerging developmental epidemiology program. *American Journal of Community Psychology, 27*, 673–710.

Caplan, G. (1964). *Principles of preventive psychiatry.* New York: Basic Books.

Carlson, J., Watts, R. E., & Maniacci, M. (2006). Consultation and psychoeducation. *Adlerian therapy: Theory and practice* (pp. 251–276). Washington, DC: American Psychological Association.

Conyne, R. K. (1987). *Primary preventive counseling: Empowering people and systems.* Muncie: IN: Accelerated Development Inc.

Conyne, R. K. (1991). Gains in primary prevention: Implications for the counseling profession. *Journal of Counseling and Development, 69*, 277–279.

Conyne, R. K. (1997). Educating students in preventive counseling. *Counselor Education and Supervision, 36*(4), 259–270.

Conyne, R. K. (2000). Prevention in counseling psychology: At long last, has the time now come? *The Counseling Psychologist, 28*(6), 838–844.

Conyne, R. K. (2004). *Preventive counseling: Helping people to become empowered in systems and settings.* New York: Brunner-Routledge.

Cowen, E. (1984). A general structural model for program development in mental health. *Personnel and Guidance Journal: Special Issue on Primary prevention in schools, 62*, 485–490.

Creswell, J. W. (2007). *Qualitative inquiry and research design: Choosing among five approaches.* Thousand Oaks, CA: Sage Publications.

Dixon, L. (1999). Providing services to families of persons with schizophrenia: Present and future. *Journal of Mental Health Policy and Economics, 2*, 3–8.

Dryfoos, J. (1990). *Adolescents at risk: Prevalence and prevention.* New York: Oxford University Press.

Durlak, J. A. (1997). *Successful prevention programs for children and adolescents.* New York: Plenum Press.

Fingeret, M. C., Warren, C. S., Cepeda-Benito, A. & Gleaves, D. H. (2006). Eating disorder prevention research: A meta-analysis. *Eating Disorders: The Journal of Prevention and Research, 14*, 191–213.

Gelso, C., & Fretz, B. (1992). *Counseling psychology* (2nd ed.). Tokyo: Harcourt College.

Greenberg, M. T., Weissberg, R. P., O'Brien, M. U., Zins, J. E., Fredericks, L., Resnik, H., & Elias, M. J. (2003). Enhancing school-based prevention and youth development through coordinated social, emotional, and academic learning. *American Psychologist, 58*, 466–481.

Grossman, J. B., & Tierney, J. P. (1998). Does mentoring work? An impact study of the Big Brothers Big Sisters program. *Evaluation Review, 22*(3), 403–426.

Hage, S. M. (2003). Reaffirming the unique identity of counseling psychology: Opting for "The road less traveled by". *The Counseling Psychologist, 31*, 555–563.

Hage, S. M., Romano, J. L., Conyne, R. K., Kenny, M., Matthews, C., Schwartz, J., & Waldo, M. (2007). Best practice guidelines on prevention, practice, research, training, and social advocacy for psychologists. *The Counseling Psychologist, 35*(4), 493–566.

Hobbs, N. (1964). Mental health's third revolution. *Journal of Orthopsychiatry, 34*, 822–833.

Johnson, S. B., & Millstein, S. G. (2003). Prevention opportunities in healthcare settings. *America Psychologist, 58*. 475–481.

Kalafat, J., & Elias, M. (1995). Suicide prevention in an educational context: Broad and narrow foci. *Suicide and Life Threatening Behavior, 25*, 123–133.

Klein, D. C., & Goldston, S. E. (1977). *Primary prevention: An idea whose time has come* (DHEW Publication No. ADM 77–747). Washington, DC: U.S. Government Printing Office.

Kumpfer, K. L., & Alvarado, R. (2003). Family-strengthening approaches for the prevention of youth problem behaviors. *American Psychologist, 58*, 457–465.

Kumpfer, K. L., Alvarado, R., Smith, P., & Bellamy, N. (2002). Cultural sensitivity and adaptation in family based interventions. *Prevention Science, 3*, 241–246.

Lehman, A., & Steinwachs, D. (1998). Translating research into practice: The Schizophrenia Patients Outcomes Research Team treatment recommendations. *Schizophrenia Bulletin, 24*, 1–10.

Leong, F., & Leach, M. M. (2007). Internationalising counseling psychology in the United States: A SWOT analysis. *Applied Psychology: An International Review, 56*(1), 165–181.

Lerner, R. M. (1995). *America's youth in crisis: Challenges and options for programs and policies.* Thousand Oaks, CA: Sage.

Lewis, C., Battistich, V., & Schaps, E. (1990). School-based primary prevention: What is an effective program? *New Directions for Child Development, 50*, 35–39.

Lewis, J. A., & Lewis, M. D. (1981). Educating counselors for primary prevention. *Counselor Education and Supervision, 20*, 172–181.

Lidchi, V. L. (2007). Reflections on training in child abuse and neglect prevention: Experiences in Brazil. *Child Abuse Review, 16*(6), 353–366.

Lopez, S. (1997). Cultural competence in psychotherapy: A guide for clinicians and their supervisors. In C. E. Watkins (Ed.), *Handbook of psychotherapy supervision* (pp. 570–587). New York: John Wiley.

Lukens, E., & McFarlane, W. (2004). Psychoeducation as evidence-based practice: Considerations for practice, research, and policy. *Brief Treatment and Crisis Intervention, 4*, 205–225.

Masten, A. S., & Coatsworth, J. D. (1998). The development of competence in favorable and unfavorable environments: Lessons form research on successful children. *American Psychologist, 53*(2), 205–220.

McEvoy, J., Scheifler, P., & Frances, A. (1999). Expert consensus guideline series: Treatment of schizophrenia. *Journal of Clinical Psychiatry, 60*, 3–80.

Morgan, M. L. (2006). International comparisons of resilience in Mexican national and Mexican immigrant populations. Doctoral dissertation, Loyola University Chicago. *Dissertation Abstracts International, 67* (9-B).

Mrazek, P. J., & Haggerty, R. J. (Eds.). (1994). *Reducing risks for mental disorders: Frontiers for preventive intervention research.* Washington, DC: National Academy Press.

Munoz, R. F., Mrazek, P. J., & Haggerty, R. J. (1996). Institute of Medicine report on prevention of mental disorders: Summary and commentary. *American Psychologist, 51*, 1116–1122.

Nation, M., Crusto, C., Wandersman, A., Kumpfer, K., Seybolt, D., Morrissey-Kane, E., et al. (2003). What works in prevention: Principles and effective prevention programs. *American Psychologist, 58*, 449–456.

National Academy of Sciences. (2002). *The future of the public's health in the 21st century.* Institute of Medicine. Washington, DC.

Newman, D., Horne, A., & Bartolomucci, L. (2000). *Bully busters: A teacher's manual for helping bullies, victims, and bystanders.* Champaign, IL: Research Press.

Newman-Carlson, D., & Horne, A. (2004). Bully busters: A psychoeducational intervention for reducing bullying behavior in middle school students. *Journal of Counseling and Development, 82*, 259–267.

O'Dea, J., & Abraham, S. (2000). Improving body image, eating attitudes, and behaviors of young male and female adolescents: A new educational approach that focuses on self-esteem. *International Journal of Eating Disorders, 28*, 43–57.

Olweus, D. (1978). *Aggression in the schools: Bullies and whipping boys.* Washington, DC: Hemisphere.

Perry, C. L., Williams, C. L., Forster, J. L., Wolfson, M., Wagenaar, A. C., Finnegan, J. R., et al. (1993). Background, conceptualization and design of a community-wide research program on adolescent alcohol use: Project Northland. *Health Education Research, 8*(1), 125–136.

Perry, C., Williams, C. L. Komro, K. A., Veblen-Mortenson, S., Stigler, M. H., Munson, K. A., Farbakhsh, K., Jones, R. M., & Forster, J. L. (2002). Project Northland: Long-term outcomes of community action to reduce adolescent alcohol use. *Health Education Research, 17*, 117–132.

Pope, K. (1990). Identifying and implementing ethical standards for primary prevention. *Prevention in Human Services, 8*, 43–64.

Portzky, G., & van Heeringen, K. (2006). Suicide prevention in adolescents: A controlled study of the effectiveness of a school-based psychoeducational program. *Journal of Child Psychology and Psychiatry, 47*, 910–918.

President's New Freedom Commission on Mental Health. (2003). *Achieving the promise: Transforming mental health care in America.* Rockville, MD: Author.

Price, R. H., Cowen, E. L., Lorion, R. P., & Ramos-McKay, J. (Eds.). (1988). *14 ounces of prevention: A casebook for practitioners.* Washington, DC: American Psychological Association.

Prilleltensky, I. (1997). Values, assumptions, and practices: Assessing the moral implications of psychological discourse and action. *American Psychologist, 52*, 517–535.

Prilleltensky, I., & Nelson, G. (1997). Community psychology: Reclaiming social justice. In D. Fox, & Prilleltensky, I. (Eds.), *Critical psychology: An introduction* (pp. 166–184). Thousand Oaks, CA: Sage.

Reese, L., & Vera, E. (2007). Culturally relevant prevention: The scientific and practical considerations of community-based programs. *The Counseling Psychologist, 35*, 763–778.

Reiss, D., & Price, R. H. (1996). National research agenda for prevention research: The National Institute of Mental Health Report. *American Psychologist, 51*, 1109–1115.

Resnicow, K., Solar, R., Braithwaite, R., Ahluwalia, J., & Butler, J. (2000). Cultural sensitivity in substance abuse prevention. *Journal of Community Psychology, 28*, 271–290.

Ripple, C. H., & Zigler, E. (2003). Research, policy, and the federal role in prevention initiative for children. *American Psychologist, 58*, 482–490.

Roche, S. E., & Sadoski, P. J. (1996). Social action for battered women. In A. R. Roberts (Ed.), *Helping battered women: New perspectives and remedies* (pp. 13–30). New York: Oxford University Press.

Romano, J. L., & Hage, S. M. (2000). Prevention and counseling psychology: Revitalizing commitments for the 21st century. *The Counseling Psychologist, 28*, 733–763.

Rouget, B., & Aubry, J. (2006). Efficacy of psychoeducational approaches on bipolar disorders: A review of the literature. *Journal of Affective Disorders, 98*, 11–27.

Rutter, M. (1987). Psychological resilience and protective mechanisms. *American Journal of Orthopsychiatry, 57*, 316–331.

Schensul, S., Nastasi, B., & Verma, R. (2006). Community-based research in India: A case example of international and transdisciplinary collaboration. *American Journal of Community Psychology, 38*, 95–111.

Spalding, J., & Balch, P. (1983). A brief history of primary prevention in the twentieth century: 1908–1980. *American Journal of Community Psychology, 11*, 59–80.

Tsarouk, T., Thompson, E. A., Herting, J. R., Walsh, E., & Randell, B. (2006). Culturally specific adaptation of a prevention intervention: An international collaborative research project. *Addictive Behaviors, 32*, 1565–1581.

Van Heeringen, C. (2001). *Understanding suicidal behavior. The process approach to research and treatment.* Chichester, UK: John Wiley & Sons.

Vera, E. M., Caldwell, J., Clarke, M., Gonzales, R., Morgan, M., & West, M. (2007). The Choices Program: Multisystemic interventions for enhancing the personal and academic effectiveness of urban adolescents of color. *The Counseling Psychologist, 35*(6), 779–796.

Vera, E. M., & Reese, L. E. (2000). Preventive interventions with school-age youth. In S. Brown, & R. Lent (Eds.), *Handbook of counseling psychology* (pp. 411–434). New York: John Wiley.

Wandersman, A., & Florin, P. (2003). Community interventions and effective prevention. *American Psychologist, 58*, 441–448.

Watkins, C. E. (1985). Counseling psychology, psychoeducation, and health psychology: A comment on Klippel and DeJoy. *Journal of Counseling Psychology, 32*(1), 147–149.

Wilezenski, R., Steegman, R., Braun, M., Feeley, F., Griffin, J., & Horowitz, T. (1994). Promoting fair play. Paper presented at the annual meeting of the National Association of School Psychologists, Seattle, WA. (ERIC Document Reproduction Service, No. ED380744).

Career Counseling

Robert C. Chope

Abstract

The field of career counseling began with a well-defined, but narrow scope. Its goal was to match a person's skills, interests, and predilections to an appropriate job. Although it offered a means of allowing people to consider new vocational options, the approach did not require the in-depth knowledge of occupations; psychological and assessment skills; the understanding of the larger contexts of ethnicity, gender, and economic and social status; and the intuitive understanding of the counseling process that have become such important parts of the field today. This chapter describes the evolution of the career counseling field, which now includes all of these aspects. Ironically, the chapter also reveals how the founder of the field, Frank Parsons, formulated an approach to vocational counseling with a social justice perspective; this perspective is currently fueling one of the fastest growing bodies of career counseling research and practice.

Keywords: assessment, career counseling, counseling process, interests, vocational counseling, social justice

This chapter is about career counseling, a discipline closely aligned with vocational psychology, a topic Larson covers earlier in this *Handbook* (2011, Chapter 6, this volume). The theories of career selection, adjustment, and satisfaction, along with theories of vocational behavior—all drawn from vocational psychology—are used in the career counseling process.

But career counseling is distinct in compelling ways and has had a storied history of over 100 years. Pope (2000) has explored this history and contextualized it by offering a social transition stage model, positing that the development of career counseling was influenced by continuing societal changes. Other approaches to the history of career counseling may be explored with Aubry (1977), Borow (1964), Brewer (1942), and Herr, Cramer, and Niles (2004).

Pope suggests that the development of the career counseling discipline can be put into perspective by enumerating six sequential stages of its history: job placement services (1890–1919), educational guidance in the schools (1920–1939), coursework in colleges and universities and the training of counselors (1940–1959), the creation of meaningful work and organizational career development (1960–1979), the independent practice of career counseling and outplacement counseling (1980–1989), and school-to-job transition, the internalization of career counseling, multicultural career counseling, and increasing sophistication in the use of technology (1990–present).

Clearly, economic expansion and contraction along with societal changes have affected the development of career counseling both within the United States and abroad. Pope contends that the enumeration of the stages of development that career counseling has undergone in the United States has the potential to assist all career professionals, regardless of where they practice, to prepare their responses to social and economic upheavals while continuing professional growth. Herr (2003) agrees to some extent with Pope, pointing out that career counseling is largely a "creature of public policy" (p. 8).

Career counseling has been characterized as the "cornerstone upon which the counseling profession was built" (Dorn, 1992, p. 176). Indeed, career counseling, known earlier by other titles such as vocational guidance or vocational counseling, has been the subject of state and federal public policy and legislation adopted to address a variety of economic, workforce, and political issues. Herr adds that legislators, along with policy developers, promoted the popular utilization of career counseling services at significant turning points in people's lives: deciding upon higher education or vocational-technical training, school-to-work transitions (STW), career change in mid-life, reentry into work, and, of course, in dealing with unemployment, job loss, and retirement.

The career counseling process, to be sure, utilizes many of the techniques of the generic, personal counseling process, covered by Hoffman (2011, Chapter 19, this volume), although the relationship between career and personal counseling has been distinguished by some thorny complications and a lack of appreciation on the part of some personal counselors. Attempts at reconciliation have been made, however. According to Zunker (2006), for the past 20 years, there has been a call for the integration of career and personal counseling. He points out that, in 1993, a portion of one issue of *The Career Development Quarterly* (*CDQ*) (Volume 42, pp. 129–173) focused upon and supported the integration of career and personal counseling by defining counseling as being concerned with problems that are a part of the many roles everyone adopts over the course of a lifetime. Highly influential theorists in the field, such as Donald Super (1993) and John Krumboltz (1993), who contributed to that perspective, agreed that a dichotomous relationship should not exist between career and personal counseling for the simple reason that career and personal problems cannot be compartmentalized.

Frank Parsons: The Origin

Unfortunately, many counseling professionals frequently view career counseling as a rather rudimentary and mechanical form of counseling. This is perhaps due to several factors. First, the origin of career counseling is typically credited to Frank Parsons (1909) and his relatively straightforward, three-pronged approach to career counseling, which included developing an awareness of the self, analyzing and understanding occupations, and using true reasoning to choose an occupation. His approach did not appear on its face to have the in-depth reflective and intuitive understanding that was to become such a hallmark of personal counseling. Instead, it involved more the matching of worker characteristics with the demands of the work environment, an approach frequently referred to as trait-factor theory or "lock and key."

In spite of the simplicity of Parson's approach, it offered a means of allowing people to consider new vocational or career-related options, although "career" was not then a term in popular usage. Parson's career counseling was enormously important at the turn of the 20th century because impoverished immigrants and farmers dwelling in urban settings were struggling to change their lots in life. Curiously, Parson's model offered an early example of the social justice influences of career counseling as a means of creating options for people living on the edges of society.

Assessing Soldiers and Veterans

After World War I and World War II, many organizational and differential psychologists were drawn together to assist in developing instrumentation for the selection and placement of military personnel (e.g., Kelly, Thorndike, Strong, Wechsler, Woodworth, Yerkes). The results of these efforts filtered into the general public with the advent of new, popular, work-related tests. These included measures of vocational interests, work personalities, aptitudes, and skills, and were brought into the career and vocational guidance process to assist with the development of self-awareness among those seeking career directions. Data extracted from military testing, of course, became especially useful to veterans seeking employment or retraining after their service. For almost a century now, researchers have continued to develop new means of gathering information on career-related worker characteristics such as aptitudes and skills, interests, values, and personality characteristics because of these early large-scale test development projects.

This "goodness of fit" information gathering process with which career counseling began led to the perception among mental health professionals and the consumers of counseling services that career counseling was an unimaginative, mechanistic experience. Furthermore, the publication of career counseling resources like the *Dictionary of Occupational Titles*, *Occupational Outlook Handbook*, and the *Guide to Occupational Information* by the Department of Labor (now replaced by links to the United States Department of Labor's *O*Net* at www.onet.org) gave a greater body of information to individuals wanting to understand the nature of work, but detracted from the psychology of career development. Certainly, career counselors use a great mass of information to become more proficient in the true reasoning process, but it has become strikingly clear that the more recent psychology of the self and the context of self-experience and meaning making have taken career counseling practitioners far beyond Parson's original vision.

Integrating Counseling and Psychotherapy

Crites (1981) takes the perspective that the incorporation of the very best from the theories of counseling and psychotherapy into the best models of career counseling results in five propositions that offer a different way of considering the integration of career and personal counseling. These propositions include:

- The need for career counseling is greater than the need for psychotherapy.
- Career counseling can be therapeutic.
- Career counseling should follow psychotherapy.
- Career counseling is more effective than psychotherapy.
- Career counseling is more difficult than psychotherapy. (pp. 14–15).

Career counseling has evolved; it incorporates self-awareness with information on occupations. The career counseling process in modern times is less focused upon the initial entry of individuals into careers and more concerned with the manner in which individuals plan a career path that will cover a variety of opportunities over the course of a lifetime. Career information is readily available in the United States and can be accessed through official portals like *O*Net* (www.onet.gov).

Life Path: The New Context

Unlike Parson's experience, in the 21st century, individuals now change jobs regularly and are in and out of new jobs and training programs as new opportunities develop and abound. Individuals can now work locally as well as globally, work face-to-face or be virtually present. In the age of information

technology (IT), certain work does not necessarily have to be done face-to-face or locally. There are more opportunities to work off-site than ever, and these opportunities continue to grow as workers plan their professional development around their choices of lifestyle and job tasks.

Career counseling motivates individuals to find work and a life path, but also assists in understanding how meaning can be put into one's life through work (Savickas, 2005). Earlier writers on career perspectives (Okun, 1984; Super, 1984) suggest that work interfaces with all of our life roles, whether with family, in hobbies and leisure activities, or in volunteer pursuits.

Career counseling is also a process that has become increasingly dynamic and is not necessarily concerned with initial job placement; instead, it focuses on the integration of various life roles and work. Accordingly, it has been recommended that career counselors be used by individual clients over the course of a lifetime, just as they use other helping professionals. Goodman (1994) has offered the *dental model* for career counselors, suggesting that consumers consult a career counselor for regular checkups, just as they regularly visit their dentists. Career counselors are quite cognizant that the work world, along with available information about work, is changing at break-neck speeds, and most individuals do not have the time or resources to pinpoint opportunities that they could avail themselves of. Career counselors can assist with this as they aid in the upward management of an individual's career.

Most of the approaches to career counseling today call attention to a field that covers the lifespan in a holistic and meaningful way. Amundson, Harris-Bowlsbey, and Niles (2009) define career counseling as a "process in which a counselor works collaboratively to help clients/students clarify, specify, implement, and adjust to work-related decisions. Career counseling addresses the interaction of work with other life roles" (p. 7).

Adding to their definition, Amundson, Harris-Bowlsbey, and Niles (2009) outline the many methods and interventions that career counselors utilize in their everyday work. Career counselors select, administer, and interpret a variety of assessment tools, gathering information on interests, values, abilities, and other personal characteristics as deemed necessary for the counseling process to be effective.

Career counselors also suggest and encourage their clients to obtain job experience and knowledge through the job shadowing process, internships, externships, or term-time employment during their secondary and higher educational experiences. Career counselors are knowledgeable about different marketing tools that job seekers need, so that they can assist with resume development, teach interviewing skills, and coach clients regarding the development of support networks. They also assist with pointing clients toward appropriate occupational information, developing career plans, and resolving work-related conflicts, including the effects of work-to-family or family-to-work spillover.

Particular approaches to career counseling have been provided by Luzzo (2000), who covers career counseling with college students. Swanson and Fouad (1999) offer a means of demonstrating the intertwining of career theory with career counseling. General theories of career development are made available by Sharf (2006).

Detecting Family Influence

In what can amount to highly personal activities in their work, career counselors also help clients to explore and understand the influence of their families in their career choices, as well as the potential links between their career choices and their cultures. To this extent, counselors must be aware of the contextual issues that influence career choice. There is a strong view that career development and career counseling must be understood from a "relational" point of view, making the developmental process dynamic since both the individual and the context are changing (Blustein, 2001; Schultheiss, 2003).

As part of these relational approaches to career counseling, career counselors must also be aware of the influence of families on career decision making. Two substantial literature reviews have been devoted to the topic of family influence on career decision making. The first, prepared by Schulenberg, Vondracek, and Crouter in 1984, summarized research findings, examining the impact of structural variables like socioeconomic status, birth order, and gender, along with process variables such as career choice modeling, parental support, and parenting styles. The review, however, lacked any material representative of the multiethnic and multicultural society evolving in the last quarter century.

A more recent review by Whiston and Keller (2004) delineated the findings of 77 studies related to the influence of the family of origin on career development. The work covered 29 different journals from various disciplines, including psychology, education, counseling and guidance, and career development. Influential family contextual factors were identified within four developmental levels from childhood through adulthood. Throughout life, structural family variables like parental places of work and process variables including warmth, support, and attachment were found to influence a variety of career constructs.

Chope (2005) offered a review of the qualitative methods for assessing influential factors in the family relative to career decision making. These included retrospective questionnaires, career genograms, career-o-grams (Thorngren & Feit, 2001), and critical incident techniques. However, it was noted that, although qualitative assessment methods can be applicable to the career counseling process, these tools are time-consuming and demand a high level of clinical skill to utilize effectively.

Still, the *career genogram* (Okiishi, 1987), a type of occupational family tree, is undeniably the most commonly recognized and frequently administered qualitative instrument for gathering information about the influence of the family in career decision making. As a postmodern tool, it allows for the understanding of career decision making in the context of the family (Dagley, 1984). More recently, there has been the establishment of the multicultural genogram (Sueyoshi, Rivera, & Ponterotto, 2001), currently used to explore how ethnicity, race, culture, and religion can affect a person's attitudes and decision making. It has been recommended that the multicultural genogram be combined with a career genogram to intensify and give a multicultural perspective to the career counseling process.

National Career Development Association

Only 4 years after Parson's seminal work, the National Career Development Association (NCDA) was founded in 1913, as the National Vocational Guidance Association (NVGA), the first national professional counseling association. The NVGA name was changed to NCDA in 1984, reflecting the greater use of the term *career counseling* in contrast to *vocational guidance*.

The NCDA website (www.ncda.org) lists the competencies required by practitioners to engage in career counseling (National Career Development Association [NCDA], 1997). These competencies include career development theory; individual and group counseling skills; individual and group assessment; career information and resources; career development program, promotion, management and implementation; coaching, consultation, and performance improvement; providing services to diverse populations; giving and receiving supervision;

knowledge of the ethical and legal issues in career counseling; knowledge for understanding research and evaluation in career counseling; and knowing how to utilize essential technology to assist clients with career planning.

Career Choice, Work Adjustment, and Job Transitions
Adjustment to Work

Career counselors clearly help individuals decide upon career and educational choices. But their work goes far beyond helping people find a job and earn a paycheck. Career counselors today are enormously concerned with a worker's current and future happiness, along with their satisfaction and adjustment in the workplace. Individuals and professionals unfamiliar with the field are often unaware of this.

People want to feel as if their work has meaning (Brief & Weiss, 2002). Blustein (2006) says that this meaning is affected by the workplace experience, in which a career identity is developed, interactions take place with other workers, and satisfaction is experienced by investment of effort, activity, and energy into work tasks.

Lent (2008) has pointed out that happy workers have a tendency to be more productive, and this can lead to greater consistency in their attendance at work, being helpful and mentoring to their coworkers, and accruing longevity on the job. This greater positive affect in the workplace can affect not only an employee's adjustment to work, but can also lead to overall improvements in both physical and mental health, even though these are known to fluctuate over time and with varying conditions (Judge & Ilies, 2004).

The adjustment to work has been studied carefully by researchers using the theory of work adjustment (TWA; Dawis & Lofquist, 1984), and it is impossible to leave this out of any material discussing career counseling. The theory matches workers' needs and skills with the reinforcers of their needs in the workplace, along with the skill requirements of the job they are currently in or hope to pursue. The correspondence between the needs of the worker with the reinforcer system of the workplace is used to predict job satisfaction. Similarly, the correspondence between the worker's skills and the skills required in the work environment are used to predict job satisfactoriness. Workers who experience both job satisfaction and job satisfactoriness are expected to accrue job tenure in their particular workplace.

The TWA is a model not unlike other "goodness-of-fit" models used by career counselors to assist individuals in entering the job market. But, in a changing and more globalized world, it has become incumbent upon career counselors to focus upon worker adaptations to a changing workplace, in which skill requirements as well as the needs of workers change over the course of their lifespan. For example, Carless and Bernath (2007) used a sample of career-changing Australian psychologists to study the antecedents to their intent to change careers. Monitoring the change of employment patterns in both Western society and their native Australia, they observed that professionals are currently redefining success, a process unheard of just a few years ago. There appears to be less interest among workers in climbing a professional, linear, corporate ladder, and more focus placed upon self fulfillment, professional engagement, and self-awareness. Whether this trend has emerged from workers engaged in life and career balancing, work-to-family spillover, or "time-sensitive" two-career families is not established.

Nevertheless, career change and reeducation to develop new career paths are now becoming common threads in the emerging, globalized work world. People who are dissatisfied with their jobs or life path tend to take more action toward change. They are more willing to tell others of their job search intentions, and to actively engage in an actual job search, culminating in a job or career change. Dissatisfied workers are more willing to engage in career planning as they seek out greater job satisfaction, in which their needs are matched by workplace reinforcers. The job changers tend to trust their own resilience as they relinquish their career identities with less than predictive discomfort and conscientiousness.

Dealing with Disappointment

The complexity of career counseling and its inherent blending with psychotherapy can be illustrated with a variety of cases, and dealing with disappointment due to barriers to opportunities stands out as one important example. There are, unfortunately, many situations that demand a career change or a rethinking of career choices when external threats to an individual's career goals arise.

This phenomenon has been studied by Pizzolato (2007) using the narratives of individuals who had to cope with looming disappointment or severe blockages to their career plans. Denial of admission to a particular professional school or being prevented from entering their chosen major illustrates their point.

Earlier, Gottfredson (1981, 2004) had studied and theorized about the nagging compromises regarding career paths that were influenced by social and economic contingencies, available resources, and support from a client's family or community. Pizzalato (2007) cites an abundance of literature describing how perceptions of achievement, competence, and self-concept are deleteriously affected by the experiences of failure. In turn, this forces compromises to plans. She goes on to articulate that many people sharing this experience do not know of or are not given information about alternative options. This is where career counselors play a significant role. Her study added to the literature on how college students cope with external threats to their career fantasies. The findings showed that threat attributions and coping strategies resulted in students either exiting or recycling through the career development process. Most importantly, the simultaneous consideration of both career goals and noncareer or personal goals led to retention or revision, as opposed to the abandonment of the highly anticipated career-possible self.

Developing Resilience

In difficult circumstances, career counselors assist clients in developing resilience as a healthy response. Moorhouse and Caltabiano (2007) examined adult resilience in the context of unemployment using a sample of 77 unemployed job seekers. They pointed out that resilience is an important ingredient in the job search process in the face of unemployment. They also advised that research has shown the unfortunate effects of unemployment on emotional well-being. Using scales for measuring resilience, depressed mood, and assertive job hunting, they found that resilience is indeed related to positive outcomes among the unemployed. Low levels of depression were also significantly correlated with high resilience, and resilience was positively and significantly correlated with the self-reported likelihood of job search assertiveness. Moorhouse and Caltabiano further noted that unemployed people who are self-reliant, independent, determined, resourceful, persevering, and resilient were more prone to be assertive in their job search.

This study demonstrated that resilience helps individuals cope with the adversity of unemployment, and lessens the likelihood of depression with repeated failures of job searching. The authors point out that the adversities of unemployment are quite different from other adversities that people confront and bring to counseling. They suggested that qualitative research might be useful to bring greater insight to what makes unemployed job seekers

remain resilient and what, in their minds, constitutes adversity. In addition, they questioned the usefulness of some job-seeking groups. It could be that, for some, remaining in groups with unsuccessful job seekers could foster feelings of helplessness, futility, and depression.

Job loss is, however, always difficult, and career counselors who work with people experiencing job loss take on a therapeutic role. In light of this truism, Blau (2007) has identified and successfully measured grieving stages during job loss in a fashion similar to that of Kubler-Ross (1969). These included negative stages—denial, anger, bargaining, and depression—as well as those that were more positive—exploration, acceptance. Greater anger was the most influential negative grieving stage, whereas acceptance was the most influential positive stage.

Evidence-based Approaches to Career Counseling

Kazdin (2008) remarks that the essential focus of evidence-based approaches to counseling is upon the extent to which empirically supported findings from research can be applied to clinical practice. He goes on to add that there remains quite a debate regarding the merits of evidence as it pertains to clinical interventions. He emphasizes that evidence-based practice (EBP) refers to "clinical practice that is informed by evidence about interventions, clinical expertise, and patient needs, values, and preferences and their integration in decision making about individual care" (p. 147). Evidence-based practice goes beyond the well-known clinical practice maxim, "Different folks benefit from different strokes" (Beutler, 1991, 2002).

The interventions that encompass the practice of career counseling have been the subject of EBP in counseling psychology for many years (Swanson, 1995; Whiston, 2002; Whitely, 1984). The selection of appropriate outcomes has been an issue for some time, although useful considerations of outcome variables have been offered years ago (Oliver, 1979). Three meta-analyses have been done regarding the general effectiveness of career counseling and indicators of EBP (Oliver & Spokane, 1988; Spokane & Oliver, 1983; Whiston, Sexton, & Lasoff, 1998). Moreover, Whiston (2002) applied the *principles of empirically supported interventions* (PESI) (Wampold, Lichtenberg, & Waehler, 2002) to research related to career counseling and interventions. Whiston highlighted the concerns over career intervention outcome investigations and pointed out that more focus needs to be given to client attribute by treatment interactions to determine which career interventions are most effective with which clients.

Although a great deal is known about the career development needs of multiethnic, multicultural, and diversified clients, an equal level of research has not explored the differing effects of career interventions with these groups, although the information contained in this chapter suggests that circumstance may be changing. Whiston also reported that the use of multiple outcome measures appears to be the norm and that the most salient evidence of EBP comes from the use of standardized instruments.

NCDA Annual Review

For the past 29 years the journal of the NCDA, *The Career Development Quarterly (CDQ)*, has produced an annual review on the subject matter of research and practice in career counseling. The annual review's authors cull the most significant articles from a calendar year's worth of career development literature and subsequently summarize the contents. The review not only provides information on evidence-based career development interventions, but appears to go beyond what Kazdin specifically defines as EBP. Moreover, Kazdin suggests that three shifts in research need to occur to fulfill his advocacy of EBP. These include giving more priority to "a) the study of the mechanisms of therapeutic change, b) the study of the moderators of change in ways that can be translated to clinical practice, and c) qualitative research" (p. 151). All of these are a part of the past research literature covered in the *CDQ* annual review.

The annual review covers the literature that addresses professional issues and provides information on those career assessment devices that were produced or updated over the course of the year. There is also an abundance of new literature that ties prominent and new career theories to innovations in practice. But, for the most part, the annual review tackles the major counseling issues of process and outcome research. Perhaps even more significantly, the annual review sets the agenda for the next avenues of career counseling research that need to be undertaken. These new roads are often a reflection of changing societal times and can be broad-based, including new interventions from the elementary school ages through higher education, and well into adulthood and retirement.

Areas that have been focused on recently include the arguments for and against emerging innovations in the practice of career counseling and the ways that work can be handled in the 21st century. These can include discussions of topics like telecommuting to work, distance learning, virtual offices, web-based career development programming, online assessments, and the use of the Internet for information gathering. All of these topics are examined from a research base. Other issues of concern include gender, work and family, and multiculturalism. The annual review allows researchers and practitioners alike to explore the variables set forth by Kazdin: the integration of client needs, the expertise of the clinician, and the needs and values of the client. From the review, counselors and researchers can choose to read the complete articles in primary sources that have been summarized.

Calls for More Evidence-based Practice

Career counseling researchers and practitioners remain interested in the science of their profession in an ever-changing world. Bernes, Bardick, and Orr (2007) recently made a call for new efficacy studies, including both experimental and longitudinal research to evaluate the impact of career counseling technique, in order to advance the field with additional EBP. They also drew attention to the need for both new and continuing EBP research with a multicultural and diversified clientele, and suggested that new techniques also be evaluated within an international context. Without a body of literature that tests career development theories and the effectiveness of various techniques, Bernes et al. suggest that we are only assuming that the work of the career counseling professional has had any lasting impact. Like others cited in the *CDQ* annual reviews over the years, they call for linking practice with theory, increasing methodological diversity, increasing field studies in outcome research, creating new experimental designs, increasing longitudinal research, constructing new instruments to operationalize new theories, internationalizing career counseling, and disseminating research findings in the literature.

Borgen and Maglio (2007) exemplify the continuing work in EBP that reflects Kazdin's statement and the issues brought forth by Bernes et al. It is important for all career counselors to know which interventions work and which do not over the course of practice with a client. But it is also important to know what seems to stay with the client over time and what does not. Swanson, Gore, Leuwerke, Achiardi, Edwards, and Edwards (2006) made it abundantly clear that clients often do not accurately recall career-related information from their counseling sessions.

With this in mind, Borgen and Maglio (2007) used the critical incident technique to understand what aided and hindered unemployed clients and career changers in implementing action plans that they had developed during the career and employment counseling process. Although action planning and goal setting have been researched in the past, empirical research on the variables that help and hinder the action planning process has been lacking. To be sure, career counseling clients frequently take action regarding their careers after they have discontinued counseling. The 23 women and 16 men who participated in the study responded to the questions, "What helped you implement your action plan?" and "What hindered you in implementing your action plan?" Data were collected in an interview format, and tapes of the interviews were transcribed. In the helping category, the following incidents and percentages of clients reporting them were recognized: positive attitude (92%); psychological support (85%); determination, seriousness, motivation (77%); self-knowledge (64%); information gathering (59%); goal focus or clarity (51%); bigger-picture perspective (44%); structured or flexible approach (38%); financial resources (31%). Incidents that were characterized as hindering action planning and the percentages of clients reporting them were: lack of goal or motivation (62%); dealing with difficult emotions (59%); difficulty with a system or discrimination (51%); lack of experience, education, or skills (46%); financial difficulties (44%); poor health in mind and body (38%); difficulty with counseling agency (36%); difficulty connecting with companies (36%); lack of support (31%).

These data suggest several ideas regarding the use of EBP in career counseling, as well as in other human services delivery systems. First, support appears to be an important ingredient in the career development process and is, unfortunately, often taken for granted. Counselors would be well served to build family or collegial support into the process. Second, it's clear that personal problems can impede the action planning or strategic implementing process, whereas psychological well-being can facilitate it. These are certainly not novel ideas, but they may not be emphasized as much as they should be in the career counseling experience. The data also suggest that there should be continuing follow-up with clients to ensure that they are proceeding with their plans and goals, and to lend support whenever possible with additional services. These can include referrals to individuals who help with life circumstances such as interfacing with the legal system or addressing needs for shelter, along with other basic human necessities.

There are, of course, continuing challenges for EBP, and some reflect new conceptual and political concerns as well as practice. Blustein, McWhirter, and Perry (2005) have questioned many of the assumptions regarding the practice of career counseling, suggesting that practitioners and researchers "look beyond the concerns of the well-educated segment toward a more activist social agenda" (p. 143). They suggest that career counseling must conduct research on members of all segments of society, along with the supports and the hindrances that affect their lives. Blustein et al. have characterized this as *emancipatory communication*. They encourage research that identifies unfair practices that have kept people from fulfilling their expectations.

Career Counseling with Culturally Diverse Populations: Attending to Race, Ethnicity, Ability, Gender, Sexual Identity

Working allows people to establish an identity that is laced with their interactions among coworkers. To that extent, work is framed within a cultural context and focused by the effort that is given to the work tasks at hand. Helms and Cook (1999) have maintained that the development of racial identity intersects with working life. For those who are privileged enough to take part in the work world, work is a life constant, often absorbing a third of a person's waking hours. On the other hand, in less privileged circumstances, work has also been called the luxury of the poor and disenfranchised (Chope & Toporek, 2007).

In the past quarter century, the populace of the United States has been witness to a dramatic transformation in its mixture of multiracial, multiethnic, and multiple-language groups. Moreover, individual and cultural identities have continued to diverge with each generation, while cultural and ethnic homogeneity have decreased with the greater frequency of intermarriage (Evans, 2008).

Career counselors have looked for models to assist with their understanding and application of career development with a multicultural perspective. For many years, Bronfenbrenner's model (Bronfenbrenner, 1977) had a particularly strong influence, especially with regard to the career counseling of women. It allowed counselors to consider influences at the micro level, such as the home and school; the exo level, which included external environments such as the workplace; the macro level, which included society at large; and the meso level, which focused upon the interactions among the different levels.

King and Madsen (2007) developed an ecological approach for understanding the contextual influences of career development among low-income African American youth. They described contextual factors "as environmental variables which interact with each individual's personal characteristics and experiences to influence career interests and choices" (p. 396). Their approach embraced the strengths of the youth rather than their deficits. Influenced by Bronfenbrenner's (1977) ecological systems theory, they used the *phenomenological variant of ecological systems theory* (PVEST; Lee, Spencer, & Harpalani, 2003) to identify the strengths and skills of low-income African American youth, advocating that this information would help counselors to facilitate these clients in the engagement of successful career development activities. The person–context model embodied in PVEST has five components: vulnerability, evaluated by considering risk and protective factors; stress engagement, including an individual's view of experiences; reactive coping strategies; stable coping responses; and life-stage coping outcomes.

Fouad and Kantamneni (2008) have also expanded upon Bronfenbrenner's model to create a new model that illustrates the many contextual influences in career counseling. Their cubic model has three dimensions: individual influences that reflected individual differences (e.g., interests, needs, values, self-efficacy), group-level influences (e.g., gender, race, ethnicity, family), and societal-level influences (e.g., acculturation, cultural values, opportunities, discrimination). All of these dimensions can be considered by practitioners as they increase their awareness of the many-faceted contextual forces that impact people's lives.

By creating competencies and performance indicators, the NCDA has had a strong presence in the development of multicultural awareness for practitioners and researchers. The NCDA Career Counseling Competencies and Performance Indicators (NCDA, 1997) include career counseling with diverse populations as one of its 11 competency categories. The knowledge and skills that are considered to be essential in relating to diverse populations, and that impact career counseling and developmental processes, include the ability to:

• Identify development models and multicultural counseling competencies.
• Identify developmental needs unique to various diverse populations, including those of different gender, sexual orientation, ethnic group, race, and physical or mental capacity.
• Define career development programs to accommodate needs unique to various diverse populations.
• Find appropriate methods or resources to communicate with limited-English-proficient individuals.
• Identify alternative approaches to meet career planning needs for individuals of various diverse populations.
• Identify community resources and establish linkages to assist clients with specific needs.
• Assist other staff members, professionals, and community members in understanding the unique needs/characteristics of diverse populations with regard to career exploration, employment expectations, and economic/social issues.
• Advocate for the career development and employment of diverse populations.
• Design and deliver career development programs and materials to hard-to-reach populations.

In identifying specific multicultural competencies, shown in the first ability above, many counselors use the multicultural counseling competencies articulated by Arredondo, Toporek, Brown, Jones, Locke, Sanchez, and Stadler (1996), which are also available on the American Counseling Association (ACA) website at www.counseling.org. These include three sections that address a counselor's awareness of his or her own cultural values and biases, an awareness of the client's worldview, and culturally appropriate intervention strategies. Each section is further divided into beliefs and attitudes, knowledge, and skills.

In August 2002, the American Psychological Association (APA) Council of representatives approved the policy on Guidelines on Multicultural Education, Training, Research, Practice, and Organizational Change for Psychologists. The Guidelines are available on the APA website at www.apa.org. The six guidelines cover attitudes and beliefs, as well as skills and knowledge similar to those presented on the ACA web site. However, the guidelines go further in encouraging practitioners, educators, and researchers to utilize constructs of multiculturalism and diversity in psychological education, training, research, and practice, as well as in facilitating organizational change.

Whether it is the NCDA, ACA, or APA, the professional counseling organizations have strived to ensure that career counseling specialists are drawn into the continuing evolution of their field, in the face of changes that are taking place both in the United States and around the world. Although neither the competencies nor guidelines are mandatory standards, they do serve to aid in assisting professionals in the provision of high-quality, appropriate, and relevant services.

The effectiveness of career counseling with multicultural, multiethnic, and diversified populations is an intricate topic. The NCDA multicultural competencies were criticized by Vera and Speight (2003) as lacking in attention to social justice issues, although Arredondo and Perez (2003) have challenged that social justice and multicultural competence are "intertwined and interdependent" (p. 282). Still, Fassinger (2008) reminds us that it is extremely demanding to unscramble the contextual effects of oppression based on racial/ethnic status from those problems prevalent among people living in conditions of poverty, with limited educational and financial resources, and with few, if any, networks of support.

Quite clearly, career decision making and planning are ultimately affected by relevant cultural factors. Thus, one primary challenge for career counselors is to develop a shared worldview with the client. The shared worldview can enhance the counseling relationship and assist in the success of the counseling process (Consoli & Chope, 2006).

The rising attention by authors toward offering new empirical data and EBP in the area of multicultural career counseling has begun to have a significant presence in the career development literature (Chope, 2008). Diversity clearly interacts with context and personal characteristics, hence influencing career choices, career development, and school-to-work transitions (Constantine, Kindaichi, & Miville, 2007; Constantine, Wallace, & Kindaichi, 2005; King & Madsen, 2007). Stead (2004) has noted that everyday activities are culturally embedded and are proved to affect an individual's career development. Gold, Rotter, and Evans (2002), with their *out-of-the-box* (OTB) model, have added that career counseling cannot be very effective without the consideration of both family and culture.

It has been of great concern to many career counseling practitioners and researchers that the authors and reviewers of career theories be sensitive to cultural inclusiveness. Career theories, developed over a period of 100 years, have not embraced the great diversity of cultural practices that can help counselors better understand the career development process

among unrepresented groups. Stead (2004) is one writer who has been critical of career theories for what he characterizes as ethnocentric views. And, Fassinger (2008) suggests that four groups of people have been disadvantaged by educational institutions and the workplace. These groups include women, people of color, sexual minorities, and people with disabilities.

To be fair, researchers and writers in the field have responded with new articles addressing these concerns. For example, Young, Marshall, and Valach (2007) took on Stead's challenge. Drawing from their 2004 paper presented at the International Association of Educational and Vocational Guidance-National Career Development Association (IAEVG-NCDA) Symposium on International Perspectives (Young et al., 2004), they orchestrated a structure for making career theories more culturally sensitive. Their approach was articulated in a fashion that is useful to both practitioners and researchers. The components of their structure include understanding culture, establishing links between career and culture, developing narrative and folk explanations for career choices, using observations in local communities, recognizing ongoing processes, and finally, subjecting observations and reports of ongoing processes to systematic analysis. Young et al. (2007) suggested that culture should be treated as more than a statistic, and that theorists as well as practitioners must work with the unambiguous links between culture and career, as well as context and history.

Recent research reflects a fresh focus on the linkage between specific cultures and career decision making. Okubo, Yeh, Lin, and Fujita (2007) showed the relationship between Asian American acculturation level and ethnic identity on the construction of career interests and aspirations. King and Madsen (2007) presented an ecological approach for understanding the contextual influence of career development on low-income African American youth. Diemer (2007) has given a perspective on the two worlds that African American men negotiate while interacting with an educational and occupational world that is predominately white. Quimby, Wolfson, and Seyala (2007), citing the growing body of new career development research, have questioned the applicability of traditional career theory to African Americans. A more extensive review of the impact of culture on career development, including Asian American culture, African American culture, African American Hispanic culture, Hispanic culture, and Appalachian culture can be found in the 2007 NCDA annual review (Chope, 2008). There are also comprehensive reviews of these and other cultures in Blustein (2006) and Leong (1995).

New contributions have been made to the career development literature with regard to those issues career counselors must understand when working with transgender clients (Kirk & Belovics, 2008). Irwin (2002) was very clear that career counselors must understand the conditions that gay, lesbian, bisexual, and transgender (GLBT) people face in the workplace as they pursue their chosen careers. Transgender employees face enormous workplace discrimination, and career counselors need to understand the clinical and legal issues, as well as legal protections, that are in place for transgender employees. In working with clients who have been marginalized in their workplace environments, career counselors must consider being advocates as well as clinicians.

Still, practical research exemplified by Hogue, Yoder, and Singleton (2007) suggest that men continue to be more likely to feel entitled to higher pay than women. Wage fairness will be a social, political, economic, and career development issue for some time. Even when men are told outright that women perform with greater competence than men on the same isolated work tasks, their study of 120 undergraduate men demonstrated that the men still felt worthy of higher wages. Women have also been discriminated against in the content of letters of support for career and educational positions. They are often described with fewer research related descriptors and they are said to be more communal and less agentic (Schmader, Whitehead, & Wysocki, 2007). Moreover, family planning and pregnancy appear to lead to discrimination, which affects the career development process for women (Cunningham & Macan, 2007). And, Masser, Grass, and Nesic (2007) provided data predicting that pregnant women are often stereotyped as warm, but incompetent, and experience workplace discrimination, especially in masculine-oriented jobs.

To incorporate the many contextual variables into the career counseling process, career counselors have begun to frequently utilize the narrative approach to the career counseling process. Conceivably, this type of approach to career counseling might be considered not just as a technique, but also as a method of understanding culture (Cochran, 1997). In addition Young et al. (2007) believe that counselors should be especially attuned to socially embedded processes that influence the psychology of working and career development, recognizing those processes that contain a longer series of activities involving cultural complexity.

Intervention Models for Career Counseling
Individual Interventions

The models of career intervention stem from the different theories of career choice and development. They can be goodness-of-fit models, like those of John Holland (1997); developmental models, like those of Donald Super (1963, 1980); constructivist approaches, like those of Mark Savickas (2005); or behavioral ones, like those of John Krumboltz (1996). Some of the great career theorists can serve as foundations for new approaches, as Krumboltz did for Kathleen Mitchell and Al Levin (Mitchell, Levin, & Krumboltz, 1999) when they "came up with" the planned happenstance theory of career counseling, an approach whereby counselors help clients learn how to create opportunities from unexpected events.

The career development processes that are discussed in most career theories are written with a particular context in mind, according to Gysbers, Heppner, and Johnston (2003). They point to five key tenets of career development theories and interventions: individualism and autonomy, affluence, structure of opportunity open to all, the centrality of work in people's lives, and the linearity, progressiveness, and rationality of the career development process. People from different cultures may not share a worldview that incorporates all of these tenets. That truism suggests that the use of any theory of career choice and the selection of interventions must be done with knowledge and the integration of multicultural perspectives.

All individual approaches use the counseling relationship to explore both individual as well as contextual variables that appear to dictate the choices that people make about their career and life plans. Career counseling clients can approach a career counselor with any number of problems. It is then incumbent on the counselor to know how to identify and hone in on the primary issue that brought the client to counseling. Along the way, the career counselor can develop hypotheses about the nature of the problem.

Using Assessments in Career Counseling

The information-gathering process can be many faceted. There are counselors who choose to gather information through the use of tests or other structured measuring devices. Some of the commonly used tests are also linked to particular theories of career choice.

The *Self-Directed Search* (SDS; Holland, 1994) is an instrument used to assess a person's career personality type and interests in six different occupational groupings (Realistic, Investigative, Artistic, Social, Enterprising, Conventional) with the goal of matching the individual to careers utilizing the same groupings. It is reflective of Holland's theory of career choice. One of the oldest and most popular measures of interests, the *Strong Interest Inventory* (Campbell, Strong, & Hansen, 1991), frames the entire interest profile of general occupational themes, basic interest scales, and occupational scales in alignment with Holland's occupational categories. With slightly different categorizations, the *Campbell Interest and Skill Survey* (Campbell, 1992) and *Harrington-O'Shea Career Decision Making System* (CDMS; Harrington & O'Shea, 2000) also use variations on Holland's scheme.

Similarly, Super's lifespan, life space theory is operationalized in the *Career Development Inventory* (CDI; Super, Thompson, Linderman, Jordan, & Myers, 1984), an instrument devoted largely to the assessment of readiness for career decision making. The *Career Maturity Inventory* (CMI; Crites & Savickas, 1995), which uses some of Savickas' thinking in career development, also explores the readiness of students in the sixth through twelfth grades to make career decisions.

Some instruments may be independent from any particular counseling theory but are concerned with those clinical issues that may hinder career planning and decision making. The *Career Thoughts Inventory* (CTI; Sampson, Peterson, Lenz, Reardon, & Saunders, 1996) makes an assessment of the irrational thoughts or dysfunctional thinking that individuals experience when making career plans, and is drawn from the theory of cognitive information processing (CIP; Peterson, Sampson, & Reardon, 1991). Likewise, the *Career Beliefs Inventory* (CBI; Krumboltz, 1991) inventories particular personal beliefs that may interfere with the clarity of perceptions about one's self and one's worldview when making career decisions; it stems from Krumboltz's learning theory of career counseling.

In the end, individual interventions come down to understanding a person's past behavior and the themes that emerge from that behavior in order to make future predictions. A person's genetic endowment, along with the contextual influences that have guided his or her life experience, need to be taken under consideration, as does the client's sense of self-concept or self-esteem. The degree to which a person has the wherewithal to develop a vocational identity also needs to be considered.

Assessment devices can be useful when there is not enough time for lengthy individual consultation and

when a client may be resistant, or not have the experience or knowledge to explore particular life themes. However, those counselors utilizing tests and other assessment devices are best served when they use instrumentation that is most consistent with their own theory of career choice and counseling. Osborn and Zunker (2006) have provided a conceptual model for career counselors using assessment results, noting that assessment in career counseling can be used for diagnosis, prediction, comparisons to others, and developmental checks over the lifespan. Their model includes an analysis of a client's needs for assessment or testing, establishing the purpose for engaging in the process, selecting the instruments, utilizing the results, and assisting the client with decision making. Assessment allows counselors to create their own data-based hypotheses about their clients and discuss these during their sessions as clients' stories unfold.

Of course, it is essential that the selection of instruments be culturally relevant, fair, and appropriate for the client's life context. Career assessment results serve as opportunities for the career counselor to engage the client in developing new hypotheses about the possibilities that are available to the client in a rapidly changing work world. They also help the counselor and client discuss complicated issues such as the client's worldview, work and life balance, vocational as well as avocational decision making, achievement needs, and career identity. In cases in which testing is accomplished with computer scoring, the test publishers frequently include additional reference material for the client to add to his or her information base. In summary, when used effectively, assessment instruments will enhance the client's self-knowledge and awareness.

Worldviews and Cognitive Predispositions

In the past, much of the counseling process considered the goodness of fit that people shared with occupations, generally using testing. Career counseling often was symbolized by a "lock and key" model. The career counseling work of the 21st century takes a much broader view of career development, one in which worldviews and cognitive predispositions are included in the clinical information gathering process. This has been characterized in Krumboltz' work, but it is also suggested by the work of Lent, Brown, and Hackett (1994) in their social cognitive career theory (SCCT). In this regard, they view the importance of the client's history of performance accomplishments, along with vicarious learning, appropriate emotional arousal, and perseverance to add to the creation of positive outcome expectations and self-efficacy. Added to this is the contextual support that comes from social persuasion or encouragement from significant others. So, the interviewing process attempts to address these variables.

Several writers have suggested that information be gathered and then integrated into a life planning process. Hansen (1997) has suggested that multiple aspects of life are interrelated, and her lifespan approach to career counseling explores the differential identities that clients have developed. She uses information that connects clients' lives to both their local and larger communities. She also promulgates the gathering of information about an individual's culture and those critical life tasks that are part of belonging to that culture.

In a vein similar to Hansen's, the systems theory framework (STF) of career development (McMahon, 2002; McMahon & Patton, 1995) is a constructivist approach to career counseling. It was originally created to manufacture a meta-theoretical frame for recognizing the contribution of many theories of career development. However, STF has been found to be useful in multicultural career counseling, qualitative career assessment, and career counselor training. Most importantly, the STF is an integrative framework that uses information from 16 intraindividual influences, six social influences, and six societal-environmental influences to assist clients.

Narratives

One of the most prominent means of gathering information in career counseling has been the use of the narrative approach. The therapeutic telling of life narratives allows career counseling clients to incorporate their personal histories in giving meaning to their evolving identities, so that they can structure their cultural and perceptual experience as they organize their thoughts about education and work. The narrative is particularly useful for career counselors to utilize in gathering information about a multicultural client's worldview (Howard, 1991). Cochran (1997) suggests that narratives in career counseling help clients share their history, current circumstances, and future goals. Some cultures actually appreciate oral histories over the written word.

Not unlike Super's idea that one's view of work is a reflection of self-concept, storytelling allows clients to become empowered as they construct new actions based on their stories. Revising a client's concept of work and life planning appears to be a major therapeutic building block, one that launches a new perceptual experience in the therapeutic process.

It allows the client to experience authenticity, by listening to an inner voice that facilitates the fullest expression of core values.

Amundson, Harris-Bowlsbey, and Niles (2009) suggest that the narrative approach can help counselors understand the context of a client's career development. Savickas (2005) has added to the narrative approach with his career styles interview. Using this approach, the focus is on vocational personality, life themes, and career adaptability. In short, individual narrative career counseling helps to create meaning in the work that individuals try to pursue. Savickas' career styles interview, formulates questions that concentrate on lifestyle and personal issues. These can include questions about role models, favorite books, magazines and newspapers, leisure activities, school subjects, mottos, and ambitions. They can also include questions, such as: What would you do if you won the super lottery?

Amundson et al. also suggest questions in a similar vein. These include gathering information about memories, knowing information about early role models, and having clients describe favorite books, movies, and television programs (p. 25).

Chope and Consoli (2006) developed a template for career counselors to consider when engaging in therapeutic storytelling related to career choice. In the narrative process of construction, deconstruction, and reauthoring, they suggest that counselors consider a number of issues to explore using an integrative, constructivist approach. The template uses the following components: client's cultural persona, acculturation modes, demographic environment, diversity within cultural groupings, legal status, language, religion, attitudes about work, rules in the family system, and gender stereotypes. Discrimination history can also be included. Using this template facilitates the establishment of a comprehensive, shared worldview between the client and counselor.

A client's narrative can capture the importance and influence of cultural identity on his or her career decision making. It also aids in considering the experiences a client may have when attempting to find work in those areas where few if any people represent the client's culture.

All acculturation modes involve a mainstream cultural context that can be supportive of other cultures or discriminating and marginalizing. Different clients will be ashamed or proud of their culture; some will wish to remain separate from their own ethnic group, while others will reject mainstream culture. Contextual interactions between the client, the family, and the social environment must be taken into consideration when seeking an under-standing of acculturation processes (Berry, 1997). Sensitivity to acculturation modes is an important feature in the process.

It is also valuable to understand the demographic environment, or the nature of the population in which the client resides. In addition, the career counselor must be sensitive, in this narrative pro-cess, to variations within a culture. For example, the broad categorization of "Latino/a" or "Hispanic" needs to be articulated further into the cultural differences between and within South American, Central American, Iberian, Cuban, Caribbean, Mexican, and other cultures.

Legal status and documentation are likely to be a sensitive topic for immigrants. Questions about status implications for career counseling can be used to deconstruct a client's story, as well as help to create additional support systems for the client. Career counselors who advocate for and empower undocumented workers through the legalization process may serve to enable all workers to compete on a level playing field.

In addition, language is a source of identity for people from all cultures. A sense of identity is devel-oped with language use, and it can reflect the dual-ism of acculturation. According to Kamasaki (2008), the desire to learn English is so pervasive in the immigrant community that, nationwide, English as a Second Language (ESL) programs for adults are overbooked. In 2006, 57.4% of ESL providers in the United States indicated that they had waiting lists for their prospective students.

Religious values also play an important role in the career choices of many. In the United States, a Protestant work ethic is thought to drive much of the economy. This ethic is often seen as anti-women and anti-immigrant, with limited multicultural applicability. Any person who follows a non-main-stream religion may feel uncomfortable on the job. Jewish workers in the United States, for example, felt for years that they couldn't ask for time off during the High Holy Days and Yom Kippur. The counselor needs to know how religion affects the client's sense of self and personal worth.

The worldview of the family and culture regard-ing work must be addressed. Some families want their children to earn money and be independent. Others want them to be high achievers, while others want them to refrain from drawing attention to themselves. Attitudes about work can also be related to earnings. Family attitudes about money, savings, and the trustworthiness of financial institutions can

speak volumes. Questions regarding this informa-tion can be asked by using a protocol developed by Chope (2006). The protocol includes six major questions that help to both guide and deepen the exploration of family influences on career choices.

- What kind of career information did the family provide?
- What tangible assistance was provided, and were any obligations attached?
- What type of emotional support was available?
- What was the impact of the client's career choice on the family?
- Were there any disruptive family events that affected the client?
- What were the actions of family members whom the client asked for help, and the actions of those who were not asked to help?

Families may have different rules about the power and influence of the extended family. Grandparents, aunts, cousins, and uncles may or may not have a role regarding career selection, depending on the culture.

Other information can be gathered and the narrative process can be enhanced with the use of a career genogram (Dagley, 1984; Okiishi, 1987). This occupational family tree can be quite useful, but it can entail gathering pertinent information from extended family members. The genogram, accompanied by good follow-up questions, allows an understanding of career expectations in the family and in the culture. Career counselors can explore dominant values in the family going back several generations. They can also accrue informa-tion on family myths, secrets, and "ghosts."

Most cultures tend to affirm some gender stereo-types regarding the roles that men and women play relative to work, educational experiences, and family responsibilities. Views on relationship status can also be influenced by the culture, the family, and the client's partner.

Group Interventions

In addition to working with individual clients, career counselors often engage in the process of career group counseling. Group interventions allow counselors to enhance their efficiency in the career counseling process by taking on more than one client per hour. Groups are particularly popular in high school and college settings, but they are also the fundamental means of intervention in adult job-seeking groups and job clubs. Groups can be used alone or in conjunction with individual career counseling. Smith, Dean, Floyd, Silva, Yamashita, Durtschi, and Heaps (2007), in a survey of 133 American College Counseling Association (ACCA) members, found that there was a need for developing more career group counseling interventions among college students.

Pyle (2000) has written extensively on the subject of career groups and has suggested that less structured groups can be useful for clients looking for direction or a change in direction. He offers a four-stage model for working with career groups. These stages include the opening, the investigation, the working stage, and the decision/operational stage. He also provides scripts for a model group career counseling program.

Groups can clearly be used as sounding boards, and they can serve to support individuals who may be struggling with career loss or unemployment. Career groups can also be useful in helping individuals to manage their career upward. They can be constructive for individuals who need to sort out their personal reasons for considering a job change as well. Having a group of listeners available in a short-term process with a positive atmosphere can be a healthy arena for career clients to discuss motivation, career satisfaction, and career disappointments. Career groups can be used for people exploring retirement options. Sullivan and Mahalik (2000) have used groups to enhance career self-efficacy by having group members focus and discuss the major components of their personal career self-efficacy: performance accomplishments, emotional arousal, vicarious experience, and verbal persuasion.

Rutter and Jones (2007) have described a time-honored group process called the *job club*. This is a group technique that uses behavioral principles and positive reinforcement contingencies to assist individuals in beginning their job search. Job clubs can be very intense, meeting several times per week. These groups have been used most frequently for new job hunters, and for those who have recently suffered a job loss or forced termination. They have also been available for career clients with severe disabilities who function best in groups with others who are sensitive to the contextual variables that affect their lives. The job club keeps job seekers from being isolated and lonely, while it also introduces a behavioral program that demands that participants engage in and document their job-seeking activities. Job clubs also emphasize empowerment and collaboration.

Shea, Ma, and Yeh (2007), noting the rapid rise in the number of Chinese immigrants in the United States and the specific challenges with which low-income Chinese immigrants must contend, developed a culturally specific career exploration group for low-income Chinese immigrant youth, Career Exploration Development and Resources (CEDAR). CEDAR includes an assessment of the participants' interests, values, abilities, and aspirations, but also recognizes the role of the family, depicted by having the participants complete career genograms. The psychological complexity of the group was appreciated through discussions about the participants' immigration experience. Guest speakers were invited to assist the group with information regarding cultural adjustment. Transition issues and perceived barriers were addressed, along with the roles of racism and sexism at work. Time was also set aside for skill building, including resume development, college application preparation, and information distribution regarding financial aid for continuing their education. In summary, CEDAR is a career group process with culturally specific career interventions that is clearly structured, content specific, and relatively straightforward to replicate.

The Increased Use of Technology As an Intervention

Once a career counselor understands a client's problem and assists him or her in creating a plan, clients generally have the expectation that the career counselor is an expert at providing information about the labor market. In the not too distant past, career counselors would refer clients to information resources that were available in the career libraries of colleges and universities, or in general libraries available to the public. As the clients gathered information, they would be encouraged to use their imagination to create a sense of direction for themselves. Clients were also encouraged to "shadow" or closely follow workers who engaged in job activities that they might be interested in. Internships or apprenticeships might also be recommended for the purposes of gathering both information and experience. Today, the Internet and the use of online websites to provide information has enabled clients work on their own.

Since the 1960s, computers have been used to enhance career counseling services, and the early work has been summarized by Super (1970). A variety of systems have been developed over the years, exemplified by the *System for Interactive Guidance Information* (SIGI; Katz, 1963), *SIGI Plus* (Educational Testing Service, 1997), and *Discover* (ACT, 2000) to name just a few. Originally, these systems were developed for high school and college students, but they are now pertinent for career clients at all levels. These systems have provided computer-based assessments of individual needs, interests, skills, and values, which then are matched to some extent with occupational and educational information found in the respective databases.

In the mid-1970s, the U.S. government established the National Occupational Information Coordinating Committee (NOICC), which was developed to lend support to the states to assist in the development of career information delivery systems. Partially in response to that effort, websites have been constructed to offer massive amounts of occupational information, including occupational outlook, nationwide and local salary levels for particular jobs, the knowledge skills and abilities that are required to enter different occupations, job availability, and the job tasks that make up different fields of employment.

There are no-fee sites, like the Department of Labor sites CareerInfoNet (www.acinet.org) and O*Net (www.onetcenter.org), along with for-fee sites like the *Kuder Career Planning System* (www.kuder.com). *CareerInfoNet* also has links to the Department of Labor's *Occupational Outlook Handbook* (www.bls.gov/oco).

The Internet and the larger Information Age have had a terrific influence on the provision of counseling services. Online employment applications and applications to educational institutions are now commonplace. Professional career counselors working in local career centers continuously gather information, as well as pertinent journal articles, over the Internet. The Internet is also available to make career and other counseling services more accessible to people through distance education, training, and counseling.

Counseling via the Internet has been defined as "web counseling" by the National Board for Certified Counselors (NBCC), although career counseling can also be done through the utilization of video conferencing and e-mail. Career information can be readily tapped through virtual career centers, and institutions can give information about in-person services and also online services such as career assessments, employer databases, and alumni databases (Amundson et al., 2009). The NBCC has proposed new ethical standards for those who utilize the web counseling experience (NBCC, 2007).

There is, however, a significant divide among people who are willing to gather online information from the Internet. Joo, Grable, and Choe (2007)

found that younger employees, along with those who participated in a defined contribution retirement plan and those who made joint personal financial decisions, were more likely to use online procedures. With regard to age, 38.5 years appeared to be the cutoff for those who used online services regularly. Nonusers were typically born before 1970 and entered their adulthood before the beginning of the explosion of Internet use. For those born after 1970, the World Wide Web has been a part of education and work life, and they are used to having information at their fingertips.

Clearly, career counselor educators have become more comfortable with teaching others how to be career counselors through online programs. They have also become more experienced in teaching students how to use the internet to engage clients in online career counseling. However, Lewis and Coursol (2007) point out the enduring and aforementioned questions about the depth of career counseling. The enthusiasm that counselor educators have for online counseling is moderated by a lingering perception that career issues are less complex than noncareer issues and, as such, are more amenable to counseling that utilizes online technology. For example, the first six of the client problems most endorsed by counselor educators tended to be of an information-generating variety. So, counselors may be more willing to respond to these issues because they are also less enduring, usually less complex, and most likely responsive to counseling.

There are, of course, many career counseling issues that are not appropriate for online counseling. These include issues like how to manage one's career upward, how to get along with coworkers and supervisors, how to assess the stress of balancing one's work and educational demands with family life, and how to address issues of self-esteem.

Career counselors must be sensitive to the fact that many potential clients use career issues as an entry into the counseling process. Quite often, these clients may be experiencing other clinical issues. And, although online counseling is moving into its adolescence, it has not developed into its adulthood. There also remains a lack of research into its effectiveness. Counselors need to be trained in online procedures, and new training guidelines and continuing ethical and legal updates for counselors will be needed. In addition, the use of other technologies like personal digital assistants, iPods, and podcasts will affect the practice of career counseling in the near future.

Zalaquett and Osborn (2007) wrote that a number of career counselor educators are developing websites to foster career information literacy among students taking graduate career classes. They remind their readers to use the Association for Counselor Education and Supervision (ACES) and the NCDA joint statement on the use of computers and the Internet in guidance and counseling (ACES/NCDA, 2000). With computer and online career information delivered on systems like O*NET and the online *Occupational Outlook Handbook* (www.bls. gov/oco), the authors suggest that counselor educators must assist students in acquiring online technical competencies.

Career Counseling in Elementary School, High School, and College

Considering the idea that career development is essentially a life-long process, Zunker (2006) has suggested the possibility that it begin as early as pre-kindergarten. Career-related programs can continue throughout the entire educational process as educational institutions prepare people for the job-related needs of their community, state, and nation. Super (1990) has been mindful of the various concepts of self that individuals have, whether they be educationally related, career related, or peer related. These various concepts remain fluid throughout life as self-concept and self-efficacy emerges with differentiating experiences. As self-esteem develops, for some, it may be related to educational endeavors, whereas for others it may be based in relationships, and for others it may be reflected in lifestyle. Gottfredson (1996) has pointed out that gender stereotypes with regard to the work world often force children to give up on particular fantasies about careers because they do not appear to be appropriate for their gender or socioeconomic class.

Elementary School

With the current interest in lifespan approaches to career counseling and the research in the contextual variables that influence the career counseling process, there is concern about developing appropriate developmental interventions for children at remarkably young ages. This interest has had support for close to 20 years. In 1992, the National Occupational Information Coordinating committee (NOICC) prepared guidelines for counselors at all levels to develop goals and methods of reaching those goals over the course of one's life (NOICC, 1992). In summary, NOICC recommended that elementary school children develop competencies in self-knowledge and awareness of growth and change, understanding the relationship between work and education, understanding how to use career information, understanding decision making, being aware of different occupations, and developing an awareness of the interrelationship of life roles.

This is a tall order. The key to having elementary school children meet the competencies suggested by NOICC lies both in the schools and in the family. Career researchers have emphasized that the family must be involved at an early age to help children understand the ramifications of career development over the lifespan. Niles and Harris-Bowlsbey (2005), for example, point to the sway parents have in their children's career choices. Parents have a profound influence on the intellectual, social, and emotional components of their children's lives (Steinberg, 2004). Their guidance is a powerful component in the decision-making process, and they expose their children to a particular variety of career choices. Brown (2003, p. 332) posits that "parents exercise more influence than any other adults on the educational and vocational choice of children."

Others have suggested that the entire family be given more focus in understanding career and life planning in the early ages (Blustein, Walbridge, Friedlander, & Palladino, 1991). More recently, the impact of siblings (Kenny & Perez, 1996), as well as extended family members, on the career decision-making process, has been suggested as a source of potential research material (Schultheiss, Kress, Manzi, & Glasscock, 2001).

So, parents, extended family members, and significant others play highly influential roles in the career decision making process, and it is incumbent upon career counselors to bring in these notable people to help in the career counseling process. They can be encouraging character models, serving as the original "network," confronting occupational stereotypes, and offering new opportunities for children to be exposed to new and challenging opportunities.

Middle School

Middle school lends itself to a strong transitioning process. Accordingly, NOICC (1992) suggested that middle school students understand the influence of a positive self-concept as they develop the skills to interact with others. It was also suggested that they know the benefits of educational achievement and career opportunities while understanding the relationship between work and learning. Career counselors need to be sensitive to the rapid developmental changes taking place as they help students with the development of significant new relationships and a personal identity. Toward the end of middle school, many counselors begin to use aptitude and interest testing to assist students in planning the future of their educational lives. Career librarians can help with the organization of appropriate career information, and schools can provide opportunities for exposure to career opportunities previously unthought-of. Counselors can assist students in experimenting with new life roles while they stimulate their imaginations, and can help them to develop new interests through exposure to new activities.

High School
In high school, career counselors assist students with a process that involves the "crystallization" of a career or vocational identity (Super, 1990). Students in high school begin to prepare themselves for the timely transition into work or vocational technical education, community college, or baccalaureate-degree colleges.

The NOICC Guidelines suggest that high school students develop the competencies to further develop their self-concept and relationship-building skills. But, most importantly, they should begin to prepare for the work world. They will need to locate, evaluate, and interpret career information, but they will also need to become job ready as they seek, obtain, maintain, and change jobs. Career planning and educational planning become essential in these years (Herr, Cramer, & Niles, 2004).

Savickas (1999) suggested that career counselors intervene to ensure that students are oriented toward career choice and become competent at planning and exploring on their own. He also suggested that group formats could be both efficient and supportive of students. Group formats could also be used to discuss any tests of vocational choice, career maturity, or concerns about work and careers.

High school also sees a greater preponderance of interest in the utilization of tests and other assessment devices. Not only are students given the opportunity to take college entrance examinations, but they will also be directed to some of the more popular instruments assessing career interests like the SDS (Holland, 1994) or the CAI (Johansson, 1986) for those who may pursue community colleges or vocational-technical education, or the SII (Campbell, Strong, & Hansen, 1991), the *Campbell Interest and Skills Survey* (CISS; Campbell, 1992), and the CDMS (Harrington & O'Shea, 2000). Popular assessments of personality like the *Myers-Briggs Type Indicator* (MBTI; Myers & Briggs, 1993) are also frequently taken at this time.

Counselors work with students to prepare them to clarify their concepts of their life roles. They encourage continued exploration and refinement of what will emerge as a vocational identity.

Higher Education
Higher education has been witness to a dramatic change in recent years, with increases in international students, students from a multicultural heritage, and students with disabilities. The NOICC has established competencies for students entering higher education and adulthood. Much of the focus of career counselors with students in higher education is the development of a strong concept of self, along with the skills to explore, enter, and participate in the educational and work worlds. Tansley, Jome, Haase, and Martens (2007) have pointed out that verbal persuasions can affect an individual's self-efficacy as well as outcome expectations, goals, and intentions. But they also suggested that, according to prospect theory, negatively framed messages can have a powerful, deleterious effect.

There will be stronger demands for the skills to not only enter new occupations, but also to make transitions from education to work, along with making future career transitions. Duffy and Sedlacek (2007) explored the presence of and search for a "calling" to the future among 3,091 first-year college students. The presence of a calling correlated positively with decidedness, comfort, self-clarity, and choice–work salience, whereas the search for a calling correlated positively with indecisiveness and a lack of educational information. To some extent, this sets the agenda for career counselors working with students in higher education and adults. Helping students to achieve cognitive clarity and refine their decision-making process will have lasting results.

Career Interventions with Marginalized Persons: A Primer on Social Justice in Career Counseling

No country, however rich, can afford the waste of its human resources. Demoralization caused by vast unemployment is our greatest extravagance. Morally it is the greatest menace to our social order.

The test of our progress is not whether we add more to the abundance of those who have much; it is whether we provide enough for those who have too little.

Franklin Delano Roosevelt's words, inscribed on his memorial in Washington, DC, characterize his thoughtfulness about social justice. Toporek and Chope (2006) conceptualized social justice in career counseling as the practice of alleviating injustice and oppression for all people, but particularly those who may be marginalized. Four areas of concern must be addressed: social justice awareness and advocacy in individual counseling, social justice program development, assisting in social entrepreneurship, and training.

A number of potential roles are available for career counselors interested in social justice and working with people who are marginalized. In individual counseling, career counselors can play a role in assisting others to learn about and pursue a career that involves social justice factors. And, career counselors can play roles as advocates for some their clients. Advocacy may be considered with clients who have had experiences that include employment and educational discrimination, sexual harassment, workplace violence or trauma, and observing wrongdoing and trying to decide whether to "blow the whistle."

Career counselors can also be involved in new program development for those who have been placed in marginalized situations. These can include people who are homeless, impoverished, undocumented, incarcerated, or physically and emotionally disabled, among others.

Probationers, parolees, and ex-offenders make up a significant population of individuals who are often underserved by the career counseling community. According to Shivy, Wu, Moon, Mann, Holland, and Eacho (2007) incarceration rates in the United States are climbing at an unprecedented rate; close to 2.2 million people are currently incarcerated. Approximately 650,000 inmates are released from prison each year, to face immense challenges with regard to returning to their communities, keeping straight, finding work, or continuing their education. Most are under some form of continuing supervision. Shivy et al. outlined several different domains of difficulties for ex-offenders including the need for education, training and practical assistance, differential challenges in obtaining and maintaining a job, and locating and obtaining available support services. Substance abuse was also an issue that affected the reentry and employment process. Shivy et al. suggested that career counselors begin to participate in relevant community activities when working with ex-offenders by visiting their social networks and the various workplaces where they are employed or seeking employment. Participation at this level can help career counselors to further understand both the internal psychological and external sociological impacts that incarceration has had on these individuals.

Career counselors can also be involved in either advising or assisting these clients in the development of new programs of an entrepreneurial nature, referred to as "social entrepreneurship." These for-profit programs are able to endure because they are divorced from the need to constantly generate income through donations and grants.

Unfortunately, one of the problems with any not-for-profit program is that it is often unable to sustain itself, given its dependence upon grants and volunteer efforts. Helms (2003) noted that one historical and structural problem in integrating social justice in counseling is that it most often relies on pro bono and volunteer work, or going beyond the scope of one's duty. Alternatively, social justice efforts have also included developing innovative, entrepreneurial, and self-sustainable organizations.

Blustein (2008) has pointed out that unemployment continues to hamper well-developed countries like the United States, with the loss of jobs to international markets. He has also identified three fundamental needs that having a job has the capacity to impact greatly: need for survival, need for relatedness, need for self-determination (Blustein, 2006). Still, the impact of characteristics of ethnicity on earning potential, mobility, and education are legion.

Accompanying the decline of strong unions and union-protected work, employers have offered workers more part-time jobs, fewer fringe benefits, and little or no job security. Reflecting on reports issued by the United States Department of Labor, Johnson (2008) notes that changes such as these are important factors contributing to rates of long-term joblessness among traditional blue-collar workers.

Diemer (2007), referenced earlier in this chapter, has a perspective on the different worlds and marginalized experiences that African American men negotiate when interfacing with predominately white educational and occupational worlds. *Two worlds* is the moniker that Diemer cites when he describes the negotiation of one's culture of origin with the predominately white opportunity structure. Using seven African American men, Diemer's well-mined qualitative data were eventually described with one category (two worlds: experience and motivation) and four subcategories (barriers in the white world, barriers in the black world, bicultural balance, bicultural skill). Participants described how they had to "move within circles" when they wanted to achieve success in the white environment without losing touch with their connection and identification with African American culture. Barriers in the white world included the obvious forms of discrimination, but also accounted for the tension that developed in different settings when one participant was asked to essentially represent all African Americans. Barriers in the black world included fears of jealousy and contempt for the success of the participants. Participants also discussed the experience of bicultural balance in their lives and the discomfort that it created. And, they pointed out the bicultural skills that were necessary to allow them to go back and forth between their two worlds. Diemer suggested that further research eagerly look at the psychological distress that individuals from all cultures experience when negotiating two environments. He also called for continuing research on the skills that make up bicultural competence, information potentially useful for clients as well as practitioners.

Diemer and Blustein (2007) offer a refreshing twist to career identity by suggesting that a new construct, "vocational hope" be considered in the mix. The authors, responsive to the few career assessment tools appropriate for urban adolescents, explored the component structure of three indices of career development with a sample of 115 females and 105 males. These indices were vocational identity, career commitment measured, and work salience. Their analyses produced a four-component solution (connection to work, vocational identity, commitment to chosen career, salience of chosen career). They pointed out that remaining connected to a vocational future or inculcating vocational hope, especially with countless barriers and pressure to disconnect, is an important consideration for career counselors and educators working with urban adolescents. Diemer and Blustein suggested that counselors provide new psychosocial and career development interventions that facilitate vocational hope. They also suggested that a new measure of the construct of vocational hope be considered for development. Perhaps the inculcating of hope is in essence of what career counselors should do best.

Conclusion

Career counseling is a unique approach to counseling because it is so intimately tied to the utilization of tests to extract information about individual clients and families and match that with jobs and career choices. But the "test 'em and tell 'em" approach to career counseling has been far less influential as the field has changed dramatically over the past 25 years. From its very narrowly conceived beginning, career counseling is now tied to a host of new approaches that attempt to link individual characteristics with contextual and relationship variables to assist individuals in the pursuit of their life goals. Career counselors may need to be more eclectic than others due to the complex nature of career counseling. Part of the counseling process with a client might call for a trait and factor approach, whereas for another part of the process a relational, contextual, or social learning approach might be used.

The interviewing process in career counseling has also changed, in that counselors ask questions that have as much to do with lifestyle as job skills. There is continuing interest in the lifespan of a client, so that clinical information about childhood, adolescence and adulthood are given equal time. This evolution in the interviewing process continues to blur the line between personal and career counseling. Career counselors may also be called upon to address particular personal issues with one's career domain, including self-esteem and self-efficacy, burnout, work–family and family–work spillover, and employment discrimination.

Providing career counseling services to the marginalized and underserved will continue to be among the greatest challenges for the career counseling profession and for professional associations such as the NCDA, the National Employment Counseling Association (NECA), the Society of Counseling Psychology-Division 17 of APA, and the Division 17 section, the Society for Vocational Psychology. In short, career counseling must return to its roots. It is indeed curious that a profession that began with the perspective of social justice envisioned by its founder, Frank Parsons, has failed to address many of the concerns that were used to create the career counseling field. The very poor, urban youth, the homeless, the imprisoned, the disabled, the marginalized, and those on probation and parole will continue to need a much greater degree of focus from the field and the professional associations. It would be wise for the professional associations to represent these various potential clients most in need of services.

Future Directions Questions

The career counseling field will confront a variety of new challenges in the future. Here, I review several of the issues that need to be taken on, along with problems that need to be resolved.

There will need to be a greater degree of international focus in the field, especially with increasing globalization and the migration of so many workers from country to country in search of new opportunities. In anticipation of this sea change in the field, Pope (2007), during his editorship of the *Career Development Quarterly* (*CDQ*), created a new section in the journal titled "Global Vision." Many contributions to the *CDQ* and the *Journal of Vocational Behavior* (*JVB*) are provided by authors living outside of the United States. Career counseling and assessment have evolved within the capitalist structure of the United States. But how do career choices evolve in socialist and communist countries? And, how might the major political changes in a country influence the career development of the citizens of that country? Some international contexts may not be friendly toward the individualistic, self-directed career development that many people experience in the United States. To address some of these emerging issues, the Society of Counseling Psychology (Division 17 of the APA) sponsored an International Counseling Psychology Conference (www.icpc2008.org) with keynote speakers from South America, Portugal, South Africa, Taiwan, and the United States, among others. Access to services around the world, honoring indigenous career models, the interface of health ethics and social science, and the future of counseling psychology were among the topics given a global perspective.

Should career counseling be seen as part of a system of health care? Although almost all of the states have licensed professional counseling laws, career counselors are not seen in the same light as other counselors providing services. Will this attitude change as people realize that clinical depression is often a by-product of job loss? More people migrate for work-related reasons than for any other phenomenon. Work-to-family and family-to-work spillover continue to disrupt marriages and relationships. Career stress leads to general anxiety problems. Career counselors are the experts in these areas, yet they are often marginalized by federal and state health care systems, not to mention HMOs, unwilling to recognize their services as fundamental to an individual's mental health.

Career counseling has been largely influenced by legislation, but will professionals in the career counseling field see the need to continue to develop advocacy models for the profession and for clients? Career professionals should continue to have a strong a relationship with the Department of Labor, along with federal, state, and local legislators, and especially with those individuals who regulate government policies. They should find a way to participate as advocates in legislation like the Employment Non-Discrimination Act (ENDA) and other legislation serving to eliminate discrimination against oppressed people. The founder of the field, Frank Parsons, engaged in advocacy over 100 years ago.

Career counselors also need to be involved in new program development and evaluation for those who have been placed in marginalized situations. These can include people who are homeless, impoverished, undocumented, incarcerated or paroled, and physically and emotionally disabled, among others. Many inner-city youth in the United States are unemployed or underemployed and not necessarily involved in job-seeking activities. Career counselors have valuable expertise in vocational program development for these and other "difficult to employ" populations. They can advise and assist in the development of new entrepreneurial programs or social entrepreneurship. These for-profit programs can directly address social problems as their central mission and endure because they are divorced from income generated only through donations and grants.

Career counselors need to prepare for the baby boomers who will be reaching retirement age soon. It is popularly known that 78 million baby boomers will reach the age of 65 in 2011. Many of these retirees will wish to explore new opportunities, and others will wish to keep working. Career counselors with training in gerontology will need to be able to provide necessary services to this group.

Finally, career counselors will need to advocate for themselves as counselors. Quite clearly, the field has changed substantially over the years, as has the workplace. As this chapter has demonstrated, contextual variables of the family, community, and culture are now included as essential ingredients in the career counseling process. Evans (2008) has suggested that there must be an integration of career counseling, personal counseling, and multicultural counseling. This integration should take place within the framework of the APA guidelines, and the NCDA and ACA competencies previously discussed. Career counselors can serve in a variety of roles: as individual practitioners, social service program developers, and advocates. They have the capacity to change lives in the area most significant in the development of a person's individual identity: the work that the person does.

References

ACT, Inc. (2000). Discover [Computer software]. Iowa City, IA: Author.

Amundson, N. E., Harris-Bowlsbey, J., & Niles, S. G. (2009). *Essential elements of career counseling: Processes and techniques.* Upper Saddle River, NJ: Pearson Education, Inc.

Arredondo, P., & Perez, P. (2003). Expanding multicultural competence through social justice leadership. *The Counseling Psychologist, 31,* 282–289.

Arrendondo, P., Toporek, R., Brown, S. P., Jones, J., Locke, D. C., Sanchez, J., & Stadler, H. (1996). Operationalization of the multicultural counseling competencies. *Journal of Multicultural Counseling and Development, 24,* 42–78.

Association for Counselor Education and Supervision/National Career Development Association. (2000). *Preparing counselors for career development in the new millennium* [ACES/NCDA position paper]. Retrieved December 18, 2006, from http://www.ncda.org/pdf/CommissionPaper.pdf.

Aubry, R. F. (1977). Historical development of guidance and counseling and implications for the future. *Personnel and Guidance Journal, 55,* 288–295.

Beutler, L. E. (1991). Have all won and must all have prizes? Revisiting Luborsky et al.'s verdict. *Journal of Consulting and Clinical Psychology, 59,* 226–232.

Beutler, L. E. (2002). The dodo bird is extinct. *Clinical Psychology: Science & Practice, 9,* 30–34.

Bernes, K. B., Bardick, A. D., & Orr, D. T. (2007). Career guidance and counselling efficacy studies: An international research agenda. *International Journal for Educational and Vocational Guidance, 7,* 81–96.

Berry, J. W. (1997). Acculturation and health. In S. Kazarian, & D. Evans (Eds.), *Cultural clinical psychology* (pp. 39–57). New York: Oxford.

Blau, G. (2007). Partially testing a process model for understanding victim responses to an anticipated worksite closure. *Journal of Vocational Behavior, 71,* 401–428.

Blustein, D. L. (2001). The interface of work and relationships: A critical knowledge base for 21st century psychology. *The Counseling Psychologist, 29,* 179–192.

Blustein, D. L. (2006). *The psychology of working: A new perspective for career development, counseling, and public policy.* Mahwah, NJ: Erlbaum.

Blustein, D. L. (2008). The role of work in psychological health and well-being. *American Psychologist, 63,* 228–240.

Blustein, D. L., McWhirter, E. H., & Perry, J. C. (2005). An emancipatory communication approach to vocational development theory, research, and practice. *The Counseling Psychologist, 33,* 141–179.

Blustein, D. L., Walbridge, M. M., Friedlander, M. L., & Palladino, D. E. (1991). Contributions of psychological separation and parental attachment to the career development process. *Journal of Counseling Psychology, 38,* 39–50.

Borgen, W. A., & Maglio, A. T. (2007). Putting action back into action planning: Experiences of career clients. *Journal of Employment Counseling, 44,* 173–184.

Borow, H. (1964). Notable events in the history of vocational guidance. In H. Borow (Ed.), *Man in a world of work* (pp. 45–64). Washington, DC: Houghton Mifflin.

Brewer, J. M. (1942). *History of vocational guidance.* New York: Harper.

Brief, A. P., & Weiss, H. M. (2002). Organizational behavior: Affect in the workplace. *Annual Review of Psychology, 53,* 279–307.

Bronfebrenner, U. (1977). Toward an experimental ecology of human development. *American Psychologist, 32,* 513–531.

Brown, D. (2003). *Career information, career counseling, and career development* (8th ed.). Boston: Allyn & Bacon.

Campbell, D. (1992). *Campbell interest and skill survey.* Minnetonka, MN: National Computer Systems.

Campbell, D., Strong, E. K., & Hansen, J. (1991). *The Strong Interest Inventory.* Palo Alto, CA: Consulting Psychologists Press.

Carless, S. A., & Bernath, L. (2007). Antecedents of intent to change careers among psychologists. *Journal of Career Development, 33,* 183–200.

Chope, R. C. (2005). Qualitatively assessing family influence in career decision making. *Journal of Career Assessment, 13,* 395–414.

Chope, R. C. (2006). *Family matters: The influence of the family in career decision making.* Austin, TX: Pro-Ed.

Chope, R. C. (2008). Practice and research in career counseling—2007. *Career Development Quarterly, 57,* 98–173.

Chope, R. C., & Consoli, A. J. (2006). A storied approach to multicultural career counseling. In K. Maree (Ed.), *Shaping the story: A guide to facilitating career counseling* (pp. 83–96). Pretoria, South Africa: Van Schaik.

Chope, R. C., & Toporek, R. L. (2007). Providing human services with a social justice perspective. In J. Z. Calderon (Ed.), *Race poverty and social justice* (pp. 148–166). Sterling, VA: Stylus.

Cochran, L. (1997). *Career counseling: A narrative approach.* Thousand Oaks, CA: Sage.

Consoli, A. J., & Chope, R. C. (2006). Contextual integrative psychotherapy: A case study. In G. Stricker, & J. Gold (Eds.), *A casebook in psychotherapy integration.* Washington, DC: APA.

Constantine, M. G., Kindaichi, M., & Miville, M. L. (2007). Factors influencing the educational and vocational transitions of Black and Latino high school students. *Professional School Counseling, 10,* 261–265.

Constantine, M. G., Wallace, B. C., & Kindaichi, M. M. (2005). Examining contextual factors in the career decision status of African American adolescents. *Journal of Career Assessment, 13,* 307–319.

Crites, J. O. (1981). *Career counseling: Models, methods, and materials.* New York: McGraw-Hill.

Crites, J. O., & Savickas, M. (1995). *Career maturity inventory.* Boulder, CO: Crites Career Consulting.

Cunningham, J., & Macan, T. (2007). Effects of applicant pregnancy on hiring decisions and interview ratings. *Sex Roles, 57,* 497–508.

Dagley, J. (1984). *A vocational genogram* (mimeograph). Athens, GA: University of Georgia.

Dawis, R. V., & Lofquist, L. (1984). *A psychological theory of work adjustment.* Minneapolis: University of Minnesota Press.

Diemer, M. A. (2007). Two worlds: African American men's negotiation of predominantly White educational and occupational worlds. *Journal of Multicultural Counseling and Development, 35,* 2–14.

Diemer, M. A., & Blustein, D. L. (2007). Vocational hope and vocational identity: Urban adolescents' career development. *Journal of Career Assessment, 15,* 98–118.

Dorn, F. J. (1992). Occupational wellness: The integration of career identity and personal identity. *Journal of Counseling & Development, 71,* 176–178.

Duffy, R. D., & Sedlacek, W. E. (2007). The presence of and search for a calling: Connections to career development. *Journal of Vocational Behavior, 70*, 590–601.

Educational Testing Service. (1997). *SIGI Plus*. Princeton, NJ: Author.

Evans, K. (2008). *Gaining cultural competence in career counseling*. Boston: Lahaska Press.

Fassinger, R. E. (2008). Workplace diversity and public policy: Challenges and opportunities for psychology. *American Psychologist, 63*, 252–268.

Fouad, N. A., & Kantamneni, N. (2008). Contextual factors in vocational psychology: Intersections of individual, group, and societal dimensions. In S. D. Brown, & R. W. Lent (Eds.), *Handbook of counseling psychology* (4th ed., pp. 408–425). Hoboken, NJ: John Wiley.

Gold, J. G., Rotter, J. C., & Evans, K. M. (2002). Out of the box: A model for counseling in the twenty-first century. In K. Evans, J. C. Rotter, & J. C. Gold (Eds.), *Synthesizing family, career, and culture: A model for counseling in the twenty-first century* (pp. 19–33). Alexandria, VA: American Counseling Association.

Goodman, J. (1994). The dental model for counseling. *American Counselor, 1*, 27–29.

Gottfredson, L. S. (1981). Circumscription and compromise: A developmental theory of occupational aspirations. *Journal of Counseling Psychology, 28*, 545–579.

Gottfredson, L. S. (1996). Gottfredson's theory of circumscription and compromise. In D. Brown, & L. Brooks (Eds.), *Career choice and development: Applying contemporary theories to practice* (3rd ed., pp. 179–232). San Francisco: Jossey-Bass.

Gottfredson, L. S. (2004). Applying Gottfredson's theory of circumscription and compromise in career guidance and counseling. In S. D. Brown, & R. W. Lent (Eds.), *Career development an counseling: Putting theory and research to work* (pp. 71–100). Hoboken, NJ: John Wiley.

Gysbers, N. C., Heppner, M. J., & Johnston, J. A. *Career counseling: Process, issues, and techniques* (2nd ed.). Boston: Allyn and Bacon.

Hansen, L. S. (1997). *Integrative life planning—Critical tasks for career development and changing life patterns*. San Francisco: Jossey-Bass.

Harrington, T., & O'Shea, A. (2000). *Harrington-O'Shea career decision making system*. Circle Pines, MN: American Guidance Service.

Helms, J. E. (2003). A pragmatic view of social justice. *The Counseling Psychologist, 31*(3), 305–313.

Helms, J. E., & Cook, D. A. (1999). *Using race and culture in counseling and psychotherapy: Theory and practice*. Boston: Allyn & Bacon.

Herr, E. L. (2003). The future of career counseling as an instrument of public policy. *Career Development Quarterly, 52*, 8–17.

Herr, E. L., Cramer, S. H., & Niles, S. G. (2004). *Career guidance and counseling through the lifespan: Systematic approaches* (6th ed.). Needham Heights, MA: Allyn & Bacon.

Hoffman, M. A. (2011). Individual counseling as an intervention. In E. M. Altmaier, & J. C. Hansen (Eds.), *The Oxford handbook of counseling psychology*. New York: Oxford University Press.

Hogue, M., Yoder, J. D., & Singleton, S. B. (2007). The gender wage gap: An explanation of men's elevated wage entitlement. *Sex Roles, 56*, 573–579.

Holland, J. L. (1994). *Self-directed search*. Odessa, FL: Psychological Assessment Resources.

Holland, J. L. (1997). *Making vocational choices: A theory of vocational personalities and work environments* (3rd ed.). Odessa, FL: Psychological Assessment Resources.

Howard, G. S. (1991). Cultural tales: A narrative approach to thinking, cross-cultural psychology, and psychotherapy. *American Psychologist, 46*, 187–197.

Irwin, J. (2002). Discrimination against gay men, lesbians, and transgender people working in Education. *Journal of Gay & Lesbian Social Services, 14*, 65–77.

Johansson, C. B. (1986). *Career assessment inventory*. Minneapolis: NCS Assessments.

Johnson, R. A. (2008). African-Americans and homelessness: Moving through history. *Journal of Black Studies, 40*, 583–605.

Joo, S., Grable, J. E., & Choe, H. (2007). Who is and who is not willing to use online employer- provided retirement investment advice. *Journal of Employment Counseling, 44*, 73–85.

Judge, T. A., & Ilies, R. (2004). Affect and job satisfaction: A study of their relationship at work and home. *Journal of Applied Psychology, 89*, 661–673.

Kamasaki, C. (2008, July). *Five facts about undocumented workers in the United States*. Keynote address presented at the National Employment Counseling Association (NECA) Workforce Development Institute II, Washington, DC.

Katz, M. (1963). *Decisions and values*. New York: College Entrance Examination Board.

Kazdin, A. E. (2008). Evidence-based treatment and practice: New opportunities to bridge clinical research and practice, enhance the knowledge base, and improve patient care. *American Psychologist, 63*, 146–159.

Kenny, M. E., & Perez, V. (1996). Attachment and psychological well being among racially and ethnically diverse first-year college students. *Journal of College Student Development, 37*, 527–535.

King, N. J., & Madsen, E. (2007). Contextual influences on the career development of low-income African American youth. *Journal of Career Development, 33*, 395–411.

Kirk, J., & Belovics, R. (2008). Understanding and counseling transgender clients. *Journal of Employment Counseling, 45*, 29–39.

Krumboltz, J. D. (1991). *The career beliefs inventory*. Palo Alto, CA: Consulting Psychologists Press.

Krumboltz, J. D. (1993). Integrating career and personal counseling. *Career Development Quarterly, 42*, 143–148.

Krumboltz, J. D. (1996). A learning theory of career counseling. In M. Savickas, & B. Walsh (Eds.), *Integrating career theory and practice* (pp. 233–280). Palo Alto, CA: Consulting Psychologists Books.

Kubler-Ross, E. (1969). *On death and dying*. New York: MacMillan.

Larson, L. M. (2011). What do we know about work life across the lifespan? In E. M. Altmaier, & J. C. Hansen (Eds.), *The Oxford handbook of counseling psychology*. New York: Oxford University Press.

Lee, C., Spencer, M. B., & Harpalani, V. (2003). Every shut eye ain't sleep: Studying how people live culturally. *Educational Leadership, 32*, 6–13.

Lent, R. W. (2008). Understanding and promoting work satisfaction: An integrative view. In S. D. Brown, & R. W. Lent (Eds.), *Handbook of counseling psychology* (4th ed., pp. 462–480). Hoboken, NJ: John Wiley.

Lent, R. W., Brown, S. D., & Hackett, G. (1994). Toward a unifying social cognitive theory of career and academic interests, choice, and performance. *Journal of Vocational Behavior, 45,* 79–122.

Leong, F. T. L. (1995). *Career development and vocational behavior of racial and ethnic minorities.* Hillsdale, NJ: Lawrence Erlbaum Associates.

Lewis, J., & Coursol, D. (2007). Addressing career issues online: Perceptions of counselor education professionals. *Journal of Employment Counseling, 44,* 146–153.

Luzzo, D. (2000). *Career counseling of college students.* Washington, DC: American Psychological Association.

Masser, B., Grass, K., & Nesic, M. (2007). "We like you, but we don't want you" the impact of pregnancy in the workplace. *Sex Roles, 57,* 703–712.

McMahon, M. (2002). The systems theory framework of career development: History and future directions. *Australian Journal of Career Development, 11,* 63–68.

McMahon, M., & Patton, W. (1995). Development of a systems theory framework of career development. *Australian Journal of Career Development, 4,* 15–20.

Mitchell, K. E., Levin, A. S., & Krumboltz, J. D. (1999). Planned happenstance: Constructing unexpected career opportunities. *Journal of Counseling and development, 77,* 115–124.

Moorhouse, A., & Caltabiano, M. L. (2007). Resilience and unemployment: Exploring risk and protective influences for the outcome variables of depression and assertive job searching. *Journal of Employment Counseling, 44,* 115–125.

Myers, I., & Briggs, K. (1993). *The Myers-Briggs type indicator.* Palo Alto, CA: Consulting Psychologists Press.

National Board of Certified Counselors. (2007). *The practice of internet counseling.* Greensboro, NC: Author.

National Career Development Association (NCDA). (1997). *Career counseling competencies.* Retrieved June 4, 2008, from www.ncda.org/pdf/counselingcompetencies.pdf.

National Occupational Information Coordinating Committee (NOICC). (1992). *The national career development guidelines project.* Washington, DC: U.S. Government Printing Office.

Niles, S. G., & Harris-Bowlsby, J. (2005). *Career development interventions in the 21st century* (2nd ed.). Upper Saddle River, NJ: Pearson Education.

Okubo, Y., Yeh, C. J., Lin, P.-Y., & Fujita, K. (2007). The career decision making process of Chinese American youth. *Journal of Counseling and Development, 85,* 440–449.

Okun, B. (1984). *Working with adults: Individual, family, and career development.* Monterey, CA: Brooks/Cole.

Okiishi, R. W. (1987). The genogram as a tool in career counseling. *Journal of Counseling and Development, 66,* 139–143.

Oliver, L. W. (1979). Outcome measurement in career counseling research. *Journal of Counseling Psychology, 26,* 217–226.

Oliver, L. W., & Spokane, A. R. (1988). Career-intervention outcome: What contributes to client gain? *Journal of Counseling Psychology, 35,* 447–462.

Osborn, D. S., & Zunker, V. G. (2006). *Using assessment results for career development.* Belmont, CA: Thompson Higher Education.

Parsons, F. (1909). *Choosing a vocation.* Boston: Houghton-Mifflin.

Peterson, G. W., Sampson, J. P., Jr., & Reardon, R. C. (1991). *Career development and services: A cognitive approach.* Pacific Grove, CA: Brooks/Cole.

Pizzolato, J. E. (2007). Impossible selves: Investigating students' persistence decisions when their career-possible selves border on impossible. *Journal of Career Development, 33,* 201–223.

Pope, M. (2000). A brief history of career counseling in the United States. *The Career Development Quarterly, 48,* 194–211.

Pope, M. (2007). Introduction to a new section: Global vision. *The Career Development Quarterly, 56,* 2–3.

Pyle, K. R. (2000). A group approach to career decision-making. In N. Peterson, & R. C. Gonzalez (Eds.), *Career counseling models for diverse populations: Hands on applications for practitioners* (pp. 121–136). Belmont, CA: Wadsworth/Thompson Learning.

Quimby, J. L., Wolfson, J. L., & Sayala, N. D. (2007). Social cognitive predictors of African American adolescents' career interests. *Journal of Career Development, 33,* 376–394.

Rutter, M. E., & Jones, J. V. (2007). The job club redux: A step forward in addressing the career development needs of counselor education students. *Career Development Quarterly, 55,* 280–288.

Sampson, J. P., Jr., Peterson, G. W., Lenz, J. G., Reardon, R. C., & Saunders, D. E. (1996). *Career thoughts inventory.* Odessa, FL: Psychological Assessment Resources.

Savickas, M. L. (1999). The transition from school to work: A developmental perspective. *Career Development Quarterly, 47,* 326–336.

Savickas, M. L. (2005). The theory and practice of career construction. In S. D. Brown, & R. W. Lent (Eds.), *Career development and counseling: Putting theory and research to work* (pp. 42–70). Hobeken, NJ: Wiley.

Schmader, T., Whitehead, J., & Wysocki, V. H. (2007). A linguistic comparison of letters of recommendation for male and female chemistry and biochemistry job applicants. *Sex Roles, 57,* 509–514.

Schulenberg, J. E., Vondracek, F., & Crouter, A. (1984). The influence of the family on vocational development. *Journal of Marriage and the Family, 46,* 129–143.

Schultheiss, D. (2003). A relational approach to career counseling: Theoretical integration and practical application. *Journal of Counseling and Development, 81,* 301–311.

Schultheiss, D., Kress, H., Manzi, A., & Glasscock, J. (2001). Relational influences in career development: A qualitative inquiry. *The Counseling Psychologist, 29,* 214–239.

Sharf, R. S. (2006). *Applying career development theory to counseling.* Belmont, CA: Thompson Higher Education.

Shea, M. M., Ma, P. W., & Yeh, C. J. (2007). Development of a culturally specific career exploration group for urban Chinese immigrant youth. *Career Development Quarterly, 56,* 62–73.

Shivy, V. A., Wu, J. J., Moon, A. E., Mann, S. C., Holland, J. G., & Eacho, C. (2007). Ex-offenders reentering the workforce. *Journal of Counseling Psychology, 54,* 466–473.

Smith, T. B., Dean, B., Floyd, S., Silva, C., Yamashita, M., Durtschi, J., & Heaps, R. A. (2007). Pressing issues in college counseling: A survey of American College Counseling Association members. *Journal of College Counseling, 10,* 64–78.

Spokane, A. R., & Oliver, L. W. (1983). The process and outcome of career counseling. In W. B. Walsh, & S. H. Osipow (Eds.), *Handbook of vocational psychology* (pp. 99–136). Hillsdale, NJ: Lawrence Erlbaum.

Stead, G. (2004). Culture and career psychology: A social constructionist perspective. *Journal of Vocational Behavior, 64,* 389–406.

Steinberg, L. (2004). *The ten basic principles of good parenting.* New York: Simon and Schuster.

Sueyoshi, L. A., Rivera, L., & Ponterro, J. G. (2001). The family genogram as a tool in multicultural career counseling.

In J. G. Ponterro, J. M. Casas, L. A. Suzuki, & C. M. Alexander (Eds.), *Handbook of multicultural counseling* (2nd ed., pp. 655–671). Thousand Oaks, CA: Sage Publications.

Sullivan, K. R., & Mahalik, J. R. (2000). Increasing career-self efficacy for women: Evaluating a group intervention. *Journal of Counseling and Development, 78,* 54–62.

Super, D. E. (1970). *Computer-assisted counseling.* New York: Teachers College, Columbia University.

Super, D. E. (1980). A life-span, life-space approach to career development. *Journal of Vocational Behavior, 16,* 282–298.

Super, D. E. (1984). Career and life development. In D. Brown, L. Brooks, et al (Eds.), *Career choice and development: Applying contemporary theories to practice* (pp. 192–234). San Francisco: Jossey-Bass.

Super, D. E. (1990). A life span, life-space approach to career development. In D. Brown, L. Brooks, et al (Eds.), *Career choice and development: Applying contemporary theories to practice* (2nd ed., pp. 197–261). San Francisco: Jossey-Bass.

Super, D. E. (1993). The two faces of counseling: Or is it three? *Career Development Quarterly, 42,* 132–136.

Super, D. E., Thompson, A. S., Lindeman, R. H., Jordan, J. P., & Myers, R. A. (1984). *Career development inventory.* Palo Alto, CA: Consulting Psychologists Press.

Swanson, J. L. (1995). The process and outcome of career counseling. In W. B. Walsh, & S. H. Osipow (Eds.), *The handbook of vocational psychology* (pp. 217–259). Mahwah, NJ: Lawrence Erlbaum.

Swanson, J., & Fouad, N. (1999). *Career theory and practice.* Thousand Oaks, CA: Sage.

Swanson, J. L., Gore, P. A., Jr., Leuwerke, W., Achiardi, C. D., Edwards, J. H., & Edwards, J. (2006). Accuracy in recalling interest inventory information in three time intervals. *Measurement and Evaluation in Counseling and Development, 38,* 236–246.

Tansley, D. P., Jome, L. M., Haase, R. F., & Martens, M. P. (2007). The effects of message framing on college students' career decision making. *Journal of Career Assessments, 15,* 301–316.

Thorngren, J. M., & Feit, S. S. (2001). The career-o-gram: A post modern career intervention. *The Career Development Quarterly, 49,* 291–303.

Toporek, R. L., & Chope, R. C. (2006). Individual, programmatic, and entrepreneurial approaches to social justice: Counseling psychologists in vocational and career counseling. In R. L. Toporek, L. Gerstein, N. A. Fouad, G. S. Roysircar, & T. Israel (Eds.), *Handbook for social justice in counseling psychology: Leadership, vision, & action* (pp. 276–293). Thousand Oaks, CA: Sage.

Vera, E. M., & Speight, S. L. (2003). Multicultural competence, social justice, and counseling psychology: Expanding our roles. *Counseling Psychologist, 31,* 253–272.

Wampold, B. E., Lichtenberg, J. W., & Waehler, C. A. (2002). Principles of empirically supported interventions in counseling psychology. *The Counseling Psychologist, 30,* 197–217.

Whiston, S. C. (2002). Application of the principles: Career counseling and interventions. *The Counseling Psychologist, 30,* 218–237.

Whiston, S. C., & Keller, B. (2004). The influences of the family of origin on career development: A review and analysis. *The Counseling Psychologist, 32,* 493–568.

Whiston, S. C., Sexton, T. L., & Lasoff, D. L. (1998). Career intervention outcome: A replication and extension. *Journal of Counseling Psychology, 45,* 150–165.

Whitely, J. M. (1984). A historical perspective on the development of counseling psychology as a profession. In S. D. Brown, & R. L. Lent (Eds.), *Handbook of counseling psychology* (pp. 3–55). New York: John Wiley.

Young, R. A., Marshall, S. K., & Valach, L. (2004, June). *Cultural sensitivity, career theory, and counseling.* Paper presented at the IAEVG-NCDA Symposium on International Perspectives in Career Development, San Francisco, CA.

Young, R. A., Marshall, S. K., & Valach, L. (2007). Making career theories more culturally sensitive: Implications for counseling. *Career Development Quarterly, 56,* 4–18.

Zalaquett, C. P., & Osborn, D. S. (2007). Fostering counseling students' career information literacy through a comprehensive career web site. *Counselor Education & Supervision, 46,* 162–171.

Zunker, V. G. (2006). *Career counseling: A holistic approach.* Belmont, CA: Thomson/Brooks Cole.

Further Reading

Amundson, N. E. (2003). *Active engagement: Enhancing the career counseling process* (2nd ed.). Richmond, BC, Canada: Ergon Communications.

Chope, R. C. (2006). *Family matters: The influence of the family in career decision making.* Austin, TX: Pro-Ed.

Evans, K. (2008). *Gaining cultural competence in career counseling.* Boston: Lahaska Press.

Harris-Bowlsbey, J., Riley Dikel, M., & Sampson, J. P., Jr. (2002). *The internet: A tool for career planning* (2nd ed.). Tulsa, OK: National Career Development Association.

John, J. (2001). *Treatment planning in career counseling.* Belmont, CA: Wadsworth/Thomson Learning.

Maree, K. (Ed.). (2007). *Shaping the story: A guide to facilitating narrative counseling.* Pretoria, South Africa: Van Schaik Publishers.

Patton, W., & McMahon, M. (1999). *Career development and systems theory: A new relationship.* Pacific Grove, CA: Brooks Cole.

Sharf, R. S. (2006). *Applying career development theory to counseling.* Belmont, CA: Thompson Higher Education.

Multicultural Counseling and Psychotherapy

Jairo N. Fuertes

Abstract

This chapter addresses three limitations to the current state of thinking and research on the topic of multicultural counseling. One, theories of multicultural counseling have not been integrated within a broader theoretical framework of counseling research and practice. Two, research in multicultural counseling has not been grounded in or directed to explain the process and outcome of psychotherapy; and three, research in multicultural counseling has not been adequately targeted at explaining or treating problems that affect racial and ethnic minority populations. The chapter also points to some potentially fruitful areas in the field of multicultural counseling, including opportunities for further theory development, research program development, and interventions that may help ameliorate conditions of injustice and human suffering.

Keywords: multicultural counseling, psychotherapy, process, outcome, ethnic racial minorities, research.

The field of multicultural counseling has now achieved a level of growth, maturation, and sophistication worth noting. Demographic changes in the United States in the last 40 years, the daily influx of immigrants to this country every day—approximately 3,000 legal immigrants a day (U.S. Department of Homeland Security, 2004), the increase and diversification of the clientele and professional corps in counseling, and the emerging interest in counseling in international markets have all contributed to an increase in thinking, research, and advocacy for the needs and services provided to immigrants, minority, and historically marginalized populations. In the last 20 years alone, numerous theories and models have been proposed on the topic of multicultural counseling; a constant flow of research has appeared on racial identity, multicultural competence, multicultural therapy, and social justice in specialized journals such as the *Journal of Multicultural Counseling and Development* and *Cultural Diversity and Ethnic*

Minority Psychology, as well as in traditional journals of psychology and counseling (see Worthington, Soth-McNett, & Moreno, 2007). New ideas and research are being presented in areas such as psychotherapy, consultation, supervision, guidance, and trainee development, and new research is being published based on constructs from multicultural counseling in related domains like medical health care delivery and public policy. The training, ethical, and accreditation guidelines of the American Psychological Association and the American Counseling Association also include numerous and important principles with respect to multicultural awareness, competence, and sensitivity, reflecting the need for practitioners to practice their craft in ways that are effective and accommodating to an increasingly diverse clientele. In essence, multicultural counseling is a field that is relevant and essential in the practice and growth of psychology and counseling. However, despite these developments, or perhaps as a consequence of them, many challenges and opportunities exist in the field of multicultural counseling with respect to service delivery, research, and training for professionals in our field. The needs in terms of service delivery center around further empirical support/evidence for multicultural approaches and theoretical/technical integration between multiculturalism and "traditional" theoretical and technical approaches to counseling. As such, these challenges parallel those that are still being discussed and addressed in "traditional" counseling, for example the search for evidence-supported treatments and the continuing goal for theoretical integration. There are also needs for evidence of efficacy for specific approaches with specific populations, for research that integrates multicultural constructs in the process of counseling, and perhaps most importantly, for data that show that multicultural approaches, including counselor multicultural competence, can decrease outcome disparities in the mental health treatment of minorities and immigrant populations in the United States.

The rationale for this chapter is the seriousness of the issues with which it relates. Besides the evidence of outcome disparities for racial/ethnic minorities who receive mental health services in the United States are the issues that affect these populations, including racism, poverty, violence, alcohol/drug abuse, teen pregnancy, and high school dropout rates. Although the evidence suggests that racial/ethnic minority groups do not experience psychiatric disorders in greater proportion or intensity than the majority population, the quality and availability of services to them is clearly a problem (Department of Health and Human Services, 2001). The problem is the lack of insurance, disproportionate poverty, and less access to and less quality of services. Furthermore, even in the event of an African American or Hispanic or immigrant patient having insurance, access, and quality of services, the Institute of Medicine and the Surgeon General (Department of Health and Human Services, 2001) concluded that racism still plays a significant part in explaining outcome disparities for these populations.

In this chapter, the focus is on individual counseling/psychotherapy (in this chapter, these terms are used interchangeably, as are the terms *counselor* and *therapist*) and on racial and ethnic minorities and immigrants in the United States, primarily those who arrive from preindustrialized nations. Despite this focus, it is possible that the content and ideas presented here will be relevant to other marginalized populations inside and outside the United States, and to other intervention modalities, such as group therapy or consultation. The intent of the chapter is to address three limitations to the current state of thinking and research on this topic. One, theories of multicultural counseling are not integrated within a broader theoretical framework of counseling research and practice; two, research in multicultural counseling has not been situated within the process and outcome of psychotherapy; and three, research in multicultural counseling has not been targeted at explaining or treating problems that affect racial and ethnic minority populations.

The chapter is organized into three broad sections. First, there is an integrated discussion of the theoretical developments in the area of multicultural counseling. This section builds primarily on the author's and his collaborators' work in identifying theories and models of multicultural counseling, and includes observations gleaned from this theoretical literature. Following this discussion, the reader will find a review of recent research on the topic of counselor multicultural competence and of the challenges and opportunities with respect to research on racial/ethnic identity. The second section also builds on previous work and presents research that appears to have implications for clinical practice. It is important to emphasize that this research does not provide evidence or support for any one approach or intervention, but tentative hypotheses are presented because of their relevance to clinical practice. The final section of the chapter presents an agenda for future research on the topic of multicultural counseling.

Definition

In a previous paper, Fuertes and Ponterotto (2003) defined multicultural competence as

> [A] counselor's ability to integrate into his or her theoretical and technical approach to assessment and intervention relevant human diversity factors that are important to the process and successful outcome of counseling. These factors may be relevant to the counselor, the client, and/or the counseling relationship. Human diversity refers to salient group-reference factors that are meaningful to the individual; these may include gender, socioeconomic background, religion, race, ethnicity, and/or regional/national origin, sexual orientation, all or any of which may inform or shape individual identity, behavior, worldviews, values, attitudes, and/or beliefs. (p. 52)

This content also provides a good definition of multicultural counseling, if one changes the text from "as a counselor's ability to integrate" to "when a counselor integrates" and leaves the rest the same. The definition is worth discussing because it contains several assumptions about multicultural counseling that can be highlighted here. One is the concept of integration, which implies that the counselor identifies and appropriately brings into the work of assessment and intervention relevant human diversity information; the other is the link between multicultural counseling and process and outcome in counseling, for example in facilitating additional therapist interventions that go toward relationship building and symptom relief. There is also the delineation of levels between counselor, client, and their relationship, meaning that multicultural material may be particularly salient at one, two, or three levels, separately or combined, such as when racial identity statuses for both counselor and client are of consequence to the work. Finally, the definition further highlights layered complexity and the variety of sources that may inform or shape the perspective of the client or counselor, and may need to be attended to if counseling is to be successful.

Theory-based Research and Related Observations

Four papers provide the bases for a synthesis of the latest thinking in the field of multicultural counseling. The first paper was published in 2000 (Ponterotto, Fuertes, & Chen), the second in 2001 (Fuertes & Gretchen), the third in 2003 (Fuertes & Ponterotto), and the fourth in 2008 (Constantine, Fuertes, Roysircar, & Kindaichi). Ponterotto et al. and Fuertes and Gretchen reviewed the theoretical underpinnings and research for 16 different theoretical papers on the topic of multicultural counseling (see Ponterotto et al., 2000; Fuertes & Gretchen, 2001 for a full review of these approaches). Fuertes and Gretchen (2001) also provided a critique and some preliminary observations with respect to theory, research, and practice, based on nine of these approaches. All 16 multicultural theories/approaches included the following: Sue et al.'s (1998) *multicultural counseling competency model*; Helms' (1990, 1995, 1996; Helms & Cook, 1999) *racial identity theory and interaction model*; Atkinson, Thompson, and Grant's (1993) *acculturation, locus of problem etiology, and goals of counseling model*; Trevino's (1996) *model of worldview and change*; Ridley, Mendoza, Kanitz, Andgermeier, and Zenk's (1994) *perceptual schemata model of cultural sensitivity*; Leong's *integrative model of cross-cultural counseling* (Leong, 1996); Fischer, Jome, & Atkinson's (1998)

common factors perspective; Sue, Ivey, and Pedersen's (1996) *theory of multicultural counseling*; Gonzalez, Biever, and Gardner's (1994) *social constructionist approach*; Ho's (1995) *perspective on internalized culture*; Coleman's (1995, 1997) *coping with diversity counseling model*; Ramirez's (1999) *multicultural model of psychotherapy*; Hanna, Bemak, and Chung's (1999) *counselor wisdom paradigm*; Locke's (1998) *model of multicultural understanding*; Herring and Walker's (1993) *cross-cultural specific model* (CSS); and Steenbarger's (1993) *multicontextual model*.

The discussion that follows builds on these previous four papers and does so by presenting observations and tentative conclusions from a review of the literature in multicultural counseling. Although it is important to begin with theory, the entire the chapter could be consumed with revisiting the theoretical papers noted above. Thus, the current discussion is limited to identifying patterns in the literature and opportunities that may provide direction for further thinking, writing, and research in this area, and the reader is referred to the original papers for in-depth reading or to the summative reviews published in the four papers noted above.

Multicultural approaches are at various stages of theoretical and empirical development, with respect to their comprehensiveness as counseling theories/models, their operationalization for testing, and their operationalization for clinical utility. A current review of the literature indicates that the amount of theoretical or empirical development on the 16 theories of multicultural counseling has been limited since 2001. The exception, however, has been continuing research on the theory of therapist multicultural competence, continued research (and considerable debate) on racial/ethnic identity development, and the development of a cultural accommodation model (Leong, 2007) based on Leong's (1996) integrative multidimensional model of cross-cultural counseling. These developments are presented below. Fuertes and Gretchen's (2001) original assessment of these approaches generated ratings that were mostly "low" to "medium" on three dimensions: comprehensiveness as counseling theory, operationalization for testing, and their operationalization for clinical utility; however, some approaches were rated as more developed than others, and have generated far more research and scholarly attention. In fact, it is quite safe to conclude that the focus of the research on multicultural counseling in the last 10 years or so has converged almost exclusively on two areas: counselor multicultural competence and racial/ethnic identity.

Why has this been true for the theories of multicultural competence and racial/ethnic identity? These are longstanding models in the literature, going back to the 1970s, and thus have been examined and reformulated by teams of scholars for some time. Another practical reason for the research conducted on these models may be that measures to assess each have been developed and submitted to review and subsequent revisions. The result is well-articulated statements with respect to their focus and structure, and fairly high psychometric properties for their respective assessment instruments, which can be readily picked up and used in research. Having said this, these theories and their measures are still a subject of attention, reformulation, and debate in the literature (see Ponterotto & Park-Taylor, 2007; Worthington et al., 2007).

Despite some of the limits of the theoretical perspectives published thus far on multicultural counseling, it is worth pointing out that they contain many compelling and thoughtful statements about the topic, and as a group, represent a diversity of perspectives that can inform the practice and research in psychotherapy. Although the theories of multicultural competence and racial identity have attracted considerable empirical testing, different researchers and thinkers have chosen specific concepts on which to develop their own thinking about multicultural counseling, and these represent viable areas that are ripe for development. For example, some (e.g., Fischer et al., 1998) have highlighted common factors of therapy, such as the relationship, to address problems in service delivery with racial and ethnic minority populations; some have highlighted differences, for example differences in worldviews (e.g., Trevino, 1996) between counselor and client and the dynamics associated with this difference in treatment; some have highlighted cognitive processes (e.g., Ramirez, 1999) of clients, and others internal dynamics evident for the counselor (e.g., Gonzalez et al., 1994) to identify mechanisms and possible venues for intervention. In sum, just as there are various theoretical approaches in "traditional" counseling, there seems to be a growing literature on ways to approach multicultural counseling. This is an important point to emphasize. Many professionals and students in our profession are genuinely interested in becoming "multiculturally sensitive" or "multiculturally competent," with the implication being that there is "one way" to do so. At this point, there are several compelling and elegant statements for conceptualizing multicultural counseling. Clearly, more work

is needed to elevate this literature to a level of prescription for practice, from additional theoretical developments to the development of measures that might allow for empirical examination. There are also possibilities for further integration and strengthening of perspectives, such as that occurring now between multicultural competence and racial identity, with more studies jointly examining these perspectives in research (e.g., Constantine, Warren, & Miville, 2005). There is also a need for theoreticians to tie their ideas and constructs to processes and targeted outcomes in counseling, particularly to the therapy relationship, which all empirical and clinical evidence suggests is fundamental to effective therapy at all stages of the helping process. The relationship in multicultural counseling is the foundation on which trust can develop, and through which respect for the person and appreciation for the dignity of the human being is communicated. It also becomes the mechanism for leverage, to help encourage and challenge clients to engage in the process of psychological growth and behavioral change. Many multicultural writers have directly or indirectly implicated the relationship in both successful and unsuccessful treatment.

Multicultural counseling approaches also delve into issues that have the potential to inform all counseling interactions. The issues raised by multicultural theories—for example, issues of identity, worldview, self-acceptance, tolerance of others, and racism—seem relevant and important, albeit to various degrees, in all counseling interactions. As the United States continues to diversify, and immigrant, majority, and minority populations clamor for shared power and adjust to increasing social and economic interdependence, the kind of issues being addressed today in multicultural counseling will become more pressing and more common. The psycho-social-cultural dimensions of living will become more accentuated and provide more fodder for counseling interactions for a greater number of people. Thus, multicultural counseling is not a fad nor likely to become passé; rather, it may increasingly represent the future of all counseling, provided that further theoretical and technical counseling interventions are developed to meet the challenges and psychological needs of the burgeoning diversity in the United States. And yet, with increasing diversity, some counseling interactions are likely to remain more multicultural in nature than others, to the extent to which cultural and social issues are at the forefront of the interactions in some counseling sessions (for example, race differences or racism, or when a U.S. born and trained psychologist treats an immigrant family), or possibly in counseling pairings that echo historical political and economic power differences, as when a European American counselor works with an African American client.

Another observation gleaned from the theories is that multicultural counseling pulls for complexity, with respect to case/person conceptualization, treatment planning, and service delivery. The professional must move beyond his or her theory of counseling to be able to adequately assess the individual not only in terms of pathology and strengths, and not only in traditional psychosocial dimensions, but in terms of sociocultural dimensions and immediate living circumstances that may be foreign to the life of the therapist. Add to this the challenge of delivering services in a way that is palpable and ultimately helpful to the person, and the complexity and challenges associated with multicultural counseling become appreciable. Although all clients tend to have social circumstances that are difficult, multicultural counseling demands very careful attention to ecology, environments, sociopolitical histories and realities, and the living circumstances of the individual person. It is a broader and deeper embrace of the person than traditional training and textbook learning would indicate. Furthermore, when multicultural issues are at the forefront of counseling interactions, the relationship becomes a social microcosm of the history and circumstances for both citizens in the dyad. Thus, the relationship might be tested and strained, and therapist might have his or her work cut out to manage and diffuse misunderstandings or tensions.

Complexity is also evident in the work of the counselor in attending to factors that pertain to racial, ethnic, national, and/or continental alliances, while at the same time attending to the individuality of the person. A balanced perspective is optimal, based on an analysis of the current circumstances, history of socialization, personality and development of the person, and the cultural, shared experiences that individuals believe they share with others like them (e.g., women and sexism, or African Americans and whites and their experiences with race differences and racism). Counselor assumptions or hypotheses cannot go unchecked, since multicultural awareness and/or sensitivity can easily be misused to stereotype the client. Even in cases in which there is appreciable group membership material relevant to counseling, the reality for the client is one of unique circumstances and concerns that have to be addressed in the context of who the client

is as an individual. The reader is directed to Locke's (1998) multicultural theory, with its emphasis on the role of the counselor being able to balance cultural presses with individual concerns of the client, and to Leong's (1996, 2007) papers, in which he delineates three dimensions of personality at the individual, group, and universal levels. Leong presents an interesting discussion in which these dimensions of personality are described, and presents a model for multicultural counseling that addresses their interplay and implications for counselors. The reader is also encouraged to read Ho's (1995) paper on internalized culture for a good treatise on the individual psychology of culture.

Current theories of multicultural counseling supplement but do not supplant other counselor techniques and skills and appear to be necessary but insufficient as standalone approaches to helping. Multicultural approaches appear to complete and enrich counseling by directing the counselor to important psychological material, interpersonal processes, and client experiences that might otherwise be missed or minimized by traditional approaches (e.g., by REBT, Gestalt, or psychoanalytic approaches). But multiculturalism does not replace effective skills in relationship building, such as Rogerian skills; nor does it replace a counselor's ability to work with issues of existence such as those addressed by Rollo May, or replace the use of helpful cognitive interventions, for example those advocated by REBT approaches, which can help people diminish perspectives that promulgate personal distress. Multiculturalism can add a dimension to effective counseling without taking away from the good skills and approaches that counselors already use. Surveys of psychologists and counselors indicate that many are eclectic and multifaceted in their approaches to assessment and intervention; thus, they are likely to further integrate into their palette of options compelling perspectives to increase their comfort and skill in dealing with the human diversity evident in their client base. By noting that these approaches play a supplemental role does not mean that their value is diminished. In my opinion, multicultural approaches highlight key pieces missing from traditional theories of counseling (e.g., the central role of race in personal identity for counselors and clients, the unquestioned reality of racism and the significant distress associated with experiencing it, and the suffering and psychological decay that can come from internalized oppression). The current argument is analogous to Leong's (2007) recommendation in his cultural accommodation model that counselors identify gaps or blind spots in existing theories of counseling, infuse in these theories relevant cultural material to address the gaps, and test the newly integrated or enhanced theory for incremental validity.

Multicultural theories tend to emphasize the external factors associated with behavior, more so than do traditional theories of counseling, personality, and psychopathology. The direct influence of contexts on individual behavior has been demonstrated beyond possible doubt by social psychology research. The implication for practitioners is the possibility that the "problem" that the client brings is not entirely intrapsychic etiologically but may be more completely understood and resolved by an analysis of the context of the individual. The context may not change, but the individual's interaction and experience in the environment can change to his or her benefit once he or she learns to identify and negotiate the surrounding challenges. Multicultural counseling demands on the part of the counselor awareness of social and political issues, historical and current events, and a progressive, affirmative posture with respect to issues of racism, race relationships, and psychological development in the context of oppression and/or possibly poverty. Furthermore, multicultural counseling demands counselor advocacy for the person. In this sense, multicultural and feminist approaches converge, in that personal issues are political issues, and the demands of the counselor may include helping clients find or use services that may help with employment, housing, or legal concerns. Similarly, counselors' personal/cultural self-awareness is important in helping them continually monitor their personal reactions or assumptions about clients, including the insidious role that racism can play in the counseling hour.

Theories of multicultural counseling also provide mixed support for the "matching hypothesis," which is the notion that clients should be matched by race/ethnicity or gender with their clients. There are equivocal findings with respect to outcome when clients are matched on the basis of race or gender. A possible explanation for the equivocal findings may be that, when matching works, the results are based not on the demographic variables of matching, but rather on matching that occurs when the talents, competence, and sensitivity of counselors dovetail the needs of their clients. I do not believe that matching on demographics is effective or even ethical as an institutional policy but that counseling is effective when counselors make serious efforts to get onto the "same page" with their clients, for example in terms of developing a working alliance in which there is agreement on the goals and tasks of treatment; effectiveness in multicultural treatment also rests on counselors being able to communicate genuine nonpossessive caring and respect for their clients. This is not to say that clients' preferences are not important, and many times clients are accommodated in counseling centers and agencies, when possible, with the type of counselor that they ask for and prefer: For example, a client may very well prefer a female counselor, or an African American counselor, or one who speaks his native language (e.g., Spanish). But as an institutional policy, this would obviously be illegal and unethical, to the extent that it amounts to discrimination.

Recent Research on Multicultural Competence

Perhaps the area of multicultural counseling that has received the greatest amount of attention and research in the last 20 years has been multicultural competence, including studies in areas such as theoretical refinement, scale development, counselor training, and correlates of competence (Worthington et al., 2007). The studies presented here as part of an integrated discussion have examined the multicultural competencies directly, with respect to counseling/therapy and counseling supervision. The reader is referred to Worthington et al. and to Hays (2008) for two excellent, recent reviews of the instrumentation and broader literature on multicultural competence.

Constantine et al. (2008) recently reviewed the literature on multicultural competence and consistently found among the empirical studies that multicultural training and education are strongly associated with increased levels of multicultural competency. When novice or experienced therapists are exposed to multicultural training, they seem to perform at a higher level with respect to multicultural competency (Arthur, 2000; Constantine, Ladany, Inman, & Ponterotto, 1996; Pope-Davis, Reynolds, Dings, & Ottavi, 1994; Sodowsky, Kuo-Jackson, Richardson, & Corey, 1998; Spanierman, Poteat, Wang, & Oh, 2008; Vereen, Hill, & McNeal, 2008). And, multicultural training works for a diverse group of counseling professionals. Even a single course in multicultural counseling leads to counselors demonstrating higher levels of multicultural competence. There is also a positive association between multicultural competence and racial identity development, as well as a positive association between multicultural competence and confidence levels in practicing multicultural counseling (see Constantine, Juby, & Liang, 2001; Cumming-McCann & Accordino, 2005; Neville, Spanierman, & Doan, 2006; Ottavi, Pope-Davis, & Dings, 1994). Professionals with higher levels of multicultural competence report feeling better prepared to work with diverse clientele. Another strand of research has shown that professionals who are minority group members have a higher interest and skill in multicultural competence (see Bernal et al., 1999; King & Howard-Hamilton, 2003; Sodowsky et al., 1998) than do European American counselors, which suggests that multicultural competence is more of a challenge for European American counselors. This is not surprising when one considers that the majority of advocates for multicultural counseling have been minority group members and women, and based on personal experience and professional interests, these advocates have gravitated to this area.

Constantine et al. (2008) also examined research that has investigated the role of counselor multicultural competence directly with counseling dyads. The results of their review, which included studies by Constantine (2002) and Fuertes and Brobst (2002), revealed a significant level of association between minority clients' ratings of counselor general and multicultural competence and between their ratings of counselor multicultural competence and satisfaction with treatment. Fuertes and Brobst (2002) further found that when comparisons were made between European American and ethnic minority clients on satisfaction, counselor multicultural competency explained a large and significant amount of variance for the ethnic minority sample only, above and beyond counselor general competency and empathy. More recently, Fuertes et al. (2006) investigated the role of counselor multicultural competency among 51 therapy dyads in counseling. These authors examined the relationship between counselor multicultural competence and several indices of counseling, such as the working alliance, counselor empathy, counselor social influence, and client and counselor satisfaction. Fuertes et al. (2006) found that, for counselors, their ratings of the working alliance but not self-ratings of multicultural competence were significantly associated with their satisfaction, along with clients' ratings of them on social influence. For clients, ratings of counselor multicultural competence were associated with their satisfaction with counseling, as well as with ratings of counselor empathy and of counselor social influence. Fuertes et al. (2006) however,

did not find a significant association between therapist multicultural competence and general competence. Taken as a whole, the findings from these studies indicate that multicultural competence is strongly associated with client satisfaction, and may be more salient for clients than are factors such as empathy and the working alliance. The research also suggests that a level of overlap exists between therapist competence, broadly defined, and multicultural competence. Fuertes, Bartolomeo, and Nichols (2001) speculated about this association and suggested that multicultural competence and general competence are associated, since multicultural competence can only be properly integrated in therapy by therapists who have a solid foundation in general competence skills, such as listening, empathy, probing, and other basic skills. In multicultural counseling, the basic and advanced skills of caring and competent counselors remain the same (e.g., empathy, or probing); it is the intent of the therapist, the content of the conversations, and the focus of the interactions that expand and deepen substantially. As a side note, a recent study examining predictors of minority patients' medical treatment adherence indicated that the only predictor of their adherence was their ratings of their physicians' multicultural competence. In explaining this result, Fuertes, Boylan, and Fontanella (in press), speculated that physician's multicultural competence communicated respect to the patients, which in turn enhanced the patients' perceptions of their doctors as competent and trustworthy, and earned the doctors the respect of their patients—thus patients complied with the treatments.

Constantine et al. (2008) also reviewed two studies that examined therapist multicultural competence using qualitative methods. Fuertes, Mueller, Chauhan, Walker, and Ladany (2002) conducted interviews with nine European-American counseling and clinical psychologists. These psychologists revealed that they generally attended to differences in race between themselves and clients directly and openly, within the first two sessions of counseling. They acknowledged this difference to convey to the client comfort and trust; psychologists also intended to engender client trust and participation in therapy. The psychologists saw race as a central component to be discussed and continually attended to in establishing and maintaining a trusting and solid working relationship. They typically saw race-related issues as relevant to clients' concerns. Fuertes et al. (2002) found that, despite wide variability in participant theoretical orientation and in clients' presenting problems, the psychologists typically reported using Rogerian core skills to engage the client and to establish the relationship. Additionally, they also typically reported using more specific and sensitive interventions to deepen and strengthen the therapy relationship. These interventions included relying on their level of racial identity development to understand the client, being attuned to the client's racial identity development and worldview, and very prominently, attending and effectively intervening to client reports of racism and oppression. This last ability, of being able to work with clients with reports of racism and oppression, was described as the most sensitive part of the work with their clients, and failing at that would have had dire consequences for the relationship or any further work in treatment.

Pope-Davis et al. (2002) used grounded theory to account for clients' perspectives of multicultural counseling. Clients were ten racially/ethnically diverse undergraduate students who had experienced individual counseling with a counselor whom they deemed culturally different from themselves. The results indicated that clients' perceptions of multicultural competence and counseling were contingent on clients' needs/issues in counseling, and that these needs were influenced by client characteristics (e.g., client expectations, role of family and support), the counseling relationship (e.g., equity and power in the relationship), client processes (e.g., salience of culture in relationships, educating the counselor), and client appraisals of the counseling experience. Pope-Davis et al. (2002) noted the importance of understanding client variables in counseling, for example by noting that clients who did not see culture as influencing their interpersonal relationships placed less importance on counselor multicultural competence. The authors underscored the importance of context for clients in order to truly understand the process and outcome of treatment for them. Findings from these two studies highlight the importance of therapist skill in the nuances of relating with their clients in sensitive and informed ways, and the importance of the discussion in therapy as being based on therapists' understanding of clients' needs, particularly with respect to the salience of race, culture, and racism in their everyday life and as possible mediating factors in their problems.

Constantine et al. (2008) also cited research on multicultural competence in relation to supervision and training. For example, they uncovered a study by Ladany, Brittan-Powell, and Pannu (1997) that found that progressive and parallel-high racial identity interactions between supervisor and supervisee were associated with greater supervisee multicultural competence, in comparison with parallel-low and regressive interactions. Constantine et al. also reported on a study by Ladany, Inman, Constantine, and Hofheinz (1997), who found that multicultural competence was associated with white and minority supervisee racial identity development, but found no significant association between supervisee multicultural competence and their multicultural case conceptualization ability. Constantine et al. also presented findings from Constantine and Ladany (2000), who found that self-report competency measures did not correlate significantly with expert-rated evaluations of case conceptualization skills. They noted that Constantine et al. (2005) had found that white supervisees in supervision dyads characterized by more advanced white racial identity schemas reported higher multicultural competence and multicultural case conceptualization skills than did whites in dyads with lower white racial identity schemas. Finally, Constantine et al. also reported on Inman (2006), who found that supervisees' ratings of their supervisors' multicultural competence were positively associated with their ratings of the supervisory working alliance and satisfaction with supervision, but negatively associated with their multicultural case conceptualization of etiology.

Recent Research on Racial and Ethnic Identity

Considerable and substantial theoretical and empirical work has been done in the areas of ethnic and racial identity. Phinney and Ong (2007) noted general parallels in both racial and ethnic identity theories. For example, both involve participants' estimations of belonging to and learning about a group, and both include values, attitudes, and behaviors associated with culture and as responses to discrimination. However, whereas the focus of racial identity has been on responses to racism and on the assessment of internalized racism, primarily using African American and white samples, Phinney and Ong (2007) point out that ethnic identity has focused on examining belonging to a culture or a heritage and exploration and commitment to its traditions, and has included a greater variety of ethnic and racial groups. In fact, a review of the recent literature shows that studies of ethnic identity tend to include a more diverse set of participants among minority groups in the United States, including subgroups of Hispanics and Asian Americans (e.g., Lee, Noh, Yoo, & Doh, 2007; Umana-Taylor & Shin, 2007). An impressive finding from studies on ethnic identity is that the construct is usually examined within complex models with clearly delineated outcomes. For example, ethnic identity has been examined as a moderating effect of psychological distress (Yip, Gee, & Takeuchi, 2008), well-being (Yoo & Lee, 2005), self-esteem (Lopez, 2008), race-related stress and quality of life (Utsey, Chae, Brown, & Kelly, 2002), situational well-being (Yoo & Lee, 2008), alcohol and marijuana use (Pugh & Bry, 2007), and depression and suicidal ideation (Walker, Wingate, Obasi, & Joiner, 2008). Ethnic identity has also been examined as a mediator with respect to delinquency and violence (Le & Stockdale, 2008), and to academic grades, prosocial behaviors, and externalizing symptoms (Schwartz, Zamboanga, & Jarvis, 2007). The results of this literature generally point to a significant effect for ethnic identity, in some instances as a buffer from psychological illness and in other instances as a contributor to distress.

Studies of racial identity tend to focus on either African Americans and/or whites, although there are also studies in the literature examining multiple racial identities (Miville, Constantine, Baysden, & So-Lloyd, 2005), Asian American racial identity (Chen, LePhuoc, Guzman, Rudem, & Dodd, 2006; Liu, 2002), and American Indian racial identity (Bryant & LaFromboise, 2005). Studies of white racial identity have by and large focused on either multicultural competence of counselors or correlates of professionals or trainees in counseling. For example, Middleton et al. (2005) and Neville et al. (2006) examined racial identity with respect to multicultural counseling competence, and Constantine et al. (2005) examined racial identity with respect to supervisees' multicultural competence. The results from these studies are unequivocal: More sophisticated statuses of racial identity are correlated with higher therapy and supervision multicultural competence. Carter, Helms, and Juby (2004) implemented a new statistical technique to develop white racial identity profiles and to discourage the conceptualization of racial identity as a linear progression of stages. They examined racial identity profiles with respect to racist attitudes for 217 white college students. Their results showed that the flat profile was the most frequently observed, and that this profile, in which no racial identity status dominates, along with a profile called Autonomy, was associated with the highest scores

on the New Racism Scale (Jacobsen, 1985), which captures a more subtle type of racism. Silvestri and Richardson (2001) examined white racial identity in relation to personality constructs, and among their findings, they reported a significant negative association between Reintegration and Agreeableness, and a significant positive association between Reintegration and Neuroticism and Openness. Gushue and Constantine (2007) examined the level of overlap between white racial identity and color-blind racial attitudes among 177 counseling and clinical psychology trainees. They reported a pattern in which attitudes that minimize racism were significantly and positively correlated with less integrated forms of racial identity.

Studies on black racial identity have focused on correlates of psychological well-being or on the adverse psychological effects of racism on African Americans. For example, Mahalik, Pierre, and Wan (2006) examined racial identity in relation to masculinity, self-esteem, and psychological distress, and found a positive relationship between more sophisticated levels of racial identity and self-esteem and a negative relationship between racial identity and psychological distress. Sellers and Shelton (2003) examined the role of racial identity in perceived racial discrimination and found, among 267 African American college students, a positive relationship among these constructs and a moderating role for racial identity between perceived discrimination and global psychological distress. Johnson and Arbona (2006) examined racial and ethnic identity (the only study that examines both jointly) and their impact on race-related stress, and found in 140 African American college students a positive association between black racial identity and ethnic identity, and that black racial identity, but not ethnic identity, was associated with race-related stress. Anglin and Wade (2007) examined racial socialization and racial identity in relation to college students' adjustment to college and found that, among 141 African American students, an internalized multicultural identity was positively associated with adjustment to college, but that an Afrocentric racial identity was negatively associated with college adjustment.

Beyond these studies, there was a recent and healthy debate with respect to racial identity, ethnic identity, and alternative conceptualizations and measures of racial and ethnic identity (Ponterotto & Park-Taylor, 2007). The essence of the arguments seem to revolve around the lack of conceptual clarity of the constructs (e.g., whether the theory is about race or racism), about the focus that each theory takes with respect to identity development (e.g., whether it examines a one-dimensional vs. multidimensional aspect of identity), and the adequacy of measurement for each (e.g., whether best practices in scale construction have been observed, such as confirmatory factor analysis). As noted by Ponterotto and Park-Taylor (2007), there are at least 22 models of racial, ethnic, and group membership identity in the literature, and the recent issue of the *Journal of Counseling Psychology* (*JCP*; Volume 54, No. 3) presented a wealth of ideas on racial and ethnic identity that might provide an alignment and redirection for future research in this area.

Ponterotto and Park-Taylor (2007) provided some excellent recommendations at the end of this special issue, in a comment article that integrated and commented on the most salient challenges and opportunities facing theory development and measurement. They suggested that researchers define their constructs more clearly, in the context of the existing literature, and provide a rationale for their selection of constructs and instrumentation. They also noted the importance of conducting reliability generalizability studies, of reporting sample characteristics and score properties, and of conducting analyses of sample selection and group data patterns. They also suggested that researchers looking to revise or develop new measures of racial and ethnic identity instruments use the published best practices guidelines available in the literature—all with a view toward improving research on racial and ethnic development. Ponterotto and Park-Taylor (2007) also provided a review of the instrumentation in this area and reviewed some of the more novel measures in the literature assessing racial and ethnic identity.

In this same special issue of *JCP*, another article provided helpful observations and suggestions for future research in the area of racial and ethnic identity. Quintana (2007) examined the research on racial and ethnic identity development and arrived at seven theoretical formulations with respect to its meaning in the broader context of developmental psychology. These formulations were derived from an analysis of empirical studies; however, it seems as if these formulations could also serve to stimulate further research on racial/ethnic identity, to either confirm or refine them. Quintana (2007) noted that racial and ethnic identity development involves exploration and crisis in early adolescence, that experiences of racism trigger racial and ethnic identity exploration, that there are benefits to positive identification with one's ethnic group and to being prepared for discrimination, and that there is a developmental hierarchy to ethnic identity development, but no support for a hierarchy of development with respect to racial identity. These observations provide a framework for future research and application in helping ethnic and racial minorities with normative problems of development and with normative problems that are exacerbated by racism and discrimination. In fact, Quintana (2007) noted the importance of school-based programs at the middle school to early high school level, when many adolescents seem to grapple with issues of identity, autonomy, and interpersonal competence and belonging. He suggested that this would be an ideal stage in which school counselors and psychologists could intervene to assess issues that are problematic with respect to identity and to facilitate a development of attitudes with respect to self that promote exploration and self-acceptance, as well as acceptance of others.

Although it seems extremely helpful to focus on school-aged populations, issues of racial identity development, racism and discrimination, and the ability of persons to effectively cope with race and racism pertain to populations beyond the school years, as is evident in counseling centers on college campuses and in work environments throughout the United States. A survey of the literature indicates that, although some research is being conducted with college students, gaps still need to be addressed by researchers who study racism, race, and racial and ethnic identity. There is a need for applied studies that examine race in the context of human problems in natural environments. That is, we need field research with targeted outcomes; for example, studies that examine efficacy of treatments that account for racial/ethnic identity of both clients and therapists. There is also a need for research that ties racial and ethnic identity to process and outcome in psychotherapy. Janet Helms's theory of regressive, parallel, and progressive racial identity interactions has not received sufficient empirical or recent theoretical attention, and could well be integrated into studies of psychotherapy with multicultural populations. There also seem to be opportunities in this particular area for multidisciplinary teams of researchers, from personality, social, and developmental psychology, to work jointly with counseling psychologists to develop a parsimonious nomological explanation of identity that accounts for personality, development, and social interactions and includes the psychology of race, racism, culture, and ethnicity.

Applied Research with Implications for Clinical Practice

A review by Fuertes and Ponterotto (2003) allowed them to distill several "knowledge" and "skill" areas that seem to come out of research studies looking at multicultural counseling effects. These areas have possible implications for practice, as well as for future research, and so they are developed here for tentative consideration and evaluation. It seems useful to connect the current research on multicultural counseling with practice, although it is emphasized that these connections are tenuous at best, and in no way represent empirical support for any of these perspectives. Clearly more research, particularly doctoral dissertations, is needed for firm conclusions to be derived with respect to research-supported multicultural practice.

KNOWLEDGE AREAS

With various perspectives in the literature on multicultural counseling, it seems likely that some constructs or concepts will be more attractive to or easily integrated by counselors, based on their approach to assessment and intervention. For example, a psychologist who works with school-aged populations may gravitate toward racial/ethnic identity theories because of the developmental nature of these theories and their focus on identity. A REBT psychologist may find Ho's (1995) perspective on internalized culture persuasive, or Gonzalez et al.'s (1994) social constructionist approach appealing since it places a great deal of emphasis on personal experience and interpretation. Parenthetically, in teaching graduate students theories of counseling, personality, and multicultural counseling, my advice to them when they ask about the best or "right" theoretical perspective in counseling is to engage in personal reflection. An important criterion for selecting a theory of counseling is whether it fits with the counselor's personality, the way a garment fits with a person's taste or body/shape. A theory is persuasive if it is consistent with who the counselor is as a person, with how she or he sees the world, with what she or he values, or with how she or he solves or approaches problems in living. This is all the more reason for exposing students in training during their formative years to the various approaches or constructs that comprise multicultural counseling, just as students are exposed to various theoretical approaches to therapy early on in graduate training. There are choices in multicultural approaches, therapists may gravitate to one or more multicultural ideas, and thus will need to work to integrate them systematically. A competent practitioner with a high percentage of racial/ethnic minority clients must know the literature in multicultural counseling, and have thought consciously about how multiculturalism fits with him or her as a person, with his or her approach to assessment and intervention, and how it can inform his or her approach to maximize effectiveness.

Counselors usually integrate new techniques or concepts such as those promoted in multicultural counseling into their wider framework for intervening, and that framework is itself often integrated with traditional approaches such as humanistic, cognitive, and behavioral interventions. For a counselor to discuss issues of racial identity or bias with a client, he or she must still rely on core skills in establishing a safe and therapeutic clinical environment, on empathy and appropriate probing skills, and on advanced skills such as challenging and interpretation, in order to help the client. Thus, the framework of multicultural counseling seems to add another dimension to effective practice, one that accounts for important and essential components. Mechanisms for service delivery in multicultural counseling will involve basic counseling skills and a host of clinical interventions that are central to the process of counseling. Since many counselors are eclectic, the issue is not whether they become multicultural and abandon everything else taught in graduate school, but how they choose multicultural principles and ideas that fit their approach to helping, and how they integrate those principles and ideas to enrich their overall framework. An example of this is the use of empathy. Some of my colleagues in the broad field of psychotherapy believe that empathy is "all you really need" to be effective. Meaning that if one can practice empathy effectively, one can experience what the client experiences, and thus empathy alone is all that is needed to understand the client and intervene accordingly. I agree that all counselors have to rely on the basic skill of empathy to understand the client, how things feel like or look like for him or her. However, even with empathy, two things are likely to happen: filtered listening and/or filtered talk. The counselor may not understand the experience of the client because it is simply too foreign or complex for the counselor to understand it, and empathy does not guarantee that the client will express everything going on with him or her to the counselor—the client may not even be aware of what is going on with him or her, due to stress or denial.

Empathy alone is not enough, nor is any one counseling skill for that matter, whether probing, immediacy, or self-disclosure, in multicultural counseling. It is the combination of these skills, along with a strong relationship and the ability of the counselor to direct the client to relevant social, interpersonal, and psychological-cultural material based on self-awareness and knowledge of the client, that allows for effective outcome. These observations are consistent with the emphasis in relational-cultural theory (RCT) on the supreme importance of the relationship in effective helping, and the emphasis in RCT on the limits of traditional Rogerian empathy on counseling interactions (Comstock, et al. 2008). Ridley, Ethington, and Heppner (2007) also discussed the important role of the relationship and of informed counselor empathy in cultural confrontation, which they proposed as the appropriate confrontation of clients whose rigid adherence to traditional beliefs or to an unhealthy developmental context run counter to their psychological well-being.

Another seemingly important bit of knowledge gleaned from the multicultural literature is that race, ethnicity, and human diversity factors are dynamic and thus are always present and relevant in the counseling session; the importance of race and ethnicity to clients is never downplayed or seen as peripheral, but rather central to the process of helping. For clients solving an array of problems, from significant relationship problems to behavioral difficulties, issues of race and identity will intermingle with other psychological factors, such self-efficacy or developmental history, and will be relevant and possibly central to the process of counseling and recovery. Issues of race or race differences, as an example, may be most pressing in the beginning and early stages of counseling, as the client assesses his or her counselor, and deals with possible (and understandable) issues of trust, ambivalence, and fear about receiving help and engaging in the process of change. Race or ethnicity will remain relevant as therapy progresses, as the client gains insight and plans venues or options for action/behavior change. Race or ethnicity may be factors and come into play for example, as the client deals with self-acceptance, or with managing racism, or with selecting a college major, or establishing intimacy, or making a decision to leave home.

All of the research examined by Fuertes and Ponterotto (2003) addressed an important common factor in multicultural counseling: Namely, the importance of core conditions of safety, support, rapport, and the relationship. Since the relationship in counseling/therapy is consistently the best predictor of outcome, it is just as important, if not more important, in multicultural counseling.

This becomes appreciable when demographic differences exist between the counselor and the client, or when the client presents with issues that are imbued with loss and pain stemming from racism, inequality, and indifference. Multicultural competence is not so much about having knowledge about various cultures of the world, although this can help in therapy and be personally valuable to counselors. The real, crucial knowledge is how racism, marginalization, or poverty can affect the individual, particularly the devastating effects that these can have on a child. This knowledge is more proximal to the needs and discomforts of the client, and is essential to the process of relationship development and the ability for counselors to intervene for their clients. In the United States, African Americans and Hispanics experience poverty rates that are 2.5 times those of whites (U.S. Bureau of the Census 2007). And while poverty-related stress affects families in similar ways across racial/ethnic groups (Wadsworth & Santiago, 2008), the disproportionate number of Hispanic and African American families who live in poverty in the United States makes it a particularly salient topic for these populations.

SKILL AREAS

There is a dearth of applied, in-session multicultural research in this area. However, Fuertes and Ponterotto (2003) and Constantine et al. (2008) examined the limited available research, and from these reviews the following tentative observations are developed here as possible skill areas for effective counseling. These represent hypotheses that are based on just a few studies, and must be examined empirically and modified/enhanced before they become prescriptive of best practice.

Effective multicultural counselors are able to establish core conditions in counseling, regardless of their preferred theoretical and technical approach to counseling. A safe, respectful, and warm environment, characterized best as being Rogerian in nature, is crucial to winning patients' trust and respect. The core conditions also promote the establishment of rapport and working relationships with clients. The reader may wonder how this is unique to multicultural counseling, since these factors are essential to all counseling interactions. The rationale is that normal issues of client trust and ambivalence can be exacerbated by seeming power differences and race or ethnic differences in the dyad. Even in dyads of the same race or ethnicity, there may be client ambivalence about who the counselor really is and the power that he or she represents.

A related skill is counselors' ability to discuss "hot button" issues with their clients, including topics associated with gender, race, ethnicity, culture, socioeconomic background, sexual orientation, and religious beliefs. A sign of ineffectiveness would be counselors writing off these issues as beyond the scope of counseling or as superfluous to the treatment that they offer. It also seems important that counselors can name or identify a client's experiences that may be of a racist or oppressive nature, even though the client is unaware of or unwilling to examine these issues. This is sensitive, since counselors also need to know when *not* to discuss race or salient cultural differences with their clients. This skill resides on clinician expertise and wisdom, and would always be a judgment call based on the best interests of the client and not on a need of the counselor. Not enough can be said about the importance of the relationship in multicultural counseling and of the core conditions being fundamental to the development of that relationship. It is crucial to establishing trust, to client involvement and empowerment, which in turn facilitates discussion of very painful and sensitive issues in multicultural counseling.

Effective multicultural counselors also need to demonstrate authentic and genuine behavior with their clients, including unconditional positive regard and an authentic acceptance and respect for the client. This goes to the importance of counselor self-awareness, integrity, and sufficient moral strength to discuss difficult issues with the client. These difficult issues include, for example, discussing racism, institutionalized racism, and challenging clients to examine internalized racism and oppression. A related skill is the ability of counselors to be genuine in their behavior and to rein in socially desirable (i.e., politically correct) behavior that may come across as a "put on." Interestingly, the broader field of counseling is beginning to examine more empirically the importance of the "real relationship" in counseling, which is comprised of realistic perceptions and genuine behaviors in treatment (Gelso, 2002). The real relationship is hypothesized to be immediate, arising when the counselor and client first make contact; it is the person-to-person relationship between the participants, and their perceptions and assessments of each other as likeable and agreeable people. The real relationship is hypothesized to precede the development of a working relationship based on trust, agreement, and client collaboration. The real relationship may have implications for the development of an effective interpersonal stance for counselors who work with an array of human diversity.

Future Research

There is a need for outcome research in several areas. First, there is a need for outcome research that examines the effectiveness of therapy with ethnic/minority clients. The reader may believe that this fact has been established, given the hundreds of outcome studies conducted in our profession over the past four decades. However, Fuertes, Mueller, Costa, and Hersch (2004) examined the outcome evidence in the most widely referenced meta-analyses and uncovered, through a random selection of articles, that the effectiveness of psychotherapy could not be ascertained from the research. Most of the studies conducted and included in the meta-analyses either did not include racial/ethnic minority group members as reported in their methods sections, or did not disclose this information at all, and no analyses were conducted by race or ethnicity. Thus, although there is anecdotal and clinical evidence of efficacy—and every reason to believe that racial/ethnic minorities benefit from therapy—research is still needed to establish the effect size of psychological interventions, and whether the effect is the same in comparison with whites or other groups. In sum, as far as the available research is concerned, it has not been established if the effect size of .80 is replicated with minority patients when using traditional approaches to helping.

Another research question is whether value is added by using enhanced or adapted methods with racial and ethnic minority clients. Griner and Smith (2006) recently published a meta-analysis of outcome for culturally adapted approaches to counseling, using a database of 76 studies and 25,225 participants. Griner and Smith (2006) included studies that involved a comparison between one culturally adapted treatment with a traditional treatment, and noted that cultural adaptation indicated that the treatment "involved explicitly including cultural values/concepts into the intervention" (p. 535), as well as matching by ethnic group and language, or included consultation with others familiar with the culture of the client, among others modifications and additions to treatment. Their findings indicated a substantial effect size of .43 for these treatments, suggesting a benefit for culturally adapted treatments versus more traditional treatments. Significant moderators included Hispanic ethnicity, particularly low-acculturation Hispanics, age (older patients did better), and treatment offered in the native language of the client. Nonsignificant moderators were gender or being African American or Asian American, or the status of the client as being either high risk, diagnosed with mental illness, or clients who represented normal problems in living. This study represented a significant step forward in beginning to ascertain the "value-added" benefit of culturally adapted treatments to outcome. As Griner and Smith (2006) noted, however, their study has limitations because many of the cultural adaptations were not described in the original studies but inferred by the researchers, and experimenter bias and allegiance effects were not controlled for in the analyses. Also, the treatments were not identified as including therapists who were either trained or exhibited multicultural competence or sensitivity. However, despite these limitations, the results from this study seem to support integrated treatment protocols that enhance services to meet the needs of racial and ethnic minority clients. Future research is warranted along this line. Griner and Smith (2006) noted the need for future research to account for therapist multicultural competence, the quality of the working relationship, and client trust in the therapist and in treatment.

There is also need for more applied research that examines outcome using the various approaches mentioned in this chapter. Although some research has examined the role of competencies with respect to client satisfaction, no research has examined the effect of multicultural competence with respect to outcome. There is still a great deal of research on multicultural competence and racial identity linking these constructs to demographic factors such as race or to ancillary factors such as comfort level and social desirability. But the research agenda for the future must include applied in-session research that examines the role of multicultural constructs to important events in counseling, particularly outcome. Data from applied outcome-oriented research may ultimately show the value added to assessment, intervention, and education when professionals are proficient in multicultural counseling. There also seems to be interest, but not much available research, on the part of health care professionals and funding agencies in knowing how multicultural counseling may improve health care practices and how it may address the irrefutable evidence showing the presence of racism in health care (Department of Health and Human Services, 2001). The emphasis on applied research does not need to take away from good research on scale development or further theoretical developments and refinements, specifically racial identity and counselor multicultural

competence. I believe that it is possible to advance the knowledge and science base in a rigorous manner while at the same time conducting research that demonstrates the relevance and external validity of our concepts and measures.

Having just written about the need to establish outcome effect sizes and the need for outcome research, there is evidence that outcome disparities exist in the treatment of mental health problems in racial/ethnic minority groups. However, these data, presented by the Surgeon General in 2001, represented sociological studies that examined factors such whether patients received free services, had insurance, the type of services they received, and other social-economic factors that tilted the balance against minority patients who received treatment. The Surgeon General's report concluded that, as in medical care, quality of care and outcome disparities exist for racial/ethnic minority patients, even when controlling for availability of insurance and patient level of education. The Surgeon General's report also concluded that *"culture counts,"* in that it influences the way people view, physically experience, and seek help for mental illness. He outlined several recommendations for service providers, professionals, and research scientists. Some of these recommendations included empirically investigating the efficacy of evidence-based treatments for minority members, exploring the ways in which different cultures experience mental illness, improving minority client access to care, eliminating barriers to and enhancing the quality of psychological services, and specifically, promoting the advancement in evidenced-based *multicultural competency training* for counselors, psychologists, psychiatrists, social workers, and other mental health professionals (Department of Health and Human Services, 2001). These challenges and opportunities for research in multicultural counseling are still valid and represent the future of a serious research agenda that is both rigorous and socially responsible.

Beyond outcome questions of efficacy or multicultural competence, research should be directed at improving the resolution of chronic problems in mental health treatment, such as the efficacy of multicultural approaches in improving longer-term outpatient participation and in improving community-based treatment for chronic and severe psychopathology. As a counseling psychologist, I would be remiss to not mention research targeting outcome indices of positive psychology that are also needed, such as the effectiveness of interventions that promote vocational development for workers at all stages of the work life-cycle, and that promote psychological growth and wellness, and the development of healthy loving families.

There are also many opportunities for process-oriented research vis à vis multicultural competence. There is a need for multicultural research that focuses on clients' experiences in counseling, and for research that describes how the relationship is established, maintained, and used as leverage to make counseling effective. A review of the literature in multicultural counseling indicates that the relationship between counselor multicultural competence and process and outcome variables in psychotherapy has not been studied, outside of the those studies noted above by Constantine, Fuertes, and their collaborators. Thus, we need to study the role of multicultural competence in counseling. Research may be directed at studying how counselor multicultural competence promotes counselor and client involvement in therapy, enhances client trust in counseling as well as client affective experiencing and insight, and promotes client satisfaction with psychological treatment. Studies that examine the relationship between multicultural competencies and culture-dependent or culturally relevant process and outcome indices (e.g., acculturation stress, amelioration of cultural conflict, internalized xenophobia) are also needed.

There is also a need for research designs that involve actual therapists and clients, such as field studies and quasi-experimental designs, and applied in-session research may highlight the value-added dimension of multicultural competence. For example, research could examine the amount of variance in process and outcome variables that is explained by counselor multicultural competence, above and beyond variance explained by more "traditional" counselor skills, such as empathy and expertness. Case studies of multicultural counseling may prove particularly revealing. For example, a cross-cultural dyad may be observed over several sessions, and these observations may yield temporal and sequential data about the role of counselor multicultural competence in facilitating the development of the therapy relationship, client progress, and counselor adaptation to the needs of the client. Consensual qualitative research and case study methodologies (Hill, Thompson, & Williams, 1997; Hill et al., 2008) also provide excellent ways of interviewing clients and counselors during or after therapy has been completed. This research could provide "thick description" to reveal how multicultural competence is manifested in therapy (i.e., the actual content of therapist interventions, the timing, and selection of these interventions), how counselors address clients' race/cultural-based concerns, and how counselors use specific interventions in counseling to defuse conflict or misunderstanding in counseling. Qualitative designs may also answer some fundamental questions central to multicultural counseling and competence, such as the type of latent and manifest components of race/culture evidenced by clients and counselors in counseling, how culture facilitates client coping and functioning, and the extent to which counseling is a social influence process and an acculturation experience for clients. Data that address these questions would have implications for practice, training, scale development, and future hypothesis-testing research in the area of multicultural competence.

Above and beyond the emphasis on process and outcome, there are opportunities for research that is informed or anchored on constructs from the broader field of psychology, but which can inform multicultural counseling assessment and interventions. For example, I have been involved in developing two models of intervention for racial/ethnic minority and immigrant clients. These two models were published recently, have not been examined empirically, but were derived rationally from the available theoretical and empirical literature, which is substantial in both areas. The first model targets problem areas for minority and immigrant children and adolescents and is anchored on the concept of self-regulation. The second model targets the needs of minority and immigrant adults and is anchored on the concept of social support. The model of self-regulation (Fuertes, Alfonso, & Schultz, 2007) includes risks and assets as two broad categories that have a potentially adverse impact on behavioral, interpersonal, and academic self-regulation. Risks are major stressors that minority and immigrant children and youth experience, such as having to learn a new language or having to face poverty or discrimination. Conversely, assets comprise a positive mechanism associated with resilience in children. Intrinsic assets are inherent qualities that, for the most part, stem from within the individual, such as level of cognitive functioning, self-efficacy, and motivation. Extrinsic assets include external influences on children that may include family members, school personnel, and caretakers and/or peers. These external assets function as supportive buffers that help children adapt and adjust to their new environment. These factors in isolation are not sole contributors to a racial or ethnic minority or immigrant child's adaptation and adjustment in school; rather, self-regulation is seen as moderating behavior and performance. The outcome of proficient self-regulation is hypothesized to be healthy adaptation to the environment, the outcome of which would be appreciable with respect to positive family relations, healthy peer relations, and successful school performance (Fuertes et al., 2007).

The model of social support (Fuertes, Alfonso, & Schultz, 2005) is analogous to the self-regulation model in that it examines risks for the adult person, internal and external resources, and targeted outcomes of interpersonal and vocational adjustment. The interest in social support stems primarily from its importance as a mediating variable between stress and mental and physical pathology. Social support also has been linked with reduction of mortality, positive rehabilitation processes, compliance and management of diabetes, protection against work strain, life satisfaction, general well-being or quality of life, and ease of migration. A fundamental assumption in developing this model of social support is the belief that humans are deeply social beings and that, without human relationships and social support people, cease to develop or even function. It is also assumed that, for racial and ethnic minorities, and for any other immigrant group, factors such as a sense of community, social support, and group belongingness become particular sources of concern as they are uprooted from their native countries and begin to adapt to a new life in the United States. Some research shows that social support helps people cope with an array of difficulties, and other research suggests that it helps people with major life transitions and migrations. In sum, there are possibilities for research to examine the viability of these concepts—self-regulation with children and adolescents—and the effective use of social support for adults—in helping them adjust, develop, and thrive. There are also opportunities, as highlighted here via these models, for researchers to avoid "re-inventing of the wheel" and instead examine, evaluate, adapt, and test ideas and interventions from the broader discipline of psychology, with a goal of developing and strengthening multicultural interventions that might work.

Conclusion

While a significant amount of work has been directed at developing the field of multicultural counseling/psychotherapy, the current state of the research in this area can be considered as a "good start". This chapter has highlighted some of the important work conducted until now, and noted some of the limitations of the research to date as well as possible areas for further work in theory development, applied research, and training.

References

Anglin, D. M., & Wade, J. C. (2007). Racial socialization, racial identity, and Black students' adjustment to college. *Cultural Diversity and Ethnic Minority Psychology, 13*, 207–215.

Arthur, N. (2000, April). *Predictive characteristics of multicultural counseling competence*. Paper presented at the annual conference of the American Educational Research Association, New Orleans, LA.

Atkinson, D. R., Thompson, C. E., & Grant, S. K. (1993). A three-dimensional model for counseling racial/ethnic minorities. *The Counseling Psychologist, 21*, 257–277.

Bernal, M. E., Sirolli, A. A., Weisser, S. K., Ruiz, J. A., Chamberlain, V. J., & Knight, G. P. (1999). Relevance of multicultural training to students' applications to clinical psychology programs. *Cultural Diversity and Ethnic Minority Psychology, 5*, 43–55.

Bryant, A., & LaFromboise, T. D. (2005). The racial identity and cultural orientation of Lumbee American Indian high school students. *Cultural Diversity and Ethnic Minority Psychology, 11*, 82–89.

Carter, R. T., Helms, J. E., & Juby, H. L. (2004). The relationship between racism and racial identity for White Americans: A profile analysis. *Journal of Multicultural Counseling and Development, 32*, 2–17.

Chen, G. A., LePhuoc, P., Guzman, M. R., Rude, S. S., & Dodd, B. G. (2006). Exploring Asian American racial identity. *Cultural Diversity and Ethnic Minority Psychology, 12*, 461–476.

Coleman, H. L. K. (1995). Strategies for coping with cultural diversity. *The Counseling Psychologist, 23*, 722–741.

Coleman, H. L. K. (1997). Conflict in multicultural counseling relationships: Source and resolution. *Journal of Multicultural Counseling and Development, 25*, 195–200.

Comstock, D. L., Hammer, T. R., Strentzsch, J., Cannon, K., Parsons, J., & Salazar, G. (2008). Relational-cultural theory: A framework for bridging relational, multicultural, and social justice competencies. *Journal of Counseling and Development, 86*, 279–287.

Constantine, M. G. (2002). Predictors of satisfaction with counseling: Racial and ethnic minority clients' attitudes toward counseling and ratings of their counselors' general and multicultural competence. *Journal of Counseling Psychology, 49*, 255–263.

Constantine, M. G., Fuertes, J. N., Roysircar, G., & Kindaichi, M. M. (2008). Multicultural competence: Clinical practice, training and supervision, and research. In W. B. Walsh (Ed.), *Biennial review of counseling psychology* Vol. 1 (pp. 97–128). New York: Routledge.

Constantine, M. G., Juby, H. L., & Liang, J. J.-C. (2001). Examining multicultural counseling competence and race-related attitudes among white marital and family therapists. *Journal of Marital and Family Therapy, 27*, 353–362.

Constantine, M. G., & Ladany, N. (2000). Self-report multicultural counseling competence scales: Their relation to social desirability attitudes and multicultural case conceptualization ability. *Journal of Counseling Psychology, 47*, 155–164.

Constantine, M. G., Ladany, N., Inman, A. G., & Ponterotto, J. G. (1996). Students' perceptions of multicultural training in counseling psychology programs. *Journal of Multicultural Counseling and Development, 24,* 241–253.

Constantine, M. G., Warren, A. K., & Miville, M. L. (2005). White racial identity dyadic interactions in supervision: Implications for supervisees' multicultural counseling competence. *Journal of Counseling Psychology, 52,* 490–496.

Cumming-McCann, A., & Accordino, M. P. (2005). An investigation of rehabilitation counselor characteristics, White racial attitudes, and self-reported multicultural counseling competencies. *Rehabilitation Counseling Bulletin, 48,* 167–176.

Department of Health and Human Services. (2001). *Mental health: Culture, race, and ethnicity: A supplement to mental health: A report of the Surgeon General.* Retrieved September 26, 2008, from http://mentalhealth.samhsa.gov/cre/ch2_racism_discrimination_and_mental_health.asp.

Fischer, A. R., Jome, L. M., & Atkinson, D. R. (1998). Reconceptualizing multicultural counseling: Universal healing conditions in a culturally specific context. *The Counseling Psychologist, 26,* 525–588.

Fuertes, J. N., Alfonso, V. C., & Schultz, J. J. (2005). Counseling South American immigrants. *Journal of Immigrant and Refugee Services, 3,* 155–169.

Fuertes, J. N., Alfonso, V. C., & Schultz, J. J. (2007). Counseling culturally and linguistically diverse children and youth: A self-regulatory approach. In G. B. Esquivel, E. C. Lopez, & S. G. Nahari (Eds.), *The handbook of multicultural school psychology* (pp. 409–427). New York: Lawrence Erlbaum.

Fuertes, J. N., Bartolomeo, M., & Nichols, C. M. (2001). Future research directions in the study of counselor multicultural competencies. *Journal of Multicultural Counseling and Development, 29,* 3–12.

Fuertes, J. N., Boylan, L. S., & Fontanella, J. A. (In press). Behavioral indices in medical care outcome: The working alliance, adherence, and related factors. *Journal of General Internal Medicine.*

Fuertes, J. N., & Brobst, K. (2002). Clients' ratings of counselor multicultural competency. *Cultural Diversity and Ethnic Minority Psychology, 8,* 214–223.

Fuertes, J. N., Costa, C., Mueller, L., & Hersh, M. (2004). Process and outcome psychotherapy research from a cultural-racial perspective. In R. Carter (Ed.), *Handbook of racial-cultural psychology and counseling* Vol. 1 (pp. 256–276). New York: Wiley.

Fuertes, J. N., & Gretchen, D. (2001). Emerging theories of multicultural counseling. In J. G. Ponterotto, J. M. Casas, L. A. Suzuki, & C. M. Alexander (Eds.), *Handbook of multicultural counseling* (pp. 509–541). Newbury Park, CA: Sage.

Fuertes, J. N., Mueller, L. N., Chauhan, R. V., Walker, J. A., Ladany, N. (2002). An investigation of Euro-American therapists' approach to counseling African-American clients. *The Counseling Psychologist, 30,* 763–788.

Fuertes, J. N., & Ponterotto, J. G. (2003). Culturally appropriate intervention strategies. In G. Roysircar, P. Arredondo, J. N. Fuertes, R. Toporek, & J. G. Ponterotto (Eds.), *2003 Multicultural counseling competencies: AMCD* (pp. 51–58). Alexandria, VA: American Counseling Association.

Fuertes, J. N., Stracuzzi, T. I., Bennett, J., Scheinholtz, J., Mislowack, A., Hersh, M., et al. (2006). Therapist multicultural competency: A study of therapy dyads. *Psychotherapy: Theory, Research, Practice, Training, 43,* 480–490.

Gelso, C. J. (2002). Real relationship: The "something more" of psychotherapy. *Journal of Contemporary Psychotherapy, 32,* 35–40.

Gonzalez, R., Biever, J. L., & Gardner, G. T. (1994). The multicultural perspective in therapy: A social constructionist approach. *Psychotherapy, 31,* 515–524.

Griner, D., & Smith, T. B. (2006). Culturally adapted mental health interventions: A meta-analytic review. *Psychotherapy: Theory, Research, Practice, Training, 43,* 531–548.

Gushue, G. V., & Constantine, M. G. (2007). Color-blind racial attitudes and White racial identity attitudes in psychology trainees. *Professional Psychology: Research and Practice, 38,* 321–328.

Hanna, F. J., Bemak, F., & Chi-Ying Chung, R. (1999). Toward a new paradigm for multicultural counseling. *Journal of Counseling and Development, 77,* 125–134.

Hays, D. G. (2008). Assessing multicultural competence in counselor trainees: A review of instrumentation and future directions. *Journal of Counseling and Development, 86,* 95–101.

Helms, J. E. (Ed.). (1990). *Black and White racial identity: Theory, research, and practice.* Westport, CT: Greenwood.

Helms, J. E. (1995). An update of Helms's White and people of color racial identity models. In J. G. Ponterotto, J. M. Casas, L. A. Suzuki, & C. M. Alexander (Eds.), *Handbook of multicultural counseling* (pp. 181–198). Thousand Oaks, CA: Sage.

Helms, J. E. (1996). Toward a methodology for measuring and assessing racial as distinguished from ethnic identity. In G. R. Sodowsky, & J. C. Impara (Eds.), *Multicultural assessment in counseling and clinical psychology* (pp. 143–192). Lincoln, NE: Buros Institute of Mental Measurements.

Helms, J. E., & Cook, D. A. (1999). *Using race and culture in counseling and psychotherapy: Theory and process.* Boston: Allyn & Bacon.

Herring, R. D., & Walker, S. S. (1993). Synergetic counseling: Toward a more holistic model with a cross-cultural specific approach. *TCA Journal, 22,* 38–53.

Hill, C. E., Sim, W., Spangler, P., Stahl, J., Sullivan, C., & Teyber, E. (2008). Therapist immediacy in brief psychotherapy: Case study II. *Psychotherapy: Theory, Research, Practice, Training, 45,* 298–315.

Hill, C. E., Thompson, B. J., & Williams, E. N. (1997). A guide to conducting consensual qualitative research. *The Counseling Psychologist, 25,* 517–572.

Ho, D. Y. F. (1995). Internalized culture, culturocentrism, and transcendence. *The Counseling Psychologist, 23,* 4–24.

Inman, A. G. (2006). Supervisor multicultural competence and its relation to supervisory process and outcome. *Journal of Marital and Family Therapy, 32,* 73–85.

Jacobsen, C. K. (1985). Resistance to affirmative action: Self interest or racism? *Journal of Conflict Resolution, 29,* 306–329.

Johnson, S. C., & Arbona, C. (2006). The relation of ethnic identity, racial identity, and race-related stress among African-American students. *Journal of College Student Development, 47,* 495–507.

King, P. A., & Howard-Hamilton, M. (2003). An assessment of multicultural competence. *NASPA Journal, 40,* 119–133.

Ladany, N., Brittan-Powell, C. S., & Pannu, R. K. (1997). The influence of supervisory racial identity interaction and racial matching on the supervisory working alliance and supervisee multicultural competence. *Counselor Education and Supervision, 36*, 284–304.

Ladany, N., Inman, A. G., Constantine, M. G., & Hofheinz, E. W. (1997). Supervisee multicultural case conceptualization ability and self-reported multicultural competence as functions of supervisee racial identity and supervisor focus. *Journal of Counseling Psychology, 44*, 284–293.

Le, T. N., & Stockdale, G. (2008). Acculturative dissonance, ethnic identity, and youth violence. *Cultural Diversity and Ethnic Minority Psychology, 14*, 1–9.

Lee, R. M., Noh, C.-Y., Yoo, H. C., & Doh, H. S. (2007). The psychology of diaspora experienced: Intergroup contact, perceived discrimination, and ethnic identity of Koreans in China. *Cultural Diversity and Ethnic Minority Psychology, 13*, 115–124.

Leong, F. T. L. (1996). Toward an integrative model for cross-cultural counseling and psychotherapy. *Applied and Preventive Psychology, 5*, 189–209.

Leong, F. T. L. (2007). Cultural accommodation as method and metaphor. *American Psychologist, 62*, 916–927.

Liu, W. M. (2002). Exploring the lives of Asian American men: Racial identity, male role norms, gender role conflict, and prejudicial attitudes. *Psychology of Men and Masculinity, 3*, 107–118.

Locke, D. C. (1998). *Increasing multicultural understanding* (2nd ed.). Newbury Park, CA: Sage.

Lopez, I. (2008). "But you don't look Puerto Rican": The moderating effect of ethnic identity on the relation between skin color and self-esteem among Puerto Rican women. *Cultural Diversity and Ethnic Minority Psychology, 14*, 102–108.

Mahalik, J. R., Pierre, M. R., & Wan, S. S. C. (2006). Examining racial identity and masculinity as correlates of self-esteem and psychological distress in Black men. *Journal of Multicultural Counseling and Development, 34*, 94–104.

Middleton, R. A., Stadler, H. A., Simpson, C., Guo, Y. J., Brown, M. J., Crow, G., et al. (2005). Mental health practitioners: The relationship between White racial identity attitudes and self-reported multicultural counseling competencies. *Journal of Counseling and Development, 83*, 444–456.

Miville, M. L., Constantine, M. G., Baysden, M. F., & So-Lloyd, G. (2005). Chameleon changes: An exploration of racial identity themes of multiracial people. *Journal of Counseling Psychology, 52*, 507–516.

Neville, H., Spanierman, L., & Doan, B.-T. (2006). Exploring the association between color-blind racial ideology and multicultural counseling competencies. *Cultural Diversity and Ethnic Minority Psychology, 12*, 275–290.

Ottavi, T. M., Pope-Davis, D. B., & Dings, J. G. (1994). Relationship between White racial identity attitudes and self-reported multicultural counseling competencies. *Journal of Counseling Psychology, 41*, 149–154.

Phinney, J. S., & Ong, A. D. (2007). Conceptualization and measurement of ethnic identity: Current status and future directions. *Journal of Counseling Psychology, 54*, 271–281.

Ponterotto, J. G., Fuertes, J. N., & Chen, E. C. (2000). Models of multicultural counseling. In S. D. Brown, & R. W. Lent (Eds.), *Handbook of counseling psychology* (3rd ed., pp. 639–669). New York: Wiley.

Ponterotto, J. G., & Park-Taylor, J. (2007). Racial and ethnic identity theory, measurement, and research in counseling psychology: Present status and future directions. *Journal of Counseling Psychology, 54*, 282–294.

Pope-Davis, D. B., Reynolds, A. L., Dings, J. G., & Ottavi, T. M. (1994). Multicultural competencies of doctoral interns at university counseling centers: An exploratory investigation. *Professional Psychology: Research and Practice, 25*, 466–470.

Pope-Davis, D. B., Toporek, R. L., Ortega-Villalobos, L., Ligiero, D. P., Brittan-Powell, C. S., Liu, W. M., et al. (2002). Client perspectives of multicultural counseling competence: A qualitative examination. *The Counseling Psychologist, 30*, 355–393.

Pugh, L. A., & Bry, B. H. (2007). The protective effects of ethnic identity for alcohol and marijuana use among Black young adults. *Cultural Diversity and Ethnic Minority Psychology, 13*, 187–193.

Quintana, S. M. (2007). Racial and ethnic identity: Developmental perspectives and research. *Journal of Counseling Psychology, 54*, 259–270.

Ramirez, M., III. (1999). *Multicultural psychotherapy: An approach to individual and cultural differences* (2nd ed.). Boston: Allyn & Bacon.

Ridley, C. R., Ethington, L. L., & Heppner, P. P. (2007). Cultural confrontation: A skill of advanced cultural empathy. In P. B. Pedersen, W. J. Lonner, J. G. Draguns, & J. E. Trimble (Eds.), *Counseling across cultures* (pp. 377–393). San Francisco: Sage.

Ridley, C. R., Mendoza, D. W., Kanitz, B. E., Angermeier, L., & Zenk, R. (1994). Cultural sensitivity in multicultural counseling: A perceptual schema model. *Journal of Counseling Psychology, 41*, 125–136.

Schwartz, S. J., Zamboanga, B. L., & Jarvis, L. H. (2007). Ethnic identity and acculturation in Hispanic early adolescents: Mediated relationships to academic grades, prosocial behaviors, and externalizing symptoms. *Cultural Diversity and Ethnic Minority Psychology, 13*, 364–373.

Sellers, R. M., & Shelton, J. N. (2003). The role of racial identity in perceived racial discrimination. *Journal of Personality and Social Psychology, 84*, 1079–1092.

Silvestri, T. J., & Richardson, T. Q. (2001). White racial identity statutes and NEO personality constructs: An exploratory analysis. *Journal of Counseling and Development, 79*, 68–76.

Sodowsky, G. R., Kuo-Jackson, P. Y., Richardson, M. F., & Corey, A. T. (1998). Correlates of self-reported multicultural competencies: Counselor multicultural social desirability, race, social inadequacy, locus of control racial ideology, and multicultural training. *Journal of Counseling Psychology, 45*, 256–264.

Spanierman, L. B., Poteat, V. P., Wang, Y. F., & Oh, E. (2008). Psychosocial costs of racism to White counselors: Predicting various dimensions of multicultural counseling competence. *Journal of Counseling Psychology, 55*, 75–88.

Steenbarger, B. N. (1993). A multicontextual model of counseling: Bridging brevity and diversity. *Journal of Counseling and Development, 72*, 8–15.

Sue, D. W., Carter, R. T., Casas, J. M., Fouad, N. A., Ivey, A. E., Jensen, M., et al. (1998). *Multicultural counseling competencies: Individual and organizational development.* Thousand Oaks, CA: Sage.

Sue, D. W., Ivey, A. E., & Pedersen, P. B. (Eds.). (1996). *A theory of multicultural counseling and therapy.* Pacific Grove, CA: Brooks/Cole.

Trevino, J. G. (1996). Worldview and change in cross-cultural counseling. *The Counseling Psychologist, 24*, 198–215.

Umana-Taylor, A. J., & Shin, N. (2007). An examination of ethnic identity and self-esteem with diverse populations: Exploring variation by ethnicity and geography. *Cultural Diversity and Ethnic Minority Psychology, 13,* 178–186.

U.S. Bureau of the Census. (2007). *Selected characteristics of racial groups and Hispanic/Latino population: 2005.* Retrieved October 10, 2008, from http://www.census.gov/compendia/statab/tables.

U.S. Department of Homeland Security. (2004). *Yearbook of immigrant statistics, 2003.* Washington, DC: Office of Immigration Statistics, National Serials Program, Library of Congress.

Utsey, S. O., Chae, M. H., Brown, C. F., & Kelly, D. (2002). Effect of ethnic group membership on ethnic identity, race-related stress, and quality of life. *Cultural Diversity and Ethnic Minority Psychology, 8,* 366–377.

Vereen, L. G., Hill, N. R., McNeal, D. T. (2008). Perceptions of multicultural counseling competency: Integration of the curricular and the practical. *Journal of Mental Health Counseling, 30,* 226–236.

Wadsworth, M. E., & Santiago, C. D. (2008). Risk and resiliency processes in ethnically diverse families in poverty. *Journal of Family Psychology, 22,* 399–410.

Walker, R. L., Wingate, L. R., Obasi, E. M., & Joiner, T. E. (2008). An empirical investigation of acculturative stress and ethnic identity as moderators for depression and suicidal ideation in college students. *Cultural Diversity and Ethnic Minority Psychology, 14,* 75–82.

Worthington, R. L., Soth-McNett, A. M., & Moreno, M. V. (2007). Multicultural counseling competencies research: A 20-year content analysis. *Journal of Counseling Psychology, 54,* 351–361.

Yip, T., Gee, G. C., & Takeuchi, D. T. (2008). Racial discrimination and psychological distress: The impact of ethnic identity and age among immigrant and United States-born Asian adults. *Developmental Psychology, 44,* 787–800.

Yoo, H. C., & Lee, R. M. (2005). Ethnic identity and approach-type coping as moderators of the racial discrimination/well-being relation in Asian Americans. *Journal of Counseling Psychology, 52,* 497–506.

Yoo, H. C., & Lee, R. M. (2008). Does ethnic identity buffer or exacerbate the effects of frequent racial discrimination on situational well-being of Asian-Americans? *Journal of Counseling Psychology, 55,* 63–74.

Spirituality, Religion, and Psychological Counseling

Thomas G. Plante *and* Carl E. Thoresen

Abstract

A substantial majority of people believe in God in some form and consider themselves to be spiritual, religious, or both. However, most psychologists and other mental health professionals perceive themselves as not religious and have little if any training in spirituality and religious diversity. Psychologists can use spiritual principles and practices to better serve clients, even if they do not share the same or any religious or spiritual perspective. We review and illustrate the emerging relationship between psychology, spirituality and religion, and its current status. Benefits of religious/spiritual engagement for physical, social, and mental health are outlined. We also comment on religious hazards to health. Spiritual tools commonly found in major religious traditions are discussed and suggested for use by counseling psychologists and others under certain conditions. A brief spiritual inquiry method is presented. Results of a spiritually focused intervention using spiritual practices serves as an example. Ethical and research issues are also discussed, along with important questions to consider.

Keywords: spirituality, religion, faith, health, counseling, psychotherapy, professional issues

We are not human beings trying to be spiritual.
Rather we are spiritual beings trying to be human.
—Jacquelyn Small

Where is the wisdom we have lost in knowledge?
Where is the knowledge we have lost in information?
—T.S. Eliot

What accounts for the growing interest of health-related disciplines and professions, such as psychology and medicine, in religion and spirituality, especially in its relationship to health, disease, and well-being? In the past decade, many professional books have been published dealing with this issue (e.g., Koenig, McCullough, & Larson, 2001; Paloutzian & Park, 2005; Plante & Thoresen, 2007). Literally hundreds of mostly empirical articles have appeared (e.g., Miller & Thoresen, 2003; McCullough, Hoyt, Larson, Koenig, & Thoresen, 2000; Thoresen & Harris, 2002) and scores of conferences and workshops have been conducted for health care professionals interested in the interplay between spirituality and health. Since 2000, the topic has been featured in almost all popular news magazines and television news programs (e.g., making its third appearance on the cover of *Time*, in February 2009). In part, this growing interest stems from a public fascinated with spirituality and its connection with health (e.g., Oprah introduced "Spirituality 101" in 2008, as a regular feature of her popular television program).

The popular interest also comes from a society seeking a greater sense of meaning, purpose, and significance in life, especially recently, in the wake of the unanticipated abrupt economic recession starting in 2008 and still lingering What really matters in life? What is sacred? Help with these questions is not readily found in today's time-pressured society, where there is less involvement in social and community groups and organizations, less involvement in developing and maintaining close personal and intimate relationships, and diminishing participation in religious organizations that provide a majority of society's "social and moral capital" (Putnam, 2000).

Current intrigue with spirituality and religion is found not only among the general population and some health care professionals but also among the psychological and counseling community as well. Although indifferent and antagonistic toward religion and spirituality for decades, psychology, among other disciplines, seems to be rediscovering its religious and spiritual roots with renewed interest (Oman & Thoresen, 2002). This renaissance seems most apparent in the professional services side of psychology (Miller & Thoresen, 2003).

In this chapter, we discuss the reviving relationship between psychology and religion and spirituality, especially as it pertains to psychological practice, such as counseling. We discuss empirical research, using some examples, of the mental and physical health benefits of spiritual and religious involvement. We also note some of its hazards to health. Spiritual and religious principles and tools are mentioned that counselors can use ethically and with sensitivity in their professional work, regardless of their personal beliefs or religious affiliation. We also mention ethical mandates and issues, as well as some empirical problems deserving consideration.

In the spirit of full disclosure, we as authors perceive ourselves as spiritually and religiously active persons. We are committed to fostering a greater overall understanding of the role of spirituality and religion in psychology as a scientific discipline and as a health-related helping profession. As empirical scholars and health professionals, we use a variety of quantitative and qualitative research methods in addition to our teaching, supervising, and consulting roles.

Definitions, Ethics, and Diversity Issues

Before continuing, we need to address three important issues. They concern defining key terms, ethical precautions, and diversity issues.

Defining Religion, Spirituality, and the Sacred

People are often confused about the definition of the words "religion" and "spirituality." Such confusion is understandable since these terms are multidimensional (e.g., social, emotional, cognitive) and multilevel concepts (e.g., processes within the

person, within local organizations, within regions, within nation states, and within the world at large). For example, the term *religion* can be used on a societal level as a social institution with organizational structures. It can also be defined on a group level as a faith community, or on an individual level as involved with the search for significance in life in ways related to what is perceived as sacred (Pargament, 2007). Emmons and Paloutzian (2003), in reviewing theory and research over past 25 years, observed that the past decade in particular has seen major changes in how religion and spirituality are conceptualized. Mention is made of changing religious landscapes in the broader culture, especially with a "new breed of spirituality that is often distinct from traditional conceptions of religion" (p. 381). Zinnbauer and Pargament (2005) offer the many pros and cons of viewing spirituality as a part of religion or viewing religion as a part of spirituality.

One of the biggest changes has been the broadening perspective of how spirituality is conceived. Essentially, the term is no longer exclusively tied directly or indirectly to religious institutions and traditions. Now, it is also applied to situations and experiences that are independent of any formal ties with religion. One of the most significant recent developments concerning spirituality has been the emerging relationship of spirituality with positive emotions viewed from an evolutionary perspective (e.g., Vaillant, 2008). We discuss this development later in the chapter.

We view *religion* broadly as a social institution with organizational and community structures that offer ways for people to understand and honor the wisdom traditions, generally through scriptures or religious writings and through rituals viewed as sacred. Religious institutions generally offer an articulated doctrine or belief structure describing the specific values and beliefs of a traditional faith community. Stated somewhat differently, religion commonly provides answers to what have been termed perennial questions about life and death (e.g., What really matters? Why do people suffer? What happens after I die?). Religion especially highlights one or more revered religious leaders or spiritual models to emulate, such as Jesus, Buddha, or Mohammed. For a comprehensive discussion of the seminal role of spiritual modeling and how spirituality is primarily "caught not taught," see Oman and Thoresen (2003, 2005) and Bandura (2003).

The world's major religious faith traditions include Christianity, Judaism, Buddhism, Hinduism,

Islam, Taoism, and Confucianism. Each tradition includes various branches, some highly similar and some quite differing from others in specific beliefs, values, and practices. For example, Christianity includes Roman Catholics, many Protestant denominations (such as Methodists and Baptists), and countless nondenominational churches not affiliated with an organized religious tradition but based on their interpretation of the Bible and the teachings of Jesus. Within the Jewish tradition, variations exists as well, such as Orthodox or Reform version of Judaism. As noted earlier, a key role of a religion as an organized faith community is to help members and others better understand and relate to what is sacred through community and through rituals, traditions, beliefs, and practices. Although some religions are quite centralized and highly structured (e.g., the Roman Catholic Church), others are very decentralized with little organizational structure (e.g., Buddhism).

We view *spirituality* primarily at the level of the individual's experiences in seeking what is perceived as sacred in life and associated in some way with the transcendent belief that a higher power or spirit exists that is greater than oneself. This connection might be to God (however defined or understood), to religious models, such as Jesus or Buddha, or to the natural world in general. The word *spirituality* comes from the Latin word, *spiritus*, meaning that which is absolutely vital to life, such as the breath or life force (Hage, 2006). William James (1936) defined spirituality in relational terms as "the feelings, acts, and experiences of individual men in their solitude, as far as they apprehend themselves to stand in relation to whatever they may consider the divine" (p. 32). In many ways, spirituality can be perceived as a blend of positive emotions mixed with prosocial behaviors, such as the joy of feeling connected to something greater than oneself or with "heartfelt" gratitude associated with feeling loved or loving another person (see Fredrickson, 2009, for an excellent overview of positive emotions).

Sacred we view as what is perceived as holy, divine, eternal, or meaningful. Pargament (2007) defines the sacred as "concepts of God, the divine, and transcendent reality, as well as other features of life that take on divine character and significance by virtue of their association with or representation of divinity . . . at the heart of the sacred lies God, divine beings, or a transcendent reality" (pp. 32–33). In effect, a person can perceive many different things and experiences as sacred. Clarifying what a person deems as sacred can help one better understand a major basis of motivation and focus in that person's life.

The phrase "spiritual but not religious" has recently become a popular way to describe some people's religious/spiritual identity. Estimates of those identifying themselves in the United States as spiritual but not religious range from 20% to 35% (Fuller, 2001; Hood, 2005). For example, in a recent study of 1,010 college students in four American universities (in west, east, and south), 30% described themselves as "spiritual but not religious," whereas 41% saw themselves as "spiritual and religious" (Oman, Thoresen, Park, Shaver, Hood, et al., 2008). Interestingly, such data compare favorably to other major studies of spirituality and religion in young adults (Astin et al., 2005).

Keep in mind that the "spiritual but not religious" designation represents a fairly heterogeneous group. Some have rejected religious organizations for many reasons, such as their perceived rigid dogma, decrees, demands to be submissive, and requirements to accept unquestioningly specific religious beliefs and traditions. For some, the connotation of being spiritual is currently perceived as quite positive, whereas being religious is viewed as fairly negative. Fewer see spirituality as a "New Age" phenomenon that is unnecessary if not antireligious and thus as very negative, with religion seen as quite positive (in the 10%–15% range).

Pargament (2007) reports that psychologists and other contemporary mental health professionals often view spirituality among their clients as a good thing, whereas religiousness is typically a bad thing. The extremely negative press associated with various religious scandals, as well as religiously inspired terrorism and violence, has contributed to the notion that organized religion is destructive, hypocritical, and outdated (e.g., Hitchens, 2007). Perhaps it is a typical American penchant to be very individualistic, such that many Americans seek and select some elements of spirituality and religion that work for them and simply reject the rest (Fuller, 2001). Yet, although some have rejected organized religion altogether, many more others have held fast to their faith traditions and communities, even following remarkable religious scandals and embarrassments (Putnam & Campbell, 2010).

It is interesting to note the results of the first major national study of spirituality and religion of the so-called "millennium generation," those born in the mid to late 1980s and now attending college (Astin et al., 2005). In this study of 112,232 college youth attending 236 American colleges and universities, a clear majority viewed themselves as both spiritual and religious. Of these students, four out of five believed in God, have attended at least one religious service in the past year, and frequently have discussed religion with friends and family. Almost one in two believe that it is "essential" or "very important" to seek ways to grow spiritually, 69% pray regularly, and over 75% reported that they are searching for greater meaning and purpose in life. These students expressed a great deal of interest in spiritually related questions, such as "What am I going to do with my life?" "What kind of person do I want to be?" "How do I know I am doing the right thing?" Almost two out of three indicated that most people can grow spiritually without being religious.

Importantly, a great deal of diversity emerged among students in different faith traditions and from attending colleges in different regions of the United States. For example, students in Southeastern colleges and universities were less likely to be interested in spirituality (cf. religion) than were students from other regions. Those who identified with more conservative denominations were less likely to be interested in social issues, such as gender and sexual orientation, as well as less interested in worldwide humanitarian issues (e.g., world hunger, poverty, discrimination; Astin et al., 2005). Clearly, the topics of spirituality and religion hold substantial interest among current young adults.

Ethical and Diversity Issues

Several ethical concerns deserve comment. First, when it comes to matters of spirituality and religion, counselors need to work within their area of competence and must not overstep professional bounds. We, as psychologists, and other professionals are obligated to perform our duties consistent with our training and experience. That means following ethical guidelines of competence as well as legal requirements that license to practices demands. Second, professionals must carefully avoid potential dual relationships, especially when their clients are members of their own faith tradition and perhaps part of the same church community. Unforeseen dual relationships and conflicts can easily emerge. One must be very sensitive to potential exploitive dual relationships, as well as to the unforeseen consequences that can unfold when working with fellow congregants. Finally, professionals must be careful to avoid potential bias by not promoting one particular religious belief system over another, especially their own.

Professionals, as well as the general population, often may have certain positive or negative perceptions about particular religious or spiritual communities. We must be, as noted earlier, very attentive to the rich diversity of beliefs and practices, even within each particular religious or spiritual tradition. We must steer clear of religious stereotyping of others, a problem that is highly prevalent in many cultures. This is especially true for those psychologists who have had little or no contact with members of particular religious group in either their professional or personal lives.

All religious and spiritual communities, along with their beliefs, rituals, and practices, exist as a part of a particular culture or subculture. Spiritual and religious customs are commonly steeped in ethnic diversity. For example, Roman Catholics from Eastern Europe may engage in different religious traditions and practices relative to Catholics from Latin America. Jews from Israel may experience their faith and cultural tradition quite differently than do those from parts of Eastern Europe or North America. Subtle and not so subtle cultural, ethnic, geographic, and political differences may be part of religious experience, customs, and traditions. In fact, many religious and spiritual beliefs and practices originated within a particular ethnic and cultural community before being adopted more broadly by a particular religious tradition. Two very simple examples: Christmas trees and Easter bunnies. The point here is that specific cultural influences are often intimately woven into religious and spiritual experience and expression (American Psychological Association [APA], 2003).

Benefits of Religious and Spiritual Engagement

Mills (2002) reported that almost 1,700 empirical studies of religion and health had been published in professional and research-oriented journals by 2000. During the same time, about 700 had been published on spiritually/spirituality and health. We suspect that since 2000, well over 4,000 articles and reports have appeared, given the exponential rate of annual publications documented by Mills (2002).

The term *health* itself has been expanding to include not only "conditions of the body" but, more importantly, "states of mind" (Ryff & Singer, 1998; Thoresen & Eagleston, 1985). Although most people still associate health with medicine, biology, and disease, many are expanding its meaning to include a person's overall life experiences. Examples include the hospice care movement, global environmental factors, and positive emotions. Some have suggested that, although in the 20th century, psychology first lost its soul and then its mind; it is now beginning to recall them both in the 21st century. In doing so, psychology may be becoming more focused on human nature and the whole person in context, rather than only focused on a person's behaviors, cognitions, or personality (Miller & Delaney, 2005).

The vast majority of high-quality research supports a positive relationship between religious involvement and beneficial health outcomes (Koenig et al., 2001; Pargament, 1997; Plante & Sherman, 2001; Plante & Thoresen, 2007; Richards & Bergin, 2005). People engaged in regular participation in a religious and spiritual tradition tend to be healthier, happier, maintain better habits, and experience more social support compared to those less active or not at all involved.

Mental Health Benefits of Spirituality and Religion

An extensive review of research involving hundreds of studies of mental health benefits of spirituality and religious involvement suggests that it is related to less anxiety, depression, chronic stress, and greater perceived well-being and self-esteem (Koenig et al., 2001; Plante & Sharma, 2001; Thoresen, 2007). Persons with religious involvement often tend to cope better with major and minor life stress. They are, for example, less likely to have alcohol and other substance abuse problems, eating disorders, be divorced, and are less likely to attempt suicide, homicide, or engage in criminal behavior. Generally, they live a healthier overall lifestyle, with better social support, usually avoiding health damaging behavior patterns. In general, they have better mental health functioning, including mood and general affect control, than do those not regularly involved religiously or spiritually.

Despite hundreds of studies, the evidence does not demonstrate or prove that religion or spirituality by itself *directly* causes better mental or physical health. Instead, the evidence clearly implicates spiritual or religious practices over time in processes involved with better physical and mental health compared with non–religiously active people. Specific causes of this beneficial relationship, however, remain unclear (Thoresen, 2007). We strongly suspect that religion and spirituality serve as a positive factor in good health and well-being but not as the only factor. Rather, spiritual and religious factors appear to serve as one of many other *indirect* but significant factors in promoting good health and well-being (see Thoresen & Harris, 2002).

Physical Health and Longevity

To date, the physical health benefits associated with spirituality and religious involvement have been impressive (Powell, Shahabi, & Thoresen, 2003). Spiritual and religiously active people tend to live longer, be less likely to develop serious medical illnesses, and recover faster from illnesses than others. In fact, meta-analytic research based on long-term prospective studies involving tens of thousands of adults show that religiously oriented people, in general, live on average 7 years longer than do non–religiously minded people. This is the case even when statistically controlling for age, gender, socioeconomic status, family history of disease, health behaviors (such as smoking, drinking alcohol, and diet), and other known risk factors for mortality, such as social support (McCullough, Hoyt, Larson, Koenig, & Thoresen, 2000; Oman & Thoresen, 2005; Powell et al., 2003). For example, Hummer, Rogers, Nam, and Ellison (1999) investigated over 21,000 adults in a national sample examining disease and mortality. They controlled for 15 likely factors that influence health outcome, such as those mentioned above, plus others. Compared to the highest religious attendance group (attending some kind of religious service more than once per week), the non–religious attendance group suffered 50% more deaths, the occasional religious attendance group (defined as once per month) had 24% more deaths, and the group attending religious services once per week group had 15% more deaths. Examining results in years of life, the highest religious attendance group lived 7.6 more years longer than nonattendees. These results provide the kind of evidence that mandates the need to clarify which factors best explain these results. Not considered in most studies, however, were indicators of quality of life and several other mental health indicators, particularly positive indicators that could shed even more light on these extraordinary findings.

When 29 independent studies of religious involvement were reviewed using meta-analysis totaling 125,826 adults and 15 potentially influencing factors were controlled, weekly or more religious attendance yielded 29% fewer deaths than did nonattendance. This figure dropped to 23% when social support was included in the analysis.

The longevity benefit for frequent church attendance was 7 additional years of life (McCullough et al., 2000). Using a review process focused on the quality of the research designs, statistical analyses used, and precision of other measures, Powell, Shahabi, and Thoresen (2003) found that, in nine highly rated studies, frequent religious attendance at services mortality rates were 25% lower than for non-attendees in general population samples of reasonably healthy adults.

In recent years, for the first time, the National Institutes of Health convened an expert panel (see Miller & Thoresen, 2003; Powell, Shahabi, & Thoresen, 2003) to conduct a critical evaluation of published clinical trials using rigorous scientific criteria. The panel concluded that "persuasive" evidence exists that active religious and spiritual involvement is significantly correlated over time in controlled prospective studies with lower all-cause mortality. The overall results indicated a 25% to 30% reduction in mortality. On average, people who are active in religious or spiritual activities can expect to live about 7 years longer than nonreligious or less religiously active people. In one major study, African Americans males lived almost 14 years longer than did nonactive African males (see Powell, Shahabi, & Thoresen, 2003). Clearly, active religious and spiritual engagement for many consistently appears to enhance their health, when broadly viewed over time.

Tragically, many mental and physical health problems are self-inflicted and thus could be prevented. Roughly 50% of all deaths in Americans and in the developed world are due to lifestyle habits and behaviors, such as smoking cigarettes, excessive eating and drinking, and lack of regular physical exercise (Centers for Disease Control, 2004). As already discussed those who are actively engaged in religious and spiritual practices live a healthier lifestyle than do those less active or not at all active. In doing so, they minimize many risks associated with the major chronic diseases, such as various cardiac diseases (e.g., Koenig et al., 2001; Oman & Thoresen, 2005; Powell, Shahabi, & Thoresen, 2003).

In response to these and other findings, the Association of American Medical Colleges has expressed the value of spirituality and religion in quality health care, stating:

Spirituality is recognized as a factor that contributes to health in many persons. The concept of spirituality is found in all cultures and societies.

It is expressed in an individual's search for ultimate meaning through participation in religion and/or belief in God . . . (and) . . . can influence how patients and health care professionals perceive health and illness and how they interact with one another.
(Association of American Medical Colleges, 1999, pp. 25–26)

Community Benefits

Many community benefits exist for active spiritual and religious involvement. Since those who tend to be religious and spiritual also tend to stay married and are less likely to engage in behaviors that could harm others, such as unsafe sexual practices, drunk driving, and criminal activity, spirituality and religiousness appear to foster a more livable and healthy community. Spiritually and religiously oriented people tend to take better care of their local as well as global community, supporting charitable causes, and especially participating in volunteerism. In fact, an added benefit of helping others in need through volunteerism is less disease and longer life (Oman & Thoresen, 2005).

To illustrate, in one major study Oman, Thoresen, and McMahon (1999) followed almost 2,000 older persons in Northern California for over two decades in terms of how many regularly volunteered to help others in the community (i.e., they received no material compensation). Roughly one-third of the sample volunteered regularly on a scheduled basis for 4 to 6 hours a month. Volunteers had 40% fewer deaths than did those who did not regularly volunteer. That difference increased to over 60% fewer deaths if the person who volunteered also was religiously active. These dramatic differences were found even after statistically controlling for over 12 known mortality risk factors. In a large nationally stratified sample, Harris and Thoresen (2005) found about 15% volunteered regularly. They experienced significantly fewer deaths, but when the other factors known to predict higher death rates were added to the analysis, only those who volunteered *and* who were regularly religiously active had significantly fewer deaths (30% fewer deaths).

Those engaged in spiritual and religious activities tend to be good citizens of the world who make the community a better place for others. In doing so, they also seem to benefit themselves by gaining a greater sense of meaning and significance in life, as well as enjoying better health and longevity along with heightened quality of life.

How Could Religious Involvement Benefit Health?

Several theories have been suggested. First, religious involvement is often conducted within a particular social structure termed a *congregation*. This social structure provides for many ready-made groups (including smaller groups) with similar interests and values to lend invaluable social and emotional support. Supportive congregational activities may help prevent mental health problems from developing or may help reduce these problems by offering better ways to cope with serious challenges and troubles. Second, spiritual and religious practices often involve activities similar to secular relaxation or mind-calming strategies. Mental health professionals often suggest various kinds of relaxation strategies to help clients cope with anxiety, depression, substance abuse, and other mental health problems. Many spiritual and religious practices, such as meditation, prayer, and attending various kinds of services, can be considered as forms of mental and physical relaxation strategies. However, such practices also offer, compared to secular relaxation practices, the added value of bolstering a diminished sense of meaning or significance in life, along with strengthening perceptions of self-efficacy about coping better with life's challenges (Oman & Thoresen, 2005). This strengthened perceived self-efficacy to cope with mental health challenges may depend on the person's perception that a relationship exists for them with a higher power or source, such as God.

McAdams (2006), for example, offers a fascinating perspective based on the study of personal narratives ("life stories") focused on Erikson's stage of generativity (the person's concern and commitment to promoting the well-being of others, such as future generations). Some who are actively involved in religion and spirituality seem to benefit greatly in having been able to reframe their suffering and pain as actually beneficial to them (sometimes called "benefit finding"). For such persons, pain and suffering is often viewed as having redemptive consequences.

We also note that the field of positive psychology, with its focus on human virtues (e.g., courage, humanity, and transcendence) and specific character strengths (e.g., hope, forgiveness, and gratitude), enhances mental health functioning (Seligman, Steen, Park, & Peterson, 2005; Snyder & Lopez, 2007). Spiritual and religious people are much more likely, for instance, to forgive others, express compassion, display gratitude, and engage in volunteerism (helping others in need without material compensation). Not surprisingly, positive psychology endorses the need for more positive emotions in daily life that may result in better mental health functioning. It is possible that the relationship between spirituality and religious involvement and positive mental health benefits and outcomes could most likely be indirectly related through a variety of causal mechanisms or pathways.

Recently, positive emotions and positive social behaviors, mentioned earlier, have been described in evolutionary terms when it comes to spirituality. For example, Keltner (2009) in *Born to Be Good*, makes a compelling case that humans survived over thousands of years not only because of their individual fitness but because of their collaborative kindness, and their spiritual and social capacities as well. That is, survival of the human species over 200 million years was not due solely to their physical genetics but more to their social and spiritual capacities, especially those selected for positive and prosocial emotions toward others. These included, for example, faith, hope, love, joy, compassion, and gratitude. One could argue that it was more of a survival of the kindest than just a survival of the fittest, especially if fitness is viewed only as physical and intellectual abilities. This spiritual evolutionary perspective finds support in several recent studies, primarily in psychology, neuroscience, ethology/animal studies, and cultural anthropology (see, for example, Brooks, 2011; Balter, 2005; Dalai Lama & Ekman, 2008; Damasio, 1994; Panksepp, 1998).

In an excellent overview, Vaillant (2008) makes a strong case that spirituality is essentially made of positive emotional experiences within social contexts—such as hope and compassion—that have evolved over the past 200 million years. Some of the major points he makes include:

- Three kinds of evolution exist—genetic, cultural, and individual—and have continually influenced each other. For example, evolving cultural changes have altered the size and functions within the brain, making it more likely to select for those living in more supportive, affiliative, and cooperative cultures characterized as fostering positive social emotions and strong social attachments.

- The human brain shares with all mammals and primates the limbic system (or paleomammalian brain), the neurophysiological home of positive emotions, empathy, and communal bonding and cooperation. This limbic system processes information from other organs of the body, coordinates emotions with past memories, and sends and receives information from the neocortex (especially the left prefrontal cortex), leading to more subtle and nuanced thoughts and motivation.

• The supremacy of words, texts, logic, and language in Western science (the primary domain of the left prefrontal cortex) have construed human experience and consciousness much too narrowly, leaving out the crucial role of emotional thinking and intuitive wisdom in understanding human experiences, perceptions, decisions, and judgments.

• Spirituality is clearly not the same as religion. Spirituality is individual-oriented, more emotional, universal in humans, more experiential, and more tolerant; religion is institutional and interpersonal-oriented, more cognitive, more culture-bound, more dogmatic, and less tolerant. Note, however, that religion is the greatest depository of spiritual resources, such as religious texts, rituals, music, and prayers/meditations.

This evolutionary perspective in highlighting the primary role of positive emotions in spirituality can help dispel the oversimplified and false dichotomy about cognitions and emotions, science and spirituality, and causes and effects.

Oman and Thoresen (2002) proposed a combination of four major causal pathways that could, in combination, explain the mental and physical health benefits of spiritual and religious factors: strong social and emotional support; health-enhancing behaviors (e.g., no or moderate drinking, not smoking); positive psychological states (e.g., faith, hope, inner peace, positive emotions); and subtle processes not yet understood scientifically (e.g., nonlocal processes, such that cognitions can be transmitted over long distances). Although contemporary science cannot at present assess some of these unidentified factors, it does not necessarily mean that they do not exit. The history of science is a story of phenomena that at one time were thought to be inconceivable, not to mention unmeasurable at the time, such as the proposition that earth revolves around the sun or that emotions are linked to certain areas of the brain or to the body's immune system.

If religious and spiritually minded people tend to live a healthier lifestyle, live more ethically, act more compassionately and forgivingly toward others and toward themselves, then they are more likely to have better psychological functioning that, in turn, could influence several physiological processes. Thus, the processes involved mutually enhance each other and other related processes. For example, engaging in daily spiritual meditation can lead to more social support and less depression which, in turn, can foster more spiritual fellowship, as well as more optimistic thoughts and expectations. All of these may impact several major organ systems of the body (e.g., immune competence, cardiovascular functioning, and metabolism) and may also, for example, impact left prefrontal cortical processes related to more positive self-perceptions, wiser decisions and judgments, and a richer consciousness.

Methodological Concerns

Conducting well-controlled studies, such as randomized experiments or prospective longitudinal studies, to examine important research and clinical questions has always been challenging. This is especially true in examining the influence of religion and spirituality on mental, social, and physical health. Researchers, for example, obviously cannot randomly assign people to different religious and nonreligious groups and then examine health outcomes. Researchers are, of course, not permitted to coerce people to engage in randomly assigned religious activities, prayer, or meditation, or to attend religious services. Therefore, most research in this area to date has been limited to correlational designs, including nonexperimental or quasi-experimental designs that do not randomize participants to different groups.

However, many important problems related to human health and well-being have been successfully studied without having to randomize some participants to the hypothesized disease condition. For example, decades of successful research in the health effects of tobacco on health did not require randomizing participants to become smokers for several years, nor has successful research on the causes and processes of morbid obesity required randomizing normal weight participants to become clinically obese over time. Science clarifies causality by gathering and critically examining patterns of evidence from a variety of sources and settings over time. There is no one best scientific method used in understanding complex human experience, such as the health effects of spiritual or religious practices, that can unequivocally establish causality. Instead, there are a variety of research designs using a variety of data and analytic techniques, depending on the specific topic, that can shed light on the role of spiritual and religious factors in health. Clearly, the almost exclusive use of self-report questionnaires or inventories is inadequate for many topics in spirituality and religion (Hill & Pargament, 2003; Oman & Thoresen, 2002). Studies need to also include behavioral observation data, for example, along with assessments of physiological markers indicative of the issue or question being studied.

To illustrate, Ironson, Solomon, Balbin, O'Creirigh, George et al. (2002) demonstrated that a comprehensive spiritual and religious self-report measure failed to directly predict mortality in HIV/AIDS patients. Instead the relationship was mediated by reduced cortisol, which in turn predicted less mortality. In the same way, the behavior of helping others significantly mediated the relationship between overall spirituality and mortality. Such studies highlight an important point cited earlier: The spirituality and religion connection with all-cause mortality exists because of several health-related factors that mediate the relationship, rather than having an independent, direct influence (Oman & Thoresen, 2002; Thoresen, Oman, & Harris, 2005).

Most studies to date have focused on questions as to whether religious people or those actively engaged in spiritual and religious practices tend to benefit overall from better mental and physical health when compared to those not engaging in spiritual and religious behaviors. This kind of correlational research is clearly worthwhile, especially longitudinal studies that assess participants more than once over time (often called *prospective designs*). However, correlational evidence has important limitations in trying to pin down possible causes of observed change, such as improved health. Well-designed prospective studies, sometimes with relatively small prospective samples ($n = 25–50$), can nevertheless shed valuable light on identifying possible causes. For example, the fascinating finding of a small study of participants' daily ratings for 1 month of how effective their spiritual coping was in reducing chronic pain that day turned out to be the most powerful predictor of actual pain experienced the very next day (Keefe et al., 2001). Such evidence encourages consideration of why this happened and how spiritual coping could be linked to reduced pain. One possibility is that reduced pain from a spiritual coping practice, such as using a short *mantram* (a short sacred word or phrase often repeated during the day), could alter the person's perception of his or her perceived competence (self-efficacy) to manage pain.

The Down Side of Religion and Health Outcomes

Are there mental and physical health hazards to health and well-being associated with religion and spirituality? The answer is yes (Pargament, 2007). For some, the policies and practices of organized religion, including the actions of religious professionals (e.g., pastors, priests, nuns, rabbis), have at times been harmful, if not devastating, to a person's or a group's health and well-being. Historically, over hundreds of years, grave abuses were authorized and sometimes implemented by religious authorities based upon a variety of reasons and doctrines. Some have noted that, even today, abuses associated with religion continue to happen (e.g., Hitchens, 2007; Plante, 2004).

One area of hazards to health associated with religion encompasses those experiencing religious struggles; that is, when a person perceives that he or she is being punished or abandoned by God in the face of a major trauma or by a perceived threat to one's existence. Although some religious beliefs and worldviews offer a greater sense of meaning, purpose, and direction in life along with sources of comfort and support, for others, certain beliefs and worldviews can create very serious problems and threats that endanger health. When a person struggles chronically with personal faith, doing so can lead to serious health problems, sometimes with fatal consequences.

For example, Edmondson, Park, Chaudoir, and Wortmann (2008) studied the negative impact of religious struggles in terminally ill heart failure patients suffering from their fear of death. Those struggling in terms of their religious beliefs were much more likely to suffer more serious depressive symptoms that were linked to their elevated fears of death. Such concerns were found to fully mediate the positive relationship of religious struggles and depression, which is serious mortality risk for those suffering from advanced cardiac diseases.

Religious involvement can be destructive to self, to others, and to the community. Tragically, religious beliefs have been used to wage war, oppress women, murder others who do not share the same religious beliefs and practices, and to instill guilt, depression, and anxiety among many. Religiousness can also be associated with harmful if not fatal health practices, such as the rejection on religious grounds to seek needed medical and psychiatric care. Religious beliefs and practices can and unfortunately continue to be used in certain areas of the world to justify, support, and enflame group conflicts as well. Curiously, religious conflicts about moral transgressions can be significant predictors of panic disorder (Trenholm, Trent, & Compton, 1998). Patients with HIV/AIDS can suffer poorer health if they hold a more rigid view of a punishing and judgmental of God, compared to a compassionate and forgiving view of God or an impersonal view of God or a higher power (Kremer & Ironson, 2007).

Clearly, empirical evidence exists that religion can be hazardous mentally and physically to health under certain circumstances. These negative effects unfortunately remain understudied and deserve more study using well-controlled research designs. Such designs need to be especially sensitive to assessing ongoing cognitive, social, and emotional experiences as well as specific contexts (e.g., time, place, others present, cultural factors, internal narratives in the setting). Methods are available to capture much of these phenomena, but seldom have been used. Tennen, Affleck, Armeli, and Carney (2000) offer, for example, useful research designs to study daily processes, such as very specific experiences. These could include specific ways to cope with distress, such as perceived spiritual support and daily spiritual self-efficacy perceptions. As mentioned, Keefe, Affleck, Lefebvre, Underwood, Caldwell et al. (2001) offer an excellent example of this kind of much-needed research.

Keep in mind that almost all of the world's major religions have urged people, for example, to avoid smoking, excessive drinking (or no use of alcohol), unsafe sexual practices, and to engage regularly in physical exercise and eat healthy foods. Although these health behaviors are vital to better health and to preventing disease, religious traditions also have long been focused on helping people cope or manage a broad variety of major and minor life stressors and distresses, which is associated with enhanced psychological functioning. These coping approaches have included optimism, positive emotions, compassion for self and others, forgiveness of others, and less anxiety, depression, and perceived stress (Plante & Thoresen, 2007).

Overall, research clearly supports the many mental, physical, and community health benefits for those who engage in spiritual and religious activities. It is likely that many spiritual and religious people generally lead lifestyles that are more health promoting and less health damaging than do those who are not actively religious or spiritual. Religions also have generally provided a variety of ways to offer social support through involvement in their faith communities, which helps people to cope with life's challenges and troubles. Finally, the focus on love, compassion, and serving others in need, along with the emphasis on ethical conduct linked to specific religious and spiritual beliefs and traditions, can have an effect of making the world a better place to live. This is especially true for the vast majority of people who live impoverished and marginalized lives. However, as discussed, there is evidence that involvement in some religious communities contributes to personal and social problems, such as anxiety, panic, obsessive compulsive symptoms, terrorism, and various forms of abuse, oppression, violence, and hatred. Typically, for most normal expressions of spiritual and religious beliefs and practices, positive mental and physical health benefits can be expected. We believe it is therefore reasonable for professionals to expect that spiritual and religious engagement could be useful, and to at least consider the role of spiritual and religious factors in an overall counseling treatment plan.

Above all, given the fact that a clear majority of Americans are religious or spiritually active, we believe that the counseling psychologist, as well as other psychologists, should at least initially broach the topic of religious and spiritual involvement with a client. But how would one do that in a way that would not be perceived as offensive or insensitive?

Barriers to Spirituality and Health Benefits in Counseling
The Public Is Religious, Psychologists Are Not

The vast majority of people in the United States and across the globe describe themselves as being spiritual, religious, or both. Most belong to a traditional faith community and are affiliated and identified with a major religious tradition. Others view themselves as spiritual but not being interested in organized religion. Most participate in regular, formalized religious services, celebrate religious holidays, and pray often or daily. In fact, over 95% of Americans report that they believe in God and 40% attend religious services once a week or more (Gallup & Lindsay, 1999). According to Gallup polls, most Americans are Christian, with 85% affiliated with either a Protestant (59%) or Catholic (26%) denomination. About 2% are Jewish, whereas Hindu, Muslim, and Buddhists together account for 3% of the population. Only 6% of Americans are not affiliated with any religious group (Gallup & Lindsay, 1999). More than 80% of Americans report that they wish to grow spiritually

(Myers, 2000). Thus, religion and spirituality is clearly an important component of life for most people.

By contrast, most psychologists are not spiritual or religious. Only 33% are affiliated with a religious tradition, only 72% report belief in God or higher power, and 51% report that religion is not important to them (Shafranske, 2000). Miller and Delaney (2005) poignantly observed that, in the 20th-century United States, of all the scientific, professional, or academic disciplines, psychology became by far one of least interested in religion and spirituality. Despite the work of some major psychologists of the 20th century (e.g., William James, Gordon Allport, and Carl Jung) on spirituality and religion, Miller and Delaney (2005) observed that, at best, "The modal response of psychologists to religion in research, practice, and training, however, became one of silence and neglect" (p. 4).

Recently, 68% of current training directors of clinical psychology internship programs state that they "never foresee religious/spiritual training being offered in their program" (Russell & Yarhouse, 2006, p. 434). Perhaps people who pursue a career as a psychologist are more secular and less religious or spiritual than the average person. Perhaps psychologists develop a "trained incapacity" in college or graduate school, such that they view religion as inherently antiscientific or spirituality as involving supernatural hocus-pocus. Shafranske (2000) suggested that most psychologists who bring this topic into their research or clinical practice do so because of a unique training experience, compared to anything systematic in their training program, or to their own personal faith commitment. Whatever the reason, the fact is that, although most people are religious, spiritual, or both, most psychologists studying or serving people are neither religious nor spiritual.

As noted, some of our famous and influential psychology forefathers, such as William James, Carl Jung, and Gordon Allport, wrote extensively about the relationship between psychology and religion (e.g., Allport, 1950; James, 1890, 1902/1936; Jung, 1938). Nevertheless, the topic of religious and spiritual beliefs, attitudes, and behavior has been largely ignored by psychological writers (Collins, 1977). Glancing through the subject index of any basic psychology text, for example, one seldom finds mention of religion or spirituality. Psychologists in the 20th century undoubtedly have been influenced by the perspectives of important leaders in the field, such as Sigmund Freud, B.F. Skinner, John Watson, and Albert Ellis. These leaders seldom had anything positive to say about religion or spirituality (e.g., Ellis, 1971; Freud, 1961; Watson, 1924/1983). For example, in *Future of an Illusion*, Freud referred to religion as an "obsessional neurosis" (Freud, 1961, p. 43). Watson referred to religion as a "bulwark of medievalism" (Watson, 1924/1983, p. 1). These and other leaders clearly implied that religious interest or concerns typically served as signs of pathology and not good health.

Psychology has long prided itself in working hard to be viewed as a rigorous, empirical, "hard science" discipline. Many psychologists appear to hold a dualistic if not stereotyped perception about religious and spiritual constructs; that is, if a construct is perceived as religious or spiritual, then it is viewed by definition as nonscientific or antiscientific. This dualistic attitude about anything religious or spiritual as antiscientific has been especially evident in the applied professional areas of psychology. For example, the recent efforts to focus on empirically supported and manualized treatments (Task Force on Promotion and Dissemination of Psychological Procedures, 1995), as well as more rigorous scientific approaches to psychological services are evidence for the continuing emphasis on science, which may have little if any interest in spiritual or religious issues.

A related issue concerns the secularization of traditional religious or spiritual practices used in interventions (e.g., procedures to manage distress, calm the body, or quiet the mind). Doing so may have been done, in part, to make them more acceptable to the professional community. For example, the field of positive psychology has categorized some topics as major *virtues* (e.g., humanity, wisdom, transcendence) and related subtopics as *specific character strengths* (e.g., love, gratitude, forgiveness). These topics have been secularized for the most part; that is, presented outside of any religious tradition or practice (see Seligman et al., 2005). The widely used mindfulness-based stress reduction (Kabit-Zinn, 1990; Shapiro & Walsh, 2007) also offers an example of secularizing of spiritual and religious practices (e.g., Buddhist meditation). Perhaps a secular approach was perceived as less controversial or more subject to empirical study than using a spiritual or religious approach.

A question worthy of attention, given that most clients or patients are religiously active and seeking greater spirituality in their lives, is to ask if spiritual practices, when secularized, have the same effectiveness as do those used within a spiritual or religious tradition. We know of few such studies.

One, however, is worthy of some detailed comment because it is based on a well-controlled randomized clinical trial design in an area lacking any such studies (Wachholtz & Pargament, 2008).

The study examined a spiritually focused meditation practice to reduce the frequency of long-term chronic migraine headaches compared with two highly similar meditations and a relaxation control procedure without any spiritual focus. Two questions were asked in the investigation: Is spiritual meditation more effective in enhancing pain tolerance and in reducing the frequency of migraine headaches over a 30-day period? Does spiritual meditation create better mental, physical, and spiritual health outcomes compared to secular meditation and relaxation techniques? Eighty-three headache sufferers were randomized to one of four conditions. One included the spiritual meditation group, in which each person selected among a list of spiritually focused meditations such as "God is love" or "God is peace." Participants in two other secular experimental groups (internal or external meditations) selected meditation statements, such as "I am joy" or "I am good" in the internal group or "Sand is soft" or "Grass is green" in the external group. Progressive muscle relaxation was used in the fourth comparison group.

After 30 consecutive days of 20-minute daily meditations, outcome results were impressive. Those in the spiritually focused experimental condition experienced significant reductions in headaches compared to modest reductions in the other three secular conditions. Reductions in pain tolerance (using the cold pressor task, in which participants place their hand in circulating freezing water until pain is too great to tolerate) were significant and dramatic as well. The baseline pain tolerance for all four groups was 45 seconds. The spiritual meditation group's pain tolerance rose to almost 2 minutes, whereas the other three groups showed either no change or modest gains up to only 20 seconds. Gains in spiritual measures, such as existential well-being and spiritual experiences, also favored the spiritual meditation group, as did reductions in trait anxiety and negative emotions.

The Wachholtz and Pargament (2008) intervention study suggests that the inclusion of a spiritual focus might enhance—if used in a sensitive, appropriate, and respectful manner—the effectiveness of psychological practices and interventions. Hopefully, other researchers will pursue this promising topic using appropriate research designs and assessments exemplified by these researchers.

Perhaps more problematic, if not destructive, is the fact that secular and nonreligious psychologists working with religiously oriented or spiritually minded clients often unwittingly preconceive or interpret their client's interest in spirituality and religion as a sign or symptom of pathology, delusion, or weakness. Or, a psychologist may be oblivious of how clients could draw upon their religious or spiritual beliefs or practices in trying to overcome problems. Are the interests of a client best served if a psychologist ignores completely anything in the spiritual and religious realm? Or, would a client be better served if a psychologist at least inquires about the client's interests and perceptions about spirituality and religion? We discuss this and other related questions later in this chapter.

Despite the long history of "silence and neglect" of spirituality and religion in modern psychology, in recent years, change has come. A greater recognition of the value of religious and spiritual concerns is under way, in psychology and in other social and behavioral sciences. This recognition seems greatest in health and disease, in which professional and public support is expanding (Hartz, 2005; Koenig et al., 2001). Many secular professional organizations, such as the Society of Behavioral Medicine, now offer special interest groups that focus on spirituality and health research and practice. Major organization such as the Templeton, Lilly, and Fetzer foundations, as well as government granting agencies such as the National Institute of Health (NIH), have also funded large research projects in this area.

The American Psychological Association (APA) has embraced these changes as well. For example, the 1999 National Multicultural Conference and Summit sponsored by the APA stated: "spirituality is a necessary condition for a psychology of human existence" and that "people are cultural and spiritual beings" (Sue, Bingham, Porche-Burke, &Vasquez, 1999, p. 1065). The ethics code for psychologists states: "Psychologists are aware of and respect cultural, individual, and role differences, including those based on age, gender, gender identity, race, ethnicity, culture, national origin, religion, sexual orientation, disability, language, and socioeconomic status and consider these factors when working with members of such groups" (APA, 2002, p. 1064). Thus, being "aware of and respect(ful)" of religious issues is now demanded by the ethics code. Finally, the APA has itself published a dozen books on psychology, spirituality and religion during the past 10 years, when previously it offered almost none.

Psychology Can Learn from Religion and Spirituality

Psychology as a scientific discipline has been around for a little more than 100 years, whereas religion and spirituality have been around for thousands of years. Perhaps psychology could learn something from its older cousin. After all, the goal of counseling and psychological services is, in part, about developing healthier strategies for living and better ways of coping with many stressful life events. Counseling seeks to help people manage their lives in a more thoughtful, significant, and healthy way. Since spiritual and religious traditions have long offered wise council on these issues for thousands of years, perhaps the counseling community could learn a few things from the collective wisdom of these faith traditions. We believe that one needs to at least consider carefully and respectfully ways to incorporate some spiritual concepts and practices into the scientific and professional work of psychology.

What concepts or practices might be considered? Some possibilities include the following: Focusing on forgiveness (self, situations, others), promoting greater acceptance of others as well as self-acceptance, using significant rituals, providing group and community support (i.e., physically, socially, emotionally, and materially), emphasizing selfless love, encouraging kindness, and volunteering regularly to serve others in need. At a broader level, the concept of learning to perceive oneself as a part of something much larger than just oneself (i.e., less egoistic) seems significant, as does the concept of enhancing a greater sense of meaning and purpose in life. Note that these and others topics have been thoughtfully considered in many ways in all of the major religious and spiritual wisdom traditions over thousands of years (Armstrong, 2006; Smith, 1991).

The field of psychology has indeed matured as an independent and international discipline, offering rigorous scientific inquiry with state-of-the-art methodologies and statistics to study many human issues, some quite challenging. The many complexities of human perception and judgment, for example, continue to be better understood by using more sophisticated concepts and methods. The study of personality is another complex, multidimensional, if not multilevel topic. The field of psychology deals with complex and challenging concepts, and it is capable of sustained commitment when dealing with the complexities of spiritual and religious concepts as they relate to health and well-being (Miller & Delaney, 2005).

Although relatively few psychologists, with the exception of those in Division 36 (Society for the Psychology of Religion and Spirituality), have studied religion or spirituality, noticeably more are now starting to do so, thus helping to expand the scope and depth of inquiry. Psychology as a discipline can and will benefit from the challenge of trying to better understand, especially empirically, the number of religious and spiritual constructs and practices involved. Psychology as a behavioral and social science discipline is known for its primary focus on the individual and the many differences within and among individuals. Spirituality is eminently personal and individual as well as experiential. It works within each person at various levels of conscious personal experiences, seasoned by a range of beliefs, emotions, and behaviors across time (past, present moment, future). Religions were created by people in part to help individuals within a perceived community deal with issues of making life more meaningful, gaining a greater sense of purpose and direction, such as how to live a "good life." Building and sustaining communities of faith that provide support for living a values-centered life is what religions seek to do. How successful they are in doing so is another issue.

As psychologists, we need to be more attentive to the broad range of diversity issues that individuals represent, such as religious and spiritual beliefs and practices. Since the APA ethics code (2002) mandates that psychologists be respectful and mindful of cultural diversity that includes religious traditions and beliefs, psychologists should not ignore or automatically pathologize religious and spiritual issues among their clients and students.

Implementing Spiritually Oriented Interventions:
What the Religious and Spiritual Traditions Offer the Counselor

Given the fact that religion and spirituality may offer many mental and physical health benefits, how might professional counselors use the research findings to enhance their clinical activities with clients? First, let us briefly introduce two important steps in ways to think about what the religious and spiritual traditions offer the professional counselor.

In the now classic book, *The World's Religions* (Smith, 1991), Huston Smith well articulates an ancient view that the world's great religions are much more similar than different. He refers to the Hindu notion that the "various religions are but different languages through which God speaks to the human heart" (p. 73). Quoting Rig-Veda (4,000 BCE), the often-quoted Hindu sage states, "Truth is one; sages call it by different names" (p. 73).

Smith provides an illustration of how to understand the world's religions that we believe can be helpful to use. He states: "It is possible to climb life's mountain from any side, when the top is reached the trails converge. At base, in the foothills of theology, ritual, and organizational structure, the religions are distinct. Differences in culture, history, geography, and collective temperament all make for diverse starting points" (p. 73). He then describes that, as we move higher, toward the top of the mountain, the world's religious traditions become one path seeking truth stating, "But beyond these differences, the same goal beckons" (p. 73). He quotes Sri Ramakrishna, a 19th-century Hindu teacher, who said, "God has made different religions to suit different aspirations, times, and countries. All doctrines are only so many paths; but a path is by no means God Himself. Indeed, one can reach God if one follows any of the paths with whole-hearted devotion. One may eat a cake with icing either straight or sideways. It all tastes sweet either way" (p. 74). At their best and most thoughtful, the religious traditions converge together and ultimately are saying much the same thing, using different languages, customs, and traditions.

Concepts from all of the major contemporary religious traditions, as well as from Greek philosophical rationalism, can be traced to the ninth century BCE, during the Axial age in four different regions of the then civilized world (Armstrong, 2006). They all struggled with similar questions and came to similar conclusions about religious, ethical, and social views. This includes "the spirit of compassion . . . lies at the core of all our traditions" (Armstrong, 2006, p. 476). However, all of the religious traditions have "fallen prey to exclusivity, cruelty, superstition, and even atrocity. But at their core, the Axial faiths share an ideal of sympathy, respect, and universal concern" (Armstrong, 2006, p. 466). The "Golden Rule," or treating others as you would like to be treated, is the main point and is well articulated in the sacred texts of all of the religious traditions (Armstrong, 2006; Pargament, 2007; Peterson, 1986). In fact, Armstrong states that the Axial sages concluded that "religion *was* the Golden Rule" (Armstrong, 2006, p. 468).

Some Spiritual Principles and Tools for the Counselor

What do religious traditions at their best offer the psychological community? At the top of the metaphorical mountain where the traditions converge, a number of highly desirable and useful principles and values are beneficial. These include a focus on the sacredness of life and of the world, ethical behavior toward others, prayer and meditation, community and service involvement, and love and respect for all. Many also conveyed the notion that God, while existing in many forms and settings, could be found within every person, regardless of their status and gender, as well as in other life and inanimate forms. The task of the person, however, was to use spiritual practices to access this divine presence within. The religious traditions emerging from the Axial age all emphasized compassion toward oneself and all others. These values and principles can be helpful to many, regardless of their particular religious traditions or affiliations, including those with no interest in any religious traditions or beliefs.

The variety of empirically supported treatment programs and protocols now available can integrate spiritual and religious tools and perspectives in services offered by psychologists and other mental health professionals. Alcoholics Anonymous (AA) is perhaps the oldest and best known self-help and peer-led program to integrate spiritual and religious perspectives in its program (Alcoholic Anonymous World Services, 1977). Of course, AA is not an empirically supported treatment program administered by mental health professionals. However, the program well illustrates the popular integration of spirituality into self-help services for alcohol and other addictions. In recent years, professionally developed empirically supported treatments have been developed and tested that integrate spiritual and religious principles in professionally administered treatment services. This includes interventions for substance abuse, eating disorders, and marital discord to name a few, and these interventions have used bibliotherapy, meditation, forgiveness training, and other spiritually and religiously based interventions with roots in all of the major religious traditions. In addition to mental health and relationship problems, interventions have also been developed to help those coping with a number of medical disorders as well, such as HIV/AIDS and coronary heart disease. A list of empirically supported treatment interventions that integrate spiritual and religious principles and tools, along with

Table 23.1. Examples of Empirically Supported Spiritual/Religious Interventions for Counseling

Name of Intervention Program	Author Reference
Opening Your Heart (Coronary heart disease and prevention)	Ornish, 1990
Christian Marriage Counseling	Worthington, 1990
Becoming a more Forgiving Christian	Worthington, 2004
Coping with Divorce	Rye and Pargament, 2003
Solace for the Soul	Murray-Swank and Pargament, 2005
Lighting the Way	Pargament, McCarthy, Shah, Anon, Tarakeshwar, et al., 2004
(Group treatment for women with HIV/AIDS)	
Spiritual Renewal (Eating disorders)	Richards, Hardman, and Berrett, 2000
Re-Creating your Life (Group treatment for serious mental illness)	Cole & Pargament, 1998
From Vice to Virtue	Ano, 2005
Eight Point Spiritual Skills Program	Easwaran, 1991
Mindfulness Meditation	Kabat-Zinn, 2003
Mantram Training	Bormann, Gifford, Shively, Smith, Redwine, et al., 2006
REACH Model for Forgiveness	Worthington, 2004

an appropriate reference for further information, is provided in Table 23.1.

Caregiving of Health Professionals: A Spiritual Practices Example

How might a practicing psychologist or other health professional use spiritual practices in a work setting? We use the example of a large Denver hospital that was seeking help to reduce perceived stress of staff and foster better care of patients and their families (Oman, Hedberg, & Thoresen, 2006). A physician connected with the hospital suggested that a comprehensive, spiritually based, nonsectarian program called the Eight Point Program (EPP) could be used

---

Box 23.1. Brief Description of Eight Point Program (EPP) of Easwaran (1991/1978)

1. Passage Meditation: Silent repetition in the mind of memorized inspirational passages from the world's great religions, such as the 23rd psalm, the Prayer of Saint Francis, or the Discourse on Good Will of the Buddha's *Sutta Nipata*. Practiced for one-half hour each morning.

2. Repetition of a Holy Word or Mantram: Silent repetition at times other than meditation of a single chosen Holy Name, hallowed phrase, or mantram from a major religious tradition.

3. Slowing Down: Setting priorities and reducing the stress and friction caused by hurry.

4. Focused/One-pointed Attention: Giving full concentration to the matter at hand.

5. Training the Senses: Overcoming conditioned habits and learning to enjoy what is beneficial.

6. Putting Others First: Gaining freedom from selfishness and separateness; finding joy in helping others.

7. Spiritual Association: Spending time regularly with others following the Eight Point Program (EPP) for mutual inspiration and support.

8. Inspirational Reading: Drawing inspiration from writings by and about the world's great spiritual figures and from the scriptures of all religions.

(Easwaran, 1991/1978; Flinders, Oman, & Flinders, 2007). Box 23.1 lists a brief description of each spiritual practice, drawn from the wisdom traditions spanning all major religions. See also an introductory primer that provides case material and narratives focusing on using the mantram, slowing down, and one-pointed attention to reduce worries, foster inner peace, and encourage kindness (Easwaran, 2005).

Working with a psychologist and other health professionals this physician, with others assisting, conducted eight weekly 2-hour sessions on the EPP for 29 professionals, with another 30 randomized to a wait group condition. A variety of assessments were conducted just before the weekly group started, at the end and at 8-week and 19-week follow-ups, spanning almost 6 months. Over 90% remained active in the study, and attendance at weekly sessions was above 85%.

Briefly, participants were mostly female (86%), had at least 5 years of full-time work experience, identified themselves as "spiritual but not religious" (50%) or "spiritual and religious" (45%), or neither (5%). Of all, 77% stated that they were very or moderately spiritual. Very few stated they were "very religious." Each session focused on one or more of the eight points, with initial attention on what is termed "passage meditation," use of the mantram, slowing down, and being more one-pointed in attention.

Results were encouraging. First, the reductions in perceived stress were impressive and were maintained through the last follow-up (roughly 6 months). Effect sizes were significant at post-treatment and at follow-ups: −0.63, −1.00, and −0.84, respectively. Translated into levels (%) for this measure in national populations samples, baseline scores for these health professionals were in the high-stress range (above 80%), whereas the immediate post-treatment score dropped to 50% or average stress level. The two follow-up levels stayed below 50%.

In addition, the Caregiving Self-Efficacy Scale (32 items tapping the perceived confidence level to do something successfully, such as "Control my temper with patients," "Help families of patients to deal with the death of patients," and "Sense the needs of other coworkers [so I can help them without being asked]") was used. Encouraging effect sizes were found in the moderately strong range (0.48, 0.59, 0.47). Improvements in other mental health indicators were less significant, but all in the desired direction. Importantly, no evidence emerged that practicing the specific eight points from a spiritual perspective was associated with any kind of negative effect on health and well-being (see Oman, Richards, Hedberg, & Thoresen, (2008) for detailed information on a qualitative, structured interview narrative study that offers some confirmation of the results cited above).

Conducting a Spiritual Inquiry in the Initial Interview

Recently, a team of psychologists, working with others, developed a simple, short, yet sensitive and respectful way to conduct a spiritual inquiry. Jean Kristeller, working with a team that included physicians, learned from survey data that a majority of physicians believed that a patient's spirituality could be important in understanding the patient's health status, but that in fact physicians seldom (less than 10%) brought the topic up with patients. When asked why, physicians often mentioned that they were unsure how to do so and did not want to be seen as imposing upon the patient's privacy. Kristeller and others developed a standardized brief protocol called the *patient-centered spirituality* protocol that could be routinely used by physicians (Kristeller, Rhodes, Cripe, & Sheets, 2005). They conducted a controlled study with 118 oncology patients to assess the effect of using this protocol with oncology patients. Patients were alternately assigned to intake with a brief spiritual inquiry group included or the usual intake interview group. Most patients were Caucasian, 55% were women with mixed diagnoses, and 81% identified themselves as being Christian in background.

Assessments of mental health factors plus patient and physician ratings of the interview were conducted just before the initial interview and 3 weeks later. Physicians rated themselves comfortable with inquiry with 85% of patients, and 76% of patients felt inquiry was somewhat or very useful. At 3-week follow-up, patients in the spiritual inquiry group showed significant improvements compared to the comparison group (at least $p < .05$) in quality of life, spiritual well-being, and perceived sense of interpersonal caring by their physician. The major steps in this protocol are as follows (with some of the suggested words used by the health professional in quotes):

1. Introduce the issue in neutral inquiring manner.

> "When dealing with this problem, many people draw on religious or spiritual beliefs to help cope with it. It would be helpful to me to know how you feel about this."

2. Inquire further, adjusting inquiry to client's initial response. If it is a:

> a. Positive-active faith response: "What have you found most helpful about your beliefs since this problem came up?"
> b. Neutral-receptive response: "How might you draw on your faith or spiritual beliefs to help you?"
> c. Spiritually-distressed response: (e.g., anger or guilt): "Many people feel that way . . . what might help you come to terms with this?"
> d. Defensive-rejecting response: "It sounds like you're uncomfortable I brought this up. What I'm really interested in is how you are coping . . . can you tell me about that?"

3. Continue to explore further as indicated:

> "I see. Can you tell me more (about . . .)?"

4. Inquire about ways of finding meaning and a sense of peace:

> "Is there some way in which you are able to find a sense of meaning or peace in the midst of this?

5. Inquire about resources.

"Whom do you have to talk to about this/these concerns?"

6. Offer assistance as appropriate and available.

"Perhaps we can arrange for you to talk to someone . . . there's a support group."

7. Bring inquiry to a close.

"I appreciate you discussing these issues with me. May I ask about it again?"

Obviously the wording would need to be modified to fit the specific mental or physical health problem (e.g., posttraumatic stress disorder, marital conflict, leadership management issues), but the general format can provide a structure that could be taught in graduate training programs and also used by practicing psychologists with some brief training. Doing so could help the client, and could also help psychologists fill the mandate of honoring the spiritual and religious diversity of their clients.

Plante (2009) outlined 13 spiritual and religious tools useful for counselors to have in their therapeutic toolbox, regardless of their interest or lack of interest in specific religious faith traditions. These include meditation; prayer; seeking a sense of vocation, meaning, purpose, and calling in life; bibliotherapy, including sacred scripture reading; attending community services, ceremonies, and rituals; volunteering and charitable works and service; ethical values and behavior with others; approaching others with forgiveness, gratitude, love, kindness, and compassion; engaging in social justice issues; learning from spiritual models; accepting oneself and others (even with faults); being part of something larger than yourself; and understanding the sacredness of life. Some of these tools are likely to be appropriate and helpful with particular clients and counselors, whereas others are not. We believe these tools can add value to the effectiveness of professional services and research offered by counseling and other psychologists involved in health care.

Conclusion
Future Directions
Religious and spiritual wisdom traditions have evolved over thousands of years. A careful reading of the history and development of these traditions indicates that all have grappled with much the same theological and philosophical issues. Wisdom traditions also offer guidance in how to live a more satisfying, happy, and meaningful life, one based on a foundation of knowing and understanding perennial human virtues and character strengths (Armstrong, 2006; Oman, Flinders & Thoresen, 2008). These traditions offer advice about learning how to discover the sacred in life and make specific suggestions about building and maintaining intimate relationships with others, including a transcendent relationship with a power or spirit greater than oneself, sometimes called God. Ways to manage major and minor stressful life events have also been recommended in dealing with common problems in the contexts of marriage, family, work, and community.

Although the wisdom accumulated in religious traditions may use different languages, customs, beliefs, and rituals about life's perennial questions, they have reached very similar conclusions over thousands of years. "When religions [traditions] are sifted for their best qualities," wrote Huston Smith (1991), the eminent scholar of the world's major religions, "they begin to look like data banks that house the winnowed wisdom of the human race" (p. 5). Undoubtedly, as human institutions, organized religions have also been a source of hatred, fear, violence, deprivation, and hypocrisy. At times, certain religious policies and practices have contradicted the essence of spirituality and the sacred, such as love, hope, and compassion. We need, however, to look beyond specific cultural differences and the dogma that goes along with very questionable practices to acknowledge and seek what religions offer at their best.

Every major religion, for example, offers life stories—in effect spiritual models—that convey admirable human qualities and character strengths (e.g., Jesus, Buddha, Gandhi, Moses, Mother Teresa). These traditions and historical spiritual exemplars also have been used to illustrate how persons faced with great challenges were able to deal with them by using spiritual practices and perspectives. We can learn from spiritual exemplars, regardless of the status of our own spiritual and religious affiliation, beliefs, and practices ("Spirituality is caught more than taught").

Empirical evidence clearly supports the view that people actively engaged in spiritual or religious activities on average are physically, socially, and mentally far better off than those seldom or not engaged. This robust empirical relationship between active involvement and health, as noted earlier, does not demonstrate that a direct and specific cause-and-effect relationship exists (e.g., that religion directly causes better health). Rather, what has been demonstrated is that a consistent relationship exists of the benefits of active spiritual and religious involvement for most people. Studies also suggest that clients prefer to have their religious and spiritual issues and traditions at least acknowledged and possibly integrated into their professional health care services.

As noted, the great wisdom traditions provide a variety of useful tools and practices used over more than three millennia. These can be employed by the competent and interested psychologist. Importantly, many of these practices can be used in a secular manner, depending on particular circumstances. For example, mindfulness-based stress reduction has been often used in secular settings, yet has roots in a particular religious tradition (Tibetan Buddhism). Although clients are not required to be religious or spiritually active to benefit from the tools derived from religious traditions, it remains unclear if use of a completely secularized practice is more or less effective than when used in a more spiritually or religiously framed manner (Wachholtz & Pargament, 2007).

Religious and spiritual beliefs and practices clearly can be harmful and hazardous to overall health. Frankly, this topic has been seldom examined rigorously, and with the needed sensitivity. Candid and comprehensive examinations of possible negative effects merit using rigorous empirical methods, and the collaboration of professional colleagues is needed in such areas such as specific religious beliefs and spiritual practices (Thoresen, Oman, & Harris, 2005).

Most people report that they are religious, spiritual, or both. Some, such as Vaillant (2008) discussed earlier believe that all humans are by nature spiritual but not religious due to cultural factors. Overall, a clear majority of people in the United States are affiliated with a religious tradition, believe in God (however defined), and pray regularly. Roughly 40% of Americans attend spiritual or religious ceremonies, services, or rituals weekly or more often. By contrast, in Northern European cultures, only a clear minority are actively religious. Interestingly, a clear majority of mental health professionals in the United States and in European cultures are not active religiously or spiritually, nor do they identify with a particular religious tradition. Furthermore, although there has been considerable focus on cultural diversity in recent years, the vast majority of graduate training programs in the mental health professions continue to ignore religious and spiritual issues, offering no instruction or training on religious diversity. The APA ethics guidelines (and other codes) in the mental health disciplines now require attention, training, and respect for religious diversity. Since a majority of clients studied and served by psychologists and other health professionals are religiously engaged and spiritually focused, we believe that it makes good professional and clinical sense for counseling psychologists and other health professionals to at least understand the role of spiritual and religious factors.

The field of counseling psychology has long history within the discipline of psychology as a specialty devoted to understanding and serving those dealing with life's inevitable "normal" problems, compared to those with severe mental, physical, or social health problems. How can the field of counseling psychology capitalize on the collective wisdom of the world's major religions discussed earlier? Much of this wisdom relates to fundamental issues of character, conduct, and consciousness. Recently, the terms *virtues* and *character strengths* have been essentially reintroduced to psychology by the positive psychology movement (e.g., Seligman et al., 2005; Snyder & Lopez, 2007). As noted earlier, these virtues (e.g., humanity, temperance, and transcendence) each involve several character strengths (e.g., humanity includes love, kindness, leadership; temperance includes forgiveness, humility, self-regulation; and transcendence includes gratitude, hope, and humor). Most would view these character strengths as important if not essential personal and social qualities.

How do people learn to be virtuous and to honor a character in their daily lives that displays such strengths as forgiveness, humility, and gratitude in their thoughts and actions? We believe that an important future direction for counseling psychology lies in focusing more on virtues and character strengths, given that many can benefit from acquiring these virtues and strengths: the person, the family, the community, and in effect, all on earth. Recent work in spiritual modeling, drawing on social cognitive theory and the distilled wisdom of all major religious traditions, offers an empirically based strategy to help people learn spiritual skills and practices that can enhance health in its broadest sense (Bandura, 2003; Oman & Thoresen, 2003, 2005).

Four important future directions for work in this area of spirituality and religion strike us as timely, in the sense of clarifying some major issues:

• Exploring the growing trend in American as well as other cultures of those who perceive themselves as "spiritual but not religious"
• Studying relationships among social, mental, and physical factors among those who are more

spiritually or religiously active compared to those less or not active.

• Identifying and understanding possible mediating factors that may help explain how a spiritual or religious factor may play a causal role in one's overall health status. Possible mediators include various forms of meditation, volunteering to serve others, attending religious or spiritual services weekly or more often, and experiencing positive social emotions.

• Consider further the evolutionary evidence that spirituality is inherently linked to positive emotions, suggesting that humans are by nature spiritual, but may need certain cultural experiences to express their spirituality in positive, prosocial ways.

We currently know little about that segment of the population who identify themselves as only spiritual. As indicated earlier, studies have found sizable numbers (from 15% to 30%) were identified as spiritual but not religious. In what ways is this group a mix of several subgroups, characterized by such factors as age, gender, socioeconomic status, educational level, ethnic identity, and geographical region? Are there significant differences among spiritual but not religious compared to other subgroups (e.g., religious only or spiritual and religious) when it comes to health? What does it mean in terms of attitudes, beliefs, and actions for someone who describes herself as spiritual but not religious? What difference exits, if any, in the kind of problems persons present for counseling services if identified as spiritual only or religious only or both or neither?

Few, if any, studies have documented the relationships among those who are very active spiritually and those less or not active in terms of physical, mental, and social health problems. Typically, studies have seldom used a variety of assessments other than survey questions; different modes of assessment (interviews, structured diaries, daily behavior ratings, ambulatory electronically based devices) are rarely used. Assessment of an individual's spiritual beliefs and practices has been usually based on one short questionnaire, and seldom have an individual's experience of what is sacred in their lives been assessed. Little has been done to gather a person's "narrative identity" with a focus on spiritual experiences, as discussed by McAdams (2006). Interviews can provide data that speaks more deeply to a person's spiritually related experiences, especially if gathered on more than one occasion. Rather than using only interviews or only surveys, using both can provide confirming evidence that survey questions could never reveal. See the Oman, Richards, Hedberg, and Thoresen (2008) study for an example of using repeated interviews to complement a variety of survey measures used on four occasions in a hospital-based spiritual intervention with health professionals.

How might a spiritual practice, such as frequent attendance at religious or spiritual services, play a causal role in reducing stress or mortality? Recall that this attendance and mortality relationship offers to date the strongest empirical evidence in the United States that spirituality and religion may enhance health in most people (Miller & Thoresen, 2003). This question reveals the impressive complexities of factors at play in seeking answers. For example, what is there about attending services that "gets under the skin" in ways that alter, at some points in time, the physiological processes that lead eventually to death? Such a question speaks to the search for mediators, factors that help explain what can be called indirect causes of an outcome, such as the connection between attendance and mortality. To date, several possible answers have been suggested involving lifestyle issues, such as health behaviors (e.g., less smoking, less high-risk behaviors), beliefs, perceptions, and emotions (e.g., believe in something greater than oneself, sense of meaning and significance), community/social and spiritual support (e.g., emotional support from congregation), and possible processes not assessable by current scientific methods. Counseling psychologists and other health professionals can help clients understand that a number of factors are at work that will help mediate the solutions to their problems. Spiritual practices and perspectives can be good candidates to serve as mediators in helping clients work out solutions to their problems of living.

As long as counseling psychologists and other health professionals are open-minded, well-trained, have access to appropriate consultation, and closely monitor ethical issues with competence, respect, integrity, and responsibility in mind, they can learn a great deal from spiritual and religious wisdom traditions. In doing so, their clients can benefit greatly as well.

References

Allport, G. W. (1950). *The individual and his religion: A psychological interpretation.* New York: Macmillan.

American Psychological Association (APA). (2002). Ethical principles of psychologists and code of conduct. *American Psychologist, 57,* 1060–1073.

American Psychological Association (APA). (2003). Guidelines on multicultural education, training, research, practice, and organizational change for psychologists. *American Psychologist*, *58*, 377–402.

Ano, G. A. (2005). *Spiritual struggles between vice and virtue: A brief psychospiritual intervention*. Unpublished doctoral dissertation, Bowling Green State University, Bowling Green, OH.

Armstrong, K. (1993). *A history of God: The 4,000 year quest of Judaism, Christianity, and Islam*. New York: Gramercy.

Armstrong, K. (2006). *The great transformation: The beginning of our religious traditions*. New York: Anchor Books.

Association of American Medical Colleges. (1999). *Report III: Contemporary issues in medicine: Communication in medicine, medical school objectives project*. Washington, DC: Association of American Medical Colleges. Retrieved August, 2007, from http://www.aamc.org/meded/msop/report3.htmtask.

Astin, A. W., Astin, H. S., Lindholm, J. A., Bryant, A. N., Calderone, S., & Szelenyi, K. (2005). *The spiritual life of college students: A national study of college students' search for meaning and purpose*. Los Angeles: Higher Education Research Institute, University of California. Retrieved from http://spirituality.ucla.edu/reports/index.html.

Balter, M. (2005). Are human brains still evolving? Brain genes show signs of selection. *Science*, *309*, 1662–1663.

Bandura, A. (2003). On the psychosocial impact and mechanisms of spiritual modeling. *The International Journal for the Psychology of Religion*, *13*, 167–174.

Bormann, J. E., Gifford, A. L., Shively, M., Smith, T. L., Redwine, L., Kelly, A., et al. (2006). Effects of spiritual mantram repetition on HIV outcomes: A randomized controlled trial. *Journal of Behavioral Medicine*, *29*, 359–376.

Brooks, D. (2009, April 7). The end of philosophy. *New York Times*, A23.

Centers for Disease Control. (2004). *National vital statistics report*. Washington, DC: Author.

Cole, B. S., & Pargament, K. I. (1998). Re-creating your life: A spiritual/psychotherapeutic intervention for people diagnosed with cancer. *Psycho-Oncology*, *8*, 395–407.

Collins, G. R. (1977). *The rebuilding of psychology: An integration of psychology and Christianity*. Wheaton, IL: Tyndale House.

Dali Lama, Ekman, P. (2008). *Emotional awareness: Overcoming the obstacles to psychological balance and compassion*. New York: Times Books.

Damasio, A. (1994). *Descartes' error*. New York: Penguin.

Easwaran, E. (1991/1978). *Meditation: A simple eight-point program for translating spiritual ideals into daily life*. Tomales, CA: Nilgiri Press. Retrieved from http://www.easwaran.org.

Easwaran, E. (2005). *Strength in the storm: Creating calm in difficult times*. Tomales, CA: Nilgiri Press.

Edmondson, D., Park, C. L., Chaudoir, S. R., & Wortmann, J. H. (2008). Death without God: Religious struggle, death concerns, and depression in the terminally ill. *Psychological Science*, *19*, 754–758.

Ellis, A. (1971). *The case against religion: A psychotherapist's view*. New York: Institute for Rational Living.

Emmons, R. A., & McCullough, M. E. (2003). Counting blessings versus burdens: Experimental studies of gratitude and subjective well-being. *Journal of Personality and Social Psychology*, *84*, 377–389.

Emmons, R. A., & Paloutzian, R. F. (2003). The psychology of religion. *Annual Review of Psychology*, *54*, 377–402.

Flinders, T., Oman, D., & Flinders, C. L. (2007). The eight-point program of passage meditation: Health effects of a comprehensive program. In T. G. Plante, & C. E. Thoresen (Eds.), *Spirit, science, and health: How the spiritual mind fuels physical wellness* (pp. 72–93). Westport, CT: Praeger/Greenwood.

Fredrickson, B. (2009). *Positivity*. New York: Random House.

Freud, S. (1961). *The future of an illusion* (J. Strachey, Ed. & Trans.). New York: Norton. (Original work published 1927 by Doubleday).

Fuller, R. C. (2001). *Spiritual but not religious*. New York: Oxford University Press.

Gallup, G., Jr., & Lindsay, D. M. (1999). *Surveying the religious landscape: Trends in U.S. beliefs*. Harrisburg, PA: Morehouse.

Hage, S. M. (2006). A closer look at the role of spirituality in psychology training. *Professional Psychology: Research and Practice*, *37*, 303–310.

Harris, A. H. S., & Thoresen, C. E. (2005). Volunteering is associated with delayed mortality in older people: Analysis of the longitudinal study of aging. *Journal of Health Psychology*, *10*, 739–752.

Hartz, G. W. (2005). *Spirituality and mental health: Clinical applications*. Binghamton, NY: Haworth Pastoral Press.

Hill, P., & Pargament, K. I. (2003). Advances in the conceptualization and measurement of religion and spirituality. *American Psychologist*, *58*, 64–74.

Hitchens, C. (2007). *God is not great: How religion poisons everything*. New York: Twelve Books.

Hood, R. W., Jr. (2005). Mystical, spiritual, and religious experiences. In R. F. Paloutzian, & C. L. Park (Eds.), *Handbook of the psychology of religion and spirituality* (pp. 348–364). New York: Guilford.

Hummer, R. A., Rogers, R. G., Nam, C. B., & Ellison, C. G. (1999). Religious involvement and U.S. adult mortality. *Demography*, *36*, 272–285.

Ironson, G., Solomon, G. F., Balbin, E. G., O'Cleirigh, C., George, A., & Kumar, M., et al. (2002). The Ironson-Woods Spirituality/Religiousness Index is associated with long survival, health behaviors, less distress, and low cortisol in people with HIV/AIDS. *Annals of Behavioral Medicine*, *24*, 34–48.

James, W. (1890). *Principles of psychology*. New York: Holt.

James, W. (1936). *The varieties of religious experience: A study in human nature*. New York: Modern Library. (Original work published 1902).

Jung, C. G. (1938). *Psychology and religion*. New Haven, CT: Yale University Press.

Kabat-Zinn, J. (1990). *Full catastrophe living*. New York: Delacourte Press.

Kabat-Zinn, J. (2003). Mindfulness-based interventions in context: Past, present, and future. *Clinical Psychology: Research and Practice*, *10*, 144–156.

Keefe, F. J., Affleck, G., Lefebvre, J., Underwood, L., Caldwell, D. S., Drew, J. (2001). Living with rheumatoid arthritis: The role of daily spirituality and daily religious and spiritual coping. *Journal of Pain*, *2*, 101–110.

Keltner, D. (2009). *Born to be good: The science of a meaningful life*. New York: Norton.

Koenig, H. G., McCullough, M. E., & Larson, D. B. (2001). *Handbook of religion and health*. New York: Oxford University Press.

Kremer, H., & Ironson, G. (2007). Spirituality and HIV/AIDS. In T. G. Plante, & C. E. Thoresen (Eds.), *Spirit, science, and* health: How the spiritual mind fuels physical wellness (pp. 176–190). Westport, CT: Praeger/Greenwood.

Kristeller, J. L., Rhodes, M., Cripe, L. D., & Sheets, V. (2005). Oncologist Assisted Spiritual Intervention Study (OASIS): Patient acceptability and initial evidence of effects. *International Journal of Psychiatry in Medicine, 35,* 329–347.

McAdams, D. P. (2006). *The redemptive self: Stories Americans live by.* New York: Oxford University Press.

McCullough, M. E., Hoyt, W. T., Larson, D. B., Koenig, H. G., & Thoresen, C. E. (2000). Religious involvement and mortality: A meta-analytic review. *Health Psychology, 19,* 211–221.

Miller W. R., & Delaney, H. D. (Eds.). (2005). *Judeo-Christian perspectives on psychology.* Washington, DC: American Psychological Association.

Miller, W. R., & Thoresen, C. E. (2003). Spirituality, religion and health: An emerging research field. *American Psychologist, 58,* 24–35.

Mills, P. J. (2002). Spirituality, religiousness, and health: From research to clinical practice. *Annals of Behavioral Medicine, 24,* 1–2.

Murray-Swank, N. A., & Argument, K. I. (2005). God, where are you? Evaluating a spiritually- integrated intervention for sexual abuse. *Mental Health, Religion & Culture, 8,* 191–203.

Myers, D. (2000). *The American paradox: Spiritual hunger in a land of plenty.* New Haven, CT: Yale University Press.

Oman, D., Hedberg, J., & Thoresen, C. E. (2006). Passage meditation reduces stress in health professionals: A randomized controlled trial. *Journal of Consulting and Clinical Psychology, 74,* 714–719.

Oman, D., Richards, T. A., Hedberg, J., & Thoresen, C. E. (2008). Passage meditation improves caregiving self-efficacy among health professionals: A randomized clinical trial. *Journal of Health Psychology, 13,* 922–1007.

Oman, D., & Thoresen, C. E. (2002). Does religion cause health? Differing interpretations and diverse meanings. *Journal of Health Psychology, 7,* 365–380.

Oman, D., & Thoresen, C. E. (2003). Spiritual modeling: A key to spiritual and religious growth? *The International Journal for the Psychology of Religion, 13,* 149–165.

Oman, D., & Thoresen, C. E. (2005). Do religion and spirituality influence health? In R. F. Paloutzian, & C. L. Park (Eds.), *Handbook of the psychology of religion and spirituality* (pp. 435–459). New York: Guilford.

Oman, D., Thoresen, C. E., & McMahon, K. (1999). Volunteerism and mortality among the community-dwelling elderly. *Journal of Health Psychology, 4,* 301–316.

Oman, D., Thoresen, C. E., Park, C. L., Shaver, P. R., Hood, R. W., & Plante, T. G. (2009). How does one become spiritual? The spiritual modeling inventory of life environments (SMILES). *Mental Health, Religion & Culture. 12,* 427–456.

Ornish, D. (1990). *Dr. Dean Ornish's program for reversing heart disease: The only system scientifically proven to reverse heart disease without drugs or surgery.* New York: Galantine Books.

Paloutzian, R. F., & Park, C. L. (Eds.). (2005). *Handbook of the psychology of religion and spirituality.* New York: Guilford.

Panksepp, J. (1998). *Affective neuroscience: The foundation of human and animal emotion.* New York: Oxford University Press.

Pargament, K. I. (1997). *The psychology of religious coping: Theory, research, practice.* New York: Guilford.

Pargament, K. I. (2007). *Spiritually integrated psychotherapy: Understanding and addressing the sacred.* New York: Guilford.

Pargament, K. I., McCarthy, S., Shah, P., Anon, G., Tarakeshwar, N., Wachholtz, A. B., et al. (2004). Religion and HIV: A review of the literature and clinical implications. *Southern Medical Journal, 97,* 1201–1209.

Peterson, R. (1986). *Everyone is right: A new look at comparative religion and its relation to science.* Marina del Ray, CA: DeVorss.

Plante, T. G. (Ed.). (2004). *Sin against the innocents: Sexual abuse by priests and the role of the Catholic Church.* Westport, CT: Praeger/Greenwood.

Plante, T. G. (2009). *Spiritual practices in psychotherapy: Thirteen tools for enhancing psychological health.* Washington, DC: American Psychological Association.

Plante, T. G., & Sharma, N. (2001). Religious faith and mental health outcomes. In T.G. Plante, & A. C. Sherman (Eds.), *Faith and health: Psychological perspectives* (pp. 240–261). New York: Guilford.

Plante, T. G., & Sherman, A. S. (Eds.). (2001). *Faith and health: Psychological perspectives.* New York: Guilford.

Plante, T. G., & Thoresen, C. E. (Eds.). (2007). *Spirit, science and health: How the spiritual mind fuels physical wellness.* Westport, CT: Praeger/Greenwood.

Powell, L., Shahabi, L., & Thoresen, C. E. (2003). Religion and spirituality: Linkages to physical health. *American Psychologist, 58,* 36–52.

Putman, R. D. (2000). *Bowling Alone: The collapse and revival of the American community.* New York: Simon & Schuster.

Putman, R. D., & Campbell, D. E. (2010) *American Grace; How religion divides and unites us.* New York: Simon & Schuster.

Richards, P. S., & Bergin, A. E. (2005). *A spiritual strategy for counseling and psychotherapy* (2nd ed.). Washington, DC: American Psychological Association.

Richards, P. S., Hardman, R. K., & Berrett, M. E. (2000). *Spiritual renewal: A journal of faith and healing.* Orem, UT: Center for Change.

Russell, S. R., & Yarhouse, M. A. (2006). Religion/ Spirituality within APA-accredited psychology predoctoral internships. *Professional Psychology: Research and Practice, 37,* 430–436.

Rye, M., & Pargament, K. I. (2003). *Coping with divorce: A journey toward forgiveness.* Unpublished manual, University of Dayton, OH.

Ryff, C. D., & Singer, B. (1998). The contours of positive human health. *Psychological Inquiry, 9,* 1–28.

Seligman, M. E. P., Steen, T. A., Park, N., & Peterson, C. (2005). Positive psychology progress: Empirical validation of interventions. *American Psychologist, 60,* 410–421.

Shafranske, E. P. (2000). Religious involvement and professional practices of psychiatrists and other mental health professionals. *Psychiatric Annals, 30,* 525–532.

Shapiro, S. L., & Walsh, R. (2007). Meditation: Exploring the farther reaches. In T. G. Plante, & C. E. Thoresen (Eds.), *Spirit, science, and health: How the spiritual mind fuels physical wellness* (pp. 57–71). Westport, CT: Praeger/Greenwood.

Smith, H. (1991). *The world's religions: Our great wisdom traditions.* San Francisco: Harper.

Snyder, C. R., & Lopez, S. J. (2007). *Positive psychology: The scientific and practical explorations of human strengths.* Thousand Oaks, CA: Sage.

Sue, D. W., Bingham, R. P., Porche-Burke, L., & Vasquez, M. (1999). The diversification of psychology: A multicultural revolution. *American Psychologist, 54*, 1061–1069.

Task Force on Promotion and Dissemination of Psychological Procedures. (1995). Training in and dissemination of empirically validated psychological treatments: Report and recommendations. *Clinical Psychologist, 48*, 3–23.

Tennen, H., Affleck, G., Armeli, S., & Carney, M. A. (2000). A daily process approach to coping: Linking theory, research, and practice. *American Psychologist, 55*, 626–636.

Thoresen, C. E. (2007). Spirituality, religion and health: What's the deal? In T. G. Plante, & C. E. Thoresen (Eds.), *Spirit, science, and health: How the spiritual mind fuels physical wellness* (pp. 3–10). Westport, CT: Praeger/Greenwood.

Thoresen, C. E., & Eagleston, J. R. (1985). Counseling for health. *The Counseling Psychologist, 13*, 15–87.

Thoresen, C. E., & Harris, A. H. S. (2002). Spirituality and health: What's the evidence and what's needed? *Annals of Behavioral Medicine, 24*, 3–13.

Thoresen, C. E., Oman, D., & Harris, A. H. S. (2005). The effects of religious practices: A focus on health. In W. R. Miller, & H. D. Delaney (Eds.), *Judeo-Christian perspectives on psychology* (pp. 205–226). Washington, DC: American Psychological Association.

Trenholm, P., Trent, J., Compton, W. C. (1998). Negative religious conflict as a predictor of panic disorder. *Journal of Clinical Psychology, 54*, 59–65.

Vaillant, G. E. (2008). *Spiritual evolution: A scientific defense of faith*. New York: Broadway.

Wachholtz, A. B., & Pargament, K. I. (2008). Migraines and meditation: Does spirituality matter? *Journal of Behavioral Medicine, 31*, 351–366.

Watson, J. B. (1983). *Psychology from the standpoint of a behaviorist*. Dover, NH: Frances Pinter (Original work published 1924).

Zinnbauer, B. J., & Pargament, K. I. (2005). Religiousness and spirituality. In R. F. Paloutzian, & C. L. Park (Eds.), *Handbook of the psychology of religion and spirituality* (pp. 21–42). New York: Guilford.

Further Reading

Brooks, D. (2011). *The Social Animal*, New York: Random House.

Fredrickson, B. (2009). *Positivity*. New York: Random House.

Miller, W. R. (Ed.). (1999). *Integrating spirituality into treatment: Resources for practitioners*. Washington, DC: American Psychological Association.

Pargament, K. I. (2007). *Spiritually integrated psychotherapy: Understanding and addressing the sacred*. New York: Guilford.

Plante, T. G. (2009). *Spiritual practices in psychotherapy: Thirteen tools for enhancing psychological health*. Washington, DC: American Psychological Association.

Plante, T. G., & Thoresen, C. E. (Eds.). (2007). *Spirit, science and health: How the spiritual mind fuels physical wellness*. Westport, CT: Praeger/Greenwood.

Richards, P. S., & Bergin, A. E. (Eds.). (2003). *Casebook for a spiritual strategy in counseling and psychotherapy*. Washington, DC: American Psychological Association.

Richards, P. S., & Bergin, A. E. (2005). *A spiritual strategy for counseling and psychotherapy* (2nd ed.). Washington, DC: American Psychological Association.

Siegel, D. J. (2010). *Mindsight: The new science of personal transformation*. New York: Bantam.

Vaillant, G. E. (2008). *Spiritual evolution: A scientific defense of faith*. New York: Broadway.

Group Counseling

Robert K. Conyne

Abstract

Three perspectives of group counseling are highlighted, leading to a suggested definition, in part, as an important therapeutic and educational method to facilitate interpersonal problem-solving processes among members as they learn how to resolve difficult but manageable problems of living and how to apply gains in the future. Group counseling's evolution across 100 years is presented. Research in key group counseling processes is examined, including therapeutic factors, group climate, and group development. Group counseling leadership research is summarized, focused on intentionality in leader tasks, roles, functions, and intervention choices. Group work standards, guidelines, and multicultural principles are addressed. Group work is expanding in contemporary society through face-to-face and online forms, leading to what might be termed an "Age of Ubiquity." The chapter concludes with research and practice suggestions for the future and an extensive reference list.

Keywords: group counseling, group work, history, therapeutic factors, group climate, group development, group leadership, standards, multicultural, online

Group counseling is a sub-set of the broad and varied field of "groups." Knowledge of that field is an important contributor to becoming a competent group counselor (Forsyth, 2011).

Indeed, group counseling is an essential intervention for counseling psychologists and other practitioners (Leszcz & Kobos, 2008). It has been found through experience and empirical research to be at least as effective as individual therapy in promoting client change while offering additional efficiencies and cost benefits (e.g., Barlow, Fuhriman, & Burlingame, 2004; Bednar & Kaul, 1994; Burlingame, Fuhriman, & Johnson, 2004; Burlingame, Kapetanovic, & Ross, 2005; Burlingame, MacKenzie, & Strauss, 2004; Dies, 1983; Fuhriman & Burlingame, 1994; Kosters, Burlingame, Nachtigall, & Strauss, 2006; Horne & Rosenthal, 1997; Johnson, 2008; McRoberts, Burlingame, & Hoag, 1998; Payne & Marcus,

2008; Shechtman, 2007; Toseland & Siporin, 1986). For instance, in one meta-analytic analysis of 23 studies investigating the comparative effectiveness of group and individual modes of helping (McRoberts et al., 1998), the group approach was found equivalent for producing client change in the areas of chemical dependency, vocational choice, and with a number of stress syndromes and V-code diagnoses.

After reviewing hundreds of studies, Barlow, Burlingame, and Fuhriman (2000) provided the following clear statement about the effectiveness of groups:

> With few exceptions (cf. Piper & McCallum, 1991), the general conclusion to be drawn from approximately 730 studies that span almost three decades is that the group format consistently produced positive effects with a number of disorders using a variety of treatment models (p. 122).

Despite the strong support for group counseling's effectiveness, MacKenzie (1995), McRoberts et al. (1998,and a number of other noted researchers (see Conyne, 2011 for extensive treatment) observe that more research is needed to specify what group treatment variables account for effectiveness, especially when the group approach is being increasingly recommended for a wide range of client problems and populations. Indeed, it is the recommendation of Burlingame et al. (2004) that future group research be directed "to measure, and hence understand, the interactive, connected, and holistic processes of group and then link these with long-term outcome" (p. 657). A summative statement on this topic might read: There remains a critical need for empirically-supported group processes and conditions, for development of more measures to accurately detect them, and for actionable group leadership that is tied to these group processes and conditions (e.g., Barlow, 2011; Brabender, 2011; Kivlighan, Miles & Paquin, 2011; McClendon & Burlingame, 2011; Schwartz, Waldo & Moravec, 2011; Stockton & Morran, 2011).

Group counseling is the subject of considerable and increasing research and scholarly activity. Several journals are devoted specifically to the intervention (e.g., *Group Dynamics: Theory, Research, and Practice*; *Journal for Specialists in Group Work*; *International Journal of Group Psychotherapy*; *Social Work with Groups*; *Group & Organization Management*; *Small Group Research*; *Group Processes and Intergroup Relations*; and *Group Facilitation: A Research and Applications Journal*), and an increasingly steady stream of books and handbooks addressing various facets of group practice has appeared over the last two decades.

In addition, exposure to group counseling is included in several subdisciplines of psychology. However, sustained attention in psychology to group training now is being moved to the postdoctoral level. By contrast, group training in graduate-level disciplines related to psychology (e.g., counselor education) occurs earlier and more consistently. In fact, master's degree-level curricular standards in counseling include required training and supervised experience in group work (CACREP, 2001). The interrelated areas of teaching, training and supervision in group counseling leadership is of great import, with many improvements needed (e. g., Brown, 2011; Riva, 2011; Shapiro, 2011).

The use of group work approaches, in general, has grown exponentially over the last two decades, finding application in the major settings of society.

These settings include education, private practice, religious organizations, social service agencies, planning boards, health care organizations, mental health care agencies, and business and industry. At the same time, successful incorporation within managed care occurs but awaits more progress.

Groups also are used frequently as an important means for reaching a wide range of targeted populations. These populations include school children, the aged, employees, members of religious congregations, college students, "baby boomers," children of divorce, those who abuse substances, people in ill health and in good health, mutual help group members, and many others.

Groups are remedial, preventive, developmental, and all points between. They are professionally led and self-help in format. They are personally oriented and task-related. They are offered within organizations, neighborhoods, and communities, within this country and around the world, face-to-face and online. In short, groups are omnipresent in contemporary life, including being made available in a multitude of settings (Kalodner & Hanus, 2011). With the above discussion as background, this chapter on group counseling is organized into sections that discuss the definition of group counseling; present a historical overview of group counseling; delineate key change processes; and examine group leadership; discuss the expansion of groups in contemporary society. The chapter concludes with some ideas for future research directions.

Definition of Group Counseling
Three Perspectives on Defining Group Counseling

Groups abound. How does group counseling fit? In fact, defining group counseling has proved to be an elusive and, some would claim, frustrating task. Perhaps this situation should be expected. After all, group counseling has emerged over decades from a number of different academic disciplines, traditions, professions, and organizations—as the following chapter section on historical evolution will illustrate. Therefore, to describe group counseling as being "multidisciplinary" would be an understatement. By contrast, to describe it as being "interdisciplinary," in which contributions from different sources are effectively inter-related and applied, would be inaccurate. Continuing to advance the interdisciplinary nature of group counseling is important, in my view.

At present, group counseling can be understood through the lenses of three related, but different, perspectives: Undifferentiated from group psychotherapy and including other group types, independent-type within group work, and overlapping therapeutic and educational goals and processes. These perspectives are described next, followed by an attempt to produce an integrative definition.

PERSPECTIVE I: GROUP COUNSELING IS UNDIFFERENTIATED FROM GROUP PSYCHOTHERAPY AND INCLUDES OTHER GROUP TYPES

Here, group counseling is viewed as being undifferentiated from group psychotherapy and—increasingly—from other group therapeutic forms, including support groups and those used for prevention, guidance, and training. Identifying terms representing this undifferentiated and comprehensive perspective include *group counseling, group psychotherapy*, and *group counseling and psychotherapy*.

This perspective is reflected in the writings of many experts (e.g., Barlow et al., 2004; Burlingame et al., 2005; Dagley, Gazda, Eppinger, & Stewart, 1994; DeLucia, Gerrity, Kalodner, & Riva, 2004; Forsyth, 2006; Fuhriman & Burlingame, 2000; Gazda, 1982) and seems generally consistent with the mission of the Association for Group Psychology and Group Psychotherapy of the American Psychological Association (APA Division 49, 2007), which is concerned with the study and practice of the broad field of group psychology and group dynamics and with group psychotherapy, particularly. John Borriello, Division President in 1996, underlined this inclusive approach in noticing that the Division's convention program titles for that year included "self-help, support, therapeutic, team building, psychosocial, behavioral-cognitive, change agent, systems-centered, and prevention" (Andronico, 2001, p. 16).

In a classic expression of group counseling and psychotherapy, group therapists or counselors use interpersonal processes to promote change in members who are dealing with psychological, behavioral, and/or emotional problems. This description generally reflects the position of the American Group Psychotherapy Association (AGPA) (2007).

However, with many new group forms and approaches appearing within the "group helping field" (Scheidlinger & Schmess, in MacKenzie, 1992, p. 17), the AGPA has extended its breadth of focus to match. Yalom and Leszcz (2005) referred to the variety of groups today as being "mind-boggling" in volume and form. They note, "Group therapy methods have proved to be so useful in so many different clinical settings that it is no longer correct to speak of group therapy. Instead, we must refer to *group therapies*" (p. 475) (italics retained). Fuhriman and Burlingame (2000, p. 31) describe group psychotherapy as "the treatment of emotional or psychological disorders or problems of adjustment through the medium of a group setting, the focal point being the interpersonal (social), intrapersonal (psychological), or behavioral change of the participating clients or group members." Burlingame et al. (2005) expands on this definition by classifying the "plethora of groups found in today's practice" (p. 388) into three categories: formal change theory used (e.g., behavioral), structural features (e.g., size, composition), and patient population (e.g., anxiety disorders).

PERSPECTIVE 2: GROUP COUNSELING IS AN INDEPENDENT GROUP TYPE WITHIN GROUP WORK

Ward (2006) observes that interest in categorizing groups into types has captured the attention of scholars for at least 25 years. Group counseling is considered by some scholars to stand as its own function, connected to other forms of group work but still unique (e.g., Conyne, Wilson, & Ward, 1997; Corey & Corey, 2006; Gladding, 6; Wilbur, Roberts-Wilbur, & Betz, 1981). Here, group counseling often is embedded within the broad definition of "group work," a conception developed within the Association for Specialists in Group Work (ASGW, 2000), a division of the American Counseling Association (ACA). Group counseling is identified as one of four major group work types, the others being psychoeducation groups, psychotherapy groups, and task groups. All types are thought to share a core set of basic processes and dynamics, with each also possessing additional distinctive characteristics.

When it is considered as an independent function, common understandings have evolved over several decades to describe aspects of group counseling. For example, stretching back to 1960, Brammer and Shostrom characterized group counseling as "educational, supportive, situational, problem-solving, conscious awareness, emphasis on 'normals,' and short-term" (p. 6). Forty-six years later, Trotzer (2006) expanded these descriptors of group counseling to include:

> [R]emedial, normal individuals, thoughts-feelings-behaviors, problem-oriented, focus de123-termined by individuals, situational, relationship important,

empathy and support is stressed, tendency toward homogeneity (common problems), verbal techniques, feelings and needs emphasized, conscious awareness, leader facilitates, present-oriented, non-medical setting, relatively short longevity. (p. 43)

Group counseling is situated in the ASGW training standards as a standalone method within the broader span of group work itself. The umbrella term of group work is defined as:

[A] broad professional practice involving the application of knowledge and skills in group facilitation to assist an interdependent collection of people to reach their mutual goals, which may be intrapersonal, interpersonal, or work related. The goals of the group may include the accomplishment of tasks related to work, education, personal development, personal and interpersonal problem solving, or remediation of mental and emotional disorders. (pp. 2–3)

As one of the four types of group work, the ASGW Standards define group counseling as:

The application of principles of normal human development and functioning through group based cognitive, affective, behavioral, or systemic intervention strategies applied in the context of here-and-now interaction that address personal and interpersonal problems of living and promote personal and interpersonal growth and development among people who may be experiencing transitory maladustment, who are at risk for the development of personal or interpersonal problems, or who seek enhancement of personal qualities and abilities. (ASGW Training Standards, p. 4)

PERSPECTIVE 3: GROUP COUNSELING, AND OTHER GROUP WORK TYPES, ARE DEFINED BY OVERLAPPING THERAPEUTIC AND EDUCATIONAL GOALS AND PROCESSES

This view, focusing on relationships among groups according to goals and processes (Gazda, Ginter, & Horne, 2001, Trotzer, 2006, Waldo & Bauman, 1998) or to purposes and methods (Conyne, 1985), tends to combine the first two perspectives discussed above. Here, a spectrum of group approaches are organized in terms of their primary emphasis on therapeutic goals and processes. For instance, Gazda et al. (2001) organized different types of groups as being either: exclusively preventive and growth engendering; primarily preventive, growth engendering, and to a lesser extent, remedial; or primarily remedial and to a lesser extent preventive and growth engendering. In this conception, group counseling

(along with some other group forms, such as T-groups and encounter groups) are viewed as being primarily preventive and growth engendering, with some aspects of remediation. Psychotherapy groups are viewed as being primarily remedial and to a lesser degree preventive and growth engendering. Group guidance/psychoeducation is viewed as being preventive and growth engendering.

Conyne (1985) suggested a "group work grid." It includes a wide array of group methods according to their emphasis on correction or enhancement (purpose) and level of group work intervention (individual, interpersonal, organization, community-population). In this schema, group counseling fit with a corrective purpose and an interpersonal level.

As mentioned, no single orientation is right or wrong, and all operate to nourish the growth of group work applications. Moreover, it may be of interest to readers that a proactive "Group Summit" was held in January 2008, attended by these and other group work organizations, to discuss possible interorganizational cooperation to promote "group." The Group Practice and Research Network (GPRN) was formed at this Summit, with members from participating organizations beginning to focus on the following initiatives: altruistic programs, guild/professional identity, exchange of member services and resources, public education, education and research, and funding.

Toward a Suggested Integrative Description of Group Counseling

As is obvious from the above discussion, developing a clear and generally acceptable definition of group counseling is challenging and complex. Ward's view (2011) of group counseling emphasizing an interpersonal, process-oriented, and strengths-based approach would seem to capture essential elements.

Drawing elements from the three perspectives discussed previously, the following definition of group counseling is offered as an attempt to integrate the foregoing material:

Group counseling is an important therapeutic and educational method that psychologists, counselors, and other helpers can use to facilitate interpersonal problem-solving processes among members as they learn how to resolve difficult but manageable problems of living and how to apply gains in the future through building on their strengths. Although being a unique service delivery method, group counseling also shares much in common with related group work approaches, including psychoeducation groups and psychotherapy groups. In general, group counseling occupies a broad middle section of the helping goals continuum where prevention, development, and remediation all play important roles, depending on member needs and situational supports and constraints.

Historical Overview of Group Counseling: 100+ Years of Development

How did these understandings of group counseling and other groups evolve? Over 100 years of history is involved. In this section, some of the significant events and persons responsible to shaping group counseling are chronicled. Let us begin by highlighting some salient quotations about group counseling and group work from over several decades.

C. Gilbert Wrenn provides a starting point; interestingly, Wrenn was a counseling "seer" who accurately predicted many future trends for counseling long before others (e.g., see Wrenn, 1962)—but he missed on this one:

First of all, counseling is personal. It cannot be
performed with a group. "Group counseling"
is a tautology; counseling is always personal.
(Wrenn, 1938, p. 119, cited in Gazda, 1982)

Rather than being inappropriate, the use of group methods in counseling and other applications increased dramatically, leading to the following prediction in 1985:

Groups will abound. . . . Group methods will be
used increasingly with families, with diverse
populations, within organizations, and even . . .
to achieve social change across all levels of systems:
in groups, organizations, communities, regions,
nations, and the world.
(Conyne, Dye, Gill, Leddick, Morran, &
Ward, 1985, p. 114)

This expansion of group applications has occurred, along with a concern about the ability to demonstrate their empirical effectiveness across settings:

The meta-analytic data from this study confirm the
general and selected diagnostic effectiveness of group
treatment, and in a day when group treatment is on
the rise, this indeed is encouraging. Nonetheless, this
is also a time when there is increased interest on the
part of service recipients and public and private
agencies for assurance that treatment will be effective,
regardless of where it takes place.
(Burlingame, Fuhriman, & Mosier, 2003, p. 11)

Running alongside the need for empirical evidence of group effectiveness (now beginning to be termed *research-supported group treatment*, RSGT; Johnson, 2008) was an awareness among many that the group circle holds particular healing value in many cultures and that it may hold particular value for reaching minority populations:

The group is the circle, the microcosm of life, where
power moves. For this reason, it may be suggested
that the group format is the most effective approach
to serving the needs of minority clients.
(Rivera, Garrett, & Crutchfield, 2004, p. 304)

The preceding quotations provide a perspective on the evolution of group counseling and companion group approaches over several decades. Met at first with a general level of disbelief, an increasing assertion developed that group approaches are essential for personal and societal change. A need for continued documentation of effectiveness emerged, as well as the realization that the circle is a basic symbol of life that informs group work, which may be, in general, the best suited of all services for multicultural practice. Signs today point to group being an omnipresent force in our society, but more about that at the end of this chapter.

Association in groups has characterized human functioning since the beginning of time. In fact, many (e.g., Foulkes & Anthony, 1957) have suggested that groups are the fundamental unit of society. Healing practices in various cultures and locations began centuries before modern advancements in group counseling or any other form of professional help-giving, and many of these practices continue to this day across cultures, with the group-circle playing an important role in several of them (e.g., Native American practices using the sweat lodge, the talking circle, and the talking stick). Garrett (2004), for instance, in considering group counseling with Native Americans, referred to group work as the "medicine of healing" (p. 173).

The following historical discussion of group counseling is based primarily, but not exclusively, on earlier historical reviews by Andronico (1999); Barlow, Burlingame, and Fuhriman (2000, 2005); Barlow et al. (2004); Bertcher (1985); Burlingame, Fuhriman, and Mosier (2003); Burlingame, Fuhriman, and Johnson (2004); Gazda (1982, 1985); Gazda et al. (2001); Forester-Miller (1998); Gladding (2002); Leddick (2008, 2011), and Scheidlinger and Schmess (in MacKenzie, 1992). Because of these reviews and the availability of several others (e.g., Blatner, 2007; Hadden, 1955;

Z. Moreno, 1966; Rosenbaum, Lakin, & Roback, 1992), the current presentation will content itself with listing some of the important milestones in the history of groups across four overlapping time periods organized and labeled by this author.

Please take note of two points. Sources, including dates, contained in the chronology to follow are presented largely without descriptive narrative and are intended for documenting historical evolution; therefore, they are not included in the chapter references. Also, I acknowledge in advance the certain degree of inevitable arbitrariness that can accompany any such effort at historical description and categorization.

A brief description of these four time periods follows. Each time period is then detailed in its own table:

• Period 1, the "Years of Development": 1900–1939, marked by early forays into working with people collectively, group work aimed at changing social conditions, and laying a foundation for the progress to come; see Table 24.1.

• Period 2, the "Years of Early Explosion": 1940–1969, a remarkable two decades beginning with accelerating the spread of group approaches following World War II and noted for innovation and experimentation; for production and organization of theory, techniques, and research; for the formation of group organizations; and for the spread of groups throughout society occurring during the human potential movement of the 1960s; see Table 24.2.

• Period 3, the "Years of Settling In": 1970–1989, two decades noted for sifting through earlier advancements and documenting what worked through substantial and influential publications, the emergence of group training in universities and elsewhere, and the formation of key group work organizations; see Table 24.3.

• Period 4, the "Years of Standardization and Further Expansion to the Age of Ubiquity": 1990–Present, a time noted for efforts to define group work and the place of group counseling in relation to it, for products intended to clarify guidelines and standards for group training and practice, for the publication of more sophisticated research into process and outcomes and for the emergence of group handbooks, for the wide expansion of group

work to fit differing populations and settings, and for experimentation of group methods into online and other electronic vehicles; see Table 24.4.

The method of group counseling has been distilled from this series of historical events that occurred over the last 100 years, from "thought-control classes" to the "Age of Ubiquity." Its successful conduct depends on effectively stimulating and using key processes for change, discussed in the next section.

Key Change Processes: Therapeutic Factors, Group Climate, and Group Development

As Yalom (Yalom & Leszcz, 2005) observes, therapeutic change in group is an "enormously complex process that occurs through an intricate interplay of human experiences" (p. 1). These human experiences are termed "therapeutic factors." Two other important partners in therapeutic change also will be addressed in this section, group climate and group development.

Therapeutic Factors

Irvin D. Yalom's seminal research and scholarly contributions in many areas of group psychotherapy have been essential in the development of seminal group therapeutic approaches. His concept of the "social microcosm," in which members enact their dominant interpersonal style and pathology within the free-flowing group itself, plays a pivotal role in group therapy. An adaptation of this process is presently occurring, connecting learning from the in-group social microcosm with both personal application and, where it fits, application aimed at system change and social justice (e.g., Jacobson & Rugeley, 2007; Orr, Wolfe, & Malley, 2008).

In addition, Yalom championed the importance of therapeutic factors in promoting change and growth in the group. Reviewing the importance of therapeutic factors, one of the concepts chiefly associated with Yalom, researchers Kivlighan and Holmes (2004) observe that, "Of Yalom's many contributions to group theory, research, and practice his delineation and description of the concept of 11 therapeutic factors as the essential elements of group-promoted change is arguably the single most influential aspect of his theoretical and research endeavors" (pp. 24–25). Readers may wish to consult the very useful history surrounding these therapeutic factors documented by Crouch, Bloch,

Table 24.1. Period 1, the Years of Development—1900–1939

Year	Event
1905	Joseph H. Pratt conducts "thought-control classes" for tuberculosis patients, realizing that something therapeutic happens by bringing them together.
1907	Jesse B. Davis focuses English classes on "vocational and moral guidance."
1910	Jane Addams, the originator of social work, uses group work processes to advance democratic principles and promote social change at Hull House in Chicago.
	In World War I, U.S. Army Alpha and Beta intelligence tests are administered in groups.
About 1919	E. W. Lazell used lecture procedures within a group to inspire schizophrenics.
	L.C. Marsh, around the same time, used multiple methods involving inspirational lecture, group discussions, and the arts with hospitalized mental patients. This approach was a forerunner to milieu therapy. He is known for his famous words, "By the crowd they have been broken; by the crowd they shall be healed."
1921	The Theater of Spontaneity (*Stegreiftheatre*) is formed by Alfred Adler; it is a precursor to psychodrama.
1922	Adler develops "collective counseling," a new form of group guidance and, later, "family councils," to help families resolve and improve their relations.
1923	The first course on group work is offered, graduate school of social work, Western Reserve University.
1925	C.R. Foster, in *Extra Curricular Activities*, urges counselors to hold "many group conferences with students on the subject of future educational or vocational plans" (p. 182).
Late 1920s	Trigant Burrow develops group analysis, emphasizing the importance of working with people in relation to the group in which they are a member.
1931	Richard D. Allen writes "A Group Guidance Curriculum in the Senior High School," published in *Education*, using the term "group counseling."
1932	Jacob Moreno coins the term "group psychotherapy."
Mid-1930s	Alcoholics Anonymous (AA), the first self-help group in the U.S. is founded by Bill Wilson and Dr. Bob Smith.
1934	A. Jones, in his *Principles of Guidance* (2nd ed.), refers to the "Boston Plan for Group Counseling in Intermediate Schools." In his review, Gazda later observed that both Allen (above) and Jones really were referring to group guidance.
1934	Maxwell Jones provided early precedent for psychoeducation to members of his large groups through lectures-in-group on psychiatric symptoms, nervous system, and other topics of relevance.
1936	Formation of the American Association for the Study of Group Work
	Progressive education movement sets the stage for group guidance movement to follow.
1936	Kurt Lewin develops field theory based on person × environment interaction. Contributions of Lewin, the "practical theorist", to group dynamics are of high importance.
1939	Lewin, Lippitt, and White's leadership field study is reported, identifying and comparing autocratic, democratic, and laissez-faire styles.

Table 24.2. Period 2, the Years of Early Explosion—1940–1969

Year	Event
1942	Carl Rogers introduces client-centered therapy, one foundation of group counseling.
1941–42	Jacob Moreno establishes the American Society of Group Psychotherapy and Psychodrama (ASGPP). Its journal, *Sociatry*, is created in 1947 (re-named *Group Psychotherapy* in 1949).
1943	Samuel Slavson forms the American Group Psychotherapy Association (AGPA). Its journal, the *International Journal of Group Psychotherapy*, is created in 1951.
1944	First Annual Conference of AGPA is held at Russell Sage Foundation, January 14–15, 1944.
	Search for more economical treatments occurs following World War II.
1946	Kurt Lewin, Leland Bradford, Kenneth Benne establish the National Training Laboratories (NTL) at Bethel, Maine, in 1946. The "Basic Skills Training Group" in 1947 changed to "T-group" (Training Group) in 1949.
1946	The Tavistock Institute of Human Relations is created.
1948	Wilfred Bion, of the Tavistock Institute, focuses on group cohesiveness, identifying group dependency, pairing, and fight–flight as basic tendencies.
1950	Study of group phenomena begins to intensify with Robert F. Bales' study of task and maintenance roles.
1951	*International Journal of Group Psychotherapy* is founded.
1953	Cartwright and Zander edit *Group Dynamics*, organizing research addressing social problems.
Mid-1950s	First International Social group workers are recognized as effective in treatment and clinical settings.
1954	Congress of Group Psychotherapy is established.
1955	Hare, Borgatta, and Bales edit *Small Groups: Studies in Social Interaction*, organizing influential social-psychological small group research.
1956	Herbert A. Thelen's *Dynamics of Groups at Work* is published.
1956	Richard Blake and Jane Mouton are among those providing a set of new group concepts with their term "developmental groups."
1958	First textbook in group work is published, *Counseling and Learning through Small-Group Discussion* (Helen J. Driver).
1961	Rudolph Dreikurs and others, such as John Bell, apply Adler's concepts to family groups. Virginia Satir and others (such as Nathan Ackerman and Gregory Bateson) continue adapting group procedures with families.
1961	Muzafer and Carolyn Sherif and colleagues conduct classic field study, "The Robbers Cave Experiment," on intergroup conflict.

Year	Event
1961	Jack Gibb develops the TORI model for groups: Trust, Openness, Realization, Interdependence.
1964	Leland Bradford, Jack Gibb, and Kenneth Benne's, *T-Group Theory and Laboratory Method: Innovation in Re-education* appears.
1964	George Bach and Fred Stoller develop marathon groups.
1965	Bruce Tuckman publishes influential group development stage model: Forming, Storming, Performing, Adjourning (later a fifth stage is added: Mourning).
1966	Eric Berne develops transactional analysis in groups.
	Some graduate programs in counselor education and psychology begin to develop group courses.
1969	William Fawcett Hill introduces *Hill Interaction Matrix* and *Learning thru Discussion*.
1960s–early 1970s	Human potential movement flourishes, with encounter groups at its center.
1967	Fritz Perls popularizes gestalt groups through his work at Esalen Institute in Big Sur, California.
1967	Wil Schutz, who developed the Fundamental Interpersonal Orientation-Behavior (FIRO-B) scale in 1958, publishes his popular book, *Joy: Expanding Human Awareness*, praising aspects of the encounter movement.
1968	*New York Times* names 1968 as "Year of the Group."
1969	Arthur Burton edits *Encounter: The Theory and Practice of Encounter Groups.*
1969	George Gazda holds the first of ten annual symposia on group counseling.

Table 24.3. Period 3, the Years of Settling In—1970–1989

	Experiential groups expand and are focused, signified by the Esalen Institute on the West Coast and the National Training Laboratories (NTL) on the East Coast.
1970	*Carl Rogers on Encounter Groups* provides person-centered substance to the human potential movement.
1970	Robert Golembiewski and Arthur Blumberg publish their edited book, *Sensitivity Training and the Laboratory Approach: Reading About Concepts and Applications.*
1970	Irvin Yalom publishes the first edition of *Theory and Practice of Group Psychotherapy,* a seminal text that now has four additional editions.
1970	Yalom identifies 11 curative (later, therapeutic) factors in groups (e.g., group cohesion, interpersonal learning), central ingredients for producing change in groups.
1971	Jane Howard publishes the wildly popular book, *Please Touch: A Guided Tour of the Human Potential Movement.*
1972	Lawrence Solomon and Betty Berzon edit *New Perspectives on Encounter Groups.*
1973	Morton Lieberman, Irvin Yalom, and Matthew Miles publish *Encounter Groups: First Facts,* which enumerates group leadership functions and styles.
1973	Association for Specialists in Group Work (ASGW) established, becoming the 11th Division of the American Personnel and Guidance Association (now known as the American Counseling Association).
Spring 1976	*Together,* the journal of ASGW is founded.
	Gerald Corey and Marianne Corey begin their continuing string of publications on group counseling.
1978	*Together* title is changed to *Journal for Specialists in Group Work.*
1978	Journal, *Social Work with Groups,* is established.
1980	*Ethical Guidelines for Group Leaders* and *Guidelines for Training Group Leaders* are approved by ASGW.
1980s	Structured groups and training for life skills begin to appear in professional literature.
1980s and beyond	Group counseling texts, articles, research increase dramatically in numbers.
	Self-help groups flourish (with Frank Riessman championing them), containing some 20 million members.
1989	ASGW *Ethical Guidelines for Group Leaders* changed to *Ethical Guidelines for Group Workers.*
1989	The Division of Group Psychology and Group Psychotherapy, the 49th Division of the American Psychological Association, is established to further the study of groups and to advance therapeutic change through groups.
	Group Dynamics appears by Forsyth, organizing research on group dynamics to examine their psychological, sociological, and personal importance.
	Books appear showcasing various ways the group method can be used, in addition to group counseling and psychotherapy.

Table 24.4. Period 4, the Years of Standardization and Further Expansion to the Age of Ubiquity—1990–present

1991	ASGW's *Professional Standards for the Training of Group Workers* is revised significantly and then is refined to include a broad definition of group work, core competencies for group work across group types, and four types of groups: task, psychoeducation, counseling, and psychotherapy.
1994	*Handbook of Group Psychotherapy* is published.
1997	APA's Division 49 (Group Psychology and Group Psychotherapy) produces the first issue of its journal, *Group Dynamics: Theory, Research, and Practice.*
1998	ASGW's *Best Practice Guidelines for Group Workers* is created and then later revised, providing ethically based guidance specific to group work.
1998	ASGW's *Principles for Diversity-Competent Group Workers* is created, providing guidance and expectations for multicultural group leadership.
	Group research becomes increasingly sophisticated into such concepts as therapeutic factors, process-outcome, group leadership, group development, group climate, group cohesion, supervision, feedback, co-leadership, situational leadership, cognitive-behavioral approach, structure, and interaction.
	Group research methodologies expand to include meta-analysis, qualitative design, focus groups, Tuckerized Growth Curve Analysis (TCGA), hierarchical linear modeling, structural analysis of group arguments, and a range of measures to study group efficacy.
	Development begins of empirical support of group approaches for many specific problems and disorders (e.g., anxiety disorders with cognitive-behavioral groups).
	Psychoeducation groups brief therapy groups, and focal groups flourish, matched to targeted populations for people with disabilities, the elderly, children, offenders, women, veterans, and many others.
2000s	In the 2000s, groups enter an "Age of Ubiquity."
	Prevention and promotion groups are described), aimed at forestalling the development of disorders and problems such as substance abuse, bullying, bereavement, trauma, and academic failure; for stimulating healthy functioning, such as problem solving, social skills, well-being; and for addressing a wide variety of health issues, such as cancer, Parkinson's disease, eating disorders, fibromyalgia, AIDS, chronic physical illness, obesity, healthy heart functioning, and many others.
	Group work for social justice assumes a renewed emphasis, in which the social microcosm concept and procedures such as community-based participatory research and action are employed.
	Post-9/11, AGPA seeks to expand from a professional guild serving professional members to include a public health resource function providing services to address trauma, grief, and community crises.
	The number and scope of groups approached a crescendo, becoming common not only in educational and mental health settings but in task environments, also. The latter settings included workplace, medical, business and industry, governmental organizations, religious settings, and in neighborhoods and the community.
	Multicultural groups address people of various cultures, including Latino/a, African American, Native American, Asians, Gay-Lesbian-Bisexual-Transgender, and others.
	E-learning tools develop (e.g., Blackboard), allowing for virtual group activity.

(Continued)

Table 24.4. Continued

2002	AGPA publishes *Guidelines for Ethics—Revised*.
2004	*Handbook of Group Counseling and Psychotherapy* is published.
2007	AGPA publishes *Practice Guidelines for Group Psychotherapists*.
	Online groups and social networking channels develop.
2008	A "Group Summit," initiated by Division 49 of APA, is held (January 10–11, 2008) to explore connections among Division 49, the Society of Consulting Psychology of APA, ASGW, AGPA, the Division of Addictions of APA, and the Division of Psychoanalysis (Group Section) of APA. At this meeting an umbrella "Group Practice and Research Network" (GPRN) is established.
2008	Research Supported Group Treatments become a focal area.

and Wanlass (1994). Kivlighan, Miles, and Paqin (2011) add that:

> Therapeutic factor research continues to lack a focus on the group itself and, more critically, to account for essential group interactional constructs.
> They urge that group theorists and researchers ground their work within the group perspective.

Yalom purports that the 11 therapeutic factors, although being arbitrary constructs, comprehensively identify the operations and mechanisms accounting for therapeutic change in groups. He indicates that they do not function independently, but are interdependent. Therapeutic factors have spawned his own research and theory, most notably represented, beginning in 1970, within the five editions of *The Theory and Practice of Group Psychotherapy*, as well as by many other research studies (e.g., reported in Crouch et al. 1994; Colijn, Hoencamp, Snijders, van der Spek, & Duivenvoorden, 1991; Shechtman & Gluk, 2005) and reviews (e.g., Kivlighan, Coleman & Anderson, 2000; Kivlighan & Holmes, 2004). In addition, one would be hard-put to find any text on the topic of group counseling and group psychotherapy that did not assign a prominent place for a discussion of these therapeutic factors.

A brief description of the 11 therapeutic factors follows. Interpersonal learning and cohesion, both marked by an asterisk in the table, are described more extensively following Table 24.5.

Table 24.5. Therapeutic Factors

Factor	Description
1) Instillation of hope	Belief of members that group participation will be helpful; member optimism in improving through group involvement
2) Universality	Members perceive that they are not alone in the world, that other members in their group share similar problems, thoughts, and feelings.
3) Imparting information	Group leader and fellow members provide information, planned theoretical inputs, didactic instruction, direct advice, and guidance.
4) Altruism	Members benefit through being of help to other members. No other helping mode provides this opportunity.
5) Corrective recapitulation of the primary family group	Members re-experience past family conflicts in a corrective way, helping to repair past damage.
6) Development of socializing techniques	Social skills are gained through an adaptive and supportive group environment.
7) Imitative behavior	Members learn by vicariously observing the leader(s) and other members.
8) *Interpersonal learning (Input and Output)	This factor is the therapeutic analogue in individual therapy of insight, working through transference, and the corrective emotional experience. A dynamic interaction emerges through which members gain personal insight (input) while permitting them to interact adaptively (output).
9) *Group cohesiveness	This factor is the therapeutic analogue to the relationship in individual therapy. The mechanism of cohesion is considered to be the most central therapeutic factor because it is a therapeutic mechanism in its own right and it also stimulates others. Cohesion appears to best define the group therapeutic relationship.
10) Catharsis	Members release emotion about past experiences and events within the group, leading them to feel better.
11) Existential factors	Members confront the challenging "givens" of life—the ultimate concerns of the human condition—learning life lessons and about their own personal responsibility for life choices.

As mentioned above, more attention is given to interpersonal learning (input and output) and to group cohesion because of their central roles in group counseling.

INTERPERSONAL LEARNING

This key group therapeutic factor is the analogue in individual therapy of insight, working through transference, and the corrective emotional experience. Interpersonal learning results when a group, acting as a social microcosm, allows for each member's personal style to be manifested within the group itself. A dynamic interaction emerges through which members gain personal insight (input) while permitting them to interact adaptively (output).

Interpersonal learning is central to group process (AGPA, 2007); Leszcz & Kobos, 2008). It can be understood as resulting from productive interpersonal relationships, the corrective emotional experience, and the group operating as a social microcosm (Yalom, 2005). In fact, according to Yalom, the critical member behavior of self-disclosure in a group is always an interpersonal act, as it occurs and is responded to within the interpersonal context.

Although individual therapy limits interpersonal sharing and feedback to the dyadic relationship of therapist and client, group counseling expands those opportunities to include not only the group leader(s) but, also all other members. Thus, the ongoing input for interpersonal learning is exponentially increased, leading to heightened possibilities for members to produce interpersonal learning that can be applied outside the group (Bernard, Burlingame, Flores, Greene, Joyce, & Kobos, 2008; Holmes & Kivlighan, 2000).

GROUP COHESIVENESS

This essential group therapeutic factor is the analogue to the relationship in individual therapy. Cohesion stems from the Latin, *cohaesus*, meaning "to cleave or stick together" (Dion, 2000). Dion proposes that group cohesion is a multidimensional construct consisting of social, task, and vertical (member to leader) cohesion, and also belongingness and attraction of members for each other and the group. To be cohesive, group members also feel a common unity and are able to coordinate their actions, much like a team (Forsyth, 2006). The mechanism of cohesion is considered to be the most central therapeutic factor because it is a therapeutic mechanism in its own right and it also stimulates others. Cohesion appears to best define the group therapeutic relationship (Burlingame, Fuhriman, &

Johnson, 2002; Yalom & Leszcz, 2005) which, in turn, is the central process cutting across all therapies (Martin, Garske, & Davis, 2000). Cohesion appears as important, if not more important, in explaining client improvement than the specific theoretical orientation practiced by the therapist (Norcross, 2002). In turn, it appears that group cohesion can be affected by the attachment style of leaders and by factors such as race, ethnicity, and sexual orientation (Marmarosh & Van Horn, 2011).

A majority of research demonstrates that a strong positive correlation exists between group cohesion and therapeutic group outcomes (Riva, Wachtel, & Lasky, 2004). For instance, Marmarosh, Holtz, and Schottenbauer (2005) studied 102 counseling center clients participating in process and theme groups. The purpose was to examine Yalom's hypothesis that group therapy cohesiveness precipitates group-derived collective self-esteem (CSE), hope for the self (HS), and psychological well-being. Path analyses reinforced the hypothesis that cohesiveness is the primary group factor and is directly related to CSE and HS.

GENERAL THERAPEUTIC FACTORS RESEARCH

As pointed out by Burlingame, Fuhriman, and Johnson (2004) most of the extensive research into therapeutic factors has used Yalom's self-report instrument, which allows for members to assign value to the factors. For instance, in a study by Colijn et al. (1991), group members generally valued catharsis, self-understanding, interpersonal learning, and cohesion while ascribing least value to the corrective family reenactment factor. This finding was consistent across gender, age, group type, or treatment and is consistent with previously conducted studies on therapeutic factors.

Yalom (Yalom & Leszcz, 2000) summarized research of homogeneous group members' choice of therapeutic factors. As a sampling, it has been found that Alcoholics Anonymous and Recovery, Inc. members emphasize instillation of hope, imparting information, universality, altruism, and some aspects of group cohesion. Spousal abusers in a psychoeducational group most valued imparting information, and members of occupational therapy groups prized cohesiveness, instillation of hope, and interpersonal learning. A pilot study (Waldo, Kerne, & Van Horn Kerne, 2007) compared male members' experiencing of therapeutic factors in domestic violence groups. Results were in predicted directions, indicating that guidance group members experienced instillation of hope, imparting information, and existential factors most frequently. In comparison, counseling group members reported experiencing universality, cohesion, and interpersonal learning most often.

Kivlighan and Holmes (2004) conducted meta-analytic studies to examine past reports ranking therapeutic factors, using cluster analysis to create a typology of groups based on their therapeutic mechanisms. They named these clusters of groups by the therapeutic factors that were rated highest and lowest in each cluster:

- Cluster 1: Affective Insight groups (e.g., containing the therapeutic factor of catharsis)
- Cluster 2: Affective Support groups (e.g., containing the therapeutic factor of instillation of hope)
- Cluster 3: Cognitive Support groups (e.g., containing the therapeutic factor of universality)
- Cluster 4: Cognitive Insight groups (e.g., containing the therapeutic factor of interpersonal learning).

Yet, the results related to therapeutic factors and type of group remain somewhat cloudy. Following a review of therapeutic factors according to type of group, Kivlighan et al. (2000) conclude that there is little evidence of consistent findings across types of groups. They observe that a lack of theoretical conceptualization exists to guide these comparisons, a point that has been made strongly before by other researchers (Beck & Lewis, 2000; Durkin, 1981; Fuhriman & Burlingame, 1994). Perhaps use of the four group work types (task, psychoeducation, counseling, and psychotherapy), defined in the ASGW training standards (ASGW, 2000) might aid in clarifying this kind of research.

THERAPEUTIC FACTORS AND GROUP DEVELOPMENT

With regard to the relationship between therapeutic factors and group development, Yalom (Yalom & Leszcz, 2005) painted the following impressionistic picture. Early in a successful group, the therapeutic factors of instillation of hope, universality, and imparting information tend to emerge. At the group's middle stage, the therapeutic factors of altruism, imitative learning, catharsis, socialization techniques, corrective recapitulation of the family experience, and cohesiveness tend to be manifested. Late in the group, the therapeutic stages of interpersonal learning and existential matters assert.

Research results reported by Kivlighan and Mullison (1988) and Kivlighan and Goldfine (1991) were used to examine the clusters of therapeutic factors (mentioned earlier) in relation to group development stages (Kivlighan & Holmes, 2004). Connecting with Tuckman's (1965) four stages of group development (forming, storming, norming, and performing), four hypotheses were generated from this research: cognitive support experiences will characterize the *forming stage* of group development, affective support experiences will predominate in the *storming stage*, cognitive insight experiences will dominate during the *norming stage*, and affective insight experiences will command the *performing stage* of group development.

Shechtman and Gluk (2005) adopted therapeutic factor clusters similar to those used by Holmes and Kivlighan (2000) in their study of adults to examine therapeutic factors in children's groups: emotional awareness-insight, relationship-climate, other-versus-self focus, and problem identification-change. The group relationship-climate was the therapeutic factor most frequently mentioned by the children, whereas the problem-identification-change factor was least appreciated, pointing to the value of relationships for children in group therapy.

After considering the large body of literature addressing the importance of therapeutic factors, Kivlighan and Holmes (2004) were led to conclude that little progress has been made in answering an initial basic question raised by Yalom: "How does group therapy help patients?" Complexities of client, therapist, and group variables—and their interaction—continue to vex efforts.

Future research into these and other areas raised in this section will help further clarify how therapeutic factors operate and how group leaders can harness their power. Perhaps incorporating a wider range of research methodologies into this search, such as qualitative designs, might yield valuable insights that could not be found by relying solely on quantitative approaches (Rubel & Atieno Okech, 2011). Developing answers to these questions is important to group counseling.

Group Climate

Group climate is the atmosphere, the culture, or the general personality of a group. It is described by MacKenzie (1983) as an environmental press that serves to facilitate or to restrict the efforts of individuals to reach their goals. Thus, group climate is thought to exert a strong effect on outcomes. Yalom (1995) holds that it is a group leader's task to establish a group culture, or climate, that is maximally conducive to effective group interaction (pp. 109–110). Through this climate therapeutic factors are stimulated, accounting for change in the group.

This contention has been supported by research. For example, Ogrodniczuk and Piper (2003) examined the association between dimensions of the common factor of group climate and treatment outcome using MacKenzie's Group Climate Questionnaire-Short From (GCQ-S; MacKenzie, 1983). In general, they found that group climate is related to positive outcome in group psychotherapy. More particularly, results showed that the dimension of engagement, reflecting a cohesive group environment and a willingness of members to participate in the group, was significantly related to positive outcome. Avoidance and conflict, conversely, were found to be inimical to development of a positive climate. Adding to the assertions of other researchers before them (e.g., Budman, Soldz, Demby, Feldstein, Springer, & Davis, 1989), the authors observe that cohesion, which can be viewed as a network of engaged relationships, likely serves a similar purpose in group therapy as the therapeutic alliance does in individual therapy.

Continuing this line of research Joyce, Piper, and Ogrodniczuk (2007) examined cohesion and therapeutic alliance (the relationship between members and leader) in relation to outcome in a time-limited psychotherapy group for complicated grief. They found alliance and cohesion to be positively correlated, but not all measures of each construct predicted outcomes. Therapeutic alliance was found in this study to be a consistently stronger predictor of member outcomes. In a study of one long-term psychoanalytically oriented group, Lorentzen (2008) found that therapeutic alliance deepened over time and that the group therapist's rating of early alliance was a positive predictor of symptom improvement in group members.

Do the findings of the Joyce et al. study throw into question the role of cohesion in affecting group outcomes? Johnson (2007), in discussing the Joyce et al. article, seeks to place the results in context. She points out that both cohesion and alliance have been defined, operationalized, and measured in different ways as increased precision is pursued. Moreover, she points out that timing in relation to measuring these factors is an important consideration, as levels of cohesion and alliance often change in relation to a group's developmental progress. Who makes what ratings deserves attention, as the best predictors of member perceptions of the therapeutic process are the fellow members, not the leaders (similar to individual therapy). Finally, Johnson points out that it matters if assessment is aimed at the individual or the group level, and if it examines both working and relational components. Results obtained, then, may need to be considered in relation to these issues.

Multilevel, structural equation models were used by Johnson, Burlingame, Olsen, Davies, and Gleave (2005) to examine four relationship constructs central to group psychotherapy: group climate, cohesion, alliance, and empathy. Data were collected from three relationship vantage points, member to member, member to group, and member to leader, involving 662 participants from 111 counseling center and personal growth groups. The research shows that nearly every measure of therapeutic relationship was significantly correlated, with the suggestion that three relationships operate in the group context: positive relational bonds, referring to the emotional connection or attachment to other members, leader, and group as a whole; positive working relationships in the group, or the collaborative engagement aimed toward goal attainment; and negative relationship factors, including aspects of process that may unfavorably impact attachments or slow therapeutic progress. In sum, group members in this study were found to distinguish their within-group relationships by relationship quality rather than by who was involved.

Following from the above study, the AGPA released the Core Battery-R (Burlingame, 2005; MacNair-Semands, 2006; Ogrodniczuk, 2005). This set of instruments is designed to help track the individual improvement of members and to assess the therapeutic relationship in groups focusing on positive relational bond, positive working relationship, and negative factors that interfere with the bond or with therapeutic work (Burlingame, Strauss, Joyce, MacNair-Semands, MacKenzie, Ogrodniczuk, & Taylor, 2006). Each of these components can be assessed from the perspective of a member's relationship with the group leader and the member's relationship with the whole group.

An earlier study tested Yalom's hypothesis that group climate mediates the relationship between group leadership and outcome (Kivlighan & Tarrant, 2001). More specifically, they explored whether the use of structure and formation of positive relationships with group members would be related to increased levels of active engagement and decreasing levels of conflict-distance. If these results occurred, the study was geared to explore if they would be related to positive member outcome. Findings supported the above hypotheses about group leadership and group climate, suggesting directions for how group leaders can build a therapeutic group climate. Based on this and previous research (e.g., Braaten, 1989; Budman et al., 1989; Kivlighan & Lilly, 1997), Kivlighan and Tarrant (2001) suggest:

> Group members will increase their active
> involvement with the group when group leaders
> refrain from doing individual therapy in the
> group and actively set goals and norms while
> maintaining a warm and supportive
> environment . . . the group leader's major task
> is to create a therapeutic group climate . . .
> unlike individual treatment, where the relationship
> between the client and therapist is tantamount,
> in group treatment leaders should probably
> de-emphasize their relationships with individual
> group members and focus on creating a therapeutic
> group climate. (p. 231).

Learning more about how group leaders can concretely promote and maintain a positive group climate is needed. Recent efforts to conceptualize "ecological group work" (Bemak & Conyne, 2004; Conyne & Bemak, 2004; Conyne, Crowell, & Newmeyer, 2008) are focused in this direction. Other work showing special promise results from several large-scale international studies (McClendon & Burlingame, 2011) organizes a 3-factor model of group climate: (a) positive bonding relationship among members, (b) positive working relationship and group climate, and (c) negative relationship and affect connected to tension, withdrawal, avoidance, and conflict.

Group Development

Group conditions evolve and fluctuate over time. The degree and direction of these shifts are dependent on many factors and their interaction, similar to most aspects of group counseling. The type of group, number of sessions, whether it is open or closed, the degree of cohesion developing early, amount of structure used, and other factors are involved. One of the factors strongly influencing functioning and later outcomes is group development (Wheelan, 2005).

The term "group development" refers to patterns of growth and change that evolve during the lifespan of a group (Forsyth, 2006). Lewin's contributions to group dynamics (e.g., Lewin, Lippitt, & White, 1939)

and to the "social field" (Lewin, 1951) provided a robust platform for considering group development. Bales (1950) made group development an area of study by developing a system for coding small group interaction using his Interaction Process Analysis. Hill's (1965) instrumentation and conceptual map for analyzing group verbal interaction developmentally advanced study in this area. Agazarian (e.g., 1999) contributed a view of group therapy as a living human system that shapes and is shaped by group development phase dynamics.

In fact, over 100 conceptual models of group development have been formulated (Conyne, 1989). These models are arranged into recurring-phase (e.g., Schutz's FIRO phase model, 1958) and sequential-stage approaches (e.g., Corey & Corey's initial-transition-working-final stages model, 2006). Regardless of approach or model, reiteration rather than linearity applies as any one group lurches along its way. Capturing this outlook, Yalom reports that Hamburg (1978) suggested the term "cyclotherapy" to refer to the kind of ebb and flow that characterizes progress in a group.

Patterns are observable when examining many groups from a distance, although chance and serendipity associated with the unique composition of a group and the often unpredictable interactions occurring among members contribute strongly to any one group's development. Still, group developmental models can be used by group leaders to assist in managing events under way in a group, to help in predicting general future events, and to guide creation of a plan for a new group (Brabender, 2011; Conyne et al., 1997, 2007; MacKenzie, 1997; Wheelan, 1997). A number of studies (e.g., Kivlighan, McGovern, & Corazzini, 1984) have shown that successful group outcome is strongly dependent on the group being able to move positively through developmental levels (Donigian & Malnati, 1997) and the capacity of a group counselor to mirror interventions with developmental progress is important (Brabender, 2011).

But, of course, there is no guarantee of such positive movement. Too many groups falter early and disband. Others may make it to the end but without successful outcomes for members. Being attuned not only to nomothetic but also to idiographic perspectives is important (Kivlighan et al., 2000).

Structuring, which plays a generally important role in group development, seems especially useful to provide pre-group preparation and growth in the early developmental stages of a group (Burlingame et al., 2004). In addition to using structure appropriately, MacKenzie (1997) provides a number of suggestions for group leaders to follow in managing positive group development, including selecting a particular group theory or format. MacKenzie (1997) and Conyne et al. (2008) both demonstrate how the purposeful selection of group techniques by leaders can be timed to group developmental stages, taking strategic advantage of their unique dynamics.

Wheelan (1997), although agreeing that group leader behavior is important for approaching success, makes the point that member behavior is of equal importance. She suggests that both leader and members need to understand the foundational dynamics and developmental patterns attending the complex system of groups for them to move to the higher stages of group development associated with positive growth. Such a level of shared understanding and participation might also support Lewin's "law" of change in groups: "It is usually easier to change individuals formed into a group than to change any one of them separately" (Lewin, 1951, cited in Forsyth, 2006, p. 525).

Group Leadership

> A leader is best
>> When people barely know he exists.
>> Not so good when people obey and acclaim him.
>> Worse when they despise him.
>> Fail to honor people, they fail to honor you;
>> But of a good leader, who talks little,
>> When his work is done, his aim fulfilled,
>> They will say, "We did this ourselves."
>
> Lao-Tse (cited in Cohen & Smith, 1976, viii).

There are many perspectives about leaders and leadership. Lao-Tse's prescient view of a leader, adapted above (from the 6th century B.C., long before the advent of sexist terminology), is no doubt one of the earliest on record. Its components mesh well with aspects of contemporary group leadership, perhaps most notably with showing caring, empathy, and respect and with the importance of collaboration.

In this section, I examine important aspects of group counseling leadership, attending to: defining this elusive ability; identifying its functions, tasks, and roles; pre-group preparation and planning in creating groups; the positive valence of the leader; stimulating and focusing here-and-now interaction; using meaning attribution; leader choice of interventions; drawing from standards, guidelines, and principles to guide effective and ethical group leadership; and a role for improvisation in group leadership.

Despite so much being written over the decades in so many disciplines, as well as in popular media, the political scientist James McGregor Burns wryly claimed that leadership is "one of the most observed and least understood phenomena on earth" (cited in Forsyth, 2006, p. 373). Is leadership related to power, to fidelity and honor? Does it involve great people doing heroic things? Is it all about motivating others? Are leaders born or made? Is it a function emerging from the structure and processes of a particular organization or environment? Is it shared by everyone in the system? Does it emerge from the wisdom of the leader?

According to Forsyth's (2006) review and summary of it, leadership is the ability to lead others by guiding them in their pursuits—often by organizing, directing, coordinating, supporting, and motivating their efforts. Although this definition seems to be generally useful, many other perspectives on leadership exist, as well. For example, some focus on leadership being a shared function of those in the system, illustrated by Raelin's (2003) notion of "leaderful" organizations. Other viewpoints focus on leadership being defined more by organizational structure than by individual behaviors (e.g., Fuqua & Newman, 2004), by the ability to facilitate effectiveness by improving process and structure (Schwarz, 2002), or by the performance of the group or team for which a leader is responsible (Kaiser, Hogan, & Craig, 2008). The Aristotelian notion of *phronesis*, in which the group leader demonstrates a "practical wisdom" (Holliday, Statler, & Flanders, 2007) combining intelligence, creativity, and knowledge aimed to better the common good (Sternberg, 2004) suggests a different perspective on leadership.

Defining Group Leadership Remains Elusive

Leading counseling groups is a particular application of leadership, as these groups are formed and conducted to benefit member growth and change. An impressive number of texts, handbooks, book chapters, journal articles, and videotapes address group counseling and its leadership. Considering texts alone, group leadership functions, tasks, competencies, interventions, strategies, techniques, challenges, principles, and more have been researched and described (e.g., Corey, 2007; Corey & Corey, 2006; Conyne et al., 2008; Conyne, Wilson, & Ward, 1997; DeLucia, Gerrity, Kalodner, & Riva, 2004; Gazda et al., 2001; Gladding, 2006;

Jacobs, Harvill, & Masson, 2006; Trotzer, 2006; Yalom & Leszcz, 2005).

However, summative concise definitions of group counseling leadership seem generally to be implied rather than explicated in the literature. Maybe this condition is due to the complexity of the activity. Type of population, leader experience, measurement methods, and other factors all contribute (Shechtman, 2007). For example, according to Higgenbotham, West, and Forsyth (1988), how much group leaders should participate in the group process remains the most significant single problem being faced by practitioners and researchers. Many other challenges persist, such as determining how leaders can effectively promote group cohesion. Therefore, it is appropriate to wonder how any one definition could capture the variety and nuances involved in group leadership.

Nonetheless, an integrative definition of group counseling leadership is suggested below, based on three central tasks of the group therapist that were identified by Yalom (Yalom & Leszcz, 2005): to create and maintain the group, to build a group culture, and to activate and illuminate the here-and-now.

Group leadership is the ability to draw from best practices and good professional judgment to:

> Create a group and, in collaboration with members, build and maintain a positive group climate that serves to nurture here-and-now interaction and its processing by leader and members, aimed at producing lasting growth and change.

Functions, Tasks, and Roles of Group Leaders

How do group leaders apply the components of the above definition or, indeed, of any definition of leadership? Results from Lewin, Lippitt, and White's (1939) famous laboratory study provided early guidance. In this social psychological experiment, 10- and 11-year-old boys met in three after-school groups to work on differing hobbies. Each group included a male leader who manifested one of three leadership styles: authoritarian, democratic, or laissez-faire. Results, although not clear cut and marked by differences in such criteria as efficiency, satisfaction, and participation, favored the democratic style, which tended to be friendlier and more group oriented.

Leaping ahead four decades, Lieberman, Yalom, and Miles (1973) reported their classic study of the processes and effects of encounter groups. Participants were 210 Stanford University students who were arranged into 18 encounter groups, each of which met for 30 hours. Ten different theoretical models and approaches were expressed through the groups: National Training Laboratory t-group, gestalt, transactional analysis, Esalen eclectic, personal growth, Synanon, psychodrama, marathon, psychoanalytically oriented, and encounter tapes—leaderless. A wide battery of tests were employed to investigate issues related to person variables, leader characteristics, leader variables, group characteristics, participants' experience, and outcome. Although this study is dated because it was conducted decades ago during a unique time of excitement about groups and social change and was comprised of college students from one campus on the West Coast, it remains as one of the most significant studies available on group leadership.

Among the results, it was found that theoretical disposition mattered little in producing member change, but leadership style was significant. Six different leadership styles were identified, each one a combination of four leadership functions. These leadership functions are: *caring*, or demonstrating empathy and a genuine concern for members; *meaning attribution*, or helping members to convert experiences occurring within the group to personal meaning; *emotional stimulation*, or catalyzing the expression of emotion and sustaining energy in the group; and *executive function*, or managing the group as an ongoing social system. The most effective group leadership style, called the "Provider," resulted from a combination of high levels of caring and meaning attribution, with moderate levels of emotional stimulation and executive functioning. Coche, Dies, and Goettelman (1991) also found that a high amount of meaning attribution and a moderate amount of executive functioning are advantageous in therapeutic groups.

These and other findings from the Lieberman et al. (1973) study have served many training programs well in preparing future group leaders. Yet, not all subsequent studies have been able to produce similar results. For instance, Tinsley, Roth, and Lease (1989), in their survey of 204 experienced group leaders, identified eight functions, not four: cognitive direction, affective direction, nonverbal exercise (leader style factor); nurturant attractiveness and charismatic expertness (leader personal qualities factor); and group functioning and personal functioning (leader objectives factor). Kivlighan (1997), in discussing situational leadership (Hershey, Blanchard, & Johnson, 1982), draws upon Dies' (1983) and Higgenbotham et al.'s analyses to suggest that a more general level of consensus is emerging that only two dimensions capture the wide variety of group leader behaviors and styles: personal, relationship dimensions and technical, task dimensions. Yet, one gets the sense that this question, as many others in group counseling, is not completely answered—due, in part, to the use of different research methodologies and research participants.

Hershey and Blanchard's situational leadership approach, mentioned above, suggests that effective leader use of task and relationship behaviors varies in relation to the developmental trajectory of the group. Task behavior is relatively more salient early in the group when rules, norms, and structure are created, with relationship behavior more important later.

Consistent with this view, Yalom (1995) maintains that the group leader's initial goals are to create a therapeutic culture drawing largely from task-oriented behaviors; this is known as the technical expert role. As the group proceeds, the leader may shift to providing increased relationship behaviors and modeling of positive attitudes and behaviors, consistent with a model-setting participant role as the group evolves. Both of these roles are important in shaping the group climate and its norms. In fact, Bauman suggests that the place to begin with training group counseling leaders is to identify what roles they will be expected to perform.

Pre-Group Preparation and Planning in Creating the Group

Pre-group preparation has been shown to be essential to promoting group cohesion, member satisfaction, and comfort with the group (e.g., Bednar & Kaul, 1994; Bowman & DeLucia, 1993; Burlingame et al., 2001, 2004; Riva et al., 2004). Pre-group preparation enjoys the strongest empirical support of all structuring approaches.

Developing an overarching group plan, within which pre-group preparation is included, provides group leaders with a valuable resource. Such a plan may include the group's underlying conceptual framework, general goals, pre-group orientation, methods, session details, the target population, recruitment and selection procedures, and evaluation, among other elements (Conyne et al., 1997, 2007). Following selection, the pre-group preparation of members helps to set expectations, establish rules, and it provides guidance about effective participation in the group. This kind of preparation

and planning, including member selection, is detailed in the Planning section of the ASGW Best Practice Guidelines (ASGW, 1998a, 2008).

Positive Valence of the Group Leader

As mentioned earlier, research has accumulated about the importance of a positive group climate in mediating growth and change in members. Likewise, research demonstrates that leaders contribute strongly to the creation and maintenance of group climate, for good or ill. Trotzer (2011) has described the group leader's positive valence as her or his "personhood." Those leaders who behave consistently with members in a caring and empathic manner, who constructively confront, and who maintain a supportive therapeutic relationship with members aid significantly in producing a positive group climate. As stated by Yalom: "The basic posture of the (group) therapist to a client must be one of concern, acceptance, genuineness, empathy. *Nothing, no technical consideration, takes precedence over this attitude*" (italics retained; Yalom & Leszcz, 2005, p. 117).

Likewise, a quote about the value of positive leader behavior from Dies (1994) is worth repeating. After reviewing 135 studies, he concluded: "Group members favor and seem to benefit more from a positive style of intervention, and that as leaders become more actively negative, they increase the possibility that participants will not only be dissatisfied, but also potentially harmed by the group experience" (cited in Riva et al., 2004, p. 40).

This positive valence of the leader contributes to the creation and maintenance of an affirming therapeutic relationship and to group cohesion. In turn, these conditions promote progress toward member goals.

Stimulating and Focusing Here-and-Now Interaction

Group counseling interaction needs to be "presentized" to be therapeutic (Bradford, Gibb, & Benne, 1964; Golembiewski & Blumberg, 1970; Zinker, 1980). As Yalom (Yalom & Leszcz, 2005) stressed, "[this is] perhaps the single most important point I make in this entire book: *the here-and-now focus, to be effective, consists of two symbiotic tiers, neither of which has therapeutic power without the other*" (p. 141) (italics retained).

In Yalom's first tier, the immediate, here-and-now interaction of members in a group session take clear precedence over those occurring in the current, outside lives of members or in their distant past. Adapting from statistical terminology to illustrate this point, in group counseling "the main effect is in the interaction" (e.g., Bronfenbrenner, 1977, cited in Conyne & Cook, 2004, p. 341). Dye (2008) referred to the introduction of the here-and-now focus in group work as the equivalent of a "tsunami" in its overall effect on how groups would henceforth function.

In the second tier, which is discussed in the next chapter section, *illumination of the process* (again, italics retained) is led to occur. This step is a kind of "doubling back" on itself, in which experience is reviewed and processed, on the way toward attribution of meaning. Continuing with Dye's analogy, if not quite the tsunami of the here-and-now, the realization that experiencing needs meaning to be genuinely valuable amounted to at least a large tidal wave.

What are some important "tier 1" skills for group leaders? They catalyze here-and-now interaction by promoting meaningful member self disclosure, feedback, appropriate use of structure, catharsis, and acquisition of social skills. These areas are associated with the group leadership function of emotional stimulation identified by Lieberman et al. (1973). Discussions of these leader skills and interventions are contained in numerous sources (e.g., Conyne et al., 2008; Corey, Corey, Callanan, & Russell, 2004; Gladding, 2006; Morran, Stockton, & Whittingham, 2004). One illustration (Trotzer, 2006) indicates the importance of leaders appropriately providing skills of reaction (e.g., active listening), interaction (e.g., linking), and action (confronting) to promote positive group and member functioning.

Tier 1 skills of group leadership also involve the proper use of positive and corrective feedback and their sequencing in a group (DeLucia-Waack & Kalodner, 2005; Hulse-Killacky & Orr, 2006; Morran, Stockton, Cline, & Teed, 1998; Morran, Stockton & Harris, 1991; Robison, Stockton, Morran, & Uhl-Wagner, 1988). In general, these studies chart the value of emphasizing positive feedback in beginning sessions of a group followed in middle and later group sessions by positive and corrective feedback. In addition, research shows (e.g., Davies & Jacobs, 1985) that the delivery of feedback within a group session should follow a sequence that is positive then corrective, or positive, then corrective, then positive all the while focusing on member behaviors that are both observable and specific (Jacobs, Jacobs, Cavior, & Burke, 1974) and giving careful consideration to member readiness to receive feedback (especially corrective feedback).

Making active use of ongoing, within-group process observations by group leaders is receiving increasing attention for group leader practice and training (e.g., Armstrong & Berg, 2005; Bieschke, Matthews, & Wade, 1996, 1998; Conyne, 1998). Group leaders learn how to observe and incorporate group processes (such as participation, task-maintenance, and decision-making; Hanson, 1972) within leader interventions. Doing so provides a way to tie leader interventions concretely to here-and-now activity, and can provide opportunities for group members to become more aware of how their group participation can influence progress and learning.

As mentioned, practice and training are critical elements in helping to produce qualified group counselors. Attention to the "personhood" (Trotzer, 2011) of the trainee also is a vital component. Finally, on-going supervision is critically important, because it can provide a continuing source of feedback, support, constructive challenge, and guidance. However, as Riva (2011) observes, the quality of supervision cannot be taken for granted. Training programs need to track client outcomes as a consequence of group leader supervision and of group leader practice under supervision.

Using Meaning Attribution

The experience of group counseling can be bewildering due to its ongoing dynamic activity. It also can be emotionally overpowering at times or, conversely, it can sap the patience of everyone involved. In any and all cases, the experience of group participation can become more understandable and meaningful, as mentioned above, when group leaders assist members in converting experience to cognition.

This lesson was learned through the empirical research of Lieberman et al. (1973) who found, among other important results, that "meaning attribution" is an essential group leader function to be performed. Yalom (Yalom & Leszcz, 2005) explained that "process illumination" promotes meaning attribution, while releasing what he terms the vital "power cell of the group." Potency surges when the "here-and-now" interaction among members is examined through a kind of "self-reflective loop," or process commentary. That is, an interpersonal experience in the group is examined by the members for its meaning. This kind of reflective process engagement sparks energy and stimulates the making of meaning. Yalom has phrased the critical question to ask in relation to an interpersonal event: "What does it tell about the interpersonal relationships of the participants?" (p. 143).

As mentioned in relation to increased attention being given to intentionality in stimulating here-and-now interaction, a similar emphasis is emerging that centers on the purposeful planning and processing of experiences in the group (Conyne, 1997, 1999; Conyne et al., 2008; Cox, Banez, Hawley, & Mostade, 2003; DeLucia-Waack, 1997; Glass & Benshoff, 1999; Kees & Jacobs, 1990; Kees & Leech, 2002; Pistole & Filer, 1991; Stockton, Morran, & Krieger, 2004; Stockton & Morran, 2011; Stockton, Morran, & Nitza, 2000; Thomas, 2006; Ward & Litchy, 2004). Group leadership is becoming a more empirically based, intentionally practiced endeavor.

Leader Choice of Interventions

Intentionality extends to the leader choice of interventions to more purposefully stimulate here-and-now experience and its meaning (e.g., Cohen & Smith, 1976; Conyne, et. al., 2008; Corey & Corey, 2006; Ivey, Pedersen, & Ivey, 2001; Jacobs, Masson, & Harvill, 2006; Stockton, Morran, & Clark, 2004; Trotzer, 2004). Stockton et al. (2004) studied the intentions of group leaders. They found four intention clusters in relation to interventions made in group sessions: promoting insight/change, planning and guiding, attending, and assessing growth.

Cohen and Smith (1976), in their critical incident growth group model, long ago provided a useful map for how to intervene and when. Their use of critical incidents is currently popular, being applied in counselor training in different spheres, including in contemporary group leader training (e.g., Tyson, Perusse, & Whitledge, 2004). The Cohen and Smith critical incident growth group model provides for 27 group leader intervention possibilities that emerge from the interaction of three intervention factors: intervention type (cognitive, experiential, structural), intervention level (group, individual, interpersonal), and intervention intensity (high, medium, low). The authors hold that cognitive-group-low intensity interventions generally are suitable early in a group, then shifting to more experiential and intensive personal and interpersonal interventions as the group progresses, then shifting back to less intense interventions as the group moves toward its conclusion. Leader flexibility (Dies, 1983; Kivlighan, 1997) is a key behavior, in that good leaders are able to adjust behavior and style to fit the developmental needs of members and of the group itself.

Building on the Cohen and Smith critical incident model, Conyne et al. (2008; Newmeyer, 2011)

integrate several additional elements thought to be important in group leadership to create the *purposeful group technique model* (PGTM). This model is used intentionally to guide the consideration and selection of group techniques. It is based on viewing a group as an ecological system. The model includes five steps:

- Identify the group type, best practice area, and group developmental stage.
- Analyze the group's ecology using the concepts of context, interconnection, collaboration, social system maintenance, meaning making, and sustainability.
- Review possible techniques considering their focus (cognitive, affective, behavioral, and structural) and level (individual, interpersonal, and group).
- Select a best-fit technique by evaluating for adequacy, appropriateness, effectiveness, efficiency, and side-effects.
- Implement and evaluate, allowing for adaptation and future change.

Practice and supervision in applying these steps can lead to an increased fluidity of use in real time.

Drawing from Standards, Guidelines, and Principles to Guide Group Leadership

The increased intentionality in group leadership has been marked by the creation and adoption of various standards, guidelines, principles, and codes that are particular to group work. It is important for group leaders to be aware of and guided by existing ethics, best practice guidelines, legal statutes, and other professional codes that are relevant to their practice (Wilson, Rapin, & Haley-Banez, 2004). In this section, we will briefly examine considerations for ethical and for diversity and multicultural practice.

ETHICAL PRACTICE

The Association for Specialists in Group Work's Best Practice Guidelines (ASGW, 1998a, 2008), the AGPA's practical guidelines for group psychotherapy (AGPA, 2007) and its ethical guidelines (2002), ASGW's professional training standards for group work (2002), and the Association for the Advancement of Social Work's standards for practice (2006) represent professional associational efforts to provide guidance and direction to effective group training and practice. For consumers, AGPA's friendly and informative brochure, *Group Works! Information About Group Psychotherapy* (n.d.a.) provides an introduction to group therapy that is both readable and understandable.

The special sections on the "ethical group psychotherapist" in the *International Journal of Group Psychotherapy* (2007), and book chapters by DeLucia-Waack and Kalodner (2005), Rapin (2004, 2011), and Rapin and Conyne (2006), addressing guidelines for the ethical and legal practice of counseling and psychotherapy groups and in group work, add further substantiation to the trend toward increased intentionality, purposefulness, and accountability in group leadership.

Sound ethical practice is accomplished through giving appropriate attention to planning, performing, and processing groups. Thorough planning, for example, can help control for committing errors in confidentiality, informed consent, and recruitment and selection of members, and to designing a group that more closely reflects the needs and culture of participants. Careful attention to performing, that is, attending to what leaders do within sessions, can enhance the effectiveness and appropriateness of leader interventions. Thoughtful processing can protect against ignoring how ethical and legal principles apply to situations being confronted, and can promote regular scrutiny and evaluation of the group being led.

In addition, Rapin (2011) suggests that ethical behavior in group counseling can be viewed as being derived from an interaction of several factors occurring within a decision-making model. These factors are: moral and ethical development, professional ethics, core knowledge and skills, specialty best practices, and legal parameters.

DIVERSITY AND MULTICULTURAL PRACTICE

Following the leads of Rapin (2004) and D'Andrea (2004), Macnair-Semands (2007) emphasizes that intentional interventions in group therapy require the group leader to be culturally competent. ASGW's diversity-competent principles (ASGW, 1998b), the APA's Multicultural Guidelines (2002), the Association for Multicultural Counseling and Diversity's multicultural competencies and standards (Sue, Arredondo, & McDavis, 1992), and scholarly contributions such as book chapters (e.g., Conyne, Tang, & Watson, 2001; Merchant, 2006; Rivera et al., 2004), books (e.g., DeLucia-Waack & Donigian, 2003; Ivey, Pedersen, & Ivey, 2008), and sections of handbooks (e.g., the extensive coverage of multicultural group applications in DeLucia-Waack et al., 2004) attest to the vital importance of group work being applied with cultural appropriateness to

an ever-expanding multicultural and diverse clientele and contexts—including internationally (e.g., Conyne, Wilson, & Tang, 2000; Conyne, Wilson, Tang, & Shi, 1999; McWhirter, J. J., McWhirter, P., McWhirter, B., & McWhirter, E. H., 2011; Walker & Conyne, 2007; Yau, 2004). Merchant (2008) is actively involved in specifying multicultural group skills that are appropriate for culturally specific groups, for groups containing members from various cultures, as well as for all groups.

Group leaders need to become comfortable and competent in providing multicultural group counseling. Specific recommendations have been provided to assist in meeting this charge (DeLucia-Waack, 2011; DeLucia-Waack & Donigian, 2003): develop awareness of the worldviews of different cultures and how these might impact group work interventions, develop self-awareness of racial identity and one's own cultural and personal worldviews, and develop a repertoire of group leader interventions that are culturally appropriate. The ASGW principles for diversity-competent group workers, referenced earlier, offer specific guidance. Three areas of multicultural competences for group leaders and group members alike are emphasized in the principles: group leader attitudes and beliefs, knowledge, and skills.

Conyne et al. (2001) underlined important aspects of diversity in therapeutic groups, including worldview, acculturation, ethnic/racial identity, and clients' differing levels of development and life style. Ritter (2011) and Keim and Olguin (2011) have elaborated on multicultural group work focused on sexual orientation and for individuals across the life span, respectively. For all these uniquely expressed groups—and for groups in general, Conyne, et al. (2001) suggest that group leaders apply the following general guideline when working with diverse groups: "Create a social ecology in the group that allows for differences to be acknowledged and respected and where commonalities can be recognized and accepted" (p. 359).

Improvisation

When all is said and done, there is more to group leadership than purposefulness and intentional behavior guided by research, theory, and standards—despite the thrust of this chapter. There is some risk involved in group leadership because leaders often cannot predict the course of events or the consequences of their own actions. Dye (2008) wryly used flying in an airplane as a metaphor.

He suggested that if group work could be thought of as flying in an airplane, then group leadership would be comparable to sky diving.

Risk acknowledged, I suggest that group leadership can be viewed as an informed improvisational art form, a creative and spontaneous act (Gladding, 2011) with at least as many similarities to the jazz musician as to the symphony orchestra conductor. Its music is an ongoing riff, not a charted score.

Nearly always, there are apparent discordances and conflicting melodies running through group interaction. At times, group interaction may "sound" cacophonous. Different members "play" idiosyncratic tunes on their own separate instruments, just as in a jazz ensemble, seemingly at times at odds with each other. Yet, underneath there often is a "matter of consistency" (Kaul, 1990)—a unison refrain, a groove, if you will—and it is the group leader's role to find it, if no one else can, to bring it home to every member's awareness. Then, leaders need to show members how their interactive participation can become harmonious even as they continue to express their individuality. Theory, research, and supervised practice contribute substantively to inform and guide group leadership, indeed; but personal factors, along with spontaneity and intuition, may be just as important.

Expansion of Groups in Contemporary Society: The "Age of Ubiquity"?

Sometimes when in the midst of a torrent of ongoing events and activities, the significance of the action can be overlooked. The Renaissance, for instance, was not experienced as a special time by Michelangelo, it is said.

I earlier noted Yalom's observation that the myriad of group therapies available today is "mind-boggling as is there application and use across the wide variety of settings in our society (Kalodner & Hanus, 2011). Although certainly not approaching the status or significance of the Renaissance, when group historians look back at the early 21st century, they may assign special notice to the variety and expanse of groups occurring in our contemporary society—whether these be called group "therapies," "group work," or some other terms. Certainly, from the beginnings of Pratt's mini-lectures, to numbers of tuberculin patients gathered together, to the present day, populated by hundreds of thousands of face-to-face and online groups, the always robust group method can be said to have entered an Age of—what? Perhaps, I suggest, "Ubiquity."

There are, of course, professionally led groups, commonly referred to as *counseling and therapy groups*. These have garnered the attention of this review chapter. As well, many specifications and adaptations exist of ASGW's four types of groups (task, psychoeducational, counseling, and psychotherapy), including a myriad of support groups and self-help/mutual-help groups. Groups are multisplendored, therefore. They are tailored to a wide range of specific populations, addressing a myriad of health and mental health care issues. Groups are offered across the lifespan and provided in brief therapy formats supported by managed care (but, alas, much more needs to be done in this arena). There are quality circle groups, community action groups, prevention groups, social justice groups, trauma groups, and the list goes on . . . and on. As a sampling, let us briefly consider brief therapy groups, mutual-help groups, social justice groups, trauma and disaster preparedness groups, and online groups.

Brief Therapy Groups

Brief group therapy (BGT) (e.g., Spitz, 1996), sometimes referred to as *focal group psychotherapy* (McKay & Paleg, 1992) is a specific form of group therapy. Most of these kinds of groups are 2 to 3 months in duration, containing 8 to 12 sessions. Thus, they are time limited.

Brief group therapy is of considerable interest for a variety of reasons. Research attests to its efficacy and wide applicability (e.g., Piper & Joyce, 2002; Spitz, 1996). In addition, BGT may be a treatment of choice for specific client problems, such as complicated grief, adjustment problems, trauma reactions, existential concerns, and more recently with medically ill patients. Combinations of BGT can be used for those with personality disorders (Piper & Ogrodniczuk, 2004).

Limitations of BGT also reflect those of groups in general. (Although I have not addressed these concerns earlier, they represent nagging roadblocks to be overcome in order to deliver group counseling more satisfactorily.) An appreciable number of people who could benefit from groups find them, at least on the surface, threatening and intimidating. Many people sometimes feel vulnerable disclosing in the presence of others they do not know or trust (at least initially) and sense that they would like more privacy than a group affords. Thus, many people are resistant to the thought of joining a therapeutic group.

Administratively, it requires more time and effort to organize a group than it does to work with people individually. Obtaining referrals to a new group, or recruiting and selecting members in other ways can be challenging. Forming groups comprised of members for whom the intended group will be useful sometimes is difficult. During the course of a group, certain members may withdraw prematurely, which may heighten the anxiety of other members about staying in the group. Developing an organized group system within agencies requires concerted dedication, commitment, and skill.

Leading groups requires a unique perspective, training, and competencies. The shorter-term focus of BGT demands that group leaders trained in longer-term methods adapt successfully. Training and supervision for leading groups is an issue needing general attention, with the demand for groups sometimes outpacing the supply of well-trained group leaders (Brown, 2011; Conyne et al., 2008;Riva, 2011; Shapiro, 2011).

Piper and Ogrodniczuk (2004) point to a unique limitation of BGT that is related to managed care. Although coverage is generally a positive factor, consumers and group leaders both sometimes question the tendency of managed care companies to prioritize efficiency and cost savings over the quality of care. Counselors also may be wary of involvement due to reimbursement concerns.

Mutual-help Groups

Klaw and Humphreys (2004) reviewed the role of peer-led mutual-help groups in enhancing well-being and health. Drawing from a national survey (Kessler, Mickelson, & Zhao, 1997) they reported that approximately 7% (about 11 million) of adults in the United States participated in a mutual-/self-help group in the year studied, and that 18% of Americans had done so at some time during their lives. Not counting self-help groups for prevention purposes (Conyne, 2004; Waldo, Schwartz, Horne, & Cote, 2011), some examples of these groups include: Mended Hearts (ischemic heart disease), Overeaters Anonymous, Young at Heart (arthritis), Narcotics Anonymous, and Make Today Count (malignant neoplasms). Klaw and Humphries point out that these kinds of groups are low-cost, participation in them can produce positive health outcomes while often lowering health care expenditures, and that professionally led groups can be improved by integrating with self-help approaches, perhaps especially if professionals leaders can collaborate with their group members (Silverman, 2011).

Social Justice Groups

The origins of counseling and social work are traced to the early 1900s and are rooted in social change efforts. For instance, Jane Addams (social work) and Jesse B. Davis (guidance) worked in the settlement house movement and in schools, respectively, using groups to introduce democratic processes, promote social support, advance learning and human development, and to seek social change. As Leddick (2008, 2011) pointed out, Addams used groups with immigrants at Hull House in Chicago, seeking to engage them in social skills, hygiene, and nutrition but also to promote larger community change.

After decades during which group work targeted person-change areas while minimizing attention to social change, the end of the last century was marked by renewed vigor in addressing change approaches aimed at social justice and community development (e.g., see Lee, 2007; Toporek, Gerstein, Fouad, Roysircar-Sodowsky, & Israel, 2005), including attention to using prevention groups (e.g., Waldo, Schwartz, Horne, & Cote, 2011) for these purposes. Examples of groups being used for social justice and system change can be found in the area of community-based participatory research and action (Finn & Jacobson, 2003; Jacobson & Rugeley, 2007), expanding learning from the group social microcosm to external system application (Orr et al., 2008), and in using empowerment groups in schools (Bemak, 2005). Using groups and group processes for social justice is emerging as an important approach, leading Hage, Mason and Kim Jung Eun (2011) to emphasize that it no longer is wise to treat or prevent human problems without incorporating attention to social problems.

Trauma and Disaster Preparedness Groups

Group-based interventions for trauma survivors were receiving attention (Burlingame & Layne, 2001) prior to the tragedy of the September 11, 2001 terrorist attacks (9/11). Following it, many professional associations in the helping fields responded through publications (e.g., Webber, Bass, & Yep, 2005; Buchele & Spitz, 2004) and provision of training and services that addressed trauma, terrorism, and recovery. For instance, in their post-9/11 initiative aimed at group interventions for trauma treatment and disaster preparedness and response, the AGPA now provides direct services to victims, survivors, witnesses, and early responders; support systems to helpers; publications; and training for mental health practitioners (Klein & Phillips, 2008). This type of program by a professional association illustrates how groups are being used to address a critically important contemporary issue. While some promising group approaches are being used with people from trauma and disaster situations, they are presently "evidence-informed" and await the generation of evidence (Foy, Drescher, & Watson, 2011).

Online Groups

Groups always have been conducted face-to-face, and nearly all of the existing research and practice knowledge is premised on that direct format. With the explosion in the creation and availability of computers and online technologies, however, a whole new arena has been opened. Although there remains concern about losing the value of personal, face-to-face groups, online formats have flourished in what was termed an "electronic frontier" (Bowman & Bowman, 1998)—an eon ago when counting in technological years.

An increasing range of possibilities exists for online group application. These include but are not limited to: interactive e-journaling (Haberstroh, Parr, Gee, & Trepal, 2006), Internet support groups (Lieberman, Wizlenberg, Golant, & Minno, 2005), synchronous and asynchronous online discussions (Romano & Cikanek, 2003), and making use of videos and computer simulations for training (Smokowski, 2003).

In general, online groups take two forms: asynchronous and synchronous. In the first case, participants join an Internet discussion at different times to post their input. In synchronous groups, members logon at the same time, and they are able to communicate with each other in real time. Regardless, most of these groups use an e-mail format in which members post to a message board or a common site. These sites are ubiquitous. Page (2004) reports that an Internet review conducted in September 2001 revealed approximately 403,000 sites for "online group counseling," and another 1,720,000 sites for "support groups online." No doubt these numbers have increased considerably today.

Research on online groups is scarce. Page (2004) also has summarized results from the few number of studies extant of online groups. For asynchronous groups, where most of the online group research exists, convenience is an attractive factor because they are available 24/7, thus permitting members to read and react at any time, including at times when no professional help would be readily available (Galinsky, Schopler, & Abell, 1997). This form of online group also has been shown to provide support generally and to individual members specifically (Winzelberg, 1997), perhaps because they are able to include therapeutic factors such as universality, instillation of hope, and cohesion (Gary & Remolino, 2000). Page's review also pointed to positive outcomes from asynchronous groups for members in alcohol treatment programs and for reduction of pain in hospitalized children (Holden, Bearison, Rode, Kapoloff, & Rosenberg, 2000; King, 1994). At the same time, concerns are raised in these groups. Information transmitted is unable to contain nonverbal behavior, such as voice tones and body language. Issues related to safety and the communication of inaccurate information can be especially problematical in these groups, too, which typically are led by peers or nonprofessionals (Finn, 1996; Galainsky, et al., 1997).

The newest wave of online groups seems to be synchronous video groups, although the research literature on them has yet to emerge, in part because the technology needed to conduct them is not widely available (it uses polycoms connected through Internet 2). Its potential is attractive, though, because these high-quality, video-based groups allow for interaction that is analogous to that occurring in face-to-face groups. Nonverbal information, as well as verbal information, becomes available in real-time situations (Page et al., 2003; Smokowski, 2003).

Ethical considerations need attention. Online communication presents some unique ethical considerations about which standards have been developed: *Standards for the Ethical Practice of Internet Counseling* (National Board for Certified Counselors [NBCC], 2007) and *Ethical Standards for Internet On-line Counseling* (American Counseling Association [ACA], 1999). The APA's *Statement on Services by Telephone, Teleconferencing, and Internet* (APA, 2008) addresses general matters of interest in this area but not online services. In general, these documents apply general ethical principles to online practice, but they do not address online *group* services specifically.

ONE EXAMPLE OF A SYNCHRONOUS ONLINE GROUP

A brief description of one such online group option, a synchronous online support groups, may give some shape to the various options that exist (Page et al., 2000). The Palace (The Palace Incorporated, 1998), downloaded Internet software, enables members to connect online in a graphical "room" to "talk" interactively by typing messages synchronously to each other. For instance, group members can be represented visually by their photographs, which are taken with a digital camera, scanned into the computer, and transferred to the prop window of The Palace. Messages are typed using one of four formatting icons (e.g., a speech bubble or a thinking bubble). These messages appear immediately and simultaneously on all members' screens, so that it is possible for group members to interact in real time. A spiked bubble allows for emotions to be communicated. Other visual cues and procedures accompany this software. Leaders skilled in the use of technology, in how to plan groups, and in group process, and who are knowledgeable about the ethical practice of Web counseling (e.g., National Board of Certified Counselors, 2007) may find this kind of option worthy of exploration and possible use.

As Page (2004) points out, one of the discrepancies between online and face-to-face groups is that traditional conceptual frameworks and labels (such as task, psychoeducation, counseling, and psychotherapy) do not appear to provide a good fit for the legions of groups populating the Internet. Online groups vary from customary groups along several dimensions. For instance, they tend to be self-help or support groups in nature, they can be synchronous or asynchronous, and many of these groups are not led by mental health professionals.

Social networking Internet formats, such as Facebook.com, Twitter.com,Academia.com, others presently in place and those that undoubtedly will mushroom in the future, appear to be rich in research opportunities. The quotation, below, addresses Facebook.com:

> [I]t is Facebook's role as a Petri dish for the social
> sciences—sociology, psychology, and political
> science—that particularly excites some scholars,
> because the site lets them examine how people,
> especially young people, are connected to one
> another—something few data sets offer,
> the scholars say.
> (Rosenbloom, 2007)

For further review of online and other forms of electronic groups, consult special journal issues dealing with the general topic of electronic group work, published in *Group Dynamics* (2002) and in the *Journal for Specialists in Group Work* (2003). A special issue of *The Counseling Psychologist (2005)* also focused on online counseling.

It seems that comprehensive group work today (Conyne et al., 1997) must include online, Internet, social networking, and other electronic possibilities. At a time in history when solid research and practice continues to accumulate about group counseling, it also is clear that the use and adaptations of both face-to-face groups and those groups provided online are proliferating. A key question is if group counselors will become involved in using these modes and, if they do, will they promote ethical practice and effective care? (Page, 2011).

Although this expansion into the online world can be concerning with regard to many currently unanswered issues of quality and measured effectiveness, the fact that groups literally are everywhere stands as good news for those who have always believed, in the end, in "giving groups away."

Conclusion

Face-to-face group counseling is effective and efficient in promoting change and growth in members. Its more than 100-year history is marked by expansion, solidification, and continued innovation. Standards, principles, and guidelines have emerged as reference points.

Group counseling and other group forms are conducted across the spectrum of remediation, development, and prevention to address a range of target populations. Groups are located in an array of settings from private practice to schools, communities, and organizations. They are professionally led and are self-help, offered face-to-face and online, they are brief or longer-term, the address trauma and wellness. Mechanisms for positive change have been identified generally, with further refinements emerging in robust research programs, being disseminated through respected scholarly vehicles. We have entered an "Age of Ubiquity," with a future full of opportunities and challenges.

Future Directions

The future of group counseling is bright. To intensify and expand its glow, the following ten points are offered, which evolve from the preceding narrative. They are arranged generally into research and practice categories:

Research

• The group research agenda needs to deepen, widen, and integrate. The promising lines of research focused on the process engines that drive groups, including cohesion, culture, and therapeutic factors are revealing important practice applications that invite deepening and focusing more closely on group phenomena (e.g., Kivlighan et al., 2000;Kivlighan, et al., 2011; Riva et al., 2004; Stockton & Morran, 2011). A widening of group research will explore multicultural, online, prevention, trauma, and other expansions of group application (Chen, Kakkad, & Balzano, 2008; DeLucia-Waack et al., 2004; Foy, Deschler & Watson, 2011; Gazda et al., 2001), and wider adoption of various credible research methodologies, such as qualitiative research, needs to occur (Rubel & Atieno Okech, 2011).

• Continued investigation of the evidence basis for group counseling needs to continue and be extended (Burlingame & Beecher, 2008). This focal area is beginning to coalesce around the designation of RSGT Barlow, 2011; (Johnson, 2008; McClendon & Burlingame, 2011). As well, RSGT efforts also need to include cultural and setting differences (Chen et al., 2008) and the whole span of group dynamics (Kivlighan, 2008).

• Adopting common conceptions of group counseling and other group formats (e.g., the ASGW delineation of group work types: task, psychoeducation, counseling, and psychotherapy (Ward, 2011); the multifaceted model of group psychotherapy described by Burlingame et al., 2005; the Group Work Grid of Conyne, 1985) would assist group research, for example, of therapeutic factors across different types of groups and settings (Kivlighan, 2008; Kivlighan & Holmes, 2004). Such definitions could emerge through coordinated attention by major professional associations in the area of groups (Brown, 2011; Rapin, 2011) such as the GPRN which presently includes the AGPA, the ASGW, the Society of Group Psychology and Group Psychotherapy of the APA, and the Association fo the Advancement of Social Work with Groups.

• The connection among group research, group training, group supervision, and group practice needs to be bridged more fully (e.g., Anderson & Wheelan, 2005; Brabender, 2011; McClendon & Burlingame, 2011; Kivlighan, Miles & Paquin, 2011; Marmarosh &Van Horn, 2011; Riva, 2011). This is a continuing challenge in virtually all areas of counseling psychology, and it certainly exists in the domain of groups. For instance, relevant research findings in social psychology need to find their way more quickly and strategically into group practice.

• Group research, practice, and training knowledge that is reported through the organs of different professional associations, and sometimes in different disciplines, needs to be interconnected by scholars, with emerging best practices made available to trainers and practitioners (Berdahl & Henry, 2005; Rapin, 2011).

• Group researchers need to study the various forms of online group systems (Williams, 2002) for efficacy, to determine what modes work best for what situations and which people. As well, tending toward practice, more group counselors need to explore the appropriate use of electronic and online vehicles in their work (McGlothlin, 2003). Ethical guidelines that are specific to these online group systems also await development (Page, 2004, 2011). Online offerings would match the daily life practice of millions of teens and adults in contemporary society.

Practice

• The "Age of Ubiquity" in group counseling means, in part, that training in counseling psychology must rearrange itself to make obvious room for group work in the curriculum (Brown, 2011; Conyne et al., 1997; Conyne & Bemak, 2004; Shapiro, 2011). Group counseling should not be a postdoctoral specialty only. In addition, it should permeate and support other counseling and psychological interventions and stand on its own as an important method, capable of delivery by a wide range of trained practitioners.

• Groups are effective (e.g., Payne & Marcus, 2008) and, of course, efficient. Group counseling advocates must build on these realities to develop concerted strategies to influence the future of health care, particularly managed care, to fully incorporate group delivery formats as reimbursable services (Spitz, 1996). Group services must become an integral part of any future renovation of the nation's health care system.

• Professionally led group methods— developed largely from group psychotherapy research with majority adults in closed groups— need to be intentionally adapted, where needed, to support work with open groups and with groups for children, minorities, the aged, for prevention, for social justice, and in international contexts (Conyne, 2004; DeLucia-Waack, 2011; Hage, et al., 2011; Keim & Olguin, 2011; McWhirter, et al., 2011; Ritter, 2011; Waldo, Schwartz, Horne, & Cote, 2011) and also to support mutual help groups (Silverman, 2011).

• Barriers against group counseling (e.g., ineffective referral processes, cumbersome processes for organizing groups within agencies, or inaccurate myths about group counseling) need to be reduced to allow groups to become more attractive and available to more people (DeLucia-Waack, 2011; Kleim & Olguin, 2011; Ritter, 2011;Trotzer, 2006).

References

Agazarian, Y. (1999). Phases of development in the system-centered group. *Small Group Research, 30*, 82–107.

American Counseling Association (ACA). (1999). *Ethical standards for Internet on-line counseling*. Retrieved December 22, 2008, from http://www.angelfire.com/co2/counseling/ethical.html.

American Group Psychotherapy Association (AGPA). (2002). *Ethical guidelines for group therapists*. Retrieved October 31, 2007, from http://agpa.org/group/ethicalguide.html.

American Group Psychotherapy Association (AGPA). (n.d.). *Group works! An introduction to group therapy*. Retrieved October 30, 2007, from http://agpa.org/group/consumers guide2000.html.

American Group Psychotherapy Association (AGPA). (2007). *Practical guidelines for group psychotherapy*. Retrieved October 31, 2007, from http://www.agpa.org/guidelines/index.html.

American Psychological Association (APA). (2002). *Guidelines on multicultural education, training, research, practice, and organization change for psychologists*. Retrieved October 31, 2007, from http://www.apa.org/pi/multiculturalguidelines.pdf.

American Psychological Association (APA). (2008). *APA statement on services provided by telephone, teleconferencing, and Internet*. Retrieved December 22, 2008, from http://www.apa.org/ethics/stmnt01.html.

American Psychological Association (APA). Division 49. Retrieved October 29, 2007, from http://www.apa49.org.

Andronico, M. (1999). A history of Division 49. In D. Dewsbury (Ed.), *Unification through division: Histories of the divisions of the American Psychological Association* (pp. 175–196). Washington, DC: American Psychological Association.

Andronico, M. (2001). A history of Division 49 (Group Psychology and Group Psychotherapy). *The Group Psychologist, 10*–18.

Anderson, G., & Wheelan, S. (2005). Integrating group research and practice. In S. Wheelan (Ed.), *The handbook of group research and practice* (pp. 545–552). Thousand Oaks, CA: Sage.

Armstrong, S., & Berg, R. (2005). Demonstrating group process using "12 Angry Men." *Journal for Specialists in Group Work, 30*, 135–144.

Association for Specialists in Group Work (ASGW). (1998a). *Best practice guidelines*. Retrieved October 30, 2007, from http://www.asgw.org/PDF/Best_Practices.pdf.

Association for Specialists in Group Work (ASGW). (1998b). *Principles for diversity-competent group workers*. Retrieved October 30, 2007, from http://www.asgw.org/PDF/Principles_for_Diversity.pdf.

Association for Specialists in Group Work (ASGW). (2000). *Professional standards for the training of group workers*. Retrieved October 31, 2007, from http://www.asgw.org/PDF/training_standards.pdf.

Association for Specialists in Group Work (ASGW). (2008). Best practice guidelines: 2007 revisions. *Journal for Specialists in Group Work, 33*, 111–117.

Association for the Advancement of Social Work with Groups, Inc. (2006). *Standards for social work practice with groups* (2nd ed.). Alexandria, VA: Author.

Bales, R. F. (1950). Interaction process analysis. Cambridge, MA: Harvard University Press.

Barlow, S. (2011). Evidence bases for group practice. In R. K. Conyne (Ed.), The Oxford handbook of group counseling. New York: Oxford University Press.

Barlow, S., Burlingame, G., & Fuhriman, A. (2000). Therapeutic applications of groups: From Pratt's "thought control classes" to modern group psychotherapy. *Group Dynamics: Theory, Research, and Practice, 4*, 115–134.

Barlow, S., Fuhriman, A., & Burlingame, G. (2004). The history of group counseling and psychotherapy. In J. DeLucia-Waack, D. Gerrity, C. Kalodner, & M. Riva (Eds.), *Handbook of group counseling and psychotherapy* (pp. 3–22). Thousand Oaks, CA: Sage.

Barlow, S., Fuhriman, A., & Burlingame, G. (2005). The history of group practice: A century of knowledge. In S. Wheelan (Ed.), *Handbook of group research and practice* (pp. 39–64). Thousand Oaks, CA: Sage.

Beck, A., & Lewis, C. (Eds.). (2000). *The process of group psychotherapy: Systems for analyzing change*. Washington, DC: American Psychological Association.

Bednar, R., & Kaul, T. (1978). Experiential group research: Current perspectives. In A. Bergin & S. Garfield (Eds.), *Handbook of psychotherapy and behavior change*. New York: Wiley.

Bednar, R., & Kaul, T. (1994). Experiential group research: Can the cannon fire? In A. Bergin, & S. Garfield (Eds.), *Handbook of psychotherapy and behavior change* (4th ed., pp. 631–663). New York: Wiley.

Bemak, F. (2005). Reflections on multiculturalism, social justice, and empowerment groups for academic success: A critical discourse for contemporary schools. *Professional School Counseling, 8*, 401–406.

Bemak, F., & Conyne, R. (2004). Ecological group work. In R. Conyne & E. Cook (Eds.), *Ecological counseling: An innovative approach to conceptualizing person-environment interaction* (pp. 195–217). Alexandria, VA: American Counseling Association.

Berdahl, J., & Henry, K. B. (2005). Contemporary issues in group research. In S. Wheelan (Ed.), *The handbook of group research and practice* (pp. 19–37). Thousand Oaks, CA: Sage.

Bernard, H., Burlingame, G., Flores, P., Greene, L., Joyce, A., & Kobos, J. (2008). Clinical practice guidelines for group psychotherapy. *International Journal of Group Psychotherapy, 58*, 455–542.

Bertcher, H. (1985). Social group work: Past, present, and future. *Journal for Specialists in Group Work: Special Issue on Critical Issues in Group Work: Now and 2001, 10*, 77–82.

Bieschke, K., Matthews, C., & Wade, J. (1996). Training group counselors: The process observer method. *Journal for Specialists in Group Work, 21*, 181–186.

Bieschke, K., Matthews, C., & Wade, J. (1998). Evaluation of the process observer method. *Journal for Specialists in Group Work, 23*, 50–65.

Blatner, A. (2007). A historical chronology of group psychotherapy and psychodrama. Retrieved December 6, 2007, from http://www.blatner.com/adam/pdntbk/hxgrprx.htm.

Bowman, R., & Bowman, V. (1998). Life on the electronic frontier: The application of technology to group work. *Journal for Specialists in Group Work, 23*, 428–445.

Bowman, V., & DeLucia-Waack, J. (1993). Preparation for group therapy: The effects of preparer and modality on group process and individual functioning. *Journal for Specialists in Group Work, 18*, 67–79.

Braaten, L. (1989). Predicting positive goal attainment and symptom reduction from early group climate dimensions. *International Journal of Group Psychotherapy, 39*, 377–387.

Brabender, V. (2011). Group development. In R. K. Conyne (Ed.), *The Oxford handbook of group counseling*. New York: Oxford University Press.

Bradford, L., Gibb, J., & Benne, K. (Eds.). (1964). *T-group theory and laboratory method: Innovation in re-education*. New York: Wiley.

Bronfenbrenner, U. (1977). Toward an experimental ecology of human development. *American Psychologist, 32*, 515–531.

Brown, N. (2011), Group leadership treaching and training: Methods and issues. In R. K. Conyne (Ed.), *The Oxford handbook of group counseling*. New York: Oxford University Press.

Buchele, B., & Spitz, H. (Eds.). (2004). *Group interventions for treatment of psychological trauma*. New York: American Group Psychotherapy Association.

Budman, S., Soldz, S., Demby, A., Feldstein, M., Springer, T., & Davis, M. (1989). Cohesion, alliance, and outcome in group psychotherapy. *Psychiatry, 52*, 339–350.

Burlingame, G. (2005). Revisiting AGPA's CORE battery: Another approach for group therapists to use in adapting to the pressure for evidence-based group practice. *Group Circle*, Winter.

Burlingame, G., & Beecher, M. (2008). Special issue: New directions and resources in group psychotherapy: Introduction to the issue. *Journal of Clinical Psychology, 64*(11), 1197–1291.

Burlingame, G., & Fuhriman, A. (Eds.). (1994). *Handbook of group psychotherapy: An empirical and clinical synthesis* (pp. 559–562). New York: Wiley.

Burlingame, G., Fuhriman, A., & Johnson, J. (2001). Cohesion in group psychotherapy. *Psychotherapy, 38*, 373–379.

Burlingame, G., Fuhriman, A., & Johnson, J. (2002). Cohesion in group psychotherapy. In J. Norcross (Ed.), *Psychotherapy relationships that work* (pp. 71–87). New York: Oxford University Press.

Burlingame, G., Fuhriman, A., & Johnson, J. (2004). Process and outcome in group counseling and psychotherapy: A perspective. In J. DeLucia-Waack, D. Gerrity, C. Kalodner, & M. Riva (Eds.), *Handbook of group counseling and psychotherapy* (pp. 49–61). Thousand Oaks, CA: Sage.

Burlingame, G., Fuhriman, A., & Mosier, J. (2003). The differential effectiveness of group psychotherapy: A meta-analytic perspective. *Group Dynamics: Theory, Research, and Practice, 7*, 3–12.

Burlingame, G., Kapetanovic, S., & Ross, S. (2005). Group psychotherapy. In S. Wheelan (Ed.), *The handbook of group research and practice* (pp. 387–406). Thousand Oaks, CA: Sage.

Burlingame, G., & Layne, C. (2001). Group-based interventions for trauma survivors: Introduction to the special issue. *Group Dynamics: Theory, Research and Practice, 5*, 243–245.

Burlingame, G., MacKenzie, K., & Strauss, B. (2004). Small group treatment: Evidence for effectiveness and mechanisms for change. In M. Lambert (Ed.), *Bergin and Garfield's handbook of psychotherapy and change* (5th ed., pp. 647–696). New York: Wiley.

Burlingame, G., Strauss, B., Joyce, A., MacNair-Semands, R., MacKenzie, K., Ogrodniczuk, J., & Taylor, S. (2006). *Core Battery-Revised*. New York: American Group Psychotherapy Association.

Chen, E., Kakkad, D., & Balzano, J. (2008). Multicultural competence and evidence- based practice in group psychotherapy. *Journal of Clinical Psychology, 64*, 1261–1278.

Council for the Accreditation of Counseling and Related Programs (CACREP). (2001). *2001 standards*. Retrieved November 1, 2007, from http://www.cacrep.org/2001Standards.html.

Coche, E., Dies, R., & Goettelman, K. (1991). Process variables mediating change in intensive group therapy training. *International Journal of Group Psychotherapy, 41*, 379–397.

Cohen, A., & Smith, R. D. (1976). *The critical incident in growth groups: Theory and technique*. La Jolla, CA: University Associates.

Colijn, S., Hoencamp, E., Snijders, H., van der Spek, M., & Duivenvoorden, H. (1991). A comparison of curative factors in different types of group psychotherapy. *International Journal of Group Psychotherapy, 41*, 365–378.

Conyne, R. (Ed.). (1985). *The group worker's handbook: Varieties of group experience*. Springfield, IL: Thomas.

Conyne, R. (1987). Developing framework for processing experiences and events in group work. *Journal for Specialists in Group Work, 22*, 167–174.

Conyne, R. (1989). *How personal growth and task groups work*. Newbury Park, CA: Sage.

Conyne, R. (1998). What to look for in groups: Helping trainees become more sensitive to multicultural influences. *Journal for Specialists in Group Work, 23*, 22–32.

Conyne, R. (1999). *Failures in group work*. Thousand Oaks, CA: Sage.

Conyne, R. (2004). Prevention groups. In J. DeLucia-Waack, D. Gerrity, C. Kalodner, & M. Riva (Eds.), *Handbook of group counseling and psychotherapy* (pp. 621–629). Thousand Oaks, CA: Sage.

Conyne, R., Wilson, F. R., & Ward, D. (1997). Comprehensive group work: What it means and how to teach it. Alexandria, VA: American Counseling Association.

Conyne, R. K. (Ed.). (2011). *The Oxford handbook of group counseling*. New York: Oxford University Press.

Conyne, R., & Bemak, F. (2004). Teaching group work from an ecological perspective. *Journal for Specialists in Group Work: Special Issue on Teaching Group Work, 29*, 7–18.

Conyne, R., & Cook, E. (Eds.). (2004). *Ecological counseling: An innovative approach to conceptualizing person-environment interaction*. Alexandria, VA: American Counseling Association.

Conyne, R., Crowell, J., & Newmeyer, M. (2008). *Purposeful group techniques: How to use them more purposefully*. Upper Saddle River, NJ: Prentice-Hall.

Conyne, R., Dye, A., Gill, S., Leddick, G., Morran, D. K., & Ward, D. (1985). A retrospective of "critical issues."

Journal for Specialists in Group Work: Special Issue on Critical Issues in Group Work: Now and 2001, 10, 112–115.

Conyne, R., Tang, M., & Watson, A. (2001). Exploring diversity in groups. In E. Welfel, & R. Ingersoll (Eds.), *The mental health desk reference* (pp. 358–364). New York: Wiley.

Conyne, R., Wilson, F. R., & Tang, M. (2000). Evolving lessons from group work involvement in China. *Journal for Specialists in Group Work, 25,* 252–268.

Conyne, R., Wilson, F. R., Tang, M., & Shi, K. (1999). Cultural similarities and differences in group work: Pilot study of a U.S.-Chinese task group comparison. *Group Dynamics: Theory, Research, and Practice, 3,* 40–50.

Conyne, R., Wilson, F. R., & Ward, D. (1997). *Comprehensive group work: What it means & how to teach it.* Alexandria, VA: American Counseling Association.

Corey, G. (2007). *Theory and practice of group counseling* (7th ed.). Pacific Grove, CA: Brooks/Cole.

Corey, M., & Corey, G. (2006). *Groups: Process and practice* (7th ed.). Pacific Grove, CA: Brooks/Cole.

Corey, G., Corey, M., Callanan, P., & Russell, J. (2004). *Group techniques* (3rd ed.). Belmont, CA: Thomson Brooks/Cole.

Cox, J., Banez, L., Hawley, L., & Mostade, J. (2003). Use of the reflecting team in the training of group workers. *Journal for Specialists in Group Work, 28,* 89–105.

Crouch, E., Bloch, S., & Wanlass, J. (1994). Therapeutic factors; Interpersonal and intrapersonal mechanisms. In A. Fuhriman, & G. Burlingame (Eds.), *Handbook of group psychotherapy: An empirical and clinical synthesis* (pp. 269–318). New York: Wiley.

Dagley, J., Gazda, G., Eppinger, S., & Stewart, E. (1994). Group psychotherapy research with children, preadolescents, and adolescents. In A. Fuhriman, & G. Burlingame (Eds.), *Handbook of group psychotherapy* (pp. 340–369). New York: Wiley.

D'Andrea, M. (2004). The impact of racial-cultural identity of group leaders and members: Theory and recommendations. In J. DeLucia-Waack, D. Gerrity, C. Kalodner, & M. Riva (Eds.), *Handbook of group counseling and psychotherapy* (pp. 265–282). Thousand Oaks, CA: Sage.

Davies, D., & Jacobs, A. (1985). Sandwiching complex interpersonal feedback. *Small Group Behavior, 16,* 387–396.

DeLucia-Waack, J. (1997). The importance of processing activities, exercises, and events to group work practitioners. *Journal for Specialists in Group Work, 22,* 82–84.

DeLucia-Waack, J. (2011). Diversity in groups. In R. K. Conyne (Ed.), *The Oxford handbook of group counseling.* New York: Oxford University Press.

DeLucia-Waack, J., & Donigian, J. (2003). *The practice of multicultural group work: Visions and perspectives from the field.* Monterey, CA: Wadsworth.

DeLucia-Waack, J., Gerrity, D., Kalodner, C., & Riva, M. (Eds.). (2004). *Handbook of group counseling and psychotherapy.* Thousand Oaks, CA: Sage.

DeLucia-Waack, J., & Kalodner, C. (2005). Contemporary issues in group practice. In S. Wheelan (Ed.), *The handbook of group research and practice* (pp. 65–84). Thousand Oaks, CA: Sage.

Dies, R. (1983). Clinical implications of research on leadership in short-term group psychotherapy. In R. Dies, & K. MacKenzie (Eds.), *Advances in group psychotherapy: Integrating research and practice* (pp. 27–75). Madison, CT: International University Press.

Dion, K. (2000). Group cohesion: From "field of forces" to multidimensional construct. *Group Dynamics: Theory, Research, and Practice: Special Issue on One hundred years of groups research, 4,* 7–26.

Donigian, J., & Malnati, R. (1997). *Systemic group therapy: A triadic model.* Pacific Grove, CA: Brooks/Cole.

Durkin, H. (1981). The group therapies and general system theory as an integrative structure. In J. Durkin (Ed.), *Living groups: Group psychotherapy and general system theory* (pp. 5–23). New York: Brunner/Mazel.

Dye, H. A. (2008, February 21). Color comments on the history of group work. In B. Bertram, & H. A. Dye, *ASGW living genogram.* Presentation at the national conference of the Association for Specialists in Group Work, St. Pete Beach, Florida.

Finn, F. (1996). Computer-based self-help groups: On-line recovery for addictions. *Computers in Human Services, 13,* 21–41.

Finn, J., & Jacobson, M. (2003). *Just practice: A social justice approach to social work.* Peosta, IA: Eddie Bowers Publishing, Inc.

Forester-Miller, H. (1998). History of the Association for Specialists in Group Work: ASGW—Timeline of significant events. *Journal for Specialists in Group Work, 23,* 335–337.

Forsyth, D. (Ed.). (2000). One hundred years of groups research [Special Issue]. *Group Dynamics: Theory, Research, and Practice, 4.*

Forsyth, D. (2006). *Group dynamics.* Belmont, CA: Thomson Wadsworth.

Forsyth, D. (2011). The nature and significance of groups. In R. K. Conyne (Ed.), *The Oxford handbook of group counseling.* New York: Oxford University Press.

Foulkes, S., & Anthony, E. (1957). *Group psychotherapy: The psychoanalytic approach.* London: Penguin Books.

Foy, D., Drescher, K., & Watson, P. (2011). Groups for trauma/disaster. In R. K. Conyne (Ed.), *The Oxford handbook of group counseling.* New York: Oxford University Press.

Fuhriman, A., & Burlingame, G. (1994). Measuring small group process: A methodological application of chaos theory. *Small Group Research, 25,* 502–519.

Fuhriman, A., & Burlingame, G. (2000). Group psychotherapy. In A. Kazdin (Ed.), *Encyclopedia of psychology* (pp. 31–35). Oxford, UK: Oxford University Press.

Fuqua, D., & Newman, J. Moving beyond the "great leader" model. *Consulting Psychology Journal: Practice and Research, 56,* 146–153.

Galinsky, M., Schopler, J., & Abell, M. (1997). Connecting group members through telephone and computer groups. *Health and social work, 22,* 181–188.

Garrett, M. T. (2004). Group counseling with Native Americans. In J. DeLucia-Waack, D. Gerrity, D. Kalodner, & M. Riva (Eds.), *Handbook of group counseling and psychotherapy* (pp. 169–182). Thousand Oaks, CA: Sage.

Gary, J., & Remolino, L. (2000). Coping with loss and grief through on-line support groups. In J. Bloom, & G. Walz (Eds.), *Cybercounseling and cyberlearning: Strategies and resources for the millennium* (pp. 95–114). Alexandria, VA: American Counseling Association.

Gazda, G. (1982). *Basic approaches to group psychotherapy and group counseling.* (3rd ed.). Springfield, IL: Thomas.

Gazda, G. (1985). Group counseling and therapy: A perspective on the future. *Journal for Specialists in Group Work: Special Issue on Critical Issues in Group Work: Now and 2001, 10,* 74–76.

Gazda, G., Ginter, E., & Horne, A. (2001). *Group counseling and group psychotherapy: Theory and application*. Boston: Allyn and Bacon.

Gladding, S. (2006). *Group work: A counseling specialty* (5th ed.). Upper Saddle River, NJ: Prentice-Hall.

Gladding, S. (2011). Creativity and spontaneity in groups. In R. K. Conyne (Ed.), *The Oxford handbook of group counseling*. New York: Oxford University Press.

Glass, J., & Benshoff, J. (1999). PARS: A processing model for beginning group leaders. *Journal for Specialists in Group Work, 24*, 15–26.

Golembiewski, R., & Blumberg, A. (Eds.). (1970). *Sensitivity training and the Laboratory approach: Readings about concepts and applications*. Oakland, CA: New Harbinger.

Haberstroh, S., Parr, G., Gee, R., & Trepal, H. (2006). Interactive E-journaling in group work: Perspectives from counselor trainees. *Journal for Specialists in Group Work, 31*, 327–337.

Hadden, S. (1955). Historic background of group psychotherapy. *International Journal of Group Psychotherapy, 5*, 62.

Hamburg, D. Personal communication. In I. Yalom, & M. Leszcz (Eds.) (2005), *The theory and practice of group psychotherapy* (5th ed., p. 320).

Hanson, P. (1972). What to look for in groups. In J. Pfeiffer, & J. Jones (Eds.), *1972 annual handbook for group facilitators* (pp. 21–24). La Jolla, CA: University Associates.

Hershey, P., Blanchard, K., & Johnson, D. (1982). *Management of organizational behavior: Utilizing human resources* (3rd ed.). Englewood Cliffs, NJ: Prentice-Hall.

Higgenbotham, H., West, S., & Forsyth, D. (1988). *Psychotherapy and behavior change: Social, cultural and methodological perspectives*. New York: Pergamon.

Hill, W. F. (1965). *HIM: Hill Interaction Matrix*. Los Angeles, CA: University of Southern California Youth Studies Center.

Holden, G., Bearison, D., Rode, D., Kapoloff, M., & Rosenberg, G. (2000). The Effects of a computer network on pediatric pain and anxiety. In J. Finn, & G. Holden (Eds.), *Human services online: A new arena for service delivery* (pp. 27–47). Binghamton, NY: Haworth.

Holliday, G., Statler, M., & Flanders, M. (2007). Developing practically wise leaders through serious play. *Consulting Psychology Journal, 59*, 126–134.

Holmes, S., & Kivlighan, D. (2000). Comparison of therapeutic factors in group and individual treatment processes. *Journal of Counseling Psychology, 47*, 478–484.

Horne, A., & Rosenthal, R. (1997). Research in group work: How did we get where we are? *Journal for Specialists in Group Work, 22*, 228–240.

Hulse-Killacky, D., & Donigian, J. (2001). *Making task groups work in your world*. Upper Saddle River, NJ: Prentice-Hall.

Hulse-Killacky, D., & Orr, J. (2006). The Corrective Feedback Instrument-Revised. *Journal for Specialists in Group Work, 31*, 263–281.

International Journal of Group Psychotherapy. (2007). Special section: The ethical group psychotherapist. *International Journal of Group Psychotherapy, 57*, 1–41.

Ivey, A., Pedersen, P., & Ivey, M. (2001). *Intentional group counseling: A microskills approach*. Pacific Grove, CA: Brooks/Cole.

Ivey, A., Pedersen, P., & Ivey, M. (2008). *Group microskills: Culture-centered group process and strategies*. Alexandria, VA: Microtraining Associates and the American Counseling Association.

Jacobs, A., Jacobs, M., Cavior, N., & Burke, J. (1974). Anonymous feedback: Credibility and desirability of structured emotional and behavioral feedback delivered in groups. *Journal of Counseling Psychology, 21*, 106–111.

Jacobs, E., Masson, R., & Harvill, R. (2006). *Group counseling: Strategies and skills* (5th ed.). Pacific Grove, CA: Brooks/Cole.

Jacobson, M., & Rugeley, C. (2007). Community-based participatory research: Group work for social justice and community change. *Social Work with Groups, 30*, 21–39.

Johnson, J. (2007). Cohesion, alliance, and outcome in group psychotherapy: Comments on Joyce, Piper, & Ogrodniczuk. *International Journal of Group Psychotherapy, 57*, 533–540.

Johnson, J. (2008). Using research-supported group treatments. *Journal of Clinical Psychology, 64*, 1206–1225.

Johnson, J., Burlingame, G., Olsen, J., Davies, D. R., & Gleave, R. (2005). Group climate, cohesion, alliance, and empathy in group psychotherapy: Multilevel structural equation models. *Journal of Counseling Psychology, 52*, 310–321.

Joyce, A., Piper, W., & Ogrodniczuk, J. (2007). Therapeutic alliance and cohesion variables as predictors of outcome in short-term group psychotherapy. *International Journal of Group Psychotherapy, 57*, 269–296.

Kaiser, R., Hogan, R., & Craig, S. B. (2008). Leadership and the fate of organizations. *American Psychologist, 63*, 96–110.

Kalodner, C., & Hanus, A. (2011). Groups across settings. In R. K. Conyne (Ed.), *The Oxford handbook of group counseling*. New York: Oxford University Press.

Kaul, T. (1990). A matter of consistency: There are just two things. *The Counseling Psychologist, 18*, 121–125.

Kees, N., & Jacobs, E. (1990). Conducting more effective groups: How to select and process group exercises. *Journal for Specialists in Group Work, 15*, 21–30.

Kees, N., & Leech, N. (2002). Using group counseling techniques to clarify and deepen the focus of supervision groups. *Journal for Specialists in Group Work, 27*, 7–15.

Keim, J., & Olguin, D. (2011). Group counseling across the life span: A psychosocial perspective. In R. K. Conyne (Ed.), *The Oxford handbook of group counseling*. New York: Oxford University Press.

Kessler, R., Michelson, K., & Humphreys, K. (1997). Patterns and correlates of self-help group membership in the United States. *Social Policy, 27*, 27–46.

King, S. (1994). Analysis of electronic support for recovering addicts. *Interpersonal Computing and Technology: An Electronic Journal for the 21st Century, 2*, 47–56.

Kivlighan, D., Jr. (1997). Leader behavior and therapeutic gain: An application of situational leadership theory. *Group Dynamics: Theory, Research, and Practice, 1*, 32–38.

Kivlighan, D., Jr. (2008). Overcoming our resistance to "doing" evidence-based group practice: A commentary. *Journal of Clinical Psychology, 64*, 1284–1291.

Kivlighan, D., Jr., Coleman, M., & Anderson, D. (2000). Process, outcome and methodology in group counseling research. In S. Brown, & R. Lent (Eds.), *Handbook of counseling psychology* (3rd ed., pp. 767–796). New York: Wiley.

Kivlighan, D., Jr., & Goldfine, D. (1991). Endorsement of therapeutic factors as a function of stage of group development and participant interpersonal attitudes. *Journal of Counseling Psychology, 38*, 150–158.

Kivlighan, D., Jr., & Holmes, S. (2004). The importance of therapeutic factors. In J. DeLucia-Waack, D. Gerrity, C. Kalodner, & M. Riva (Eds.), *Handbook of group counseling and psychotherapy* (pp. 23–36). Thousand Oaks, CA: Sage.

Kivlighan, D., Jr., & Lilly, R. (1997). Developmental changes in group climate as they relate to therapeutic gain. *Group Dynamics: Theory, Research, and Practice, 1,* 208–221.

Kivlighan, D., Jr., McGovern, T., & Corazzini, J. (1984). The effects of the content and timing of structuring interventions on group therapy process and outcome. *Journal of Counseling Psychology, 31,* 363–370.

Kivlighan, D., Jr., Miles, J., & Paquin, J. (2011). Therapeutic factors in group counseling: Asking new questions. In R. K. Conyne (Ed.), *The Oxford handbook of group counseling.* New York: Oxford University Press.

Kivlighan, D., Jr., & Mullinson, D. (1988). Participants' perception of therapeutic factors in group counseling: The role of interpersonal style and stage of development. *Small Group Behavior, 19,* 452–468.

Kivlighan, D., Jr., & Tarrant, J. (2001). Does group climate mediate the group leadership-group outcome relationship? A test of Yalom's hypotheses about leadership priorities. *Group Dynamics: Theory, Research, and Practice, 5,* 220–234.

Klaw, E., & Humphreys, K. (2004). The role of peer-led mutual help groups in promoting health and well-being. In J. DeLucia-Waack, D. Gerrity, C. Kalodner, & M. Riva (Eds.), *Handbook of group counseling and psychotherapy* (pp. 630–640). Thousand Oaks, CA: Sage.

Klein, R., & Phillips, S. (Eds.). (2008). *Group interventions for disaster preparedness and response.* New York: American Group Psychotherapy Association.

Kosters, M., Burlingame, G., Nachtigall, C., & Strauss, B. (2006). A meta-analytic review of the effectiveness of inpatient group psychotherapy. *Group Dynamics: Theory, Research, and Practice, 10,* 146–163.

Leddick, G. (2008, February 22). *Illustrated history of group work.* Presentation at the national conference of the Association for Specialists in Group Work, St. Pete Beach, Florida.

Leddick, G. (2011). The history of group counseling. In R. K. Conyne (Ed.), *The Oxford handbook of group counseling.* New York: Oxford University Press.

Lee, C. (2007). *Counseling for social justice* (2nd ed.). Alexandria, VA: American Counseling Association.

Leszcz, M., & Kobos, J. (2008). Evidence-based group psychotherapy: Using AGPA's practice guidelines to enhance clinical effectiveness. *Journal of Clinical Psychology, 64,* 1238–1260.

Lewin, K. (1951). *Field theory in social science.* New York: Harper.

Lewin, K., Lippitt, R., & White, R. (1939). Patterns of aggressive behavior in experimentally created "social climates." *Journal of Social Psychology, 10,* 271–299.

Lieberman, M., Wizlenberg, A., Golant, M., & Minno, M. (2005). The impact of group composition on Internet support groups: Homogeneous versus heterogeneous Parkinson's groups. *Group Dynamics: Theory, Research, and Practice, 9,* 239–250.

Lieberman, M., Yalom, I., & Miles, M. (1973). *Encounter groups: First facts.* New York: Basic Books.

Lorentzen, S. (2008). Cohesion, alliance, and outcome in group psychotherapy: Comments on Joyce et al. (2007) and Johnson (2007). *International Journal of group psychotherapy, 58,* 403–409.

Macnair-Semands, R. (2007). Attending to the spirit of social justice as an ethical approach in group therapy. *International Journal of Group Psychotherapy, 57,* 61–66.

Marmarosh, C., Holtz, A., & Schottenbauer, M. (2005). Group cohesiveness, group-derived collective self-esteem, group-derived hope, and the well-being of group therapy members. *Group Dynamics: Theory, Research, and Practice, 9,* 32–44.

MacKenzie, K. R. (1983). The clinical application of a group climate measure. In R. Dies, & K. MacKenzie (Eds.), *Advances in group psychotherapy: Integrating research and practice* (pp. 159–170). Madison, CT: International Universities Press.

MacKenzie, K. R. (1995). Rationale for group psychotherapy in managed care. In K. MacKenzie (Ed.), *Effective use of group therapy in managed care* (pp. 1–26). Washington, DC: American Psychiatric Press.

MacKenzie, K. R. (1997). Clinical application of group development ideas. *Group Dynamics: Theory, Research, and Practice, 1,* 275–287.

MacNair-Semands, R. (2006). CORE-R battery: Group selection and pre-group preparation. *Group Circle* (pp. 3–5), Winter.

Martin, D., Garske, J., & Davis, M. (2000). Relation of the therapeutic alliance with outcome and other variables: A meta-analytic review. *Journal of Consulting and Clinical Psychology, 68,* 438–450.

McGlothlin, J. (2003). Response to the mini special issue on technology and group work. *Journal for Specialists in Group Work, 28,* 42–47.

McKay, M., & Paleg, K. (Eds.). (1992). *Focal group psychotherapy.* Oakland, CA: New Harbinger.

McKenna, Y., & Green, A. (2002). Virtual group dynamics. *Group Dynamics: Theory, Research, and Practice: Special Issue on Groups and the Internet, 6,* 116–127.

McRoberts, C., Burlingame, G., & Hoag, M. (1998). Comparative efficacy of individual and group psychotherapy: A meta-analytic perspective. *Group Dynamics: Theory, Research, and Practice, 2,* 101–117.

McWhirter, J. J., McWhirter, P., McWhirter, B., & McWhirter, E. H. (2011). International group counseling. In R. K. Conyne (Ed.), *The Oxford handbook of group counseling.* New York: Oxford University Press.

Merchant, N. (2006). Multicultural and diversity-competent group work. In J. Trotzer (Ed.), *The counselor and the group: Integrating theory, training, and practice* (4th ed., pp. 319–349). New York: Brunner-Routledge.

Merchant, N. (2008, February 22). *Types of multicultural group work: A closer look.* Key Note Address at national conference of the Association for Specialists in Group Work, St. Pete Beach, Florida.

Morran, D. K., Stockton, R., Cline, R., & Teed, C. (1998). Facilitating feedback exchange in groups: Leader interventions. *Journal for Specialists in Group Work, 23,* 257–268.

Morran, D. K., Stockton, R., & Harris, M. (1991). Analysis of group leader and member feedback messages. *Journal of Group Psychotherapy, Psychodrama, and Sociometry, 44,* 126–135.

Morran, D. K., Stockton, R., & Whittingham, M. (2004). Effective leader interventions for counseling and psychotherapy groups. In J. DeLucia-Waack, D. Gerrity, C. Kalodner, & M. Riva (Eds.), *Handbook of group counseling and psychotherapy* (pp. 91–103). Thousand Oaks, CA: Sage.

National Board of Certified Counselors. (2007). *The practice of Internet counseling.* Retrieved December 22, 2008, from http://www.nbcc.org/webethics2.

Norcross, J. (Ed.). (2002). *Psychotherapy relationships that work.* New York: Oxford University Press.

Ogrodniczuk, J. (2005). CORE-R battery: Assessment of group therapy outcomes. *Group Circle* (pp. 4–5), Spring.

Ogrodniczuk, J., & Piper, W. (2003). The effect of group climate on outcome in two forms of short-term group therapy. *Group Dynamics: Theory, Research, and Practice, 7*, 64–76.

Orr, J., Wolfe, A., & Malley, J. (2008, February 22). *From ripple to wave: Using social microcosms in group to address systemic change.* Presentation at the national conference of the Association for Specialists in Group Work, St. Pete Beach, Florida.

Page, B. (2003). Introduction to using technology in group work. *Journal for Specialists in Group Work, 28*, 7–8.

Page, B. (Ed.). (2003). Technology and group work [Special issue]. *Journal for Specialists in Group Work, 28.*

Page, B. (2004). Online group counseling. In J. DeLucia-Waack, D. Gerrity, C. Kalodner, & M. Riva (Eds.), *Handbook of group counseling and psychotherapy* (pp. 609–620). Thousand Oaks, CA: Sage.

Page, B. (2011). Online groups. In R. K. Conyne (Ed.), *The Oxford handbook of group counseling.* New York: Oxford University Press.

Page, B., Delmonico, D., Walsh, J., L'Amoreauz, N., Danninhirsh, C., Thompson, R., et al. (2000). Setting up on-line support groups using The Palace software. *Journal for Specialists in Group Work, 25*, 133–145.

Page, B., Jencius, M., Rehfuss, M., Foss, L., Dean, E., Petruzzi, M., et al. (2003). PalTalk online groups: Process and reflections on students' experience. *Journal for Specialists in Group Work, 28*, 35–41.

Payne, K., & Marcus, D. (2008). The efficacy of group psychotherapy for older adult clients: A meta-analysis. *Group Dynamics: Theory, Research, and Practice, 12*, 268–278.

Piper, W., & Joyce, A. S. (2002). Time-limited groups. In D. Brook & H. Spitz (Eds.), *The group therapy of substance abuse.* Binghanton, NY: Haworth Press.

Piper, W., & McCallum, M. (1991). Group interventions for those who have experienced loss. *Group Analysis, 24*, 363–373.

Piper, W., & Ogrodniczuk, J. (2004). Brief group therapy. In J. DeLucia-Waack, D. Gerrity, C. Kalodner, & M. Riva (Eds.), *Handbook of group counseling and psychotherapy* (pp. 641–660). Thousand Oaks, CA: Sage.

Pistole, C., & Filer, R. (1991). Evaluating experiential elements and stimulating research in the teaching of group counseling. *Journal for Specialists in Group Work, 16*, 40–45.

Raelin, J. (2003). *Creating leaderful organizations: How to bring out leadership in everyone.* San Francisco: Jossey-Bass.

Rapin, L. (2004). Guidelines for ethical and legal practice in counseling and psychotherapy groups. In J. DeLucia-Waack, D. Gerrity, C. Kalodner, & M. Riva (Eds.), *Handbook of group counseling and psychotherapy* (pp. 151–165). Thousand Oaks, CA: Sage.

Rapin, L. (2011). Ethics, best practices and law in group counseling. In R. K. Conyne (Ed.), *The Oxford handbook of group counseling.* New York: Oxford University Press.

Rapin, L., & Conyne, R. (2006). Best practices in group work. In J. Trotzer (Ed.), *The counselor and the group: Integrating theory, training, and practice* (4th ed., pp. 291–318).

Ritter, K. (2011). Group counseling with sexual minorities. In R. K. Conyne (Ed.), *The Oxford handbook of group counseling.* New York: Oxford University Press.

Riva, M. (2011). Supervision of group counseling. In R. K. Conyne (Ed.), *The Oxford handbook of group counseling.* New York: Oxford University Press.

Riva, M., Wachtel, M., & Lasky, G. (2004). Effective leadership in group counseling and psychotherapy. In J. DeLucia-Waack, D. Gerrity, C. Kalodner, & M. Riva (Eds.), *Handbook of group counseling and psychotherapy* (pp. 37–48). Thousand Oaks, CA: Sage.

Rivera, E. T., Garrett, M. T., & Crutchfield, L. B. (2004). Multicultural interventions in groups: The use of indigenous methods. In J. DeLucia-Waack, D. Gerrity, C. Kalodner, & M. Riva (Eds.), *Handbook of group counseling and psychotherapy* (pp. 295–306). Thousand Oaks, CA: Sage.

Robison, F., Stockton, R., Morran, D. K., & Uhl-Wagner, A. (1988). Anticipated consequences of communicating corrective feedback during early counseling group development. *Small Group Behavior, 19*, 469–484.

Romano, J., & Cikanek, K. (2003). Group work and computer applications: Instructional components for graduate students. *Journal for Specialists in Group Work, 28*, 23–34.

Rosenbaum, M., Lakin, M., & Roback, H. (1992). In D. Freedharm (Ed.), *History of psychotherapy: A century of change.* Washington, DC: American Psychological Association.

Rosenbloom, S. (2007, December 17). On Facebook, scholars link up with data. *New York Times.* Retrieved December 17, 2007, from http://www.nytimes.com/2007/12/17/style/17facebook.html?_r=1&ref=todayspaper&oref=slogin.

Rubel, D., & Atieno Okech, J. E. (2011). Qualitative research approaches and group counseling. In R. K. Conyne (Ed.), *The Oxford handbook of group counseling.* New York: Oxford University Press.

Scheidlinger, S., & Schmess, G. Fifty Years of AGPA 1942–1992: An overview. In K. R. MacKenzie (Ed.). (1992). *Classics in group psychotherapy* (pp. 1–22). New York: Guilford. Retrieved November 1, 2007, from http://agpa.org/pubs/50%20Years%20of%20AGPA.pdf.

Schutz, W. (1958). *FIRO: A three-dimensional theory of interpersonal behavior.* New York: Rinehart.

Schwarz, R. (2002). *The skilled facilitator: A comprehensive resource for consultants, facilitators, managers, trainers, and coaches* (2nd ed.). San Francisco, CA: Jossey-Bass.

Schwartz, J., Waldo, M., & Moravec, M. S. (2011). Assessing groups. In R. K. Conyne (Ed.), *The Oxford handbook of group counseling.* New York: Oxford University Press.

Shapiro, J. (2011). Brief group treatment. In R. K. Conyne (Ed.), *The Oxford handbook of group counseling.* New York: Oxford University Press.

Shechtman, Z. (2007). How does group process research inform leaders of counseling and psychotherapy groups? *Group Dynamics: Theory, Research, and Practice: Special Issue on Groups in educational settings, 11*, 293–304.

Shechtman, Z., & Gluk, O. (2005). An investigation of therapeutic factors in children's groups. *Group Dynamics: Theory, Research, an Practice, 9*, 127–134.

Silverman, P. (2011). Mutual help groups: What are they and what makes them work? In R. K. Conyne (Ed.), *The Oxford handbook of group counseling.* New York: Oxford University Press.

Smokowski, P. (2003). Using technology to enhance modeling and behavioral rehearsal in group work practice. *Journal for Specialists in Group Work, 28*, 9–22.

Spitz, H. (1996). *Group psychotherapy and managed mental health care: A clinical guide for providers.* New York: Brunner/Mazel.

Sternberg, R. (2004). Words to the wise about wisdom? *Human Development, 47*, 286–289.

Stockton, R., & Morran, D. K. (2011). General research models. In R. K. Conyne (Ed.), *The Oxford handbook of group counseling.* New York: Oxford University Press.

Stockton, R., Morran, D. K., & Clark, M. (2004). An investigation of group leaders' intentions. *Group Dynamics: Theory, Research, and Practice, 8,* 196–206.

Stockton, R., Morran, D. K., & Krieger, K. (2004). An overview of current research and best practices for training beginning group leaders. In J. DeLucia-Waack, D. Gerrity, C. Kalodner, & M. Riva (Eds.), *Handbook of group counseling and psychotherapy* (pp. 65–75). Thousand Oaks, CA: Sage.

Stockton, R., Morran, D. K., & Nitza, A. (2000). Processing group events: A conceptual map for leaders. *Journal for Specialists in Group Work, 25,* 343–355.

Sue, D. W., Arredondo, P., & McDavis, R. (1992). Multicultural counseling competencies and standards: A call to the profession. *Journal of Counseling & Development, 70,* 477–486.

The Counseling Psychologist. (2005). In M. Mallen & D. Vogel (Eds.), Online counseling: Challenges for the information era [Special Issue]. *The Counseling Psychologist, 33.*

The Palace Incorporated. (1998). The Palace (Version 3.4.2). [Computer Software]. Cupertino, CA: Electric Communities Company.

Thomas, G. (2006). Facilitator education: Learning from counselor education. *Group Facilitation: A Research and Applications Journal, 7,* 3–12.

Tinsley, H., Roth, J., & Lease, S. (1989). Dimensions of leadership and leadership style among group leadership specialists. *Journal of Counseling Psychology, 36,* 48–53.

Toporek, R., Gerstein, L., Fouad, N., Roysircar-Sodowsky, G., & Israel, T. (Eds.). (2005). *Handbook for social justice in counseling psychology.* Thousand Oaks, CA: Sage.

Toseland, R., & Siporin, M. (1986). When to recommend group treatment: A review of the clinical and research literature. *International Journal of Group Psychotherapy, 36,* 171–201.

Trotzer, J. (2004). Conducting a group: Guidelines for choosing and using activities. In J. DeLucia-Waack, D. Gerrity, C. Kalodner, & M. Riva (Eds.), *Handbook of group counseling and psychotherapy* (pp. 76–90). Thousand Oaks, CA: Sage.

Trotzer, J. (2006). *The counselor and the group: Integrating theory, training, and Practice* (4th ed.). New York: Routledge.

Trotzer, J. (2011). Personhood of the leader. In R. K. Conyne (Ed.), *The Oxford handbook of group counseling.* New York: Oxford University Press.

Tuckman, B., & Jensen, M. (1977). Stages of small group development revisited. *Group & Organizational Studies, 2,* 419–427.

Tyson, L., Perusse, R., & Whitledge, J. (Eds.). (2004). *Critical incidents in group counseling.* Alexandria, VA: American Counseling Association.

Waldo, M., & Bauman, S. (1998). Regrouping the categorization of group work: A goals and process (GAP) Matrix for groups. *Journal for Specialists in Group Work, 23,* 164–176.

Waldo, M., Kerne, P., IV, & Van Horn Kerne, V. (2007). *Journal for Specialists in Group Work, 32,* 346–361.

Walker, L., & Conyne, R. (2007). Group work with international students. In H. Singaravelu, & M. Pope (Eds.), *A handbook for counseling international students in the United States* (pp. 299–310). Alexandria, VA: American Counseling Association.

Ward, D. (2006). Editorial: Classification of groups. *Journal for Specialists in Group Work, 31,* 93–97.

Ward, D. (2011). Definition of group counseling. In R. K. Conyne (Ed.), *The Oxford handbook of group counseling.* New York: Oxford University Press.

Ward, D., & Litchy, M. (2004). The effective use of processing in groups. In J. DeLucia-Waack, D. Gerrity, C. Kalodner, & M. Riva (Eds.), *Handbook of group counseling and psychotherapy* (pp. 104–119). Thousand Oaks, CA: Sage.

Webber, J., Bass, D., & Yep, R. (2005). *Terrorism, trauma, and tragedy* (2nd ed.). Alexandria, VA: American Counseling Association.

Wheelan, S. (1997). Group development and the practice of group psychotherapy. *Group Dynamics: Theory, Research, and Practice, 1,* 288–293.

Wheelan, S. (2005). The developmental perspective. In S. Wheelan (Ed.), *The handbook of group research and practice.* Thousand Oaks, CA: Sage.

Wheelan, S. (Ed.). (2005). *The handbook of group research and practice.* Thousand Oaks, CA: Sage.

Wilbur, M., Roberts-Wilbur, J., & Betz, R. (1981). Leader and member behaviors in three group modalities: A typology. *Journal for Specialists in Group Work, 6,* 224–234.

Williams, K. (Ed.). (2002). Groups and the Internet. [Special issue]. *Group Dynamics: Theory, Research, and Practice, 6*(1).

Wilson, F. R., Rapin, L., & Haley-Banez, L. (2004). How teaching group work can be guided by foundational documents: Best practice guidelines, diversity principles, training standards. *Journal for Specialists in Group Work: Special Issue on Teaching group work, 29,* 19–29.

Winzelberg, A. (1997). The analysis of an electronic support group for individuals with eating disorders. *Computers in human behavior, 13,* 393–407.

Wrenn, C. G. (1938). Counseling with students. In G. Whipple (Ed.), *Guidance in educational institutions,* Part I, *National Society for the Study of Education.* Bloomington, IL: Bloomington Public School Publishing Co.

Wrenn, C. G. (1962). *The counselor in a changing world.* Washington, DC: American Personnel and Guidance Association.

Yao, T. (2004). Guidelines for facilitating groups with international college students. In J. DeLucia-Waack, D. Gerrity, C. Kalodner, & M. Riva (Eds.), *Handbook of group counseling and psychotherapy* (pp. 253–264). Thousand Oaks, CA: Sage.

Yalom, I. (1970). *The theory and practice of group psychotherapy.* New York: Basic Books.

Yalom, I. (1995). *The theory and practice of group psychotherapy* (4th ed.). New York: Basic Books.

Yalom, I., & Leszcz, M. (2005). *The theory and practice of group psychotherapy* (5th ed.). New York: Basic Books.

Zinker, J. (1980). *Beyond the hot seat.* Gouldsboro, ME: Gestalt Journal Press.

Further Reading
Group Journals

Group counseling is a multi-disciplinary intervention that has emerged through and continues to be informed by numerous sources. Continuous streams of knowledge flow forth, which find their way into disciplinary-specific vehicles, such as journals and conference presentations. Advancements in group work will come from those who become aware of these cross-disciplinary and cross-profession knowledge bases and are able to effectively span them. The journals listed earlier in this chapter can provide exposure to important sources to obtain the contemporaneous, interdisciplinary information and perspective that will be invaluable.

Key Chapter References

Bradford, L., Gibb, J., & Benne, K. (Eds.). (1964). *T-group theory and laboratory method: Innovation in re-education.* New York: Wiley.

Burlingame, G., & Fuhriman, A. (Eds.). (1994). *Handbook of group psychotherapy: An empirical and clinical synthesis.* New York: Wiley.

Conyne, R. (Ed.). (1985). *The group workers' handbook: Varieties of group experience.* Springfield, IL: Thomas.

Corey, M., & Corey, G. (2006). *Groups: Process and practice* (7th ed.). Pacific Grove, CA: Brooks/Cole.

DeLucia-Waack, J., Gerrity, D., Kalodner, C., & Riva, M. (Eds.). (2004). *Handbook of group counseling and psychotherapy.* Thousand Oaks, CA: Sage.

Gazda, G. (1982). *Basic approaches to group psychotherapy and group counseling* (3rd ed.). Springfield, IL: Thomas.

Gladding, S. (2002). *Group work: A counseling specialty* (4th ed.). Upper Saddle River, NJ: Prentice-Hall.

Kivlighan, D., Jr., Coleman, M., & Anderson, D. C. (2000). Process, outcome, and methodology in group counseling research. In S. Brown, & R. Lent (Eds.), *Handbook of counseling psychology* (3rd ed., pp. 767–796). New York: Wiley.

Lieberman, M., Yalom, I., & Miles, M. (1973). *Encounter groups: First facts.* New York: Basic Books.

Wheelan, S. (Ed.). (2005). *The handbook of group research and practice.* Thousand Oaks, CA: Sage.

Yalom, I., & Leszcz, M. (2005). *The theory and practice of group psychotherapy* (5th ed.). New York: Basic Books.

Couple and Family Therapy

Myrna L. Friedlander *and* Gary M. Diamond

Abstract

The conceptual underpinnings, fundamental assumptions, and interventions used in couple and family therapy (CFT) are consistent with counseling psychology's traditional emphasis on normative development and person–environment fit, and its focus on clients' problems in living, resilience, and cultural context rather than psychiatric diagnoses. In this chapter, we begin by outlining the history of the couple and family therapy movement, identifying the central systems constructs and assumptions, and providing an overview of several classic and contemporary approaches to conjoint treatment. Next, we describe eight exemplary programs of efficacy research that address the question, "For whom does CFT work?" Finally, addressing the question, "How does CFT work?," we summarize the theory and research on three basic mechanisms of change in conjoint treatment: therapeutic alliance, reframing, and enactment. The chapter concludes with recommended future directions for the field—theoretical, empirical, and practical.

Keywords: couple and family therapy, systems theory, psychotherapy outcome, psychotherapy process, therapeutic alliance, enactment, reframing

Although couple and family therapy did not originate within the field of counseling psychology, it might well have. Unlike early clinical psychologists, who embraced the medical model, locating symptoms within individuals and paying little attention to a client's psychosocial context, counseling psychologists took a broader view (Gelso & Fretz, 2001). Traditionally, counseling psychologists worked in schools and outpatient settings with clients who had problems in living (e.g., test anxiety, divorce, career indecision, bereavement) rather than psychiatric diagnoses. Even when contemporary counseling psychologists see clients suffering from diagnosable emotional disorders, they are more likely to view emotional distress as integrally related to person–environment fit and to psychosocial development, in much the same way that couple and family therapists conceptualize problems.

Moreover, long before clinical psychologists (e.g., Seligman & Csikszentmihalyi, 2000) began writing about positive psychology, counseling psychologists were being trained to assess emotional problems from a strengths-based perspective (Gelso & Fretz, 2001). That is, not only noting clients' difficulties and deficiencies, counseling psychologists also inquire about past successes, coping strategies, and environmental supports. Like a solution-focused family therapist, a counseling psychologist would consider close ties with adult children, a solid work history, and multiple leisure avocations as integral to the assessment and treatment of a depressed, middle-aged man whose wife had died 5 years prior. The client's depressive symptoms would not be overlooked, of course, but treatment planning would also take into account the client's aspirations and adjustment to each of his life roles since his wife's death.

Paying attention to person–environment fit is but a short step to working directly with family systems. In treating family problems, it is essential to consider the broad social and cultural context, the family's developmental stage (e.g., recently married, raising young children, transitioning to retirement), the current developmental tasks of each member of the family, and the family's unique strengths and resources (e.g., religious commitment, community involvement, ties with extended family). Thus, although family therapy as a treatment model did not originate within counseling psychology, working clinically with couples and families is a natural fit for counseling psychologists.

What distinguishes a "family therapist" from a "therapist who sees families"? Although in common parlance these terms are interchangeable, at a conceptual level the distinction is more than semantic. Family therapists consider familial relationships to be "the client"; they design interventions to shift power dynamics between and among family members, and they view changes within individuals as both catalysts and markers of fundamental system shifts. Therapists who "see families," on the other hand, bring family members into the session to help the troubled individual who is the identified focus of concern, and these "extra" family members often see themselves as consultants or witnesses to the recovery process of their child or partner (Friedlander, Escudero, & Heatherington, 2006a).

Moreover, what distinguishes couple and family therapy (CFT) from individual therapy is not readily identifiable. That is, CFT is not defined by who or how many family members attend a therapy session, nor by the presenting problems or even the treatment goals. To illustrate, a "family therapist" may work solely with an isolated, depressed single mother, but that therapy is likely to look quite different from the one offered to the same client by an "individual" therapist. Although both clinicians may have as a goal to reduce the client's isolation and depression, their conceptualizations and treatment strategies are likely to be strikingly different. A cognitive-behavioral therapist might challenge this client's negative self-appraisals, encourage her to engage in more pleasurable activities, and teach her parenting skills. A psychoanalytic therapist might explore the client's sense of self, her internal representations of significant others, her fantasies and dreams, her memories and childhood attachment history. A "family therapist," on the other hand, might encourage the client to renew ties with her estranged family of origin, negotiate a better relationship with her children's father and his family, establish clearer emotional boundaries with her children, promote the children's sibling relationships, and explore ways to bring other caring adults into her children's lives.

In other words, the family therapist would assume that by restoring this overburdened mother's competence as head of household and guiding her to help her children become closer siblings and better functioning individuals, her depression could be reduced and her desire to attend to her personal life goals could be increased.

Take a different example. A "therapist who sees families" agrees to work with a 10-year-old girl who is doing poorly in school, has no friends, and responds explosively to parental demands. The therapist asks the mother, and sometimes the father, to attend sessions in which behavioral goals (doing chores, finishing homework, increasing physical activity) are planned, using charts, therapy "homework," and rewards for good behavior. In other words, the parent serves as the coach, helping the therapist carry out the treatment plan at home.

A "family therapist" approaches the situation differently. This therapist takes note of the parents' distancing from one another, their focus on the 10-year-old to the exclusion of their marriage or their individual pursuits, and the father's contempt of his wife, which is mirrored by the 13-year-old sister's contempt of the 10-year-old "identified patient." The family therapist's strategies include empowering the mother's relationships with both daughters, suggesting that she resume working or volunteering outside the home, encouraging the older sister to go away to summer camp, recommending a smaller school, a religious youth group, or a team sport for the 10-year-old, and (eventually) working with the parents to improve their relationship and connect with their families of origin. All of these strategies are designed to simultaneously reduce the family's isolation by bringing in new systems (work, camp, school, youth group, team, extended family), rebalance the family's power dynamics, improve the spousal relationship, give the two girls some space from each other, and eliminate the intense focus on the younger child. In other words, systems change begets individual change, and individual changes beget systems change.

In this chapter, we begin by summarizing the history of CFT from a theoretical perspective, including a review of several classic approaches to CFT.[1] We then present a brief overview of selected empirically supported couple and family therapies. This overview serves as a backdrop for the next, more detailed discussion of the unique challenges of working clinically from a family systems perspective and investigating the effectiveness of CFT. Specifically, we describe three critically important process phenomena—the therapeutic alliance, reframing, and enactment: their purported role in the change process and how they have been subjected to empirical inquiry. The chapter concludes with suggested future directions to increase our understanding of CFT as a unique treatment format.

Brief History of Couple and Family Therapy
Early Influences

Working independently in the mid-20th century, pioneers such as Nathan Ackerman (1958), Don Jackson (1965), John Bell (1961), Virginia Satir (1964), and Murray Bowen (1961) felt constrained by the psychoanalytic injunction against meeting with a patient's family members. Psychoanalysis, the prevailing treatment approach at that time, was a highly intimate and private experience. It was believed that a patient's transference to the analyst, crucial for treatment success, would be irrevocably contaminated by the presence of other family members (Nichols & Schwartz, 2007).

In the 1950s and 1960s, some of the most disturbed psychiatric patients in "mental hospitals" were the first to experience conjoint family therapy. A few analysts cautiously began involving family members in treatment after noticing that the patients, who had seemingly recovered in the hospital, relapsed on returning home. These analysts also noted the curious phenomenon that, when a patient's mental health improved, another family member's would often deteriorate (Nichols & Schwartz, 2007).

Seeing the family as the context for emotional problems was not unique to psychiatrists. Social workers had long recognized family (and community) factors in causing and maintaining mental illness (Nichols & Schwartz, 2007). In fact, since the early 1900s, social workers described their clients as "cases," a term that refers to an individual within a specific family and neighborhood context. Caseworkers often visited patients in their homes, and early social workers wrote about concentric levels of influence on the individual, a concept that foreshadowed later theorizing about the interrelations of systems (Nichols & Schwartz, 2007).

Two other influences outside mainstream psychiatry also propelled the family therapy movement forward (Nichols & Schwartz, 2007). First, in the early 20th century, religious leaders, teachers, and attorneys began offering "professional marriage counseling" to couples in distress who were not likely to seek help from mental health providers.

Beginning with a few marriage counseling centers, the family relations profession gave birth in 1945 to the American Association of Marriage Counselors. Second, workers in child guidance centers, which were created throughout the country to help prevent childhood mental disorders, began treating families when they saw children's emotional disorders as expressions of family dysfunction.

Perhaps the most influential contribution to CFT began with research on human and animal communication. The "Palo Alto group," an interdisciplinary team with scientists Gregory Bateson, Jay Haley, and John Weakland, joined by psychiatrists Don Jackson and William Fry, began extrapolating from basic research on humor, the behavior of otters, and patterns of communication between indigenous South Pacific tribes to the family interactions of young adults with schizophrenia (Nichols & Schwartz, 2007). In developing their *double-bind theory*, Bateson and colleagues (Bateson, Jackson, Haley, & Weakland, 1956) promoted the radical idea that mental illness was caused and maintained by repetitive and pernicious patterns of parent–child interaction, which paradoxically stabilized family relationships. In other words, psychotic behavior was seen as functional within a disturbed family system by preventing change, which the family perceived as threatening. According to the theory, a child who continually receives punishing, demanding, and contradictory messages ("Show me that you love me"/"Bad boy, I'll punish you for touching me") learns to make "insane" responses because either protesting the contradiction or escaping is forbidden. Over time, the child begins responding to any aspect of a double-bind message with rage or panic (Bateson et al., 1956). Although later discredited as the cause of schizophrenia, the double-bind theory opened the door for treatments focusing on modifying dysfunctional patterns of family interaction.

Early family therapists were also heavily influenced by general systems theories (Bertalanffy, 1950) and cybernetics (Wiener, 1948) in the fields of engineering, physics, and mathematics (Nichols & Schwartz, 2007). Systems theorists discovered that, from the smallest to the most complex, entities (or systems) have interlocking parts that function as organized units. Understanding a system cannot be accomplished by examining its parts individually, and when a unit's properties are not maintained, it breaks down.

From cybernetics, family theorists (e.g., Jackson, 1959) adopted the notion of *feedback loops*, which refer to processes by which a system self-regulates, either by compensating to maintain a steady state (called *homeostasis*) or by evolving to an entirely new state (called *second-order change*). Extrapolating to families, early theorists applied these concepts to explain how emotional problems, located within an individual, are expressions of systemic (i.e., family) dysregulation. A young adolescent's chronic refusal to eat, for example, is not a mental illness, but rather a habitual pattern of behavior that stabilizes her parents' dysfunctional marriage (Minuchin, Rosman, & Baker, 1978). (Note that the term "stabilize" does not refer to psychological stability but rather to homeostasis.) That is, by worrying, commiserating together, and focusing exclusively on their daughter's anorexia, mother and father avoid facing the dangerous, unspoken tensions within their marriage.

By conceptualizing families as functioning like machines, which have moving parts but no mental consciousness, many early family theorists eschewed all notions of psyche. In other words, whether individuals' behaviors are conscious or unconscious is irrelevant. From a purely behavioral perspective, the child's self-starvation and the parents' conflict avoidance are mutually reinforcing, a behavioral feedback loop that keeps a homeostatic balance in the family and prevents change. Because of this circular causality, freeing the daughter from her self-destructive behavior cannot be accomplished without a corresponding shift in the parents' behavior toward her and toward each other. If a therapeutic change can be accomplished, there will be a second-order change, a new family system that behaves differently and has family members who think and feel differently about themselves and each other.

Classic Models of Family Therapy

It is no surprise, then, that some of the earliest theoretical approaches to CFT were uniquely focused on modifying interpersonal behavior. Structural family therapist Salvador Minuchin (1974; Minuchin & Fishman, 1981; Minuchin et al., 1978) was arguably the theorist whose approach most closely reflected the principles of general systems theory. According to Minuchin (1974), families are systems that go awry when their structure is dysfunctional, and repetitive patterns of interaction reveal these dysfunctional structures. When boundaries between individuals are too diffuse (or "enmeshed"), family members cannot operate autonomously. At the other extreme, when interpersonal boundaries are too rigid (or "disengaged"), the family has no sense of "we-ness." In some dysfunctional families, the

parents no longer function as "executives;" rather, the children have too much power. In other families, one parent may form a "coalition" with a child to discredit or control the other parent.

In the case of families with anorexia, the tensions in the marital "subsystem" are said to be "detoured" onto the starving child, who has come to have too much power in the family system. Freeing family members from symptoms, even severe symptoms like anorexia, requires modifying boundaries by changing how people interact with each other (Minuchin et al., 1978). The daughter, with the help of professionals, is put in charge of maintaining a healthy weight, and the parents are relieved of this burden (Sargent, Liebman, & Silver, 1985). Instead, they are encouraged to assert their parental authority, work out their marital problems, and begin pursuing individual interests. In a family session, the structural therapist might encourage an *enactment*, in which the parents are asked to discuss something of importance and the child is constrained from interrupting. Such therapeutic strategies are designed to disrupt parent–child enmeshment and break the circular causality (self-starvation → avoidance of marital problems → self-starvation). Theoretically, when the family's behavioral interactions reflect a healthier structure, and when family relationships become more functional and mutually rewarding, individuals' emotional disorders will disappear (Minuchin & Fishman, 1981).

Another early family therapy approach, which later combined with structural therapy, applied Gregory Bateson's patterns of communication to the understanding and treatment of families. Strategic therapists Jay Haley (1963) and Cloe Madanes (1981), members of the Mental Research Institute group (Fisch, Weakland, & Segal, 1982; Watzlawick, Weakland, & Fisch, 1974), and the Milan (Italy) associates (Selvini Palazzoli, Boscolo, Cecchin, & Prata, 1978), worked uniquely with family behavior, with minimal focus on clients' cognitions or emotions. Using constructs from cybernetics, these problem-focused theorists assess the covert "rules" that function as feedback loops to keep family systems in a homeostatic state. Like structural therapists, strategic therapists view the attempted solution to the problem (cajoling a starving daughter to eat) as maintaining the problem (marital distancing) in a circular fashion. The cybernetic solution for this kind of impasse is to create a "positive feedback loop," which can interrupt the "negative feedback loop" (i.e., vicious cycle) that maintains the problem.

Theoretically, it is not necessary for family members to understand the mutually reinforcing cycle that keeps them stuck. Rather, the strategic therapist creates a ritual or ordeal that disrupts the system. Often using consulting teams observing behind a one-way mirror, strategic therapists use their authoritative power to impose creative interventions that will disrupt homeostatic cycles. Because families resist change, strategic therapists cleverly devise "therapeutic double-binds," paradoxical interventions that force behavioral shifts. The Milan group (Selvini Palazzoli, 1986), for example, might prescribe a parental vacation for the overbearing, worried parents of symptomatic young adults. The parents, whose overprotection reinforces their child's extreme dependence, would be told to leave the child alone in the home for an extended period of time, sometimes weeks. This "prescription" would be designed to force the young adult to become self-reliant and to put the parents in a situation where they could not avoid dealing directly with one another.

Although in Murray Bowen's family systems theory (Bowen, 1966, 1976; Kerr & Bowen, 1988) the central construct, *differentiation of self*, refers to individual experience, this theory is based on general systems concepts. Differentiation of self refers to an individual's ability to separate and balance thinking and feeling, on the intrapsychic level, and autonomy and closeness, on the interpersonal level (Bowen, 1976). According to Bowen, highly differentiated individuals are effective problem solvers. In the face of an emotional crisis, they are able to acknowledge their feelings but also think through the alternatives and decide on the best course of action. Poorly differentiated individuals, on the other hand, either become flooded with emotion or are so cut off from their feelings that they cannot function well in anxiety-laden situations, and at other times, they have difficulty behaving in a mature manner. Whether they remain "fused" with others or "reactively distance," these individuals behave in ways to reduce intolerable levels of stress.

Poorly differentiated people characteristically create emotional triangles with others, which stabilize otherwise immature relationships (Bowen, 1976). Take the example of a wife who has an exciting affair with a coworker. By distancing from her husband in this way, the couple avoids discussing the husband's impotence due to alcohol abuse. Aware of his wife's infidelity, the husband does not confront her because of his personal shame (impotence) and guilt (alcoholism). As illustrated in Figure 25.1, the triangles of Wife-Husband-Lover and Wife-Husband-Alcohol interlock, so that change is extremely difficult. Two other triangles, Wife-Husband-Rebellious Son and Wife-Grandmother-Son, further freeze the system. That is, when Wife is upset with Husband or Son, she turns to Lover or Grandmother. Similarly, when Husband is distressed by Wife or Son, he turns to Alcohol. When Son sees his parents argue, he acts out. The system is stable but highly dysfunctional.

By forming emotional triangles, family members remain locked in dysfunctional patterns that, according to Bowen (1976; Kerr & Bowen, 1988), are passed down through generations in the behavior of individual family members. In a family's life cycle (Carter & McGoldrick, 1999), certain developmental tasks create emotional stress that activates triangles through increased fusion or distancing. Consider the family described above. When newly married, the wife finds herself unable to separate enough from her own mother to fully commit to her new relationship. Possibly, her mother was divorced and lonely, or maybe her mother's marriage was stable but stale. The husband, who had been attracted to his wife because of her emotional availability, begins distancing from her in the same way that his parents distanced from him and from each other. When the first child is born, the Wife-Husband-Baby triangle interlocks with the Wife-Grandmother-Baby triangle to further push the young husband away. Eventually, the wife's intense focus on her child, which compensates for the increasing coldness she feels from her spouse, repeats the pattern in her own family. The husband, feeling pushed out of the marriage by his son, distances through alcohol, mirroring what occurred in his parents' marriage. Eventually, when the boy becomes a pre-teen, he rebels fiercely. The wife takes a lover, and the husband becomes an alcoholic.

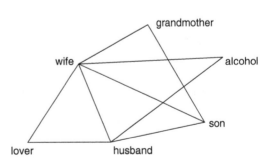

Fig. 25.1 Example of interlocking emotional triangles.

In contrast to structural therapists, who encourage in-session enactments, Bowenian family systems therapists (Kerr & Bowen, 1988) discourage clients from interacting directly with each other in the therapy sessions. Rather, these therapists work to promote an understanding of the family forces that constrain individual behavior and healthy relationships. Insight, rather than action, is said to be the key to treatment success. To facilitate insight, Bowenian therapists stay as neutral as possible, striving to reduce the emotionality in the system and enhance individuals' self-reflection. In fact, Bowen maintained that family systems therapy was best accomplished by working solely with the most differentiated individual in the family, the one who is most able to reflect on and then begin "detriangulating" from the nuclear family's "emotional process."

Not all of the first-wave family therapists embraced systems thinking, however. One of the pioneers in the field, Nathan Ackerman (1958), stayed closer to his psychoanalytic roots than other analysts, e.g., Jackson (1959) and Bowen (1976). Experiential family therapists, notably Carl Whitaker (Whitaker & Keith, 1981) and Virginia Satir (1964), immersed themselves in their clients' emotional world, believing that caring attunement and personal involvement gave families the courage to change. Behavioral family therapists used learning theory to teach parents how to extinguish their children's misbehavior (Boardman, 1962; Patterson, 1971; Williams, 1959) or facilitate new behavior (Risley & Wolf, 1967). Spouses were used as coaches in anxiety management (Wolpe, 1958). Contingency management (Stuart, 1969) and social learning principles (Liberman, 1970) were applied to couples' problems in other early behavioral approaches to CFT.

Later Developments

From the late 1970s through the 1980s, the predominant approach to couples treatment was behavioral marital therapy (Jacobson, 1977; Jacobson & Margolin, 1979), whereas the major therapies for families were structural-strategic (e.g., Haley, 1976; Minuchin & Fishman, 1981), functional family therapy (Alexander & Parsons, 1982), and parent management training (e.g., Kazdin, 1987; Patterson, 1982). In the late 1980s into the 1990s, family therapists took a step away from the general systems and behavioral interaction theories that predominated a decade earlier. One impetus was the feminist challenge (e.g., Luepnitz, 1988) to the highly paternalistic conceptualizations and interventions of

structural-strategic therapists. Urging therapists to adopt a warmer, more collaborative stance with families, feminists moved the field forward in a different direction.

By the late 1990s, family therapists were demonstrating a strong interest in the cognitive and emotional problems that sustain couple and family problems. From strategic, problem-focused therapy came solution-focused therapy (de Shazer, 1985), which rejected the focus on problem-maintaining behavioral cycles in favor of helping families imagine, hope for, and work toward a more fulfilling life. Adopting the postmodern, social constructionist perspective on human problems—that people are constrained by life stories that derive from oppressive social forces (Foucault, 1965)—narrative therapists Michael White (1995) and David Epston (White & Epston, 1990) taught clients to "re-author" their lives by viewing their problems as external to themselves and then finding ways to struggle against them. On the psychoanalytic front, the increasingly popular object relations theory was integrated with couple and family work (Scharff & Scharff, 1987; Slipp, 1984). Using this approach, therapists help family members develop insight into how their unrealistic internal representations of each other play out in destructive ways. Traditional behavioral therapists, as well, began to focus on cognitive processes. Recognizing that behavioral marital therapy was limited for many couples, Jacobson and Christensen (1996; Jacobson, Christensen, Prince, Cordova, & Eldridge, 2000) devised integrative couple therapy. This approach moved beyond teaching behavior exchange and communication skills to help couples change their destructive patterns and find mutual acceptance. Explicitly focusing on emotion, Greenberg and Johnson (1988) created emotion-focused therapy for couples, which evolved from experiential individual therapy and systemic family theory. By encouraging partners to access and communicate their need for attachment and intimacy, emotion-focused therapists help couples move from blame and defensiveness to expressions of underlying, primary emotions, such as hurt and sadness.

Contemporary Family Therapy

Over the past two decades, the parameters of family therapy have expanded greatly. Notably, there has been a blurring of boundaries between theories, as well as the development of treatment models that integrate different approaches (Nichols & Schwartz, 2007). We have also seen a proliferation of CFT therapies tailored for specific client problems, such as infertility, children's behavior disorders, substance abuse, depression, and juvenile offending, as well as interventions designed to prevent psychosocial difficulties (e.g., Tolan, 2003). Contemporary family therapists are also being encouraged to pay close attention to ethnic and cultural norms that suggest important differences in how diverse families define dysfunction and in how these families should be assessed and treated (Nichols & Schwartz, 2007).

Whereas early theorists and practitioners focused almost exclusively on family dynamics and on understanding the problem as functional within the family system, it is now clear that problems are multiply determined—influenced not only by family but also by individual, biological, and extrafamilial factors (i.e., peer group, school, etc.). Consequently, current family therapists often intervene in multiple life domains (Liddle, 2005; Schoenwald & Henggeler, 2005), no longer confining their efforts to the behavioral interactions of the nuclear family.

Take the example of a therapist who is treating a boy with attention deficit hyperactivity disorder. The therapist might begin by providing both parents and child with psychoeducation about the disorder. As the parents and siblings begin to understand the origins of certain behaviors, family interactions and relationships are likely to change. That is, rather than interpreting the child's unresponsiveness as defiance, family members come to understand it as related to neurological deficits in attentional and behavioral control, and their responses to the boy become more empathic and supportive. The therapist is then positioned to help family members understand how their own behaviors contribute to escalating conflict ("When you yell directions from the other room, he is not very likely to register them and respond. You then become frustrated and angry. He feels frustrated because he has no memory of being asked to complete the task and so becomes defiant. This gets you even angrier and leads to extreme punitive behavior and his sense of injustice and hopelessness"). At the same time, the therapist coaches the parents to teach their son compensatory strategies, which the child can use in school and with peers. Finally, the therapist may encourage parents to consult with a physician about medication and begin developing collaborative relationships with important extrafamilial systems or agents. For instance, therapist and parent(s) might meet with the school psychologist and teachers to engineer a school environment that provides the best chance for the child to succeed. This multifaceted approach to treatment exemplifies how the field has moved beyond a singular focus on family dynamics.

Another development that has changed the landscape of family therapy practice is the use of manuals for specific treatment approaches. Typically, these evidence-based approaches are informed by theory and research from a wide range of domains, including normative development, developmental psychopathology, cognition and emotion, and have a clearly articulated conceptualization of the forces maintaining the disorder of interest, the optimal change strategies, and the corresponding interventions. As a result, contemporary family-based treatments have become more systematic, standardized, and targeted.

The next sections of this chapter focus on the empirical evidence that informs CFT practice. First, we review a number of exemplary research programs that address the outcome question, "Which approaches to CFT work for specific kinds of clients?" Then, we turn our attention to process research that addresses "how" CFT works, focusing on three specific mechanisms of change in actual clinical settings.

Current Evidence-based Treatment Programs

By the late 1990s, several comprehensive reviews of the outcome literature (e.g., Baucom, Shoham, Mueser, Daiuto, & Stickle, 1998; Dunn & Schwebel, 1995; Pinsof, Wynne, & Hambright, 1996) concluded that couple and family treatments were as effective as no-treatment or wait-list controls. An influential meta-analysis of 71 studies (Shadish, Ragsdale, Glaser, & Montgomery, 1995) showed that clients in CFT treatments did, on average, approximately half a standard deviation better than untreated controls, and the effect sizes for CFT were comparable to those reported for individual therapies. Moreover, in studies that compared CFT to individual treatment, the differences in outcome were negligible (Shadish et al., 1995).

Although there is substantial evidence, generally, for the efficacy of CFT, some disorders and clinical populations have been more extensively researched. In the following section, we summarize the findings from recent clinical trials of prominent CFT approaches that target specific client problems or disorders.

Conjoint Couples Therapy
INTEGRATIVE BEHAVIORAL COUPLE THERAPY
Beginning with Stuart's (1969) classic report on applying behavioral reinforcement to the treatment of couples' problems, *traditional behavioral couple*

therapy (TBCT) has been the most widely studied approach for treating marital distress, with over 20 randomized clinical trials demonstrating its relative efficacy and clinical significance (Baucom, Shoham, Mueser, Daiuto, & Stickle, 1998; Jacobson, Christensen, Prince, Cordova, & Eldridge, 2000). However, as Jacobson et al. (2000) pointed out, despite positive results, at least one-third of couples remain clinically distressed at the end of treatment and, even among those who improve, many do not maintain their gains beyond 2 years.

In an effort to improve the effectiveness of the model, Andrew Christensen and Neil Jacobson (Christensen, Jacobson, & Babcock, 1995; Jacobson & Christensen, 1996) developed *integrative behavioral couple therapy* (IBCT), which added humanistic elements to the traditional change-oriented strategies of TBCT. ICBT's acceptance-based interventions are designed to help partners accept aspects of each other that are intransigent and considered intolerable. Emphasizing a contextual, functional analysis of the couple's problems, ICBT therapists work with the naturally occurring contingencies in couples' lives rather than inventing new reinforcers, as was done in TBCT contingency contracts (Gollan & Jacobson, 2002). In addition to promoting an understanding of destructive patterns and partners' mutual acceptance, ICBT therapists "promote empathic joining or unified detachment with the goal of turning problem areas into sources of renewed intimacy" (Gollan & Jacobson, 2002, p. 111).

The efficacy of IBCT was demonstrated in two early studies (Christensen, Jacobson, & Babcock, 1995; Christensen & Heavey, 1999). In a subsequent, large clinical trial comparing IBCT to TBCT, Christensen and colleagues (Christensen et al., 2004) randomly assigned 134 seriously and chronically distressed couples to one of the two treatments. Results indicated that, at post-treatment, the two treatments produced similar levels of clinically meaningful improvement (71% for IBCT, 59% for TBCT). Interestingly, couples receiving TBCT improved more quickly, although their gains tended to plateau, whereas couples receiving IBCT improved steadily over time.

One question raised by the authors was whether these differential trajectories had implications for long-term outcome. In a later study examining couple functioning 2 years post-treatment, Christensen et al. (2006) found that both treatments produced substantial and similar rates of clinically significant improvement (ICBT 69%; TBCT 60%).

EMOTION-FOCUSED THERAPY

Another couple therapy that has been extensively researched and applied is *emotion focused therapy* (EFT; Greenberg & Johnson, 1988; Johnson & Greenberg, 1985). Developed from humanistic and systemic theories, EFT focuses on couples' negative interaction cycles and poor communication patterns that result from the disowning of primary needs for attachment. As mentioned earlier, by identifying and working with negative cycles, EFT therapists help partners to access underlying, primary emotions (hurt, sadness) and communicate their attachment needs clearly before generating solutions for specific problems. In contrast to ICBT, EFT specifically targets attachment as the key to emotional intimacy.

Based on a number of randomized clinical trials conducted throughout the 1990s (Johnson, 1998), EFT has been recognized as one of the foremost empirically supported treatments for couples. Over the past few years, clinical researchers have continued to explore the use of EFT with a wide range of clinical populations. For example, in one small, exploratory study (MacIntosh & Johnson, 2008), ten couples with a partner reporting childhood sexual abuse received an average of 19 sessions of EFT. Results indicated that half of the couples reported clinically significant increases in relationship satisfaction and decreases in trauma symptoms at post-treatment. In another small, open trial in which 24 couples with a partner who reported an attachment injury (e.g., perceived betrayal, abandonment, etc.) received, on average, 13 sessions of EFT, 15 of the 24 couples were identified as being resolved by the end of treatment (Makinen & Johnson, 2006).

Conjoint Family Therapy

In the field of family therapy, no area has received as much attention or has been researched as thoroughly as adolescent substance abuse and problem behaviors (i.e., delinquency and conduct disorder). A number of groups have established impressive, longstanding, systematic research programs to develop, test, adapt, and transport these family-based treatments to community clinics. All of these models are based, to some degree, on structural and strategic principles and intervention strategies; they address not only the adolescent's functioning but also the nature and quality of adolescent-parental relationships. Furthermore, all of these treatments address, to varying degrees, ecological factors (e.g., school, peers) that are known to have an impact on the adolescent's functioning.

BRIEF STRATEGIC FAMILY THERAPY

One influential treatment approach is *brief strategic family therapy* (BSFT), developed by José Szapocznik and colleagues (Szapocznik et al., 2002) at the University of Miami. Brief strategic family therapy combines elements from structural and strategic theories, with the goal of changing dysfunctional family patterns that maintain teen drug use. Interventions with school officials and other systems are used to reduce risk and enhance protective factors.

Throughout the 1980s and 1990s, a number of clinical trials demonstrated that BSFT was efficacious in reducing Hispanic adolescents' drug use and problem behaviors (see Robbins, Szapocznik, & Perez, 2007 for a review). A number of recent studies provide further evidence regarding the model's efficacy. For example, in one study, 126 Hispanic families were randomly assigned to either BSFT or a problem-solving group treatment. Adolescents who received BSFT showed greater pre- to post-treatment improvements on parent-reported conduct problems and delinquency, adolescents' report of marijuana use, and observers' reports of family functioning (Santisteban et al., 2003). In another study, Robbins et al. (2008) found that a family-based ecological approach, integrating BSFT with a school assessment and intervention, with the teen's peer group and with juvenile justice, was more effective in reducing Hispanic adolescents' drug use than traditional BSFT or a community treatment-as-usual comparison group. The same effect was not found for African American adolescents, however. An ambitious, ongoing, multisite trial with diverse samples is investigating changes in family functioning as a mediator of BSFT's treatment effectiveness (Shoham, Rohrbaugh, Robbins, Szapocznik, & Feaster, 2003).

MULTIDIMENSIONAL FAMILY THERAPY

Another well developed and researched conjoint approach is *multidimensional family therapy* (MDFT; Liddle, 2005), which combines elements from strategic and structural family therapy, developmental psychology, and ecological principles. In this approach, adolescents' symptoms are targeted and their prosocial behaviors are increased when the therapist focuses on normative, developmentally appropriate behavior, peer relations, identity, attachment to school, and autonomy in relation to parents. Interventions delivered to parents separately focus on improving parenting strategies, and meetings commonly take place with extended family members and members of other influential social groups.

In 2008 Multidimensional family therapy was recognized—along with functional family therapy (Alexander & Parsons, 1982)—as one of only two family treatments considered "well established" for treating adolescent substance abusers (Waldron & Turner, 2008). In the first large-scale study of the model (Liddle et al., 2001), 182 racially diverse, marijuana and alcohol abusing adolescents were randomly assigned to MDFT, adolescent group therapy, or a multifamily educational intervention. Although adolescents in all three treatments improved from intake to termination, those receiving MDFT showed the most improvement on drug use and family functioning. Furthermore, participants receiving MDFT showed the highest rates of clinically significant change 12 months post-treatment (Liddle et al., 2001).

In a second study (Liddle, Dakof, Turner, Henderson, & Greenbaum, 2008), 224 primarily African American, substance using male adolescents were randomly assigned to 3 months of MDFT or individual cognitive-behavioral therapy for drug use. Both treatments were associated with significant and similar reductions in frequency of marijuana use over the course of treatment and at 6 months follow-up. However, MDFT was more effective in reducing drug use, with these effects continuing to remain significant at the 12-month follow-up.

In yet another study (Dennis et al., 2004), MDFT was one of five treatment conditions in a multisite Cannabis Youth Treatment Study. Although all five treatments evidenced significant post-treatment gains on the two primary outcome measures (days of abstinence and percent of adolescents in recovery), there were no between-treatment differences.

Other studies have shown that MDFT can be transported to community clinics and effectively administered by front-line clinicians. In one study (Liddle, Rowe, Dakof, Ungaro & Henderson, 2004) conducted at a nonprofit community drug abuse clinic, 80 urban, low-income, ethnically diverse substance abusing and problem behavior adolescents were randomly assigned to MDFT or group therapy. Assessments at 6 weeks and at discharge showed that MDFT was more effective at reducing drug use and various risk factors (e.g., delinquent peer involvement) as well as promoting protective factors, such as family cohesion. At the 12-month follow-up (Liddle, Rowe, Dakof, Henderson, & Greenbaum, in press), clients receiving MDFT evidenced less substance use, substance use problems, delinquency, internalized distress, and family, peer and school risk factors.

MULTISYSTEMIC THERAPY

Today, *multisystemic therapy* (MST; Bourduin, Henggeler, Blaske, & Stein, 1990; Henggeler, Schoenwald, Bourduin, Rowland, & Cunningham, 1998) is one of the most established and effective treatments for criminal, delinquent, and substance use behaviors among adolescents. Like MDFT, MST addresses individual development, family structure and functioning, and the key social systems in adolescents' lives. Because of its intensity, therapists using this model tend to see a small number of families, working closely with all of the systems involved in the teen's life and managing crises as they occur.

Results from the first set of randomized clinical trials conducted in the 1990s found that MST was particularly effective in increasing abstinence from marijuana and reducing re-arrests, criminal activity, out-of-home placements, and self-reported drug and alcohol use (Borduin et al., 1995; Henggeler, Melton, & Smith, 1992; Henggeler, Melton, Brondino, Scherer, & Hanley, 1997; Henggeler, Pickerel, & Brondino, 1999). Furthermore, most of these gains were maintained up to 4 years post-treatment (Borduin, Henggeler, Blaske, & Stein, 1990; Borduin, et al., 1995; Henggeler, et al., 1991; Henggeler, Melton, & Smith, 1992; Henggeler, Melton, Smith, Schoenwald, & Hanley, 1993).

Over the past few years, a number of investigations examined the long-term results of some of the earlier studies. Henggeler, Clingempeel, Brondino, and Pickrel (2002), for example, assessed the 4-year outcomes of 80 substance abusing juvenile offenders who had participated in a randomized clinical trial comparing MST to usual community services. The adolescents who had received MST evidenced lower rates of aggressive criminal activity, but not property crimes. Analyses of urine and hair samples indicated that the teens in the MST treatment showed greater marijuana abstinence, although there were no treatment differences in self-reported drug use.

In one of the most impressive follow-up studies conducted to date, Schaeffer and Borduin (2005) examined arrest and incarceration data from 176 seriously offending youths who had received either MST or individual therapy 12–15 years prior (Borduin et al., 1995). Even after such a lengthy time period, participants who had received MST showed lower rates of recidivism (50% vs. 81% for individual therapy), fewer arrests, and fewer days of confinement.

More recently, MST has been examined by independent investigators, both within and outside the United States. In a randomized clinical trial conducted in Norway (Ogden & Halliday-Boykins, 2004), 100 adolescents referred for severe behavior problems received either MST or regular child welfare services. Results indicated that MST was more effective in reducing out-of-home placements and behavior problems at termination and at 2 years post-treatment (Ogden & Hagen, 2006). In the first randomized clinical trial conducted in the United States without the direct oversight of the model developers, Timmons-Mitchell, Bender, Kishna, and Mitchell (2006) randomly assigned 93 juvenile offenders to either MST or usual child welfare services. Importantly, this effectiveness study took place in a community setting with master's degree-level therapists. It was found that adolescents who participated in MST evidenced lower recidivism rates and higher functioning at home, school, and in the community than did the teens who received treatment as usual.

Multisystemic therapy has also been successfully used with psychiatric patients (Henggeler et al., 1999; Huey et al., 2005; Rowland, 2005; Schoenwald, Ward, Henggler & Rowland, 2000), children with health disorders, such as type I diabetes (Ellis et al., 2007; Naar-King et al., 2007), and children with perinatally acquired HIV (Ellis, Naar-King, Cunningham, & Secord, 2006).

FAMILY-FOCUSED TREATMENT

Over the past decade, Miklowitz and colleagues (Miklowitz & Goldstein, 1990) have developed and tested *family-focused treatment* (FFT) for patients suffering from bipolar disorder and their families. Originally created for adults (Miklowitz & Goldstein, 1997), this approach has also been used effectively with adolescents (Miklowitz et al., 2004) as well as younger children (Pavuluri et al., 2004). The treatment is designed to reduce family criticism and conflict and consists of three phases: psychoeducation, the learning of effective communication skills, and training in problem solving. Family members learn about the disorder, share coping strategies, and attempt to reduce emotional reactivity. With younger children, the unique symptoms of pediatric bipolar disorder are emphasized (Pavuluri et al., 2004).

In the first large scale randomized clinical trial (Miklowitz et al., 2000), 101 bipolar adult patients were randomly assigned to either 21 sessions of FFT or to two family education sessions with follow-up crisis management. Both groups received ongoing mood stabilizing medication. Patients who received FFT had fewer relapses and longer periods of time between relapses at the 1-year evaluation. These patients also showed greater improvement in family communication and in depressive, but not manic, symptoms. Results at 2 years post-randomization showed that patients receiving FFT continued to be less likely to relapse, and benefited from longer intervals prior to relapse, than the patients who received crisis management (Miklowitz, George, Richards, Simoneau & Suddath, 2003).

In a second, more rigorously designed study, Rea at al. (2003) compared FFT to an individually focused therapy, which included psychoeducation, case management and problem solving, for a sample of recently hospitalized adult manic patients. Again, both groups received concurrent mood stabilizing medication. Compared to those receiving individual treatment, patients receiving FFT were less likely to be re-hospitalized or to experience mood disorder relapses over the two year period including active treatment (1 year) and follow-up (1 year).

Finally, a large-scale (N = 293), multisite study (Miklowitz et al., 2007) examined the benefit of medication plus one of four psychosocial interventions. Results indicated that patients receiving FFT, interpersonal and social rhythm therapy, or cognitive therapy had better recovery rates, less time to recovery, better total functioning, better relationship functioning, and greater life satisfaction than patients receiving brief collaborative care (i.e., three sessions of psychoeducation).

FAMILY-BASED TREATMENT FOR ANOREXIA

Over the course of the 1990s, a group of clinical researchers at Maudsley Hospital in London (Dare, Eisler, Russell, Treasure & Dodge, 2001; Dare & Eisler, 1995) developed and successfully tested a family therapy model for treating anorexia nervosa in adolescents (Eisler, Lock, le Grange, 2007). The treatment first involves defining the anorexia as a severe psychiatric illness and subsequently helps parents to take control of their adolescent's eating behavior. Once the lost weight has been restored, the adolescent is helped to manage his or her own eating habits and cope with the development tasks of adolescence (school, peer relations, etc.).

In a series of studies (Dare, Eisler, Russell, & Szmukler, 1990; Russell, Szmukler, Dare, & Eisler, 1987; Eisler et al., 1997; Robin, Siegel, Koepke,

Moye, & Tice, 1994), investigators showed that this family therapy approach was efficacious and potentially superior to individual therapy for adolescents suffering from anorexia nervosa. More recently, a study was conducted in which 40 families received either 1 year of conjoint or separated family therapy (SFT), a treatment in which the therapist meets with family members separately (Eisler, Dare, Hodes, Russell, Dodge, & Le Grange, 2000). A randomized, stratified design was used to account for level of maternal criticism. Overall, there were significant reductions in anorexic symptoms, as well as gains in psychological and family functioning, across the two treatments, with nearly two-thirds of the adolescents achieving a normal weight. As might be expected, SFT was more efficacious for families high in maternal criticism, whereas there were no treatment differences for families with low levels of emotional reactivity. A follow-up study found that the gains were maintained 5 years post-treatment, with more than 75% of patients demonstrating no eating disorder symptoms (Eisler, Simic, Russell, & Dare, 2007). Notably, high maternal criticism continued to be associated with poor outcome at the 5-year follow-up.

Researchers at Stanford University (Lock, Agras, Bryson, & Kraemer, 2005) explored the role of dose and length of Dare and colleagues' Maudsley treatment model. Lock et al. (2005) randomly assigned 86 adolescents to either 10 therapy sessions over the course of 6 months, or 20 sessions over the course of 1 year. Results indicated that although 96% of the patients showed improvement and 67% could conservatively be described as remitters, there were no significant treatment effects, suggesting that the shorter course of therapy was sufficient. In a subsequent study that examined the effects of this treatment at, on average, 4 years post-therapy, 89% of the sample weighed 90% of more of their ideal body weight and 74% did not evidence any eating disorder symptoms (Lock, Couturier, & Agras, 2006). Again, no significant differences were found between the short- and long-term therapy conditions.

Although most studies of family therapy for anorexia have focused on adolescents, Dare, Eisler, Russell, Treasure and Dodge (2001) examined the comparative efficacy of 1 year of family therapy, 1 year of focal psychoanalytic psychotherapy, 7 months of cognitive-analytic therapy, and 1 year of low-contact, routine treatment for young adults suffering from anorexia nervosa. Results showed that, across treatments, there was modest symptomatic improvement over the course of the year.

However, in contrast to studies on adolescents, more than two-thirds of patients remained abnormally underweight at the end of treatment. Family therapy and focal psychoanalytic therapy were found to be equally effective and more effective in producing weight gain than the control treatment.

In contrast to its utility for treating anorexia nervosa, family therapy may not be the treatment of choice for adolescents suffering from bulimia nervosa. In the only published study to date, Schmidt et al. (2007) found that after 6 months of treatment, adolescents receiving individual cognitive-behavioral therapy reported less binging behavior than those receiving Eisler et al's (2005) family therapy model. These group differences, however, disappeared at 12-month follow-up, at which time patients maintained their treatment gains or improved.

ATTACHMENT-BASED FAMILY THERAPY

Diamond and colleagues (Diamond, Siqueland & Diamond, 2003; Diamond, 2005) at the Children's Hospital of Philadelphia have developed and gathered efficacy data for *attachment-based family therapy* (ABFT), the first manualized family therapy approach specifically designed to treat seriously depressed and suicidal adolescents. The model is based on structural family therapy, MDFT, attachment theory, adolescent development research, and emotion-focused principles and intervention strategies. The model is structured as a series of specific, interrelated treatment tasks. The first task is to shift the focus of therapy from one of behavioral control or management to a focus on the quality of the adolescent–parent attachment relationship. The therapist then typically meets with the adolescent and then the parent alone. In the session with the adolescent, the therapist aims to identify conflicts that, from the adolescent's perspective, have damaged the family's attachment bond. Sessions alone with the parents aim to deepen their commitment to repairing attachment and facilitating meaningful communication with their child. Once this foundation has been set, the family is brought back together to discuss core conflicts that have damaged trust. Sometimes, these conflicts arise from the stress of normal family life; however, often these conflicts stem from a history of abuse or neglect. The working through process occurs in the context of conjoint enactments, or reattachment episodes. Once the attachment ruptures have been resolved, the therapy focuses on helping parents support and guide the adolescent as she or he gets back on track

with normal developmental tasks (i.e., school, peer relationships).

In the initial pilot randomized clinical study of ABFT (Diamond, Reiss, Diamond, Siqueland, & Isaacs, 2002), 32 depressed adolescents, primarily female and African American, were assigned to either 12 weeks of ABFT or 6 weeks of a minimal wait-list control condition. At the end of treatment, 81% of the adolescent clients no longer met criteria for major depressive disorder, as compared to 47% of those on the waiting list. Furthermore, adolescents who received ABFT showed greater reductions in anxiety symptoms and family conflict. Of the 15 ABFT cases assessed at follow-up, 13 (87%) continued not to meet the criteria for major depressive disorder 6 months post-treatment.

In a larger, recently completed study (Diamond, Winterstein, Brown, Gallop, Shelef, Diamond, & Levy, under review), 66 adolescents with severe suicidal ideation and moderate to severe depressive symptoms were randomly assigned to either 14 weeks of ABFT or 14 weeks of enhanced usual care. Over the active phase of treatment, adolescents in ABFT showed significantly more rapid reductions of suicidal ideation. These relative gains were maintained over follow-up assessments. In addition, rates of clinical recovery were higher for patients in ABFT across all time points. Patients in ABFT also experienced greater initial reductions in depression. These findings were true even when looking at the subsample of adolescents who met criteria for a diagnosis of depression and/or reported a history of sexual abuse.

As indicated by these eight exemplary research programs, there is now substantial evidence for the efficacy and effectiveness of CFT for a number of specific problems and diagnosable mental disorders. However, less is known about "how" CFT works. More research is needed to examine the CFT therapy process in order to understand how, specifically, change comes about in conjoint treatment.

What Makes Couple and Family Therapy Work?

To move psychotherapy research forward, Greenberg (1986) advocated studying specific change processes. Greenberg's advocacy for "change process research" differentiated this kind of study from traditional process research. That is, rather than simply describing what takes place in therapy sessions, change process research seeks to identify specific mechanisms of change. In other words, the focus of this kind of research is what, specifically, produces a meaningful shift in clients' psychosocial problems.

Describing change process research, Greenberg (1986) described concentric levels of therapeutic influence. If we envision the therapy process as layers of an onion, at the most micro level, or the center, is *content*—what is discussed in treatment. Examples include dreams, irrational thoughts, or coping strategies. Although informative, content has less to do with facilitating change than the next process level, *speech acts* (Greenberg, 1986). By studying speech acts, or therapeutic techniques (e.g., interpretation, confrontation, reframing), we can discover what "works" across content areas. When the topic under discussion is the client's hostility, for example, is the most effective technique confrontation, reflection of feelings, or interpretation? At the next process level is the *episode*, or event. That is, content and technique occur within a period of time in which a specific task is the focus. Like a chapter in a book, a therapeutic episode has a beginning, middle, and end (Greenberg, 1986). In individual therapy, for example, an episode might involve an entire session (or more) that is specifically focused on the client's "unfinished business" with a deceased parent (Greenberg & Malcolm, 2002). In couple therapy, an episode might be half a session devoted to working out an equitable balance of household chores during which the partners are encouraged to negotiate with each other and achieve a compromise. Finally, at the highest process level (the outer layer of the onion) is the *therapeutic relationship*, most often studied as the working alliance. That is, in the context of purposeful collaboration between therapist and client(s), we might study how specific episodes and techniques bring about therapeutic change. Or, when the therapeutic relationship is not firmly established, we could investigate what takes place in session to enhance it.

In a 1994 article, Friedlander, Wildman, Heatherington, and Skowron used Greenberg's (1986) model of change process research to review the published studies to date in CFT. At that time, research at the intervention, or technique, level predominated (Friedlander et al., 1994). In the two decades since that publication, many CFT researchers have turned their attention to the therapeutic relationship and to episodes of change, also called *change events*.

In selecting CFT process areas to review for this chapter, we decided to focus on three core

components or change mechanisms in CFT: the therapeutic alliance (at the relationship level), reframing (at the speech act level), and enactment (at the event level). In the following sections, a definition of each construct is followed by an explanation of its purported role in the change process, its complexity and uniqueness in CFT and relevant ethical considerations. We then review the empirical research in each area, highlighting not only the results of published studies but also the methodological challenges for future research.

Therapeutic Alliance

It is widely accepted that, in individual treatment, a strong therapeutic alliance between client and therapist plays an important role in outcome, especially when the alliance is assessed from the client's perspective (Horvath & Bedi, 2002; Horvath & Symonds, 1991). Far less has been written about the nature or importance of the working alliance in conjoint CFT. As described previously, early family theorists (e.g., Minuchin & Fishman, 1981; Watzlawick et al., 1967) focused on designing strategies to disrupt rigid and dysfunctional family patterns, the result being that the therapeutic relationship took a back seat to technique.

What is the therapeutic alliance? This construct has its roots in early psychoanalytic writings (Freud, 1912/1940; Sterba, 1934) that emphasized the importance of analyst–analysand (i.e., patient) collaboration. In 1967, Greenson distinguished the "working alliance" from transference and the "real relationship" between analyst and patient. It was Bordin (1979, 1994), however, who popularized the construct by defining it in a way that could be operationalized for empirical research.

According to Bordin (1979, 1994), the working, or therapeutic, alliance has three related components. First, client and therapist mutually negotiate the goals of treatment—what the client wishes to achieve from psychotherapy. Examples include reducing depression, overcoming test anxiety, or managing anger. The second component is mutual agreement about the tasks of therapy—what will take place in session and between sessions. Will the therapist assign "homework?" Ask the client to free associate or analyze dreams? Use an empty chair to facilitate emotional catharsis? Third, the working alliance requires a strong emotional bond. The bond is more than simply rapport. To do the hard work necessary for therapeutic change, the client needs to care for, trust, and respect the therapist, and the therapist needs to care about and communicate deep empathy for the client.

Beginning with Pinsof and Catherall's (1986) seminal work on the alliance in CFT, theory and research on this construct has steadily increased over the past two decades. As a common factor in CFT, the alliance cuts across theoretical boundaries (Sprenkle & Blow, 2004). That is, just as in individual therapy, the alliance in conjoint CFT treatment is not theory specific. Its importance for treatment retention and outcome has been demonstrated in solution-focused family therapy (Beck, Escudero, & Friedlander, 2006; Escudero, Friedlander, Varela, & Abascal, 2008), MFT (Shelef, Diamond, Diamond, & Liddle, 2005; Robbins et al., 2006), functional family therapy (Robbins et al., 2003), integrative problem solving (Knobloch-Fedders, Pinsof, & Mann, 2004), EFT for couples (S. M. Johnson & Talitman, 1997), and BSFT (Robbins, Mayorga, Mitrani, Szapocznik, Turner, & Alexander, 2008), as well as nonmanualized couple and family "treatment-as-usual" (Friedlander, Lambert, & Muñiz de la Peña, 2008; L. N. Johnson, Wright, & Ketring, 2002; Symonds & Horvath, 2004)(see Friedlander, Escudero, Heatherington, & Diamond (2011) for a meta-analysis of alliance-outcome research).

However, in conjoint CFT, the alliance–outcome relationship is not as straightforward as it is in individual therapy (Friedlander et al., 2008). Research suggests that the degree to which each individual's alliance with the therapist affects retention and outcome depends on the quality of other family members' alliances. Robbins et al. (2003), for example, found that the discrepancy between adolescents' and parents' alliances with the therapist had greater predictive value than their alliances considered independently. Symonds and Horvath (2004) reported that a couple's agreement on the alliance, regardless of its strength, was more influential than either partner's individual alliance alone. In contrast, Knobloch-Fedders et al. (2004) found that outcomes were better when husbands' alliances surpassed those of their wives, but the opposite pattern was found in another study of couples (Quinn, Dotson, & Jordan, 1997).

Despite these contradictions, it seems clear that "split" family alliances; that is, considerable discrepancies in the self-reported alliances of different family members (Beck et al., 2006; Friedlander et al., 2006a; Heatherington & Friedlander, 1990; Mamodhoussen, Wright, Tremblay, & Poitras-Wright, 2005; Muñiz de la Peña, Friedlander, & Escudero, 2009; Pinsof & Catherall, 1986; Quinn et al., 1997), are common

occurrences in both couples and family treatment. Splits can be predicted both by individual and marital distress (Knobloch-Fedders et al., 2004; Mamodhoussen et al., 2005; Symonds & Horvath, 2004), and their "repair" is said to be essential for treatment to be successful (Friedlander et al., 2006a; Muñiz de la Peña et al., 2009; Pinsof, 1995).

What makes CFT alliances unique? It goes without saying that complexity is inherent when working with multiple couples simultaneously. Aside from that, in conjoint treatment, family members observe each other responding to the therapist (Heatherington & Friedlander, 1990; Pinsof & Catherall, 1986; Rait, 2000), and these observations can have reverberating effects. A husband, for example, finds that a male therapist takes his wife seriously (when he, himself, does not), so that the wife's alliance with the therapist is affected not only by her own bond with him but also by her husband's new attitude toward her. As another example, a mother may not be impressed by the therapist but may nonetheless be pleased with the progress made by her son, who does apparently like and trust the therapist.

These examples illustrate why CFT alliances differ from therapeutic alliances in individual treatment. As explained by Friedlander et al. (2006a), family members often have differing motivation levels and agendas. People usually seek conjoint therapy when conflicts between them are insurmountable, and they naturally expect the therapist to take sides. Adults and children are at different developmental levels, and family members may have different capacities for taking risks, tolerating anxiety, or expressing emotions. Perhaps more importantly, clients in conjoint therapy generally have less control over what is said, or what is said about them, than do clients in individual therapy. The private thoughts, feelings, or secrets that may be revealed in a conjoint therapy session cannot be as easily pushed aside after the session. A woman comes to therapy to improve her relationship with her partner but finds out that the partner is planning to leave her. A mother brings her depressed daughter to a therapist, only to discover that her husband, the girl's stepfather, has been molesting her regularly.

Ethical considerations play a role in developing and maintaining strong alliances with couples and families. Relationships are inevitably affected when the therapist is mandated to report suspected child abuse, for example. Consider a couple who came to treatment to work out some marital difficulties, which had escalated after the birth of their second child.

Therapy was proceeding fairly well until the husband brought in photographs of the toddler's bruises, which he said were caused by his wife. Although the wife admitted to restraining the child "too forcefully," she minimized the injuries. Although the therapist did his best to retain the couple in treatment after calling Child Protective Services (CPS), the alliance with the husband was strengthened but the alliance with the wife deteriorated. She refused to return to treatment, despite the fact that the CPS worker found no conclusive evidence of abuse.

Another ethical issue arises when secrets are revealed, a not uncommon occurrence in CFT. Clients reveal secrets when they need the therapist to serve as a buffer or protector. That is, for many clients, telling a secret in the consulting room is far safer than revealing it at home, where other family members might react extremely. If the secret involves harm, such as ongoing molestation, the therapist is mandated to report it to authorities. Although the consequences may be similar to those in the earlier example, sometimes taking such action can strengthen the family's ties with the therapist (see Friedlander et al., 2006a, for some clinical examples).

A secret may challenge the therapeutic alliance in other ways. To illustrate, consider another couples case. A woman calls the therapist between sessions to explain that she is having an ongoing, secret love affair. Although she wants the therapist to have this information, she does not want it revealed to her partner. This bid to align with the therapist creates a dysfunctional emotional triangle that puts the alliance at risk and is counterproductive for treatment and for the couple's well-being.

Although confidentiality is an ethical principle, for the therapist to keep this secret would be harmful to the partner, to the couple's relationship, and to the therapeutic alliance. On the other hand, revealing it without the client's consent would not only be unethical but also would destroy the client's faith in the therapist. One strategy would be to give the client a choice—she can inform her partner, either at home or in the next therapy session because, otherwise, the conjoint therapy has little chance of success. However, if the client refuses either alternative, discontinuing the treatment without divulging the reason risks damaging both clients' trust in the therapist—and perhaps in all mental health providers.

As Butler, Harper, and Seedall (2009) pointed out, infidelity damages attachment bonds and obstructs authentic intimacy. Therapists who collude to keep infidelity secrets violate the ethic of "doing no harm" since people have the right to know and act on vital information about their own intimate relationships. In these authors' words, "[I]t is inconsistent and contradictory for couple therapists to ostensibly affirm ethics of justice, equality, and individual rights in relationships while at the same time accommodating and/or facilitating clients in keeping relationship-relevant information from a spouse" (p. 127). Citing data indicating that most couples who address infidelity in treatment do, in fact, stay together, Butler et al. (2009) argued for "facilitated disclosure," by which the "aggrieved partner" is told (preferably by the "offending partner") that there is some relevant information of which he or she is unaware. Then the recipient has the choice to ask or not ask for disclosure of the secret. This intervention, which is designed to respect the individual's right to privacy, requires the therapist to explain the need for disclosure and, once the infidelity is disclosed, to focus intensively on the healing process (Butler, Seedall, & Harper, 2008).

We see, then, that alliances in CFT are complex. They can shift dramatically over time, based on what happens in the family's life outside therapy or by who chooses to come (or not come) to a therapy session. For these reasons, advancing our understanding of the alliance through empirical study is essential.

To study the development, maintenance, and effects of the alliance in CFT, researchers must first consider the nature of their alliance measures and also decide what constitutes a "family alliance." Taking Bordin's (1979) classic conceptualization of the alliance (an emotional bond with the therapist and mutually agreed upon goals and therapy tasks) as a point of departure, Pinsof and Catherall (1986) developed couple and family alliance measures, in which clients were asked to report on the alliance (goals, tasks, and bonds) from their own perspective, from the perspective of "other family members," and from the perspective of the "group as a whole." Subsequently, Pinsof (1994, 1995; Pinsof, Zinbarg, & Knobloch-Fedders, 2008) added the "within-system alliance," which other authors (Friedlander et al., 2006a, 2008; Friedlander, Escudero, Horvath, Heatherington, Cabero, & Martens, 2006b) term the family's "shared sense of purpose," or the degree to which family members concur on the need, purpose, and value of conjoint treatment.

When multiple family members report on their alliances with the therapist, the question becomes: How should these individual scores be analyzed? Averaging family members' scores "washes out" individual differences, making it impossible to identify split alliances. Subtracting alliance scores (e.g., the father's score minus the son's score) does allow splits to be identified but fails to take into account the alliances' relative strength (e.g., a discrepancy score of 5 could reflect family scores of 30 and 35 as well as scores of 12 and 17).

For these reasons, Friedlander and colleagues (2006a, 2006b) developed an observational rating system, the System for Observing Family Therapy Alliances (SOFTA-o), to assess the strength of the alliance from in-session behavior, specifically family members' individual interactions with the therapist and with each other. A corresponding self-report measure (SOFTA-s; Escudero et al., 2008; Friedlander et al., 2006a; Muñiz de la Peña et al., 2009) asks individuals to report on their own alliance with the therapist and their perceptions of the entire family's shared sense of purpose; that is, the alliance between and among family members irrespective of the therapist. An example of a shared sense of purpose item is, "Each of us in the family helps the others get what they want out of therapy" (Friedlander et al., 2006a, p. 298). By assessing the within-system alliance in this way, the SOFTA-s avoids the problem some authors (Beck et al., 2006; L. N. Johnson et al., 2002) reported with Pinsof and Catherall's (1986) measures—that clients often do not know how their family members feel about the therapist.

Like the SOFTA-s, the SOFTA-o contains two dimensions that reflect Bordin's (1979, 1994) perspective on the alliance, *engagement in the therapeutic process* (which includes client–therapist agreement on goals and tasks) and *emotional connection with the therapist* (which is similar to Bordin's emotional bond). Two other dimensions reflect the uniqueness of CFT. *Shared sense of purpose within the family* has behavioral items that are both positive ("Family members offer to compromise," "Family members validate each other's point of view") and negative ("Family members try to align with the therapist against each other") (Friedlander et al., 2006a, p. 274). The other unique SOFTA dimension is *safety within the therapeutic system*. Although safety is important in all forms of therapy, in CFT it is unique because clients need to take risks and discuss intimate topics in front of other family members, with whom they are likely to be in conflict. Like shared sense of purpose, safety behaviors are both positive ("Client directly asks other family members for feedback about his/her behavior or about herself/himself as a person," "Client reveals a secret or

something that other family members didn't know") and negative ("Client refuses or is reluctant to respond when directly addressed by another family member") (Friedlander et al., 2006a, p. 273).

After observing a live or video-taped session and considering the number, valence, intensity, and clinical context of the observed behaviors, trained raters make global judgments of each dimension on a −3 (*extremely problematic*) to +3 (*extremely strong*) scale, where 0 = *unremarkable or neutral*. Based on specific rating guidelines, family members are judged individually on engagement, emotional connection, and safety, whereas the entire family or couple is rated as a unit on shared sense of purpose. The assumption underlying the SOFTA-o is that external observers can make judgments about the quality and strength of the alliance from observing specific alliance-related client behaviors, just as clinicians make inferences about their relationships with clients from the behavior that unfolds in front of them in a session (Friedlander et al., 2006a, 2006b).

Research with the SOFTA-o, and its self-report version, the SOFTA-s, suggests that the two unique aspects of the alliance, safety and shared sense of purpose, are of particular importance. In intensive analyses of individual families (Beck et al., 2006; Friedlander, Lambert, Escudero, & Cragun, 2008), poor outcome cases were distinguished from good outcome cases by low ratings on these two observed variables. In a study of 22 low-income families (Friedlander, Lambert, & Muñiz de la Peña, 2008), the parents' degree of safety predicted the family's shared sense of purpose in session 1, which in turn predicted parent reports of improvement-so-far after session 3. In another study (Escudero et al., 2008), shared sense of purpose was the alliance dimension that most consistently predicted therapeutic progress, and it was the only dimension that improved significantly over time in therapy.

To date, there have been few empirical studies of effective alliance repair in CFT. In the first exploratory investigation, five improving and five deteriorating alliances with adolescents were compared. Results showed that the therapists in the improving cases were more likely to ally with the adolescent, focusing on his or her experience and suggesting therapy goals that were of personal interest to the teen (Diamond, Liddle, Hogue, & Dakof, 1999). However, this study focused uniquely on improving the adolescent's initially poor alliance with the therapist. Repairing a "split" alliance requires simultaneous attention to the discrepant alliances of two or more family members. How can a therapist best repair a split alliance—by encouraging the parents to engage the teen in working for systemic change? Research on this complex change process has yet to be conducted.

In terms of other future directions, it is time for researchers to move beyond alliance-outcome investigations. It is abundantly clear that poor within-family alliances and differences in how individual family members view the therapist have negative consequences for retention and treatment outcome. At this point, it seems worthwhile to investigate the factors, both individual and systemic, that contribute to poor family alliances. Since split alliances seem to be most likely when clients begin therapy with high levels of individual, marital, and family-of-origin distress (Knobloch-Fedders et al., 2004; Mamodhoussen et al., 2005; Symonds & Horvath, 2004), investigators might well study family members' attachment styles and relational patterns. When both partners in a couple are highly avoidant, for example, their ability to form a strong bond with the therapist is likely to be difficult. What interventions can help make therapy a safe place for these clients to take emotional risks? Partners with highly anxious attachment styles, on the other hand, may relate quite well to the therapist but poorly with each other. How can a therapist use a strong therapeutic bond to disrupt a couple's rigid and dysfunctional interactions?

We should also begin studying the episodes and speech acts that contribute to strong (and problematic) family alliances. For example, how do effective therapists build alliances with couples and families who see their presenting problems in terms of winning or losing? Which techniques are most helpful when a family begins treatment with a poor sense of shared purpose? Investigating questions like these would move family alliance research away from global predictions of outcome to more practitioner-friendly studies of effective interventions for therapeutic change.

Finally, although an abundance of research findings demonstrates the link between alliance and outcome in CFT (Friedlander et al., 2011), one important but understudied question is *how*, exactly, the alliance facilitates the change process in conjoint therapy. Certainly, the therapist's support, recognition, and validation can increase each family member's sense of self-esteem, agency, and hopefulness, which in itself may promote change (Satir, 1964; Shirk & Russell, 1996). However, many CFT theorists do not view the client–therapist relationship as the primary change vehicle. Rather, the therapeutic

alliance is conceived of as a necessary, preliminary step in the change process: the development of a platform or safe base from which family members draw the courage and confidence to risk relating to one another in a different manner. It is a sufficiently strong therapeutic alliance that allows the therapist to challenge clients to be more direct and assertive, more vulnerable and less defensive. The two specific change mechanisms described in the following sections, reframing and enactment, require solid therapeutic alliances with all participating clients in a couple or family in order to be effective.

Reframing

Reaching agreement on the goals and tasks of therapy in CFT is arguably more complicated than in individual psychotherapy. Often family members present for treatment with different goals in mind. For example, although the mother of an adolescent daughter may come to therapy looking for ways to get her 16-year-old daughter to be more obedient, her daughter may hope that treatment helps to get her mother "off her back." In the context of couple therapy, it is not unusual for one partner to think that the other is not sufficiently committed to the relationship or emotionally available. When this person seeks greater closeness, the other partner may feel that she or he is being smothered and, consequently, seeks more psychological-emotional distance. Under such circumstances, it may appear that there is no way to formulate a mutually agreed upon treatment goal toward which all members of the system can work in concert.

One method for creating a shared goal or sense of purpose about attending therapy is through reframing (Friedlander et al., 2006a), an intervention that is common to many forms of CFT. In the words of Watzlawick et al. (1974), "to reframe . . . means to change the conceptual and/or emotional setting or viewpoint in relation to which a situation is experienced and to place it in another frame which fits the "facts' of the same concrete situation equally well or even better and thereby changes its entire meaning" (p. 94). According to structural therapists Minuchin and Fishman (1981), "the therapist's task is to . . . convince the family members that reality as they have mapped it can be expanded or modified" (p. 76).

As a speech act, reframing can be accomplished using a wide variety of interventions, including positive attributions ("It is wonderful how the two of you protect each other from feeling pain. When your wife becomes emotional, you focus her attention on problem solving. When you become emotional, she focuses your attention on other problems"), paradox ("I would like you to devote 15 minutes each evening to worrying about your relationship"), metaphor ("In many ways, the two of you remind me of a teeter-totter: one must be down so that the other is up") or externalization of symptoms ("The two of you are in a fight against this thing called depression which has invaded your lives. I'll help you stand together against it") (White & Epston, 1990), among others.

Each of these interventions places the problem in a different light, either in terms of the motivation behind or function of a person's behavior, the degree to which the behavior is controllable, intentional, or harmful. By changing the scope and/or meaning of the problem or impasse, the goals and tasks of therapy change as well. The emergence of new frames offers people the opportunity to construct new treatment goals—goals that supersede and bridge what initially appear to be family members' conflicting aims. For example, the mother and daughter described above seemingly want different, incongruous outcomes: The mother wants the daughter to be more obedient, the daughter wants more autonomy. In systemic terms, these goals can be characterized as attempts at "first order" change or "more of the same." However, by reframing the conflict in developmental, relational terms, a third option emerges, which may resonate for both mother and daughter. The therapist might explain, for example, "Clearly your relationship is important, and it's not hard to see the love you have for one another. However, it seems to me that you are trying to beat each other into concession rather than work together to help Karie grow up, and this battle has undermined one of the most important things in your lives—your relationship." This intervention speaks to the underlying attachment themes, while reframing the problem as a difficulty in how the two go about managing the developmentally normative process of negotiating autonomy in a collaborative fashion. In other words, the goal changes from two individuals wanting to "get their way" to, instead, finding a mutually acceptable method to work together—one that strengthens rather than undermines their personal relationship.

Not only can reframing facilitate the formation of the therapeutic alliance, but systemic reframes can also reduce criticism, blame, and negativity between and among family members (Friedlander, Heatherington, & Marrs, 2000). That is, when the problem at hand is framed in relational terms (e.g., "We don't seem to understand one another"),

the issue becomes the nature of the interaction or relationship itself, not one partner or family member.

In a study examining the impact of reframe interventions in functional family therapy for delinquent adolescents, Robbins and colleagues (Robbins, Alexander, Newell & Turner, 1996) found that adolescents responded to reframes more positively than to other types of interventions. This finding is particularly important in light of the fact that behavior disordered, other-referred adolescents typically present for therapy reluctantly (Taylor, Adelman, & Kaiser-Boyd, 1985) and have high levels of negativity (Robbins et al., 1996). Further analyses of this same sample revealed that reframes actually served to disrupt defensive or negative family interactions. More specifically, when therapists used reframes in response to family members' defensive statements, such as sarcasm or blame, family members were less likely to respond with defensive behavior than when therapists used reflection, structuring, or information gathering interventions (Robbins, Alexander & Turner, 2000).

Two studies examined the impact of relational reframes in ABFT for depressed adolescents. In the first study, Diamond and colleagues (Moran, Diamond, & Diamond, 2005) found that reframes led parents to adopt an *inter*personal, rather than an *intra*personal construction of the problem. Interpersonal constructions promote a sense of shared responsibility and possibilities for change, whereas intrapersonal constructions refer to an individual's personality or other constitutional factors, which are hard to change and connote blame. Not surprisingly, results from the second study (Moran & Diamond, 2008) found that following a relational reframe, parents were more likely to exhibit neutral or even positive attitudes toward their depressed adolescent rather than negativity. This finding is particularly important in light of the pernicious role played by parental criticism in the development and maintenance of depression during adolescence (Sheeber, Hyman, & Davis, 2001).

Clinical experience and research findings suggest that reframing can influence not only clients' cognitive constructions and behaviors, but also their emotional experience. For example, after listening to a husband and wife battle for the first 10 minutes of a session, the therapist might ask, "I wonder if the two of you miss those times when you felt supported, understood, and close to one another and wish it could be like that again? Maybe your fights allow you to find a way, even if it's a negative way, to bring some strong emotion back into your relationship?" Such reframing interventions, which shift clients' attention away from blame and anger and onto underlying or emergent vulnerable emotions that fuel conflict, typically lead to a dramatic shift in the emotional tone of the session: anger and acrimony are suddenly replaced by sadness and longing (Diamond & Liddle, 1996).

Indeed, reframing seems to be a powerful clinical tool when partners or family members blame one another in session. Friedlander et al. (2000) analyzed therapeutic interactions following blaming sequences in videotaped family therapy sessions with experts in narrative, solution-focused, and constructivist family therapy. Results showed that reframing was a frequent therapeutic intervention following within-family blame. Reframes took the form of focusing on competence, focusing on the positive, using metaphors, redefining or reinterpreting, and expanding the theme to bring in a new perspective. For example, one therapist reframed a child's silence, another therapist pointed to a child's competence in the face of her mother's criticism, and yet another therapist interpreted a couple's argument as due to their being "under a spell" that they needed to fight against (Friedlander et al., 2000).

In another study of constructivist family therapy (Sluzki, 1992), Coulehan, Friedlander, and Heatherington (1998) found that, during intake sessions, the therapist's exploration of positive attributes of individuals and the family unit was associated, not only with shifts from intrapersonal to interpersonal, relational constructions of the presenting problem, but also with a shift from negative to positive emotions. In the "old story," parents described the child as the "identified patient," the one who was being brought to therapy to be "fixed." Using circular questioning (e.g., "How does his misbehavior affect your marital relationship?"), asking about exceptions to the problem ("Tell me about a time when Sean did what you asked without a fuss"), and stimulating hope, the therapists in this study helped bring about a "new story" for four families. In one of these cases, a father declared at the end of the interview, "I guess we need a little more respect all around" (Coulehan et al., 1998). This comment suggested that, at least for him, the presenting problem was not his daughter but rather a problem shared throughout the family.

A number of important yet unstudied questions remain. For example, do reframes increase clients' hope, motivation for change and productive participation in treatment? In theory, after a successful reframe, clients should be more willing to engage in certain behaviors/tasks that they may previously have been reluctant to try. Other questions have to do with what constitutes an effective reframe and how it should be formulated. Good reframing requires substantial competence. It involves observing and understanding the couple or family dynamic, as well as the personality and level of defensiveness of each family member. As with interpretations in individual therapy, a premature, overly threatening, or poorly delivered reframe will not resonate with family members; in some instances, it may even generate resistance or undermine the therapeutic alliance. In contrast, effective reframes echo the underlying, core relational themes that are fueling the family's conflict or disengagement and are delivered in a manner in which family members feel heard and deeply understood.

Enactment

The therapeutic alliance in general, and the formulation of interpersonal, systemic therapy goals in particular, are preludes to a second core feature of most CFT approaches: transforming family/couple interactions in a session through enactment. The importance of enactment as a therapeutic event is reflected in one of the central tenets of CFT: that problem behaviors are the function of, or at least influenced by, family interaction patterns. Indeed, there is voluminous research on the association between couple and family functioning and a wide range of psychopathologies and problems in living, including anxiety (Rapee, 1997) and conduct disorders (Snyder, Cramer, Afrank, & Patterson, 2005), adolescent drug use (Fletcher, Darling, & Steinberg, 1995), adult alcoholism and marital violence (Foran & O'Leary, 2008), depression (Rehman, Gollan, & Mortimer, 2008; Sheeber, Hymans, & Davis, 2001) and severe mental illness, including bipolar disorder and schizophrenia (Miklowitz, 2008). Moreover, a number of studies have found that when family relations improve over the course of treatment, treatment outcomes are better (Huey, Henggeler, Brondini & Pickrell, 2000; Schmidt, Liddle & Dakof, 1996). Unfortunately, however, there are, as yet, few studies that support the proposition that changes in parent–child or partner interactions mediate treatment outcomes.

Enactment is a unique and powerful method for transforming couple/family relationships through in-session, face to face encounters between family members. Essentially, therapeutic enactments are in-session experiential events during which the therapist encourages family members to generate and experiment with new, more functional interactions (Minuchin & Fishman, 1981). In some cases, enactment involves introducing structural changes, such as helping a daughter to speak directly to her father rather than communicate to him through her mother. In other cases, enactment involves introducing and sustaining focused, explicit conversation about previously avoided topics or themes, such as a husband's fear that he no longer interests his wife. In yet other cases, enactment involves changing the process or rules of the conversations. For example, partners who regularly fight about how much time they do or do not spend with their in-laws may be encouraged to, alternately, refrain from trying to persuade or defend their position and, instead, listen carefully and with curiosity to their partner's experience.

Many times, such changes create a therapeutic space in which new themes, underlying feelings, and previously unformulated and unarticulated thoughts emerge. Without having to defend himself, the husband may, for the first time, become aware of and express his concern that if he does not visit his parents every Saturday, he is a "bad, uncaring son." This type of revelation expands his wife's experience of and empathy for her husband, reducing conflict and increasing the couple's motivation for problem solving and compromise.

Enactments may also involve challenging partners or family members to successfully finish a task that they have previously not been able to complete. In one example from Minuchin and Fishman's (1981) book on structural technique, Minuchin tells the mother of a disruptive, oppositional girl to find a way to make the child play independently in a different area of the treatment room so that he can speak with the couple without being interrupted. When the mother is not able to accomplish the task, Minuchin simply tells her to "make it happen" (Minuchin & Fishman, 1981). In this way, therapists can simultaneously push and support family members to try out new ways of relating.

Through enactments, therapists instruct and guide family members to interact with one another, rather than channeling the interaction through themselves (Davis & Butler, 2004). Indeed, the role of the therapist is to initiate conversations, behaviors, and generally new ways of interacting and then to get out of the way, intervening only when the interaction becomes stuck or unproductive. Typically, the process is one of successive approximation. Initially, as family members take risks and

become more vulnerable and direct with each other, the slightest sign of invalidation or criticism can lead family members to retreat to earlier behaviors. In other words, the process is one of two steps forward, one step backward, with the therapist marking positive changes and using them to shape future behavior.

In theory, effective enactments produce change via multiple pathways simultaneously. When family members change their behavior (i.e., listen more, divulge previously undisclosed information about themselves that puts them in a vulnerable position, express love or caring in a new and different way), other family members' attributions, emotional experience, and interactional patterns are influenced. For example, when a newly divorced mother explains to her daughter that she never spoke about being abused by the girl's father so as not to negatively influence her daughter's feelings for him, the daughter's resentment about the divorce may subside. Suddenly, the daughter sees her mother as caring and protective, rather than as selfish and insensitive, and feelings of appreciation and warmth begin to surface. Furthermore, the daughter's self-representation is likely to change. Whereas before she thought that her mother disregarded her needs, she now sees how important she is to her mother. Reinforced by such positive responses, both mother and daughter engage in further disclosure and approach behaviors. In this sense, changes in interactions are both a change target and a change mechanism (Davis & Butler, 2004).

Although enactment is a common and potentially potent CFT intervention, it requires a great deal of skill to conduct effectively (Butler, Davis & Seedal, 2008). In some instances, habitual negative interactional patterns between partners or family members can escalate quickly when "hot topics" are introduced. In order for therapy not to become a retraumatizing experience, it is essential that the therapist work to modulate, draw meaning from, and transform negative interactions into reparative experiences. In other instances, family members may resist speaking with one another about conflictual topics, afraid to re-experience the frustration and or pain they felt in the past when trying to discuss such topics at home (Nichols & Fellenberg, 2000). Frequently, family members try to enlist the therapist as an ally to support or validate their own side or conception of the problem by, for example, only addressing the therapist and avoiding speaking directly to other family members. Effective enactment demands that the therapist be prepared for such occurrences with specific intervention strategies.

Two papers offer general guidelines for promoting successful enactments. First, Nichols and Fellenberg (2000) conducted a discovery-oriented study of successful versus unsuccessful enactments. These authors found that in successful enactments therapists instructed clients how to talk to one another (e.g., "Ask her how she feels" or "Instead of explaining what was going on for you, just listen to what he has to say") and specified a topic. Once the enactment was initiated, successful facilitation involved not interrupting family members and repeatedly directing them to continue speaking to one another, either explicitly or nonverbally, for example, by leaning backward or breaking eye contact. When such conversations stalled or became less productive, therapists either challenged family members to be clearer or more explicit about their feelings or probed for deeper, underlying affect. Finally, successful closure of enactments involved helping clients make sense of their experience by describing the interactional dynamic that was fueling the impasse and praising family members for their courage and ability to relate differently.

In a later study, Davis and Butler (2004) presented a similar model. Importantly, they emphasized how critical it is to evaluate the enactment once it has ended. In the true spirit of enactment, these authors suggested that the post-enactment processing should occur between family members, not between the therapist and individuals. However, the therapist may remind family members of their goals for the enactment and how these goals relate to aspirations for changing their relationship. The therapist may also invite clients to reflect on what went well or was helpful, commend them for their successes and express gratitude, note how the interaction may have gone even better, and commit to working further to improve their relationship.

In addition to these pantheoretical guidelines for conducting enactments, a number of clinical researchers have outlined specific moment-by-moment intervention models for facilitating productive, clinically significant interpersonal processes within a given therapeutic approach and task. Perhaps the most well known and well researched of these models involves promoting connection (i.e., attachment) in the context of EFT for couples (Greenberg & Johnson, 1988; Johnson, 1998). In most cases, the expression of vulnerable emotions and needs elicits by one partner nurturance and understanding on the part of the other partner, thereby transforming contentious, negative interpersonal interactions into safe, satisfying, attachment-promoting interactions.

Quite a few task analytic studies support the validity of a three-stage enactment sequence in EFT (Greenberg, Ford, Alden & Johnson, 1993; Makinen & Johnson, 2006), as outlined by Johnson and Greenberg (2006). In stage 1, a strong therapeutic alliance is established with each member of the couple by exploring their emotional experience in the relationship and their attempts to meet attachment needs for safety, security and comfort. The therapist works with each partner to access previously unacknowledged, underlying emotions that fuel interpersonal behaviors. In doing so, the therapist reframes the problematic interactional cycle as the partners' ineffective attempts to get their attachment needs met. In stage 2, the therapist actively restructures the couple's in-session interactions to help the partners become more accessible and responsive to each other's attachment needs. For example, the therapist may turn to a wife and say, "When your husband criticizes you, you feel ashamed and worthless, which makes you even more anxious about how safe you are in the relationship. Can you turn to him and tell him how afraid you are?" During such events, the disengaged, avoidant partner typically becomes more engaged and, in response, the aggrieved, blaming partner tends to become softer and more forgiving, The result is the formation of a more secure emotional bond. Finally, in stage 3—consolidation and integration— the therapist facilitates the emergence of new solutions to old relationship problems: solutions based on acknowledging each member's underlying attachment needs. The therapist also helps the couple recognize the benefits of being open and persevering in expressing fears and attachment needs.

Enactment has also been shown to be effective for resolving therapeutic impasses in the context of MDFT for adolescent substance abusers (Diamond & Liddle, 1996). In-session impasses are defined as conflictual, negative, escalating parent-adolescent arguments about behavioral issues, such as curfew, chores, etc. (Diamond & Liddle, 1999). Such impasses are said to result from ruptures in the adolescent–parent attachment relationship. Theoretically, the opposition, acrimony, and anger that are characteristic of such conflicts derive, at least in part, from failures in the attachment system— lapses in trust and care associated with a history of betrayal, neglect, abandonment, and abuse. Such ruptures are repaired by shifting family members' focus from the behavioral conflict to the underlying attachment-related themes and emotions fueling the conflict.

The therapist plays a central role in generating and maintaining this shift, typically by first eliciting or highlighting feelings of regret, loss or sadness regarding the quality of the adolescent-parent relationship. For example, the therapist might say to a father, "I wonder if somewhere inside you also feel sad that your relationship with your son has become so distant and angry—if you had thought or hoped it would be different?" Then, when the parent adopts a more reflective and softer posture, the therapist turns to the adolescent to ask if she or he also feels regret. Once both family members are on-board regarding their desire for things to be different between them, the enactment starts. That is, therapist asks the parent to find out from the adolescent why he or she is so angry or detached. As long as the parent is sincere and nondefensive, the adolescent is likely to respond by expressing long-standing grievances, such as abandonment, abuse, or neglect. At this point, the therapist works to help the parent contain and acknowledge the child's experience without explaining, justifying, or correcting. This simple but profound act of validation and care is the first step in re-establishing trust and an emotional bond (Diamond & Liddle, 1996, 1999; Liddle, 2005).

Basing their work with MDFT (Liddle, 2005) and Emotion-Focused Therapy (Greenberg & Johnson, 1988), Diamond and colleagues articulated a step-by-step approach to preparing and conducting reattachment episodes or enactments to repair relational ruptures between depressed and suicidal adolescents and their parents (Diamond, Diamond, & Liddle, 2000; Diamond & Siqueland, 1995, 1998; Diamond & Stern, 2003). Results from a task analytic study (Diamond & Stern, 2003) suggested that successful reattachment enactments were characterized by parents' affiliative focus on their adolescent's experience and expressions and the aggrieved adolescent's focus on her- or himself. This pattern reflects the parental empathic holding and validation promoted by the reattachment task and purported to positively influence adolescent attachment schema and behavior.

Yet another microanalytic enactment model was described in a task analytic study (Friedlander, Heatherington, Johnson, & Skowron, 1994) of the process by which therapists help families move from disengagement to sustained, productive engagement in problem solving. The authors found that when families were able to generate sustained engagement, the first therapeutic step was to help family members get in touch with underlying emotions and cognitions that were contributing to their relational impasse, such as a sense of hopelessness or anger. In step 2, the therapists helped the clients describe these heretofor unexpressed feelings or thoughts to each other. Such revelations often led to the emergence of softer emotions and more benevolent attributions. In step 3, the therapists worked to keep family members focused on and to validate each other's experience. In step 4, family members' attributions regarding the impasse and understanding of each other's motivations and feelings seemed to lead to good will, empathy, and flexibility. Throughout the process, the therapists highlighted the importance and potential benefits of family members sustaining engagement with each other (Friedlander, Heatherington et al., 1994).

Enactment is a particularly potent intervention. When employed skillfully, it has the potential to affect dramatic, therapeutic changes in the manner in how family members experience themselves and others. However, negative interactional processes between family members, such as attack and withdrawal behaviors, can escalate quickly among volatile, highly reactive couples and families. When left unchecked, enactments can deteriorate and end up replicating the highly negative, traumatic experiences that brought the family to therapy in the first place. The last thing a therapist wants to have happen is for partners to demean or somehow act destructively toward one another and then leave the consulting room feeling worse and more demoralized than when they arrived.

Therefore, the ethical, responsible use of enactment involves careful assessment and continuous monitoring of the level of volatility/reactivity/receptivity of each family member, and a corresponding level of therapist involvement or directiveness. Indeed, Davis and Butler (2004) presented a well-articulated, five-stage developmental model for conducting enactments in which the degree to which family members speak directly toward one another (vs. through the therapist), the level of emotional intensity and amount of verbal autonomy (i.e., how freely they interact) corresponds to the level of relationship distress, emotional reactivity, and interactional volatility. In short, initiating and managing enactments in a constructive, therapeutic manner requires a great deal of training, practice, and supervision.

Whereas considerable progress has been made in delineating the sequence of client and therapist behaviors associated with resolving interpersonal conflict, attachment injuries, and so on, a number of important questions remain. For example, what is the minimum level of emotional arousal required to facilitate change, and at what point is the emotional arousal too high to allow for productive discussion and information processing? Every family therapist has wondered, at one time or another, whether the emotion being expressed in the session—particularly anger—has become too intense and therefore unproductive or, alternatively, whether family members are not sufficiently engaged or connected to their feelings. More research is needed to identify and quantify the optimal range of emotional arousal for effecting cognitive and behavioral change in the context of in-session enactments. Such research may benefit from including continuous, objective measures of physiological arousal, along with observer and client self-report measures.

Another understudied question relates to both the immediate and longer-term impact of successful enactments on clients' subsequent cognitive schema, emotions, and behavior. For example, do successful enactments in attachment-based, emotion-focused treatments actually lead to changes in family members' attachment schema (i.e., how trusting they are of one another)? Do effective enactments actually promote more approaching, affiliative behaviors on the part of family members, not only in the consulting room but also in the family's daily life? Are family members better able to solve problems, resolve conflicts, disclose vulnerable emotions, and turn to each other for support and help after a powerful enactment or series of enactments?

The Future of Couple and Family Therapy

Conjoint psychotherapy began as an experiment. Now, roughly 50 years later, the field is thriving. No longer an "also ran," CFT has been shown to work as well as individual psychotherapy, and for some clinical problems it surpasses individual treatment in effectiveness.

The challenges faced by families in the second millennium were inconceivable when Sigmund Freud began treating individual patients for psychological problems. Early psychoanalysts conceptualized emotional disorders in light of patients' childhood histories, paying notably less attention to the sociocultural factors that affect individual functioning. At that time, culture arguably played a smaller role in an individual's mental health than it does now, 100 years later. As globalization is rapidly affecting cultural norms around the world, academics and professionals across disciplines are responding to the problems of our increasingly heterogeneous societies. Having traditionally examined psychosocial well-being contextually, counseling psychologists are in a position to make an important, unique contribution to the understanding and treatment of couples and families from diverse cultures.

To do so, we need to move further away from the medical model, with its "top-down" approach to theory, research, and practice, in which standard treatments are tested for their efficacy with various client groups. Rather, by applying our knowledge of contextual factors, we can develop couple and family interventions "from the bottom up," that is to say, by focusing on the specific needs of different clientele. In our view, it is more desirable to create (and investigate) new treatments, or to substantially modify existing ones, for specific populations rather than to simply apply the tried-and-true methods to various client groups.

One intervention that exemplifies the "bottom-up" approach is a filial therapy group that was designed specifically for first-generation Chinese parents in Toronto who were experiencing acculturative strains with their children (Chau & Landreth, 1997). Culture-specific family interventions like this are essential because many of the immigrants and refugees needing mental health services have within-family conflicts arising from cultural mistrust, bicultural identities, acculturative stress, and social class mobility. Moreover, immigrants and refugees from Asia, Latin America, Africa, and the Middle East come from collectivist societies, in which family well-being is crucial for individual well-being.

In addition to developing or adapting culturally sensitive treatment models, our future agenda should include a better integration of what we now know about psychopathology, development, personality, and empirically supported individual interventions with couple and family treatments. Although the early pioneers of family therapy emphasized (perhaps overemphasized) the role and impact of systemic forces in order to differentiate CFT from the individually based models that preceded it, contemporary authors are rediscovering and acknowledging the power and impact of intrapsychic forces on the individual and on the family or couple system. This relatively new focus in the CFT field has led to the development of multisystemic and multidimensional family-based treatments that target intrapersonal as well as interpersonal concerns.

However, more work is needed to integrate specific individual and systems treatment models. For example, it would be wise to offer individual therapy to an adolescent who was raped along with conjoint family sessions to prevent her from being isolated by family members who are secondarily traumatized. Likewise, exposure therapy with a husband who suffers from obsessive-compulsive disorder could alternate with couples sessions in which the origins and nature of the disorder are explained and the wife is helped to recognize and avoid safety behaviors that work against her husband's recovery.

Becoming a competent couple and family therapist requires a substantial knowledge base and extensive supervised training. Given our field's traditional focus on individual young adults, most counseling psychology programs do not sufficiently prepare students to become CFT therapists. Programs that offer one or perhaps two courses in couple and family therapy do just enough for entry-level therapists to recognize and appreciate the complexity of systems work. In our experience, however, it takes at least 2 to 3 years of training (theoretical and practical) to become a relatively competent CFT practitioner.

To expand our students' skills in this area, we encourage counseling psychology programs to recruit faculty who are interested and skilled in CFT and expand practicum options to allow students to gain focused, supervised experience in systems-based treatments. One possible training model is to offer a subspecialty or certificate that could be pursued by students who are interested in CFT. This focused experience should include four to six systems-oriented courses, including relational assessment, a review of empirically supported CFT approaches, and intensive supervised practica in CFT. We have found that counseling psychology students, who have a broad knowledge base in psychology, can be competitive for internships with a specialized family track. Moreover, these students tend to be quite successful in these internships because of their background in normative development, person–environment fit, and strengths-based assessment and intervention.

As counseling psychologists, we have a unique perspective on human functioning that has yet to be realized the broader CFT field. With continued theorizing and empirical attention to the uniqueness and promise of CFT as a treatment modality, counseling psychologists will be better equipped to address the myriad challenges facing contemporary couples and families.

Notes

1. Although we view couple and family therapy as a way of conceptualizing and treating emotional problems, which can be accomplished with a single individual, the focus of this chapter is on conjoint CFT—i.e., therapy in which two or more partners or family members are physically present in the session.

2. We use the word "patient" (rather than "client") because psychoanalysis evolved from and embraced the medical model of diagnosis and treatment, locating emotional disturbances within an individual's psyche.

3. In a therapist version for the SOFTA-o, the therapist's behavioral contributions to the therapeutic alliance are rated along the same four dimensions (Friedlander et al., 2006a).

References

Ackerman, N. W. (1958). *The psychodynamics of family life.* New York: Basic Books.

Alexander, J., & Parsons, B. (1982). *Functional family therapy.* Monterey, CA: Brooks Cole.

Bateson, G., Jackson, D. D., Haley, J., & Weakland, J. (1956). Toward a theory of schizophrenia. *Behavioral Sciences, 1,* 251–264.

Baucom, D. H., Shoham, V., Mueser, K. T., Daiuto, A. D., & Stickle, T. R. (1998). Empirically supported couple and family interventions for marital distress and adult mental health problems. *Journal of Consulting and Clinical Psychology, 66,* 53–88.

Beck, M., Friedlander, M. L., & Escudero, V. (2006). Three perspectives on clients' experiences of the therapeutic alliance: A discovery-oriented investigation. *Journal of Marital and Family Therapy, 32,* 355–368.

Bell, J. E. (1961). *Family group therapy.* Public Health Monograph No. 64. Washington, DC: U.S. Government Printing Office.

Berg, I. K. (1994). *Family-based services: A solution-focused approach.* New York: Norton.

Bertalanffy, L. von. (1950). An outline of general systems theory. *British Journal of Philosophy of Science, 1,* 139–164.

Boardman, W. K. (1962). Rusty: A brief behavior disorder. *Journal of Consulting Psychology, 26,* 293–297.

Bordin, E. S. (1979). The generalizability of the psychoanalytic concept of the working alliance. *Psychotherapy, 16,* 252–260.

Bordin, E. S. (1994). Theory and research on the therapeutic working alliance: New directions. In A. O. Horvath, & L. S. Greenberg (Eds.), *The working alliance: Theory, research, and practice.* (pp. 13–37). New York: John Wiley & Sons, Inc.

Bourduin, C. M., Mann, B. J., Cone, L. T., Henggeler, S. W., Fucci, B. R., Blaske, D. M., & Williams, R. A. (1995). Multisystemic treatment of serious juvenile offenders: Long-term prevention of criminality and violence. *Journal of Clinical and Consulting Psychology, 63,* 569–578.

Bowen, M. (1966). The use of family theory in clinical practice. *Comprehensive Psychiatry, 7,* 345–374.

Bowen, M. (1976). Theory in the practice of psychotherapy. In P. J. Guerin (Ed.), *Family therapy: Theory and practice* (pp. 42–90). New York: Gardner Press.

Butler, M. H., Davis, S. D., & Seedall, R. B. (2008). Common pitfalls of beginning therapists utilizing enactments. *Journal of Marital and Family Therapy, 34,* 329–352.

Butler, M. H., Harper, J. M., & Seedall, R. B. (2009). Facilitated disclosure versus clinical accommodation of infidelity secrets: An early pivot point in couple therapy. Part 1: Couple relationship ethics, pragmatics, and attachment. *Journal of Marital and Family Therapy, 35,* 125–143.

Butler, M. H., Seedall, R. B., & Harper, J. M. (2008). Facilitated disclosure vs. clinical accommodation of infidelity secrets: An early pivot point in couple therapy. Part 2: Therapy ethics, pragmatics, and protocol. *American Journal of Family Therapy, 36,* 265–283.

Carter, B., & McGoldrick, M. (1999). *The expanded family life cycle* (3rd ed.). Boston: Allyn & Bacon.

Chau, I. Y., & Landreth, G. L. (1997). Filial therapy with Chinese parents: Effects on parental empathic interactions, parental acceptance of child and parental stress. *International Journal of Play Therapy, 6,* 75–92.

Christensen, A., Atkins, D. C., Berns, S., Wheeler, J., Baucom, D. H., & Simpson, L. E. (2004). Traditional versus integrative behavioral couple therapy for significantly and chronically distressed married couples. *Journal of Consulting and Clinical Psychology, 72,* 176–191.

Christensen, A., Atkins, D. C., Yi, J., Baucom, D. H., & George, W. H. (2006). Couple and individual adjustment for 2 years following a randomized clinical trial comparing traditional versus integrative behavioral couple therapy. *Journal of Consulting and Clinical Psychology, 74,* 1180–1191.

Christensen, A., & Heavey, C. L. (1999). Interventions for couples. *Annual Review of Psychology, 50,* 165–190.

Christensen, A., Jacobson, N. S., & Babcock, J. C. (1995). Integrative behavioral couple therapy. In N. S. Jacobson, & A. S. Gurman (Eds.), *Clinical handbook of couple therapy* (pp. 31–62). New York: Guilford Press.

Coulehan, R., Friedlander, M. L., & Heatherington, L. (1998). Transforming narratives: A change event in constructivist family therapy. *Family Process, 37,* 465–481.

de Shazer, S. (1985). *Keys to solutions in brief therapy.* New York: Norton.

Dare, C., & Eisler, I. (1995). Family therapy. In G. I. Szmukler, C. Dare, & J. Treasure (Eds.), *Handbook of eating disorders: Theory, treatment and research.* London: Wiley.

Dare, C., Eisler, I., Russell, G. F., & Szmukler, G. I. (1990). The clinical and theoretical impact of a controlled trial of family therapy in anorexia nervosa. *Journal of Marital and Family Therapy, 16,* 39–57.

Dare, C., & Eisler, I., Russell, G., Treasure, J., Dodge, L. (2001). Psychological therapies for adults with anorexia nervosa. *British Journal of Psychiatry, 178,* 216–221.

Davis, S. D., & Butler, M. H. (2004). Enacting relationships in marriage and family therapy: A conceptual and operational definition of an enactment. *Journal of Marital and Family Therapy, 30,* 319–333.

Dennis, M., Godley, S. H., Diamond, G. S., Tims, F. M., Babor, T., Donaldson, J., Liddle, H., Titus, J. C., Kaminer, Y., Webb, C., Hamilton, N., & Funk, R. (2004). The cannabis youth treatment (CYT) study: Main findings from two randomized trials. *Journal of Substance Abuse Treatment, 27,* 197–213.

Diamond, G. M., Diamond, G. S., & Liddle, H. A. (2000). The therapist-parent alliance in family-based therapy for adolescents. *Journal of Clinical Psychology, 56,* 1037–1050.

Diamond, G. M., Hogue, A., Liddle, H. A., & Dakof, G. A. (1999). Alliance-building interventions with adolescents in family therapy: A process study. *Psychotherapy, 36,* 355–368.

Diamond, G. S. (2005). Attachment-based family therapy for depressed and anxious adolescents. In J. L. Lebow (Ed.), *Handbook of clinical family therapy* (pp. 17–41). Hoboken, NJ: Wiley & Sons.

Diamond, G. S., & Liddle, H. A. (1996). Resolving and therapeutic impasse between parents and adolescents in multidimensional family therapy. *Journal of Consulting and Clinical Psychology, 64,* 481–488.

Diamond, G. S., & Liddle, H. A. (1999). Transforming negative parent-adolescent interactions: From impasse to dialogue. *Family Process, 38,* 5–26.

Diamond, G. S., Reis, B. F., Diamond, G. M., Siqueland, L., & Isaacs, L. (2002). Attachment-based family therapy for depressed adolescents: A treatment development study. *Journal of the American Academy of Child and Adolescent Psychiatry, 41,* 1190–1196.

Diamond, G. S., & Siqueland, L. (1995). Family therapy for the treatment of depressed adolescents. *Psychotherapy: Theory, research, practice, training, 32,* 77–90.

Diamond, G. S., & Siqueland, L. (1998). Emotions, attachment and the relational reframe: The first session. *Journal of Systemic Therapies, 17,* 36–50.

Diamond, G. S., Siqueland, L., & Diamond, G. M. (2003). Attachment-based family therapy for depressed adolescents: Programmatic treatment development. *Clinical Child and Family Psychology Review, 6,* 107–127.

Diamond, G. S., & Stern, R. (2003). Attachment-based family therapy for depressed adolescents: Repairing attachment failures. In V. E. Whiffen, & S. M. Johnson (Eds.), *Attachment processes in couple and family therapy* (pp. 191–212). New York: Guilford.

Dennis, M., Godley, S. H., Diamond, G. S., Tims, F. M., Babor, T., Donaldson, J., et al. (2004). The cannabis youth treatment (CYT) study: Main findings from two randomized trials. *Journal of Substance Abuse Treatment, 27,* 197–213.

Dunn, R. L., & Schwebel, A. I. (1995). Meta-analytic review of marital therapy outcome research. *Journal of Family Psychology, 9,* 58–68.

Eisler, I., Dare, C., Hodes, M., Russell, G., Dodge, E., & LeGrange, D. (2000). Family therapy for adolescent anorexia nervosa: The results of a controlled comparison of two family interventions. *Journal of Child Psychology and Psychiatry, 42,* 727–736.

Eisler, I., Dare, C., Russell, G. F., Szmukler, G. I., le Grange, D., & Dodge, E. (1997). Family and individual therapy in anorexia. A 5-year follow-up. *Archives of General Psychiatry, 54,* 1025–1030.

Eisler, I., Lock, J., & le Grange, D. (2007). Family-based treatments for adolescents with anorexia nervosa: Single-family and multi-family approaches. In C. Grilo, & J. Mitchell (Eds.), *The treatment of eating disorders.* New York: Guilford.

Eisler, I., Simic, M., Russell, G. F. M., & Dare, C. (2007). A randomized controlled treatment trial of two forms of family therapy in adolescent anorexia nervosa: A five-year follow-up. *Journal of Child Psychology and Psychiatry, 48*, 552–560.

Ellis, D. A., Naar-King, S., Cunningham, P. B., & Secord, E. (2006). Use of multisystemic therapy to improve antiretroviral adherence and health outcomes in HIV-infected pediatric patients: Evaluation of a pilot program. *AIDS Patient Care and STDs, 20*, 112–121.

Ellis, D. A., Templin, T., Naar-King, S., Frey, M. A., Cunningham, P. B., Podolski, C., & Cakan, N. (2007). Multisystemic therapy for adolescents with poorly controlled Type I diabetes: Stability of treatment effects in a randomized controlled trial. *Journal of Consulting and Clinical Psychology, 75*, 168–174.

Escudero, V., Friedlander, M. L., Varela, N., & Abascal, A. (2008). Observing the therapeutic alliance in family therapy: Associations with participants' perceptions and therapeutic outcomes. *Journal of Family Therapy, 30*, 194–204.

Fisch, R., Weakland, J., & Segal, L. (1982). *The tactics of change*. San Francisco: Jossey Bass.

Fletcher, A. C., Darling, N., & Steinberg, L. (1995). Parental monitoring and peer influences on adolescent substance use. In J. McCord (Ed.), *Coercion and punishment in long-term perspectives* (pp. 259–271). New York: Cambridge.

Foran, H. M., & O'Leary, K. D. (2008). Alcohol and intimate partner violence: A meta-analytic review. *Clinical Psychology Review, 28*, 1222–1234.

Foucault, M. (1965). *Madness and civilization: A history of insanity in the age of reason*. New York: Random House.

Freud, S. (1912/1940). The dynamics of transference. In J. Strachey (Ed.), *Standard edition of the complete psychological works of Sigmund Freud* Vol. 12 (pp. 122–144). London: Hogarth. (Original work published 1912).

Friedlander, M. L., Escudero, V., and Heatherington, L. (2006a). *Therapeutic alliances in couple and family therapy: An empirically informed guide to practice*. Washington, DC: American Psychological Association.

Friedlander, M. L., Escudero, V., Horvath, S., Heatherington, L., Cabero, A., & Martens, M. P. (2006b). System for observing family therapy alliances: A tool for research and practice. *Journal of Counseling Psychology, 53*, 214–224.

Friedlander, M. L., Escudero, V., Heatherington, L., & Diamond, G. M. (2011). Alliance in couple and family therapy. *Psychotherapy, 48*, 25–33.

Friedlander, M. L., Heatherington, L., Johnson, B., & Skowron, E. A. (1994). "Sustaining engagement": A change event in family therapy. *Journal of Counseling Psychology, 41*, 438–448.

Friedlander, M. L., Heatherington, L., & Marrs, A. (2000). Responding to blame in family therapy: A narrative/constructionist perspective. *American Journal of Family Therapy, 28*, 133–146.

Friedlander, M. L., Lambert, J. E., Escudero, V., & Cragun, C. (2008). How do therapists enhance family alliances? Sequential analyses of therapist → client behavior in two contrasting cases. *Psychotherapy: Theory, Research, Practice, Training, 45*, 75–87.

Friedlander, M. L., Lambert, J. E., & Muñiz de la Peña, C. (2008). A step towards disentangling the alliance/improvement cycle in family therapy. *Journal of Counseling Psychology, 55*, 118–124.

Friedlander, M. L., Wildman, J., Heatherington, L., & Skowron, E. A. (1994). What we do and do not know about the process of family therapy. *Journal of Family Psychology, 8*, 390–416.

Gelso, C., & Fretz, B. (2001). *Counseling psychology* (2nd ed.). Belmont, CA: Wadsworth/Thompson Learning.

Gollan, J. K., & Jacobson, N. S. (2002). Developments in couple therapy research. In H. A. Liddle, D. A. Santisteban, R. F. Levant, & J. H. Bray (Eds.), *Family psychology: Science-based interventions* (pp. 105–122). Washington, DC: American Psychological Association.

Greenberg, L. S. (1986). Change process research. *Journal of Consulting and Clinical Psychology, 54*, 4–9.

Greenberg, L. S., Ford, C. L., Alden, L., & Johnson, S. M. (1993). In-session change in emotionally focused therapy. *Journal of Consulting and Clinical Psychology, 61*, 78–84.

Greenberg, L. S., & Johnson, S. M. (1988). *Emotionally focused therapy for couples*. New York: Guilford Press.

Greenberg, L. S., & Malcolm, W. (2002). Resolving unfinished business: Relating process to outcome. *Journal of Consulting and Clinical Psychology, 70*, 406–416.

Greenson, R. (1967). *The technique and practice of psychoanalysis*. New York: International Universities Press.

Haley, J. (1963). *Strategies of psychotherapy*. New York: Grune & Stratton.

Haley, J. (1976). *Problem-solving therapy*. San Francisco: Jossey-Bass.

Heatherington, L., & Friedlander, M. L. (1990). Couple and family therapy alliance scales: Empirical considerations. *Journal of Marital and Family Therapy, 16*, 299–306.

Henggeler, S. W., Borduin, C. M., Melton, G. B., Mann, B. J., Smith, L. A., Hall, J. A., et al. (1991). Effects of multisystemic therapy on drug use and abuse in serious juvenile offenders: A progress report from two outcome studies. *Family Dynamics of Addiction Quarterly, 1*, 40–51.

Henggeler, S. W., Clingempeel, W. G., Brondino, M. J., & Pickrel, S. G. (2002). Four-year follow-up of multisystemic therapy with substance-abusing and substance-dependent juvenile offenders. *Journal of the American Academy of Child and Adolescent Psychiatry, 41*, 868–874.

Henggeler, S. W., Melton, G. B., Brondino, M. J., Scherer, D. G., & Hanley, J. H. (1997). Multisystemic therapy with violent and chronic juvenile offenders and their families: The role of treatment fidelity in successful dissemination. *Journal of Consulting and Clinical Psychology, 60*, 821–833.

Henggeler, S. W., Melton, G. B., & Smith, L. A. (1992). Family preservation using multisystemic therapy: An effective alternative to incarcerating serious juvenile offenders. *Journal of Consulting and Clinical Psychology, 60*, 953–961.

Henggeler, S. W., Melton, G. B., Smith, L. A., Schoenwald, S. K., & Hanley, J. (1993). Family preservation using multisystemic therapy: Long-term follow-up to a clinical trial with serious juvenile offenders. *Journal of Child and Family Studies, 2*, 283–293.

Henggeler, S. W., Pickrel, S. G., & Brondino, M. J. (1999). Multisystemic treatment of substance abusing and dependent delinquents: Outcomes, treatment fidelity, and transportability. *Mental Health Services Review, 1*, 171–184.

Henggeler, S. W., Rowland, M. D., Randall, J., Ward, D., Pickrel, S. G., Cunningham, P. B., et al. (1999). Home-based multisystemic therapy as an alternative to the hospitalization of youth in psychiatric crisis: Clinical outcomes. *Journal of the American Academy of Child and Adolescent Psychiatry, 38*, 1331–1339.

Henggeler, S. W., Schoenwald, S. K., Borduin, C. M., Rowland, M. D., & Cunningham, P. B. (1998). *Multisystemic treatment for antisocial behavior in youth*. New York: Guilford Press.

Horvath, A. O., & Bedi, R. P. (2002). The alliance. In J. C. Norcross (Ed.), *Psychotherapy relationships that work: Therapist contributions and responsiveness to patients* (pp. 37–69). New York: Oxford University Press.

Huey, S. J., Henggeler, S. W., Brondino, M. J., & Pickrel, S. G. (2000). Mechanisms of change in multisystemic therapy: Reducing delinquent behavior through therapist adherence and improved family and peer functioning. *Journal of Consulting and Clinical Psychology, 68*, 451–467.

Huey, S. J., Henggeler, S. W., Rowland, M. D., Halliday-Boykins, C. A., Cunninghham, P. B., Pickrel, S. G., & James, E. (2005). Multisystemic therapy effects on attempted suicide by youths presenting psychiatric emergencies. *Journal of the American Academy of Child and Adolescent Psychiatry, 43*, 183–190.

Horvath, A. O., & Symonds, B. D. (1991). Relation between working alliance and outcome in psychotherapy: A meta-analysis. *Journal of Counseling Psychology, 38*, 139–149.

Kerr, M., & Bowen, M. (1988). *Family evaluation*. New York: Norton.

Jackson, D. D. (1965). Family rules: The marital quid pro quo. *Archives of General Psychiatry, 12*, 589–594.

Jacobson, N. S. (1977). Problem solving and contingency contracting in the treatment of marital discord. *Journal of Consulting and Clinical Psychology, 45*, 92–100.

Jacobson, N. S., & Christensen, A. (1998). *Acceptance and change in couple therapy: A therapist's guide to transforming relationships*. New York: Norton.

Jacobson, N. S., Christensen, A., Prince, S. E., Cordova, J., & Eldridge, K. (2000). Integrative behavioral couple therapy: An acceptance-based, promising new treatment for couple discord. *Journal of Consulting and Clinical Psychology, 68*, 351–355.

Jacobson, N. S., & Margolin, G. (1979). *Marital therapy: Strategies based on social learning and behavior exchange principles*. New York: Brunner/Mazel.

Johnson, S. (1998). Emotion focused couple therapy. In F. M. Dattilio (Ed.), *Case studies in couple and family therapy: Systemic and cognitive perspectives* (pp. 450–472). New York: Guilford.

Johnson, S. M., & Greenberg, L. S. (1985). Emotionally focused couples therapy: An outcome study. *Journal of Marital and Family Therapy, 11*, 313–317.

Johnson, S. M., & Greenman, P. S. (2006). The path to a secure bond: Emotionally focused couple therapy. *Journal of Clinical Psychology, 62*, 597–609.

Johnson, L. N., Wright, D. W., & Ketring, S. A. (2002). The therapeutic alliance in home-based family therapy: Is it predictive of outcome? *Journal of Marital and Family Therapy, 28*, 93–102.

Johnson, S. N., & Talitman, E. (1997). Predictors of success in emotion focused marital therapy. *Journal of Marital and Family Therapy, 23*, 135–152.

Kazdin, A. E. (1987). *Conduct disorders in childhood and adolescence*. Newbury Park, CA: Sage.

Knobloch-Fedders, L. M., Pinsof, W. M., & Mann, B. J. (2004). The formation of the therapeutic alliance in couple therapy. *Family Process, 43*, 425–442.

Liberman, R. P. (1970). Behavioral approaches to family and couple therapy. *American Journal of Orthopsychiatry, 40*, 106–118.

Liddle, H. A. (2005). Multidimensional family therapy: A science-based treatment for adolescent drug abuse. In J. L. Lebow (Ed.), *Handbook of clinical family therapy* (pp. 128–163). Hoboken, NJ: Wiley & Sons.

Liddle, H. A., Dakof, G. A., Parker, K., Diamond, G. S., Barrett, K., & Tejeda, M. (2001). Multidimensional family therapy for adolescent drug abuse: Results of a randomized clinical trial. *American Journal of Drug and Alcohol Abuse, 27*, 651–688.

Liddle, H. A., Dakof, G. A., Turner, R. M., Henderson, C. E., & Greenbaum, P. E. (2008). Treating adolescent drug abuse: A randomized trial comparing multidimensional family therapy and cognitive behavior therapy. *Addiction, 103*, 1660–1670.

Liddle, H. A., Rowe, C. R., Dakof, G. A., Henderson, C. E., & Greenbaum, P. E. (in press). Multidimensional family therapy for young adolescent substance abuse: Twelve month outcomes of a randomized controlled trial. *Journal of Consulting and Clinical Psychology*. Forthcoming.

Liddle, H. A., Rowe, C. R., Dakof, G. A., Ungaro, R. A., & Henderson, C. E. (2004). Early intervention for adolescent substance abuse: Pretreatment to posttreatment outcomes of a randomized clinical trial comparing multidimensional family therapy and peer group treatment. *Journal of Psychoactive Drugs, 36*, 49–63.

Lock, J., Agras, W. S., Bryson, S., & Kraemer, H. C. (2005). A comparison of short- and long-term therapy for adolescent anorexia nervosa. *Journal of the American Academy of Child and Adolescent Psychiatry, 44*, 632–639.

Lock, J., Couturier, J., & Agras, W. S. (2006). Comparison of long-term outcomes in adolescents with anorexia nervosa treated with family therapy. *Journal of the American Academy of Child and Adolescent Psychiatry, 45*, 666–672.

Luepnitz, D. (1988). *The family interpreted: Feminist theory in clinical practice*. New York: Basic Books.

MacIntosh, H. B., & Johnson, S. (2008). Emotionally focused therapy for couples and childhood sexual abuse survivors. *Journal of Marital and Family Therapy, 34*, 298–315.

Madanes, C. (1981). *Strategic family therapy*. San Francisco: Jossey Bass.

Makinen, J. A., & Johnson, S. M. (2006). Resolving attachment injuries in couples using emotionally focused therapy: Steps toward forgiveness and reconciliation. *Journal of Consulting and Clinical Psychology, 74*, 1055–1064.

Mamodhoussen, S., Wright, J., Tremblay, N., & Poitras-Wright, H. (2005). Impact of marital and psychological distress on therapeutic alliance in couples undergoing couple therapy. *Journal of Marital and Family Therapy, 31*, 159–169.

Miklowitz, D. J. (2008). *Bipolar disorder: A family–focused treatment approach* (2nd ed.). New York: Guilford.

Miklowitz, D. J., George, E. L., Axelson, D. A., Kim, E. Y., Birmaher, B., Schneck, C., et al. (2004). Family-focused treatment for adolescents with bipolar disorder. *Journal of Affective Disorders, 82*, S113–S128.

Miklowitz, D. J., George, E. L., Richards, J. A., Simoneau, T. L., & Suddath, R. L. (2003). A randomized study of family-focused psychoeducation and pharmacotherapy in the outpatient management of bipolar disorder. *Archives of General Psychiatry, 60*, 904–912.

Miklowitz, D. J., & Goldstein, M. J. (1990). Behavioral family treatment for patients with bipolar affective disorder. *Behavior Modification, 14,* 457–489.

Miklowitz, D. J., & Goldstein, M. J. (1997). *Bipolar disorder: A family-focused treatment approach.* New York: Guilford Press.

Miklowitz, D. J., Otto, M. W., Frank, E., Reilly-Harrington, N. A., Wisniewski, S. R., Kogan, J. N., et al. (2007). Psychosocial treatments for bipolar depression: A 1-year randomized trial from the Systematic Treatment Enhancement Program. *Archives of General Psychiatry, 64,* 419–427.

Miklowitz, D. J., Simoneau, T. L., George, E. L., Richards, J. A., Kalbag, A., Sachs-Ericsson, N., & Suddath, R. (2000). Family-focused treatment of bipolar disorder: 1-year effects of a psychoeducational program in conjunction with pharmacotherapy. *Biological Psychiatry, 48,* 582–592.

Minuchin, S. (1974). *Families and family therapy.* Cambridge, MA: Harvard University Press.

Minuchin, S., & Fishman, H. C. (1981). *Family therapy techniques.* Cambridge, MA: Harvard University Press.

Minuchin, S., Rosman, B., & Baker, L. (1978). *Psychosomatic families: Anorexia nervosa in context.* Cambridge, MA: Harvard University Press.

Moran, G., & Diamond, G. M. (2008). Generating nonnegative attitudes among parents of depressed adolescents: The power of empathy, concern, and positive regard. *Psychotherapy Research, 18,* 97–107.

Moran, G., Diamond, G. M., & Diamond, G. S. (2005). The relational reframe and parents' problem constructions in attachment-based family therapy. *Psychotherapy Research, 15,* 226–235.

Muñiz de la Peña, C., Friedlander, M. L., & Escudero, V. (in press). Frequency, severity, and evolution of split family alliances: How observable are they? *Psychotherapy Research.* Forthcoming.

Naar-King, S., Ellis, D. A., Idalski, A., Frey, M. A., & Cunningham, P. (2007). Multisystemic therapy decreases parental overestimation of adolescent responsibility for Type I diabetes management in urban youth. *Families, Systems & Health, 25,* 178–189.

Nichols, M. P., & Fellenberg, S. (2000). The effective use of enactments in family therapy: A discovery-oriented process study. *Journal of Marital and Family Therapy, 26,* 143–152.

Nichols, M. P., & Schwartz, R. C. (2007). *Family therapy: Concepts and methods* (7th ed.). Boston, MA: Pearson Education, Inc.

Ogden, T., & Hagen, K. A. (2006). Multisystemic treatment of serious behavior problems in youth: Sustainability of effectiveness two years after intake. *Child and Adolescent Mental Health, 11,* 142–149.

Ogden, T., & Halliday-Boykins, C. A. (2004). Multisystemic treatment of antisocial adolescents in Norway: Replication of clinical outcomes outside of the US. *Child and Adolescent Mental Health Volume, 9,* 77–83.

Patterson, G. R. (1971). *Families: Application of social learning theory to family life.* Champaign, IL: Research Press.

Patterson, G. R. (1982). *Coercive family process.* Eugene, OR: Castalia.

Pavuluri, M. N., Grazyk, P. A., Henry, D. B., Carbray, J. A., Heidenreich, J., & Miklowitz, D. J. (2004). Child- and family-focused cognitive behavioral therapy for pediatric bipolar disorder: Development and preliminary results. *Journal of the American Academy of Child and Adolescent Psychiatry, 43,* 528–537.

Pinsof, W. M. (1994). An integrative systems perspective on the therapeutic alliance: Theoretical, clinical, and research implications. In A. O. Horvath, & L. S. Greenberg (Eds.), *The working alliance: Theory, research, and practice* (pp. 173–195). New York: Wiley & Sons.

Pinsof, W. M. (1995). *Integrative problem-centered therapy.* New York: Basic Books.

Pinsof, W. M., & Catherall, D. R. (1986). The integrative psychotherapy alliance: Family, couple and individual therapy scales. *Journal of Marital and Family Therapy, 12,* 137–151.

Pinsof, W. M., Wynne, L. C., & Hambright, A. B. (1996). The outcomes of couple and family therapy: Findings, conclusions, and recommendations. *Psychotherapy: Theory, Research, Practice, Training, 33,* 321–331.

Pinsof, W. M., Zinbarg, R., & Knobloch-Fedders, L. M. (2008). Factorial and construct validity of the revised short form Integrative Psychotherapy Alliance Scales for family, couple, and individual therapy. *Family Process, 43,* 281–301.

Quinn, W., Dotson, D., & Jordan, K. (1997). Dimensions of therapeutic alliance and their associations with outcome in family therapy. *Psychotherapy Research, 7,* 429–438.

Rait, D. S. (2000). The therapeutic alliance in couples and family therapy. *In Session: Psychotherapy in Practice, 56,* 211–224.

Rapee, R. M. (1997). Perceived threat and perceived control a predictors of the degree of fear in physical and social situations. *Journal of Anxiety Disorders, 11,* 455–461.

Rea, M. M., Tompson, M. C., Miklowitz, D. J., Goldstein, M. J., Hwang, S., & Mintz, J. (2003). Family-focused treatment versus individual treatment for bipolar disorder: Results of a randomized clinical trial. *Journal of Consulting and Clinical Psychology, 71,* 482–492.

Rehman, U. S., Gollan, J., & Mortimer, A. R. (2008). The marital context of depression: Research, limitations, and new directions. *Clinical Psychology Review, 28,* 179–198.

Robbins, M. S., Alexander, J. F., Newell, R. M., & Turner, C. W. (1996). The immediate effect of reframing on client attitude in family therapy. *Journal of Family Psychology, 10,* 28–34.

Robbins, M. S., Alexander, J. F., & Turner, C. W. (2000). Disrupting defensive family interactions in family therapy with delinquent adolescents. *Journal of Family Psychology, 14,* 688–701.

Robbins, M. S., Liddle, H. A., Turner, C. W., Dakof, G. A., Alexander, J. F., & Kogan, S. M. (2006). Adolescent and parent therapeutic alliances as predictors of dropout in multidimensional family therapy. *Journal of Family Psychology, 20,* 108–116.

Robbins, M. S., Mayorga, C. C., Mitrani, V. B., Szapocznik, J., Turner, C. W., & Alexander, J. F. (2008). Adolescent and parent alliances with therapists in brief strategic family therapy with drug-using Hispanic adolescents. *Journal of Marital and Family Therapy, 34,* 316–328.

Robbins, M. S., Szapocnik, J., Dillooon, F. R., Turner, C. W., Mitrani, B. B., & Feaster, D. J. (2008). The efficacy of structural ecosystems therapy with drug-abusing/dependent African American and Hispanic American adolescents. *Journal of Family Psychology, 22,* 51–61.

Robbins, M. S., Szapocznik, J., & Perez, G. A. (2007). Brief strategic family therapy. In L. L'Abate, & N. Kazantzis (Eds.), *Handbook of homework assignments in psychotherapy: Research, practice, prevention.* New York: Springer.

Robbins, M. S., Turner, C. W., Alexander, J. F., & Perez, G. A. (2003). Alliance and dropout in family therapy for adolescents with behavior problems: Individual and systemic effects. *Journal of Family Psychology, 17,* 534–544.

Robin, A. L., Siegal, P. T., Koepke, T., Moye, A. W., & Tice, S. (1994). Family therapy versus individual therapy for adolescent females with anorexia nervosa. *Developmental and Behavioral Pediatrics, 15,* 111–116.

Rowland, M. D., Halliday-Boykins, C. A., Henggeler, S. W., Cunningham, P. B., Lee, T. G., Kruesi, M. J. P., & Shapiro, S. B. (2005). A randomized trial of multisystemic therapy with Hawaii's Felix class youths. *Journal of Emotional and Behavioral Disorders, 13,* 13–23.

Russell, G. F. M., Szmukler, G. I., Dare, C., & Eisler, I. (1987). An evaluation of family therapy in anorexia nervosa and bulimia nervosa. *Archives of General Psychiatry, 44,* 1047–1056.

Santisteban, D. A., Coatsworth, J. D., Perez-Vidal, A., Kurtines, W. M., Schwartz, S. J., LaPerriere, A., & Szapocnik, J. (2003). Efficacy of brief strategic family therapy in modifying Hispanic adolescent behavior problems and substance use. *Journal of Family Psychology, 17,* 121–133.

Sargent, J., Liebman, R., & Silver, M. (1985). Family therapy for anorexia. In J. Harkaway (Ed.), *Family therapy for eating disorders: Vol. 20. Family therapy collection.* Rockville, MD: Aspen Systems.

Satir, V. (1964). *Conjoint family therapy.* Palo Alto, CA: Science and Behavior Books.

Schaeffer, C. M., & Borduin, C. M. (2005). Long-term follow-up to a randomized clinical trial of multisystemic therapy with serious and violent juvenile offenders. *Journal of Consulting and Clinical Psychology, 73,* 445–453.

Scharff, D., & Scharff, J. (1987). *Object relations family therapy.* New York: Jason Aronson.

Schmidt, S. E., Liddle, H. A., & Dakof, G. A. (1996). Changes in parenting practices and adolescent drug abuse during multidimensional family therapy. *Journal of Family Psychology, 10,* 12–27.

Schmidt, U., Lee, S., Beecham, J., Perkins, S., Treasure, J., Yi, I., et al. (2007). A randomized controlled trial of family therapy and cognitive behavior therapy guided self-care for adolescents with bulimia nervosa and related disorders. *American Journal of Psychiatry, 164,* 591–598.

Schoenwald, S. K., & Hengeller, S. W. (2005). Multisystemic therapy for adolescents with serious externalizing problems. In J. L. Lebow (Ed.), *Handbook of clinical family therapy* (pp. 103–127). Hoboken, NJ: Wiley & Sons.

Schoenwald, S. K., Ward, D. M., Henggeler, S. W., & Rowland, M. D. (2000). Multisystemic therapy versus hospitalization for crisis stabilization of youth: Placement outcomes 4 months postreferral. *Mental Health Services Research, 2,* 3–12.

Seligman, M. E. P., & Csikszentmihalyi, M. (2000). Positive psychology: An introduction. *American Psychologist, 55,* 5–14.

Selvini Palazzoli, M., Boscolo, L., Cecchin, G., & Prata, G. (1978). *Paradox and counterparadox.* New York: Jason Aronson.

Shadish, W. R., Ragsdale, K., Glaser, R. R., & Montgomery, L. M. (1995). The efficacy and effectiveness of marital and family therapy: A perspective from meta-analysis. *Journal of Marital and Family Therapy, 21,* 345–360.

Sheeber, L., Hyman, H., & Davis, B. (2001). Family processes in adolescent depression. *Clinical Child and Family Psychology Review, 4,* 19–35.

Shelef, K., Diamond, G. M., Diamond, G. S., & Liddle, H. A. (2005). Adolescent and parent alliance and treatment outcome in multidimensional family therapy. *Journal of Consulting and Clinical Psychology, 73,* 689–698.

Shoham, V., Rohrbaugh, M. J., Robbins, M. R., Szapocznik, J., & Feaster, D. (2003). *Mediators and moderators of Brief Strategic Family Therapy (BSFT) for adolescent drug use.* Award R01 DA17539 from National Institute on Drug Abuse, Rockville MD.

Slipp, S. (1984). *Object relations: A dynamic bridge between individual and family treatment.* New York: Jason Aronson.

Sluzki, C. (1992). Transformations: A blueprint for narrative changes in therapy. *Family Process, 31,* 217–230.

Snyder, J., Cramer, A., Afrank, J., & Patterson, G. R. (2005). The contributions of ineffective discipline and parental hostile attributions of child misbehavior to the development of conduct problems at home and school. *Developmental Psychology, 41,* 30–41.

Sprenkle, D. H., & Blow, A. J. (2004). Common factors and our sacred models. *Journal of Marital and Family Therapy, 30,* 113–129.

Sterba, R. (1934). The fate of the ego in analytic therapy. *International Journal of Psychoanalysis, 15,* 117–125.

Stuart, R. B. (1969). An operant-interpersonal treatment for marital discord. *Journal of Consulting and Clinical Psychology, 33,* 675–682.

Symonds, D., & Horvath, A. O. (2004). Optimizing the alliance in couple therapy. *Family Process, 43,* 443–455.

Szapocznik, J., Robbins, M. S., Mitrani, B. B., Santisteban, D. A., Hervis, O., & Williams, R. A. (2002). Brief strategic family therapy. In F. W. Kaslow (Ed.), *Comprehensive handbook of psychotherapy: Integrative/eclectic* Vol 4 (pp. 83–109). Hoboken, NJ: Wiley & Sons.

Taylor, T., Adelman, H. S., & Kaser-Boyd, N. (1985). Exploring minors' reluctance and dissatisfaction with psychotherapy. *Professional Psychology: Research and Practice, 16,* 418–425.

Timmons-Mitchell, J., Bender, M. B., Kishna, M. A., & Mitchell, C. C. (2006). An independent effectiveness trial of multisystemic therapy with juvenile justice youth. *Journal of Clinical Child and Adolescent Psychology, 35,* 227–236.

Tolan, P. H. (2003). Family-focused prevention research: "Tough but tender." In H. A. Liddle, D. A. Santisteban, R. F. Levant, & J. H. Bray (Eds.), *Family psychology: Science-based interventions* (pp. 197–213). Washington, DC: American Psychological Association.

von Bertalanffy, L. (1950). An outline of general systems theory. *British Journal of Philosophy of Science, 1,* 139–164.

Waldron, H. B., & Turner, C. W. (2008). Evidence-based psychosocial treatments for adolescent substance abuse. *Journal of Clinical child and Adolescent Psychology, 37,* 238–261.

Watzlawick, P., Beavin, J., & Jackson, D. (1967). *Pragmatics of human communication.* New York: Norton.

Watzlawick, P., Weakland, J., & Fisch, R. (1974). *Change: Principles of problem formation and problem resolution.* New York: Norton.

Whitaker, C. A., & Keith, D. V. (1981). Symbolic-experiential family therapy. In A. S. Gurman, & D. P. Kniskern (Eds.), *Handbook of family therapy* (pp. 187–225). New York: Brunner/Mazel.

White, M., & Epston, D. (1990). *Narrative means to therapeutic ends.* New York: Norton.

Wiener, N. (1948). *Cybernetics or control and communication in the animal and the machine.* Cambridge, MA: MIT Press.

Williams, C. D. (1959). The elimination of tantrum behavior by extinction procedures. *Journal of Abnormal and Social Psychology, 59,* 269.

Wolpe, J. (1958). *Psychotherapy by reciprocal inhibition.* New York: Pergamon Press.

PART 5

Intersections

Rehabilitation Psychology

Timothy R. Elliott *and* Joseph F. Rath

Abstract

As one of the oldest psychology specialties active in interdisciplinary medical centers and health and public policy, rehabilitation psychology focuses on the optimal adjustment of individuals with disabilities, their families, and primary support systems. The wide array of circumstances confronting individuals with disabilities demands a broad skill set and flexibility in the rehabilitation psychologist's approach. Throughout its 50-year history, the field has been shaped and informed by theory and research drawn from other academic and practice areas of psychology including social, clinical, and counseling psychology, rehabilitation counseling, behavioral neuroscience, and neuropsychology. This rich heritage contributes to the specialty's resilience and potential to address current challenges facing American health care, including the aging of the baby boom generation and the unprecedented numbers of wounded veterans returning to society with injuries that may require life-long services.

Keywords: Rehabilitation psychology, disability, chronic illness, health care, assessment and intervention

In a current statement, the Division of Rehabilitation Psychology within the American Psychological Association (APA) offered this definition of rehabilitation psychology:

> Rehabilitation Psychology is the study and application of psychological principles on behalf of persons with physical, sensory, cognitive, developmental or emotional disabilities. People with disabilities, including those with loss of function due to chronic illness, may face personal, social, or situational barriers to healthy and satisfying lifestyles. Some barriers are inherent in the disabling condition, while others arise from the environment, including social myths that contribute to devaluation of persons who are different. Through clinical interventions, research, and advocacy, rehabilitation psychologists seek to improve health and functioning and broaden opportunities available to persons with disabilities.

(Scherer et al., 2004, p. 801)

With over 50 years of organized professional involvement, rehabilitation psychology is one of the oldest psychological specialties active in interdisciplinary medical settings, health and public policy, and the study of and service to persons with chronic and disabling health conditions. Rehabilitation psychologists are active in a wide range of institutions serving individuals living with disabling conditions, including hospitals, universities, medical schools, schools, nonprofit organizations, and federal and state agencies.

In this chapter, we review the history of rehabilitation psychology and the various theoretical systems that have shaped and informed the specialty, both historically and in the present. We will comment on major streams of research and identify the clinical practices that typify rehabilitation psychology practice. Finally, we will comment on training and emerging issues that now shape the field.

History and Background

Unlike the primary areas of psychology that have strong roots in academia, rehabilitation psychology was born on the fields of public and health policy. Unlike the primary practice disciplines of professional psychology that originally focused on mental health issues, rehabilitation psychology was among the first specialties to operate in health care settings and focus on personal health and optimal adjustment in social, personal, and vocational roles among people with disabilities and chronic health problems.

Public attention and federal policies to rehabilitate and retrain injured workers in late 19th- and early 20th-century American cities provided an essential backdrop for the field. Most landmark activities germane to vocational rehabilitation and psychology have been discussed (in varying levels of detail) in other places (e.g., Elliott & Leung, 2005; Larson & Sachs, 2000; Oberman, 1965; Peterson & Aguiar, 2004; Rubin & Roessler, 2001). In general terms, the Industrial Revolution is recognized as the major precursor to federal and public policies concerning rehabilitation. As workers incurred disabling injuries in rapidly expanding industrial enterprises, the need to provide support, assistance, education, and training for those injured became evident. Several charitable and nonprofit agencies (e.g., Goodwill Industries, B'nai B'rith) tried to address these needs, while others developed specialized services for the vocational assessment and guidance of injured workers.

At the end of the 19th century, ongoing industrialization of the American workforce, combined with pressures ensuing from immigration, urbanization, and advocacy from the Populist and Progressive political movements, led to a greater recognition of the complexity of social issues germane to welfare and the economy. Social welfare concerns pressed into the federal agenda during Theodore Roosevelt's administration. In 1908, a presidential committee concluded that public health was a responsibility of the federal government, being too much of a responsibility for private charities to address alone (Oberman, 1965). For example, the number of workers left disabled by the high rate of industrial accidents was too great for private agencies to accommodate, leaving many injured workers with no opportunity for rehabilitation or retraining for the workforce. With passage of the Federal Employees Compensation Act of 1908, the first worker's compensation legislation was enacted to assist federal workers employed in hazardous occupations. By 1921, most states had enacted legislation to provide disabled workers with some form of compensation.

Organized labor and increased urbanization of the workforce also created a need for relevant training and vocational education programs. Often, workers lacked skills or possessed skills rendered obsolete by new technology and industry. The Smith–Hughes Act of 1917 provided states with matching funds to develop vocational education programs, and the Federal Board of Vocational Education was created to administer vocational rehabilitation (VR) programs under this same legislation.

World Wars and Rehabilitation

The aftermath of World War I led to several important legislative policies designed to address the needs of returning soldiers. The Soldiers Rehabilitation Act (1918) provided funds to rehabilitate disabled veterans, with the Federal Board for Vocational Education administering these services. In 1921, the Veterans Bureau was created, and in time, evolved into the Department of Veterans Affairs.

Following World War II, the need for psychology service providers increased exponentially as armed services personnel returned to society. The demand for professionals in every area of psychology was greater than at any time in the nation's history (Buchanon, 2003; Pickren, 2005). This unprecedented need exceeded the available supply; consequently, individuals from various specialties within psychology, as well as from the larger field of education, took clinical positions providing a variety of services. For example, one of the early leaders of the Division of Rehabilitation Psychology within the APA—Beatrice Wright—completed her graduate training in social psychology with Kurt Lewin at the University of Iowa. She then worked as a counselor with the United States Employment Service helping veterans and learning about "jobs and factories and hard-to-place people [and the] . . . *Dictionary of Occupational Titles*" (Hollingsworth, Johnson, & Cook, 1989, p. 385).

The overwhelming need for specialized services for returning veterans prompted federal policy makers to promote specialization in various professions. Federal policies contributed to the medical specialization of physiatry. Medical management of cases that involved disability, neurological trauma, and long-term medical management necessitated particular expertise in "physical medicine and rehabilitation," which was recognized in 1947 as a specialty board by the American Medical Association (Allan, 1958).

Many physicians who served in the medical corps during World War II returned to work in hospital settings and advocated for the needs of their patients. The Vocational Rehabilitation Act of 1954 provided funds to colleges and universities for training rehabilitation service providers and "qualified rehabilitation personnel." In essence, this act created the field of rehabilitation counseling. The legislation also stipulated the model of VR services in which the rehabilitation counselor served as the primary service coordinator.

Bringing Rehabilitation Psychology into Being

Federal support to professional psychology was less obvious, but present nonetheless. Many psychologists were hired as VR specialists to work in medical facilities operated by the Veterans Administration (Larson & Sachs, 2000). Furthermore, federal agencies identified with VR—the Department of Health, Education, and Welfare (in 1958) and the Office of Vocation Rehabilitation (in 1959)—financially supported conferences for psychologists interested in rehabilitation. These conferences were sponsored, in part, because of the influence and support of James Garrett, who was then associate director of the Office of Vocational Rehabilitation (OVR) in the Department of Health, Education, and Welfare (Larson & Sachs, 2000).

Two conferences in particular were vital to organizing rehabilitation psychology research, practice, and training. The first, conducted in Princeton, New Jersey in 1958, typically is acknowledged as the formal beginning of rehabilitation psychology (Wright, 1959). A second conference, held in Miami the following year, was convened to determine the possible contributions of the broader domains of psychology to rehabilitation research and practice (Lofquist, 1960). Prior to these founding conferences, psychologists and counselors who identified with the field of rehabilitation had organized as the National Council on the Psychological Aspects of Disability (NCPAD). NCPAD, which became a special interest group of APA in 1949 (Wright, 1993), met at several APA conventions and published a newsletter. The Princeton and Miami conferences, along with NCPAD, provided an organizational springboard that contributed in part to the development of the Division of Rehabilitation Psychology within APA.

A mix of academicians, clinicians, federal agency administrators, and representatives from other professions (e.g., social work, nursing, physical therapy,

occupational therapy) attended the Princeton conference. Several attendees are well known for their contributions in other areas of psychology (see Table 26.1 for a selective listing of participants). Counseling psychology, for example, was well represented and representatives from the specialty played influential roles in these formative days of rehabilitation psychology. One participant, John McGowan, a counseling psychologist from the University of Missouri, would later be the lead author of one of the most influential books in VR (*An Introduction to the Vocational Rehabilitation Process: A Training Manual;* McGowan & Porter, 1967. The book was published by the federal government.). Attendees Anne Roe, John G. Darley, and Lloyd H. Lofquist were well known for their work in vocational psychology and career development theory. In the ensuing years, Lofquist's work in developing the Minnesota Theory of Work Adjustment was supported by funding from the Rehabilitation Services Administration and other federal and state vocational rehabilitation agencies (Dawis & Lofquist, 1984).

Table 26.1.   Select Participants at the 1958 Princeton Conference and Their Historical Area of Contributions to Professional Psychology

Name	Historical Area of Contributions
John G. Darley	Counseling Psychology
Tamara Dembo	Social Psychology
Leonard Diller	Neuropsychological Rehabilitation
Salvatore DiMichael	Vocational Rehabilitation
James Garrett	Department of Health, Education and
	Welfare, World Rehabilitation Fund
Lloyd H. Lofquist	Counseling Psychology
John McGowan	Counseling Psychology
Lee Meyerson	Rehabilitation Psychology
Victor Raimy	Clinical Psychology
Anne Roe	Counseling and Vocational Psychology
Harold Seashore	Founder, The Psychological Corporation
Beatrice A. Wright	Rehabilitation and Social Psychology

In contrast to the Princeton conference, psychologists "visible" in areas other than rehabilitation were invited to the Miami conference to assist in developing a research agenda of interest to psychology as a whole that would inform and advance rehabilitation. Counseling psychologists were again well represented among conference planners and workgroup members (see Table 26.2). Leona Tyler, Cecil

Table 26.2.   Planning Committee Members and Work Group Members at the 1960 Miami Conference

Planning Committee Members

Emory L. Cowen	Lee Meyerson
John G. Darley	Howard L. Roy
Erasmus L. Hoch	Morton Seidenfeld
Harold H. Kelley	Franklin Shontz
Lloyd H. Lofquist	

Work Group I: Cognition: Sensory and Perceptual Organization

Franklin Shontz	Seymour Wapner
Tamara Dembo	Cecil H. Patterson
Martin Scheerer	

Work Group II: Career Development

George W. England	Leona E. Tyler
Lee J. Cronbach	Abraham Jacobs
Donald G. Patterson	

Work Group III: Learning

Lee Meyerson	Charles E. Osgood
John L. Michael	Arthur W. Staats
O. Hobart Mowrer	

Work Group IV: Personality Theory and Motivation

Emory L. Cowen	Morton Wiener
Richard S. Lazarus	O. Bruce Thomason
Abraham S. Luchins	

Work Group V: Social Psychology

Harold H. Kelley	John W. Thibaut
Albert H. Hastorf	William M. Usdane
Edward E. Jones	

From Lofquist, 1960, pp. 2–5.

Patterson, George England, Donald Patterson, as well as Darley and Lofquist, worked with other figures renowned for their achievements in social psychology (Lazarus, Kelley, Hastorf, Jones, Thibaut), learning theory (Mowrer, Osgood), and psychometrics (Cronbach). These workgroup themes remain viable in contemporary rehabilitation psychology.

These conferences concluded that a unique specialty for rehabilitation was not needed for psychologists, primarily because the field was much too broad, and all branches of psychology could make meaningful contributions to the research base and inform clinical practice and public policy. Participants agreed that doctoral-level training in psychology was required for work in rehabilitation settings. In addition, both conferences laid out a research agenda that relied on psychological expertise and also recommended funding from federal granting agencies to support the research enterprise, as it represented important public and health policy priorities.

Decisions from these conferences concerning research, scholarship, policy, and training in rehabilitation psychology had tremendous influence on the development and health of the field that persists to this day. In the following section, we will summarize the major strands of these influences.

Defining the Literature Base

Rehabilitation psychology remains a field steeped in interdisciplinary endeavors, and as such, its literature base is heavily dependent upon various threads of scholarship within psychology, as well as from research conducted by other professions invested in the health and rehabilitation of persons living with disabilities. In the decades following the Princeton and Miami conferences, we can trace the particular impact of research from boarder areas of psychology, including social, clinical, and counseling psychology, rehabilitation counseling, behavioral neuroscience, and neuropsychology.

Social Psychology

The influence of academic social psychology was immediately apparent at the Princeton and Miami conferences. Beatrice Wright, one of the enduring pioneers of rehabilitation psychology, studied with faculty noted for their outstanding contributions to social psychology (Kurt Lewin, Tamara Dembo, Solomon Asch) and with others recognized for their contributions to clinical psychology (Kenneth Spence, Carl Rogers, Abraham Maslow; Dunn & Elliott, 2005). She participated in a faculty-student discussion group (the "Topological Group") that included Margaret Mead, Henry Murray, Erik Erikson, and Fritz Heider (Hollingsworth, Johnson, & Cook, 1989). Her field research with Roger Barker, funded by the Social Science Research Council in 1946, resulted in a landmark critique of the extant literature on adjustment following illness and disability (Barker, Wright, Meyerson, & Gonick, 1953). After serving as chronicler of the Princeton conference (Wright, 1959), Wright published the seminal *Physical Disability: A Psychological Approach* (1960), the first theory-driven psychological statement from rehabilitation psychology, grounded in the best scholarly traditions, informed by the extant literature, and enriched with applications and illustrations to inform both academicians and clinicians.

In her book, Wright (1960) persuasively argued for appreciating disability within context, relying heavily on Lewian field theory (in which $B = f(P, E)$; Lewin, 1935) to depict disability as a social psychological phenomenon in which any atypical appearance, physique, or behavior attracts the attention of, and stimulates inferences from, observers. In doing so, she extended previous work with Tamara Dembo to draw explicit ramifications for understanding behaviors and issues presented by clients in clinical settings (see Dembo, Leviton, & Wright, 1956).

Wright's contributions ran parallel to other work informed by social psychological perspectives that appeared in the literature throughout the formative years of rehabilitation psychology. For example, in 1948, Lee Meyerson—a contemporary and collaborator of Wright's—edited a special issue of the *Journal of Social Issues* entitled "The Social Psychology of Disability" that, in part, surmised the Barker research program to that time and drew implications for theory and policy. Decades later, in an update and review of the relevant research in this area, Fine and Asch (1988) asserted that Meyerson's 1948 publication had a lasting and fundamental influence on social policy concerning disability and rehabilitation. In addition to addressing subtle and blatant matters of stigma and discrimination concerning persons with disability, Meyerson's contribution also provided considerable scholarly and intellectual heft to the emerging area of disability rights, advocacy, and disability studies.

Indeed, the study of social stigma associated with disability was informed by scholarly essays (notably Goffman, 1960) and experimental analogue research (e.g., "kindness norm" work [Kleck,1968; Kleck, Ono, & Hastorf, 1966], and "attitude amplification"

research [Katz, Farber, Glass, Lucido, & Emswiller, 1978]), and it expanded with the development of the popular Attitudes Toward Disabilities Scale (Yuker, Block, & Younng, 1966), which was used in scores of empirical—albeit mostly correlational—studies (Yuker, 1988; Yuker & Block, 1986).

Wright's book (1960) appeared at a time when the newly minted rehabilitation counseling training programs needed contemporary texts for their curricula. The book, along with its later revision (Wright, 1983) proved immensely influential: The first edition was the second most frequently cited work published prior to 1973 in articles that appeared in three volumes of two major rehabilitation counseling journals (*Rehabilitation Counseling Bulletin, Journal of Applied Rehabilitation Counseling*; Elliott, Byrd, & Nichols, 1987), and the second edition (Wright, 1983) was the second most frequently cited work published after 1973 in articles in these same volumes. The first edition also was the most frequently cited publication in articles appearing in three volumes of *Rehabilitation Psychology* (Vols. 27–29; Elliott & Byrd, 1986).

The direct influence of Wright's books may have dimmed in recent years: In a survey of board-certified rehabilitation psychologists, neither edition was listed among the influential readings identified by this relatively small and restricted sample (Ryan & Tree, 2004). Nevertheless, Wright's work has remained influential in the emerging area of positive psychology, particularly as her work pertains to assessment of deficits and assets, and the impact of context on assessment, generally (Wright, 1991; Wright & Lopez, 2002). Current interest in positive psychology may serve to regenerate social psychological applications in rehabilitation psychology for a number of reasons. In particular, many theoretical positions concerning growth, happiness, gratitude, life satisfaction, and well-being often are tested and refined in rigorous, real-life applications; therefore, many empirical tests are conducted among persons who have incurred or live with severe disabilities (e.g., Emmons & McCullough, 2003, study 4; Lucas, 2007; for integrative summaries, see Dunn, Uswatte, & Elliott, 2009; Elliott, Kurylo, & Rivera, 2002). Current perspectives on subjective well-being following disability using sophisticated prospective methodologies now inform theoretical models of adjustment over time (e.g., Resch et al., 2009).

An enduring contribution of social psychology may be found in the disability studies literature of the past few decades. Spurred on by Fine and

Asch's (1988) update of Meyerson's earlier work, several scholars have advanced a scholarly understanding of the "insider's" perspective and experience of disability (Nosek, Howland, Rintala, Young, & Chanpong, 2001; Vash, 1981). Consumers of rehabilitative services and their advocates tend to be much more sensitive to the demands and issues centered in the environment in which behavior is framed than are service providers (Olkin, 1999). To a great extent, federal funding priorities have been influenced by these perspectives (e.g., at the National Institute on Disability Rehabilitation and Research; Olkin & Pledger, 2003). To a lesser extent, psychology doctoral training programs also have been influenced, albeit only among those few training programs that address disability as a minority experience (Olkin, 2002). Despite this influence, contemporary disability studies programs seem to be more aligned in content and mission with academic public health than with conventional doctoral training programs in clinical and counseling psychology.

Clinical Psychology

Clinical psychology has steadily and powerfully grown in significance to the core of rehabilitation psychology practice and research. Although this influence may not have been readily apparent at the Princeton and Miami conferences, many clinical psychologists were working in medical settings that provided services to persons with acquired disabilities. Some, like Wilbert E. Fordyce, were in departments specifically created to meet the medical needs of these patients. Others, like Jerome Siller, were in academic departments, and their roles were often consultative, providing liaison services to medical teams and agencies providing therapeutic services and assistive devices. Colleagues in these roles were compelled to understand and improve services to the cases they routinely encountered.

Fordyce entered the clinical rehabilitation environment with expertise in personality assessment (evidenced in his early published work concerning the MMPI) and an apparent high regard for behavioral learning theories. Although clinical anecdotes about personality and disability were prevalent during these times (many emanating from psychiatry), Fordyce conducted one of the earliest empirical studies of personality and disability in his examination of MMPI profiles and manner of disability onset among patients with spinal cord injuries (SCI; Fordyce, 1964). This work was among the first to demonstrate the thoughtful, judicious

use of appropriate comparison groups in studying self-report data in rehabilitation psychology, and it provided some of the first evidence that certain behavioral patterns—notably, "imprudent, impulsive, and excitement seeking" tendencies that can jeopardize health in risk-taking activities prior to injury—may be important clinical factors in understanding adjustment and well-being following disability. This study also revealed relatively low levels of psychopathology, generally, in the sample. Many of these same themes—the study of self-report assessment devices; use of appropriate samples, comparison groups, and normative data; and investigations into psychopathology, behavioral patterns, and well-being—are ongoing hallmarks of contemporary rehabilitation psychology literature.

Fordyce's application of operant conditioning theory to understanding the dynamics and contingencies that shape and reinforce "pain behavior" (Fordyce, 1971) and suffering following disability (Fordyce, 1988) had a broad, sweeping impact on research, practice, and policy. His 1976 book, entitled *Behavioral Methods for Chronic Pain and Illness*, is a classic in the rehabilitation and health psychology literature (Elliott & Byrd, 1986; Patterson, 2005). In his conceptualization, pain behaviors are conditioned by a patient's interpersonal and social environment, and these environmental reactions serve to maintain or increase pain behaviors. Applying operant learning theory, Fordyce also argued persuasively about the dangers of "as needed" medication schedules and advocated use of time-contingent schedules to prevent acquisition of maladaptive behavioral patterns, with the additional benefit of maintaining steady medication levels in the patient (Patterson, 2005). This model also was central in illuminating the value of exercise and activity at regular intervals by taking into account the initial "punishing" aspects of this activity in terms of increased pain, which may contribute to faulty learning patterns and decreased activity levels that reward pain behavior over time.

In direct contrast to Fordyce, who relied on behavioral-learning theory in his wide-ranging work on assessment and intervention strategies in rehabilitation psychology, Jerome Siller extrapolated many of his ideas from psychoanalytic theory. Leaning on logic and clinical experience, Siller refined existing "stage models" of adjustment that could enlighten understanding of acceptance and adjustment following the acute onset of severe disability (Siller, 1969, 1988). Certain features of stage models would vary, but to a degree, many of these Freudian-based extrapolations posited that the ego would likely feel a sense of "castration" at the loss of a limb or motor function. Losses accompanying disability would deal a severe blow to the individual's inherent narcissism, and most individuals would use denial to defend against the anxiety precipitated by the loss. As the ego became able to permit experience of the loss, denial would be replaced by depression. Presumably, for individuals with a strong enough ego, depression eventually would be replaced by acceptance of the reality of their permanent injury.

Siller's writings on this model were revisited and reworked over the years by others in rehabilitation (Cubbage & Thomas, 1989; Grzesiak & Hicock, 1994), and he expanded his thinking to incorporate contemporary ideas from object relations theory (Thomas & Siller, 1999). Unfortunately, these theoretical models generated very little empirical research (although recent evidence indicates that certain constructs from self-psychology models can account for significant variance in clinical outcomes following acquired disability; Elliott, Uswatte, Lewis, & Palmatier, 2000). Siller and his colleagues also developed measures of attitudes toward disability and adaptation to disability based on classical psychoanalytic theory (Siller, Chipman, Ferguson, & Vann, 1967), but this work, too, failed to stimulate rigorous, sustained empirical scrutiny from others. Nevertheless, the intuitive, clinical appeal of stage models influenced—and continue to influence—many clinical conceptualizations of adjustment following disability.

The attention to clinical assessment and theoretical models to improve practice and predict outcomes—evident in the diverse contributions of Fordyce and Siller—characterize the bulk of modern rehabilitation psychology research and practice. Traditionally, psychologists in rehabilitation settings spend the majority of their time conducting assessments of intelligence, personality, adjustment, and neuropsychological functioning (Eisenberg & Jansen, 1987; Grzesiak, 1979; Jansen & Fulcher, 1982). The clinical psychology heritage undoubtedly has made the most pronounced and long-lasting impression on the field.

Counseling Psychology and Rehabilitation Counseling

One of the more remarkable and intriguing stories in the evolution of rehabilitation psychology is the rise and demise of contributions from counseling psychology to the field, and its ambivalent relationship with the highly influential rehabilitation counseling profession (indeed, to this day, many psychologists in some specialty areas mistakenly equate rehabilitation psychology with rehabilitation counseling). As we have seen, many academic counseling psychologists were key figures at the Princeton and Miami conferences. Their presence supplied expertise in areas of vocational psychology, career development, and training. During the "golden years" of VR (Rusalem, 1976), these counseling psychologists maintained their identity in their academic "home" of counseling psychology and assumed leadership roles in rehabilitation psychology, primarily in their training and research activities. Often, these activities were centered in the graduate programs that they (e.g., John McGowan, Cecil Patterson, and others) developed to train rehabilitation counselors, using financial support from state and federal agencies. Virtually all of these training programs were housed in colleges of education. For many years, a significant number of APA Division 22 (i.e., Division of Rehabilitation Psychology) members had earned their doctoral degrees in rehabilitation counseling (Jansen & Fulcher, 1982; Neff, 1971).

The chief mission of rehabilitation counseling programs, however, was dictated by the 1954 rehabilitation legislation that created the field. This legislation dictated a model of VR services in which the rehabilitation counselor was at the core as the primary coordinator. Many rehabilitation counseling programs flourished when federal support was provided to colleges and universities to train rehabilitation service providers and "qualified rehabilitation personnel" to administer and coordinate programs. Rehabilitation counseling subsequently has been considered "synonymous with . . . the State-Federal rehabilitation program" (Jenkins, Patterson, & Szymanski, 1997, p. 1). In a seminal text, George N. Wright (1980, p. 22) acknowledged the academic roots of the rehabilitation counseling profession in counseling psychology, but asserted that, although counseling was an integral part of the VR process, rehabilitation counselors were uniquely skilled to meet the needs of persons with disabilities and address the psychosocial issues that they encounter.

Counseling psychologists in attendance at the Princeton and Miami conferences clearly were familiar with psychology training models and the use of theory-driven research and practice; they conducted research programs and produced scholarly materials that informed training and counseling strategies. For example, the development of the Minnesota Theory of Work Adjustment

(Dawis & Lofquist, 1984) at the University of Minnesota resulted in many instruments for use with a VR clientele. Other counseling psychologists, some of whom were working in the Veterans Administration health care system, used established instruments in vocational psychology to develop appropriate norms and study specific behaviors. As an example, patterns in vocational interest profiles indicative of specific personality characteristics and behavioral patterns were associated with how a disability was acquired ("accident proneness;" Kunce & Worley, 1966), a finding consistent with Fordyce's earlier work using the MMPI.

Academic counseling psychology's interest in disability and rehabilitation generally waned over time, however. Peterson and Elliott (2008) reported that disability-related topics (physical, intellectual, and sensory disabilities and associated services) appeared in the titles of 18 articles published in the ten volumes of the *Journal of Counseling Psychology* published from 1970 to 1979, but the next 18 articles on disability accumulated slowly over the ensuing 27 volumes (volumes 27–53, published from 1980 to 2006). Perusal of recent Division of Rehabilitation Psychology membership rosters (maintained by APA) indicates that a very small percentage of division members have earned doctorates in counseling psychology (7.8% in the 2008 report), and fewer still had joint membership in APA's Society of Counseling Psychology (4%).

Rehabilitation counseling itself faced unique problems and professional identity issues at the end of the 20th century that still persist. Many practitioners were skeptical of the relevance of psychological coursework and theory in the VR enterprise (Olshansky & Hart, 1967). Increased workload (requiring additional time commitments with job placement activities, case management, and interactions with employers) typically left little time or expectation for rehabilitation counselors to provide adjustment "counseling" (Thomas & Parker, 1981). Consequently, rehabilitation counseling drifted away from the broader field of counseling psychology toward a more distinct and separate profession, characterized by administrative and managerial duties (Thomas & Parker, 1984). Training models for rehabilitation counseling subsequently shifted away from their academic roots in response to, and with increased dependence upon, federal legislation and its accompanying financial support (Hershenson, 1988; Thomas, 1991). Thomas (1991) was particularly critical of rehabilitation counseling's dependence upon federal money for training and its

ongoing identification with state VR agencies, noting that clinical psychology was not considered synonymous with the Veterans Administration despite clear support from that branch of the federal government over the years. Finally, doctoral graduates of rehabilitation counseling programs found it increasingly difficult to obtain psychology licenses in most states, as licensing boards created strict standards for applicants to meet concerning accredited training programs, internships, and postdoctoral experiences.

Behavioral Neuroscience and Neuropsychology

According to the reports from the Miami conference (Lofquist, 1960), considerable weight was placed on the potential of learning theory to further understanding about conditioned responses and improvements in learning and rehabilitative therapies. Several members of the Learning workgroup (see Table 26.2) had extensive experience with animal models of behavior and were familiar with existing paradigms in psychophysiology. It was recommended that advanced students steeped in these models and paradigms should be given financial support and ample opportunity to "rub their noses in . . . rehabilitation problems in facilities where they can come face to face with the behavioral problems involved" in rehabilitation (Lofquist, 1960, p. 71).

Neal Miller experienced this very scenario when his students (Bernard Brucker, Lawrence Ince) convinced him of the unique opportunities for applying classical and operant conditioning theory to the study of visceral, reflex, and motor responses in the "clinical laboratory" of the rehabilitation hospital (Brucker & Ince, 1977; Ince, Brucker, & Alba, 1978; Miller & Brucker, 1979). In a series of creative, yet rigorous, single-case designs, this research team obtained sufficient evidence to establish biofeedback as an empirically based technique for use with persons with disabling conditions, and to cultivate a great appreciation for using behavioral strategies to augment rehabilitation therapies, enhance adjustment, and condition responses previously thought to be autonomic (Ince, 1980).

A contemporary extension of this work, grounded in state-of-the-art behavioral neuroscience, is evident in Edward Taub's theory of learned nonuse of motor behavior (Taub & Uswatte, 2000), which stems directly from animal models of behavior. The resulting strategy—constraint-induced movement therapy (CIMT)—derived from laboratory and clinical studies of learned nonuse, has immense implications for researchers' understanding of brain–behavior relationships and neuroplasticity that extend far beyond the walls of the rehabilitation setting. Notably, the intervention strategy—like the model developed by Fordyce for chronic pain rehabilitation programs—is implemented by the multidisciplinary treatment team, and not by the psychologist, per se, in face-to-face interactions.

The contributions of neuropsychology to the rehabilitation enterprise may sound less dramatic in the telling, but the steady application of contemporary assessment procedures, careful observations, and empirical studies has grown in proportion with the number of neurological disabilities that occur in modern society. Leonard Diller, a participant at the Princeton conference and founder of scientifically based cognitive rehabilitation (Goldstein, 2009), remarked that he "stumbled" into his position in the Rusk Institute of Rehabilitation Medicine at the New York University School of Medicine. He described having "almost nobody to talk to" about the everyday clinical problems he encountered until he read Tamara Dembo's seminal work describing the problems experienced by individuals with acquired disabilities (Brownsberger, 2003, p. 12). He credited interactions and collaborations with Dembo and other colleagues at the Princeton conference with helping him develop his early notions of neuropsychological rehabilitation.

In traditional approaches to clinical neuropsychology, the psychologist's role stopped at assessment and interpretation, and patients were "handed over to the speech, occupational, and physical therapists for rehabilitation" (Goldstein, 2009, p. 141). Diller was instrumental in developing informed, tailored interventions to help patients with acquired brain injuries and their families compensate for cognitive and psychosocial deficits. In 1970, Diller and colleagues at the Rusk Institute published two landmark research papers: *Accidents in Hemiplegia* (Diller & Weinberg, 1970) and *Relationships Between Initial Competence and Ability to Profit from Cues in Brain-Injured Individuals* (Ben-Yishay, Diller, Gerstman, & Gordon, 1970), which firmly established the contribution of neuropsychology to the field of rehabilitation (Goldstein, 2009).

Funded by grants from the Department of Education, the National Institutes of Health (NIH), and other public and private agencies, Diller led a series of seminal research programs that advanced understanding of the nature of cognitive impairments that typically follow brain injury and other neurological insults (e.g., problems in attention, learning, memory, planning, organization, emotional self-regulation, and other "executive-function" skills). These empirical studies led to the development and clinical application of strategies to ameliorate these deficits and improve function, techniques now known collectively as *cognitive rehabilitation* and *cognitive remediation* (Ben-Yishay & Diller, 1983; Gordon & Hibbard, 1991). Eventually, Diller's clinical and research programs at the Rusk Institute would provide training experiences in cognitive rehabilitation to over 400 students, interns, and postdoctoral fellows (Brownsberger, 2003).

Over the years, neuropsychology has grown tremendously in influence and appearance in rehabilitation psychology. Brain injuries and stroke are among the most frequent disabilities in society, so it is understandable that many rehabilitation psychologists encounter some form of neurological deficit in clinical practice. Currently, data from the APA indicate that 51% of the members of the Division of Rehabilitation Psychology also have membership in the Division of Clinical Neuropsychology (Division 40). This is one of the highest percentages of dual membership among APA divisions.

Summarizing the Literature Base

Over 25 years ago, in an attempt to distinguish rehabilitation psychology from the emerging areas of health psychology and behavioral medicine, Jansen and Eisenberg (1982) observed that rehabilitation psychology often "seemed isolated from the mainstream of psychology" (p. 3), due in part to the publication of important research and training articles in nonpsychological journals (Shontz & Wright, 1980). Leaders in the field were certainly prolific, and as we have seen, they made many lasting contributions that have benefited several core areas of psychology, far beyond the rehabilitation environment. However, the literature base did not have a periodical that served as a "centerpiece" for the field.

Scholars in rehabilitation counseling contributed to outlets published by their professional associations and, in the process, arguably established their own literature base. These peer-review outlets included the *Rehabilitation Counseling Bulletin*, the *Journal of Rehabilitation*, and the *Journal of Applied Rehabilitation Counseling*. Prior to the 1980s, many counseling psychologists published studies relevant to rehabilitation practice and training in the *Journal of Counseling Psychology*. Psychologists housed in medical schools tended to be "team players" in their choice of outlets, striving to advance the interdisciplinary enterprise of rehabilitation, inform colleagues of their work, advance knowledge, and show their home institutions in the best light. This required publishing in medical outlets, including the leading journal in the field, the *Archives of Physical Medicine and Rehabilitation (APMR)*. Currently, several members of the Division of Rehabilitation Psychology serve as associate editors for *APMR*. As specialties in rehabilitation grew, multidisciplinary journals devoted to specific diagnostic conditions emerged. As of this writing, members of the Division of Rehabilitation Psychology serve as editor-in-chief of the *Journal of Head Trauma Rehabilitation*, *Brain Injury*, and *Neuro Rehabilitation*.

Such commitments to multidisciplinary outlets activity drained energy and contributions from the divisional journal, *Rehabilitation Psychology* (now published by the APA). Now in its 53rd volume, *Rehabilitation Psychology* began as a division newsletter and evolved into a peer-reviewed outlet. Given its small circulation and lack of currency among the health professions active in the rehabilitation enterprise, the journal has yet to receive the same level of enthusiastic and scholarly support enjoyed by the more senior publications in the broader, multidisciplinary rehabilitation literature.

The multidisciplinary nature of rehabilitation also has influenced the scope and parameters in which a unique "rehabilitation psychology" literature developed. Rehabilitation research often is dependent upon external funds for support, and interdisciplinary collaborations are paramount in the pursuit of federal funds. Consequently, rehabilitation psychologists often are well positioned to address stated national priorities and health and public policy needs (e.g., rehabilitation of veterans returning from international conflicts, facilitating vocational rehabilitation of persons with acquired disabilities; Elliott & Leung, 2005; Larson & Sachs, 2000). Such opportunities place a premium on multidisciplinary collaborations and applied, pragmatic solutions. These activities reward practical products or services, but esoteric, jargonized academic theories that are difficult to communicate to colleagues from other disciplines are viewed as impractical or professionally self-serving (Dunn & Elliott, 2008). There are a few well-identified, theory-driven research programs readily identifiable in the contemporary rehabilitation psychology literature.

Indeed, the most influential, long-lasting theoretical and clinical contributions from rehabilitation psychology emphasize the ways that multidisciplinary team members (including nurses, physiatrists, and physical therapists) work collaboratively

to modify patient behavior to promote skill acquisition, health, and adjustment (Fordyce, 1976; Taub & Uswatte, 2000). VR research and practice also has championed multidisciplinary collaborations, and this is readily visible in the utility of supported employment as a job placement strategy (Anthony & Blanch, 1987; Wehman, 1988; Wehman, Sale, & Parent, 1992). This model, influenced considerably by teaching strategies in special education (particularly the individualized approaches pioneered by Gold, 1974) has enjoyed substantial empirical support. At least 12 published randomized clinical trials (RCTs) have demonstrated the effectiveness of this job placement strategy for persons with psychiatric disorders (Bond, 2004; Cook, Leff, et al., 2005; Cook, Lehman, et al., 2005; Mueser et al., 2004). Supported employment is recognized as an evidence-based practice. Finally, the unique value that rehabilitation psychology places on multidisciplinary collaborations is manifested in contemporary applications of virtual reality technologies to train patients in activities of daily living, driving skills, and as an adjunct treatment for adjustment problems (Hoffman, Patterson, & Carrougher, 2000; Schultheis & Rizzo, 2001).

Issues in the Research and Evidentiary Base

In an interview published in the Division 22 newsletter, Leonard Diller—an early leader of the division—reflected that rehabilitation started as a "compromise between vocational/education forces and medicine" (Brownsberger, 2003, p. 12). The major funding for rehabilitation efforts following World War II came from the Department of Education (with a subsequent emphasis on education, retraining, and labor needs), and other money was directed from the Office of Special Education to support medical inpatient programs to ensure excellence in medical management for persons with understudied and underserved conditions (Diller, 2008). A lasting consequence of the compromise between education and medicine is evident in the historic ties between the rehabilitation professions and the Office of Special Education (and the Rehabilitation Services Administration, the National Institute for Disability Rehabilitation and Research [NIDRR]) and the longstanding lack of presence at—and a lack of support from—NIH.

Disability advocates and various agencies lobbied the Department of Education for a systematic, collaborative, and coordinated database across sites to inform and improve clinical care and service delivery to persons with complicated, high-cost, low-incidence disabilities. This resulted in the establishment of the federally funded Model Systems of Care program in the mid-1970s. Each center in the Model Systems was to provide comprehensive services within a defined catchment area and feature five components of care: emergency medical services, acute care, physical rehabilitation, psychosocial and vocational services, and ongoing follow-up and evaluation (Thomas, 1995). Participating sites also offered improved accessibility to care, coordination of clinical services from emergency to acute to post-discharge settings, a critical volume of patients and referrals for service, ongoing research and evaluation of services and clientele, education and training for staff and consumers, and community outreach and advocacy services for persons with specific disabilities designated by the project (Thomas, 1995).

The first Model Systems program addressed SCI, and others were developed to study and treat traumatic brain injuries (TBI) and burn injuries. Initially, these programs emphasized the collection of demographic and medical information pertinent to the clinical management of these disabilities and associated complications. However, as consumer involvement increased, and as outcome data implicated social and behavioral mechanisms in the occurrence of disability and secondary complications, more research has been directed to psychosocial factors and adjustment. Additional grant programs by NIDRR funded Research and Training Centers to support projects that increasingly attended to behavioral and social factors (e.g., return-to-work, family support, community integration).

These collaborative projects enriched the knowledge base concerning the rehabilitation enterprise, generally, but the study of effective, efficacious psychological interventions was not funded by these agencies in any meaningful, systematic fashion. To be fair, relatively few RCTs of rehabilitation interventions exist, generally, and this poses considerable problems for identifying evidence-based practices in medical rehabilitation as well (Johnstone, 2003). With the high premium currently placed on evidence-based treatments, rehabilitation psychologists now assist in establishing evidence for multidisciplinary practices in medical rehabilitation (cf. Cicerone et al., 2005), while facing increasing expectations to provide evidence for psychological interventions in rehabilitation settings for people with various disabling conditions. These are not necessarily complementary activities: One review of interventions for treatment of depression following SCI found no RCTs for either antidepressant medication or psychological interventions in the peer-reviewed literature (Elliott & Kennedy, 2004). Unfortunately, an expert panel—composed of colleagues representing several professions active in medical rehabilitation—had previously reviewed this literature and granted the highest grade of evidence to psychopharmacological therapies and gave a much lower evidence grade to psychological interventions (Consortium for Spinal Cord Medicine, 1998).

Obtaining and grading empirical evidence for evidence-based practice (EBP) remains a conundrum for all professions involved in rehabilitation. Interdisciplinary treatments are often tailored to individuals in medical rehabilitation settings, and there are considerable difficulties obtaining participants from low-incidence disability conditions in numbers sufficient to impress review panels (Dijkers et al., 2009). It is difficult to construe meaningful control or "placebo" conditions for RCTs in rehabilitation, as there are often no "treatment as usual" conditions to approximate, and the provision of any clinical attention may be above and beyond routine experience (Dijkers et al., 2009; Elliott, 2007).

Many outcomes following disability are influenced by a wide range of social, behavioral, and demographic factors that are not amenable to any single intervention (Elliott & Warren, 2007) or adequately controlled by randomization, particularly when the number of participants may be relatively low. The impact of factors that impinge upon measurable outcomes, independent of methodological and statistical controls, assure that practically any psychological intervention in rehabilitation will likely have effects sizes that range from small to moderate at best. Large effect sizes may be realized in rigorous research designs that examine tailored interventions for specific problems of great personal importance to the individual. Although consonant with the rehabilitation ideal, this does not translate well into the kind of multisite clinical trial of a manualized protocol with numbers large enough to impress most policy makers and third-party payers.

Finally, RCTs are especially problematic for psychological interventions in rehabilitation as these designs are usually disinterested in theoretical models of change; we already know from prior study of behavioral contingencies and family dynamics that some behavioral problems may exacerbate before improvement is observed. Behavior following disability is best studied with theoretical models that anticipate the various mediators and moderators of change over time, rather than a linear model of change often associated with drug therapies for specific symptoms (for which RCTs are better suited; Tucker & Reed, 2008).

The present market value on EBP and the divided loyalties that rehabilitation psychology researchers face in medical and multidisciplinary settings may eventually result in greater scrutiny of many psychological interventions that have documented support. Such interventions as hypnosis for burn pain (Patterson, Everett, Burns, & Marvin, 1992); biofeedback to enhance self-regulation for persons with SCI (Brucker, 1980); and group interventions to improve social skills (Glueckauf & Quittner, 1992), problem-solving abilities (Rath, Simon, Langenbahn, Sherr, & Diller, 2003), coping skills (King & Kennedy, 1999), and general adjustment (Wegener, Mackenzie, Ephraim, Ehde, & Williams, 2009) following disability may best be construed as empirically supported treatments. Understandably, many critics of the false premiums placed on RCTs have urged an expansion of the evidentiary base to appreciate contributions of alternative research designs, sound theory, sophisticated meta-analytic techniques, and cumulative evidence across studies and designs (Dijkers et al., 2009; Dunn & Elliott, 2008; Horn & Gassaway, 2007; Tucker & Reed, 2008).

Professional Training

Throughout its existence, rehabilitation psychology has experienced difficulties in training and mentoring future colleagues. This is due, in part, to the lack of doctoral training programs in rehabilitation psychology, and to the longstanding lack of attention in clinical and counseling psychology doctoral programs to disability- and rehabilitation-related issues in coursework and practica. Very few members of the Division of Rehabilitation Psychology hold academic positions in APA-approved doctoral training

programs. Only a few programs state an explicit identification with rehabilitation psychology, and to date, none of these have APA accreditation.

In the late 20th century, the debate concerning professional training and identity renewed. Several advocates—notable because of their pivotal roles in the formation of the division and the specialty— tried to distinguish rehabilitation psychology from the emerging and popular areas of health psychology and behavioral medicine (Shontz & Wright, 1980). However, empirical descriptions of actual practice demonstrated considerable overlap between rehabilitation psychology activities and clinical health psychology (Eisenberg & Jansen, 1987; Jansen & Fulcher, 1982). Consequently, other colleagues advocated for core training common to APA-approved doctoral programs in clinical and counseling psychology with subsequent specialization in practica, internship, and postdoctoral training (Elliott & Gramling, 1990; Glueckauf, 2000). Despite these well-intentioned assertions, there is some indication that most APA-approved doctoral training programs provide no more exposure to rehabilitation- and disability-relevant issues now (Olkin, 1999, 2002) than they did in the past (Leung, Sakata, & Ostby, 1990; Spear & Schoepke, 1981).

An understandable shift to guidelines for training experiences at the internship and postdoctoral level initially appeared promising (Patterson & Hanson, 1995). These training guidelines were particularly timely and congruent with the competencies identified by the American Board of Rehabilitation Psychology (ABRP; established under the auspices of the American Board of Professional Psychology; Hibbard & Cox, 2010). These competencies are contained in Table 26.3.

Table 26.3. Required and Supplemental Competencies for the American Board of Rehabilitation

Psychology
ASSESSMENT
Required
Adjustment to Disability: Patient
Adjustment to Disability: Family
Assessment of extent and nature of disability and preserved abilities
Assessment as it relates to educational and/or vocational capacities
Personality and emotional assessment

(Continued)

Table 26.3. Continued

Cognitive testing

Competency evaluation

Sexual functioning assessment

Pain assessment

Substance use/abuse

Social and behavioral functioning assessment

INTERVENTION

Required

Individual therapeutic intervention as it relates to adjustment to disability

Family/couples therapeutic intervention as related to adjustment to disability

Behavioral Management

Sexual Counseling with disabled population(s)

Supplemental

Pain management

Cognitive retraining

Group therapeutic intervention as it relates to adjustment to disability

CONSULTATION

Required

Behavioral functioning improvement

Cognitive Functioning

Vocational and/or Education Considerations

Personality/Emotional Factors

Substance Abuse Identification and Management

Sexual Functioning and Disability

Supplemental

Improvements in physical functioning

Integration of assistive technology for enhancement of cognitive, sensory, and physical functioning

COMPETENCE IN CONSUMER PROTECTION

Required

State laws of practice

Laws related to and including ADA

APA Ethical Principles

(Continued)

Table 26.3. Continued

Awareness and sensitivity to multicultural and diversity factors
Issues related to patient confidentiality and privacy (e.g., HIPAA)
Supplemental
Advance directives/Wish to Die
Abuse/Exploitation (sexual, financial, physical, psychological)
Prevention e.g. Advocacy of legislative policy changes, Education
Establishment of Standards of Care/Practice in Rehabilitation
PROFESSIONAL DEVELOPMENT COMPETENCE
Required
Continuing education: must include documented CE credits in
rehabilitation psychology areas within the previous 2 years.
Supplemental
Professional presentation - local, state, national levels
Publications
Teaching
Involvement in advocacy groups
Gain expertise in related subspecialty areas (e.g., supervision, workshops)

The ABRP recognizes that qualified applicants may have an earned doctorate in clinical, counseling, or school psychology, neuropsychology, or health psychology (Hibbard & Cox, 2010). Therefore, the basic, fundamental skills underpinning these competencies ideally are acquired during doctoral training in any of these programs. The specific competencies unique to rehabilitation may be refined in internship and postdoctoral experiences.

Recent survey research suggests that relatively few internship and postdoctoral training programs are providing training experiences that meet the expectations for competency as delineated by the ABRP (Stiers & Stucky, 2008). These data also indicate that, among the responding programs that had outcome data, trainees were as likely to pursue board certification in clinical neuropsychology (15%) as in rehabilitation psychology (12%). Although current programs seem to be providing more training experiences in rehabilitation psychology principles and competencies than previously documented, the overall quality and type of training remains less than ideal, and perhaps too low to meet current labor demands and opportunities (Stiers & Stucky, 2008).

Clinical Practice
Populations Served

Rehabilitation psychologists provide services to individuals with a wide range of disorders typically encountered in medical rehabilitation settings, including traumatic injuries (e.g., SCI), catastrophic illness (e.g., cancer), and chronic disabling conditions (impaired vision, deafness and hearing loss; Scherer et al., in press; Warschausky, Kaufman, & Stiers, 2008). However, it is not uncommon for rehabilitation psychologists to cover a particular area or unit of an inpatient or outpatient setting representing a specific diagnostic group or to choose to specialize in work with one particular patient population (e.g., individuals with amputations, chronic pain, or brain injuries) or age group (e.g., children, older adults).

Conditions commonly addressed range from neurologic (e.g., traumatic brain injury [TBI], SCI, Guillain-Barré syndrome) to orthopedic (e.g., fractures, joint replacements) to general medical (e.g., HIV/AIDS, multiple sclerosis, vestibular disorders) to psychiatric (e.g., schizophrenia, major depression) to developmental (e.g., mental retardation, cerebral palsy) to any combination of these (e.g., polytrauma secondary to motor vehicle accidents). Conditions may be acute (e.g., stroke, TBI) or chronic (e.g., fibromyalgia, rheumatoid arthritis, diabetes), static, or progressive. Substance use disorders are considered elsewhere in this volume; however, they are certainly prevalent in medical rehabilitation settings (e.g., alcohol abuse, dependence on pain medication). Such disorders may contribute to the onset of disability, development of preventable secondary complications following disability (e.g., ER visits, infections, skin ulcers), and poor outcome (Heinemann, 1993). Regardless of type, severity, or duration of disability, people with disabilities may receive services from rehabilitation psychologists to help address limitations in psychological, familial, social, and vocational aspects of their lives due to physical, cognitive, and/or emotional aspects of their conditions.

Practice Settings

Rehabilitation psychologists practice in a wide variety of inpatient and outpatient settings that serve individuals with disabilities and chronic illnesses. Common settings are public and private acute- and postacute care hospitals, other postacute inpatient settings (i.e., skilled nursing facilities and intermediate care facilities), comprehensive outpatient rehabilitation facilities, specialty clinics (e.g., cardiac rehabilitation), and private practice, but also include schools, universities, nonprofit organizations, and state and federal agencies (Scherer et al., in press). In hospitals and other institutional practice settings, rehabilitation psychologists almost always work within interdisciplinary teams. Depending on the particular setting and the individual's needs, teams generally include some combination of the following disciplines: physiatrists (physicians specializing in rehabilitation medicine), nurses, physical therapists (PT), occupational therapists (OT), speech and language pathologists (SLP), social workers, audiologists, vocational counselors, and recreational therapists, as well as consulting physicians such as neurologists, orthopedists, psychiatrists, internists, and others (Strasser, Uomoto, & Smits, 2008).

Over the past 15 years, there has been a trend for rehabilitation resources to be reallocated from traditional acute and post-acute inpatient settings to outpatient and home-based programs (Elliott & Jackson, 2005). In addition, new initiatives such as telehealth approaches are being developed to augment ongoing treatment after discharge from acute and postacute treatment facilities and return to the community (Glueckauf et al., 2003). Individuals may qualify for educational and/or vocational assistance from state or private agencies that will then participate in the rehabilitation process.

Scope of Practice

Regardless of the specific disability or practice setting, the wide array of circumstances confronting individuals with disabilities demands a broad skill set and flexibility in the rehabilitation psychologist's approach. For example, in many general rehabilitation settings, on any given day, a psychologist may be engaged in consultation with nursing staff regarding behavioral management of a patient with TBI, offering supportive psychotherapy to a polytrauma patient grieving the loss of a loved one, and providing sexual counseling to the spouse of a patient with SCI with questions about sexual functioning. Consistent with the historical background of the field, rehabilitation psychologists routinely provide services informed by other academic and practice areas of psychology including, but not limited to, social, clinical, and counseling psychology; rehabilitation counseling; behavioral neuroscience; and neuropsychology. In their case conceptualizations, they balance traditional field-theory perspectives on disability (i.e., Wright, 1960, 1983) with an understanding of the major impact that preinjury behaviors (e.g., substance abuse) have on physical and psychological adjustment (cf. Elliott & Gramling, 1990).

In planning clinical services, rehabilitation psychologists are sensitive to issues of social stigmatization due to disability, confidentiality, and consumer protection (e.g., laws related to the Americans with Disabilities Act), as well as multicultural and diversity issues (e.g., race/ethnicity, age, gender, sexual orientation; Hanjorgiris, Rath, & O'Neill, 2004). In addition, they take into account limitations that may be imposed by such factors as geographic location, socioeconomic status, and architectural barriers; they are knowledgeable about, and recommend as necessary, relevant environmental modifications and assistive technologies, devices, products, and services.

Services typically provided by rehabilitation psychologists can be divided into three broad categories (Elliott & Gramling, 1990): assessment (e.g., psychological, neuropsychological, and psychosocial), intervention (e.g., counseling/psychotherapy, psychoeducation, behavioral management, family interventions, sexual counseling, cognitive remediation), and consultation (e.g., with interdisciplinary teams, primary caregivers, and/or outside parties and regulatory systems).

Assessment

Rehabilitation psychologists are involved in the formal psychometric assessment of intelligence, cognition, personality, mood, social functioning, and/or outcome. In addition, they use a variety of standardized and nonstandardized methods, including structured and unstructured interviews, rating scales, and questionnaires to assess aspects of adjustment such as extent and nature of disability, sexual functioning, pain level, and substance use. Regardless of the setting or specific disability, assessment often involves adaptations of traditional tests for patients with mobility and sensory limitations (e.g., Caplan & Shechter, 2008). Rehabilitation psychologists are thus acutely aware of, and skilled in, issues such as test selection, administration and interpretation issues, and threats to test validity that may exist in a given case. They use a flexible approach to balance proper test administration with effective accommodations for specific disabilities. A primary concern is making evaluation data relevant to the individual's functional life skills, including, but not limited to, educational and/or vocational capacities.

Inpatient rehabilitation settings typically require rapid assessment of cognitive and emotional functioning, preexisting and reactive psychopathology, and motivation for treatment. In situations in which the individual is experiencing extreme distress, the rehabilitation psychologist may be called upon to differentiate between situational and characterological sources of psychological symptoms. Especially in acute inpatient settings, but in other settings as well, rehabilitation psychologists also use both formal and informal methods to assess family and caregiver adjustment.

When developing treatment plans for individuals with cognitive deficits due to TBI, stroke, or other conditions that impact neurological functioning, rehabilitation psychologists typically employ a process approach to assess patients' strengths and limitations. A comprehensive neuropsychological evaluation typically is completed to identify specific cognitive deficits, preserved abilities, and measurable goals to guide treatment planning. Once again, a primary concern is making the assessment data relevant to the patient's functional life skills (Wilson, 1997).

Consultation

Rehabilitation psychologists routinely provide consultations regarding patient behavior, especially in inpatient settings. Consultations address such diverse issues as adherence to treatment regimens, behavioral disturbances, vocational potential, motivational issues, and family concerns (Elliott & Gramling, 1990). Rehabilitation psychologists provide guidance to the treatment team regarding the patient's specific learning style, needed accommodations, motivational needs, cognitive abilities, and emotional reactions. Such collaboration can help the interdisciplinary team establish realistic treatment goals.

Psychologists may consult individually with certain staff members or develop larger-scale psychoeducational interventions (see below) for staff. In many practice settings, rehabilitation psychologists formally communicate with team members during weekly meetings, but are available for informal consultation between meetings. In addition to working directly with interdisciplinary teams, rehabilitation psychologists play a key role in providing consultations to authorized outside parties, such as family members, attorneys, courts, governmental and social-service agencies, schools, employers, and insurance companies.

Intervention

In rehabilitation psychology practice, interventions focus on the provision of therapeutic strategies designed to assist individuals, their families, and primary support systems cope with, and adapt to, the effects of disability. Rehabilitation psychologists address the implications of disability in the context of the individual's life circumstances, both currently and developmentally, as the person's needs change over time. They are skilled in a variety of psychotherapeutic strategies and treatment options appropriate to various stages of adaptation to physical injury or disabling illness. Intervention techniques and modalities include, but are not limited to, individual and group counseling/psychotherapy, behavioral intervention/ management, cognitive remediation/rehabilitation, couples' counseling and family therapy, psychoeducation, sexual counseling, pain management, biofeedback, and clinical hypnosis.

In inpatient counseling/psychotherapy, the rehabilitation psychologist's interventions often are focused on facilitating psychological adjustment to new physical disability, traumatic injury, or catastrophic illness. Depending on theoretical orientation, the psychologist may incorporate psychodynamic formulations or learning theory, as well as specific cognitive-behavioral interventions (Chan, Berven, & Thomas, 2004). Regardless of orientation, rehabilitation psychologists stress the development of flexible coping and problem-solving approaches.

Throughout the course of treatment, rehabilitation psychologists tailor psychotherapeutic strategies and treatment options to the individual's stages of adaptation to injury or illness. For example, to further a patient's overall rehabilitation goals, the psychologist initially might focus on maintaining day-to-day motivation, but then later address issues of long-term adjustment to disability and future educational/vocational goals. Sexual counseling may include educational and counseling strategies to encourage communication, increase sexual pleasure, and lessen the impact of disability (Schover & Jensen, 1988). When providing sexual counseling services, rehabilitation psychologists are mindful not to limit their interventions to married couples or presume heterosexuality. Similarly, they are sensitive to the sexual concerns of individuals who are not in relationships and may be struggling with issues related to stigma and disability.

To address maladaptive behaviors, rehabilitation psychologists employee a variety of behavioral management techniques, such as positive reinforcement, shaping, time-outs, and modeling (Stoll, 2004). Behavioral intervention techniques may be especially useful in reducing impulsivity and improving self-control in patients with TBI, and addressing aggressive or disruptive behavior in general. When implementing behavioral management plans, rehabilitation psychologists typically work closely with interdisciplinary team members, including nursing, PT, OT, and SLP.

When working with individuals with TBI, stroke, and other conditions that affect brain function, rehabilitation psychologists typically employ cognitive remediation, a systematic intervention designed to improve functional abilities and increase levels of independence (Ben-Yishay & Prigatano, 1990). There are two general approaches to cognitive remediation: restoration and compensation (cf. Wilson, 1997). The restoration approach is based on the premise that repetitive exercise can restore compromised cognitive abilities. Techniques include visual and auditory exercises, numerical tasks, computer-assisted exercises, and feedback on performance, practice, and reinforcement. The compensation approach reinforces the individual's preserved cognitive strengths, while teaching strategies to circumvent (or compensate for) impaired cognitive abilities, with the goal of increasing independent functioning. Compensatory strategies include the use of cues, written instructions, notes, calendars, and date books, and electronic devices such as beepers and pagers. The individual is taught to minimize distractions, break complex tasks down into steps, and to self-monitor and self-regulate behavior. The two approaches are not mutually exclusive; both techniques are usually employed as necessary, depending upon the individual's needs (NIH Consensus Development Panel on Rehabilitation of Persons with TBI, 1999).

Disability and chronic illness affect not only the individual with the disability, but also the individual's primary caregivers and support systems. Rehabilitation psychology practice therefore includes provision of psychoeducational and counseling/psychotherapy services to family members and primary caregivers (Kosciulek, 2004; Padrone, 1999). Rehabilitation psychologists are proficient in engaging couples and families, and formulating and executing systemic interventions. Typical interventions might include stress management and/or problem-solving training (with emerging evidence from randomized clinical trials that these may be effectively provided in the home using long-distance technologies; Grant, Elliott, Weaver, Bartolucci, & Giger, 2002; Elliott, Brossart, Berry, & Fine, 2008; Rivera, Elliott, Berry, & Grant, 2008).

Rehabilitation psychologists offer psychoeducational services to provide family caregivers with specific information about the particular disability or chronic illness, along with skills for coping with their family member's disabling condition. Similarly, psychoeducational training programs may be provided for interdisciplinary team members to improve coping and practical skills. Psychoeducational groups also can be used to bring together individuals coping with the same type of disability or chronic illness. Learning that occurs through the group process of sharing similar concerns and strategies for overcoming them may be more effective than direct didactic transmission of information (Hale & Cowls, 2009).

Finally, rehabilitation psychologists may incorporate any number of specialized intervention methods tailored to individual patient needs. For example, when working with patients with chronic pain, rehabilitation psychologists may utilize clinical hypnosis or biofeedback, in addition to more routine pain and anxiety management treatment strategies (e.g., visualization, progressive muscle relaxation, diaphragmatic breathing). In some settings, biofeedback therapy may be provided for individuals with such diverse conditions as migraine, diabetes, Guillain-Barré syndrome, and fibromyalgia (e.g., Huyser, Buckelew, Hewett, & Johnson, 1997), as well as orthopedic and neurological cnditions such as SCI,

TBI, stroke, and cerebral palsy (e.g., Ince, Leon, & Christidis, 1987). Overall, across practice settings, rehabilitation psychologists use a broad skill set and a flexible approach while working with patients, families, and interdisciplinary teams to facilitate maximal functioning and adjustment.

Conclusion
Future Directions and Challenges
Throughout its history, rehabilitation psychology has been responsive to and shaped by contextual and economic events in larger society. It has maintained involvement in the larger interdisciplinary enterprise of rehabilitation (as conducted in medical settings, primarily). Unlike other psychological specialties, it is a long-time participant in policy-relevant activities with federal agencies (the National Institute of Disability Research and Rehabilitation, the Centers for Disease Control, the National Center for Medical Rehabilitation Research within NIH) and consumer groups (e.g., the Paralyzed Veterans of America). This rich heritage contributes to the resilience and far-reaching influence that rehabilitation psychology has demonstrated for several decades.

Undoubtedly, rehabilitation psychology also will be shaped by the current times and challenges. Current changes sweeping across the landscape of American health care are dramatic and uncompromising. The primary drivers of these changes will have a tremendous impact on professional psychology, generally, and rehabilitation psychology, specifically. The aging of the baby boomers in American society is one major factor, but this demographic trend does not account for other forces that are in play.

The number of people living with chronic health conditions in American society has increased steadily over the past 50 years. In fact, for the first time in the nation's recorded history, almost half of all Americans live with a chronic health condition (i.e., condition that lasts longer than a year, limits a person's activities, and may require ongoing medical care to manage symptoms), and almost half of this number has more than one condition (Partnerships for Solutions, 2004). This increase is due, in part, to drastic improvements in emergency care and technologies that have increased the likelihood of survival following motor vehicle accidents, acts of violence, and other forms of trauma. Some diseases, such as HIV/AIDS or Lyme disease, stem from infectious processes, but other chronic diseases (e.g., hypertension, heart disease, and diabetes) often have genetic predispositions that can increase susceptibility, with risk increased by behavioral and social factors. Pharmacological interventions have had a radical effect on increased longevity of life, permitting individuals to manage their symptoms and curtail disease progression. Similarly, advanced medical technologies have increased the life expectancy of persons with acquired and congenital physical disabilities.

People with chronic health conditions account for two-thirds of prescribed medication use, and they have the highest rates of hospitalization and office visits (Partnerships for Solutions, 2004). In 2001, the care they received accounted for 83% of all health care expenditures. Individuals with multiple chronic conditions account for 96% of Medicare expenditures. It should be noted that the majority of persons with chronic health conditions are of working age (younger than 65 years of age; Partnerships for Solutions, 2004). Persons who acquire physical disabilities (e.g., SCI, TBI) with considerable life expectancies often require life-long commitments from a family member to perform caregiving duties (Lollar & Crews, 2003). Therefore, the health and well-being of family caregivers—and the subsequent ability to assist their care recipients— is a public health priority (Talley & Crews, 2007). Healthy People 2010 (US Department of Health and Human Services, 2000) recognized the need for behavioral and social initiatives to promote the health and quality of life of persons with disabilities and their family caregivers.

Finally, the number of wounded veterans returning to society from the international conflicts in Iraq and Afghanistan present with conditions that may require a lifetime of assistance and health care service. Many returning service personnel from the Operation Iraqi Freedom/Operation Enduring Freedom theatres have documented problems with depression and posttraumatic stress disorder (PTSD). The rates of depression and PTSD are complicated further by the high incidence of acquired brain injuries incurred by personnel in these theatres: Depression is a common complication of acquired brain injury, and the high rate of concomitant PTSD with brain injury among returning personnel is without precedent in the extant literature. Increased anger, agitation, fatigue, and impulsivity commonly accompany these injuries. The veteran's decreased functioning and increased emotional fragility can be a source of immense distress for families. The loss of this supportive safety net may increase the vulnerability of the veteran and place a greater responsibility for care on the health system (Eibner, 2008). The long-lasting physical and emotional concomitants of these wounds will also tax social and legal services for some time (Stern, 2004; Tanielian, 2009).

In sum, the ensuing costs to American society are enormous. American health care systems are overwhelmed by the sheer number of persons presenting with chronic conditions, their accompanying behavioral and social needs (which may extend over the course of a lifetime), and the complexity of managing multiple symptoms across primary and specialty care. This dilemma has been called the "epidemic of survival" (Oeffinger, Eshelman, Tomlinson, & Buchanan, 1998). These factors, combined with the aging of the baby boom generation and the two wars, may "produce the largest population of persons with disabilities in this century" (Johnson, 2008, p. 182).

As in post-World War II America, the demand for professionals with expertise regarding behavioral and social issues in health care will exceed the available supply. Furthermore, the subsequent demands on health care systems to support and provide appropriate services will not sustain doctoral-level service provision at a rate required to meet the needs of these individuals and their families throughout urban, rural, and suburban American communities.

To meet these challenges, many rehabilitation psychologists may respond by embracing a more public health perspective of disability and other chronic health conditions (Elliott, 2002). Ideally, such a perspective is chiefly concerned with "large-scale behavior change to address social problems" and influence public policy in the process (McKnight, Sechrest, & McKnight, 2005, p. 559). Psychological science can be used to inform and direct decisions about meaningful policy, particularly when it demonstrates the potential for large-scale changes rather than relatively expensive, time-consuming, face-to-face interventions that involve doctoral-level service providers.

Consequently, programs will be developed to provide ongoing, community-based assistance that fully embraces the reality that an individual's lifestyle and day-to-day choices—and the immediate social factors that influence these behaviors—have more impact on the course of their health than do services offered by any single health profession (Glass & McAtee, 2006). This will necessitate a conscious move away from a patient-oriented "paternalistic" medical model of service delivery to one that promotes a "participatory ethic" (Mechanic, 1998, p. 283). This ethic is considered essential in

developing collaborative partnerships with people who live with disabilities and other chronic health problems, as it recognizes and seeks to empower their active role in their ongoing health and well-being (Israel, Schulz, Parker, & Becker, 1998). Effective program and policy development for persons with disabilities and their families may be realized when these people are recognized as experts on their service needs, and they can exercise an element of choice, control, and direction in the delivery of services (Kosciulek, 2000; Turnbull & Stowe, 2001). These programs will circumvent environmentally imposed limitations and restrictions that contribute to health disparities among persons with disabilities (Lollar, 2008). To be cost-effective, they will likely involve the use of low-cost, non–doctoral level service providers in programs administered and/or supervised by psychologists (Callahan, 2010).

The role of rehabilitation psychology in medical settings will likely entail more applications of neuropsychological skills, as illustrated in many of the ABRP competencies. These skills already are valued in the medical setting for assessment and consultation, but decreasing support and reimbursement for psychological interventions will limit therapeutic activities in the inpatient environment. As we have seen, many rehabilitation psychologists already have some identity with neuropsychology, and preliminary survey data indicate that postdoctoral trainees may place greater value on board certification in neuropsychology than rehabilitation psychology. At least one recent review of neuropsychological rehabilitation places heavy weight on neuropsychological practice with little or no reference to rehabilitation psychology's contributions to the area (Wilson, 2008), despite listing values that are remarkably similar to those historically espoused by rehabilitation psychology (e.g., Wright, 1972).

Rehabilitation psychologists who focus on community approaches and those who identify with certain medical specialties may have different reactions to the increasingly popular reconceptualization of disability defined in the International Classification of Functioning (ICF; World Health Organization, 2001). The ICF conceptualizes *disability* as an over-arching term that refers to any impairments, activity limitations, or participation restrictions, or "the outcome or result of a complex relationship between an individual's health condition and personal factors, and of the external factors that represent the circumstances in which the individual lives" (WHO, 2001, p. 17). This perspective places a greater recognition on the disabling features of the environment and the person–environment interaction in a fashion consistent with the social psychological heritage of rehabilitation psychology, and it is quite compatible with the views of most disability advocates (Pledger, 2003). However, it poses conceptual and practical challenges for many medical specialties that are dedicated in service and research to specific diagnostic conditions, and by extension, to those health professions that do likewise.

Psychologists who are wedded to medical specialties in research and in practice implicitly and explicitly embrace a medical model that champions assessment and diagnosis essential to the specialty practice, and promotes services deemed essential by the specialty. Community-residing consumers are more likely to prefer services that are accessible and meaningful to their everyday lives. With the steady influx of neuropsychologists into rehabilitation settings, it is likely that these psychologists will likely assume most of the rehabilitation psychology positions in medical settings along with other doctoral-level specialties that champion assessment, diagnosis, and expert interventions from medical perspectives. Psychologists who are more generalists in outlook and competence will be more likely to participate in public health programs to promote the health and well-being of community-residing individuals with disabling conditions, generally, regardless of the specific medical or psychological diagnosis, in a manner congruent with the ICF. These dynamics will undoubtedly shape the next iteration of the rehabilitation psychology specialty.

References

Allan, W. S. (1958). *Rehabilitation: A community challenge.* New York: Wiley.

Anthony, W. A., & Blanch, A. (1987). Supported employment for persons who are psychiatrically disabled: A historical and conceptual perspective. *Psychosocial Rehabilitation Journal, 11,* 5–23.

Barker, R. G., Wright, B. A., Meyerson, L., & Gonick, M. R. (1953). *Adjustment to physical handicap and illness: A survey of the social psychology of physique and disability.* New York: Social Science Research Council.

Ben-Yishay, Y., & Diller, L. (1983). Cognitive remediation. In M. Rosenthal, E. R. Griffith, M. R. Bond, & J. D. Miller (Eds.), *Rehabilitation of the head injured adult* (pp. 167–183). Philadelphia: F. A. Davis.

Ben-Yishay, Y., Diller, L., Gerstman, L. J., & Gordon, W. A. (1970). Relationships between initial competence and ability to profit from cues in brain damaged individuals. *Journal of Abnormal Psychology, 75,* 248–259.

Ben-Yishay, Y., & Prigatano, G. P. (1990). Cognitive remediation. In M. Rosenthal, E. R. Griffith, M. R. Bond, & J. D. Miller (Eds.), *Rehabilitation of the adult and child with traumatic brain injury* (2nd ed., pp. 393–409). Philadelphia: F. A. Davis.

Bond, G. R. (2004). Supported employment: Evidence for an evidence-based practice. *Psychiatric Rehabilitation Journal, 27,* 345–359.

Brucker, B. S. (1980). Biofeedback and rehabilitation. In L. P. Ince (Ed.), *Behavioral psychology in rehabilitation medicine: Clinical applications* (pp. 188–217). Baltimore: Williams & Wilkins.

Brucker, B. S., & Ince, L. P. (1977). Biofeedback as an experimental treatment for postural hypotension in a patient with a spinal cord lesion. *Archives of Physical Medicine and Rehabilitation, 58,* 49–53.

Brownsberger, M. G. (2003, Fall). Interview with Leonard Diller, Ph.D. *Division 22 Newsletter, 31*(1), 12–13.

Buchanon, R. (2003). Legislative warriors: American psychiatrists, psychologists, and competing claims over psychotherapy in the 1950s. *Journal of the History of the Behavioral Sciences, 39,* 225–249.

Callahan, C. (2010). Rehabilitating the health care organization: Administering psychology's opportunity. In R. G. Frank, M. Rosenthal, & B. Caplan (Eds.), *Handbook of rehabilitation psychology* (2nd ed., pp. 459–466). Washington, DC: American Psychological Association.

Caplan, B., & Shechter, J. (2008). Test accommodations for the geriatric patient. *NeuroRehabilitation, 23,* 395–402.

Chan, F., Berven, N. L., & Thomas, K. R. (Eds.). (2004). *Counseling theories and techniques for rehabilitation health professionals.* New York: Springer.

Cicerone, K. D., Dahlberg, C., Malec, J. F., Langenbahn, D. M., Felicetti, T., Kneipp, S., et al. (2005). Evidence-based cognitive rehabilitation: Updated review of the literature from 1998 through 2002. *Archives of Physical Medicine and Rehabilitation, 86,* 1681–1692.

Consortium for Spinal Cord Medicine. (1998). *Depression following spinal cord injury: A clinical practice guideline for primary care physicians.* Washington, DC: Paralyzed Veterans of America.

Cook, J. A., Leff, H. S., Blyler, C. R., Gold, P. B., Goldberg, R. W., et al. (2005). Results of a multisite randomized trial of supported employment interventions for individuals with severe mental illness. *Archives of General Psychiatry, 62,* 505–512.

Cook, J. A., Lehman, A. F., Drake, R., McFarlane, W. R., Gold, P. B., Leff, H. S., et al. (2005). Integration of psychiatric and vocational services: A multisite randomized, controlled trial of supported employment. *American Journal of Psychiatry, 162,* 1948–1956.

Cubbage, M. E., & Thomas, K. R. (1989). Freud and disability. *Rehabilitation Psychology, 34,* 161–173.

Dawis, R. V., & Lofquist, L. H. (1984). *A psychological theory of work adjustment.* Minneapolis: University of Minnesota Press.

Dembo, T., Leviton, G. L., & Wright, B. A. (1956). Adjustment to misfortune: A problem of social-psychological rehabilitation. *Artificial Limbs, 3*(2), 4–62.

Dijkers, M. P. J. M. for the NCDDR Task Force on Systematic Review and Guidelines. (2009). *When the best is the enemy of the good: The nature of research evidence used in systematic reviews and guidelines.* Austin, TX: SEDL. Retrieved from http://www.ncddr.org/kt/products/tfpapers/.

Diller, L. (2008, February). *Rehabilitation psychology: A subjective view.* Paper presented at the annual Rehabilitation Psychology conference, Jacksonville, FL.

Diller, L., & Weinberg, J. (1970). Accidents in hemiplegia. *Archives of Physical Medicine and Rehabilitation, 51,* 358–363.

Dunn, D. S. (2009). The social psychology of disability. In R. G. Frank, B. Caplan, & M. Rosenthal (Eds.), *Handbook of rehabilitation psychology* (2nd ed.). Washington, DC: American Psychological Association.

Dunn, D., & Elliott, T. R. (2005). Revisiting a constructive classic: Wright's Physical disability: A psychosocial approach. *Rehabilitation Psychology, 50*, 183–189.

Dunn, D., & Elliott, T. R. (2008). The place and promise of theory in rehabilitation psychology research. *Rehabilitation Psychology, 53*, 254–267.

Dunn, D. S., Uswatte, G., & Elliott, T. R. (2009). Happiness, resilience and positive growth following disability: Issues for understanding, research, and therapeutic intervention. In S. J. Lopez (Ed.), *The handbook of positive psychology* (2nd ed., pp. 651–664). New York: Oxford University Press.

Eibner, C. (2008, June). *Invisible wounds of war: Quantifying the societal costs of psychological and cognitive injuries.* Santa Monica, CA: Rand Corporation. Retrieved from http://www.rand.org/pubs/testimonies/CT309/.

Eisenberg, M., & Jansen, M. A. (1987). Rehabilitation psychologists in medical settings: A unique specialty or a redundant one? *Professional Psychology: Research and Practice, 18*, 475–478.

Elliott, T. R. (2007). Registering randomized clinical trials and the case for CONSORT. *Experimental and Clinical Psychopharmacology, 15*, 511–518.

Elliott, T. R., Brossart, D., Berry, J. W., & Fine, P. R. (2008). Problem-solving training via videoconferencing for family caregivers of persons with spinal cord injuries: A randomized controlled trial. *Behaviour Research and Therapy, 46*, 1220–1229.

Elliott, T. R., & Byrd, E. K. (1986). Frequently cited works, authors, and sources of research in Rehabilitation Psychology. *Rehabilitation Psychology, 31*, 112–115.

Elliott, T. R., Byrd, E. K., & Nichols, R. (1987). Influential publications and authors in contemporary rehabilitation counseling research. *Journal of Applied Rehabilitation Counseling, 18*(3), 45–48.

Elliott, T. R., & Gramling, S. (1990). Psychologists and rehabilitation: New roles and old training models. *American Psychologist, 45*, 762–765.

Elliott, T. R., & Jackson, W. T. (2005). Cognitive-behavioral therapy in rehabilitation psychology. In A. Freeman (Ed.), *Encyclopedia of cognitive behavior therapy* (pp. 324–327). New York: Springer Science + Business Media.

Elliott, T. R., & Kennedy, P. (2004). Treatment of depression following spinal cord injury: An evidence-based review. *Rehabilitation Psychology, 49*, 134–139.

Elliott, T. R., Kurylo, M., & Rivera, P. (2002). Positive growth following acquired physical disability. In C. R. Snyder, & S. J. Lopez (Eds.), *Handbook of positive psychology* (pp. 687–699). New York: Oxford University Press.

Elliott, T. R., & Leung, P. (2005). Vocational rehabilitation: History and practice. In W. B. Walsh, & M. Savickas (Eds.), *Handbook of vocational psychology* (3rd ed., pp. 319–343). New York: Lawrence Erlbaum Press.

Elliott, T. R., Uswatte, G., Lewis, L., & Palmatier, A. (2000). Goal instability and adjustment to physical disability. *Journal of Counseling Psychology, 47*, 251–265.

Elliott, T. R., & Warren, A. M. (2007). Why psychological issues are important. In P. Kennedy (Ed.), *Psychological management of physical disabilities: A practitioner's guide* (pp. 16–39). London: Brunner-Rutledge Press.

Emmons, R. A., & McCullough, M. E. (2003). Counting blessings versus burdens: An experimental investigation of gratitude and subjective well-being in daily life. *Journal of Personality and Social Psychology, 84*, 377–389.

Fine, M., & Asch, A. (1988). Disability beyond stigma: Social interaction, discrimination, and activism. *Journal of Social Issues, 44*, 3–21.

Fordyce, W. E. (1964). Personality characteristics in men with spinal cord injury as related to manner of onset of disability. *Archives of Physical Medicine and Rehabilitation, 45*, 321–325.

Fordyce, W. E. (1971). Behavioral methods in rehabilitation. In W. S. Neff (Ed.), *Rehabilitation psychology* (pp. 74–108). Washington, DC: American Psychological Association.

Fordyce, W. E. (1976). *Behavioral methods for chronic pain and illness.* Saint Louis, MO: C. V. Mosby Company.

Fordyce, W. E. (1988). Pain and suffering. *American Psychologist, 43*, 276–283.

Glass, T. A., & McAtee, M. (2006). Behavioral science at the crossroads in public health: Extending horizons, envisioning the future. *Social Science and Medicine, 62*, 1650–1671.

Glueckauf, R. L. (2000). Doctoral education in rehabilitation and health care psychology: Principles and strategies for unifying subspecialty training. In R. G. Frank, & T. R. Elliott (Eds.), *Handbook of rehabilitation psychology* (pp. 615–627). Washington, DC: American Psychological Association.

Glueckauf, R. L., Pickett, T. C., Ketterson, T. U., Loomis, J. S., & Rozensky, R. H. (2003). Preparation for the delivery of telehealth services: A self-study framework for expansion of practice. *Professional Psychology: Research and Practice, 34*, 159–163.

Glueckauf, R. L., & Quittner, A. L. (1992). Assertiveness training for disabled adults in wheelchairs: Self-report, role-play, and activity pattern outcomes. *Journal of Consulting and Clinical Psychology, 60*, 419–425.

Goffman, E. (1960). *Stigma: Notes on management of a spoiled identity.* Englewood Cliffs, NJ: Prentice Hall.

Gold, M. (1974). Breaking the expectancy cycle. *Education and Training of the Mentally Retarded, 9*, 37–40.

Goldstein, G. (2009). Neuropsychology in New York City (1930–1960). *Archives of Clinical Neuropsychology, 24*, 137–143.

Gordon, W. A., & Hibbard, M. R. (1991). The theory and practice of cognitive remediation. In J. Kreutzer, & P. Wehman (Eds.), *Cognitive rehabilitation for persons with traumatic brain injury: A functional approach* (pp. 13–22). Baltimore: Paul H. Brookes.

Grant, J., Elliott, T., Weaver, M., Bartolucci, A., & Giger, J. (2002). A telephone intervention with family caregivers of stroke survivors after hospital discharge. *Stroke, 33*, 2060–2065.

Grzesiak, R. (1979). Psychological services in rehabilitation medicine: Clinical aspects of rehabilitation psychology. *Professional Psychology, 10*, 511–520.

Grzesiak, R. C., & Hicock, D. A. (1994). A brief history of psychotherapy in physical disability. *American Journal of Psychotherapy, 48*, 240–250.

Hale, S., & Cowls, J. (2009). Psychoeducational groups. In I. Soderback (Ed.), *International handbook of occupational therapy interventions* (pp. 255–260). New York: Springer Science.

Hanjorgiris, W. F., Rath, J. F., & O'Neill, J. H. (2004). Gay men living with chronic illness or disability: A sociocultural, minority group perspective on mental health. In B. Lipton (Ed.),

Gay men living with chronic illnesses and disabilities: From crisis to crossroads (pp. 25–42). Binghamton, NY: Haworth Press.

Heinemann, A. W. (Ed.). (1993). *Substance abuse and physical disability*. Binghamton, NY: Haworth Press.

Hershenson, D. (1988). Along for the ride: The evolution of rehabilitation counselor education. *Rehabilitation Counseling Bulletin, 31*, 204–217.

Hibbard, M. R., & Cox, D. R. (2010). Competencies of a rehabilitation psychologist. In R. G. Frank, M. Rosenthal, & B. Caplan (Eds.), *Handbook of rehabilitation psychology* (2nd ed., pp. 467–475). Washington, DC: American Psychological Association.

Hoffman, H. G., Patterson, D. R., & Carrougher, G. J. (2000). Use of virtual reality for adjunctive treatment of adult burn pain during physical therapy: A controlled study. *The Clinical Journal of Pain, 16*, 244–250.

Hollingsworth, D. K., Johnson, W. C., Jr., & Cook, S. W. (1989). Beatrice A. Wright: Broad lens, sharp focus. *Journal of Counseling and Development, 67*, 384–393.

Horn, S. D., & Gassaway, J. (2007). Practice-based evidence study design for comparative effectiveness research. *Medical Care, 45*(10 Supplement 2), S50–S57.

Huyser, B., Buckelew, S. P., Hewett, J. E., & Johnson, J. C. (1997). Factors affecting adherence to rehabilitation interventions for individuals with fibromyalgia. *Rehabilitation Psychology, 42*, 75–91.

Ince, L. P. (1980). *Behavioral psychology in rehabilitation medicine*. Baltimore: Williams & Wilkins.

Ince, L. P., Brucker, B. S., & Alba, A. (1978). Reflex conditioning in a spinal man. *Journal of Comparative and Physiological Psychology, 92*, 796–802.

Ince, L. P., Leon, M. S., & Christidis, D. (1987). EMG biofeedback with the upper extremity: A critical review of experimental foundations of clinical treatment with the disabled. *Rehabilitation Psychology, 32*, 77–91.

Israel, B. A., Schulz, A. J., Parker, E. A., & Becker, A. B. (1998). Review of community-based research: Assessing partnership approaches to improve public health. *Annual Review of Public Health, 19*, 173–202.

Jansen, M. A., & Fulcher, R. (1982). Rehabilitation psychologists: Characteristics and scope of practice [Comment]. *American Psychologist, 37*, 1282–1283.

Jenkins, W. H., Patterson, J. B., & Szymanski, E. M. (1997). Philosophical, historical, and legislative aspects of the rehabilitation counseling profession. In R. M. Parker, & E. M. Szymanski (Eds.), *Rehabilitation counseling: Basics and beyond* (pp. 1–31). Austin, TX: Pro-Ed.

Johnson, W. G. (2008). There is a difference between differences and disparities. *Disability and Health Journal, 1*, 181–183.

Johnston, M. V. (2003). Desiderata for clinical trials in medical rehabilitation. *American Journal of Physical Medicine & Rehabilitation, 82*(10 Suppl.), S3–S7.

Katz, I., Farber, J., Glass, D. C., Lucido, D., & Emswiller, T. (1978). When courtesy offends: Effects of positive and negative behavior by the physically disabled on altruism and anger in normals. *Journal of Personality, 46*, 506–518.

King, C., & Kennedy, P. (1999). Coping effectiveness training for people with spinal cord injury: Preliminary results of a controlled trial. *British Journal of Clinical Psychology, 38*, 5–14.

Kleck, R. E. (1968). Physical stigma and nonverbal cues emitted in face to face interactions. *Human Relations, 21, 19–28*.

Kleck, R. E., Ono, H., & Hastorf, A. (1966). The effects of physical deviance upon face-to-face interaction. *Human Relations, 19*, 425–436.

Kosciulek, J. F. (2000). Implications of consumer direction for disability policy development and rehabilitation service delivery. *Journal of Disability Policy Studies, 11*(2), 82–89.

Kosciulek, J. F. (2004). Family counseling. In F. Chan, N. L. Berven, & K. R. Thomas (Eds.), *Counseling theories and techniques for rehabilitation health professionals* (pp. 264–281). New York: Springer.

Kunce, J. T., & Worley, B. H. (1966). Interest patterns, accidents, and disability. *Journal of Clinical Psychology, 22*, 105–107.

Larson, P., & Sachs, P. (2000). A history of Division 22. In D. A. Dewsbury (Ed.), *Unification through division: Histories of the divisions of the American Psychological Association* (pp. 33–58). Washington, DC: American Psychological Association.

Laurenceau, J. P., Hayes, A. M., & Feldman, G. C. (2007). Some methodological and statistical issues in the study of change processes in psychotherapy. *Clinical Psychological Review, 27*, 682–695.

Leung, P., Sakata, R., & Ostby, S. (1990). Rehabilitation psychology professional training: A survey of APA accredited programs. *Rehabilitation Education, 4*, 177–183.

Lewin, K. (1935). *A dynamic theory of personality*. New York: McGraw-Hill.

Lofquist, L. H. (1960). *Psychological research and rehabilitation*. Washington, DC: American Psychological Association.

Lollar, D. (2008). Rehabilitation psychology and public health: Commonalities, barriers, and bridges. *Rehabilitation Psychology, 53*, 122–127.

Lollar, D. E., & Crews, J. (2003). Redefining the role of public health in disability. *Annual Review of Public Health, 24*, 195–208.

Lucas, R. E. (2007). Long-term disability is associated with lasting changes in subjective well-being: Evidence from two nationally representative longitudinal studies. *Journal of Personality and Social Psychology, 92*, 717–730.

McGowan, J., & Porter, T. (1967). *An introduction to the vocational rehabilitation process: A training manual*. Washington, DC: U. S. Department of Health, Education, and Welfare, Vocational Rehabilitation Administration.

Mechanic, D. (1998). Public trust and initiatives for new health care partnerships. *The Milbank Quarterly, 76*, 281–302.

Meyerson, L. (Ed.). (1948). The social psychology of physical disability [Special Issue]. *Journal of Social Issues. 4*(4).

Miller, N. E., & Brucker, B. S. (1979). A learned visceral response apparently independent of skeletal ones in patients paralyzed by spinal lesions. In N. Birbaumer, & H. D. Kimmel (Eds.), *Biofeedback and self-regulation* (pp. 287–304). Hillside, NJ: Erlbaum.

Mueser, K. T., Clark, R. E., Haines, M., Drake, R. E., McHugo, G. J., Bond, G. R., et al. (2004). The Hartford Study of supported employment for persons with severe mental illness. *Journal of Consulting and Clinical Psychology, 72*, 479–490.

National Institutes of Health Consensus Development Panel on Rehabilitation of Persons With Traumatic Brain Injury. (1999). Rehabilitation of persons with traumatic brain injury. *JAMA, 282*, 974–983.

Neff, W. (1971). *Rehabilitation psychology*. Washington, DC: American Psychological Association.

Nosek, M. A., Howland, C. A., Rintala, D. H., Young, M. E., & Chanpong, G. F. (2001). National study of women with physical disabilities: Final report. *Sexuality and Disability, 19*(1), 5–39.

Oberman, C. E. (1965). *A history of vocational rehabilitation in America.* Minneapolis: T. S. Denison.

Oeffinger, K. C., Eshelman, D., Tomlinson, G., & Buchanan, G. R. (1998). Programs for adult survivors of childhood cancer. *Journal of Clinical Oncology, 16,* 2864–2867.

Olkin, R. (1999). *What psychotherapists should know about disability.* New York: Guilford Press.

Olkin, R. (2002). Could you hold the door for me? Including disability in diversity. *Cultural Diversity and Ethnic Minority Psychology, 8,* 130–137.

Olkin, R., & Pledger, C. (2003). Can disability studies and psychology join hands? *American Psychologist, 58,* 296–304.

Olshanksy, S., & Hart, W. R. (1967). Psychologists in vocational rehabilitation or vocational rehabilitation counselors? *Journal of Rehabilitation, 33*(2), 28–29.

Padrone, F. J. (1999). Treating family members. In K. G. Langer, L. Laatsch, & L. Lewis (Eds.), *Psychotherapeutic interventions for adults with brain injury or stroke: A clinician's treatment resource* (pp. 191–209). Madison, CT: Psychosocial Press.

Partnerships for Solutions. (2004). *Chronic conditions: Making the case for ongoing care.* Baltimore: Johns Hopkins University Press.

Patterson, D. R. (2005). Behavioral methods for chronic pain and illness: A reconsideration and appreciation. *Rehabilitation Psychology, 50,* 312–315.

Patterson, D. R., Everett, J. J., Burns, G. L., & Marvin, J. A. (1992). Hypnosis for the treatment of burn pain. *Journal of Consulting and Clinical Psychology, 60,* 713–717.

Patterson, D. R., & Hanson, S. (1995). Joint Division 22 and ACRM guidelines for post-doctoral training in rehabilitation psychology. *Rehabilitation Psychology, 40,* 299–310.

Peterson, D. B., & Aguiar, L. (2004). History & systems: United States. In T. F. Riggar, & D. R. Maki (Eds.), *The handbook of rehabilitation counseling* (pp. 50–75). New York: Springer.

Peterson, D. B., & Elliott, T. (2008). Advances in conceptualizing and studying disability. In R. Lent, & S. Brown (Eds.), *Handbook of counseling psychology* (4th ed., pp. 212–230). New York: Sage.

Pickren, W. E. (2005). Science, practice, and policy: An introduction to the history of psychology and the National Institute of Mental Health. In W. E. Pickren, & S. F. Schneider (Eds.), *Psychology and the National Institute of Mental Health: A historical analysis of science, practice, and policy* (pp. 3–15). Washington, DC: APA Books.

Pledger, C. (2003). Discourse on disability and rehabilitation issues: Opportunities for psychology. *American Psychologist, 58,* 279–284.

Rath, J. F., Simon, D., Langenbahn, D., Sherr, R., & Diller, L. (2003). Group treatment of problem-solving deficits in outpatients with traumatic brain injury: A randomized outcome study. *Neuropsychological Rehabilitation, 13,* 461–488.

Reed, G. M., Olkin, R., Spaulding, W. D., Elliott, T. R., Olivera Roulet, G., Di Nanno, A. E., et al. (in press). Psychological and counselling services. In *World report on disability and rehabilitation.* Geneva: World Health Organization.

Resch, J. A., Villareal, V., Johnson, C., Elliott, T., Kwok, O., Berry, J., & Underhill, A. (2009). Trajectories of life satisfaction in the first five years following traumatic brain injury. *Rehabilitation Psychology, 54,* 51–59.

Rivera, P., Elliott, T., Berry, J., & Grant, J. (2008). Problem-solving training for family caregivers of persons with traumatic brain injuries: A randomized controlled trial. *Archives of Physical Medicine and Rehabilitation, 89,* 931–941.

Rubin, S. E., & Roessler, R. T. (2001). *Foundations of the vocational rehabilitation process* (5th ed.). Austin, TX: Pro-Ed.

Rusalem, H. (1976). A personalized recent history of vocational rehabilitation in America. In H. Rusalem, & D. Malikin (Eds.), *Contemporary vocational rehabilitation* (pp. 29–45). New York: New York University Press.

Ryan, J. J., & Tree, H. A. (2004). Essential readings in rehabilitation psychology. *Teaching of Psychology, 31,* 138–140.

Scherer, M. J., Blair, K. L., Banks, M. E., Brucker, B., Corrigan, J., & Wegener, S. H. (2004). Rehabilitation psychology. In W. E. Craighead, & C. B. Nemeroff (Eds.), *The concise Corsini encyclopedia of psychology and behavioral science* (3rd ed., pp. 801–802). Hoboken, NJ: Wiley.

Scherer, M. J., Blair, K. L., Bost, R., Hanson, S., Hough, S., Kurylo, M., et al. (in press). Rehabilitation psychology. In I. B. Weiner, & W. E. Craighead (Eds.), *The concise Corsini encyclopedia of psychology and behavioral science* (4th ed.). Hoboken, NJ: Wiley. Forthcoming.

Schultheis, M. R., & Rizzo, A. A. (2001). The application of virtual reality technology in rehabilitation. *Rehabilitation Psychology, 46,* 296–311.

Schover, L. R., & Jensen, S. B. (1988). *Sexuality and chronic illness: A comprehensive approach.* New York: Guilford.

Shontz, F., & Wright, B. A. (1980). The distinctiveness of rehabilitation psychology. *Professional Psychology, 11,* 919–924.

Siller, J. (1969). Psychological situation of the disabled with spinal cord injuries. *Rehabilitation Literature, 30,* 290–296.

Siller, J. (1988). Intrapsychic aspects of attitudes toward persons with disabilities. In H. E. Yuker (Ed.), *Attitudes toward persons with disabilities* (pp. 58–67). Springer: New York.

Siller, J., Chipman, A., Ferguson, L. T., & Vann, D. H. (1967). *Attitudes of the nondisabled toward the physically disabled.* New York: New York University School of Education.

Spear, J., & Schoepke, J. (1981). Psychologists and rehabilitation: Mandates and current training practices. *Professional Psychology, 12,* 606–612.

Stern, J. M. (2004). Traumatic brain injury: An effect and cause of domestic violence and child abuse. *Current Neurology and Neuroscience Reports, 4,* 179–181.

Stiers, W., & Stucky, K. (2008). A survey of training in rehabilitation psychology practice in the United States and Canada: 2007. *Rehabilitation Psychology, 53,* 536–543.

Stoll, J. L. (2004). Behavior therapy. In F. Chan, N. L. Berven, & K. R. Thomas (Eds.), *Counseling theories and techniques for rehabilitation health professionals* (pp. 136–176). New York: Springer.

Strasser, D. C., Uomoto, J. M., & Smits, S. J. (2008). The interdisciplinary team and polytrauma rehabilitation: Prescription for partnership. *Archives of Physical Medicine and Rehabilitation, 89,* 179–181.

Talley, R. C., & Crews, J. E. (2007). Framing the public health of caregiving. *American Journal of Public Health, 97,* 224–228.

Tanielian, T. (2009). *Assessing combat exposure and post-traumatic stress disorder in troops and estimating the costs to society: Implications from the RAND invisible wounds of war study.* Santa Monica, CA: Rand Corporation. Retrieved from http://www.rand.org/pubs/testimonies/2009/RAND_CT321.pdf.

Taub, E., & Uswatte, G. (2000). Constraint-induced movement therapy based on behavioral neuroscience. In R. G. Frank, & T. R. Elliott (Eds.), *Handbook of rehabilitation psychology* (pp. 475–496). Washington, DC: American Psychological Association.

Thomas, J. P. (1995). The model spinal cord injury concept: Development and implementation. In S. L. Stover, J. DeLisa, & G. Whiteneck (Eds.), *Spinal cord injury: Clinical outcomes from the model systems* (pp. 1–9). Gaithersburg, MD: Aspen Publishers.

Thomas, K. R., & Associates. (1991). *Rehabilitation counseling: A profession in transition*. Athens, GA: Elliott & Fitzpatrick.

Thomas, K., & Parker, R. (1981). Promoting counseling in rehabilitation settings. *Journal of Applied Rehabilitation Counseling, 12*(2), 101–103.

Thomas, K., & Parker, R. (1984). Counseling interventions. *Journal of Applied Rehabilitation Counseling, 15*(3), 15–19.

Thomas, K. R., & Siller, J. (1999). Object loss, mourning, and adjustment to disability. *Psychoanalytic Psychology, 16*, 179–197.

Tucker, J. A., & Reed, G. (2008). Evidentiary pluralism as a strategy for research and evidence-based practice in rehabilitation psychology. *Rehabilitation Psychology, 53*, 279–293.

Turnbull, H. R., & Stowe, M. J. (2001). A taxonomy for organizing the core concepts according to their underlying principles. *Journal of Disability Policy Studies, 12*, 177–197.

U. S. Department of Health and Human Services. (2000). *Healthy people 2010*. Washington, DC: Author.

Vash, C. L. (1981). *The psychology of disability*. New York: Springer.

Wegener, S. T., Mackenzie, E. J., Ephraim, P., Ehde, D., & Williams, R. (2009). Self-management improves outcomes in persons with limb loss. *Archives of Physical Medicine and Rehabilitation, 90*, 373–380.

Wehman, P. (1988). Supported employment: Toward zero exclusion of persons with severe disabilities. In P. Wehman, & M. S. Moon (Eds.), *Vocational rehabilitation and supported employment* (pp. 3–16). Baltimore: Brookes Publishing.

Wehman, P., Sale, P., & Parent, W. (1992). *Supported employment: Strategies for integration of workers with disabilities*. Boston: Andover Medical Publishers.

Wilson, B. A. (1997). Cognitive rehabilitation: How it is and how it might be. *Journal of the International Neuropsychological Society, 3*, 487–496.

Wilson, B. A. (2008). Neuropsychological rehabilitation. *Annual Review of Clinical Psychology, 4*, 141–162.

World Health Organization. (2001). *ICF: International classification of functioning, disability and health*. Geneva, Switzerland: Author.

World Health Organization. (2002). *Innovative care for chronic conditions: Building blocks for action*. Geneva, Switzerland: Author.

Wright, B. A. (1959). *Psychology and rehabilitation*. Washington, DC: American Psychological Association.

Wright, B. A. (1960). *Physical disability: A psychological approach*. New York: Harper & Row.

Wright, B. A. (1972). Value-laden beliefs and principles for rehabilitation psychology. *Rehabilitation Psychology, 19*, 38–45.

Wright, B. A. (1980). Developing constructive views of life with a disability. *Rehabilitation Literature, 41*, 274–279.

Wright, B. A. (1983). *Physical disability: A psychosocial approach* (2nd ed.). New York: Harper & Row.

Wright, B. A. (1991). Labeling: The need for greater person–environment individuation. In C. R. Snyder, & D. R. Forsyth (Eds.), *Handbook of social and clinical psychology* (pp. 469–487). New York: Pergamon Press.

Wright, B. A., & Lopez, S. J. (2002). Widening the diagnostic focus: A case for including human strengths and environmental resources. In C. R. Snyder, & S. J. Lopez (Eds.), *Handbook of positive psychology* (pp. 26–44). New York: Oxford University Press.

Wright, G. N. (1980). *Total rehabilitation*. Boston: Little, Brown, & Co.

Yuker, H. E. (Ed.). (1988). *Attitudes toward persons with disabilities*. New York: Springer.

Yuker, H. E., & Block, J. (1986). *Research with the attitudes toward disabled persons scales*. Hempstead, NY: Hofstra University.

Yuker, H. E., Block, J., & Younng, J. (1966). *The measurement of attitudes toward disabled persons*. Albertson, NY: Human Resources Center.

School-based Prevention of Peer Relationship Problems

Dorothy L. Espelage *and* V. Paul Poteat

Abstract

Research on bullying, social/relational aggression, and prejudice are reviewed with some guidance for ways in which schools can begin to prevent these phenomena and how counseling psychology can enter the very important conversation that will lead to making our schools safer. Bullying is verbal, physical, or social in nature, and is seen as repeated acts of aggression that differs from normal peer conflict. Relational aggression includes behaviors that damage relationships and feelings of acceptance, friendship, or group inclusion, and that seeks to exclude a person from making or maintaining one or more relationships. Prejudiced attitudes toward student's racial/ethnic affiliation or sexual orientation are often used as a basis to exclude, harass, and humiliate. Recommendations are provided for school-based efforts to prevent these disruptive attitudes and behaviors.

Keywords: Bullying, social aggression, relational aggression, homophobia, racial prejudicial, school-based prevention

Children and adolescents face many psychosocial challenges, but perhaps at the forefront are the basic needs to develop a positive identity and to establish rewarding social relations with peers (Rubin, Bukowski, Parker, & Bowker, 2008). Interactions among peers are focused on the goal of developing mutual friendships, which sometimes involves establishing dominance through competitiveness and sometimes exclusion and teasing. As children enter adolescence, being accepted and "fitting in" are central goals that contribute to the establishment of social hierarchies (Rodkin, 2004). As such, children with less social power may develop feelings of anger and/or contempt toward peers, and these emotions can exacerbate rejection, bullying, and social aggression (Crick, Bigbee, & Howes, 1996; Espelage, Holt, & Henkel, 2003). In addition, the development of stereotypes, prejudiced attitudes, and engagement in discriminatory behavior also represent critical social issues that must be addressed

during the earlier developmental periods of childhood and adolescence (Aboud, 2005; Fishbein, 1996). Emerging findings have begun to note the interconnections between these two prominent issues of bullying and prejudice, including their combined impact on mental health, their similar associations with dominance and establishments of social hierarchies, and the influence that peers have on the socialization of attitudes and behaviors related to bullying and prejudice (D'Augelli, Pilkington, & Hershberger, 2002; Espelage et al., 2003; Pellegrini & Long, 2002; Poteat, 2007; Poteat, Espelage, & Green, 2007; Snyder et al., 2003).

Counseling psychologists are well-positioned to be strong assets to schools looking to develop prevention programs to address peer- and school-related adjustment issues. Although much work needs to be conducted to increase the presence of counseling psychology in school-based prevention and intervention work, there has been a growing trend for faculty and graduate students within counseling psychology programs across the United States to focus their research and practice on child/adolescent developmental issues. These scholars, who have expertise in theories of human development and employ a lens toward prevention, play a critical role in educating teachers, administrators, and parents about the importance of intervening early and often. Counseling psychologists also understand the importance of designing prevention programs that consider multiple contexts and are sensitive to individual differences (e.g., gender, race, socioeconomic status). Counseling psychologists can also play a direct role in improving the social and emotional climate in schools by influencing school policy and the implementation of outreach programs for students. Furthermore, Walsh, Galassi, Murphy, and Park-Taylor (2002) note the extraordinary expertise characteristic of counseling psychology—the knowledge base of multicultural issues—an especially critical area given the demographic changes in contemporary American schools. In this chapter, the research on bullying, social/relational aggression, and prejudice will be reviewed with some guidance for ways in which schools can begin to prevent these phenomena and how counseling psychology can enter the very important conversation that will lead to making our schools safer.

Bullying

Olweus spearheaded a nationwide Scandinavian campaign against bullying in the 1970s, and set forth the following definition of bullying, which remains current today: "A student is being bullied or victimized when he or she is exposed, repeatedly and over time, to negative actions on the part of one or more students" (Olweus, 1993). This definition highlights the aggressive component of bullying, its associated inherent power imbalance, and its repetitive nature. However, in recent years, scholars have recognized the wide range of behaviors consistent with bullying, including both physical and relational manifestations, cyber-bullying, and bullying in dating relationships. Smith and Sharp noted "a student is being bullied or picked on when another student says nasty and unpleasant things to him or her. It is also bullying when a student is hit, kicked, threatened, locked inside a room, sent nasty notes, and when no one ever talks to him" (Sharp & Smith, 1991, p.1). *Cyber-bullying* has emerged as a common occurrence among children and adolescents. Cyber-bullying has also been called: e-bullying, electronic bullying, cyberviolence, digital bullying, and the like. A recent definition of cyber-bullying posited by Ybarra and Mitchell (2004) is "intentional and overt act of aggression toward another person online."

PREVALENCE

Bullying may be the most prevalent type of school violence (Batsche & Porter, 2006). Worldwide incidence rates for bullying among school-aged youth range from 10% of secondary students to 27% of middle school students who report being bullied often (Whitney & Smith, 1993). Studies in the United States have yielded slightly higher rates of bullying, ranging from a low of 10% for "extreme victims" of bullying (Perry, Kusel, & Perry, 1988) to a high of 75% who reported being bullied at least one time during their school years (Hoover, Oliver, & Hazler, 1992). In a nationally representative study of American students in grades 6 through 10, Nansel and colleagues (2001) reported that 17% had been bullied with some regularity (several times or more within the semester) and 19% had bullied others. Bullying is not a part of normative development for children and adolescents and should be considered a precursor to more serious aggressive behaviors (Nansel et al., 2001).

Since Olweus' seminal work on bullying in Norway, significant changes have emerged in how children and adolescents interact with technology and how technology is used to bully others. For example, Pew Internet and American Life (2005) reported that 87% of U.S. teenagers (aged 12 through 17) currently use the Internet, and a Forrester report (2007) found that nearly 80% of youth between these same ages use MySpace (networking site) at least weekly. A more recent Pew Internet and American Life (2007) study reports that the preferred modality of communication is instant messaging (IM); 75% of teens between the ages of 12 and 17 years used IM and of these teens, 48% report using IM at least every day. These environments are social in nature; however, they do not involve face-to-face interactions. Thus, these social environments are not immune to the various negative interactions that are encountered in schools, families, and neighborhoods. Studies have found that 10% –33% of youth between the ages of 11 and 19 have experienced being the target of aggression/bullying online (Finn, 2004; Patchin & Hinduja, 2006), and more than 15% of youth reported being perpetrators of such behaviors (Patchin & Hinduja, 2006). The influx of technology in the lives of children and adolescents is a relatively new field, but it is likely that it will have a major impact on how teens interact with each other and may impact the development of social skills (see Swearer, Espelage, & Napolitano, 2009, for discussion).

ASSOCIATIONS WITH OUTCOMES

Bullying, in its many forms, is a serious problem that can harm students' school performance in the form of school avoidance, lower levels of academic achievement, and more conflictual relations with teachers and students. A recent study by Glew and colleagues (2005) found an association between certain bullying experiences and low academic achievement. Among third-, fourth-, and fifth-grade students, victims (adjusted odds ratio [AOR] 0.8; 95% confidence interval [CI] 0.7–0.9) and bully–victims (AOR 0.8; 95% CI 0.6–1.0) were less likely to be high achievers in school (measured by a composite score including reading, math, and listening) as compared to bystanders, although the finding for bully–victims was borderline significant (Glew, Fan, Katon, Rivara, & Kernic, 2005). A bully–victim is a child who is both a bully and a recipient of bullying behavior. A more recent study by Glew and colleagues (2008) of seventh-, ninth-, and eleventh-graders in an urban public school district found that for each 1-point rise in grade point average (GPA), the odds of being a victim versus a bystander decreased by 10% (Glew, Fan, Katon, & Rivara, 2008). A study of 930 sixth-graders in the first year of middle school found that students who were bullies, victims, or bully–victims showed poorer school adjustment (e.g., doing well on schoolwork, getting along with classmates, following rules, doing homework) than their uninvolved peers over three assessments into the end of the seventh grade (Nansel, Haynie, & Simons-Morton, 2003).

Bullying can also result in negative psychological, emotional, and behavioral outcomes. Victims, bullies, and bully–victims often report adverse psychological effects and poor school adjustment as a result of their involvement in bullying, which might also lead to subsequent victimization or perpetration (Juvoven, Nishina, & Graham, 2000). Nansel et al., 2003). For example, targets of bullying evidence more loneliness and depression, greater school avoidance, more suicidal ideation, and less self-esteem than their nonbullied peers (Hawker & Boulton, 2000; Kaltiala-Heino, Rimpelae, & Rantanen, 2001; Kochenderfer & Ladd, 1996; Olweus, 1992; Rigby, 2001). Whereas victims tend to report more internalizing behaviors, bullies are more likely than their peers to engage in externalizing behaviors like anger, to experience conduct problems, and to be delinquent (Haynie, Nansel, & Eitel, 2001; Nansel et al., 2001). Furthermore, long-term outcomes for bullies can be serious; compared to their peers, bullies are more likely to be convicted of crimes in adulthood in Norway/Sweden (Olweus, 1993). Bully–victims demonstrate more externalizing behaviors, are more hyperactive, and have a greater probability of being referred for psychiatric consultation than do their peers (Kumpulainen, Rasanen, & Henttonen, 1998; Nansel et al., 2001, 2003).

SCHOOL-BASED PREVENTION EFFORTS FOR BULLYING

Although some evaluation efforts of school-based prevention programs for bullying have offered promising findings, results of a recent meta-analysis of 14 whole-school antibullying programs provide a more modest assessment (Smith, Schneider, Smith, & Ananiadou, 2004). These programs were based on the Olweus Bullying Prevention Program (OBPP, Olweus, 1993), which has yet to demonstrate consistent efficacy within U.S. schools (as measured by being published in peer-reviewed journals). Results indicated that there were moderate effect sizes on self-reported victimization that students experienced from bullies (e.g., being teased, called names, shoved or hit) and small to negligible effects on self-reported bullying perpetration (e.g., teasing, name-calling, hitting or pushing others). The authors concluded that significant caution should be observed when implementing school-wide programs. However, very few of the studies under investigation looked beyond mean level differences and examined how effects varied across individuals and schools. Thus, Guerra, Boxer, and Cook (2006) called for the prevention field to examine potential moderators of effectiveness, including baseline levels of aggression among students, classroom practices that promote aggression, peer social status, and implementation rates.

Indeed, educators and researchers have been charged by the 2001 No Child Left Behind Act (NCLB) to use data to guide the selection of programs and implementation methods. Although 200 violence prevention programs are available, less than one-fourth of these are empirically validated (Howard, Flora, & Griffin, 1999). What has been learned to date is that zero-tolerance policies (policies that provide for punishment regardless of the basis of the problem behavior) are not effective in curbing aggressive behaviors (Casella, 2003), and expulsion appears to be equally ineffective (Morrison, Redding, Fisher, & Peterson, 2006). Thus, interventions that have been typically employed in school settings (group treatment, zero-tolerance, and expulsion) are ineffective in dealing with bullying.

Additionally, intervention programs designed to combat bullying have tended to allocate more resources to identifying individual bullies and addressing their behavior than to developing universal programs that address the entire student body. Furlong, Morrison, and Grief (2003) noted that, despite the value of taking a relational approach to bullying, most formalized legislation addressing bullying and peer aggression in schools continues to emphasize taking action with bullies to the exclusion of addressing the needs of victims or addressing the larger school climate. A relational approach dictates that responses to bullies need to rely less on the traditional punitive approach and more on targeting the patterns of behavior of both bullies and their victims, with attention to the noninvolved bystanders of the schools, as well as the classroom/school climate (Furlong et al., 2003; Orpinas & Horne, 2006).

As we become increasingly knowledgeable about how bullying overlaps with other problem behaviors, intervention strategies should consequently shift to a more comprehensive approach. Research has demonstrated that problem behaviors tend to be interrelated and share common risk factors (Donovan, Jessor, & Costa, 1991; Jessor, 1991), suggesting the need for prevention programs that implement a coordinated set of interventions to target and reduce overlapping risk factors, rather than programs that focus on specific problems or separate disorders (Kenny, Waldo, Warter, & Barton, 2002).

Rather than a discussion of specific bullying prevention or intervention programs, we provide general suggestions for program planning. Consistently, the effectiveness of a prevention/intervention program within a school environment relies on tailoring prevention to school needs. Therefore, the first suggestion is for school personnel to systematically assess the nature and frequency of the bullying and other forms of aggression that exists within their school. These data can be used to tailor the intervention efforts to address the unique aspects of the school. For example, one school might determine through an anonymous survey that students are engaging in bullying through text messaging. This school then might select a prevention program that addresses both within-school and online bullying experiences.

Many schools have to select from a number of marketed programs. Thus, a second suggestion is for schools to be smart consumers of these products.

Programs should be research-based, promote ethical behavioral principles, and advocate prosocial behavior and include skills training (Beard, Colvin, Hagan, Sprague, & Tobin, 1998). Prosocial behavior change includes promoting forgiveness and empathy, examining perceptions of the school climate and social hierarchy, and promoting problem-solving and social skills (Cupach & Willer, in press). Problem-solving skills training effectively reduces aggressive behaviors (Kazdin, 1996) and results in decreased reports of externalizing behaviors in schools (Rothman & Teglasi, 1999). Anger management is also important. Students reported that they believe they react to provocative instances less aggressively following anger management training (Dwivedi & Gupta, 2003). Programs should also be longitudinal and developmentally based, thus targeting behaviors common to each group. Finally, as schools are determining which programs to adopt, peer mediation strategies are counterproductive to their objective (Cavell & Hughes, 1999).

A third suggestion relates to how to address a specific bullying incident. When a specific bullying incident arises, it is essential to be mindful of the appropriate intervention techniques to utilize. Antibullying programs typically encourage interventions in a group model, but this method is not always successful (Dishion, McCord, & Poulin, 1999). Therefore, staff and counselors involved with the intervention must determine the need for a group- or individual-based intervention, depending on the specificity of the given situation. Typically, it is most effective for the counselor to assess separately each individual involved in a particular incident and subsequently evaluate the severity of the issue at hand; thereafter a decision may be better made regarding the potential effectiveness, and safety, of a group intervention. Whatever the preferred form of intervention, constant communication among staff members and counselors is crucial (Cupach & Willer, in press).

Regardless of the program adopted, some additional suggestions will increase the efficacy of the prevention program (Cupach & Willer, in press):

• Create an open-door policy for all students to report instances of bullying and aggression (emphasize confidentiality).
• Develop a uniform code of conduct for responding to incidents (this should address the need to intervene immediately).
• Create an open-door policy for teachers and staff to report instances.

- Train teachers and school counselors to address both incidents of victimization and the possible internalizing effects (i.e., depression, anxiety).
- Counselor interventions should include an assessment for anxiety and depression in both perpetrator and target. Counseling should be individualized for each group involved in the aggression, including perpetrator, target, bystander, and supportive bystander.
- Include bullying topics in educational curricula whenever applicable.

Relational Aggression

Three subcategories of nonphysical aggressive behavior have been noted in the literature: relational, indirect, and social. The term "relational aggression" was initially used to describe the bullying behaviors of female adolescents that primarily focused on damaging a peer's social connections within a given peer group (Crick & Grotpeter, 1995). Relational aggression includes acts that "harm others through damage (or the threat of damage) to relationships or feelings of acceptance, friendship, or group inclusion" and seeks to exclude a person from making or maintaining one or more relationships (Bjoerkqvist, Kaukiainen, & Lagerspetz, 1992). Relationally aggressive behavior is defined by the use of a relationship as a weapon or collateral. The threat of the destruction of the relationship by the perpetrator is inherent to the action taken against the target. Relational aggression includes behaviors such as friendship manipulation, social exclusion, negative gossip or backstabbing, using negative body language, and ignoring someone for vengeful reasons (Crick et al., 1996).

Socially aggressive behaviors intend to damage the social status of an individual within a peer group, or possibly within a greater environmental context (e.g., school, summer camp, etc.). Social aggression consists primarily of indirect forms of victimization, such as rumor spreading and social exclusion (Crick, 1996). The act of excluding an individual from normal peer activities and social relations is the key component to social aggression. It is distinct from both relational and indirect aggressive behaviors in that the relationship harm can result from both direct and indirect actions (Archer & Coyne, 2005) and may include nonverbal forms of exclusion (Galen & Underwood, 1997). However, as a result of the overlap of behavioral characteristics, relational aggression and social aggression are in many aspects synonymous, and therefore will be combined unless otherwise stated for the remainder of this chapter. Children's and adolescents' preference for nonphysical aggression may surface when the costs of more direct targeting are high (e.g., punishment; Archer & Coyne, 2005). Both relationally and socially aggressive behavior tends to be subtle and insidious, often making the identification of the perpetrators difficult for observers.

In sum, social or relational forms of aggression can include rejection (e.g., relational termination, social ostracism), humiliation (e.g., pranks, actively undermining target), betrayal (e.g., revealing a peer's secret/revoking confidence, spreading false rumors), personal attack (e.g., insults, spiteful teasing, gossip), relational manipulation (e.g., flirting with target's boyfriend/girlfriend/romantic interest, disparaging target to this individual), relational depreciation (e.g., declining closeness or commitment), and cyberbullying (i.e., any of the aforementioned behaviors exerted via communication technologies).

PREVALENCE

In one of the earliest studies of relational aggression, Crick and Grotpeter (1995) found that 2% of boys and 17% of girls in grades 3 through 6 (n = 491) reported rates of relational aggression perpetration over 1 standard deviation above the mean. Among some 4,496 third-graders in Maine, 34% of the students reported being left out on purpose at least once a month (Silvernail, Thompson, Yang, & Kopp, 2000). Along with knowledge of the possible adverse effects on young people due to aggressive behaviors, it is crucial for educators to remain aware of certain indicators, or "red flags," that are apparent in the classroom and that may be a sign of relational and social aggression. A partial list of such indicators includes: negative body language or physical gestures toward an individual (e.g., pointing, whispering, laughing, eye-rolling, increase in glancing); covert, exclusive communication (e.g., note passing, texting, etc.); noticeable change in social groups (e.g., partner changing, group shifting, seating changes); noticeable change in potential target's mood, demeanor, expression, physicality; and decrease in class participation or GPA.

From the initial onset of research investigating nonphysical forms of aggression, those who spearheaded the studies focused solely on females' tendency toward the behavior. The results of these beginning studies showed that girls were more relationally victimized, whereas boys were more overtly, and often physically, victimized (Crick & Bigbee, 1998). When investigating the aggressive behavioral patterns of middle school students in Canada, the results indicated that males reported more acts of physical aggression than did other comparison groups (Craig, 1998). When asked what actions are instigated when there is intent to harm another, boys reported fewer accounts of typical relationally aggressive behaviors (Crick et al., 1996).

Other research results have shown that both boys and girls report equal frequencies of social aggression (Espelage, Mebane, Swearer, & Turner, 2004). In a recent study of the aggression trajectories of adolescents living in rural areas, it was found that boys perpetrated more physical aggression than did girls, but there was no difference in the perpetration of social aggression between boys and girls (Ennett, Foshee, Karriker-Jaffe, & Suchindran, 2008). However, girls tend to think about the instances of social aggression more frequently and were more distressed by them. Also, the instances of social aggression were more strongly related to girls' self-concepts than to those of boys' (Paquette & Underwood, 1999). Therefore, it appears that the effect of social and relational victimization is stronger for young females than for males, which might be related to the greater importance that girls place on their friendships in comparison to boys (Underwood, 2003).

Adolescents of both genders utilize sexualized peer abuse as a form of nonphysical aggression, specifically social aggression. Gossip and rumors can often target an individual's physical development, involvement in sexual relations, and general sexual experience and maturity (Levy, 2005). Adolescents have shown tendencies to utilize rumors of sexual activity, both heterosexual and homosexual in nature, as a way to ostracize and reject a classmate from his or her previous social standing within the school (Levy, 2005).

When working with children and adolescents in a classroom setting, it is imperative to not only observe and recognize victimizing behaviors but to possess the tools necessary to predict the behaviors before they come to fruition. With this in mind, recent research has focused on the influence peer and friendship groups have on a young person's likelihood to exhibit relational and social aggression. Although there are numerous studies documenting the socialization of bullying among friendship groups (Espelage et al., 2003 for an example), only a handful of studies examining this possible behavioral predictor exist for relational aggression. For girls, having a friend who exhibited high levels of relationally aggressive behavior predicted substantial increases in the target girls' relationally aggressive

behavior and joint exhibitions of this nonphysical aggression may in fact strengthen the relationship between the two girls: "When two friends collaborate in the use of relational aggression against another person . . . [it] might actually promote cohesiveness, or otherwise strengthen the ties between the two friends" (Crick & Werner, 2004, p. 499). Indeed, girls' friendship cohesion tends to be more strongly related to exclusive remarks and exclusive gestures than are boys' friendship cohesions. Also, the exclusivity of a peer relationship may be positively related to the pairing's involvement in relationally aggressive behaviors (Sebanc, 2003). This was especially true of girls' friendships. As young females strive to gain and maintain intimacy within their relationships, they tend to favor the social exclusion of others to uphold this intimacy. To girls, the more exclusive the relationship, the more unattainable for others, and thus the more prized. In a study of 406 7-year-old twins, a genetic–environment interaction was found for predicting social aggression; genetics plus friends' social aggressiveness had direct effects on children's tendency toward social aggression (Brendgen et al., 2008). These findings highlight the need to carefully observe children's and adolescents' peer involvements, as the relationships may indicate an affinity for certain negative social behaviors; therefore, teachers, administrators, and school personnel may be better able to prevent relational and social aggression in their classrooms.

ASSOCIATIONS WITH OUTCOMES

Knowledge and understanding of the possible effects and risks associated with relational and social aggression are critical for two reasons. First, calling attention to relational and social aggression highlights the urgency and severity of a behavior that has commonly been viewed as innocuous, or even "phase"-like. Second, possessing awareness of the possible correlating symptoms of such victimization or perpetration can better assist school personnel in identifying students involved in each. Children and adolescents who engage in relational and/or social aggression either as perpetrators or victims are at risk for developing social, behavioral, emotional, and academic problems, including peer rejection, depression, loneliness, and anxiety (Underwood, Galen, & Paquette, 2001). These youth may also be at risk for eating disorders, borderline personality as adults, substance abuse, school refusal, poor self-esteem, gang involvement, social isolation (Crick, Casas, & Nelson, 2002), and social withdrawal (Hodges & Perry, 1999). Peer victimization in kindergarten is connected to later loneliness and school avoidance (Kochenderfer & Ladd, 1996), whereas experiences of rejection and isolation predicted instances of social anxiety and depression (Abwender, Beery, Ewell, & Vernberg, 1992). Specifically in adolescent females, experiences of victimization can lead to self-injury (Levenkron, 1998) and potential involvement in dating violence (Downey & Purdie, 2000). It has been surmised that the victimization that may condition a young woman to remain passive in a relationally aggressive situation may influence her to become submissive in future, more physically and/or sexually threatening relationships.

Relational aggression is related to both social skills deficits and increased child psychopathology (see Crick & Zahn-Waxler, 2003). Moreover, recent research also demonstrates that relational aggression is associated with negative school outcomes. Relational aggression is associated with lack of school engagement, poor academic achievement, teacher–student conflict, and health-risk behaviors that are indirectly related to school performance (i.e., substance use) (Murray-Close, Ostrov, & Crick, 2007; Sullivan, Farrell, & Kliewer, 2006; Woods & Wolke, 2004). Additionally, exposure to relational aggression at school negatively impacts the social, emotional, and psychological climate of schools, resulting in students' perceiving school as unsafe (Boxer, Edwards-Leeper, Goldstein, Musher-Eizenman, & Dubow, 2003; Glew et al., 2008; Goldstein, Young, & Boyd, 2008) and leading to declines in classroom participation and increases in school avoidance over time (Buhs, Ladd, & Herald, 2006).

SCHOOL-BASED PREVENTION EFFORTS FOR SOCIAL AGGRESSION

The nature of relational and social aggression among children and adolescents is usually covert; thus, these behaviors can often remain all but invisible to teachers and school administrators (Underwood, 2003). Therefore, it is essential not only to assess and identify potentially aggressive situations as they arise, but to also implement appropriate preventative techniques within the school. Although there is a widespread acknowledgment of the short- and long-term consequences of bullying, the tendency of schools to address incidences as they arise allows more indirect aggression to go gravely unnoticed. Children and adolescents have also reported that, in many cases, schools' and adults' attempts at intervention may increase cases of social aggression rather than reduce them (Underwood, 2003).

Much of the research conducted on the sustainability and effectiveness of general bullying prevention programs has not specifically addressed relational aggression (Espelage & Swearer, 2003). Therefore, a need exists to develop more effective programming within schools that targets more covertly aggressive behaviors among students (Barton, Taiariol, & Yoon, 2004). Existing programs may be modified to specifically target socially and relationally aggressive behaviors. However, the research that has been done on relational and social aggression programs conveys the need for schools to develop systematic approaches to better prevent these behaviors.

The first systematic study of a theory-based social aggression prevention program (SAPP) for preadolescent girls in public schools found that the effort had a positive impact on students' social problem-solving ability (Cappella & Weinstein, 2006). Teachers reported that the implementation of this small-group curriculum increased the participants' prosocial behaviors. Researchers indicated that a concentrated focus on social conflict resolution skills, from various perspectives (including target, perpetrator, bystander), may significantly contribute to the success and productivity of such a program. It has also been noted that, when working with female adolescents, specifically, a focus on peer intervention and social assertiveness may help reduce relationally aggressive behaviors (Underwood, 2003). Data have also shown that in addition to addressing conflict resolution, programs should address students' aggressiveness within a social-cognitive information-processing framework (Boxer & Dubow, 2001).

M. Underwood, a leading scholar of social aggression, offers a developmental approach to the prevention of social aggression (Underwood, 2003). When working with preschool-aged children, Underwood stresses the importance of explicitly acknowledging the negative and unacceptable nature of social aggression, as children in this age bracket frequently report that socially aggressive behavior is often acceptable. This theory posits that the more children recognize the apparent wrongfulness of a certain behavior, the more likely they are to report it. With school-aged children, it is important to assist individuals to recognize their own paranoid and self-negative thinking in social situations, as young people often have the tendency to interpret benign instances as direct attacks. The most critical aspect of social aggression prevention is the promotion of positive assertiveness within peer relations. Children and adolescents should learn to express their needs and emotions in positive ways and to accept that relational conflict is natural (Underwood, 2003). Encouraging bystander and peer intervention may also help diminish the frequency and effects of victimization.

Addressing Prejudice Through School Programming

Childhood and adolescence have been considered critical and formative periods for the development and expression of stereotypes, prejudiced attitudes, and discriminatory behavior (Aboud, 2005; Fishbein, 1996). However, relative to the research conducted among adult populations, fewer studies and interventions have focused on prejudice among younger age groups. Increasingly, scholars have discussed the need for prejudice prevention and intervention programming during these earlier developmental periods (Bigler & Liben, 2006; Salzman & D'Andrea, 2001). Bigler and Liben (2006) argued that, although changing the stereotypes and prejudiced attitudes of children may be difficult, the level of difficulty in achieving this task can be even greater among adults. This underscores the need for a greater focus on both prevention and toward early development. Although programming can and should be provided across the multiple social settings in which children and adolescents interact, the school setting represents a particularly important and central social context considering the proportion of time most individuals spend in this environment, the degree of interaction among individuals, and the growing student diversity within school systems.

Specific to the school system, the expression of prejudice and the marginalization of racial and sexual minorities (i.e., lesbian, gay, bisexual, and transgender youth; LGBT) remains a prominent concern among administrators, students, practitioners, and policy makers. For example, legal cases involving homophobic victimization of sexual minority youth while at school have ruled school administrators as partially responsible for such occurrences (see American Civil Liberties Union, 2005, for a review of recent lawsuits). A number of students have labeled homophobic bullying as a form of sexual harassment (Fineran, 2002). Of the range of verbal content used as part of many bullying episodes, students have indicated homophobic language to be among the most disturbing to them (American Association of University Women, 2001; Thurlow, 2001). Policy makers and practitioners also have commented on the prevalence of prejudiced behavior and its effects

on students, while concomitantly noting the absence of established programs and policies within the schools that are specific to this social concern and the lack of resources that have been made available to racial and sexual minority students (Kosciw, Diaz, & Greytak, 2008; Muller, 2000).

An interdisciplinary approach is especially needed as counseling psychologists become more involved in providing school-based prevention and intervention services to address prejudice. This can include collaborating with scholars in related subdisciplines of psychology (e.g., developmental, school, social, or community psychology), as well as with scholars in other fields (e.g., social work or education). The growing attention to multicultural counseling competencies within the field of counseling psychology and its attention to best practices and guidelines for working with diverse clients (American Psychological Association, 2003) could significantly contribute to and inform the research and programming that has been conducted within related disciplines. Similarly, it is important for counseling psychologists to be aware of the current prevention and intervention programs that have been developed. In this section, we focus on two forms of diversity, sexual orientation and race, to highlight the current state of school-based intervention research and practice as it relates to prejudice.

Prejudiced Attitudes and Behavior in Schools

For counseling psychologists to provide effective school-based interventions to address prejudice, it is important to have some knowledge of the extent to which individuals hold prejudiced attitudes during earlier developmental periods, the general prevalence of prejudiced behavior among students, and the reasons why students engage in this behavior. In this section, we provide an overview of the extant research on each of these issues.

PREJUDICE DURING EARLY DEVELOPMENT

Few studies have been conducted to examine the development of and changes in prejudice among children and adolescents. Those studies examining homophobic attitudes have presented inconsistent findings with regard to age and grade differences. Among white adolescents, Hoover and Fishbein (1999) noted a trend in which students in grades 7 and 11 reported lower levels of homophobic attitudes than did students in grade 9. This suggested that an increase, followed by a decrease, in homophobic attitudes occurred during adolescence. However, only the difference between ninth- and eleventh-grade students was identified to be significant. A continued decreasing pattern also was noted between students in grade 11 and college students, although this difference also was not significant. In an earlier study testing for gender differences, Baker and Fishbein (1998) noted a nonsignificant trend among boys, in which boys in grade 11 reported more homophobic attitudes than did boys in grade 9. In contrast, girls in grade 11 reported lower homophobic attitudes than did girls in grade 9. More recently, Horn (2006) noted similar cohort differences among adolescents and young adults. Specifically, students in grade 10 reported more homophobic attitudes than did students in grade 12 or college students. This added support to the non-significant decreasing trend in homophobic attitudes noted by Hoover and Fishbein (1999).

Specific to racial and ethnic prejudice, Black-Gutman and Hickson (1996) found that Anglo-Australian children aged 7–9 reported less bias toward Aborigines than did children aged 5–6, and that children aged 10–12 reported greater perceived similarity between groups than did children in the youngest (i.e., ages 5–6 years) and middle (i.e., ages 7–9 years) age groups. However, the oldest age group did not differ significantly from the middle age group on negative evaluations of Aborigines. Also documenting age cohort differences, Nesdale and Brown (2004) found that, among Anglo-Australian 6-, 9-, and 12-year-old children, 6-year-old children reported more likability for an in-group (Anglo-Australian) member than an out-group (Chinese) member described in a vignette, whereas this difference was not evident among 12-year-old children. Furthermore, 12-year-old children remembered more positive traits of the out-group member compared to 6-year-old children. Although findings from studies examining homophobic and racist attitudes suggest the potential for changes in prejudiced attitudes across childhood and adolescence, the interpretation and validity of these findings remain limited due to cross-sectional design confounds. However, regardless of the specific patterns of change, the documentation of various levels of stereotyping, in-group preference, and prejudice among children and adolescents further indicates the need for school-based prevention programs to be developed and implemented during these early developmental periods.

PREVALENCE AND FUNCTIONS OF PREJUDICED BEHAVIOR

Many LGBT students continue to report experiencing victimization and discrimination while at school, including physical and verbal harassment, isolation and stigmatization, and physical assault (Kosciw et al., 2008; Pilkington & D'Augilli, 1995; Rivers, 2001). Despite attempts to address homophobia within the school system, rates of discrimination while at school have changed little over the past decade (Kosciw et al., 2008; Pilkington & D'Augelli, 1995). For example, in a recent national survey of LGBT youth, approximately 85% reported experiencing some form of bullying or harassment while at school (Kosciw et al., 2008). The most frequent specific forms of victimization experienced by LGBT youth have included name-calling, assault, rumor spreading, and teasing (82%, 60%, 59%, and 58%, respectively; Rivers, 2001). Most often, LGBT students report being bullied by groups of students, as opposed to single individuals (Rivers, 2001). Although research has focused primarily on homophobic bullying and the use of homophobic epithets among boys, studies have found that adolescent girls also engage in this behavior (Poteat & Espelage, 2005; Rivers, 2001). In addition to discrimination perpetuated by other students, LGBT youth report that school administrators, staff, and teachers can contribute to creating or perpetuating a negative school climate (Chesir-Teran, 2003; Sears, 1991). Level of perceived support and acceptance from teachers was a significant predictor of academic performance for sexual minority youth (Russell, Seif, & Truong, 2001). Finally, a majority of LGBT youth (64%) have reported feeling unsafe while at school (Kosciw, 2004).

Of equal importance to documenting the prevalence of prejudiced behavior among students is an understanding of its underlying function and intent. The use of homophobic and racist language and engagement in other forms of prejudiced behavior against marginalized groups of students can perhaps most clearly be seen as an expression of homophobic and racist attitudes. However, researchers also have noted that homophobic and racist language can serve multiple additional functions, which can include enforcing peer norms, gaining status and attention within peer groups, and establishing dominance hierarchies (Connolly, 2000; Guerin, 2003; Korobov, 2004; Phoenix, Frosh, & Pattman, 2003; Poteat & Espelage, 2005). Among children and adolescents, homophobic behavior often is used to assert their masculinity and heterosexuality, to challenge the masculinity of other boys, or to enforce gender-normative behavior among peers (Kimmel, 1997; Korobov, 2004; Phillips, 2007; Phoenix, Frosh, & Pattman, 2003; Plummer, 2001; Stoudt, 2006).

Based on these additional functions, students can be targets of homophobic epithets regardless of their actual or perceived sexual orientation. Male young adults have reported that their engagement in homophobic behavior during adolescence was not always a comment on the targeted individual's actual or perceived sexual orientation, but rather was intended to attack the targeted individual's masculinity (Plummer, 2001). However, it should be noted that students who identify as or who are perceived to be LGBT remain more frequently targeted than their heterosexual peers (Espelage, Aragon, Birkett, & Koenig, 2008; Poteat & Espelage, 2005). Similarly, the use of racist language has been documented within children's peer groups (Connolly, 2000), and adolescents use racist language as a way to gain the attention of their peers and in some situations to elevate their status within the peer group (Guerin, 2003). Guerin has noted that individuals can often minimize any potential repercussions of their use of racist language through humor (e.g., "it was only a joke"). However, research has consistently documented the seriousness of such behavior and its negative psychological and social effects on targeted individuals (Burchinal, Roberts, Zeisel, & Rowley, 2008; D'Augelli, Pilkington, & Hershberger, 2002; Mattison & Aber, 2007; Poteat, Aragon, Espelage, & Koenig, 2009).

Psychosocial Consequences of Prejudice in the Schools

The negative consequences of racism in the schools continue to be documented with regard to the academic performance and mental health of students of color (Burchinal et al., 2008; Mattison & Aber, 2007). Following the transition from elementary school to middle school, the expectation of experiencing racial discrimination was identified as a factor that could negatively impact the academic achievement and social adjustment among African American children (Burchinal et al., 2008). Similar findings have been documented among high school students, in whom the perception of a positive racial climate within the school was associated with better academic performance (Mattison & Aber, 2007). Higher reported internalizing and externalizing mental health and behavioral concerns also have been documented for African American students who experienced more frequent discrimination (Clark, Coleman, & Novak, 2004). Concurrently, however, scholars have noted that racial minority students frequently are under-represented and overlooked in the provision of school-based counseling

services (Muller, 2000). This disconnect represents an important area of service that could be provided by counseling psychologists.

Experiences of homophobic victimization can contribute to increased mental health and social concerns among sexual minority youth. A number of studies have documented concerns such as anxiety, depression, and suicidal ideation (D'Augelli et al., 2002; Herek, Gillis, & Cogan, 1999), stigmatization from peers (Nichols, 1999), and substance use (Garofalo, Wolf, Kessel, Palfrey, & DuRant, 1998; Jordan, 2000; Marshal et al., 2008). Yet, when sexual minority youth perceive the school climate to be positive, this can act as a buffer against the experience of negative psychological and social concerns (Espelage, Aragon, Birkett, & Koenig, 2008). Of interest, homophobic victimization also has been found to predict higher levels of psychosocial concerns among targeted heterosexual students (Poteat & Espelage, 2007).

However, scholars also have indicated the need for caution in how the psychological and social experiences of sexual minority youth are described and how comparisons to heterosexual youth are made (Poteat et al., 2009; Savin-Williams, 2001). Broad group comparisons between heterosexual and sexual minority youth, when significant, often are qualified by relatively small effect sizes (Poteat et al., 2009; Rosario, Schrimshaw, & Hunter, 2004; Williams et al., 2005). Similarly, a common limitation in many studies among sexual minority youth is the use of smaller convenience samples, and limited generalizability to the broader population of sexual minority youth (Savin-Williams, 2001, 2008). Scholars also have highlighted the need to consider the diversity within the sexual minority youth community with regard to the intersection of sexual orientation, gender, and racial identity (Balsam, Huang, Fieland, Simoni, & Walters, 2004; Poteat et al., 2009; Rosario et al., 2004). Programming could be more effective if tailored to the unique needs of specific subgroups within the sexual minority community, including sexual minority youth of color, bisexual and transgender youth, and youth who are questioning their sexual orientation identity (Hollander, 2000; Mulick & Wright, 2002; Poteat et al., 2009; Rosario et al., 2004).

Finally, additional research is needed with a greater emphasis on resilience for both racial minority and sexual minority youth. Counseling psychologists in particular have advocated strongly for this approach in both providing services for clients and in conducting research. Several factors promoting resilience have received attention in the literature, including various sources of social support (Anderson, 1998; Elias & Haynes, 2008; Hammack, Richards, Luo, Edlynn, & Roy, 2004; Li, Nussbaum, & Richards, 2007; Nesmith, Burton, & Cosgrove, 1999; Shin, Daly, & Vera, 2007), adaptive coping styles (Clauss-Ehlers, 2008; Yeh, Kim, Pituc, & Atkins, 2008), and positive self-esteem and identity development (Grossman & Kerner, 1998; Shin et al., 2007). The integration of resilience-based models in the development and provision of programming to address prejudice and its psychosocial effects within the schools could be a significant and distinct contribution made by counseling psychologists.

Types of School-based Interventions for Prejudice

School-based interventions and programs have targeted prejudiced attitudes and behavior using a variety of approaches grounded in the theoretical and empirical literature. Many interventions have been based on cognitive information-processing, social contact theories, and ecological models (e.g., Allport, 1954; Bronfenbrenner, 1977; Evans & Prilleltensky, 2007; Tajfel & Turner, 1979). The focus, strategies, and activities of intervention programs can vary according to the models on which they are based. For example, interventions grounded in cognitive theories attempt to decrease prejudice by changing cognitive schemas, the ways in which children categorize individuals into groups, how students encode and interpret social information about minority groups, and by correcting stereotypes (e.g., Aboud & Doyle, 1996; Bigler & Liben, 1992). Programs based on social contact encourage extended interpersonal interaction among students from different groups (e.g., sexual orientation, racial, or ethnic groups) and cooperative learning or group projects as part of the educational process (e.g., Molina & Wittig, 2006; Turner, Hewstone, & Voci, 2007; Walker & Crogan, 1998). Broader ecological approaches may include attention to factors at both the individual level and within the broader social context (Evans & Prilleltensky, 2007), such as attention to the overall school climate (Benner, Graham, & Mistry, 2008). Additional initiatives under this approach might extend beyond the immediate school environment to include family systems (e.g., addressing parental prejudiced attitudes) and the connections among schools and other community-based contexts in which students interact. Across these various approaches, it is important that prevention and intervention programming take into consideration relevant developmental factors during childhood and adolescence. Several authors have provided comprehensive reviews of the advances in cognitive and social development in general (e.g., Collins & Steinberg, 2006; Rubin, Bukowski, & Parker, 2006) and in relation to stereotyping and prejudice (e.g., Bigler & Liben, 2006) during these developmental periods. Counseling psychologists interested in developing prejudice prevention and intervention programs for children and adolescents should consult these resources to ensure that their activities and materials are developmentally appropriate.

A number of school-based interventions have been implemented and evaluated on their effectiveness to decrease prejudiced attitudes and behavior and to increase appreciation for diversity. Evaluation research has demonstrated that programs and interventions with either cognitive or social emphases have positive effects on reducing prejudiced attitudes (Aboud & Doyle, 1996; Aboud & Fenwick, 1999; Molina & Wittig, 2006; Pettigrew & Tropp, 2000; Turner et al., 2007; Walker & Crogan, 1998). From an 11-week classroom program among fifth-grade students that included group, dyadic, and individual activities, Aboud and Fenwick (1999) found that white students in the intervention group, who initially expressed high levels of racial prejudice, reported lower levels of prejudice 2 months after the intervention, whereas high-prejudiced white students in the control group did not report a decrease in their prejudiced attitudes. Also, low-prejudiced white students in the intervention group did not increase their prejudiced attitudes. Similarly, Aboud and Doyle (1996) found that white children, ages 8 through 11, who initially expressed high levels of racial prejudice later reported lower levels of prejudice after talking about racial issues with a friend who initially expressed low levels of racial prejudice. In addition to providing more structured programming, research also suggests that promoting positive cross-cultural friendships among students could contribute to lower prejudiced attitudes among children. Among elementary school students, Turner et al. (2007) found that self-disclosure and empathy expressed within cross-racial friendships were mediators of more positive racial attitudes among white children. Furthermore, because peers can contribute to the socialization of prejudiced attitudes during adolescence (Poteat, 2007), school-based interventions might focus specifically on developing programming that addresses intergroup relations within peer groups. Paluck (2006) found that providing diversity training to a select group of students led to some measurable positive effects on other students with whom these individuals interacted. Also, Molina and Wittig (2006) found that providing opportunities for personal interactions and social contact, and promoting interdependence among racially diverse groups of students can reduce prejudiced attitudes and facilitate the development of a common in-group identity among high school students.

The impact of Gay-Straight Alliances (GSAs) on levels of homophobia, discrimination against LGBT students, and academic achievement of LGBT students also has been examined (California Safe Schools Coalition, 2004; Lee, 2002; Russell, Kostroski, McGuire, Laub, & Manke, 2006). Students in schools with GSAs reported higher levels of perceived safety than did students in schools without GSAs (California Safe Schools Coalition, 2004). As these data suggest, the involvement of heterosexual student allies (e.g., heterosexual students who support their LGBT peers or counter the homophobic attitudes and behaviors of other peers in schools) can significantly contribute to creating safer schools and promoting understanding and appreciation of sexual minority youth among other students. However, although the process of ally development has been explored (Anzaldua, 2000; Broido, 2000), little research has been conducted on the effectiveness of ally training models for adolescents and the influence of heterosexual youth allies on reducing prejudice among peers. This highlights a current need in the school intervention literature addressing prejudice. Relative to the documentation of students' engagement in prejudiced behavior, less research has focused on students' engagement in antiprejudice and social justice behavior. Furthermore, students who reported that LGBT issues were included in school curriculum reported higher levels of perceived safety in school (Russell et al., 2006). Similarly, LGBT students who attended schools that had support groups reported lower victimization and suicidality (Goodenow, Szalacha, & Westheimer, 2006). Generally, interactive and experiential activities have greater effects on student attitudes and behaviors than do more didactic and less participatory curriculum and instruction (Slavin & Madden, 1979; Spencer, 1998; Turner & Brown, 2008).

School-based interventions also can involve working with minority group members. This approach has been grounded in several frameworks, such as participatory action and liberation and empowerment frameworks within psychology. Researchers involved in participatory action research work closely and in collaboration with participants to develop projects to address the issues relevant to the specific group of participants (Kidd & Kral, 2005). Similarly, empowerment and liberation frameworks focus on addressing both the structural forms of oppression and the empowerment of marginalized groups within society (Prilleltensky & Prilleltensky, 2003). These programs often focus on student empowerment, build critical awareness of institutional and cultural oppression, focus on healthy psychosocial development, and emphasize the strengths and resources available to students to buffer against the psychosocial risks associated with victimization and discrimination (Balcazar, Tandon, & Kaplan, 2001; Diemer, Kauffman, Koenig, Trahan, & Hsieh, 2006; Lee, 2002; McKown, 2005). For example, among a sample of predominantly racial minority students in an urban school, students who perceived support among their peers and other adults to challenge racism and sexism also reported greater critical consciousness of these issues (Diemer et al., 2006). In addition, researchers have commented on the positive effects of school-based psychoeducational dialogue groups in which students can discuss and process issues around race, such as racial identity development and experiences of discrimination (Candelario & Huber, 2002). Similarly, psychoeducational groups also have been proposed to promote social justice awareness and engagement for elementary school through high school students (Portman & Portman, 2002).

In addition to working with students, school-based intervention and training programs should involve administrators and teachers for a more comprehensive approach to prejudice reduction and prevention (McFarland & Dupuis, 2001; Pickett, 1995; Suyemoto & Tree, 2006; Walters & Hayes, 1998). These programs often include educational modules and activities intended to promote multicultural knowledge and awareness, empathy, and perspective-taking; to highlight terminology, relevant laws, and school policies regarding diversity and discrimination; and to identify effective ways to intervene when incidences of prejudice and discrimination occur (Cho & DeCastro-Ambrosetti, 2005; Paluck, 2006; Rivers, Duncan, & Besag, 2007). The provision of these training modules is also needed among preservice teachers (Cho & DeCastro-Ambrosetti, 2005). Cho and DeCastro-Ambrosetti found that classes addressing multicultural issues contributed to the development of multicultural awareness and knowledge among preservice teachers in a way that could inform their work with students in the school system. Researchers also have emphasized the importance for teachers and administrators to model appreciation and respect for diversity and multiculturalism for students within the school (Onyekwuluje, 2000). Furthermore, developmental research suggests that educators might reconsider how they use certain social categories among children. For example, the functional use of gender in classrooms (e.g., dividing the class according to gender or assigning individuals to groups based on gender) led to higher levels of occupational gender stereotyping among elementary school children in this condition compared to children in control group conditions (Bigler, 1995).

Intervention Programs and Resources

In this section, we provide information on several current programs and resources at the national level that have been used or are currently being tested as part of school-based interventions to address prejudice. Additional information about each program, as well as accessible materials for practitioners, students, teachers, and parents may be accessed through the website of each organization.

Many professional and nonprofit national organizations offer resources to address diversity issues and prejudice in the schools. Many of these organizations provide material targeted toward teachers and administrators, students, and parents. However, these materials also can be used by counseling psychologists and other mental health practitioners who are interested in providing programming around prejudice prevention and reduction in schools. Additionally, many of these organizations provide a range of resources tailored to be appropriate for elementary school students through high school students. The National Education Association (NEA; www.nea.org) provides resources and activities for a number of diversity topics and social issues around sexual orientation, race, gender, social class, and English-language learners. For example, this includes their *Diversity Toolkit*, which provides recommendations and activities that educators can use to promote appreciation for diversity and social justice within the school system. The Teaching Tolerance program (www.tolerance.org), formed through the Southern Poverty Law Center, also provides a substantial number of resources, including handbooks, curricula, and activities for teachers to use in classrooms to address prejudice and intergroup relations. Also, this program includes additional sections specifically for parents, children, and teenagers that discuss how to address prejudice, and these sections contain activities, stories, and news items related to diversity. For example, the parenting section includes the handbook, *Beyond the Golden Rule: A Parent's Guide to Preventing and Responding to Prejudice*. The Anti-Defamation League (ADL; www.adl.org/education) offers online educational material appropriate for use with children through adolescents that address various forms of prejudice and offer ways to build appreciation for diversity (e.g., A Classroom of Difference™ curriculum), as well as professional development material for educators. Their Curriculum Connections resources offer educators lesson plans and activities that can be used to address prejudice, diversity, and social justice. Examples of specific issues include bullying, racial diversity, religious diversity, Native Americans and Indigenous People, people with disabilities, and gender diversity.

One of the largest national organizations to provide educational resources and research on LGBT issues in the schools is the Gay, Lesbian, and Straight Education Network (GLSEN; www.glsen.org). Its research publications include the biennial National School Climate Survey (NSCS) and other research briefs on current LGBT issues in schools. Using a national sample of LGBT youth, the NSCS provides data on the prevalence of homophobia and homophobic bullying within the school system, while also including additional information on academic and mental health issues among LGBT youth, as well as the availability of school policies and support programs. The organization also provides resources such as lesson plans, training program kits, and various materials for educators, students, and parents that can be accessed through their website. Some cities have local GLSEN chapters that can be contacted for additional materials or training opportunities. Other prominent national organizations that include a focus on LGBT issues in schools include Parents, Families, and Friends of Lesbians and Gays (PFLAG; www.pflag.org) and the Human Rights Campaign (HRC; www.hrc.org). Current intervention and educational programming for LGBT issues include the Respect for All Project (www.groundspark.org) and the Welcoming Schools project (www.welcomingschools.org). Comprising the Respect for All Project are several educational films on LGBT issues in education (*It's Elementary*), homophobic bullying (*Let's Get Real*), family diversity (*That's a Family!*), and gender norms and homophobia (*Straightlaced*), as well as accompanying curricula and activity guides and workshops.

The Welcoming Schools pilot program was initiated through the HRC to address LGBT issues in elementary schools, and includes lesson plans, professional development for teachers and administrators, and additional educational resources for families.

Conclusion

Interactions with peers during childhood and adolescence are formative in the development of healthy relationships, a secure identity, and a strong, resilient personality. As noted in this chapter, children and adolescents are often exposed to bullying and relational aggression. Furthermore, bullying and other forms of aggression are often connected with prejudice. All of these are preventable, but it will take a concerted effort on the part of schools and communities to tackle these growing problems. Rather than seeing these phenomena in isolation, it is time that these peer-related problems are seen as symptomatic of school climates in which disrespect and exclusion are fostered by school-wide policies, lack of teacher/staff training, and ineffective teacher and staff responses to peer problems. Furthermore, future prevention and intervention efforts need to also consider how the school community is influenced by other social contexts, such as families, neighborhoods, and media.

It is time for counseling psychology to contribute to the research and practice of school-based prevention efforts. Indeed, Walsh and colleagues (2002) stated that, upon consideration of all the applied subfields within psychology, only school psychology emerges as one that has maintained an emphasis on K–12 education. This is unfortunate, given the strength of counseling psychologists in developing and evaluating large-scale investigations. Counseling psychology programs should include graduate coursework in human development, prevention science, and training in randomized clinical trials.

Future Directions

As highlighted throughout this chapter, there are many future directions for school-based prevention and intervention programming in relation to addressing aggression and prejudice. In this section, we review several of these directions for counseling psychologists.

Continued research is needed to evaluate prevention and intervention programs for their effectiveness. As part of this effort, clearer criteria and standards are needed for assessing and quantifying the degree of program effectiveness. This should also include the identification of the specific components of programs that contribute to their effectiveness, identifying the conditions under which programs are more effective, and for whom these programs are more effective. Generally stated, research is needed to identify the moderators of program efficacy.

Issues such as aggression and prejudice within the schools, far from being isolated and distinct problems, have complex associations with myriad other individual and social concerns (Clark et al., 2004; D'Augelli et al., 2002; Donovan et al., 1991; Jessor, 1991; Nansel et al., 2001). This necessitates the implementation of more comprehensive programming that also addresses common underlying risk and causal factors that contribute to the development and perpetuation of these interrelated concerns (Kenny et al., 2002). For example, programs addressing homophobic behavior would likely need to incorporate the discussion of a variety of issues that are associated with this behavior, including sexual minority stereotypes and homophobic attitudes, the pressure to conform to rigid expectations for gender-normative behavior, addressing its connection to bullying and aggression, and discussing how this behavior negatively affects all students.

Finally, as counseling psychologists become involved in school-based prevention and intervention, it is critical that we form committed and collaborative partnerships with school administrators, teachers, and students. Through both research and practice, counseling psychologists must attend to the unique needs of these schools, and translate our research into practice and services that will directly benefit the individuals within these schools. Walsh et al. (2002) have highlighted the importance of counseling psychologists becoming more involved in schools. Long-term partnerships are needed in this area, as our understanding of these social concerns within schools and the impact and efficacy of our programs cannot be determined based on single time point approaches. These long-term commitments can also contribute to addressing the impact of such programs on attitudes, behaviors, and mental health outcomes later in adulthood. Ultimately, the involvement of counseling psychologists in school-based intervention and prevention programming expands upon the growing commitment of our field to addressing social justice issues in our community and society.

References

Aboud, F. E. (2005). The development of prejudice in childhood and adolescence. In J. F. Dovidio, P. Glick, & L. A. Rudman (Eds.), *On the nature of prejudice: Fifty years after Allport* (pp. 310–326). Malden, MA: Blackwell Publishing.

Aboud, F. E., & Doyle, A. B. (1996). Does talk of race foster prejudice or tolerance in children? *Canadian Journal of Behavioural Science, 28,* 161–170.

Aboud, F. E., & Fenwick, V. (1999). Exploring and evaluating school-based interventions to reduce prejudice. *Journal of Social Issues, 55,* 767–786.

Abwender, D. A., Beery, S. H., Ewell, K. K., & Vernberg, E. M. (1992). Social anxiety and peer relationships in early adolescence: A prospective analysis. *Journal of Clinical Child and Adolescent Psychology, 21,* 189–196.

Allport, G. (1954). *The nature of prejudice.* Cambridge, MA: Addison-Wesley.

American Association of University Women. (2001). *Hostile hallways: Bullying, teasing, and sexual harassment in school.* Washington, DC: American Association of University Women.

American Civil Liberties Union. (2005, June 20). *Summary of school harassment lawsuits.* Retrieved August 5, 2008, from http://www.aclu.org/lgbt/youth/11898res20050620.html.

American Psychological Association. (2003). Guidelines on multicultural education, training, research, practice and organizational change for psychologists. *American Psychologist, 58,* 377–402.

Anderson, A. L. (1998). Strengths of gay male youth: An untold story. *Child and Adolescent Social Work Journal, 15,* 55–71.

Anzaldua, G. (2000). Allies. In M. Adams, W. J. Blumenfeld, R. Castaneda, H. Hackman, M. Peters, & X. Zuniga (Eds.), *Readings for diversity and social justice* (pp. 475–477). New York: Routledge.

Archer, J., & Coyne, S. M. (2005). An integrated review of indirect, relational, and social aggression. *Personality and Social Psychology Review, 9*(3), 212–230.

Baker, J., & Fishbein, H. (1998). The development of prejudice towards gays and lesbians by adolescents. *Journal of Homosexuality, 36,* 89–100.

Balcazar, F., Tandon, D., & Kaplan, D. (2001). A classroom-based approach for promoting critical consciousness among African American youth. *The Community Psychologist, 34,* 30–32.

Balsam, K. F., Huang, B., Fieland, K. C., Simoni, J. M., & Walters, K. L. (2004). Culture, trauma, and wellness: A comparison of heterosexual and lesbian, gay, bisexual, and two-spirit Native Americans. *Cultural Diversity and Ethnic Minority Psychology, 10,* 287–301.

Barton, E., Taiariol, J., & Yoon, J. S. (2004). Relational aggression in middle school: Educational implications of developmental research. *The Journal of Early Adolescence, 24*(3), 303–318.

Batsche, G. M., & Porter, L. J. (2006). Bullying. In G. G. Bear, & K. M. Minke (Eds.), *Children's needs III: Development, prevention, and intervention* (pp. 135–148). Washington, DC: National Association of School Psychologists.

Beard, K., Colvin, G., Hagan, S., Sprague, J., & Tobin, T. (1998). The school bully: Assessing the problem, developing interventions, and future research directions. *Journal of Behavioral Education, 8*(3), 293–319.

Bigler, R. S. (1995). The role of classification skill in moderating environmental influences on children's gender stereotyping: A study of the functional use of gender in the classroom. *Child Development, 66,* 1072–1087.

Bigler, R. S., & Liben, L. S. (1992). Cognitive mechanisms in children's gender stereotyping: Theoretical and educational implications of a cognitive-based intervention. *Child Development, 63,* 1351–1363.

Bigler, R. S., & Liben, L. S. (2006). A developmental intergroup theory of social stereotypes and prejudice. In R. Kail (Ed.), *Advances in child development and behavior Vol. 34* (pp. 39–89). New York: Academic Press.

Bjoerkqvist, K., Kaukiainen, A., & Lagerspetz, K. M. J. (1992). Do girls manipulate and boys fight? Developmental trends in regard to direct and indirect aggression. *Aggressive Behavior, 18,* 117–127.

Black-Gutman, D., & Hickson, F. (1996). The relationship between racial attitudes and social-cognitive development in children: An Australian study. *Developmental Psychology, 32,* 448–456.

Boxer, P., & Dubow, E. F. (2001). A social-cognitive information-processing model for school-based aggression reduction and prevention programs: Issues for research and practice. *Applied and Preventative Psychology, 10*(3), 177–192.

Boxer, P., Edwards-Leeper, L., Goldstein, S. E., Musher-Eizenman, D., & Dubow, E. F. (2003). Exposure to "low-level" aggression in school: Associations with aggressive behavior, future expectations, and perceived safety. *Violence and Victims, 18*(6), 691–704.

Benner, A. D., Graham, S., & Mistry, R. S. (2008). Discerning direct and mediated effects of ecological structures and processes on adolescents' educational outcomes. *Developmental Psychology, 44,* 840–854.

Brendgen, M., Boivin, M., Vitaro, F., Bukowski, W. M., Dionne, G., Tremblay, R. E., & Perusse, D. (2008). Linkages between children's and their friends' social and physical aggression: Evidence for a gene-environment interaction? *Child Development, 79*(1), 13–29.

Broido, E. M. (2000). The development of social justice allies during college: A phenomenological investigation. *Journal of College Student Development, 41,* 3–18.

Bronfenbrenner, U. (1977). Toward an experimental ecology of human development. *American Psychologist, 32,* 513–531.

Buhs, E. S., Ladd, G. W., & Herald, S. L. (2006). Peer exclusion and victimization: Processes that mediate the relation between peer group rejection and children's classroom engagement and achievement? *Journal of Educational Psychology, 98*(1), 1–13.

Burchinal, M. R., Roberts, J. E., Zeisel, S. A., & Rowley, S. J. (2008). Social risk and protective factors for African American children's academic achievement and adjustment during the transition to middle school. *Developmental Psychology, 44,* 286–292.

California Safe Schools Coalition, & 4-H Center for Youth Development, University of California, Davis. (2004). *Consequences of harassment based on actual or perceived sexual orientation and gender non-conformity and steps for making schools safer.*

Candelario, N., & Huber, H. (2002). A school-based group experience on racial identity and race relations. *Smith College Studies in Social Work, 73,* 51–72.

Cappella, E., & Weinstein, R. (2006). The prevention of social aggression among girls. *Social Development, 15*(3), 434–462.

Casella, R. (2003). Zero tolerance policy in schools: Rationale, consequences, and alternatives. *Teachers College Record, 105,* 872–892.

Cavell, T. A., & Hughes, J. N. (1999). Secondary prevention as a context for assessing change processes in aggressive children. *Journal of School Psychology, 38,* 199–235.

Chesir-Teran, D. (2003). Conceptualizing and addressing heterosexism in high schools: A setting-level approach. *American Journal of Community Psychology, 31*, 269–279.

Cho, G., & DeCastro-Ambrosetti, D. (2005). Is ignorance bliss? Pre-service teachers' attitudes toward multicultural education. *The High School Journal, 89*, 24–28.

Clark, R., Coleman, A. P., & Novak, J. D. (2004). Initial psychometric properties of the everyday discrimination scale in black adolescents. *Journal of Adolescence, 27*, 363–368.

Clauss-Ehlers, C. S. (2008). Sociocultural factors, resilience, and coping: Support for a culturally sensitive measure of resilience. *Journal of Applied Developmental Psychology, 29*, 197–212.

Collins, W. A., & Steinberg, L. (2006). Adolescent development in interpersonal context. In N. Eisenberg, W. Damon, & R. M. Lerner (Eds.), *Handbook of child psychology: Vol. 3. Social emotional and personality development* (6th ed., pp. 1003–1067). Hoboken, NJ: John Wiley & Sons.

Connolly, P. (2000). Racism and young girls' peer-group relations: The experiences of South Asian girls. *Sociology, 34*, 499–519.

Craig, W. M. (1998). The relationship among bullying, victimization, depression, anxiety, and aggression in elementary school children. *Personality and Individual Differences, 24*, 123–130.

Crick, N. R. (1996). The role of overt aggression, relational aggression, and prosocial behavior in the prediction of children's future social adjustment. *Child Development, 67*, 2317–2327.

Crick, N. R., & Bigbee, M. A. (1998). Relational and overt forms of peer victimization: A multi-informant approach. *Journal of Consulting and Clinical Psychology, 66*, 337–347.

Crick, N. R., Bigbee, M. A., & Howes, C. (1996). Gender differences in children's normative beliefs about aggression: How do I hurt thee? Let me count the ways. *Child Development, 67*, 1003–1014.

Crick, N. R., Casas, J. F., & Nelson, D. A. (2002). Toward a more comprehensive understanding of peer maltreatment: Studies of relational victimization. *Current Directions in Psychological Science, 11*(3), 98–101.

Crick, N. R., & Grotpeter, J. K. (1995). Relational aggression, gender, and social-psychological adjustment. *Child Development, 66*, 710–722.

Crick, N. R., & Werner, N. E. (2004). Maladaptive peer relationships and the development of relational and physical aggression during middle childhood. *Social Development, 13*, 495–514.

Crick, N. R., & Zahn-Waxler, C. (2003). The development of psychopathology in females and males: Current progress and future challenges. *Development and Psychopathology: Special Issue on Conceptual, Methodological, and Statistical Issues in Developmental Psychopathology, 15*(3), 719–742.

Cupach, W. R., & Willer, E. K. (in press). When sugar and spice turn to fire and ice: Factors affecting the adverse consequences of relational aggression among adolescent girls. *Communication Studies*. Forthcoming.

D'Augelli, A. R., Pilkington, N. W., & Hershberger, S. L. (2002). Incidence and mental health impact of sexual orientation victimization of lesbian, gay, and bisexual youths in high school. *School Psychology Quarterly, 17*, 148–167.

Diemer, M. A., Kauffman, A., Koenig, N., Trahan, E., & Hsieh, C. A. (2006). Challenging racism, sexism, and social injustice: Support for urban adolescents' critical consciousness development. *Cultural Diversity and Ethnic Minority Psychology, 12*, 444–460.

Dishion, T. J., McCord, J., & Poulin, F. (1999). When interventions harm: Peer groups and problem behavior. *American Psychologist, 54*, 755–764.

Donovan, J. E., Jessor, R., & Costa, F. (1991). Adolescent health behavior and conventionality - unconventionality: An extension of problem-behavior theory. *Health Psychology, 10*, 2–61.

Downey, G., & Purdie, V. (2000). Rejection sensitivity and adolescent girls' vulnerability to relationship-centered difficulties. *Child Maltreatment, 5*, 338–349.

Dwivedi, K., & Gupta, A. (2003). Keeping cool: Anger management through group work. *Support for Learning, 15*, 76–81.

Elias, M. J., & Haynes, N. M. (2008). Social competence, social support, and academic achievement in minority, low-income, urban elementary school children. *School Psychology Quarterly, 23*, 474–495.

Ennett, S. T., Foshee, V. A., Karriker-Jaffe, K. J., & Suchindran, C. (2008). The development of aggression during adolescence: Sex differences in trajectories of physical and social aggression among youth in rural areas. *Journal of Abnormal Child Psychology, 36*(8), 1227–1236.

Espelage, D. L., Aragon, S. R., Birkett, M., & Koenig, B. W. (2008). Homophobic teasing, psychological outcomes, and sexual orientation among high school students: What influence do parents and schools have? *School Psychology Review, 37*, 202–216.

Espelage, D. L., Holt, M. K., & Henkel, R. R. (2003). Examination of peer-group contextual effects on aggression during early adolescence. *Child Development, 74*, 205–220.

Espelage, D. L., & Swearer, S. M. (2003). Research on school bullying and victimization: What have we learned and where do we go from here? *School Psychology Review, 32*, 365–383.

Espelage, D. L., Mebane, S. E., Swearer, S. M., & Turner, R. (2004). Gender differences in bullying: Moving beyond mean level differences. In D. L. Espelage, & S. M. Swearer (Eds.), *Bullying in American schools: A social-ecological perspective on prevention and intervention* (pp. 15–35). Mahwah, NJ: Erlbaum.

Evans, S. D., & Prilleltensky, I. (2007). Youth and democracy: Participation for personal, relational, and collective well-being. *Journal of Community Psychology, 35*, 681–692.

Fineran, S. (2002). Sexual harassment between same-sex peers: Intersection of mental health, homophobia, and sexual violence in schools. *Social Work, 47*, 65–74.

Finn, J. (2004). A survey of online harassment at a university campus. *Journal of Interpersonal Violence, 19*(4), 468–483.

Fishbein, H. D. (1996). *Peer prejudice and discrimination: Evolutionary, cultural, and developmental dynamics*. Boulder, CO: Westview Press.

Forrester Research. (2007, July 11). Retrieved October 23, 2007, from http://www.forrester.com/ER/Research/Survey/Excerpt/1,5449,535,00.html.

Furlong, M. J., Morrison, G. M., & Grief, J. L. (2003). Reaching an American consensus: Reactions to the special issue on school bullying. *School Psychology Review, 32*, 456–470.

Galen, B., & Underwood, J. K. (1997). A developmental investigation of social aggression among children. *Developmental Psychology, 33*, 589–600.

Garofalo, R., Wolf, R. C., Kessel, S., Palfrey, J., & DuRant, R. H. (1998). The association between health risk behaviors and sexual orientation among a school-based sample of adolescents. *Pediatrics, 101*, 895–902.

Glew, G. M., Fan, M., Katon, W., Rivara, F. P., & Kernic, M. A. (2005). Bullying, psychosocial adjustment, and academic performance in elementary school. *Archives of Pediatric Adolescent Medicine, 159*, 1026–1031.

Glew, G. M., Fan, M., Katon, W., & Rivara, F. P. (2008). Bullying and school safety. *The Journal of Pediatrics, 152*, 123–128.

Goldstein, S. E., Young, A., & Boyd, C. (2008). Relational aggression at school: Associations with school safety and social climate. *Journal of Youth and Adolescence, 37*(6), 641–654.

Goodenow, C., Szalacha, L., & Westheimer, K. (2006). School support groups, other school factors, and the safety of sexual minority adolescents. *Psychology in the Schools, 43*, 573–589.

Grossman, A. H., & Kerner, M. S. (1998). Self-esteem and supportiveness as predictors of emotional distress in gay male and lesbian youth. *Journal of Homosexuality, 35*, 25–39.

Guerin, B. (2003). Combating prejudice and racism: New interventions from a functional analysis of racist language. *Journal of Community and Applied Social Psychology, 13*, 29–45.

Guerra, N. G., Boxer, P., & Cook, C. R. (2006). What works (and what does not) in youth violence prevention: Rethinking the questions and finding new answers. In C. Hudley, & R. N. Parker (Eds.), *Pitfalls and pratfalls: Null and negative findings* (pp. 59–71). Monograph from New Directions for Evaluation, 110.

Hammack, P. L., Richards, M. H., Luo, Z., Edlynn, E. S., & Roy, K. (2004). Social support factors as moderators of community violence exposure among inner-city African American young adolescents. *Journal of Clinical Child and Adolescent Psychology, 33*, 450–462.

Hawker, D. S. J., & Boulton, M. J. (2000). Twenty years' research on peer victimization and psychosocial maladjustment: A meta-analytic review of cross-sectional studies. *Journal of Child Psychology and Psychiatry and Allied Disciplines, 41*, 441–455.

Haynie, D. L., Nansel, T., & Eitel, P. (2001). Bullies, victims, and bully/victims: Distinct groups of at-risk youth. *Journal of Early Adolescence, 21*, 29–49.

Herek, G. M., Gillis, J. R., & Cogan, J. C. (1999). Psychological sequelae of hate-crime victimization among lesbian, gay, and bisexual adults. *Journal of Consulting and Clinical Psychology, 67*, 945–951.

Hodges, E. V. E., & Perry, D. G. (1999). Personal and interpersonal antecedents and consequences of victimization by peers. *Journal of Personality and Social Psychology, 76*, 677–685.

Hollander, G. (2000). Questioning youth: Challenges to working with youths forming identities. *School Psychology Review, 29*, 173–179.

Hoover, J. H., Oliver, R., & Hazler, R. (1992). *Causal attributions: From cognitive processes to collective beliefs*. Oxford, UK: Blackwell.

Hoover, R., & Fishbein, H. D. (1999). The development of prejudice and sex role stereotyping in White adolescents and White young adults. *Journal of Applied Developmental Psychology, 20*, 431–448.

Horn, S. S. (2006). Heterosexual adolescents' attitudes and beliefs about homosexuality and gay and lesbian peers. *Cognitive Development, 21*, 420–440.

Howard, K. A., Flora, J., & Griffin, M. (1999). Violence-prevention programs in schools: State of the science and implications for future research. *Applied and Preventative Psychology, 8*, 197–215.

Jessor, R. (1991). Risk behavior in adolescence: A psychosocial framework for understanding and action. *Journal of Adolescent Health, 12*, 597–605.

Jordan, K. M. (2000). Substance abuse among gay, lesbian, bisexual, transgender, and questioning adolescents. *School Psychology Review, 29*, 201–206.

Juvoven, J., Nishina, A., & Graham, S. (2000). Self-views versus peer perceptions of victim status among early adolescents. In J. Juvonen, & S. Graham (Eds.), *Peer harassment in schools: The plight of the vulnerable and victimized* (pp. 105–124). New York: The Guilford Press.

Kaltiala-Heino, R., Rimpelae, M., & Rantanen, P. (2001). Bullying at school: An indicator for adolescents at risk for mental disorders. *Journal of Adolescence, 23*, 661–674.

Kazdin. A. E. (1996). Parent management training: Evidence, outcomes, and issues. *Journal of the American Academy of Child & Adolescent Psychiatry, 36*, 1349–1356.

Kenny, M. E., Waldo, M., Warter, E. H., & Barton, C. (2002). School-linked prevention: Theory, science and practice for enhancing the lives of children and youth. *Counseling Psychologist, 30*, 726–748.

Kidd, S. A., & Kral, M. J. (2005). Practicing participatory action research. *Journal of Counseling Psychology, 52*, 187–195.

Kimmel, M. S. (1997). Masculinity as homophobia: Fear, shame, and silence in the construction of gender identity. In M. M. Gergen, & S. N. Davis (Eds.), *Toward a new psychology of gender* (pp. 223–242). Florence, KY: Taylor & Frances.

Kochenderfer, B. J., & Ladd, G. W. (1996). Peer victimization: Cause or consequence of school maladjustment? *Child Development, 67*, 1305–1317.

Korobov, N. (2004). Inoculating against prejudice: A discursive approach to homophobia and sexism in adolescent male talk. *Psychology of Men and Masculinity, 5*, 178–189.

Kosciw, J. G. (2004). *The 2003 national school climate survey: The school-related experiences of our nation's lesbian, gay, bisexual, and transgender youth*. New York: GLSEN.

Kosciw, J. G., Diaz, E. M., & Greytak, E. A. (2008). *The 2007 national school climate survey: The experiences of lesbian, gay, bisexual, and transgender youth in our nation's schools*. New York: GLSEN.

Kumpulainen, K., Rasanen, E., & Henttonen, I. (1998). Children involved in bullying: Psychological disturbance and the persistence of the involvement. *Child Abuse & Neglect, 23*, 1253–1262.

Lee, C. (2002). The impact of belonging to a high school gay/straight alliance. *The High School Journal, 85*, 13–26.

Levenkron, S. (1998). *Cutting: Understanding and overcoming self-mutilation* (pp. 40–83). New York: W.W. Norton & Company, Ltd.

Levy, A. (2005). *Female chauvinist pigs: Women and the rise of raunch culture* (pp. 139–170). New York: Free Press.

Li, S. T., Nussbaum, K. M., & Richards, M. H. (2007). Risk and protective factors for urban African-American youth. *American Journal of Community Psychology, 39*, 21–35.

Marshal, M. P., Friedman, M. S., Stall, R., King, K. M., Miles, J., Gold, M. A., et al. (2008). Sexual orientation and adolescent substance use: A meta-analysis and methodological review. *Addiction, 103*, 546–556.

Mattison, E., & Aber, M. S. (2007). Closing the achievement gap: The association of racial climate with achievement and behavioral outcomes. *American Journal of Community Psychology, 40*, 1–12.

McFarland, W. P., & Dupuis, M. (2001). The legal duty to protect gay and lesbian students from violence in school. *Professional School Counseling, 4*, 171–179.

McKown, C. (2005). Applying ecological theory to advance the science and practice of school-based prejudice reduction interventions. *Educational Psychologist, 40*, 177–189.

Molina, L. E., & Wittig, M. A. (2006). Relative importance of contact conditions in explaining prejudice reduction in a classroom context: Separate and equal? *Journal of Social Issues, 62*, 489–509.

Morrison, G. M., Redding, M., Fisher, E., & Peterson, R. (2006). Assessing school discipline. In S. R. Jimerson, & M. Furlong (Eds.), *Handbook of school violence and school safety: From research to practice* (pp. 211–220). Mahwah, NJ: Erlbaum.

Mulick, P. S., & Wright, L. W. (2002). Examining the existence of biphobia in the heterosexual and homosexual populations. *Journal of Bisexuality, 2*, 45–64.

Muller, L. E. (2000). A 12-session, European-American-led counseling group for African-American females. *Professional School Counseling, 3*, 264–269.

Murray-Close, D., Ostrov, J. M., & Crick, N. R. (2007). A short-term longitudinal study of growth of relational aggression during middle childhood: Associations with gender, friendship intimacy, and internalizing problems. *Development and Psychopathology, 19*(1), 187–203.

Nansel, T. R., Haynie, D. L., & Simons-Morton, B. G. (2003). The association of bullying and victimization with middle school adjustment. *Journal of Applied School Psychology, 19*, 45–61.

Nansel, T. R., Overpeck, M., Pilla, R. S., Ruan, W. J., Simons-Morton, B. G., & Scheidt, P. (2001). Bullying behaviors among US youth: Prevalence and association with psychosocial adjustment. *Journal of the American Medical Association, 285*, 2094–2100.

Nesdale, D., & Brown, K. (2004). Children's attitudes towards an atypical member of an ethnic in-group. *International Journal of Behavioral Development, 28*, 328–335.

Nesmith, A. A., Burton, D. L., & Cosgrove, T. J. (1999). Gay, lesbian, and bisexual youth and young adults: Social support in their own words. *Journal of Homosexuality, 37*, 95–108.

Nichols, S. L. (1999). Gay, lesbian, and bisexual youth: Understanding diversity and promoting tolerance in schools. *The Elementary School Journal, 99*, 505–519.

Olweus, D. (1992). Bullying among schoolchildren: Intervention and prevention. In R. D. Peters, R. J. McMahon, & V. L. Quinse (Eds.), *Aggression and violence throughout the life span* (pp. 100–125). London: Sage.

Olweus, D. (1993). Bully/victim problems among schoolchildren: Long-term consequences and an effective intervention program. In S. Hodgins (Ed.), *Mental disorder and crime* (pp. 317–349). Thousand Oaks, CA: Sage.

Onyekwuluje, A. B. (2000). Adult role models: Needed voices for adolescents, multiculturalism, diversity, and race relations. *Urban Review, 32*, 67–85.

Orpinas, P., & Horne, A. M. (2006). *Bullying prevention: Creating a positive school climate and developing social competence.* Washington, DC: American Psychological Association.

Paluck, E. L. (2006). Diversity training and intergroup contact: A call to action research. *Journal of Social Issues, 62*, 577–595.

Paquette, J. A., & Underwood, M. K. (1999). Gender differences in young adolescents' experiences of peer victimization: Social and physical aggression. *Merrill-Palmer Quarterly, 48*.

Patchin, J. W., & Hinduja, S. (2006). Bullies move beyond the schoolyard: A preliminary look at cyberbullying. *Youth Violence & Juvenile Justice, 4*, 148–169.

Pellegrini, A. D., & Long, J. D. (2002). A longitudinal study of bullying, dominance, and victimization during the transition from primary school through secondary school. *British Journal of Developmental Psychology, 20*, 259–280.

Perry, D. G., Kusel, S. J., & Perry, C. L. (1988). Victims of peer aggression. *Developmental Psychology, 24*, 807–814.

Pettigrew, T. F., & Tropp, L. R. (2000). Does intergroup contact reduce prejudice? Recent meta-analytic findings. In S. Oskamp (Ed.), *Reducing prejudice and discrimination* (pp. 93–114). Mahwah, NJ: Lawrence Erlbaum Associates, Inc.

Pew Internet. (2005, July 25). *Teens forge forward with the Internet and other new technologies.* Retrieved October 23, 2007, from http://www.pewinternet.org/press_release.asp?r=109.

Pew Internet & American Life Project, February 15–March 7, 2007 http://www.pewinternet.org/trends/User_Demo_6.15.07.htm.

Phillips, D. A. (2007). Punking and bullying: Strategies in middle school, high school, and beyond. *Journal of Interpersonal Violence, 22*, 158–178.

Phoenix, A., Frosh, S., & Pattman, R. (2003). Producing contradictory masculine subject positions: Narratives of threat, homophobia, and bullying in 11–14 year old boys. *Journal of Social Issues, 59*, 179–195.

Pickett, L. (1995). Multicultural training workshops for teachers. *Transactional Analysis Journal, 25*, 250–258.

Pilkington, N. W., & D'Augelli, A. R. (1995). Victimization of lesbian, gay, and bisexual youth in community settings. *Journal of Community Psychology, 23*, 34–56.

Plummer, D. C. (2001). The quest for modern manhood: Masculine stereotypes, peer culture and the social significance of homophobia. *Journal of Adolescence, 24*, 15–23.

Portman, T. A. A., & Portman, G. L. (2002). Empowering students for social justice (ES²J): A structured group approach. *Journal for Specialists in Group Work, 27*, 16–31.

Poteat, V. P. (2007). Peer group socialization of homophobic attitudes and behavior during adolescence. *Child Development, 78*, 1830–1842.

Poteat, V. P., Aragon, S. R., Espelage, D. L., & Koenig, B. W. (2009). Psychosocial concerns of sexual minority youth: Complexity and caution in group differences. *Journal of Consulting and Clinical Psychology, 77*, 196–201.

Poteat, V. P., & Espelage, D. L. (2005). Exploring the relation between bullying and homophobic verbal content: The Homophobic Content Agent Target (HCAT) scale. *Violence and Victims, 20*, 513–528.

Poteat, V. P., & Espelage, D. L. (2007). Predicting psychosocial consequences of homophobic victimization in middle school students. *Journal of Early Adolescence, 27*, 175–191.

Poteat, V. P., Espelage, D. L., & Green, H. D. (2007). The socialization of dominance: Peer group contextual effects on homophobic and dominance attitudes. *Journal of Personality and Social Psychology, 92*, 1040–1050.

Prilleltensky, I., & Prilleltensky, O. (2003). Synergies for wellness and liberation in counseling psychology. *The Counseling Psychologist, 31*, 273–281.

Rigby, K. (2001). Health consequences of bullying and its prevention in schools. In J. Juvonen, & S. Graham (Eds.),

Peer harassment in school: The plight of the vulnerable and victimized (pp. 310–331). New York: Guilford Press.

Rivers, I. (2001). The bullying of sexual minorities at school: Its nature and long-term correlates. *Educational and Child Psychology, 18*, 32–46.

Rivers, I., Duncan, N., & Besag, V. E. (2007). *Bullying: A handbook for educators and parents.* Westport, CT: Praeger Publishers.

Rodkin, P. (2004). Peer ecologies and bullying. In D. L. Espelage, & S. M. Swearer (Eds.), *Bullying in American schools: A social-ecological perspective on prevention and intervention.* Mahwah, NJ: Erlbaum.

Rosario, M., Schrimshaw, E. W., & Hunter, J. (2004). Ethnic/racial differences in the coming-out process of lesbian, gay, and bisexual youths: A comparison of sexual identity development over time. *Cultural Diversity and Ethnic Minority Psychology, 10*, 215–228.

Rothman, L., & Teglasi, H. (1999). Stories: A classroom-based program to reduce aggressive behavior. *Journal of School Psychology, 39*, 71–94.

Rubin, K. H., Bukowski, W. M., & Parker, J. G. (2006). Peer interactions, relationships, and groups. In W. Damon, R. M. Lerner, & N. Eisenberg (Eds.), *Handbook of child psychology, volume 3, social emotional and personality development* (6th Ed., pp. 1003–1067). Hoboken, NJ: John Wiley & Sons.

Rubin, K. H., Bukowski, W. M., Parker, J. G., & Bowker, J. C. (2008). Peer interactions, relationships, and groups. In W. Damon, & R. Lerner (Eds.), *Child and adolescent development: An advanced course.* Hoboken, NJ: Wiley.

Russell, S. T., Kostroski, O., McGuire, J. K., Laub, C., & Manke, E. (2006). *LGBT issues in the curriculum promotes school safety. California Safe Schools Coalition research brief no. 4.* San Francisco: California Safe Schools Coalition.

Russell, S. T., Seif, H., & Truong, N. L. (2001). School outcomes of sexual minority youth in the United States: Evidence from a national study. *Journal of Adolescence, 24*, 111–127.

Salzman, M., & D'Andrea, M. (2001). Assessing the impact of a prejudice prevention project. *Journal of Counseling and Development, 79*, 341–346.

Sears, J. T. (1991). Educators, homosexuality, and homosexual students: Are personal feelings related to professional beliefs? *Journal of Homosexuality, 22*, 29–79.

Sebanc, A. M. (2003). The friendship features of preschool children: Links with prosocial behavior and aggression. *Social Development, 12*, 249–268.

Sharp, S., & Smith, P. K. (1991). Bullying in UK schools: The DES Sheffield bullying project. *Early Child Development and Care, 77*, 47–55.

Shin, R., Daly, B., & Vera, E. (2007). The relationships of peer norms, ethnic identity, and peer support to school engagement in urban youth. *Professional School Counseling, 10*, 379–388.

Silvernail, D. L., Thompson, A. M., Yang, Z., & Kopp, H. J. P. (2000). *A survey of bullying behavior among Maine third graders.* Retrieved February 20, 2005, from http://lincoln.midcoast.com/~wps/against/bullying.html.

Savin-Williams, R. C. (2001). Suicide attempts among sexual minority youths: Population and measurement issues. *Journal of Consulting and Clinical Psychology, 69*, 983–991.

Savin-Williams, R. C. (2008). Then and now: Recruiting, definition, diversity, and positive attributes of same-sex populations. *Developmental Psychology, 44*, 135–138.

Slavin, R. E., & Madden, N. A. (1979). School practices that improve race relations. *American Educational Research Journal, 16*, 169–180.

Smith, J. D., Schneider, B. H., Smith, P. K., & Ananiadou, K. (2004). The effectiveness of whole-school antibullying programs: A synthesis of evaluation research. *School Psychology Review, 33*(4), 547–560.

Snyder, J., Brooker, M., Patrick, M. R., Snyder, A., Schrepferman, L., & Stoolmiller, M. (2003). Observed peer victimization during early elementary school: Continuity, growth, and relation to risk for child antisocial and depressive behavior. *Child Development, 74*, 1881–1898.

Spencer, M. S. (1998). Reducing racism in schools: Moving beyond the rhetoric. *Social Work in Education, 20*, 25–36.

Stoudt, B. G. (2006). "You're either in or you're out": School violence, peer discipline, and the (re)production of hegemonic masculinity. *Men and Masculinities, 8*, 273–287.

Sullivan, T. N., Farrell, A. D., & Kliewer, W. (2006). Peer victimization in early adolescence: Association between physical and relational victimization and drug use, aggression, and delinquent behaviors among urban middle school students. *Development and Psychopathology, 18*(1), 119–137.

Suyemoto, K. L., & Tree, C. A. F. (2006). Building bridges across differences to meet social action goals: Being and creating allies among people of color. *American Journal of Community Psychology, 37*, 237–246.

Swearer, S. M., Espelage, D. L., & Napolitano, S. A. (2009). *Bullying prevention and intervention Realistic strategies for schools.* New York: Guilford Publications.

Tajfel, H., & Turner, J. C. (1979). An integrative theory of intergroup conflict. In W. G. Austin, & S. Worchel (Eds.), *The social psychology of intergroup relations* (pp. 33–48). Monterey, CA: Brooks Cole.

Thurlow, C. (2001). Naming the "outsider within": Homophobic pejoratives and the verbal abuse of lesbian, gay and bisexual high-school pupils. *Journal of Adolescence, 24*, 25–38.

Turner, R. N., & Brown, R. (2008). Improving children's attitudes toward refugees: An evaluation of a school-based multicultural curriculum and an anti-racist intervention. *Journal of Applied Social Psychology, 38*, 1295–1328.

Turner, R. N., Hewstone, M., & Voci, A. (2007). Reducing explicit and implicit outgroup prejudice via direct and extended contact: The mediating role of self-disclosure and intergroup anxiety. *Journal of Personality and Social Psychology, 93*, 369–388.

Underwood, M. K. (2003). Preventing and reducing social aggression among girls. *The Brown University Child and Adolescent Behavior Letter, 19*, 6–12.

Underwood, M. K., Galen, B. R., & Paquette, J. A. (2001). Top ten challenges for understanding gender aggression in children: Why can't we all just get along? *Social Development, 10*, 248–266.

Walker, I., & Crogan, M. (1998). Academic performance, prejudice, and the jigsaw classroom: New pieces to the puzzle. *Journal of Community and Applied Social Psychology, 8*, 381–393.

Walsh, M. E., Galassi, J. P., Murphy, J. A., & Park-Taylor, J. (2002). A conceptual framework for counseling psychologists in schools. *The Counseling Psychologist, 30*, 682–704.

Walters, A. S., & Hayes, D. M. (1998). Homophobia within schools: Challenging the culturally sanctioned dismissal of gay students and colleagues. *Journal of Homosexuality, 35*, 1–23.

Whitney, I., & Smith, P. K. (1993). A survey of the nature and extent of bullying in junior/middle and secondary schools. *Educational Research, 35,* 3–25.

Williams, T., Connolly, J., Pepler, D., & Craig, W. (2005). Peer victimization, social support, and psychosocial adjustment of sexual minority adolescents. *Journal of Youth and Adolescence, 34,* 471–482.

Woods, S., & Wolke, D. (2004). Direct and relational bullying among primary school children and academic achievement. *Journal of School Psychology, 42,* 135–155.

Ybarra, M. L., & Mitchell, K. J. (2004). Online aggressors/targets, aggressors, and targets: A comparison of associated youth characteristics. *Journal of Child Psychology and Psychiatry, 45,* 1308–1316.

Yeh, C. J., Kim, A. B., Pituc, S. T., & Atkins, M. (2008). Poverty, loss, and resilience: The story of Chinese immigrant youth. *Journal of Counseling Psychology, 55,* 34–48.

Counseling Health Psychology

Margit I. Berman *and* Larry C. James

Abstract

Although the involvement of counseling psychologists in health care has raised questions about our professional identity since the beginning of our field, counseling psychology has made important contributions to health. Counseling health psychologists have provided theory, interventions, and research initiatives to enhance primary care and the treatment of pain, chronic illness, and injury; improve physical rehabilitation; and augment care in cancer, HIV/AIDS, other life-threatening illnesses, and other health issues. Multicultural expertise, social justice values, and a focus on health promotion and disease prevention have distinguished counseling health psychology (CHP) as a developing field. A conceptual framework for CHP is presented, which draws upon core themes of positive health and wellness, patient-centeredness, and a systems perspective to make recommendations for theory, research, practice, and advocacy.

Keywords: counseling health psychology, health psychology, health promotion, disease prevention, wellness, positive health

Health care in the United States and throughout the world has changed dramatically since the birth of counseling psychology. In 1946, when Division 17 was formed, five of the top ten causes of death in the United States were either accidents, infections, or diseases associated with infection, such as nephritis (National Center for Health Statistics, n.d.). But medicine was rapidly changing: The fields of epidemiology and public health, and the biomedical model of disease—themselves only about a century old—were gathering steam. By 1946, young public health departments around the world were beginning to analyze statistics and change laws to prevent deaths by accident or infection—helped by vaccines for smallpox, anthrax, rabies, yellow fever, tuberculosis, and mumps, which by then had all been developed. Bacterial infections had a new enemy in the form of sulfa antibiotics. Penicillin was not yet widely available; polio was still a menace. Although psychologists played important roles in

helping people adjust to the effects of illness and injury (vocational rehabilitation of disabled returning soldiers was a major early activity for counseling psychologists), it may have seemed, in 1946, that there was little role for the new discipline in understanding or treating physical illness itself.

Today, however, the world has changed. Although acute infections remain a major killer both in the United States and worldwide, particularly in low-income countries, diseases with multiple causes and a chronic course, such as heart disease, stroke, chronic obstructive pulmonary disease, and lung cancer, now claim many more lives (World Health Organization, 2008). The role of behavioral variables, such as smoking, sexual behavior, psychological stress and strain, or failure to engage in positive self-care, are more evident in the current most common causes of death than they may have been when bacterial infections claimed millions of lives.

Several authors have observed that counseling psychologists have much to offer when it comes to improving health care in a complex world (Alcorn, 1991; Klippel & DeJoy, 1984), including holistic attention to the ecologies or systems in which an individual's health is embedded; a focus on human strengths, well-being, and the concept of "positive health" rather than the absence of disease; interest in diverse and underserved populations; and a developmental lifespan perspective. We also have specific skills that may be useful in enhancing health care, such as interpersonal and relationship-building skills that may enhance patient compliance, or behavioral interventions that may target health-related behaviors. Although the involvement of counseling psychologists in health care has raised questions about our identity as counseling psychologists and our interface with clinical psychology since the beginning of our field (cf. Scott, 1980), we believe that counseling psychology can make and in fact has made and continues to make an important contribution to human health.

With this thesis, in this chapter, we first summarize the history of counseling health psychology (CHP) and some of the major theoretical perspectives counseling psychologists have offered to understand human health and illness. We then present an overview of major health areas in which counseling psychologists are making contributions, including in primary care and in the understanding and treatment of specific diseases. Next, we consider two traditional areas of strength for CHP, specifically our attention to multicultural counseling and social justice issues related to health disparities, and our focus on positive health promotion and disease prevention. The chapter concludes with recommendations for research, training, and practice.

A Brief History of Counseling Health Psychology

Counseling psychologists have frequently considered professional involvement in health care, disease prevention and health promotion, or behavioral medicine activities as nontraditional or innovative activities, distinct from more typical professional roles. Some authors have even expressed concern that counseling psychologists working in health care settings may be subject to a loss of professional identity, given the distinct role they play and its differences from "traditional" counseling psychology (Mrdjenovich & Moore, 2004).

In fact, both professional involvement in health and medical care, and also professional tension and concern about the relevance of such involvement for counseling psychologists, have been present since the very beginnings of the field. In the original draft bylaws of Division 17, composed by John G. Darley and distributed to the provisional membership of the division in 1946, several purposes were delineated for the emerging division, including: "to collaborate with those clinical psychologists who are primarily attached to medical activities in arriving at definitions and working relationships between these related psychological specialties" (Scott, 1980). This aim captures both the presence of counseling psychologists in medical settings, and their multidisciplinary, diffuse, and sometimes problematic professional identity.[1]

Neither the presence of nor the tensions inherent to counseling psychologists in medical settings at the beginnings of our field should be surprising. It was in a medical setting—the Veterans Administration (VA) hospital system—that applied psychology, both counseling and clinical, developed (Cranston, 1986). After World War II, thousands of veterans returned with physical and psychiatric problems: 40,000 of them were hospitalized for psychiatric conditions alone. Millions of veterans applied for training under the G.I. Bill; about 10% of them had disabilities and would require additional rehabilitation and counseling. The need for psychological services was profound, and a VA-based training program in clinical psychology—a discipline that prior to that time served mainly children, not adults—was established in 1946. At the same time, counseling psychologists were providing vocational and personal guidance to healthy veterans through the VA system, as well as vocational rehabilitation services to disabled veterans, but their duties were largely limited to these more traditional counseling psychology tasks (Cranston, 1986).

In 1952, however, the VA launched a training program in counseling psychology similar to that offered 6 years earlier for clinical psychologists (Cranston, 1986). The launch of this formal training program, as well as a number of other concurrent and related changes in counseling psychology as a field, served to open up for counselors greater involvement in a variety of roles, including in health care and non-VA hospital settings. In 1953, Division 17 changed its name from the Division of Counseling and Guidance to the Division of Counseling Psychology, emphasizing a shift in focus away from educational and vocational guidance and toward broader roles (Scott, 1980). With the launch of the VA training program, the doctorate also became required for counseling psychology at the VA, with the rationale that only doctoral-level psychologists would be equipped to handle vocational rehabilitation for profoundly disabled veterans (Cranston, 1986), a move that emphasizes the link between counseling psychology's growth as a profession and our involvement with health and recovery. These changes were controversial: By the early 1960s, some Division 17 past presidents were lamenting the lack of distinction between clinical and counseling psychology and the loss of focus on more purely vocational or guidance concerns (Scott, 1980). Mitchell Dreese, president of Division 17 in 1952–1953, noted specifically that the fact that clinical psychologists practiced mainly in medical settings was one of the remaining thin lines of demarcation between the two fields (as cited in Scott, 1980).

Obscured in these early concerns about the demarcation of counseling and clinical psychology in health care was the soon-to-be-growing interest among psychologists of all kinds in applying psychological principles to health concerns. In 1969, William Schofield wrote a seminal *American Psychologist* article that launched the field of health psychology via the argument that psychology is a health science, and that applied psychologists were health professionals (Altmeier, Johnson, & Paulson, 1998; Matarozzo, 1980). In the 1970s, psychology as a whole took up his charge and became more significantly involved in health issues. The American Psychological Association (APA) established a task force on health research (chaired by Schofield). Division 18 began a section on health research that rapidly grew and was formally recognized as a division of its own (38; Health Psychology) in 1978. The first doctoral training program in health psychology was established in 1977, at the University of California, San Francisco. By the 1980s, psychologists were considering the definitions and limits of health psychology (Matarrozzo, 1980; Millon, 1982; Singer & Krantz, 1982), and training programs continued to grow, such that by the late 1990s, 50 institutions offered some formal training opportunity in health psychology (Altmeier, Johnson, & Paulson, 1998).

Meanwhile, the controversial line between clinical and counseling psychologists in the VA system grew even more diffuse. By the 1980s, VA counseling psychologists worked in all the same areas as clinical psychologists, with the possible exception of acute psychiatric care. Many of these new roles involved health care: By the 1980s, counseling psychologists in VA hospitals were working as generic health psychologists, as behavioral medicine specialists, in physical rehabilitation as well as vocational rehabilitation, in neuropsychology, in gerontology, in patient education, and in pain management, among other roles (Bernard, 1992). Counseling psychologists, like other psychologists, had begun to be interested in health care. The 1979 Annual Review of Psychology article on counseling included for the first time a section on "Health Related Outcomes" including issues such as insomnia, smoking cessation, chronic pain, and weight loss (Krumboltz, Becker-Haven, & Burnett, 1979). A chapter on health psychology was included, albeit in the "Special Issues and Emerging Areas" section, in the first edition of the *Handbook of Counseling Psychology* (Thoresen & Eagleston, 1984). The same authors wrote a major contribution on "Counseling for Health" for *The Counseling Psychologist* the following year (Thoresen & Eagleston, 1985).

In the midst of this scholarly activity within psychology, counseling psychologists with experience in health issues were beginning to emerge out of VA internships and postdoctoral fellowships into other hospital and health care settings. In longitudinal surveys of counseling psychology training programs, a consistent trend across time has been increasing placement of both predoctoral interns and counseling psychology graduates seeking their first jobs into hospital settings. This is not the result of growth in the VA system: The percentage of counseling psychologists completing internships or taking first jobs at VA settings has remained relatively steady since the 1970s, with about 20% of counseling psychology students having internship placements and about 5%–6% taking their first jobs in a VA hospital. Internships and first job placements in non-VA hospital settings, in contrast, have increased since the 1970s, such that by 1998, about 23% of counseling psychology interns were placed in non-VA hospital settings, and nearly 10% took their first jobs in such settings (Neimeyer, Bowman, & Stewart 2001). Counseling psychology has responded to this growth in health psychology with both excitement about the contributions counseling psychologists can make to health care (e.g., Alcorn, 1991; Altmeier, 1991), as well as fear of a loss of professional identity or a merger of counseling with clinical psychology (Fitzgerald & Osipow, 1986; Lent, 1990). At the institutional level, Division 17 has reflected the growth of CHP with the development and steady growth of a health psychology section. Bylaws for the Division 17 Health Psychology Section were developed in 1995;

by 2002, the section had 140 members (Mrdjenovich & Moore, 2004). Theoretical approaches to CHP have also developed along with this institutional growth, emphasizing a perspective on health concerns that provides a counterpoint to biomedical models of disease and pathology.

Theoretical Approaches to Counseling Health Psychology

Since the pathogenic theory of disease revolutionized medicine beginning in the mid-19th century, a biomedical model of disease and health has held sway among physicians and in hospitals, and for good reason. But as diseases caused by pathogens have succumbed, at least in part, to the incredible advances in medication, vaccination, hygiene, and public health made possible by the biomedical model, physicians and researchers have identified the limits of this model for understanding illness and wellness, and have articulated the need for a more holistic model of medicine that incorporates psychosocial and biomedical aspects of health (Engel, 1977; Schwartz, 1982). Counseling psychologists have responded to this demand for a biopsychosocial view of health and disease with a variety of theoretical models that bring traditional counseling values and strengths to our understanding of illness and health.

Seeman (1989) applied cybernetics theory and a focus on what he described as "positive health" to elaborate and extend systems theory in health psychology (Schwartz, 1982). In this model, living systems such as human beings are conceptualized as made up of hierarchically organized subsystems that interact with one another bidirectionally across time, using cybernetic processes of communication and control to coordinate the subsystems, often in "feedback loop" systems that promote regulation or dysregulation. For a human system to achieve health, all the subsystems must function and communicate effectively; dysregulation in any part of the system must be communicated and responded to effectively by the other elements of the system, a state that Seeman described as *organismic integration*. The system hierarchy includes ecological, interpersonal, environmental, cognitive, perceptual, physiological, and biochemical subsystems interacting bidirectionally to communicate and control the individual system; developmental processes are also included, as the system interacts and develops complexly over time. From this perspective, individual health can be assessed at any stage of wellness or disease, and positive health can be promoted regardless of an individual's current health status by strengthening

any conveniently modifiable subsystem, which then is posited to communicate and control related subsystems at other layers of the hierarchy to improve health.

Similarly, Hoffman and Driscoll's (2000) *concentric biopsychosocial model of health status* focuses on the development of positive health and wellness, as well as on the amelioration of disease, via a concentric circles model that emphasizes the interactions among and between a variety of variables at three different levels of analysis to influence health status (both good health and presence or absence of diseases). Their model rejects an explicitly hierarchical approach, with bidirectional interactions between elements of the system, in favor of a more complex systems approach that emphasizes the role of psychosocial factors as mediators and moderators between biomedical and biosocial variables that affect health status. Psychosocial contributors included in the model are both intrapersonal and interpersonal, including cognitions, attitudes, moods, affect, coping style, behaviors, interpersonal and functional roles, and interpersonal and institutional supports. They also identify biosocial contributors as distinct from biomedical contributors, including variables with both biomedical and socially constructed aspects, such as culture, race, ethnicity, gender, socioeconomic status (SES), environmental factors, and sexual orientation. Like the positive health model (Seeman, 1989), the concentric biopsychosocial model includes a systemic, interactive approach and focuses on positive health promotion, not only the absence or amelioration of disease. It also emphasizes the complexity of determinants of health outcomes, and the need for interventions at all levels of the system to create change.

These two models do not represent the limits of counseling psychologists' contribution to a systems-based understanding of human health; additional similar models have been proposed that add to this basic approach a more nuanced awareness of feedforward as well as feedback mechanisms, additional dysregulatory and developmental processes, and an awareness of human beings' tendency to actively self-organize and self-construct their own systems toward health and illness (Ford, 1987, 1990; Nicholas & Gobble, 1990).

In addition to these theoretical models, counseling psychologists (Alcorn, 1991; Bor, Miller, Latz & Salt, 1998; Thoresen & Eagleston, 1985) have also suggested a variety of other theoretical perspectives traditional to our field that should be brought to bear on an understanding of health psychology, such as the adoption of a developmental, lifespan perspective on health; attention to relationship variables, such as attachment to caregivers or health care providers; attention to attitudes and beliefs as they impact health and health care; use of a cognitive social learning model for understanding and intervening with health concerns; and a focus on our strengths as providers of educational, rather than medical or remedial interventions, to promote positive health. Counseling psychologists have also generally raised cautions about deterministic models of health and well-being in favor of dynamic models that express hope for human growth and change even under conditions of disease and adversity (Elliott & Shewchuk, 1996).

Using these and similar theoretical perspectives to ground their work, counseling health psychologists have offered innovative benefits in a variety of medical and hospital settings, to address a variety of health problems. The work of these psychologists is considered next, first in a section discussing the role of counseling psychologists in primary care, and next in a section considering the application of CHP to a variety of specific health concerns.

Counseling Psychologists in Primary Care

When Americans have problems in living, many of them do not seek out the services of a psychologist. In fact, most Americans receive mental health services from their primary care provider (Narrow, Reiger, Rae, Manderscheid, & Locke, 1993), rather than from either a psychologist or a psychiatrist. Primary care physicians prescribe 67% of all psychotropic medications, and as many as 70% of all primary care patient visits have a primary underlying psychosocial basis rather than a medical cause for the presenting symptoms (James, 2006). Several authors (Cummings, Cummings, & Johnson, 1997; James & Folen, 2005; O'Donohue, Byrd, Cummings, & Henderson, 2005; Strosahl, 2005) have therefore concluded that the primary care setting is the largest de facto mental health care system in the United States. Although primary care clinics may not be the obvious or currently the ideal setting for mental health services, traditional mental health care in the United States is also plagued with difficulties. Mental health services in the United States are disorganized, and care is often fragmented; attrition rates are high, and the great majority of psychologically distressed individuals receive no mental health care even when care is free (Regier et al., 1993; Ware, Manning, Duan, Wells, & Newhouse, 1984).

One important advantage to integrating psychological services with primary care is that coordinating and delivering mental health services in primary care can reduce patient attrition while simultaneously increasing access, as patients are already familiar with the clinic, and may prefer to have access to psychological services in a familiar, nonspecialty setting. If patients are seeking psychological services in primary care clinics, it may be reasonable for counseling health psychologists to provide services there. And, once integrated within a primary care setting, there may be unique opportunities for counseling health psychologists to enhance not only mental health treatment, but overall health care for patients seen in the integrated setting.

Counseling psychology training and experiences may be uniquely well suited to primary care service delivery, particularly because counseling psychologists are traditionally trained to see health, strength, and resilience in our patients. Counseling psychologists may also be well trained in prevention, in the promotion of well-being, and in behavioral interventions. Because patients often come to primary care clinics for regular health maintenance, patients seen there are often diagnosed with both physical and mental health problems relatively early in the disease process, when strengths-based and preventive interventions may be more effective and problems may be more amenable to change. For example, many type 2 diabetics are seen and identified at the prediabetes stage by their primary care provider. At this juncture in the disease process, psychoeducation and healthy lifestyle interventions delivered by a well-trained counseling health psychologist can be efficacious. Similarly, identifying and intervening with difficulties in mood in response to a major life stressor soon after the event, rather than when the problem has escalated to a major depressive episode and the patient presents in a mental health clinic, may permit more rapid improvement in psychological symptoms, as well as effective use of shorter, focal interventions.

What does a counseling health psychologist do in a primary care clinic? James and Folen (2005, adapting the work of Frank, McDaniel, Bray, & Heldring, 2004) have defined primary care psychology as "the provision of integrated care that includes the prevention of disease and the promotion of health behaviors in individuals, families and communities via the primary care setting. Primary Care Psychologists are experts in: (a) assessment & evaluation of common psychosocial symptoms seen in the primary care setting; (b) able to distinguish between symptoms associated with a medical disease and a mental health condition; (c) collaborate with primary care teams; (d) have the knowledge to triage appropriately; (e) have an understanding of biomedical conditions commonly seen in primary care and applicable pharmacological interventions." Primary care counseling health psychologists play several roles. They serve as the primary care clinic's resident consultants on patient behavioral health, behavior management, interpersonal communication skills, and mental health resources and referral. They may teach, supervise medical residents, or conduct research. Primary care counseling health psychologists also provide direct patient care, usually from a brief, consultative model.

Rowan and Runyan (2005) provided a model for the conceptual organization of a 30-minute primary care CHP treatment session. This brief session is divided into three parts: introduction and assessment, intervention, and follow-up. In the *introduction and assessment phase* the psychologist sets the conceptual framework for the office visit. The introduction and assessment phase has two goals; first, to help patients understand that the appointments are brief and goal-oriented, and second, to ascertain the patient's needs, whether for referral to longer-term therapy, psychoeducational interventions, or access to other resources, such as support groups. A critical part of the assessment phase is prescreening: Patients are given self-report questionnaires at every session to screen for suicidal ideation and major psychiatric disorders and to quantify the patient's progress. Instruments such as the OQ-45 can be administered in 8–10 minutes on a computer, a PDA, or in paper and pencil form. The psychologist quickly reviews the results of these screening measures to help guide and focus the discussion on the patient's most pressing concerns. The second phase is the *intervention phase*. In this phase, the psychologist provides the patient with brief cognitive-behavioral coping strategies and bibliotherapy in the form of handouts, books, or websites to help patients manage their concerns independently. In the *follow-up phase*, the psychologist integrates the information obtained from the referring physician and the patient and devises a plan in the form of a "prescription." This prescription may be written on the familiar physician's prescription pad, and may list goals for the patient, websites, and/or the critical things to be done prior to the next visit. Feedback is also provided to the physician in this phase; ideally, at the conclusion of the initial appointment, the psychologist and patient actually walk next door to the patient's physician to share information about the patient's diagnosis, treatment plan, goals, and recommendations.

One question that arises in considering the integration of CHP with primary care is: Is this effective? A series of pilot projects conducted in the Kaiser Health System in California and a Native Hawaiian Community Health Clinic in Hawaii suggested that integrating psychological services into primary care could offer cost-effective and efficacious service to address primary care patients' mental and physical health concerns from a behavioral medicine perspective (Cummings, et al., 1997). Patient satisfaction increased, access to mental health care improved, and primary care providers (PCPs) were pleased with being able to consult with the psychologists whose offices were now colocated with them.

Since these initial studies, counseling health psychologists have continued to integrate an ever-expanding array of services into the primary care setting, including interventions for obesity and weight loss (Bacho, Myhre, & James, 2008; James et al., 1997; James, Folen, Page, Noce, & Britton, 1999), diabetes (Earles, 2005), insomnia (Isler, Peterson, & Isler, 2005), depression (Jarrett, 2008), heart disease (Kop, 2005), smoking cessation (Lavin, 2008), HIV/AIDS (Law & Buermeyer, 2005), improved medication adherence (Levensky, 2005), pain management (Otis, Reid, & Kerns, 2005), and women's health (Poleshuck, 2005). Several authors have also suggested that primary care counseling interventions need not be limited to adults. Clay and Stern (2005) and Etherage (2005) have conceptualized pediatric clinics as part of the primary care psychology model. Etherage provided six case examples of providing primary behavioral health services to children in pediatric clinics. Etherage described the conceptual framework for the delivery of services in this setting, as well as criteria for an effective pediatric primary care consultant. McDaniel and Hepworth (2004) described the delivery of family therapy in the primary care setting.

Although counseling health psychologists in primary care settings provide enormous opportunities for improved patient care and enhanced health and well-being, there are also pitfalls for counselors working and researching in this setting. Training resources and opportunities specific to the needs of counseling psychologists in primary care are scant or nonexistent, and counseling psychologists must therefore adapt more general training materials in health psychology. Many of the core competency areas for a psychologist in primary care, such as competence in the interaction of biology and behavior, human anatomy, physiology, pharmacology, and pathophysiology (McDaniel, Hargrove, Belar, Schroeder, & Freeman, 2004), may not be available even as electives in counseling psychology training programs or even in hospital- or clinic-based psychology internships and postdoctoral fellowships.

Issues of professional identity can also be problematic for the counseling health psychologist practicing in primary care. Altmaier (1998) highlighted many of the pitfalls with professional identity for psychologists working in medical settings. The lure of the "white lab coat" may create confusion in professional identity or raise colleagues' concerns. James (2009), for example, described the initial impressions of the senior psychologists in his department when he returned from an inpatient surgery ward wearing a lab coat. His colleagues were chagrined and alarmed and could not apprehend why any psychologists would wear a lab coat. James was told "after all, you're not a doctor," by a senior member of his department. It is common for primary care departments to have one lone psychologist, which can lead to professional and personal feelings of isolation. Without a plan to stay connected to the psychology department, primary care psychologists' professional identity can begin to shift away from psychology. Attending psychology grand rounds, supervising psychology interns, and retaining formal and service links to a hospital psychology department can help lessen this isolation and loss of identity.

Ethical concerns also arise for counseling health psychologists in primary care. In a medical clinic setting, psychologists need basic knowledge of psychopharmacology, pathophysiology, anatomy, and how to interpret laboratory studies. However, there may be pressure to use medical information or to practice in ways that extend beyond our competencies as psychologists. For example, some primary care physicians lack confidence in prescribing psychotropic medications, and may seek guidance from resident counseling health psychologists; counseling health psychologists have to be careful to respect the limits of their knowledge and facilitate consultation with appropriate professionals (e.g., a psychiatrist) when asked for advice that goes beyond our professional competencies.

Despite the potential pitfalls that face counseling health psychologists in primary care, the opportunity to provide innovative services in this setting may offer tremendous potential to use traditional counseling skills in positive psychology and prevention to enhance human health and well-being. DeLeon, Rossmando, and Smedley (2004) envisioned a future in which the services that psychologists provide will take on a larger role in health care, prevention, medicine, and daily living for all Americans, leading to more affordable and quality health care that is available to more people. Some counseling health psychologists (James & Follen, 1999) even envision that we may become the primary health care managers and coordinators of the future, as we employ our unique skills to enhance health-related behaviors, provide behavioral consultation to individual and organizations, and use research to inform practice to become invaluable contributors to health care of the future.

Counseling Psychology and Specific Health Concerns

In addition to expanding involvement in primary care settings, counseling health psychologists have applied counseling psychology methods, values, research, and conceptual models to tackle serious and chronic health concerns that extend beyond the scope of primary care. A review of every disease or specific health issue that counseling psychologists have addressed in research or practice is beyond the scope of this chapter. However, in this section, we provide an overview of some major diseases and health issues with which counseling psychology has been concerned, highlighting changes over time as well as specific contributions counseling psychologists have made. We make no effort here to provide a comprehensive review of research in each area; instead, we highlight illustrative studies to demonstrate CHP's unique contribution to knowledge and social change in each area. We conclude this section by identifying themes, values, and areas of strength in these contributions by counseling psychology, to set the stage for our consideration of our professional strengths and values in more detail in the following sections.

PAIN

Counseling psychologists have been interested in chronic pain for decades; the 1979 *Annual Review of Psychology* article on counseling psychology (Krumboltz et al., 1979) included pain control (along with insomnia, weight control, and smoking cessation) in a section on health-related outcomes of importance to counselors, stating in its summary of the research to date that "Counselors can help clients to control the perception of physical pain by teaching them how to relax and how to use relevant cognitive coping strategies" (p. 567). Since that initial summary, counseling psychologists have focused on developing and testing treatments for chronic physical pain. One experimental trial, for example, compared standard inpatient rehabilitation and physical therapy with standard therapy enriched with training in relaxation, coping skills, and contingency management for exercise behavior, finding that both treatments were effective (Altmaier, Lehmann, Russell, Weinstein, & Kao, 1992). Counseling psychologists have also conducted research to identify the components or mechanisms of effective treatment for chronic pain, demonstrating, for example, that imagery and relaxation training are particularly powerful elements of stress inoculation therapy for increasing pain tolerance (Hackett & Horan, 1980; Worthington & Shumate, 1981) or that increases in self-efficacy beliefs during treatment for chronic pain predicted long-term outcome (Altmaier, Russell, Kao, Lehmann, & Weinstein, 1993). Fewer studies of chronic pain have appeared in counseling psychology journals in recent years, as the field of behavioral pain management has matured and become more specialized; counselors continue to do this work, and to provide guidance about how to address chronic pain with cognitive behavioral interventions (Okey, 1998).

CHRONIC ILLNESS, INJURY, AND REHABILITATION

Counseling psychology has a long history in the rehabilitation of disabled individuals. Vocational rehabilitation of disabled returning soldiers in World War II was a foundational initial activity for the field, as previously noted. Even apart from vocational rehabilitation, counseling psychologists have provided services in substantial numbers in rehabilitation settings for decades (Parker & Chan, 1990). The advantages that have been described for counseling psychologists in rehabilitation echo those for counseling health psychologists in general. Counseling psychologists' background in vocational psychology, multicultural and social justice issues, and developmental, lifespan concerns make them uniquely well-suited to working with individuals adjusting to disability, who may face vocational challenges, discrimination and oppression based on their disability or other factors, and changes in their abilities to navigate developmental tasks (Chwalisz, 1998). These traditional counseling psychology strengths may make counseling health psychologists well-poised to enhance rehabilitation for individuals

with disabilities because they may prepare us to adopt a social/educational rather than medical model of disability, and to understand and incorporate the "new paradigm" of disability, which repudiates a medical model of disability and emphasizes issues of oppression, power, civil rights, and the social construction of ability and disability, while focusing on enhancing independent living (National Institute on Disability and Rehabilitation Research, 1999). Psychologists have been criticized for their failure to develop knowledge and skills reflective of the new paradigm, instead treating the presence of physical disabilities in their clients as a "medical condition" requiring the services of a rehabilitation specialist, instead of an aspect of human identity and development with which all psychologists should be concerned and familiar (Olkin & Pledger, 2003).

Although counseling psychology graduate training programs continue to do a poor job of providing training in disability, with few courses in disability available and fewer still that approach disability from a new paradigm perspective (Olkin & Pledger, 2003), there is some evidence that counseling psychology could emerge as a leader in a new paradigm approach to human disability. Counseling health psychologists have been active in emphasizing the degree to which disability and chronic illness are normal developmental tasks eventually faced by most adults, and in identifying the intersection between work and chronic illness or disability as a typical midcareer challenge that counseling psychologists must address (Chwalisz, 2008). Counseling health psychologists have helped define the ways that disability is imposed on our clients through environmental, personal, and social factors that limit their full participation in all aspects of life, rather than as the result of a disease or injury per se (Peterson & Elliott, 2008).

Research in vocational psychology in particular has begun to attend to disability from a new paradigm perspective, as counseling psychologists learn more about disability as one of a number of intersecting elements of identity that shape career development. Mpofu and Harley (2006), for example, reviewed the intersection of African American and disability elements of identity as they affect career development, whereas Noonan et al. (2004) conducted a qualitative study of highly achieving women with disabilities. In both cases, these researchers emphasized the complex interactive nature of various aspects of identity (including disability) with the world of work, and also identified specific ways that these multiple identities could be used as assets or strengths, as well as the basis of oppression and discrimination in the world of work.

CANCER AND OTHER LIFE-THREATENING ILLNESSES

Early CHP research on cancer tended to focus on the process of death and dying, as viewed from both patient and counselor perspectives, finding, for example, that religiosity and previous experience with death and dying were related to less fear of death among indigent cancer patients (Gibbs & Achterberg-Lawliss, 1978), or that terminal cancer patients had less death anxiety overall and over time than those with other chronic but non–life-threatening illnesses (Dougherty, Templer, & Brown, 1986). Fear of cancer was also identified as an important variable to explain why counselors in experimental settings were less helpful with patients with cancer than with clients with other comparably serious disabilities (Pinkerton & McAleer, 1976).

More recent research, however, has emphasized adaptive means for cancer patients to adjust to and even grow from their experience with life-threatening disease. Merluzzi and Sanchez (1998) described a developmental model of coping with cancer and life-threatening illnesses in order to inform counselors about the processes required to cope adaptively at each stage, from diagnosis through treatment and post-treatment (although their model did not include a stage for terminal or end-of-life coping, which they acknowledge as a limitation). For example, they describe the diagnosis phase in cancer as one in which uncertainty and anxiety are often very high, and may be ameliorated somewhat by the process of committing to a treatment plan, whereas in the treatment phase, chemotherapy drugs themselves may cause psychological symptoms that may overwhelm previously psychologically healthy clients. At post-treatment, even when treatment is successful, fear of recurrence and/or adjustment to changes in functioning may cause difficulties. These researchers point out that demands may overwhelm coping resources at any phase in this process, and they developed a model of successful adjustment to life-threatening illness to conceptualize how counselors could foster such adjustment.

In this model (Merluzzi & Sanchez, 1998), a variety of psychological, disease, treatment, social, and environmental factors, such as premorbid psychiatric problems, disease stage at diagnosis, treatment aggressiveness, social support, optimism, and other life events, lead to changes in self-efficacy to cope with the demands of the illness at various stages in the disease process. Self-efficacy in turn affects the individual's adjustment, quality of life, and longevity. Although this model is overly simplistic in terms of explanatory power (e.g., we would expect disease stage at diagnosis to have direct as well as mediated effects on longevity), it serves as a valuable guide for counselors, who can assess the variety of factors that may impact an individual's sense of self-efficacy in coping with life-threatening illness, and then bolster self-efficacy indirectly through improving these factors or directly via interventions designed to increase clients' confidence in their ability to cope with illness.

In addition to self-efficacy, counseling health psychologists have also investigated other psychological factors and means of coping that may assist individuals with their progress through life-threatening illness, making medical decisions, and healing from or adjusting to disease. Depth of processing information relevant to making a decision about medical treatment, for example, has been shown to be associated with how well cancer patients cope with illness. When an important medical decision arises, cancer patients who engaged in thoughtful, effortful processing of relevant information, seeking out information on their own, and actively choosing an approach for their treatment, used more effective, active coping strategies, had greater positive focus, and were better able to find meaning in their situations, than were those who simply followed their doctors' advice. This was true regardless of the stage of cancer diagnosis or the prognosis, suggesting that patients who most readily accept advice from their physicians (and may be perceived as "good" patients) may be at increased risk of difficulty adjusting to illness at any stage of treatment (Petersen, Heesacker, & Marsh, 2001).

Being able to find benefits and meaning in the experience of life-threatening illness has been found to be more generally important, predicting both better psychological and physical functioning in bone marrow transplant patients, for example, 2 years later (Tallman, Altmaier, & Garcia, 2007). Using religious beliefs and resources (e.g., church ties) to cope is also beneficial: Religious coping strategies were associated with improved adjustment both concurrently and over time among both kidney transplant patients and their spouses (Tix & Frazier, 1998). Social support is well-known as an important element of positive health, but counseling health psychologists have pointed out that the quality of the relationship in which the support is enacted may matter more for recovery from life-threatening illness than the support behaviors or perceptions of support themselves (Frazier, Tix, & Barnett, 2003). One problem with the literature on effective coping with life-threatening illness is the lack of theoretical consensus regarding the relations among various variables known to be adaptive for cancer sufferers. Social support, for example, has been described as a predictor of an important mediator (e.g., self-efficacy, Merluzzi & Sanchez, 1998), a mediating variable (e.g., between religiosity and adjustment, Tix & Frazier), and an outcome (e.g., of better depth of processing of medical decisions, Petersen et al., 2001).

HIV/AIDS

As with cancer and other life-threatening illness, early CHP research and theory about HIV/AIDS focused on end-of-life issues and controversies, such as "rational suicide" (Rogers & Britton, 1994; Werth, 1992), and on counselors' fear of HIV and their consequent anxiety and discomfort in working with affected individuals (Hayes & Gelso, 1993). Important parallels between HIV/AIDS and cancer or other life-threatening illnesses were identified, with some authors suggesting that the process of coping with the course of these illnesses, as well as adaptive coping behaviors, should be similar (Merluzzi & Sanchez, 1998). However, early researchers also identified important differences in the needs of persons with HIV (PWHIV) compared to persons with other life-threatening illnesses.

Hoffman's early work on PWHIV in particular (Hoffman, 1991, 1993) emphasized the psychosocial and multicultural elements unique to HIV/AIDS at the beginning of the epidemic. Her psychosocial model of HIV infection encouraged counselors to consider the special characteristics unique to HIV/AIDS infection, such as the disruption created by the (then rapidly progressive and fatal) disease for young people's developmental life course and timing, as well as the profound legal and social stigma experienced by seropositive individuals early in the epidemic, when, for example, nearly half of Americans surveyed reported that they would refuse to work with an individual with AIDS (Blendon & Donelan, 1988).

Hoffman (1993) also considered multicultural issues and the intersection of identity in prescient detail, describing how AIDS diagnosis and progression affected individuals from a variety of cultural groups differently. As she described, for white gay men who lived in metropolitan areas with access to social communities of other gay men, AIDS could serve as an impetus to homophobia and targeted violence or other negative impacts from stigma; could serve to "out" individuals who were previously closeted, causing distress or exposure to violence; could trigger feelings of grief as valued members of gay communities became ill ("AIDS-related bereavement"); or could permit positive outcomes, such as improved access to medical care and social support via clinics and activist groups comprised of and for gay men. For women, people of color, heterosexuals, or IV drug users, on the other hand, AIDS could serve to further isolate or inhibit access to health care and social support, while raising issues of misidentification, stigma, and shame.

Since this early seminal work, CHP research, theory, and practice relevant to PWHIV have continued to evolve to reflect changes in the spread and treatment of HIV. The development of highly active antiretroviral therapy (HAART) as a treatment for HIV in the mid-1990s dramatically shifted the outcome of HIV from almost certain progression to AIDS and death, to a more manageable chronic illness, such that patients taking HAART drugs can remain essentially free of HIV virus indefinitely, as long as they remain on the medications. However, HAART comes with serious challenges, including high financial cost, complicated drug regimens (sometimes requiring combining three or more different drugs at multiple, specific times each day), and potentially serious side effects. The provision of HAART therapy thus raises both behavioral (e.g., medication adherence) and social justice (e.g., considerations of how or whether to provide medication to those who cannot afford it) issues of interest to counseling health psychologists.

The spread of the epidemic has also changed in ways of importance to counselors seeking to understand or help PWHIV. In the United States, initial HIV infections were mainly among white gay men, intravenous drug users, and people who had received contaminated blood products through medical care. Currently, however, new HIV infections in the United States disproportionately affect African Americans. Nearly 50% of new HIV infections in 2005 were in African American men and women, and 70% of infants born with HIV were African American. HIV infections in women are also growing rapidly, such that women now account for 31% of new infections (Werth, Borges, McNally, Maguire, & Britton, 2008a). Worldwide, women now account for 50% of the world's new

HIV infections in adults; half of all new HIV infections are in children and young people under age 25 (Joint United Nations Programme on HIV/AIDS, 2008).

As it has spread, HIV has increasingly emerged as a social justice issue, in that who acquires HIV infection, and how the infection proceeds once it has been acquired, is strongly and increasingly influenced by socioeconomic class and access to commodities associated with class and other forms of privilege, such as health care, economic means to pay for medication, and freedom from rape or otherwise coercive or economically motivated sexual interactions. Members of traditionally disenfranchised groups are at increased risk of acquiring HIV infection, and may become more disenfranchised as a result of the infection itself, via economic deprivation, discrimination, disability, or other negative outcomes (Werth, Borges, McNally, Maguire, & Britton, 2008b)

As a result, counseling health psychologists have grown increasingly interested in HIV as a social justice issue and as an arena with potential to unite a variety of traditional counseling psychology values and concerns. Recently, counseling psychologists with interest in the interface of health and vocational concerns have pointed out that even though our traditional interests and values as counseling psychologists, such as multiculturalism, vocational development, strengths-based interventions, and social justice, lend themselves well to addressing the holistic needs of individuals with chronic health concerns, in practice we have done a relatively poor job of integrating these traditional values to help people and cause community- and social-level change (Werth, Borges, McNally, Maguire, & Britton, et al. 2008b).

These psychologists have offered HIV and PWHIV as a case study example in which CHP, PWHIV, and our broader communities would benefit by increased integration of core counseling psychology interests and values (Werth, Borges, McNally, Maguire, & Britton 2008a, b). Furthermore, these psychologists describe how counseling health psychologists can both increase our understanding of HIV and promote the dissemination of the counseling psychology knowledge base for positive social change, via a variety of methods. Participatory, action research paradigms and qualitative research methods (Maguire, McNally, Britton, Werth, & Borges, 2008), training-research-service partnerships between community agencies serving PWHIV and counseling psychology training

programs (Schmidt, Hoffman, & Taylor, 2006), and direct political advocacy (Werth, Borges, McNally, Maguire, & Britton, 2008b) have all been used to enhance our understanding of PWHIV, as well as to promote vocational, psychological, and physical health and wellness for PWHIV.

Multicultural and Social Justice Values in Counseling Health Psychology

As the foregoing review of CHP involvement in primary care and in the prevention, understanding, and treatment of various specific health concerns makes clear, CHP may be distinguished from other health disciplines and from health psychology in general by its emphasis on bringing core counseling strengths and values to the health arena. In the following sections, we explore these values and strengths in more depth. In this section, we focus on multicultural and social justice values as they inform CHP. In the next section, we focus on health promotion and prevention as guiding principles that have shaped—and we hope will continue to shape—counseling's contribution to human health in the future.

Social justice is a core value for counseling psychologists and integral to both the history and current aims of the field. Frank Parsons, the father of vocational psychology, focused in the 1900s on vocational counseling as a tool for sociopolitical change and access to equity for young men in impoverished areas of Boston (Fouad, Gerstein, & Toporek, 2006). Similar concerns and interests informed counseling psychologists working with veterans in the 1940s and 1950s, with homelessness and community mental health in the 1960s, and with civil rights and feminism in the 1960s and 1970s (Fouad, Gerstein, & Toporek, 2006). This interest in social justice endures. At the 2001 National Counseling Psychology Conference in Houston, for example, more than 40% of conference attendees signed up for one or more social action groups, which worked throughout the conference and beyond developing action plans to address issues such as racism, domestic abuse, and violence; 88% of conference attendees indicated strong support for social justice activities as important to the field of counseling psychology (Fouad et al., 2004).

Because social justice is inherently concerned with the equitable distribution of advantages and disadvantages among individuals and groups in society, counseling psychologists' interest in social justice has often been closely linked to our traditional expertise in multicultural counseling (Fouad et al., 2006). Counseling psychologists have a considerable strength in multicultural counseling and therapy. The field has been at the forefront of developing, training, and researching cultural competence in counseling and psychotherapy; writing essential and widely adopted texts in the area (e.g., Sue & Sue, 1999); and demonstrating leadership in developing guidelines for multicultural competence for psychologists as a whole (e.g., American Psychological Association, 2003).

These strengths in social justice and multicultural issues are of exceptional importance in health care. There is abundant evidence that simply belonging to various groups, as well as specific experiences of group-based oppression, bias, and discrimination, negatively impact health and health care. For example, African American patients are more likely than whites to experience amputations (Gornick et al., 1996), but less likely to receive analgesics when they are seen in emergency rooms for bone fractures (Todd, Deaton, D'Adamo, & Goe, 2000). Whites and men are more likely to be referred for cardiac catheterization to diagnose heart disease than African Americans and women (Schulman et al., 1999). Medicare recipients who are least affluent are much less likely to receive mammograms or influenza immunizations compared to the most affluent (Gornick et al., 1996.). Women from a variety of ethnic groups have as much as a 200% greater risk of mortality following a breast cancer diagnosis than do non-Hispanic white women (Li, Malone, & Daling, 2003). Differences by racial or ethnic group, gender, SES, and other group memberships (e.g., sexual orientation, geographic location) have been demonstrated across the developmental spectrum of health care, from variables that may affect need for health care, such as health knowledge; to health behaviors such as smoking or exercise, or attitudes toward medical care; to access to and cost of care; to bias and poor treatment once in the medical system in terms of diagnosis, recommendations, referrals, and treatment received; to outcomes such as life expectancy, morbidity, and mortality from disease (Tucker, Ferdinand, et al., 2007). As a result, there has been both increased research and increased federal funding for research to eliminate these group-based health disparities.

Some authors have observed that the stark injustice revealed by research into health disparities should compel counseling psychologists to become involved in this area, whereas our traditional skills in providing multiculturally competent health care

assure that we have something necessary to offer our health care colleagues (Tucker, Ferdinand, et al., 2007). Specifically, these authors suggest that counseling psychologists can ameliorate health disparities by using their unique expertise in health care settings to take on roles such as health care staff trainer and consultant (with a special focus on training health care colleagues in culturally competent health care delivery), patient and community health empowerment coach (including facilitating contact and collaboration between indigenous health care providers and more traditional medical providers), public policy advocate, health counselor and psychotherapist, and health care researcher.

Indeed, counseling health psychologists have already begun to develop important theory, research, training, interventions, and assessments designed to understand and eliminate health disparities. In the process, they have also generated important critiques of existing research and health practice as it affects individuals from a variety of cultural groups. They have identified a variety of variables that contribute to the existence and maintenance of health disparities for people from diverse groups and have made efforts to explain how aspects of culture may influence health outcomes.

Factors that influence health for group members may be divided into biological variables, behavioral and psychological variables, and social or environmental variables (Anderson, 1998, as cited in Tucker, Ferdinand et al., 2007). Biological, behavioral, and psychological variables, in turn, may be classified as "micro" or individual factors affecting health for group members, whereas social and environmental variables are "macro" or systemic factors (Hopps & Liu, 2006). In the broader literature on health disparities, extensive and programmatic attention has been paid to understanding and developing interventions to address micro factors. Counseling health psychologists have also been involved in innovative ways in addressing micro-level variables, including biological and genetic variables, and incorporating these into a lifespan developmental, biopsychosocial approach; for example, in developing a CHP approach to genetic counseling (Kaut, 2006).

However, counseling health psychologists also have pointed out that intense attention on micro factors, although obviously useful, is nevertheless problematic for several reasons, including potentially diverting attention from macro factors that may be the primary cause of health disparities, "blaming the victim" through the implication that minority groups affected by health disparities are inferior biologically or psychologically, reifying racial or other group-based stereotypes, or attempting to change intractable individual-level behaviors, which, even if improved, would not affect larger sociopolitical imbalances (e.g., if micro-level differences such as increased smoking among low-SES individuals were eliminated through research or intervention, low SES would remain and continue to cause health disparities in other areas; Tucker, Ferdinand et al., 2007; Hopps & Liu, 2006).

Instead, counseling health psychologists have called for a focus on systemic, macro variables as mechanisms to explain health disparities, while also giving appropriate attention to micro-level, and particularly psychological, variables that may affect health. Social class has been one area of particular interest for researchers interested in health disparities, because SES consistently emerges as one of the strongest predictors of morbidity and mortality (Angell, 1993), and because SES operates as an influence on health in an intriguing, graded fashion, such that even within social classes, those at the lower end of the class continuum are less healthy than those of higher status. In other words, not only is it the case that those in poverty are less healthy than those whose basic needs are met, but even among the wealthy, the very wealthiest are healthier than the less wealthy (Adler & Conner Snibbe, 2003). Counseling health psychologists have pointed out that several micro-level variables have emerged as important mediators of this relationship between social class and health, including patterns of health risk behaviors; feelings of control, security, and ability to cope; social support; negative cognitions; and self-perceptions of social status (Herman et al., 2007; Hopps & Liu, 2006).

By comparison, macro-level variables have received relatively little research or intervention attention as mechanisms to explain health disparities. Interactions between micro- and macro-level variables have received even less attention. Nevertheless, certain systemic variables have emerged as important for various groups. Experiences of oppression, for example, may account for the relationship between perceived control or stress and health for minority groups. Racism and discrimination may also exert direct effects on health; racial discrimination is linked to hypertension in African Americans, for example (Williams & Neighbors, 2001). These macro-level factors likely interact with micro-level variables complexly: For example, discrimination may lead to decreased perceived control, with both variables affecting health directly and in interaction. For social justice–oriented counseling health psychologists, the social and political community in which people live must be seen as part of any given health problem, to be considered independently as a consumer or participant for research or intervention (Roysircar, 2006).

Because there is a risk that the health care community may replicate aspects of the social environment that create health disparities for diverse groups (Herman et al., 2007), recent CHP attention has focused on identifying and reviewing macro-level social and environmental characteristics of the health care environment that contribute to health disparities. Tucker, Ferdinand et al. (2007) identified several aspects of the health care environment already demonstrated to contribute to health disparities. These included health care quality factors (such as evidence that low-income ethnic and racial minority groups receive poorer quality of health care even when they have health insurance and similar health problems compared to others; Institute of Medicine, 2003) and access to care factors. Access to care factors include impaired entry into the health care system because of lack of insurance or lack of a usual source of health care; structural barriers to care within the health system, such as lack of geographic availability of health care, lack of transportation or work-convenient hours; difficulties with patient–provider communication because of language barriers, inappropriate language use by providers, illiteracy or difficulties with health literacy, differences in health-related beliefs between patients and providers; and lack of provider cultural competence and cultural sensitivity.

Counseling health psychologists have demonstrated leadership in attending to both macro- and micro-level variables (and their interactions) in understanding and intervening upon health problems, as well as in creating positive health and well-being. However, they have also contended with a variety of difficult conceptual and practical problems in their efforts to eliminate health disparities. Counseling health psychologists have joined with other health professionals in calling for the provision of multiculturally competent and sensitive health care (Herman et al., 2007: Institute of Medicine, 2003), but they have also described how the lack of a clear definition of "cultural competence" or "cultural sensitivity" create barriers to achieving this goal. In addition, counseling health psychologists have highlighted the overfocus in the cultural competence literature on the health care provider as the center of cultural competence, rather than paying attention to cultural competence as a function of the interaction among the patient, provider, and health care environment. Both of these problems—lack of clear definitions of cultural sensitivity and an overfocus on health care providers as a source of such sensitivity—have impeded effective research, training, and implementation of culturally competent health care to address health disparities (Herman et al., 2007).

Terms such as "cultural sensitivity," "cultural competence," and "culturally responsive" have all been used in the counseling and health care literature; although these terms have been distinguished from one another in various ways, their definitions also overlap, and counseling psychologists have also critiqued these terms. The term *cultural sensitivity*, for example, has been criticized by counselors because it has various meanings and has been used interchangeably with the other terms mentioned above, its elements are poorly described and specified, it lacks theoretical grounding, and we have poor means of measuring or assessing it (Ridley, Mendoza, Kanitz, Angermeier, & Zent, 1994). Definitions of *cultural competence*, which focus on understanding and integrating information specific to each patient population served, also risk inadvertently promoting or reifying culturally based stereotypes, and have difficulty accounting for the fact that all patients have identities that intersect with multiple cultural memberships (e.g., an African American lesbian or a deaf, upper-class Latino man). Also missing from all definitions of cultural competence, sensitivity, or responsiveness, is any consideration of the multicultural patients' perspective (Herman et al., 2007). Culturally competent, responsive, and sensitive health care has been defined by experts and located as a property of expert health-care providers, rather than emerging out of the provider behaviors, attitudes, knowledge, and health-care environments that patients from diverse cultures or underserved groups consider to be evidence of respect for their culture or evidence of good care. Thus, counseling health psychologists have recently moved to defining, researching, and implementing patient-centered, culturally sensitive health care, which has also been described as "cultural competence plus" (Herman et al., 2007). Patient-centered culturally sensitive health care will be described in more detail later, when considering CHP efforts to address health disparities.

Aside from conceptual barriers to understanding or ameliorating health disparities, practical barriers also make participating in socially just efforts to improve health for diverse populations more difficult. These barriers include those common to counseling psychology in any health care setting, such as perceived lack of role fit between counseling and medicine, either by medical providers or by counseling psychologists themselves; lack of adequate power or status to effect change in medical settings; and lack of funding for psychologists to take a research, consultative, or interventive role to implement interventions (Tucker, Ferdinand et al., 2007). Lack of access to communities and individuals who do not present for health care may also be a problem (Roysircar, 2006). Counseling health psychologists may also be daunted in their efforts to provide culturally competent or sensitive health care by the need to know detailed cultural information about all groups and intersections among groups that occur in individual patients who may present for care.

Counseling health psychologists have been creative in addressing these barriers and in encouraging colleagues to take on the challenge of provisioning social justice in health care settings. In particular, they have emphasized that, although the Society for Counseling Psychology has an important role to play in fostering training opportunities and positive relationships between medicine and counseling psychology, individual psychologists can circumvent difficulties with inadequate acceptance in medical settings by calling attention to the empirical basis of our work, offering relevant training experiences and continuing medical education credits to our colleagues in medicine, publishing research in medical journals, and including medical professional colleagues in our research and publication efforts. They point out that federal funding for research into health disparities remains relatively abundant, and that counseling health psychologists have not taken full advantage of our skills in tapping these funding sources (Tucker, Ferdinand et al., 2007).

Community–university partnerships, as well as involving members of underserved communities in research and intervention efforts, have been used to circumvent access barriers for psychologists (Roysircar, 2006; Schmidt et al., 2006). In considering how to address the potentially daunting task of providing culturally sensitive health care to all cultural groups, some researchers have suggested that a patient-centered approach might uncover that diverse patient groups have relatively modest needs, including universally desirable health care characteristics such as individualized attention and basic respect, as well as functional mechanisms for patients to provide feedback about their health care needs and wishes and the quality of the care they receive (Tucker, Herman et al., 2007).

Despite the practical and conceptual challenges involved in enhancing social justice by eliminating health disparities, counseling health psychologists have been involved in a variety research and intervention projects that address health disparities and social justice in health care. Schmidt, Hoffman, and Taylor (2006) described a *university and community agency partnership* (U-CAP) model to create social justice and liberate and empower communities serving people with HIV/AIDS by offering university counseling psychology department resources to community agencies that serve PWHIV in reciprocal needs assessment, research, program implementation, and evaluation.

Huynh and Roysircar (2006) provided a case study of development of a community health promotion curriculum designed to enhance health education, self- and preventative health care, and linkages between indigenous health practice and Western medical care among Southeast Asian refugees. The program built working alliances with community agencies and indigenous leaders serving Southeast Asian refugees in a large U.S. city, and provided a psychoeducational curriculum for participants that focused on medical and psychiatric conditions that are highly prevalent in Southeast Asian refugee communities. The 6-week course covered topics including good versus bad health from a Southeast Asian perspective; the importance of health education and prevention of disease; the importance of the doctor–patient relationship; heart problems; other physical health problems common in Southeast Asian refugee populations (e.g., hypertension, liver disease, stomach cancer); behaviors such as relaxation, smoking, and nutrition; mental health; medication; and participant questions. Instruction was provided by a health professional with specific expertise in refugee mental health and experience working with Southeast Asian refugees, and a translator. Informed consent forms, psychoeducational materials, and assessments were provided in Vietnamese and Kru/Khmer. In a pretest–posttest design pilot study with 25 Vietnamese and Cambodian refugee participants, significant improvement in health confidence was found for participants at the end of the class. Although this research is obviously preliminary, with inadequate sample size and limited study-designed assessments, it provides an example of CHP research and intervention with underserved community populations.

Buki and her colleagues (Buki, 1999; Buki, Borrayo, Feigal, & Carrillo, 2004; Schiffner & Buki, 2006) have developed a program of research designed to increase the rate of breast and cervical cancer screening among Latina women via qualitative and quantitative research into Latina beliefs about cancer and sexual health, as well as cultural and environmental barriers to cancer screening. Particularly striking about this program of research is the emphasis on the differences as well as similarities among Latina women of various ancestries; for example, one qualitative study found that embarrassment about touching their own breasts was a barrier for older Mexican-American women engaging in breast self-exams, whereas older South American women who had migrated to the United States felt comfortable with this type of self-touching (Buki, et al., 2004).

Tucker and her colleagues (Tucker, Herman et al., 2007; Tucker et al., 2003) have developed an ambitious program including intervention and assessment tools as well as a theoretical model of CHP to address health disparities. This intervention includes training health care providers and office staff to engage in behaviors and display attitudes that help patients feel comfortable, trusting, and culturally respected; changing the physical clinic environment in ways that patients report enhance their sense of belonging and comfort in the clinic; and empowering patients directly, via training in health-promoting lifestyles and in how to obtain desired changes from their health care providers and health care environment.

The *patient-centered culturally sensitive health care* model (Tucker, Herman et al., 2007; Tucker et al., 2003) specifies theoretical links between this intervention program and patient-centered culturally sensitive changes in the physical environment where health care is received, health care provider behaviors, and patient behaviors. These changes interact with one another to produce increased patient-perceived cultural sensitivity and interpersonal control, which interact to improve patient health-promoting lifestyles and patient satisfaction. Patient satisfaction leads to improved treatment adherence; improved adherence and enhanced health-promoting lifestyles, in turn, are theorized to improve patients' health status and outcomes. To date, this research program has included qualitative research with African American, Hispanic, and non-Hispanic white focus groups to identify behaviors, attitudes, and aspects of health care considered helpful and culturally affirming (Tucker et al., 2003); development and initial psychometric evaluation of the Tucker Culturally Sensitive Health Care Inventories for these cultural groups for patients to evaluate their health care, as well as parallel forms for providers and staff to self-evaluate their behaviors; and pilot-testing of the above-described intervention (Tucker, Herman, et al., 2007). This program of research, although still in its early stages, shows tremendous promise in terms of determining cultural competence from culturally diverse patients' perspectives, as well as for providing specific training and intervention for patients, providers, staff, and health care environments to enhance culturally competent service delivery and eliminate health disparities.

All of the research, training, and intervention efforts just described share a focus on serving underserved populations, empowering members of traditionally oppressed and marginalized groups to achieve better health, and enhancing social justice in human health. All of these programs also share a focus on health promotion and prevention rather than on amelioration of health problems after they have arisen. This interest in health promotion and prevention represents another core CHP value, which we will consider next.

Health Promotion and Disease Prevention in Counseling Psychology

It may seem that the prevention of problems in normal, healthy individuals, and the promotion of human health and well-being, ought to be foundational to the discipline of counseling psychology. Several authors, however, have observed that prevention and health promotion activities have been long neglected in counseling psychology (Adams, 2007; Krumboltz et al., 1979; Romano & Hage, 2000a). Krumboltz et al. famously said that prevention activities occupied "last place in the hearts of counseling psychologists." Although the current summary archival description of counseling psychology provided by the American Psychological Association (APA) as a means of recognizing and identifying the specialty states that "Counseling psychology is a general practice and health service provider specialty [which] . . . centers on typical or normal developmental issues as well as atypical or disordered development [and] . . . help[s] people . . . improve well-being" (APA, n.d, paragraph 1), and specifically states that counseling psychology interventions may be "preventive, skill-enhancing or

remedial" (paragraph 8), the field of counseling psychology continues to emphasize remedial, individual interventions to address problems rather than preventive or systemic efforts at promotion of health (Romano & Hage).

The requirements for licensure as a psychologist, accreditation requirements for training programs, and payment for the practice of psychology have all focused heavily on individual remediation, psychopathology, and crisis intervention at the expense of systemic or preventive interventions (Romano & Hage, 2000a). This neglect has also extended to research; a 2002 review of four major counseling journals found that fewer than 2% of articles published in the 1980s and 1990s focused on primary prevention (O'Byrne, Brammer, Davidson, & Poston, 2002). The impact of this neglect in research and training may be noted in the daily practice of counseling psychologists. Only a quarter of one random sample of counseling psychologists reported any regular involvement in prevention or outreach activities; among those who did involve themselves in this work, it occupied only about 10% of their time on average (Goodyear et al., 2008). More troublesome still is the evidence that this may in fact represent a substantial decrease over time in involvement in prevention by counseling psychologists (Hage et al., 2007).

Nevertheless, there is some evidence that counseling psychologists, along with other psychologists, may be again increasing their attention to prevention. Romano and Hage (2000a) noted that primary prevention had significantly advanced in the 1990s, with the launch by the APA of a peer-reviewed electronic journal, *Prevention and Treatment*, devoted to the topic, and an APA convention, in 1998, which took prevention as its theme. Although this new journal had ceased publication by 2003, counseling psychologists have continued to show new interest in prevention issues. Although *The Counseling Psychologist* did not publish a major contribution on prevention until 2000 (Romano & Hage, 2000a), it has made up for lost time, with two additional major contributions on the topic in 2007 alone (Hage et al., 2007; Reese & Vera, 2007). All editions of the *Handbook of Counseling Psychology* have included a section devoted to prevention; the last three editions included chapters on health promotion and disease prevention specifically (Altmaier & Johnson, 1992; Chwalisz & Obasi, 2008; Hoffman & Driscoll, 2000). Division 17 has active sections on prevention and on the related and emerging field of positive psychology.

Nevertheless, it is clear that prevention and health promotion activities are not currently central activities for most counseling psychologists.

Adams (2007) conceptualized the field of counseling psychology as resistant to change in terms of adopting prevention science as a focus of the field, and used the *transtheoretical stages of change model* (Prochaska & DiClemente, 2005) to conceptualize the field's resistance. She suggested that Romano and Hage's (2000a) major contribution moved counseling psychology from the precontemplation to the contemplation stage of change with respect to involving itself in prevention more deeply, and that later research and theory has placed us at the preparation stage. However, she indicated that both barriers to and benefits of changing our field to include more prevention work must be identified to tip the field into the action stage of change.

Adams (2007) identified barriers to culturally responsive prevention work in counseling psychology, which included the greater interest of counseling psychologists in understanding and intervening with individuals, rather than systems; the emotionally draining and difficult nature of preventive or community interventions; lack of reimbursement by insurers for prevention; lack of funding for prevention research; the time-intensive nature of prevention research and the lack of respect for this activity among tenure committees; the emphasis in training programs on individual remediation; counselors' discomfort with the unfamiliar community settings that may be most appropriate for prevention interventions; and the quantity of required coursework in counseling psychology training programs that leads to resistance to creation of new courses.

The conceptual and theoretical difficulties in defining prevention, and the resulting controversies inside and outside the field of prevention science, although not mentioned as a barrier by Adams (2007), may also make it more difficult for counseling health psychologists to enter the field. Classic descriptions of prevention research capture the difficulties, describing the field as "a friendly and virtuous territory of high abstraction and low practicality" (Bower, 1977, p. 24) or a conceptual swamp that "lures the unwary into quagmires" (Kessler & Albee, 1975, p. 558).

One major difficulty in defining prevention is separating it from remediation. Early mental health efforts to clarify prevention activities delineated primary, secondary, and tertiary forms of prevention, in which primary efforts reduced the number of new incidences of disorder, secondary efforts targeted individuals at risk for or in the early stages of a disorder, and tertiary efforts focused on decreasing the negative impact of a disorder already acquired (Caplan, 1964). However, conceptually distinguishing tertiary prevention from remediation is difficult, particularly when the onset or cause of the problem is unclear. In addition, it can be difficult to distinguish whether a given intervention is in fact primary, secondary, or tertiary prevention, especially when it is broadly applied to a large group, in which some individuals may not have the problem, and others may have it severely (Romano & Hage, 2000a).

Nevertheless, more recent efforts to define the field have provided some navigational guidance to counseling psychologists. Counseling psychologists have encouraged a broad but clearly elaborated definition of prevention that includes efforts to stop a problem behavior from ever occurring; delay the onset of a problem behavior; reduce the impact of a problem behavior; strengthen knowledge, attitudes, and behaviors that promote emotional and physical well-being; and promote institutional, community, and government policies that further physical, social, and emotional well-being. Prevention in counseling psychology thus may include risk reduction, wellness or strengths-based, or social justice efforts and approaches (Hage et al., 2007; Romano & Hage, 2000a). Counseling psychologists have also recently produced detailed guidelines for psychology as a field to define best practice in prevention practice, research, training, and social advocacy (Hage et al., 2007). These 15 best-practice guidelines are intended to provide both clear standards and a vision for prevention work by psychologists, and to move psychologists toward improving health and well-being for more individuals and communities. As such, they are likely to be useful to counseling health psychologists in developing a set of principles to guide health promotion and disease prevention efforts.

Some counseling psychologists have suggested that, since initial efforts to define prevention mainly took place in departments of epidemiology and public health and focused on physical health concerns, these definitions might be better suited to CHP interests, at least in comparison to mental disorders or other complex psychological or social ills (Romano & Hage, 2000a). However, many of the same conceptual difficulties in defining prevention efforts extend to physical health concerns. As previously noted, the etiologies of many of the most serious and prevalent physical health concerns, such as heart disease or cancer, are complex, with behavioral and psychological variables interacting with other mechanisms to produce illness. For many of the most common physical illnesses, although numerous risk factors have been identified that correlate with disease, it remains unclear how well these risk factors prospectively predict disease acquisition, morbidity, or mortality. For example, the well-known Framingham Risk Score, which uses a collection of risk factors to determine individuals' risk of coronary heart disease, has demonstrated poor predictive power and specificity both in elderly (Koller et al., 2007) and young (Berry, Lloyd-Jones, Garside, & Greenland, 2007) populations.

In addition, even when risk factors do predict disease, it is unclear that altering them actually reduces the negative impact of disease. For example, heart health programs that target multiple risk factors for cardiovascular disease do demonstrate successful (albeit small) changes in risk factors; however, these programs have no impact on disease mortality (Ebrahim, Beswick, Burke, Davey, & Smith, 2006). One of the largest experimental studies of dietary modification ever conducted, The Women's Health Initiative Dietary Modification Trial, provides a similar cautionary example. More than 48,000 postmenopausal women were enrolled in this study; they were followed for a mean of more than 8 years. Women in the experimental arm of the study underwent an intensive behavioral intervention that successfully reduced their dietary fat intake and increased their intake of vegetables, fruits, and grains, compared to a control group of women who ate their usual diet. However, these dietary changes did not significantly reduce the participants' risk of heart disease, stroke, or most forms of cancer (Beresford et al., 2006; Howard, Van Horn, et al., 2006; Prentice et al., 2006). In addition, despite successfully maintaining significant caloric restriction compared to controls throughout the study, the women enrolled in the experimental arm of the study had lost an average of only 1 pound compared to controls at the study endpoint (Howard, Manson, et al., 2006). Promoting health and preventing disease is of obvious major importance, and it is likely and in many cases evident that alterable social, psychological, and behavioral factors in which counseling health psychologists have expertise cause or contribute to ill health. However, altering these factors in a fashion that decreases the impact of disease is conceptually and practically difficult.

Despite the barriers to participation in prevention efforts and the challenges of successful health promotion and disease prevention, counseling health psychologists are beginning to be active and innovative in developing prevention science, practice, training, and advocacy. The importance of theory and model development to guide creation, dissemination, and research into disease prevention and health promotion interventions by counseling psychologists has been noted (Hage et al., 2007). Hoffman and Driscoll's (2000) concentric biopsychosocial model of health status, previously described, represents one example of a theoretical model developed to help guide disease prevention and health promotion intervention development. The *theory of reasoned action and planned behavior* (TRA/PB) has also been applied to prevention science within counseling psychology (Romano & Netland, 2008). Romano and Netland provide an example of how TRA/PB could be used to guide a program of research and intervention designed to prevent violence among school-aged children.

Counseling health psychologists have developed and implemented a variety of preventive interventions to prevent diverse health problems or promote general health and well-being. Adams (2007) describes a U.S.–Mexico border health class offered at New Mexico State University that leads to a community-based behavioral health practicum in which students provide multidisciplinary health care with family medicine residents in a primary care clinic to support systemic change in health care service delivery among this patient population. D'Andrea (2004) developed an intriguing community-and-school-based violence prevention program that used a theoretical model of comprehensive school-based violence prevention programming (D'Andrea & Daniels, 1999; Daniels, Arredondo, & D'Andrea, 1999) to develop a graduate-level course in school-based violence prevention that was offered to administrators, counselors, and teachers at four targeted elementary schools in Hawaii. Course participants used the training they received to develop violence prevention efforts in their schools that targeted students and the school community itself both directly (e.g., through support groups or classroom-based interventions) and indirectly (e.g. via community outreach or policy change). This intervention had effects beyond the four schools initially included; for example, course participants collaborated with local officials to organize a community Peace Day, which was ultimately attended by more than 3,000 elementary school students in Hawaii. Kenny, Waldo, Warter, and Barton (2002) describe another elementary school-based intervention, the Gardner Extended Service School, where counseling psychologists have collaborated with other stakeholders in an urban community to enhance a variety of outcomes, including children's physical health and well-being. The intervention uses developmental psychological principles to reduce student risk and enhance resiliency by extending school services to address children's biopsychosocial developmental needs via changes in the context in which they live.

Counseling health psychologists have also used research and consultation expertise to help measure physician performance in cognitive and noncognitive aspects of job performance using a job analysis and critical incident interview methodology (Tarico, Smith, Altmaier, Franken, & VanVelzen, 1984). This line of research, which has been shown to generalize across a number of specialties and training sites (Altmaier et al., 1990; Altmaier, From, Pearson, Garbatenko-Roth, & Ugolini, 1997; Altmaier, Johnson, Tarico, & Laube, 1988), has been used to develop behaviorally based selection interviews that better predict medical resident success than traditional interview procedures (Altmaier, Smith, O'Halloran, & Franken, 1992; Wood, Smith, Altmaier, Tarico, & Franken, 1990), an important outcome for medical care and education.

Education and training within counseling psychology training programs can also advance health promotion or disease prevention. Hage et al. (2007) describe a graduate course that used problem-based learning principles to teach prevention science and practice to trainees through their participation in developing proposals for a grant-funded Summer Prevention Academy whose focus was on promoting healthy schools and families in the community. Students, individually and in teams, developed a poster conference to highlight community needs and best practices in prevention, and local experts chose the best projects for implementation.

Just as the value of multiculturalism and social justice has supported and encouraged a focus on prevention and health promotion, so too have counseling psychologists interested in prevention urged involvement in social justice and political advocacy as an essential aspect of counseling psychologists' work. Indeed, the Best Practice Guidelines on Prevention include the specific statement that "Psychologists are encouraged to engage in governmental,

legislative, and political advocacy activities that enhance the health and well-being of the broader population served" (Hage et al., 2007, p. 550). Several authors have observed that disease prevention, human wellness, and social justice must include political advocacy, because many social and health ills may have sociopolitical injustice as a root cause (Albee, 2000a; Prilleltensky & Prilleletensky, 2003). Albee (2000a) noted that some research suggests that countries with the smallest gap between the average incomes of the rich and poor had the best longevity, as well as the best mental health (Wilkinson, 1996); therefore, he noted, psychologists interested in disease prevention and health promotion should advocate for congressional interventions, such as doubling the minimum wage. He observed that effective prevention interventions will include efforts to address injustice and political changes that may be controversial. Whether individual counseling health psychologists agree with Albee's (2000) specific policy prescriptions or not, it is clear that for the field, our core values of social justice and multiculturalism support and enhance our efforts to improve human health through preventive and ameliorative means.

Conclusion
Recommendations for Research, Training, Practice, and Advocacy
The serious and ongoing human health problems and health disparities identified by Albee (2000a) and others make it clear that work in CHP has only just begun. Even though, as we have reviewed, efforts to date to eliminate unjust health disparities, to enhance physical health and well-being, and to prevent and ameliorate disease are intriguing and in many cases of obvious utility, it is clear that counseling psychology's involvement in these issues has not reached its full potential. Whereas there is some evidence that CHP as a field is picking up speed and increasing its efforts in all these areas, in other cases, we also echo and extend Adams' (2007) formulation that counseling psychology has sometimes demonstrated resistance to change and growth. The various calls to action (e.g., Altmaier, 1991; Romano & Hage, 2000b) to counseling psychologists to involve themselves more deeply in health promotion and disease prevention and amelioration have been unevenly, if sometimes enthusiastically, heeded.

Others have already noted that counseling psychology has unique expertise and values to promote and improve human health (Altmaier, 1991). In this conclusion, we hope to enhance the field's readiness to extend our skills to address ongoing human health needs by highlighting these strengths and values as a means to enhance our motivation to move forward. Toward that end, we will first provide a summary of three themes (and associated subthemes) elaborated in this chapter that we believe represent core strengths and areas of value for CHP and that we believe can and should be extended to aid the broader enterprise of enhancing human health. For each of these positive themes, and their subthemes, all identified in italics below, we offer relevant recommendations for research, training, practice, and advocacy. We also discuss two barrier themes identified in the chapter (and also noted below in italics) that prevent the ongoing improvement and development of CHP as a field.

We conclude by drawing upon these positive themes to create a conceptual framework for CHP, displayed in Figure 28.1, which we hope can be used to circumvent the identified barriers. This conceptual framework seeks to provide a graphical representation of the field in terms of prototypical professional activities and attitudes held by many counseling health psychologists. We do not intend these themes or the conceptual framework to be exhaustive or prescriptive of what counseling health psychologists do or ought to do. Instead, we believe these themes reflect our unique strengths as counseling health psychologists, and serve as resources to draw upon. We are hopeful that these themes, embedded in a conceptual framework such as that presented here, can enhance both theory, research, practice, and advocacy in health psychology, as well as strengthen the professional identity of counseling health psychologists.

One major theme in this chapter and for CHP as a whole is our value of and expertise in *positive health and wellness*, rather than only the amelioration of disease. Because of this emphasis on positive health, we are uniquely well suited to developing and testing interventions and identifying advocacy efforts that are likely to be of greatest value in *preventing disease and promoting good health*. Among individuals with disabilities and chronic illnesses, an emphasis on positive health and wellness also suggests that we reject an individualistic, deterministic,

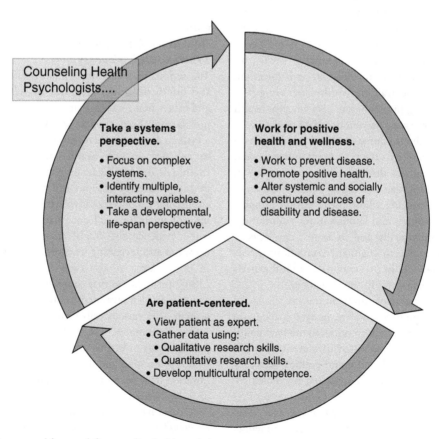

Fig. 28.1 A conceptual framework for counseling health psychology.

medical model of disability and disease, instead promoting and advancing a "new paradigm" that focuses *on altering systemic and socially constructed sources of disability and disease.*

What does this theme of *positive health and wellness* imply for research, training, practice, and advocacy in CHP? One important implication is that human health problems cannot be solved exclusively or even mainly by treatment (Albee, 2000a). Treatment resources are always limited in comparison to the incidence of problems, leading to the public health aphorism that "no disorder or disease has ever been treated out of existence" (Albee, 2000b). Thus, in research, practice, and training of future counseling health psychologists, a focus on disease prevention and promotion of good health is of major practical importance. If the aim is to enhance human health and wellness, we can no longer afford to train students or conduct research or practice solely with an eye toward curing disorders or diseases. Professional involvement in political advocacy by counseling health psychologists should also be encouraged and supported, given that political and systemic changes at the level of the community may have the strongest positive impact on human health and well-being (Hage et al., 2007).

Students in counseling psychology have been identified as a possible barrier to effective prevention work, as they may "self-select" into counseling psychology because of an interest in individual treatment or with hopes of making high incomes in the private practice of psychotherapy (Albee, 2000a). However, the first author was struck by the systems-level ambitions identified by advanced counseling psychology graduate students in a consultation practicum she taught at the University of Maryland. Asked to write a personal mission statement for their future consultation work, students' responses reflected profound interest in advancing a preventive, positive health agenda. Prototypical student mission statements included advocacy and wellness as main themes, such as: "advocating for those whose needs have been underserved"; "fighting for girls' and women's rights"; and "changing the image of mental health" (C. Risco, personal communication, April 16, 2008; H. Ganginis & K. McGann, personal communication, April 1, 2008). Training in CHP would benefit if these ambitions were nurtured in practica and courses that permitted students to learn the challenges and rewards of health promotion and disease prevention.

Although the crowded nature of counseling psychology graduate program curricula and the multiple requirements for training posed by licensure and accreditation authorities are well-known barriers to enhanced training in preventive interventions (Romano & Hage, 2000a), an integration of a positive health and wellness orientation into existing coursework is possible. Several authors have provided examples or guidelines for how prevention interventions, health promotion projects, and efforts to alter systemic or socially constructed sources of disease and disability can be integrated into counseling practica (e.g., Adams, 2007; Schmidt et al., 2006). Problem-based or service-learning pedagogical approaches can be integrated into a variety of typical counseling courses (e.g., multicultural counseling, history and systems) to permit enhanced training in preventive or systemic intervention (Hage et al., 2007).

A second important theme and area of value and expertise for CHPs is our *patient-centeredness.* As counseling psychologists, we have traditionally looked to the people we serve as the primary source of expertise informing how we may be helpful. We use our traditional *strengths in both qualitative and quantitative research* to better access and understand the experiences of the people we serve. These methodological skills are a resource we can offer colleagues in other health professions as we collaborate to identify and assist with the health needs of individuals and groups. Counseling psychology's leadership in developing and defining *multicultural competence* is another extension of our traditional respect for and focus on the individual needs and wishes of the people we serve.

How can *patient-centeredness* be used to enhance research, training, practice, and advocacy in CHP? The patient-centered approach to multicultural sensitivity and multicultural competence developed by Tucker and her colleagues (Tucker, Herman, et al., 2007) is an ambitious program that shows tremendous promise for addressing and ameliorating health disparities among traditionally underserved groups. More broadly, the insight that current definitions of culturally competent health care are not grounded in patients' perspectives or experiences of health care is of major importance in delineating a CHP agenda for research and practice to address health disparities (Herman et al., 2007). Research on patient groups affected by health disparities to identify their specific health needs and barriers to good health is in its infancy and is an area in which counseling health psychologists can contribute; qualitative research methods are particularly underused in identifying patient perspectives on health disparities.

Several authors have noted that skills in research methodology, multicultural service delivery, and patient-centered interpersonal communication are a resource we can offer to allied health professionals (Altmaier, 1991; Tucker, Ferdinand, et al., 2007). Altmaier and colleagues' program of research using critical incident interviewing to improve selection of the most competent medical residents, nearly all of which has been published in medical journals, is an excellent example of using counseling psychology research methods to improve human health (Altmaier et al., 1992; Wood et al., 1990). Similarly, D'Andrea provides an example of using counseling psychology theory and training programs to create systemic change in exposure to violence among school children (2004). Counseling health psychologists should follow these examples, using their creativity to consider how their typical daily activities in academic, counseling, psychiatric, or medical settings can be extended into the communities in which they live and work.

A final theme developed in this chapter and in CHP is our *systems perspective*, and our interest in the operation of complex systems and multiple variables interacting to produce health or disease. Counseling health psychologists have developed models of human health and health promotion that eschew simple or deterministic relations among factors in favor of highlighting the interactive and holistic operation of complex biopsychosocial systems in determining wellness (e.g., Hoffman & Driscoll, 2000; Seeman, 1989). A related CHP focus is our *developmental, lifespan perspective*, which offers value to the enterprise of health promotion and disease prevention in a variety of ways. For example, counseling health psychologists are likely to identify disability as a normal developmental task faced by most adults, rather than evidence of abnormality or atypicality, or to focus on how the experience of illness or disease alters developmental tasks and timing.

How should counseling health psychologists do research, provide training, practice, or conduct advocacy informed by a *systems perspective*? We agree with other authors that systemic, macro-level variables affecting health have been seriously neglected in research and intervention efforts, and that CHP is well-poised to address this deficiency (Tucker, Ferdinand et al., 2007; Hopps & Liu, 2006). Research on how macro-level variables affect health should be prioritized so that a programmatic research base comparable to that still developing for micro- individual-level variables can be developed.

As we described above, nurturing the ambitions of students to engender systems-level change is also important and should be addressed through the integration of such opportunities into coursework and practica.

Comparative research that tests the impact on health outcomes of altering macro- versus micro-level variables would also be helpful for model and theory development. The comprehensive school-based violence programming theoretical model (D'Andrea & Daniels, 1999; Daniels et al., 1999), for example, includes service and intervention components that target both micro-level (e.g., services offered directly to troubled students) and macro-level (e.g., services intended to indirectly impact an entire school, such as political advocacy) variables. Experimental research that compares these elements of the model for their impact on subsequent incidence of student violence in affected schools would shed light on how elements of the model interrelate, as well as which level of analysis is most fruitfully targeted for intervention.

Counseling health psychologists have demonstrated leadership in developing systemic models of human health and wellness. However, in some cases, CHP models of health are overly simplistic, with poorly specified relations among components of the model, or a lack of research effort to operationalize the components or test their proposed relations. In contrast, the patient-centered culturally sensitive health care model (Tucker, Herman, et al., 2007) provides a high-quality example of how model development, measurement, intervention, and practice could be conducted in CHP. The model describes a complex system with multiple components in a nuanced, empirically informed fashion, and sequential, well-organized, programmatic efforts have already been made to test the model through the development of potentially useful interventions, qualitative research, and measure development. More research that is similarly programmatic, theoretically and empirically driven, and relevant is much needed.

The three themes—positive health and wellness, patient-centeredness, and a systems perspective—as well as their subthemes detailed above, represent professional attitudes and behaviors that counseling health psychologists can use as a resource. As such, we have embedded them into a conceptual framework for CHP displayed in Figure 28.1. All three of the CHP themes developed thus far, as well as the conceptual framework, represent positive areas of expertise and professional values that counseling health psychologists can and should draw upon in their efforts to enhance human health. These themes are not entirely novel; others have noted similar areas of strength and potential for CHP (Altmaier, 1991; Mrdjenovich & Moore, 2004). However, in addition to these positive themes, some themes can also be identified that describe barriers or problems that prevent CHP from making a complete contribution to human health. The two most important barrier themes we would like to highlight here include *limited resources* for CHP and counseling health psychologists' *insecure professional identity*.

Several authors have described the various practical and resource barriers that prevent counseling health psychologists from becoming more fully involved in improving human health, including limited opportunities for new or enhanced courses in CHP in crowded counseling psychology training programs, limited funding for health psychology research, lack of reimbursement for preventive interventions, or limited access to community settings where CHP may occur most usefully (Adams, 2007; Tucker, Ferdinand, et al., 2007).

Problems arising from counseling health psychologists' insecure professional identity may come from within counseling psychology and from psychologist colleagues, or it may come from within medicine and from medical professional colleagues. Several authors have described the pressures and barriers to effective CHP that may arise from colleagues in medicine, such as a lack of professional respect or parity with physicians, lack of power to effect change in medical settings, or role confusion and a lack of role fit between what counseling health psychologists have to offer and what medical professionals see as their needs (Good, 1992; Tucker, Ferdinand et al., 2007). In addition, as previously reviewed, counseling psychologists have expressed concerns about involvement in health care and hospital settings and about the diffusion of responsibility demarcating counseling from clinical psychology since virtually the beginning of the field (Scott, 1980). Although larger numbers of counseling psychologists are training and working in health care settings (Neimeyer et al., 2001), psychologists continue to express concerns about the potential loss of professional identity that counseling health psychologists may experience when they enter medical settings (Altmaier et al., 1998; Fitzgerald & Osipow, 1986; Mrdjenovich & Moore, 2004). These authors identify a number of concerns, such as the possibility of professional isolation; lack of connection to counseling psychology organizations, research, or values; and ethical concerns, such as the possibility that counseling health psychologists will be asked to practice outside their competencies by virtue of their isolation in medical settings.

Even when these concerns are ameliorated, one professional identity barrier may arise simply because counseling psychologists may not think of health psychology as a natural and typical extension of their work. Unlike departments of psychiatry, which are housed in medical schools and therefore clearly linked with the enterprise of enhancing human health, counseling psychology programs are housed in departments of education or psychology, where colleagues' interests and resources may be geared toward other or more diverse concerns. Physical health may also be a minor proportion of client presenting concerns in college counseling centers; clients with either acute or chronic (e.g., a disability) physical health concerns who do present at counseling centers may be referred to other campus agencies, such as disability services or a student health service. Similarly, research conducted in counseling programs often uses healthy college students as participants, a pool that does not lend itself well to most studies of disease prevention or health promotion, since physical health status is likely to be less variable among this group. In addition, the movement in both counseling psychology and psychology as a whole toward greater professional diversity and specialization may have led counseling psychologists interested in health away from counseling and toward other professional "homes." Between seven and nine divisions per decade were formed within APA from the 1960s through the 1990s, and currently there are 54 divisions. Many divisions publish their own journals, and counseling psychologists interested in health psychology may have closer professional ties to Division 38 and *Health Psychology* or medical journals than to Division 17 and the *Journal of Counseling Psychology* or *The Counseling Psychologist*. Perhaps it is partly for this reason that little health research is currently published in the flagship counseling journals.

We have not included these barrier themes in our conceptual framework for CHP, but, in the tradition of strengths-based counseling (Smith, 2006), which encourages clients to use their strengths to circumvent weaknesses and solve problems, we suggest that CHP would benefit from using the strengths identified in the conceptual framework to address these barriers, strengthening our professional identity and enlarging our influence in health promotion and disease prevention and recovery.

For example, the blurring of professional identity between counseling and clinical psychology, or between counseling psychology and allied professions such as medicine or psychiatry, may have arisen in part because counseling psychologists practicing in medical and psychiatric settings adopt a medical model or other approaches borrowed from allied fields to address patient problems. Although this may be often appropriate and helpful in the context of interdisciplinary collaboration, in many cases, this adoption of the medical model may occur when counseling health psychologists lack a clear, unique, and persuasive counseling perspective to offer allied colleagues.

Instead, counseling health psychologists could use the conceptual framework presented here to describe, promote, and offer their unique strengths to professionals in other health service fields. As others have noted, promoting our unique skills and strengths, such as in multiculturally competent service delivery or qualitative and quantitative measurement, may enhance our influence and enlarge the resources available to us to promote human health. In so doing, both individuals and organizations that represent CHP can strengthen our identity and expand our reach. (Tucker, Ferdinand, et al., 2007). Counseling health psychologists also need to use their systems perspective to advocate for public policy and other social change that would facilitate the integration of health issues with counseling. For example, counselors should advocate for funding and reimbursement mechanisms for outreach and prevention activities, and for changes in accreditation requirements to permit more training in systemic and preventive interventions. Counseling health psychologists should also build tighter professional ties and market our skills to medical schools, hospitals, and departments of public health.

With this conceptual model for CHP as a core element of their professional identity, we are hopeful that counseling health psychologists may continue to develop language, shared values, and motivation to retain their ties to counseling psychology and indeed provide leadership to the field. The *wellness-liberation model* (Prilleltensky & Prilleltensky, 2003) provides a synergistic example of how adoption of these CHP themes could be used to enhance the field. By using our unique skills in defining ourselves as counseling health psychologists, we may strengthen our professional identity and expand our influence and reach, leading to enhanced wellness for the field. By adhering to our core values in defining ourselves as counseling health psychologists, we may liberate ourselves from those aspects of allied fields, such as a medical model or a focus on individual-level change, that limit our professional influence. This growing wellness and liberation as a field may operate synergistically, permitting us to improve the well-being of and advance justice for the people we serve, allowing an expanding cycle of health and social change for CHP and for community and individual health.

Note

1. I am indebted to Mrdjenovich and Moore (2004) for the broad outlines of the historical background of counseling health psychology sketched here.

References

Adams, E. M. (2007). Moving from contemplation to preparation: Is counseling psychology ready to embrace culturally responsive prevention? *The Counseling Psychologist, 35*, 840–849.

Adler, N. E., & Conner Snibbe, A. (2003). The role of psychosocial processes in explaining the gradient between socioeconomic status and health. *Current Directions in Psychological Science, 12*, 119–123.

Albee, G. W. (2000a). Commentary on prevention and counseling psychology. *The Counseling Psychologist, 28*, 845–853.

Albee, G. W. (2000b). Critique of psychotherapy in American society. In C. R. Snyder, & R. E. Ingram (Eds.), *Handbook of psychological change: Psychotherapy process and practices for the 21st century* (pp. 689–706). New York: Wiley.

Alcorn, J. D. (1991). Counseling psychology and health applications. *The Counseling Psychologist, 19*, 325–341.

Altmaier, E. M. (1991). Research and practice roles for counseling psychologists in health care settings. *The Counseling Psychologist, 19*, 342–364.

Altmaier, E. M., From, R. P., Pearson, K. S., Gorbatenko-Roth, K. G.,& Ugolini, K. A. (1997). A prospective study to select and evaluate anesthesiology residents: Phase I, the critical incident technique. *Journal of Clinical Anesthesia, 9*, 629–636.

Altmaier, E. M., & Johnson, B. D. (1992). Health-related applications of counseling psychology: Toward health promotion and disease prevention across the life span. In S. D. Brown, & R. W. Lent Eds., *Handbook of counseling psychology* (pp. 315–347). New York: Wiley.

Altmaier, E. M., Johnson, B. D., & Paulsen, J. S. (1998). Issues in professional identity. In S. Roth-Roemer, S. E. R. Kurpius, & C. Carmin (Eds.), *The emerging role of counseling psychology in health care* (pp. 7–29). New York: W.W. Norton & Company.

Altmaier, E. M., Johnson, S. R., Tarico, V. S., & Laube, D. (1988). An empirical specification of residency performance dimensions. *Obstetrics and Gynecology, 72*, 126–130.

Altmaier, E. M, Lehmann, T. R., Russell, D. W., Weinstein, J. N., & Kao, C. F. (1992). The effectiveness of psychological interventions for the rehabilitation of low back pain: A randomized controlled trial evaluation. *Pain, 49*, 329–335.

Altmaier, E. M., McGuinness, G., Wood, P. S., Ross, R. R., Bartley, J., & Smith, W. L. (1990). Defining successful performance among pediatric residents. *Pediatrics, 85,* 139–143.

Altmaier, E. M., Russell, D. W., Kao, C. F., Lehmann, T. R., & Weinstein, J. N. (1993). Role of self-efficacy in rehabilitation outcome among chronic low back pain patients. *Journal of Counseling Psychology, 40,* 335–339.

Altmaier, E. M., Smith, W. L., O'Halloran, C. M., & Franken, E. A. (1992). The predictive utility of behavior-based interviewing compared with traditional interviewing in the selection of radiology residents. *Investigative Radiology, 27,* 385–389.

American Psychological Association. (n.d.). *Archival description of counseling psychology.* Retrieved July 19, 2009, from http://www.apa.org/crsppp/counseling.html.

American Psychological Association. (2003). Guidelines on multicultural education, training, research, practice, and organizational change for psychologists. *American Psychologist, 58,* 377–402.

Angell, M. (1993). Privilege and health: What is the connection? *New England Journal of Medicine, 329,* 126–127.

Bacho, E., Myhre, J., & James, L. C. (2008). An integrative approach to treating obesity and comorbid disorders. In R. Kessler, & D. Stafford (Eds.), *Collaborative medicine case studies: Evidence in practice* (pp. 287–298). New York: Springer.

Beresford, S. A. A., Johnson, K. C., Ritenbaugh, C., Lasser, N. L., Snetselaar, L. G., Black, H. R., et al. (2006). Low-fat dietary pattern and risk of colorectal cancer: The Women's Health Initiative Randomized Controlled Dietary Modification Trial. *Journal of the American Medical Association, 295,* 643–654.

Bernard, C. B. (1992). Counseling psychologists in general hospital settings: The continued quest for balance and challenge. *The Counseling Psychologist, 20,* 74–81.

Berry, J. D., Lloyd-Jones, D. M., Garside, D. B., & Greenland, P. (2007). Framingham risk score and prediction of coronary heart disease death in young men. *American Heart Journal, 154,* 80–86.

Blendon, R. J., & Donelan, K. (1988). Discrimination against people with AIDS: The public's perspective. *New England Journal of Medicine, 319,* 1022–1026.

Bor, R., Miller, R., Latz, M., & Salt, H. (1998). Counselling in health care settings: Some theoretical and practical considerations. *Counselling Psychology Review, 13,* 26, 34.

Bower, E. (1977). Mythologies, realities, and possibilities. In G. W. Albee, & J. M. Joffe (Eds.), *Primary prevention of psychopathology: Vol. 1. The issues* (pp. 18–41). Hanover, NH: University Press of New England.

Buki, L. P. (1999). Early detection of breast and cervical cancer among medically underserved Latinas. In M. Sotomayor, & A. Garcia (Eds.), *La familia: Traditions and realities* (pp. 67–85). Washington DC: National Hispanic Council on Aging.

Buki, L. P., Borrayo, E. A., Feigal, B. M., & Carrillo, I. Y. (2004). Are all Latinas the same? Perceived breast cancer screening barriers and facilitative conditions. *Psychology of Women Quarterly, 28,* 400–411.

Caplan, G. (1964). *Principles of preventive psychiatry.* New York: Basic Books.

Chwalisz, K. (1998). Rehabilitation medicine. In S. Roth-Roemer, S. E. R. Kurpius, & C. Carmin (Eds.), *The emerging role of counseling psychology in health care* (pp. 210–231). New York: W.W. Norton & Company.

Chwalisz, K. (2008). The future of counseling psychology: Improving quality of life for persons with chronic health issues. *The Counseling Psychologist, 36,* 98–107.

Chwalisz, K., & Obasi, E. (2008). Promoting health and preventing and reducing disease. In S. D. Brown, & R. W. Lent (Eds.), *Handbook of counseling psychology* (4th ed., pp. 517–534). New York: Wiley.

Clay, D. L., & Stern, M. (2005). Pediatric psychology in primary care. In L. C. James, & R. A. Folen (Eds.), *The primary care consultant: The next frontier for psychologists in hospitals and clinics* (pp. 155–172). Washington, DC: American Psychological Association Press.

Cranston, A. (1986). Psychology in the Veteran's Administration: A storied history, a vital failure. *American Psychologist, 41,* 990–995.

Cummings, N. A., Cummings, J. L., & Johnson, J. N. (1997). *Behavioral health in primary care: A guide for clinical integration.* Madison, CT: Psychosocial Press.

D'Andrea, M. (2004). Comprehensive school-based violence prevention training: A developmental-ecological training model. *Journal of Counseling and Development, 82,* 277–286.

D'Andrea, M., & Daniels, J. (1999). Exploring the psychology of White racism through naturalistic inquiry. *Journal of Counseling & Development, 77,* 93–101.

Daniels, J., Arredondo, P., & D'Andrea, M. (1999). Expanding counselors' thinking about the problem of violence. *Counseling Today, 41,* 12–17.

DeLeon, P. H., Rossmando, N. P., & Smedley, B. D. (2004). The future is primary care. In R. Frank, S. McDaniel, J. Bray, & M. Heldring (Eds.), *Primary care psychology* (pp. 63–92). Washington, DC: American Psychological Association Press.

Dougherty, K., Templer, D. I., & Brown, R. (1986). Psychological states in terminal cancer patients as measured over time. *Journal of Counseling Psychology, 33,* 357–359.

Earles, J. E. (2005). Innovative strategies for treating diabetes mellitus. In L. C. James, & R. A. Folen (Eds.), *The primary care consultant: The next frontier for psychologists in hospitals and clinics.* (pp. 105–120). Washington, DC: American Psychological Association Press.

Ebrahim, S., Beswick, A., Burke, M., & Davey Smith, G. (2006). Multiple risk factor interventions for primary prevention of coronary heart disease. *Cochrane Database of Systematic Reviews, 4,* CD001561.

Elliott, T. R., & Shewchuk, R. M. (1996). Defining health and well-being for the future of counseling psychology. *The Counseling Psychologist, 24,* 743–750.

Engel, G. L. (1977). The need for a new medical model: A challenge for biomedicine. *Science, 196,* 129–136.

Etherage, J. (2005). Pediatric behavioral health consultation: A new model for primary care. In L. C. James, & R. A. Folen (Eds.), *The primary care consultant: The next frontier for psychologists in hospitals and clinics* (pp. 173–190). Washington, DC: American Psychological Association Press.

Fitzgerald, L. F., & Osipow, S. H. (1986). An occupational analysis of counseling psychology: How special is the specialty? *American Psychologist, 41,* 535–544.

Ford, D. H. (1987). *Humans as self-constructing living systems: A developmental perspective on personality and behavior.* Hillsdale, NJ: Erlbaum.

Ford, D. H. (1990). Positive health and living system frameworks. *American Psychologist, 45,* 980–981.

Fouad, N. A., Gerstein, L. H., & Toporek, R. L. (2006). Social justice and counseling psychology in context.

In R. L. Toporek, L. H. Gerstein, N. A. Fouad, G. Roysircar, & T. Israel (Eds.), *Handbook for social justice in counseling psychology* (pp. 1–16). Thousand Oaks, CA: Sage.

Fouad, N. A., McPherson, R. H., Gerstein, L., Blustein, D. L., Elman, N., Helledy, K. I., & Metz, A. J. (2004). Houston, 2001: Context and legacy. *The Counseling Psychologist, 32,* 15–77.

Frank, R. G., McDaniel, S. H., Bray, J. H., & Heldring, M. (2004). *Primary care psychology.* Washington, DC: American Psychological Association Press.

Frazier, P. A., Tix, A. P., & Barnett, C. L. (2003). The relational context of social support: Relationship satisfaction moderates the relations between enacted support and distress. *Personality and Social Psychology Bulletin, 29,* 1133–1146.

Gibbs, H. W., & Achterberg-Lawlis, J. (1978). Spiritual values and death anxiety: Implications for counseling with terminal cancer patients. *Journal of Counseling Psychology, 25,* 563–569.

Good, G. E. (1992). Counseling psychologists in hospital/medical settings: Dilemmas facing new professionals. *The Counseling Psychologist, 20,* 67–73.

Goodyear, R. K., Murdock, N., Lichtenberg, J. W., McPherson, R., Koetting, K., & Petren, S. (2008). Stability and change in counseling psychologists' identities, roles, functions, and career satisfaction across 15 years. *The Counseling Psychologist, 36,* 220–249.

Gornick, M. E., Eggers, P. W., Reilly, T. W., Mentnech, R. M., Fitterman, L. K., Kucken, L. E., & Vladeck, B. C. (1996). Effects of race and income on mortality and use of services among Medicare beneficiaries. *New England Journal of Medicine, 335,* 791–799.

Hackett, G., & Horan, J. J. (1980). Stress inoculation for pain: What's really going on? *Journal of Counseling Psychology, 27,* 107–116.

Hage, S. M., Romano, J. L., Conyne, R. K., Kenny, M., Matthews, C., Schwartz, J. P., & Waldo, M. (2007). Best practice guidelines on prevention practice, research, training, and social advocacy for psychologists. *The Counseling Psychologist, 35,* 493–566.

Hayes, J. A., & Gelso, C. J. (1993). Male counselors' discomfort with gay and HIV-infected clients. *Journal of Counseling Psychology, 40,* 86–93.

Herman, K. C., Tucker, C. M., Ferdinand, L. A., Mirsu-Paun, A., Hasan, N. T., & Beato, C. (2007). Culturally sensitive health care and counseling psychology: An overview. *The Counseling Psychologist, 35,* 633–649.

Hoffman, M. A. (1991). Counseling the HIV-infected client: A psychosocial model for assessment and intervention. *The Counseling Psychologist, 19,* 467–542.

Hoffman, M. A. (1993). Multiculturalism as a force in counseling clients with HIV-related concerns. *The Counseling Psychologist, 21,* 712–731.

Hoffman, M. A., & Driscoll, J. M. (2000). Health promotion and disease prevention: A concentric biopsychosocial model of health status. In S. D. Brown, & R. W. Lent (Eds.), *Handbook of counseling psychology* (3rd ed., pp. 532–570). New York: Wiley.

Hopps, J. A., & Liu, W. M. (2006). Working for social justice from within the health care system: The role of social class in psychology. In R. L. Toporek, L. H. Gerstein, N. A. Fouad, G. Roysircar, & T. Israel (Eds.), *Handbook for social justice in counseling psychology* (pp. 318–337). Thousand Oaks, CA: Sage.

Howard, B. V., Manson, J. E., Stefanick, M. L., Beresford, S. A., Frank, G., Jones, B., et al. (2006). Low-fat dietary pattern and weight change over 7 years: The Women's Health Initiative Dietary Modification Trial. *Journal of the American Medical Association, 295,* 39–49.

Howard, B. V., Van Horn, L., Hsia, J., Manson, J. E., Stefanick, M. L., Wassertheil-Smoller, S., et al. (2006). Low-fat dietary pattern and risk of cardiovascular disease: The Women's Health Initiative Randomized Controlled Dietary Modification Trial. *Journal of the American Medical Association, 295,* 655–666.

Huynh, U. K., & Roysircar, G. (2006). Community health promotion curriculum: A case study of Southeast Asian refugees. In R. L. Toporek, L. H. Gerstein, N. A. Fouad, G. Roysircar, & T. Israel (Eds.), *Handbook for social justice in counseling psychology* (pp. 338–357). Thousand Oaks, CA: Sage.

Institute of Medicine Committee on Understanding and Eliminating Racial and Ethnic Disparities in Health Care. (2003). *Unequal treatment: Confronting racial and ethnic disparities in health care.* Washington, DC: National Academy of Science.

Isler III, W. C., Peterson, A. L., & Isler, D. E. (2005). Behavioral treatment of insomnia in primary care. In L. C. James, & R. A. Folen (Eds.), *The primary care consultant: The next frontier for psychologists in hospitals and clinics* (pp. 155–172). Washington, DC: American Psychological Association Press.

James, L. C. (2006). Integrating clinical psychology into primary care settings. *Journal of Clinical Psychology, 62,* 1207–1212.

James, L. C. (2009, January 9). *Integrating mental health services into the primary care setting.* Workshop presented at Walter Reed Army Medical Center, Washington, DC.

James, L. C., & Folen, R. (1999). A paradigm shift in the scope of practice for health psychologists: Training health psychologists to be primary care case managers. *Professional Psychology: Research and Practice, 30,* 352–356.

James, L. C., & Folen, R. A. (2005). *The primary care consultant: The next frontier for psychologists in hospitals and clinics.* Washington, DC: American Psychological Association Press.

James, L. C., Folen, R. A., Garland, F., Noce, M., Edwards, C., Gohdes, D., et al. (1997). The Tripler LEAN Program: A healthy lifestyle model for the treatment of obesity. *Military Medicine, 162,* 328–332.

James, L. C., Folen, R. A., Page, H., Noce, M., & Britton, C. (1999). The Tripler LEAN Program: A two-year follow-up report. *Military Medicine, 164,* 389–395.

Jarrett, E. M. (2008). Treating depression in the primary care setting. In L. C. James, & W. T. O'Donohue (Eds.), *The primary care toolkit* (pp. 133–168). New York: Springer.

Joint United Nations Programme on HIV/AIDS. (2008). *2008 report on the global AIDS epidemic.* Retrieved June 26, 2009, from http://www.unaids.org/en/KnowledgeCentre/HIVData/GlobalReport/2008/2008_Global_report.asp.

Kaut, K. P. (2006). Counseling psychology in the era of genetic testing: Considerations for practice, research, and training. *The Counseling Psychologist, 34,* 461–488.

Kenny, M. E., Waldo, M., Warter, E. H., & Barton, C. (2002). School-linked prevention: Theory, science, and practice for enhancing the lives of children and youth. *The Counseling Psychologist, 30,* 726–748.

Kessler, M., & Albee, G. W. (1975). Primary prevention. *Annual Review of Psychology, 26,* 557–591.

Koller, M. T., Steyerberg, E. W., Wolbers, M., Stijnen, T., Bucher, H. C., Hunink, M. G. M., & Witteman, J. C. M. (2007). Validity of the Framingham point scores in the elderly: Results from the Rotterdam study. *American Heart Journal, 154,* 87–93.

Kop, W. J. (2005). Psychological interventions with coronary heart disease. In L. C. James, & R. A. Folen (Eds.), *The primary care consultant: The next frontier for psychologists in hospitals and clinics* (pp. 61–82). Washington, DC: American Psychological Association Press.

Krumboltz, J. D., Becker-Haven, J. F., & Burnett, K. F. (1979). Counseling psychology. *Annual Review of Psychology, 30,* 355–402.

Lavin, D. (2008). Smoking. In L. C. James, & W. T. O'Donohue (Eds.), *The primary care toolkit* (pp. 277–290). New York: Springer.

Law, W. A., & Buermeyer, C. (2005). Management and treatment of HIV/AIDS in primary care. In L. C. James, & R. A. Folen (Eds.), *The primary care consultant: The next frontier for psychologists in hospitals and clinics* (pp. 83–104). Washington, DC: American Psychological Association Press.

Lent, R. W. (1990). Further reflections on the public image of counseling psychology. *The Counseling Psychologist, 18,* 324–332.

Levensky, E. (2005). Increasing medication adherence in chronic illness: Guidelines for behavioral health-care clinicians working in the primary care setting. In W. T. O'Donohue, M. R. Byrd, N. A. Cummings, & D. A. Henderson (Eds.), *Behavioral integrative care: Treatments that work in primary care* (pp. 347–366). New York: Brunner-Routledge.

Li, C. I., Malone, K. E., & Daling, J. R. (2003). Differences in breast cancer stage, treatment, and survival by race and ethnicity. *Archives of Internal Medicine, 163,* 49–56.

Maguire, C. P., McNally, C. J., Britton, P. J., Werth, J. L., Jr., & Borges, N. J. (2008). Challenges of work: Voices of persons with HIV disease. *The Counseling Psychologist, 36,* 42–89.

Matarazzo, J. D. (1980). Behavioral health and behavioral medicine: Frontiers for a new health psychology. *American Psychologist, 35,* 807–817.

McDaniel, S. H., Hargrove, D. S., Belar, C. D., Schroeder, C. S., & Freeman, E. L. (2004). Recommendations for education and training in primary care. In R. Frank, S. H. McDaniel, J. Bray, & M. Heldring (Eds.), *Primary care psychology* (pp. 63–92). Washington, DC: American Psychological Association Press.

McDaniel, S. H., & Hepworth, J. (2004). Family psychology in primary care: Managing issues of power and dependence through collaboration. In R. Frank, S. H. McDaniel, J. Bray, & M. Heldring (Eds.), *Primary care psychology* (pp. 113–132). Washington, DC: American Psychological Association Press.

Merluzzi, T. V., & Sanchez, M. A. M. (1998). Psychological perspectives on life-threatening illness: Cancer and AIDS. In S. Roth-Roemer, S. E. R. Kurpius, & C. Carmin (Eds.), *The emerging role of counseling psychology in health care* (pp. 157–190). New York: W.W. Norton & Company.

Millon, T. (1982). On the nature of clinical health psychology. In T. Millon, C. J. Green, R. B. Meagher (Eds.), *Handbook of clinical health psychology.* New York: Plenum.

Mpofu, E., & Harley, D. A. (2006). Racial and disability identity: Implications for the career counseling of African Americans with disabilities. *Rehabilitation Counseling Bulletin, 50,* 14–23.

Mrdjenovich, A. J., & Moore, B. A. (2004). The professional identity of counselling psychologists in health care: A review and call for research. *Counselling Psychology Quarterly, 17,* 69–79.

Narrow, W. E., Reiger, D. A., Rae, D. S., Manderscheid, R. W., & Locke, B. Z. (1993). Use of services by persons with mental and addictive disorders: Findings from the National Institute of Mental Health Epidemiological Catchment Area Program. *Archives of General Psychiatry, 50,* 95–107.

National Center for Health Statistics. (n.d.). *Leading causes of death 1900–1998.* Retrieved June 6, 2009, from http://www.cdc.gov/nchs/data/dvs/lead1900_98.pdf.

National Institute on Disability & Rehabilitation Research. (1999). *NIDRR long-range plan.* Washington, DC: Office of Special Education and Rehabilitation Services.

Neimeyer, G. J., Bowman, J., & Stewart, A. E. (2001). Internship and initial job placements in counseling psychology: A 26-year retrospective. *The Counseling Psychologist, 7,* 82–85.

Nicholas, D. R., & Gobble, D. C. (1990). On the importance of disregulatory processes in models of health. *American Psychologist, 45,* 981–982.

Noonan, B. M., Gallor, S. M., Hensler-McGinnis, N. F., Fassinger, R. E., Wang, S., & Goodman, J. (2004). Challenge and success: A qualitative study of the career development of highly achieving women with physical and sensory disabilities. *Journal of Counseling Psychology, 51,* 68–80.

O'Byrne, K. K., Brammer, S. K., Davidson, M. M., & Poston, W. S. C. (2002). Primary prevention in counseling psychology: Back to the future. *The Counseling Psychologist, 30,* 330–344.

O'Donohue, W. T., Byrd, M. R., Cummings, N. A., & Henderson, D. A. (2005). *Behavioral integrative care: Treatments that work in primary care.* New York: Brunner-Routledge.

Okey, J. L. (1998). Pain management. In S. Roth-Roemer, S. E. R. Kurpius, & C. Carmin (Eds.), *The emerging role of counseling psychology in health care* (pp. 191–209). New York: W. W. Norton & Company.

Olkin, R., & Pledger, C. (2003). Can disability studies and psychology join hands? *American Psychologist, 58,* 296–304.

Otis, J. D., Reid, M. C., & Kerns, R. D. (2005). Multidisciplinary approaches to pain management in primary care settings. In L. C. James, & R. A. Folen (Eds.), *The primary care consultant: The next frontier for psychologists in hospitals and clinics* (pp. 41–60). Washington, DC: American Psychological Association Press.

Parker, H. J., & Chan, F. (1990). Psychologists in rehabilitation. Preparation and experience. *Rehabilitation Psychology, 35,* 239–248.

Peterson, D. B., & Elliott, T. R. (2008). Advances in conceptualizing and studying disability. In R. Lent, & S. Brown (Eds.), *Handbook of counseling psychology* (4th ed., pp. 212–230). New York: John Wiley & Sons.

Petersen, S., Heesacker, M., & Marsh, R. D. (2001). Medical decision making among cancer patients. *Journal of Counseling Psychology, 48,* 239–244.

Pinkerton, S. S., & McAleer, C. A. (1976). Influence of client diagnosis–cancer–on counselor decisions. *Journal of Counseling Psychology, 23,* 575–578.

Poleshuck, E. L. (2005). Women's health and the role in primary care psychology. In L. C. James, & R. A. Folen (Eds.),

The primary care consultant: The next frontier for psychologists in hospitals and clinics (pp. 217–242). Washington, DC: American Psychological Association Press.

Prentice, R. L., Caan, B., Chlebowski, R. T., Patterson, R., Kuller, L. H., Ockene, J. K., et al. (2006). Low-fat dietary pattern and risk of invasive breast cancer: The Women's Health Initiative Randomized Controlled Dietary Modification Trial. *Journal of the American Medical Association, 295,* 629–642.

Prilleltensky, I., & Prilleltensky, O. (2003). Synergies for wellness and liberation in counseling psychology. *The Counseling Psychologist, 31,* 273–281.

Prochaska, J. O., & DiClemente, C. C. (2005). The transtheoretical approach. In J. C. Norcross, & M. R. Goldfried (Eds.), *Handbook of psychotherapy integration* (pp. 147–171). New York: Oxford University Press.

Reese, L. E., & Vera, E. M. (2007). Culturally relevant prevention: The scientific and practical considerations of community-based programs. *The Counseling Psychologist, 35,* 763–778.

Regier, D. A., Narrow, W. E., Rae, D. S., Manderscheid, R. W., Locke, B. Z., & Goodwin F. K. (1993). The de facto US mental and addictive disorders service system: Epidemiologic catchment area prospective 1-year prevalence rates of disorders and services. *Archives of General Psychiatry, 50,* 85–94.

Ridley, C. R., Mendoza, D. W., Kanitz, B. E., Angermeier, L., & Zent, R. (1994). Cultural sensitivity in multicultural counseling: A perceptual schema model. *Journal of Counseling Psychology, 41,* 125–136.

Rogers, J. R., & Britton, P. J. (1994). AIDS and rational suicide: A counseling psychology perspective or a slide on the slippery slope. *The Counseling Psychologist, 22,* 171–178.

Romano, J. L., & Hage, S. M. (2000a). Prevention and counseling psychology: Revitalizing commitments for the 21st century. *The Counseling Psychologist, 28,* 733–763.

Romano. J. L., & Hage, S. M. (2000b). Prevention: A call to action. *The Counseling Psychologist, 28,* 854–856.

Romano, J. L., & Netland, J. D. (2008). The application of the theory of reasoned action and planned behavior to prevention science in counseling psychology. *The Counseling Psychologist, 36,* 777–806.

Rowan, A., & Runyan, C. N. (2005). A primer on the consultation model of primary care behavioral health integration. In L. C. James, & R. A. Folen (Eds.), *The primary care consultant: The next frontier for psychologists in hospitals and clinics* (pp. 9–28). Washington, DC: American Psychological Association Press.

Roysircar, G. (2006). Counseling health psychology's collaborative role in the community. In R. L. Toporek, L. H. Gerstein, N. A. Fouad, G. Roysircar, & T. Israel (Eds.), *Handbook for social justice in counseling psychology* (pp. 313–317). Thousand Oaks, CA: Sage.

Schiffner, T., & Buki, L. P. (2006). Latina college students' sexual health beliefs about HPV. *Cultural Diversity and Ethnic Minority Psychology, 12,* 687–696.

Schmidt, C. K., Hoffman, M. A., & Taylor, N. (2006). Social justice related to working with HIV/AIDS from a counseling health psychology perspective. In R. L. Toporek, L. H. Gerstein, N. A. Fouad, G. Roysircar, & T. Israel (Eds.), *Handbook for social justice in counseling psychology* (pp. 358–374). Thousand Oaks, CA: Sage.

Schofield, W. (1969). The role of psychology in the delivery of health services. *American Psychologist, 24,* 565–584.

Schulman, K. A., Berlin, J. A., Harless, W., Kerner, J. F., Sistrunk, S., Gersh, B. J., et al. (1999). The effect of race and sex on physicians' recommendations for cardiac catheterization. *New England Journal of Medicine, 340,* 618–626.

Schwartz, G. E. (1982). Testing the biopsychosocial model: The ultimate challenge facing behavioral medicine? *Journal of Consulting and Clinical Psychology, 50,* 1040–1053.

Scott, C. W. (1980). History of the division of counseling psychology: 1945–1963. In J. M. Whiteley (Ed.), *The history of counseling psychology* (pp. 25–40). Monterey, CA: Brooks/Cole.

Seeman, J. (1989). Toward a model of positive health. *American Psychologist, 44,* 1099–1109.

Singer, J. E., & Krantz, D. S. (1982). Perspectives on the interface between psychology and public health. *American Psychologist, 37,* 955–960.

Smith, E. J. (2006). The strengths-based counseling model. *The Counseling Psychologist, 34,* 13–79.

Strosahl, K. (2005). Training behavioral health and primary care providers for integrated care: A core competence approach. In W. T. O'Donohue, M. R. Byrd, N. A. Cummings, & D. A. Henderson (Eds.), *Behavioral integrative care: Treatments that work in the primary care setting* (pp. 15–52). New York: Brunner-Routledge.

Sue, D. W., & Sue, D. (1999). *Counseling the culturally different: Theory and practice* (3rd ed.). Hoboken, NJ: John Wiley & Sons Inc.

Tallman, B. A., Altmaier, E., & Garcia, C. (2007). Finding benefit from cancer. *Journal of Counseling Psychology, 54,* 481–487.

Tarico, V., Smith, W. L., Altmaier, E. M., Franken, E. A., & VanVelzen, D. R. (1984). Critical incident interviewing in evaluation of residency performance. *Radiology, 152,* 327–329.

Thoresen, C. E., & Eagleston, J. R. (1984). Counseling, health, and psychology. In S. D. Brown, & R. W. Lent (Eds.), *Handbook of counseling psychology* (pp. 930–955). New York: Wiley.

Thoresen, C. E., & Eagleston, J. R. (1985). Counseling for health. *The Counseling Psychologist, 13,* 15–87.

Tix, A. P., & Frazier, P. A. (1998). The use of religious coping during stressful life events: Main effects, moderation, and mediation. *Journal of Consulting and Clinical Psychology, 66,* 411–422.

Todd, K. H., Deaton, C., D'Adamo, A. P., & Goe, L. (2000). Ethnicity and analgesic practice. *Annals of Emergency Medicine, 35,* 11–16.

Tucker, C. M., Ferdinand, L. A., Mirsu-Paun, A., Herman, K. C., Delgado-Romero, E., van den Berg, J. J., & Jones, J. D. (2007). The roles of counseling psychologists in reducing health disparities. *The Counseling Psychologist, 35,* 650–678.

Tucker, C. M., Herman, K. C., Pedersen, T. R., Higley, B., Montrichard, M., & Ivery, P. (2003). Cultural sensitivity in physician-patients relationships: Perspectives of an ethnically diverse sample of low-income primary care patients. *Medical Care, 41,* 859–870.

Tucker, C. M., Herman, K. C., Ferdinand, L. A., Bailey, T. R., Lopez, M. T., Beato, C., et al. (2007). Providing patient-centered culturally sensitive health care: A formative model. *The Counseling Psychologist, 35,* 679–705.

Ware, J. E., Manning, W. G., Duan, N., Wells, K. B., & Newhouse, J. P. (1984). Health status and the use of outpatient mental health services. *American Psychologist, 39,* 1090–1100.

Werth, J. L., Jr. (1992). Rational suicide and AIDS: Considerations for the psychotherapist. *The Counseling Psychologist, 20,* 645–659.

Werth, J. L., Jr., Borges, N. J., McNally, C. J., Maguire, C. P., & Britton, P. J. (2008a). Integrating health and vocational psychology: HIV and employment. *The Counseling Psychologist, 36,* 8–15.

Werth, J. L., Jr., Borges, N. J., McNally, C. J., Maguire, C. P., & Britton, P. J. (2008b). The intersections of work, health, diversity, and social justice: Helping people living with HIV disease. *The Counseling Psychologist, 36,* 16–41.

Wilkinson, R. G. (1996). *Unhealthy societies: The afflictions of inequity.* London: Routledge.

Williams, D. R., & Neighbors, H. W. (2001). Racism, discrimination, and hypertension: Evidence and needed research. *Ethnicity and Disease, 11,* 800–816.

Wood, P. S., Smith, W. L., Altmaier, E. M., Tarico, V. S., & Franken, E. A. (1990). A prospective study of cognitive and noncognitive selection criteria as predictors of resident performance. *Investigative Radiology, 25,* 855–859.

World Health Organization. (2008). *The top 10 causes of death.* Retrieved June 6, 2009, from http://www.who.int/mediacentre/factsheets/fs310/en/index.html.

Worthington, E. L., Jr., & Shumate, M. (1981). Imagery and verbal counseling methods in stress inoculation training for pain control. *Journal of Counseling Psychology, 28,* 1–6.

Counseling Psychology and Occupational Health Psychology

Donald E. Eggerth *and* Thomas R. Cunningham

Abstract

Given its historical roots in vocational psychology and its current emphases on multiculturalism, positive psychology and social justice, counseling psychology is uniquely poised to contribute to the emerging, interdisciplinary field of occupational health psychology (OHP). Despite a halving of work-related injury rates in recent decades, work remains the sixth leading cause of death in the United States. The goal of OHP is to protect and promote the health of workers and of their families, and to improve the quality of work life. Occupational health psychology has a threefold focus on the work environment, the individual worker, and the interface between work and family. Specific topics that OHP is attempting to address include work-related stress; occupational health disparities related to gender, age, ethnicity or race, work–family interface; increasing intervention effectiveness; improving safety climate; job design; and work organization.

Keywords: Occupational health psychology, work stress, occupational health disparities, burnout, safety climate, work–family interface, person–environment fit

As a field, counseling psychology never seems afraid to take on big challenges. This should not be surprising, given its roots in Frank Parsons' visionary efforts to improve the lives of the huge cohort of recent immigrants to the United States at the turn of the 20th century. In subsequent decades, counseling psychology repeatedly proved itself robust and relevant enough to successfully contribute to addressing emergent social concerns including the Great Depression, the Civil Rights Movement, Women's Liberation and Gay Pride—not to mention the world wars.

The current breadth of counseling psychology applications may be seen in Bingham's (2001) categorization of the field around four core themes: vocational psychology, positive psychology, multicultural psychology, and social justice. Positive psychology, multicultural psychology, and social justice are frequently viewed as more recent structures built upon the foundation of vocational psychology. However, if one looks at the intent of the founders of

the field (allowing for differences in terminology), vocational psychology, positive psychology, multicultural psychology, and social justice were all present from the start and were not viewed as separate themes, but as facets of a common goal—the betterment of the individual and society (Eggerth, 2008). For these founders, work was the powerful vehicle by which self-, economic, political, and social empowerments were attained. Indeed, Frank Parsons, the individual considered by most to be the father of vocational psychology, and therefore a "grandfather" of counseling psychology, was very much concerned with all of these topics (Blustein, McWhirter, & Perry, 2005; O'Brien, 2001). Parsons hoped to improve the overall quality of life of poor immigrant workers and their families by more thoughtfully matching workers with jobs. Careful matching of job skills to employment led to job security and therefore financial security, the foundation upon which all else could be built.

Subsequent generations of vocational psychologists developed more sophisticated tools and models to meet the needs of adult workers. Many of the approaches used in the first college counseling centers were adapted from those developed during the Great Depression to facilitate matching unemployed adults with new jobs. In this first generation of counseling centers, vocational psychologists sought to further empower Parsons' immigrant families by facilitating the success of their children at colleges and universities (Williamson, 1939). The need for the military to classify and train millions of new recruits during World War II provided a huge boost to the development of vocational psychology. These newly developed models and methods were further refined in campus settings as returning servicemen took advantage of G.I. Bill benefits and sought college degrees in unprecedented numbers.

Clearly, during these very productive early decades, meeting the needs of adult workers set the agenda for vocational psychologists. These models were then fruitfully adapted for use with students. However, in subsequent decades, the primary emphasis of the field shifted toward meeting the needs of students, with only indirect consideration of adult workers. For many, vocational psychology is now virtually synonymous with career guidance performed in campus settings. Choosing a college major has become the proxy for an actual job or career.

A number of interconnected factors likely led to this shift in emphasis. Prominent among these factors was the postwar economic boom. Unemployment was low and union membership was at all-time highs—adult workers simply did not need the level of assistance they had in prior decades. At the same time, their children, the demographic bulge of the "baby boom," were working their way through the educational system. Sheer numbers, coupled with an economic prosperity that allowed many to be the first in their families to attend college, greatly increased enrollment at colleges and universities. Civil rights advances opened the doors of higher education to yet more students and further swelled enrollment. It is no wonder that vocational psychology focused on successfully assimilating this mass of new students.

Globalization

In the 1980s, the economic phenomena now referred to as *globalization* first began to adversely impact businesses and workers in industrialized countries. As technology and international agreements increasingly rendered distance and borders less relevant, "First World" manufacturing jobs were shifting to less developed countries. Corporations scrambled to maintain a competitive edge through a flurry of mergers and/or downsizings (National Institute for Occupational Safety and Health; NIOSH, 2002). New management models, such as just-in-time production, lean management, multitasking, outsourcing, and an ever-increasing use of contractors or temporary employees, were embraced. Union membership steadily declined. The bonds of loyalty between employer and worker broke down. Workers no longer expected, nor could realistically expect, to work their entire careers for a single employer. Making a virtue out of necessity, workers were encouraged to view themselves as entrepreneurs who moved frequently from job to job on the road to independence and self-sufficiency.

Although these many changes positively benefited corporate bottom lines, they exacted great costs from workers. Many workers found themselves needing to switch employment, if not careers, often at lower incomes, in their forties and fifties—ages that previously were associated with stable employment and peak earning potential. All of these changes were accompanied by stress, both for workers losing or changing jobs and for those retaining employment, but needing to adapt to new contingencies. Citing the results from several surveys, the National Institute for Occupational Safety and Health (NIOSH; 1999) reported that between 26% and 40% of American workers consider themselves to be very stressed at work.

Work-related stress has now become one of the leading occupational health problems in the United States (NIOSH, 2004). In 2001, workers with anxiety, stress, or neurotic disorders lost a median of 25 workdays, as compared to a median of 6 workdays for all other sources of nonfatal occupational injury and illness. Over 42% of workers with anxiety, stress, or neurotic disorders were away from work more than 30 days, as compared to only 22% of workers suffering from all other sources of occupational injury and illnesses. Clearly, on a case-by-case basis, stress-related disorders have the potential to cost businesses far more than other sources of occupational injury and illness. Of course, these statistics do not even touch upon the "ripple effect" of stress-related disorders on family and friends.

Emergence of Occupational Health Psychology

Although its earliest roots can be traced back a century, occupational health psychology (OHP) largely emerged, as a discipline, in response to the human costs associated with the changes to work organization and structure that were first implemented in the 1980s and continued through the 1990s to the present (Barling & Griffiths, 2003). Professionals in medicine, public health, and behavioral sciences could not help but to take notice of the accumulative costs of work-related stress upon workers and their families. The term *occupational health psychology* was introduced by Raymond, Wood, and Patrick (1990) in their seminal paper arguing for the creation of doctoral-level training programs that integrated health psychology and public health, and which incorporated elements of occupational medicine, nursing, preventative medicine, behavioral medicine, political science, sociology and business.

The goal of OHP is to improve the quality of work life, and to protect and promote the health of workers and of their families (Quick, 1999). Occupational health psychology is interdisciplinary, involving most areas of psychology and drawing upon fields such as public health, sociology, medicine, and industrial engineering. Occupational health psychology is typically characterized as having a threefold focus on the work environment, the individual worker, and the interface between work and family. Interventions and/or research range across all three levels (primary, secondary, and tertiary) of the public health model of prevention. Although work-related stress continues to be of central interest to OHP, the scope of the field has expanded to address a wide range of behavior interactions and consequences related to reducing the number of workers injured or killed and/or increasing worker well-being. Examples of these areas include worker decision processes concerning the use of personal protective equipment (PPE), such as safety glasses and helmets; the managerial decision processes related to providing PPE and other occupational safety and health (OSH) resources; risk perception and risk acceptance; improving the impact of OSH training and occupational health disparities related to gender, age, ethnicity, or race; the impact of work upon family life in an era during which the barriers between work and home are dissolving; safety climate; and safety culture.

Connecting Counseling Psychology and Occupational Health Psychology
Given its roots in addressing the needs of working adults, it would seem that OHP would be a natural fit for counseling psychology. However, counseling psychology as a whole has been slow to perceive the relevance OHP. In 1992, NIOSH partnered with the American Psychological Association (APA) to develop postdoctoral training in OHP. NIOSH has funded (through APA) the development of OHP training programs at 12 universities across the United States. To date, only one of these programs (University of Minnesota) is based within a counseling psychology program. The other programs are affiliated with industrial/organizational, clinical and/or social psychology programs, schools of public health, and schools of medicine.

Exceptional among counseling psychologists, more than a decade ago in her presidential address to the Society of Counseling Psychology, Jo-Ida Hansen (1995) called for counseling psychology to recognize and address the ever-increasing levels of work stress and ever-decreasing levels of job satisfaction experienced by American workers. Hansen made a clear case for the expanding conceptualization of career guidance beyond mere choice of career and into the realm of ongoing work adjustment by addressing topics such as the impact of corporate restructuring on worker well-being, the work–family interface, and the incursion of work upon leisure time through advances in communication technologies. Hansen called for the development of counseling psychology training programs and research agendas to address these and other occupational health issues. She is a founding member of the Society for Occupational Health Psychology, and it is due to her leadership that the University of Minnesota became the only counseling psychology program in the United States to take advantage of APA/NIOSH funding for the development of OHP training programs.

Lawrence Jones (1996) was another early voice for OHP concerns in counseling psychology. Jones argued forcefully that, in an increasingly insecure world of work, career counselors were doing their clients a disservice by only focusing on the "positive" aspects of a given occupation. Jones argued that the "negative" aspects should also be taken into account. For example, a student contemplating medical school should not just be allowed to view it as an opportunity to express interests and skills in science or to meet values related to altruism, social esteem, or income. This same student should be made aware of the risks from exposures to diseases, such as blood-borne pathogens, the very long work hours, high levels of work-related stress, and the attendant toll upon families, including a high divorce rate.

More recently, David Blustein (2006) called for broadening the focus of vocational psychology from matching college students with majors, which presumably lead to related careers, to the entire spectrum of how work impacts individuals and society. He termed to this new perspective the *psychology of work*. Blustein used Maslow's hierarchy of needs as a framework within which to discuss all of the reasons people work. He argues that vocational psychology has focused too much on meeting higher-level needs related to self-actualization and self-expression and has largely ignored the plight of individuals who work to meet basic survival needs—food, shelter, security.

Before further exploring connections between counseling psychology and OHP, let us first explore the scope of OSH problems and delve deeper into the historical roots of OHP.

The Impact of Occupational Safety and Health failures

Despite a nearly 50% decrease in the rate of work-related injuries since the Occupational Safety and Health Act of 1970 was implemented (NIOSH, 2004), working for a living remains the sixth leading cause of death in the United States (Pickle, Mongiole, Jones, & White, 1996). Although the number of work-related mortalities is not nearly as high as the deaths attributable to heart disease, strokes, or lung cancer (first, second, and third leading causes of death, respectively), it is larger than those of "higher-profile" causes of death, such as diabetes (seventh), motor vehicle accidents (eighth), breast cancer (ninth), suicide (tenth), and HIV/AIDS (eleventh), all of which have been the targets of ongoing public health prevention campaigns. NIOSH (2003) estimates that each day (7 days a week/365 days a year) in American workplaces, there are 9,000 disabling injuries and 16 deaths from injuries. An additional 137 people die each day from work-related diseases.

Due to underreporting and miscategorizations, it is extremely difficult to estimate the true costs of OSH failures to the United States economy (Schulte, 2005). The most comprehensive study of the burden of occupational injury and disease (Leigh, Markowitz, Fahs, Shin, & Landigan, 1997) is now over a decade old. However, even when unadjusted for inflation, the economic cost remains staggering. Leigh et al. estimated the annual cost (in 1992 dollars) of OSH failures in the United States to be $171 billion, of which injuries cost $145 billion and illnesses $26 billion. In comparison, the cost for all forms of cancer was $171 billion, $164 billion for heart disease, $67 billion for Alzheimer's disease, and $30 billion for HIV/AIDS. It is significant to note that Leigh et al. estimated that 6%–10% of all cancers and 5%–10% of heart disease are likely attributable to occupational causes. These illnesses can take many years to develop prior to medical diagnosis; in some instances, the individual may have long since changed employment and consequently no connection is made between past workplace exposures and current medical conditions. This time lag further complicates efforts to calculate the monetary costs of OSH failures and suggests that the $26 billion estimate for illnesses may be low.

The economic burden of OSH failures is so large for two reasons. One is the sheer number of people involved. Most adults have jobs. The second reason is the enormous impact of disabling injuries and work-related diseases. Disabled workers may be off their jobs for days, weeks, months, or years. Some never return to work. Their injury-related expenses include initial and long-term medical costs, rehabilitation, lost productivity, and in some cases, medical retirements.

Work-related diseases are often the result of toxic exposures and can involve years of convalescence prior to death. Of course, these statistics do not even begin to quantify the nonmonetary costs of OSH failures. For workers, these losses may include well-being, work identity, and family role. For family members, these costs may include adverse impact upon career goals due to the demands of caregiving, increased stress levels, role reassignment within the family, or even the emotional toll of watching a loved one die slowly, and perhaps painfully.

As discussed previously, the number of lost work days for workers with anxiety, stress, and neurotic disorders was, on average, more than four times greater than the number of workdays lost for all nonfatal injuries or illnesses together (NIOSH, 2004). So, although the prevalence of these disorders was low in comparison to other types of illnesses and injuries, on a case-by-case basis, anxiety, stress, and neurotic disorders have the potential to be far more costly than other work-related injuries or illnesses. Goetzel et al. (1998) reported that health care costs were nearly 50% greater for workers who report high levels of stress. Stress also costs businesses in other ways. Atkinson (2004) reported that stress was a contributing factor in 80% of all work-related injuries and in 40% of workplace turnovers. A recent survey of more than 7,600 U.S.

workers found that 78% say they feel burned-out, 46% feel their workload has increased over the past 6 months, and 45% describe their current workload as "heavy" or "too heavy" (Harris Interactive, 2008).

Traditionally, OSH has been viewed as the domain of industrial hygienists, toxicologists, and engineers. Until recently, the only behavioral scientists contributing to OSH were human factors specialists. However, with recognition of the importance of work-related stress and the subsequent emergence of the field of OHP, it is now recognized that all psychologists can play an important role in reducing the incidence and impact of OSH failures.

Historical Roots of Occupational Health Psychology

Barling and Griffiths (2003) suggest that the roots of OHP may be found in efforts to understand and later to remedy the impact of application of Frederick Taylor's management principles on factory workers. Early in the last century, Taylor argued that industrial productivity can be improved by simplifying, compartmentalizing, and standardizing worker tasks. Taylor's approach came to be termed *scientific management*. Taylor advocated the separation of "thinking" about work from the actual "doing" of work. Thinking about work was considered the domain of industrial engineers, who designed processes that were then implemented by managers. Doing the actual work, without thinking, was the role of workers. In its purest form, scientific management aimed to make workers interchangeable, and consideration of the emotional responses of workers was thought to interfere with productivity.

Although scientific management seemed to hold great economic promise, managers quickly realized that its implementation did not guarantee increases in production (Barling & Griffiths, 2003). It did however, tend to lower employee morale and increase the physical and mental health problems of workers. In addition, research guided by Taylor's principles found that, contrary to expectations, workers feelings and perceptions did impact productivity. One early finding is famously known as the *Hawthorne effect*. The Hawthorne effect is typically presented as the principal finding from a series of studies in which researchers varied illumination levels in an effort to determine optimal lighting levels for an assembly line (Gottfredson, 1996). Contrary to expectations, productivity increased with each change in lighting. The Hawthorne effect is frequently presented as a classic illustration of the impact of observation upon

research participants. However, what is glossed over in such a presentation of study findings is that at each stage of the study, workers were given feedback on performance and productivity. Parson's (1991) interpreted the Hawthorne results from an operant conditioning perspective and suggested that the feedback served as a consequence that reinforced (motivated) improved performance. Gottfredson concludes that the evidence most strongly supports a long-term learning effect, because in subsequent phases of the study, when manipulation of break periods caused unhappiness among workers, productivity did drop, but at all times remained well above baseline levels.

As a result of many such findings, researchers began to look more closely at the role of worker motivation and satisfaction in productivity and found that many of the same factors associated with physical and mental health (stimulation, variety, task control, autonomy, etc.) are also associated with higher levels of job performance (Barling & Griffiths, 2003). Job design theorists proposed that worker motivation and job satisfaction could be increased through skill use, challenge, and/or recognition. Karasek's (1979) paper describing the relationships between job demands, worker decision making latitude, and job stress has been particularly influential.

Paralleling these American efforts, and indeed, often leading the way, were important research programs in Europe, particularly Britain and the Scandinavian countries (Barling & Griffiths, 2003). In important early work, Trist and Bamforth (1951) found that British coal miners experienced high levels of anxiety, anger, and depression when shifted from autonomous workgroups doing a wide range of interrelated tasks to a mechanized system in which they only performed segmented job tasks, and in which their ability to complete these tasks was contingent on the output of other workgroups.

Bertil Gardell, Lennart Levi, and Töres Theorell were among the most important Scandinavian researchers (Barling & Griffiths, 2003). Gardell and his colleagues at the University of Stockholm investigated the relationship between new technologies, autonomy, participation, and worker mental health, finding that machine-paced work, monotonous work, lack of control, and fragmented and isolated work all had adverse effects upon workers. After having studied with the pioneering stress researcher Hans Selye, Levi returned to Sweden to establish a stress research lab at the Karolinska Institute. Levi and his colleagues conducted foundational work investigating the relationship between working conditions and physical health, and the psycho-physiological mechanisms associated with stressful conditions, and argued for the importance of consideration of psychosocial factors from a more global perspective in connection with worker health. Levi went on to found, and to serve as the first director of, the Institute for Psychosocial Factors and Health. Theorell, a younger colleague of Levi, was a cardiologist interested in the impact of stressful life events on health. Theorell's work laid the solid foundation upon which Karasek and other OHP stress researchers have since built.

American Developments

In the United States, NIOSH has been a leader in researching work-related stress. Although OSH often seems to only concern itself with traumatic injuries and toxic exposures, it is significant that the Occupational Safety and Health Act of 1970 which created NIOSH, specifically recognized the need to investigate the role of "psychological factors" related to OSH. As was mentioned earlier, the term *occupational health psychology* was first introduced by Raymond, Wood, and Patrick (1990) in their seminal paper arguing for the creation of doctoral-level training programs that integrated health psychology and public health, and which incorporated elements of occupational medicine, nursing, preventative medicine, behavioral medicine, political science, sociology, and business. This proposed training was to follow a scientist–practitioner model and would prepare graduates to function in interdisciplinary settings researching and/or remedying occupational health concerns.

Another watershed moment for the emerging field of OHP was the 1990 conference titled *Work and Well-Being: An Agenda for the 1990s* that was cosponsored by NIOSH and the APA (Schneider, Camara, Tetrick, & Stenberg, 1999). The success of the conference led to a second conference, *Work, Stress, and Well-being*, and NIOSH/APA partnership to develop postdoctoral training in OHP, both in 1992. Building upon the success of these initial ventures, NIOSH funded (through APA) the development of OHP training programs at universities across the United States. Twelve university programs have participated in this project, with results ranging from OHP curriculum development to formal graduate minors. The momentum surrounding these activities also led to the founding of the *Journal of Occupational Health Psychology* (published by APA) and the Society for Occupational Health Psychology.

The Current Status of Occupational Health Psychology

As was discussed earlier, the roots of OHP can be traced to investigations of the impact of Taylor management principles on the emotional and physical health of workers. However, in recent decades, the focus of OHP has broadened considerably. As the result of globalization, there have been significant changes in the structure of work in both the United States and Europe. Many manufacturing jobs were lost, and economies shifted toward service jobs. Corporate mergers and downsizing left many workers needing to switch employment, at ages (forties and fifties) that previously were associated with stable employment and peak earning potential (NIOSH, 2002). Companies moved away from making long-term commitments to employees, relying instead upon temporary workers and/or contractors. Correspondingly, there has been an increase in the number of self-employed people. All of these changes were accompanied by stress, both for workers losing or changing jobs and for those retaining employment, but needing to adapt to new contingencies.

In addition to the structural changes discussed above, to remain competitive, many employers significantly changed management systems, supervisory practices, and production processes (NIOSH, 2002). Among these changes were compressed work schedules, flexible work schedules, home-based work, lean management, and an increased reliance on technology. These practices are intended to increase the ability of companies to respond quickly and efficiently to changing production demands without compromising quality. However, following implementation of these practices, employees work longer and harder, and often bear greater responsibility for outcomes, although not always with increased decision-making latitude. Learning new processes and new technologies places increased cognitive demands on workers, leading to stress that has been tied to negative health effects.

Organization of Work

Within OHP, the term *organization of work* is used to denote the interactive network of relationships discussed above. NIOSH (2002) proposed a three-tiered model for the study of the organization of work. The highest level of this "top-down" model is termed the *external context*. The external context includes factors such as economic, legal, political, technological, and demographic forces acting at the national and international level. Examples include the advent of globalization, the signing of the North American Free Trade Agreement (NAFTA), and the development of high-speed computer networks. The second level of this model is termed the *organizational context*. This level includes the management structures, supervisory practices, production methods, and human resources policies that are typically made in response to changes in the external context. The final level of the model is the *work context*. This includes job characteristics, job demands, and conditions in the workplace.

As a field, it is beyond the power of OHP to have a significant impact upon factors related to the external context. However, the organizational and work contexts are within reach. Consequently, much OHP research has focused upon *organizational practices* (management and production methods and human resources policies), *work processes* (the way jobs are designed and performed), and the impact of these two areas upon worker well-being (work-related stress levels) and occupational injury rates.

Work Stress

After having written at some length about the importance and impact of work-related stress, it is somewhat awkward to now admit how difficult this concept is to fully define and operationalize. Hans Selye (1950), the father of modern stress research defined stress as "the nonspecific response of the body to any demand for change." One might be tempted to view this definition as deceptively simple or so broad as to be meaningless. In a sense it is both and neither. As pointed out by Quick, Quick, Nelson, and Hurrell (1997), the term "stress" is a rubric for a complex series of physiological and psychological reactions. On the physical level, stress involves a cascade of interrelated events including increased heart rate, respiration, and perspiration; elevated blood pressure; release of hormones; and the tightening of large muscle groups. Psychological aspects of stress can include affective responses such as anxiety, fear, anger, or depression, and cognitive symptoms such as inability to concentrate, rumination, or distractibility.

Obviously, this familiar term covers a lot of ground and means many things, often to many different people. Consequently, stress has been operationally defined in different ways by different researchers depending both upon discipline and professional bias. Researchers grounded in the biological sciences tend to define stress in terms of objectively measured physiological markers such as hormone

levels, blood pressure, and heart rate. Researchers grounded in the social sciences tend to define it in terms of self-report measures focusing on affect, cognitions, and self-perceptions. These differences in approach would be relatively unimportant if the research findings dovetailed nicely, but unfortunately they do not. Physiological markers of stress do not always correlate significantly with self-report measures of perceived stress.

One reason for this lack of correspondence may be found in the distinction between *eustress* and *distress* (Quick, Quick, Nelson, & Hurrell, 1997). Eustress can be thought of as a healthy or positive stress response. Eustress is experienced when one successfully marshals one's resources to rise to a challenge. Although objectively, from a physiological standpoint, one is experiencing stress, from an affective standpoint one is likely experiencing the thrill of competition or a satisfying sense of accomplishment from rising to the occasion. From a cognitive standpoint, one might be experiencing a period of sharpened focus and enhanced concentration. Distress may be thought of as a negative or unhealthy stress response, with the sort of affective and cognitive experiences more commonly associated with the term "stress." Here, one is far more likely to feel threatened or overwhelmed than challenged. Physiologically, eustress and distress may be manifested similarly, but their subjective psychological experiences are very different.

Quick, Quick, Nelson, and Hurrell (1997) relate eustress and distress to the familiar performance curve of the Yerkes-Dodson Law. Very low and very high levels of stress are associated with low levels of performance. Optimal levels of performance are typically associated with moderate levels of stress. Moderate levels of stress will likely be associated with eustress, whereas high levels of stress will be associated with distress.

Person–Environment Fit

As might be expected for so complex a construct, a number of different theoretical models have been developed to describe work-related stress. One group of theories is *person–environment (P–E) fit* models of stress. Many current P–E fit models, such as the NIOSH stress model, are refinements of a model of job stress originally developed by researchers at the University of Michigan (Landsbergis, Schnall, Scwartz, Warren, & Pickering, 1995). Like the person–environment fit models used in career guidance, these models attempt to characterize salient features in both the work environment and the worker.

Job stress is hypothesized to arise from a mismatch between the skills and abilities of the worker and the pressures and demands of the work environment (Spielberger, Vagg, & Wasala, 2003). Lack of fit can lead to both physical and psychological strain, which in turn can be expected to lead to behavioral consequences such as lowered production, absenteeism, turnover, or health-related problems. Although P–E fit models are praised by some (Landsbergis et al., 1995) for their descriptive richness, others have faulted them for lacking specificity and for failing to distinguish between different types of fit (Spielberger et al., 2003). Vogel and Feldman (2009) state that most P–E fit research has focused on either person–organization fit or person–job fit and has tended to neglect related, but distinct variables such person–vocation fit and person–group fit.

Demand–Control Model

One of the most influential job stress models is Karasek's (1979) *demand–control* model. The demand–control model focuses on the interaction between the psychological demands of a job and the decision latitude (control) that a worker has to meet those demands (Radmacher & Sheridan, 1995). This interaction gives rise to four categories of job strain: *low strain* (low demand and high control), *active* (high demand and high control), *passive* (low demand and low control), and *high strain* (high demand and low control). High-strain jobs are expected to have the most negative health effects, a finding that has been borne out by numerous studies. However, as Theorell (2003) acknowledges, this finding seems to be stronger for cardiovascular problems than for other work-related health problems such as musculoskeletal disorders. Research support has been consistent in finding a main effect for both demand and control, but support for the hypothesized interaction effect is somewhat mixed (Landsbergis et al., 1995; Radmacher & Sheridan, 1995).

Cognitive-Behavioral Models

Lazarus' extension of the *transactional process* model to occupational stress takes into account both the worker's emotional reaction to a given stressor and cognitive appraisal of the level of threat represented by the stressor (Spielberger et al., 2003). By allowing for individual differences in responding to the same stressor, Lazarus' model accounts for why some workers will perceive a given stressor as a challenge and consequently experience eustress when coping with it and others will perceive the same stressor as a threat and experience distress (Quick et al., 1997). Given its grounding in a mainstream cognitive-behavioral therapy approach, Lazarus' model may well offer more guidance for interventions than other models of job stress.

Speilberger's *state-trait process* (STP) model of occupational stress attempts to integrate his widely known state-trait conception of anxiety and anger with Lazarus' transactional process model (Spielberger et al., 2003). The STP model focuses on perceived severity and frequency of occurrence of two major categories of work-related stressors—job pressures and lack of support. Like Lazarus' model, the STP model allows for individual differences in appraisal of threats. If a threat is judged to be severe and occurs frequently, it can be expected to lead to a range of negative behavior and/or health outcomes.

Responsibility for Stress and Coping

Work-related stress can be viewed as either "personal trouble" related to personality characteristics or a "public concern" related to work characteristics and the epidemiology of occupational health (Kenny & Cooper, 2003). How one approaches interventions to manage occupational stress will vary depending on which conceptualization is endorsed. NIOSH (1999) characterizes this dichotomy as *worker characteristics* and *work conditions*. Traditionally, OSH professionals have considered providing a safe work environment to be an obligation employers owe to workers. For work hazards involving the risk of injury or illness from toxic exposures, this seems a fairly straightforward approach. For example, if an employee is working on a potentially dangerous piece of equipment, such as a table saw, the business owner clearly should have safety features such as blade guards in place. In addition, the business owner should provide PPE, such as safety glasses and respirators, as needed. Given this perspective, nearly all responsibility for OSH lies with the company. The worker need only show up for work, use provided PPE, and perform his or her work safely—as they have been trained (by the employer) to do. Placing any other obligation for OSH upon workers risked being labeled "blaming the victim."

However, with an occupational hazard such as work-related stress, in which the research indicates individual worker response plays a key role in outcomes, the lines of responsibility become somewhat blurry. NIOSH (1999) acknowledges the role that individual differences make in responding to workplace stressors, but emphasizes that it is preferable to address working conditions rather than worker characteristics for the simple reason that research has identified a number of workplace practices that increase the risk for adverse stress reactions for all workers. Examples of these include long work hours, backward rotating work shifts, and a breaking down of barriers between work and home life (Caruso et al., 2006). Addressing these factors alleviates current stress levels and prevents future work stress problems for all workers in that company. Moreover, there is a question regarding the ethics of training a worker to cope with what would otherwise be unreasonable workplace demands. Who benefits most? The worker—for being able to continue on the job? Or, the employer—who can now make greater demands of the worker? Or, is it a "win-win" situation for both? Should workers be asked to change themselves to adapt to work demands that could be remedied in other ways? In particular, should workers be asked to undergo what in other circumstances might be considered psychotherapy to successfully cope with demands at work?

Work Stress Interventions

As indicated in the discussion above, work stress management interventions can be aimed at work conditions or worker characteristics. Ivancevich et al. (1990) identified three potential targets for intervention: the intensity of stressors in the workplace, the employee's appraisal of stressful situations, or the employee's ability to cope with the outcomes.

Following the public health model of prevention, work stress interventions can be classified as primary, secondary, or tertiary (Quick, 1999; Richardson & Rothstein, 2008). *Primary interventions* aim to alter the sources of stress and may include redesigning job roles, increasing individuals' decision-making authority, or organizing coworker support groups. *Secondary interventions* attempt to reduce severity of stress symptoms in the individual before significant health problems arise and may include cognitive-behavioral skills training, meditation, relaxation, deep breathing, exercise, journaling, time management, and goal setting. *Tertiary interventions* treat individuals' existing stress-related mental health conditions via access to mental health professionals, often in the form of free and confidential employee assistance programs.

Reviews of the work stress intervention literature indicate that secondary interventions are the most often used and among these interventions the most effective is cognitive-behavioral (van der Klink, Blonk, Schene, & van Dijk, 2001; Richardson &

Rothstein, 2008). Cognitive-behavioral interventions are intended to alter individuals' appraisal of stressful situations and their responses to them by providing education on the role played by one's thoughts and emotions in response to stressful events and teaching skills to modify thoughts and improve coping effectiveness. Another effective intervention is teaching relaxation and meditation techniques. These approaches work by evoking a physiological state that is the opposite of stress. Multimodal interventions that included a mix of cognitive-behavioral, relaxation, and/or organizational interventions were also found to be effective. However, organizational interventions alone were found to be the least effective.

A meta-analysis conducted by van der Klink et al. (2001) found an effect size of 0.68 for cognitive-behavioral interventions, 0.51 for multimodal interventions, 0.35 for relaxation interventions, and 0.08 for organizational interventions. All effect sizes were statistically significant except for organizational interventions. A follow-up meta-analysis conducted by Richardson and Rothstein (2008) found a similar pattern, although somewhat larger effect sizes. The effect size for cognitive-behavioral interventions was 1.164; for relaxation, 0.497; for multimodal, 0.239; and for organizational, it was 0.1444. Once again, all effect sizes were statistically significant except for organizational interventions. Richardson and Rothstein also included a category they labeled "Alternative" that included a "grab bag" of worker interventions (exercise, journaling, and time management) that did not fit well into the other categories. This alternative category fared well, with an effect size of 0.909.

It would seem with findings like these that work stress interventions aimed at worker characteristics, particularly cognitive-behavioral and relaxation/meditation interventions, would be the clear methods of choice. However, the case is far from closed. Semmer (2003), arguing strongly for organizational interventions, points out that effective organizational interventions are far more difficult to conduct because they involve changing a large and complex social system. Individual worker interventions are far less disruptive to the functioning of the company because they do not involve significant organizational changes. Semmer (2003) points out that no matter how successful individual worker interventions may be, they ultimately do nothing to address the primary sources of work stress. It is almost definitional that worker interventions can be secondary prevention at best as the ongoing environmental contributors toward work stress remain unchanged.

Each new worker will need to be "inoculated" against stressful conditions that might otherwise be alleviated by organizational changes. Only by eliminating these organizational sources of work stress can one truly do primary prevention. Moreover, as discussed above, there exists the ethical question of who is more obligated to change—the worker or the employer. Semmer and many others would argue that it is the employer.

Burnout

Burnout is a chronic pattern of negative affective responses associated with reduced job satisfaction, lower job performance, absenteeism, and turnover (Quick et al., 1997). Most burnout research has focused on the "helping professions"—occupations such as physician, nurse, social worker, teacher, and therapist. Miller (1998) cautioned that not only can the *compassion fatigue* of doing challenging psychotherapy produce burnout among mental health providers, but that the stresses inherent to doing therapy, particularly with trauma victims, can sometimes produce posttraumatic stress disorder (PTSD) in the therapist as well.

Maslach (1982) proposed that burnout consists of three dimensions. *Emotional exhaustion* consists of feelings of being depleted of one's emotional resources, emotionally overextended, and drained by interactions with others. *Depersonalization* is a negative, cynical, and detached response to other people at work, in particular toward those seeking one's services. *Reduced personal accomplishment* refers to feelings of reduced professional competence, productivity, and self-efficacy.

Maslach developed a burnout inventory using these three dimensions that is the most widely used instrument for assessing burnout in empirical research (Shirom, 2003). The three dimensions of Maslach's model were identified by conducting factor analyses of burnout symptoms. There is no theoretical rationale for the co-occurrence of these three clusters of symptoms. Consequently, other researchers have challenged this conceptualization of burnout. Some argue that emotional exhaustion is the central characteristic of burnout. Others argue that these three dimensions are really a single factor, not three separate factors. Yet others challenge the notion that reduced professional competency is really a symptom of burnout, but rather a natural consequence of the condition (Schaufeli, Keijers, & Miranda, 1995).

Some researchers conceptualize burnout as being the logical endpoint for individuals working in organizations without stress management programs (Shirom, 2003). Others consider burnout so extreme as to be qualitatively different from common stress reactions. As of yet, researchers looking toward individual personality traits as a predisposing factor for burnout have found no clear patterns. Some question whether it is even meaningful to differentiate burnout from depression (Schonfeld, 1992), considering the high degree of overlap between items found on scales assessing burnout and on those assessing depression.

In a review of the burnout literature, Shirom (2003) points out that, although burnout was initially conceptualized in terms of the helping professions, it is now recognized that individuals in other occupations who suffer from chronic stressors, such as high demand and low social support, can develop burnout. Conceptually, it is now recognized that one could suffer burnout in nonwork life domains such as family and marriage. The terminology used to describe two of the dimensions of burnout has also been modified. Depersonalization is now frequently referred to as *cynicism* and reduced personal accomplishment is referred to as *inefficacy*.

Individual Treatment Approaches

The treatment of burnout has tended to be focused on the affected individual (Le Blanc, Hox, Schaufel, Taris, & Peeters, 2007; Shirom, 2003). In part, this is a reflection of the empirical literature, which has largely focused on burnout as an individual phenomenon rather than attempting to identify organizational practices contributing to its development. No doubt, this also reflects Semmer's (2003) observation regarding the difficulty of conducting organizational interventions. In any event, individual treatment for burnout tends to very closely resemble the cognitive-behavioral approaches used to address other work stress problems and/or depression (Shirom, 2003).

Review of the treatment literature suggests that burnout interventions are most effective in reducing symptoms of emotional exhaustion, but typically have little or no impact on depersonalization or professional efficacy. Van Dierondonck, Garssen, and Visser (2005) suggested that these findings might arise from nearly all interventions being cognitive-behaviorally oriented. Positing that a more holistic therapy model would address a broader range of burnout symptoms, they developed an intervention based upon Assagioli's (1965) psychosynthesis model. The intervention included activities such as meditation, group discussions, guided imagery, and education on relevant aspects of the psychosynthesis model. In a sample consisting primarily of engineers, the study found both a significant decrease in emotional exhaustion and an increase in professional efficacy. However, depersonalization remained unchanged.

Salmela-Aro, Naatanen, and Nurmi (2004) also tested non–cognitive-behavioral burnout interventions on a sample of workers suffering from severe burnout. Over the course of a year, workers in the treatment condition received 16 group therapy sessions. Half of the workers in the treatment condition participated in psychoanalytically oriented group therapy based upon free association within the groups. Therapeutic interpretations were provided by group facilitators. The remaining workers participated in group therapy based primarily upon psycho-dramatic techniques such as role-playing. Compared to a control group, both treatment groups experienced decreases in their level of burnout, particularly symptoms of emotional exhaustion. However, these differences were not statistically significant.

Shapiro, Astin, Bishop, and Cordova (2005) used a mindfulness-based stress reduction program with a sample of health care providers. Over the course of 8 weeks, participants were taught meditation, yoga, and other techniques intended to raise their awareness of body sensations, thoughts, and emotions. Compared to a control group, study participants experienced significant increases in life satisfaction and self-compassion and decreases in perceived stress. Although the treatment group did experience a reduction in burnout symptoms, it was not statistically significant.

Along more cognitive-behaviorally oriented lines, Van Dierenconck, Schaufeli, and Buunk (1998) tested an intervention that conceptualized burnout in terms of perceived inequity, on the part of the worker, between their efforts and contributions on the job and outcomes such as recognition, status, and/or pay. The intervention encouraged workers to restore their perceptions of equity in one of three ways: by identifying strategies to change either their own contributions and/or to elicit more desired outcomes from the workplace, by changing their perceptions of contributions and/or outcomes to better match, and by leaving the job to pursue a more congruent work situation elsewhere. In a study sample of direct-care professionals working with mentally disabled individuals, this study found a significant effect for the reduction of emotional exhaustion and a moderating effect for social support. However, similar to other studies, it found neither a reduction in depersonalization nor an increase in professional efficacy.

Westman and Eden (1997) explored whether a simple respite from the work environment had an impact on work stress and burnout. They tracked a sample of workers before, during, and after a vacation. As might be expected, these workers reported a reduction in stress and burnout symptoms during their vacations. However, this effect was fleeting as workers had returned to their baseline levels of stress and burnout within 3 weeks after returning to work.

Organizational Treatment Approaches

Semmer (2003) argued that organizational interventions represent primary prevention, as opposed to the secondary, if not tertiary prevention of individual interventions. Consequently, despite the considerable challenges inherent to attempting organizational interventions, from a public health perspective, they clearly remain a more desirable approach. Recent publications in the empirical literature eloquently testify to both the promise and the frustrations of organizational treatment approaches.

Le Blanc et al. (2007) worked with the staffs from 29 oncology wards over a 6-month period. Nine wards were randomly selected to participate in an intervention program consisting of monthly 3-hour training sessions facilitated by program counselors. Training topics included the emergence of unwanted collective behaviors, communication, social support, and emotional investment in one's job. The workers in the treatment condition experienced significantly less emotional exhaustion and less depersonalization than did those in the control condition.

In what might be viewed as a mixed individual/organizational approach, Hatinen, Kinnunen, Pekkonen, and Kalimo (2007) compared traditional intervention with a participatory intervention with a group of female professionals. The traditional treatment intervention consisted primarily of individual and group therapy, and education regarding individual responses to stress, depression, and burnout. In addition, individuals in the traditional treatment intervention participated in a small number of group and individual therapy sessions focusing on work-related factors. The individuals in the participatory intervention received the same treatment package as those in traditional treatment. However, on two occasions, representatives from their workplaces participated in their treatment to identify ways to improve conditions and climate at work. At a 1-year follow-up, individuals in the participatory intervention reported significant improvements in both emotional exhaustion and depersonalization.

Individuals in the traditional treatment reported some improvement, but it was not statistically significant.

On a less hopeful note, Elo, Ervast, Kuosma, and Mattila (2008) reported the findings of an ambitious, 2-year organizational intervention in a public services organization in Finland. Interventions included training on relevant topics for both workers and managers and a series of "work conferences" in which participants discussed work organization factors and strategies for improving the climate in their organization. Despite earlier work finding significant effects for the individual treatment components of this study, no statistically significant results were found for the overall field study.

Burnout and Counseling Psychology

Maslach (2003) characterizes burnout as arising from the chronic stress due to incongruence, or misfit, between worker and job. Given this definition, it is dismaying that most interventions in the literature are aimed not at correcting this incongruence but at helping the worker to better adapt to it. It is also a definition that suggests counseling psychology might hold the key to the most powerful of primary prevention interventions for burnout—a well-informed, thoughtful career choice. Occupational health psychology reminds counseling psychology that a good initial choice of career has an impact on far more than college major. It helps to preserve quality of life many decades later.

Work–Family Balance

The term *work–family balance* refers to the impact that work and family have upon one another. Although work–family balance has been identified as one of three areas of primary interest to OHP (Quick, 1999), it has received far less research attention than the other two areas (the individual worker and the work environment). Among the earliest, and still one of the most common, conceptualizations of the work–family balance is the *spillover*

effect—the transfer of reactions to work to other life domains (Kelloway & Barling, 1994). Implicit to most conceptualizations of work–family balance is the notion of a "zero sum" game. Individuals are considered to have finite levels of time and energy, which if used in one life domain are no longer available for use in another (Greenhaus & Parasuraman, 2002).

Frone (2003) suggested that the term *work–family balance*, although widely used in the literature, was not consistently defined nor understood. Although spillover from one domain to the another has always been conceptualized as either positive or negative, the work in this area has focused almost exclusively on negative impact—work demands upon family life or family demands upon work. Aiming at both balance and clarification, Frone proposed a model of work–family balance (see Table 29.1). One dimension is work-to-family/family-to-work. The other is conflict–facilitation. The interaction of these dimensions yields four cells: work-to-family conflict, family-to-work conflict, work-to-family facilitation, and family-to-work facilitation. Conflict represents negative impact and facilitation positive impact. Citing what little facilitation research there is in the literature, Frone states that there is evidence for family-to-work facilitation, but little for work-to-family facilitation.

Sources of Conflict

In the last half century, ever-increasing numbers of women have sought employment and careers (Marshall & Barnett, 1994). The rise in the number of dual-income families has been paralleled by a rise in divorce rates and consequently single-parent families. Both situations leave parents with less time to accomplish necessary domestic tasks and to raise children. Despite significant social, political, and economic advances by women in the last several decades, within the home, tasks still tend to be divided along traditional gender lines. Although research indicates that married men and women

Table 29.1. Dimensions of Work–Family Balance

		Type of Effect	
		Conflict	Facilitation
Direction of Influence	*Work-to-Family Conflict*	Work-to-Family Conflict ↓	Work-to-Family Facilitation ↑
	Family-to-Work Conflict	Family-to-Work Conflict ↓	Family-to-Work Facilitation ↑

From Frone, M.R. (2003). Work–family balance. In J.C. Quick & L.E. Tetrick (Eds.), *Handbook of OHP*, American Psychological Association. Reprinted with permission.

tend to work about the same number of hours per week on domestic activities, the tasks performed by women tend to have significantly lower levels of control than those performed by men. For example, feeding and bathing of children takes place daily at more or less the same times. Mowing the lawn can be put off without significant consequences.

An often overlooked source of stress is eldercare (Jarvik & Small, 1988). Medical advances are keeping individuals with significant physical and/or cognitive impairments alive far longer than in decades past. Their middle-aged children are increasingly called upon to serve as their primary caregiver and/ or legal decision maker. Given the famously transient American lifestyle, many children live hundreds if not thousands of miles from their aging parents, adding further complications to an already stressful situation.

It is important to realize that work–family conflict does not only adversely impact the individual employee experiencing the conflict. Tetrick et al. (1994) reported that in a sample of nearly 3,000 respondents, 28% reported that the childcare obligations of coworkers had adversely impacted their own job performance. In addition, the impact of stressful work conditions upon the family is not simply limited to reducing the emotional quality of life of a family. A study by Dompierre and Lavoie (1994) found relationships between work stress and family violence.

Promoting Work–Family Balance

In recent decades, many workplaces have introduced a range of "family-friendly" policies (Marshall & Barnett, 1994; Frone, 2003). These policies include facilitating dependent care (onsite daycare, subsidies for child- or eldercare, referral services), flexible work arrangements (flexible starting and ending times, work-at-home, reduced or compressed work schedules), flexible leave policies (maternity leave, leave to care for sick family members), and employee assistance programs offering an increasing number of services related to family concerns. Although well-intended and costly, there has been little research to support the efficacy of such programs. In a broad survey of workers, Marshall and Barnett (1994) found a fair amount of variability across industries and occupations in terms of family-friendly benefits, but found no relationship between the availability of these benefits and job satisfaction, work conflict, and the mental health of respondents. However, as pointed out by these and other researchers, just having these benefits does not necessarily alleviate

stress for workers. One must actually be in immediate need of these family-friendly policies to benefit from them. Consequently, a study by Tetrick et al. (1994) that looked only at parents found that those with childcare difficulties (both male and female) suffered from more frequent and larger losses of productivity than did parents with reliable childcare. In a study based upon Karasek's (1979) demand–control model, Kelloway and Barling (1994) found that simply increasing worker job control did little to ameliorate work–family stress. They concluded that to be effective, work–family interventions needed to be more comprehensive and tailored to individual need.

Occupational Health Disparities

Any differences in disease incidence, mental illness, or morbidity and mortality that exist among specific populations due to work-related causes are termed an *occupational health disparity*. For reasons beyond actual OSH needs, the bulk of research efforts have focused on three groups: women, aging workers, and Hispanic immigrant workers. Clearly, women, aging workers, and Hispanic immigrants are not the only groups worthy of study. Rather, they represent the response in the literature to fairly specific sociopolitical pressures: the success of the women's movement, the aging of the baby boom, and the massive influx of undocumented Hispanic immigrants into the United States in recent decades.

Other groups also suffer occupational health disparities, but have not received nearly as much attention. For example, despite being barred from the most hazardous jobs by law, young workers (19 and younger), particularly male, are killed on the job at rates twice those of adults (NIOSH, 2004). African Americans comprise 9.8% of the American workforce, but suffer 11.9% of work-related nonfatal injuries and illnesses and have a fatality rate (1.4 per 100,000) significantly higher than the population average (1.0). Asians are sometimes referred to as the "model minority" because so many achieve a higher degree of success than the population average. However, this characterization ignores the 1.5 million undocumented Asian immigrants in the United States (Passel, 2006). Many of these immigrants work in low-paying jobs and are socially marginalized because they speak Cantonese, not Mandarin, the dialect of the educated classes in Chinese societies (Fujishiro et al., 2009). Although the OSH literature is beginning to address the needs of young workers, it is sparse for African American workers and there is almost nothing concerning Asian immigrant workers.

It is important to recognize that occupational health disparities are not just an American concern. Within the European Union, most legal barriers to the flow of workers from one country to another have been eliminated. Some European Union countries have also experienced an influx of undocumented workers. The large influx non-native workers—both documented and unauthorized—has left many European Union countries struggling to overcome the barriers of language, culture, and legal status that can leave immigrant workers vulnerable to exploitation. An example is Ireland, with a population of less than 5 million, but with the same proportion of non-native workers as the United States (Beggs, Mangan, Concagh, & Pollock, 2005). Whereas the United States has been challenged to simply meet the needs of Spanish-speaking immigrants, Ireland must attempt to overcome barriers of language and culture for a dozen nationalities.

Women Workers

In the decades following World War II, ever-increasing numbers of women have sought employment and careers (Stellman & Mailman, 1999). The successes of the women's movement in the 1960s and 1970s further increased the number of women working. Barriers were broken down, and women entered occupations that previously had been closed to them and began to regularly rise to heights in organizational leadership seldom previously attained.

Unfortunately, these hard-fought advances did not come without ongoing costs. Quick et al. (1997) reported research from a number of studies indicating that work-related stress takes a significant toll among female managers. As a group, female managers smoked more, and took more tranquilizers, antidepressants, and sleeping pills than did their male counterparts. The rise in dual-income families have left parents struggling to balance the often conflicting demands of work and family. The great workplace gains of the past several decades have not been matched by a significant shift in traditional family roles. Women still bear the responsibility of the majority of childrearing, cooking, cleaning, and laundry (Marshall & Barnett, 1994). Research indicates that married men and women tend to work about the same number of hours per week on domestic activities. However, the tasks performed by women tend to have significantly lower levels of control than those performed by men. This can be expected to lead to higher levels of stress and more work–family conflicts.

Violence Against Women Workers

Although it would cause dismay, it would likely not greatly surprise most to learn that roughly 50% of women can expect to be sexually harassed at some point in their work or academic lives (Bell, Cycyota, & Quick, 2002). However, most would be surprised that homicide was the leading cause of death on the job among women, accounting for roughly 40% of all work-related fatalities (NIOSH, 1995). Hoskins (2005) reports that female homicide victims are far more likely to have been killed by a family member than are male victims. Domestic violence spills over into the workplace in less lethal ways as well. Three-quarters of battered women report having been harassed at work by their batterer (Friedman, Tucker, Neville, & Imperial, 1996). In addition, 20% reported having been late for work because of the interference of their partners, and more than half reported missing an average of 3 workdays a month because of injuries, emotional responses, or appointments with physicians and/or lawyers. More than half reported having lost a job as a direct result of domestic violence. Nicoletti and Spooner (1996) report that domestic violence and stalking violence now account for more workplace injuries and deaths than violence committed by disgruntled or ex-employees.

Equipment and Exposures

As women continue to move into fields traditionally dominated by men, OSH professionals are faced with re-evaluating longstanding recommendations and practices. For example, exposure to some workplace toxins at levels thought to be safe for men are known to be hazardous for a developing fetus (Messing & de Grosbois, 2001). Safety professionals and business owners are faced with either trying to reduce exposure levels even further or banning women of child-bearing years from working in certain work settings. In fields such as construction and manufacturing, women find that most of the PPE is manufactured in sizes appropriate for men and is too large for them to use (NIOSH, 1999; Ontario Women's Directorate and the Industrial Accident Prevention Association, 2006). In addition, tools and equipment are also sized for men, making it difficult or even hazardous for many women to use them.

Musculoskeletal Disorders

Musculoskeletal disorders (MSDs), ranging from repetitive strain to back injuries, were the leading source of nonfatal, work-related health problems for women (Hoskins, 2005). Women are much more likely to develop MSDs than men (Stellman & Mailman, 1999). In part, this may be due to the nature of the work of traditionally female-dominated fields. For example, in nursing, back injuries occur at very high rates due to activities such as lifting and positioning patients (Trinkoff, Lipscomb, Geiger-Brown, & Brady, 2002). Clerical work is notorious for high rates of repetitive strain injuries. However, as pointed out by Stellman and Mailman (1999), women working in nonclerical fields, such as assembly and retail trade, actually suffer from higher rates of repetitive strain injuries. They suggest that a major factor in this counterintuitive finding is, as discussed above, that women frequently have to use tools and equipment sized for men. The awkward and/or stressful positions women must put themselves in to perform job tasks using inappropriately sized tools or equipment significantly elevates their risks of developing MSDs.

Aging Workers

The workforce in many industrialized countries is aging (Wegman, 1999). In part, this shift simply reflects the demographics of the baby boom. Other factors are in play as well. With advances in medical science, people are healthy and fit later in life, and some choose to continue working past the age at which they are eligible for retirement benefits. However, due to economic downturns, retirement accounts have suffered and companies have defaulted on employee pension plans. Consequently, many are working due to economic necessity. In the United States, the eligibility age for Social Security retirement benefits has been incrementally raised, so that many current workers need to work until they are nearly 70 to receive full benefits. Much of Western Europe has experienced declining birthrates since World War II. There are simply not enough replacement workers being born. Consequently, there is great interest in keeping older workers healthy and satisfied enough to remain working (Barling & Griffiths, 2003). In some European countries, such as Finland, this has been a major factor in the development of OHP.

It is interesting to note how quickly 65 became enshrined as the typical retirement age. Wegman (1999) points out that prior to World War II, most people died while still in their fifties. People simply worked as long as they were able. However, following the war, with lifespans increasing dramatically, governments, in a sense, defined old age by setting the age for most retirement benefits at 65 in an effort to encourage older workers to retire, thereby opening positions for younger workers and reducing unemployment. This somewhat arbitrary line of demarcation is reflected in much of the literature regarding aging workers and because of its reification through widespread practice, it goes unquestioned.

Arbitrary definitions aside, there are some significant differences between aging workers and their younger colleagues. Kisner and Pratt (1997) found that the workplace fatality rate for workers 65 and older was 2.6 times that of workers aged 16–64 (14.1 per 100,000 vs. 5.4). Significant gender differences were found for older workers. Men 65 and over had a fatality rate nearly ten times that of women 65 and over (22.1 per 100,000 vs. 2.3). This compares to a rate of 9.0 per 100,000 for men aged 16–64 and 0.7 per 100,000 for women aged 16–64. For older men, the most prevalent cause of death was accidents involving machines, followed by motor vehicle accidents, falls, and homicides. For older women, the most prevalent causes of death were homicide and motor vehicle accidents. By far, the most dangerous industry area for older workers was agriculture/forestry/fishing, with fatality rates six times higher than the next highest industry category (transportation/communications/public utilities).

It is widely recognized that older workers are affected by age-related declines in strength and endurance and consequently are less robust physically than their younger colleagues (Wegam & McGee, 2004). However, as Wegman (1999) points out, these physical declines may not be as occupationally relevant as one might suppose. These are declines in maximum performance, and even physically demanding jobs tend to only require submaximal effort.

Wegman divided jobs in four broad categories: age-enhanced, age-neutral, age-counteracted, and age-impaired. Age-enhanced jobs involve knowledge-based decision making without time pressures. Given that older workers can bring the wisdom of decades to a job, Wegman argues that they can outperform younger workers in such activities. Age-neutral jobs involve relatively undemanding tasks and are not expected to be impacted significantly by age. Age-counteracted jobs involve skilled manual work. Here, any decrements in physical capacity can be expected to be counteracted by the enhanced skills and expertise acquired from years performing the job. Age-impaired jobs involve continuous high-pace data processing and are the only category in which older workers can be expected to suffer age-related deficits in job performance.

Accommodating Older Workers

Although the overall job performance for older workers is the same, if not better, in most categories of work as compared to younger workers (Wegman, 1999), there are some age-related factors that can have an impact on job performance, but which can be easily addressed in most workplaces (Wegman & McGee, 2004). Most of these factors are environmental. Aging diminishes the sensitivity of the eyes, so older workers may benefit from higher levels of lighting in work areas than needed by younger workers. Older workers also tend to be far more sensitive to extremes of temperature than younger workers. If environmental modifications cannot be easily made, managers might consider assigning older employees to tasks that avoid extremes of temperature. Older workers may also be less tolerant of background noise than younger workers. This can make it more difficult for them to hear important auditory signals. If minimizing background noise levels cannot be accomplished, managers might consider using different or redundant signal channels. For example, instead of using an auditory tone, substitute a warning light or better yet, use both. Research indicates that older workers are less able to adapt to shift work than younger workers. However, they tend to wake earlier than younger workers and perform better in morning hours (Wegman, 1999). Consequently, managers should attempt to assign older workers early morning hours and day shifts, avoiding evening and night shifts. In those instances in which retired individuals return to work out of economic need, they frequently find themselves working in low-level service industry jobs, often with colleagues and managers who are many years younger. If older workers are subjected to stereotypes about the elderly or disrespect due to the unskilled nature of their current employment, they will likely begin to suffer from unacceptable levels of work-related stress. Organizational interventions addressing attitudes toward older workers could help to alleviate such situations.

Hispanic Immigrant Workers

Currently, over 42 million persons of Hispanic descent are living in the United States, approximately half of whom are foreign-born (U.S. Census Bureau 2005, 2006). Hispanics recently became the largest minority group in the United States. It is estimated that by 2050, 15% of the American workforce will be Hispanic. It is estimated that 12 million of these Hispanics are in the country unauthorized (Passel, 2006). Areas of the United States, such as the Southeast and the Midwest, that have not traditionally been destinations for Hispanic immigrant workers have experienced explosive growth in the size of their Hispanic communities since the early 1990s (Passel, 2005). In addition to political issues and legal consequences related to their undocumented status, Hispanic immigrants in these "new settlement areas" are further socially marginalized and subject to exploitation due to lack of a Spanish-speaking public and/or social services infrastructure (Passel, Capps, & Fix, 2002).

The Hispanic population in the United States represents many unique challenges for OSH. Trainers are challenged by barriers of both language and culture (O'Connor, 2003). Regulatory officers are challenged by distrust on the part of the many undocumented Hispanic immigrant workers for any government official. These problems are compounded because Hispanic immigrant workers tend to be employed in the least desirable, poorest paid, and most dangerous occupations, so that they are at increased risk to suffer from negative health consequences (Dong & Platner, 2004; Loh & Richardson, 2004; Richardson, Ruser, & Saurez, 2003).

The popular perception of undocumented Hispanic immigrants is that most work in agriculture or as day laborers. This is far from reality. Approximately 4% work in agriculture (Passel, 2006) and less than 1% of Hispanic immigrants work as day laborers (Valenzuela, Theodore, Melendez, & Gonzalez, 2006). The remainder work for companies ranging in size from small businesses to international corporations. Almost a third work in service industries (e.g., cleaning & food preparation), nearly a fifth work in construction or mining, and 15% work in manufacturing, installation and repair (Passel, 2006).

Fatal Injury Rates

Between 1996 and 2000, the number of foreign-born workers in the United States grew 22%, but the fatal injury rate for these workers increased by 43% (Loh & Richardson, 2004). During this same period, the overall injury rate for all U.S. workers declined by 5%. In 2001, the fatality rate for all U.S. workers decreased to a low of 4.3 per 100,000 workers. However, the fatality rate for foreign-born workers increased to a high of 5.7 per 100,000 workers. In 2000, 51.6% of all foreign-born workers in the United States were from Latin American countries (Loh & Richardson, 2004). However, they suffered 61.2% of fatal work-related injuries. This disparity does not appear to be directly related to being Hispanic. Richardson, Ruser, and Suarez (2003) reported that, between 1995 and 2000, the fatal work injury rate for all workers in the United States was 4.6 per 100,000 workers. This compares to a rate of 4.5 per 100,000 for native-born Hispanics and 6.1 per 100,000 for foreign-born Hispanics. Most of this disparity in fatal injury rates arises from injuries to Mexican-born workers (Loh & Richardson, 2004). Mexicans account for 27.3% of all foreign-born workers in the United States, but suffer 42.1% of all fatal work-related injuries.

Nonfatal Injuries and Illnesses

Between 1998 and 2000, Hispanic men had the highest overall relative risk (1.51 per 100,000) of nonfatal occupational injuries and illnesses (Richardson et al., 2003). This compares to a relative risk of 1.07 per 100,000 for white, non-Hispanic men and of 1.40 for black, non-Hispanic men. Although Hispanic women were not at greater risk (1.0 per 100,000) when compared to all working women (1.0 per 100,000), they were at greater risk when compared to white, non-Hispanic women (0.76 per 100,000). However, Hispanic women were at slightly lower risk than black, non-Hispanic women (1.06 per 100,000).

Safety Culture and Safety Climate

In the OHP literature, the concept of *safety climate* is frequently, but incorrectly, used interchangeably with the related, but distinct, concept of *safety culture* (Zohar, 2003). Safety culture is defined as the embodiment of the values, beliefs, and underlying assumptions of an organization about safety (Flin, Mearns, O'Connor, & Bryden, 2000). Defined thusly, safety culture is simply one facet of *organizational culture*. Quick et al. (1997) consider organizational culture as a "top-down" emanation of the values and practices promoted by the top leaders of an organization.

In contrast, safety climate is considered to be "an emergent property, characterizing groups of individuals" (Zohar, 2003, p. 124) and has been defined as the shared perceptions regarding safety policies, procedures, and practices among groups of workers. Zohar (1980) was the first to introduce the concept of safety climate. He proposed there were eight dimensions to safety climate: perceived importance of safety training, perceived management attitudes toward safety, perceived effects of safe conduct on promotion, perceived level of risk in the workplace, perceived effects of work pace on safety, perceived

status of the safety officer, perceived effects of safe conduct on social status, and perceived status of the safety committee.

Safety climate is essentially a workgroup's consensus on how seriously management takes and how consistently management enforces safe work practices. A workplace that holds employees to a high standard of safety conduct during periods of normal production, but which orders workers to "cut corners" in terms of safety in order to meet production goals during periods of high demand is likely to have a poor safety climate even though the "crunch periods" may only constitute a very small percentage of total production time over the course of a year (Zohar, 2003). Workers in this situation realize that safety is considered optional depending upon the immediate needs of management. On the other hand, if a company refuses to compromise safety standards during periods of high demand, it will likely have a very good safety climate as workers here realize that here indeed, "Safety comes first." Workers in a good safety climate are more likely to use proper safety equipment, even when not closely supervised. They are more likely to monitor coworkers' safety behaviors and to assist them in performing safely. These workers will bring previously unidentified workplace hazards to the attention of management and will sometimes propose even safer ways of doing a hazardous task. In short, these workers are actively invested in thinking about, maintaining, and improving workplace safety. Workers in organizations with poor safety climates can be expected to perform few or none of these behaviors.

The "Structure" of Safety Climate

In the decades since Zohar first introduced the concept of safety climate, researchers have found varying degrees of support for his eight proposed dimensions (Neal & Griffin, 2004). Some researchers have identified as few as two or three dimensions, whereas others have found an intermediate number of dimensions. The number of dimensions found by a given study seems to arise from an interaction between study instrumentation, sample characteristics, and the statistical procedures used to analyze the data. It is of fundamental importance to recognize that the research does not call into question the existence or importance of safety climate. It merely argues over how its constituent parts are clustered.

Based upon a review of the literature and their own research, Neal and Griffin (2004) proposed a comprehensive, hierarchical model that can be used to characterize safety climate. In many respects, this model reconciles previous contradictory findings regarding the number of dimensions. This model contains two broad dimensions, which can be thought of as higher-order factors. These dimensions each have a number of component elements or lower-order factors. One dimension is organizational policies and procedures and has three component elements: perceived management commitment to safety, human resource practices (which impact safety), and perceived quality of existing safety systems. The other dimension is local work conditions and practices, which has five component elements: perceived supervisor support (for safety), internal group processes (communication and cohesion), perceived quality of communications between the workgroup and others regarding safety, perceptions of risk magnitude for work tasks, and work pressure (at the expense of safety).

Microclimates

It is important to recognize that safety climate may not be homogenous throughout an organization. Neal and Griffin (2004) suggest that, in some organizations, there may be more than one safety climate depending upon the worker groups being considered. Some work groups may be isolated from others in the organization due to location or the differing nature of their work tasks (i.e., factory line workers as compared to factory office workers). The safety climates of these smaller groups are sometimes referred to as *safety microclimates*. For example, given the barriers of language and culture experienced by most Hispanic immigrant workers working in the United States, these workers likely have their own safety microclimate within the larger organizations that employ them.

Counseling Psychology and Safety Climate

At first glance, the concepts of organizational culture and safety climate seem relatively distant from counseling psychology. However, if one views them as representing a cataloging of salient aspects of a given work environment, then connections can quickly be made among organizational culture, safety climate, and the rich vocational psychology heritage of person–environment fit models. Vogel and Feldman (2009) remind us that person–environment fit is a generic term given meaning from specific comparisons: person–organization fit, person–vocation fit, person–job fit, and person–group fit. Currently, in counseling psychology most applications of P–E fit are used to predict person–vocation fit.

However, one of counseling psychology's earliest efforts to characterize environments was at the level of person–organization fit. The *environmental assessment technique* (EAT; Astin & Holland, 1961; Astin 1962, 1963a,b, 1965a,b, 1968) classified environments in terms of size, average intelligence of inhabitants, and a census of Holland vocational personality types in the environment. The EAT was successfully used to categorize university settings and to differentially predict student performance in these settings. Counseling psychologists must move beyond viewing the work-related interests and activities characterized by Holland's six vocational types (Holland, 1997) and/or the occupational reinforcers and work values of the theory of work adjustment (Dawis & Lofquist, 1984) as representing the whole of the work environment, but rather as facets of a greater whole.

Counselor Psychologists As Agents of Change

Counseling psychologists, who have been trained to "save the world one person at a time," usually do not receive any training in organizational interventions and may feel somewhat at a loss regarding how to develop and implement interventions on the organizational level. Although counseling psychologists working in isolation would find it difficult to shift the culture of an organization, as part of an interdisciplinary team, they can play a key role in facilitating change. However, even when working on the level of the individual worker, counseling psychology can help to initiate a "ripple effect" that has the potential to impact on the broader organization in a manner analogous to the positive impact of therapy upon the individual benefiting family and friends. For example, addressing the needs of an individual with substance abuse issues or an anxiety disorder undoubtedly also serves the needs of the family and support system. Similarly, assisting an individual worker in developing better safety and health practices also indirectly affects the safety climate of that individual's coworkers. Safety culture and climate measures are group-level indicators that arise from the actions of groups of individuals. Consequently, the safety culture of the organization can be affected by the work of counseling psychologists with individual workers.

Occupational Safety and Health Interventions

It has long been accepted in the OSH community that it is better to eliminate a hazard than it is to attempt to control it (Smith, Karsh, Carayon, &

Conway, 2003). If a hazard cannot be entirely eliminated, then access to it should be blocked. If a hazard can be neither eliminated entirely nor access to it blocked, then employees should be warned of the hazard and trained to avoid it. In the case of toxic substances or potentially dangerous machinery, the elimination or blocking of access has typically fallen within the realm of *engineering controls*. As its name implies, this approach tends to be guided by engineers, and it attempts to achieve goals through redesign of manufacturing processes and/or machinery. For example, a process may be redesigned to no longer require the use of a hazardous substance or to use a nontoxic or less toxic substitute. A machine may be redesigned so that a formerly dangerous part (e.g., saw blade) can no longer be reached by a worker. Common sense alone dictates that in those instances where engineering controls can be practically implemented, they are preferable to relying upon the impact of warnings and training upon the workers. However, despite tremendous reductions in work-related injuries and mortalities since the adoption of the Occupational Safety and Health Act of 1970 (NIOSH, 2004), work remains the sixth leading cause of death in the United States (Pickle et al., 1996).

Clearly, much more remains to be done. If these safety efforts cannot be fully accomplished through engineering controls, then one must rely upon OSH interventions with workers—a realm in which behavioral scientists should have far more to offer than engineers. However, even the implementation of engineering controls is not without room for behavioral sciences. After all, the managers who make decisions about whether to devote resources to implementing these controls are subject to the same influences upon their decision-making processes as other humans. Examination of this decision-making process clearly falls within the realm of OHP. Among the most common worker OSH interventions are training and behavior-based safety programs.

Occupational Safety and Health Training
Colligan and Cohen (2004) argue that learning new information is a process that occurs so frequently, and often so effortlessly, we tend to take its efficacy for granted. However, if one looks at the massive public health information campaigns concerning smoking, safe sex, exercise, and driving while intoxicated, one must conclude that information alone is not the answer. In their comprehensive review of the OSH training literature, Cohen and Colligan (1998) concluded that OSH training can indeed

have a significant impact, but cautioned that training does not occur in a vacuum, and it alone will not result in a safer workplace. Counseling psychology can make significant contributions to improving workplace health and safety by helping both managers and workers better understand and overcome the challenges inherent to any attempt to change human behavior—in the workplace or elsewhere.

Training Factors
In broad terms, the factors impacting the effectiveness of training may be divided into three categories: the training model, the work context that the worker returns to, and the individual worker. Colligan and Cohen (2004) point out that two of the most obviously important variables impacting training effectiveness—frequency and duration of training—are also among the least studied. Many companies base their training schedules on Occupational Safety and Health Administration regulations and/or insurance carrier minimum requirements. In many instances, this consists of an initial training when starting a new job, followed by annual refresher training. Colligan and Cohen report, as might be expected, the literature indicates more frequent and lengthier training is more effective. However, there is little in the literature to guide optimal frequencies or length of training. As might be expected, more complex functions that are seldom performed deteriorate more quickly than those requiring simple manual operations. This suggests that those complex functions that are critical to emergency response, but only performed during an emergency, should be practiced far more frequently than those that are not. For example, respirator usage, which requires not only a proper device fit, but correct selection of appropriate filters, should be practiced more frequently than less complex behaviors, such as evacuating a building during a fire drill.

Colligan and Cohen (2004) suggested the more interactive and "hands-on," the more effective training will be. Support for this contention is found in the recent meta-analysis of OSH training effectiveness conducted by Burke et al. (2006). Burke et al. found that training effectiveness was related to the *level of engagement* of the training. Low-engagement training consists of activities such as lecture or film presentations that are not followed by any discussion. Medium-engagement might consist of a lecture followed by an interactive discussion of content. High-engagement training typically has "hands-on" opportunities and allows for a high degree of interaction between participants and instructors.

Work Environment

Unfortunately, no matter how much is learned in training, the safety recommendations can only be practiced to the extent that the work setting allows or endorses a given practice (Colligan & Cohen, 2004). In some settings, the proper PPE is not provided. In others, the actual physical layout of the facility will not allow proper practices to be implemented. An example of this would be a warehouse shipping facility that was so arranged that ergonomically recommended lifting and carrying practices could not be used. Perhaps the most important factor influencing actual implementation of safety practices on the job is management support or safety climate. As discussed earlier, the workers in a company that consistently requires safe work practices, without compromise during periods of high production demand, are more likely to use proper safety equipment, even when not closely supervised and will identify ways to improve safety of their own initiative (Zohar, 2003). In contrast, a company that compromises safe work practices during periods of high demand will tend to have workers who are less likely to follow safe work practices even during periods of normal work load.

The Worker

Another important factor related to compliance with training recommendations is worker motivation (Colligan & Cohen, 2004). A worker who knows the correct practice may simply choose not to do it. Campbell, McCloy, Oppler, and Sager (1993) characterized the difference between knowledge and motivation as "can do" versus "will do." Worker motivation at the individual level has received little attention in the OSH literature. In part, this reflects the traditional OSH bias against approaches that have the potential to "blame the victim"—after all, poor motivation could easily be characterized as a character flaw. However, it does seem clear from the discussion above that improving a company's safety climate would be an excellent way to improve worker motivation. Referring back to the core components of counseling psychology, there is clearly a role for positive psychology here. Focusing on identifying the critical positive health and safety behaviors and providing contingencies to increase and maintain those critical behaviors is the primary aim of behavior-based safety processes and should be the lens through which worker motivation challenges are viewed.

Behavior-based Safety

Behavior-based safety processes are one widely used approach to maintain recommended safety behaviors following training. These programs usually consist of an initial safety training that is then followed by implementation of a monitoring system (Geller, 2001). A safe practices monitoring system typically consists of systematic observation and recording of the targeted behaviors (e.g., proper use of PPE), followed by feedback to workers regarding the frequency or percentage of safe versus at-risk behaviors observed. These programs may also include goal setting, commitment strategies, and/or incentives to encourage participation.

Critics of behavior-based safety programs claim the widespread use of incentives has the potential to turn OSH into a "numbers game," in which the number of observations completed and percentage of safe behavior are manipulated so that individuals and/or work groups will achieve program goals—at least on paper—and thereby qualify for an award (Geller, 2001). In response to these criticisms, Geller (2005) developed an approach he dubbed *people-based safety*. This approach melds aspects of behavior-based safety programs with a focus on individual worker feelings and thoughts regarding safety and a strong management commitment to a safe workplace. In many respects, Geller's people-based safety approach is intended as a mechanism by which an organization can positively transform its safety climate.

Transforming the safety climate in a given work environment requires not only increasing critical health and safety behaviors, but also influencing the attitudes of workers to hold safety as a *value*, and not just a temporary *priority*. Geller's (2005) people-based safety approach directly targets workers' thoughts about safety, so that attitude change and behavior change are impacted simultaneously, rather than one following from the other. This is analogous to cognitive-behavioral therapy for the organization. Counselors can support these kinds of group-level intervention processes by providing additional targeted intervention for individuals who are less responsive than their coworkers.

Health Promotion Interventions

For decades, many European public health agencies have been taking advantage of the "captive audience" provided by the workplace and using it as a forum for broader public health initiatives, such as weight loss and smoking cessation. However, it is only in the last decade, in response to increasing health care costs, that this strategy has been implemented in American workplaces. NIOSH (2009) has launched the WorkLife Initiative (WLI). The WLI views the division of health concerns into "at home" or "at work" as being artificial and inefficient. The WLI seeks to improve overall work health through better work-based programs, policies, practices, and benefits.

Weight Control and Physical Fitness

One of the most common health concerns addressed by work-based health promotion programs is weight control. Similar to the success of occupational safety training initiatives, most research supports the positive effect of worksite physical activity programs for increasing physical activity and reducing musculo-skeletal disorders (Proper et al., 2003). A differentiation is made between physical activity and exercise. Physical activity refers broadly to bodily movement produced by contraction of skeletal muscles, which substantially increases energy expenditure. Exercise refers to a subset of physical activity that is planned, structured, and includes repetitive bodily movement done to improve or maintain components of physical fitness (Pratt, 1999). Physical activity refers to any sort of moderate level of continuous movement (e.g., walking, bowling, playing Nintendo Wii©), whereas exercise refers specifically to aerobic activity in which one engages in moderate- to high-intensity activity with sustained increases in heart rate and respiration (e.g., running, swimming, cardio-boxing).

Although most recommendations for worksite interventions suggest increasing physical activity along with improving diet through education and nutrition counseling, research shows significant reductions in overweight and obesity conditions and increases in fitness are realized only when interventions include a high dose level of some type of aerobic exercise (Church, Earnest, Skinner, & Blair, 2007). This is not to say that physical activity is ineffective in low and moderate doses, but rather that there is a dose–response relationship that can be characterized as "Even a little is good; more may be better!" (Lee, 2007, p. 2139).

Disease Prevention

Exercise and nutrition interventions may also be applied in work settings for disease prevention outcomes. Worksite health interventions may be targeted for specific types of disease, including cancer, diabetes, and cardiovascular disease. Many of these efforts can be characterized as "lifestyle change" interventions, as they tend to require participants to not only change their behavior at work, but also at home and with family.

Cardiovascular disease is of particular concern in the realm of disease prevention as it remains the number one cause of death in the United States (National Center for Health Statistics, 2007). The most effective work-based cardiovascular disease prevention interventions address multiple factors (i.e., controlling hypertension, reducing cholesterol, managing stress, quitting smoking) rather than focusing solely on reducing one targeted risk factor, as these interventions allow different employees to benefit from the program in different ways (Pelletier, 2005). A review of multifactorial cardiovascular intervention programs also found providing opportunities for individualized cardiovascular risk reduction counseling for high-risk employees to be a critical component of successful interventions, as well as gradually increasing dose–response relative to risk (Pelletier, 2005).

A Framework for Occupational Health Psychology

Clearly, OHP is a field that is interested in many topics: the individual worker, the work organization, job design, work stress, person–environment fit, gender, aging, racial/ethnic group differences, social climate, prevention, remediation, learning, motivation, compliance, and the work–family interface. In part, this list reflects the interests of the many disciplines involved in OHP, but to a greater extent this list reflects just how cross-cutting work is.

In an effort to better frame OHP, Quick (1999) proposed an organizational matrix for OHP. This framework crosses the public health levels of prevention—primary, secondary, and tertiary—with the three primary emphasis areas of OHP—work environment, individual worker, and the work–family interface. The crossing of levels of prevention with areas of interest in this model yields nine cells, each of which represents a different set of challenges and solutions (see Table 29.2).

In public health, *primary prevention* refers to activities intended to prevent problems from ever occurring (Quick, 1999). *Secondary prevention* refers to activities intended to remedy problems after they have already occurred, but are not yet at the level of crisis. *Tertiary prevention* is somewhat of a misnomer as it refers to activities intended to control the damage of problems that have reached the point of crisis. In Quick's model, the *work environment* refers to virtually everything on the job other than the individual worker. For example, this broad category includes the job tasks, the equipment used, the physical environment, supervision received,

Table 29.2. An Intervention Framework for Occupational Health Psychology

Level of Prevention	Workplace	Individual	Work–family Interface
Primary	job design or redesign, organizational culture	time management, learned optimism	flexi-time, flexi-place, daycare, elder care
Secondary	social supports, team building	physical fitness, relaxation training	family leave policies, family support systems
Tertiary	task revision, EAP	psychotherapy, education, career counseling	health insurance, family counseling

From Quick, J.C. (1999). Occupational health psychology: The convergence of health and clinical psychology with public health and preventative medicine in an organizational context. *Professional Psychology: Research and Practice*, 30, 123–128. American Psychological Association. Reprinted with permission.

company policies, and corporate decision making. The *individual* refers to everything a given worker brings to a job—work history, education, skills, attitudes, habits, expectations, and motivations. The *work–family interface* refers to the overlapping of life domains, in this case work and family. This dynamic construct recognizes that, not only does work impact family life in ways such as mandatory overtime, shift work, business travel, the carrying home of work-related stress—but that family needs and events impact work. Examples include the availability of child or elder care, dual-career households, and the chronic illness of a family member.

Finding Common Ground

Quick (1999) predicates this model on two principles: individual health and organizational health are interdependent, and organizational leaders have responsibility for individual and organizational health. Given that, in many companies, there is a history of conflict between management and workers, the first challenge for an occupational health psychologist may be to help management and workers find common ground upon which to ease into the cooperation implied by these principles.

Indeed, it has long been conventional wisdom that an inherent tension exists between meeting the needs of the organization and meeting the needs of workers. This is reflected in the traditional emphases of the two disciplines working in the area of vocational psychology. Industrial/organizational psychologists have typically approached problems from the perspective of the company. Counseling psychologists have focused on the needs of the individual. In OHP, this division is recognized, but is not viewed from an "either/or" perspective; rather, the needs of both parties are considered so intertwined that both require attention for any solution

to achieve long-term success. Quick (1999) suggests that one important way to build a bridge between management and workers is to use P–E fit models.

By definition, P–E fit models describe the work environment and individuals using shared dimensions and attempt to identify optimal matches between the two—typically viewed as being of benefit to both. However, in practice, most applications have followed the division of interests discussed above. For example, industrial/organizational psychologists might use Holland types for selection purposes, without consideration of the needs of the individual. Similarly, counseling psychologists use the same Holland types to guide students toward college majors without consideration of the larger context in which they will spend their working years. Even in isolation, both approaches have proven useful enough to become nearly ubiquitous in their respective settings. However, OHP challenges and inspires us to consider how much more powerful P–E fit models could be if used to simultaneously meet the needs of both work environments and workers.

The Theory of Work Adjustment

Perhaps the P–E fit model best positioned for use in OHP is the *theory of work adjustment* (TWA; Dawis, 2004; Dawis & Lofquist, 1984). Hesketh and Griffin (2005) observed that few theories are comprehensive enough to be applied to career choice, selection, training, and organizational interventions. The TWA accomplishes this by placing equal emphasis on satisfying the worker and the workplace and by using symmetrical processes to describe both.

The TWA views work as an interactive and reciprocal process between the individual and the work environment (Dawis, 2004; Dawis & Lofquist, 1984). In simplest terms, the individual may be viewed as fulfilling the labor requirements of the work environment, in exchange for which the work environment fulfills a wide range of financial, social, and psychological needs for the individual. The TWA provides a framework within which to predict the outcomes of the match between individual and work environment and to describe the ongoing process of interaction (work adjustment) between worker and work environment.

In his review of P–E fit models, Tinsley (2000) opined that TWA had accumulated the most evidence of validity of all P–E fit models and that its instrumentation was an exemplar of psychometric rigor. The NIOSH job stress model that conceptualizes job stress as arising from a mismatch between job demands and/or rewards with worker skills and/or needs was directly influenced by TWA (Lawrence R. Murphy, personal communication). In addition, the core variables of the TWA prediction model were adopted by the *Occupational Information Network* (*O*NET*), the United States Department of Labor's online database that is the successor to the *Dictionary of Occupational Titles*. The O*NET database is being increasingly used by OHP researchers to define important work-related variables. Interested readers should refer to Larson (2011, Chapter 6, this volume) for a more thorough discussion of P–E fit models and TWA.

Counseling Psychology and Occupational Health Psychology

Even with the benefit of Quick's organizational framework and powerful P–E fit models such as TWA, the sprawling field of OHP still is far from unified and seamless. Of the disciplines most actively involved in OHP, none can come close to addressing all the cells of Quick's matrix. Indeed, most can claim expertise in only one or two and relevance to few more. However, counseling psychology, which has been minimally involved in OHP to date, arguably has the potential to provide expertise and relevant input to nearly all the cells in Quick's matrix.

At the primary intervention level, starting with the workplace, counseling psychology does not have the ergonomic expertise to assist in the physical aspects of job design. However, counseling psychology could certainly contribute to the psychological aspects of job design. For example, simple application of Holland types would guide the sort of primary activities that were assigned to a position. By clustering activities that were of the same or adjacent Holland types, one has the potential to eliminate sources of job dissatisfaction and work

stress. At the secondary prevention level for the workplace, counseling psychologists would surely have the background to contribute to the fostering of social support networks within a work setting. At the tertiary level of prevention, the general counseling background every counseling psychologist receives would certainly be congruent with employee assistance programs, and any skills useful for initial job design would also be applicable to job redesign.

Let us now look at the individual. At the primary prevention level, counseling psychology, which prides itself on having practiced positive psychology before it was ever labeled as such, could surely teach learned optimism. Also, what could be a better primary prevention measure at the individual level for job dissatisfaction and work stress than appropriate initial choice of career? At the secondary level of prevention, relaxation training and cognitive-behavior interventions for work stress are clearly within the potential scope of practice of counseling psychologists. Finally, at the tertiary level of prevention, psychotherapy, education, and counseling for career change are already common practice among counseling psychologists.

The primary prevention level of the work–family interface may initially appear to be in the realm of managerial policy setting. However, counseling psychology could provide input to the process. Similar input could also be provided at the secondary level regarding the development of family-friendly policies for the workplace. Finally, at the tertiary level, one finds family counseling, as another area in which many counseling psychologists are already practicing.

Recent Developments in Counseling Psychology

One might get the impression that many counseling psychologists have already been working in the field of OHP—but did not realize they were doing so. Imagine the impact they could have if their efforts were coordinated! A recent special section in *American Psychologist* (see 2008, vol. 63, no. 4) on work and career written by several of the most prominent counseling psychologists currently active in the field seems to have initiated just such a call.

Citing findings from the positive, vocational, multicultural, and clinical psychology literatures, Blustein (2008) argued strongly for the centrality of work to well-being and called for breaking down artificial barriers between vocational psychology and other areas of psychology. Blustein identified OHP as being congruent with both the historical and current goals of vocational psychology and the psychology of work. He suggested that a conscious and purposeful linkage of these three "would yield a powerfully compelling scholarly and public policy agenda" (Blustein, 2008, p. 236).

Arguing along similar lines, Fouad and Bynner (2008) suggest that vocational psychology has focused primarily on the transition from school to work and has tended to turn a blind eye to the many transitions workers experience in the remainder of their working lives. Some of these transitions are voluntary and are largely associated with positive outcomes. Examples include advancement within one's field through promotion or accepting a new job that offers greater benefits and satisfactions. Other transitions are involuntary and associated with significant stress. Examples of stressful transitions include the loss of employment due to corporate downsizing, merger, or closure. Fouad and Bynner state that it is not possible to separate the impact of work transitions from other life domains. For example, the financial security (or lack thereof) of one's job impacts decisions such as marriage, having children, and purchasing a home. Work-related stress clearly impacts one's functioning as a life partner and/or a parent. Even "positive" transitions are likely to generate stress for both the individual and their family. For example, an exciting new job may require moving to another city, uprooting children from school, and initiating a job search for a working spouse. Although Fouad and Bynner discuss these concerns without reference to OHP, clearly these are all topics that have long been of interest to OHP.

In a third paper, Fassinger (2008) explored the interconnections between the core counseling psychology themes of vocational psychology, multiculturalism, and social justice within Blustein's (2006) psychology of work framework. The implications of Fassinger's paper are a powerful argument that the barriers separating the study of work from the remainder of life are not only arbitrary, but counterproductive. Ultimately, Fassinger concluded her paper with a call for action that pushes counseling psychology toward issues (occupational health disparities, organization of work, and work–family interface) that are of central interest to OHP.

Future Directions

At the beginning of this chapter, Bingham's (2001) categorization of counseling psychology into the four core areas of vocational psychology, positive psychology, multicultural psychology, and social justice was discussed. If this is an apt characterization, then counseling psychology and OHP share considerable overlap. Vocational psychology has relevance to better understanding the psychological aspects of job design and redesign, the work–family interface, work stress, and person–environment fit models. However, to be most useful, it will need to be the vocational psychology of the working class, not just the college educated. It will need to be the vocational psychology of adult workers, not just college undergraduates. It will need to be the vocational psychology that sees work not just as an opportunity for self-expression, but as an essential tool for survival, advancement, and empowerment.

Positive psychology, the study of well-being, has clear implications for guiding the development of organizational culture, work stress prevention programs and interventions, and family-friendly policies. It will be a positive psychology that identifies commonalities in high-functioning organizations and develops methods to implement these practices in less functional settings. It will be a positive psychology that embraces that most powerful of primary prevention interventions for work stress—a well-informed, thoughtful career choice.

Multiculturalism can assist organizations to engender policies and an organizational culture that truly embraces diversity and views it as an advantage in a competitive, increasingly global world of business. Multiculturalism can also contribute much to better understanding and then eliminating occupational health disparities. It will need to be a multiculturalism that places less emphasis on cataloging discrimination and victimization, and more on achieving and maintaining social, economic, and political power.

Social justice is, in many respects, a paradox. On one hand, it is the most ephemeral of these core values and at the same time the most concrete in its final impact. It is far easier to recognize its absence than its presence. However, it provides counseling psychology and OHP with a powerful moral compass pointing us toward the question of why simply working for a living, something we all have to do to survive—barring being born to wealth or winning the lottery—should remain a leading cause of injury and death. Social justice can be the force that does not ask why employers are hiring undocumented immigrants, but why these immigrants are killed and injured at two to three times the rate of American-born workers. Social justice can help us to explore the ethical issues related to choosing between the immense resources required to change work organizations to stress workers less versus the far more modest resources needed to train workers to better cope with higher levels of stress.

Conclusion
A Return to Our Roots

In many respects, the counseling psychology described above represents a return to the roots of our field, a field that viewed vocational psychology, positive psychology, multicultural psychology, and social justice not as four separate themes, but inseparably interconnected and intertwined. This was a counseling psychology that viewed the workplace, for better or worse, as the venue in which social betterment, economic advantage, and political empowerment were obtained.

It is just this vision from our past that is OHP's future. As a field, OHP has matured enough that it is no longer merely cataloguing the adverse impact of organizational practices upon worker health and well-being. It is increasingly interested in developing both interventions to remedy current problems and best-practices guidelines that organizations can use to prevent problems from ever occurring. In both the United States and the European Union, occupational health psychologists have recognized the importance of the work–life interface and of alleviating occupational health disparities. With both globalization and advances in technologies rendering distances and borders less relevant, OHP will become of increasingly relevance to the remainder of the world as well, in part, to help developing countries to learn to avoid repeating our mistakes and in part, to remedy mistakes already made in the course of their rapid industrialization.

The fit between counseling psychology and OHP is so obvious that there is no doubt that some counseling psychologists will play a leading role in OHP. The question is whether as a field, counseling psychology recognizes and embraces OHP as being of the same intellectual and moral lineage and "become(s) not just part of the mainstream, but *the* mainstream of this movement toward the science and application of occupational health" (Hansen, 1995, p. 137).

Acknowledgments

The views and opinions expressed in this manuscript are those of the authors and do not represent official policies or findings of the National Institute for Occupational Safety and Health.

References

Assagioli, R. (1965). *Psychosynthesis: A manual of principles and techniques.* New York: The Viking Press.

Astin, A. W. (1962). An empirical characterization of higher education institutions. *Journal of Educational Psychology,* 53(5), 224–235.

Astin, A. W. (1963a). Differential college effects on the motivation of talented students to obtain the PhD. *Journal of Educational Psychology,* 54(1), 63–71.

Astin, A. W. (1963b). Further validation of the environmental assessment technique. *Journal of Educational Psychology,* 54(4), 217–226.

Astin, A. W. (1965a). Effects of different college environments on the vocational choices of high aptitude students. *Journal of Counseling Psychology,* 12(1), 28–34.

Astin, A. W. (1965b). *Who goes where to college?* Chicago: Science Research Associates.

Astin, A. W. (1968). *The college environment.* Washington, DC: The American Council on Education.

Astin, A. W., & Holland, J. L. (1961). The environmental assessment technique: A way to measure college environments. *Journal of Educational Psychology,* 53(6), 308–316.

Atkinson, W. (2004). Stress: Risk management's most serious challenge? *Risk Management,* 51(6), 20–24.

Barling, J., & Griffiths, A. (2003). A history of occupational health psychology. In J. C. Quick, & L. E. Tetrick (Eds.), *Handbook of occupational health psychology* (pp. 19–33), Washington, DC: American Psychological Association.

Beggs, J., Mangan, O., Concagh, G., & Pollock, J. (2005). *Non-national workers in the Irish economy.* Dublin, Ireland: AIB Global Treasury Economic Research.

Bell, M. P., Cycyota, C. S., & Quick, J. C. (2002). An affirmative defense: The preventive management of sexual harassment. In D. L., Nelson, & R. J. Burke (Eds.), *Gender, work stress, and health* (pp. 191–210). Washington, DC: American Psychological Association.

Bingham, R. P. (2001). *Counseling psychology: Looking to the future.* Paper presented at the American Psychological Association Annual Conference, Chicago, IL.

Blustein, D. L. (2006). *The psychology of working: A new perspective for career development, counseling, and public policy.* Mahwah, NJ: Lawrence Erlbaum.

Blustein, D. L. (2008). The role of work in psychological health and well-being: A conceptual, historical and public policy perspective. *American Psychologist,* 63(4), 228–240.

Blustein, D. L., McWhirter, E. H., & Perry, J. C. (2005). An emancipatory communitarian approach to vocational development theory, research, and practice. *The Counseling Psychologist,* 33, 141–179.

Burke, M. J., Sarpy, S. A., Smith-Crowe, K., Chan-Serafin, S., Salvador, R. O., & Islam, G. (2006). Relative effectiveness of worker safety and health training methods. *American Journal of Public Health,* 96(2), 315–324.

Campbell, J. P., McCloy, R. A., Oppler, S. H., & Sager, C. E. (1993). A theory of performance. In N. Schmitt, & W. C. Borman (Eds.), *Personnel selection in organizations.* San Francisco: Jossey-Bates.

Caruso, C. C., Bushnell, T., Eggerth, D., Heitmann, A., Kojola, B., Newman, K., et al. (2006). Long working hours, safety, and health: Toward a national research agenda. *American Journal of Industrial Medicine,* 49, 930–942.

Center to Protect Workers' Rights. (2002). *The construction chart book: The U.S. construction industry and Its workers* (3rd ed.). Silver Spring, MD: Author.

Church, T. S., Earnest, C. P., Skinner, J. S., & Blair, S. N. (2007). Effects of different doses of physical activity on cardiorespiratory fitness among sedentary, overweight or obese postmenopausal women with elevated blood pressure: A randomized controlled trial. *JAMA, 297*(19), 2081–2091.

Cohen, A., & Colligan, M. (1998). *Assessing occupational safety and health training* (No. 98–145). Wasington, DC: National Institute for Occupational Safety and Health.

Colligan, M. J., & Cohen, A. (2004). The role of training in promoting workplace safety and health. In J. Barling, & M. R. Frone (Eds.), *The psychology of workplace safety* (pp. 223–248). Washington, DC: American Psychological Association.

Dawis, R. V. (2004). The Minnesota Theory of Work Adjustment. In S. D. Brown, & R. W. Lent (Eds.), *Career development: putting theory and research into practice* (pp. 3–23). Hoboken, NJ: Wiley.

Dawis, R. V., & Lofquist, L. H. (1984). *A psychological theory of work adjustment*. Minneapolis: University of Minnesota Press.

Dompierre, J., & Lavoie, F. (1994). Subjective work stress and family violence. In G. P. Keita, & J. J. Hurrell (Eds.), *Job stress in a changing workforce: Investigating gender, diversity, and family issues* (pp. 213–228). Washington, DC: American Psychological Association.

Dong, X., & Platner, J. W. (2004). Occupational fatalities of Hispanic construction workers from 1992 to 2000. *American Journal of Industrial Medicine, 45*, 45–54.

Eggerth, D. E. (2008). From theory of work adjustment fit to person-environment correspondence counseling: Vocational psychology as positive psychology. *Journal of Career Assessment, 16*(1), 60–74.

Elo, A., Ervasti, J., Kuosma, E., & Mattila, P. (2008). Evaluation of an organizational stress management program in a municipal public workers organization. *Journal of Occupational Health Psychology, 13*(1), 10–23.

Fassinger, R. E. Workplace diversity and public policy: Challenges and opportunities for psychology. *American Psychologist, 63*(4), 252–268.

Flin, R., Mearns, K., O'Connor, P., & Bryden, R. (2000). Measuring safety climate: Identifying the common features. *Safety Science, 34*, 177–192.

Fouad, N. A., & Bynner, J. (2008). Work transitions. *American Psychologist, 63*(4), 241–251.

Friedman, L. N., Tucker, S. B., Neville, P. R., & Imperial, M. (1996). The impact of domestic violence on the workplace. In G. R. VandenBos, & E. Q. Bulatao (Eds.), *Violence on the job: Identifying risks and developing solutions* (pp. 153–161). Washington, DC: American Psychological Association.

Frone, M. R. (2003). Work-family balance. In J. C. Quick, & L. E. Tetrick (Eds.), *Handbook of occupational health psychology* (pp. 143–162). Washington, DC: American Psychological Association.

Fujishiro, K., Gong, F., Baron, S., Jacobson, J. C., DeLaney, S., Flynn, M., & Eggerth, D. E. (2009). Translating questionnaire items for a multi-lingual worker population: The iterative process of translations and cognitive interviews with English-, Spanish-, and Chinese-speaking workers. *American Journal of Industrial Medicine*.

Geller, E. S. (2001). *The psychology of safety handbook*. Boca Raton, FL: CRC Press.

Geller, E. S. (2005). *People-based safety: The source*. Virginia Beach, VA: Coastal Training Technologies.

Goetzel, R. Z., Anderson, D. R., Whitmer, R. W., Ozminkowski, R. J., Dunn, R. L., & Wasserman, J. (1998). The relationship between modifiable health risks and health care expenditures: An analysis of the multi-employer HERO health risk and cost database. *Journal of Occupational and Environmental Medicine, 40*(10), 843–854.

Gottfredson, G. D. (1996). The Hawthorne misunderstanding (and how to get the Hawthorne effect in action research). *Journal of Research in Crime and Delinquency, 33*(1), 28–48.

Greenhaus, J. H., & Parasuraman, S. (2002). The allocation of time to work and family roles. In D. L. Nelson, & R. J. Burke (Eds.), *Gender, work stress and health* (pp. 115–128). Washington, DC: American Psychological Association.

Hansen, J. C. (1995). No one ever died wishing they had spent more time in the office. *The Counseling Psychologist, 23*(1), 129–141.

Harris Interactive. (2008). *Poll: 78% of U.S. workers burned out*. Rochester, NY: Author.

Hatinen, M., Kinnunen, U., Pekkonen, M., & Kalimo, R. (2007). Comparing two burnout interventions: Perceived job control mediates decreases in burnout. *International Journal of Stress Management, 14*(3), 227–248.

Hesketh, B., & Griffin, B. (2005). Work adjustment. In W. B. Walsh, & M. L. Savickas (Eds.), *Handbook of vocational psychology* (3rd ed., pp. 245–266). Mahwah, NJ: Lawrence Earlbaum.

Holland, J. L. (1997). *Making vocational choices* (3rd ed.). Odessa, FL: Psychological Assessment Resources.

Hoskins, A. B. (2005). Occupational injuries, illnesses, and fatalities among women. *Monthly Labor Review, 128*(10), 31–37.

Ivancevitch, J. M., Matteson, M. T., Freedman, S. M., & Phillips, J. S. (1990). Worksite stress management interventions. *American Psychologist, 45*, 252–261.

Jarvik, L. F., & Small, G. W. (1988). *Parentcare: A commonsense guide for adult children*. New York: Crown Publishing.

Jones, L. K. (1996). A harsh and challenging world of work: Implications for counselors. *Journal of Counseling and Development, 74*, 453–459.

Karasek, R. (1979). Job decision latitude, job demands and mental strain: Implications for job redesign. *Administrative Science Quarterly, 24*, 285–307.

Kelloway, E. K., & Barling, J. (1994). Stress, control, well-being, and marital functioning: A causal correlational analysis. In G. P. Keita, & J. J. Hurrell (Eds.), *Job stress in a changing workforce: Investigating gender, diversity, and family issues* (pp. 241–252). Washington, DC: American Psychological Association.

Kenny, D. T. & Cooper, C. L. (2003). Introduction: Occupational stress and its management. *International Journal of Stress Management, 10*(4), 275–279.

Kisner, S. M., & Prat, S. G. (1997). Occupational fatalities among older workers in the United States: 1980–1991. *Journal of Occupational and Environmental Medicine, 39*(8), 715–721.

Landsbergis, P. A., Schnall, P. L., Scwartz, J. E., Warren, K., & Pickering, T. G. (1995). Job-strain, hypertension, and cardiovascular disease: Empirical evidence, methodological issues, and recommendations for future research. In S. L. Sauter, & L. R. Murphy (Eds.), *Organizational risk factors for job stress* (pp. 97–112). Washington, DC: American Psychological Association.

Larson, L. M. (2011). What do we know about worklife across the lifespan. In E. M. Altmaier, & J. C. Hansen (Eds.), *The Oxford handbook of counseling psychology*. New York: Oxford University Press.

Le Blanc, P. M., Hox, J. J., Schaufeli, W. B., Taris, T. W., & Peeters, M. C. W. (2007). Take care! The evaluation of a team-based burnout intervention program for oncology care providers. *Journal of Applied Psychology, 92,* 213–227.

Lee, I. M. (2007). Dose-response relation between physical activity and fitness: Even a little is good; more is better. *Journal of the American Medical Association, 297*(19), 2137–2139.

Leigh, P. J., Markowitz, S. B., Fahs, M., Shin, C., & Landigan, P. J. (1997). Occupational injury and illness in the United States. *Archives of Internal Medicine, 157,* 1557–1568.

Loh, K., & Richardson, S. (2004). Foreign-born workers: Trends in fatal occupational injuries, 1996–2001. *Monthly Labor Review, 127*(6), 42–53.

Marshall, N. L., & Barnett, R. C. (1994). Family-friendly workplaces, work-family interface and worker health. In G. P. Keita, & J. J. Hurrell (Eds.), *Job stress in a changing workforce: Investigating gender, diversity, and family issues* (pp. 253–264). Washington, DC: American Psychological Association.

Maslach, C. (1982). *Burnout: The cost of caring.* Englewood Cliffs, NJ: Prentice-Hall.

Maslach, C. (2003). Job burnout: New directions in research and intervention. *Current Directions in Psychological Science, 12*(5), 189–192.

Messing, K., & de Grosbois, S. (2001). Women workers confront one-eyed science: Building alliances to improve women's occupational health. *Women and Health, 33,* 125–141.

Miller, L. (1998). Our own medicine: Traumatized psychotherapists and the stresses of doing therapy. *Psychotherapy, 35*(2), 137–146.

National Center for Health Statistics (2007). *Health, United States, 2007 With Chartbook on Trends in the Health of Americans.* Hyattsville, MD: Author.

National Institute for Occupational Safety and Health. (1995). *Preventing homicide in the workplace* (DHHS/NIOSH Publication No. 93–109). Washington, DC: Author.

National Institute for Occupational Safety and Health. (1999). *Providing safety and health protection for a diverse construction workforce: Issues and ideas* (DHHS/NIOSH Publication No. 99–140). Washington, DC: Author.

National Institute for Occupational Safety and Health. (1999). *Stress . . . at work* (DHHS/NIOSH Publication No. 99–101). Washington, DC: Author.

National Institute for Occupational Safety and Health. (2002). *The changing organization of work and safety and the health of working people: Knowledge gaps and research directions* (DHHS/NIOSH Publication No. 2002–116). Washington, DC: Author.

National Institute for Occupational Safety and Health. (2003). *National occupational research agenda, Update 2003* (DHHS/NIOSH Publication No. 2003–148). Washington, DC: Author.

National Institute for Occupational Safety and Health. (2004). *Worker health chartbook, 2004* (DHHS/NIOSH Publication No. 2004–146). Washington, DC: Author.

National Institute for Occupational Safety and Health. (2009). *The WorkLive Initiative* (DHHS/NIOSH Publication No. 2009–146). Washington, DC: Author.

Neal, A., & Griffin, M. A. (2004). Safety climate and safety at work. In J. Barling, & M. R. Frone (Eds.), *The psychology of workplace safety* (pp. 15–34). Washington, DC: American Psychological Association.

Nicoletti, J., & Spooner, K. (1996). Violence in the workplace: Response and intervention strategies. In G. R. VandenBos, & E. Q. Bulatao (Eds.), *Violence on the job: Identifying risks and developing solutions* (pp. 267–282). Washington, DC: American Psychological Association.

O'Brien, K. M. (2001). The legacy of Parson: Career counselors and vocational psychologists as agents of change. *Career Development Quarterly, 50,* 66–76.

O'Connor, T. (2003). Reaching Spanish-speaking workers and employers with occupational safety and health information. In *Safety is Seguridad* (pp. 93–111). Washington, DC: The National Academies Press.

Ontario Women's Directorate and the Industrial Accident Prevention Association. (2006). *Personal protective equipment for women: Addressing the need.* Toronto, Canada: Industrial Accident Prevention Association.

Parsons, H. M. (1991). Hawthorne: An early OBM experiment. *Journal of Organizational Behavior Management, 12*(1), 27–43.

Passel, J. S. (2005). *Estimates of the size and characteristics of the undocumented population.* Washington, DC: Pew Research Center.

Passel, J. S. (2006). *The size and characteristics of the unauthorized migrant population in the U.S. estimates based on the March 2005 current population survey.* Washington, DC: Pew Research Center.

Passel, J. S., Capps, R., & Fix, M. E. (2002). *The dispersal of Immigrants in the 1990s.* Immigrant families and workers: Facts and perspectives, Brief no. 2. Washington, DC: Urban Institute.

Pelletier, K. (2005). A review and analysis of the clinical and cost-effectiveness studies of comprehensive health promotion and disease management programs at the worksite: Update VI 2000–2004. *Journal of Occupational and Environmental Medicine, 47*(10), 1051–1058.

Pickle, L. W., Mongiole, M., Jones, G. K., & White, A. A. (1996). *Atlas of United States mortality* (DHHS Publication No. 97–1015). Hyattsville, MD: National Center for Health Statistics.

Pratt, M. (1999). Benefits of lifestyle activity vs. structured exercise. *Journal of the American Medical Association, 281*(4), 375–376.

Proper, K., Koning, M., Van der Beek, A., Hildebrandt, V., Bosscher, R., & van Mechelen, W. (2003). The effectiveness of worksite physical activity programs on physical activity, physical fitness, and health. *Clinical Journal of Sport Medicine, 12,* 106–117.

Quick, J. C. (1999). Occupational health psychology: The convergence of health and clinical psychology with public health and preventative medicine in an organizational context. *Professional Psychology: Research and Practice, 30,* 123–128.

Quick, J. C., Quick, J. D., Nelson, D. L., & Hurrell, J. J. (1997). *Preventive stress management in organizations.* Washington, DC: American Psychological Association.

Radmacher, S. A., & Sheridan, C. L. (1995). An investigation of the demand-control model of job strain. In S. L. Sauter, &

L. R. Murphy (Eds.), *Organizational risk factors for job stress* (pp. 127–138). Washington, DC: American Psychological Association.

Raymond, J. S., Wood, D. W., & Patrick, W. K. (1990). Psychology doctoral training in work and health. *American Psychologist, 45*, 1159–1161.

Richardson, K. M., & Rothstein, H. R. (2008). Effects of occupational stress management intervention programs: A meta-analysis. *Journal of Occupational Health Psychology, 13*, 69–93.

Richardson, S., Ruser, R., & Suarez, P. (2003). Hispanic workers in the United States: An analysis of employment distributions, fatal occupational injuries, and non-fatal occupational injuries and illnesses. In *Safety is Seguridad* (pp. 43–82). Washington, DC: The National Academies.

Salmela-Aro, K., Naatanen, P., & Nurmi, J. (2004). The role of work-related personal projects during two burnout interventions: A longitudinal study. *Work & Stress, 18*(3), 208–230.

Schaufeli, W. B., Keijsers, G. B., & Miranda, D. R. (1995). Burnout, technology use and ICU performance. In S. L. Sauter, & L. R. Murphy (Eds.), *Organizational risk factors for job stress* (pp. 259–272). Washington, DC: American Psychological Association.

Schneider, D. L., Camara, W. J., Tetrick, L. E., & Stenberg, C. R. (1999). Training in occupational health psychology: Initial efforts and alternative models. *Professional Psychology: Research and Practice, 30*, 138–142.

Schonfeld, I. S. (1992). Assessing stress in teachers: Depressive symptom scales and neutral self-reports of the work environment. In J. C. Quick, L. R. Murphy, & J. J. Hurrell (Eds.), *Stress and well-being at work: Assessments and interventions for occupational mental health* (pp. 270–285). Washington, DC: American Psychological Association.

Schulte, P. A. (2005). Characterizing the burden of occupational injury and disease. *Journal of Occupational and Environmental Medicine, 47*, 607–622.

Selye, H. (1950). Diseases of adaptation. *Wisconsin Medical Journal, 49*(6), 515–516.

Semmer, N. K. (2003). Job stress interventions and organization of work. In J. C. Quick, & L. E. Tetrick (Eds.), *Handbook of occupational health psychology* (pp. 325–353). Washington, DC: American Psychological Association.

Shapiro, S. L., Astin, J. A., & Cordova, M. (2005). Mindfulness-based stress reduction for health care professionals: Results from a randomized trial. *International Journal of Stress Management, 12*(2), 164–176.

Shirom, A. (2003). Job-related burnout: A review. In J. C. Quick, & L. E. Tetrick (Eds.), *Handbook of occupational health psychology* (pp. 245–264). Washington, DC: American Psychological Association.

Smith, M. J., Karsh, B., Carayon, P., & Conway, F. T. (2003). Controlling occupational safety and health hazards. In J. C. Quick, & L. E. Tetrick (Eds.), *Handbook of occupational health psychology* (pp. 35–68). Washington, DC: American Psychological Association.

Spielberger, C. D., Vagg, P. R., & Wasala, C. F. (2003). Occupational stress: Job pressures and lack of support. In J. C. Quick, & L. E. Tetrick (Eds.), *Handbook of occupational health psychology* (pp. 185–200). Washington, DC: American Psychological Association.

Stellman, J. M., & Mailman, J. L. (1999). Women workers: The social construction of a special population. *Occupational Medicine: State of the Art Reviews, 14*, 559–580.

Tetrick, L. E., Miles, R. L., Marcil, L., & Van Dosen, C. M. (1994). Child-care difficulties and the impact on concentration, stress, and productivity among single and nonsingle mothers and fathers In G. P. Keita, & J. J. Hurrell (Eds.), *Job stress in a changing workforce: Investigating gender, diversity, and family issues* (pp. 229–240). Washington, DC: American Psychological Association.

Theorell, T. (2003). To be able to exert control over one's own situation: A necessary condition for coping with stressors. In J. C. Quick, & L. E. Tetrick (Eds.), *Handbook of occupational health psychology* (pp. 201–219). Washington, DC: American Psychological Association.

Tinsely, H. E. A. (2000). The congruence myth: An analysis of the efficacy of the person-environment fit model. *Journal of Vocational Behavior, 56*, 147–179.

Trinkoff, A. M., Lipscomb, J. A., Geiger-Brown, J., & Brady, B. (2002). Musculoskeletal problems of the neck, shoulder, and back and functional consequences in nurses. *American Journal of Industrial Medicine, 41*, 170–178.

Trist, E. L., & Bamforth, K. W. (1951). Some social and psychological consequences of the longwall methods of coal-getting. *Human Relations, 14*, 3–38.

U.S. Census Bureau. (2005). *Facts of features: Hispanic heritage month 2005.* Retrieved September 8, 2005, from http://www.census.gov/.

U.S. Census Bureau. (2006). *Current population survey: Annual social and economic supplement.* Retrieved January 8, 2008, from http://www.census.gov/.

Valenzuela, A., Theodore, N., Melendez, E., & Gonzalez, A. L. (2006). *On the corner: Day labor in the United States.* Los Angeles: UCLA Center for the Study of Urban Poverty.

van der Klink, J. C. L., Blonk, R. W. B., Schene, A. H., & van Dijk, F. J. H. (2001). The benefits of interventions for work-related stress. *American Journal of Public Health, 91*(2), 270–276.

van Dierendonck, D., Garssen, B., Visser, A. (2005). Burnout prevention through personal growth. *International Journal of Stress Management, 12*(1), 62–77.

van Dierendonck, D., Schaufeli, W. B., & Buunk, B. P. (1998). The evaluation of an individual burnout intervention program: The role of inequity and social support. *Journal of Applied Psychology, 83*(1), 392–407.

Vogel, R. M., & Feldman, D. C. (2009). Integrating levels of person-environment fit: The roles of vocational fit and group fit. *Journal of Vocational Behavior, 75*(1), 68–81.

Wegman, D. H. (1999). Older workers. *Occupational Medicine: State of the Art Reviews, 14*(3), 537–557.

Wegman, D. H., & McGee, J. P. (2004). *Health and safety needs of older workers.* Washington, DC: The National Academies Press.

Westman, M., & Eden, D. (1997). Effects of a respite from work on burnout: Vacation relief and face-out. *Journal of Applied Psychology, 82*(4), 516–527.

Williamson, E. G. (1939). *How to counsel students.* New York: McGraw-Hill.

Zohar, D. (1980). Safety climate in industrial organizations: Theoretical and applied implications. *Journal of Applied Psychology, 65*, 96–102.

Zohar, D. (2003). Safety climate: Conceptual and measurement issues. In J. C. Quick, & L. E. Tetrick (Eds.), *Handbook of occupational health psychology.* Washington, DC: American Psychological Association.

Trent A. Petrie *and* Robert J. Harmison

Abstract

Although sport psychology is an interdisciplinary field, it has a natural and strong philosophical and historical connection to counseling psychology. With this connection as the foundation, we discuss sport psychology's history and identify the current issues in the field, such as graduate training and professional certification. We define mental toughness and identify the skills and strategies consultants use to assist athletes, teams, and coaches in attaining it and improving their performances. Several clinical issues are then discussed in the context of the uniqueness of the sport environment. Given the centrality of training to the field, we present an ideal training model for students and professionals who want to be applied sport psychologists. Finally, we identify the issues that we believe will define the future of applied sport psychology and offer suggestions on how to address them.

Keywords: sport psychology, mental toughness, applied training, eating disorders, athletic injury, professional issues, sport psychology values, performance enhancement interventions

In the last 40 years, sport psychology has become more applied as athletes, teams, coaches, and parents have sought professionals who can assist them with gaining the mental edge to improve performances and increase the likelihood of winning competitions (Smith, 1989). With this shift to service delivery, psychologists have become more involved in the field, working with athletes of all levels (e.g., elite, college, youth) and using their skills and knowledge of human behavior to help athletes reach their performance goals, work more effectively as a unit, and enjoy the process of learning new and improving existing skills (Petrie & Diehl, 1995; Petrie, Diehl, & Watkins, 1995). Although some professionals have argued that sport psychology is simply a subfield of psychology and that those working in the field should be trained as psychologists (e.g., Nideffer, 1984), the reality is that sport psychology is an interdisciplinary field whose historical roots are embedded within departments of physical

education, kinesiology, and exercise science (Lutz, 1990; Petrie & Watkins, 1994). Even today, professional organizations (e.g., Association for Applied Sport Psychology [AASP]) recognize the interdisciplinary nature of the field, offering certification to those who have training in both psychology and exercise/sport science.

We begin this chapter by providing an overview of the history and current perspectives in sport psychology. In doing so, we identify the key events and figures that represent modern-day applications of sport psychology and discuss the field's current status in terms of graduate training, national organizations, and professional certification and status. In this discussion, we affirm our respect for sport psychology as an interdisciplinary field, yet, like others (e.g., Howard, 1993; Petitpas, Giges, & Danish, 1999), argue that counseling psychology's values, training, and philosophy are ideally suited for working in the sport environment and for counseling/consulting with athletes of all levels. Second, we define mental toughness and then discuss the psychological skills and strategies that have been identified by athletes and coaches as essential for their success, and how such strategies can be used to help athletes be mentally tougher performers. Third, we identify clinical issues that occur with some regularity among athletes, and then discuss how these issues are affected by unique factors of the sport environment. Fourth, we present what we believe is an ideal model for training applied sport psychologists. Consistent with our view that counseling psychology's values and philosophy are an excellent fit with athletes' needs and the demands of the sport environment, the foundational training program is housed within counseling psychology. Throughout this chapter, we rely not only on relevant empirical research and literature in the field, but also our combined 35 years of working with athletes, teams, coaches, and organizations at all competitive levels.

A Brief History of (and Current Perspectives in) Sport Psychology

Sport psychology has been defined as "the educational, scientific, and professional contributions of psychology to the promotion, maintenance, and enhancement of sport-related behaviors . . ." (p. 239, Rejeski & Brawley, 1988). Division 47 (Exercise and Sport Psychology) of the American Psychological Association (APA) has suggested that sport psychologists are interested in "helping athletes use psychological principles to achieve optimal mental health and to improve performance (performance enhancement) . . ." (APA, n.d.). Although these definitions highlight the centrality of "psychology" in the field, its roots do not lie solely within this discipline. The reality is that, historically, sport psychology has connections to the early work of psychologists who did field work on sport performances and to exercise/sport scientists who defined it as a subdiscipline within their then departments of physical education.

Historical Roots

Singer (1989) identified two psychologists—Norman Triplett and Coleman Griffith—whose work represented the origins of what is now modern-day sport psychology. In 1898, Triplett studied how the presence of others affected physical performances, such as bicycle racing, and set the stage for future work on social facilitation and inhibition. Coleman Griffith's work occurred during the 1920s and early 1930s at the University of Illinois. He is credited with establishing the first sport psychology laboratory in the United States (Joyce & Baker, 2008), and his career is a prophetic illustration of what we now refer to as the scientist–practitioner—he conducted laboratory and field research, wrote two influential books (*Psychology of Coaching*; Griffith, 1926; *Psychology and Athletics*; Griffith, 1928), and consulted with professional sport teams on psychological methods to improve their performances (Singer). Joyce and Baker, in their review of the history of sport psychology, affirmed the importance of Triplett and Griffith, but also noted the collaborative work psychologists Graves and Miles did with Stanford football coach, Glenn "Pop" Warner during the 1920s. They suggested that Graves and Miles' studies represented another example of how psychological research methods and principles were applied within sport settings with the intent purpose of improving performance.

Although these individuals are historical icons and represent the origins of the field, their direct legacies were limited because they lacked students to carry on their work. Thus, it was not until the 1960s that sport psychology really emerged, both in academia and the world of sport. In colleges and universities, sport psychology was becoming an accepted academic subdiscipline within then departments of physical education (Feltz, 1987), solidifying its connection to the exercise/sport sciences. Furthermore, Singer (1989) suggested that the book, *Problem Athletes and How to Handle Them* (Ogilvie & Tutko, 1966), put sport psychology back into the public's eye and renewed athletes' and coaches' interests in how psychological issues could influence physical performances. The fact that the two authors were psychologists represented a continuation of sport psychology's early connection to psychology.

Professionalization of Sport Psychology

Over the last four decades, sport psychology has undergone tremendous change and experienced many of the growing pains associated with the emergence and definition of a new professional field, including: development of professional organizations and journals, credentialing and service provision, and graduate training. For example, during this time, sport psychology organizations have been formed (e.g., North American Society for the Psychology of Sport and Physical Activity [NASPSPA] in 1967) and have splintered, such as when members of NASPSPA formed a new professional organization in 1985 (i.e., AASP) whose focus was more applied than experimental. The APA's Division 47 also was formed in the 1980s and provided another anchoring point to psychology. In addition to the formation of organizations that would help to define and represent the field's professional interests, journals were started to disseminate research findings and promote a discussion of professional issues. Currently, there are over 15 sport- and exercise-related journals, such as: *Journal of Sport & Exercise Psychology, The Sport Psychologist, Journal of Applied Sport Psychology, Journal of Clinical Sport Psychology, Medicine and Science in Sport and Exercise, Research Quarterly for Sport and Exercise, Journal of Sport Behavior, Sport, Exercise and Performance Psychology*, and *Psychology of Sport and Exercise*, to name a few. Many of these journals are indexed within traditional psychology databases (e.g., PsychInfo) and are published by organizations that represent a membership beyond just sport psychologists (e.g., American College of Sports Medicine [ACSM]; American Alliance for Health, Physical Education, Recreation and Dance [AAHPERD]), suggesting that sport psychology has become an increasingly recognized and accepted discipline within psychology and exercise/sport sciences.

SERVICE PROVISION

As sport psychology has developed from a primarily lab- or experimentally based discipline to a professional, applied field, it has had to contend with issues concerning who should provide services and how those professionals should be credentialed. Although the majority of leading sport psychologists from the 1960s through the early 1980s were trained in and graduated from departments of exercise/sport science and practiced as "educational" sport psychologists (Straub & Hinman, 1992), over the last two decades, psychologists have become increasingly involved in the provision of sport psychology services to athletes and other performers (Hays, 2002, 2006; Leffingwell, Wiechman, Smith, Smoll, & Christenson, 2001; Petrie & Diehl, 1995; Petrie et al., 1995). In their study of APA Division 17 counseling psychologists, Petrie et al. found that 38% and 68%, respectively, reported consulting with athletes and sport teams and counseling athletes in individual therapy. Furthermore, these professional interactions were not limited to traditional counseling/clinical areas (e.g., inter-/intrapersonal concerns, depression), but also focused on sport specific issues, such as performance enhancement, anxiety and stress related to performances, and team dynamics. Studies such as these (e.g., Petrie & Diehl, 1995) have shown that psychologists are being sought to provide not only counseling/therapeutic

services to athletes, but to consult with them (and with sport teams) on issues (e.g., teaching imagery) and in areas (e.g., team cohesion) that would best be described as performance enhancement and that previously had been considered the sole province of exercise/sport science–trained sport psychologists.

Psychologists increasing involvement in the provision of sport psychology services has been a double-edged sword for the field. On the one hand, there are many more licensed psychologists (and other licensed mental health professionals) than traditional sport psychologists, and these licensed professionals have an extensive understanding of human behavior and are experts in promoting change, growth, and improvement in performance. So, having psychologists available to provide counseling and consulting services increases the opportunities for athletes, coaches, and sport teams to receive assistance, such as developing preperformance routines, regulating emotions, communicating effectively, or coping with stress and anxiety. This more "etic" perspective suggests that general training in counseling or clinical psychology is sufficient to work competently with sport performers; interdisciplinary training would not be necessary. On the other hand, sport performers, from the youth to the elite level, represent a subgroup whose environment, experiences, and needs are unique and specialized. Thus, psychologists who lack interdisciplinary training may not have the knowledge, skills, or understanding to provide the highest level of service to sport performers. This "emic" perspective suggests that training as a psychologist is an important, but not sufficient, condition for providing competent and ethical services (Petrie et al., 1995). Psychologists who want to work in the field need also to have had training in the exercise/sport sciences (e.g., motor learning, exercise physiology), and have received supervision for their applied work (Danish, Petitpas, & Hale, 1993). Despite the promotion of interdisciplinary training by professional organizations (e.g., AASP), few counseling or clinical psychologists have pursued this option (Petrie & Diehl, 1995; Petrie et al., 1995), whether that involves formal training (i.e., coursework) or supervision of applied sport psychology work.

CREDENTIALING

This state of the field—psychologists interested in and actually working with sport performers but also lacking what some view as necessary interdisciplinary training—has served as a catalyst for organizations to address the issue of professional credentials.

Although limited options are available for established psychologists who want to demonstrate their competency in sport psychology, there is agreement among the major sport psychology organizations (e.g., AASP, APA Division 47) that interdisciplinary training in psychology (e.g., counseling) and exercise/sport sciences is necessary for competent practice. Currently, AASP offers the only process in which professionals, through a review of their coursework and practical experiences (a portfolio-based approach), can achieve a credential in the field (designation of Certified Consultant, AASP). Although AASP's credentialing criteria are ideal for current students because they offer a model for how to structure graduate training so as to achieve certification, its portfolio-based approach represents a substantial barrier to established, practicing psychologists who do not have the time, energy, nor inclination to return to school to take courses in the exercise/sport sciences. Thus, the total number of active AASP certified sport psychology professionals remains small (only 275 as of 2011; personal communication, Sarah Castillo, April 17, 2011), limiting its benefit to the profession and public. Furthermore, because the scope of practice defined in the AASP certification criteria is somewhat limited (e.g., teaching goal setting skills, enhancing team cohesion, etc., and not counseling athletes regarding personal issues, psychometric assessment of athletes, etc.), it is not clear what benefit this certification provides to those who are licensed mental health providers (e.g., psychologists).

The United States Olympic Committee (USOC) offers another type of "credential" through membership on its Sport Psychology Registry. Professionals seeking membership on the Registry (and thus a recommended referral source for Olympic level athletes), though, must be a Certified Consultant, AASP, be a member of APA, and have their application reviewed and approved by the USOC Sport Sciences committee. Thus, this credential has similar limitations in not being practical for a larger pool of psychologists.

APA Division 47 also has been involved in the issue of credentialing, developing a proficiency statement for sport psychology in the profession of psychology that was recognized in 2003 (APA, n.d.). This designation provides psychologists with information on the knowledge and experiences that are deemed necessary to practice competently in this specialized area, but does not offer a formal or approved process for signifying one has achieved proficiency (or specialization) in the field. Although these three credentialing processes represent advances in identifying the scope, limits, and ethics of practicing as a sport psychologist; establishing a designation that defines minimum levels of training, education, and experience needed; and offering some protections for consumers by promoting these designations to the public, AASP and APA Division 47 have recognized the limitations of these credentials, particularly for established and currently practicing psychologists. Thus, the executive committees of these two professional organizations continue to work on developing other mechanisms (e.g., examination-based processes) for defining competency and protecting the public from professionals who are providing services, but who also may lack the necessary training.

GRADUATE TRAINING

The existing credentialing processes, and the fact that all the major professional organizations have formally recognized sport psychology's interdisciplinary basis, have influenced graduate training in the United States as well as in other countries. In the 1980s, doctoral graduates in sport psychology came almost solely from departments of exercise/sport science (e.g., kinesiology; Waite & Pettit, 1993). In the 1990s, though, increasing numbers of doctoral students in sport psychology were graduating from departments of psychology, in particular from counseling and clinical psychology programs (Andersen, Williams, Aldridge, & Taylor, 1997; Williams & Scherzer, 2003), and the majority of these graduates were completing two or more semesters of practica devoted solely to working with athletes and sport teams and taking the necessary exercise/sport science courses to meet the criteria for AASP certification (Williams & Scherzer). Furthermore, over 60% of the directors of APA-accredited counseling psychology programs could identify at least one student in their programs who had sport psychology interests (Petrie & Watkins, 1994). This increase in the number of counseling psychology doctoral graduates who have specialized in sport psychology reflects counseling psychology program's openness to, support of, and interest in the field. Although almost no APA-accredited counseling psychology programs reported offering actual sport psychology courses, over 40% stated that they had sport psychology practica available to their doctoral students (Petrie & Watkins, 1994). Furthermore, these programs deemed it very acceptable for their doctoral students to want to specialize in sport psychology, propose a sport psychology research topic for their dissertation, and take exercise/sport sciences courses in addition to their general program requirements.

CURRENT JOB MARKET

These shifts in graduate training in applied sport psychology also have been influenced by financial factors and by the demands and realities of the current job market. Although the percentage of income from sport-related sources is greater for unlicensed, exercise/sport science trained sport psychology professionals in comparison to licensed sport psychologists (i.e., licensed psychologists who have specialized in sport psychology), the licensed sport psychologists' overall income is up to three times greater than their unlicensed counterparts (Meyers, Coleman, Whelan, & Mehlenbeck, 2001). Thus, psychologists, who are not limited to only working with athletes and sport teams from an educational perspective, have earning potentials that are substantially greater than their unlicensed counterparts. Regarding the broader job market, recent trends suggest that sport organizations—professional teams, the USOC, university athletic departments—are hiring sport psychologists who also are licensed mental health providers. For example, all the sport psychologists employed by the USOC are licensed psychologists (USOC, n.d.), and recent sport psychology jobs at universities across the United States (e.g., University of Oklahoma, University of Kansas, University of Arizona) have been filled by licensed psychologists who have specialized in sport psychology (e.g., Kansas Jayhawks, n.d.; Winerman, 2005).

Staffing an athletic department or sport organization with licensed sport psychologists makes sense for two major reasons. First, athletes, like nonathletes, experience myriad mental health concerns (e.g., depression, relationship concerns, eating disorders; Brewer & Petrie, 2002) that, on their own, can be highly distressing, but also can significantly undermine successful sport performances. In fact, licensed sport psychologists who have worked at major sport competitions suggest that athletes seek assistance primarily for psychological concerns and, secondarily, for performance enhancement issues (Meyers, 1997). Second, athletes initially may present with performance enhancement concerns, but the underlying cause of these decrements may be psychological distress or dysfunction and, even if not, the ability to differentially determine the etiology is essential for planning and implementing effective treatments. Sport psychologists who are not trained as mental health providers may not recognize the psychological problems that exist or,

if recognized, not be able to treat them (or if they tried to, which sometimes occurs, would be practicing outside of their bounds of competence, a clear ethical violation). For organizations that want a sport psychologist to oversee the health, well-being, and performance of their athletes, having a professional who has the training to provide not only educational performance enhancement services, but work with the wide range of psychological problems that may arise (e.g., depression, eating disorders, anxiety, interpersonal problems) makes practical and financial sense. Why would an organization *not* hire someone who has the training to work effectively in both the performance enhancement and mental health domains? In making this observation, we acknowledge that there are some very competent and highly skilled exercise/sport science trained sport psychology practitioners. We are fortunate to have them as colleagues. However, in the current professional environment, in which interdisciplinary training is the acknowledged standard and available to graduate students, we believe that students wanting to be applied sport psychologists would be best served by selecting an applied psychology program (i.e., counseling psychology) as their foundational academic discipline and then take courses in exercise/sport science and practica in sport psychology while pursuing their doctorates. In other words, the ideal *academic training environment*, which we discuss in more detail later in the chapter, would be interdisciplinary with counseling psychology as its foundation.

The Sport Psychology–Counseling Psychology Interface

A primary reason that counseling psychology, as opposed to other applied psychology programs or other exercise/sport science–based programs, represents the ideal environment for applied sport psychology is because the values that long have been a part of counseling psychology's history and define its "worldview" are an excellent match with the realities and demands of the sport environment and the work sport psychologists generally do with athletes, teams, and organizations. Howard (1992), in his conceptual and philosophical evaluation of counseling psychology's history, identified 14 such values. Eight of these values seem to be particularly relevant to sport psychology:

• *Solid, positive interpersonal relationships are important.* Between teammates, a coach and an athlete, and/or players and their parents, the quality of the relationship often determines whether a performance is successful, new skills or strategies are learned, or athletes even stay involved in sports. Applied sport psychologists often work to improve communication between coach and athlete, increase the social and task cohesion of a team, or educate parents on how to create a positive, supportive sport environment for their children, so that they can have fun and stay involved in athletics. Being able to form positive, solid, working relationships is the hallmark of a successful applied sport psychologist (Orlick & Partington, 1987).

• *Viewing human problems through a developmental/growth lens.* Because athletes often are involved in sports for many years, some over the course of their lifetimes, it is important to understand the general developmental changes that occur as children become adolescents and then move into adulthood. In addition, the longer athletes are involved in sports, the more likely they will be to experience sport-specific developmental changes and challenges. For example, the focus of training and challenges will be very different for a 5-year-old youth soccer player than for a collegiate basketball player. At age 5, the focus should be on having fun, learning new skills, and making new friends. But, years later, as athletes continues to play and their skills have solidified, they will become more focused on and challenged by learning how to train in practice. Still later in their development, their attention is likely to shift to learning how to compete and win. Thus, sport psychologists, by understanding the general and sports-specific changes that occur as athletes participate in sports over time, are able to develop and implement interventions that take into account the developmental needs, issues, and challenges that are specific to different ages and experience levels.

• *Understanding the influences of the environment on human functioning and problems.* Athletes are embedded in multiple environments that strongly influence their behaviors, such as those created by their sport organization (e.g., high school team), their coaches, their teammates, their parents, and even their opponents during competition. Applied sport psychologists try to understand such contextual factors, and help athletes, coaches, and teams work effectively with them, even modifying the environments (e.g., changing location of training, having parents not yell at their children during competitions) if such changes would lead to improved performances.

• *The multiple and diverse ways in which counseling psychologists can intervene.* In working with athletes and sport teams, applied sport psychologists have to understand situations from multiple perspectives (e.g., athlete, coach, parent) and be able to intervene on multiple levels. Sometimes, the intervention may be at the group level (e.g., improving team communication) or at the level of the group leader (e.g., helping the coach understand the personality of a star player). At other times, the sport psychologist may work at the individual level and, even there, the intervention will vary depending on whether the focus is more on general counseling issues or solely on performance enhancement. Being able to take an eclectic, multifaceted approach is a key for successfully intervening.

• *Counseling psychologists work to increase individual's ability to solve problems, make decisions, and cope more effectively with stress and life demands.* Athletes generally view themselves as healthy individuals who are in control and able to successfully handle the demands in their lives. They recognize that training can be stressful and demanding, but they do not shrink from it and, when they encounter obstacles, work in a direct manner to solve the problem that is interfering with their progress. Applied sport psychologists often take a very direct, solution-focused approach when working with athletes. They attempt to build on the athletes' existing strengths, set goals for what they want to achieve, teach new psychological skills/strategies, and/or develop new and effective ways to cope so the athletes can perform at their best. Sport competition is the stressor that athletes learn how to handle.

• *Prevention is valued over remediation.* In sports, a major focus of athletes, coaches, and teams is predicting the problems that might arise in training and upcoming competitions, and then preparing for those in advance to either minimize their effect or eliminate their occurrence completely. This approach is referred to as developing a training regimen and preparing a "game plan" for an upcoming competition. Applied sport psychologists work from this perspective when they teach athletes to use imagery to "practice" events that might occur in future competitions (but are difficult to simulate in live practices) or have athletes plan for and think through the challenges that will exist when they go to their first national/international competition (e.g., world championship). Prepared, conditioned, trained athletes increase their chances of having successful performances.

- *A holistic approach that acknowledges the entire person and recognizes the connection between mind, body, and environment.* Athletes, because of what they do, can view themselves primarily from a physical perspective and believe that they are valued, such as by their coaches, only for what their bodies can do or for the results of their most recent physical performance. Sport psychologists, though, offer athletes a broader perspective on who they are (multiple identities, such as student, worker, son/daughter) and often help them appreciate or plan for other successes in their lives (e.g., graduating from college), while still helping them achieve their athletic goals. Through interventions, such as positive thinking, emotion regulation, and relaxation, sport psychologists help athletes understand the connections between their emotions and thoughts and how these interact to affect their bodies and their physical performances.

- *An appreciation of and respect for diversity.* Sports represent a venue through which individuals from all different areas/spectrums of life (e.g., race/ethnicity) come together to set, work toward, and, in many instances, achieve, a common goal. For some athletes, sport is the one place where they interact with individuals who are different from themselves in some meaningful way (e.g., race/ethnicity, socioeconomic status). In fact, in many high-profile sports, such as basketball and football, racial/ethnic minority players are represented at rates higher than exist in the general population (Coakley, 2009). Each sport, in its own right, also has a history and culture that is unique and is passed down from coach to player and so on. In addition, each team, within a sport, has its own separate culture that is determined by the demands of that specific sport, the training that this set of coaches require, the traditions of this team, and the current set of athletes (and their experiences and values) that comprise the team at this point in time. Applied sport psychologists who work successfully with athletes and sport teams have an understanding not only of broad issues of diversity, such as gender and race/ethnicity, that exist and likely are to be encountered in sports, but also of the diversity that is represented at the level of the sport (e.g., badminton vs. rugby) and of a particular team.

We are not the only counseling psychologists who have noted the interface between counseling and sport psychology and have argued that counseling psychology's philosophy was aligned with the values of sport and the work sport psychologists traditionally do in athletics (Danish et al., 1993; Howard, 1993; Petitpas, Giges, & Danish, 1999). For example, Petitpas et al. (1999) suggested that counseling psychology's focus on psychoeducation and development, goal attainment, and prevention were some of what distinguished it from clinical psychology and made it an ideal approach for working with athletes and sport teams who were healthy and wanted to improve on their existing strengths. Furthermore, they argued that it was time for a paradigm shift in applied sport psychology training, one that embraced not only the teaching of cognitive-behaviorally based skills but one that focused on the development, growth, and self-awareness of the sport psychology consultant. From this perspective, sport psychology would become more like counseling psychology, a profession that views a positive working relationship as the primary agent of change and improvement (Andersen, 2000, 2005). In a subsequent section, we elaborate on this idea of counseling psychology (and its values) being the ideal foundational academic environment by offering an ideal model for training applied sport psychologists.

Intervening with Performance Issues

The optimization of athletic performance is an area of great interest to many applied sport psychologists, and issues related to intervention/performance enhancement have received considerable attention. Thorough discussions of all relevant performance issues have been provided elsewhere (e.g., Hardy, Jones, & Gould, 1996; Weinberg & Gould, 2007), and it is not our intention to do the same here. Rather, in this section, we present several topics of current interest that sample the array of performance issues addressed by most applied sport psychologists, are consistent with our view of the scope of sport psychology practice, and reflect the interface between counseling psychology and sport psychology related to the core values described earlier.

Mental Toughness

Although mental toughness has long been considered one of the most important characteristics for athletes to possess, only recently have sport psychologists defined it. Through a series of interviews and focus group work with elite-level athletes, Jones, Hanton, and Connaughton (2002) defined mental toughness as a natural or learned psychological edge that allows athletes to cope better than their opponents with the demands of their sport (e.g., training, competition, lifestyle); and more specifically, be better and more consistent than their opponents in remaining determined, focused, confident, and in control under pressure. In addition, they identified the attributes of the mentally tough performer: self-belief, desire/motivation, handling competition-related pressure (external) and anxiety (internal), performance-related focus, lifestyle-related focus, and dealing with physical and emotional pain/hardship.

Although criticisms have surfaced regarding the clarity of Jones et al.'s (2002) definition (Crust, 2007; Middleton, Marsh, Martin, Richards, & Perry, 2004), other researchers have provided support for this conceptualization (e.g., Bull, Shambrook, James, & Brooks, 2005; Connaughton, Wadey, Hanton, & Jones, 2008; Harmison & Roth, 2006). In addition, Mischel and Shoda's (1995) social-cognitive model of personality functioning, also referred to as the *cognitive-affective processing system* (CAPS), can be applied to add precision to its definition. The CAPS model views personality as a dynamic network of five types of processing and behavior-generation units: encodings (e.g., personal constructs for the self, people, events, and situations), expectancies and beliefs (e.g., beliefs about the self, the world, and "how things are"), affects (e.g., cognitive and physiological emotional responses), goals and values (e.g., short- and long-term desired and undesired outcomes), and self-regulation skills (e.g., cognitive, affective, and behavioral capabilities to respond and influence). Not only do these CAPS units respond to and activate or inhibit one another, the units also collectively interact with situational factors to produce the expression of one's personality, in what is referred to as *behavioral signatures*.

From this model, mental toughness can be construed as a personality construct characterized by the distinctive organization of the athletes' cognitions and affects, the interrelations among the athletes' cognitions and affects, and the relationship between athletes' cognitions/affects and the psychological features of the competitive situation (Harmison, Hehn, Sims, & Poupeney, 2007; Smith 2006). For example, if a woman's basketball player perceives herself as capable of being one of the very best at her position (encodings), then she likely has strong beliefs in her ability to respond successfully to challenging, competitive situation (expectancies and beliefs). This self-belief may be connected to the importance she places on her grit and determination in such situations, as well as to the enjoyment that mastering such challenges brings to her (goals and values). Also, if this truly is her self-belief, she will feel confident in her ability to be successful even during a critical game when she is not playing well (affects), which may be the result of her ability to remain optimistic and hopeful despite some failure and set-backs (self-regulation skills).

Interventions with Individual Athletes

A major thrust of applied sport psychologists' work with individual athletes is to teach them psychological skills (referred to as *mental skills* in the sport psychology literature) in an effort to improve their mental toughness and enhance their sport performances (Petrie et al., 1995). Successful, mentally tough athletes possess a certain set of cognitive and behavioral skills (e.g., thought control strategies, arousal management techniques, attentional control) that, in the end, facilitate performance (Krane & Williams, 2006; Vealey, 2007). Since a complete review of all of the mental training strategies and techniques utilized by successful athletes is beyond the scope of this chapter, we introduce the four primary mental skills from the applied sport psychology canon—goal setting, imagery, physical relaxation, and self-talk.

BASIC MENTAL SKILLS

Goal setting is a popular technique used by coaches and athletes at all competitive levels to help them achieve performance success. Goal setting is thought to work because goals provide motivation (e.g., mobilize effort and enhance persistence) and regulate behavior (i.e., planning and adapting thoughts, emotions, and actions to achieve goals) (Weinberg, Harmison, Rosenkranz, & Hookom, 2005). Effective goal setting strategies include setting specific goals, challenging yet realistic goals, and a combination of short-term and long-term goals; developing goal achievement strategies; utilizing outcome, performance, and process types of goals; and providing support for and feedback on athletes' goal achievement efforts. A number of systematic goal setting approaches can be found in the literature to guide sport psychology professionals as well (e.g., Burton, Naylor, & Holliday, 2001; Weinberg et al., 2005).

Imagery can be defined as a polysensory experience that occurs in the absence of external stimuli that includes recreating external events or past experiences or creating new internal pictures in one's mind from memory (Vealey & Greenleaf, 2006).

Athletes use imagery for myriad motivational (e.g., achieving specific goals, mastering challenging situations, managing emotions) and cognitive (e.g., learning specific sport skills, rehearsing competition strategies) purposes in hopes of improving performance (Hall, Mack, Paivio, & Hausenblas, 1998). Imagery appears to work because it enhances the learning and performance of sport skills and helps athletes regulate competition-related thoughts and emotions (e.g., confidence, motivation, anxiety) related to successful performance (Vealey & Greenleaf, 2006). Traditional explanations for how imagery improves the learning and performance of sport skills have focused on the psychoneuromuscular theory (i.e., imagery enhances performance by increasing muscle memory), symbolic learning theory (i.e., imagery enhances performance by increasing familiarity and automaticity of movements), and bioinformational theory (i.e., imagery enhances performance by providing a template for overt responding), and recent advances have included a cognitive neuroscience approach using functional equivalence theory to better integrate the strengths and limitations of these theoretical explanations (Murphy, Nordin, & Cumming, 2008). Useful guidelines can be found in the literature for imagery work with athletes as well. For example, the PETTLEP model (Holmes & Collins, 2001) emphasizes the use of various elements (e.g., physical, timing, emotion) in imagery scripts to activate selected brain structures, and a model of imagery use (Martin, Moritz, & Hall, 1999) suggests that different types of imagery (e.g., motivational specific, cognitive general) should be used by athletes to obtain specific results (e.g., increased motivation to achieve a goal, rehearse competition strategies).

Applied sport psychologists (e.g., Krane & Williams, 2006) typically advocate the use of physical relaxation techniques by athletes to regulate arousal levels, in particular, competitive state anxiety, which is defined as the subjective, consciously perceived feelings of worry and physical nervousness related to competition (Weinberg & Gould, 2007). Learning to relax helps athletes self-regulate their physiological (e.g., muscle tension, increased heart rate), psychological (e.g., worry, doubt), and behavioral (e.g., fatigue, loss of coordination) anxiety-related responses to various competitive stressors. Specific approaches to relaxation include muscle-to-mind techniques, such as deep breathing and progressive muscle relaxation, and mind-to-muscle techniques, such as meditation and imagery (Williams & Harris, 2006). It is recommended that

athletes master both types of techniques to develop the ability to deal with multiple types of anxiety simultaneously (e.g., excessive muscle tension, overwhelming self-doubt) (Burton, 1990).

Finally, self-talk consists of interpretive and content-specific verbalizations or statements addressed to the self, is multidimensional and dynamic in nature, and serves both instructional and motivational functions (similar to those of imagery) (Hardy, 2006; Hardy, Gammage, & Hall, 2001). Despite the common use of self-talk by athletes and the understanding that cognitive processes are critical determinants of sport performance, very little theory-based research exists to adequately account for the reasons why self-talk may improve performance. Some researchers have suggested that self-talk facilitates performance by improving an athlete's attentional focus, whereas others have indicated that perhaps self-talk serves to improve information processing to enhance performance (e.g., Landin, 1994; Ziegler, 1987). The available research does suggest that athletes would be wise to rely on positive, rational, and task-focused self-talk and learn how to modify maladaptive, irrational, and task-irrelevant self-talk (Hardy et al., 1996).

EFFICACY OF MENTAL SKILLS TRAINING INTERVENTIONS

Qualitative literature reviews (e.g., Meyers, Whelan, & Murphy, 1996; Vealey, 2007) have provided evidence for the efficacy of goal setting, imagery, physical relaxation, and self-talk to enhance the psychological state of athletes and improve their performance. In addition, three quantitative reviews (Greenspan & Feltz, 1989; Martin, Vause, & Schwartzman, 2005; Meyers et al., 1996) also support the effectiveness of applied sport psychology interventions. Specifically, a meta-analysis of 56 published intervention studies yielded an average effect size of .62 (standard deviation [SD] = .85) for cognitive-behavioral interventions compared to the control group (Whelan, Meyers, & Berman, as cited in Meyers et al., 1996). In addition, Greenspan and Feltz (1989) reviewed intervention research that only utilized athlete-participants in noncontrived competitive situations and found positive results on performance for 20 out of 23 (87%) interventions. Eliminating studies that assessed performance in mock competitions, relied on athlete self-reports of their performance as the dependent variable, or failed to incorporate an acceptable between-groups research or appropriate single-subject design, Martin et al. (2005) found a positive effect on performance for 14 out of 15 (93%) interventions, with nine showing a substantial impact (i.e., mean improvement ranged from 3%–80% over baseline or control). Criticisms (e.g., Gardner & Moore, 2006; Morgan, 1997) of this research include a very limited number of experimental studies, lack of external validity (e.g., non–sport research setting), inadequate experimental designs (e.g., lack of a control group), behavioral artifacts (e.g., halo effect), and a large number of equivocal findings, leading some sport psychology professionals to suggest that practitioners should proceed with caution in the absence of confirming, supportive research.

Interventions with Teams

Applied sport psychologists also strive to enhance mental toughness in teams by providing performance enhancement services to groups of athletes. The nature of these services range from enhancing group mental skills (e.g., team goal setting) to addressing various group dynamics (e.g., cohesion, communication). Fortunately, a number of useful texts are available for practitioners with interests in working with teams to increase a more collective mental toughness (e.g., Carron, Hausenblas, & Eys, 2005; Dosil, 2006). A particularly important group dynamic, group cohesion, often is placed at the center of the conceptual framework in the understanding of the psychology of sport teams (Carron et al., 2005).

GROUP COHESION

Group cohesion in sports is defined as the tendency for a team to stick together and remain unified in the pursuit of the team's task-related goals and/or for the satisfaction of team members' affective needs (Carron, Brawley, & Widmeyer, 1998). It is a dynamic process that is multidimensional in nature, consisting of both task (i.e., teamwork) and social (i.e., team spirit) aspects, and based on individual team member's attraction to the team as well as to their perceptions of the team overall (Carron, Widmeyer, & Brawley, 1985). Historically, qualitative literature reviews of the relationship between group cohesion and team performance have been inconclusive and sometimes contradictory (e.g., Gill, 1986). More recent meta-analyses (Carron, Colman, Wheeler, & Stevens, 2002; Mullen & Cooper, 1994), however, have revealed the existence of a positive linear relationship between cohesion and performance. When the cohesion–performance relationship is examined exclusively within a sport setting, a significant, moderate to large, and positive

relationship between cohesion and team success is found; both task and social cohesion is significantly correlated to team performance; team success and cohesion are both predictive of one another; and cohesion is related to better performance in both team (e.g., basketball) and individual (e.g., bowling) sports (Carron et al., 2002).

TEAM BUILDING

Many applied sport psychologists engage teams in activities designed to enhance group cohesion. These activities commonly are referred to as *team building*, which is defined as a method of helping a team increase its effectiveness, meet the needs of team members, or improve training or competition environmental conditions (Brawley & Paskevich, 1997). When delivering team building interventions, applied sport psychologists generally take either a direct or indirect services approach. A direct services approach (e.g., Yukelson, 1997) involves a coach or sport psychology professional implementing the team building intervention (e.g., team goal setting) directly with the team. By contrast a typical indirect services approach (e.g., Carron, Spink, & Prapavessis, 1997) consists of the sport psychology professional providing a coaching staff with insights and strategies to enhance team productivity and satisfy team members' needs and then equipping them with the skills, strategies, and/or knowledge to carry out the team building interventions themselves.

Despite the intuitive appeal and popular use of team building interventions, very little research exists to guide practitioners in their implementation. A review of the available research, though, sheds some positive light on the efficacy of team building interventions. Specifically, athlete self-reports related to the effectiveness of multicomponent, season-long team building programs suggest that these interventions may lead to improved team performance, team unity and harmony, role definition, accountability, team communication, focus on team goals, and motivation (Bloom & Stevens, 2002; Voight & Callaghan, 2001). Also, brief team building interventions in which personal disclosure/mutual sharing among team members is emphasized can result in self-reported enhanced understanding of others and self, increased cohesion (e.g., closeness, playing for each other), and more confidence (e.g., trust in self and teammates and feelings of invincibility) (Dunn & Holt, 2004; Holt & Dunn, 2006). However, other findings suggest that less-than-clear conclusions can be drawn regarding the efficacy of team building interventions. Season-long team building interventions have revealed initial improvements in task and/or social cohesion that were not maintained over the entire course of the teams' competitive season (Cogan & Petrie, 1995; Stevens & Bloom, 2003), maintenance but not improvement in both task and social cohesion over the course of an entire competitive season (Senécal, Loughead, & Bloom, 2008), and no effect on cohesion whatsoever (Bloom & Stevens, 2002; Prapavessis, Carron, & Spink, 1996).

Interventions with Coaches

A final area in which applied sport psychologists address the development of mental toughness is related to their consultation work with coaches at all levels of sport, and intervention programs with youth sport coaches have been subject to the most extensive empirical investigation. Research suggests that the attributes of mental toughness described earlier begin forming with athletes' initial involvement in sport at a very young age, and their coaches' leadership and behaviors throughout their youth sport's experience play a crucial role in its ultimate development (Connaughton et al., 2008). Thus, intervention programs with young athletes, such as *coach effectiveness training* (CET; Smith, Smoll, & Curtis, 1979), that have a growth/developmental focus and place a high value on the prevention of undesirable coaching behaviors would appear to be effective approaches to be used by applied sport psychologists to promote the development of mental toughness in athletes.

COACH EFFECTIVENESS TRAINING

Coach effectiveness training is based on a mediational model of the psychosocial impact of coaching behaviors on athletes (Smoll & Smith, 1984) that suggests coaching behaviors influence athletes' perceptions and recall of their sport experiences, which in turn impacts the athletes' evaluation of and attitudes toward their sport experiences. The crux of the model rests on athletes' perceptions of their coaches' behavior, and the key objectives of CET include helping coaches become more aware of their behaviors, increase their desire to generate positive consequences for their athletes, and enhance their ability to perform desirable coaching behaviors more effectively (Smith et al., 1979). Coach effectiveness training teaches coaches to reward their players for good plays and not take their efforts for granted; encourage players immediately following their mistakes, provide corrective instruction, and avoid punishment; prevent misbehaving by establishing clear expectations, rewarding wanted behaviors, and avoiding nagging or threatening actions to keep control; and provide spontaneous instruction and encouragement to get positive things to happen with their players. In addition, coaches are encouraged to adopt a philosophy of winning that emphasizes "doing your best" and "having fun" versus a "winning at all costs."

Coach effectiveness training has been found to positively change youth sport coaching behaviors, influence young athletes' perceptions of their coaches, increase young athletes' positive perceptions of themselves, and enhance the motivational climate of youth sport participants. More specifically, CET-trained coaches engage in more observable reward/reinforcement behaviors than do non–CET-trained coaches (Smith et al., 1979), an effect that has been found to be moderate to large (Conroy & Coatsworth, 2004). In addition, youth sport athletes perceive CET-trained coaches as displaying more desirable coaching behaviors (e.g., reinforcement, encouragement, instruction) and less undesirable coaching behaviors (e.g., nonreinforcement, punishment; Smith et al., 1979; Smith, Smoll, & Barnett, 1995; Smoll, Smith, Barnett, & Everett, 1993). Similarly, youth who played for CET-trained coaches have demonstrated increased perceptions of self-esteem, more enjoyment, and greater positive relationships with teammates (Coatsworth & Conroy, 2006; Smith et al., 1979, 1995; Smoll et al., 1993). Finally, with regard to motivational climate, young athletes have reported experiencing lower levels of performance anxiety (Smith et al., 1995) and a rate of attrition from sport that was five times lower (Barnett, Smoll, & Smith, 1992) as a result of playing for CET-trained coaches.

Characteristics of Successful Applied Sport Psychologists

The previous discussion of mental toughness and mental skills focused on the nature of the intervention, but ignored the potential influence of athlete and applied sport psychologist characteristics. We agree, though, with Smith's (1989) assertion that the evaluation of a change program goes beyond a simple determination of whether a specific intervention is effective or not and further believe that the nature of the relationship between the athlete and applied sport psychologist is a critical component in the effectiveness of any intervention. Fortunately, anecdotal accounts (e.g., Dorfman, 1990; Halliwell, 1990), survey evidence (e.g., Gould, Murphy, Tammen, & May, 1991; Orlick & Partington, 1987), and empirical studies exist to provide an idea of what personal and professional characteristics are important in the effective provision of sport psychology services.

In sum, the literature suggests that successful applied sport psychologists not only possess excellent technical knowledge and skills related to the psychology of sport, but they also have highly developed interpersonal skills with the ability to establish good working relationships with athletes and coaches. They are perceived as likeable, trustworthy, positive, caring, and warm by athletes and coaches, and are people-oriented helpers with a clear understanding of themselves, a genuine willingness to learn from athletes and coaches, and an ability to fit within a team environment. This evidence has led some sport psychology professionals (e.g., Tod & Andersen, 2005) to conclude that the relationship between the applied sport psychologist and the athlete/coach is the actual intervention and the sport psychologist is the primary consulting tool whose main responsibility is to form a collaborative relationship and strong working alliance. In other words, it is through the relationship that change occurs.

Counseling/Clinical Issues in Sport Performance

The optimization of sport performances does not occur solely by teaching athletes mental skills/strategies; it also happens through the prevention and remediation of personal and clinical issues. The reality is that athletes (and coaches for that matter) experience inter- and intrapersonal concerns, and these personal and clinical issues, which can range from problems in romantic relationships to mood disorders (Petrie et al., 1995), can significantly interfere with sport performances. Likewise, how well athletes or coaches perform in their sport can exacerbate underlying mental health problems and affect core issues of self-worth, self-identity, interpersonal relationships, and family dynamics (Barber & Krane, 2005). Thus, being able to assist athletes in resolving personal and clinical issues can be a primary and necessary focus for applied sport psychologists.

It is beyond the scope of this chapter to review all possible clinical issues/concerns that could affect athletes' performances, and there are recent reviews concerning the presence of psychopathology among athletes and within sport and exercise settings that interested professionals can peruse (see Brewer & Petrie, 2002). Thus, in this section, we focus on three specific issues/concerns—eating disorders, reactions to and coping with athletic injury, and transitions from sport (i.e., ending a career)—that may be common among athletes, may be complicated by aspects of the sport environment or the sport experience, and/or have been the focus of specific interventions within the sport environment. Consistent with counseling psychology's core values, interventions associated with these concerns have focused not only on the amelioration of existing symptoms but also on preventing their occurrence.

Eating Disorders

Although athletes generally are more body satisfied than nonathletes (Hausenblas & Symons Downs, 2001), which is a protective factor when considering the development of eating disorders (Stice, 2002), the reality is that athletes experience higher levels of disordered eating in comparison to their nonathletic counterparts (Hausenblas & Carron, 1999; Smolak, Murnen, & Ruble, 2000). For example, in samples of male and female collegiate athletes, respectively, Petrie and his colleagues (Petrie, Greenleaf, Reel, & Carter, 2008; Greenleaf, Petrie, Carter, & Reel, 2009) found that 0.0% and 2.0% could be categorized as having a clinical eating disorder, whereas another 19.2% and 25.5% engaged in behaviors that were symptomatic (subclinical). Furthermore, in a study of elite athletes, Sundgot-Borgen and Torstveit (2004) reported that the male and female athletes were three times more likely to have a subclinical or clinical eating disorder than were a matched group of nonathletes. The female athletes, as is found in the general population, had higher prevalence rates than the male athletes, regardless of how severe the disordered eating symptoms. Often occurring in tandem with disordered eating for female athletes are high levels of amenorrhea (Sanborn, Horea, Siemers, & Dieringer, 2000) and less frequently, osteoporosis (or osteopenia). Together, this cluster of events is known as the *female athlete triad*. In addition to the general physical and psychological symptoms associated with disordered eating, athletes who have the triad may experience increased bone fractures, increased skeletal fragility, and permanent bone loss (Sanborn et al., 2000).

Like nonathletes, athletes are exposed to the general sociocultural pressures concerning attractiveness and media images about the ideal male or female body, yet they also experience weight- and body-related pressures unique to the sport environment that may increase their risk of developing disordered eating attitudes and behaviors (Petrie, Greenleaf,

Reel, & Carter, 2009). First, some athletes experience pressures from judges to have a certain "look" (e.g., thin) and thus may believe that to succeed in their sport, they must diet or exercise more to achieve this "required" body type/style. Second, the uniforms of certain sports, such as swimming/diving, triathlons, volleyball, wrestling, and gymnastics, are form-fitting and revealing and may contribute to athletes feeling self-conscious and uncomfortable with their bodies. Thus, athletes may be motivated to reduce excess body fat and, for males, gain lean muscle mass, often through extreme measures (e.g., excessive exercise, vomiting, steroids), to look better in their uniforms. Third, characteristics of disordered eating (in particular, anorexia nervosa), when displayed in the sport environment, may be viewed as normal and even reinforced by coaches. Are athletes who pursue excellence in sport no matter what the cost, comply with all coaches' requests, train/compete despite pain or discomfort, and exercise/train excessively to improve simply demonstrating their devotion to sport and desire to improve, or are these the traits of a person with an eating disorder (Thompson & Sherman, 1999)? Fourth, health status often is secondary to weight loss and performance because many coaches mistakenly believe that being lighter is associated with improved performance (Griffin & Harris, 1996). Coaches may send direct or subtle messages to their athletes that they should diet, increase exercise loads, and/or engage in other pathogenic weight control techniques (e.g., vomit, take steroids) to become leaner, gain strength/muscle mass, and achieve a performance body ideal. These messages communicate that the highest value is placed on sport performance, no matter what the personal, physical, and/or psychological costs may be to the athlete.

Although providing individual counseling to athletes with eating disorders will follow many of the same treatment principles used with nonathletes (e.g., Stein et al., 2001), several issues are unique to the sport environment that must be considered as well. First, depending on the severity of the eating disorder, the issue of continuing to practice and/or compete must be addressed. Often, athletes' participation in their sport is the primary thing of value in their lives, so the decision to prohibit involvement must be made thoughtfully and in consultation with the treatment team (e.g., psychologist, physician, nutritionist). If athletes can continue to train/compete and it not be detrimental to their physical health, then allowing them to do so may be an advantage in treatment. If training compromises health, though, then limitations need to be considered. Second, athletes are part of integrated systems in which multiple individuals—coaches, athletic trainers, general managers, etc.—may be privy to personal and medical information and may be in the position to refer them for treatment. Thus, confidentiality, including its limits and who should be made aware of the athletes' treatment, needs to be discussed in advance. In such discussions, the issues of informed consent and best interest of the client (i.e., athlete) must be kept at the forefront. Third, depending on the athletes' competitive level, their participation may be very public. In fact, at the college, elite, and professional levels (and nowadays, even at the high school level), athletes and their performances come under daily scrutiny and coverage by the media. Thus, if athletes are restricted from practice/competition because participation would be health-compromising, then it may become necessary to discuss how this public absence from the team will be explained to the media (and possibly to teammates). For more information on working with these and other issues that may arise when counseling athletes with eating disorders, see Petrie and Sherman (2000) and Thompson and Sherman (2010).

In the last decade, research on eating disorder prevention (e.g., Stice, Presnell, Gau, & Shaw, 2007) suggests that body-dissatisfied women's risk can be reduced through a variety of interventions, including cognitive dissonance-based approaches. Studies such as that by Stice et al. have shown that women who participate in 1-hour weekly meetings during which they critique the societal thin ideal, both verbally and behaviorally, report decreases in internalization of societal beauty ideals, body dissatisfaction, dieting, and negative affect, to name a few, that can last for years. Recently, such programs have been undertaken with athletes, showing initial promise as effective and efficient ways to reduce eating disorder risk among this group of women. For example, Smith and Petrie (2008) tested a modification of the Stice et al. dissonance program with female collegiate athletes and found that the women showed decreases in sadness/depression and internalization of the physically fit and in-shape body type and increases in their levels of body satisfaction over the course of the 3-week intervention. Prevention programs such as the one used by Smith and Petrie represent an important avenue of continued study with athletes, given their elevated risk for disordered eating. In addition, such programming should be tested with male athletes, although such interventions would need to be modified to address the concerns most relevant to men, including muscle dysmorphia, pressures to gain weight and muscle, and ingestion of muscle building products (e.g., steroids).

Athletic Injury

Injury is an unfortunate, but very real, part of the sport environment. Every year, tens of millions of athletes, from recreational to competitive levels, suffer sport injuries (American Sports Data, 2003). Injury rates among male and female athletes tend to be relatively equal (Centers for Disease Control [CDC], 2006; Hootman, Dick, & Agel, 2007), although injuries occur more frequently in competitions than practices, and in contact sports, such as football, wrestling, and ice hockey (men's and women's), and noncontact sports, such as soccer, volleyball, basketball, and gymnastics, than in other sports (Hootman et al., 2007). Thus, at some point in time, applied sport psychologists are likely to have an athlete under their care who has suffered injury and, depending on its severity, may require surgery and extensive rehabilitation.

Injury often is viewed solely as a physical/physiological event, yet psychological factors, such as life stress, social support, coping skills, and sport anxiety, do in fact contribute to athletes' risk of becoming injured and can influence how athletes' respond once injured (Petrie & Utley-Hamson, in press). Furthermore, injury rehabilitation is not solely a physical process. Athletes must recover from not only the physical trauma they have experienced, but also cope with the extreme negative emotions (e.g., anger, confusion, anxiety, depression) that may occur in association with their injury (Albinson & Petrie, 2003). Although initial injury response models took a simple "stage" approach, subsequent formulations have conceptualized it as an individualized, interactional process in which personal, social, and environmental factors influence how athletes respond emotionally, cognitively, and behaviorally to their injuries and engage in the recovery process. The etiology of and responses to injury is a complex, interactive, multifactorial process in which both physical and psychological factors play an important role (see Petrie & Utley-Hamson, in press, for a review of the psychological etiology and responses to injury).

There are two primary routes through which applied sport psychologists can intervene in the area of athletic injury (Petrie & Perna, 2004). First, because physical training and psychological factors do increase athletes' risk of injury (e.g., Petrie, 1993),

interventions can help athletes (1) adapt to and recover from the high intensity training regimens that are a necessary part of sport, and (2) reduce negative psychosocial factors that exist (e.g., life stress), increase positive psychosocial factors (e.g., social support), modify psychological appraisals of situations, and learn to reduce anxiety, worry, and stress responses that occur. Recent research has shown that cognitive-behaviorally based interventions that employ techniques such as relaxation, cognitive-restructuring, and imagery can reduce injury rates, days missed due to injury, and number of illnesses and health center visits (Johnson, Ekengren, & Andersen, 2005; Maddison & Prapavessis, 2005; Perna, Antoni, Baum, Gordon, & Schneiderman, 2003). Although these initial results suggest that athletes who are taught a variety of psychologically based skills can better manage their stress, alleviate their negative mood, and reduce their risk of injury and illness than those who have not, more research is needed in this area, specifically testing other interventions and examining their effectiveness over longer periods of time.

Second, some athletes will be injured during their seasons and may experience psychological distress in relation to their being out of sport (including a loss of confidence) and may behave in ways that are counterproductive to their rehabilitation and recovery. For example, an athlete who has experienced a season- or career-ending injury may become depressed and withdrawn, and then may not attend rehabilitation sessions, may not put forth sufficient effort when in session, and/or may not do assigned rehabilitation homework. The end result is that the athlete's recovery will be slower and longer than needed. In such instances, working cooperatively with the athlete's physical therapist and helping the athlete become reengaged in and motivated about the rehabilitation process will be an important step. In addition, some athletes may experience a loss of sport confidence due to not being able to physically train and/or a fear of reinjury. Thus, some medically cleared athletes may not immediately return to play because of psychological factors. Many of the same cognitive-behavioral skills that reduce injury rates, such as relaxation and imagery, can be used to help athletes' cope more effectively when injured (for a review, see Petrie & Utley-Jordan, in press). Such skills can be taught during individual counseling sessions; however, group counseling may be particularly effective because it provides the added dimension of peer social support, which may be missing among injured athletes who are not as centrally involved with their teams due to their injured status (see Petrie, 2007, for a review on working with injured athletes).

Transitions from Sport

Athletes transition out of sports at all ages and for any number of reasons. The common factor, though, is that at some point all athletes will leave their primary sport, being unable to compete at the level they once did. Even if athletes stay involved in another capacity (e.g., coaching), they still must adjust to life away from competition and their sport, and research suggests that upward of 20% of them experience psychological distress associated with this transition (Grove, Lavallee, Gordon, & Harvey, 1998). How athletes adjust to this "career" transition can be influenced by three factors: the reason the athlete is transitioning out of sport (i.e., what is the cause of the career termination?), the current developmental or life factors (e.g., age, relationship status, level of athletic identity) that are present for the athlete, and the internal (e.g., coping skills) and external (e.g., social support) resources that exist for the athlete (Lavallee & Andersen, 2000). Like athletic injury, applied sport psychologists are likely to work with athletes who are facing or are undergoing a transition from sport while under their care, so being aware of and able to work with these factors will be important when intervening.

Athletes leave sports for voluntary (e.g., no longer enjoy participating) and involuntary (e.g., cut from team) reasons. A voluntary or planned departure may produce less psychological distress and be easier to handle. Many transitions from sport, though, are sudden or involuntary in nature, resulting from athletic injury, declining physical abilities, and/or being cut from the team for financial reasons. Because termination from sport will occur at some point in time, athletes may benefit from discussing and planning for this transition before it occurs. Applied sport psychologists can assist athletes (particularly those who are at the college level and beyond) by helping them define their after-sport career goals and begin preparing themselves now for that change. Although athletes who are currently performing well initially may resist discussions concerning the end of their career, planning in advance may be a particularly important coping strategy for successfully weathering the transition when it occurs (Lavallee & Andersen, 2000).

Developmental and life factors also will influence athletes' transition from sports. How old is the athlete, and what other general developmental issues

might be present? How long has the athlete been involved in sport? How strongly is the athlete identified with the athlete role, and does the athlete have any other areas in which he or she has a strong identity? Brewer, Van Raalte, and Petitpas (2000) have suggested that athletic identity, particularly when it has been foreclosed, can contribute to distress during the transition from sport. Athletes who see themselves primarily in that role and do not have any other well-defined and informed identities may struggle with the idea of not being involved in sport. For them, the question becomes, "Who am I if I am not an athlete?" Applied sport psychologists can assist athletes with this identity issue by helping them internalize the other important roles in their lives, such as student, son/daughter, romantic partner, friend, and more. Athletes whose identities are multiply determined are likely to transition most successfully from sport to other careers and life pursuits.

Internal and external resources can influence how athletes' cognitively appraise the transition from sport and thus affect their emotional and behavioral reactions. For example, athletes who are optimistic, self-confident, and instrumental in their approach to life, who are able to cope effectively with life stressors, and who have broad and deep social support systems may appraise the transition in a more positive manner, viewing it as an opportunity to try a new role in their lives or as a time to reconnect with friends and family. Thus, applied sport psychologists who are working with athletes in transition will need to assess a wide range of personal and situational factors to accurately assess the resources that are available to the athlete. Lavallee and Andersen (2000) provided a list of questions applied sport psychologists might ask when working with athletes in transition, such as how the athlete has coped with prior transitions and to what extent the athlete has achieved sport-competition goals. Keeping these questions in mind can facilitate the counseling process. In addition to working individually with athletes who actually are undergoing a career transition, applied sport psychologists could intervene proactively by providing them with career workshops and training while they still are playing in their sport, to get them thinking about and preparing for what is an inevitable transition.

An Ideal Training Model for Applied Sport Psychology

As discussed previously, applied sport psychology is an interdisciplinary profession that requires training, knowledge, skills, and experience in the practice and science of both psychology and the exercise/sport sciences (McCullagh & Noble, 2002; Zizzi, Zaichkowsky, & Perna, 2002). Although there is agreement that sport psychology is an interdisciplinary field, there is no uniform consensus regarding the specific coursework, training experiences, and necessary credentialing that should be required. In this section, we discuss current career possibilities and explore the issues of accreditation of training programs. We conclude by offering an ideal training program in applied sport psychology. In doing so, we acknowledge that other models and pathways for training exist, yet we have based ours within counseling psychology because we believe its values and training are best suited, as a foundational academic environment, for training applied sport psychologists.

Current Career Possibilities

Unlike other professions in psychology, detailed data on applied sport psychology as an occupation are limited. However, three survey studies of sport psychology professionals and recent graduates (Andersen et al., 1997; Meyers et al., 2001; Williams & Scherzer, 2003) indicate that their primary work environment appears to be equally split between academic (i.e., faculty positions in departments of psychology or exercise/sport science) and applied (e.g., private practice, hospital) settings. In addition, these surveys revealed that professionals with a full-time interest in sport psychology-related activities primarily are employed in exercise/sport science academic positions, and that psychology-trained professionals do indeed work with athletes and in sport settings. Direct applied work with athletes, though, does not constitute a major portion of either the academic's or the practitioner's income or time spent in their jobs, regardless of the professional's academic background.

Despite these findings, there are full-time, applied sport psychology professionals making a living (e.g., Taylor, 2008; USOC, n.d.; Winerman, 2005; Wysocki, 2005), and there has been, and likely will be in the future, some growth in the availability of full-time consulting positions at universities and among professional sport organizations. The current market, though, is not likely to be able to support a large number of full-time applied sport psychology practitioners, so professionals who desire a career in this field would be wise to consider doing so, at least initially, on a supplemental, part-time basis. This reality also has implications for a model

of applied sport psychology training. Ideally, sport psychology professionals-in-training would acquire a broad knowledge base, develop a diverse set of skills, and be eligible for whatever credentialing is available to them to increase their career options and job marketability. Doctoral graduates from counseling psychology programs who have taken sport psychology and exercise/sport science coursework and been a part of extensive, supervised sport psychology practica would be ideally suited for entering and being successful in the applied sport psychology job market.

Current Perspectives on Accreditation

A major development toward the identification of a set of educational standards occurred in 1989, when the AASP approved an interdisciplinary certification program that was based on obtaining a graduate degree in exercise/sport science or psychology; completing coursework in sport psychology, psychology/counseling, sport science, ethics, and research design/statistics or assessment; demonstrating competence in sport; and receiving supervision in sport psychology practice (AASP, n.d.). The certification of applied sport psychology professionals generally is lauded as necessary and fundamental to increase the accountability of training, recognition of professionals, credibility of the field, preparation of professionals, and public awareness (Zaichkowsky & Perna, 1992). As discussed previously, though, AASP's portfolio-based certification program presents considerable challenges to established psychologists who want to demonstrate their competence in sport psychology.

In psychology, a relatively direct link exists between matriculating from an APA-accredited training program and being approved to sit for a state licensure exam (or ultimately having the opportunity to be "credentialed"). In sport psychology, however, there is no such mechanism in place (i.e., professional organization) for accrediting programs, and thus there is no established pathway or set of educational criteria for training in applied sport psychology. As a result, graduate program accreditation could be a useful mechanism for improving applied sport psychology training. Silva, Conroy, and Zizzi (1999) presented a compelling argument in favor of program accreditation, citing a number of potential benefits to the profession of sport psychology (e.g., raising of standards of training for future professionals, strengthening of certification/licensure criteria, and creation of graduate programs with stronger identities and greater clarity of focus). Others have been more critical of the need for sport psychology program accreditation, though, suggesting it is premature to pursue the issue before a greater need for sport psychology services has been established, with sport psychology having limited status in most graduate training programs, and with high political, financial, and psychological costs associated with obtaining accreditation (Hale & Danish, 1999). Consistent with this position, in a curricular review of 79 sport psychology graduate programs, Van Raalte et al. (2000) found that most training programs did not offer all the courses or experiences that would be necessary to meet existing credentialing criteria (i.e., AASP). Currently, there are no plans among the primary sport psychology organizations (i.e., AASP, APA Division 47) to develop accreditation guidelines or criteria. Thus, current graduate students are somewhat left on their own to determine what constitutes an ideal applied sport psychology training program that would prepare them to function competently and ethically as a professional in the field.

An "Ideal" Applied Sport Psychology Training Model

Because a universally accepted educational pathway leading to sport psychology professional qualification currently does not exist, and there are no current plans for any professional sport psychology organization to develop and institute an accreditation process, we offer a model of training in applied sport psychology that is interdisciplinary, has an identified set of core values, and emphasizes practical training in both general mental health issues and specific sport psychology interventions (e.g., performance enhancement). This model can serve as a guide for the preparation of future applied sport psychology professionals, for the acquisition of the necessary knowledge and skills, and ultimately, to be eligible for existing professional credentials. In presenting this model, we acknowledge the previous work completed by the sport psychology professionals who established the AASP certification program, because these criteria are an integral part of the model's curriculum. However, we also incorporate the additional knowledge base and skill sets suggested by APA Division 47 and consider the realities of the current job market in applied sport psychology.

In offering this training model, we also acknowledge that several different options currently are available to students who want careers in applied sport psychology. Most notably, these options include obtaining a master's or doctoral-level degree in sport psychology from an exercise/sport science based training program. These programs historically have prepared students rather well for careers in academia, with opportunities to do some part-time performance enhancement consulting work with athletes and teams, and in some rare cases, full-time consulting work. In addition, exercise/sport science-based training programs recently have begun to surface that allow students to meet AASP certification criteria and also be eligible to obtain licensure/certification as master's level professional counselors. However, each of these training options restrict graduates in some form or another, such as limiting their competence (e.g., sport science trained not able to ethically provide counseling services), reducing their marketability (e.g., master's degree-level counselors not eligible for jobs requiring licensure as a psychologist), and requiring additional characteristics, knowledge, and skills for success (e.g., entrepreneurial spirit, service product development, marketing). Thus, we define doctoral-level training in applied sport psychology as the sine qua non of the field, including the need for licensure, and make the case for why we believe a doctoral program in counseling psychology is an ideal training environment. We are fully aware of the potential implications this training model could have on other academic programs. That being said, we believe that the principles, values, and educational experiences that form the foundation of our model can be integrated into existing training programs as well, resulting in the best possible training even for those students with primary (sole) interests in performance enhancement consulting work and/or a lesser desire or resources to pursue a doctoral degree.

Our training model consists of a set of eight core values, eight learning/knowledge areas, and four primary training outcomes (see Figure 30.1). For us, any training model must have a defined set of values that describe what is important, influence decisions regarding students' training experiences, and impact the course of action taken by program directors; in our model, those values come from counseling psychology. Enveloped by this set of core values are the specific learning/knowledge areas that represent the coursework, scholarly activity, and applied experiences that define the students' training. Students' mastery of these eight learning/knowledge area results in the outcomes presented in the center of the model. We discuss each level below.

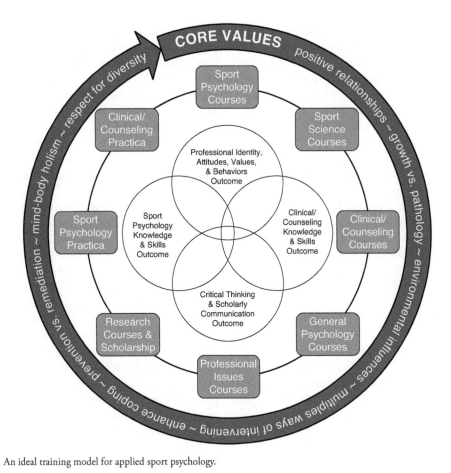

Fig. 30.1 An ideal training model for applied sport psychology.

CORE VALUES

In the outer ring of the figure are the eight core values from counseling psychology (defined earlier in the chapter) that provide the foundation for students' training experiences. These values also are very consistent with what applied sport psychology encompasses (Danish et al., 1993), including: optimization of performance by eliminating obstacles and building on existing strengths; counseling of athletes to work through the daily challenges of life; remediation of more severe clinical issues that may emerge; development of life skills through psychoeducation and generalization/transfer of sport experiences; prevention of and, when necessary, psychological rehabilitation from, athletic injury; facilitating systemic change in sport organizations, sport teams, and coaching staffs; and promoting involvement in and enjoyment of sport throughout the lifespan. Because of this connection, students who choose counseling psychology as their foundational educational degree (the area in which they receive their doctorate) would be trained in and thus incorporate these values into their professional

identities, and thus have the worldview that is consistent with the environmental demands of sport and the experiences of athletes.

LEARNING/KNOWLEDGE AREAS

On the inner ring of the figure are the eight learning/knowledge areas that encompass training in the essential knowledge, skills, attitudes, and behaviors for professional practice. These areas include an understanding and application of applied sport psychology principles and practices; physical, technical, and social aspects of sport behavior; abnormal aspects of human behavior and counseling interventions; general human cognitions, affect, and behavior; professional issues and ethics; scientific methodology and scholarship activity; individual and group clinical/counseling skills; and individual and group sport psychology skills. Although we present each learning/knowledge area separately, they are not independent areas. Rather, we view them as reciprocally interacting knowledge areas that increase individuals' understanding of and ability to work effectively with individuals.

1. *Sport psychology core.* Applied sport psychology is a discipline of study that is distinct but not separate from the psychological and sport sciences, and as such, a firm understanding of the principles and practices related to sport psychology is one of the core learning/knowledge areas. Thus, a combination of courses in applied sport psychology would provide students with a broad foundation of the science and practice of sport psychology. These courses should cover the content areas of intervention/performance enhancement, social psychology in sport, and health/exercise psychology and serve as a theoretical and empirical base for practice. Examples of specific courses include sport psychology theory and research, applied sport psychology interventions, team dynamics in sport, and psychological aspects of athletic injury.

2. *Exercise/sport science core.* Applied sport psychologists must have a basic understanding of how socio-environmental, physiological, and biomechanical factors influence sport performance if they are to differentiate the causes of performance decrements, such as whether a baseball player's poor hitting is due to poor swing mechanics or worry that is disrupting his attentional focus (or a combination of the two). Thus, courses in the physiological, biomechanical, motor, social, and/or philosophical bases of sport behavior would provide a foundation of general human performance principles. Examples of specific courses include exercise physiology, biomechanics of human movement, motor learning, and history of physical education.

3. *Counseling/clinical core.* The third core learning/knowledge area concerns having a firm understanding of personality and abnormal human behavior, problems in daily living, human development and issues that exist across the lifespan, and counseling theory and interventions. A combination of courses in this area provides students with a foundation in human psycho-pathology, assessment of psychopathology, and counseling interventions that emphasize human development from a positive, growth-oriented perspective. Examples of specific courses include abnormal psychology, psychological assessment, theories of counseling, cognitive-behavioral therapy, human development, and counseling methods and skills.

4. *General psychology core.* Just as it would limiting to only have knowledge about the psychology of sport behavior, it would be insufficient to only be exposed to courses and experiences in counseling and clinical psychology. Thus, a basic understanding of the complexity of human beings and the myriad factors that influence human cognitive processes, emotions, and actions is the fourth core learning/knowledge. Courses in the biological, cognitive-affective, and social bases of human behavior, as well as an understanding of historical and philosophical perspectives in psychology, would provide students with a foundation in this area. Examples of specific courses include physiological psychology, learning and emotion, and social psychology.

5. *Professional issues.* Together, training in ethics, diversity, and other professional issues is the fifth learning/knowledge area. Courses in ethics, legal issues, and professional standards of behavior, and courses that provide learning opportunities on understanding diversity in a multicultural world and expanding one's own self-awareness and worldview would provide students with a foundation in the essential attitudes, values, and behaviors of professional practice. Examples of specific courses include ethical and legal issues, professional orientation, and multicultural counseling.

6. *Research and scholarship.* The sixth knowledge/learning area concerns training in quantitative and qualitative research methods, the use of statistics to analyze data, the ability to think critically about complex issues/information, and the skills to communicate findings in a coherent and scholarly manner. Thus, courses in research design and statistics in combination with supervised scholarly/research activities, such as the completion of a doctoral dissertation, is a central part of our model. Not only do these experiences teach students critical thinking skills, scientific methodology, and the ability to evaluate data, but the process of doing their dissertation is the pathway to becoming an expert on a specific topic and an opportunity to make a professional and scientific contribution within the field. Examples of specific courses include applied research methods, multivariate statistical methods, and qualitative research design and analysis. Examples of scholarly activities include conducting original research, developing theoretical position papers, writing critical reviews of literature, creating innovative intervention programs, and evaluating outcomes of existing intervention programs.

7. *Counseling/clinical practica.* The seventh knowledge/learning area centers on the

development of individual and group counseling/ therapy skills in the general mental health area. This area represents the translation of theory and research into actual intervention activities and is what most applied psychologists consider to be the central part of their training. These experiences with "live" clients should be supervised to guide students in their work and provide them with opportunities to gain self-understanding and awareness and acquire counseling skills in intervening with individuals, couples, families, and groups who may be experiencing a wide range of mental health issues. Specific competencies to be developed in this area include the ability to appropriately assess and conceptualize case material, evaluate one's own reactions to client issues and therapeutic interactions, plan and implement individual and group interventions, and evaluate the effectiveness of said interventions. Students may benefit from having a broad range of experiences (e.g., type of mental health service, age/gender or client, mental health issue) and a diverse group of supervisors (e.g., theoretical orientation), particularly in their predoctoral practica. Predoctoral internship may offer students an opportunity to pursue more in-depth training in a specific domain (e.g., college counseling centers) or therapeutic approach (e.g., cognitive-behavioral, interpersonal).

8. *Sport psychology practica.* The eighth knowledge/learning area concerns sport psychology specific practica training. Although meeting the requirements of this core area may be difficult, we believe it is important for students to have supervised applied sport psychology training experiences that are nearly equal to their general counseling practica in terms of depth and breadth. These applied experiences provide students with opportunities to gain experience and acquire individual and group performance enhancement, counseling/clinical, and/or consultation skills with athletes and teams. In addition, these experiences will help students understand the connection between general mental health issues and performance decrements and learn to discern when the intervention's focus should be on general performance enhancement skills and when consultants need to help athletes address their inter-/intrapersonal concerns. Furthermore, these experiences, if with teams or organizations, can provide important opportunities to learn how systems work and how components within

a system influence one another. Like general counseling practica, it is important for students to have experiences across modalities (e.g., individual, team, organization), level of sport (e.g., youth, collegiate), sport team (e.g., basketball, soccer), and gender if at all possible. These experiences, of course, should be supervised, and the supervisor should be experienced in applied sport psychology, preferably holding one of the existing credentials (e.g., Certified Consultant, AASP), within the field.

TRAINING OUTCOMES

At the center of the figure is a set of intersecting circles that designate the four outcomes that ideally result from integrated training in the eight core areas. The intersecting circles denote that the outcomes are linked and interact with one another, and it is the successful demonstration of the four training outcomes that represents the competently trained applied sport psychology professional. Two of the training outcomes—sport psychology and clinical/counseling knowledge and skills—result from the requisite knowledge bases and skill sets needed for effective sport psychology practice. Consistent with the interdisciplinary focus of our model, applied sport psychologists need to demonstrate that they are knowledgeable and skilled in the principles and practices of both sport psychology and clinical/counseling psychology. Meeting these two training outcomes will not only ensure competent, broadly defined sport psychology practice, but it will result in a more marketable practitioner eligible to be licensed as a psychologist and credentialed as a sport psychology consultant.

With the third outcome, the demonstration of a professional identity and essential attitudes, values, and behaviors for professional practice, we suggest that future applied sport psychologists need more than just knowledge and skills to be effective practitioners. Rather, a healthy professional identity, an attitude of openness and respect for others, an internalization of the foundational values, and conscientious and responsible ethical behavior are among the other requirements for competent professional practice in sport psychology. Finally, effective sport psychology practice should be based in sound theoretical and empirical science, and the fourth training outcome of our model highlights the importance of applied sport psychology professional being good scholars/scientists as well. Specifically, future applied sport psychologists need to demonstrate critical thinking in the application of their knowledge with clients, in addition to being able to communicate their understanding, both orally and in writing, in a scholarly and informed way.

MODEL SUMMARY

Although we promote doctoral-level training program in counseling psychology as the foundational educational environment because it prepares graduates for the necessary credentialing (i.e., licensure as a psychologist) and puts them in the most marketable position for applied sport psychology jobs, we recognize and appreciate the value of different models of applied sport psychology training (e.g., exercise/sport science based, master's level licensure/certification). In addition, we know that not every student interested in applied sport psychology will pursue a Ph.D. in counseling psychology, so we identified and included the core values and knowledge/learning areas in it, so that students in other training programs (e.g., exercise/sport science) could have the opportunity to obtain the types of training experiences that may lead to the development of ethical, knowledgeable, competent, and self-aware practitioners.

Future Directions

Based on our review of the literature and our many years in the field, we offer the following suggestions/comments about the issues that are pressing in the field and about what we think can be done to advance sport psychology as a profession.

Separate "Exercise" from Applied Sport Psychology

Over 20 years ago, Rejeski and Brawley (1988) made the argument that sport psychology was poorly defined, often overlapping with exercise, health, and rehabilitation psychology. In their article, they offered clear definitions of each field, compelling arguments concerning the benefits that would come with definitional clarity, and mechanisms for determining in which area research would best fit. Unfortunately, little has changed in that sport psychology still remains linked to exercise psychology despite their different foci. Such linkages seem part of the fabric of the field, and professional organizations (e.g., Division 47, Exercise and Sport Psychology, of the American Psychological Association) and journals (e.g., *Journal of Sport & Exercise Psychology*) are illustrations of this questionable alliance. From our perspective, both fields suffer from this marriage. For example, this linkage likely creates unneeded confusion for the public about what sport and exercise psychologists actually do and who they might want to seek for assistance with performance-based sport problems. Instead of being linked as they are, sport psychology, which involves both science and practice, needs to be defined and pursued as its own field, one that recognizes that its aims, goals, theories, and services are different from exercise psychology. A clear distinction between the two fields, as we are suggesting, would benefit both fields, in particular applied sport psychology, as it moves to establish itself as a needed resource for athletes and coaches.

Define the Scope and Practice of Sport Psychology.

Following the separation of the fields, professional organizations, particularly those closely affiliated with the parent discipline of psychology (i.e., Division 47), need to more clearly define the scope and practice of the field. What do sport psychologists actually do? With what populations do they work? How do they bring about change and growth in their clientele? What interventions are effective with which clients under what circumstances? What defines competent practice? What makes working with athletes and within the sport environment unique? What training is needed to become a competent applied sport psychologist? What ethical issues and practices are unique to sport and must be considered in ways perhaps different from traditional psychology? Questions such as these will be important to answer. In addition, like counseling psychology, sport psychology must recognize the importance of both science/research and applied practice, and encourage open communication between those who identify primarily as researchers and those who make their livings as practitioners. Such collaborations are crucial to advance knowledge, develop and test theories, implement and evaluate treatments, and establish applied sport psychology as a needed resource for athletes, coaches, and sport organizations.

Define, Evaluate, and Support Ideal Models of Training

Although we have offered a training model in this chapter, we recognize its limitations in scope and ability to effect change. But we do hope it serves as a catalyst for academics in psychology and exercise/sport science departments (and in counseling psychology programs) to work across departmental boundaries to create dynamic, content-based training opportunities that reflect what sport psychologists ultimately do. We also hope that models such as ours can help us move beyond the artificial dichotomy that exists between performance enhancement and counseling/clinical issues. As a field, we have too long fought that battle, and the reality is that it likely is more of an issue to us than to our consumers. There is diversity in the training that professionals in sport psychology have, and everything applied sport psychologists do, whether dealing with a relational issue or helping an athlete develop a preperformance routine, is geared toward improving performance. The broader, and more important, question is whether professionals are practicing within the boundaries of their training and competence.

Lack of Influence

In comparison to other fields, such as athletic training and strength and conditioning, applied sport psychology's role and influence in the world of sport appears relatively limited. Although applied sport psychology services are used at all levels of sport, there has yet to be substantial public understanding of (and support for) what sport psychology is, how it plays an essential role in any sport performance, and its value (in terms of time and money spent on it) to an athlete, team, or sport organization. This lack of influence in the public sphere may be due to several factors, including the unneeded connection between sport and exercise psychology, the lack of one voice (in terms of professional organizations) that speaks for the field, and the fact that there is no accepted and influential credential defining competence. From our perspective, a viable strategy would be for applied sport psychologist to consider rallying behind a single professional organization that has the necessary power, infrastructure, and influence to effect change and raise the status and visibility of the field. In our mind, there are two such influential organizations, the AASP and APA Division 47. Perhaps it is time for these organizations to merge or at least consider mechanisms for pooling resources in some meaningful way for the broader benefits to the field. Although we understand that this suggestion is anathema to some, we hope that a conversation can be started to look at all viable options for how our professional organizations can advance the standing and influence of the field.

Credentialing (or Recognition) of Training Programs

Although some (e.g., Hale & Danish, 1999) have argued that credentialing is premature, given the lack of need for and public recognition of applied sport psychology services, in reality, these issues need to be addressed simultaneously. First, professional organizations, as we mentioned previously, need to define the scope and practice of applied sport psychology and, through that, provide a de facto training curriculum/model that university programs can use in developing their programs. Second, professional organizations need to establish a system through which training programs' curricula can be evaluated. Third, professional organizations need to promote applied sport psychology as a necessary component in the health, wellness, and performance of athletes and sport teams. Fourth, professional organizations need to help sport teams and organizations understand the value of applied sport psychologists having certain training (or coming from certain credentialed programs) and holding specific credentials. If these steps are taken in concert with one another, they can promote growth and influence in the field.

Evaluation of Treatments/Interventions

At present, very few applied sport psychology interventions have been evaluated to determine their efficacy (Greenspan & Feltz, 1989; Martin et al., 2005). More evaluation research is needed, and the work of Ron Smith and his colleagues at the University of Washington provide a model for how that can be done (e.g., Smith et al., 1995). If the field is going to advance and raise the value of what it has to offer, applied sport psychologists and researchers must learn to collaborate, not only with each other, but with coaches and sport organizations. Applied sport psychologists must understand the need to test and document what they do, and academic researchers must be willing to get out into the field and learn from practitioners. Although experimental designs will remain the sine qua non of scientific research, much can be learned through quasi-experimental and N-of-one methods that are conducted in the field. Applied sport psychologist must work to convince coaches, parents, and other gatekeepers of the value associated with participating in research while practicing or competing.

Conclusion

Applied sport psychology is an interdisciplinary field with roots in the exercise/sport sciences and strong ties to psychology. Over the past 40 years, as sport psychology has moved increasingly out of the laboratory and onto the playing field and, through that, recognized the importance of applied training in psychology, the field has faced many challenges to its identity. These challenges—which have ranged from the establishment of professional organizations able to address the practice issues to credentialing and titling to graduate training—have served as a catalyst for growth as professionals within the field have struggled to establish guidelines for ethical practice and define its future. There is a depth, breadth, and complexity within the field of applied sport psychology that belies its historical youth.

Although we support the historical and present interdisciplinary structure of sport psychology, we believe that individuals wanting to engage in the practice of sport psychology should be trained within a curriculum that is grounded in counseling psychology and its values, training, and philosophy. In particular, counseling psychology values are consistent with the breadth of issues that athletes present across the performance enhancement and clinical/interpersonal domains. That counseling psychology values strengths-based interventions and prevention fits well with athletes and their focus on performance outcome. Counseling psychology values also address the developmental issues and ethical nuances inherent in effective applied sport psychology practice. As we illustrate in Figure 30.1, counseling psychology's core values provide the foundational structure that supports individuals' pursuit of the interdisciplinary training that defines the field. Such training and internalization of these values can lead to outcomes that we associate with competent and ethical practice.

As sports become more important and popular and as athletes and coaches continue to search for the "edge" that will improve their performances, applied sport psychology will continue to grow as a field. Counseling psychology can be at the vanguard of this growth by collaborating with departments of exercise/sport science at their universities to create the interdisciplinary curriculum that is necessary to train competent, ethical applied sport psychologists. Current counseling psychologists, by seeking additional training in the exercise/sport sciences and supervision from appropriately trained colleagues, also can become more involved in the field, bringing their expertise and understanding of human growth and development, appreciation of diversity, and commitment to proactive intervention to this unique population. It is exciting to consider that applied sport psychology's ideal "home" may be within counseling psychology.

References

Albinson, C., & Petrie, T. (2003). Cognitive appraisals, stress, and coping: Preinjury and postinjury factors influencing psychological adjustment to sport injury. *Journal of Sport Rehabilitation, 12*, 306–322.

American Psychological Association (APA). (n.d.). *Summary: Sport psychology a proficiency in professional psychology*. Retrieved November 24, 2008, from http://www.apa.org/crsppp/ archsportpsych.html.

American Sports Data. (2003, June). *A comprehensive study of sports injuries in the U.S.* Retrieved June 6, 2008, from http://www.americansportsdata.com/sports_injury1.asp.

Andersen, M. (Ed.) (2000). *Doing sport psychology*. Champaign, IL: Human Kinetics.

Andersen, M. (Ed.) (2005). *Sport psychology in practice*. Champaign, IL: Human Kinetics.

Andersen, M., Williams, J., Aldridge, T., & Taylor, J. (1997). Tracking the training and careers of graduates of advanced degree programs in sport psychology, 1989 to 1994. *The Sport Psychologist, 11*, 326–344.

Association for Applied Sport Psychology. (n.d.). *Become a certified consultant*. Retrieved October 31, 2008, from http://appliedsportpsych.org/consultants/become-certified.

Barber, H., & Krane, V. (2005). The elephant in the locker room: Opening the dialogue about sexual orientation on women's sports teams. In M. Andersen (Ed.), *Sport psychology in practice* (pp. 265–285). Champaign, IL: Human Kinetics.

Barnett, N., Smoll, F., & Smith, R. (1992). Effects of enhancing coach-athlete relationships on youth sport attrition. *The Sport Psychologist, 6*, 111–127.

Bloom, G., & Stevens, D. (2002). Case study: A team-building mental skills training program with an intercollegiate equestrian team. *Athletic Insight, 4*. Retrieved from www.athleticinsight.com/Vol4Iss1/EquestrianTeamBuilding.htm.

Brawley, L., & Paskevich, D. (1997). Conducting team-building research in the context of sport and exercise. *Journal of Applied Sport Psychology, 9*, 11–40.

Brewer, B., & Petrie, T. (2002). Psychopathology in sport and exercise. In J. Van Raalte, & B. Brewer (Eds.), *Exploring sport and exercise psychology* (pp. 307–323). Washington, DC: American Psychological Association.

Brewer, B., Van Raalte, J., & Petitpas, A. (2000). Self-identify issues in sport career transitions. In D. Lavallee, & P. Wylleman (Eds.), *Career transitions in sport: International perspectives* (pp. 29–43). Morgantown, WV: Fitness Information Technologies.

Bull, S., Shambrook, C., James, W., & Brooks, J. (2005). Towards an understanding of mental toughness in elite English cricketers. *Journal of Applied Sport Psychology, 17*, 209–227.

Burton, D. (1990). Multimodal stress management in sport: Current status and future directions. In J. Jones, & L. Hardy (Eds.), *Stress and performance in sport* (pp. 171–201). New York: John Wiley & Sons.

Burton, D., Naylor, S., & Holliday, B. (2001). Goal-setting in sport: Investigating the goal effectiveness paradox. In R. Singer, H. Hausenblas, & C. Janelle (Eds.), *Handbook of sport psychology* (pp. 497–528), New York: Wiley.

Carron, A., Brawley, L., & Widmeyer, W. (1998). The measurement of cohesiveness in sport groups. In J. Duda (Ed.), *Advancements in sport and exercise measurement* (pp. 213–226). Morgantown, WV: Fitness Information Technology.

Carron, A., Colman, M., Wheeler, J., & Stevens, D. (2002). Cohesion and performance in sport: A meta analysis. *Journal of Sport & Exercise Psychology, 24*, 168–188.

Carron, A., Hausenblas, H., & Eys, M. (2005). *Group dynamics in sport.* Morgantown, WV: Fitness Information Technology.

Carron, A., Spink, K., & Prapavessis, H. (1997). Team-building and cohesiveness in the sport and exercise setting: Use of indirect interventions. *Journal of Applied Sport Psychology, 9*, 61–72.

Carron, A., Widmeyer, W., & Brawley, L. (1985). The development of an instrument to assess cohesion in sport teams: The group environment questionnaire. *Journal of Sport Psychology, 7*, 244–266.

Centers for Disease Control. (2006). Sports-related injuries among high school athletes United States, 2005–06 school year. *Morbidity and Mortality Weekly Report, 55*, 1037–1040. Retrieved November 6, 2008, from http://www.cdc.gov/mmwr/preview/mmwrhtml/mm5538a1.htm.

Coakley, J. (2009). *Sports in society: Issues and Controversies* (10th ed.). New York, NY: McGraw-Hill.

Coatsworth, J., & Conroy, D. (2006). Enhancing the self-esteem of youth swimmers through coach training: Gender and age effects. *Psychology of Sport & Exercise, 7*, 173–192.

Cogan, K., & Petrie, T. (1995). Sport consultation: An evaluation of a season-long intervention with female college gymnasts. *The Sport Psychologist, 9*, 282–296.

Connaughton, D., Wadey, R., Hanton, S., & Jones, G. (2008). The development and maintenance of mental toughness: Perceptions of elite performers. *Journal of Sports Sciences, 26*, 83–95.

Conroy, D., & Coatsworth, J. (2004). The effects of coach training on fear of failure in youth swimmers: A latent growth curve analysis from a randomized, controlled trial. *Journal of Applied Developmental Psychology, 25*, 193–214.

Crust, L. (2007). Mental toughness in sport: A review. *International Journal of Sport & Exercise Psychology, 5*, 270–290.

Danish, S., Petitpas, A., & Hale, B. (1993). Life development interventions for athletes: Life skills through sport. *The Counseling Psychologist, 21*, 352–385.

Dorfman, H. (1990). Reflections on providing personal and performance enhancement consulting services in professional baseball. *The Sport Psychologist, 4*, 341–346.

Dosil, J. (2006). *The sport psychologist's handbook: A guide for sport-specific performance enhancement.* Chichester, UK: John Wiley & Sons.

Dunn, J., & Holt, N. (2004). A qualitative investigation of a personal-disclosure mutual-sharing team building activity. *The Sport Psychologist, 18*, 363–380.

Feltz, D. (1987). The future of graduate education in sport and exercise science: A sport psychology perspective. *Quest, 39*, 217–223.

Gardner, F., & Moore, Z. (2006). *Clinical sport psychology.* Champaign, IL: Human Kinetics.

Gill, D. (1986). *Psychological dynamics of sport.* Champaign, IL: Human Kinetics.

Gould, D., Murphy, S., Tammen, V., & May, J. (1991). An evaluation of U.S. Olympic sport psychology consultant effectiveness. *The Sport Psychologist, 5*, 111–127.

Greenleaf, C., Petrie, T., Carter, J., & Reel, J. (2009). Female collegiate athletes: Prevalence of eating disorders and disordered eating behaviors. *Journal of American College Health, 57*, 489–495.

Greenspan, M., & Feltz, D. (1989). Psychological interventions with athletes in competitive situations: A review. *The Sport Psychologist, 3*, 219–236.

Griffin, J., & Harris, M. (1996). Coaches' attitudes, knowledge, experiences, and recommendations regarding weight control. *The Sport Psychologist, 10*, 180–194.

Griffith, C. (1926). *Psychology of coaching.* New York: Scribners.

Griffith, C. (1928). *Psychology of athletics.* New York: Scribners.

Grove, J., Lavallee, D., Gordon, S., & Harvey, J. (1998). Account-making: A model for understanding and resolving distressful reactions to retirement from sport. *The Sport Psychologist, 12*, 52–67.

Hale, B., & Danish, S. (1999). Putting the accreditation cart before the AAASP horse: A reply to Silva, Conroy, and Zizzi. *Journal of Applied Sport Psychology, 11*, 321–328.

Hall, C. R., Mack, D. E., Paivio, A., & Hausenblas, H. A. (1998). Imagery use by athletes: Development of the sport imagery questionnaire. *International Journal of Sport Psychology, 29*, 73–89.

Halliwell, W. (1990). Providing sport psychology consulting services in professional hockey. *The Sport Psychologist, 4*, 369–377.

Hardy, J. (2006). Speaking clearly: A critical review of the self-talk literature. *Psychology of Sport and Exercise, 7*, 81–97.

Hardy, J., Gammage, K., & Hall, C. (2001). A descriptive study of athlete self-talk. *The Sport Psychologist, 15*, 306–318.

Hardy, L., Jones, G., & Gould, D. (1996). *Understanding psychological preparation for sport: Theory and practice of elite performance.* New York: John Wiley & Sons.

Harmison, R., Hehn, M., Sims, N., & Poupeney, N. (2007, October). Understanding and developing mental toughness in sport: An application of the CAPS approach and preliminary investigation. In R. Stratton (Chair), *Understanding and developing mental toughness in sport.* Symposium presented at the 22nd annual meeting of the Association for Applied Sport Psychology, Louisville, KY.

Harmison, R., & Roth, R. (2006, September). *Mental toughness: Developing determined, focused, and confident athletes that perform under pressure.* Colloquium presented at the 21st annual meeting of the Association for the Advancement of Applied Sport Psychology, Miami, FL.

Hausenblas, H. A., & Carron, A. V. (1999). Eating disorder indices and athletes: An integration. *Journal of Sport & Exercise Psychology, 21*, 230–258.

Hausenblas, H., & Symons Downs, D. (2001). Comparison of body image between athletes and nonathletes: A meta-analytic review. *Journal of Applied Sport Psychology, 13*, 323–339.

Hays, K. (2002). Putting sport psychology into (your) practice. *Professional Psychology: Research and Practice, 26*, 33–40.

Hays, K. (2006). Being fit: The ethics of practice diversification in performance psychology. *Professional Psychology: Research and Practice, 37*, 223–232.

Holmes, P., & Collins, D. (2001). The PETTLEP approach to motor imagery: A functional equivalence model for sport psychologists. *Journal of Applied Sport Psychology, 13*, 60–83.

Holt, N., & Dunn, J. (2006). Guidelines for delivering personal-disclosure mutual-sharing team building interventions. *The Sport Psychologist, 20*, 348–367.

Hootman, J., Dick, R., & Agel, J. (2007). Epidemiology of collegiate injuries for 15 sports: Summary and recommendations for injury prevention initiatives. *Journal of Athletic Training, 42*, 311–319.

Howard, G. (1992). Behold our creation! What counseling psychology has become and might yet become. *Journal of Counseling Psychology, 39*, 419–442.

Howard, G. (1993). Sport psychology: An emerging domain for counseling psychologists. *The Counseling Psychologist, 21*, 349–351.

Johnson, U., Ekengren, J., & Andersen, M. (2005). Injury prevention in Sweden: Helping soccer players at risk. *Journal of Sport & Exercise Psychology, 27*, 32–38.

Jones, G., Hanton, S., & Connaughton, D. (2002). What is this thing called mental toughness? An investigation of elite sport performers. *Journal of Applied Sport Psychology, 14*, 205–218.

Joyce, N., & Baker, D. (2008). The early days of sport psychology. *Monitor on Psychology, 39*(7), 28–29.

Kansas Jayhawks. (n.d.). *Sports psychologist joins Kansas Athletics.* Retrieved November 27, 2008, from http://kuathletics.cstv.com/genrel/042706aab.html.

Krane, V., & Williams, J. (2006). Psychological characteristics of peak performance. In J. Williams (Ed.), *Applied sport psychology: Personal growth to peak performance* (pp. 207–227). New York: McGraw-Hill.

Landin, D. (1994). The role of verbal cues in skill learning. *Quest, 46*, 299–313.

Lavallee, D., & Andersen, M. (2000). Leaving sport: Easing career transitions. In M. Andersen (Ed.), *Doing sport psychology* (pp. 249–260). Champaign, IL: Human Kinetics.

Leffingwell, T., Wiechman, S., Smith, R., Smoll, F., & Christensen, D. (2001). Sport psychology training within a clinical psychology training program and a department of intercollegiate athletics. *Professional Psychology: Research and Practice, 32*, 531–536.

Lutz, D. (1990). An overview of training models in sport psychology. *The Sport Psychologist, 4*, 62–71.

Maddison, R., & Prapavessis, H. (2005). A psychological approach to the prediction and prevention of athletic injury. *Journal of Sport & Exercise Psychology, 27*, 289–310.

Martin, K., Moritz, S., & Hall, C. (1999). Imagery use in sport: A literature review and applied model. *The Sport Psychologist, 13*, 245–268.

Martin, G., Vause, T., & Schwartzman, L. (2005). Experimental studies of psychological interventions with athletes in competitions: Why so few? *Behavior Modification, 29*, 615–641.

McCullagh, P., & Noble, J. (2002). Education for becoming a sport psychologist. In J. Van Raalte, & B. Brewer (Eds.), *Exploring sport and exercise psychology* (pp. 439–457). Washington, DC: American Psychological Association.

Meyers, A. (1997). Sport psychology service to the United States Olympic Festival: An experiential account. *The Sport Psychologist, 11*, 454–468.

Meyers, A., Coleman, J., Whelan, J., & Mehlenbeck, R. (2001). Examining careers in sport psychology: Who is working and who is making money? *Professional Psychology: Research and Practice, 32*, 5–11.

Meyers, A., Whelan, J., & Murphy, S. (1996). Cognitive behavioral strategies in athletic performance enhancement. In M. Hersen, R. Eisler, & P. Miller (Eds.), *Progress in behavior modification* (pp. 137–164). Pacific Grove, CA: Brooks/Cole.

Middleton, S., Marsh, H., Martin, A., Richards, G., & Perry, C. (2004). *Discovering mental toughness: A qualitative study of mental toughness in elite athletes.* Self Research Centre Biannual Conference, Berlin. Retrieved from http://self.uws.edu.ou/Conferences/2004_Middleton_Marsh_Martin-Richards_Perryb.pdf.

Mischel, W., & Shoda, Y. (1995). A cognitive-affective system theory of personality: Reconceptualizing situations, dispositions, dynamics, and invariance in personality structure. *Psychological Review, 102*, 246–268.

Morgan, W. (1997). Mind games: The psychology of sport. In D. Lamb, & R. Murray (Eds.), *Optimizing sport performance* (pp. 1–62). Carmel, IN: Cooper.

Mullen, B., & Cooper, C. (1994). The relation between group cohesiveness and performance: An integration. *Psychological Bulletin, 115*, 210–227.

Murphy, S., Nordin, S., & Cumming, J. (2008). Imagery in sport, exercise, and dance. In T. S. Horn (Ed.), *Advances in sport psychology* (pp. 297–324). Champaign, IL: Human Kinetics.

Nideffer, R. (1984). Current concerns in sport psychology. In J. Silva, & R. Weinberg (Eds.), *Psychological foundations of sport* (pp. 35–44). Champaign, IL: Human Kinetics.

Ogilvie, B., & Tutko, T. (1966). *Problem athletes and how to handle them.* London: Pelham.

Orlick, T., & Partington, J. (1987). The sport psychology consultant: Analysis of critical components as viewed by Canadian Olympic athletes. *The Sport Psychologist, 1*, 4–17.

Perna, F. M., Antoni, M. H., Baum, A., Gordon, P., & Schneiderman, N. (2003). Cognitive behavioral stress management effects on injury and illness among competitive athletes: A randomized clinical trial. *Annals of Behavioral Medicine, 25*, 66–73.

Petitpas, A., Giges, B., & Danish, S. (1999). The sport psychologist – athlete relationship: Implication for training. *The Sport Psychologist, 13*, 344–357.

Petrie, T. (1993). Coping resources, competitive trait anxiety, and playing status: Moderating effects on the life stress-injury relationship. *Journal of Sport & Exercise Psychology, 15*, 261–274.

Petrie, T. (2007). Using counseling groups in the rehabilitation of athletic injury. In D. Pargman (Ed.), *Psychological bases of sport injuries* (pp. 191–216). Morgantown, WV: Fitness Information Technology.

Petrie, T., & Diehl, N. (1995). Sport psychology in the profession of psychology. *Professional Psychology: Research and Practice, 26*, 288–291.

Petrie, T., Diehl, N., & Watkins, C. (1995). Sport psychology: An emerging domain in the counseling psychology profession? *The Counseling Psychologist, 23*, 535–545.

Petrie, T., Greenleaf, C., Reel, J., & Carter, J. (2008). Prevalence of eating disorders and disordered eating behaviors among male collegiate athletes. *Psychology of Men and Masculinity, 9*, 267–277.

Petrie, T., Greenleaf, C., Reel, J., & Carter, J. (in press). An examination of psychosocial correlates of disordered eating among female collegiate athletes. *Research Quarterly for Exercise & Sport, 80*, 621–632.

Petrie, T., & Perna, F. (2004). Psychology of injury: Theory, research, and practice. In T. Morris & J. Summers (Eds.), *Sport psychology: Theory, applications and issues* (pp. 547–571). Queensland, Australia: Wiley & Sons.

Petrie, T., & Sherman, R. (2000). Counseling athletes with eating disorders: A case example. In M. Andersen (Ed.), *Doing sport psychology* (pp. 121–138). Champaign, IL: Human Kinetics.

Petrie, T., & Utley-Hamson, J. (in press). Psychosocial antecedents of and responses to athletic injury. In T. Morris, & P. Terry (Eds.), *Sport psychology: Theory, applications and issues* (3rd ed.). Morgantown, WV: Fitness Information Technologies.

Petrie, T., & Watkins, C. (1994). Sport psychology training in counseling psychology programs: Is there room at the inn? *The Counseling Psychologist, 22*, 335–341.

Prapavessis, H., Carron, A., & Spink, K. (1996). Team-building in sport. *International Journal of Sport Psychology, 27*, 269–285.

Rejeski, W., & Brawley, L. (1988). Defining the boundaries of sport psychology. *The Sport Psychologist, 2*, 231–242.

Sanborn, C., Horea, M., Siemers, B., & Dieringer, K. (2000). Disordered eating and the female athlete triad. *Clinics in Sport Medicine, 19*, 199–213.

Senécal, J., Loughead, T., & Bloom, G. (2008). A season-long team-building intervention: Examining the effect of team goal setting on cohesion. *Journal of Sport & Exercise Psychology, 30*, 186–199.

Silva, J., Conroy, D., & Zizzi, S. (1999). Critical issues confronting the advancement of applied sport psychology. *Journal of Applied Sport Psychology, 11*, 298–320.

Singer, R. (1989). Applied sport psychology in the United States. *Journal of Applied Sport Psychology, 1*, 61–80.

Smith, A., & Petrie, T. (2008). Reducing the risk of disordered eating among female athletes: A test of alternative interventions. *Journal of Applied Sport Psychology, 20*, 392–407.

Smith, R. (1989). Applied sport psychology in the age of accountability. *Journal of Applied Sport Psychology, 1*, 166–180.

Smith, R. (2006). Understanding sport behavior: A cognitive-affective processing systems approach. *Journal of Applied Sport Psychology, 18*, 1–27.

Smith, R., Smoll, F., & Barnett, N. (1995). Reduction of children's sport performance anxiety through social support and stress-reduction training for coaches. *Journal of Applied Developmental Psychology, 16*, 125–142.

Smith, R., Smoll, F., & Curtis, B. (1979). Coach effectiveness training: A cognitive-behavioral approach to enhancing relationship skills in youth sport coaches. *Journal of Sport Psychology, 1*, 59–75.

Smolak, L., Murnen, S. K., & Ruble, A. E. (2000). Female athletes and eating problems: A meta-analysis. *International Journal of Eating Disorders, 27*, 371–380.

Smoll, F., & Smith, R. (1984). Leadership research in youth sports. In J. Silva, & R. Weinberg (Eds.), *Psychological foundations of sport* (pp. 371–386). Champaign, IL: Human Kinetics.

Smoll, F., Smith, R., Barnett, N., & Everett, J. (1993). Enhancement of children's self-esteem through social support training for youth sport coaches. *Journal of Applied Psychology, 78*, 602–610.

Stein, R., Saelens, B., Dounchis, J., Lewczyk, C., Swenson, A., & Wifley, D. (2001). Treatment of eating disorders in women. *The Counseling Psychologist, 29*, 695–732.

Stevens, D., & Bloom, G. (2003). The effect of team building on cohesion. *Avante, 9*, 43–54.

Stice, E. (2002). Risk and maintenance factors for eating pathology: A meta-analytic review. *Psychological Bulletin, 128*, 825–848.

Stice, E., Presnell, K., Gau, J., & Shaw, H. (2007). Testing mediators of intervention effects in randomized controlled trials: An evaluation of two eating disorder prevention programs. *Journal of Consulting and Clinical Psychology, 75*, 20–32.

Straub, W., & Hinman, D. (1992). Profiles and professional perspectives of 10 leading sport psychologists. *The Sport Psychologist, 6*, 297–312.

Sundgot-Borgen, J., & Torstveit, M. K. (2004). Prevalence of eating disorders in elite athletes is higher than in the general population. *Clinical Journal of Sports Medicine, 14*, 25–32.

Taylor, J. (2008). Prepare to succeed. Private consulting in applied sport psychology. *Journal of Clinical Sport Psychology, 2*, 160–177.

Thompson, R., & Sherman, R. (1999). "Good athlete" traits and characteristics of anorexia nervosa: Are they similar? *Eating Disorders, 7*, 181–190.

Thompson, R., & Sherman, R. (2010). *Eating disorders in sport.* New York: Routledge.

Tod, D., & Andersen, M. (2005). Success in sport psych: Effective sport psychologists. In S. Murphy (Ed.), *The sport psychology handbook* (pp. 305–314). Champaign, IL: Human Kinetics.

Van Raalte, J., Brown, T., Brewer, B., Avondoglio, J., Hartmann, W., & Scherzer, C. (2000). An on-line survey of graduate course offerings satisfying AAASP certification criteria. *The Sport Psychologist, 14*, 98–104.

Vealey, R. (2007). Mental skills training in sport. In G. Tenenbaum, & R. C. Eklund (Eds.), *Handbook of sport psychology* (pp. 287–309). Hoboken, NJ: John Wiley & Sons.

Vealey, R., & Greenleaf, C. (2006). Seeing is believing: Understanding and using imagery in sport. In J. Williams (Ed.), *Applied sport psychology: Personal growth to peak performance* (pp. 306–348). New York: McGraw-Hill.

Voight, M., & Callaghan, J. (2001). A team building intervention program: Application and evaluation with two university soccer teams. *Journal of Sport Behavior, 24*, 420–431.

Waite, B., & Pettit, M. (1993). Work experiences of graduates from doctoral programs in sport psychology. *Journal of Applied Sport Psychology, 5*, 234–250.

Weinberg, R., & Gould, D. (2007). *Foundations of sport and exercise psychology.* Champaign, IL: Human Kinetics.

Weinberg, R., Harmison, R., Rosenkranz, R., & Hookom, S. (2005). Goal setting. In J. Taylor, & G. Wilson (Eds.), *Applying sport psychology: Four perspectives* (pp. 101–116). Champaign, IL: Human Kinetics.

Williams, J., & Harris, D. (2006). Relaxation and energizing techniques for regulation of arousal. In J. Williams (Ed.), *Applied sport psychology: Personal growth to peak performance* (pp. 285–305). New York: McGraw-Hill.

Williams, J., & Scherzer, C. (2003). Tracking the training and careers of graduate of advanced degree programs in sport psychology, 1994 to 1999. *Journal of Applied Sport Psychology, 15*, 335–353.

Winerman, L. (2005). Psychology in the stadium. *Monitor on Psychology, 36*, 50.

Wysocki, B. (2005, September, 25). It's a living: For a sports psychologist, life is a nonstop consultation. *Wall Street Journal*, p. B1.

Yukelson, D. (1997). Principles of effective team building interventions in sport: A direct services approach at Penn State University. *Journal of Applied Sport Psychology, 9*, 73–96.

Zaichkowsky, L., & Perna, F. (1992). Certification of consultants in sport psychology: A rebuttal to Anshel. *The Sport Psychologist, 6,* 287–296.

Ziegler, T. (1987). Effects of stimulus cueing on the acquisition of groundstrokes by beginning tennis players. *Journal of Applied Behavior Analysis, 20,* 405–411.

Zizzi, S., Zaichkowsky, L., & Perna, F. (2002). Certification in sport and exercise psychology. In J. L. Van Raalte, & B. W. Brewer (Eds.), *Exploring sport and exercise psychology* (pp. 459–477). Washington, DC: American Psychological Association.

Trauma Psychology

Patricia A. Frazier

Abstract

The purpose of this chapter is to review research on the prevalence of traumatic life events, risk factors for exposure to traumatic events, the psychological effects of traumatic life events, risk factors for posttraumatic stress disorder (PTSD), the effectiveness of interventions for PTSD, and posttraumatic growth. This research suggests that virtually everyone experiences a traumatic event in their lifetime, although some individuals are more at risk for exposure than are others (e.g., members of racial minority groups). Although the vast majority of people exposed to traumatic events do not develop PTSD, several individual (e.g., gender), trauma-related (e.g., event type), and posttrauma (e.g., social support) factors are reliably associated with greater risk. There are several effective psychotherapeutic interventions for PTSD, including exposure therapies and cognitive-behavioral therapies (CBT). Most individuals who have experienced traumatic events report that the event led to positive changes in their lives, although recent evidence suggests that self-reported growth may not be associated with actual positive changes from pre- to posttrauma. Future research directions related to each of these topics are discussed.

Keywords: trauma, posttraumatic stress disorder, posttraumatic growth

Many people grow up believing that bad things do not happen to good people. Unfortunately, bad things happen to everyone. Friends and loved ones die. Life-threatening illnesses develop. Long-term marriages dissolve, sometimes unexpectedly.

The purpose of this chapter is to review research on the prevalence of these kinds of traumatic life events, who is most at risk of experiencing traumatic events, how these events affect people for better or for worse, factors that are related to better or worse adjustment to traumatic events, and the effectiveness of interventions that have been developed to help people overcome the effects of traumatic events. The chapter will conclude with a discussion of future directions in research on these topics.

These topics are particularly relevant to counseling psychology for several reasons. As this chapter will illustrate, virtually everyone experiences at least one traumatic event in his or her lifetime.

These events often happen to "normal" people, and most people recover from them without developing diagnosable psychological disorders. As a result, the study of the prevalence and effects of traumatic events fits squarely within counseling psychology's emphasis on the normal range of human functioning and positive adaptation. In addition, because of the ubiquity of trauma, counseling psychologists in practice are almost certain to work with trauma survivors, and several psychotherapeutic interventions that can be delivered by counseling psychologists are effective in ameliorating the effects of trauma. Thus, to be effective practitioners, it is imperative for counseling psychologists to be knowledgeable about the prevalence and effects of, and interventions for, trauma (Courtois & Gold, 2009).

The literature on trauma is vast. For example, a PsychInfo search using the keyword "trauma" conducted in February 2009 yielded 15,668 hits just since 2002. Thus, the coverage of topics within the broad areas mentioned above necessarily will be selective. In choosing topics to cover within each section, research and issues congruent with the traditional foci of counseling psychology, such as diversity, strengths, and individual differences, are highlighted. The focus also is on research on longer-term effects of trauma rather than immediate reactions. Within particular topics, the goal was to introduce the reader to the key studies in the area and the most recent meta-analyses, when available.

Brief History of Research on Trauma

Although the effects of traumatic events on people have been noted in literature throughout history (Friedman, Resick, & Keane, 2007; van der Kolk, 2007), interest in the effects of trauma within psychology and psychiatry is more recent and has waxed and waned, even within this more recent history (Courtois & Gold, 2009; van der Kolk, 2007). The first edition of the *Diagnostic and Statistical Manual of Mental Disorders* (DSM-I; American Psychiatric Association [APA], 1952) contained the diagnosis of *gross stress reaction* for people who were previously well-adjusted but who had symptoms following extreme stressors such as combat. Interestingly, this diagnosis was dropped from the DSM-II (APA, 1968), which was published at the height of the Vietnam War. During the 1970s, several factors converged to bring increased attention to the issues faced by trauma survivors. Most notable among these was recognition of the problems faced by Vietnam veterans returning from the war and recognition, spurred by the women's movement, of the prevalence of violence against women (e.g., sexual assault, sexual abuse, domestic violence).

Because the symptoms and problems reported by female survivors of sexual violence were very similar to those reported by Vietnam veterans, when the posttraumatic stress disorder (PTSD) diagnosis was first introduced in the DSM-III (1980), reactions to all traumatic events were described under one category. Traumatic events were defined as events that were outside the range of usual human experience that would be very distressing to almost anyone, and symptom criteria were outlined and further refined in the DSM-III-R (APA, 1987). The definition of a trauma was changed in the DSM-IV (APA, 1994) and DSM-IV-TR (APA, 2000) to focus on the subjective experience of the event. Specifically, according to the DSM-IV-TR, an individual has been exposed to a traumatic event if she or he "has experienced, witnessed, or was confronted with an event or events that involved actual or threatened death or serious injury, or a threat to the physical integrity of self or others" (Criterion A1) and "the person's response involved intense fear, helplessness, or horror" (Criterion A2) (APA, 2000, p. 467). Several examples of qualifying events are listed in the DSM-IV-TR for the three categories of directly experienced (e.g., combat, violent personal assault, life-threatening illness), witnessed (e.g., observing the serious injury or unnatural death of another person due to violent assault or accident), and confronted events (e.g., serious accident, sudden unexpected death of a close friend or family member).

Trauma Prevalence

The following section contains a review of the results of large-scale epidemiological studies of trauma prevalence among community samples (see Table 31.1). To narrow the scope, studies of children and adolescents were excluded, as were studies that focused only on specific events, such as spousal abuse. Studies of life events that generally are not considered traumatic (e.g., repeating a grade in school) also were excluded. Because many counseling psychologists work in educational settings as faculty members or as counselors (Munley, Pate, & Duncan, 2008), studies of trauma prevalence among undergraduate students also are reviewed (see Table 31.2). Studies that assess exposure using traumatic event checklists rather than studies that ask a screening question (e.g., Have you ever experienced something traumatic?) will be highlighted because the former method yields higher and presumably more accurate trauma prevalence rates than does the latter (Breslau, 2002; see Peirce, Burke, Stoller, Neufeld, & Brooner, 2009, for a comparison of the two methods). Using trauma checklist measures also is now standard practice in the field (Breslau, 2002). This section concludes with a summary and critique of studies on trauma prevalence.

Trauma Prevalence in Community Samples

One of the largest and best-known studies of trauma prevalence in the United States is the National Comorbidity Survey (NCS; Kessler, Sonnega, Bromet, Hughes, & Nelson, 1995). In the NCS, a nationally representative sample of adults in the United States was surveyed regarding various mental disorders, including PTSD. As part of the assessment of PTSD, respondents were asked whether they had experienced several traumatic events (e.g., combat, rape), all of which qualified as traumas according to the DSM-III-R (APA, 1987). Sixty-one percent of the male respondents and 51% of the

Table 51.1. Epidemiological Studies of Trauma and Posttraumatic Stress Disorder (PTSD) Prevalence

Authors	Sample	Trauma Measure	Trauma Prevalence	PTSD Measure	PTSD Prevalence for Exposed Sample	PTSD Prevalence for Total Sample
Breslau et al. (1998)	Random sample of 2,181 adults aged 18–45 in Detroit, MI (N = 2,181)	19 events grouped into 4 categories	90%	DIS DSM-IV	Lifetime, for random event (9%); for worst event (14%)	N/A
Creamer et al. (2001)	Representative sample of 10,641 adults in Australia	9 events plus "other" event and any "confronted" event	men 64%, women 49%	CIDI DSM-IV PTSD module	N/A	12-month, for worst event (1%)
Elliott (1997)	National, stratified, random sample of 505 adults aged 18–90 in U.S.	13 events grouped into 3 categories	72%	N/A	N/A	N/A
Frans et al. (2005)	Random sample of 1,824 adults aged 18–70 in Sweden	7 events plus "other" event	81%	PTSD Checklist (PCL) DSM-IV	Lifetime, for worst event (7%)	Lifetime, for worst event (6%)
Kessler et al. (1995)	Stratified random sample of 5,887 adults aged 15–54 in U.S.	11 events plus 1 "other" event	men 61%, women 51%	Revised DIS DSM-III-R	Lifetime for worst event (8% for men, 20% for women)	Lifetime for worst event (8%)
Kessler, Berglund, et al. (2005)	Stratified random sample of 5,692 adults over age 18 in U.S.	9 events plus "other" event and any "confronted" event	N/A	CIDI DSM-IV PTSD module	N/A	Lifetime for worst event (7%)
Kessler, Chiu, et al. (2005)	Stratified random sample of 5,692 adults over age 18 in U.S.	9 events plus "other" event and any "confronted" event	N/A	CIDI DSM-IV PTSD module	N/A	12-month, worst event (4%)
Norris (1992)	1000 adults over age 18 in 4 cities in SE U.S. affected by Hurricane Hugo	9 events (besides Hurricane Hugo)	69%	Nonstandard measure; DSM-III-R	Lifetime (7%)	Lifetime (6%)
Perkonigg et al. (2000)	Random sample of 3,021 adolescents and young adults aged 14–24 in Munich, Germany	10 events plus "other" event	21%	CIDI DSM-IV PTSD module	Lifetime, for worst event (8%)	Worst event, lifetime (1%); past 12-months (1%)
Resnick et al. (1993)	Representative sample of 4,008 women age 18 or older in the U.S.	4 types of crime and one category of noncrime events	69%	NWS PTSD module - DSM-III-R	Lifetime (18%); past 6-month (7%)	Lifetime (12%); past 6-months (5%)
Stein et al. (1997)	Random sample of 1,002 adults age 18 or older in Winnipeg, Manitoba, Canada	11 events plus "other" event	women 74%, men 81%	Modified PTSD Symptom Scale, DSM-IV	N/A	Past month, worst event (1% for men, 3% for women)

DIS, Diagnostic Interview Schedule; CIDI, Composite International Diagnostic Interview; NWS, National Women's Study.

Table 31.2. Studies of Trauma and Posttraumatic Stress Disorder (PTSD) Prevalence in Undergraduate Samples

Authors	Sample	Trauma Measure	Trauma Prevalence	PTSD Measure	PTSD Prevalence For Exposed Sample	PTSD Prevalence for Total Sample
Amir and Sol (1999)	Ben Gurion University, Israel (N = 983)	10 events (many military-related), plus other event	67%	Self-report PTSD measure, DSM-IV	Past month (6%)	Past month (4%)
Bernat et al. (1998)	University of Georgia (N = 937)	17 events	67%	Impact of Event Scale-Revised, DSM-IV	Past week, worst event (12%)	Past week, worst event (4%)
Daugherty (1998)	Freshman male military students (N = 515)	24 unspecified events	91%	Modified PTSD symptom scale	N/A	N/A
Frazier, Anders, et al. 2009	Four Universities in US (N = 1,528)	22 events plus "other" event	85%	PTSD Checklist - Specific Version, DSM-IV	Past 2 weeks, worst event (6%)	Past 2 weeks, worst event (5%)
Goodman et al. (1998)	Large Eastern University (N = 202)	11 events and 2 "other" events	72%	N/A	N/A	N/A
Green et al. (2000)	Sophomore women at 6 colleges in Washington DC area (N = 2,507)	11 events and 2 "other" events	65%	Trauma Symptom Inventory	N/A	N/A
Kirk and Dollar (2002)	Rural University in Georgia (N = 234)	11 events	68%	N/A	N/A	N/A
Owens and Chard (2006)	Southern University (N = 221)	10 events	52%	Modified PTSD symptom scale, DSM-IV	N/A	N/A

Scarpa (2001)	Rural Western college (N = 476)	16 witnessed and 9 experienced events of community violence	96% (witnessed); 82% (experienced)	N/A	N/A	N/A
Scarpa et al. (2002)	Unspecified University (N = 518)	16 witnessed and 9 experienced events of community violence	93% (witnessed); 76% (experienced)	N/A	N/A	N/A
Vrana and Lauterbach (1994)	Unspecified University (N = 440)	11 events plus 2 "other" events	84%	Impact of Event Scale, Mississippi Scale, DSM-III-R	N/A	N/A
Watson and Haynes (2007)	University of Hawaii, female students seeking medical care (N = 339)	22 events plus "other" event	94%	Distressing Event Questionnaire, DSM-IV	Past month, worst event (12%)	N/A

Unless stated otherwise, samples include male and female students in United States.

female respondents reported having experienced at least one of these events in their lifetime, and most had experienced more than one event. The most common events were witnessing someone being badly injured or killed; experiencing a fire, flood or disaster; or being involved in a life-threatening accident. Other studies that have assessed nationally representative samples in the United States also reveal high rates (69%–72%) of trauma exposure (Elliott, 1997; Resnick, Kilpatrick, Dansky, Saunders, & Best, 1993).

Other studies have assessed trauma exposure in random samples of adults in cities in the United States and Canada (as opposed to national samples). For example, Breslau et al. (1998) surveyed a large community sample of adults in the Detroit metropolitan area regarding exposure to 19 different events. Using this list of events, 90% of the sample reported experiencing at least one event, with an average of almost five lifetime events. The higher rate of trauma exposure in this study was likely due to the inclusion of sudden death of a close loved one, which was reported by 60% of the sample. Studies in the southeastern United States (Norris, 1992) and in Winnipeg, Canada (Stein, Walker, Hazen, & Forde, 1997) also yielded high (69%–81%) trauma exposure rates.

Three other studies have assessed trauma prevalence in representative samples outside of the United States and Canada. Studies in Australia (Creamer, Burgess, & McFarlane, 2001) and Sweden (Frans, Rimmö, Åberg, & Fredrikson, 2005) yielded fairly high rates of trauma exposure (49%–81%). The trauma prevalence rate in a study of young adults (aged 14–24) in Munich, Germany (Perkonigg, Kessler, Storz, & Wittchen, 2000) was much lower (21%). The authors attributed this to the fact that Germany has few natural disasters, very restrictive weapons laws, and much lower crime rates than the United States.

Trauma Prevalence in Undergraduate Samples

There have been no studies of trauma exposure among undergraduate students in the United States using nationally representative samples (see Table 31.2). Most studies of the prevalence of traumatic events among undergraduate students sample students in one geographic area, and typically at one campus.

One of the largest studies of trauma prevalence among undergraduate students was recently completed by a multisite team of investigators (Frazier, Anders, et al., 2009). In this study, 1,528 students at four U.S. universities completed a validated trauma checklist measure that assessed a wide range of events. The vast majority of the sample (85%) reported experiencing at least one event during their lifetime. The unexpected death of a close friend or loved one, a life-threatening event that happened to a loved one, and witnessing family violence were the most common events. The average number of lifetime events reported was 2.79.

Approximately ten other studies have assessed lifetime trauma prevalence among undergraduate students, primarily in the United States. All of these studies indicated that the majority of students (52%–96%) reported having experienced a traumatic event in their life time. High rates (76%–96%) were reported in two studies that assessed witnessing or experiencing community violence (Scarpa, 2001; Scarpa et al., 2002), and in two studies that assessed a broad range of traumatic events (Vrana & Lauterbach, 1994; Watson & Haynes, 2007). Somewhat lower trauma prevalence rates (52%–72%) were reported in six studies that assessed a narrower range of potentially traumatic events (Amir & Sol, 1999; Bernat, Ronfeldt, Calhoun, & Arias, 1998; Goodman, Corcoran, Turner, Yuan, & Green, 1998; Green et al., 2000; Kirk & Dollar, 2002; Owens & Chard, 2006). For example, Owens and Chard did not include any events that happened to close friends or family members (e.g., life-threatening illness, unexpected death).

Summary and Critique

It is clear from this review that most people report having experienced a traumatic event in their lifetime and that many people report having experienced more than one traumatic event. However, the lifetime trauma prevalence rates do vary considerably. For example, in large-scale epidemiological studies in the United States, trauma prevalence rates ranged from 51% of women in the NCS (Kessler et al., 1995) to 90% of the total sample in the Detroit area study (Breslau et al., 1998). Similarly, in studies of college students, rates ranged from approximately 50% (Owens & Chard, 2006) to over 90% (Daugherty, 1998; Scarpa, 2001, 2002; Watson & Haynes, 2007). Because the specific events that were assessed varied across studies, it is difficult to say which events were most common.

Part of this variability in trauma prevalence rates owes to the lack of consistency across studies in how traumas are defined and assessed. Which specific events are assessed greatly influences overall trauma prevalence rates. For example, studies that do not include the sudden death of a loved one as a trauma report much lower trauma prevalence rates because sudden death is the most commonly reported event in studies that do assess it (see e.g., Breslau et al., 1998; Frazier, Anders, et al., 2009). More consistent use of validated trauma checklists would greatly facilitate comparison of trauma prevalence across studies. Even unvalidated checklists are preferable to open-ended screening questions that ask whether the respondent has experienced anything traumatic which, as noted, result in much lower trauma prevalence rates (e.g., 39%; Breslau, Davis, Andreski, & Peterson, 1991). Using a validated checklist resulted in a nine-times higher trauma prevalence rate than did using an open-ended screening question in one recent study (Peirce et al., 2009).

Another limitation of most studies of trauma prevalence is that they assess lifetime event exposure retrospectively. This is problematic because individuals may not accurately remember what they have experienced (see Rubin, Berntsen, & Bohni, 2008, for a review of research related to memory and PTSD). For example, in a study in which soldiers were asked to report on stressful experiences while in the military both after their return and a few years later, reports of stressful-event exposure increased over time, particularly among those who had more PTSD symptoms (Roemer, Litz, Orsillo, Ehlich, & Friedman, 1998). This illustrates both the inaccuracy of memory and the effect of current distress on retrospective recall. Not surprisingly, consistency in reporting over time varies by event (Krinsley, Gallagher, Weathers, Kutter, & Kaloupek, 2003). For example, directly experienced events were more likely to be remembered than were witnessed events.

Very few studies have assessed trauma exposure prospectively, asking people to describe the events they have experienced over a specific period of time. Although these reports may still be influenced by memory problems and the effects of current mood, they may be more accurate than reports of exposure over a lifetime. They also provide useful data on who is most at risk for experiencing traumatic life events because risk factors can be measured prior to trauma exposure. Frazier, Anders et al. (2009) assessed trauma exposure prospectively in their multisite study and found that 21% of their undergraduate student sample reported experiencing a traumatic event during a 2-month period. Other prospective studies that have assessed trauma exposure over 3- to 4-year periods have found similar rates of trauma exposure (Breslau, Davis, & Andreski, 1995; Stein et al., 2002).

In summary, although these studies consistently suggest that the majority of people experience at least one and probably multiple traumatic events in their lifetime, additional studies are needed that assess trauma exposure in representative samples; that assess a wide range of traumatic events, including the sudden unexpected death of close friends or relatives; that use well-validated trauma exposure measures; and that assess trauma exposure both retrospectively and prospectively.

Individual Differences in Trauma Exposure

Even though overall trauma prevalence rates are high, it is nevertheless the case that some people are at greater risk for trauma exposure than are others. Because of the strong interest among counseling psychologists in issues related to diversity, differences in trauma exposure related to gender, ethnicity, socioeconomic status (SES), and age are highlighted. Information about the demographic distribution of stressful life events can help to identify groups at greatest risk of exposure, which can then guide further research and prevention efforts.

Gender Differences in Trauma Exposure

There is a great deal of interest in gender differences in trauma exposure, because as discussed later, women are much more likely to be diagnosed with PTSD than are men. Gender differences in trauma exposure were assessed in a recent meta-analysis (Tolin & Foa, 2006). Across 19 studies, men were significantly more likely to report having experienced a traumatic event than were women. This was especially true in more rigorous studies (e.g., those that used interviews vs. questionnaires, and epidemiological vs. convenience samples). Tolin and Foa also examined whether men and women differed with regard to exposure to specific events. Specifically, they analyzed 64 studies with 482 independent gender comparisons of the frequency of exposure to nine categories of traumatic events. Men were more likely to report six of the nine events: accidents; nonsexual assault; combat, war, or terrorism; disaster or fire; witnessing death or injury; and illness or unspecified injury. However, women were six times more likely to report having experienced adult sexual assault and were almost three times more likely to report having experienced child sexual abuse. These differences were robust and unaffected by methodological characteristics of the studies. There was no gender difference in reported exposure to nonsexual child abuse or neglect. Thus, whether there is an overall gender difference in trauma prevalence in a specific study will depend on what kinds of traumatic events are assessed. Tolin and Foa did not assess gender differences in reporting the sudden or unexpected death of a loved one, but other studies have not found gender differences in exposure to this event (e.g., Breslau et al., 1998; Frazier, Anders, et al., 2009; Vrana & Lauterbach, 1994).

Racial and Ethnic Group Differences in Trauma Exposure

Data on ethnic and racial group differences in trauma exposure are surprisingly sparse and somewhat inconsistent. In their large-scale epidemiological study, Breslau et al. (1998) examined differences between whites and nonwhites for four classes of events (i.e., assaultive violence, nonassaultive traumas, trauma to others, and unexpected death). Nonwhites reported almost twice as much exposure to assaultive violence as did whites, controlling for several other demographic factors (e.g., education, income). Differences in exposure to other events were small. Another study that compared lifetime exposure to nine traumatic events found that a higher percentage of whites (77%) than African Americans (61%) reported having experienced the traumatic events assessed, even though whites were far more advantaged socioeconomically (Norris, 1992). Differences were significant for four of the nine events (e.g., robbery, physical assault). In a study that compared four specific ethnic groups (i.e., Cubans, Caribbean Basin Hispanics, African Americans, and non-Hispanic whites), non-Hispanic whites reported the highest rates of sexual molestation and physical abuse by someone other than a partner or parent, whereas African Americans reported the highest rates of being threatened or injured with a deadly weapon (Turner & Lloyd, 2004). African Americans reported all six witnessed events (e.g., witnessed someone being killed) more frequently than did the other ethnic groups. African Americans also reported more traumatic events among loved ones (e.g., loved one being attacked or killed with a deadly weapon), whereas hearing of the suicide or rape of someone they knew was more prevalent among white non-Hispanic participants. Overall, African Americans reported the highest number of adversities.

The only study to examine racial/ethnic differences in trauma exposure among undergraduate students found that racial minorities reported significantly more lifetime traumatic events than did white students (Frazier, Anders, et al., 2009).

With regard to specific events, racial minorities were more likely to report having witnessed family violence, having witnessed a beating, having been sexually or physically abused as a child, and having lived in a war zone.

Thus, whether studies find racial/ethnic group differences in trauma exposure depends on a number of factors, including the specific ethnic groups included in the sample, whether or not all ethnic groups were combined into one "minority" group, and the types of events studied. In their review of research on ethnic and racial group differences in exposure to stressful and traumatic life events, Hatch and Dohrenwend (2007) concluded that when racial and ethnic group differences in experiencing prejudice and discrimination are included, African Americans (and perhaps members of other minority groups) tend to experience more stressful events than do whites.

Socioeconomic Status Differences in Trauma Exposure

The data on SES differences in trauma exposure are consistent in showing that individuals from lower SES groups tend to report more traumatic (and stressful) life events than do individuals from higher SES groups (Hatch & Dohrenwend, 2007). For example, the risk of experiencing assaultive violence was approximately twice as high for those with less than high school education (compared to college graduates) and for those with annual incomes of less than $25,000 (compared to those with annual incomes of $75,000 or more; Breslau et al., 1998). Turner and Avison (2003) found that those in the lowest third of the SES distribution reported more lifetime traumas, more witnessed violence, more traumas to people they knew, and more deaths of close associates than did those in the middle or upper third of the SES distribution. In every event category, lower SES was associated with greater stress exposure.

Age Differences in Trauma Exposure

The data regarding age differences in trauma exposure also are consistent across studies. Somewhat surprisingly, younger individuals tend to report more traumatic events than do older individuals (Hatch & Dohrenwend, 2007). For example, in the Detroit area study, the highest risk age for exposure was 16–20, particularly for trauma to others and assaultive violence (Breslau et al., 1998). The only event type that was not most frequent in this age group was the unexpected death of a close friend or family member. Norris (1992) compared lifetime and past-year trauma exposure for younger (18–39), middle-aged (40–59), and older (60+) adults. The three groups did not differ in terms of the overall percentage who reported lifetime trauma exposure (67%–72% across groups), but there were differences in exposure to some specific events. In addition, younger (27%) and middle-aged (21%) adults reported more traumatic events in the past year than did older adults (14%). For example, younger and middle-aged adults were more likely than older adults to report having been physically or sexually assaulted in their lifetime and in the past year. It was not clear whether these differences were due to cohort effects (i.e., young people now are more at risk of violence than were young people in previous generations) or whether older individuals report fewer events because they have forgotten events that happened a long time ago.

Summary and Critique

More research has been conducted on gender differences in trauma exposure than on other types of diversity. This research indicates that men are more likely to experience several types of traumatic events (e.g., accidents) than are women, but that women are much more likely to experience sexual violence. Studies also fairly consistently show that younger individuals and those from lower SES groups are more likely to report traumatic events. To facilitate prevention efforts, the reasons behind the higher rates in these samples need to be explored. For example, Hatch and Dohrenwend (2007) concluded that, to understand why younger individuals report more traumatic events than do older individuals, long-term longitudinal studies are needed in which trauma exposure is assessed over time within individuals using methods that can improve recall of events (see Turner & Lloyd, 2004, for an example). Research on racial and ethnic group differences in trauma exposure is surprisingly sparse and inconsistent.

Effects of Traumatic Life Events

The research reviewed thus far suggests that, when exposure to traumatic events is measured using checklists that assess a broad range of traumatic events, the vast majority of people report having experienced a traumatic event in their lifetime. The obvious next question is: How are people affected by these events? To answer this question, the prevalence of PTSD in the large-scale epidemiological studies of trauma exposure and the studies of trauma exposure in undergraduate students reviewed previously will be highlighted. Although traumatic events can lead to other psychological problems, such as depression and other anxiety disorders (e.g., Krupnick et al., 2004; Turner & Lloyd, 2004), most of the large-scale studies of trauma focus on PTSD.

Diagnostic Criteria for Posttraumatic Stress Disorder

The diagnostic criteria for PTSD in the *DSM-IV-TR* (APA, 2000) consist of five additional criteria (Criteria B–F) besides Criterion A (which defines qualifying traumas). To meet the criteria for a diagnosis of PTSD, individuals who have been exposed to a Criterion A event must report at least one re-experiencing symptom, such as recurrent distressing dreams (Criterion B); at least 3 symptoms reflecting avoidance of stimuli associated with the trauma (e.g., avoiding activities, places, or people) or numbing (e.g., feelings of detachment from others) (Criterion C); and at least two symptoms reflecting increased arousal, such as irritability or difficulty concentrating (Criterion D). The symptoms described in Criteria B, C, and D have to last for at least 1 month (Criterion E), and cause significant distress or impairment in functioning (Criterion F).

Posttraumatic Stress Disorder Prevalence in Epidemiological Studies

Table 31.1 includes the PTSD prevalence rates in large-scale epidemiological studies. As indicated, some studies report the overall lifetime PTSD prevalence rate for the entire sample and some report it for the trauma-exposed sample. Some also report current or past 12-month prevalence rates (vs. lifetime rates). The methods by which PTSD was assessed are included in the table. Most of these studies used structured diagnostic interviews, which is the preferred method of assessment (Weathers, Keane, & Foa, 2009). Lifetime PTSD prevalence rates for those exposed to traumatic events ranged from 7% to 8% for studies conducted outside of the United States (Frans et al., 2005; Perkonigg et al., 2000) to 14% for men and women in Detroit (Breslau et al., 1998), to 18% for a national sample of women in the United States (Resnick et al., 1993). PTSD prevalence rates for representative samples of the U.S. population (regardless of trauma exposure) were very similar in the NCS (8%; Kessler et al., 1995) and in the NCS replication study (7%; Kessler, Berglund, et al., 2005). A similar rate was reported in a national sample in Sweden (6%; Frans et al., 2005), whereas population rates were lower in Munich (1%; Perkonnig et al., 2000) and higher among women in the United States (12%; Resnick et al., 1993).

It is more difficult to compare current (vs. lifetime) PTSD prevalence rates because researchers have used different time frames to define "current" (e.g., past month vs. past year). Nonetheless, current PTSD rates in the population (regardless of trauma exposure) were low (Creamer et al., 2001; Kessler, Chiu, Demler, & Walters, 2005; Resnick et al., 1993; Stein et al., 1997), ranging from 1% of nationally representative samples in Australia (Creamer et al., 2001) and Germany (Perkonnig et al., 2000) to 5% of women in the United States (Resnick et al., 1993). Current PTSD prevalence rates were slightly higher (7%) among trauma-exposed women (Resnick et al., 1993).

Posttraumatic Stress Disorder Prevalence in Undergraduate Samples

Unlike the large-scale epidemiological studies, only four studies of undergraduate students reported PTSD prevalence rates, and all four reported current (vs. lifetime) rates (Amir & Sol, 1999; Bernat et al., 1998; Frazier, Anders, et al., 2009; Watson & Haynes, 2007). None used structured diagnostic interviews to assess all of the diagnostic criteria for PTSD. Rather, probable PTSD prevalence rates were estimated based on responses to self-report measures that assess the PTSD symptoms listed in the DSM-IV. Only two studies (Frazier, Anders, et al., 2009; Watson & Haynes, 2007) used established cutpoints to determine PTSD rates. Current PTSD prevalence rates for trauma-exposed samples ranged from 6% (Amir & Sol, 1999; Frazier, Anders, et al., 2009) to 12% (Bernat et al., 1998; Watson & Haynes, 2007). Current PTSD prevalence for the total samples (including trauma-exposed and nonexposed groups) ranged from 4% to 5% (Amir & Sol, 1999; Bernat et al., 1998; Frazier, Anders, et al., 2009).

Summary and Critique

The evidence reviewed clearly suggests that most people do not develop PTSD following traumatic life events. Lifetime prevalence rates for individuals who have experienced traumatic events ranged from 7% to 18% in large-scale epidemiological studies. Current PTSD prevalence rates were 6%–12% in trauma-exposed undergraduate samples. However, several limitations of these studies are discussed below.

The typical method of assessing PTSD in both community and student samples is to ask respondents if they have experienced each of several traumatic events and, if they have experienced more than one

(which most people have), to pick the worst event and report on PTSD symptoms related to that event. One problem with this method is that it can overestimate the probability of PTSD following traumatic events because these "worst" events might be more likely to result in PTSD than more "typical" events. To address this question, Breslau et al. (1998) compared PTSD prevalence rates for individuals' self-nominated worst events and an event randomly selected from all traumatic events reported. The PTSD prevalence rate was lower for the randomly selected events (9%) than for the self-selected worst events (14%). Thus, the typical method of assessing the effects of self-nominated "worst" events may overestimate the risk of PTSD.

Another issue is that not all studies use structured interviews to assess PTSD. This is particularly true of studies of undergraduate students, but it applies to some epidemiological studies as well (e.g., Norris, 1992). Studies that use self-report measures often do not assess all the criteria necessary to make a diagnosis of PTSD (e.g., impairment). This makes it difficult to compare PTSD prevalence rates across studies because studies using these different methods are not really assessing the same thing.

A final issue with regard to assessing the effects of trauma in terms of PTSD is that, because some PTSD symptoms are linked to a traumatic event (e.g., recurrent thoughts about an event), it is very difficult to compare PTSD symptoms in groups who have and have not experienced traumatic events. Traumatic events can be compared to each other in terms of risk of PTSD, but it is very difficult to know whether individuals experience similar kinds of symptoms without having experienced traumatic events. One study addressed this issue by asking participants (who were all seeking treatment for major depressive disorder) about PTSD symptoms, even if they denied experiencing any traumatic events (Bodkin, Pope, Detke, & Hudson, 2007). Specifically, participants who denied having any traumatic events were asked if they had any thoughts, worries, or fears that had troubled them, and were then asked about PTSD symptoms with regard to these thoughts, worries, or fears. Surprisingly, the PTSD rates did not differ between those who had and those who had not experienced a traumatic event (78% for both groups). This suggests that PTSD symptoms may not be specific to traumatic events.

Risk Factors for Posttraumatic Stress Disorder

The previous review indicates that most people do not develop diagnosable PTSD following traumatic events. However, these overall prevalence rates are averages that combine rates across a range of events and people. One of the central questions in trauma research concerns identifying who is most (and least) at risk of developing PTSD (or more severe PTSD symptoms). Categories of potential risk factors include personal characteristics and background, the nature of the event experienced, subjective reactions to the event, and others' reactions after the event.

Meta-analyses of Risk Factors for Posttraumatic Stress Disorder

To date, two meta-analyses have summarized the results of studies assessing general risk factors for PTSD (Brewin, Andrews, & Valentine, 2000; Ozer, Best, Lipsey, & Weiss, 2003). The goal of Brewin et al.'s meta-analysis was to provide a quantitative estimate of the absolute and relative effect sizes associated with various risk factors for PTSD. They identified 77 studies containing 85 separate datasets that examined the relation between a risk factor and either a PTSD diagnosis or PTSD symptom severity. They included risk factors in their meta-analysis that had been assessed in at least four studies, for a total of 14 factors. These variables can generally be divided into demographic characteristics (i.e., gender, age at trauma, SES, education, intelligence, race), prior history (i.e., previous psychiatric history, prior traumas, childhood abuse, other adverse childhood experiences, family history of psychiatric disorder), event characteristics (i.e., trauma severity), and posttrauma experiences (i.e., life stress, social support).

The relations between all 14 risk factors and PTSD were significant. The effect sizes for the demographic variables were small to moderate (ranging from $r = .05$ for race to $r = .18$ for low intelligence). The effect sizes for the prior history characteristics also were small to moderate and ranged from $r = .11$ (prior psychiatric history) to $r = .19$ (other adverse childhood experiences). The effect size associated with trauma severity was $r = .23$. The largest effect sizes were for the posttrauma variables: posttrauma life stress ($r = .23$) and posttrauma social support ($r = .40$). Thus, the three trauma or posttrauma factors (i.e., greater trauma severity, less social support, more subsequent life stress) were most strongly associated with greater risk of PTSD.

Although all 14 effects were significant, 11 differed significantly across studies. (The three predictors that had similar effect sizes across studies were psychiatric history, childhood abuse, and family psychiatric history.) To explore what might explain the differences in effect sizes across studies, Brewin, Andrews, and Valentine (2000) examined the impact of six sample and study characteristics on the relations between the risk factors and PTSD (e.g., type of trauma, retrospective vs. prospective design). The main conclusion from these analyses was that the relations between many of the risk factors and PTSD differed as a function of these sample and study characteristics. For example, the relation between age at trauma and PTSD was significant in retrospective but not prospective studies. As a result of these complex findings, Brewin et al. concluded that we cannot assume that risk factors are the same across different samples (e.g., men and women; civilian vs. military) or that a single model of risk for PTSD can be developed. Race was one of the few demographic variables that weakly predicted PTSD across all of the studies. However, because race was coded as white majority versus minority group, and the minority category included a wide range of ethnic groups, Brewin et al. warned against drawing any conclusions about the role of race in predicting PTSD.

The other recent meta-analysis (Ozer et al., 2003) focused more specifically on factors that were either characteristics of the person related to psychological processing of the traumatic event (i.e., prior psychological adjustment, family history of psychopathology, prior trauma) or trauma/posttrauma factors (i.e., perceived life-threat, peritraumatic emotions, peritraumatic dissociation, social support). Thus, there was quite a bit of overlap in the risk factors assessed in these two meta-analyses, although Ozer et al. did not include demographic characteristics and Brewin et al. did not include peritraumatic emotions or dissociation. The Ozer et al. meta-analysis included 68 studies, 21 of which were not included in the previous meta-analysis (Brewin, Andrews, & Valentine, 2000). All seven factors were assessed in a minimum of five studies and with at least 600 participants.

As in the previous meta-analysis, all seven factors were significantly related to PTSD. The three person-related variables all had effect sizes (r's) of .17, slightly higher than the effect sizes in the previous meta-analysis for similar factors. The effect size for perceived threat was $r = .26$ (similar to the .23 for trauma severity reported by Brewin, Andrews, & Valentine, 2000). The effect size for social support ($r = .28$) was somewhat smaller than the effect size ($r = .40$) reported by Brewin et al. The effect size for peritraumatic emotions (i.e., negative emotions during or immediately following the trauma) was $r = .26$ and the strongest effect size was for peritraumatic dissociation ($r = .35$).

Ozer et al. (2003) examined four factors that might affect the relations between a given risk factor and PTSD: sample, time since trauma, type of trauma, and method of PTSD assessment (self-report versus interview). Type of trauma was the most consistent moderator: It affected the size of the relation between the risk factors and PTSD for five of the seven risk factors. The basic pattern of findings was that the effect sizes were stronger if the trauma involved noncombat interpersonal violence. In other words, five of the risk factors (e.g., life-threat) were more strongly related to PTSD if the trauma involved interpersonal violence versus other kinds of traumas.

Ozer et al. (2003) concluded their meta-analysis by stating that if they had to "bet" on only one variable in predicting PTSD they would bet on peritraumatic responses (emotions and dissociation). The importance of dissociation was confirmed in a recent meta-analysis, in which the average relation between peritraumatic dissociation and PTSD across 59 studies was .40 (Lensvelt-Mulders et al., 2008). However, the authors of this latter meta-analysis stressed that these significant relations do not necessarily mean that dissociation is causally related to the development of PTSD.

Type of Trauma and Risk for Posttraumatic Stress Disorder

One factor not examined in these meta-analyses is the effect on PTSD rates of the type of trauma experienced (although this was examined as a moderator of the relation between other risk factors and PTSD). Even though overall rates of PTSD are low, some events might be associated with higher PTSD rates than others. Events that are particularly likely to lead to PTSD might be good targets for prevention or outreach efforts. However, differences across events in PTSD prevalence rates are difficult to summarize for a few reasons. First, there is little consistency in the measurement of traumatic events across studies. Second, because studies usually assess multiple (i.e., 10 to 20) events, researchers often do not report statistical comparisons across events. Third, when researchers do report statistical comparisons across event types, they typically combine events into larger categories that may mask the effects of specific events. For example, directly (e.g., life-threatening illness) and indirectly (e.g., witnessing an assault) experienced events are sometimes grouped together

as non-interpersonal traumas, even though these are very different kinds of events. Finally, events may be more likely to lead to PTSD in some groups (e.g., women) than in others (e.g., men), making it difficult to identify an absolute level of risk associated with any given event.

Despite these issues, some consistent findings emerge across studies. Probably the most consistent finding is that sexual assault is associated with among the highest—or the highest—PTSD rates in epidemiological studies. For example, in the NCS (Kessler et al., 1995), rape was associated with higher rates of PTSD for men (65%) than any other event. In one study (Breslau et al., 1991), the PTSD rate for rape was as high as 80% among women. Even when PTSD was assessed with regard to a randomly selected event (vs. a self-nominated worst event), the PTSD rate was higher (49%) for rape than for all other events except being held captive, tortured, or kidnapped (54%; Breslau et al., 1998). In the Swedish study, experiencing sexual assault was associated with a five-times higher risk of developing PTSD (Frans et al., 2005). The same holds true in college student samples: In the Frazier, Anders, et al. (2009) study, sexual assault was associated with the highest current probable PTSD rate (13%). Physical assaults also are associated with high rates of PTSD, especially for women (39% in Resnick et al., 1993; 49% in Kessler et al., 1995). In contrast, some of the events associated with the lowest rates of lifetime PTSD include natural disasters, with PTSD rates of 4%–5% (Breslau et al., 1998; Kessler et al., 1995), and witnessed events, with PTSD rates of 6%–7% (Breslau et al., 1998; Kessler et al., 1995). Thus, although overall PTSD prevalence rates are low, this is somewhat misleading because the probability of developing PTSD depends greatly on what specific traumatic event a person has experienced. The majority of people may develop PTSD following some events, such as rape.

In addition to reporting the risk of PTSD following different events, Breslau et al. (1998) reported the percentage of PTSD cases that were attributable to different events. For example, an event may carry a high risk of PTSD, but if that event is very rare it will not account for a very high proportion of PTSD cases overall. This analysis indicated that the single event that was responsible for the most cases of PTSD was the sudden unexpected death of a close friend or relative. Almost one-third (31%) of all cases of PTSD were attributable to this event because it was the single most common event (reported by 60% of the sample) and because it carried a moderate risk of

PTSD (14%) when randomly selected as the index trauma for PTSD assessment. As a category, assaultive violence accounted for 39% of the PTSD cases. In the NCS, rape and sexual molestation accounted for almost half (49%) of the PTSD diagnoses among women (Kessler et al., 1995).

As mentioned previously, it can be difficult to say which events are most likely to lead to PTSD because PTSD rates may vary across individuals even following the same events. For example, in the NCS, the PTSD prevalence rates differed significantly between men and women for seven of the 12 events (Kessler et al., 1995). Tolin and Foa (2006) examined this issue by assessing the size of the gender difference in PTSD symptoms in 216 studies that compared men and women who had experienced the same events. This analysis also addressed the question of whether gender differences in PTSD remained when differences in the events experienced by men and women were controlled. Their analysis showed that, even when men and women had experienced the same events, women reported more PTSD symptoms ($d = .29$). They also found that, in general, women were two times more likely to meet criteria for PTSD than were men (see Olff, Langeland, Draijer, & Gersons, 2007, for a qualitative review of research on possible factors underlying gender differences in PTSD).

Although it is important to compare PTSD prevalence rates across specific discrete events, due to the number of different traumatic events that can be experienced, this can quickly become unwieldy. Thus, another approach is to identify the underlying dimensions that might discriminate among events and compare events along these dimensions. One such dimension is whether the event was directly or indirectly experienced. The description of Criterion A in the DSM-IV-TR (APA, 2000) explicitly mentions that traumatic events can be directly experienced, witnessed, or can involve learning that a loved one experienced a traumatic event. Surprisingly few studies have directly compared events that vary along this dimension. For example, one study found higher rates of probable PTSD (based on a self-report measure of PTSD symptoms) for events that involved injuries or life-threat to the respondent (19%–24%) than for events that involved injuries or life-threat to someone else (10%–13%) in two undergraduate samples (Bedard-Gilligan & Zoellner, 2008). However, this difference was not apparent in a small community sample of women with trauma histories in the same study (probable PTSD rates of 74% for directly experienced events and 70% for indirectly experienced events). In the Detroit area study, PTSD rates were 21% for directly experienced assaultive violence compared to 2% for learning about events that happened to others (Breslau et al., 1998). However, PTSD rates for all directly experienced events and all indirectly experienced events were not directly compared. This is important because some directly experienced events (e.g., natural disasters) are associated with much lower PTSD rates than are assaultive violence. Two studies that have statistically compared directly and indirectly experienced events have yielded mixed results. In a community sample of 894 women, directly experienced events were associated with an almost four times greater risk of PTSD than were indirectly experienced events (Anders, Frazier, & Frankfurt, 2011). However, in an undergraduate sample, directly experienced events were not associated with higher levels of PTSD symptoms (Frazier, Anders, et al., 2009).

Thus, although the data are not entirely consistent, they generally suggest that directly experienced events are associated with more PTSD symptoms than are indirectly experienced events. Relatedly, perceived life-threat, which would be more likely for directly experienced events, was associated with more PTSD symptoms in Ozer et al.'s (2003) meta-analysis.

Another event characteristic that is not explicitly mentioned in the description of Criterion A in the DSM-IV-TR (APA, 2000) is whether the event was intentionally or unintentionally perpetrated. Events involving intentional harm may be especially likely to shatter one's views about the world and lead to PTSD. For example, one of the reasons why assaultive violence is more associated with PTSD symptoms than are natural disasters may be because the former involves the intentional infliction of harm. Again, few studies have assessed the importance of this event dimension in predicting PTSD. In one national study of injured trauma survivors seen in hospitals around the United States, the risk of probable PTSD (based on a self-report measure) was 1.69 times higher among those who experienced intentional (e.g., physical assaults) versus unintentional (e.g., motor vehicle accidents) injuries (Zatzick et al., 2007). In their study of undergraduate students who had experienced a range of traumatic events, Frazier, Anders, et al. (2009) also found that intentionally perpetrated events were associated with more PTSD symptoms. Although the effect size was small, whether the event was intentionally versus unintentionally perpetrated was as strongly related to PTSD symptoms as was whether or not the event met Criterion A2 (i.e., caused fear, helplessness, or horror).

Other Important Risk Factors for Posttraumatic Stress Disorder

Although the two meta-analyses described above (Brewin, Andrews, & Valentine, 2000; Ozer et al., 2003) were very helpful in identifying the strength of the relation between various risk factors and PTSD, they both also left out some important variables. This is partly because there has been an enormous amount of research on PTSD since these meta-analyses were conducted. A thorough review of this research is beyond the scope of the chapter (for reviews see McKeefer & Huff, 2003; Olff et al., 2007; Ozer & Weiss, 2004). However, factors that appear to hold particular promise for understanding who develops PTSD (or more severe PTSD symptoms) will be highlighted. Although biological factors clearly are important, the focus will be on psychosocial factors that are amenable to change through psychotherapeutic interventions. Several other sources review biological risk factors for PTSD (see e.g., McKeever & Huff, 2003; Nemeroff et al., 2006; Olff et al., 2007; Ozer & Weiss, 2004; Yehuda, 2004).

Appraisals

The two primary meta-analyses (Brewin, Andrews, & Valentine, 2000; Ozer et al., 2003) of general risk factors for PTSD suggested that how the event is appraised by the individual is a key aspect of how the individual will be affected by the event. In fact, subjective reactions to the event in terms of whether it caused fear, helplessness, or horror are part of the criteria for a diagnosis of PTSD (i.e., Criterion A2). According to Olff et al.'s (2007) conceptual model of the development of PTSD, "the appraisal process, reflecting a person's subjective perception, interpretation, and evaluation of the traumatic event, is the crucial first step in the cascade of psychobiological responses that can eventually lead to pathological symptoms" (p. 187). Similarly, in her review, Yehuda (2004) noted that the development of PTSD is not just associated with exposure to trauma, but with how the event is interpreted and how the person acts in the immediate aftermath of the trauma. The primary variables most closely related to appraisals included in the previous meta-analyses were perceived life-threat and peritraumatic emotions. The latter was primarily assessed in terms of Criterion A2 (fear, helplessness, or horror). Both had small to

medium effect sizes in terms of their relations to PTSD. However, many other aspects of the appraisal process may be important in addition to perceived threat and fear, some of which are reviewed below. Cognitive appraisals will be highlighted, consistent with the efficacy of cognitive behavioral approaches to the treatment of PTSD, discussed in a later section.

Ehlers and Clark (2000) developed a cognitive model of PTSD that described numerous types of appraisals that can maintain PTSD symptoms. The basic thesis of their model was that persistent PTSD develops if the way in which individuals appraise the event or its sequelae produces a sense of a serious current threat. Their model includes cognitive processing during the event (e.g., mental defeat), negative appraisals of reactions (e.g., negative appraisals of actions taken during the event), and negative appraisals of event sequelae (e.g., negative appraisals of initial PTSD symptoms).

Dunmore, Clark, and Ehlers (2001) tested this model in a longitudinal study of recent survivors of physical or sexual assault. Cognitive variables were used to predict later PTSD symptoms, controlling for earlier PTSD symptoms. The cognitive variable that was most consistently related to later PTSD symptom severity was negative appraisal of initial PTSD symptoms. Negative appraisals of symptoms involve believing that having PTSD symptoms, such as lack of concentration, mean that one is going crazy or is permanently damaged, as opposed to experiencing a normal reaction to a traumatic event (see also Ehlers, Mayou, & Bryant, 1998).

The Posttraumatic Cognitions Inventory (PTCI; Foa, Ehlers, Clark, Tolin, & Orsillo, 1999) was developed to measure individual differences in appraisals of traumatic events and their sequelae. It includes three subscales: negative cognitions about self, negative cognitions about the world, and self-blame. Respondents answer the questions with regard to thoughts they may have had after the traumatic experience. All three subscales had very high correlations (greater than .56) with a measure of PTSD symptoms in a sample that had experienced a variety of traumatic events. However, in a sample of motor vehicle accident survivors, the negative cognitions about self and world subscales were again highly correlated with PTSD symptoms, but the relation between self-blame and PTSD symptoms was essentially zero (Beck, Coffey, Palyo, Gudmundsdottir, Miller, & Colder, 2004), suggesting that the relations between appraisals and PTSD symptoms may differ across events. One limitation of the PTCI is that the negative cognitions about the self scale, in particular, includes a wide range of items, some of which are appraisals (e.g., "My reactions since the event mean that I am going crazy") and some of which seem to reflect symptoms or consequences of the event (e.g., "I have no future"). Thus, high correlations between this subscale and PTSD may be due to overlap in item content with PTSD measures (which also include items about having a foreshortened future).

Perceived Control

Another aspect of trauma appraisal that is mentioned in many reviews and theoretical accounts is the appraisal of the controllability of the trauma. For example, Foa, Zinbarg, and Rothbaum (1992) developed a theoretical model of the etiology of PTSD that focuses on control. Based on animal research showing that exposure to uncontrollable and unpredictable aversive events leads to PTSD-like symptoms, Foa et al. hypothesized that events that are less controllable and predictable are more likely to lead to PTSD in humans as well. They stressed, however, that perceptions of control are more important than actual contingencies. Foa et al. argued that the perceived uncontrollability and unpredictability of an event are so important that they should be incorporated into the definition of a traumatic event in the DSM. In Olff et al.'s (2007) conceptual model, appraisals that include greater loss of control also are thought to contribute to PTSD.

Despite the importance of control in current theories of the etiology of PTSD and other trauma-related disorders, the ways in which control is conceptualized in these theories do not reflect the complexity of the construct. That is, these theories tend to discuss event controllability as a unitary construct, whereas, in fact, there are various aspects of events over which people can perceive that they have control. In fact, Skinner (1996) identified more than 100 control-related constructs that differ along several dimensions. According to Frazier, Berman, and Steward (2002), the temporal dimension (i.e., past, present, and future) is particularly important for understanding the role of control in adjustment to traumatic life events. Specifically, past control refers to the perception that the occurrence of the event itself was controllable, present control refers to perceived control over the current impact of the event (i.e., current symptoms), and future control refers to perceived control over the event happening again.

Frazier et al.'s (2002) review of the literature using a temporal framework suggested that past, present, and future control had very different relations with measures of posttrauma adjustment and that, contrary to the truism "control is good," perceived control was not always adaptive. That is, past control generally was either not associated with distress or was associated with more distress, present control was nearly always associated with less distress and fewer PTSD symptoms, and future control was generally (although not always) associated with fewer PTSD symptoms. Studies that examined the relation between perceived control and PTSD were rare, however. Subsequent research has confirmed that perceived present control (operationalized as control over the recovery process) was associated with less PTSD symptom severity in survivors of sexual assault and bereavement (Frazier, Steward, & Mortensen, 2004). Moreover, present control was a stronger predictor of PTSD than was either past or future control, and predicted PTSD symptoms controlling for several other important factors such as neuroticism. A measure that assesses these three aspects of perceived control, as well as the perceived likelihood that the event will happen again, has been developed (Frazier, Keenan, et al., 2011). Across several studies conducted in the process of developing this measure, perceived present control had the strongest relations with PTSD symptoms of any of the aspects of control, with effect sizes generally in the medium to large range (Frazier, Keenan, et al., 2011). Thus, individuals who perceive that they have more control over their thoughts, feelings, and reactions to the event report fewer PTSD symptoms. Importantly, unlike the past or the future, the present is something over which one does actually have some control.

Coping

Conceptual models of the development of PTSD often link appraisals, including control appraisals, to the methods individuals use to cope with the traumatic event. For example, in Olff et al.'s (2007) model, "appraisals that include greater threat or loss of control perceptions may contribute to PTSD . . . because they direct coping toward excessive emotional regulation and divert it from problem solving" (p. 185). Negative appraisals are thought to be associated with coping strategies such as disengagement, social isolation, self-destructive behaviors, denial, rumination, and blaming others that consistently have been associated with more posttrauma distress (Olff et al., 2007). Ehlers and Clark (2000) also outlined the coping strategies that follow from specific kinds of negative appraisals. For example, if individuals negatively appraise posttrauma symptoms (e.g., "If I think about the trauma, I will fall apart") they may engage in dysfunctional coping strategies (e.g., trying hard not to think about the trauma, drinking) that may in turn prevent them from developing more positive appraisals. In an empirical test of their model, Dunmore et al. (2001) assessed two forms of dysfunctional cognitive/behavioral coping strategies: avoidance/safety seeking (e.g., avoiding thoughts and activities associated with the trauma) and undoing (i.e., attempts to mentally erase or alter memories of the event). Only the avoidance/safety seeking behaviors predicted later PTSD symptoms, controlling for earlier symptoms. However, as mentioned in relation to the PTCI, there is overlap between the items in the avoidance/safety seeking scale and PTSD symptoms, especially the avoidance symptoms. Thus, although there are consistent relations between avoidance coping and PTSD in the literature, the extent to which the relations are due to item overlap is unclear. In addition, Dunmore et al. did not assess the relations between appraisals and coping. Other studies suggest, however, that control appraisals are associated with coping strategies and that coping mediates the relation between control appraisals and distress. For example, in two samples of sexual assault survivors, self-blame was associated with more distress primarily because it was associated with greater social withdrawal (Frazier, Mortensen, & Steward, 2005). Conversely, present control (perceived control over the recovery process) was associated with less distress because it was associated with less social withdrawal.

Personality

Given the crucial role of appraisals in understanding who develops PTSD, it also is important to identify factors that may put individuals at risk of making more negative appraisals of traumatic events and their sequelae or of perceiving events as less controllable. Identifying pretrauma characteristics that predict appraisals could help us to intervene with at-risk individuals and perhaps teach them skills to appraise events less negatively.

The personality trait of neuroticism has received the most attention in the PTSD literature. Neuroticism is defined as a relatively stable tendency to respond to threat, frustration, or loss with negative emotion (Lahey, 2009). In a recent review of research on neuroticism, Lahey reviewed evidence suggesting that individuals who score higher on measures of neuroticism respond to laboratory and daily stressors with more negative affect. In fact, Lahey noted that "the construct of neuroticism would have little meaning if persons high in neuroticism did not respond with negative emotions more frequently and intensely when they experience stressful life events" (p. 248). With regard to PTSD, in one study, neuroticism significantly predicted PTSD symptoms after controlling for several other important factors (e.g., history of affective disorder, history of multiple trauma exposure; Cox, MacPherson, Enns, & McWilliams, 2004). For women, neuroticism was the only significant predictor of PTSD when other factors were controlled. Both neuroticism and self-criticism were significant in the final model for men. Although this study examined cross-sectional relations between neuroticism and PTSD, prospective studies also have consistently found that neuroticism assessed prior to the trauma predicts higher levels of PTSD following a subsequent trauma (e.g., Bramsen, Dirkzwager, & van der Ploeg, 2000; Engelhard, Huijding, van den Hout, & de Jong, 2007; Frazier, Gavian, et al., 2011; Hodgins, Creamer, & Bell, 2001; Parslow, Jorm, & Christensen, 2006). Individuals higher in pretrauma neuroticism also have been found to appraise subsequent events as more distressing and to perceive that they have less control over their reactions to the event (Frazier, Gavian, et al., 2011).

The relations between other personality-related variables and PTSD also have been established prospectively. For example, in four prospective studies, individuals with higher self-esteem or more positive self-views assessed prior to a trauma reported fewer PTSD symptoms following a subsequent trauma (Bryant & Guthrie, 2005; Card, 1987; Frazier, Gavian, et al., 2011; Lengua, Long, Smith, & Meltzoff, 2005). Pretrauma optimism was identified as a protective factor in two prospective studies (Frazier, Gavian, et al., 2011; Oxlad & Wade, 2008). Both self-esteem (e.g., Adams & Boscarino, 2006) and optimism (e.g., Zoellner, Rabe, Karl, & Maercker, 2008) also were related to lower PTSD symptoms in cross-sectional studies. In their review of cognitive vulnerabilities for PTSD, Elwood and colleagues (2009) identified several personality-related factors that may put individuals at risk for PTSD, including negative attributional style, anxiety sensitivity, and looming cognitive style. However, it was not clear whether any of the relations between these factors and PTSD had been established prospectively. Finally, general self-efficacy beliefs, which involve beliefs that one can control one's environment and cope effectively with challenge, also were related to lower PTSD symptoms (see Luszczynska, Benight, & Cieslak, 2009, for a meta-analysis of studies on self-efficacy and PTSD following collective trauma).

Summary and Critique

In summary, numerous factors have been found to be related to greater risk of PTSD including pretrauma background characteristics of the person, characteristics of the trauma and reactions to it, and posttrauma factors. Among pretrauma factors, neuroticism is one of the most firmly established risk factors, having been established in several prospective studies. Female gender is also a consistent risk factor, with women being twice as likely to develop PTSD as men. The reasons behind this consistent gender difference are not yet fully understood (see Olff et al., 2007; Tolin & Foa, 2006). Several characteristics of the traumatic event itself also are associated with greater risk of PTSD, including whether it was directly (vs. indirectly) experienced and whether it was intentionally (vs. unintentionally) perpetrated. Interpersonal violence, especially sexual assault, is consistently associated with the highest rates of PTSD. More research is needed to understand the factors that make sexual assault so much more distressing than other events. In addition to these objective characteristics, subjective reactions are very important, including subjective appraisals of the event and emotional reactions during the event (e.g., dissociation). Finally, several posttrauma factors are important, including social support following the event (see Charuvastra & Cloitre, 2008, for a recent review of research in this area) and the related constructs of posttrauma appraisals of symptoms and perceived control over one's reactions to the event. Posttrauma factors generally are thought to be more strongly related to PTSD symptoms than are pretrauma factors, but this could be because they are caused by PTSD symptoms as well as cause them. The direction of the relations between posttrauma factors and PTSD symptoms cannot be established using typical cross-sectional designs.

As this last statement suggests, one of the major limitations of research on risk factors for PTSD is that the vast majority of studies assess risk factors retrospectively, after the trauma, at the same time as PTSD symptoms are measured. This is problematic because the effects of the trauma may influence the reporting of pretrauma factors. For example, individuals with more posttrauma distress may retrospectively report more pretrauma distress. Assessing pretrauma factors prior to the event provides a much stronger test of which factors are associated with more or less risk for PTSD. Even if posttrauma factors truly are more important than pretrauma factors, they likely reflect the effects of pretrauma factors (e.g., someone who is more neurotic may be less likely to have adequate social support, which in turn is associated with greater PTSD symptom severity). Knowledge of these pretrauma factors can help us identify individuals who are more at risk of appraising events negatively, perceiving a lack of control, or having inadequate support posttrauma. Thus, knowledge of pretrauma factors can help us identify those most at risk.

Interventions for Posttraumatic Stress Disorder

Even though most people who have experienced traumatic events do not develop PTSD, it is still a relatively common disorder, with an estimated lifetime population prevalence of approximately 7% in the United States (Kessler, Berglund, et al., 2005). In addition, individuals with PTSD are at greater risk for other disorders, including depression, other anxiety disorders, and substance abuse disorders (Breslau, 2002). Fortunately, several forms of psychotherapy and some medications have been found to be effective for PTSD. Prior to describing research on the efficacy of these interventions for PTSD, research on early interventions for trauma survivors, guidelines for the assessment of trauma and PTSD, and theories that inform the interventions for PTSD will be reviewed.

Early Interventions

In their review of research on early interventions for trauma, Litz and Maguen (2007) distinguished among three phases of the posttrauma recovery process. The first phase is the immediate phase (0–48 hours posttrauma). Many people who have experienced a trauma are severely distressed during this phase. The next period is the acute phase, which lasts from a few days to 1 month following the trauma. Distress diminishes greatly between the immediate and acute period for most people. As discussed, even fewer people (less than 10%) develop chronic PTSD with significant symptoms lasting for more than 1 month and sometimes many years following the trauma (chronic phase).

Because many people experience significant distress in the immediate aftermath of trauma, interventions have been developed to decrease distress and prevent chronic PTSD from developing. These immediate interventions are called *psychological debriefing* (PD). The most commonly used form of PD is critical incident stress debriefing (CISD). CISD is typically a single-session intervention lasting 3–4 hours that includes both psychoeducation about stress reactions and emotional processing of the event. Despite its intuitive appeal, expert treatment guidelines have concluded that there is no evidence that single-session PD is effective for preventing the development of PTSD symptoms (Foa, Keane, Friedman, & Cohen, 2009a). Rather, these guidelines recommend that, shortly after a trauma, individuals should be provided with practical psychological support and information about possible stress reactions, how to help themselves, how to access support, and where to get further help if needed. Litz and Maguen (2007) describe this as "psychological first aid." The primary difference between PD and psychological first aid is that the latter does not include emotional processing of the event. For individuals who continue to experience significant distress beyond the immediate posttrauma period, 5 to 12 weekly sessions of CBT is recommended in the acute period (Foa et al., 2009a; Litz & Maguen, 2007). However, at present, the optimal time for intervening is not known. What does seem to be clear is that, because most people recover on their own, it is not appropriate to intervene with everyone. Individuals at high risk, based on the factors outlined previously, should be screened and monitored, and offered CBT if they remain distressed.

Assessment

The assessment of trauma exposure and PTSD symptoms can serve different purposes in different contexts. The specific assessment tools used will vary as a function of the assessment goals, the population and the assessment context, and available resources (Weathers et al., 2009). For example, as noted in the previous discussion of early interventions, one purpose of assessment is to identify traumatized individuals who continue to experience significant distress, and thus may be at greater risk of developing chronic PTSD and may benefit from CBT in the acute posttrauma period. In the more typical general counseling context, given the high prevalence of trauma exposure, it is important to assess lifetime trauma on a routine basis (Weathers et al., 2009). If an individual reports a significant trauma, a comprehensive diagnostic evaluation is needed to determine the presence of PTSD and whether the

PTSD symptoms are the prominent issue (Foa, Keane, Friedman, & Cohen, 2009b). Even if an individual comes to counseling to deal with a specific discrete event (e.g., a sudden death), it is useful to conduct a thorough trauma history because individuals are likely to have experienced more than one traumatic event. The assessment of trauma exposure and PTSD is also done in forensic contexts when, for example, individuals sue for psychological damages following a traumatic event such as a motor vehicle accident.

In their treatment guidelines for the assessment of PTSD, Weathers et al. (2009) reviewed interview and self-report measures of PTSD symptoms that can be used in these various contexts. The National Center for PTSD web site (www.ncptsd.va.gov) also has very useful lists of self-report and interview measures of both trauma exposure and PTSD (see also Keane, Brief, Pratt, & Miller, 2007; Wilson & Keane, 2004). With regard to the assessment of PTSD, Weathers et al. recommended that structured interviews be used whenever possible. If a structured interview is not feasible, self-report measures that assess all of the PTSD diagnostic criteria (e.g., the Posttraumatic Diagnostic Scale; Foa, Cashman, Jaycox, & Perry, 1997) are preferred. Weathers et al. also recommended using multiple assessments whenever possible. They described a typical comprehensive protocol as including a trauma exposure measure, a structured diagnostic interview for PTSD, one or more self-report PTSD measures, a multiscale inventory (such as the Minnesota Multiphasic Personality Inventory [MMPI]) that assesses response bias, and possibly a psychophysiological assessment. This type of comprehensive approach seems particularly important for assessing PTSD in a forensic context but would not be feasible in all settings or contexts.

Theories of the Development of Posttraumatic Stress Disorder

Prior to reviewing evidence regarding the effectiveness of various interventions for PTSD, it is useful to review prominent theories regarding the development of PTSD. These theories inform interventions and must be able to account for the efficacy of interventions. In their review and critique of various theories of PTSD, Cahill and Foa (2007) noted that any adequate theory of PTSD must be able to account for the specific symptoms of PTSD such as re-experiencing and avoidance; the natural course of posttraumatic reactions, including that most people have symptoms immediately posttrauma but do not develop chronic PTSD; and the efficacy of CBT for PTSD.

Cahill and Foa (2007) reviewed five categories of theories of PTSD: conditioning theories, schema theories, emotional processing theory, cognitive theories, and theories positing multiple representation structures. Some of these theories, such as Ehlers and Clark's (2000) cognitive theory of PTSD, have been mentioned in the previous description of research on risk factors for PTSD. The key features of these models are described below (see Cahill & Foa, 2007, for more information).

Conditioning theories (e.g., Keane, Zimerling, & Caddell, 1985) explain the development of PTSD through the processes of classical and operant conditioning. Specifically, fear is acquired through the process of classical conditioning because previously neutral stimuli (e.g., time of day, smells) that were present during the trauma become associated with intense anxiety. Avoidant symptoms are acquired through the process of operant conditioning. In other words, because the trauma memory and other stimuli elicit fear and anxiety, they are avoided. This avoidance in turn reduces fear and anxiety. However, this avoidance also prevents the extinction of the link between the previously neutral stimuli and anxiety.

Schema (also called social-cognitive) theories (e.g., Horowitz, 1986; Janoff-Bulman, 1992) draw from theories in personality and social psychology rather than from learning theories. These theories focus on the impact of traumatic events on people's preexisting schemas (i.e., core assumptions and beliefs) about the world and the self. Often these theories assume that a traumatic event shatters preexisting positive beliefs, such as that the world is safe, people are good, and the self is strong and competent. Information about self and the world emanating from the trauma that is inconsistent with these preexisting positive beliefs must be assimilated into existing beliefs, or existing beliefs must be accommodated to incorporate information about the self and world learned from the trauma. The recovery process involves repetitive efforts to integrate these two sources of information, which is thought to explain the reexperiencing symptoms of PTSD. Competing with this is the tendency to avoid the distress caused by the reexperiencing symptoms, which accounts for the avoidance symptoms of PTSD. However, avoidance prevents the resolution of the discrepancy between existing beliefs and trauma-related information.

Emotional processing theory was originally developed to explain the development of anxiety disorders (e.g., Foa & Kozak, 1986) but was later expanded to include a comprehensive theory of PTSD (Foa & Jaycox, 1999). The two main premises of emotional processing theory are that anxiety disorders (including PTSD) reflect the presence of pathological fear structures in memory and that successful treatment involves modifying these fear structures so that stimuli that once evoked anxiety no longer do so. Natural recovery results from activation of the trauma memory through engaging trauma-related thoughts and feelings, talking about the trauma with others, and being confronted with reminders of the trauma. All of these processes will result in the trauma survivor being confronted with information that is inconsistent with information in the fear structure, such as that the world is dangerous. The development of PTSD is thought to result from a failure to process the trauma adequately.

Cognitive theories of PTSD, like cognitive theories of depression and anxiety, focus on individuals' interpretation of a traumatic event. According to Ehlers and Clark's (2000) cognitive theory, PTSD results when an individual's interpretation of the event or its consequences leads to a sense of current threat. The nature of the traumatic memory can also lead to a sense of current threat in this model. For example, fragmented trauma memories, the perception of the memory as happening in the present, and lack of incorporation of the trauma memory with other memories are thought to explain why a past event can cause a sense of current threat.

Theories positing multiple representation structures derive from research in cognition and cognitive neuroscience. These theories describe different memory systems that can in turn explain different types of PTSD symptoms. One impetus for these theories is the belief that the concept of a single emotional memory is too narrow to explain the symptoms of PTSD. One example of this type of theory is dual-representation theory (Brewin, Dalgleish, & Joseph, 1996), which posits two memory systems: verbally accessible memory and situationally accessible memory. As the name implies, verbally accessible memories contain information about the traumatic event and its meaning that can be deliberately retrieved and communicated. Situationally accessible memories cannot be deliberately recalled but are triggered by reminders of the trauma and are responsible for the re-experiencing and arousal symptoms of PTSD. According to this theory, emotional processing of the event involves activating the situationally accessible memories, so that they can be altered or replaced and changing the verbally accessible memories to reconcile discrepancies between preexisting beliefs and trauma-related information (similar to schema theories).

In sum, although the theories differ, they all propose that the reduction of PTSD symptoms involves exposure to the event (e.g., to change fear structures or memories) and reinterpretation of the event and its meaning (e.g., reconciling the trauma with existing beliefs). Thus, it is not surprising that effective treatments for PTSD involve exposure and CBT, as described below.

Psychosocial Interventions for Posttraumatic Stress Disorder

Two meta-analyses describe the evidence for both the absolute and relative efficacy of psychotherapeutic interventions for PTSD (Bisson et al., 2007; Bradley, Greene, Russ, Dutra, & Westen, 2005). Although the two reviews differed somewhat in the comparisons they reported and how they categorized treatments, some general conclusions can be drawn. First, with regard to absolute efficacy, several treatments have been shown to be more effective than wait-list or supportive counseling control conditions. These include exposure therapy, CBT, exposure plus CBT, and eye movement and desensitization and reprocessing (EMDR). The effect sizes for comparisons of these treatments to wait-list control groups were large (ds = 1.11 to 1.53) in both meta-analyses. In other words, on average individuals who received one of these treatments scored more than 1 standard deviation lower on measures of PTSD symptoms than did individuals on a wait-list who received no treatment. Effect sizes for comparisons to supportive counseling control conditions were somewhat lower (ds = .75 to 1.01) but still large (Bradley et al., 2005). Effect sizes associated with pre- to post-treatment reductions (vs. comparisons to control groups) in symptoms also were large for these treatments (ds = 1.43 to 1.66; Bradley et al., 2005). The pre- to post-treatment effect size was .59 for the supportive counseling control conditions (and these conditions did not differ from wait-list control conditions, d = -.01). Across active treatments, 67% of those who completed treatment no longer met criteria for PTSD at the end of treatment, although many of those who no longer met PTSD criteria remained symptomatic (Bradley et al., 2005). Second, with regard to relative effectiveness, in both meta-analyses differences between treatments were small (see also Benish, Imel, & Wampold, 2008). For example, studies that directly compared exposure therapy to other kinds of treatment yielded

an average effect size of d = .11. Although differences between treatments were small, there tended to be more studies that have established the effectiveness of exposure, CBT, or exposure plus CBT than studies that have established the effectiveness of EMDR.

Another excellent resource for information on the efficacy of various interventions for PTSD is the set of treatment guidelines developed by a task force of the International Society for Traumatic Stress Studies (ISTSS; Foa et al., 2009a). This book contains chapters summarizing evidence regarding the efficacy of various forms of treatments for PTSD for adults, children, and adolescents, followed by briefer treatment guidelines. The review was not limited to empirically supported treatments and the evidence for each form of intervention was graded in terms of six levels, reflecting the strength of the evidence. Consistent with the results of the meta-analyses described previously, these treatment guidelines recommended CBT (which includes exposure therapy) as the first-line treatment for both acute and chronic PTSD. According to Friedman et al. (2007), all clinical practice guidelines identify CBT as the treatment of choice for PTSD.

The ISTSS guidelines also provide information for practitioners to use in treatment planning. In terms of treatment duration, they offered a general guideline of 8 to 12 sessions lasting 60 to 120 minutes each, administered once or twice weekly. They also concluded that there was more evidence for the efficacy of individual than of group therapy. The guidelines also stressed the importance of establishing a trusting relationship with the client, assessing the client's safety, providing education and reassurance regarding PTSD symptoms, monitoring the client's symptoms and functioning over time, and identifying and addressing any comorbid problems and issues. Assessing and addressing readiness for treatment also is important. Because avoidance is one of the hallmark features of PTSD, many clients are reluctant to seek help that may involve confronting the trauma. They may need to be educated and reassured about the treatment process. Engaging clients with PTSD in the therapy process is a crucial first stage in treatment (Friedman, Cohen, Foa, & Keane, 2009).

The ISTSS guidelines also reviewed evidence regarding whether the effectiveness of PTSD treatment varies as a function of various factors (Foa et al., 2009b; Friedman et al., 2009). This review suggested there was no conclusive evidence that the effectiveness of PTSD treatment depends on the type of trauma that caused the PTSD, whether the PTSD was due to single or multiple traumas, or the client's gender or age at time of trauma exposure. However, there generally is little research on these issues. Research also has not reached the point at which we can identify specific types of treatments that are more effective for certain types of clients. The guidelines do, however, provide some guidance on choosing among treatment approaches by, for example, considering client preferences, cultural acceptability, cost, and availability of resources (Friedman et al., 2009, pp. 632–634). Data on the most effective combinations of treatments also are lacking, although, again, some guidelines are provided regarding how to most effectively combine treatments (Friedman et al., 2009, pp. 635–637). The authors also acknowledged that little is known about the treatment of PTSD for people in nonindustrialized countries.

Pharmacological Interventions

Evidence regarding the effectiveness of psychotropic medications for treating PTSD is less conclusive than the evidence for the effectiveness of psychotherapeutic interventions. In one recent review of randomized controlled trials of pharmacotherapy for PTSD, symptom severity was significantly reduced in 17 of the 35 trials (Stein, Ipser, & Seedat, 2006). There was most evidence for the efficacy of selective serotonin reuptake inhibitors (SSRIs). The PTSD treatment guidelines developed by ISTSS (Foa et al., 2009a) concluded that both SSRIs and serotonin-norepinephrine reuptake inhibitors (SNRIs) can be recommended as first-line treatments for PTSD. However, they also concluded that these medications are not as effective as CBT and that relapse is more likely after discontinuing medications than after completing psychotherapy. Other evidence-based guidelines have concluded that medications should not be used as a routine first-line treatment for PTSD in adults (National Collaborating Centre for Mental Health, 2005).

Posttraumatic Growth

Thus far, the focus has been on PTSD as the primary outcome of trauma. However, a growing body of research focuses on the positive transformations that can occur in individuals' lives following traumatic events. This phenomenon is referred to as *posttraumatic growth, stress-related growth, benefit-finding,* and *positive life change* in the literature. The term posttraumatic growth (PTG) will be used here, which tends to be most common. Using these search terms in the PsychInfo database resulted in 434 hits

just between 2002 and 2009. There are also frequent anecdotal reports in the media regarding positive life transformations following traumatic events. In the following, evidence regarding the prevalence and correlates of self-reported PTG will be reviewed, followed by a discussion of some concerns that have been raised about the validity of self-reported growth. Tedeschi and Calhoun (2004) and Joseph and Linley (2005) provide theoretical accounts of the development of PTG.

Substantial evidence suggests that most people who have experienced traumatic events report experiencing positive life changes as a result of those events. For example, more than 80% of women with cancer (Sears, Stanton, & Danoff-Burg, 2003) and HIV/AIDS (Siegel & Schrimshaw, 2003) reported at least one positive change in their life resulting from their illness. Similar findings have been reported in individuals who have experienced other events including bereavement (Davis, Nolen-Hoeksema, & Larson, 1998), disasters (McMillen, Smith, & Fisher, 1997), and sexual assault (Frazier, Conlon, & Glaser, 2001). The positive changes most frequently reported include greater life appreciation, closer relationships with family and friends, changed priorities (e.g., more concern for others, more compassion), greater spirituality and religiousness, and positive self-changes (e.g., feeling stronger).

A recent meta-analysis reviewed 87 studies reporting data on correlates of PTG and relations between measures of PTG and distress or well-being (Helgeson, Reynolds, & Tomich, 2006). Research on correlates of PTG addresses the question of whether certain types of people are more likely to report growth following traumatic events or whether certain types of events are more likely to lead to growth. Specifically, their review focused on four categories of variables that have often been examined as correlates of PTG: demographic factors ($n = 5$), stressor characteristics ($n = 3$), personality-related variables ($n = 3$), and coping strategies ($n = 3$). Of the 14 variables assessed, ten had significant relations with PTG although the relations generally were small. For example, of the five demographic variables the strongest relation ($r = -.08$) indicated that women reported more PTG than did men. Of the three stressor characteristics, perceived stressor severity had the strongest relation with PTG ($r = .14$) indicating that individuals who perceived the events they experienced as more stressful reported more growth. With regard to personality, neuroticism ($r = -.05$) was not associated with PTG, but individuals who were more optimistic ($r = .27$) and more religious ($r = .17$)

reported more growth. Positive reappraisal coping had the strongest relation with PTG ($r = .38$), which is not surprising given that positive reappraisal involves finding benefits in difficult events.

The Helgeson et al. (2006) meta-analysis also addressed the important question of the relation between measures of PTG and more traditional measures of distress and well-being posttrauma. If PTG is an adaptive response to trauma one would expect individuals who report more growth to report less distress. Conversely, if growth is more likely following more stressful events, and arises from dealing with event-related distress, one might expect positive relations between PTG and distress. Or, growth and distress may be separate outcomes that are essentially unrelated to each other. Helgeson et al., in fact, found complicated relations between measures of PTG and distress and well-being in their meta-analysis. For example, PTG was negatively related to depression ($r = -.09$), unrelated to anxiety ($r = -.02$), and positively related to the PTSD symptoms of intrusion and avoidance ($r = .18$). Moreover, these effects differed significantly across studies and were moderated by several variables, including time since the trauma occurred. For example, intrusive thoughts were more related to PTG in studies in which the trauma was more recent ($r = .23$) than in studies in which the trauma was less recent ($r = .08$).

Helgeson et al. (2006) concluded that one reason for the inconsistent relations between measures of PTG and distress was the lack of clarity regarding what PTG measures actually assess. That is, does self-reported PTG reflect actual change in people's lives, or does it reflect a cognitive strategy of coping with distress not necessarily reflective of actual change? Because virtually all data on PTG consist of survivors' reports that they have experienced various positive life changes, concerns about whether these reports reflect actual life changes are increasingly being raised.

There are several reasons to suspect that reports of PTG may not represent actual life changes. First, people may describe the positive things that came out of a trauma because they want to appear to be coping well or because they think that is what others want to hear. This cultural script may be particularly prevalent in the United States (Steger, Frazier, & Zacchanini, 2008). Second, reports of growth may reflect motivated illusions. McFarland and Alvaro (2000) presented convincing evidence that people report that they have changed as a result of traumatic events not because they have actually grown but because they derogate their past selves. Third, some

survivors actually report decreases over time in self-reported growth (Frazier et al., 2001). "Growth" that does not last would not seem to reflect actual growth. Finally, research in other domains suggests that people generally are not very accurate in assessing the degree to which they have changed over time. For example, assessments of perceived personality change have small correlations with actual personality change in longitudinal studies (e.g., Robins, Noftle, Trzesniewski, & Roberts, 2005). Such assessments of change are what measures of PTG require.

Several methods have been used to assess the validity of self-reported PTG and studies using these methods generally do not find strong evidence that reports of growth reflect actual life change. For example, studies that assess whether significant others corroborate growth reports show only modest concordance between trauma survivors and their significant others (McMillen & Cook, 2003; Park, Cohen, & Murch, 1996). If individuals have truly changed, significant others should recognize and report the change as well. Another approach involves comparing the well-being of individuals who experienced a trauma to a matched comparison group of individuals who did not experience a trauma. A variation of this approach involves comparing the well-being of individuals who reported growth from a trauma to that of their counterparts who reported no growth. Frazier and Kaler (2006) used both approaches and found little evidence to support the validity of self-reported PTG. For example, there were no significant differences in well-being between undergraduate students who said that something positive had come out of their worst stressor and those who reported no positives. Finally, a recent study found only modest (r's = .04 to .22) correlations between self-reported PTG and actual change from pre- to post-cancer treatment (Ransom, Sheldon, & Jacobsen, 2008). If self-reported PTG reflects actual positive change, one would expect a stronger correlation.

Although these studies yield useful information about the correlates of perceived growth, the best way to assess whether perceived growth corresponds to actual growth is to conduct a prospective study in which self-reported growth is compared to actual growth from pre- to posttrauma. Such a study recently was conducted, which is the first in the literature (Frazier, Tennen, et al., 2009). To assess pretrauma functioning, a large group of undergraduate students was assessed at baseline and 2 months later. The expectation was that a small percentage would experience a major trauma over that time period.

If a participant reported a traumatic event during that time, their pre- and posttrauma scores on various PTG-related domains (to measure actual growth) were compared to their scores on a self-report measure of PTG (to measure perceived growth) after the trauma. The self-report measure used was the Posttraumatic Growth Inventory (PTGI; Tedeschi & Calhoun, 1996). If the PTGI measures actual growth, the two scores should be at least moderately correlated. However, the correlation between actual posttraumatic growth and PTGI scores was fairly small ($r = .22$). In addition, higher scores on the PTGI (perceived growth) were related to greater increases in distress from pre- to posttrauma and more positive reappraisal coping posttrauma, suggesting that the PTGI may be measuring coping as opposed to actual growth. In contrast, actual growth from pre- to posttrauma (e.g., improved relationships) was associated with decreases in distress from pre- to posttrauma. In a follow-up study, there were much stronger relations between perceived and actual growth among trauma survivors who were less distressed posttrauma than in those who were more distressed posttrauma, supporting the notion that reporting PTG may be a strategy for coping with distress (Gunty, Frazier, Tennen, Tashiro, & Tomich, 2011).

The previous section should not be taken to imply that some people do not grow following traumatic events. Clearly they do. In the prospective study described above (Frazier, Tennen, et al., 2009), 25% of the sample reported reliable increases in life satisfaction from pre- to posttrauma (although those increases were not necessarily due to the trauma). The accumulating data do suggest, however, that retrospective self-reports of growth following trauma do not necessarily reflect actual growth from pre- to posttrauma. As a result, some researchers have commented that propagating the notion that most people experience actual growth can have adverse effects on trauma survivors (e.g., Wortman, 2004). This is illustrated in a book, written by a cancer survivor, who said "For at least a year after I had breast cancer, my friends would ask me what I'd learned from it. And I admit I fell prey to the media hype a little. I did think there ought to be something I could point to . . . I hated to let everyone down" (Lewis, 2008, p. 9). This is not another burden we want to add to individuals struggling to cope with traumatic life events.

Future Directions in Trauma Research

This final section outlines some of the most pressing questions and issues that need to be addressed in future research on trauma. Issues related to each of the broad topics reviewed previously will be highlighted. This list is by no means exhaustive but does provide some directions for future research.

Trauma Prevalence

As mentioned previously, trauma prevalence rates depend greatly on how traumatic events are measured and defined. One definition of a "traumatic" event is that contained in PTSD Criterion A in the DSM-IV, which focuses on whether the event was life-threatening. However, there is considerable debate in the literature regarding whether events need to meet Criterion A to lead to PTSD (see Rosen & Lilienfeld, 2007, for a review). In fact, several studies have found that events that do not meet Criterion A1 are just as likely (Anders et al., 2011; Green et al., 2000) or more likely (e.g., Gold, Marx, Soler-Baillo & Sloan, 2005) to lead to PTSD than are Criterion A1 events. Thus, Criterion A1 may be changed, or even eliminated, in the upcoming DSM-V. Criterion A2 (experiencing fear, helplessness, or horror) also is problematic and may be changed or eliminated because other emotions (e.g., guilt, shame, anger) may be as or more important in predicting who develops PTSD (Brewin, Andrews, & Rose, 2000). Unless researchers assess non-Criterion A1 events and emotions besides fear, helplessness, or horror, we will not have a complete picture of which events are most distressing or which peritraumatic emotions are most important. One category of event that deserves further attention is the category of interpersonal traumas, such as ostracism, discrimination, and betrayal. Even though these typically do not involve life-threat, there is a great deal of evidence suggesting that they are very distressing and threaten basic belongingness needs (see Smart Richman & Leary, 2009). Researchers also need to take into account the fact that there are cultural variations in what is considered traumatic. For example, in one study of Tibetan refugees, the destruction of religious sites (e.g., temples) and signs was rated as the worst possible event that could ever happen (Terheggen, Stroebe, & Kleber, 2001). Such an event would not count as a trauma according to Western definitions.

Risk of Trauma Exposure

The previous review focused on demographic difference in risk for trauma exposure. This review revealed a need for more research on risk for trauma exposure among specific ethnic groups and research exploring the reasons behind the counterintuitive finding that younger individuals report more lifetime traumas than do older individuals. Additional studies also are needed that move beyond the assessment of demographic differences in risk of trauma exposure. Prospective studies in which risk factors are assessed prior to trauma exposure are most useful. When "risk" factors are assessed at the same time as lifetime trauma exposure, the risk factors (e.g., neuroticism) may influence the reporting of past traumatic events. Further research also is needed that explores risk factors for different types of events. For example, the predictors of traumatic events in childhood differ from the predictors of traumatic events in adulthood (Breslau, Davis, & Andreski, 1995). Hatch and Dohwenrend (2007) distinguished between fateful events and events that may have been brought about by the behavior of the individual, which also may have different predictors. Finally, we need effective interventions for preventing traumatic events, particularly those that, like sexual assault, carry a high risk for PTSD. Most sexual assault prevention programs focus on changing attitudes on the assumption that changed attitudes will result in changed behavior but few programs have been shown to reduce the actual risk of perpetration or victimization (Anderson & Whiston, 2005).

Effects of Trauma

The 2008 and 2009 conferences of the ISTSS contained a great deal of programming related to possible changes to the PTSD criteria in the DSM-V. These changes include whether PTSD will continue to be classified as an anxiety disorder or whether there will be a new category of trauma-related disorders. Given that the DSM is a diagnostic classification scheme used around the world, one recurring theme in these discussions was the need for cross-cultural research on the effects of trauma that assesses both universal and cultural-specific symptoms. According to Miller (2006), "a strict reliance on the language and constructs of Western psychiatry risks inappropriately prioritizing psychiatric syndromes that are familiar to Western practitioners, such as . . . PTSD, but that may be of secondary concern or simply lack meaning to non-Western populations for whom local idioms of distress are more salient" (p. 423). For example, studies that move beyond Western paradigms have identified unique symptoms of distress among Africans that differ from those recognized in Western psychology including "crawling" beneath or on the scalp, intense heat in the body or head, and perceived sudden movements of the heart (e.g., "heart flying out") (Rasmussen, Smith, & Keller, 2007).

Risk Factors for Posttraumatic Stress Disorder

One conclusion drawn by several authors who have reviewed the literature on PTSD risk factors is that more complex models of the development of PTSD need to be developed and tested (Brewin, Andrews, & Valentine, 2000; Elwood et al., 2009; Ozer et al., 2003; Ozer & Weiss, 2004). These models could involve either interactions (moderator effects) among risk factors or the posttrauma mechanisms (mediator effects) by which pretrauma risk factor are associated with greater symptom severity. The need for examining moderator effects was illustrated by the findings of both meta-analyses (Brewin, Andrews, & Valentine, 2000; Ozer et al., 2003) that the relations between risk factors and PTSD symptom depended on (i.e., were moderated by) other factors (e.g., gender, type of trauma). For example, McKeever and Huff (2003) have developed a diathesis-stress model of PTSD in which biological (e.g., genetic) and ecological (e.g., personal history, social support) factors interact with each other and with trauma severity in predicting PTSD (see also Olff et al., 2007). With regard to mediators, the mechanisms by which pretrauma factors (ideally measured prior to the trauma) are related to the development of PTSD need to be identified (see Engelhard, van den Hout, Kindt, Arntz, & Schouten, 2003; Frazier, Gavian, et al., 2011; Lengua, Long, & Meltzoff, 2006, for examples).

Interventions

As mentioned, several treatments have been identified that are effective in treating PTSD, such as exposure therapy and CBT. Bradley et al. (2005) described some of the limitations of existing PTSD treatment efficacy studies. One limitation is the lack of systematic data on comorbidity in patient samples. Given that comorbidity is the rule rather than the exception in individuals with PTSD (Breslau, 2002), lack of data on this issue makes it difficult to assess the generalizability of treatment findings.

Rather than review the limitations of existing treatment outcome studies, the need for innovative treatments and service delivery formats that can reach individuals who may not be interested in traditional psychotherapy is highlighted. This includes veterans who may find seeking help too stigmatizing, individuals from cultures in which psychotherapy is not commonly used, or individuals who have experienced traumas they may not wish to disclose, such as sexual assault. All the best treatments in the world will not help if the barriers to using them are too great. For example, the Department of Defense and the Veteran's Administration have funded a project to develop and implement an Internet-based intervention for veterans that reduces many of the barriers to treatment-seeking among this group (e.g., stigma). The ISTSS treatment guidelines for PTSD (Foa et al., 2009a) concluded that technological innovations in service delivery (e.g., virtual reality, Internet-based interventions) show promise in making treatments more readily available. The National Institute on Drug Abuse has funded a study to evaluate the effectiveness of brief video-based interventions for sexual assault survivors in the emergency room, one of which has been found to be effective in a previous study (Resnick, Acierno, Holmes, Kilpatrick, & Jager, 1999). Because many sexual assault survivors do not return for follow-up services (Rosenberger, Frazier, & Moore, 2000), the emergency room may be the one chance to intervene with survivors. Finally, a qualitative study with Somali refugees is being conducted to understand the reasons behind the low service utilization rates for this group and to develop more culturally appropriate interventions. For example, even though many Somali refugees have been tortured, very few (less than 1%) requested or accepted referrals for Western mental health services (Jaranson et al., 2004).

Posttraumatic Growth

As suggested by the previous review of research on PTG, one of the most important tasks is to further explore what scores on PTG inventories actually represent. Frazier and Kaler (2006) outlined a future research agenda for PTG that included the need for studies in which data are collected prospectively prior to the trauma to assess actual change from pre- to posttrauma, studies that assess whether self-reports of growth are evident in actual behaviors either in laboratory or real-life situations, and studies that examine whether individuals who report that they have grown from a traumatic event are better able to cope with future traumas. Research also is needed on the antecedents and consequences of both perceived and actual growth, which may very well differ. Even if measures of perceived growth do not measure actual growth, they still may predict important outcomes.

Conclusion

Given that almost everyone experiences a traumatic event in their lifetime, counseling psychologists in practice are going to see clients who have experienced traumatic events. Thus, it is imperative that counseling psychologists are aware of research related to trauma and are trained to work with trauma survivors. According to Courtois and Gold (2009), training in trauma-related topics has been largely ignored in psychology or offered in specialty courses outside of the main curricula. Given the prevalence and effects of trauma, Courtois and Gold decry this situation, stating that "the noninclusion of information in psychology about trauma as a major aspect of human experience and as a substantive contributor to derailment of normative development and the development of psychopathology defies logic" (p. 12). They propose that basic information about trauma be integrated throughout the psychology curriculum, beginning at the undergraduate level and continuing through all aspects of graduate training (e.g., coursework, practica, research). Their article also provides information on existing training programs and resources.

As argued at the beginning of the chapter, counseling psychology is particularly well-suited to contribute to the understanding and treatment of trauma-related problems. As shown in this chapter, these events happen to almost everyone, and most people recover from them without developing diagnosable psychological disorders such as PTSD. Thus, trauma psychology fits well within counseling psychology's emphasis on normal human functioning and positive adaptation. However, at this point, trauma research is not well-represented in counseling journals. Hopefully, this chapter will serve to encourage more counseling psychologists to contribute to this important area of research and practice and to focus on the normative processes of resilience following traumatic life events.

References

Adams, R. E., & Boscarino, J. A. (2006). Predictors of PTSD and delayed PTSD after disaster: The impact of exposure and psychosocial resources. *Journal of Nervous and Mental Disease, 194*, 485–493.

American Psychiatric Association (APA). (1952). *Diagnostic and statistical manual of mental disorders*. Washington, DC: Author.

American Psychiatric Association (APA). (1968). *Diagnostic and statistical manual of mental disorders* (2nd ed.). Washington, DC: Author.

American Psychiatric Association (APA). (1980). *Diagnostic and statistical manual of mental disorders* (3rd ed.). Washington, DC: Author.

American Psychiatric Association (APA). (1987). *Diagnostic and statistical manual of mental disorders* (3rd ed., text rev.). Washington, DC: Author.

American Psychiatric Association (APA). (1994). *Diagnostic and statistical manual of mental disorders* (4th ed.). Washington, DC: Author.

American Psychiatric Association (APA). (2000). *Diagnostic and statistical manual of mental disorders* (4th ed., text rev.). Washington, DC: Author.

Amir, M., & Sol, O. (1999). Psychological impact and prevalence of traumatic events in a student sample in Israel: The effect of multiple traumatic events and physical injury. *Journal of Traumatic Stress, 12*(1), 139–154.

Anders, S., Frazier, P., & Frankfurt, S. (2011). Variations in Criterion A and PTSD prevalence rates in a community sample of women. *Journal of Anxiety Disorders, 26*, 176–184.

Anderson, L. A., Whiston, S. C. (2005). Sexual assault education programs: A meta-analytic examination of their effectiveness. *Psychology of Women Quarterly, 29*(4), 374–388.

Beck, J. G., Coffey, S. F., Palyo, S. A., Gudmundsdottir, B., Miller, L. M., & Colder, C. R. (2004). Psychometric properties of the Posttraumatic Cognitions Inventory (PTCI): A replication with motor vehicle accident survivors. *Psychological Assessment, 16*, 289–298.

Bedard-Gilligan, M., & Zoellner, L. A. (2008). The utility of the A1 and A2 criteria in the diagnosis of PTSD. *Behavior Research and Therapy, 46*, 1062–1069.

Benish, S. G., Imel, Z. E., & Wampold, B. E. (2008). The relative efficacy of bona fide psychotherapies for treating post-traumatic stress disorder: A meta-analysis of direct comparisons. *Clinical Psychology Review, 28*(5), 746–758.

Bernat, J. A., Ronfeldt, H. M., Calhoun, K. S., & Arias, I. (1998). Prevalence of traumatic events and peritraumatic predictors of posttraumatic stress symptoms in a nonclinical sample of college students. *Journal of Traumatic Stress, 11*, 645–664.

Bisson, J. I., Ehlers, A., Matthews, R., Pilling, S., Richards, D., & Turner, S. (2007). Psychological treatments for chronic post-traumatic stress disorder: Systematic review and meta-analysis. *British Journal of Psychiatry, 190*(2), 97–104.

Bodkin, J. A., Pope, H. G., Detke, M. J., & Hudson, J. I. (2007). Is PTSD caused by traumatic stress? *Journal of Anxiety Disorders, 21*, 176–182.

Bradley, R., Greene, J., Russ, E., Dutra, L., & Westen, D. (2005). A multidimensional meta-analysis of psychotherapy for PTSD. *American Journal of Psychiatry, 162*(2), 214–227.

Bramsen, I., Dirkzwager, A. J. E., & van der Ploeg, H. M. (2000). Predeployment personality traits and exposure to trauma as predictors of posttraumatic stress symptoms: A prospective study of former peacekeepers. *American Journal of Psychiatry, 157*, 1115–1119.

Breslau, N. (2002). Epidemiologic studies of trauma, posttraumatic stress disorder, and other psychiatric disorders. *Canadian Journal of Psychiatry, 47*, 923–929.

Breslau, N., Davis, G. C., & Andreski, P. (1995). Risk factors for PTSD-related traumatic events: A prospective analysis. *American Journal of Psychiatry, 152*(4), 529–535.

Breslau, N., Davis, G. C., Andreski, P., & Peterson, E. (1991). Traumatic events and posttraumatic stress disorder in an urban population of young adults. *Archives of General Psychiatry, 48*, 216–222.

Breslau, N., Kessler, R. C., Chilcoat, H. D., Schultz, L. R., Davis, G. C., & Andreski, P. (1998). Trauma and posttraumatic stress disorder in the community: The 1996 Detroit area survey of trauma. *Archives of General Psychiatry, 55*, 626–632.

Brewin, C. R., Andrews, B., & Rose, S. (2000). Fear, helplessness, and horror in posttraumatic stress disorder: Investigating the DSM-IV Criterion A2 in victims of violent crime. *Journal of Traumatic Stress, 13*, 499–509.

Brewin, C. R., Andrews, B., & Valentine, J. D. (2000). Meta-analysis of risk factors of posttraumatic stress disorder in trauma-exposed adults. *Journal of Consulting and Clinical Psychology, 68*, 748–766.

Brewin, C., Dalgleish, T., & Joseph, S. (1996). A dual representation theory of posttraumatic stress disorder. *Psychological Review, 103*, 670–686.

Bryant, R., & Guthrie, R. (2005). Maladaptive appraisals as a risk factor for posttraumatic stress: A study of trainee firefighters. *Psychological Science, 16*, 749–752.

Cahill, S. P., & Foa, E. B. (2007). Psychological theories of PTSD. In M. J. Friedman, T. M. Keane, & P. A. Resick (Eds.), *Handbook of PTSD: Science and practice* (pp. 55–77). New York: Guilford Press.

Card, J. (1987). Epidemiology of PTSD in a national cohort of Vietnam veterans. *Journal of Clinical Psychology, 43*, 6–17.

Charuvastra, A., & Cloitre, M. (2008). Social bonds and posttraumatic stress disorder. *Annual Review of Psychology, 59*, 301–328.

Courtois, C. A., & Gold, S. N. (2009). The need for inclusion of psychological trauma in the professional curriculum: A call to action. *Psychological Trauma: Theory, Research, Practice, and Policy, 1*, 3–23.

Cox, B. J., MacPherson, P. S. R., Enns, M. W., & McWilliams, L. A. (2004). Neuroticism and self-criticism associated with posttraumatic stress disorder in a nationally representative sample. *Behaviour Research and Therapy, 42*, 105–114.

Creamer, M., Burgess, P., & McFarlane, A. C. (2001). Post-traumatic stress disorder: Findings from the Australian National Survey of Mental Health and Well-being. *Psychological Medicine, 31*, 1237–1247.

Daugherty, T. K. (1998). Childhood trauma and current anxiety among college men. *Psychological Reports, 83*, 667–673.

Davis, C., Nolen-Hoeksema, S., & Larson, J. (1998). Making sense of loss and benefiting from the experience: Two construals of meaning. *Journal of Personality and Social Psychology, 75*, 561–574.

Dunmore, E., Clark, D. M., & Ehlers, A. (2001). A prospective investigation of the role of cognitive factors in persistent Posttraumatic Stress Disorder (PTSD) after physical or sexual assault. *Behaviour Research and Therapy, 39*, 1063–1084.

Ehlers, A., & Clark, D. M. (2000). A cognitive model of post-traumatic stress disorder. *Behaviour Research and Therapy, 38*, 319–345.

Ehlers, A., Mayou, R. A., & Bryant, B. (1998). Psychological predictors of chronic posttraumatic stress disorder after motor vehicle accidents. *Journal of Abnormal Psychology, 107*, 508–519.

Elliott, D. M. (1997). Traumatic events: Prevalence and delayed recall in the general population. *Journal of Consulting and Clinical Psychology, 65*, 811–820.

Elwood, L. S., Hahn, K. S., Olatunji, B. O., & Williams, N. L. (2009). Cognitive vulnerabilities to the development of PTSD: A review of four vulnerabilities and the proposal of an integrative vulnerability model. *Clinical Psychology Review, 29*(1), 87–100.

Engelhard, I. M., Huijding, J., van den Hout, M. A., & de Jong, P. J. (2007). Vulnerability associations and symptoms of posttraumatic stress disorder in soldiers deployed to Iraq. *Behaviour Research and Therapy, 45*, 2317–2325.

Engelhard, I. M., van den Hout, M. A., Kindt, M., Arntz, A., & Schouten, E. (2003). Peritraumatic dissociation and post-traumatic stress after pregnancy loss: A prospective study. *Behaviour Research and Therapy, 41*, 67–78.

Foa, E. B., Cashman, L., Jaycox, L., & Perry, K. (1997). The validation of a self-report measure of posttraumatic stress disorder: The Posttraumatic Diagnostic Scale. *Psychological Assessment, 9*, 445–451.

Foa, E. B., Ehlers, A., Clark, D. M., Tolin, D. F., & Orsillo, S. M. (1999). The Posttraumatic Cognitions Inventory (PTCI): Development and validation. *Psychological Assessment, 11*(3), 303–314.

Foa, E. B., & Jaycox, L. H. (1999). Cognitive-behavioral theory and treatment of posttraumatic stress disorder. In D. Spiegel (Ed.), *Efficacy and cost-effectiveness of psychotherapy* (pp. 23–61). Washington, DC: American Psychiatric Press.

Foa, E. B., Keane, T. M., Friedman, M. J., & Cohen, J. A. (2009a). (Eds.). *Effective treatments for PTSD: Practice guidelines from the International Society for Traumatic Stress Studies* (2nd ed.). New York: Guilford Press.

Foa, E. B., Keane, T. M., Friedman, M. J., & Cohen, J. A. (2009b). Introduction. In E. B. Foa, T. M. Keane, M. J. Friedman, & J. A. Cohen (Eds.), *Effective treatments for PTSD: Practice guidelines from the International Society for Traumatic Stress Studies* (2nd ed., pp. 1–20). New York: Guilford Press.

Foa, E. B., & Kozak, M. J. (1986). Emotional processing of fear: Exposure to corrective information. *Psychological Bulletin, 99*, 20–35.

Foa, E. B., Zinbarg, R., & Rothbaum, B. O. (1992). Uncontrollability and unpredictability in posttraumatic stress disorder: An animal model. *Psychological Bulletin, 112*, 218–238.

Frans, Ö, Rimmö, P.-A., Åberg, L., & Fredrickson, M. (2005). Trauma exposure and post-traumatic stress disorder in the general population. *Acta Psychiatrica Scandinavica, 111*, 291–299.

Frazier, P., Anders, S., Perera, S., Tomich, P., Tennen, H., Park, C., & Tashiro, T. (2009). Traumatic events among undergraduate students: Prevalence and associated symptoms. *Journal of Counseling Psychology, 56*, 450–460.

Frazier, P., Berman, M., & Steward, J. (2002). Perceived control and posttraumatic stress: A temporal model. *Applied & Preventive Psychology, 10*, 207–223.

Frazier, P., Conlon, A., & Glaser, T. (2001). Positive and negative life changes following sexual assault. *Journal of Consulting and Clinical Psychology, 69*, 1048–1055.

Frazier, P., Gavian, M., Hirai, R., Park, C., Tennen, H., Tomich, P., & Tashiro, T. (2011). Prospective predictors of PTSD symptoms: Direct and mediated relations. *Psychological Trauma: Theory, Research, Practice, and Policy, 3*, 27–36.

Frazier, P. A., & Kaler, M. E. (2006). Assessing the validity of self-reported stress-related growth. *Journal of Consulting and Clinical Psychology, 74*, 859–869.

Frazier, P., Keenan, N., Anders, S., Perera, S., Shallcross, S. & Hintz, S. (2001). Perceived past, present, and future control and adjustment to stressful life events. *Journal of Personality and Social Psychology, 100*, 749–765.

Frazier, P., Mortensen, H., & Steward, J. (2005). Coping strategies as mediators of the relations among perceived control and distress in sexual assault survivors. *Journal of Counseling Psychology, 52*, 267–278.

Frazier, P., Steward, J., & Mortensen, H. (2004). Perceived control and adjustment to trauma: A comparison across events. *Journal of Social and Clinical Psychology, 23*, 303–324.

Frazier, P., Tennen, H., Gavian, M., Park, C., Tomich, P., & Tashiro, T. (2009). Does self-reported post-traumatic growth reflect genuine positive change? *Psychological Science, 20*, 912–919.

Friedman, M. J., Cohen, J. A., Foa, E. B., & Keane, T. M. (2009). Integration and summary. In E. B. Foa, T. M. Keane, M. J. Friedman, & J. A. Cohen (Eds.), *Effective treatments for PTSD: Practice guidelines from the International Society for Traumatic Stress Studies* (2nd ed., pp. 617–642). New York: Guilford Press.

Friedman, M., Resick, P., & Keane, T. (2007). Twenty-five years of progress and challenge. In M. Friedman, T. Keane, & P. Resick (Eds.), *Handbook of PTSD: Science and practice* (pp. 3–18). New York: Guilford Press.

Gold, S. D., Marx, B. P., Soler-Baillo, J. M., & Sloan, D. M. (2005). Is life stress more traumatic than traumatic stress? *Anxiety Disorders, 19*, 687–698.

Goodman, L. A., Corcoran, C., Turner, K., Yuan, N., & Green, B. L. (1998). Assessing traumatic event exposure: General issues and preliminary findings for the stressful life events screening questionnaire. *Journal of Traumatic Stress, 11*, 521–542.

Green, B. L., Goodman, L. A., Krupnick, J. L., Corcoran, C. B., Petty, R. M., Stockton, P., & Stern, N. M. (2000). Outcomes of single versus multiple trauma exposure in a screening sample. *Journal of Traumatic Stress, 13*, 271–286.

Gunty, A., Frazier, P., Tennen, H., Tomich, P., Tashiro, T., & Park, C. (2011). Moderators of the relation between perceived and actual posttraumatic growth. *Psychological Trauma: Theory, Research, Practice, and Policy, 3*, 61–66.

Hatch, S. L., & Dohrenwend, B. P. (2007). Distribution of traumatic and other stressful life events by race/ethnicity, gender, SES and age: A review of the research. *American Journal of Community Psychology, 40*, 313–332.

Helgeson, V. S., Reynolds, K. A., & Tomich, P. L. (2006). A meta-analytic review of benefit finding and growth. *Journal of Consulting and Clinical Psychology, 74*, 797–816.

Hodgins, G. A., Creamer, M., & Bell, R. (2001). Risk factors for posttrauma reactions in police officers: A longitudinal study. *Journal of Nervous and Mental Disease, 189*, 541–547.

Horowitz, M. J. (1986). *Stress response syndromes* (2nd ed.). Northvale, NJ: Aronson.

Janoff-Bulman, R. (1992). *Shattered assumptions: Towards a new psychology of trauma.* New York: Free Press.

Jaranson, J., Butcher, J., Halcon, L., Johnson, D., Robertson, C., Savik, K., et al. (2004). Somali and Oromo refugees: Correlates of torture and trauma. *American Journal of Public Health, 94*, 591–598.

Joseph, S., & Linley, P. A. (2005). Positive adjustment to threatening events: An organismic valuing theory of growth through adversity. *Review of General Psychology, 9*, 262–280.

Keane, T. M., Brief, D. J., Pratt, E. M., & Miller, M. W. (2007). Assessment of PTSD and its comorbidities in adults. In M. J. Friedman, T. M. Keane, & P. A. Resick (Eds.), *Handbook of PTSD: Science and practice* (pp. 279–305). New York: Guilford Press.

Keane, T. M., Zimering, R. T., & Caddell, J. M. (1985). A behavioral formulation of posttraumatic stress disorder. *Behavior Therapist, 8*, 9–12.

Kessler, R. C., Berglund, P., Demler, O., Jin, R., Merikangas, K. R., & Walters, E. E. (2005). Lifetime prevalence and age-of-onset distributions of DSM-IV disorders in the National Comorbidity Survey Replication. *Archives of General Psychiatry, 62,* 593–602.

Kessler, R. C., Chiu, W. R., Demler, O., Walters, E. E. (2005). Prevalence, severity, and comorbidity of 12-Month DSM-IV disorders in the National Comorbidity Survey Replication. *Archives of General Psychiatry, 62,* 617–627.

Kessler, R. C., Sonnega, A., Bromet, E., Hughes, M., & Nelson, C. B. (1995). Posttraumatic stress disorder in the National Comorbidity Survey. *Archives of General Psychiatry, 52,* 1048–1060.

Kirk, A., & Dollar, S. C. (2002). Prevalence of traumatic events and PTSD symptomatology among a selected sample of undergraduate students. *Journal of Social Work in Disability & Rehabilitation, 1,* 53–65.

Krinsley, K. E., Gallagher, J. G., Weathers, F. W., Kutter, C. J., & Kaloupek, D. G. (2003). Consistency of retrospective reporting about exposure to traumatic events. *Journal of Traumatic Stress, 16,* 399–409.

Krupnick, J. L., Green, B. L., Stockton, P., Goodman, L., Corcoran, C., & Petty, R. (2004). Mental health effects of adolescent trauma exposure in a female college sample: Exploring differential outcomes based on experiences of unique trauma types and dimensions. *Psychiatry, 67,* 264–279.

Lahey, B. (2009). Public health significance of neuroticism. *American Psychologist, 64,* 241–256.

Lengua, L. J., Long, A. C., & Meltzoff, A. N. (2006). Preattack stress-load, appraisals, and coping in children's responses to the 9/11 terrorist attacks. *Journal of Child Psychology and Psychiatry, 47,* 1219–1227.

Lengua, L. J., Long, A. C., Smith, K. I., & Meltzoff, A. N. (2005). Preattack symptomatology and temperament as predictors of children's responses to the September 11 terrorist attacks. *Journal of Child Psychology and Psychiatry, 46,* 631–645.

Lensvelt Mulders, G., van Der Hart, O., van Ochten, J. M., van Son, M. J. M., Steele, K., & Breeman, L. (2008). Relations among peritraumatic dissociation and posttraumatic stress: A meta-analysis. *Clinical Psychology Review, 28*(7), 1138–1151.

Lewis, S. (2008). *Five lessons I didn't learn from breast cancer (and one big one I did).* New York: New American Library.

Litz, B. T., & Maguen, S. (2007). Early intervention for trauma. In M. J. Friedman, T. M. Keane, & P. A. Resick (Eds.), *Handbook of PTSD: Science and practice* (pp. 306–329). New York: Guilford Press.

Luszczynska, A., Benight, C. C., & Cieslak, R. (2009). Self-efficacy and health-related outcomes of collective trauma: A systematic review. *European Psychologist, 14*(1), 51–62.

McFarland, C., & Alvaro, C. (2000). The impact of motivation on temporal comparisons: Coping with traumatic events by perceiving personal growth. *Journal of Personality and Social Psychology, 79,* 327–343.

McKeever, V. M., & Huff, M. E. (2003). A diathesis-stress model of posttraumatic stress disorder: Ecological, biological, and residual stress pathways. *Review of General Psychology, 7*(3), 237–250.

McMillen, J. C., & Cook, C. L. (2003). The positive by-products of spinal cord injury and their correlates. *Rehabilitation Psychology, 48,* 77–85.

McMillen, J. C., Smith, E., & Fisher, R. (1997). Perceived benefit and mental health after three types of disaster. *Journal of Consulting and Clinical Psychology, 65,* 733–739.

Miller, K., Omidian, P., Quraishy, A., Quraishy, N., Nasiry, M., et al. (2006). The Afghan symptom checklist: A culturally grounded approach to mental health assessment in a conflict zone. *American Journal of Orthopsychiatry, 76,* 423–233.

Munley, P. H., Pate, W. E., II, & Duncan, L. E. (2008). Demographic, educational, employment, and professional characteristics of counseling psychologist. *The Counseling Psychologist, 36,* 250–280.

National Collaborating Centre for Mental Health. (2005). *Posttraumatic stress disorder: The management of PTSD in adults and children in primary and secondary care.* London: National Institute for Clinical Excellence (NICE).

Nemeroff, C. B., Bremner, J. D., Foa, E. B., Mayberg, H. S., North, C. S., & Stein, M. B. (2006). Posttraumatic stress disorder: A state-of-the-science review. *Journal of Psychiatric Research, 40*(1), 1–21.

Norris, F. H. (1992). Epidemiology of trauma: Frequency and impact of different potentially traumatic events on different demographic groups. *Journal of Consulting and Clinical Psychology, 60,* 409–418.

Olff, M., Langeland, W., Draijer, N., & Gersons, B. P. R. (2007). Gender differences in posttraumatic stress disorder. *Psychological Bulletin, 133*(2), 183–204.

Owens, G. P., & Chard, K. M. (2006). PTSD severity and cognitive reactions to trauma among a college sample: An exploratory study. *Journal of Aggression, Maltreatment, & Trauma, 13,* 23–36.

Oxlad, M., & Wade, T. D. (2008). Longitudinal risk factors for adverse psychological functioning six months after coronary artery bypass graft surgery. *Journal of Health Psychology, 13,* 79–92.

Ozer, E., Best, S., Lipsey, T., & Weiss, D. (2003). Predictors of posttraumatic stress disorder and symptoms in adults: A meta-analysis. *Psychological Bulletin, 129,* 52–73.

Ozer, E. J., & Weiss, D. S. (2004). Who develops posttraumatic stress disorder? *Current Directions in Psychological Science, 13,* 169–172.

Park, C. L., Cohen, L. H., & Murch, R. L. (1996). Assessment and prediction of stress-related growth. *Journal of Personality, 64,* 71–105.

Parslow, R., Jorm, A., & Christensen, H. (2006). Associations of pretrauma attributes and trauma exposure with screening positive for PTSD: Analysis of a community-based study of 2085 young adults. *Psychological Medicine, 36,* 387–395.

Peirce, J. M., Burke, C. K., Stoller, K. B., Neufeld, K. J., & Brooner, R. K. (2009). Assessing traumatic event exposure: Comparing the traumatic life events questionnaire to the structured clinical interview for DSM-IV. *Psychological Assessment, 21*(2), 210–218.

Perkonigg, A., Kessler, R. C., Storz, S., & Wittchen, H. (2000). Traumatic events and post-traumatic stress disorder in the community: Prevalence, risk factors and comorbidity. *Acta Psychiatrica Scandinavica, 101*(1), 46–59.

Ransom, S., Sheldon, K., & Jacobsen, P. (2008). Actual change and inaccurate recall contribute to posttraumatic growth following radiotherapy. *Journal of Clinical and Consulting Psychology, 76,* 811–819.

Rasmussen, A., Smith, H., & Keller, A. (2007). Factor structure of PTSD symptoms among West and Central African refugees. *Journal of Traumatic Stress, 20,* 271–280.

Resnick, H., Acierno, R., Holmes, M., Kilpatrick, D., & Jager, N. (1999). Prevention of post rape psychopathology: Preliminary evaluation of an acute rape treatment. *Journal of Anxiety Disorders, 13*, 359–370.

Resnick, H. S., Kilpatrick, D. G., Dansky, B. S., Saunders, B. E., & Best, C. L. (1993). Prevalence of civilian trauma and post-traumatic stress disorder in a representative national sample of women. *Journal of Consulting and Clinical Psychology, 61*, 984–991.

Robins, R. W., Noftle, E. E., Trzesniewski, K. H., & Roberts, B. W. (2005). Do people know how their personality has changed? Correlates of perceived and actual personality change in young adulthood. *Journal of Personality, 73*, 489–521.

Roemer, L., Litz, B. T., Orsillo, S. M., Ehlich, P. J., & Friedman, M. J. (1998). Increases in retrospective accounts of war-zone exposure over time: The role of PTSD symptom severity. *Journal of Traumatic Stress, 11*, 597–605.

Rosen, G. M., & Lilienfeld, S. O. (2007). Posttraumatic stress disorder: An empirical evaluation of core assumptions. *Clinical Psychology Review, 28*, 837–868.

Rosenberger, S., Frazier, P., & Moore, N. (2000, August). *Correlates of service utilization among sexual assault survivors.* Poster presented at the annual meeting of the American Psychological Association, Washington, DC.

Rubin, D. C., Berntsen, D., & Bohni, M. K. (2008). A memory-based model of posttraumatic stress disorder: Evaluating basic assumptions underlying the PTSD diagnosis. *Psychological Review, 115*(4), 985–1011.

Scarpa, A. (2001). Community violence exposure in a young adult sample. *Journal of Interpersonal Violence, 16*, 36–53.

Scarpa, A., Fikretoglu, D., Bowser, F., Hurley, J. D., Pappert, C. A., Romero, N., & Van Voorhees, E. (2002). Community violence exposure in university students. *Journal of Interpersonal Violence, 17*, 253–272.

Sears, S. R., Stanton, A. L., & Danoff-Burg, S. (2003). The yellow brick road and the emerald city: Benefit finding, positive reappraisal coping, and posttraumatic growth in women with early-stage breast cancer. *Health Psychology, 22*, 487–497.

Siegel, K., & Schrimshaw, E. W. (2003). Reasons for adopting celibacy among older men and women living with HIV/AIDS. *Journal of Sex Research, 40*, 189–200.

Skinner, E. A. (1996). A guide to constructs of control. *Journal of Personality and Social Psychology, 71*, 549–570.

Smart Richman, L., & Leary, M. R. (2009). Reactions to discrimination, stigmatization, ostracism, and other forms of interpersonal rejection: A multimotive model. *Psychological Review, 116*, 365–383.

Steger, M., Frazier, P., & Zacchanini, J. L. (2008). Terrorism in two cultures: Stress and growth following September 11th and the Madrid train bombings. *Journal of Loss and Trauma, 13*, 511–527.

Stein, D. J., Ipser, J. C., & Seedat, S. (2006). Pharmacotherapy for post traumatic stress disorder (PTSD). *Cochrane Database of Systematic Reviews, 1*, Art. No.: CD002795. DOI: 10.1002/14651858.CD002795.pub2.

Stein, M. B., Hofler, M., Perkonigg, A., Lieb, R., Pfister, H., Maercker, A., et al. (2002). Patterns of incidence and psychiatric risk factors for traumatic events. *International Journal of Methods in Psychiatric Research, 11*(4), 143–153.

Stein, M. B., Walker, J. R., Hazen, A. L., & Forde, D. R. (1997). Full and partial posttraumatic stress disorder: Findings from a community survey. *American Journal of Psychiatry, 154*, 1114–1119.

Tedeschi, R., & Calhoun, L. (2004). Posttraumatic growth: Conceptual foundations and empirical evidence. *Psychological Inquiry, 15*, 1–18.

Tedeschi, R. G., & Calhoun, L. G. (1996). The Posttraumatic Growth Inventory: Measuring the positive legacy of trauma. *Journal of Traumatic Stress, 9*, 455–472.

Terheggen, M., Stroebe, M., & Kleber, R. (2001). Western conceptualizations and Eastern experience: A cross-cultural study of traumatic stress reactions among Tibetan refugees in India. *Journal of Traumatic Stress, 14*(2), 391–403.

Tolin, D. F., & Foa, E. B. (2006). Sex differences in trauma and posttraumatic stress disorder: A quantitative review of 25 years of research. *Psychological Bulletin, 132*, 959–992.

Turner, R. J., & Avison, W. R. (2003). Status variations in stress exposure: Implications for the interpretation of research on race, socioeconomic status and gender. *Journal of Health and Social Behavior, 44*, 488–505.

Turner, R. J., & Lloyd, D. A. (2004). Stress burden and the lifetime incidence of psychiatric disorder in young adults. *Archives of General Psychiatry, 61*, 481–488.

van der Kolk, B. A. (2007). The history of trauma in psychiatry. In M. J. Friedman, T. M. Keane, & P. A. Resick (Eds.), *Handbook of PTSD: Science and practice* (pp. 19–36). New York: Guilford Press.

Vrana, S., & Lauterbach, D. (1994). Prevalence of traumatic events and post-traumatic psychological symptoms in a non-clinical sample of college students. *Journal of Traumatic Stress, 7*, 289–302.

Watson, S. B., & Haynes, S. N. (2007). Brief screening for traumatic life events in female undergraduate health service patients. *International Journal of Clinical and Health Psychology, 7*, 261–282.

Weathers, F. W., Keane, T. M., & Foa, E. B. (2009). In E. B. Foa, T. M. Keane, M. J. Friedman, & J. A. Cohen (Eds.), *Effective treatments for PTSD: Practice guidelines from the International Society for Traumatic Stress Studies* (2nd ed., pp. 23–61). New York: Guilford Press.

Wilson, J. P., & Keane, T. M. (2004). *Assessing psychological trauma and PTSD* (2nd ed.). New York: Guilford Press.

Wortman, C. B. (2004). Posttraumatic growth: Progress and problems. *Psychological Inquiry, 15*, 81–90.

Yehuda, R. (2004). Risk and resilience in posttraumatic stress disorder. *Journal of Clinical Psychiatry, 65*, 29–36.

Zatzick, D., Rivara, F., Nathens, A., Jurkovich, G., Wang, J., Fan, M., et al. (2007). A nationwide US study of post-traumatic stress after hospitalization for physical injury. *Psychological Medicine, 37*, 1469–1480.

Zoellner, T., Rabe, S., Karl, A., & Maercker, A. (2008). Posttraumatic growth in accident survivors: Openness and optimism as predictors of its constructive or illusory sides. *Journal of Clinical Psychology, 64*, 245–263.

Further Reading

Bradley, R., Greene, J., Russ, E., Dutra, L., & Westen, D. (2005). A multidimensional meta-analysis of psychotherapy for PTSD. *American Journal of Psychiatry, 162*, 214–227.

Breslau, N., Kessler, R. C., Chilcoat, H. D., Schultz, L. R., Davis, G. C., & Andreski, P. (1998). Trauma and posttraumatic stress disorder in the community: The 1996 Detroit area survey of trauma. *Archives of General Psychiatry, 55,* 626–632.

Foa, E., Keane, T., Friedman, M., & Cohen, J. (2009). (Eds.). *Effective treatments for PTSD: Practice guidelines from the International Society for Traumatic Stress Studies* (2nd ed.). New York: Guilford Press.

Friedman, M., Keane, T., & Resick, P. (Eds.). (2007). *Handbook of PTSD: Science and practice.* New York: Guilford Press.

Kessler, R. C., Sonnega, A., Bromet, E., Hughes, M., & Nelson, C. B. (1995). Posttraumatic stress disorder in the National Comorbidity Survey. *Archives of General Psychiatry, 52,* 1048–1060.

McKeever, V. M., & Huff, M. E. (2003). A diathesis-stress model of posttraumatic stress disorder: Ecological, biological, and residual stress pathways. *Review of General Psychology, 7,* 237–250.

Ozer, E., Best, S., Lipsey, T., & Weiss, D. (2003). Predictors of posttraumatic stress disorder and symptoms in adults: A meta-analysis. *Psychological Bulletin, 129,* 52–73.

Rubin, D. C., Berntsen, D., & Bohni, M. K. (2008). A memory-based model of posttraumatic stress disorder: Evaluating basic assumptions underlying the PTSD diagnosis. *Psychological Review, 115,* 985–1011.

Counseling Psychologists As Consultants

Stewart E. Cooper *and* Sandra L. Shullman

Abstract

The new American Psychological Association (APA) guidelines on education and training (Rodolfa, Bent, Eisman, Nelson, Rehm, & Ritchie (2005) list consultation as one of the five key competencies for applied psychologists in general. All counseling psychologists engage in consultation as one of their primary work activities, with the specifics being influenced by setting, population, and particular job responsibilities. The purpose of this chapter is to enhance understanding of the concepts and skills associated with the professional role, type of consultation, and focus of consulting processes for counseling psychologists serving as consultants. Additionally, suggested direction for further development of consultation for counseling psychologists is presented.

Keywords: consultant, consulting, consultation, mental health consultation, school consultation, organizational consultation

Psychologically based consultation is a primary professional activity, engaged in by virtually all counseling psychologists, whether or not they consciously consider and/or label the activity as consultation. Moreover, consultation as an expected professional role for psychologists is now more formally considered as a highly significant professional activity. For example, consultation and education has been recently recognized as one of seven core competencies needed by all professional psychologists, along with relationship, assessment, intervention, research and evaluation, management and supervision, and diversity (Rodolfa, Bent, Eisman, Nelson, Rehm, & Ritchie, 2005).

The purpose of this chapter is to assist counseling psychologists in learning more about consultation as a professional role and about the range of possible consultation types and focus areas. The chapter is divided into six sections. The first section covers the essentials of psychologically based consultation and examples of counseling psychologists working as consultants. This incorporates common characteristics,

key roles, and requisite skills for counseling psychologists as consultants. The second section focuses on consultation theory and research. The third addresses multicultural issues and the practice of consultation. The fourth presents a generic model of consultation, along with three specific applied models of consultation: mental health consultation, school consultation, and organizational consultation. The fifth section presents the current status (and dearth) of training on this key professional psychology competency. Finally, the last section presents some best practices for counseling psychologists who aspire to engage or are currently engaged in psychologically based consultation and suggests some needed steps for the immediate future of this area of practice.

Essentials of Psychologically Based Consultation: Common Characteristics, Roles, and Skill Sets of Consultation
Common Characteristics
Dougherty (2009a) presents ten common aspects or characteristics of psychologically based consultation

that can be used to differentiate this service modality from other modalities: the role of a human services professional; a focus on a problem-solving process; work that is triadic in nature; a helping relationship; work done either internally or externally; efforts involving all voluntary parties; relationships of peers; marked collaboration, regardless of what consultation role best fits the needs of the consultee and client system; temporary rather than ongoing engagement; and focus on either remedial or developmental needs. The following illustrate each of these ten characteristics as they might play out for counseling psychologists in consultation roles.

Consultation by a human services professional differs from consultation by other professions in the need for flexible adaptation of the interventions based on an interactive process between the consultant and the consultee. For example, a counseling psychologist who had delivered several team building consultations to the leadership team of a non-profit organization going through significant expansion and change shifted to working on developing and revising job descriptions and to supporting the onboarding process for new hires to the team. The need from this shift emerged from a series of discussions with the CEO based on the progress already made through the previous consultations in the face of new challenges that had emerged for the organization.

Consultation involves a focus on the care-taking/work-related role of the consultee rather than their mental health issues. For example, a counseling psychologist meets four times with a teacher who would appear to be having control-based frustrations with an oppositional student. Instead of focusing on the history and dynamics of the teacher and the teacher's need for control, the psychologist could work with the teacher to develop new strategies that give options to the student as well, putting emphasis on increasing the cooperation level of the student with the teacher.

Consultation typically involves a triadic and indirect connection, in which the consultant relates through the consultee to the client system. For example, a director of a number of community behaviorally oriented group homes for developmentally delayed adults participates in a 3-day intensive training experience in advanced behavior modification strategies, taught by three counseling psychologists with expertise in these methods.

Consultation is fundamentally a helping relationship. For example, a counseling psychologist employed as a leadership development specialist

for an upper-level manager (consultee) by a large corporation also has client relationship responsibilities with the upper-level manager's boss and the organization. In this situation, the consultant ensures that the information emerging from the work with the consultee (upper-level manager) benefits not only that individual but the organization as well. This requires clarification at the beginning with all parties.

Consultations can be internal or external to the consultee or can be a hybrid of the two. For example, a counseling center director does team building with the staff of the career center at the same university. The director, who is a counseling psychologist, is an internal consultant in that the director and the career center staff both work at the same university and both are in the student affairs division. Yet, the psychologist is an external consultant, as the career center and its staff is a distinct unit, with only a moderate number of cross-referrals and interactions.

Consultation is engaged in on a voluntary basis. For example, a counseling psychologist employed in an employee assistance program (EAP) is contacted by a line manager having a problem with a staff member. The human resources (HR) office suggested that the manager contact the EAP office, but it was an option offered to the manager to pursue voluntarily. This example shows how easy it can be to intentionally or unintentionally put significant pressure on an individual or a team to become a consultee by using "recommended" consulting services.

Consultation is a relationship of peers. In consultation, although the consultee and the consultant may have different knowledge and skills, both come together as equals to develop and select interventions to benefit the client system and then to implement these interventions with adjustments to meet these goals. The consultee often brings a much better awareness of the client system and its context than does the consultant, whereas the consultant often has specific in-depth expertise in processes to assist the consultee in achieving success and/or professional growth. For example, a counseling psychologist working in the defense industry works with a section chief to develop ways to be a more effective leader. The work is sufficiently complicated, and the section manager may have a good deal of information that cannot be shared due to national security concerns. The consultant can focus on effective leadership processes and rely on the client to apply learning without revealing protected information.

Consultation is marked by collaboration, regardless of consultation role and fit with consultee/client system needs. This point can be confusing because consultation and collaboration are related yet distinct professional activities. As discussed earlier, consultation, regardless of consultant role taken and consulting approach used, must be collaborative to be successful. This is due to several of the characteristics described above, including the concepts of relationship between peers and viewing consultation as a voluntary relationship. In this sense, the collaboration inherent in consultation is somewhat different than the relationship between supervisor and supervisee and between teacher and student. Both of these latter relationships involve a power differential and an evaluative component. (A professional gatekeeping function is often present as well.) In contrast, for example, a counseling psychologist is hired to do a program evaluation of a community methadone clinic. Although the consultant has the expertise needed to do such program evaluation, a good deal of discussion and collaboration is needed between the consultant and the director of the program to identify the components to be evaluated and the staff resources available to gather and assemble the data.

Consultation is temporary rather than ongoing. Some consultation projects, particularly those that are complex and involve teams of consultants with specialized expertise areas, can continue for a sustained period of time. Similarly, executive coaching, due to its nature, can go on for several months or years. Most consultation, however, is short term, focused on specific problems, and is done when the goals are satisfactorily met or when no additional resources can be used to support further work. For example, a counseling psychologist is hired to provide coaching to the director of a large urban hospital with 2,000 employees, a great deal of complexity, and major economic challenges. The psychologist consultant and the director agree that a 3-month contract for weekly consultation should provide some needed support to make changes helpful to the hospital organization and its very diverse constituencies, each with its own focus. They may also agree to review where they are at the end of each month and at the end of the 3-month period.

Consultation is focused on either remedial or developmental needs. Remedial needs would represent situations in which moderate or more serious concerns exist about the current performance level of client system and/or the consultee. Developmental needs represent situations in which the goal is to anticipate or prevent a problem or to learn to function at a higher or different level of effectiveness.

For example, a counseling psychologist who has developed a school safety program provides seminars to administrators, teachers, and professional staff in districts within a large regional area. The psychologist employs an educational approach. A developmentally focused program helps the administrators, teachers, and professional staff apply what they have learned to create new and creative approaches to school safety within their specific schools. In contrast, a remedial program helps them identify previous deficiencies in their school safety programs to bring them up to minimum standards.

Consultation Roles

Counseling psychologists delivering psychologically based consultation typically take on one or more of six roles: expert, trainer/educator, collaborator, fact-finder, process specialist, advocate (Dougherty, 2009a).

During the time of their training and subsequent to graduation, counseling psychologists typically develop, by plan or circumstances, several areas of expertise, thereby becoming an *expert*. These areas of early expertise often become the basis of future professional work. Furthermore, it is common to develop consultation activities in areas of expertise. A few examples of such a transition to *expert* are provided to further explain this process. For example, a counseling psychologist trained in a Veterans Administration (VA) internship to do therapy for veterans with posttraumatic stress disorder (PTSD) is asked to give testimony at a congressional committee meeting on what is needed to successfully assist such persons. As a second example, a counseling psychologist who has done a good deal of student suicide prevention work on campus goes on to develop and deliver workshops to campus administrators. Third, a counseling psychologist with advanced business training works with corporate leadership teams within a company to enhance success in areas for which individual team leaders have responsibility.

Counseling psychologists who use the *expert* role as their primary role in a particular consultation situation do so when the consultee believes they have a clearly identified need, requiring specialized knowledge and experience that the consultant possesses. Often, however, the need they have identified may not be either the best or only need, and other, more important needs emerge as the consultation process develops. Additionally, consultees who are seeking expert consultants do not develop their own problem-solving skills when sometimes doing so would be to their advantage. There is perhaps a potential parallel here to the situation in which mental health clients may look for experts to tell them how to fix their mental health issues rather than learning to handle these issues themselves. It is incumbent on the consultant to clearly define and clarify areas of expertise for potential consultees.

The *trainer/educator* consultation role is one that is close to the expert role just described. It is perhaps the most common consultation role that counseling psychologists use (Cooper, 2003). The goal is for the consultant to assist the consultee in the development of new knowledge and skills, to help the client systems with whom they work. Training and education can be formal or informal, and training requires the counseling psychologist consultant to have specific skills, expertise, and facilitation/teaching skills. Education requires the counseling psychologist consultant to possess a high-level knowledge base and strong teaching ability. For example, a counseling psychologist provides ongoing training to a police department to help line officers better respond to situations involving a person with significant mental illness. As a second example, a counseling psychologist provides a workshop on behavioral strategies and then follows-up with group consultation to bachelors' level staff at group homes for emotionally disabled children. Or, a counseling psychologist delivers a half-day workshop to campus student affairs administrators on campus strategies for suicide prevention. The trainer/educator approach is most useful when the information or skills imparted to the consultee can be easily implemented and put into practice to support the client system. Typically, however, formal assessment of such implementation does not take place (Dougherty, 2009a).

The *collaborator* role of consultation is likely to be one of the two consultation roles of most familiarity and preference for counseling psychologists (Cooper, 2003; Pryzwansky & White, 1983). The collaborator role requires that the consultee has the requisite knowledge and skills to be able to bring these to bear in meeting the needs of the client system, yet needs the assistance of the consultant, for various reasons, to have the best outcomes. Typically, the consultant first solicits the consultee's perspectives about his or her direct service issues and goals, and his or her ideas about how to achieve them. The consultant then provides assistance in generating and tentatively suggesting solutions, determining the promoting and restraining influences on these options, and facilitating consultee decision making. It is the consultee who determines the course of action selected and the responsibility for its implementation. The benefit of the collaborator approach to consultation is that it maximizes the consultee's professional growth. The caution is that the consultant can overestimate the level of the consultee's knowledge and skills, especially if he or she is talented interpersonally. As an example, a counseling psychologist assists a mental health counselor in making choices about which therapy interventions are most likely to be successful, subsequent to assisting the consultee in conducting an interpersonally based treatment formulation. For a second example, a counseling psychologist engages in collaborative consultation with the CEO of a local YMCA and its leadership team to optimize the opportunities provided by their move to a new facility. Or, a counseling psychologist working in a school district consults collaboratively with the special education team in one of the area high schools. The purpose of this collaborative consultation is to help this team evaluate the quality of the services they provide, with the intention of using the results to improve the services received by students and their families.

The *fact-finder* is another role that counseling psychologist consultants can use to help consultees assist their own client systems. The background and training experiences in assessment and program evaluation that counseling psychologists receive in their doctoral studies and postdoctoral professional development are well suited to this fact-finder role. The most common process is for the consultant in the fact-finder role to gather, analyze, and synthesize information and to provide feedback to the consultee (Dougherty, 2009a). Such information can be simple or complex, take a long or short time, and can focus information gathering on an individual, individuals, a group, or the entire organization. Sources of information range over a wide variety of topics and are selected depending upon the purposes and needs of the consultation. Both naturalistic and standardized methods can be employed (Cooper & O'Connor, 1993). Naturalistic techniques may include nonintrusive observation, use of existing records, interviews, and informal assessments. Standardized methods would consist of validated and reliable inventories and substantiated qualitative methods. An excellent initial question for the consultant being asked to take on a fact-finding role is to discern why they, rather than the consultee, is being asked to collect, analyze, and evaluate the results. Often, consultation is requested because of lack of existing expertise or lack of time or other resources (Schein, 1999).

The *process specialist* consultation role is one that is a strong fit with the training of counseling psychologists. It is the least directive of all the six roles (Lippit & Lippit, 1986). In the process specialist role, the consultant focuses more on the questions of "how" rather than "what," and on process rather than content. Edgar Schein was the architect of this approach (Schein, 1969, 1978, 1987, 1988, 1999). Two subcomponents of process consultation were defined—a process observer role and a process facilitator role (Kormanski & Eschbach, 1997). The relative balance of these two for the counseling psychologist engaged in consultation depends on the needs, goals, and preexisting skills of the consultees with whom they are working. For example, a counseling psychologist is brought into a large company to assist a mid-level team that is exhibiting difficulties in communication and decision making during their weekly 2-hour meetings. As a second example, a large firm that has a high rate of dissatisfaction among its front-line employees hires a counseling psychologist to observe front-line manager behavior and to meet with each one to discuss observations. A third example might involve a counseling psychologist who is brought into a large community mental health center to facilitate discussion among group therapy leaders and administrators, following discovery that the group program is evaluated as not working well. For counseling psychologists, their education and experience in working with groups provides them with a strong skill set for using this process specialist role in consultation (Corey, Corey, & Corey, 2010). A common pitfall in such a process consultation role, however, can occur when consultants put too much focus on resolving interpersonal issues (Schein, 1988). It is critical to know when to make referrals for therapy rather than moving over that boundary in the consulting process (Schein, 1990).

Other paradigms for categorizing consulting roles exist; these are helpful and often utilize a roles continuum (Dougherty, 2009a). The most popular categorization approach still used was developed earlier by Lippit and Lippit (1986). In their approach, the consultants' roles lie on a continuum ranging from *directive* to *nondirective roles*. In directive roles, the consultant is something of a technical expert, whereas in nondirective roles, consultants tend to facilitate the consultee's expertise. (Lippitt & Lippitt, 1986). Another popular approach to consultants' roles, developed in the 1970s, includes *task roles* (those related to expertise) at one end of a continuum and *process roles* (those related to facilitation at the other; Margulies & Raia, 1972; Schein, 1999). Consultation roles often appear to be categorized by the balance of involvement and control in the process between the consultant and the consultee (Dougherty, 2009a). There is an obvious parallel here to the counseling process, in which the counseling psychologist's role of involvement and control is balanced in interaction with the counseling client's psychological and situational resources.

There are several key factors in selecting the primary, secondary, and perhaps tertiary roles to be assumed in a particular consultation situation (Dougherty, 2009b). These key factors involve the nature of the problem itself, the purpose of the consultation and its desired outcomes, and the consultant's and consultee's skill sets (Dougherty, 2009b). Given the enhanced complexity of the triadic nature of consultation relative to the complexities of dyadic services, such as individual counseling, it is often helpful to have co-consultants or a "shadow consultant" brainstorm about best roles and approaches to particular consultation situations (Kilburg, 2002).

Consultant Skill Sets
Recent efforts have been made to define specific competencies and skill sets for psychologists in consultation roles (O'Roark, 1999). Specifically, Division 13 of the American Psychological Association (APA), the Society for Consulting Psychology, developed a set of consulting competencies for training consulting psychologists, which were adopted as APA Guidelines (APA, 2007; O'Roark, Lloyd, & Cooper, 2005). These are presented in Table 32.1. Shullman (2002) discussed the relationship of the consulting competencies for training consulting psychologists with the training of counseling psychologists. Although several attempts have been made to define essential skill sets for consultants (Cooper, Monarch, Serviss, Gordick, & Skipton, 2007), Dougherty (2009) has developed a set of seven skill domains, each of which is composed of nine skills (see Dougherty, 2009a, pp. 25–31 for a more detailed description of these 63 skills). The seven domains are communications skills, interpersonal skills, problem-solving skills, organization analysis skills, group work, cultural competence skills, and ethical/legal knowledge and competency. The overlap between essential skill sets for counseling psychologists as therapists and

Table 32.1. Competencies for Postdoctoral level Organizational Consulting Psychologists

A. Primarily Individual-Level Core Competencies

    (1) Individual assessment for purposes of career and vocational assessment
    (2) Individual assessment for purposes of employee selection or development
    (3) Job analysis for purposes of individual assessment
    (4) Executive and individual coaching
    (5) Individual-level intervention for job and career-related problems

B. Primarily Group-Level Core Competencies

    (1) Group assessment
    (2) Assessment of the functional and dysfunctional group behavior
    (3) Assessment and development of teams
    (4) Creating group level teams in organizations (e.g., self-directed work groups)
    (5) Inter-group assessment and intervention
    (6) Group boundary assessment and intervention
    (7) Identity group (racial, gender, ethnic) management in the organizational context

C. Primarily Organizational/Systemic-Level Core Competencies

    (1) Organizational diagnosis including systemic assessment of the entire organization or large component parts of the organization
    (2) Attitude, climate, and satisfaction surveys
    (3) Evaluation of corporate management philosophy, organizational culture and nature of systemic stressors
    (4) Work-flow and project planning activities
    (5) Identification of aggregate performance measures
    (6) Assessment of organizational values and management practices
    (7) Organizational level interventions
    (8) Change management of organizational systems

counseling psychologists as consultants is significant. The largest differences are in focus when applying these skills and in attention to organizational context (Shullman, 2002).

Essentials of Consultation Theory and Research Understanding Psychologically Based Consultation

A number of counseling psychologists have identified psychologically based consultation as an important role. In 1974, Morrill, Oetting, and Hurst developed a three-dimensional "cube" model for categorizing a broad range of counseling interventions. They identified one to four possible targets of intervention (individual, primary group, association group, and institution or community); one of three possible purposes (remediation, prevention, and development); and one of three possible methods of intervention (direct service, consultation, and media). Thus, their model explicitly cited consultation as one of the three counseling intervention methods listed. The cube model stimulated further work having a direct bearing on consultation.

One approach involved revising the cube to become a more systems and interactional model (Pace, Stamler, Yarris, & June, 1996). Kurpius and Fuqua (1993) advanced the field when they served as authors and editors of a double special issue of the *Journal of Counseling & Development* entitled "Consultation: A Paradigm for Helping." Atkinson, Thompson, and Grant (1993) articulated eight roles for counseling psychologists. They also presented their work as a cube-like model, in which consultation was one of these eight roles. Similarly, the community psychology model placed a large emphasis on the use of consultation as an indirect (triadic) service mode (Lewis, Lewis, Daniels, & D'Andrea, 2003). Caplan's mental health consultation model (1970) has also received significant attention. In his model, mental health consultation was considered an alternative means of delivering primary care interventions, with a large emphasis on a power-free relationship between consultant and consultee and a focus on the client's ecological system. The mental health collaboration approach later emerged to address some of the control and responsibility issues questioned in the original model. (Caplan, Caplan, & Erchul, 1994). Thus, the mental health consultation approach was considerably revised later as a result of critiques of the model based on resulting research (Caplan & Caplan, 1993).

Although the various forms of consultation employed by psychologists have not received a great deal of attention, several texts clarify both the overlap and distinctiveness of consultation in relation to counseling and psychotherapy (e.g., Bellman, 1990; Dougherty, 2009a; Lippitt & Lippitt, 1986). To understand these commonalities and differences, it is helpful to distinguish consultation terms from related clinical terms. Dougherty (2009a) presents concise definitions of four critical terms, designated as the "4 Cs": consultation, consultee, consultant, and client system.

- *Consultation*: A type of helping relationship in which a human service professional (consultant) delivers assistance to another person (consultee) so as to solve a work-related or caretaking-related problem the consultee has with a client system (a person, group, organization, or community).
- *Consultant*: A person, typically a human service professional, who delivers direct service to another person (consultee) who has a work-related or caretaking-related problem with a client system.
- *Consultee*: The person, often a human service professional or a caretaker (for example, a parent, teacher, or supervisor), to whom the consultant provides assistance with a work-related or caretaking-related problem. One of the goals of consultation is to improve the current and future functioning of the consultee.
- *Client system*: The person, group, organization, or community with whom the consultee is having work-related or caretaking-related problem. One of the goals of consultation is to improve the functioning of the client system (Dougherty, 2009a).

Dougherty (2009a) views consultation as dealing exclusively with the consultee's work-related or caregiving-related problems, and is collaborative. The consultant and consultee work together in solving the problems defined by consultation. The word "challenge" rather than "problem" may convey a more positive connotation that could be helpful to the consultee (Foster & Lloyd, 2007).

Although nearly all consultation involves a consultant, consultee, and a client system, the particulars of the content and focus of consultation can differ tremendously. Additionally, the major distinction in consultation focuses on whether the primary emphasis of the consultation is on the consultee's work-related role versus a caretaking-related role. (Dougherty, 2009a). An example of a counseling psychologist helping a consultee with a work-related role could be an executive coaching situation. In such a situation, an upper-level administrator may help an individual redirect leadership behaviors that are likely interfering with the direction and effectiveness of those who work for them. Such situations are dexribed in detail elsewhere (Kampa-Kokesch & Anderson, 2001). Alternatively, an example of a counseling psychologist helping a consultee with a caretaking role could be a consultant hired to conduct a program evaluation of a campus suicide prevention effort, working with and through a task force created to address this issue. In this situation, the consultant and task force might meet to discuss the results of the evaluation, and the task force may make decisions concerning changes in the program, based on the interaction with the consultant.

The idea of a triadic relationship is common to most concepts of psychologically based consultation (Bell & Nadler, 1985). The consultant interacts directly with the consultee who, in turn, is seeking to enhance a targeted area of functioning of the individual, the group, or the organization. Often, the effectiveness of the consultant with the client system is indirect, via the actions of the consultee (Knoff, Hines, & Kromrey, 1995). At times, however, the consultant may interact directly with the client system (Peterson, 2010). For example, the counseling psychologist consultant may conduct an assessment of a person for selection or may assist him or her with leadership development. Such selection and/or leadership development will likely have a considerable effect on the individual's team, agency, or organization. Systems evaluation and observation are other examples of direct contact between the consultant and the client system. Such limited direct contact of the consultant with the client system differs from what is labeled collaboration (Caplan et al., 1994). This distinction will be addressed later in this chapter.

Psychologically based mental health, school-based, and organizational consultation offer differential approaches to mental health therapy. Mental health–focused consultation differs from psychotherapy not so much in the goal of change for the client system, but in the triadic nature of how this is accomplished (Caplan & Caplan, 1993). For example, a consultant with expertise in PTSD may be brought in to help mental health workers better assist those affected by trauma. In this situation, the consultant does not work directly with those in need of services, but with those who are trying to help them.

The differences between mental health therapy and school-based consultation focus on the priority given to the student's educational attainment over other areas of his or her life functioning and on the triadic rather than dyadic/direct nature of the service (Rosenfield, 2002). For example, a counseling psychologist with additional training as a school psychologist may gather information from formalized testing of the student, from the informal and behavioral assessments and observations of others, and from interviews with parents and teachers. The psychologist, as consultant, then makes recommendations on class placement and educational interventions that others will implement.

The differences between mental health therapy and organizational consultation provide perhaps the largest contrast (Schein, 2006).The overall goal of organizational consultations is to assist the organization in achieving its goals. A consultant who focuses too heavily on the mental health issues of a consultee, at the cost of focusing on his or her work functioning and the organizational context, could quite possibly cause damage to that individual and the organization. This error of overfocusing on the individual and his mental health issues is one that trained counseling psychologists need to guard against, given the many experiences they have had in analyzing and diagnosing mental health issues in persons and then intervening to assist them. One particular model utilizes a process approach to consultation, relying on counseling skills but focusing the content much differently than in personal counseling (Schein, 1999).

Psychologically based consultation differs from vocational therapy in the scope of its focus and the nature of who is served and why (Blustein, 2006). Specifically, vocational therapy has primarily emphasized the study of vocational development and the phases of occupational decision making. Decades of research and practice have focused on this, and it remains a vibrant area of research (Dawis, 1996; (Fouad, 2007). More recently, this focus has been expanding as more is understood about the life-long nature of changes in the work people do, changes some make by choice, and, more and more, because of circumstances (Wasylyshyn, 2001). A good deal

of consultation in organizational settings focuses on individual work issues, although often the focus for organizational consultation is on teams and the organization as a whole. Even when the focus of the consultation is on an individual, the goals of the individual's organization are at least equal or perhaps more important than the goals of the individual person. Thus, compared to the individual making an occupational choice, counseling psychologists engaged in organizational consultation focus on enhancing the functioning of the organization itself, by improving the functioning of individuals and groups within the organization or by changing the organization's structures and processes. Thus, although the consultation work may be being done with an individual—as in executive coaching or talent development—the objective of the work in organizational consultation is primarily about how the organization benefits (and hopefully the individual, too) (Levinson, 2009).

Research by counseling psychologists on consultation process or practice is far less than for psychotherapy. Plus, the majority of articles that counseling psychologists have authored are conceptual in approach rather than being quantitative- or qualitative-based research (Cooper, 2008). Perhaps the main reason for this paucity of investigation is that consulting psychology is currently neither a specialization nor proficiency, and most working in the field are practitioners (Blanton, 2000). To find existing literature, the most likely psychology journal outlets for these publications are the *Consulting Psychology Journal, Journal of Educational and Psychological Consultation, Journal of Consulting and Clinical Psychology, Journal of School Psychology*, the *School Counselor, Elementary School Guidance and Counseling*, and the *Journal of Applied Behavioral Science*. Several nonpsychology journals may contain articles on psychologically based consultation. They include the *Harvard Business Review, Journal of Management, the Leadership and Organizational Development Journal*, and the *Training and Development Journal*.

The *Journal of Counseling and Development* published a double special issue on consultation (Kurpius & Fuqua, 1993). The first part focused on conceptual, structural, and operational definitions. The second part focused on prevention, preparation, and key issues. These special issues were updates of earlier articles published in the *Personal and Guidance Journal*.

Two main domains of scholarship on consultation are of relevance to counseling psychologists.

The primary one is conceptual and applied. As illustrations of such scholarship, *Consulting Psychology Journal* has released a number of special issues on select topics such as executive coaching (Diedrich, 2008); leadership (Leonard, 2003; Quick & Nelson, 2008); workplace mobbing (Sperry, 2009); and culture, race, and ethnicity in organizational consulting psychology (2008).

Empirical research on consultation has a 40-year history, but the methods of investigation used have not been sophisticated (Dougherty, 2009a). Lowman (2008) calls for high-quality literature reviews, avoidance of authoritatively presented hypotheses, and both theoretical and empirical rigor in both data-based and case studies. Given the highly applied nature of consultation and that most reports come from practitioners, case studies and quasi-scientific studies have been the dominant form of research, with less work that is scientifically or meta-analysis based (Armenakis & Burdg, 1988). Consultation appears to result in moderately positive outcomes (Gibson & Chard, 1994) in approximately three-fourths of the studies (Sheridan, Welch, & Orme, 1996).

Essentials of Psychologically Based Consultation: Multiculturalism in Consultation

Racial, ethnic, religious, and national diversity is increasing rapidly in the United States and many other countries of the world (Cooper & Leong, 2008). This results from a number of factors, such as immigration and emigration and from differential birthrates among different populations. The increased interaction among diverse persons in a global, flat world is increasing even more rapidly. Additionally, more organizations and industries are operating cross-culturally and internationally. The sharing of information around the world via the Internet and other form of electronic communication has grown exponentially (Cooper & Leong, 2008).

A combination of these factors has led to applied psychology's growing attention to professionals who work with clients who are different from themselves and the need to provide competent and helpful consultation. Counseling psychology has been a leader in the multicultural movement in psychology. For example, Division 17 was one of the co-founding APA divisions of the National Multicultural Conference and Summit (Sue, Bingham, Porsche-Burke & Vasquez, 1999). A significant proportion of the scholarly articles published recently in the *Journal of Counseling Psychology* and *The Counseling Psychologist* have some element of multiculturalism as a central focus or variable in the study. Other APA Divisions such as the Society for the Psychological Study of Ethnic Minority Issues (Division 45), the Society for the Psychological Study of Lesbian, Gay, Bisexual, and Transgender Issues (Division 44), the Society for the Psychology of Women (Division 35), and the Division of International Psychology (Division 52) have been equally active.

The case can easily be made that working with issues of diversity and multiculturalism in consultation is inherently even more complicated due to its triadic nature. There is an added component when the diversity of the consultant, the diversity of the consultee, and the diversity of the client system all have to come together. For example, such issues are being addressed in the training of those working in community mental health centers (Parker-Taylor, Kim, Budianto, Laidlaw, Sakurai & Pfeifer, 2009). When there are multiple consultants, multiple consultees, and a complex client system, the importance of attending to multicultural issues is geometrically significant.

Steward (1996) called for consultants to attend to workplace diversity issues. He affirmed that important progress could be accomplished by focusing on organizational infrastructure, job satisfaction, relationships among staff, and work productivity. Similarly, Plummer (1998) argued that attending to diversity consultation is a must, given the increasing diversity in the workplace. Dealing with issues of awareness, sociopolitical implications, open dialogue, cultural competence, and cultural norms is vital if organizations are to accomplish enhanced diversity functioning. Unfortunately, relatively little empirical work has been conducted in this area to date Cooper & Leong, 2008). Yet, the presses of internationalization and diversity within and external to organizations continue to push for consultants to incorporate a "multicultural and racially sensitive consultation approach" (Cooper, Wilson-Stark, Peterson, & O'Roark, 2008, p. 200).

Although few empirical studies have been conducted, some of the literature provides prescriptive suggestions to the consultant. Dougherty (2009a) noted nine skills related to incorporating the salience of multicultural factors into successful consultation. Several additional frameworks exist that can assist the consultant and the consultee in functioning with cultural competence. Hofstede (2005) has conducted a long-term study of cultural differences around the globe. His model includes five factors (2005):

- *Power distance* reflects the extent to which the less powerful members of institutions and organizations within a country expect and accept that power is distributed unequally. *Individualism* pertains to societies in which the ties between individuals are loose: Everyone is expected to look after himself or herself and his or her immediate family.
- *Collectivism*, the opposite of individualism, pertains to societies in which people from birth onward are integrated into strong in-groups, which throughout people's lifetimes continue to protect them in exchange for unquestioning loyalty.
- A *masculine society* has gender roles that are clearly distinct: Men are supposed to be assertive, tough, and focused on materials success, whereas women are supposed to be nonassertive, tender, and concerned with the quality of life. In contrast, a *feminine society* has emotional gender roles that overlap: Both men and women are supposed to be modest, tender, and concerned with the quality of life.
- *Uncertainty avoidance* is defined as the extent to which the members of a culture feel threatened by ambiguous or unknown situations.
- A *long-term orientation* focuses on the fostering of virtues oriented toward future rewards—in particular, perseverance and thrift. Its opposite, a *short-term orientation*, stands for the following of virtues related to the past and present—in particular, respect for tradition, preservation of "face," and fulfilling social obligations.

Hofstede's research has explored a nation-based analysis of differences on these dimensions in areas such as work life, personal beliefs, student–teacher relationships, etc. On a general, "emic" (universal) perspective, knowing the ratings for a given country can help the consultant work more effectively in that country or with people who came from that country. Always, however, an individual, "etic" (group) approach must be kept in mind by the consultant for both the consultee and the client system. Although Hofstede's model was developed primarily for international application, it is useful for addressing within-country diversity as well (Hofstede, 2005).

Similar to Hofstede's approach, the Center for Creative Leadership (CCL, 1998) has developed a seven-factor model (Prince & Hoppe, 2007). The seven factors CCL uses in leadership training are: source and expression of identity (collective vs. individual), source and expression of authority (equal vs. unequal), means and goals of achievement (tender–work to live vs. tough–live to work), response to uncertainty and change (dynamic vs. stable), means of knowledge acquisition (reflective vs. active), orientation to time (scarce–linear vs. plentiful–cyclical), and response to natural and social environment (being–harmony vs. doing–mastery).

Like Hofstede's work, researchers using the CCL model have collected data regarding where different countries fall on a continuum of each of these factors. Consultants can utilize these factors to help the consultant work better with consultees or client systems that are multiculturally different, whether these differences of diversity are within the United States or occur cross-nationally.

Another significant resource to assist consultants to consult with multicultural competence is the *Guidelines on Multicultural Education, Training, Research, Practice, and Organizational Change for Psychologists* (APA, 2003). The latter two sections of this document are particularly appropriate. Guideline 5 pertains to practice. The Guideline states: "Psychologists strive to apply culturally appropriate skills in clinical and other applied psychological practices" (APA, 2003, p. 390). Specifically, "culturally appropriate psychological applications assume awareness and knowledge about one's worldview as a cultural being and as a professional psychologist, and the worldview of others' particularly as influenced by ethnic/racial heritage" (APA, 2003, p. 390). This Guideline refers to applying that awareness and knowledge in psychological practice.

It is not necessary to develop an entirely new repertoire of psychological skills to practice in a culture-centered manner. Rather, it is helpful for psychologists to realize that there will likely be situations in which culture-centered adaptations in interventions and practices will be more effective (Cooper & Leong, 2008). Psychological practice is defined here as the use of psychological skills in a variety of settings and for a variety of purposes, encompassing counseling, clinical, school, consulting, and organizational psychology. This guideline further suggests that, regardless of our practice site and purview of practice, psychologists are responsive to the Ethics Code (APA, 1992; 2002). In the

Preamble to the Ethics Code is language that advocates behavior that values human welfare and basic human rights. Most of the initial work on Guideline 5 was on clinical work, but it would appear to be equally, if not more, suitable for consulting activity.

Guideline 6 advocates significant use of organizational consultation as a means of achieving meaningful change. The Guideline reads "psychologists are encouraged to use organizational change processes to support culturally informed organizational (policy) development and practices" (APA, 2003, p. 392). Guideline 6 is based on the advocate role of the consultant, in which the consultant is assisting organizations as consultees/client systems to develop new ways of functioning that are congruent with a pluralistic work and social environment. Specifically, Guideline 6 is designed to inform psychologists about the following: the contemporary and future contexts that provide motivators for psychologists' proactive behavior with organizational change processes, perspectives about psychologists in transition, frameworks and models to facilitate multicultural organizational development, and examples of processes and practices reflective of psychologists' leadership in the development of culture-centered organizations (APA, 2003).

Given the paucity of literature on this topic, Cooper and Leong (2008) co-edited a special issue of the *Consulting Psychology Journal* entitled "Culture, Race, and Ethnicity in Organizational Consulting Psychology." This special issue adopted a qualitative approach to the topic from leaders in this field, as well as an article summarizing themes (Cooper, Wilson-Stark, Peterson, & O'Roark, 2008) and a detailed bibliography with sections on general diversity issues, diversity management and intercultural communication, culture specific issues, racism and prejudice, and cross-cultural and international issues (Leong, Cooper, & Huang, 2008).

Cooper et al. (2008) employed a consensual qualitative research method of developing summaries of findings based on narratives from consultants' perspectives of integrating attention and priority to diversity issues within their work and then presenting these back to those who contributed for affirmation, change, or addition. The final seven consultation themes developed by this reiterative process were:

- *Theme 1*: Culture, race, and ethnicity matters.
- *Theme 2*: Networking and mentoring are more challenging for nonmajority managers and leaders to obtain.

- *Theme 3*: Use of language between the consultant and consultee may be a challenge or an issue when diversity is greater.
- *Theme 4*: Combining an emic (universal), etic (group), and unique (person) approach to organizational consulting with consultees is recommended.
- *Theme 5*: It is best to bring up differences of culture, race, and ethnicity directly and into the open.
- *Theme 6*: It takes concentrated effort to avoid cultural myopia and colonialism.
- *Theme 7*: When the consultant and the consultee are of differing culture, race, or ethnicity, more time is likely to be needed to build trust and to develop the consulting relationship. (Cooper, Wilson-Stark, Peterson, & O'Roark, 2008, pp. 199–200)

> With effort, study, practice and mentoring, organizational consultants can gain knowledge, attitude, and behavioral skills needed to have reasonable and effective cultural competence when consulting with consultees and client systems that differ culturally, racially or ethnically from the consultant. With further scientific study, we can deepen our understanding of consulting effectively in this increasingly multicultural world. The need for enhancement of both practice and science on this topic is great.
> (Cooper et al., 2008, p. 200)

A Transtheoretical Model for Psychologically Based Consultation

Dougherty (2009) has developed a detailed generic approach to consulting that counseling psychologists might find very useful in the consultation work they do—mental health, school, behavioral, or organizational consultation. It also works well whether it is a relatively simple consultation (i.e., one consultee and one client), or a very complex consultation with multiple consultants, consultees, and client system targets at the individual, group, and organizational levels.

Dougherty's generic approach is divided into four phases: entry, diagnosis, implementation, and disengagement. Furthermore, each phase is divided into four stages. Although his approach appears to be a linear process, there is interaction and overlap among the stages in each phase and among the phases as well, especially the first three. The amount of time and detail needed varies tremendously depending on the nature of the problem to be resolved and the dynamics of each particular psychologically based consultation. For most consultations that counseling psychologists do, relatively little time is needed to go through the entire process, but for some, the opposite is the case.

Entry occurs when the consultant develops a professional relationship with the consultee and explores the presenting problem, along with formulating a formal or informal contract. This involves beginning to physically and psychologically enter the system of the consultee and his or her agency or organization. Dougherty defines entry as "the general process by which the consultant enters the system in which consultation is to occur" (Dougherty, 2009a, p. 53). In the entry stage, the counseling psychologist consultant focuses on four phases: exploring organizational needs (McLean, 2006; Stroh & Johnson, 2006), contracting (APA, 2003 see Ethical Code Standard 3.11); physically entering the system (Gallessich, 1982; McLean, 2006), and psychologically entering the system.

According to Dougherty (2009a), the *diagnostic stage* involves the process of defining and specifying the work-related or care-taking problem to be resolved. This initially involves gathering, analyzing, and discussing information and data. The consultatee and consultant move on to goal setting and brainstorming of implementation strategies. Similar to counseling and therapy, diagnosis is essential in determining the course of action to be taken, in this case by the consultant and consultee. The thoroughness of the diagnostic process depends on the purpose of the consultation and, in some consultations, feedback about the results of the diagnosis is the main outcome. In other consultations with a different goal, there are interrelationships among diagnosis, data collecting, and intervention. In the diagnostic stage, the counseling psychologist consultant focuses on four phases: gathering information (Dougherty, 2009a), defining the problem, setting goals (Curtis & Stollar; Egan, 2006; Locke & Latham, 2002), and generating possible interventions (Egan, 2006, 2007).

The third phase of Dougherty's generic model is *implementation* and begins with the selection of interventions. This is followed by the consultee engaging in action with the support of the consultant. A reiterative process is involved with the plan. Changes are made depending on the level of goal attainment for the client system. Whereas the major purpose of the first two stages of the consultation process is to set the stage for action for the consultee or consultees to make change to help their client(s),

teams, or organizations, the role of the consultant during the implementation phase typically involves those of being a resource person and/or trainer (Dougherty, 2009a). In the implementation stage, the counseling psychologist consultant focuses on four phases: choosing an intervention, which involves selection (Gutkin & Curtis, 1999) and modality, for example, third-party peacemaking (Gelembiewski & Rauschenberg, 1993); formulating a plan (Egan, 1985); implementing the plan; and evaluating the plan.

The final phase of Dougherty's generic model, *disengagement*, constitutes a winding down process. The more involved the consultation, in terms of length and intensity, the more length of time and effort is needed to end the consultation successfully. Disengagement typically starts with collection and discussion of the summative evaluation data. Prior to this, the evaluations conducted throughout and at the end of the entry, diagnosis, and implementation phases were process-oriented and often brief and qualitative in nature.

As with counseling and therapy, disengagement is a critical part of the helping process and one that is far too often done badly. The effects of such a badly done disengagement process can adversely affect a consultation that has gone very well through all the first three stages. When done very poorly, the consultant–consultee relationship is irreparably damaged, and there can be intense negative emotions for the consultee(s). The disengagement stage proceeds through evaluating the process of consultation, using both summative and process evaluation methods; postconsultation planning; reduced contact; follow-up (see Myrick, 2003, for a listing of benefits); and termination (Teyber & McClure, 2011). Much greater detail on Dougherty's generic model is available in part II of his book, *Psychological Consultation and Collaboration in School and Community Settings* (5th ed.).

The relationship between counseling psychologists using the integrative model of consultation versus use of a specific model or particular approach to consultation is identical to the relationship between counseling psychologists who use systemic, eclectic, or transtheoretical models of counseling versus those who choose use of a specific theoretical model or approach. Generally, most counseling psychologists engaging in consultation will find the generic approach to be more flexible to adapt to the particular consultation needed. However, some consultants find it easier working within a specific model or with any of the approaches that are part of that model. Sometimes, the parameters of a situation or setting may elicit the use of a particular consultation approach. One difference between consultation and counseling is the relatively smaller number of current models and approaches. For psychologically based consultation, four main models are mental health, behavioral, school, and organizational (Dougherty, 2009a).

Mental Health Consultation

For counseling psychologists who engage in consulting, the closest consultation model is the mental health consultation model developed by Caplan (1970, 1993). The focus of mental health consultation is to help the therapist or the administrator work more effectively with clients and programs, respectively. Although some of the above may seem identical to clinical supervision (particularly when the focus is on helping a counselor be more helpful to their client), there are a number of differences between consultation and clinical supervision (Haynes, Corey, & Moulton, 2003). Supervision involves a hierarchical relationship that addresses evaluation of the student.

Within the mental health model, there are four main approaches: client-centered case, consultee-centered case, program-centered administrative, and consultee-centered administrative (Caplan, 1970). A two-dimensional figure can be visualized, in which one dimension is the target of the consultation (an individual vs. a program) and the other dimension is focus (more on the client or more on the consultee).

In client-centered case consultation, the counseling psychologist consultant focuses on helping a consultee with a client (with the consultant having no or minimal contact with the consultee). In consultee-centered case consultation, the counseling psychologist consultant considers work-related problems to reside in the consultee and helps the consultee by focusing on a specific case. In program-centered administrative consultation, the counseling psychologist consultant helps an administrator fix a program-related problem. Caplan and Caplan (1993) added a fifth approach, ecological, which aims at the human–environment interface, a systemic perspective.

The behavioral model of consultation is based on various behavioral models, but especially on social learning, instrumental conditioning, and cognitive-behavioral therapy (CBT) theories (Dougherty, 2009a). There are three main approaches within

this model: case (Bergin & Kratochwill, 1990), technology training (Vernberg & Reppucci, 1986), and system (Lewis & Newcomer, 2002).

In behavioral case consultation, the counseling psychologist consultant helps a consultee apply behavioral technology to a case (Kratochwill, 2007). In behavioral technology training, the counseling psychologist consultant trains consultees to improve their general and/or specific skill areas of behavioral technology. In behavioral system consultation, the counseling psychologist consultant assists an organization in being more effective by using behavioral technology.

For the school consultation model, there are three main approaches. These approaches include: Adlerian (Carlson, Watts, & Maniacci, 2006; Dinkmeyer, 2006), instructional (Rosenfield, 2002), and organizational development change (Cowan, 2007; Dougherty, 2009a; Flashpohler, 2007). In Adlerian consultation, the counseling psychologist consultant uses Adlerian principles to help teachers individually or, in a C-group, to assist a student or students. In instructional consultation, the counseling psychologist consultant focuses on modifying the teacher's behavior to create a better learning environment. In organizational development change consultation, the counseling psychologist consultant helps the school improve its functioning on a system-wide basis.

The organizational model of consultation emerged outside the mental health and school fields of study, but it has influenced both profoundly. Dougherty (2009a), based on earlier work by Schein (1988, 1999, 2006), describes four approaches within the organizational model: educational/training (Arredondo, 1996), program consultation (Gallesich, 1982), doctor–patient (Schein, 1990), and process (Schein, 1990).

In educational/training consultation (Arredondo, 1996), the counseling psychologist consultant trains or educates consultees to be more effective in some area. In program consultation (Staton, Bensen, Briggs, Cowen, Echterling, Evans, et al., 2007), the counseling psychologist consultant assists a program, frequently via program evaluation. In doctor–patient consultation (Schein, 1990), the counseling psychologist consultant enters an organization, diagnoses a problem, and prescribes a solution. In process consultation (Schein, 1990), the counseling psychologist consultant assists consultees in becoming better decision makers and problem solvers in the future. See Table 32.2 for a summary of these four approaches.

Table 32.2. Consultation Approaches and Areas of Emphasis

Mental Health	
Client-Centered Case	Helping a consultee with a client (with minimal contact with the consultee)
Consultee-Centered Case	Considers work-related problem to reside in the consultee; helping consultee by focusing on case
Program-Centered Administrative	Helping an administrator fix a program-related problem
Consultee-Centered Administrative	Helping an administrator and other consultees develop their skills to improve the mental health aspects of the organization and its programs
Ecological	Changing the human–environment interface
Behavioral	
Case	Helping a consultee apply behavioral technology to a case
Training	Training consultees to improve their general and/or specific skill areas of behavioral technology
System	Assisting an organization in being more effective by using behavioral technology
School	
Adlerian	Using Adlerian principles to help teachers individually or in a C-group
Instructional	Focuses on modifying the teacher's behavior to create a better learning environment.
Organizational Development Change	Helping the school improve its functioning on a system-wide basis
Organizational	
Educational/Training	Training or educating consultees to be more effective in some area
Program	Assisting a program, frequently evaluation
Doctor–Patient	Entering an organization, diagnosing a problem, and prescribing a solution
Process	Assisting consultees in becoming better decision makers and problem solvers in the future

The Status of Training and Research on Psychologically Based Consultation

Consultation is recognized as one of six main functional competency domains for counseling psychologists (Rodolfa, et al., 2005). Yet, graduate counseling psychology programs place very limited curricular time toward instruction on consultation. The authors of this chapter conducted an e-survey of the directors of APA-accredited programs in counseling psychology in July 2009. Although the number of respondents was not large ($N = 13$), half of the programs were consistent in how content on psychologically based consultation was covered. Specifically, half of these programs provided a combined supervision/consultation course. One program focused on consultation in rural settings and combined this with a course on program evaluation. Another program combined consultation-focused content in a course on community prevention and intervention, and yet another incorporated consultation into their professional development and assessment courses. Two of the responder schools offered no coursework in consultation, and one school, which has historically offered a combined supervision/consultation class, is in the process of moving toward a standalone consultation course.

The APA Guidelines and Principles for Accreditation of Programs in Professional Psychology (http://www.apa.org/ed/accreditation/qrg_doctoral.html, 2009) list specific criteria that all accredited programs must meet. Standard B.3 (c) is the standard that most directly addresses the consultation area. "Diagnosing or defining problems through assessment and implementing intervention strategies (including empirically supported procedures) including exposure to the current body of knowledge in at least the following areas: (a) Theories and methods of assessment and diagnosis, (b) Effective intervention, (c) Consultation and supervision, and (d) Evaluating the efficacy of interventions." Given the increasing importance of consultation as a key competency, the limited amount of attention current programs build into their required curriculum seems insufficient (Rodolfa, Bent, Eisman, Nelson, Rehm, & Ritchie, 2005).

The APA accreditation standards for internship sites reflect the increased attention to consultation given in the current program accreditation standards (see APA, Guidelines and Principles for Accreditation of Programs in Professional Psychology, 2009). Specifically, Standard 4 (c) reads "In achieving its objectives, the program requires that all interns demonstrate an intermediate to advanced level of professional psychological skills, abilities, proficiencies, competencies, and knowledge in the areas of: (c) Theories and/or methods of consultation, evaluation, and supervision;" (APA, http://www.apa.org/ed/accreditation/intern. html, 2009). Each program is required to document how this standard is being met via the expectations and experiences that are built into the training requirements. Given the combination of consultation, evaluation, and supervision that are all combined in this single standard, however, it is unlikely that significant attention is given to enhancing consultation knowledge and skill acquisition at most internship sites.

Best Practices for Enhancing Psychologically Based Consultation Education and Training

Although neither counseling psychology nor other branches of applied psychology have focused significant resources on education, training, and research on the practice of consultation, sufficient work has been done to be able to suggest best practices for enhancing education and training, as well as research. Suggestions for counseling psychologists who want to become or are engaged in psychologically based consultation are given first. This is followed by suggestions on improving research-related to consultation.

The seven skill sets that effective consultants use were described earlier (Dougherty, 2009a). The micro-skills in each of these skills sets could serve as the basis for educational curriculum and outcomes assessment. Another valuable conceptual framework for developing best practices is the organizational consultation competencies that were passed as official APA Guidelines in 2005 (APA, 2007). These consist of a number of different competency areas nested respectively under individual, group, and organizational levels. As official APA-approved guidelines, these represent work that involved a highly reviewed and quality-controlled process. The outcomes are considered to represent best practice. In general, APA has approved only a handful of such guidelines, as they represent officially sanctioned perspectives.

The educational curriculum of most counseling psychology programs already targets the acquisition of several of the individual- and group-level core competencies that are part of these Guidelines. For counseling psychologists, the historical inclusion of vocational counseling as a root of counseling psychology gives the field a significant advantage for consultation over the curriculums of the other "clinically focused" graduate programs (Shullman, 2002). What would most be needed for counseling psychology programs to better prepare their students to provide high-quality consultation would be to find textbook and in-class examples of consultations within organizational settings, to be presented along with the clinical setting examples that currently prevail in both book resources and classroom discourse. Additionally, programs moving toward a standalone consultation course instead of the combined supervision/consultation course, required currently by many programs, would double the attention paid to the development of consultation as a core competency. Furthermore, most counseling psychology programs do not focus on the organizational level of intervention, despite a strongly held value within counseling psychology toward prevention and community enhancement (Shullman, 2002). Expansion of the curriculum to include this molar emphasis could best be achieved via a curriculum infusion process rather than by the development of new courses to be taught by already overstretched counseling psychology faculty.

Cooper (2002) edited a special issue of the *Consulting Psychology Journal* on "Training and Education in Organizational Consulting Psychology." This special issue included reaction pieces from several counseling psychologists. Fuqua and Newman (2002) focused on doctoral-level curricula. They stated that the Guidelines provide four important advantages: They focus on competencies rather than on course activities; they place an emphasis on the utilization of applied research skills; they prioritize process and summative evaluation; and they endorse the scientist–practitioner approach to professional work (now reframed as the evidence-based practice model). In their reaction piece, Fuqua and Newman (2002) questioned the level of actual attention that would be paid to developing a solid, underlying science for consulting, and expressed concern about practices being taken without sufficient foundation. They also questioned the level of distinctiveness of consultation from therapy focused skills. Concerning this distinctiveness, the concept of two overlapping Venn diagrams, in which consultation and counseling share many of the same skills sets, yet differ in how these are utilized, would seem to portray the most accurate picture. The main difference that offsets consultation is that it is triadic, indirectly targeting improvement in the client, group, or organization; it has a work- or caretaking-related focus; and the consultant–consultee relationship differs from the therapist–client relationship. Fuqua and Newman (2002) presaged the current discussion of changes in the APA Model Professional Psychology Practice Act by speculating about what the future might bring in the relationship of the Guidelines to professional practice and licensure. As currently proposed, the APA Model Practice Act will encompass the work of all professional psychologists, both clinical and applied. Practice within the domain of one's demonstrated competencies, as acquired by curricular and applied experiences, is a central component of the proposed act.

Shullman (2002) supported a congruence of most counseling psychology doctoral curriculum with the individual and group levels of the Guidelines. Yet, she also described several aspects of the consulting competencies in which counseling psychology students could benefit from greater exposure. An example at the individual level is a greater utilization of a strengths-based rather than solely a deficits-based approach, an approach typically used in counseling vocational psychology. Examples at the group level are uses of tools to assess and assist workgroups and to facilitate intergroup problem solving, to identity groups and intergroup relations, and to align groups with organizational objectives. Shullman (2002) asserted that the largest area of deficit in the training of counseling psychologists is at the organizational/systemic level. She articulated that counseling psychology's emphases on person–environment fit and multiculturalism provide the basis for a broader individual-group-organizational model that could incorporate therapy, consultation, and the other four core applied psychology domains.

These suggestions would take place within the doctoral program of studies. A best practice that would assist the development of consultation competency at the practicum and predoctoral levels would be the creation of communication networks among these sites that share trainee expectations and developmental experiences that aim to improve the student's understanding and skills in consulting. Use of organizations such as the Association of Psychology Postdoctoral and Internship Centers (APPIC) that already have extensive networking among the training coordinators would require relatively little effort.

Cooper, Monarch, Serviss, Gordick, and Leonard (2007) focused on post-degree learning experiences that psychologists wanting to work as consultants could seek as a means of acquiring the requisite knowledge, skills, and supervised applied experiences. These learning experiences were viewed as needing to fit into a developmental model for those doing consultation, with the stages increasing from beginning to entry to mid-level to senior psychologists. These suggestions cross the developmental level of the psychologist with the individual-group-organizational consultation competencies model. A report presenting each of these suggestions is available from the Society of Consulting Psychology's website at http://www.div13.org/Reports/PresidentialTaskForce.htm. The report was a product of a Presidential Task Force on Professional Preparation and Continuing Education for Beginning, Entry, Mid-level, and Senior Consulting Psychologists.

Best Practices for Enhancing Psychologically Based Consultation Research

Several best practices targeted at improving consultation-focused research emerge from the work done by APA on evidence-based psychology practice (APA, 2005). Specifically, the recommendations generated by the APA Task Force on Empirically Based Practice provide a context for examining research on consultation process and practice (APA, 2005). In relation to the methodologies used to study consultation, the primary methodologies scholars have employed have been clinical observation, qualitative research (most of which have been very simplistic and have not used contemporary rigorous qualitative methods), and studies of interventions as delivered in naturalistic settings. Some consultation studies (e.g., Cooper & Newbold, 1994) have employed single-case experimental designs. Such single-case design studies are more prevalent in behavioral (see Kratochwill, Elliot, & Callan-Soiber, 2002) and school-based consultations (Rosenfield, 2002). A few meta-analyses of organization-wide interventions (e.g., Gibson & Chard, 1994) have been conducted. Systematic case study, process outcome studies, and randomized clinical trail studies have rarely been employed (Dougherty, 2009a). With randomized controlled trials, both lack of funding and the highly idiographic nature of consultation have been barriers. Few studies of consultation with diverse consultees or client populations have been carried out (Cooper & Leong, 2008). Rodney Lowman, the current editor of *Consulting Psychology Journal*, wrote:

> The Society's [APA Div.13] flagship journal: *Consulting Psychology: Practice and Research* is one outlet for creating the new knowledge base but it is

far from the only one. Consulting Psychology will need carefully to note and master the research that is published in related disciplines on our field's areas of special expertise (e.g., coaching, assessment and group-organizational interventions). Needed are "bread and butter" studies that do the necessarily detailed work to validate operating premises such as approaches to assessment and intervention. Unfortunately we have very few graduate training programs in consulting psychology so there is not a large amount of research and theory emanating from the usual sources and with the usual support mechanisms. If we wish as a profession to expand the research base of our discipline we must support the expansion of such graduate programs, to create internships and post-docs in these areas with research expectations and we must facilitate the expansion of journals and other publication outlets. By promoting jobs in this area of psychological practice and reasonable methods of licensure, we may be able to attract more graduate programs and more students and in turn more faculty and research. Encouraging consulting firms to take on research agendas also provide an outlet. (Personal communication, Lowman, 2009)

Conclusion

Consulting psychology is a major area of psychological practice that is currently neither a specialty or proficiency. Although longstanding in practice, consulting psychological practice is still lacking in empirical rigor. To paraphrase the language of the 2005 APA Task Force on Evidence-Based Practice in Psychology (APA, 2005), evidence-based practice is the integration of the best available research with consultant expertise in the context of consultee and individual, group, and organizational client characteristics, culture, and preferences. A fertile field is open to counseling psychologists for developing both the science and the practice components of this equation.

References

American Psychological Association (APA). (2003). Guidelines on multicultural education, training, research, practice, and organizational change for psychologists. *American Psychologist*, 58, 377–402.

American Psychological Association (APA). (2005). *American Psychological Association policy statement on evidence-based practice in psychology*. Retrieved from http://search.apa.org/search?query=evidence-based%20practice.

American Psychological Association (APA). (2007). Guidelines for education and training at the doctoral and postdoctoral levels in consulting psychology/organizational consulting psychology. *American Psychologist*, 62, 980–992.

American Psychological Association (APA). (2009). *Guidelines and principles for accreditation of programs in professional psychology*. Retrieved from http://www.apa.org/ed/accreditation/qrg_doctoral.html.

Armenakis, A. A., & Burdig, H. B. (1988). Consultation research: Contributions to practice and directions for improvement. *Journal of Management*, 14, 339–365.

Arredondo, P. (1996). *Successful diversity management initiatives*. Thousand Oaks, CA: Sage.

Atkinson, D. R., Thompson, C. E., & Grant, S. K. (1993). A three-dimensional model for counseling racial/ethnic minorities. *The Counseling Psychologist*, 21, 257–277.

Bell, C. R., & Nadler, L. (1985). *Clients and consultants*. Houston, TX: Gulf.

Bellman, G. M. (1990). *The consultants calling*. San Francisco: Josey-Bass.

Bergin, J. R., & Kratochwill, T. R. (1990). *Behavioral consultation and therapy*. New York: Plenum.

Blanton, J. S. (2000). Why consultants don't apply psychological research. *Consulting Psychology Journal: Practice and Research*, 52, 235–247.

Blustein, D. L. (2006). *The psychology of working: A new perspective for career development, counseling, and public policy*. Mahwah, NJ: Lawrence Erlbaum Associates.

Caplan, G., & Caplan, R. B. (1993). *Mental health consultation and collaboration*. San Francisco: Josey-Bass.

Caplan, G., Caplan, R. B., & Erchul, W. P. (1994). Caplanian mental health consultation: Historical background and current status. *Consulting Psychology Journal: Practice and Research*, 46, 2–12.

Civiello, C. L. (2009). Introduction to the special issue on organizational consulting in national security contexts. *Consulting Psychology Journal: Practice and Research*, 61(1), 1–4.

Cooper, S. E. (2002). Training and education in organizational consulting psychology. *Consulting Psychology Journal: Practice and Research (special issue)*, 54, 211–278.

Cooper, S. E. (2003). College counseling centers as internal organizational consultants to universities. *Consulting Psychology Journal: Practice and Research*, 55, 230–238.

Cooper, S. E. (2008, August). *Enhancing the practice, craft, and science of psychologically-based consultation*. Presidential Address for Division 13 at the annual convention of the American Psychological Association. Boston, Massachusetts.

Cooper, S. E., & Leong F. T. L. (2008). Introduction to the special issue on culture, race, and ethnicity in organizational consulting psychology. *Consulting Psychology Journal: Practice and Research: Special Issue on Culture, race and ethnicity in organizational consulting psychology*, 60(2), 133–138.

Cooper, S. E., Monarch, N., Serviss, S. T., Gordick, D., & Skipton, L. H. (2007). Professional preparation and continuing education for beginning, entry, midlevel, and senior consulting psychologists. *Consulting Psychology Journal: Practice and Research*, 59, 1–16.

Cooper, S. E., & Newbold, R. C. (1994). Combining external and internal behavioral system consultation to enhance plant safety. *The Consulting Psychologist*, 46, 32–41.

Cooper, S. E., & O'Connor, R. M. (1993). Standards for organizational consultation assessment and evaluation instruments. *Journal of Counseling & Development: Special issue on Consultation: A paradigm for helping: Consultation I: Conceptual, structural, and operational dimensions*, 71, 651–660.

Cooper, S. E., Wilson-Stark, K., Peterson, D., O'Roark, A. M. & Pennington, G. (2008). Consulting competently in multicultural contexts. *Consulting Psychology Journal: Practice and Research, 60,* 186–202.

Corey, M. S., Corey, G., & Corey, C. (2010). *Groups: Process and Practice* (8th ed.). Pacific Grove, CA: Brooks/Cole.

Dawis, R. V. (1996). Vocational psychology, vocational adjustment, and the workforce: Some familiar and unanticipated consequences. *Psychology, Public Policy, and Law, 2*(2), 229–248.

Diedrich, R. C. (Ed.). (2008). More about executive coaching: Practice and research. Special issue. *Consulting Psychology Journal: Practice and Research, 60*(1), 4–131.

Dinkmeyer, D. Jr. (2006). School consultation using individual psychology. *Journal of individual psychology, 62,* 180–187.

Dougherty, A. M. (2009a). *Psychological consultation and collaboration in school and community settings* (5th ed.). Belmont, CA: Brooks/Cole.

Dougherty, A. M. (2009b). *Psychological consultation and collaboration in school and community settings: A casebook* (5th ed.). Pacific Grove, CA: Brooks/Cole.

Foster, S. L., & Lloyd, P. (2007). Positive psychology principles applied to consulting psychology at the individual and group level. *Journal of Consulting Psychology, 59*(1), 30–40.

Fouad, N. A. (2007). Work and vocational psychology: Theory, research, and applications. *Annual Review of Psychology, 58,* 543–564. doi:10.1146/annurev.psych.58.110405.085713.

Gallesich, J. (1982). *The profession and practice of consultation.* San Francisco: Josey-Bass.

Gibson, G., & Chard, K. M. (1994). Quantifying the effects of community mental health consultation interventions. *Consulting Psychology Journal: Practice and Research, 46,* 13–25.

Haynes, R., Corey, G., Moulton, P. (2003). *Clinical supervision in the helping professions.* Pacific Grove, CA: Thompson Brooks/Cole.

Hofstede, G. (2005). *Cultures and organizations: Software of the mind.* Columbus, OH: McGraw-Hill.

Kampa-Kokesch, S., & Anderson, M. Z. (2001). Executive coaching: A comprehensive review of the literature. *Consulting Psychology Journal: Practice and Research, 53*(4), 205–228.

Kilburg, R. R. (2002) Shadow consultation: A reflective approach for preventing practice disasters. *Consulting Psychology Journal: Practice and Research, 54,* 75–92.

Knoff, H. M., Hines, C. V., & Kromrey, J. D. (1995). Finalizing the Consultant Effectiveness Scale: An analysis and validation of the characteristics of effective consultants. *School Psychology Review, 24,* 480–496.

Kratochwill, T. R. (2007). Preparing psychologists for evidence-based school practice: Lessons learned and challenges ahead. *American Psychologist, 62*(8), 829–843.

Kratochwill, T. R., Elliot, S. N., & Callan-Stoiber, K. (2002). Best practices in school-based problem-solving consultation. In A. Thomas and J. Grimes (Eds.), *Best practices in school psychology* (4th ed., pp. 583–608). Washington, DC: National Association of School Psychologists.

Kurpius, D. J., & Fuqua, D. R. (1993). Fundamental issues in defining consultation. *Journal of Counseling & Development, 71,* 598–600.

Leonard, H. S. (2003). Leadership development: New perspectives. *Consulting Psychology Journal. 55*(1).

Leong, F. T. L., Cooper, S., & Huang, J. L. (2008). Selected bibliography on diversity consulting: psychology. *Consulting Psychology Journal: Practice and Research, 60,* 215–226.

Levinson, H. (2009). Reciprocation: The relationship between man and organization. In H. Levinson, A. M. Freedman (Ed.), & K. H. Bradt (Ed.). *Consulting psychology: Selected articles by Harry Levinson* (pp. 31–47). Washington, DC: American Psychological Association.

Lewis, V. A., Lewis, M. D., Daniels, J. A., & D'Andrea, M. J. (2003). *Community counseling: Empowerment strategies for a diverse society* (3rd ed.). Pacific Grove, CA: Brooks/Cole Publishing.

Lippit, G. L., & Lippit, R. (1986). *The consulting process in practice.* (2nd ed.). La Jolla, CA: University Associates.

Locke, E. A., & Latham, G. P. (2002). Building a practically useful theory of goal setting and task motivation: A 35 year odyssey. *American Psychologist, 57,* 705–717.

Lowman, R. L. (2008). Editorial policy of the Consulting Psychology Journal: Practice and Research. *Consulting Psychology Journal: Practice and Research, 60,* 1–3.

McCauley, C. D., Moxley, R. S., & Van Vesslor, E. (Eds.). (1998). *Center for Creative Leadership handbook of leadership development.* San Francisco: Jossey-Bass.

McLean, G. N. (2006). *Organization development.* San Francisco: Berrett-Koehler Publishers.

National Council of Schools and Programs in Professional Psychology. (2008). *Competency developmental achievement levels (DALs) of the National Council of Schools and Programs in Professional Psychology.* Retrieved July 25, 2009, from http://www.ncspp.info/.

O'Roark, A. M. (1999). A History of Division 13 initiatives on education and training in consulting psychology. *Consulting Psychology Journal: Practice and Research, 51*(4), 218–225.

O'Roark, A. M., Lloyd, P. J., & Cooper, S. E. (2005, February 20). *Guidelines for education and training at the doctoral and postdoctoral level in consulting psychology/organizational consulting psychology.* Retrieved August 14, 2009, from http://www.apa.org/governance/cpm/div13guidelines.pdf.

Pace, D., Stamler, V. L., Yarris, E., & June, L. (1996). Rounding out the cube: Evolution to a global model for counseling centers. *Journal of Counseling & Development, 74,* 321–325.

Park-Taylor, J., Kim, G. S., Lina, B., Gary, P., Phillip, L., Mariko, S., & Jessica, P. (2009). Toward reflective practice: A multicultural competence training model from a community mental health center. *Professional Psychology: Research and Practice, 4*(1), 88–95.

Peterson, D. B. (2010). Executive coaching: A critical review and recommendations for advancing the practice. In S. Zedeck (Ed.), *APA handbook of industrial and organizational psychology: Vol. 2. Selecting and developing members for the organization* (pp. 527–566). Washington, DC: American Psychological Association.

Prince, D. W., & Hoppe, M. H. (2007). *Communicating across cultures (J-B CCL Center for Creative Leadership).* Greensboro, NC: Center for Creative Leadership.

Pryzwansky, W. B., & White, G. W. (1983). The influence of consultee characteristics on preferences for consultation approaches. *Professional Psychology: Research and Practice, 14*(4), 457–461.

Quick, J. C., & Nelson, D. L. (2008). Emerging issues in leadership development consultation. Special issue. *Consulting Psychology Journal: Practice and Research, 60*(4).

Rodolfa, E., Bent, R., Eisman, E., Nelson, P., Rehm, L., & Ritchie, P. (2005). A cube model for competency development: Implications for psychology educators and regulators. *Professional Psychology: Research and Practice, 36,* 347–354.

Schein, E. H. (1969). *Process consultation: Its role in organization development* (1st ed.). Reading, MA: Addison-Wesley.

Schein, E. H. (1978). The role of the consultant: Content expert or process facilitator? *Personnel and Guidance Journal, 56,* 339–343.

Schein, E. H. (1987). *Process consultation: Lessons for managers and consultants* (Vol. 2). Reading, MA: Addison-Wesley.

Schein, E. H., (1988). *Process consultation: Its role in organization development* (Vol 1, 2nd ed.). Reading, MA: Addison-Wesley.

Schein, E. H. (1999). *Process consultation revisited: Building the helping relationship.* Reading, MA: Addison-Wesley.

Schein, E. H. (2006). Consultation and coaching revisited. In M. Goldsmith, & L. S. Lyons (Eds.), *Coaching for leadership* (2nd ed., pp. 17–25). San Francisco: Wiley.

Sheridan, S. M., Welch, M., & Orme, S. F. (1996). Is consultation effective? A review of outcome research. *Remedial and Special Education, 17,* 341–354.

Shullman, S. L. (2002). Reflections of a counseling psychologist: Implications for the principles for education and training at the doctoral and postdoctoral level in consulting psychology for the practice of counseling psychology. *Consulting Psychology Journal: Practice and Research, 54*(4), 242–251.

Sperry, L. (2009). Workplace mobbing and bullying. Special issue. *Consulting Psychology Journal, 61*(3).

Steward, R. J. (1996). Training consulting psychologists to be sensitive to multicultural issues in organanizational consultation. *Consulting Psychology Journal: Practice and Research, 48,* 180–189.

Sue, S. (1998). In search of cultural competence in psychotherapy and counseling. *American Psychologist, 53,* 440–448.

Sue, D. W., Bingham, R. P., Porché-Burke, L., Vasquez, M. (1999). The diversification of psychology: A multicultural revolution. *American Psychologist, 54,* 1061–1069.

Teyber, E. & McClure, F. H. (2011). Interpersonal Process in Therapy: An Integrative Model. (6th ed.). Belmont, CA: Brooks/Cole.

Wasylshyn, K. M. (2001). On the full actualization of psychology in business. *Consulting Psychology Journal: Practice and Research, 53,* 10–21.

Social Justice in Counseling Psychology

Nadya A. Fouad *and* Jeffrey P. Prince

Abstract

This chapter traces the historical roots of social justice in counseling psychology and reviews social justice in counseling psychology practice, training, and research. Social justice advocacy in counseling psychology urges counseling psychologists to use their knowledge and expertise to actively create new opportunities for clients, to change the systems that perpetuate injustice, and to advocate for new policies that will institutionalize equity and fairness. We also identify the challenges and barriers to conducting social justice work, and we highlight some of the ethical issues and dilemmas of social justice work. Finally, we make some recommendations for policy and legislation, and suggest next steps for counseling psychologists to be social justice agents.

Keywords: social justice, multicultural training, multicultural counseling, multicultural research, advocacy

Counseling psychology, as a discipline, has long placed an emphasis on prevention, on understanding the role that individual and cultural differences play in clients' lives, and on normal, developmental concerns. For example, counseling psychologists have proposed prevention interventions (Romano & Netland, 2008), have sought to understand racial identity development for black youth (Nicolas, Helms, Jernigan, Sass, Skrzypek, & DeSilva, 2008), and have examined individuals' work and career-related decisions (Blustein & Fouad, 2008). The underlying philosophical assumption, that counseling psychology research and practice can help to make conditions more equitable and fair, coincides with philosophical premises underlying social justice work that dates back to Greek philosophers.

More recently, social workers and community psychologists have written extensively about the philosophical underpinnings determining fair distribution of resources. Counseling psychologists owe a great deal to the scholars who have eloquently argued

for the role that psychologists can, and should play in the redistribution of resources in the United States. A review of that history is well beyond the scope of this chapter, but readers are referred to Fox, Prilleltensky, and Austin (2009) and Prilleltensky (in press). This chapter will briefly trace the historical roots of social justice in counseling psychology and review social justice in counseling psychology practice, training, and research. In each area, we will also identify the challenges and barriers to conducting social justice work. We conclude the chapter by highlighting some of the ethical issues and dilemmas of social justice work, make some recommendations for policy and legislation, and finally suggest next steps for counseling psychology.

Social justice advocacy in counseling psychology urges counseling psychologists to use their knowledge and expertise to actively create new opportunities for clients, to change the systems that perpetuate injustice, and to advocate for new policies that will institutionalize equity and fairness. Vera and

Speight (2003) argued that counseling psychologists need to do more than examine factors that contribute to, or are the results of, injustice. Rather, counseling psychologists need to actively work for societal change. Goodman, Liang, Helms, Latta, Sparks, and Weintraub (2004a) defined social justice as "scholarship and professional action designed to change social values, structures, policies, and practices" (p. 795). Fouad, Gerstein, and Toporek (2006) characterized social justice in counseling psychology as "helping to ensure that opportunities and resources are distributed fairly and helping to ensure equity when resources are distributed unfairly" (p. 1). Using these definitions, activities that may be viewed as social justice actions for counseling psychologists include using individual therapy to empower clients struggling with racism, sexism, or homophobia; intervening to ameliorate institutional barriers to equal opportunities; and advocating to influence legislation. To successfully accomplish social justice actions like these, counseling psychologists must understand and work to systemically change the root causes of societal problems that affect the well-being of clients and their families.

Counseling psychology's commitment and involvement in social justice activities may be traced back to its earliest days, but the field's commitment to social justice has been uneven. For example, early pioneers of counseling psychology, such as Frank Parsons, advocated for social change through career guidance, believing that work could serve as a social equalizer (O'Brien, 2001). Counseling psychologists continued to advocate for social change in their work with veterans after World War II. Counseling psychologists campaigned actively for civil rights during the 1960s, and vigorously worked to create equal opportunities for women in the 1970s. But, although some counseling psychologists continued to advocate for change, particularly highlighting the effects of racism, sexism, and homophobia, the market forces of managed care in the 1980s changed the reward structures for counseling psychologists. Individual therapy and remediation were rewarded, whereas prevention and social advocacy were not. Managed care companies required clients to have a diagnosis and treatment plan in order for psychologists to be reimbursed. As Speight and Vera (2008) note, prevention care is rarely, if ever, reimbursed by a third party.

Reward structures in universities also changed during the 1980s, with more pressure for faculty to publish rigorous empirical articles in journals with high-impact ratings and to secure external funding. External funding agencies were much more likely to focus on problems and areas of remediation, rather than on prevention or community partnerships. Many journal editors were concerned about studies with high internal validity, and generalizability and practical implications were less important considerations. Community partnerships take time to build and sustain, and faculty spent less time on collaboration and more time on individual studies that led to peer-reviewed publications. The net effect was less focus on community work, more focus on studies that were easy to conduct, and less interdisciplinary work.

Social justice has, though, been very much in the forefront of the field for the past 10 years. A number of initiatives have come together to highlight the need for counseling psychologists to play a more active role in advocating for social change. One of these factors has been the increased emphasis on contextual influences of behavior. Researchers have moved away from the uniformity myth that all individuals are the same, regardless of gender or culture, or treating gender, race, or sexual orientation as nuisance variables. Rather, scholars have begun to examine individuals' behavior as shaped by the context that includes many dimensions of diversity (e.g., gender, race/ethnicity, sexual orientation, religion, disability, social class). Another factor was the increased emphasis in universities and funding agencies on interdisciplinary collaboration and community partnerships. Faculty began to be rewarded for building and sustaining social justice programs.

Another factor in the renewed focus on social justice has been successful organizational initiatives within the American Psychological Association (APA), the American Counseling Association (ACA), and the Society of Counseling Psychology (Division 17 of APA). For example, counseling psychologists played key roles in writing the *Multicultural Guidelines on Education and Training, Research, Practice, and Organizational Change* that were adopted as policy by APA in 2003 (APA, 2003), and to develop *Advocacy Competencies* that were adopted as policy by ACA in 2002 (Lewis, Arnold, House, & Toporek, 2002). The ACA and Psychologists for Social Responsibility have co-sponsored the development of an electronic journal, called the *Journal for Social Action in Counseling and Psychology*, highlighting the work that counselors and psychologists may play as community change agents. These initiatives have given an impetus to encouraging counseling psychologists to be agents of social change.

At the same time that counseling psychologists were involved in these organizational initiatives, they were planning for the 2001 National Counseling Psychology Conference. The theme of the conference was "Making a Difference," with social action groups focusing on a number of social advocacy plans (Fouad, McPherson, Gerstein, Blustein, Elman, Helledy, & Metz, 2004). One of the outcomes of the conference was the development of the *Handbook of Social Justice in Counseling Psychology* (Toporek, Gerstein, Fouad, Roysircar, & Israel, 2006). Another outcome was the decision by Robert Carter, the editor of *The Counseling Psychologist*, to create a social justice forum, encouraging major contributions on social justice. A third outcome was the development of the Social Justice Award, sponsored by the authors of the *Handbook*, awarded for "a sustained commitment to the specialty, to community involvement, to recognizing diversity, and to demonstrating evidence of achieving community or organizational change that supports disenfranchised, disempowered, less privileged, or oppressed groups and has a larger impact on practice, research, and scholarship in the field." The first award was presented in 2007 to Maria de Lourdes Prendes-Lintel for her community work with immigrant and refugee families in Nebraska. Finally, under William Parham's presidency of the Society, a committee was formed to give back to the communities in which the annual APA convention is held. Community activities, such as serving at a homeless shelter, were sponsored in San Francisco in 2007 and in Boston in 2008. Thus, the past decade has seen renewed emphasis on social justice in counseling psychology, with articles, committees, books, awards, and a journal calling for counseling psychologists to be more active as agents of change. This chapter will focus on social justice activities of counseling psychologists, and highlight that work in practice settings, training, and research.

Social Justice Practice

The practice of social justice in counseling psychology builds on decades of work from other areas of psychology, such as community and social psychology, as well as from the long history of the practice of social justice in other disciplines such as social work, law, medicine, religion, education, and economics. Counseling psychologists have developed models of practice that integrate key concepts of social justice into the core domains of counseling psychology to address inequities encountered by a wide range of marginalized populations. However, often, they have

not labeled their efforts specifically as social justice work.

More recently, there has been renewed attention paid to highlighting social justice as a central component to the practice of counseling psychology. For example, as noted in the introduction, counseling psychologists were instrumental in guiding the development of APA practice guidelines for marginalized and underserved populations, such as the *Guidelines on Multicultural Education, Training, Research, Practice and Organizational Change* (American Psychological Association [APA], 2003) and the *Guidelines for Psychotherapy with Lesbian, Gay and Bisexual Clients* (APA, 2000). The development of multicultural counseling competencies (Arredondo et al., 1996) has been an especially important contribution from counseling psychology. These competencies provide guidance for counselors working with racial and ethnic minority clients. The development of these competencies has been in itself an important step toward the practice of social justice. However, a number of authors (Constantine, Hage, Kindaichi, & Bryant, 2007; Toporek & Reza, 2001; Vera & Speight, 2003) have argued that the implementation of multicultural competencies is not sufficient; that there is a need for a stronger emphasis on linking multicultural counseling to a broader commitment of practicing social justice. They have emphasized a need to expand beyond competencies in individual counseling to the full range of counseling psychology practice, and to function as an advocate and social change agent at organizational, institutional, and societal levels. Martin-Baro (1994) stated even more strongly that psychologists motivated to address social justice need to go beyond understanding the world to seeking to transform it.

As we noted earlier, such directions are not new for the practice of counseling psychology. The profession's philosophical foundation emphasizes prevention, the development of strengths, and a holistic view of a person interacting within an environment. Similarly, the skill sets of counseling psychologists have routinely included functions that are critical to the work of social justice, such as group facilitation, consultation, assessment, program evaluation, and the integration of science and practice. Recently, however, counseling psychologists have begun to define the skills and actions needed to practice social justice, and several theoretical models have been proposed to organize and guide practice in this domain. These models are in their early theoretical stage of development and have limited empirical support at this time, but they provide useful guidance for conceptualizing and counseling clients, particularly those from marginalized populations. They share a common framework for addressing both the individual and contextual forces that are critical to understanding and changing the lives and situations of marginalized individuals.

MODELS OF SOCIAL JUSTICE PRACTICE

Atkinson, Thompson, and Grant (1993) were pioneers in developing a model for the practice of social justice. They offered a model for working with diverse populations that argued for expanding the roles of counseling psychologists beyond the traditional functions of counselor and psychotherapist. They identified the following eight roles for broadening the repertoire of counseling psychologists:

- *Facilitator of indigenous healing methods.* Counselors need to consider referring clients to healers from the clients' culture or apply these healing methods directly if trained appropriately.
- *Facilitator of indigenous support systems.* It is important for counselors to know what support systems are available in the client's culture and how to assist the client in using them.
- *Advisor.* Counselors at times need to offer direct advice to clients on how to remedy potential problems and to describe how others have managed to address them.
- *Advocate.* Sometimes counselors need to speak on behalf of clients, especially those who are low in acculturation or have limited English-language skills, to remediate problems that result from discrimination.
- *Change agent.* Counselors need to work toward changing environments that are oppressive and discriminatory, whether or not a particular client is involved.
- *Consultant.* Counselors can help clients to anticipate and strategize how to minimize effects of discrimination and racism in various environments.
- *Counselor.* This role is one of traditional counseling that focuses on preventing problems and on addressing developmental and educational needs of clients. It incorporates an awareness of the influence of cultural and environmental factors that contribute to clients' clients needs.
- *Psychotherapist.* The traditional psychotherapist role is deemed appropriate only to clients with high acculturation who want relief from an existing problem; this role needs to be

carried out with vigilance for the environmental forces that may be contributing to the problem.

Each role involved takes into account three factors: client level of acculturation, locus of the etiology of client's presenting concerns (i.e., stemming from internal, dynamic sources or from environmental sources), and goals or desired outcomes of the intervention. This model was the first to specify methods of incorporating cultural variables into counseling to ensure that services would be more effective and relevant to clients from diverse cultures.

Goodman et al. (2004a) built on Atkinson, Thompson and Grant's model by adding a theoretical structure derived from feminist and multicultural counseling models to guide how a counselor might take on the expanded roles needed for social justice work. Their model emphasizes that the practice of social justice occurs on three levels: micro (i.e., individuals), meso (communities and organizations), and macro (social structures and policies). They proposed the following set of principles to assist counseling psychologists in attending to each level:

- *Ongoing self-examination*: To engage in critical self-assessment and to acknowledge hidden biases and preconceived notions toward clients from culturally diverse populations. This principle stresses the need for counselors and practitioners to recognize the role that power plays in how they are perceived across interpersonal interactions and practice settings, particularly given the variation in power attached to social position, race, gender, and culture.
- *Sharing power*: To engage in consensual decision making where possible. The practitioner's contribution is presented as just one source of information, not the expert or best source. The goal of this principle is for both partners to gain from the interaction through a collaborative, co-learning relationship, and to avoid the practitioner behaving as the only expert who directs, teaches, or controls the client.
- *Giving voice*: To amplify the needs, perspectives, and strengths of oppressed groups by advocating for them both within and outside the counseling office.
- *Consciousness raising*: To help clients understand the role of historical, political, and social forces—such as discrimination, racism, sexism, and homophobia—that contribute to an individual's difficulties. The goal of this

principle is to empower clients through identifying the source of distress outside of themselves in social institutions and norms.

• *Focus on strengths*: To facilitate growth and development through helping clients to recognize their competencies, skills, and talents, and their capacity to find solutions to their problems.

• *Leaving clients tools*: To avoid dependence and to emphasize indigenous strengths and support systems that will continue to develop and sustain self-determination, empowerment, and growth after the relationship ends and over time.

One criticism of this model is its limited scope (Kiselica, 2004; Palmer, 2004; Thompson & Shermis, 2004). It places a strong emphasis on helping individuals but it does not fully address changing broader systems and communities.

Another model for practicing social justice has been proposed by Toporek and colleagues (Toporek & Chope, 2006; Toporek & Liu, 2001). This model complements the models previously described through its emphasis on the knowledge base that practitioners need to acquire to effectively carry out the roles and principles of social justice. Furthermore, this model expands upon previous models with its strong emphasis on the need for practitioners to engage in a broad range of advocacy roles, functions that have not been traditionally part of the repertoire of counseling psychologists.

These authors highlight four particular areas of knowledge that form the foundation of social justice practice:

• *Interdisciplinary contributions*: Becoming familiar with social justice work in other disciplines and developing partnerships with other community professionals with similar goals.

• *Cultural competence*: Developing an awareness of personal beliefs, values, and biases to understand how they influence interventions and to ensure that they are directed toward the best interest of the client.

• *Complex roles*: Gaining an understanding of how a practitioner's role may vary along a continuum from individual empowerment to social action depending on the situation and the strengths of the psychologist and client.

• *Social justice resources*: Becoming adequately familiar with resources that can address clients' needs, such as financial resources, legal resources, and others.

Advocacy competencies that follow from this model were endorsed by the American Counseling Association (Lewis et al., 2002). Competencies were classified according to three types of practice: individual counseling, community work, and social change. Furthermore, they were organized according to six domains of advocacy, varying from a focus on micro- to macro-level actions, and according to whether they are carried out either in action with the client or in action on behalf of the client. Individual practice is represented at the micro level of advocacy, community work at the middle level, and social change at the macro level. Advocacy may take place at all three levels through acting either *with* agents (e.g., working with clients or with a community agency) or *on behalf of* agents (e.g., systems advocacy). Thus, this classification results in six domains for practicing advocacy: client empowerment, client advocacy, community collaboration, systems advocacy, public information, and social/political advocacy. Each of the six domains has specific competencies.

Client empowerment begins with an understanding of the influences of social, political, economic, and cultural contexts on individual clients. Counseling psychologists must be able to identify the client's strengths and resources, identify his or her contextual factors, and understand the role that internalized oppression may play in a client's life. The psychologist must then be able to help the client identify external barriers, help him or her develop self-advocacy skills and action plans, and help the client to carry out the action plan.

Client advocacy goes beyond helping a client develop self-advocacy skills to acting as an advocate on behalf of the client. Competencies include negotiating services on behalf of clients, helping clients access resources, identifying barriers to the well-being of clients, developing an action plan for confronting these barriers, identifying potential allies for confronting the barriers, and carrying out the action plan.

The third domain of advocacy is community collaboration, in which the counseling psychologist helps to identify barriers within communities and serves as an ally to facilitate systemic change. Competencies include the ability to identify recurring themes within a community, skills to alert community groups to the concerns, and mechanisms to facilitate that change. The latter includes skills to develop alliances within the community, and skills to listen and respect the group's goals while still advocating for change.

Systems advocacy, the fourth competency, includes the skills to facilitate systemic change, thereby altering the status quo. In this domain, counseling psychologists are able to identify factors influencing clients' development, help gather and interpret data to support their findings, and help community stakeholders develop a vision for change. Embedded in systems advocacy is the ability to analyze the political and social sources of power within the community, build alliances to facilitate change, and help communities develop a plan to implement change. Counseling psychologists also need to be able to analyze potential sources of resistance to change and know how to overcome that resistance.

The fifth competency is the ability to communicate publicly about systemic areas of oppression. Counseling psychologists develop skills to recognize oppression, identify environmental factors that may help to ameliorate oppression, and prepare materials that help to publicize these. This includes the ability to communicate in ways ethical for the community and collaborating with allies to help disseminate information broadly.

Finally, the last competency is social and political advocacy, in which counseling psychologists act as agents to change public policies. This includes recognizing which problems may be addressed by social or political action, identifying ways to address those problems, establishing relationships with allies, preparing rationales for change, and lobbying policy makers to facilitate change.

PRACTICE ARENAS

To practice counseling psychology—and to deliver mental health services generally—in a way that addresses social justice requires an acknowledgment that accessibility to services is itself a critical concern. Seeking counseling and psychotherapy for many cultural groups is highly stigmatized and a violation of cultural norms. Even if individuals seek out these services, they may not be accessible due to location or cost. Furthermore, services may be viewed with distrust due to past practices of discrimination or inadequate care (Vera, Daly, Gonzales, Morgan, & Thankral, 2006). Consequently, the practice of counseling psychology, in any setting, frequently needs to be carried out in nontraditional ways if it is to serve the needs of oppressed communities.

Counseling psychologists have translated principles of social justice through the development of interventions and programs in a number of core practice areas. A number of model programs in school, health care, and work settings have been implemented with a wide array of disenfranchised communities. They have demonstrated the commitment and potential that counseling psychologists bring to combating oppression through action.

Schools

Davidson, Waldo, and Adams (2006) have pointed out that elementary and secondary school systems are ideal settings for the practice of social justice given the existence of schools within every geographic area and across all social and economic levels. They have stressed the importance of both the connection and the distinction between social justice and prevention. For example, prevention efforts typically attempt to reduce risks for individuals or groups, but many do not address the broader context of underlying societal inequities and hierarchies that are the target of social justice efforts. These authors have implemented interventions that achieved social changes in public school environments though implementing service learning activities, educating teachers, and training school personnel.

Similarly, Thompson, Alfred, Edwards, and Garcia (2006) have presented a framework for racial-social activism based on Helms' *racial identity interaction model* (Helms, 1995) to address racial injustice through a school-based effort within one community. This project, the Heritage Project, was designed to address racism constructively with parents, teachers, students, and community members, and to facilitate the racial identity development of students in a predominantly white school system. Strategies for effecting change included a wide array of activities including classroom instruction, community consultations, and workshops.

Health Care

Many counseling psychologists practice within hospitals and health centers that are located within poor and disenfranchised communities. However, location alone does not guarantee adequate care. The U.S. Surgeon General's report in 2001 (U.S. Department of Health and Human Services, 2001) documented significant disparities in mental health care for racial and ethnic groups in the United States. The report showed that minorities had less access to services, were less likely to receive care, and received poorer quality care. The practice of social justice within health care settings requires focused attention to these inequities and active collaboration with the communities in which counseling psychologists work. Furthermore, the integration of indigenous beliefs and health practices is imperative to ensure that the community interests are being served (Roysicar, 2006).

One example of how social justice can be addressed within this setting was illustrated by Huynh and Roysircar (2006). They described a pilot program designed by the Harvard Program in Refugee Trauma that addressed the psychological health of Southeast Asian refugees by promoting a biopsychosocial health education model to help maximize available resources. This effort involved building working alliances with civic organizations and local ethnic community leaders to develop services and clinical competencies that were appropriate to the clients' cultural context. Similarly, Schmidt, Hoffman, and Taylor (2006) described a social justice approach to working with individuals with HIV/AIDS that illustrated the impact that counseling psychologists can have not only with individuals, but with global communities. They stressed the importance of collaborating with community agencies to better understand sexual behaviors, substance use, stigma, and sexual orientation, among other variables, to develop reciprocal, mutually beneficial opportunities for social justice work.

Work

Counseling psychology has a long history of attending to the vocational and career development needs of disenfranchised groups. In fact, many of the strongest examples of social justice work within counseling psychology have occurred within the vocational domain. Early efforts that set the groundwork for current practice include Frank Parsons' vocational interventions with poor boys in Boston in the early 1900s (Pope, 2000) and post-World War II vocational guidance programs that attended to the needs of returning veterans and the changing roles of women in the workplace (Sundberg & Littman, 1994; Thompson, Super, & Napoli, 1955). More recently, vocational counseling psychologists have advocated for equal access and higher-quality career development services for a number of underserved and marginalized populations, including women (Betz & Fitzgerald, 1987; Fitzgerald & Harmon, 2001), racial and ethnic minorities (Fouad & Bingham, 1995; Leong 1995), gays and lesbians (Chung 2003; Croteau, Anderson, Distefano, & Kampa-Kokesch, 2000), and poor and working-class individuals (Blustein, 2006; Fouad & Brown, 2000). Toporek and Chope (2006) have described common examples of workplace injustice; they have detailed strategies that counseling psychologists can use to

specifically address discrimination and harassment on both an individual and institutional level. These authors caution that interventions appropriate to the culture of one community may be inappropriate for a different community. They have illustrated this point in documenting vocational intervention programs in San Francisco that targeted homelessness and poverty. Juntunen, Cavett, Clow, Rempel, Darrow, and Guilmino (2006) have provided a similarly detailed description of a welfare-to-work program that stresses the importance of refocusing the responsibility for change from individuals to employers, policy makers, and community leaders. Some counseling psychologists (e.g., Fassinger & Gallor, 2006) have argued that such efforts are not enough, however, and have advocated for a full dismantling and rebuilding of the occupational structure within the United States to remedy the patriarchal hierarchies that maintain workplace inequities. Obviously their goal is idealistic. Nevertheless, these authors emphasize the parallel to remodeling a house one plank at a time. Oppressive structures in the workplace and in schools can be remodeled to address inequities across gender, sexuality, race, and abilities through collaborations and coalitions that target legal, policy, and professional changes a step at a time.

CHALLENGES AND BARRIERS TO SOCIAL JUSTICE PRACTICE

Although much work has been done to guide and develop the practice of counseling psychology toward an emphasis on social justice, this focus remains limited within the field overall. The practice of social justice, for a number of reasons, has yet to be fully emphasized and integrated into the broad practice of counseling psychology. One barrier to the practice of social justice is simply economic. Insurance payments, for example, will typically reimburse practitioners for individual psychotherapy, but not for the expanded functions of prevention, advocacy, and community work that a social justice perspective entails (Vera & Speight, 2003). Even in those practice settings that do not rely on third-party payments from insurance companies, such as college and university counseling centers and community mental health clinics, rarely are social justice models integrated into practice models. The missions of these agencies may be to serve the broad psychological and developmental needs of all the members of their communities, but in recent times, most of these services have reduced their focus on prevention and advocacy. Instead, many have redirected their limited resources toward responding to increasing demands for individual clinical care, to reducing wait-lists, and to remaining accessible to individuals in crisis (Gallagher, 2007; Ivey & Collins, 2003). Prevention work and programs that address the needs of under-represented groups may be funded instead through secondary income sources such as time-limited and competitive government grants (Davidson, Waldo, & Adams, 2006).

Perhaps the most significant challenge to integrating social justice into the core practice of counseling psychology is the call for of expanding the scope of our discipline beyond its historic emphasis on helping individuals, couples, families, and small groups. Only recently have counseling psychologists begun to define the guiding principles of social justice work; we have yet to fully develop and refine the skill sets needed for working with communities and larger systems through interdisciplinary collaborations (Davidson et al., 2006; Goodman et al., 2004a).

Social justice work can be extremely rewarding personally and professionally. At the same time, it challenges practitioners emotionally in ways that traditional counseling and consulting do not. The work can be time-consuming and draining, and the outcomes can be small compared to the large social problems being addressed. Helms (2003) highlighted how often social justice work relies on volunteer work and is conducted in addition to a psychologist's full-time job duties. To sustain social justice work, practitioners need the availability of strong professional support structures and supportive colleagues or supervisors. These supports can provide needed encouragement, recognition, and consultation. Most importantly, they can help combat the common corollaries of this work, such as burnout, hopelessness, and anger.

Social Justice Training

Scholars writing about social justice have frequently given specific suggestions for training (e.g., Aldarondo, 2007; Ali, Liu, Mahmood, & Arguello, 2008; Lee, 2007; Toporek et al., 2006). The suggestions and recommendations range from overhauling the entire training program, to adding specific components to training, to providing concrete suggestions of activities or projects that may be incorporated into a class. Each defines social justice somewhat differently, but most define social justice training as different from training in multicultural competence. However, Pieterse, Evans, Risner-Butner, Collins, and Mason (2009) reviewed multicultural counseling course syllabi and found that social justice was often included as an objective in the course, but few of the instructors included exploration of actual strategies for social change. In this section, we will review the literature on social justice training and highlight challenges and barriers for social justice training. The two questions of concern in social justice training are *what* knowledge and skills students need to learn and *how* to include this knowledge acquisition in training.

SOCIAL JUSTICE KNOWLEDGE AND ADVOCACY COMPETENCE

What exactly is social justice training? In general, there is a consensus that social justice training builds on training for multicultural competence (Arredondo & Rosen, 2007; Goodman et al., 2004a; McWhirter & McWhirter, 2007; Toporek et al., 2006; Vera & Speight, 2003). Students must have self-awareness and must have knowledge of cultural groups, but training for social justice involves more action on the part of the student. Students must learn to conceptualize structural explanations for clients' concerns and know how to systemically intervene to ameliorate their concerns.

Consistent with the first and second APA (2003) *Guidelines on Multicultural Education, Training, Research, Practice and Organizational Change for Psychologists*, students need to learn an appreciation and respect for diversity, gain knowledge about marginalized and oppressed groups, and learn an understanding of oppression. Indeed, Toporek and Pope-Davis (2005) found that students with multicultural training were more likely to have structural, rather than individual, explanations for poverty. Beyond attitude change, however, Toporek et al. recommended that social justice training helps students to learn about roles for counseling psychologists other than that of individual therapy. Thus, students need to learn to collaborate with other professionals, learn advocacy skills, learn to ethically conduct research in community-based settings, and to ethically build and sustain community partnerships.

One of the questions about social justice training is how to help students build competencies needed for ethical advocacy. Advocacy is a core competency for psychologists defined as "Actions targeting the impact of social, political, economic or cultural factors to promote change at the individual (client), institutional, and/or systems level" (Fouad et al., 2009, p. S24).

Two essential components comprise the advocacy competence: empowerment and systems change. Students need to learn how to empower their clients and how to promote systems change. Developmentally, training begins with building students' awareness of the need for empowerment and systems change and then builds their competence in contextual analysis and finally, helping students to develop skills to intervene appropriately.

Skills for advocacy are developed sequentially across levels of training. At the first developmental level for empowerment, students are expected to be able to articulate social, political, economic, or cultural factors that may have an impact on human development and functioning. By the time students are ready for internship, they should know how to use that awareness in the context of service provision, as evidenced by their ability to identify specific barriers to client improvement, such as lack of access to resources or exposure to discrimination, and to assist clients in the development of self-advocacy plans. By the time students are ready to enter the profession, they should be able to intervene with clients to promote action on those barriers, knowing how to promote client self-advocacy and how to assess the client's implementation and outcome of that self-advocacy.

The second essential component in advocacy is systems change. Early in their training, students are expected to understand the differences between individual- and institutional-level interventions and systems level change. This is evidenced by their ability to articulate the role of therapist as a change agent outside of direct patient contact. By the time they are ready for internship, students should be able to promote change to enhance the functioning of individuals. Students are able to specify the concern, formulate and engage in a plan for action, and demonstrate an understanding of appropriate boundaries to advocate on behalf of the client. At the final level of training, students should be qualified to promote change at the level of institutions, community, or society. This will be evidenced by their ability to develop alliances with relevant individuals and groups and by their ability to engage with groups with differing viewpoints around issues to promote change.

Thus, in addition to learning the traditional skills to be a counseling psychologist (e.g., building relationships, conducting assessment and interventions), students are encouraged to learn advocacy skills. Some authors suggest that social justice training must de-emphasize developing the skills to be an individual therapist. For example, Vera and Speight (2003) argued that "clients need more than [individual] counseling and communities need

services other than remedial interventions" (p. 269), and students need to be trained to think more systemically about their work as psychologists. They do not specifically suggest that students should not be trained to be competent at remedial, individually focused interventions. Rather, they discuss the potential for student stress and burnout when students emphasize therapy as the avenue for change, when clients are embedded in a social context that needs to be changed. They recommended that training activities foster a passion for social justice (an affective component), provide students with knowledge of history of oppression and the psychological affects of oppression (intellectual component), and most critically, provide students with the skills and tools to effectively intervene as social change agents (a component that moves them to action).

SOCIAL JUSTICE TRAINING MODELS

The second question in social justice training is how programs can help students to develop these skills. Several authors have described the development of social justice–oriented training programs in counseling psychology. Goodman et al.'s (2004a) six core themes were described more fully in the previous section on practice; Goodman et al. also applied these to training. Briefly, these themes include helping students to build an awareness of power dynamics; understand how to share power and foster empowerment; learn how to "give voice" to others' experiences, particularly to those with less power; raise clients' consciousness of the extent to which difficulties are embedded in societal contexts; learn how to foster clients' strengths and resources; and leave clients with the tools to continue growing.

Training Models

McWhirter and McWhirter (2007) described the counseling psychology program at the University of Oregon. They outlined the shift in the program over the last 10 years from training students to do individual interventions to giving students the skills to be systemic change agents. They help students build these skills through practica designed to help them understand contextual influences on clients, including a practicum in which students conduct home and school visits. Specifically, they assume that "counseling psychologists are responsible for working to reduce or eliminate risk factors, develop protective interventions that contribute to resilience . . . and support and strengthen aspects of the community" (p. 395). The authors delineate various readings that are integrated into courses, the infusion of multicultural competence throughout the curriculum, and ways that students are engaged in the community through practica and community-based research.

Burns and Manese (2008) described implementation of social justice training as part of an APA-accredited internship located at the University of California-San Diego University Counseling Center. The internship provides opportunities for interns to engage in consultation, outreach, and preventative activities outside the campus community, in addition to the individual and group counseling typical of internship training. The authors analyzed their program within the six tenets identified by Goodman et al. (2004a), providing perspectives from both the training director and a previous intern. The authors conclude with several recommendations for internship programs, including: select interns who have an interest in social justice activities, assess the commitment of training staff to social justice activities, provide training and support for staff on an ongoing basis, and develop training opportunities that are commensurate with the interns' skills. Interns with higher levels of skills are able to develop, implement, and evaluate their own programs, whereas interns with less developed skills are able to observe workshops or participate in discussion. The authors noted, in particular, the need to use a strengths-based perspective to avoid putting interns into positions in which they feel inadequate, or staff in positions in which they feel burned out.

The training programs described above are, themselves, examples of systemic change in the training programs. Common across these examples are key leaders who articulated the need to shift to a social justice training model and invested a great deal in developing strong community partnerships that benefited both the university and the community site. Training activities were designed to provide students with the opportunities to learn advocacy skills in a real-life setting. Each model also described the difficulties in creating such change. The authors delineate the importance of lengthy faculty/staff discussions of how and what to change in the curriculum, of faculty/staff engagement, and faculty/staff commitment. Implementing a program-wide commitment to social justice training begins with a deep faculty commitment to establishing and maintaining strong community partnerships. Goodman, Liang, Weintraub, Helms, and Latta (2004b) noted not only the intensive amount of time to develop and sustain community partnerships, but the

additional course load for students. Although students and faculty at Boston College valued a social justice curriculum, this curriculum was in addition to the activities of the typical counseling psychology training expected in an APA-accredited program.

Ali, Liu, Mahmood, and Arguello (2008) commented on the importance of social justice training in counseling psychology as a philosophical stance, as well, and described two concrete methods for teaching social justice, through courses that offer service learning (e.g., community-based experiences as part of a course) or through focused practicum experiences that emphasize social justice work. Goodman et al. (2004a) also described service learning as a mechanism for teaching social justice and having students participate in extended community–faculty partnerships. Green, McCollum, and Hays (2008) suggested several ways to teach students the skills for advocacy counseling, including helping students to develop an advocacy plan for a community need, or having students participate in the orientation sessions of local community organizations.

CHALLENGES AND BARRIERS

The central difficulty in social justice training is that community needs and training needs do not always coincide. Traditional training programs help students build competence in quarter- or semester-long intervals. But the need for advocacy within the community may occur at any time of the year, and not necessarily when the faculty believe that the students are ready to be advocates. Clearly, community and client needs for advocacy may not coincide with the training schedule. Ethically, training programs cannot extend opportunities for advocacy for the semester, and then abandon efforts until the next semester starts. Thus, many programs find that they can build awareness of the need for social justice and build knowledge of ways to implement social justice, but may not be able to build social justice skills.

Ali et al. (2008) also acknowledged the practical difficulty of implementing a social justice agenda, particularly the very real problem of asking faculty to add to their workload. As mentioned above, creating and sustaining community partnerships take a great deal of faculty time. Time is needed to listen to community concerns, and time is needed to create training models and activities that meet community needs. These activities must also help students become competent psychologists. Faculty must often rethink their courses and instructional strategies, which also takes time. Faculty may not want to invest the time in these changes for a variety of reasons. They may not agree with the philosophical shifts to a social justice model, they may have their own pressures to publish to be successful, and they may, themselves, be fatigued with community efforts.

Talleyrand, Chung, and Bemak (2006) had several suggestions to help programs that were interested in incorporating social justice training, including holding faculty retreats, ensuring additional training for adjunct faculty and supervisors, empowering students to have a voice in the program, partnering with local community-based services, and ensuring consistent assessment and evaluation of the training. But, Burns and Manese (2008) also point out the difficulty of mandating that faculty and staff participate in social justice activities if they are not prepared or are burned out or have compassion fatigue. Also, programs may be in danger of marginalizing faculty or staff who have not developed those skills, or who do not want to engage in community service. Thus, program faculty and staff need to determine if their training mission includes the development of advocacy skills, in addition to awareness and knowledge related to advocacy.

Social Justice Research

Social justice research may be viewed in two ways: research on the effectiveness of social justice practice or training, and research that, as Sedlacek (2007) suggested, "[is] making a difference in bringing about social change" (p. 223). Few studies have been done on the former at this point, and clearly this is an area for future research. How do we know that we are, in fact, making a difference by integrating a social justice perspective in our practice or training? Are some activities more helpful than others in creating advocacy skills in students? Are some attitudes so essential in developing social justice skills that training programs need to select students on those attitudes? What traditional and nontraditional healing practices are the most critical in helping empower clients? Speight and Vera (2008) note that research on factors leading to mental health disparities (and ways to redress this) are a type of social justice research, and Toporek et al. (2006) suggest that research could focus on factors that lead to perpetuating injustice, including studies on oppressors, rather than the oppressed. Research results may guide program development to help ensure that a social justice perspective does no harm to clients or communities.

Much more has been written about developing mechanisms to use research for social justice purposes.

Counseling psychologists have a number of skills to collect and analyze data that can be of great help to communities. For example, counseling psychologists may help to document the existence of a problem, may help to design systems of data collection to argue the need for more resources, or to help community partners evaluate and document the effectiveness of services. Fassinger and Gallor (2006) suggest that research documenting fiscal need for services may be the most important advocacy tool we have. But, the most critical issue is to ask questions that are important to the community. This requires time and patience to understand what issues are important to community partners, who may not be versed in the language of operational definitions that translate into research studies. In other words, community partners are knowledgeable about the work they are doing, the problems of the community, and the possible solutions, but may not know how to create a way to examine these problems or solutions. Counseling psychologists can bring their skills to help develop evaluation or research studies, but it must be a collaborative process (Vera & Speight, 2003). Listening and developing socially relevant questions is best done as part of a systemic partnership that will benefit all parties involved. As we have noted several times in this chapter, this takes time, persistence, and patience. Toporek et al. (2006) suggest, as well, that we need to develop new and collaborative multidisciplinary mechanisms of doing research, including participatory action research. They recommend that counseling psychologists can learn from community-centered research paradigms that have been developed by social workers and community psychologists.

It is also important to be broad in the dissemination of social justice research. Developing sound methodological research will help enable studies to be published in counseling psychology journals, but community partners are not likely to read and be influenced by those journals. Identifying outlets to write about the practical implications for the community is important. This is similar to the call for translational research in health sciences, to bridge the gap between basic research and the clinical implications. Counseling psychologists also need to learn to write succinct summaries of their research to provide information to legislators and policy makers.

CHALLENGES AND BARRIERS

The collaborative nature of social justice research also brings a few dilemmas. When research does not support the community partner's perspective, the question may arise, who owns the data? Do counseling psychologists have an obligation to publish the results of studies that may not be in favor of community initiatives? Do they have an obligation to support the community partner's perspective, even if the data do not support it? This becomes more of a concern when considering the pressure that many academic counseling psychologists are under to publish. Whose needs are met when research results cause a conflict?

Academic psychologists may also be in universities in which community work is not supported, or in which community partnerships are expected, but are not rewarded. Tenure policies that emphasize publications in academic journals with high impact ratings may differentially reinforce scholarship in narrow avenues of research and not reward faculty who are involved in community-based partnerships. By the same token, programs that try to protect junior faculty from community-based partnerships may overburden senior faculty and may prevent community partners from benefiting from new faculty perspectives and ideas.

Ethics

The practice of social justice requires an understanding of underlying ethical considerations and carries with it unique ethical challenges. Social justice work is complex work and is often filled with ethical dilemmas. It involves an ongoing process of self-examination, of power dynamics and negotiating multiple levels of individual, organizational, and community interactions. A number of authors (Goodman et al., 2004a; Kiselica, 2004), drawing from feminist and multicultural psychology, have emphasized two broad ethical mandates for the practice of social justice: to reflect our personal values and those values of the organizations and systems in which we operate, and to empower and collaborate rather than to exploit and objectify.

Carrying out such mandates is not straightforward; difficult self-reflection and ethical conflicts are necessary components. For example, clashes can occur when the cultural values and worldviews of psychologists are incongruent with the cultural values of their clients or client groups. Such conflicts underscore the need for psychologists to be attentive to their motives as well as to their positions of power and privilege compared to those of their clients, and the need to avoid acting in ways that are paternalistic and reinforcing of clients' feelings of helplessness. Similarly, Kiselica and Robinson (2001) have cautioned that since social justice work often requires

taking on nontraditional roles in nontraditional settings, counseling psychologists may need to cautiously engage in dual roles with clients and to work within a broader definition of professional boundaries. Practitioners need to actively and consistently seek out supervision and peer consultation to help identify and negotiate these challenges. Similarly, training programs need to incorporate case studies and offer supervision in social justice practice to assist students in identifying and responding to these unique ethical dilemmas.

We highlighted earlier some of the ethical dilemmas that counseling psychologists confront when they incorporate social justice into their training and research, particularly the ethical dilemma when training or research needs conflict with the advocacy needs of a community. The ethical mandates from our professional codes of practice require doing no harm to clients, ensuring competence, and providing informed consent. These principles become even more critical when students are involved in advocacy work with vulnerable populations. Consider the potential ethical dilemmas in social justice training. Faculty may have a conflict between training students to be competent and doing no harm to clients. What happens when the best solution for clients is to pull a student from the training site, but the best solution for students is to keep them at the site to develop their skills? Whose needs are best met in this situation? What happens when students are not yet competent to provide services in a community partnership, but the site is depending on those services? Whose needs are met in this situation, particularly if the university wants to continue the partnership in the future, or the faculty member is conducting research at the site? Clearly, these ethical dilemmas need to be considered when faculty are creating partnerships to enable their students to develop advocacy competencies.

Toporek and her colleagues have written extensively on the topic of ethics in social justice work (Toporek & Chope, 2006; Toporek & Williams, 2006). They have identified three practical ethical issues that are related to both research and practice: the need for psychologists to provide informed consent not only to individuals, but to communities as well; the need to acknowledge limits to a psychologist's competence with community work, and the necessity of working collaboratively with other agencies and professionals to ensure the client's needs are best addressed; and the importance of balancing conflicting goals, such as a clash between the goals of a client and the need for social change.

For example, there is an ethical responsibility to maintain a client's goal as foremost, when a client chooses to not take action in the face of injustice.

Toporek and Williams (2006) have called for an expansion of the APA's ethical standards (APA, 2002), so that attention to social justice is embedded in the fundamentals of all ethical psychological practice. They have distilled a number of themes specific to social justice from the ethical standards of a number of professions and organizations, and have recommended that the following three themes be incorporated into the current APA ethical principles and code of conduct (APA, 2002):

- *Respect.* Psychologists need to acquire adequate knowledge of a culture's customs and structures before engaging in any work with a community. This knowledge should serve as a base for identifying a community's strengths and as a guide for the psychologist's behavior within that community.
- *Responsibility.* Not only do psychologists need to recognize that all persons are entitled to equal access and equal quality of psychological services; psychologists also need to work toward ending discrimination, oppression, and other forms of social justice. Furthermore, psychologists have a responsibility to engage in research and practice that serves oppressed groups and eliminates oppression.
- *Social action.* Psychologists should be expected to confront injustice, to correct discriminatory and unjust practices, and to expand opportunities for vulnerable, disadvantaged, and oppressed people.

Policy and Legislation

Advocates of social justice point out how essential it is for counseling psychologists to network, to lobby, and to actively work toward modifying policies and structures that create inequities and oppression in the United States and globally. Nevertheless, many counseling psychologists, although committed to the values of social justice, are uncomfortable becoming involved at the macro level of organizational and political action. For some, this may reflect a personal preference, disillusionment with the lengthy process of social change, or perhaps a desire to avoid dual relationships within specific communities. For many, however, reluctance may be due largely to not knowing how to do such work. Where and how does a counseling psychologist trained and skilled in the helping of individuals begin to influence policy and legislation? Counseling psychology training programs have not yet routinely addressed the teaching and practicing of specific skills that would enable new professionals to influence large organizations, social policies, and legislatures.

Nevertheless, counseling psychologists have an array of core proficiencies, including interpersonal relations, research, counseling, administration, teaching, and consultation, that have vast potential for influencing policy makers and legislators. Furthermore, numerous counseling psychologists have shown through their writings and by example how to influence macro-level social and political changes through their exercise of the knowledge and skills that are central to our field. For example, Haldeman (2003) has made significant contributions to inform national leaders on misguided and discriminatory programs in conversion therapy for gays and lesbians; Winerman (2004) has helped to oppose discrimination against same-sex parents and to support same-sex marriage; and several authors have outlined ways to address workplace inequities (Blustein, 2006; Fassinger & Gallor, 2006; Toporek & Reza 2001). Counseling psychologists have advocated for changes in social policy through a variety of roles, including drafting legislation to promote funding for mental health of college students (Ablasser, 2004), testifying before legislative bodies to advocate for equal rights for women, and even serving as an elected public official, as did Ted Strickland, the first psychologist (counseling psychologist) elected to the U. S. Congress (Shullman, Celeste, & Strickland, 2006).

Counseling psychologists also have been instrumental in influencing social policies in international arenas. For example, Norsworthy and her colleagues have described their consulting and peace-building efforts in Southeast Asia, and have stressed the importance of counseling psychologists working with nonpsychologist, international partners to successfully address justice worldwide (Norsworthy, 2006). Similarly, Gerstein and Kirkpatrick (2006) have identified through their efforts in Tibet some critical roles that counseling psychologists can assume to reduce international violence. For example, counseling psychologists can serve as group leaders, program planners, trainers, and evaluators on multidisciplinary teams to help integrate indigenous strategies toward peaceful solutions. Furthermore, many nonprofit and international organizations hire psychologists to study and address the reasons and consequences for violence.

These examples underscore the innumerable opportunities for counseling psychologists to become involved and to commit to action in a tangible way. Although most counseling psychologists will not run for office or create international programs, we can begin to influence social policies through becoming more informed about basic legislative and policy-making structures, learning how state and federal bills are introduced and passed, and sending letters of support for bills that address social injustice to representatives in state and federal legislatures.

The APA and the ACA have a number of divisions, sections, committees, and task groups that work toward supporting and educating psychologists interested in influencing social policy. The APA has a Public Policy Office that actively engages in shaping federal policy, as well as a Directorate for Public Interest that promotes the advancement of human welfare. In addition, the APA formed a coalition for social justice in 1999, Divisions for Social Justice, that is comprised of representatives from a number of APA divisions and focuses on supporting and encouraging social justice initiatives across divisions through sponsoring symposia and town hall meetings at conventions. Similarly, the ACA has formed a division devoted to addressing social justice issues. Both organizations have created a range of opportunities for members to lobby legislative bodies and to share data and research findings with legislators that can be used to craft and support bills that address social justice needs.

Shullman et al. (2006) offered these nine suggestions for different ways in which counseling psychologists can become more involved in the political and policy making process:

- Support social advocacy efforts of national professional organizations, such as APA, ACA, the Association of Black Psychologists, the Latino/Latina Psychological Association, and the Association of Asian Psychologists.
- Support public policy efforts of professional organizations of psychologists at state and local levels.
- Support independent political action groups that support social justice issues.
- Become directly involved in dialogues with policy makers through sharing professional knowledge on social justice issues.
- Focus efforts on getting to know specific policy makers and on influencing a specific social justice topic.

- Help policy makers prepare materials and frame arguments through serving as a staff member or advisor to public officials or through an appointment to public policy boards, committees, and commissions.
- Support and encourage other psychologists who are involved in public debates about social justice.
- Engage in lobbying and raising money for candidates and political action committees that support social justice causes.
- Educate and prepare psychologists for social advocacy work through professional seminars that address real-world ethical dilemmas in shaping and forming public policy.

The challenges to influencing policies and legislators from local to global levels are immense. Nevertheless, as larger numbers of counseling psychologists become engaged in such advocacy, large-scale social and political changes will occur. The potential for counseling psychology to contribute to social change and to address community, societal, and global injustices has only begun to be recognized.

Conclusion
Future Directions
Strengthening the practice of social justice in counseling psychology will require efforts on a number of fronts. Counseling psychology has only begun to develop culturally sensitive and internationally effective models related to various forms of social oppression. Incorporating theories from other disciplines such as anthropology, sociology, and political science, among others, will be a challenge but an essential component to developing our knowledge base and to creating more culturally informed, interdisciplinary, and systemically focused models.

Some training programs have incorporated social justice as part of the curriculum, but as Pieterse et al. (2009) have shown, many programs combine social justice training with training in multicultural competence. More information is needed on minimal competencies for social justice effectiveness. Stronger collaborative partnerships in research, training, and practice between universities and community agencies need to be developed across domains of psychology, across professional disciplines, and across communities and nations. For both practical and ethical reasons, these collaborations need to be developed with an eye toward respecting the strengths of community stakeholders affected by oppression and with the assumption that these stakeholders hold the knowledge that will lead to solutions. Counseling psychologists can begin to develop such collaborative relationships through becoming more involved in established interdisciplinary organizations working toward social justice, such as the United Nations, diplomatic services, and human rights groups.

Most importantly, a shift in our professional standards is needed to ensure that our practice settings embrace social justice and that our training programs mirror the broader roles required for social justice work. Accreditation standards for our academic and training programs, for example, need revision to ensure they include courses, experiences, and interventions specific to developing social justice skills. Similarly, professional licensure requirements need to be expanded if practitioners are to be held accountable for incorporating social justice into the fabric of their work. The field of counseling psychology is at a crossroads. The work of a handful of counseling psychologists has paved the way for a transformation of our profession, one that encompasses a broader, more direct and more collaborative approach to confronting social injustice.

References

Ablasser, C. (2004). Creating healthy campuses: APA members successfully promote psychological services at colleges and universities. *APA Monitor on Psychology, 5*(10), 66–67.

Aldarondo, E. (Ed.). (2007). *Advancing social justice through clinical practice.* Mahwah, NJ: Lawrence Erlbaum Associates.

Ali, S. R., Liu, W. M., Mahmood, A., & Arguello, J. (2008). Social justice and applied psychology: Practical ideas for training the next generation of psychologists. *Journal for Social Action in Counseling and Psychology, 1*(2), 1–13.

American Psychological Association (APA). (2000). Guidelines for psychotherapy with lesbian, gay and bisexual clients. *American Psychologist, 55,* 1440–1451.

American Psychological Association (APA). (2002). Ethical principles of psychologists and code of conduct. *American Psychologist, 57,* 1060–1073.

American Psychological Association (APA). (2003). Guidelines on multicultural education, training, research, practice, and organizational change for psychologists. *American Psychologist, 58,* 377–402.

Arredondo, P., Toporek, R., Brown, S. P., Jones, J., Sanchez, J., & Stadler, H. (1996). Operationalization of the multicultural counseling competencies. *Journal of Multicultural Counseling and Development, 24,* 42–78.

Arredondo, P., & Rosen, D. C. (2007). Applying principles of multicultural competencies, social justice, and leadership in training and supervision. In E. Aldarondo (Ed), *Advancing social justice through clinical practice* (pp. 443–458). Mahwah, NJ: Lawrence Erlbaum Associates.

Atkinson, D. R., Thompson, C. E., & Grant, S. K. (1993). A three-dimensional model for counseling racial/ethnic minorities. *The Counseling Psychologist, 21*(2), 257–277.

Betz, N. E., & Fitzgerald, L. F. (1987). *The career psychology of women.* San Diego: Academic Press.

Blustein, D. L. (2006). *The Psychology of working.* Mahwah NJ: Lawrence Erlbaum Associates.

Blustein, D. L., & Fouad, N. A. (2008). Changing face of vocational psychology: The transforming world of work. In W. B. Walsh (Ed.), *Biennial review of counseling psychology* Vol. 1 (pp. 129–155). New York: Routledge/Taylor & Francis Group.

Burnes, T. R., & Manese, J. E. (2008). Social justice in an accredited internship in professional psychology: Answering the call. *Training and Education in Professional Psychology, 2,* 176–181. doi: 10.1037/1931–3918.2.3.176.

Chung, Y. B. (2003). Career counseling with lesbian, gay, bisexual, and transgendered persons: The next decade. *Career Development Quarterly, 52,* 78–85.

Constantine, M. G., Hage, S. M., Kindaichi, M. M., & Bryant, R. M. (2007). Social justice and multicultural issues: Implications for the practice and training of counselors and counseling psychologists. *Journal of Counseling and Development, 85,* 24–29.

Croteau, J. M., Anderson, M. Z., Distefano, T. M., & Kampa-Kokesch, S. (2000). Lesbian, gay and bisexual vocational psychology: Reviewing foundations and planning construction. In R. M. Perez, K. A. DeBord, & D. J. Bieschke (Eds.), *Handbook of counseling and psychotherapy with lesbian, gay and bisexual clients* (pp. 383–408). Washington, DC: American Psychological Association.

Davidson, M. M., Waldo, M., & Adams, E. M. (2006). Promoting social justice through preventive interventions in schools. . In R. L. Toporek, L. Gerstein, N. A. Fouad, G. Roysircar, & T. Israel (Eds.), *Handbook for social justice in counseling psychology: Leadership, vision, and action* (pp. 117–129). Thousand Oaks, CA: Sage.

Fassinger, R. E., & Gallor, S. M. (2006). Tools for remodeling the master's house: Advocacy and social justice in education and work. In R. L. Toporek, L. Gerstein, N. A. Fouad, G. Roysircar, & T. Israel (Eds.), *Handbook for social justice in counseling psychology: Leadership, vision, and action* (pp. 256–275). Thousand Oaks, CA: Sage.

Fitzgerald, L. F., & Harmon, L. W. (2001). Women's career development: A postmodern update. In F. T. L. Leong, & A. Barak (Eds.), *Contemporary models in vocational psychology: A volume in honor of Samuel H. Osipow* (pp. 207–230). Mahwah, NJ: Lawrence Erlbaum.

Fouad, N. A., & Bingham, R. (1995). Career counseling with racial/ethnic minorities. In B. Walsh, & S. Osipow (Eds.), *Handbook of vocational psychology* (2nd ed., pp. 331–366). Hillsdale, NJ: Lawrence Erlbaum.

Fouad, N. A., & Brown, M. T. (2000). The role of race and class in development: Implications for counseling psychology. In S. D. Brown, & R. W. Lent (Eds.), *Handbook of counseling psychology* (3rd ed., pp. 379–408). New York: Wiley.

Fouad, N. A., Grus, C. L., Hatcher, R. L., Kaslow, N. L., Hutchings, P. S., Madson, M., et al. (2009). Competency benchmarks: A developmental model for understanding and measuring competence in professional psychology. *Training and Education in Professional Psychology,* Vol. 3 (4, Suppl), S5–S26.

Fouad, N. A., McPherson, R. H., Gerstein, L., Blustein, D. L., Elman, N., Helledy, K. I., & Metz, A. J. (2004). Houston, 2001: Context and Legacy. *Counseling Psychologist, 32,* 15–77.

Fouad, N. A., Gerstein, L. H., & Toporek, R. L. (2006). Social justice and counseling psychology in context. In R. L. Toporek, L. Gerstein, N. A. Fouad, G. Roysircar, & T. Israel (Eds.), *Handbook for social justice in counseling psychology: Leadership, vision, and action* (pp. 1–16). Thousand Oaks, CA: Sage.

Fox, D., Prilleltensky, I., & Austin, S. (Eds.). (2009). *Critical psychology: An introduction* (2nd ed.). London: Sage.

Gallagher, R. (2007). *National survey of counseling center directors 2006.* Washington DC: International Association of Counseling Services Inc.

Gerstein, L. H., & Kirkpatrick, D. (2006). Counseling psychology and non-violent activism: Independence for Tibet!. In R. L. Toporek, L. Gerstein, N. A. Fouad, G. Roysircar, & T. Israel (Eds.), *Handbook for social justice in counseling psychology: Leadership, vision, and action* (pp. 442–471). Thousand Oaks, CA: Sage.

Goodman, L. A., Liang, B., Helms, J. E., Latta, R. E., Sparks, E., & Weintraub, S. R. (2004a). Training counseling psychologists as social justice agents: Feminist and multicultural principles in action. *Counseling Psychologist, 32,* 793–837. doi: 10.1177/0011000004268802.

Goodman, L. A., Liang, B., Weintraub, S. R., Helms, J. E., & Latta, R. E. (2004b). Warts and all: Personal reflections on social justice in counseling psychology. Reply to Kiselica, Palmer, Thompson and Shermis, and Watts. *Counseling Psychologist, 32,* 886–899.

Green, E. J., McCollum, V. C., & Hays, D. G. (2008). Teaching advocacy counseling within a social justice framework: Implications for school counselors and educators. *Journal for Social Action in Counseling and Psychology, 1*(2), 14–30.

Haledman, D. C. (2003). The practice and ethics of sexual orientation conversion therapy. In L. D. Garnets, & D. C. Kimmel (Eds.), *Psychological perspectives on lesbian, gay, and bisexual experiences* (2nd ed., pp. 681–698). New York: Columbia University Press.

Helms, J. E. (1995). An update of Helm's White and people of color racial identity models. In J. Ponterotto, J. M. Casas, L. A. Suzuki, & C. M. Alexander (Eds.), *Handbook of multicultural counseling* (pp. 181–198). Thousand Oaks, CA: Sage.

Helms, J. E. (2003). A pragmatic view of social justice. *The Counseling Psychologist, 31,* 305–313.

Huynh, U. K., & Roysircar, G. (2006). Community health promotion curriculum: A case study of Southeast Asian refugees. In R. L. Toporek, L. Gerstein, N. A. Fouad, G. Roysircar, & T. Israel (Eds.), *Handbook for social justice in counseling psychology: Leadership, vision, and action* (pp. 338–357). Thousand Oaks, CA: Sage.

Ivey, A. E., & Collins, N. M. (2003). Social justice: A long-term challenge for counseling psychology. *The Counseling Psychologist, 31,* 290–298.

Juntunen, C. L., Cavett, A. M., Clow, R. B., Rempel, V., Darrow, R. E., & Guilmino, A. (2006). Social justice through self-sufficiency: Vocational psychology and the transition from welfare to work. In R. L. Toporek, L. Gerstein, N. A. Fouad, G. Roysircar, & T. Israel (Eds.), *Handbook for social justice in counseling psychology: Leadership, vision, and action* (pp. 294–309). Thousand Oaks, CA: Sage.

Kiselica, M. S. (2004). When duty calls: The implications of social justice work for policy, education, and practice in the mental health professions. *The Counseling Psychologist, 32,* 838–854.

Kiselica, M. S., & Robinson, M. (2001). Bringing advocacy counseling to life: The history, issues, and human dramas of social justice work in counseling. *Journal of Counseling & Development, 70,* 387–397.

Lee, C. C. (Ed.). (2007). *Counseling for social justice* (2nd ed.). Alexandria, VA: American Counseling Association.

Leong, R. T. L. (Ed.). (1995). *Career development and vocational behavior of racial and ethnic minorities.* Hillsdale, NJ: Lawrence Erlbaum.

Lewis, J., Arnold, M., House, R., & Toporek, R. (2002). *American Counseling Association advocacy competencies.* Alexandria, VA: American Counseling Association.

Martin-Baro, I. (1994). War and mental health. In A. Aron, & S. Corne (Eds.), *Writings for liberation psychology: Ignacio Martin-Baro* (pp. 108–121). Cambridge, MA: Harvard University Press.

McWhirter, E. H., & McWhirter, B. T. (2007). Grounding clinical training and supervision in an empowerment model. In E. Aldarondo (Ed.), *Advancing social justice through clinical practice* (pp. 417–442). Mahwah, NJ: Lawrence Erlbaum Associates.

Nicolas, G., Helms, J. E., Jernigan, M. M., Sass, T., Skrzypek, A., & DeSilva, A. M. (2008). A conceptual framework for understanding the strengths of Black youths. *Journal of Black Psychology, 34,* 261–280. doi: 10.1177/0095798408316794.

Norsworthy, K. L. (2006). Bringing social justice to international practices of counseling psychology. In R. L. Toporek, L. Gerstein, N. A. Fouad, G. Roysircar, & T. Israel (Eds.), *Handbook for social justice in counseling psychology: Leadership, vision, and action* (pp. 421–441). Thousand Oaks, CA: Sage.

O'Brien, K. M. (2001). The legacy of Parsons: Career counselors and vocational psychologists as agents of social change. *The Career Development Quarterly, 50,* 66–76.

Palmer, L. K. (2004). The Call to Social Justice: A Multidiscipline Agenda. *The Counseling Psychologist, 32,* 879–885.

Pieterse, A. L., Evans, S. A., Risner-Butner, A., Collins, N. M., & Mason, L. B. (2009). Multicultural competence and social justice training in counseling psychology and counselor education: A review and analysis of a sample of multicultural course syllabi. *The Counseling Psychologist, 37,* 93–115.

Pope, M. (2000). A brief history of career counseling in the United States. *Career Development Quarterly, 48,* 194–211.

Prilleltensky, I. (in press). Justice in the helping professions: A brief guide. In M. Constantine (Ed.), *Social justice and empowerment initiatives in psychology and education.* Washington DC: American Psychological Association.

Romano, J. L., & Netland, J. D. (2008). The application of the theory of reasoned action and planned behavior to prevention science in counseling psychology. *Counseling Psychologist, 36,* 777–806.

Roysircar, G. (2006). Counseling Health Psychology's Collaborative Role in the Community. In R. L. Toporek, L. Gerstein, N. A. Fouad, G. Roysircar, & T. Israel (Eds.), *Handbook for social justice in counseling psychology: Leadership, vision, and action* (pp. 313–317). Thousand Oaks, CA: Sage.

Schmidt, C. K., Hoffman, M. A., & Taylor, N. (2006). Social justice related to working with HIV/AIDS from a counseling health psychology perspective. In R. L. Toporek, L. Gerstein, N. A. Fouad, G. Roysircar, & T. Israel (Eds.), *Handbook for social justice in counseling psychology: Leadership, vision, and action* (pp. 44–58). Thousand Oaks, CA: Sage.

Sedlacek, W. E. (2007). Conducting research that makes a difference. In C. C. Lee (Ed.), *Counseling for social justice* (2nd ed., pp. 223–237). Alexandria, VA: American Counseling Association.

Shullman, S. L., Celeste, B. L., & Strickland, T. (2006). Extending the Parsons legacy: Applications of counseling psychology in pursuit of social justice through the development of public policy. In R. L. Toporek, L. Gerstein, N. A. Fouad, G. Roysircar, & T. Israel (Eds.), *Handbook for social justice in counseling psychology: Leadership, vision, and action* (pp. 499–513). Thousand Oaks, CA: Sage.

Speight, S. L., & Vera, E. M. (2008). Social justice and counseling psychology: A challenge to the profession. In S. D. Brown, & R. W. Lent (Eds.), *Handbook of counseling psychology* (4th ed., pp. 54–67). New York: Wiley.

Sundberg, N. D., & Littman, R. A. (1994). Leona Elizabeth Tyler (1906–1993). *American Psychologist, 49*(3), 211–212.

Talleyrand, R. M., Chi-yung, R., & Bemak, F. (2006). Incorporating social justice in counselor training programs: A case study example. In R. L. Toporek, L. Gerstein, N. A. Fouad, G. Roysircar, & T. Israel (Eds.), *Handbook for social justice in counseling psychology: Leadership, vision, and action* (pp. 44–58). Thousand Oaks, CA.: Sage.

Thompson, C. E., Alfred, D. M., Edwards, S. L., & Garcia, P. G. (2006). Transformative endeavors: Implementing Helms's racial identity theory to a school-based heritage project. In R. L. Toporek, L. Gerstein, N. A. Fouad, G. Roysircar, & T. Israel (Eds.), *Handbook for social justice in counseling psychology: Leadership, vision, and action* (pp. 100–116). Thousand Oaks, CA: Sage.

Thompson, C. E., & Shermis, S. S. (2004). Tapping the Talents Within: A Reaction to Goodman, Liang, Helms, Latta, Sparks, and Weintraub. *The Counseling Psychologist, 32*, 866–878.

Thompson, A. S., Super, D. E., & Napoli, P. J. (1955). Developing a VA counseling psychology training program: A case history of university-hospital cooperation. *American Psychologist, 10*, 283–288.

Toporek, R. L., & Chope, R. C. (2006). Individual, programmatic, and entrepreneurial approaches to social justice. In R. L. Toporek, L. Gerstein, N. A. Fouad, G. Roysircar, & T. Israel (Eds.), *Handbook for social justice in counseling psychology: Leadership, vision, and action* (pp. 276–293). Thousand Oaks, CA: Sage.

Toporek, R. L., Gerstein, L., Fouad, N. A., Roysircar, G., & Israel, T. (Eds.). (2006). *Handbook for social justice in counseling psychology: Leadership, vision, and action.* Thousand Oaks, CA: Sage.

Toporek, R. L., & Liu, W. M. (2001). Advocacy in counseling: Addressing race, class, and gender oppression. In D. B. Pope-Davis, & H. L. K. Coleman (Eds.), *The intersection of race, class and gender in multicultural counseling* (pp. 285–413). Thousand Oaks, CA: Sage.

Toporek, R. L., & Pope-Davis, D. B. (2005). Exploring the relationships between multicultural training, racial attitudes, and attributions of poverty among graduate counseling trainees. *Cultural Diversity and Ethnic Minority Psychology, 11*, 259–271. doi: 10.1037/1099–9809.11.3.259.

Toporek, R. L., & Reza, J. V. (2001). Context as a critical dimension of multicultural counseling: Articulating personal, professional, and institutional competence. *Journal of Multicultural Counseling and Development, 29*(1), 13–30.

Toporek, R. L., & Williams, R. A. (2006). Ethics and professional issues related to the practice of social justice in counseling psychology. In R. L. Toporek, L. Gerstein, N. A. Fouad, G. Roysircar, & T. Israel (Eds.), *Handbook for social justice in counseling psychology: Leadership, vision, and action* (pp. 17–34). Thousand Oaks, CA: Sage.

U.S. Department of Health and Human Services. (2001). *Mental health: Culture, race and ethnicity–a supplement to mental health: A report of the Surgeon General.* Rockville, MD: U. S. Department of Health and Human Services, Public Health Office, Office of the Surgeon General.

Vera, E. M., & Speight, S. L. (2003). Multicultural competence, social justice, and counseling psychology: Expanding our roles. *Counseling Psychologist, 31*, 253–272. doi: 10.1177/0011000003031003001.

Vera, E., Daly, B., Gonzales, R., Morgan, M., & Thakral, C. (2006). Prevention and outreach with underserved populations: Building multisystemic youth development programs for urban youth. In R. L. Toporek, L. Gerstein, N. A. Fouad, G. Roysircar, & T. Israel (Eds.), *Handbook for social justice in counseling psychology: Leadership, vision, and action* (pp. 86–99). Thousand Oaks, CA: Sage.

Winerman, L. (2004). Timely action. *APA Monitor on Psychology, 35*(1), 48.

Internationalization of Counseling Psychology

Lawrence H. Gerstein *and* Stefanía Ægisdóttir

Abstract

This chapter discusses the consequences of exporting U.S. models and strategies of counseling to other countries, and it presents a few ethical issues linked with the internationalization of the field. Additionally, an in-depth discussion and analysis of specific lines of cross-cultural research in psychology and counseling (i.e., emotions, coping, and psychological help-seeking) is included and evaluated in terms of its cross-cultural validity and applicability to diverse cultures. Methodological challenges of cross-cultural research, theory, and practice are also highlighted, as are alternative approaches to performing cross-cultural research. The chapter ends with a brief discussion about the importance of cross-cultural collaboration and future opportunities for counseling professionals.

Keywords: cross-cultural research, cross-cultural validity, internationalization, emotions, coping, help-seeking, culture, methodology, collaboration

From almost its very inception, the discipline of psychology in the United States has been connected to some degree with professionals outside the U.S. borders. In the 1800s, for instance, there was a close association between U.S. and European psychologists (Brehm, 2008). The interest of U.S. counseling psychologists in international issues can be traced to the 1940s. At this time, a number of pioneers in the early days of the profession engaged in work outside the United States. Such luminaries in the profession as H. Borow, L. Brammer, W. Lloyd, D. Super, and E. G. Williamson collaborated with education faculty in Japan in helping to establish counseling services. In the 1960s, other leaders of the profession (e.g., F. Robinson, C. G. Wrenn) assisted with launching the counseling profession in England (Heppner, Leong, & Chiao, 2008a), while Donald Super and his associates began conducting international research on work values and career choice. The U.S. counseling profession's interest in international topics blossomed, however, in the first decade of the 21st century. Gerstein, Heppner, Ægisdóttir,

Leung, and Norsworthy (2009a) and Heppner et al. (2008a) provided an in-depth discussion of the history of this interest for the counseling and psychology professions in the United States.

In this chapter, we discuss the consequences of exporting U.S. models and strategies of counseling to other countries, and we present a few ethical issues linked with the internationalization of the field. Additionally, an in-depth discussion and analysis of specific lines of cross-cultural research in psychology and counseling is included (i.e., emotions, coping, and psychological help-seeking) and evaluated in terms of its applicability to diverse cultures. Methodological challenges of cross-cultural research, theory, and practice are also highlighted, as are alternative approaches to performing cross-cultural research. The chapter ends with a brief discussion about the importance of cross-cultural collaboration and future opportunities for counseling professionals.

Before discussing these topics, it is essential to first define four terms that appear throughout this chapter, to provide clarity and uniformity in their use. Frequently, these terms are either not defined or are inconsistently defined in the counseling literature. The concept of *internationalization* has been defined in many ways in the counseling literature (Gerstein et al., 2009a). Here, the definition offered by Leung, Clawson, Tena, Szilagyi, and Norsworthy (2009) will be employed. These scholars claimed that internationalization is an ongoing process of synthesizing research and information derived from counseling practices tied to various cultures. The knowledge gained from this endeavor is used to solve issues locally and globally. Furthermore, internationalization involves taking steps to indigenize counseling worldwide, so that theories, practices, and systems are developed and grounded in the local culture. *Globalization* is another term inconsistently used in the counseling literature, with its use varying with the context of analyses. In this chapter, it refers to interdependent transactions across borders that affect economic, social, cultural, and political aspects of life (United Nations ESSAP, 1999).

In the late 1980s and early 1990s, the multicultural counseling movement, first called the cross-cultural counseling movement (see Gerstein et al., 2009a), emerged as an important focus in the counseling profession. Historically, since the terms multicultural and cross-cultural counseling have been used synonymously and often defined inconsistently (Gerstein et al., 2009a; Heppner, Ægisdóttir, Leung, Duan, Helms, Gerstein, & Pedersen, 2009), it is essential to also clarify their definitions for the purposes of this chapter. Basically, multicultural counseling involves helping individuals, groups, organizations, and communities through the use of universal and cultural specific strategies that are consistent with the cultural values and experiences of the target clientele (Sue & Torino, 1994). More specifically, the multicultural counseling movement emphasizes the importance of offering a host of appropriate and effective services to diverse groups of people including persons of various ethnic and racial origins, socioeconomic status, sexual orientation, and physical ability. Serving international populations in and outside the United States was also emphasized early on in the movement, although it was not a high priority or central to the mission.

As mentioned above, in the initial stages of the emergence of the multicultural counseling movement, the terms *multicultural counseling* and *cross-cultural counseling* were frequently used interchangeably. This has led to some confusion among counseling professionals, especially recently, as more persons have pursued international work both in and outside the United States. Counseling professionals engaged in such work have wondered whether to call their activities multicultural or cross-cultural counseling. In trying to resolve this confusion, Gerstein et al. (2009a) introduced a new, unique definition of cross-cultural counseling in order to differentiate this concept from multicultural counseling. These authors defined cross-cultural counseling as the "pursuit and application of universal and indigenous theories, strategies (e.g., direct service, consultation, training, education, prevention), and research paradigms of counseling and mental health help-seeking grounded in an in-depth examination, understanding, and appreciation of the cultural and epistemological underpinnings of countries located worldwide" (p. 6). Gerstein et al. (2009a) also introduced another new term, *cross-national counseling*, to capture a unique set of specific international activities apart from those linked with cross-cultural counseling. They defined cross-national counseling as "collaborative professional activities (e.g., program development and implementation, training, teaching, consultation) jointly pursued by mental health professionals residing in at least two countries" (p. 6). Heppner et al. (2009) introduced another new term, *cross-national movement*, to help further crystallize and clarify the international nomenclature in the U.S. counseling profession. They defined cross-national movement as "the evolution of thought about culturally sensitive collaboration about all aspects of the counseling profession among counseling professionals across countries" (pp. 33–34).

Clearly, many terms are associated with cultural and international counseling activities. Regardless of the term or its definition, however, the more recent increased interest in international topics in the counseling profession can be traced to numerous innovative developments in the multicultural counseling movement and many professionals who were either directly or indirectly affected by this movement (Heppner et al., 2009). Although serving international domestic populations has been perceived by most U.S. counseling professionals to be a component of the multicultural movement, activities involving populations in other countries frequently have not been considered under the rubric of multicultural counseling.

It not surprising, therefore, that a certain degree of tension has existed between the U.S. multicultural and cross-national counseling movements (Gerstein, Heppner, Stockton, Leong, & Ægisdóttir, 2009b;

Heppner et al., 2009), or between the counseling professionals interested in domestic versus international cultural issues. In general, members affiliated with both movements are concerned, albeit to differing degrees, about resource allocation, educational opportunities, and meeting the needs of diverse and large populations (Gerstein et al., 2009b; Heppner et al., 2009). Heppner et al. (2009) provided an extensive discussion about the tensions, similarities, and differences between the two movements, and also the benefits of strengthening collaboration between the two groups.

Clashing Cultural and Counseling Paradigms

The internationalization of the U.S. counseling profession has led to many new lines of research, collaborative cross-national relationships, consulting opportunities, developments in methodology, and intervention strategies. It has also resulted in a stronger network of counseling professionals worldwide, and a deeper understanding and respect for cultural diversity and uniqueness. Although the U.S. cross-national counseling movement has enriched numerous professionals and others in the United States and abroad, and has helped meet the needs of various international clientele, many scholars (Gerstein et al., 2009a; Gerstein & Ægisdóttir, 2005a, 2005b; Gerstein & Ægisdóttir, 2007; Heppner, 2006; Heppner et al., 2008a; Leong & Ponterotto, 2003; Leong & Blustein, 2000; Leung, 2003; Pedersen, 2003; Pedersen & Leong, 1997) have seriously questioned the appropriateness, validity, relevance, and impact of countries embracing U.S. paradigms of counseling. Historically, these paradigm have been either exported to other countries by U.S. counseling professionals and international scholars and international students returning home, or imported by non-U.S. professionals enamored of the presumedly scientific, theoretical, and applied superiority of the U.S. models.

In fact, these paradigms and those linked with U.S. psychology have been called *ethnocentric* (Cheung, 2000; Heppner, 2006; Heppner et al., 2008a; Heppner, Leong, & Gerstein, 2008b; Leong & Leach, 2007; Leung, 2003; Marsella, 1998; Norsworthy, 2006; Pedersen & Leong, 1997; Takooshian, 2003; Stevens & Wedding, 2004), *U.S.-centric* (Leong & Ponterotto, 2003), or *Anglo-centric* (Cheung, 2000; Trimble, 2001) because they are grounded in U.S. cultural values, beliefs, and behaviors, and assume that persons and contexts from other countries and cultures share this background.

Furthermore, some counseling professionals have assumed these paradigms can be employed to accurately conceptualize the emotions, cognitions, and behaviors of individuals living in other countries, and also used to design and implement effective interventions. There is a growing awareness among counseling professionals worldwide (Gerstein et al., 2009a; Ægisdóttir, Gerstein, Leung, Kwan, & Lonner, 2009), however, that such assumptions are inaccurate and potentially harmful to the cultural integrity and survival of countries around the globe.

Other scholars have voiced even stronger concerns about the exportation and importation of U.S. counseling models to other countries, claiming that this was yet another example of Western Eurocentric domination, psychological hegemony (control or domination of one person or group over another, particularly one society or nation over others), cultural imperialism (a more powerful nation or society enforces its stance of superiority through domination and control; Said, 1993), and/or neocolonialism (dominance, usually by a Western nation, over another nation that is politically independent but weak economically and dependent on trade with the more powerful nation) that could deepen inequities among countries and destroy indigenous cultures (Norsworthy, Heppner, Ægisdóttir, Gerstein, & Pedersen, 2009a). Lugones and Spelmann (1983) went so far as to state that Western psychologists working outside of the West were inclined to engage in a type of psychological colonization (system of domination depicted by social patterns or mechanisms of control that maintain oppression and that vary from context to context; Moane, 1994) or neocolonialism.

To overcome the ethnocentric, U.S.-centric, or Anglo-centric exportation and importation of U.S. counseling paradigms, and the potential for psychological hegemony, imperialism, colonialism, and neocolonialism, it is essential that U.S. counseling professionals become more mindful of the implications of employing their paradigms elsewhere, and most importantly, that they learn how, by recognizing internalized attitudes and behaviors linked with positions of privilege and oppression, they can avoid perpetuating dominant–subordinate relationships (Norsworthy et al., 2009a). This also requires counseling professionals to respect, listen, and learn from each other; commit to distributing and sharing power, and establish and maintain equitable relationships with one another worldwide. This can lead to greater understanding of various cultures around the world, and a deeper appreciation of the similarities and unique differences in how people think, feel, and behave. It also can potentially facilitate a clearer understanding for counseling professionals of the "conscientization" process (Freire, 1970). That is, these therapists can develop an awareness and comprehension about the dynamics of colonization, domination, and subordination, and their own attitudes, feelings, and behaviors linked with such dynamics (Norsworthy et al., 2009a). Acquiring this awareness and genuine conscientization requires counseling professionals to enact solutions to change existing oppressive conditions. Additionally, it requires professionals to learn how to liberate themselves from a colonized mentality and set of behaviors so that they may creatively collaborate and partner with one another (Norsworthy et al., 2009a).

Although taking the steps outlined above cannot ensure that U.S. models of counseling will no longer be indiscriminately exported and imported around the world, it is likely that following this path will increase counseling professionals' cultural sensitivity and understanding, deepen their recognition of being culturally encapsulated (Wrenn, 1962), and increase the potential that they can be liberated from a colonized mentality (Norsworthy et al., 2009a). Taking this path should also enhance professionals' awareness, knowledge, and respect for diverse, rich, and unique models of counseling embraced worldwide, including indigenous paradigms. In so doing, there is a much greater probability that counseling professionals will rely on culturally appropriate, valid, and effective theories and strategies of counseling when assisting diverse clientele around the world.

Professional Issues Worldwide
Definition, Role, and Function of Counseling

Although the terms *psychologist* and *counselor* are somewhat common throughout the world, Abi-Hashem (1997) claimed that, when these terms do exist, they are defined differently than in Western countries. The title *counseling psychologist* and the counseling psychology field, in contrast, exists in only a few nations (e.g., United States, Canada, Hong Kong, South Africa, Australia, Taiwan, Thailand, Puerto Rico), and is thought to be unique to the United States. In fact, counseling psychology cannot be found in most European countries and in the Southern Hemisphere.

The role and function of a counselor and psychologist (see Rosenzweig, 1982) also varies greatly worldwide. For instance, in some countries (e.g., Sweden, Portugal), the title *psychologist* only refers to professors teaching psychology and/ or researchers conducting psychological studies. In other countries (e.g., United States, Canada), the title of psychologist can characterize individuals engaged in clinical, counseling, educational, or industrial work, for example, as well as persons who teach and/ or conduct research.

There is also variation in the role and function of counseling psychologists in countries where the title exists (Gerstein et al., 2009a; Heppner et al., 2008b; Savickas, 2007). In the United States, counseling psychologists' "participate in a range of activities including teaching, research, psychotherapeutic and counseling practice, career development, assessment, supervision, and consultation. They employ a variety of methods closely tied to theory and research to help individuals, groups and organizations function optimally as well as to mediate dysfunction. Interventions may be either brief or long-term; they are often problem-specific and goal-directed. These activities are guided by a philosophy that values individual differences and diversity and a focus on prevention, development, and adjustment across the lifespan, which includes vocational concerns" (see www.div17.org/students_defining.html). Counseling psychologists in the United States are employed in a many settings (e.g., universities, independent practice, mental health centers, medical facilities, rehabilitation agencies, business and industrial organizations, and consulting firms).

A somewhat similar definition can be found in Australia. The Australian Psychological Society (2007a) reported, "Counselling psychologists employ a wide range of therapeutic methods, each of which places a significant emphasis on the quality of the relationship between the client and the psychologist. They assist individuals, families, and groups in areas related to personal well-being, interpersonal relationships, work, recreation, and health. They are also trained to assist people experiencing both acute and chronic life crises." These professionals are employed in health and community agencies, educational institutions, property and business organizations, and government and administrative offices (Australian Bureau of Statistics, 2003).

The definition of counseling psychology in Canada is also quite specific. Young and Nicol (2007) stated the Colleges of Psychologists of Ontario (CPO) defined this term as "the fostering and improving of normal human functioning by helping people solve problems, make decisions, and cope with stresses of everyday life" (p. 21). The CPO is the organization that licenses psychologists. Similar to counseling psychologists in the United States, Canadian professionals are engaged in many activities (e.g., counseling, prevention, research, training, supervision, policy development and implementation) with a diverse clientele (e.g., individuals, families, groups, organizations) that vary in their concerns and needs. These professionals are employed in a host of settings (e.g., educational institutions, social service agencies, government offices, private practice, business and industry) (Young & Nicol, 2007).

In contrast to the employment opportunities available to counseling psychologists in the countries already discussed, in South Africa, very few work settings are available to these professionals (Naidoo & Kagee, 2009). Almost all these individuals are affiliated with a private practice. Some are employed, however, by nongovernmental organizations that offer counseling services (e.g., career interventions, health development, prevention, and economic empowerment) to economically disadvantaged individuals living with HIV/AIDS, or to those who have survived trauma, rape, or crime. The definition of a counselling psychologist in South Africa is somewhat vague as compared to the one adopted in the United States and Australia. According to the scope of practice statement issued by the Health Professions Council of South Africa (2011), "Counselling psychologists assist relatively well-adjusted people in dealing with normal problems of life concerning all stages and aspects of a person's existence in order to facilitate desirable psychological adjustment, growth, and maturity." South African counselling psychologists engage in assessment, intervention, policy development, program design, research, training, and supervision.

In Hong Kong, the recently formed Division of Counseling Psychology of the Hong Kong Psychological Society introduced a new definition of counseling psychology. Like South Africa, this definition is somewhat general: "the application of psychological knowledge, psychotherapeutic skills, and professional judgment to facilitate enhanced human functioning and quality of life" (Leung, Chan, & Leahy, 2007, p. 53). This definition assumes counseling psychologists assist diverse populations, work in a host of settings, employ growth- and strengths-oriented strategies linked to psychotherapeutic and developmental perspectives, consider context and systems, use preventive interventions, and conduct research (Leung et al., 2007). In Hong Kong, counseling psychologists are infrequently employed by governmental agencies, and instead, they work in schools, universities, health care settings, social service agencies, private enterprises, and in business (Leung et al., 2007).

Regardless of the country or the specific psychological title (e.g., clinical psychologist, counseling psychologist, school psychologist) employed, psychologists in many locations are involved in some type of professional activity closely connected to psychology and not some other discipline or content area. Furthermore, to become a psychologist, an individual must complete some form of academic training. In the United States, a psychologist must earn a doctoral degree, whereas in most other countries a master's degree or an equivalent diploma is required for a practicing psychologist (Europe, South Africa, Taiwan, China, Korea, Japan, Uganda), and a doctoral degree for an academic psychologist (Gerstein et al., 2009a). In many regions of the world (South, Latin, and Central America), it is possible to become a practicing psychologist with the equivalent of a bachelor's degree (Gerstein et al., 2009a).

There is even greater divergence in how the title, role, and function of a counselor are defined worldwide, and in the case of the title, how it is used (Gerstein et al., 2009a; Heppner & Gerstein, 2008). In some countries (e.g., India), the title *counselor* is utilized by indigenous healers, and by persons who offer financial advice (e.g., bankers), legal services (i.e., lawyers), or medical care (e.g., physicians, nurses). In other countries, only individuals engaged in psychological activities employ the title. For example, professional counselors offering psychological services exist in Taiwan, China, Japan, South Korea, Thailand, Malaysia, Hong Kong, Singapore, the Philippines, Israel, Lebanon, Saudi Arabia, Egypt, Jordan, Kuwait, the United Arab Emirates (UAE), the Palestinian territory, Turkey, Iran, Greece, Uganda, Ghana, Kenya, Nigeria, Botswana, South Africa, Italy, The Netherlands, Ireland, Great Britain, Ukraine, Slovakia, Portugal, France, Hungary, South Korea, and New Zealand.

To become a professional counselor in different countries, similarly to becoming a psychologist, an individual must complete some type of academic training. In the United States, a professional counselor must earn a master's degree, whereas in many other countries a bachelor's degree is sufficient to become a counselor (e.g., Australia, United Arab Emirates). There are also some countries where a person can become a professional counselor with less than a college education (e.g., the Ukraine).

Finally, it should be mentioned that worldwide, some amount of advanced academic coursework is required to be a professional counselor or psychologist. For both occupations, however, countries vary in their requirements to complete counseling practica or field experiences, and/or an internship as part of the training program. Licensure requirements also vary greatly worldwide. Some countries license counselors (e.g., Japan, Lebanon, United States, Malaysia) and psychologists (e.g., Taiwan, Greece, South Africa, Iceland, Portugal, Ireland, Canada, United States, Colombia, Venezuela, Argentina, Puerto Rico), whereas others (e.g., New Zealand, Fiji, Turkey, Iran, Uganda, Ghana, Italy, Great Britain, Slovakia, South Korea, Turkey, Greece, Nigeria, United Arab Emirates) have no laws to regulate these titles or the services provided by individuals in such professions.

Ethics of International Work

A growing number of counseling organizations worldwide have adopted an ethical code. These codes were developed and endorsed by counseling and psychology organizations to provide guiding principles and standards, in part, for the ethical practice of counseling, and to promote the conducting of cross-culturally and culturally valid research. Ethical codes are expressions of values (Diener & Grandall, 1978; Gerstein et al., 2009c) and are constructed in a specific cultural context. For instance, Pedersen (1995, 1997) argued the ethical codes endorsed by U.S. counseling and psychology associations (i.e., American Psychological Association [APA], American Counseling Association) were based on a dominant U.S. cultural perspective, and therefore ignored or minimized the cultural context in ethical decision-making regarding minority groups in the United States Several books have emphasized the importance of considering cultural factors in ethical decision making (e.g., Houser, Wilczenski, & Ham, 2006). These books offer counseling professionals information on how different worldviews can influence and guide this process.

Many counseling and psychology organizations around the world have developed ethical codes and guidelines for the practice of psychology in their country (see e.g., Leach, 2008) grounded in their unique cultural context. Yet, in other countries, no ethical code exists. To address this gap, the General Assembly of the International Union of Psychological Science (IUPsyS), and the International Association of Applied Psychology (IAAP) developed and adopted a "universal declaration of ethical

principles for psychologists" (see http://www.iupsys.org/ethics) to promote ethical ideals in the psychology profession. These principles are based on shared global values (e.g., respect for dignity, maximize benefits and minimize harm to individuals, families, and communities, integrity, and being responsible to society) that are moral and aspirational, without prescribing specific behaviors that are influenced by cultural values and laws (Gauthier, 2008).

Although many countries have ethical codes and regulations guiding counseling professionals' work in general, fewer have specific guidelines regarding psychological tests and testing (Iliescu, Ispas, & Harris, 2009). Leach and Oakland (2007) compared ethical standards affecting the development of tests and their use across 31 ethical codes in 35 countries. They discovered that these standards were valuable in that they provided mental health professionals with guidelines for practicing with competence.

Some specific policies have been influential with respect to the ethics of testing. In this regard, the APA has continuously pursued the creation of such policies, with the latest being the "Standards for Educational and Psychological Testing" (AERA, APA, NCME, 1999). Yet, in spite of this policy's wide reach and importance, it is "tributary to local values, customs, and practices and do [sic] not bring about adherence from psychologists around the world" (Iliescu et al., 2009, n.p.). An important step, however, was taken by the International Test Commission (ITC) when addressing the unique testing issues faced by professionals outside the United States. Three documents in this regard are of great importance. First, the ITC International Guidelines on Test Use (International Test Commission, 2000) focuses on the fair and ethical use of tests worldwide and the competence of test users. Second, the ITC Guidelines on Test Adaptation (e.g., van de Vijver & Hambleton, 1996) addresses the selection, translation, adaptation, and interpretation of psychological tests employed outside their culture/country of origin. And the third document, the ITC Guidelines on Computer-based and Internet Delivered Testing (Bartram & Coyne, 2005), focuses on issues and best practices in the use of technology in test administration, the security of tests and test results, and the control over the testing process.

Given the contextual influence on ethical practices, the ITC International Guidelines for Test Use (Bartram, 2001) and the Universal Declaration of Ethical Principles for Psychologists (Gauthier, 2008) are extremely valuable documents for counseling professionals engaged in psychological testing in an international arena for several reasons. For example, countries differ greatly in the degree, if any, of legal control over psychological testing and those tested. Therefore, the ethical guidelines outlined in these documents may offer a degree of support to national associations interested in developing such standards where they are lacking. These guidelines also may help provide direction to professionals practicing in countries where no statutory control exists. Consistent with this observation, we concur with Iliescu et al. (2009), who stated that, in a situation in which there are few if any laws about psychological tests, and where none is internationally binding, for a test or testing procedure to be considered ethical, it should adhere to the Universal Declaration of Ethical Principles for Psychologists.

Relevance of Cross-cultural Research to Counseling

Along with having an influence on ethical practices worldwide, context and culture also may differentially impact important variables of interest to counseling professionals. As a result, it is critical to discuss a few lines of research and the corresponding relevant potential challenges. Here, we will focus on emotions, coping, and help-seeking to highlight what is known about these topics from an international perspective, the challenges connected with each, and possible solutions that counseling professionals might pursue to conduct culturally and cross-culturally valid and appropriate research. Each of these topics is salient to both the practice and science of counseling worldwide.

Culture and Emotions: An Overview

In the United States and many other countries, emotions have been central to the science and practice of counseling. From the early days of the pioneers in psychotherapy (e.g., Freud, Jung, Rank, Reich, Adler) to the more contemporary giants of our profession (e.g., Rogers, Perls, Frankl), the emotional life of individuals has occupied much of our training, practice, and pursuit of research. Even theorists (e.g., Beck, Ellis) whose psychotherapeutic approaches were grounded in understanding and changing cognition placed great importance on comprehending the role of emotion, particularly as it effected cognition. Without a doubt, a large number of counseling professionals worldwide continue to structure their work whether it be, for instance, direct service, prevention, training, or research, around the identification, assessment, conceptualization, and/or treatment of the emotions of individuals, couples, families, and groups. In fact, an overwhelming number of our U.S. graduate-level master's training programs in counseling continue to emphasize the acquisition of basic helping skills linked with the recognition and reflection of clients' emotions. Developing these skills is also considered important to the establishment of an effective counseling relationship with all clients, regardless of their ethnic, cultural, racial, and/or national background. Furthermore, displaying these skills is thought to be an essential prerequisite for learning theories and strategies tied to most all therapeutic approaches.

Although emotions have occupied a central role in the counseling profession throughout the world, the profession itself has not given much thought to the generalizability and cross-cultural validity of U.S. theories designed to explain these constructs, nor has it focused much attention on the role of such constructs in individuals' everyday life. Instead, the prevailing assumption in the field basically has been that all individuals experience and express emotions in a similar fashion, and that these constructs serve a similar role across cultures and countries.

Interestingly, the broader profession of psychology in the United States and elsewhere has a long history of both exploring and questioning these assumptions. Perhaps, Darwin was the first to investigate this topic and provide a foundation for the study of emotional expressions across culture (Matsumoto, 2009). Darwin argued, "the communication of emotion, both its expression and its recognition, is part of our biological heritage" (Russell, 1991, p. 427). He also claimed that people throughout the world were consistent in how they expressed some emotions and that this could be understood by looking at their faces (Matsumoto, 2009).

Numerous social scientists later questioned Darwin's observations. According to Matsumoto (2009), Margaret Mead and Ray Birdwhistell were vocal critiques of Darwin, claiming that expressive behaviors across cultures varied greatly, and as such, it was not possible to consider facial expressions universal. Mead and Birdwhistell thought emotional expressions were learned differently in every culture. Moreover, they stated that "just as different cultures have different languages, they must have different languages of the face" (Matsumoto, p. 264). Since the time of Darwin's work, and Mead and Birdwhistell's pointed criticism, there has been an enormous amount of research on the universality of the expression of emotion and the corresponding facial behavior of individuals across cultures. The early work of psychologists investigating the relationship between culture and emotions was also driven by an interest in determining if facial expressions for specific "basic" emotions were universal (Soto, Levenson, & Ebling, 2005). Before summarizing the extensive research on this topic, it is necessary to highlight the current discussion in the psychology literature on the operational definition of emotion.

Definitions and Precursors of Emotions

According to Matsumoto, Yoo, Fontaine et al. (2008a), "emotions are neurophysiological and psychological reactions that aid in adapting to social coordination problems" (p. 58) that incorporate intra- and interpersonal functions (Keltner & Haidt, 1999; Levenson, 1999). Matsumoto (2009) also claimed the fundamental system of emotions people possess at birth operates as a central processor, modified for a variety of functions within specific cultures. Put another way, emotions are critical to "'managing relationships with other persons, defining the self, maintaining the self's worth or dignity and organizing appropriate action in many social situations'" (Kitayama, Markus, & Matsumoto 1995, p. 442). Some researchers (Matsumoto) claimed that, in the early years of life, individuals learn to have emotions linked with situations they encounter. These emotions are thought to be specific to the persons' culture and themselves. Consequently, there are cultural and individual differences in the experience and expression of emotions, although some investigators have claimed there are seven (plus or minus two) basic universal emotions (e.g., happiness, fear, anger, disgust, sadness). Matsumoto further stated, "One of the functions of culture, for instance, is to ascribe meaning to the various events that occur in our lives that are not part of our evolutionary past" (p. 275).

Mesquita and Walker (2003) also argued that, by nature, emotions were sociocultural and biological. Galati, Schmidt, Sini et al. (2005) claimed, in the late 1970s, that many investigators (e.g., Boucher, 1979, 1983) were interested in distinguishing universal antecedents of the fundamental emotions such as joy, surprise, fear, anger, disgust, and sadness as a way to show that emotions were based in biology, and as such, that they were basically innate responses. Some researchers (Kitayama & Markus, 1994; Mesquita & Frijda, 1992; Mesquita & Walker) have reported that most of the cross-cultural research on emotions has centered on the universal, biological features of the construct. In contrast, until recently, psychology has paid little attention to the sociocultural or cross-cultural facets of emotion. A summary of this line of research is presented later.

There are several components of emotions, including self-awareness, self-expression, self-regulation, and the recognition and identification of emotions in others. Emotional responding through expressive behavior serves an essential function of communication in that it helps regulate interpersonal interactions (Matsumoto et al., 2008a). The expression of emotion is an aspect of emotional behavior defined as outward expressions and actions linked with emotional experience (Mesquita & Frijda, 1992; Mesquita, Frijda, & Scherer, 1997). Emotional regulation, on the other hand, "is the ability to manage and modify one's emotional reactions to achieve goal-directed outcomes" (Matsumoto, 2006, p. 421).

Some writers (Menon, 2000) have indicated that emotions are cognitive appraisals derived from cultural values, beliefs, and norms. As such, culture shapes what persons should feel and experience, and emotions are culturally relative and affect individuals' relationships. Individuals' cognitive appraisals of situations and relationships determine what emotions they experience (Lynch, 1990; Menon, 2000). Cultures also establish rules, guidelines, and norms about the regulation of emotions since emotions, for example, play a critical role in social interactions (Keltner, Ekman, Gonzaga, & Beer, 2003).

Cultural psychologists offer another perspective on the nature of emotions. These psychologists (e.g., Menon, 2000; Shweder, 1991, 1993) are inclined to perceive emotions as scripts or narratives comprised of several features. Such scripts are considered appraisals of specific events or situations (Menon, 2000). From this viewpoint, Shweder (1993) argued that, when conducting cross-cultural research on emotional functioning, it is beneficial to separate an emotion-script into its specific narrative features. This strategy renders it possible to draw comparisons between the differences and similarities in the specific features of individuals' emotional script. In so doing, it also permits an assessment of the commonalities in the pattern of how persons from various cultures evaluate different events or circumstances.

Matsumoto et al. (2008a) also argued that culture shapes the norms connected to the experience and expression of emotions, and consequently, informs the display rules guiding emotional expressions (see also Ekman & Friesen, 1969; Izard, 1980). Some investigators (e.g., Eid & Diener, 2001) have argued, however, that there have been a limited number of quantitative cross-cultural studies on the norms for experiencing emotions. Some highlights of various aspects of this line of research follow.

DISPLAY RULES

Ekman and Friesen (1969) introduced the concept of *display rules* more than 35 years ago. According to Ekman and Friesen and others (Saarni, 1999), individuals learn display rules early in their life. Once emotions are elicited, these rules inform and guide people in how they might express themselves emotionally, given specific social situations. Investigators often rely on these rules when characterizing cultural differences in the display of emotions (Matsumoto, 2009). In fact, in the 1980s, researchers started to assess cultures and ethnicities in terms of their display rules (Matsumoto, 1990, 1993), although Ekman and Friesen had earlier argued that such rules could be used to explain variations in facial expressions of emotions across cultures. The most recent extensive study on this topic (Matsumoto et al., 2008a) examined display rules in more than 30 cultures worldwide. The overall results indicated that display rule norms of less expressivity were more common in collectivistic as compared to individualistic cultures. Based on these findings, Matsumoto et al. concluded that the regulation of expressing all emotions was vital to preserving the social order in these cultures.

In addition to display rules, some writers have discussed similar rules known as *feeling rules*. Hochschild (1983) claimed these rules represent social norms prescribing how persons should feel in specific situations (e.g., wedding or funeral). Clearly, these rules also can vary by culture. There are numerous cultural differences in the display or expression of emotions. Matsumoto (2009) claimed that two processes are responsible for this variation. First, a culture's display rules or differences in the cultural norms linked with managing and regulating the expression of emotion contributes to this variation. And second, cultural differences in the antecedent circumstances that elicit emotions contribute to cultural variations in how individuals will express their emotions.

THE LANGUAGE OF EMOTION

One of the most important aspects and challenges of understanding emotions across cultures is examining the vocabulary or language structure used by a culture to capture and convey the experience and expression of feelings and emotions. Therefore, it is not surprising that researchers (e.g., Matsumoto & Assar, 1992; Russell, 1991) have reported that the vocabulary of languages varies in how well it captures the expression of emotional concepts. For instance, for native English speakers the verb "to feel" is linked with emotions and intimately associated with emotional expression and experience (Menon, 2000). In contrast, there is no exact equivalent for the verb "to feel" in most South Asian languages, and yet, South Asians do not miss this verb when they experience and express their emotions (Lynch, 1990).

Not only are there differences in the presence of the verb "to feel" in some languages, there are also major differences in whether certain feeling or emotion words appear in various languages, and if the concept of *emotion* even exists in all cultures (Russell, 1991). In a study by Brandt and Boucher (1986), for example, it was discovered that the concept emotion and a term for this concept existed in the targeted languages of the study (Indonesian, Japanese, Korean, Malay, Spanish, and Sinhalese). Matsuyama et al. (1978), however, discovered something very different for the Japanese language. They reported that, in this language, the word for emotion, *jodo*, includes being angry, happy, sad, and ashamed, and also includes terms not considered emotions (e.g., considerate, motivated, lucky). Other investigators, in contrast, have claimed that some cultures have no concept or word for emotion. For instance, this was reported to be the case for the Tahitians (Levy, 1973), the Bimin-Kuskusmin of Papua, New Guinea (Poole, 1985), the Gidjingali aborigines of Australia (Hiatt, 1978), the Ifalukians of Micronesia (Lutz, 1980, 1983), the Chewong of Malaysia (Howell, 1981), and the Samoans (Gerber, 1975).

Although the concept or word *emotion* might not exist in certain cultures, there is evidence that in some of these cultures the concept is implicit (Russell, 1991). Furthermore, similar words may be used, or words not recognized by English speakers might be employed to communicate the term *emotion* (Russell, 1991). Moreover, as Russell stated, "Some English emotion words have no equivalent in some other language" (p. 430), words such as love, anger, sadness, and fear. Similarly, some emotion words in non-English languages have no equivalent word in the English language.

Even if the concept or word *emotion* appears in a particular culture, researchers have discovered major differences in how such concepts or words are interpreted and understood. For example, Hupka, Lenton, and Hutchison (1999) reported that for approximately 20% of the world's languages, no distinction is made between envy and jealousy. In these languages, one word captures both concepts. Similarly, Leff (1973) claimed that only one word described anger and sadness in some African languages, whereas Russell (1991) stated this was also the case for the Ilongot in the Philippines and the Ifaluk who reside on a coral atoll in the Caroline Islands. A number of cultures also do not distinguish between shame and other emotions such as fear (Gidjingali aborigines of Australia; Hiatt, 1978) and embarrassment (Japanese: Lebra, 1983; Tahitians: Levy, 1973; Ifalukians:- Lutz, 1980; Indonesians: Keeler, 1983; Newars of Nepal: Levy, 1983). In other cultures (e.g., Ilongot, Javanese, Pintupi), one word captures shame and other emotions (e.g., timidity, embarrassment, awe, obedience, respect, guilt, shyness) at the same time (see Geertz, 1959; Myers, 1979; M. Z. Rosaldo, 1983). Cultures also vary in their cognitive schemas of emotions (Levy, 1983, 1984; Mesquita & Frijda, 1992).

The concept of depression has posed challenges for cultural investigations as well. Researchers have faced difficulties with defining this concept and understanding its meaning (Marsella, 1980). In fact, when summarizing cross-cultural studies of depression, some writers (Marsella, 1980; Kleinman, 1977) have suggested that the ethnocentric conceptualization of depression has led to challenges when conducting research. Other researchers (e.g., Brandt & Boucher, 1986; Marsella, 1980), when reviewing previous studies, have concluded that a number of non-Western societies have no emotion terms similar to the concept of depression used in the English language. In their study of this observation, Brandt and Boucher discovered that, as an organizing concept, depression was present in one of three Western (United States) and three of five non-Western (Indonesia, Japan, and Sri Lanka) countries. The researchers concluded from this "that the broad classification of cultures into dichotomous groups— Western vs. non-Western—cannot account for the occurrence (and nonoccurrence) of depression clusters" (p. 330). Furthermore, they reported that for the countries just mentioned, "depression was a sufficiently salient semantic organizing concept . . . despite their cultural and linguistic differences" (p. 341). Last, Brandt and Boucher argued that, unlike the *Diagnostic and Statistical Manual* (DSM-III) that described a depressive episode as "either a dysphoric mood or loss of interest or pleasure in usual activities and pastimes," their "samples did not view depression as an either-or-phenomenon" (p. 343).

Other researchers have reported that there is no single word for depression in certain cultures. This is true, for instance, for the Yoruba of Nigeria (Leighton et al., 1963), some North American Indian Nations (Termansen & Ryan, 1970), the Malay (Resner & Hartog, 1970), the Chinese (Chan, 1990; Tseng & Hsu, 1969), the Eskimos (Leff, 1973), the Fulani in Africa (Riesman, 1977), the Kaluli of Papua New Guinea (Schieffelin, 1985), and the Xhosa of Southern Africa (Cheetham & Cheetham, 1976).

Along with depression, a fair amount of cultural research has been conducted on semantic structures of emotions. Russell (1991) reported on an extensive review of this literature, stating, among other observations, that words for emotions in different languages cannot be accurately translated one-to-one. Russell cautioned, however, that this conclusion needed to be further explored since the earlier research had been based on ethnographic methods. Interestingly, two later studies on the cultural universals in the semantic structure of emotion terms, in general, found that emotion concepts were comparable across cultures (Church, Katigbak, Reyes, & Jensen, 1998; Romney, Moore, & Rusch, 1997). Similarly, when studying 25 emotional clusters (e.g., adoration, agony, anger, depression, envy, guilt, pride, relief) across 64 languages, Hupka et al. (1999) discovered the "naming of emotion categories was relatively uniform across languages when English terms were used as the referents and when the establishment of the universal developmental sequence of the emotion lexicon was based on emotion category terms that all sampled languages had encoded" (p. 260).

Regardless of these findings, it is rather difficult to accurately investigate how language depicts the emotions of various cultures. Complicating this task even further is the fact that criteria are lacking to judge the equivalence of words to describe emotions, making it difficult to compare the equivalence or nonequivalence of emotions between cultures (Mesquita & Frijda, 1992). This task is further complicated by the recognition that languages vary in the number of words they use to classify emotions (Russell, 1991). For instance, Wallace and Carson (1973) reported that over 2,000 words in the English language were used to classify emotions, whereas Hoekstra (1986) discovered 1,501 words in Dutch, Boucher (1979) found 750 words in Taiwanese Chinese and 230 words in Malay, and Howell (1981) reported seven words in Chewong linked with categories of emotion.

Additionally, it has been discovered that there is the possibility that emotions "may lose some of their meaning across cultural boundaries" (Elfenbein & Ambady, 2002, p. 228). Consistent with this assumption, Menon (2000) reported, "Glossing emotion terms across cultural and linguistic boundaries will rarely make the emotional experiences they represent intelligible" (p. 48). As stated earlier, Menon argued that if we want to comprehend the similarities and differences in emotional functioning between cultures, we must separate emotion scripts into their specific elements.

Moore, Romney, Hsia, and Rusch (1999) did exactly this when examining the structure of emotion terms for Chinese, English, and Japanese. They found a similar structure for emotion terms for the three languages. These researchers, like others (Romney et al., 1997; Rusch, 1996), also reported that Chinese, English, and Japanese shared a similar cognitive semantic structure of emotion terms.

Kim and Hupka (2002), on the other hand, investigated the cross-cultural comparability of emotions from a different perspective. They studied the free associations to five emotion concepts of university students in Korea and the United States. Although they discovered some minor differences, for both samples there were similarities in about one-third of the associations to anger, envy, fear, jealousy, or sadness. Kim and Hupka concluded there might be universals in the primary structural components of the language of emotion. They also thought their results corroborated earlier findings of universals in, for instance, semantics (Herrmann & Raybeck, 1981; Ullman, 1963/1966), phonology, grammar, lexicon, kinship terminology (Greenberg, 1966), the utilization of antonyms (Raybeck & Herrmann, 1996), the appraisal process linked with emotions (Scherer, 1997a), and the conceptual organization of emotion terms (Russell, 1983).

Looking at emotion terms from yet another perspective, based on the results of two mixed-methods studies, Semin, Görts, Nandram, and Semin-Goossens (2002) discovered emotion terms served as relationship-markers, and emotion events were symbolized by employing concrete linguistic terms in cultures that valued relationships and interdependence, as contrasted with cultures emphasizing the value of the individual. In the latter cultures, emotion terms were also found to operate mainly as self-markers symbolized by the greater use of, for instance, adjectives and nouns. Semin et al. concluded, "If the manner in which emotion is marked (relationship vs. self) differs systematically, as do the

situations that give rise to it, then it is likely that there are subtle differences in the way interdependent and independent cultures engage in talking about emotions" (p. 26). Moreover, they stated that their results suggested emotion-talk has greater implications for action in an interdependent culture (i.e., pursue or do something collaboratively) as compared to in an independent culture, in which emotion-talk might just be analytic in nature. Semin et al. urged investigators to further research these conclusions.

Finally, it is important to note that, in some cultures, emotions are exclusively linked with physical sensations or specific bodily organs (Mesquita & Frijda, 1992), and as such, the language used to describe an emotion is associated with a physical attribute. Rosaldo (1980), for example, reported that the Ilongot of the Philippines depicted motions of the heart when describing emotions, whereas Soto et al. (2005) proposed that the Chinese displayed emotions as physical symptoms linked with illness, and as such, they somatised their emotions. In general, researchers have claimed that there are cultural differences in the salience of physical sensations when describing and experiencing emotions and also the number of physical responses linked with reports of emotions (Mesquita & Frijda).

METHODS FOR STUDYING EMOTION

Before discussing in further detail the cross-cultural research on the experience, expression, regulation, and recognition of emotions, it is important to briefly highlight a few of the major methodologies employed to investigate these topics. Historically, the most common strategy employed by researchers has been extrapolating emotions from facial expressions and movements. In the early 1970s, a number of investigators introduced observational coding systems to distinguish facial expressions, in general, and to varying degrees specific facial movements assumed to be linked with different emotions. Ekman, Friesen, and Tomkins (1971) were the first to do this when they developed the Facial Action Scoring Technique. Soon thereafter, Ekman and Friesen (1976, 1978) constructed the Facial Action Coding System (FACS). Following this, a number of other methods were introduced, including the Maximally Discriminative Facial Movement Coding System (Izard, 1979), Monadic Phases (Tronick, Als, & Brazelton, 1980), Emotion FACS (EMFACS; Ekman & Friesen, 1982), and A System for Identifying Affect Expressions by Holistic Judgment (Izard, Dougherty, & Hembree, 1983). It should be noted the EMFACS is a technique for employing the FACS to specifically assess facial movements presumed to be connected to identifying emotions. Strategies to investigate the relationship between electrical activity in the muscles of the face and emotions also have been developed (Ekman, 1993). Ekman (1982) provided an excellent review of the early work on the various methodologies to measure facial movements considered to be relevant to emotional activity.

To date, the FACS is the most frequently used and researched methodology for assessing and describing facial expressions in many diverse fields (e.g., computer vision and graphics; neuroscience; developmental, social, and clinical psychology), and it is considered the "criterion measure of facial behavior" (Sayette, Cohn, Wertz, Perrott, & Parrott, 2001, p. 168). This technique offers a framework to assess all visually distinctive, observable facial movements. It also can be used to identify the "'basic emotions'" of happiness, sadness, surprise, disgust, anger, and fear through coding specific muscles in the face tied to facial behaviors (Ekman & Friesen, 1978). Ekman and Friesen referred to each facial movement as an action unit (AU) (Ekman, Friesen, & Hager, 2002). It appeared from the most current FACS manual that there are 46 AUs (Ekman et al., 2002); however, over the years, investigators have generated a range of AUs (e.g., 30–58) based on the purpose of their projects and the data obtained.

Since its introduction, the FACS has been used to investigate thousands of photographs, films, and videotapes of facial expressions (Ekman, 2003). Reliability and validity for the system has been established by Ekman and his colleagues (see Ekman et al., 2002). Reliability also has been shown in conjunction with hundreds of other projects designed to study a host of topics linked with facial behavior. Perhaps the most comprehensive examination of the FACS's reliability was conducted by Sayette et al. (2001), who reported good to excellent reliability for various aspects of the system.

As stated above, the EMFACS identifies specific AUs that are thought to be connected to facial expressions linked with emotions. According to Matsumoto and Willingham (2006), the validity for this system has been supported by investigations of spontaneous expression and judgments of expressions (Ekman, Davidson, & Friesen, 1990; Ekman & Friesen, 1971; Ekman, Friesen, & Ancoli, 1980; Ekman, Friesen, & Ellsworth, 1972; Ekman, Friesen, & O'Sullivan, 1988; Ekman, Sorenson, & Friesen, 1969). Investigators employing the EMPACS have

established reliability (e.g., inter-rater, interobserver) based on the unique data collected in their own studies.

As mentioned earlier, researchers have often also assessed display rules. Such rules have been measured in many ways, but only a few of the techniques employed have been rendered sound in terms of their psychometrics (Matsumoto, Yoo, Hirayama, & Petrova, 2005). In some of the earliest research designed to investigate display rules, the investigators (Ekman, 1972; Friesen, 1972) did not actually assess the rules with a psychometric instrument. Instead, differences in facial responses of individuals from two cultures were assessed and compared, and interpretations of the findings were guided by theory and not an empirical construct (Matsumoto et al., 2005).

Much of the early work (e.g., Saarni, 1979) on assessing display rules was conducted with children by exposing them to stories about social situations that would elicit their emotional responses. Until recently, the measures employed in such studies were not validated. In the early part of this century, two devices with sound psychometric properties were introduced and employed to examine the emotional expressivity of children: Children's Sadness Management Scale (CSMS; Zeman, Shipman, & Penza-Clyve, 2001) and the Emotion Expression Scale for Children (EESC; Penza-Clyve & Zeman, 2002). The CSMS measures the inhibition of the expression of sadness, emotion regulation coping, and dysregulated expression, whereas the EESC assesses two components of deficiencies in expressing emotions: lack of emotion awareness and lack of motivation to express negative emotion.

A number of adult measures of display rules and the management of emotional expressions with satisfactory psychometric qualities began to appear in the 1980s. However, like the devices designed for children, almost all of these instruments were constructed to investigate individual differences in the emotional expressivity, emotional control, or emotion regulation of adults along a single dimension of expression management, such as suppression or inhibition (Matsumoto et al., 2005). Some examples of these adult scales include the Courtauld Emotional Control Scale (Watson & Greer, 1983) that assesses the emotional control of Anger, Depressed Mood, and Anxiety; the Emotion Control Questionnaire (Roger & Najarian, 1989; Roger & Nesshoever, 1987) that measures the inclination to inhibit the expression of emotional responses (i.e., emotional inhibition, aggression control, and benign control); the Emotional Expressiveness Questionnaire (King & Emmons, 1990) that assesses emotional expressiveness in terms of the expression of positive emotion, expression of intimacy, and expression of negative emotion; the Emotional Expressivity Scale (Kring et al., 1994) that simply measures emotional expressiveness; the Berkeley Expressivity Questionnaire (BEQ) (Gross & John, 1995, 1997) that assesses emotional expressivity with regard to general expressivity, impulse strength, positive expressivity, and negative expressivity; and the Emotion Regulation Questionnaire (Gross & John, 2003) that measures the reappraisal and suppression of emotion or the ability to control the expression and experience of emotions. Matsumoto et al. (2005) provided a fairly comprehensive review of all the child and adult instruments constructed to assess display rules and emotional expressiveness.

Matsumoto, Takeuchi, Andayani, Kouznetsova, and Krupp (1998) introduced a different type of scale to measure display rules. Their device, the Display Rule Assessment Inventory (DRAI), unlike previous measures, was designed to capture the complexity of the behavioral repertoire linked with display rules instead of simply the suppression or inhibition of emotions. As such, it attempted to account for various behavioral responses when individuals experience different emotions in a host of social relationships. Seven emotions considered universally displayed in the face (i.e., anger, contempt, disgust, fear, happiness, sadness, and surprise along with a synonym for each) were linked with four types of social relationships (family members, close friends, work colleagues, and strangers). Participants were asked to report what they might do in terms of seven behavioral responses if they experienced each of these emotions in each social relationship. Six of the behavioral responses corresponded with Ekman and Friesen's (1969; 1975) original assumptions about how expressions might be managed when emotions are aroused: Express the feeling as is with no inhibitions (express); express the feeling, but with less intensity than one's true feelings (deamplify); express the feeling, but with more intensity than one's true feelings (amplify); try to remain neutral, express nothing (neutralize); express the feeling, but together with a smile to qualify one's feelings (qualify); and smile only, with no trace of anything else, in order to hide one's true feelings (mask). The seventh option allowed participants to share some other response. This measure was given to four different populations worldwide, and it was written in four languages (i.e., English, Japanese, Russian, and Korean).

Because of how it was constructed, it was not possible to perform a factor analysis on participants' responses. Instead, the researchers conducted multidimensional scaling. Although the six expected strategies to manage emotions were obtained from this process, this study failed to provide extensive evidence for the validity of the DRAI, and it did not measure the scale's reliability.

Matsumoto et al. (2005) conducted two studies to more closely investigate the psychometric properties of the DRAI. In the first, participants were from the United States, Russia, and Japan. Based on factor analysis, five factors were retained: express, deamplify, amplify, mask, and qualify. The investigators argued this result was the first to empirically support Ekman and Friesen's (1969) theoretical assumption about various unique expressive modes for facial expressions. Convergent validity and internal reliability were also explored and found to be satisfactory. The second study further investigated the validity and reliability of the measure with a sample of U.S. and non-U.S. participants. The findings supported the scale's convergent and predictive validity, and also its internal and test-retest reliability.

Cross-cultural Research on Emotions: Some Themes Relevant to Counseling Psychology

By now, it is rather apparent how daunting the challenge is for psychologists to operationally define the recognition, experience, and expression of emotions; to understand how language is used in the context of identifying, labeling, and communicating emotion; and to employ valid and reliable methods designed to capture the complexity of this construct, especially across cultures. An even more insurmountable task, however, is to effectively and accurately summarize the enormous amount of research conducted worldwide on various cultural and cross-cultural features of emotions. This is particularly difficult given the extensive, inconsistent results reported in this body of literature. In fact, attempting to discuss this entire line of research is beyond the scope of this chapter. Instead, some highlights of a few important themes found in this literature that are relevant to counseling professionals will be presented.

EXPERIENCING EMOTIONS
Perhaps the most frequently researched topic appearing in this literature is whether there are similarities and/or differences in how individuals from various cultures experience, express, and recognize emotions. Stated another way, investigators have explored the

universality versus uniqueness of the experience, expression, and recognition of emotions across and within cultures. One of the first to study this topic was Ekman, whose often-cited project in New Guinea (Ekman, 1972) suggested that the expression and recognition of emotion was universal (Matsumoto, 2009). Other studies by Ekman and his colleagues further supported this conclusion (Ekman & Friesen, 1971; Ekman et al., 1969) by discovering that persons from a host of diverse cultures were able to correctly and consistently identify emotions (e.g., anger, disgust, fear, happiness, sadness, and surprise) displayed in facial expressions and that individuals from different cultures could spontaneously exhibit the same expressions when these emotions were generated (Matsumoto). According to Matsumoto, Keltner, O'Sullivan, and Frank (2006), approximately 74 studies since Ekman's (1972) seminal investigation have basically confirmed the facial configurations first theorized by Darwin and later verified by Ekman and his associates (Ekman, 2003; Ekman & Friesen, 1971, 1975, 1986; Ekman et al., 1969).

Matsumoto (2009) argued, however, that simply because facial expressions of emotion appeared to be universal, this discovery did not account for the root of this universality. Matsumoto theorized the source of this universality could be attributed to "culture constant learning," whereby individuals worldwide learn to spontaneously display similar facial features for the same emotions. A second source for the universality of facial expressions of emotion proposed by Matsumoto (2009) is biology and evolution. Matsumoto claimed, and others have discovered, that facial configurations connected to emotions for persons throughout the world are innately biological. This association also has been found for nonhuman primates (de Waal, 2003).

It should be noted that the extensive research on the universality of facial expressions of emotions performed by Ekman and his associates prior to 2003 was based on controlled laboratory studies. Therefore, the findings from these studies might not generalize to naturalistic environments (Matsumoto, 2009). To address this limitation, Matsumoto and Willingham (2006) conducted a study with athletes who were participating in the 2004 Athens Olympic Games. The spontaneous facial expressions of emotions of 84 athletes when receiving their medals were investigated. These athletes represented 35 countries and six continents. Overall, the results paralleled emotions predicted by the EMFACS dictionary and suggested that the expression of emotion did not differ based on culture, thus supporting the universality of emotional expressions found in the large body of laboratory research on this topic. For example, when receiving their medals, the athletes smiling behavior seemed consistent across cultures even though this expression was displayed in an emotionally charged, naturalistic setting.

As will be discussed later in the chapter, although a substantial amount of research documents the cross-cultural similarity of facial expressions and emotions, there is also research indicating cross-cultural differences. Commenting on this, Matsumoto reported, "cultural differences in emotional expressions are produced because members of different cultures learn to have different emotional reactions to different culturally available events in the first place" (p. 276).

ANTECEDENTS OF EMOTIONS

Many studies have examined the factors that elicit emotions across cultures (Soto et al., 2005). Galati and associates found similarities in the antecedents of emotions for Africans and Italians (Galati, 1989) and persons from Northern and Southern Italy (Galati & Sciaky, 1995). Cultural differences in the antecedents of emotions (e.g., anger, disgust, fear, joy, sadness, surprise) also have been reported, as have individuals' beliefs about when and how emotions should be experienced and shared (e.g., Ekman, 1972; Galati et al., 2005; Hochschild, 1979; Mesquita & Frijda, 1992; Shweder, 1993). Some researchers (van Hemert, Poortinga, & van de Vijver, 2007) have claimed that persons from cultures with fewer restrictions on behavior and with more open social norms are more likely to freely express their emotions. As an example, Rosenblatt, Walsh, and Jackson (1976) reported that, during the entire mourning time after a loved one had died, persons from Bali were not permitted to cry. Others have found that, in certain cultures, displaying intense emotions (e.g., crying) was condemned or only permitted in specific situations (e.g., Becht & Vingerhoets, 2002; Georges, 1995; Wellenkamp, 1995). For the Utku Eskimos, for example, it is socially inappropriate to express anger (Briggs, 1970). In contrast, the Kaluli of Papua New Guinea are expected to display their anger (Schieffelin, 1983).

INTERPRETING EMOTIONS

According to Yuki, Maddux, and Masuda (2007), researchers have also discovered cultural differences in how emotions are interpreted (Elfenbein & Ambady, 2002, 2003; Elfenbein, Mandal, Ambady,

Harizuka, & Kumar, 2004; Marsh, Elfenbein, & Ambady, 2003; Matsumoto, 1989; Matsumoto & Ekman, 1989) although other investigators (e.g., Matsumoto & Kishimoto, 1983; Russell, 1991; van Bezooijen, Otto, & Heenan, 1983) have claimed that facial expressions (e.g., smiles, frowns) are attributed the same meaning across cultures and languages. For instance, Wilkins and Gareis (2006) in an exploratory study found that stating "I love you" varied between cultures. In some cultures, the phrase was uttered only in romantic relationships, whereas in others it was expressed with friends, family, lovers, and others. Furthermore, non-native English-speaking persons reported saying, "I love you" more frequently in English than their native language.

INDIVIDUALISTIC VERSUS COLLECTIVISTIC CULTURES AND EMOTIONS

Mesquita and Walker (2003) claimed that, in general, cultural differences in the occurrence of emotional expressions and behaviors reflected variations in cultural structures. In fact, a good deal of research has explored differences in the expression of emotions in individualistic versus collectivistic cultures. Investigators have reported that in individualistic cultures, it is more common for persons to directly and explicitly express their emotions (e.g., Markus & Kitayama, 1991), whereas in collectivistic cultures (e.g., Japan, China, and Korea) individuals control and subdue their emotional expressions since to do so is to help maintain harmonious relationships (Heine et al., 1999; Markus & Kitayama; Yuki et al., 2007) or because there is little social significance attached to expressing emotions (Potter, 1988). In one collectivistic culture, Mexico, however, researchers have theorized (Garza, 1978; Guerra, 1970; Ramirez & Castaneda, 1974) and discovered (Tsai & Levenson, 1997) that emotions are openly expressed, accepted, and valued.

In Western individualistic cultures, to express one's emotions is also considered being true to one's self (Heine et al., 1999; Markus & Kitayama, 1991). Yuki et al. (2007) claimed that the findings in the literature on facial expressions supported the results just highlighted in the previous paragraphs. That is, individuals from collectivistic cultures suppressed their negative emotions in the presence of others more so than did persons from individualistic cultures. Matsumoto et al. (1998) also discovered that Japanese persons, when compared to Americans, engaged in greater control of both their expression of negative emotions and their feelings of happiness.

Therefore, it is not surprising that some researchers have discovered that guilt is of greater importance in collectivistic as compared to individualistic cultures (Eid & Diener, 2001). It should be noted, though, that Matsumoto et al. (2009) reported a different result. They discovered that greater intensities of shame or guilt were not linked with collectivistic cultures. Furthermore, in one study, unlike what would have been expected, Americans as compared to Chinese college students were found to experience greater degrees of shame in certain situations (Tang, Wang, Qian, Gao, & Zhang, 2008).

Cultural differences in the experience of pride also have been reported. For instance, Stipek (1998) found differences in the experience of pride between U.S. and Chinese persons. For the Chinese participants, pride was considered more acceptable for achievements benefiting others as compared to achievements resulting from personal accomplishments. Eid and Diener (2001) in their cross-cultural study of 1,846 participants from two individualistic (United States, Australia) and two collectivistic (China, Taiwan) countries also discovered that pride was more important in individualistic versus collectivistic cultures.

Additionally, based on the results of their study, Eid and Diener (2001) reported larger cross-cultural differences in the self-conscious or self-reflective emotions (i.e., emotions connected to an individual's own actions). The investigators stated, in part, that individualistic cultures believe self-reflective emotions about persons performing well are good, whereas collectivistic cultures, such as Confucian cultures of the Pacific Rim, think self-reflective emotions conveying individuals' controllable actions are wrong or insufficient. The latter conclusion is considered desirable as well.

Eid and Diener's (2001) findings also indicated that both culture-specific and universal kinds of norms were connected to the experience of emotions. Furthermore, collectivistic cultures were found to have intranational variability in their norms for emotions, whereas individualistic cultures were very consistent in such norms, especially in terms of pleasant emotions. More specifically, Australia and the United States were found to be relatively tight nations in terms of their norms for positive affect. According to Eid and Diener, the norms in cultures that are tight are very homogeneous, and persons in such cultures are pressured to adhere to the norms. In contrast, loose cultures lack such homogeneous norms, and they tolerate variations in behavior. Given this explanation, Eid and Diener claimed individuals in the United States and Australia may experience pressure to be happy, joyful, and full of love and pride. Furthermore, they might "make use of their constitutional right to the pursuit of happiness" (p. 880). When unhappy, Eid and Diener argued, persons from these countries would be expected to become happy through, for example, seeking counseling. Eid and Diener's results also suggested that the collectivistic cultures in their study, China and Taiwan, were looser in their norms for positive emotions. They found China to have a wide range of norms. For instance, they reported some Chinese might find being unhappy acceptable, whereas others would not since they perceived positive emotions as undesirable. Similarly, many of the Chinese and Taiwanese in their study viewed pride as undesirable, but others thought it was acceptable.

Another set of findings from Eid and Diener's study with regard to Taiwan must be mentioned. In terms of almost every positive emotion investigated except pride, Taiwan was quite similar to Australia and the United States. With respect to the frequency of negative emotions, however, Taiwan was similar to Australia and the United States, but differed from these countries in the intensity of negative emotions. The Taiwanese experienced less intense negative emotions than did individuals from Australia and the United States.

Eid and Diener's findings, in part, contradicted an earlier less well-designed and smaller study conducted by Sommers (1984). Sommers found the emotions of love, happiness, and joy were valued across the cultures investigated (United States, China, Greece, and West Indies), whereas hate, terror, and rage were viewed as dangerous and destructive, and guilt, frustration, fear, shame, and embarrassment were perceived as aversive in these cultures. Sommers also discovered differences in the experience of emotions between the cultures. Persons from the United States greatly treasured enthusiasm, individuals from Greece prized respect, and West Indians valued pride, whereas the Chinese viewed more negative emotions as useful and constructive as compared to respondents from the other three cultures.

The results of a more recent large-scale, carefully designed study by Matsumoto et al. (2008a) on the topic of emotions might help explain the inconsistency in these results. In this project, the responses of 5,000 individuals from 32 countries were investigated. In general, the findings revealed that persons from both individualistic and collectivistic cultures were more inclined to express emotions to people in their own versus another culture. Furthermore, persons from individualistic cultures were more likely to endorse expressivity norms, especially those related to the expression of positive emotions. Individuals from collectivistic cultures, in contrast, were less inclined to express their emotions to people in their own culture. Additionally, the researchers discovered that interindividual variability ("individual differences in overall expressivity norms across contexts and emotions" p. 59) was negatively linked with individualistic cultures. That is, the increased freedom to express emotions in such cultures was correlated with a smaller (not larger) continuum of possible ways that individuals could express themselves. One conclusion that Matsumoto et al. presented was that the expression of emotions across cultures fluctuated as a result of the specific emotion, the type of interactants, and the degree of emotional expressivity sanctioned by a particular culture. This conclusion was consistent with Eid and Diener (2001), who urged cross-cultural researchers to pay careful attention to both within and between cultural differences in the variability associated with the norms connected to emotion. Based on their results, these investigators claimed that even when norms are similar, emotional experiences vary by nation. Given this, Eid and Diener concluded, "it appears that factors such as genetics or life circumstances also influence emotional experiences beyond the influence of norms" (p. 882).

Perhaps another explanation for the inconsistent results reported thus far in terms of the emotions experienced by persons in individualistic versus collectivistic cultures is related to the role of harmonious relationships in various cultures. Numerous writers have reported that most Asian cultures deeply value harmonious relationships between people rather than pursuits that are self-fulfilling at the expense of such relationships. Mesquita and Walker (2003) even claimed that these cultures frown on persons "occupying too much space in the relationship, both figuratively and literally" (p. 786). These researchers also argued that in cultures valuing harmonious relationships the expression of happiness is discouraged. The expression of anger is also seen in some cultures as disrupting social relationships (Bender, Spada, Seitz, Swoboda, & Traber, 2007). Bender et al. discovered that persons from Tonga expressed less anger than did individuals from Western countries for this very reason.

Cultures within nations also have been found to vary in emotional expressivity. For example, European Americans typically value expressing emotions (Kim & Sherman, 2007; Matsumoto, 1990), whereas Asian Americans consider such expressions less acceptable with their acquaintances (Matsumoto, 1993). U.S. males and females of European, African, Asian, and Hispanic descent have been found to also vary in their emotional expressivity. Results of three studies conducted by Durik, Hyde, Marks, Roy, Anaya, and Schultz (2006) indicated that stereotypes embraced by European American men suggested they expressed more pride than women, whereas stereotypes of African American men indicated that they were similar to women in their expression of this emotion. Furthermore, smaller gender differences were discovered between Hispanic and Asian Americans in terms of their expression of love as compared to European Americans, in whom women, as contrasted with men, were thought to display greater degrees of this emotion. Other studies have discovered gender differences in the emotional responses of Japanese and European Americans (Frymier, Klopf, & Ishii, 1990; Zahn-Waxler, Friedman, Cole, Mizula, & Hiruma, 1996). Based on their own findings and those of others, Durik et al. concluded that "different norms may pose challenges for inter-cultural interactions, and they point to the importance of considering both gender and ethnicity simultaneously in the study of emotions" (p. 429).

EMOTIONAL REGULATION

In addition to examining cultural differences in the experience and expression of emotions, researchers have investigated cultural variations in the regulation of emotions. Recall that emotional regulation has been defined as being able to manage and change emotional reactions to fulfill specific outcomes (Matsumoto, 2006). According to Gross and associates (1998; Gross & John, 2003), reappraisal and suppression are components of emotion regulation. Reappraisal is defined as the way persons construe an emotion-eliciting situation to modify its effect on their emotional experience, whereas suppression is thought to inhibit emotionally expressive behaviors.

Several studies have discovered cross-cultural differences in processes and factors linked with emotional regulation. For instance, cultural differences have been found for emotion-related appraisals (Matsumoto, Kudoh, Scherer, & Wallbott, 1988; Mauro, Sato, & Tucker, 1992; Roseman, Dhawan, Rettek, & Naidu, 1995; Scherer, 1997a, 1997b); coping, which is connected to reappraisal

(Morling, Kitayama, & Miyamoto, 2003; Taylor, Sherman, Kim, Jarcho, & Takagi, 2004; Tweed, White, & Lehman, 2004; Yeh & Inose, 2002); and display rules, which are linked to suppression (Matsumoto, 1990, 1993; Matsumoto et al., 1998, 2005). A substantial amount of previous research also has discovered that the suppression of emotions was linked with increased physiological responding for European Americans (Butler et al., 2003; Gross & Levenson, 1993, 1997). In contrast, suppressing emotions was found to be relatively normative and automated for Asian American women (Butler, Lee, & Gross, 2007, 2009).

In a direct study of the emotional regulation components of reappraisal and suppression in 23 countries, Matsumoto, Yoo, Nakagawa et al. (2008b) found cultures valuing social order (i.e., long-term oriented, embeddedness, and hierarchy) like China, Japan, and Korea were more inclined to have higher suppression scores, and a positive correlation between suppression and reappraisal. On the other hand, cultures emphasizing affective autonomy and egalitarianism (e.g., United States, Canada, Italy) were more likely to have lower suppression scores, and a negative correlation between these two components of emotional regulation.

Differences in the expected direction in suppression, reappraisal, and a more general assessment of emotional regulation were also found in a study comparing Japanese and U.S. respondents (Matsumoto, 2006). Of particular interest is the fact that Matsumoto discovered that the personality traits of extraversion, neuroticism, and conscientiousness mediated the differences in the three emotion regulation variables for the target populations. Matsumoto concluded that these differences might not be related to culture, but to the possibility that persons in the United States have personalities with a greater likelihood to engage in reappraisal, whereas the Japanese were more inclined to have personalities that employ suppression. Assuming the results of Matsumoto's study are replicated and extended, it would seem critical that future research includes personality variables when investigating potential cross-cultural differences in emotional regulation.

Universal norms for emotional expression regulation also have been reported in the literature. In a large-scale study involving the facial display rules in 32 countries, Matsumoto et al. (2008a) discovered little variation in the overall facial expression of emotions, leading the researchers to conclude that there was a universal norm for the regulation of emotional expressions.

RECOGNITION OF EMOTION

Cultural variations and similarities in the recognition of emotion is another topic widely investigated. Researchers have focused on examining facial expressions since they are considered a basic way of communicating emotions (Yuki et al., 2007). Much of the extensive evidence, including meta-analytical studies (Elfenbein & Ambady, 2002, 2003), has indicated, in general, a universal recognition of emotions based on facial expressions (Ekman, 1989, 1992; Matsumoto, 2001, 2009; Yuki et. al., 2007). Even so, researchers have also reported cross-cultural differences in emotion recognition explained by moderators (see Mesquita & Frijda, 1992; Russell, 1994; Scherer, 1997a; Scherer & Wallbott, 1994), such as exposure between cultures, majority or minority status in the culture, attributes of studies, and demographics (Elfenbein & Ambady).

More specifically, in their meta-analysis, Elfenbein and Ambady (2002) discovered it was easier for persons to identify the basic emotions of individuals from their own as compared to another ethnicity, nationality, or regional group. This finding, however, seemed to be connected to the accuracy of individuals judging the emotions of persons from their same culture. In this regard, investigators have discovered that the greater the knowledge about ones' culture, or exposure to a particular culture, the more accurate persons are in identifying emotions in that culture (Elfenbein & Ambady, 2002, 2003; Elfenbein et al., 2004; Marsh et al., 2003; Shimoda, Argyle, & Ricci Bitti, 1978). van Hemert et al. (2007), in their meta-analytic study, discovered somewhat similar results, reporting that differences in emotions were greater in cross-national as compared to intranational studies.

Based on their findings, Elfenbein and Ambady (2002) concluded that specific aspects of emotions are universal and probably biological, and that the expression of emotions can lose some meaning across cultures. Furthermore, they concluded that the ability of persons from various cultures to comprehend the emotions of other individuals is not consistently symmetric. Drawing on their findings, Elfenbein and Ambady indicated that members of a minority group displayed greater accuracy when judging the emotions of majority group members than did majority group persons when assessing the emotions of individuals from a minority group.

One other methodologically sophisticated emotion recognition cross-cultural study needs to be mentioned. In this large-scale study (Matsumoto, Olide, Schug, Willingham, & Callan, 2009) designed to examine whether 548 observers (U.S.-born and -raised Americans, immigrants to the United States, Japanese, and British) of spontaneous displays of emotion could accurately recognize emotions, the participants were asked to assess the emotional expressions of the athletes involved in Matsumoto and Willingham's (2006) study discussed earlier. A unique aspect of this study, as compared to previous research, was its focus on the spontaneous display of facial expressions rather than a still photograph. Another unique feature was that it was the first to investigate cross-cultural spontaneous facial expressions of emotion assessed by persons from different cultures. In general, the findings suggested that observers, regardless of their cultural background, were able to accurately and consistently recognize the emotions expressed by the Olympic medal–winning athletes representing the various countries.

SUMMARY OF RESEARCH ON EMOTIONS

Although it is impossible to draw any definitive conclusions about the extensive cross-cultural research on various aspects of emotions, based on a meta-analysis of 190 published studies from 1967 to 2000, van Hemert et al. (2007) claimed that any differences in emotional expression, types of emotions, and the recognition of facial expressions might be overestimated due to statistical artifacts and method-related factors. The investigators discovered, however, differences in "broad patterns in emotions" connected to positive and negative emotions, and emotional recognition. In an earlier publication, Russell (1991) reached a somewhat similar conclusion as a result of reviewing a large body of literature on emotions. He reported "studies on what is similar in how emotions are understood across cultures point principally to bipolar dimensions: pleasure-displeasure surely, arousal-sleepiness and dominance-submissiveness probably" (p. 440).

Based on the results of their study, Matsumoto et al. (2009) reached a different conclusion. They reported that the variance explained by country or culture in their study was not very large and best attributed to differences in individuals instead of cultures. Furthermore, they claimed that when differences in emotions by country did exist, such differences could be linked with a specific culture. In a thorough recent review of the cross-cultural literature on emotions, Matsumoto (2009) eloquently captured the essence of the complex, inconsistent previously reported findings when he stated, "Because different events occur in different cultures or have different meanings in different cultures, individuals learn to have different emotional reactions across cultures, thus producing different expressions" (p. 271).

Consistent with one of Matsumoto et al's (2009) conclusions, Mesquita and Frijda (1992), in another extensive literature review on emotions cautioned that, "global statements about cross-cultural universality of emotion, or about their cultural determination, are inappropriate. Rather, any evaluation of biological or cultural determinants should start from an analytical approach of the emotion process, distinguishing the determinants for different components. Within each component, moreover, differences in level of analysis of the phenomena also appear to be decisive for the kind of conclusions drawn" (p. 198). The authors also concluded, however, that there are universal features of emotions, such as emotional reactions (i.e., modes of action readiness), specific types of responses (e.g., facial expressions, voice intonations, physiological responses, inhibition), antecedents arousing emotions (e.g., loss of close individual, rejection of social group), and methods of appraising and reappraising emotions (e.g., self-blame, hope, other-blame, outcome uncertainty, controllability, and modifiability). Mesquita and Walker (2003), in their literature review, reached a very different conclusion about emotional responses. Drawing on the research of other investigators (Mesquita, 2003; Mesquita et al., 1997), they claimed, "there are cultural differences in the prevalent, modal, and normative emotional responses" (p. 777). This observation was thought to have important implications for assessing emotional disturbances defined as "'excesses' in emotions, 'deficits' in emotions, or the lack of coherence in emotional components" (Kring, 2001, p. 337). Perhaps the best way to summarize the numerous lines of inconsistent results linked with various aspects of emotions is to recognize that communicating emotions is central to being a human being, regardless of membership in a specific culture (Russell, 1991). As Russell (1991) stated, to conclude anything else is to embrace findings that are open to a range of interpretations.

IMPLICATIONS FOR THE COUNSELING PROFESSION

Given the breadth, complexity, and inconsistency in the literature on emotions, it is impossible to offer the counseling profession highly specific, concrete recommendations concerning practice, training, and research. Rather, we can extrapolate from the literature a few global and general suggestions that can provide a framework for the field to embrace a more focused and informed perspective on the complexity of emotions, especially across cultures. Obviously, given their job responsibilities, it behooves counseling professionals and students to further enhance their knowledge of the psychological and cross-cultural literature on emotions.

As pointed out previously, it is critical that counseling professionals and students be extremely cautious in assuming that all people experience the same emotions; report the same antecedents for their emotions; express, regulate, and interpret their emotions in a similar fashion; and are comparable in their ability to recognize emotions in other persons. Although the literature suggested that universal features of emotions exist, it also suggested unique components to this concept in particular cultures and countries. It was discovered that the structure of the culture (i.e., collectivistic vs. individualistic) has a great influence on what emotions are experienced, expressed, and/or recognized, and how emotions may be interpreted. The literature also indicated there could be differences in components of the emotional phenomena depending upon the nature of this structure. Regardless of the structure, however, the research revealed that culture shapes the norms linked with all aspects of emotions including, for example, whether it is appropriate to express anger or sadness. The norms of a culture, in general, influence not only the experience of specific emotions, but also the regulation of emotions in terms of emotional suppression and reappraisal.

One other study not reported earlier might help illustrate the importance of culture with respect to norms associated with emotions. In this study, self-report data were gathered from over 4,000 males and females residing in 30 countries (Becht & Vingerhoets, 2002). Based on the results of a regression analysis, as expected, it was discovered that masculinity–femininity, national income, shame, and the frequency of crying predicted changes in mood. Extrapolating from these results, Becht and Vingerhoets concluded that how individuals feel after crying is a function of how common crying is in a person's culture and also in an individual's feelings of shame about crying.

The literature reviewed earlier also suggested that various features of emotions differ by gender, ethnicity, and personality characteristics, and these variables may interact with the structure of the culture, affecting how emotions are, for instance, experienced and expressed. It is essential, therefore, that counseling professionals and students understand the structure of their client's culture, the function of emotions in that culture, and also the universal and potentially unique ways that emotions are experienced, expressed, regulated, and interpreted by males, females, persons with different personality characteristics, and individuals of different ethnicities in the client's culture.

To strengthen counseling professionals cultural understanding of emotions, it seems beneficial for graduate counseling training programs to teach students the different methods (e.g., observations and rating systems of facial expressions, self-report inventories) of studying emotions and the host of available tools (e.g., FACS, EMFACS) to accomplish this objective. Acquiring knowledge about the literature on display rules and the instrumentation and strategies (e.g., DRAI, Emotional Expressivity Scale, Emotion Regulation Questionnaire) to investigate these rules, for instance, could greatly enrich students' basic repertoire of counseling skills, particularly their cross-cultural and multicultural counseling skills. Possessing this knowledge and demonstrating the skills linked with understanding the complexity of display rules, including how they were shaped by the client's culture would certainly strengthen students' ability to accurately and effectively recognize, code, assess, conceptualize, and reflect their clients' emotions. Furthermore, it would enhance students' ability to correctly interpret excesses and deficits in emotions, and the normal range of emotions, given their client's cultural background.

Counseling professionals and students must also accept the reality that some individuals may be from cultures that do not have a clear vocabulary or language of emotions, and if there is such a language, its lexicon and structure might not directly, overtly, and/or clearly convey emotional terms or concepts. As documented in the literature, for example, some languages do not have a word for depression or anger. Other languages use phrases and not simply one word to communicate the concept of depression or anger. Even if a language has a word(s) for depression, anger, or some other emotion, counseling professionals and students must be aware that a direct one-to-one translation of such a word(s) might not be accurate. Moreover, talking about emotions in counseling for some languages and cultures might be connected to eventually taking some form of action, whereas in other cultures it may be simply talking for the sake of talking! Individuals from still other cultures may not talk about or express their emotions at all in counseling. Instead,

their emotions might be noticed and displayed through physical cues or symptoms that these individuals and their mental health providers' recognize. A study mentioned earlier in this chapter illustrates this possibility. Butler et al. (2009) investigated whether expressing emotions raised or lowered blood pressure for 32 European Americans and Asian Americans. Their results indicated that expressing emotions was inversely related to blood pressure for European American dyads, but positively related for Asian American dyads. Therefore, they concluded that cultural context might moderate this relationship. The investigators also concluded that the expression of emotion "is culturally condoned in most European American contexts but may be socially problematic for Asian Americans, and that this results in different physiological response patterns when such expression does occur" (p. 514).

Because the language or vocabulary of emotion varies worldwide, it is also critical that counseling professionals and students become knowledgeable about how their client's culture or country employs language to convey, understand, and interpret emotions. Professionals and students do not necessarily need to learn their client's language, although that would be ideal. Instead, they need to understand how the client's native language communicates emotions and how this might be different or similar to the language being used in the counseling context. One way to accomplish this is for professionals and students to immerse themselves in the client's culture and to seek opportunities to experience many diverse cultures. This is especially critical since the previous reported research indicated that people are better able to identify emotions of individuals from their own culture, ethnicity, and nationality.

All of the recommendations offered take on even greater importance when counseling professionals and students are working with individuals from a cultural context or country not their own. What is absolutely clear from the literature is that mental health professionals and students must carefully assess and balance their assumptions and knowledge about and skills linked with addressing emotions with the specific cultural context and language of the client being served. Similar to other topics discussed in the counseling literature, counseling professionals and students should strive to embrace and implement culturally appropriate and effective conceptual models and interventions that are tailored to the unique and universal emotional characteristics of the clients receiving services.

Obviously, the study of emotions offers a rich array of potential projects for persons in the counseling profession. Many of the studies discussed in this chapter could be easily replicated with counseling professionals and students as the participants, as well as with individuals seeking different types of services. Performing such studies would contribute to further exploration of the validity and reliability of the previous results and assumptions, along with further investigating the psychometrics of the previously employed methods and instruments. A few more specific recommendations to members of the counseling profession who are interested in conducting research on emotions follow.

Given the importance of emotions in almost every model of counseling and training paradigm employed to prepare counselors and psychologists, it would be revealing to conduct a study that compared a traditional form of training (e.g., human relations skills) with an educational approach that taught students the skills to effectively assess display rules and facial expressions. The two groups could be compared in their ability to accurately and correctly identify and interpret emotions of persons in their own culture and also another culture or nation. A similar study could be done with professionals. Furthermore, counseling professionals and students who learned these skills could be compared in their ability to recognize emotions with samples of individuals or students not in the mental health field but who also learned display skills. Presumably, the counseling professionals and students who were taught the skills would be better able to correctly recognize and interpret emotions than other persons who had not learned this skill set. Moreover, the former group, if offering traditional counseling services, should be less likely to misdiagnose a client's presenting concern compared to the latter group.

Another potential study could compare counseling professionals and students who had and had not been taught the skills on their effectiveness in delivering services to diverse clients. Not only could the outcome of the service be analyzed, but also the process variables connected to offering the service. Additionally, client and mental health provider satisfaction could be compared for both groups. Again, the assumption would be that mental health providers who received the training would be more effective, their clients would be more satisfied, and the process linked with the delivery of service would be more positively perceived. The providers should also be more satisfied with their clients, and with the process and outcome of the service they offered.

Finally, persons in our profession might pursue some basic research on emotions. Matsumoto (2009) shared some suggestions that are relevant in this regard. He reported a need for research on defining which specific cultures deamplify emotions, whereas others neutralize or mask emotions. Furthermore, he suggested a need to determine the situations in which these outcomes occur and why. Matsumoto also called for research on the degree of agreement in a culture between display rules and individual differences in emotional expressive behavior. Additionally, he urged investigators to identify those events that are and are not cultural and how such events are connected to the cultures' emotion system. Moreover, he recommended conducting studies on the links between these events, the emotional systems, and the response systems, including emotional expressions, and determining if these linkages are similar or different for various events.

Culture and Coping: An Overview

Like the study of emotions, coping also has been a widely researched construct in the United States and worldwide over the last three decades. *Coping* refers to individuals' cognitive and behavioral efforts to overcome, reduce, or tolerate the stress considered to be taxing or exceeding to their resources and jeopardizing their well-being (Lazarus & Folkman, 1984). It is a construct, therefore of extreme relevance for counseling professionals. Successful coping reflects strategies that reduce the emotional distress of the person, whereas maladaptive coping strategies increase the distress (Lyons, Mickelson, Sullivan, & Coyne, 1998). Several theories and conceptual models have been proposed about stress and coping. Lazarus and Folkman's (1984) transactional theory of coping is probably the one most widely studied within and across cultures and countries (Rexrode, Petersen, & O'Toole, 2008). In this theory, the relationship between the person and the environment is emphasized, in that the coping strategies used are dependent on the appraisal of the stressful event. Lazarus and Folkman (1984) differentiated between two categories of coping strategies: problem-focused and emotion-focused. In problem-focused coping, the individual strives to change the stressful situation by problem solving and using direct instrumental methods to change the stressful event. In emotion-focused coping, in contrast, the individual uses cognitive coping strategies to regulate distressing emotions. These two dimensions have also been referred to as primary and secondary coping (e.g., Heppner, 2006).

Several instruments have been developed to measure coping, and most incorporate problem-focused or action-oriented coping, and also emotion-focused coping. The Ways of Coping Scale (WOCS; Folkman & Lazarus, 1988), which is based on the transactional theory of coping, is considered one of the most widely used measures of coping (e.g., De Ridder, 1997; Parker & Endler, 1992). For this discussion, it serves as a prototype for the U.S. and Western conceptualization of coping.

The WOCS measures eight specific coping strategies that persons may employ when encountering a specific stressful event. Two scales assess problem-focused (primary) coping geared toward altering the stressful situation (confrontive coping, planful problem-solving) and six scales measure emotion-focused (secondary) coping (distancing, self-controlling, accepting responsibility, escape-avoidance, positive reappraisal, seeking social support). One of the major findings from the coping research in the United States is that problem-focused coping or any type of action-oriented coping is related to more positive psychological outcomes for an individual, whereas emotion-focused coping strategies, such as avoidance, are connected with poorer mental health (Wong, Wong, & Scott, 2006).

Although a number of studies have examined ethnic and cultural differences in coping, this research has been criticized for lacking an incorporation of contextual factors (Chun, Moos, & Cronkite, 2006). That is, much of this research compared coping strategies used between cultural groups in which the coping construct was defined based on theories and instruments (e.g., WOCS) developed in the United States. Thus, the conceptualization of coping, for instance, as problem- (primary) and emotion- (secondary) focused may not always be appropriate worldwide as this framework is based on cultural values appropriate and salient in the United States. These theories and instruments, therefore, might not capture coping mechanisms used in countries and cultures under investigation. In fact, Wong et al. (2006) maintained that the lack of progress when understanding stress and coping could be attributed to the theoretical and methodological limitations of past research and the domination of European American conceptualizations of coping. Stated differently, the lack of progress in understanding coping and stress across cultures was the focus of previous research on measurement equivalence instead of construct equivalence of the coping scales employed (e.g., using a translated version of a U.S. instrument in China). This focus raises serious concerns about the cross-cultural validity of past research on coping.

Theoretical constructs and their measurement are linked with cultural values, worldviews, and ideologies of the specific cultures in which they are developed (Gerstein et al., 2009a; Norsworthy et al., 2009a; Ægisdóttir et al., 2009). For instance, in the United States, individual freedom and individual uniqueness (i.e., individualism and independent self-construal) are highly valued and are reflected in theoretical constructs such as coping (e.g., problem-focused and emotion-focused). Furthermore, viewing coping in relation to change in an individual's distress (i.e., adaptive vs. maladaptive coping based on the outcome for the person) is highly culture bound and reflects an emphasis on the individual and the self (Lyons et al., 1998; Lyons, Sullivan, Ritvo, & Coyne 1995). Such an individual focus may not apply to more interdependent cultures. Because of these limitations and a lack of universal coping theories and measurement devices, Wong et al. (2006) concluded that, without the proper conceptualization of coping in non-Western cultures, valid inferences about cultural similarities and differences could not be derived.

A recent and important development in the literature on coping in the United States, however, is the addition of a new concept called *relation-focused* or *communal coping* to the existing dimensions of problem- and emotion-focused coping (Lyons et al., 1998). Communal coping is a process whereby a stressful event is evaluated and responded to in the context of close relationships. That is, the problem is viewed as shared with others ("our" vs. "my" problem), and the corresponding coping strategies are shared or collaborative (e.g., help/support seeking). Thus, coping is viewed as a means to facilitating group cohesion through three functions: relationship maintenance and development, the well-being of significant others, and for the benefit of the collective. This new concept extends current understanding of coping, thus potentially enhancing the cross-cultural validity of the concept of coping worldwide.

Yeh, Chang, Leong, Arora, and Kim's (2004; cited in Yeh, Arora, & Wu, 2006) research also can increase the cross-cultural validity of the concept of coping since it focused on characteristics (e.g., collectivistic cultures and values, and interdependence) that were more salient in non-Western cultures. These investigators developed the Collectivistic Coping Scale (CCS) to represent coping strategies of persons with interdependent self-construal.

The CCS conceptualizes coping as consisting of seven factors: respect for authority (coping by relying on elders and mentors), forbearance (coping by refraining from sharing problems), social activity (coping by using social networks), intracultural coping (coping by using supportive networks of racially similar individuals), relational universality (coping by seeking relationships with persons sharing similar experiences), fatalism (coping by regarding problems as one's fate), and family support (coping by seeking help from family members).

Heppner et al. (2006) also relied on features of collectivistic cultures and values when developing the Collectivistic Coping Styles Inventory (CCSI) with a Taiwanese sample. This instrument consists of five coping constructs: acceptance, reframing, and striving (focusing on accepting the problem, reframe its meaning, and perceived efficacy to resolve the problem); family support (seeking support from family and respected elders); religion-spirituality (coping by aligning with spiritual and religious institutions, beliefs and rituals); avoidance and detachment (coping by avoiding the problem and not sharing it); and private emotional outlet (coping by seeking advice from professionals).

The two measures of collectivistic ways of coping (i.e., CCS and CCSI) just discussed stress a reliance on support networks (e.g., family, authority, spirituality), and accepting, reframing, and forbearing one's problems, instead of actively changing one's surrounding context to relieve a problem. The latter strategy is best characterized by individualistic ways of coping (e.g., problem-focused coping). These additional collectivistic techniques greatly enrich the conceptualization and potential investigation of coping strategies employed by individuals associated with diverse cultures. Furthermore, these techniques represent strategies not included in traditional U.S. measures of coping (e.g., WOC). Therefore, the inclusion of these techniques provides a more valid representation of ways to cope in collectivistic cultures inside and outside the United States.

Zhang and Long (2006) also emphasized seeking support and relational and communal coping (e.g., O'Brien & DeLongis, 1996) when developing the Collective Coping Scale. Additionally, the instrument developers relied on the WOC scale (Folkman & Lazarus, 1988) and the Chinese Ways of Coping Questionnaire (Chan, 1994) when constructing their inventory based on responses from Chinese professionals working overseas. In specific, the Collective Coping Scale has three factors: collective coping (seeking support from one's group),

engagement coping (focusing on changing ones perspective), and disengagement (ignoring the stressful event and making less of it).

Although these additional conceptualizations of coping add tremendously to the individualistic U.S. conceptualization of coping as comprising problem-focused and emotion-focused components, and therefore potentially enhance the validity of the coping construct in diverse cultures, more work is needed to fully understand how persons around the world cope with adversities (Wong et al., 2006). Chen (2006a), speaking from a Buddhist perspective, for instance, challenged the use of the term "stress" in the stress and coping research paradigm as this term reflects the pressure of *external* forces on the person. Instead, Chen emphasized a framework of suffering and stress that emerges from *within* individuals and stated, "it is the psychological mechanism of craving and aversion and the ignorance about its workings that are responsible for most of our troubles and difficulties in life" (p. 75). Thus, the emphasis should not be on changing events residing outside the person, but instead on changing the psychology of the person. Furthermore, Chen stated that, according to Buddhist philosophy, coping is not just a reaction to a stressful situation, but a path toward freedom from the things that trouble a person. Coping therefore, based on Buddhism, involves the *personal* transformation to be free of stress and suffering that is accomplished through mindfulness and learning. This transformation involves the individual learning to accept both pain and pleasure, instead of avoiding pain and holding on to pleasure (Chen, 2006a).

Similar to Buddhism, the Taoist perspective of coping involves *personal* transformation (Chen, 2006b). Taoism, as does Buddhism, embraces the view that all things coexist in opposites (e.g., internal–external locus of control, pain–pleasure) and one cannot exist without the other. Instead of suffering and pleasure being two polar opposites on one dimension, these two strong polar emotions represent two coexisting entities forming a whole. Things, events, and experiences are also perceived in a cyclical fashion, in which everything eventually turns to its opposite. Once suffering has reached its peak, pleasure follows (Chen, 2006b). In addition to representing transformational coping, the Taoist perspective emphasizes a proactive, in contrast to a reactive stance, whereby a balance between the opposite forces is valued (moderate pleasure and suffering) and, if the balance is compromised, one is prepared to cope with change (extreme suffering) by recognizing the cyclic path of the opposites. Furthermore, the Taoist philosophy emphasizes the position of "doing nothing" as a way of coping. This refers to letting go of striving to change events, but instead recognizing and embracing the opposite forces as a dualistic pair that balance and complement each other (Chen, 2006b). Therefore, coping by "doing nothing" refers to letting nature take its course and recognizing and accepting that the negative and positive are an integrated whole. One can simultaneously experience great pleasure and pain and perceive control of an event while simultaneously attributing its locus to an external source. Thus, instead of striving to change one's feelings or situation, one does nothing and accepts things as they are (Chen, 2006b).

Finally, conceptualizing coping as a spiritual and existential construct might also aid in understanding how persons cope around the world. Frankl (1984, 1986) emphasized the "will to meaning" as a fundamental motive for coping and survival. In Frankl's view, coping consisted of searching for meaning in one's distress. Likewise, spirituality and spiritual coping may involve creating meaning out of stressful situations, as well as seeking comfort and relationship with spiritual and religious organizations and entities. In some cultures, spirituality may represent the most valued and most commonly used coping strategy (e.g., Klaassen, McDonald, & James, 2006; Pargament, Keoning, & Peres, 2000; Siegel & Schrimshaw, 2002).

As may seem obvious at this point, a broader and more inclusive conceptualization of coping— one incorporating more diverse worldviews than the one embraced in the United States and the Western world is necessary to increase one's understanding of how persons around the world cope with adversities, stress, and suffering. A more diverse conceptualization of coping can not only provide a better understanding of cultural similarities and differences in coping, but can also enhance how counseling psychologists approach their practice. One would expect that teaching clients to employ multiple coping strategies and to consider multiple perspectives when appraising adversities could be beneficial. For instance, in a culture that values individualism, and also instrumental and direct coping techniques when such strategies cannot be used or are ineffective (e.g., terminal disease), transformational coping might enhance a person's well-being. In contrast, in a culture valuing collectivism and the stance of doing nothing, under extreme circumstances in which injustice takes place, a person might

be empowered to actively work against changing the situation to eliminate the stressor. Understanding coping from different philosophies and worldviews also has implications for measurement. For instance, the nonlinear, circular view of human existence and experiences represented in Buddhism and Taoism requires one to measure opposite entities not as polar opposites in a one-dimensional scale reflecting high or low scores, but instead as separate scales or dimensions on which a person can score highly on both opposite entities (e.g., high on both internal and external locus of control).

The increased understanding of how culture affects stress and coping has led to many new ways that coping can be conceptualized and researched. Given the importance of this construct to counseling professionals, we urge such professionals to continue research on this topic and to explore various dimensions of coping. For instance, it is important to examine the contribution of relational, problem-solving, and emotion-focused coping to individuals' emotional and physical well-being. It is also important to investigate the process and outcome of teaching clients diverse coping strategies based on various worldviews. Although many different aspects of coping could be researched, it is essential that studies focus on enhancing and expanding theories and related measures linked with this construct.

Psychological Help-seeking

Another way in which persons may cope with their stress or problem is to seek help from mental health professionals. Whereas professional counseling in the United States has a long history (e.g., Dixon, 1987), and as such, a large number of people are comfortable turning to these professionals, in many other countries, professional counseling is just now in its early developmental stages. Flum (1998), for instance, reported that Chinese, Japanese, and Korean international students in the United States perceived counseling in their home country as "underdeveloped" and utilized less frequently than are counseling services in the United States. With professional counseling services becoming more prevalent in countries outside of the United States, one may ask how persons in these countries view mental health counseling. In the United States, scholars have often sought an answer to this question by investigating persons' attitudes toward counseling (e.g., Fischer & Turner, 1970; Morgan, Ness, & Robinson, 2003). Such a question is in line with Fishbein and Ajzen's theory of planned behavior (1975; Ajzen, 1985; Ajzen & Fishbein, 1980) that argues a person's attitude toward performing a behavior (attitudes toward seeking psychological help) is a strong predictor of the individual actually emitting that behavior (seeking psychological help). It is not surprising, therefore, that scholars abroad have begun investigating counseling attitudes to understand how persons in their home country view professional counseling. Counseling attitudes of international students and immigrant and refugee groups in the United States have also been examined with the intent to comprehend how professional counseling services are perceived by persons from countries outside the United States.

An understanding of how persons residing outside the United States view professional psychological help is extremely important, given that U.S. models of counseling theory and practice are sometimes uncritically imported to other countries (e.g., Heppner et al., 2009; Gerstein & Ægisdóttir, 2007; Gerstein et al., 2009a; Norsworthy et al., 2009a). Also, because of the increased exportation of U.S. counseling models to countries worldwide, it is imperative that studies be performed aimed at investigating the influence of culture on attitudes toward professional counseling. Such studies might also provide insight into whether U.S. models of counseling and measurement are feasible in the country of interest. Therefore, a critical examination of the current literature on studies examining counseling attitudes of international persons is imperative. This will not only provide scholars with an understanding of the role of culture and counseling attitudes, but will also offer some insight into the validity of the current cross-cultural and international literature on counseling attitudes.

An examination of the empirical literature on U.S. and non-U.S. persons' counseling attitudes revealed that, most of the time, this attitude construct was measured by the short (10-item) or long (29-item) versions of the Attitudes Toward Seeking Professional Psychological Help scale (ATSPPH; Fischer & Turner, 1970; Fischer & Farina, 1995). Thus, by employing this measure in its English-language form or translated into a target language, attitudes toward seeking professional psychological help have been investigated in relation to numerous cultural, demographic, background, and adjustment variables.

Looking at the influence of culture on this attitude construct, many studies that targeted foreign nationals living in the United States (i.e., international students, immigrants, and refugees) investigated how acculturation affects attitudes toward counseling.

In the studies we reviewed, the researchers expected a positive relationship between acculturation and more positive counseling attitudes. A perusal of these studies, however, indicated conflicting results. Whereas some studies found that the more acculturated persons were to the United States, the more positive were their attitudes about seeking professional counseling (Dadfar & Friedlander, 1982; Harik-Williams, 2003; Ly, 2002; Sharma, 1995; Sheikh, 2001; Zhang & Dixon, 2003), almost as many studies did not find this relationship (Fang, 1999; Haque-Kan, 1997; Khoie, 2002; Vensa, 2002; Wong, 1998). Similarly conflicting results were obtained when nationality was used to conceptualize culture. Whereas Atkinson, Ponterotto, and Sanchez (1984) focused on refugees from Vietnam, and Todd and Shapira's (1974) focused on British college students, both studies found these persons expressed less positive attitudes toward counseling than the U.S. persons did. However, studies comparing U.S. nationals to persons from Eritrea (Gebreyesus, 2001), the Caribbean, Puerto Rico (Vensa, 2002), and Korea (Yoo, 1997) did not discover any cultural difference connected to these attitudes. Yet, when examining international students in the United States, Dadfar and Friedlander (1982) and Harik-Williams (2003) found Western students (Europe and Latin America) expressed more positive attitudes than did non-Western students (Africa and Asia). Furthermore, Baysden (2003) discovered that the better international students adjusted to college, the more positive were their counseling attitudes.

Other cultural variables and factors related to U.S. cultural values also have been investigated in relation to attitudes toward counseling. Here, culture has been conceptualized and measured in terms of personality structures rather than as behavioral (e.g., acculturation) or background (e.g., nationality, ethnicity) variables that have been suggested as a more effective and valid method when investigating cultural influences on psychological functioning (e.g., Adamopoulus & Lonner, 2001). Collectively, it has been discovered that, in fact, culture influences persons' counseling attitudes. Harik-Williams (2003), for instance, when studying international students, found that persons who were more long-term-goal oriented were more positive in their attitudes toward professional counseling. Furthermore, others have discovered that the more independent versus interdependent Chinese and Malaysian immigrants' self-construal was (Yeh, 2001), the more positive these persons' attitudes were toward counseling.

When looking at the international literature on counseling attitudes, it is important to compare what has been found in the United States with discoveries reported from countries outside the United States, and on international samples within the United States. Such comparisons can provide insight into both universal and culture-specific trends in relation to the attitude variable. Gender has often been investigated in relation to counseling attitudes of both U.S. and international samples, and the results have shed light on the similarities and differences in males' and females' counseling attitudes.

Numerous studies involving U.S. nationals (e.g., Fischer & Farina, 1995; Fischer & Turner, 1970; Kelly & Achter, 1995; Lopez et al., 1998; Price & McNeill, 1992; Tata & Leong, 1994, Vogel & Wester, 2003; Ægisdóttir & Gerstein, 2009) have revealed that women reported more positive attitudes toward counseling than did men. This finding has been interpreted in line with gender differences in socialization and in relation to women more commonly using counseling than men. Similar gender differences in counseling attitudes have been reported for some international samples. For instance, it has been found that women from Korea (Yoo, 1997), Taiwan (Yeh, 2002), New Zealand (Surgenor, 1985), China, Malaysia (Lim, 2001), Iran (Khoie, 2002), the Caribbean, and Puerto Rico (Vensa, 2002) expressed more positive counseling attitudes than did men from these countries. This similar effect for gender found across cultures (U.S. and non-U.S. participants) indicates that, in many countries, there may be comparable expectations of each gender and also forces of socialization that supersede other cultural and national factors, resulting in women expressing more positive attitudes toward seeking counseling services than men. For instance, it is conceivable that in the countries represented in these studies, women were socialized to be more emotionally expressive than men were, and as a result, they may have felt more comfortable engaging in such behavior with a counselor. Therefore, they reported more positive attitudes. It is important to note, though, that these gender differences were not found among Eritreans (Gebreyesus, 2001), Indians, and Pakistanis (Sheikh, 2001).

Another variable often investigated in relation to counseling attitudes within the United States and internationally is previous counseling experience. Within the United States, it has been found that persons with prior counseling experience (e.g., Fischer & Farina, 1995; Fischer & Turner, 1970; Halgin, Weaver, Edell, & Spencer, 1987; Vogel & Wester, 2003; Ægisdóttir & Gerstein, 2009) express more positive attitudes toward counseling than do persons without such experience. Similarly, persons from countries such as New Zealand (Carlton & Deane, 2000; Deane, Skogstad, & Williams, 1999; Surgenor, 1985), the United Kingdom (Asian and white British; Furnham & Andrew, 1996), Israel (Raviv, Raviv, & Yonovitz, 1989), and Korea (Yoo; 1997), and international students in the United States (Dadfar & Friedlander, 1982) who have sought counseling services reported more positive attitudes than did individuals without such experiences. Thus, the relationship between prior counseling experience and counseling attitudes may transcend culture. Yet, the universality of this relationship can only be tentatively stated, given the scarcity of countries represented. Furthermore, a deeper understanding of cause and effect in this relationship has not yet been established.

Finally, several studies conducted outside the United States have found a relationship between psychological distress and counseling attitudes. Al-Darmaki (2003) focusing on Arabs in the United Arab Emirates discovered that the more depressed people were and the lower their self-esteem, the more negative their attitudes were about counseling. Similarly, Carlton and Deane (2000) found the more suicidal New Zealand adolescents were, the more negative their psychological help seeking attitudes. Additionally, Furnham and Andrew discovered a relationship between the severity of somatization and counseling attitudes among Asian immigrants in the United Kingdom, whereas Todd and Shapira (1974), who studied British college students, failed to find a relationship between anxiety and counseling attitudes.

The Use of ATSPPH in International Research on Counseling Attitudes and Expectations

As stated earlier, both the short and long versions of the ATSPPH (1970; Fischer & Farina 1995) are widely used measures of counseling attitudes both in the United States and elsewhere. Yet, despite their widespread use, both instruments have some methodological limitations that may limit the findings they produce. The ATTSPH has, for example, been criticized for its diverse item content (Choi, 2008; Ægisdóttir & Gerstein, 2009). For example, very often, when using the ATTSPH, researchers are interested in persons' attitudes toward seeking psychological services from certain mental health professionals (e.g., counselors or psychologists). The items, however, include statements referring to a wide variety of professionals, such as psychiatrist, clergy, or unknown professionals or staff at a "mental hospital." Ægisdóttir and Gerstein (2009) noted that this diversity of helpers represented in the scale may make the attitude represented blurred and inconsistent. They also noted that many of the ATSPPH items included an outdated terminology, and that some items did not seem to be directly related to attitudes toward seeking psychological services, but instead seemed to measure persons' ego strength and coping mechanism when feeling distressed. Additionally, the factor structure of the ATSPPH has been questioned (e.g., Fisher & Farina, 1995; Ægisdóttir & Gerstein, 2009). For this reason, scholars have used the shorter unidimensional version of the ATSPPH, which may lack the multiplicity of the attitude construct and, therefore, may not fully capture it (Ægisdóttir & Gerstein, 2009). To address this limitation, Ægisdóttir and Gerstein developed the Beliefs About Psychological Services (BAPS) scale. It measures three distinct constructs connected to help-seeking attitudes that are tied to the theory of planned behavior (Ajzen, 1985; Ajzen & Fishbein, 1980): intent (intent to seek psychological services), stigma tolerance (stigma and negative beliefs about psychotherapy), and expertness (merits of professional counseling due to psychologists' education).

The general limitations of the ATSPPH (Fischer & Farina, 1995; Fischer & Turner, 1970) just mentioned apply to using the scale in the United States and internationally. In fact, these limitations may account for some inconsistencies in the literature on attitudes toward seeking psychological help. Moreover, using these instruments on an international sample of participants poses a whole new set of issues that must be considered. When reviewing the international studies on counseling attitudes, it became apparent that, in most cases, insufficient attention was paid to these limitations when employing the ATSPPH.

Whereas the studies on help-seeking attitudes listed earlier provide important information regarding cultural variations in psychological help-seeking attitudes, to some degree, the validity of these findings may be questioned. For instance, there are questions about the thoroughness of the translation methods employed in converting an instrument such as the ATSPPH for use in another language (e.g., Ægisdóttir et al., 2008). Furthermore, it can be questioned if issues of construct equivalence were considered. For example, were the ATSPPH items appropriate for use in the other country? Similarly, was there a need for additional or different items that might be more representative of the attitude constructs found in the target country (e.g., van de Vijver & Leung, 1997a; Ægisdóttir et al., 2008), thereby increasing the accuracy of measured construct?

Issues about the structural and measurement equivalence are also of concern (van de Vijver & Leung, 1997a). For example, does the factor structure of the scale hold up cross-culturally, or does the construct yield different dimensions? Such findings may indicate cultural differences on the structure of the construct. Likewise, it is critical to determine if additional psychometrics of the scale, such as reliability and validity of the translated measures, were comparable to the original language versions of the instrument. Finally, in any type of cross-cultural and international research, it is essential to obtain information on whether responding to a paper-and-pencil scale is an appropriate method of inquiry to assess persons' attitudes in a particular country. Acquiring this information would help determine if there were any method biases when gathering data in such a fashion in the country or culture of interest.

Unfortunately, in few if any of the studies examining attitudes toward seeking psychological help-seeking were issues of cross-cultural validity examined. In most instances, the items linked with the ATSPPH were translated verbatim to the target language. In some of the studies, the psychometric properties of the non-English language version of the measure were reported (e.g., factor structure, reliability, validity), but in none of the projects did the investigators question the cross-cultural validity of the ATSPPH items or determine that it was best to replace items with other items. Finally, in none of the studies did the researchers include additional items that could be considered unique to the attitude construct in the target country. Integrating such items might have enhanced the constructs' validity and reliability and also helped to minimize construct bias.

Although conducting a translation of an existing research instrument, such as the ATSPPH, to assess psychological help-seeking internationally may seem an appropriate way to compare and contrast cultures, even after having determined that the construct being measured is functionally equivalent and that the survey method makes sense in the target cultures, there may still be problems. First, translated instruments were developed in a certain culture and therefore they include culture-specific items. As a result, the instrument may only depict the construct as it is perceived in the culture from which it originated. This same problem has been observed in research on coping (e.g., Wong et al., 2006). Second, instruments are usually developed from a specific model that may be indigenous to a culture. For instance, the ATSPPH was developed to assess attitudes toward counseling as they are held in the United States. Therefore, the meaning respondents associated with the terms referred to on the instrument (e.g., psychotherapy) may differ from one nation to another. Third, there may be items or portions of the construct in the target culture that are not included in the original version of the instrument, thus leading to an incomplete coverage of the construct. This lack of coverage of the relevant domain may leave out important information about what and how different sociological, cultural, and personality factors may affect this particular attitude construct.

Finally, items that are translated to be used in another country may refer to behaviors uncommon or unknown in the country of interest, making the scale look strange and foreign to respondents. This may result in participants' frustration and lack of cooperation with the research. These are all indicators of a construct bias that needs to be attended to when exporting instruments and models to be used outside their culture of origin. For more in-depth information about performing cross-culturally valid research and conducting an appropriate back-translation procedure, we suggest the work of Ægisdóttir et al. (2008), Brislin (1986), van de Vijver and Leung (1997), and Ægisdóttir et al. (2009).

In sum, because none of the studies on counseling attitudes that we reviewed employed a rigorous and cross-culturally valid methodology, it is difficult to accurately understand how persons across countries perceive counseling. It is necessary, therefore, for future researchers interested in counseling attitudes to adopt a more rigorous and internally valid methodology to better comprehend how persons of diverse cultures view counseling, and also how models of counseling across cultures may be adapted or developed to better address the specific needs of persons from different cultures.

Despite the limitations of the studies discussed in this section of the chapter, some tentative general implications can be drawn from this body of research. It appears that counseling attitudes as *theorized* and *measured* in the United States do not seem to vary much across countries. It should be mentioned though that, in general, this was not found when culture was conceptualized as acculturation or

nationality. It is also noteworthy that, in the few studies that conceptualized culture as an interaction between personality and cultural variables (e.g., self-construal, time orientation), some cultural variations were discovered indicating greater positive attitudes in relation to U.S.-held cultural values. Also of note was that variables commonly found to influence counseling attitudes in the United States also influenced counseling attitudes of international participants. These were prior counseling experience and gender. Whereas these findings suggest that these factors transcend cultures, it may also be that these findings are an artifact of the measures that were used (ATSPPH) as they were developed in the United States and with U.S. counseling models in mind.

To better understand counseling attitudes of international persons, more culturally sensitive instruments need to be developed and utilized. Furthermore, replications of the studies reported here need to be performed using more valid attitude measures. When more programmatic research is conducted on international persons' attitudes toward counseling services, then and only then, will counseling scholars understand how individuals worldwide perceive counseling services.

Methodological Challenges in Cultural and Cross-cultural Research

Designing more culturally sensitive scales is not the only challenge of conducting cross-culturally valid and appropriate research on concepts of interest to counseling professionals (e.g., emotions, coping, and help-seeking). Cross-cultural comparative and cultural research with international samples on a large array of topics is urgently needed to advance the science and practice of counseling psychology. However, debates about how to best perform such research and how to operationally define the construct of culture have challenged psychology and anthropology for decades (Adamopoulos & Lonner, 2001; Gerstein, Rountree, & Ordonez, 2007; Hunt, 2007; Ægisdóttir et al., 2009). There are basically two schools of thought on how to conceptualize and study culture and cultural influences on behavior. One is the *relativistic stance*, in which it is believed that persons can only be studied in their cultural context by using *emic* (culture-specific) constructs. The term "emic" comes from linguistics and is extracted from the word "phonemics," which focuses on the meaning and context of words (Pike, 1967). Those adhering to the relativistic school of thought, such as cultural psychologists, focus their studies on the meaning of constructs as understood by natives, often employing ethnographic and qualitative research methods. Cross-cultural comparisons are generally not of interest to such scholars and may not make sense, given the aims of this field of inquiry (Ægisdóttir et al., 2009). Within this school, culture is considered a human construction and an inseparable part of the mind (Adamapoulos & Lonner, 2001).

The cultural relativism approach has sometimes been accused of not being scientific (e.g., Heilfrich, 1999; Hunt, 2007) as it often defies the comparative paradigm. As stated in the previous paragraph, given that the aim of cultural psychology is studying the meaning of a construct within a culture (see Gerstein et al., 2009a), qualitative approaches and methods rooted in anthropology are often used. This is a discovery-oriented approach in which prior conceptualizations of constructs are avoided and issues of biases in data collection and interpretation are the main challenges in enhancing its scientific rigor (e.g., Hunt, 2007; Ægisdóttir et al., 2009). Many insights and discoveries in psychology, however, have been made by focusing on emic constructs and using qualitative methodologies.

The other school of thought on how to conceptualize and study culture and cultural influences on behavior is called *universalism* or the *cross-cultural approach*. For this approach, the goal is to discover universal laws of behavior and psychological functioning. In this regard, cultural influences on psychological functioning are discerned by studying cultural similarities and differences by comparing two or more cultural groups. *Etic* constructs, or constructs considered universal are the main interest to scholars aligning with this stance (Adamopoulos & Lonner, 2001; Ægisdóttir et al., 2009). The term "etic" is derived from the linguistic term "phonetics," which refers to universal sounds used in language, regardless of their meaning, in a particular language (Pike, 1967). In psychology and anthropology, therefore, the use of etic constructs refers to using concepts and categories that have meaning to scientific observers, in order that they might understand cultural influences on behavior (Helfrich, 1999; Ægisdóttir et al., 2009). Within this comparative approach, culture is treated as an independent variable (e.g., cultural groups, self-construal, cultural syndrome) either moderating or mediating behavior. The main methodological problems linked with cross-cultural comparisons are related to bias and equivalence (van de Vijver & Leung, 1997a, b; Ægisdóttir et al., 2008, 2009).

The cross-cultural comparative approach has also been criticized for its lack of cultural sensitivity. For this approach, the hypothetico-deductive paradigm is used in discerning cultural influences on individuals using etic constructs. As mentioned earlier, in comparative research, culture is "elevated" to the status of a quasi-independent variable that may either mediate or moderate behavior (Adamopoulos & Lonner, 2001). Given that, with this approach, cultural groups are compared on a particular variable, eliminating measurement artifacts as alternative explanations of cultural differences is the main challenge. These artifacts are issues of bias and equivalence. In cross-cultural comparisons, there are two competing explanations about what may account for observed differences between cultural groups. One has to do with culture (i.e., cultural differences on underlying traits or characteristics) and the other deals with bias. The challenge is ruling out bias and ensuring equivalence; these challenges are discussed in the paragraphs to follow. Unfortunately, many cross-cultural studies have been published that failed to pay sufficient attention to bias (e.g., Berry, Poortinga, Segall, & Dasen, 2002; van de Vijver and Tanzer, 2004; Ægisdóttir et al., 2008).

van de Vijver and Leung (1997) identified three main types of bias: *construct bias*, when the construct measured is not the same across cultures; *method bias*, when aspects of an instrument or its administration elicit diverse responses from members of a different culture; and *item bias*, which is caused by inaccurate item translation or the use of test items that are inappropriate or irrelevant (e.g., items describing unfamiliar experiences or activities) to some of the cultural groups under study. To eliminate or minimize these different types of bias, researchers must be careful when selecting and adapting scales for use in cross-cultural research, and they need to employ techniques and statistical methods recommended in the literature (e.g., Brislin, Lonner, & Thorndike, 1973; van de Vijver & Leung, 1997a; Ægisdóttir et al., 2008, 2009). One important issue to consider when employing the same methods or measures in multiple languages is to implement a thorough translation-adaptation procedure. Numerous scholars have written about translation and back-translation methods (e.g.,; Brislin, 1973, 1986; Hambleton & de Jong, 2003; Shiraev & Levy, 2006; van de Vijver & Hambleton, 1996; van de Vijver & Leung,1997a; Ægisdóttir et al., 2008, 2009) that are reflected in the standards of the ITC.

In short, the following procedures have been recommended:

• Employ bilingual persons who are familiar with test construction, the construct under study, and the cultures of interest to perform the translation from the original to the target language(s).

• Use a committee of persons rather than a single individual who performs the translation independently of one another. This will help reduce biases of a specific person.

• Compare each individual translation and develop the best single translated version of the instrument based on the consensus agreement of the translators.

• Employ other bilingual individual(s) to perform a back-translation of the original language of the final translated version of the instrument.

• Have the translation committee then compare the back-translated version of the measure to the original version and make corresponding modifications to increase linguistic equivalence.

• Pretest the translated version by, for instance, administering both language versions of the instrument to bilingual individuals (in the two target languages) to determine language equivalence (see also Ægisdóttir et al., 2008).

• Measure the translated instruments' reliability and validity and potential bias, and compare it to measured properties of the original language version.

• Document and include in published articles the translation procedures used, the challenges involved, and the evidence for the translated versions' equivalence.

In summary, bias is a major threat to the validity in cross-cultural comparisons. The greater the cultural distance (e.g., language, social structure, political structure, climate, human development index) between the cultures under investigation, the greater the potential for bias (Triandis, 2001; Ægisdóttir et al., 2008). Counseling researchers must identify the types of biases that are likely to exert an influence on their studies and design them so as to minimize such threats and to enhance equivalence of the protocols used.

Equivalence, another important concept in cross-cultural comparisons, has been conceptualized in at least two ways. Lonner (1985) discussed four types: functional, conceptual, metric, and linguistic. Functional equivalence refers to the functions tied to constructs across cultures. If different functions are connected to behaviors or activities across cultures, their parameters cannot be used for cross-cultural comparison. A classic example is pet ownership. In the United States, dogs and cats are often treated as family members, whereas in other cultures they may be an annoyance. Issues of *functional equivalence* can often be resolved during the translation of scales (Ægisdóttir et al., 2009). *Conceptual equivalence* refers to the meaning associated with a construct. Effective coping with a difficulty may, for instance, mean actively doing something to solve the problem in one culture, whereas it could mean forbearance in another. *Metric equivalence* has to do with the psychometric properties (validity, reliability, item distribution) of the measures used in cross-cultural research, whereas *linguistic equivalence* refers to the form, structure, reading difficulty, and naturalness of the items and questions used to assess the construct under study (Lonner, 1985, van de Vijver & Leung,1997a; Ægisdóttir et al., 2008).

van de Vijver and Leung (1997a,b) expanded the discussion of equivalence. They distinguished between four levels of equivalence: construct nonequivalence, construct (structural) equivalence, measurement-unit equivalence, and scalar equivalence. *Construct nonequivalence* refers to constructs being so dissimilar or nonexistent across cultures (e.g., culture-bound syndromes) that they cannot be compared. Next and at the lowest level of equivalence is *construct* or *structural equivalence*. It has to do with the meaning attached to the construct compared across cultures and its nomological network (convergent and divergent validity; e.g., Ægisdóttir et al., 2008). At this level, a construct might have the same definition and meaning (e.g., coping) across cultures, yet the operational definition of the construct may differ, such that different items (activities) are to be used to measure the construct (e.g., Ægisdóttir et al., 2009). At this level, only indirect comparisons can be performed. The next level is *measurement-unit equivalence* (van de Vijver 2001; van de Vijver & Leung, 1997a). Here, the scales used to measure the concept are equivalent across groups, but their origins differ. In some instances, a known constant can be applied to one of the measures to make them equivalent. A classic example is the measure of temperature using the Kelvin and Celsius scales (e.g., van de Vijver & Leung, 1997a). To make these two measures of temperature comparable, one needs to add a constant of 273 degrees to the Kelvin scale. In counseling psychology, because of bias, different cut-scores on psychological inventories are sometimes used to identify psychological characteristics (e.g., personality traits) of individuals from different groups (Ægisdóttir et al., 2008). Thus, different scores on a measure represent the same quality (meaning) based on group memberships. However, comparing raw scores on these inventories using mean score comparison is not valid unless they are made more comparable by applying the correction or constant making the origin the same. Also, a bias originating in different cultural groups' interpretation of or response style on rating scales (e.g., extreme responses, acquiescence bias) can render the origins of a scale different across cultural groups.

The highest level of equivalence is scalar equivalence. At this level, mean score comparability is considered valid. It is achieved if the same scale is employed as a measure across cultures, using an equivalent unit of measurement (e.g., either ratio or interval) and bias has been ruled out. Establishing scalar equivalence often involves the use of psychometric procedures (e.g., van de Vijver & Leung, 1997a,b; van de Vijver & Tanser, 2004; Ægisdóttir et al., 2008). Obviously, equivalence of observations and scales can never be assumed, and those involved in cross-cultural research need to assess, document, and report the methods and strategies used to establish equivalence of their cross-cultural comparisons.

Despite the methodological challenges with the cross-cultural comparative framework in understanding cultural influences on psychological functioning, numerous studies have been performed across cultures that are methodologically sophisticated and that provide relevant results to counseling psychology. Furthermore, in recent years, researchers have encouraged employing mixed methodologies, using both emic and etic constructs to understand persons in their cultural context (e.g., Helfrich, 1999; Ægisdóttir et al., 2008, 2009). Although the approaches used by cultural relativists are informative, and the study of meaning of constructs within a culture has contributed to the knowledge base of counseling psychology, we contend that, for the science of counseling psychology to advance, it is essential that cross-cultural investigations and the cross-cultural comparative approach be embraced. We agree with Hunter (2007), a cultural anthropologist challenging cultural relativism in his field, who stated, "if there is no comparability of empirical observations, there can be no science" (p. 1). That is, for counseling psychology to advance as a science, it is important it examine the universality of its constructs and theories, as well as differences and similarities in behavior, cognitions, and emotions.

Clearly, there are challenges and benefits to both the cultural (relativistic) and the cross-cultural (universal) approaches to conceptualizing and studying culture and cultural influences on behavior. In fact, these approaches actually complement one another as they investigate and conceptualize culture from unique angles. Both are grounded in different epistemological and ontological frameworks, the relative approach in post-modernistic constructivism, whereas the cross-cultural approach is rooted in positivism and post-positivism (Ægisdóttir et al., 2009). For a more in-depth discussion of each, including their strengths and shortcomings, we recommend reading van de Vijver and Leung (1997), van de Vijver (2001), Ægisdóttir et al. (2009), and Hunt (2007).

Conclusion

As discussed in this chapter, there has been a steady, growing interest in international issues connected to the field of counseling. The profession has emerged and thrived in many countries. Boundaries between professional associations and also among professionals throughout the world have become more fluid and flexible, leading to greater and more effective communication and understanding. Serious questions have been raised as well about the cross-cultural validity and applicability of concepts, theories, strategies, and research methods once thought to be acceptable, appropriate, and useful. As a result, counseling professionals around the globe are carefully rethinking many aspects of their work, be it practice, research, and/or training, to determine the relevance and validity of exporting and importing U.S. paradigms presumed to be generalizable and valid. Although not stated earlier in this chapter, this has led to the emergence of, and recommitment to, indigenous models, perspectives, strategies, and concepts linked with the science and practice of psychology and counseling (see Draguns, 2004, 2007; Tanaka-Matsumi, 2008). Given these developments, it is not surprising that some scholars (Gerstein et al., 2009a) have claimed that we are in the midst of a renaissance period in the counseling profession; a period in which ethnocentric and U.S.-centric frameworks and values of science and practice are being questioned and discarded, and either modified or replaced with more culturally appropriate, relevant, and valid paradigms, assumptions, and beliefs.

In the years ahead, there will be a dramatic increase in the number of research studies that explore indigenous constructs and approaches. Hopefully, these projects will be grounded in the principles and methods mentioned earlier in this chapter for conducting culturally and/or cross-culturally appropriate and valid studies. Additionally, these projects, as well as others that investigate universal constructs, should employ more informative and rigorous mixed methodologies that capture the richness of diverse data. To conduct such studies, at times, it will be essential that professionals develop even more effective collaborative global relationships. That is, relationships based on equality, respect, shared responsibility, and a commitment to honoring both the universal and unique features of one another's culture, values, and professional paradigms. A growing body of literature has called for the establishment and maintenance of such relationships to pursue not only research projects but also a litany of other opportunities (e.g., consultation, training, program development, policy formulation and implementation) designed to effectively serve diverse populations (see Gerstein & Kirkpatrick, 2005; Gerstein et al., 2009b; Heppner et al., 2009; Norsworthy, 2006; Norsworthy, Leung, Heppner, & Wang, 2009b; Wang & Heppner, 2009).

Assuming that the field of counseling will continue to grow worldwide and the need for international collaboration will increase, there will be an astronomical spike in the career opportunities for people in our profession. We are already witnessing, for example, the availability of a greater number of academic and counseling center positions for counseling professionals in many countries. Through e-mail and websites, our awareness of these positions has increased. Technology (e.g., Skype) also has made it possible to easily consult with our colleagues worldwide on research, training, and service projects, for instance. This has led to many more speaking, teaching, consulting, and collaborative global opportunities.

With the anticipated growth in such opportunities and the importance of preparing future professionals to effectively perform in many countries, our training programs around the world will require modification, so that our students acquire the necessary knowledge base and skill set. Some scholars have begun to articulate how we might alter our training programs to accomplish this objective (Gerstein et al., 2009b; Gerstein & Ægisdóttir, 2007; Hall, 2006; Heppner et al., 2008b; Ægisdóttir & Gerstein, 2010). A major challenge for programs in the United States has been offering a manageable curriculum with an international focus that meets the standards for accreditation enforced by the APA. For instance, programs struggle with how to accept practicum and internship experiences outside the United States that may not meet these standards. Furthermore, programs struggle with how to offer practicum and internship experiences in other countries while at the same time having their students graduate in a timely fashion. Creative solutions are definitely required to resolve these dilemmas, especially since, in the United States, a growing number of students have expressed a strong desire to incorporate an out-of-country educational experience as part of their program of study. In fact, many persons inquire about this when applying to graduate programs, perhaps because many of them have already traveled abroad as part of their undergraduate programs and were deeply enriched by the experience.

In conclusion, there is great potential for enhancing the cross-cultural validity of the science and practice of counseling. This chapter discussed some ways that the counseling profession can contribute to this critical mission. The literature on a few important constructs (i.e., psychological help-seeking, emotions, coping) relevant to our profession was reviewed and briefly critiqued in this regard. Specific recommendations were offered concerning how to conduct more cross-culturally valid future research on these constructs. Counseling professionals worldwide have both the responsibility and opportunity to pursue this type of research and other projects through collaborative endeavors across diverse national and cultural borders. Ultimately, the outcome of such efforts will further reduce the boundaries and misunderstandings among counseling professionals around the world, and strengthen their relationships and the identity of our profession. The clients we all serve also will definitely benefit from these efforts, as they will receive more culturally valid and appropriate services, structured to affirm their cultural framework and their unique individual characteristics.

It is quite exciting and invigorating to be a member of the counseling profession during this renaissance period in our existence. The opportunities for growth and global travel and collaboration abound, as do the challenges to respectfully and effectively engage in international pursuits. In the years ahead, many new frontiers will emerge, presenting counseling professionals and students with a chance to enhance the quality of life of persons from diverse contexts, cultures, and countries. Our profession is in its infancy, establishing the foundation to operate as a truly unified, valid, and efficacious scientist–practitioner international discipline. Much more work is required to investigate the universal and individual dimensions of the human experience, so that we may eventually become genuinely effective cross-cultural scientist–practitioners. Our path to achieve this outcome is as diverse as those who are on it. Yet, our commitment is shared and motivation unquestionable: affirming, respecting, and celebrating our differences, and embracing and honoring our similarities as people and professionals.

Acknowledgments

The authors want to thank Laura Walker for her library research connected to this chapter.

References

Abi-Hashem, N. (1997). Reflections on international perspectives in psychology. *American Psychologist, 52*, 569–573.

Adamopolous, J., & Lonner, W. J. (2001). Culture and psychology at a crossroad: Historical perspective and theoretical analysis. In D. Matsumoto (Ed.), *Handbook of culture and psychology* (pp. 11–34). New York: Oxford University Press.

AERA, APA, NCME. (1999). *Standards for educational and psychological testing.* Washington, DC: AERA.

Ajzen, I. (1985). From intention to action: A theory of planned behavior. In J. Kuhl & J. Beckman (Eds.), *Action – control: From cognition to behavior* (pp. 11–39). Heidelberg: Springer.

Ajzen, I., & Fishbein, M. (1980). *Understanding Attitudes and Predicting Social Behavior.* Engelwood Cliffs, NJ: Prentice-Hall.

Al-Darmaki, F. R. (2003). Attitudes towards seeking professional psychological help: What really counts for United Arab Emirates university students. *Social Behavior and Personality, 31*, 497–508.

Atkinson, D. R., Ponterotto, J. G., & Sanchez, A. R. (1984). Attitudes of Vietnamese and Anglo-American students toward counseling. *Journal of College Student Personnel, 25*, 448–452.

Australian Bureau of Statistics. (2003). *Labour force survey.* Canberra, AU: Author.

Australian Psychological Society. (2007). *APS member groups.* Retrieved 29 May, 2007, from http://www.psychology.org.au.

Bartram, D. (2001). Guidelines for test users: A review of national and international initiatives. *European Journal of Psychological Assessment, 17*, 173–186.

Bartram, D., & Coyne, I. (2005). *International guidelines on computer-based and internet-delivered testing.* Punta Gorda, FL: ITC.

Baysden, M. F., Jr. (2003). International and United States citizen student adaptation to college, opinions about mental illness, and attitudes toward seeking professional counseling help. *Dissertation Abstracts International, 64*(2-A), 393.

Becht, M., & Vingerhoets, J. (2002). Crying and mood change: A cross-cultural study. *Cognition &Emotion, 16*(1), 87–101.

Bender, A., Spada, H., Seitz, S., Swoboda, H., & Traber, S. (2007). Anger and rank in Tonga and Germany: Cognition, emotion, and context. *Ethos, 35*(2), 196–234.

Berry, J. W., Poortinga, Y. H., Segall, M. H. & Dasen, P. R. (2002). *Cross-cultural psychology: Research and applications.* New York, NY: Cambridge University Press.

Boucher, J. D. (1979). Culture and emotion. In A. J. Marsella, R. G. Tharp, & T. V. Ciborowski (Eds.), *Perspectives on cross-cultural psychology* (pp. 159–178). San Diego: Academic Press.

Boucher, J. D. (1983). Antecedents of emotions across cultures. In S. H. Irvine, & J. W. Berry (Eds.), *Human assessment and cultural factors* (pp. 407–420). New York: Plenum Press.

Brandt, M., & Boucher, J. (1986). Concepts of depression in emotion lexicons of eight cultures. *International Journal of Intercultural Relations, 10*(3), 321–346.

Brehm, S. S. (2008). Looking ahead: The future of psychology and APA. *American Psychologist, 63*, 337–344.

Briggs, J. L. (1970). *Never in anger: Portrait of an Eskimo family.* Cambridge, MA: Harvard University Press.

Brislin, R. W. (1976). Comparative research methodology: Cross cultural studies. *International Journal of Psychology, 11*, 213–229.

Brislin, R. W. (1986). The wording and translation of research instruments. In W. J. Lonner, & J. W. Berry (Eds.), *Field methods in cross-cultural research* (pp. 137–164). Beverly Hills, CA: Sage.

Brislin, R. W., Lonner, W. J., & Thorndike, R. M. (1973). *Cross-cultural research methods.* New York: John Wiley & Sons.

Butler, E. A., Egloff, B., Wilhelm, F. H., Smith, N. C., Erickson, E. A., & Gross, J. J. (2003). The social consequences of expressive suppression. *Emotion, 3*, 48–67.

Butler, E., Lee, T., & Gross, J. (2007). Emotion regulation and culture: Are the social consequences of emotion suppression culture-specific?. *Emotion, 7*, 30–48.

Butler, E. A., Lee, T. L., & Gross, J. J. (2009). Does expressing your emotions raise or lower your blood pressure? The answer depends. on cultural context. *Journal of Cross-Cultural Psychology, 40*, 510–517.

Carlton, P. A., & Deane, F. P. (2000). Impact of attitudes and suicidal ideation on adolescents' intentions to seek professional psychological help. *Journal of Adolescence, 23*, 35–45.

Chan, D. W. (1990). The meaning of depression: Chinese word associations. *Psychologia: An International Journal of Psychology in the Orient, 33*, 191–196.

Chan, D. W. (1994). The Chinese ways of Coping Questionnaire: Assessing coping in secondary school teachers and students in Hong Kong. *Psychological Assessment, 6*, 101–116.

Cheetham, W. S., & Cheetham, R. J. (1976). Concepts of mental illness amongst the Xhosa people in South Africa. *Australian and New Zealand Journal of Psychiatry, 10*, 39–45.

Chen, Y.-H. (2006a). Coping with suffering: The Buddhist perspective. In P. T. P. Wong, & L. C. J. Wong (Eds.), *Handbook of multicultural perspectives on stress and coping* (pp. 73–90). New York: Springer.

Chen, Y.-H. (2006b). The way of nature as a healing power. In P. T. P. Wong, & L. C. J. Wong (Eds.), *Handbook of multicultural perspectives on stress and coping* (pp. 91–104). New York: Springer.

Cheung, F. M. (2000). Deconstructing counseling in a cultural context. *The Counseling Psychologist, 28*, 123–132.

Choi, S. (2008). *Measurement of attitudes toward counseling: Scale development.* Unpublished dissertation. Ball State University (Muncie, Indiana).

Chun, C.-A., Moos, R. H., & Cronkite, R. C. (2006). Culture: A fundamental context for the stress and coping paradigm. In P. T. P. Wong, & L. C. J. Wong (Eds.), *Handbook of multicultural perspectives on stress and coping* (pp. 29–53). New York: Springer.

Church, A. T., Katigbak, M. S., Reyes, J. A. S., & Jensen, S. M. (1998). Language and organization of Filipino emotion concepts: Comparing emotion concepts and dimensions across cultures. *Cognition and Emotion, 12*(1), 63–92.

Dadfar, S., & Friedlander, M. L. (1982). Differential attitudes of international students toward seeking professional psychological help. *Journal of Counseling Psychology, 29*, 335–338.

Deane, F. P., Skogstad, P., & Williams, M. W. (1999). Impact of attitudes, ethnicity, and quality of prior therapy on New Zealand male prisoners' intentions to seek professional psychological help. *International Journal for the Advancement of Counseling, 21*, 55–67.

De Ridder, D. (1997). What is wrong with coping assessment? A review of conceptual and methodological issues. *Psychology and Health, 12*, 417–431.

de Waal, F. B. M. (2003). Darwin's legacy and the study of primate visual communication. In P. Ekman, J. Campos, R. J. Davidson, & F. B. M. De Waal (Eds.), *Emotions inside out: 130 years after Darwin's the expression of emotion in man and animals* (pp. 7–31). New York: New York Academy of Sciences.

Diener, E., & Crandall, R. (1978). *Ethics in social and behavioral research*. Chicago: University of Chicago Press.

Dixon, D. N. (1987). From Parsons to profession: The history of guidance and counseling psychology. In J. A. Glover & R. R. Ronning (Eds). *Historical Foundations of Educational Psychology* (pp. 107–120). New York: Plenum Publishing Co.

Draguns, J. G. (2004). From speculation through description toward investigation: A prospective glimpse at cultural research in psychotherapy. In U. P. Gielen, J. M. Fish, & J. G. Draguns (Eds.), *Handbook of culture, therapy, and healing* (pp. 369–387). Mahwah, NJ: Lawrence Erlbaum Associates.

Draguns, J. G. (2007). Psychotherapeutic and related interventions for a global psychology. In M. J. Stevens, & U. P. Gielen (Eds.), *Toward a global psychology: Theory, research, intervention, and pedagogy* (pp. 233–266). Mahwah, NJ: Lawrence Erlbaum Associates.

Durik, A., Hyde, J., Marks, A., Roy, A., Anaya, D., & Schultz, G. (2006). Ethnicity and gender stereotypes of emotion. *Sex Roles, 54*(7), 429–445.

Eid, M., & Diener, E. (2001). Norms for experiencing emotions in different cultures: Inter- and intranational differences. *Journal of Personality and Social Psychology, 81*, 869–885.

Ekman, P. (1972). Universal and cultural differences in facial expression of emotion. In J. R. Cole (Ed.), *Nebraska Symposium on Motivation, 1971* (pp. 207–283). Lincoln, NE: Nebraska University Press.

Ekman, P. (Ed.). (1982). *Emotion in the human face*. Cambridge, UK: Cambridge University Press.

Ekman, P. (1989). The argument and evidence about universals in facial expressions of emotion. In H. Wagner, & A. Manstead (Eds.), *Handbook of social psychophysiology* (pp. 143–164). Chichester, UK: Wiley.

Ekman, P. (1992). Are there basic emotions? *Psychological Review, 99*, 550–553.

Ekman, P. (1993). Facial expression and emotion. *American Psychologist, 48*, 384–392.

Ekman, P. (2003). *Emotions revealed: Recognizing faces and feelings to improve communication and emotional life*. New York: Times Books.

Ekman, P., Davidson, R. J., & Friesen, W. V. (1990). The Duchenne smile: Emotional expression and brain physiology: II. *Journal of Personality and Social Psychology, 58*, 342–353.

Ekman, P., & Friesen, W. V. (1969). The repertoire of nonverbal behavior: Categories, origins, usage, and coding. *Semiotica, 1*, 49–98.

Ekman, P., & Friesen, W. (1971). Constants across cultures in the face and emotion. *Journal of Personality and Social Psychology, 17*, 124–129.

Ekman, P., & Friesen, W. V. (1975). *Unmasking the face; a guide to recognizing emotions from facial clues*. Englewood Cliffs, NJ: Prentice Hall.

Ekman, P., & Friesen, W. V. (1976). *Pictures of facial affect*. Palo Alto, CA: Consulting Psychologists Press.

Ekman, P., & Friesen, W. V. (1978). *Facial action coding system: Investigator's guide*. Palo Alto, CA: Consulting Psychologists Press.

Ekman, P., & Friesen, W. V. (1982). *EMFACS*. Unpublished manuscript, San Francisco, CA.

Ekman, P., & Friesen, W. (1986). A new pan-cultural facial expression of emotion. *Motivation and Emotion, 10*, 159–168.

Ekman, P., Friesen, W., & Ancoli, S. (1980). Facial signs of emotional experience. *Journal of Personality and Social Psychology, 39*, 1125–1134.

Ekman, P., Friesen, W. V., & Ellsworth, P. (1972). *Emotion in the human face: Guidelines for research and an integration of findings*. New York: Pergamon Press.

Ekman, P., Friesen, W. V., & Hager, J. C. (2002). *Facial Action Coding System (FACS)*. Salt Lake City, UT: A Human Face.

Ekman, P., Friesen, W. V., & O'Sullivan, M. (1988). Smiles when lying. *Journal of Personality and Social Psychology, 54*, 414–420.

Ekman, P., Friesen, W. V., & Tomkins, S. S. (1971). Facial Affect Scoring Technique (FAST): A first validity study. *Semiotica, 3*, 37–58.

Ekman, P., Sorenson, E., & Friesen, W. (1969). Pan-cultural elements in facial displays of emotion. *Science, 164*(3875), 86–88.

Elfenbein, H., & Ambady, N. (2002). On the universality and cultural specificity of emotion recognition: A meta-analysis. *Psychological Bulletin, 128*, 203–235.

Elfenbein, H., & Ambady, N. (2003). When familiarity breeds accuracy: Cultural exposure and facial emotion recognition. *Journal of Personality and Social Psychology, 85*, 276–290.

Elfenbein, H., Mandal, M., Ambady, N., Harizuka, S., & Kumar, S. (2004). Hemifacial differences in the in-group advantage in emotion recognition. *Cognition & Emotion, 18*(5), 613–629.

Fang, K. B. (1999). Acculturation as a predictor of attitudes toward seeking professional psychological help in the Hmong community. *Dissertation Abstract International, 60*(6-B), 2939.

Fischer, E. H., & Farina, A. (1995). Attitudes toward seeking psychological help: A shortened form and considerations for research. *Journal of College Student Development, 36*, 368–373.

Fischer, E. H., & Turner, J. LeB. (1970). Orientations to seeking professional help: Development and research utility of an attitude scale. *Journal of Consulting and Clinical Psychology, 35*, 79–90.

Flum, M. E. (1998). Attitudes toward mental health and help-seeking preferences of Chinese, Japanese, and Korean international college students. *Dissertation Abstracts International, 59*(5-A), 1470.

Folkman, S., & Lazarus, R. S. (1988). *Manual for the Ways of Coping Scale*. Palo Alto, CA: Consulting Psychology Press.

Frankl, V. E. (1984). *Man's search for meaning*. New York: Washington Square Press.

Frankl, V. E. (1986). *The doctor and the soul: From psychotherapy to logotherapy*. New York: Vintage Books.

Freire, P. (1970). *Pedagogy of the oppressed*. New York: Herder & Herder.

Friesen, W. V. (1972). *Cultural differences in facial expressions in a social situation: An experimental test of the concept of display rules*. Unpublished doctoral dissertation, University of California, San Francisco.

Frymier, A. B., Klopf, D. W., & Ishii, S. (1990). Japanese and Americans compared on the affect orientation construct. *Psychological Reports, 66*, 985–986.

Furnham, A., & Andrew, R. (1996). A cross-cultural study of attitudes towards seeking psychological help. *Psychological Reports, 79*, 289–290.

Galati, D. (1989). La valutazione di antecedenti situazionali delle emozioni e la sua variabilità culturale [The evaluation of meaning of emotional antecedents and its cultural variability]. *Ricerche di Psicologia, 4*, 41–71.

Galati, D., & Sciaky, R. (1995). The representation of antecedents of emotions in the North and South of Italy. *Journal of Cross-Cultural Psychology, 26*, 123–140.

Galati, D., Schmidt, S., Sini, B., Tinti, C., Manzano, M., Roca, M., et al. (2005). Emotional experience in Italy, Spain, and Cuba: A cross-cultural comparison. *Psychologia: An International Journal of Psychology in the Orient, 48*(4), 268–287.

Garza, R. T. (1978). Affective and associative qualities in the learning styles of Chicanos and Anglos. *Psychology in the Schools, 15*, 111–115.

Gauthier, J. (2008). Universal declaration of ethical principles for psychologists. In J. E. Hall, & E. M. Altmaier (Eds.), *Global promise: Quality assurance and accountability in professional psychology* (pp. 98–105). New York: Oxford University Press.

Gebreyesus, S. (2001). An examination of self-construal, gender, and attitudes toward seeking professional psychological help, between Eritrean immigrant and American college students. *Dissertation Abstract International, 62*(3-A), 910.

Geertz, H. (1959). The vocabulary of emotion: A study of Javanese socialization process. *Psychiatry, 22*, 225–237.

Georges, E. (1995). A cultural and historical perspective on confession. In J. W. Pennebaker (Ed.), *Emotion, disclosure, and health* (pp. 11–22). Washington, DC: American Psychological Association.

Gerber, E. (1975). *The cultural patterning of emotions in Samoa*. Unpublished doctoral dissertation, University of California, San Diego.

Gerstein, L. H., Heppner, P. P., Ægisdóttir, S., Leung, S.-M. A., & K. L. Norsworthy. (2009a). Cross-cultural counseling: History, challenges, and rationale. In L. H. Gerstein, P. P. Heppner, S. Ægisdóttir, S.-M. A. Leung, & K. L. Norsworthy (Eds.), *International handbook of cross-cultural counseling: Cultural assumptions and practices worldwide* (pp. 3–32). Thousand Oaks, CA: Sage.

Gerstein, L. H., Heppner, P. P., Stockton, R., Leong, F. T. L., & Ægisdóttir, S. (2009b). The counseling profession in- and outside the United States. In L. H. Gerstein, P. P. Heppner, S. Ægisdóttir, S.-M. A. Leung, & K. L. Norsworthy (Eds.), *International handbook of cross-cultural counseling: Cultural assumptions and practices worldwide* (pp. 53–67). Thousand Oaks, CA: Sage.

Gerstein, L. H., Heppner, P. P., Ægisdóttir, S., Leng, S.-M. A., & Norsworthy, K. L. (2009c). A global vision for the future of cross-cultural counseling: Theory, collaboration, research, and training. In L. H. Gerstein, P. P. Heppner, S. Ægisdóttir, S.-M. A. Leung, & K. L. Norsworthy (Eds.), *International handbook of cross-cultural counseling: Cultural assumptions and practices worldwide* (pp. 503–522). Thousand Oaks, CA: Sage.

Gerstein, L. H., & Kirkpatrick, D. (2005). Counseling psychology and nonviolent activism: Independence for Tibet! In R. L. Toporek, L. H. Gerstein, N. A. Fouad, G. Roysircar-Sodowsky, & T. Israel (Eds.), *Handbook for social justice in counseling psychology: Leadership, vision, and action* (pp. 442–471). Thousand Oaks, CA: Sage.

Gerstein, L. H., Rountree, C., & Ordonez, M. A. (2007). An anthropological perspective on multicultural counselling. *Counselling Psychology Quarterly, 20*, 375–400.

Gerstein, L. H., & Ægisdóttir, S. (Eds.). (2005a). Counseling around the world [Special issue]. *Journal of Mental Health Counseling, 27*, 95–184.

Gerstein, L. H., & Ægisdóttir, S. (Eds.). (2005b). Counseling outside of the United States: Looking in and reaching out [Special section]. *Journal of Mental Health Counseling, 27*, 221–281.

Gerstein, L. H., & Ægisdóttir, S. (2007). Training international social change agents: Transcending a U.S. counseling paradigm. *Counselor Education and Supervision, 47*, 123–139.

Greenberg, J. H. (1966). *Language universals*. The Hague, The Netherlands: Mouton.

Gross, J. J. (1998). Antecedent- and response-focused emotion regulation: Divergent consequences for experience, expression, and physiology. *Journal of Personality and Social Psychology, 74*, 224–237.

Gross, J. J., & John, O. P. (1995). Facets of emotional expressivity: Three self-report factors and their correlates. *Personality & Individual Differences, 19*, 558–568.

Gross, J. J., & John, O. P. (1997). Revealing feelings: Facets of emotional expressivity in self-reports, peer ratings, and behavior. *Journal of Personality and Social Psychology, 72*, 435–448.

Gross, J. J., & John, O. P. (2003). Individual differences in two emotion regulation processes: Implications for affect, relationships, and well-being. *Journal of Personality and Social Psychology, 85*, 348–362.

Gross, J. J., & Levenson, R. W. (1993). Emotional suppression: Physiology, self-report, and expressive behavior. *Journal of Personality and Social Psychology, 64*, 970–986.

Gross, J. J., & Levenson, R. W. (1997). Hiding feelings: The acute effects of inhibiting positive and negative emotions. *Journal of Abnormal Psychology, 106*, 95–103.

Guerra, M. H. (1970). The retention of Mexican-American students in higher education with special reference to bicultural and bilingual problems. In H. S. Johnson, & W. J. Hernandez (Eds.), *Educating the Mexican-American* (pp. 124–144). Philadelphia: Johnson Press.

Halgin, R. P., Weaver, D. D., Edell, W. S., & Spencer, P. G. (1987). Relation of depression and help seeking history to attitudes toward seeking professional psychological help. *Journal of Counseling Psychology, 34*, 177–185.

Hall, J. (2006). Working in cross-cultural and international settings. In J. Hall, & S. Llewelyn (Eds.), *What is clinical psychology?* (4th ed., pp. 313–330). Oxford, UK: Oxford University Press.

Hambleton, R. K., & de Jong, J. H. A. L. (2003). Advances in translating and adapting educational and psychological tests. *Language Testing, 20*, 127–134.

Harik-Williams, N. (2003). Willingness of international students to seek counseling. *Dissertation Abstracts International, 64*(3-B), 1492.

Haque-Khan, A. (1997). Muslim women's voices: Generation, acculturation, and faith in the perceptions of mental health and psychological help. *Dissertation Abstract International, 58*(5-B), 2676.

Health Professions Council of South Africa. (2011). *Practice framework adopted by the Professional Board for Psychology.* Retrieved 27 April, 2011 from http://www.hpcsa.co.za/board_psychology.php.

Heilfrich, H. (1999). Beyond the dilemma of cross-cultural psychology: Resolving the tension between etic and emic approaches. *Culture and Psychology*, 5, 131–153.

Heine, S. J., Lehman, D. R., Markus, H. R., & Kitayama, S. (1999). Is there a universal need for positive self-regard? *Psychological Review, 106*, 766–794.

Heppner, P. P. (2006). The benefits and challenges of becoming cross-culturally competent counseling psychologists: Presidential address. *The Counseling Psychologist, 34*, 147–172.

Heppner, P. P., & Gerstein, L. H. (2008). International developments in counseling psychology. In E. Altmaier, & B. D. Johnson (Eds.), *Encyclopedia of counseling: Changes and challenges for counseling in the 21st century* Vol. 1 (pp. 260–266). Thousand Oaks, CA: Sage.

Heppner, P. P., Heppner, M. J., Lee, D.-G., Wang, Y.-W., Park, H.-J., & Wang, L.-F. (2006). Development and validation of a collectivistic coping styles inventory. *Journal of Counseling Psychology, 53*, 107–125.

Heppner, P. P., Leong, F. T. L., & Chiao, H. (2008a). A growing internationalization of counseling psychology. In S. D. Brown, & R. W. Lent (Eds.), *Handbook of counseling psychology* (4th ed., pp. 68–85). Hoboken, NJ: Wiley.

Heppner, P. P., Leong, F. T. L., & Gerstein, L. H. (2008b). Counseling within a changing world: Meeting the psychological needs of societies and the world. In W. B. Walsh (Ed.), *Biennial review in counseling psychology* (pp. 231–258). Thousand Oaks, CA: Sage.

Heppner, P. P., Ægisdóttir, S., Leung, S.-M. A., Duan, C., Helms, J. E., Gerstein, L. H., & Pedersen, P. B. (2009). The intersection of multicultural and cross-national movements in the United States: A complementary role to promote culturally sensitive research, training, and practice. In L. H. Gerstein, P. P. Heppner, S. Ægisdóttir, S.-M. A. Leung, & K. L. Norsworthy (Eds.), *International handbook of cross-cultural counseling: Cultural assumptions and practices worldwide* (pp. 33–52). Thousand Oaks, CA: Sage.

Herrmann, D. J., & Raybeck, D. (1981). Similarities and differences in meaning in six cultures. *Journal of Cross-Cultural Psychology, 12*, 194–206.

Hiatt, L. R. (1978). Classification of the emotions. In L. R. Hiatt (Ed.), *Australian aboriginal concepts* (pp. 182–187). Princeton, NJ: Humanities Press.

Hochschild, A. R. (1979). Emotion work, feeling rules, and social structure. *American Journal of Sociology, 84*, 551–575.

Hochschild, R. (1983). *The managed heart.* Berkeley, CA: University of California Press.

Hoekstra, H. A. (1986). *Cognition and affect in the appraisal of events.* Groningen. The Netherlands: Rijksuniversiteit te Groningen.

Houser, R., Wilczenski, F. L., & Ham, M. A. (2006). *Culturally relevant ethical decision-making in counseling.* Thousand Oaks, CA: Sage.

Howell, S. (1981). Rules not words. In P. Heelas, & A. Lock (Eds.), *Indigenous psychologies: The anthropology of the self* (pp. 133–143). San Diego: Academic Press.

Hunt, R. C. (2007). *Beyond relativism: Rethinking comparability in cultural anthropology.* New York: Alta Mira Press.

Hupka, R., Lenton, A., & Hutchison, K. (1999). Universal development of emotion categories in natural language. *Journal of Personality and Social Psychology, 77*, 247–278.

Iliescu, D., Ispas, D., & Harris, M. (2009). Social implications and ethics of testing. International Test Commission: Online readings of the International Test Commission (ORTA). Retrieved August 21, 2009, from http://www.intestcom.org/Publications/ORTA/Social%20implications%20and%20ethics%20of%20testing.php.

International Test Commission. (2000). *International guidelines for test use: Version 2000.* Retrieved March 31 2009, from http://www.intestcom.org/guidelines/index.php.

International Test Commission (ITC). (2000). *International guidelines for test use.* Retrieved June 1 2009, from http://www.intestcom.org/itc_projects.htm.

Izard, C. E. (1979). *The maximally discriminative facial movement coding system (MAX).* Unpublished manuscript, Instructional Resource Center, University of Delaware, Newark, DE.

Izard, C. E. (1980). Cross-cultural perspectives on emotion and emotion communication. In H. C. Triandis, & W. Lonner (Eds.), *Handbook of cross-cultural psychology* Vol. 3 (pp. 185–221). Boston: Allyn & Bacon.

Izard, C. E., Dougherty, L. M., & Hembree, E. A. (1983). *A system for identifying affect expressions by holistic judgments.* Unpublished Manuscript, University of Delaware.

Keeler, W. (1983). Shame and stage fright in Java. *Ethos, 11*, 152–165.

Kelly, A. E., & Achter, J. A. (1995). Self-concealment and attitudes toward counseling in university students. *Journal of Counseling Psychology, 42*, 40–46.

Keltner, D., Ekman, P., Gonzaga, G. C., & Beer, J. (2003). Facial expressions of emotion. In R. J. Davidson, K. G. Scherer, & H. H. Goldsmith (Eds.), *Handbook of affective sciences* (pp. 415–432). New York: Oxford University Press.

Keltner, D., & Haidt, J. (1999). Social functions of emotion at four levels of analysis. *Cognition and Emotion, 13*, 505–521.

Khoie, K. (2002). Predictors of attitudes of Iranian males toward seeking psychological help. *Dissertation Abstracts International, 63*(2-B), 1032.

Kim, H.-J. J., & Hupka, R. (2002). Comparison of associative meaning of the concepts of anger, envy, fear, romantic jealousy, and sadness between English and Korean. *Cross-Cultural Research: The Journal of Comparative Social Science, 36*(3), 229–255.

Kim, H. S., & Sherman, D. K. (2007). "Express yourself": Culture and the effect of self-expression on choice. *Journal of Personality and Social Psychology, 92*, 1–11.

King, L. A., & Emmons, R. A. (1990). Conflict over emotional expression: Psychological and physical correlates. *Journal of Personality and Social Psychology, 58*, 864–877.

Kitayama, S., & Markus, H. R. (1994). *Emotion and culture: Empirical studies of mutual influence.* Washington, DC: American Psychological Association.

Kitayama, S., Markus, H. R., & Matsumoto, H. (1995). Culture, self, and emotion: A cultural perspective on "self-conscious" emotions. In J. P. Tangney, & K. W. Fischer (Eds.), *Self-conscious emotions: The psychology of shame, guilt, embarrassment, and pride* (pp. 439–464). New York: Guilford Press.

Kring, A. M., Smith, D. A., & Neale, J. M. (1994). Individual differences in dispositional expressiveness: Development and validation of the Emotional Expressivity Scale. *Journal of Personality and Social Psychology, 66*, 934–949.

Klaassen, D. W., McDonald, M. J., & James, S. (2006). Advance in the study of religious and spiritual coping. In P. T. P. Wong, & L. C. J. Wong (Eds.), *Handbook of multicultural perspectives on stress and coping* (pp. 105–132). New York: Springer.

Kleinman, A. (1977). Depression, somatization and the new cross-cultural psychiatry. *Social Science and Medicine, 11*, 3–10.

Kring, A. M. (2001). Emotion and psychopathology. In T. J. Mayne, & G. A. Bonanno (Eds.), *Emotions* (pp. 337–360). New York: Guilford Press.

Lazarus, R. S., & Folkman, S. (1984). *Stress, appraisal and coping.* New York: Springer.

Leach, M. M. (2008). Compendium: Codes of ethics of national psychology associations around the world. *International Union of Psychological Sciences.* http://www.am.org/iupsys/ethics/index.html.

Leach, M. M., & Oakland, T. (2007). Ethics standards impacting test development and use: A review of 31 ethics codes impacting practices in 35 countries. *International Journal of Testing, 7*, 71–88.

Lebra, T. S. (1983). Shame and guilt: A psychocultural view of the Japanese self. *Ethos, 11*, 192–209.

Leff, J. (1973). Culture and the differentiation of emotional states. *British Journal of Psychiatry, 123*, 299–306.

Leighton, A., Lambo, T., Hughes, C., Leigton, D., Murphy, J., & Macklin, D. (1963). *Psychiatric disorder among the Yoruba.* Ithaca, N Y: Cornell University.

Leong, F. T. L., & Blustein, D. L. (2000). Toward a global vision of counseling psychology. *The Counseling Psychologist, 28*, 5–9.

Leong, F. T. L., & Leach, M. M. (2007). Internalizing counseling psychology in the United States: A SWOT analysis. *Applied Psychology: An International Review, 56*, 165–181.

Leong, F. T. L., & Ponterotto, J. G. (2003). A proposal for internationalizing counseling psychology in the United States: Rationale, recommendations and challenges. *The Counseling Psychologist, 31*, 381–395.

Leung, S. A. (2003). A journey worth traveling: Globalization of counseling psychology. *The Counseling Psychologist, 31*, 412–419.

Leung, S. A., Chan, C. C., & Leahy, T. (2007). Counseling psychology in Hong Kong: A germinating discipline. *Applied Psychology: An International Review, 56*(1), 51–68.

Leung, S. M. A., Clawson, T., Norsworthy, K., Tena, A., Szilagyi, A., & Rogers, J. (2009). Internationalization of the counseling profession: An indigenous perspective. In L. H. Gerstein, P. P. Heppner, S. Ægisdóttir, S. M. A. Leung, & K. Norsworthy (Eds.), *International handbook of cross-cultural counseling: Cultural assumptions and practices worldwide* (pp. 111–123). Thousand Oaks, CA: Sage.

Levenson, R. W. (1999). The intrapersonal functions of emotion. *Cognition and Emotion, 13*(5), 481–504.

Levy, R. I. (1973). *Tahitians: Mind and experience in the Society Islands.* Chicago: University of Chicago Press.

Levy, R. I. (1983). Introduction: Self and emotion. *Ethos, 11*, 128–134.

Levy, R. I. (1984). Emotion, knowing, and culture. In R. A. Shweder, A. R. A. LeVine (Eds.), *Culture theory: Issues on mind, self and emotion* (pp. 214–237). Cambridge, UK: Cambridge University Press.

Lim, B. K. H. (2001). Conflict resolution styles, somatization, and marital satisfaction in Chinese couples: The moderating effect of forgiveness and willingness to seek professional help. *Dissertation Abstracts International, 61*(7-B), 3902.

Lonner, W. J. (1985). Issues in testing and assessment in cross-cultural counseling. *The Counseling Psychologist, 13*, 599–614.

Lugones, M. C., & Spelmann, E. V. (1983). Have we got a theory for you! Feminist theory, cultural imperialism and the demand for "the woman's voice." *Women's Studies International Forum, 6*, 573–581.

Lutz, C. (1980). *Emotion words and emotional development on Ifaluk Atoll.* Unpublished doctoral dissertation, Harvard University.

Lutz, C. (1983). Parental goals, ethnopsychology, and the development of emotional meaning. *Ethos, 11*, 246–262.

Ly, P. H. (2002). Acculturation and attitudes toward the utilization of mental health services among Vietnamese refugees. *Dissertation Abstracts International, 63*(1-B), 536.

Lynch, O. (Ed.). (1990). *Divine Passions: The social construction of emotion in India.* Berkeley: University of California Press.

Lyons, R. F., Mickelson, K. D., Sullivan, M. J. L., & Coyne, J. C. (1998). Coping as a communal process. *Journal of Social and Personal Relationships, 15*, 579–605.

Lyons, R., Sullivan, M., Ritvo, P., & Coyne, J. (1995). *Relationship in chronic illness and disability.* Thousand Oaks, CA: Sage.

Markus, H. R., & Kitayama, S. (1991). Culture and the self: Implications for cognition, emotion, and motivation. *Psychological Review, 98*, 224–253.

Marsella, A. (1980). Depressive experience and disorders across cultures. In H. Triandis, & J. Draguns (Eds.), *Handbook of cross-cultural psychology: Vol. 6. Mental health* (pp. 237–289). Boston: Allyn & Bacon.

Marsella, A. J. (1998). Toward a "global-community psychology": Meeting the needs of a changing world. *American Psychologist, 53*, 1282–1291.

Marsh, A., Elfenbein, H., & Ambady, N. (2003). Nonverbal "accents": Cultural differences in facial expressions of emotion. *Psychological Science, 14*(4), 373–376.

Matsumoto, D. (1990). Cultural similarities and differences in display rules. *Motivation & Emotion, 14*(3), 195–214.

Matsumoto, D. (1993). Ethnic differences in affect intensity, emotion judgments, display rule attitudes, and self-reported emotional expression in an American sample. *Motivation and Emotion, 17*(2), 107–123.

Matsumoto, D. (2001). Culture and emotion. In D. Matsumoto (Ed.), *The handbook of culture and psychology* (pp. 171–194). New York: Oxford University Press.

Matsumoto, D. (2006). Are cultural differences in emotion regulation mediated by personality traits? *Journal of Cross-Cultural Psychology, 37*, 421–437.

Matsumoto, D. (2009). Culture and emotional expression. In C. Y. Chiu, Y. Y. Hong, S. Shavitt, & R. S. Wyer (Eds.), *Problems and solutions in cross-cultural theory, research, and application* (pp. 271–287). New York: Psychology Press.

Matsumoto, D., & Assar, M. (1992). The effects of language on judgments of universal facial expressions of emotion. *Journal of Nonverbal Behavior, 16*(2), 85–99.

Matsumoto, D., & Ekman, P. (1989). American-Japanese cultural differences in intensity ratings of facial expressions of emotion. *Motivation and Emotion, 13*(2), 143–157.

Matsumoto, D., & Kishimoto, H. (1983). Developmental characteristics in judgments of emotion from nonverbal vocal cues. *International Journal of Intercultural Relations, 7*, 415–424.

Matsumoto, D., Keltner, D., O'Sullivan, M., & Frank, M. G. (2006). *What's in a face? Facial expressions as signals of discrete emotions.* Manuscript submitted for publication.

Matsumoto, D., Kudoh, T., Scherer, K., & Wallbott, H. (1988). Antecedents of and reactions to emotions in the United States and Japan. *Journal of Cross-Cultural Psychology, 19*, 267–286.

Matsumoto, D., Olide, A., Schug, J., Willingham, B., & Callan, M. (2009). Cross-cultural judgments of spontaneous facial expressions of emotion. *Journal of Nonverbal Behavior, 33*, 213–238.

Matsumoto, D., Takeuchi, S., Andayani, S., Kouznetsova, N., & Krupp, D. (1998). The contribution of individualism-collectivism to cross-national differences in display rules. *Asian Journal of Social Psychology, 1*, 147–165.

Matsumoto, D., & Willingham, B. (2006). The thrill of victory and the agony of defeat: Spontaneous expressions of medal winners of the 2004 Athens Olympic games. *Journal of Personality and Social Psychology, 91*, 568–581.

Matsumoto, D., Yoo, S., Fontaine, J., et al. (2008a). Mapping expressive differences around the world: The Relationship between emotional display rules and individualism versus collectivism. *Journal of Cross-Cultural Psychology, 39*, 55–74.

Matsumoto, D., Yoo, S. H., Hirayama, S., & Petrova, G. (2005). Validation of an individual-level measure of display rules: The Display Rule Assessment Inventory (DRAI). *Emotion, 5*, 23–40.

Matsumoto, D., Yoo, S., Nakagawa, S., et al. (2008b). Culture, emotion regulation, and adjustment. *Journal of Personality and Social Psychology, 94*, 925–937.

Matsuyama, Y., Kama, H., Kawamura, Y., & Mine, H. (1978). An analysis of emotional words. *The Japanese Journal of Psychology, 49*, 229–232.

Mauro, R., Sato, K., & Tucker, J. (1992). The role of appraisal in human emotions: A cross-cultural study. *Journal of Personality and Social Psychology, 62*, 301–317.

Menon, U. (2000). Analyzing emotions as culturally constructed scripts. *Culture & Psychology, 6*(1), 40–50.

Mesquita, B., & Frijda, N. (1992). Cultural variations in emotions: A review. *Psychological Bulletin, 112*, 179–204.

Mesquita, B., Frijda, N. H., & Scherer, K. R. (1997). Culture and emotion. In P. Dasen, & T. S. Saraswathi (Eds.), *Handbook of cross-cultural psychology* Vol. 2 (pp. 255–297). Boston: Allyn and Bacon.

Mesquita, B., & Walker, R. (2003). Cultural differences in emotions: A context for interpreting emotional experiences. *Behaviour Research and Therapy, 41*, 777–793.

Moane, G. (1994). A psychological analysis of colonialism in an Irish context. *The Irish Journal of Psychology, 15*(2 & 3), 250–265.

Moore, C. C., Romney, A. K., Hsia, T., & Rusch, C. D. (1999). The universality of the semantic structure of emotion terms: Methods for the study of inter- and intra-cultural variability. *American Anthropologist, 101*, 529–546.

Morgan, T., Ness, D., & Robinson, M. (2003). Students' help-seeking behaviors by gender, racial background, and student status. *Canadian Journal of Counselling, 37*, 151–166.

Morling, B., Kitayama, S., & Miyamoto, Y. (2003). American and Japanese women use different coping strategies during normal pregnancy. *Personality and Social Psychology Bulletin, 29*, 1533–1546.

Myers, F. (1979). Emotions and the self. *Ethos, 7*, 343–370.

Naidoo, A. V., & Kagee, A. (2009). The quest for relevance: Counseling psychology in South Africa. In L. H. Gerstein, P. P. Heppner, S. Ægisdóttir, S.-M. A. Leung, & K. L. Norsworthy (Eds.), *International handbook of cross-cultural counseling: Cultural assumptions and practices worldwide* (pp. 421–433). Thousand Oaks, CA: Sage.

Norsworthy, K. L. (2006). Bringing social justice to international practices of counseling psychology. In R. L. Toporek, L. H. Gerstein, N. A. Fouad, G. Roysircar-Sodowsky, & T. Israel (Eds.), *Handbook of social justice in counseling psychology: Leadership, vision, and action* (pp. 421–441). Thousand Oaks, CA: Sage.

Norsworthy, K. L., Heppner, P. P., Ægisdóttir, S., Gerstein, L. H., & Pedersen, P. B. (2009a). Exportation of U.S.-based models of counseling and counseling psychology: A critical analysis. In L. H. Gerstein, P. P. Heppner, S. Ægisdóttir, S.-M. A. Leung, & K. L. Norsworthy (Eds.), *International handbook of cross-cultural counseling: Cultural assumptions and practices worldwide* (pp. 69–88). Thousand Oaks, CA: Sage.

Norsworthy, K. L., Leung, S.-M. A., Heppner, P. P., & Wang, L. (2009b). Crossing borders in collaboration. In L. H. Gerstein, P. P. Heppner, S. Ægisdóttir, S.-M. A. Leung, & K. L. Norsworthy (Eds.), *International handbook of cross-cultural counseling: Cultural assumptions and practices worldwide* (pp. 125–139). Thousand Oaks, CA: Sage.

O'Brien, T. B., & DeLongis, A. (1996). The interactional context of problem-, emotion-, and relationship-focused coping: The role of the big five personality factors. *Journal of Personality, 64*, 775–813.

Pargament, K. I., Koenig, H. G., & Perez, L. M. (2000). The many methods of religious coping: Development and initial validation of the RCOPE. *Journal of Clinical Psychology, 56*, 519–543.

Parker, J. D. A., & Endler, N. S. (1992). Coping with coping assessment: A critical review. *European Journal of Personality, 6*, 321–344.

Pedersen, P. B. (1995). Culture-centered ethical guidelines for counselors. In J. G. Ponterotto, J. M. Casas, L. A. Susuki, & C. M. Alexander (Eds), *Handbook of multicultural counseling* (pp. 34–49). Thousand Oaks, CA: Sage.

Pedersen, P. B. (1997). The cultural context of American Counseling Association code of ethics. *Journal of Counseling and Development, 76*, 23–28.

Pedersen, P. B. (2003). Culturally biased assumptions in counseling psychology. *The Counseling Psychologist, 31*, 396–403.

Pedersen, P. B., & Leong, F. (1997). Counseling in an international context. *The Counseling Psychologist, 25*, 117–122.

Penza-Clyve, S., & Zeman, J. (2002). Initial validation of the Emotion Expression Scale for Children (EESC). *Journal of Clinical Child and Adolescent Psychology, 31*, 540–547.

Pike, K. L. (1967). *Language in relation to a unified theory of structure of human behavior* (2nd ed.). The Hague, Netherlands: Mouton.

Poole, F. J. P. (1985). Coming into social being: Cultural images of infants in Bimin-Kuskusmin folk psychology. In G. M. White, & J. Kirkpatrick (Eds.), *Person, self, and experience: Exploring Pacific ethnopsychologies* (pp. 183–242). Berkeley, CA: University of California Press.

Potter, S. H. (1988). The cultural construction of emotion in rural Chinese social life. *Ethos, 16*, 181–208.

Price, B. K., & McNeill, B. W. (1992). Cultural commitment and attitudes toward seeking services in American Indian college students. *Professional Psychology: Research and Practice, 23*, 376–381.

Ramirez, M., & Castaneda, A. (1974). *Cultural democracy, biocognitive development and education.* New York: Academic Press.

Raviv, A., Raviv, A., & Yonovitz, R. (1989). Radio psychology and psychotherapy: Comparison of client attitudes and expectations. *Professional Psychology Research and Practice, 20*, 67–72.

Raybeck, D., & Herrmann, D. (1996). Antonymy and semantic relations: The case for a linguistic universal. *Cross-Cultural Research, 30*(2), 154–183.

Resner, G., & Hartog, J. (1970). Concepts and terminology of mental disorder among Malays. *Journal of Cross-Cultural Psychology, 1*, 369–381.

Rexrode, K. R., Petersen, S., & O'Toole, S. (2008). The Ways of Coping Scale: A reliability generalization study. *Educational and Psychological Measurement, 68*, 262–280.

Riesman, P. (1977). *Freedom in Fulani social life: An introspective ethnography* (M. Fuller, Trans.). Chicago: University of Chicago Press. (Original work published 1974).

Roger, D., & Najarian, B. (1989). The construction and validation of a new scale for measuring emotion control. *Personality & Individual Differences, 10*, 845–853.

Roger, D., & Nesshoever, W. (1987). The construction and preliminary validation of a scale for measuring emotional control. *Personality & Individual Differences, 8*, 527–534.

Romney, A. K., Moore, C. C., & Rusch, C. D. (1997). Cultural universals: Measuring the semantic structure of emotion terms in English and Japanese. *Proceedings of the National Academy of Sciences of the USA, 94*, 5489–5494.

Roseman, I. J., Dhawan, N., Rettek, S. I., & Naidu, R. K. (1995). Cultural differences and cross-cultural similarities in appraisals and emotional responses. *Journal of Cross-Cultural Psychology, 26*, 23–48.

Rosaldo, M. Z. (1980). *Knowledge and passion: Ilongot notions of self and social life.* Cambridge, UK: Cambridge University Press.

Rosaldo, M. Z. (1983). The shame of headhunters and the autonomy of self. *Ethos, 11*, 135–151.

Rosenblatt, P. C., Walsh, R. P., & Jackson, D. A. (1976). *Grief and mourning in cross-cultural perspective.* New Haven, CT: HRAF Press.

Rosenzweig, M. R. (1982). Trends in development and status of psychology: An international perspective. *International Journal of Psychology, 17*, 117–140.

Rusch, C. D. (1996). *The effects of bilingualism on cognitive semantic structure in the subjective lexicon: The case of emotions in Japanese and English.* Unpublished doctoral dissertation, University of California, Irvine.

Russell, J. (1983). Pancultural aspects of the human conceptual organization of emotions. *Journal of Personality and Social Psychology, 45*, 1281–1288.

Russell, J. (1991). Culture and the categorization of emotions. *Psychological Bulletin, 110*, 426–450.

Russell, J. (1994). Is there universal recognition of emotion from facial expressions? A review of the cross-cultural studies. *Psychological Bulletin, 115*, 102–141.

Saarni, C. (1979). Children's understanding of display rules for expressive behavior. *Developmental Psychology, 15*, 424–429.

Saarni, C. (1999). *The development of emotional competence.* New York: Guilford.

Said, E. W. (1993). *Culture and imperialism.* New York: Knopf.

Savickas, M. L. (2007). Internationalisation of counseling psychology: Constructing cross-national consensus and collaboration. *Applied Psychology: An International Review, 56*(1), 182–188.

Sayette, M. A., Cohn, J. F., Wertz, J. M., Perrott, M. A., & Parrott, D. J. (2001). A psychometric evaluation of the Facial Action Coding System for assessing spontaneous expression. *Journal of Nonverbal Behavior, 25*, 167–186.

Scherer, K. (1997a). The role of culture in emotion-antecedent appraisal. *Journal of Personality and Social Psychology, 73*, 902–922.

Scherer, K. (1997b). Profiles of emotion-antecedent appraisal: Testing theoretical predictions across cultures. *Cognition & Emotion, 11*(2), 113–150.

Scherer, K. R., & Wallbott, H. (1994). Evidence for universality and cultural variation of differential emotion response-patterning. *Journal of Personality and Social Psychology, 66*, 310–328.

Schieffelin, E. D. (1983). Anger and shame in the tropical forest: An affect as a cultural system in Papua New Guinea. *Ethos, 11*, 181–191.

Schieffelin, E. L. (1985). The cultural analysis of depressive affect: An example from New Guinea. In K. Kleinman, & B. Good (Eds.), *Culture and depression: Studies in anthropology and psychiatry of affect and disorder* (pp. 101–133). Berkeley, CA: University of California Press.

Semin, G., Görts, C., Nandram, S., & Semin-Goossens, A. (2002). Cultural perspectives on the linguistic representation of emotion and emotion events. *Cognition & Emotion, 16*(1), 11–28.

Sharma, P. (1995). Asian Indian attitudes toward seeking professional psychological help. *Dissertation Abstract International, 55*(10-B), 4614.

Sheikh, A. J. (2001). Gender and levels of acculturation as predictors of attitudes toward seeking professional psychological help and attitudes toward women among Indians and Pakistanis in America. *Dissertation Abstract International, 61*(910-B), 5581.

Shimoda, K., Argyle, M., & Ricci Bitti, P. (1978). The intercultural recognition of emotional expressions by three national racial groups: English, Italian and Japanese. *European Journal of Social Psychology, 8*(2), 169–179.

Shiraev, E., & Levy, D. (2006). *Cross-cultural psychology: Critical thinking and contemporary applications* (3rd ed.). Boston: Allyn & Bacon.

Shweder, R. A. (1991). *Thinking through cultures.* Cambridge, MA: Harvard University Press.

Shweder, R. A. (1993). The cultural psychology of the emotions. In M. Lewis, & J. Haviland (Eds.), *Handbook of emotions* (pp. 417–434). New York: Guilford.

Siegel, K., & Schrimshaw, E. W. (2002). The perceived benefits of religious and spiritual coping among older adults living with HIV/Aids. *Journal of the Scientific Study of Religion, 41*, 91–102.

Sommers, S. (1984). Adults evaluating their emotions: A cross-cultural perspective. In C. Z. Malatesta, & C. Izard (Eds.), *Emotions in adult development* (pp. 319–338). Beverly Hills, CA: Sage.

Soto, J., Levenson, R., & Ebling, R. (2005). Cultures of moderation and expression: Emotional experience, behavior, and physiology in Chinese Americans and Mexican Americans. *Emotion, 5,* 154–165.

Stevens, M. J., & Wedding, D. (Eds.). (2004). *Handbook of international psychology.* New York: Brunner-Routledge.

Stipek, D. (1998). Differences between Americans and Chinese in the circumstances evoking pride, shame, and guilt. *Journal of Cross-Cultural Psychology, 29,* 616–629.

Sue, D. W., & Torino, G. C. (1994). Racial-cultural competence: Awareness, knowledge, and skills. In R. T. Carter (Ed.), *Handbook of racial-cultural psychology and counseling, Training and Practice* Vol. 2 (pp. 3–18), New York: Wiley.

Surgenor, L. J. (1985). Attitudes toward seeking professional psychological help. *New Zealand Journal of Psychology, 14,* 27–33.

Takooshian, H. (2003). Counseling psychology's wide new horizons. *The Counseling Psychologist, 31,* 420–426.

Tanaka-Matsumi, J. (2008). Functional approaches to evidence-based practice in multicultural counseling and therapy. In U. P. Gielen, J. G. Draguns, & J. M. Fish (Eds.), *Principles of multicultural counseling and therapy* (pp. 169–198). New York: Taylor & Francis Group.

Tang, M., Wang, Z., Qian, M., Gao, J., & Zhang, L. (2008). Transferred shame in the cultures of interdependent-self and independent self. *Journal of Cognition and Culture, 8*(1), 163–178.

Tata, P. S., & Leong, F. T. L. (1994). Individualism-collectivism, social network orientation, and acculturation as predictors of attitudes toward seeking professional psychological help among Chinese Americans. *Journal of Counseling Psychology, 41,* 280–287.

Taylor, S. E., Sherman, D. K., Kim, H. S., Jarcho, J., & Takagi, K. (2004). Culture and social support: Who seeks it and why? *Journal of Personality and Social Psychology, 87,* 354–362.

Termansen, R. E., & Ryan, J. (1970). Health and disease in a British Columbian Indian community. *Canadian Psychiatric Association Journal, 15,* 121–127.

Todd, J. L., & Shapira, A. (1974). U.S. and British self-disclosure, anxiety, empathy, and attitudes to psychotherapy. *Journal of Cross-Cultural Psychology, 5,* 364–369.

Triandis, H. C. (2001). Individualism and collectivism: Past, present, and future. In D. Matsumoto (Ed.), *Handbook of culture and psychology* (pp. 35–50). New York: Oxford University Press.

Trimble, J. E. (2001). A quest for discovering ethnocultural themes in psychology. In J. G. Ponterotto, J. M. Casas, L. A. Suzuki, & C. M. Alexander (Eds.), *Handbook of multicultural counseling* (2nd ed., pp. 3–13). Thousand Oaks, CA: Sage.

Tronick, E., Als, H., & Brazelton, T. B. (1980). Monadic phases: A structural descriptive analysis of infant-mother face-to-face interaction. *Merrill-Palmer Quarterly of Behavior and Development, 26,* 3–24.

Tsai, J., & Levenson, R. (2007). Cultural influences on emotional responding: Chinese American and European American dating couples during conflict. *Journal of Cross-Cultural Psychology, 28,* 600–625.

Tseng, W.-S., & Hsu, J. (1969). Chinese culture, personality formation and mental illness. *International Journal of Social Psychiatry, 16,* 5–14.

Tweed, R. G., White, K., & Lehman, D. R. (2004). Culture, stress, and coping: Internally- and externally-targeted control strategies of European Canadians, East Asian Canadians, and Japanese. *Journal of Cross-Cultural Psychology, 35,* 652–668.

Ullmann, S. (1963/1966). Semantic universals. In J. H. Greenberg (Ed.), *Universals of Language* (pp. 217–262). Cambridge, MA: MIT Press.

United Nations Economic and Social Survey of Asia and the Pacific (UNESSAP). (1999). *Part two: Asia and the Pacific into the twenty-first century.* Bangkok, Thailand: Poverty and Development Division.

Van Bezooijen, R., Otto, S. A., & Heenan, T. A. (1983). Recognition of vocal expressions of emotion: A three-nation study to identify universal characteristics. *Journal of Cross-Cultural Psychology, 14,* 387–406.

van de Vijver, F. J. R. (2001). The evolution of cross-cultural research methods. In D. Matsumoto (Ed.), *Handbook of culture and psychology* (pp. 77–97). New York: Oxford University Press.

van de Vijver, F. J. R., & Hambleton, R. K. (1996). Translating tests: Some practical guidelines. *European Psychologist, 1,* 89–99.

van de Vijver, F. J. R., & Leung, K. (1997a). *Methods and data analysis for cross-cultural research.* Thousand Oaks, CA: Sage Publications.

van de Vijver, F. J. R., & Leung, K. (1997b). Methods and data analysis of comparative research. In J. W. Berry, Y. H. Poortinga, & Pandey, J. (Eds.), *Handbook of cross cultural psychology: Vol. 1. Theory and Method* (pp. 257–300). Boston: Allyn & Bacon.

van de Vijver, F. J. R., & Tanzer, N. K. (2004). Bias and equivalence in cross-cultural assessment: An overview. *European Review of Applied Psychology, 47,* 263–279.

van Hemert, D., Poortinga, Y., & van de Vijver, F. (2007). Emotion and culture: A meta-analysis. *Cognition & Emotion, 21*(5), 913–943.

Vensa. J. (2002). A cross-cultural examination of attitudes and intentions toward seeking professional psychological help: The relationship of attachment, acculturation, psychological distress, and social desirability. *Dissertation Abstracts International, 63*(4-B), 2079.

Vogel, D. L., & Wester, S. R. (2003). To seek help or not to seek help: The risk of self-disclosure. *Journal of Counseling Psychology, 50,* 351–361.

Wallace, A. E. C., & Carson, M. T. (1973). Sharing and diversity in emotion terminology. *Ethos, 1,* 1–29.

Wang, L., & Heppner, P. P. (2009). Cross-cultural collaboration: Developing cross-cultural competencies and yuan-fen. In L. H. Gerstein, P. P. Heppner, S. Ægisdóttir, S.-M. A. Leung, & K. L. Norsworthy (Eds.), *International handbook of cross-cultural counseling: Cultural assumptions and practices worldwide* (pp. 141–154). Thousand Oaks, CA: Sage.

Watson, M., & Greer, S. (1983). Development of a questionnaire measure of emotional control. *Journal of Psychosomatic Research, 27,* 299–305.

Wellenkamp, J. (1995). Cultural similarities and differences regarding emotional disclosure: Some examples from Indonesia and the Pacific. In J. W. Pennebaker (Ed.), *Emotion, disclosure and health* (pp. 293–312). Washington, DC: APA.

Wilkins, R., & Gareis, E. (2006). Emotion expression and the locution "I love you": A cross-cultural study. *International Journal of Intercultural Relations, 30*(1), 51–75.

Wong, P. T. P., Wong, L. C. J., & Scott, C. (2006). Beyond stress and coping: The positive psychology of transformation. In P. T. P. Wong, & L. C. J. Wong (Eds.), *Handbook of multicultural perspectives on stress and coping* (pp. 1–26). New York: Springer.

Wong, V. L. (1998). Relationships among degree of acculturation, opinions about mental illness, selected sociodemographic variables, and attitudes toward seeking professional psychological help among Chinese college students. *Dissertation Abstracts International, 58*(7-B), 3552.

Wrenn, C. G. (1962). The culturally encapsulated counselor. *Harvard Educational Review, 32,* 111–119.

Yeh, C. J. (2001). Taiwanese students' gender, age interdependent and independent self-construal, and collective self-esteem as predictors of professional psychological help-seeking attitudes. *Diversity and Ethnic Minority Psychology, 81,* 19–29.

Yeh, C. J., Arora, A. K., & Wu, K. A. (2006). A new theoretical model of collectivistic coping. In P. T. P. Wong, & L. C. J. Wong (Eds.), *Handbook of multicultural perspectives on stress and coping* (pp. 55–72). New York: Springer.

Yeh, C., & Inose, M. (2002). Difficulties and coping strategies of Chinese, Japanese and Korean immigrant students. *Adolescence, 37,* 69–82.

Yoo, S. K. (1997). Individualism-collectivism, attribution styles of mental illness, depression symptomatology, and attitudes toward seeking professional help: A comparative study between Koreans and Americans. *Dissertation Abstracts International, 57*(12-B), 7748.

Young, R. A., & Nicol, J. J. (2007). Counselling psychology in Canada: Advancing psychology for all. *Applied Psychology: An International Review, 56*(1), 20–32.

Yuki, M., Maddux, W., & Masuda, T. (2007). Are the windows to the soul the same in the East and West? Cultural differences in using the eyes and mouth as cues to recognize emotions in Japan and the United States. *Journal of Experimental Social Psychology, 43,* 303–311.

Zahn-Waxler, C., Friedman, R. J., Cole, P. M., Mizula, I., & Hiruma, N. (1996). Japanese and United States preschool children's responses to conflict and distress. *Child Development, 67,* 2462–2477.

Zhang, D., & Long, B. C. (2006). A multicultural perspective on work-related stress: Development of a collective coping scale. In P. T. P. Wong, & L. C. J. Wong (Eds.), *Handbook of multicultural perspectives on stress and coping* (pp. 555–578). New York: Springer.

Zeman, J., Shipman, K., & Penza-Clyve, S. (2001). Development and initial validation of the Children's Sadness Management Scale. *Journal of Nonverbal Behavior, 25,* 187–205.

Zhang, N., & Dixon, D. N. (2003). Acculturation and attitudes of Asian international students toward seeking psychological help. *Journal of Multicultural Counseling and Development, 31,* 205–222.

Ægisdóttir, S., & Gerstein, L. H. (2009). Beliefs About Psychological Services (BAPS): Development & psychometric properties. *Counselling Psychology Quarterly, 22,* 197–219.

Ægisdóttir, S., & Gerstein, L. H. (2010). International counseling competencies: A new frontier in multicultural training. In J. C. Ponterotto, J. M. Casas, L. A. Suzuki, & C. A. Alexander (Eds.), *Handbook of multicultural counseling* (3rd ed., pp. 175–188). Thousand Oaks, CA: Sage.

Ægisdóttir, S., Gerstein, L. H., Leung, S.-M. A., Kwan, K.-L. K., & Lonner, W. J. (2009). Theoretical and methodological issues when studying culture. In L. H. Gerstein, P. P. Heppner, S. Ægisdóttir, S.-M. A. Leung, & K. L. Norsworthy (Eds.), *International handbook of cross-cultural counseling: Cultural assumptions and practices worldwide* (pp. 89–109). Thousand Oaks, CA: Sage.

Ægisdóttir, S., Gerstein, L. H., Cinarbas, D. C. (2008). Methodological issues in cross-cultural counseling research: Equivalence, bias and translations. *The Counseling Psychologist, 36,* 188–219.

PART 6

Conclusions

Contemporary Counseling Psychology

Jo-Ida C. Hansen

Abstract

Yogi Berra warned "It's always risky to make predictions—especially about the future" (cited in Taylor, 2010, p. 218). Nonetheless, in this chapter, I reflect on five areas toward which the discipline of psychology is moving, that also are of importance to counseling psychology and counseling psychologists. These five directions include a *focus on individual differences*, a long tradition in counseling psychology, that is highlighted in the *Handbook* in the context of attention to diversity or under-represented populations or multicultural issues; *globalization and internationalization* and their increasing societal implications, for which counseling psychology is well positioned; the *development of translational research*, essential for closing the practice–research gap; *technological advances* that will dramatically change our science and our practice; and *knowledge about neural mechanisms and genotypes* that will have important implications for understanding interventions, processes, and outcomes in counseling psychology. These five areas are a thin slice of the emerging opportunities that the future will present for counseling psychology. In today's parlance, ours is a nimble field, with practitioners, researchers, educators, and policy makers who have the skills and dexterity necessary to change with an evolving future and to continue to contribute to the well-being of society and to scientific knowledge.

Keywords: individual differences, diversity, technology, globalization, neurobiology

Several themes that represent the bedrock, as well as the cutting edge, of counseling psychology emerge across almost every chapter prepared for this *Handbook of Counseling Psychology*. These themes, as explicated by the authors, are embedded in the historical links, the current status, and the future directions of their chapters. The most pervasive theme is a focus on individual differences—often presented in the context of attention to diversity or under-represented populations or multicultural issues. Also underlying each *Handbook* chapter is the core counseling psychology principle that values individual differences and promotes applications that focus on the individual or groups of individuals. Several chapters were commissioned specifically to focus on areas of diversity in which counseling psychology has been particularly visible. Other chapters point

to counseling psychology's diversity in research methodology. The diversity of the field of counseling psychology also is noteworthy in the range of settings populated and studied by counseling psychologists, as well as in the range of approaches to intervention that counseling psychologists employ.

As Baker and Subich noted (2008), counseling psychology was one of the first areas within applied psychology to devote attention to issues of diversity, social action, and justice; this tradition continues with diversity broadly defined. Although we know more than we did two decades ago, each chapter in the *Handbook* demonstrates that much work has yet to be done to understand fully the impact of diversity on counseling psychology's interventions, assessment tools, theories, training, and research methods.

Undergirding all aspects of counseling psychology is the need for diversity training that informs both research and practice. Much has been written about—and guidelines have been developed to—create awareness of the need for multicultural competency of practitioners. But, a broad definition of diversity competency is needed to advance both research and practice. To engage in either domain in a space devoid of diversity competencies will not serve the profession well.

Global Counseling Psychology

In *The World is Flat*, Friedman (2005) articulated the ways in which technology, transportation, and communication have shrunk the world. The interconnectedness of the world affects individuals, families, human rights, social structures and cultural traditions, economies, and the corporate world. As Wrenn noted in *The Counselor in a Changing World* (1962), the professional skills of counseling psychologists will continue to evolve to meet new opportunities but, like early counseling psychologists, the professionals of the future will continue to help "people find a place in the world, regardless of their condition, physical, emotional or otherwise" (Baker & Subich, 2008, p. 19).

Migration, international trade, and technological advances in communications and travel are contributing factors to the globalization of counseling psychology. Although differences in roles and functions of counseling psychologists and in professional credentials exist across countries, counseling psychology is present worldwide (Heppner, Leong, & Gerstein, 2008; Hohenshil, 2010), and globalization and internationalization will be important ingredients in the future of counseling psychology. International collaborations and exchanges are occurring on research, practice, and training fronts. These projects are by definition complex and often require substantially more time to complete than do locally conducted projects. Nonetheless, the importance of international collaborations for counseling psychology's knowledge base cannot be denied.

Counseling psychology's investment in diversity and multicultural competency provides skills critical for international research, practice, and training. Listening, asking questions, developing relationships, and being nonjudgmental are those strengths of counseling psychology professionals essential to international collaborations. Participation in international conferences and seeking out international attendees at North American conferences provide opportunities to develop lasting partnerships that will lead to collaborative research, enhance the integration of multiple cultural viewpoints into practice and science, and provide learning and exchange opportunities on effective practice and research models. Promoting student and faculty exchange programs, rethinking and internationalizing the curriculum, the inclusion of migration and immigration in diversity discussions, the development of international definitions of practice competencies, and working with a worldwide community of practitioners and researchers, are among the grassroots efforts that can contribute to the internationalization of, and a global perspective for, counseling psychology (Belar, 2007; Miller, 2007). In many ways, the social justice movement advanced by counseling psychology, which seeks equal political, economic, and social rights and opportunities, goes hand in hand with a global perspective of counseling psychology.

Science and Practice

The integration of science and practice, an emphasis within counseling psychology for many decades, will continue to be important as the field strives to develop psychosocial interventions, to promote compliance with medical and safety procedures, and to promote growth in services to under-represented populations. In the same vein, defining and measuring effective outcomes will be essential both to demonstrate the way in which psychological treatment can reduce overall health care costs as well as to develop practice guidelines for counseling psychology (Gelso & Fretz, 2001).

One of the challenges for counseling psychology, one that ultimately will enhance the integration of science and practice, is to develop programs of translational research—simply put, the research needs to be translated into meaningful applications. Conversely, practitioner-driven research questions may serve to make research more relevant and may help to address demands for accountability and evidence-based intervention models (DeAngelis, 2010).

The Role of Technology

Technological advances already are having an influence on the research, training, and practice of psychology, and technology is going to continue to be a major driver in the future. Education has embraced digital classroom presentations (e.g. Smart Boards, PowerPoint, Keynote, Google Presentations), course management systems (e.g., Web Vista, Moodle), Facebook Groups, Ning, Skype, Portfolios (to hold and share academic materials), student response systems (i.e., clickers), Wimba Voice Tools (for audio-based discussions and testing), Wikis and Google docs (for collaborative writing), blogs, and Twitter—all of which were largely unavailable at the turn of the century. Technology also provides mechanisms for promoting academic integrity, such as TurnItIn to check academic integrity on papers and Respondus to lock-down browsers for online testing (personal communication, Jen Mein, September, 2010).

Inevitably, the impact of technology on counseling psychology practice and research will increase, whether the demand is for electronic record keeping or for psychological interventions (Martin, 2009). For example, the movement to digitize health care records to reduce costs and to improve patient care creates the need for counseling psychologists to use electronic health care records. All things electronic, of course, raise questions about security and data privacy and the need to develop tiered levels of access. The net effect of electronic health records may be to increase and enhance communications among health care professionals. This ease of communication may mean that counseling psychologists are more often included in patient treatment plans and, ultimately, more easily included in future health care systems, where they will work closely with physicians and other health care professionals (Chamberlin, 2009). Yet, for counseling psychologists who do not practice in an integrated health care setting, the cost of electronic records (i.e., technology challenges, security issues) may seem to outweigh the benefits.

Technology also has the potential to enhance counseling psychologists' work with clients. Telepsychology—which includes video counseling, using technology such as Skype and language translation software, and employing e-mail to communicate with clients (Chamberlin, 2009)—will have a far-reaching impact on many aspects of practice. Although technology may bring psychotherapy to clients who would not otherwise have access to care, technology also raises questions about regulations for therapy across state or national borders, ethical and legal concerns about privacy, the need for electronic security measures, the coverage of malpractice insurance, and 24/7 expectations of clients.

Nonetheless, research is showing the potential for technology to advance the effectiveness of psychological treatment. Online interventions, for example, are being assessed for efficacy for such presenting problems as depression, panic disorder, anxiety, insomnia, and binge drinking prevention (Carlbring, Nilsson-Ihrfelt & Waara, 2005; Caspar & Berger, 2005; Clarke, Eubanks, & Reid, 2005; Kenwright & Marks, 2004; Mallen, Vogel, Rochlen, & Day, 2005; Moore, Soderquist & Werch, 2005; Strom, Petterson, & Anderson, 2004). The results also appear promising for online cognitive-behavioral interventions for adjustment of children after traumatic brain injuries (TBI; Wade, Carey, & Wolfe, 2006). As another example, virtual reality technology has been used in intervention studies to activate a person's fear structure prior to reconditioning of the original frightening stimulus (Rizzo, 2009). Work is ongoing to determine if such virtual reality techniques may be effective for conditions, traditionally resistant to treatment, such as phobias, posttraumatic stress disorder, and panic disorder. Virtual reality therapy approaches, however, are not intended to be administered as self-help programs; rather, such interventions must be administered "within the context of appropriate care via a thoughtful professional appreciation of the complexity and impact of the disorders" (Rizzo, et al., 2009, p. 394). Both the practice and science of counseling psychology will play an important role in establishing the efficacy of technology-based interventions and in assuming that the techniques are administered in an ethical and professionally responsible manner.

The Brain

Brain imaging technology, applied to the study of human behavior, has the potential to make tremendous contributions to knowledge about the biological bases of affective behavior. Functional magnetic resonance imaging (fMRI) research, which monitors the blood flow in the brain to portray neural activity (Conkle, 2009), provides the foundation for understanding relations among brain activity and emotions, personality, and even activity preferences (i.e., leisure and vocational interests). Often, the reaction to early work that attempted to identify regions of the brain related to psychological constructs was "so what?" Nonetheless, in 2001, Davidson predicted that "the science of emotion is likely to look very different a decade from now" (p. 29). Recent work using fMRI to study the personality of healthy adults (DeYoung et al., 2010) suggests that the progress Davidson predicted is occurring. And, with increased understanding of the biological basis of behavior, translation of science to application is happening.

Work in the arena of affective neuroscience is contributing, through the use of fMRI, to basic science knowledge about social variables that may influence brain development (Siegel, 1999), the biological basis of empathy (Decety & Jackson, 2004; Jackson & Decety, 2004), and depression (Davidson, Pizzagalli, Nitschke, & Putnam, 2002). Some fMRI work shows that, for culturally diverse groups (e.g., American and Korean participants), neural regions correlate with the experience of feeling persuaded (Falk et al., 2009). And research on the neural mechanisms underlying women's math performance has been linked to research on stereotype threat (Krendl, Richeson, Kelley, & Heatherton, 2008). Although competing explanations have been presented (Gauthier, Tarr, Anderson, Skudlarski, & Gore, 1999), the work of Kanwisher and colleagues (1997; Epstein & Kanwisher, 1998; Downing, Jiang, Shuman, & Kanwisher, 2001) has identified regions of the brain that may process faces, visual scenes depicting places, and images of the human body. Similarly, areas of the brain hypothesized to specialize in thinking about what others are thinking (Saxe & Kanwisher, 2003) and that show brain sensitivity to social rejection (Drevets et al, 1997; Somerville, Heatherton, & Kelley, 2006) have been identified.

Thus, neuroscience is beginning to provide the framework necessary for understanding the relations between counseling interventions and efficacy, as well as interventions matched to client types and diagnoses. The developmental orientation of counseling psychology meshes well with neuroscience that has identified the ways in which changes over the lifespan have an impact on the development of the brain. Theories of neuroplasticity (the development of new neural networks) and neurogenesis (building of new neurons) suggest that counseling interventions may stimulate the development of new neural networks (Ivey, Ivey, & Zalaquett, 2007) and that knowing the neurocircuitry of clients and therapists eventually may help therapists to identify dysfunctional patterns and to tailor treatments to disorders (Good & Beitman, 2006). As fMRI technology improves and allows the brain to be viewed with increasing precision, work in neuroscience has the potential to provide knowledge about the circuitry that supports emotional processing, as well as an understanding of why interventions work and ways in which counseling psychologists can hone skills to understand what clients are feeling. Armed with this knowledge, counseling psychologists will be better able to develop models of intervention that match techniques with the responses of involved brain regions.

Genetics

Mapping the human genome is another area of biological research that promises to advance understanding of psychological disorders and healthy behavior and to inform the development of interventions that capitalize on knowledge of gene–environment interactions (Reiss, 2010a, b). Gene–environment interactions (G × E) are defined as instances in which individual differences in sensitivity to specific environments are genetically influenced. Much behavior genetics research has concluded that population variance can be partitioned into separate additive and nonadditive genetic components and shared and nonshared environmental effects (Rutter & Silberg, 2002). A growing trend, however, is to recognize the role that gene–environment interactions play in sensitivity to risk and protective processes. For example, research with participants who are twins has found an association between adolescents' risk for substance abuse and parental substance abuse (suggesting genetic risk) as well as a relation with affiliation with deviant peers (suggesting environmental risk). A significant interaction also was found, such that family risk was elevated in the presence of high environmental risk (implying G × E; Legrand, McGue, & Iacona, 1999).

Although continued research that studies psychological risks within the context of biological processes is needed to investigate behaviors that moderate the gene–environment connection, genetic analyses are beginning to inform interventions. The identification of gene-influenced sensitivities has led to research exploring the extent to which the genotypes of an individual moderate responsiveness (i.e., more or less responsive) to interventions (Leve, Harold, Ge, Neiderhiser, & Patterson, 2010). In the case of family interventions, for example, behavioral genetics research can provide an understanding of the role individual differences play in the adaptation of children to various environments and the way in which adaptation may vary during different developmental stages. This knowledge, in turn, can inform the design of preventive and treatment interventions. Research to better understand why some people benefit more from physical exercise than do others also has been linked to G × E interactions (Nicklas, 2010). The angiotensin-1 converting enzyme (ACE) gene appears to be associated with physical responses to exercise (e.g., individual differences in muscle strength improvement and endurance improvement for people engaged in combined walking and resistance exercise). Knowing a person's genotype could lead to more effective interventions for motivating people to engage in exercise (or other healthy behaviors), under the assumption that people who respond positively to an intervention are likely to adhere to the treatment plan.

Integrating behavioral interventions and genetic analyses has the potential to lead to a better understanding of individual differences in response to interventions and thus, to more precise selections of interventions to match client diagnosis or client developmental or educational need. The time is opportune to move ahead with translational research that can inform intervention design and improve outcomes by identifying individuals who may benefit most from, or be harmed by, an approach (Plomin & Haworth, 2010).

Conclusion

The counseling psychology model of scientist–practitioner training—grounded in its traditions of assessment, individual differences, and a focus on strengths and assets (Hansen, 1995)—prepares counseling psychology professionals to apply their skills and knowledge to specialties that intersect with other subfields in psychology and to emerging areas within research and practice. This is evident in the work counseling psychologists do in specialties featured in Part Four: Applications—rehabilitation psychology, school-based counseling, health psychology, occupational health psychology, sport psychology, trauma research, and consulting psychology. Tyler, Tiedeman, and Wrenn (1980) noted that the "scientific and professional interests of members of Division 17 [counseling psychology] are multiple and complex"; it is not surprising that counseling psychologists are making important contributions to these areas that flow easily from the foundations of counseling psychology.

Given widespread access to cell phones, mobile devices, and wireless networks, technology-related issues may be at the forefront of emerging client presenting problems. Practitioners report increased incidence of Internet addiction and abuse, Internet pornography, impaired communication skills, information overload, cyber affairs, and cyber-bullying. A broad range of psychological, physical, and social trauma also is increasing demand for interventions and for research that provides an understanding of complicated interactions. Traumatic stress, for example, encompasses problems related to posttraumatic stress disorders following military combat as well as environmental emergencies such as hurricanes, tornadoes, and earthquakes. The psychological effects

of institutional oppression and mental health issues related to job stress, including workplace violence, unemployment, and underemployment, also are on the upswing. Older adults, a rapidly increasing population, are increasingly amenable to mental health services. Correlated with these emerging issues is increased demand for skilled practitioners who use science to inform practice and researchers engaged in scientific inquiry who have the skills necessary to translate research results into applications (DeAngelis, 2008; Keita, 2010; Rollins, 2008). As argued in the beginning of this chapter and throughout the *Handbook*, the core and foundations of counseling psychology are especially well suited to the demand for scientific inquiry and interventions in these emerging areas.

References

Baker, D. B., & Subich, L. M. (2008). Counseling psychology historical perspectives. In W. B. Walsh (Ed.), *Biennial review of counseling psychology* (pp. 1–26). New York: Routledge.

Belar, C. (2007). Toward the globalization and internationalization of psychology. *The Educator, 5*, 1–4.

Carlbring, P., Nilsson-Ihrfeldt, E., & Warra, J. (2005). Treatment of panic disorder: Live therapy vs. self-help via the Internet. *Behavior Research Therapy, 43*, 1321–1333.

Caspar, F., & Berger, T. (2005). The future is bright: How can we optimize online counseling, and how can we know whether we have done so? *The Counseling Psychologist, 33*, 900–909.

Chamberlin, J. (2009). Smart charts. *Monitor on Psychology, 40*(9), 74–75.

Clarke, G., Eubanks, D., Reid, E., Kelleher, C., O'Connor, E., DeBar, L., et al. (2005). Overcoming Depression on the Internet (ODIN) (2): A randomized trial of a self-help depression skills program with reminders. *Journal of Medical Internet Research, 7*(2), e16.

Conkle, A. (2009). Sharpening the focus on brain function. *Observer, 22*, 7–9.

Davidson, R. J., Pizzagalli, D., Nitschke, J. B., & Putnam, K. (2001). Depression: Perspectives from affective neuroscience. *Annual Review of Psychology, 53*, 545–574.

DeAngelis, T. (2008). Psychology's growth careers. *Monitor on Psychology, 39*(4), 64–71.

DeAngelis, T. (2010). Closing the gap between practice and research. *Monitor on Psychology, 41*(6), 42–43, 46.

Decety, J., & Jackson, P. L. (2004). The functional architecture of human empathy. *Behavioral and Cognitive Neuroscience Reviews, 3*, 71–100.

DeYoung, C. G., Hirsh, J. B., Shane, M. S., Papademetris, X., Rejeevan, N., & Gray, J. R. (2010). Testing predictions from personality neuroscience: Brain structure and the big five. *Psychological Science, 21*, 820–828.

Downing, P. E., Jiang, Y., Shuman, M., & Kanwisher, N. (2001). A cortical area selective for visual processing of the human body. *Science, 293*, 2470–2473.

Drevets, W. C., Price, J. L., Simpson, J. R., Todd, R. D., Reich, T., Vanier, M., & Raichle, M. E. (1997). Subgenual prefrontal cortex abnormalities in mood disorders. *Nature, 386*, 824–827.

Epstein, R., & Kanwisher, N. (1998). A cortical representation of the local visual environment. *Nature, 392*, 598–601.

Falk, E. B., Rameson, L., Berkman, E. T., Liao, B., Kang, Y., Inagaki, T. K., & Lieberman, M. D. (2009). The neural correlates of persuasion: A common network across cultures and media. *Journal of Cognitive Neuroscience, 22*, 2447–2459.

Friedman, T. L. (2005). *The world is flat: A brief history of the twenty-first century.* New York: Farrar, Straus & Giroux.

Gauthier, I., Tarr, M. J., Anderson, A. W., Skudlarski, P., & Gore, J. C. (1999). Activation of the middle fusiform "face area" increases with expertise in recognizing novel objects. *Nature Neuroscience, 2*, 568–573.

Gelso, C., & Fretz, B. (2001). *Counseling psychology* (2nd ed.). Belmont, CA: Thomson Wordsworth.

Good, G. E., & Beitman, B. (2006). *Counseling and psychotherapy essentials: Integrating theories, skills and practices.* New York: WW Norton & Co.

Hansen, J. C. (1995). No one ever died wishing they had spent more time in the office. *The Counseling Psychologist, 23*, 129–141.

Heppner, P. P., Leong, F. T. L., & Gerstein, L. H. (2008). Counseling within a changing world: Meeting the psychological needs of societies and the world. In W. B. Walsh (Ed.), *Biennial review of counseling psychology* (pp. 231–258). New York: Routledge.

Hohenshil, T. H. (2010). International counseling introduction. *Journal of Counseling and Development, 88*, 3.

Ivey, A., Ivey, M. B., & Zalaquett, C. (2007). *Intentional interviewing and counseling: Facilitating client development in a multicultural society.* Belmont, CA: Brooks/Cole/Cengage.

Jackson, P. L., & Decety, J. (2004). Motor cognition: A new paradigm to study self other interactions. *Current Opinions in Neurobiology, 14*, 259–263.

Kanwisher, N., McDermott, J., & Chun, M. M. (1997). The fusiform face area: A module in human extrastriate cortex specialized for face perception. *The Journal of Neuroscience, 17*, 4302–4311.

Keita, G. P. (2010). Calling more attention to worker stress. *Monitor on Psychology, 41*(4), 56.

Kenwright, M., & Marks, I. M. (2004). Computer-aided self-help for phobia/panic via Internet at home: A pilot study. *Journal of Psychiatry, 184*, 448–449.

Krendl, A. C., Richeson, J. A., Kelley, W. M., & Heatherton, T. F. (2008). The negative consequences of threat: A functional resonance imaging investigation of the neural mechanisms underlying women's underperformance in math. *Psychological Science, 19*, 168–175.

Legrand, L. N., McGue, M., & Iacona, W. G. (1999). Searching for interactive effects in the etiology of early onset substance use. *Behavioral Genetics, 29*, 433–444.

Leve, L. D., Harold, G. T., Ge, X., Neiderhiser, J. M., & Patterson, G. (2010). Refining intervention targets in family-based research: Lessons from quantitative behavioral genetics. *Perspectives on Psychological Science, 5*, 516–526.

Mallen, M. J., Vogel, D. L., Rochlen, A. B., & Day, S. X. (2005). Online counseling: Review of the literature from a counseling psychology framework. *The Counseling Psychologist, 33*, 819–871.

Martin, S. (2009). Embrace the future. *Monitor on Psychology, 40*(9), 74–75.

Miller, T. W. (2007). Trauma, change, and psychological health in the 21st century. *American Psychologist, 62*, 889–898.

Moore, M. J., Soderquist, J., & Werch, C. (2005). Feasibility and efficacy of a binge drinking prevention intervention for college students delivered via the Internet versus postal mail. *Journal of American College Health, 54*, 38–44.

Nicklas, B. J. (2010). Heterogeneity of physical function responses to exercise in older adults: Possible contribution of variation in the angiotensin-1 converting enzyme (ACE) gene? *Perspectives in Psychological Science, 5*, 575–584.

Plomin, R., & Haworth, C. M. A. (2010). Genetics and intervention research. *Perspectives on Psychological Science, 5*, 557–563.

Reiss, D. (2010a). Genetic thinking in the study of social relationships: Five points of entry. *Perspectives on Psychological Science, 5*, 502–515.

Reiss, D. (2010b). Introduction to the special issue: Genetics, personalized medicine, and behavioral intervention–can this combination improve patient care? *Perspectives on Psychological Science, 5*, 499–501.

Rizzo, A., Reger, G., Grahm, G., Difede, J., & Rothbaum, B. O. (2009). Virtual reality exposure therapy for combat related PTSD. In P. J. Shiromani, T. Keane, & J. LeDoux (Eds.), *Post-traumatic stress disorder: Basic science and clinical practice.* Totowa, NJ: Humana Press.

Rollins, J. (2008). Emerging client issues. *Counseling Today,* July, 30–41.

Rutter, M., & Sitberg, J. (2002). Gene-environment interplay in relation to emotional and behavioral disturbance. *Annual Review of Psychology, 53*, 463–490.

Saxe, R., & Kanwisher, N. (2003). People thinking about thinking people: The role of the temporo-parietal junction in "theory of mind." *Neuroimage, 19*, 1835–1842.

Siegel, D. J. (1999). *The developing mind: Toward a neurobiology of interpersonal experience.* New York: Guilford Press.

Somerville, L. H., Heatherton, T. F., & Kelley, W. M. (2006). Dissociating expectancy violation from social rejection. *Nature Neuroscience, 9*, 1007–1008.

Strom, L., Petterson, R., & Anderson, G. (2004). Internet-based treatments for insomnia: A controlled evaluation. *Journal of Consulting and Clinical Psychology, 72*, 113–120.

Taylor, M. C. (2010). *Crisis on campus.* New York: Alfred A. Knopf.

Tyler, L., Tiedeman, D., & Wrenn, C. G. (1980). The current status of counseling psychology. In J. M. Whitely (Ed.), *The history of counseling psychology* (pp. 114–124). Monterey, CA: Brooks/Cole.

Wade, S. L., Carey, J., & Wolfe, C. R. (2006). The efficacy of online cognitive-behavioral family intervention in improving child behavior and social competence following pediatric brain injury. *Rehabilitation Psychology, 51*, 179–189.

Wrenn, C. G. (1962). *The counselor in a changing world.* Washington, DC: American Personnel and Guidance Association.

INDEX

Note: Page numbers followed by "*f*" and "*t*" denote figures and tables, respectively.

cross-cultural approach, 901
cross-cultural counseling. *See also* multiculturalism
  definition of, 874
  emotions and, 879–80, 891–93
  research in, 879–80
crossed relationship, 308
cross-national counseling, 874
cross-national movement, 874
Cross Racial Identity Scale (CRIS), 295–96, 310–12
cross-validation, 246, 248
Croteau, J. M., 410, 418, 424, 427
Crouch, E., 616, 623
Crowell, J., 628
CRSPPP. *See* Commission on Recognition of Specialties
  and Proficiencies in Professional Psychology
Crunkleton, A., 46
crying, 891
CSE. *See* collective self-esteem
Csikszentmihalyi, M., 354
CSMS. *See* Children's Sadness Management Scale
CSTs. *See* clinical support tools
CTI. *See* Career Thoughts Inventory
Cuddy, A. J. C., 348
Cudeck, R., 252, 253
cultural competence, 736. *See also* multiculturalism
"Culturally Relevant Prevention," 532, 534
cultural paranoia, 417
cultural relativism, 900–901
cultural relevance, 538
cultural sensitivity, 736
culture
  hip-hop, 318–19
  individualistic *vs.* collectivistic, 887–89
  organizational, 768
  research on, 900–903
  safety, 768
"Culture, Race, and Ethnicity in Organizational
  Consulting Psychology," 847
Cummings, D. L., 274
Cummings, N. A., 97
Cummins, A. G., 447
Curriculum Connections, 715
Curry, K. T., 55
custody evaluations, 278–79
CWB. *See* counterproductive work behaviors
cyber-bullying, 704
cybernetics, 650, 651
cyclotherapy, 627

D

DADT. *See* "Don't Ask—Don't Tell"
D'Andrea, M., 740
Daniels, K., 292
Danish, S., 786
Danziger, P. R., 60
Daras, M. D., 114, 117
Darcy, M. U. A., 133
Darley, John G., 681, 682, 724
Darrow, R. E., 862
Darwin, Charles, 208, 879
D-AT. *See* disability-affirmative therapy
Davidson, J., 46
Davidson, M. M., 861
Davies, D. R., 626
Davis, G. C., 812, 814, 816, 818
Davis, Jesse B., 617*t*, 635
Davis, K. M., 508
Davis, S. D., 667
Davison, G. C., 85, 87
Dawes, René, 129, 130, 145, 168
Day, J., 272, 273
Day, S. X., 41, 133, 158
Dean, B., 559
Deane, F. P., 898
death rates, 377
Deaux, K., 359
DeBlaere, C., 411, 425
DeCastro-Ambrosetti, D., 714
DECIDES model, 144
deconstruction, 439
Deepening Psychotherapy with Men (Rabinowitz and
  Cochran, S. V.), 393
Defense of Marriage Acts (DOMA), 414
DeLeon, P. H., 729

demand-control model, 759
Dembo, Tamara, 681, 683, 687
dementia, 483, 489
DeMers, S. T., 285
DeNeve, K. M., 246
Department of Defense, U.S. (DOD), 414
Department of Education, U.S. (USDOE), 15, 25, 688
Department of Medicine and Surgery, of the Veterans
  Administration (VA), 13
Department of Veteran Affairs, U.S., 23
dependent variables (DVs), 243
depersonalization, 761, 762
depression
  CBT for, 505, 516
  CFT for, 658
  counseling psychology for, 516
  internationally, 882
  masked, 389
  among older adults, 481, 483, 485, 487–88, 491
  reframing for, 664–65
Depression Collaborative Research Program, 58
descriptive statistics, 240
desensitization, 85
designation, 15, 16, 17
Designation Project, 17–18
Diagnostic and Statistical Manual (DSM), 81, 100,
  808, 830
  gender and, 351–52, 366, 444
Diamond, L. M., 413, 419
Diemer, M. A., 554, 563, 564
Dies, R., 629, 630
Dies, R. R., 224
differential item functioning (DIF), 214
differentiation, of self, 651
Dik, B., 253
Dik, B. J., 147
Diller, Leonard, 681, 687, 688
Dillon, F. R., 421
DiMichael, Salvatore, 681
Dion, K., 624
direct effects parameter, 255
direct oblimin, 251
disability. *See also* rehabilitation psychology
  anger with, 467–68
  attitudes about, 466
  boundaries with, 468
  case formulation with, 473–74
  as central characteristic, 466
  CHP with, 730–31
  community, 474
  definition of, 461, 697–98
  employment with, 476
  hidden, 460–61
  language for, 466–67
  legal issues with, 469–70
  models of, 461–62, 463*t*, 464, 465*t*, 466, 471
  of older adults, 487
  requirement of mourning for, 467
  stigma of, 468–69
  supervision with, 462–64, 474–75
  testing with, 473
  therapy with, 471, 472*t*, 473–74
  training in, 462–64, 474–75
  vulnerability awareness with, 468
disability-affirmative therapy (D-AT), 460, 471–74
discriminant analysis, 247–48
discrimination
  interpersonal, 349, 352
  occupational, 159
  racism, 436
  with sex, 356–57
  sexist, 349–51, 436
  in testing, 213–14
  violence and, 350–51, 353
  workplace, 349–50, 352–53, 365
discrimination model, 186
Dishion, T. J., 120
Disorder of the Self: Male Type, 391
Display Rule Assessment Inventory (DRAI), 885
display rules, 881, 884
distance education, 24, 25. *See also* education
Distefano, T. M., 427
distress, 758
distribution, normal, 240

Diversity Toolkit, 715
Division of Counseling and Guidance, 3
Division of Counseling Psychology of
  the Hong Kong Psychological Society, 877
divorce, 120, 278–79
Dixon, D. N., 226
Dixon, L., 536
Doan, B.-T., 578
doctoral programs, in counseling psychology, 12, 725
  accreditation, 14, 15, 16
  designated, 16, 17–18
  practicum, 18
  sequence of, 15*f*
  training for, 18, 180
  unaccredited, 16–17
DOD. *See* Department of Defense, U.S.
Dodo bird effect, 80, 107
Dohrenwend, B. P., 814, 830
Dollard, J., 34, 82
DOMA. *See* Defense of Marriage Acts
DOMA Watch, 414
Domene, J. E., 260, 261
Dompierre, J., 764
"Don't Ask—Don't Tell" (DADT), 414–15
Dorn, F. J., 54
dose-effect model, 106
dose-effect studies, 517, 518
double-bind theory, 649, 651
Dougherty, A. M., 837–38, 841, 843, 845, 847, 848
Dover, C., 261
Dovidio, J. F., 60
Downing, N. E., 359, 360
Doyle, A. B., 713
Dozier, M., 118, 120, 121
DRAI. *See* Display Rule Assessment Inventory
Draijer, N., 820, 821
Drasgow, F., 227
Dreese, Mitchell, 725
Dreikurs, Rudolph, 618*t*
Driscoll, J. M., 726, 740
Driver, Helen J., 618*t*
Drum, D. J., 14
DSM. *See* Diagnostic and Statistical Manual
dual-representation theory, 825
Duan, C., 874, 875
Duckworth, Jane, 54–55, 222–23, 224
Dudley, N. M., 150, 151, 152
Dunkle, J. H., 48
Dunmore, E., 820, 822
Dunn, R. L., 755
Dunston, K., 330, 331
Durtschi, J., 559
Dutra, L., 830
DVs. *See* dependent variables
Dye, H. A., 631, 633–34
Dynamics of Groups at Work (Thelen), 618*t*

E

EAC. *See* Expectations About Counseling measure
Eagle, M. N., 121
EAT. *See* environmental assessment technique
eating disorders
  anorexia, 657–58
  feminist approach to, 448–49
  prevention of, 537–38
  in sport psychology, 791–93
  of women, 791, 792
EBP. *See* evidence-based practice
EBPP. *See* evidence-based practice in psychology
EBTs. *See* empirically based treatments
Eby, L. T., 153, 161
eclecticism, 520
Eccles, J. S., 141
ecological systems model, 5–6, 553
economic cultures (ECs), 332
economics, hierarchy of, 327–28
ECs. *See* economic cultures
Eden, D., 762
education. *See also* psychoeducation; school psychology;
  schools; specific forms of education
  achievement in, 141–43
  of African Americans, 156
  of Asian Americans, 159–60

Gordon, W. A., 687
Gormally, J., 511
Gottfredson, L. S., 129, 130, 139, 140, 549–50, 561
GPA. *See* grade point average
GPRN. *See* Group Practice and Research Network
grade point average (GPA), 141–42
Graduate Management Admission Test (GMAT), 141–42
Graff, H., 47
Granic, I., 120
Grant, S. K., 842, 859
Grass, K., 555
Grawe, K., 508
GRC. *See* gender role conflict
GRCS. *See* Gender Role Conflict Scale
GRC Scale for Adolescents (GRCS-A), 387*t*
Great Depression, 753
Green, E. J., 865
Greenberg, L. S., 42, 513, 521, 652, 659
Greenberg, Leslie, 512
Greene, J., 830
Greenson, R., 659
Greenspan, M., 788
Grencavage, L. M., 509–10
Gretchen, D., 572
Grey Panthers, 485
Greystone Conference, 13, 271, 504
grief, stages of, 550
Grieger, I., 266
Griffen, M. A., 768–69
Griffith, Coleman, 781
Griffiths, A., 756
Griner, D., 582–83
Groden, J., 361
Gross, J. J., 892
gross stress reaction, 808
grounded theory, 257, 263, 577
group centroids, 248
group climate, 625–27
group cohesion, sports, 789
group cohesiveness, 624, 626
group consciousness, 364–65
group counseling
    Age of Ubiquity in, 616, 621*t*, 634
    BGT, 634–35
    climate in, 625–27
    definitions of, 612–15
    development in, 626, 627–28
    efficacy of, 611–12
    ethics in, 632–33, 636
    feedback in, 631
    focal group psychotherapy, 634
    in group work, 613–14, 625
    here-and-now interactions in, 630–31
    history of, 615–16, 617*t*, 618*t*, 619*t*, 620*t*, 621*t*, 622*t*
    on Internet, 636–37
    leadership in, 628–34
    models of, 627
    multiculturalism in, 633
    mutual-help, 635
    with Native Americans, 615
    research on, 637–38
    self-disclosure in, 624
    social justice, 635
    in sport psychology, 789–90
    supervision with, 631
    therapeutic factors in, 616, 623, 623*t*, 624–25, 626
    training for, 612, 638
    trauma, 635–36
    working alliance in, 626
Group Dynamics, 618*t*, 620*t*
Group Dynamics: Theory, Research, and Practice., 621*t*
group identity of, 364–65
group leadership
    defining, 628–29
    functions, 629–30
    improvisation in, 633–34
    intervention choice by, 632
    meaning attribution in, 631–32
    positive valence in, 630
    preparation for, 630
    standards for, 632–33
Group Practice and Research Network (GPRN), 614
Group Summit, 614

group work, 613–14, 625
Group Works! Information About Group Psychotherapy, 631–32
GSAs. *See* Gay-Straight Alliances
Guber, B., 464, 475
Guidelines for Defining a Doctoral Program in Psychology, 16, 17
Guidelines for Training Group Leaders, 620*t*
Guilmino, A., 862
Gumbley, S. J., 86
Gunnar, M. R., 120, 121
Gurin, P., 364, 365
Gushue, G. V., 364
Gustad, J. W., 4
Gysbers, N. C., 53

H

HA. *See* Penn Helping Alliance scales
HAART. *See* highly active antiretroviral therapy
Hackett, G., 129, 130, 134, 135, 136, 142, 161, 556–57
Hackler, A. H., 507
Hage, S. M., 530, 531–32, 738, 739, 741
Hager, J. C., 884
Haggarty, D. J., 21
Hahn, K., 822
Hahn, Milton E., 504
Haldeman, D. C., 868
Haley, Jay, 649
Hall, J. E., 14, 21, 23, 24, 28, 272
Hall, W. S., 309
Halpert, S. C., 427
Ham, M., 283
Hamburg, D., 627
HAM-D. *See* Hamilton Depression Rating Scale
Hamel, D. A., 144
Hamilton Depression Rating Scale (HAM-D), 115, 116
Hammers, D., 233
Hancock, G. R., 42
Handbook of Group Counseling and Psychotherapy, 622*t*
Handbook of Group Psychotherapy, 621*t*
Handbook of Psychotherapy and Behavior Change, 36
Handbook of Social Justice in Counseling Psychology, 858
handicap, 461
Handler, L., 227
Hansen, J. C., 253
Hansen, Jo-Ida, 754
Hansen, L. S., 557
Hanson, W. E., 55
Hanton, S., 786–87
Hardiman, R., 293, 298, 301, 302
Hardin, S. I., 46
Hardy, G., 513
Hardy, G. E., 509
Harley, D. A., 731
Hartley's *F* max test, 241
Harper, J. M., 661
Harper, R. A., 504
Harren, V. A., 144
Harrington-O'Shea Career Decision Making System (CDMS), 556
Harris-Bowlsbey, J., 547, 557, 561
Harrison, D. A., 151, 153
Harry Benjamin International Gender Dysphoria (HBIGD) Standards of Care, 423
Hartung, P. J., 223
Harvard program in Refugee Trauma, 862
Hatch, S. L., 814, 830
Hatinen, M., 762
Haverkamp, B. E., 265
Hawkins, E. J., 106
Hawthorne effect, 756
Hayes, A. M., 96
Hayes, J. A., 36–37, 39, 44, 45, 50, 60
Hays, D. G., 865
H&B codes. *See* health and behavior assessment and intervention service codes
HBIGD. *See* Harry Benjamin International Gender Dysphoria Standards of Care
health. *See also* counseling health psychology; occupational health psychology; rehabilitation psychology; stress; specific health issues
    of African Americans, 733, 734
    behavioral variables in, 723

    definition of, 592–93
    disparities in, 734–35
    ethnicity and, 482
    of immigrants, 737
    multiculturalism and, 736–38
    of older adults, 480–81, 482–84, 485
    prevention in, 738–41, 772
    in psychology, 23
    religion/spirituality and, 593–98
    risk factors with, 740
    SES and, 735
    social justice in, 861–62
    of women, 740, 765–66
health and behavior assessment and intervention service codes (H & B codes), 494
Health Insurance Portability and Accountability Act (HIPAA), 278, 279
Health Professions Council of South Africa, 877
"Health Related Outcomes," 725
Health Service Provider in Psychology, 22
Health Service Provider in Psychology (HSPP), 15*f*
"Healthy People 2010," 531
Healthy Personality Inventory (HPI), 244, 245*t*, 251, 252, 252*t*
Healy, C. C., 54
Heaps, R. A., 559
Heatherington, L., 41, 660, 662, 665
Heaton, K. J., 44–45
hegemonic masculinity paradigm, 379
Heggestad, E. D., 165, 166, 167
Helgeson, V. S., 365, 828
Helm, K., 312
Helms, J. E., 281, 301, 307–8, 310, 313, 363, 552, 563, 578, 857, 859, 861, 864, 865, 874, 875
Helms, Janet, 291, 296, 297, 307, 579
helper intentions, 183
helping skills, taxonomy of, 511
help-seeking
    factors in, 506–7
    internationally, 896–98
    by men, 392–93, 394, 398, 400–401, 898
    in U.S., 896, 898
    by women, 898
Hendricks, F., 53
Henry, W. P., 51, 87, 120
Hensler-McGinnis, N. F., 731–32
Heppner, M. J., 53
Heppner, P. P., 59, 873, 874, 875
Hepworth, J., 728
Herek, G. M., 416
Herink, R., 74
heritability, 160–61
Heritage Project, 861
Hermann, K., 254*t*
Hersh, M., 576, 582
Hess, S. A., 260, 261
Hesson-McInnis, M., 253
heterosexist bias, 416
heterosexuality, 412
heuristic model of nonoppressive interpersonal development (HMNID), 191
Hickson, F., 711
Highlen, P. S., 46
highly active antiretroviral therapy (HAART), 732
Hill, C. E., 38, 44–45, 46, 50, 53, 57, 183, 184, 260, 261, 511, 513–14
Hill, Clara, 511
Hill, M., 441
Hill, M. S., 360
Hill, R. D., 480
Hill, S., 380
Hill, W. F., 619*t*, 627
Hilliard, R. B., 120
Hill Interaction Matrix, 619*t*
Hinrichsen, 491
HIPAA. *See* Health Insurance Portability and Accountability Act
hip-hop culture, 318–19
Hirsch, L., 380
Hispanic Americans, 156. *See also* Latinas; Latinos
    OHP with, 767–68
    as older adults, 486
hit rate, 248
HIV/AIDS, 273, 597, 598, 732–33, 737

modification indices, 256
Mohr, J. J., 45, 416–17, 418
Moliero, C. M., 118
Molinaro, M., 50
Monarch, N., 852
Moore, M., 105
Moos, R., 75
Moradi, B., 309, 411, 416–17, 418, 425
Moradi, B. Subich, L. M., 442
moral model, 462, 463*t*, 464, 465*t*
Moreland, K. L., 224
Moreno, Jacob, 618*t*
Morgeson, F. P., 51, 153–54
Morin, S. F., 416
Morris, J. F., 283
Morrison, K., 97
Morrow, S. L., 257, 264–65
Morrow-Bradley, C., 87
Morten, G., 293, 297, 300, 301
Morton, R. J., 86
motivation, worker, 771
motivational enhancement therapy (MET), 111
motivational interviewing, 85
Mount, M. K., 142, 150, 165
Mouton, Jane, 618*t*
Moyer, J., 508
Mpofu, E., 731
MPQ Primary Scales, 166–67, 167*f*, 168*f*
MRNS. *See* Male Role Norm Scale
MS. *See* mean squares
MSDs. *See* musculoskeletal disorders
MST. *See* multisystemic therapy
Mueller, L., 582
Mueller, L. N., 576–77
Muhammad, G., 292
Mullen, E. J., 87
Mullison, D., 625
multicultural genogram, 548
multiculturalism, 6. *See also* specific ethnicities; specific races
   with assessment, 227–28
   in career counseling, 552–55, 557–58, 563–64
   in CFT, 669–70
   in CHP, 734, 735–38
   competence in, 197, 281, 570, 571–72, 575–77, 581–82, 584, 736, 743, 745
   in consultation, 845–47
   in counseling relationship, 53, 55–63, 581
   definition of, 874
   empathy and, 60
   expectations with, 46–47
   feminism and, 361, 435–36
   in group counseling, 633
   health and, 736–38
   language of, 425–26
   with LGBTs, 425–26
   men and, 390, 394
   in OHP, 775
   of older adults, 486–87
   poverty and, 581
   in prevention, 538–39
   research on, 572, 573, 575–85
   self-awareness in, 181
   sexual orientation with, 411–12, 421–22
   in social justice, 858
   with supervision, 190–91, 577
   theories of, 572–75, 579, 584–85
   training in, 180–81, 575, 580
   womanist identity and, 363–64
multicultural knowledge, skills, and awareness model (KSA), 422
multidimensional family therapy (MDFT), 655–56, 668
multidimensional inventory of black identity (MIBI), 312–13
Multidimensional Model of Racial Identity (MMRI), 299–300
Multidimensional Personality Questionnaire, 163
multidimensional scaling (MDS), 253
multigroup ethnic identity measure (MEIM), 316–17, 319
multiple regression, 246
multisystemic therapy (MST), 656
multitrait-multimethod matrix, 220

multivariate analysis of variation (MANOVA), 241, 243–44, 247–48
multiway frequency analysis (MFA), 248
Multon, K. D., 53, 136–37, 514
Murphy, J. A., 716
Murphy, M. D., 105
Murphy, M. J., 24
musculoskeletal disorders (MSDs), 765–66
mutual-help groups, 635
Mutual Recognition Agreement, 28
MVs. *See* measured variables
Myers, 491
Myers, Roger, 56

N

Naatanen, P., 762
NAFTA. *See* North American Free Trade Agreement
Naglieri, J. A., 227
Nahrgang, J. D., 51, 153–54
Napoli, P. J., 861
Narducci, J., 51
narrative exposure therapy (NET), 103
narrative therapy, 505
   with career counseling, 557–58
   feminism in, 448–50
narratology, 257–58, 263
Nash, M. R., 105
National Association of Social Workers (NASW), 282
National Board for Certified Counselors (NBCC), 560
National Career Development Association (NCDA), 548, 551, 553, 561
National Comorbidity Survey (NCS), 808, 815
National Conference on Counseling Psychology (2001), 281
National Conference on Postdoctoral Fellowship Training in Applied Psychology, 19
National Council for Schools and Programs of Professional Psychology (NCSPP), 180
National Council on the Psychological Aspects of Disability (NCPAD), 681
National Counseling Psychology Conference, 505, 858
National Education Association (NEA), 715
National Gay and Lesbian Task Force (NGLTF), 415
national health insurance, 97, 99
National Health Interview Survey (NHIS), 481
National Institute for Occupational Safety and Health (NIOSH), 753, 754, 757, 759–60, 771, 774
National Institute of Mental Health (NIMH)
   National Prevention Conference, 531
   Research Task Force, 74
   Treatment of Depression Collaborative Research Program, 508, 510
National Institute on Drug Abuse, 831
National Multicultural Conference and Summit (NCMS), 451, 600
National Occupational Information Coordinating Committee (NOICC), 560, 561, 562
National Register of Health Service Providers in Psychology, 17, 18, 22, 23, 29
National School Climate Survey (NSCS), 715
National Science Foundation, 159
National Training Laboratories (NTL), 618*t*, 620*t*
National Transgender Discrimination Survey, 415
National Vocational Guidance Association (NVGA), 548
Native Americans
   group counseling with, 615
   as older adults, 486
Nature, 71
NBCC. *See* National Board for Certified Counselors
NCDA. *See* National Career Development Association
NCLB. *See* No Child Left Behind Act
NCMS. *See* National Multicultural Conference and Summit
NCPAD. *See* National Council on the Psychological Aspects of Disability
NCS. *See* National Comorbidity Survey
NCSPP. *See* National Council for Schools and Programs of Professional Psychology
NEA. *See* National Education Association
Neal, A., 768–69
Necowitz, L., 256
Neely, L. C., 62
Negromachy model, 293–94

"The Negro-To-Black Conversion Experience" (Cross, W.), 294
Neimeyer, G. J., 86
Nelson, D. L., 758, 765, 768
Nelson, D. W., 60
Nelson, M. L., 48
Nelson, P., 180
Nesic, M., 555
NET. *See* narrative exposure therapy
Netland, J. D., 740
Netzky, W., 46
Neuner, F., 103
neuroimaging, 113, 115–17, 919–20
neuropsychology, 225, 686–87
neuroticism, 822
Neville, H., 578
The New Handbook of Psychotherapy and Counseling with Men (Brooks, G. R., and Good), 392
Newman, D. A., 151, 153
Newman, M. G., 520
Newmeyer, M., 628
New Perspectives on Encounter Groups, 620*t*
A New Psychotherapy for Traditional Men (Brooks, G. R.), 393
The New Psychotherapy with Men (Pollack and Levant), 392
New Racism Scale, 578
Newsweek, 71
New York Times, 619*t*
New Zealand, 28
Ng, T. W. H., 153, 161
NGLTF. *See* National Gay and Lesbian Task Force
NHIS. *See* National Health Interview Survey
NHST. *See* null hypothesis significance testing
Nichols, M. P., 667
Nicol, J. J., 876
Nicoletti, J., 765
Nielson, S. L., 106–7
Nigrescence model, 293, 294–96, 300, 309
Nigro, T., 50
Niles, S. G., 54, 547, 557, 561
NIMH. *See* National Institute of Mental Health
NIOSH. *See* National Institute for Occupational Safety and Health
NNFI. *See* Bentler-Bonnett non-normed fit index
Noble, S., 36, 48, 49, 50, 52, 57, 61
nocebo effect, 510
No Child Left Behind Act (NCLB), 705
NOICC. *See* National Occupational Information Coordinating Committee
Noland, R. M., 228
nominal scales, 211
nomological network, 210
nondisclosures, 193
nonverbal communication, 182
Noonan, B. M., 731–32
Norcross, J. C., 17, 506, 509–10
normative discontent, 353
normative sample, 214
norms, 214
Norris, F. H., 814–15
Norsworthy, K. L., 873, 874
North American Free Trade Agreement (NAFTA), 28
Northwestern Conference, 504
Northwestern University, 13, 271
Norway, 51
Notice of Privacy Practice forms, 278
Novy, D. M., 141
NSCS. *See* National School Climate Survey
NTL. *See* National Training Laboratories
null hypothesis significance testing (NHST), 241–42
Nunnally, J. C., 212
Nurmi, J., 762
Nutt-Williams, E., 44–45, 50
NVGA. *See* National Vocational Guidance Association

O

Oakley, D., 361
Obama, Barack, 291
objectification, sexual, 353–54
objectification theory, 353–54
object relations theory, 652
oblique rotation, 251–52
OBPP. *See* Olweus Bullying Prevention Program

Printed in Australia
AUHW011507160822
367680AU00003B/3